Microsoft Office XP

Post Advanced Concepts and Techniques

COURSE THREE

Gary B. Shelly
Thomas J. Cashman
Misty E. Vermaat

Contributing Authors
Mary Z. Last
Philip J. Pratt
James S. Quasney
Jeffrey J. Quasney
Susan L. Sebok
Joy L. Starks

COURSE TECHNOLOGY
THOMSON LEARNING

COURSE TECHNOLOGY
25 THOMSON PLACE
BOSTON MA 02210

SHELLY CASHMAN SERIES®

Australia • Canada • Denmark • Japan • Mexico • New Zealand • Philippines • Puerto Rico • Singapore
South Africa • Spain • United Kingdom • United States

COURSE TECHNOLOGY
THOMSON LEARNING™

Printed in the United States of America

Asia (excluding Japan)
Thomson Learning
60 Albert Street, #15-01
Albert Complex
Singapore 189969

Japan
Thomson Learning
Palaceside Building 5F
1-1-1 Hitotsubashi, Chiyoda-ku
Tokyo 100 0003 Japan

Australia/New Zealand
Nelson/Thomson Learning
102 Dodds Street
Southbank, Victoria 3006
Australia

Latin America
Thomson Learning
Seneca, 53
Colonia Polanco
11560 Mexico D.F. Mexico

South Africa
Thomson Learning
15 Brookwood Street
P.O. Box 1722
Soverset West 7120
South Africa

Canada
Nelson/Thomson Learning
1120 Birchmount Road
Scarborough, Ontario
Canada M1K 5G4

UK/Europe/Middle East
Thomson Learning
Berkshire House
168-173 High Holborn
London, WC1V 7AA United Kingdom

Spain
Thomson Learning
Calle Magallanes, 25
28015-MADRID
ESPANA

For more information, contact Course Technology, 25 Thomson Place, Boston, MA 02210.

Or visit our Internet site at www.course.com

PHOTO CREDITS: **Microsoft Word 2002** *Project 8, pages WD 8.02-03* Young graduates, graduation cap, college graduation, Courtesy of PhotoDisc, Inc.; *Project 9, pages WD 9.02-03* Keyboard and notebook, young man at computer, hand holding pencil, woman in library, young business woman, Courtesy of PhotoDisc, Inc.; **Microsoft Excel 2002** *Project 7, pages E 7.02-03* Young couple, Courtesy of Dynamic Graphics, Inc.; people at piano, Courtesy of Corel Professional Photos; *Project 8, pages E 8.02-03* Woman chef, Courtesy of PhotoDisc, Inc.; child eating, volunteer servers, Courtesy of Union Rescue Mission, Los Angeles, California; baby in overalls, Courtesy of Digital Stock.; **Microsoft Access 2002** *Project 7, pages A 7.02-03* Clown, Courtesy of Rubber Ball Productions; tickets, Courtesy of PhotoDisc, Inc.; *Project 8 A 8.02-03* Fruit and vegetables, Courtesy of KPT Metatools; *Project 9, pages A 9.02-03* Women using fitness equipment, FitLinxx monitor, Courtesy of FitLinxx, Inc.; cartoon people exercising, Courtesy of Corel.; **Microsoft PowerPoint 2002** *Project 5, pages PP 5.02-03* Hands typing on keyboard, monitor cable image, Courtesy of PhotoDisc, Inc.; background image, business people working, woman talking on telephone, Courtesy of Dynamic Graphics, Inc.; *Project 6, pages PP 6.02-03* Margi Presenter-to-Go™ Courtesy of MARGI SYSTEMS, INC

ISBN 0-7895-6291-X

1 2 3 4 5 6 7 8 9 10 BC 06 05 04 03 02

Microsoft Office XP

Post Advanced Concepts and Techniques

COURSE THREE

WORD 2002 EXCEL 2002 ACCESS 2002 POWERPOINT 2002

Contents

Microsoft Word 2002

7 PROJECT SEVEN

Creating an Online Form

8 PROJECT EIGHT

Working with Macros and Visual Basic for Applications (VBA)

9 PROJECT NINE

WORKING WITH A MASTER DOCUMENT, AN INDEX, AND A TABLE OF CONTENTS

INTEGRATION FEATURE

LINKING AN EXCEL WORKSHEET AND CHARTING ITS DATA IN WORD

Microsoft Excel 2002

7 PROJECT SEVEN

USING MACROS AND VISUAL BASIC FOR APPLICATIONS (VBA) WITH EXCEL

8 PROJECT EIGHT

Formula Auditing, Data Validation, and Complex Problem Solving

9 PROJECT NINE

Importing Data, Routing Changes, PivotCharts, PivotTables, and Trendlines

WEB FEATURE

Creating a PivotTable List Web Page Using Excel

Microsoft Access 2002

7 PROJECT SEVEN

Creating a Report Using Design View

8 PROJECT EIGHT

Using Visual Basic for Applications (VBA) and Advanced Form Techniques

9 PROJECT NINE

Administering a Database System

INTEGRATION FEATURE

Grouped Data Access Pages, PivotTables, and PivotCharts

Microsoft PowerPoint 2002

5 PROJECT FIVE

Working with Macros and Visual Basic for Applications (VBA)

6 PROJECT SIX

Creating a Self-Running Presentation Containing Interactive Documents

Preface

The Shelly Cashman Series® offers the finest textbooks in computer education. We are proud of the fact that our series of Microsoft Office 4.3, Microsoft Office 95, Microsoft Office 97, and Microsoft Office 2000 textbooks have been the most widely used books in education. With each new edition of our Office books, we have made improvements based on the software and comments made by the instructors and students. The *Microsoft Office XP* books continue with the innovation, quality, and reliability that you have come to expect from the Shelly Cashman Series.

Office XP is the most significant upgrade ever to the Office suite. It provides a much smarter work experience for users. Microsoft has enhanced Office XP in the following areas: (1) streamlined user interface; (2) smart tags and task panes to help simplify the way people work; (3) speech and handwriting recognition; (4) an improved Help system; (5) enhanced Web capabilities; and (6) application-specific features. Each one of these enhancements is part of Microsoft Office XP and is discussed in detail.

In this *Microsoft Office XP* book, you will find an educationally sound and easy-to-follow pedagogy that combines a step-by-step approach with corresponding screens. All projects and exercises in this book are designed to take full advantage of the Office XP enhancements. The popular Other Ways and More About features offer in-depth knowledge of Microsoft Office XP. The new Learn It Online page presents a wealth of additional exercises to ensure your students have all the reinforcement they need. The project openers provide a fascinating perspective of the subject covered in the project. The project material is developed carefully to ensure that students will see the importance of learning the Office applications for future coursework.

Objectives of This Textbook

Microsoft Office XP: Post Advanced Concepts and Techniques is intended for a one-quarter or one-semester post-advanced computer applications course. This book assumes that students are familiar with the fundamentals of Microsoft Word, Microsoft Excel, Microsoft Access, and Microsoft PowerPoint. These topics are covered in the companion textbooks *Microsoft Office XP: Introductory Concepts and Techniques* and *Microsoft Office XP: Advanced Concepts and Techniques*. The objectives of this book are:

- To extend students' basic knowledge of Microsoft Word 2002, Microsoft Excel 2002, Microsoft Access 2002, and Microsoft PowerPoint 2002.
- To help students demonstrate their proficiency in the Microsoft Office XP applications by preparing them to pass the Expert-level Microsoft Office User Specialist Exam for Microsoft Word 2002, Microsoft Excel 2002, and Microsoft Access 2002, and the Comprehensive-level Microsoft Office User Specialist Exam for Microsoft PowerPoint 2002.
- To acquaint students with the proper procedures to create more advanced documents, workbooks, databases, and presentations suitable for course work, professional purposes, and personal use
- To develop an exercise-oriented approach that allows students to learn by example
- To encourage independent study, and help those who are working alone in a distance education environment

Approved by Microsoft as Courseware for the Microsoft Office User Specialist Program Expert and Comprehensive Levels

Microsoft Office XP: Post Advanced Concepts and Techniques, when used in combination with the companion textbooks *Microsoft Office XP: Introductory Concepts and Techniques* and *Microsoft Office XP: Advanced Concepts and Techniques* in a three-semester sequence, has been approved by Microsoft as courseware for the Microsoft Office User Specialist (MOUS) program. After completing the projects and exercises in this book and its companion books, students will be prepared to take the Expert-level Microsoft Office User Specialist Exams for Microsoft Word 2002, Microsoft Excel 2002, and Microsoft Access 2002, and the Comprehensive-level Microsoft Office User Specialist Exam for Microsoft PowerPoint 2002. By passing the certification exam for a Microsoft software program, students demonstrate their proficiency in that program to employers. This exam is offered at participating centers, participating corporations, and participating employment agencies. See Appendix E for additional information on the MOUS program and for a table that includes the Word 2002, Excel 2002, Access 2002, and PowerPoint 2002 MOUS skill sets and corresponding page numbers on which a skill is discussed in the book and can be practiced, or visit the Web site mous.net. To purchase a Microsoft Office User Specialist certification exam, visit desktopiq.com.

The Shelly Cashman Series Microsoft Office User Specialist Center Web page (Figure 1) has more than fifteen Web pages you can visit to obtain additional information on the MOUS Certification program. The Web page scsite.com.offxp/cert.htm includes links to general information on certification, choosing an application for certification, preparing for the certification exam, and taking and passing the certification exam.

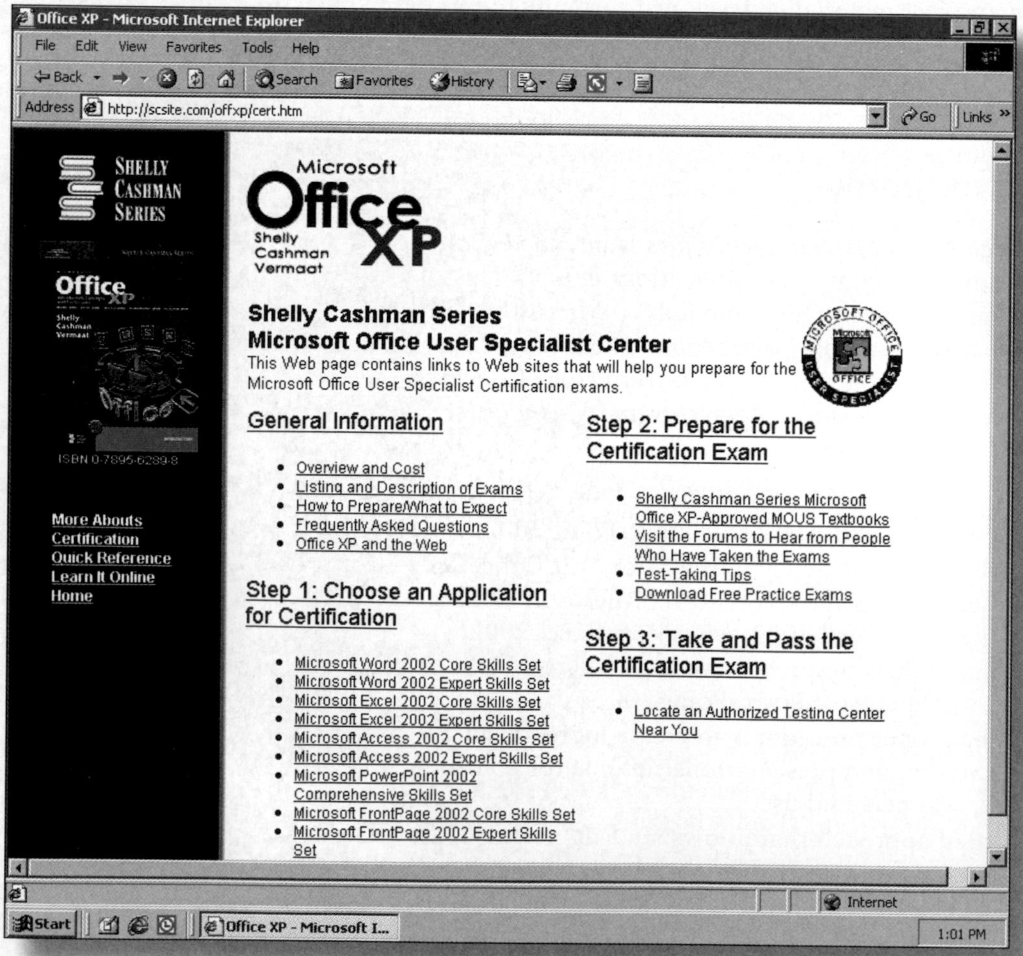

FIGURE 1 The Shelly Cashman Series Microsoft Office User Specialist Center Web Page

The Shelly Cashman Approach

Features of the Shelly Cashman Series *Microsoft Office XP* books include:

- **Project Orientation:** Each project in the book presents a practical problem and complete solution in an easy-to-understand approach.
- **Step-by-Step, Screen-by-Screen Instructions:** Each of the tasks required to complete a project is identified throughout the project. Full-color screens accompany the steps.
- **Thoroughly Tested Projects:** Every screen in the book is correct because it is produced by the author only after performing a step, resulting in unprecedented quality.
- **Other Ways Boxes and Quick Reference Summary:** Office XP provides a variety of ways to carry out a given task. The Other Ways boxes displayed at the end of most of the step-by-step sequences specify the other ways to do the task completed in the steps. Thus, the steps and the Other Ways box make a comprehensive reference unit. A Quick Reference Summary that summarizes the way specific tasks can be completed can be found at the back of this book or on the Web at scsite.com/offxp/qr.htm.
- **More About Feature:** These marginal annotations provide background information and tips that complement the topics covered, adding depth and perspective to the learning experience.
- **Integration of the World Wide Web:** The World Wide Web is integrated into the Office XP learning experience by (1) More About annotations that send students to Web sites for up-to-date information and alternative approaches to tasks; (2) a MOUS information Web page so students can prepare for the MOUS Certification examinations; (3) an Office XP Quick Reference Summary Web page that summarizes the ways to complete tasks (mouse, menu, shortcut menu, and keyboard); and (4) the Learn It Online page at the end of each project, which has project reinforcement exercises, learning games, and other types of student activities.

Other Ways

1. On Tools menu click Options, click Security tab, enter password, on File menu click Save As
2. In Voice Command mode, say "Tools, Options, Security, [type password], OK, File, Save As"

More About

Importing External Data

Excel assigns a name to each external data range. You can view these names by clicking the Name box arrow in the formula bar. External data ranges from text files are named with the text file name. External data ranges from databases are named with the name of the query. External data ranges from Web queries are named with the name of the Web page from which the data was retrieved.

Organization of This Textbook

Microsoft Office XP: Post Advanced Concepts and Techniques consists of three projects each on Microsoft Word 2002, Microsoft Excel 2002, and Microsoft Access 2002, two projects on Microsoft PowerPoint 2002, four short special features, one following each application, five appendices, and a Quick Reference Summary. A brief description of each follows.

Microsoft Word 2002

This textbook begins by providing detailed instruction on how to use the advanced commands and techniques of Microsoft Word 2002. The material is divided into three projects and an Integration Feature.

Project 7 – Creating an Online Form In Project 7, students learn how to create an online form and then use Word to fill in the form. Topics include creating a document template; highlighting text; inserting a table into a form; inserting text form fields, drop-down form fields, and check box form fields; formatting form fields; using the Format Painter button; adding Help text to form fields; drawing a rectangle; filling a drawing object with a texture; formatting a drawing object; animating text; protecting a form; saving form data in a text file; opening a text file in Word; and modifying the location of workgroup templates.

Project 8 – Working with Macros and Visual Basic for Applications (VBA) In Project 8, students enhance an online form by modifying its appearance, adding macros, and inserting an ActiveX control. Topics include setting security levels in Word; creating and applying a new style; formatting a drawing object; recording and executing a macro; assigning a macro to a toolbar button; copying, renaming, and deleting macros; viewing a macro's VBA code; adding comments and VBA code statements to a macro; attaching a macro to the exit property of a form field; inserting, formatting, and setting properties of an ActiveX control; writing VBA code statements for an ActiveX control; and attaching a digital signature.

Project 9 – Working with a Master Document, an Index, and a Table of Contents In Project 9, students learn how to organize and work with a long document. Topics include e-mailing a document for review; inserting, reviewing, and deleting comments; tracking changes; accepting and rejecting tracked changes; comparing and merging documents; saving multiple versions; adding a caption; creating a cross-reference; password-protecting a document; working with a master document and subdocuments; inserting and formatting a diagram; creating a table of figures; marking index entries; building an index; creating a table of contents; adding a bookmark; creating alternating headers and footers; setting a gutter margin; and using the Document Map.

Integration Feature – Linking an Excel Worksheet and Charting Its Data in Word In this Integration Feature, students are introduced to linking Excel data to a Word document. Topics include linking an Excel worksheet to a Word document; creating a chart; linking Excel data to the chart; and editing a linked object.

Microsoft Excel 2002

Following the three advanced projects and integration feature on Microsoft Word 2002, this textbook presents three advanced projects and a Web Feature on Microsoft Excel 2002.

Project 7 – Using Macros and Visual Basic for Applications (VBA) with Excel In Project 7, students learn how to automate tasks by incorporating VBA into their workbooks. Topics include protecting worksheets with passwords; using the macro recorder; executing macros; security; adding buttons to toolbars and commands to menus; creating a user interface by adding controls to a worksheet; setting properties; writing VBA code; using the Visual Basic Editor; validating incoming data; and using event-driven programs.

Project 8 – Formula Auditing, Data Validation, and Complex Problem Solving In Project 8, students learn how to go about solving complex problems. Topics include using the Formula Auditing toolbar; using data validation; goal seeking; using Solver to solve multiple problems; saving multiple scenarios with Scenario Manager; analysis of Solver answers and multiple scenarios; and workbook properties.

Project 9 – Importing Data, Routing Changes, PivotCharts, PivotTables, and Trendlines In Project 9, students learn how to import data into an Excel workbook, collaboration techniques, and advanced data analysis techniques. Topics include importing data from a text file, an Access database, a Web page, and an XML file; turning tracking changes on and off; accepting and rejecting changes; serially routing a workbook to recipients; creating a PivotChart and PivotTable; analyzing a worksheet database using a PivotChart and PivotTable; sharing and merging workbooks; and creating a trendline on a chart.

Web Feature - Creating a PivolTable List Web Page Using Excel In this Web Feature, students learn how to create and manipulate a PivotTable list. Topics include saving a worksheet database as a PivotTable list; viewing the PivotTable list using a browser;

changing the view of the PivotTable list; adding summary totals; sorting columns of data; filtering techniques; removing fields and adding fields to a PivotTable list; and improving the appearance of a PivotTable list.

Microsoft Access 2002

Following the three advanced projects and Web Feature on Microsoft Excel 2002, this textbook provides detailed instruction on advanced topics in Microsoft Access 2002. The topics are divided into three projects and an Integration Feature.

Project 7 – Creating a Report Using Design View In Project 7, students learn to use Design view to create complex reports involving data from queries that join multiple tables. Topics include relating multiple tables; changing join properties in a query; changing field properties in a query; filtering a query's recordset; creating and running a parameter query; grouping and sorting in a report; adding fields to a report; including a subreport in a report; adding a date and page number to a report; and creating and printing mailing labels.

Project 8 – Using Visual Basic for Applications (VBA) and Advanced Form Techniques In Project 8, students learn to use Visual Basic for Applications (VBA) as well as advanced techniques for creating forms. Topics include adding command buttons to forms; modifying VBA code associated with a command button; adding a combo box to a form that will be used for searching; modifying the properties of the combo box; using the combo box to search; general VBA concepts; creating functions in a standard module in VBA; testing functions; using functions in queries and forms; associating code with events; creating Sub procedures in VBA; creating functions to run commands; creating a form using Design view; adding a tab control to a form; adding a subform control to a form; adding charts to a form; and adding an ActiveX control to a form.

Project 9 – Administering a Database System In Project 9, students learn the issues and techniques involved in administering a database system. Topics include converting a database to other versions of Access; using the Table Analyzer, Performance Analyzer, and Documenter; creating a custom input mask; specifying referential integrity options; setting startup options; setting and removing passwords; encrypting a database; creating and presenting information in PivotTable view and PivotChart view; creating and using a replica; synchronizing a Design Master and a replica; creating and running SQL commands; splitting a database; creating an MDE file; and specifying user-level security.

Integration Feature – Grouped Data Access Pages, PivotTables, and PivotCharts In this Integration Feature, students learn how to create grouped data access pages as well as data access pages containing PivotTables and PivotCharts. Topics include creating a grouped data access page in Design view; using a grouped data access page, creating a data access page containing a PivotTable; using a data access page containing a PivotTable; saving a PivotChart as a data access page; and using a data access page containing a PivotChart.

Microsoft PowerPoint 2002

The final Microsoft Office XP software application covered in this textbook is Microsoft PowerPoint 2002. The material is presented in two advanced projects and a Web Feature.

Project 5 – Working with Macros and Visual Basic for Applications (VBA) In Project 5, students use VBA to develop an electronic career portfolio designed for viewing during a job interview. The slides are customized for each interview and include a digital picture and a video clip. Topics include creating a new toolbar and adding buttons; using the macro recorder to create a macro that prints a pure black and white handout displaying four slides per page; assigning the macro to a command on the File menu; and creating a user interface.

Project 6 – Creating a Self-Running Presentation Containing Interactive Documents In Project 6, students create a self-running presentation to view at a kiosk. The slides contain action buttons and hyperlinks to a Visual Basic program, an Excel chart, and a Word table. Topics include inserting a slide from another presentation; applying custom animation; using guides to position objects; setting slide timings manually; and inserting, formatting, and animating a diagram and an AutoShape.

Web Feature – Importing Clips and Templates from the Microsoft Web Site In this Web Feature, students are introduced to downloading clips and design templates from a source on the Internet and adding them to a presentation. Topics include connecting to the Microsoft Web site; searching for and downloading clips and templates; and importing clips into a presentation.

Appendices

The book includes five appendices. Appendix A presents an introduction to the Microsoft Office XP Help system. Appendix B describes how to use the speech and handwriting recognition capabilities of Office XP. Appendix C explains how to publish Web pages to a Web server. Appendix D shows how to reset the menus and toolbars. Appendix E introduces students to the Microsoft Office User Specialist (MOUS) Certification program.

Quick Reference Summary

In Office XP, you can accomplish a task in a number of ways, such as using the mouse, menu, shortcut menu, and keyboard. The Quick Reference Summary at the back of the book provides a quick reference to each task presented in this book and its companion books *Microsoft Office XP: Introductory Concepts and Techniques* and *Microsoft Office XP: Advanced Concepts and Techniques*.

End-of-Project Student Activities

A notable strength of the Shelly Cashman Series *Microsoft Office XP* books is the extensive student activities at the end of each project. Well-structured student activities can make the difference between students merely participating in a class and students retaining the information they learn. The activities in the Shelly Cashman Series *Microsoft Office XP* books include the following:

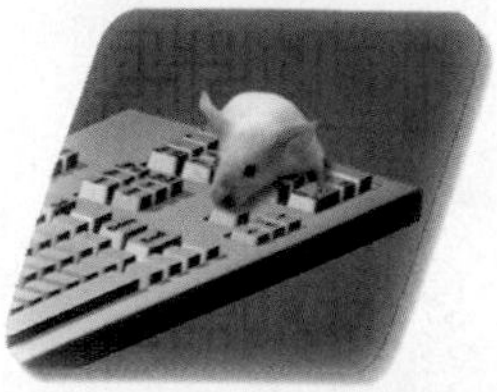

- What You Should Know A listing of the tasks completed within a project together with the pages on which the step-by-step, screen-by-screen explanations appear.
- Learn It Online Every project features a Learn It Online page comprised of ten exercises. These exercises include True/False, Multiple Choice, Short Answer, Flash Cards, Practice Test, Learning Games, Tips and Tricks, Newsgroup usage, Expanding Your Horizons, and Search Sleuth.
- Apply Your Knowledge This exercise usually requires students to open and manipulate a file on the Data Disk. To obtain a copy of the Data Disk, follow the instructions on the inside back cover of this textbook.
- In the Lab Three in-depth assignments per project require students to apply the knowledge gained in the project to solve problems on a computer.
- Cases and Places Up to seven unique real-world case-study situations.

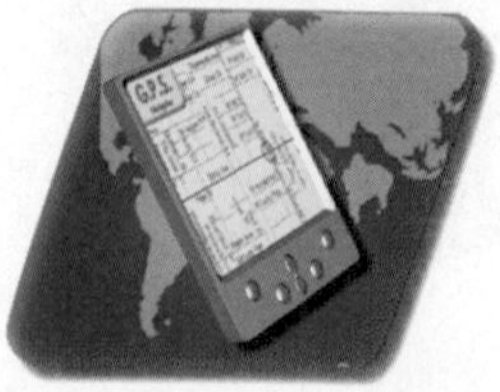

Shelly Cashman Series Teaching Tools

The three basic ancillaries that accompany this textbook are: Teaching Tools (ISBN 0-7895-6323-1), Course Presenter (ISBN 0-7895-6466-1), and MyCourse.com. These ancillaries are available to adopters through your Course Technology representative or by calling one of the following telephone numbers: Colleges and Universities, 1-800-648-7450; High Schools, 1-800-824-5179; Private Career Colleges, 1-800-477-3692; Canada, 1-800-268-2222; and Corporations and Government Agencies, 1-800-340-7450.

Teaching Tools

The contents of the Teaching Tools CD-ROM are listed below.

- **Instructor's Manual** The Instructor's Manual includes the following for each project: project objectives; project overview; detailed lesson plans with page number references; teacher notes and activities; answers to the end-of-project exercises; a test bank of 110 questions for every project (25 multiple-choice, 50 true/false, and 35 fill-in-the-blank) with page number references; and transparency references. The transparencies are available through the Figures in the Book. The test bank questions are the same as in ExamView and Course Test Manager.
- **Figures in the Book** Illustrations for every screen and table in the textbook are available in electronic form. Use this ancillary to present a slide show in lecture or to print transparencies for use in lecture with an overhead projector.
- **ExamView** ExamView is a state-of-the-art test builder that is easy to use. With ExamView, you quickly can create printed tests, Internet tests, and computer (LAN-based) tests. You can enter your own test questions or use the test bank that accompanies ExamView. The test bank is the same as the one described in the Instructor's Manual section. Instructors who want to continue to use our earlier generation test builder, Course Test Manager, rather than ExamView, can call Customer Service at 1-800-648-7450 for a copy of the Course Test Manager database for this book.
- **Course Syllabus** Any instructor who has been assigned a course at the last minute knows how difficult it is to come up with a course syllabus. For this reason, sample syllabi are included that can be customized easily to a course.
- **Lecture Success System** Lecture Success System files are used to explain and illustrate the step-by-step, screen-by-screen development of a project in the textbook without entering large amounts of data.
- **Instructor's Lab Solutions** Solutions and required files for all the In the Lab assignments at the end of each project are available. Solutions also are available for any Cases and Places assignment that supplies data.
- **Lab Tests/Test Outs** Tests that parallel the In the Lab assignments are supplied for the purpose of testing students in the laboratory on the material covered in the project or testing students out of the course.
- **Project Reinforcement** True/false, multiple choice, and short answer questions.
- **Student Files** All the files that are required by students to complete the Apply Your Knowledge exercises are included.
- **Interactive Labs** Eighteen completely updated, hands-on Interactive Labs that take students from ten to fifteen minutes each to step through help solidify and reinforce mouse and keyboard usage and computer concepts. Student assessment is available.

Course Presenter

Course Presenter is a lecture presentation system that provides PowerPoint slides for each project. Presentations are based on the projects' objectives. Use this presentation system to present well-organized lectures that are both interesting and knowledge-based. Course Presenter provides consistent coverage at schools that use multiple lecturers in their applications courses.

MyCourse.com

MyCourse.com offers instructors and students an opportunity to supplement classroom learning with additional course content. You can use MyCourse.com to expand on traditional learning by completing readings, tests, and other assignments through the customized, comprehensive Web site. For additional information, visit MyCourse.com and click the Help button.

SAM XP

SAM XP is a powerful skills-based testing and reporting tool that measures your students' proficiency in Microsoft Office applications through real-world, performance-based questions. SAM XP is available for a minimal cost.

TOM, Training Online Manager for Microsoft Office XP

TOM is Course Technology's MOUS-approved training tool for Microsoft Office XP. Available via the World Wide Web and CD-ROM, TOM allows students to actively learn Office XP concepts and skills by delivering realistic practice through both guided and self-directed simulated instruction.

Acknowledgments

The Shelly Cashman Series would not be the leading computer education series without the contributions of outstanding publishing professionals. First, and foremost, among them is Becky Herrington, director of production and designer. She is the heart and soul of the Shelly Cashman Series, and it is only through her leadership, dedication, and tireless efforts that superior products are made possible.

Under Becky's direction, the following individuals made significant contributions to these books: Doug Cowley, production manager; Ginny Harvey, series specialist and developmental editor; Ken Russo, senior Web and graphic designer; Mike Bodnar, associate production manager; Mark Norton, Web designer; Betty Hopkins and Richard Herrera, interior design; Michelle French, Christy Otten, Kellee LaVars, Stephanie Nance, Chris Schneider, Sharon Lee Nelson, Sarah Boger, Amanda Lotter, Michael Greco, and Ryan Ung, graphic artists; Jeanne Black and Betty Hopkins, QuarkXPress compositors; Lyn Markowicz, Nancy Lamm, Kim Kosmatka, Pam Baxter, Eva Kandarpa, Ellana Russo, and Marilyn Martin, copy editors/proofreaders; Cristina Haley, proofreader/indexer; Sarah Evertson of Image Quest, photo researcher; and Ginny Harvey, Rich Hansberger, Kim Clark, Nancy Smith, contributing writers; and Richard Herrera, cover art.

Finally, we would like to thank Richard Keaveny, associate publisher; Cheryl Ouellette, managing editor; Jim Quasney, series consulting editor; Alexandra Arnold, product manager; Erin Runyon, associate product manager; Francis Schurgot and Marc Ouellette, Web product managers; Rachel VanKirk, marketing manager; and Reed Cotter, editorial assistant.

Gary B. Shelly Thomas J. Cashman Misty E. Vermaat

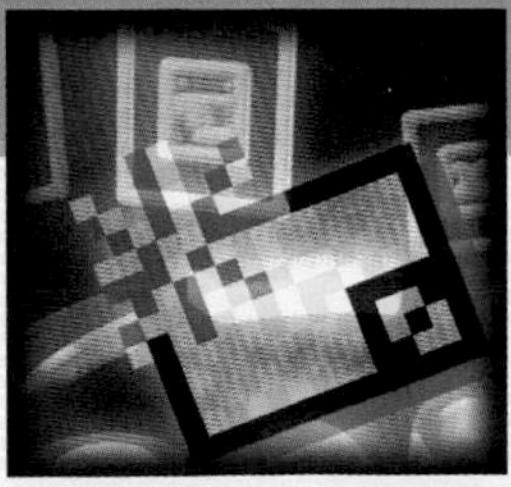

Microsoft Word 2002

PROJECT 7

Creating an Online Form

You will have mastered the material in this project when you can:

OBJECTIVES

- Design an online form
- Create a document template
- Highlight text
- Insert a table into a form
- Insert a text form field into a form
- Insert a drop-down form field into a form
- Insert a check box into a form
- Format form fields
- Use the Format Painter button
- Add Help text to form fields
- Insert and format a rectangle drawing object
- Animate text
- Protect a form
- Open a new document based on a template
- Fill out a form
- Save data on a form in a text file
- Modify the location of workgroup templates

Virtual Shoppers

Find the Perfect Fit

Today's virtual individual enjoys the convenience of Internet shopping; communicating with friends, family, and colleagues via e-mail; researching information for school projects and work assignments; and participating in a myriad of other online activities.

No other facet of the Internet has garnered more interest than e-commerce. With hunderds of e-consumers attracted to the vast numbers of sales channels from e-retail to e-financial, sales are in the billions of dollars. Buying online is a bit more complicated, however, when it comes to purchasing clothing. Without the ability to try on the selected garments, how can you be sure of the fit?

This logistical problem can be frustrating to shoppers who are expected to spend $13 billion online for apparel by 2003.

Lands' End has come up with a solution to these virtual shopping woes. This Wisconsin-based direct merchant of traditional, casual clothes has developed Your Personal Model, a personalized 3-D representation of female customers that selects the most flattering clothes for their figures, suggests specific outfits for various occasions, and provides an online dressing room to try on the garments.

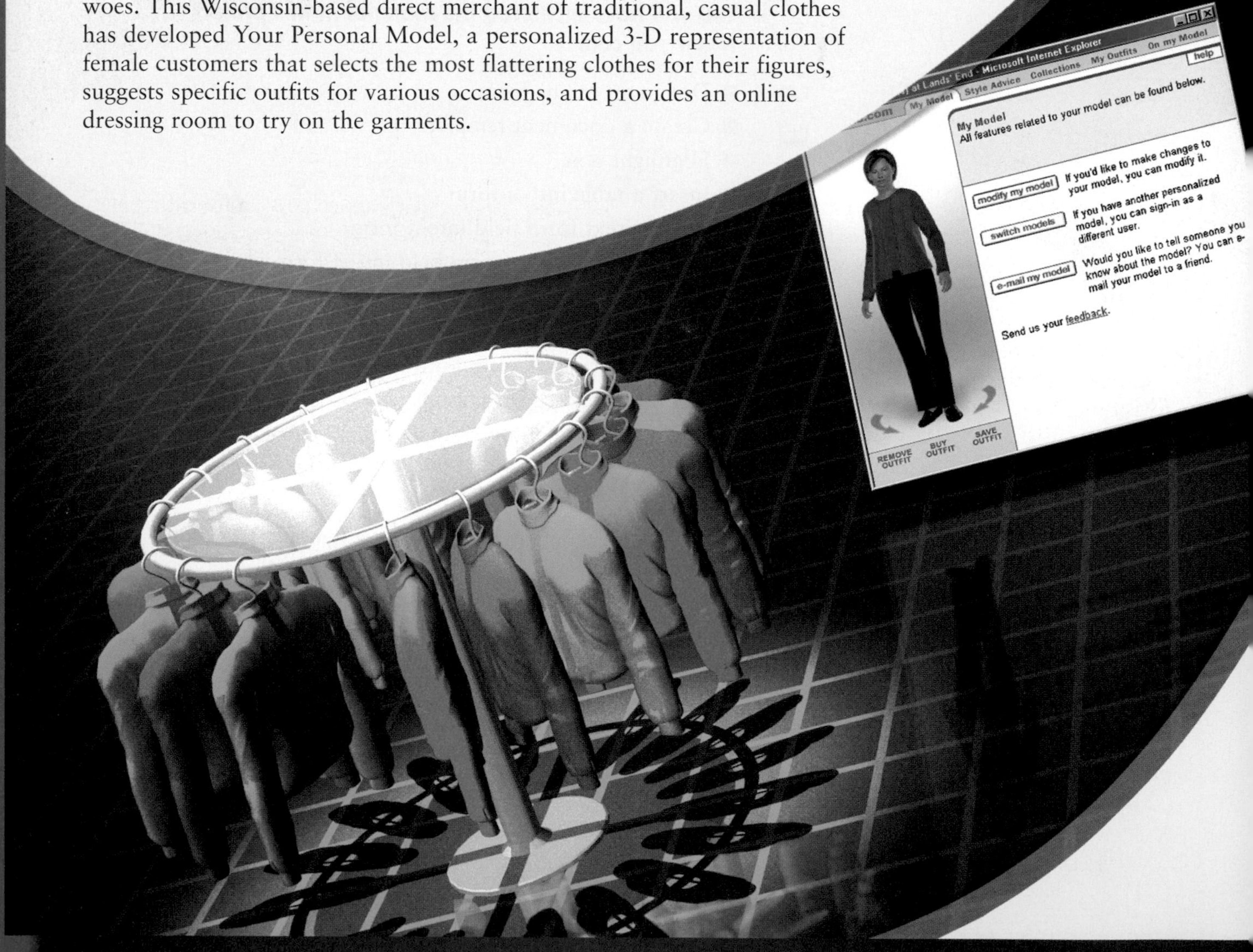

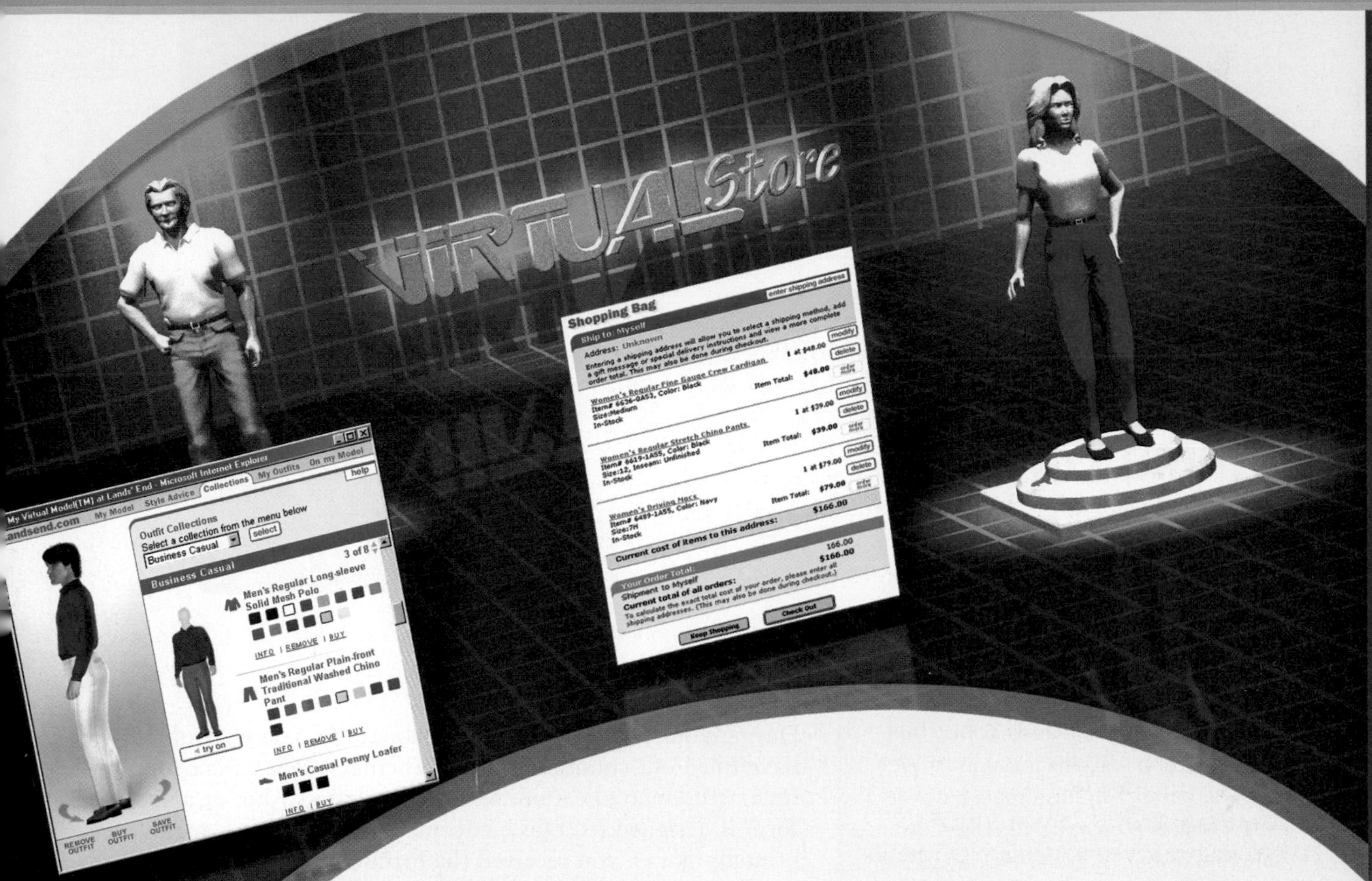

Shoppers begin their Your Personal Model shopping adventure by answering several questions regarding their physical features, such as specific skin tones, face shapes, hairstyles, and hair colors. They save their profiles for future shopping sprees, and proceed to the Welcome Page.

At this point, their models appear along with custom outfits designed for their bodies and for their lifestyles. The site may make suggestions for specific occasions such as gray Chinos and a beige sweater set for a casual workplace and a simple black knit dress for an informal weekend party.

The next step is to take these garments to The Dressing Room. There, the shoppers can view the particular clothes on their models. The site gives advice on choosing the proper size and then places the items in the customers' virtual shopping carts.

Ordering is easy. If they use Your Personal Model, the contents of their shopping carts display automatically in an order form.

Gary C. Comer, an avid sailor and advertising copywriter, founded Lands' End in 1961 in Chicago to sell sailing equipment and hardware via a catalog. In the 1970s, the company's focus switched to clothing. Today, Lands' End is the second largest apparel mail-order company with sales of more than $1.37 billion to its 6.1 million customers. The Lands' End Web site (www.landsend.com) was unveiled in 1995 and receives 15 million visitors yearly.

Internet shopping has created an important focus for the use of forms and online communication. In Project 7, you will develop a form by creating a template in Word 2002. The form will be structured as a survey in order to gather information and opinions from Web customers of Brim's Blooming Boutique. Survey information will provide an assessment of order types, customer satisfaction, and online convenience. As a result of the survey, changes may be implemented and successes enhanced.

With increasingly more people using computers in the home, school, and workplace, the use of well-thought-out online forms provides the ability to complete successfully many aspects of course work, vocational activities, and personal interests.

Microsoft Word 2002

Creating an Online Form

PROJECT 7

CASE PERSPECTIVE

For the past two years, Brim's Blooming Boutique has allowed customers to order flowers, plants, teddy bears, fruit baskets, and other gifts through its Web site. The number of customers placing orders online is growing rapidly. Carol Brim, the owner of Brim's Blooming Boutique, believes the Web site is easy to use. She wants to be sure, however, that customers have the same opinion. Carol knows that a satisfied customer is one who will return for more business.

Today, you receive a call from Carol, who is Aunt Carol to you. She knows you are majoring in Office Automation at school and wonders if you could create a survey to e-mail to all Web customers. The survey should ask for the customer's name, an opinion of the Web site navigation, the time it takes to shop, and the type of orders placed on the Web. You welcome the opportunity to help Aunt Carol. Designing and distributing the surveys will be fun. Once the completed surveys are returned, you will tabulate the responses and print them in a report for your favorite aunt.

Introduction

During your personal and professional life, you undoubtedly have filled out countless forms. Whether a federal tax form, a time card, an application, an order, a deposit slip, or a survey, a form is designed to collect information. In the past, forms were printed; that is, you received the form on a piece of paper, filled it in with a pen or pencil, and then returned it manually.

Today, people are concerned with using resources efficiently. To minimize waste of paper, save the world's trees, improve office efficiency, and improve access to data, many businesses attempt to become a paperless office. Thus, the online form has emerged. With an **online form**, you access the form using your computer, fill it out using the computer, and then return it via the computer. You may access the form at a Web site, on your company's intranet, or from your inbox if you receive it via e-mail.

Not only does an online form reduce the need for paper, it saves the time spent duplicating a form and distributing it. With more and more people owning a home computer, online forms have become a popular means of collecting personal information, as well. In Word, you easily can create an online form for distribution electronically, which then can be filled in using Word.

Project Seven — Online Form

Project 7 uses Word to create the online form shown in Figure 7-1. The form is a survey e-mailed to all Web customers of Brim's Blooming Boutique. Upon receipt of the form, customers fill it in, save it, and then e-mail it back to the boutique. Figure 7-1a shows how the form displays on a customer's screen initially (as a blank form); Figure 7-1b shows the form partially filled in by one customer; and Figure 7-1c shows how the customer filled in the entire form.

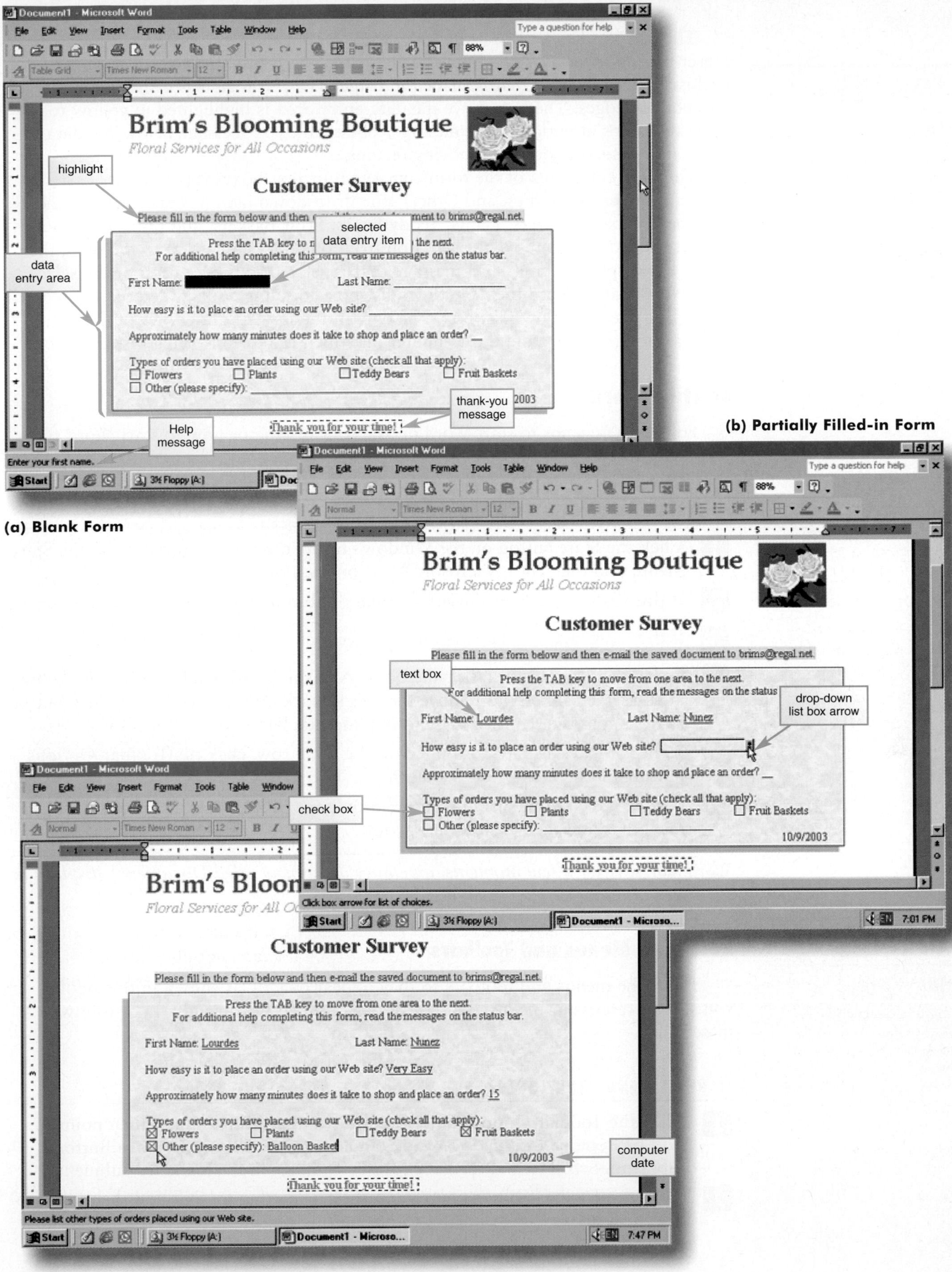

(a) Blank Form

(b) Partially Filled-in Form

(c) Filled-In Form

FIGURE 7-1

The form is designed so it fits completely within the Word window — without a user having to scroll while filling in the form. The **data entry area** of the form is enclosed by a rectangle that is shaded in beige. The rectangle has a shadow on its left and bottom edges. The line above the data entry area is highlighted in yellow to draw the user's attention to the message. The thank-you message below the data entry area is surrounded by a moving rectangle.

The data entry area of the form contains four text boxes (First Name, Last Name, number of minutes, and Other), one drop-down list box (ease of use), and five check boxes (Flowers, Plants, Teddy Bears, Fruit Baskets, and Other). As a user presses the TAB key to move the selection from one data entry item to the next, the status bar displays a brief Help message that is related to the location of the selection. Note that in Word the drop-down list box does not display the box arrow until you tab to the drop-down list box. The date in the lower-right corner of the data entry area is the date from the computer on which the form is being displayed.

> More About
>
> **Online Forms**
>
> For a sample online form on the Web, visit the Word 2002 More About Web page (www.scsite.com/wd2002/more.htm) and then click Sample Online Form.

Starting Word

Follow these steps to start Word or ask your instructor how to start Word for your system.

TO START AND CUSTOMIZE WORD

1. Click the Start button on the Windows taskbar, point to Programs on the Start menu, and then click Microsoft Word on the Programs submenu.
2. If the Word window is not maximized, double-click its title bar to maximize it.
3. If the Language bar displays on the screen, click its Minimize button.
4. If the New Document task pane displays in the Word window, click the Show at startup check box to remove the check mark and then click the Close button in the upper-right corner of the task pane title bar.
5. If the toolbars display positioned on the same row, click the Toolbar Options button and then click Show Buttons on Two Rows.
6. If your screen differs from Figure 7-3 on page WD 7.09, click View on the menu bar and then click Print Layout.

Word starts. After a few moments, an empty document titled Document1 displays in the Word window (shown in Figure 7-3).

> More About
>
> **Fields**
>
> For more information about fields, visit the Word 2002 More About Web page (www.scsite.com/wd2002/more.htm) and then click Fields.

Resetting Menus and Toolbars

To set the menus and toolbars so they appear exactly as shown in this book, you should reset your menus and toolbars as outlined in Appendix D or follow these steps.

TO RESET MENUS AND TOOLBARS

1. Click the Toolbar Options button on the Standard toolbar and then point to Add or Remove Buttons. Point to Standard on the Add or Remove Buttons submenu. Scroll to and then click Reset Toolbar on the Standard submenu.
2. Click the Toolbar Options button on the Formatting toolbar and then point to Add or Remove Buttons. Point to Formatting on the Add or Remove Buttons submenu. Scroll to and then click Reset Toolbar on the Formatting submenu.

3 Click the Toolbar Options button on the Standard toolbar and then point to Add or Remove Buttons. Click Customize on the Add or Remove Buttons submenu.

4 When the Customize dialog box displays, if necessary, click the Options tab and then click the Reset my usage data button. When the Microsoft Word dialog box displays, click the Yes button. Click the Close button in the Customize dialog box.

Word resets the menus and toolbars.

Displaying Formatting Marks

It is helpful to display formatting marks that indicate where in the document you pressed the ENTER key, SPACEBAR, and other keys. Perform the following step to display formatting marks.

TO DISPLAY FORMATTING MARKS

1 If the Show/Hide ¶ button on the Standard toolbar is not selected already, click it.

Word displays formatting marks in the document window, and the Show/Hide ¶ button on the Standard toolbar is selected (shown in Figure 7-3 on page WD 7.09).

Zooming Page Width

When you zoom page width, Word displays the page on the screen as large as possible in print layout view. Perform the following steps to zoom page width.

TO ZOOM PAGE WIDTH

1 Click the Zoom box arrow on the Standard toolbar.

2 Click Page Width in the Zoom list.

Word computes the zoom percentage and displays it in the Zoom box (shown in Figure 7-3). Your percentage may be different depending on your computer.

Designing an Online Form

To minimize the time spent creating a form on the computer, you should sketch it on a piece of paper first. A design for the online form in this project is shown in Figure 7-2 on the next page.

During the **form design**, you should create a well-thought-out draft of the form that attempts to include all essential form elements. These elements include the form's title, placement of text and graphics, instructions for users of the form, and field specifications. A **field** is a placeholder for data. A **field specification** defines characteristics of a field such as the field's type, length, format, and a list of possible values that may be entered into the field. Many designers place Xs in fields where a user will be allowed to enter any type of character, and 9s in fields where a user will be allowed to enter numbers only. For example, in Figure 7-2, a user can enter up to 15 of any type of character in the First Name text box and up to two numbers in the number of minutes text box.

More About

Forms

Both Microsoft Word and Microsoft Access allow you to create forms and templates that contain complex formatting, pictures, check boxes, drop-down lists, or text areas. You can assign specific data types, formatting, and default text. You also can set conditions for adding data to a form, include macros that run automatically, and provide Help messages that make it easier for others to complete a form. Both programs allow you to create forms for online use, as well as forms to print on paper.

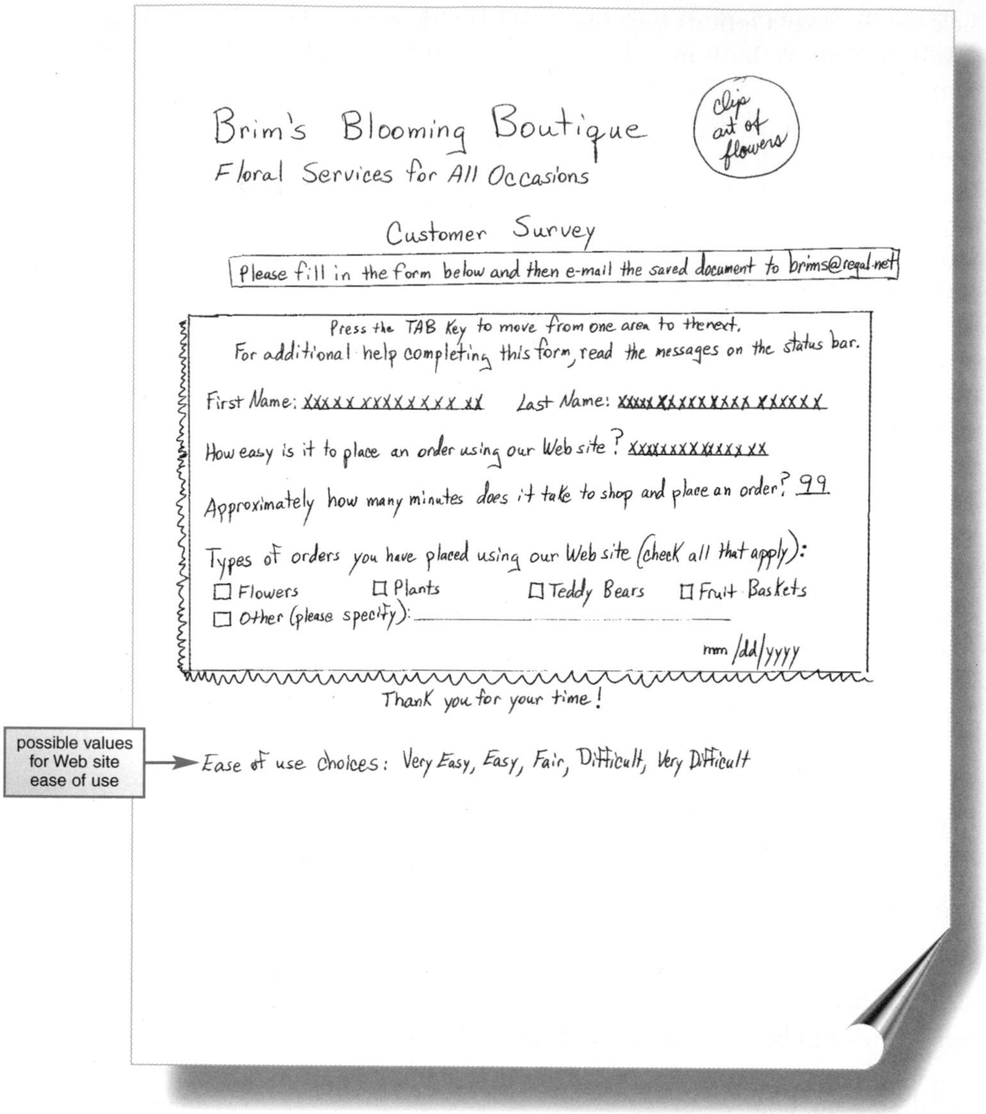

Brim's Blooming Boutique
Floral Services for All Occasions
clip art of flowers
Customer Survey
Please fill in the form below and then e-mail the saved document to brims@regal.net
Press the TAB Key to move from one area to the next.
For additional help completing this form, read the messages on the status bar.
First Name: XXXXX XXXXXXXXX XX
Last Name: XXXXXXXXXXXXXX XXXXXX
How easy is it to place an order using our Web site? XXXXXXXXXXXXXX
Approximately how many minutes does it take to shop and place an order? 99
Types of orders you have placed using our Web site (check all that apply):
Flowers
Plants
Teddy Bears
Fruit Baskets
Other (please specify):
mm/dd/yyyy
Thank you for your time!
possible values for Web site ease of use
Ease of use choices: Very Easy, Easy, Fair, Difficult, Very Difficult

FIGURE 7-2

With this draft of the form in hand, the next step is to create the form in Word.

> **More About**
>
> **Protected Forms**
>
> If you open an existing form that has been protected, Word will not allow you to modify the form's appearance until you unprotect it. To unprotect a document, click Tools on the menu bar and then click Unprotect Document. If the form has been password-protected, you will be asked to enter a password when you invoke the Unprotect Document command.

Creating an Online Form

The process of creating an online form begins with creating a template. Next, you insert and format any text, graphics, and fields where data is to be entered on the form. Finally, before you save the form for electronic distribution, you protect it. With a **protected form**, users can enter data only where you have placed form fields; that is, they will not be able to modify any other items on the form. Many menu commands and toolbar buttons are dimmed, and thus unavailable, in a protected form. The steps on the following pages illustrate how to create an online form.

Creating a Template

A **template** is a file that contains the definition of the appearance of a Word document, including items such as default font, font size, margin settings, and line spacing; available styles; and even placement of text. Every Word document you create is based on a template. When you select Blank Document in the New Document task pane or when you click the New Blank Document button on the Standard toolbar, Word creates a document based on the Normal template. Word also provides other templates for more specific types of documents such as memos, letters, and fax cover sheets. Creating a document based on these templates can improve your productivity because Word has defined much of the document's appearance for you.

If you create and save an online form as a Word document that is based on the Normal template, users will be required to open that Word document to display the form on the screen. Next, they will fill in the form. Then, to preserve the content of the original form, they will have to save the form with a new file name. If they accidentally click the Save button on the Standard toolbar, Word will replace the original blank form with a filled-in form.

If you create and save the online form as a **document template** instead, users will open a new document window that is based on that template. This displays the form on the screen as a brand new Word document; that is, the document does not have a file name. Thus, the user fills in the form and then simply saves it. By using a template for the form, the original form remains intact when the user clicks the Save button.

Perform the following steps to create a document template to be used for the online form and then save the template with the name Brim's Survey.

> **More About**
>
> **Templates**
>
> Most documents have a file name and a three-character file extension. When a file extension displays, it is separated from the file name with a period. The extension, sometimes called the file type, often is assigned by an application, which helps Windows open the file with the correct software. For example, a Word document has an extension of doc, and a Word template has an extension of dot. Thus, a file named Finance Report.doc is a Word document, and a file named Learning Survey.dot is a Word template.

Steps To Create a Document Template

1 Click File on the menu bar and then click New. When the New Document task pane displays, click General Templates. When the Templates dialog box displays, if necessary, click the General tab. Click the Blank Document icon and then click Template in the Create New area. Point to the OK button.

Word displays the Templates dialog box (Figure 7-3). The Template option button instructs Word to create a new template, instead of a new Word document.

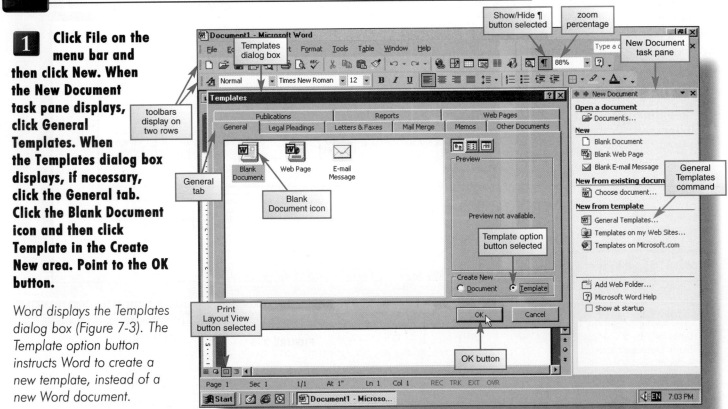

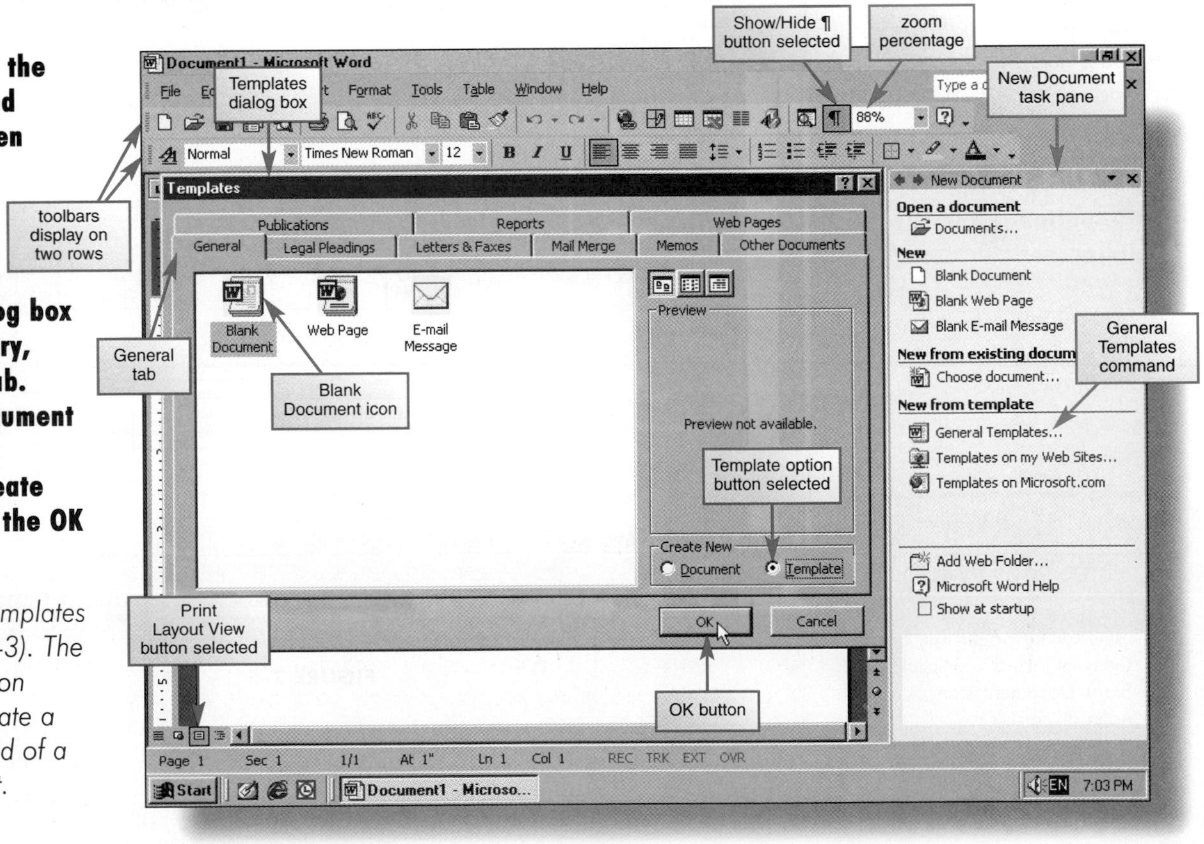

FIGURE 7-3

2 **Click the OK button.**

Word displays a blank template titled Template1 in the Word window (Figure 7-4).

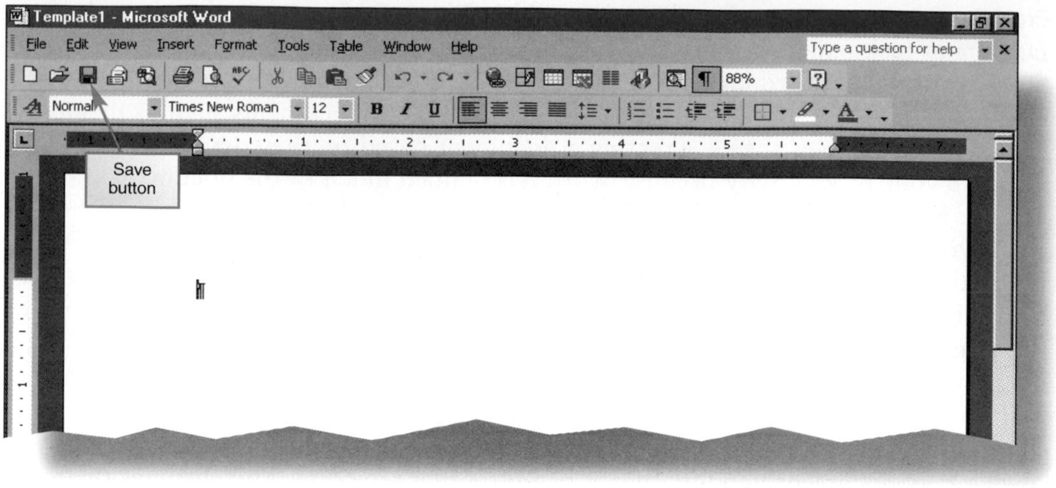

FIGURE 7-4

3 **With a disk in drive A, click the Save button on the Standard toolbar. Type** `Brim's Survey` **in the File name text box. If necessary, click the Save in box arrow and then click 3½ Floppy (A:). Point to the Save button in the Save As dialog box.**

Word displays the Save As dialog box with Document Template listed in the Save as type box (Figure 7-5).

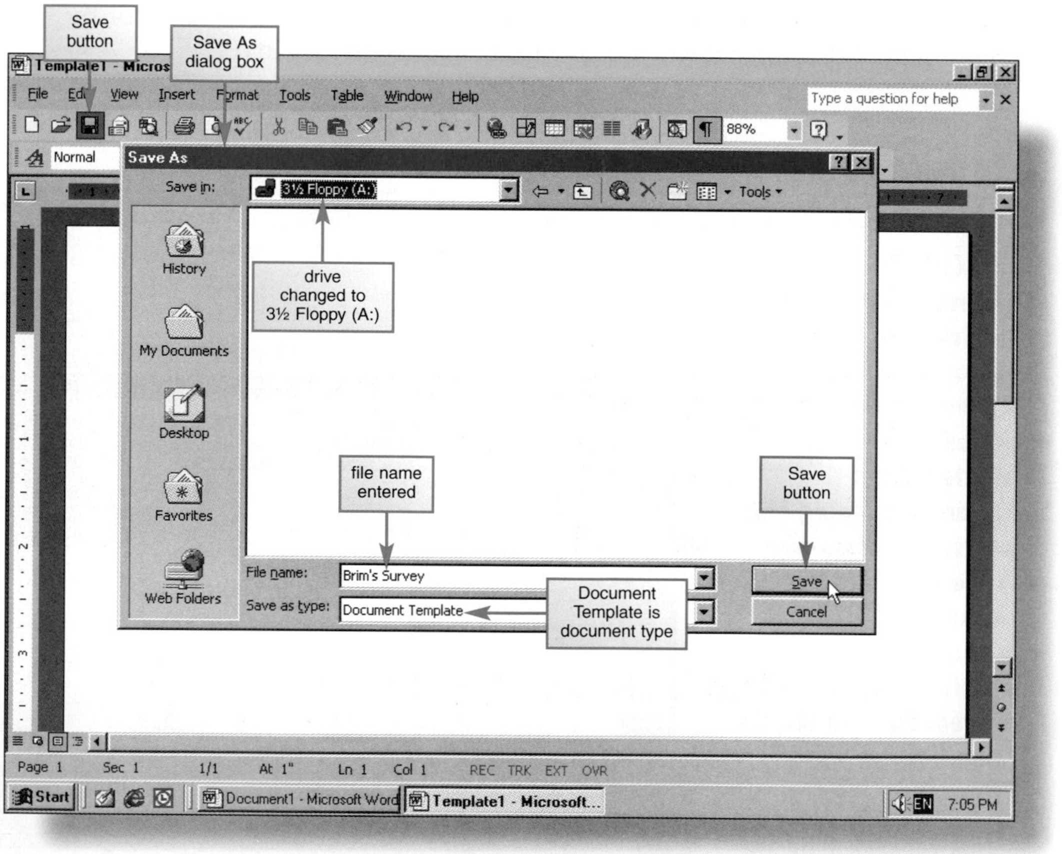

FIGURE 7-5

4 **Click the Save button in the Save As dialog box.**

Word saves the template on the floppy disk in drive A with the file name, Brim's Survey (shown in Figure 7-6).

Other Ways

1. Click Start button on Windows taskbar, click New Office Document, click General tab, double-click Blank Document icon
2. Right-click Start button on Windows taskbar, click Open, double-click New Office Document, click General tab, double-click Blank Document icon
3. With task pane displaying, in Voice Command mode, say "General Templates, General, [select Blank Document icon], OK"

The next step in creating the online form is to enter the text, graphics, and fields into the template. Perform the following steps to format and enter the boutique name, business tag line, and survey title.

TO ENTER AND FORMAT TEXT

1. Click the Font box arrow on the Formatting toolbar, scroll to and then click Book Antiqua. Click the Font Size box arrow on the Formatting toolbar and then click 28. Click the Font Color button arrow on the Formatting toolbar and then click Violet. Press CTRL+B to turn on bold formatting. Type `Brim's Blooming Boutique` and then press CTRL+B to turn off bold formatting. Press the ENTER key.
2. Click the Font box arrow on the Formatting toolbar and then click Times New Roman. Click the Font Size box arrow on the Formatting toolbar and then click 16. Click the Font Color button arrow on the Formatting toolbar and then click Sea Green. Press CTRL+I to turn on italic formatting. Type `Floral Services for All Occasions` and then press CTRL+I to turn off italic formatting. Press the ENTER key twice.
3. Click the Font Size box arrow on the Formatting toolbar and then click 22. Click the Font Color button arrow on the Formatting toolbar and then click Violet. Press CTRL+B to turn on bold formatting. Press CTRL+E to center the paragraph. Type `Customer Survey` and then press CTRL+B to turn off bold formatting. Press the ENTER key.

The boutique name, business tag line, and survey title display as shown in Figure 7-6.

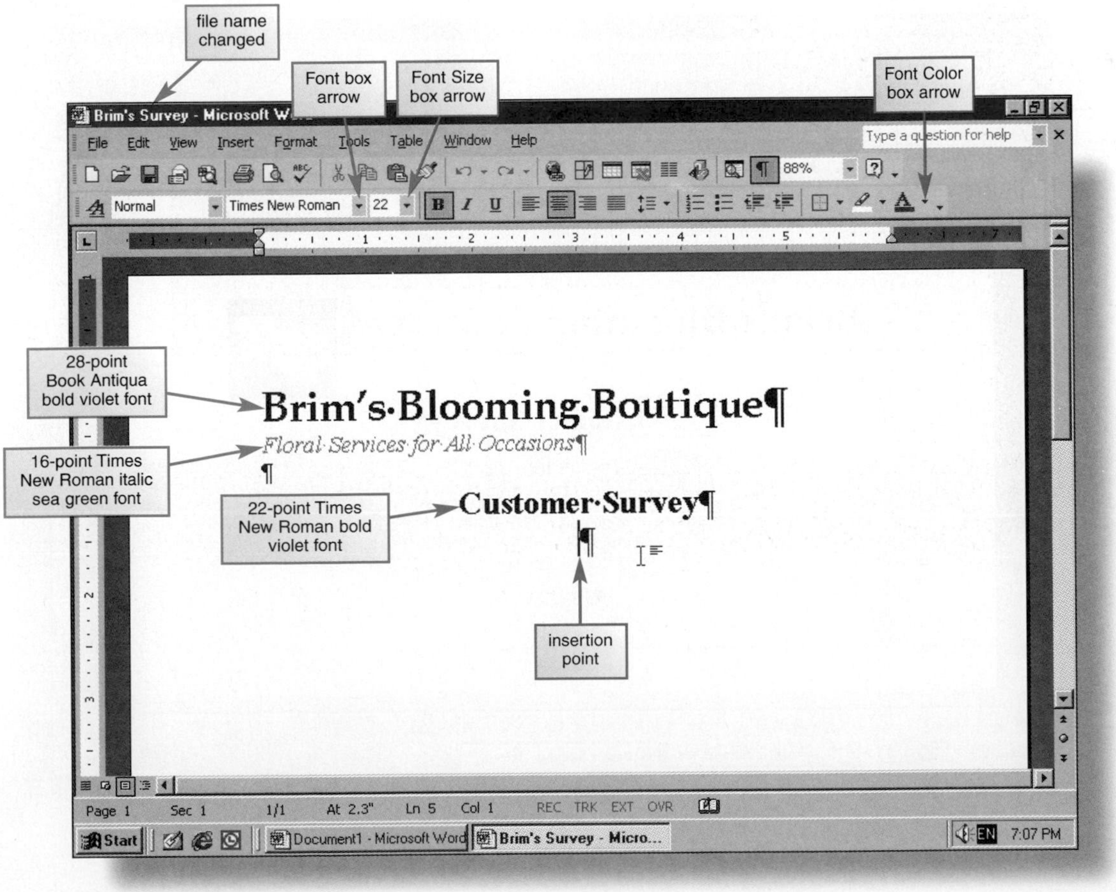

FIGURE 7-6

The next step is to insert the clip art of the flowers. Word inserts clip art as an inline graphic; that is, part of the current paragraph. You want to position the image of the flowers to the right of the boutique name (Figure 7-1 on page WD 7.05). Thus, the graphic needs to be a floating graphic instead of an inline graphic. Also, the graphic is too large for this form. Thus, after you insert the graphic you will reduce its size and change its wrapping style to Square, as described in the following steps.

More About

Designing Questionnaires

For more information on how to design a good questionnaire, visit the Word 2002 More About Web page (www.scsite.com/wd2002/more.htm) and then click Designing Questionnaires.

TO INSERT AND FORMAT CLIP ART

1. With the insertion point on line 5, click Insert on the menu bar, point to Picture, and then click Clip Art. When the Insert Clip Art task pane displays, drag through any text in the Search text text box. Type `flowers` and then press the ENTER key.
2. Point to the clip of the flowers that matches the one shown in Figure 7-7. Click the box arrow that displays to the right of the clip and then click Insert on the menu. Click the Close button on the Insert Clip Art task pane title bar.
3. Double-click the graphic. When the Format Picture dialog box displays, if necessary, click the Size tab. Change the Height and Width in the Scale area to 50%.
4. Click the Layout tab and then click Square in the Wrapping style area. Click the OK button. Drag the flowers graphic to the right of the boutique name as shown in Figure 7-7.
5. Position the insertion point on the paragraph mark on line 5.

The graphic displays on the form, as shown in Figure 7-7.

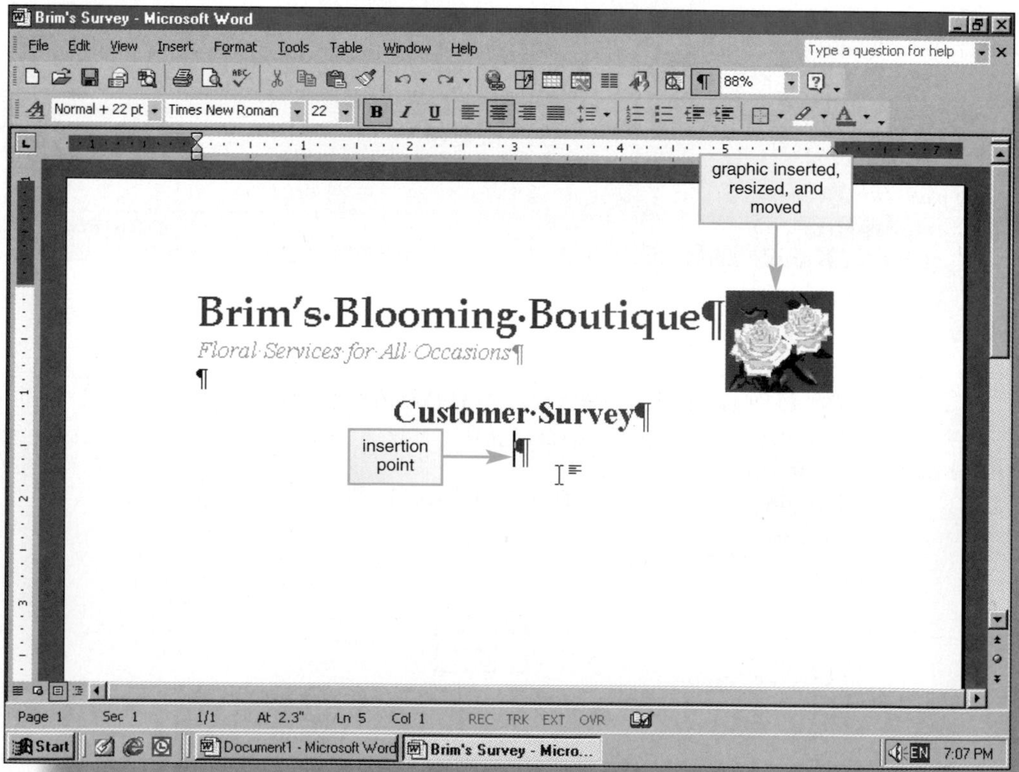

FIGURE 7-7

The next step is to enter the instructions and then highlight them in yellow.

Highlighting Text

You **highlight** text in an online document to alert the reader to the text's importance, much like a highlight marker does in a book. You want to draw attention to the instructions that specify where to mail the completed form. Thus, you highlight this line.

Perform the following steps to highlight text in a document.

More About

Removing Highlights

To remove all highlights from a document, click Edit on the menu bar, click Select All, click the Highlight button arrow, and then click None. To remove an individual highlight, select the text from which you wish to remove the highlight, click the Highlight button arrow, and then click None.

Steps To Highlight Text

1 Click the Font Size box arrow on the Formatting toolbar and then click 12. Click the Font Color button arrow on the Formatting toolbar and then click Automatic. Press the ENTER key. Type `Please fill in the form below and then e-mail the saved document to brims@regal.net.` **Press the ENTER key. Right-click the hyperlink and then click Remove Hyperlink on the shortcut menu. If the Highlight button on the Formatting toolbar displays yellow on its face, click the Highlight button; otherwise, click the Highlight button arrow and then click Yellow. Position the mouse pointer in the document window.**

The Highlight button is selected and displays yellow on its face (Figure 7-8). The mouse pointer displays as an I-beam with a highlighter attached to it.

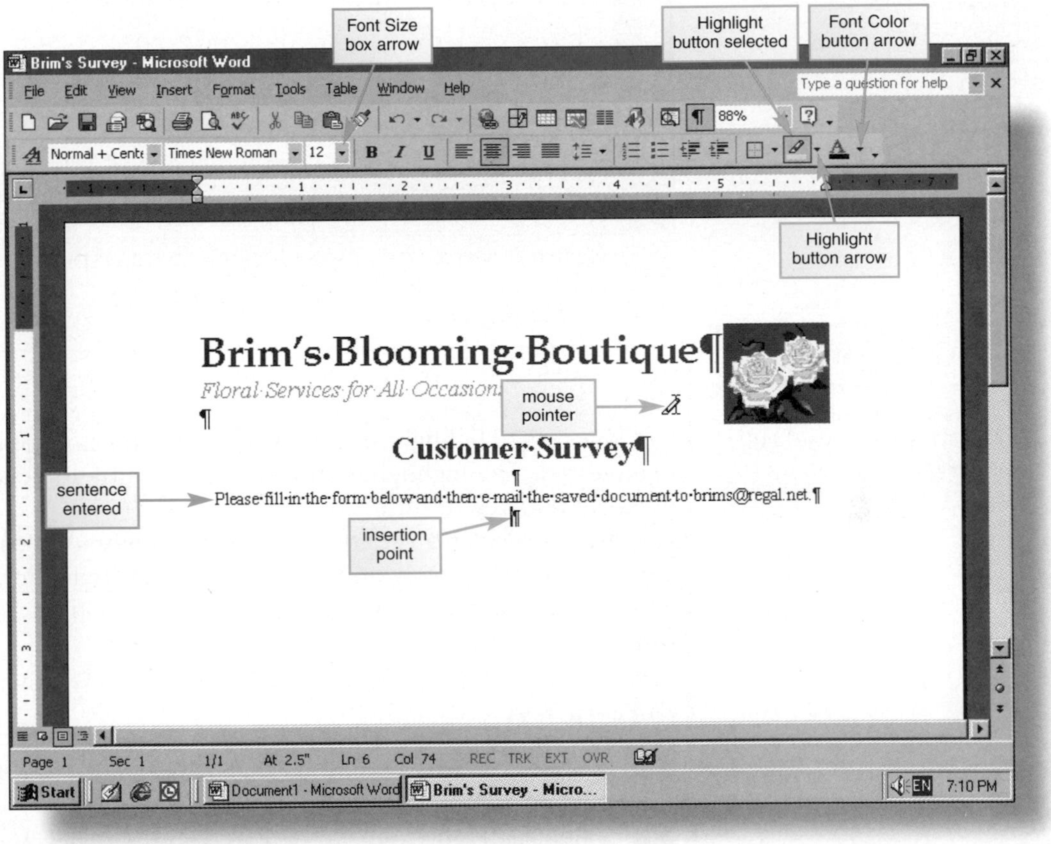

FIGURE 7-8

2 **Click to the left of the sentence or drag through the sentence to highlight it.**

Word highlights the selected text in yellow (Figure 7-9). The Highlight button remains selected.

3 **Click the Highlight button on the Formatting toolbar to turn highlighting off (shown in Figure 7-10).**

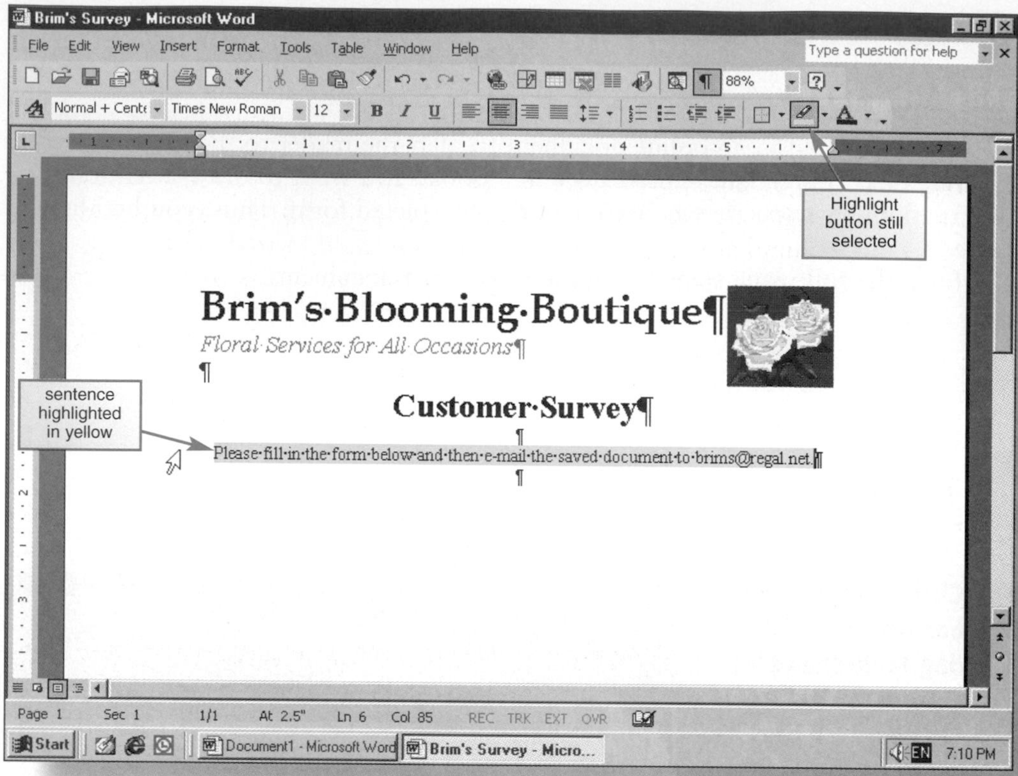

FIGURE 7-9

Other Ways

1. In Voice Command mode, say "Highlight, [select text], Highlight"

When the Highlight button is selected, you can continue to select text to be highlighted. The highlighter remains active until you click the Highlight button or press the ESC key to turn it off.

Word provides a variety of highlighter colors. To change the color, click the Highlight button arrow and then click the desired color.

The next step is to enter the instructions for filling in the data entry area of the form, as described in the following steps.

TO ENTER TEXT

1. Position the insertion point on the paragraph mark below the highlighted text and then press the ENTER key.
2. Click the Font Color box arrow and then click Violet. Type `Press the TAB key to move from one area to the next.` Press the ENTER key.
3. Type `For additional help completing this form, read the messages on the status bar.` Press the ENTER key twice.
4. Press CTRL+L to left-align the current paragraph.

The data entry area instructions are entered (shown in Figure 7-11 on page WD 7.16).

The next step is to insert a table to hold the fields in the data entry area of the form.

Inserting a Table into a Form

The first line of data entry in the form consists of the First Name text box, which begins at the left margin, and the Last Name text box, which begins at the center point. Although you could set tab stops to align the data in a form, it is easier to insert a table. For example, the first line could be a 1 × 2 table; that is, a table with one row and two columns. By inserting a 1 × 2 table, Word automatically positions the second column at the center point. Using tables in forms also keeps the data entered within the same region of the form, in case the user enters data that wraps to the next line on the screen.

When you insert a table, Word automatically surrounds it with a border. You do not want borders on tables in forms. Perform the following steps to enter a 1 × 2 table into the form and then remove its border.

More About

Using Tables in Forms

At first glance, it might seem easier to set a tab stop wherever you would like a form field to display. Actually, it can become a complex task. Consider a row with three form fields. To space them evenly you must calculate where each tab stop should begin based on the width of the page and the margins. If you insert a 1 × 3 table instead, Word automatically calculates the size of three evenly spaced columns.

Steps To Insert a Borderless Table into a Form

1 If the Forms toolbar does not display on the screen, click View on the menu bar, point to Toolbars, and then click Forms. If necessary, scroll up so that the boutique name is positioned at the top of the document window. With the insertion point on line 11, click the Insert Table button on the Forms toolbar. Point to the cell in the first row and second column of the grid.

Word displays a grid to define the dimension of the desired table (Figure 7-10). Word will insert the table immediately above the insertion point.

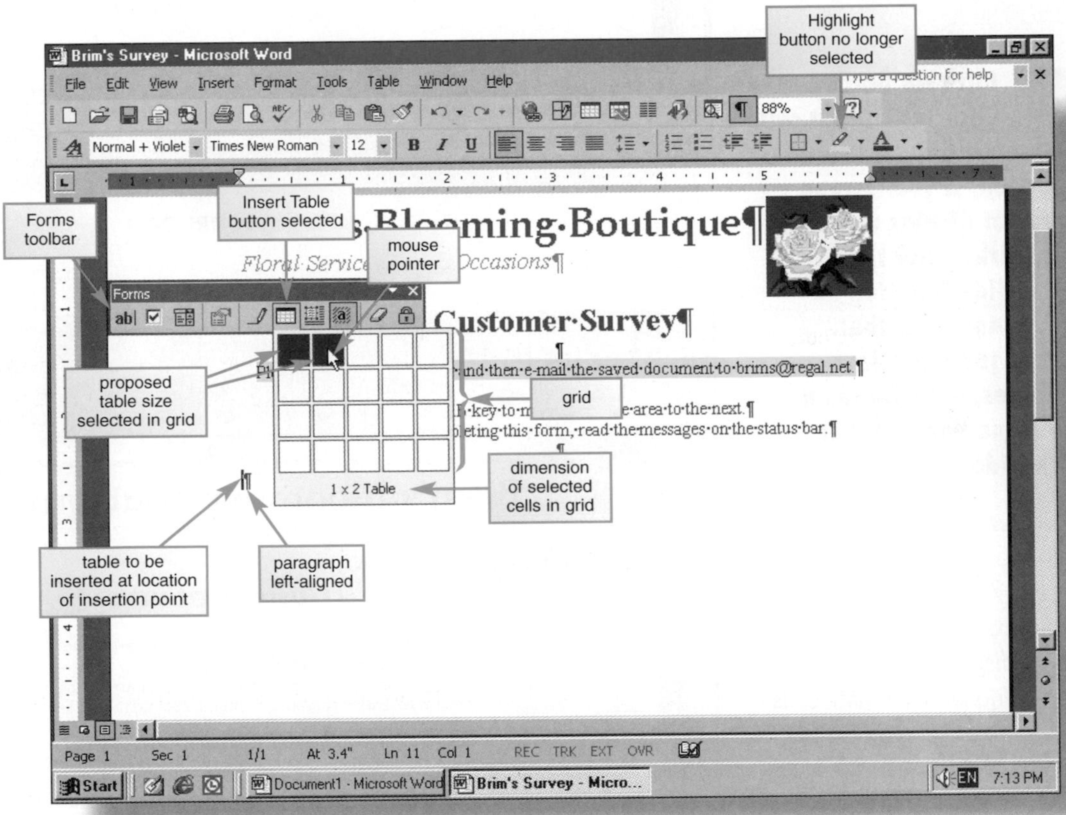

FIGURE 7-10

2 Click the cell in the first row and second column of the grid.

Word inserts an empty 1 × 2 table into the form. The insertion point is in the first cell (row 1 and column 1) of the table (shown in Figure 7-11 on the next page).

3 When the table displays, point to the first cell and then, when the table move handle displays, click the table move handle to select the table. Click the Border button arrow on the Formatting toolbar and then point to No Border on the border palette.

Word displays a list of border types on the border palette (Figure 7-11). The table is selected in the document.

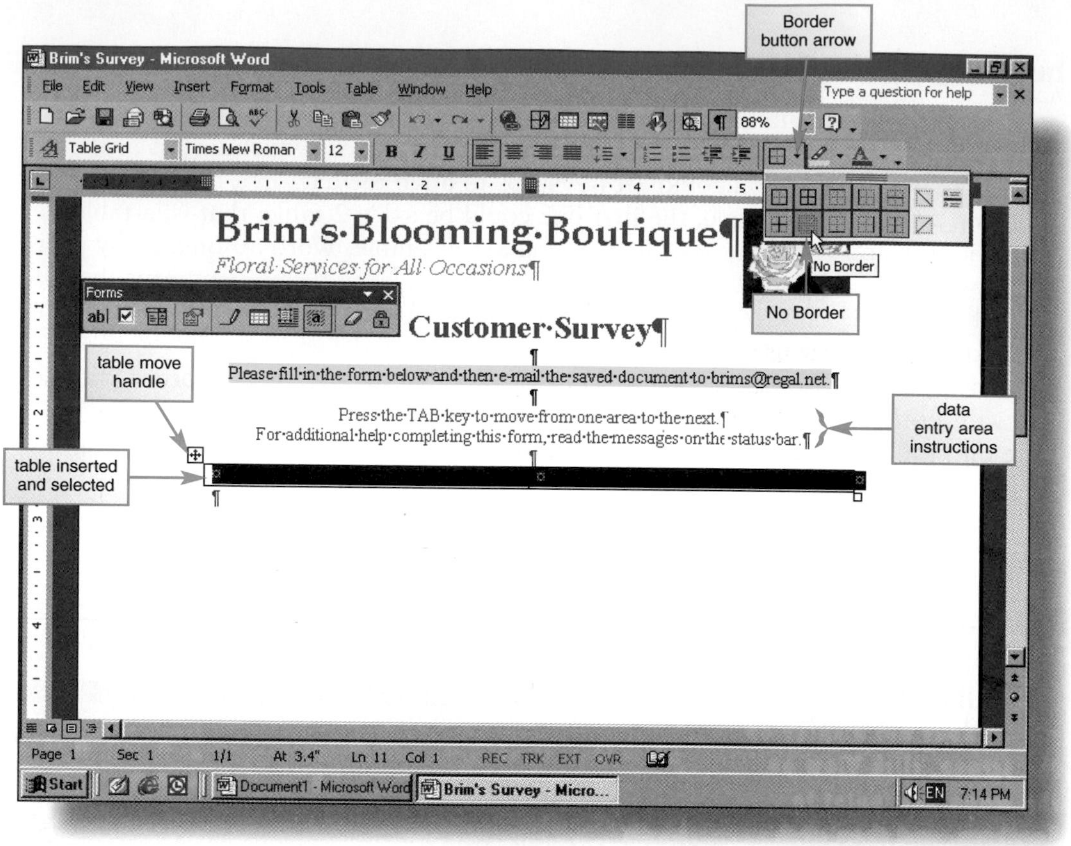

FIGURE 7-11

4 Click No Border. Click in the first cell of the table to remove the selection. If your screen does not display end-of-cell marks, click the Show/Hide ¶ button on the Standard toolbar. If your table displays gridlines, click Table on the menu bar and then click Hide Gridlines.

Word removes the border from the cells in the table (Figure 7-12). Only the end-of-row and end-of-cell marks display in the document window to identify cells in the table.

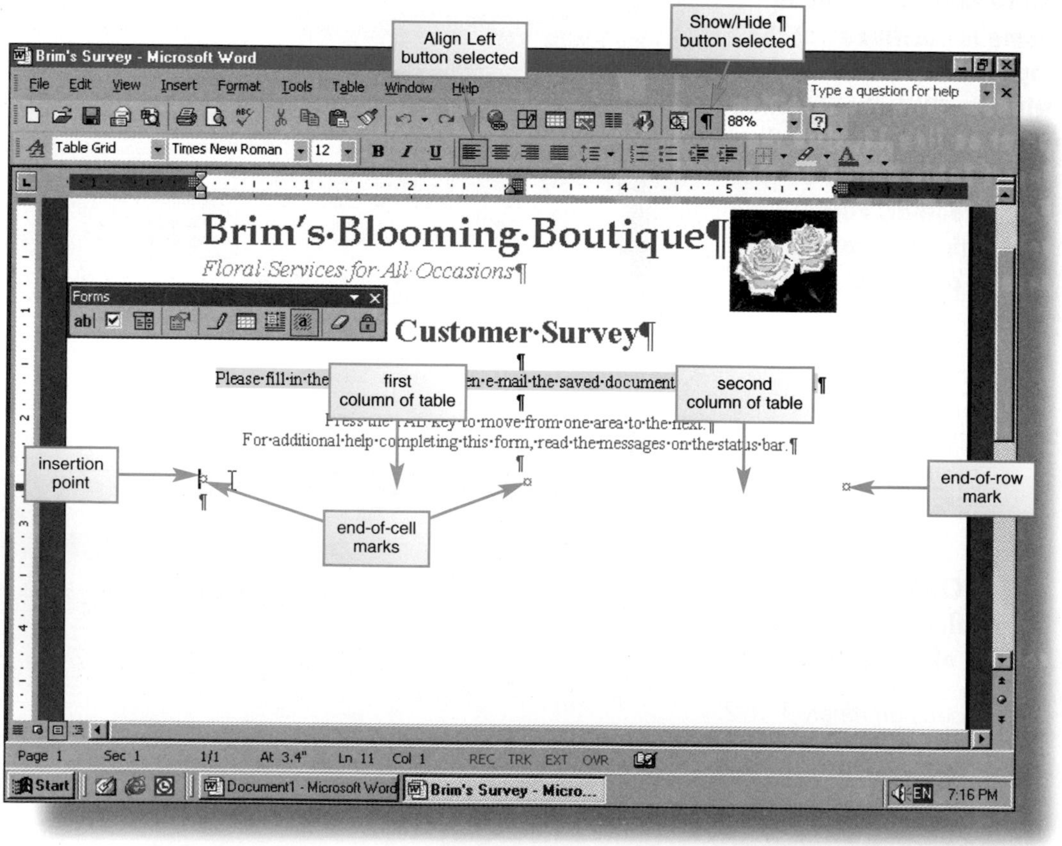

FIGURE 7-12

Other Ways

1. Click Insert Table button on Standard toolbar, click grid
2. On Table menu point to Insert, click Table, enter number of columns, enter number of rows, click OK button
3. In Voice Command mode, say "Table, Insert, Table, [enter number of columns and rows], OK"

Each row of a table has an end-of-row mark, and each cell has an end-of-cell mark. The end-of-cell marks in Figure 7-12 are left-aligned because the cells are formatted as left-aligned. The data you enter within a cell wordwraps in that cell just as text does between the margins of a document. To place data into a cell, click the cell and then type. To advance rightward from one cell to the next, press the TAB key.

The next step is to enter fields into the cells of the table.

More About

Gridlines

If you want to see the table gridlines while developing a form, click Table on the menu bar and then click Show Gridlines. Gridlines are formatting marks that do not print. They are designed to help users easily identify table cells, rows, and columns.

Inserting a Text Form Field that Accepts any Text

The first item that users enter on the Customer Survey is their first name. The field caption text, First Name, is to display to the left of a text box. A **field caption** is the text on the screen that informs the user what to enter into the field. Often a colon or some other character follows a field caption to separate the field caption from a text box or other data entry field.

To place a text box in the document, you insert a text form field. A **text form field** allows users to enter letters, numbers, and other characters into the field.

Perform the following steps to insert the field caption and the text form field into the first cell of the table.

Steps To Insert a Text Form Field

1 With the insertion point in the first cell of the table as shown in Figure 7-12, type `First Name` **and then press the COLON (:) key. Press the SPACEBAR. Point to the Text Form Field button on the Forms toolbar.**

Word places the field caption into the first cell of the table (Figure 7-13).

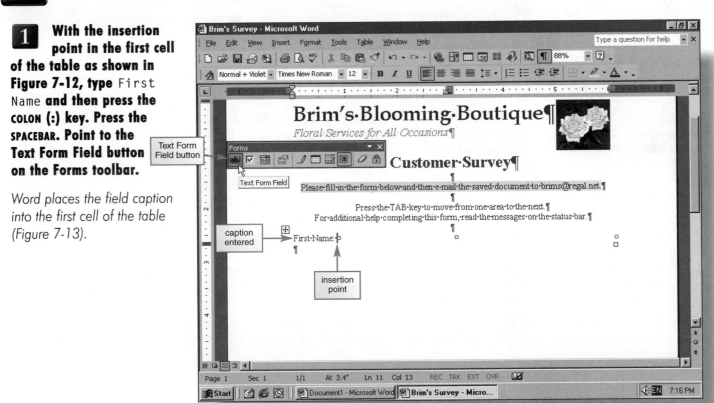

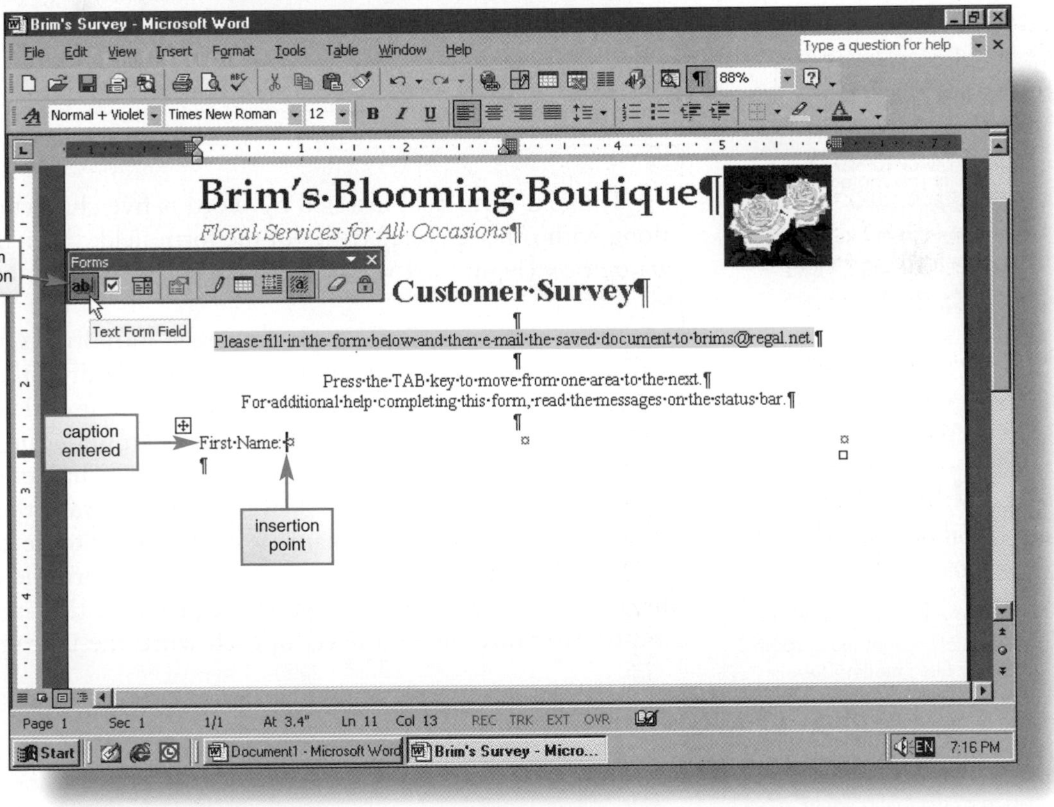

FIGURE 7-13

2 Click the Text Form Field button. If the form field does not display shaded in gray, click the Form Field Shading button on the Forms toolbar.

Word inserts a text form field at the location of the insertion point (Figure 7-14). The form field displays shaded in gray.

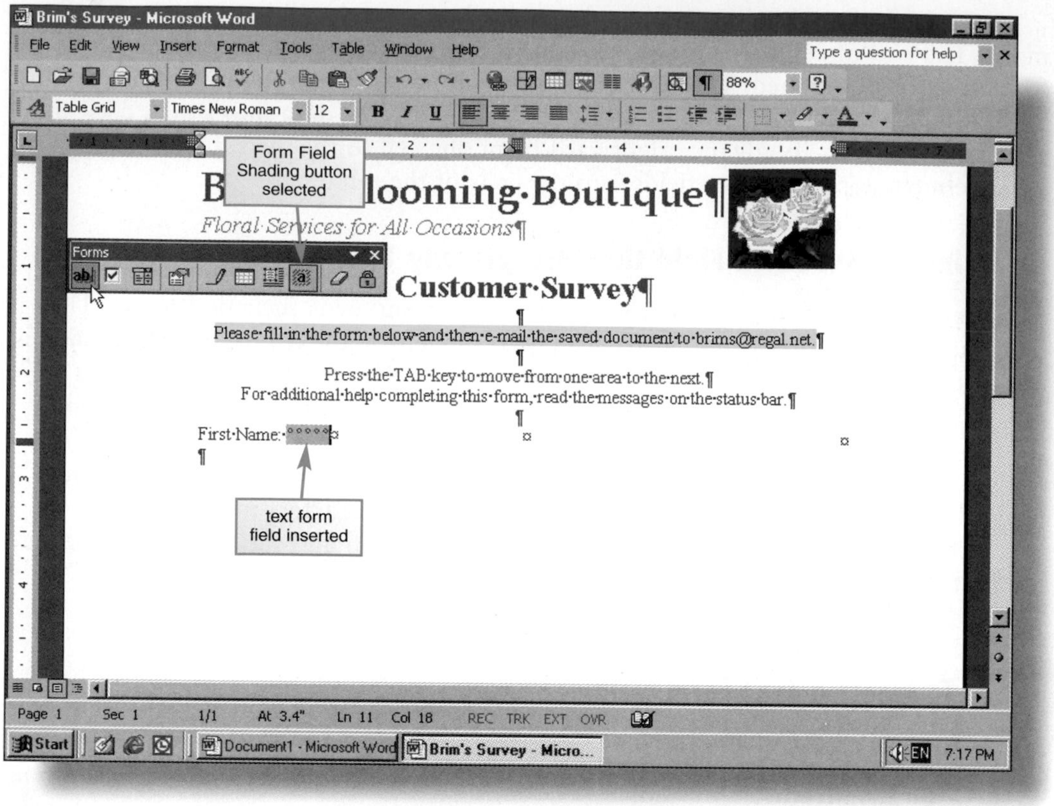

FIGURE 7-14

Other Ways

1. With Forms toolbar displaying, in Voice Command mode, say "Text Form Field" or say "Edit Box"

More About

Field Lengths

The standard width for a first name field is 15 characters. Even though it may not accommodate all people, most businesses allow that much room in their files, mailing labels, and forms. The standard width for last name gradually is increasing. The Internal Revenue Service will increase its last name field width to 25 characters with the 2003 tax season, to accommodate the longer hyphenated names that are becoming so popular.

The text form field inserted by Word is five characters wide. You change its width, along with other characteristics of the form field, through the Text Form Field Options dialog box (Figure 7-15). You display this dialog box by double-clicking the text form field.

When this form displays on the screen initially (as a blank form), you want the text form fields to display an underline that signifies the data entry area. The text displayed initially in a field is called the **default text**. Thus, the default text for the text form fields on the Customer Survey is an underline.

You want to limit a user's entry for the first name to 15 characters. Thus, the underline should consume 15 spaces. You also want the first letter of each word that a user enters into the First Name text form field to be capitalized.

Perform the following steps to set the text form field for the first name so it displays 15 underscores as default text, to limit the user's entry to 15 characters, and to capitalize the first letter of each word the user enters.

Steps To Specify Text Form Field Options

1 Double-click the text form field (shown in Figure 7-14). When Word displays the Text Form Field Options dialog box, press the UNDERSCORE (_) key 15 times in the Default text text box. Double-click the Maximum length text box and then type 15 as the length. Click the Text format box arrow and then click First capital. Point to the OK button.

Word displays the Text Form Field Options dialog box (Figure 7-15).

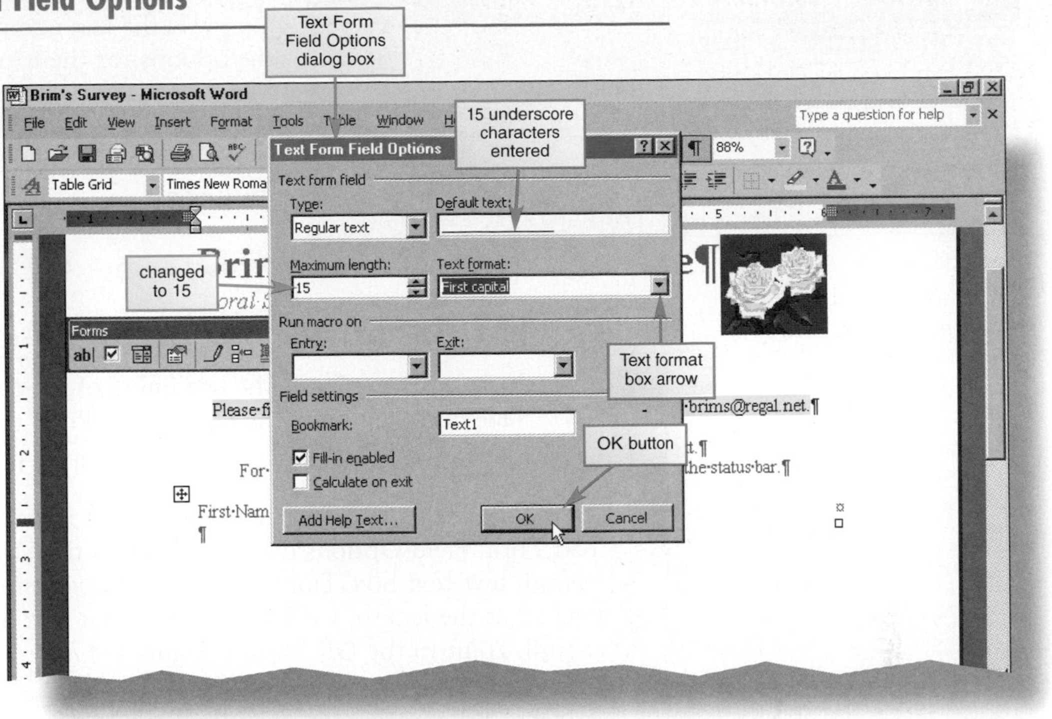

FIGURE 7-15

2 Click the OK button. Press the TAB key to move the insertion point to the beginning of the next cell in the table.

The text form field options are set (Figure 7-16).

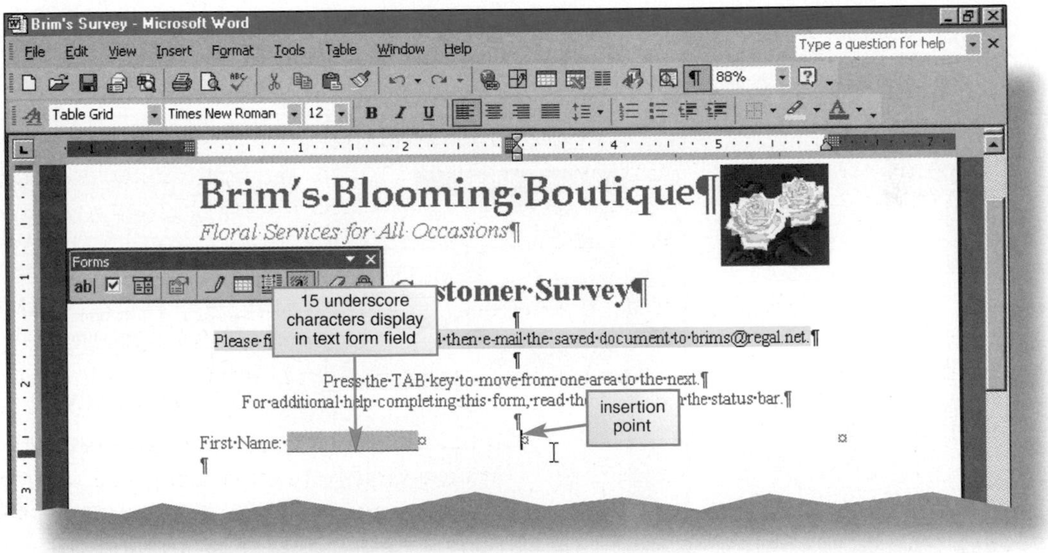

FIGURE 7-16

When you click the Text format box arrow in the Text Form Field Options dialog box (Figure 7-15), four choices display: Uppercase, Lowercase, First capital, and Title case. If you select one of these options, Word displays a user's entry according to your selection — after the user presses the TAB key to advance out of the form field. Table 7-1 on the next page illustrates how each option displays text that a user enters into the form field.

Other Ways

1. Click Form Field Options button on Forms toolbar
2. Right-click form field, click Properties on shortcut menu
3. With Forms toolbar displaying, in Voice Command mode, say "Form Field Options" or say "Properties"

Table 7-1 Text Formats for Text Form Fields

TEXT FORMAT	*EXAMPLE*
Uppercase	ALL LETTERS IN ALL WORDS ARE CAPITALIZED.
Lowercase	all letters in all words display as lowercase letters.
First capital	The first letter of the first word is capitalized.
Title case	The First Letter Of Every Word Is Capitalized.

The next form field to enter into the Customer Survey is the last name. The only difference between the options for the form fields for the last name and first name is that the last name allows up to 20 characters, instead of 15. Perform the following steps to insert and specify options for another text form field.

TO INSERT AND SPECIFY OPTIONS FOR A TEXT FORM FIELD

1. With the insertion point at the beginning of the second cell of the table, type `Last Name` and then press the COLON key. Press the SPACEBAR.
2. Click the Text Form Field button on the Forms toolbar.
3. Double-click the text form field for the last name. When Word displays the Text Form Field Options dialog box, press the UNDERSCORE key 20 times in the Default text text box. Double-click the Maximum length text box and then type `20` as the length. Click the Text format box arrow and then click First capital. Point to the OK button (Figure 7-17).
4. Click the OK button.

Word displays the form field for the last name according to the settings in the Text Form Field Options dialog box (shown in Figure 7-18).

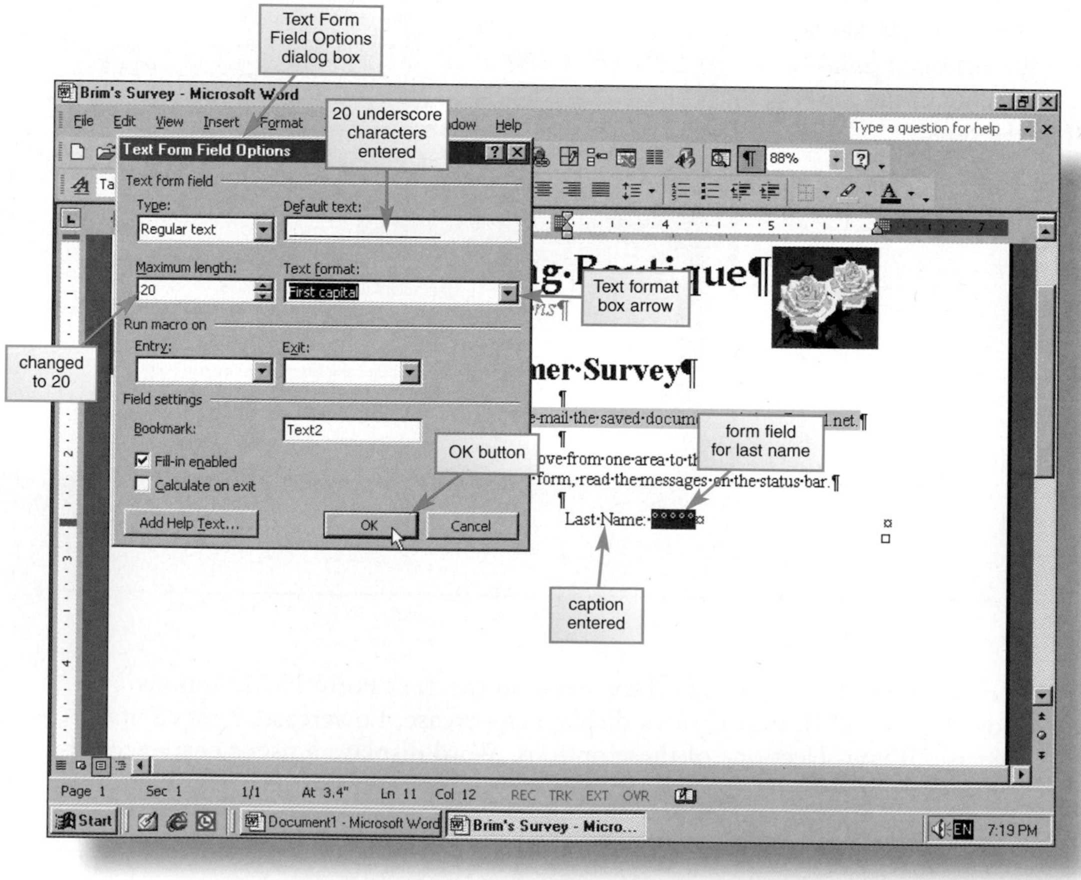

FIGURE 7-17

The next step in creating the Customer Survey is to insert a drop-down form field.

Inserting a Drop-Down Form Field

You use a **drop-down form field** when you want to present a set of choices to a user in the form of a drop-down list box. To view the set of choices, the user clicks an arrow that displays at the right edge of the form field, which displays a list box (Figure 7-1b on page WD 7.05). In this online form, the drop-down form field to be inserted is to contain the customer's opinion on how easy the Web site is to use. The valid choices to be presented to the user are Very Easy, Easy, Fair, Difficult, and Very Difficult.

Perform the following steps to insert a drop-down form field into the Customer Survey.

Steps To Insert a Drop-Down Form Field

1 Click the paragraph mark below the table to position the insertion point below the First Name caption and then press the ENTER key. Type `How easy is it to place an order using our Web site?` **and then press the SPACEBAR. Point to the Drop-Down Form Field button on the Forms toolbar.**

Word displays the field caption (Figure 7-18).

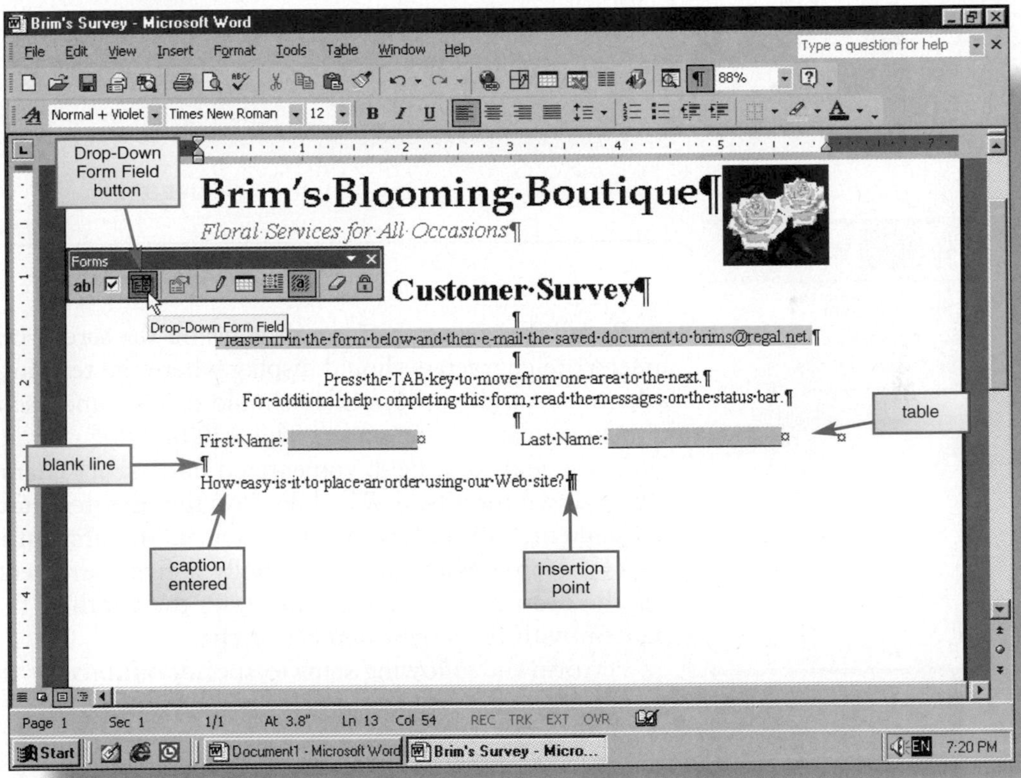

FIGURE 7-18

2 Click the Drop-Down Form Field button.

Word inserts a drop-down form field at the location of the insertion point (Figure 7-19). The form field displays shaded in gray.

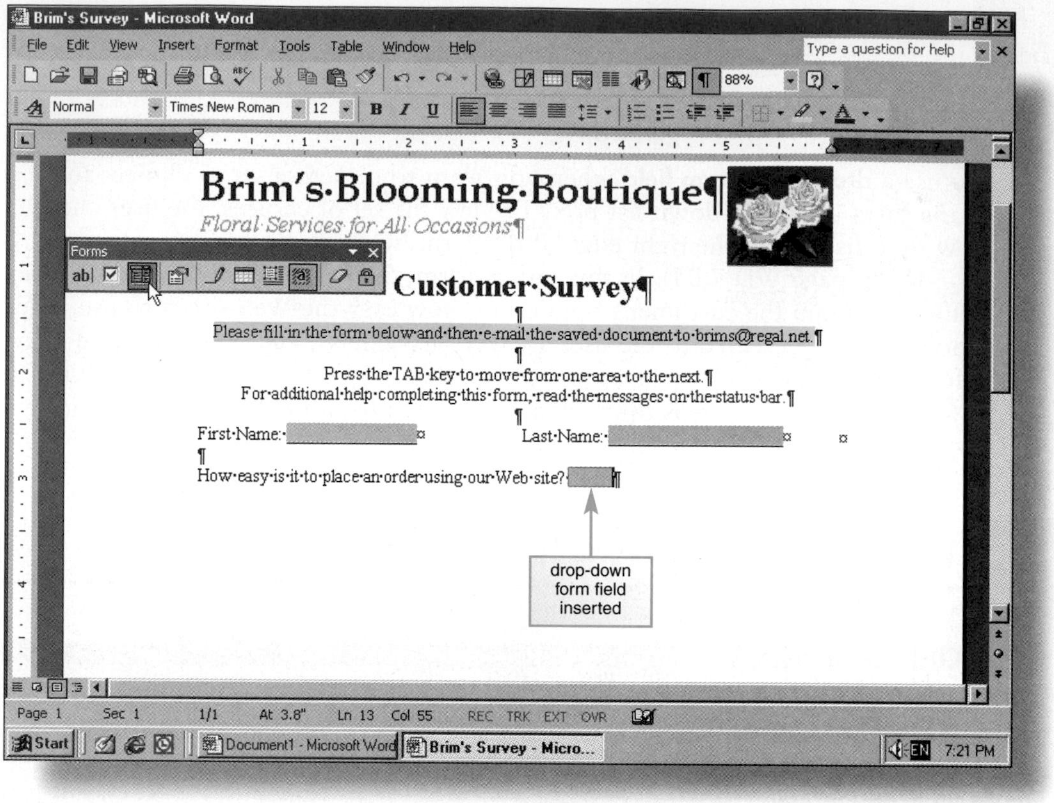
Brim's Survey - Microsoft Word
Brim's·Blooming·Boutique¶
Floral·Services·for·All·Occasions¶
Forms
Customer·Survey¶
Please·fill·in·the·form·below·and·then·e-mail·the·saved·document·to·brims@regal.net.¶
Press·the·TAB·key·to·move·from·one·area·to·the·next.¶
For·additional·help·completing·this·form,·read·the·messages·on·the·status·bar.¶
First·Name:·
Last·Name:·
How·easy·is·it·to·place·an·order·using·our·Web·site?
drop-down form field inserted

FIGURE 7-19

Other Ways

1. With Forms toolbar displaying, in Voice Command mode, say "Combo Box" or say "Drop-Down Form Field"

More About

Drop-Down Form Fields

Instead of clicking the Add button in the Drop-Down Form Field Options dialog box (as shown in Figure 7-20) to move an item from the Drop-down item text box to the Items in drop-down list box, you can press the ENTER key.

Recall that when the form displays on the screen initially (as a blank form), underscore characters should display where the text form fields are located. Similarly, the drop-down form field should display underscore characters when the form initially displays on the screen. This will help the user identify all the data entry areas.

In the text form field, you entered underscore characters as the default text. With a drop-down form field, Word displays the first item in the list on a blank form. Thus, you will enter 15 underscore characters as the first list item.

The drop-down form field initially is five characters wide. As you enter items into the drop-down list, Word increases the width of the form field to accommodate the item with the largest number of characters.

Perform the following steps to specify options for the drop-down form field.

Steps To Specify Drop-Down Form Field Options

1 Double-click the drop-down form field. When Word displays the Drop-Down Form Field Options dialog box, press the UNDERSCORE key 15 times in the Drop-down item text box and then point to the Add button.

Word displays the Drop-Down Form Field Options dialog box (Figure 7-20).

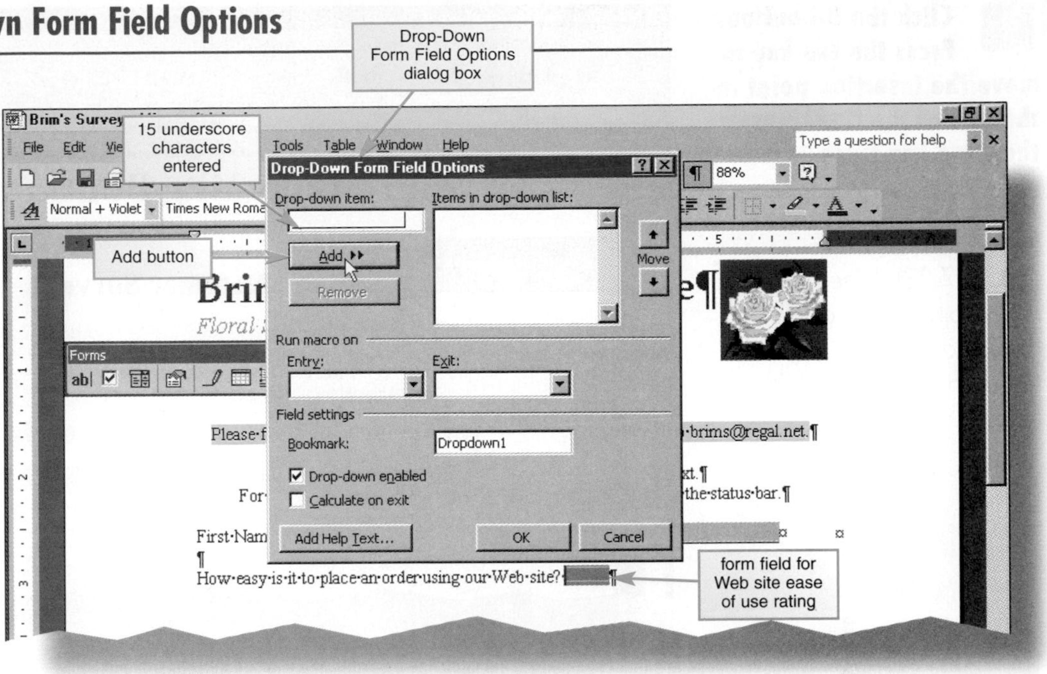

FIGURE 7-20

2 Click the Add button.

Word places the 15 underscore characters as the first item in the Items in drop-down list list (Figure 7-21). The Drop-down item text box now is empty, awaiting the next entry.

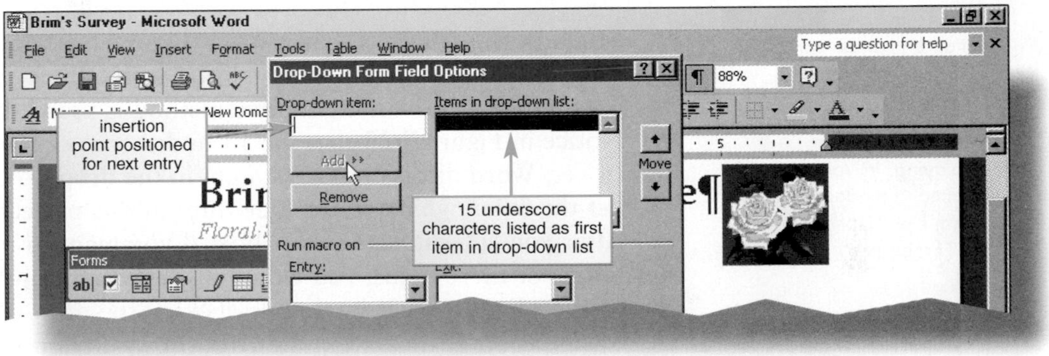

FIGURE 7-21

3 With the insertion point positioned in the Drop-down item text box, type `Very Easy` **and then click the Add button. Type** `Easy` **and then click the Add button. Type** `Fair` **and then click the Add button. Type** `Difficult` **and then click the Add button. Type** `Very Difficult` **and then click the Add button. Point to the OK button.**

The items in the drop-down list are entered (Figure 7-22).

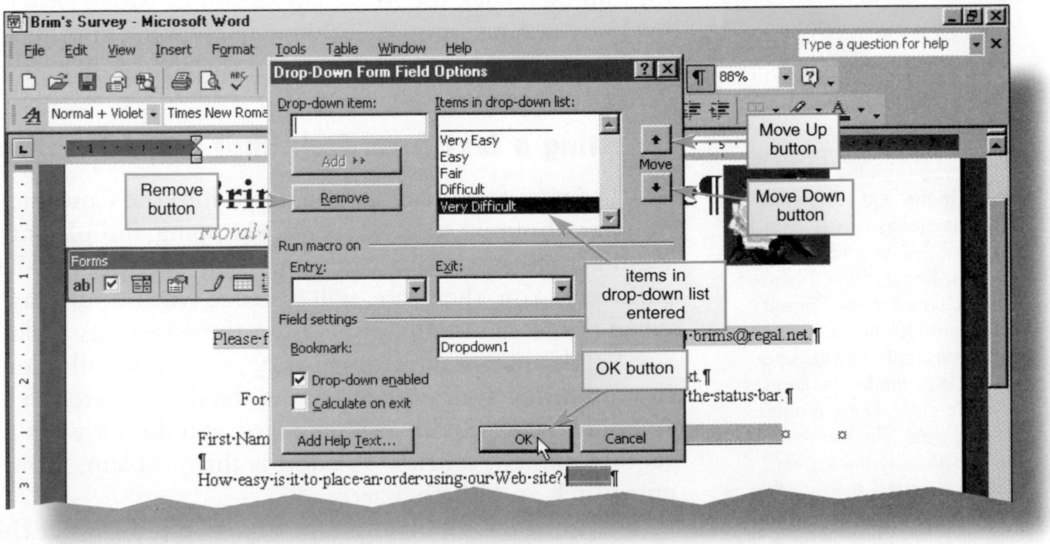

FIGURE 7-22

4 **Click the OK button. Press the END key to move the insertion point to the end of the line. Press the ENTER key twice.**

The list for the drop-down form field is defined (Figure 7-23). When you fill in the form, a box arrow will display at the right edge of the drop-down form field.

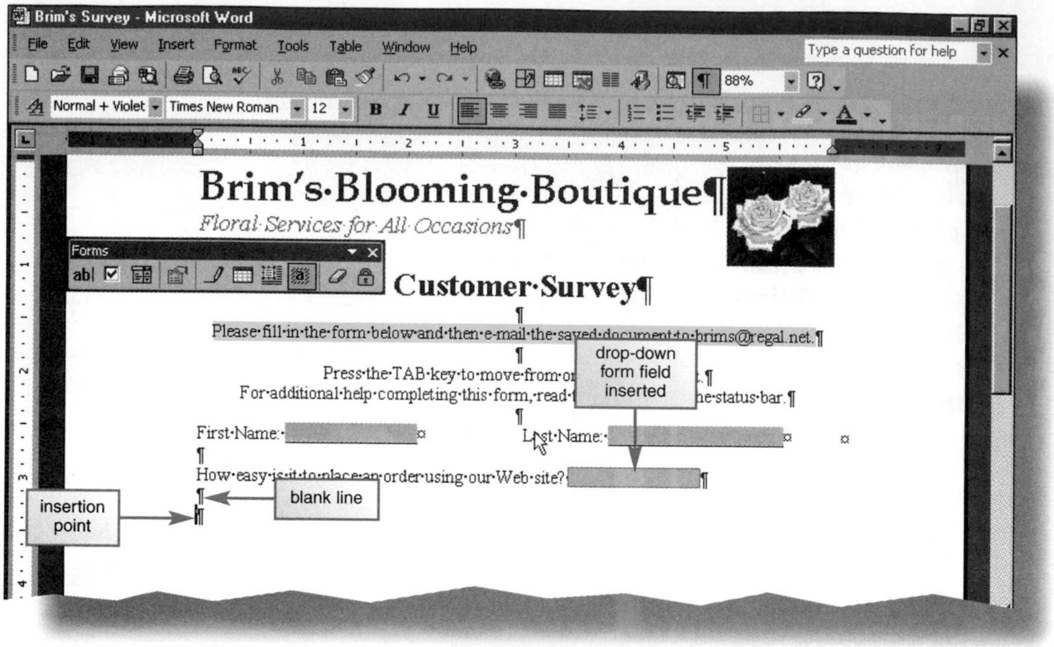

FIGURE 7-23

Other Ways

1. Click Form Field Options button on Forms toolbar
2. Right-click form field, click Properties on shortcut menu
3. With Forms toolbar displaying, in Voice Command mode, say "Form Field Options" or say "Properties"

Instead of clicking the Add button (Figure 7-20 on the previous page) to move items from the Drop-down item text box to the Items in drop-down list, you can press the ENTER key. This alternative method is used later in this project.

Notice in Figure 7-23 that the 15 underscore characters do not display on the screen yet. Word displays the first item in the drop-down list on the screen when you protect the form, which you will do later in this project.

After you enter items in a list box, if you want to modify their order, or add or delete one or more items, you would display the Drop-Down Form Field Options dialog box (Figure 7-22) by double-clicking the drop-down form field. To add more items, simply enter the text in the Drop-down item text box and then click the OK button. To remove an item, click it in the Items in drop-down list list and then click the Remove button. To reorder the list, click an item in the Items in drop-down list list and then click the Move Up button or Move Down button to move the item up or down one position each time you click the appropriate button.

The next step is to insert a text form field that requires a number.

More About

Text Form Field Types

When you click the Type box arrow in the Text Form Field Options dialog box (shown in Figure 7-24), you have six options: Regular text, Number, Date, Current date, Current time, and Calculations. Regular text accepts any keyboard character. Number requires a numeric entry. Date requires a valid date. The last three options display the system date, the system time, or the result of a calculation, and do not allow a user to change the resulting displayed value.

Inserting a Text Form Field that Requires a Number

The next form field to be entered into the Customer Survey is for the approximate number of minutes a user spends shopping and placing an order. Most users easily would complete an order in fewer than 100 minutes. Thus, a two-digit input area is sufficient. You, therefore, will instruct Word to display two underscore characters when the form initially displays on the screen (as a blank form).

Valid minutes entered will vary greatly, but all minutes entered should be numeric. If you ultimately will be analyzing the data entered in a form with another type of software package such as a database, you do not want non-numeric data in fields that require numeric entries. To address this problem, Word can convert a non-numeric entry such as ABC to a zero.

Perform the following steps to insert and format this text form field.

TO INSERT AND SPECIFY OPTIONS FOR A TEXT FORM FIELD

1. With the insertion point positioned two lines below the previous entry, as shown in Figure 7-23, type `Approximately how many minutes does it take to shop and place an order?` and then press the SPACEBAR.
2. Click the Text Form Field button on the Forms toolbar.
3. Double-click the newly inserted text form field for the number of minutes. When Word displays the Text Form Field Options dialog box, click the Type box arrow and then click Number. Press the TAB key to position the insertion point in the Maximum length text box and then type `2` as the length. Press the TAB key to position the insertion point in the Default number text box and then press the UNDERSCORE key two times. Point to the OK button (Figure 7-24).
4. Click the OK button.

Word displays the text form field for the number of minutes according to the settings in the Text Form Field Options dialog box (shown in Figure 7-25 on the next page).

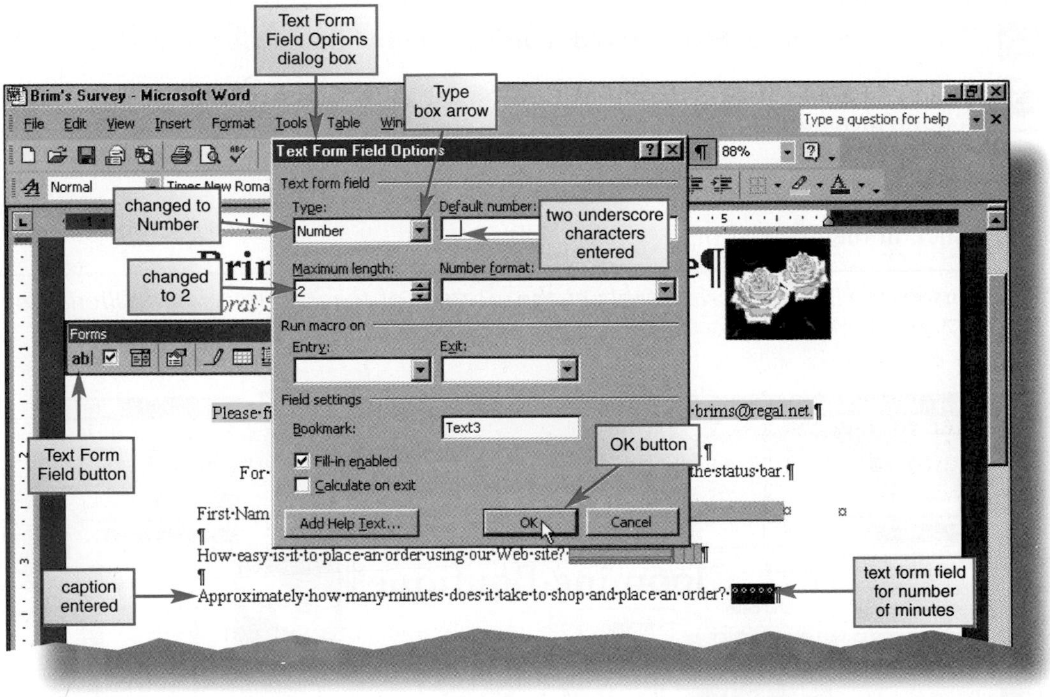

FIGURE 7-24

By changing the Type box to Number (Figure 7-24), Word will convert any non-numeric entry in this form field to a zero. Other valid text form field types are discussed later in this project.

The next step is to enter the check boxes into the Customer Survey.

Inserting a Check Box

The bottom of the data entry area of the Customer Survey contains five check boxes, one each for Flowers, Plants, Teddy Bears, Fruit Baskets, and Other. The Other check box also has a text form field to its right, which allows a user to explain further. Above the check boxes is a line of instructions pertaining to the check boxes. The following pages explain how to enter this section of the form.

The first step is to enter the line of text containing instructions for the check boxes. Perform the steps on the next page to enter this line of text.

More About

Check Boxes

If you want an X to display in a check box when the form initially displays on the screen (as a blank form), double-click the check box form field. When the Check Box Form Field Options dialog box displays, click Checked in the Default value area, and then click the OK button.

TO ENTER TEXT

1. Press the END key to move the insertion point to the end of the line. Press the ENTER key twice. Type `Types of orders you have placed using our Web site (check all that apply)` and then press the COLON key.
2. Press the ENTER key.

The instructions for the check boxes display (shown in Figure 7-25).

You want four check boxes to display horizontally below the check box instructions. To do this and align the check boxes evenly across the line, insert a 1 × 4 borderless table; that is, a table with one row and four columns. Perform the following steps to insert a 1 × 4 table into the form.

TO INSERT A BORDERLESS TABLE INTO A FORM

1. With the insertion point on the paragraph mark below the check box instructions, click the Insert Table button on the Forms toolbar and then point to the cell in the first row and fourth column of the grid (Figure 7-25).
2. Click the cell in the first row and fourth column of the grid.
3. When the table displays, point to the first cell and then, when the table move handle displays, click the table move handle to select the table. Click the Border button arrow on the Formatting toolbar and then click No Border on the border palette.
4. Click in the first cell of the table.

Word inserts a 1 × 4 borderless table at the location of the insertion point (shown in Figure 7-26).

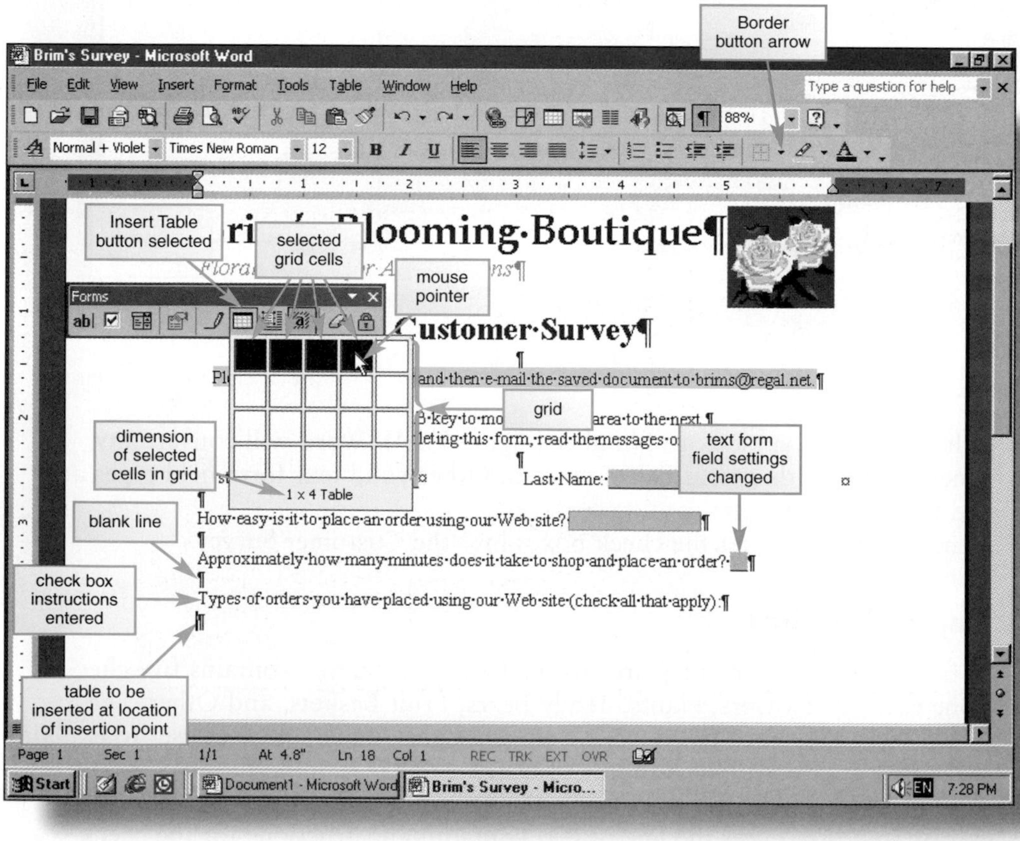

FIGURE 7-25

The next step is to insert the first check box into the first cell of the table as shown in the following steps.

Steps To Insert a Check Box

1 With the insertion point in the first cell of the table, point to the Check Box Form Field button on the Forms toolbar (Figure 7-26).

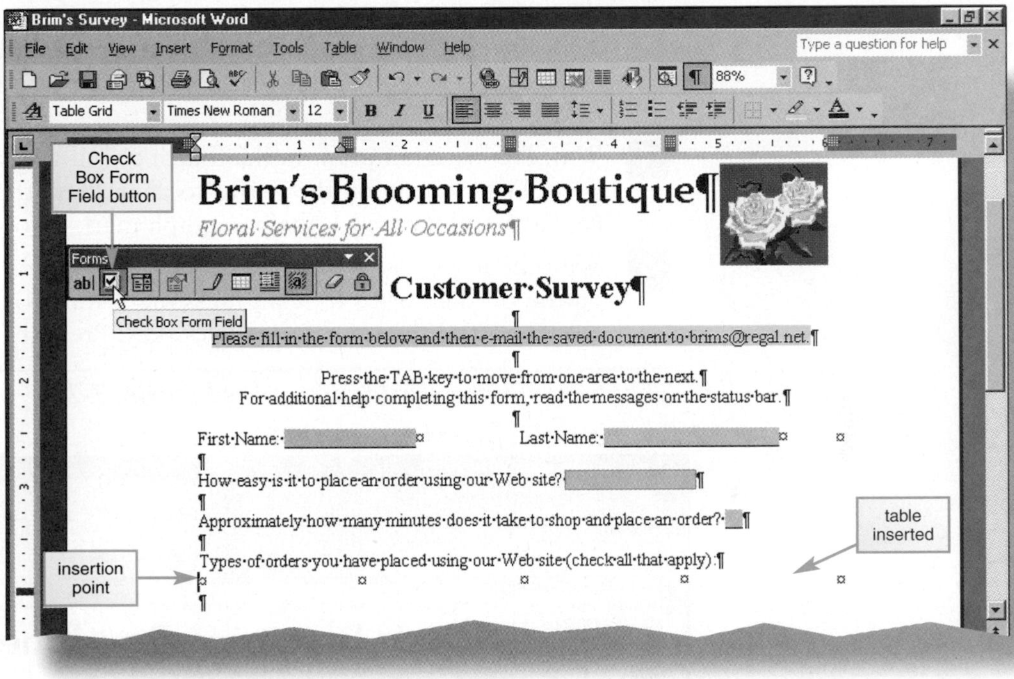
Brim's Survey - Microsoft Word
Check Box Form Field button
Brim's·Blooming·Boutique¶
Floral·Services·for·All·Occasions¶
Forms
Check Box Form Field
Customer·Survey¶
Please·fill·in·the·form·below·and·then·e-mail·the·saved·document·to·brims@regal.net.¶
Press·the·TAB·key·to·move·from·one·area·to·the·next.¶
For·additional·help·completing·this·form,·read·the·messages·on·the·status·bar.¶
First·Name:·
Last·Name:·
How·easy·is·it·to·place·an·order·using·our·Web·site?·
Approximately·how·many·minutes·does·it·take·to·shop·and·place·an·order?·
Types·of·orders·you·have·placed·using·our·Web·site·(check·all·that·apply):¶
table inserted
insertion point

FIGURE 7-26

2 Click the Check Box Form Field button. Press the SPACEBAR. Type `Flowers` and then press the TAB key.

Word inserts a check box form field followed by its caption in the first cell of the table (Figure 7-27).

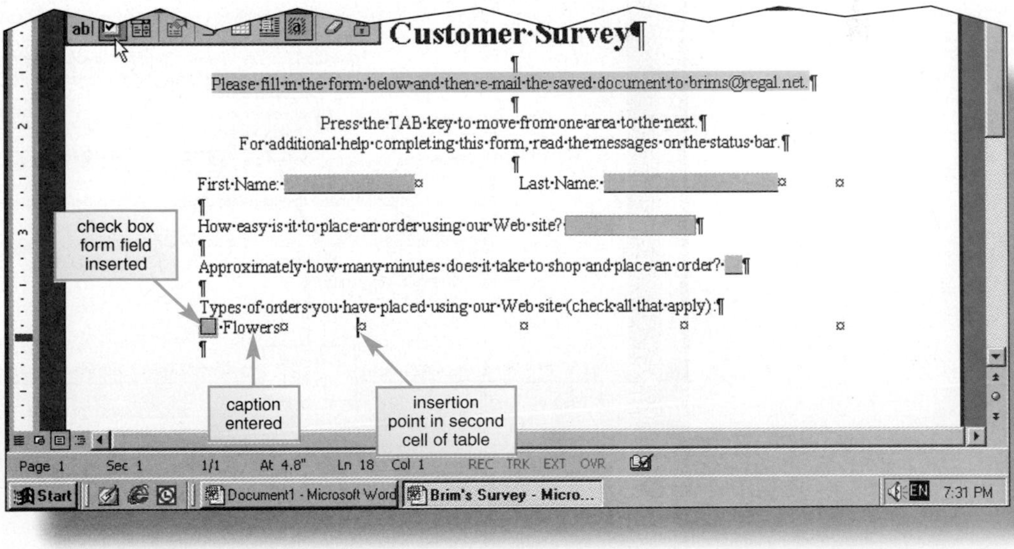
Customer·Survey¶
Please·fill·in·the·form·below·and·then·e-mail·the·saved·document·to·brims@regal.net.¶
Press·the·TAB·key·to·move·from·one·area·to·the·next.¶
For·additional·help·completing·this·form,·read·the·messages·on·the·status·bar.¶
First·Name:·
Last·Name:·
How·easy·is·it·to·place·an·order·using·our·Web·site?·
Approximately·how·many·minutes·does·it·take·to·shop·and·place·an·order?·
Types·of·orders·you·have·placed·using·our·Web·site·(check·all·that·apply):¶
·Flowers
check box form field inserted
caption entered
insertion point in second cell of table
Page 1 Sec 1 1/1 At 4.8" Ln 18 Col 1 REC TRK EXT OVR
Start
Document1 - Microsoft Word
Brim's Survey - Micro...
7:31 PM

FIGURE 7-27

Other Ways

1. With Forms toolbar displaying, in Voice Command mode, say "Check Box"

The next step is to enter the remaining check box fields in the form, as described in the following steps.

TO INSERT ADDITIONAL CHECK BOX FORM FIELDS

1. With the insertion point in the second cell of the table, click the Check Box Form Field button on the Forms toolbar. Press the SPACEBAR. Type `Plants` and then press the TAB key.
2. With the insertion point in the third cell of the table, click the Check Box Form Field button on the Forms toolbar. Press the SPACEBAR. Type `Teddy Bears` and then press the TAB key.
3. With the insertion point in the fourth cell of the table, click the Check Box Form Field button on the Forms toolbar. Press the SPACEBAR. Type `Fruit Baskets` and then click the paragraph mark below the table.
4. With the insertion point below the table, click the Check Box Form Field button on the Forms toolbar. Press the SPACEBAR. Type `Other (please specify)` and then press the COLON key. Press the SPACEBAR.

The check box form fields are inserted (Figure 7-28).

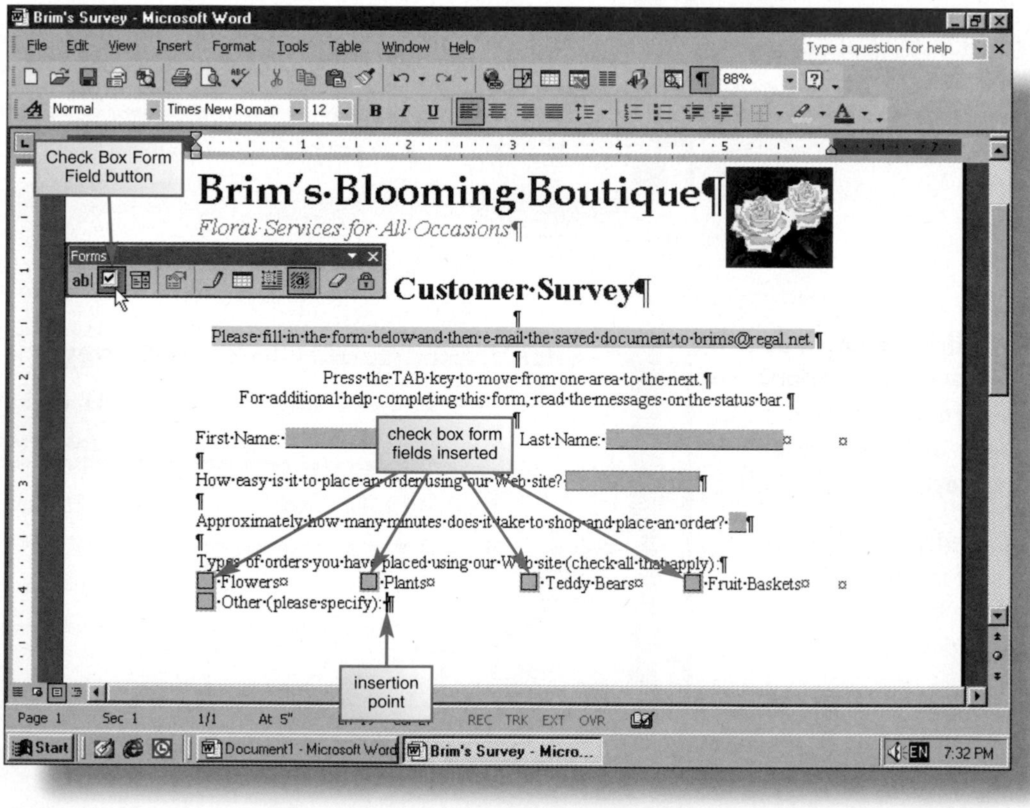

FIGURE 7-28

If users select the check box with the Other caption, you want them to explain the other type of order they placed using the Web site. To allow this, you insert a text form field as described in the following steps.

TO INSERT AND SPECIFY OPTIONS FOR A TEXT FORM FIELD

1. Click the Text Form Field button on the Forms toolbar.
2. Double-click the text form field for Other (please specify). When Word displays the Text Form Field Options dialog box, press the UNDERSCORE key 30 times in the Default text text box. Point to the OK button (Figure 7-29).
3. Click the OK button.

Word displays the text form field for the other types of orders according to the settings in the Text Form Field Options dialog box.

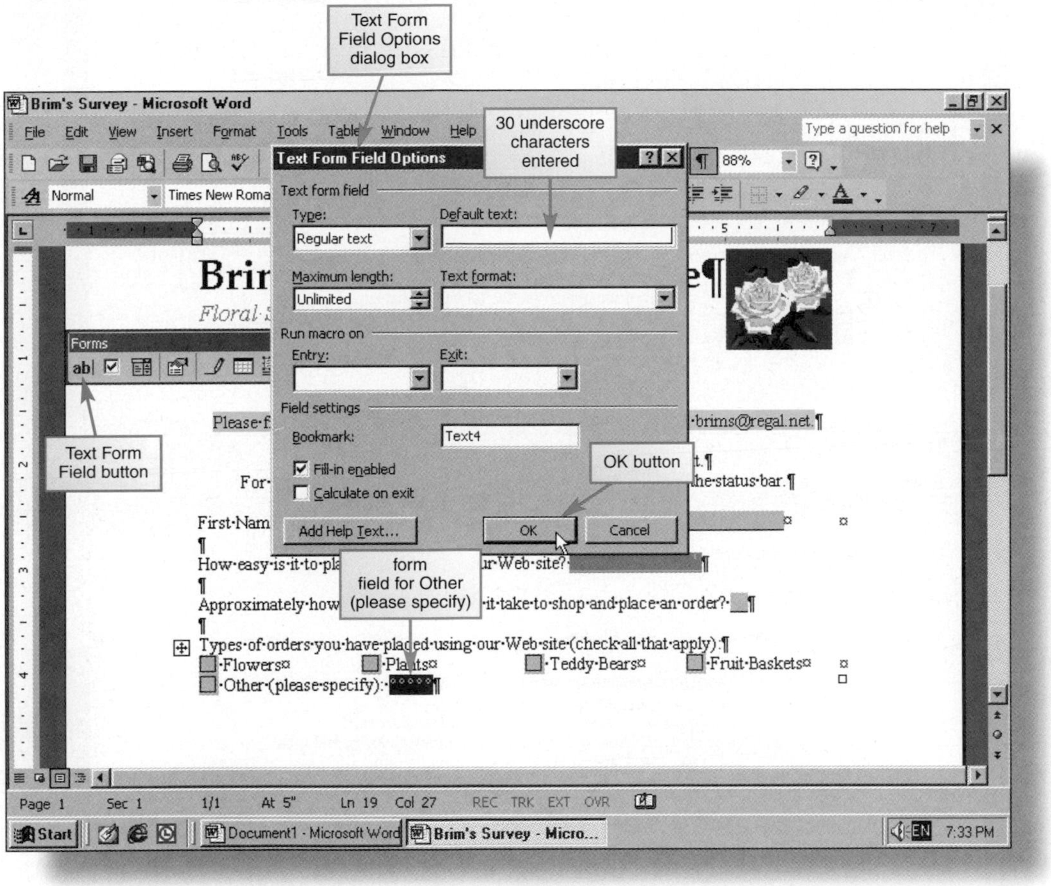

FIGURE 7-29

More About

Text Form Fields

If the Maximum length box is set to Unlimited, as shown in Figure 7-29, the user can enter a maximum of 255 characters into the text box.

The next step is to display the current date on the form.

Inserting a Text Form Field that Displays the Current Date

The next form field to be entered into the Customer Survey is the current date. You do not want the user to enter the date; instead, you simply want the current date to display on the form. When a user fills in and e-mails the completed form, the date the user completed the form will display automatically.

You could insert the current date as a field by clicking Insert on the menu bar and then clicking Date and Time. If, however, you plan to analyze the data later using a database or some other software and you want the current date to be part of the data saved with the form, then you must insert a text form field that displays the current date. Perform the steps on the next page to insert and specify options for this text form field as the current date.

Steps To Insert and Specify Options for a Text Form Field as the Current Date

1 **Click at the end of the last text form field entered and then press the ENTER key. Press CTRL+R to right-align the paragraph. Click the Text Form Field button on the Forms toolbar. Double-click the new text form field that displays. When Word displays the Text Form Field Options dialog box, click the Type box arrow and then click Current date. Click the Date format box arrow and then click M/d/yyyy. Point to the OK button (Figure 7-30).**

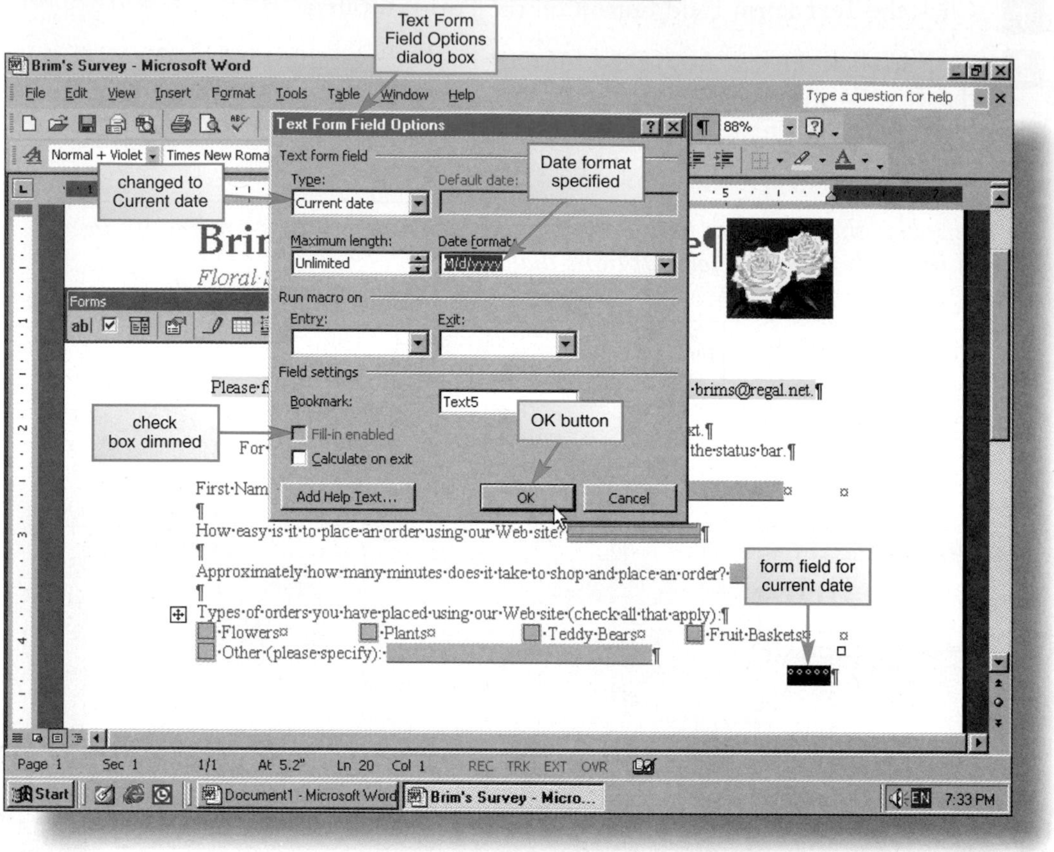

FIGURE 7-30

2 **Click the OK button. Click outside the field to remove the selection.**

Word displays the current date in the form field (Figure 7-31). Your date displayed will be different.

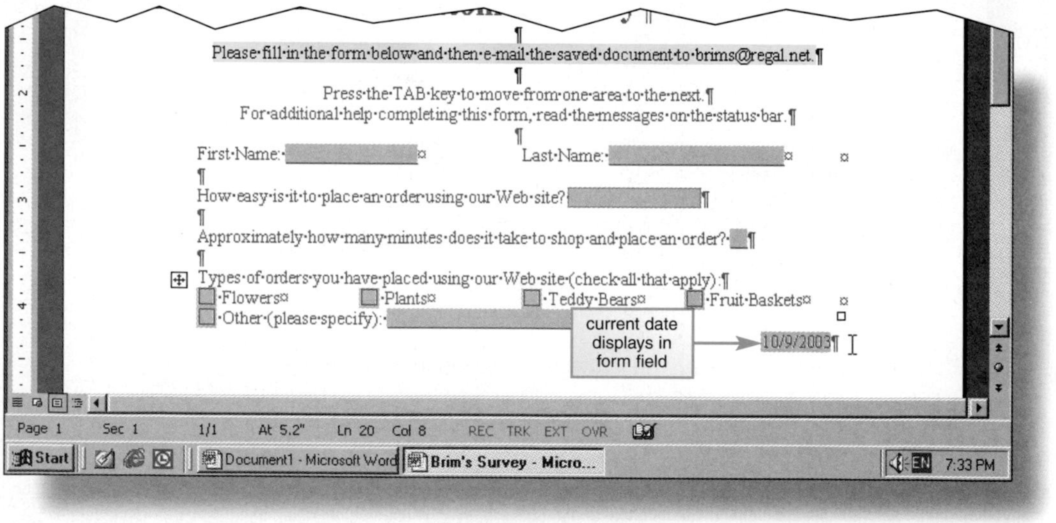

FIGURE 7-31

Other Ways

1. With the Forms toolbar displaying, in Voice Command mode, say "Text Form Field" or say "Edit Box"

Notice in the Text Form Field Options dialog box shown in Figure 7-30 that the Fill-in enabled check box in the Field settings area is dimmed. Word automatically dims this check box when you select Current date as the field type. When this check box is dimmed, a user is not allowed to modify the contents of the field when it displays on the screen. If you want a user to enter a date, you would select Date in the Type list instead of Current date.

Two other options in the Type list that also dim the Fill-in enabled check box are Current time and Calculation. That is, if you select Current time as the field type, Word displays the current time on the screen – so a user cannot change the time displayed. If you select Calculation as the field type, Word displays the result of a formula you enter.

The next step is to format the data entry fields.

> **More About**
>
> **Date and Time**
>
> If a text form field type has been changed to Current date (Figure 7-30) or Current time and you intend to print the form, you should ensure that the date and time are current, or updated, before printing. To do this, click Tools on the menu bar, click Options, click the Print tab, place a check mark in the Update fields check box, and then click the OK button.

Formatting Form Fields

As users enter data into the text form fields and the drop-down form field on the form, you want the characters they type to be underlined in violet. Word prevents users from formatting data they enter into form fields. Thus, specify any desired field formatting to fields on the form template. To format a field, select the field and then format it as you do any other text. In this case, you use the Font dialog box to specify an underline color.

Perform the following steps to underline the field for the first name in violet.

Steps To Underline in Color

1 **Click the text form field for the first name to select it. Right-click the selection and then point to Font on the shortcut menu (Figure 7-32).**

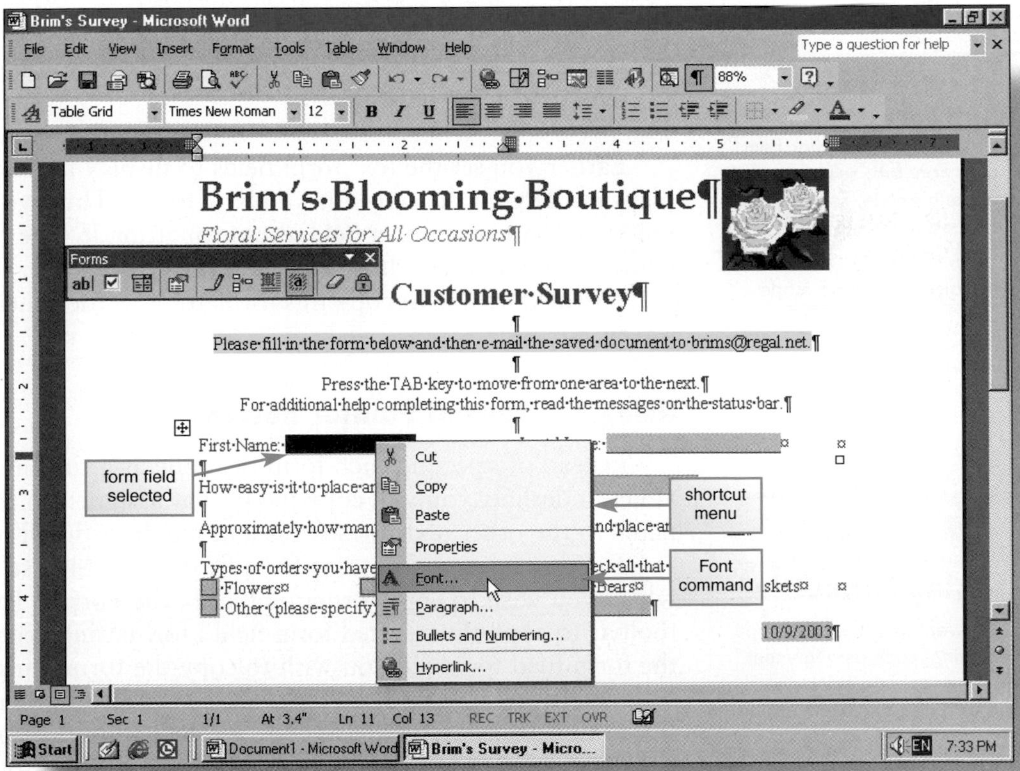

FIGURE 7-32

2 Click Font. When the Font dialog box displays, if necessary, click the Font tab. Click the Underline style box arrow and then click the first underline in the list. Click the Underline color box arrow and then click Violet. Point to the OK button.

Word displays the Font dialog box (Figure 7-33).

3 Click the OK button.

Word formats the data entry for the field to 12-point Times New Roman underlined violet font (shown in Figure 7-34).

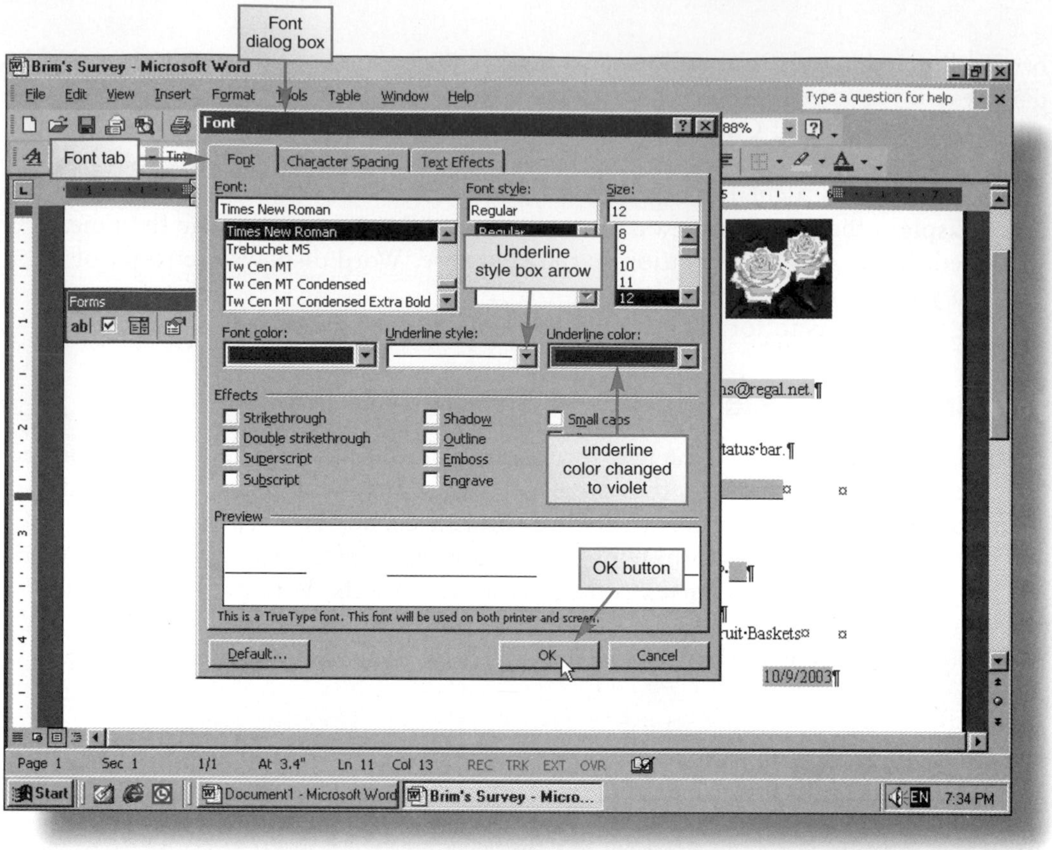

FIGURE 7-33

Other Ways

1. On Format menu click Font, click Font tab, select desired underline style, select desired underline color, click OK button
2. In Voice Command mode, say "Format, Font, Font, [select underline style and color], OK"

More About

Copying Formatting

If you want to copy paragraph formatting, such as alignment and line spacing, select the paragraph mark at the end of the paragraph prior to clicking the Format Painter button. If you want to copy just character formatting, such as fonts and font sizes, do not select the paragraph mark.

Earlier you set the text form fields to display an underline when the form displays initially on the screen (as a blank form). Thus, you will not notice a change to the First Name text form field after formatting it. The formatting options will take effect when you enter data into the form.

The next step is to copy this formatting to the other data entry fields on the screen.

Using the Format Painter Button

Instead of selecting each form field one at a time and then formatting it with the violet underline, you will copy the format assigned to the form field for the first name to the other text form fields and the drop-down form field.

To copy formats from one form field to another, select the form field from which you wish to copy formatting, click the Format Painter button on the Standard toolbar to copy the selected form field's formatting specifications, and then select the form field to which you wish to copy the formatting. To select a text form field, simply click it or drag through it. To select a drop-down form field, drag through it.

In this project, you are to copy formats from one form field to multiple form fields. Thus, you double-click the Format Painter button so that the format painter remains active until you turn it off, as shown in the following steps.

Steps To Use the Format Painter Button

1 **With the text form field for the first name selected, double-click the Format Painter button on the Standard toolbar. Move the mouse pointer into the document window.**

Word attaches a paintbrush to the mouse pointer when the Format Painter button is selected (Figure 7-34). The 12-point Times New Roman underlined violet font has been copied by the format painter.

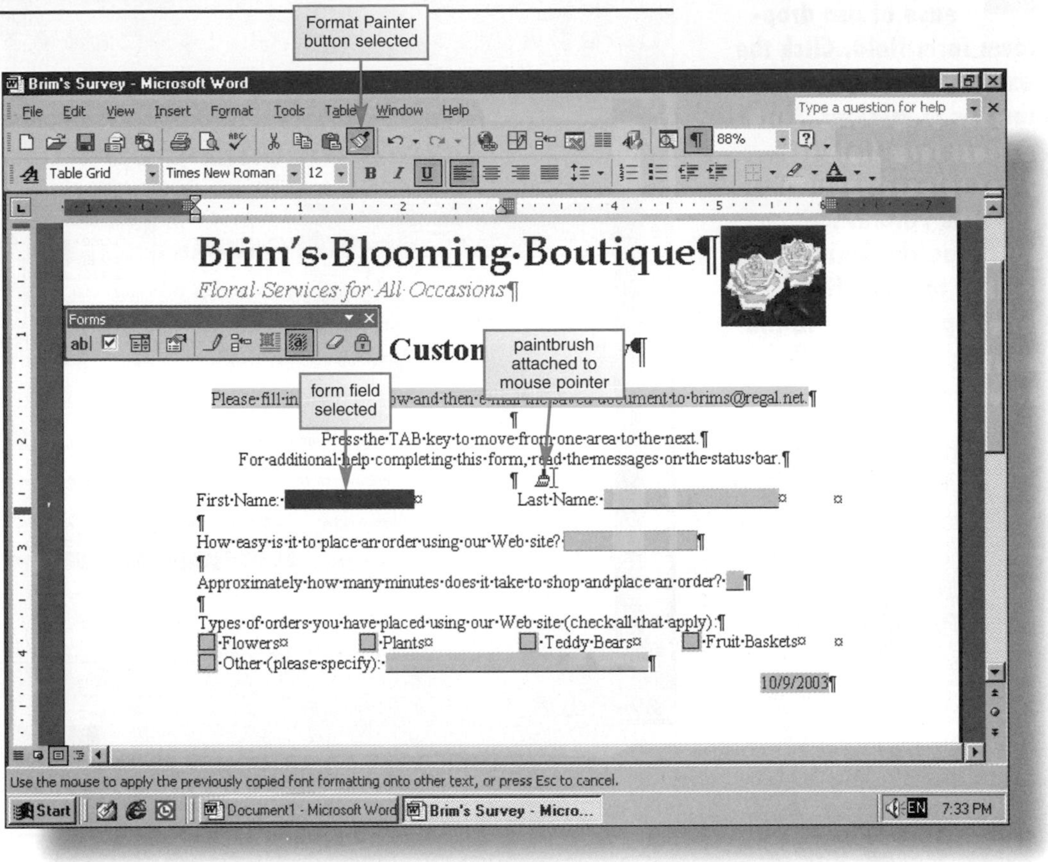

FIGURE 7-34

2 **Click the text form field for the last name.**

Word copies the 12-point Times New Roman underlined violet font to the text form field for the last name (Figure 7-35). The last name field is selected, and the format painter remains active, allowing you to select more fields to which you wish to copy the format.

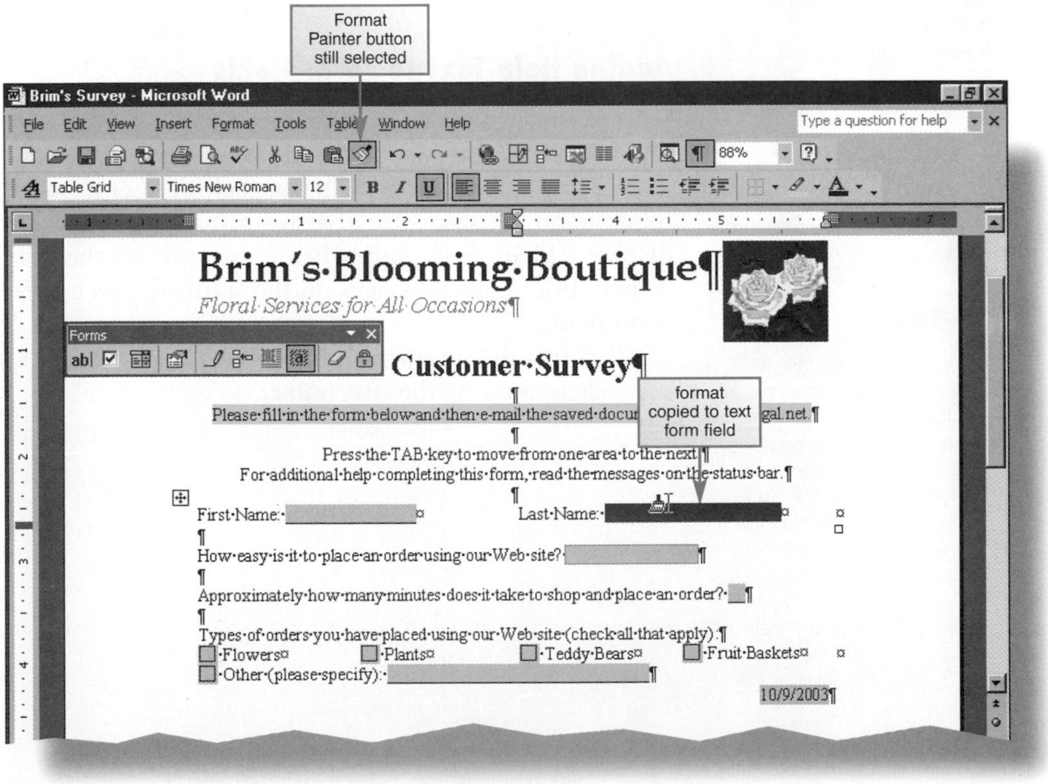

FIGURE 7-35

3 **Drag through the ease of use drop-down form field. Click the text form field for the number of minutes. Click the text form field for Other (please specify). Click the Format Painter button on the Standard toolbar to turn off the format painter. Move the mouse pointer into the document window.**

The format in the text form field for the first name is copied to all other text form fields and to the drop-down form field (Figure 7-36). The Format Painter button no longer is selected.

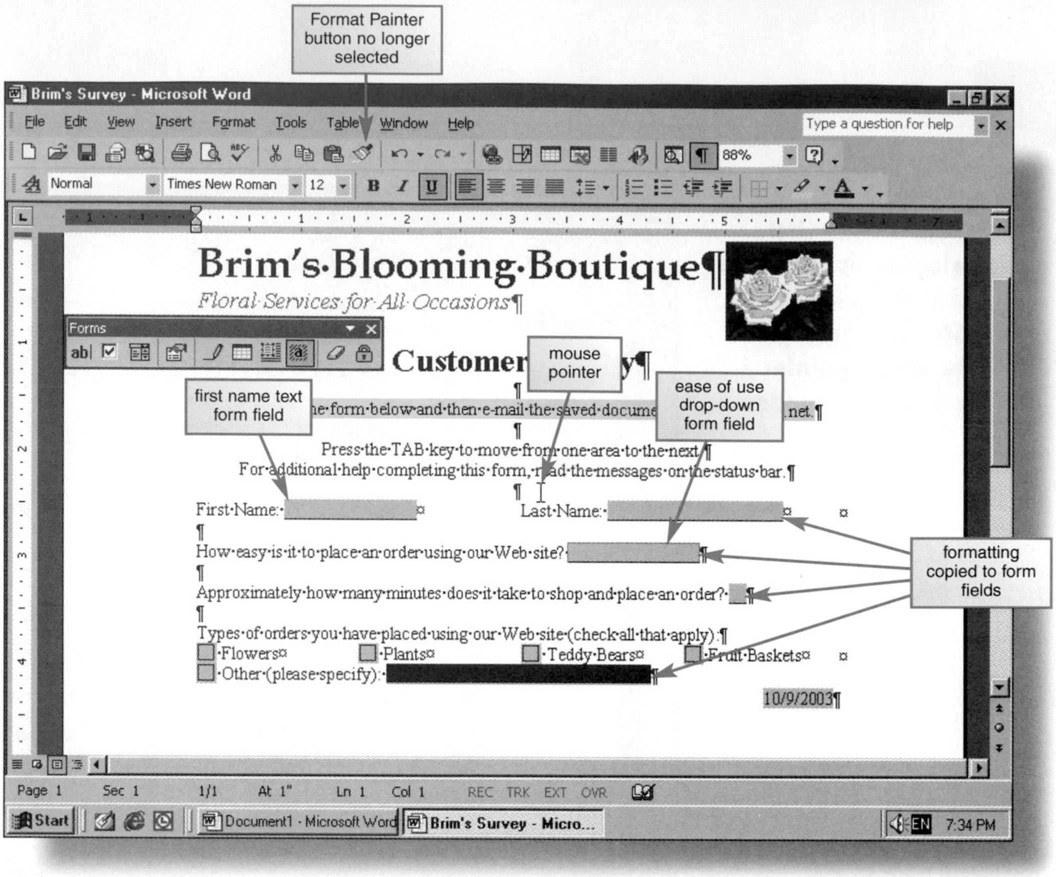

FIGURE 7-36

Other Ways

1. In Voice Command mode, say "[select text to copy from], Format Painter, [select text to copy formatting to]"

The next step is to add help for users to the form.

Adding Help Text to Form Fields

As users enter data into form fields, they may have a question about the purpose or function of a particular field. Thus, Word provides two Help mechanisms by which you can assist users during their data entry process. You can display a Help message on the status bar that relates to the current data entry field and/or you can display a Help dialog box when a user presses the F1 key. In this project, you want to display brief Help messages on the status bar as a user moves from form field to form field.

Perform the following steps to display a Help message on the status bar when the user is entering the first name.

More About

Help Text

When you enter Help text to display on the status bar, you are limited to 138 characters. You can create longer Help text, up to 255 characters, for those that display in a dialog box when the user presses the F1 key. A good practice is to provide users as much help as possible; thus, you may wish to create both status bar Help text and dialog box Help text.

Steps To Add Help Text to a Form Field

1 **Double-click the text form field for the first name (shown in Figure 7-36). When the Text Form Field Options dialog box displays, point to the Add Help Text button (Figure 7-37).**

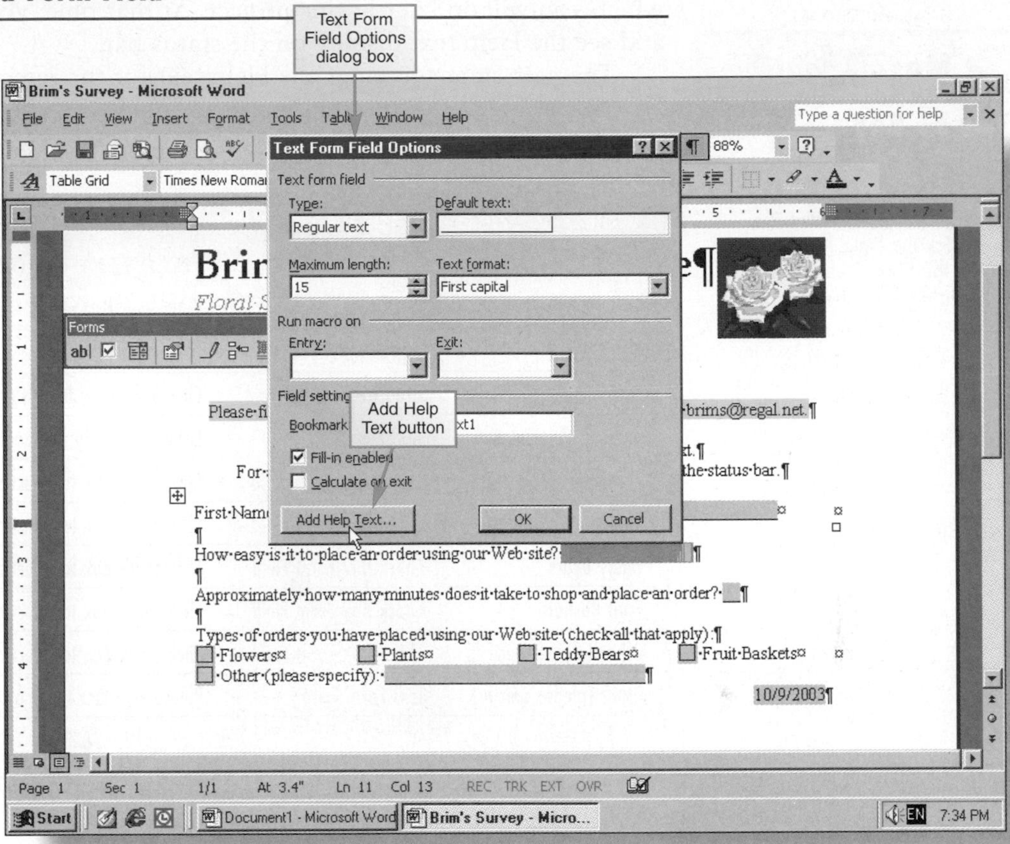

FIGURE 7-37

2 **Click the Add Help Text button. When the Form Field Help Text dialog box displays, if necessary, click the Status Bar tab. Click Type your own. Type** `Enter your first name.` **Point to the OK button.**

Word displays the Form Field Help Text dialog box (Figure 7-38).

3 **Click the OK button. Click the OK button in the Text Form Field Options dialog box.**

The Help text is entered for the first name text form field.

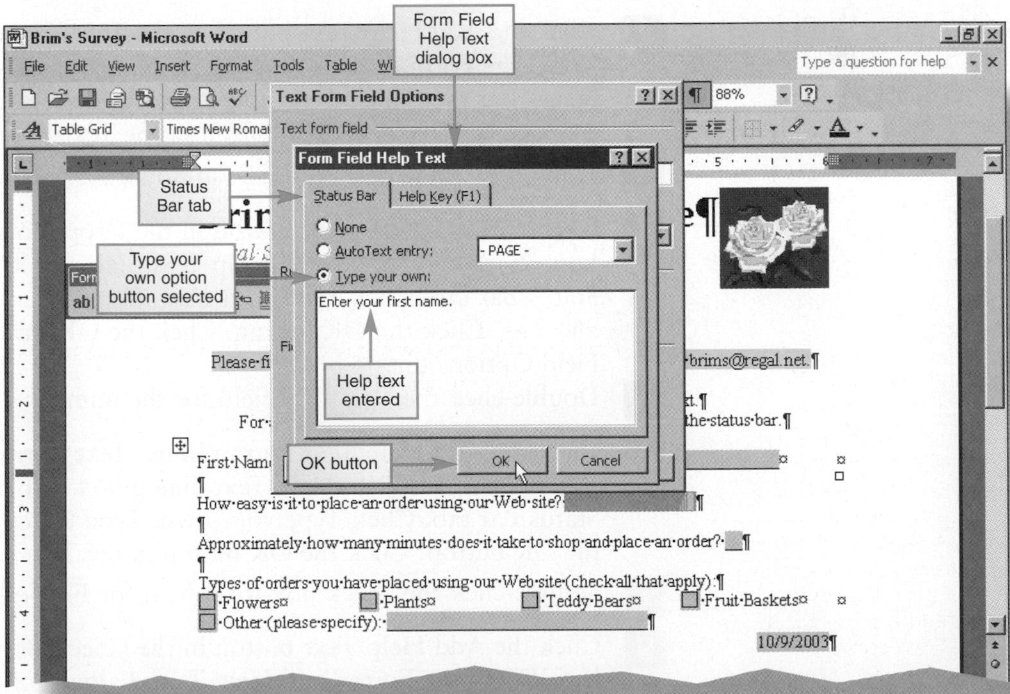

FIGURE 7-38

More About

The F1 Key

If you want to enter Help text in a dialog box that displays when a user presses the F1 key, click the Help Key (F1) tab in the Form Field Help Text dialog box (shown in Figure 7-38 on the previous page). You enter Help text in the Help Key (F1) sheet in the same manner as in the Status Bar sheet.

The Help text does not display on the status bar until you protect the form, which you will do later in this project. At that time, you will enter data into the form and see the Help text display on the status bar.

The next step is to enter the Help text for the remaining form fields in the form. You repeat the procedure on the previous page for each data entry field on the form. The Help text for each field on the Customer Survey is shown in Table 7-2.

Table 7-2 Help Text for Fields on the Form

FIELD	*FIELD TYPE*	*HELP TEXT TO DISPLAY ON STATUS BAR*
First Name	Text Form Field	Enter your first name.
Last Name	Text Form Field	Enter your last name.
ease of use	Drop-Down Form Field	Click box arrow for list of choices.
number of minutes	Text Form Field	Enter minutes in numbers.
Flowers	Check Box Form Field	Click check box to select or deselect.
Plants	Check Box Form Field	Click check box to select or deselect.
Teddy Bears	Check Box Form Field	Click check box to select or deselect.
Fruit Baskets	Check Box Form Field	Click check box to select or deselect.
Other (please specify)	Check Box Form Field	Click check box to select or deselect.
Other (please specify)	Text Form Field	Please list other types of orders placed using our Web site.

The following steps describe how to add the Help text shown in Table 7-2.

TO ADD MORE HELP TEXT

1. Double-click the text form field for the last name.
2. Click the Add Help Text button in the Text Form Field Options dialog box. When the Form Field Help Text dialog box displays, if necessary, click the Status Bar tab. Click Type your own. Type `Enter your last name.` Click the OK button. Click the OK button in the Text Form Field Options dialog box.
3. Double-click the ease of use drop-down form field.
4. Click the Add Help Text button in the Drop-Down Form Field Options dialog box. When the Form Field Help Text dialog box displays, if necessary, click the Status Bar tab. Click Type your own. Type `Click box arrow for list of choices.` Click the OK button. Click the OK button in the Drop-Down Form Field Options dialog box.
5. Double-click the text form field for the number of minutes.
6. Click the Add Help Text button in the Text Form Field Options dialog box. When the Form Field Help Text dialog box displays, if necessary, click the Status Bar tab. Click Type your own. Type `Enter minutes in numbers.` Click the OK button. Click the OK button in the Text Form Field Options dialog box.
7. Double-click the check box form field for Flowers.
8. Click the Add Help Text button in the Check Box Form Field Options dialog box. When the Form Field Help Text dialog box displays, if necessary, click the Status Bar tab. Click Type your own. Type `Click check box to select or deselect.` Click the OK button. Click the OK button in the Check Box Form Field Options dialog box.
9. Double-click the check box form field for Plants. Repeat Step 8.

10 Double-click the check box form field for Teddy Bears. Repeat Step 8.

11 Double-click the check box form field for Fruit Baskets. Repeat Step 8.

12 Double-click the check box form field for Other (please specify). Repeat Step 8.

13 Double-click the text form field for Other (please specify).

14 Click the Add Help Text button in the Text Form Field Options dialog box. When the Form Field Help Text dialog box displays, if necessary, click the Status Bar tab. Click Type your own. Type `Please list other types of orders placed using our Web site`. Click the OK button. Click the OK button in the Text Form Field Options dialog box.

15 Click outside the selected text to remove the selection.

Help text is entered for all data entry fields according to Table 7-2.

If you would like to change the Help text for any of the form fields, simply double-click the form field and then click the Add Help Text button in the dialog box. When the Form Field Help Text dialog box displays, if necessary, click the Status Bar tab. Make any necessary changes to the existing Help text and then click the OK button in the dialog boxes.

The next step is to remove the form field shading.

> **More About**
>
> **Form Field Shading**
>
> If you print a form that displays form field shading, the shading will not print. To add shading to a field on a printed form, you must select the form field, click the Shading Color button arrow on the Tables and Borders toolbar, and then click the desired shading color. Likewise, if you want a border surrounding a field, select the form field, click the Border button arrow on the Tables and Borders toolbar, and then click the Outside Border button.

Removing Form Field Shading

The fields on the form currently are shaded (Figure 7-39). During the design of a form, it is helpful to display field shading so you easily can identify the fields. You do not want the fields to be shaded, however, when a user is entering data into a form. Thus, perform the following steps to remove form field shading.

Steps To Remove Form Field Shading

1 **Point to the Form Field Shading button on the Forms toolbar (Figure 7-39).**

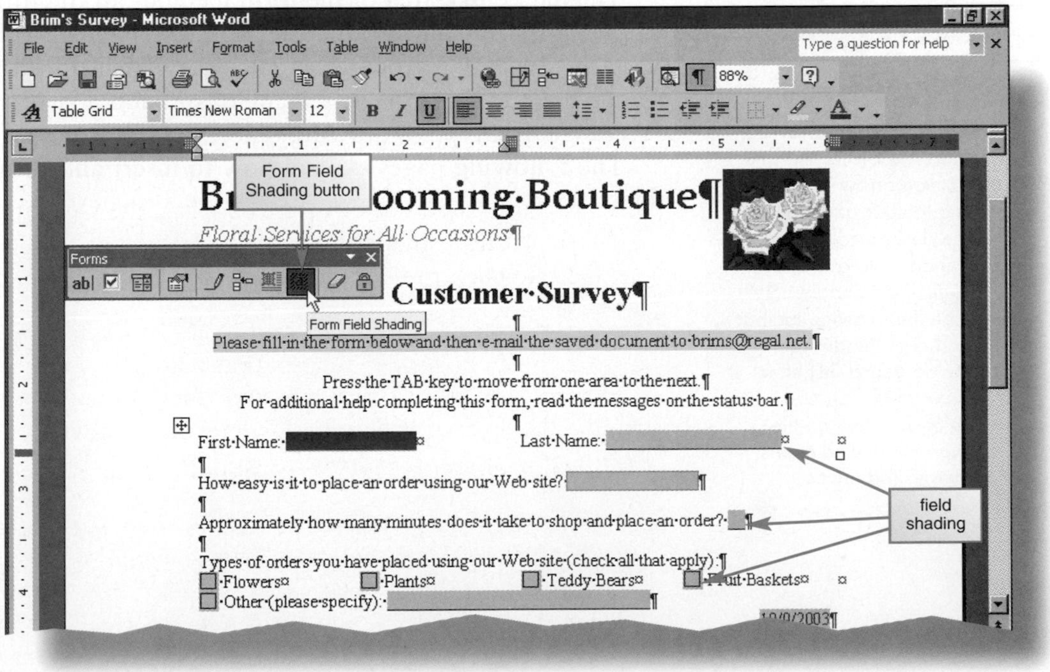
Brim's Survey - Microsoft Word
Form Field Shading button
Forms
Form Field Shading
Customer·Survey¶
Please·fill·in·the·form·below·and·then·e-mail·the·saved·document·to·brims@regal.net.¶
Press·the·TAB·key·to·move·from·one·area·to·the·next.¶
For·additional·help·completing·this·form,·read·the·messages·on·the·status·bar.¶
First·Name:·
Last·Name:·
How·easy·is·it·to·place·an·order·using·our·Web·site?
Approximately·how·many·minutes·does·it·take·to·shop·and·place·an·order?·
Types·of·orders·you·have·placed·using·our·Web·site·(check·all·that·apply):¶
·Flowers
·Plants
·Teddy·Bears
·Other·(please·specify):·
field shading

FIGURE 7-39

2 **Click the Form Field Shading button.**

Word removes the shading from the form fields (Figure 7-40).

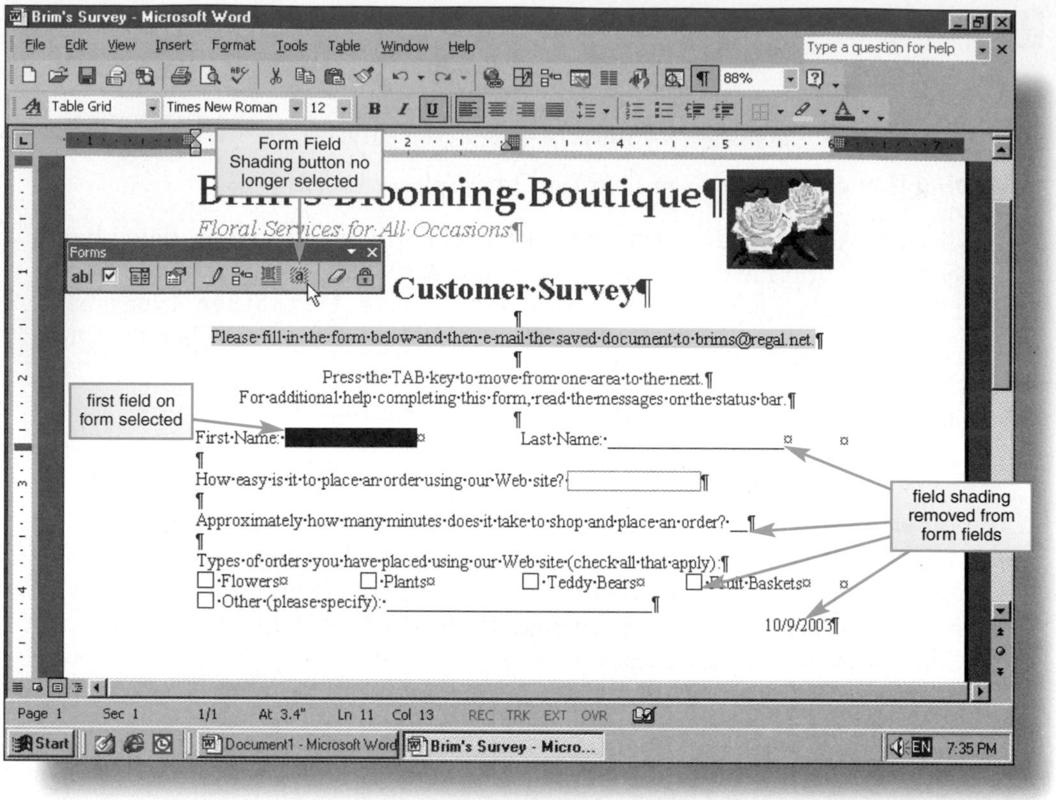
Brim's Survey - Microsoft Word
Form Field Shading button no longer selected
Brim's Blooming Boutique¶
Floral Services for All Occasions¶
Forms
Customer Survey¶
Please fill in the form below and then e-mail the saved document to brims@regal.net.¶
Press the TAB key to move from one area to the next.¶
For additional help completing this form, read the messages on the status bar.¶
first field on form selected
First Name:
Last Name:
How easy is it to place an order using our Web site?
Approximately how many minutes does it take to shop and place an order?
Types of orders you have placed using our Web site (check all that apply):¶
Flowers
Plants
Teddy Bears
Fruit Baskets
Other (please specify):
10/9/2003¶
field shading removed from form fields

FIGURE 7-40

Other Ways

1. In Voice Command mode, say "Form Field Shading"

More About

Drawing Objects

To change the color of a drawing object, click the Line Color button arrow on the Drawing toolbar and then click the desired color. To add a shadow to a drawing object, click the Shadow Style button on the Drawing toolbar and then click the desired shadow. To add a 3-D effect to a drawing object, click the 3-D Style button on the Drawing toolbar and then click the desired effect.

The next step is to emphasize the data entry area of the form.

Inserting and Formatting a Rectangle Drawing Object

The data entry area of the form includes all the form fields into which a user enters data. You want to call attention to this area of the form. Thus, you decide to place a rectangle around the data entry area, fill the rectangle with a texture, change the line color of the rectangle, and add a shadow to the rectangle. In Word, a rectangle is a type of drawing object.

The following pages explain how to insert and format a rectangle drawing object.

Steps To Draw a Rectangle

1 Click at the end of the form, positioning the insertion point after the date field. If the Drawing toolbar does not display on the screen, click the Drawing button on the Standard toolbar. Point to the Rectangle button on the Drawing toolbar (Figure 7-41).

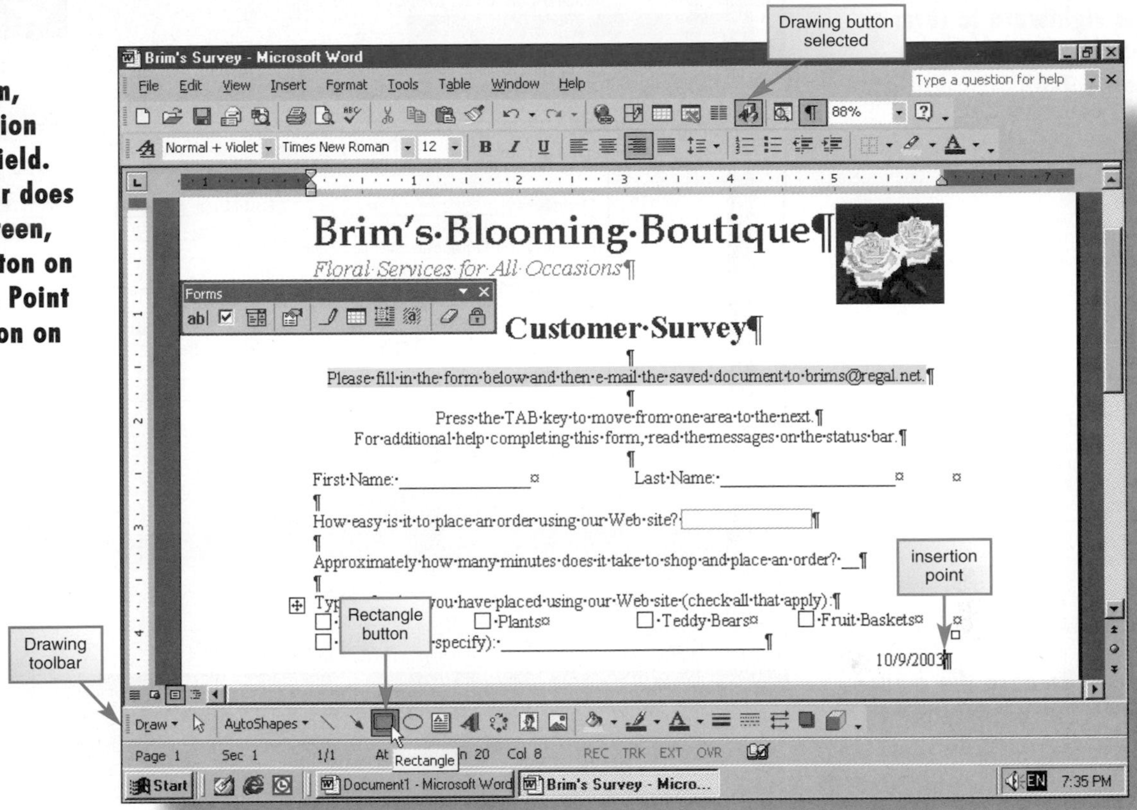
Drawing button selected
Brim's Survey - Microsoft Word
Brim's·Blooming·Boutique¶
Floral·Services·for·All·Occasions¶
Customer·Survey¶
Please·fill·in·the·form·below·and·then·e-mail·the·saved·document·to·brims@regal.net.¶
Press·the·TAB·key·to·move·from·one·area·to·the·next.¶
For·additional·help·completing·this·form,·read·the·messages·on·the·status·bar.¶
insertion point
Rectangle button
Drawing toolbar
Rectangle

FIGURE 7-41

2 Click the Rectangle button. When Word inserts the drawing canvas, scroll above the drawing canvas to display the form fields completely. Position the crosshair mouse pointer as shown in Figure 7-42.

Word displays the mouse pointer as a crosshair, which you drag to form the size of the rectangle. Recall that the drawing canvas is a container that helps you resize and arrange shapes on the page. You do not want the AutoShape on the drawing canvas.

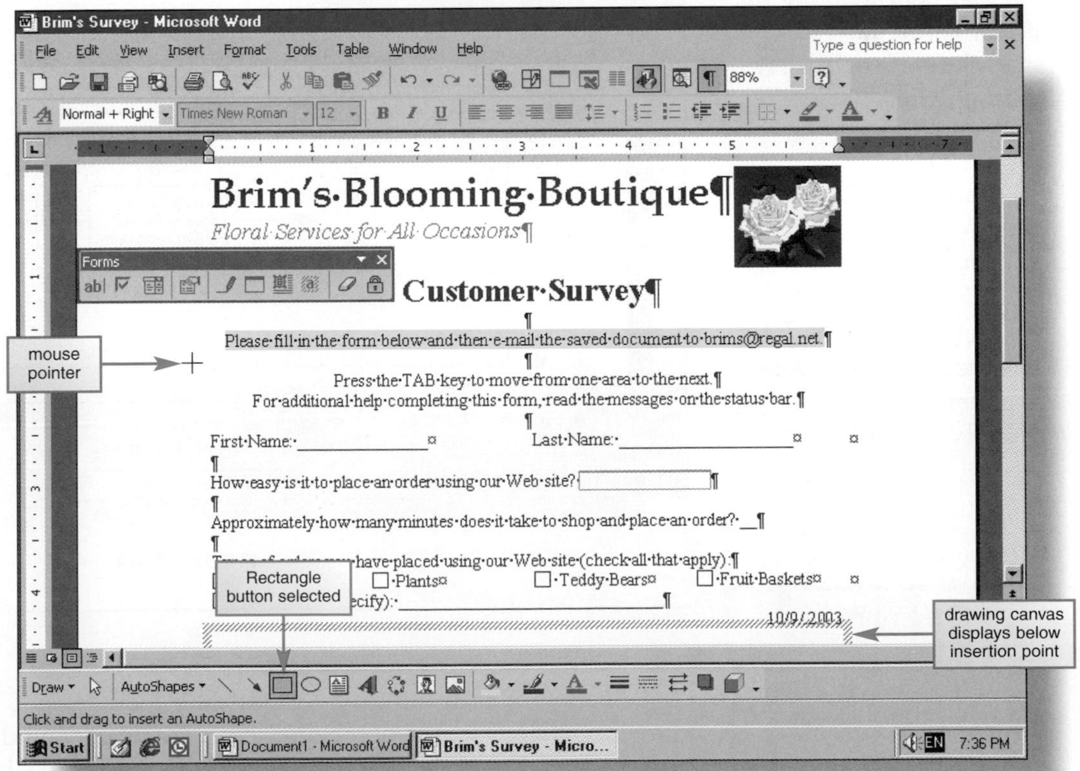
Brim's Survey - Microsoft Word
mouse pointer
Rectangle button selected
drawing canvas displays below insertion point
Click and drag to insert an AutoShape.

FIGURE 7-42

3 Drag the mouse pointer downward and rightward to form a rectangle as shown in Figure 7-43.

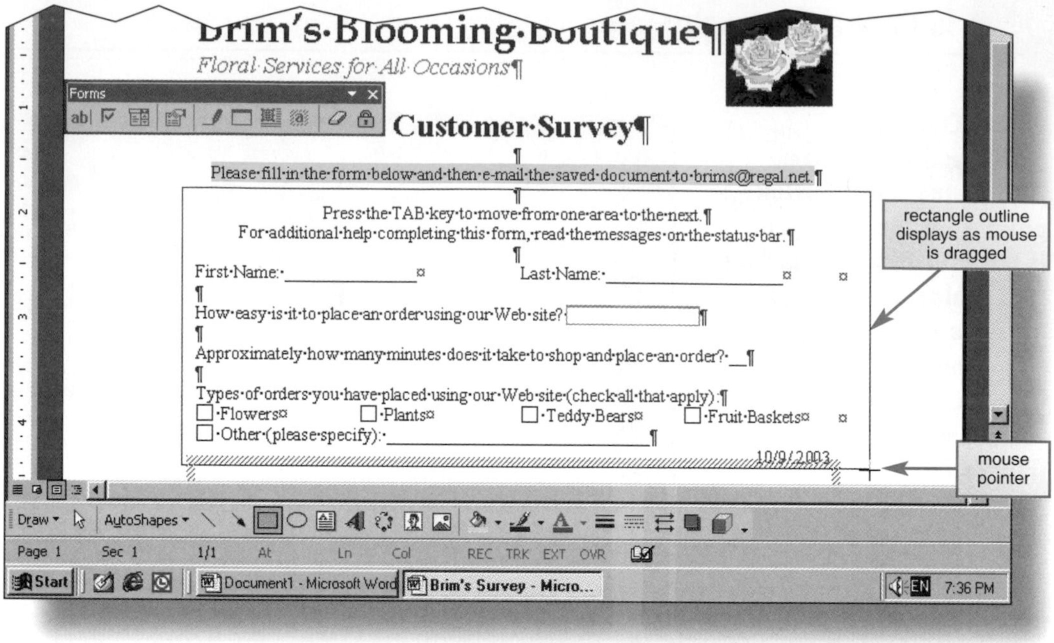
Brim's·Blooming·Boutique¶
Floral·Services·for·All·Occasions¶
Forms
Customer·Survey¶
Please·fill·in·the·form·below·and·then·e-mail·the·saved·document·to·brims@regal.net.¶
Press·the·TAB·key·to·move·from·one·area·to·the·next.¶
For·additional·help·completing·this·form,·read·the·messages·on·the·status·bar.¶
First·Name:·
Last·Name:·
How·easy·is·it·to·place·an·order·using·our·Web·site?
Approximately·how·many·minutes·does·it·take·to·shop·and·place·an·order?·
Types·of·orders·you·have·placed·using·our·Web·site·(check·all·that·apply):¶
·Flowers
·Plants
·Teddy·Bears
·Fruit·Baskets
·Other·(please·specify):·
10/9/2003
rectangle outline displays as mouse is dragged
mouse pointer
Draw
AutoShapes
Page 1
Sec 1
1/1
At
Ln
Col
REC
TRK
EXT
OVR
Start
Document1 - Microsoft Word
Brim's Survey - Micro...
7:36 PM

FIGURE 7-43

4 Release the mouse button. If Word positions the form text below the rectangle, click Format on the menu bar, click AutoShape, click the Layout tab, click In front of text, and then click the OK button. If you need to resize the rectangle after it is drawn, simply drag the sizing handles.

When you release the mouse button, Word positions the rectangle on top of the text, thus hiding the data entry area from view (Figure 7-44). Once the rectangle is drawn, Word removes the drawing canvas from the screen.

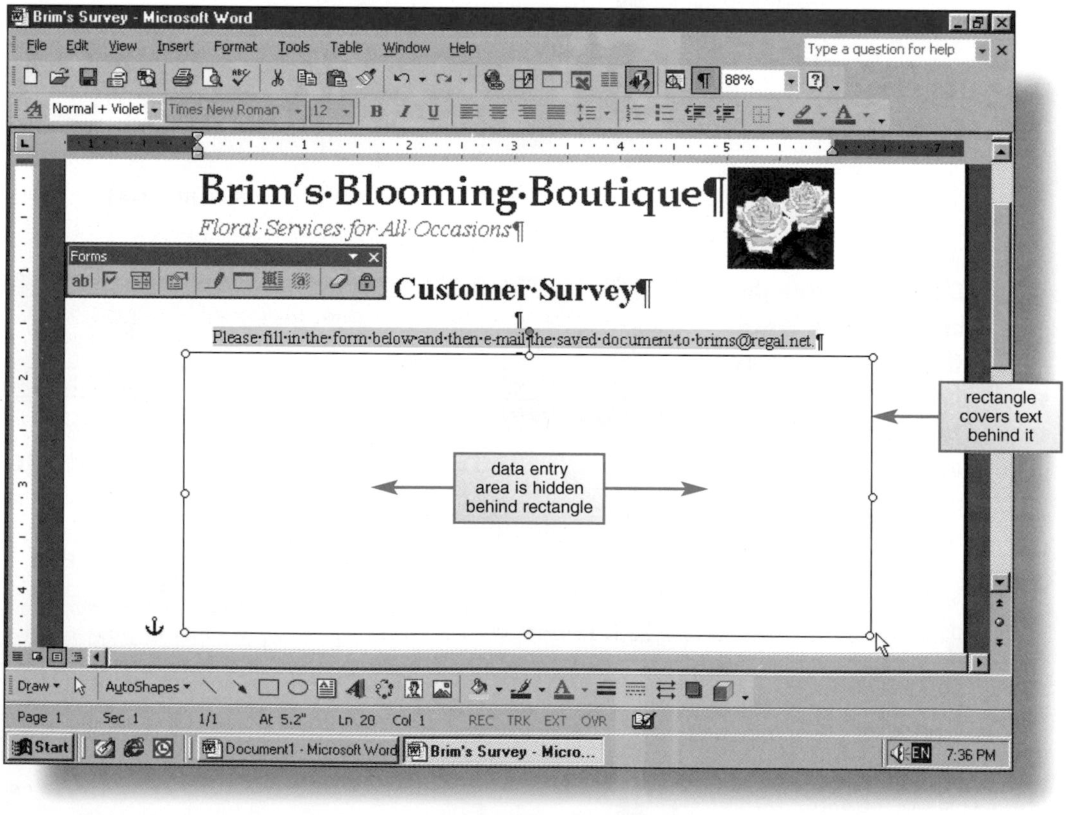
Brim's Survey - Microsoft Word
File
Edit
View
Insert
Format
Tools
Table
Window
Help
Type a question for help
88%
Normal + Violet
Times New Roman
12
Brim's·Blooming·Boutique¶
Floral·Services·for·All·Occasions¶
Forms
Customer·Survey¶
Please·fill·in·the·form·below·and·then·e-mail·the·saved·document·to·brims@regal.net.¶
rectangle covers text behind it
data entry area is hidden behind rectangle
Draw
AutoShapes
Page 1
Sec 1
1/1
At 5.2"
Ln 20
Col 1
REC
TRK
EXT
OVR
Start
Document1 - Microsoft Word
Brim's Survey - Micro...
7:36 PM

FIGURE 7-44

Other Ways

1. With Drawing toolbar displaying, in Voice Command mode, say "Rectangle, [draw rectangle]"

When you insert a drawing object into a document, Word initially places the drawing object in front of, or on top of, any text behind it. You can change the stacking order of the drawing object so that it displays behind the text, as shown in the following steps.

Steps To Send a Drawing Object behind Text

1 Point to the edge of the drawing object (in this case, the rectangle) until the mouse pointer displays a four-headed arrow and then right-click. Point to Order on the shortcut menu and then point to Send Behind Text (Figure 7-45).

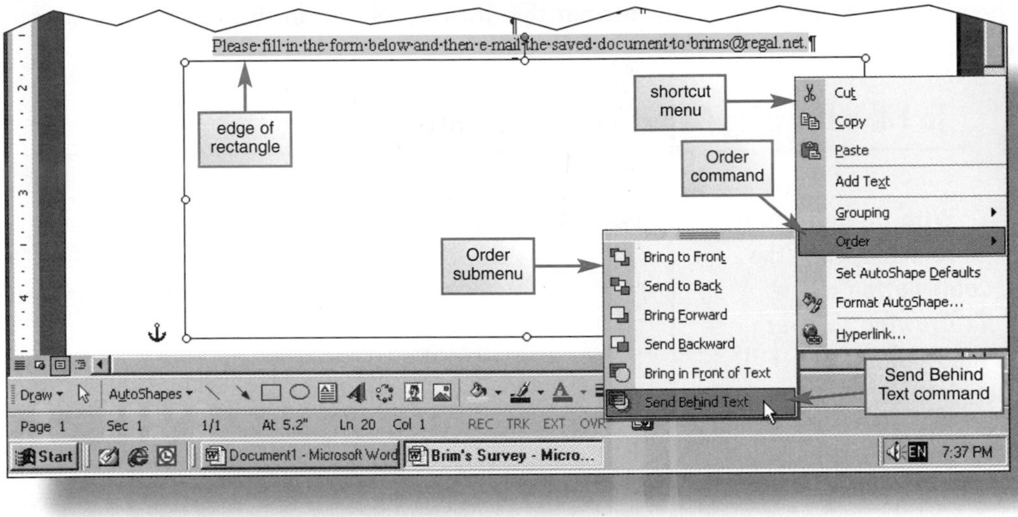

Please·fill·in·the·form·below·and·then·e-mail·the·saved·document·to·brims@regal.net.¶
edge of rectangle
shortcut menu
Order command
Order submenu
Cut
Copy
Paste
Add Text
Grouping
Order
Set AutoShape Defaults
Format AutoShape...
Hyperlink...
Bring to Front
Send to Back
Bring Forward
Send Backward
Bring in Front of Text
Send Behind Text
Send Behind Text command

FIGURE 7-45

2 Click Send Behind Text.

Word positions the rectangle drawing object behind the text (Figure 7-46). The data entry area is visible again.

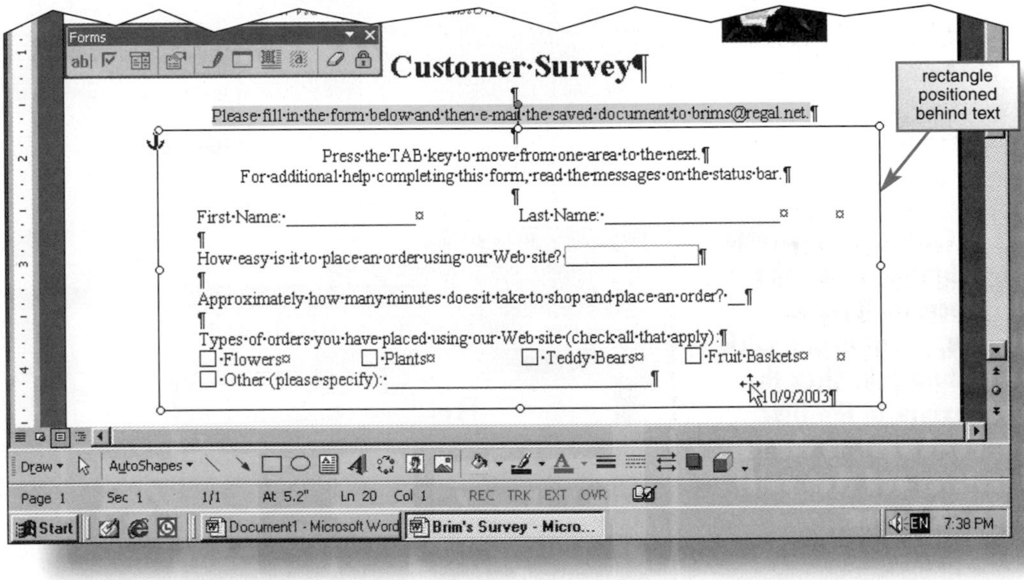

Customer·Survey¶
Please·fill·in·the·form·below·and·then·e-mail·the·saved·document·to·brims@regal.net.¶
rectangle positioned behind text
Press·the·TAB·key·to·move·from·one·area·to·the·next.¶
For·additional·help·completing·this·form,·read·the·messages·on·the·status·bar.¶
First·Name:·
Last·Name:·
How·easy·is·it·to·place·an·order·using·our·Web·site?
Approximately·how·many·minutes·does·it·take·to·shop·and·place·an·order?·
Types·of·orders·you·have·placed·using·our·Web·site·(check·all·that·apply):¶
·Flowers
·Plants
·Teddy·Bears
·Fruit·Baskets
·Other·(please·specify):·
10/9/2003¶

FIGURE 7-46

If you want to bring the drawing object on top of the text again, right-click one of its edges, point to Order on the shortcut menu, and then click Bring in Front of Text (Figure 7-45).

If you have multiple graphics displaying on the screen and would like them to overlap, you can change their stacking order by right-clicking the graphic to reorder, pointing to Order on the shortcut menu, and then clicking one of the first four commands on the Order submenu (Figure 7-45). The Bring to Front command displays the selected object at the top of the stack, and the Send to Back command displays the selected object at the bottom of the stack. The Bring Forward and Send Backward commands each move the drawing object forward or backward one layer in the stack.

Other Ways

1. Click drawing object, on Format menu click AutoShape, click Layout tab, click Behind text, click OK button
2. With drawing object selected, in Voice Command mode, say "Format, AutoShape, Layout, Behind text, OK"

The next step is to fill the inside of the rectangle. In Word, you can **fill**, or paint, the inside of a drawing object with a color or with an effect. **Fill effects** include gradient (two-toned) colors, textures, patterns, and pictures. Perform the following steps to format the drawing object, in this case the rectangle, using a texture fill effect.

Steps To Fill a Drawing Object with a Texture

1 With the rectangle selected, click the Fill Color button arrow on the Drawing toolbar and then point to the Fill Effects button.

The available predefined fill colors display, as well as the More Fill Colors and Fill Effects buttons (Figure 7-47).

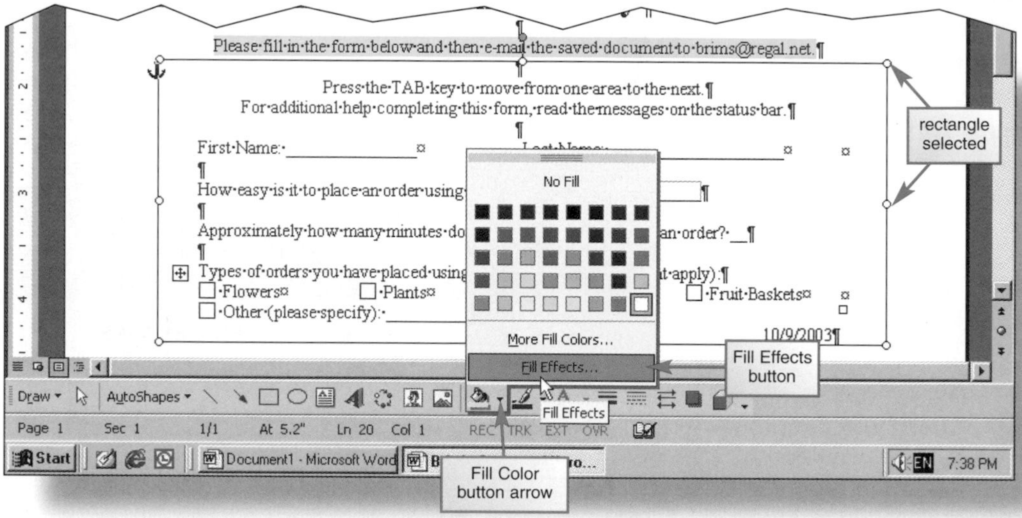

FIGURE 7-47

2 Click the Fill Effects button. When the Fill Effects dialog box displays, if necessary, click the Texture tab. Click the third texture in the first row, Parchment, in the list of textures and then point to the OK button.

Word displays the Fill Effects dialog box (Figure 7-48). The selected texture name displays below the textures.

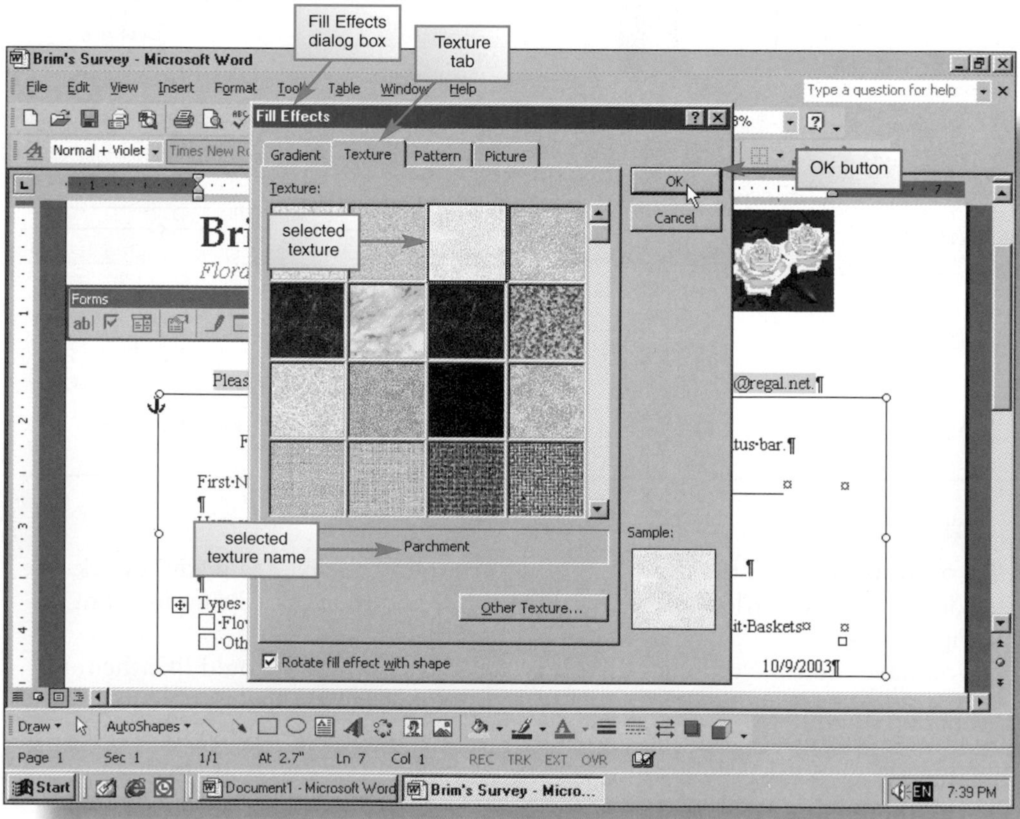

FIGURE 7-48

3 Click the OK button.

Word fills the rectangle with the Parchment texture (Figure 7-49).

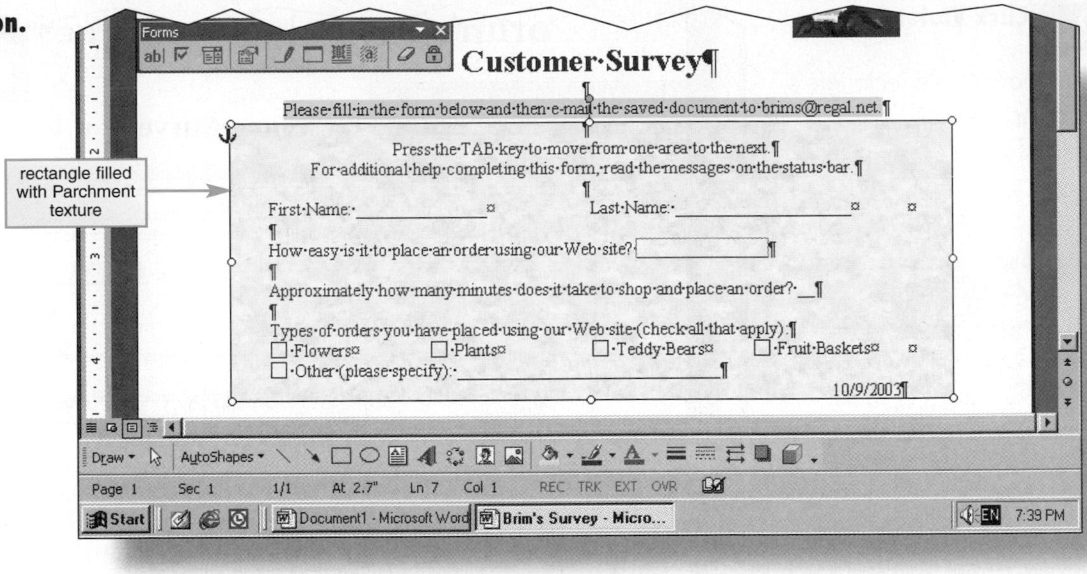
rectangle filled with Parchment texture
Customer Survey
Please fill in the form below and then e-mail the saved document to brims@regal.net.
Press the TAB key to move from one area to the next.
For additional help completing this form, read the messages on the status bar.
First Name:
Last Name:
How easy is it to place an order using our Web site?
Approximately how many minutes does it take to shop and place an order?
Types of orders you have placed using our Web site (check all that apply):
Flowers
Plants
Teddy Bears
Fruit Baskets
Other (please specify):
10/9/2003

FIGURE 7-49

Other Ways

1. With drawing object selected, in Voice Command mode, say "Format, AutoShape, Colors and Lines, Fill Color, Fill Effects, Texture, [select desired texture], OK, OK"

The next step is to change the line color of the rectangle from the default color, black, to violet, which matches the color of the text. Perform the following steps to change the line color of the rectangle drawing object.

Steps To Change the Line Color of a Drawing Object

1 With the rectangle selected, click the Line Color button arrow on the Drawing toolbar and then point to Violet.

The available predefined line colors display, as well as the More Line Colors and Patterned Lines buttons (Figure 7-50).

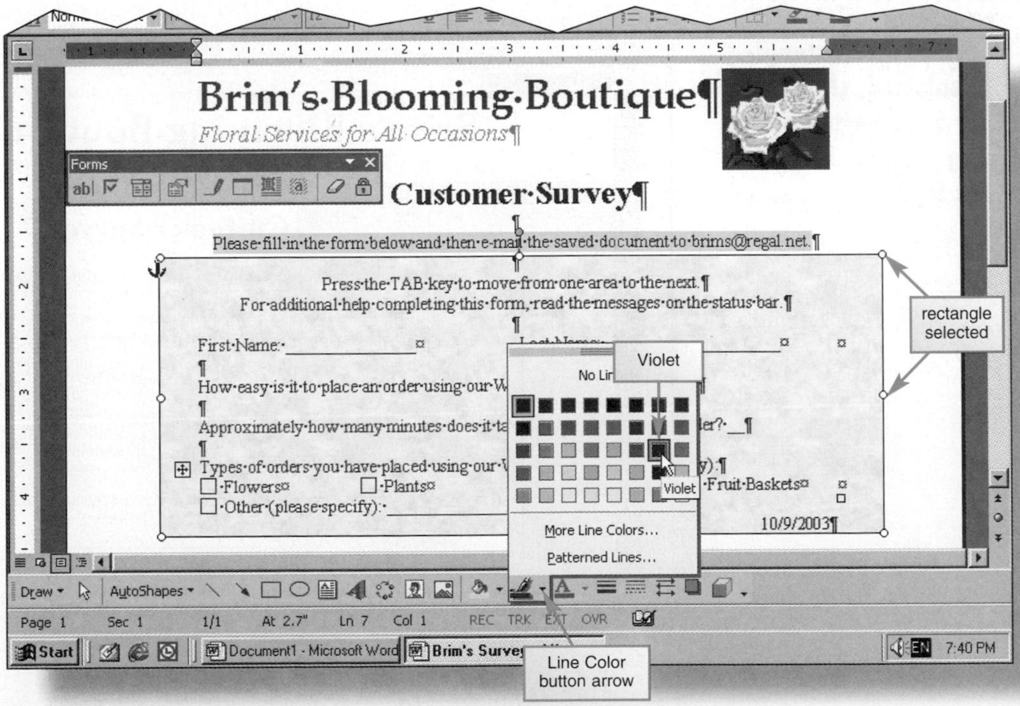
Brim's Blooming Boutique
Floral Services for All Occasions
Customer Survey
rectangle selected
Violet
No Line
More Line Colors...
Patterned Lines...
Line Color button arrow

FIGURE 7-50

2 Click Violet.

Word changes the rectangle's line color to violet (Figure 7-51).

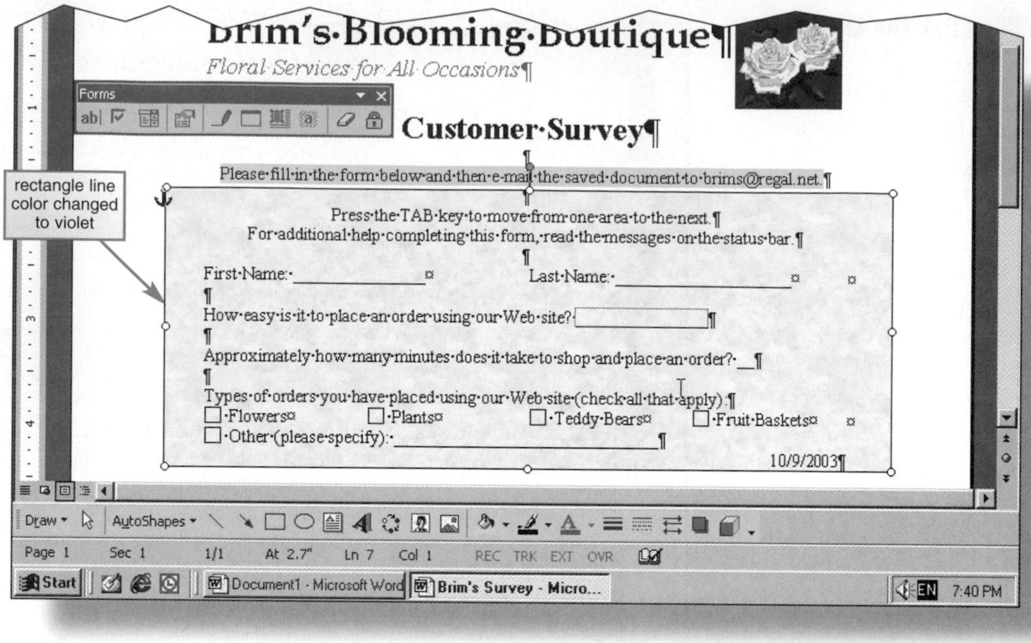

FIGURE 7-51

Other Ways

1. Select drawing object, click AutoShape on Format menu, click Colors and Lines tab, click Color button arrow in Line area, click desired color, click OK button
2. Right-click edge of drawing object, click Format AutoShape on shortcut menu, click Colors and Lines tab, click Color button arrow in Line area, click desired color, click OK button
3. With drawing object selected, in Voice Command mode, say "Format, AutoShape, Colors and Lines, Line Color, [select color], OK"

The next step is to add a shadow to the drawing object (in this case, the rectangle), as shown in the following steps.

Steps To Add a Shadow to a Drawing Object

1 With the rectangle selected, click the Shadow Style button on the Drawing toolbar. Point to Shadow Style 5.

The available predefined shadow styles display, as well as the Shadow Settings button (Figure 7-52).

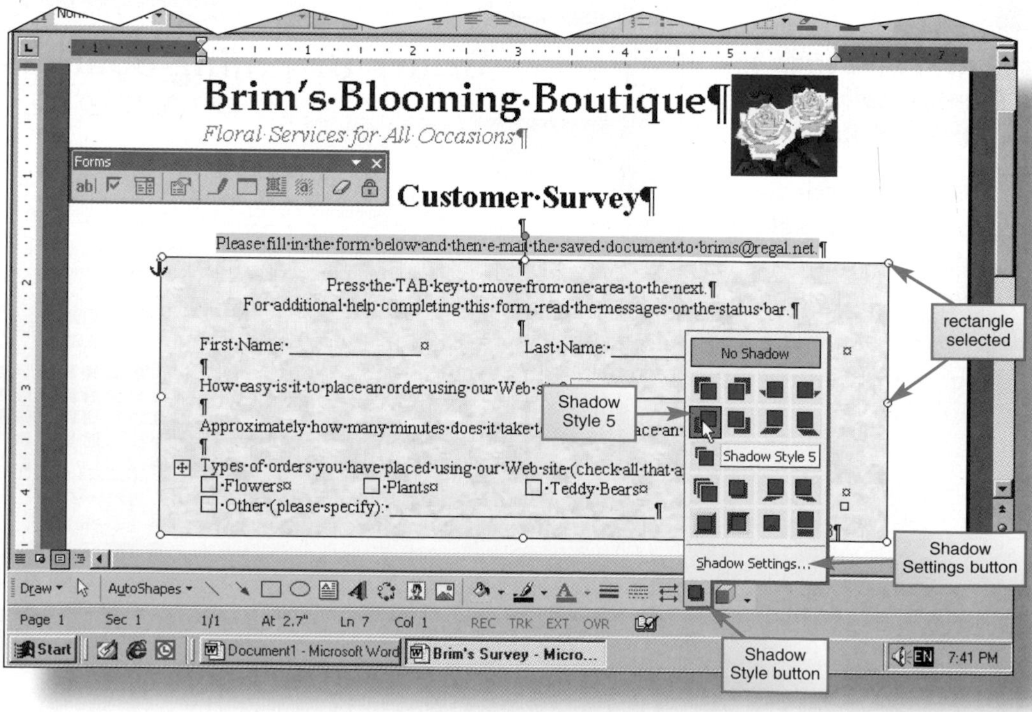

FIGURE 7-52

2 Click Shadow Style 5. Click the Drawing button on the Standard toolbar to remove the Drawing toolbar. Click inside the selected rectangle to remove the selection. If necessary, scroll up to position the boutique name at the top of the document window.

Word adds a shadow to the left and bottom of the rectangle (Figure 7-53). Turning off the Drawing toolbar allows you to see the entire form on the screen.

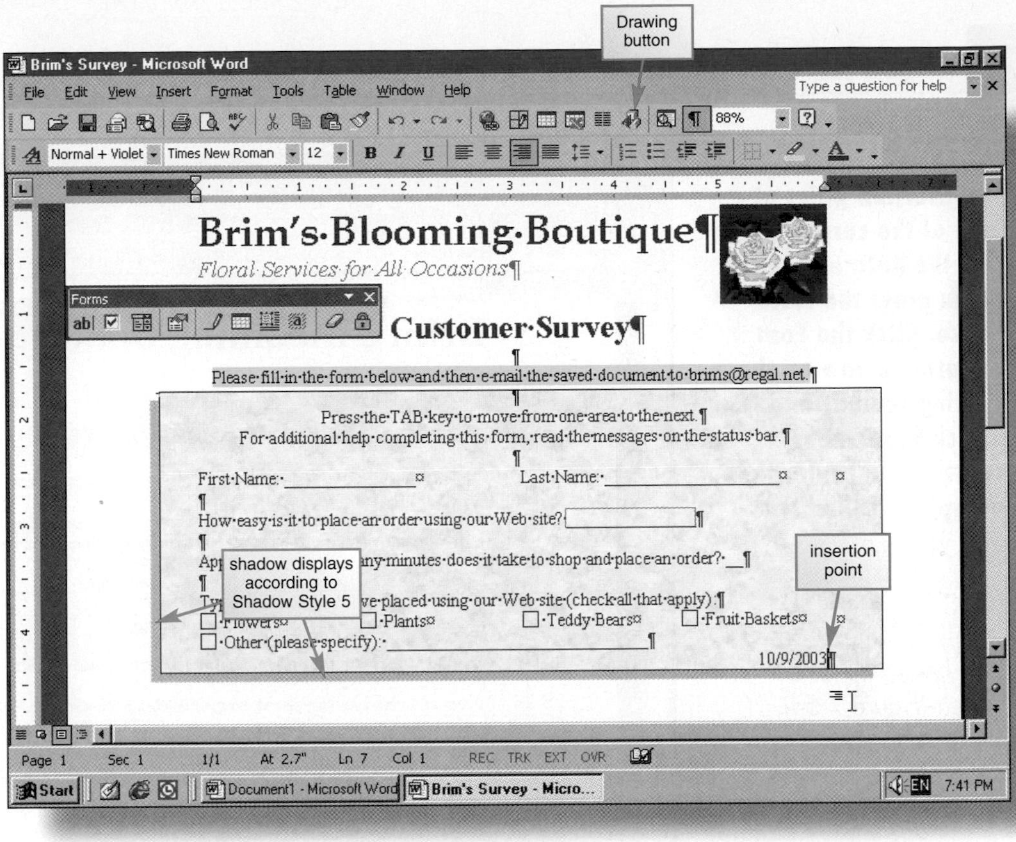
Drawing button
Brim's Survey - Microsoft Word
Brim's·Blooming·Boutique¶
Floral·Services·for·All·Occasions¶
Customer·Survey¶
Please·fill·in·the·form·below·and·then·e-mail·the·saved·document·to·brims@regal.net.¶
Press·the·TAB·key·to·move·from·one·area·to·the·next.¶
For·additional·help·completing·this·form,·read·the·messages·on·the·status·bar.¶
First·Name:·
Last·Name:·
How·easy·is·it·to·place·an·order·using·our·Web·site?
shadow displays according to Shadow Style 5
insertion point
Plants
Teddy·Bears
Fruit·Baskets
Other·(please·specify):·
10/9/2003¶

FIGURE 7-53

Other Ways

1. With Drawing toolbar displaying, in Voice Command mode, say "Shadow Style, [select shadow style]"

When clicked, the Shadow Settings button (Figure 7-52) displays the Shadow Settings toolbar. If you want Word to display a wider or narrower shadow, you may move the shadow up, down, left, or right, by clicking any of the four Nudge Shadow buttons on the Shadow Settings toolbar to create the effect you want. Each time you click Nudge Shadow, the shadow moves one point in the specified direction.

The next step is to enter and format the thank-you message below the data entry area.

Animating Text

In an online document, you can animate text in order to draw the reader's attention to it. When you **animate text**, it has the appearance of motion. To animate text in Word, you select it and then apply one of the predefined text effects in the Font dialog box.

For this form, you want the thank-you message below the data entry area to have a moving black rectangle around it, which is called the Marching Black Ants animation in the Font dialog box. Perform the steps on the next page to animate the thank-you message on the online form.

More About

Animated Text

Animated text can distract readers; thus, you should use it sparingly. If a reader wants to hide animated text, he or she can click Tools on the menu bar, click Options, click the View tab, remove the check mark from the Animated text check box, and then click the OK button. Animated text does not print on a hard copy.

Steps To Animate Text

1 **Position the insertion point at the end of the current date in the data entry area and then press the ENTER key twice. Click the Font Color button arrow on the Formatting toolbar and then click Sea Green. Press CTRL+E to center the paragraph and then type** `Thank you for your time!`

The thank-you message displays below the data entry area (Figure 7-54).

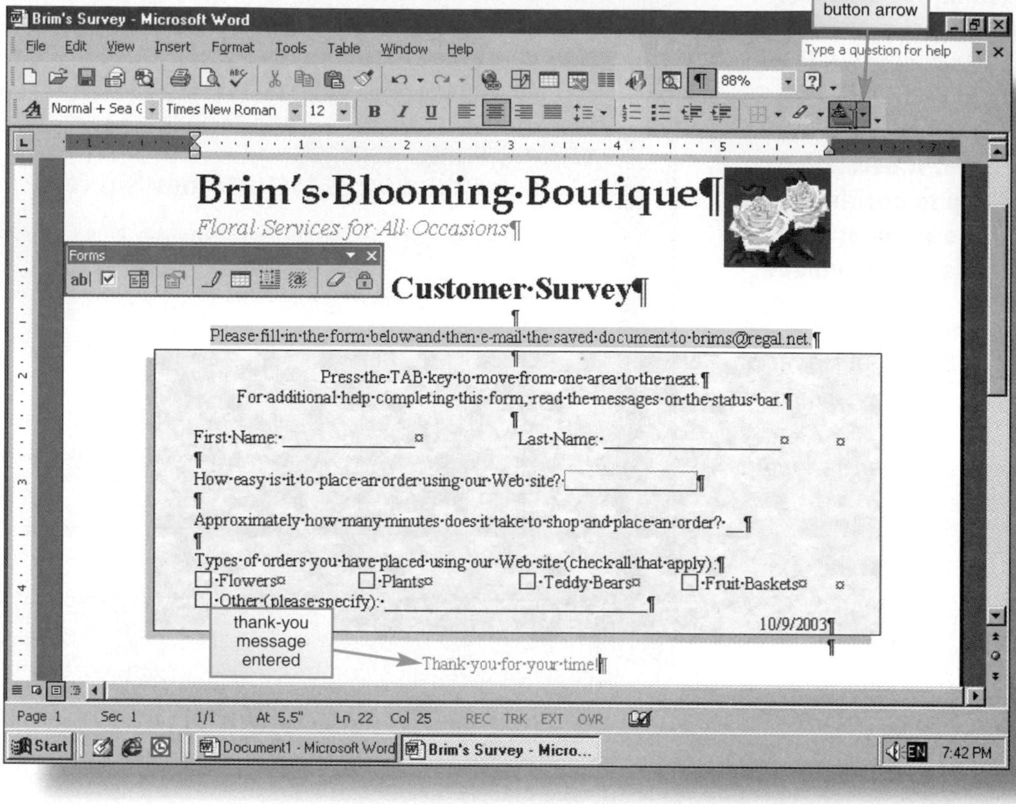

FIGURE 7-54

2 **Select the sentence just entered. Right-click the selection and then click Font on the shortcut menu. When the Font dialog box displays, if necessary, click the Text Effects tab. Click Marching Black Ants in the Animations list. Point to the OK button.**

Word displays the Font dialog box (Figure 7-55). The Preview area shows a sample of the selected animation.

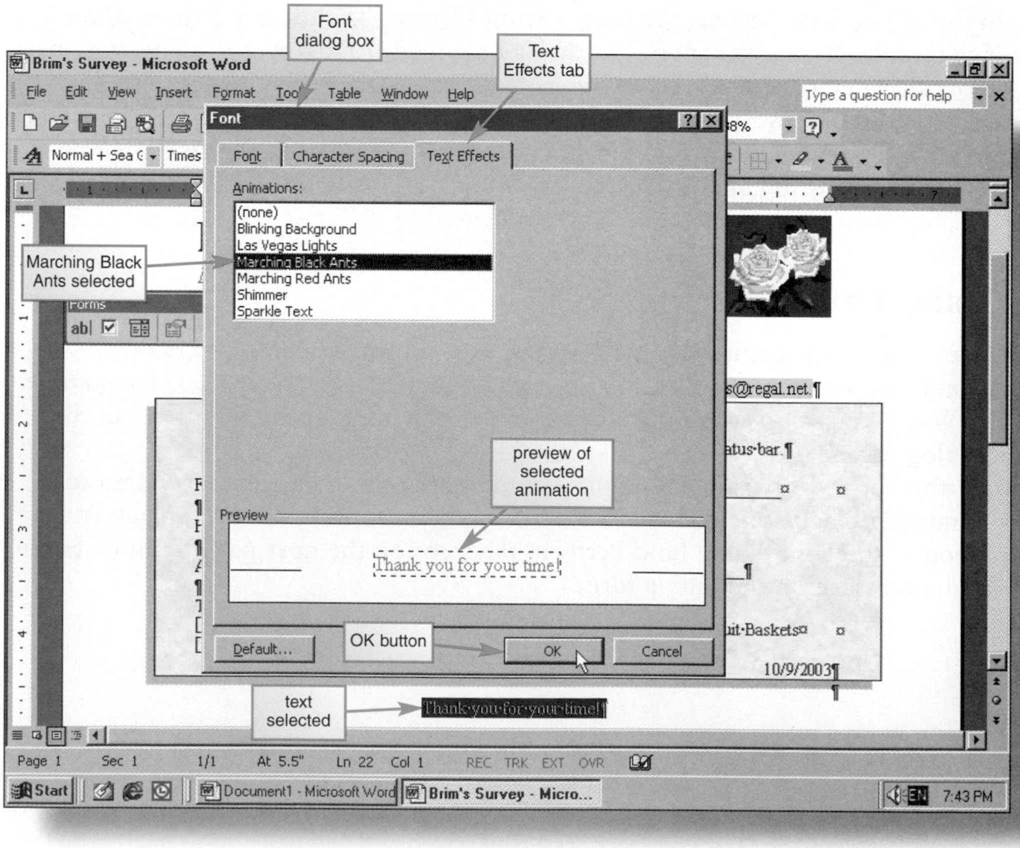

FIGURE 7-55

3 Click the OK button. Click outside the selected text to remove the selection.

Word applies the animation to the selected text (Figure 7-56).

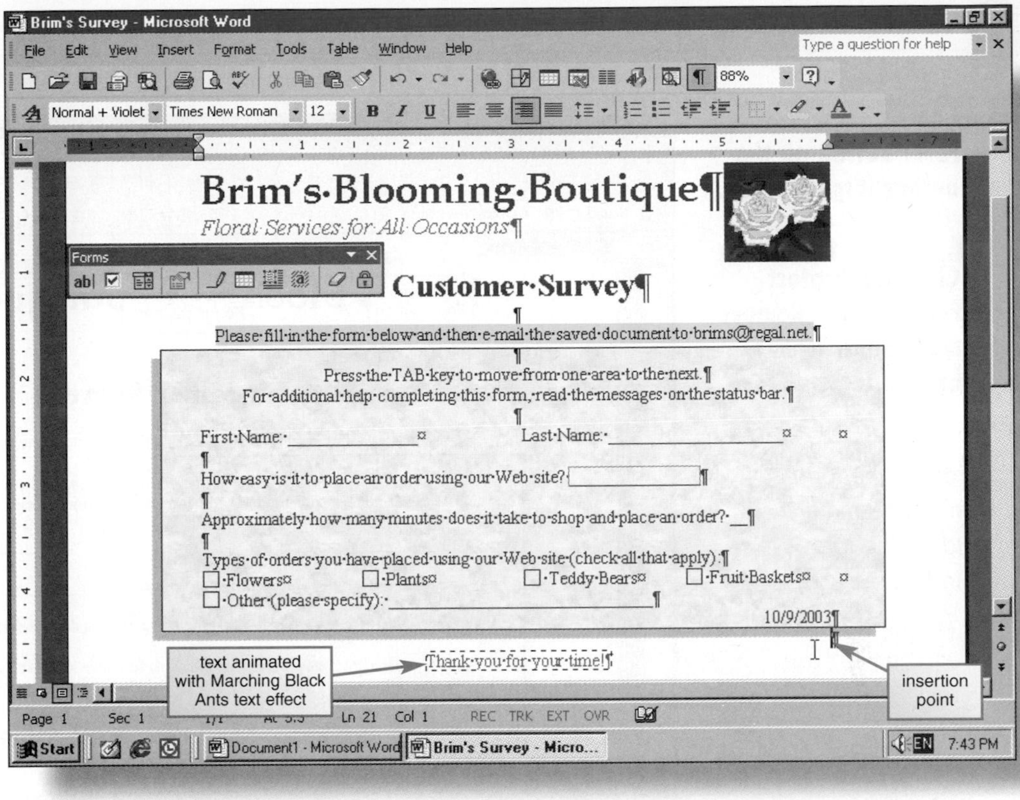

Brim's Survey - Microsoft Word
Brim's·Blooming·Boutique¶
Floral·Services·for·All·Occasions¶
Customer·Survey¶
Please·fill·in·the·form·below·and·then·e-mail·the·saved·document·to·brims@regal.net.¶
Press·the·TAB·key·to·move·from·one·area·to·the·next.¶
For·additional·help·completing·this·form,·read·the·messages·on·the·status·bar.¶
First·Name:·
Last·Name:·
How·easy·is·it·to·place·an·order·using·our·Web·site?
Approximately·how·many·minutes·does·it·take·to·shop·and·place·an·order?·
Types·of·orders·you·have·placed·using·our·Web·site·(check·all·that·apply):¶
·Flowers
·Plants
·Teddy·Bears
·Fruit·Baskets
·Other·(please·specify):·
10/9/2003¶
Thank·you·for·your·time!¶
text animated with Marching Black Ants text effect
insertion point

FIGURE 7-56

Other Ways

1. Select text, click Font on Format menu, click Text Effects tab, click desired animation, click OK button
2. In Voice Command mode, say "Format, Font, Text Effects, [select desired animation], OK"

If you want to remove an animation from text, select the text, right-click the selection, click Font on the shortcut menu, click the Text Effects tab, click (none) in the Animations list, and then click the OK button.

If you print a document that contains animated text, the animations do not show on the hard copy; instead, the text prints as regular text. Thus, animations are designed specifically for documents that will be viewed online.

The next step in this project is to protect the Customer Survey.

Protecting a Form

It is crucial that you protect a form before making it available to users. When you **protect a form**, you are allowing users to enter data only in designated areas — specifically, the form fields that are enabled.

Perform the steps on the next page to protect the Customer Survey.

More About

Protecting Forms

If you want only authorized users to be able to unprotect a form, you should password-protect the form. To do this, click Tools on the menu bar, click Protect Document, click Forms in the Protect document for area, type the password in the Password (optional) text box, and then click the OK button. Then, reenter the password in the Confirm Password dialog box.

Steps To Protect a Form

1 Point to the Protect Form button on the Forms toolbar (Figure 7-57).

2 Click the Protect Form button. Remove the Forms toolbar from the screen by clicking its Close button.

Word protects the form and then selects the first form field on the form (shown in Figure 7-58).

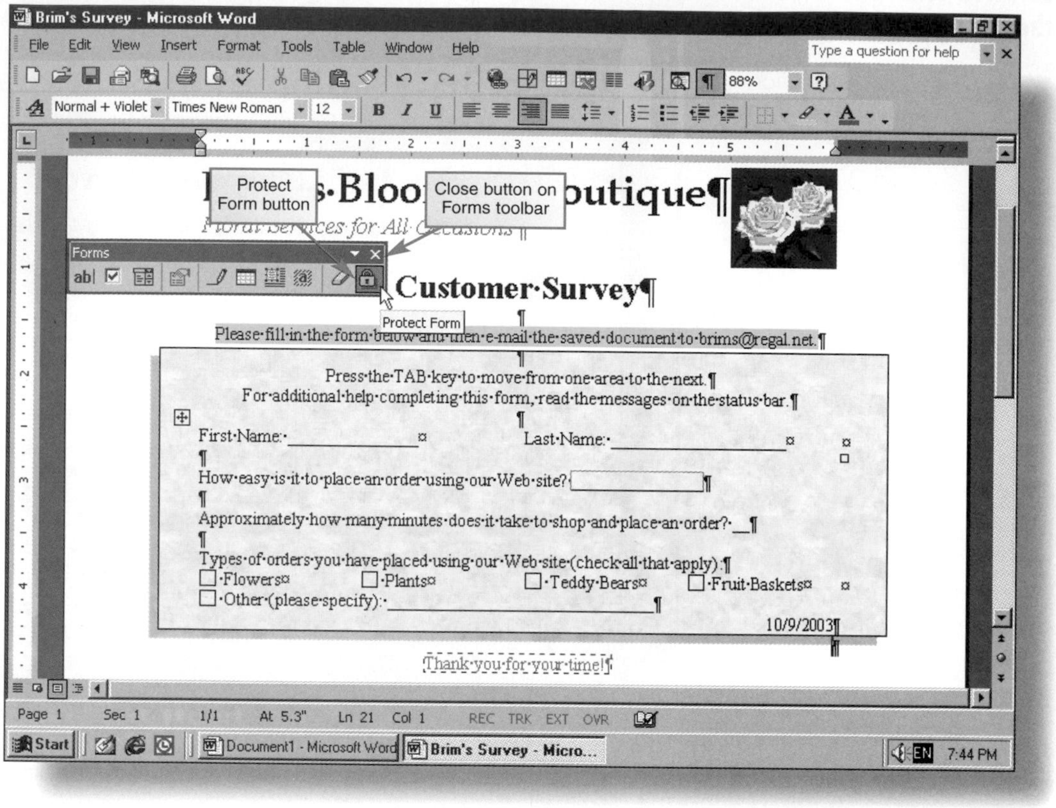

Brim's Survey - Microsoft Word
Protect Form button
Close button on Forms toolbar
Forms
Protect Form
Customer Survey
Please fill in the form below and then e-mail the saved document to brims@regal.net.
Press the TAB key to move from one area to the next.
For additional help completing this form, read the messages on the status bar.
First Name:
Last Name:
How easy is it to place an order using our Web site?
Approximately how many minutes does it take to shop and place an order?
Types of orders you have placed using our Web site (check all that apply):
Flowers
Plants
Teddy Bears
Fruit Baskets
Other (please specify):
10/9/2003
Thank you for your time!

FIGURE 7-57

Other Ways

1. On Tools menu click Protect Document, click Forms, click OK button
2. In Voice Command mode, say "Protect Form"

When the form is protected, the selection displays in the first form field. To advance to the next form field, press the TAB key. To move to a previous form field, press SHIFT+TAB. You will enter data into this form later in the project.

The next step is to turn off the display of formatting marks. You do not want them on the form when a user opens it. Perform the following step to hide formatting marks.

TO HIDE FORMATTING MARKS

1 If the Show/Hide ¶ button on the Standard toolbar is selected, click it.

Word hides the formatting marks (Figure 7-58).

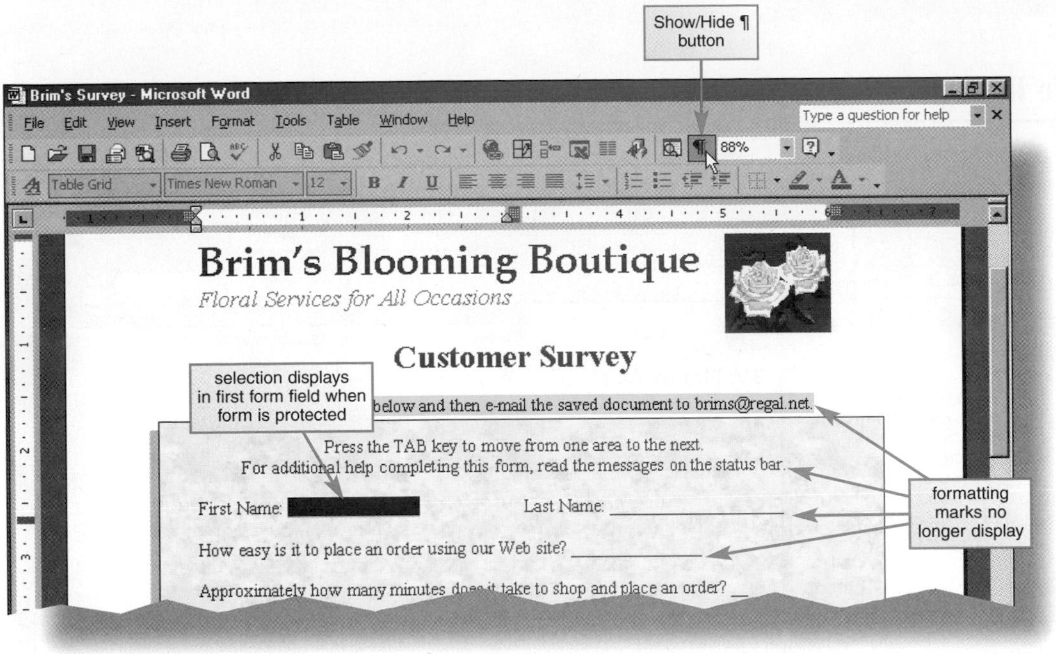
Show/Hide ¶ button
Brim's Survey - Microsoft Word
File Edit View Insert Format Tools Table Window Help
Type a question for help
88%
Table Grid
Times New Roman
12
Brim's Blooming Boutique
Floral Services for All Occasions
Customer Survey
selection displays in first form field when form is protected
below and then e-mail the saved document to brims@regal.net.
Press the TAB key to move from one area to the next.
For additional help completing this form, read the messages on the status bar.
First Name:
Last Name:
How easy is it to place an order using our Web site?
Approximately how many minutes does it take to shop and place an order?
formatting marks no longer display

FIGURE 7-58

The online form template for this project now is complete. Perform the following steps to save it again and then quit Word.

TO SAVE THE DOCUMENT AGAIN

1. Click the Save button on the Standard toolbar.

Word saves the template with the same file name, Brim's Survey.

TO QUIT WORD

1. Click File on the menu bar and then click Exit.

The Word window closes.

Working with an Online Form

Once you have created a template, you then can make it available to users. Users do not open templates with the Open button on the Standard toolbar in Word. A developer of a template uses the Open button to open the template so it can be modified. A user, by contrast, starts a new Word document that is based on the template. That is, when a user accesses a template, the title bar displays the default file name, Document1 (or a similar name). Instead of the Word window being blank, however, it contains text and formatting associated with the template that the user accesses. For example, Word provides a variety of templates such as those for memos, letters, fax cover sheets, and resumes. If a user accesses a memo template, Word displays the contents of a basic memo in a new document window.

When you save the template to a disk in drive A, as instructed earlier in this project, a user can access your template through the My Computer window or Windows Explorer. Perform the steps on the next page to display a new Word document window that is based on the Brim's Survey template.

More About

Web Forms

Online forms frequently are used on Web pages to collect and provide data. For example, you might create a form on a Web page that allows users to search a database you have stored on a Web server or collect data from visitors. A Web form typically contains a Submit button to send the information back to the host computer. The Submit button and other Web form controls are available on the Web Tools toolbar.

Steps To Access a Template through Windows Explorer

1 **Right-click the My Computer icon on the Windows desktop and then click Explore on the shortcut menu. When the Explorer window opens, if necessary, double-click its title bar to maximize the window. Click the Address text box to select it. Type** a: **and then press the ENTER key.**

The Explorer window opens (Figure 7-59). Notice the icon for the Brim's Survey template has a small yellow bar at its top. Your Explorer window may display differently.

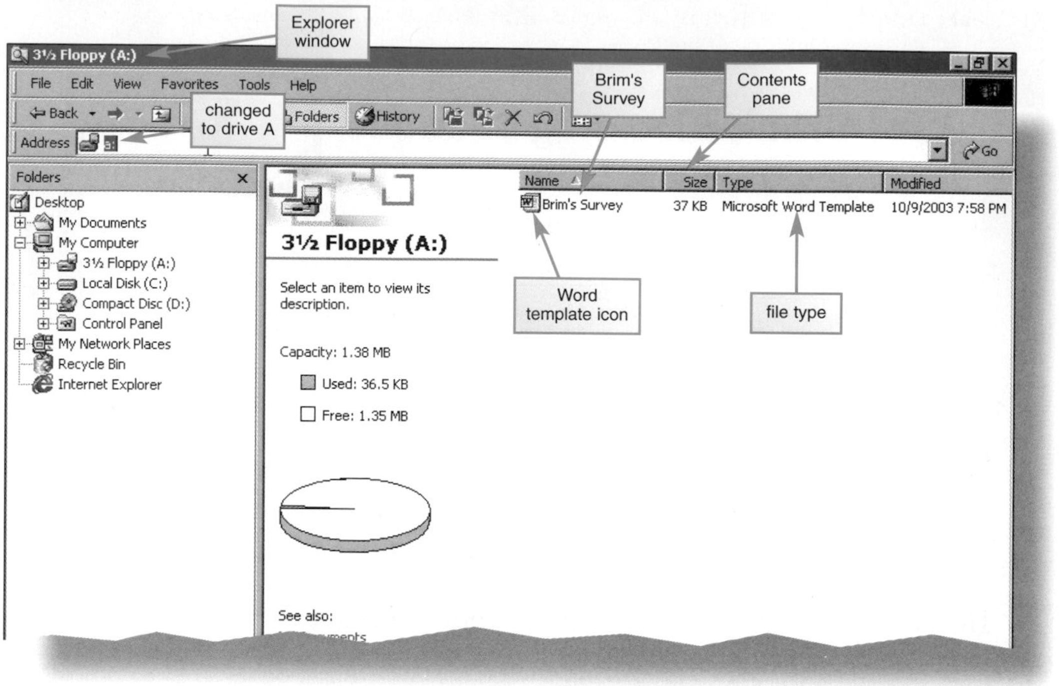

FIGURE 7-59

2 **Double-click the Brim's Survey icon in the Contents pane. When Word starts, if necessary, maximize the Word window. If the Show/Hide ¶ button on the Standard toolbar is selected, click it. Zoom to Page Width. If gridlines display, click Table on the menu bar and then click Hide Gridlines. Scroll down so the entire form displays in the Word window.**

Windows starts Word and displays a new document window that is based on the contents of the Brim's Survey template (Figure 7-60). The selection displays in the first form field, ready for a user's data entry. The corresponding Help message displays on the status bar.

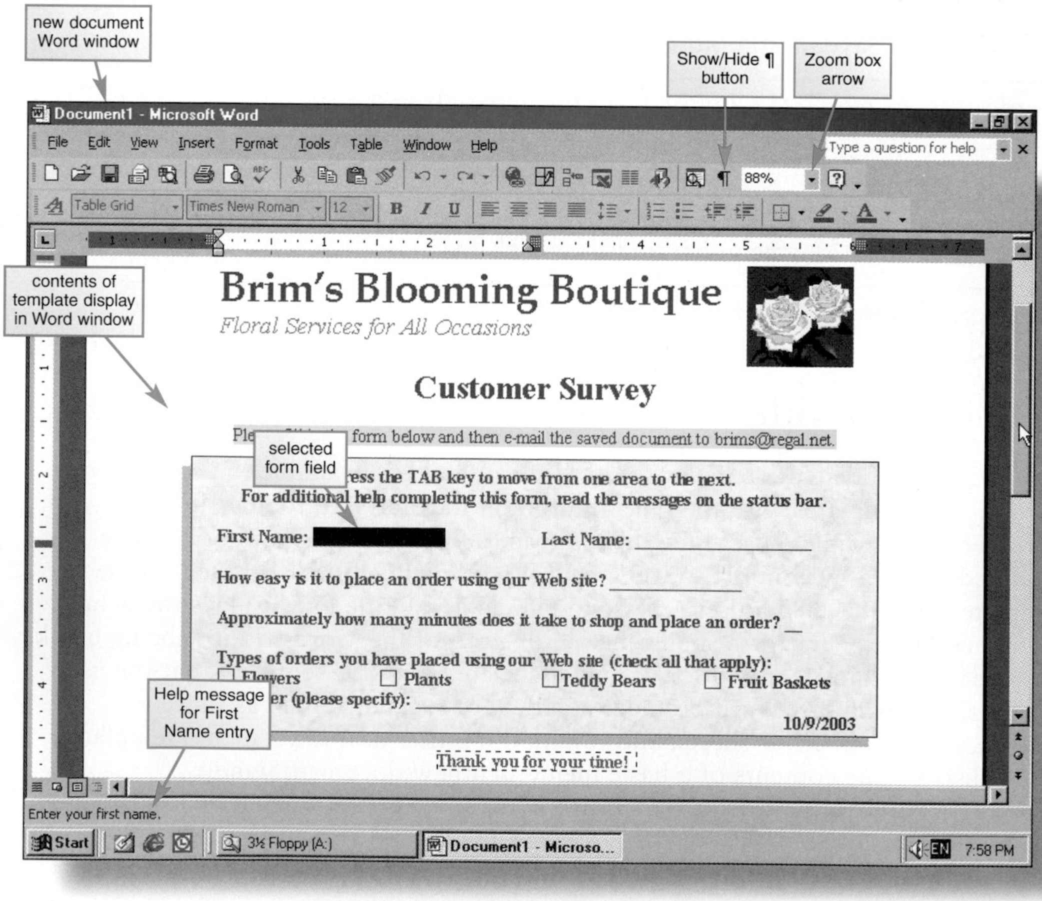

FIGURE 7-60

The next step is to enter data into the form. To advance to the next form field, a user presses the TAB key. To move to a previous form field, a user presses SHIFT+TAB. As a user tabs from one form field to the next, the status bar displays the Help messages related to the current field.

Perform the following steps to fill out the Customer Survey.

Steps To Fill Out a Form

1 **With the First Name form field selected, type** `Lourdes` **and then press the TAB key. Type** `Nunez` **in the Last Name form field. Press the TAB key to select the ease of use form field and display its box arrow. Click the box arrow and then point to Very Easy.**

The drop-down list displays (Figure 7-61).

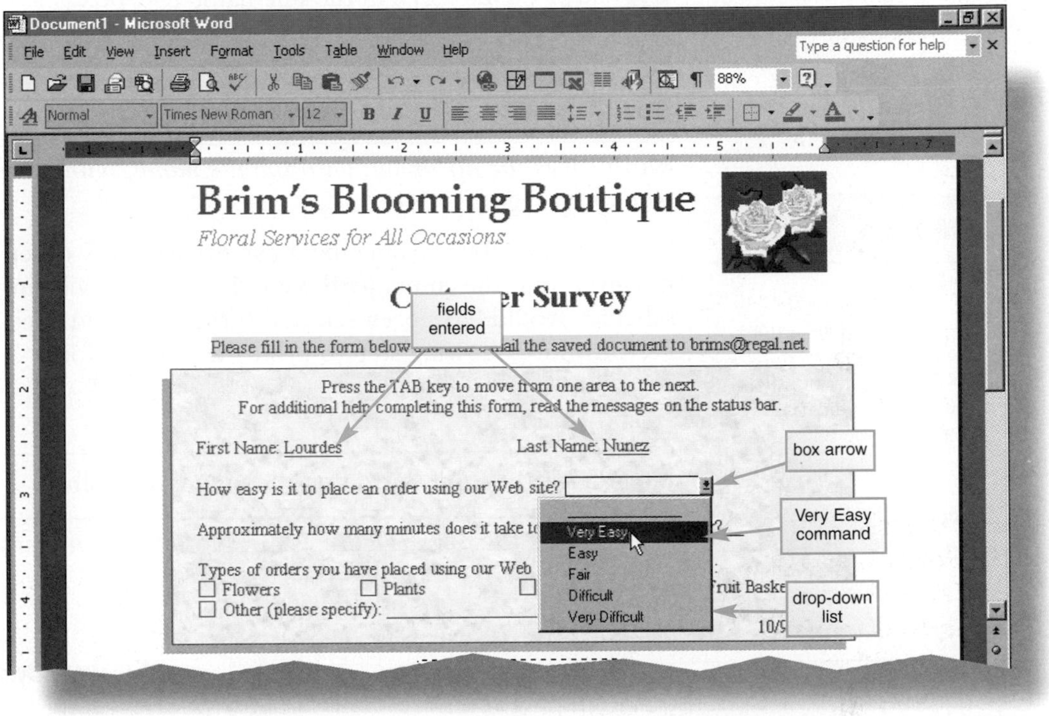

FIGURE 7-61

2 **Click Very Easy and then press the TAB key. Type** `15` **in the number of minutes text box. Press the TAB key. Click the following check boxes: Flowers, Fruit Baskets, and Other. Press the TAB key. Type** `Balloon Basket` **in the Other text box.**

The form is filled in (Figure 7-62). Notice that the text box and drop-down list box entries are underlined in violet.

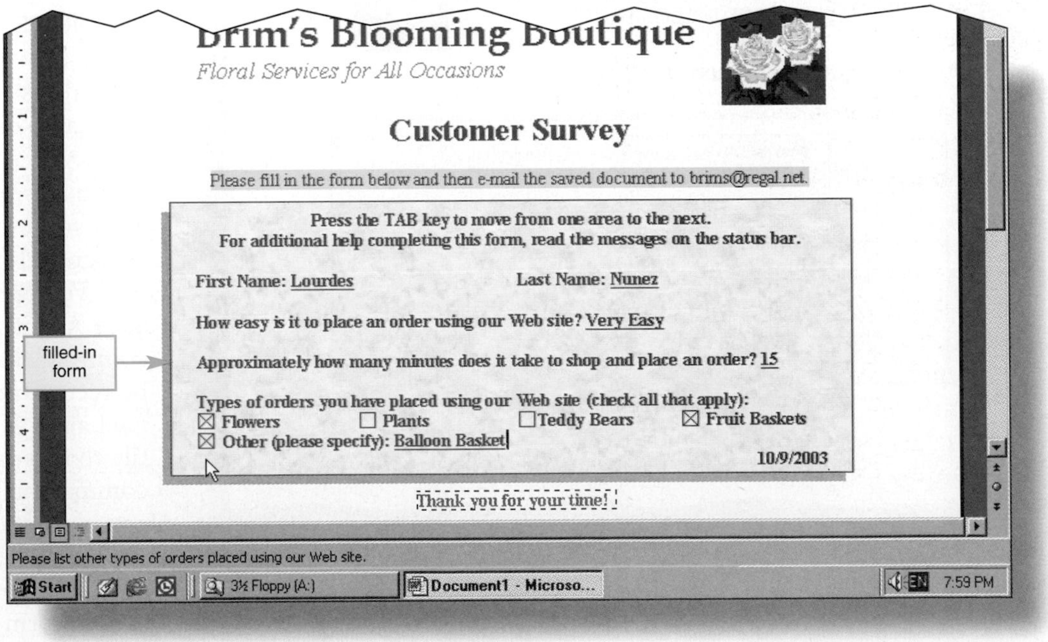

FIGURE 7-62

With the form filled in, a user can save it by clicking the Save button on the Standard toolbar. By basing the new document on a template, the blank Customer Survey remains unchanged because users are saving a new document instead of saving a modification to the survey. Perform the following steps to save the document that contains your responses.

TO SAVE A DOCUMENT

1. With a floppy disk in drive A, click the Save button on the Standard toolbar.
2. Type `Nunez Form` in the File name text box.
3. If necessary, click the Save in box arrow and then click 3½ Floppy (A:).
4. Click the Save button in the Save As dialog box.

Word saves the document with the file name, Nunez Form, on a disk in drive A (shown in Figure 7-64).

More About

Printing

If you want to save ink, print faster, or decrease printer overrun errors, print a draft. Click File on the menu bar and then click Print. Click the Options button, place a check mark in the Draft output check box, and then click the OK button in each dialog box.

You can print the document as you print any other document. Keep in mind, however, that the colors used were designed for viewing online. Thus, different color schemes would have been selected if the form had been designed for a printout. Perform the following step to print the filled-in form.

TO PRINT A FORM

1. Click the Print button on the Standard toolbar.

Word prints the form (Figure 7-63). Notice the animation on the thank-you message does not print.

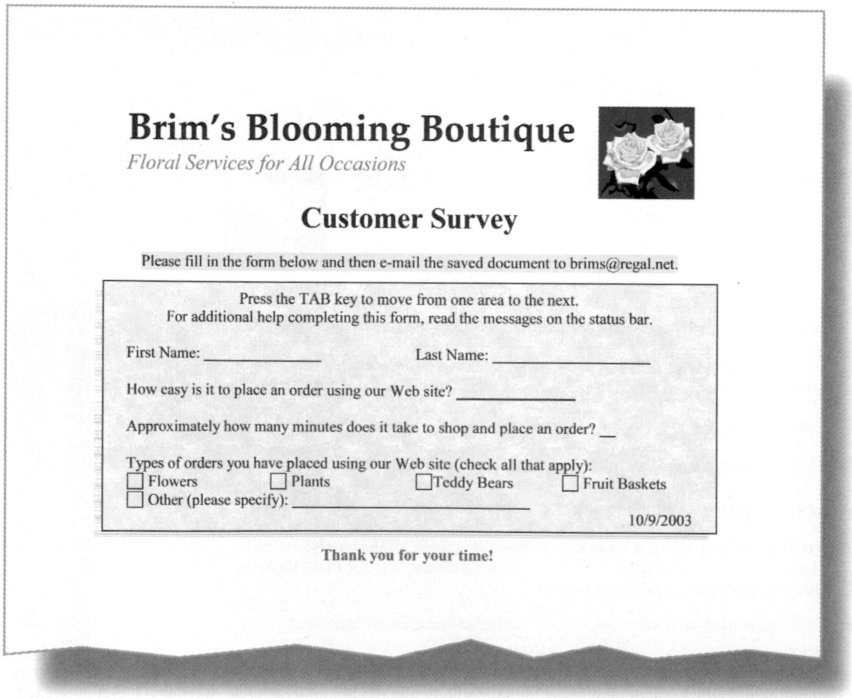
Brim's Blooming Boutique
Floral Services for All Occasions

Customer Survey

Please fill in the form below and then e-mail the saved document to brims@regal.net.

Press the TAB key to move from one area to the next.
For additional help completing this form, read the messages on the status bar.

First Name: ____________ Last Name: ______________

How easy is it to place an order using our Web site? ____________

Approximately how many minutes does it take to shop and place an order? __

Types of orders you have placed using our Web site (check all that apply):
☐ Flowers ☐ Plants ☐ Teddy Bears ☐ Fruit Baskets
☐ Other (please specify): ______________________

10/9/2003

Thank you for your time!

FIGURE 7-63

Saving Data on the Form

You may wish to gather the responses from the completed surveys and analyze them. Depending on the number of forms completed, tabulating the data manually could be a time-consuming and monumental task. One alternative is to use database software, such as Access, to assist you in analyzing the responses. To do this, you must save the data on each survey in a manner that will be recognized by the database software.

Word provides a means through the Save As dialog box to save the data in a comma-delimited text file so that it can be recognized by database software packages. A **comma-delimited text file** is a file that separates each data item with a comma and places quotation marks around text data items. Figure 7-69 on page WD 7.56 shows an example of a comma-delimited text file.

Perform the following steps to save the data from the form in a text file.

Steps To Save Form Data in a Text File

1 Click File on the menu bar and then click Save As. When the Save As dialog box displays, click the Tools button and then point to Save Options.

Word displays the Save As dialog box (Figure 7-64).

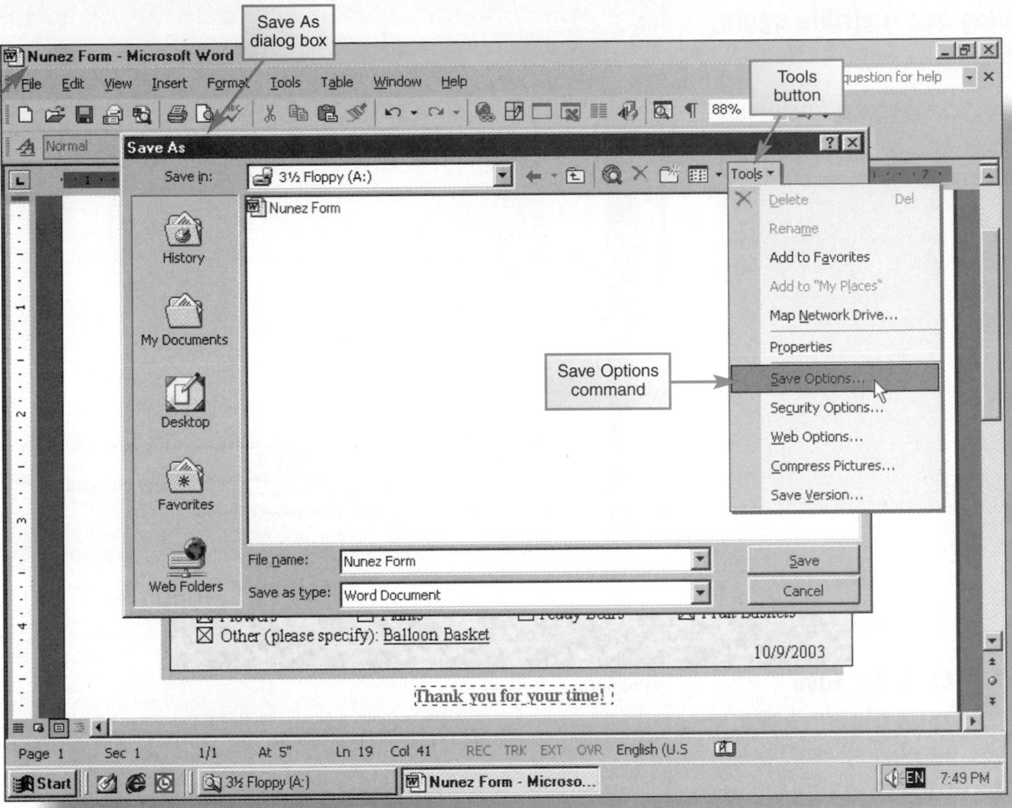

FIGURE 7-64

2 Click Save Options. When the Save dialog box displays, place a check mark in the Save data only for forms check box and then point to the OK button.

Word displays the Save dialog box (Figure 7-65).

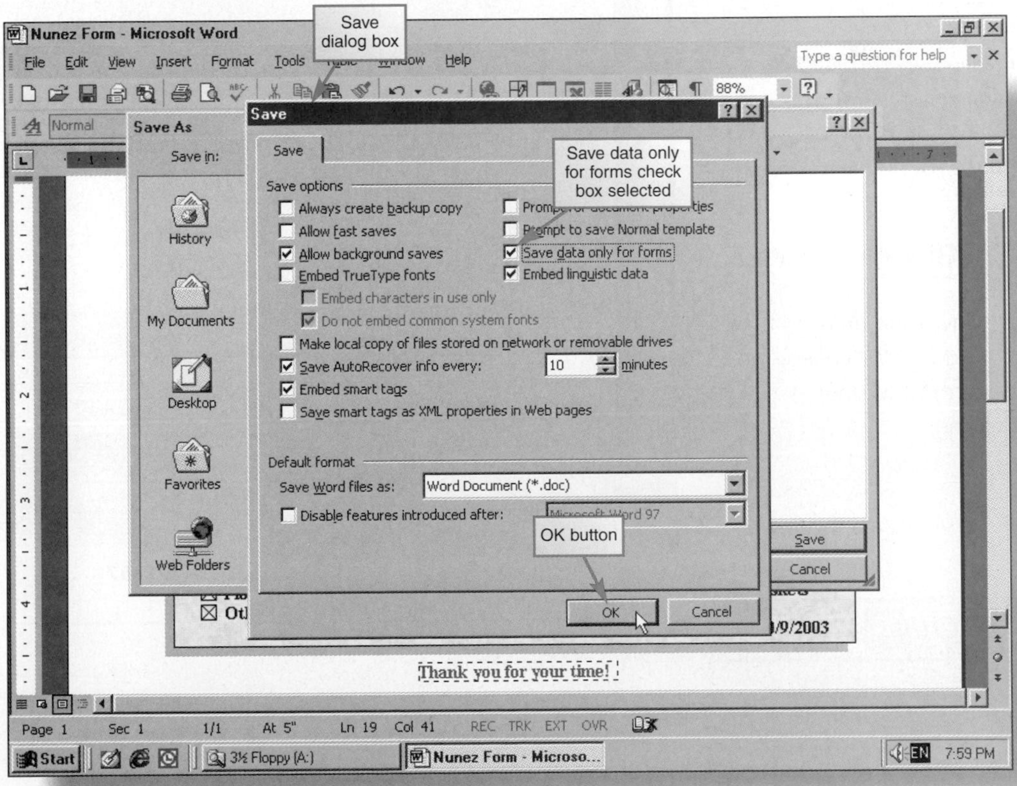

FIGURE 7-65

3 **Click the OK button. When the Save As dialog box is visible again, point to its Save button.**

Word changes the document type in the Save as type box to Plain Text (Figure 7-66).

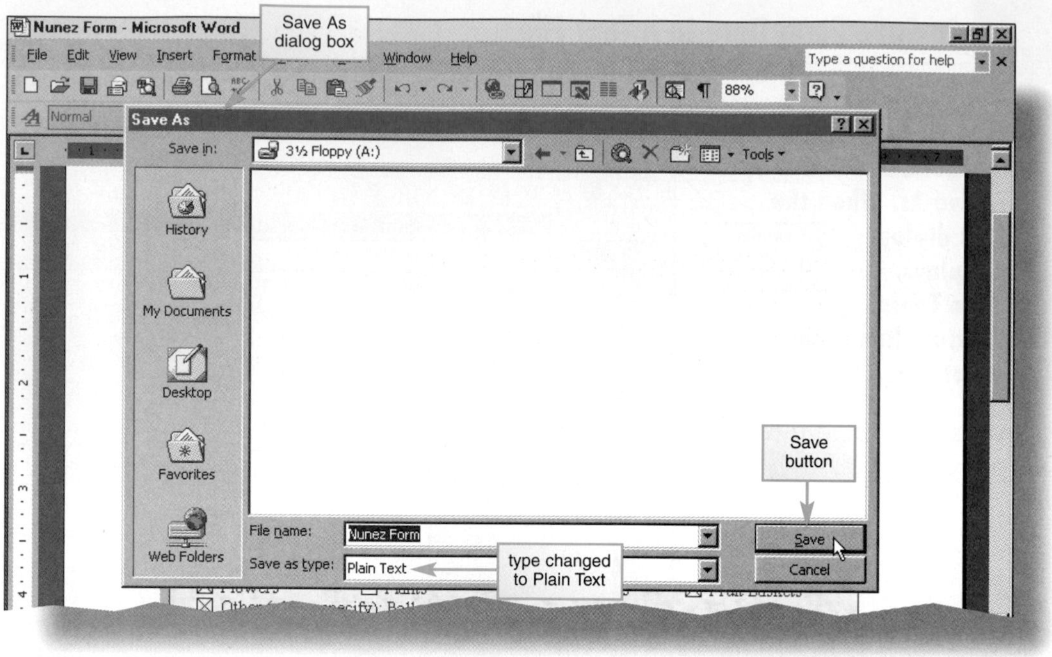

FIGURE 7-66

4 **Click the Save button in the Save As dialog box. When Word displays the File Conversion - Nunez Form dialog box, point to the OK button.**

The File Conversion - Nunez Form dialog box displays, indicating that some formatting may be lost (Figure 7-67).

5 **Click the OK button.**

Word saves the data on the form in a text file called, Nunez Form, without formatting.

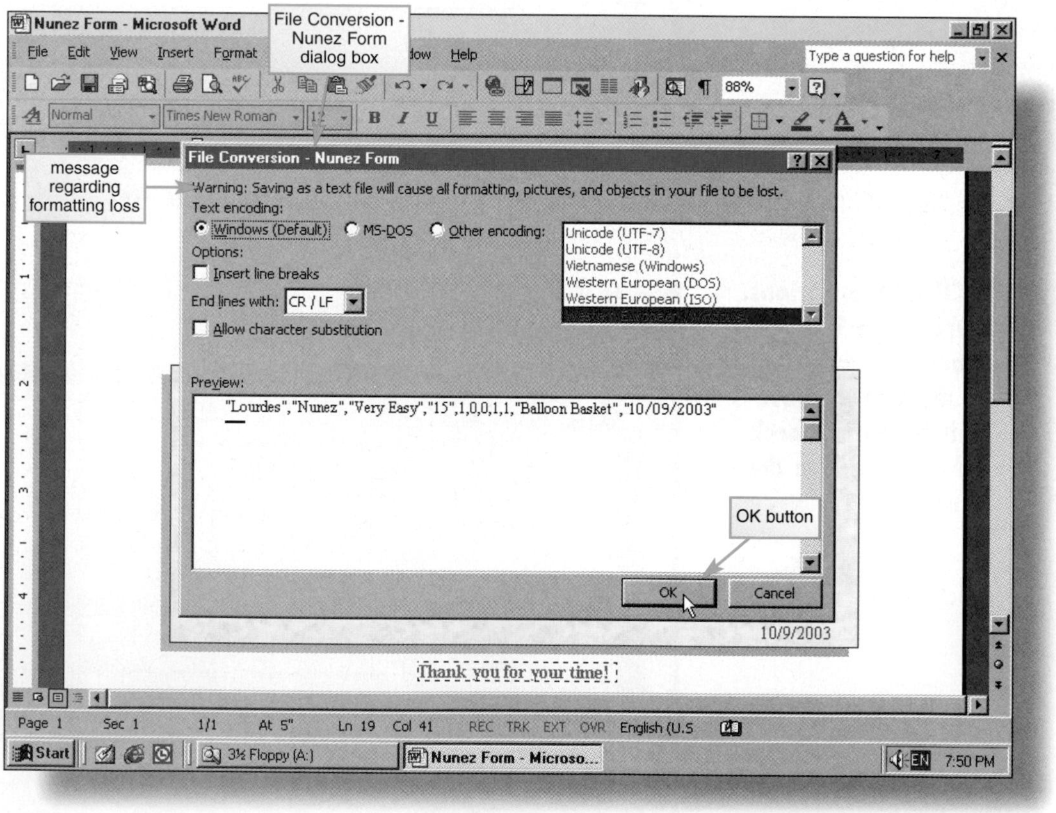

FIGURE 7-67

Other Ways

1. In Voice Command mode, say "Tools, Options, Save, Save data only for forms, OK, File, Save copy As, Save"

After you save the data to a text file, you should remove the check mark from the Save data only for forms check box so that Word will save the entire form the next time you save the document.

Perform the following steps to uncheck the Save data only for forms check box.

TO UNCHECK THE SAVE DATA ONLY FOR FORMS CHECK BOX

1. Click Tools on the menu bar and then click Options. When the Options dialog box displays, click the Save tab.
2. Click the Save data only for forms check box to remove the check mark. Click the OK button.

In the future, the entire form will be saved.

If you wanted to view the contents of the text file, you could open it in Word by performing the following steps.

More About

Microsoft Access 2002

For more information on features of Access in analyzing data, visit the Word 2002 More About Web page (www.scsite.com/wd2002/more.htm) and then click Microsoft Access 2002.

Steps To Open a Text File in Word

1 Click the Open button on the Standard toolbar. When the Open dialog box displays, if necessary, click the Files of type box arrow and then click All Files. Click the text file called Nunez Form in the list and then point to the Open button in the dialog box.

Word displays the Open dialog box (Figure 7-68). The icon for a text file looks like a piece of paper with writing on it. Depending on previous settings, your screen may not show a preview of the file.

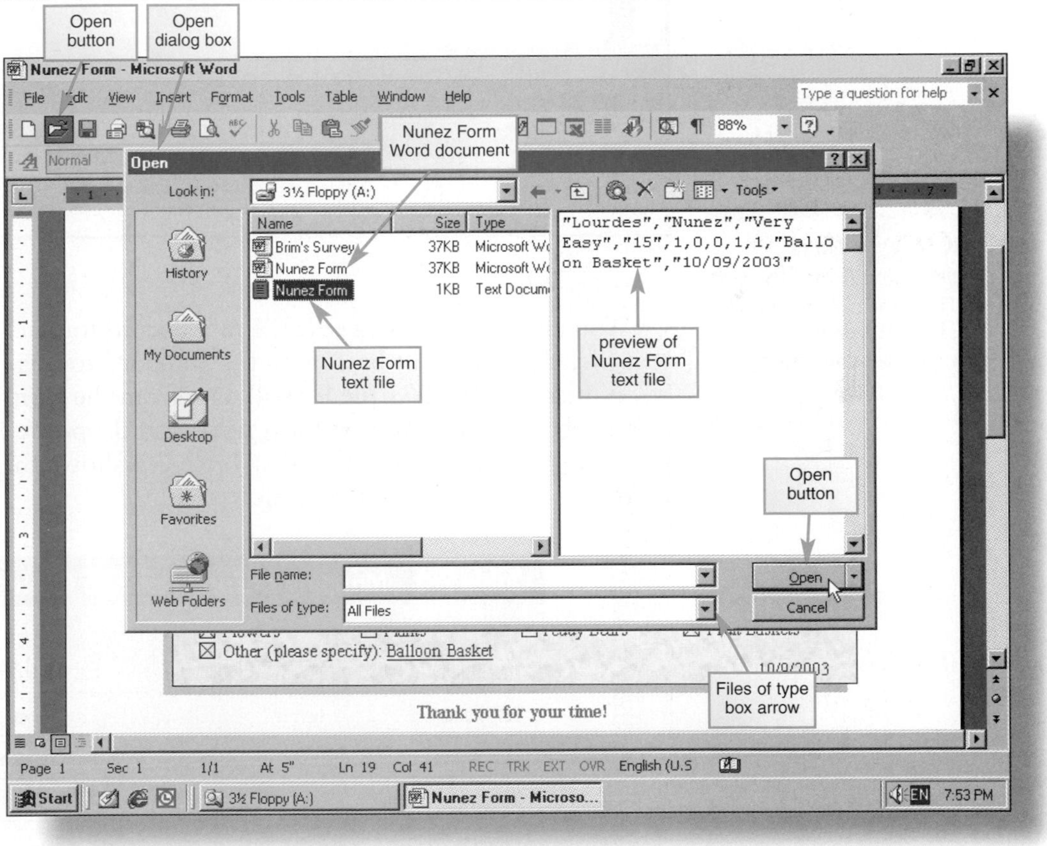

FIGURE 7-68

2 Click the Open button in the Open dialog box.

The text file displays in the Word window (Figure 7-69).

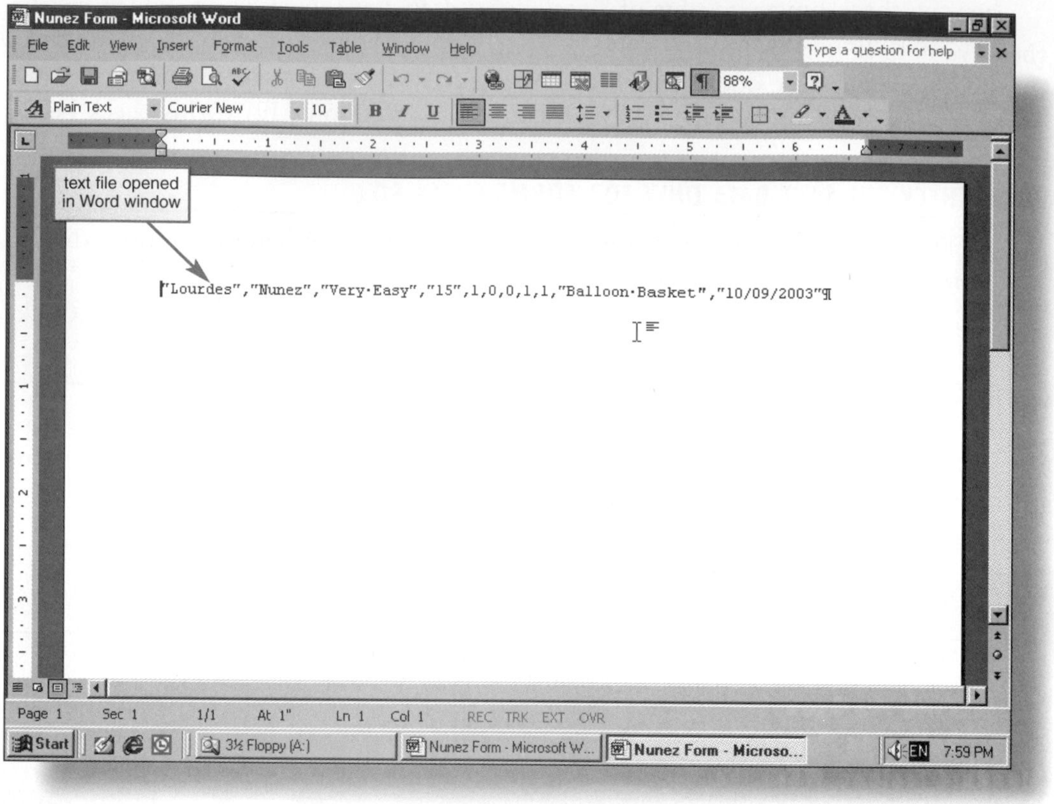

FIGURE 7-69

Other Ways

1. On File menu click Open, click Files of type box arrow, click All Files, double-click text file name
2. In Voice Command mode, say "File, Open, Files of type, All Files, [select file name], OK"

You also can display a text file in a text editor such as Notepad. To print the text file, click the Print button on the Standard toolbar.

Notice that the text file lists all data from the form fields, separating each form field with a comma. All text form fields and drop-down list form field entries are surrounded with quotation marks. Table 7-3 shows the form field and the corresponding entry in the text file.

Table 7-3 Mapping of Form Fields to Contents of Text File

FORM FIELD	FORM FIELD TYPE	TEXT FILE ENTRY
First Name	Text	"Lourdes"
Last Name	Text	"Nunez"
Ease of use	Drop-Down List	"Very Easy"
Number of minutes	Text	"15"
Flowers	Check Box	1
Plants	Check Box	0
Teddy Bears	Check Box	0
Fruit Baskets	Check Box	1
Other	Check Box	1
Other	Text	"Balloon Basket"
	Date	"10/09/2003"

For the check boxes, a value of 1 (one) indicates that the user selected the check box, and a value of 0 (zero) indicates that a user did not select the check box. The text file is ready to be imported into a database table.

Perform the following step to close the window displaying the text file.

TO CLOSE A WINDOW

1. Click File on the menu bar and then click Close.

Word closes the window displaying the text file.

Working with Templates

If you want to modify the template, open it by clicking the Open button on the Standard toolbar, clicking the template name, and then clicking the Open button in the dialog box. Then, you must unprotect the form by clicking the Protect Form button on the Forms toolbar or by clicking Tools on the menu bar and then clicking Unprotect Document.

When you created the template in this project, you saved it on a floppy disk in drive A. In environments other than an academic setting, you would not save the template on a floppy disk. Instead, you would save it in the Templates folder, which is the folder Word initially displays in the Save As dialog box for a document template file type. When you save a template in the Templates folder, Word places an icon for the template in the General sheet in the Templates dialog box. Thus, to open a new Word document that is based on a template that has been saved in the Templates folder, you click File on the menu bar, and then click New. When the New Document task pane displays, click General Templates, and then, in the General sheet, double-click the template icon. Figure 7-70 shows the template icon for Brim's Survey in the General sheet in the Templates dialog box.

More About

The Templates Folder

If you want a template to display in a tabbed sheet other than the General Sheet, save the template in the appropriate subfolder of the Templates folder. If you wish to create a custom tabbed sheet, create a new subfolder in the Templates folder. The subfolder name will be the name of the tabbed sheet.

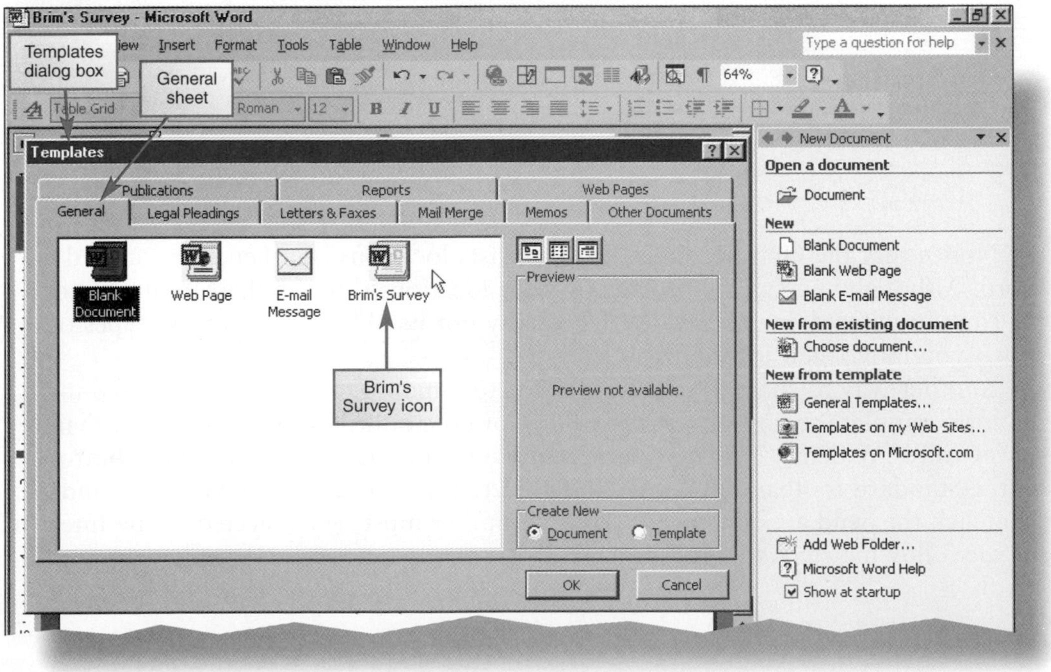

FIGURE 7-70

You also can make templates available on a network so others can share them. These templates, called **workgroup templates**, typically are stored on the network server by the network administrator as read-only files, which prevents users from inadvertently modifying them. You can change the location of workgroup templates in the Options dialog box (Figure 7-71) by clicking Tools on the menu bar, clicking Options, clicking the File Locations tab, clicking Workgroup templates in the File types list, and then clicking the Modify button. Locate the folder assigned to workgroup templates (as specified by the network administrator), and then click the OK button. With the workgroup template location specified, these templates also display in the General sheet in the Templates dialog box.

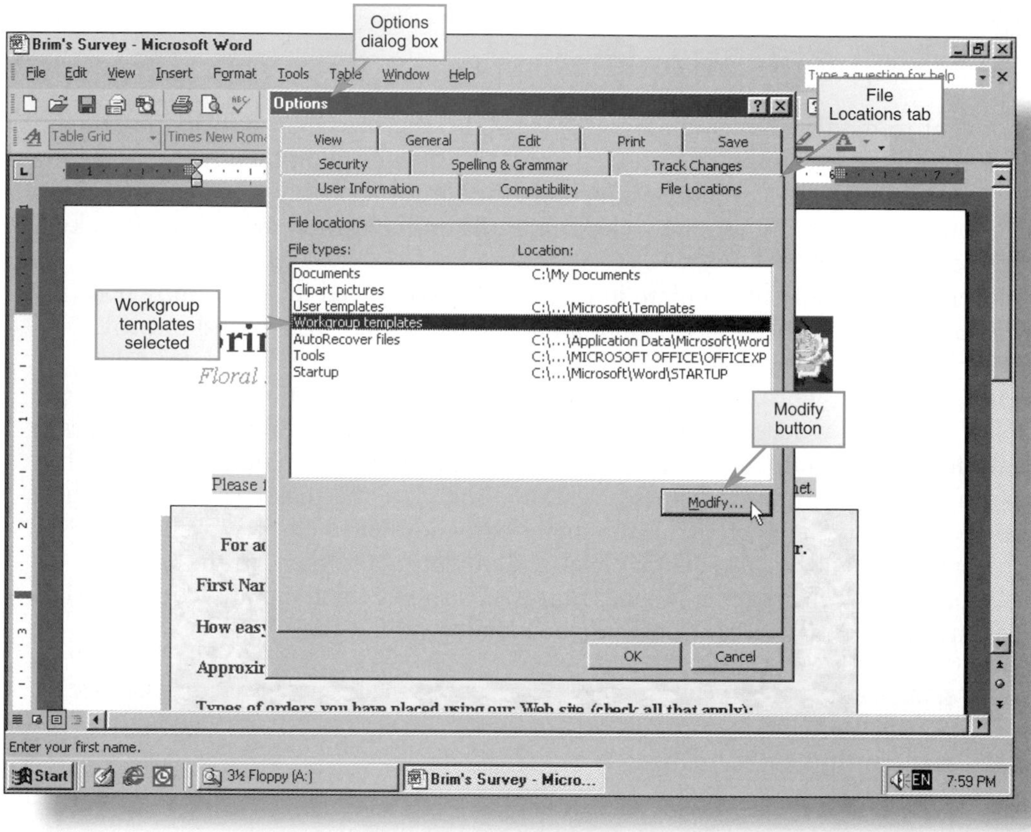

FIGURE 7-71

Notice that the Options dialog box also lists locations of other files accessed by Word. Although you can change any of these locations through the Modify button, use caution when doing so because Word may not be able to access these types of files if you move their location.

Another way to share a form template is to e-mail it. You might want to e-mail the form template to co-workers for editing or collaboration, or you might e-mail a survey to respondents. To send a form template via e-mail, click the E-mail button on the Standard toolbar. Fill in the To, Subject, and Introduction text boxes, and then click the Send a Copy button. Your computer must be connected to the Internet for the following steps to work properly.

More About

Quick Reference

For a table that lists how to complete tasks covered in this book using the mouse, menu, shortcut menu, and keyboard, see the Quick Reference Summary at the back of this book or visit the Shelly Cashman Series Office XP Web page (scsite.com/offxp/qr.htm) and then click Microsoft Word 2002.

TO E-MAIL A FORM

1. With the filled-in Customer Survey displaying, click the E-mail button on the Standard toolbar.
2. Type your instructor's e-mail address in the To text box if your instructor gives you permission to do so. Type `Customer Survey` in the Subject text box. If an Introduction text box displays, type `Attached is the Customer Survey Form Template` in the Introduction text box.
3. If instructed to do so, click the Send a Copy button; otherwise, if you want to cancel the e-mail operation, click the E-mail button again.

The form template is e-mailed to the recipient named in the To text box.

The final steps are to quit Word and close Windows Explorer.

TO QUIT WORD

1. Click File on the menu bar and then click Exit.

The Word window closes.

TO CLOSE WINDOWS EXPLORER

1. Click the Close button on the Exploring - 3½ Floppy (A:) window's title bar.

The Explorer window closes, and the desktop displays.

CASE PERSPECTIVE SUMMARY

You e-mail the Customer Survey to 100 customers who have placed recent orders. Of the 100, you receive 61 completed forms. You decide to use Access to analyze the customer responses. Thus, you save each completed form as a text file.

You create an Access database that contains a table named Brim's Survey Results. The table contains one field for each form field on the survey. After you import the data from each text file into the table, you create a report that lists the total number of customers that selected each option on the form. From this report, you create an average customer response list for Aunt Carol at Brim's Blooming Boutique.

Project Summary

Project 7 introduced you to creating an online form. You created a document template as the basis for the form. Then, you added text form fields, a drop-down list form field, and check boxes to the form. You added Help text to each of these form fields. On the form, you also highlighted text, animated text, and added a rectangle drawing object around the data entry area. After you protected the form, you opened a new document based on the template and filled out the form. You also learned how to save the data on a form in a text file and how to modify the location of workgroup templates.

What You Should Know

Having completed this project, you should now be able to perform the following tasks:

- Access a Template through Windows Explorer *(WD 7.50)*
- Add a Shadow to a Drawing Object *(WD 7.44)*
- Add Help Text to a Form Field *(WD 7.35)*
- Add More Help Text *(WD 7.36)*
- Animate Text *(WD 7.46)*
- Change the Line Color of a Drawing Object *(WD 7.43)*
- Close a Window *(WD 7.57)*
- Close Windows Explorer *(WD 7.59)*
- Create a Document Template *(WD 7.09)*
- Display Formatting Marks *(WD 7.07)*
- Draw a Rectangle *(WD 7.39)*
- E-Mail a Form *(WD 7.59)*
- Enter and Format Text *(WD 7.11)*
- Enter Text *(WD 7.14, WD 7.26)*
- Fill a Drawing Object with a Texture *(WD 7.42)*
- Fill Out a Form *(WD 7.51)*
- Hide Formatting Marks *(WD 7.48)*
- Highlight Text *(WD 7.13)*
- Insert a Borderless Table into a Form *(WD 7.15, WD 7.26)*
- Insert a Check Box *(WD 7.27)*
- Insert a Drop-Down Form Field *(WD 7.21)*
- Insert a Text Form Field *(WD 7.17)*
- Insert Additional Check Box Form Fields *(WD 7.28)*
- Insert and Format Clip Art *(WD 7.12)*
- Insert and Specify Options for a Text Form Field *(WD 7.20, WD 7.25, WD 7.29)*
- Insert and Specify Options for a Text Form Field as the Current Date *(WD 7.30)*
- Open a Text File in Word *(WD 7.50)*
- Print a Form *(WD 7.52)*
- Protect a Form *(WD 7.48)*
- Quit Word *(WD 7.49, WD 7.59)*
- Remove Form Field Shading *(WD 7.37)*
- Reset Menus and Toolbars *(WD 7.06)*
- Save a Document *(WD 7.52)*
- Save Form Data in a Text File *(WD 7.53)*
- Save the Document Again *(WD 7.49)*
- Send a Drawing Object behind Text *(WD 7.41)*
- Specify Drop-Down Form Field Options *(WD 7.23)*
- Specify Text Form Field Options *(WD 7.19)*
- Start and Customize Word *(WD 7.06)*
- Uncheck the Save Data Only for Forms Check Box *(WD 7.55)*
- Underline in Color *(WD 7.31)*
- Use the Format Painter Button *(WD 7.33)*
- Zoom Page Width *(WD 7.07)*

More About

Microsoft Certification

The Microsoft Office User Specialist (MOUS) Certification program provides an opportunity for you to obtain a valuable industry credential — proof that you have the Word 2002 skills required by employers. For more information, see Appendix E or visit the Shelly Cashman Series MOUS Web page at scsite.com/offxp/cert.htm.

Learn It Online

Instructions: To complete the Learn It Online exercises, start your browser, click the Address bar, and then enter `scsite.com/offxp/exs.htm`. When the Office XP Learn It Online page displays, follow the instructions in the exercises below.

1 Project Reinforcement

TF, MC, and SA
Below Word Project 7, click the Project Reinforcement link. Print the quiz by clicking Print on the File menu. Answer each question. Write your first and last name at the top of each page, and then hand in the printout to your instructor.

2 Flash Cards

Below Word Project 7, click the Flash Cards link. When Flash Cards displays, read the instructions. Type `20` (or a number specified by your instructor) in the Number of Playing Cards text box, type your name in the Name text box, and then click the Flip Card button. When the flash card displays, read the question and then click the Answer box arrow to select an answer. Flip through Flash Cards. Click Print on the File menu to print the last flash card if your score is 15 (75%) correct or greater and then hand it in to your instructor. If your score is less than 15 (75%) correct, then redo this exercise by clicking the Replay button.

3 Practice Test

Below Word Project 7, click the Practice Test link. Answer each question, enter your first and last name at the bottom of the page, and then click the Grade Test button. When the graded practice test displays on your screen, click Print on the File menu to print a hard copy. Continue to take practice tests until you score 80% or better. Hand in a printout of the final practice test to your instructor.

4 Who Wants to Be a Computer Genius?

Below Word Project 7, click the Computer Genius link. Read the instructions, enter your first and last name at the bottom of the page, and then click the Play button. Hand in your score to your instructor.

5 Wheel of Terms

Below Word Project 7, click the Wheel of Terms link. Read the instructions, and then enter your first and last name and your school name. Click the Play button. Hand in your score to your instructor.

6 Crossword Puzzle Challenge

Below Word Project 7, click the Crossword Puzzle Challenge link. Read the instructions, and then enter your first and last name. Click the Play button. Work the crossword puzzle. When you are finished, click the Submit button. When the crossword puzzle redisplays, click the Print button. Hand in the printout.

7 Tips and Tricks

Below Word Project 7, click the Tips and Tricks link. Click a topic that pertains to Project 7. Right-click the information and then click Print on the shortcut menu. Construct a brief example of what the information relates to in Word to confirm you understand how to use the tip or trick. Hand in the example and printed information.

8 Newsgroups

Below Word Project 7, click the Newsgroups link. Click a topic that pertains to Project 7. Print three comments. Hand in the comments to your instructor.

9 Expanding Your Horizons

Below Word Project 7, click the Articles for Microsoft Word link. Click a topic that pertains to Project 7. Print the information. Construct a brief example of what the information relates to in Word to confirm you understand the contents of the article. Hand in the example and printed information to your instructor.

10 Search Sleuth

Below Word Project 7, click the Search Sleuth link. To search for a term that pertains to this project, select a term below the Project 7 title and then use the Google search engine at google.com (or any major search engine) to display and print two Web pages that present information on the term. Hand in the printouts to your instructor.

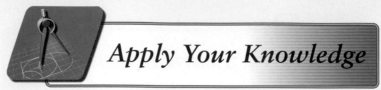

Apply Your Knowledge

1 Filling Out a Form

Instructions: In this assignment, you access a template through Windows Explorer. As shown in Figure 7-72, the template contains an online form. You are to fill in the form, save it, and print it. The template is located on the Data Disk. If you did not download the Data Disk, see the inside backcover for instructions for downloading the Data Disk or see your instructor.

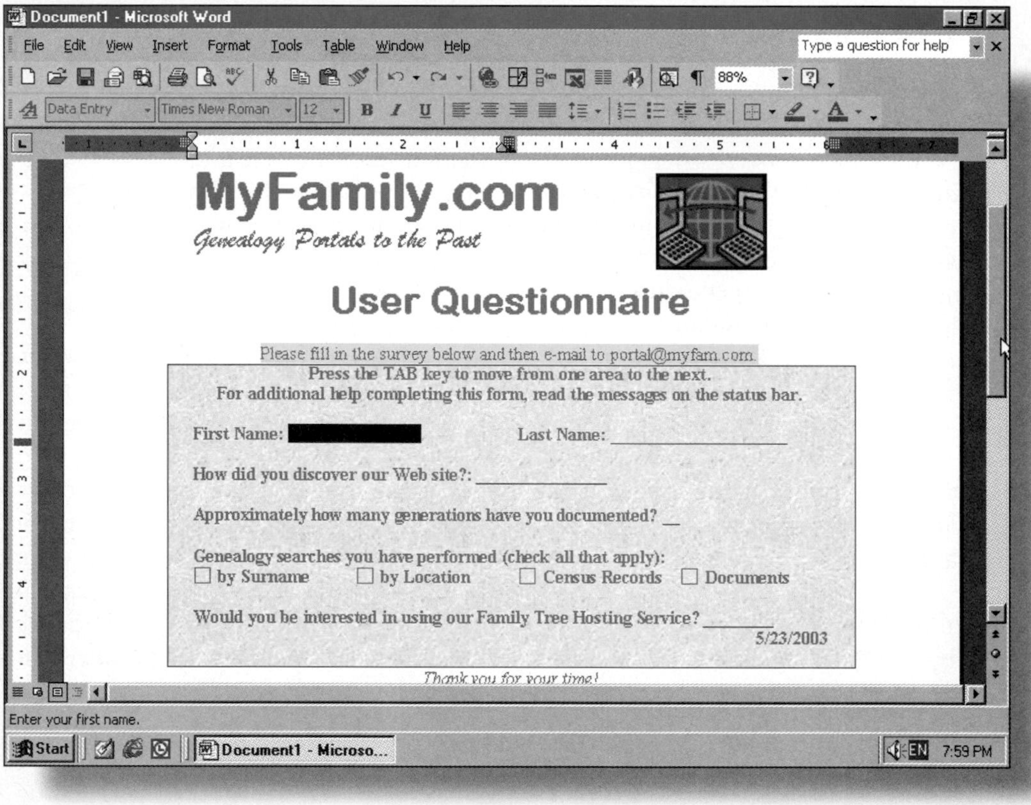

FIGURE 7-72

Perform the following steps.

1. Right-click the My Computer icon on the Windows desktop and then click Explore on the shortcut menu. When the Exploring window displays, click the Address text box to select it. With the Data Disk in drive A, type `a:` and then press the ENTER key. Double-click the MyFamily Questionnaire icon in the Contents pane.
2. When Word displays a new document based on the MyFamily Questionnaire template, scroll down so the entire form fits in the Word window. If the Show/Hide ¶ button on the Standard toolbar is selected, click it.
3. With the First Name text box selected, type `Marsha` and then press the TAB key.
4. With the Last Name text box selected, type `Louks` and then press the TAB key.
5. With the drop-down list box selected, click the box arrow. Click Search Engine in the How did you discover our Web site? drop-down list. Press the TAB key.
6. Type `5` in response to Approximately how many generations have you documented? Press the TAB key.
7. Place an X in the by Surname and Census Records check boxes by clicking them. Press the TAB key twice.

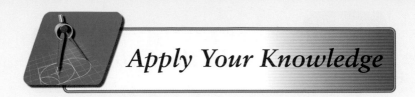

Apply Your Knowledge

8. With the drop-down list box selected, click the box arrow. Click Yes in the Would you be interested in using our Family Tree Hosting Service? drop-down list.
9. Save the file with the name Louks Form. Print the form.
10. Click File on the menu bar and then click Save As. When the Save As dialog box displays, click the Tools button and then click Save Options. When the Save dialog box displays, place a check mark in the Save data only for forms check box and then click the OK button. Click the Save button in the Save As dialog box. When Word displays the File Conversion dialog box, click the OK button.
11. Click Tools on the menu bar and then click Options. When the Options dialog box displays, click the Save tab. Click the Save data only for forms check box to remove the check mark. Click the OK button.
12. Click the Open button on the Standard toolbar. When the Open dialog box displays, click the Files of type box arrow and then click All Files. Click the text file called Louks Form in the list and then click the Open button in the dialog box. Print the text file.

In the Lab

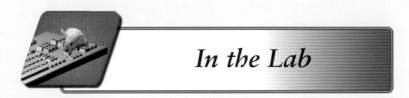

1 Creating an Online Form with a Texture Fill Effect

Problem: You work part-time for Web Management, a company specializing in hosting Web pages and wireless connections. Recently, Web Management has begun to offer customers a user portal, which is a highly-personalized browser interface, complete with free e-mail, file storage, and worldwide access. Your supervisor has asked you to prepare an online survey for Web customers. The survey should obtain the following information from the customer: first name, last name, whether they currently use a portal, the average time it takes for them to log on from home, and the kinds of services they think a portal should provide. You prepare the online form shown in Figure 7-73 on the next page.

Instructions:

1. Create a template called Portal Questionnaire for the online form.
2. Enter and format the company name, clip art, business tag line, and form title as shown in Figure 7-73.
3. Enter the form instructions and highlight them in yellow.
4. Enter the instructions in the data entry area, form field captions, and form fields as shown in Figure 7-73. First Name and Last Name are text form fields. Do you currently use a personal portal on the Internet? is a drop-down form field with these choices: Yes, No, and Uncertain. The Average time it takes you to log onto the Web from Home (in minutes) is a text field requiring numeric input. The choices below What services do you think a portal should offer? are check boxes. ***Hint:*** use a 2 × 3 borderless table. The Other check box also has a text form field to its right for further explanation. When the form initially displays on the screen as a blank form, the text form fields and drop-down form field should display underlines in dark blue.

(continued)

In the Lab

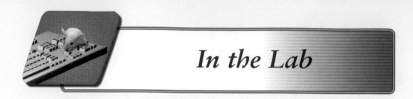

Creating an Online Form with a Texture Fill Effect *(continued)*

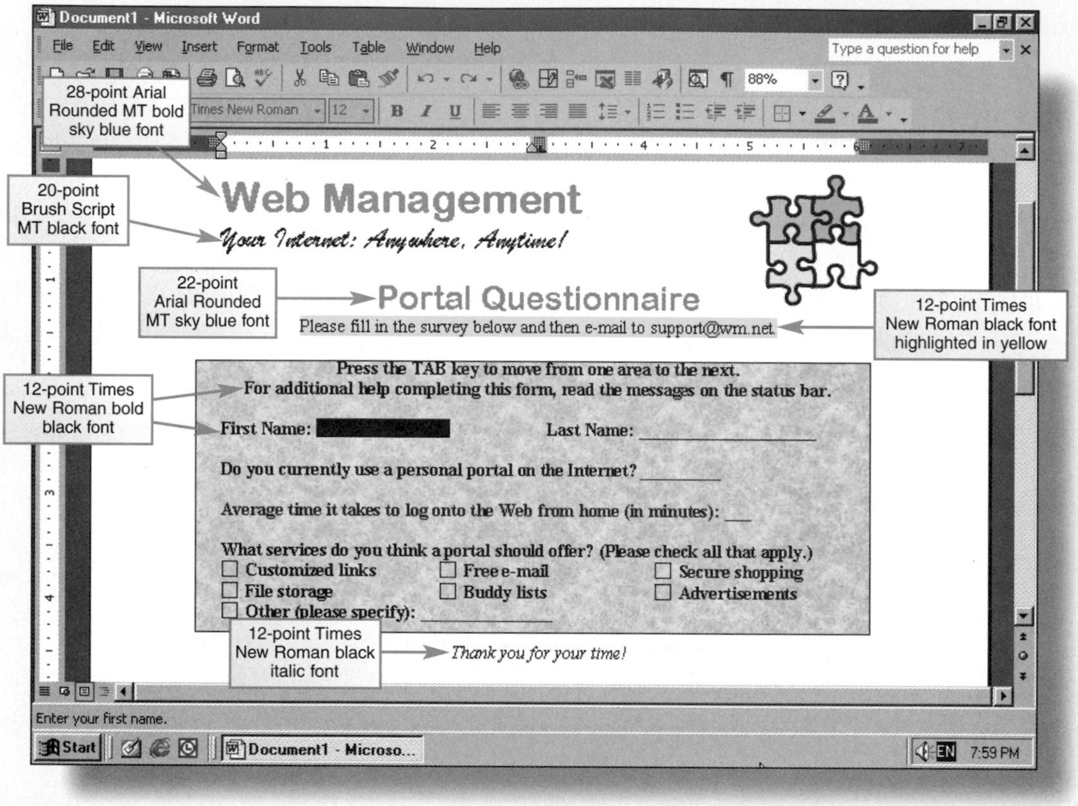

FIGURE 7-73

5. Enter the thank-you message as shown in Figure 7-73.
6. Insert a rectangle drawing object around the data entry area. Fill the rectangle drawing object with the Bouquet texture.
7. Add Help text to all the form fields.
8. Check the spelling of the form. Protect the form. Save the form again. Print the blank form.
9. Access the template through Windows Explorer. Fill out the form. Save the filled-out form. Print the filled-out form.

2 Creating an Online Form with a Gradient Fill Effect and Nudged Shadow

Problem: You work part-time for College Technical Support Services at Montgomery Community College. Your supervisor has asked you to prepare an online survey to be distributed to students who use the lab. The survey should obtain the following information from the students: first name, last name, how they would rate the computers, average time they have to wait to find an open station, and the types of computer applications they use. You prepare the online form shown in Figure 7-74.

In the Lab

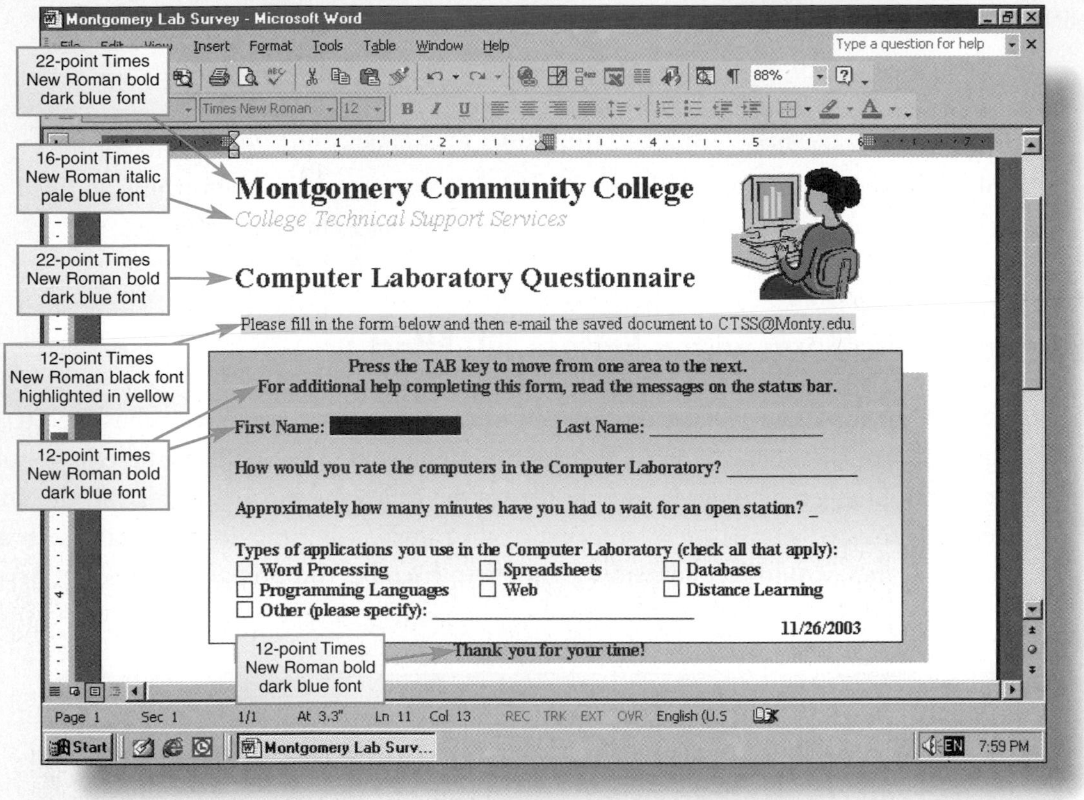

FIGURE 7-74

Instructions:

1. Create a template called Montgomery Lab Survey for the online form.
2. Enter and format the college name, department name, clip art, and form title as shown in Figure 7-74.
3. Enter the form instructions and highlight them in yellow.
4. Enter the instructions in the data entry area, form field captions, and form fields as shown in Figure 7-74. First Name and Last Name are text form fields. Rating the computers is a drop-down form field with these choices: Excellent, Good, Fair, Poor, No Opinion. The number of minutes students have to wait is a text form field that allows only a numeric entry. The types of applications are check boxes. The Other field is both a check box and a text form field. When the form initially displays on the screen as a blank form, the text form fields and drop-down form field should display underlines in dark blue.
5. Enter the thank-you message as shown in Figure 7-74.
6. Insert a rectangle drawing object around the data entry area. Change the rectangle line color to dark blue. Fill the rectangle with a two-color gradient of light blue to white. *Hint:* Click the Gradient tab in the Fill Effects dialog box.
7. Add Shadow Style 6 to the rectangle. With the rectangle selected, click the Shadow Style button, and then click Shadow settings. Click the Nudge Shadow Down button several times, so that the thank-you message displays in the rectangle's shadow. Click the Nudge Shadow Right button approximately the same number of times to even out the shadow on both the right and the bottom.

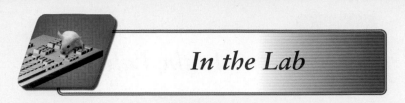

(continued)

In the Lab

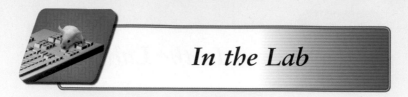

Creating an Online Form with a Gradient Fill Effect and Nudged Shadow *(continued)*

8. Add Help text to all the form fields.
9. Check the spelling of the form. Protect the form. Save the form again. Print the blank form.
10. Access the template through Windows Explorer. Fill out the form. Save and then print the filled-out form.
11. E-mail the template to your instructor, if your instructor gives you permission to do so.

3 Creating an Online Form with a Pattern Fill Effect

Problem: A new K&F Premier Movie Theater has opened in your town and you have been hired to help with public relations. Your supervisor has asked you to prepare an online survey asking Backstage Pass holders for their opinions on the recent premier. The survey should obtain the following information from the attendees: first name, last name, age group of viewer, opinion rating of the movie, other movies they have seen at this K&F theater, and whether or not they would recommend the movie to friends. You prepare the online form shown in Figure 7-75.

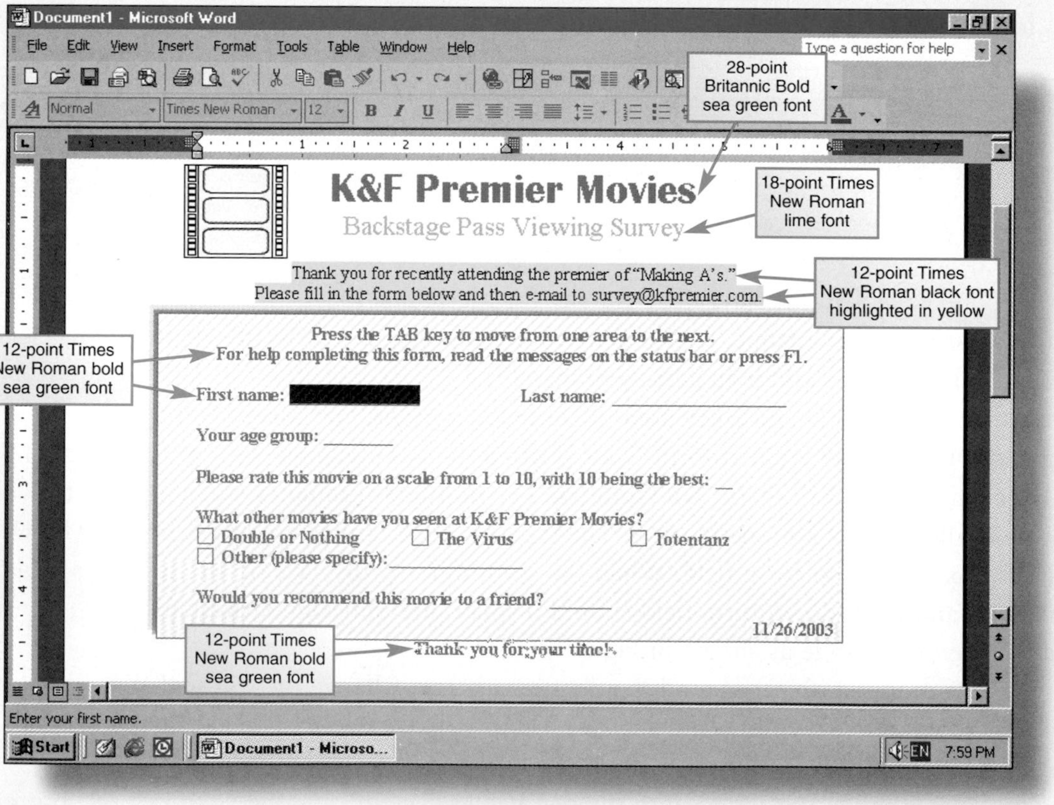

FIGURE 7-75

In the Lab

Instructions:

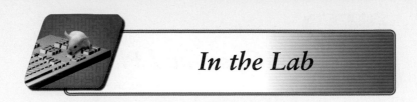

1. Create a template called Premier Movie Feedback for the online form.
2. Enter and format the company name, clip art, and form title as shown in Figure 7-75.
3. Enter the form instructions and highlight them in yellow.
4. Enter the instructions in the data entry area, form field captions, and form fields as shown in Figure 7-75. First name and Last name are text form fields. The age group should be a drop-down form field with these choices: 18-30, 31-49, 50-65, 66 or older. The rating is a text form field requiring a numeric entry. Other movies they have seen include three choices of movies as check boxes. Other is a check box followed by a text form field. The question, Would you recommend this movie to a friend? is followed by a drop-down form field containing the choices, Yes, No, and Unsure. The current date is a text form field. When the form initially displays on the screen as a blank form, the text form fields and drop-down form fields should display underlines in sea green.
5. Enter the thank-you message as shown in Figure 7-75. Animate the message using Sparkle Text.
6. Insert a rectangle drawing object around the data entry area. Change the rectangle line color to Sea Green. Fill the rectangle with a Wide upward diagonal pattern that has a foreground color of yellow. ***Hint:*** Click the Gradient tab in the Fill Effects dialog box. Add a shadow to the rectangle using Shadow Style 13.
7. Add Help text to all the form fields. The Help should display on the status bar, as well as when the user presses the F1 key.
8. Check the spelling of the form. Protect the form. Save the form again. Print the blank form.
9. Access the template through Windows Explorer. Fill out the form. Save the filled-out form. Print the filled-out form.
10. If you have access to a Web server or FTP site, save the template to the server or site (see Appendix C for instructions). Access the template from the Web site or FTP site.

Cases and Places

The difficulty of these case studies varies:
◗ are the least difficult; ◗◗ are more difficult; and ◗◗◗ are the most difficult.

1 ◗ You and a friend are starting a desktop publishing service, which includes products such as stationery, business and greeting cards, business forms, newsletters, and brochures. You decide to send a survey to all your friends (at least those with e-mail addresses) asking the types of products that might interest them. The top of the survey should list the name of your new company, Publisher It Here, along with the title of the survey, Customer Preference Survey. Insert an appropriate graphic of a computer from the Clip Organizer. Immediately above the data entry area, the following sentence should be highlighted: Please fill in the form below and then e-mail the saved document to survey@pih.com. The data entry area contains the following two sentences of instructions: Press the TAB key to move from one area to the next. For help completing this form, read the messages on the status bar or press the F1 key. The data entry area should request the customer's first name and last name. Display check boxes for the types of publications in which they might be interested (from list above and a check box for Other with a text box for users to enter other types of publications). Include a numeric data field for the maximum price they would be willing to pay for a personalized greeting card, and a drop-down list (Yes, No, Unsure) asking if they would buy supplies such as greeting cards over the Web. The form should contain the current date as a form field. The data entry area should be surrounded by a rectangle filled in with an appropriate fill effect. Below the form, place an animated thank-you message. All data entry fields should have Help text that displays on the status bar, as well as when the user presses the F1 key. Use the concepts and techniques presented in this project to create and format this online form.

2 ◗◗ As a student worker in the Computer Technology department at your school, you have been asked to send a survey to all students requesting feedback on the Distance Learning courses. Because each DL student on campus has an e-mail account, you decide to send an online form. The form should contain text boxes for the name of the online class they chose, their expected grade for the course, and the name of the teacher. Include drop-down list boxes asking the students the browser they use and the speed of their modem. Include check boxes for the type of equipment they needed for the course, such as scanner, microphone, fax machine, video camera, or other. The form should contain the current date as a form field. Use the concepts and techniques presented in this project to create and format the online form. Be sure to include an appropriate graphic from the Clip Organizer. If you have access to a Web server or FTP site, save the template to the server or site (see Appendix C for instructions). Access the template from the Web site or FTP site.

3 ◗◗ As a part-time assistant for your school's bookstore, you have been asked to send a survey to all customers requesting their opinion of the online order process. You decide to send an online form because each student has an e-mail account. The form should ask for customer opinions and preferences on various aspects of the bookstore's Web site. Enter user instructions. Use text boxes for items such as the name and class standing. Use a drop-down list for the time of day they usually shop with choices such as Morning, Afternoon, Evening, Late Night, Times Vary. Create check boxes to determine how students shop at the bookstore: Browse aisles, Order online, Mail order, and Other. Use the concepts and techniques presented in this project to create and format the online form. Be sure to include an appropriate graphic(s) from the Clip Organizer. E-mail the form template to your instructor, if your instructor gives you permission to do so.

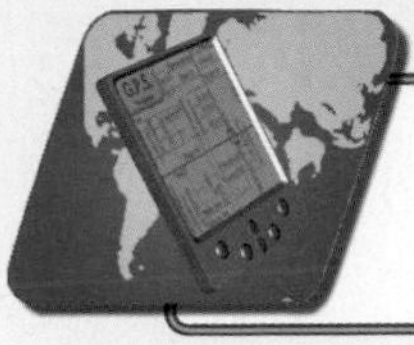

Cases and Places

4 ▶▶ Many banks now offer Web Banking. Write a letter to a fictitious bank discussing the process of sending out Web site surveys to its customers. Suggest possible inclusions for text fields, drop-down lists, and check boxes. Use Microsoft Word Help to find information about automatic calculations and macros in forms. In your letter, list at least two ways the bank could use these form features. E-mail the letter to your instructor, if your instructor gives you permission to do so.

5 ▶▶▶ If Microsoft Access is installed on your computer, you can use it to create a database table and then use that table to analyze the data from Word forms. Your supervisor at Brim's Blooming Boutique would like to analyze the results of the surveys sent using Microsoft Access. To generate data for the database table, fill out the Project 7 Word form (Figure 7-1a on page WD 7.05) five times (acting as five separate customers) and save the form data for each filled-in form in a separate text file. Start Access. Click File on the menu bar and then click New. When the New File task pane displays, click Blank Database. Name the database, Brim's Customers. Click File on the menu bar, point to Get External Data, and then click Import. When the Import dialog box displays, change the file type to Text Files, locate the text file that contains one of the form's data, and then click the Import button. Use the Import Text Wizard to create a table for the form in Figure 7-1. Data in the text file is comma-delimited. Use field names that match the field captions on the form. Each form field, including the current date, should have a field name. When the Import Text Wizard prompts you, choose no primary key field. Name the table, Customer Survey Table. Repeat the process to import each of the remaining four text files into the existing table. After the table contains the five records, generate a report in Access that lists all the data collected from the forms.

6 ▶▶▶ If Microsoft Access is installed on your computer, you can use it to create a database table and then use that table to analyze the data from Word forms. Your supervisor at MyFamily.com would like to analyze the results of the surveys sent using Microsoft Access. To generate data for the database table, fill out the Apply Your Knowledge Exercise form (Figure 7-72 on page WD 7.62) five times (acting as five separate Web site visitors) and save the form data for each filled-in form in a separate text file. Start Access. Click File on the menu bar and then click New. When the New File task pane displays, click Blank Database. Name the database, MyFamily Customers. Click File on the menu bar, point to Get External Data, and then click Import. When the Import dialog box displays, change the file type to Text Files, locate the text file that contains one of the form's data, and then click the Import button. Use the Import Text Wizard to create a table for the form in Figure 7-72. Data in the text file is comma-delimited. Use field names that match the field captions on the form. Each form field, including the current date, should have a field name. When the Import Text Wizard prompts you, choose no primary key field. Name the table, Web Site Survey Table. Repeat the process to import each of the remaining four text files into the existing table. After the table contains the five records, generate a report in Access that lists all the data collected from the forms.

Microsoft Word 2002

PROJECT 8

Working With Macros and Visual Basic for Applications (VBA)

OBJECTIVES

You will have mastered the material in this project when you can:

- Unprotect a document
- Set a security level in Word
- Create a new style with a shortcut key
- Fill a drawing object with a gradient effect
- Add a 3-D effect to a drawing object
- Record and execute a macro
- Assign a macro to a toolbar button
- Record an automatic macro
- View a macro's VBA code
- Add comments to a macro's VBA code
- Modify a macro's VBA code
- Add code statements to a macro's VBA code
- Insert a VBA procedure
- Plan a VBA procedure
- Enter code statements in a VBA procedure
- Run a macro when a user exits a form field
- Insert an ActiveX control
- Format and set properties for an ActiveX control
- Write a VBA procedure for an ActiveX control
- Attach a digital signature

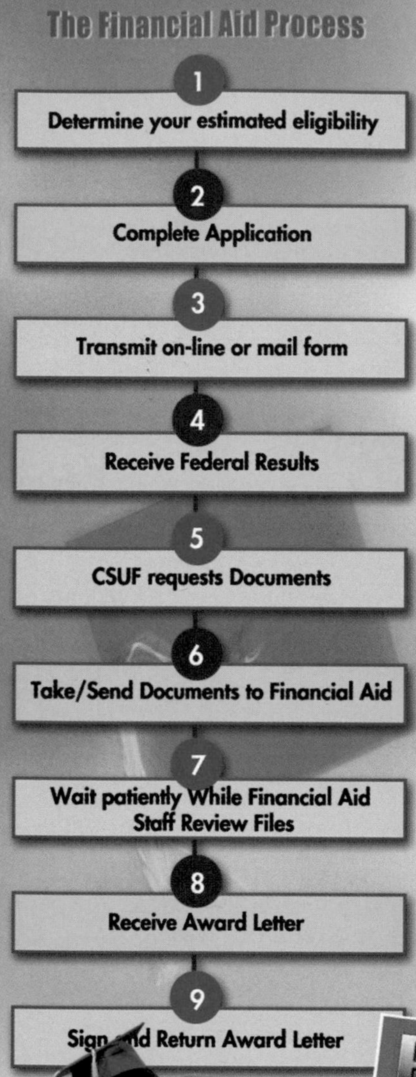
The Financial Aid Process
1
Determine your estimated eligibility
2
Complete Application
3
Transmit on-line or mail form
4
Receive Federal Results
5
CSUF requests Documents
6
Take/Send Documents to Financial Aid
7
Wait patiently While Financial Aid Staff Review Files
8
Receive Award Letter
9
Sign and Return Award Letter

A Class Act

Broadening Educational Opportunities

Some of the United States' more prestigious universities owe their beginnings to a brilliant piece of federal legislature signed into law by President Abraham Lincoln on July 2, 1862. The Morrill Act, otherwise known as the Land-Grant College Act of 1862, was introduced by Justin Morrill of Vermont, who had been working to pass it since 1857. The Act provided funding for institutions of higher learning in each state. Ever since colonial times, basic education had been an important principle of American democratic thinking. By the 1860s, higher education was becoming more accessible, and educators and politicians desired to make some sort of advanced education available to all young Americans.

The act gave every state that had remained in the Union, a grant of 30,000 acres of public land for every member of its congressional delegation. Even the smallest state received 90,000 acres due to the fact that under the Constitution, every state had at least two senators and one representative. The states were directed to sell this land, using the proceeds to establish colleges in engineering, agriculture, and military science. More than 70 land grant colleges were established under the original Morrill Act.

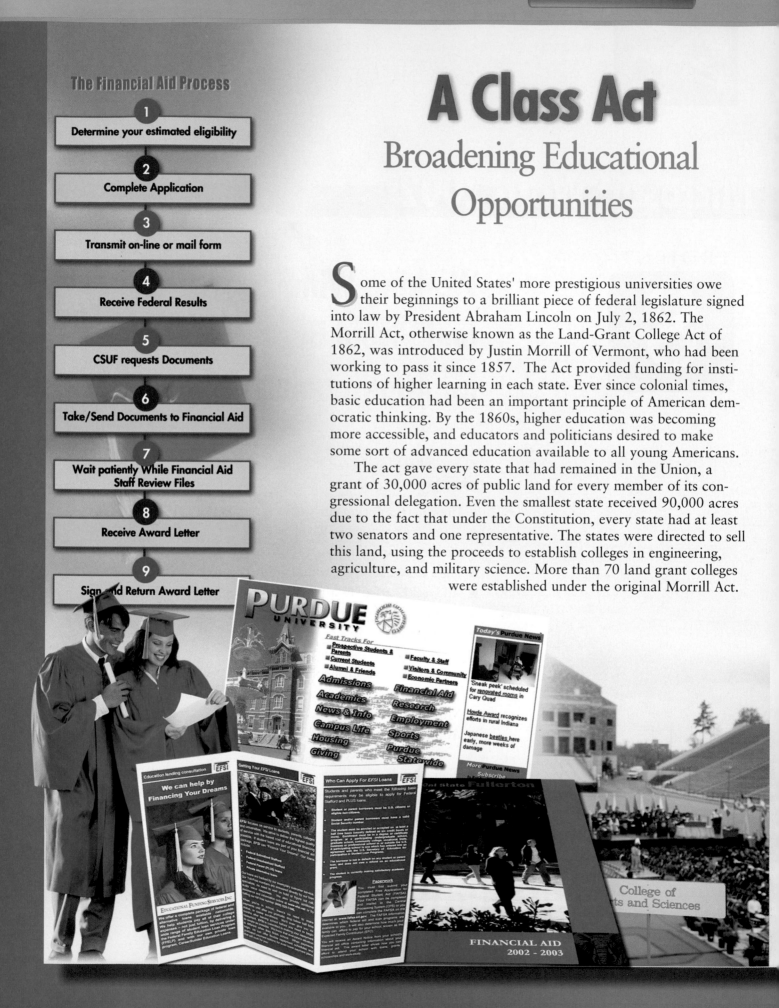

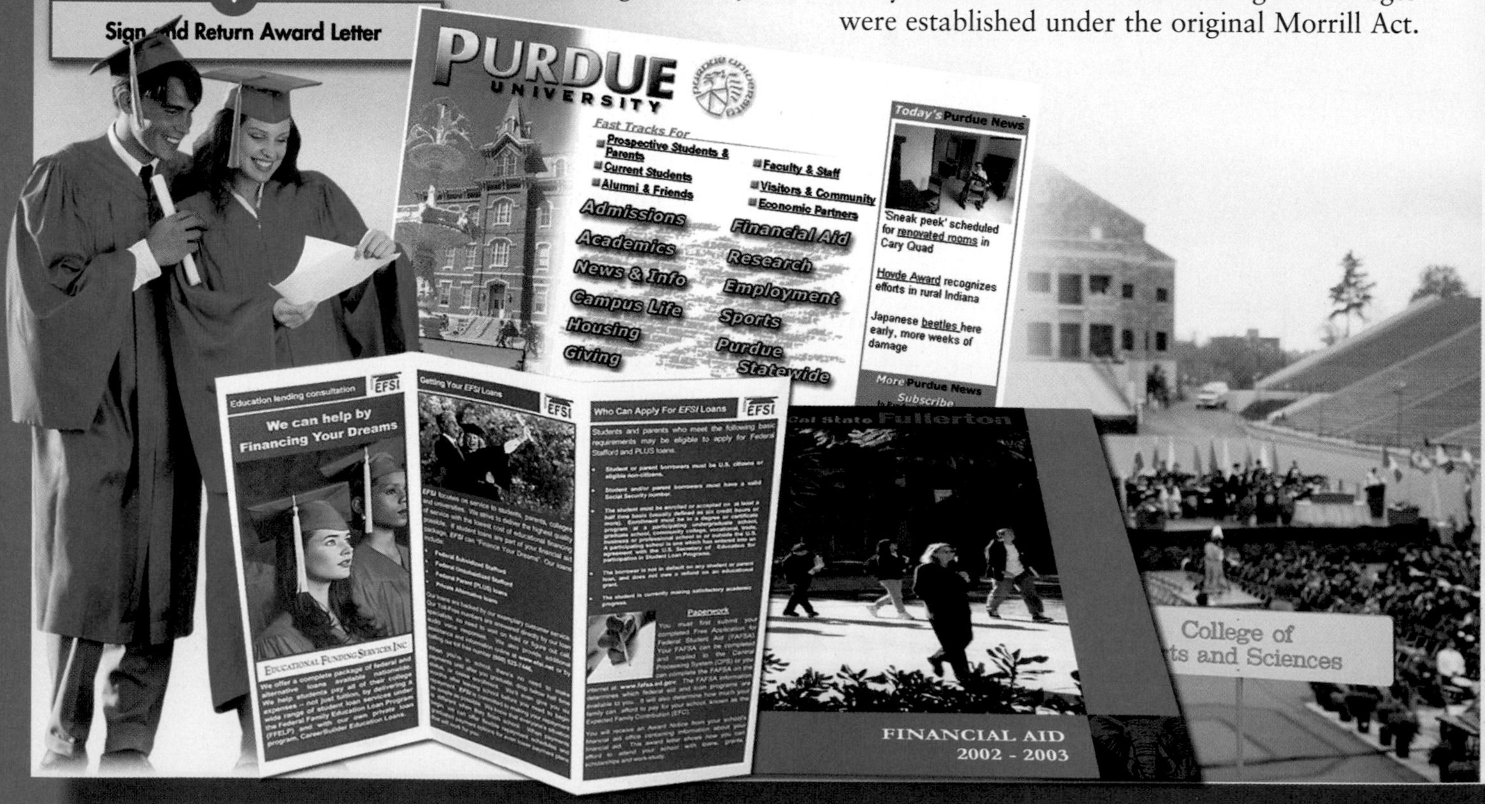

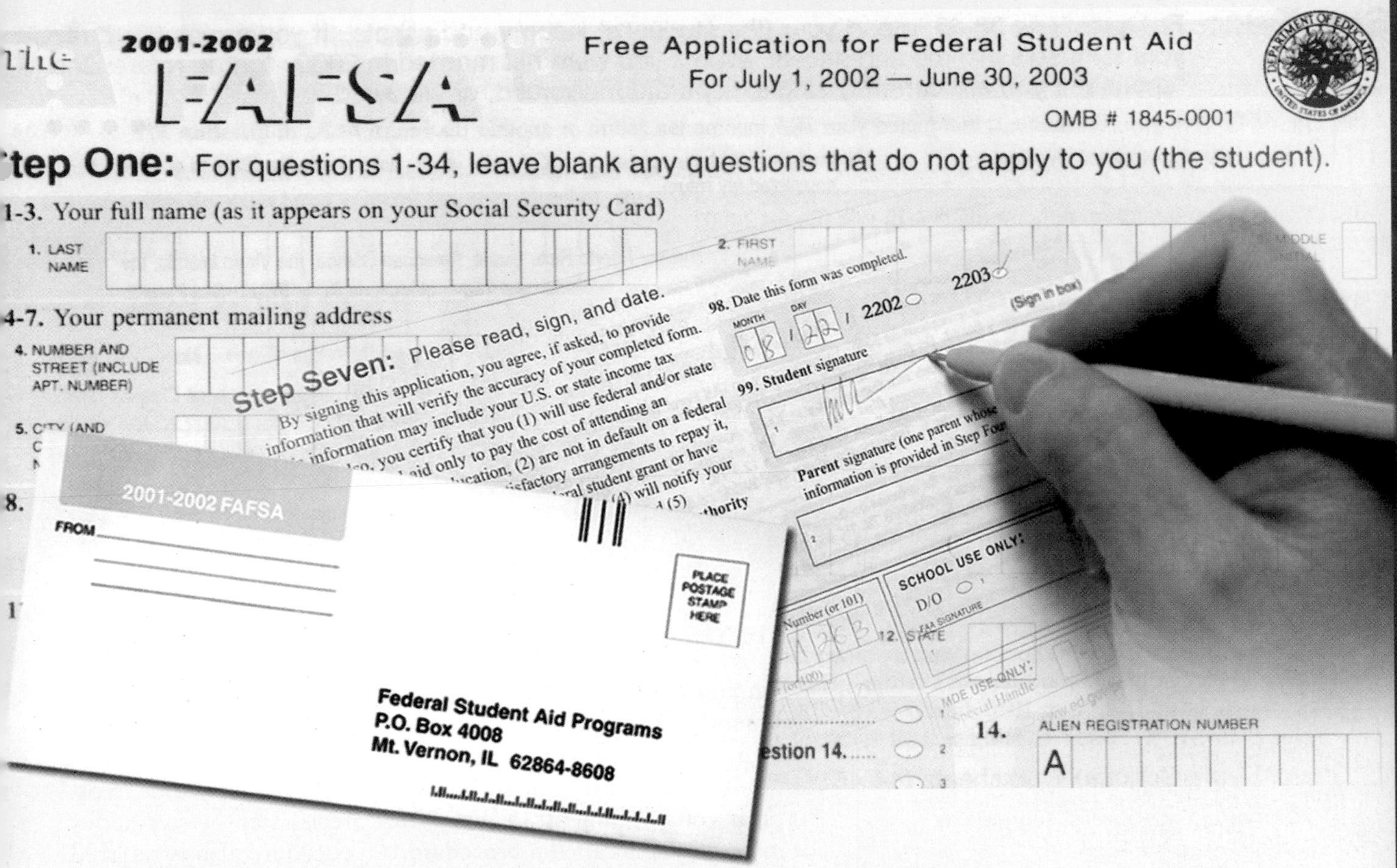

A second act in 1890 extended the land grant provisions to include the sixteen southern states.

Purdue University, one of the original land-grant colleges, began classes on September 16, 1874 with six instructors and 39 students. Five years earlier, the Indiana assembly accepted $150,000 from Lafayette civic leader, John Purdue, $50,000 from Tippecanoe County, and 100 acres of land from local citizens. In appreciation, the legislators decided that the university should be located in West Lafayette and named Purdue University.

Today, Purdue's buildings dwarf the original three structures. Current semester enrollment is more than 37,700, and graduates number more than 410,000, accounting for Purdue's reputation as one of America's top universities. Applying to Purdue is made more convenient by using the online forms available on Purdue's Web site (purdue.edu).

Semester fees and tuition for full-time enrollment grow at an exponential rate. The price tag for attending Purdue and similar universities may be financially out of reach for many potential students. Fortunately, Purdue and other colleges work with the U.S. Department of Education to help fund students' education through the Student Financial Assistance Program, the largest source of student aid in America. The Free Application for Federal Student Aid (FAFSA) offers online application forms for grants, loans, and work-study assistance. These online forms are crisp, clear, and convenient.

To make online forms viable, the designers must fine-tune them until they are practical, easy-to-use, and eye-catching. Similarly in this project, you will improve upon the online form created in Project 7, allowing you to produce a more efficient and visually pleasing form.

The importance of the land grant colleges cannot be overemphasized. Although originally slated as agricultural and technical schools, many of them grew into large universities, which over the years have educated millions of individuals. Submitting applications to these colleges and niversities and applying for student loans, is made convenient through the use of the Internet and online forms.

Microsoft Word 2002

Working with Macros and Visual Basic for Applications (VBA)

PROJECT 8

CASE PERSPECTIVE

You recently designed the online survey for the owner of Brim's Blooming Boutique, who happens to be your Aunt Carol. Before showing your aunt the form, you decide to show it to your Web Page Design instructor for his opinion. He has several suggestions for improving the form.

First, he suggests changing the color scheme and graphics on the form. Second, the form should display without formatting marks showing and be positioned properly in the Word window without the user having to scroll. Third, if a user enters a letter or other nonnumeric value into the number of minutes text box, the form should display an error message. Fourth, if a user enters text into the Other text box, the form automatically should place an X in the Other check box. Finally, he suggests you add a button to the Standard toolbar that instructs Word to save only the data when you save the form. This button will save you many extra steps in analyzing customer responses.

To complete this project, you will need the online form template created in Project 7. (If you did not create the template, see your instructor for a copy.)

Introduction

When you issue an instruction to Word by clicking a button or a command, Word must have a step-by-step description of the task to be accomplished. For example, when you click the Print button on the Standard toolbar, Word follows a precise set of steps to print your document. In Word, this precise step-by-step series of instructions is called a **procedure**. A procedure also is referred to as a **program** or **code**.

The process of writing a procedure is called **computer programming**. Every Word command on a menu and button on a toolbar has a corresponding procedure that executes when you click the command or button. **Execute** means that the computer carries out the step-by-step instructions. In a Windows environment, an event causes the instructions associated with a task to be executed. An **event** is an action such as clicking a button, clicking a command, dragging a scroll box, or right-clicking selected text.

Although Word has many toolbar buttons and menu commands, it does not include a command or button for every possible task. Thus, Microsoft has included with Word a powerful programming language called Visual Basic for Applications. The **Visual Basic for Applications** (**VBA**) programming language allows you to customize and extend the capabilities of Word.

Project Eight — Working with Macros and Visual Basic for Applications

In this project, you improve upon the online form created in Project 7 (shown in Figure 7-1 on page WD 7.05). Figure 8-1a shows the revised blank form, in which the fonts, font sizes, graphic, highlight color, and fill effect in the drawing object are changed. Figure 8-1b shows an error message box that displays if

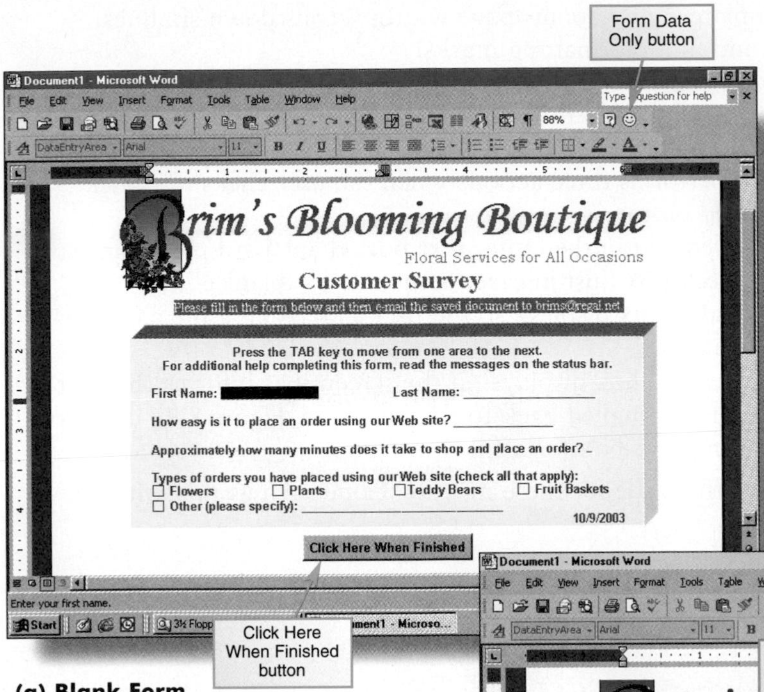
Form Data Only button
Brim's Blooming Boutique
Floral Services for All Occasions
Customer Survey
Please fill in the form below and then e-mail the saved document to brims@regal.net
Press the TAB key to move from one area to the next.
For additional help completing this form, read the messages on the status bar.
First Name:
Last Name:
How easy is it to place an order using our Web site?
Approximately how many minutes does it take to shop and place an order?
Types of orders you have placed using our Web site (check all that apply):
Flowers
Plants
Teddy Bears
Fruit Baskets
Other (please specify):
10/9/2003
Click Here When Finished
Enter your first name.
Click Here When Finished button

(a) Blank Form

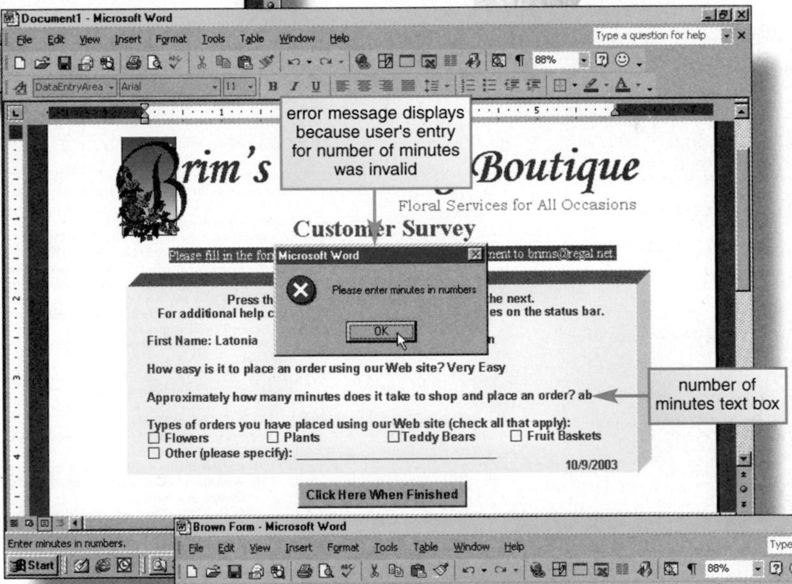
error message displays because user's entry for number of minutes was invalid
Microsoft Word
Please enter minutes in numbers
OK
First Name: Latonia
How easy is it to place an order using our Web site? Very Easy
Approximately how many minutes does it take to shop and place an order? ab
number of minutes text box
Click Here When Finished
Enter minutes in numbers.

(b) Error Message Dialog Box

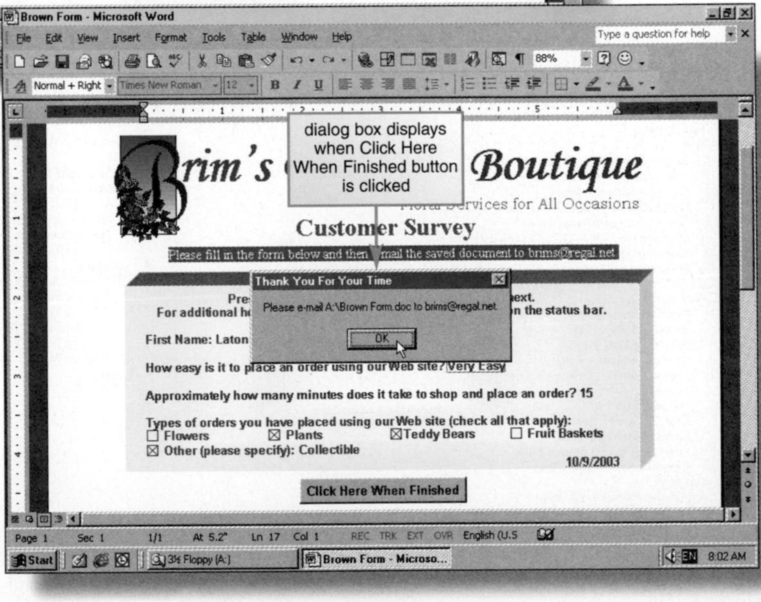
Brown Form - Microsoft Word
dialog box displays when Click Here When Finished button is clicked
Thank You For Your Time
Please e-mail A:\Brown Form.doc to brims@regal.net
OK
Approximately how many minutes does it take to shop and place an order? 15
Other (please specify): Collectible
Click Here When Finished

(c) Thank-You Message Dialog Box

FIGURE 8-1

a user makes an invalid entry, and Figure 8-1c shows a thank-you message box that displays when the user clicks the button at the bottom of the form.

Four macros are saved with the template file so that they can be used while the template, or a document based on the template, displays in the Word window. A **macro** is a procedure made up of VBA code. The four macros are designed to make the form more efficient:

1. The first macro places a check mark in the Save data only for forms check box in the Save sheet in the Options dialog box. With this check box selected, the next time you click the Save button, Word will save the form data in a comma-delimited text file. Additionally, the Standard toolbar contains a new button called the Form Data Only button (Figure 8-1a). When you click the Form Data Only button or press ALT+D (the shortcut key assigned to the button), Word places a check mark in the Save data only for forms check box in the Save sheet in the Options dialog box.

2. The second macro controls how the form initially displays on the screen (as a blank form). When a user starts a new Word document that is based on the form template, Word zooms page width, scrolls down six lines, hides gridlines, and hides formatting marks.
3. The third macro displays an error message if the user leaves the number of minutes text box blank or enters a nonnumeric entry in the text box. Figure 8-1b on the previous page displays the error message.
4. The fourth macro performs three actions when the user clicks the Click Here When Finished button:
   a. If the user entered text in the Other text box, then Word places an X in the Other check box (just in case the user left it blank).
   b. The Save As dialog box displays so the user can assign a file name to the filled-in form.
   c. A thank-you message box displays on the screen that informs the user what file should be e-mailed back to the boutique. Figure 8-1c displays the thank-you message box for a filled-in form.

Figure 8-2 shows the VBA code for these macros. Code such as this, often is called a computer program.

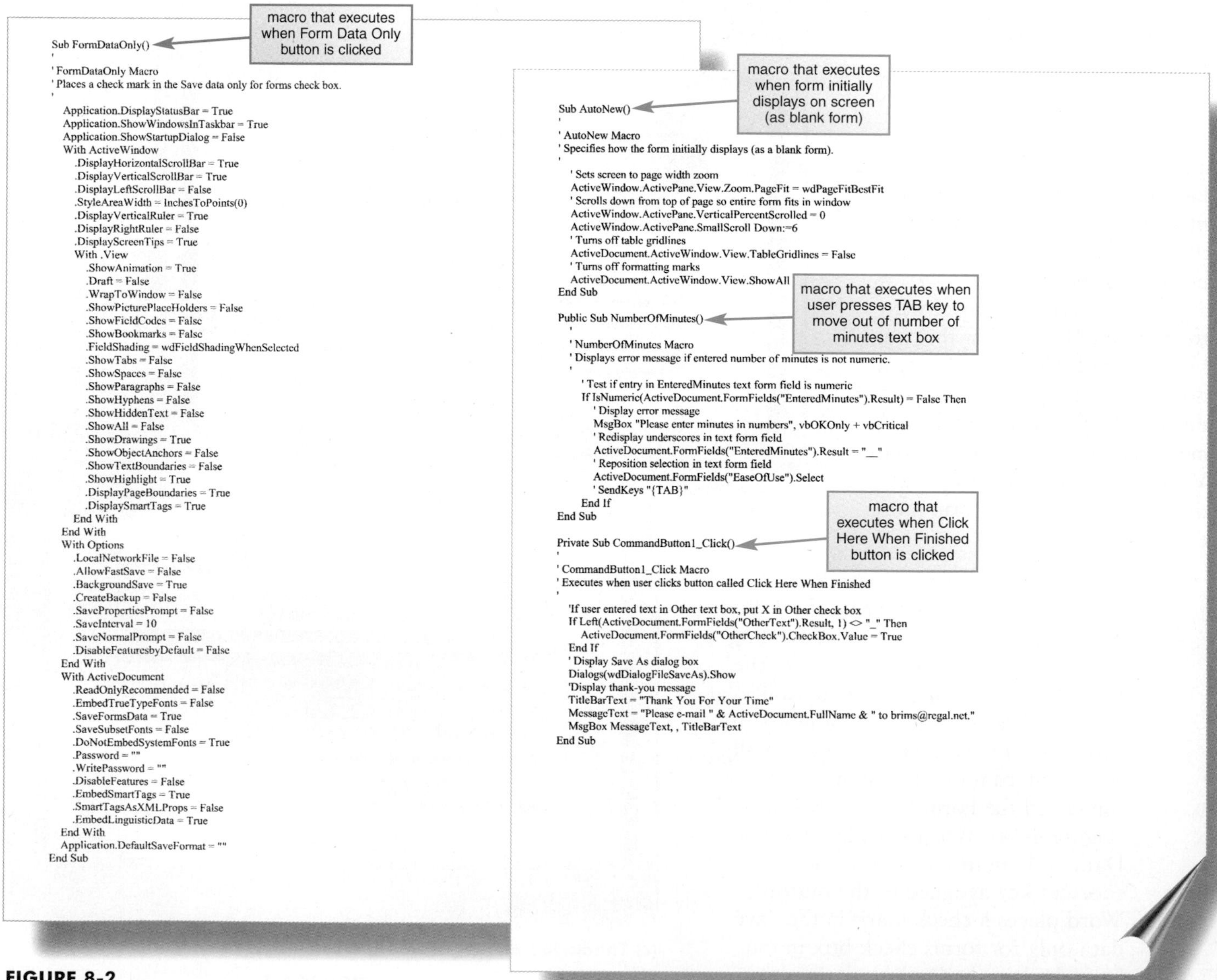


```
Sub FormDataOnly()
'
' FormDataOnly Macro
' Places a check mark in the Save data only for forms check box.
'
   Application.DisplayStatusBar = True
   Application.ShowWindowsInTaskbar = True
   Application.ShowStartupDialog = False
   With ActiveWindow
      .DisplayHorizontalScrollBar = True
      .DisplayVerticalScrollBar = True
      .DisplayLeftScrollBar = False
      .StyleAreaWidth = InchesToPoints(0)
      .DisplayVerticalRuler = True
      .DisplayRightRuler = False
      .DisplayScreenTips = True
      With .View
         .ShowAnimation = True
         .Draft = False
         .WrapToWindow = False
         .ShowPicturePlaceHolders = False
         .ShowFieldCodes = False
         .ShowBookmarks = False
         .FieldShading = wdFieldShadingWhenSelected
         .ShowTabs = False
         .ShowSpaces = False
         .ShowParagraphs = False
         .ShowHyphens = False
         .ShowHiddenText = False
         .ShowAll = False
         .ShowDrawings = True
         .ShowObjectAnchors = False
         .ShowTextBoundaries = False
         .ShowHighlight = True
         .DisplayPageBoundaries = True
         .DisplaySmartTags = True
      End With
   End With
   With Options
      .LocalNetworkFile = False
      .AllowFastSave = False
      .BackgroundSave = True
      .CreateBackup = False
      .SavePropertiesPrompt = False
      .SaveInterval = 10
      .SaveNormalPrompt = False
      .DisableFeaturesbyDefault = False
   End With
   With ActiveDocument
      .ReadOnlyRecommended = False
      .EmbedTrueTypeFonts = False
      .SaveFormsData = True
      .SaveSubsetFonts = False
      .DoNotEmbedSystemFonts = True
      .Password = ""
      .WritePassword = ""
      .DisableFeatures = False
      .EmbedSmartTags = True
      .SmartTagsAsXMLProps = False
      .EmbedLinguisticData = True
   End With
   Application.DefaultSaveFormat = ""
End Sub
```

```
Sub AutoNew()
'
' AutoNew Macro
' Specifies how the form initially displays (as a blank form).
'
   ' Sets screen to page width zoom
   ActiveWindow.ActivePane.View.Zoom.PageFit = wdPageFitBestFit
   ' Scrolls down from top of page so entire form fits in window
   ActiveWindow.ActivePane.VerticalPercentScrolled = 0
   ActiveWindow.ActivePane.SmallScroll Down:=6
   ' Turns off table gridlines
   ActiveDocument.ActiveWindow.View.TableGridlines = False
   ' Turns off formatting marks
   ActiveDocument.ActiveWindow.View.ShowAll
End Sub

Public Sub NumberOfMinutes()
   '
   ' NumberOfMinutes Macro
   ' Displays error message if entered number of minutes is not numeric.
   '
      ' Test if entry in EnteredMinutes text form field is numeric
      If IsNumeric(ActiveDocument.FormFields("EnteredMinutes").Result) = False Then
         ' Display error message
         MsgBox "Please enter minutes in numbers", vbOKOnly + vbCritical
         ' Redisplay underscores in text form field
         ActiveDocument.FormFields("EnteredMinutes").Result = "__"
         ' Reposition selection in text form field
         ActiveDocument.FormFields("EaseOfUse").Select
         ' SendKeys "{TAB}"
      End If
End Sub

Private Sub CommandButton1_Click()
'
' CommandButton1_Click Macro
' Executes when user clicks button called Click Here When Finished
'
   'If user entered text in Other text box, put X in Other check box
   If Left(ActiveDocument.FormFields("OtherText").Result, 1) <> "_" Then
      ActiveDocument.FormFields("OtherCheck").CheckBox.Value = True
   End If
   ' Display Save As dialog box
   Dialogs(wdDialogFileSaveAs).Show
   'Display thank-you message
   TitleBarText = "Thank You For Your Time"
   MessageText = "Please e-mail " & ActiveDocument.FullName & " to brims@regal.net."
   MsgBox MessageText, , TitleBarText
End Sub
```

FIGURE 8-2

Starting Word and Opening an Office Document

The first step in this project is to open the template for the online form that was created in Project 7 so that you can modify it. (If you did not create the template, see your instructor for a copy.) Perform the following steps to start Word and then open the Brim's Survey file.

TO START AND CUSTOMIZE WORD AND OPEN AN OFFICE DOCUMENT

1. Click the Start button on the Windows taskbar, point to Programs on the Start menu, and then click Microsoft Word on the Programs submenu.
2. If the Word window is not maximized, double-click its title bar to maximize it.
3. If the Language bar displays on the screen, click its Minimize button.
4. If the New Document task pane displays in the Word window, click the Show at startup check box to remove the check mark and then click the Close button in the upper-right corner of the task pane title bar.
5. If the toolbars display positioned on the same row, click the Toolbar Options button and then click Show Buttons on Two Rows.
6. Click View on the menu bar and then click Print Layout.
7. With the disk containing the Brim's Survey template file in drive A, click File on the menu bar and then click Open. When the Open dialog box displays, if necessary, click the Look in box arrow and then click 3½ Floppy (A:). Click the Files of type box arrow and then click Document Templates.
8. Double-click the template named, Brim's Survey. Scroll down so the entire form displays in the Word window.

The online form titled, Brim's Survey, displays in the Word window.

Because this project uses floating graphics, you will use print layout view. Thus, the Print Layout View button on the horizontal scroll bar is selected.

More About

Online Forms

For a sample online form on the Web, visit the Word 2002 More About Web page (scsite.com/wd2002/more.htm) and then click Sample Online Form.

Saving the Document with a New File Name

To preserve the contents of the Brim's Survey template file created in Project 7, save a copy of it with a new file name as described in the following steps.

TO SAVE A DOCUMENT WITH A NEW FILE NAME

1. With a floppy disk in drive A, click File on the menu bar and then click Save As.
2. Type `Brim's New Survey` in the File name text box. Do not press the ENTER key.
3. Click the Save as type box arrow and then click Document Template. If necessary, click the Save in box arrow and then click 3½ Floppy (A:).
4. Click the Save button in the Save As dialog box.

Word saves the document on a floppy disk in drive A with the new file name, Brim's New Survey (shown in Figure 8-3 on the next page).

Unprotecting a Document

The template for the Customer Survey online form is protected. When a document is **protected**, users cannot modify it in any manner — except for entering values into form fields placed on the form. Thus, before you can modify the online form, you must unprotect the form, as described in the following steps.

TO UNPROTECT A DOCUMENT

1. Click Tools on the menu bar and then point to Unprotect Document (Figure 8-3).
2. Click Unprotect Document.

Word unprotects the Brim's New Survey template.

More About

Unprotecting Documents

If Word requests a password when you attempt to unprotect a document, you must enter a password in order to unprotect and then change the document. If you do not know the password, you cannot change the look of the form; you can enter data into its form fields, however.

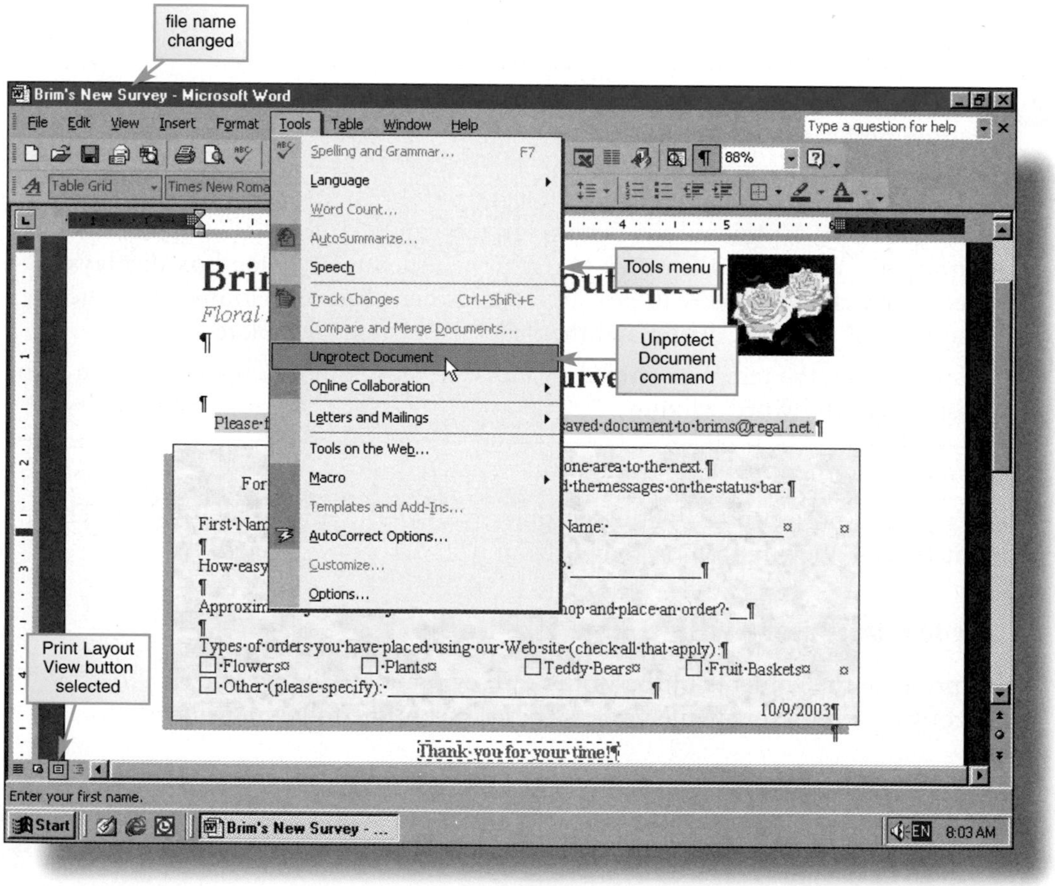

FIGURE 8-3

With the template unprotected, you can change its contents. Later in this project, after you have completed the modifications, you will protect the document again.

Resetting Menus and Toolbars

To set the menus and toolbars so they appear exactly as shown in this book, reset your menus and toolbars as outlined in Appendix D or follow these steps.

TO RESET MENUS AND TOOLBARS

1. Click the Toolbar Options button on the Standard toolbar and then point to Add or Remove Buttons. Point to Standard on the Add or Remove Buttons submenu. Scroll to and then click Reset Toolbar on the Standard submenu.
2. Click the Toolbar Options button on the Formatting toolbar and then point to Add or Remove Buttons. Point to Formatting on the Add or Remove Buttons submenu. Scroll to and then click Reset Toolbar on the Formatting submenu.
3. Click the Toolbar Options button on the Standard toolbar and then point to Add or Remove Buttons. Click Customize on the Add or Remove Buttons submenu.
4. When the Customize dialog box displays, if necessary, click the Options tab and then click the Reset my usage data button. When the Microsoft Word dialog box displays, click the Yes button. Click the Close button in the Customize dialog box.

Word resets the menus and toolbars.

Displaying Formatting Marks

It is helpful to display formatting marks that indicate where in the document you pressed the ENTER key, SPACEBAR, and other keys. Perform the following step to display formatting marks.

TO DISPLAY FORMATTING MARKS

1. If the Show/Hide ¶ button on the Standard toolbar is not selected already, click it.

Word displays formatting marks in the document window, and the Show/Hide ¶ button on the Standard toolbar is selected (shown in Figure 8-4 on the next page).

Zooming Page Width

When you zoom page width, Word displays the page on the screen as large as possible in print layout view. Perform the following steps to zoom page width.

TO ZOOM PAGE WIDTH

1. Click the Zoom box arrow on the Standard toolbar.
2. Click Page Width.

Word computes the zoom percentage and displays it in the Zoom box (shown in Figure 8-4). Your percentage may be different depending on your computer.

Setting a Security Level in Word

A **computer virus** is a potentially damaging computer program designed to affect, or infect, your computer negatively by altering the way it works without your knowledge or permission. Currently, more than 53,000 known computer viruses exist and an estimated six new viruses are discovered each day. The increased use of networks, the Internet, and e-mail has accelerated the spread of computer viruses.

More About

Viruses

For more information about viruses, visit the Word 2002 More About Web page (scsite.com/wd2002/more.htm) and then click Viruses.

To combat this evil, most computer users run antivirus programs that search for viruses and destroy them before they ever have a chance to infect the computer. Macros are a known carrier of viruses, because of the ease with which a person can write code for a macro. For this reason, you can reduce the chance your computer will be infected with a macro virus by setting a **security level** in Word. These security levels allow you to enable or disable macros. An enabled macro is a macro that Word will execute, and a **disabled macro** is a macro that is unavailable to Word. Table 8-1 summarizes the three available security levels in Word.

More About

Macro Security

All templates, add-ins, and macros shipped with Office XP are digitally signed by Microsoft. If you add Microsoft to your list of trusted sources for one of these installed files, all subsequent interaction with these files will not display security dialog boxes.

Table 8-1 Word Security Levels

SECURITY LEVEL	*CONDITION*
High	Word will execute only macros that are digitally signed. All other macros are disabled when the document is opened.
Medium	Upon opening a document that contains macros from an unknown source, Word displays a dialog box asking if you wish to enable the macros.
Low	Word turns off macro virus protection. The document is opened with all macros enabled, including those from unknown sources.

If Word security is set to high and you attach a macro to a document, Word will disable that macro when you open the document. Because you will be creating macros in this project, you should ensure that your security level is set to medium. Thus, each time you open this Word document or any other document that contains a macro from an unknown source, Word displays a dialog box warning that a macro is attached and allows you to enable or disable the macros. If you are confident of the source (author) of the document and macros, you should click the Enable Macros button in the dialog box. If you are uncertain about the reliability of the source of the document and macros, you should click the Disable Macros button.

Perform the following steps to set Word's security level to medium.

Steps To Set a Security Level in Word

1 Click Tools on the menu bar, point to Macro, and then point to Security on the Macro submenu (Figure 8-4).

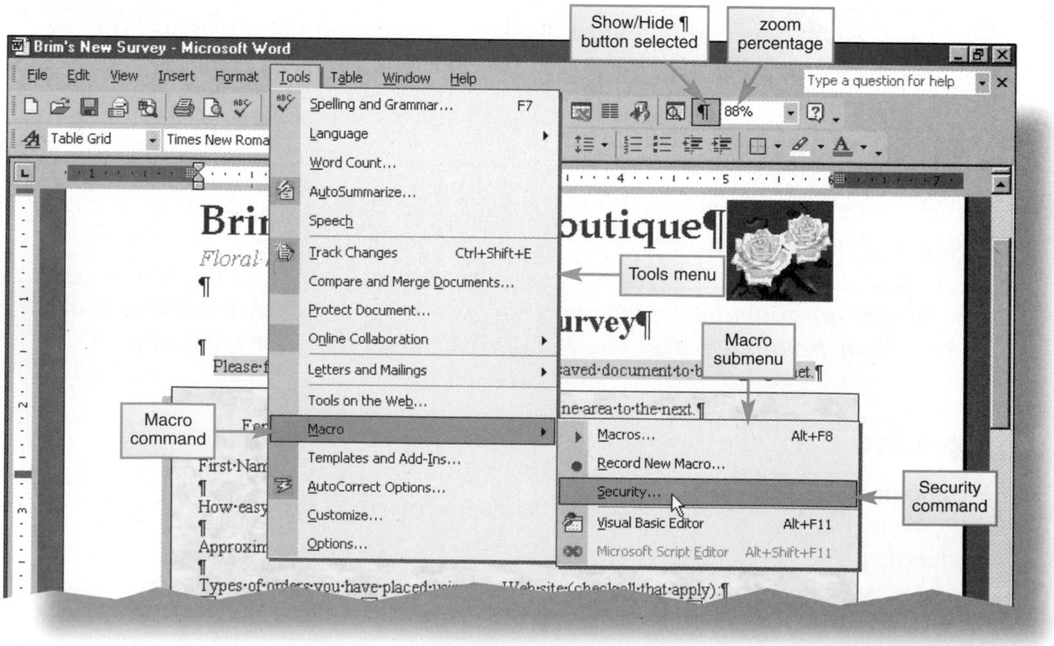

FIGURE 8-4

2 Click Security. When the Security dialog box displays, if necessary, click the Security Level tab. Click Medium and then point to the OK button.

Word displays the Security dialog box (Figure 8-5). The Medium option button is selected.

3 Click the OK button.

Word sets its security level to medium.

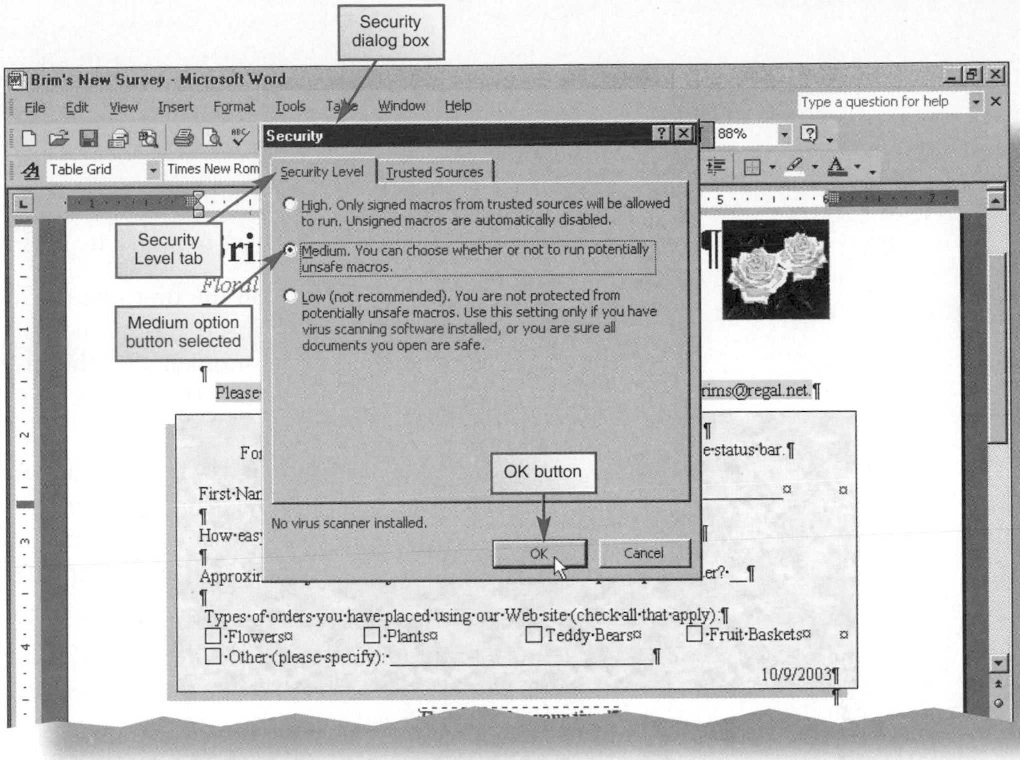

FIGURE 8-5

The next time you open a document that contains a macro from an unauthorized source, Word will ask if you wish to enable or disable the macro.

Other Ways

1. In Voice Command mode, say "Tools, Macro, Security, Medium, OK"

Modifying a Form

As suggested by your instructor, you will change the look of the Customer Survey. You will change the graphic, insert the headings into a text box, and then modify the fonts, font colors, font sizes, and alignment. You also will change the highlight color and the fill inside the rectangle drawing object. The following pages discuss how you modify the online form.

Modifying the Graphic

The first step in modifying the online form is to remove the existing graphic of the flowers and insert a new decorative graphic of the letter B to replace the first letter in Brim's. The new clip art image is available on the Web. If you do not have access to the Web, you may insert the graphic from a file on the Data Disk that accompanies this book. First, you will reduce the size of the inserted image. Then, you will change it from an inline object to a floating object. Finally, you will move the graphic to the left of the boutique name to use it as the first letter of the company name.

Perform the steps on the next page to delete the graphic on the form, insert a clip art image from the Web into the Word document, and then modify the graphic.

More About

Macro Viruses

If Word's security level is set to low, Word does not warn you that a file contains a macro, thus leaving your computer open for macro viruses. A macro virus is a type of computer virus that is stored in a macro within a file, template, or add-in. If Word's security level is set to medium, Word warns you before opening a document containing a macro. For the best protection against macro viruses, purchase and install specialized antivirus software. For more information about using antivirus software, visit the Word 2002 More About Web Page (scsite.com/wd2002/more.htm) and then click Antivirus Software.

Note: The following steps assume your computer is connected to the Internet. If it is not, go directly to the shaded steps at the top of page WD 8.13.

TO CHANGE THE GRAPHIC

1. Click the graphic of the flowers to select it. Press the DELETE key.
2. Position the insertion point on the first line of the form, immediately to the left of the capital letter B. Click Insert on the menu bar, point to Picture, and then click Clip Art on the Picture submenu. In the Insert Clip Art task pane, drag through any text in the Search text text box to select the text. Type b and then press the ENTER key.
3. When Word displays thumbnails of clips that match the description, point to the clip shown in Figure 8-6. The globe icon in the lower-left corner of a thumbnail indicates the clip art is located on the Web.
4. Click the box arrow that displays to the right of the clip. Click Insert on the menu and then click the Close button in the Insert Clip Art task pane title bar.
5. When the graphic displays in the document, double-click the graphic. When the Format Picture dialog box displays, if necessary, click the Size tab. Change the height and width values in the Scale area to 58%.
6. Click the Layout tab and then click Square. Click the OK button.
7. Drag the graphic to the left so it is aligned approximately with the left side of the rectangle below it, as shown in Figure 8-6.
8. Click outside the graphic to deselect it. If necessary, drag the scroll box on the vertical scroll bar to display the entire form in the document window.

The graphic is resized and positioned as shown in Figure 8-6.

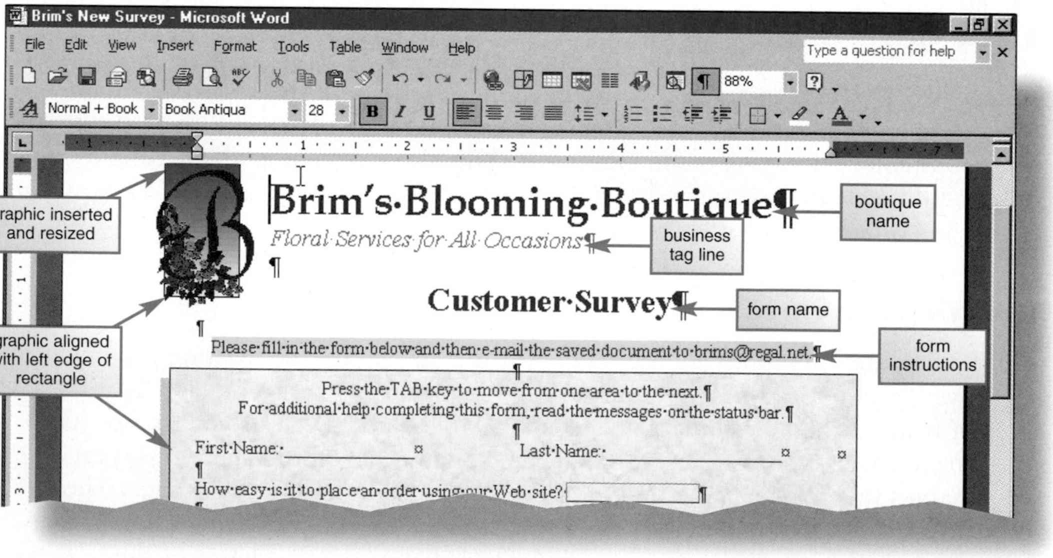

FIGURE 8-6

If you do not have access to the Web, you can insert the clip art file into the Word document from the Data Disk, as described in the following steps. If you did not download the Data Disk, see the inside back cover for instructions for downloading the Data Disk or see your instructor.

TO INSERT A GRAPHIC FILE FROM THE DATA DISK

1. With the insertion point at the beginning of the form, click Insert on the menu bar, point to Picture, and then click From File.
2. Insert the Data Disk into drive A. When the Insert Picture dialog box displays, click the Look in box arrow and then click 3½ Floppy (A:). Click the file name, letterB, and then click the Insert button.
3. When the graphic displays in the document, double-click the graphic. When the Format Picture dialog box displays, if necessary, click the Size tab. Change the height and width values in the Scale area to 58%.
4. Click the Layout tab and then click Square. Click the OK button.
5. Drag the graphic to the left so it approximately is aligned with the left side of the rectangle below it, as shown in Figure 8-6.
6. Click outside the graphic to deselect it.

Word inserts the clip into your document and resizes it (shown in Figure 8-6).

The next step in modifying the Customer Survey is to insert the boutique name, business tag line, and form name (Figure 8-6) into a text box and then change the alignment, font, font style, font size, and font color.

Inserting a Text Box and Formatting Text

To use the new graphical B as the first letter in Brim's Blooming Boutique, you need to delete the letter B and then move the text close to the graphic. Inserting the text into a text box allows you to move the text closer to the graphic. Perform the following steps to delete the letter B, and then insert and format the text box.

TO INSERT AND FORMAT A TEXT BOX

1. Select the first letter of Brim's and then press the DELETE key to remove the capital B. Press the DOWN ARROW key to position the insertion point on line 2. If necessary, right-click the green wavy underline below rim's and then click Ignore Once on the shortcut menu.
2. On the third line, delete the paragraph mark to remove the blank line. Also, delete the paragraph mark below the text, Customer Survey, to remove that blank line.
3. Select the first three lines of text that include the boutique name, the business tag line, and the form name. If the Drawing toolbar does not display on the screen, click the Drawing button on the Standard toolbar to display the Drawing toolbar. Click the Text Box button on the Drawing toolbar to place a text box around the selected text. (You will fix the cluttered appearance next.)
4. Click the Fill Color button arrow on the Drawing toolbar and then click No Fill. Click the Line Color button arrow on the Drawing toolbar and then click No Line.
5. Drag the text box to the right so that no text overlaps the graphic. Drag the right-middle sizing handle of the text box to approximately the 6 inch mark on the horizontal ruler, as shown in Figure 8-7 on the next page. If the form instructions line that is highlighted yellow below the text box wraps to a second line, drag the bottom-middle sizing handle on the text box down until the instructions display on a single line. You may need to move the text box around a bit to make your screen look like Figure 8-7.

More About

Text Boxes

Text boxes and frames are both containers for text that can be positioned on a page and then sized. Earlier versions of Word used frames to wrap text around a graphic. With Word 2002, you can use text boxes to manipulate text and take advantage of new graphical effects. Text boxes provide nearly all the advantages of frames, plus they provide many additional advantages. You can use the Drawing toolbar to enhance text boxes with effects such as fill color - just as you can with any other drawing object.

6 Click the Drawing button on the Standard toolbar to remove the Drawing toolbar from the screen. Scroll as necessary to display the entire form.

Word inserts and formats the text box.

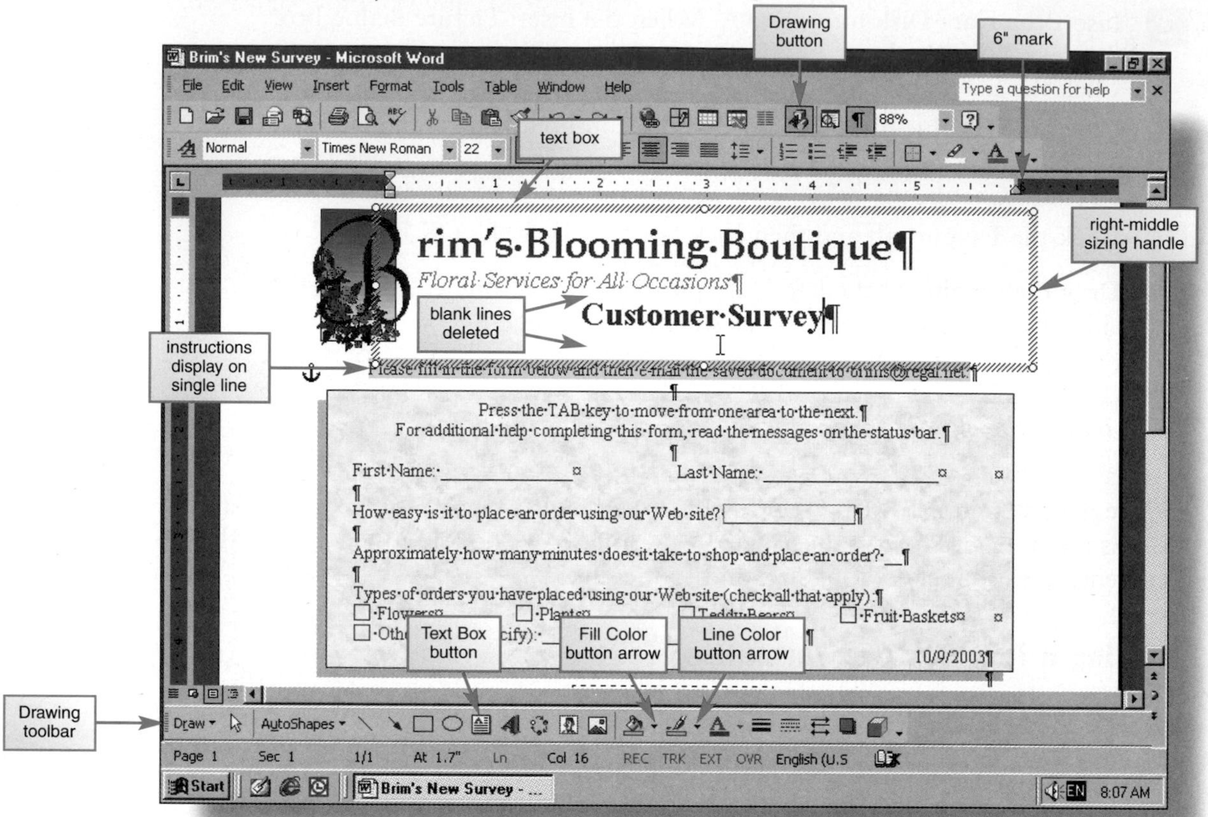

FIGURE 8-7

The next step is to format the text in the text box, as described in the steps below.

TO FORMAT TEXT IN A TEXT BOX

1. Select the first line of text in the text box, rim's Blooming Boutique. Click the Font box arrow on the Formatting toolbar. Scroll to and then click Monotype Corsiva. Click the Font Size box arrow on the Formatting toolbar. Scroll to and then click 48. Click the Font Color button arrow on the Formatting toolbar and then click Indigo.
2. Click the Align Right button on the Formatting toolbar to right-align the first line in the text box. If necessary, drag the left-middle sizing handle on the text box to the left so the entire company name displays on a single line.
3. Select the second line of text in the text box, which contains the business tag line: Floral Services for All Occasions. Click the Font box arrow on the Formatting toolbar. Scroll to and then click Bookman Old Style. Click the Font Size box on the Formatting toolbar and then click 14. Click the Italic button on the Formatting toolbar to turn off italic formatting. Click the Font Color button arrow on the Formatting toolbar and then click Orange.
4. Click the Align Right button on the Formatting toolbar to right-align the second line of text in the text box.

5 Select the third line of text in the text box, which contains the form name, Customer Survey. Click the Font Color button arrow on the Formatting toolbar and then click Green.

6 If necessary, drag the Left Indent marker on the horizontal ruler one-half inch to the left to center the form name above the rectangle.

7 If necessary, drag the text box closer to the graphic to facilitate reading the decorative B as the first letter in the boutique name.

The boutique name, business tag line, and form name display as shown in Figure 8-8.

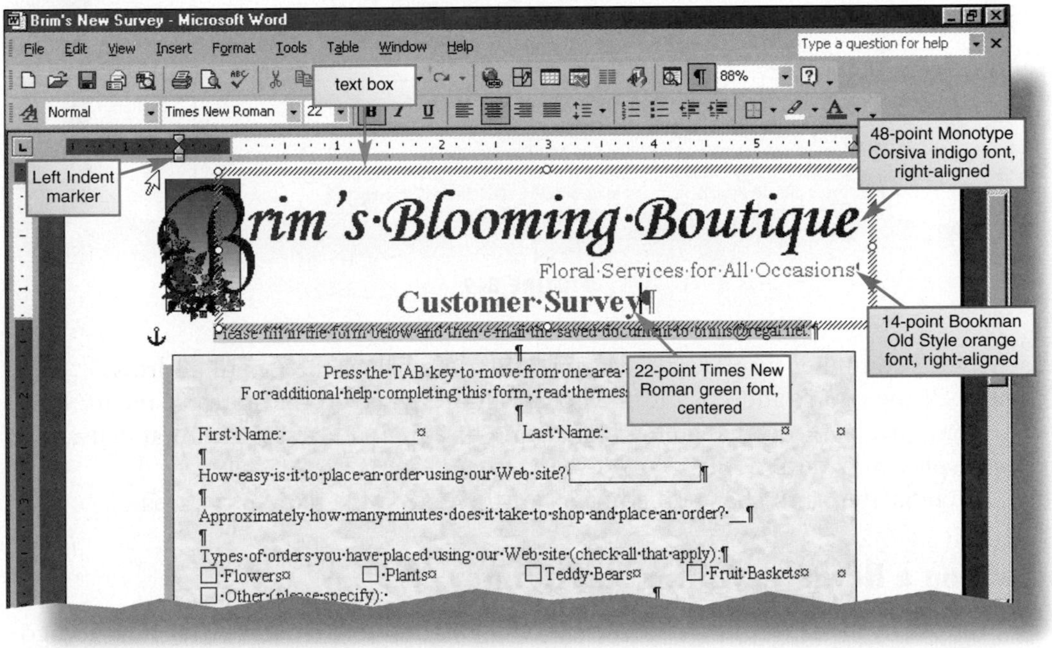

FIGURE 8-8

The next step is to format the form instructions. You will change the highlight color of the form instructions from yellow to green and then change the font color to white. You will right-align the text and then insert a blank line below the instructions in preparation for changes to the rectangle.

TO FORMAT THE FORM INSTRUCTIONS

1 Select the form instructions that currently are highlighted in yellow.

2 Click the Highlight button arrow on the Formatting toolbar and then click Green.

3 Click the Font Color button arrow on the Formatting toolbar and then click White.

4 Click the Center button on the Formatting toolbar.

5 Click the blank line below the instructions. Press the ENTER key to create a second blank line.

Word changes the highlight on the form instructions from yellow to green (Figure 8-9 on the next page). The font color changes to white, and the line is centered. Two blank lines display below the instructions.

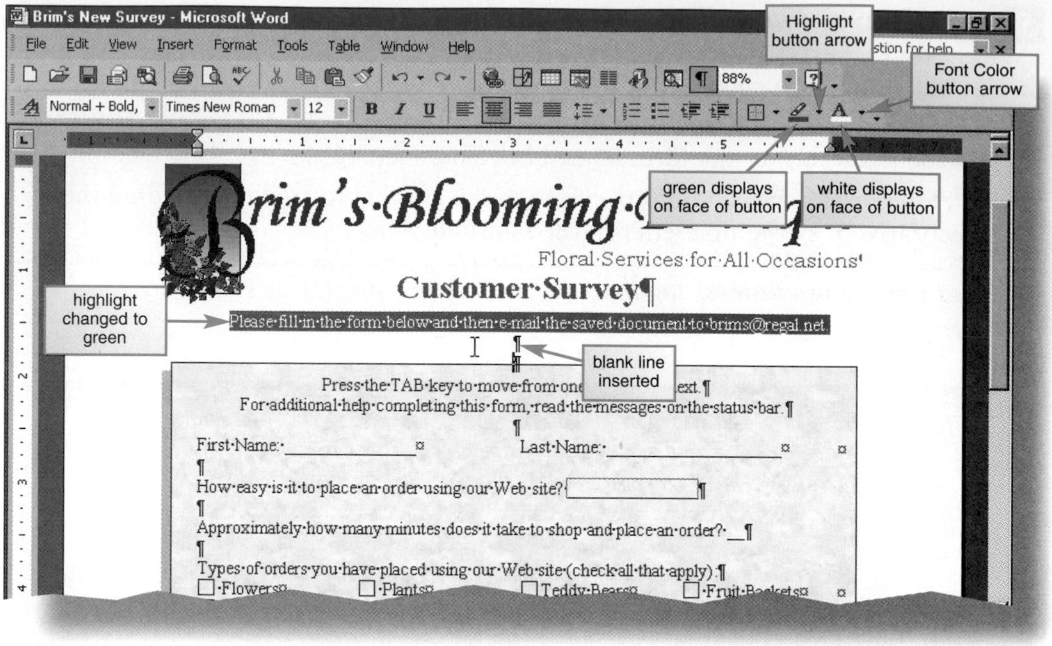

FIGURE 8-9

If your computer displays a red wavy underline below the e-mail address, right-click the e-mail address and then click Ignore Once on the shortcut menu. If your computer is set to change the formatting of e-mail addresses automatically, your display may differ.

The next step is to change the format of the text in the data entry area.

Creating a New Style with a Shortcut Key

All text in the data entry area should be formatted to 11-point Arial bold indigo font. You could select each text item in the data entry area, one at a time, and change its font to Arial, its font size to 11, its font style to bold, and its font color to indigo. A timesaving alternative, however, is to use a style. A **style** is a customized format that you can apply to text. Although Word has many built-in styles, none of them is an 11-point Arial bold indigo font. You can create your own new style, however, and then apply this style to the text in the data entry area of the form.

Word has two types of styles: character and paragraph. A **character style** defines attributes for selected text, such as font, font size, and font style. A **paragraph style** defines formatting for a paragraph, such as line spacing, text alignment, and borders. Paragraph styles can include a character style definition. In the data entry area of this form, you want to change text to 11-point Arial bold indigo font. Thus, you will create a character style.

Recall that shortcut keys are one or more keys you press on the keyboard to complete a task. Rather than selecting the newly created character style from a long list, using a keystroke combination gives you the advantage of not having to move your hands away from the keyboard to position the mouse on a different part of the screen and clicking and scrolling to locate the desired style. You can customize shortcut keys in Word by assigning the keystrokes to commands that do not have them already, removing shortcut keys that you do not want, or returning to the default shortcut key settings at anytime.

Perform the following steps to create a new character style, called DataEntryArea, which formats selected text to 11-point Arial bold indigo font. You will assign the shortcut, ALT+C, to the new character style.

More About

Creating Styles

To create a character style, click the New Style button in the Styles and Formatting task pane. When the New Style dialog box displays, click the Style type box arrow and then click Character. To create a paragraph style, click the Style type box arrow in the New Style dialog box and then click Paragraph. If you accidentally create a paragraph style rather than a character style, all current paragraph formatting will be applied to the selected text. In the case of Figure 8-10 for example, a paragraph style would include the centered format.

Steps To Create a Style That Has a Shortcut Key

1 Click the Styles and Formatting button on the Formatting toolbar. When the Styles and Formatting task pane displays, point to the New Style button.

Word displays the Styles and Formatting task pane (Figure 8-10). Your list of formats may be different.

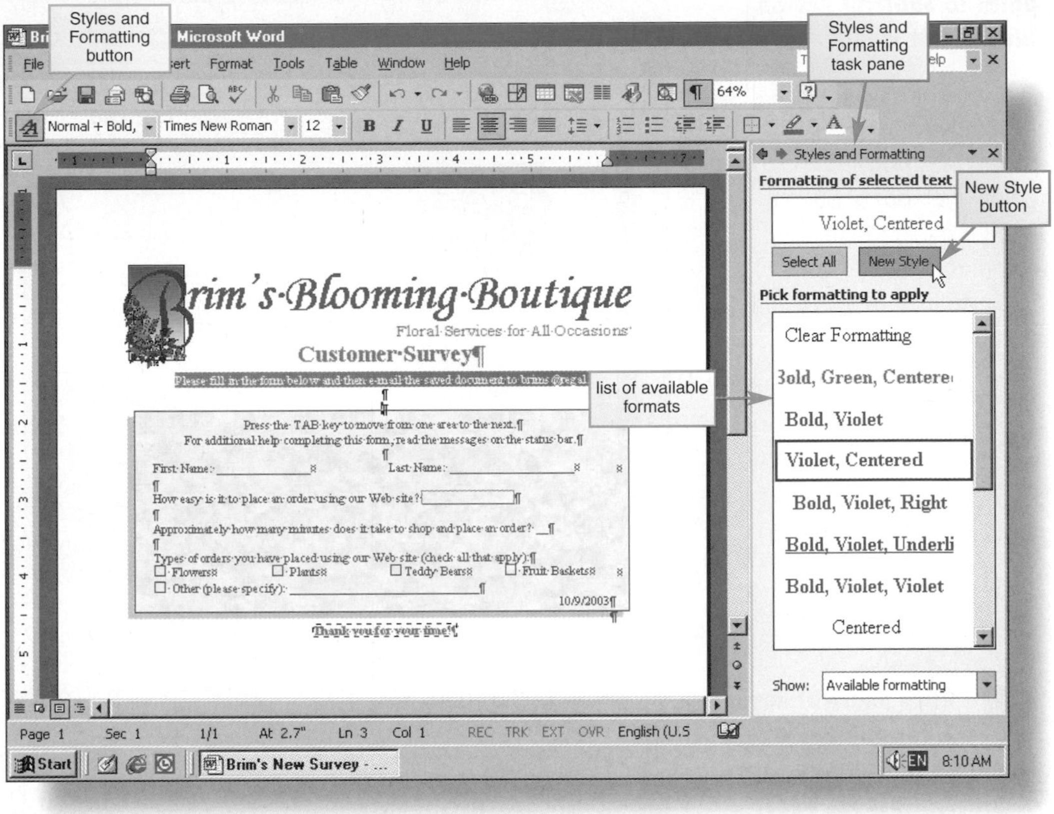

FIGURE 8-10

2 Click the New Style button. When the New Style dialog box displays, type `DataEntryArea` **in the Name text box. Click the Style type box arrow and then click Character. In the Formatting area, click the Font box arrow and then click Arial; click the Font Size box arrow and then click 11; click the Bold button; click the Font Color button arrow and then click Indigo. Point to the Format button.**

Word displays the New Style dialog box (Figure 8-11).

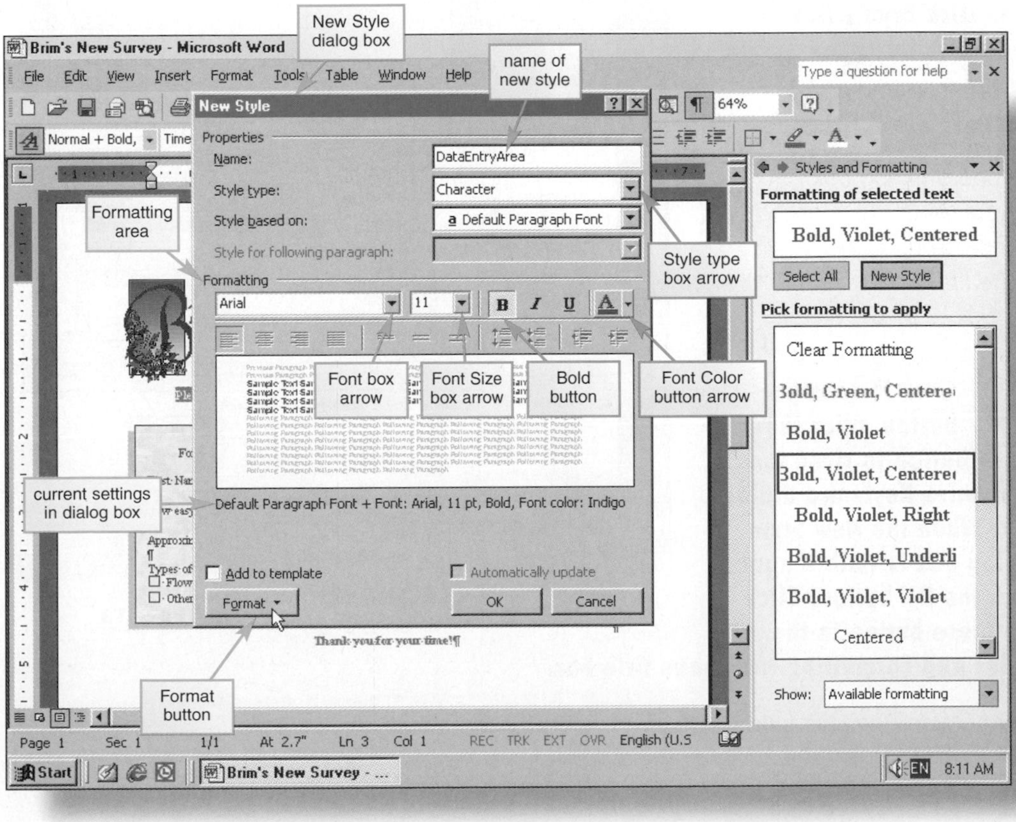

FIGURE 8-11

3 Click the Format button and then point to Shortcut key on the Format menu.

Word displays a list of available formatting commands above or below the Format button (Figure 8-12). Some commands are dimmed because they relate to paragraph styles.

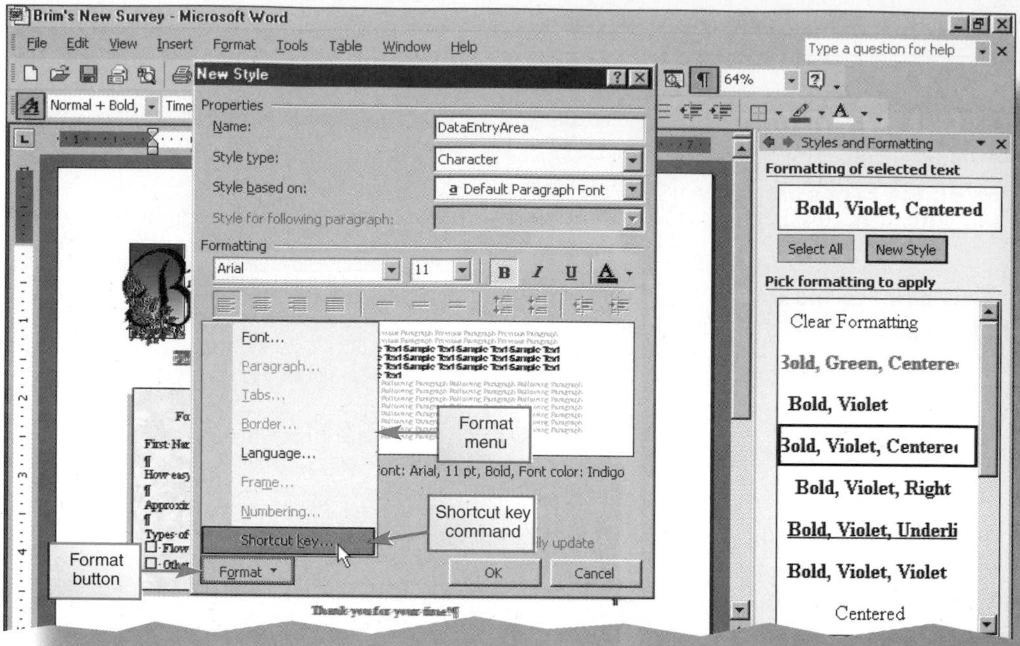

FIGURE 8-12

4 Click Shortcut key. When the Customize Keyboard dialog box displays, press ALT+C. If necessary, click the Save changes in box arrow and then click Brim's New Survey. Point to the Assign button.

Word displays the Customize Keyboard dialog box (Figure 8-13). The characters you pressed, ALT+C, display in the Press new shortcut key text box.

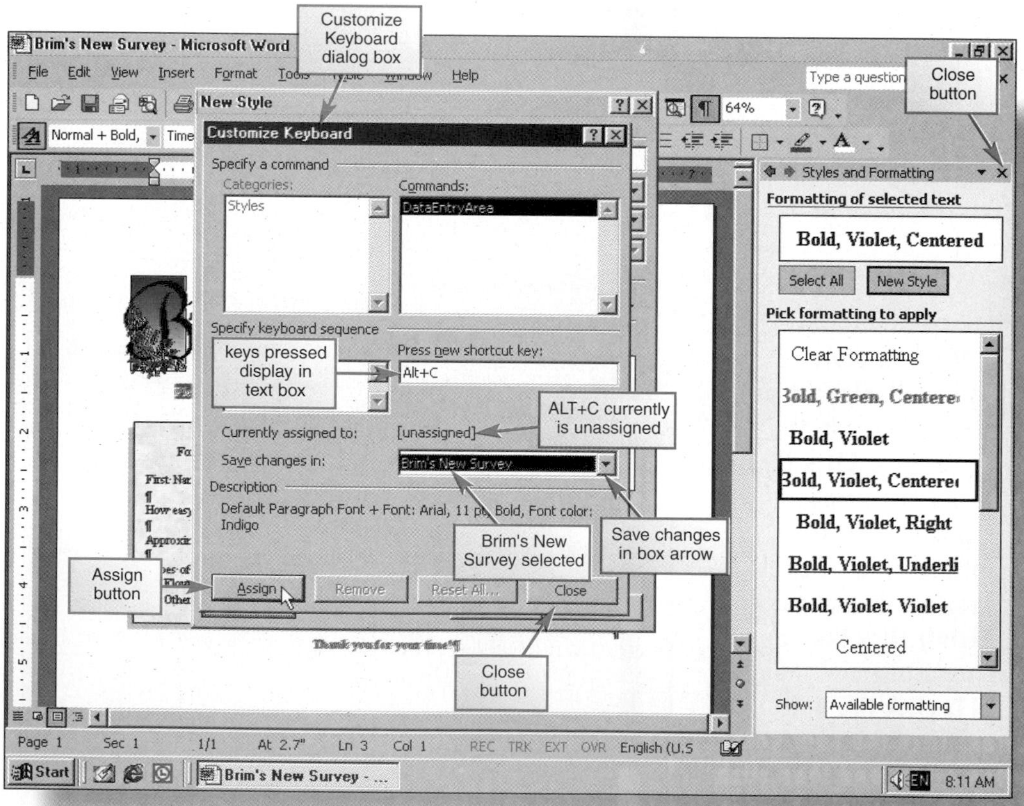

FIGURE 8-13

5 Click the Assign button. Click the Close button to close the Customize Keyboard dialog box. When the New Style dialog box is visible again, click the OK button. Click the Close button in the Styles and Formatting task pane title bar.

Word creates the DataEntryArea style along with its shortcut key, ALT+C.

To apply a character style, select the text to be formatted and then apply the style. To apply a paragraph style, you do not need to select text before applying the style — simply click in the paragraph to be formatted and then apply the style.

In the previous steps, you created a shortcut key of ALT+C for the DataEntryArea style. Instead of using the Style box on the Formatting toolbar to apply the DataEntryArea style to text in the data entry area of the Customer Survey, you will use the shortcut key. Perform the following step to apply a style using a shortcut key.

More About

Applying Styles

If you click the Style box arrow on the Formatting toolbar to apply styles, paragraph style names display a proofreader's paragraph mark, and character style names display an underlined letter a.

Steps To Apply a Style Using a Shortcut Key

1 If necessary, scroll to display the entire form in the document window. Drag through all of the text within the rectangle to select it and then press ALT+C. Click outside the selected text to remove the selection.

All of the text within the rectangle now is formatted with the new style; that is, 11-point Arial bold indigo font (Figure 8-14).

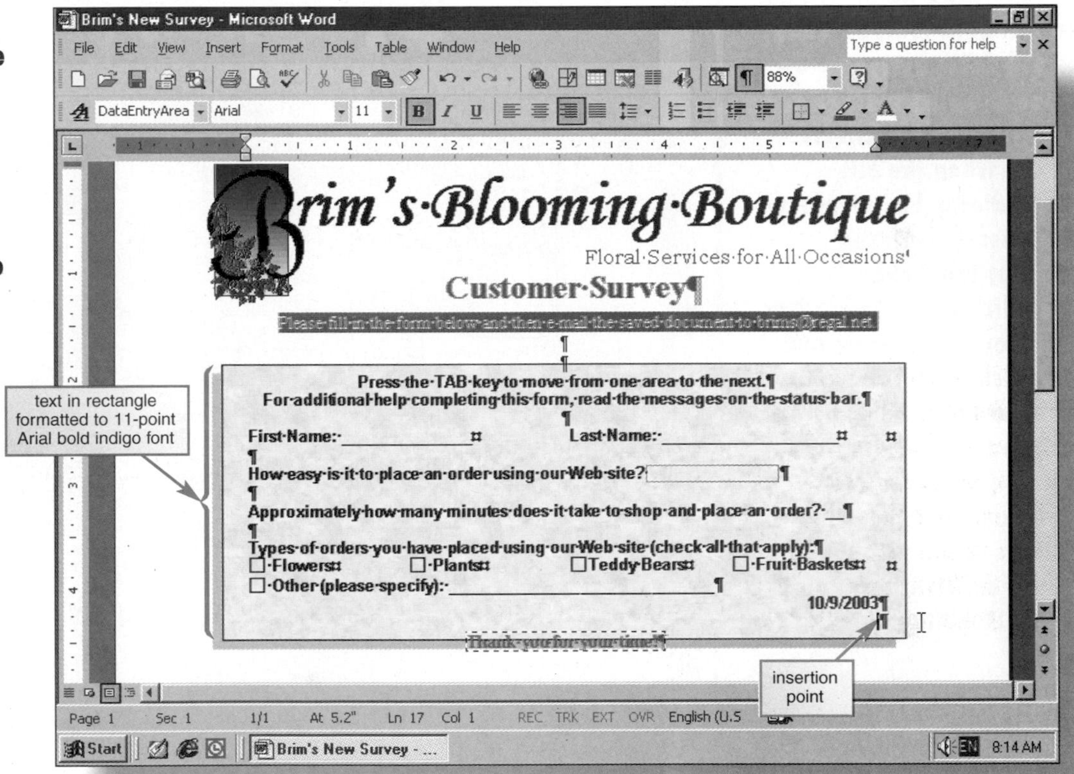

FIGURE 8-14

Other Ways

1. Click Style box arrow on Formatting toolbar, click style name
2. On Format menu click Styles and Formatting, click style name
3. In Voice Command mode, say "Format, Styles, [style name]"

The next step is to add a gradient fill effect to the rectangle.

Filling a Drawing Object with a Gradient Effect

The data entry area in the form is surrounded with a rectangle drawing object, which currently is filled with the parchment texture. Other available fill effects include solid colors, gradient colors, patterns, and pictures. This project requires a gradient fill effect in the rectangle drawing object. **Gradient** means a gradual progression of colors and shades, usually from one color to another color, or from one shade to another shade of the same color.

Perform the steps on the next page to fill the rectangle drawing object with a gradient fill effect.

Steps To Fill a Drawing Object with a Gradient Fill Effect

1 Select the rectangle by pointing to an edge of the rectangle and clicking when the mouse pointer has a four-headed arrow attached to it. If the Drawing toolbar does not display on your screen, click the Drawing button on the Standard toolbar. Click the Fill Color button arrow on the Drawing toolbar and then click the Fill Effects button. When the Fill Effects dialog box displays, if necessary, click the Gradient tab. In the Colors area, click Two colors. Click the Color 1 box arrow and then click Light Yellow. Click the Color 2 box arrow and then click White. In the Shading styles area, click From center. In the Variants area, click the variant on the right. Point to the OK button.

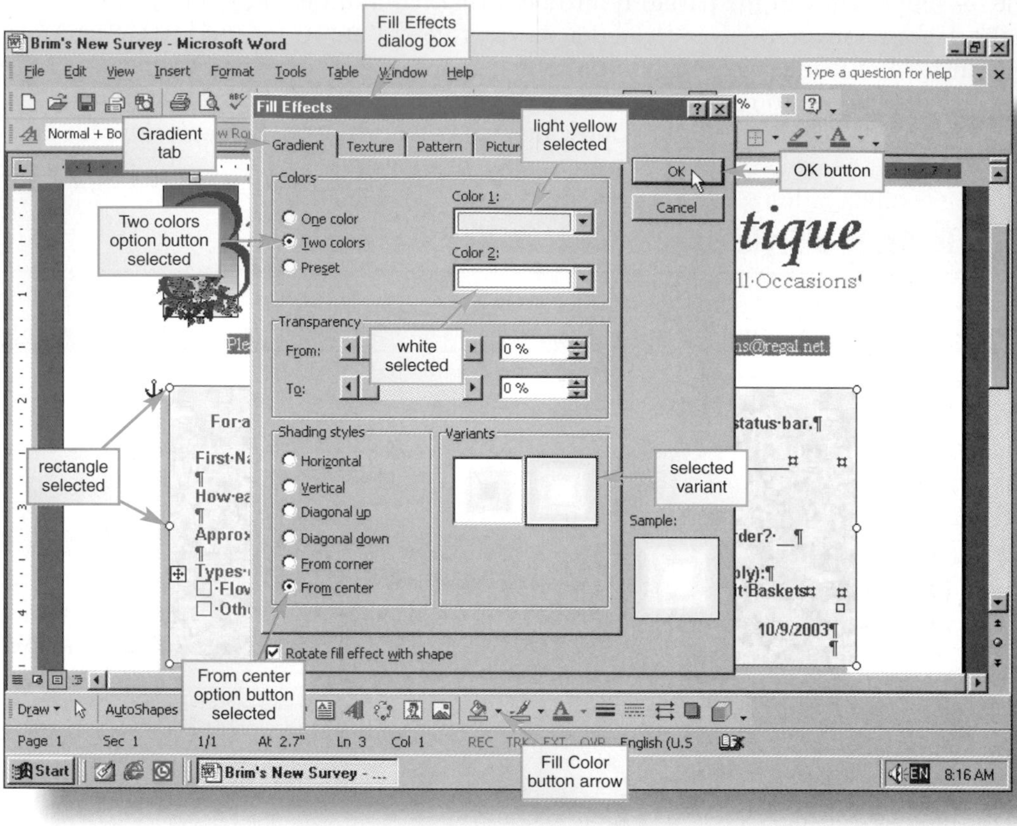

FIGURE 8-15

The Fill Effects dialog box displays (Figure 8-15).

2 Click the OK button.

Word fills the rectangle with the light yellow and white gradient effect (Figure 8-16).

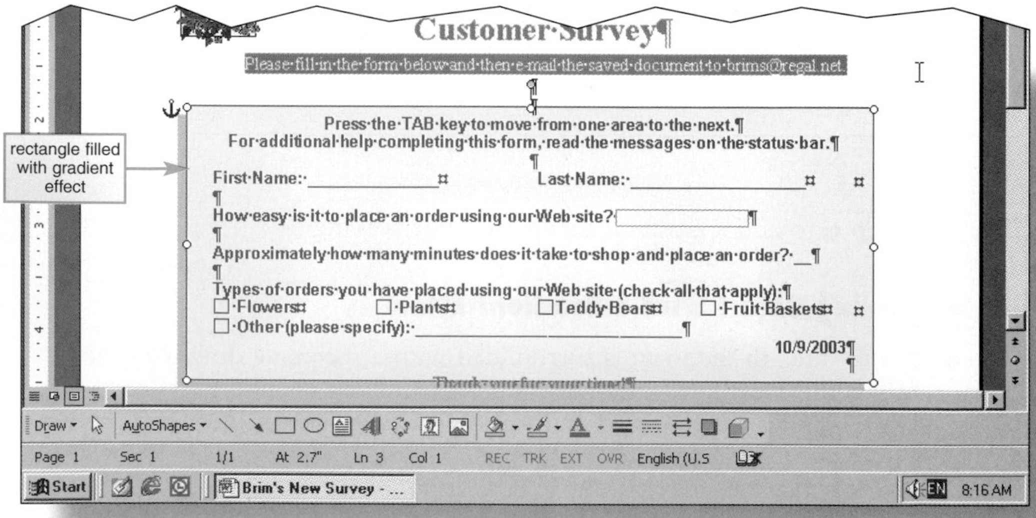

FIGURE 8-16

Other Ways

1. Right-click edge of drawing object, click Format AutoShape on shortcut menu, click Colors and Lines tab, click Color button arrow in Fill area, click Fill Effects button, click Gradient tab
2. Select drawing object, click AutoShape on Format menu, click Colors and Lines tab, click Fill Color button arrow, click Fill Effects button, click Gradient tab

Notice in Figure 8-16 that the gradient fill is white in the center and gradually fills the entire drawing object to a solid yellow at the edges. This is because you selected From center in the Gradient sheet in the Fill Effects dialog box (Figure 8-15).

The next step is to add a 3-D effect to the rectangle drawing object.

Adding a 3-D Effect to a Drawing Object

You can add a 3-D effect to a drawing object by using the 3-D button on the Drawing toolbar. Adding a **3-D effect** changes the depth of the drawing object, its shadow color, the angle, the direction of lighting, and the surface reflection. When you add a 3-D effect, Word removes any previously applied shadow. Perform the following steps to add a 3-D effect to the rectangle drawing object that surrounds the data entry area of the Customer Survey.

More About

3-D Effects

You can change the color, rotation, depth, lighting, or texture of a 3-D effect by using the 3-D Settings toolbar. To display this toolbar, click the 3-D button on the Drawing toolbar and then click the 3-D Settings button in the list.

Steps To Add a 3-D Effect

1 **With the rectangle still selected, click the 3-D Style button on the Drawing toolbar and then point to 3-D Style 1 (Figure 8-17).**

2 **Click 3-D Style 1.**

Word adds the 3-D Style 1 effect to the rectangle drawing object (shown in Figure 8-18 on the next page).

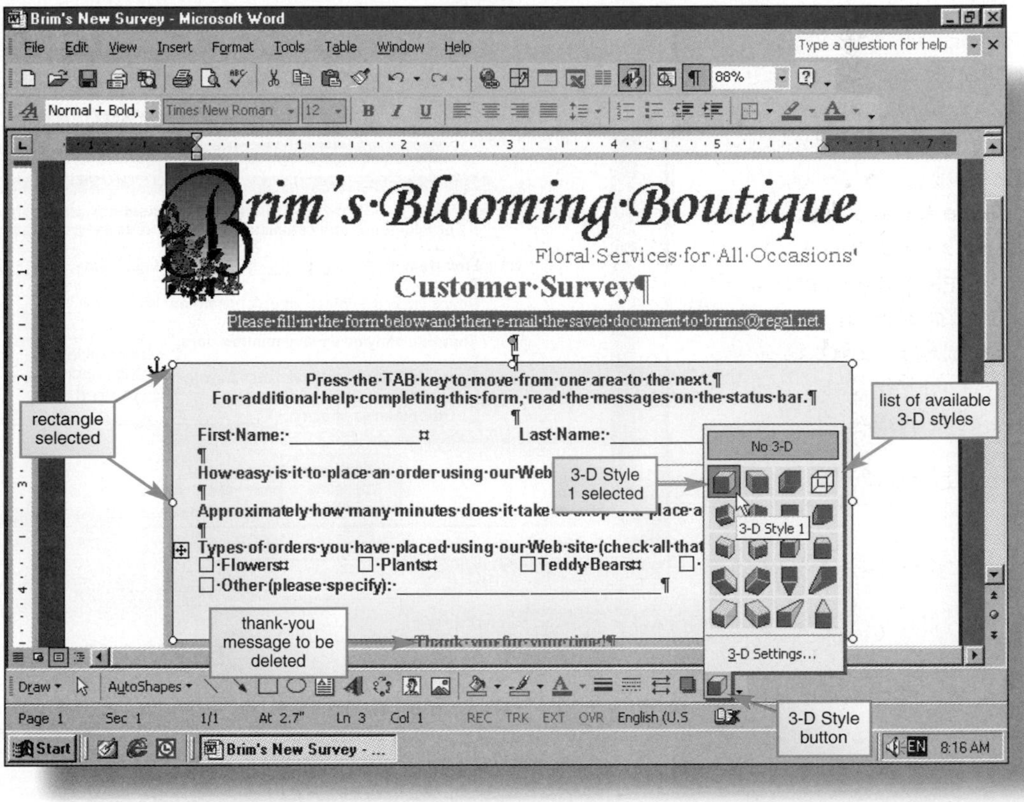
Brim's New Survey - Microsoft Word
Brim's·Blooming·Boutique
Floral·Services·for·All·Occasions
Customer·Survey¶
Please·fill·in·the·form·below·and·then·e-mail·the·saved·document·to·brims@regal.net
Press·the·TAB·key·to·move·from·one·area·to·the·next.¶
For·additional·help·completing·this·form,·read·the·messages·on·the·status·bar.¶
First·Name:
Last·Name:
How·easy·is·it·to·place·an·order·using·our·Web
Approximately·how·many·minutes·does·it·take
Types·of·orders·you·have·placed·using·our·Web·site·(check·all·that
Flowers
Plants
Teddy·Bears
Other·(please·specify):
rectangle selected
3-D Style 1 selected
list of available 3-D styles
No 3-D
3-D Style 1
3-D Settings...
thank-you message to be deleted
3-D Style button

FIGURE 8-17

Other Ways

1. In Voice Command mode, say "3 D Style, [style name]"

The final step in modifying the form is to delete the thank-you message and resize the rectangle.

TO DELETE THE THANK-YOU MESSAGE AND RESIZE THE RECTANGLE

1. Select the line below the data entry area that contains the thank-you message and then press the DELETE key.
2. Point to an edge of the rectangle and click when the mouse pointer has a four-headed arrow attached to it. Drag the bottom-middle sizing handle on the rectangle up until the bottom of the rectangle is immediately below the date.
3. Click the Drawing button on the Standard toolbar to remove the Drawing toolbar from the screen. Scroll as necessary to display the entire form in the document window.

The online form displays as shown in Figure 8-18.

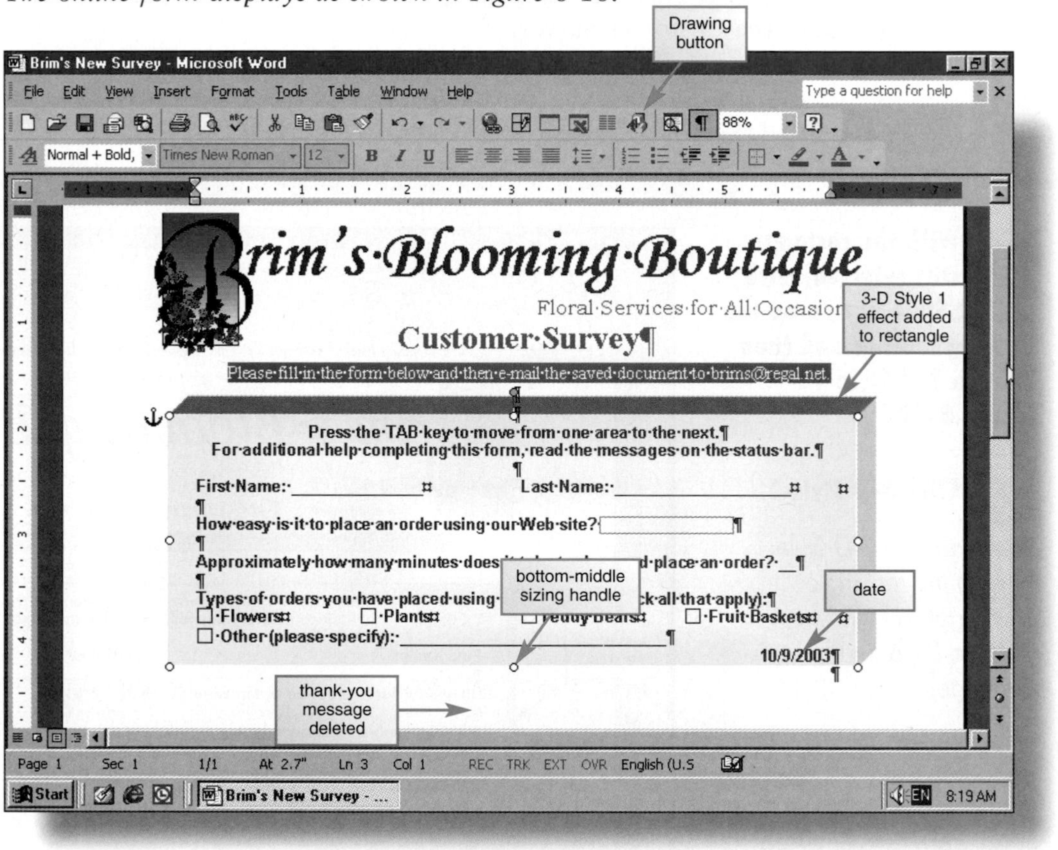
Drawing button
Brim's New Survey - Microsoft Word
Brim's·Blooming·Boutique
Floral·Services·for·All·Occasions
Customer·Survey¶
3-D Style 1 effect added to rectangle
Please·fill·in·the·form·below·and·then·e-mail·the·saved·document·to·brims@regal.net.
Press·the·TAB·key·to·move·from·one·area·to·the·next.¶
For·additional·help·completing·this·form,·read·the·messages·on·the·status·bar.¶
First·Name:·
Last·Name:·
How·easy·is·it·to·place·an·order·using·our·Web·site?
bottom-middle sizing handle
date
·Flowers
·Plants
·Fruit·Baskets
·Other·(please·specify):·
10/9/2003¶
thank-you message deleted

FIGURE 8-18

Because you have performed many formatting tasks thus far, perform the following step to save the form again.

TO SAVE A DOCUMENT

1. Click the Save button on the Standard toolbar.

Word saves the Brim's New Survey document on a floppy disk in drive A.

Using a Macro to Automate a Task

As previously discussed, a macro consists of a series of Word commands or instructions that are grouped together as a single command. This single command is a convenient way to automate a difficult or lengthy task. Macros often are used for formatting or editing activities, to combine multiple commands into a single command, or to select an option in a dialog box with a single keystroke.

To create a macro, you can use the macro recorder or the Visual Basic Editor. The following pages discuss how to use the macro recorder to create a macro. Later in this project, you use the Visual Basic Editor to create a macro.

More About

Naming Macros

If you give a new macro the same name as an existing built-in command in Microsoft Word, the new macro actions will replace the existing actions. Thus, you should be careful not to name a macro FileSave or after any other menu commands. To view a list of built-in macros in Word, point to Macro on the Tools menu, and then click Macros. Click the Macros in box arrow and then click Word Commands.

Recording and Executing a Macro

When you receive filled-in forms from users, your next step will be to analyze the data on the forms. Often, you want to use database software, such as Access, to assist you in analyzing the responses on the forms. As discussed in Project 7, you must save the data on each survey in a comma-delimited text file so that Access can use the data. To do this, you must place a check mark in the Save data only for forms check box in the Save sheet in the Options dialog box — prior to clicking the Save button on the Standard toolbar.

If you receive 70 completed forms, you will be performing the following steps 70 times: click Tools on the menu bar, click Options, click the Save tab, place a check mark in the Save data only for forms check box, and then click the OK button. A timesaving alternative is to create a macro that places the check mark in the check box. Then, you simply execute the macro and click the Save button. Thus, the purpose of the first macro you create in this project is to select an option in a dialog box.

Word has a **macro recorder** that creates a macro automatically based on a series of actions you perform while it is recording. The macro recorder is similar to a video camera in that it records all actions you perform on a document during a period of time. Once you turn on the macro recorder, it records your activities; when you are finished recording activities, turn off the macro recorder to stop the recording. After you have recorded a macro, you can **execute the macro**, or play it back, anytime you want to perform that same set of actions.

To create the macro that will place a check mark in the Save data only for forms check box, you will follow this sequence of steps:

1. Start the macro recorder and specify options about the macro.
2. Place a check mark in the Save data only for forms check box in the Save sheet in the Options dialog box.
3. Stop the macro recorder.

The impressive feature of the macro recorder is that you actually step through the task as you create the macro — allowing you to see exactly what the macro will do before you use it.

When you first create the macro, you have to name it. The name for this macro is FormDataOnly. **Macro names** can be up to 255 characters long; they can contain numbers, letters, and underscores; they cannot contain spaces or other punctuation.

Earlier in this project, you assigned a shortcut key to a style. Likewise, you can assign a shortcut key to a macro, which allows you to run the macro by using its name or by pressing the shortcut key. Perform the steps on the next page to record the macro and assign ALT+D as its shortcut key.

Steps To Record a Macro and Assign It a Shortcut Key

1 **Double-click the REC status indicator on the status bar. When the Record Macro dialog box displays, type** `FormDataOnly` **in the Macro name text box. Click the Store macro in box arrow and then click Documents Based On Brim's New Survey. Select the text in the Description text box and then type** `Places a check mark in the Save data only for forms check box.` **Point to the Keyboard button.**

Word displays the Record Macro dialog box (Figure 8-19).

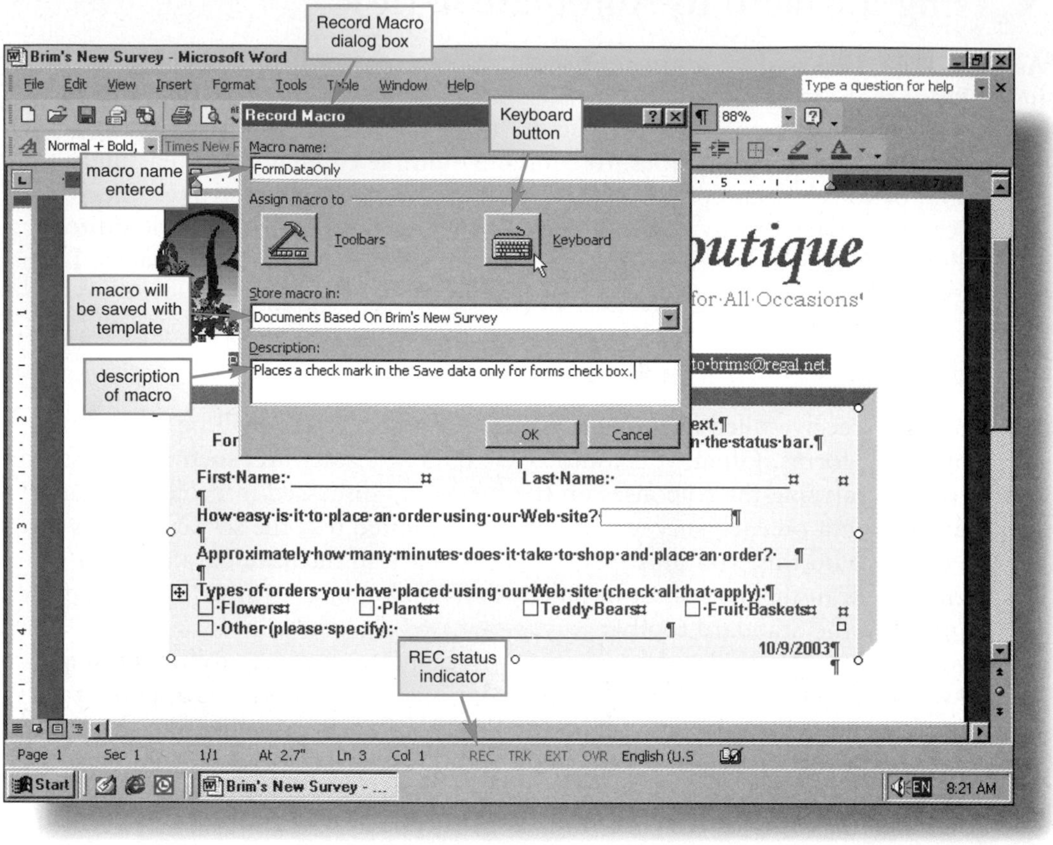

FIGURE 8-19

2 **Click the Keyboard button. When the Customize Keyboard dialog box displays, press ALT+D. Point to the Assign button.**

Word displays the Customize Keyboard dialog box (Figure 8-20). The characters you pressed, ALT+D, display in the Press new shortcut key text box.

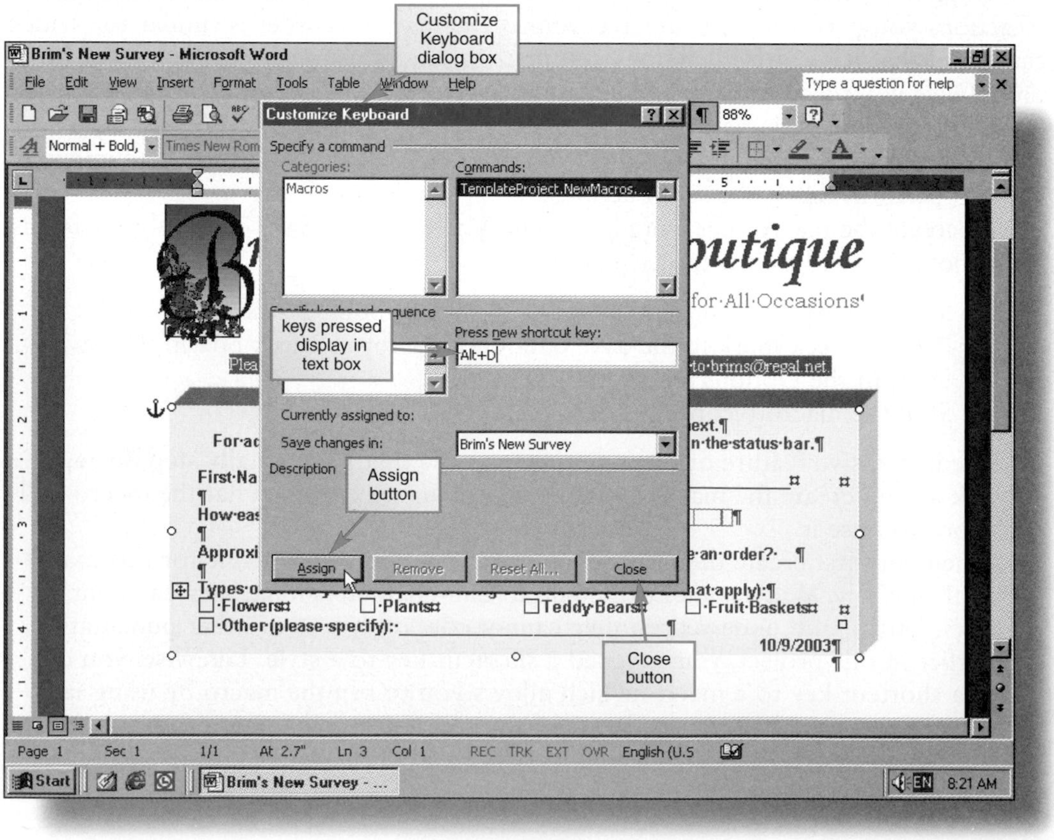

FIGURE 8-20

3 **Click the Assign button. Click the Close button in the Customize Keyboard dialog box.**

Word assigns the shortcut key, ALT+D, to the FormDataOnly macro, closes the Customize Keyboard and Record Macro dialog boxes, darkens the REC status indicator on the status bar, and then displays the Stop Recording toolbar in the document window (Figure 8-21). The mouse pointer displays with a tape icon to remind you that you are recording. Any task you do will be part of the macro. When you are finished recording the macro, you will click the Stop Recording button on the Stop Recording toolbar.

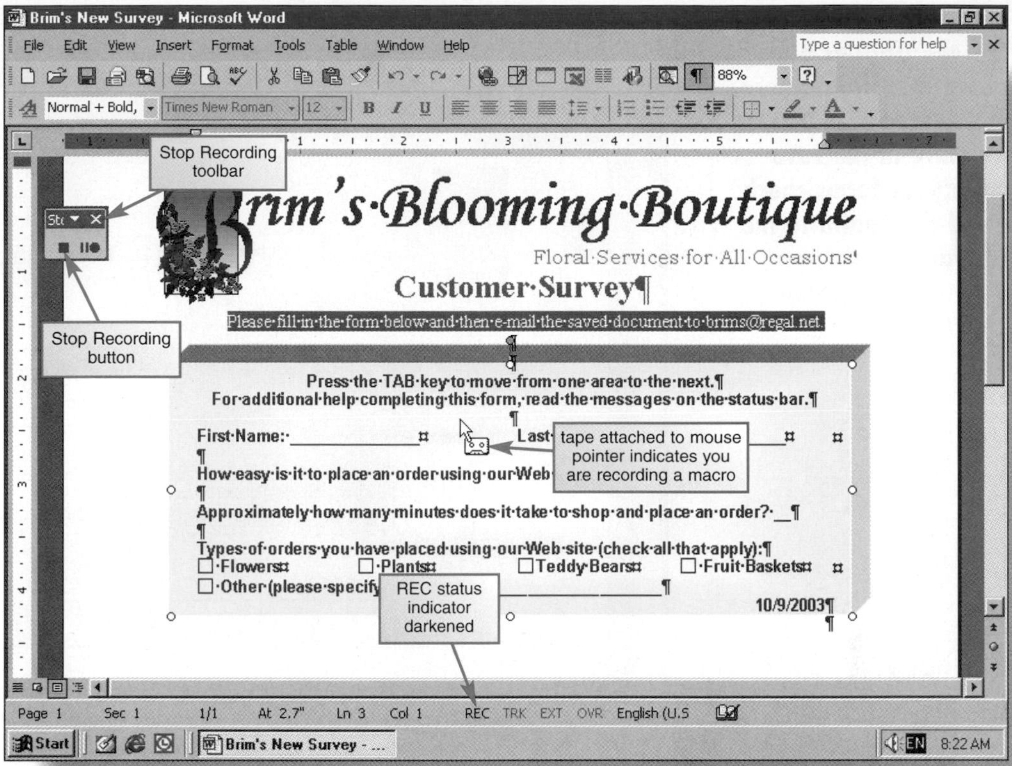

FIGURE 8-21

4 **Click Tools on the menu bar and then point to Options.**

When you are recording a macro and the mouse pointer is in a menu or pointing to a toolbar button, the tape icon does not display next to the pointer (Figure 8-22).

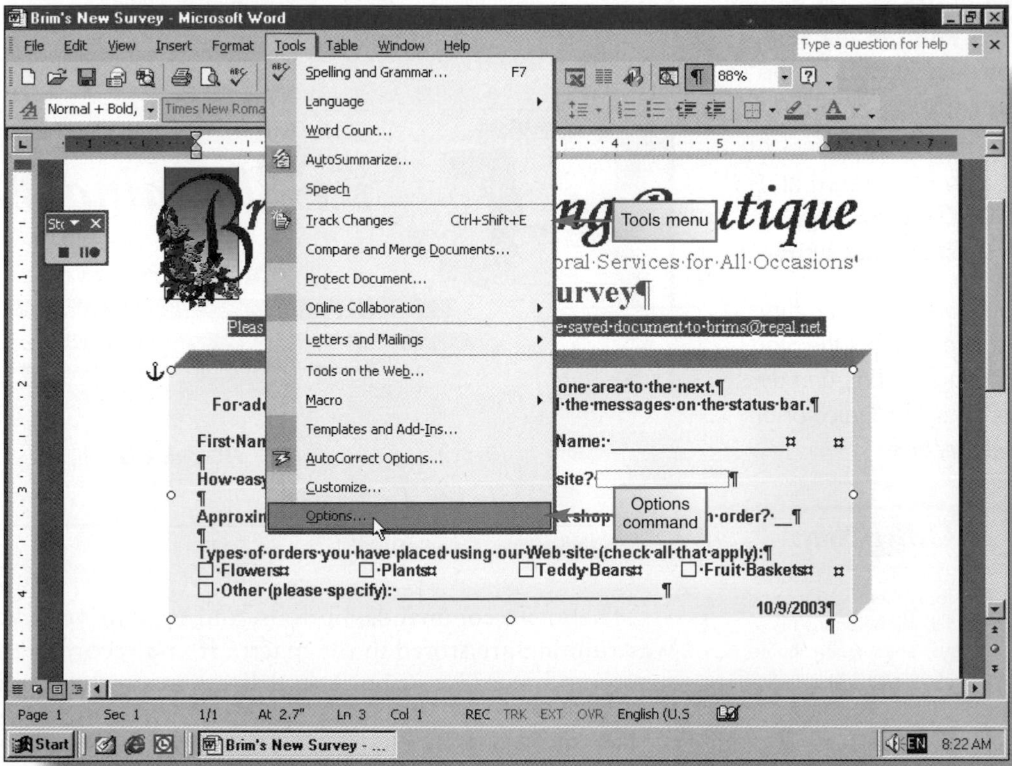

FIGURE 8-22

5 Click Options. When the Options dialog box displays, if necessary, click the Save tab. Place a check mark in the Save data only for forms check box and then point to the OK button.

The Options dialog box displays as shown in Figure 8-23.

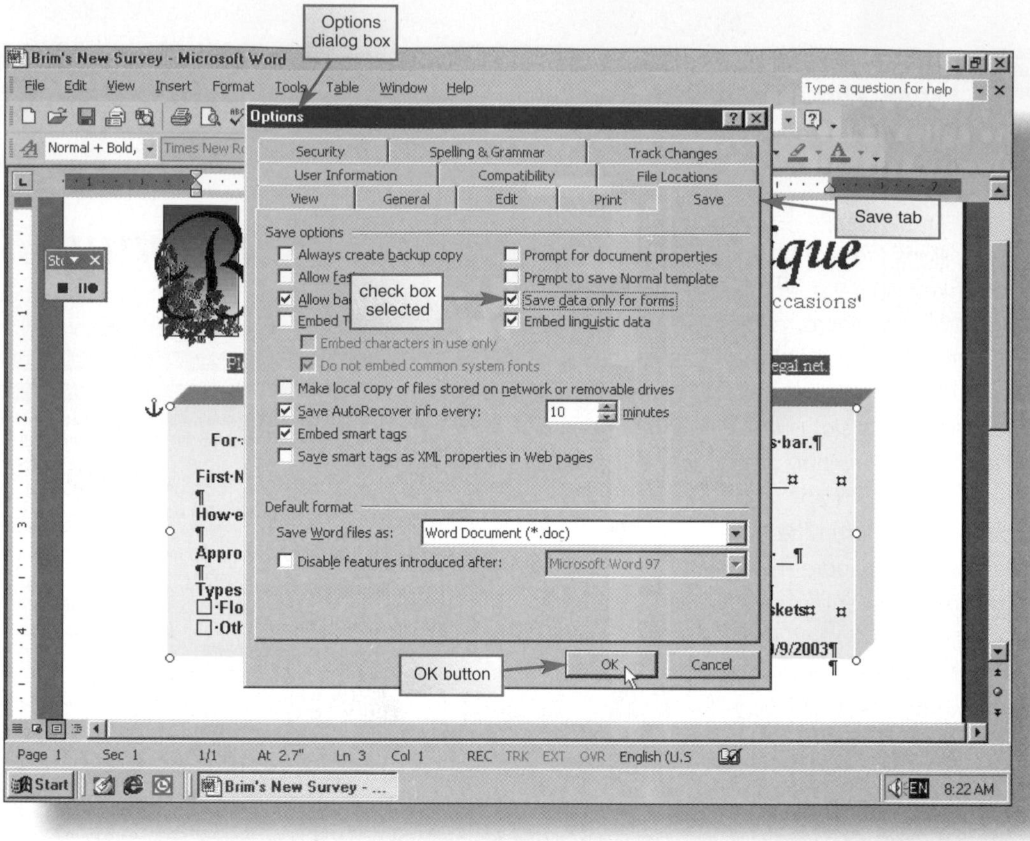

FIGURE 8-23

6 Click the OK button. Point to the Stop Recording button on the Stop Recording toolbar (Figure 8-24).

7 Click the Stop Recording button.

Word stops recording the keystrokes, closes the Stop Recording toolbar, and dims the REC status indicator on the status bar.

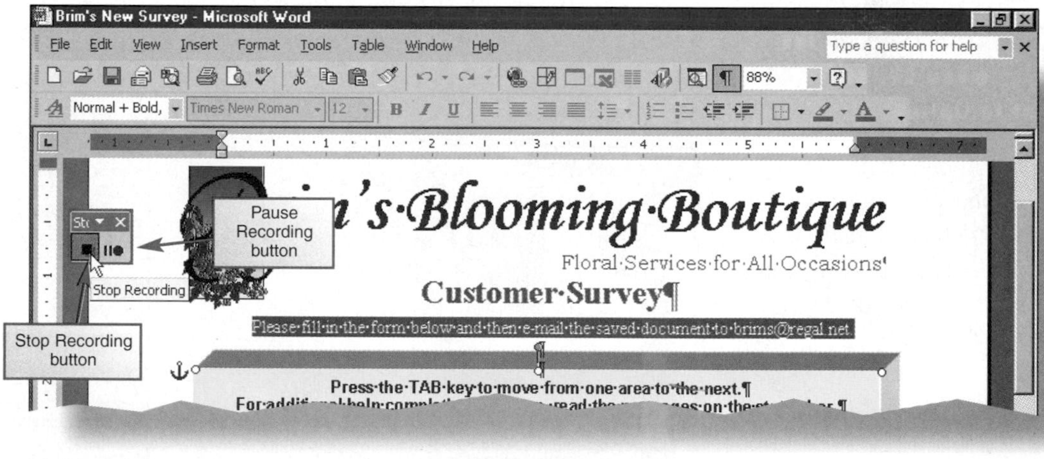

FIGURE 8-24

Other Ways

1. On Tools menu point to Macro, click Record New Macro, enter macro name, click Keyboard button, press shortcut keys, click Assign button, click Close button, record macro, click Stop Recording button on Stop Recording toolbar
2. In Voice Command mode, say "Tools, Macro, Record New Macro"

The menu commands, buttons, and options you clicked while the macro recorder was running are stored in the macro. If you recorded the wrong actions, delete the macro and record it again. You delete a macro by clicking Tools on the menu bar, pointing to Macro on the Tools menu, and then clicking Macros on the Macro submenu. When the Macro dialog box displays, click the name of the macro (FormDataOnly), click the Delete button, and then click the Yes button. Finally, record the macro again.

If, while recording a macro, you want to perform some actions that should not be part of the macro, click the Pause Recording button on the Stop Recording toolbar (Figure 8-24) to suspend the macro recorder. The Pause Recording button changes to a Resume Recording button that you click when you want to continue recording.

In the Record Macro dialog box (Figure 8-19 on WD 8.24), you selected the location to store the macro in the Store macro in box. If you wanted a macro to be available to all documents you create that are based on the normal template, you would select All Documents (Normal.dot) in the Store macro in list. Most macros created with the macro recorder, however, are document specific, and thus are stored in the current template or document.

The next step is to execute, or run, the macro to ensure that it works. Recall that you assigned the shortcut key, ALT+D, to this macro. Perform the following steps to run the macro.

More About

Macro Locations

In the Record Macro dialog box (Figure 8-19 on page WD 8.24), you indicate where Word should save the macro by selecting the appropriate location in the Store macro in list. When you store a macro with a document or a template, it is available only when the document or template is open. When you store a macro in All Documents (Normal.dot), the macro is always available in Word, regardless of the document you have open.

Steps To Run a Macro

1 Click Tools on the menu bar and then click Options. When the Options dialog box displays, if necessary, click the Save tab. Remove the check mark from the Save data only for forms check box and then click the OK button. Press ALT+D.

Word performs the instructions stored in the FormDataOnly macro.

2 To verify that the macro worked properly, display the Options dialog box by clicking Tools on the menu bar and then click Options. When the Options dialog box displays, if necessary, click the Save tab. Point to the OK button.

A check mark displays in the Save data only for forms check box, indicating that the macro executed properly (Figure 8-25).

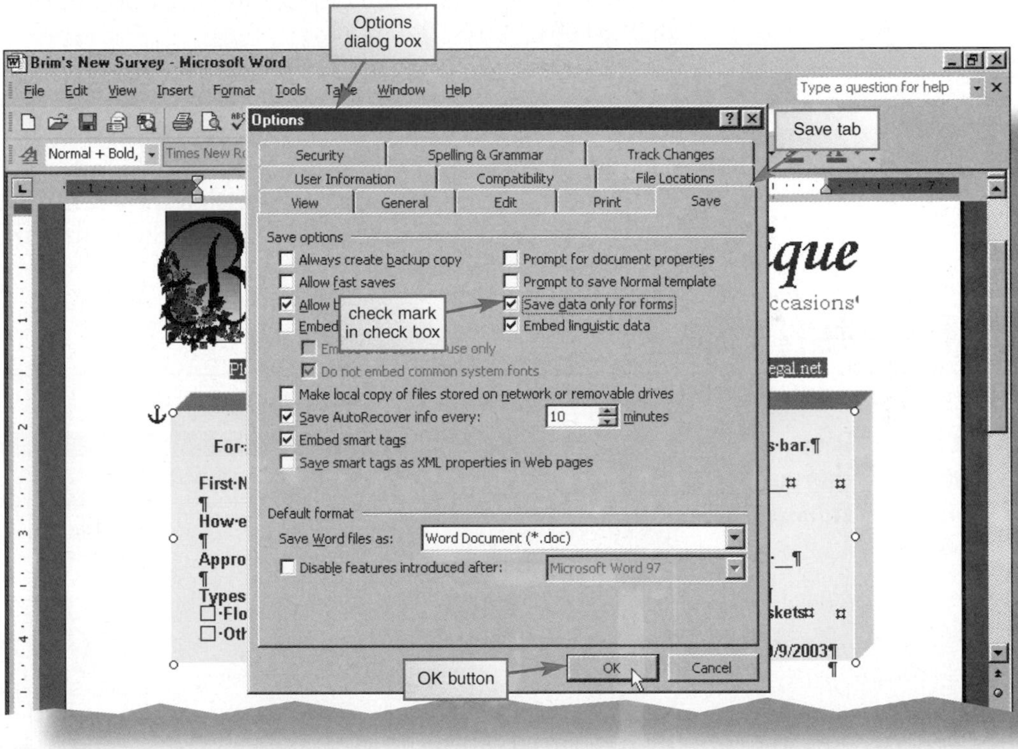

FIGURE 8-25

3 Click the OK button.

Other Ways

1. On Tools menu point to Macro, click Macros, click macro name in Macro name list, click Run button
2. Press ALT+F8, click macro name in Macro name list, click Run button
3. In Voice Command mode, say, "Tools, Macro, [select macro], Run"

You should remove the check mark from the Save data only for forms check box so that future saves will save the entire form.

More About

Customizing Word

In addition to customizing toolbars and their buttons, you can customize menus using the Customize dialog box. To add a command to a menu, for example, click Commands in the Categories list in the Commands sheet and then drag the desired command to the appropriate menu name.

TO UNCHECK THE SAVE DATA ONLY FOR FORMS CHECK BOX

1. Click Tools on the menu bar and then click Options. When the Options dialog box displays, if necessary, click the Save tab.
2. Remove the check mark from the Save data only for forms check box. Click the OK button.

Word removes the check mark from the Save data only for forms check box.

Assigning a Macro to a Toolbar Button

You can customize toolbars by adding buttons, deleting buttons, and changing the function or appearance of buttons. You also can assign a macro to a button. In this project, you want to create a toolbar button for the FormDataOnly macro so that instead of pressing the shortcut keys, you can click the button to place a check mark in the Save data only for forms check box in the Save sheet in the Options dialog box.

You customize a toolbar using the Customize command on the Tools menu. The key to understanding how to customize a toolbar is to recognize that when you have the Customize dialog box open, Word's toolbars and menus are in Edit mode. **Edit mode** allows you to modify the toolbars and menus.

Perform the following steps to assign the FormDataOnly macro to a new button on the Standard toolbar and then change the button image.

Steps To Customize a Toolbar

1 Click Tools on the menu bar and then point to Customize (Figure 8-26).

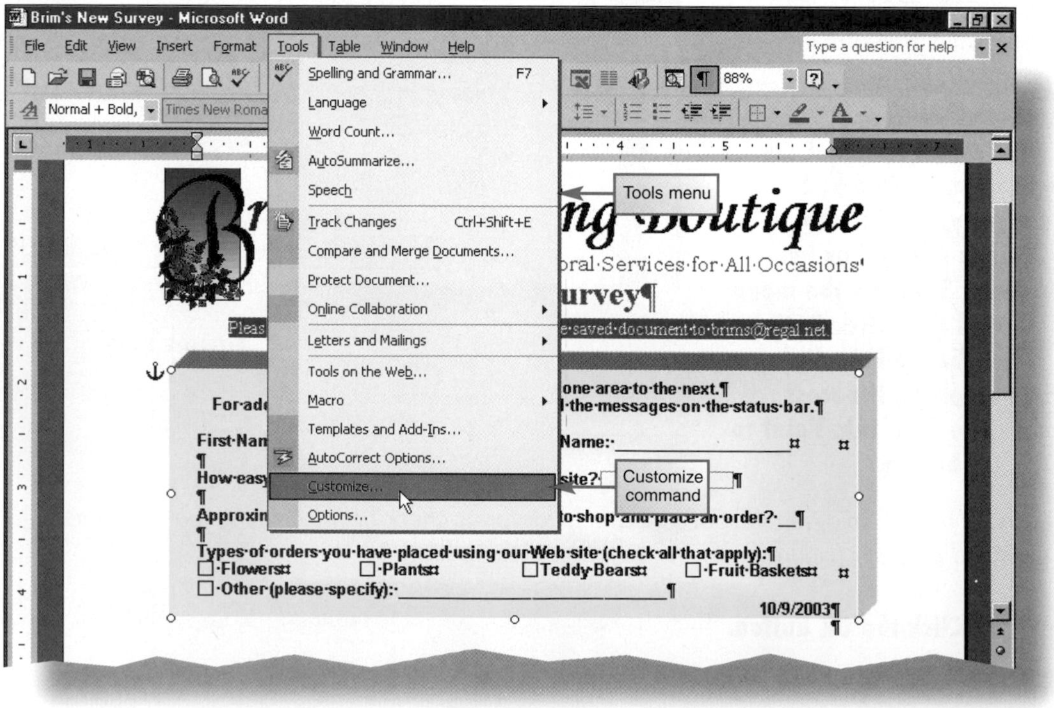

FIGURE 8-26

2 Click Customize. When the Customize dialog box displays, if necessary, click the Commands tab. Scroll to and then click Macros in the Categories list. Click TemplateProject. NewMacros.FormDataOnly in the Commands list.

The Customize dialog box displays (Figure 8-27).

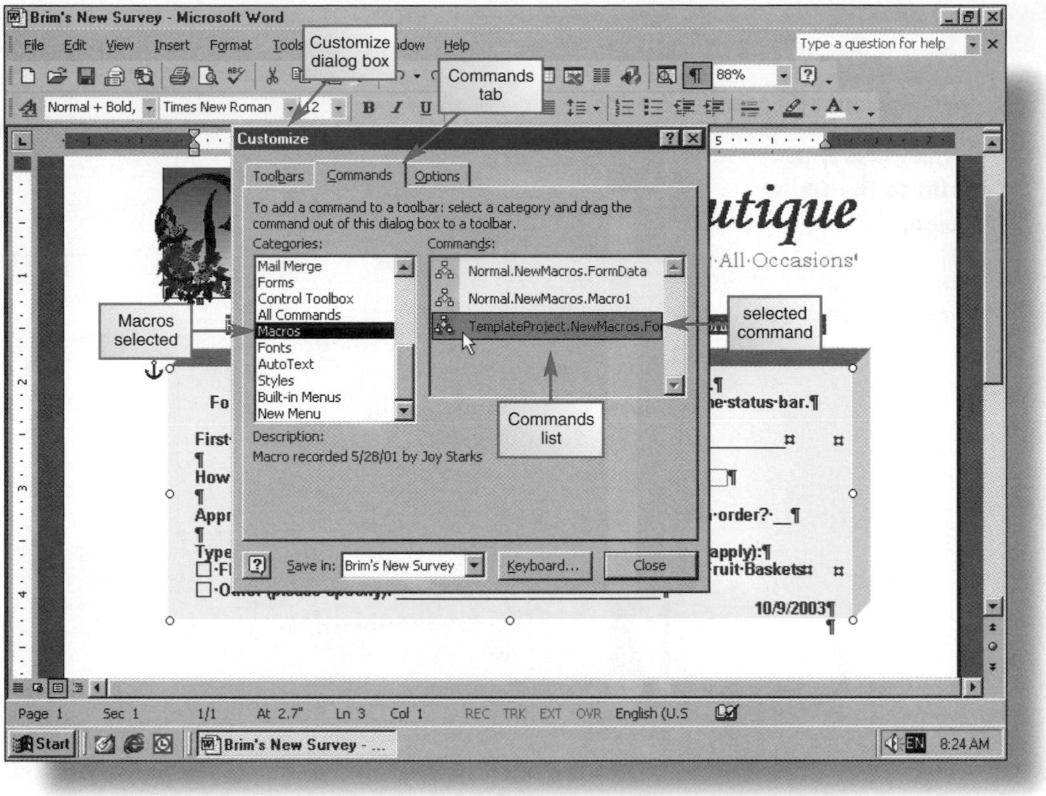

FIGURE 8-27

3 Drag the selected command in the Commands list to the right of the Microsoft Word Help button on the Standard toolbar.

A button containing the text, TemplateProject.NewMacros. FormDataOnly, displays next to the Microsoft Word Help button on the Standard toolbar (Figure 8-28). The toolbar may wrap to two lines because the button is so long. A thick border surrounds the new button indicating Word is in Edit mode.

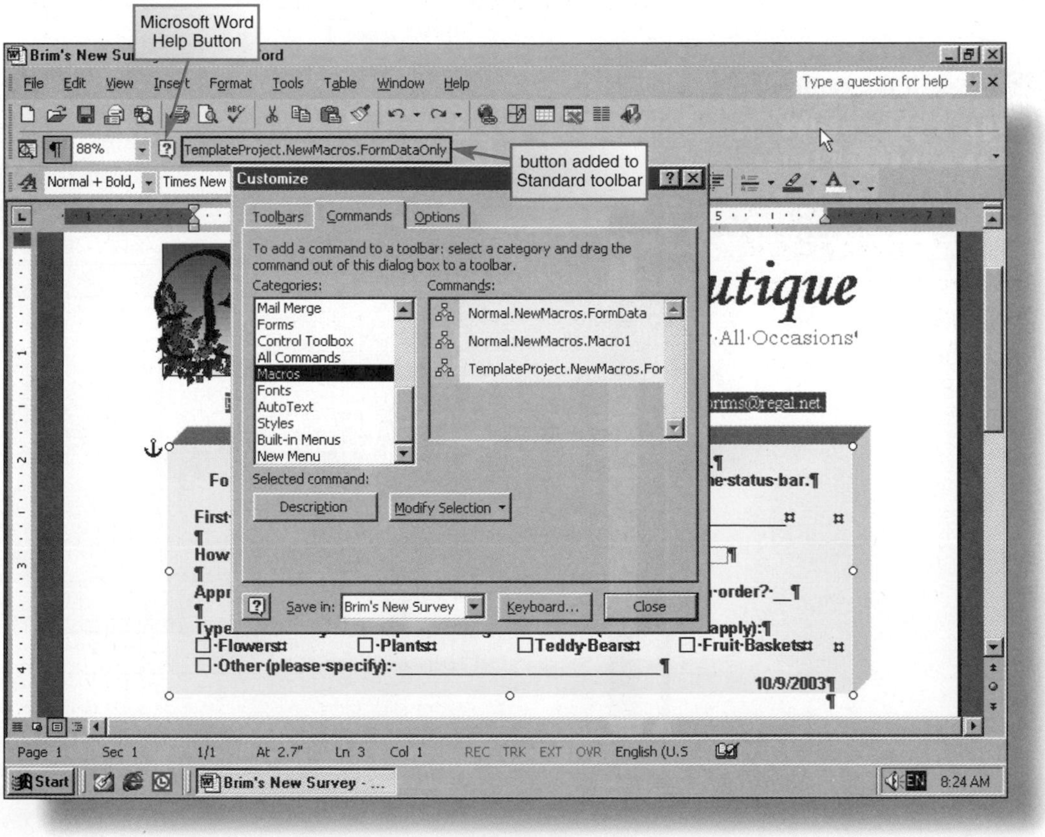

FIGURE 8-28

4 **Right-click the button just added to the Standard toolbar, point to Change Button Image on the shortcut menu, and then point to the smiley face image.**

Word displays a palette of button images from which you can select (Figure 8-29).

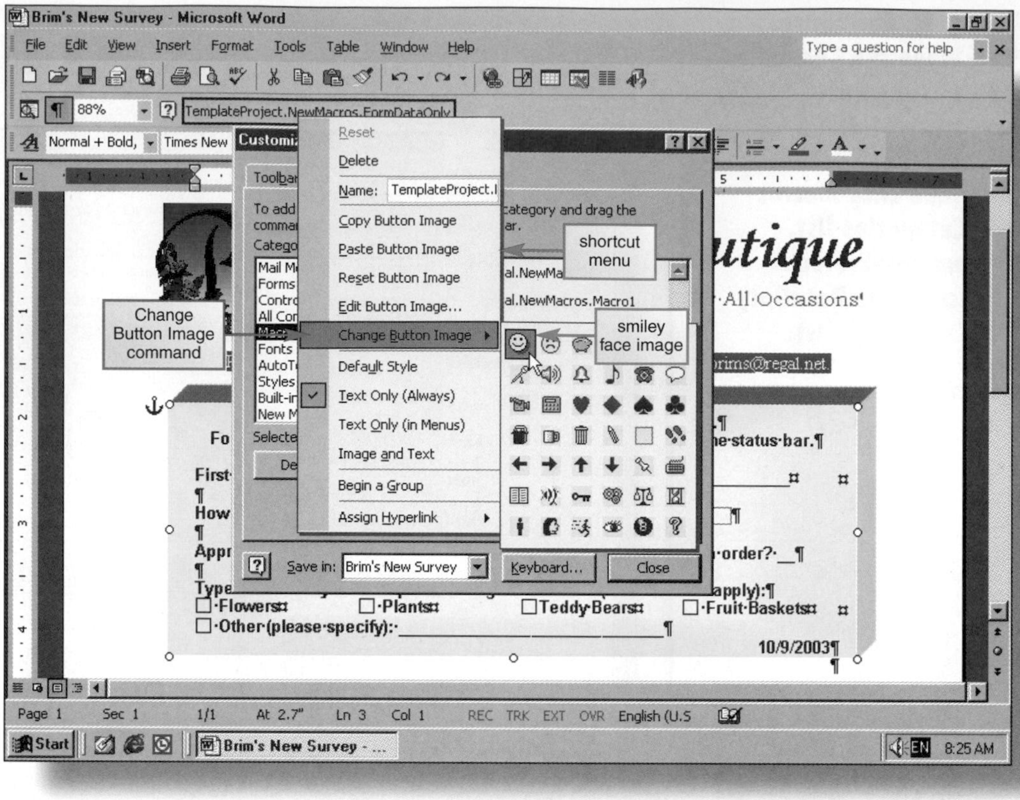

FIGURE 8-29

5 **Click the button with the smiley face image. Right-click the button just added to the Standard toolbar. Point to Text Only (in Menus) on the shortcut menu.**

Word places the smiley face image on the button (Figure 8-30).

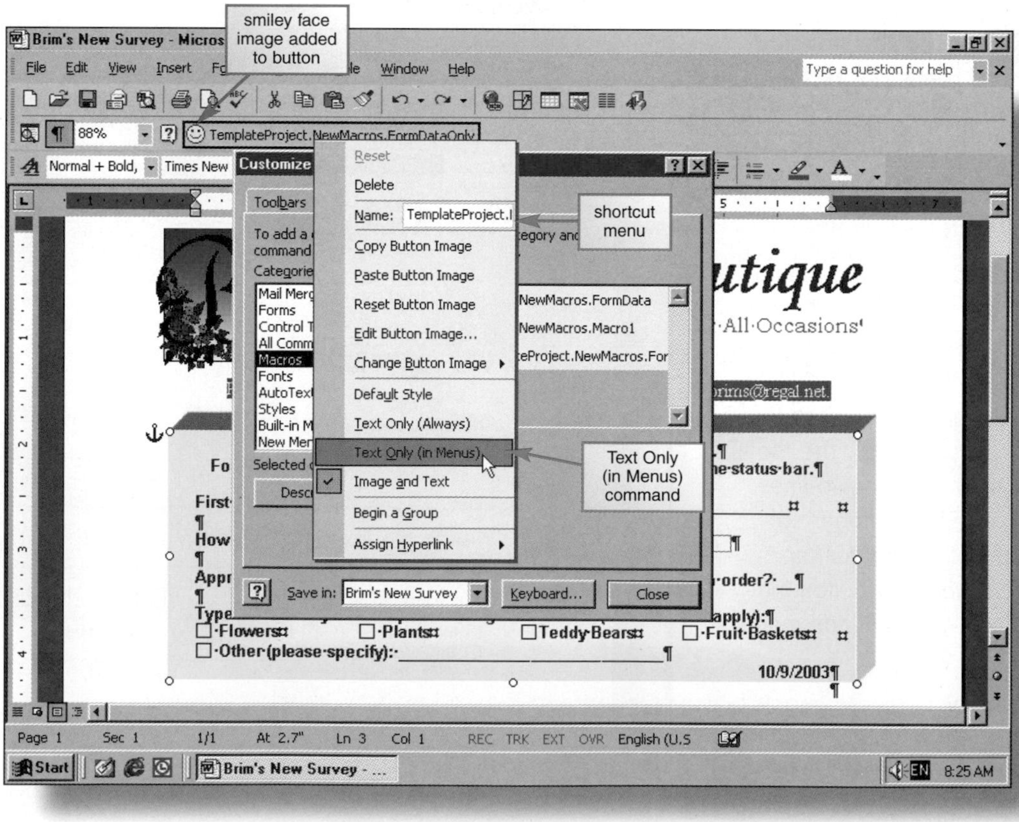

FIGURE 8-30

6 Click Text Only (in Menus). Point to the Close button in the Customize dialog box.

The text, TemplateProject. NewMacros.FormDataOnly, no longer displays on the button (Figure 8-31). If you add the macro to a menu at a later time, the text will display in the menu.

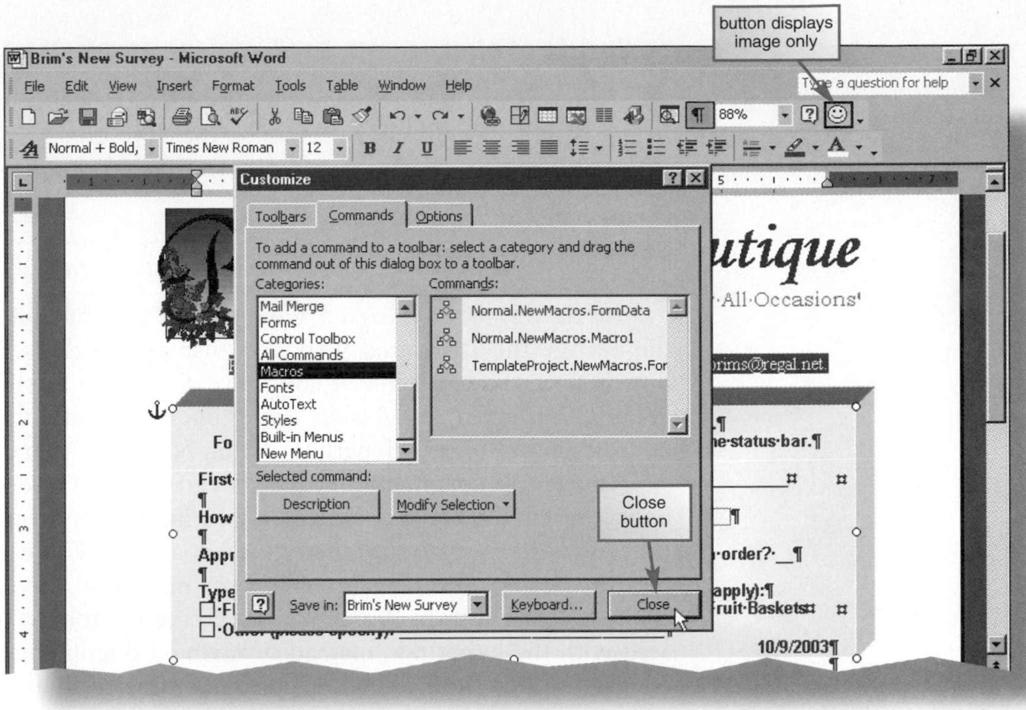

FIGURE 8-31

7 Click the Close button in the Customize dialog box. Point to the Form Data Only button on the Standard toolbar.

Word quits Edit mode. The Form Data Only button displays on the Standard toolbar with the ScreenTip, Form Data Only (Figure 8-32).

FIGURE 8-32

8 Click the Form Data Only button on the Standard toolbar.

Word places a check mark in the Save data only for forms check box in the Save sheet in the Options dialog box.

Other Ways

1. On View menu click Toolbars, click Customize, click Commands tab
2. Right-click toolbar, click Customize on shortcut menu, click Commands tab
3. In Voice Command mode, say "View, Toolbars, Customize"

You can verify that the Form Data Only button works properly by clicking Tools on the menu bar, clicking Options, clicking the Save tab, and then confirming that a check mark displays in the Save data only for forms check box. You do not want the check mark in the check box now. Thus, remove the check mark as described in the steps on the next page.

TO UNCHECK THE SAVE DATA ONLY FOR FORMS CHECK BOX

1. Click Tools on the menu bar and then click Options. When the Options dialog box displays, if necessary, click the Save tab.
2. Remove the check mark from the Save data only for forms check box. Click the OK button.

Word removes the check mark from the Save data only for forms check box.

If you wanted to assign a Web address to a button so that when the user clicks the button, the associated Web page displays on the screen, you would right-click the button with the Customize dialog box displaying as shown in Figure 8-30 on page WD 8.30, point to the Assign Hyperlink command, click Open, enter the Web address in the Assign Hyperlink dialog box, and then click the OK button.

You can add as many buttons as you want to a toolbar. You also can change the image on any button or change an existing button's function. For example, when in Edit mode (the Customize dialog box is active), you can right-click the Save button on the Standard toolbar and assign it a macro or a hyperlink. The next time you click the Save button, Word would execute the macro or start the application associated with the hyperlink, instead of saving a document.

As you add buttons, other buttons on the toolbar will be demoted to the More Buttons list. You also can create new toolbars. To create a new toolbar, click the Toolbars tab in the Customize dialog box and then click the New button.

To remove a button from a toolbar, while in Edit mode, right-click the button and then click Delete on the shortcut menu.

You reset the toolbars to their installation default by clicking the Toolbars tab in the Customize dialog box, selecting the toolbar name in the Toolbars list, and then clicking the Reset button. Each project in this book begins by resetting the toolbars because it is so easy to change the buttons on a toolbar.

You also can customize menus using a procedure similar to the one for customizing a toolbar. For example, to add a command to a menu, click a name in the Categories list in the Customize dialog box (Figure 8-27 on page WD 8.29) and drag the command name in the Commands list to the menu name on the menu bar. Then, when the menu displays, drag the command to the desired location in the menu list of commands. For additional information, see Appendix D.

More About

Automatic Macros

A document can contain only one AutoClose, AutoNew, and AutoOpen macro. The AutoExec and AutoExit macro, however, are not stored with the document; instead, they must be stored in the Normal template. Thus, only one AutoExec and only one AutoExit macro can exist for all Word documents.

Recording an Automatic Macro

In the previous section, you created a macro, assigned it a unique name (FormDataOnly), and then created a toolbar button that executed the macro. Word also has five prenamed macros, called **automatic macros**, which execute automatically when a certain event occurs. Table 8-2 lists the name and function of these automatic macros.

Table 8-2 Automatic Macros

MACRO	NAME RUNS
AutoClose	When you close a document containing the macro
AutoExec	When you start Word
AutoExit	When you quit Word
AutoNew	When you create a new document based on a template containing the macro
AutoOpen	When you open a document containing the macro

The name you use for an automatic macro depends on when you want certain actions to occur. In this project, when a user creates a new Word document that is based on the Brim's New Survey template, you want the online form to display properly in the Word window. Thus, you will create an AutoNew macro using the macro recorder.

The form displays properly when the zoom is set to page width. Thus, you will record the steps to zoom to page width. Also, you want the entire form to display in the Word window so the user does not have to scroll to position the form. When you display the form in the Word window, the top of the form displays. Thus, you will go to the top of the page by dragging the scroll box to the top of the vertical scroll bar and then click the scroll arrow at the bottom of the vertical scroll bar several times to position the form properly.

Perform the following steps to create an AutoNew macro.

Steps To Create an Automatic Macro

1 **Double-click the REC status indicator on the status bar. When the Record Macro dialog box displays, type** `AutoNew` **in the Macro name text box. Click the Store macro in box arrow and then click Documents Based On Brim's New Survey. In the Description text box, type** `Specifies how the form initially displays (as a blank form).` **Point to the OK button.**

Word displays the Record Macro dialog box (Figure 8-33).

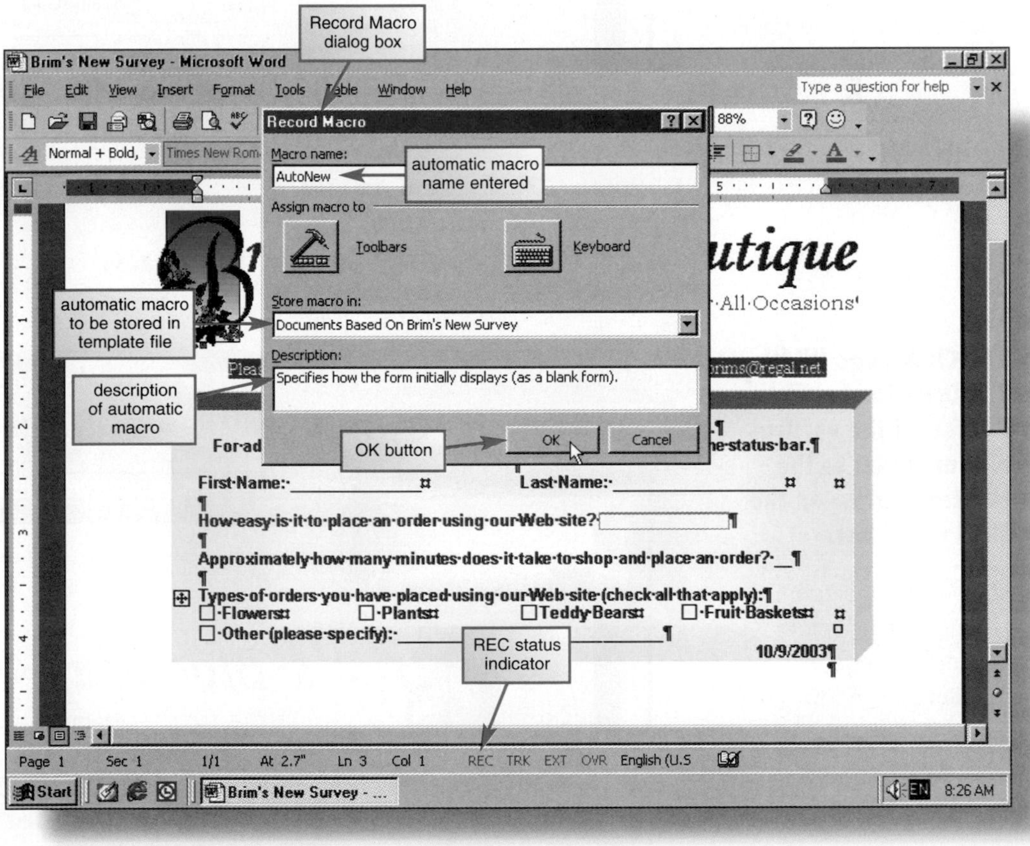

FIGURE 8-33

2 Click the OK button.

Word closes the Record Macro dialog box and then displays the Stop Recording toolbar in the document window.

3 Click the Zoom box arrow and then point to Page Width.

Recall that when you are recording a macro and the mouse pointer is in a menu or pointing to a toolbar button, the tape icon does not display next to the pointer (Figure 8-34).

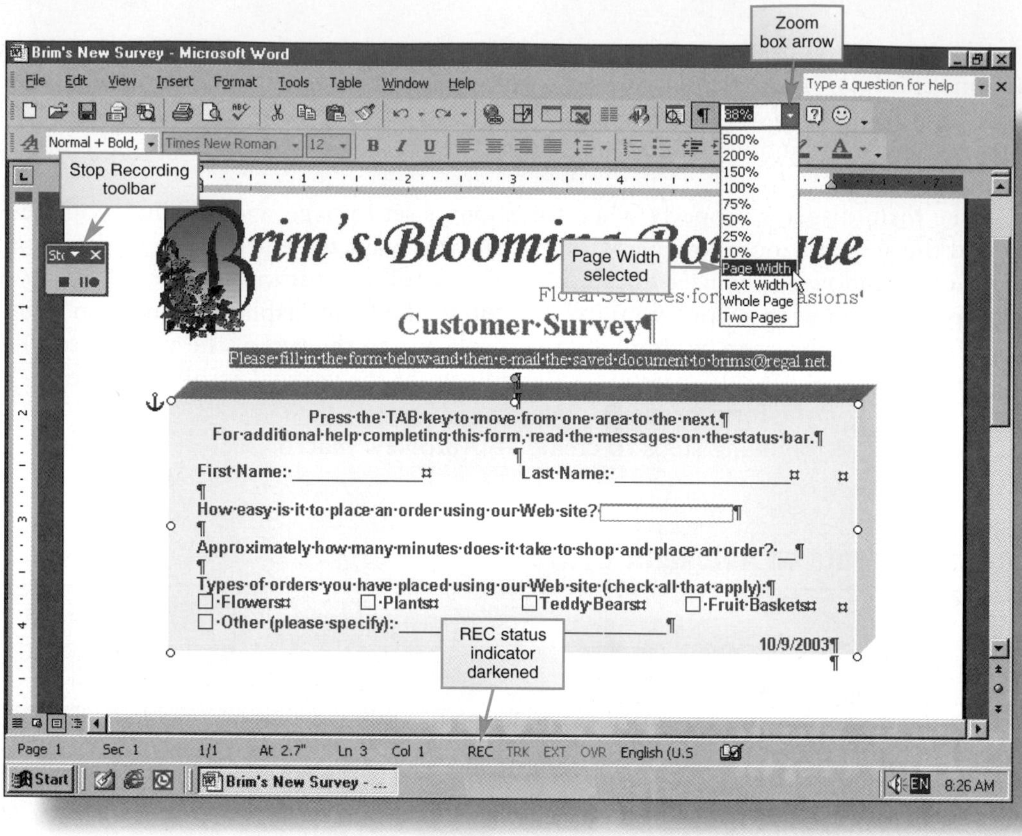

FIGURE 8-34

4 Click Page Width. Drag the scroll box to the top of the vertical scroll bar. Point to the down scroll arrow on the vertical scroll bar.

Word changes the zoom percentage and displays the top of the page in the document window (Figure 8-35).

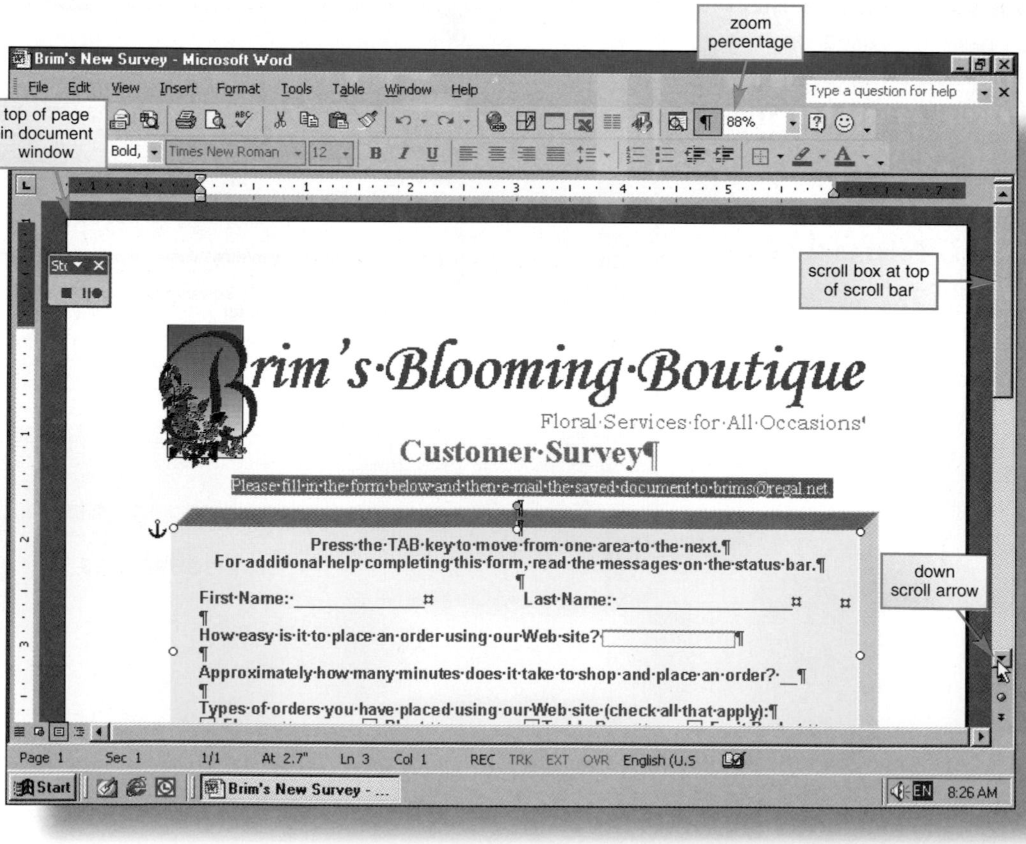

FIGURE 8-35

5 **Click the down scroll arrow on the vertical scroll bar five times. Point to the Stop Recording button on the Stop Recording toolbar.**

The online form displays as shown in Figure 8-36.

6 **Click the Stop Recording button.**

Word stops recording the keystrokes, closes the Stop Recording toolbar, and dims the REC status indicator on the status bar.

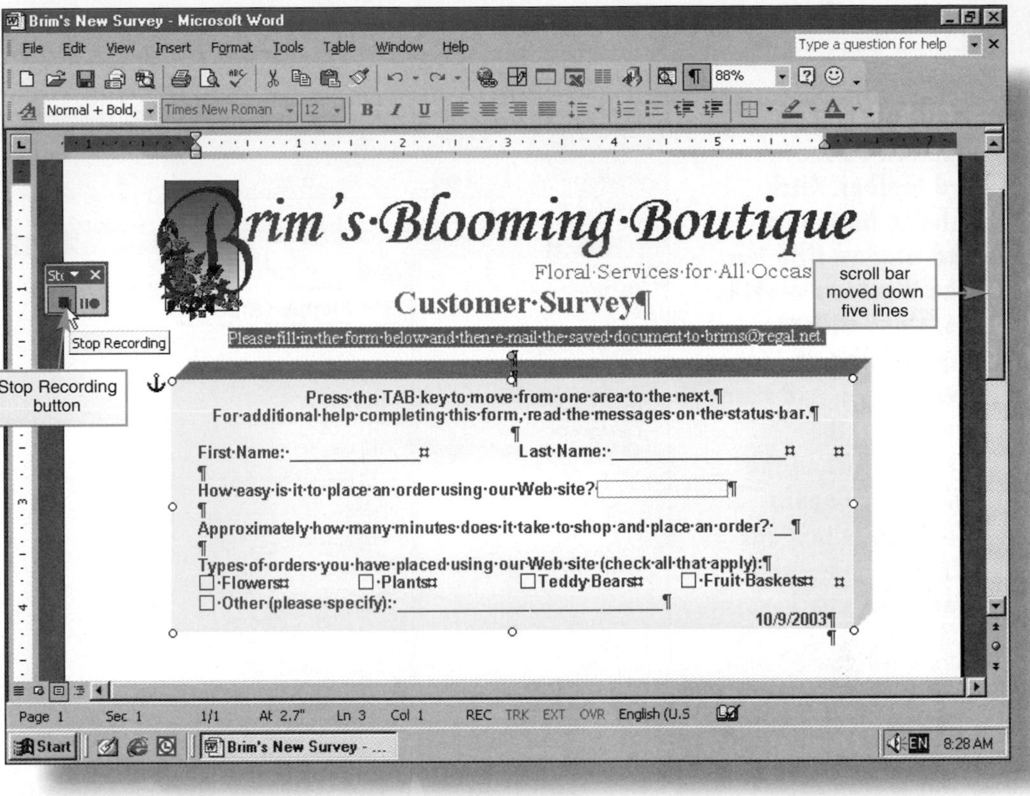
Brim's New Survey - Microsoft Word
File Edit View Insert Format Tools Table Window Help
Type a question for help
Brim's·Blooming·Boutique
Floral·Services·for·All·Occas
Customer·Survey¶
Please·fill·in·the·form·below·and·then·e-mail·the·saved·document·to·brims@regal.net.
Press·the·TAB·key·to·move·from·one·area·to·the·next.¶
For·additional·help·completing·this·form,·read·the·messages·on·the·status·bar.¶
First·Name:·
Last·Name:·
How·easy·is·it·to·place·an·order·using·our·Web·site?
Approximately·how·many·minutes·does·it·take·to·shop·and·place·an·order?·
Types·of·orders·you·have·placed·using·our·Web·site·(check·all·that·apply):¶
·Flowers
·Plants
Teddy·Bears
·Fruit·Baskets
·Other·(please·specify):·
10/9/2003¶
Stop Recording
Stop Recording button
scroll bar moved down five lines
Page 1 Sec 1 1/1 At 2.7" Ln 3 Col 1 REC TRK EXT OVR English (U.S
Start
Brim's New Survey - ...
8:28 AM

FIGURE 8-36

To test the automatic macro, you activate the event that causes the macro to execute. For example, the AutoNew macro runs whenever you create a new Word document that is based on the template. As discussed in Project 7, when you save a template to a disk in drive A, a user can create a Word document based on a template through the My Computer window or Windows Explorer.

Perform the steps on the next page to display a new Word document window that is based on the Brim's New Survey template.

Other Ways

1. In Voice Command mode, say "Tools, Macro, Record New Macro"

More About

Recording and Running Macros

If Word does not allow you to record or run a macro in a document, the document probably is marked as read-only. To record or run a macro in this document, save it with a new name using the Save As dialog box and then record or run the macro in the newly named document.

Steps To Test the AutoNew Macro

1 Click the Save button on the Standard toolbar. Click the Minimize button on the Word window title bar. When the Windows desktop displays, right-click the My Computer icon on the Windows desktop and then click Explore on the shortcut menu. When the Explorer window opens, click the Address text box to select it. Type a: **and then press the ENTER key.**

The Explorer window opens (Figure 8-37). Word still is running.

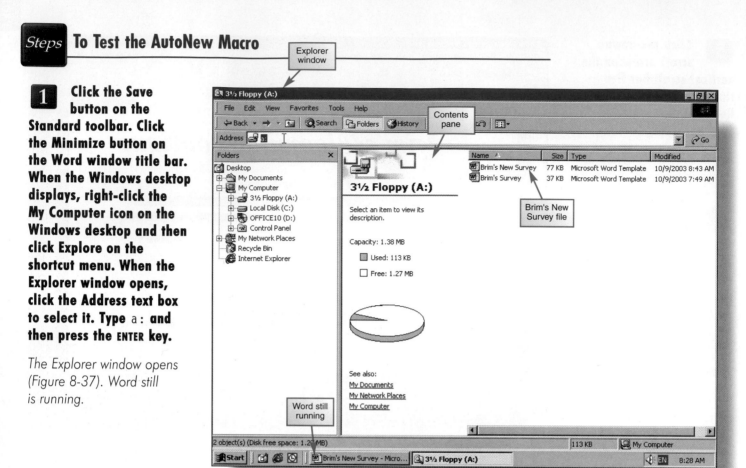

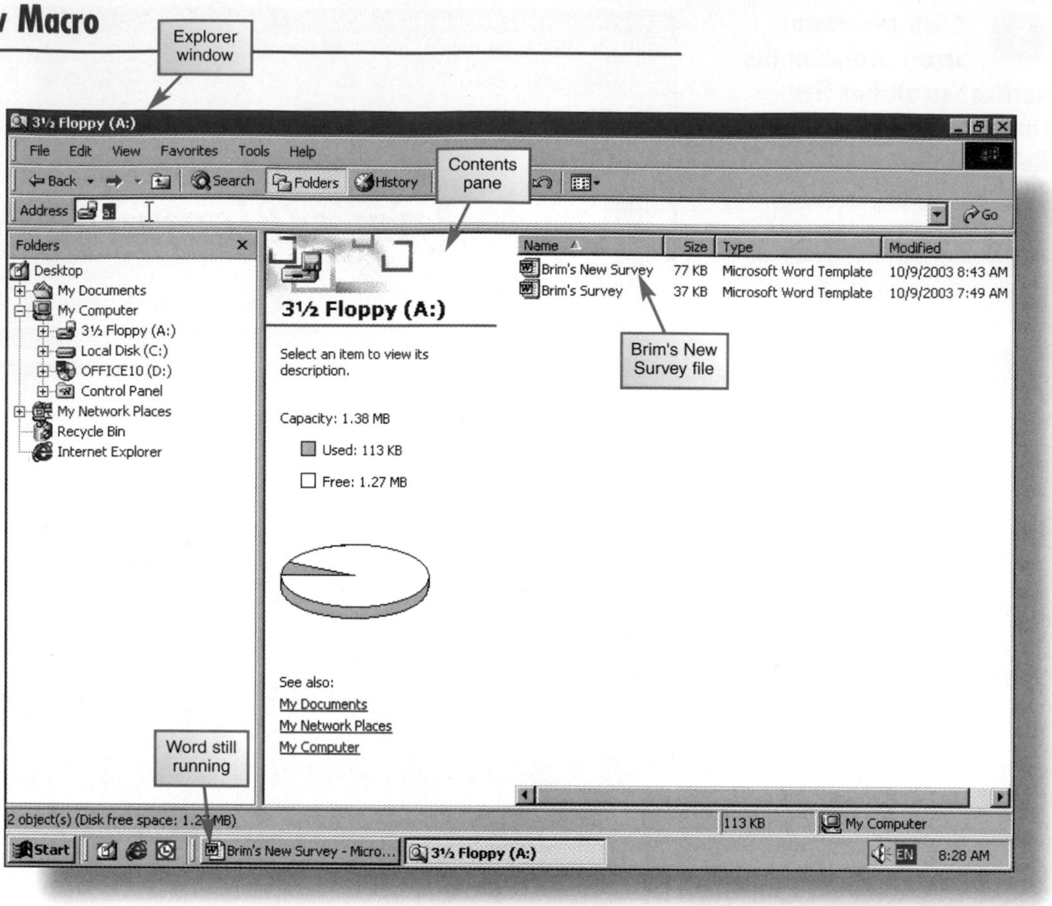

FIGURE 8-37

2 Double-click the Brim's New Survey icon in the Contents pane.

Word opens a new document window that is based on the contents of the Brim's New Survey (Figure 8-38). The zoom is set to page width, and the screen scrolls down five lines as instructed by the AutoNew macro.

3 Click the Close button at the right edge of the Word title bar. If necessary, click the Brim's New Survey - Microsoft Word program button on the taskbar.

The new document window closes. The Brim's New Survey template displays on the screen.

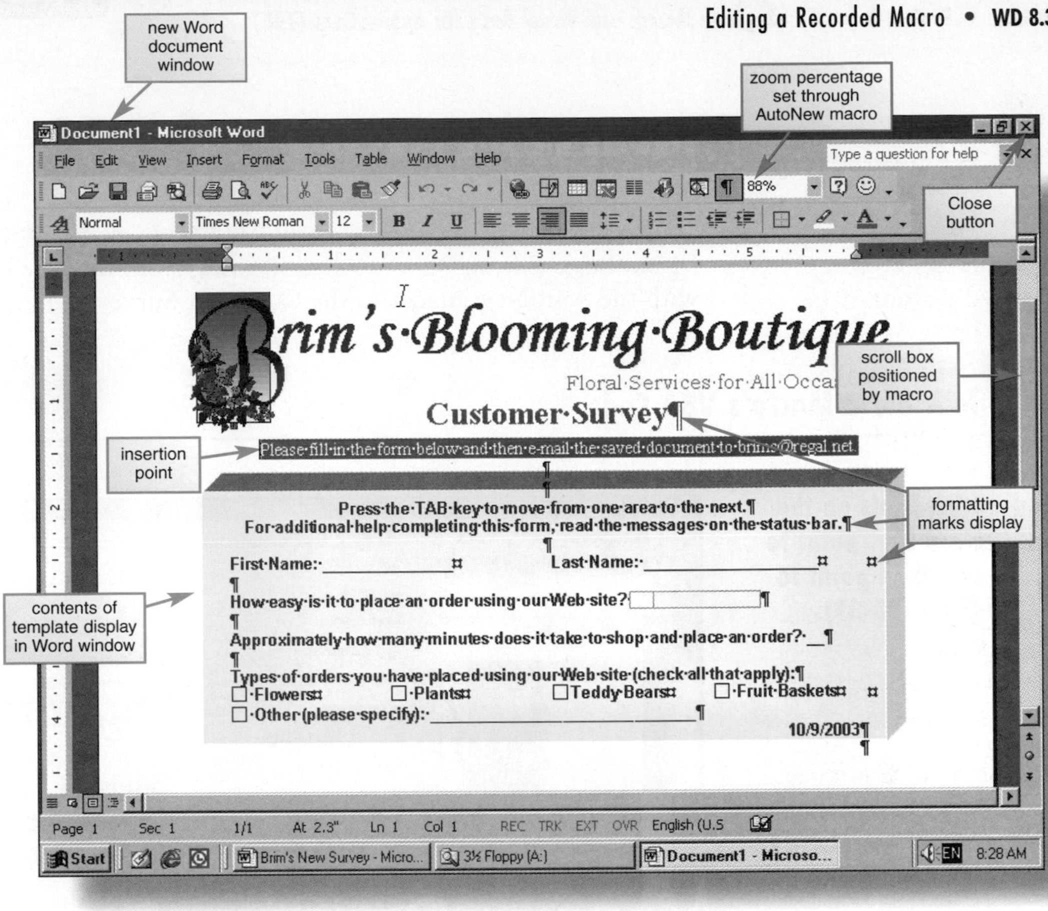
new Word document window
zoom percentage set through AutoNew macro
Close button
scroll box positioned by macro
insertion point
formatting marks display
contents of template display in Word window
Document1 - Microsoft Word
Brim's·Blooming·Boutique
Customer·Survey¶
Please·fill·in·the·form·below·and·then·e-mail·the·saved·document·to·brims@regal.net.
Press·the·TAB·key·to·move·from·one·area·to·the·next.¶
For·additional·help·completing·this·form,·read·the·messages·on·the·status·bar.¶
First·Name:·
Last·Name:·
How·easy·is·it·to·place·an·order·using·our·Web·site?
Approximately·how·many·minutes·does·it·take·to·shop·and·place·an·order?·
Types·of·orders·you·have·placed·using·our·Web·site·(check·all·that·apply):¶
·Flowers
·Plants
Teddy·Bears
·Fruit·Baskets
·Other·(please·specify):·
10/9/2003¶

FIGURE 8-38

Notice in Figure 8-38 that the insertion point is at the beginning of the form instructions below the text box. Recall that when you make a form available for users to access, you first protect the form. Protecting a form places the selection in the first form field and allows users to access only the form fields. You did not protect the form yet because you are not finished modifying it. You simply tested the AutoNew macro to be sure it worked properly.

When testing the AutoNew macro, you noticed that the formatting marks displayed on the screen (Figure 8-38). You also noticed that the screen actually should scroll down one more line so it fits better in the Word window. Thus, you want to edit this macro.

Editing a Recorded Macro

The next step in this project is to edit the AutoNew macro. Word uses VBA to store a macro's instructions. Thus, to edit a recorded macro, you use the Visual Basic Editor. All Office applications use the Visual Basic Editor to enter, modify, and view VBA code associated with a document. The following pages explain how to use the Visual Basic Editor to view, enter, and modify VBA code.

More About

Using VBA

For more information about using Visual Basic for Applications, visit the Word 2002 More About Web page (scsite.com/wd2002/more.htm) and then click Using VBA.

Viewing a Macro's VBA Code

As described earlier, a macro consists of VBA code, which the macro recorder automatically creates. You view the VBA code assigned to a macro through the Visual Basic Editor. Perform the following steps to view the VBA code associated with the AutoNew macro in the Customer Survey.

Steps To View a Macro's VBA Code

1 **Click Tools on the menu bar, point to Macro, and then point to Macros (Figure 8-39).**

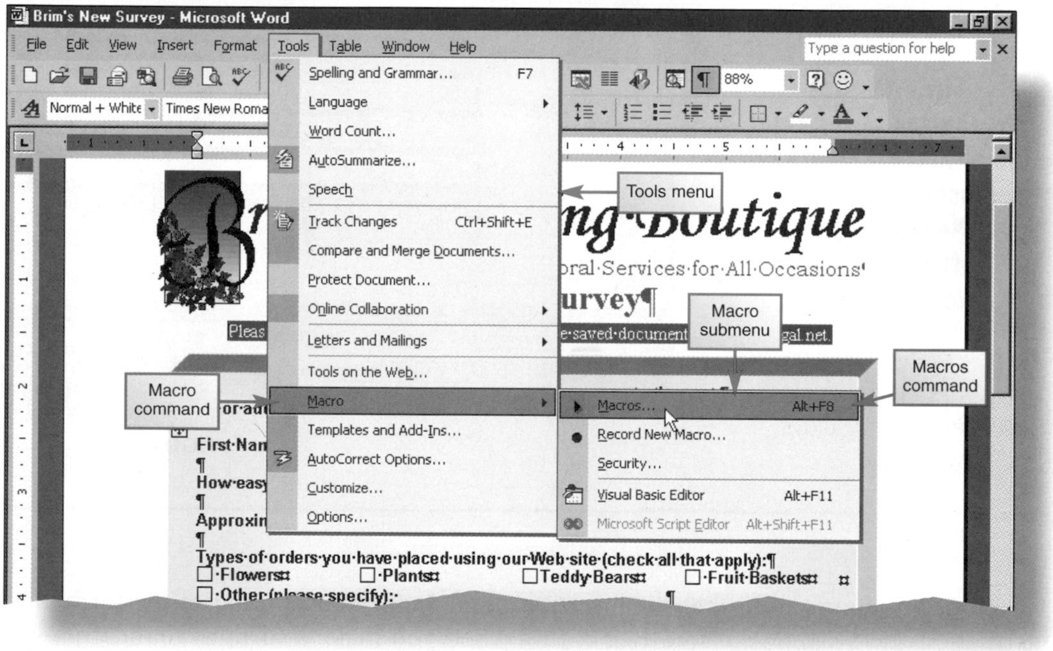

FIGURE 8-39

2 **Click Macros. When the Macros dialog box displays, click the Macros in box arrow and then click Brim's New Survey (template). If necessary, click AutoNew in the Macro name list and then point to the Edit button.**

The Macros dialog box displays (Figure 8-40).

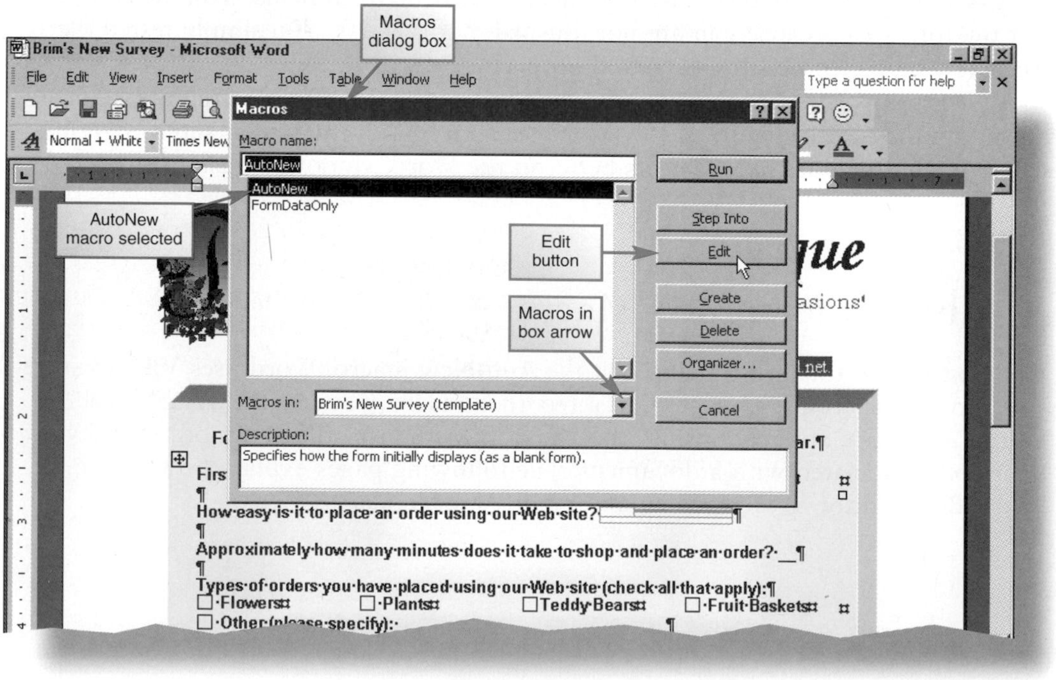

FIGURE 8-40

3 Click the Edit button. If the Code window does not display, click View on the menu bar and then click Code. If the Project Explorer window displays, click its Close button. If the Properties window displays, click its Close button. If the Code window is not maximized, double-click its title bar.

The Visual Basic Editor starts and displays the VBA code for the AutoNew macro in the Code window (Figure 8-41). Your screen may display differently depending on previous Visual Basic Editor settings.

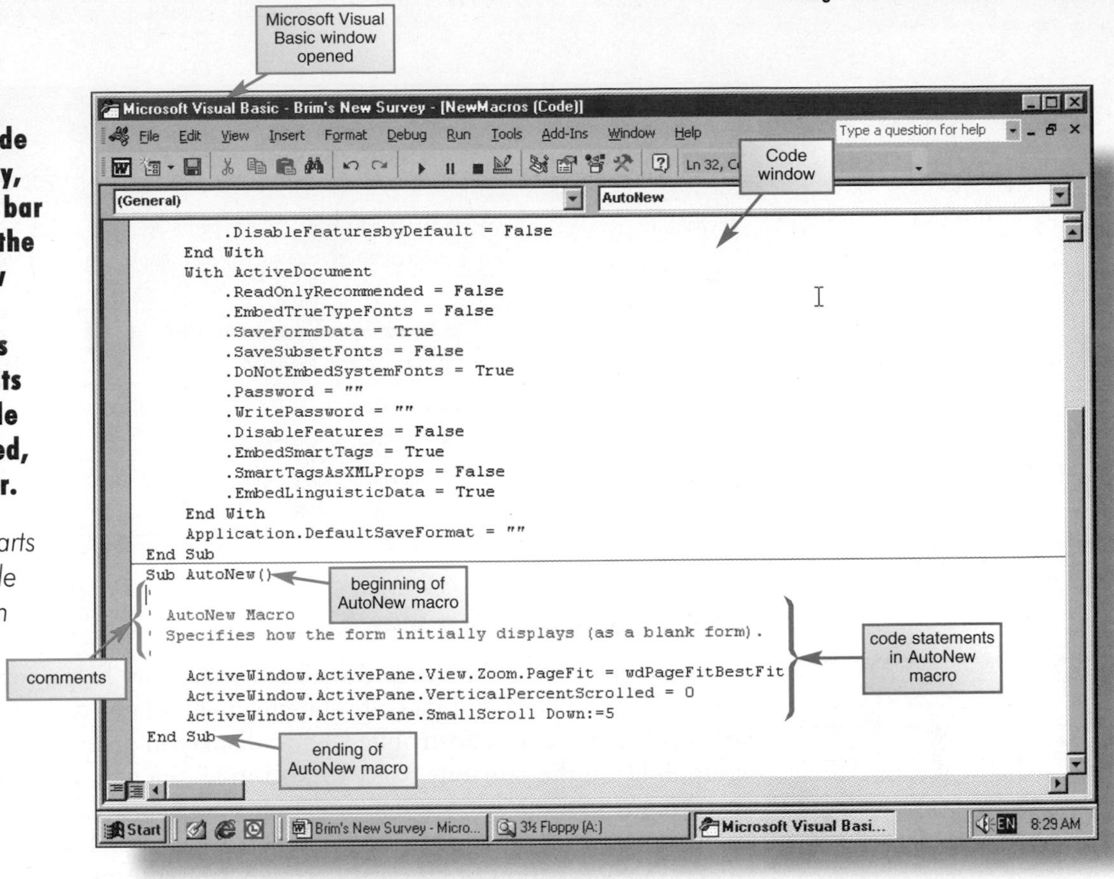

FIGURE 8-41

Other Ways

1. On Tools menu point to Macro, click Visual Basic Editor, scroll to desired procedure
2. Press ALT+F11, scroll to desired procedure
3. In Voice Command mode, say "Tools, Macro, Visual Basic Editor"

The named set of instructions associated with a macro is called a **procedure**. It is this set of instructions — beginning with the words Sub AutoNew in Figure 8-41 and continuing sequentially to the line with the words End Sub — that executes when you run the macro.

If you scroll up the Code window, you will see the code associated with the FormDataOnly macro. By scrolling through the two procedures of VBA code, you can see that the macro recorder generated many instructions.

The instructions within a procedure are called **code statements**. Each code statement can contain keywords, variables, constants, and operators. Table 8-3 on the next page explains the function of each of these elements of a code statement.

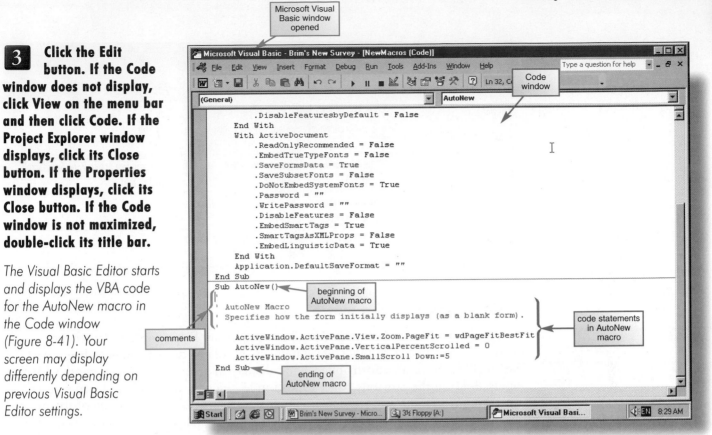

A procedure begins with a **Sub statement** and ends with an **End Sub statement**. As shown in Figure 8-41, the Sub statement is followed by the name of the procedure, which is the macro name (AutoNew). The parentheses following the macro name in the Sub statement are required. They indicate that arguments can be passed from one procedure to another. Passing arguments is beyond the scope of this project, but the parentheses still are required. The End Sub statement signifies the end of the procedure and returns control to Word. For clarity, code statement lines between the Sub statement and End Sub statement are indented four spaces.

Table 8-3 Elements of a Code Statement

CODE STATEMENT ELEMENT	DEFINITION	EXAMPLES
Keyword	Recognized by Visual Basic as part of its programming language. Keywords display in blue in the Code window.	Sub End Sub
Variable	An item whose value can be modified during program execution.	ActiveWindow.Active.Pane.SmallScroll TitleBar Text
Constant	An item whose value remains unchanged during program execution.	5
Operator	A symbol that indicates a specific action.	= +

Adding Comments to a Macro

Adding comments before and within a procedure helps you remember the purpose of the macro and its code statements at a later date. **Comments** begin with the word, Rem, or an apostrophe (') and display in green in the Code window. In Figure 8-41 on the previous page, for example, the macro recorder placed four comment lines below the Sub statement. These comments display the name of the macro and its description, as entered in the Record Macro dialog box. Comments have no effect on the execution of a procedure; they simply provide information about the procedure, such as its name and description.

The macro recorder, however, does not add comments to the executable code statements in the procedures. Any code statement that is not a comment is considered an **executable code statement**. The AutoNew procedure in Figure 8-41 contains three executable code statements. The first,

```
ActiveWindow.ActivePane.View.Zoom.PageFit = wdPageFitBestFit,
```

changes the zoom percentage to page width. The macro recorder generated this code statement when you clicked the Zoom box arrow on the Standard toolbar and then clicked Page Width.

The next two code statements scroll the screen downward five lines from the top of the page. The macro recorder generated these code statements when you dragged the scroll box to the top of the vertical scroll bar and then clicked the down scroll arrow on the vertical scroll bar five times.

You would like to enter comments that explain the purpose of executable code statements in the AutoNew procedure. You make changes such as these using the Visual Basic Editor. The Visual Basic Editor is a full-screen editor, which allows you to enter a procedure by typing lines of VBA code as if you were using word processing software. At the end of a line, you press the ENTER key or use the DOWN ARROW key to move to the next line. If you make a mistake in a code statement, you can use the ARROW keys and the DELETE or BACKSPACE keys to correct it. You also can move the insertion point to lines requiring corrections.

Perform the following steps to add comments above the executable code statements in the AutoNew procedure.

More About

VBA Statements

Instead of a long VBA statement on a single line, you can continue a VBA statement on the next line by placing an underscore character (_) at the end of the line to be continued and then pressing the ENTER key. To place multiple VBA statements on the same line, place a colon (:) between each statement.

Steps To Add Comments to a Procedure

1 **Click to the left of the letter A in the first code statement beginning with the word ActiveWindow in the AutoNew procedure and then press the ENTER key to add a blank line above the code statement. Press the UP ARROW key. Type** `'Sets screen to page width zoom` **and then press the DOWN ARROW key. Make sure you type the apostrophe at the beginning of the comment.**

The first comment is entered and displays in green (Figure 8-42).

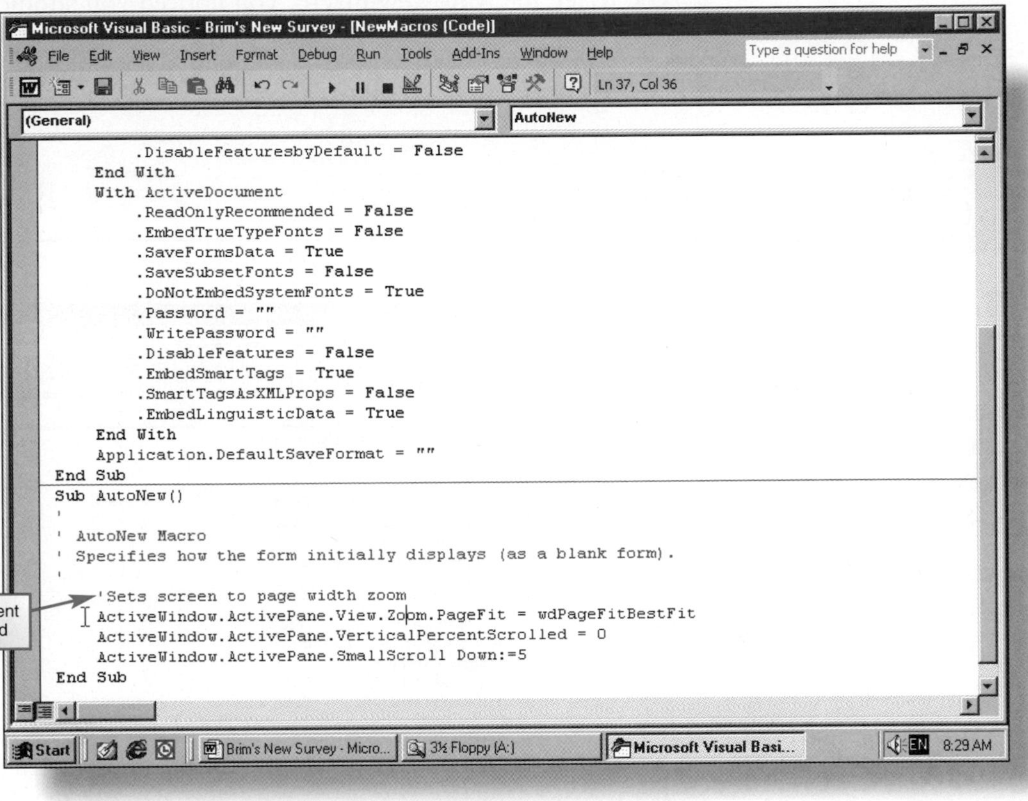

FIGURE 8-42

2 **Click to the left of the letter A in the second code statement beginning with the word ActiveWindow and then press the ENTER key to add one blank line above the code statement. Press the UP ARROW key. Type** `'Scrolls down from top of page so entire form fits in window` **and then press the DOWN ARROW key. Make sure you type the apostrophe at the beginning of the comment.**

The second comment is entered and displays in green (Figure 8-43).

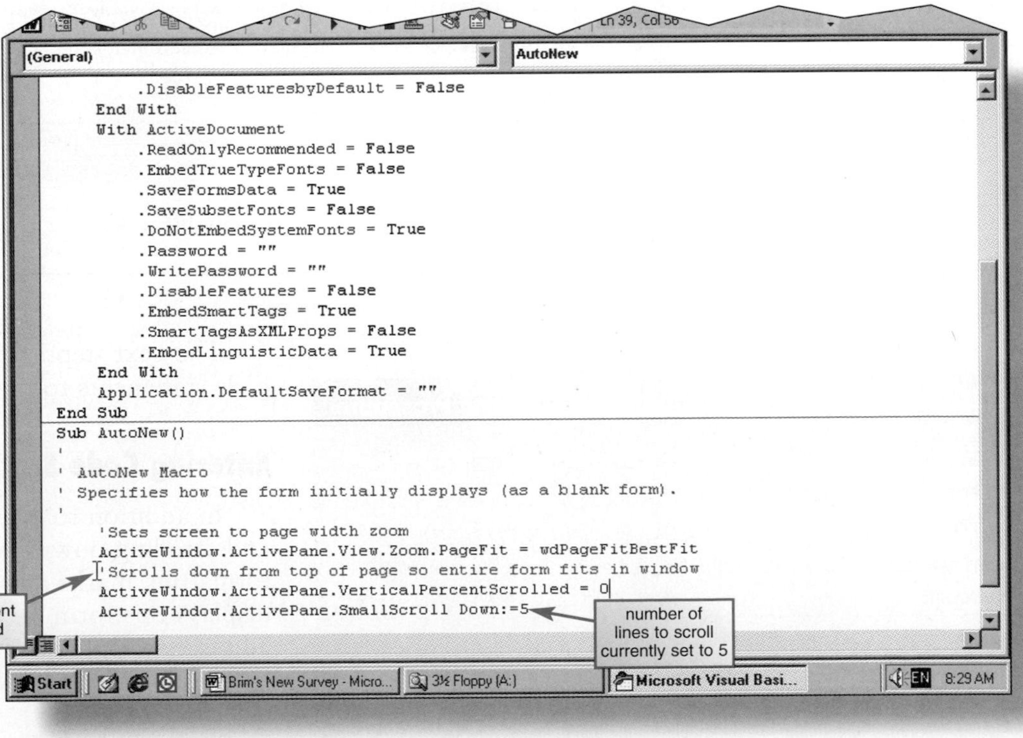

FIGURE 8-43

Modifying Existing Code in a Macro

The next step is to modify existing code in the AutoNew macro. Recall that when you tested the AutoNew macro, you noticed you should scroll down one more line so the boutique name displays closer to the top of the screen (shown in Figure 8-38 on page WD 8.37). Thus, you should change the 5 in the third executable code statement in the AutoNew procedure to a 6, as shown in the following step.

Steps To Modify Existing Code

1 Double-click the 5 at the end of the executable code statement above the End Sub statement. Type 6 **as the new number of lines to scroll.**

The code statement is modified (Figure 8-44).

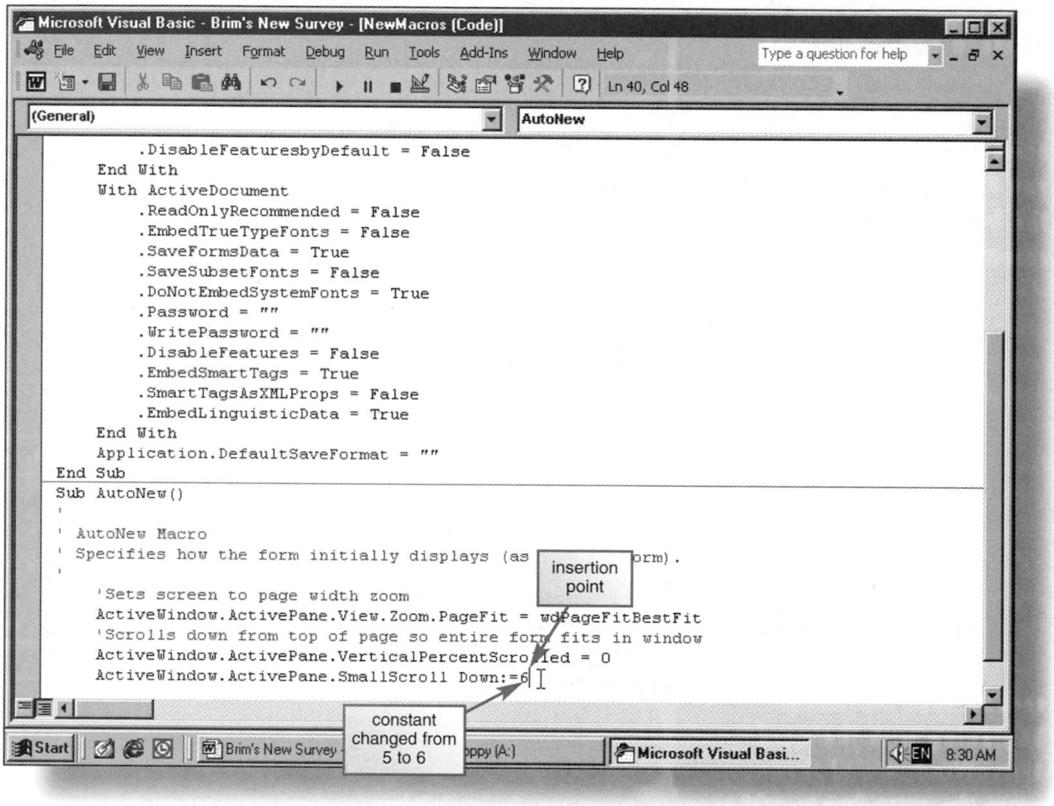

FIGURE 8-44

Table 8-4 Code Statements Added to AutoNew Procedure	
ORDER	*CODE STATEMENT*
First new code statement	'Turns off table gridlines
Second new code statement	ActiveDocument.ActiveWindow.View.TableGridlines = False
Third new code statement	'Turns off formatting marks
Fourth new code statement	ActiveDocument.ActiveWindow.View.ShowAll = False

The next step is to add two more executable code statements to the AutoNew macro.

Entering Code Statements

In addition to changing the zoom to page width and scrolling down six lines, you would like to hide formatting marks and gridlines when a user initially displays this form (as a blank form). Thus, you will add two executable code statements, each preceded by a comment. Table 8-4 shows the code statements to be entered.

Perform the following step to add these code statements to the procedure.

Steps To Add Code Statements to a Procedure

1 With the insertion point following the 6 as shown in Figure 8-44, press the ENTER key. Type the first new code statement shown in Table 8-4. Press the ENTER key. Enter the remaining three code statements shown in Table 8-4. Make sure you type an apostrophe at the beginning of both comment lines. Ignore any shortcut menus that display as you type.

The new code statements are entered into the AutoNew procedure (Figure 8-45).

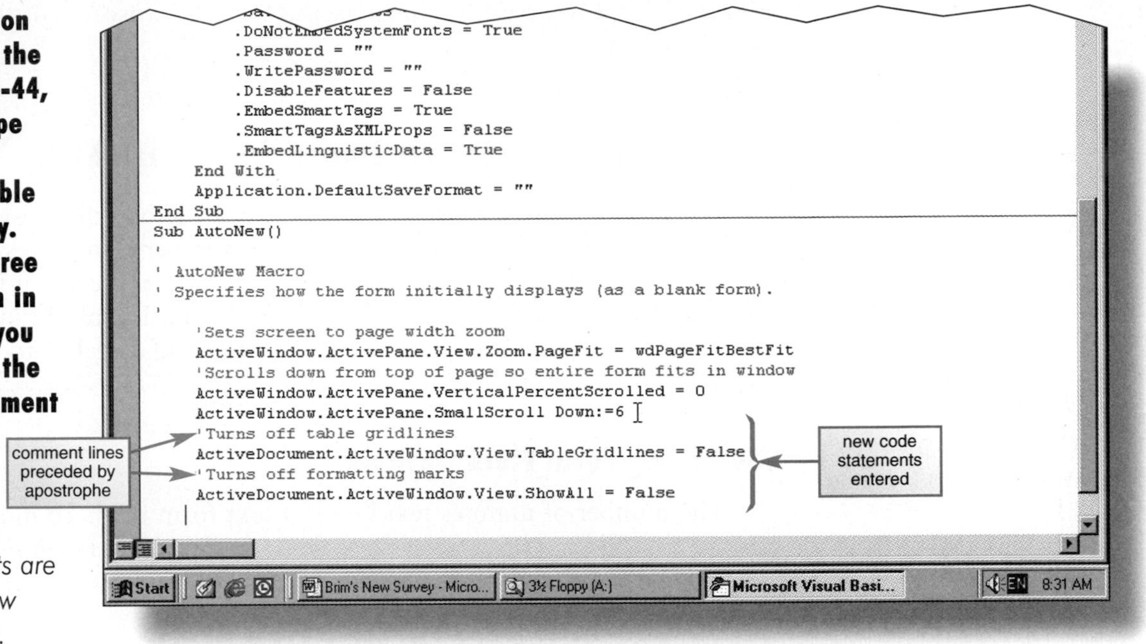
.DoNotEmbedSystemFonts = True
.Password = ""
.WritePassword = ""
.DisableFeatures = False
.EmbedSmartTags = True
.SmartTagsAsXMLProps = False
.EmbedLinguisticData = True
End With
Application.DefaultSaveFormat = ""
End Sub
Sub AutoNew()
' AutoNew Macro
' Specifies how the form initially displays (as a blank form).
'Sets screen to page width zoom
ActiveWindow.ActivePane.View.Zoom.PageFit = wdPageFitBestFit
'Scrolls down from top of page so entire form fits in window
ActiveWindow.ActivePane.VerticalPercentScrolled = 0
ActiveWindow.ActivePane.SmallScroll Down:=6
'Turns off table gridlines
ActiveDocument.ActiveWindow.View.TableGridlines = False
'Turns off formatting marks
ActiveDocument.ActiveWindow.View.ShowAll = False
comment lines preceded by apostrophe
new code statements entered
Start
Brim's New Survey - Micro...
3½ Floppy (A:)
Microsoft Visual Basi...
8:31 AM

FIGURE 8-45

You could add many more statements to this procedure to ensure the initial screen displays properly. For example, you could close any open toolbars. For purposes of this project, you now are finished modifying the AutoNew macro. Thus, perform the following steps to quit the Visual Basic Editor and return control to Word.

Steps To Quit the Visual Basic Editor

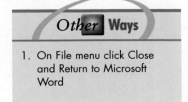

1 Point to the Close button on the right edge of the Microsoft Visual Basic title bar (Figure 8-46).

2 Click the Close button.

The Visual Basic Editor window closes and control returns to Word.

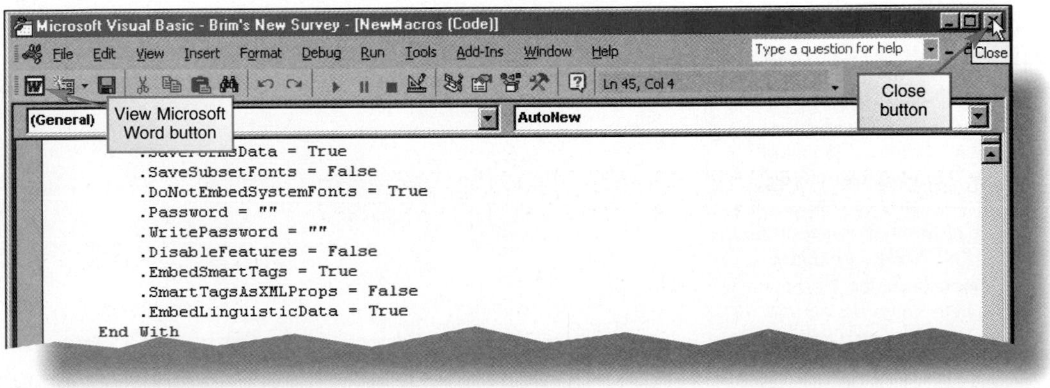
Microsoft Visual Basic - Brim's New Survey - [NewMacros (Code)]
File Edit View Insert Format Debug Run Tools Add-Ins Window Help
Type a question for help
Close
Ln 45, Col 4
Close button
(General)
View Microsoft Word button
AutoNew
.SaveSubsetFonts = False
.DoNotEmbedSystemFonts = True
.Password = ""
.WritePassword = ""
.DisableFeatures = False
.EmbedSmartTags = True
.SmartTagsAsXMLProps = False
.EmbedLinguisticData = True
End With

FIGURE 8-46

Other Ways

1. On File menu click Close and Return to Microsoft Word

Instead of closing the Visual Basic Editor, you can click the **View Microsoft Word button** on the Visual Basic toolbar (Figure 8-46 on the previous page) to minimize the Visual Basic Editor and return control to Word. If you plan to switch between Word and the Visual Basic Editor, then use the View Microsoft Word button; otherwise use the Close button.

Creating a Macro from Scratch Using VBA

The next macro to be created in this project is the one that displays an error message if the user enters a nonnumeric value in the number of minutes text box (shown in Figure 8-1b on page WD 8.05). The macro is to execute when the user presses the TAB key to move the insertion point out of the number of minutes text box. The following pages explain how to create this macro and attach it to the text form field for the number of minutes.

Modifying Form Field Options

The number of minutes text box is a text form field. To modify a text form field, you double-click the text form field to display the Text Form Field Options dialog box. Two changes are to be made in the dialog box: change the type and enter a bookmark.

In Project 7, you wanted only numbers to display in the text form field. Thus, you changed the text form field's type to Number. Doing so ensured that if a user entered a nonnumeric value in the text form field during data entry, the entry automatically was converted to a zero. In this project, you want to display an error message if the user enters a nonnumeric value. Thus, you must change the text form field's type back to Regular text so that you can display an error message if a user makes an incorrect entry.

You also want to change the bookmark for this text form field because you will be writing VBA code that references this text form field. A **bookmark** is an item in a document that you name for future reference. Currently, the bookmark is Text3, which is not very descriptive. A more meaningful bookmark would be EnteredMinutes. Notice this new bookmark does not have a space between the words, Entered and Minutes. This is because a bookmark cannot contain any spaces; a bookmark also must begin with a letter.

Perform the following steps to change the text form field type and edit the bookmark.

More About

Bookmark Names

Each time you create a form field, Word assigns it a sequential default bookmark name. For example, the first text form field has a bookmark name of Text1, the second text form field has a bookmark name of Text2, the third text form field has a bookmark name of Text3, and so on.

Steps To Change Options for a Text Form Field

1 Double-click the text form field for number of minutes. When the Text Form Field Options dialog box displays, point to the Type box arrow.

Word displays the Text Form Field Options dialog box (Figure 8-47).

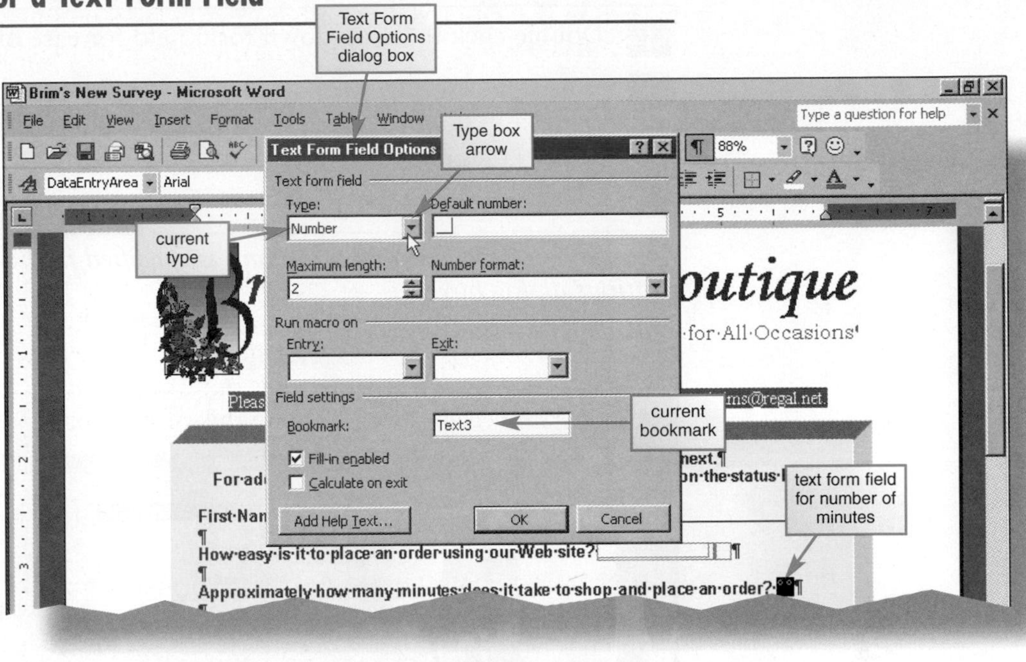

FIGURE 8-47

2 Click the Type box arrow and then click Regular text. Double-click the text in the Bookmark text box and then type `EnteredMinutes` **as the new bookmark. Point to the OK button.**

The form field options display as shown in Figure 8-48.

3 Click the OK button.

Word changes the form field options as specified in the Text Form Field Options dialog box.

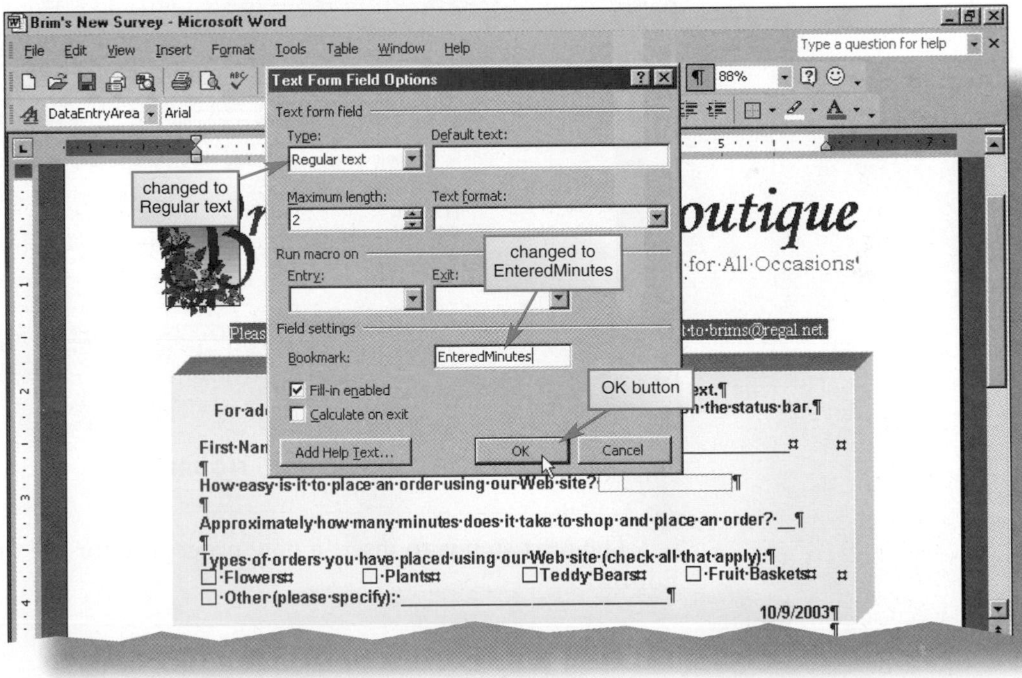

FIGURE 8-48

Other Ways

1. Click Form Field Options button on Forms toolbar
2. Right-click form field, click Properties on shortcut menu
3. With Forms toolbar displaying, in Voice Command mode, say "Form Field Options" or say "Properties"

The next step is to change the bookmark for the drop-down form field for the ease of use from Dropdown3 to a more meaningful name, because this form field also will be referenced in the VBA code. Perform the steps on the next page to change the bookmark for the drop-down form field.

TO CHANGE A BOOKMARK FOR A DROP-DOWN FORM FIELD

1. Double-click the drop-down form field for ease of use.
2. When the Drop-Down Form Field Options dialog box displays, double-click the text in the Bookmark text box and then type `EaseOfUse` as the new bookmark. Point to the OK button (Figure 8-49).
3. Click the OK button.

Word changes the form field options as specified in the Drop-Down Form Field Options dialog box.

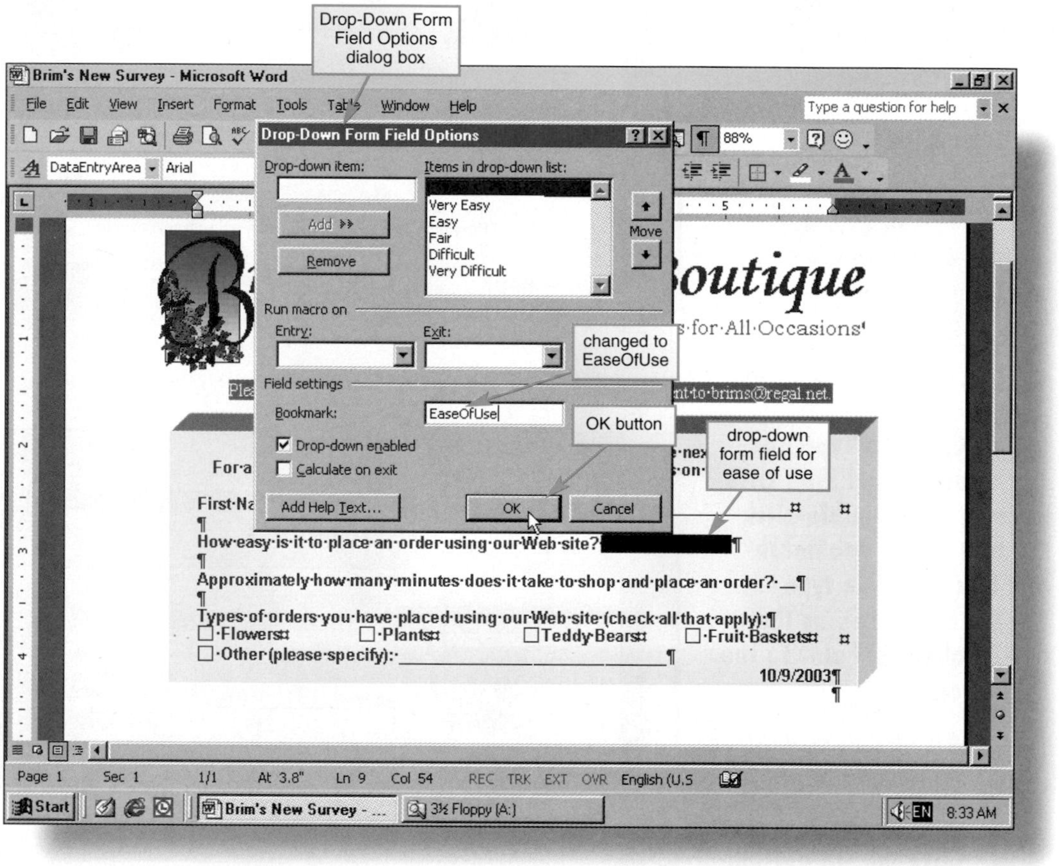

FIGURE 8-49

The next step is to insert a new procedure for the macro using the Visual Basic Editor.

Inserting a Procedure for the Macro

For the previous two macros, you used the macro recorder to create the macros, which generated corresponding VBA code from your actions. For this macro, you cannot record the displaying of the error message, because an error message for this text form field does not exist. Thus, you must write the VBA code for this macro using the Visual Basic Editor. To do this, you insert a procedure.

Perform the following steps to insert a new empty procedure named NumberOfMinutes.

Steps To Insert a Visual Basic Procedure

1 Press ALT+F11 to open the Visual Basic Editor in a new window. If the Project Explorer displays, click its Close button. If the Properties window displays, click its Close button. If the Code window does not display, click View on the menu bar and then click Code. If necessary, maximize the Code window. Click the Insert UserForm button arrow and then point to Procedure.

The Visual Basic Editor displays as shown in Figure 8-50.

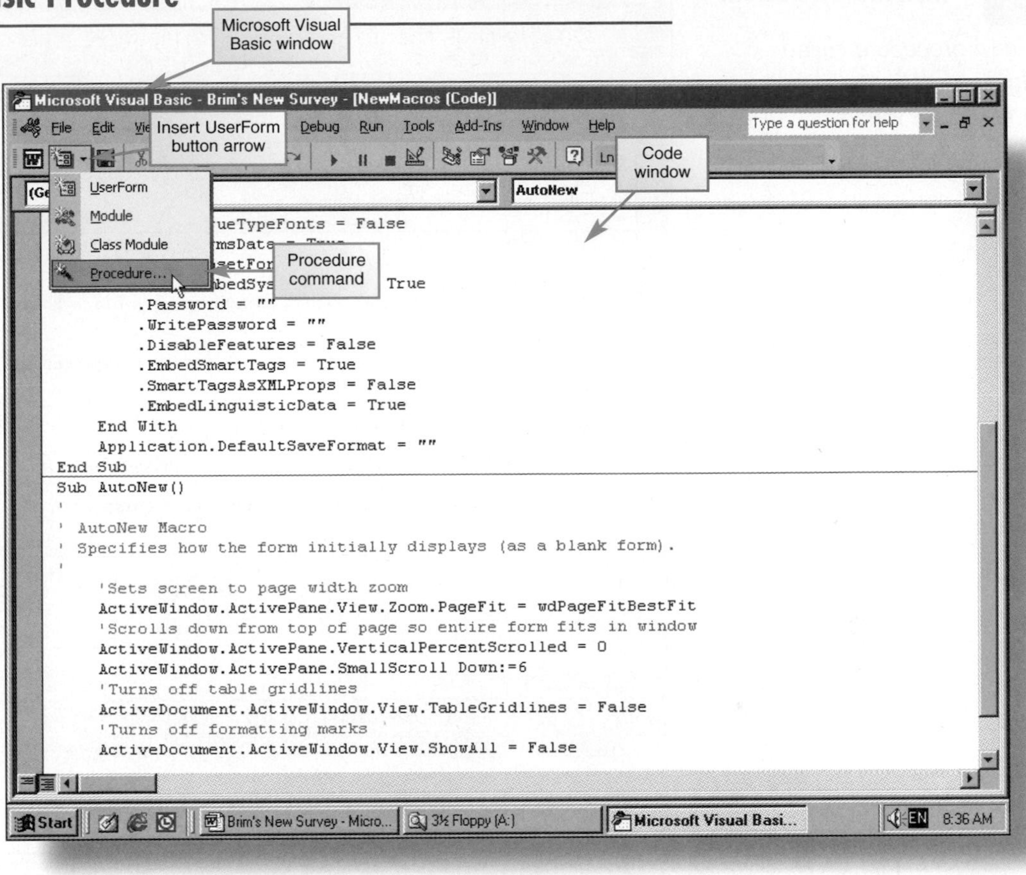

FIGURE 8-50

2 Click Procedure. When Word displays the Add Procedure dialog box, type `NumberOfMinutes` **in the Name text box and then point to the OK button.**

The Add Procedure dialog box displays (Figure 8-51).

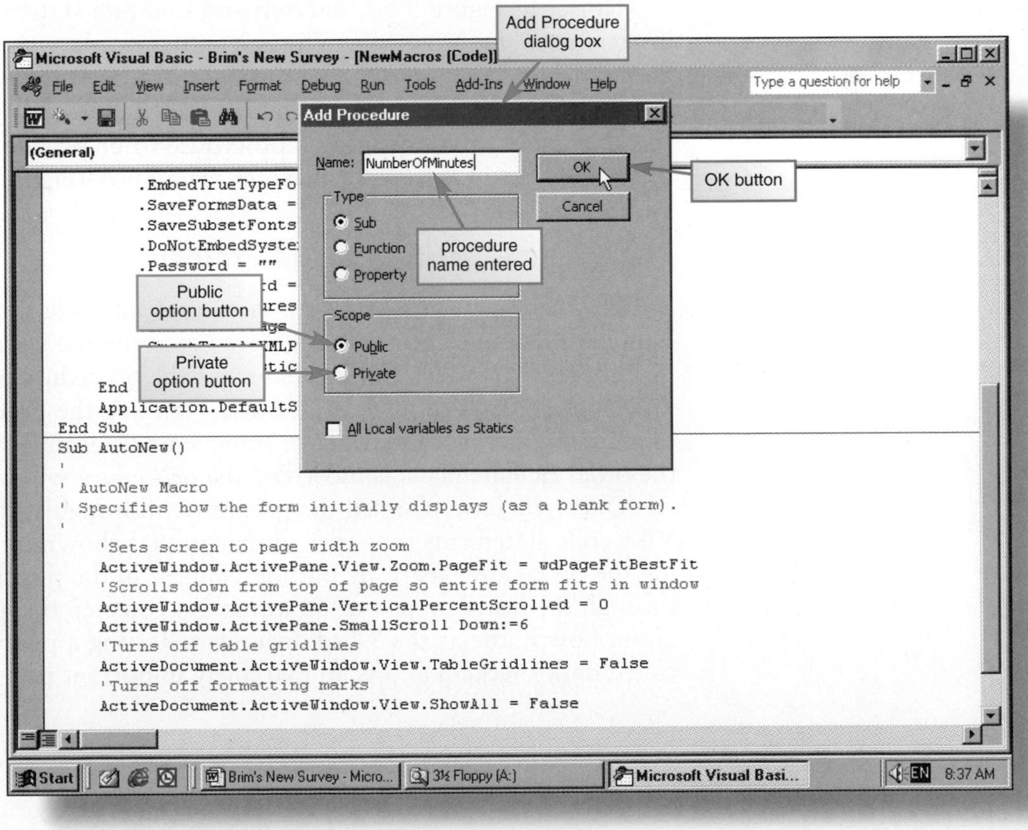

FIGURE 8-51

3 Click the OK button.

A new procedure called NumberOfMinutes displays in the Code window (Figure 8-52).

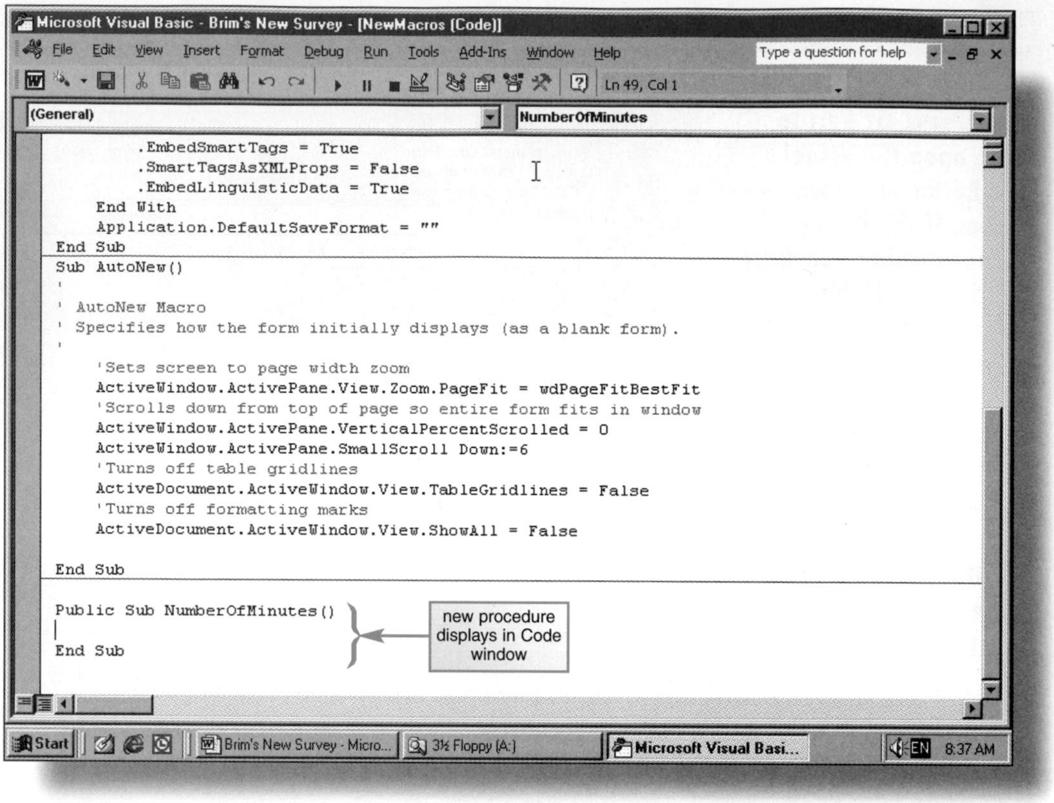

FIGURE 8-52

Other Ways

1. On Insert menu click Procedure, enter procedure name, click OK button
2. In Voice Command mode, say "Insert, Procedure"

Notice in Figure 8-52 that Sub and End Sub statements automatically are inserted into the procedure. The Sub statement, however, begins with the keyword Public, which means that this procedure can be executed from other documents or programs. Private, by contrast, means that the procedure can be executed only from this document. If you wanted a procedure to be private, you would click Private in the Scope area in the Add Procedure dialog box (Figure 8-51 on the previous page).

Planning and Writing a VBA Procedure

The next step is to write and then enter the code statements for the newly created NumberOfMinutes procedure. Before you write the statements, you should plan the procedure; that is, determine what tasks the procedure is to accomplish and the order in which the tasks should be executed. Planning the procedure is an extremely important activity because the order of statements determines the sequence of execution. If the order of statements is incorrect, the procedure will not execute properly.

Once you have planned the procedure thoroughly, the next step is to write the VBA code statements on paper similar to that shown in Table 8-5. Then, before entering the procedure, test it by putting yourself in the position of Word and stepping through the instructions one at a time. As you step through the procedure, think about how it affects the Word document. Testing a procedure before entering it is called **desk checking** and is an extremely important part of the development process.

Table 8-5 Code Statements for NumberOfMinutes Procedure

LINE	*VBA CODE STATEMENT*
1	`Public Sub NumberOfMinutes()`
2	`'`
3	`' NumberOfMinutes Macro`
4	`' Displays error message if entered number of minutes is not numeric.`
5	`'`
6	`    'Test if entry in EnteredMinutes text form field is numeric`
7	`    If IsNumeric(ActiveDocument.FormFields("EnteredMinutes").Result) = False Then`
8	`        'Display error message`
9	`        MsgBox "Please enter minutes in numbers", vbOKOnly + vbCritical`
10	`        'Redisplay underscores in text form field`
11	`        ActiveDocument.FormFields("EnteredMinutes").Result = "___"`
12	`        'Reposition selection in text form field`
13	`        ActiveDocument.FormFields("EaseOfUse").Select`
14	`        'SendKeys "{TAB}"`
15	`    End If`
16	`End Sub`

In the code statements shown in Table 8-5, lines 2, 3, 4, 5, 6, 8, 10, 12, and 14 are comments. Lines 1 and 16 contain the Sub and End Sub statements that were inserted automatically when you created the procedure. Line 7 is the first executable code statement. It is called an If...Then statement because it executes the line(s) of code up to the End If statement if the result of a condition is true. The condition in line 7 is IsNumeric(ActiveDocument.FormFields("EnteredMinutes").Result) = False. In nonprogramming terms, this condition is testing whether the user entered a number in the EnteredMinutes form field. (Recall that earlier in this project, you changed the bookmark for this form field to EnteredMinutes.) If not, then the statements up to the End If statement will be executed. If the user did enter a number, then the statements up to the End If statement are not executed and control returns to Word.

If the user entered a nonnumeric value in the EnteredMinutes form field, the next executable code statement is in line 9, which uses the MsgBox keyword to display a message box on the screen. The text inside the quotation marks displays inside the message box; vbOKOnly places an OK button in the message box, and vbCritical places an icon of an X in the dialog box. Table 8-6 lists the types of icons that can display in a message box.

After a user reads the message in the message box and clicks the OK button, the next executable code statement is in line 11, which replaces the user's invalid entry with underscore characters. Then, line 13 positions the selection in the EaseOfUse drop-down form field. Some later versions of Word may need line 14, which presses the TAB key so that the selection is positioned in the EnteredMinutes text form field — ready for the user to make another entry in the number of minutes text box. Currently the line is commented; that is, it begins with an apostrophe so VBA ignores the command. Later in the project, when you execute the macro, if the selection does not display in the number of minutes text form field, remove the apostrophe.

Having desk checked the code statements on paper, you now are ready to enter them into the Visual Basic Editor. Perform the steps on the next page to enter the code statements into the NumberOfMinutes procedure.

More About

InputBox

A MsgBox displays a message and one or more buttons that the user can click. If you would like the user to enter information that you can use in the VBA procedure, you should display an InputBox. An InputBox displays a message, a text box, and one or more buttons that the user can click. If the user clicks the OK button, the entered text is saved for use later in the procedure.

Table 8-6 Types of Icons for a Message Box

ICON	*VISUAL BASIC CONSTANT*
Letter X	vbCritical
Question mark	vbQuestion
Exclamation point	vbExclamation
Information symbol	vbInformation

Steps To Enter the NumberOfMinutes Procedure

1 **With the insertion point on the blank line between the Sub and End Sub statements in the Code window, type the code statements shown in lines 2 through 15 in Table 8-5 on the previous page. Make sure you enter an apostrophe at the beginning of each comment line. For clarity, indent code statements as shown in Table 8-5.**

The NumberOfMinutes procedure is entered (Figure 8-53).

2 **Verify your code statements by comparing them to Figure 8-53.**

3 **Click the Close button on the right edge of the Microsoft Visual Basic title bar to return to the template.**

The Microsoft Visual Basic window closes and control returns to Word.

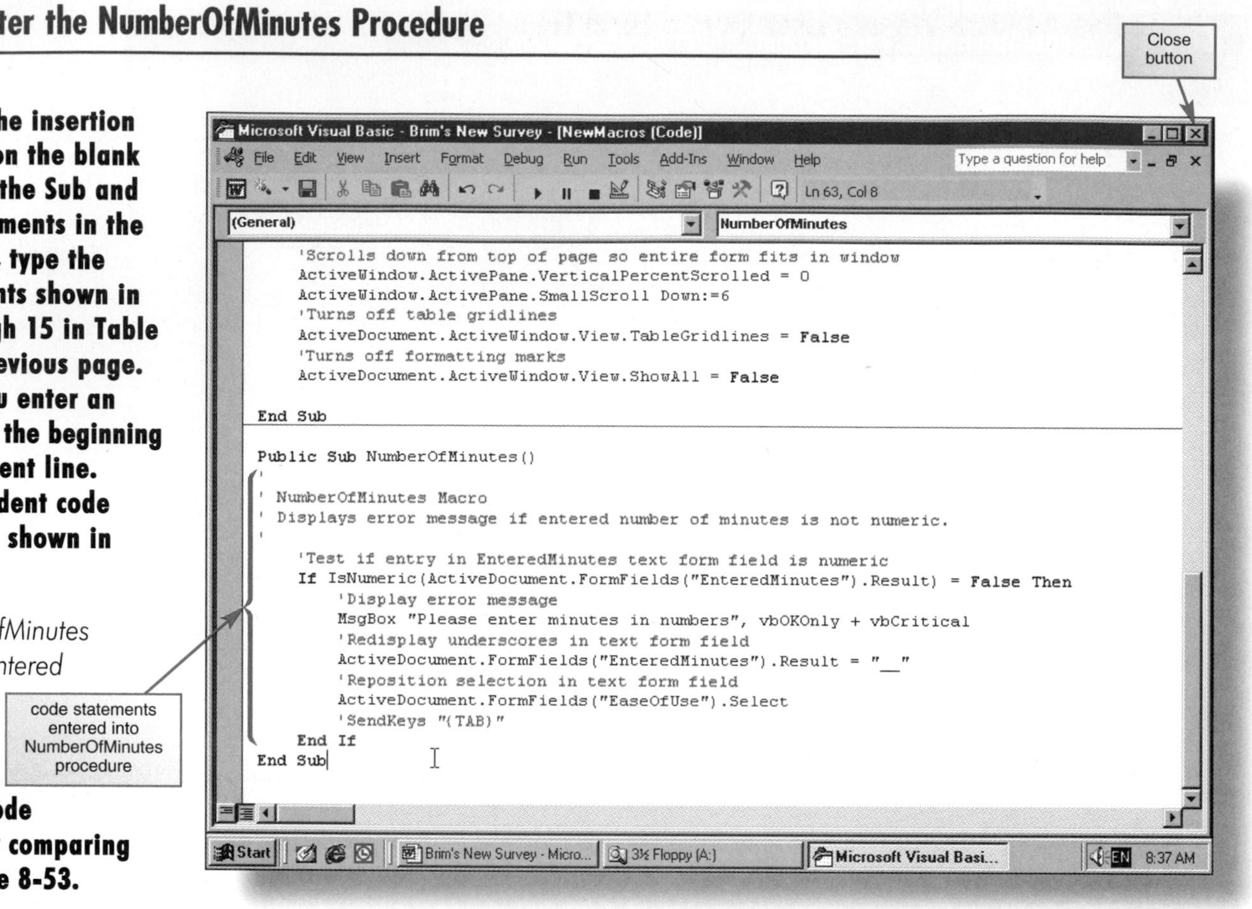

FIGURE 8-53

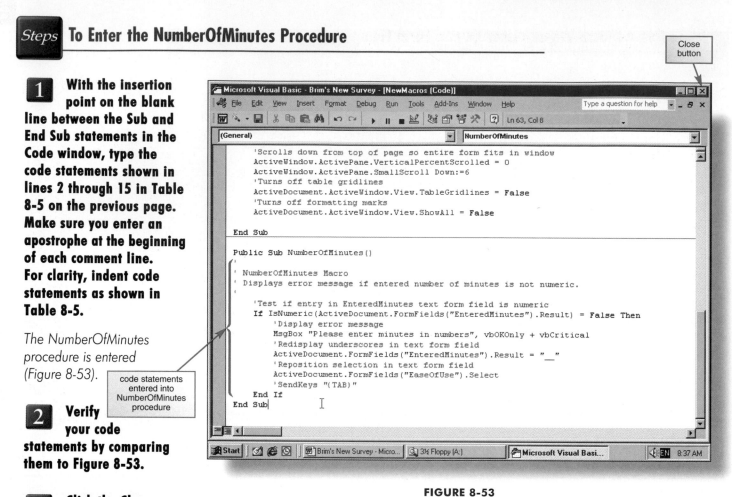

The next step is to attach this procedure for the macro to the text form field for the number of minutes.

Running a Macro When a User Exits a Form Field

The NumberOfMinutes macro that you just created in the Visual Basic Editor should execute whenever a user presses the TAB key to move the insertion point out of the number of minutes text form field. That is, pressing the TAB key out of the number of minutes text form field is the event that is to trigger execution of the procedure. With respect to form fields, Word allows you to execute a macro under these two circumstances: (1) when the user enters a form field, and (2) when the user exits the form field. You specify when the macro should run through the Text Form Field Options dialog box. Perform the following steps to instruct Word to execute the NumberOfMinutes macro when a user exits the text form field for the number of minutes.

Steps To Run a Macro When a User Exits a Form Field

1 Double-click the text form field for the number of minutes. When the Text Form Field Options dialog box displays, click the Exit box arrow, and then click NumberOfMinutes. Point to the OK button.

Word displays the Text Form Field Options dialog box (Figure 8-54). The selected macro name displays in the Exit box.

2 Click the OK button.

The form field options are set as specified in the Text Form Field Options dialog box.

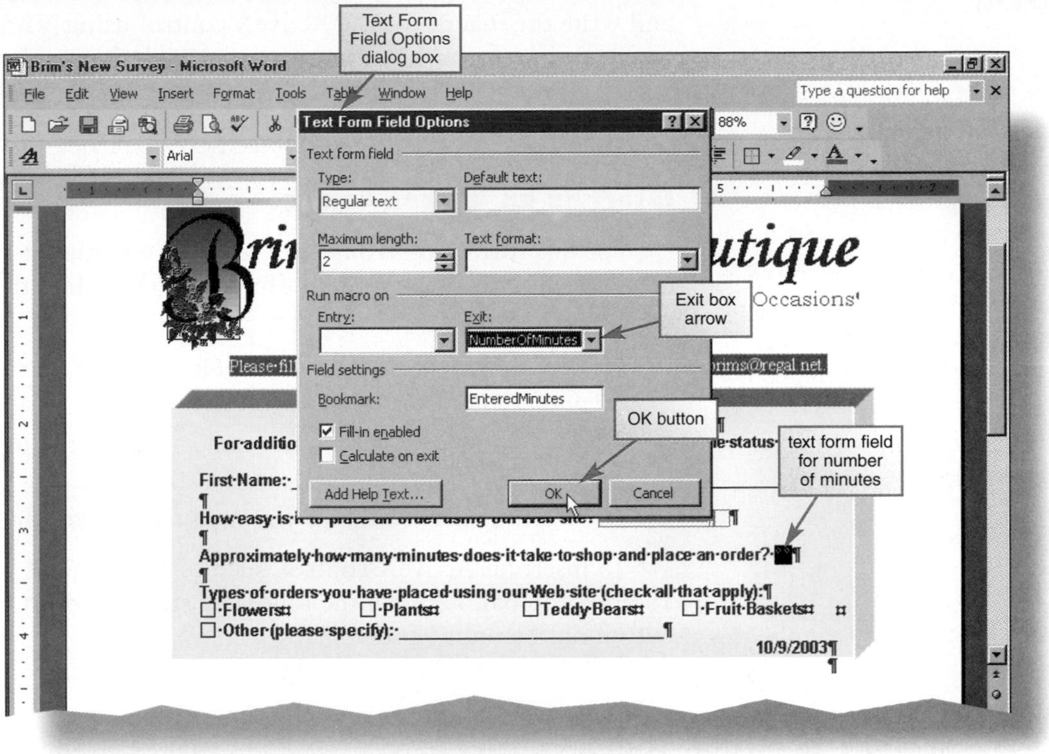

FIGURE 8-54

When you click the Entry or Exit box arrow in the Run macro on area in the Text Form Field Options dialog box, Word displays all available macros. You can select any one macro to run when the user enters or exits each form field in the form.

The NumberOfMinutes macro is complete. You will test this macro at the end of this project, after you create the next VBA procedure.

Adding an ActiveX Control to a Form

In addition to the form fields available on the Forms toolbar, you can insert an ActiveX control on a Word form. An **ActiveX control** is an object, such as a button or check box, which can be included in a form to be published on the World Wide Web. The major difference between a form field and an ActiveX control is that form fields require the use of Word, whereas ActiveX controls do not. Thus, if you intend to create a Web page form, you should place ActiveX controls on the form instead of form fields.

ActiveX controls have the appearance and functionality of Windows controls. For example, the check box ActiveX control displays like any check box in any Windows dialog box. A check box form field, by contrast, has an appearance unique to Word. That is, it displays an X (instead of a check mark). Users that are familiar with Windows applications will find it easier to work with ActiveX controls than working with form fields. With form fields, a user has to press the TAB key to move the insertion point from one form field to another. With an ActiveX control, the user can click in the form field or press the TAB key to move to it.

More About

ActiveX

For more information about ActiveX, visit the Word More About Web page (scsite.com/wd2002/more.htm) and then click ActiveX.

Adding an ActiveX control to a form involves four major activities: insert the ActiveX control, set properties of the ActiveX control, format the ActiveX control, and write the macro for the ActiveX control using VBA. Word refers to the time in which you perform these four activities as **design mode**. When you run the form (fill it in) as a user does, by contrast, you are in **run mode**. The following pages explain how to add an ActiveX control to an online form.

Inserting an ActiveX Control

For this form, you would like to insert a command button that users click when they are finished filling in the form. When they click the button, three actions should occur:

1. If the user entered text in the Other text box, then Word places an X in the Other check box (in case the user forgot to place an X in the check box).
2. Word displays the Save As dialog box so the user can assign a file name to the filled-in form.
3. Word displays a thank-you message box on the screen.

To insert an ActiveX control, such as a command button, you use the Control Toolbox toolbar. Perform the following steps to insert an ActiveX control command button on the online form.

Steps To Insert an ActiveX Control

1 If the Control Toolbox toolbar does not display on the screen already, click View on the menu bar, point to Toolbars, and then click Control Toolbox. Click the paragraph mark at the end of the form and then press the ENTER key. Center the paragraph mark. Position the insertion point on the centered paragraph mark below the data entry area. Point to the Command Button button on the Control Toolbox toolbar (Figure 8-55).

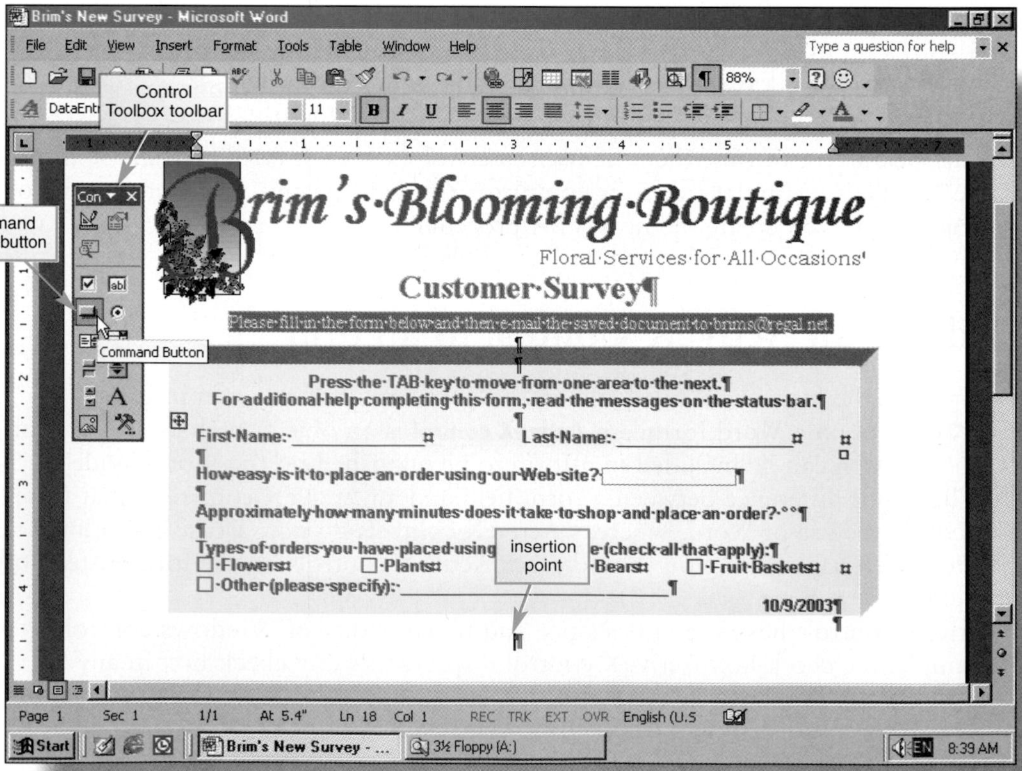

FIGURE 8-55

2 Click the Command Button button.

Word inserts a standard-sized command button at the location of the insertion point and switches to design mode (Figure 8-56). The text CommandButton1 partially displays on the face of the button. The button is selected and is surrounded by sizing handles.

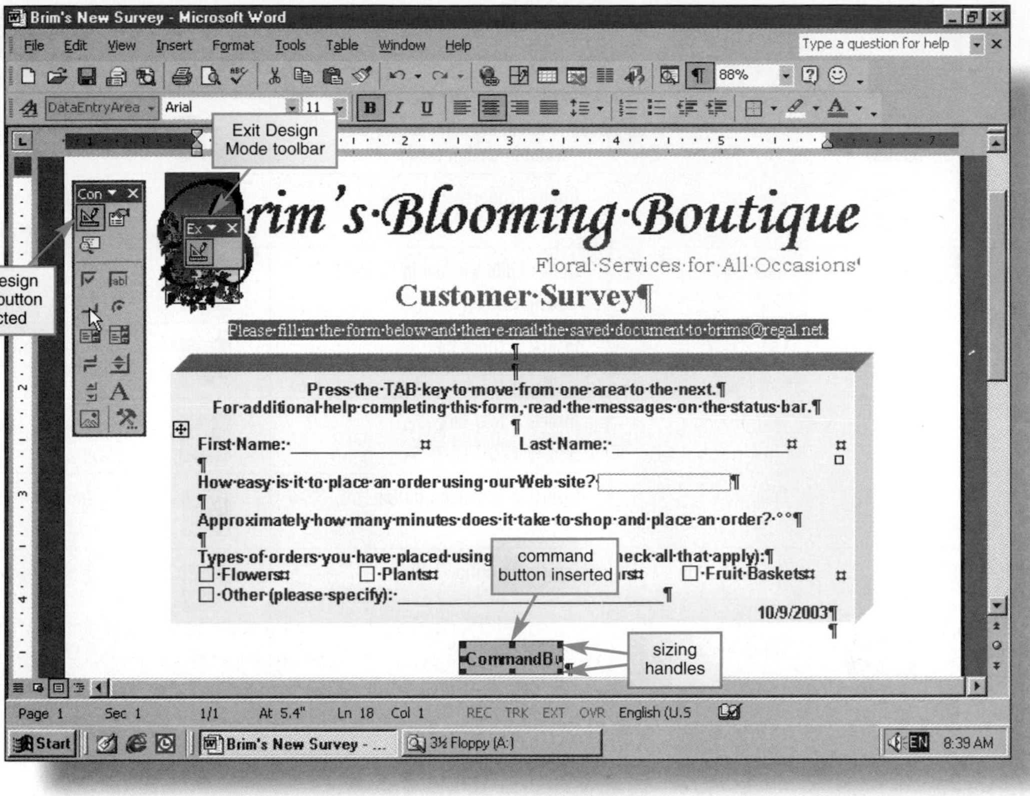

FIGURE 8-56

When you click a button on the Control Toolbox toolbar, Word automatically switches to design mode, changes the Design Mode button on the Control Toolbox toolbar to an Exit Design Mode button, and selects the Exit Design Mode button. Word also may display an Exit Design Mode toolbar. The Control Toolbox toolbar buttons are summarized in Table 8-7 on the next page.

The next step is to set the properties of the ActiveX control.

Setting Properties of an ActiveX Control

In Word, a command button ActiveX control has 20 different properties (shown in Figure 8-58 on page WD 8.55), such as the caption (the words on the face of the button), background color, foreground color, height, width, font, and so on. After you insert a command button into a form, you can change any one of the 20 properties to improve the button's appearance and modify its function. For this command button, you are to change its caption to the text, Click Here When Finished.

Other Ways

1. Click Design Mode button on Visual Basic toolbar
2. In Voice Command mode, say "Command Button"

More About

VBA Help

For help with VBA, code statements, and properties, type `VBA help` in the Ask a question box and then press the ENTER key. When the topics display, click Get Help for Visual Basic for Applications in Word.

Table 8-7 Summary of Buttons on the Control Toolbox Toolbar

BUTTON	NAME	FUNCTION	BUTTON	NAME	FUNCTION
	Design Mode button	Changes to Exit Design Mode button when in design mode		Combo Box	Inserts a drop-down list box
	Properties	Opens Properties window		Toggle Button	Inserts a toggle button
	View Code	Opens Code window in Visual Basic Editor		Spin Button	Inserts a spin button
	Check Box	Inserts a check box		Scroll Bar	Inserts a scroll bar
	Text Box	Inserts a text box		Label	Inserts a label
	Command Button	Inserts a command button		Image	Inserts an image
	Option Button	Inserts an option button		More Controls	Displays a list of additional controls
	List Box	Inserts a list box			

Perform the following steps to change the Caption property of an ActiveX control.

Steps To Set Properties of an ActiveX Control

1 **With the command button selected and Word in design mode, point to the Properties button on the Control Toolbox toolbar (Figure 8-57).**

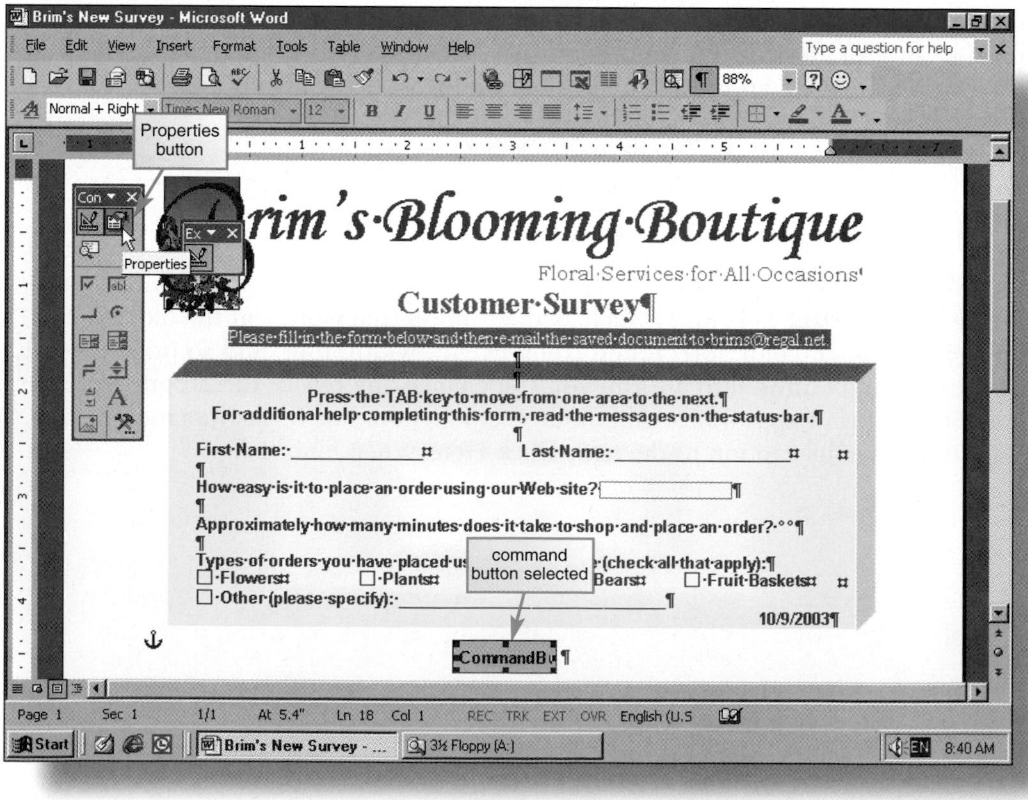

FIGURE 8-57

2 **Click the Properties button. When the Properties window opens, if necessary, click the Properties box arrow and then click CommandButton1 in the list. If necessary, click the Alphabetic tab. In the list, click Caption in the left column and then double-click CommandButton1 in the right column.**

The Property names display on the left, and the data for each property displays on the right (Figure 8-58).

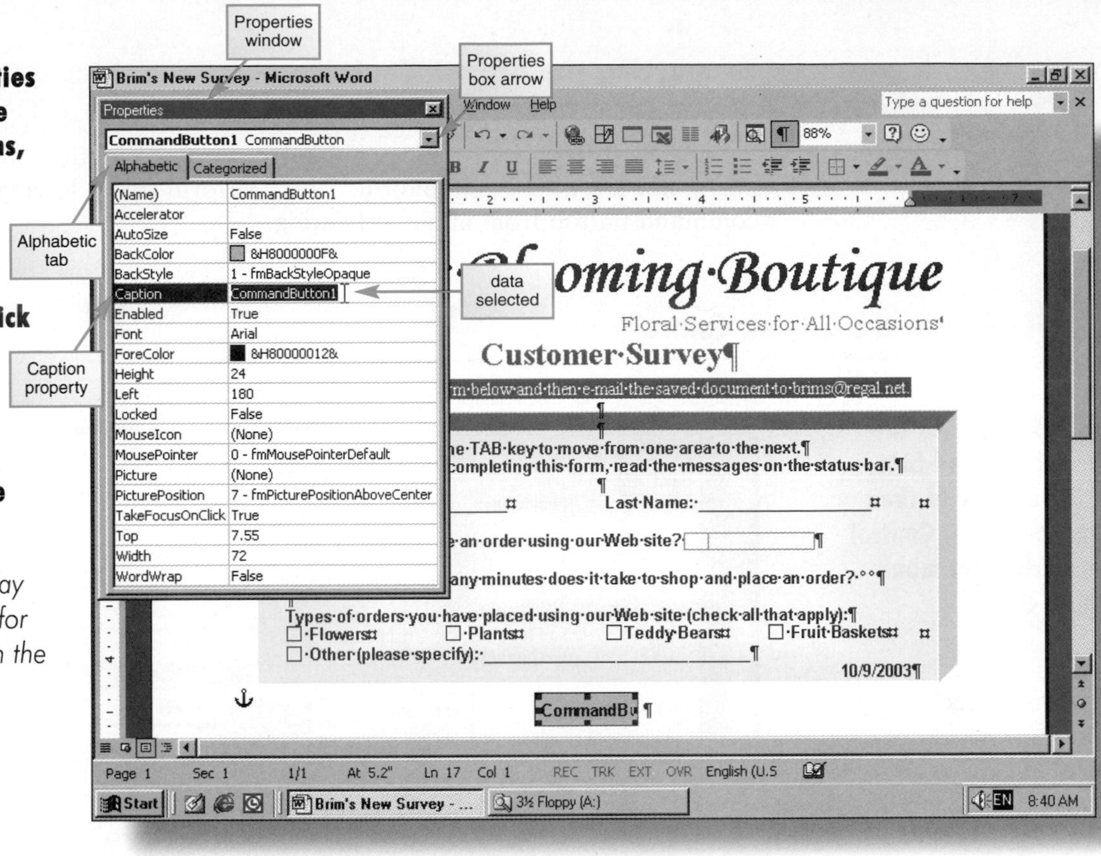

FIGURE 8-58

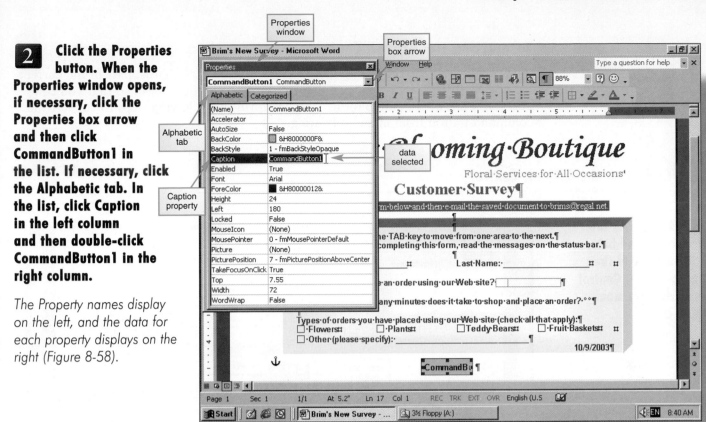

3 **Type** `Click Here When Finished` **as the new caption. Point to the Close button on the Properties window title bar.**

The Caption property is changed (Figure 8-59).

4 **Click the Close button on the Properties window title bar.**

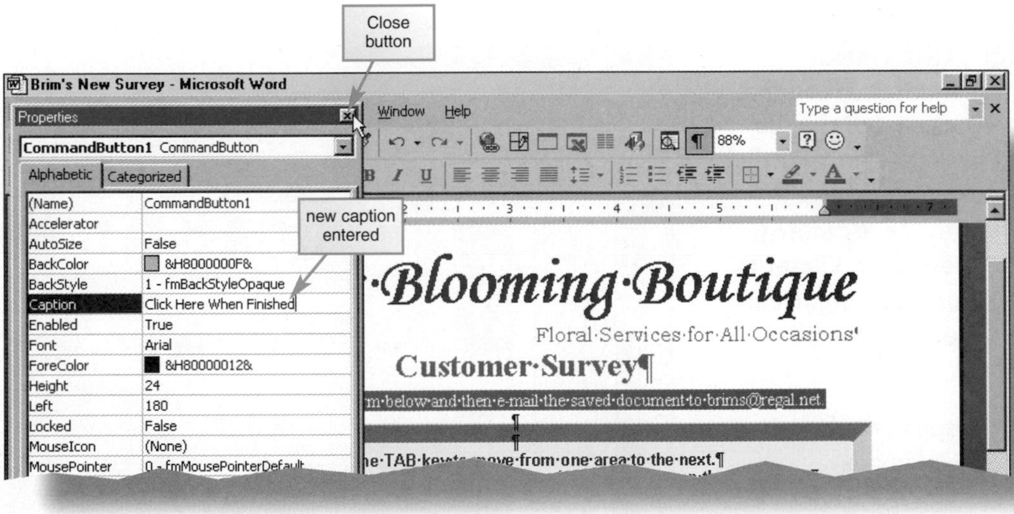

FIGURE 8-59

Other Ways

1. In design mode, right-click control, click Properties on shortcut menu
2. Click Properties Window button on toolbar when Visual Basic Editor is active
3. In Voice Command mode, say "Properties"

The Properties window (Figure 8-58) has two tabs, Alphabetic and Categorized. The **Alphabetic sheet** displays the properties in alphabetical order. The **Categorized sheet** displays the properties by subject, such as appearance, behavior, font, and miscellaneous.

The next step is to format the ActiveX control so it is a floating object and then resize it. You resize an ActiveX control the same way you resize any other object — by dragging its sizing handles.

Formatting the ActiveX Control

Word inserts the command button as an inline object; that is, part of the current paragraph. You want the command button to be a floating object so that you can position it anywhere on the form. Thus, perform the following steps to convert the command button from inline to floating.

Steps To Format the ActiveX Control

1 Right-click the command button just inserted and then point to Format Control on the shortcut menu (Figure 8-60).

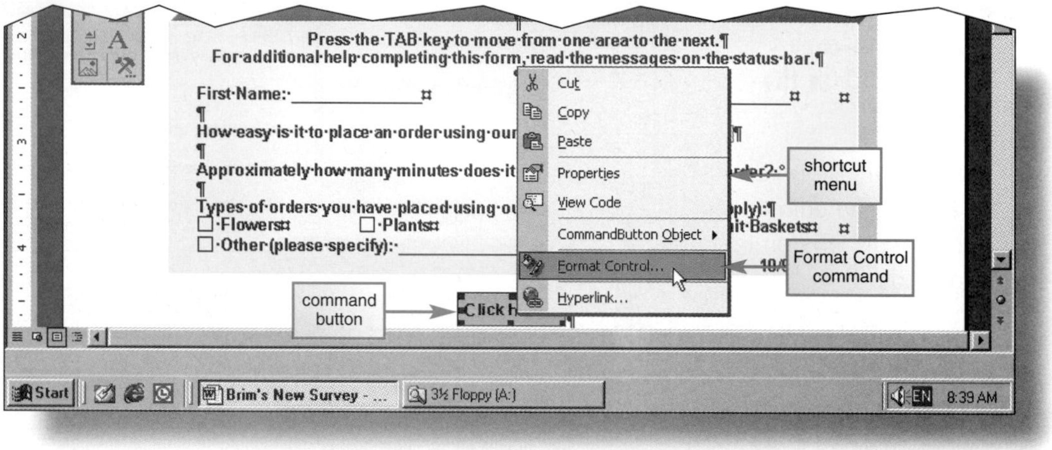

FIGURE 8-60

2 Click Format Control. When the Format Object dialog box displays, if necessary, click the Layout tab. Click Square in the Wrapping style area. Click Center in the Horizontal alignment area. Point to the OK button.

Word displays the Format Object dialog box (Figure 8-61). A square wrapping style changes an object to floating.

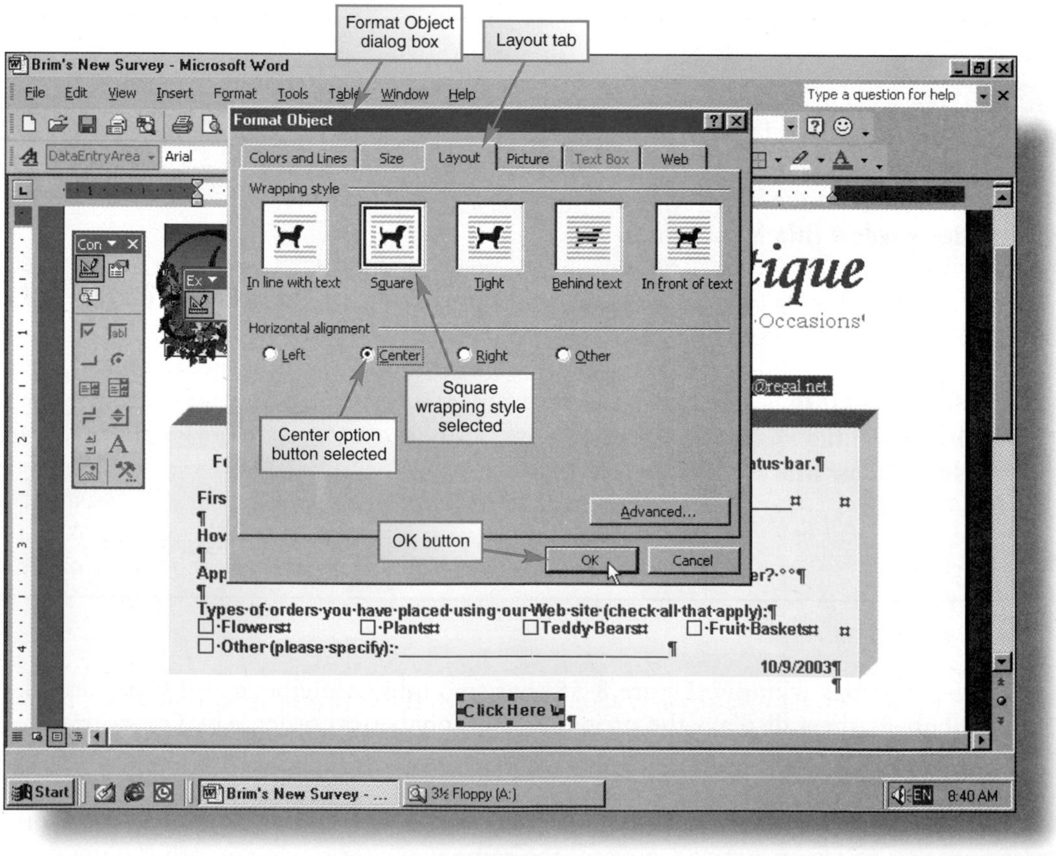

FIGURE 8-61

3 Click the OK button. If necessary, drag the right-middle sizing handle to display the entire caption. Drag the control so that approximately one-quarter inch displays between the top of the command button and the bottom of the data entry area.

The command button is positioned as shown in Figure 8-62.

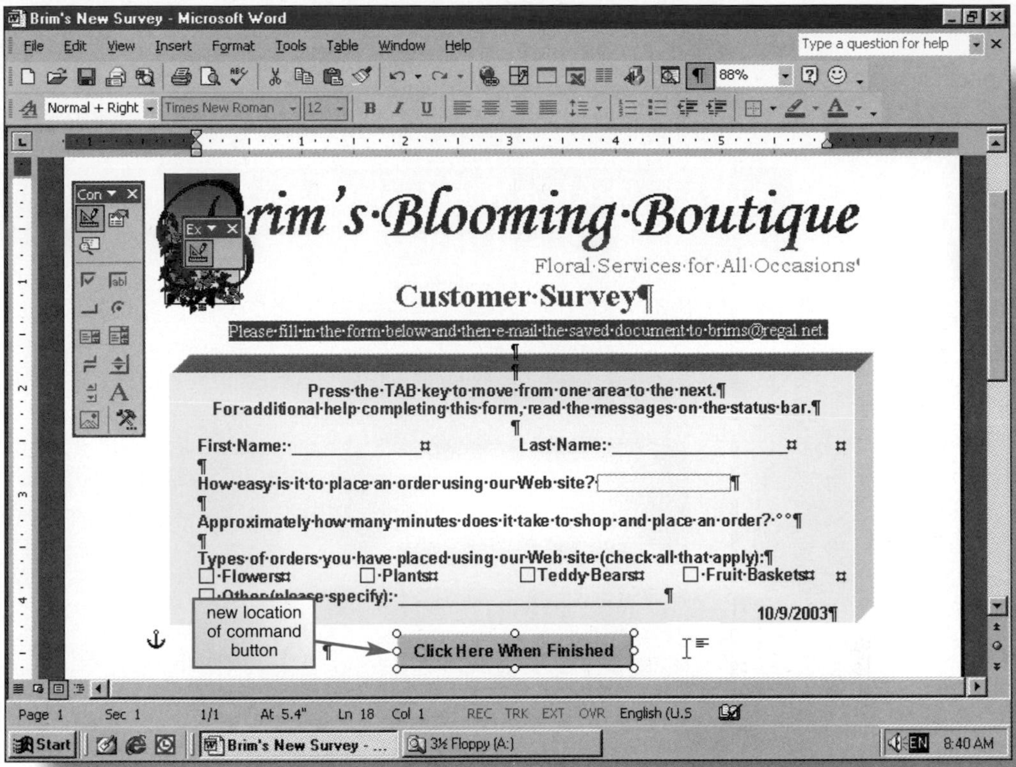

Brim's New Survey - Microsoft Word
Brim's Blooming Boutique
Floral·Services·for·All·Occasions
Customer·Survey¶
Please·fill·in·the·form·below·and·then·e-mail·the·saved·document·to·brims@regal.net.
Press·the·TAB·key·to·move·from·one·area·to·the·next.¶
For·additional·help·completing·this·form,·read·the·messages·on·the·status·bar.¶
First·Name:·
Last·Name:·
How·easy·is·it·to·place·an·order·using·our·Web·site?
Approximately·how·many·minutes·does·it·take·to·shop·and·place·an·order?
Types·of·orders·you·have·placed·using·our·Web·site·(check·all·that·apply):¶
Flowers
Plants
Teddy·Bears
Fruit·Baskets
10/9/2003¶
new location of command button
Click Here When Finished

FIGURE 8-62

Writing the Macro for the ActiveX Control

The next step is to write and then enter the procedure for the macro that will execute when a user clicks the Click Here When Finished button. Clicking the button is the event that triggers execution of the macro.

As mentioned earlier, you should plan a procedure by writing its VBA code on paper similar to that shown in Table 8-8 on the next page. Then, before entering the procedure into the computer, desk check it.

Notice in line 1 that the name of the procedure in the Sub statement is CommandButton1_Click, which Word determines from the name of the button (shown in Figure 8-64 on page WD 8.59), and the event that causes the procedure to execute (Click).

The first executable code statement is an If...Then statement in line 7. This statement tests if the user entered text in the Other text box, which will have a bookmark of OtherText. If it does, then line 8 instructs Word to place an X in the Other check box, which will have a bookmark of OtherCheck; otherwise, Word skips lines 8 and 9 and then proceeds to line 10.

The next executable code statement is in line 11, which displays the Save As dialog box on the screen — allowing the user to save the form. Finally, line 15 displays a message box that contains two variables. The first is for the message text, which is defined in line 14; and the second is for the title bar text, which is defined in line 13. Variables are used to define these elements of the message box, because the text for the title bar and message is so long.

As illustrated earlier in this project, you use the Visual Basic Editor to enter code statements into a procedure. With Word in design mode and the ActiveX control selected, you can click the View Code button on the Control Toolbox toolbar to display the control's procedure in the Code window of the Visual Basic Editor.

Table 8-8 Click Here When Finished Button Procedure

LINE	*VBA CODE STATEMENT*
1	`Private Sub CommandButton1_Click()`
2	`'`
3	`' CommandButton1_Click Macro`
4	`' Executes when user clicks button called Click Here When Finished.`
5	`'`
6	`   'If user entered text in Other text box, put X in Other check box`
7	`   If Left(ActiveDocument.FormFields("OtherText").Result, 1) <> "_" Then`
8	`      ActiveDocument.FormFields("OtherCheck").CheckBox.Value = True`
9	`   End If`
10	`   'Display Save As dialog box`
11	`   Dialogs(wdDialogFileSaveAs).Show`
12	`   'Display thank-you message`
13	`   TitleBarText = "Thank You For Your Time"`
14	`   MessageText = "Please e-mail " & ActiveDocument.FullName & " to brims@regal.net."`
15	`   MsgBox MessageText, , TitleBarText`
16	`End Sub`

The code statements in lines 7 and 8 use bookmarks that need to be defined. You enter a bookmark in the Form Field Options dialog box. Perform the following steps to change the default bookmarks for the Other check box form field and the Other text form field.

TO CHANGE BOOKMARKS FOR FORM FIELDS

1. Double-click the check box form field for Other (shown in Figure 8-63).
2. When the Check Box Form Field Options dialog box displays, double-click the text in the Bookmark text box and then type `OtherCheck` as the new bookmark. Click the OK button.
3. Double-click the text form field for Other (shown in Figure 8-63).
4. When the Text Form Field Options dialog box displays, double-click the text in the Bookmark text box and then type `OtherText` as the new bookmark. Click the OK button.

Word changes form field options as specified in the Form Field Options dialog boxes.

Perform the following steps to enter the code statements for the procedure for the macro that will execute when a user clicks the Click Here When Finished button.

Steps To Enter the Click Here When Finished Button Procedure

1 **With Word in design mode, click the Click Here When Finished button and then point to the View Code button on the Control Toolbox toolbar (Figure 8-63).**

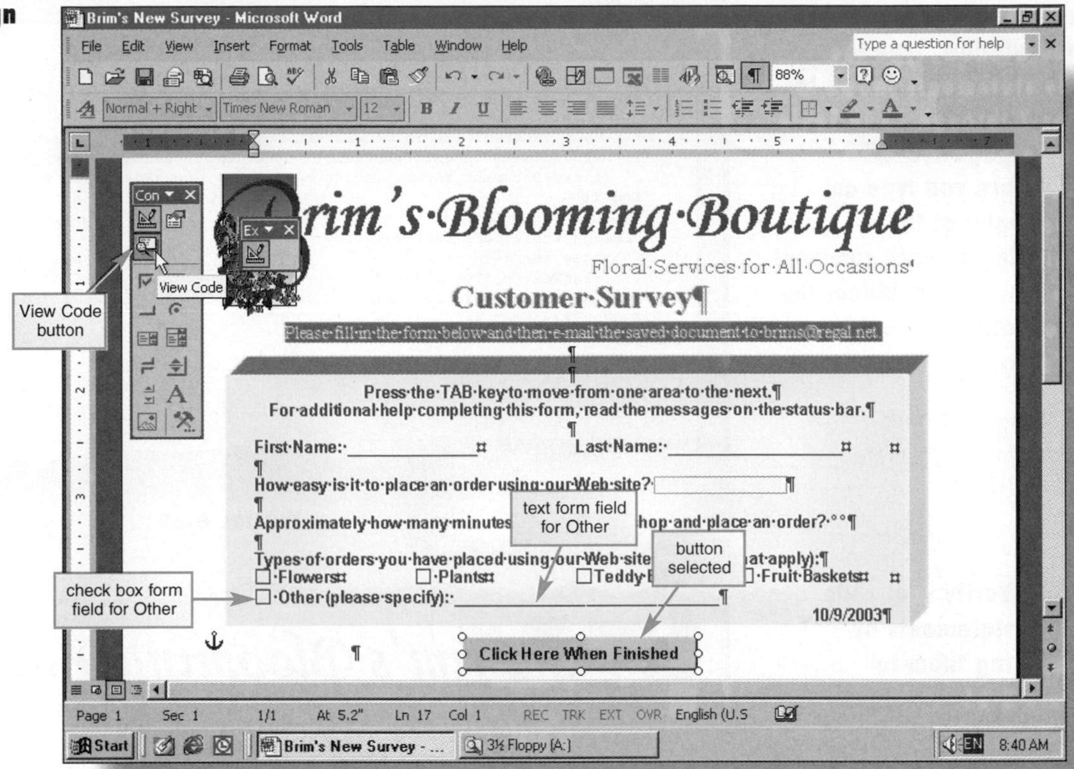

FIGURE 8-63

2 **Click the View Code button. If the Project Explorer window opens, click its Close button. When the Visual Basic Editor window opens, if necessary, double-click the Code window title bar to maximize the window.**

Word starts the Visual Basic Editor and opens the Microsoft Visual Basic window (Figure 8-64). The Visual Basic Editor automatically inserts the Sub and End Sub statements and positions the insertion point between the two statements.

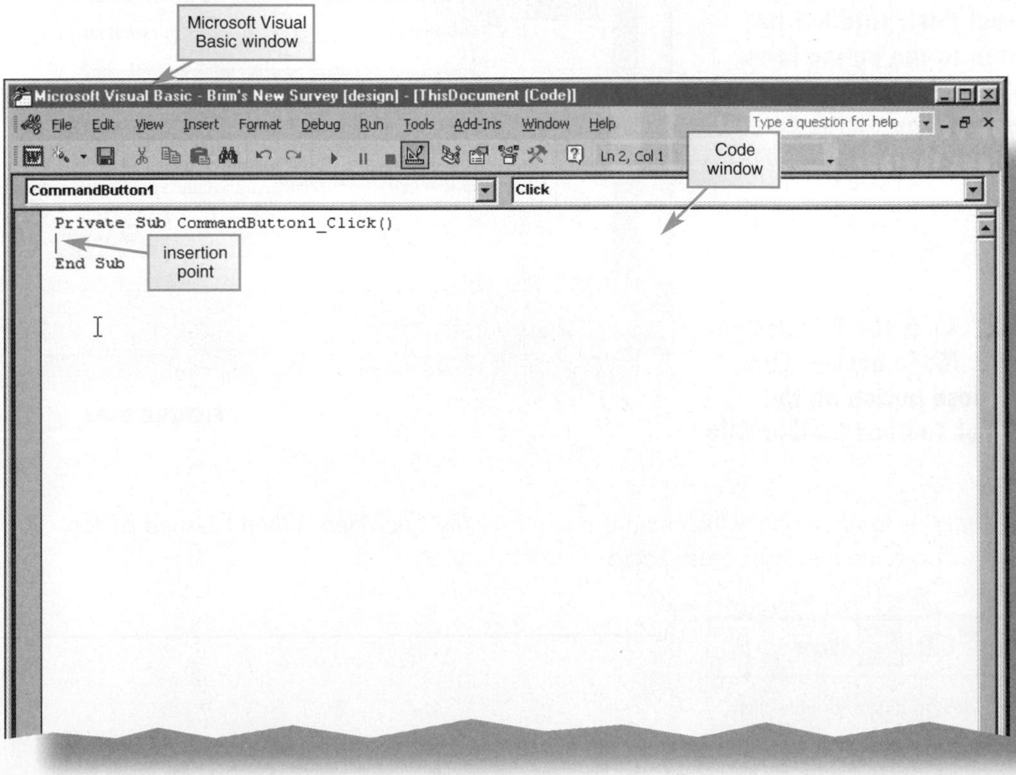

FIGURE 8-64

3 **With the insertion point on the blank line between the Sub and End Sub statements in the Code window, type the code statements shown in lines 2 through 15 in Table 8-8 on page WD 8.58. Make sure you type an apostrophe at the beginning of each comment line. For clarity, indent the code statements as shown in Table 8-8.**

The command button procedure is complete (Figure 8-65).

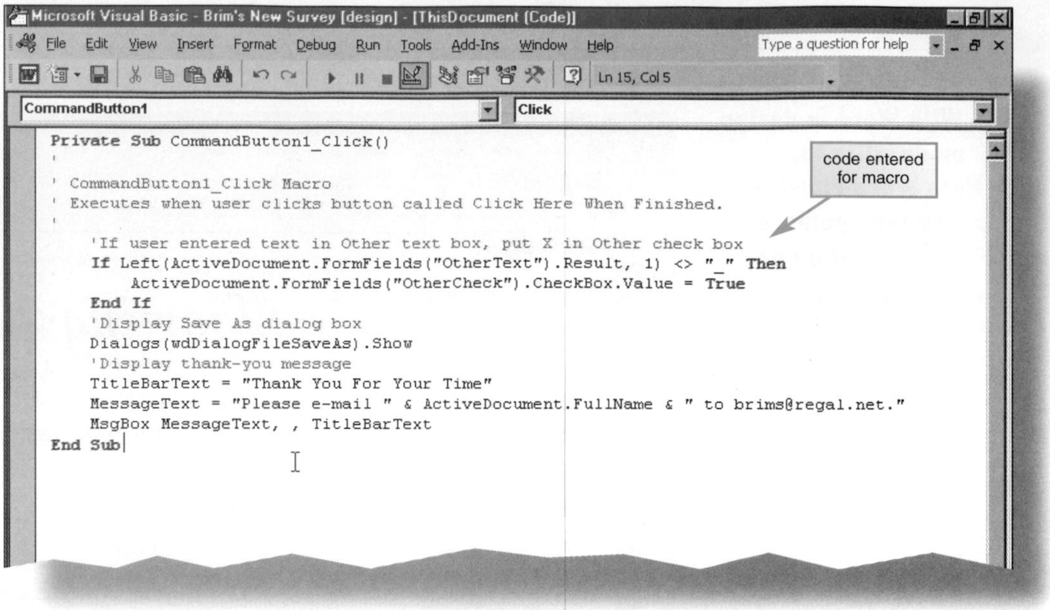

FIGURE 8-65

4 **Verify your code statements by comparing them to Figure 8-65.**

5 **Click the Close button on the right edge of the Microsoft Visual Basic title bar to return to the online form. Point to the Exit Design Mode button on the Control Toolbox toolbar.**

The online form displays as shown in Figure 8-66.

6 **Click the Exit Design Mode button. Click the Close button on the Control Toolbox toolbar title bar.**

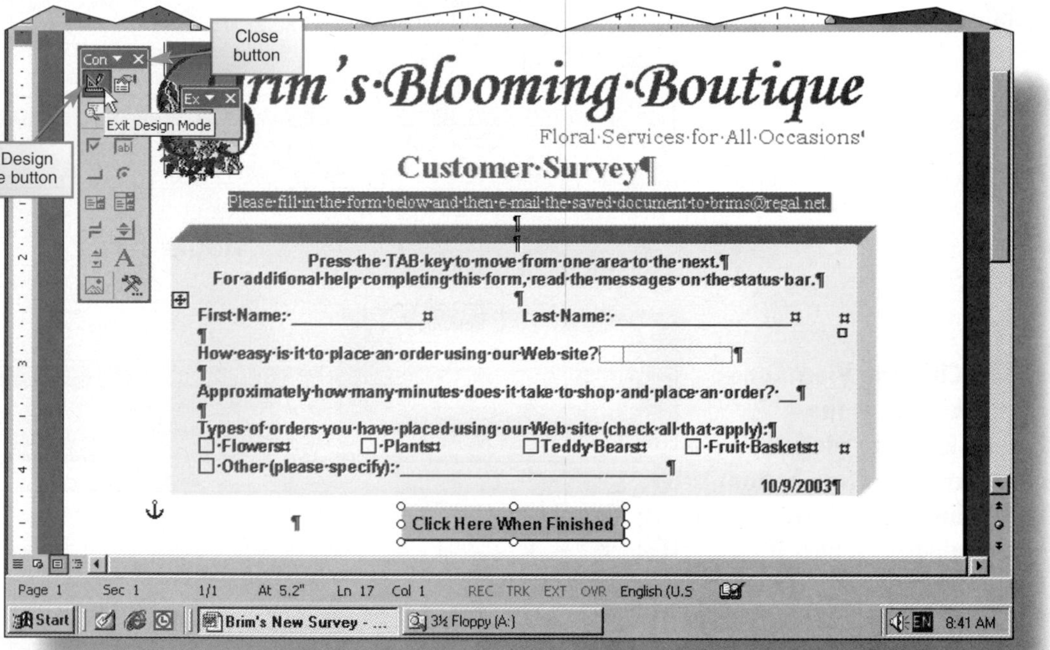

FIGURE 8-66

Word returns to run mode, which means if you click the Click Here When Finished button, Word will execute the associated macro.

Other Ways

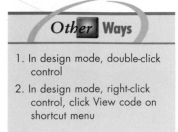

1. In design mode, double-click control
2. In design mode, right-click control, click View code on shortcut menu

More About Visual Basic for Applications

Visual Basic for Applications uses many more statements than those presented in this project. These statements, however, should help you understand the basic composition of a Visual Basic statement. For example, the code statement in line 11 of Table 8-8 on page WD 8.58 that displays the Save As dialog box includes a period. The entry on the left side of the period tells Word which object you want to affect (in this case, the dialog box). An object can be a document, a form field, a bookmark, a dialog box, a button, or any other control on a form. The entry on the right side of the period tells Word what you want to do to the object (in this case, display it).

Earlier you were shown how to change an object's properties using the Properties window (Figure 8-58 on page WD 8.55). This code statement from the NumberOfMinutes macro changed an object's property during execution of a procedure:

```
ActiveDocument.ActiveWindow.View.TableGridlines = False
```

This statement changes the TableGridlines property of the View object in the ActiveWindow object in the ActiveDocument object to false; that is, it hides table gridlines. An equal sign in a code statement instructs Word to make an assignment to a property, variable, or other object. In the previous code statement, the TableGridlines property was set to False.

Now that you have completed the macros, you once again should protect the form and save it, as shown in the following steps.

TO PROTECT THE FORM

1. Click Tools on the menu bar and then click Protect Document.
2. When the Protect Document dialog box displays, click Forms in the Protect document for area, and then click the OK button.

Word protects the form.

TO SAVE A DOCUMENT

1. Click the Save button on the Standard toolbar.

Word saves the template with the same file name, Brim's New Survey.

More About

Web Forms

If you intend to publish a form on the World Wide Web, you should limit ActiveX controls to the standard HTML controls, which include the following: check box, drop-down list box, text box, submit and reset password, option button, list box, text area, submit with image, and hidden.

More About

Printing

If you want to print a form and wish to save ink, print faster, or minimize printer overrun errors, print a draft. Click File on the menu bar, click Print, click the Options button, place a check mark in the Draft output check box, and then click the OK button in each dialog box.

Testing the Online Form

The modifications and macros for the Brim's New Survey file are complete. You now are ready to test the form.

Perform the steps on the next page to test the form.

Steps To Test the Form

1 Click the Explorer program button on the taskbar to display Windows Explorer and then double-click the Brim's New Survey icon in the Contents pane to display a new Word document based on the contents of the Customer Survey. If Word displays a Security Warning dialog box, click the Enable Macros button.

As instructed by the AutoNew macro, the Word document zooms page width, scrolls down six lines, hides table gridlines, and hides formatting marks (Figure 8-67).

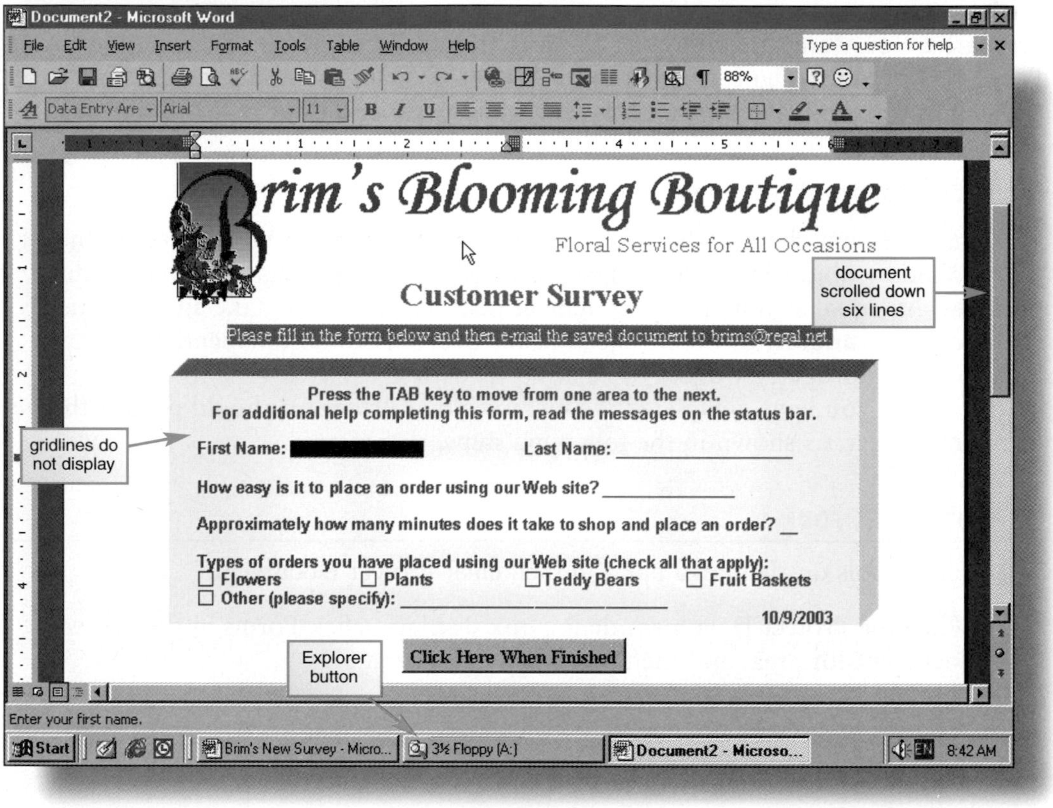
Document2 - Microsoft Word
File Edit View Insert Format Tools Table Window Help
Type a question for help
Brim's Blooming Boutique
Floral Services for All Occasions
Customer Survey
Please fill in the form below and then e-mail the saved document to brims@regal.net.
document scrolled down six lines
Press the TAB key to move from one area to the next.
For additional help completing this form, read the messages on the status bar.
gridlines do not display
First Name:
Last Name:
How easy is it to place an order using our Web site?
Approximately how many minutes does it take to shop and place an order?
Types of orders you have placed using our Web site (check all that apply):
Flowers
Plants
Teddy Bears
Fruit Baskets
Other (please specify):
10/9/2003
Explorer button
Click Here When Finished
Enter your first name.
Start
Brim's New Survey - Micro...
3½ Floppy (A:)
Document2 - Microso...
8:42 AM

FIGURE 8-67

2 **With the selection in the First Name text box, type** Latonia **and then press the TAB key. Type** Brown **in the Last Name text box. Press the TAB key to select the ease of use drop-down list box and display its box arrow. Click the ease of use box arrow and then click Very Easy. Press the TAB key. Type** ab **in the number of minutes text box. Press the TAB key. When the error message displays, point to the OK button.**

As instructed by the NumberOfMinutes macro, an error message displays (Figure 8-68).

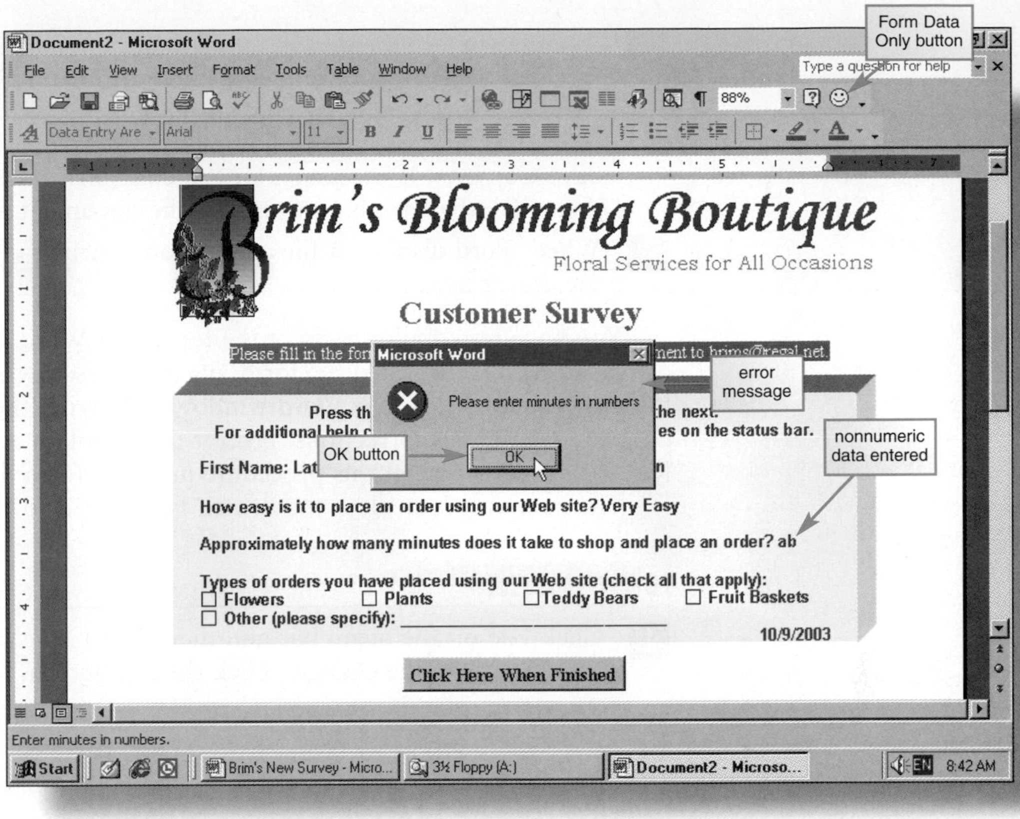

FIGURE 8-68

3 **Click the OK button in the message box. Type** 15 **in the number of minutes text box. Press the TAB key. Click the following check boxes: Plants and Teddy Bears. Press the TAB key three times to position the selection in the Other text box. Type** Collectible **in the Other text box.**

The data is entered.

To finish testing the online form, you will test the form's command button as well as the Form Data Only button in the Standard toolbar.

TO FINISH TESTING THE ONLINE FORM

1. Click the Click Here When Finished button.
2. As defined by the CommandButton1_Click procedure, Word displays the Save As dialog box. Change the Save in location to 3½ Floppy (A:). Type `Brown Form` in the File name text box and then click the Save button in the Save As dialog box.
3. When the save process is complete, the CommandButton1_Click procedure then displays a thank-you message box that indicates the name and location of the file the user should e-mail back to the boutique (shown in Figure 8-1c on page WD 8.05).
4. Click the OK button in the message box. Notice that Word placed an X in the Other check box.

5. Assume you are the person tabulating the form results at the boutique and just received the Brown Form. Click the Form Data Only button on the Standard toolbar, which instructs Word to place a check mark in the Save form data only check box in the Options dialog box. Click File on the menu bar and then click Save Copy As. If necessary, type `Brown Form` in the File name text box and then click the Save button to save the document as a text file.
6. When Word displays a file conversion warning message, click the OK button in the dialog box.

You have tested all aspects of the form. If a Word or Visual Basic error message displayed while you tested the form, make necessary corrections and then retest the form. To do this, close the Word window displaying the Brown Form. Unprotect the template. Make the corrections. Protect the template again. Save the template again. Retest the form. Repeat this procedure until the form displays as intended.

The next step is to close the Brown Form file and then close Windows Explorer.

TO CLOSE A FILE

1. Click File on the menu bar and then click Close. If a Word dialog box displays asking to save the changes, click the No button.

Word closes the Brown Form file.

TO CLOSE WINDOWS EXPLORER

1. Click the Close button on the Explorer window's title bar.

Windows Explorer closes.

Digital Signatures

More About

Certified Digital Signatures

Several companies provide authenticated, certified digital signatures via the Web. For more information about digital signatures, visit the Word 2002 More About Web Page (scsite.com/wd2002/more.htm) and then click Certified Digital Signatures.

Some users prefer to attach a digital signature to verify the authenticity of a document. A **digital signature** is an electronic, encrypted, and secure stamp of authentication on a document. This signature confirms that the file originated from the signer (file developer) and that it has not been altered.

A digital signature references a digital certificate. A **digital certificate** is an attachment to a file, macro project, or e-mail message that vouches for its authenticity, provides secure encryption, or supplies a verifiable signature. Many users who receive online forms enable the macros based on whether they are digitally signed by a developer on the user's list of trusted sources.

You can obtain a digital certificate from a commercial **certification authority**, from your network administrator, or you can create a digital signature yourself. A digital certificate you create yourself is not issued by a formal certification authority. Thus, signed macros using such a certificate are referred to as **self-signed projects**. Certificates you create yourself are considered unauthenticated and still will generate a warning when opened if the security level is set to high or medium. Many users, however, consider self-signed projects safer to open than those with no certificates at all.

Attaching a Digital Signature to a File

A **file digital signature** is a digital signature that displays when you e-mail a document from Word. Word will display the digital signature whenever the document is opened. In the following steps, you will digitally sign a file from the Data Disk that accompanies this book. If you did not download the Data Disk, see the inside back cover for instructions for downloading the Data Disk or see your instructor.

Perform the following steps to open the file from the Data Disk and then save it with a new name.

More About

Digital Signatures

When you attach a digital signature to a macro project, Word will display the digital signature when the user of the file is asked to enable macros. When you modify code in a signed macro project, its digital signature usually is removed. For this reason, you should digitally sign macros only after your solution has been saved, tested, and is ready for distribution.

TO OPEN A FILE FROM THE DATA DISK AND SAVE IT WITH A NEW NAME

1. With the Data Disk in drive A, click the Open button on the Standard toolbar.
2. When the Open dialog box displays, click 3½ Floppy (A:) in the Look in list. When the list of files displays, double-click the MyFamily Questionnaire icon in the Contents pane.
3. When the file displays, click the Zoom box arrow and then click Page Width. Scroll down so the complete form displays on the screen.
4. Click Tools on the menu bar and then click Unprotect Document.
5. Click File on the menu bar and then click Save As.
6. When the Save As dialog box displays, if necessary, click 3½ Floppy (A:) in the Look in list. Type `Revised Questionnaire` in the File name text box and then click the Save button in the Save As dialog box.

The file is saved on the floppy disk with the name, Revised Questionnaire.

Perform the following steps to digitally sign the file.

Steps To Digitally Sign a File

1. **Click Tools on the menu bar, and then click Options. When the Options dialog box displays, if necessary, click the Security tab. Point to the Digital Signatures button.**

The Security sheet displays options for passwords and protection, as well as digital signatures (Figure 8-69).

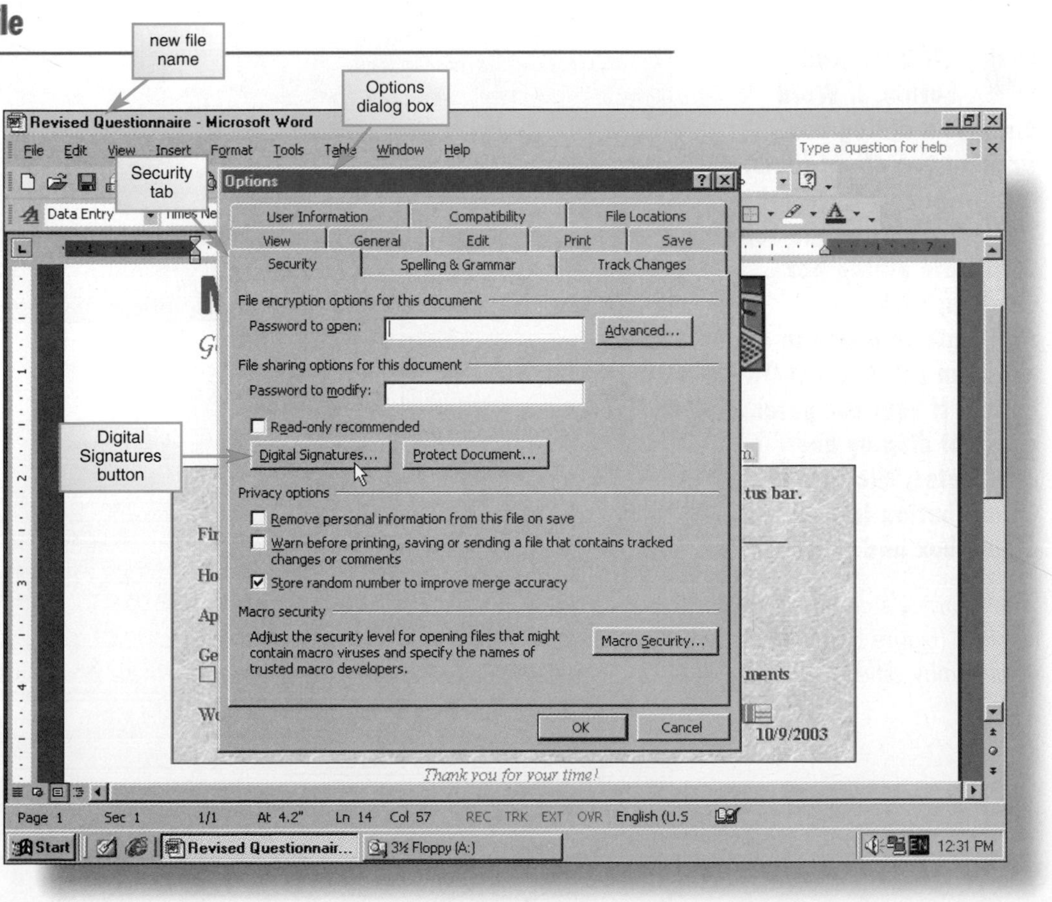

FIGURE 8-69

2 **Click the Digital Signatures button. When the Digital Signature dialog box displays, point to the Add button.**

Your Signer list may display previous certificates (Figure 8-70).

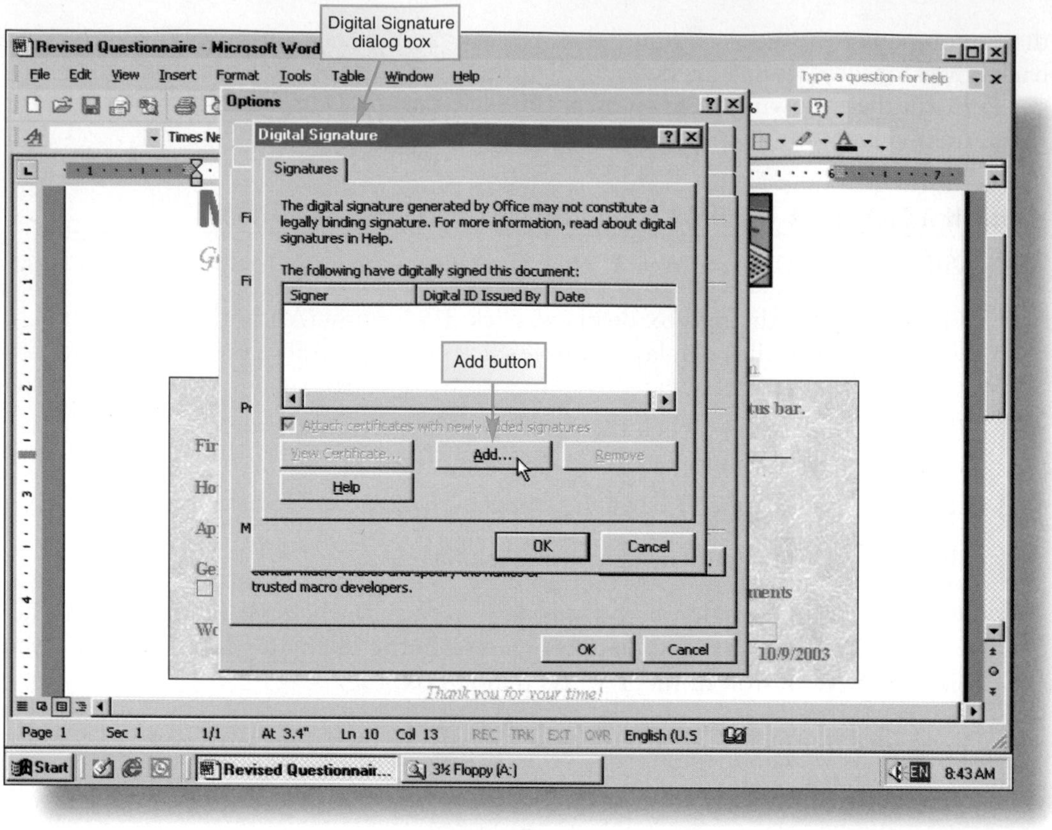

FIGURE 8-70

3 **Click the Add button. If Word displays a dialog box, warning you about fonts, text, or pictures, click the Yes button. When the Select Certificate dialog box displays, click the certificate you wish to add and then point to the OK button. If your computer does not display any certificates, click the Cancel button in each dialog box and skip Step 4.**

The boutique's certificate displays (Figure 8-71). Your display may differ.

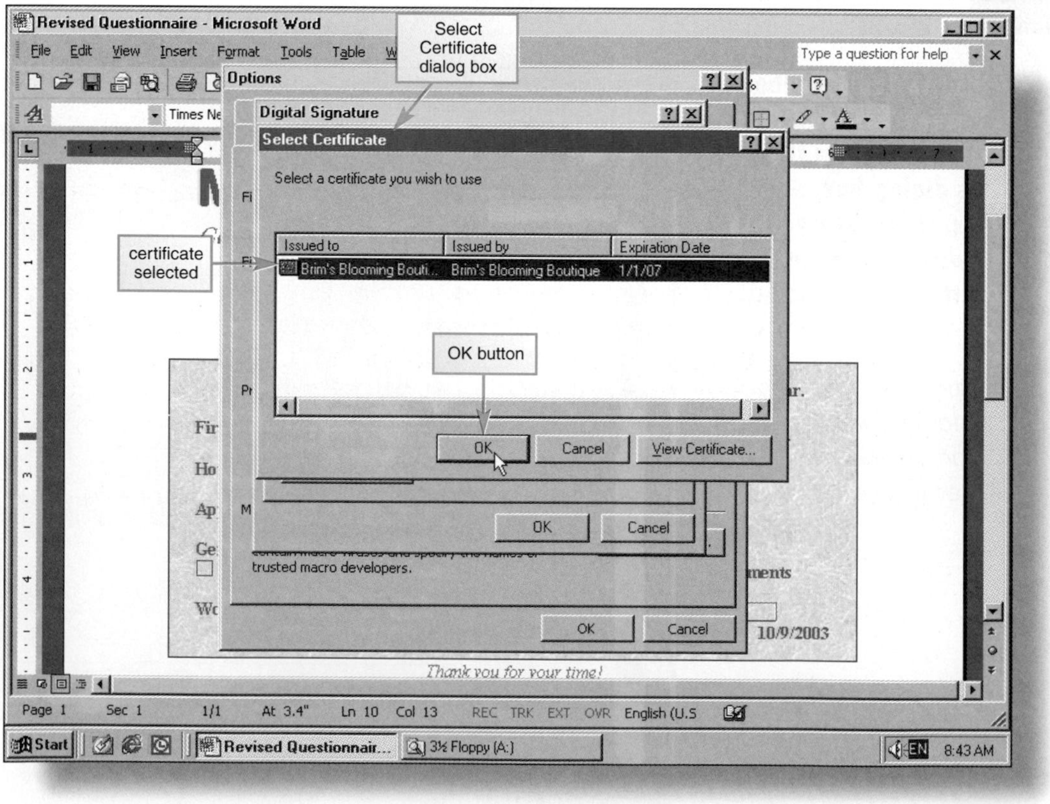

FIGURE 8-71

4 Click the OK button. When the Digital Signature dialog box is visible again, click the OK button. When the Options dialog box is visible again, click the OK button.

A certificate icon displays on the status bar, and the title bar displays (Signed) after the file name (Figure 8-72).

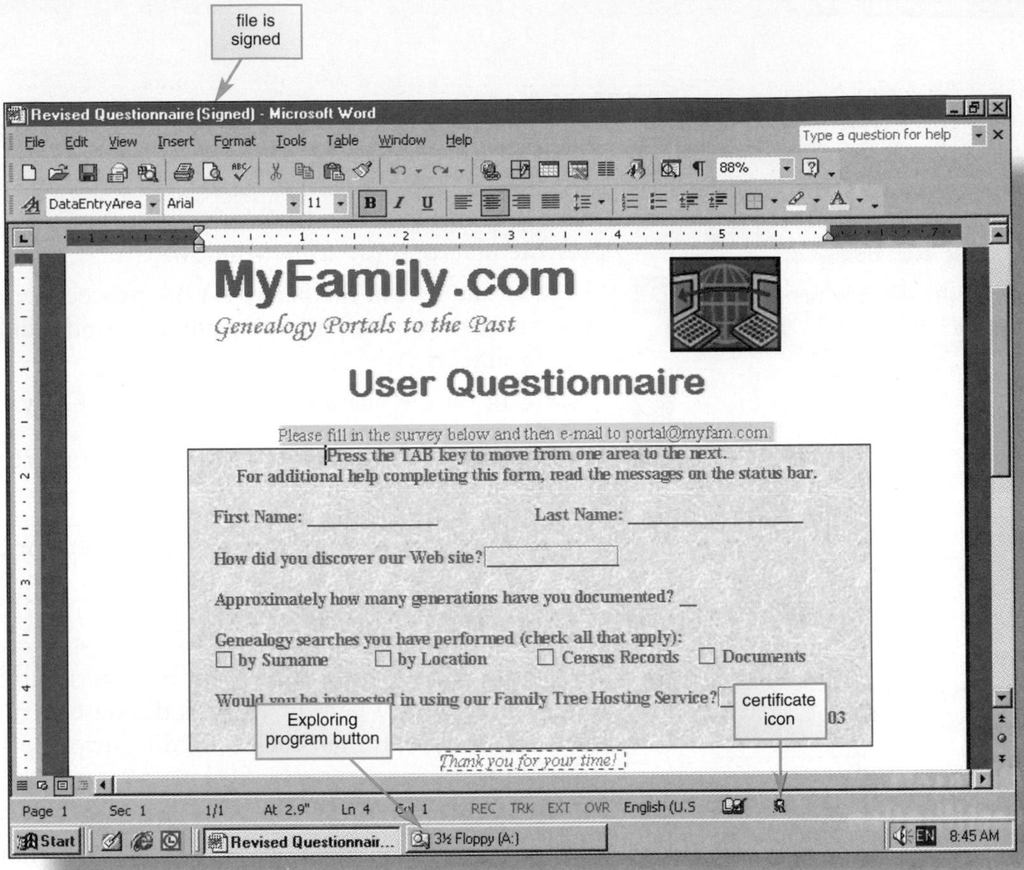

FIGURE 8-72

When you open a digitally signed document, Word displays a message announcing the signature on the status bar while the file opens. Once the file is opened, Word displays a certification icon on the status bar. You can double-click the icon to find out who digitally signed the document. The word, (Signed), also displays on the title bar, indicating the document is digitally signed.

If you do not have any digital certificates on your computer, you can create one by running a program named **Selfcert.exe** that is supplied with your Office program. Be aware that running this program multiple times can create duplicate digital signatures on the computer. You cannot remove duplicate digital signatures using Word.

You are finished with the form. Perform the following step to quit Word and close Windows Explorer.

> **More About**
>
> **Self Certification**
>
> Microsoft Office XP uses Microsoft Authenticode technology to enable you to sign a file or a macro project digitally by using a digital certificate. The Selfcert.exe program is supplied with Office XP. The certificate used to create this signature confirms that the macro or document originated from the signer, and the signature confirms that it has not been altered.

TO QUIT WORD

1. Click File on the menu bar and then click Exit.

The Word window closes.

Copying, Renaming, and Deleting Macros

You may find it necessary to copy a macro, rename a macro, or delete a macro. Macros cannot be copied or renamed from Word; instead, you must use the Visual Basic Editor. You can, however, delete a macro from Word.

More About

Quick Reference

For a table that lists how to complete tasks covered in this book using the mouse, menu, shortcut menu, and keyboard see the Quick Reference Summary at the back of this book or visit the Shelly Cashman Series Office XP Web page (scsite.com/offxp/qr.htm) and then click Microsoft Word 2002.

More About

Microsoft Certification

The Microsoft Office User Specialist (MOUS) Certification program provides an opportunity for you to obtain a valuable industry credential — proof that you have the Word 2002 skills required by employers. For more information, see Appendix E or visit the Shelly Cashman Series MOUSE Web page at scsite.com/offxp/cert.htm.

TO COPY A MACRO

1. Click Tools on the menu bar, point to Macro, and then click Macros on the Macro submenu. When the Macros dialog box displays, click the macro name to copy, and then click the Edit button to start the Visual Basic Editor and display the macro in the Code window.
2. Select all the text in the macro's VBA procedure; that is, drag from the Sub statement to the End Sub statement (including the Sub and End Sub statements).
3. Click Edit on the menu bar and then click Copy.
4. Position the insertion point in the destination area. Click Edit on the menu bar and then click Paste.

You can paste a macro into the same document or a different document.

TO RENAME A MACRO

1. Click Tools on the menu bar, point to Macro, and then click Macros on the Macro submenu. When the Macros dialog box displays, click the macro name to be renamed, and then click the Edit button to start the Visual Basic Editor and display the macro in the Code window.
2. Select the macro name following the keyword Sub at the beginning of the macro's procedure and then type a new macro name.

The macro will be renamed in the Macros dialog box.

TO DELETE A MACRO

1. Click Tools on the menu bar, point to Macro, and then click Macros on the Macro submenu.
2. When the Macros dialog box displays, click the macro name to be deleted, and then click the Delete button.
3. Click the Yes button in the Microsoft Word dialog box.

CASE PERSPECTIVE SUMMARY

Before showing the modified Brim's New Survey to your aunt, you decide to have two of your fellow students test it to be sure it works properly. They find one error. You unprotect the template, fix the error, protect the form again, and then test it one final time, just to be sure the error is fixed. Then, you e-mail the Customer Survey to Aunt Carol for her review. She is quite pleased with the results. Realizing the power of macros and Visual Basic for Applications, she asks you to train three members of her staff on how to create macros and VBA procedures in Word.

Project Summary

Project 8 introduced you to working with macros and Visual Basic for Applications (VBA). You modified the template for the online form created in Project 7. To change its appearance, you inserted a graphic from the Web, changed the text by creating and applying a new style, filled the drawing object with a gradient effect, and then added a 3-D effect to the rectangle drawing object. Then, you created a macro using the macro recorder and assigned the macro to a toolbar button. Next, you recorded an automatic macro. You viewed the macro's code using the Visual Basic Editor and added comments and code statements to the macro. You created another macro that executed when the user exits a form field. After inserting an ActiveX control, you set its properties, formatted it, and wrote a VBA procedure for it. Finally, you attached a digital signature.

What You Should Know

Having completed this project, you should now be able to perform the following tasks:

- Add a 3-D Effect *(WD 8.21)*
- Add Code Statements to a Procedure *(WD 8.43)*
- Add Comments to a Procedure *(WD 8.41)*
- Apply a Style Using a Shortcut Key *(WD 8.19)*
- Change a Bookmark for a Drop-Down Form Field *(WD 8.46)*
- Change Bookmarks for Form Fields *(WD 8.58)*
- Change the Graphic *(WD 8.12)*
- Change Options for a Text Form Field *(WD 8.45)*
- Close a File *(WD 8.64)*
- Close Windows Explorer *(WD 8.64)*
- Copy a Macro *(WD 8.68)*
- Create a Style That Has a Shortcut Key *(WD 8.17)*
- Create an Automatic Macro *(WD 8.33)*
- Customize a Toolbar *(WD 8.28)*
- Delete a Macro *(WD 8.68)*
- Delete the Thank-You Message and Resize the Rectangle *(WD 8.21)*
- Digitally Sign a File *(WD 8.65)*
- Display Formatting Marks *(WD 8.09)*
- Enter the Click Here When Finished Button Procedure *(WD 8.59)*
- Enter the NumberOfMinutes Procedure *(WD 8.50)*
- Fill a Drawing Object with a Gradient Fill Effect *(WD 8.20)*
- Finish Testing the Online Form *(WD 8.63)*
- Format Text in a Text Box *(WD 8.14)*
- Format the ActiveX Control *(WD 8.56)*
- Format the Form Instructions *(WD 8.15)*
- Insert a Graphic File from the Data Disk *(WD 8.13)*
- Insert a Visual Basic Procedure *(WD 8.47)*
- Insert an ActiveX Control *(WD 8.52)*
- Insert and Format a Text Box *(WD 8.13)*
- Modify Existing Code *(WD 8.42)*
- Open a File from the Data Disk and Save It with a New Name *(WD 8.65)*
- Protect the Form *(WD 8.61)*
- Quit the Visual Basic Editor *(WD 8.43)*
- Quit Word *(WD 8.67)*
- Record a Macro and Assign It a Shortcut Key *(WD 8.24)*
- Rename a Macro *(WD 8.68)*
- Reset Menus and Toolbars *(WD 8.09)*
- Run a Macro *(WD 8.27)*
- Run a Macro When a User Exits a Form Field *(WD 8.51)*
- Save a Document *(WD 8.22, WD 8.61)*
- Save a Document with a New File Name *(WD 8.07)*
- Set a Security Level in Word *(WD 8.10)*
- Set Properties of an ActiveX Control *(WD 8.54)*
- Start and Customize Word and Open an Office Document *(WD 8.07)*
- Test the AutoNew Macro *(WD 8.36)*
- Test the Form *(WD 8.62)*
- Uncheck the Save Data Only for Forms Check Box *(WD 8.28, WD 8.32)*
- Unprotect a Document *(WD 8.08)*
- View a Macro's VBA Code *(WD 8.38)*
- Zoom Page Width *(WD 8.09)*

Learn It Online

Instructions: To complete exercises 1 through 6, start your browser, click the Address bar, and then enter `scsite.com/offxp/exs.htm`. When the Office XP Learn It Online page displays, follow the instructions in the exercises.

1 Project Reinforcement TF, MC, and SA

Below Word Project 8, click the Project Reinforcement link. Print the quiz by clicking Print on the File menu. Answer each question. Write your first and last name at the top of each page, and then hand in the printout to your instructor.

2 Flash Cards

Below Word Project 8, click the Flash Cards link. When Flash Cards displays, read the instructions. Type `20` (or a number specified by your instructor) in the Number of Playing Cards text box, type your name in the Name text box, and then click the Flip Card button. When the flash card displays, read the question and then click the Answer box arrow to select an answer. Flip through Flash Cards. Click Print on the File menu to print the last flash card if your score is 15 (75%) correct or greater and then hand it in to your instructor. If your score is less than 15 (75%) correct, then redo this exercise by clicking the Replay button.

3 Practice Test

Below Word Project 8, click the Practice Test link. Answer each question, enter your first and last name at the bottom of the page, and then click the Grade Test button. When the graded practice test displays on your screen, click Print on the File menu to print a hard copy. Continue to take practice tests until you score 80% or better. Hand in a printout of the final practice test to your instructor.

4 Who Wants to Be a Computer Genius?

Below Word Project 8, click the Computer Genius link. Read the instructions, enter your first and last name at the bottom of the page, and then click the Play button. Hand in your score to your instructor.

5 Wheel of Terms

Below Word Project 8, click the Wheel of Terms link. Read the instructions, and then enter your first and last name and your school name. Click the Play button. Hand in your score to your instructor.

6 Crossword Puzzle Challenge

Below Word Project 8, click the Crossword Puzzle Challenge link. Read the instructions, and then enter your first and last name. Click the Play button. Work the crossword puzzle. When you are finished, click the Submit button. When the crossword puzzle redisplays, click the Print button. Hand in the printout.

7 Tips and Tricks

Below Word Project 8, click the Tips and Tricks link. Click a topic that pertains to Project 8. Right-click the information and then click Print on the shortcut menu. Construct a brief example of what the information relates to in Word to confirm you understand how to use the tip or trick. Hand in the example and printed information.

online

8 Newsgroups

Below Word Project 8, click the Newsgroups link. Click a topic that pertains to Project 8. Print three comments. Hand in the comments to your instructor.

9 Expanding Your Horizons

Below Word Project 8, click the Articles for Microsoft Word link. Click a topic that pertains to Project 8. Print the information. Construct a brief example of what the information relates to in Word to confirm you understand the contents of the article. Hand in the example and printed information to your instructor.

10 Search Sleuth

Below Word Project 8, click the Search Sleuth link. To search for a term that pertains to this project, select a term below the Project 8 title and then use the Google search engine at google.com (or any major search engine) to display and print two Web pages that present information on the term. Hand in the printouts to your instructor.

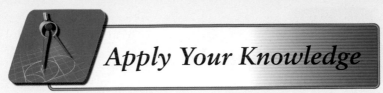

Apply Your Knowledge

1 Debugging VBA Code

Instructions: In this assignment, you access a template through Windows Explorer. As shown in Figure 8-73, the template contains an online form. The form contains two macros: one that executes when you initially display the form on the screen, and another that executes when you click the command button at the bottom of the screen. Each macro contains one coding error. You are to test the code by filling in the form. Then, correct the Visual Basic errors as they display on the screen.

The template is located on the Data Disk. If you did not download the Data Disk, see the inside back cover for instructions for downloading the Data Disk or see your instructor.

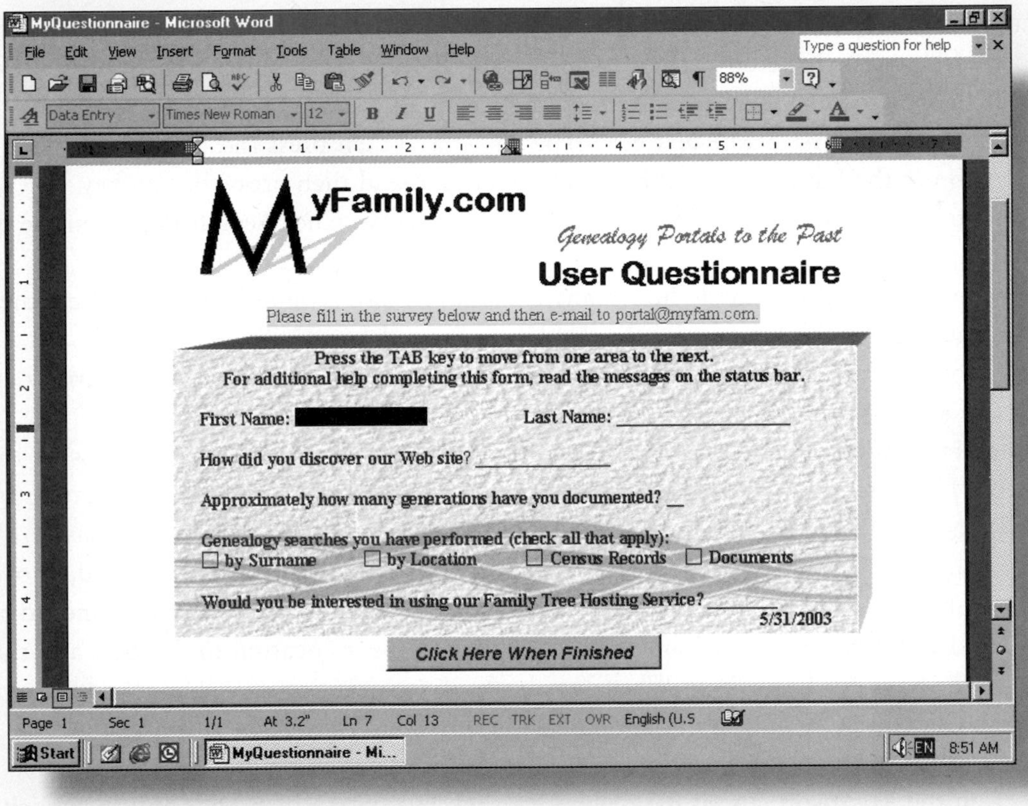

FIGURE 8-73

(continued)

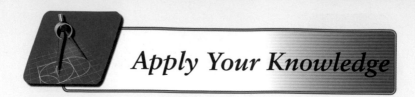

Apply Your Knowledge

Debugging VBA Code *(continued)*

Perform the following tasks:

1. Right-click the My Computer icon on the Windows desktop and then click Explore on the shortcut menu. When the Explorer window opens, click the Address text box to select it. With the Data Disk in drive A, type `a:` and then press the ENTER key. Double-click the MyQuestionnaire icon in the contents pane to display a new document based on the MyQuestionnaire template.
2. When Word displays a dialog box about macros, click the Enable Macros button.
3. When a Microsoft Visual Basic error message displays, click its OK button. If necessary, maximize the Microsoft Visual Basic window. Notice the text, .ZoomPageFit =, is highlighted because Visual Basic did not recognize it. The text should say, .Zoom.PageFit = (it is missing the period). Click the selected text and insert the period between the letters m and P. Then, click the Continue button on the Visual Basic Standard toolbar. Close the Microsoft Visual Basic window by clicking its Close button.
4. With the selection in the First Name text box, type `Heinz` and then press the TAB key.
5. With the selection in the Last Name text box, type `Dortmund` and then press the TAB key.
6. With the selection in the drop-down list box, click the box arrow. Click Search Engine in the drop-down list. Press the TAB key.
7. Type `12` in response to Approximately how many generations have you documented? Press the TAB key.
8. Place an X in each of the check boxes by clicking them. Press the TAB key.
9. With the selection on the drop-down list box at the bottom of the form, click the box arrow and then click Yes.
10. Click the Click Here When Finished button. When the Microsoft Visual Basic error message displays, click the OK button. If necessary, click the Microsoft Visual Basic - MyQuestionnaire program button on the taskbar to display the Visual Basic Editor. Notice the code statement that displays the Save As dialog box is highlighted as an error. To the right of the text, Dialogs(wdDialogFileSaveAs)., the word, Show, is missing. Type the word `Show` after the period. Click the Continue button on the Visual Basic Standard toolbar.
11. Type `Dortmund Form` in the Save As dialog box, change the Save in location to drive A, and then click the Save button in the Save As dialog box. When Word asks if you want to save changes to the template, click the No button. Click the OK button in the Thank You For Your Time message box.
12. Print the filled-in form.
13. Press ALT+F11. In the Microsoft Visual Basic window, click File on the menu bar and then click Print. When the Print dialog box displays, click Current Project and then click the OK button.

In the Lab

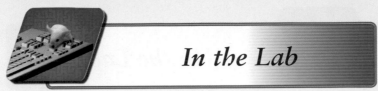

1 Creating an Automatic Macro for an Online Form

Problem: You created the online form shown in Figure 7-73 on page WD 7.64 for Web Management. Your supervisor has asked you to change its appearance and create a macro for the form so it displays properly on the screen when a user first displays it (as a blank form). You modify the form so it looks like the one shown in Figure 8-74.

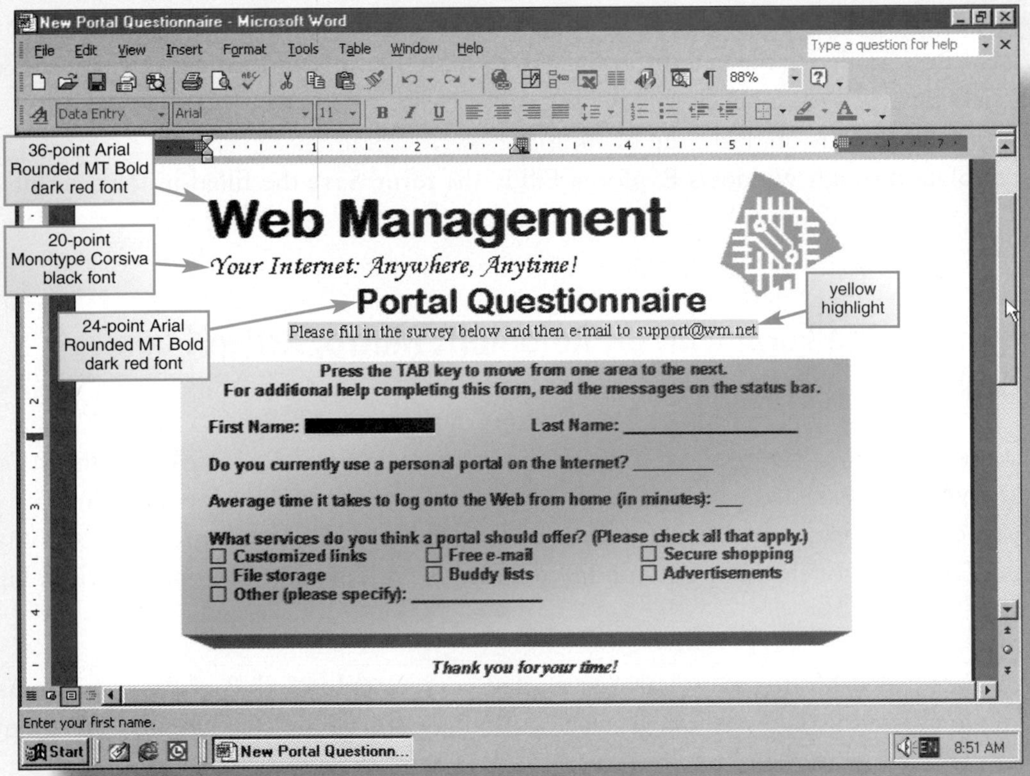

FIGURE 8-74

Instructions:

1. Open the template called Portal Questionnaire that you created in Lab 1 of Project 7 on page WD 7.64. Save the survey with a new file name of New Portal Questionnaire. If you did not complete this lab, see your instructor for a copy.
2. Modify the formats of the company name, business tag line, form title, form instructions, and thank-you message as shown in Figure 8-74. Remove the current clip art and insert the one shown in Figure 8-74. Resize the clip art image to 60 percent of its original size.
3. Change the fill effect in the rectangle drawing object to a two-tone gradient with pale blue and light turquoise. Choose the Diagonal up Shading Style and the lower-right Variant. Add the 3-D effect called 3-D Style 7.

(continued)

In the Lab

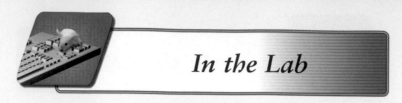

Creating an Automatic Macro for an Online Form *(continued)*

4. Create a new character style called DataEntryArea that is formatted with an 11-point Arial bold black font. Assign a shortcut key of ALT+D. Apply the style to all text in the data entry area.
5. Create an automatic macro called AutoNew using the macro recorder. The macro should change the zoom to page width and scroll down so the entire form fits in the document window. Run the macro to be sure it works.
6. Modify (edit) the macro in the Visual Basic Editor so that it also hides formatting marks and table gridlines. Also, modify the number of lines it scrolls down, if necessary. Run the macro again.
7. Print the Visual Basic code for the macro (in the Visual Basic Editor window, click File on the menu bar, click Print, click Current Project, click the OK button).
8. Protect the form. Save the form. Print the blank form.
9. Access the template through Windows Explorer. Fill in the form. Save the filled-in form. Print the filled-in form.

2 Creating an Online Form with an Automatic Macro, ActiveX Control, and Digital Signature

Problem: You created the online form shown in Figure 7-74 on page WD 7.65 for Montgomery Community College. Your supervisor has asked you to change its appearance, create a macro for the form so it displays properly on the screen when a user first displays it (as a blank form), and add a button that automatically displays the Save As dialog box for the user. You modify the form so it looks like the one shown in Figure 8-75.

Instructions:

1. Open the template called Montgomery Lab Survey that you created in Lab 2 of Project 7 on page WD 7.65. If you did not complete this lab, see your instructor for a copy. Save the survey with a new file name of ML Survey.
2. Remove the current clip art and insert a decorative M graphic from the Web as shown in Figure 8-75. If you do not have access to the Web, the graphic is on the Data Disk in a file called letterM. Resize the graphic to 45 percent of its original size. Delete the M in Montgomery and insert the first three lines of text into a text box. Modify the formats of the college name, form title, and form instructions as shown in Figure 8-75. Left-align the college name. Reposition it, if necessary.
3. Change the fill effect in the rectangle drawing object to the parchment texture. Add the 3-D effect called 3-D Style 19.
4. Create a new character style called DataEntryArea that is formatted with an 11-point Arial bold green font. Assign a shortcut key of ALT+D. Apply the style to all text in the data entry area.
5. Create an automatic macro called AutoNew using the macro recorder. The macro should change the zoom percentage to page width and scroll down so the entire form fits in the document window. Run the macro to be sure it works.
6. Modify (edit) the macro in the Visual Basic Editor so that it also hides formatting marks and table gridlines. Also, modify the number of lines it scrolls down, if necessary. Run the macro again.

In the Lab

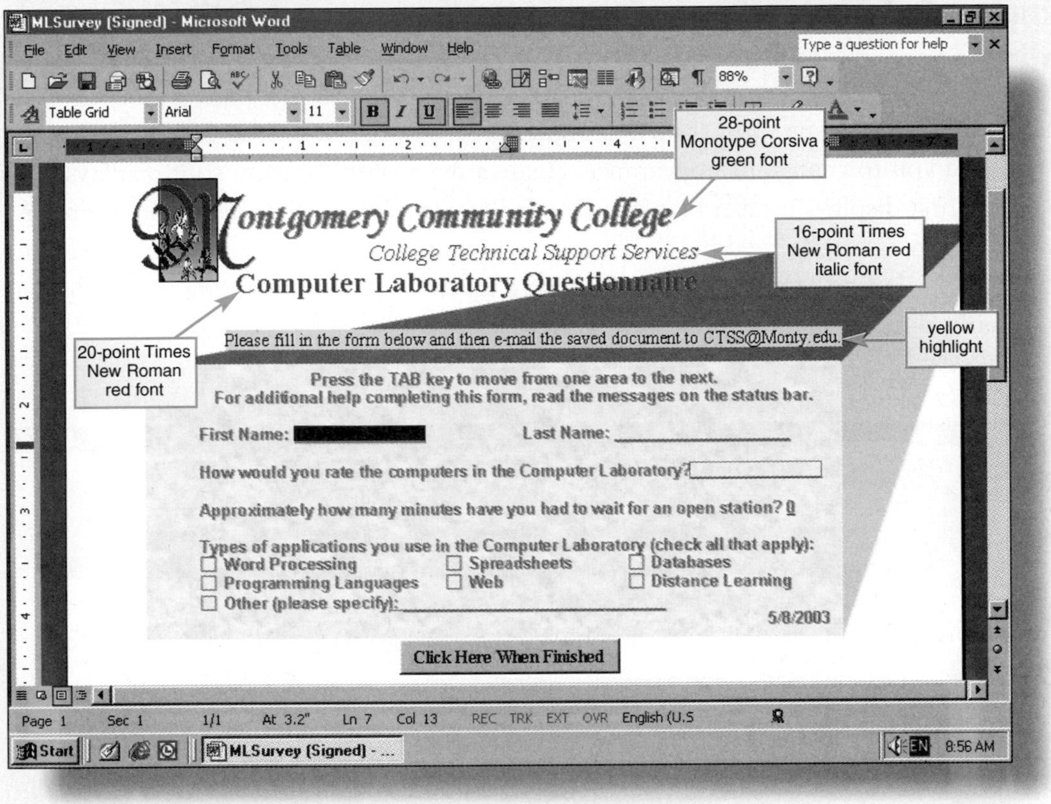

FIGURE 8-75

7. Remove the thank-you message line. Insert a command button ActiveX control. Format the command button as a floating object. Change its caption property to the text, Click Here When Finished. Change its Font property to 12-point Times New Roman bold font. Resize the button so the entire caption displays. Add code to the button so that when the user clicks the button it displays the Save As dialog box and displays a thank-you message.
8. Print the Visual Basic code for the macros (in the Visual Basic Editor window, click File on the menu bar, click Print, click Current Project, click the OK button).
9. Protect the form. Save the form. Print the blank form.
10. Attach a digital signature to the form.
11. Access the template through Windows Explorer. Fill in the form. Save the filled-in form. Print the filled-in form.

In the Lab

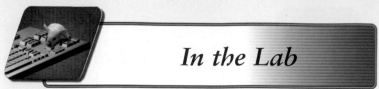

3 Creating an Automatic Macro, Data Entry Macros, and ActiveX Control for an Online Form

Problem: You created the online form shown in Figure 7-75 on page WD 7.66 for K&F Premier Movies. Your supervisor has asked you to change its appearance, create a macro for the form so it displays properly on the screen when a user first displays it (as a blank form), and create a macro that displays an error message when the user leaves the numeric rating field blank or enters a nonnumeric entry. Add a button that automatically displays the Save As dialog box for the user, and create a macro and corresponding button on the toolbar that places a check mark in the Save form data only check box. You modify the form so it looks like the one shown in Figure 8-76.

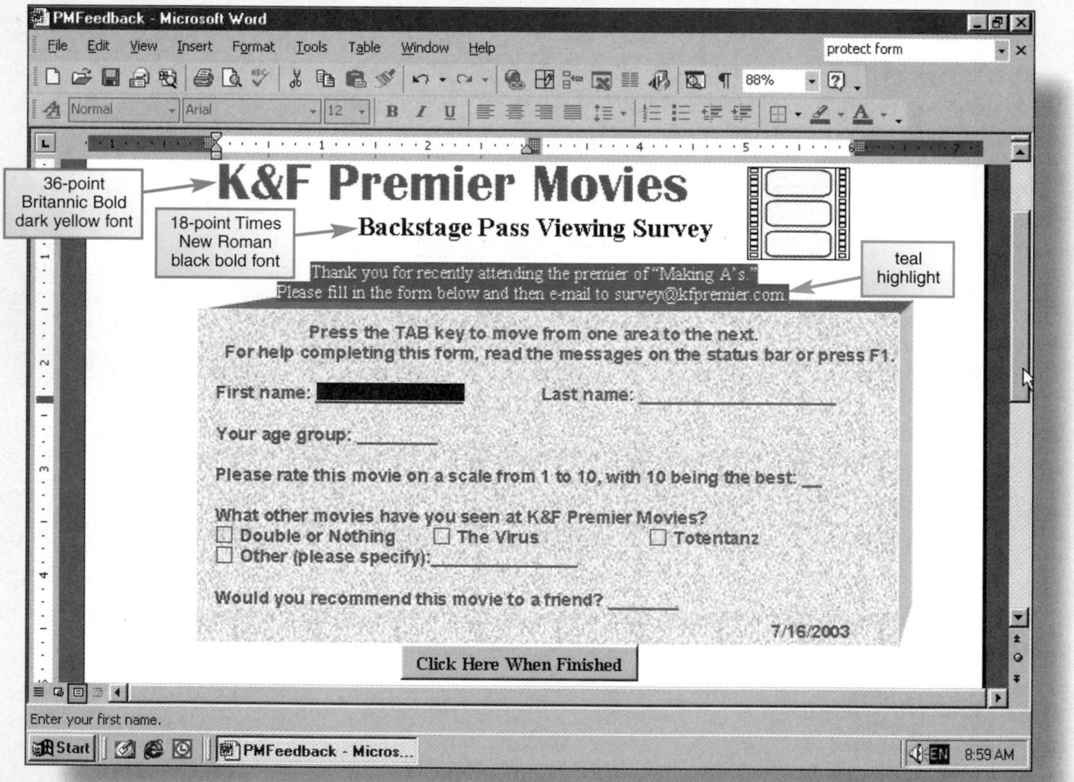

FIGURE 8-76

Instructions:

1. Open the template called Premier Movie Feedback that you created in Lab 3 of Project 7 on page WD 7.66. If you did not complete this lab, see your instructor for a copy. Save the survey with a new file name of PM Feedback.
2. Modify the formats of the company name, form title, and form instructions as shown in Figure 8-76. Move the current clip art to the right of the title as shown in Figure 8-76. Left-align the company name. Reposition it, if necessary.

In the Lab

3. Change the fill effect in the rectangle drawing object to the newsprint texture. Add the 3-D effect called 3-D Style 11.
4. Create a new character style called DataEntryArea that is formatted with a 12-point Arial bold teal font. Assign a shortcut key of ALT+D. Apply the style to all text in the data entry area.
5. Create an automatic macro called AutoNew using the macro recorder. The macro should change the zoom percentage to page width and scroll down so the entire form fits in the document window. Run the macro to be sure it works.
6. Modify (edit) the macro in the Visual Basic Editor so that it also hides formatting marks and table gridlines. Also, modify the number of lines it scrolls down, if necessary. Run the macro again.
7. Create a macro that displays an error message when the user exits the rating field if the user leaves the entry blank or enters a nonnumeric entry.
8. Remove the thank-you message line. Insert a command button ActiveX control. Format the command button as a floating object. Change its caption property to the text, Click Here When Finished. If necessary, change its Font property to 12-point Times New Roman bold font. Resize the button so the entire caption displays. Add code to the button so that when the user clicks the button, it displays the Save As dialog box and displays a thank-you message.
9. Record a macro that places a check mark in the Save data only for forms check box in the Save sheet in the Options dialog box. Create a toolbar button for this macro; use the image of a coffee cup for the button. Also, add a command to the Tools menu for this macro. (For information on adding commands to menus, also see Appendix D.)
10. Copy the AutoNew macro to a macro called TestMacro. Change the TestMacro name to the name MacroTest.
11. Print the Visual Basic code for the macros (in the Visual Basic Editor window, click File on the menu bar, click Print, click Current Project, and then click the OK button).
12. Delete the macro called MacroTest.
13. Delete the coffee cup button from the toolbar. Delete the macro command from the Tools menu.
14. Protect the form. Save the form. Print the blank form.
15. Access the template through Windows Explorer. Fill in the form. Save and then print the filled-in form.

Cases and Places

The difficulty of these case studies varies:
◗ are the least difficult; ◗◗ are more difficult; and ◗◗◗ are the most difficult.

1 ◗ You created the online form for the desktop publishing service that was defined in Cases and Places Assignment 1 in Project 7 on page WD 7.68. You decide to change its appearance; that is, change its fonts, font sizes, fill effects, colors, and clip art, and use a graphic from the Web in the company name. You also decide that the form should include the following:

1. When the form initially displays on the screen (as a blank document), Word zooms page width, scrolls down to display the entire form in the Word window, hides formatting marks, and hides gridlines.
2. If the user leaves the text box containing the price they would be willing to pay for a card blank or enters a nonnumeric entry, an error message should display.
3. The form should contain a Click Here When Finished button that when clicked does the following:
   a. If the user entered text in the Other text box, then Word places an X in the Other check box (just in case the user left it blank).
   b. The Save As dialog box displays so the user can assign a file name to the filled-in form.
   c. A thank-you message displays on the screen that informs the user what file should be e-mailed back to the service.

2 ◗◗ You created the survey for the Computer Technology Department at your school that was defined in Cases and Places Assignment 2 in Project 7 on page WD 7.68. The department chair has asked you to change the survey's appearance (all fonts, font sizes, colors, graphics, and fill effects), create a macro for the form so it displays properly on the screen when a user first displays it (as a blank form), and add a button that when clicked automatically displays the Save As dialog box for the user and then displays a thank-you message. Use the concepts and techniques presented in this project to modify the online form. Attach a digital signature to the document.

3 ◗◗ You created the survey for your school's bookstore that was defined in Cases and Places Assignment 3 in Project 7 on page WD 7.68. The director of the bookstore has asked you to change the survey's appearance (use a text box and change all fonts, font sizes, colors, graphics, and fill effects), create a macro for the form so it displays properly on the screen when a user first displays it (as a blank form), and add a button that when clicked automatically displays the Save As dialog box for the user and then displays a thank-you message. Use the concepts and techniques presented in this project to modify the online form. Be sure to use a different graphic from the Clip Organizer or from the Web.

Cases and Places

4 ▶▶ Search the Web for companies that certify digital signatures, such as VeriSign, Inc. Use Word to create a list of companies you find, the kinds of information they require their customers to submit, and the cost. Search each certification company's Web site for customers they have certified in the past, and list two for each company. Ask an IT professional at your school or place of employment if he or she can provide you with an internal certificate. Write a paragraph describing what you learned. Finally, write a paragraph describing your definition of trusted sources, based on your research. Save the report and then attach a digital certificate to it. E-mail the report to your instructor, if your instructor gives you permission to do so.

5 ▶▶▶ An Internet Service Provider's online survey asks business users what percentage of their business comes via Web-based technologies. These business users are asked to enter a decimal percentage rate for that percentage; however, many users enter a whole number, such as 7, instead of a decimal, such as .07. Write the code, including appropriate comments, for a macro that tests the field for a numeric value greater than 1 and then converts it to a decimal by multiplying it by .01. Use the concepts and techniques presented in this project to write an If...Then statement to test the field's value. Then, use Microsoft Word Help to look up automatic calculations and assign a new value to form fields.

6 ▶▶▶ The owner of Brim's Blooming Boutique would like to publish the Customer Survey (Figure 8-1 on page WD 8.05) on the Web. Thus, all of the form fields must be changed to ActiveX controls; that is, you have to delete the Word form fields and insert similar ActiveX controls. Also, she would like every text box and drop-down list box to display an error message if the user leaves the entry blank, which means you will write a VBA procedure for each of the objects. Use the concepts and techniques presented in this project to modify the online form.

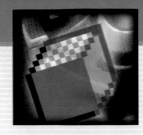

Microsoft Word 2002

PROJECT

9

Working with a Master Document, an Index, and a Table of Contents

OBJECTIVES

You will have mastered the material in this project when you can:

- Insert, modify, review, and delete comments
- Track changes in a document
- Save multiple versions of a document
- Accept and reject tracked changes
- Add and modify a caption
- Create a cross-reference
- Mark index entries
- Password-protect a document
- Work with a master document and subdocuments
- Create and modify an outline
- Insert and format a diagram
- Create a table of figures
- Build and modify an index
- Create and modify a table of contents
- Add a bookmark
- Create alternating headers
- Set a gutter margin
- Use the Document Map

Smooth Styles

Penning the Perfect Paper

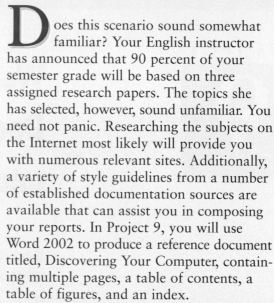

Does this scenario sound somewhat familiar? Your English instructor has announced that 90 percent of your semester grade will be based on three assigned research papers. The topics she has selected, however, sound unfamiliar. You need not panic. Researching the subjects on the Internet most likely will provide you with numerous relevant sites. Additionally, a variety of style guidelines from a number of established documentation sources are available that can assist you in composing your reports. In Project 9, you will use Word 2002 to produce a reference document titled, Discovering Your Computer, containing multiple pages, a table of contents, a table of figures, and an index.

After selecting a topic, the work begins: researching your subject, finding reference materials, taking notes, and outlining. Then, you write a series of drafts, check language and style, rewrite the final paper, and maybe more than once! To ensure that the reader of your paper can navigate easily, you need a table of contents and an index. It is a good habit to verify your references and make certain that all of your sources are given the appropriate credit. The citation procedure may seem tedious, but it is the way your readers know how to find additional information on the subjects and the way you ethically give credit to the individuals who have researched these topics before you.

Finally, you must consider the type of binding. You do not want your hard work misplaced or lost. Although folders or

other kinds of binders are a nice final addition, some instructors have certain preferences for handing in your completed work, and you always should be aware of their requirements.

In academia, three major style systems for writers of research and scientific papers generally are recognized. Scholars in the humanities use The Modern Language Association (MLA). The MLA style is organized in the *MLA Handbook for Writers of Research Papers*. Researchers in the social sciences use another popular style developed by the American Psychological Association (APA). The APA style is documented in the *Publication Manual of the American Psychological Association*. The third style is the number system used by the Council of Biology Editors (CBE). The CBE manual, *Scientific Style and Format*, describes the citation-sequence system and the name-year system used by writers in the applied sciences.

Writers also consult other style handbooks such as *The Chicago Manual of Style,* the *American Chemical Society Handbook for Authors,* the *Microsoft Manual of Style for Technical Writers,* and others.

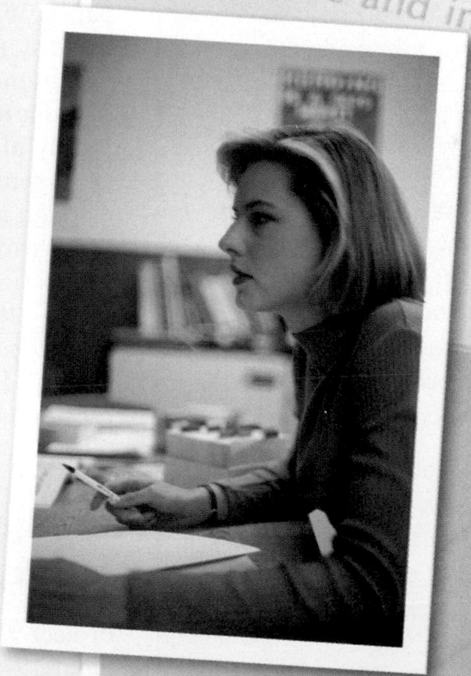

Teams of instructors and scholars develop the style guidelines in each of these major publications. The *MLA Handbook,* for example, originated in 1951 for MLA members, and later was expanded to become a guide for undergraduates. Subsequent revisions are published on a regular basis. The MLA makes the guide available on the Internet, which includes up-to-date conventions for documenting sources on the World Wide Web. You can visit MLA online (www.mla.org).

Because style systems frequently are revised, it is essential to utilize the latest revision. Fortunately, many of the major documentation sources can be accessed on the Web, providing direction on formatting headings, works cited, tables, statistics, and more. For additional information, visit the Word 2002 More About Web page (scsite.com/wd2002/more.htm).

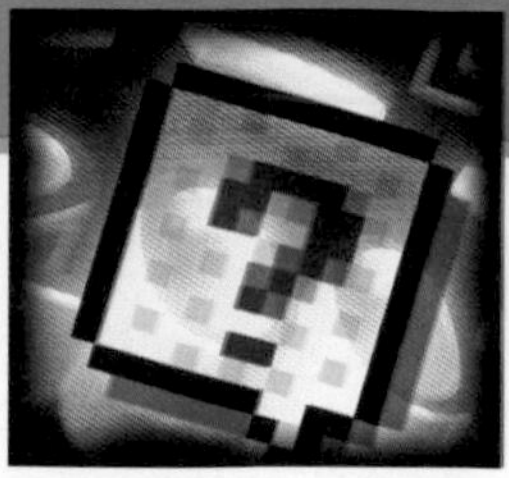

Microsoft Word 2002

Working with a Master Document, an Index, and a Table of Contents

PROJECT

9

CASE PERSPECTIVE

As a public service, the Clark County Public Library develops and prints multipage documents that contain information it feels may be helpful to community members. One of its series, titled Discovering Your Computer, presents a brief overview of some aspect of computers.

Keith Bettenhaus, library director, included a public opinion survey about the Discovering Your Computer series in its last pamphlet. Comments were very positive. Suggestions were made, however, that the documents could be more organized including items such as a table of contents and index, and be made available online.

Employees in the technical services department assemble these documents, with assistance from employees in other departments. For example, the office automation staff assists with the content for the Discovering Your Computer series. In coordinating all the comments and edits of these documents, Keith has noticed much inefficiency. As a part-time computer specialist in the technical services department for the library, you have been assigned the task of redesigning the production of these documents.

Introduction

During the course of your academic studies and professional endeavors, you may find it necessary to compose a document that is many pages in length or even one that is hundreds of pages. When composing a long document, you must ensure that the document is organized so a reader easily can locate material within the document. Sometimes a document of this nature is called a **reference document**.

By placing a table of contents at the beginning of the document and an index at the end, you help a reader navigate through a long document. If a document contains several illustrations, each illustration should have a caption. In addition, the illustrations could be listed in a table, called a table of figures, which identifies the location of each figure in the document. For long documents that will be viewed online, you should incorporate hyperlinks so a user can click the link to jump from one portion of the document to another.

Project Nine — Master Document, Index, and Table of Contents

Project 9 uses Word to produce the reference document shown in Figure 9-1. The document, called Discovering Your Computer, is a public information guide that is distributed by the Clark County Public Library to interested employees and patrons. Notice that the inner margin between facing pages has extra space to allow duplicated copies of the document to be bound — without the binding covering the words.

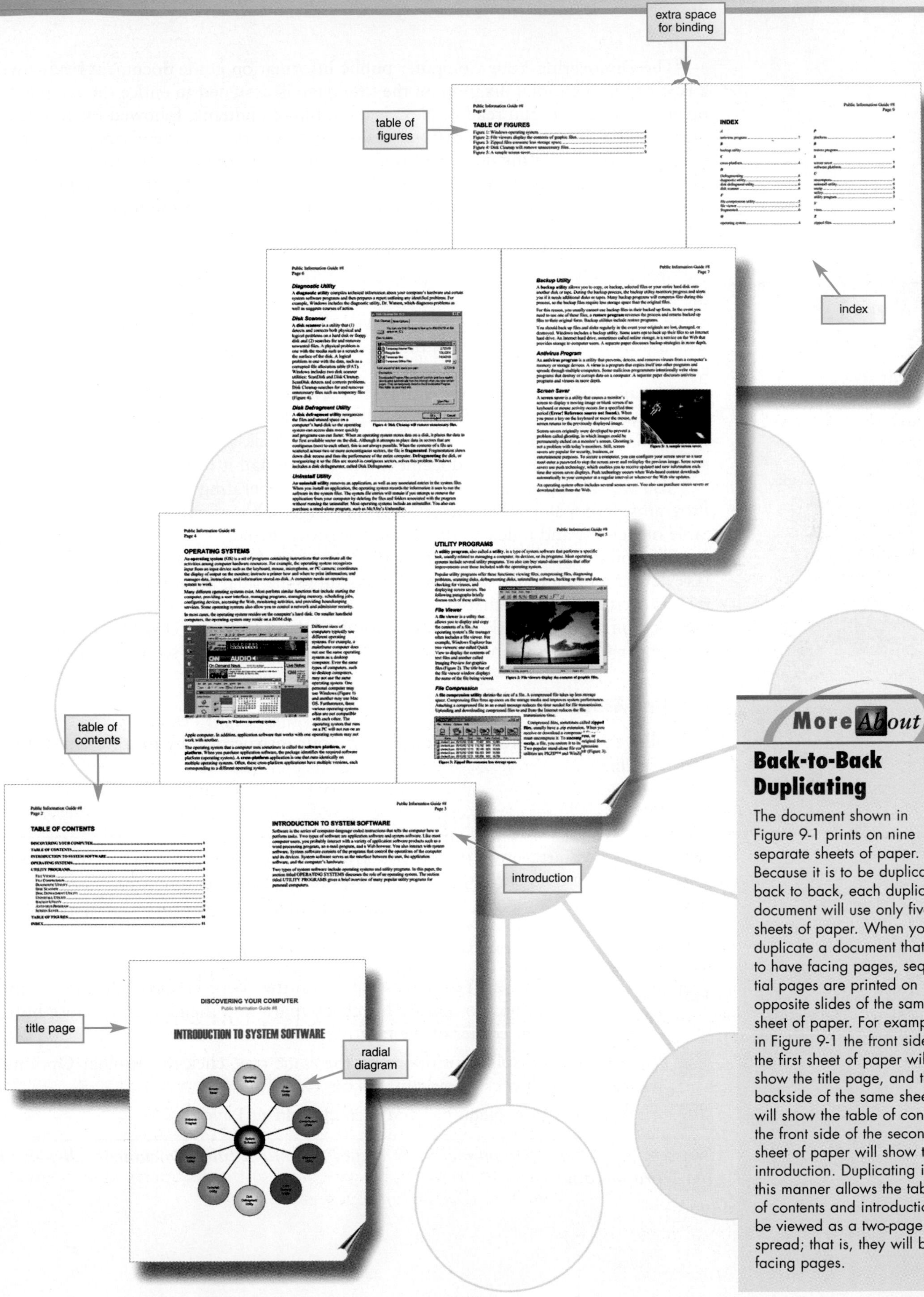

More About

Back-to-Back Duplicating

The document shown in Figure 9-1 prints on nine separate sheets of paper. Because it is to be duplicated back to back, each duplicated document will use only five sheets of paper. When you duplicate a document that is to have facing pages, sequential pages are printed on opposite slides of the same sheet of paper. For example, in Figure 9-1 the front side of the first sheet of paper will show the title page, and the backside of the same sheet will show the table of contents; the front side of the second sheet of paper will show the introduction. Duplicating in this manner allows the table of contents and introduction to be viewed as a two-page spread; that is, they will be facing pages.

FIGURE 9-1

The Discovering Your Computer public information guide document begins with a title page. The radial diagram on the title page is designed to entice the recipient to open the document and read it. Next is the table of contents, followed by an introduction. The document then discusses two topics: operating systems and utility programs. At the end of the document is a table of figures and an index to assist readers in locating information. A miniature version of the Discovering Your Computer public information guide document is shown in Figure 9-1 on the previous page; for a more readable view, visit scsite.com/wd2002/project9.htm.

You have asked employees in the office automation area to write the content for the operating systems and utility programs sections of the document and then e-mail the files to you for inclusion in the Discovering Your Computer public information guide document. You already have received the completed Utility Programs section, which now is ready to include in the Discovering Your Computer public information guide document.

Joy, an office automation specialist, has written a first draft of the Operating Systems section and e-mailed it to her supervisor Keith, and her co-workers Anita, Donna, and Patti, for review. After Joy receives it back from them, she will make any necessary adjustments to the document and then e-mail it to you.

You will incorporate the two completed files, Operating Systems and Utility Programs, into a single file and create a title page, table of contents, introduction, table of figures, and index so the document is organized.

The following pages explain how the Operating Systems section of the document is reviewed and modified and how you assemble the final document. For purposes of this project, certain files that are e-mailed to various people or departments are included on the Data Disk. If you did not download the Data Disk, see the inside back cover for instructions for downloading the Data Disk or see your instructor.

More About

Reference Documents

For a sample reference document on the Web that contains elements commonly found in long documents, visit the Word 2002 More About Web page (scsite.com/wd2002/more.htm) and then click Sample Reference Document.

Starting Word

Follow these steps to start Word or ask your instructor how to start Word for your system.

TO START AND CUSTOMIZE WORD

1. Click the Start button on the Windows taskbar, point to Programs on the Start menu, and then click Microsoft Word on the Programs submenu.
2. If the Word window is not maximized, double-click its title bar to maximize it.
3. If the Language bar displays on the screen, click its Minimize button.
4. If the New Document task pane displays in the Word window, click the Show at startup check box to remove the check mark and then click the Close button in the upper-right corner of the task pane title bar.
5. If the toolbars display positioned on the same row, click the Toolbar Options button and then click Show Buttons on Two Rows.
6. Click View on the menu bar and then click Print Layout.

Word starts. After a few moments, an empty document titled Document1 displays in the Word window.

Resetting Menus and Toolbars

To set the menus and toolbars so they appear exactly as shown in this book, reset your menus and toolbars as outlined in Appendix D or follow these steps.

TO RESET MENUS AND TOOLBARS

1. Click the Toolbar Options button on the Standard toolbar and then point to Add or Remove Buttons. Point to Standard on the Add or Remove Buttons submenu. Scroll to and then click Reset Toolbar on the Standard submenu.
2. Click the Toolbar Options button on the Formatting toolbar and then point to Add or Remove Buttons. Point to Formatting on the Add or Remove Buttons submenu. Scroll to and then click Reset Toolbar on the Formatting submenu.
3. Click the Toolbar Options button on the Standard toolbar and then point to Add or Remove Buttons. Click Customize on the Add or Remove Buttons submenu.
4. When the Customize dialog box displays, if necessary, click the Options tab and then click the Reset my usage data button. When the Microsoft Word dialog box displays, click the Yes button. Click the Close button in the Customize dialog box.

Word resets the menus and toolbars.

Displaying Formatting Marks

Recall that it is helpful to display formatting marks that indicate where in the document you pressed the ENTER key, SPACEBAR, and other keys. Perform the following step to display formatting marks.

TO DISPLAY FORMATTING MARKS

1. If the Show/Hide ¶ button on the Standard toolbar is not selected already, click it.

Word displays formatting marks in the document window, and the Show/Hide ¶ button on the Standard toolbar is selected (shown in Figure 9-2 on the next page).

Zooming Page Width

When you zoom page width, Word displays the page on the screen as large as possible in print layout view. Perform the following steps to zoom page width.

TO ZOOM PAGE WIDTH

1. Click the Zoom box arrow on the Standard toolbar.
2. Click Page Width in the Zoom list.

Word computes the zoom percentage and displays it in the Zoom box (shown in Figure 9-2). Your percentage may be different.

Reviewing a Document

Reviewing a document is one of the collaborative tools provided in Word. One person creates the document; other people make changes to the same document. Those changes then display on the screen with options for reviewers to accept or reject them. For demonstration purposes, this project illustrates how both an originator (author) and a reviewer work with a document.

The following pages illustrate the reviewing features of Word.

More About

Proofreading Marks

For more information on marks and abbreviations used by proofreaders, visit the Word 2002 More About Web page (scsite.com/wd2002/more.htm) and then click Proofreading Marks.

E-Mailing a Document for Review

The first step in e-mailing a document for review is to open it. Joy has written a first draft of the Operating Systems section of the Discovering Your Computer public information guide document. She is ready to e-mail this draft to her supervisor, Keith, for review.

For this project, the Operating Systems Draft file that Keith is to review is located on the Data Disk. If you did not download the Data Disk, see the inside back cover for instructions for downloading the Data Disk or see your instructor.

Open the Operating Systems Draft file, as described in the following steps.

Steps To Open and E-Mail a Document for Review

1 Click the Open button on the Standard toolbar. When the Open dialog box displays, click the Look in box arrow and then click 3½ Floppy (A:). Click Operating Systems Draft in the list and then click the Open button in the dialog box. When the Operating System Draft file displays in the document window, click File on the menu bar, point to Send To, and then point to Mail Recipient (for Review) on the Send To submenu (Figure 9-2).

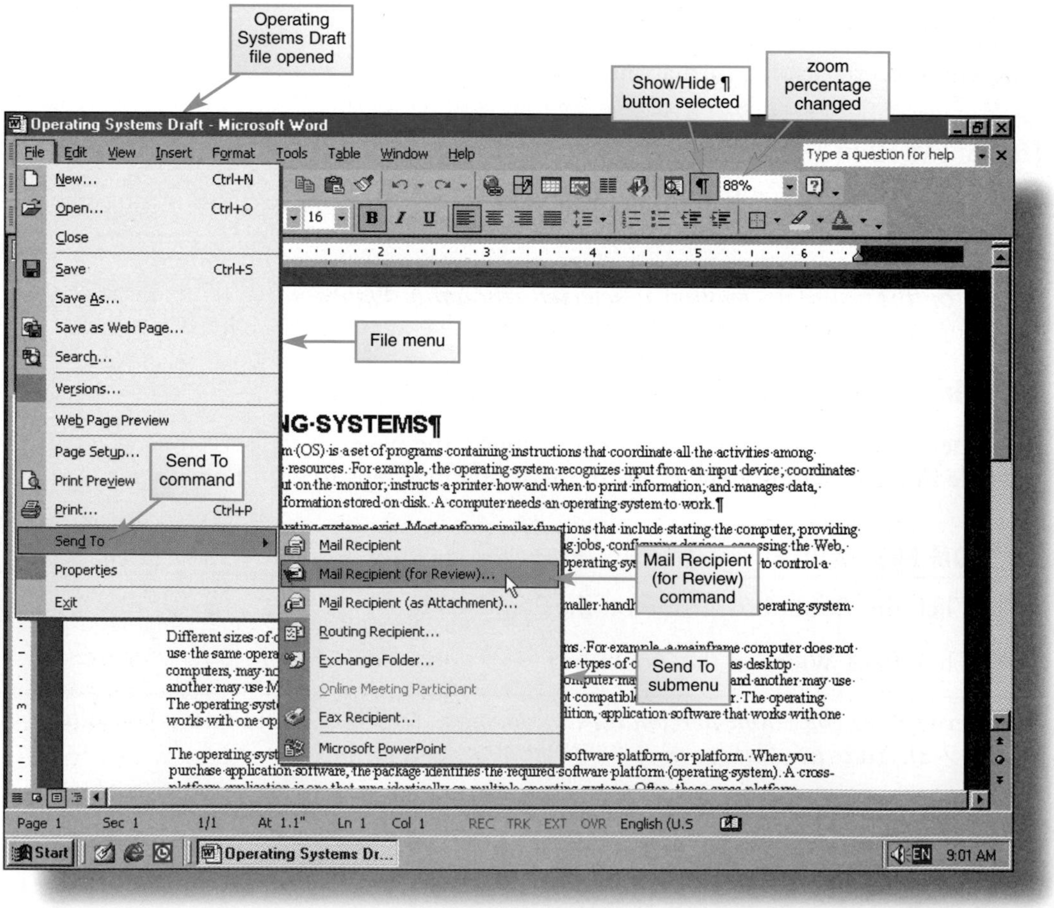

FIGURE 9-2

2 Click Mail Recipient (for Review). When the Please review 'Operating Systems Draft' window displays, type your e-mail address in the To text box, or type an address provided by your instructor. Point to the Send button.

Word displays the Please review 'Operating Systems Draft' window for the mail message (Figure 9-3). Notice the mail message automatically displays a message in the Subject text box and includes the Operating Systems Draft file as an attachment.

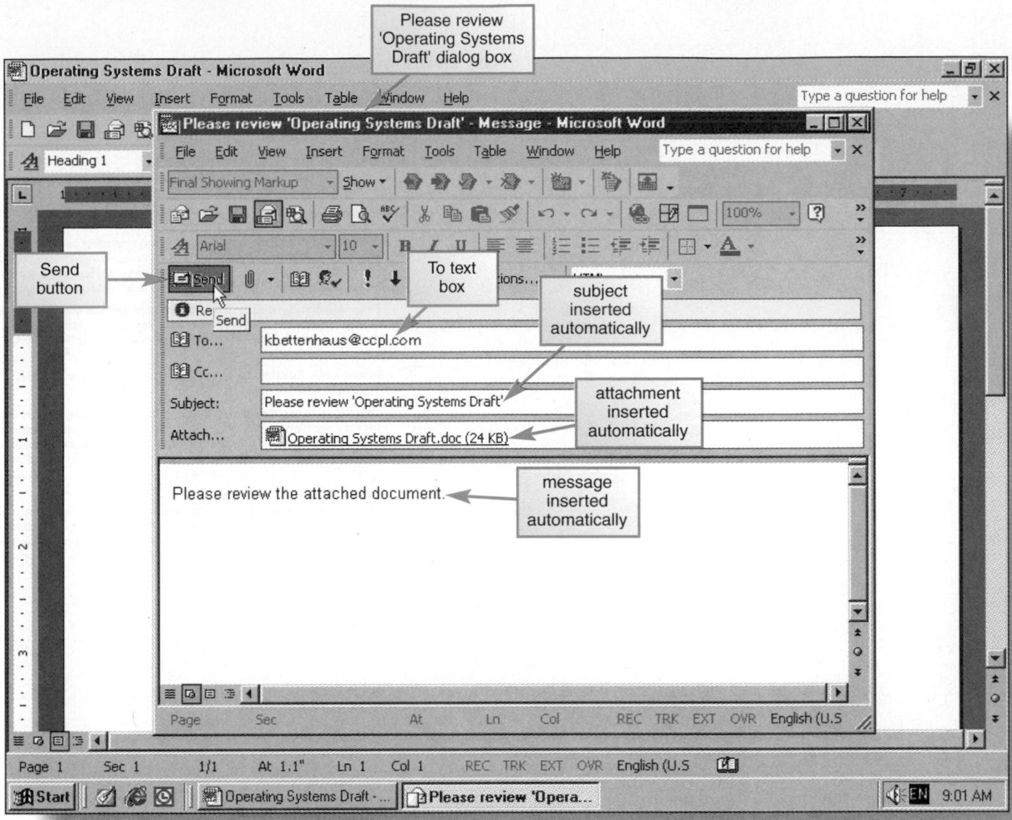

FIGURE 9-3

3 Click the Send button, if directed to do so by your instructor.

Word sends the document shown in Figure 9-4a on the next page to the named recipient in the To text box. The Reviewing toolbar also may automatically display in the Word window (shown in Figure 9-5 on page WD 9.11).

Other Ways

1. In Exploring window, right-click file, point to Send To on shortcut menu, click Mail Recipient on Send To submenu
2. In Voice Command mode, say "File, Send To, Mail Recipient for Review, [enter e-mail address], Send"

When a reviewer receives a document e-mailed for review, the subject line in the e-mail program shows the name of the attached file and a paper clip displays to denote the attachment. The reviewer simply double-clicks the document attachment in the mail message to start the application and open the document.

Reviewing the Document

After reading through the Operating Systems Draft file, Keith has some suggested changes. Keith could print a copy of the document and write his suggested changes using proofreader's revision marks, as shown in Figure 9-4a. Instead of writing his suggestions on the printed draft copy, however, Keith plans to use Word's **change-tracking feature** and enter his suggested changes directly into the document. Then, Joy can choose to accept or reject each of the changes online. As a comparison, Figure 9-4b on the next page shows the final copy of the Operating Systems file, after Joy reviews the changes suggested by Keith and modifies the document accordingly. When comparing Figures 9-4 a and 9-4b, notice that Joy makes most of the changes suggested by Keith.

(a) Draft of Operating Systems File with Suggested Changes

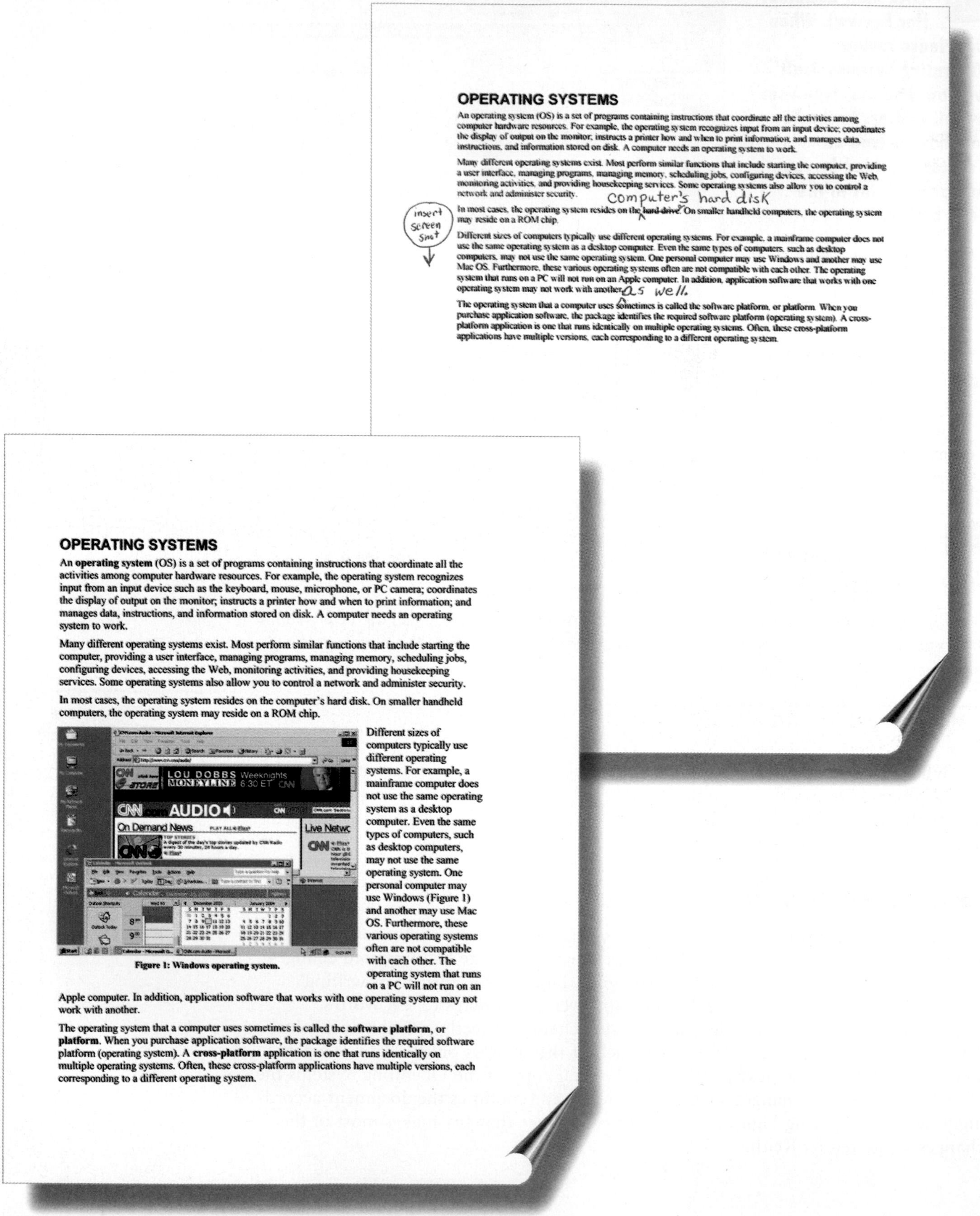

OPERATING SYSTEMS

An operating system (OS) is a set of programs containing instructions that coordinate all the activities among computer hardware resources. For example, the operating system recognizes input from an input device; coordinates the display of output on the monitor; instructs a printer how and when to print information, and manages data, instructions, and information stored on disk. A computer needs an operating system to work.

Many different operating systems exist. Most perform similar functions that include starting the computer, providing a user interface, managing programs, managing memory, scheduling jobs, configuring devices, accessing the Web, monitoring activities, and providing housekeeping services. Some operating systems also allow you to control a network and administer security.

computer's hard disk

insert screen shot

In most cases, the operating system resides on the ~~hard drive~~. On smaller handheld computers, the operating system may reside on a ROM chip.

Different sizes of computers typically use different operating systems. For example, a mainframe computer does not use the same operating system as a desktop computer. Even the same types of computers, such as desktop computers, may not use the same operating system. One personal computer may use Windows and another may use Mac OS. Furthermore, these various operating systems often are not compatible with each other. The operating system that runs on a PC will not run on an Apple computer. In addition, application software that works with one operating system may not work with another. as well.

The operating system that a computer uses sometimes is called the software platform, or platform. When you purchase application software, the package identifies the required software platform (operating system). A cross-platform application is one that runs identically on multiple operating systems. Often, these cross-platform applications have multiple versions, each corresponding to a different operating system.

OPERATING SYSTEMS

An **operating system** (OS) is a set of programs containing instructions that coordinate all the activities among computer hardware resources. For example, the operating system recognizes input from an input device such as the keyboard, mouse, microphone, or PC camera; coordinates the display of output on the monitor; instructs a printer how and when to print information; and manages data, instructions, and information stored on disk. A computer needs an operating system to work.

Many different operating systems exist. Most perform similar functions that include starting the computer, providing a user interface, managing programs, managing memory, scheduling jobs, configuring devices, accessing the Web, monitoring activities, and providing housekeeping services. Some operating systems also allow you to control a network and administer security.

In most cases, the operating system resides on the computer's hard disk. On smaller handheld computers, the operating system may reside on a ROM chip.

Figure 1: Windows operating system.

Different sizes of computers typically use different operating systems. For example, a mainframe computer does not use the same operating system as a desktop computer. Even the same types of computers, such as desktop computers, may not use the same operating system. One personal computer may use Windows (Figure 1) and another may use Mac OS. Furthermore, these various operating systems often are not compatible with each other. The operating system that runs on a PC will not run on an Apple computer. In addition, application software that works with one operating system may not work with another.

The operating system that a computer uses sometimes is called the **software platform**, or **platform**. When you purchase application software, the package identifies the required software platform (operating system). A **cross-platform** application is one that runs identically on multiple operating systems. Often, these cross-platform applications have multiple versions, each corresponding to a different operating system.

(b) Final Version of Operating Systems File

FIGURE 9-4

Saving a Document with a New File Name

To preserve the contents of the original Operating Systems Draft file, save a copy of it with a new file name, as described in the following steps.

TO SAVE A DOCUMENT WITH A NEW FILE NAME

1. With a floppy disk in drive A, click File on the menu bar and then click Save As.
2. Type `Operating Systems` in the File name text box. Do not press the ENTER key.
3. If necessary, click the Save in box arrow and then click 3½ Floppy (A:).
4. Click the Save button in the Save As dialog box.

Word saves the document on a floppy disk in drive A with the file name, Operating Systems (shown in Figure 9-5).

Inserting Comments

A **comment**, or annotation, is a note inserted into a document that does not affect the text of the document. Reviewers often use comments to communicate suggestions, tips, and other messages to the author of a document. For example, Keith believes that the document would have more impact if it included a figure showing a screen shot of Windows. Perform the following steps, as a reviewer, to insert a comment of this nature into the document.

More About

Comments

If you have a pen-equipped computer, you can insert pen comments that become drawing objects in the document. Likewise, if your computer has a microphone and sound card, you can record voice comments that are attached to the document as recordings.

Steps To Insert a Comment

1 **Select the text on which you wish to comment (in this case, the word, Windows, in the fourth paragraph). Click Insert on the menu bar and then point to Comment (Figure 9-5).**

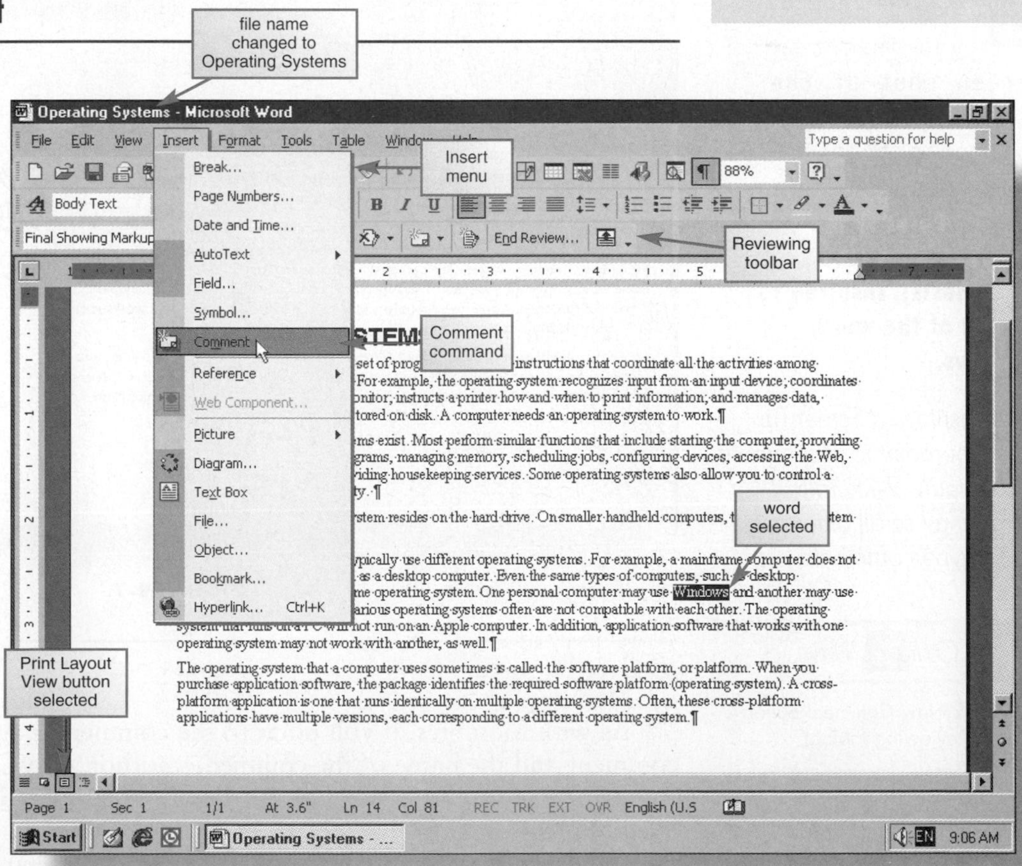

FIGURE 9-5

2 **Click Comment. Click Zoom box arrow on the Standard toolbar and then click 100%. Click the right scroll arrow on the horizontal scroll bar to view completely the comment balloon.**

*Word displays a **comment balloon** to the right of the text on the page and displays **comment marks** as parentheses around the selected text in the document window (Figure 9-6). The insertion point is positioned in the comment balloon to the right of the word, Comment.*

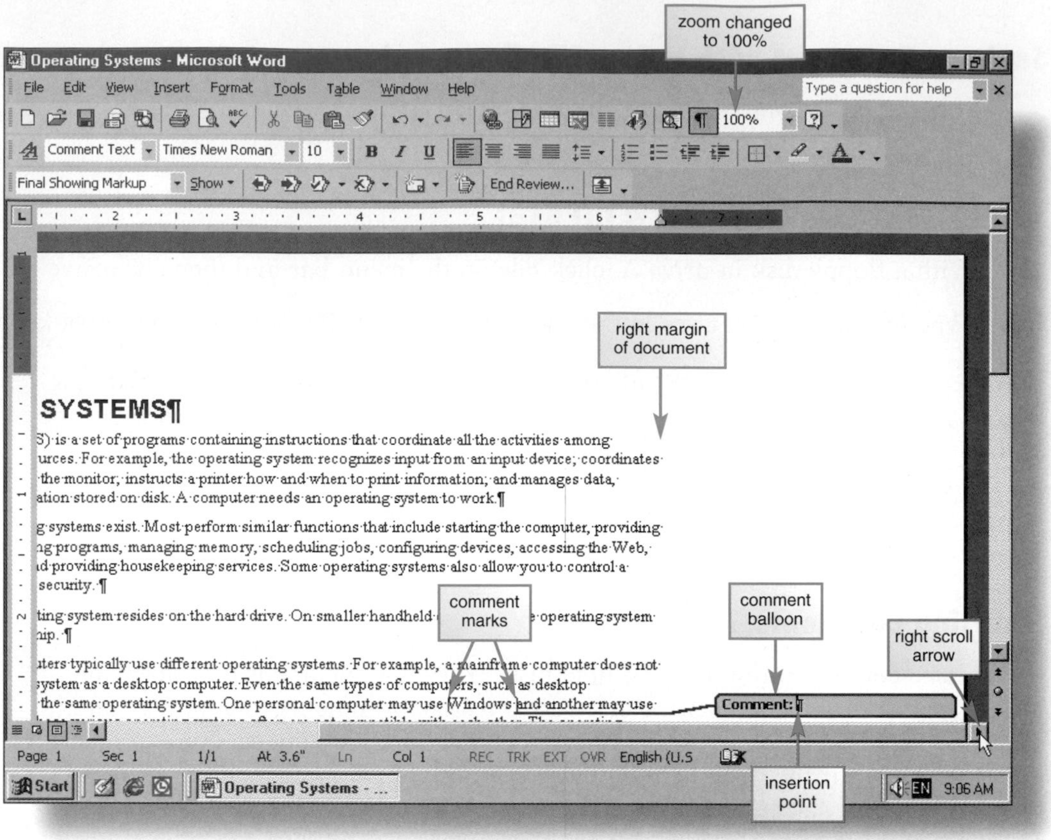

FIGURE 9-6

3 **Type** `I suggest you insert a screen shot of the Windows desktop here to emphasize the importance of this topic.` **Point to the comment mark (the parenthesis), inserted to the left of the word, Windows.**

Word displays a ScreenTip when you point to a comment mark (Figure 9-7). Your screen may scroll differently as you type comments.

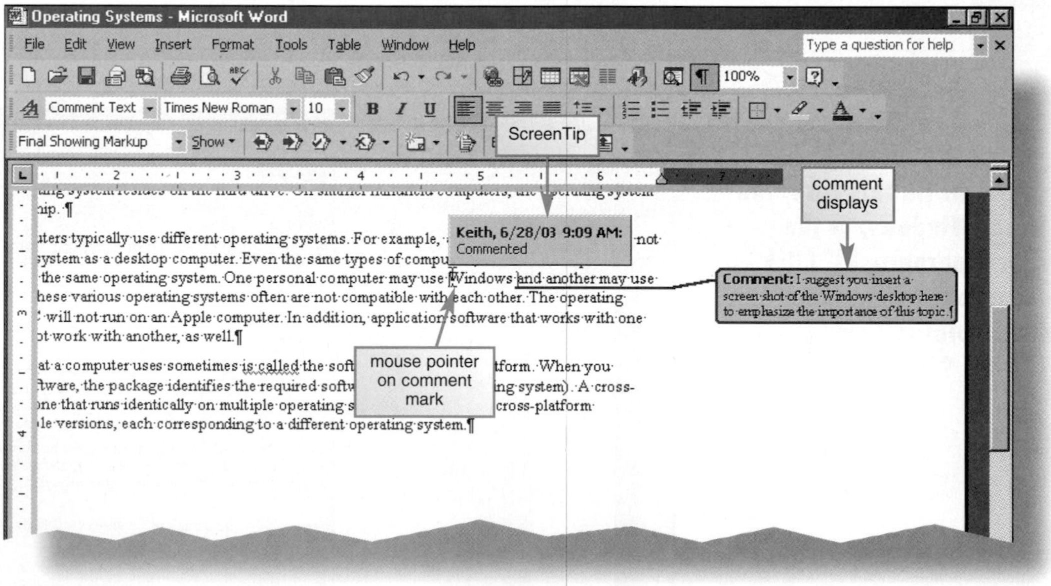

FIGURE 9-7

Other Ways

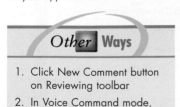

1. Click New Comment button on Reviewing toolbar
2. In Voice Command mode, say "Insert, Comment"

As with footnotes, if you point to the comment mark, Word displays the comment and the name of the comment's author above the comment mark as a ScreenTip. Comments display in comment balloons in both print layout and Web layout views.

Word uses predefined settings for the reviewer's name that display in the ScreenTip. If the name that displays is not correct, you can change it by clicking

Tools on the menu bar, clicking Options, clicking the User Information tab, and entering the correct name. In addition to the reviewer's name, each reviewer's comments are shaded in a different color to help you visually differentiate among multiple reviewers' comments.

Instead of selecting text on which you wish to comment (as shown in Step 1 on page WD 9.11), you simply can click at the location where you want to insert the comment. In this case, the comment marks (parenthesis) display side by side at the location of the insertion point.

Word always cannot display the complete text of a comment in the comment balloon. To see longer comments, to view comments in normal view, or to see items such as inserted or deleted graphics and text boxes, use the **Reviewing Pane**. Figure 9-8 shows the Reviewing Pane that contains the comment just added, as well as the changes to be made in the next series of steps.

To display the Reviewing Pane, click the Reviewing Pane button on the Reviewing toolbar or right-click the TRK status indicator on the status bar and then click Reviewing Pane on the shortcut menu. To close the Reviewing Pane, click the Reviewing Pane button on the Reviewing toolbar again.

> **More About**
>
> **The Reviewing Toolbar**
>
> To display the Reviewing toolbar, click View on the menu bar, point to Toolbars, and then click Reviewing. The Reviewing toolbar contains buttons that enable you to work with comments and tracked changes.

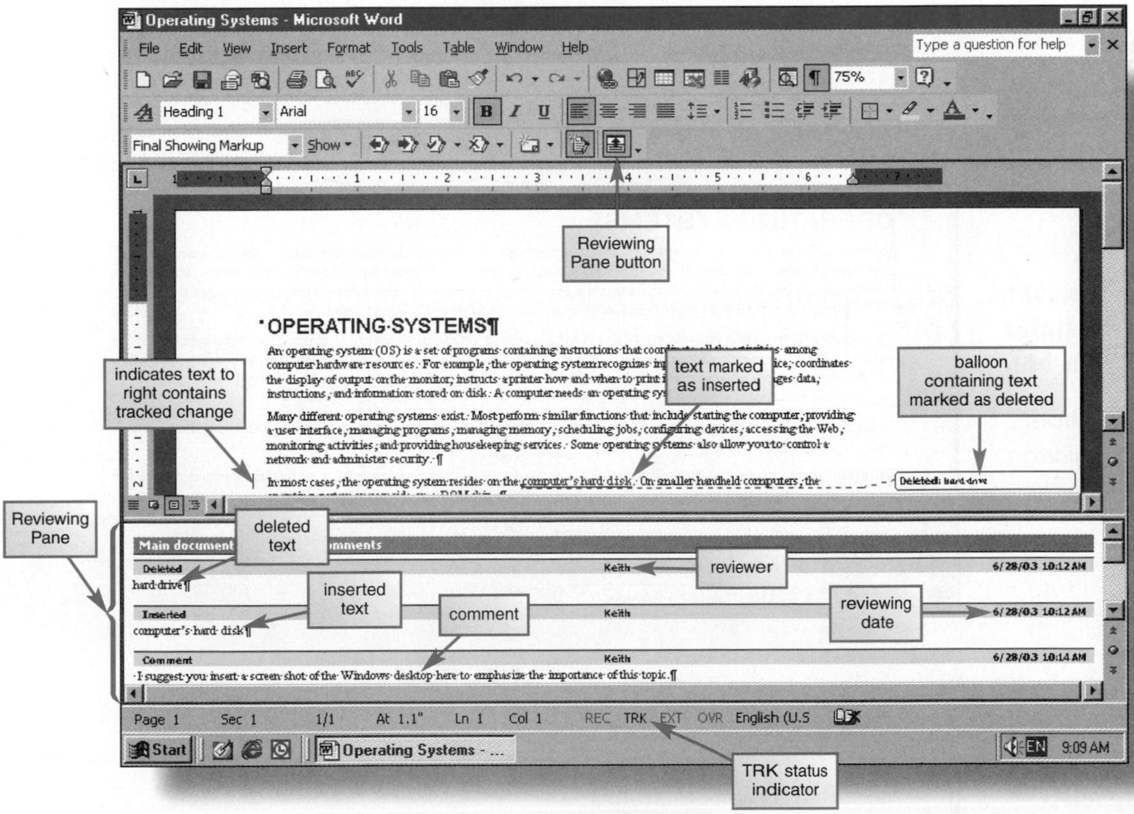

FIGURE 9-8

You modify comments by clicking inside the comment balloon and editing as you edit text in the document window. To edit comments in the Reviewing Pane, click the comment in the Reviewing Pane and then edit the comment as you would any Word text.

When you print a document with comments, Word by default, chooses the zoom percentage and page orientation to best display the comments in the printed document. If you want to print the comments only (without printing the document), click File on the menu bar, click Print, click the Print what box arrow, click List of markup, and then click the OK button. If you want to print the document without

More About

Color of Tracked Changes

If multiple reviewers track changes to a document, the changes of each reviewer are marked in a different color. To change the color or other aspects of reviewer marks, right-click the TRK status indicator on the status bar, click Options on the shortcut menu, adjust settings in the Track Changes dialog box, and then click the OK button.

comments, click File on the menu bar, click Print, click the Print what box arrow, click Document, and then click the OK button.

The next step is to track changes while editing the document.

Tracking Changes

Keith has two suggested changes for the Operating Systems document: (1) in the third paragraph change the phrase, hard drive, to the phrase, computer's hard disk, and (2) insert the words, as well, at the end of the fourth paragraph. To track changes in a document, you turn on the change-tracking feature by double-clicking the TRK status indicator on the status bar. When you edit a document that has the change-tracking feature enabled, Word marks all text or graphics that you insert, delete, or modify and calls the revised version a **markup**. Thus, an author can identify the changes a reviewer has made by looking at the markup in the document. The author also has the ability to accept or reject any change that a reviewer has made to a document.

The following pages illustrate how a reviewer tracks changes to a document and then how the author (originator) reviews the tracked changes made to the document.

Steps To Track Changes

1 Press CTRL+HOME to position the insertion point at the beginning of the document. Double-click the TRK status indicator on the status bar.

Word darkens the characters in the TRK status indicator on the status bar (Figure 9-9).

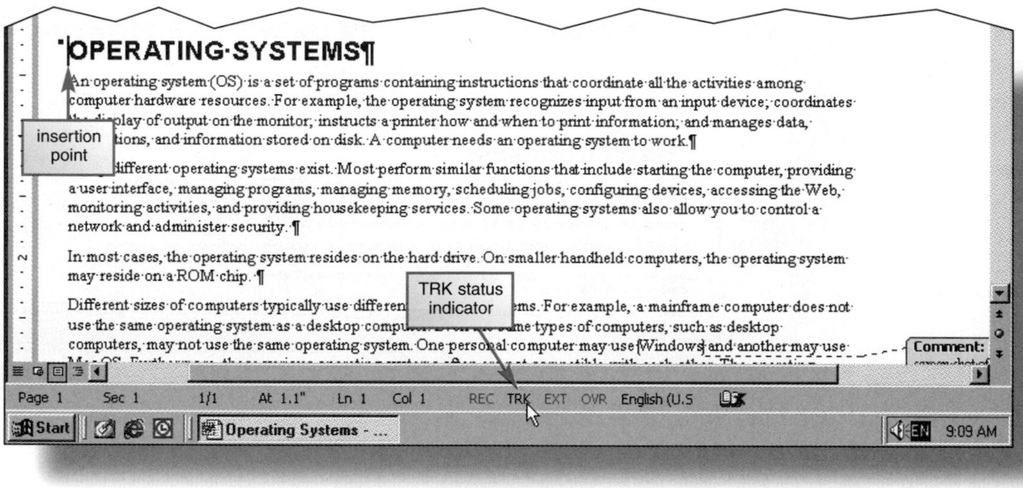

FIGURE 9-9

2 In the third paragraph, select the text, hard drive (Figure 9-10).

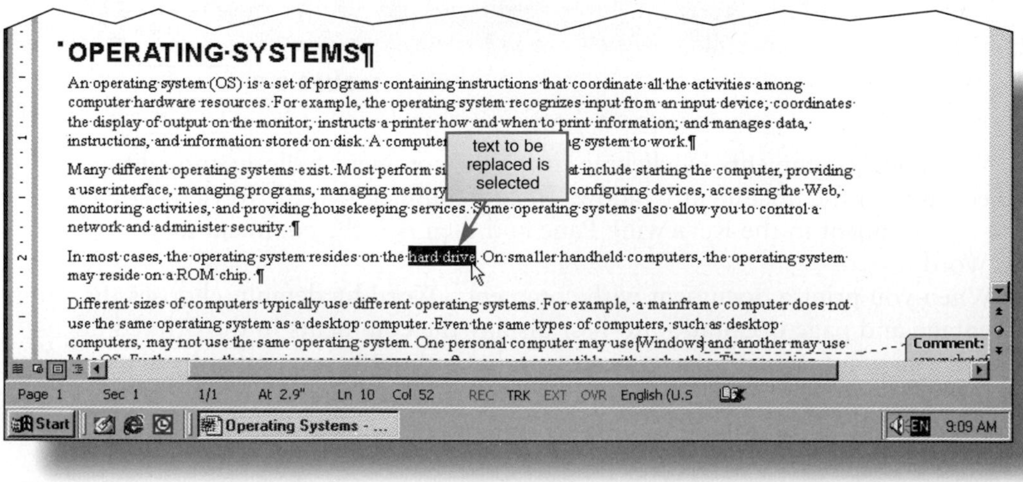

FIGURE 9-10

3 **With the text still selected, type** `computer's hard disk` **as the replacement text. Click the right scroll arrow to display the markup balloon.**

Word marks the selection, hard disk, as deleted, and marks the words, computer's hard disk, as inserted (Figure 9-11). Deleted text displays in a ***markup balloon****, and inserted text displays in the document in color and underlined.*

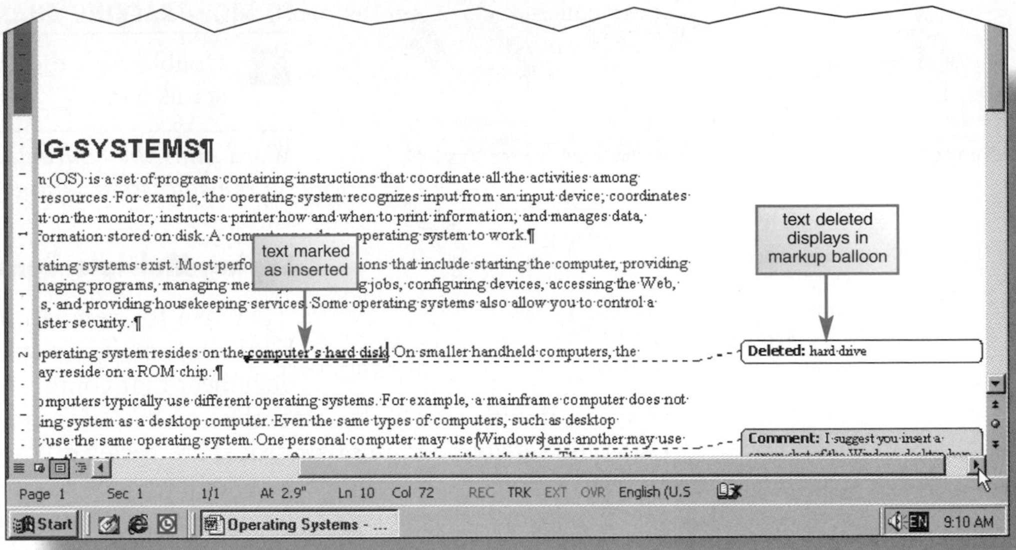

FIGURE 9-11

4 **Scroll down to display the end of the fourth paragraph. Click to the left of the period at the end of the last sentence in the paragraph. Press the SPACEBAR and then type** `as well` **at the end of the sentence.**

Word marks the inserted text, as well, as inserted (Figure 9-12). That is, it displays in color and underlined.

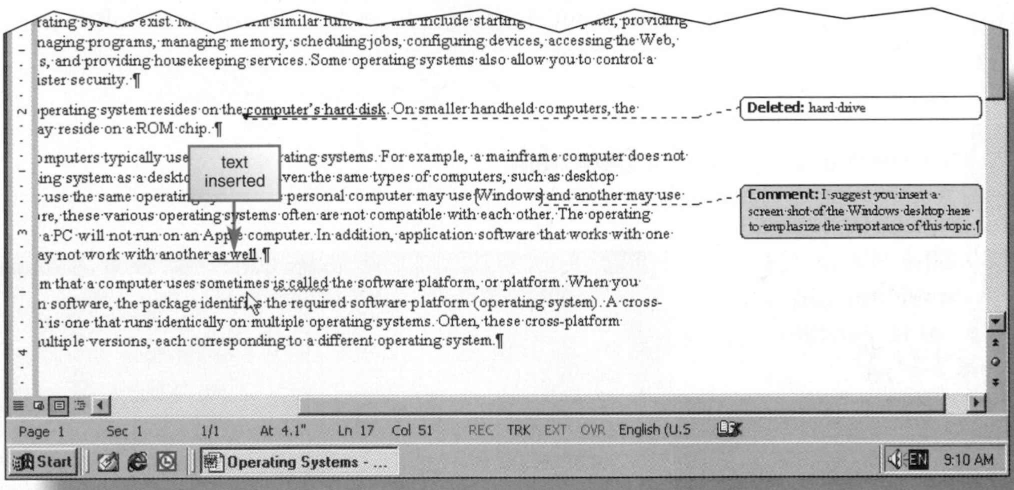

FIGURE 9-12

Other Ways

1. Click Track Changes button on Reviewing toolbar
2. On Tools menu click Track Changes
3. Press CTRL+SHIFT+E
4. In Voice Command mode, say "Tools, Track Changes"

Tracked changes display in markup balloons in both print layout and Web layout views. These changes are called **revision marks**. In normal view, tracked changes display as **strikethroughs** for deleted text and underlined for inserted text. Word places a **changed line** (a vertical bar) at the left edge of each line that contains a tracked change. In any view, if you point to a tracked change, Word displays a ScreenTip that identifies the reviewer's name and the type of change made by that reviewer. As with comments, Microsoft Word cannot always display the complete text of a tracked change in a markup balloon. Use the Reviewing Pane to view longer revisions.

The Reviewing toolbar contains buttons and boxes to view versions of documents; show specific kinds of changes or specific reviewers; review, accept, or delete each change in sequence; edit comments; and turn on or off review features. Figure 9-13 on the next page identifies each of these buttons and boxes.

The next step is to turn off the change-tracking feature, as described in the step on the next page.

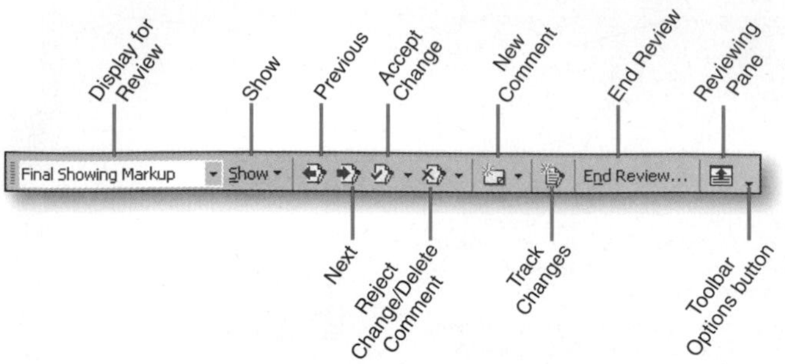

FIGURE 9-13

TO STOP TRACKING CHANGES

1 Double-click the TRK status indicator on the status bar.

Word dims the characters in the TRK status indicator on the status bar (shown in Figure 9-14).

Saving Multiple Versions of a Document

When Joy receives the reviewed document from Keith via e-mail, she wants to preserve a copy of the document that contains the tracked changes. Instead of saving it with a new file name, she opts to save a separate version of the document. Using the version feature saves disk space because Word saves only the changes among versions — as opposed to a complete copy of the file. The downside is that you cannot modify a version; you only can open and print versions.

When saving a **version** of a document, you insert a description of the version so you can identify it at a later time. The version represents the current state, or snapshot, of the document.

For purposes of this project, you will save a version of the Operating Systems document that is on your disk. Perform the following steps to save a version of a document.

Steps To Save a Version of a Document

1 Click File on the menu bar and then point to Versions (Figure 9-14).

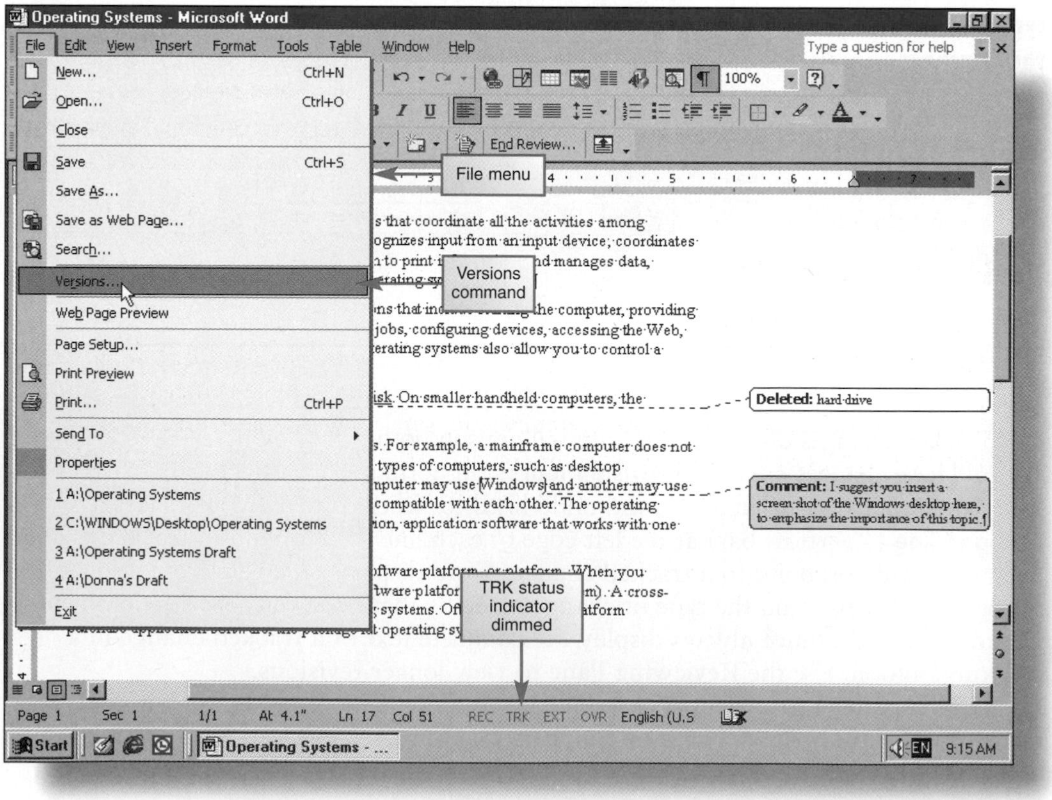

FIGURE 9-14

2 **Click Versions. When the Versions in Operating Systems dialog box displays, click the Save Now button. When Word displays the Save Version dialog box, type** `Contains comments and tracked changes from Keith.` **Point to the OK button.**

Word displays the Versions in Operating Systems dialog box, followed by the Save Version dialog box (Figure 9-15).

3 **Click the OK button.**

Word saves the current state of the document along with the entered comment.

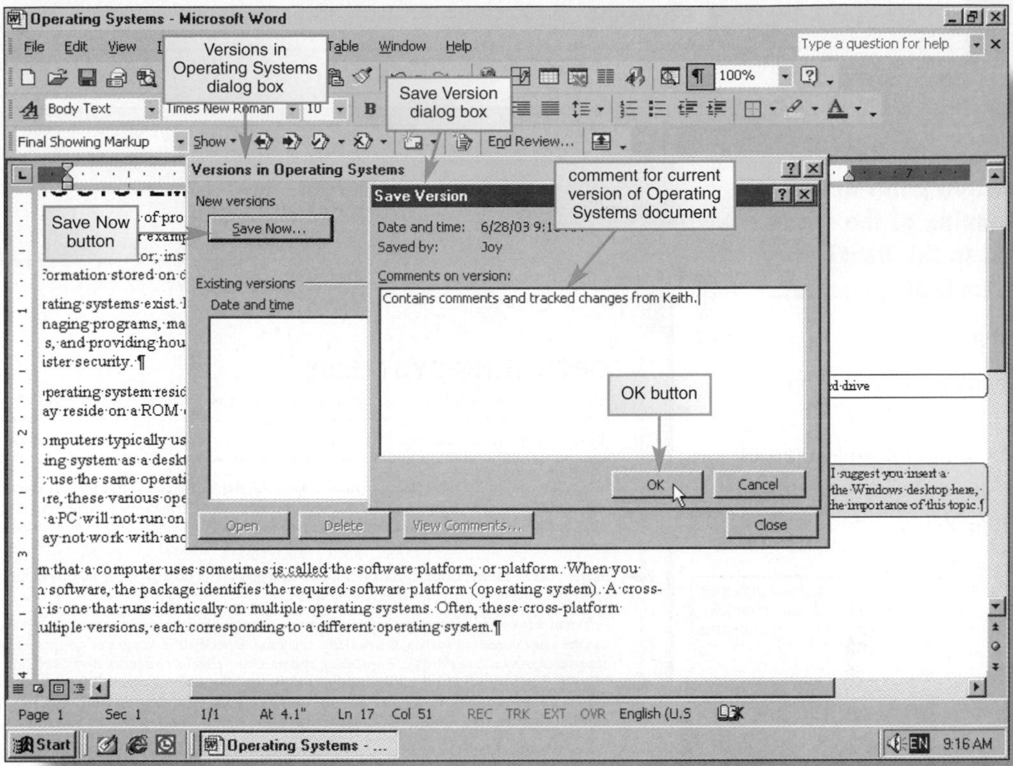

FIGURE 9-15

Other Ways

1. In Voice Command mode, say "File, Versions, Save Now, [type comment], OK"

To open a previous version of a document, click File on the menu bar, click Versions, click the version you wish to open in the Existing versions list, and then click the Open button in the Versions in [file name] dialog box. If, for some reason, you wanted to edit a previous version of a document, you would open it and then save it with a new file name.

Reviewing Tracked Changes

Next, Joy would like to read the tracked changes and comments from Keith. She could scroll through the document and point to each markup to read it, but she might overlook one or more changes using this technique. A more efficient method is to use the Reviewing toolbar to review the changes and comments one at a time, deciding whether to accept, modify, or delete them. To do this, be sure the markups display on the screen. If they do not, click View on the menu bar and then click Markup.

Perform the steps on the next page to review the changes and comments from Keith.

More *About*

Versions

To automatically save a version of a document when you close the document, click File on the menu bar, click Versions, place a check mark in the Automatically save a version on close check box, and then click the Close button.

Steps To Review Tracked Changes

1 Press CTRL+HOME to position the insertion point at the beginning of the document. Point to the Next button on the Reviewing toolbar.

With the insertion point at the beginning of the document, the review of tracked changes and comments will begin at the top of the document (Figure 9-16).

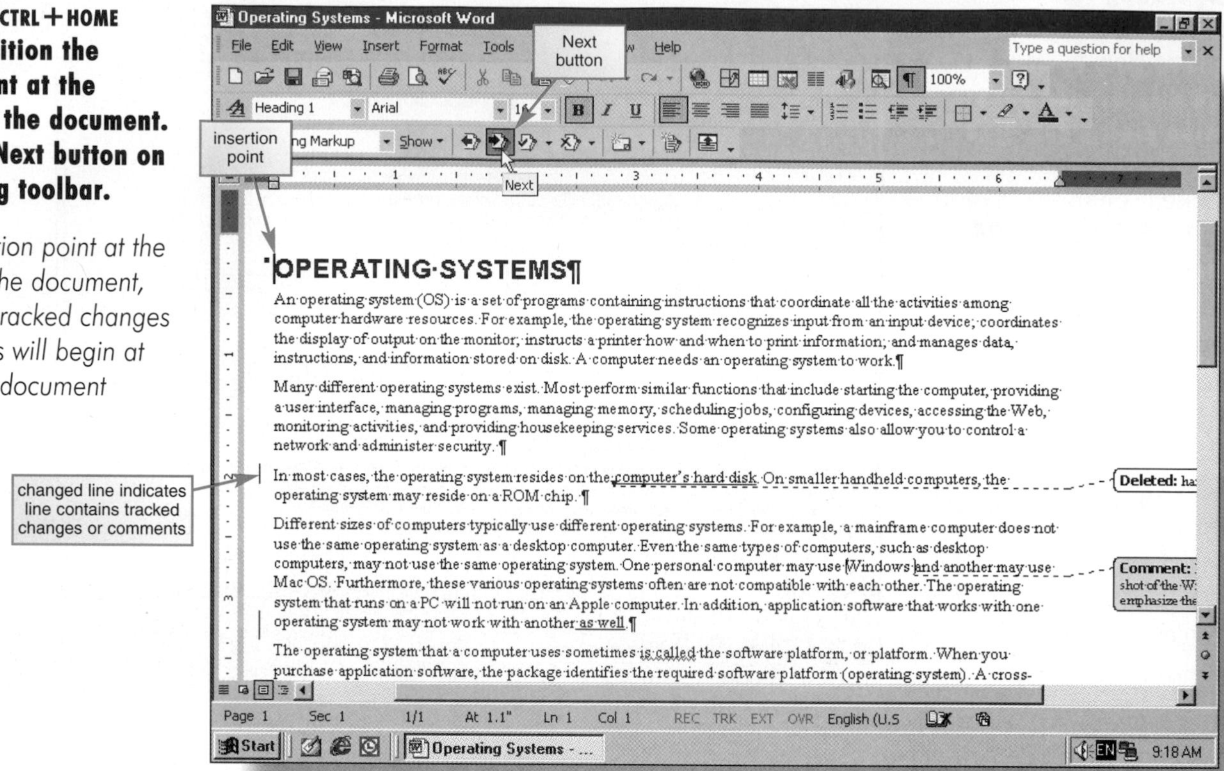

FIGURE 9-16

2 Click the Next button. If necessary, click the right scroll arrow on the horizontal scroll bar so that the markup balloon is visible. Point to the Accept Change button on the Reviewing toolbar.

Word selects the tracked change, which is the deleted text (Figure 9-17). You will accept this change.

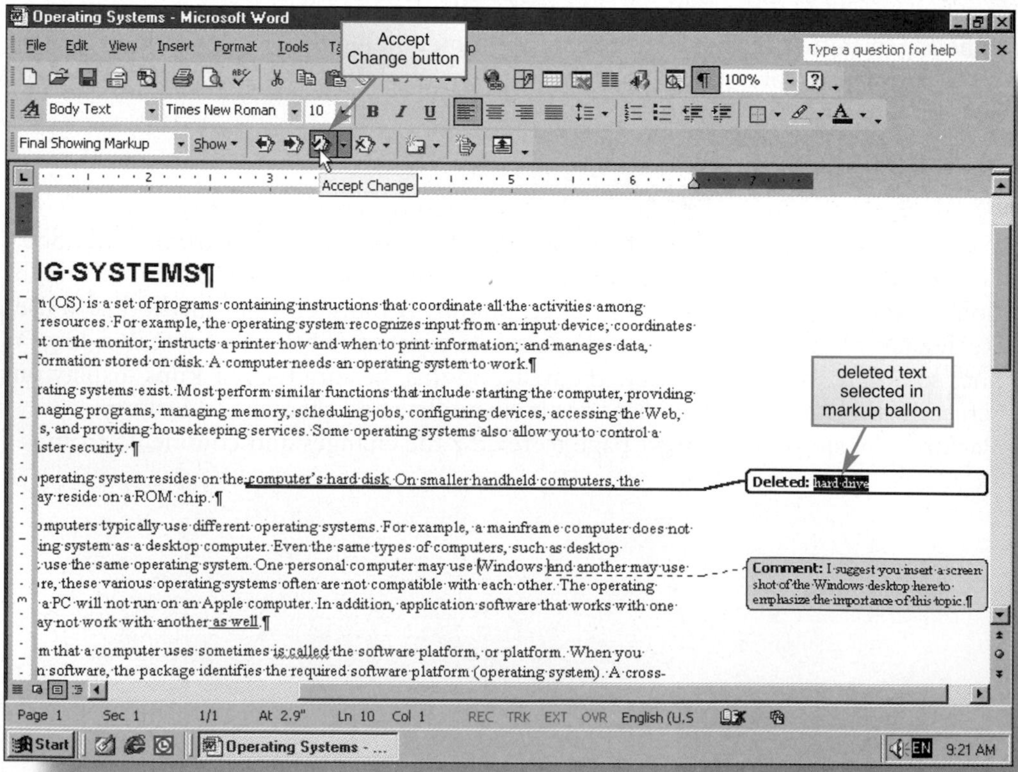

FIGURE 9-17

3 Click the Accept Change button and then click the Next button on the Reviewing toolbar.

Word accepts the deletion and selects the next change, the inserted text (Figure 9-18).

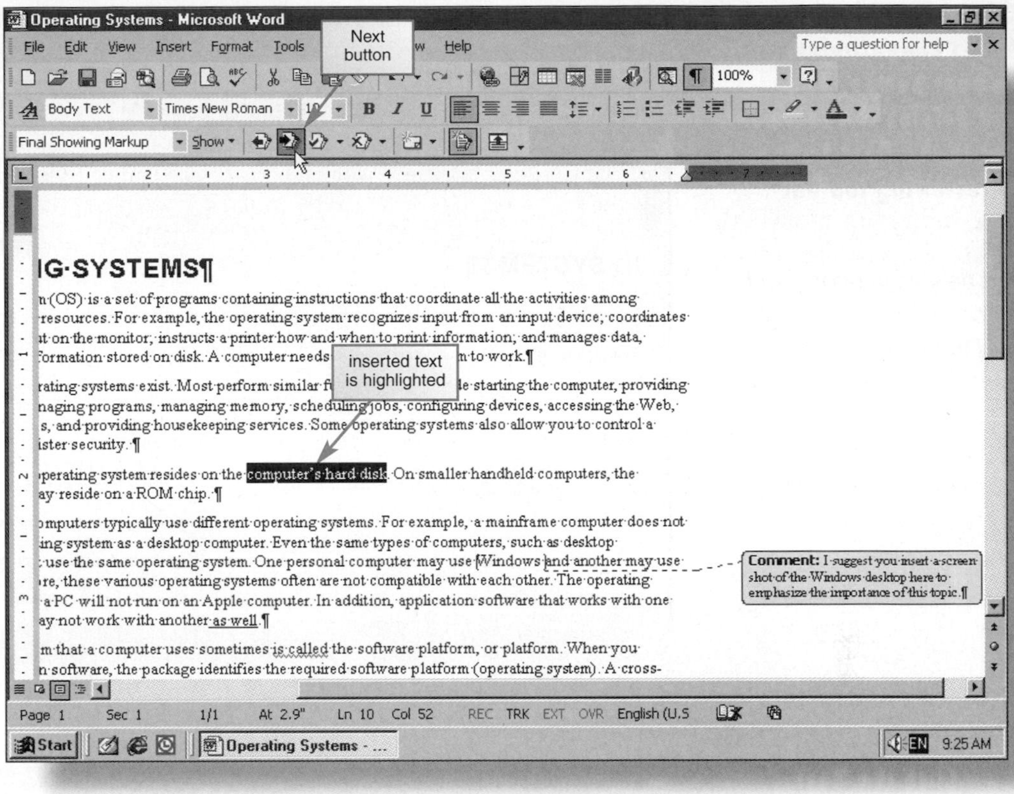

FIGURE 9-18

4 Click the Accept Change button and then click the Next button on the Reviewing toolbar. When Word displays the insertion point in the comment balloon, point to the Reject Change/Delete Comment button on the Reviewing toolbar.

The previous insertion is accepted, and now the comment is selected (Figure 9-19).

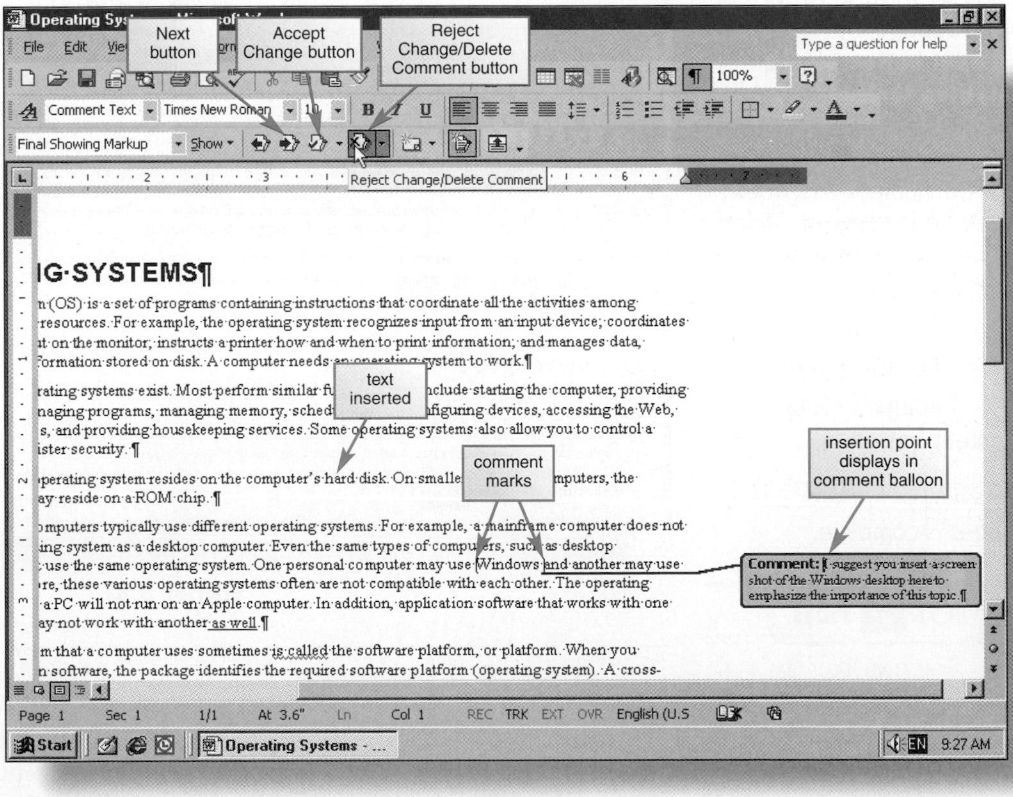

FIGURE 9-19

5 **Click the Reject Change/Delete Comment button. After Word deletes the comment, point to the Next button on the Reviewing toolbar again.**

Word deletes the comment balloon and the comment marks in the document (Figure 9-20).

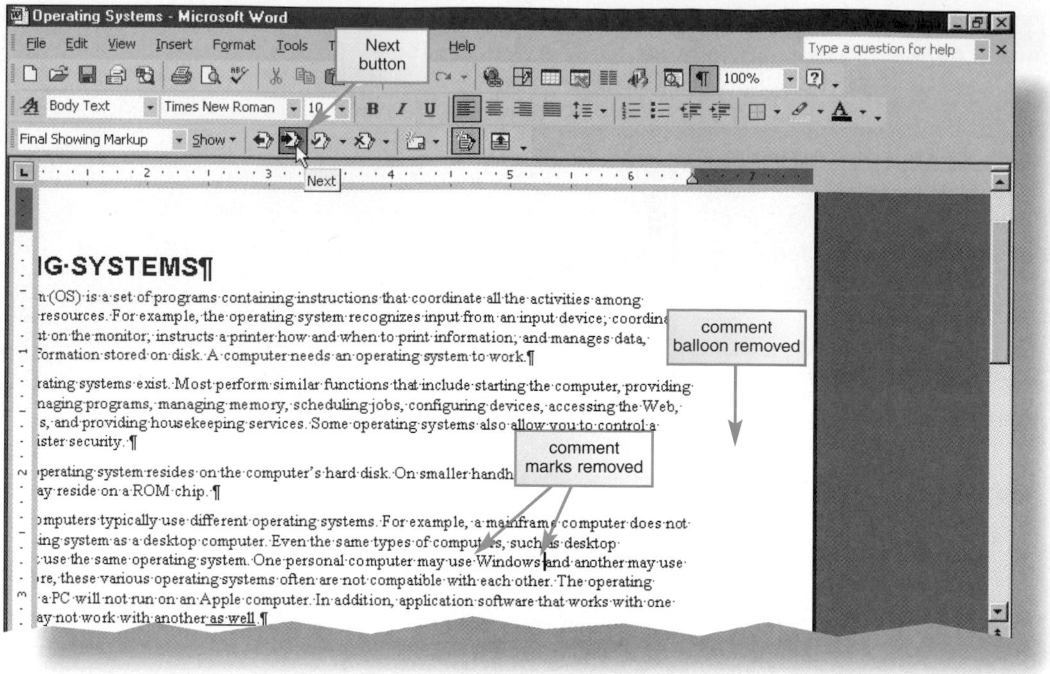

FIGURE 9-20

6 **Click the Next button. When Word selects the insertion of the words, as well, point to the Reject Change/Delete Comment button on the Reviewing toolbar.**

The words, as well, are selected (Figure 9-21). You do not want to accept this change because the words are unnecessary.

7 **Click the Reject Change/Delete Comment button.**

The review of tracked changes is complete.

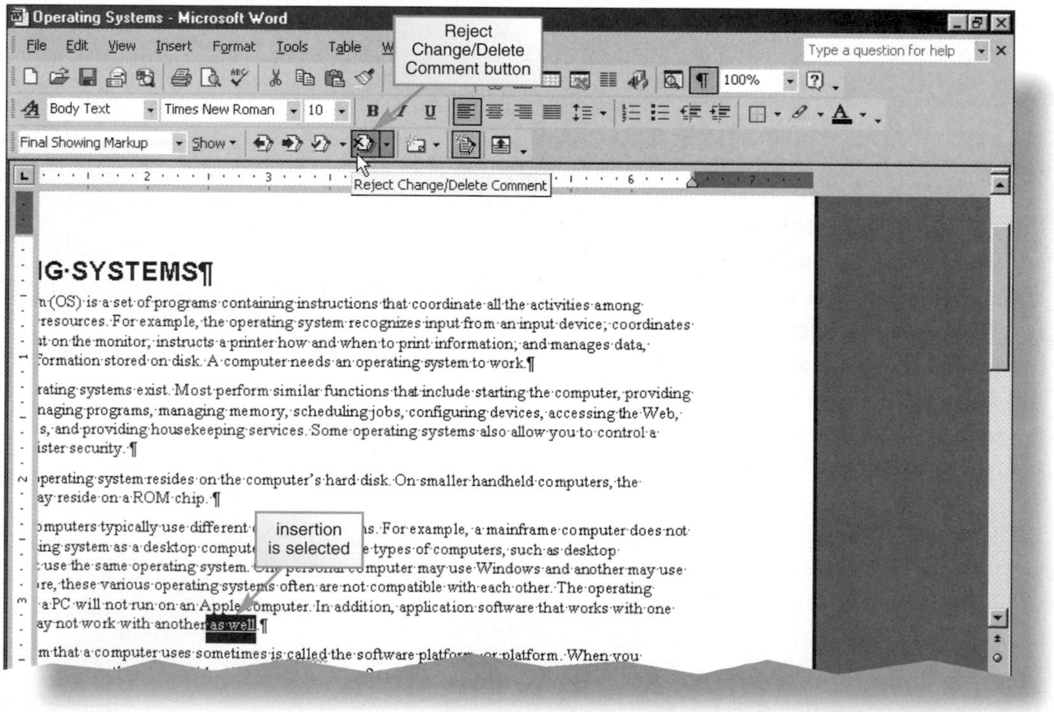

FIGURE 9-21

Other Ways

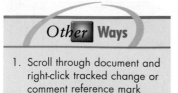

1. Scroll through document and right-click tracked change or comment reference mark
2. On File menu click Print, click Print what box arrow, click Document showing markup
3. In Voice Command mode, say "Track Changes"

You also may accept or reject a change or comment by right-clicking it. On the shortcut menu, choices display that allow you to accept or reject the changes.

If you are certain you plan to accept all changes in a document containing tracked changes, you can accept all the changes at once by clicking the Accept Change button arrow on the Reviewing toolbar and then clicking Accept All

Changes in Document. Likewise, you can click the Reject Change/Delete Comment button arrow on the Reviewing toolbar and then click Reject All Changes in Document or Delete All Comments in Document to reject all the changes or delete all the comments at once. If you click either of these commands by mistake, you can click the Undo button on the Standard toolbar to undo the action.

If you click the Next button and no tracked changes remain, a dialog box displays informing you the document contains no more changes. If this occurs, click the OK button.

To see how a document will look if you accept all the changes, without actually accepting them, click Markup on the View menu or click the Display for Review button on the Reviewing toolbar and then click Final. To print a hard copy that shows how the document will look if you accept all the changes, click Markup on the View menu so the tracked changes do not display, and then print in the usual manner.

> **More About**
>
> **Displaying Comments**
>
> If a comment's text does not display in a ScreenTip when you point to the comment reference mark, click Tools on the menu bar, click Options, click the View tab, place a check mark in the ScreenTips check box, and then click the OK button.

Comparing and Merging Documents

When a document has multiple reviewers, you can use Word's Compare and Merge feature to compare any two documents. Word shows the differences among the documents as tracked changes that you can accept or reject. The changes display the reviewer's name in the ScreenTip.

Joy has sent the document to her co-workers, Anita, Donna, and Patti. You want to compare and merge each of the changed documents to Joy's document. Each co-worker's document is saved on the Data Disk that accompanies this book. If you did not download the Data Disk, see the inside back cover for instructions for downloading the Data Disk or see your instructor.

Perform the following steps to compare and merge documents.

Steps To Compare and Merge Documents

1 Insert the Data Disk into drive A. With the Operating Systems document still displaying in the Word window, press CTRL+HOME to position the insertion point at the beginning of the document. Click the Zoom box arrow on the Standard toolbar and then click Page Width. Click Tools on the menu bar and then point to Compare and Merge Documents (Figure 9-22).

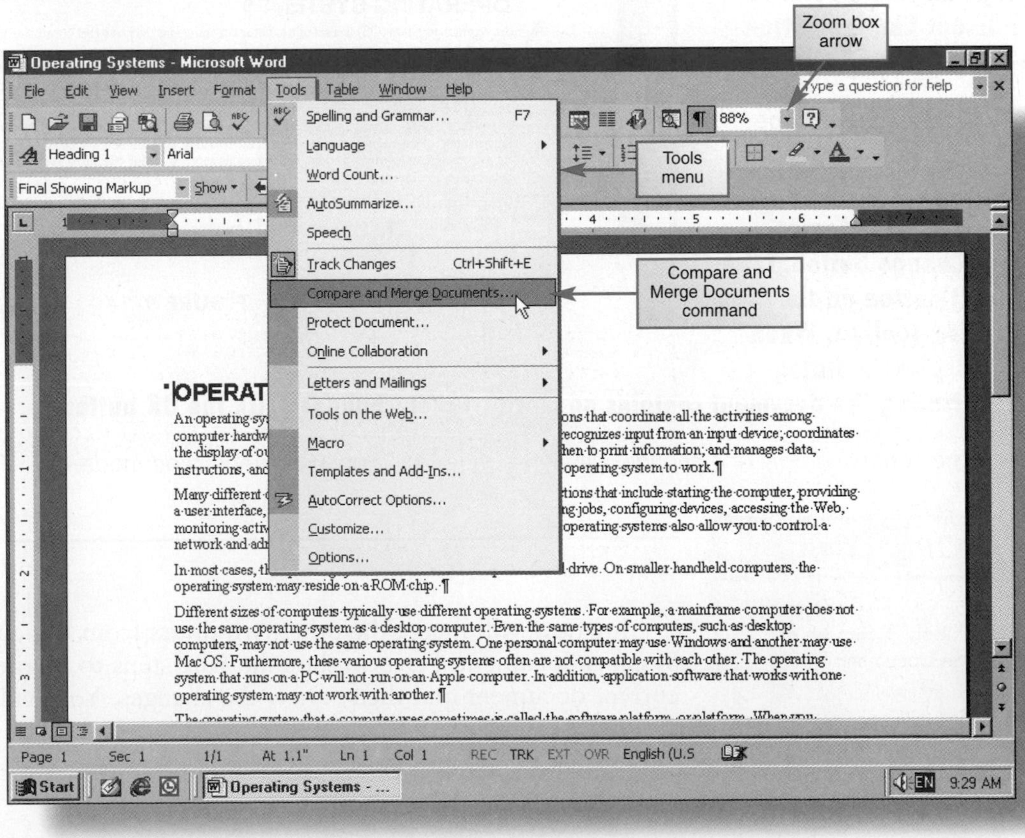

FIGURE 9-22

2 **Click Compare and Merge Documents. When the Compare and Merge Documents dialog box displays, if necessary click the Look in box arrow and then click 3½ Floppy (A:). Click Anita's Draft in the list. Click the Merge button arrow and then point to Merge into current document.**

The Merge menu displays three commands: Merge, Merge into current document, and Merge into new document (Figure 9-23).

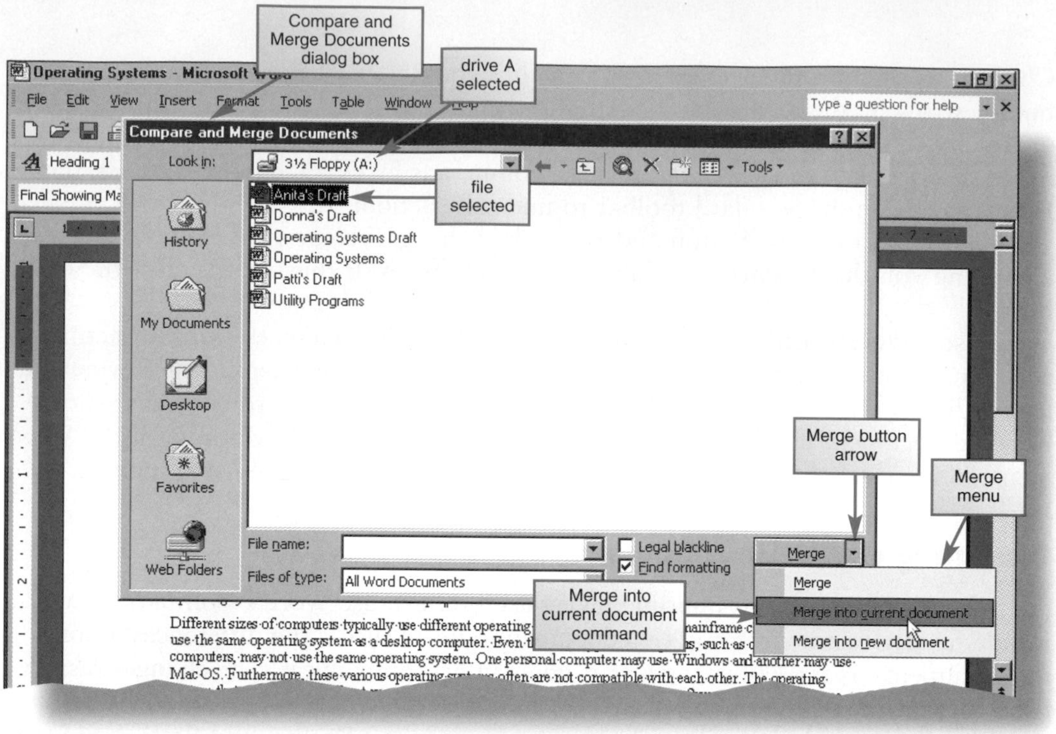

FIGURE 9-23

3 **Click Merge into current document. When the document again is visible, click the Next button on the Reviewing toolbar. When the first change displays, point to the Accept Change button on the Reviewing toolbar.**

You will accept the change (Figure 9-24).

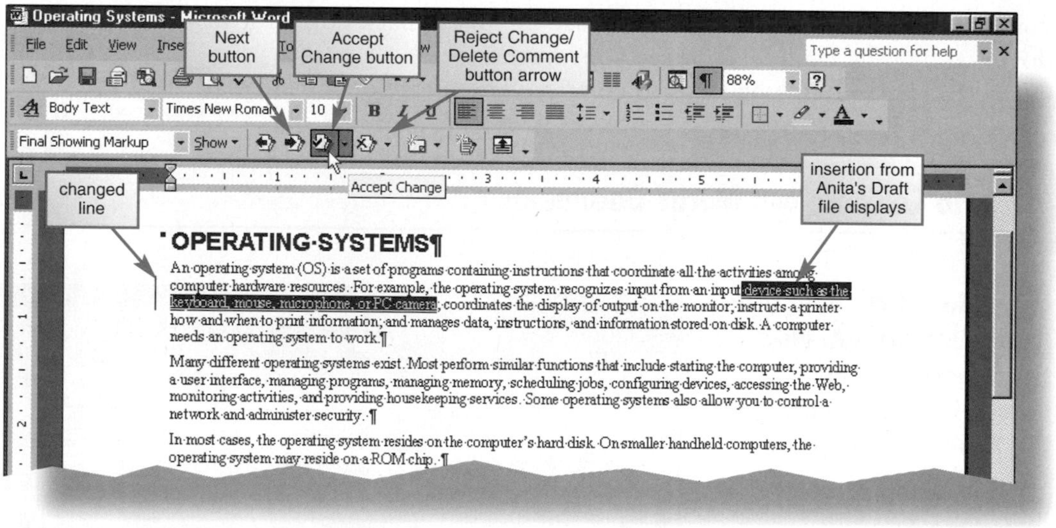

FIGURE 9-24

4 **Click the Accept Change button. Click the Next button on the Reviewing toolbar. When Word displays a dialog box indicating the document contains no more tracked changes, click the OK button.**

The merge contained only one change. Anita's change to the document has been made.

Other Ways

1. In Voice Command mode, say "Tools, Compare and Merge Documents"

Joy now will merge the other two drafts from her co-workers into the Operating Systems document. Perform the following steps to merge both documents into the current document and then review the changes. You will reject all the changes from the two drafts.

TO COMPARE AND MERGE, REJECTING CHANGES

1. With the Data Disk in drive A, click Tools on the menu bar and then click Compare and Merge Documents.
2. When the Compare and Merge Documents dialog box displays, if necessary click the Look in box arrow and then click 3½ Floppy (A:). Click Donna's Draft in the list. Click the Merge button arrow and then click Merge into current document.
3. Repeat Steps 1 and 2 to merge Patti's Draft from the Data Disk.
4. When the document again displays, read through all the tracked changes. Click the Reject Change/Delete Comment button arrow on the Reviewing toolbar and then click Reject All Changes in Document.

The document displays with no changes accepted from either the Donna's Draft or Patti's Draft files.

Even if a reviewer does not remember to use the change-tracking feature while editing a document, you can use Word's Compare and Merge feature to compare the reviewer's document to your original document. Word will track changes to display all differences between the two documents — which you can accept or reject later.

Because you now are finished tracking changes, you can hide the Reviewing toolbar, as shown in the following steps.

TO HIDE THE REVIEWING TOOLBAR

1. Right-click the Reviewing toolbar.
2. Click Reviewing on the shortcut menu.

Word hides the Reviewing toolbar. Thus, it no longer displays in the Word window.

Preparing a Document to Be Included in a Longer Document

Joy is not finished with the Operating Systems file yet. Based on the comment from Keith, Joy needs to include a screen shot of Windows. After the screen shot is inserted, she needs to add a figure caption to the graphic — because public information guide documents always have figure captions. Then, she will modify the text so it references the figure. The last page of all public information guide documents is an index, so Joy will mark any words in the Operating Systems document that should be listed in the index. As a precaution, she will ensure that single lines of any paragraph do not display by themselves on a page. Finally, Joy will save the document with a password, which will allow only authorized individuals to open and modify the file in the future.

The following pages outline these changes to the Operating Systems document. The final copy of the document is shown in Figure 9-4b on page WD 9.10.

More About

Screen Shots

Many computer application programs exist to help capture screen images. For information on a screen capture program, visit the Word 2002 More About Web page (scsite.com/wd2002/more.htm) and then click Capture Screen Images.

Inserting and Formatting a Graphic

The graphic you will insert in the Operating Systems document is located on the Data Disk that accompanies this book. If you did not download the Data Disk, see the inside back cover for instructions for downloading the Data Disk or see your instructor. The graphic displays a screen shot of Windows. A **screen shot** is a picture of the screen captured either by pressing the PRINT SCREEN key on the keyboard or by using special screen capturing software. You will insert the screen shot graphic, resize it, and then change it from an inline graphic to a floating graphic.

Perform the following steps to insert the screen shot graphic from the file on the Data Disk.

TO INSERT A GRAPHIC

1. Position the insertion point at the beginning of the fourth paragraph in the Operating Systems file. Click Insert on the menu bar, point to Picture, and then click From File on the Picture submenu.
2. When the Insert Picture dialog box displays, click the Look in box arrow and then click 3½ Floppy (A:).
3. Click Windows Screen Shot in the list of files and then click the Insert button.

Word inserts the screen shot graphic into the document.

> **More About**
> **Graphics**
> Two basic types of graphics that you can use to enhance your documents are drawing objects and pictures. Drawing objects include AutoShapes, diagrams, curves, lines, and WordArt drawing objects — all of which become part of your Word document. Pictures are graphics created from another file, which include bitmaps, scanned pictures, photographs, and clip art.

You want the screen shot graphic to be smaller in the document. Thus, perform the following steps to resize the graphic.

TO RESIZE A GRAPHIC

1. Double-click the graphic.
2. When the Format Picture dialog box displays, click the Size tab. Change the height and width values in the Scale area to 55%.
3. Click the OK button.

Word reduces the size of the screen shot graphic to 55 percent of its original size (Figure 9-25).

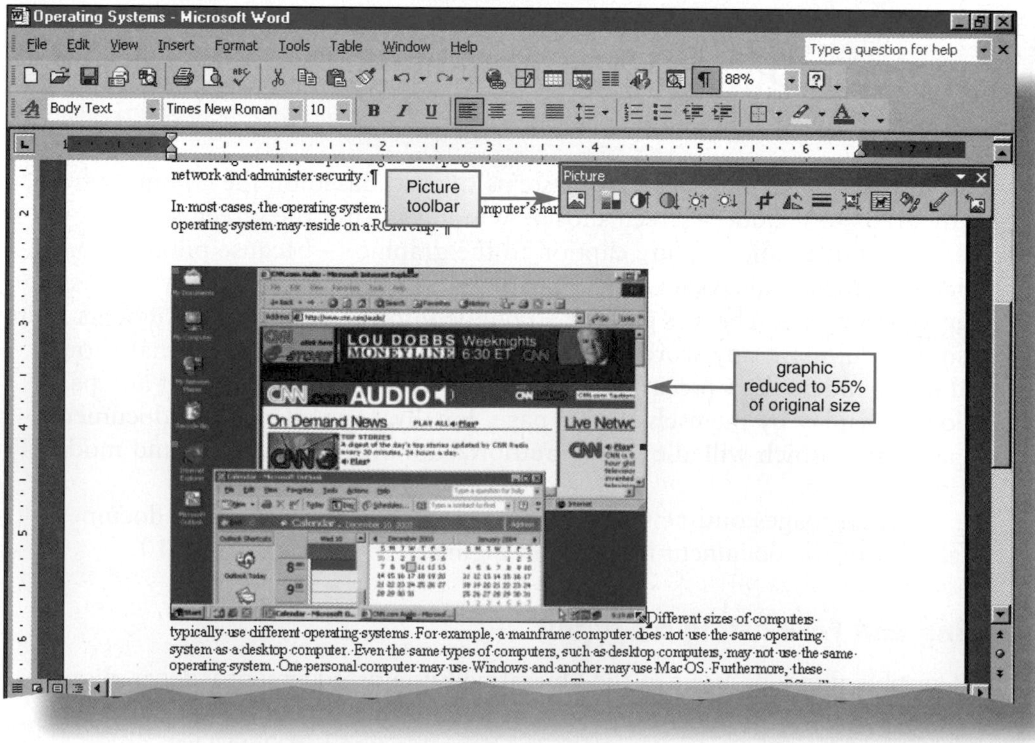

FIGURE 9-25

Notice in Figure 9-25 that the screen shot graphic is inline; that is, the graphic is part of the current paragraph. You want to position the graphic to the left of the paragraph and have the text wrap to the right of the graphic. Thus, the graphic needs to be a floating graphic instead of an inline graphic. To accomplish this, change the graphic's wrapping style to square, as shown in the following steps.

More About

Editing Graphics

Use the Drawing toolbar to edit drawing objects using color, patterns, borders, and other effects. Use the Picture toolbar and color and shading buttons on the Drawing toolbar to edit pictures. In some cases, you must ungroup and convert a picture to a drawing object before you can use many of the other Drawing toolbar options.

TO CHANGE AN INLINE GRAPHIC TO A FLOATING GRAPHIC

1. If the Picture toolbar does not display, right-click the graphic, and then click Show Picture Toolbar on the shortcut menu. With the graphic still selected, click the Text Wrapping button on the Picture toolbar and then point to Square (Figure 9-26).
2. Click Square.
3. If necessary, scroll down to display the graphic and then drag the graphic to the left of the paragraph to position the graphic as shown in Figure 9-27 on the next page.

Word converts the graphic from inline to floating so you can position it anywhere on the page.

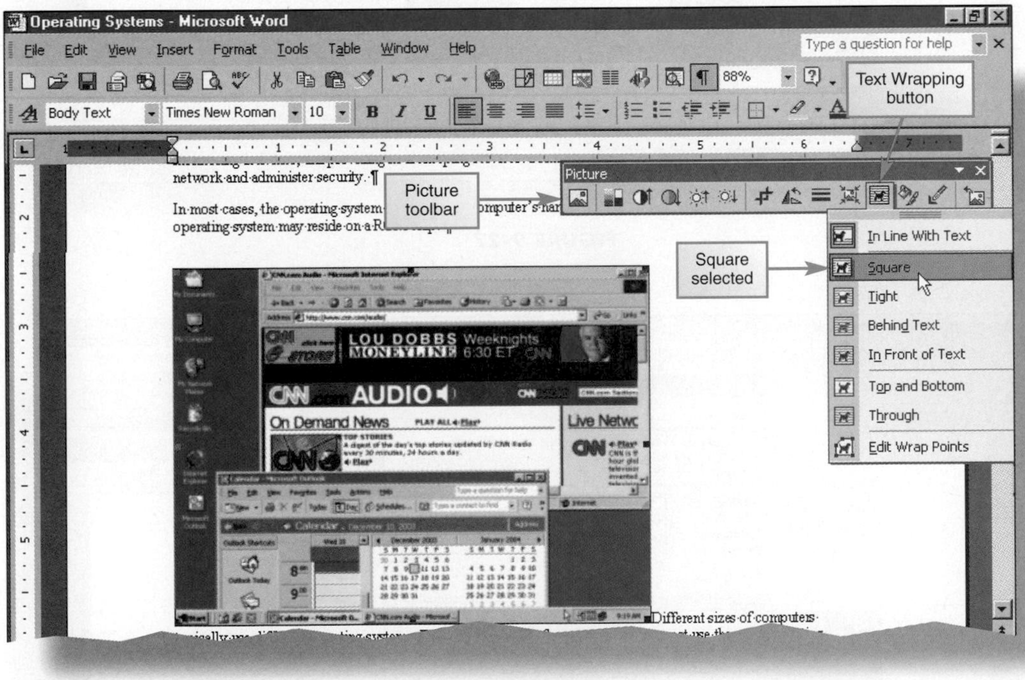

FIGURE 9-26

The next step is to add a caption to the graphic.

Adding a Caption

At the end of all public information guide documents is a table of figures, which lists all figures and their corresponding page numbers. Word generates this table of figures from the captions in the document. A **caption** is a numbered label, such as Figure 1, that you can add to a table, figure, equation, or other item. If you move, delete, or add captions in a document, Word renumbers remaining captions in the document automatically.

Perform the steps on the next page to add a caption to the graphic.

More About

Captions

If your caption displays with extra characters inside curly braces {}, Word is displaying field codes instead of field results. Press ALT+F9 to display the caption correctly as field results. If your caption prints field codes, click Tools on the menu bar, click Options, click the Print tab, remove the check mark from the Field codes check box, click the OK button, and then print the document again.

Steps To Add a Caption

1 **With the graphic still selected, click Insert on the menu bar, point to Reference, and then point to Caption on the Reference submenu (Figure 9-27).**

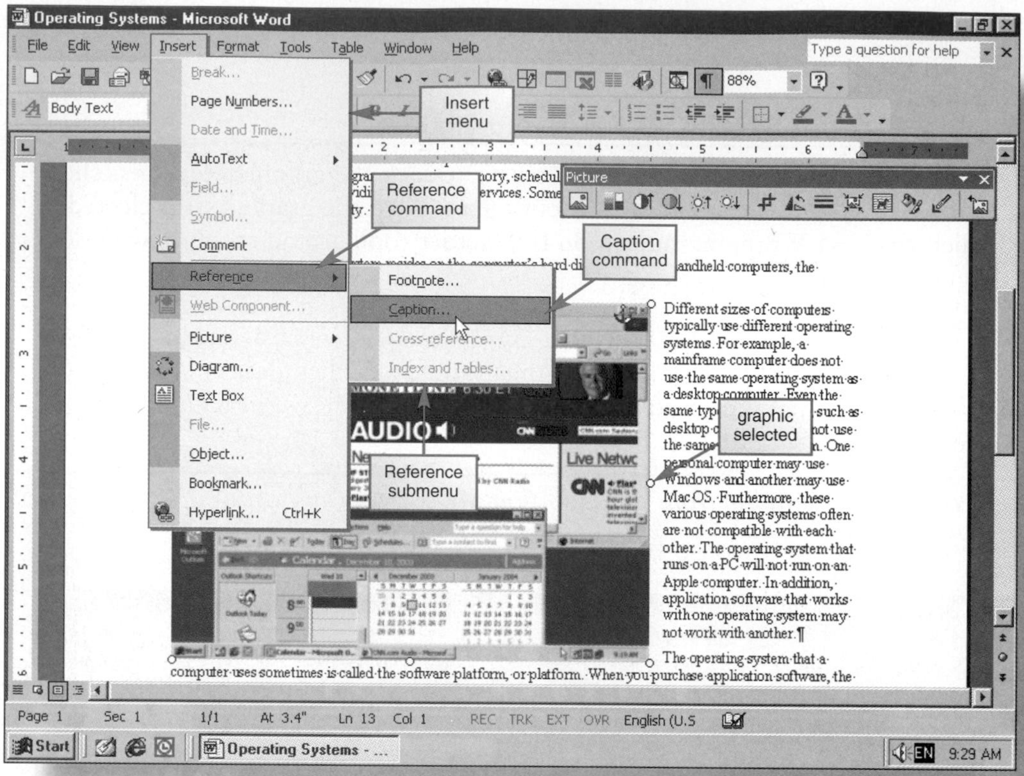

FIGURE 9-27

2 **Click Caption. When the Caption dialog box displays, if necessary, click the Caption text box to position the insertion point after the text, Figure 1. Press the COLON (:) key and then press the SPACEBAR. Type** `Windows operating system.` **Point to the OK button.**

Word displays the Caption dialog box (Figure 9-28). Word will position the caption for this figure below the graphic.

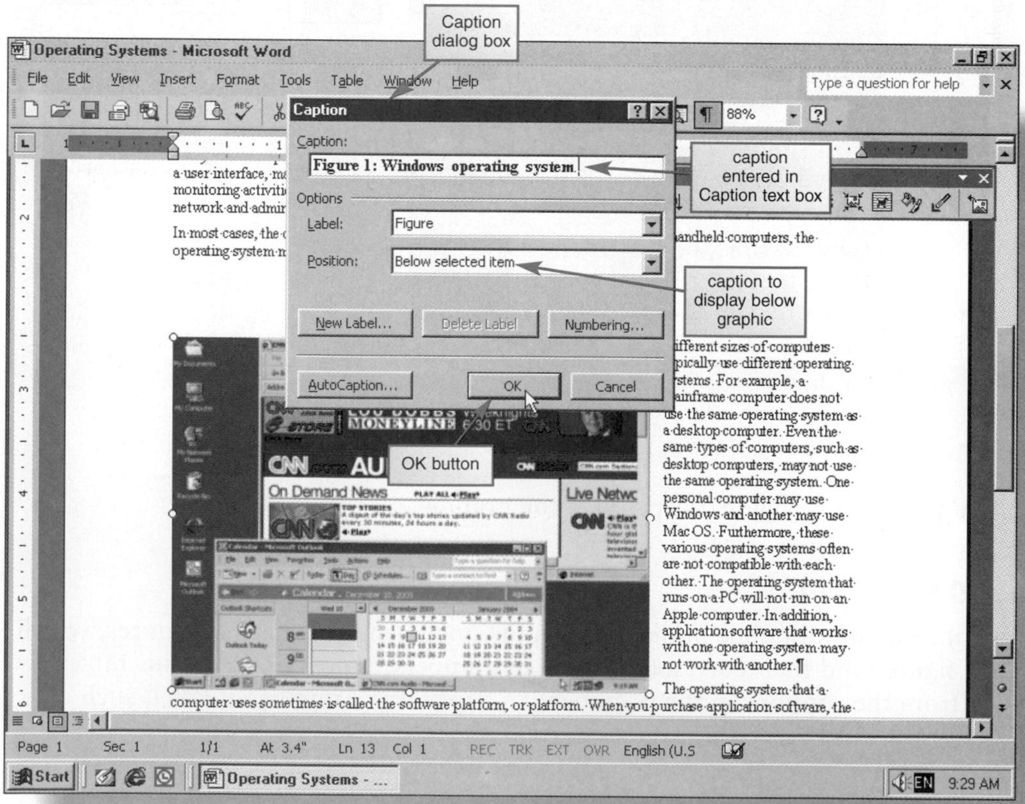

FIGURE 9-28

3 **Click the OK button.**

Word inserts the caption in a text box below the selected graphic (Figure 9-29).

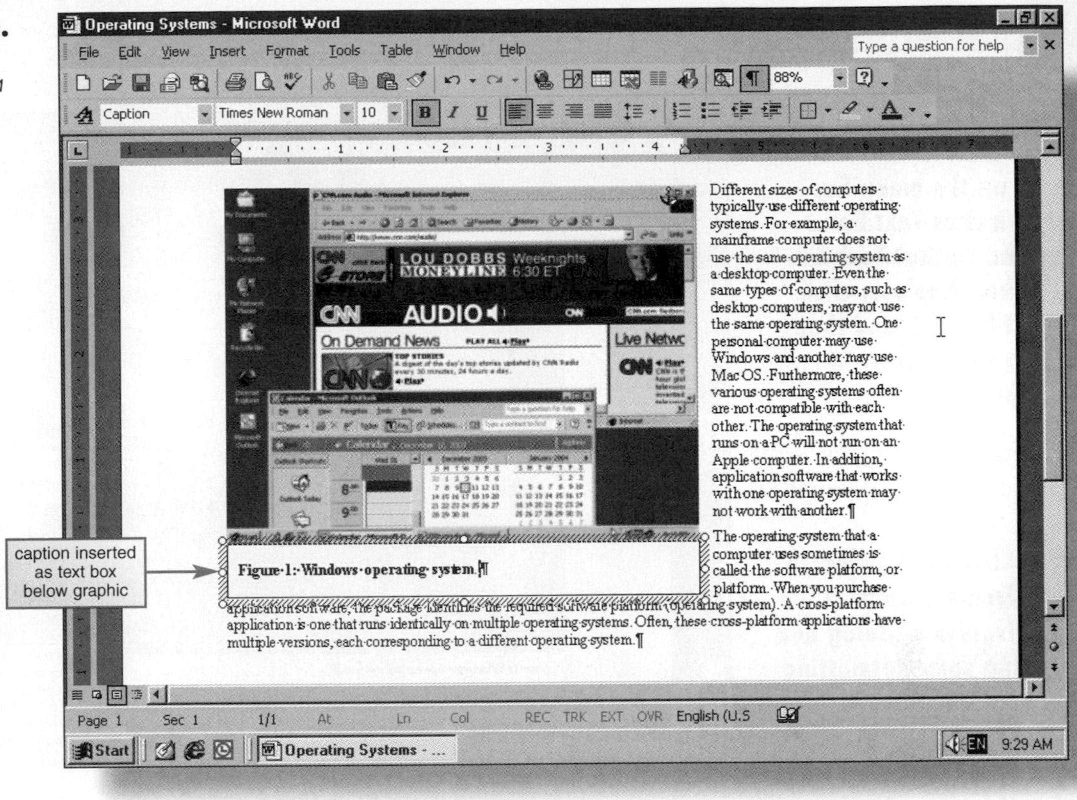

FIGURE 9-29

Other Ways

1. In Voice Command mode, say "Insert, Reference, Caption"

If, at a later time, you insert a new item with a caption, or move or delete items containing captions, Word automatically updates caption numbers throughout the document.

A caption contains a field. In Word, a **field** is a placeholder for data that you expect might change in a document. Examples of fields you have used in previous projects are page numbers, merge fields, IF fields, form fields, and the current date.

Because the caption number is a field, you update it using the same technique used to update a field. That is, to update all caption numbers, select the entire document and then press the F9 key or right-click the selection and then click Update Field on the shortcut menu. When you print a document, Word updates the caption numbers automatically, whether or not the document window displays the updated caption numbers.

When you add a caption to an inline graphic, the caption is not inserted in a text box. As just illustrated, however, the caption for a floating graphic is inserted in a text box. If you plan to generate a table of figures for a document, a caption cannot be in a text box. Instead, it must be in a frame. Perform the steps on the next page to convert the text box to a frame.

Steps To Convert a Text Box to a Frame

1 With the text box selected, click Format on the menu bar and then click Text Box. When the Format Text Box dialog box displays, click the Text Box tab and then point to the Convert to Frame button.

Word displays the Format Text Box dialog box (Figure 9-30).

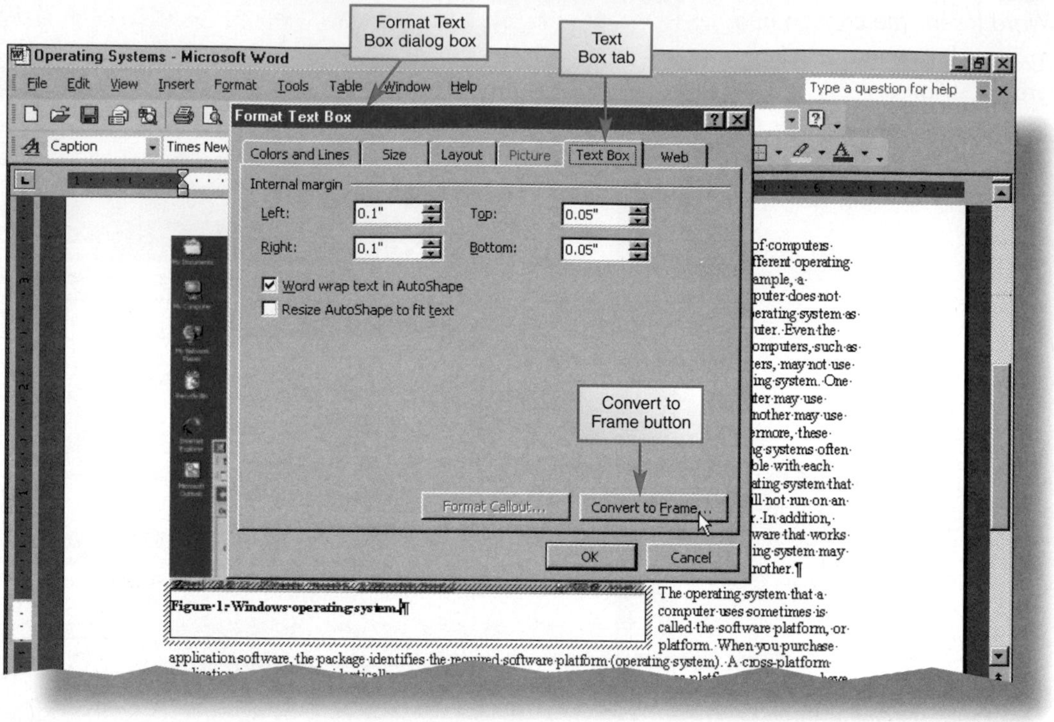

FIGURE 9-30

2 Click the Convert to Frame button. When Word displays a dialog box indicating some formatting of the frame may be lost, click the OK button. If Word displays a dialog box asking if you want a Frame command on the Insert menu, click the Cancel button.

Word converts the text box to a frame. You did not format the text box; thus, you will not lose any formatting in the conversion from a text box to a frame.

Other Ways

1. Right-click text box, click Format Text Box on shortcut menu, click Text Box tab, click Convert to Frame button
2. In Voice Command mode, say "Format, Text Box, Text Box, Convert to Frame, OK"

Notice in Figure 9-29 on the previous page that the caption has a border around it. This is because Word automatically placed a border around the caption when it was a text box. You do not want the border around the caption. You also want to center the contents of the caption. Perform the following steps to modify the caption.

TO MODIFY THE CAPTION

1. With the caption frame selected, click the Border button arrow on the Formatting toolbar and then click No Border.
2. Click in the caption text and then click the Center button on the Formatting toolbar.

Word modifies the caption (shown in Figure 9-31).

The next step is to add a reference to the new figure in the document text.

Creating a Cross-Reference

In public information guide documents, the text always makes a specific reference to a figure and explains the contents of the figure. Thus, you want to enter a phrase into the document that refers to the figure of the screen shot graphic. Recall that the Operating Systems file will be inserted into a larger file. You do not know what the figure number of the graphic will be in the new document. In Word, you can create a **cross-reference**, which is a link to an item such as a heading, caption, or footnote in a document. By creating a cross-reference to the caption, the text that mentions the figure will update whenever the caption to the figure updates.

Perform the following steps to create a cross-reference.

Steps To Create a Cross-Reference

1 Position the insertion point so that it is immediately to the left of the text, and another may use, in the fourth paragraph. Press the LEFT PARENTHESIS (() key. Click Insert on the menu bar, point to Reference, and then point to Cross-reference on the Reference submenu (Figure 9-31).

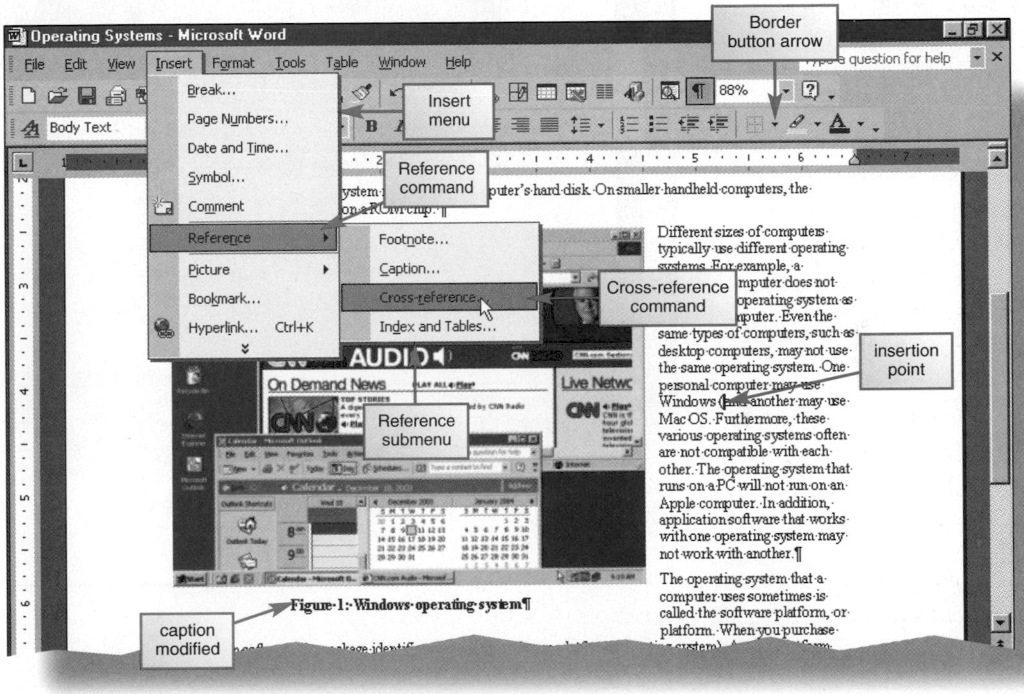

FIGURE 9-31

2 Click Cross-reference. When the Cross-reference dialog box displays, click the Reference type box arrow and then click Figure. Click the Insert reference to box arrow and then click Only label and number. If the Insert as hyperlink check box contains a check mark, remove the check mark. Point to the Insert button.

Word displays the Cross-reference dialog box (Figure 9-32). You want the text to display only the label (the word, Figure) and the label number (the figure number).

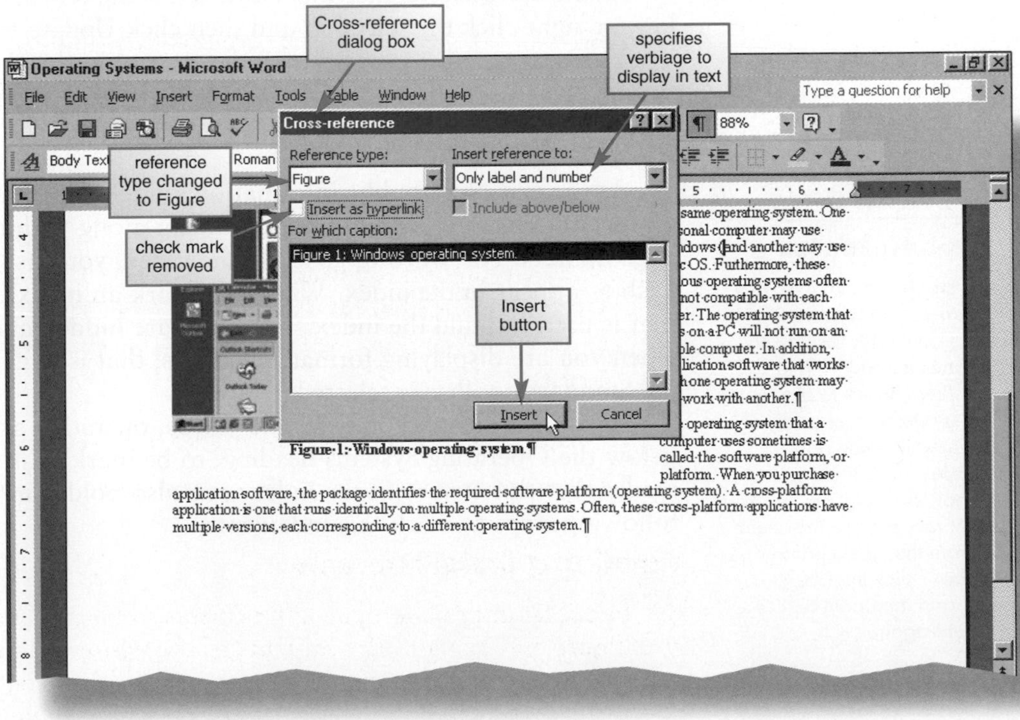

FIGURE 9-32

3 **Click the Insert button. Click the Close button in the Cross-reference dialog box. Press the RIGHT PARENTHESIS ()) key and then press the SPACEBAR.**

Word inserts the cross-reference to the figure into the document text (Figure 9-33). Because the figure number in the document is a field, Word may shade it gray — depending on your Word settings.

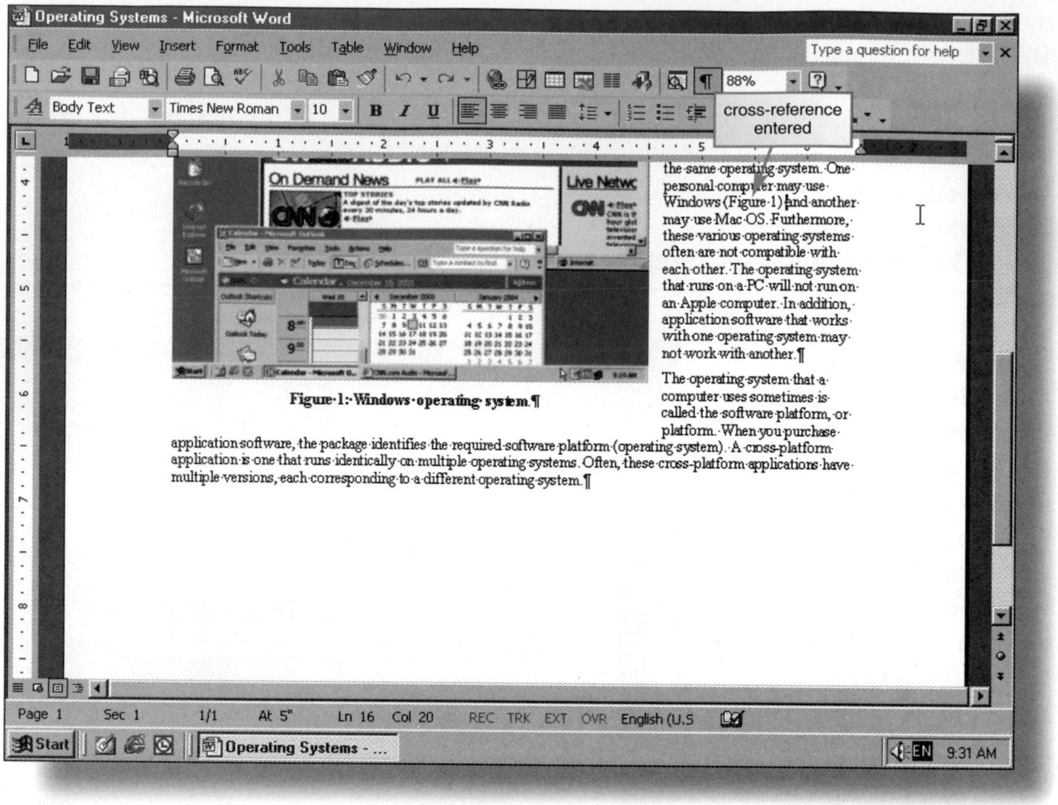

FIGURE 9-33

Other Ways

1. In Voice Command mode, say "Insert, Reference, Cross-reference"

Like caption numbers, a cross-reference is a field. In many cases, Word automatically updates cross-references in a document if the item it refers to changes. To update a cross-reference manually, select the cross-reference and then press the F9 key, or right-click the selection and then click Update Field on the shortcut menu.

The next step is to mark any index entries in this document.

Marking Index Entries

At the end of all public information guide documents is an index, which lists important terms discussed in the document along with each term's corresponding page number. For Word to generate the index, you first must mark any item you wish to appear in the index. When you mark an index entry, Word creates a field that is used to build the index. The fields are hidden and display on the screen only when you are displaying formatting marks; that is, when the Show/Hide ¶ button on the Standard toolbar is selected.

In this document, you want the words, operating system, in the first sentence below the Operating Systems heading, to be marked as an index entry. To alert the reader that this term is in the index, you also bold it in the document. Perform the following steps to mark this index entry.

More About

Cross-References

If your cross-reference displays odd characters inside curly braces {}, Word is displaying field codes instead of field results. Press ALT+F9 to display the cross-reference correctly. If your cross-reference prints field codes, click Tools on the menu bar, click Options, click the Print tab, remove the check mark from the Field codes check box, click the OK button, and then print the document again.

Steps To Mark an Index Entry

1 **Press CTRL+HOME to position the insertion point at the beginning of the document. Select the text you wish to appear in the index (the words, operating system, in this case). Press ALT+SHIFT+X. When the Mark Index Entry dialog box displays, point to the Mark button.**

Word displays the Mark Index Entry dialog box (Figure 9-34).

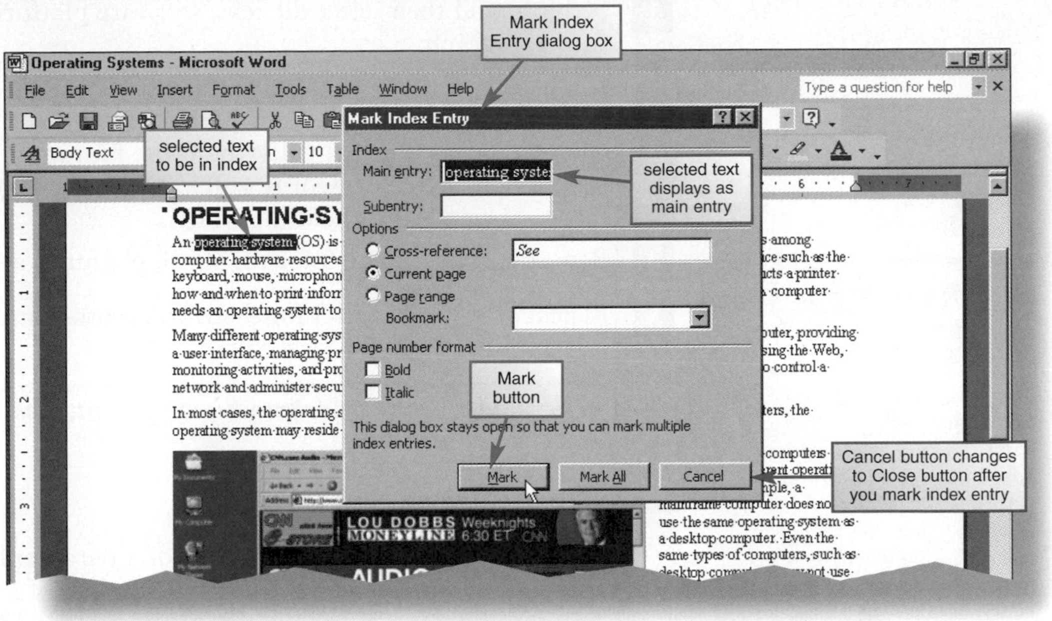

FIGURE 9-34

2 **Click the Mark button. Click the Close button in the Mark Index Entry dialog box. Again, select the words, operating system, to the left of the left brace and then press CTRL+B to apply bold formatting.**

Word inserts an index entry field into the document (Figure 9-35). These fields display on the screen only when the Show/Hide ¶ button on the Standard toolbar is selected.

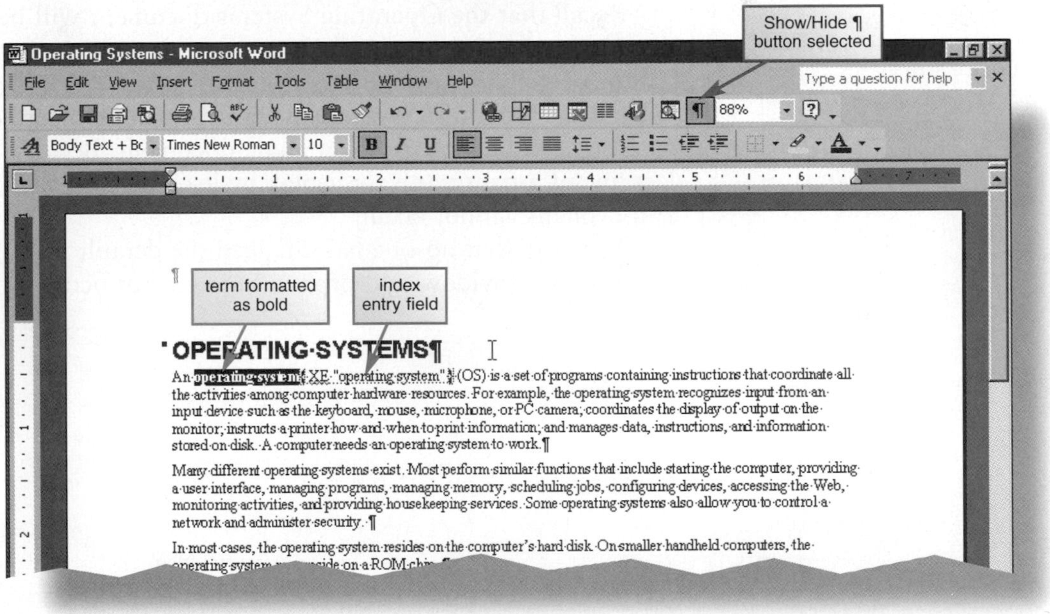

FIGURE 9-35

Word leaves the Mark Index Entry dialog box open until you close it, which allows you to mark multiple index entries without having to reopen the dialog box repeatedly. To mark multiple index entries, click in the document window, scroll to and select the next index entry, click the Main entry text box in the Mark Index Entry dialog box (shown in Figure 9-34), and then click the Mark button.

Perform the steps on the next page to mark more index entries and bold them.

Other Ways

1. Select text, on Insert menu point to Reference, click Index and Tables on Reference submenu, click Index tab, click Mark Entry button, click Mark button, click Close button
2. In Voice Command mode, say "Insert, Reference, Cross-reference"

TO MARK MORE INDEX ENTRIES AND BOLD THEM

1. Scroll to and then select the text, software platform, in the first sentence of the fifth paragraph.
2. Press ALT+SHIFT+X.
3. Click the Mark button. Click the Close button in the Mark Index Entry dialog box. Again, select the words, software platform, to the left of the left brace and then press CTRL+B to bold the words.
4. Repeat Steps 1, 2, and 3 for the word, platform, at the end of the same sentence.
5. Repeat Steps 1, 2, and 3 for the word, cross-platform, later in the same paragraph.

Word inserts index entry fields into the document. The terms display in bold.

More About

Index Entries

Index entries may include a switch, which is a slash followed by a letter inserted after the field text. Switches include \b to apply bold formatting to the entry's page number, \f to define an entry type, \i to make the entry's page number italic, \r to insert a range of pages numbers, \t to insert specified text in place of a page number, and \y to specify that the subsequent text defines the yomi or pronunciation for the index entry. A colon in an index entry precedes a subentry keyword in the index.

Controlling Widows and Orphans

A **widow** is created when the last line of a paragraph displays by itself at the top of a page, and an **orphan** occurs when the first line of a paragraph displays by itself at the bottom of a page. Word, by default, prevents widows and orphans from occurring in a document.

Recall that the Operating Systems document will be incorporated into a larger document, the Discovering Your Computer public information guide document. Although the Operating Systems document fits on a single page now, Joy is unsure as to how the Operating Systems document will be inserted into the Discovering Your Computer public information guide document. Because she does not want the first or last line of a paragraph to display by itself on any page, Joy will ensure that widows and orphans cannot occur.

To verify that no one has changed the default setting, perform the following steps to ensure that widow and orphan lines cannot occur.

Steps To Verify the Widow and Orphan Setting

1 Press CTRL+HOME to position the insertion point at the beginning of the document. Press CTRL+A to select all the paragraphs in the document. Right-click the selection and then click Paragraph on the shortcut menu. When the Paragraph dialog box displays, click the Line and Page Breaks tab and then ensure that the Widow/Orphan control check box contains a check mark. Point to the OK button.

Word displays the Paragraph dialog box (Figure 9-36). A check mark displays in the Widow/Orphan control check box.

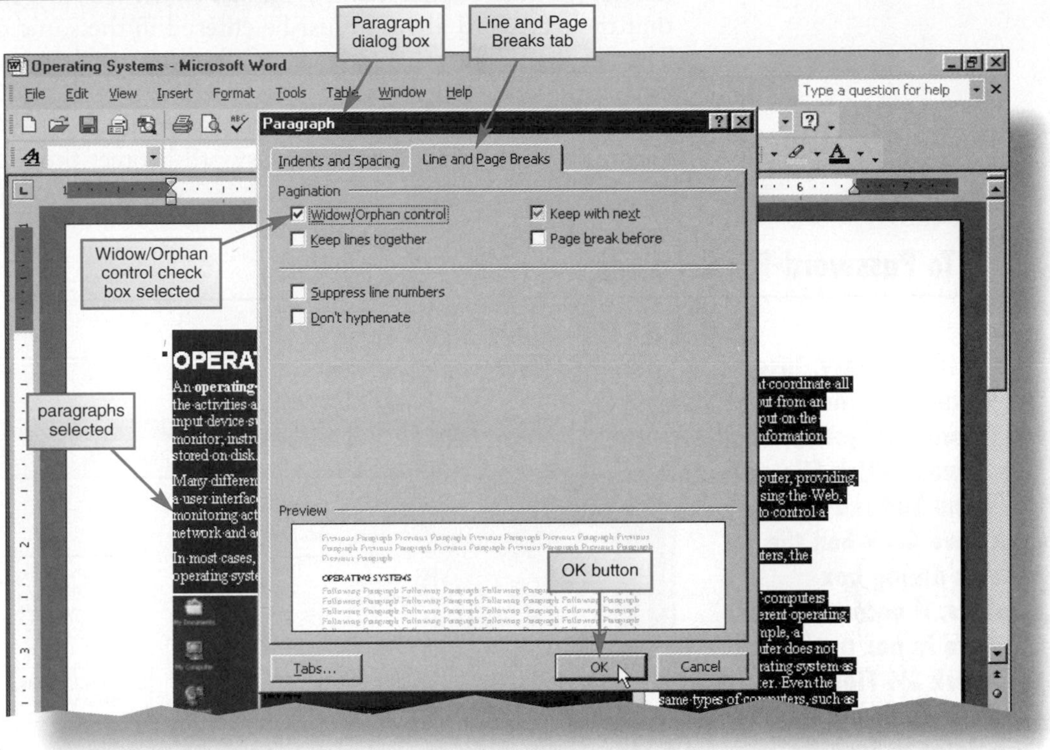

FIGURE 9-36

2 Click the OK button. Click anywhere in the document to remove the selection.

Word ensures that no widows or orphans can occur in this document.

Other Ways

1. On Format menu click Paragraph, click Line and Page Breaks tab, click Widow/Orphan control, click OK button
2. In Voice Command mode, say "Format, Paragraph, Line and Page Breaks, Widow/Orphan Control, OK"

The options in the Line and Page Breaks sheet in the Paragraph dialog box (Figure 9-36) are designed to provide you with options in how lines and paragraphs print. The Keep lines together check box can be used to ensure that a page break does not occur within a single paragraph, by positioning the insertion point in the appropriate paragraph and then selecting the check box. If you do not want a page break to occur between two paragraphs, click in the appropriate paragraph and then place a check mark in the Keep with next check box. Similarly, if you want a page break to occur immediately before a paragraph, place a check mark in the Page break before check box.

If, for some reason, you wanted to allow a widow or an orphan in a document, you would position the insertion point in the appropriate paragraph, display the Line and Page Breaks sheet in the Paragraph dialog box, and then remove the check mark from the Widow/Orphan control check box.

Password-Protecting a File

Joy is finished with the Operating Systems file and is ready to send it to Keith for inclusion in the Discovering Your Computer public information guide document. Keith, her supervisor, has specified that all incoming documents be password-protected. A **password-protected document** is a document that requires a password to open or modify it. Password protecting the document helps to ensure that the document has been modified by only authorized individuals.

In Word, a password may be up to 15 characters in length and can include letters, numbers, spaces, and symbols. Passwords are **case-sensitive**, which means that the password always must be entered in the same case in which it was saved. That is, if you enter a password in all uppercase letters, it must be entered in uppercase letters when the file is opened or modified.

Keith has suggested using the password, computer (in lowercase), for the file. Perform the following steps to password-protect the file.

Steps To Password-Protect a File

1 If necessary, insert the disk containing the Operating Systems file into drive A. Click File on the menu bar and then click Save As. When the Save As dialog box displays, if necessary, click the Save in box arrow and then click 3½ Floppy (A:). Click the Tools button and then point to Security Options.

Word displays the Save As dialog box (Figure 9-37).

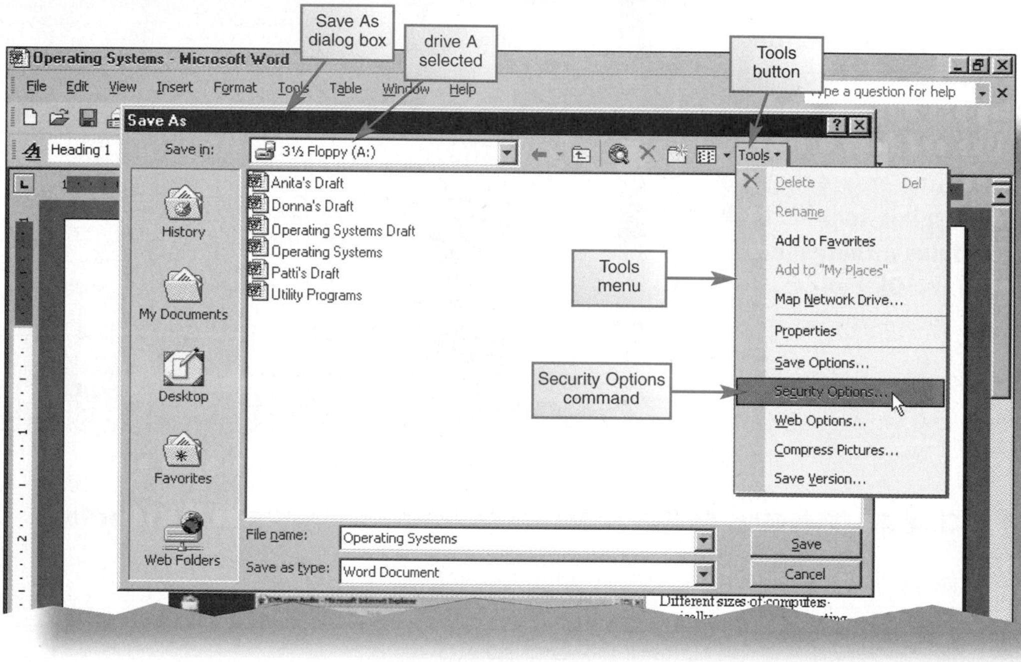

FIGURE 9-37

2 Click Security Options. When the Security dialog box displays, type `computer` **in the Password to open text box. Point to the OK button.**

Word displays the Security dialog box (Figure 9-38). When you type the password, computer, Word displays a series of asterisks (*) instead of the actual characters you type.

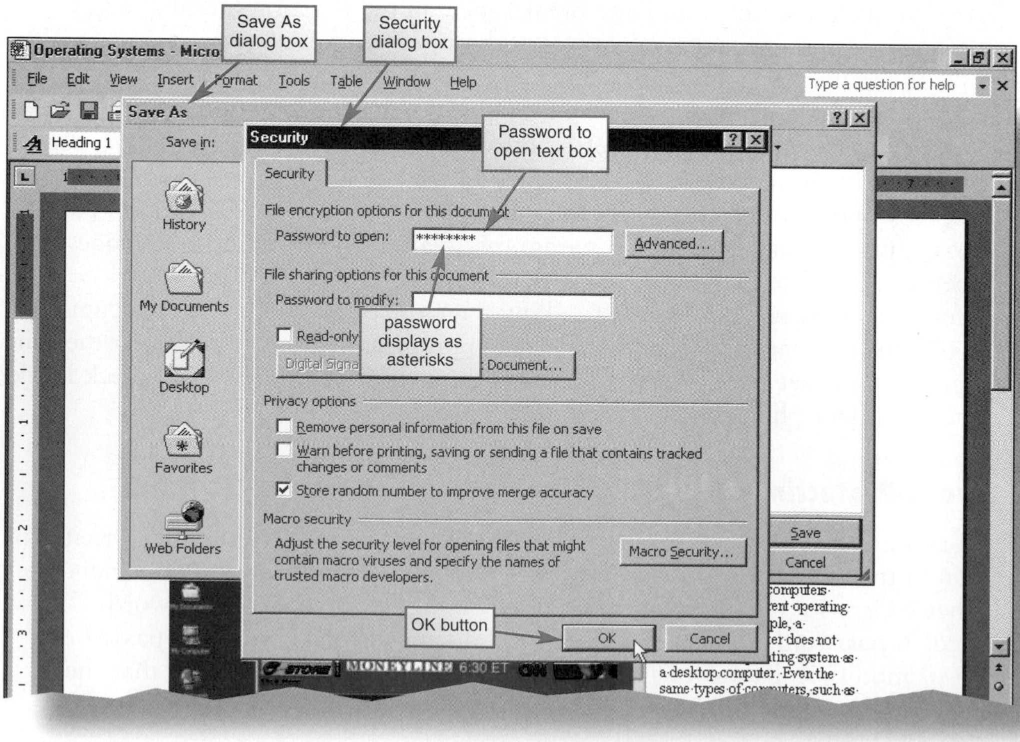

FIGURE 9-38

3 **Click the OK button. When Word displays the Confirm Password dialog box, type** `computer` **in the Reenter password to open text box. Point to the OK button in the Confirm Password dialog box.**

Word displays the Confirm Password dialog box (Figure 9-39). Again, the password displays as a series of asterisks (*) instead of the actual characters you type.

4 **Click the OK button. When the Save As dialog box is visible again, click its Save button.**

Word saves the document with the password, computer.

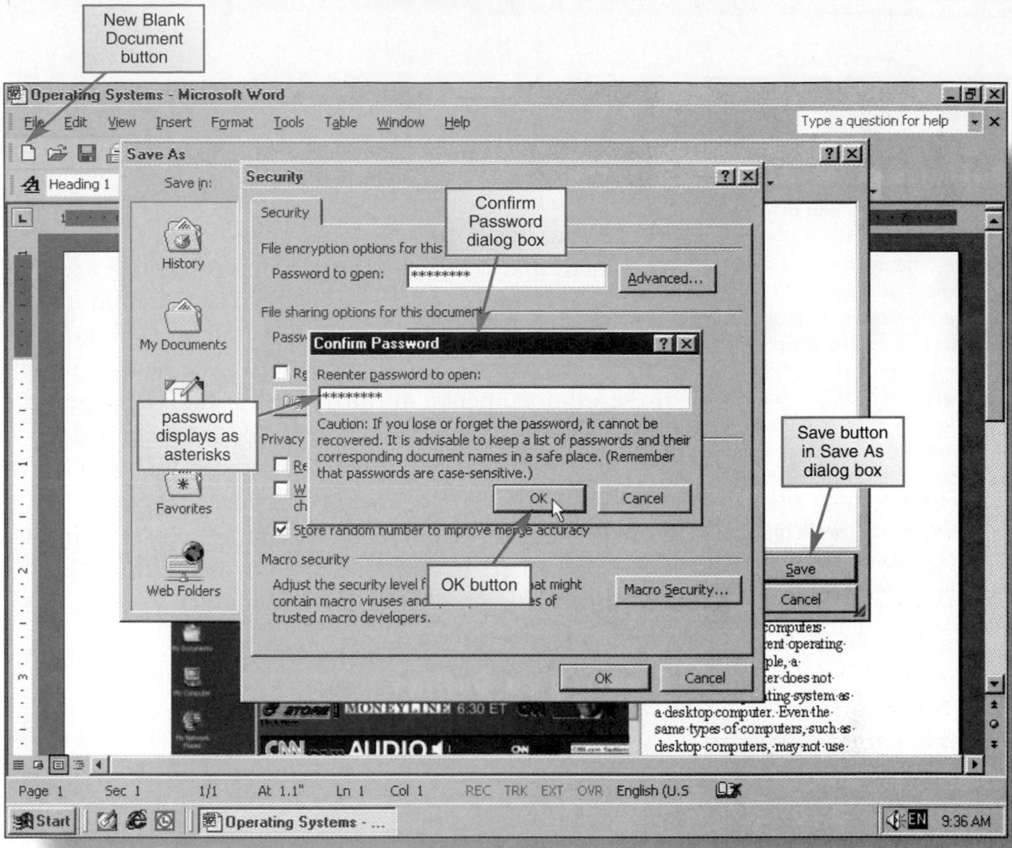

FIGURE 9-39

When someone attempts to open the document in the future, he or she will be prompted to enter the password.

The Operating Systems file is complete. Perform the following steps to close the file.

TO CLOSE THE DOCUMENT

1. Click File on the menu bar and then click Close.
2. If a Document1 program button displays on the taskbar, click it to display a blank document in the document window. If you do not have a Document1 button on the taskbar, click the New Blank Document button on the Standard toolbar.

Word closes the Operating Systems file and displays a blank document in the document window.

Joy e-mails the Operating Systems document to you for inclusion in the Discovering Your Computer public information guide document. For purposes of this project, you will use the document you just saved on your disk.

Other Ways

1. On Tools menu click Options, click Security tab, enter password, on File menu click Save As
2. In Voice Command mode, say "Tools, Options, Security, [type password], OK, File, Save As"

More About

Selecting Passwords

For more information on selecting good passwords, visit the Word 2002 More About Web page (scsite.com/wd2002/more.htm) and then click Selecting Passwords.

More About

Master Documents

Master documents can be used when multiple people prepare different sections of a document or when a document contains separate elements such as the chapters in a book. If multiple people in a network need to work on the same document, divide the document into subdocuments and store the master document on the network server. Then, multiple users can work on different sections of the document simultaneously.

More About

Outlines

If you wanted to rearrange the headings in an outline, for example move one up, you would drag its outline symbol in the direction you wanted to move it.

Working with a Master Document

When you are creating a document from a series of other documents, you may want to create a master document to organize all the documents. A **master document** is simply a document that contains other documents, which are called the **subdocuments**. In addition to subdocuments, a master document can contain its own text and graphics.

In this project, the master document file is named DC #8, which stands for Discovering Your Computer public information guide #8. The file DC #8 contains three subdocuments: an Introduction file, the Operating Systems file, and the Utility Programs file. The first has yet to be created, and the latter two (Operating Systems and Utility Programs) have been written by other individuals and e-mailed for inclusion in the DC #8 document. The master document also contains other items: a title page, a table of contents, a table of figures, and an index. The following pages illustrate how to create this master document and insert the necessary elements into the document to create the DC #8 document.

Creating an Outline

To create a master document, you must be in outline view. You then enter the headings of the document as an outline using Word's built-in heading styles. As discussed in previous projects, a style is a customized format that you can apply to text. Word has nine heading styles named Heading 1, Heading 2, and so on. Each contains different formatting that you can apply to headings in a document.

In an outline, the major heading displays at the left margin with each subordinate, or lower-level, heading indented. In Word, the built-in Heading 1 style displays at the left margin in outline view. Heading 2 style is indented, Heading 3 style is indented further, and so on.

You do not want to use a built-in heading style for the paragraphs of text within the document because when you create a table of contents, Word places all lines formatted using the built-in heading styles in the table of contents. Thus, the text below each heading is formatted using the Body Text style. By using styles in the document, all pages will be formatted similarly — even though various people create them.

The DC #8 document contains the following seven major headings: Discovering Your Computer, Table of Contents, Introduction to System Software, Operating Systems, Utility Programs, Table of Figures, and Index (shown in Figure 9-1 on page WD 9.05). Two of these headings (Operating Systems and Utility Programs) are not entered in the outline; instead, they are part of the subdocuments that you insert into the master document in the next section.

You want each heading to print at the top of a new page. You might want to format the pages within a heading differently from those pages in other headings. Thus, you will insert next page section breaks between each heading.

Perform the following steps to create an outline that contains headings to be used in the master document.

Steps To Create an Outline

1 With a new document window displaying, click the Outline View button on the horizontal scroll bar. If your screen does not display the Outlining toolbar, click View on the menu bar, point to Toolbars, and then click Outlining. If the three buttons identified on the Outlining toolbar in this figure are not selected on your screen, click the button(s).

Word switches to outline view (Figure 9-40). An outline symbol displays to the left of each paragraph. You use outline symbols to rearrange text or display and hide text.

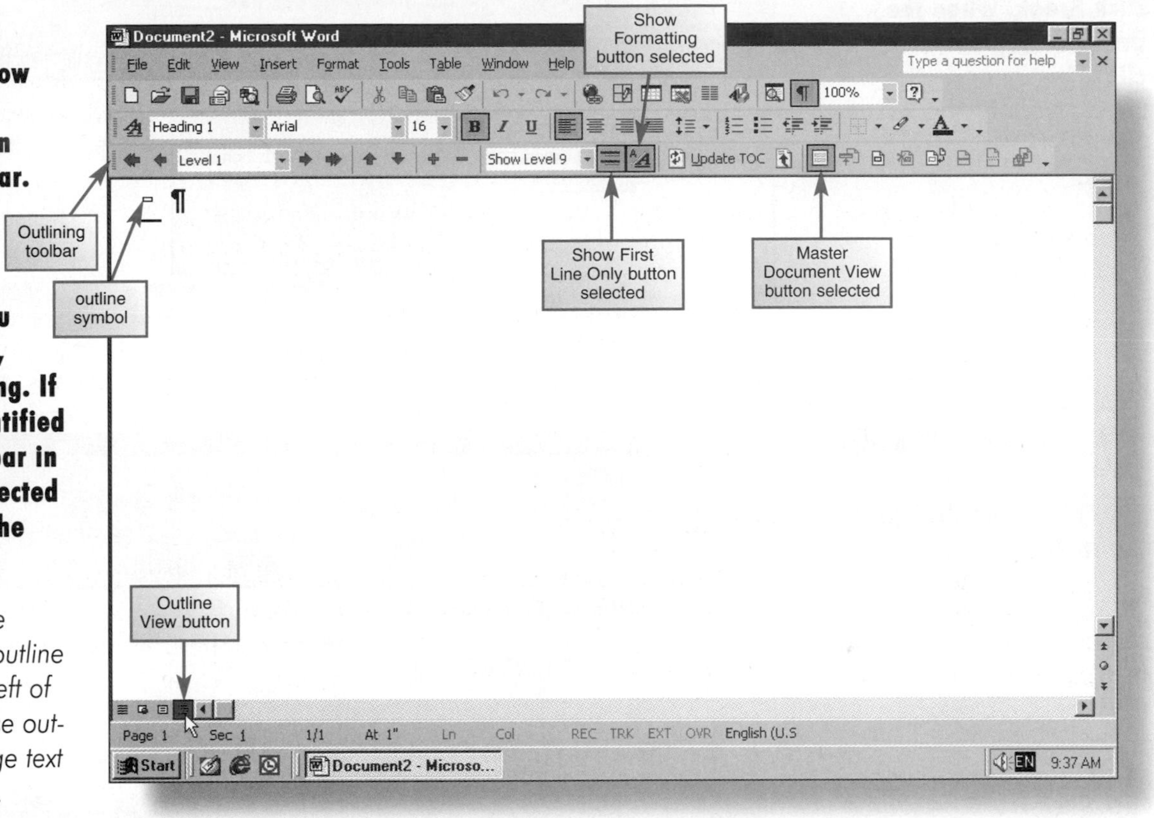

FIGURE 9-40

2 Type DISCOVERING YOUR COMPUTER **and then press the ENTER key.**

Word enters the first heading using the built-in Heading 1 style (Figure 9-41).

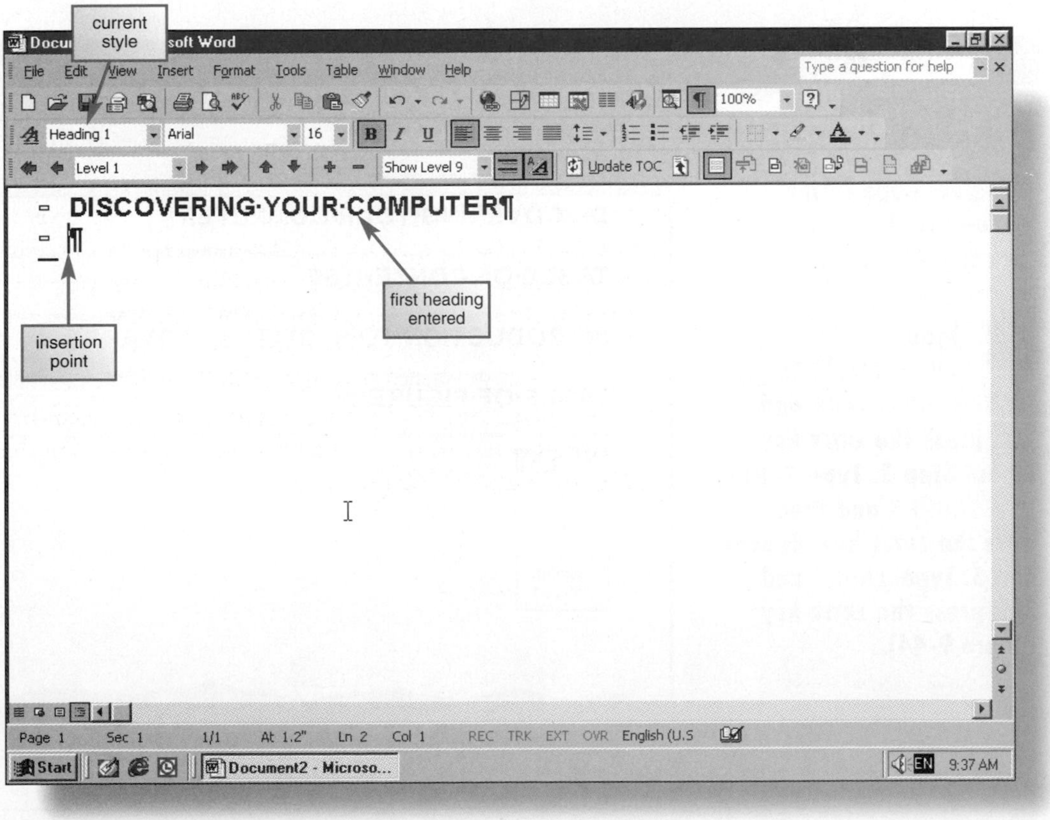

FIGURE 9-41

3 **Click Insert on the menu bar and then click Break. When the Break dialog box displays, click Next page in the Section break types area and then point to the OK button.**

The Break dialog box displays (Figure 9-42).

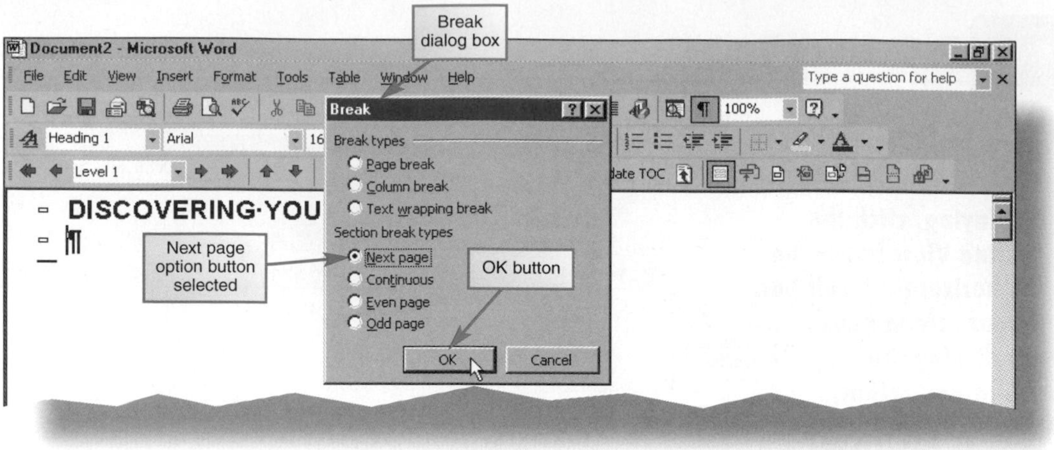

FIGURE 9-42

4 **Click the OK button. Type** TABLE OF CONTENTS **and then press the ENTER key.**

Word inserts a next page section break below the first heading (Figure 9-43). The new text also displays.

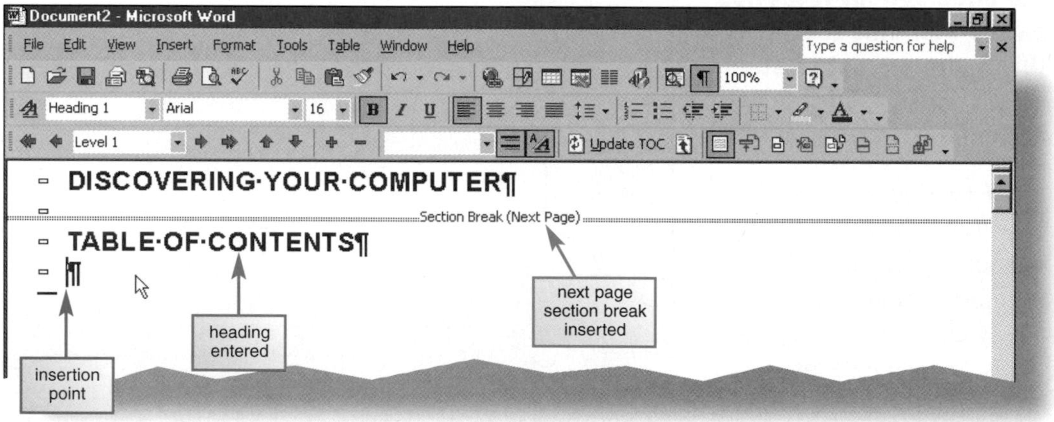

FIGURE 9-43

5 **Click Insert on the menu bar and then click Break. When the Break dialog box displays, click Next page in the Section break types area. Click the OK button.**

6 **Type** INTRODUCTION TO SYSTEM SOFTWARE **and then press the ENTER key. Repeat Step 5. Type** TABLE OF FIGURES **and then press the ENTER key. Repeat Step 5. Type** INDEX **and then press the ENTER key (Figure 9-44).**

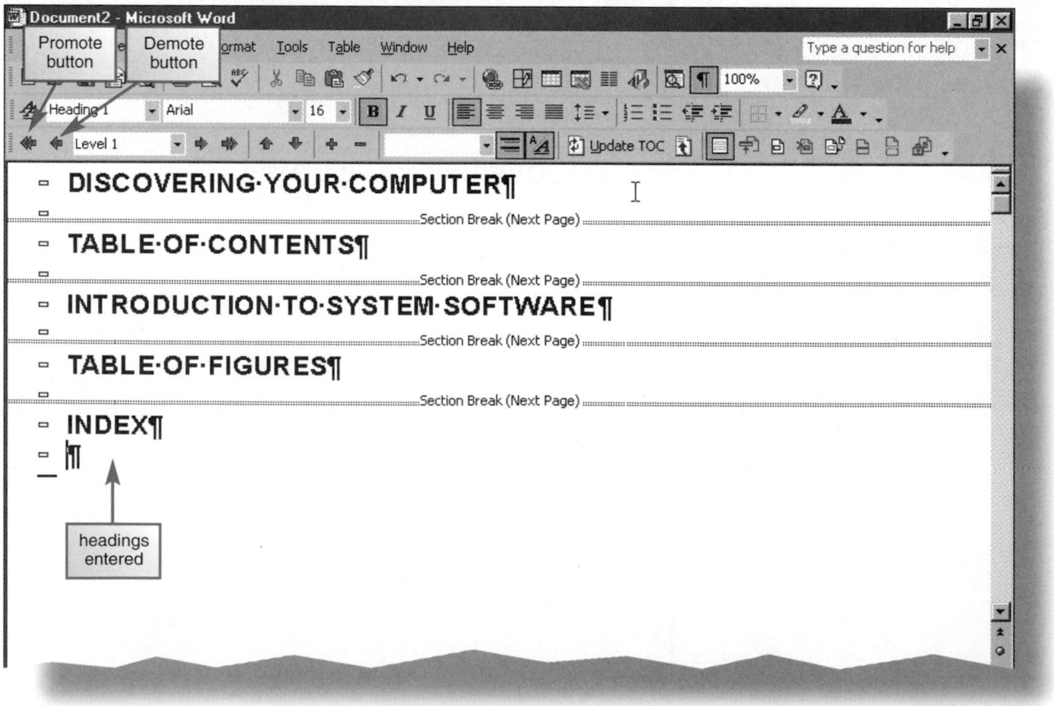

FIGURE 9-44

The Next Page section break between each heading will cause each heading to begin at the top of a new page.

The Outlining toolbar contains buttons and boxes for promoting and demoting items in the outline, changing the outline level, as well as buttons to update and display the table of contents. Figure 9-45 identifies the buttons and boxes on the Outlining toolbar.

The two other major headings, Operating Systems and Utility Programs, will be inserted as subdocuments, as discussed in the following pages. When you insert these files as subdocuments, the headings will become part of the outline.

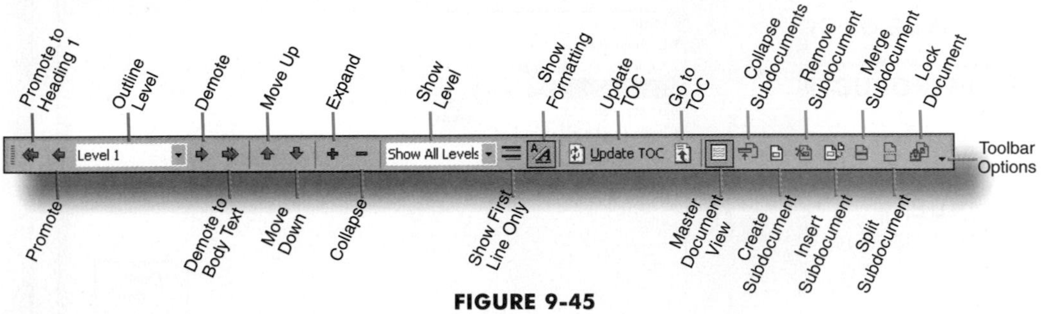

FIGURE 9-45

Inserting a Subdocument in a Master Document

The next step is to insert one of the subdocuments into the master document. Word places the first line of text in the subdocument at the first heading level because it is defined using the Heading 1 style. Nonheading text uses the Body Text style. Figure 9-46 shows the Operating Systems subdocument and identifies the styles used in the document.

The subdocument to be inserted is the Operating Systems file that you modified earlier in this project. Recall that you saved the document with the password, computer. Thus, you will enter that password when prompted by Word, as shown in the steps on the next page.

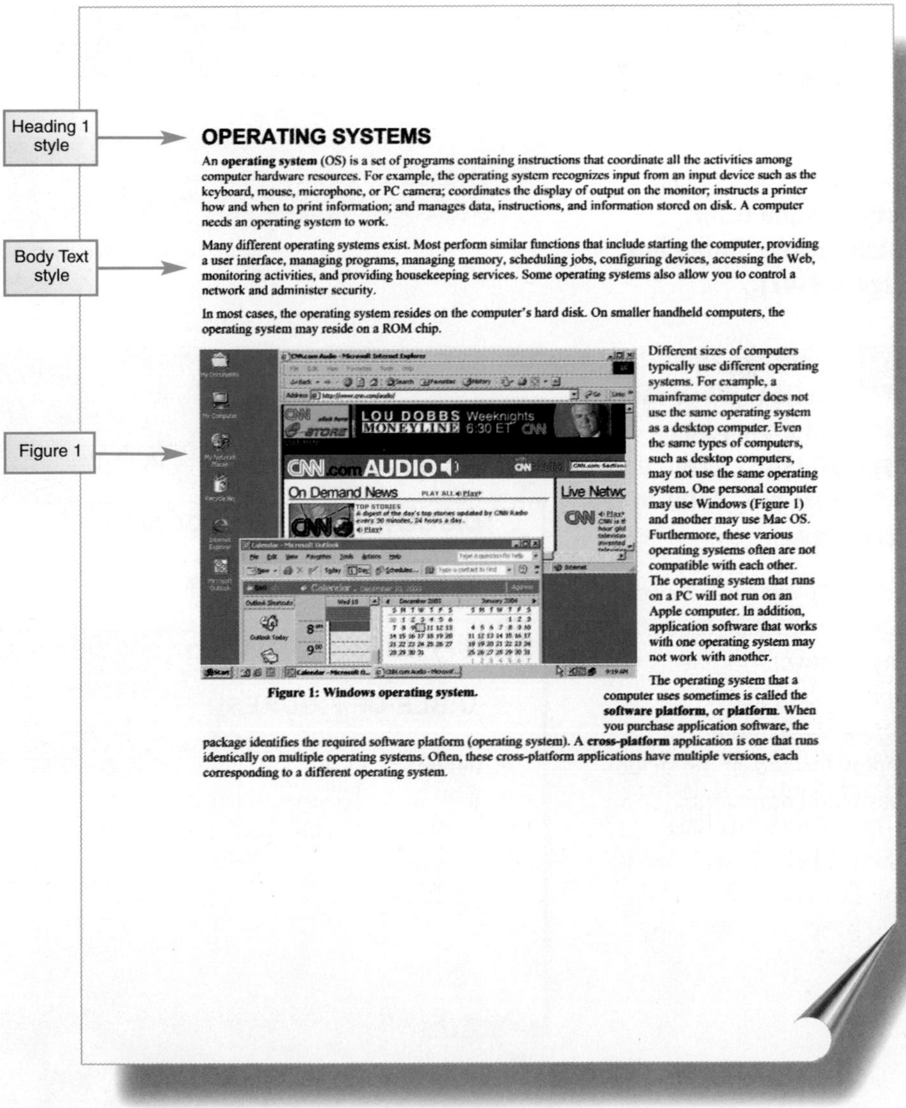

OPERATING SYSTEMS

An **operating system** (OS) is a set of programs containing instructions that coordinate all the activities among computer hardware resources. For example, the operating system recognizes input from an input device such as the keyboard, mouse, microphone, or PC camera; coordinates the display of output on the monitor; instructs a printer how and when to print information; and manages data, instructions, and information stored on disk. A computer needs an operating system to work.

Many different operating systems exist. Most perform similar functions that include starting the computer, providing a user interface, managing programs, managing memory, scheduling jobs, configuring devices, accessing the Web, monitoring activities, and providing housekeeping services. Some operating systems also allow you to control a network and administer security.

In most cases, the operating system resides on the computer's hard disk. On smaller handheld computers, the operating system may reside on a ROM chip.

Different sizes of computers typically use different operating systems. For example, a mainframe computer does not use the same operating system as a desktop computer. Even the same types of computers, such as desktop computers, may not use the same operating system. One personal computer may use Windows (Figure 1) and another may use Mac OS. Furthermore, these various operating systems often are not compatible with each other. The operating system that runs on a PC will not run on an Apple computer. In addition, application software that works with one operating system may not work with another.

Figure 1: Windows operating system.

The operating system that a computer uses sometimes is called the **software platform**, or **platform**. When you purchase application software, the package identifies the required software platform (operating system). A **cross-platform** application is one that runs identically on multiple operating systems. Often, these cross-platform applications have multiple versions, each corresponding to a different operating system.

FIGURE 9-46

Steps To Insert a Password-Protected File as a Subdocument

1 **If necessary, insert into drive A the floppy disk containing the Operating Systems file. Position the insertion point where you want to insert the subdocument (on the section break between the INTRODUCTION TO SYSTEM SOFTWARE and TABLE OF FIGURES headings). Click the Insert Subdocument button on the Outlining toolbar. When the Insert Subdocument dialog box displays, if necessary, click the Look in box arrow and then click 3½ Floppy (A:). Click the file name, Operating Systems, and then point to the Open button in the Insert Subdocument dialog box (Figure 9-47).**

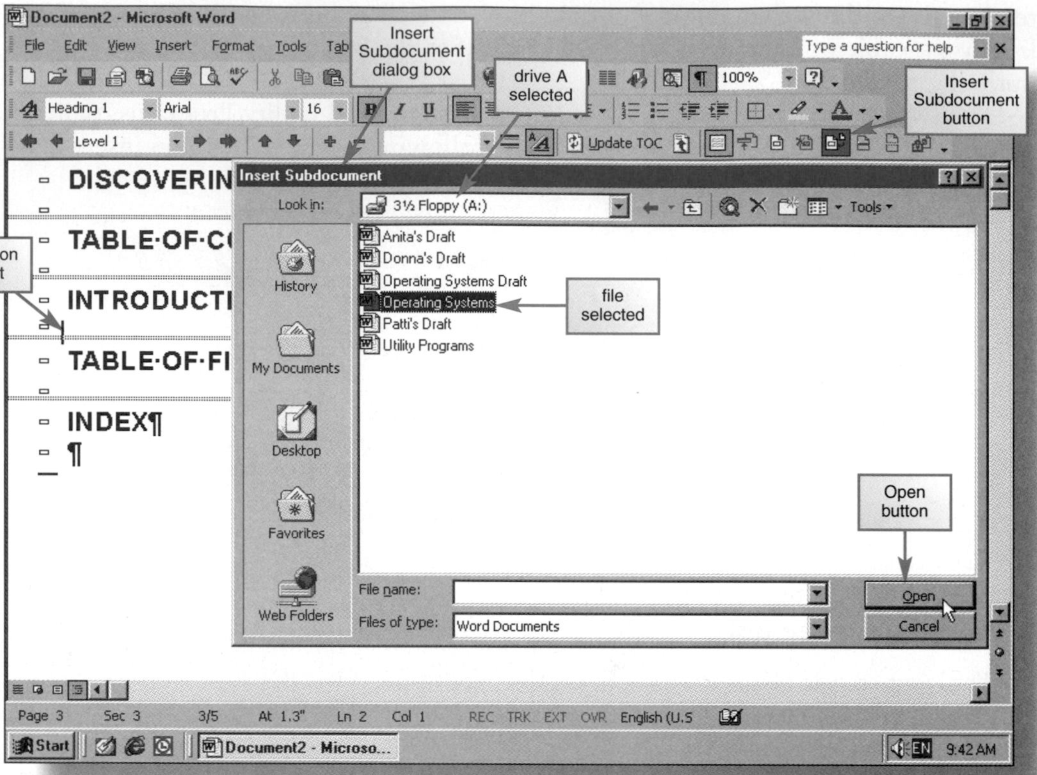

FIGURE 9-47

2 **Click the Open button. When the Password dialog box displays, type** `computer` **in the text box. Point to the OK button.**

Word displays the Password dialog box, which requests your password for the Operating Systems file (Figure 9-48). Asterisks display instead of the actual password characters.

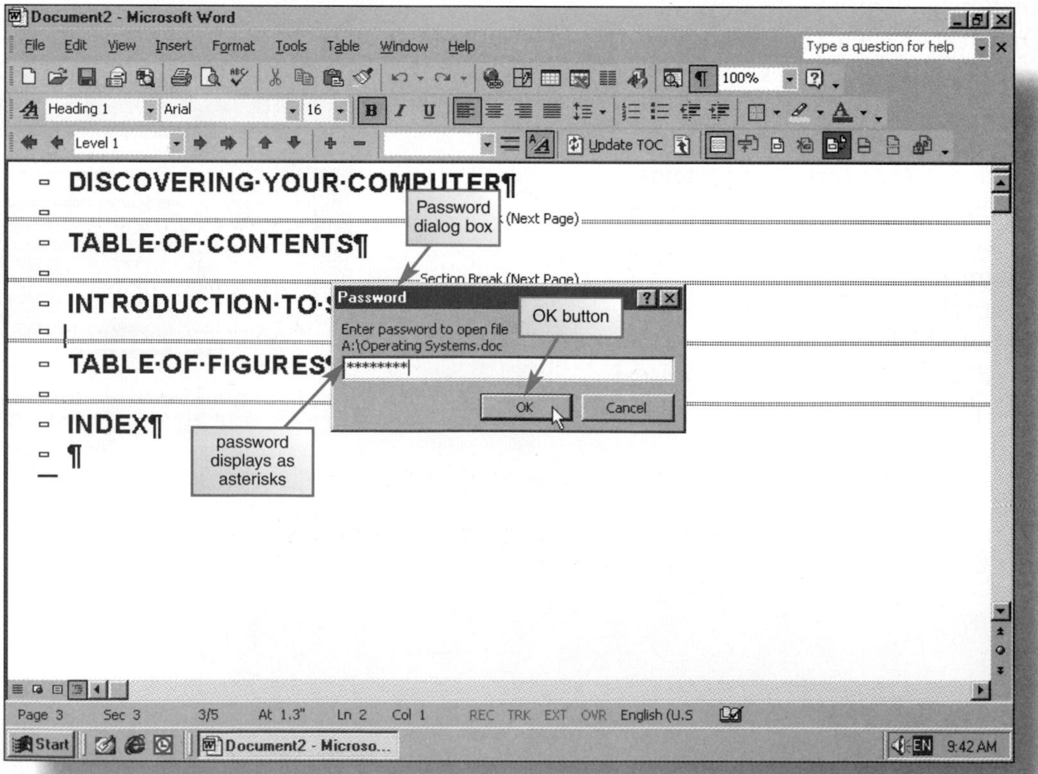

FIGURE 9-48

3 Click the OK button.

Word inserts the Operating Systems file into the document (Figure 9-49). Notice the document contains marked index entries. Only the first line of each paragraph displays because the Show First Line Only button on the Outlining toolbar is selected.

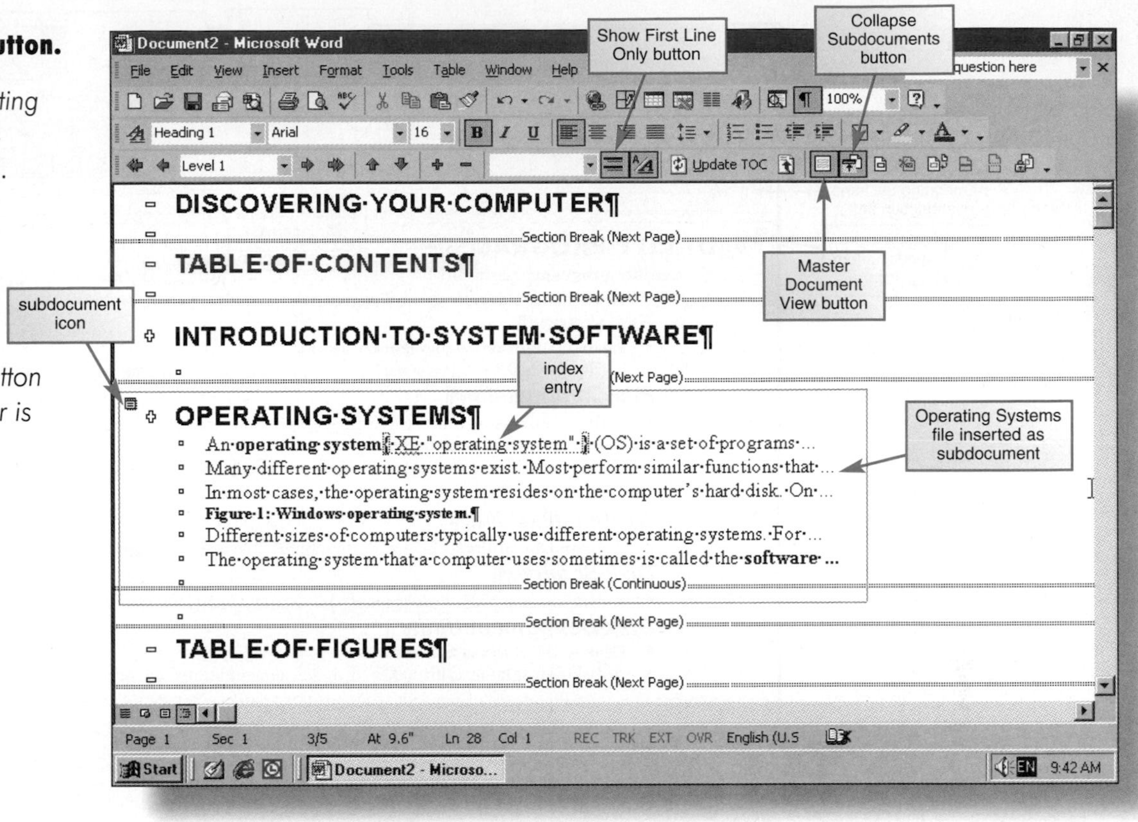

FIGURE 9-49

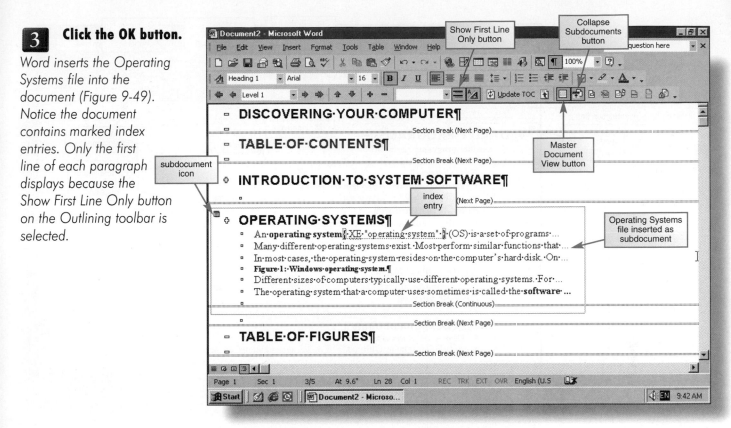

The next step is to insert another subdocument below the Operating Systems subdocument. The next subdocument to be inserted is named Utility Programs and is located on the Data Disk. If you did not download the Data Disk, see the inside back cover for instructions for downloading the Data Disk or see your instructor.

Perform the following steps to insert another subdocument.

TO INSERT ANOTHER SUBDOCUMENT

1. Insert the Data Disk into drive A. Scroll down and, if necessary, position the insertion point on the next page section break above the Table of Figures heading. Click the Insert Subdocument button on the Outlining toolbar.
2. When the Insert Subdocument dialog box displays, if necessary, click the Look in box arrow and then click 3½ Floppy (A:). Click the Utility Programs file name in the Look in list and then click the Open button in the Insert Subdocument dialog box.
3. Scroll up to display the top of the inserted subdocument.

Word inserts the Utility Programs file into the outline below the Operating Systems subdocument (Figure 9-50 on the next page).

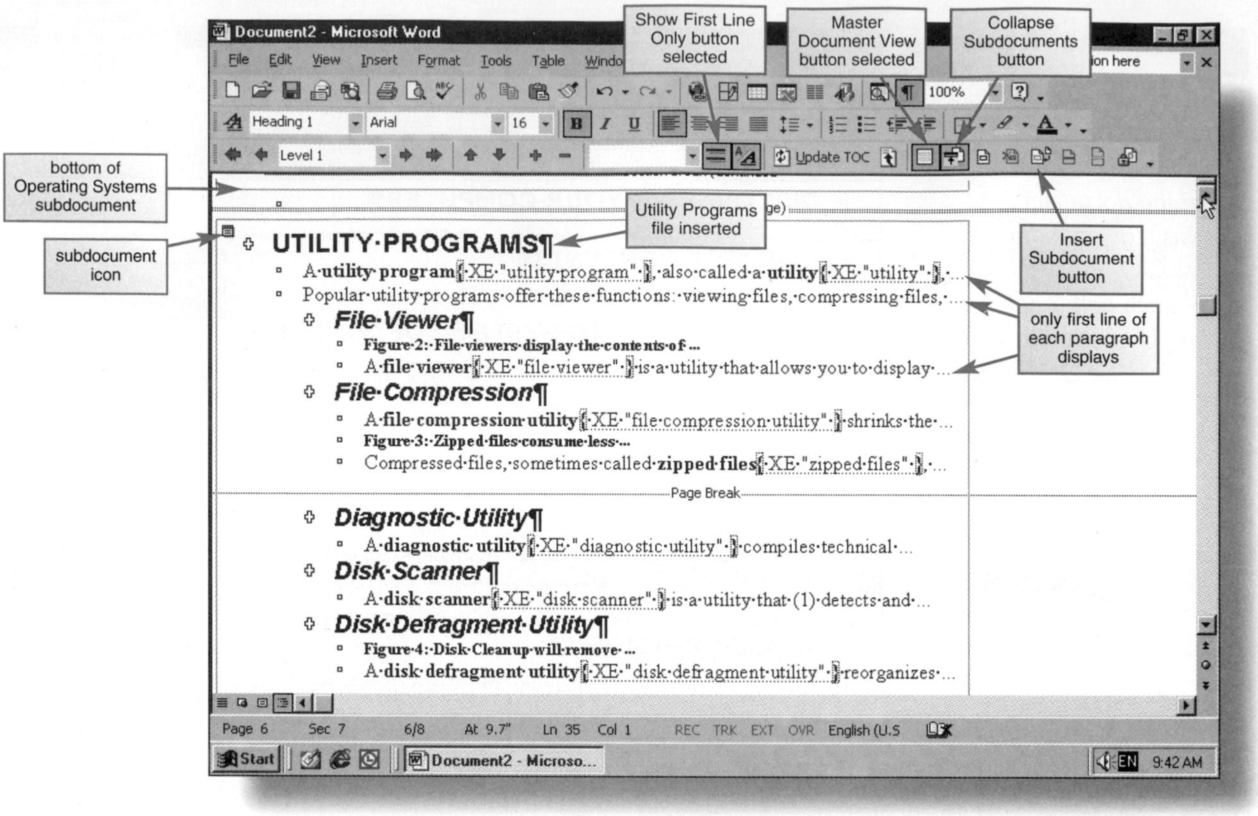

FIGURE 9-50

The inserted file shown in Figure 9-50 is the same document shown on pages 5, 6, and 7 in Figure 9-1 on page WD 9.05. Notice that in Figure 9-50 only the first line of each paragraph displays. This is because the Show First Line Only button on the Outlining toolbar is selected. If you wanted to display all lines in all paragraphs, you would click the Show First Line Only button so it is not selected.

The master document shown in Figure 9-50 is expanded. When in outline view, an expanded document is one that displays the contents of its subdocuments. A collapsed document, by contrast, displays subdocuments as hyperlinks; that is, instead of displaying the contents of the subdocuments, Word displays the name of the subdocuments in blue and underlined. Later in this project, you work with a collapsed document.

To collapse an expanded document and display subdocuments as hyperlinks, click the Collapse Subdocuments button on the Outlining toolbar. To expand subdocuments, click the Expand Subdocuments button on the Outlining toolbar.

You can open a subdocument in a separate document window and modify it. To open a collapsed subdocument, click the hyperlink. To open an expanded subdocument, double-click the subdocument icon (Figure 9-50) to the left of the document heading. If the subdocument icon does not display on the screen, click the Master Document View button on the Outlining toolbar. When you are finished working on a subdocument, close it and return to the master document by clicking File on the menu bar and then clicking Close.

You have performed several tasks. Thus, you should save the document as described in the following steps.

More About

The Lock Icon

If a lock icon displays next to a subdocument's name, either the master document is collapsed or the subdocument is locked. If the master document is collapsed, simply click the Expand Subdocuments button on the Outlining toolbar. If the subdocument is locked, you will be able to open the subdocument but will not be able to modify it.

TO SAVE A DOCUMENT

1. With your floppy disk in drive A, click the Save button on the Standard toolbar.
2. Type DC #8 in the File name text box. Do not press the ENTER key after typing the file name.
3. If necessary, click the Save in box arrow and then click 3½ Floppy (A:). Click the Save button in the Save As dialog box. If a Microsoft Word dialog box displays, click the OK button.

Word saves the document on a floppy disk in drive A with the file name, DC #8 (shown in Figure 9-51).

When you save a master document, Word also saves the subdocument files on the disk. Thus, the DC #8 file, the Operating Systems file, and the Utility Programs file all are saved when you save the DC #8 file.

More About

Creating Subdocuments

If the Create Subdocument button is dimmed, you need to expand subdocuments by clicking the Expand Subdocuments button on the Outlining toolbar. Then, the Create Subdocument button should be available.

Creating a Subdocument from a Master Document

The next step is to create a new subdocument for the INTRODUCTION TO SYSTEM SOFTWARE section of the DC #8 document. Perform the following steps to create a subdocument.

Steps To Create a New Subdocument

1. **Press CTRL+HOME. Point to the plus outline symbol to the left of the heading, INTRODUCTION TO SYSTEM SOFTWARE, and then click when the mouse pointer changes to a four-headed arrow to select the heading. Point to the Create Subdocument button on the Outlining toolbar (Figure 9-51).**

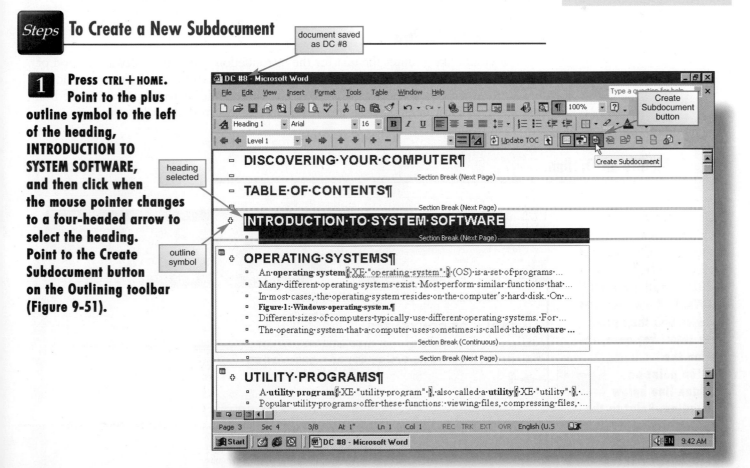

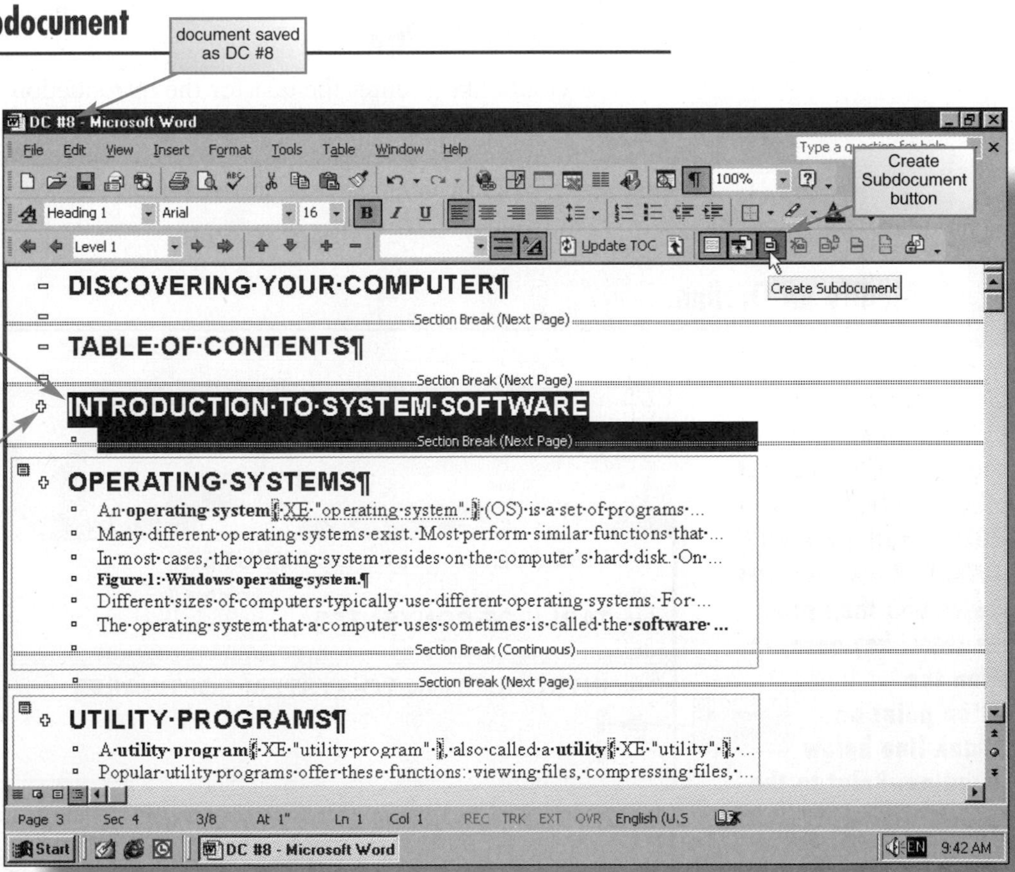

FIGURE 9-51

2 Click the Create Subdocument button.

Word creates a subdocument for the INTRODUCTION TO SYSTEM SOFTWARE heading (Figure 9-52). If Word places a continuous section break above or below the subdocument, do not remove this section break.

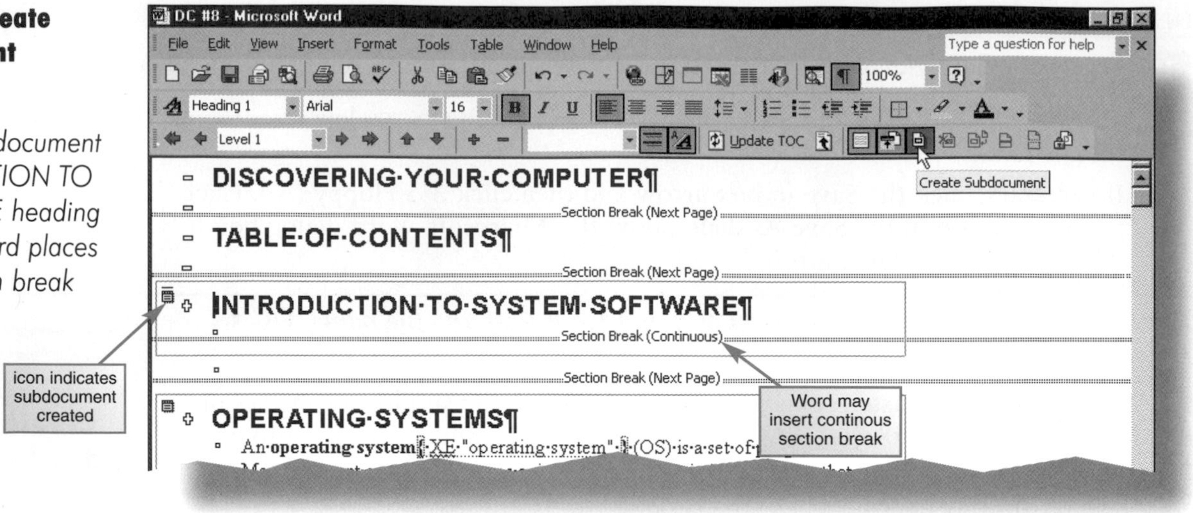

FIGURE 9-52

Other Ways

1. To create a subdocument, in Voice Command mode, say "Create Subdocument"

The next time you save the DC #8 document, Word will create another document called INTRODUCTION TO SYSTEM SOFTWARE on your disk.

Modifying an Outline

You would like to enter the text for the Introduction to System Software section of the document. The paragraphs of text in the Introduction to System Software section should not use a built-in heading style; instead, they should be formatted using the Body Text style. You can enter the text in outline view, as shown in the following steps.

Steps To Modify an Outline

1 Position the insertion point immediately after the last E in the heading, INTRODUCTION TO SYSTEM SOFTWARE. Press the ENTER key twice and then press the UP ARROW key once, to position the insertion point on the blank line below the heading. Point to the Demote to Body Text button on the Outlining toolbar (Figure 9-53).

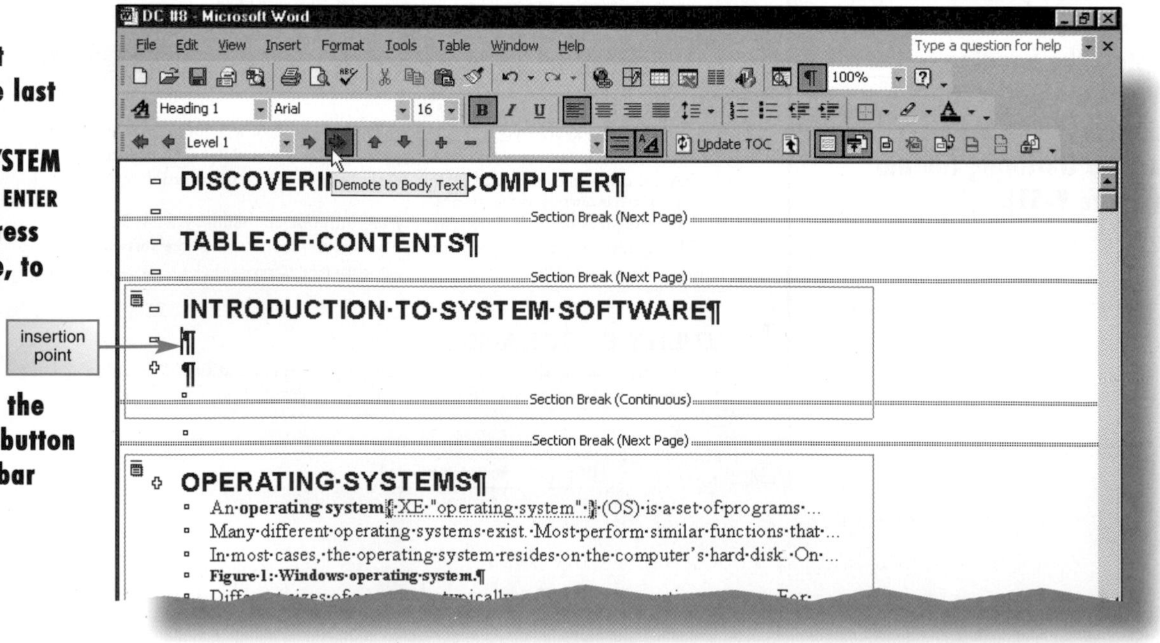

FIGURE 9-53

2 **Click the Demote to Body Text button.**

Word changes the style of the current line from Heading 1 to Body Text (Figure 9-54).

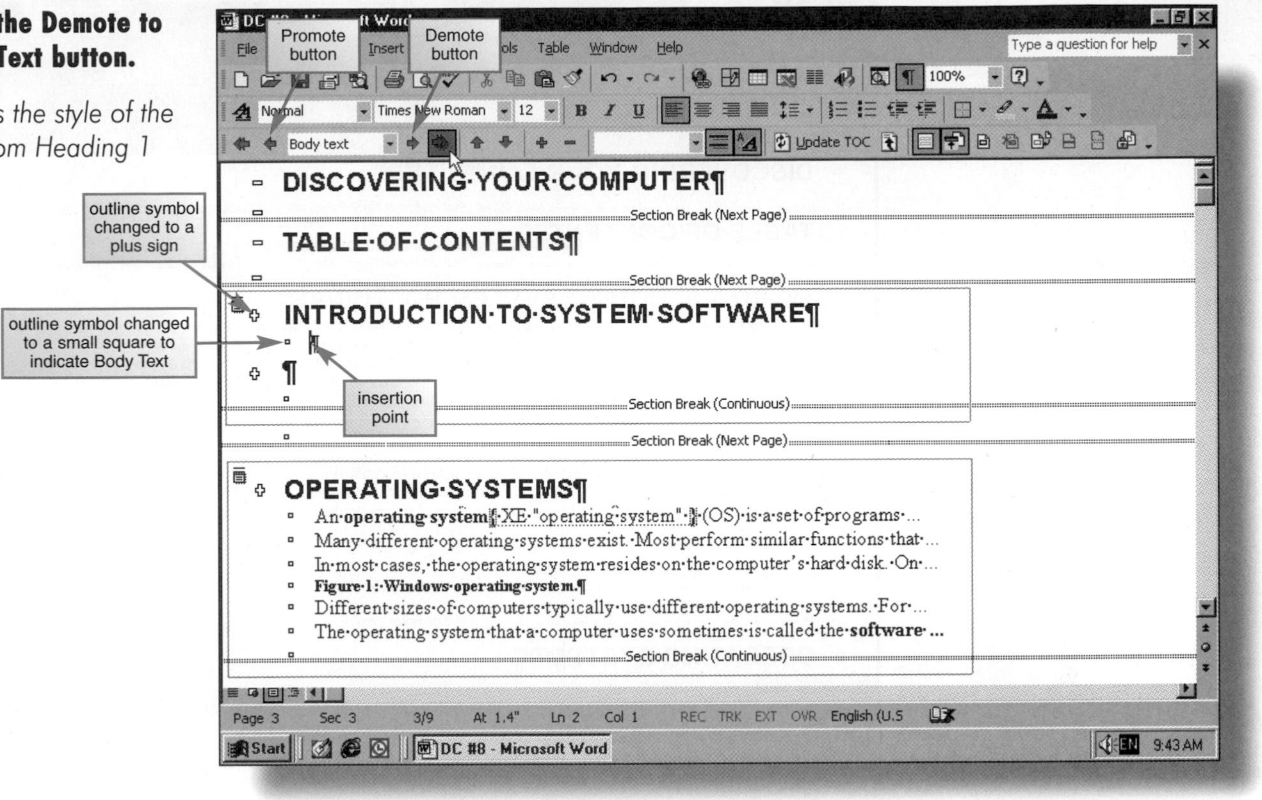

FIGURE 9-54

Notice in Figure 9-54 that the outline symbols changed. The outline symbol to the left of the INTRODUCTION TO SYSTEM SOFTWARE heading changed from a minus sign to a plus sign, indicating the heading has subordinate text. The outline symbol below the heading changed from a minus sign to a small square, indicating it is formatted using the Body Text style.

If you wanted to change a heading to a lower-level, or subordinate, heading style instead of to the Body Text style, such as for a subheading, you would press the TAB key or click the Demote button on the Outlining toolbar; or you can drag the outline symbol to the right. Likewise, to change a heading to a higher-level heading, you would press the SHIFT+TAB keys or click the Promote button on the Outlining toolbar (as you did previously); or you can drag the outline symbol to the left.

The next step is to enter the text of the introduction as described in the following steps.

TO ENTER BODY TEXT INTO AN OUTLINE

1. If the Show First Line Only button on the Outlining toolbar is selected, click it. Click the Style box arrow on the Formatting toolbar and then click Body Text.
2. With the insertion point on the line below the INTRODUCTION TO SYSTEM SOFTWARE heading (shown in Figure 9-54), type the first paragraph shown in Figure 9-55 on the next page. Press the ENTER key.
3. Type the second paragraph shown in Figure 9-55.

The INTRODUCTION TO SYSTEM SOFTWARE section is complete (Figure 9-55).

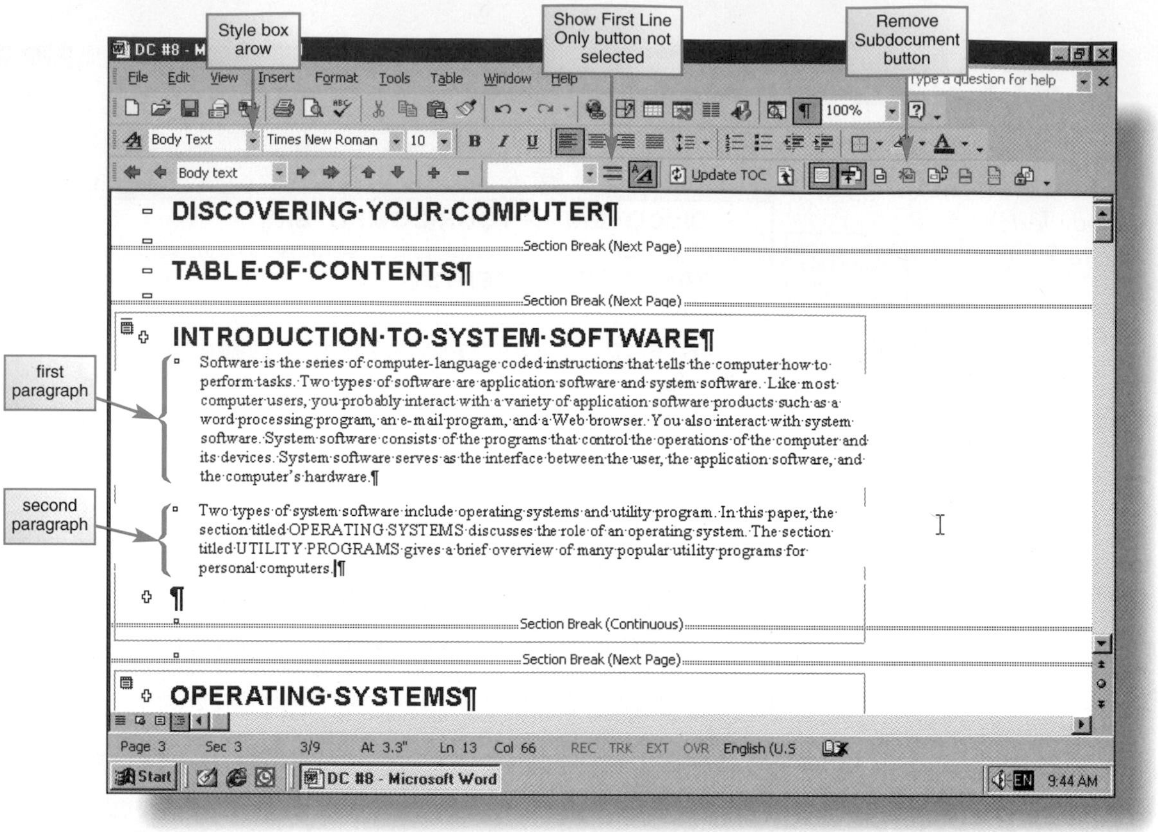

FIGURE 9-55

In outline view, text does not display formatted. Instead, each subheading is indented below the previous heading. Text formatted using the Body Text style, such as that shown in Figure 9-55, also displays indented. To display text properly formatted, switch to print layout view.

If, for some reason, you wanted to remove a subdocument from a master document, you would expand the subdocuments, click the subdocument icon to the left of the subdocument's first heading, and then press the DELETE key. Although Word removes the subdocument from the master document, the subdocument file remains on disk.

Occasionally, you may want to convert a subdocument to part of the master document — breaking the connection between the text in the master document and the subdocument. To do this, expand the subdocuments, click the subdocument icon, and then click the Remove Subdocument button on the Outlining toolbar.

> **More About**
>
> **Outline View**
>
> When the Show First Line Only button on the Outline toolbar is selected, only the first line of each paragraph displays. When the button is not selected, all text associated with the paragraph displays.

Entering Text and Graphics as Part of the Master Document

The next step is to create the title page for the DC #8 document. The completed title page is shown in Figure 9-56. You decide not to create a subdocument for the title page; instead you will enter the text as part of the master document. The title page contains graphics. Thus, you will work in print layout view as opposed to outline view.

On the title page, you want only the first line of text (DISCOVERING YOUR COMPUTER) to show up in the table of contents. Thus, only the first line should be the Heading 1 style. The remaining lines will be formatted using the Body Text style. To be sure that all text below the Heading 1 style is formatted to the Body Text style, demote the blank line below the heading to body text as described in the following steps.

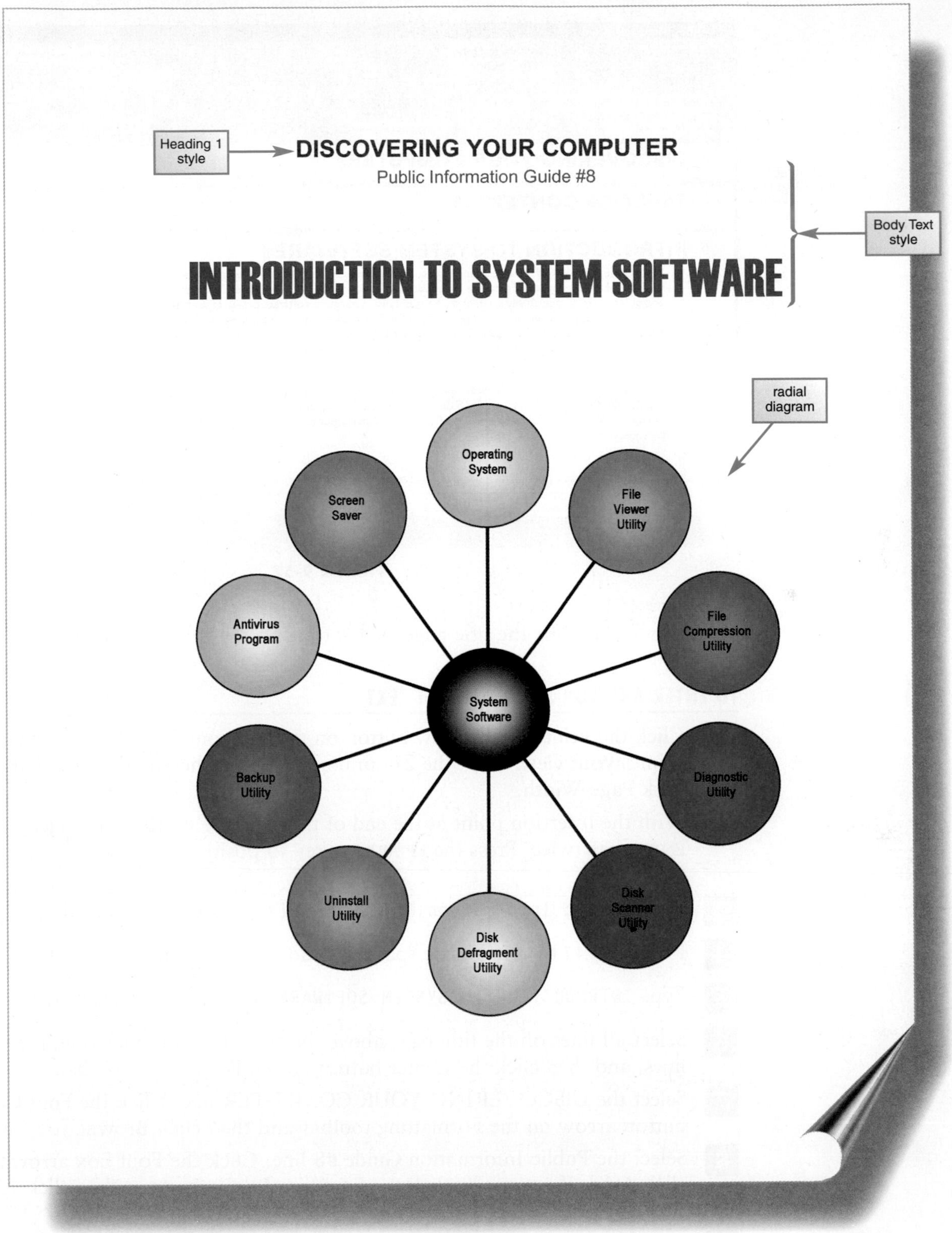

FIGURE 9-56

TO DEMOTE A LINE TO BODY TEXT

1. In outline view, position the insertion point on the section break below the DISCOVERING YOUR COMPUTER heading.
2. Click the Demote to Body Text button on the Outlining toolbar.

Word changes the current line from Heading 1 style to Body Text style (Figure 9-57 on the next page).

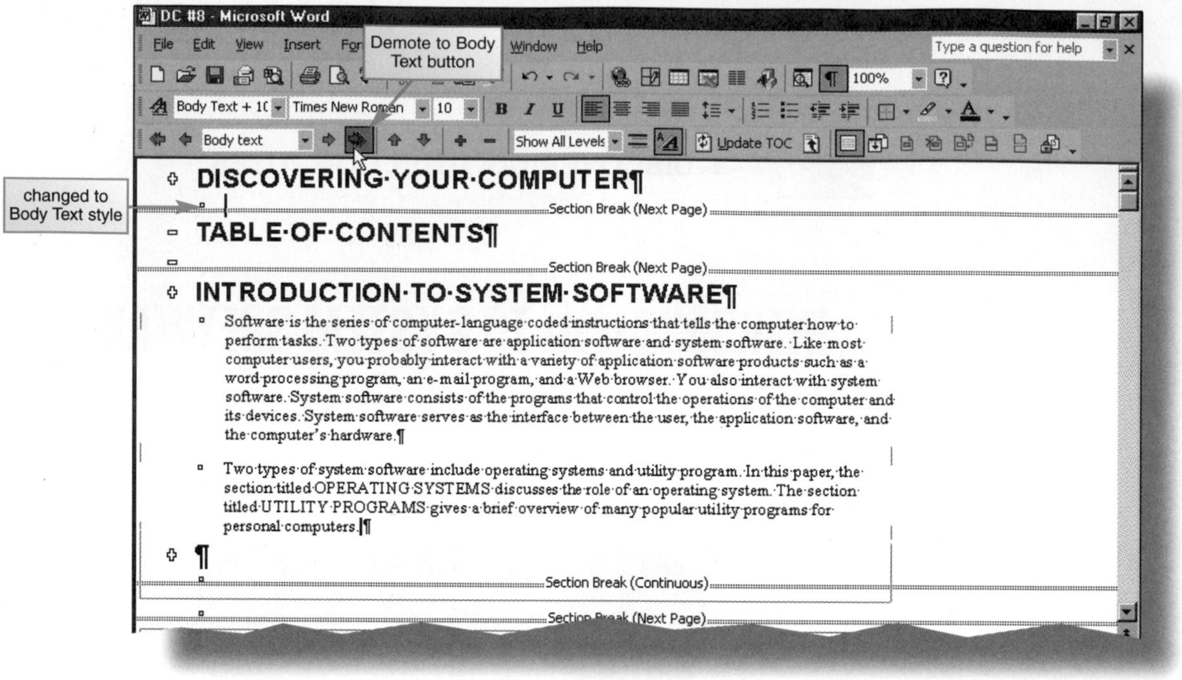

FIGURE 9-57

Enter the text for the title page as described in the following steps.

TO ENTER AND FORMAT TITLE PAGE TEXT

1. Click the Print Layout View button on the horizontal scroll bar to switch to print layout view. Click the Zoom box arrow on the Standard toolbar and then click Page Width.
2. With the insertion point at the end of the first line on the title page, press the ENTER key twice. Press the UP ARROW key to position the insertion point on the blank line.
3. Type `Public Information Guide #8` and then press the ENTER key.
4. Press CTRL+2 to change line spacing to double. Press the ENTER key.
5. Type `INTRODUCTION TO SYSTEM SOFTWARE` and then press the ENTER key.
6. Select all lines on the title page above the section break, including the blank lines, and then click the Center button on the Formatting toolbar.
7. Select the DISCOVERING YOUR COMPUTER line. Click the Font Color button arrow on the Formatting toolbar and then click Brown.
8. Select the Public Information Guide #8 line. Click the Font box arrow and then click Arial. If necessary, click the Font Size box arrow and then click 12. Click the Font Color button arrow and then click Orange.
9. Select the line, INTRODUCTION TO SYSTEM SOFTWARE. Click the Font box arrow and then click Haettenschweiler. Click the Font Size box arrow and then click 36. Click the Font Color button arrow and then click Red. Click to the left of the section break.

The title page displays as shown in Figure 9-58.

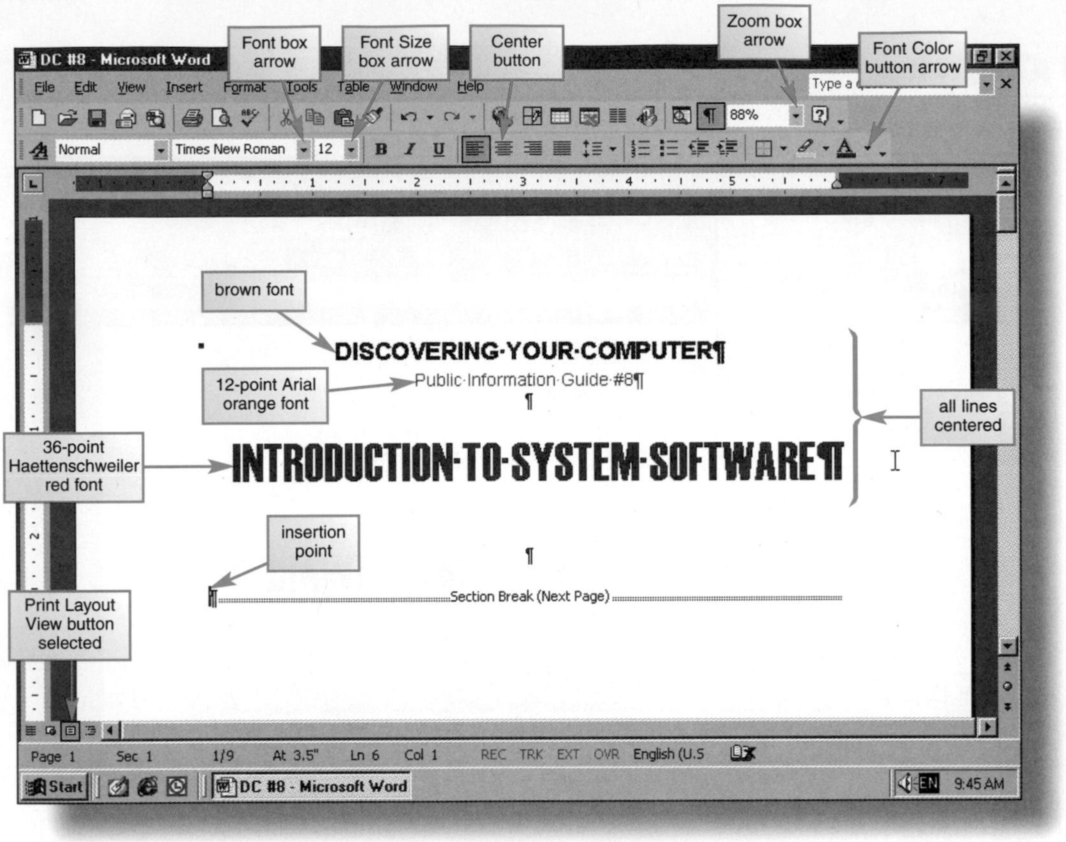

FIGURE 9-58

The next step is to add a radial diagram to the title page.

Inserting a Diagram

You can insert two types of graphics into a Word document: a picture and a drawing object. A **picture** is a graphic that was created in another program. Examples of pictures are scanned images, photographs, and clip art. A **drawing object** is a graphic that you create using Word. You can modify or enhance drawing objects using the Drawing toolbar. Examples of drawing objects include diagrams, AutoShapes, curves, lines, and WordArt.

In this project, you add a **diagram**, which is a predefined shape or shapes in Word. Word provides a Diagram Gallery (shown in Figure 9-60 on the next page) with diagrams such as organization charts, cycle diagrams, radial diagrams, pyramid diagrams, Venn diagrams, and target diagrams. Each diagram contains embedded text boxes with instructions that indicate where to click to add text. The DC #8 title page includes a radial diagram, which is used to show relationships of a core element. The core element, or main idea, displays in the middle of the diagram. Spokes lead outward to subtopics. Each element, or shape, may include text and formatting. The text for the core element and each subtopic in the project is listed in Table 9-1. The completed diagram is shown in Figure 9-56 on page WD 9.47.

Perform the steps on the next page to insert the radial diagram, format it, and then insert and format the text in each element.

Table 9-1 Radial Diagram Text

ELEMENT *(subtopic elements begin at the top and proceed clockwise)*	*TEXT*
Center element	System Software
Element 1	Operating System
Element 2	File Viewer Utility
Element 3	File Compression Utility
Element 4	Diagnostic Utility
Element 5	Disk Scanner Utility
Element 6	Disk Defragment Utility
Element 7	Uninstall Utility
Element 8	Backup Utility
Element 9	Antivirus Program
Element 10	Screen Saver

Steps To Insert and Format a Diagram

1 With the insertion point positioned as shown in Figure 9-59, click Insert on the menu bar and then point to Diagram (Figure 9-59).

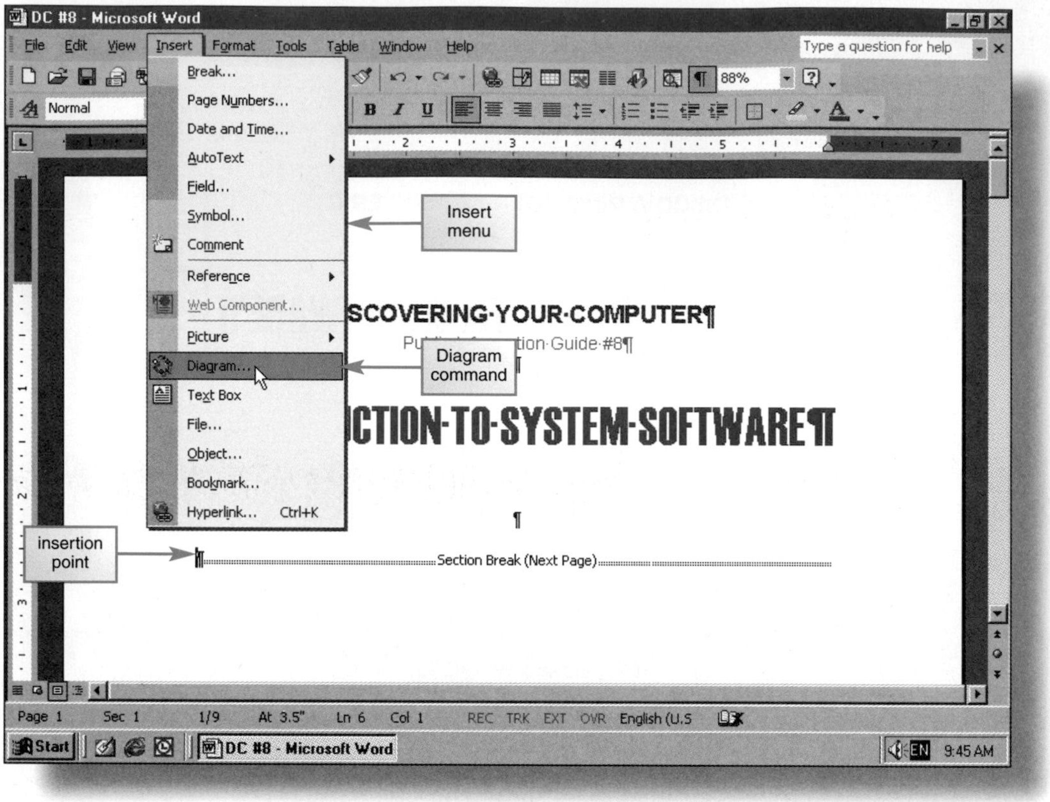

FIGURE 9-59

2 Click Diagram. When the Diagram Gallery dialog box displays, click Radial Diagram and then point to the OK button.

The Diagram Gallery dialog box displays a brief description of the selected diagram type (Figure 9-60).

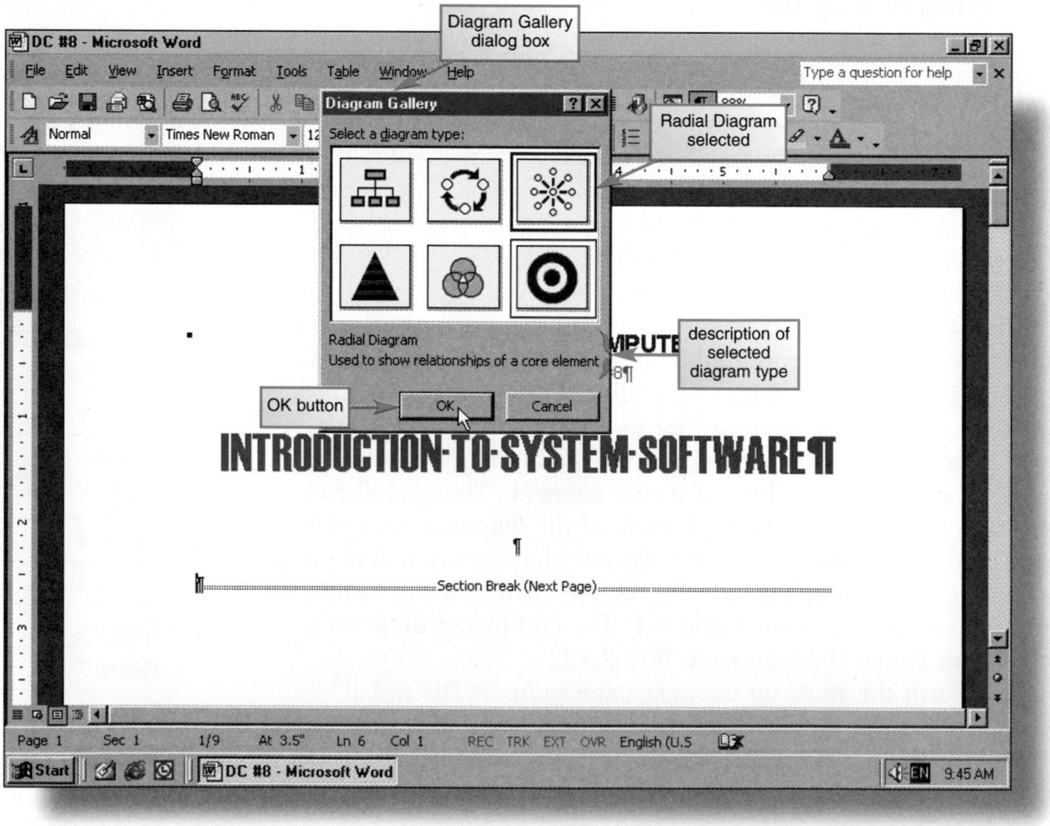

FIGURE 9-60

3 **Click the OK button. Point to the Insert Shape button on the Diagram toolbar.**

The radial diagram displays as an inline graphic with three spokes (Figure 9-61). Word automatically displays the drawing canvas, the Diagram toolbar, and the Drawing toolbar.

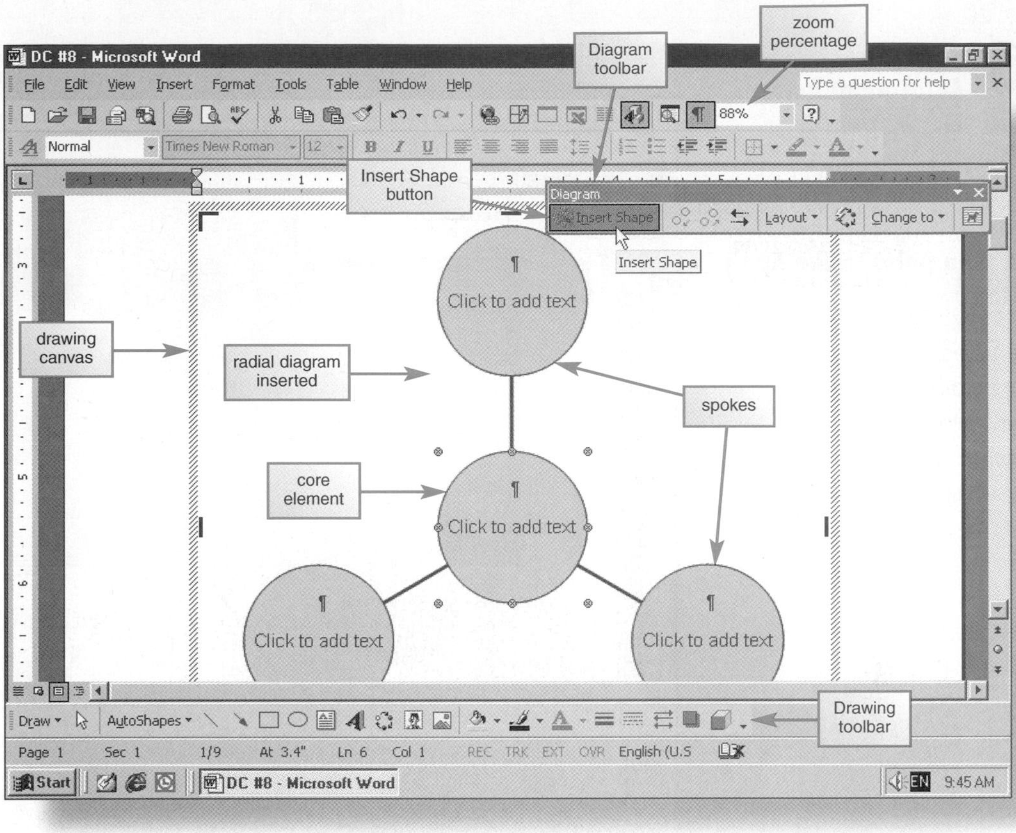

FIGURE 9-61

4 **Click the Insert Shape button seven times to create a total of ten spokes. Point to the AutoFormat button on the Diagram toolbar.**

As you insert more shapes or elements to a radial diagram, Word automatically resizes the diagram and spaces the elements evenly (Figure 9-62).

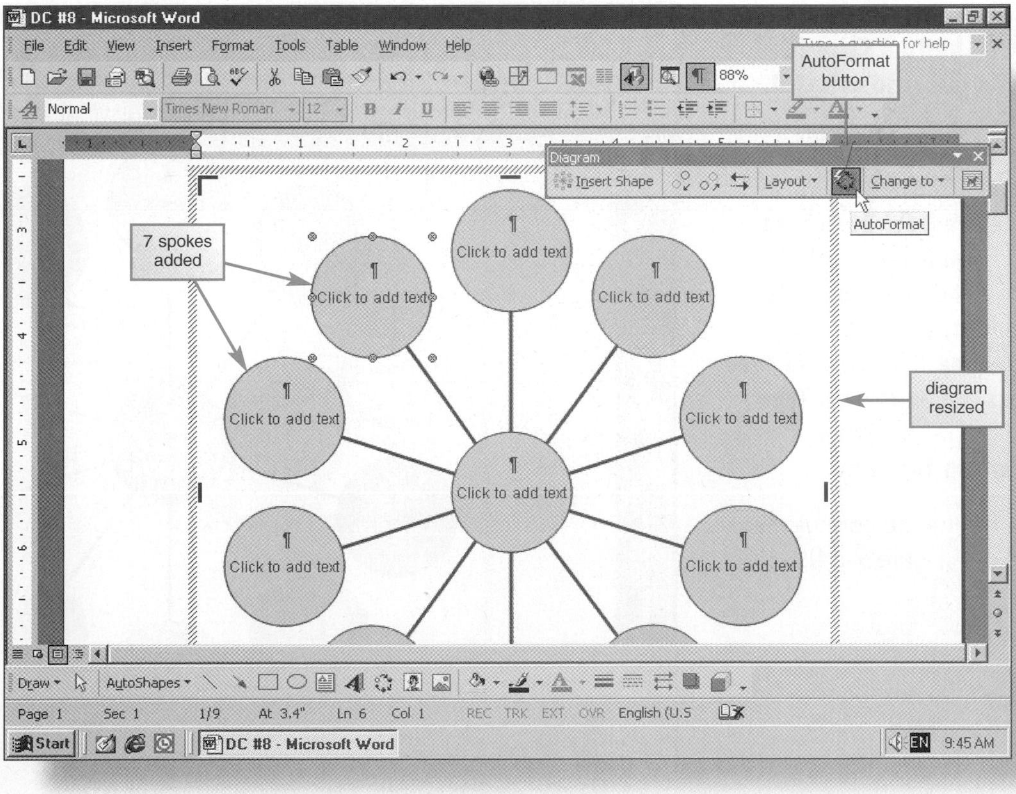

FIGURE 9-62

5 Click the AutoFormat button. When the Diagram Style Gallery dialog box displays, click Fire in the Select a Diagram Style list and then point to the Apply button.

The Select a Diagram Style list contains a variety of radial diagram styles (Figure 9-63). A preview of the selected style displays.

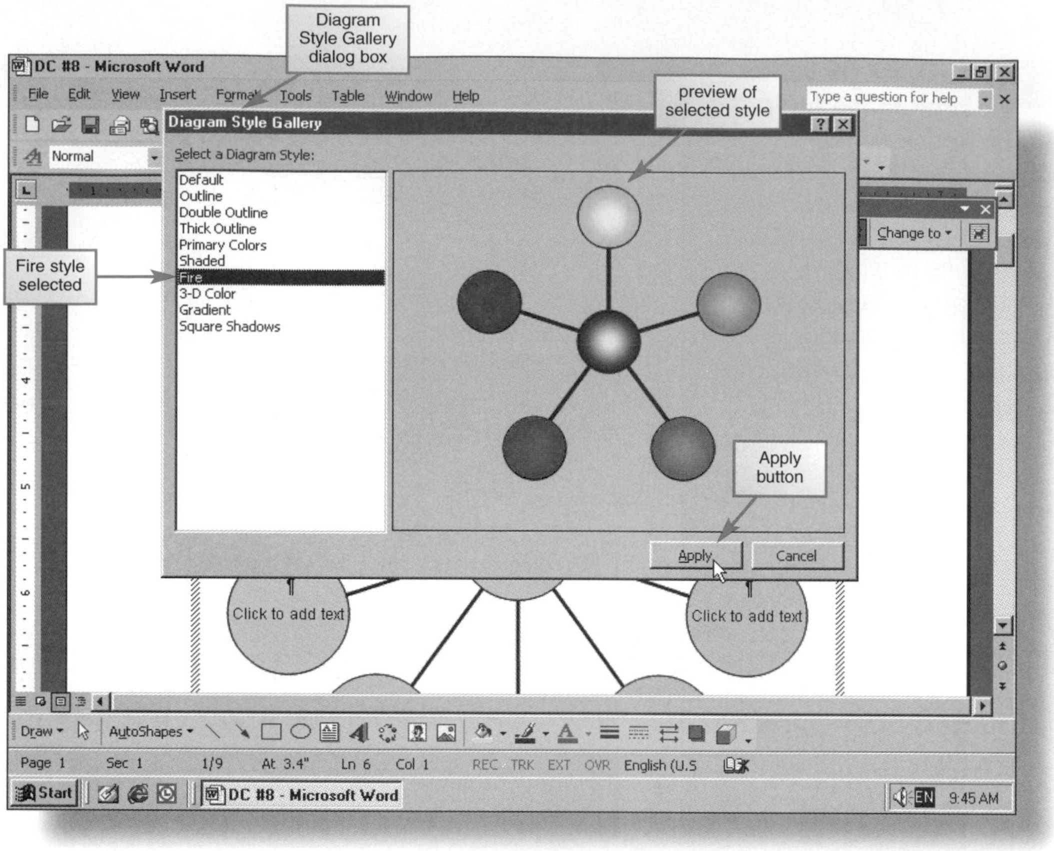

FIGURE 9-63

6 Click the Apply button. Click the center circle to select it. Click the Font box arrow on the Formatting toolbar and then click Arial Narrow. Click the Bold button on the Formatting toolbar. When the insertion point displays, press the ENTER key. Type `System` **and then press the ENTER key. Type** `Software` **to finish inserting the text.**

The text for the core element displays (Figure 9-64).

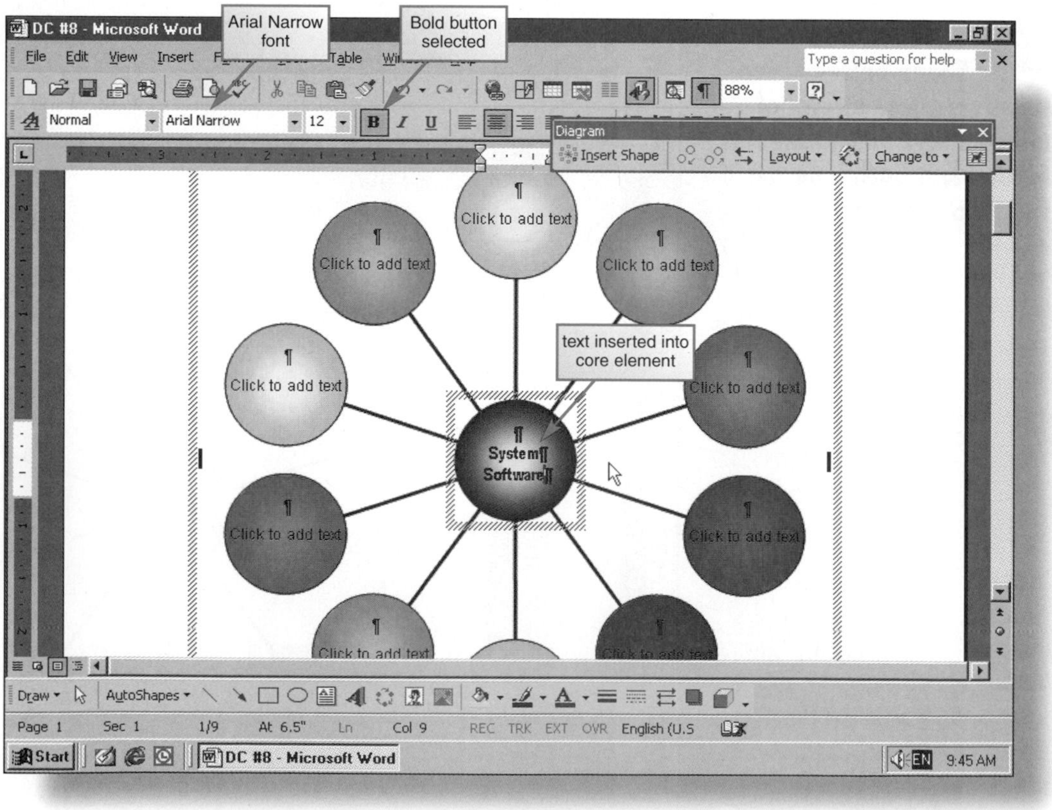

FIGURE 9-64

7 One at a time, beginning with the top center circle and moving clockwise, click each circle to add the text from Table 9-1 on page WD 9.49. In each circle, first press the ENTER key and then type the text, pressing the ENTER key between each word.

The completed text displays in each circle (Figure 9-65). Some words may wrap to two lines or only partially display. You will format the text in the next steps.

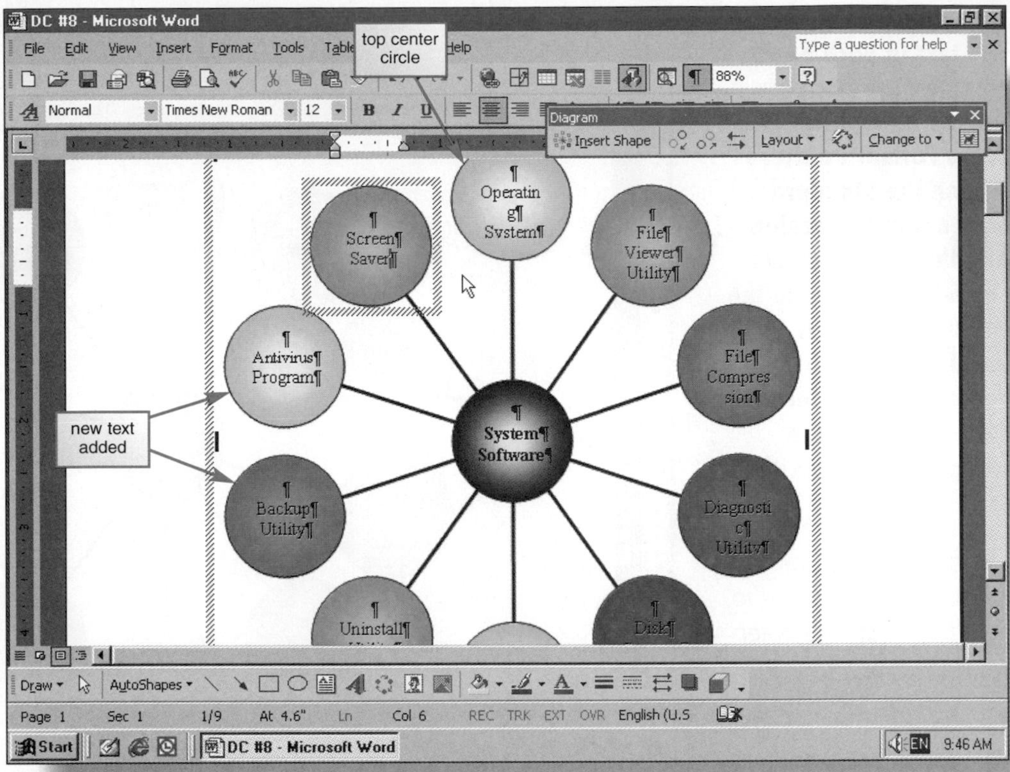

FIGURE 9-65

8 Drag through the text in the top center circle to select its text. Click the Font box arrow on the Formatting toolbar and then click Arial Narrow in the list. Click the Font Size box on the Formatting toolbar and then click 9 in the list. Click the Bold button on the Formatting toolbar. Double-click the Format Painter button on the Standard toolbar.

The text in the top-center circle is 9-point Arial Narrow bold font (Figure 9-66). You will copy the format of the text in this circle to the remaining circles in the diagram.

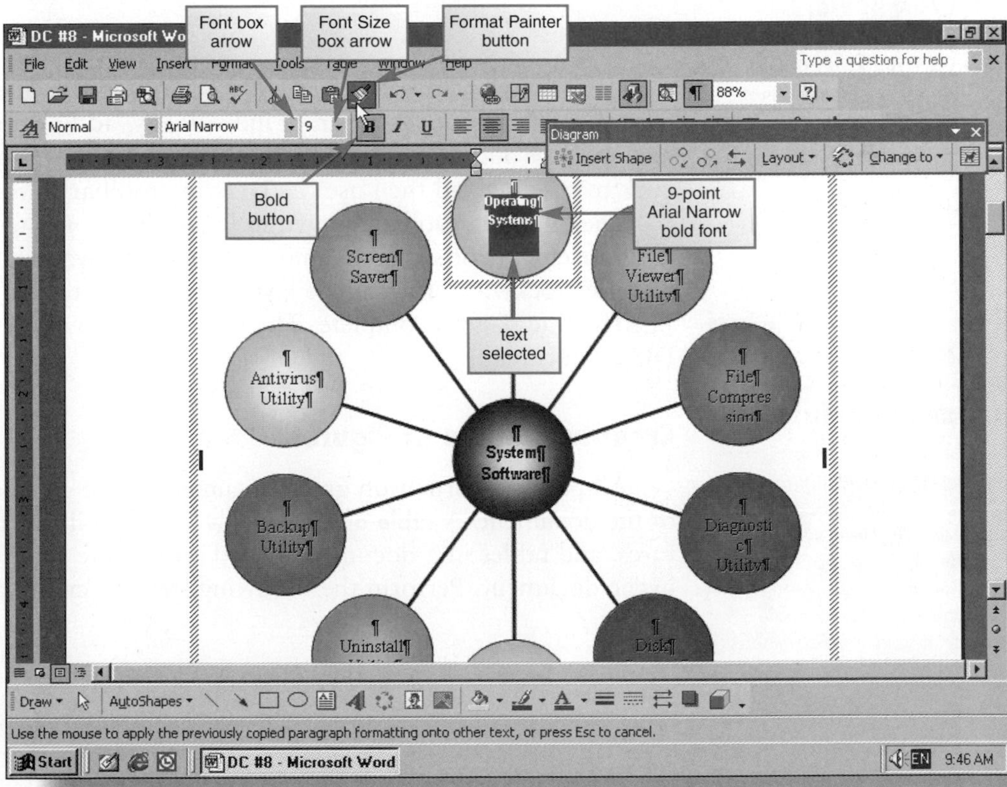

FIGURE 9-66

9 Drag through the text in each of the remaining nine circles. When you have finished, click the Format Painter button on the Standard toolbar again to deselect it, and then click outside the drawing canvas, so the diagram no longer is selected. Click the Drawing button on the Standard toolbar to remove the Drawing toolbar from the screen.

The formatting from the text in the top circle is applied to each of the remaining outer circles (Figure 9-67).

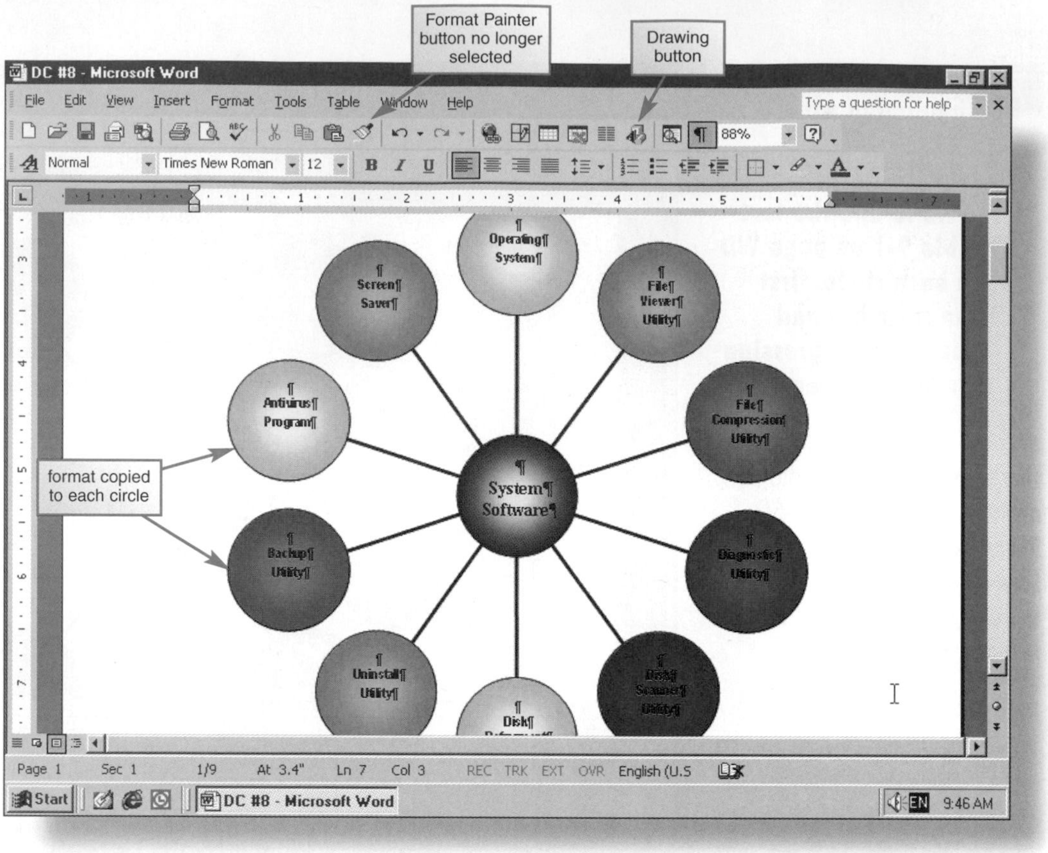

FIGURE 9-67

Other Ways

1. To format diagram, right-click diagram, click Format Diagram on shortcut menu
2. To insert diagram, in Voice Command mode, say "Insert, Diagram"

You formatted the diagram with a preset style named, Fire. Alternately, you can format the pieces of the diagram individually, adding color, changing line weights and style, or adding fills, textures, and backgrounds. To format an individual shape, click to select it and then use the Drawing toolbar to format it individually.

The Diagram toolbar, shown in Figure 9-61 on page WD 9.51, contains buttons to add elements or segments, move elements forward (clockwise) or backward (counterclockwise), format the layout, and wrap text.

The title page is complete. The next step is to create the table of figures for the DC #8 document.

More About

Indexes and Tables

If your index, table of contents, or table of figures displays odd characters inside curly braces {}, then Word is displaying field codes instead of field results. Press ALT+F9 to display the index or table correctly. If your index or table prints field codes, click Tools on the menu bar, click Options, click the Print tab, remove the check mark from the Field codes check box, click the OK button, and then print the document again.

Creating a Table of Figures

All public information guide documents have a table of figures following the text of the document. A **table of figures** is a list of all illustrations such as graphics, pictures, and tables in a document. Word creates the table of figures from the captions in the document. Perform the following steps to create a table of figures.

Steps To Create a Table of Figures

1 **If it is selected, click the Show/Hide ¶ button on the Standard toolbar to hide formatting marks. Scroll down to display the TABLE OF FIGURES heading. Position the insertion point at the end of the heading. Press the ENTER key. Click Insert on the menu bar, point to Reference and then point to Index and Tables on the Reference submenu (Figure 9-68).**

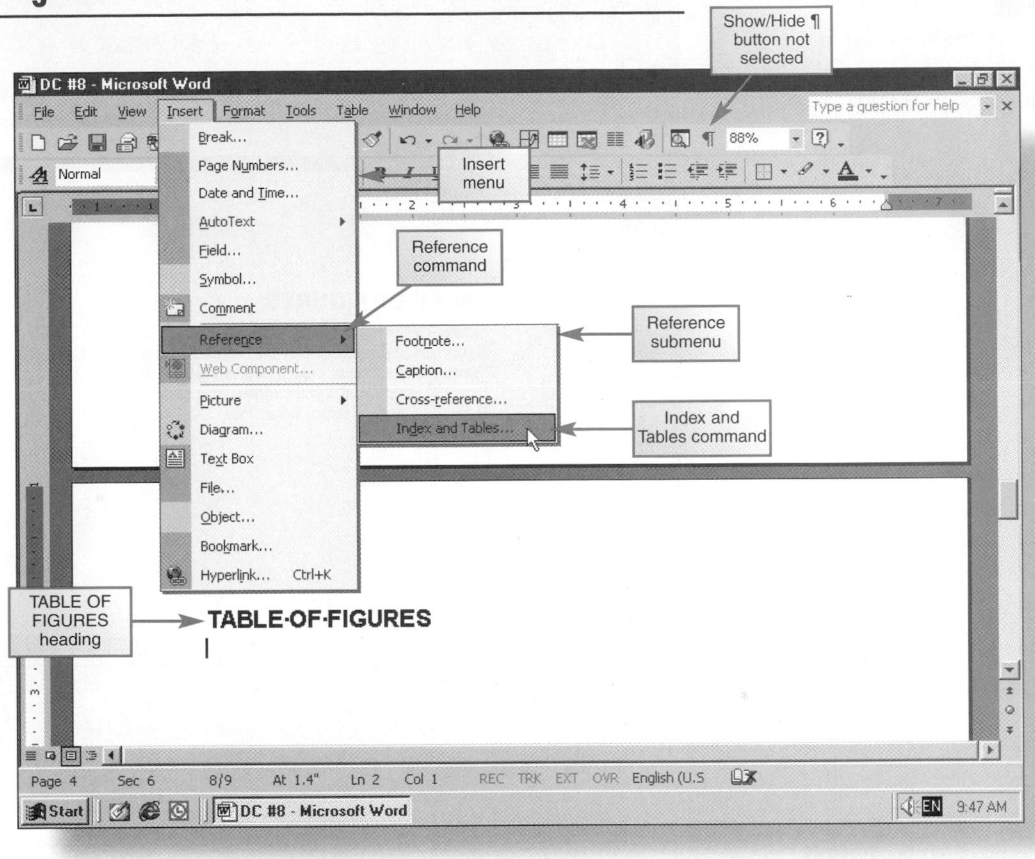

FIGURE 9-68

2 **Click Index and Tables. If a Microsoft Word dialog box displays asking you to open the subdocuments, click the Yes button. When the Index and Tables dialog box displays, if necessary, click the Table of Figures tab. Be sure that all check boxes in the dialog box contain check marks. Point to the OK button.**

Word displays the Table of Figures sheet in the Index and Tables dialog box (Figure 9-69).

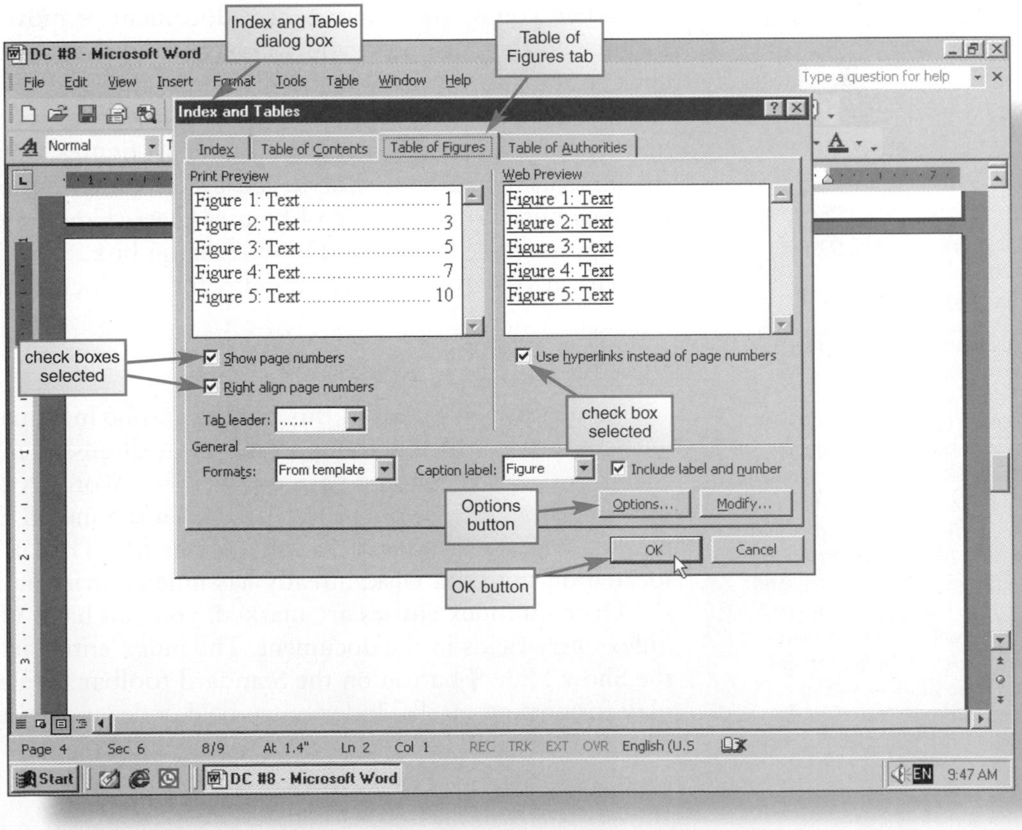

FIGURE 9-69

3 Click the OK button.

Word creates a table of figures at the location of the insertion point (Figure 9-70).

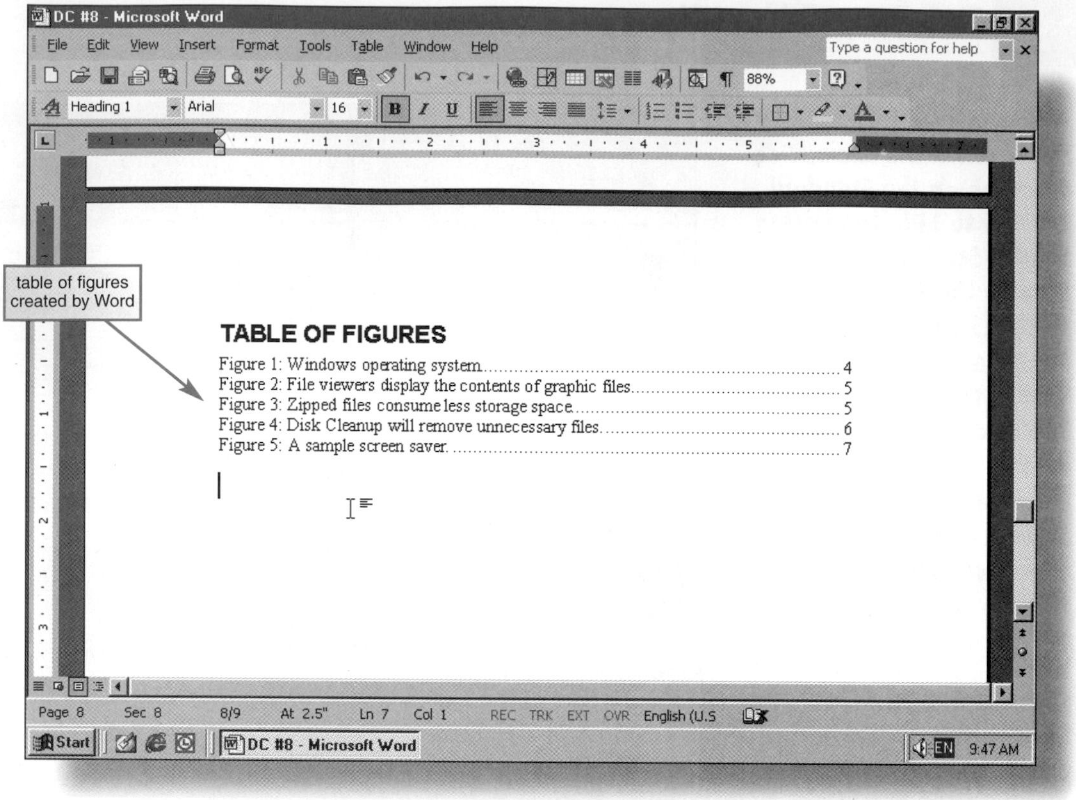

FIGURE 9-70

Other Ways

1. In Voice Command mode, say "Insert, Reference, Index and Tables"

More About

Index Entries

Instead of marking index entries in a document, you can create a concordance file, which Word uses to mark index entries automatically. The concordance file contains two columns: (1) the first column identifies the text in the document you want Word to mark as an index entry, and (2) the second column lists the index entries to be generated from the text in the first column. To mark entries in the concordance file, click the AutoMark button in the Index and Tables dialog box.

When you modify captions in a document or move illustrations to a different location in the document, you will have to update the table of figures. To do this, click to the left of the table and then press the F9 key.

If you did not use captions to create labels for your illustrations in a document and would like Word to generate a table of figures, you can instruct Word to create the table using the built-in style you used for the captions. To do this, click the Options button in the Table of Figures sheet (Figure 9-69 on the previous page) to display the Table of Figures Options dialog box.

The next step is to build an index for the document.

Building an Index

As mentioned earlier in this project, public information guide documents end with an index, which lists important terms discussed in the document along with each term's corresponding page number. For Word to generate the index, you first must mark any item you wish to appear in the index. Earlier in this project, you marked an entry in the Operating Systems file. The Utility Programs file, which is located on the Data Disk, already has index entries marked.

Once all index entries are marked, you can have Word build the index from the index entry fields in the document. The index entry fields display on the screen when the Show/Hide ¶ button on the Standard toolbar is selected; that is, when you display formatting marks. Index entry field codes may alter the document pagination. Thus, you should hide field codes before building an index.

Perform the following steps to build an index.

Steps To Build an Index

1 Scroll down and click to the right of the INDEX heading and then press the ENTER key. If the Show/Hide ¶ button on the Standard toolbar is selected, click it. Click Insert on the menu bar, point to Reference, and then click Index and Tables on the Reference submenu. When the Index and Tables dialog box displays, if necessary, click the Index tab. Click the Formats box arrow. Scroll to and then click Formal. Point to the OK button.

Word displays the Index sheet in the Index and Tables dialog box (Figure 9-71). The Formats box contains a variety of available index styles.

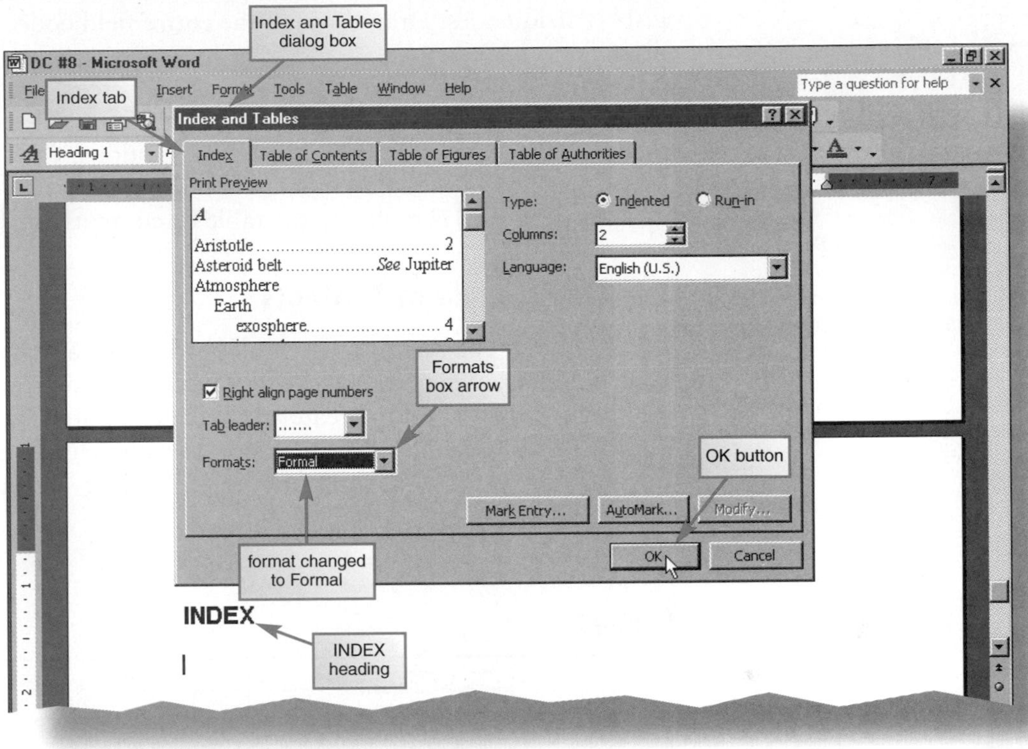

FIGURE 9-71

2 Click the OK button. If necessary, click outside the index to remove the selection.

Word creates a formal index at the location of the insertion point (Figure 9-72).

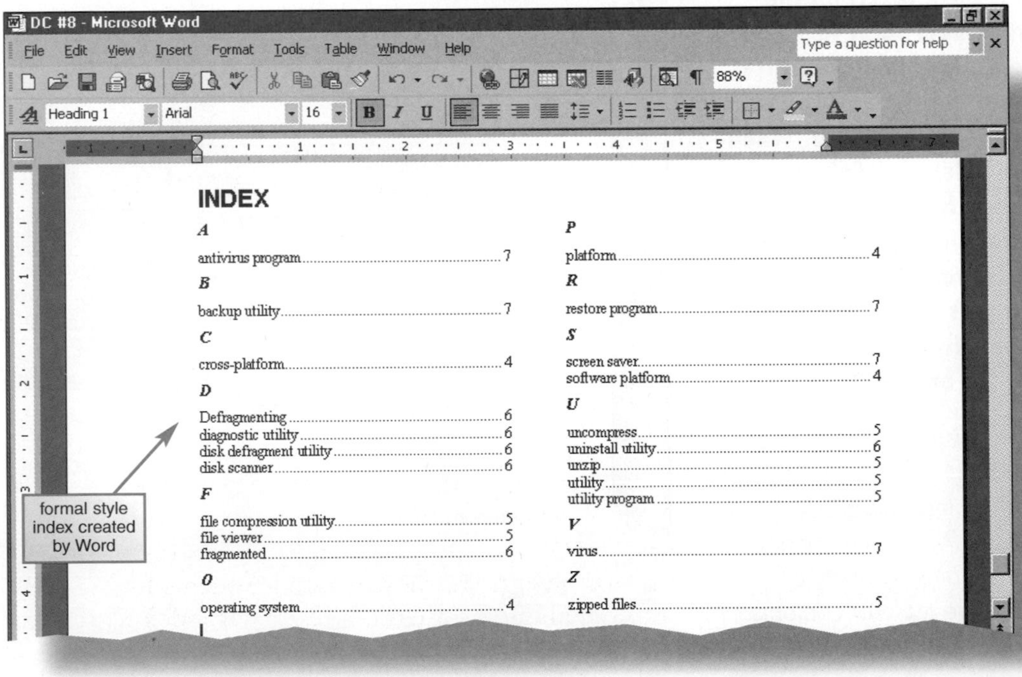

FIGURE 9-72

Other Ways

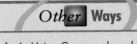

1. In Voice Command mode, say "Insert, Reference, Index and Tables"

To update an index, click to the left of the index to select it and then press the F9 key. To delete an index, click to the left of the index and then press SHIFT+F9 to display field codes. Drag through the entire field code, including the braces, and then press the DELETE key.

When you display the document on the screen, the index entries may still appear — even with the Show/Hide ¶ button not selected. If you want to remove them, click Tools on the menu bar, click Options, click the View tab, remove the check mark from the Hidden text check box, and then click the OK button.

The next step is to create the table of contents for the DC #8 document.

More About

Modifying a Table of Contents

The table of contents that Word generates may contain a heading that you do not want. To remove a heading from the table of contents, you should change the style applied to the heading from a built-in heading to a non-heading style. Then, update the table of contents.

Creating a Table of Contents

A table of contents is a list of all headings in a document and their associated page numbers. When you use Word's built-in heading styles (for example, Heading 1), you can instruct Word to create a table of contents from these headings. In the DC #8 document, the heading of each section uses the Heading 1 style, and subheadings use the Heading 2 style. Thus, perform the following steps to create a table of contents from heading styles.

Steps To Create a Table of Contents

1 Scroll up and click to the right of the TABLE OF CONTENTS heading. Press the ENTER key. Click Insert on the menu bar, point to Reference, and then click Index and Tables on the Reference submenu. When the Index and Tables dialog box displays, if necessary, click the Table of Contents tab. Click the Formats box arrow and then click Formal. Point to the OK button.

Word displays the Table of Contents sheet in the Index and Tables dialog box (Figure 9-73). The Formats list contains a variety of available table of contents styles.

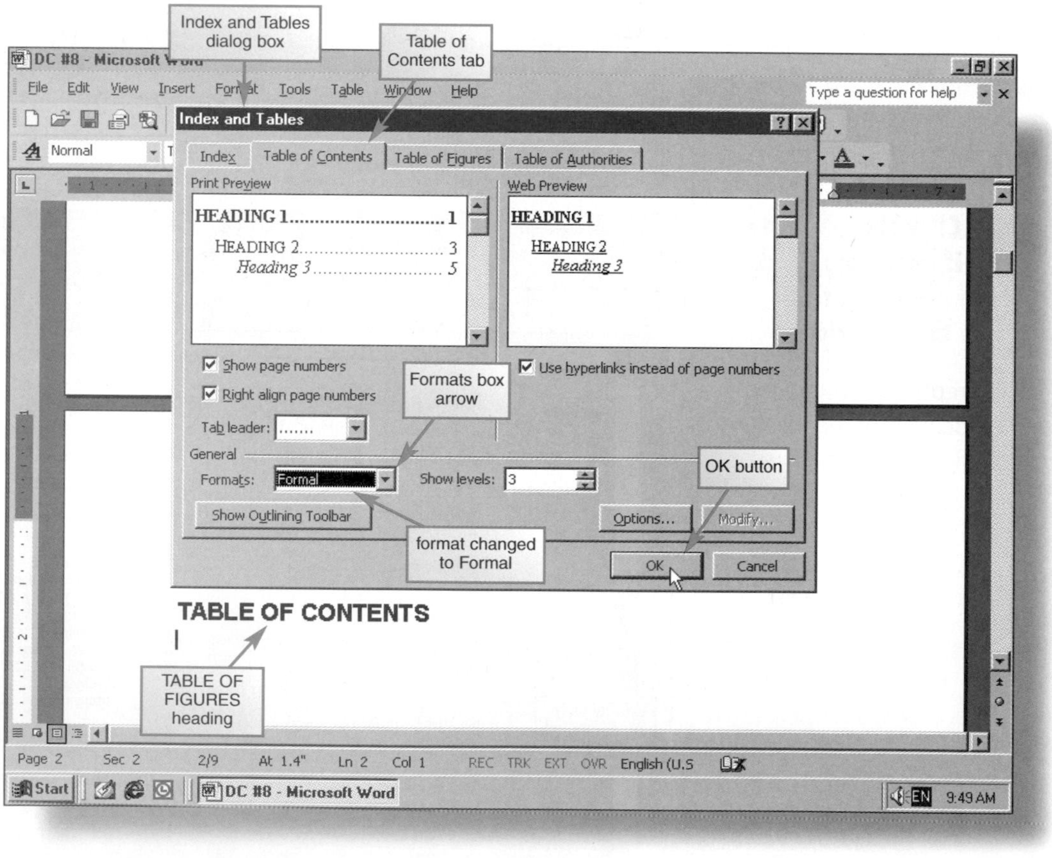

FIGURE 9-73

2 **Click the OK button. If a dialog box displays asking if you want to replace the selected table of contents, click the No button.**

Word creates a formal table of contents at the location of the insertion point (Figure 9-74).

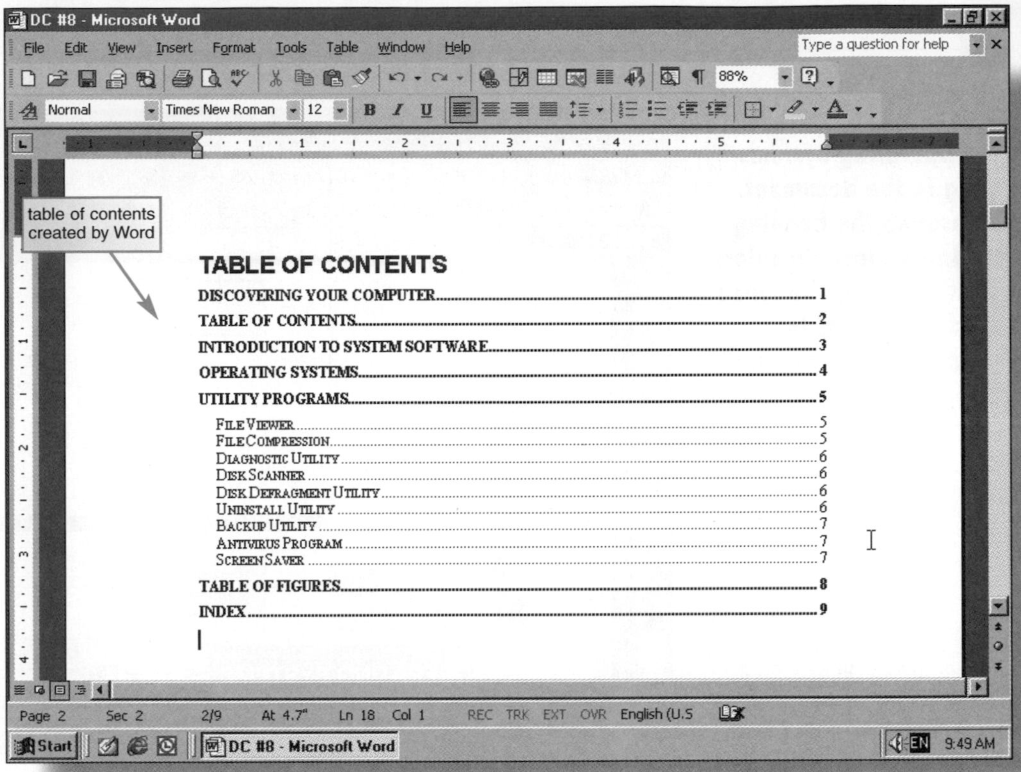

FIGURE 9-74

> ***Other Ways***
>
> 1. In Voice Command mode, say "Insert, Reference, Index and Tables"

When you change headings or text in a document, you should update its associated table of contents. To update a table of contents, click to the left of the table of contents to select it and then press the F9 key.

In a document that contains a table of contents or a table of figures, you can use these tables to navigate through a document. When you CTRL+click any of the entries in either table, Word displays the associated text or graphics in the document window. For example, if you CTRL+click Screen Saver in the table of contents, Word displays the page containing the Screen Saver section.

The next step is to add bookmarks to the document.

> ***More About***
>
> **Bookmarks**
>
> To show bookmarks in a document, click Tools on the menu bar, click Options, click the View tab, place a check mark in the Bookmarks check box, and then click the OK button. If your bookmark displays an error message, select the entire document and then press the F9 key to update the fields in the document.

Adding Bookmarks

To further assist users in navigating through a document, you can add bookmarks. A bookmark is an item in a document that you name for future reference. For example, you could bookmark the two headings, Operating Systems and Utility Programs, so users easily could jump to these two areas of the document. Perform the steps on the next page to add these bookmarks.

Steps To Add a Bookmark

1 Scroll to the Operating Systems heading in the document. Drag through the heading Operating Systems to select it. Click Insert on the menu bar and then point to Bookmark (Figure 9-75).

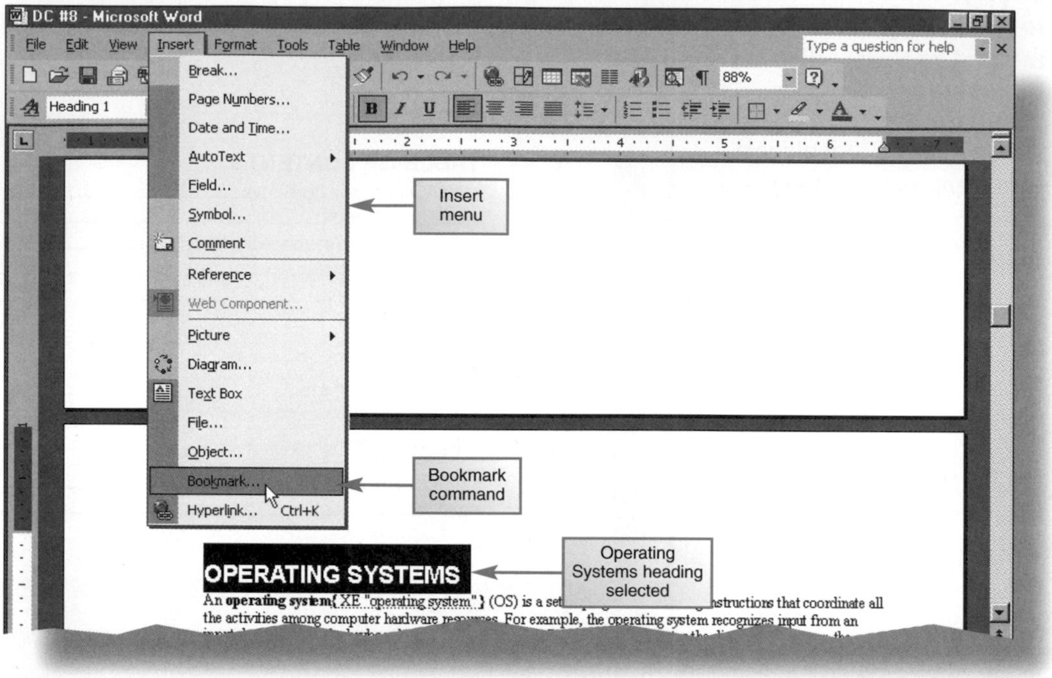

FIGURE 9-75

2 Click Bookmark. When the Bookmark dialog box displays, type `OperatingSystems` **in the Bookmark name text box and then point to the Add button.**

Word displays the Bookmark dialog box (Figure 9-76). Bookmark names can contain only letters, numbers, and the underscore character (_). They also must begin with a letter and contain no spaces.

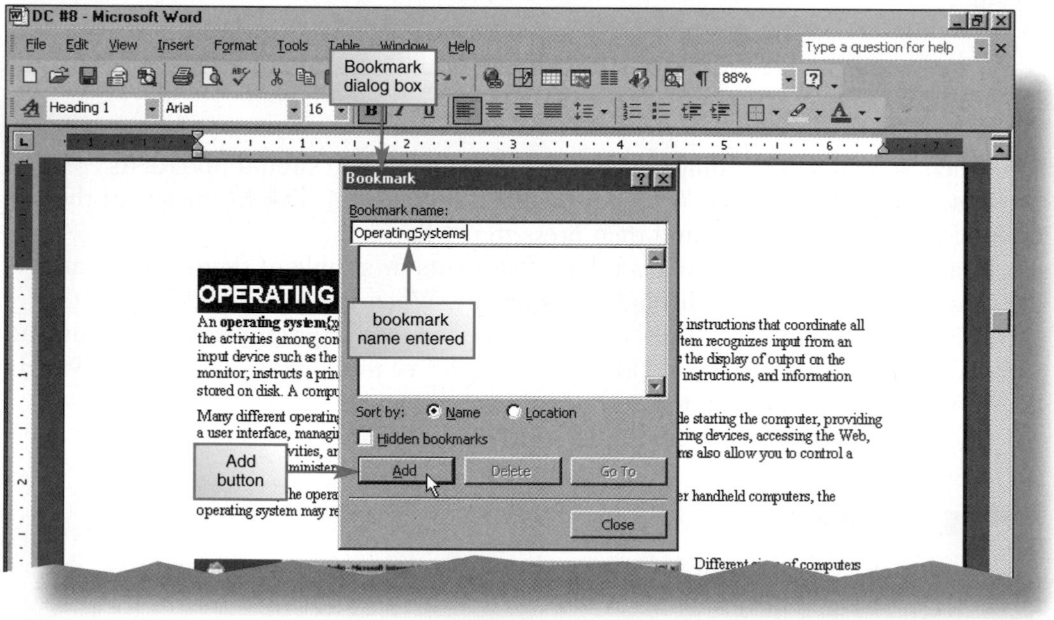

FIGURE 9-76

3 Click the Add button.

Word adds the bookmark name to the list of existing bookmarks for the document.

4 Repeat Steps 1 through 3 for the Utility Programs heading in the document, using the bookmark name of UtilityPrograms.

Other Ways

1. In Voice Command mode, say "Insert, Bookmark"

Once you have added bookmarks, you can jump to a bookmark by displaying the Bookmark dialog box (shown in Figure 9-76), clicking the bookmark name in the list, and then clicking the Go To button; or by pressing the F5 key to display the Go To dialog box, clicking bookmark in the list, selecting the bookmark name, and then clicking the Go To button.

The text of the document now is complete. The next step is to place a header on all pages of the document, except the title page.

More About

Publishing and Graphic Arts Terms

For more information on terms used in publishing and graphic arts, visit the Word 2002 More About Web page (scsite.com/wd2002/more.htm) and then click Publishing and Graphic Arts Terms.

Creating Alternating Headers and Footers

Public information guide documents are designed so that they can be duplicated back-to-back. That is, the document prints on nine separate pages. When you duplicate it, however, pages one and two are printed on opposite sides of the same sheet of paper. Thus, the nine page document when printed back-to-back only uses five sheets of paper.

In many books and documents that have facing pages, the page number is on the outside edges of the pages. In Word, you accomplish this task by specifying one type of header for even-numbered pages and another type of header for odd-numbered pages.

Perform the following steps to create alternating headers beginning with the second page of the document.

Steps To Create Alternating Headers

1 Position the insertion point in the Table of Contents heading (section 2 of the document). Click View on the menu bar and then click Header and Footer. Click the Page Setup button on the Header and Footer toolbar. When the Page Setup dialog box displays, if necessary, click the Layout tab. Click Different odd and even. Click the Apply to box arrow and then click This point forward. Point to the OK button.

Word displays the Page Setup dialog box (Figure 9-77).

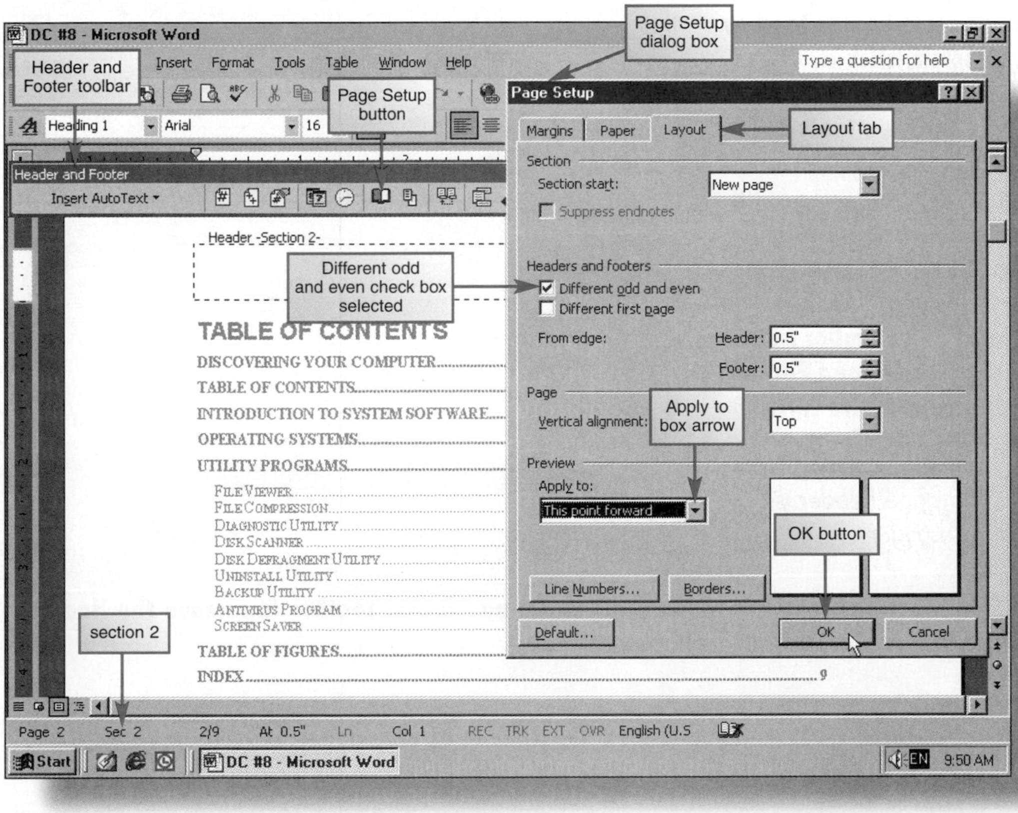

FIGURE 9-77

2 **Click the OK button. If the Same as Previous button on the Header and Footer toolbar is selected, click it. Type** `Public Information Guide #8` **and then press the ENTER key. Type** `Page` **and then press the SPACEBAR. Click the Insert Page Number button on the Header and Footer toolbar. Press the ENTER key. Point to the Show Next button on the Header and Footer toolbar.**

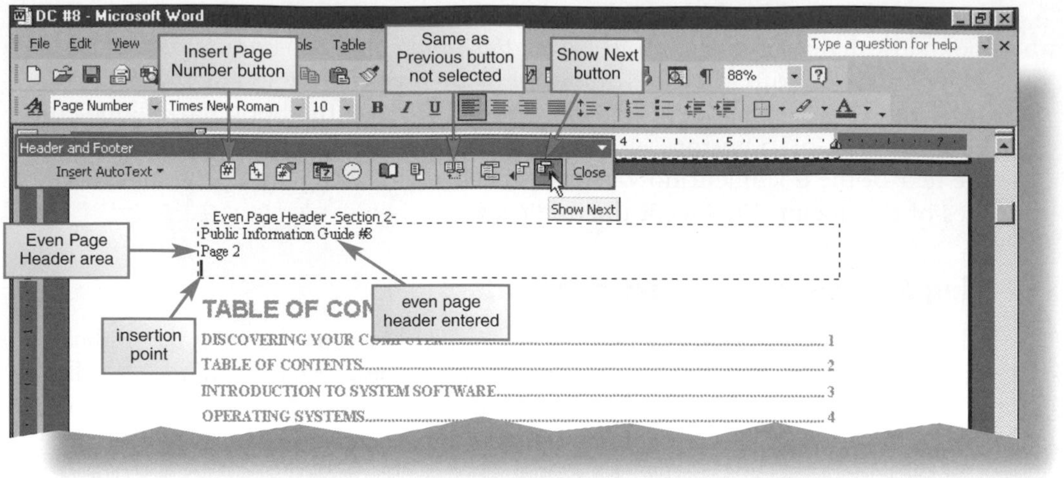

FIGURE 9-78

Word displays the Even Page Header area (Figure 9-78). You want text on even page numbers to be left-aligned and text on odd page numbers to be right-aligned. The Show Next button will display the Odd Page Header area.

3 **Click the Show Next button. If the Same as Previous button on the Header and Footer toolbar is selected, click it. Click the Align Right button on the Formatting toolbar. Type** `Public Information Guide #8` **and then press the ENTER key. Type** `Page` **and then press the SPACEBAR. Click the Insert Page Number button on the Header and Footer toolbar. Press the ENTER key.**

The odd page header is complete (Figure 9-79).

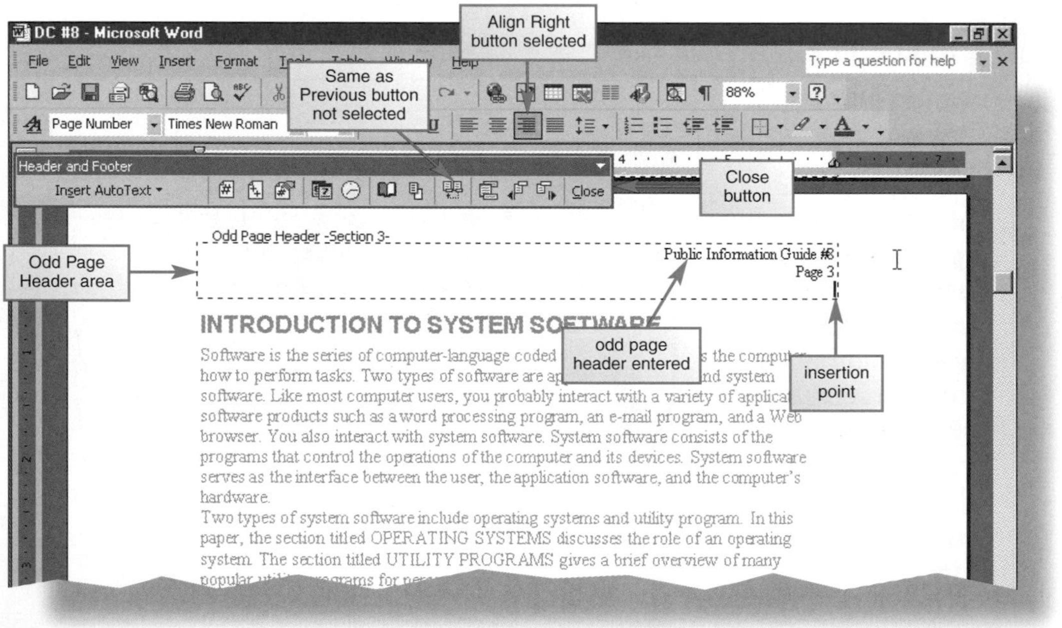

FIGURE 9-79

4 **Click the Close button on the Header and Footer toolbar to remove the Header and Footer toolbar from the screen.**

Other Ways

1. In Voice Command mode, say "View, Header and Footer, Page Setup"

To create alternating footers, follow the same basic procedure as you would to create alternating headers, except enter text in the footer area instead of the header area.

The next step is to set a gutter margin for the document.

Setting a Gutter Margin

Public information guide documents are designed so that the inner margin between facing pages has extra space to allow printed versions of the documents to be bound (such as stapled) — without the binding covering the words. This extra space in the inner margin is called the gutter margin.

Perform the following steps to set a three-quarter inch left and right margin and a one-half inch gutter margin.

Steps To Set a Gutter Margin

1 Click File on the menu bar and then click Page Setup. When the Page Setup dialog box displays, if necessary, click the Margins tab. Type .75 **in the Left text box,** .75 **in the Right text box, and** .5 **in the Gutter text box. Click the Apply to box arrow and then click Whole document. Point to the OK button.**

Word displays the Page Setup dialog box (Figure 9-80). The Preview area illustrates the position of the gutter margin.

2 Click the OK button.

Word sets the gutter margin for the entire document.

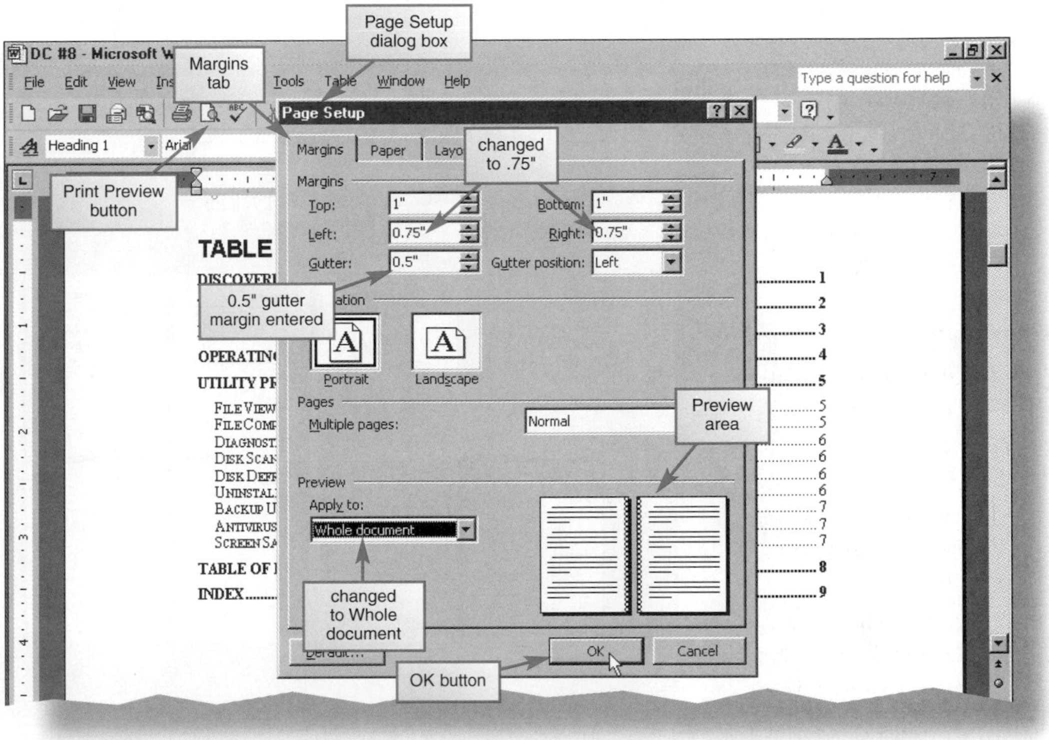

FIGURE 9-80

Other Ways

1. In Voice Command mode, say "File, Page Setup"

You notice that the Body Text style uses a 10-point font. You prefer a 12-point font. Perform the following steps to change the Body Text style from 10 to 12 point.

TO MODIFY A STYLE

1. Position the insertion point in the body text in the INTRODUCTION TO SYSTEM SOFTWARE section. Click the Styles and Formatting button on the Formatting toolbar to display the Styles and Formatting task pane.
2. Point to Body Text in the Styles and Formatting task pane and then click the box arrow that displays to the right of Body Text. Click Modify in the menu. When the Modify Style dialog box displays, if necessary, click the Font Size box arrow in the dialog box and then click 12. Click the OK button. Click the Close button on the Styles and Formatting task pane.

Word changes all text formatted using the Body Text style in the document from 10 to 12 point.

To view the layout of all the pages in the document, display all the pages in print preview as described in the following steps.

TO DISPLAY SEVERAL PAGES IN PRINT PREVIEW

1. Click the Print Preview button on the Standard toolbar.
2. Click the Multiple Pages button on the Print Preview toolbar. Click the right-bottom icon in the grid (when the description reads 2 x 6 pages) to display the pages in the Discovering Your Computer public information guide document as shown in Figure 9-81.
3. Click the Close button on the Print Preview toolbar.

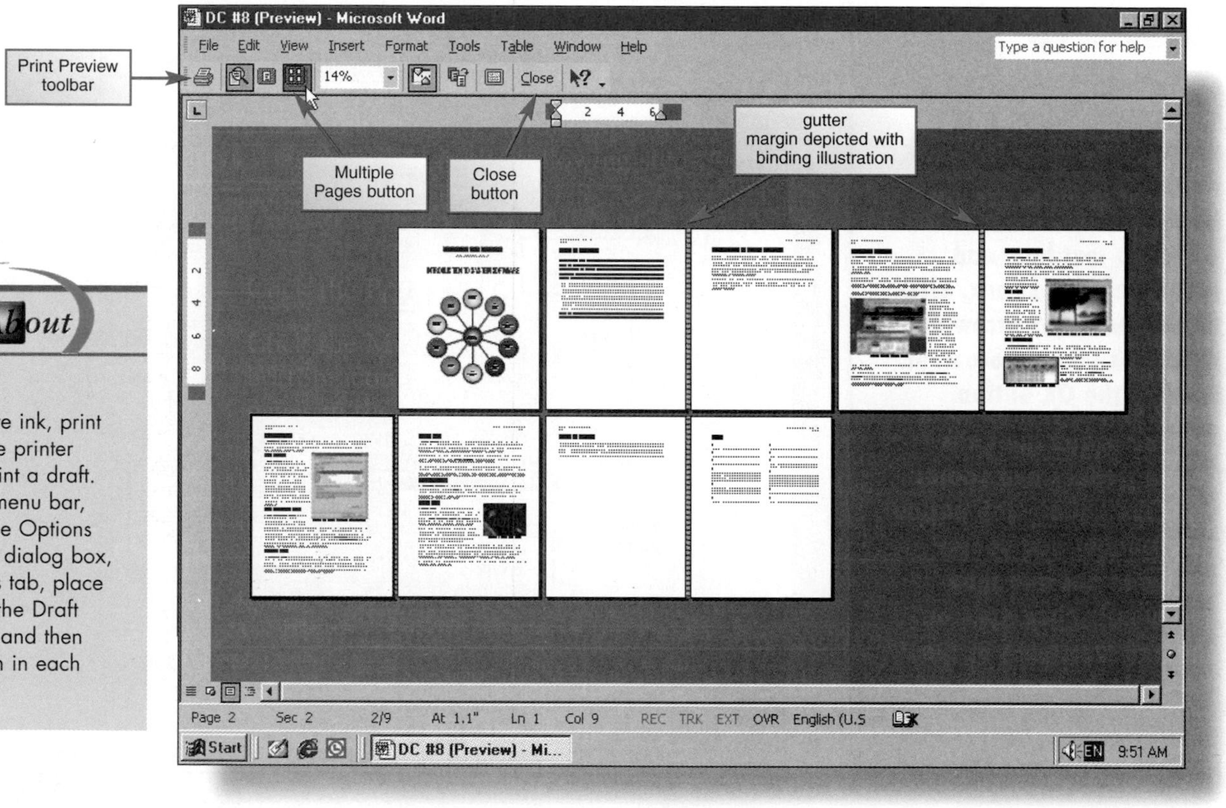

FIGURE 9-81

More About

Printing

If you want to save ink, print faster, or minimize printer overrun errors, print a draft. Click File on the menu bar, click Print, click the Options button in the Print dialog box, click the Graphics tab, place a check mark in the Draft output check box and then click the OK button in each dialog box.

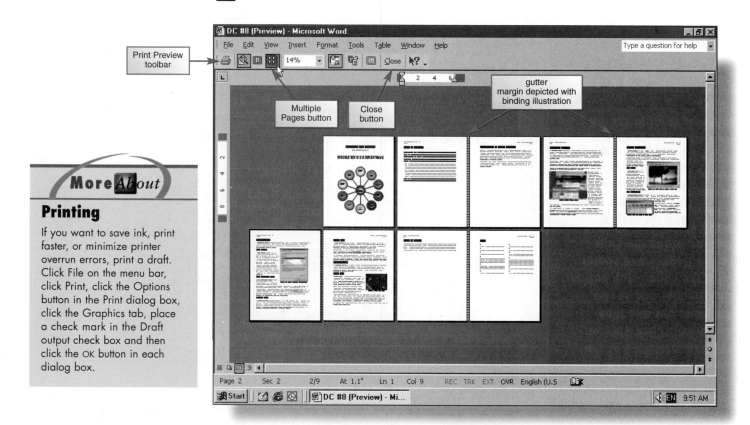

The reference master document for this project now is complete. Perform the following steps to save it again, print it, and then close the document.

TO SAVE AND PRINT THE DOCUMENT

1. Click the Save button on the Standard toolbar.
2. Click the Print button on the Standard toolbar.

Word saves the document with the same file name, DC #8. The completed document prints each page shown in Figure 9-1 on page WD 9.05 on a separate piece of paper.

TO CLOSE THE DOCUMENT

1. Click File on the menu bar and then click Close.

Opening a Master Document

You may wish to open a master document at a later date to edit or print its contents. When you open the master document, the subdocuments are collapsed; that is, the subdocuments display as hyperlinks. Thus, switch to outline view and expand the subdocuments, as shown in the following steps.

Steps To Open a Master Document

1 Open the DC #8 document. Click the Outline View button on the horizontal scroll bar. Be sure the Show/Hide ¶ button on the Standard toolbar is selected. Make sure the Show First Line Only button on the Outlining toolbar is not selected. Scroll down to display the hyperlinks. Point to the Expand Subdocuments button on the Outlining toolbar.

Word displays the DC #8 document in outline view (Figure 9-82).

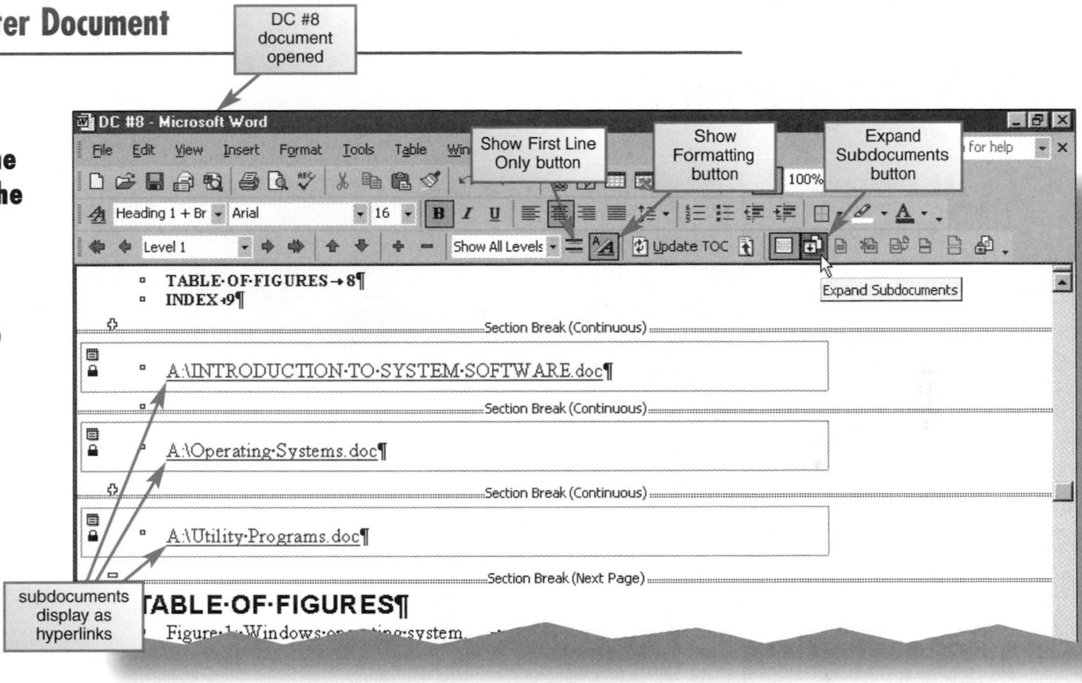

FIGURE 9-82

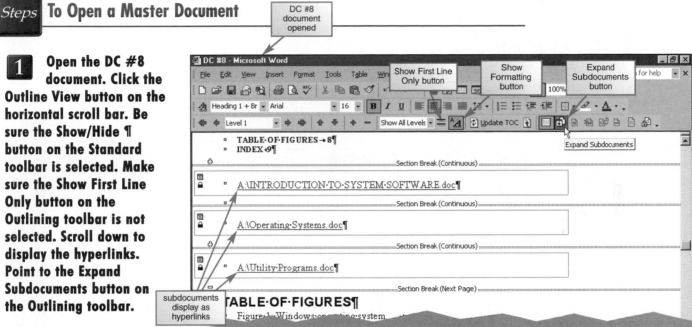

2 Click the Expand Subdocuments button. When the Password dialog box displays, type `computer` **and then click the OK button. Scroll down to display the subdocuments.**

Word displays the contents of the subdocuments in the master document (Figure 9-83).

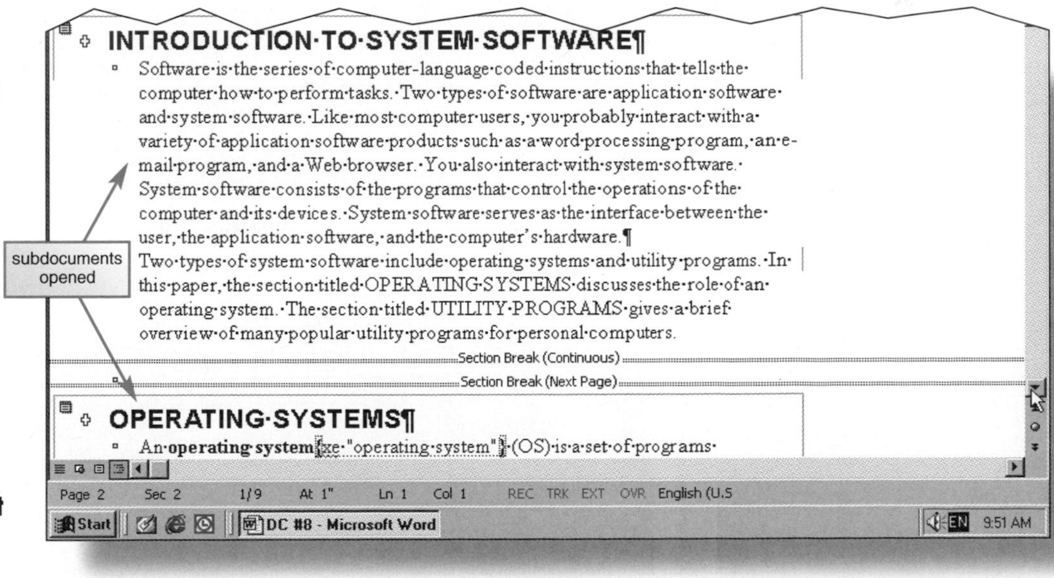

FIGURE 9-83

3 Click the Print Layout View button on the horizontal scroll bar.

The master document is ready to be printed or modified.

Other Ways

1. In Voice Command mode, say "File, Open, [select file], OK, Outline View"

Using the Document Map

When you use Word's built-in heading styles in a document, you can use the Document Map to navigate quickly through the document. The **Document Map** is a separate area at the left edge of the Word window that displays these headings in an outline format. When you click a heading in the Document Map, Word scrolls to and displays that heading in the document window.

Perform the following steps to use the Document Map.

Steps To Use the Document Map

1 If the Show/Hide ¶ button on the Standard toolbar is selected, click it. Click the Document Map button on the Standard toolbar. Right-click the Document Map and then click All on the shortcut menu to ensure that all headings display.

Word displays the Document Map in a separate pane at the left edge of the Word window (Figure 9-84). The Document Map lists all headings that are formatted using Word's built-in heading styles. Your document map may show some blank lines between headings.

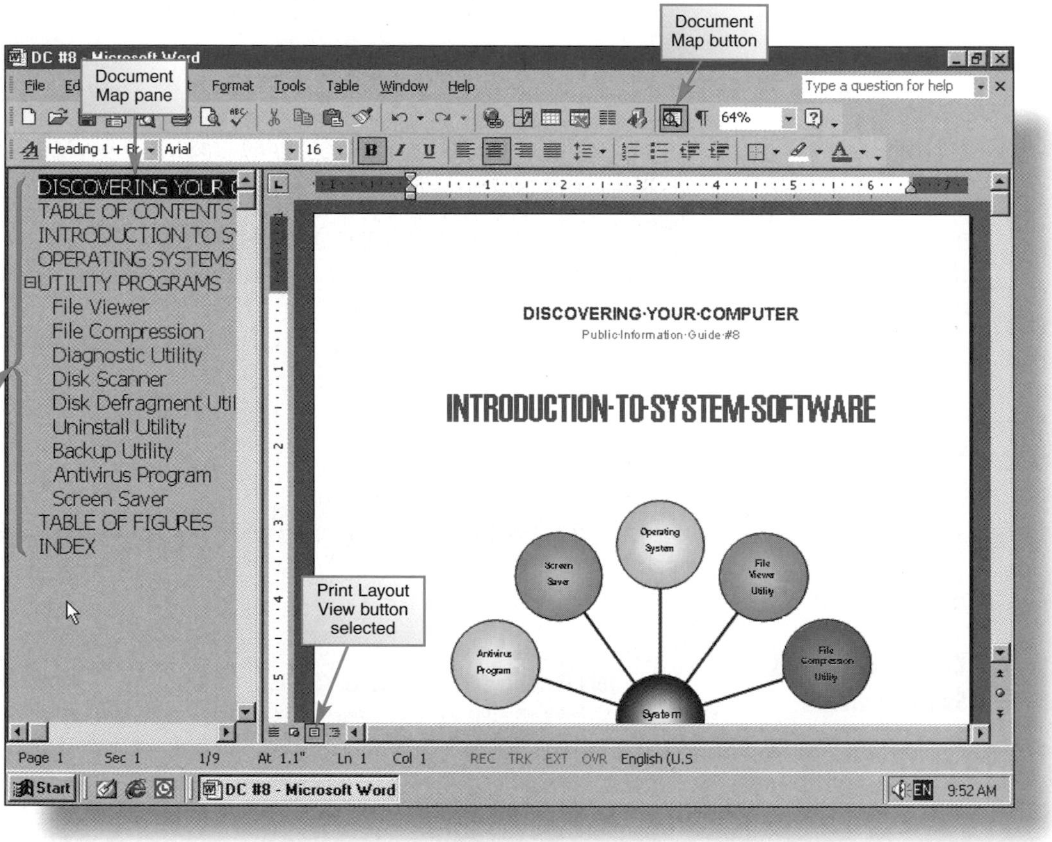

FIGURE 9-84

2 Click TABLE OF CONTENTS in the Document Map pane.

Word scrolls to and displays the TABLE OF CONTENTS heading at the top of the document window (Figure 9-85).

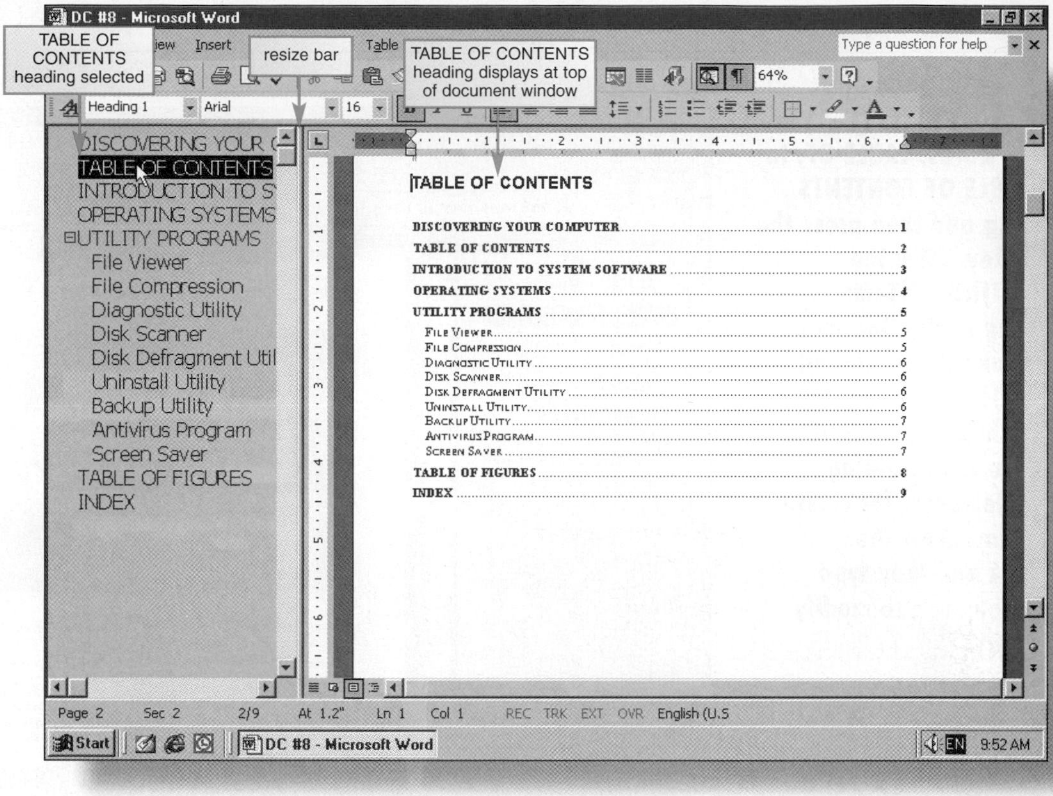

FIGURE 9-85

Other Ways

1. In Voice Command mode, say "Document Map"

To display any subheadings below a heading, click the plus sign (+) to the left of the heading. Likewise, to hide any subheadings, click the minus sign (–) to the left of the heading.

If a heading is too wide for the Document Map pane, you do not need to make the Document Map pane wider — simply point to the heading to display a ScreenTip that shows the complete title. You can change the width of the Document Map pane, however, by dragging the resize bar to the left or right.

Modifying the Table of Contents and Index

Assume you wanted to change the title of the TABLE OF CONTENTS to just the word, CONTENTS. Assume also that you want to change the index entry for cross-platform to the phrase, cross-platform application. After making these changes to the document, you must update the table of contents and the index as shown in the steps on the next page.

More About

Subdocuments

If you want to change the name of a subdocument, you cannot use Windows Explorer. Instead, display the document in outline view, click the Collapse Subdocuments button on the Outlining toolbar, and then click the hyperlink of the document to be renamed. When the subdocument displays in its own Word window, click File on the menu bar, click Save As, change the document name, and then click the Save button in the dialog box. Then, return to the master document by clicking File on the menu bar and then clicking Close.

Steps To Modify a Table of Contents and Index

1 **Drag through the words, TABLE OF, in the TABLE OF CONTENTS heading and then press the DELETE key. Click the OPERATING SYSTEMS heading in the Document Map pane. Scroll to and then click immediately to the right of the m inside the braces containing the index entry for cross-platform. Press the SPACEBAR and then type** `application` **to modify the entry.**

The document is modified (Figure 9-86).

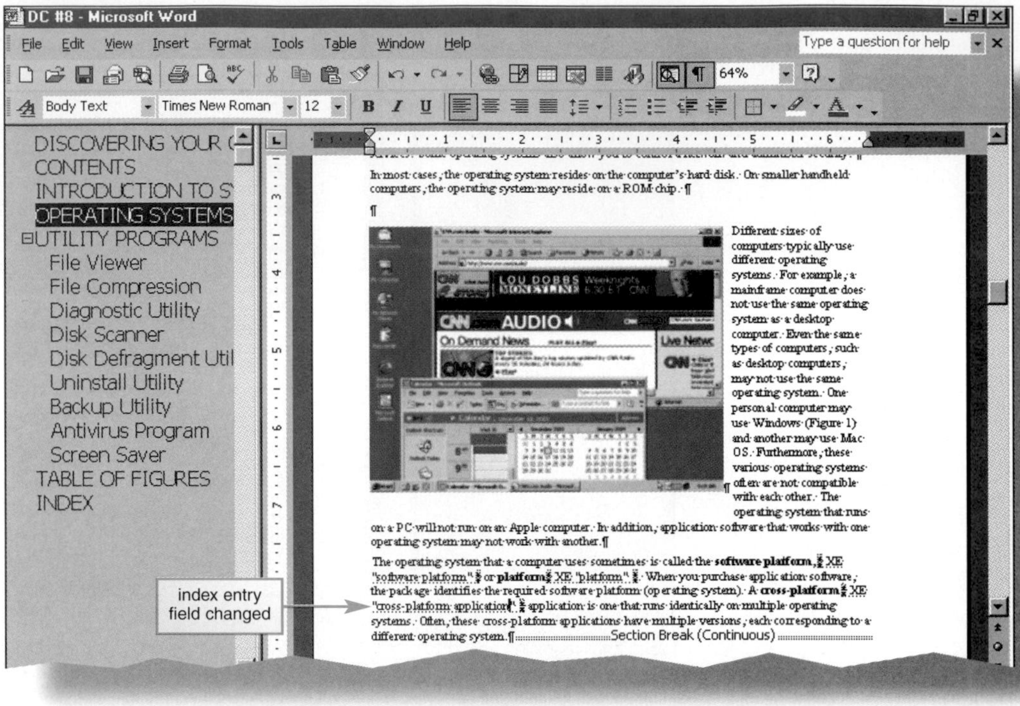

FIGURE 9-86

2 **If the Show/Hide ¶ button on the Standard toolbar is selected, click it. In the Document Map pane, click CONTENTS and then click the contents listing in the document window to select the table. Press the F9 key. When the Update Table of Contents dialog box displays, click Update entire table and then point to the OK button.**

Word displays the Update Table of Contents dialog box (Figure 9-87).

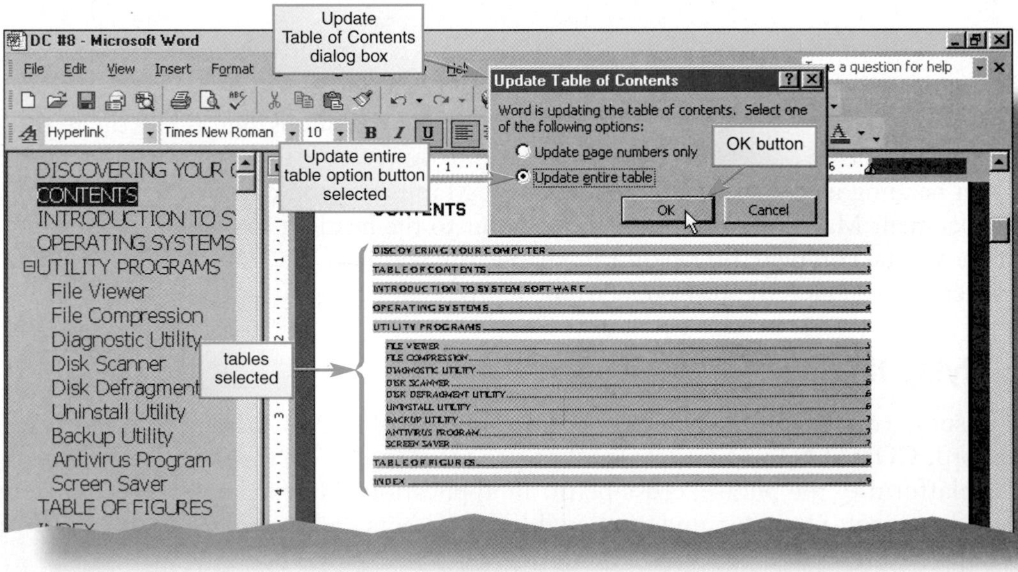

FIGURE 9-87

3 **Click the OK button. Repeat Step 2, clicking INDEX in the Document Map pane. Word will update the index when you press the F9 key.**

Word updates the index, changing the index entry from cross-platform to cross-platform application.

Other Ways

1. Click Update TOC button on Outlining toolbar
2. In Voice Command mode, say "Update Table of Contents"

By selecting the entire table of contents or index and then pressing the F9 key, you are instructing Word to update all fields in the document. If you want to update a single field, select it and then press the F9 key.

The next step is to hide the Document Map, as described in the following step.

TO HIDE THE DOCUMENT MAP

1. Click the Document Map button on the Standard toolbar.

Word removes the Document Map pane from the Word window.

You also can hide the Document Map by double-clicking the resize bar to its right (shown in Figure 9-85 on page WD 9.67).

You are finished modifying the document. Perform the following step to quit Word.

TO QUIT WORD

1. Click the Close button on the Word title bar. When Word displays a dialog box asking if you wish to save changes, click the No button.

The Word window closes.

More About

Quick Reference

For a table that lists how to complete tasks covered in this book using the mouse, menu, shortcut menu, and keyboard, see the Quick Reference Summary at the back of this book or visit the Shelly Cashman Series Office XP Web page (scsite.com/offxp/qr.htm) and then click Microsoft Word 2002.

CASE PERSPECTIVE SUMMARY

You send the redesigned public information guide document to Keith for his approval. He is thrilled with the new design. The table of contents, table of figures, and index really organize the document for a reader. He gives you approval to duplicate and distribute the document.

Keith would like you to conduct training classes for company employees on the change-tracking features of Word. You send an e-mail announcing the schedule and topic of the training classes. Next, you write a set of instructions to distribute to each attendee at the training classes. Your first class is tomorrow — it will be nice to be on the other side of the podium!

More About

Microsoft Certification

The Microsoft Office User Specialist (MOUS) Certification program provides an opportunity for you to obtain a valuable industry credential — proof that you have the Word 2002 skills required by employers. For more information, see Appendix E or visit the Shelly Cashman Series MOUS Web page at scsite.com/offxp/cert.htm.

Project Summary

Project 9 introduced you to creating a long document with a table of contents, a table of figures, and an index. You inserted, modified, reviewed, and deleted comments. You also tracked changes, and accepted and rejected the tracked changes. You learned how to save multiple versions of a document, add and modify a caption, insert a diagram, create a cross-reference, mark index entries, add a bookmark, verify the widow/orphan setting, password-protect a document, create alternating headers, and set a gutter margin. You also worked with master documents and subdocuments. Finally, you used the Document Map to navigate through the document.

What You Should Know

Having completed this project, you should now be able to perform the following tasks:

- Add a Bookmark *(WD 9.60)*
- Add a Caption *(WD 9.26)*
- Build an Index *(WD 9.57)*
- Change an Inline Graphic to a Floating Graphic *(WD 9.25)*
- Close the Document *(WD 9.35, WD 9.64)*
- Compare and Merge Documents *(WD 9.21)*
- Compare and Merge, Rejecting Changes *(WD 9.23)*
- Convert a Text Box to a Frame *(WD 9.28)*
- Create a Cross-Reference *(WD 9.29)*
- Create a New Subdocument *(WD 9.43)*
- Create a Table of Contents *(WD 9.58)*
- Create a Table of Figures *(WD 9.55)*
- Create Alternating Headers *(WD 9.61)*
- Create an Outline *(WD 9.37)*
- Demote a Line to Body Text *(WD 9.47)*
- Display Formatting Marks *(WD 9.07)*
- Display Several Pages in Print Preview *(WD 9.64)*
- Enter and Format Title Page Text *(WD 9.48)*
- Enter Body Text into an Outline *(WD 9.45)*
- Hide the Document Map *(WD 9.69)*
- Hide the Reviewing Toolbar *(WD 9.23)*
- Insert a Comment *(WD 9.11)*
- Insert a Graphic *(WD 9.24)*
- Insert a Password-Protected File as a Subdocument *(WD 9.40)*
- Insert and Format a Diagram *(WD 9.50)*
- Insert Another Subdocument *(WD 9.41)*
- Mark an Index Entry *(WD 9.31)*
- Mark More Index Entries and Bold Them *(WD 9.32)*
- Modify a Style *(WD 9.63)*
- Modify a Table of Contents and Index *(WD 9.68)*
- Modify an Outline *(WD 9.44)*
- Modify the Caption *(WD 9.28)*
- Open and E-Mail a Document for Review *(WD 9.08)*
- Open a Master Document *(WD 9.65)*
- Password-Protect a File *(WD 9.34)*
- Quit Word *(WD 9.69)*
- Reset Menus and Toolbars *(WD 9.07)*
- Resize a Graphic *(WD 9.24)*
- Review Tracked Changes *(WD 9.18)*
- Save a Document *(WD 9.43)*
- Save a Document with a New File Name *(WD 9.11)*
- Save a Version of a Document *(WD 9.16)*
- Save and Print the Document *(WD 9.64)*
- Set a Gutter Margin *(WD 9.63)*
- Start and Customize Word *(WD 9.06)*
- Stop Tracking Changes *(WD 9.16)*
- Track Changes *(WD 9.14)*
- Use the Document Map *(WD 9.66)*
- Verify the Widow and Orphan Setting *(WD 9.33)*
- Zoom Page Width *(WD 9.07)*

Learn It Online

Instructions: To complete the Learn It Online exercises, start your browser, click the Address bar, and then enter `scsite.com/offxp/exs.htm`. When the Office XP Learn It Online page displays, follow the instructions in the exercises below.

1 Project Reinforcement

TF, MC, and SA

Below Word Project 9, click the Project Reinforcement link. Print the quiz by clicking Print on the File menu. Answer each question. Write your first and last name at the top of each page, and then hand in the printout to your instructor.

2 Flash Cards

Below Word Project 9, click the Flash Cards link. When Flash Cards displays, read the instructions. Type `20` (or a number specified by your instructor) in the Number of Playing Cards text box, type your name in the Name text box, and then click the Flip Card button. When the flash card displays, read the question and then click the Answer box arrow to select an answer. Flip through Flash Cards. Click Print on the File menu to print the last flash card if your score is 15 (75%) correct or greater and then hand it in to your instructor. If your score is less than 15 (75%) correct, then redo this exercise by clicking the Replay button.

3 Practice Test

Below Word Project 9, click the Practice Test link. Answer each question, enter your first and last name at the bottom of the page, and then click the Grade Test button. When the graded practice test displays on your screen, click Print on the File menu to print a hard copy. Continue to take practice tests until you score 80% or better. Hand in a printout of the final practice test to your instructor.

4 Who Wants to Be a Computer Genius?

Below Word Project 9, click the Computer Genius link. Read the instructions, enter your first and last name at the bottom of the page, and then click the Play button. Hand in your score to your instructor.

5 Wheel of Terms

Below Word Project 9, click the Wheel of Terms link. Read the instructions, and then enter your first and last name and your school name. Click the Play button. Hand in your score to your instructor.

6 Crossword Puzzle Challenge

Below Word Project 9, click the Crossword Puzzle Challenge link. Read the instructions, and then enter your first and last name. Click the Play button. Work the crossword puzzle. When you are finished, click the Submit button. When the crossword puzzle redisplays, click the Print button. Hand in the printout.

7 Tips and Tricks

Below Word Project 9, click the Tips and Tricks link. Click a topic that pertains to Project 9. Right-click the information and then click Print on the shortcut menu. Construct a brief example of what the information relates to in Word to confirm you understand how to use the tip or trick. Hand in the example and printed information.

8 Newsgroups

Below Word Project 9, click the Newsgroups link. Click a topic that pertains to Project 9. Print three comments. Hand in the comments to your instructor.

9 Expanding Your Horizons

Below Word Project 9, click the Articles for Microsoft Word link. Click a topic that pertains to Project 9. Print the information. Construct a brief example of what the information relates to in Word to confirm you understand the contents of the article. Hand in the example and printed information to your instructor.

10 Search Sleuth

Below Word Project 9, click the Search Sleuth link. To search for a term that pertains to this project, select a term below the Project 9 title and then use the Google search engine at google.com (or any major search engine) to display and print two Web pages that present information on the term. Hand in the printouts to your instructor.

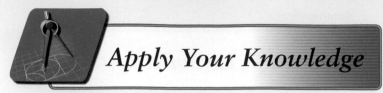

Apply Your Knowledge

1 Using Word's Change-Tracking Feature

Instructions: Start Word. Open the document, Client Server Concepts Draft, on the Data Disk. If you did not download the Data Disk, see the inside back cover for instructions for downloading the Data Disk or see your instructor.

As shown in Figure 9-88, the document contains reviewer's comments and tracked changes. You are to review and delete the comments and then accept or reject each of the tracked changes.

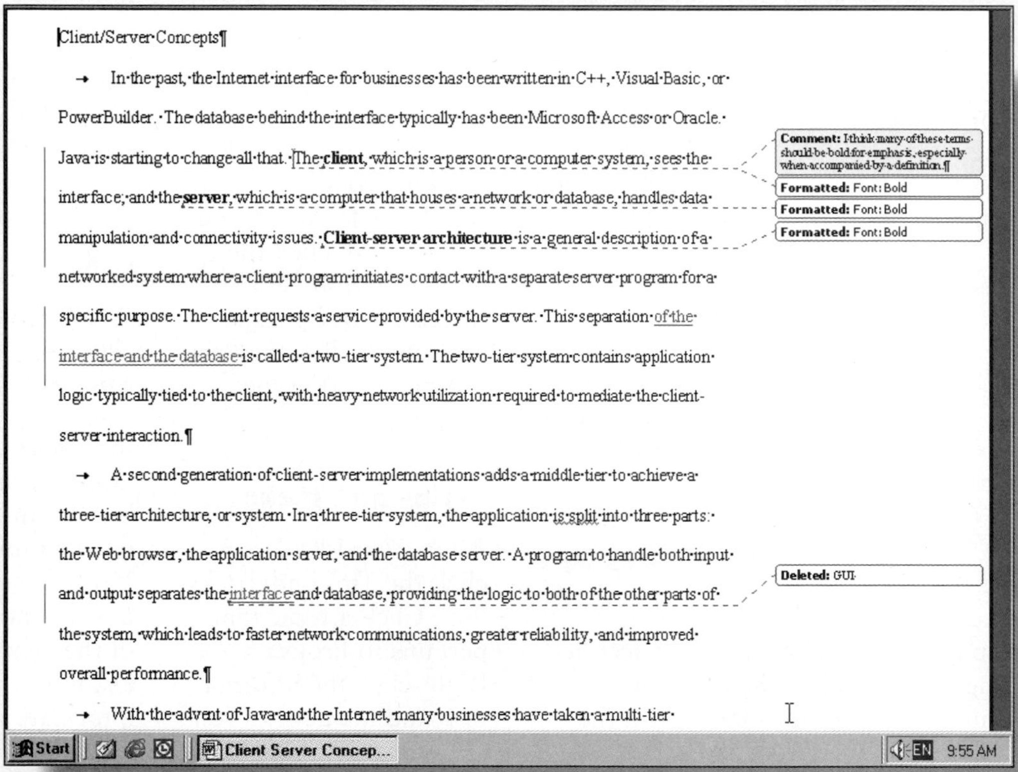

FIGURE 9-88

Perform the following tasks:

1. Click the Print Layout View button on the horizontal scroll bar. If the Reviewing toolbar does not display, click View on the menu bar, point to Toolbars, and then click Reviewing. If the TRK status indicator on the status bar displays darkened double-click it to dim it.
2. Click File on the menu bar, click Print, click the Print what box arrow, and then click Document showing markup in the list. Click the OK button to print the document with tracked changes and comments. Click File on the menu bar, click Print, click the Print what box arrow, and then click Document in the list. Click the OK button to print the document with all marked changes made.
3. Press CTRL+HOME. Click the Next button on the Reviewing toolbar. Read the comment. Right-click the comment balloon and then click Delete Comment on the shortcut menu to delete the comment.

Apply Your Knowledge

4. Click the Next button on the Reviewing toolbar. If necessary, scroll to display the markup balloon. Click the Accept Change button to accept the bold formatting.
5. Repeat Step 4 twice, to accept the next two formatting changes.
6. Click the Next button on the Reviewing toolbar. Click the Accept Change button to accept the insertion of the phrase (of the interface and the database).
7. Click the Next button. If necessary, scroll to display the markup balloon. Click the Accept Change button twice to accept the replacement of the word, GUI, with the word, interface.
8. Click the Next button on the Reviewing toolbar. If necessary, scroll to display the tracked change balloon. Click the Accept Change button to accept the insertion of the word, therefore.
9. Click the Next button on the Reviewing toolbar. If necessary, scroll to display the comment balloon. Read the comment. Right-click the comment balloon and then click Delete Comment on the shortcut menu. Right-click the inserted phrase (such as JavaScript or CGI) and then click Accept Insertion on the shortcut menu.
10. Click the Next button. Scroll, if necessary to display the tracked change balloon. Click the Reject Change/Delete Comment button to reject the insertion of the word, substantial.
11. At the end of the document, insert the following comment: Tracked changes accepted and rejected.
12. Save the reviewed document with the name, Client Server Concepts Revised. Print the document with comments.

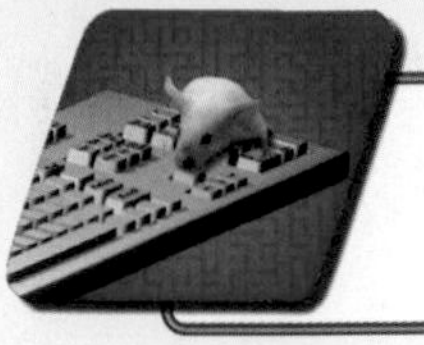

In the Lab

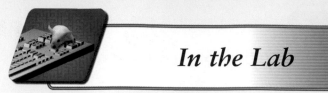

1 Working with a Master Document, Table of Contents, and Index

Problem: You are an editor for Dixon Publishing, a national company that publishes how-to manuals. You are to begin assembling Chapter 3 of a desktop publishing manual. You design chapters of the books as master documents and insert subdocuments as you receive chapter text from authors. You are responsible for inserting figure captions, creating the table of contents and index, and formatting the chapter. A miniature version of the Chapter 3 document is shown in Figure 9-89; for a more readable view, visit scsite.com/ wd2002/ project9.htm.

You just received the first subdocument for Chapter 3. Thus, you lay out the master document for the chapter. The subdocument used in this lab is on the Data Disk. If you did not download the Data Disk, see the inside back cover for instructions for downloading the Data Disk or see your instructor.

Instructions:

1. Open the document, Chapter 3 Creating Brochures Draft, from the Data Disk. Save the document with a new file name, Chapter 3 Creating Brochures.
2. If necessary, switch to print layout view. Add the following caption to the first figure: Page 1 of the Scholarship Brochure. Add the following caption to the second figure: Page 2 of the Scholarship Brochure.
3. Below the first graphic, the paragraph should end with the phrase, as shown in Figure 1, with the text Figure 1 being a cross-reference. Modify the sentence accordingly. Make a similar change to the text about the second figure.
4. Mark each bold term as an index entry.
5. Save the Chapter 3 Creating Brochures file again and then close the file.
6. Start a new Word document. Switch to outline view. Enter the following Heading 1 headings on separate lines of the outline: Chapter 3 — Creating Brochures, Table of Contents, and Index. Insert a next page section break between the headings.
7. Save the master document with the file name, Desktop Publishing. Between the Table of Contents and Index headings, insert the Chapter 3 Creating Brochures file as a subdocument.
8. If necessary, switch to print layout view. On page 1 (the title page) below the Chapter 3 — Creating Brochures heading, enter this line double-spaced in 20-point Times New Roman: `Confidential Work in Progress`. Below that text, insert a clip art image of a book. Below the graphic, enter these lines double-spaced in 20-point Times New Roman underlined: `Authors: J. Reneau and M. Louks; Editor: D. Montgomery; Proofreader: B. Arslanian`. On the next line, type `Date to Film: 10/22/2003` and then press the ENTER key. Type `Bound Book Date: 11/19/2003` as the last line. Center all text and graphics on the title page.
9. Build an index for the document. In the Index sheet, use the formal format for the index and place a check mark in the Right align page numbers check box. Remember to hide formatting marks prior to building the index.
10. Create a table of contents for the document. Use the Formal format.
11. Beginning on the second page (the table of contents), create a header as follows: print the words, Chapter 3 Page, followed by the page number at the right margin. The title page does not have a header. Note: Because you do not want facing pages in this document, you do not create alternating headers.
12. Change all margins to 1" with a gutter margin of .5". Be sure to change the Apply to box to Whole document.
13. Verify that the following headings begin on a new page: Table of Contents, Introduction, and Index. If any do not, insert a next page section break.
14. Because you modified the margins, update the table of contents and index.
15. Save the document again. Print the document. Staple the document along the gutter margin.

In the Lab

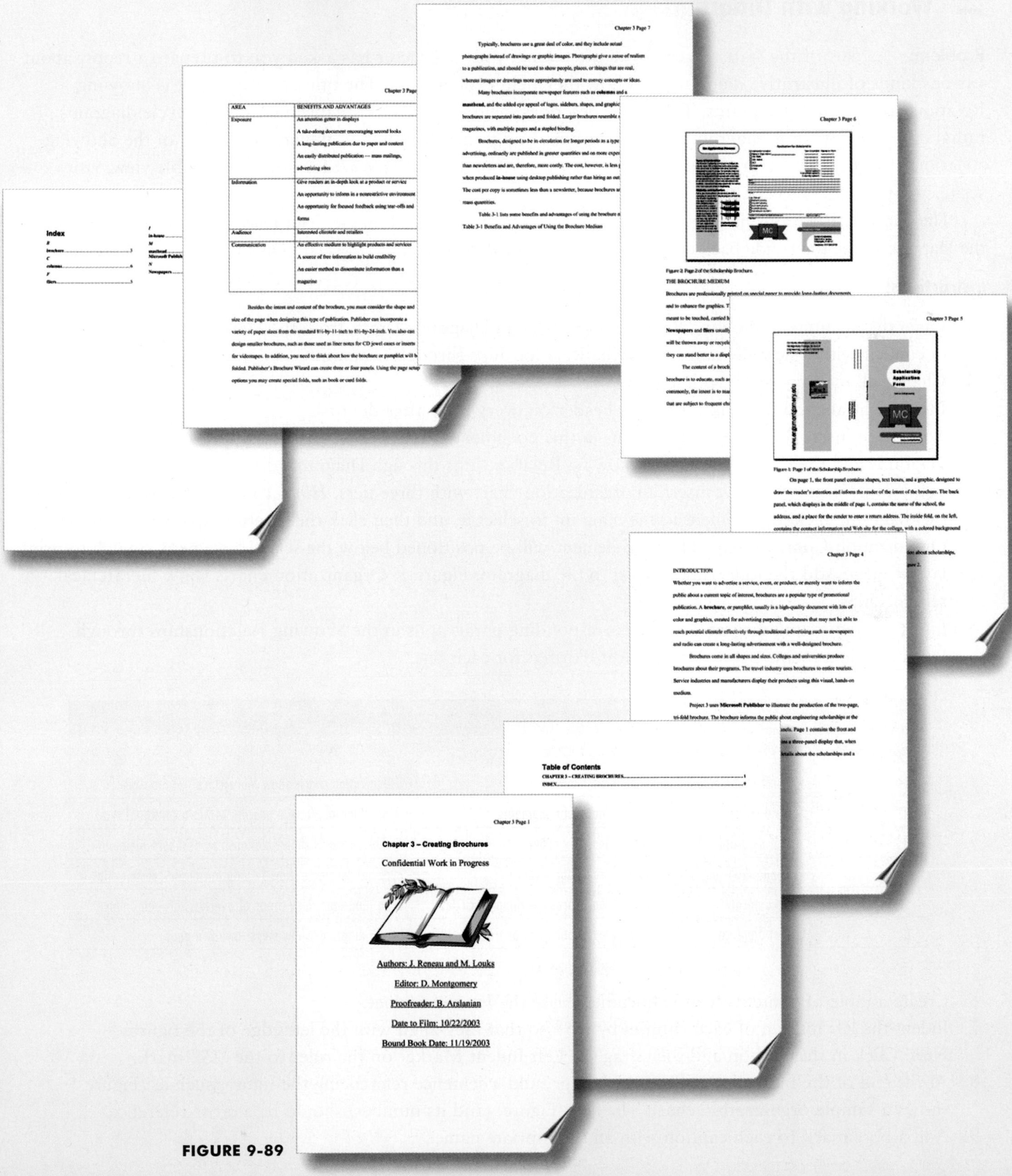

FIGURE 9-89

In the Lab

2 Working with Diagrams

Problem: As part of the statistics class you are taking, your instructor has asked you to prepare a report about various kinds of illustrative diagrams and how they help explain data. The title of your report is Showing Relationships through Diagrams. The report describes diagrams such as organization charts, cycle diagrams, radial diagrams, pyramid diagrams, Venn diagrams, and target diagrams. A miniature version of the Showing Relationships through Diagrams is shown in Figure 9-90 on page WD 9.77; for a more readable view, visit scsite.com/wd2002/project9.htm.

The Showing Relationships through Diagrams document is located on the Data Disk. If you did not download the Data Disk, see the inside back cover for instructions for downloading the Data Disk or see your instructor.

Instructions:

1. Open the document, Showing Relationships through Diagrams Draft, from the Data Disk. Save the document with a new file name, Showing Relationships through Diagrams.
2. Change all margins to 1" with a gutter margin of .5".
3. Insert right-aligned page numbers as a header on every page after the first.
4. You are to insert diagrams and captions in this document. Table 9-2 on the next page displays the types of diagrams and their captions. In the Showing Relationships through Diagrams document, below the paragraph in item number one, insert an organization chart with three tiers. ***Hint***: To insert a new element into the diagram, click any element in the diagram to select it, and then click the Insert Shape button on the Organization Chart toolbar. The new element will be positioned below the selected element. Switch to print layout view. Add the following caption to the diagram: Figure 1: Organization charts show hierarchical relationships.
5. Insert the remaining diagrams in the corresponding paragraphs in the Showing Relationships through Diagrams document. Use a different AutoFormat for each one.

Table 9-2 Diagrams and Captions

NUMBER	*DIAGRAM*	*INSTRUCTIONS*	*CAPTION*
1	organization chart	Create at least three tiers	Organization charts show hierarchical relationships
2	cycle diagram	Create at least four segments	Cycle diagrams show a process within a continual cycle
3	radial diagram	Create at least six spokes	Radial diagrams show relationships of a core element
4	pyramid diagram	Create at least four levels	Pyramid diagrams show foundation-based relationships
5	Venn diagram	Create at least three overlapping circles	Venn diagrams show areas of overlap between elements
6	target diagram	Create at least four rings or tracks	Target diagrams show steps toward a goal

6. Create a table of contents for the document. Use the Formal format.
7. Indent the left margin of each caption by .25" so that they align with the left edge of the figures. ***Hint:*** Click in the caption and then drag the Left Indent Marker on the ruler to the .25" mark.
8. At the end of the first paragraph on each page, add a sentence referencing the figure, such as: Figure 1 shows a sample organization chart. The text, Figure, (and its number) should be a cross-reference.
9. Add a bookmark to each caption with an appropriate name.

In the Lab

10. Verify that widows and orphans cannot occur.
11. Mark the following text as index entries: organization chart, cycle diagram, radial diagram, pyramid diagram, Venn diagram, and target diagram. You will find each phrase in the first sentence of each numbered paragraph. After marking the entries, bold them in the text.
12. Insert a page break at the end of the document. Change the style of the first line on the new page from List Number to Heading 1. On the new page, type the heading `Index` using the Heading 1 style. Below the heading, build an index for the document. Use the Formal format for the index. Remember to hide formatting marks prior to building the index.
13. Modify the document as follows: mark all figure captions as index entries.
14. Update the index. Remember to hide formatting marks prior to rebuilding the index.
15. Go to the bookmark using the Go To dialog box.
16. Save the document again. Print the document. Staple the document along the gutter margin.

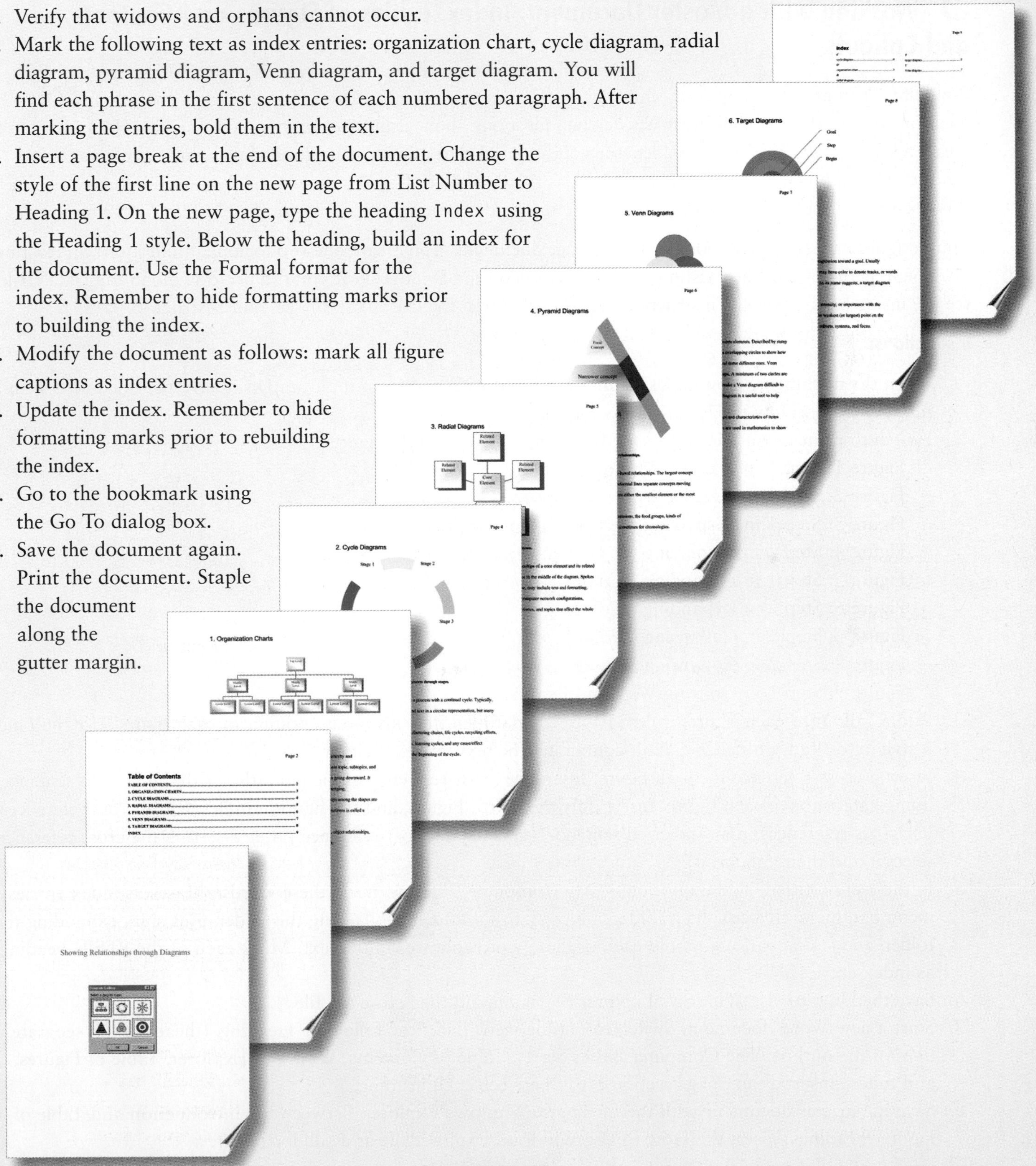

FIGURE 9-90

In the Lab

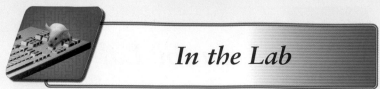

3 Working with a Master Document, Index, Tables of Figures and Contents, and Callouts

Problem: You are the computer technician at the Plattsburg Youth Center. The director of youth programs mentions to you that he constantly is receiving questions about using the computers in the lab. He wants you to create a series of instructional booklets for youths, similar to miniature user manuals, which explains various aspects of computers. The first one you create is titled, How to Use Windows Explorer. A miniature version of this document is shown in Figure 9-91; for a more readable view, visit scsite.com/wd2002/project9.htm.

You design the instructional booklet as a master document. You create one subdocument and insert an existing document as the other. The existing subdocument is on the Data Disk. If you did not download the Data Disk, see the inside back cover for instructions for downloading the Data Disk or see your instructor.

Instructions:

1. Open the document, How to Use Windows Explorer Draft, from the Data Disk. Save the document with a new file name, How to Use Windows Explorer.
2. Switch to print layout view. Add the following captions to the figures:
   Figure 1: Step 1 in Starting Windows Explorer
   Figure 2: Step 2 in Starting Windows Explorer
   Figure 3: Step 1 in Displaying the Contents of a Folder
   Figure 4: Step 2 in Displaying the Contents of a Folder
   Figure 5: Step 1 in Expanding a Folder
   Figure 6: Step 2 in Expanding a Folder
   Figure 7: Step 1 in Collapsing a Folder
   Figure 8: Step 2 in Collapsing a Folder
   Figure 9: Step 1 in Quitting Windows Explorer
3. Add a callout to each figure, except Figure 2, that identifies the mouse pointer in each figure. Use the Line 3 style of callout with each callout containing the text, mouse pointer.
4. Insert a cross-reference for each figure. Insert the cross-reference in the parentheses that end each sentence immediately above each figure. Insert only the word, Figure, and the figure number as the cross-reference. For cross-references in an italicized sentence, italicize the cross-reference (after inserting the cross-reference, select it and then italicize it).
5. In the section titled, The Exploring — My Computer Window, mark these words/phrases as index entries: menu bar, hierarchy, contents, folder, minus sign, subfolders, collapsing the folder, plus sign, expanding the folder, and status bar. Also, bold each of these words/phrases in the text. Mark each of the STEPS headings as index entries.
6. Save the How to Use Windows Explorer file again and then close the file.
7. Start a new Word document. Switch to outline view. Enter the following Heading 1 headings on separate lines of the outline: The Computer Basics Series, Table of Contents, Windows Explorer, Table of Figures, and Index. Insert a next page section break between each heading.
8. Save the master document with the file name, Windows Explorer. Between the Introduction and Table of Figures headings, insert the How to Use Windows Explorer file as a subdocument.

In the Lab

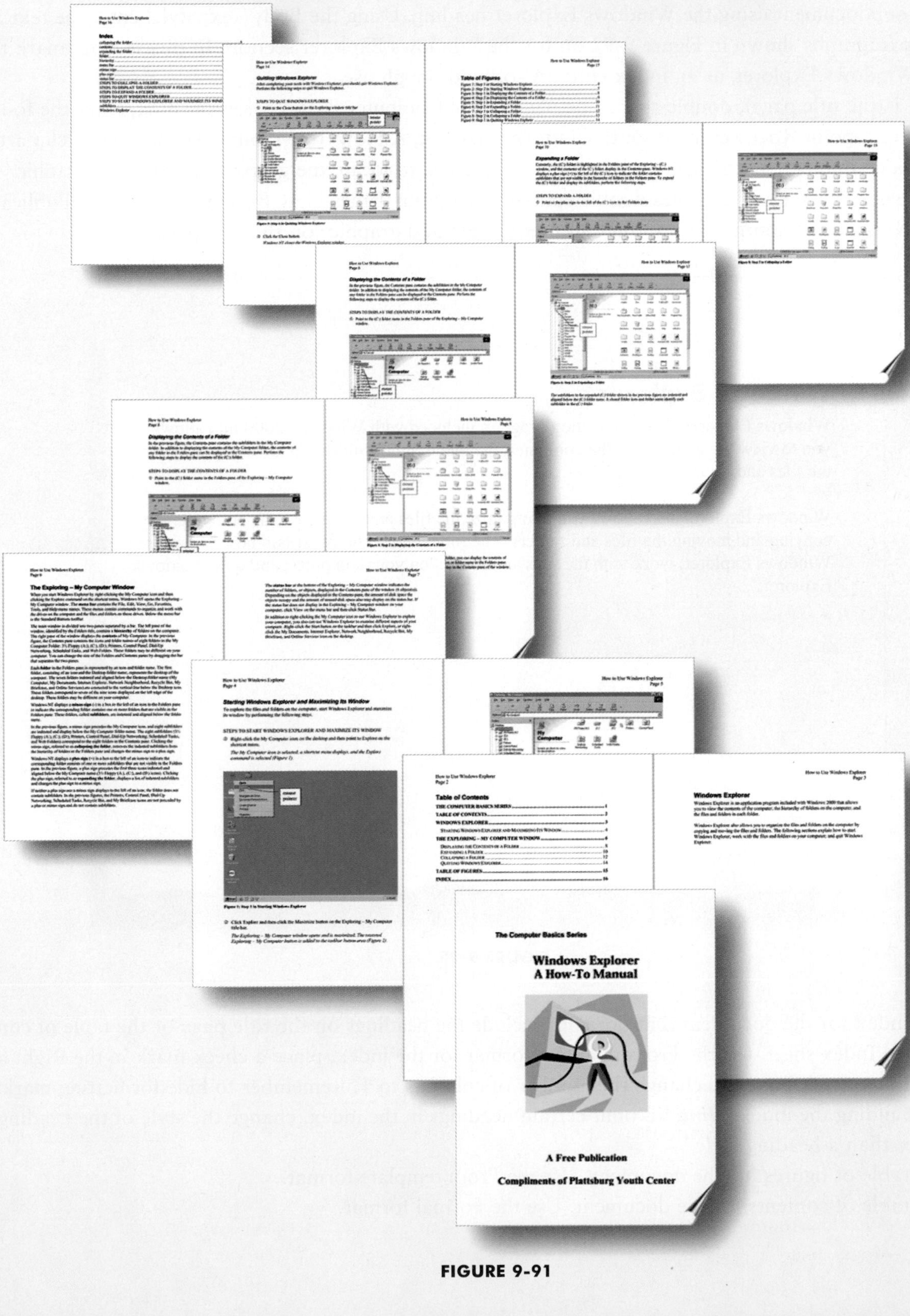

FIGURE 9-91

(continued)

In the Lab

9. Create a subdocument using the Windows Explorer heading. Using the Body Text style, enter the text for the two paragraphs shown in Figure 9-92 on for the Windows Explorer section. In this section, mark the phrase, Windows Explorer, as an index entry. Also, bold the phrase.
10. On page 1 (the title page), double-spaced below the The Computer Basics Series heading, enter the following text in 28-point Rockwell bold font: Windows Explorer, A How-To Manual. Then, insert a clip art image of a computer. Use the keywords, computer cartoon, to locate the graphic. Enlarge the graphic. Below the graphic, enter these lines double-spaced in 24-point Times New Roman font: A Free Publication, Compliments of Plattsburg Youth Center. Center all text and graphics on the title page.

Windows Explorer

Windows Explorer is an application program included with Windows 2000 that allows you to view the contents of the computer, the hierarchy of folders on the computer, and the files and folders in each folder.

Windows Explorer also allows you to organize the files and folders on the computer by copying and moving the files and folders. The following sections explain how to start Windows Explorer; work with the files and folders on your computer; and quit Windows Explorer.

FIGURE 9-92

11. Build an index for the document that does not include the headings on the title page or the table of contents page. In the Index sheet, use the From template format for the index, place a check mark in the Right align page numbers check box, and change the number of columns to 1. Remember to hide formatting marks prior to building the index. ***Hint***: To omit certain headings in the index, change the style of the heading to a style other than a heading style.
12. Create a table of figures for the document. Use the From template format.
13. Create a table of contents for the document. Use the Formal format.

In the Lab

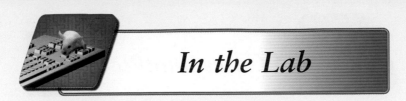

14. Beginning on the second page (the table of contents), create alternating headings as follows: even-numbered pages should print at the left margin the words, How to Use Windows Explorer, on the first line and Page, followed by the page number on the second line. Odd-numbered pages should print the same text at the right margin. The title page does not have a header.
15. For the entire document, set the left and right margins to 1" and set a gutter margin of .5".
16. Verify that the following headings begin on a new page: Table of Contents, Windows Explorer, Starting Windows Explorer and Maximizing Its Window, The Exploring - My Computer Window, Table of Figures, and Index. If any do not, insert a next page section break.
17. Because margins have changed, update the fields, table of contents, and index by selecting the entire document and then pressing the F9 key.
18. Save the document again. Print the document. If you have access to a copy machine, duplicate the document back-to-back.

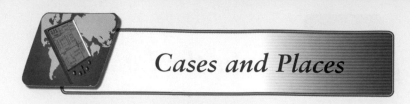

Cases and Places

The difficulty of these case studies varies:
◗ are the least difficult; ◗◗ are more difficult; and ◗◗◗ are the most difficult.

1 ◗ As editor for the school newspaper, you review all articles before they are published. One section of the newspaper spotlights a student of the week. For the next issue, the author has prepared an article about an interesting student and sent it to you for review. The article, named Jim Williamson Candidate, is located on the Data Disk. If you did not download the Data Disk, see the inside back cover for instructions for downloading the Data Disk or see your instructor. When you review the article, you find several areas where you wish to make changes and offer suggestions. You are to use Word's change-tracking feature to insert, delete, and replace text in the article. Make at least 10 changes to the article and add at least three comments. Print the article with tracked changes showing and without tracked changes showing. Also, print comments. Save the article containing the tracked changes as a version. Assume you are the author of the article and have received it back from the editor. Delete the comments and accept all the changes in the document. Obtain the tracked changes documents from three other students in your class. Compare and merge the documents from these students into your document. Save the merged document using the password, merge. If your instructor permits, e-mail the merged document for his or her review.

2 ◗ You are an editor for Dixon Publishing, a national company that publishes how-to manuals. The chapter you are working on is called Project 4. You design the chapters as master documents and insert subdocuments as you receive chapter text from authors. You are responsible for creating the table of contents and index and formatting the chapter. You just received the first subdocument for Project 4. The article, named Tracking Changes, is located on the Data Disk. If you did not download the Data Disk, see the inside back cover for instructions for downloading the Data Disk or see your instructor. Set up a master document that contains the following: title page, table of contents, reviewing a document file as a subdocument, table of figures, and index. Use the concepts and techniques presented in this project to format the document.

3 ◗◗ Your instructor in CIS 216 has distributed notes about object-oriented terminology and concepts. The notes are in a Word document named OO Terminology, which is located on the Data Disk. If you did not download the Data Disk, see the inside back cover for instructions for downloading the Data Disk or see your instructor. Your assignment is to insert a diagram that illustrates the relationship of object types, supertypes, and subtypes. Read the article and then choose an object with which you are familiar, such as a mode of transportation, an article of clothing, or a food item. Use a three-level organization chart available in the Diagram Gallery. Your diagram should have one element at the top, three in the second level, and six in the third level. To add a new element to the diagram, click any element in the diagram and then click Insert Shape on the Organization Chart toolbar to insert a new subelement. Place your object in the second level of the diagram and then fill in examples for each of the other elements. Choose an appropriate AutoFormat. Insert a caption below the chart and a reference to the figure in the text. Use the concepts and techniques presented in this project to format the document.

Cases and Places

4 ▶▶ As your final project in CIS 286, your instructor has asked you to prepare a master document that has at least one subdocument, a title page, a table of contents, a table of figures, and an index. The subdocument is to contain the text and figures on pages WD 9.36 through WD 9.38 in this project. To capture a screen shot, display the screen on your computer and then press the PRINT SCREEN key. To include the screen shot in your Word document, click the Paste button on the Standard toolbar in the Word window. Use the concepts and techniques presented in this project to format the document.

5 ▶▶▶ You are a trainer with the Computer Support Services at the college. Your supervisor has asked you to create a series of instructional booklets, similar to miniature user manuals, for lab assistants that explain the various aspects of computers. The first instructional booklet you prepared is shown in Figure 9-91 on page WD 9.79. Your assignment is to prepare the next instructional booklet for the lab assistants. Write the instructional booklet on a software application with which you are familiar and to which you have access. Use the software application's Help system, textbooks, and other instructional books for reference. The booklet is to be a how-to type of document that includes screen shots. To capture a screen shot, display the screen on your computer and then press the PRINT SCREEN key. To include the screen shot in your Word document, click the Paste button on the Standard toolbar in the Word window. The figures should contain captions. The document should contain the following sections: title page, table of contents, how-to discussion, table of figures, and index. Use the concepts and techniques presented in this project to format the document.

6 ▶▶▶ You are a student peer advisor for the School of Technology. Several students have asked you about MOUS (Microsoft Office User Specialist) certification. Because you also are interested in the MOUS certification, you decide to prepare a document outlining information about the exam (cost, description, how to prepare, where to take the exam, etc.). You obtain most of your information through links at the Shelly Cashman Series MOUS Web page at scsite.com/offxp/cert.htm. Because the document will be quite lengthy with many headings and subheadings, you organize it as a master document. In addition to information about MOUS, the document also contains the following: title page, table of contents, and index. Include at least one screen shot as a figure. To capture a screen shot, display the screen on your computer and then press the PRINT SCREEN key. To include the screen shot in your Word document, click the Paste button on the Standard toolbar in the Word window. All figures should contain captions. Use the concepts and techniques presented in this project to format the document.

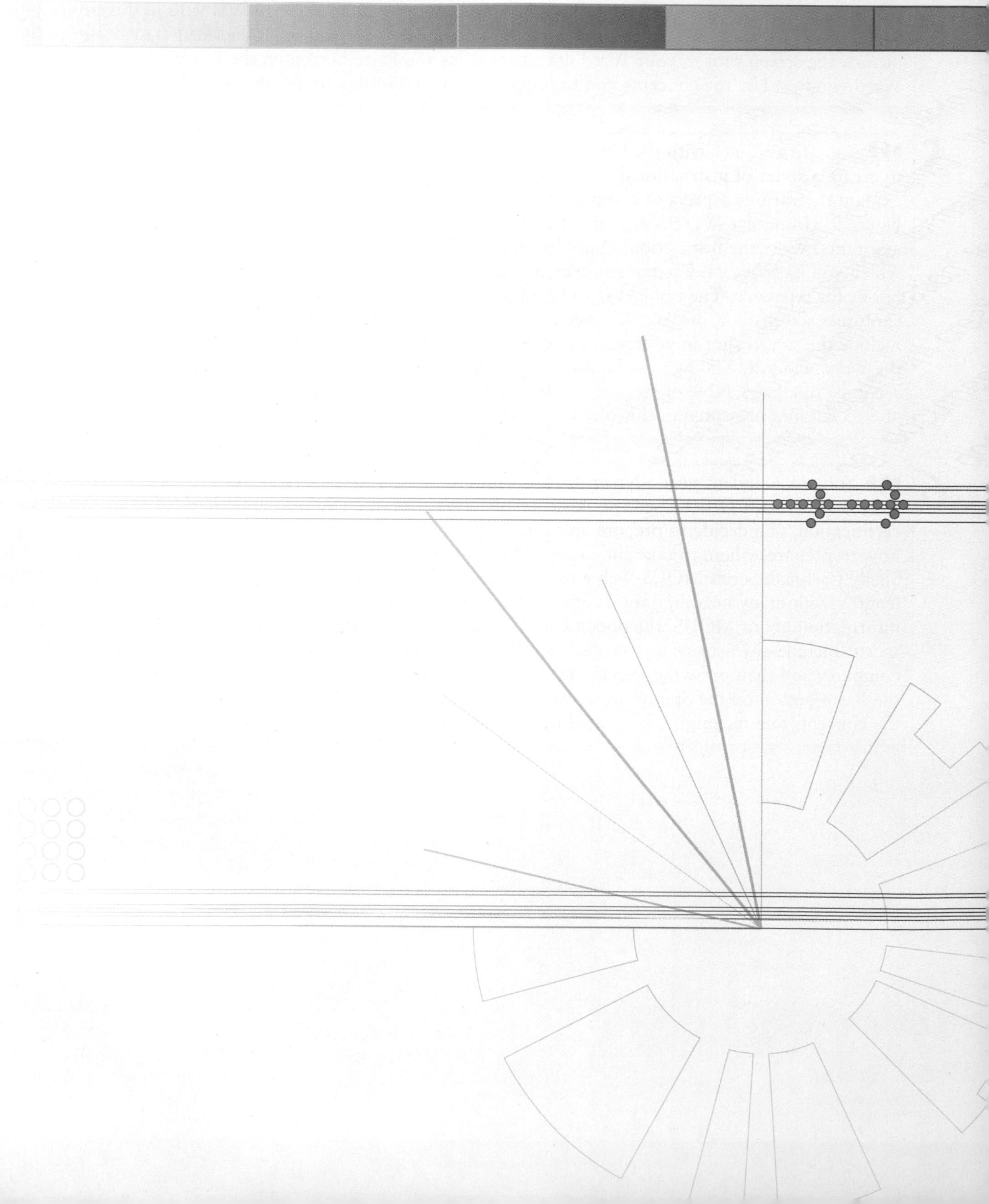

Microsoft Word 2002

Linking an Excel Worksheet and Charting Its Data in Word

CASE PERSPECTIVE

At a recent faculty meeting of the computer information systems department at Edwards College, an agenda item about the recent fund-raising campaign led to a discussion about results of the campaign. The campaign raised money in four categories: scholarships, computer laboratories, faculty support, and curriculum development. Campaign donors selected a category to which they wished their money directed.

Faculty members were very interested in the results of the campaign. Specifically, they wanted to know the total number of donors, as well as the total amount pledged in each donation category. Jamie Daraska, department head, indicated she would contact the administrative affairs office for the exact numbers and then distribute the results in memo form to all department faculty.

One week later, Jamie received the figures from administrative affairs in an Excel worksheet. As her assistant, Jamie has asked you to create a memo that links the Excel worksheet to the memo. She also would like a chart of the Excel worksheet to show graphically the donation pledges by category.

Introduction

With Microsoft Office XP products, you can insert part or all of a document, called an **object**, created in one application into a document created in another application. For example, you could insert an Excel worksheet into a Word document. In this case, the Excel worksheet (the object) is called the **source document** (inserted from) and the Word document is called the **destination document** (inserted into). You can use one of three techniques to insert objects from one application to another: copy and paste, embed, or link.

When you copy an object by clicking the Copy button on the Standard toolbar and then paste it by clicking the Paste button on the Standard toolbar, the source document becomes part of the destination document. You edit a **pasted object** using editing features of the destination application. For example, an Excel worksheet would become a Word table that you can edit in Word.

Similarly, an embedded object becomes part of a destination document. The difference between an embedded object and a pasted object is that you edit the contents of an **embedded object** using the editing features of the source application. For example, an embedded Excel worksheet remains as an Excel worksheet in the Word document. To edit the worksheet in the Word document, double-click the worksheet to display Excel menus and toolbars in the Word window. If you edit the Excel worksheet by opening the worksheet from within Excel, however, the embedded object will not be updated in the Word document.

A **linked object**, by contrast, does not become a part of the destination document even though it appears to be a part of it. Rather, a connection is established between the source and destination documents so that when you open the destination document, the linked object displays as part of it. When you edit a linked object, the source application starts and opens the source document that contains the linked object. For example, a linked

Excel worksheet remains as an Excel worksheet. To edit the worksheet from the Word document, double-click the worksheet to start Excel and display the worksheet file in an Excel window. Unlike an embedded object, if you edit the Excel worksheet by opening it from Excel, the linked object will be updated in the Word document, too.

You would use the link method when the contents of an object are likely to change and you want to ensure that the most current version of the object displays in the source document. Another reason to link an object is if the object is large, such as a video clip or a sound clip.

As shown in Figure 1, this integration feature links an Excel worksheet to a Word document (a memo) and then links a Word chart to the Excel worksheet data. That is, the Excel worksheet is inserted into the Word document in the form of an Excel worksheet. Word also charts the data in the Excel worksheet. Because the data is inserted into the Word document as a link, anytime you open the memo in Word, the latest version of the Excel worksheet data displays in the memo. Figure 1a shows the memo draft (without any links to Excel); Figure 1b shows the Excel worksheet; and Figure 1c shows the final copy of the memo with links to the Excel worksheet and its data.

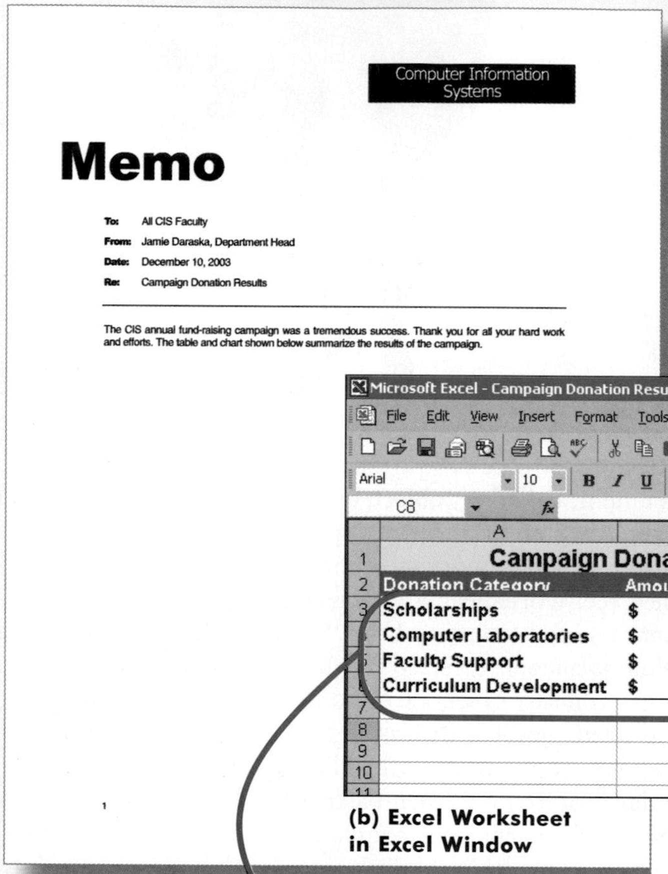

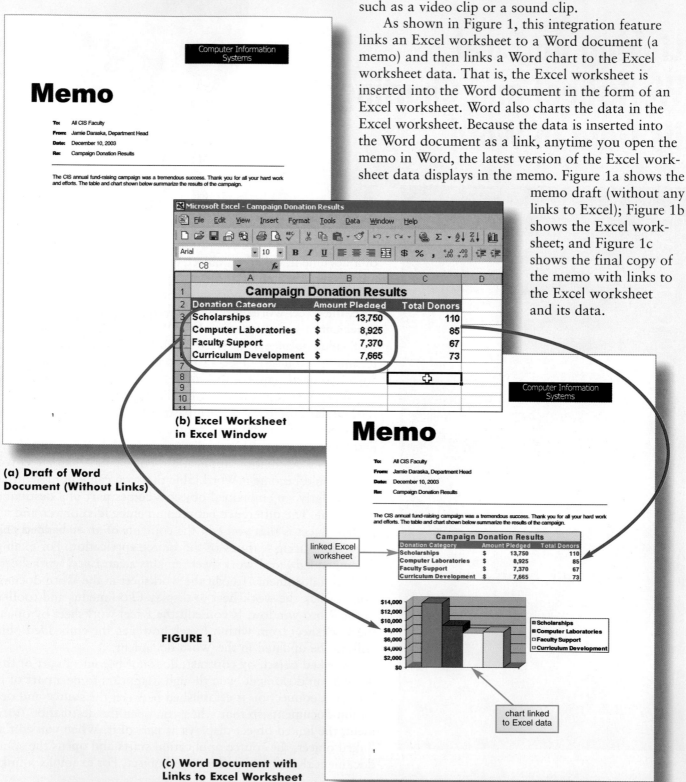

(a) Draft of Word Document (Without Links)

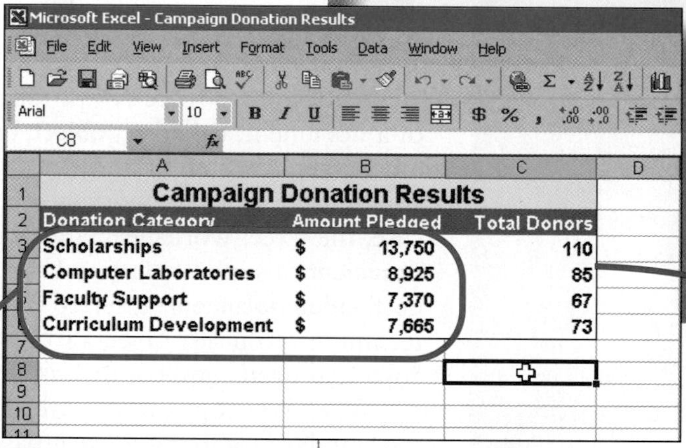

(b) Excel Worksheet in Excel Window

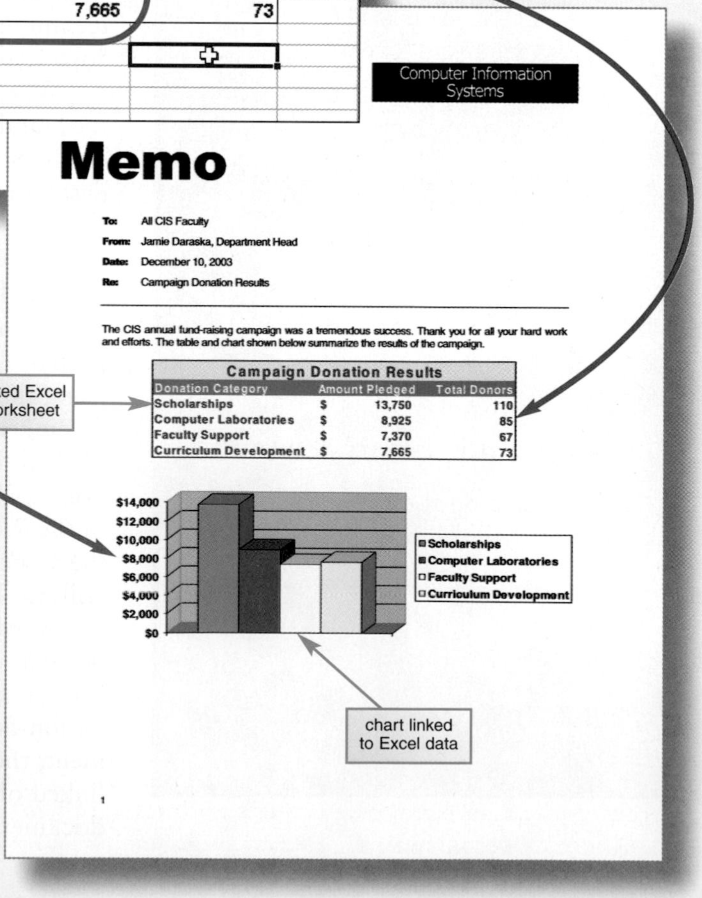

FIGURE 1

(c) Word Document with Links to Excel Worksheet

Starting Word and Opening a Document

The first step in this integration feature is to open the draft of the memo that is to include the linked worksheet data. The memo file, named Campaign Memo Draft, is located on the Data Disk. If you did not download the Data Disk, see the inside back cover for instructions for downloading the Data Disk or see your instructor.

Perform the following steps to open the memo.

TO START AND CUSTOMIZE WORD AND OPEN A DOCUMENT

1. Click the Start button on the Windows taskbar, point to Programs on the Start menu, and then click Microsoft Word on the Programs submenu.
2. If the Word window is not maximized, double-click its title bar to maximize it.
3. If the Language bar displays on the screen, click its Minimize button.
4. If the New Document task pane displays in the Word window, click the Show at startup check box to remove the check mark and then click the Close button in the upper-right corner of the task pane title bar.
5. If the toolbars display positioned on the same row, click the Toolbar Options button and then click Show Buttons on Two Rows. Reset the toolbars as described in Appendix D.
6. With the Data Disk in drive A, click the Open button on the Standard toolbar. When the Open dialog box displays, if necessary, click the Look in box arrow and then click 3½ Floppy (A:). Double-click the file named Campaign Memo Draft.
7. Click View on the menu bar and then click Print Layout. If the Show/Hide ¶ button on the Standard toolbar is not selected, click it.

Word starts and opens the Campaign Memo Draft file.

More About

Office XP

For more information on the features of Microsoft Office XP, visit the Word 2002 More About Web page (scsite.com/wd2002/more.htm) and then click Microsoft Office XP Features.

Saving the Document with a New File Name

To preserve the contents of the original Campaign Memo Draft file, save a copy of it on the Data Disk with a new file name as described in the following steps.

TO PRESERVE THE CONTENTS OF AN ORIGINAL FILE

1. With the Data Disk in drive A, click File on the menu bar and then click Save As.
2. Type `Campaign Memo` in the File name text box. Do not press the ENTER key.
3. If necessary, click the Save in box arrow and then click 3½ Floppy (A:).
4. Click the Save button in the Save As dialog box.

Word saves the document on the Data Disk in drive A with a new file name of Campaign Memo (shown in Figure 2 on the next page).

More About

Saving Linked Documents

When working with linked documents on floppy disks, both the source and destination documents must be saved on the same disk. If they reside on different disks, Word will display an error message indicating it cannot find the destination file when it attempts to save or open the source file.

Linking an Excel Worksheet

The next step in this integration feature is to insert the Excel worksheet (source document) in the Campaign Memo (destination document) as a linked object. The Excel worksheet (Campaign Donation Results) is located on the Data Disk.

Perform the following steps to link the Excel worksheet to the Word document.

Steps To Link an Excel Worksheet to a Word Document

1 **Position the insertion point on the paragraph mark at the end of the memo (below the paragraph of text). Click Insert on the menu bar and then point to Object (Figure 2).**

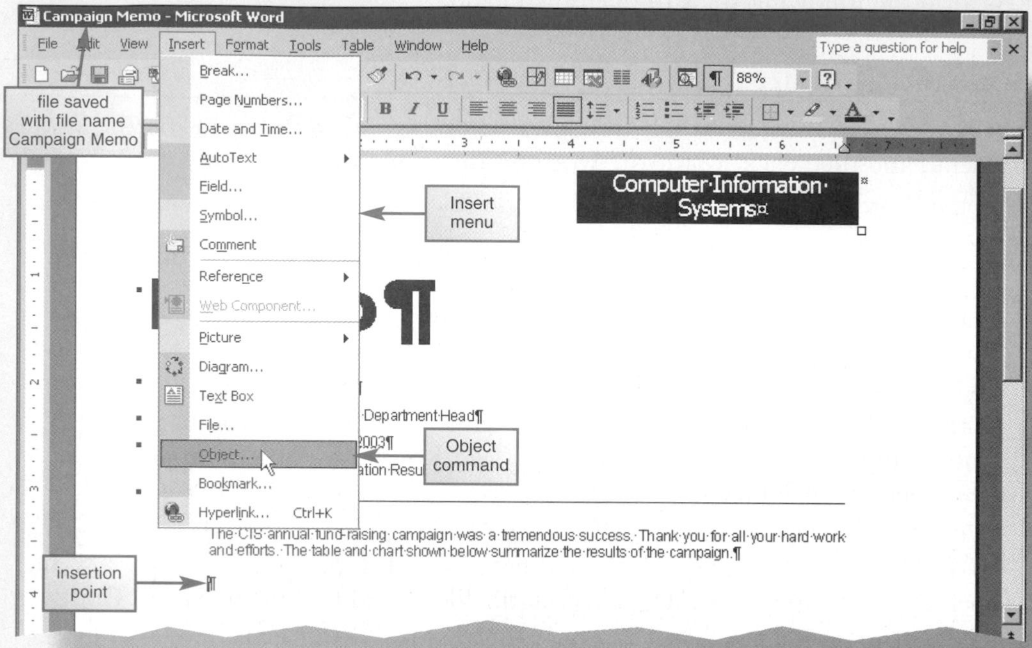

FIGURE 2

2 **Click Object. When the Object dialog box displays, if necessary, click the Create from File tab. With the Data Disk in drive A, click the Browse button. When the Browse dialog box displays, locate on the Data Disk the Excel file called Campaign Donation Results. Click Campaign Donation Results in the list and then point to the Insert button in the Browse dialog box.**

Word displays the Object dialog box and then the Browse dialog box (Figure 3).

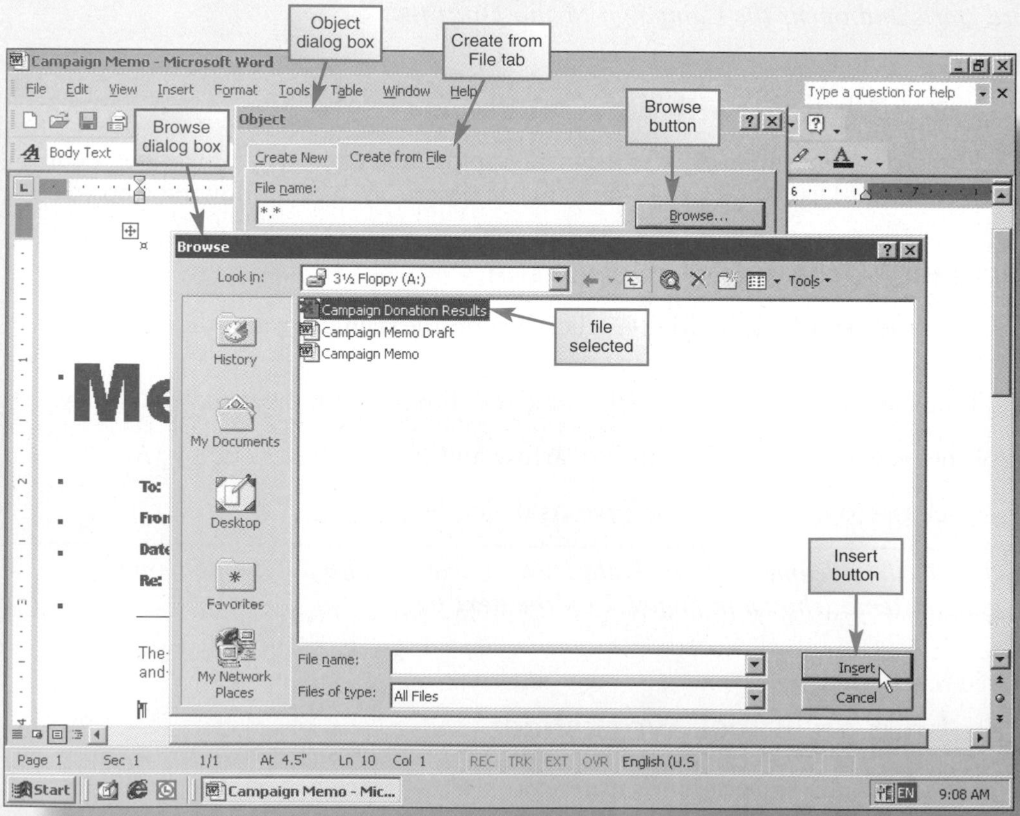

FIGURE 3

3 **Click the Insert button. When the Browse dialog box closes and the entire Object dialog box is visible again, place a check mark in the Link to file check box and then point to the OK button.**

The Object dialog box displays the name of the selected file in the File name text box (Figure 4). The xls following the file name, Campaign Donation Results, identifies the file as an Excel worksheet.

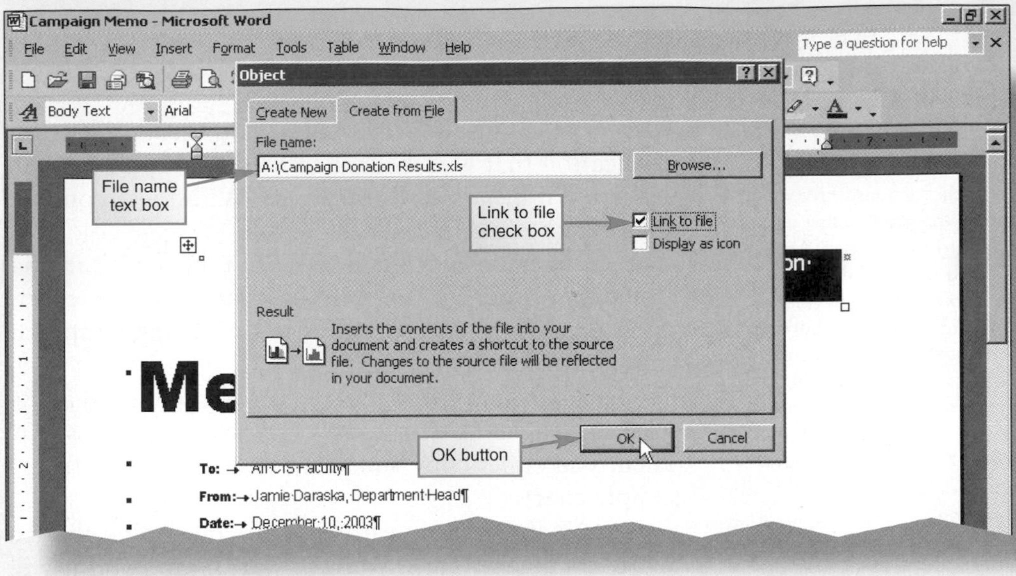

FIGURE 4

4 **Click the OK button. Click the Center button on the Formatting toolbar. If necessary, scroll down so the Excel table displays in the document window.**

Word inserts the Excel worksheet as a linked object at the location of the insertion point (Figure 5). The object is centered between the document margins.

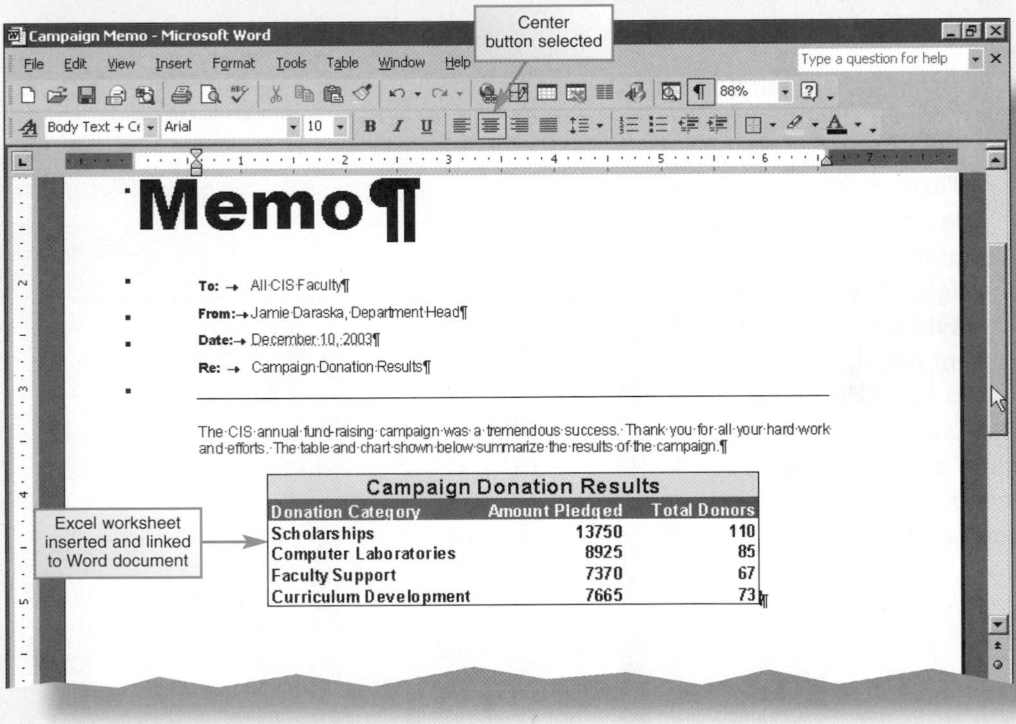

FIGURE 5

The Excel worksheet now is linked to the Word document. If you save the Word document and reopen it, the worksheet will display just as it does in Figure 5. If you wanted to delete the worksheet, you would select it and then press the DELETE key.

If you wanted to embed an Excel worksheet instead of link it, you would not place a check mark in the Link to file check box in the Object dialog box (Figure 4).

Other Ways

1. Copy object in source application to the Clipboard; in destination application, on Edit menu click Paste Special, click Paste link, click Microsoft Excel Worksheet Object, click OK button

More About

Excel Worksheets

To insert a blank Excel worksheet into a Word document, click the Insert Microsoft Excel Worksheet button on the Standard toolbar and then click the grid at the location that represents the number of rows and columns to be in the worksheet. The menus and toolbars change to Excel menus and toolbars. To redisplay Word menus and toolbars, click outside the Excel worksheet in the Word document.

Creating a Chart from an Excel Worksheet

You easily can use Word to chart data through **Microsoft Graph 2002**, a charting application that is embedded in Word. Graph is an embedded application. Thus, it has its own menus and commands. With these commands, you can modify the appearance of the chart.

Graph can chart data in a Word table or it can chart data from another Office application, such as Excel. If you want Graph to chart data that is in a Word table, select the data to be charted prior to starting Graph, and then Graph automatically will chart the selected data.

To chart data from another application, such as Excel, start Graph without selecting any data. This causes Graph to create a sample chart with sample data. Then, you either copy and paste or link the data from another application to the sample chart.

In this integration feature, you want to link the Excel data to the chart in the Word document. Thus, you will start Graph and it will create a sample chart. Then, you will link the Excel data to the chart.

Perform the following steps to start Graph.

Steps To Create a Sample Chart

1 Position the insertion point on the paragraph mark to the right of the Excel worksheet in the Word document and then press the ENTER key. Click Insert on the menu bar, point to Picture, and then point to Chart on the Picture submenu (Figure 6).

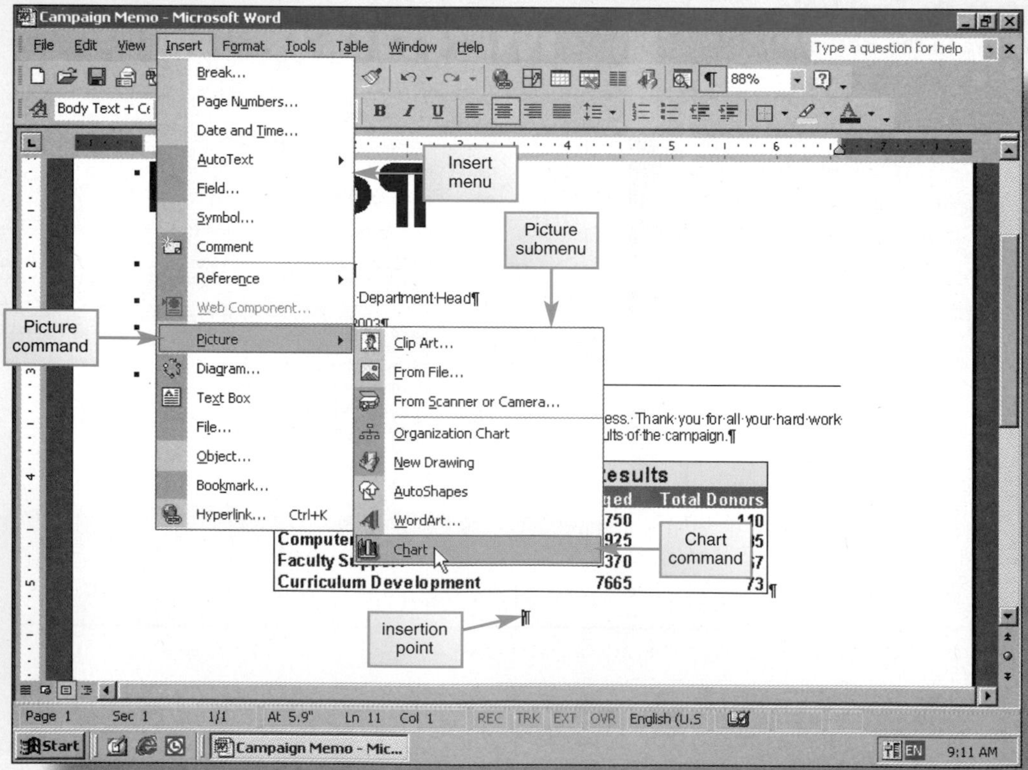

FIGURE 6

2 Click Chart. If your screen does not display a Datasheet window, click the View Datasheet button on the Standard toolbar.

Word starts the Microsoft Graph 2002 application (Figure 7). Graph creates a sample chart at the location of the insertion point and displays sample data in the Datasheet window.

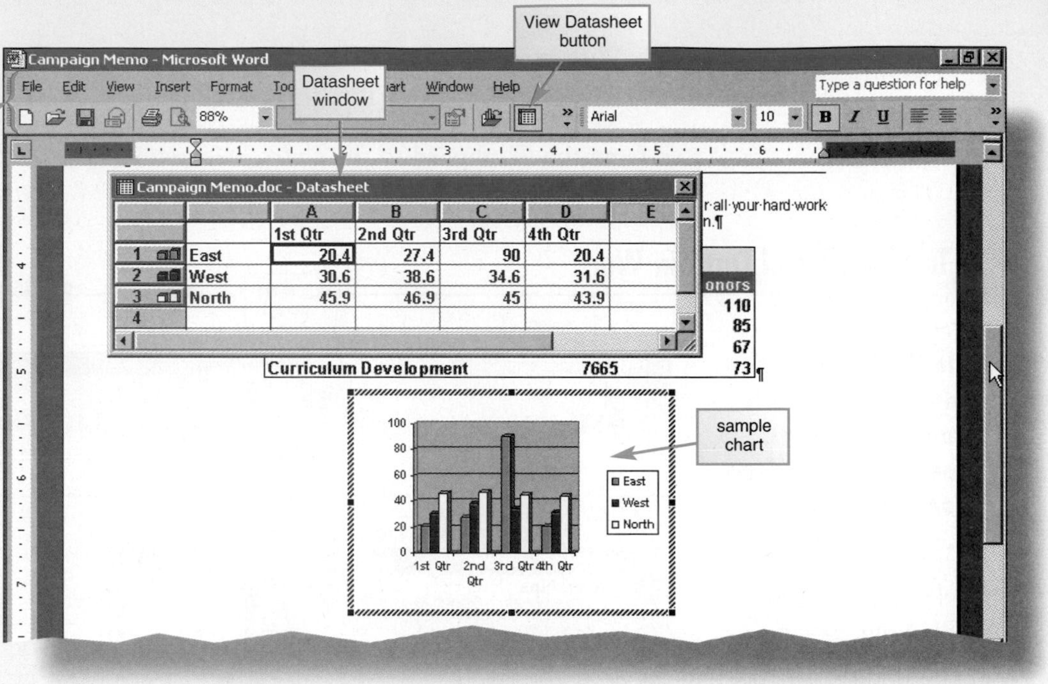

FIGURE 7

Other Ways

1. In Voice Command mode, say "Insert, Picture, Chart"

The menus on the menu bar and buttons on the toolbars change to Graph menus and toolbars. That is, the Graph program is running inside the Word program.

You can copy and paste data from an Excel worksheet into the sample chart or you can link the Excel data to the sample chart. In this integration feature, you link the data to the chart. To link the data, start Excel and display the workbook containing the worksheet data to be linked, copy the data in the worksheet to the Clipboard, and then use Graph's Paste Link command to link the data on the Clipboard to the Word document.

Thus, the first step in linking the data from the Excel worksheet to the Word chart is to open the Excel workbook that contains the worksheet data to be charted. The Excel workbook that contains the data to be linked to the chart is the Campaign Donation Results workbook file, which is located on the Data Disk.

Perform the following steps to start Excel and open a workbook.

More About

Starting Excel

If a Word document that displays on the screen contains a linked Excel worksheet, you also can start Excel by double-clicking the Excel worksheet in the Word document. For example, if you double-click the Campaign Donation Results worksheet in the Word document, Excel starts and then displays the associated Excel workbook in an Excel window.

TO START AND CUSTOMIZE EXCEL AND OPEN AN EXCEL WORKBOOK

1. Click the Start button on the Windows taskbar, point to Programs on the Start menu, and then click Microsoft Excel on the Programs submenu.
2. If the Excel window is not maximized, double-click its title bar to maximize it.
3. If the Language bar displays on the screen, click its Minimize button.
4. If the New Workbook task pane displays, click its Close button.
5. With the Data Disk in Drive A, click the Open button on the Standard toolbar. When the Open dialog box displays, if necessary, click the Look in box arrow and then click 3½ Floppy (A:). Double-click the Excel file named Campaign Donation Results.
6. Reset Excel toolbars as described in Appendix D.

Excel starts and displays the Campaign Donation Results file in the Excel window (shown in Figure 8 on the next page).

With both Word and Excel open, you can switch between the applications by clicking the appropriate program button on the taskbar.

Next, copy to the Clipboard the Excel data to be charted and then paste link it from the Clipboard to the chart, as shown in the following steps.

Steps To Chart Excel Data in Word

1 In the Excel window, drag through cells in the range A3:B6 to select them. Click the Copy button on the Standard toolbar.

The Excel window is active (Figure 8). A marquee displays around the range A3:B6, which has been copied to the Clipboard.

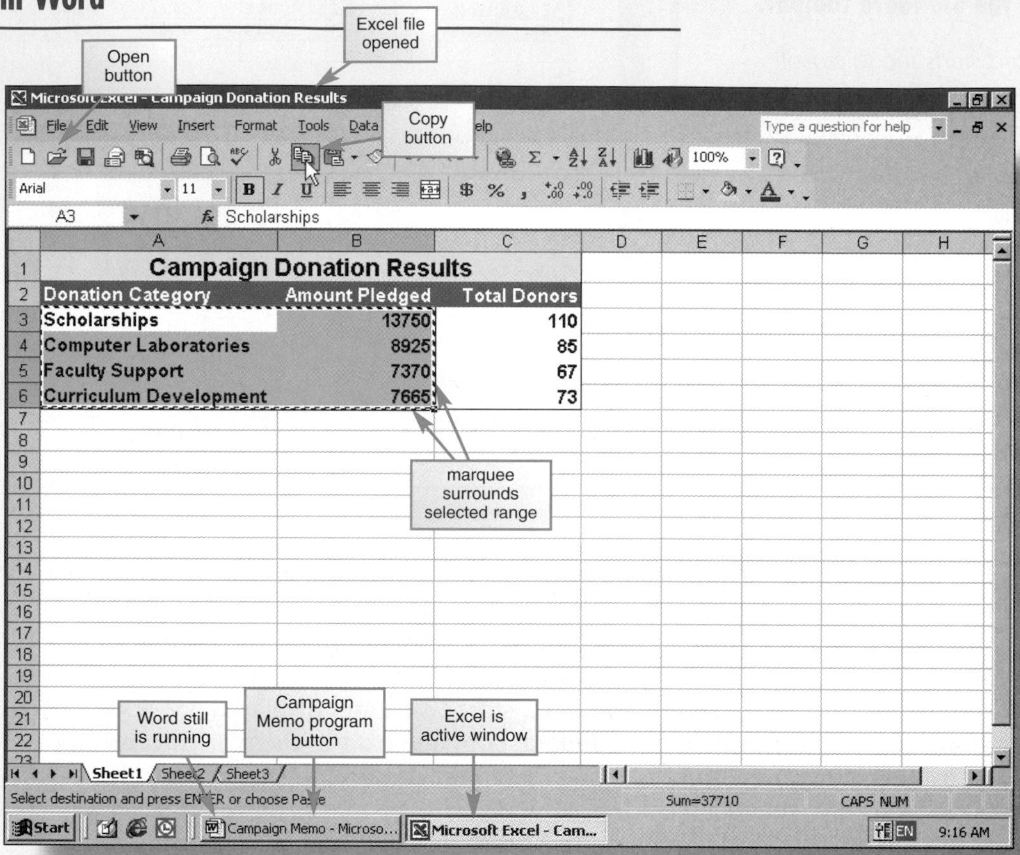

FIGURE 8

2 **Click the Campaign Memo - Microsoft Word program button on the taskbar. Click anywhere in the Datasheet window. (If Graph is not active in the Word window, double-click the chart.) Click Edit on the menu bar and then point to Paste Link.**

Graph still is active within Word (Figure 9).

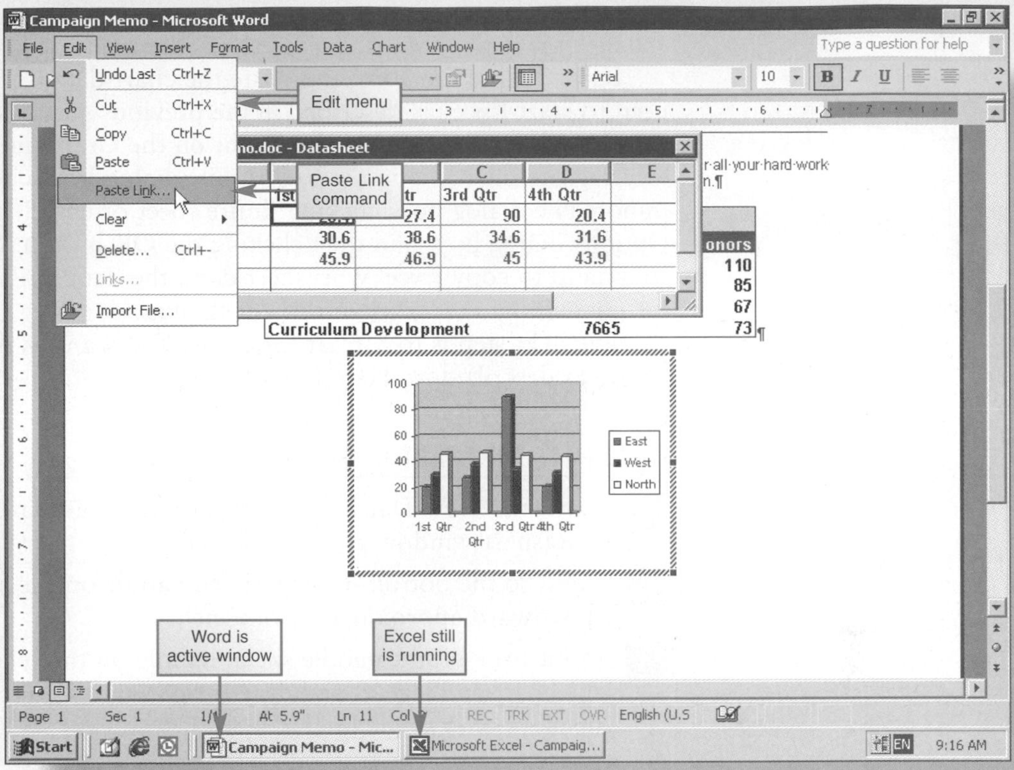

FIGURE 9

3 **Click Paste Link. When Graph displays a dialog box indicating the linked data will replace existing data, click the OK button.**

Graph copies the data from the Clipboard into the Datasheet window, replacing the sample data currently in the Datasheet window (Figure 10). Graph then charts the contents of the Datasheet window.

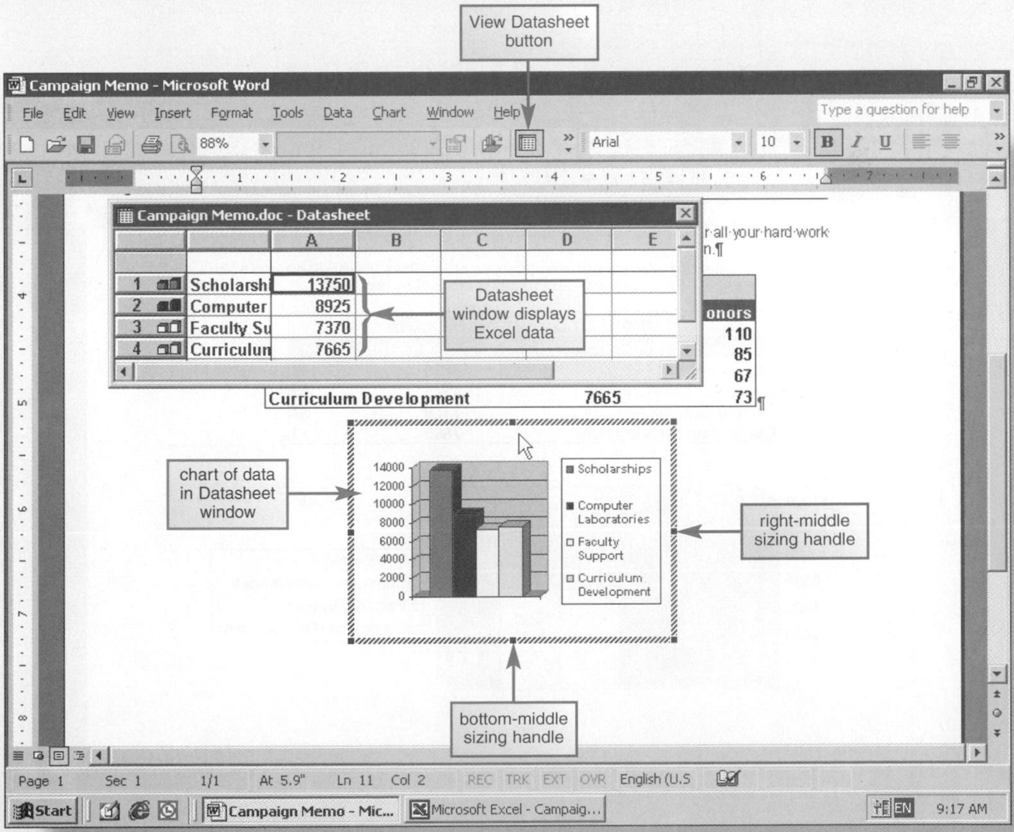

FIGURE 10

Graph charts the Excel data. The Excel data is linked to the chart. Thus, if you change any of the data in the Excel worksheet, it will be reflected in the chart.

If you wanted to copy and paste the chart data, instead of link it, you would not need to start Excel as described in the previous steps. After starting Graph, copy the Excel worksheet data by clicking Edit on the Graph menu bar, clicking Import File, locating the file name in the Import File dialog box, clicking the Open button in the Import File dialog box, clicking Entire sheet or entering the range in the Import File Options dialog box, and then clicking the OK button. When you use the Import File command to copy Excel worksheet data, the data in the chart will not be updated if the contents of the Excel worksheet change.

The next step is to format the chart. You want to make the size of the chart larger, as described in the following steps.

TO FORMAT THE CHART IN GRAPH

1. Click the View Datasheet button on the Standard toolbar to remove the Datasheet window from the screen.
2. Point to the bottom-middle sizing handle on the selection rectangle and drag it downward approximately one inch.
3. Point to the right-middle sizing handle on the selection rectangle that surrounds the chart and legend and drag it rightward until each item in the legend displays on a single line.

Graph resizes the chart.

You are finished modifying the chart. The next step is to exit Graph and return to Word.

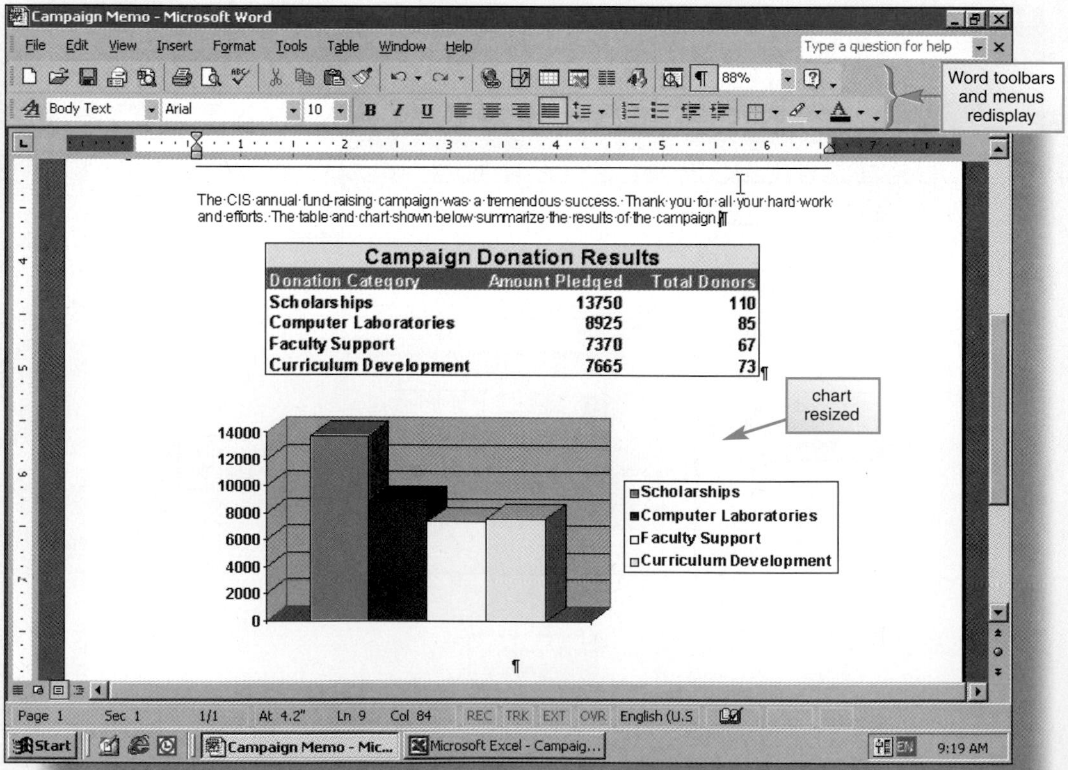

FIGURE 11

TO EXIT GRAPH AND RETURN TO WORD

1. Click somewhere outside the chart.

Word closes the Graph application (Figure 11). Word's menus and toolbars redisplay below the title bar.

If, for some reason, you wanted to modify an existing chart in a document, you would double-click the chart to reopen the Microsoft Graph 2002 application. Then, you can make any necessary changes to the chart. When you are finished making changes to the chart, click anywhere outside the chart to return to Word.

You are finished with the memo. Save the document again, print it, and then quit Word as described in the following steps.

TO SAVE A DOCUMENT

1. With the Data Disk in drive A, click the Save button on the Standard toolbar.

Word saves the document on the Data Disk in drive A.

TO QUIT WORD

1. Click the Close button on Word's title bar.

The Word window closes.

More About

Linking Excel Data

If you want to display a linked worksheet as an icon, instead of as the worksheet itself, do the following: copy the data to be linked in Excel, switch to Word, click Edit on the menu bar, click Paste Special, click Paste link, click the desired option in the As list, place a check mark in the Display as icon check box, and then click the OK button.

Editing a Linked Worksheet

At a later time, you may find it necessary to change the data in the Excel worksheet. Any changes you make to the Excel worksheet while in Excel will be reflected in the Excel table and chart in the Word document because the objects are linked.

Perform the following steps to change the format of the dollar amounts in the amount pledged cells to currency.

Steps To Edit a Linked Object

1. **With the Excel worksheet displaying on the screen, drag through cells B3:B6 to select them. Click the Currency Style button on the Formatting toolbar. Click the Decrease Decimal button on the Formatting toolbar twice.**

The format of the numbers in cells B3:B6 changes from general to currency (Figure 12).

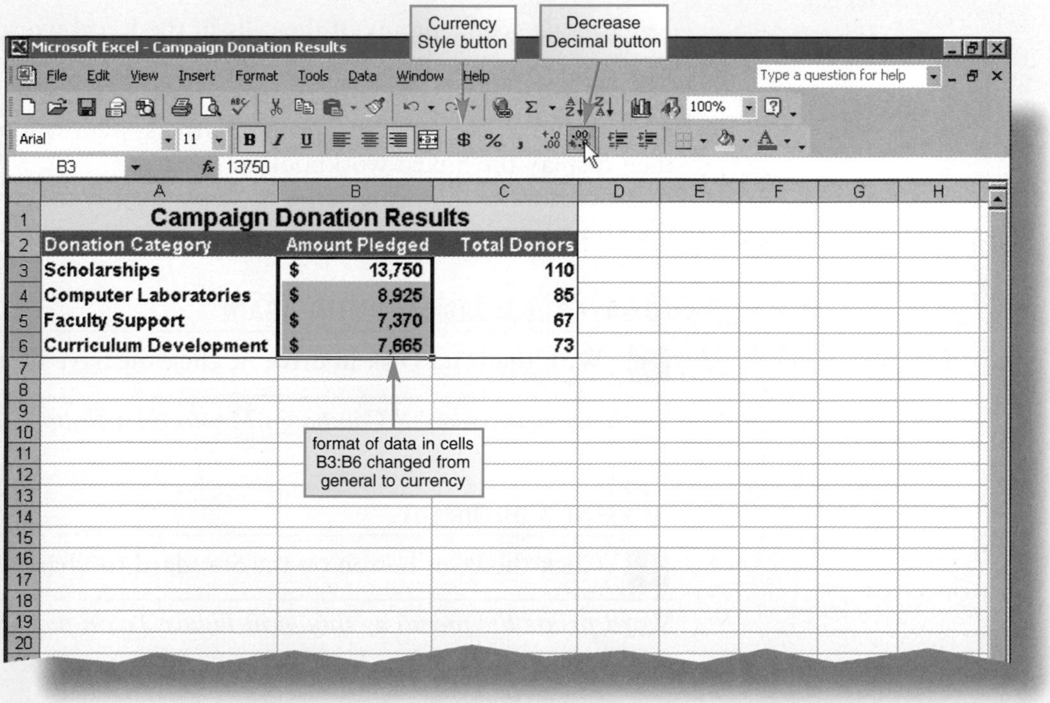

FIGURE 12

2 **Click in cell C8 to remove the selection from the worksheet. Click the Save button on the Standard toolbar. Click the Close button at the right edge of Excel's title bar.**

Excel saves the changes to the worksheet. The Excel window closes.

3 **Start Word and then open the Campaign Memo document on the Data Disk. If the table does not display the updated data format, click it and then press the F9 key. If the chart does not display updated data, double-click the chart and then click outside the chart to exit Graph.**

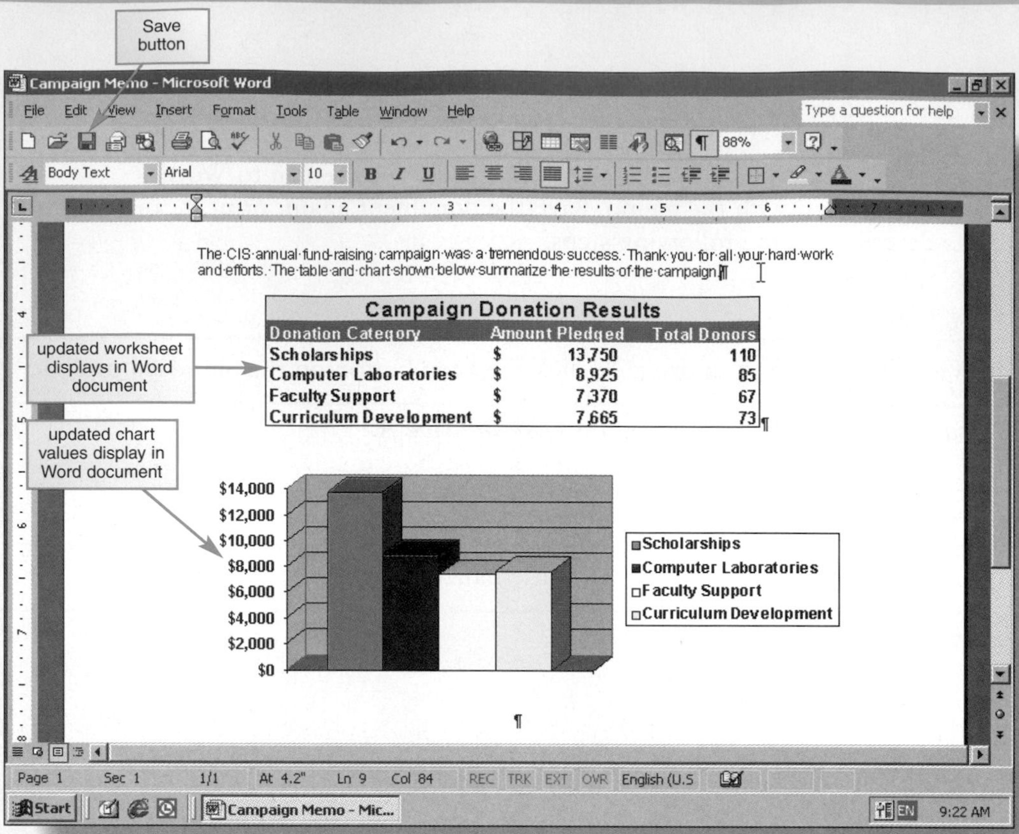

FIGURE 13

The Word document displays the updates to the Excel worksheet object and chart object (Figure 13).

You also can edit any of the cells in the Excel worksheet (the object) while it displays as part of the Word document. To edit the worksheet, double-click it. If Excel is running already, the computer will switch to it and display the linked workbook in Excel. If Excel is not running, the system will start Excel automatically and then display the linked workbook in Excel.

Perform the following series of steps to save and print the Word document and then quit Word.

TO SAVE THE WORD DOCUMENT AGAIN

1 With the Data Disk in drive A, click the Save button on the Standard toolbar.

Word saves the revised Campaign Memo on a floppy disk in drive A.

TO PRINT A DOCUMENT

1 Click the Print button on the Standard toolbar.

Word prints the memo as shown in Figure 1c on page WDI 2.02.

TO QUIT WORD

1. Click the Close button at the right edge of Word's title bar.

The Word window closes.

CASE PERSPECTIVE SUMMARY

Jamie distributes the memo to the department faculty so they can review it prior to the department meeting. At the meeting, they quickly conclude from the memo that the majority of donors contributed to scholarships. Thus, they decide to post scholarship information in advisors' offices.

Two weeks later, the manager of administrative affairs asks Jamie how she included the table and chart in the memo. Jamie confesses that she did not compose the memo and directs him to you so that you can show him how to link documents between applications.

Integration Feature Summary

This Integration Feature introduced you to linking an Excel worksheet to a Word document. You also charted Excel data in Word using an embedded Microsoft Graph charting application. Then, you modified the linked worksheet to see the changes reflected in the Word document.

What You Should Know

Having completed this Integration Feature, you now should be able to perform the following tasks:

- Chart Excel Data in Word *(WDI 2.08)*
- Create a Sample Chart *(WDI 2.06)*
- Edit a Linked Object *(WDI 2.11)*
- Exit Graph and Return to Word *(WDI 2.10)*
- Format the Chart in Graph *(WDI 2.10)*
- Link an Excel Worksheet to a Word Document *(WDI 2.04)*
- Preserve the Contents of an Original File *(WDI 2.03)*
- Print a Document *(WDI 2.12)*
- Quit Word *(WDI 2.11, WDI 2.13)*
- Save a Document *(WDI 2.11)*
- Save the Word Document Again *(WDI 2.12)*
- Start and Customize Excel and Open an Excel Workbook *(WDI 2.07)*
- Start and Customize Word and Open a Document *(WDI 2.03)*

More About

Quick Reference

For a table that lists how to complete tasks covered in this book using the mouse, menu, shortcut menu, and keyboard, see the Quick Reference Summary at the back of this book or visit the Shelly Cashman Series Office XP Web page (scsite.com/offxp/qr.htm) and then click Microsoft Access 2002.

More About

Microsoft Certification

The Microsoft Office User Specialist (MOUS) Certification program provides an opportunity for you to obtain a valuable industry credential — proof that you have the Word 2002 skills required by employers. For more information, see Appendix E or visit the Shelly Cashman Series MOUS Web page at scsite.com/offxp/cert.htm.

In the Lab

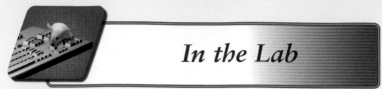

1 Linking an Excel Table to a Word Document

Problem: Marty Yonkovich, director of admissions at River Community College, has created an Excel worksheet that lists the number of full-time and part-time students majoring in each department on campus. He would like you to prepare a memo that includes the Excel worksheet.

Instructions:

1. Create a memo using a memo template. Save the memo using the file name, Department Major Memo. The memo is to all department heads, from Marty Yonkovich, and should have a subject of Full-Time and Part-Time Student Distribution by Department. In the memo, type the following sentence: `The table shown below lists the total number of full-time and part-time students in each department on campus. Please call me if you have any questions.`
2. Link the Students by Major Excel worksheet, which is on the Data Disk to the Word memo file.
3. Save the Word memo file again.
4. Print the Word memo file.

2 Linking Data from an Excel Worksheet to a Word Chart

Problem: Marty Yonkovich, director of admissions at River Community College, has created an Excel worksheet that lists the number of full-time and part-time students majoring in each department on campus. He would like you to prepare a memo that includes a chart of the Excel worksheet data.

Instructions:

1. Create a memo using a memo template. Save the memo using the file name, Department Major Memo with Chart. The memo is to all department heads, from Marty Yonkovich, and should have a subject of Full-Time and Part-Time Student Distribution by Department. In the memo, type the following sentence: `The chart shown below shows the total number of full-time and part-time students in each department on campus. Please call me if you have any questions.`
2. Link the Students by Major Excel worksheet data, which is on the Data Disk, to a Word chart.
3. Save the Word memo file again.
4. Print the Word memo file.

3 Creating an Excel Worksheet and Linking It to a Word Document

Problem: Your science instructor, Mr. Edwards, has requested that you collect the daily high and low temperatures for a 10-day period and create an Excel worksheet that lists the data. Then, you are to prepare a memo that links the Excel worksheet to the memo and includes a chart of the Excel data.

Instructions: Create a memo to Mr. Edwards using a memo template. Explain the contents of the worksheet and chart in the memo. Link the Excel worksheet to the Word memo file. Link the Excel worksheet data to a Word chart. Save the Word memo file again. Print the Word memo file. Close Word. In Excel, change the high and low temperatures for two of the days. Open the Word memo file, be sure the linked table and chart data are updated, and then print the updated memo.

Microsoft Excel 2002

PROJECT 7

Using Macros and Visual Basic for Applications (VBA) with Excel

OBJECTIVES

You will have mastered the material in this project when you can:

- Use the Undo button to undo multiple changes
- Use passwords to assign protected and unprotected status to a workbook
- Use the macro recorder to create a macro
- Execute a macro
- Understand Visual Basic for Applications code
- Customize a toolbar by adding a button
- Customize a menu by adding a command
- Add controls to a worksheet, such as command buttons, scroll bars, check boxes, and spin buttons
- Assign properties to controls
- Use VBA to write a procedure to automate data entry into a worksheet
- Understand Do-While and If-Then-Else statements
- Test and validate incoming data
- Explain event-driven programs

Plan Today, Enjoy Tomorrow

Retire in Style

"If you would be wealthy, think of saving as well as getting."
Benjamin Franklin

The good news? Americans now can expect to live longer, healthier lives than ever before. The bad news? Although a current survey indicates that 63 percent of Americans believe they will be able to save enough money to retire comfortably, the number of Americans who no longer share this confidence recently jumped from 10 to 17 percent.

Some experts recommend starting retirement savings with the very first paycheck. But how can you save for retirement when you have tuition payments, a car loan, utility bills, and rent or mortgage payments? The answer is careful planning, starting right now.

Workers are retiring earlier and living longer than ever before. Considering that the average person spends 18 years in retirement, you need to plan for that time early in your career. During your retirement, you will be faced with buying new cars, replacing your appliances, putting a new roof on your home, and needing prescription drugs and hearing aids.

Unfortunately, fewer than half of all American workers have calculated how much money they will need to retire comfortably. Although the number of Americans who devote some portion of their income to retirement savings has increased dramatically in recent years, most Americans are

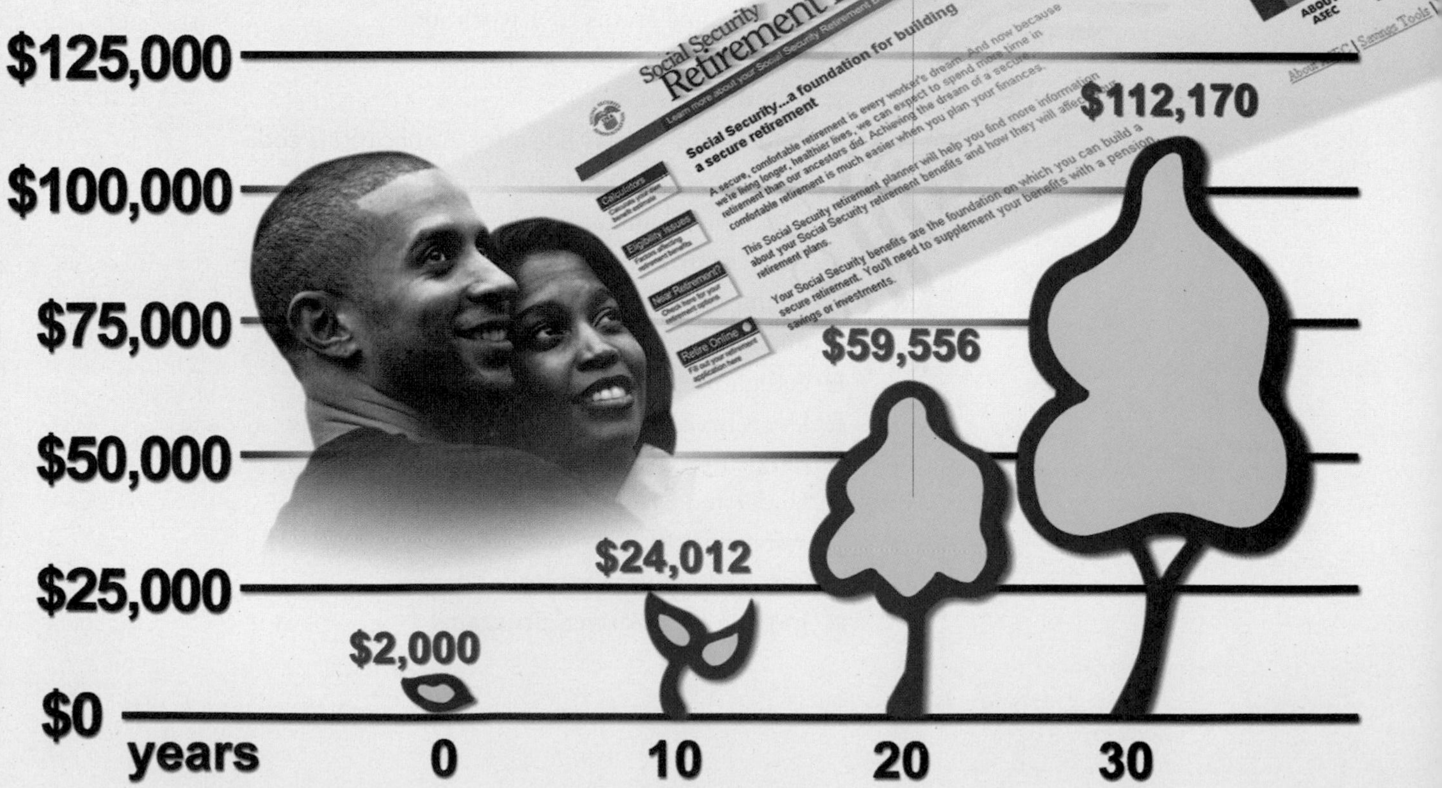

unaware that simply saving is not enough. To save money effectively, you need to calculate how much money you will need after your retirement and implement a retirement savings plan to meet your needs.

At a minimum, a retirement needs calculation should take into account your current annual income, expected retirement age, inflation, your monthly living expenses after retirement, and the types of monthly income you expect to receive after retirement.

The percent of your annual income you devote to retirement savings will vary based on these types of factors, but consider the following example. If your average annual salary is $30,000 a year, and you save 6 percent of your salary each month, or $150, starting at age 30, a 10 percent average annual return on your investments will yield $574,242 by the time you reach age 65. On the other hand, if you do not start saving until age 55, you would realize only $30,983 ten years later.

Although that amount may seem large, consider that inflation also is an important factor. If you spend $25,000 on living expenses the year you retire, you will need $56,000 for these same expenses 20 years later if inflation rises four percent annually.

In this Excel project, you will see just how advantageous retirement plans can be. You will use the Visual Basic for Applications programming language to build the Master Software Employment Retirement Savings Plan worksheet. You then will input current salary, employee investment, employer match, rate of return, and years of service. You will see that regular contributions to this retirement plan for 45 years could yield close to $2 million, even without receiving salary increases.

So where do you start planning for your retirement? The Internet abounds with sites brimming with financial calculators and investment strategies. Begin with the Social Security Administration's site (www.ssa.gov) and find a link to the Social Security Benefits Planner that calculates your potential Social Security payments. Other sites, such as the Administration on Aging (www.aoa.dhhs.gov/retirement), the American Savings Education Council (www.asec.org), and SmartMoney (www.smartmoney.com), have a multitude of interactive tools and worksheets.

No matter your investment strategy, plans today will reap rewards tomorrow. A sound retirement plan can provide you and your family with a firm financial foundation after your retirement.

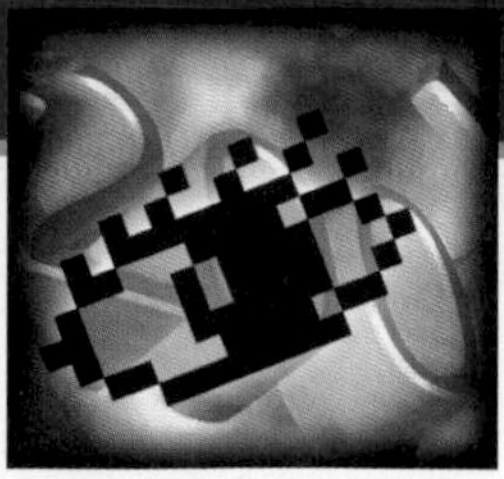

Microsoft Excel 2002

Using Macros and Visual Basic for Applications (VBA) with Excel

PROJECT 7

CASE PERSPECTIVE

Louis Pankros is the director of the human resource department for Master Software, a small but growing software provider. One of Louis's main tasks is to convince potential and current employees that Master Software offers excellent benefits.

Master Software's most lucrative benefit is an employee retirement savings plan. This plan is similar to a 401(k) plan. A 401(k) plan is a retirement savings program that allows employees to invest pretax dollars through payroll deductions.

Louis has a planning workbook. Any change to the data causes the planning workbook to recalculate all formulas instantaneously, thus showing the results of investing in the company's employee retirement savings plan.

Louis wants to put the workbook on the company's intranet so potential and current employees easily can determine the financial advantages of the retirement plan. The problem is that without an easy-to-use interface that steps the user through the entry of data, there is too much room for error and confusion. Louis has asked you to use Visual Basic for Applications to create a user-friendly interface for entering data into the workbook in three phases.

Introduction

Before a computer can take an action and produce a desired result, it must have a step-by-step description of the task to be accomplished. The step-by-step description is a series of precise instructions called a **procedure**. A procedure also is called a **program** or **code**. The process of writing a procedure is called **computer programming**. Every Excel command on a menu and button on a toolbar has a corresponding procedure that executes when you click the command or button. **Execute** means that the computer carries out the step-by-step instructions. In a Windows environment, the instructions associated with a task are executed when an **event** takes place, such as clicking a button, clicking a command, dragging a scroll box, or right-clicking a screen element.

Because a command or button in Excel does not exist for every possible worksheet task, Microsoft has included a powerful programming language called Visual Basic for Applications. The **Visual Basic for Applications** (**VBA**) programming language allows you to customize and extend the capabilities of Excel. Commonly used combinations of tasks can be grouped together using VBA and then reused at a later time. In this project, you will learn how to create macros using a code generator called a **macro recorder**. A **macro** is a procedure composed of VBA code. It is called a macro, rather than a procedure, because it is created using the macro recorder. You also will learn how to add buttons to toolbars and commands to menus and associate these with macros. Finally, you will learn the basics of VBA, including creating the interface, setting the properties, and writing the code.

Project Seven — Master Software Employee Retirement Savings Plan Worksheet

Master Software has determined the following needs and source of data.

Needs: The easy-to-use interface for the employee retirement savings plan workbook will be implemented in three phases:

Phase 1 — Create a macro using the macro recorder that prints the worksheet in portrait orientation using the Fit to option. Assign the macro to a button on the Standard toolbar (Figure 7-1a) and to a command on the File menu so the user can execute the macro by clicking the button or the command.

Phase 2 — Create a button on the worksheet as shown in Figure 7-1a, assign the button properties, and write an associated procedure (Figure 7-1b) that steps the user through entering the required data in the range D5:D10.

Phase 3 — Create an area on the worksheet called Adjustment Center (Figure 7-2 on the next page) that allows the user to enter his or her name and annual salary using a button and the remaining data using scroll bars, a check box, and spin buttons. Verify that the annual salary entered is positive.

Source of Data: The workbook shown in Figure 7-1a, without the button on the worksheet and the button on the toolbar, is available on the Data Disk with the file name Master Software.

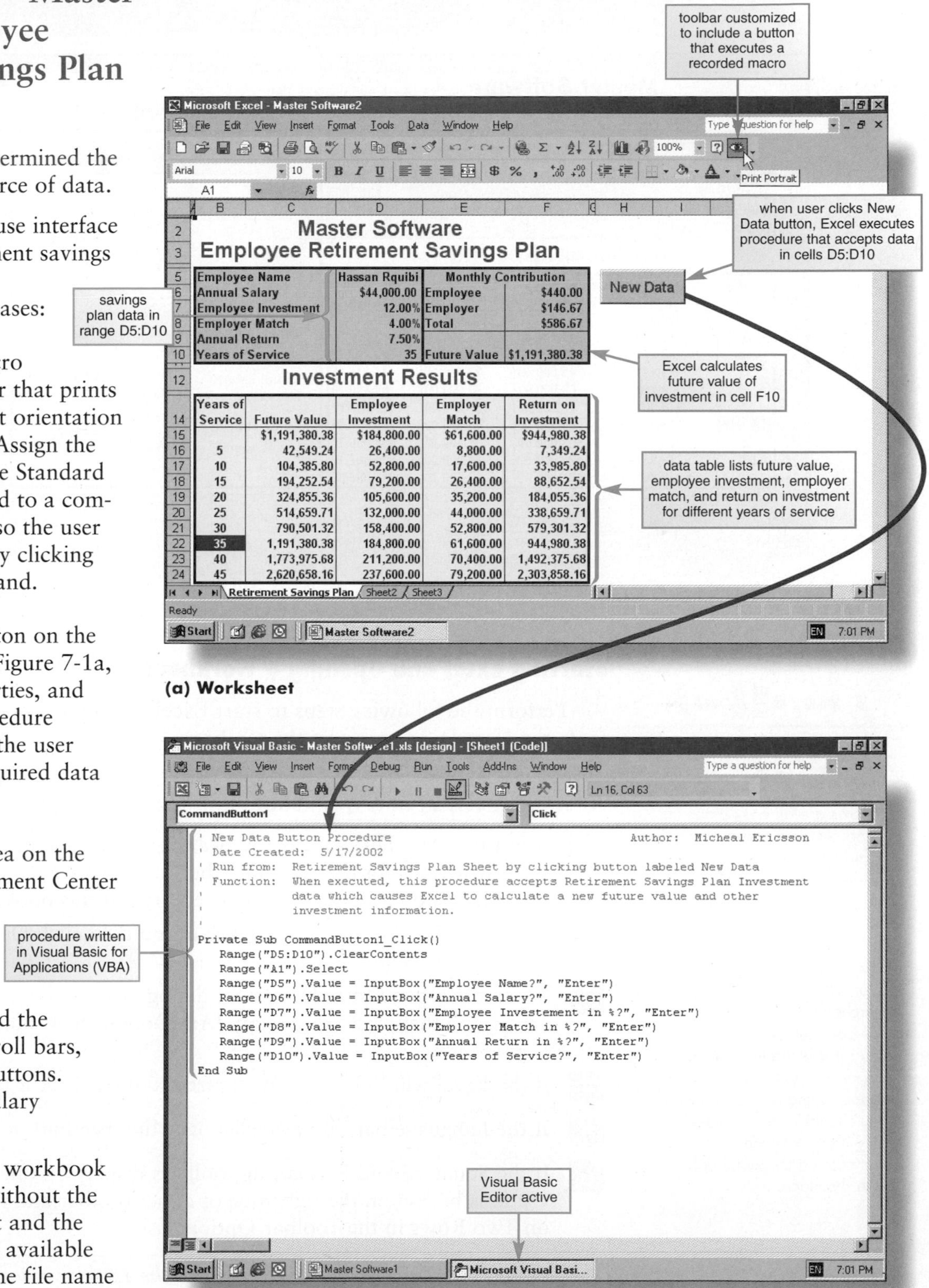

toolbar customized to include a button that executes a recorded macro
Microsoft Excel - Master Software2
Print Portrait
when user clicks New Data button, Excel executes procedure that accepts data in cells D5:D10
Master Software
Employee Retirement Savings Plan
savings plan data in range D5:D10
New Data
Excel calculates future value of investment in cell F10
Investment Results
data table lists future value, employee investment, employer match, and return on investment for different years of service
Retirement Savings Plan
Microsoft Visual Basic - Master Software1.xls [design] - [Sheet1 (Code)]
CommandButton1
Click
' New Data Button Procedure   Author: Micheal Ericsson
' Date Created: 5/17/2002
' Run from: Retirement Savings Plan Sheet by clicking button labeled New Data
' Function: When executed, this procedure accepts Retirement Savings Plan Investment
'   data which causes Excel to calculate a new future value and other
'   investment information.
Private Sub CommandButton1_Click()
Range("D5:D10").ClearContents
Range("A1").Select
Range("D5").Value = InputBox("Employee Name?", "Enter")
Range("D6").Value = InputBox("Annual Salary?", "Enter")
Range("D7").Value = InputBox("Employee Investement in %?", "Enter")
Range("D8").Value = InputBox("Employer Match in %?", "Enter")
Range("D9").Value = InputBox("Annual Return in %?", "Enter")
Range("D10").Value = InputBox("Years of Service?", "Enter")
End Sub
procedure written in Visual Basic for Applications (VBA)
Visual Basic Editor active

(a) Worksheet

(b) Visual Basic for Applications

FIGURE 7-1

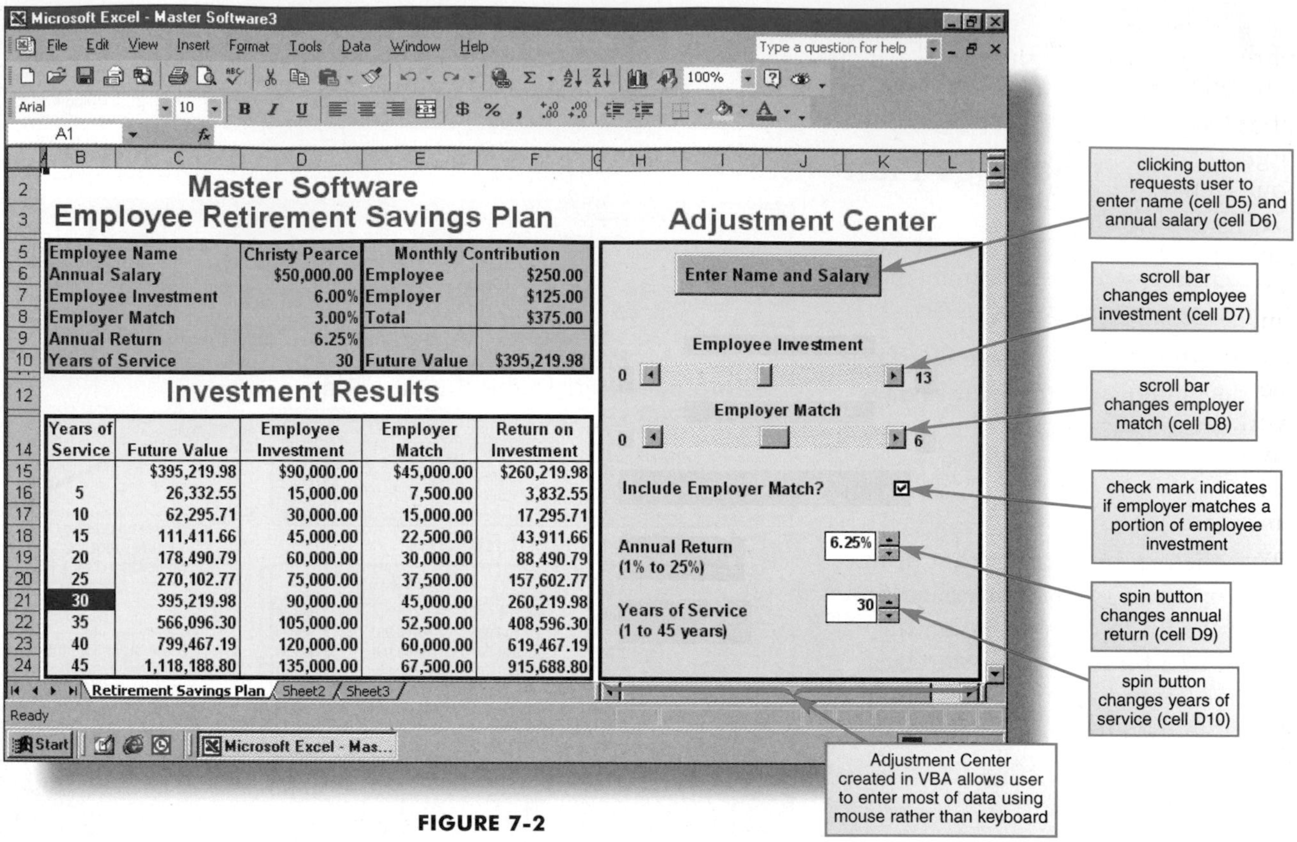

FIGURE 7-2

Starting Excel and Opening a Workbook

Perform the following steps to start Excel, open the workbook Master Software from the Data Disk, and reset the toolbars.

TO START EXCEL, OPEN A WORKBOOK, AND CUSTOMIZE EXCEL

1. Insert the Data Disk in drive A. See the inside back cover of this book for instructions for downloading the Data Disk or see your instructor for information on accessing the files required in this book.
2. Click the Start button on the taskbar and then click Open Office Document on the Start menu.
3. When the Open Office Document dialog box displays, click the Look in box arrow and then click 3½ Floppy (A:). Double-click Master Software in the Look in list.
4. If the Excel window is not maximized, double-click its title bar to maximize it.
5. If the Language bar displays, click its Minimize button.
6. If the Standard and Formatting toolbars display on one row, click the Toolbar Options button on the right side of either toolbar and then click Show Buttons on Two Rows in the Toolbar Options list.

The Master Software workbook displays in the Excel window (Figure 7-3).

The Retirement Savings Plan worksheet in the Master Software workbook is divided into two parts (Figure 7-3). The top part contains the data (range D5:D10) and the results (range F6:F10). The key cell is F10, which displays the future value of the investment.

More About

Opening Workbooks

Macros are an easy place for computer virus programmers to hide computer viruses. For this reason, Excel 2002 displays a dialog box whenever you open a workbook that contains a macro. The dialog box requires that you choose to enable or disable the attached macro before it will open the workbook. If you disable the macro and the macro contains a virus, it cannot damage your system. You should enable macros only if you trust the author that created the workbook with the macro.

The bottom part of the worksheet is a data table that varies the years of service in column B and organizes the results of four formulas in the range C15:F24 — future value (column C), employee investment (column D), employer match (column E), and return on investment (column F). In this worksheet, the return on investment is the future value less the sum of the employee and employer investment.

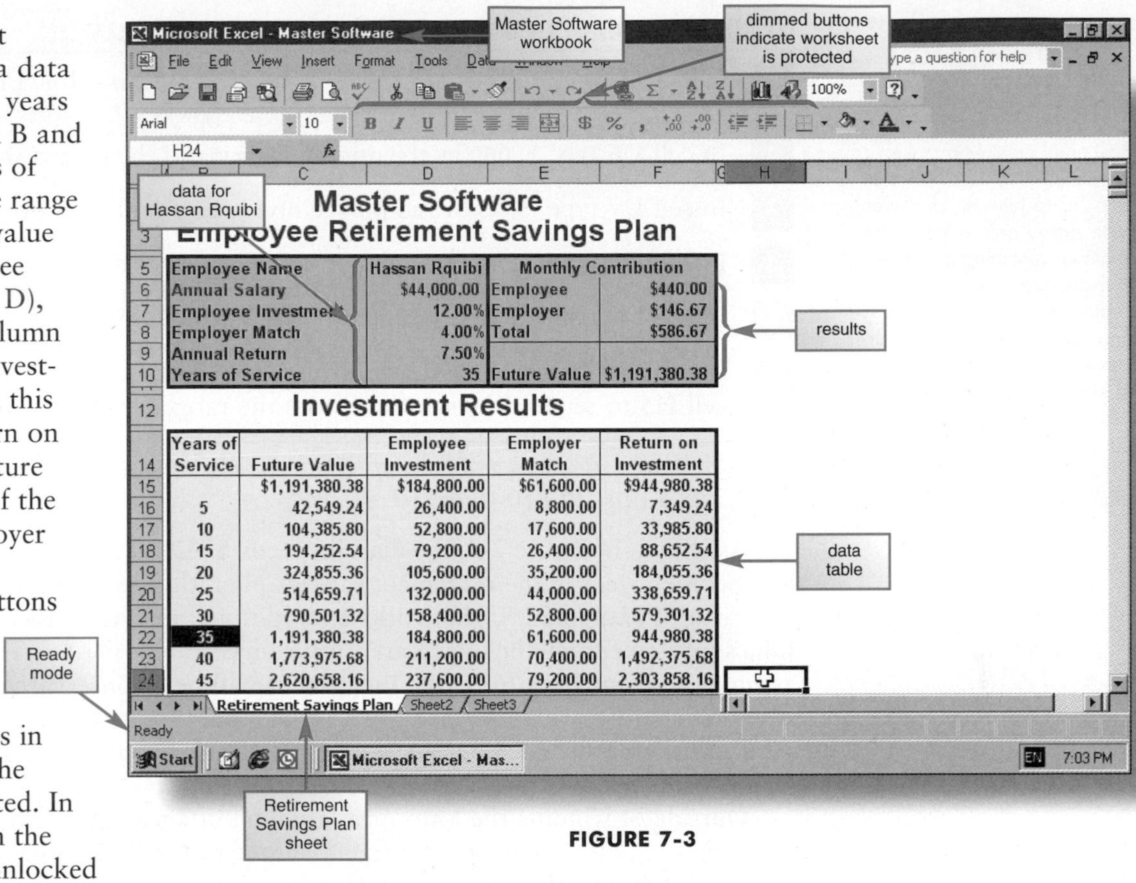

FIGURE 7-3

Many of the buttons on the toolbars are dimmed. When buttons are dimmed and Excel is in Ready mode, then the worksheet is protected. In this case, the cells in the range D5:D10 are unlocked so users can enter data, but the rest of the cells in the worksheet are protected and, therefore, cannot be changed. Later in this project, the worksheet will be unprotected so that changes can be made to it.

Gaining Confidence in a Workbook Created by Someone Else

When you modify a workbook created by someone else, such as the Master Software workbook, you should learn as much as you can about the workbook before you modify it. You can learn more about a workbook by doing the following:

1. Press CTRL+ACCENT MARK (`) to display the formulas version to gain an understanding of what formulas and functions are used in the worksheet, and which cells are referenced by the formulas and functions.
2. Use Range Finder or the auditing commands to show which cells are referenced in formulas and functions. You double-click a cell with a formula or function to activate Range Finder.
3. Check which cells are locked and which cells are unlocked. Usually all cells in a workbook are locked, except for those in which you enter data. For example, on the Retirement Savings Plan worksheet in Master Software, only the cells in the range D5:D10 are unlocked.
4. Enter sample data and verify the results.

To illustrate the entry of sample data, the following employee data will be used: Employee Name (cell D5) – Julia Hin; Annual Salary (cell D6) – $76,000.00; Employee Investment (cell D7) – 7.00%; Employer Match (cell D8) – 3.00%; Annual Return (cell D9) – 6.00%; and Years of Service (cell D10) – 35. Before entering the data, select the range D5:D10 so that Excel automatically makes the next cell in the range the active one when you complete a cell entry by pressing the enter key.

Perform the steps on the next page to enter the sample data.

More About

Gaining Confidence in a Workbook

Some Excel commands provide additional ways to uncover details of workbooks created by another author. For example, the Page Setup command on the File menu, the Print Preview command on the File menu, and Options command on the Tools menu can tell you if the author used any unusual settings. To list the macros in the workbook, point to Macro on the Tools menu and then click Macros on the Macro submenu.

More About

Retirement Plans

Most employers who make contributions to 401(k) or similar plans require an employee to be vested before the employer matching contributions are granted to the employee. Usually a company requires three to five years of continuous employment before an employee is completely vested. Virtually all 401(k) plans, however, can be transferred from one employer to another.

TO AUTOMATE DATA ENTRY BY SELECTING A RANGE OF CELLS

1. Click cell D5 and then select the range D5:D10. In cell D5 type `Julia Hin` as the employee name and then press the ENTER key.
2. In cell D6 type `76000` as the annual salary and then press the ENTER key.
3. In cell D7 type `7%` as the employee investment and then press the ENTER key.
4. In cell D8 type `3%` as the employer match and then press the ENTER key.
5. In cell D9 type `6%` as the annual return and then press the ENTER key.
6. In cell D10, type `35` as the years of service and then press the ENTER key. Click cell H5 to remove the selection from the range D5:D10.

The worksheet displays with the updated results, including a new future value of $902,316.52 in cell F10 (Figure 7-4).

As shown in Figure 7-4, if Julia Hin earns $76,000 a year and invests 7% of her income a year in the retirement savings plan, then in 35 years her investment will be worth $902,316.52. If she works an additional ten years, then cell C24 shows Julia's investment will be worth an astonishing $1,745,461.99. These future values assume the annual return on the investment will be a conservative 6%. They also assume that Julia will never get a raise, which means the investment could be worth significantly more if she does get raises, because she is investing a percentage of her income, rather than a fixed amount.

Outside of winning the lotto or a large inheritance, a retirement saving plan is the easiest way for a person on a fixed income to legally become a millionaire at some point in his or her lifetime. A significant benefit of the plan is that participants usually do not pay taxes on the money that they invest into the plan. Once you start drawing funds from the plan, you are required to pay taxes on what you withdraw. Plans usually have penalties for withdrawing funds before you are 59½ years old. For example, you may pay a 10 percent penalty on withdrawals before you are 59½ years old.

As shown in the previous set of steps, when you select a range before entering data, Excel automatically advances one cell downward when you press the ENTER key. If the worksheet consists of multiple columns and you enter the last value in a column, then Excel moves to the top of the next column.

Follow these steps to change the data in the range D5:D10 back to its original values.

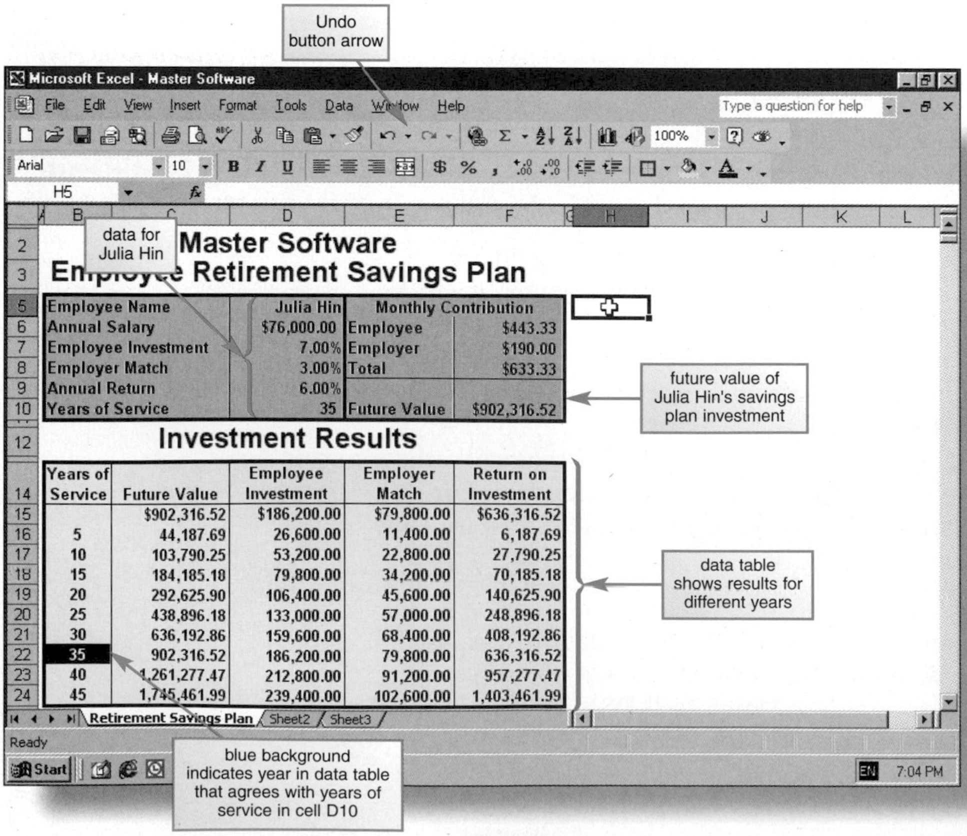

FIGURE 7-4

TO UNDO A GROUP OF ENTRIES USING THE UNDO BUTTON

1. Click the Undo button arrow on the Standard toolbar (Figure 7-4).
2. When the Undo list displays, drag from the top down through Julia Hin and then release the left mouse button. Click cell H5.

Excel changes the range D5:D10 back to its original values and recalculates all formulas and the data table. The Retirement Savings Plan worksheet displays as shown earlier in Figure 7-3 on page E 7.07.

More About

The Undo Button

To undo recent actions one at a time, click the Undo button on the Standard toolbar. To undo several actions, click the Undo button arrow and select from the list. Excel will undo the selected action, as well as all the actions above it.

Unprotecting a Password-Protected Worksheet

The Retirement Savings Plan worksheet in the Master Software workbook is protected. When a worksheet is protected, users cannot change data in locked cells or modify the worksheet in any manner. Thus, before modifying the worksheet in the three phases, it must be unprotected. A **password** ensures that users will not unprotect the worksheet by using the Unprotect command. The Retirement Savings Plan worksheet password is planright.

A password, such as planright, can contain any combination of letters, numerals, spaces, and symbols, and it can be up to 15 characters long. Passwords are case-sensitive, so if you vary the capitalization when you assign the password, you must type the same capitalization later when you unprotect the worksheet.

The following steps show how to unprotect the password-protected worksheet.

Steps To Unprotect a Password-Protected Worksheet

1. **Click Tools on the menu bar, point to Protection, and then point to Unprotect Sheet on the Protection submenu.**

The Tools menu and Protection submenu display (Figure 7-5).

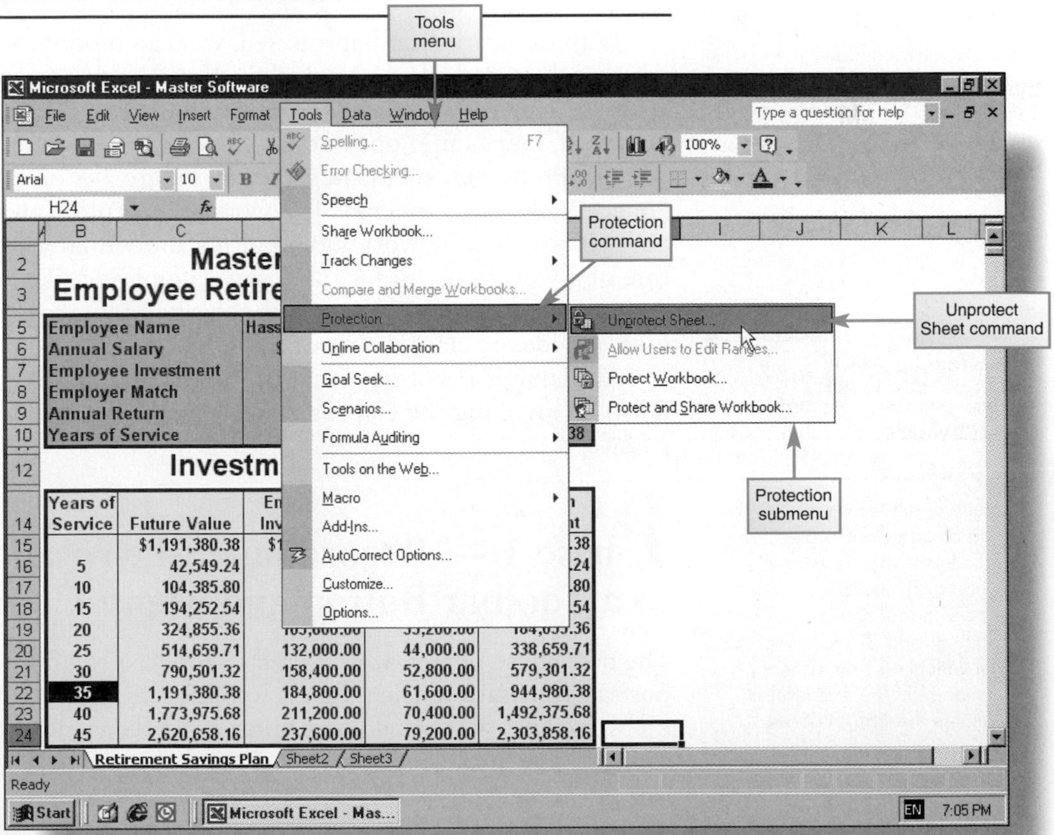

FIGURE 7-5

2 **Click Unprotect Sheet. When the Unprotect Sheet dialog box displays, type** `planright` **in the Password text box and then point to the OK button.**

The Unprotect Sheet dialog box displays (Figure 7-6). Excel displays asterisks in place of the password planright so no one can look over your shoulder and copy the password.

3 **Click the OK button.**

Excel unprotects the Retirement Savings Plan worksheet.

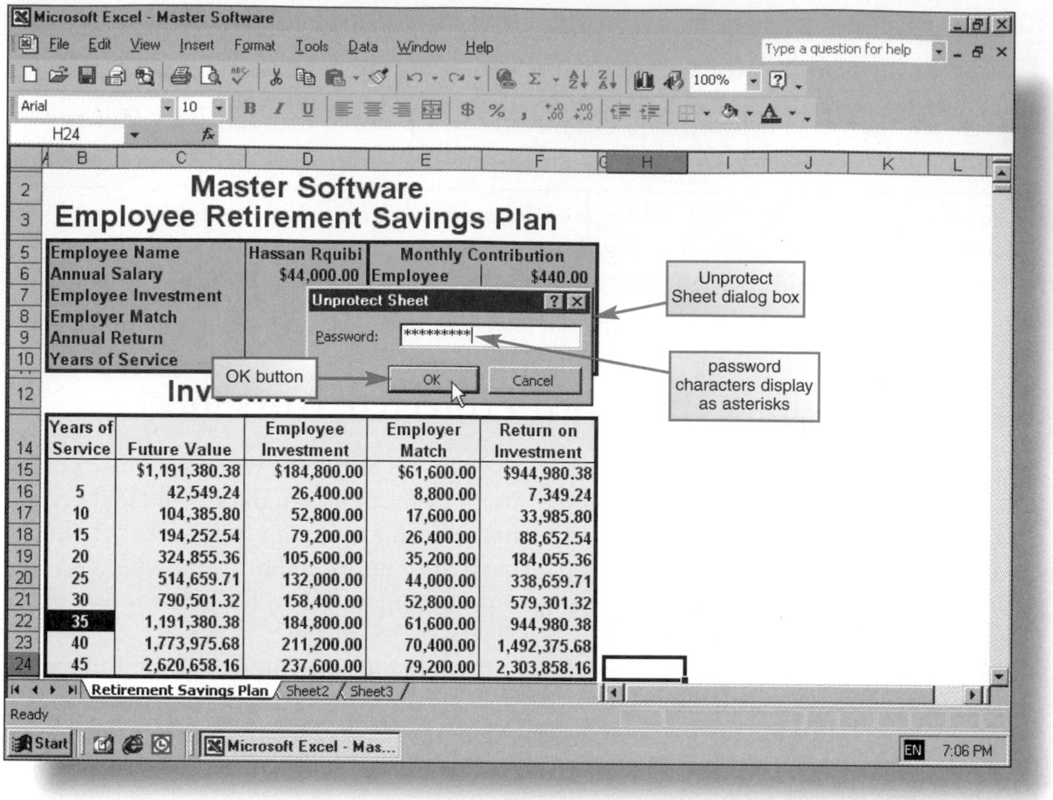

FIGURE 7-6

Other Ways

1. Press ALT+T, P, P
2. In Voice Command mode, say "Tools, Protection, Unprotect, [type password] OK"

With the worksheet unprotected, you can modify the contents of cells regardless of whether they are locked or unlocked. If you decide to password-protect a worksheet, make sure you write down the password and keep it in a secure place. If you lose the password, you cannot open or gain access to the password-protected worksheet.

The Protection submenu shown in Figure 7-5 on the previous page also has a **Protect Workbook command.** The workbook protection level protects the structure and windows of the workbook, but not individual worksheets. Protecting the structure of a workbook means that users cannot add, delete, move, hide, unhide, or rename sheets. Protecting a workbook's windows means users cannot move, resize, hide, unhide, or close the workbook's windows.

Although it is not necessary in this project to unprotect the workbook, you can do so by invoking the Unprotect Workbook command and using planright as the password.

More About

Password Protection

Excel offers three basic levels of password protection: 1) file level when you save it to disk; 2) workbook level so the window cannot be modified; and 3) worksheet level so locked cells cannot be changed. The first level is available through the Save As command on the File menu. The second and third levels are available through the Protection command on the Tools menu.

Phase 1 — Recording a Macro and Assigning It to a Toolbar Button and Menu Command

The first phase of this project creates a macro to automate printing the worksheet in portrait orientation using the Fit to option. Recall that the Fit to option ensures that the worksheet will fit on one printed page. The orientation for the printout was set to landscape in Master Software. The planned macro will change the orientation from landscape to portrait and use the Fit to option to force it to fit on one page. It then will reset the print settings back to their original settings.

The purpose of this macro is to give users the option of printing the worksheet in landscape orientation by clicking the Print button on the Standard toolbar or executing the macro to print the worksheet in portrait orientation. Once the macro is created, it will be assigned to a button on the Standard toolbar and a command on the File menu.

Recording a Macro

Excel has a **macro recorder** that creates a macro automatically based on a series of actions you perform while it is recording. As with a video recorder, the macro recorder records everything you do to a workbook over time. The macro recorder can be turned on, during which time it records your activities, and then turned off to stop the recording. Once the macro is recorded, it can be played back, or executed, as often as you want.

It is easy to create a macro. Simply turn on the macro recorder and carry out the steps to be recorded.

1. If necessary, switch from landscape orientation to portrait orientation and from 100% normal size printing to fit to one page.
2. Print the worksheet.
3. Switch from portrait orientation to landscape orientation and from fit to one page to 100% normal size printing.
4. Stop the macro recorder.

What is impressive about the macro recorder is that you actually step through the task as you create the macro. Therefore, you see exactly what the macro will do before you use it.

When you first create the macro, you must name it. The name is used later to reference the macro when you want to execute it. Executing a macro causes Excel to step through all of the recorded steps. The macro name in this project is PrintPortrait. **Macro names** can be up to 255 characters long; they can contain numbers, letters, and underscores; they cannot contain spaces and other punctuation.

Perform the following steps to record the macro.

More About

The Macro Recorder

The macro recorder is unforgiving. Once it is turned on, Excel records every action you take. If you make a mistake, you must start over. For this reason, you need to plan carefully from start to finish what you intend to do before you turn the macro recorder on.

Steps: To Record a Macro to Print the Worksheet in Portrait Orientation Using the Fit to Option

1 Click Tools on the menu bar. Point to Macro and then point to Record New Macro on the Macro submenu.

The Tools menu and Macro submenu display (Figure 7-7).

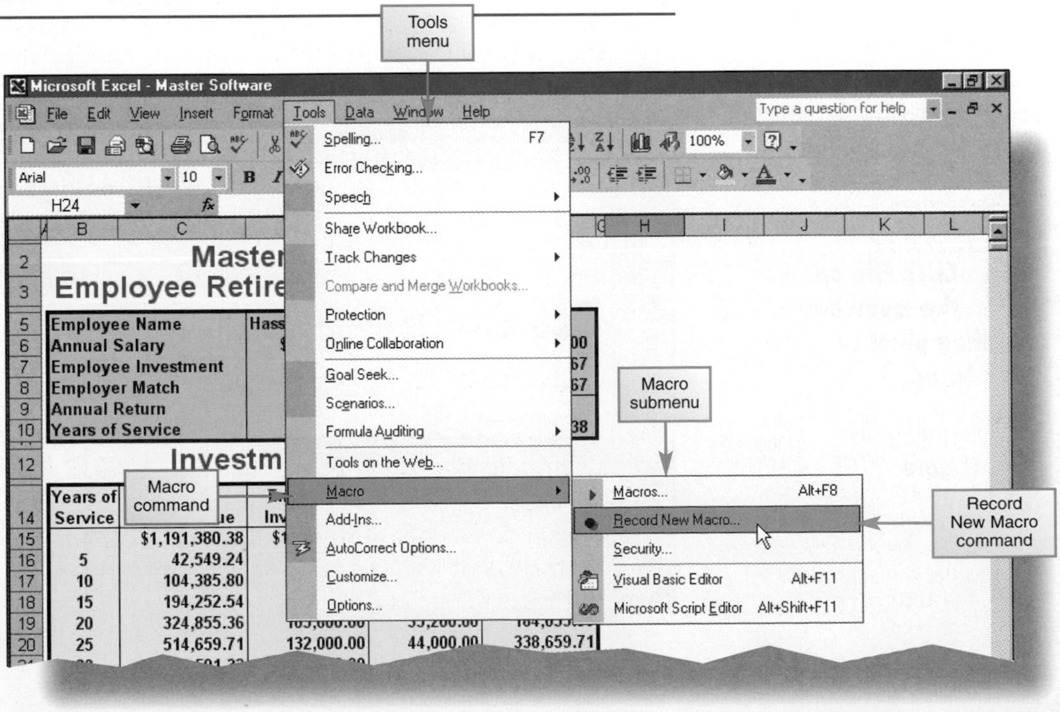

FIGURE 7-7

2 **Click Record New Macro. When the Record Macro dialog box displays, type** `PrintPortrait` **in the Macro name text box. Type** `r` **in the Shortcut key text box, and then type** `Macro prints worksheet in portrait orientation on one page` **in the Description text box. Make sure the Store macro in box displays This Workbook. Point to the OK button.**

The Record Macro dialog box displays as shown in Figure 7-8. The shortcut key for executing the macro is CTRL+R.

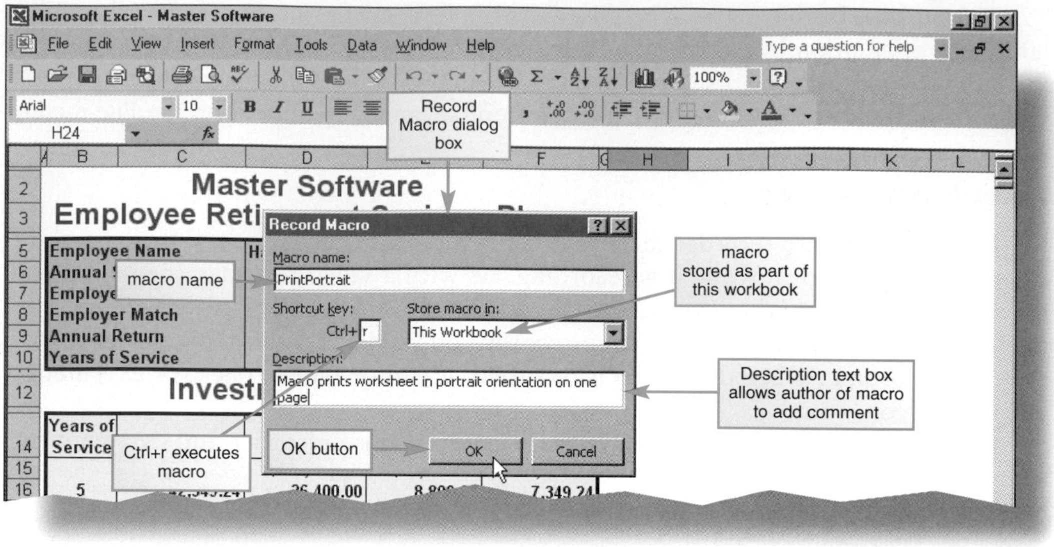

FIGURE 7-8

3 **Click the OK button. If the Stop Recording toolbar does not display, click View on the main menu, then select Stop Recording on the Toolbars submenu.**

The Stop Recording toolbar displays (Figure 7-9). Any task you perform in Excel will be part of the macro. When you are finished recording the macro, clicking the Stop Recording button on the Stop Recording toolbar ends the recording.

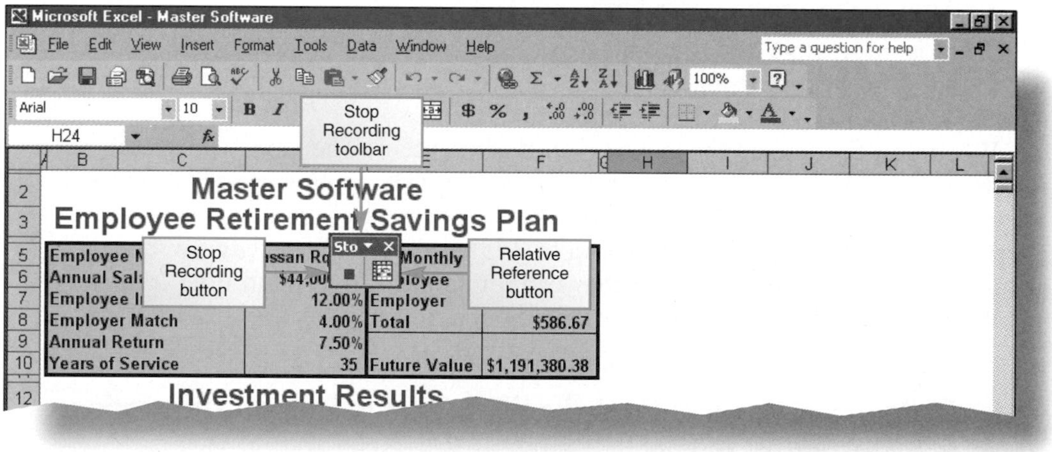

FIGURE 7-9

4 **Click File on the menu bar and then point to Page Setup.**

The File menu displays (Figure 7-10).

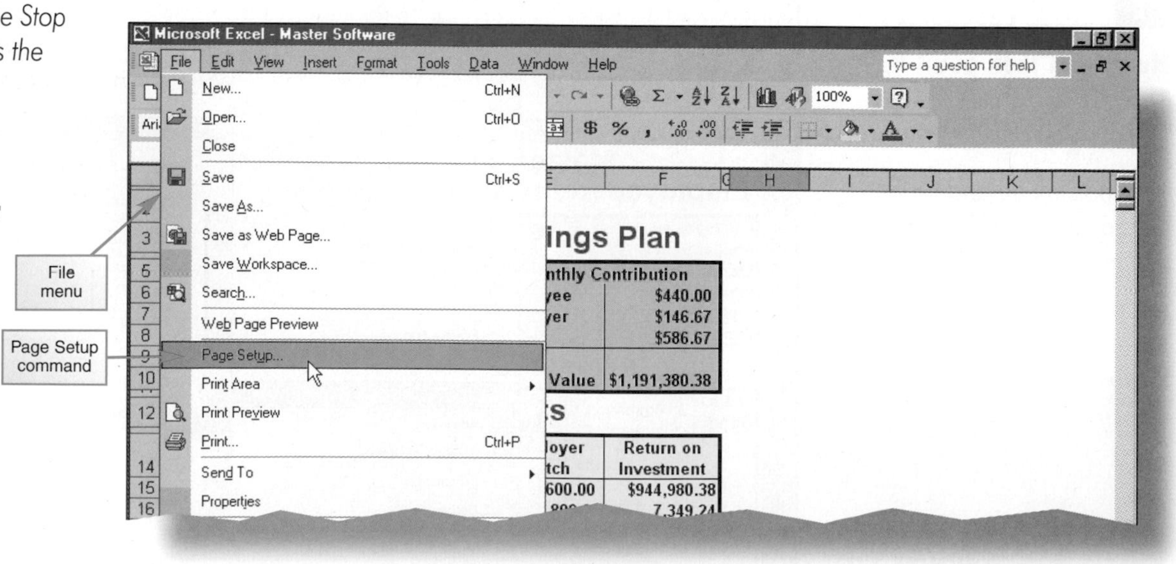

FIGURE 7-10

5 **Click Page Setup. When the Page Setup dialog box displays, click the Page tab, click Portrait in the Orientation area if necessary, click Fit to in the Scaling area, and then point to the Print button.**

The Page Setup dialog box displays as shown in Figure 7-11.

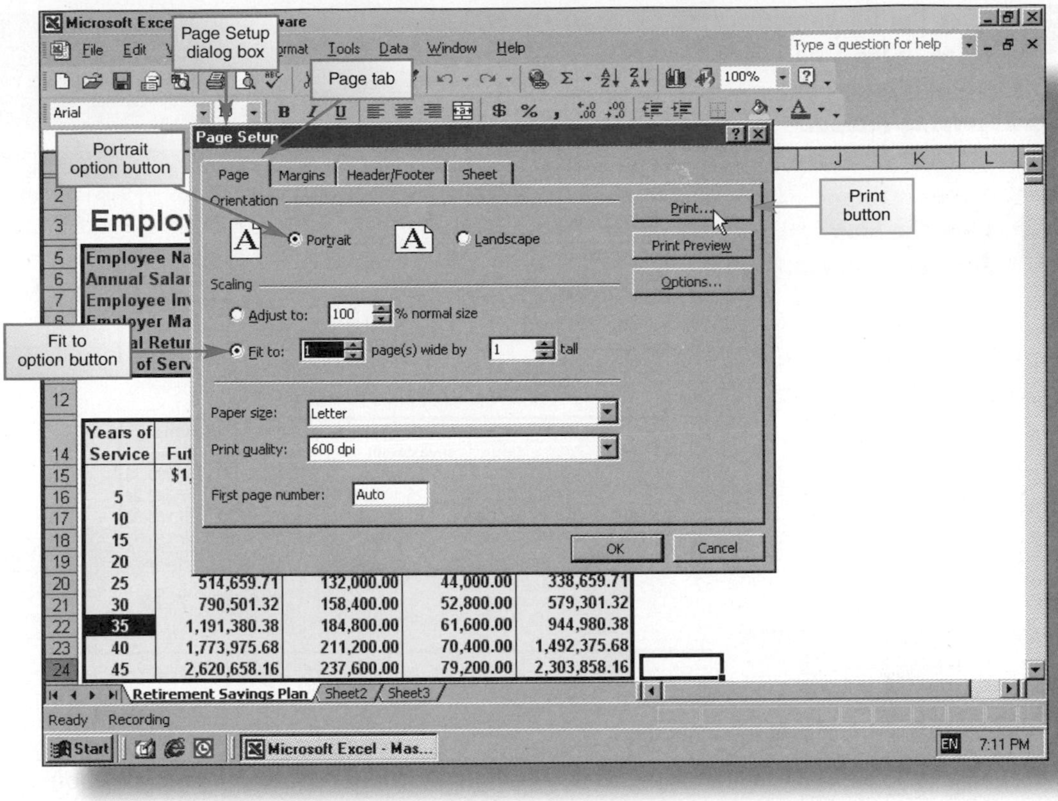

FIGURE 7-11

6 **Click the Print button. When the Print dialog box displays, click the OK button. Click File on the menu bar and then click Page Setup. When the Page Setup dialog box displays, if necessary, click the Page tab, click Landscape in the Orientation area, click Adjust to in the Scaling area, type** 100 **in the % normal size box, and then point to the OK button.**

After the worksheet prints in portrait orientation on one page, the Page Setup dialog box displays as shown in Figure 7-12.

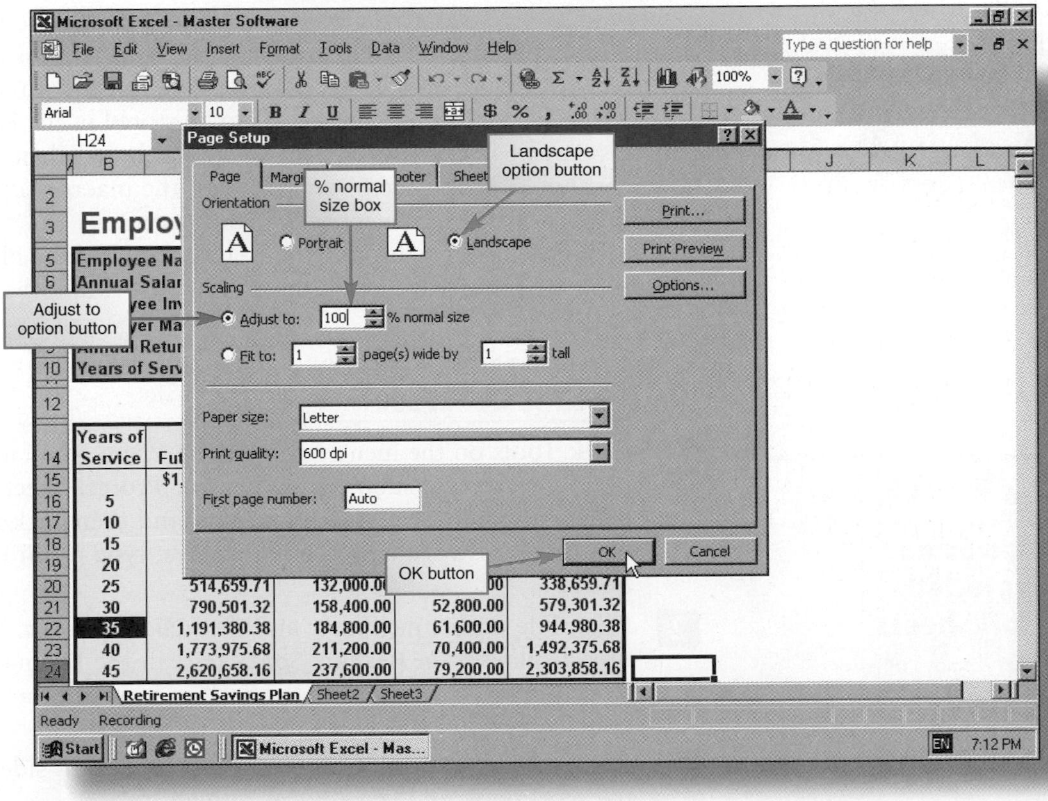

FIGURE 7-12

7 **Click the OK button. Point to the Stop Recording button on the Stop Recording toolbar (Figure 7-13).**

8 **Click the Stop Recording button.**

Excel stops recording the worksheet activities and hides the Stop Recording toolbar.

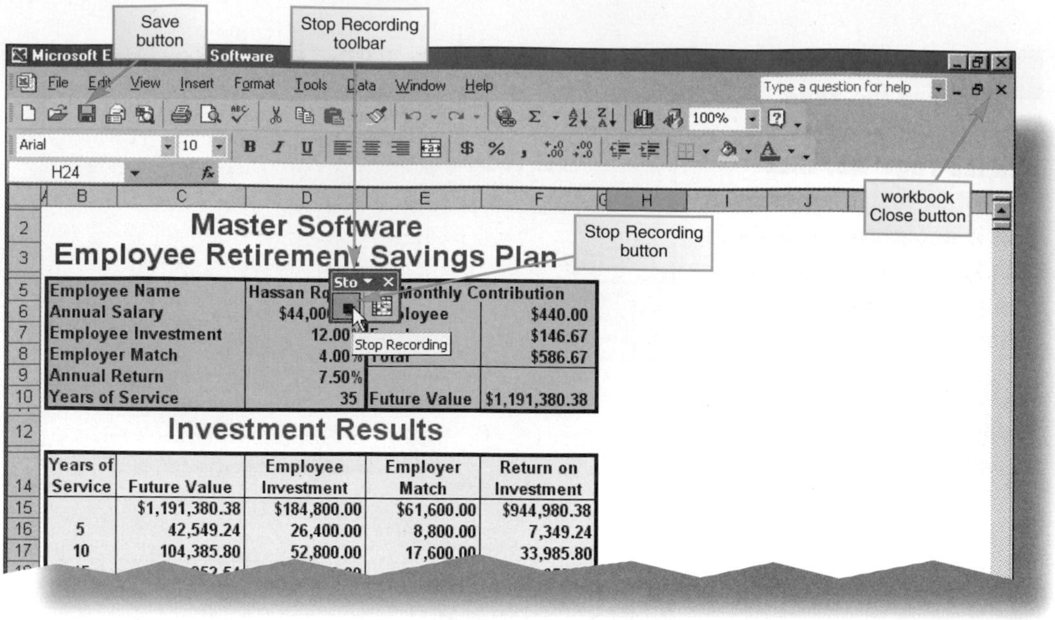

FIGURE 7-13

Other Ways

1. Click Record Macro button on Visual Basic toolbar
2. Press ALT+T, M, R
3. In Voice Command mode, say "Tools, Macro, Record"

More About

Displaying the Stop Recording Toolbar

If the Stop Recording toolbar does not display when you begin to record a macro, right-click a toolbar and then click Stop Recording on the shortcut menu.

More About

Macros and Protected Worksheets

Excel displays an error message if you execute a macro that attempts to modify a protected worksheet. If you want to modify a protected worksheet using a macro, have the macro unprotect the worksheet at the beginning, and then have the macro protect the worksheet at the end.

If you recorded the wrong actions, delete the macro and record it again. You delete a macro by clicking Tools on the menu bar, pointing to Macro on the Tools menu, and then clicking Macros on the Macro submenu. When the Macro dialog box displays, click the name of the macro (PrintPortrait) and then click the Delete button. Finally, record the macro again.

In the Record Macro dialog box (Figure 7-8 on page E 7.12), you select the location to store the macro in the Store macro in box. If you want a macro to be available whenever you use Microsoft Excel, select Personal Macro Workbook in the Store macro in list. This selection causes the macro to be stored in the **Personal Macro Workbook**, which is part of Excel. If you click New Workbook, then Excel stores the macro in a new workbook. Most macros created with the macro recorder are workbook-specific, and thus, are stored in the active workbook.

The following steps protect the Retirement Savings Plan worksheet, save the workbook using the file name Master Software1, and then close the workbook.

TO PASSWORD-PROTECT THE WORKSHEET, SAVE THE WORKBOOK, AND CLOSE THE WORKBOOK

1. Click Tools on the menu bar, point to Protection, and then click Protect Sheet on the Protection submenu. When the Protect Sheet dialog box displays, type `planright` in the Password text box and then click the OK button. When the Confirm Password dialog box displays, type `planright` and then click the OK button.
2. Click File on the menu bar and then click Save As. When the Save As dialog box displays, type `Master Software1` in the File name text box. Make sure 3½ Floppy (A:) displays in the Save in box and then click the Save button in the Save As dialog box.
3. Click the workbook's Close button on the right side of its menu bar to close the workbook and leave Excel active.

Excel protects the worksheet, saves the workbook to drive A, and closes the Master Software1 workbook.

Opening a Workbook with a Macro and Executing the Macro

A **computer virus** is a potentially damaging computer program designed to affect, or infect, your computer negatively by altering the way it works without your knowledge or permission. Currently, more than 15,000 known computer viruses exist and an estimated 200 more are created each month. The increased use of networks, the Internet, and e-mail has accelerated the spread of computer viruses.

To combat this menace, most computer users run antivirus programs that search for viruses and destroy them before they ever have a chance to infect the computer. Macros are a known carriers of viruses, because of the ease with which a person can add programming code to macros. For this reason, each time you open a workbook with an associated macro, Excel displays a Microsoft Excel dialog box warning that a macro is attached and that macros can contain viruses. Table 7-1 summarizes the buttons users can select from to continue the process of opening a workbook with macros.

Table 7-1 Buttons in the Microsoft Excel Dialog Box When Opening a Workbook with Macros

BUTTONS	DESCRIPTION
Disable Macros	Macros are unavailable to the user
Enable Macros	Macros are available to the user to execute
More Info	Opens the Microsoft Excel Help window and displays information on viruses and workbook macros

If you are confident of the source (author) of the workbook and macros, click the Enable Macros button. If you are uncertain about the reliability of the source of the workbook and macros, then click the Disable Macros button. For more information on this topic, click the More Info button.

The following steps open the Master Software1 workbook to illustrate the Microsoft Excel dialog box that displays when a workbook contains a macro. The steps then show how to execute the recorded macro PrintPortrait by using the shortcut key CTRL+R. Recall that the shortcut key was established in Step 2 of the previous set of steps.

More About

Macro Viruses

To guard against macro viruses in workbooks created by someone else, you should purchase antivirus software that is designed to detect and repair files infected with a virus. For more information on antivirus software, visit the Excel Web page (www.scsite.com/ex2002/more.htm) and click Antivirus Software.

More About

Security

If your antivirus software is compatible with Office XP, you can select the lowest level of security in the Security dialog box. You display the Security dialog box by clicking Tools on the menu bar, Macro on the Tools menu, and Security on the Macro submenu. The antivirus software will scan all incoming workbooks for viruses, regardless of the level of security you choose.

Steps To Open a Workbook with a Macro and Execute the Macro

1 **With Excel active, click File on the menu bar and then click Open. When the Open dialog box displays, click the Look in box arrow, and then click 3½ Floppy (A:). Double-click the file name Master Software1.**

The Microsoft Excel dialog displays (Figure 7-14).

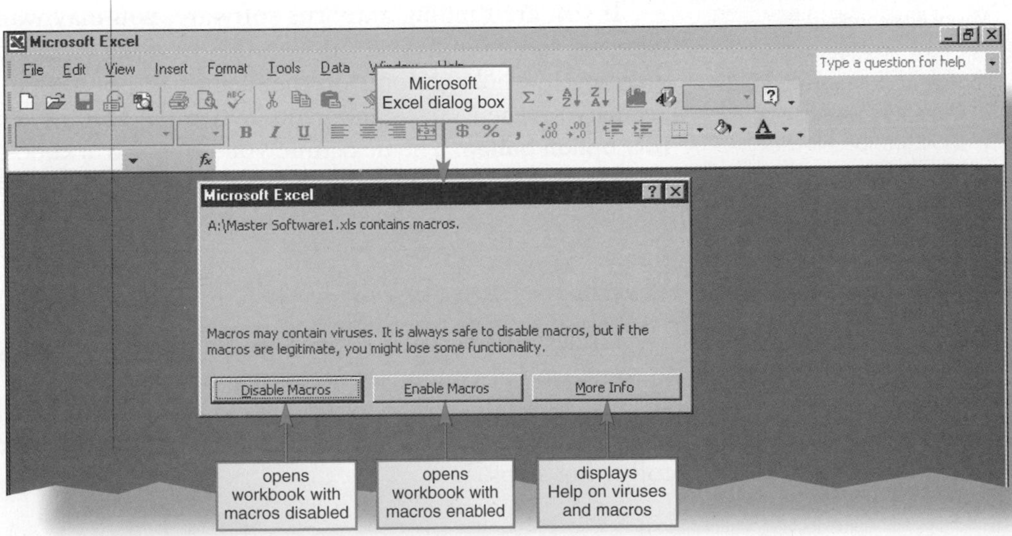

FIGURE 7-14

2 **Click the Enable Macros button. When the Retirement Savings Plan worksheet in the Master Software1 workbook displays, press CTRL+R.**

Excel opens the workbook Master Software1. The Excel window blinks for several seconds as the macro executes. The report prints as shown in Figure 7-15.

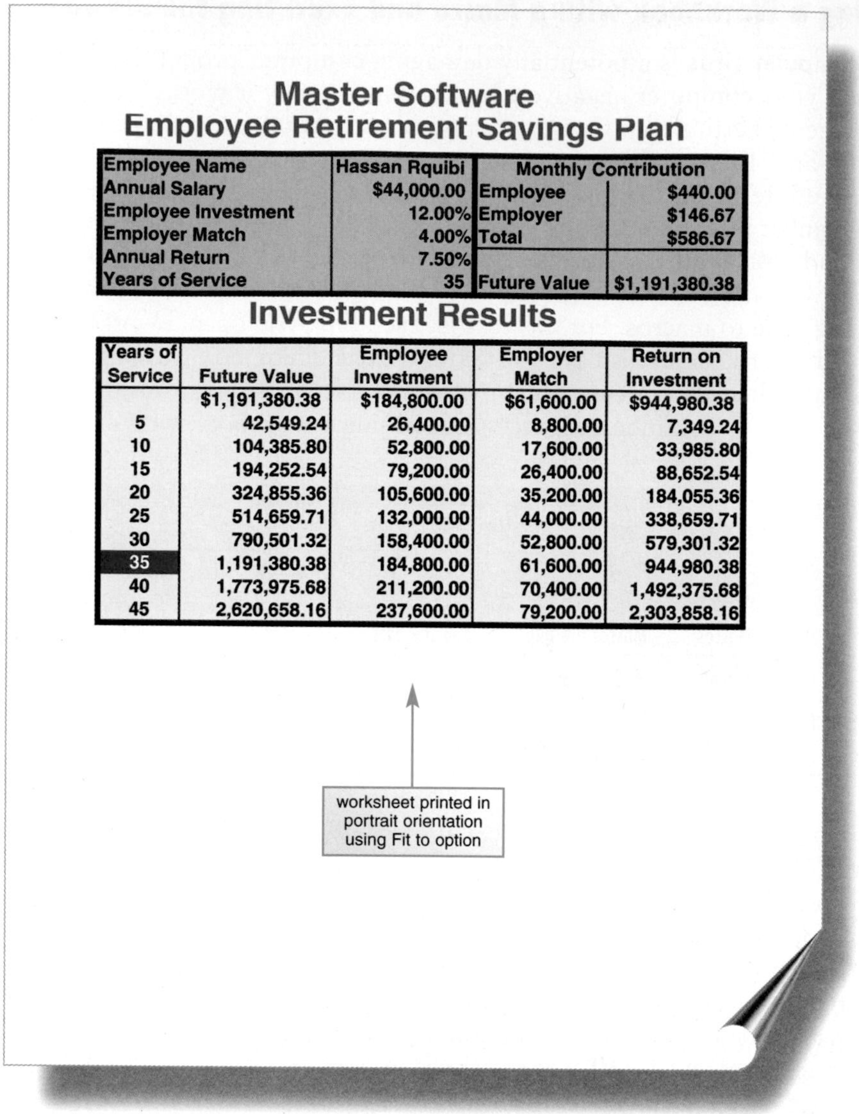

Master Software
Employee Retirement Savings Plan

		Monthly Contribution	
Employee Name	Hassan Rquibi		
Annual Salary	$44,000.00	Employee	$440.00
Employee Investment	12.00%	Employer	$146.67
Employer Match	4.00%	Total	$586.67
Annual Return	7.50%		
Years of Service	35	Future Value	$1,191,380.38

Investment Results

Years of Service	Future Value	Employee Investment	Employer Match	Return on Investment
	$1,191,380.38	$184,800.00	$61,600.00	$944,980.38
5	42,549.24	26,400.00	8,800.00	7,349.24
10	104,385.80	52,800.00	17,600.00	33,985.80
15	194,252.54	79,200.00	26,400.00	88,652.54
20	324,855.36	105,600.00	35,200.00	184,055.36
25	514,659.71	132,000.00	44,000.00	338,659.71
30	790,501.32	158,400.00	52,800.00	579,301.32
35	1,191,380.38	184,800.00	61,600.00	944,980.38
40	1,773,975.68	211,200.00	70,400.00	1,492,375.68
45	2,620,658.16	237,600.00	79,200.00	2,303,858.16

FIGURE 7-15

Other Ways

1. Click Run Macro button on Visual Basic toolbar
2. On Tools menu point to Macro, click Macros, double-click macro name
3. Press ALT+F8, double-click macro name
4. In Voice Command mode, say "Tools, Macro, Macros, [click macro name], OK"

If you are running antivirus software, you may want to turn off the security warning shown in Figure 7-14 on the previous page. You can turn off the security warning by clicking Tools on the menu bar, pointing to Macro, and then clicking Security on the Macros submenu. When the **Security dialog box** displays, click the **Low option button**. The next time you open a workbook that includes a macro, Excel will open the workbook immediately, rather than display the dialog box shown in Figure 7-14.

Viewing a Macro's VBA Code

As described earlier, a macro is comprised of VBA code, which is created automatically by the macro recorder. You can view the VBA code through the Visual Basic Editor. The **Visual Basic Editor** is used by all Office applications to enter, modify, and view VBA code. To view the macro's VBA code, complete the following steps.

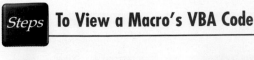

Steps To View a Macro's VBA Code

1 Click Tools on the menu bar. Point to Macro on the Tools menu and then point to Macros on the Macro submenu.

The Tools menu and Macro submenu display (Figure 7-16).

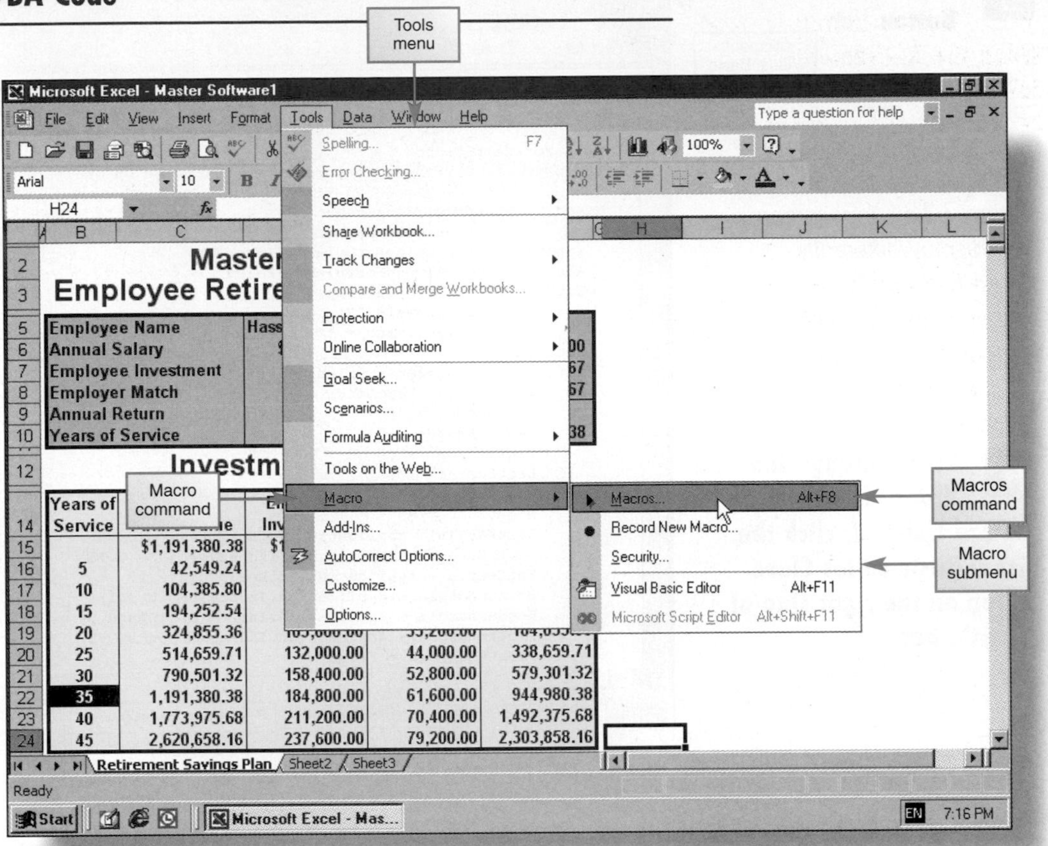

FIGURE 7-16

2 Click Macros. When the Macro dialog box displays, click PrintPortrait in the list, and then point to the Edit button.

The Macro dialog box displays as shown in Figure 7-17.

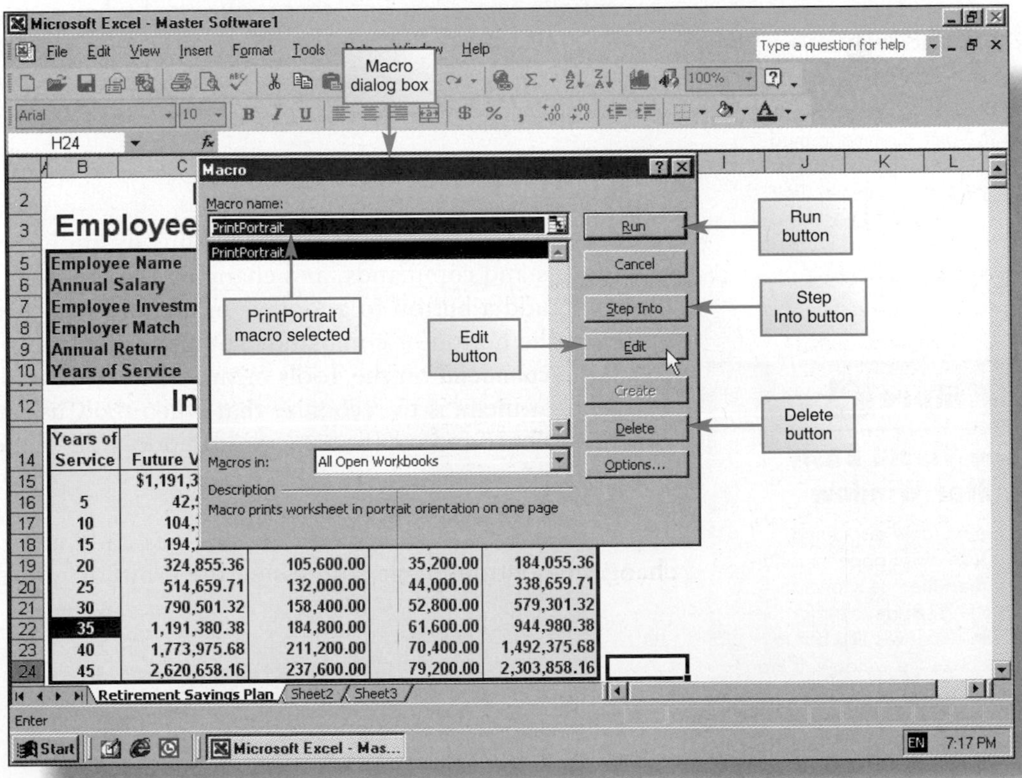

FIGURE 7-17

3 Click the Edit button.

The Visual Basic Editor starts and displays the VBA code in the macro PrintPortrait (Figure 7-18). Your screen may display differently depending on how it displayed the last time the Visual Basic Editor was activated.

4 Scroll through the VBA code. When you are finished, click the Visual Basic Editor Close button on the right side of the title bar.

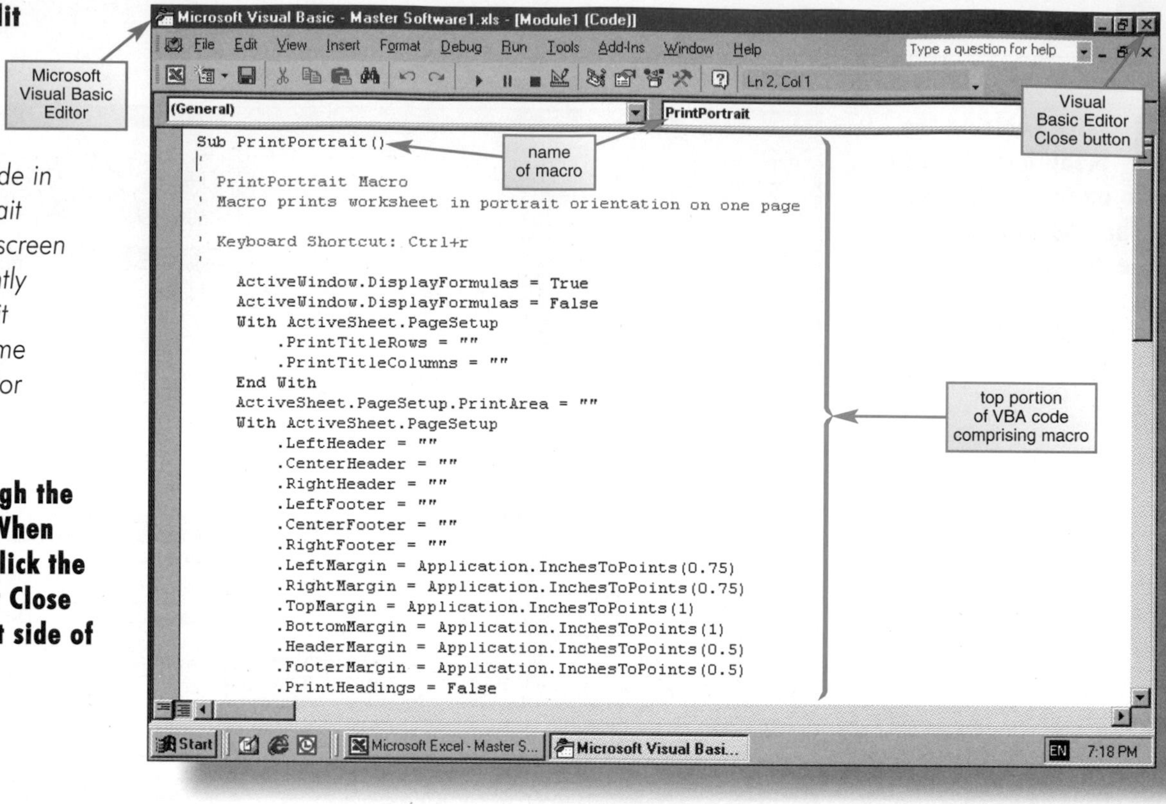

FIGURE 7-18

Other Ways

1. Click Visual Basic Editor button on Visual Basic toolbar
2. Right-click the worksheet tab, click View Code
3. Press ALT+F8, click Edit
4. In Voice Command mode, say "Tools, Macro, Macros, [click macro name], Edit"

It is this set of instructions, beginning with line 1 in Figure 7-18 and continuing sequentially to the last line, that is executed when you invoke the macro. By scrolling through the VBA code, you can see that the macro recorder generates a lot of instructions. In this case, 75 lines of code are generated to print the worksheet in portrait orientation using the Fit to option.

Customizing Toolbars and Menus

You can customize toolbars and menus by adding buttons and commands, deleting buttons and commands, and changing the function of buttons and commands. Once you add a button to a toolbar or a command to a menu, you can assign a macro to the button or command. You customize a toolbar or menu by invoking the **Customize command** on the Tools menu. The key to understanding how to customize a toolbar or menu is to recognize that when the Customize dialog box is open, Excel's toolbars and menus are in Edit mode. Edit mode allows you to modify the toolbars and menus.

CUSTOMIZING A TOOLBAR The following steps add a button to the Standard toolbar, change the button image, and assign the PrintPortrait macro to the button.

More About

The Visual Basic Editor Window

If the window displaying the VBA code appears different than the one shown in Figure 7-18, double-click the Code window's title bar to maximize the window. If the Project window or Properties window displays on the left side of the Visual Basic Editor window, click its Close button.

Steps To Add a Button to a Toolbar, Assign the Button a Macro, and Use the Button

1 Click Tools on the menu bar, and then point to Customize.

The Tools menu displays (Figure 7-19).

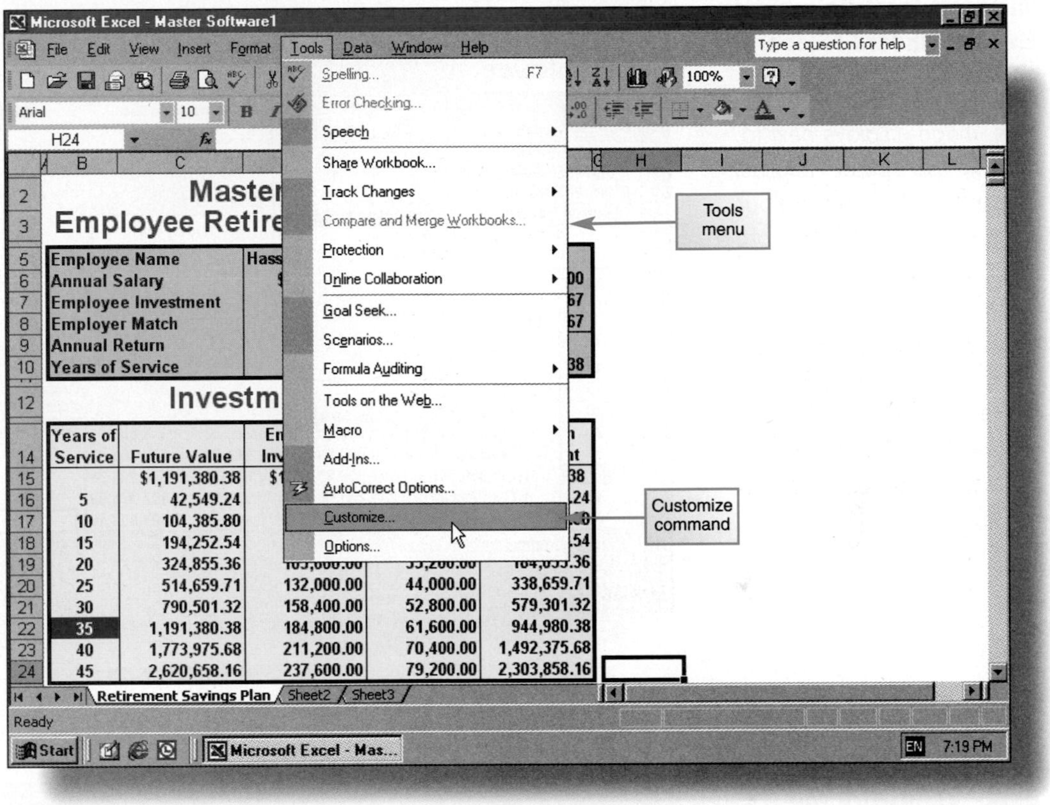

FIGURE 7-19

2 Click Customize. When the Customize dialog box opens, click the Commands tab. Scroll down in the Categories list and then click Macros.

The Customize dialog box displays as shown in Figure 7-20. The two items in the Command list for the Macro category are Custom Menu Item and Custom Button.

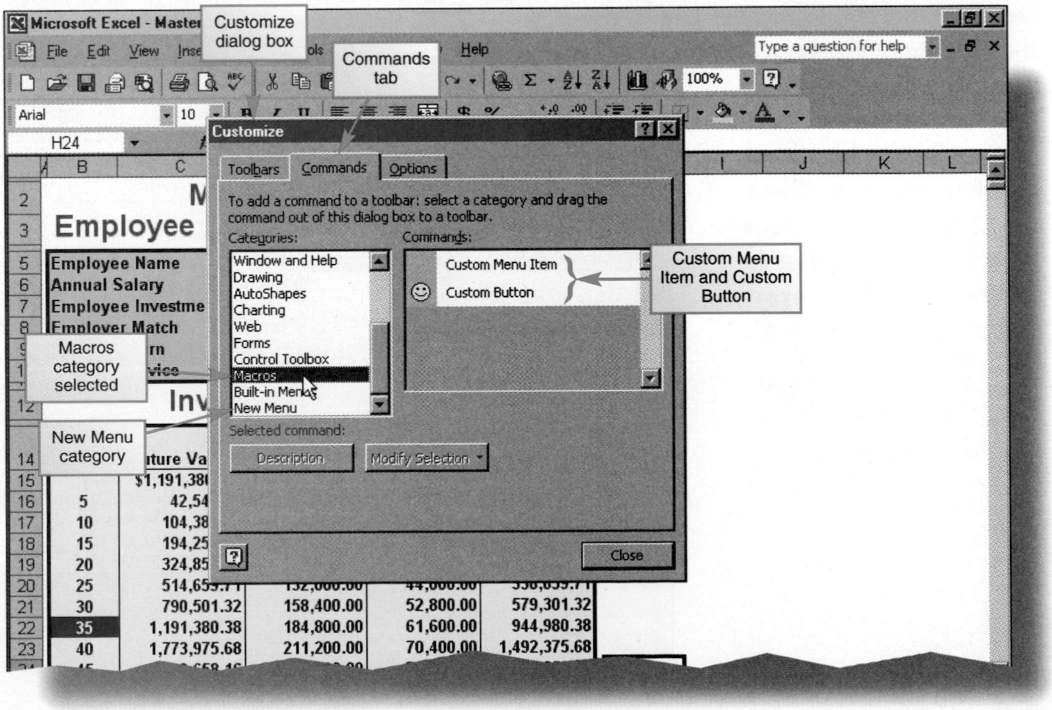

FIGURE 7-20

3 **Drag the button with the smiley face image in the Commands list to the right of the Microsoft Excel Help button on the Standard toolbar.**

The button with the smiley face image displays next to the Microsoft Excel Help button on the Standard toolbar (Figure 7-21). A heavy border surrounds the button with the smiley face image, indicating Excel is in Edit mode.

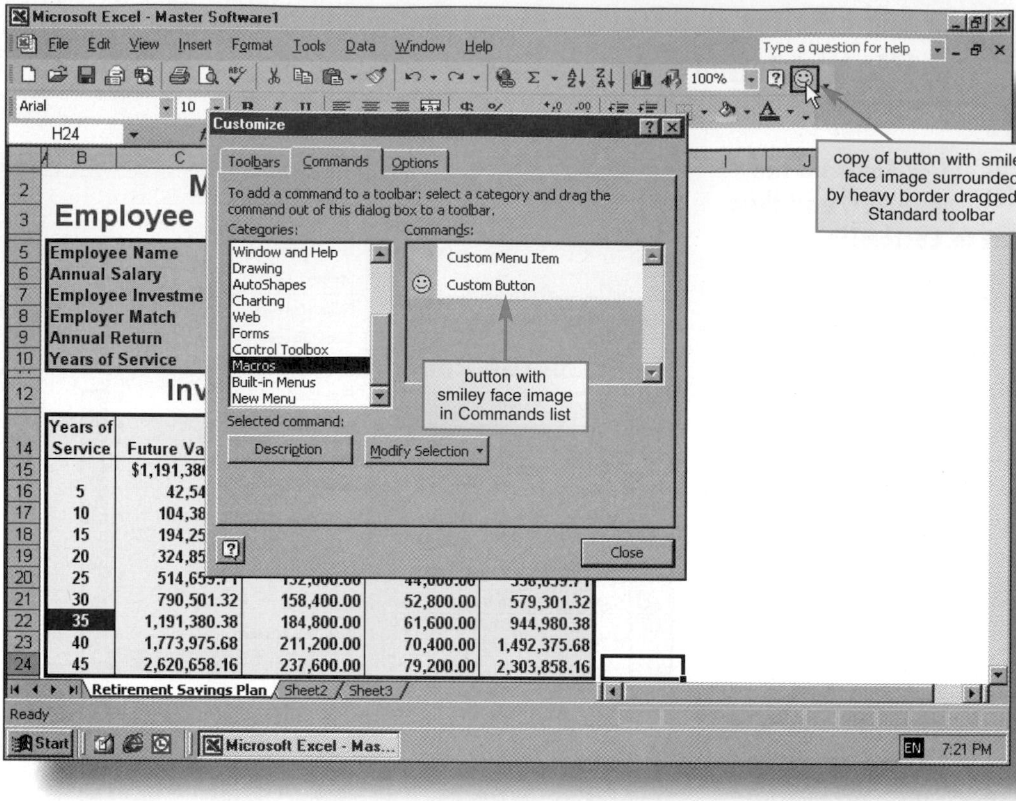

FIGURE 7-21

4 **Right-click the button with the smiley face image on the Standard toolbar. When the shortcut menu displays, type** `Print Portrait` **in the Name text box. Point to Change Button Image on the shortcut menu. When the Change Button Image palette displays, point to the button with the eye image (row 7, column 4).**

Excel displays a palette of button images from which to choose (Figure 7-22).

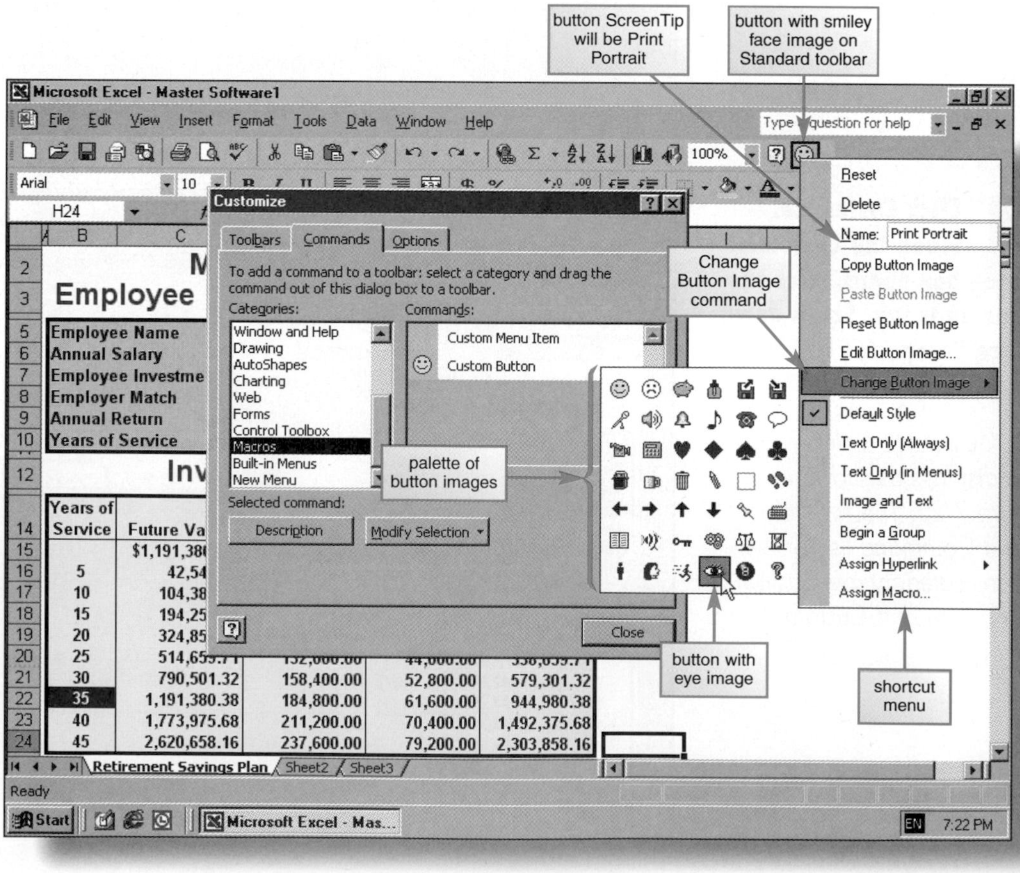

FIGURE 7-22

5 Click the button with the eye image. Right-click the button with the eye image on the Standard toolbar and then point to Assign Macro on the shortcut menu.

Excel replaces the button with the smiley face image on the Standard toolbar with the button with the eye image (Figure 7-23) and the shortcut menu displays.

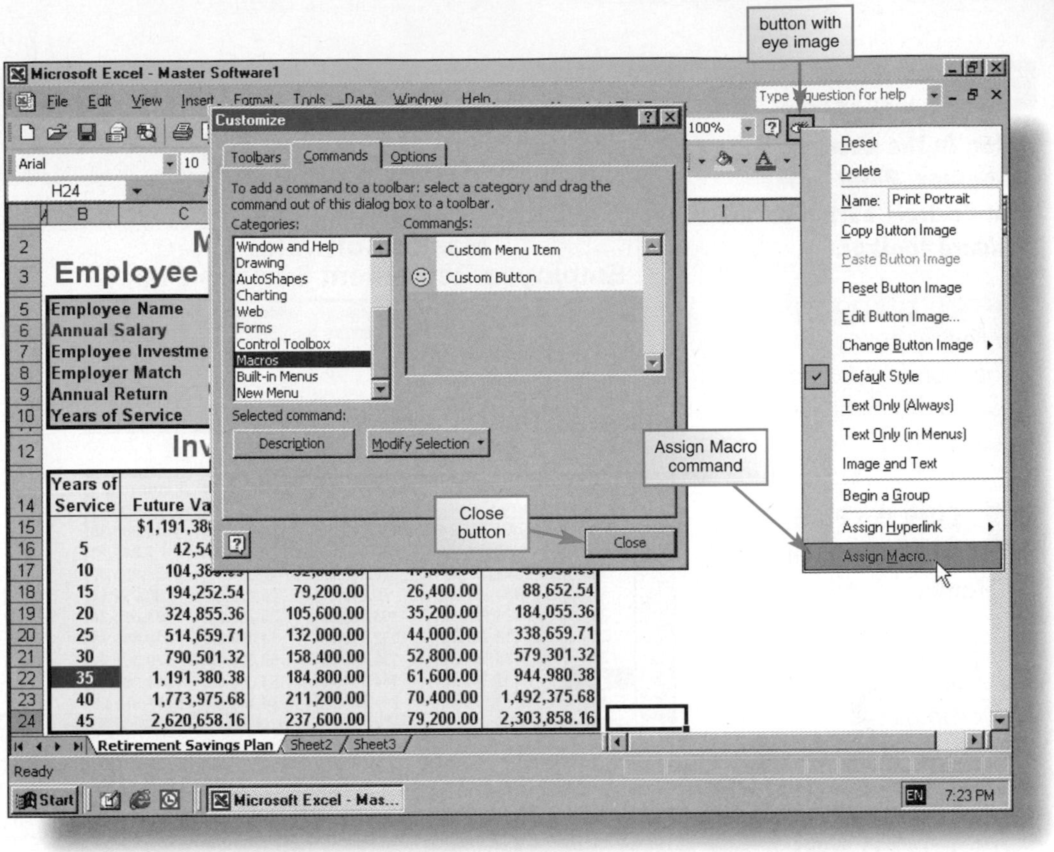

FIGURE 7-23

6 Click Assign Macro on the shortcut menu. When the Assign Macro dialog box displays, click PrintPortrait, and then point to the OK button.

The Assign Macro dialog box displays as shown in Figure 7-24.

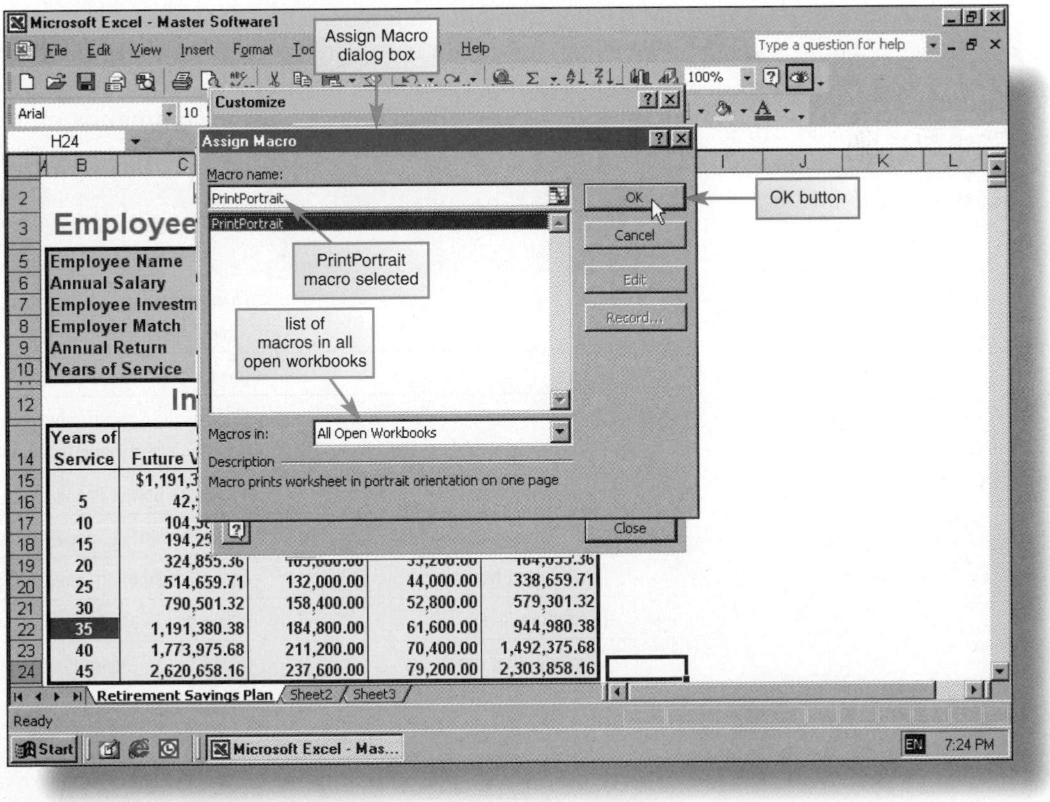

FIGURE 7-24

7 Click the OK button. Click the Close button in the Customize dialog box. Point to the Print Portrait button on the Standard toolbar.

Excel quits Edit mode. The Print Portrait button displays on the Standard toolbar with the ScreenTip, Print Portrait (Figure 7-25).

8 Click the Print Portrait button on the Standard toolbar.

After a few seconds, the worksheet prints in portrait orientation as shown in Figure 7-15 on page E 7.16.

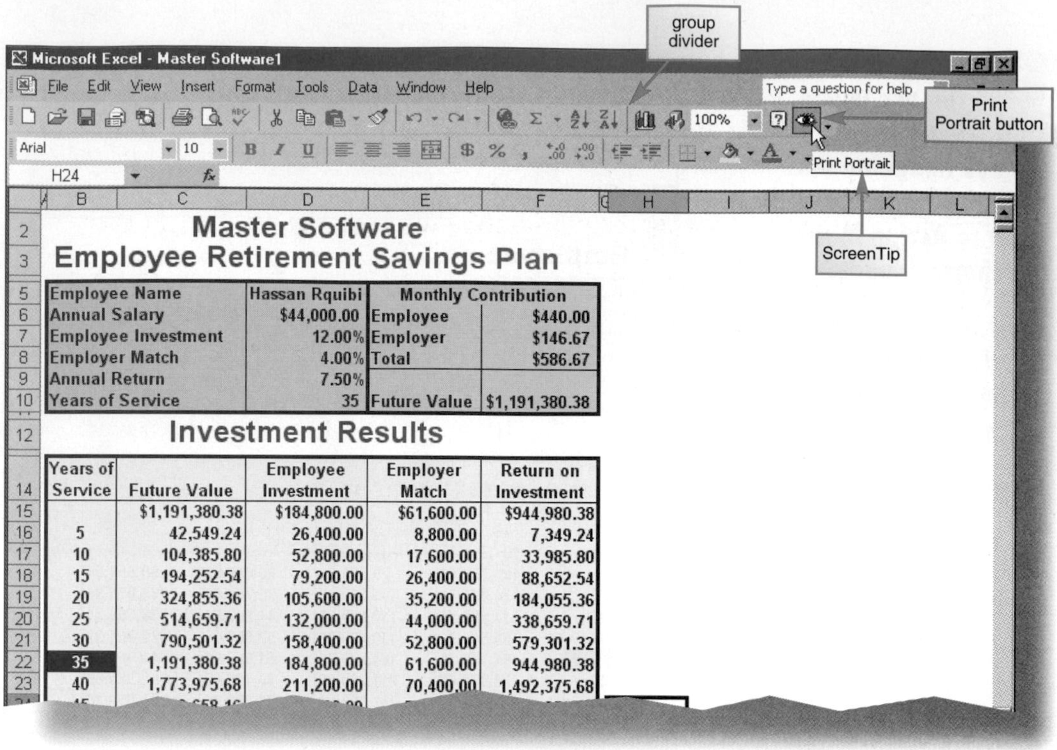

FIGURE 7-25

Other Ways

1. On View menu click Toolbars, click Customize, click Commands tab
2. Right-click toolbar, click Customize on the shortcut menu, click Commands tab
3. Press ALT+V, T, C
4. Click Modify Selection button in Customize dialog box
5. In Voice Command mode, say "Tools, Customize," click the Commands tab

The previous steps illustrate how easy it is in Excel to add a button to a toolbar and assign the button a macro.

Excel includes a complete repertoire of commands for editing buttons on a toolbar as shown on the shortcut menu in Figure 7-23 on the previous page. Table 7-2 briefly describes each of the commands on the shortcut menu.

Table 7-2 Summary of Commands on the Button Shortcut Menu

COMMAND	DESCRIPTION
Reset	Changes the icon on the selected button to the original icon and disassociates the macro with the button
Delete	Deletes the selected button
Name	Changes the ScreenTip for a button and changes the command name for a command on a menu
Copy Button Image	Copies the button image to the Office Clipboard
Paste Button Image	Pastes the button image on the Office Clipboard to the selected button
Reset Button Image	Changes the button image back to the original image
Edit Button Image	Allows you to edit the button image
Change Button Image	Allows you to choose a new button image
Default Style;Text Only (Always); Text Only (in Menus); Image and Text	Allows you to choose one of the four styles to indicate how the button should look
Begin a Group	Groups buttons by drawing a vertical line (divider) on the toolbar (see the group divider line in Figure 7-25)
Assign Hyperlink	Assigns a hyperlink to a Web page or Office document to the button
Assign Macro	Assigns a macro to the button

You can add as many buttons as you want to a toolbar. You also can change the image on any button or change a button's function. For example, when in Edit mode (the Customize dialog box is active) you can right-click the Save button on the Standard toolbar and assign it a macro or hyperlink. The next time you click the Save button, the macro will execute or Excel will launch the application associated with the hyperlink, rather than saving the workbook. You reset the toolbars to their installation default by clicking the Toolbars tab in the Customize dialog box, selecting the toolbar in the Toolbars box, and then clicking the Reset button. Because it is so easy to change the buttons on a toolbar, each project in this book begins by resetting the toolbars.

As you add buttons, other buttons on the toolbar will be demoted to the More Buttons box.

More About

Creating Toolbars

You can create new toolbars and add buttons to it, rather than adding buttons to current toolbars. To create a new toolbar, click the Toolbars tab in the Customize dialog box and then click the New button. You can display the Customize dialog box by right clicking any menu, and then clicking Customize.

CUSTOMIZING A MENU Up to this point, you have been introduced to using a shortcut key and button to execute a macro. Excel also allows you to add commands to a menu. The following steps show how to add a command to the File menu to execute the PrintPortrait macro.

Steps To Add a Command to a Menu, Assign the Command a Macro, and Invoke the Command

1 Click Tools on the menu bar, and then click Customize. When the Customize dialog box displays, if necessary, click the Commands tab. Scroll down in the Categories box and then click Macros. Click File on the menu bar to display the File menu.

The Customize dialog box and File menu display as shown in Figure 7-26.

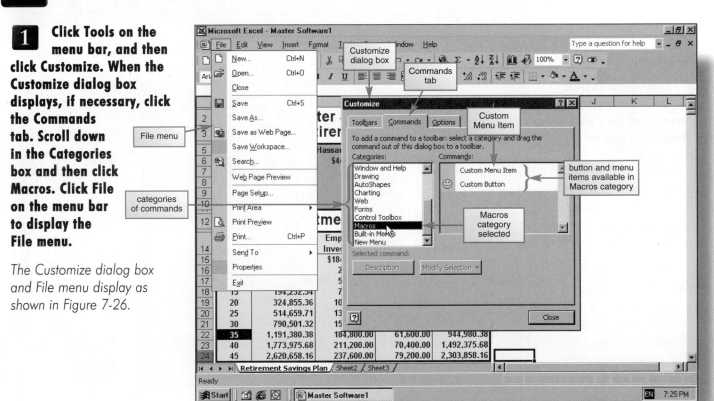

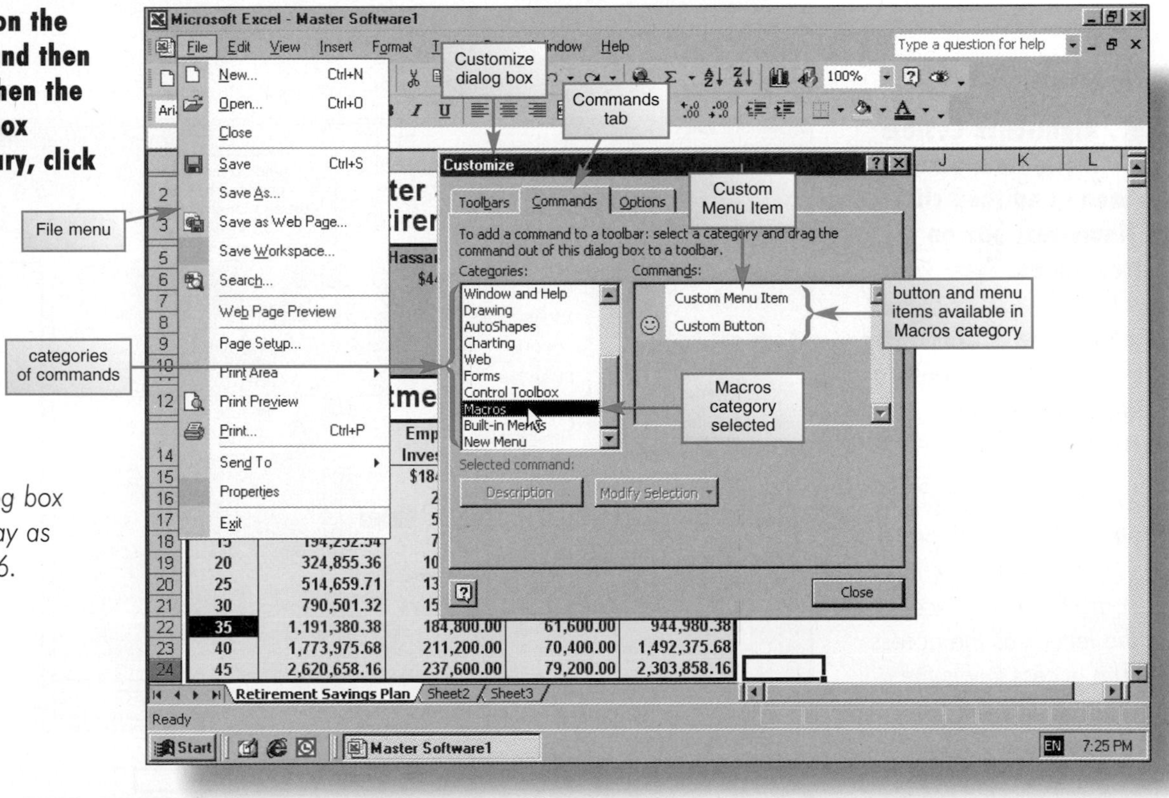

FIGURE 7-26

2 **Drag the Custom Menu Item entry from the Commands list in the Customize dialog box immediately below the Print command on the File menu.**

Excel adds Custom Menu Item to the File menu (Figure 7-27). A heavy border surrounds Custom Menu Item on the File menu, indicating it is in the Edit mode.

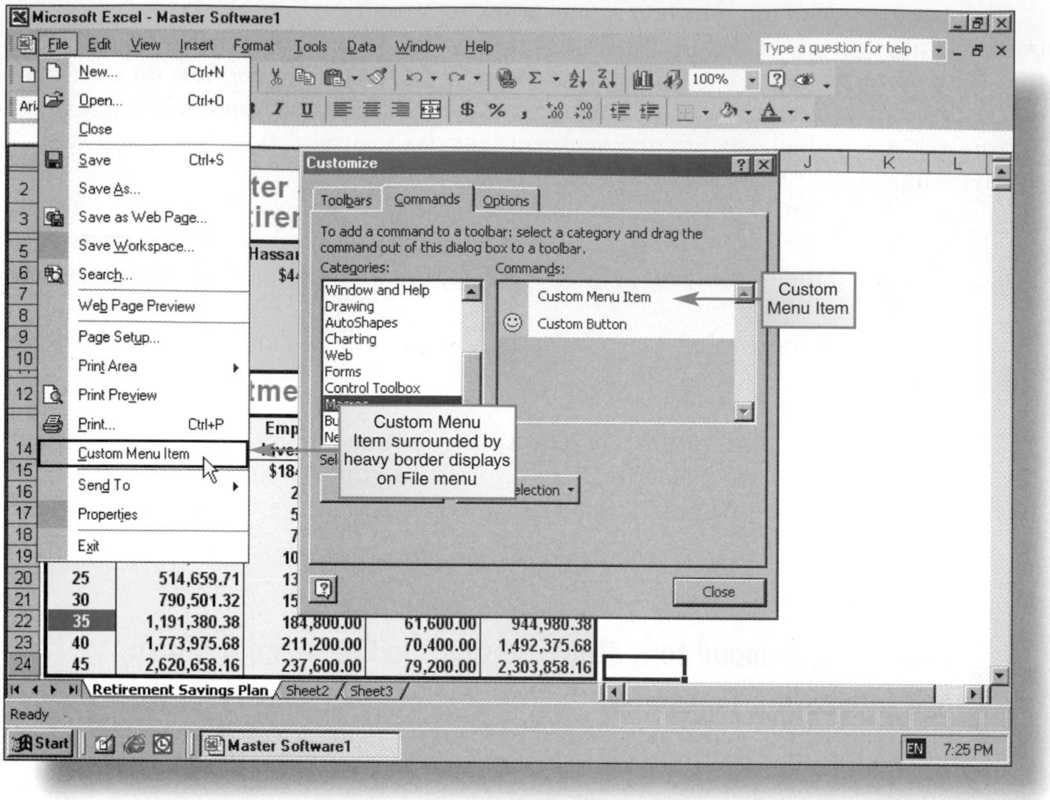

FIGURE 7-27

3 **Right-click Custom Menu Item on the File menu and then click the Name text box on the shortcut menu. Type** `Print Po&rtrait Ctrl+R` **as the new name of this entry on the File menu. Point to Assign Macro on the shortcut menu.**

The shortcut menu displays (Figure 7-28). The ampersand (&) preceding the letter r in Portrait instructs Excel to use the letter r as the access key. The access key is the underlined letter that you can press to invoke the command when the menu displays.

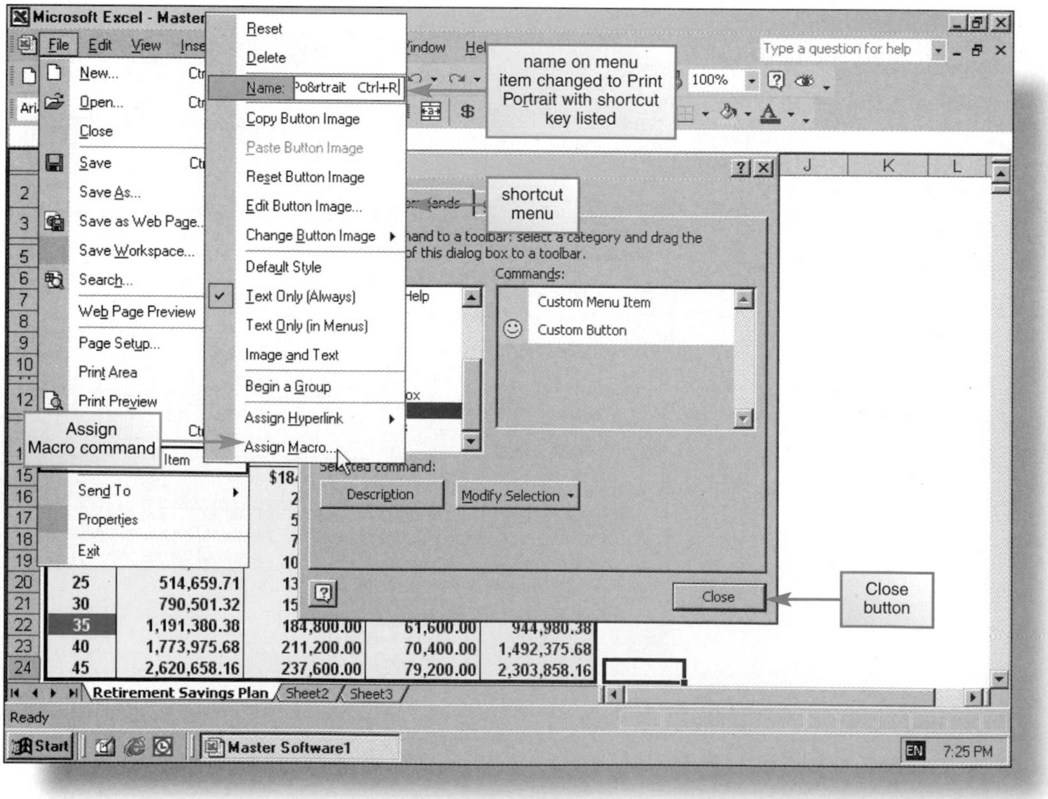

FIGURE 7-28

4 **Click Assign Macro on the shortcut menu. When the Assign Macro dialog box displays, double-click PrintPortrait. Click the Close button at the bottom of the Customize dialog box. Click File on the menu bar and then point to Print Portrait.**

Excel exits Edit mode. The File menu displays with the new command Print Portrait on the menu (Figure 7-29). The underlined letter r in Portrait is the access key.

5 **Click Print Portrait on the File menu.**

After several seconds, the worksheet prints in portrait orientation as shown in Figure 7-15 on page E 7.16.

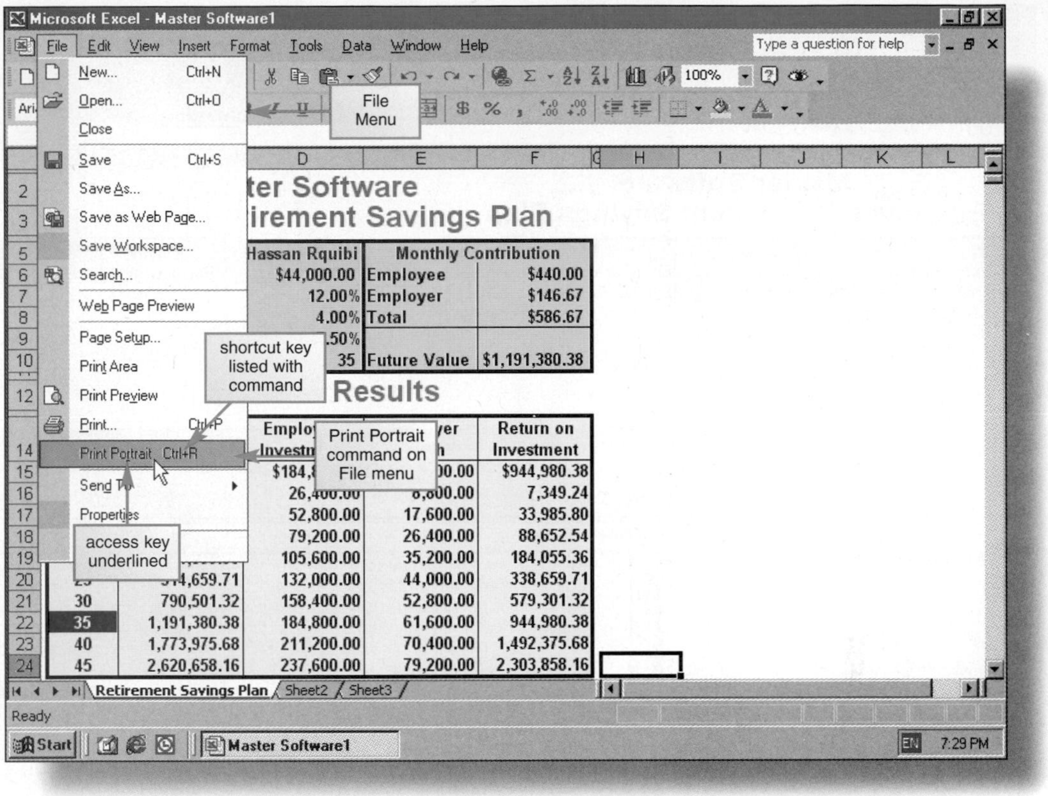

FIGURE 7-29

6 **Click the Save button on the Standard toolbar to save the workbook using the file name Master Software1.**

You have the same customization capabilities with menus as you do with toolbars. All of the shortcut commands described in Table 7-2 on page E 7.22 apply to menus as well. The commands specific to buttons pertain to editing the button image on the left side of a command on a menu.

An alternative to adding a command to a menu is to add a new menu name to the menu bar and add commands to its menu. You can add a new menu name to the menu bar by selecting New Menu in the Categories list of the Customize dialog box (Figure 7-27) and dragging it to the menu bar.

Phase 2 — Creating a Procedure to Automate the Retirement Savings Plan Data Entry

Earlier in this project on page E 7.08, the data for Julia Hin was entered to calculate new future value information. A novice user, however, might not know what cells to select or how much retirement savings plan data is required to obtain the desired results. To facilitate entering the savings plan data, Phase 2 calls for creating a Command Button control (Figure 7-30a on the next page) and an associated procedure (Figure 7-30b on the next page) that steps the user through entering the data using dialog boxes.

Other Ways

1. On View menu click Toolbars, click Customize, click Commands tab
2. Right-click toolbar, click Customize, click Commands tab
3. In Voice Command mode, say "Tools, Customize," click the Commands tab

More About

Creating New Menus

You can create an entire new menu on the menu bar by dragging New Menu from the Categories box in the Customize dialog box to the menu bar. You can then add new commands to the new menu using the procedure described in the previous set of steps. You can display the Customize dialog box by right clicking any menu, and then clicking Customize.

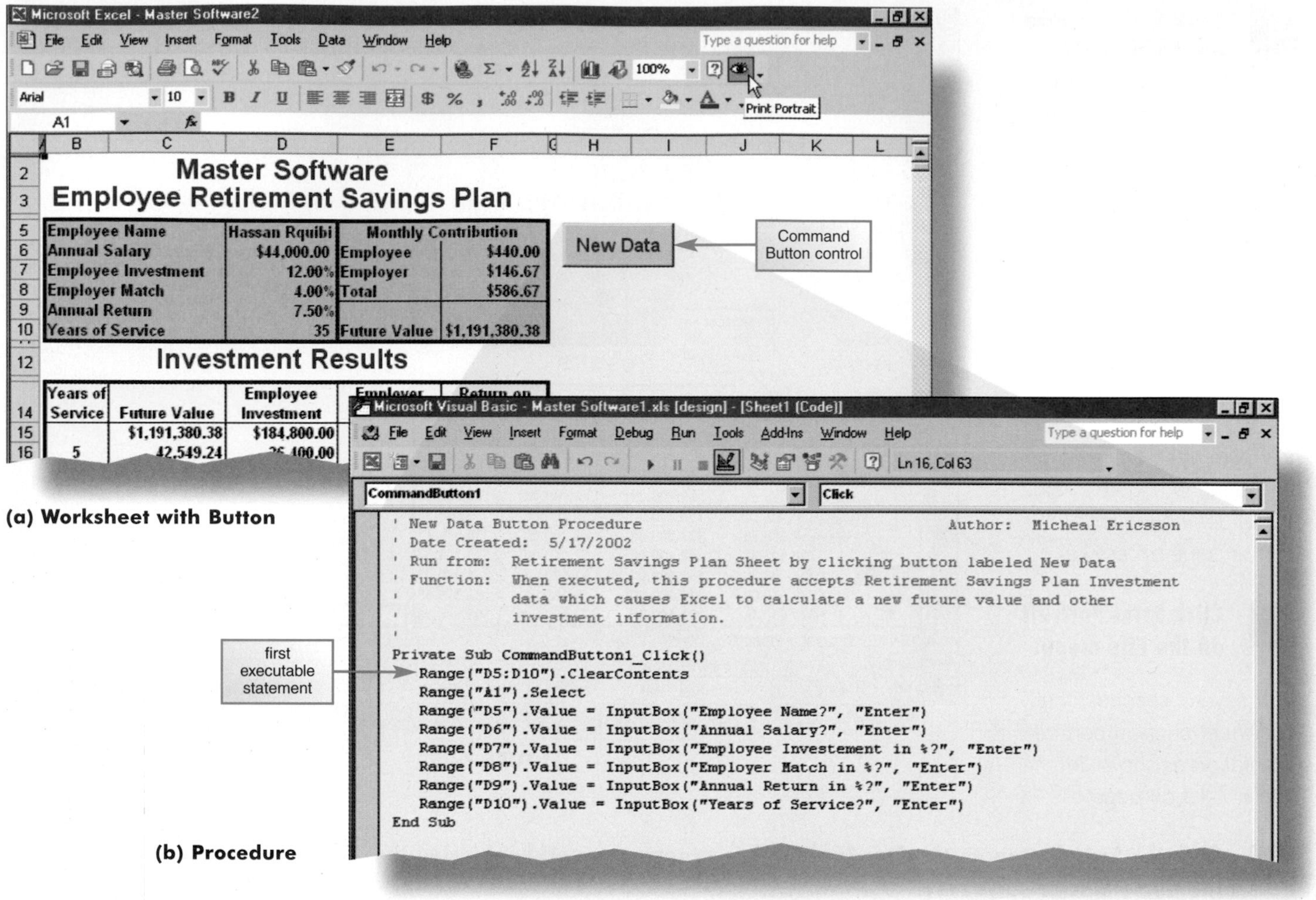
Microsoft Excel - Master Software2
Print Portrait
Master Software
Employee Retirement Savings Plan
Employee Name
Hassan Rquibi
Monthly Contribution
Annual Salary
$44,000.00
Employee
$440.00
Employee Investment
12.00%
Employer
$146.67
Employer Match
4.00%
Total
$586.67
Annual Return
7.50%
Years of Service
35
Future Value
$1,191,380.38
Investment Results
New Data
Command Button control
(a) Worksheet with Button
Microsoft Visual Basic - Master Software1.xls [design] - [Sheet1 (Code)]
CommandButton1
Click
' New Data Button Procedure   Author: Micheal Ericsson
' Date Created: 5/17/2002
' Run from: Retirement Savings Plan Sheet by clicking button labeled New Data
' Function: When executed, this procedure accepts Retirement Savings Plan Investment
' data which causes Excel to calculate a new future value and other
' investment information.
Private Sub CommandButton1_Click()
Range("D5:D10").ClearContents
Range("A1").Select
Range("D5").Value = InputBox("Employee Name?", "Enter")
Range("D6").Value = InputBox("Annual Salary?", "Enter")
Range("D7").Value = InputBox("Employee Investement in %?", "Enter")
Range("D8").Value = InputBox("Employer Match in %?", "Enter")
Range("D9").Value = InputBox("Annual Return in %?", "Enter")
Range("D10").Value = InputBox("Years of Service?", "Enter")
End Sub
first executable statement
(b) Procedure

FIGURE 7-30

> **More About**
>
> **Visual Basic for Applications**
>
> All of the applications in Office XP (Word, Excel, Access, and PowerPoint) use Visual Basic for Applications. Thus, what you learn in this project applies to the other applications as well. Today, Visual Basic for Applications is the most widely used Windows applications programming language.

A **Command Button control** is different from a toolbar button in that it is an object you draw on the worksheet. Once you trigger the event by clicking the Command Button control, the instructions in the associated procedure guide the user through entering the required savings plan data in the range D5:D10. The Command Button control also is the user interface. The **user interface** can be as simple as a button and as complex as a series of windows that accept data and display results. The user interface, together with the procedure, is called an **application**. Thus, the name Visual Basic for Applications.

If you step through the procedure (Figure 7-30b) beginning at the line just below Private Sub CommandButton1_Click(), you can see how a procedure methodically steps the user through entering the data in the range D5:D10.

1. The first line clears the range D5:D10.
2. The second line selects cell A1.
3. Lines three through eight accept data for the cells in the range D5:D10, one cell at a time.

Applications are built using the three-step process shown in Figure 7-31: (1) create the user interface; (2) set the properties; and (3) write the VBA code. Before you can create the user interface, the Retirement Savings Plan worksheet in the Master Software1 workbook must be unprotected. The following steps unprotect the worksheet.

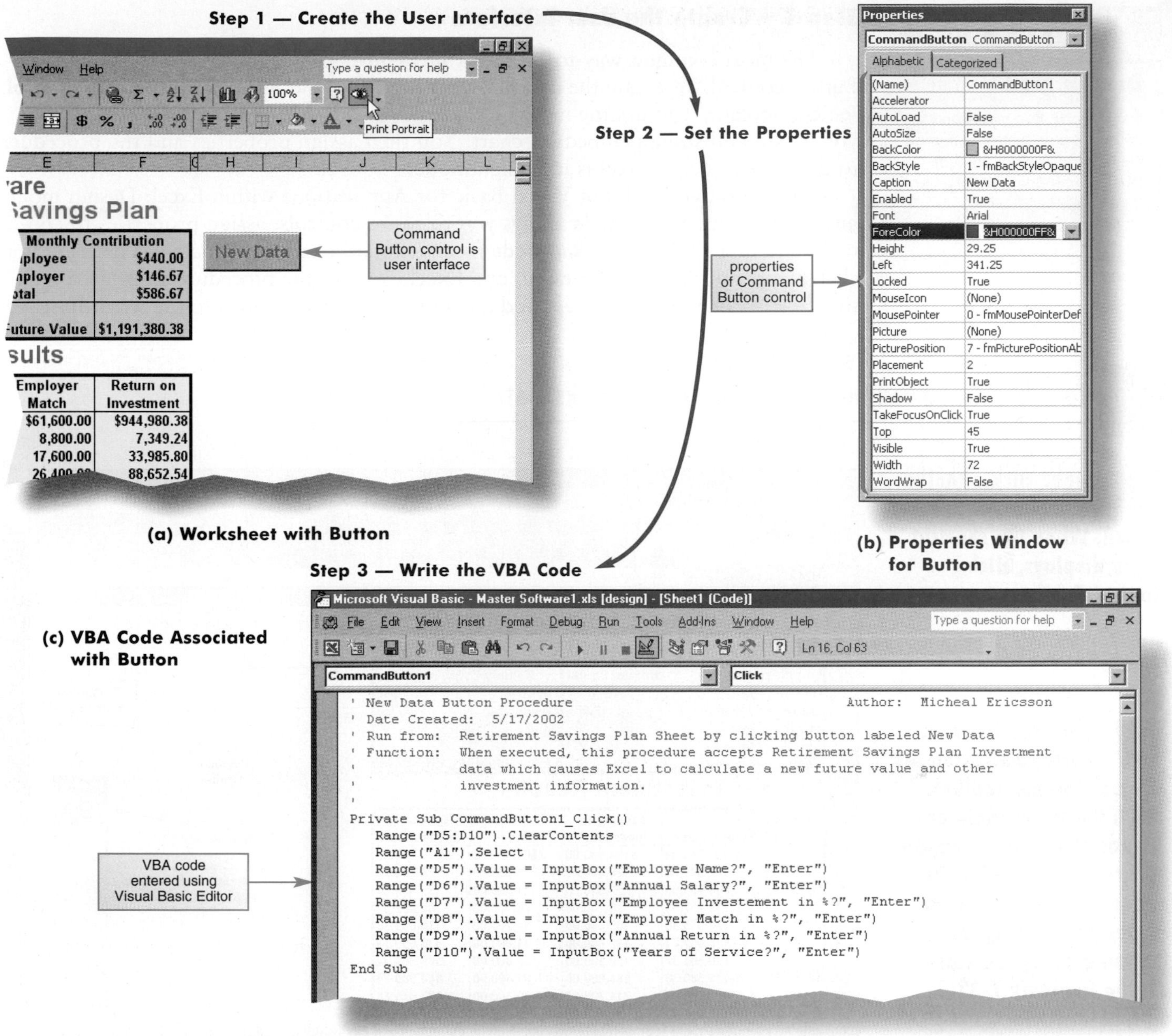

FIGURE 7-31

TO UNPROTECT A PASSWORD-PROTECTED WORKSHEET

1. With the Master Software1 workbook open, click Tools on the menu bar, point to Protection, and then click Unprotect Sheet on the Protection submenu.
2. When the Unprotect Sheet dialog box displays, type `planright` as the password and then click the OK button.

Excel unprotects the worksheet and toolbar buttons become active.

More About

Earlier Excel Version Macros

Some earlier versions of Excel use a language called XLM, rather than VBA, for its macros. Excel 2002 supports both languages. That is, you can execute macros created using XLM. Excel 2002, however, will not allow you to create macros in XLM.

More About

Design Mode

If Excel is in Run mode and you click any control button on the Control Toolbox toolbar, Excel immediately switches to Design mode.

Step 1 – Create the User Interface

The most common way to execute a procedure in Excel is to create a Command Button control. To create the control, click the **Command Button button** on the **Control Toolbox toolbar**. You use the mouse to locate and size the control in the same way you locate and size an embedded chart. You then assign properties and the procedure to the control while Excel is in Design mode.

There are two modes of Visual Basic for Applications within Excel: Design mode and Run mode. **Design mode** allows you to resize controls, assign properties to controls, and enter VBA code. **Run mode** means that all controls are active. That is, if you click a control it triggers the event, and Excel executes the procedure associated with the control. The following steps add a Command Button control to the worksheet.

Steps To Add a Command Button Control to the Worksheet

1 Right-click a toolbar at the top of the screen. When the shortcut menu displays, click Control Toolbox.

The Control Toolbox toolbar displays.

2 Click the Command Button button on the Control Toolbox toolbar. Move the mouse pointer (a cross hair) to the upper-left corner of cell H5. Drag the mouse pointer so the rectangle defining the button area appears as shown in Figure 7-32 and hold.

A light border surrounds the proposed button area in the worksheet (Figure 7-32). When you click the Command Button button, Excel automatically switches to Design mode.

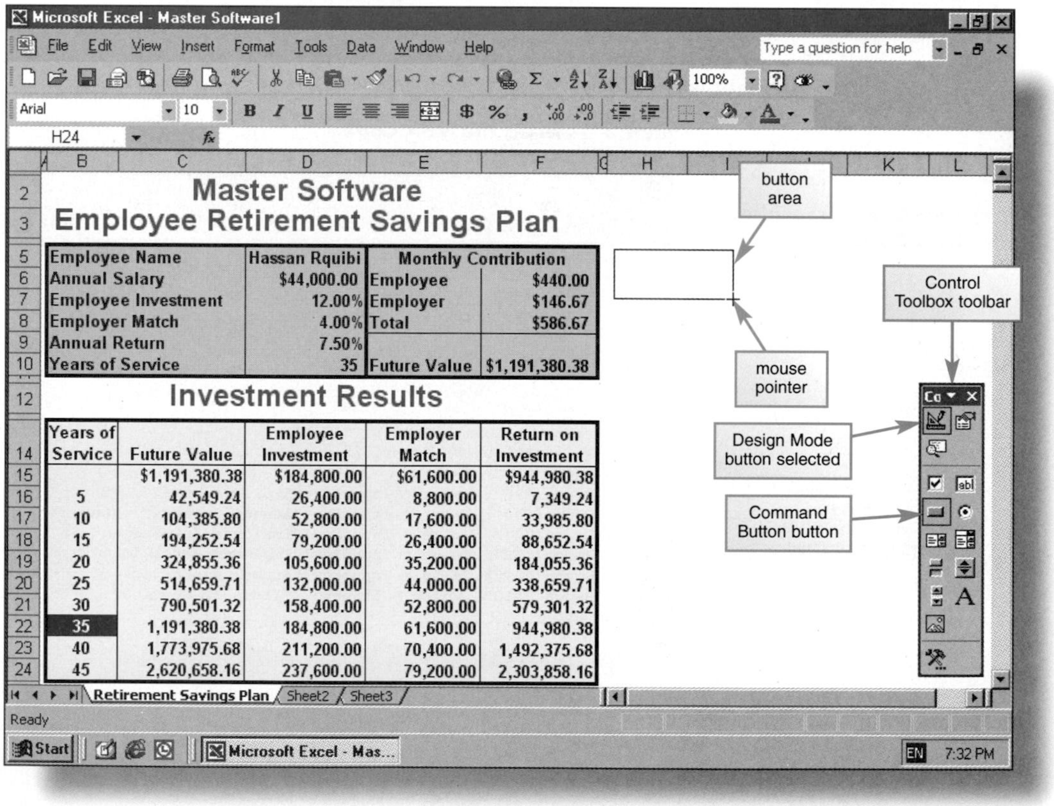

FIGURE 7-32

3 Release the left mouse button.

Excel displays the button with the default caption CommandButton1 (Figure 7-33). Because Excel is in Design mode and the button is selected, the button is surrounded by sizing handles.

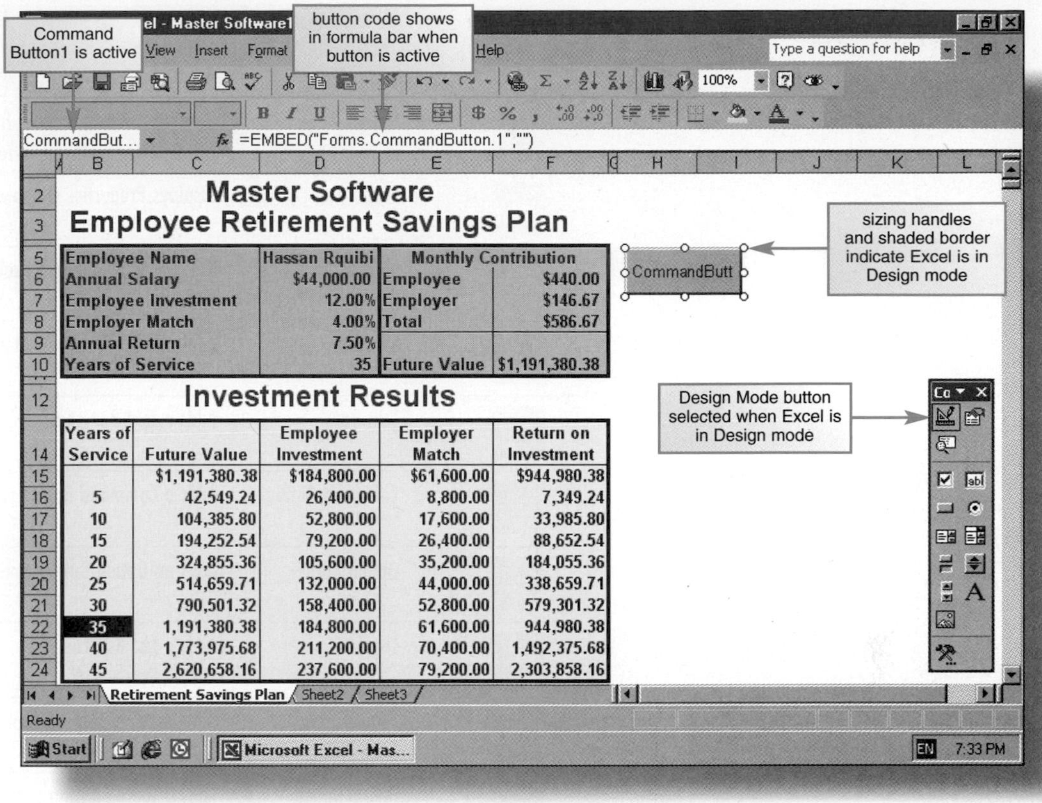

FIGURE 7-33

Other Ways

1. Click Design Mode button on Visual Basic toolbar

The Control Toolbox toolbar buttons are summarized in Table 7-3 on the next page. Many of the buttons allow you to add controls to the worksheet that you have worked with previously in Excel, such as check boxes, list boxes, and scroll bars.

Another toolbar that may be helpful as you use Visual Basic for Applications is the **Visual Basic toolbar**. The Visual Basic toolbar is shown in Figure 7-34. You can display the Visual Basic toolbar by right-clicking a toolbar and then clicking Visual Basic on the shortcut menu.

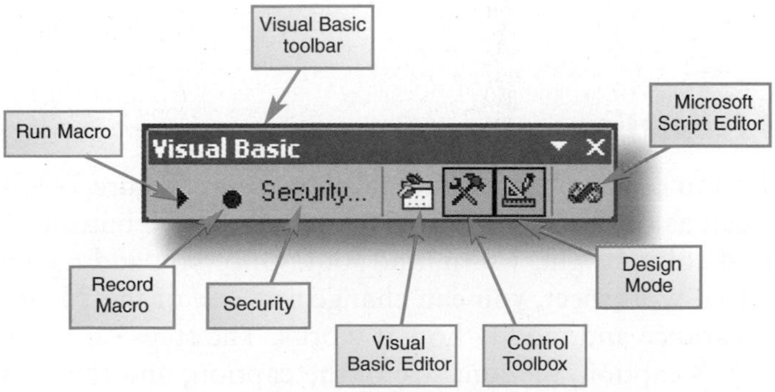

FIGURE 7-34

More About

The User Interface

You can use graphics, such as clip art, rather than a Command Button button to serve as the control that you click to trigger the event.

Table 7-3 Summary of Buttons on the Control Toolbox Toolbar

BUTTON	NAME	FUNCTION
	Design Mode	Changes to design mode; Design Mode button changes to Exit Design Mode button when in design mode
	Properties	Displays Properties window
	View Code	Displays VBA code in Visual Basic Editor
	Check Box	Adds a Check Box control
	Text Box	Adds a Text Box control
	Command Button	Adds a Command Button control
	Option Button	Adds an Option Button control
	List Box	Adds a List Box control
	Combo Box	Adds a Combo Box control
	Toggle Button	Adds a Toggle Button control
	Spin Button	Adds a Spin Button control
	Scroll Bar	Adds a Scroll Bar control
	Label	Adds a Label control
	Image	Adds an Image control
	More Controls	Displays a list of additional controls

More About

More Controls

The last button described in Table 7-3 is the More Controls button. If you click this button, nearly 200 additional controls, similar to those in Table 7-3, are available to incorporate in a user interface. The controls will vary depending on the software that is installed on your computer.

Step 2 – Set Properties

A Command Button control has 25 different **properties** (Figure 7-31b on page E 7.27), such as caption (the words on the face of the button), background color, foreground color, height, width, and font. Once you add a Command Button control to a worksheet, you can change any one of the 25 properties to improve its appearance and modify how it works. The steps on the next page change the button's caption, the font size of the caption, and the color of the caption.

Steps To Set the Command Button Control Properties

1 **With the Command Button control selected and Excel in Design mode, click the Properties button on the Control Toolbox toolbar. When the Properties window displays, if necessary, click the Alphabetic tab, click Caption, and then type** `New Data` **as the caption. Click ForeColor, click the ForeColor arrow, click the Palette tab, and then point to the color red (column 2, row 3).**

Excel displays the Properties window for the Command Button control (Figure 7-35). The Caption property is New Data and the ForeColor Palette sheet displays.

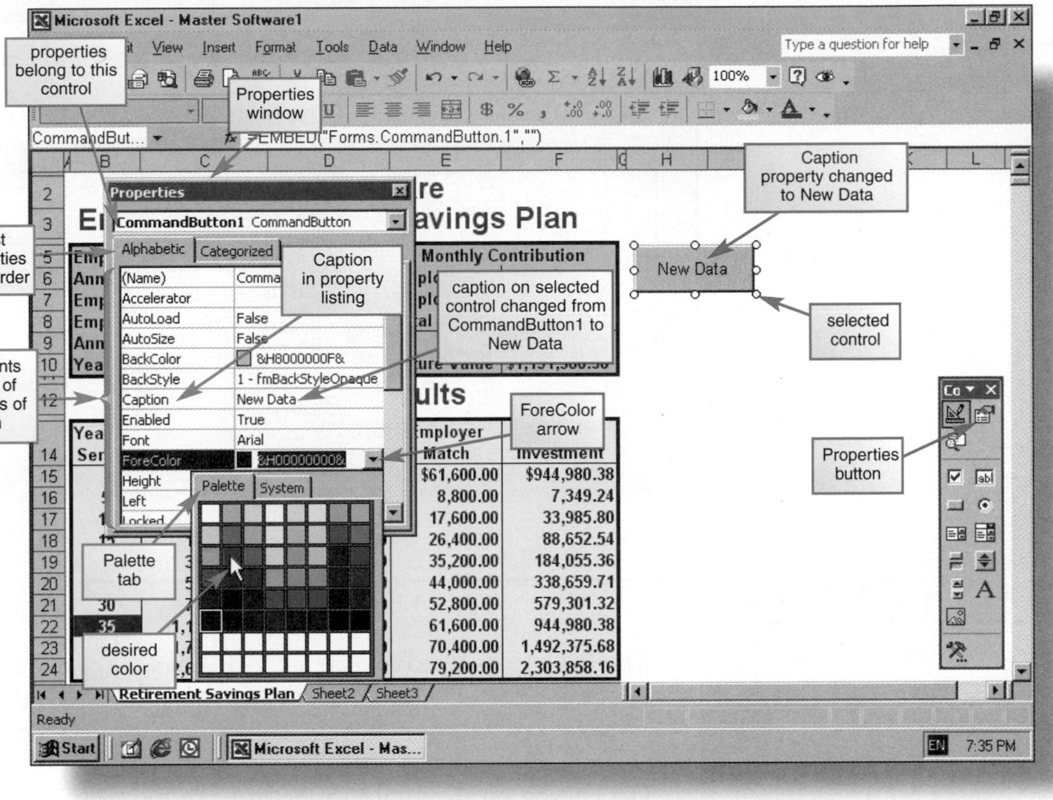

FIGURE 7-35

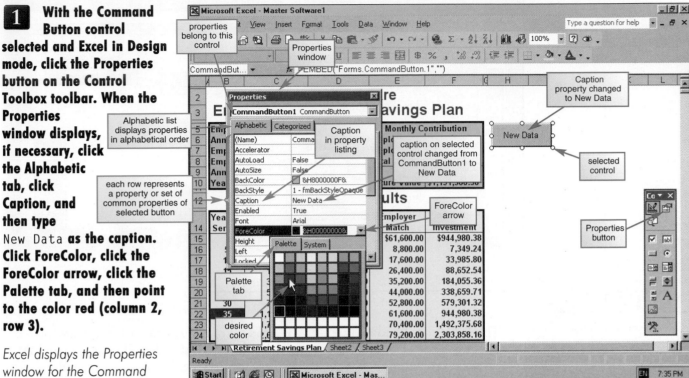

2 **Click red on the color palette. Click Font in the Properties window and then click the Font button. When the Font dialog box displays, click Bold in the Font style list and 12 in the Size list. Point to the OK button.**

The Properties window and Font dialog box display as shown in Figure 7-36.

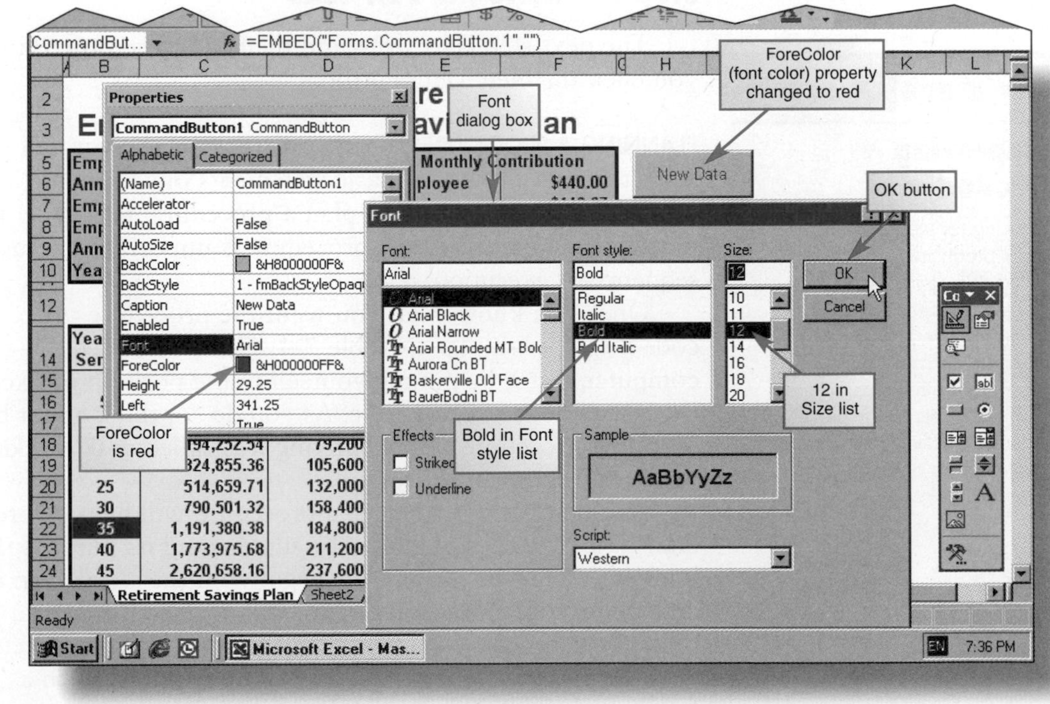

FIGURE 7-36

3 **Click the OK button.**

The Command Button control and its Properties window display as shown in Figure 7-37.

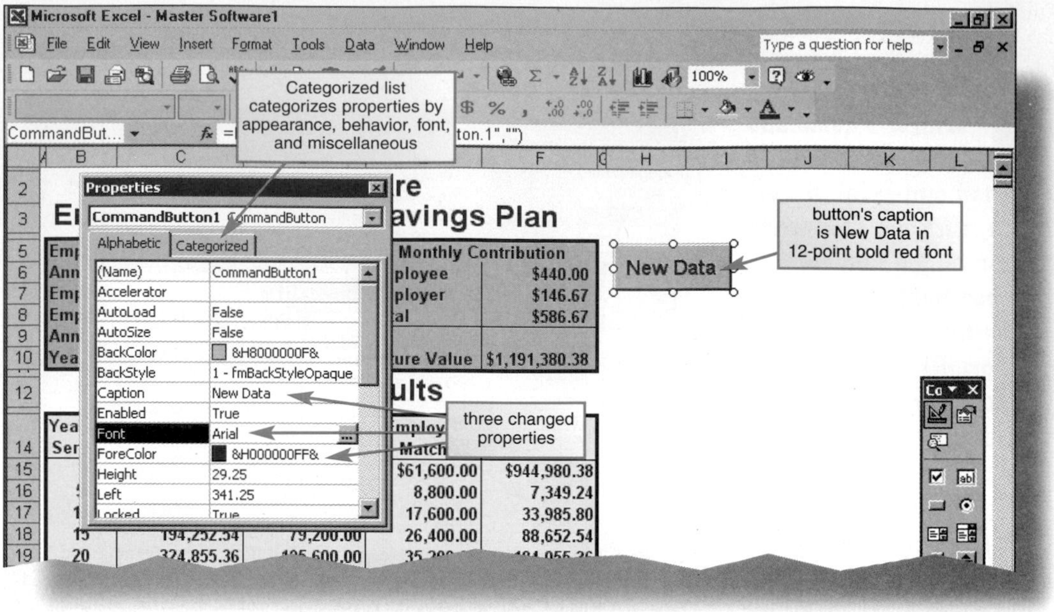

FIGURE 7-37

Other Ways

1. Click Properties Window button on toolbar when Visual Basic Editor is active
2. In Design mode, right-click control, click Properties on shortcut menu
3. In Design mode, right-click control, in Voice Command mode, say "Properties"

The Properties window (Figure 7-37) has two tabs, Alphabetic and Categorized. The **Alphabetic list** displays the properties in alphabetical order. The **Categorized list** displays the properties in categories, such as appearance, behavior, font, and miscellaneous.

Depending on the application, you can modify any one of the Command Button control properties shown in Figure 7-35 on the previous page, much like you changed the Caption and Font properties in the previous steps.

Step 3 – Write the VBA Code

The next step is to write and then enter the procedure that will execute when you click the New Data button.

PLANNING A PROCEDURE When you trigger the event that executes a procedure, Excel steps through the Visual Basic statements one at a time, beginning at the top of the procedure. Thus, when you plan a procedure, remember that the order in which you place the statements in the procedure is important because the order determines the sequence of execution.

Once you know what you want the procedure to accomplish, write the VBA code on paper similar to Table 7-4. Then, before entering the procedure into the computer, test it by putting yourself in the position of Excel and stepping through the instructions one at a time. As you do so, think about how it affects the worksheet. Testing a procedure before entering it is called **desk checking** and is an important part of the development process.

Adding comments before a procedure will help you remember its purpose at a later date or help somebody else understand its purpose. In Table 7-4, the first seven lines are comments. **Comments** begin with the word Rem or an apostrophe ('). These comments contain overall documentation and are placed before the procedure, above the Sub statement. Comments have no effect on the execution of a procedure; they simply provide information about the procedure, such as name, creation date, and function. Comments also can be placed in between lines of code or at the end of a line of code as long as the comment begins with an apostrophe (').

More About

Improving Productivity

Looking for ways to improve your productivity? If you find yourself entering the same series of Excel commands over and over, you can use the macro recorder or VBA to complete the steps automatically. This can improve your productivity by eliminating routine tasks and simplifying complex tasks.

Table 7-4 New Data Button Procedure

LINE *VBA CODE*

```
1   ' New Data Button Procedure                           Author:  Micheal Ericsson
2   ' Date Created:  5/17/2002
3   ' Run from:                 Retirement Savings Plan Sheet by clicking button labeled New Data
4   ' Function:                 When executed, this procedure accepts Retirement Savings Plan
5   '                           Investment data which causes Excel to calculate a new future
6   '                           value and other investment information.
7   '
8   Private Sub CommandButton1_Click()
9      Range("D5:D10").ClearContents
10     Range("A1").Select
11     Range("D5").Value = InputBox("Employee Name?", "Enter")
12     Range("D6").Value = InputBox("Annual Salary?", "Enter")
13     Range("D7").Value = InputBox("Employee Investment in %?”, "Enter")
14     Range(“D8").Value = InputBox("Employer Match in %?", "Enter")
15     Range("D9").Value = InputBox("Annual Return in %?", "Enter")
16     Range("D10").Value = InputBox(“Years of Service?", "Enter")
17  End Sub
```

A procedure begins with a Sub statement and ends with an End Sub statement (lines 8 and 17 in Table 7-4). The **Sub statement** includes the keyword Private or Public followed by the name of the procedure, which Excel determines from the name of the button (CommandButton1), and the event that causes the procedure to execute (Click). **Private** means that the procedure can be executed only from this workbook. **Public** means that it can be executed from other workbooks or programs. Thus, the name of the Command Button control procedure is CommandButton1_Click.

The parentheses following the keyword Click in the Sub statement in line 8 are required. They indicate that arguments can be passed from one procedure to another. Passing arguments is beyond the scope of this project, but the parentheses still are required. The **End Sub statement** signifies the end of the procedure and returns Excel to Ready mode.

The first executable statement in Table 7-4 is line 9, which clears the cells in the range D5:D10. Line 10 selects cell A1 to remove clutter from the screen. One at a time, lines 11 through 16 accept data from the user and assign the data to the cells in the range D5:D10. Each one of the six statements handles one cell each. To the right of the equal sign in lines 11 through 16 is the InputBox function. A **function** returns a value to the program. In this case, the InputBox function displays a dialog box and returns the value entered by the user. For example, in line 11 the InputBox function displays a dialog box with the message, "Employee Name?" When the user responds and enters a name, the InputBox function returns the value entered to the program and assigns it to cell D5.

To enter a procedure, you use the Visual Basic Editor. To activate the Visual Basic Editor, Excel must be in Design mode. With the control selected, you click the **View Code button** on the Control Toolbox toolbar.

The **Visual Basic Editor** is a full-screen editor, which allows you to enter a procedure by typing the lines of VBA code as if you were using word processing software. At the end of a line, you press the ENTER key or use the DOWN ARROW key to move to the next line. If you make a mistake in a statement, you can use the arrow keys and the DELETE or BACKSPACE key to correct it. You also can move the insertion point to previous lines to make corrections.

More About

Entering VBA Comments

If a horizontal line displays between the comment and Sub Statement, press the ENTER key after the last comment to begin a new line. Then press the DELETE key to delete the horizontal line.

USING THE VISUAL BASIC EDITOR TO ENTER A PROCEDURE The following steps activate the Visual Basic Editor and create the procedure for the New Data button.

Steps To Enter the New Data Button Procedure

1 With Excel in Design mode and the New Data button selected, point to the View Code button on the Control Toolbox toolbar.

The selected New Data button and Control Toolbox toolbar display as shown in Figure 7-38.

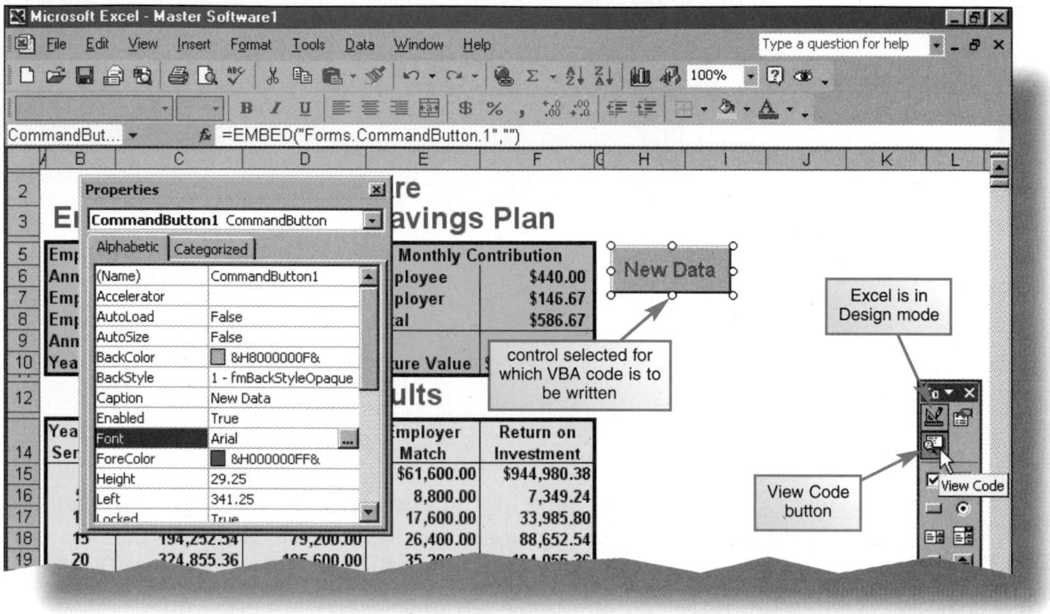

FIGURE 7-38

2 Click the View Code button. When the Visual Basic Editor starts, if the Project Explorer window displays on the left, click its Close button. Double-click the title bar to maximize the window on the right.

Excel starts the Visual Basic Editor and opens the Microsoft Visual Basic window (Figure 7-39). The Visual Basic Editor automatically inserts the Sub and End Sub statements and positions the insertion point between the two statements as shown.

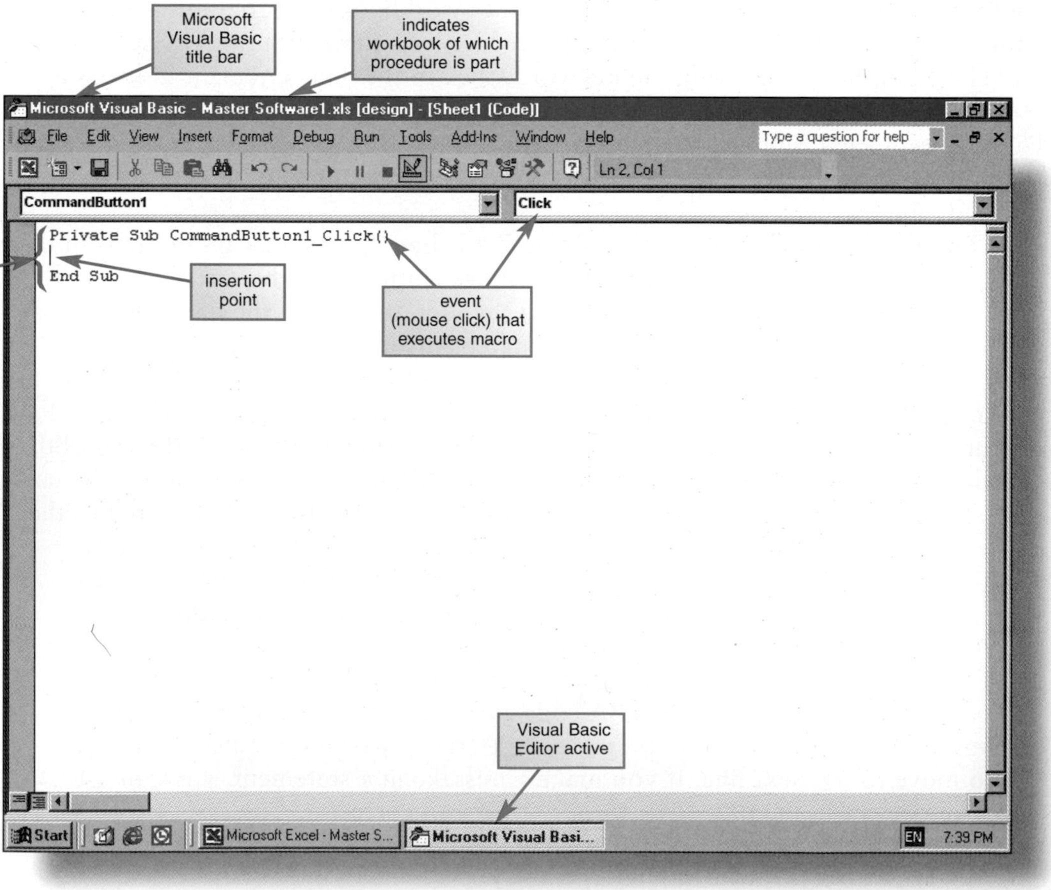

FIGURE 7-39

3 **Click to the left of the letter P in the word Private on the first line and press the ENTER key to add a blank line before the Sub statement. Move the insertion point to the blank line and then type the seven comment statements (lines 1 through 7) in Table 7-4 on page E 7.33. Make sure you enter an apostrophe (') at the beginning of each comment line.**

Excel automatically displays the comment lines in green (Figure 7-40).

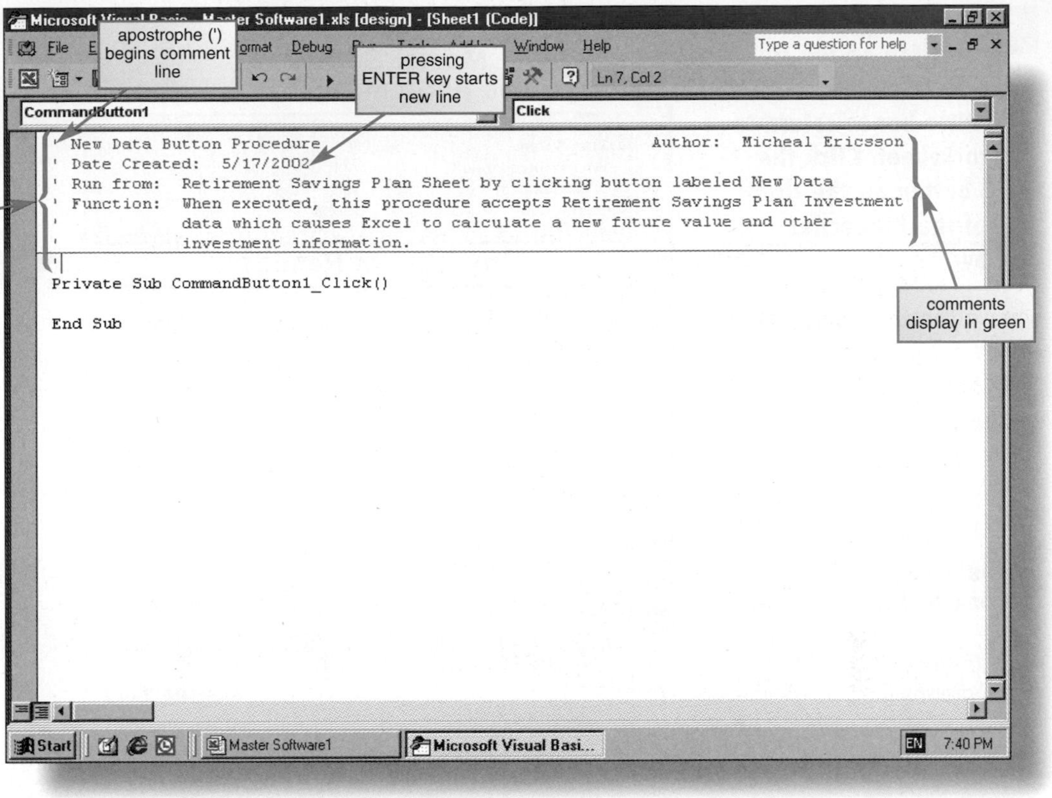
Microsoft Visual Basic - Master Software1.xls [design] - [Sheet1 (Code)]
apostrophe (') begins comment line
pressing ENTER key starts new line
comment lines
comments display in green
Ln 7, Col 2
CommandButton1
Click
' New Data Button Procedure   Author: Micheal Ericsson
' Date Created: 5/17/2002
' Run from: Retirement Savings Plan Sheet by clicking button labeled New Data
' Function: When executed, this procedure accepts Retirement Savings Plan Investment
'   data which causes Excel to calculate a new future value and other
'   investment information.
'
Private Sub CommandButton1_Click()
End Sub

FIGURE 7-40

4 **Position the insertion point on the blank line between the Sub and End Sub statements. Enter lines 9 through 16 in Table 7-4 on page E 7.33. For clarity, indent all lines between the Sub statement and End Sub statement by three spaces.**

The Command Button control procedure is complete (Figure 7-41).

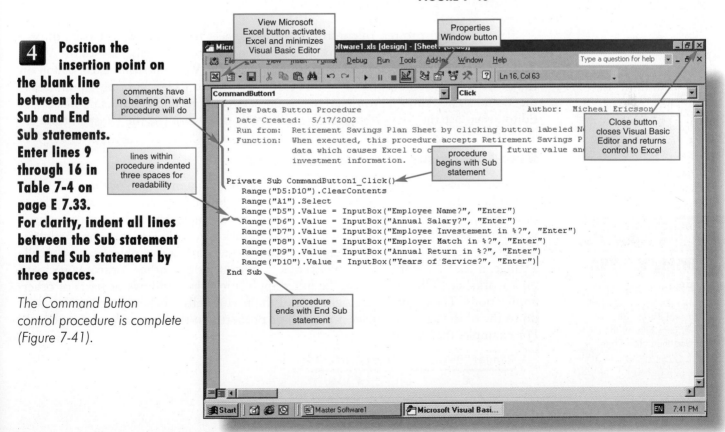

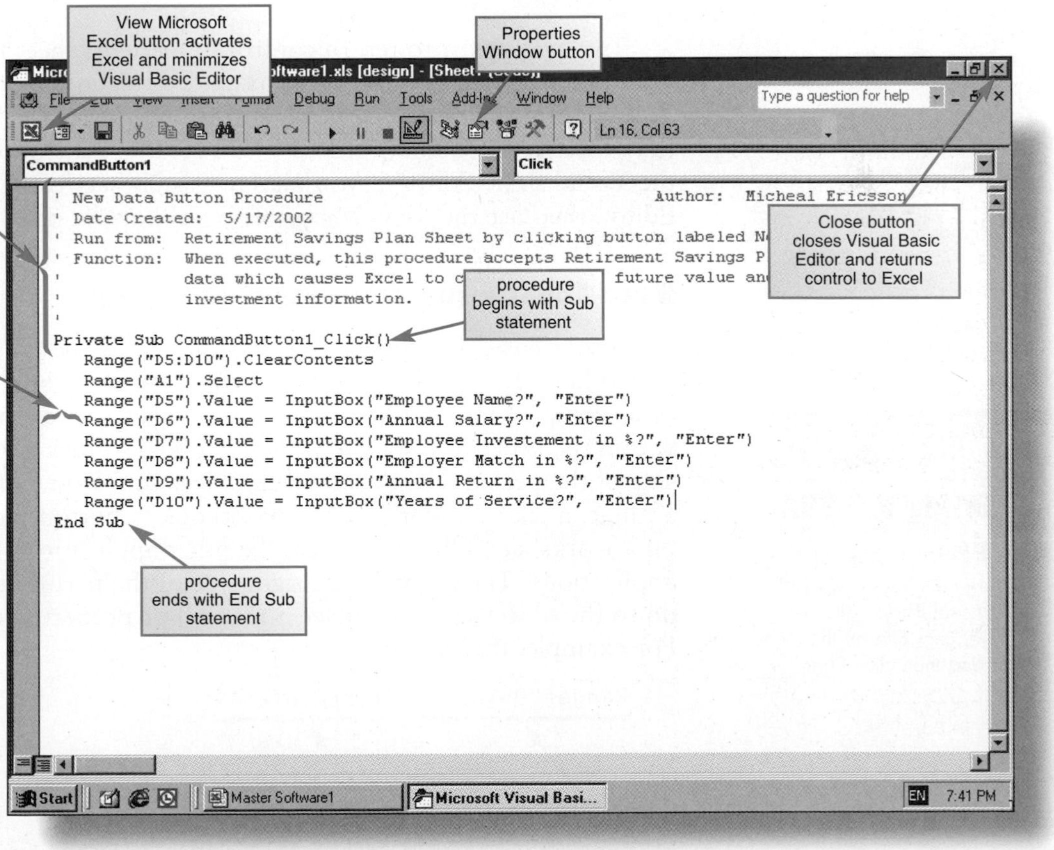
View Microsoft Excel button activates Excel and minimizes Visual Basic Editor
Properties Window button
comments have no bearing on what procedure will do
lines within procedure indented three spaces for readability
Close button closes Visual Basic Editor and returns control to Excel
procedure begins with Sub statement
procedure ends with End Sub statement
Ln 16, Col 63
CommandButton1
Click
Private Sub CommandButton1_Click()
   Range("D5:D10").ClearContents
   Range("A1").Select
   Range("D5").Value = InputBox("Employee Name?", "Enter")
   Range("D6").Value = InputBox("Annual Salary?", "Enter")
   Range("D7").Value = InputBox("Employee Investement in %?", "Enter")
   Range("D8").Value = InputBox("Employer Match in %?", "Enter")
   Range("D9").Value = InputBox("Annual Return in %?", "Enter")
   Range("D10").Value = InputBox("Years of Service?", "Enter")
End Sub

FIGURE 7-41

5 **Click the Close button on the right side of the Microsoft Visual Basic title bar to return to the worksheet. Click the Close button on the right side of the Properties window.**

The worksheet displays as shown in Figure 7-42.

6 **Click the Exit Design Mode button on the Control Toolbox toolbar. Click the Close button on the right side of the Control Toolbox toolbar title bar.**

Excel returns to Run mode, which means if you click the New Data button, Excel will execute the associated procedure.

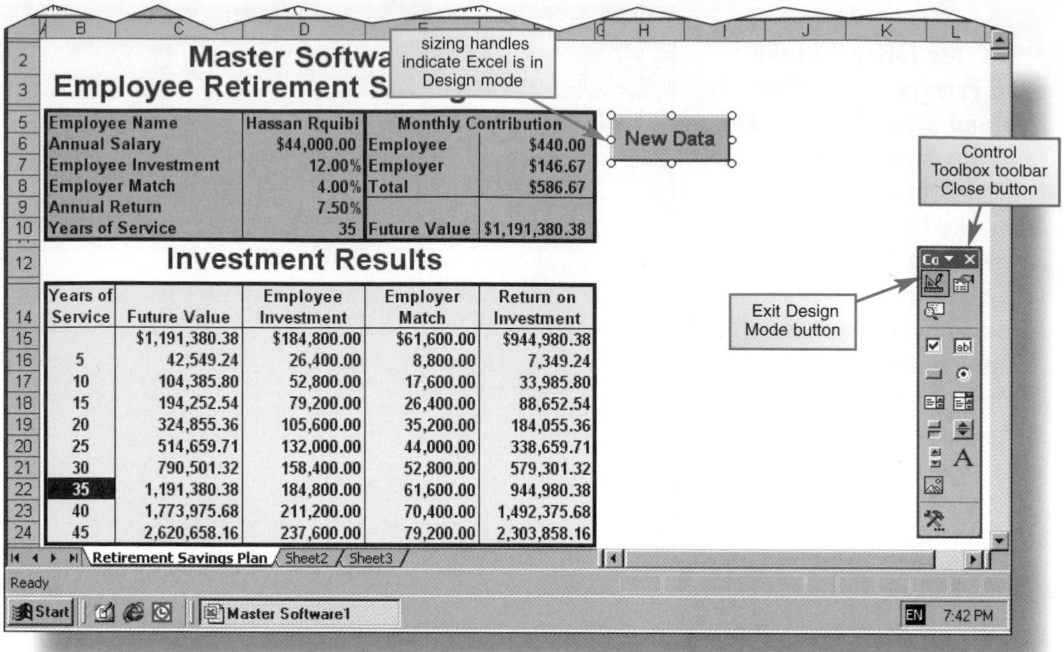

FIGURE 7-42

Other Ways

1. Click Visual Basic Editor button on Visual Basic toolbar
2. In Design mode, right-click control, click View Code on shortcut menu
3. In Design mode, right-click control, in Voice Command mode, say "View Code"

More About

Printing the VBA Code

To print the VBA code while the Visual Basic Editor is active, click File on the menu bar and then click Print.

Two ways exist to return control to the worksheet from the Visual Basic Editor. The Close button on the title bar (Figure 7-41 on the previous page) closes the Visual Basic Editor and returns control to the worksheet. The **View Microsoft Excel button** on the Visual Basic toolbar (Figure 7-41), returns control to Excel, but only minimizes the Visual Basic Editor. If you plan to switch between Excel and the Visual Basic Editor, then use the View Microsoft Excel button, otherwise use the Close button.

More About Visual Basic for Applications

Visual Basic for Applications includes many more statements than those presented here. Even this simple procedure, however, should help you understand the basic composition of a Visual Basic statement. For example, each of the statements within the procedure shown in Figure 7-41 includes a period. The entry on the left side of the period tells Excel which object you want to affect. An **object** can be a cell, a range, a chart, a worksheet, a workbook, a button, or any other control you create on a worksheet. Objects also can be other applications in Windows or parts of other applications. The entry on the right side of the period tells Excel what you want to do to the object. You can place a method or property on the right side of the period. For example, the statement

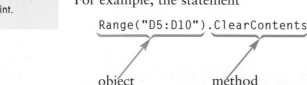

```
Range("D5:D10").ClearContents
```

object   method

clears the range D5:D10. You use a **method**, such as ClearContents, to change an object's behavior. In this case, the method ClearContents is changing the behavior of the range by deleting its contents.

You previously were shown how to change an object's properties using the Properties window (Figure 7-35 on page E 7.31). The following example shows that you also can change an object's properties during execution of a procedure. The object in this case is a Command Button control.

```
CommandButton1.Caption = "Savings Plan Data"
```

name of control — property

This statement changes the Caption property of the button to Savings Plan Data during execution of the procedure.

The second statement in the procedure in Figure 7-41

```
Range("A1").Select
```

selects cell A1, which, in effect, hides the heavy border that surrounds the active cell. Several of the statements in the procedure also include equal signs. An **equal sign** instructs Excel to make an assignment to a cell. For example, when executed as part of the procedure

```
Range("D5").Value = InputBox("Employee Name?", "Enter")
```

the equal sign instructs Excel to display a dialog box called Enter with the prompt message, Employee Name?, and then assigns cell D5 the value entered by the user in response to the dialog box. Thus, the first argument in the InputBox function is the message to the user and the second argument identifies the dialog box in its title bar.

More About

Running Procedures

Always save a workbook before you execute a procedure in case something unexpected occurs. This is especially true when testing a procedure.

Testing the Retirement Savings Plan Data Entry Procedure

Perform the steps below to enter the following Retirement Savings Plan data: Employee Name (cell D5) – Meg Bell; Annual Salary (cell D6) - $68,500.00; Employee Investment (cell D7) – 9.00%; Employer Match (cell D8) – 4.00%; Annual Return (cell D9) – 8.00%; and Years of Service (cell D10) – 40. Before attempting to enter data using the New Data button, it is important that you exit Design mode and close the Control Toolbox toolbar as indicated in Step 6 of the previous set of steps.

Steps To Enter Retirement Savings Plan Data Using the New Data Button

1 Click the New Data button. When Excel displays the first Enter dialog box with the prompt message, Employee Name?, type `Meg Bell` **in the text box. Point to the OK button.**

Excel clears the range D5:D10 and then selects cell A1. Next, it displays the Enter dialog box shown in Figure 7-43.

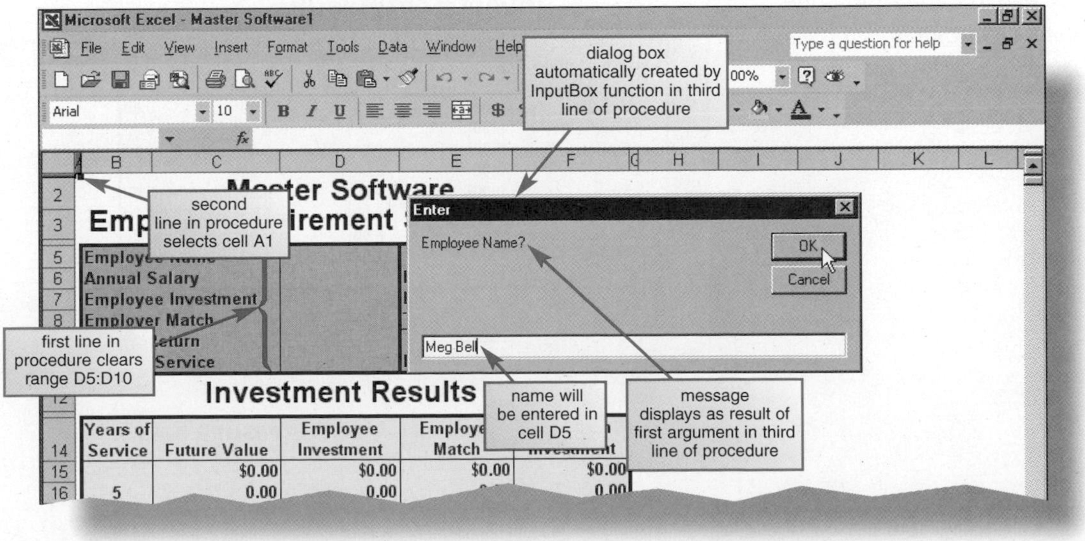

FIGURE 7-43

2 **Click the OK button or press the ENTER key. When Excel displays the next Enter dialog box with the prompt message, Annual Salary?, type** 68500 **in the text box. Point to the OK button.**

Excel assigns the text Meg Bell to cell D5 and displays the second Enter dialog box as shown in Figure 7-44.

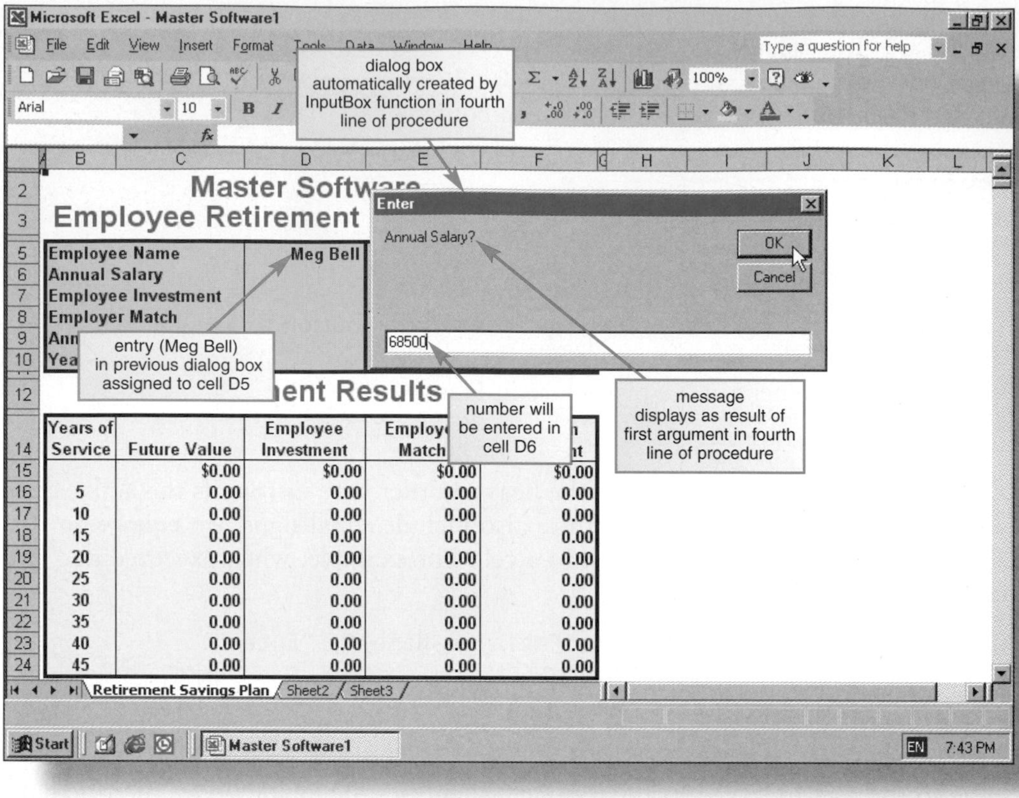

FIGURE 7-44

3 **Click the OK button. When Excel displays the next Enter dialog box with the prompt message, Employee Investment in %?, type** 9% **in the text box, making certain to type the percent (%) sign. Point to the OK button.**

Excel assigns the $68,500.00 to cell D6 and displays the third Enter dialog box as shown in Figure 7-45.

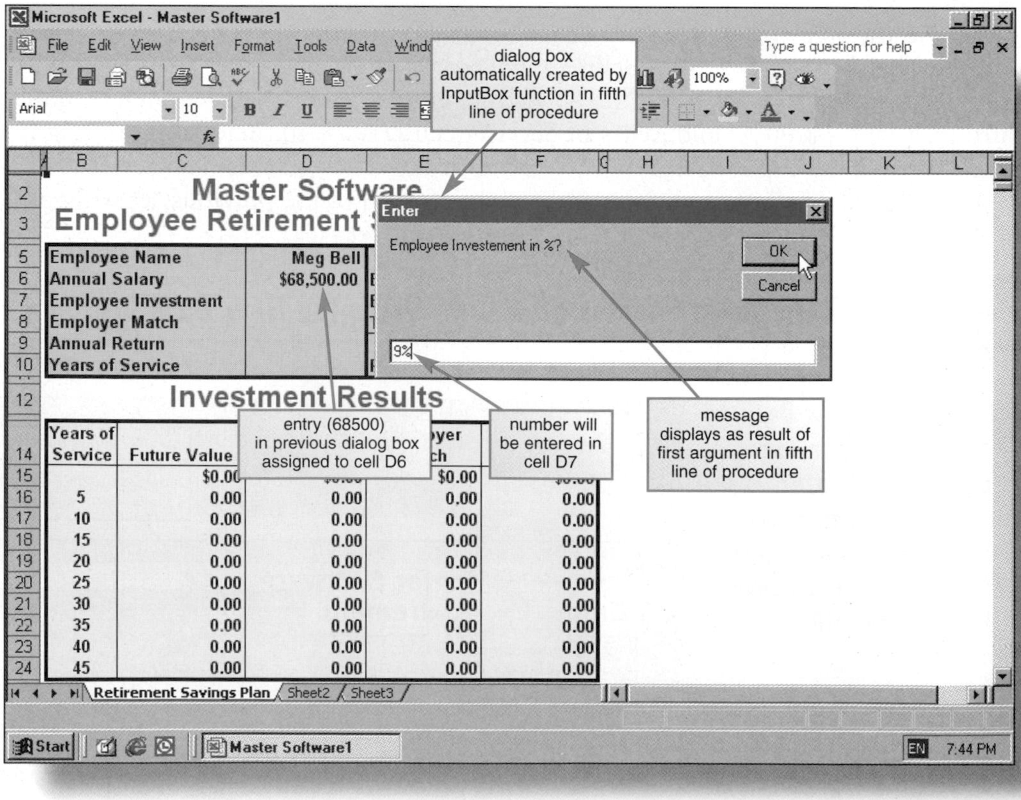

FIGURE 7-45

4 Click the OK button. When Excel displays the next Enter dialog box with the prompt message, Employer Match in %?, type 4% **in the text box. Point to the OK button.**

Excel assigns the 9.00% to cell D7 and displays the fourth Enter dialog box as shown in Figure 7-46.

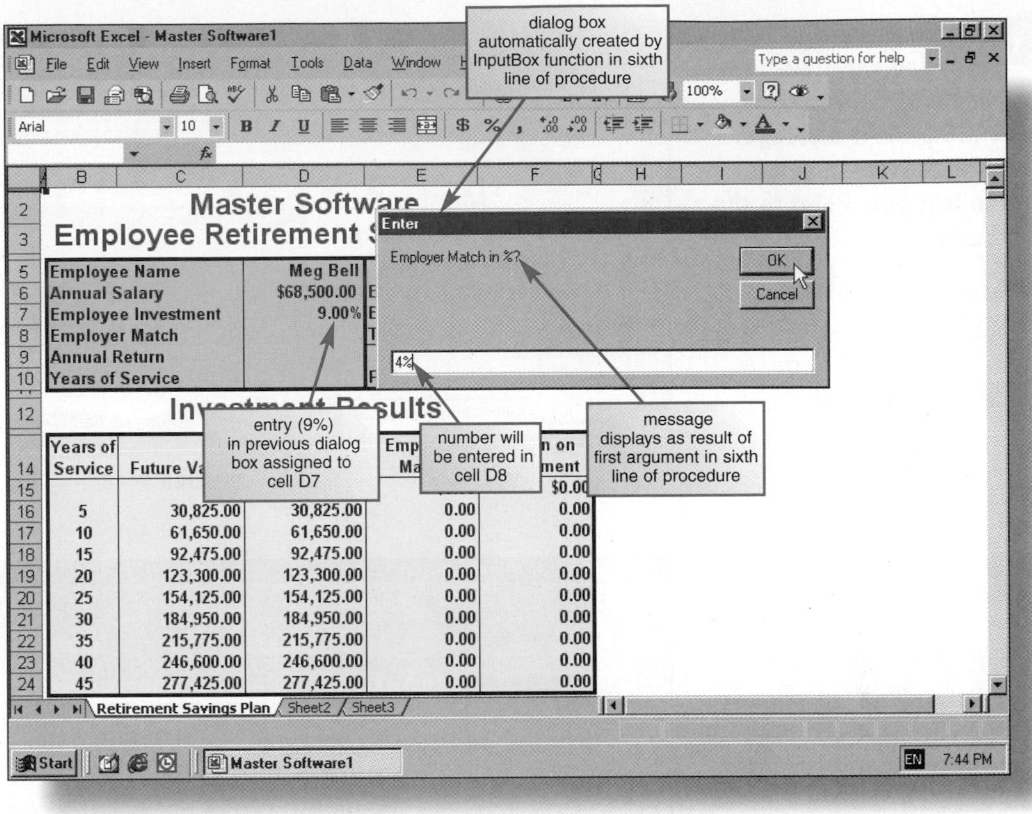

FIGURE 7-46

5 Click the OK button. When Excel displays the next Enter dialog box with the prompt message, Annual Return in %?, type 8% **in the text box. Point to the OK button.**

Excel assigns 4.00% to cell D8 and displays the fifth Enter dialog box as shown in Figure 7-47.

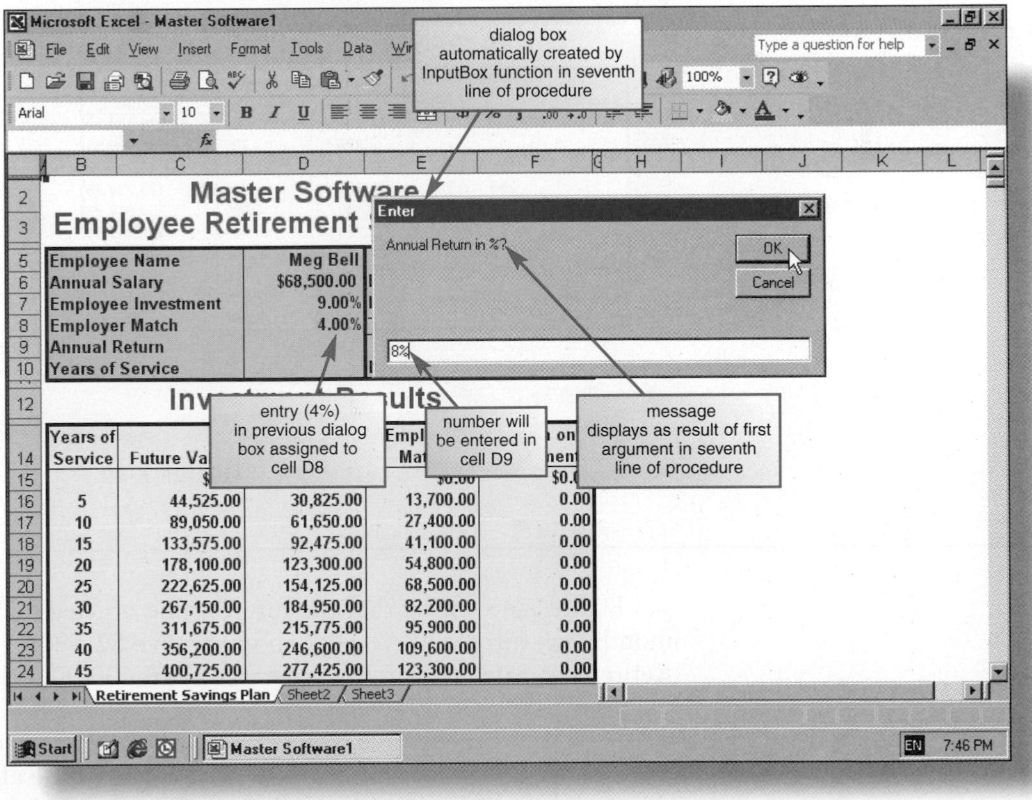

FIGURE 7-47

6 Click the OK button. When Excel displays the next Enter dialog box with the prompt message, Years of Service?, type 40 **in the text box. Point to the OK button.**

Excel assigns 8.00% to cell D9 and displays the sixth Enter dialog box as shown in Figure 7-48.

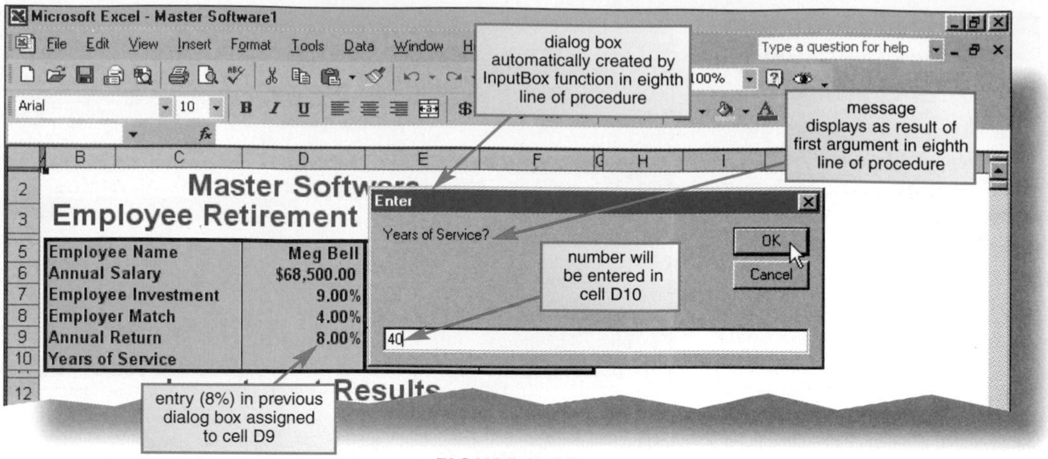

FIGURE 7-48

7 Click the OK button.

Excel assigns 40 to cell D10 and displays the results for Meg Bell in the range F6:F10 (Figure 7-49). Excel also recalculates the data table.

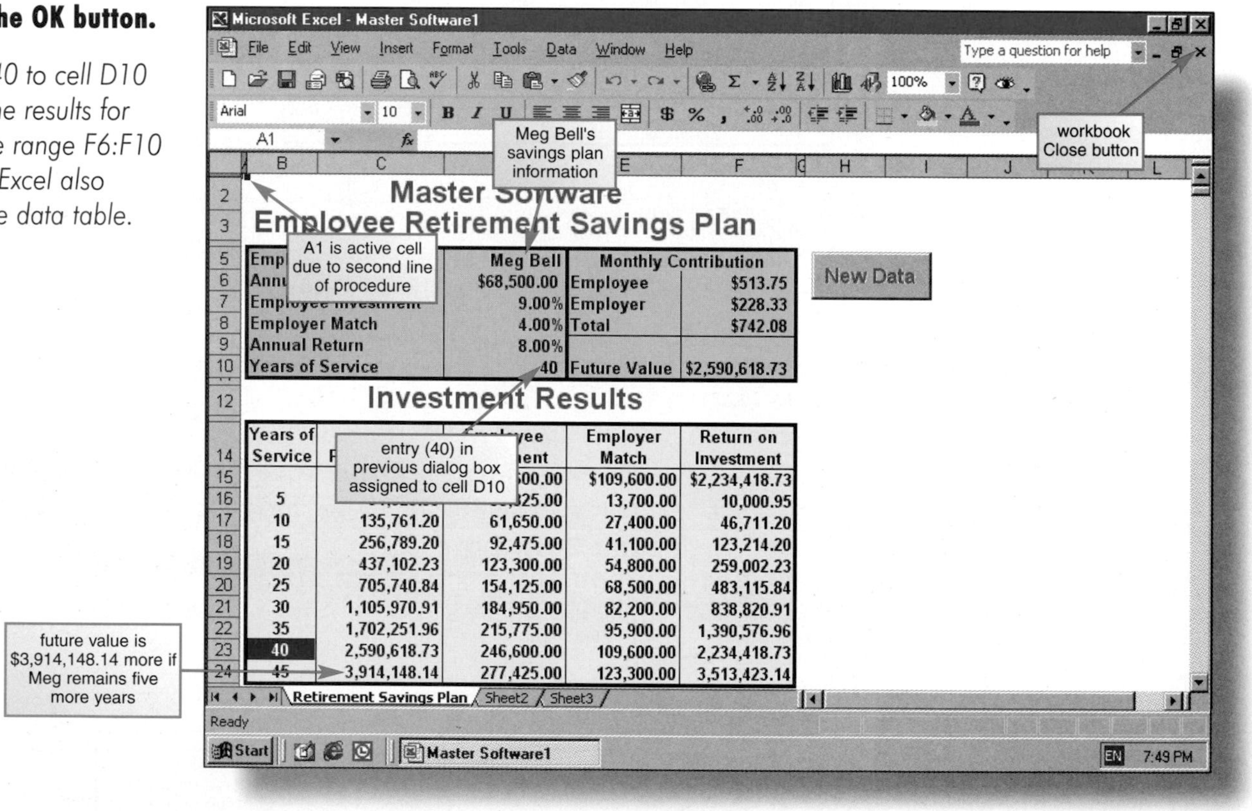

FIGURE 7-49

Figure 7-49 shows that the future value of Meg Bell's investment of $513.75 per month (cell F6) for 40 years is an impressive $2,590,618.73 (cell C23). Meg's total Retirement Savings Plan investment is $246,600.00 (cell D23) and the total employer match is $109,600.00 (cell E23).

Based on this example, you can see the significance of using a VBA to automate the worksheet tasks, especially if the users know little about computers. In this worksheet, each time the user clicks the New Data button, the procedure guides him or her through entering the Retirement Savings Plan data and placing it in the correct cells.

With Phase 2 of this project complete, the final step is to protect the worksheet and save the workbook.

TO PROTECT A WORKSHEET AND SAVE THE WORKBOOK

1. Click Tools on the menu bar, point to Protection, and then click Protect Sheet on the Protection submenu.
2. When the Protect Sheet dialog box displays, type `planright` in the Password text box and then click the OK button. When the Confirm Password dialog box displays, type `planright` and then click the OK button.
3. Click File on the menu bar and then click Save As. When the Save As dialog box displays, type `Master Software2` in the File name text box. Make sure 3½ Floppy (A:) displays in the Save in box and then click the Save button.
4. Click the Close button on the right side of the menu bar to close the Master Software2 workbook.

Phase 2 of this project is complete.

Phase 3 — Creating an Adjustment Center to Automate the Retirement Savings Plan Data Entry

The final phase of this project requires that you add more controls to the worksheet to automate the Retirement Savings Plan data entry. In Phase 2, all of the data was entered using input dialog boxes that displayed one after the other when you triggered the event by clicking the New Data button. This phase uses input dialog boxes for only the name and annual salary. The remaining data (employee investment, employer match, annual return, and years of service) is entered using scroll bars, a check box, and spin buttons.

Consider the Adjustment Center in Figure 7-50. When you click the Enter Name and Salary button, Excel displays input dialog boxes to accept the employee name for cell D5 and the annual salary for cell D6.

The Employee Investment scroll bar immediately below the Enter Name and Salary button allows you to set the employee investment in cell D7. Recall that a scroll bar is made up of three separate areas you can click or drag — the **scroll arrows** on each side that you can click; the **scroll box** between the scroll buttons that you can drag; and the **scroll bar** that you can click that extends from one scroll arrow to the other.

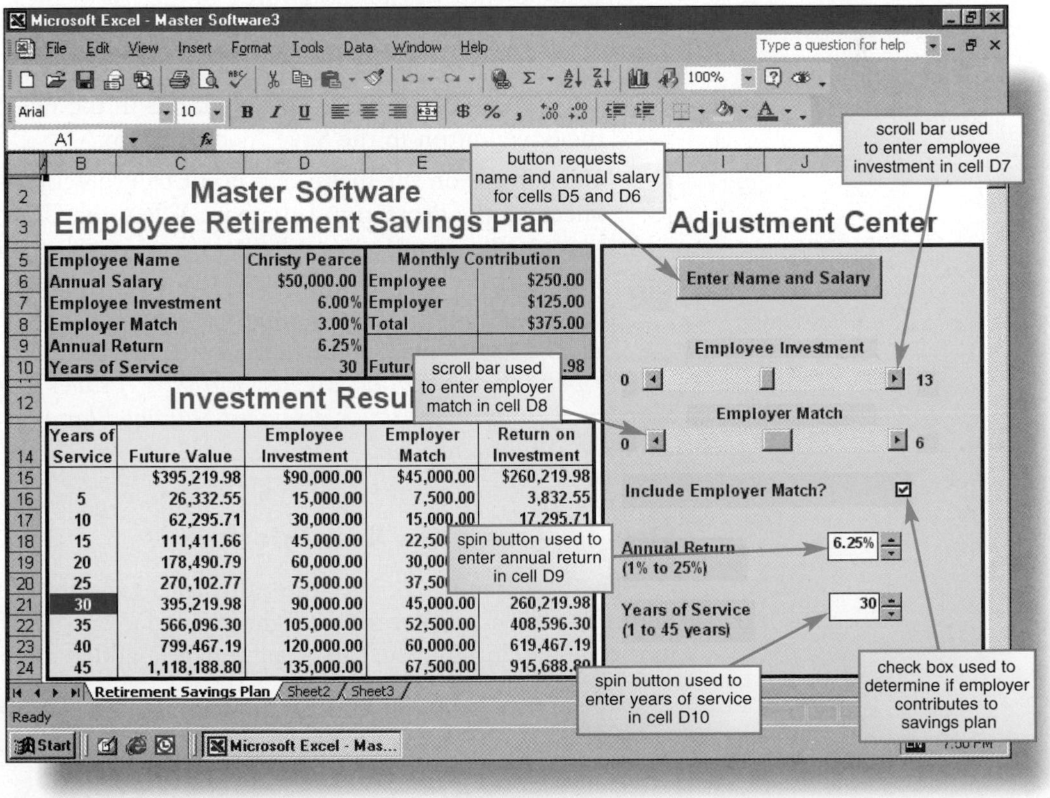

FIGURE 7-50

> **More About**
>
> **Data Validation**
>
> The VBA code entered in Step 4 on page E 7.39 does not check the incoming data to be sure it is reasonable. For example, if a user enters a negative value for the Years of Service in Step 6 on the previous page, Excel will calculate an incorrect Future Value. In the next phase of this project, you will learn how to write VBA code that will ensure that unreasonable numbers are rejected. See the VBA code in Figure 7-80 on page E 7.64 for an example.

More About

Visual Basic for Applications Jobs

Visual Basic for Applications is the most popular programming language used in the computer field today. If you are interested in pursuing a high-paying programmer/analyst career, visit the Excel 2002 Web page (www.scsite.com/ex2002/more.htm) and click Visual Basic Jobs.

More About

Visual Basic for Applications

To learn Visual Basic for Applications, visit the Excel 2002 Web page (www.scsite.com/ex2002/more.htm) and click Visual Basic Development Exchange.

The Employee Investment scroll bar has a minimum value of 0% and a maximum value of 13%. When you click one of its scroll arrows, the employee investment percent in cell D7 increases or decreases by 0.5%, depending on which scroll arrow you click. If you click the scroll bar on either side of the scroll box, the employee investment percent in cell D7 increases or decreases by 1%. Finally, you can drag the scroll box to the right or left to increase or decrease the employee investment percent in cell D7.

The Employer Match scroll bar (middle right in Figure 7-50 on the previous page) works the same way, except that the change in the employer match is 0.25% when you click a scroll arrow, and the scroll bar runs from 0% to 6%.

The Include Employer Match? check box in the middle of the Adjustment Center in Figure 7-50 indicates if the Employer Match scroll bar is enabled or disabled. If the check mark is present, then the scroll bar below the check box is enabled. If the check mark is removed, then cell D8 is set equal to 0% and the scroll bar is disabled.

The Annual Return spin button in the lower portion of the Adjustment Center increases or decreases the annual return in cell D9 by 0.25% each time you click a spin button arrow. A **spin button** has two buttons, one to increment and one to decrement the value in the cell with which it is associated. The Years of Service spin button in the lower portion of the Adjustment Center increases or decreases the years of service in cell D10 by one each time you click a spin button arrow.

The following steps open the workbook Master Software1, save it using the file name Master Software3, unprotect the Retirement Savings Plan worksheet, and display the Control Toolbox toolbar.

TO OPEN A WORKBOOK, UNPROTECT A WORKSHEET, AND DISPLAY THE CONTROL TOOLBOX TOOLBAR

1. Click the Open button on the Standard toolbar. When the Open dialog box displays, if necessary, click the Look in box arrow and click 3½ Floppy (A:). Double-click Master Software1 in the list of files. If necessary, click Enable Macros on the Microsoft Excel dialog box.
2. Click File on the menu bar and then click Save As. When the Save As dialog box displays, type `Master Software3` in the File name text box and then click the Save button in the Save As dialog box.
3. Click Tools on the menu bar, point to Protection, and then click Unprotect Sheet on the Protection submenu. When the Unprotect Sheet dialog box displays, type `planright` in the Password text box and then click the OK button.
4. Right-click a toolbar and then click Control Toolbox. Drag the Control Toolbox toolbar to the middle of the window.

Excel opens the workbook Master Software1, saves it using the file name Master Software3, unprotects the Retirement Savings Plan worksheet, and displays the Control Toolbox toolbar.

Step 1 – Create the User Interface

The first step is to create the Adjustment Center user interface shown in Figure 7-50. After creating the light green background for the Adjustment Center in the range H5:L24, the following must be added to it:

1. A Command Button control
2. Two Scroll Bar controls
3. A Check Box control
4. Two Spin Button controls
5. Label controls to identify controls and display data

When you first create a user interface, you position the controls as close as you can to their final location on the screen, and then after setting the properties you finalize the locations of the controls. Therefore, the following steps make no attempt to position the controls exactly in the locations shown in Figure 7-50 on page 7-41.

Steps To Add Controls to a User Interface

1 **Select the range H5:L24. Click the Fill Color button arrow on the Formatting toolbar and then click Light Green (column 4, row 5) on the Fill Color palette. Click the Borders button arrow on the Formatting toolbar and then click Thick Box Border (column 4, row 3) on the Borders palette.**

2 **Click the Command Button button on the Control Toolbox toolbar and then drag the mouse pointer so the control displays as shown in Figure 7-51.**

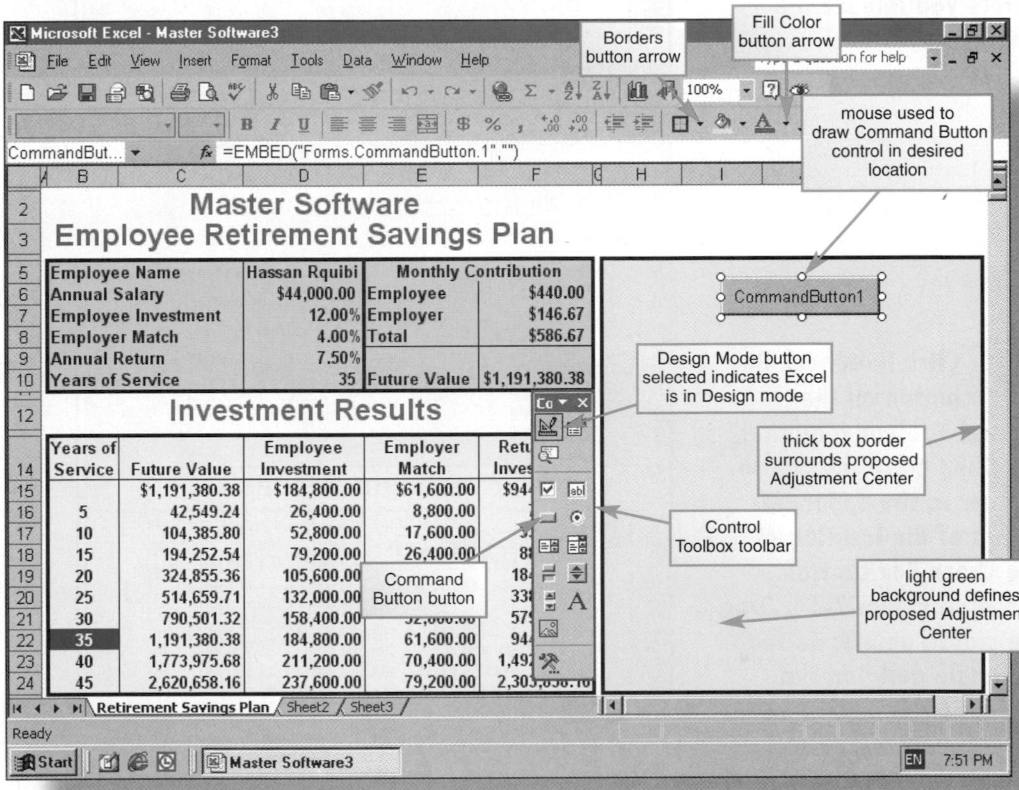

FIGURE 7-51

3 **Click the Scroll Bar button on the Control Toolbox toolbar and then move the mouse pointer to approximately the left of cell I12. Drag the mouse pointer so the Scroll Bar control displays as shown in Figure 7-52.**

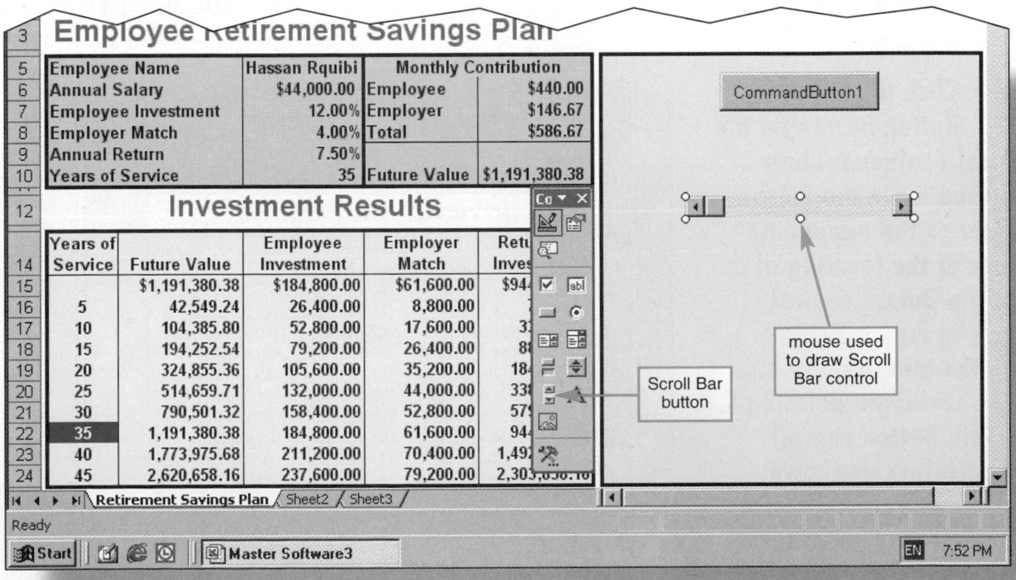

FIGURE 7-52

4 **Point to the Scroll Bar control. Hold down the CTRL key and drag a copy of the Scroll Bar control to the location shown in Figure 7-53. It is important that you release the left mouse button before you release the CTRL key.**

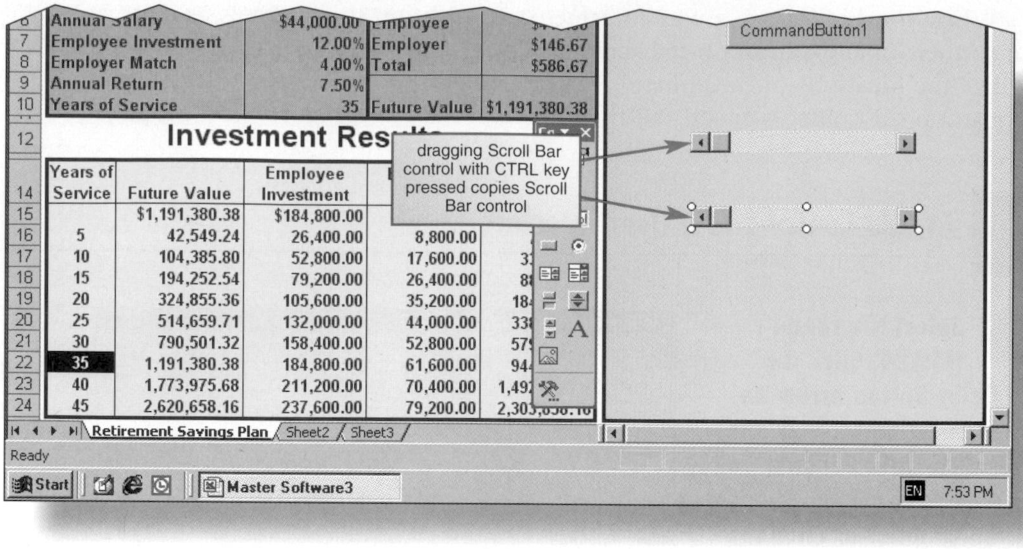

FIGURE 7-53

5 **Click the Check Box button on the Control Toolbox toolbar and then move the mouse pointer to the upper-left corner of the location of the Check Box control shown in Figure 7-54. Drag the mouse pointer so the rectangle defining the Check Box control area displays with half of the word CheckBox1 showing.**

The check box will be resized after its caption is changed later in this project.

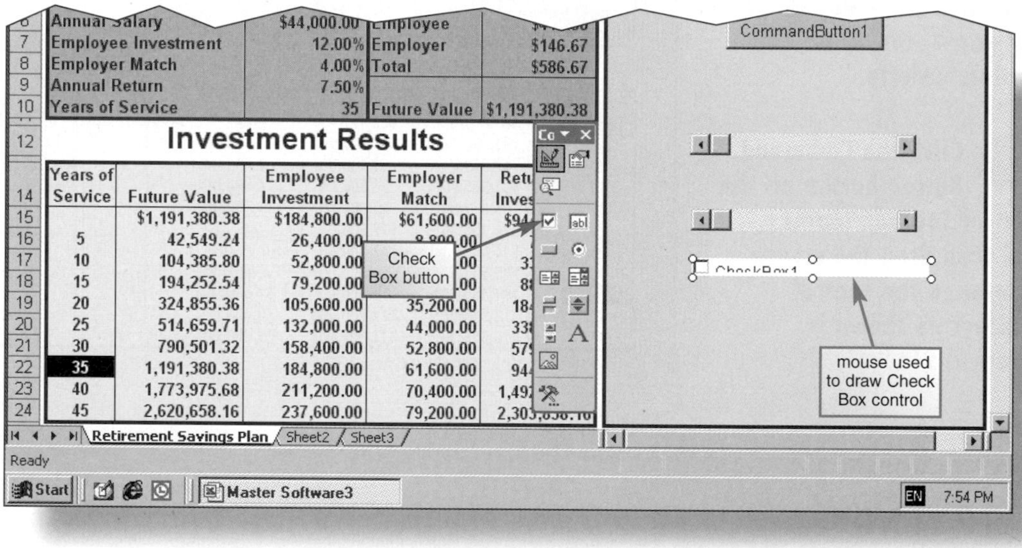

FIGURE 7-54

6 **Click the Spin Button button on the Control Toolbox toolbar and then move the mouse pointer to the upper-left corner of the location of the Spin Button control shown in Figure 7-55. Drag the mouse pointer so the rectangle defining the Spin Button control area displays as shown in Figure 7-55.**

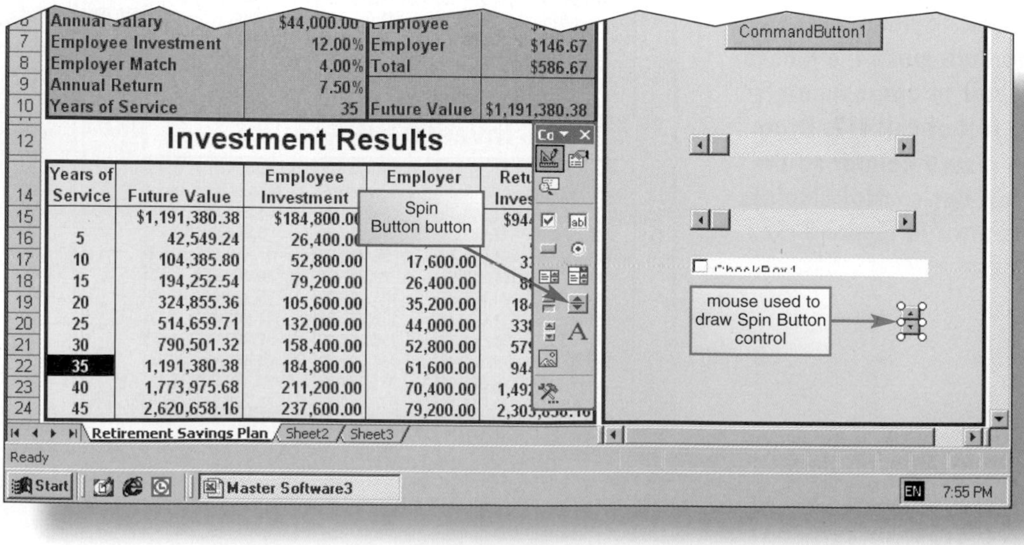

FIGURE 7-55

7 **Point to the Spin Button control in the Adjustment Center. Hold down the CTRL key and drag a copy of the Spin Button control to the second location shown in Figure 7-56. It is important that you release the left mouse button before you release the CTRL key.**

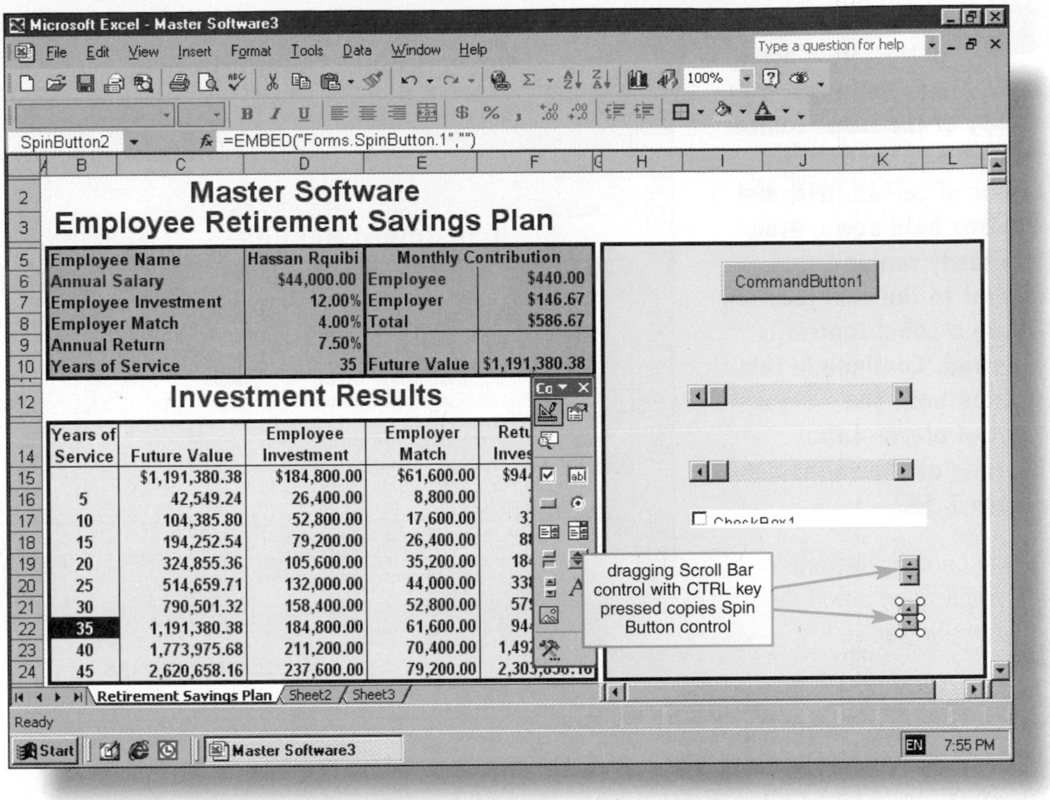

FIGURE 7-56

8 **Click the Label button on the Control Toolbox toolbar and then move the mouse pointer to the left of the Scroll Bar control below the CommandButton1 button. Drag the mouse pointer so the rectangle defining the Label control displays as shown in Figure 7-57.**

This Label control is used to indicate the lowest value (zero) on the scroll bar.

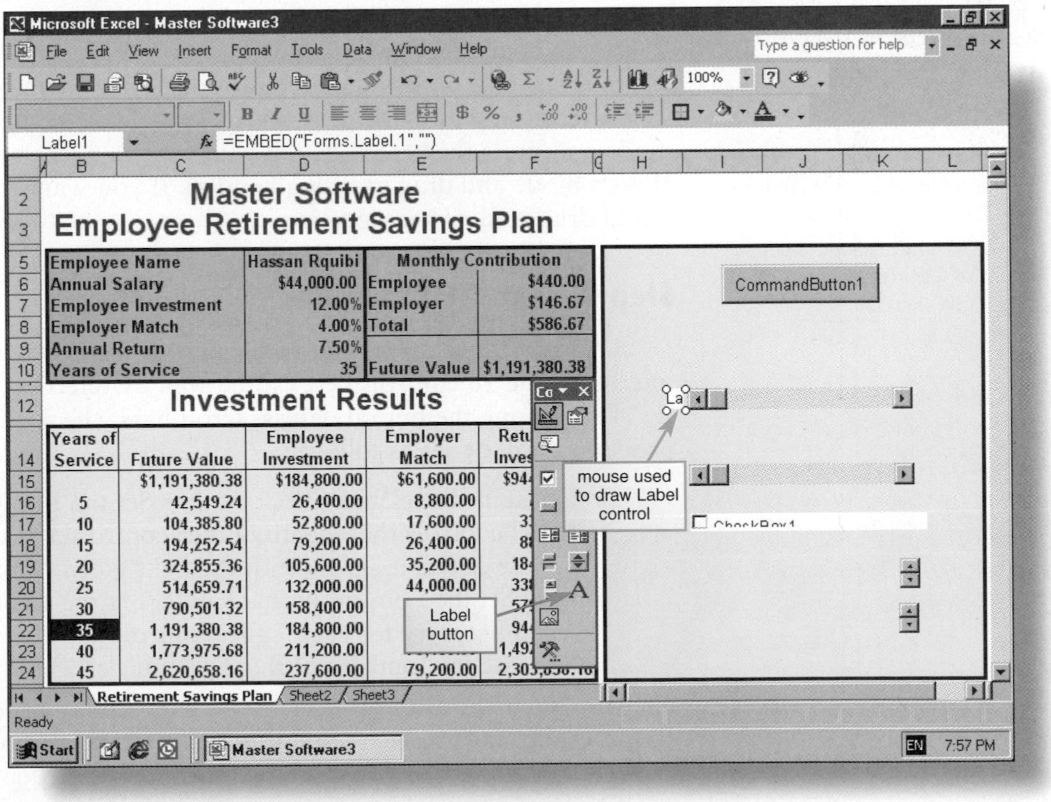

FIGURE 7-57

9 **Point to the Label control. Hold down the CTRL key and then drag a copy of the Label control created in Step 8 to the center of cell J3. With the CTRL key held down, drag the newly copied Label control to the next location where a Label control is required. Continue in this fashion until you have a total of eleven Label controls as shown in Figure 7-58.**

All the controls needed for this application are in the Adjustment Center.

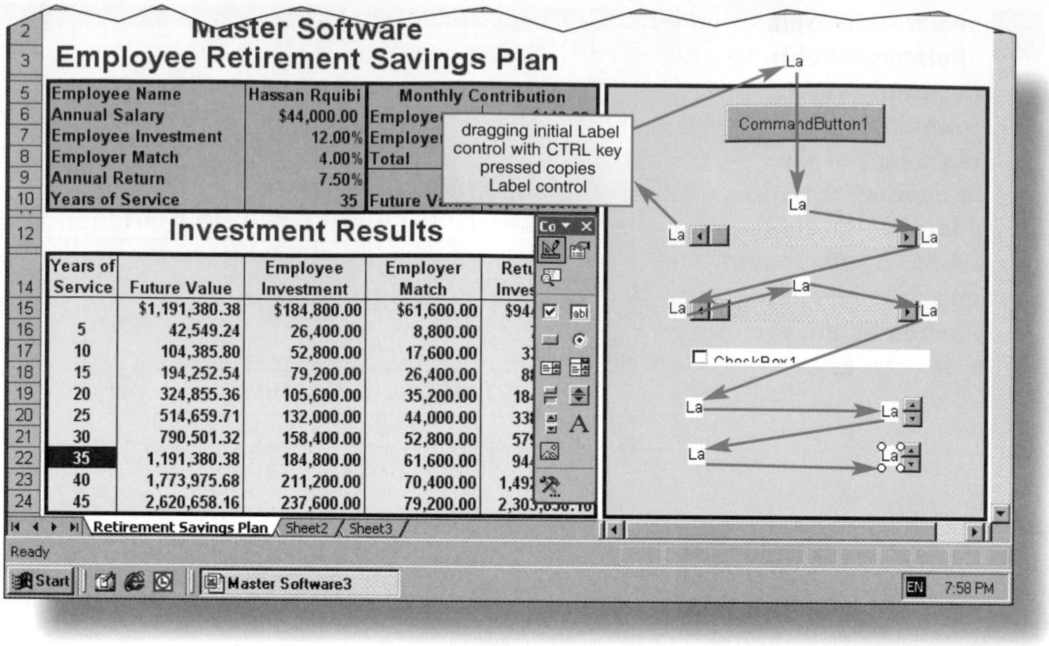

FIGURE 7-58

Other Ways

1. Select control, click Copy button on Standard toolbar; click Paste button on Standard toolbar
2. Select control, on Edit menu click Copy, on Edit menu click Paste
3. Right-click control, click Copy on shortcut menu, click Paste on shortcut menu
4. Select control, click CTRL+C to copy, click CTRL+V to paste
5. In Voice Command mode, say "Copy" to copy, say "Paste" to paste

When you create a Label control, a caption is associated with it. The Caption property for the first Label control is Label1. For the next Label control you create, the Caption property is Label2, and so on. Because of the size of the Label controls in Figure 7-58, you can see only two characters of the caption, the La.

If you compare Figure 7-58 with 7-50 on page 7.41, you will notice that except for captions and some minor repositioning of the controls, the Adjustment Center user interface is complete. If you want to delete a control, select it while in Design mode and press the DELETE key. If you want to resize a control, select it while in Design mode and drag its sizing handles. If you want to reposition a control, select it and drag it to its new location.

Step 2 – Set the Properties

The next step is to set the properties for the 16 controls that make up the user interface. The 16 controls best can be seen by referring to Figure 7-50 on page E 7.41 counting the button, labels, scroll bars, check box, and spin buttons. The properties will be set as follows:

1. **Constant Label and Check Box** — Set the BackColor property of the Label controls that identify other controls and the Check Box control to light green so it agrees with the light green background of the user interface. Set the Font property to Bold. Set the Caption property and Text Align property for each Label control that identifies another control. Increase the font size of the Adjustment Center title to size 18.
2. **Command Button** — Change the Caption property to Enter Name and Salary and resize the button so the entire caption shows.
3. **Employee Investment Scroll Bar** — Change the Name property to scrEmployeeInvest, the SmallChange property to 50 (0.5%), the LargeChange property to 100 (1%), the Min property to 0 (0%), and the Max property to 1300 (13%).

4. **Employer Match Scroll Bar** — Change the Name property to scrEmployerMatch, the SmallChange property to 25 (0.25%), the LargeChange property to 100 (1%), the Min property to 0 (0%), and the Max property to 600 (6%).
5. **Employer Match Check Box** — Change the Name property to chkEmployerMatch and the Caption property to Include Employer Match?. Resize the check box so the new caption displays. Change the SpecialEffect to fmButtonEffectFlat. Change the alignment to fmAlignLeft.
6. **Annual Return Spin Button** — Change the Name property to spnAnnualReturn, the SmallChange property to 25 (0.25%), the Min property to 0 (0%), and the Max property to 10000 (100%).
7. **Years of Service Spin Button** — Change the Name property to spnYearsofService, the SmallChange property to 1, the Min property to 1, and the Max property to 45.
8. **Annual Return Label** — Change the Name property to lblAnnualReturn, the Caption property to 5%, the Font property to Bold, the TextAlign property to align right, and the BorderStyle property to single.
9. **Years of Service Label** — Change the Name property to lblYearsofService, the Caption property to 10, the Font property to Bold, the TextAlign property to align right, and the BorderStyle property to single.

More About

Determining Properties

It is best to have all of your properties determined before you sit down at the computer. Using a grid, or graph paper, is often the best way to layout a screen by hand and set properties such as height, width, and location. Other properties should be determined in this manner, as well. Often, this design is detailed in a formal document called a functional specification, which is reviewed and approved by users of the finished worksheet.

Excel automatically assigns the first Command Button control the name CommandButton1. If you create a second Command Button control, Excel will call it CommandButton2, and so on. In the controls just listed, some will have their Name property changed as indicated, while others will not. Usually, you do not change the Name property of Label controls that identify other controls in the user interface. On the other hand, controls that are referenced in the VBA code should be given names that help you recall the control. Table 7-5 summarizes the controls whose Name property will be changed because they will be referenced in the VBA code.

The name of a control, such as scrEmployeeInvest, must begin with a letter, cannot exceed 255 characters, and cannot have a space, period, exclamation point, or the characters @, &, $, or #. You should develop a naming convention of your own and then use it consistently to name controls. In this book, the first three characters of the name identify the type of control. For example: scr stands for scroll bar; chk stands for check box; and spn stands for spin button. Following the three characters are words that identify what the control is controlling. In this case, scrEmployeeInvest is a scroll bar controlling the value in cell D7, the Employee Investment. You also must make sure that the names are unique in an application, because duplicate names are not allowed.

Table 7-5 Referenced Controls and Their Names

CONTROL	*NAME*
Employee Investment Scroll Bar	scrEmployeeInvest
Employer Match Scroll Bar	scrEmployerMatch
Employer Match Check Box	chkEmployerMatch
Annual Return Spin Button	spnAnnualReturn
Years of Service Spin Button	spnYearsofService
Annual Return Label	lblAnnualReturn
Years of Service Label	lblYearsofService

SETTING THE CONSTANT LABELS AND CHECK BOX PROPERTIES When you create a Label control, it has a white background. If the Label control identifies another control, the background color is changed so it becomes part of the user interface background. If the Label control is going to display a value that varies, the background is left white. The following steps use the SHIFT key to select all the Label controls that identify other controls and the Check Box control so that the BackColor property can be changed for all selected items at once. The Font property of the selected controls also is changed to bold. After the BackColor and Font are changed, then each Label control is selected and the properties are set.

Steps To Set Properties of the Constant Label Controls and Check Box Control

1 With Excel in Design mode, click the Label control in the top-right of the user interface. Hold down the SHIFT key and then one at a time click the Label controls that will remain constant and the Check Box control (right of Figure 7-59). Release the SHIFT key. Click the Properties button on the Control Toolbox toolbar. When the Properties window opens, click BackColor, click the BackColor arrow, if necessary, click the Palette tab, and then point to light green in the list.

The selected Label controls, the Check Box control, and the Properties window display as shown in Figure 7-59.

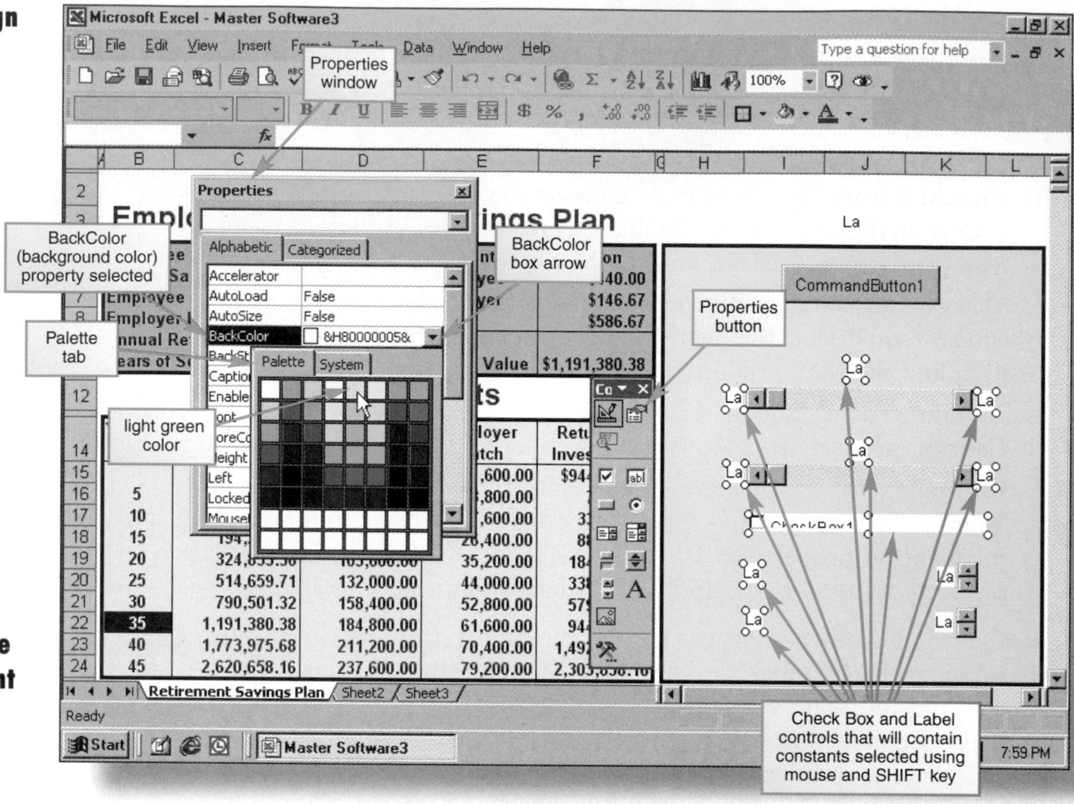

FIGURE 7-59

2 Click light green. Click Font in the Properties window and then click the Font button arrow. When the Font dialog box displays, click Bold in the Font style list and then point to the OK button.

The Properties window and Font dialog box display as shown in Figure 7-60. The selected Label controls and Check Box control have a light green background.

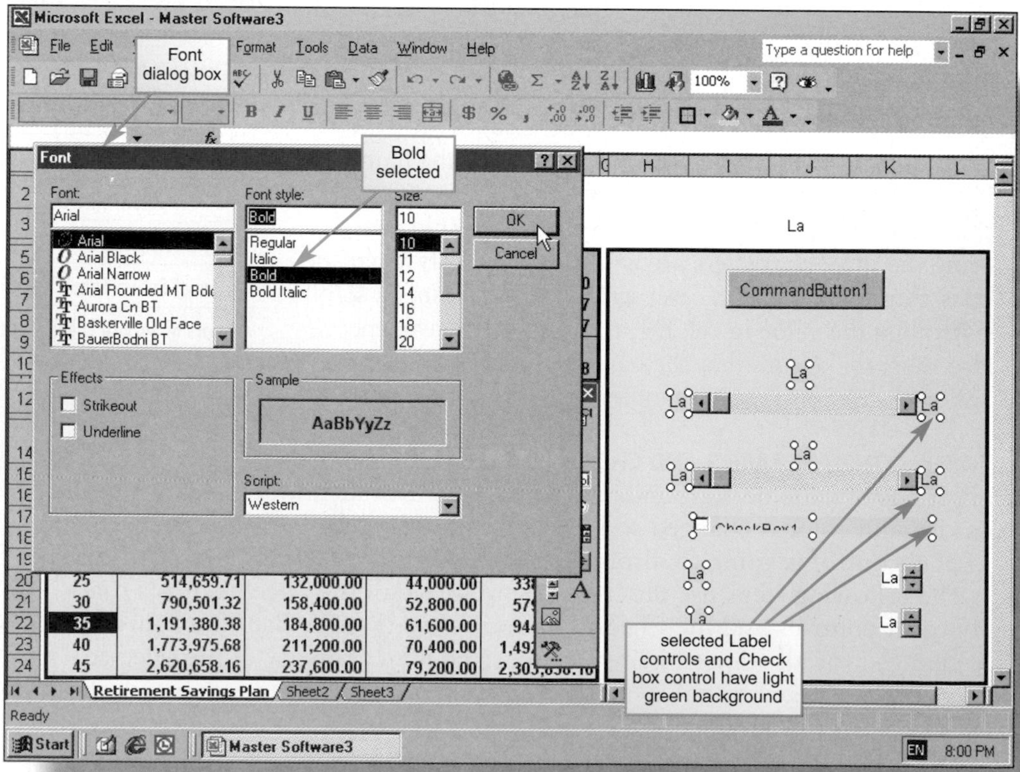

FIGURE 7-60

3 **Click the OK button. Click anywhere in the Adjustment Center area to deselect the Label controls and Check Box control. Click the Label control to the left of the Employee Investment scroll bar. Click Caption in the Properties window and then type** 0 **as the caption. Click TextAlign in the Properties window, click the TextAlign box arrow, and then click 2 - fmTextAlignCenter.**

The Label control in to the left if the top scroll bar is selected and the Properties window displays its properties as shown in Figure 7-61.

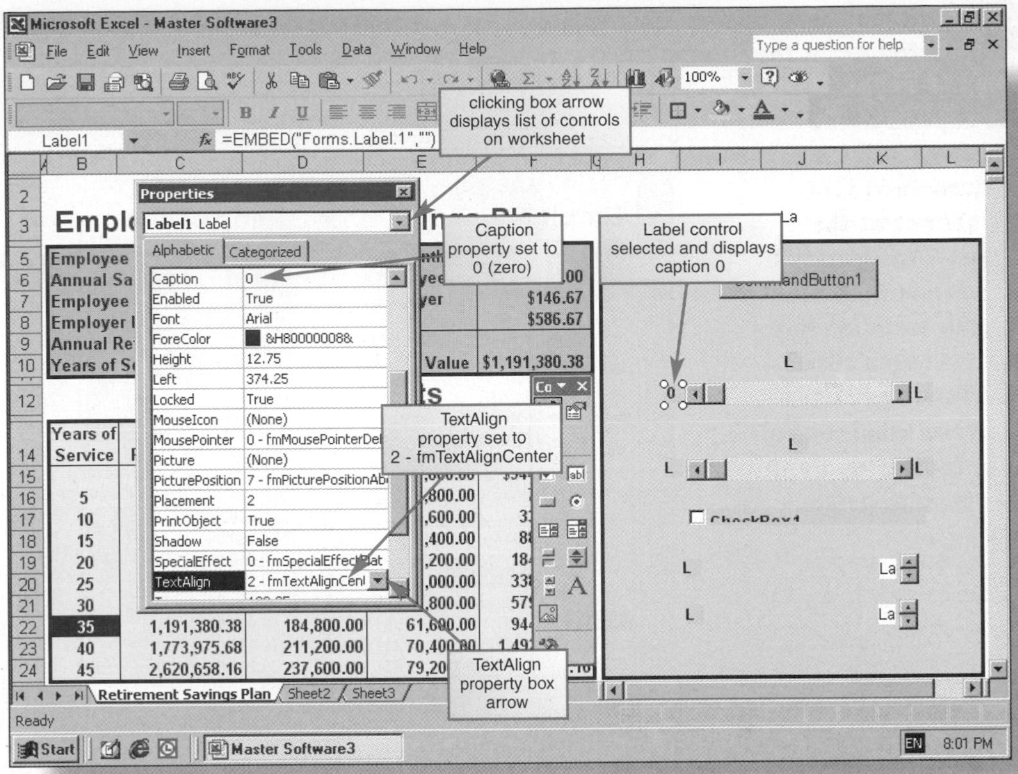

FIGURE 7-61

4 **Click the Label control to the right of the Employee Investment scroll bar. Click Caption in the Properties window and then type** 13 **as the caption. Click TextAlign in the Properties window, click the TextAlign arrow, and then click number 2 - fmTextAlignCenter. If necessary, resize the Label control so the caption 13 is visible.**

The Properties window for the selected Label control displays as shown in Figure 7-62.

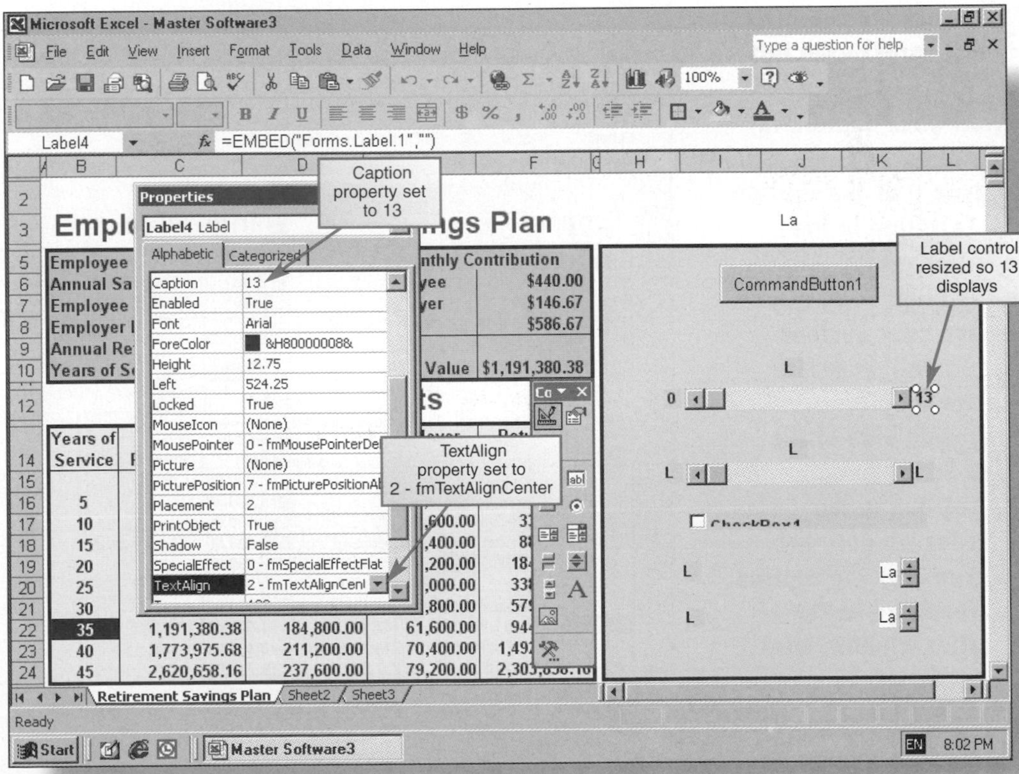

FIGURE 7-62

5 Click the Label control under the Command Button control. Click Caption in the Properties window and then type `Employee Investment` **as the caption. Click TextAlign in the Properties window. Click the TextAlign box arrow and then click 2 - fmTextAlignCenter. Resize the Label control so the caption Employee Investment is visible.**

The Properties window displays as shown in Figure 7-63.

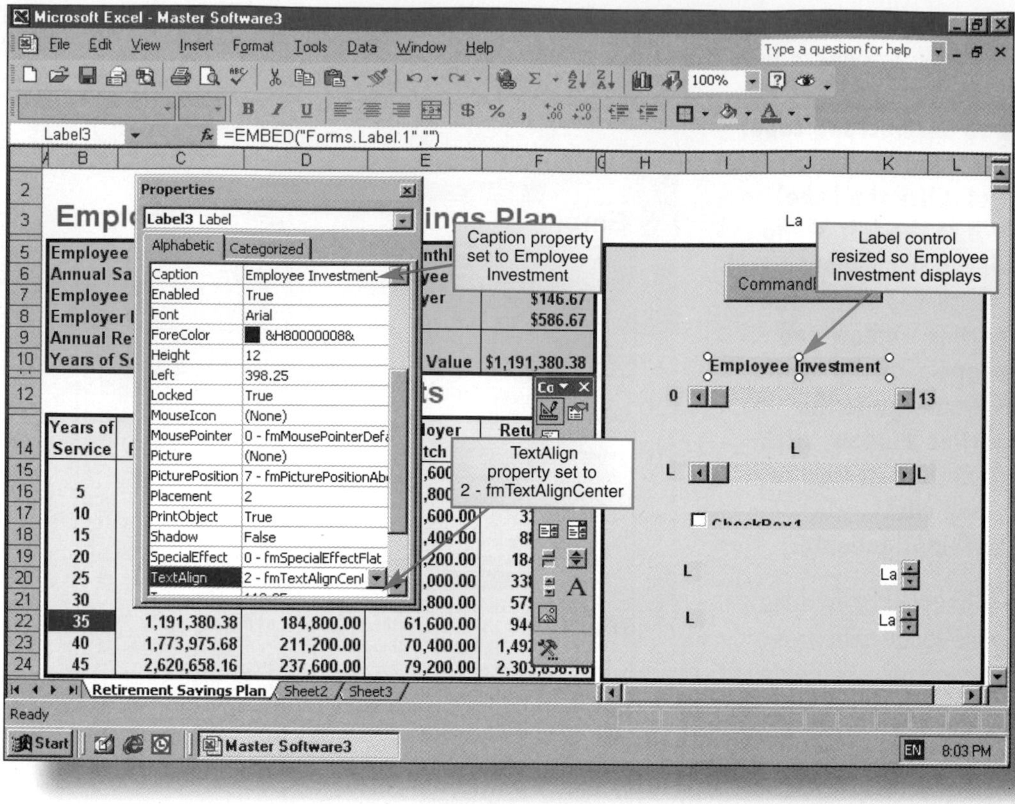

FIGURE 7-63

6 Click the Label control to the left of the second Scroll Bar control. Click Caption in the Properties window and then type 0 **as the caption. Click TextAlign in the Properties window, click the TextAlign box arrow, and then click number 2 - fmTextAlignCenter. Click the Label control on the right side of the second Scroll Bar control. Click Caption in the Properties window and then type** 6 **as the caption. Click TextAlign in the Properties window, click the TextAlign box arrow, and then click number 2 - fmTextAlignCenter.**

The Properties window for the selected Label control displays as shown in Figure 7-64.

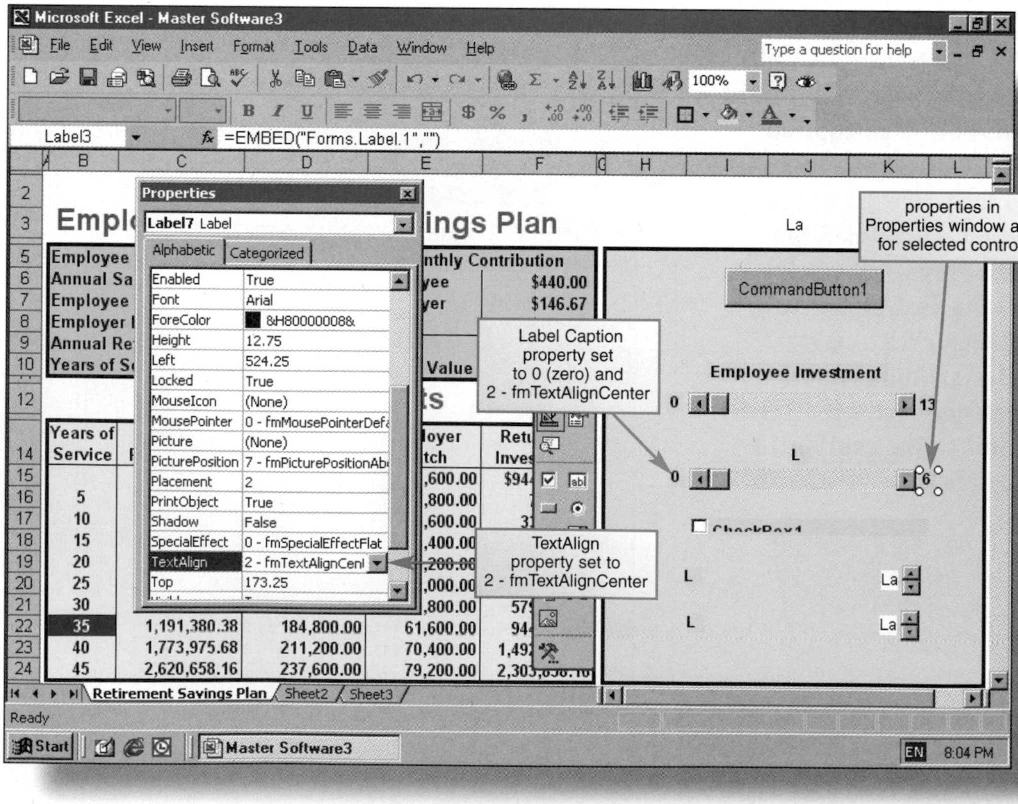

FIGURE 7-64

7 **Click the Label control above the Adjustment Center area. Click Caption in the Properties window and then type** `Adjustment Center` **as the caption. Click TextAlign in the Properties window, click the TextAlign box arrow, and then click 2 - fmTextAlignCenter. Click Font in the Properties window and then click the Font button. When the Font dialog box displays, click 18 in the Size list and then click the OK button. Resize the Label control so the caption displays in its entirety.**

The Properties window for the selected Label control displays as shown in Figure 7-65.

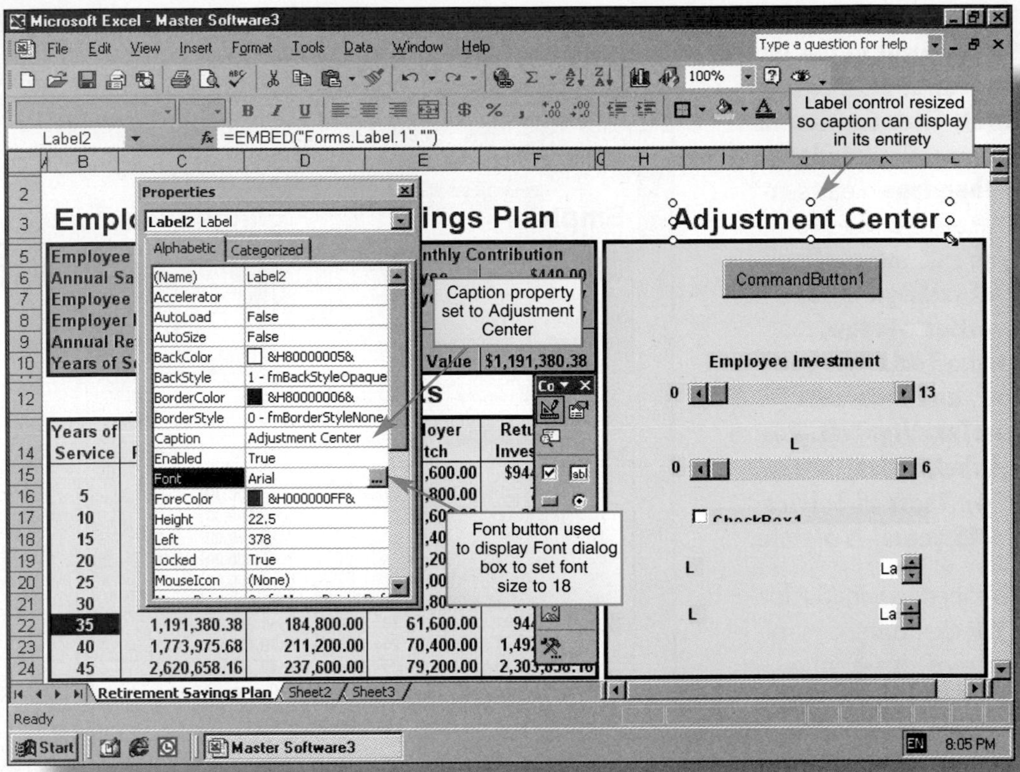

FIGURE 7-65

8 **Click the Label control below the upper Scroll Bar control. Click Caption in the Properties window and then type** `Employer Match` **as the caption. Click TextAlign in the Properties window, click the TextAlign box arrow, and then click number 2 - fmTextAlignCenter. Resize the Label control so the caption displays in its entirety. Click the Label control to the left of the top Spin Button control. Click Caption in the Properties window and then type** `Annual Return (1% to 25%)` **as the caption. Click TextAlign in the Properties window, click the TextAlign box arrow, and then, if necessary, click number 1 - fmTextAlignLeft. Resize the Label control so the caption Annual Return (1% to 25%) is visible.**

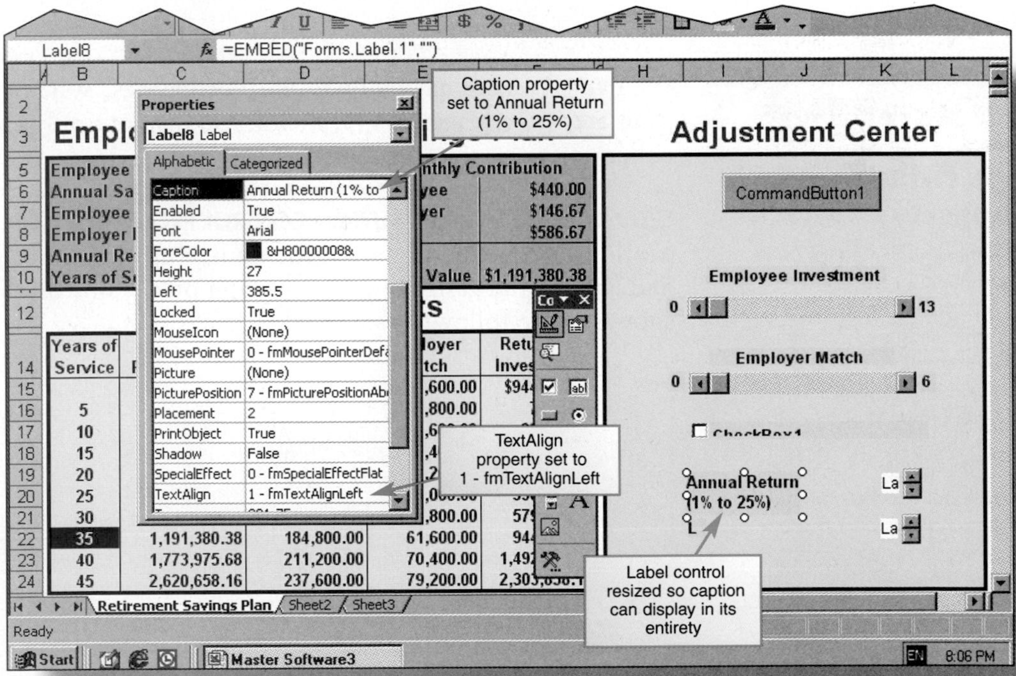

FIGURE 7-66

The Properties window for the selected Label control displays as shown in Figure 7-66.

9 **Click the Label control to the left of the lower Spin Button control. Click Caption in the Properties window and then type** `Years of Service (1 to 45 years)` **as the caption. Click TextAlign in the Properties window, click the TextAlign box arrow, and then click 1 - fmTextAlignLeft. Resize the Label control so the caption Years of Service (1 to 45 years) is visible.**

The Properties window for the selected Label control displays as shown in Figure 7-67.

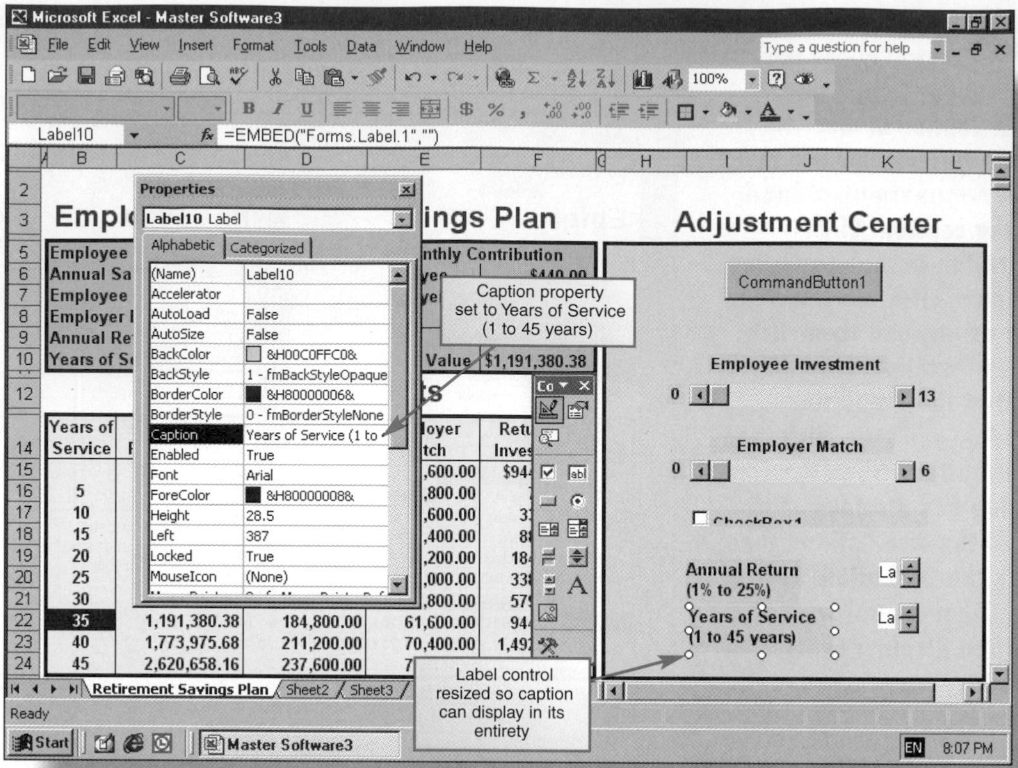

FIGURE 7-67

More About

The Picture Property

The Picture property of the CommandButton control allows you to display a graphic image on a button, allowing you to create a richer user interface. The PicturePosition property offers eight choices of where you want the graphic positioned on the button. You can make a button that has only a graphic, or you can include text on the button along with the graphic.

Every control has its own set of properties. When you select multiple controls as in Step 1 on page E 7.48, then Excel displays only those properties that are common to the controls selected.

SETTING THE COMMAND BUTTON CONTROL PROPERTIES The next step is to change the caption on the Command Button control from CommandButton1 to Enter Name and Salary, and resize it so the caption on the button displays in its entirety, as shown in the following step.

Steps To Set the Command Button Control Properties

1 With Excel in Design mode, click the Command Button control in the Adjustment Center. Click Caption in the Properties window and then type `Enter Name and Salary` **as the caption. Drag one of the sizing handles surrounding the Command Button control so that the caption displays in its entirety.**

The button and its properties display as shown in Figure 7-68.

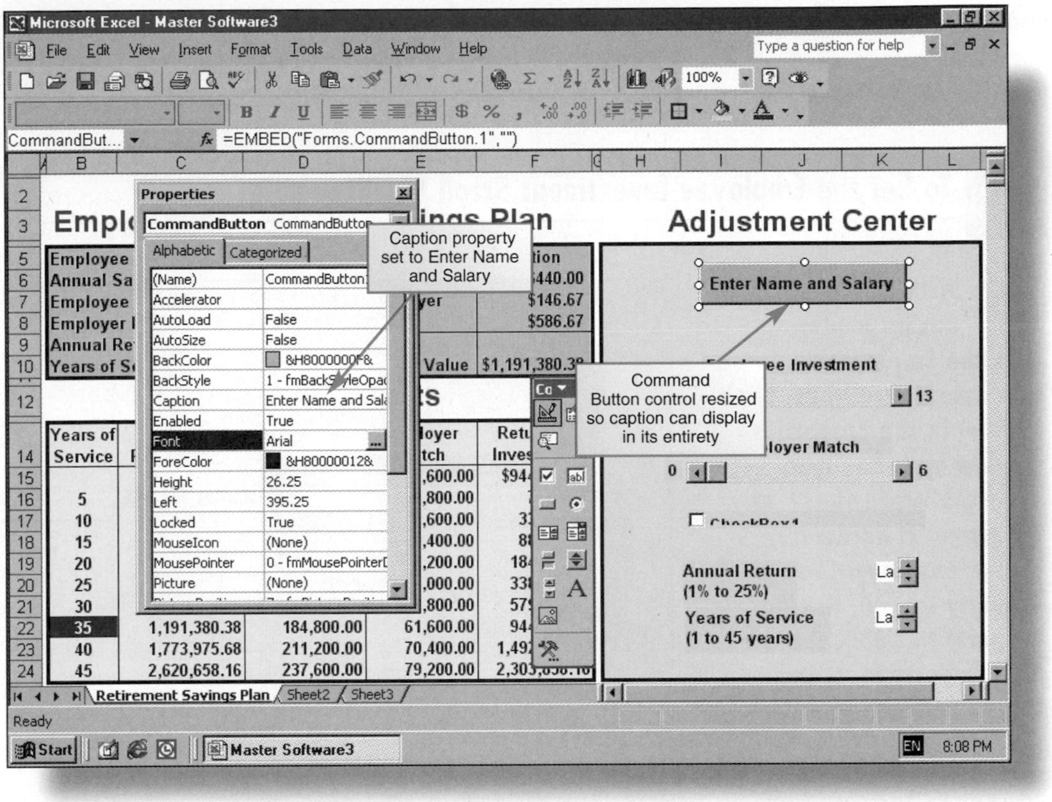

FIGURE 7-68

As you can see from the Properties window shown in Figure 7-68, a Command Button control has many different properties. One that may interest you that is not used in this project is the MousePointer property. If you click MousePointer in the Properties window and then click the MousePointer arrow, you will see several mouse pointers listed, many that you are familiar with from your experiences in Excel. If you change the MousePointer property, the mouse pointer will change when you point to the button. You can choose from the Hour Glass, I-beam, arrow, and cross.

SETTING THE EMPLOYEE INVESTMENT SCROLL BAR PROPERTIES The next step is to set the Employee Investment Scroll Bar properties. The function of this Scroll Bar control is to assign cell D7 a value. When you use a control, such as a scroll bar, you must set the Min and Max properties. The **Min property** is the least value the control can register. The **Max property** is the maximum value the control can register. You also have to set the SmallChange and LargeChange values. The **SmallChange property** is the value the control will change by each time you click the scroll arrow. The **LargeChange** property is the value the control will change by each time you click the scroll bar.

You can assign only whole numbers for these four properties. This increases the complexity of the VBA code because the cell in question must be assigned a decimal number. Thus, to assign the cell the maximum value 0.13 (13%), you actually must set the Maximum property to 1300, and then later in the VBA code divide by 10000 to assign the cell a value of 0.13.

Perform the following step to set the Employee Investment Scroll Bar properties.

Steps To Set the Employee Investment Scroll Bar Properties

1 With Excel in Design mode, click the Employee Investment scroll bar. Click (Name) in the Properties window and then type `scrEmployeeInvest` **as the name. If necessary, change the LargeChange property to** `100`**, the Max property to** `1300`**, the Min property to** `0`**, and the SmallChange property to** `50`**.**

The Employee Investment scroll bar Properties window displays as shown in Figure 7-69

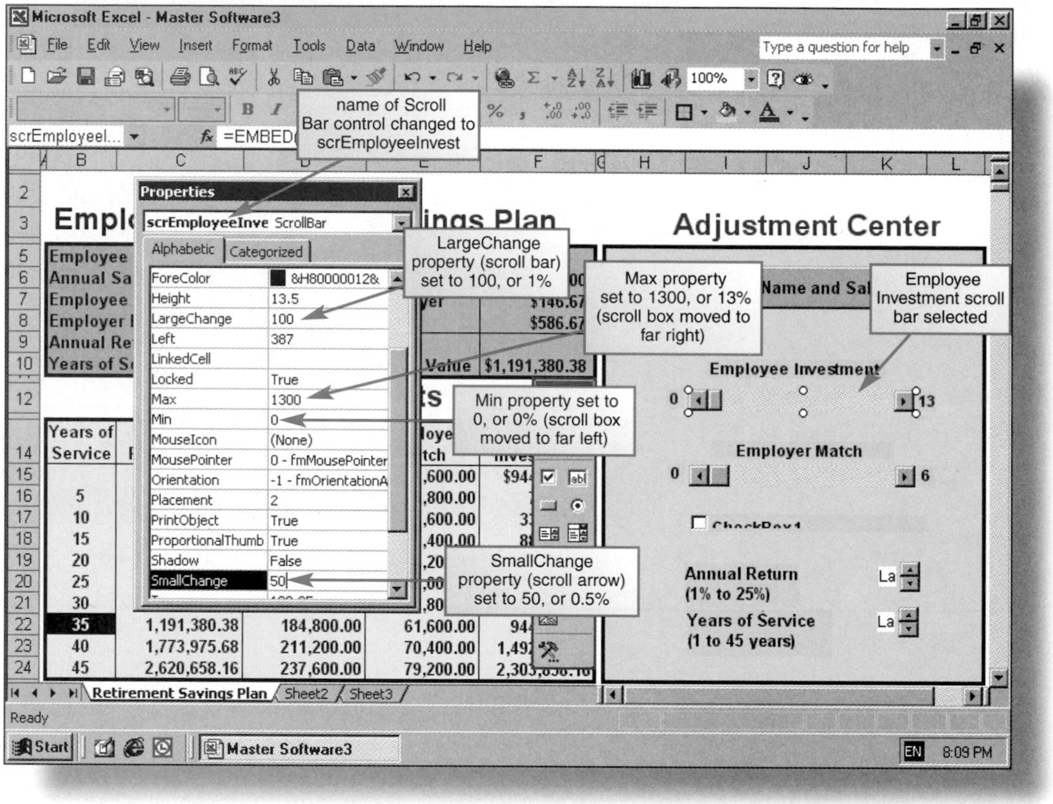

FIGURE 7-69

> **More About**
>
> **The Max Property**
>
> One of the more difficult concepts to understand about scroll bars is why the Max property is set to such a large number (600 in Figure 7-70), when the maximum value of the scroll bar is only 6% (.06). The two reasons are (1) the Max property can be set equal to only a whole number; and (2) the large number allows you to assign reasonable increments to the SmallChange and LargeChange properties of the scroll bar.

Excel automatically will determine how far to move the scroll button on the scroll bar when you click the scroll button (small change) and when you click the scroll boxes (large change) from the four numeric values entered in Step 1.

SETTING THE EMPLOYER MATCH SCROLL BAR PROPERTIES The next step sets the Employer Match Scroll Bar properties. The property settings are similar to those assigned to the Employee Investment scroll bar. Once the VBA code is written, this scroll bar will assign a value to cell D8.

Steps To Set the Employer Match Scroll Bar Properties

1 **With Excel in design mode, click the Employer Match scroll bar. Click (Name) in the Properties window and then type** `scrEmployerMatch` **as the name. Change the LargeChange property to** `100`**, the Max property to** `600`**, the Min property to** `0`**, and the SmallChange property to** `25`**.**

The Employer Match scroll bar Properties window displays as shown in Figure 7-70.

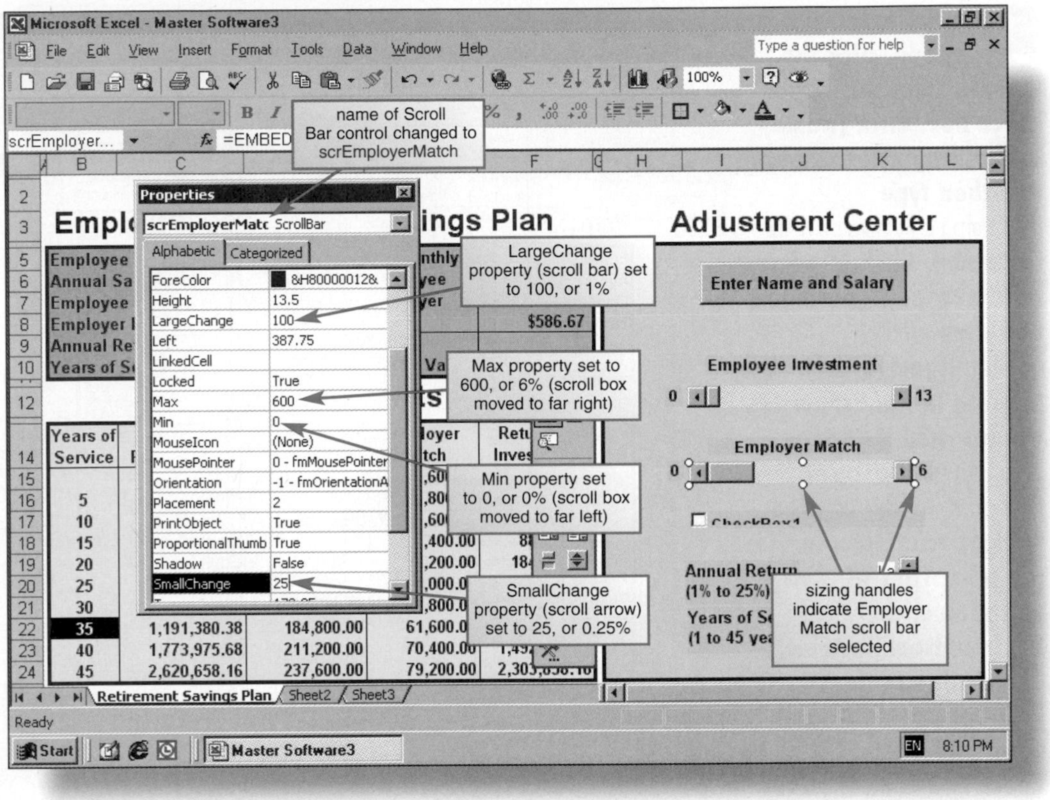

FIGURE 7-70

SETTING THE EMPLOYER MATCH CHECK BOX PROPERTIES The Employer Match check box enables or disables the Employer Match Scroll Bar control. If the Employer Match check box contains a check mark, then the Employer Match scroll bar is enabled and it can be used to change the value in cell D8. If the check box is empty, then the Employer Match Scroll Bar control is disabled. The VBA code will enable or disable the Scroll Bar based on the check box status. The following step sets the Include Employer Match check box properties.

More About

Properties

Many properties, such as the Value property (Figure 7-71), can be only one of two states — True or False. If it is True, the property is turned on. If it is False, the property is turned off. For example, assigning the Value property the value True, means that the check mark will display in the Employer Match check box.

Steps To Set the Employer Match Check Box Properties

1 With Excel in Design mode, click the Include Employer Match check box. Click (Name) in the Properties window and then type `chkEmployerMatch` **as the name. Click Alignment in the Properties window and then click 0 - fmAlignmentLeft. Click Caption in the Properties window and then type** `Include Employer Match?` **as the caption. Click SpecialEffect in the properties window and then click 0 - fmButtonEffectFlat. Click Value in the Properties window and then type** `True`**. Resize the Check Box control so the caption Include Employer Match? is visible.**

The Include Employer Match check box Properties window displays as shown in Figure 7-71.

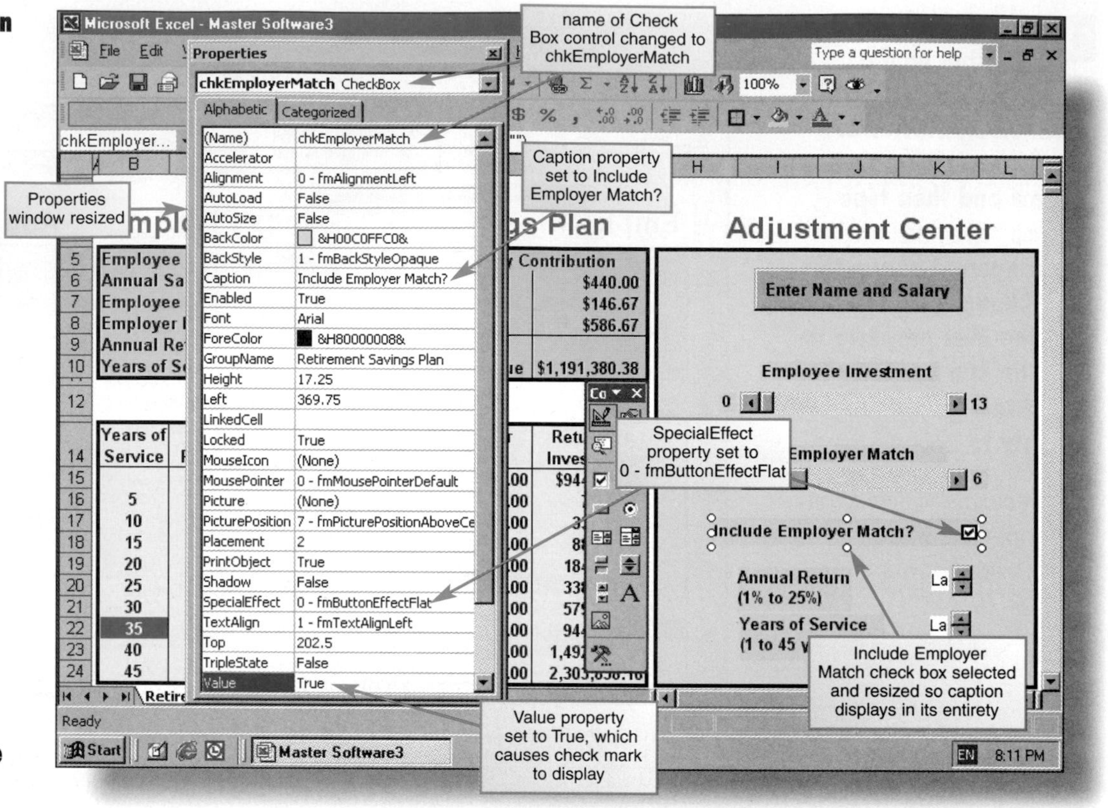

FIGURE 7-71

Setting the Value property to True inserts a check mark in the Include Employer Match check box.

SETTING THE ANNUAL RETURN AND YEARS OF SERVICE SPIN BUTTON PROPERTIES The Annual Return spin button increments or decrements the value in cell D9 by 0.25%. The Years of Service spin button increments or decrements the value in cell D10 by one. With a spin button, the up arrow increases the value, and the down arrow decreases the value. The Label controls to the left of the Spin Button controls (Figure 7-71) indicate the values assigned to the associated cells. The Min, Max, and SmallChange properties must be set. The SmallChange property indicates the change each time you click an arrow.

The following steps set the properties for the Annual Return and Years of Service spin buttons.

Steps To Set Properties for Annual Return and Years of Service Spin Buttons

1 **With Excel in Design mode, click the Annual Return spin button. Click (Name) in the Properties window and then type** `spnAnnualReturn` **as the name. If necessary, change the Max property to** `10000`**, the Min property to** `0`**, and the SmallChange property to** `25`**.**

The Annual Return Spin Button Properties window displays as shown in Figure 7-72.

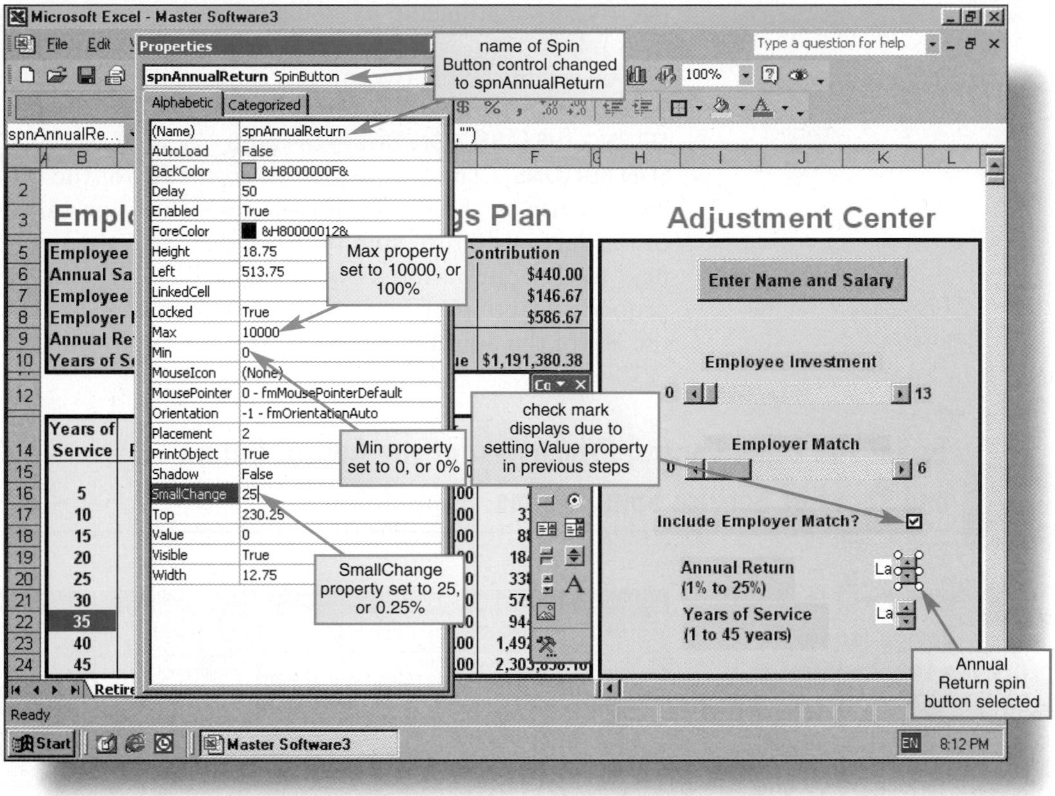

FIGURE 7-72

2 **Click the Years of Service spin button. Click (Name) in the Properties window and then type** `spnYearsofService` **as the name. Change the Max property to** `45`**, the Min property to** `1`**, and the SmallChange property to** `1`**.**

The Years of Service Spin Button Properties window displays as shown in Figure 7-73.

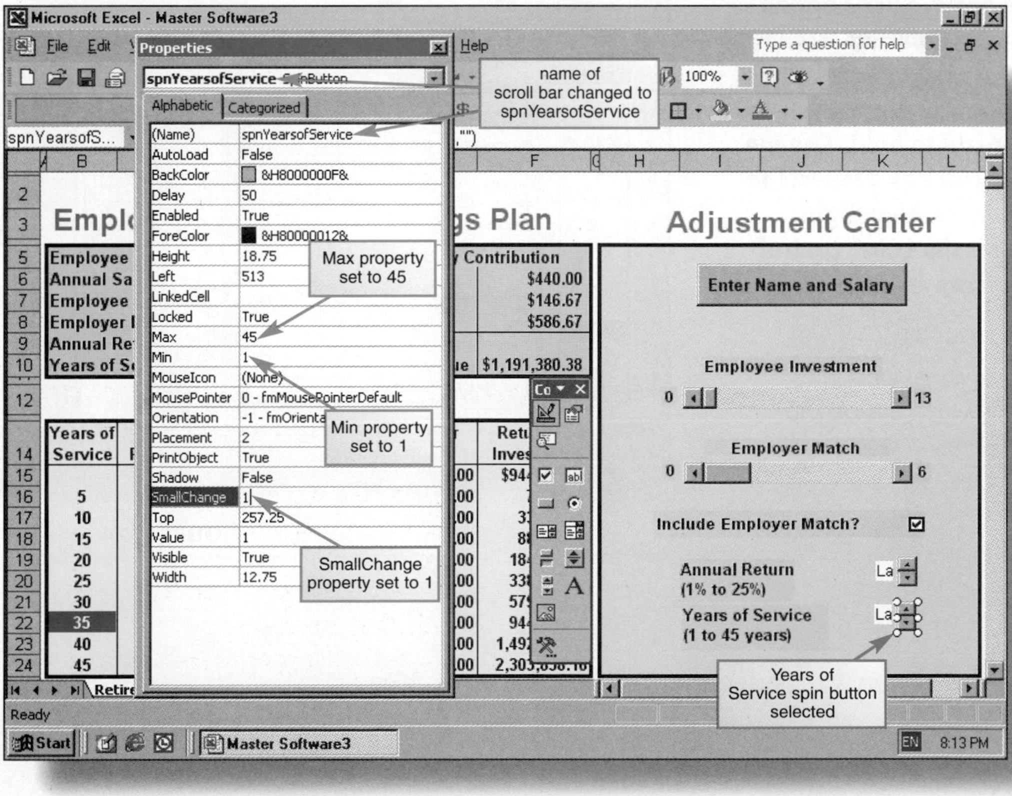

FIGURE 7-73

The least value the Annual Return spin button can be set to is 0 (0%). The greatest value is 10000 (100%). Once the VBA code is written, each time you click a button, the annual return in cell D9 will change by 0.25%. At this point in the project, no relationship exists between the Annual Return spin button and cell D9. This relationship will be established later in the VBA code. A similar relationship will be established between the Years of Service spin button and cell D10.

SETTING THE LABEL CONTROL PROPERTIES FOR THE ANNUAL RETURN AND YEARS OF SERVICE SPIN BUTTONS The Label controls to the left of the two Spin Button controls will be used to display the values of their respective spin buttons. Thus, when you click one of the Annual Return spin buttons, the new value will display in the Label control next to the spin button as well as in cell D9. The following steps set the Name property, Caption property, and TextAlign property for the two Label controls to the left of the Spin Button controls.

Steps To Set the Label Control Properties for the Annual Return and Years of Service Spin Buttons

1 **With Excel in Design mode, click the Label control to the left of the Annual Return spin button. Click (Name) in the Properties window and then type** `lblAnnualReturn` **as the name. Click Caption in the Properties window and then type** `5%` **as the caption. Change the Font property to bold. Change the TextAlign property to 3 - fmTextAlignRight. Resize the Label control as shown in Figure 7-74.**

The Annual Return Spin Button Label Properties window displays as shown in Figure 7-74.

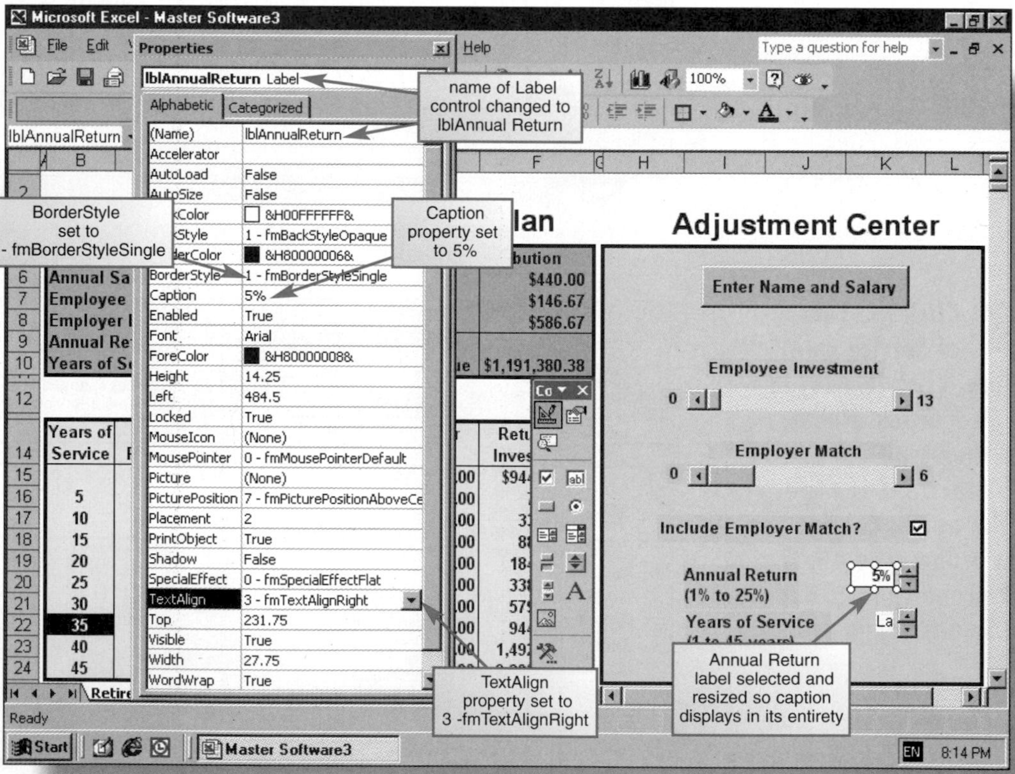

FIGURE 7-74

2 **Click the Label control to the left of the Years of Service Spin Button control. Click (Name) in the Properties window and then type** `lblYearsofService` **as the name. Change the Font property to bold. Click Caption in the Properties window and then type** `10` **as the caption. Change the TextAlign property to 3 - fmTextAlignRight. Resize the Label control as shown in Figure 7-75.**

The Years of Service Spin Button Label Properties window displays as shown in Figure 7-75.

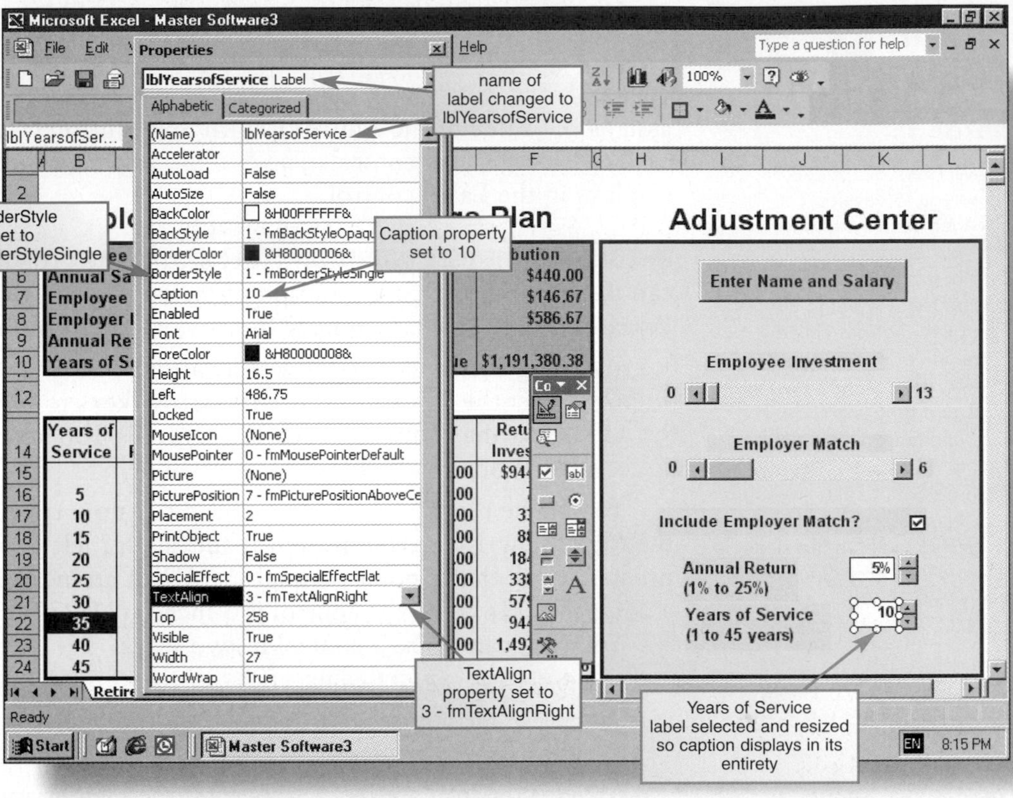

FIGURE 7-75

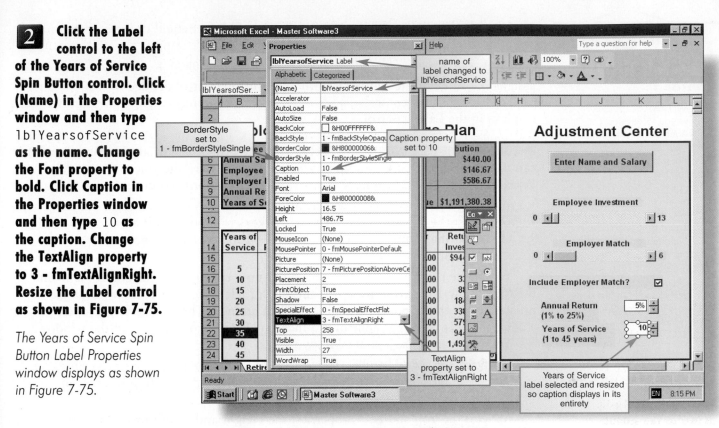

3 **Click the Close button on the right side of the Properties window title bar.**

The Adjustment Center displays as shown in Figure 7-76.

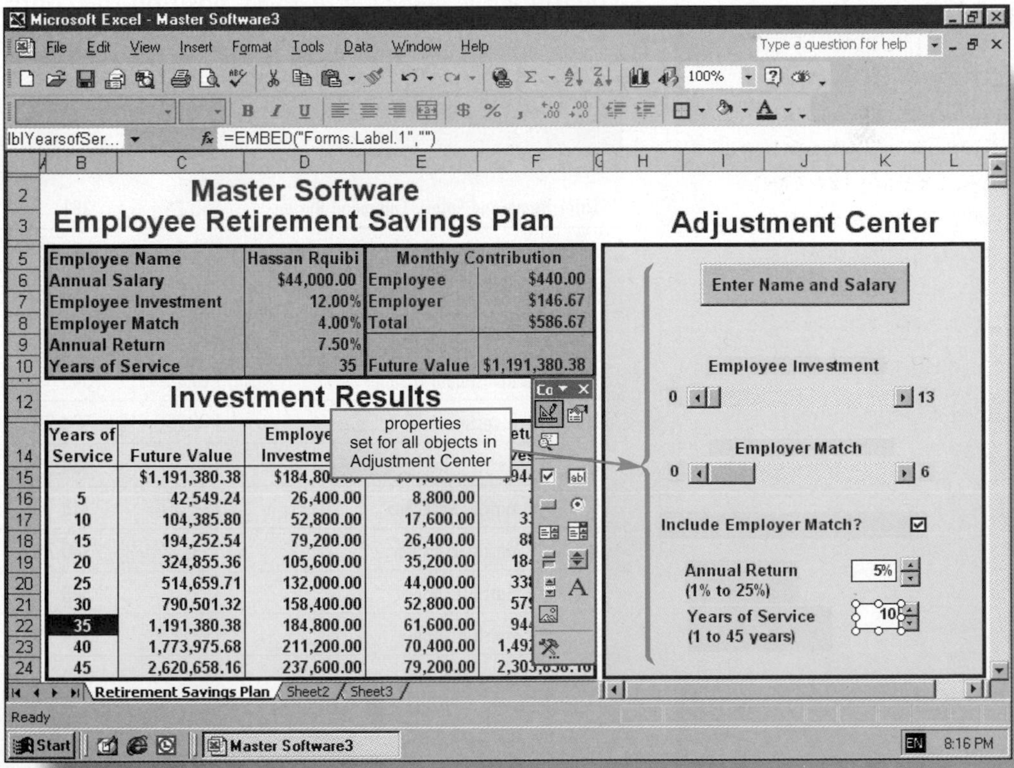

FIGURE 7-76

More About

Microsoft Script Editor

The Microsoft Script Editor allows you to develop complex Web pages that interact with your company's data, whether the data is in Excel or a database. The Script Editor generates what are called Active Server Pages. These Web pages contain both HTML and program code. For more information, click Tools, point to Macro, and click Microsoft Script Editor. When the Microsoft Script Editor opens click Help on the menu bar, and then click Contents on the Help menu.

Later in the VBA code, the Label controls will be set equal to the corresponding Spin Button controls through the use of the names. For example, the VBA statement

```
lblAnnualReturn = spnAnnualReturn.Value / 10000 & "%"
```

assigns the value of the Annual Return Spin Button control divided by 10000 to its corresponding Label control. The & "%" appends a percent sign to the number that displays in the Label control.

FINE-TUNING THE USER INTERFACE After setting the properties for all the controls, you can fine-tune the size and location of the controls in the Adjustment Center. With Excel in Design mode, you have three ways to reposition a control:

1. Drag the control to its new location.
2. Select the control and use the arrow keys to reposition it.
3. Select the control and set the control's Top and Left properties in the Properties window.

To use the third technique, you need to know the distance the control is from the top of row 1 (column headings) and the far left of column A (row headings) in points. Recall that a point is equal to 1/72 of an inch. Thus, if the Top property of a control is 216, then the control is 3 inches (216/72) from the top of the window.

You also can resize a control in two ways:

1. Drag the sizing handles.
2. Select the control and set the control's Height and Width properties in the Properties window.

As with the Top and Left properties, the Height and Width properties are measured in points. Table 7-6 lists the exact points for the Top, Left, Height, and Width properties of each of the controls in the Adjustment Center.

The following steps resize and reposition the controls in the Adjustment Center using the values in Table 7-6.

Table 7-6 Exact Locations of Controls in Adjustment Center

CONTROL	TOP	LEFT	HEIGHT	WIDTH
Enter Name and Salary Command Button	50.25	381	26.25	123.75
Adjustment Center Label	19.5	377.25	22.5	165
Employee Investment Label	99	386.25	14.25	119.75
Employee Investment Scroll Bar	116.25	360.75	14.25	157.5
Employee Investment 0 Label	116.25	348	13.5	6.75
Employee Investment 13 Label	116.25	524.25	13.5	14.25
Employer Match Label	138	386.25	14.25	114.75
Employer Match Check Box	179.25	348	21.75	174.75
Employer Match Scroll Bar	153	360.75	14.25	157.5
Employer Match 0 Label	153	348	13.5	6.75
Employer Match 6 Label	153	524.25	13.5	6.75
Annual Return Label	218.25	348	27	75
Annual Return Spin Button	215.25	502.5	18	13.5
Annual Return Label	215.25	471	18	31.5
Years of Service Label	255.75	348	27	79.75
Years of Service Spin Button	252	502.5	18	13.5
Years of Service Label	252	471	18	31.5

Steps To Resize and Reposition the Controls in the Adjustment Center

1 Click the Properties button on the Control Toolbox toolbar. Drag the Properties window to the left side of the Excel window. Click the Enter Name and Salary button. Change its Top, Left, Height, and Width properties to those listed in Table 7-6.

The Name and Salary Command Button control Properties window displays as shown in Figure 7-77.

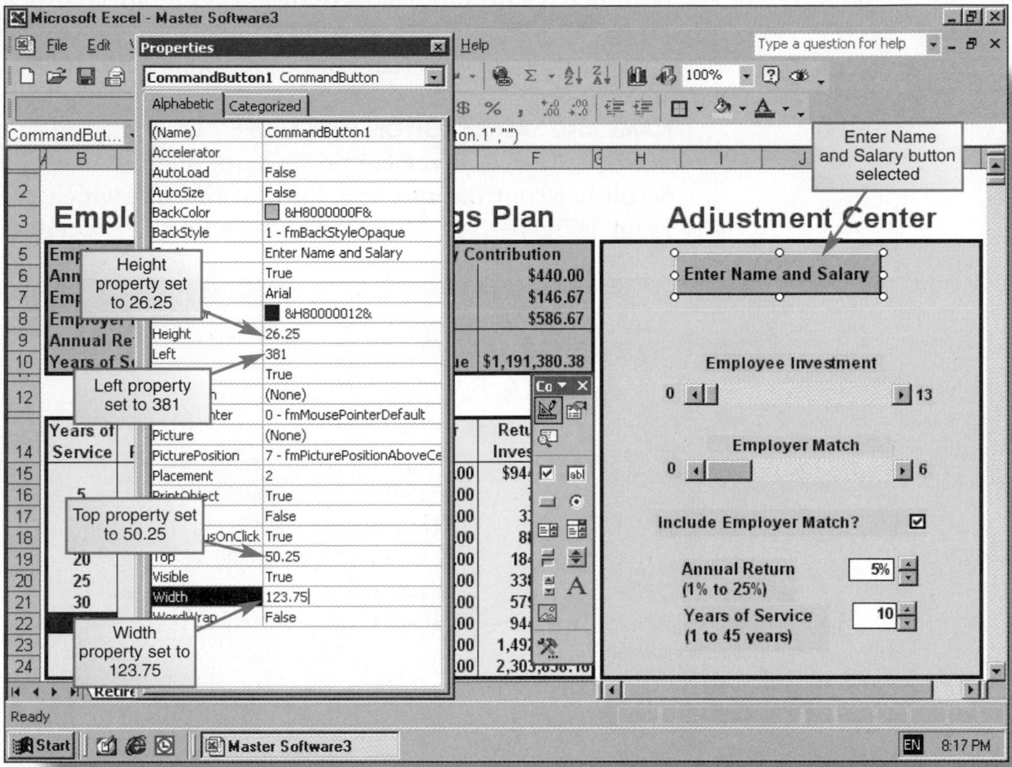

FIGURE 7-77

2 One at a time, select the controls and change their Top, Left, Height, and Width properties to those listed in Table 7-6. Close the Properties window and then deselect the Years of Service (1 to 45 years) label by clicking cell A1.

The Adjustment Center displays as shown in Figure 7-78.

3 Click the Save button on the Standard toolbar.

Excel saves the workbook using the file name Master Software3.

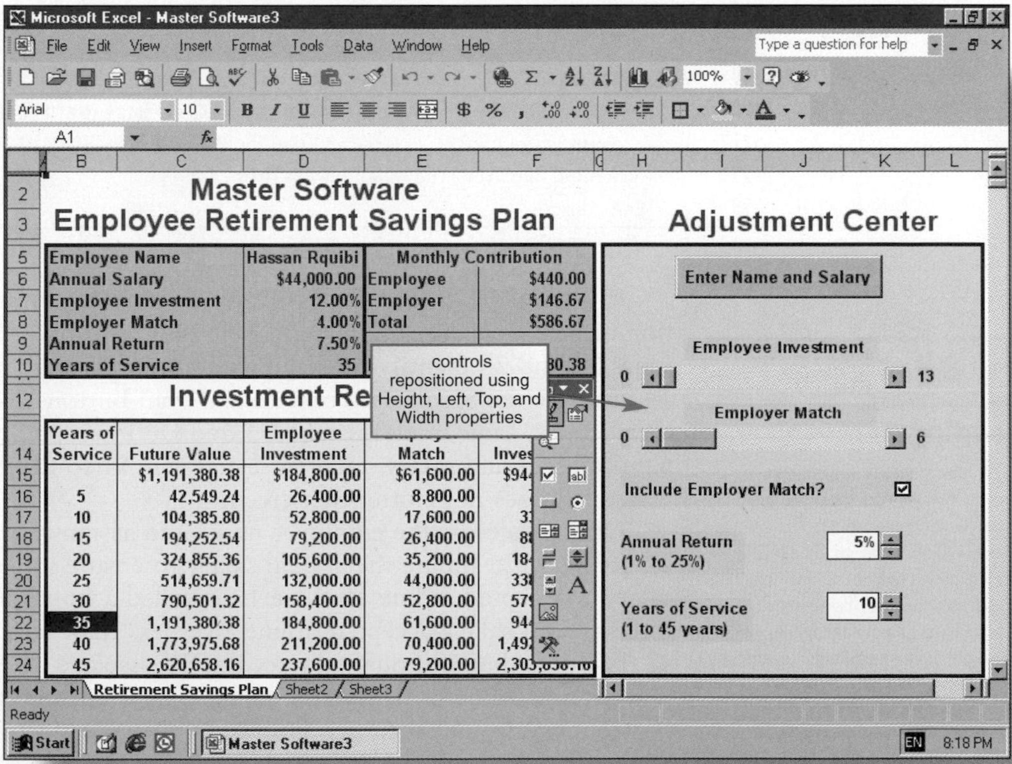

FIGURE 7-78

Step 3 — Write the Code

The next step is to write a procedure for each of the following six controls: (1) Enter Name and Salary Button; (2) Employee Investment Scroll Bar; (3) Include Employer Match Check Box; (4) Employer Match Scroll Bar; (5) Annual Return Spin Button; and (6) Years of Service Spin Button.

NAME AND SALARY BUTTON PROCEDURE The function of the Enter Name and Salary button is to accept the employee name and annual salary. It also assigns values to the Scroll Bar controls and Spin Button controls, which in turn resets the values in the range D7:D10. The Name and Salary Button procedure is shown in Table 7-7.

Table 7-7 Enter Name and Salary Button Procedure

LINE *VBA CODE*

```
1   ' Name and Salary Button Procedure                 Author:   Micheal Ericsson
2   ' Date Created:   5/17/2002
3   ' Run from:       Employee Retirement Savings Plan Model Sheet by clicking button
4   '                 labeled Enter Name and Salary
5   ' Function:       This procedure initializes the scroll bars and spin buttons,
6   '                 clears the range D5:D6, selects cell A1, accepts the employee
7   '                 name (cell D5) and annual salary (cell D6), and validates the
8   '                 annual salary before assigning it to cell D6.
9   '
10  Private Sub CommandButton1_Click()
11    scrEmployeeInvest = 100
12    scrEmployerMatch = 0
13    spnAnnualReturn = 500
14    spnYearsofService = 10
15    Range("D5:D6").ClearContents
16    Range("A1").Select
17    Range("D5").Value = InputBox("Employee Name?", "Enter")
18    AnnualSalary = InputBox("Annual Salary?", "Enter")
19    Do While AnnualSalary <= 0
20    AnnualSalary = InputBox("Annual salary must be > zero.", "Please Re-enter")
21    Loop
22    Range("D6").Value = AnnualSalary
23  End Sub
```

In Table 7-7, lines 1 through 9 are comments and have no bearing on the execution of this procedure. Comments help you remember the function of a procedure. Lines 10 and 23 identify the beginning and end of the procedure. Lines 11 through 14 initialize the Scroll Bar controls and Spin Buttons controls by assigning values to their names. Line 15 clears cells D5 and D6 in preparation to receive the employee name and annual salary. Line 16 selects cell A1 so the heavy border surrounding the active cell does not clutter the screen.

Line 17 accepts the employee name and assigns it to cell D5. Lines 18 through 22 accept and validate the annual salary to ensure it is greater than zero. The annual salary is accepted in line 18. Line 19 is called a **Do-While statement**. It tests to see if the annual salary accepted in line 18 is less than or equal to zero. If the annual salary is less than or equal to zero, line 20 displays an error message and requests that the user re-enter the annual salary. The **Loop statement** in line 21 transfers control back to the corresponding Do-While statement in line 19, which tests the annual salary again.

More About

Looping

VBA has several statements that allow you to loop through a series of statements. They are the Do-While or Do-Until, which loops while or until a condition is True; For-Next, which uses a counter to repeat statements a specified number of times; and For Each-Next, which repeats a group of statements for each object in a collection.

The VBA code in lines 19 through 21 is called a **loop**. If the variable Annual Salary is greater than zero, then the Do-While statement in line 19 transfers control to line 22, which assigns the value of AnnualSalary to cell D6. Line 23 halts execution of the procedure and returns Excel to Ready mode.

The variable AnnualSalary first was used in line 18. A **variable** is a location in the computer's memory whose value can change as the program executes. You create variables in VBA code as you need them. In this case, a variable is needed to hold the value accepted from the user in lines 18 and 20. Variable names follow the same rules as control names (see page E 7.47).

The following steps enter the Enter Name and Salary Button procedure shown in Table 7-7.

Steps To Enter the Enter Name and Salary Button Procedure

1 **With Excel in design mode, click the View Code button on the Control Toolbar toolbar (Figure 7-38 on page E 7.34). Click the Object box arrow at the top of the window and then click CommandButton1 in the alphabetical list.**

The Visual Basic Editor starts. When the CommandButton1 control is selected, the Visual Basic Editor displays the Sub and End Sub statements for the procedure and positions the insertion point between the two statements (Figure 7-79).

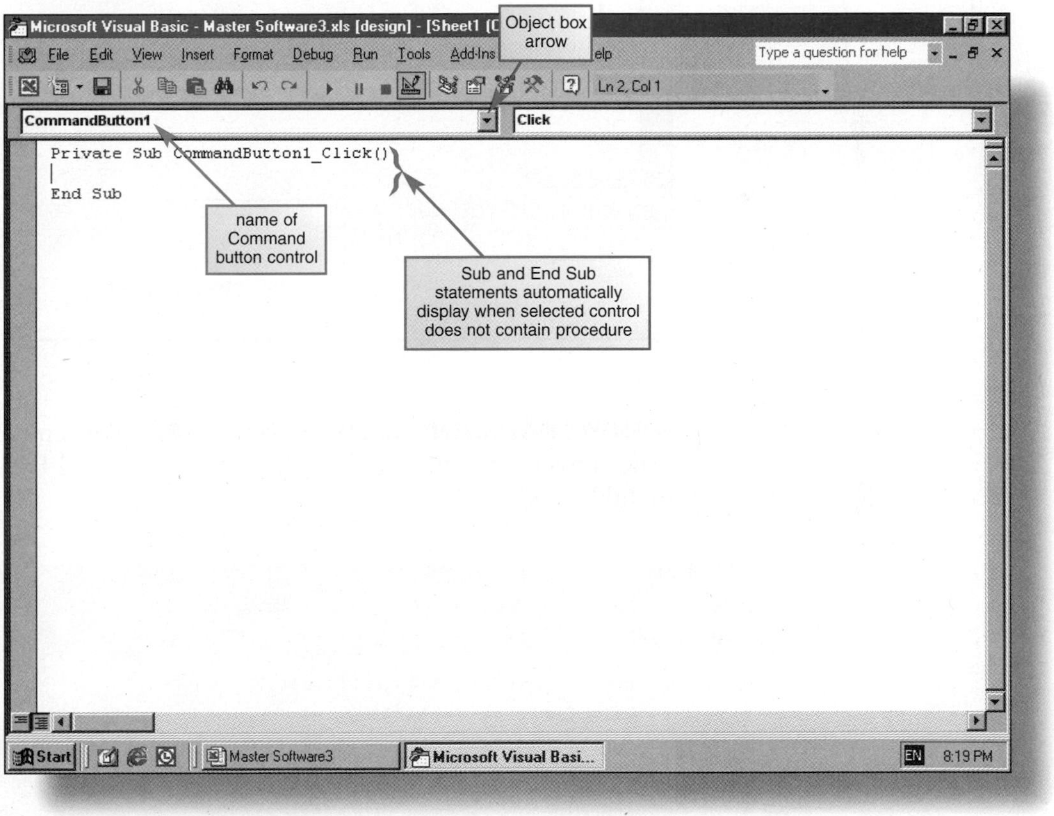

FIGURE 7-79

2 Click before the P in Private and then press the ENTER key. Enter the lines 1 through 9 in Table 7-7 on page E 7.62. Click the blank line between the Sub and End Sub statements. Enter lines 11 through 22 in Table 7-7.

The Name and Salary Button procedure displays as shown in Figure 7-80.

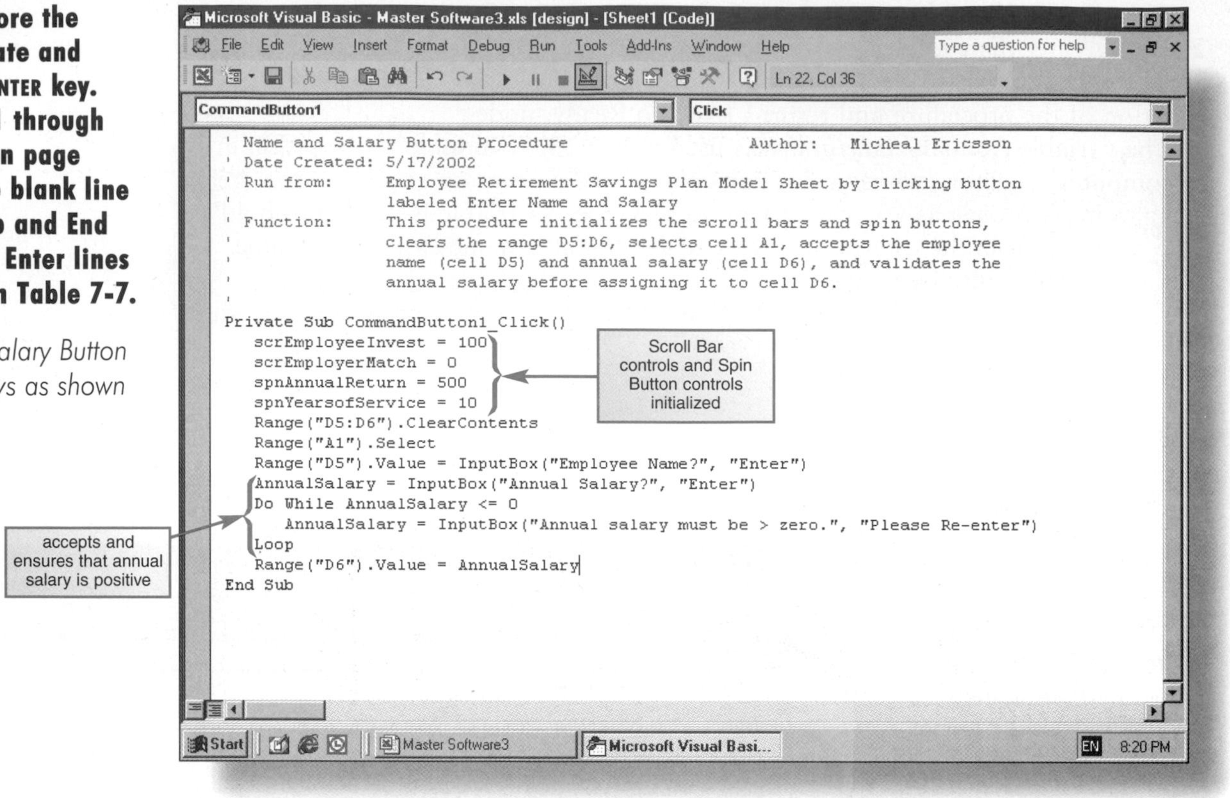

FIGURE 7-80

EMPLOYEE INVESTMENT SCROLL BAR PROCEDURE The Employee Investment Scroll Bar procedure assigns the value of the scroll bar to cell D7. The procedure is shown in Table 7-8.

Table 7-8 Employee Investment Scroll Bar Procedure

LINE	STATEMENT
1	`' Employee Investment Scroll Bar Procedure          Author:   Micheal Ericsson`
2	`' Date Created:  5/17/2002`
3	`' Run from:      Employee Retirement Savings Plan Model Sheet by clicking the`
4	`'                scroll bar labeled Employee Investment`
5	`' Function:      This procedure assigns the value of the Employee Investment scroll`
6	`'                bar to cell D7.`
7	`'`
8	`Private Sub scrEmployeeInvest_Change()`
9	`   Range("D7").Value = scrEmployeeInvest.Value / 10000`
10	`End Sub`

In Table 7-8, the first seven lines are comments. Lines 8 and 10 define the beginning and end of the procedure. Line 9 assigns the value of the Scroll Bar control (scrEmployeeInvest) divided by 10000 to cell D7. Recall that the scroll bar was assigned a Max property of 1300, which is equivalent to 130,000%. Thus, the value of scrEmployeeInvest must be divided by 10000 to assign the correct percentage value to cell D7. The following steps enter the Employee Investment Scroll Bar procedure shown in Table 7-8.

Steps To Enter the Employee Investment Scroll Bar Procedure

1 With the Visual Basic Editor active, click the Object box arrow at the top of the window and then click scrEmployeeInvest.

The Visual Basic Editor displays the Sub and End Sub statements for this procedure and positions the insertion point between the two statements.

2 Enter the VBA code shown in Table 7-8.

The Employee Investment Scroll Bar procedure displays as shown in Figure 7-81.

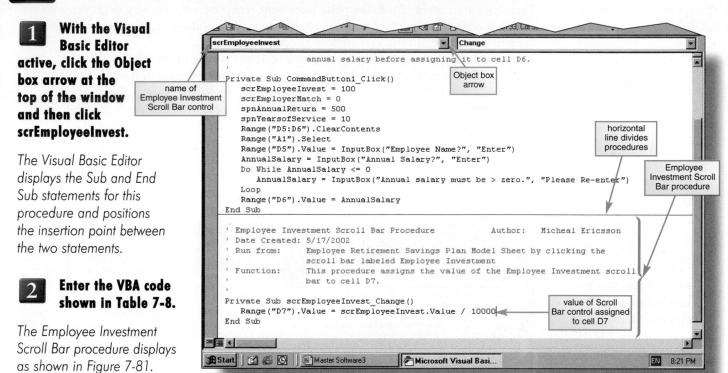

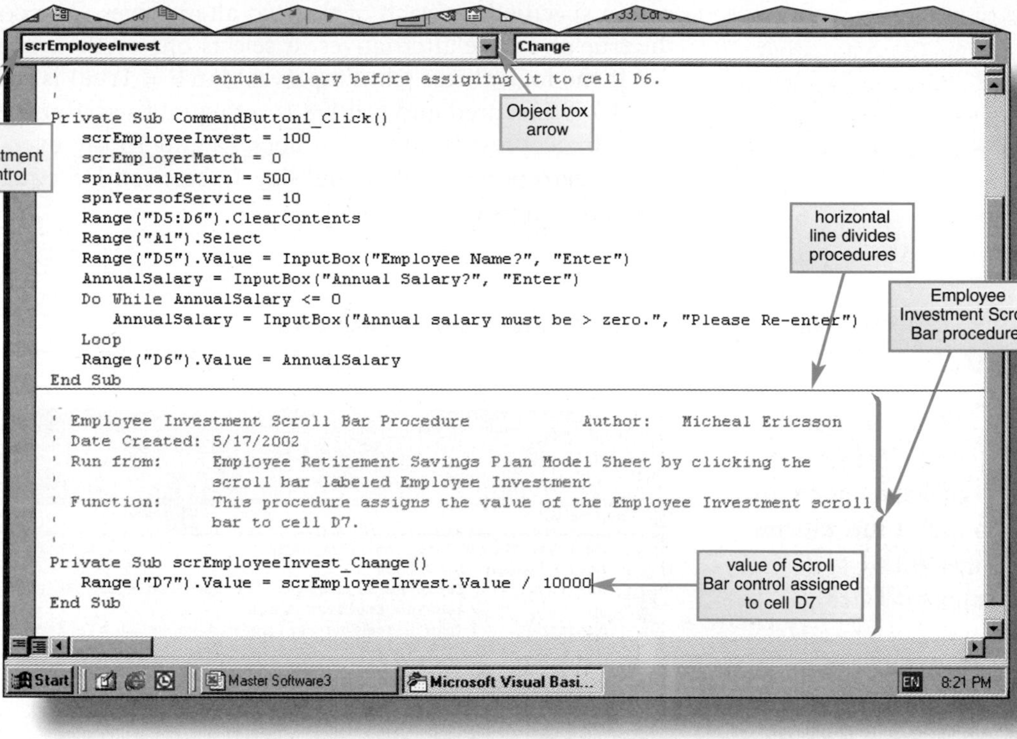

FIGURE 7-81

EMPLOYER MATCH CHECK BOX PROCEDURE As with the other procedures, the Employer Match Check Box procedure executes only when you click the check box. If the check box is checked, then the name of the check box (chkEmployerMatch) is equal to the logical value True. If the check box is unchecked, then the name of the check box is equal to the logical value False. Adding a check mark or removing a check mark triggers the event that executes the Employee Match Check Box procedure shown in Table 7-9.

Table 7-9 Employer Match Check Box Procedure

LINE	STATEMENT
1	' Employer Match Check Box Procedure Author: Micheal Ericsson
2	' Date Created: 5/17/2002
3	' Run from: Employee Retirement Savings Plan Model Sheet by clicking check box
4	' labeled Employer Match
5	' Function: This procedure assigns the value of the Employer Match scroll bar
6	' or 0 (zero) to cell D8.
7	'
8	Private Sub chkEmployerMatch_Click()
9	If chkEmployerMatch.Value = True Then
10	Range("D8").Value = scrEmployerMatch.Value / 10000
11	Else
12	scrEmployerMatch = 0
13	Range("D8").Value = 0
14	End If
15	End Sub

In Table 7-9 on the previous page, lines 1 through 7 are comments. Lines 8 and 15 define the beginning and end of the procedure. Lines 9 through 14 include an If-Then-Else statement. An **If-Then-Else statement** represents a two-way decision with action specified for each of the two alternatives. The computer never executes both the true and false alternatives. It selects one or the other.

If the logical test (chkEmployerMatch = True) is true in line 9 of Table 7-9, then line 10 is executed and cell D8 is set equal to scrEmployerMatch divided by 10000. If the logical test is false, then lines 12 and 13 are executed. Line 12 sets the scroll box to zero percent (0%), and line 13 sets cell D8 equal to zero percent (0%). The following steps enter the code.

Steps To Enter the Employer Match Check Box Procedure

1 With the Visual Basic Editor active, click the Object box arrow at the top of the window and then click chkEmployerMatch.

The Visual Basic Editor displays the Sub and End Sub statements for this procedure and positions the insertion point between the two statements.

2 Enter the VBA code shown in Table 7-9.

The Employer Match Check Box procedure displays as shown in Figure 7-82.

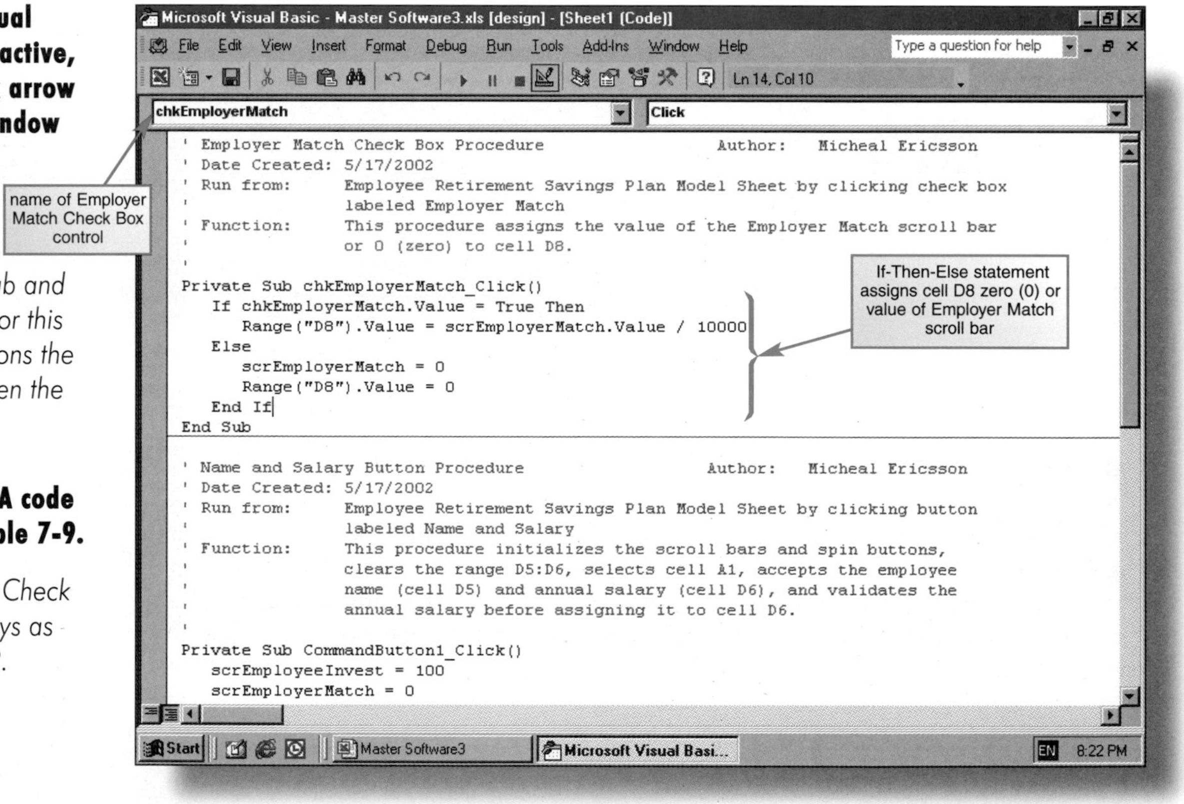

FIGURE 7-82

EMPLOYER MATCH SCROLL BAR PROCEDURE The Employer Match Scroll Bar procedure executes whenever you use the Scroll Bar control below the check box. The Scroll Bar control is active only when the Employer Match Check Box control is checked. The Scroll Bar control event assigns the value of scrEmployerMatch to cell D8. The Employer Match Scroll Bar procedure is shown in Table 7-10.

In Table 7-10, line 10 in the If-Then statement assigns the value of the scroll bar (scrEmployerMatch) divided by 10000 to cell D8. This statement, however, is executed only if the logical test in line 9 (chkEmployerMatch =True) is true. Thus, the Employer Match Check Box control determines whether the Scroll Bar control is active. The following steps enter the code.

Table 7-10 Employer Match Scroll Bar Procedure

LINE *STATEMENT*

```
' Employer Match Scroll Bar Procedure                  Author:   Micheal Ericsson
' Date Created:   5/17/2002
' Run from:       Employee Retirement Savings Plan Model Sheet by clicking the
'                 scroll bar labeled Employer Match
' Function:       This procedure assigns the value of the Employer Match scroll bar
'                 to cell D8.
'
Private Sub scrEmployerMatch_Change()
   If chkEmployerMatch.Value = True Then
      Range("D8").Value = scrEmployerMatch.Value / 10000
   End If
End Sub
```

Steps To Enter the Employer Match Scroll Bar Procedure

1 With the Visual Basic Editor active, click the Object box arrow at the top of the window and then click scrEmployerMatch.

The Visual Basic Editor displays the Sub and End Sub statements for this procedure and positions the insertion point between the two statements.

2 Enter the VBA code shown in Table 7-10.

The Employer Match Scroll Bar procedure displays as shown in Figure 7-83.

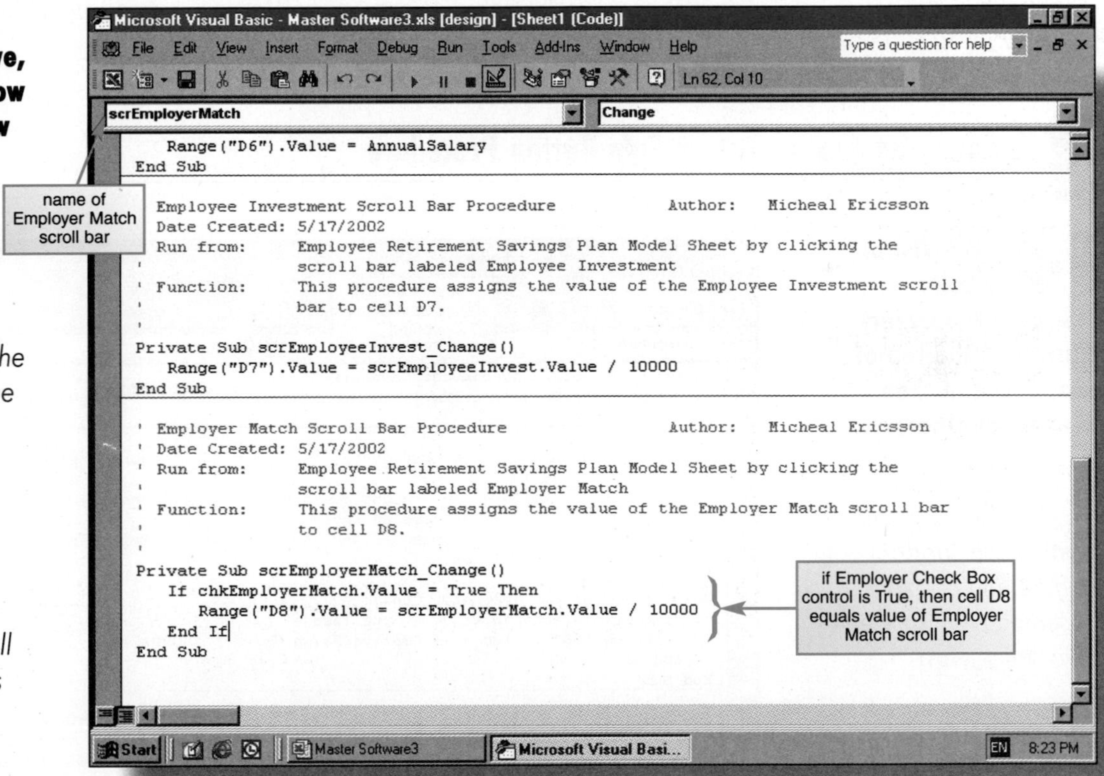

FIGURE 7-83

ANNUAL RETURN SPIN BUTTON PROCEDURE The Annual Return Spin Button procedure executes whenever you click one of it buttons. Its function is to set the percent value in cell D9 and in the corresponding Label control. Recall that you set the SmallChange property to 25, which when divided by 10000 equals 0.25%. The Annual Return Spin Button Control procedure is shown in Table 7-11.

Table 7-11 Annual Return Spin Button Procedure

LINE	STATEMENT
1	`' Annual Return Spin Button Procedure          Author:    Micheal Ericsson`
2	`' Date Created:  5/17/2002`
3	`' Run from:      Retirement Savings Plan Model Sheet by clicking the spin`
4	`'                button labeled Annual Return`
5	`' Function:      This procedure assigns the value of the Annual Return spin button`
6	`'                to cell D9.`
7	`'`
8	`Private Sub spnAnnualReturn_Change()`
9	`   lblAnnualReturn = spnAnnualReturn.Value / 100 & "%"`
10	`   Range("D9").Value = spnAnnualReturn.Value / 10000`
11	`End Sub`

In Table 7-11, line 9 uses the names of the two controls to assign the value of the Spin Button control to the Label control. In this case, spnAnnualReturn is divided by 100 because a percent should display as a whole number percent in the Label control. The & "%" at the end of line 9 appends a percent sign to the value. Line 10 assigns the value of spnAnnualReturn divided by 10000 to cell D9. The following steps enter the code.

Steps To Enter the Annual Return Spin Button Procedure

1 With the Visual Basic Editor active, click the Object box arrow at the top of the window and then click spnAnnualReturn.

The Visual Basic Editor displays the Sub and End Sub statements for this procedure and positions the insertion point between the two statements.

2 Enter the VBA code shown in Table 7-11.

The Annual Return Spin Button procedure displays as shown in Figure 7-84.

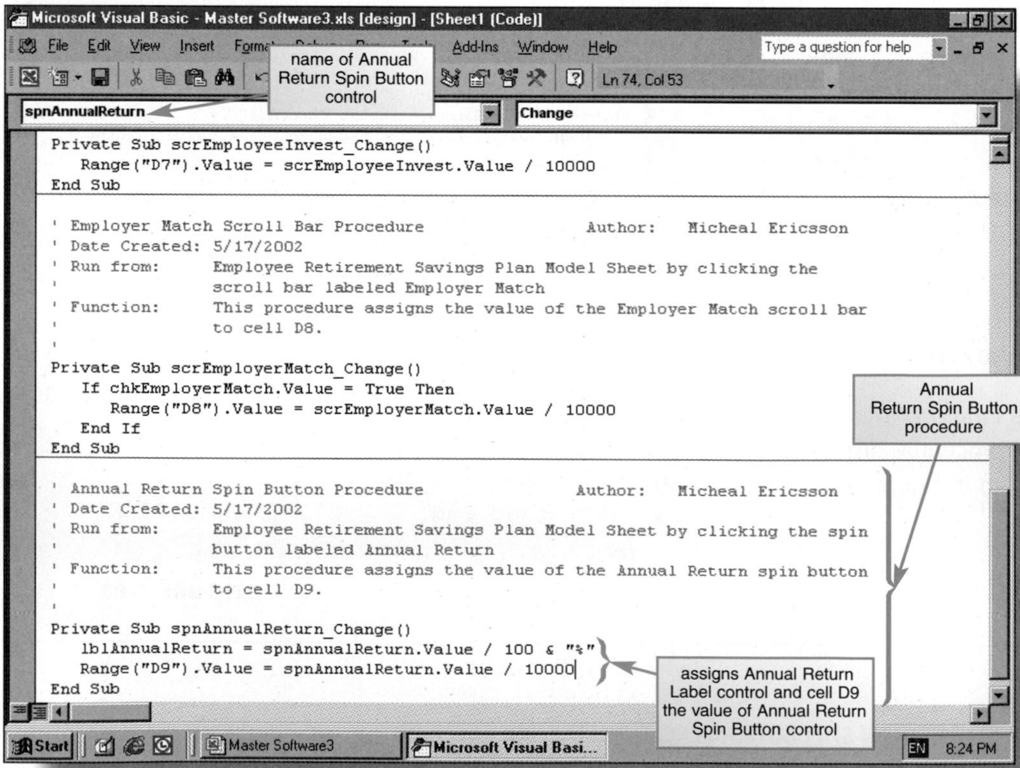

FIGURE 7-84

YEARS OF SERVICE SPIN BUTTON PROCEDURE The Years of Service Spin Button procedure determines the value assigned to cell D10 and in the corresponding Label control and is executed by Excel when the user clicks one of the buttons making up the spin button control. The procedure is shown in Table 7-12.

Table 7-12 Years of Service Spin Button Procedure

LINE	*STATEMENT*
1	`' Years of Service Spin Button Procedure          Author:   Micheal Ericsson`
2	`' Date Created:     5/17/2002`
3	`' Run from:         Employee Retirement Savings Plan Model Sheet by clicking the spin`
4	`'                   button labeled Years of Service`
5	`' Function:         This procedure assigns the value of the Years of Service spin`
6	`'                   button to cell D10.`
7	`'`
8	`Private Sub spnYearsofService_Change()`
9	`   lblYearsofService = spnYearsofService`
10	`   Range("D10").Value = spnYearsofService`
11	`End Sub`

In Table 7-12, line 9 assigns spnYearsofService (value of the Spin Button control) to the corresponding Label control. Line 10 assigns the value of spnYearsofService to cell D10. The following steps enter the code.

Steps To Enter the Years of Service Spin Button Procedure

1 With the Visual Basic Editor active, click the Object box arrow at the top of the window and then click spnYearsofService.

The Visual Basic Editor displays the Sub and End Sub statements for this procedure and positions the insertion point between the two statements.

2 Enter the VBA code shown in Table 7-12.

The Years of Service Spin Button procedure displays as shown in Figure 7-85.

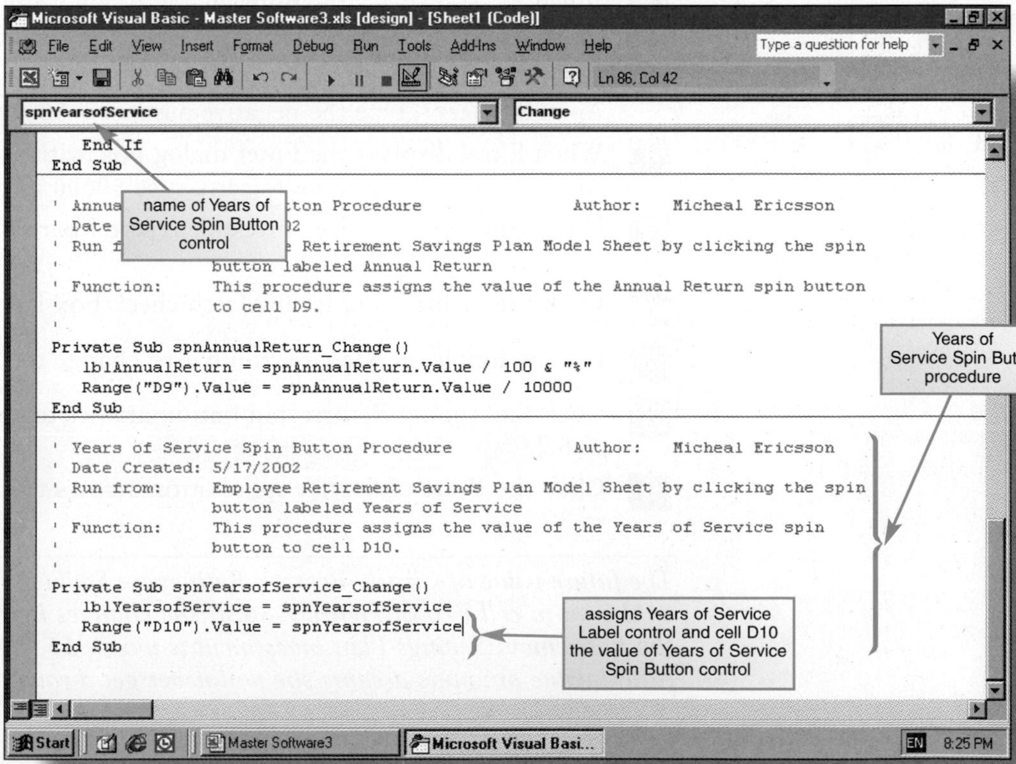

FIGURE 7-85

More About

Debugging VBA Code

The Visual Basic Editor allows you to locate the source of errors in your code through the use of the Debug menu. You can set breakpoints in your code that will cause Excel to stop executing your code at a certain point. At that time, Excel shows the current executing code in the editor. You can point at variables in your code to make sure they are correctly set. Or you can step through your code line by line to make sure the code is getting executed in the order that you expect it to. Click Microsoft Visual Basic Help on the Help menu in the Visual Basic Editor window for more information about debugging.

More About

The Visual Basic Editor

When you open the Visual Basic Editor, the same windows display that displayed when you closed it the last time.

The VBA code is complete. The following steps close the Visual Basic Editor, quit Design mode, protect the worksheet, and save the workbook. Before closing the Visual Basic Editor, you should verify your code by comparing it with Figures 7-80 through 7-85 on pages E 7.64 through E 7.69.

TO CLOSE THE VISUAL BASIC EDITOR, PROTECT THE WORKSHEET, AND SAVE THE WORKBOOK

1. Click the Close button on the right side of the Visual Basic Editor title bar.
2. When the Excel window displays, click the Exit Design Mode button on the Control Toolbox toolbar. Close the Control Toolbox toolbar.
3. Click Tools on the menu bar, point to Protection, and then click Protect Sheet. When the Protect Sheet dialog box displays, type `planright` in the Password to unprotect sheet text box. Verify the password when prompted by clicking OK.
4. Click the Save button on the Standard toolbar to save the workbook using the file name Master Software3.

Testing the Controls

The final step is to test the controls in the Adjustment Center. Use the following data: Employee Name – Christy Pearce; Annual Salary (cell D6) – $50,000.00; Employee Investment (cell D7) – 6%; Employer Match (cell D8) – 3%; Annual Return (cell D9) – 6.25%; and Years of Service (cell D10) – 30.

TO TEST THE CONTROLS IN THE ADJUSTMENT CENTER USER INTERFACE

1. Click the Enter Name and Salary button in the Adjustment Center.
2. When Excel displays the Enter dialog box with the prompt message, Employee Name?, type `Christy Pearce` as the employee name.
3. When Excel displays the Enter dialog box with the prompt message, Annual Salary?, type the negative number `-50000` as the annual salary.
4. When Excel displays the Enter dialog box with the prompt message, Annual salary must be >= to zero, type `50000` as the annual salary.
5. Use the includeEmployee Investment scroll bar to change the value in cell D7 to 6%.
6. Click the Include Employer Match check box if it does not have a check mark.
7. Use the Employer Match scroll bar to change the value in cell D8 to 3%.
8. Click the Annual Return spin button arrows to change the value in cell D9 to 6.25%.
9. Click the Years of Service spin button arrows to change the value in cell D10 to 30.

The future value of Christy Pearce's Retirement Savings Plan investment is $395,219.98 as shown in cell F10 of Figure 7-86. If she changes her years of service to 45 years, the Retirement Savings Plan investment is worth $1,118,188.80 (cell C24). Both future value amounts assume she will never get a raise.

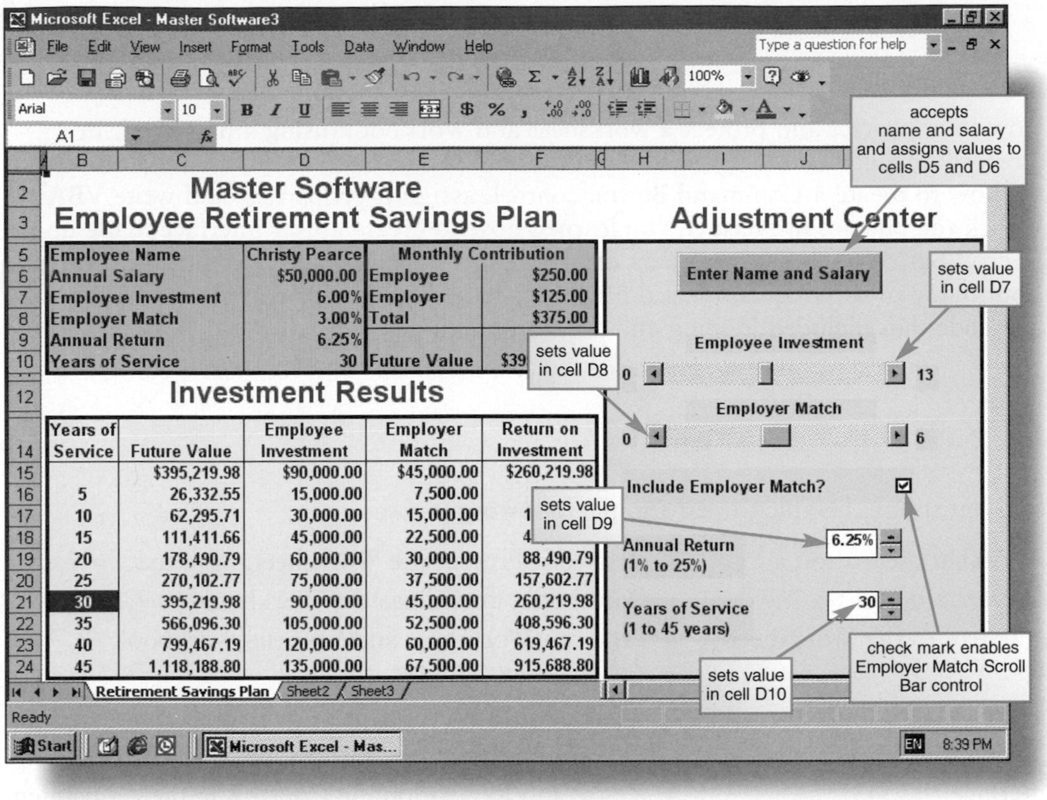

FIGURE 7-86

If the controls in the Adjustment Center do not work as indicated here, then unprotect the worksheet, display the Control Toolbox toolbar, click the Design Mode button on the Control Toolbox toolbar, and check the controls' properties and VBA code.

Quitting Excel

The project is complete. To quit Excel, follow the steps below.

TO QUIT EXCEL

1. Click the Close button on the right side of the title bar.
2. If the Microsoft Excel dialog box displays, click the No button.
3. If you wish to reset the toolbar and File menu to remove the items added in this project, click Tools on the menu bar, and then click Customize. When the Customize dialog box displays, click the Reset my usage data button, and then click the Yes button.

More About

Quick Reference

For a table that lists how to complete the tasks covered in this book using the mouse, menu, shortcut menu, and keyboard, see the Quick Reference Summary at the back of this book or visit the Shelly Cashman Series Office site (scsite.com/offxp/qr.htm), and click the application name.

More About

Microsoft Certification

The Microsoft Office User Specialist (MOUS) Certification program provides an opportunity for you to obtain a valuable industry credential — proof that you have the Excel 2002 skills required by employers. For more information, see Appendix E or visit the Shelly Cashman Series MOUS Web page at scsite.com/offxp/cert.htm.

CASE PERSPECTIVE SUMMARY

With the three workbooks developed in this project, Louis Pankros can post the new workbook to the intranet as you complete each phase. The final phase, Master Software3, includes the easy-to-use Adjustment Center that allows the user to enter any reasonable Retirement Savings Plan data with ease and quickly determine the future value of the investment.

Project Summary

In this project, you learned how to unprotect and protect a worksheet and workbook using a password. In Phase 1, you learned how to record a macro and assign it to a button on a toolbar and to a command on a menu. In Phase 2, you learned how to create a Command Button control, assign it properties, and write VBA code that executes when you click the button. In Phase 3, you learned how to create a user interface made up of a Command Button control, Scroll Bar controls, a Check Box control, Label controls, and Spin Button controls. In this phase, you learned about many of the frequently used properties in Visual Basic for Applications. You also learned how to write VBA code that included looping and decision-making.

What You Should Know

Having completed this project, you should be able to perform the following tasks:

- Add a Button to a Toolbar, Assign the Button a Macro, and Use the Button *(E 7.19)*
- Add a Command Button Control to the Worksheet *(E 7.28)*
- Add a Command to a Menu, Assign the Command a Macro, and Invoke the Command *(E 7.23)*
- Add Controls to a User Interface *(E 7.43)*
- Automate Data Entry by Selecting a Range of Cells *(E 7.08)*
- Close the Visual Basic Editor, Protect the Worksheet, and Save the Workbook *(E 7.70)*
- Enter Retirement Savings Plan Data Using the New Data Button *(E 7.37)*
- Enter the Annual Return Spin Button Procedure *(E 7.68)*
- Enter the Employee Investment Scroll Bar Procedure *(E 7.65)*
- Enter the Employer Match Check Box Procedure *(E 7.66)*
- Enter the Employer Match Scroll Bar Procedure *(E 7.67)*
- Enter the Enter Name and Salary Button Procedure *(E 7.63)*
- Enter the New Data Button Procedure *(E 7.34)*
- Enter the Years of Service Spin Button Procedure *(E 7.69)*
- Open a Workbook with a Macro and Execute the Macro *(E 7.15)*
- Open a Workbook, Unprotect a Worksheet, and Display the Control Toolbox Toolbar *(E 7.42)*
- Password-Protect the Worksheet, Save the Workbook, and Close the Workbook *(E 7.14)*
- Protect a Worksheet and Save the Workbook *(E 7.41)*
- Quit Excel *(E 7.71)*
- Record a Macro to Print the Worksheet in Portrait Orientation Using the Fit to Option *(E 7.11)*
- Resize and Reposition the Controls in the Adjustment Center *(E 7.61)*
- Set Properties for the Annual Return and Years of Service Spin Buttons *(E 7.57)*
- Set Properties of the Constant Label Controls and Check Box Control *(E 7.48)*
- Set the Command Button Control Properties *(E 7.31, E 7.53)*
- Set the Employee Investment Scroll Bar Properties *(E 7.54)*
- Set the Employer Match Check Box Properties *(E 7.56)*
- Set the Employer Match Scroll Bar Properties *(E 7.55)*
- Set the Label Control Properties for the Annual Return and Years of Service Spin Buttons *(E 7.58)*
- Start Excel, Open a Workbook, and Customize Excel (*E 7.06*)
- Test the Controls in the Adjustment Center User Interface *(E 7.70)*
- Undo a Group of Entries Using the Undo Button *(E 7.09)*
- Unprotect a Password-Protected Worksheet *(E 7.09, E 7.27)*
- View a Macro's VBA Code *(E 7.17)*

Learn It Online

Instructions: To complete the Learn It Online exercises, start your browser, click the Address bar, and then enter `scsite.com/offxp/exs.htm`. When the Office XP Learn It Online page displays, follow the instructions in the exercises below.

1 Project Reinforcement TF, MC, and SA

Below Excel Project 7, click the Project Reinforcement link. Print the quiz by clicking Print on the File menu. Answer each question. Write your first and last name at the top of each page, and then hand in the printout to your instructor.

2 Flash Cards

Below Excel Project 7, click the Flash Cards link. When Flash Cards displays, read the instructions. Type 20 (or a number specified by your instructor) in the Number of Playing Cards text box, type your name in the Name text box, and then click the Flip Card button. When the flash card displays, read the question and then click the Answer box arrow to select an answer. Flip through Flash Cards. Click Print on the File menu to print the last flash card if your score is 15 (75%) correct or greater and then hand it in to your instructor. If your score is less than 15 (75%) correct, then redo this exercise by clicking the Replay button.

3 Practice Test

Below Excel Project 7, click the Practice Test link. Answer each question, enter your first and last name at the bottom of the page, and then click the Grade Test button. When the graded practice test displays on your screen, click Print on the File menu to print a hard copy. Continue to take practice tests until you score 80% or better. Hand in a printout of the final practice test to your instructor.

4 Who Wants to Be a Computer Genius?

Below Excel Project 7, click the Computer Genius link. Read the instructions, enter your first and last name at the bottom of the page, and then click the Play button. Hand in your score to your instructor.

5 Wheel of Terms

Below Excel Project 7, click the Wheel of Terms link. Read the instructions, and then enter your first and last name and your school name. Click the Play button. Hand in your score to your instructor.

6 Crossword Puzzle Challenge

Below Excel Project 7, click the Crossword Puzzle Challenge link. Read the instructions, and then enter your first and last name. Click the Play button. Work the crossword puzzle. When you are finished, click the Submit button. When the crossword puzzle redisplays, click the Print button. Hand in the printout.

7 Tips and Tricks

Below Excel Project 7, click the Tips and Tricks link. Click a topic that pertains to Project 7. Right-click the information and then click Print on the shortcut menu. Construct a brief example of what the information relates to in Excel to confirm you understand how to use the tip or trick. Hand in the example and printed information.

online

8 Newsgroups

Below Excel Project 7, click the Newsgroups link. Click a topic that pertains to Project 7. Print three comments. Hand in the comments to your instructor.

9 Expanding Your Horizons

Below Excel Project 7, click the Articles for Microsoft Excel link. Click a topic that pertains to Project 7. Print the information. Construct a brief example of what the information relates to in Excel to confirm you understand the contents of the article. Hand in the example and printed information to your instructor.

10 Search Sleuth

Below Excel Project 7, click the Search Sleuth link. To search for a term that pertains to this project, select a term below the Project 7 title and then use the Google search engine at google.com (or any major search engine) to display and print two Web pages that present information on the term. Hand in the printouts to your instructor.

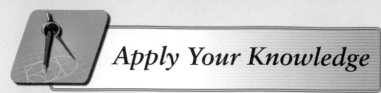

Apply Your Knowledge

1 Creating Macros and Customizing Menus and Toolbars

Instructions: Start Excel and perform the following tasks.

1. Open the workbook Whitewater Plumbing (Figure 7-87a) from the Data Disk. See the inside back cover of this book for instructions for downloading the Data Disk or see your instructor for information on accessing the files required in this book.
2. Reset the toolbars to their installation settings (see Step 6 on page E 7.06).
3. Unprotect the worksheet. The password is dripdrip.
4. Enter your name, course, laboratory assignment number (Apply 7-1), date, and instructor name in the range A11:A15.
5. Use the Record New Macro command to create a macro that prints the range A2:B8. Call the macro PrintNameAndRate, use the shortcut CTRL+N, change the name of the author in the Description box to your name, and store the macro in this workbook. When the Stop Recording toolbar displays, do the following: (a) select the range A2:B8; (b) click File on the menu bar, and then click Print; (c) click the Selection option in the Print what area of the Print dialog box; (d) click the OK button; and (e) click the Stop Recording button on the Stop Recording toolbar. If the Stop Recording toolbar does not display, click View on the main menu, then select Stop Recording on the Toolbars submenu.
6. Press ALT+F8 to display the Macro dialog box. Run the PrintNameAndRate macro. Press ALT+F8 to display the Macro dialog box a second time. Select the PrintNameAndRate macro and then click the Edit button. When the Visual Basic Editor displays the macro, click File on the menu bar and then click Print. Hand in both printouts to your instructor.
7. Add a button to the Standard toolbar (Figure 7-87a) and a command to the File menu (Figure 7-87b). Assign the button and command the PrintNameAndRate macro.
8. Run the macro as follows: (a) click the button you added to the Standard toolbar; (b) on the File menu, click the Print Name and Rate command; and (c) press CTRL+N. Hand in the three printouts to your instructor.
9. Protect the worksheet. Use the first six characters of your last name as the password. Save the workbook using the file name Whitewater Plumbing1.
10. Reset the toolbars to their installation settings (see Step 6 on page E 7.06).

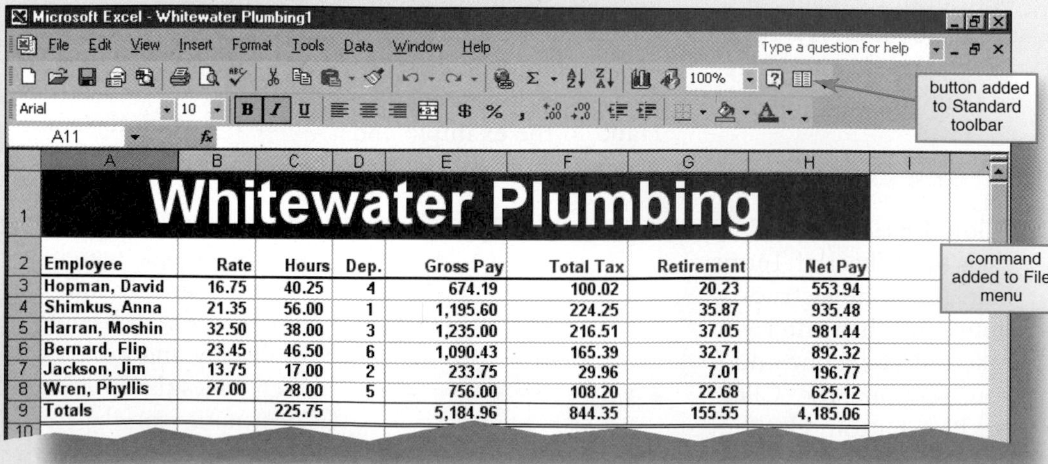

(a) Worksheet

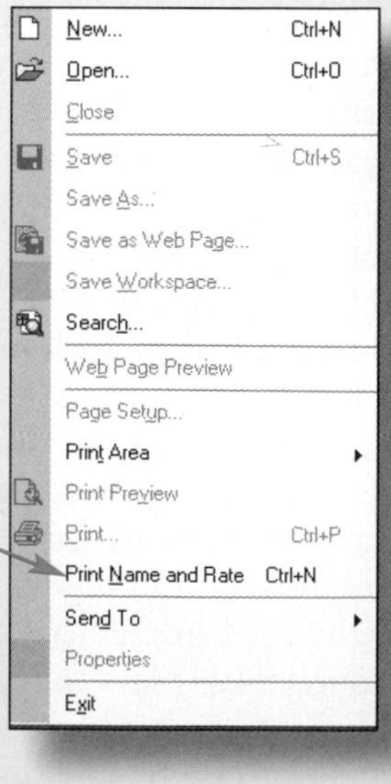

(b) File Menu

FIGURE 7-87

In the Lab

1 Automating a Mortgage Worksheet

Problem: Holiday Mortgage specializes in mortgages for local vacation properties. The president, Eliza Harrison, has asked you to automate the entry of mortgage data into a Mortgage Analysis worksheet.

Instructions Part 1: Start Excel and perform the following tasks.

1. Open the Holiday Mortgage workbook from the Data Disk. See the inside back cover of this book for instructions for downloading the Data Disk or see your instructor for information on accessing the files required in this book.
2. Reset the toolbars to their installation settings (see Step 3 on page E 7.71).
3. Unprotect the Mortgage Analysis worksheet. The password is norent.
4. Display the Control Toolbox toolbar. Click the Command Button button on the Control Toolbox toolbar. Draw the button in the range D3:D5 as shown in Figure 7-88a.
5. With the Command Button control selected, click the Properties button on the Control Toolbox toolbar. Change the following properties: (a) Caption = Mortgage Data; (b) Font = Regular; and (c) PrintObject = False.
6. Click the View Code button on the Control Toolbox toolbar. Enter the procedure shown in Figure 7-88b. Check your code carefully. On the File menu, click Print to print the procedure.
7. Close the Visual Basic Editor window. Click the Exit Design Mode button on the Control Toolbox toolbar. Close the Control Toolbox toolbar. Close the Properties window.
8. Enter your name, course, laboratory assignment number (Lab 7-1), date, and instructor name in the range G3:G7.
9. Use the newly created button to determine the monthly payment for the following mortgage data and print the worksheet for each data set: (a) Price = $149,000; Down Payment = $20,000; Interest Rate = 8.25%; and Years = 15; (b) Price = $129,000; Down Payment = $15,000; Interest Rate = 8.75%; and Years = 12. The Monthly Payment for (a) is $1,251.48 and for (b) is $1,281.36.
10. Protect the worksheet. Use the password norent. Save the workbook using the file name Holiday Mortgage Automated and close the workbook.

Instructions Part 2: With the workbook Holiday Mortgage Automated created in Part 1 open, do the following:

1. Unprotect the worksheet. The password is norent.
2. Use the Record New Macro command to create a macro that prints the formulas version of the worksheet. Call the macro PrintFormulas, use the shortcut CTRL+F, change the name of the author in the Description box to your name, and store the macro in this workbook.
3. With the Stop Recording toolbar on the screen, do the following: (a) Press CTRL+ACCENT MARK (`); (b) On the File menu, click Page Setup, click Landscape option, click Fit to option, click the Print button in the Page Setup dialog box, and then click the OK button; (c) Press CTRL+ACCENT MARK (`); (d) On the File menu, click Page Setup, click Portrait option, click Adjust to option, type 100 in the Adjust to box, and then click the OK button; and (e) Click the Stop Recording button on the Stop Recording toolbar.

(continued)

In the Lab

Automating a Mortgage Worksheet *(continued)*

4. Press ALT+F8 to display the Macro dialog box. Run the PrintFormulas macro. Press ALT+F8 to display the Macro dialog box a second time. Select the PrintFormulas macro and then click the Edit button. When the Visual Basic Editor displays the macro, click File on the menu bar and then click Print. Hand in both printouts to your instructor.
5. Add a button to the Standard toolbar (Figure 7-88a) and a command to the File menu (Figure 7-88c). Assign the button and command the PrintFormulas macro.
6. Run the macro as follows: (a) click the button you added to the Standard toolbar; (b) on the File menu, click the Print Formulas; and (c) press CTRL+F. Hand in the three printouts to your instructor. The button will not print as part of the worksheet because PrintObject was set to False earlier.
7. Do not protect the worksheet because the Print Formulas macro will not work with a protected worksheet. Save the workbook using the file name Holiday Mortgage Automated2 and close the workbook.

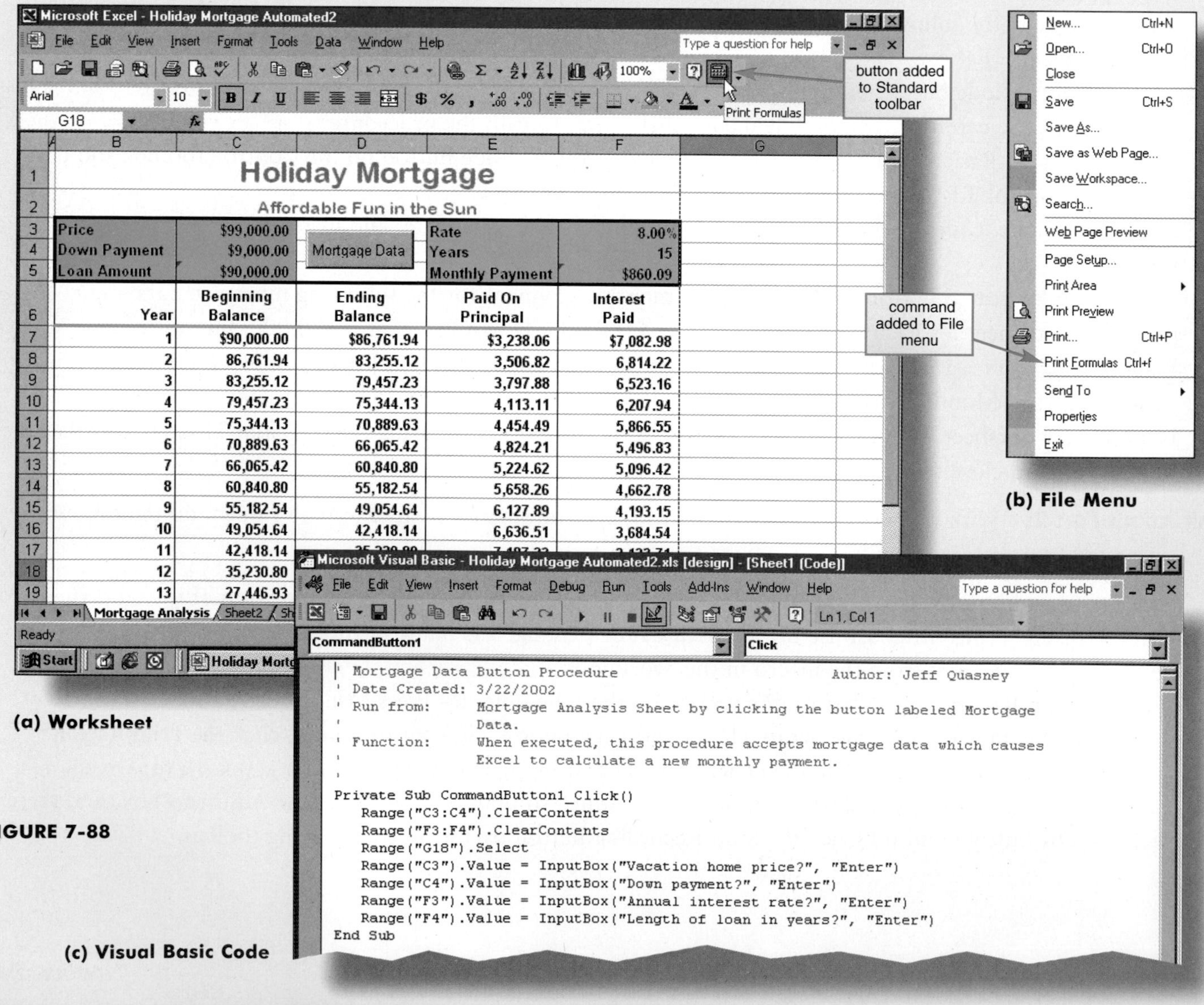

(a) Worksheet

(b) File Menu

(c) Visual Basic Code

FIGURE 7-88

In the Lab

2 Automating a Five-Year Projected Financial Statement

Problem: As the spreadsheet specialist at Executive Chairs, you have been asked to use your Visual Basic for Applications skills to automate the Five-Year Projected Financial Statement worksheet as shown in Figure 7-89. The objective is to simplify data entry for the company's financial analysts. This worksheet projects financial information for a five-year period based on the previous year's sales and additional data. The user interface on the right side of the screen accepts the assumptions in the range I6:I10. The numbers in the range B5:F18 are based on these assumptions.

The user interface has two buttons, one spin button, and three scroll bars. The Reset Assumptions button resets the assumptions as follows: (a) cell I6 = 50,000; (b) cell I7 = $355.00; (c) I8 = 10%; (d) I9 = 5%; and (e) I10 = 60%. The Chairs Sold in 2002 button accepts and ensures the units sold in 2002 is greater than zero and then assigns it to cell I6. The Unit Cost spin button changes the unit cost in cell I7. The Annual Sales Growth scroll bar changes the annual sales growth in cell I8. The Annual Price Decrease scroll bar changes the annual price decrease in cell I9. The Margin scroll bar changes the margin in cell I10.

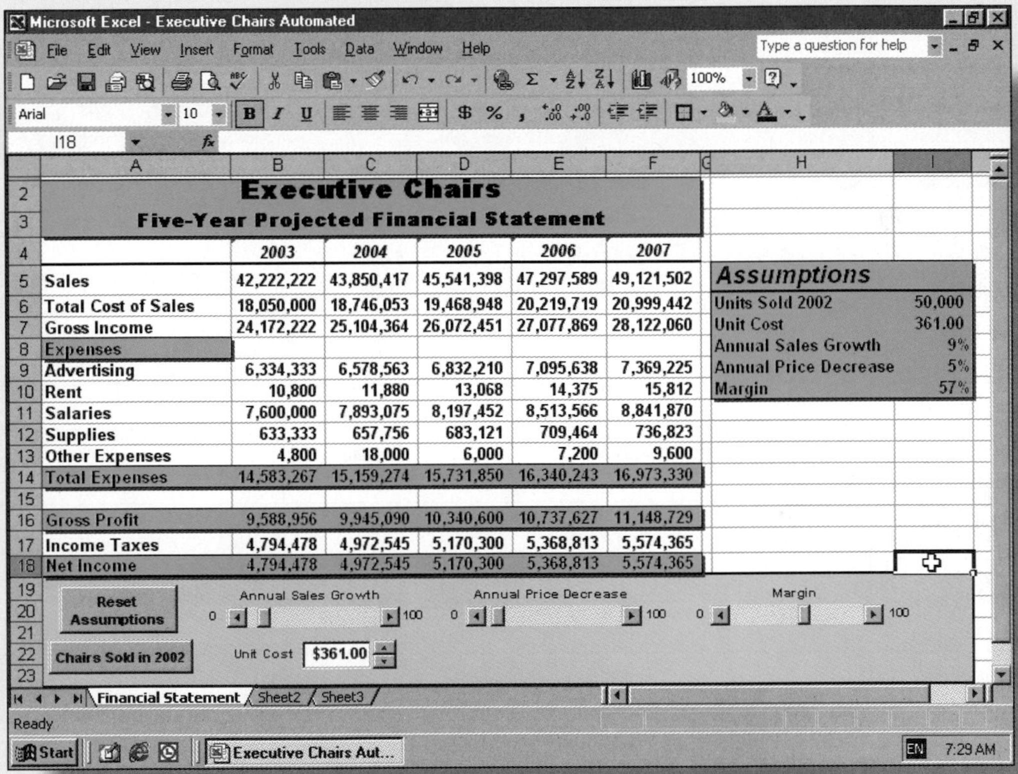

FIGURE 7-89

Instructions: Start Excel and complete the following tasks.

1. Open the Executive Chairs workbook from the Data Disk. See the inside back cover of this book for instructions for downloading the Data Disk or see your instructor for information on accessing the files required in this book.
2. Reset the toolbars to their installation settings (see Step 3 on page E 7.71).
3. Unprotect the Financial Statement worksheet. The password is chairs.

(continued)

In the Lab

Automating a Five-Year Projected Financial Statement *(continued)*

4. Color the background of the range A19:I23 turquoise (column 5, row 4 on the Fill Color palette). Draw a thick box border (column 4, row 3 on the Borders palette) around the range A19:I23.
5. Display the Control Toolbox toolbar. Use the concepts and techniques developed in this project to add the 17 controls shown on the bottom of Figure 7-89.
6. Modify the properties of the 17 controls as described in Table 7-13.

Table 7-13 Controls and Their Properties

CONTROL	NAME	CAPTION	BACK COLOR	FONT	TEXT ALIGN	WORD WRAP	SPECIAL EFFECT	MAX	MIN	SMALL CHG	LARGE CHG
Reset Assumptions Button	btnReset	Reset Assumptions		8-point bold	True						
Chairs Sold in 2002 Button	btnChairsSold	Chairs Sold in 2002		8-point bold							
Unit Cost Label		Unit Cost	Turquoise	8-point bold	Right						
Unit Cost Spin Button	spnUnitCost							100000	0	100	
Unit Cost Spin Button Label		$320.00		10-point bold	Right		Sunken				
All three 0 Labels		0	Turquoise	8-point bold	Center						
All three 100 Labels		100	Turquoise	8-point bold	Center						
Annual Sales Growth Label		Annual Sales Growth	Turquoise	8-point bold	Center						
Annual Sales Growth Scroll Bar	scrAnnualSalesGrowth						10000	0	25	100	
Annual Price Decrease Label		Annual Price Decrease	Turquoise	8-point bold	Center						
Annual Price Decrease Scroll Bar	scrAnnualPriceDecrease						10000	0	25	100	
Margin Label		Margin	Turquoise	8-point bold	Center						
Margin Scroll Bar	scrMargin							10000	0	25	100

In the Lab

7. Enter your name, course, laboratory assignment number (Lab 7-2), date, and instructor name in the range H12:H16. Save the workbook using the file name Executive Chairs Automated.
8. The Reset Assumptions Button procedure resets the assumptions as follows:

```
Range("I6").Value = 50000
spnUnitCost = 35000
scrAnnualSalesGrowth = 1000
scrAnnualPriceDecrease = 500
scrMargin = 6000
Range("I10").Select
```

9. The Chairs Sold in 2002 Button procedure accepts and validates the number of chairs sold in 2002 in cell I6 as follows:

```
ChairsSold = InputBox("Chairs Sold in 2002?", "Enter")
Do While ChairsSold <= 0
   ChairsSold = InputBox("Chairs Sold in 2002 must be > zero.", "Please Re-enter")
Loop
Range("I6").Value = ChairsSold
```

10. The Unit Cost Spin Button procedure enters the unit cost in the Unit Cost Spin Button Label control and in cell I7 as follows:

```
lblUnitCost = Format$(spnUnitCost.Value / 100, "currency")
Range("I7").Value = spnUnitCost.Value / 100
```

The Format$ function in the first line formats the result that will display in the Unit Cost Spin Button Label control to include a floating dollar sign and two decimal positions to the right of the decimal.

11. The Annual Sales Growth Scroll Bar procedure changes the annual sales growth in cell I8 as follows:

```
Range("I8").Value = scrAnnualSalesGrowth.Value / 10000
```

12. The Annual Price Decrease Scroll Bar procedure and the Margin Scroll Bar procedure work in a fashion similar to the Annual Sales Growth scroll bar, except that they assign values to cells I9 and I10, respectively.
13. Click the Microsoft Excel button on the taskbar. Click the Exit Design Mode button on the Control Toolbox toolbar. Close the Control Toolbox toolbar. Print the worksheet.
14. Use the newly designed interface to determine the five year projections based on the following assumptions and print the worksheet for each data set: (a) Units Sold in 2002 = 45,000; Unit Cost = $41.70; Annual Sales Growth = 17%; Annual Price Decrease = 4%; and Margin = 58.5%. (b) Units Sold in 2002 = 37,000; Unit Cost = $395.00; Annual Sales Growth = 12.5%; Annual Price Decrease = 3.5%; and Margin = 52%. The Net Income for the year 2007 in cell F18 for (a) is $7,063,302 and for (b) is $3,687,503.
15. Click the Visual Basic Editor button on the taskbar. On the File menu, click Print to print the VBA code. Close the Visual Basic Editor.
16. Protect the worksheet. Use the password, chairs. Click the Save button on the Standard toolbar to save the workbook using the file name Executive Chairs Automated.

In the Lab

3 Automating a Projected Income Statement

Problem: You work in the strategic planning office of E&R, Inc., a local manufacturer. Your boss needs a workbook (Figure 7-90) automated to make it easier for her accountants to use. Because you are taking an advanced Excel course that includes Visual Basic for Applications, she has asked you to automate the data entry in cells D4 (Units Sold); D5 (Price per Unit); D14 (Material Cost per Unit); and D16 (Manufacturing Cost per Unit). All other cells in the worksheet use formulas.

Instructions: Start Excel and complete the following tasks.

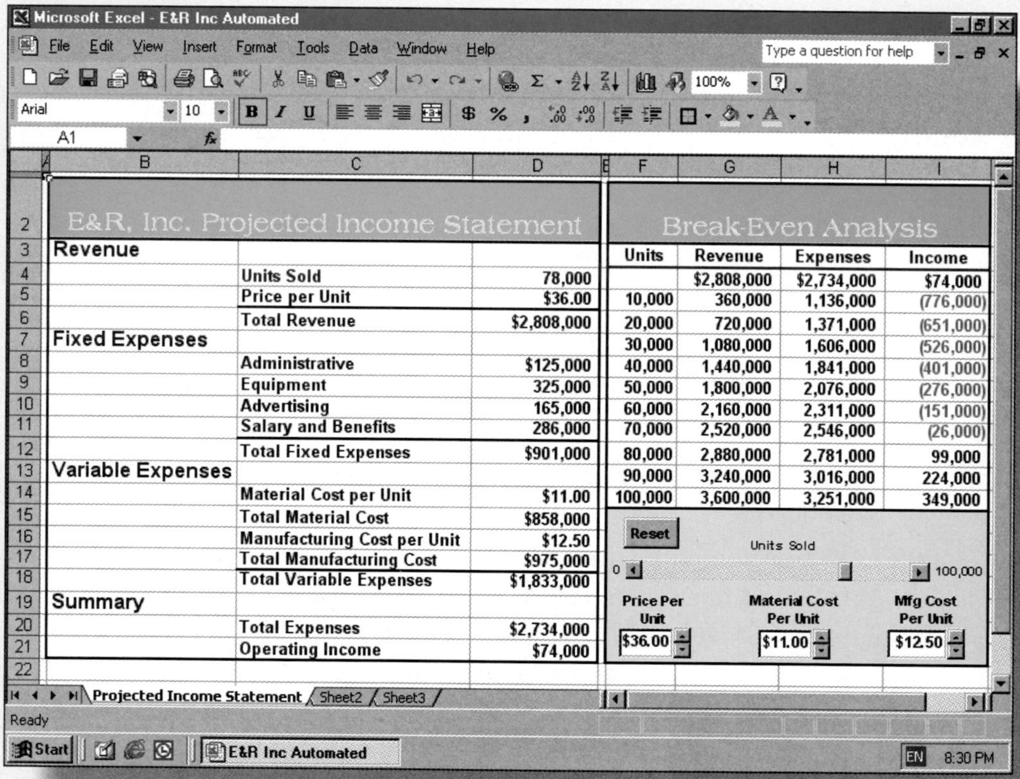

FIGURE 7-90

1. Open the E&R Inc workbook from the Data Disk. See the inside back cover of this book for instructions for downloading the Data Disk or see your instructor for information on accessing the files required in this book.
2. Reset the toolbars to their installation settings (see Step 3 on page E 7.71).
3. Unprotect the Projected Income Statement worksheet. The password is erinc.
4. Color the background of the range F15:I21 yellow (column 3, row 4 on the Fill Color palette). Draw a thick box border (column 4, row 3 on the Borders palette) around the range F15:I21.
5. Display the Control Toolbox toolbar. Use the concepts and techniques developed in this project to add the 14 controls shown in the lower-right corner of Figure 7-90. The Units Sold scroll bar should assign a value to cell D4. The Price Per Unit spin button should assign a value to cell D5. The Material Cost Per Unit spin button should assign a value to cell D14. The Mfg Cost Per Unit spin button should assign a value to cell D16.
6. Modify the properties of the 14 controls as described in Table 7-14.

In the Lab

Table 7-14 Controls and Their Properties

CONTROL	NAME	CAPTION	BACK COLOR	FONT	TEXT ALIGN	WORD WRAP	SPECIAL EFFECT	MAX	MIN	SMALL CHG	LARGE CHG
Reset Button	btnReset	Reset		8-point bold							
0 Label		0	Yellow	8-point bold	Center						
Units Sold Label		Units Sold	Yellow	8-point bold	Center						
100,000 Label		100,000	Yellow	8-Point bold	Center						
Units Sold Scroll Bar	scrUnitsSold							100000	0	100	1000
Price Per Unit Label		Price Per Unit	Yellow	8-point bold	Center	True					
Price Per Unit Spin Button	spnPrice							9999	0	10	
Price Per Unit Spin Button Label		$36.00		10-point bold	Right		Sunken				
Material Cost Per Unit Label		Material Cost Per Unit	Yellow	8-point bold	Center	True					
Material Cost Per Unit Spin Button	spnMaterialCost							9999	0	10	
Material Cost Per Unit Spin Button Label		$11.50		10-point bold	Right		Sunken				
Mfg Cost Per Unit Label	Mfg Cost	Yellow Per Unit	8-point	Center bold	True						
Mfg Cost Per Unit Spin Button	spnMfgCost							9999	0	10	
Mfg Cost Per Unit Spin Button Label		$12.50		10-point bold	Right		Sunken				

7. Enter your name, course, laboratory assignment number (Lab 7-3), date, and instructor name in the range B23:B27. Save the workbook using the file name E&R Inc Automated.
8. The Reset Button procedure should set the Units Sold scroll bar (scrUnitsSold) to 78000; the Price Per Unit Spin Button (spnPrice) to 40000; the Material Cost Per Unit (spnMaterialCost) to 10000; and the Mfg Cost Per Unit (spnMfgCost) to 10000. It also should select cell A1.
9. The Units Sold Scroll Bar procedure should assign the value of the scroll bar (scrUnitsSold) to cell D4. For example,

```
Range("D4").Value = scrUnitsSold.Value
```

(continued)

In the Lab

Automating a Projected Income Statement *(continued)*

10. The Price Per Unit Spin Button procedure should assign the value of spnPrice / 100, formatted to the Currency style, to the Price Per Unit Spin Button Label control. It also should assign the value of spnPrice / 100 to cell D5. For example,

    ```
    lblPrice = Format$(spnPrice.Value / 100, "currency")
    Range("D5").Value = spnPrice.Value / 100
    ```

    The Format$ function in the first line formats the result that will display in the Price Per Unit Spin Button Label control to include a floating dollar sign and two decimal positions to the right of the decimal. The value assigned to cell D5 will display in the same format because the cell was formatted to the Currency style as part of the normal worksheet formatting.
11. The Material Cost Per Unit Spin Button procedure should assign the value of spnMaterialCost / 100, formatted to the Currency style, to the Material Cost Per Unit Spin Button Label control. It also should assign the value of spnMaterialCost / 100 to cell D14. For example,

    ```
    lblMaterialCost = Format$(spnMaterialCost.Value / 100, "currency")
    Range("D14").Value = spnMaterialCost.Value / 100
    ```

12. The Mfg Cost Per Unit Spin Button procedure should assign the value of the spnMfgCost / 100, formatted to the Currency style, to the Mfg Cost Per Unit Spin Button Label control. It also should assign the value of spnMfgCost / 100 to cell D16. For example,

    ```
    lblMfgCost = Format$(spnMfgCost.Value / 100, "currency")
    Range("D16").Value = spnMfgCost.Value / 100
    ```

13. Click the Microsoft Excel button on the taskbar. Click the Exit Design Mode button on the Control Toolbox toolbar. Hide the Control Toolbox toolbar. Print the worksheet.
14. Use the newly designed user interface to determine the operating income for the following projections and print the worksheet for each data set: (a) Units Sold = 55,000; Price per Unit = $40.00; Material Cost per Unit = $15.50; and Manufacturing Cost per Unit = $12.00. (b) Units Sold = 70,000; Price per Unit = $42.00; Material Cost per Unit = $11.50; and Manufacturing Cost per Unit = $12.00. The Operating Income in cell D21 for (a) is $(213,500) and for (b) is $394,000.
15. Click the Visual Basic Editor button on the taskbar. On the File menu, click Print to print the VBA code. Close the Visual Basic Editor.
16. Protect the worksheet. Use the password, erinc. Click the Save button on the Standard toolbar to save the workbook using the file name E&R Inc Automated.

Cases and Places

The difficulty of these case studies varies:
◗ are the least difficult; ◗◗ are more difficult; and ◗◗◗ are the most difficult.

1 ◗ Open the workbook MaxGlass from the Data Disk. Create a Command Button control below the Assumptions box. Change the button's caption to Assumptions. Write a procedure for the Command Button control that accepts data for each of the five assumptions in the range B21:B25. Print the Forecast worksheet. Print the Command Button control procedure. Use the Assumptions button to enter the following data sets and then print the worksheet for each data set: (a) Manufacturing = 43%; R & D = 9%; Marketing = 18%; Corporate = 17%; Commissions = 12%. (b) Manufacturing = 35%; R & D = 6%; Marketing = 20%; Corporate = 18%; Commissions = 15%. The Total Net Income in cell E18 for (a) is $59,299.10 and for (b) is $355,794.60. Save the workbook with the name MaxGlass1. Hand in the four printouts to your instructor.

2 ◗ Open the workbook MaxGlass from the Data Disk. Print the Forecast worksheet. Create a macro that prints the cell formulas version of the Forecast worksheet in landscape orientation using the Fit to option. Make sure that the macro resets the Page Setup options before terminating. Execute the macro. Print the macro VBA code. Save the workbook with the name MaxGlass2. Hand in the three printouts to your instructor.

3 ◗ Using a Web search engine, such as Google, type the keywords Visual Basic for Applications. Visit three Web pages that show VBA code solving a problem. Print each Web page. Hand in the three printouts to your instructor.

4 ◗◗ Open the workbook MaxGlass from the Data Disk. Create a well-balanced user interface made up of a Reset button and five scroll bars, one for each of the cells in the range B21:B25. Have the Reset button set the five assumptions to 45%, 8%, 12%, 12%, and 10%, respectively. The scroll bars should range from 0% to 100% and increment by 0.25% (scroll arrows) and 1% (scroll bars). Use the titles in the Assumptions box in the range A21:A25 for the names of the scroll bars. Print the worksheet. Use the interface to enter the data specified in Cases and Places Exercise 1 above. Save the workbook with the name MaxGlass3. Hand in the printout to your instructor.

5 ◗◗◗ Open the workbook Sky Mortgage Analysis from the Data Disk. Modify the procedure associated with the New Mortgage button on the worksheet so that it validates the price, down payment, interest rate, and years as follows: (a) the price must be between $20,000 and $150,000 inclusive; (b) the down payment must be between $2,000 and $150,000 inclusive; (c) the interest rate must be between 4% and 20% inclusive; and (d) the years must be between 1 and 15 inclusive. Print the procedure. Create and enter two sets of valid test data. Print the worksheet for each set. Hand in the three printouts to your instructor.

Cases and Places

6 ▸▸▸ Open the workbook MaxGlass from the Data Disk. Create a well-balanced user interface that allows the user to change the quarter (months) that the workbook is being used for. The first prompt should ask the user to enter which quarter the data is for. After accepting a valid number (1 through 4), the Visual Basic code should update cells A2, B4, C4, and D4 with appropriate labels.

7 ▸▸▸ Open the workbook Sky Mortgage Analysis from the Data Disk. Remove the New Mortgage command button. Create a well-balanced user interface that allows input for the value in the cells C3, C4, C5, C7, and C8. Use at least one text box control, at least one scroll bar control, and at least one spin button control. Use the same validation rules as detailed in Cases and Places Exercise 5 above. Include a text box control that is labeled as the Maximum Requested Monthly Payment. At the end of each procedure that you create for the controls, include a check that determines if the Monthly Payment in cell C9 is greater than the Maximum Requested Monthly Payment. If so, set the font color in the cell to red by using the Visual Basic statement Range("C9").Font.Color = RGB(255, 0, 0). If the value in C9 is less than or equal to the Maximum Requested Monthly Payment, then set the color in cell C9 to black by using the Visual Basic statement Range("C9").Font.Color = RGB(0, 0, 0). The value of cell C9 must be compared to a numeric value. Use the syntax CDBL(txtMaxPayment.Value) to make the Maximum Requested Monthly Payment a numeric value.

Microsoft Excel 2002

PROJECT

8

Formula Auditing, Data Validation, and Complex Problem Solving

OBJECTIVES

You will have mastered the material in this project when you can:

- Use the Formula Auditing toolbar to analyze a worksheet
- Trace precedents and dependents
- Add data validation rules to cells
- Use trial and error to solve a problem on a worksheet
- Use goal seeking to solve a problem
- Use Excel's Solver to solve a complex problem
- Password-protect a workbook file
- Use Excel's Scenario Manager to record and save different sets of what-if assumptions and the corresponding results
- Create a Scenario Summary of scenarios
- Create a Scenario PivotTable
- Set and change the properties of a workbook

Sustaining the Hungry

Spreadsheet Solutions for Food Distribution

Across America, many dedicated people have joined together to end hunger. In soup kitchens and food banks, at churches and local community centers, approximately one out of every ten Americans seeks help from these committed individuals every year. Nearly half of those seeking assistance are children, and almost 40 percent include households where the primary providers are employed but do not earn enough money to buy the basic foods they need.

Although difficult to comprehend, it is estimated that 30 million Americans are in danger of going hungry. In large part, these families and individuals are helped through the efforts of America's Second Harvest, the nation's largest domestic hunger-relief organization. Corporate donors, local businesses, and individuals provide surplus food to the food banks, which then is distributed to more than 50,000 charitable agencies. A network of more than 200 food banks serves all 50 states and Puerto Rico, and distributes more than 1.5 billion pounds of donated food and groceries each year.

One of Second Harvest's food banks is the Greater Chicago Food Depository. The Food Depository collects donated surplus food from wholesale food manufacturers, produce growers and distributors, food store chains, and restaurants. After gathering the food, Food depository drivers deliver the provisions

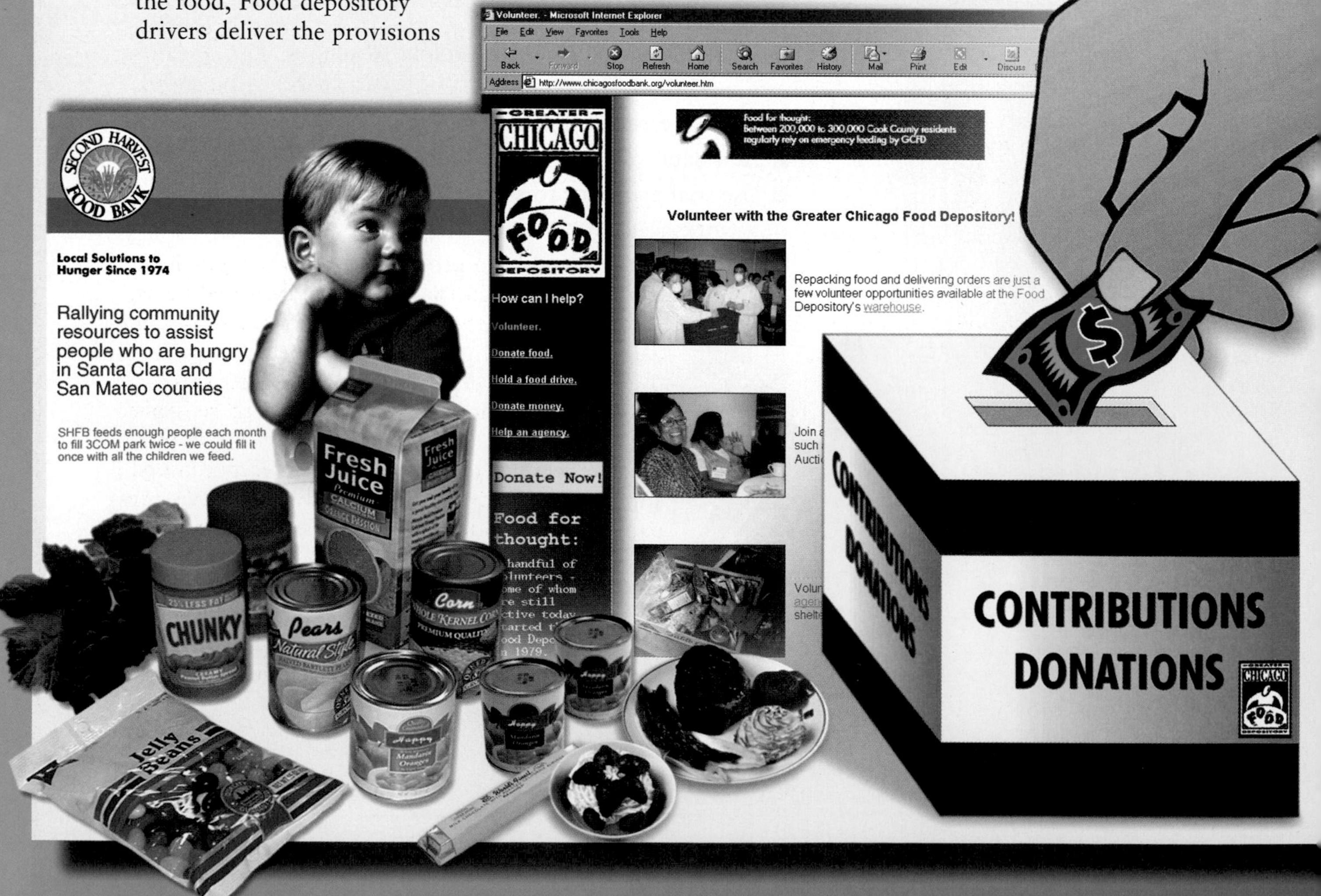

to warehouses where the products are distributed later to charitable food pantries, soup kitchens, and shelters throughout the Chicago area.

With the huge distribution of food each year, employees needed a more efficient method of keeping track of these goods than using manual methods. Given the ease with which Excel can audit and analyze data, the Food Depository developed Excel worksheets, similar to the worksheets developed in this project.

In Project 8, the management of Northland Instrument Distributors requires an Excel spreadsheet that can analyze complex data in order to provide practical solutions for managing shipments of its products to wholesalers around the country. In the project, you will learn to use Excel's capabilities to evaluate various constraints imposed by both shipping companies and by the management at Northland Instrument Distributors. The formulas will help you determine the most economical combination of products that can be shipped, given the allowable maximum weight and available space on a limited number of trucks.

The Food Depository uses Excel worksheets to organize, tabulate, and summarize hundreds of pallets and thousands of pounds of food shipped each week to its warehouses. Last year alone, employees at the Food Depository needed to coordinate the distribution of 32.4 million pounds of food, valued at more than $54 million, which they estimate to be the equivalent of 67,000 meals a day, 365 days a year. Excel worksheets help to ensure that distribution centers receive food deliveries just when they need it, which in turn helps to minimize food surpluses at warehouses.

As inventory arrives at a warehouse, employees can enter the quantity and type of delivered items, which facilitates the instant analysis of storage and distribution needs. If items arrive in a damaged or disarrayed state, employees also can enter this information in the spreadsheet so that these items are not included inappropriately in the count of available inventory. Workers can generate reports, study the worksheets to determine their needs, prepare for the amounts of food expected to arrive the following day, and survey how much warehouse space is needed to ensure sufficient room for the products.

Whether your needs are large or small, Excel delivers spreadsheet solutions that improve productivity.

Microsoft Excel 2002

Formula Auditing, Data Validation, and Complex Problem Solving

PROJECT 8

CASE PERSPECTIVE

Shipping costs comprise a significant portion of expenses for many small businesses. Northland Instrument Distributors receives large shipments of musical instruments from manufacturers, which it then distributes to musical instrument wholesalers around the country. To ship its goods, the company purchases extra space on trucks from trucking firms. Before the company makes a shipment to a particular city, it contacts trucking firms asking whether they have spare capacity on trucks going to that city. Typically, the company receives weight and volume limitations to which they must adhere if they are to ship goods on the truck. As the assistant shipping manager, you are required to prepare a worksheet that will select the most economical mix of products to fill the space on a truck. In addition, you must maximize the company's profit on each shipment.

Marsha Gresham, your manager, has given you a list of products, their dimensions, and weight. You also have the profit per instrument that the company can make on each item. Both Marsha and the trucking companies also want documentation that shows the requirements have been satisfied.

Introduction

This project introduces you to formula auditing a worksheet, data validation, and solving complex problems. Formula auditing allows you to check both the cells being referenced in a formula and the formulas that reference a cell. Formula auditing a worksheet is helpful especially when you want to learn more about a workbook created by someone else or you want to verify the formulas in a newly created workbook.

Data validation allows you to define cells in such a way that only certain values are accepted. This feature also lets you display a prompt message when the user selects the cell and an error message if the user attempts to enter a value outside of a valid range that you define.

The majority of this project introduces you to solving complex problems that involve changing values of cells to arrive at a solution, while abiding by constraints imposed on the changing values. The worksheet in Figure 8-1a on page E 8.06 shows the details of the shipping requirements for this project as described in the Case Perspective. Columns B, C, and D each refer to one of the three instrument types currently in stock, Guitars, Keyboards, and Tubas, that must ship. The row titles in rows 4 through 7 in column A refer to the characteristics of each instrument, such as Item Volume in Cubic Feet, Item Weight in Pounds, Profit per Item, and Amount in Stock. Row 9 is where you enter the number of each instrument to ship. In this case, the number of instruments must be more than one and less than the number in stock. Once you enter the shipment number of each instrument in cells B9, C9, and D9, Excel determines the results of the suggested shipment in rows 11 through 13, Total Shipment Volume, Total Shipment Weight, and Total Shipment Profit. The objective is to maximize the profit while filling up as much of the truck as possible. The constraints given for the current truck under consideration for the shipment are in cells B16 and B17.

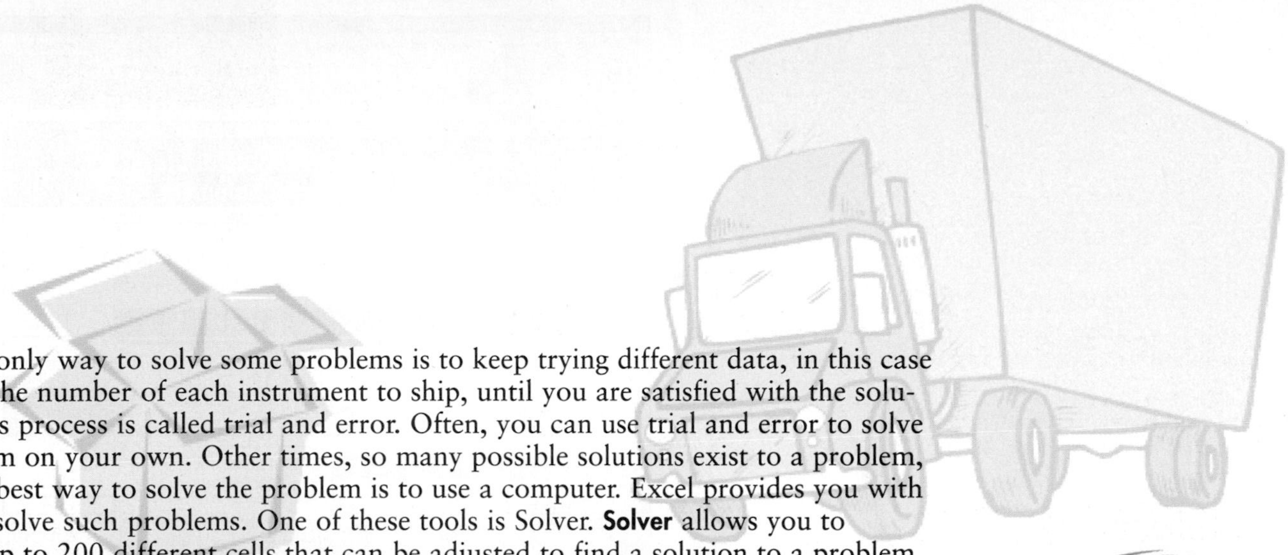

The only way to solve some problems is to keep trying different data, in this case varying the number of each instrument to ship, until you are satisfied with the solution. This process is called trial and error. Often, you can use trial and error to solve a problem on your own. Other times, so many possible solutions exist to a problem, that the best way to solve the problem is to use a computer. Excel provides you with tools to solve such problems. One of these tools is Solver. **Solver** allows you to specify up to 200 different cells that can be adjusted to find a solution to a problem. It also lets you place constraints on the variables. A **constraint** is a limitation on the possible values that a cell can contain. Once you define the constraints and instruct Solver what to look for, it will try many possible solutions until it finds the best one.

In Figure 8-1b on the next page, the values of cells B9, C9, and D9 have been modified by Solver to find the best combination of instruments to ship on a particular truck. When Solver finishes solving a problem, you can instruct it to create an Answer Report. An Answer Report (Figures 8-1c and 8-1e on page E 8.07) shows the answer that Solver found, the values that were manipulated by Solver to find the answer, and the constraints that were used to solve the problem.

Excel's **Scenario Manager** is a what-if analysis tool that allows you to record and save different sets of what-if assumptions used to forecast the outcome of a worksheet model. You will use Scenario Manager to manage two different sets of Solver data. Figure 8-1d on the next page shows a scenario where accordions have been substituted for guitars as an instrument available to ship. Scenario Manager also allows you to create reports that summarize the scenarios on your worksheet. Figure 8-1f on page E 8.07 shows a Scenario Summary and Scenario PivotTable that concisely report the differences in the two scenarios in Figures 8-1b and 8-1d.

> **More About**
>
> **Constraints**
>
> The constraints of a problem are the rules that you must follow to solve a given problem. You even may add constraints to cells that are not referenced in the formulas you are solving. Solver will modify these types of cells to meet the constraints, but they will not affect the solution. For example, you can change row or column headers, or worksheet headers to better explain to the user the results of a Solver solution.

Project Eight — Northland Instrument Distributors Weekly Shipping Worksheet

To create the Northland Instrument Distributors weekly shipping worksheet, you determine the following needs and source of data.

Needs: The Macon Trucking Company has a truck leaving today that is making a delivery very close to the Northland's East Coast distribution center. The truck has spare space that Macon Trucking would like to fill. You are to determine the best mix of items to ship that includes at least one of each item, because that is what the distribution center on the East coast requires. The shipment must fit within the constraints of the current truck under consideration: 400 cubic feet and 600 pounds. When determining the best mix of products to ship, you must maximize the profit to Northland while operating within the constraints that the trucking company has placed on you.

Finally, reports need to be generated for the trucking company that indicate the volume and weight constraints have been met. In addition, a second shipment that includes accordions must be analyzed and compared with the shipment that includes guitars.

> **More About**
>
> **The Solver Add-In**
>
> If you do not have Solver installed on your computer, see your instructor about obtaining the Microsoft Office XP CD-ROMs. To install the Solver Add-In, use the Add-Ins command on the Tools menu, check the Solver option box, and then follow the instructions.

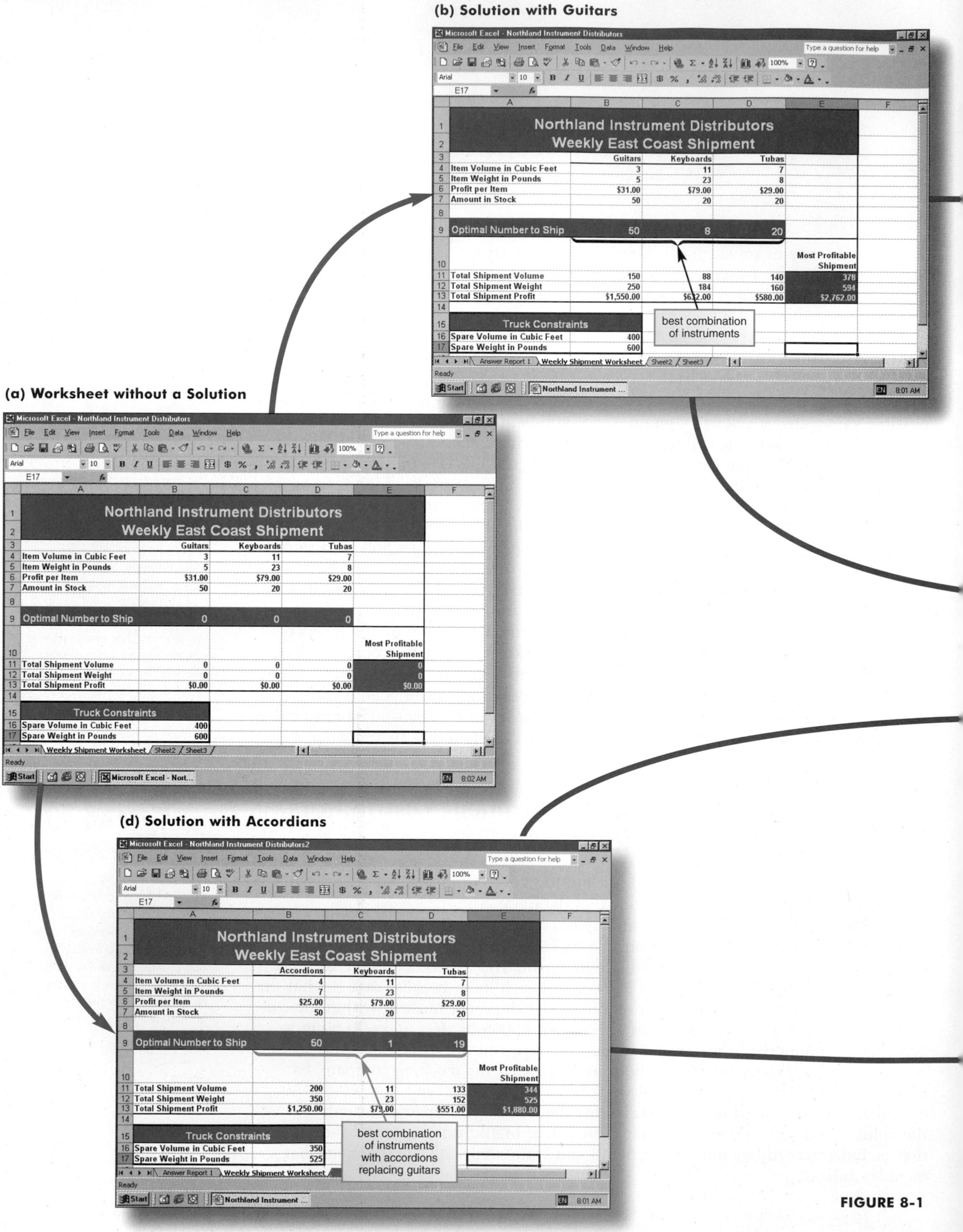

(a) Worksheet without a Solution

	Guitars	Keyboards	Tubas	
Item Volume in Cubic Feet	3	11	7	
Item Weight in Pounds	5	23	8	
Profit per Item	$31.00	$79.00	$29.00	
Amount in Stock	50	20	20	
Optimal Number to Ship	0	0	0	Most Profitable Shipment
Total Shipment Volume	0	0	0	0
Total Shipment Weight	0	0	0	0
Total Shipment Profit	$0.00	$0.00	$0.00	$0.00
Truck Constraints				
Spare Volume in Cubic Feet	400			
Spare Weight in Pounds	600			

(b) Solution with Guitars

	Guitars	Keyboards	Tubas	
Item Volume in Cubic Feet	3	11	7	
Item Weight in Pounds	5	23	8	
Profit per Item	$31.00	$79.00	$29.00	
Amount in Stock	50	20	20	
Optimal Number to Ship	50	8	20	Most Profitable Shipment
Total Shipment Volume	150	88	140	378
Total Shipment Weight	250	184	160	594
Total Shipment Profit	$1,550.00	$632.00	$580.00	$2,762.00
Truck Constraints				
Spare Volume in Cubic Feet	400			
Spare Weight in Pounds	600			

(d) Solution with Accordians

	Accordions	Keyboards	Tubas	
Item Volume in Cubic Feet	4	11	7	
Item Weight in Pounds	7	23	8	
Profit per Item	$25.00	$79.00	$29.00	
Amount in Stock	50	20	20	
Optimal Number to Ship	50	1	19	Most Profitable Shipment
Total Shipment Volume	200	11	133	344
Total Shipment Weight	350	23	152	525
Total Shipment Profit	$1,250.00	$79.00	$551.00	$1,880.00
Truck Constraints				
Spare Volume in Cubic Feet	350			
Spare Weight in Pounds	525			

Northland Instrument Distributors
Weekly East Coast Shipment

FIGURE 8-1

(c) Answer Report with Guitars

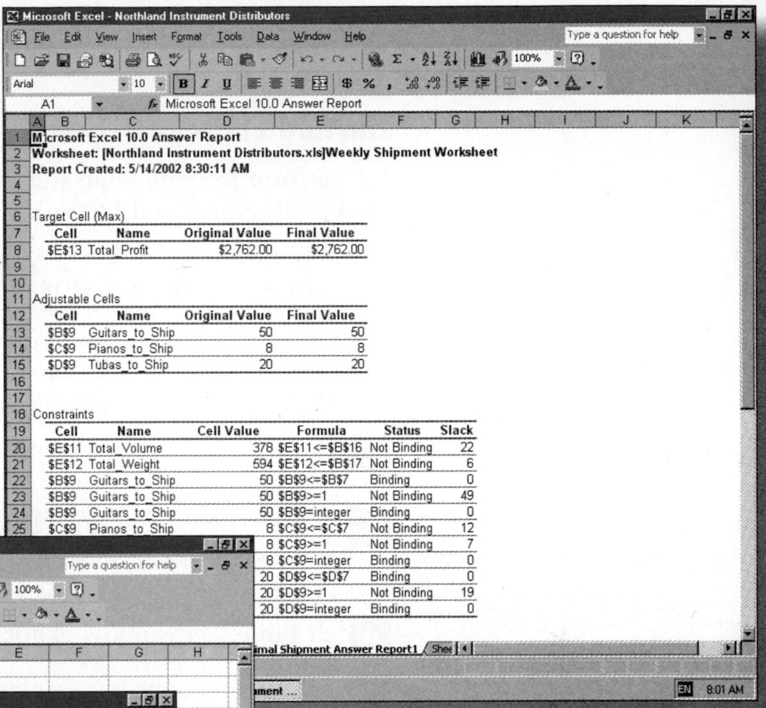

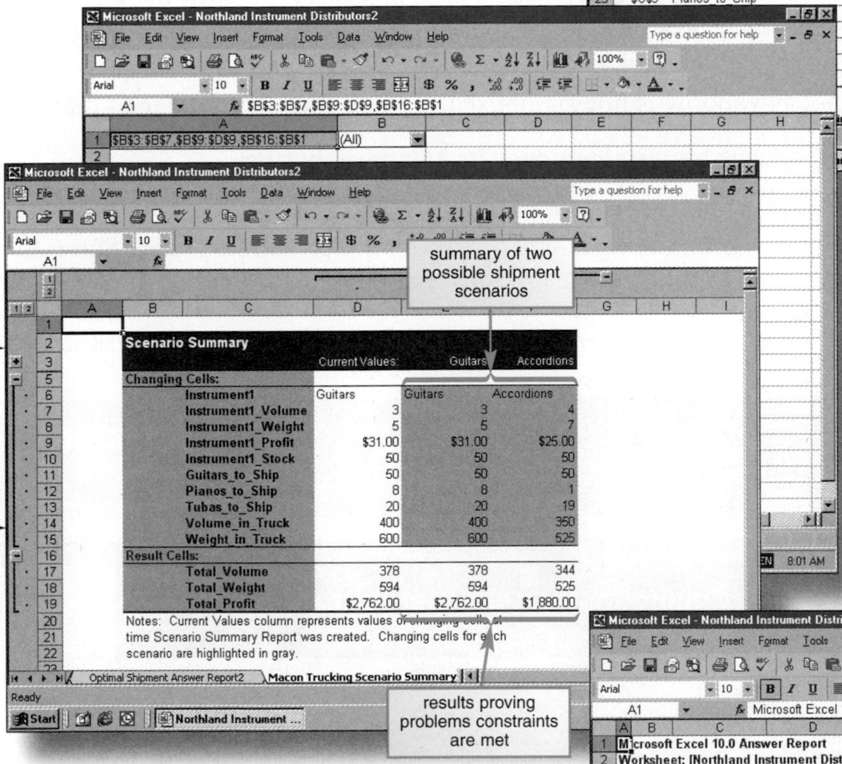

(f) Scenario Summary and Scenario PivotTable of Solutions

(e) Answer Report with Accordians

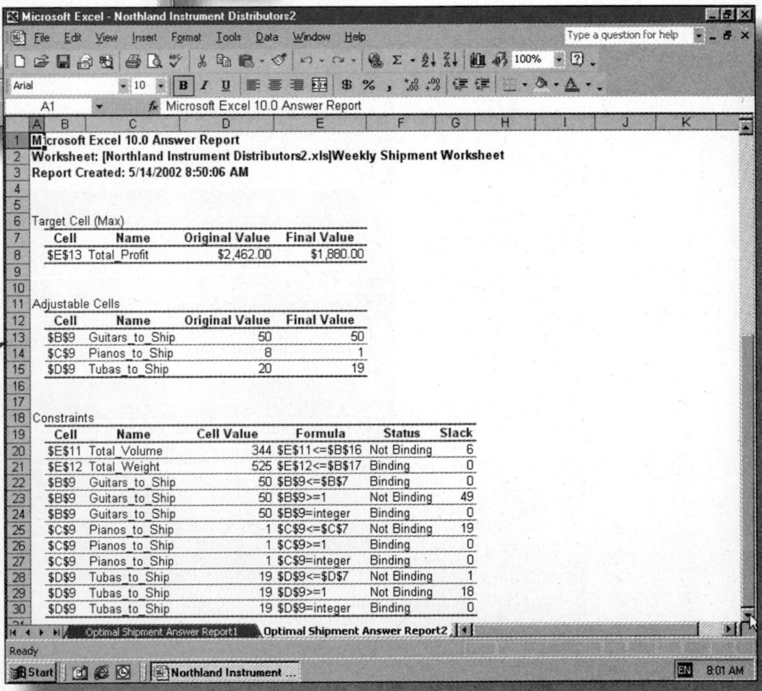

Source of Data: The workbook shown in Figure 8-1a on page E 8.06 is available on the Data Disk with the file name, Northland Instrument Distributors.

Starting Excel and Opening a Workbook

Perform the following steps to start Excel, reset the toolbars, and open the workbook Northland Instrument Distributors from the Data Disk.

TO START EXCEL, OPEN A WORKBOOK, AND CUSTOMIZE EXCEL

1. Insert the Data Disk in drive A. See the inside back cover of this book for instructions for downloading the Data Disk or see your instructor for information on accessing the files required in this book.
2. Click the Start button on the Windows taskbar and then click Open Office Document.
3. When the Open Office Document dialog box displays, click the Look in box arrow and then click 3½ Floppy (A:). Double-click Northland Instrument Distributors in the Look in list.
4. If the Excel window is not maximized, double-click its title bar to maximize it.
5. If the Language bar displays, click its Minimize button.
6. If the Standard and Formatting toolbars display on one row, click the Toolbar Options button on the right side of either toolbar and then click Show Buttons on Two Rows in the Toolbar Options list.

The Weekly Shipment Worksheet displays in the Excel window (Figure 8-2).

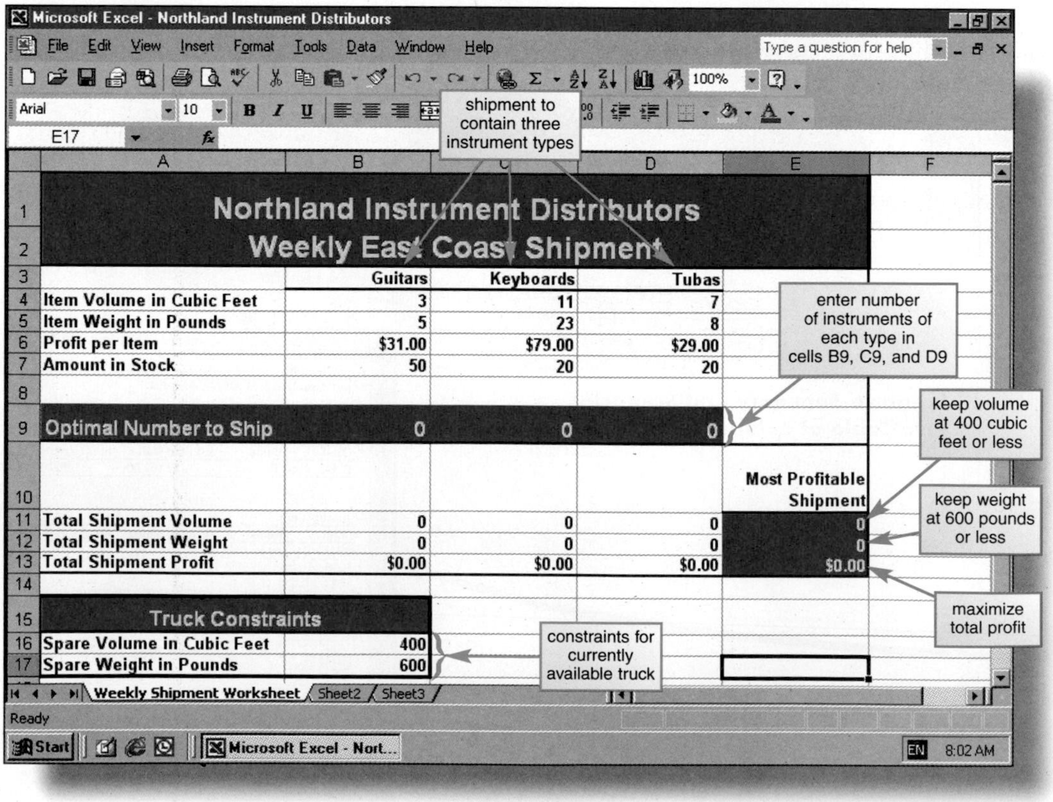

FIGURE 8-2

The Weekly Shipment Worksheet shown in Figure 8-2 consists of information for three types of instruments. Rows 4 through 7 show the information for each type of instrument. Row 9 contains the optimal combination of instruments, which is the information that needs to be determined in this project. Rows 11 through 13 show the totals for each instrument based on the number of instruments entered in the range B9:D9. As cells B9, C9, and D9 change, the values in the range B11:D13 are updated. Finally, the grand totals for the entire shipment are calculated in the range E11:E13. The goals are to keep the total volume of the shipment (cell E11) less than or equal to 400 (cell B16), keep the total weight of the shipment (cell E12) less than or equal to 600 (cell B17), and maximize the total profit made on the shipment (cell E13).

The current worksheet displays guitars as one of the instruments. One of the requirements is to create shipments within the constraints for both guitars and accordions. Therefore, the information in column B needs to be modified later in the project to reflect the volume, weight, profit, and stock of accordions.

Formula Auditing

The term **formula auditing** refers to the practice of proving the correctness of a worksheet. The **Formula Auditing toolbar** supplies several tools that you can use to analyze the formulas in a worksheet.

Formula auditing is useful both for analyzing a complex worksheet and for finding the source of errors that may occur in your worksheet. Excel provides visual auditing tools that display cues to help you understand the worksheet. These cues take the form of tracer arrows and circles around worksheet cells. **Tracer arrows** are blue arrows that point from cell to cell and let you know what cells are referenced in a formula in a particular cell. Tracer arrows display red when one of the cells referenced contains an error.

More About

Auditing

Auditing is a very important job function in corporations and government. For more information about auditing, visit the Excel 2002 More About Web page (www.scite.com/offxp/more.htm) and then click Auditing.

Displaying the Formula Auditing Toolbar

When you want to audit a worksheet, you can display the Formula Auditing toolbar. The Formula Auditing toolbar contains buttons that allow you to trace the details of a formula or locate the source of errors in a worksheet. To display the Formula Auditing toolbar, complete the steps on the next page.

Steps To Display the Formula Auditing Toolbar

1 Click Tools on the menu bar, point to Formula Auditing, and then point to Show Formula Auditing Toolbar on the Formula Auditing submenu.

The Tools menu and Formula Auditing submenu display (Figure 8-3).

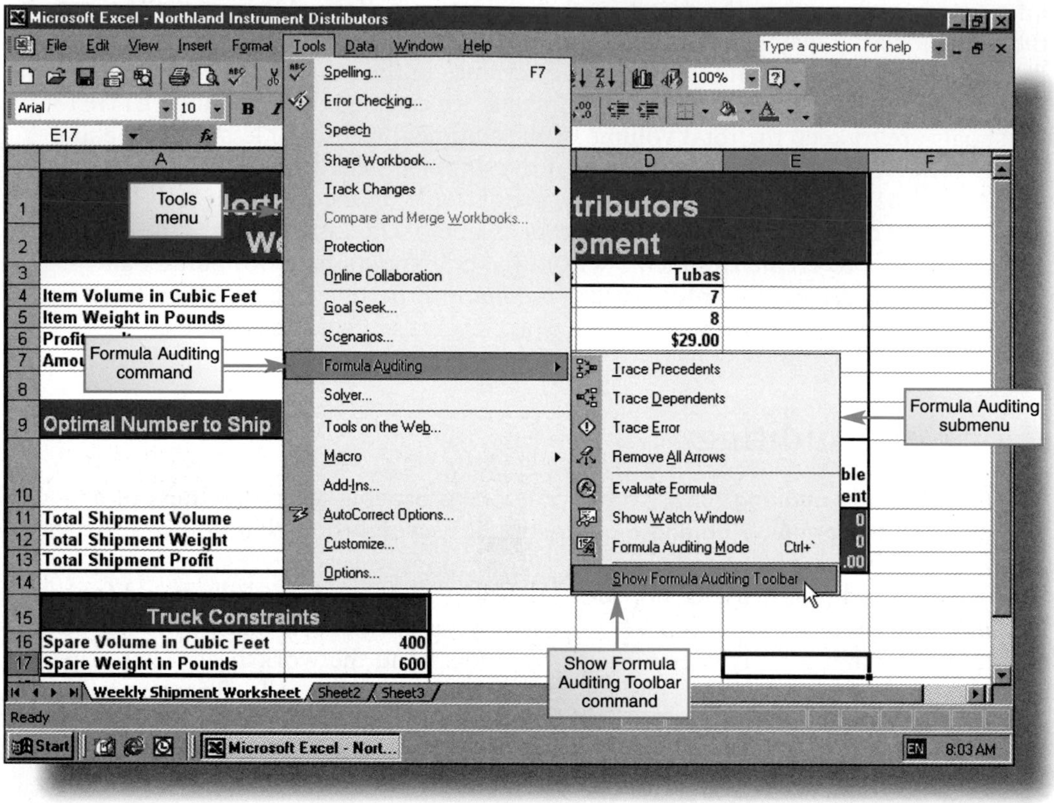

FIGURE 8-3

2 Click Show Formula Auditing Toolbar.

The Formula Auditing toolbar displays (Figure 8-4). Excel displays the Formula Auditing toolbar on the screen in the same location and with the same shape as it displayed the last time it was used.

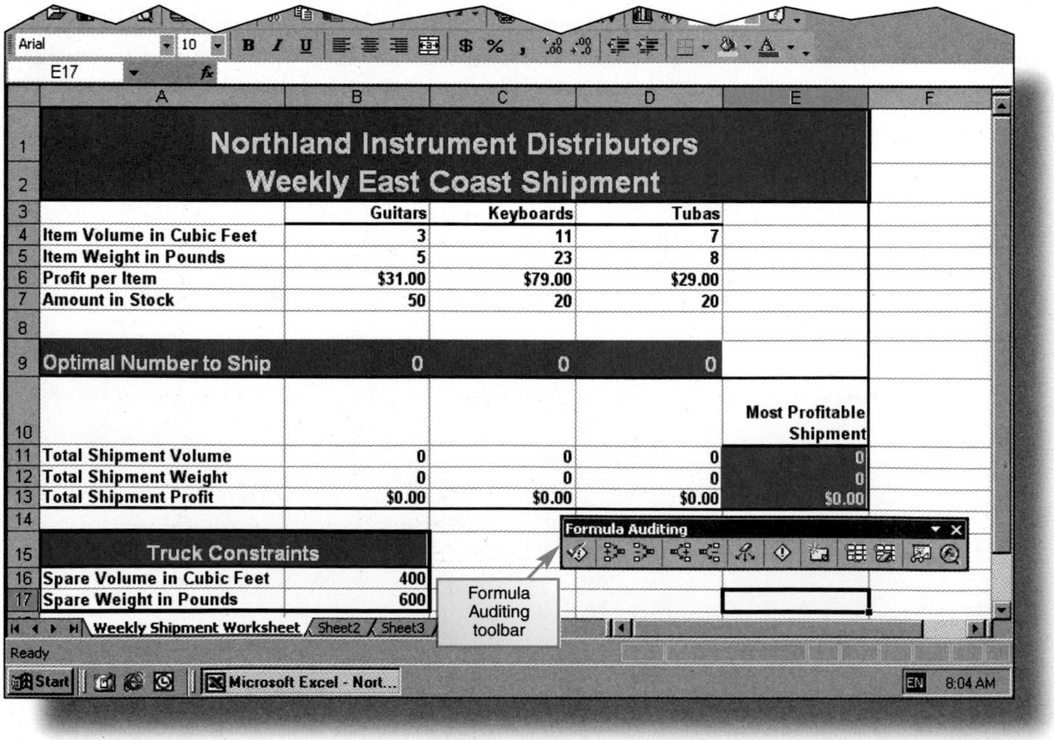

FIGURE 8-4

Other Ways

1. Right-click Standard or Formatting toolbar, click Formula Auditing
2. Press ALT+T, U, S
3. In Voice Command mode, say "Tools, Formula Auditing, Show Formula Auditing Toolbar"

Tracing Precedents with the Formula Auditing Toolbar

A formula that relies on other cells for a computation is said to have precedents. **Precedents** are cells that are referenced in a formula. For example, if you assign cell A5 the formula =A1+A2, then cells A1 and A2 are precedents of cell A5. Tracing precedent cells shows you how a particular cell is calculated. Often a precedent cell has precedents itself. For instance, in the previous example, if you assign cell A1 the formula =B1+B2, then cell A1, which is a precedent of cell A5, also has precedents. Excel also allows you to trace the precedents of precedents; however, you can audit only one cell at a time. That is, Excel does not allow you to audit ranges. The following steps show the precedent cells for the total profit of the best shipment in cell E13.

Steps To Trace Precedents

1 Click cell E13 and then click the Trace Precedents button on the Formula Auditing toolbar.

Excel draws an arrow across the range B13:E13.

2 Click the Trace Precedents button again.

Excel draws arrows indicating the precedents of cells B13:D13 (Figure 8-5).

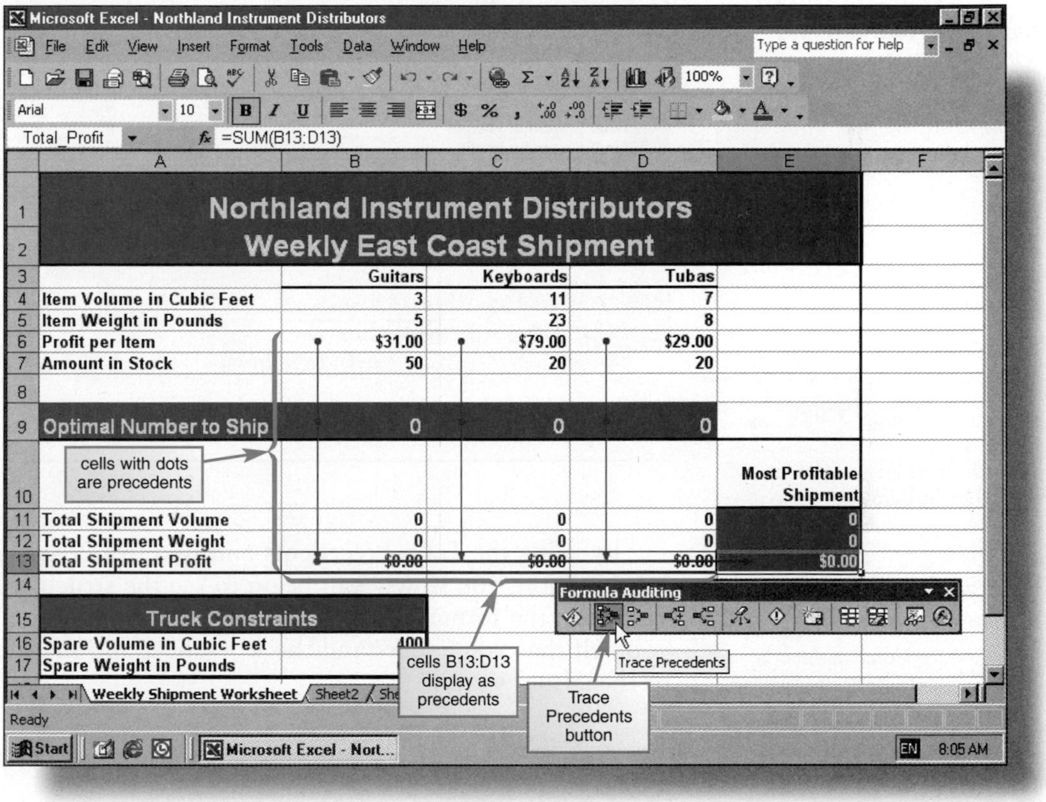

FIGURE 8-5

The arrows in Figure 8-5 have arrowheads on cells that are traced, and dots on cells that are direct precedents of the cells with arrowheads. For example, cell B13 is a precedent of cell E13, the total profit cell, and B13 has precedents above it in cells B6 and B9. As you click the Trace Precedents button, you can visually follow the levels of precedents through the worksheet.

Other Ways

1. On Tools menu point to Formula Auditing, click Trace Precedents
2. Press ALT+T, U, T
3. In Voice Command mode, say "Tools, Formula Auditing, Trace Precedents"

Removing Precedents Arrows with the Formula Auditing Toolbar

After understanding the precedents of a particular cell, you can remove the precedent arrows one level at a time, as shown in the steps on the next page.

Steps To Remove the Trace Precedents Arrows

1 Click the Remove Precedent Arrows button on the Formula Auditing toolbar.

Excel removes the arrows across the range B6:D9, the last level of precedent arrows added.

2 Click the Remove Precedents Arrows button on the Formula Auditing toolbar again.

Excel removes the remaining precedent arrows (Figure 8-6).

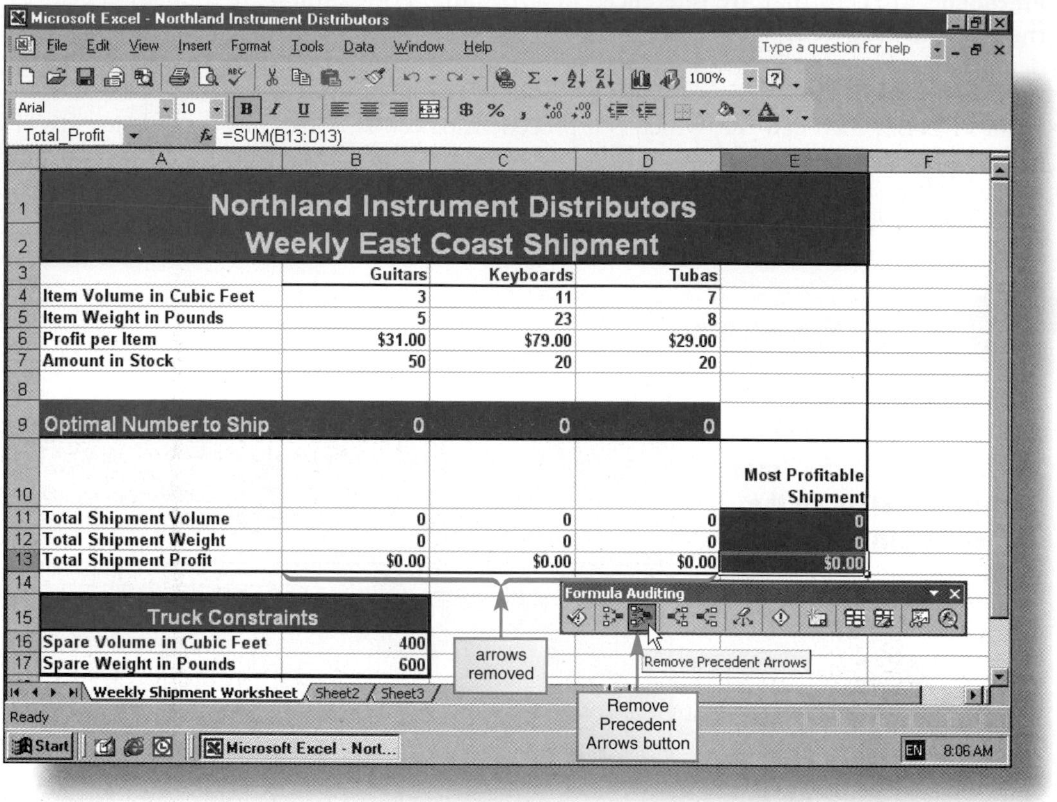

FIGURE 8-6

Other Ways

1. On Tools menu point to Formula Auditing, click Remove All Arrows
2. On Formula Auditing toolbar, click Remove All Arrows
3. Press ALT+T, U, A
4. In Voice Command mode, say "Tools, Formula Auditing, Remove All Arrows"

More About

Tracing Precedents and Dependents

When no more levels of precedents are available on the worksheet, Excel will beep if you try to trace another level. If you double-click a tracer arrow, the cell at the end of the arrow will be selected. This is useful on complex worksheets where the destination of an arrow may not be easy to ascertain.

By using the Trace Precedents and Remove Precedent Arrows buttons in combination, you slowly can begin to see the structure of the worksheet that is hidden in the formulas within the cells. By doing more analysis, you can assure yourself that you understand the worksheet and that no obvious errors are apparent to the casual viewer.

Tracing Dependents with the Formula Auditing Toolbar

A cell is a **dependent** if it is referenced in a formula in another cell. Often, it is useful to find out where a cell is being used in a worksheet to perform subsequent calculations. In other words, you can discover which cells in the worksheet use the cell in question. The following steps trace the dependents of the optimal number of guitars to ship in cell B9.

Steps To Trace Dependents

1 Click cell B9 and then click the Trace Dependents button on the Formula Auditing toolbar.

Excel draws arrows to cells B11, B12, and B13.

2 Click the Trace Dependents button once more.

Excel draws arrows indicating the remaining dependents of cell B9 (Figure 8-7).

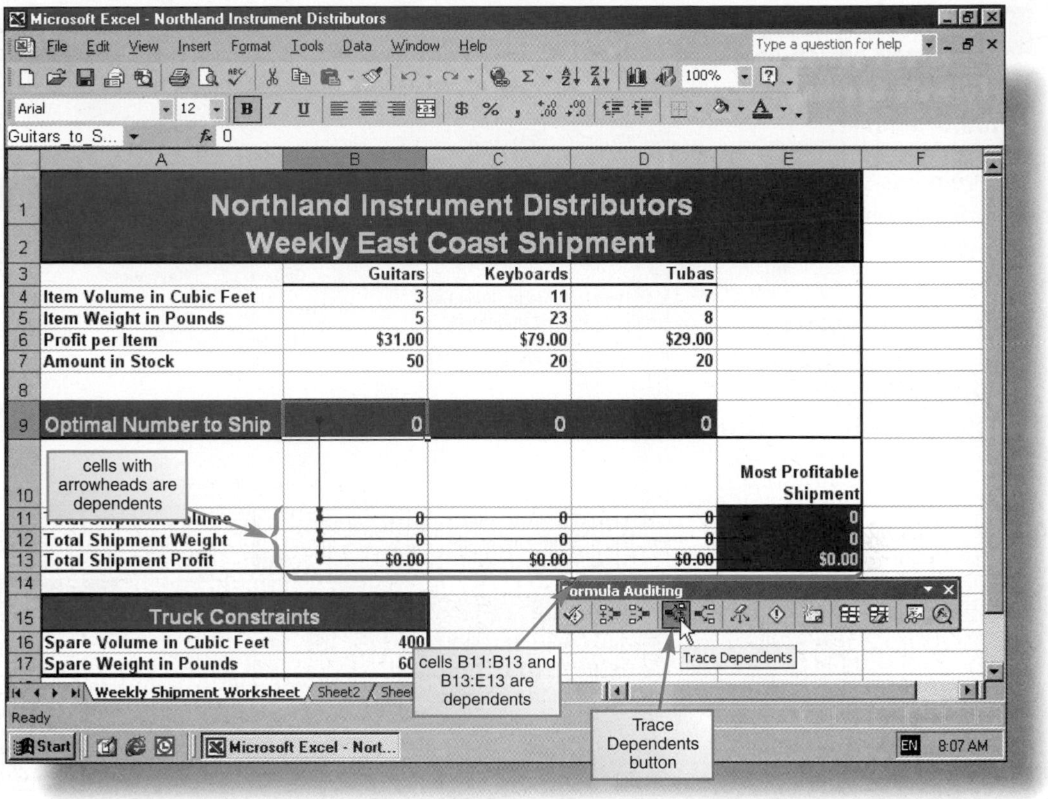

FIGURE 8-7

Other Ways

1. On Tools menu point to Auditing, click Trace Dependents
2. Press ALT+T, U, D
3. In Voice Command mode, say "Tools, Formula Auditing, Trace Dependents"

Figure 8-7 indicates that cells B11, B12, and B13 depend on cell B9. Subsequently, the range E11:E13 depends on those cells. Clearly, before any results can be computed in the range E11:E13, cell B9 must have a value.

Removing All Arrows with the Formula Auditing Toolbar

When you have finished auditing the worksheet with the Formula Auditing toolbar, the easiest way to clear all of the trace arrows is to use the Remove All Arrows button on the Formula Auditing toolbar, as shown in the steps on the next page.

Steps To Remove the Trace Dependents Arrows

1 Click the Remove All Arrows button on the Formula Auditing toolbar.

Excel removes all of the trace dependents arrows (Figure 8-8).

2 Click the Close button on the right side of the Formula Auditing toolbar to close it.

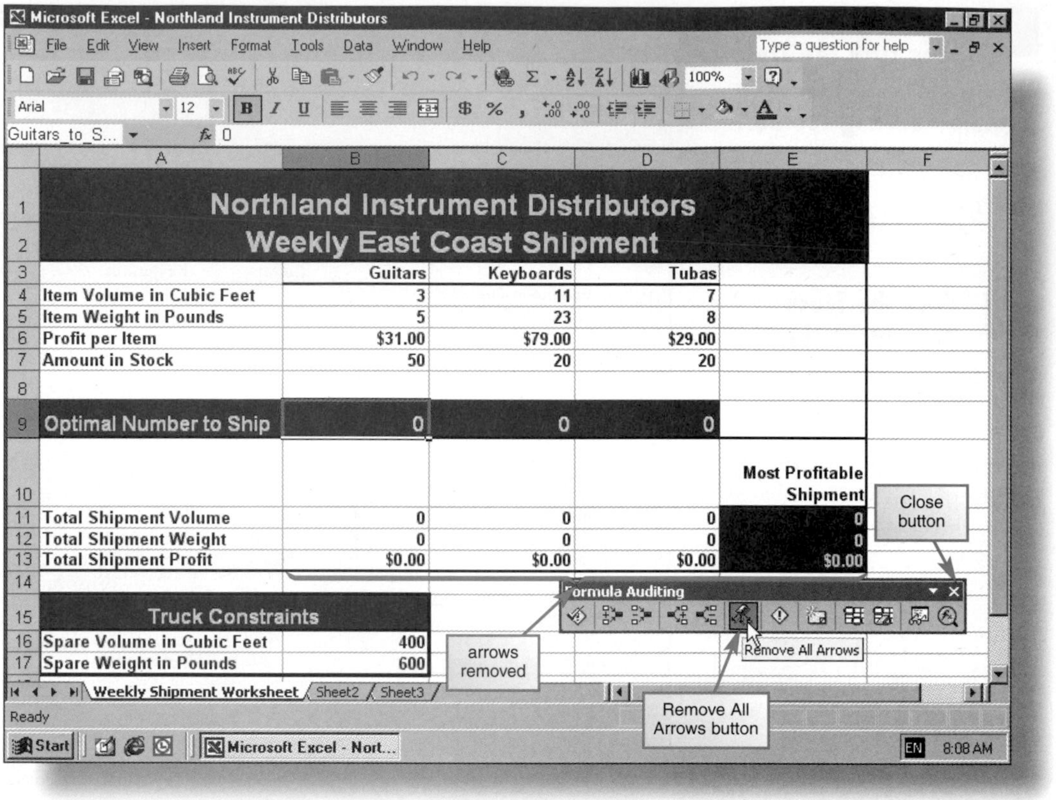

FIGURE 8-8

Other Ways

1. On Tools menu point to Auditing, click Remove All Arrows
2. Press ALT+T, U, A
3. In Voice Command mode, say "Tools, Formula Auditing, Remove All Arrows"

Sometimes, a cell has precedents or dependents on other worksheets or in other workbooks. In this case, Excel draws a dashed arrow to an icon of a worksheet to indicate that the precedent or dependent is outside of the current worksheet. If you click the dashed arrow and the workbook that contains the precedent or dependent is open, Excel displays the Go To dialog box that allows you to navigate to that location.

Figure 8-9 shows the buttons of the Formula Auditing Toolbar. Table 8-1 summarizes the buttons on the Formula Auditing Toolbar.

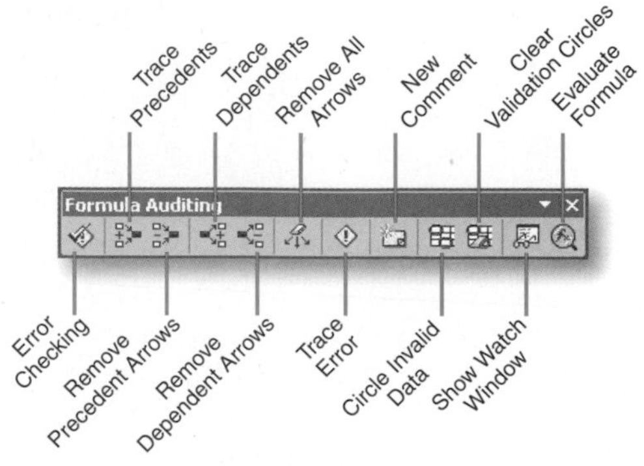

FIGURE 8-9

The **Trace Error button** is used when you see an error in a cell and want to trace the source of the error. If you see an error in a cell, including #DIV/0!, #NAME?, #NA, #NULL!, #NUM!, #REF!, and #VALUE!, the Trace Error button will display red tracer arrows to inform you of the precedents of the cell that contains the error. You then can inspect the precedent cells to see if you can determine the cause of the error and correct it. The **Error Checking button** will search the current worksheet for any errors and then display the Error Checking dialog box to help you take corrective action.

Table 8-1 Summary of Buttons on the Formula Auditing Toolbar

BUTTON	*NAME*	*FUNCTION*
	Error Checking	Checks the entire worksheet for errors.
	Trace Precedents	Draws tracer arrows from the cells that affect the formula in the current cell.
	Remove Precedent Arrows	Removes tracer arrows from one level of dependents on the active worksheet.
	Trace Dependents	Draws tracer arrows to the cells that use the current cell in their formula.
	Remove Dependent Arrows	Removes tracer arows from one level of dependents on the active worksheet.
	Remove All Arrows	Removes all tracer arrows drawn with the Trace Precedents and Trace Dependents buttons.
	Trace Error	If the active cell contains an error value, draw tracer arrows to the cells that may be causing the error value to appear.
	New Comment	Attach a comment to the active cell.
	Circle Invalid Data	Draw circles around the cells that contain values outside of the limits defined through the Validation command on the Data menu.
	Clear Validation Circles	Clears the circles drawn by the Circle Invalid Data button
	Show Watch Window	Shows a window that displays cells and their formulas that you select to monitor.
	Evaluate Formula	Allows you to debug complex formulas by monitoring the formula step by step.

The **New Comment button** allows you to place comments in cells so that you can make notes to yourself or to others about questionable data in the worksheet. For example, if you are auditing someone else's worksheet and you believe that a cell should be the precedent of a particular cell, you can make a note that will display when the other user opens the worksheet. Comments are discussed further in Project 9.

The **Circle Invalid Data button** and **Clear Validation Circles button** are used in combination with Excel's data validation capability discussed in the next section. If a cell contains data validation parameters and the current data in the cell is outside of those validation criteria, the Circle Invalid Data button draws a circle around the cell. The Clear Validation Circles button is used to clear these circles.

The **Show Watch Window button** displays the Watch Window. The **Watch Window** allows you to monitor cells and formulas as you work on a worksheet. The **Evaluate Formula button** displays the **Evaluate Formula dialog box**, which allows you to debug or understand complex formulas in a worksheet, much in the manner that programmers debug source code. See Project 7 in this book for a more in-depth discussion of programming in Excel.

Data Validation, Trial and Error, and Goal Seek

Often, it is necessary to limit the values that should be placed in a particular cell. Excel allows you to place limitations on the values of cells by using data validation. **Data validation** restricts the values that may be entered into a cell by the worksheet user. Excel allows you to determine the restrictions placed on data entered into a cell, set an input message that the user will see when selecting the cell, and set an error message that displays when a user violates the restrictions placed on the cell. By implementing these features, you limit the possibilities for error on a worksheet by giving the user as much information as possible about how to use the worksheet properly.

One important aspect of Excel's data validation is that the rules apply only when the user enters data into the cell manually. That is, if a cell is calculated by a formula or set in a way other than direct input by the user, Excel does not check the validation rules.

More About

Validation Circles

Validation circles display in red to indicate that these cells contain error values. Excel will display a maximum of 256 invalid data circles at a time.

More About

Data Validation

If you have the Office Assistant turned on, Data Validation input and error messages will be displayed as part of the assistant. Input and error messages can be up to 255 characters in length.

Adding Data Validation to Cells

Recall from the Needs section for this project on page E 8.05, shipment amounts must be whole numbers and at least one of each type of instrument must be included in each shipment, but no more than are in stock of each type of instrument. By examining the worksheet, you can see that cells B9, C9, and D9 must have these restrictions. Data validation is added to cells by using the **Validation command** on the Data menu.

Perform the following steps to add data validation to cells B9, C9, and D9.

Steps To Add Data Validation

1 Select the range B9:D9. Click Data on the menu bar and then point to Validation.

The Data menu displays (Figure 8-10).

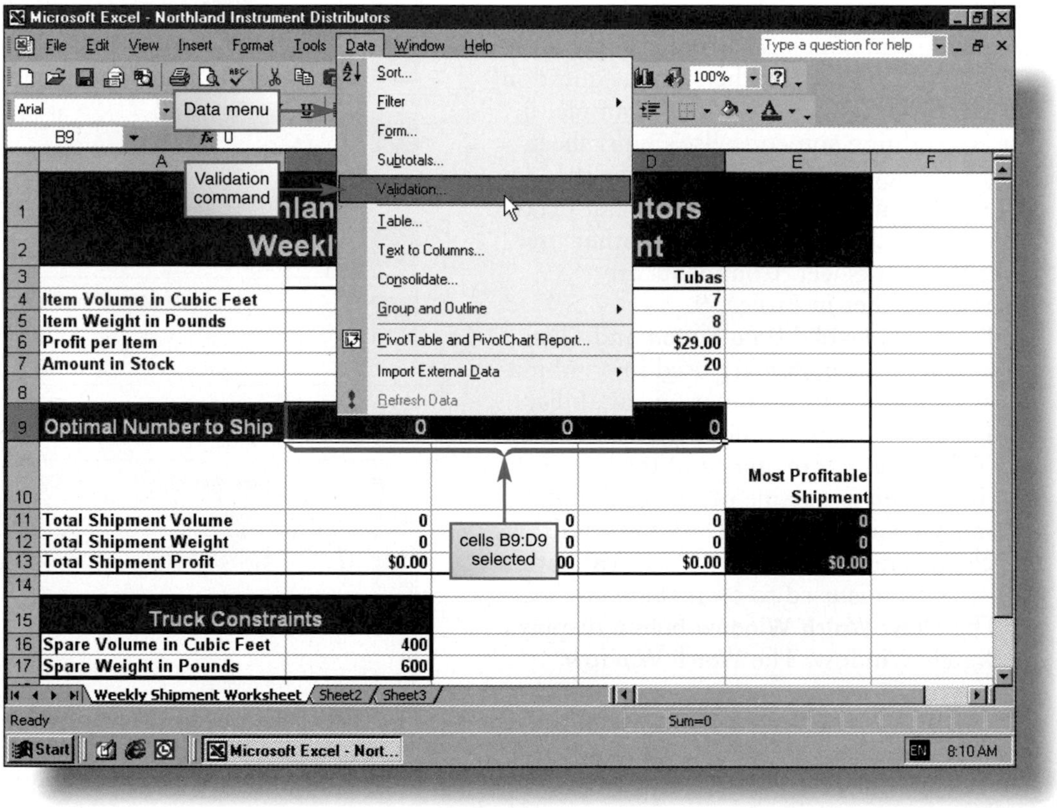

FIGURE 8-10

2 **Click Validation. When the Data Validation dialog box displays, click the Allow box arrow and then click Whole number. Click the Data box arrow and then, if necessary, click between. Type** `1` **in the Minimum box. Select the Maximum box and click cell B7. Point to the Input Message tab.**

The Data Validation dialog box displays (Figure 8-11).

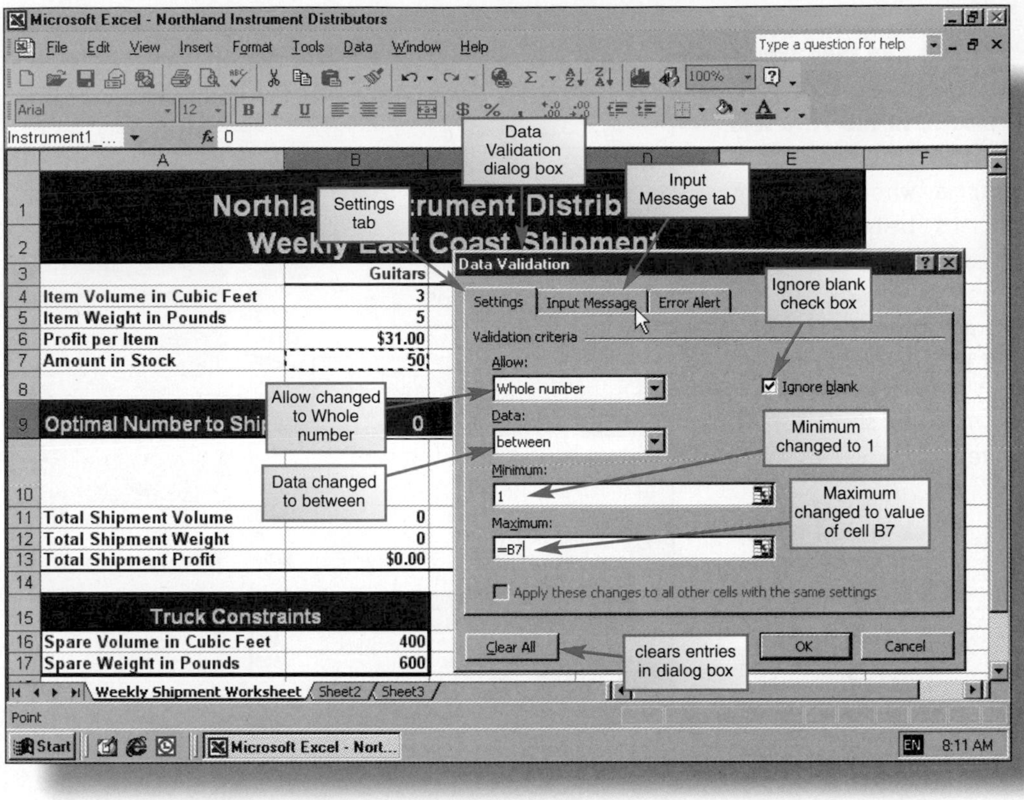

FIGURE 8-11

3 **Click the Input Message tab and then type** `Items to Ship` **in the Title text box. Type** `Enter the number of items to include in this shipment. The number must be greater than zero and less than or equal to the number of items in stock.` **in the Input message box. Point to the Error Alert tab.**

The Input Message sheet displays (Figure 8-12).

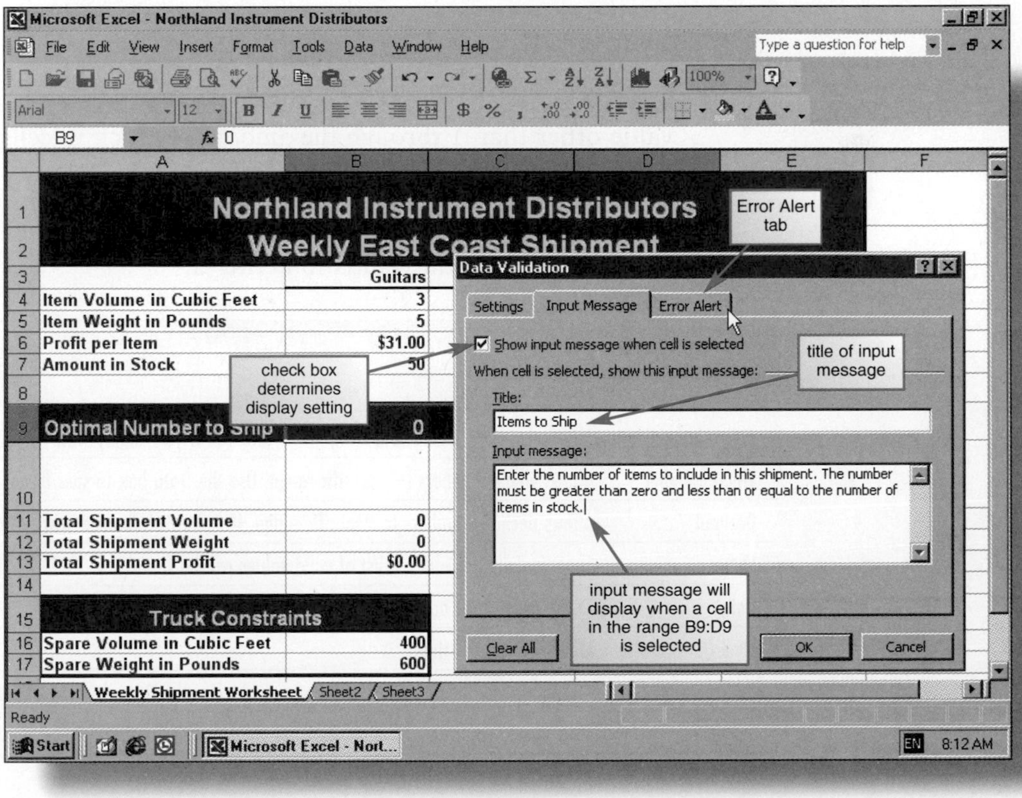

FIGURE 8-12

4 **Click the Error Alert tab and then type** `Input Error in Shipment` **in the Title text box. Type** `You must enter a whole number that is between zero and the number of items in stock.` **in the Error message text box. Point to the OK button.**

The Error Alert sheet displays (Figure 8-13).

5 **Click the OK button.**

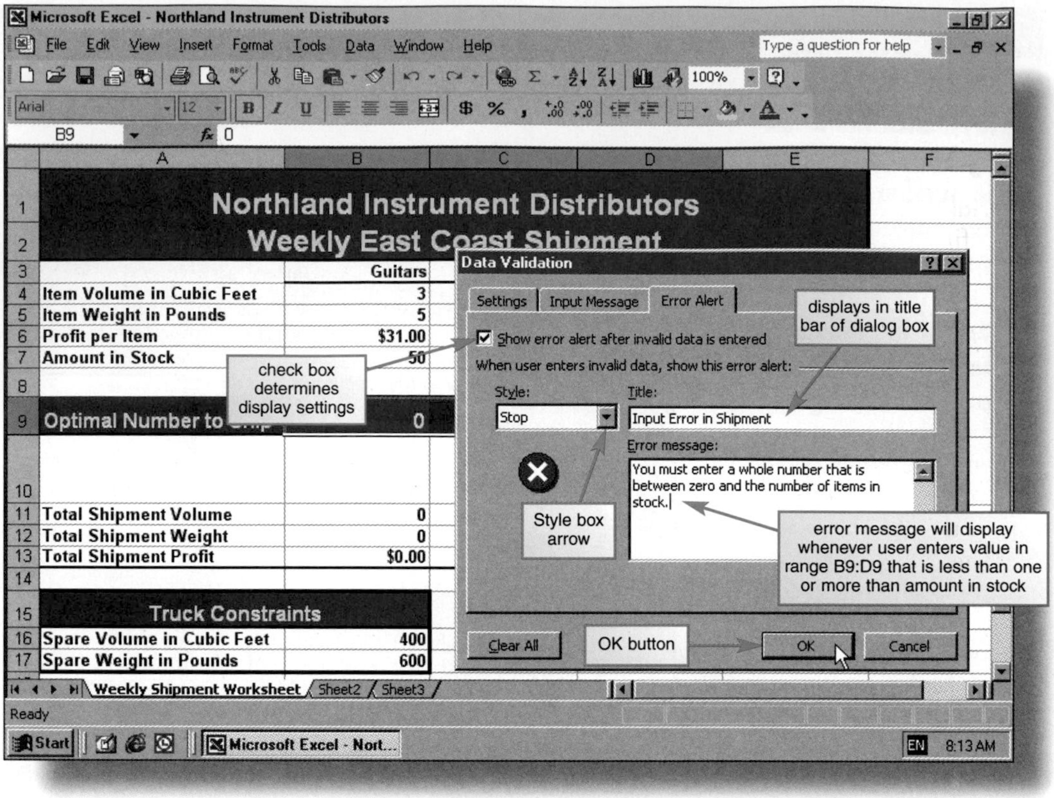

FIGURE 8-13

Other Ways

1. Press ALT+D, L
2. In Voice Command mode, say "Data, Validation"

When the user selects one of the cells in the range B9:D9, Excel displays the input message defined in Figure 8-12 on the previous page. When the user enters a value other than 1 through the amount in stock in cells B9:D9, the error message defined in Figure 8-13 displays.

Excel allows several types of validation to be done in the Validation criteria area shown in Figure 8-11 on the previous page. Table 8-2 shows the various criteria types available in the Validation criteria.

TABLE 8-2 Types of Validation Criteria Allowed

ALLOW	*MEANING*
Any value	Allows the user to enter anything in the cell. Use if you simply want to display an input message.
Whole number	Allows whole numbers in a specific range. Use the Data box to specify how the validation takes place.
Decimal	Allows decimal numbers in a specific range. Use the Data box to specify how the validation takes place.
List	Specifies a range where a list of valid values can be found.
Date	Allows a range of dates.
Time	Allows a range of times.
Text length	Allows a certain length text string to be input. Use the Data drop-down list to specify how the validation takes place.
Custom	Allows you to specify a formula that will validate the data entered by the user.

The Ignore blank check box should be cleared if you want to require that the user enter data in the cell. By leaving the Ignore blank check box selected, Excel allows the user to select the cell, and then leave the cell with no data being entered.

Using Trial and Error to Solve a Complex Problem

Trial and error refers to the practice of adjusting cells in a worksheet manually to try to find a solution to a problem. In the Weekly Shipment Worksheet, you could adjust cells B9, C9, and D9 until the criteria for volume and weight are met. While many combinations of possible values exist, you could try keeping one or two of the values constant while adjusting the others.

Trial and error is more than just guessing. Because you understand the constraints on the problem and the goals, you use logic to make subsequent trials better than the previous. For example, if you increase the number of keyboards by five and it causes the total weight of the shipment to exceed 600 pounds, you may instead try to increase the number of keyboards by one to see if that keeps the totals within the constraints.

The following steps illustrate using trial and error to solve a problem.

More About

Validation Types

When using the Custom validation type, you can use a formula that evaluates to either true or false. If the value is false, data may not be entered in the cell by the user. Suppose, for example, you have a cell that contains an employee's salary. If the salary is zero, which indicates the employee no longer is with the company, you may want to prohibit the user from entering a percentage in another cell that contains the employee's raise for the year.

Steps To Use Trial and Error to Attempt to Solve a Complex Problem

1 Click cell B9 and type 60 **as the number of guitars to ship and then press the ENTER key. Point to the Retry button.**

The Input Error in Shipment dialog box displays (Figure 8-14), because 60 is outside the limits of acceptable values for this cell. The Items to Ship ScreenTip displays because cell B9 is selected.

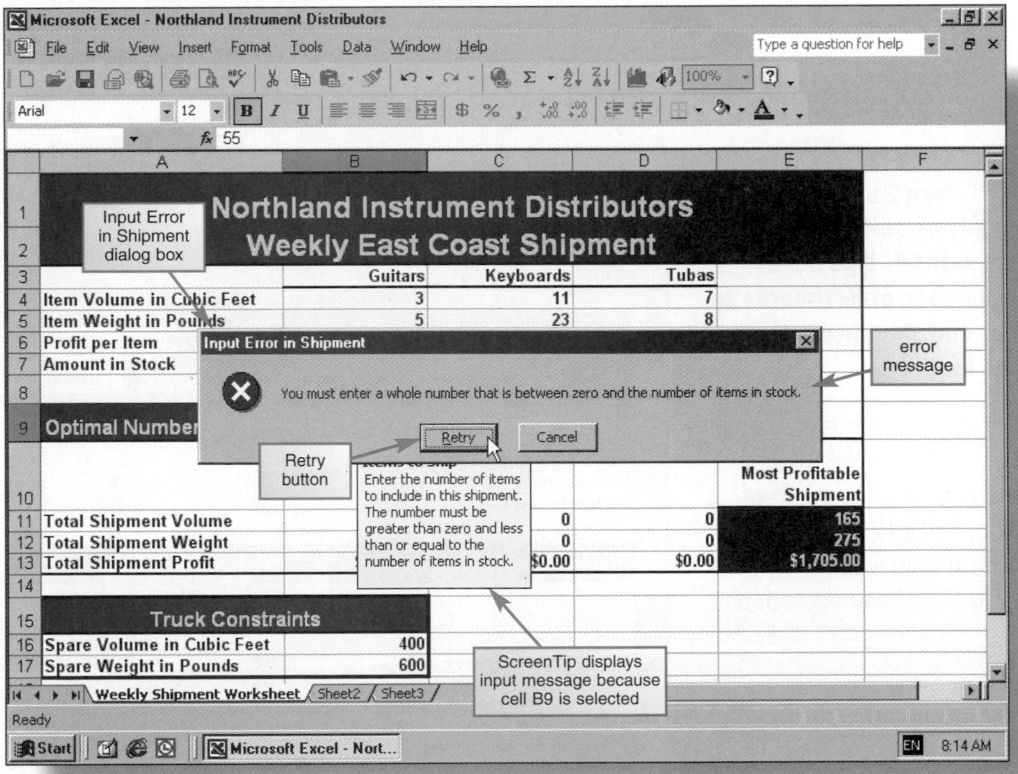

FIGURE 8-14

2 **Click the Retry button. Type** 47 **as the number of guitars to ship in cell B9. Click cell C9 and type** 18 **as the number of keyboards to ship. Click cell D9, type** 18 **as the number of tubas to ship and then press the ENTER key.**

Excel displays the new values and updates the totals in the range B11:E13 as shown in Figure 8-15. The value of 465 in cell E11 indicates that the maximum volume for the shipment of 400 cubic feet (cell B16) has been exceeded.

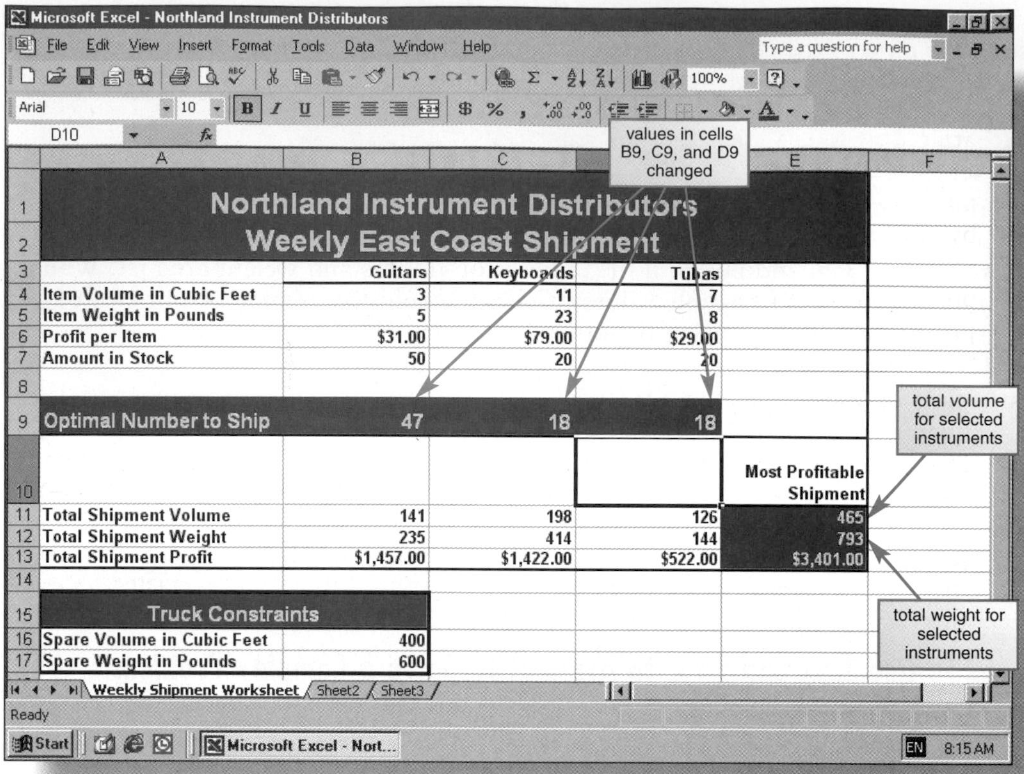

FIGURE 8-15

3 **Click cell B9 and type** 35 **as the number of guitars to ship. Click cell C9, type** 15 **as the number of keyboards to ship, and then press the ENTER key.**

Excel displays the recalculated values for the worksheet (Figure 8-16). The value of 664 in cell E12 indicates that the maximum weight of 600 pounds has been exceeded.

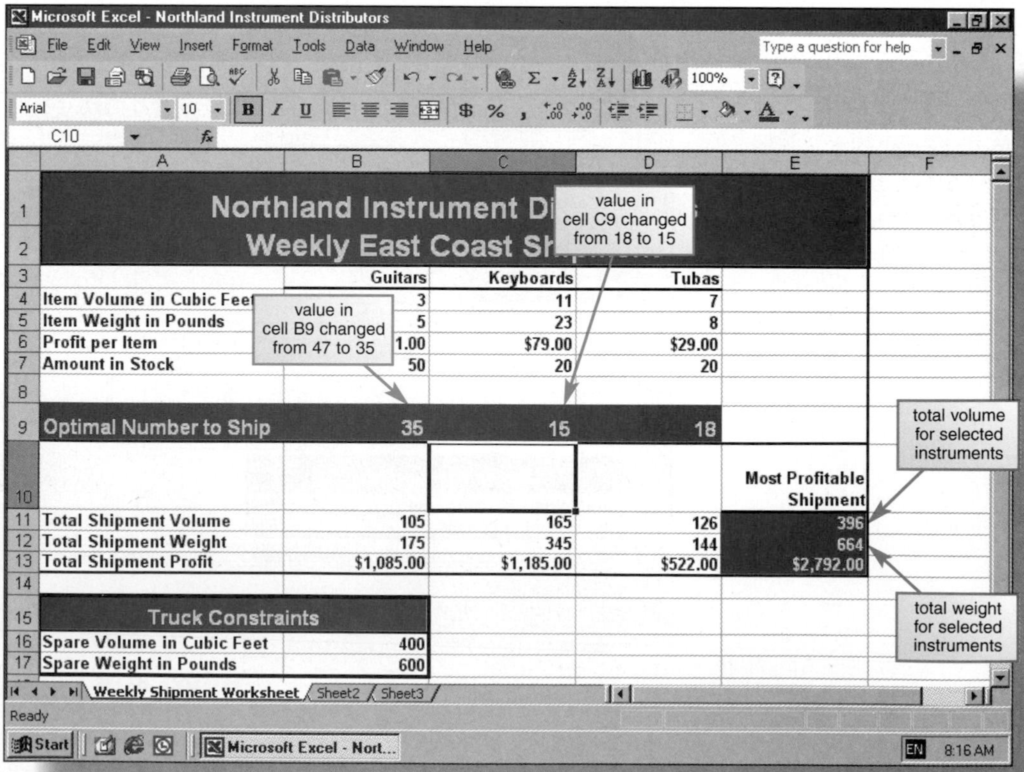

FIGURE 8-16

Trial and error can be used on simple problems in many cases. Trial and error, however, has many limitations. The Weekly Shipment Worksheet has three cells (B9, C9, and D9) that can be adjusted to solve the problem. Because each cell can contain a value between 1 and the amount in stock, many different combinations are possible that you could try, many of which may give the proper volume and weight to the shipment. The biggest drawback to using trial and error in this situation is that you must maximize the profit while meeting the other conditions. It is difficult to determine by casual observation if the profit has been maximized. Rather than using trial and error to test all possible shipment combinations and see which one produces the most profit while meeting the truck constraints, Excel provides other tools to help solve problems where cells can contain a number of values.

Goal Seeking to Solve a Complex Problem

If you know the result you want a formula to produce, you can use **goal seeking** to determine the value of a cell on which a formula depends. In the Weekly Shipment Worksheet, the total volume for the shipment is one result that can be sought by varying the number of one of the instruments. Goal seeking takes trial and error one step further by automatically changing the value of a cell until a single criteria is met in another cell. In this case, suppose you suspect that by varying the number of tubas, you can achieve the goal of 400 cubic feet for the shipment. In doing this, you hope that the other constraints of the problem also are satisfied.

The following steps show how goal seek can be used to alter the number of tubas to keep the total volume at less than or equal to 400 cubic feet.

More About

Goal Seeking

Goal seeking is a methodology in which you know what value you want a formula in a cell to result in but you do not know the value to place in a cell that is involved in the formula. You can goal seek by changing the value in a cell that is used indirectly in the formula.

Steps To Use the Goal Seek Command to Attempt to Solve a Complex Problem

1 Click cell E11, the cell that contains the total volume for the shipment. Click Tools on the menu bar and then point to Goal Seek.

The Tools menu displays (Figure 8-17).

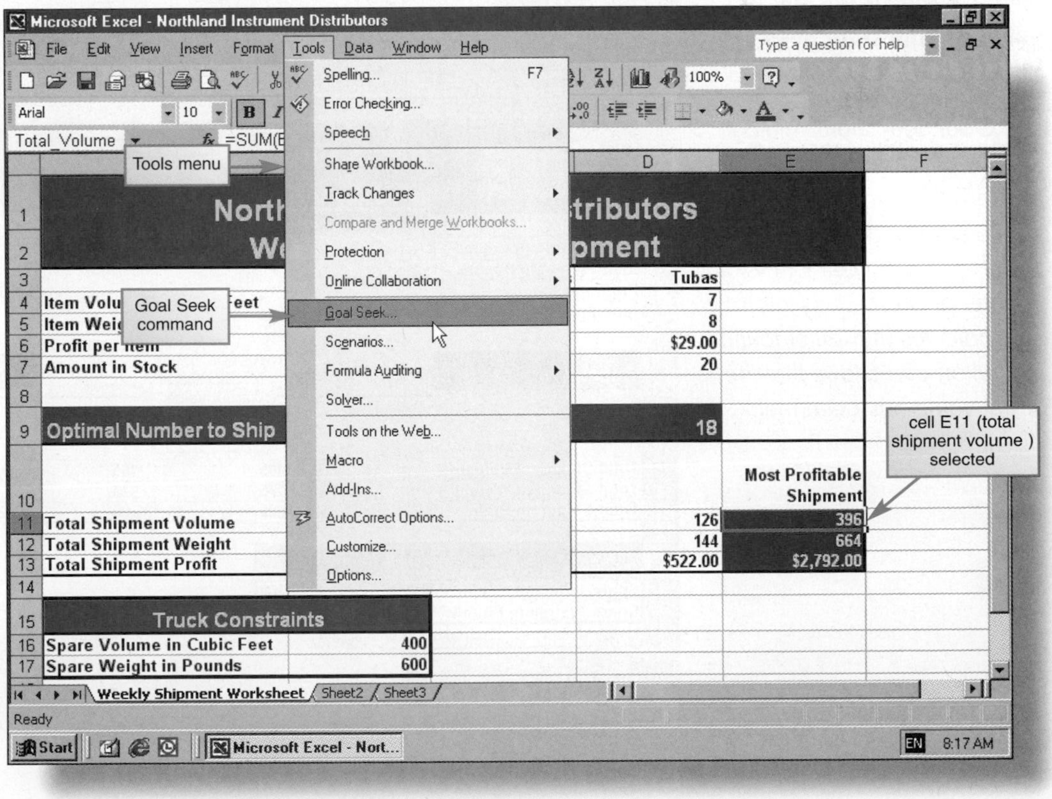

FIGURE 8-17

2 Click Goal Seek.

The Goal Seek dialog box displays. The Set cell box is assigned the cell reference of the active cell in the worksheet (cell E11) automatically.

3 Click the To value text box. Type 400 **and then click the By changing cell box. Click cell D9 on the worksheet. Point to the OK button.**

The ***Goal Seek dialog box*** *displays as shown in Figure 8-18. A marquee displays around cell D9.*

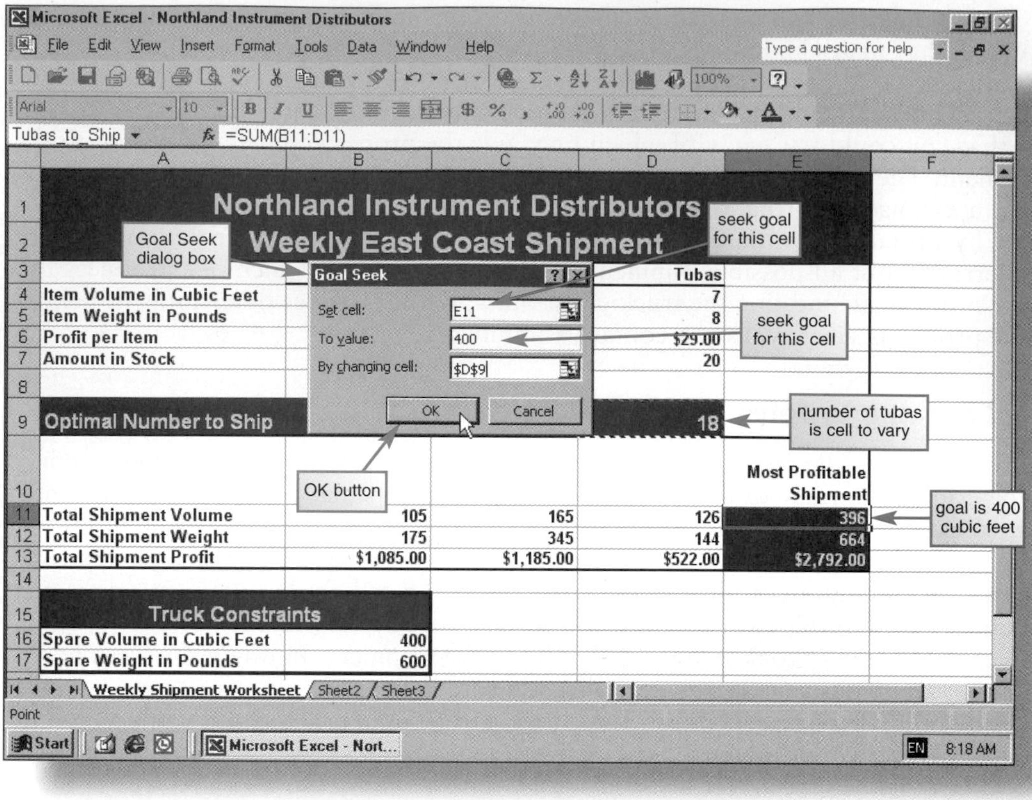

FIGURE 8-18

4 Click the OK button. Point to the OK button in the Goal Seek Status dialog box.

The ***Goal Seek Status dialog box*** *displays as shown in Figure 8-19. Excel changes the number in cell D9 to 19, and the value in cell E11 is updated to 400. The dialog box indicates that Excel found a solution and shows that the target value has been met.*

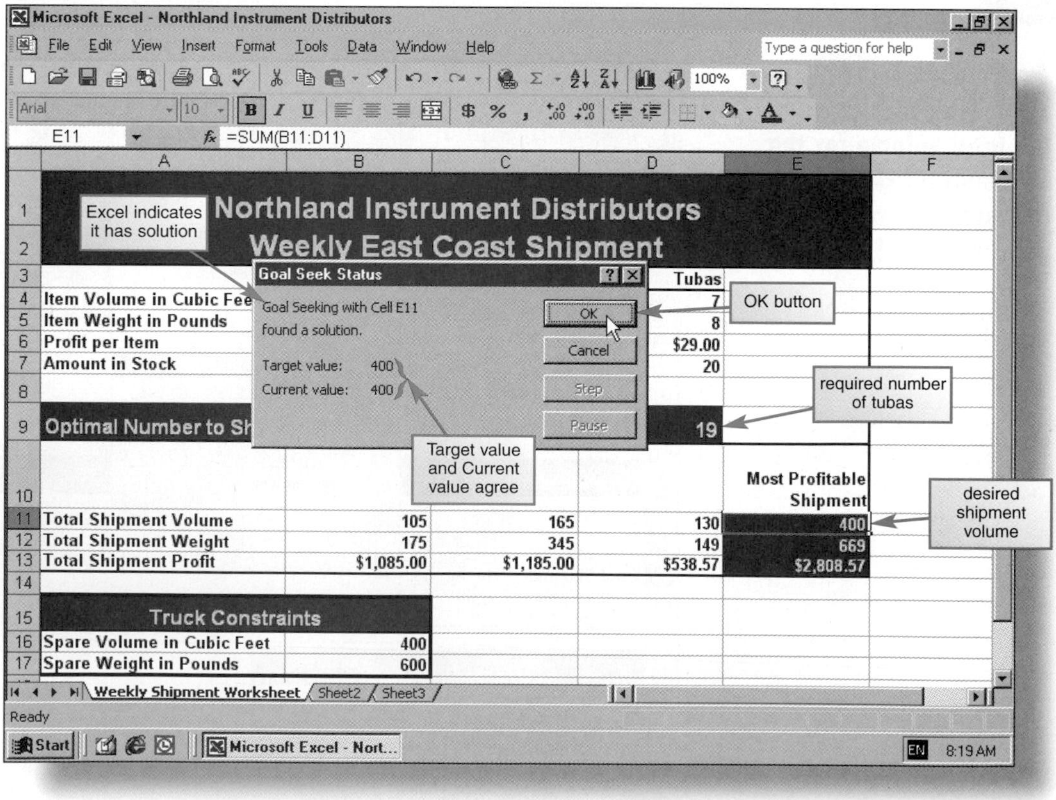

FIGURE 8-19

5 Click the OK button. Click cell E17 to deselect cell E11.

The Goal Seek Status dialog box closes, and Excel displays the updated worksheet (Figure 8-20).

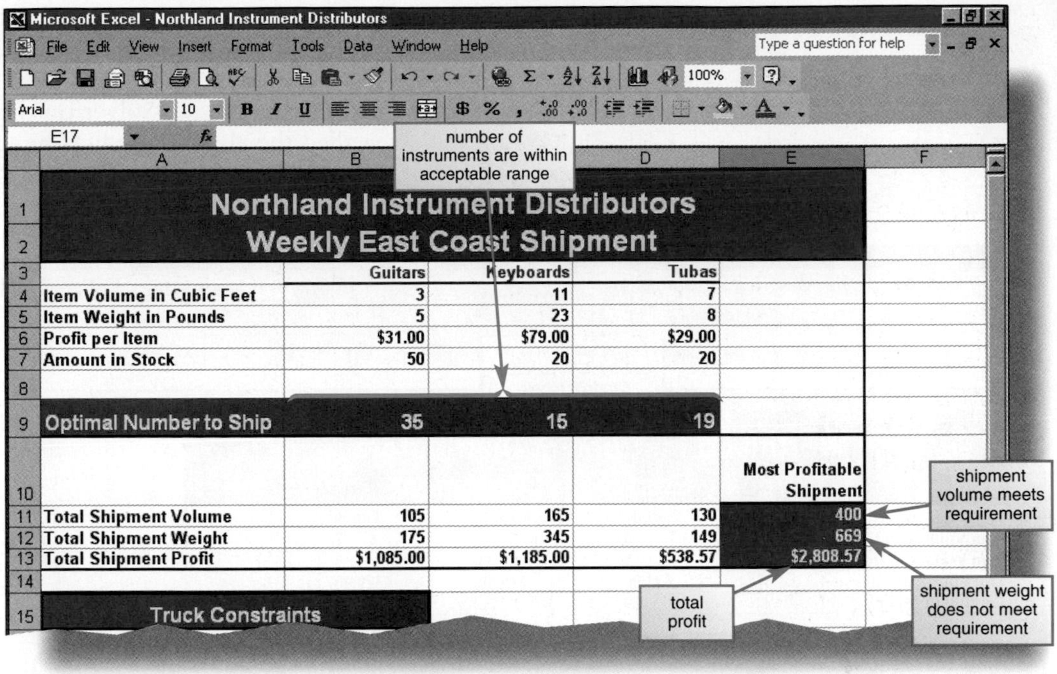

FIGURE 8-20

Other Ways

1. Press ALT+T, G
2. In Voice Command mode, say "Tools, Goal Seek"

Goal seeking assumes you can change the value of only one cell referenced directly or indirectly. In this example, to change the total volume in the shipment to 400 cubic feet, the number of tubas must change to 19. This assumes that the numbers of other instruments shipped do not change.

The value of 19 in cell D9 is actually a decimal value, but is formatted as a whole number. Goal Seeking disallows placing a whole number constraint on a changing cell. This is yet another reason that Goal Seeking may not be the best way to solve this particular problem.

As you learned previously, you do not have to reference directly the cell to vary in the formula or function. The total volume is calculated as a sum of the cells in the range B11:D11. The formula does not include a direct reference to the number of tubas in cell D9. Because the total volume of tubas is dependent on the number of tubas shipped, however, Excel is able to goal seek on the total volume of the shipment by varying the number of tubas.

The total volume for the shipment (cell E11) and the total weight for the shipment (cell E12) may satisfy the requirements of the trucking company. Still, you have no way of knowing whether the constraint of maximizing profit (cell E13) has been achieved. Your manager requires that total profit be maximized while satisfying the weight and volume limitations of the trucking company. Surely, other combinations of the three instruments satisfy the shipping requirements and produce total profit that is maximized.

Using Solver to Solve Complex Problems

Solver allows you to solve complex problems where a number of variables can be changed in a worksheet in order meet a goal in a particular cell. As just stated, goal seeking allows you to change only one cell, and trial and error requires too much uncertainty and time to solve complex problems adequately.

Solver uses a technique called linear programming to solve problems. **Linear programming** is a complex mathematical process used to solve problems that include

More About

Linear Programming

For more information about linear programming, visit the Excel 2002 More About Web page (www.scite.com/offxp/more.htm) and then click Linear Programming.

multiple variables and the minimizing or maximizing of result values. Solver essentially tries as many possible combinations of solutions as it can. On each attempt to solve the problem, Solver checks to see if it has found a solution.

Figure 8-21a shows the results of using Solver on the Weekly Shipment Worksheet. Cells B9, C9, and D9 are called the changing cells. **Changing cells** are those cells that will be modified by Solver to solve the problem. The total profit in cell E13 serves as the **target cell**, which means that Solver will attempt to meet some criteria (maximize profit) in this cell by varying the changing cells. **Constraints** are the requirements that have been placed on certain values in the problem. For example, the total volume of the shipment must not exceed 400 cubic feet (cell B16), and the total weight of the shipment must not exceed 600 pounds (cell B17).

Figure 8-21b shows a Solver Answer Report. An **Answer Report** is

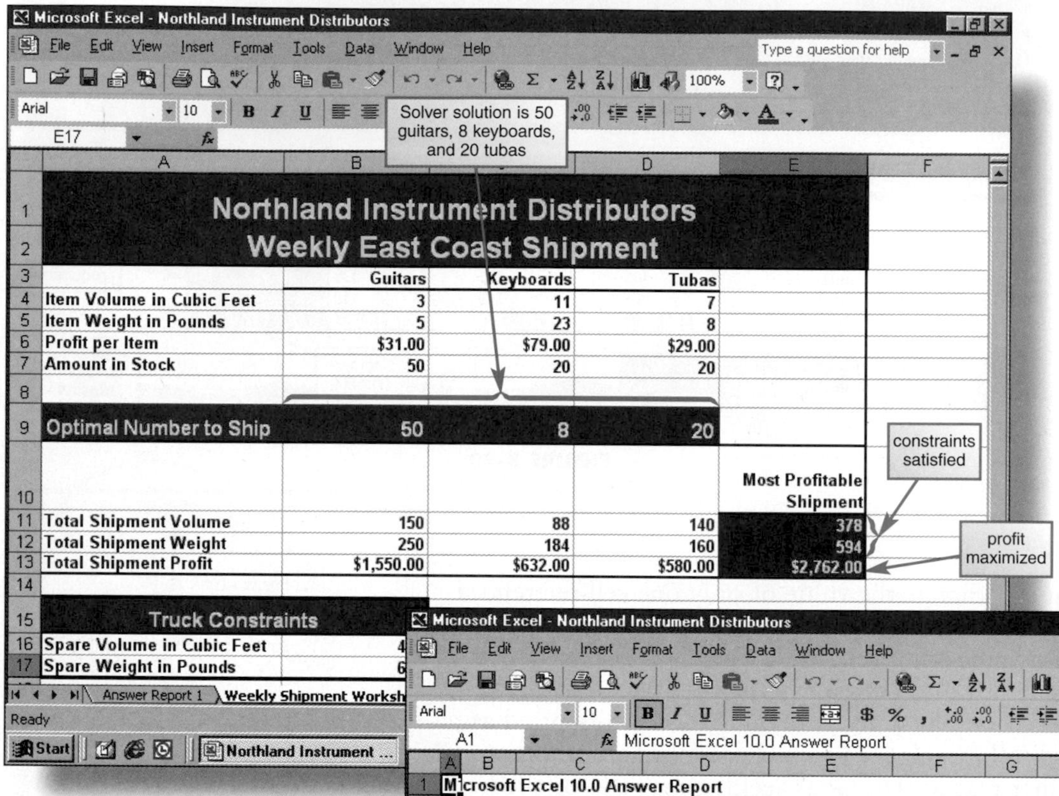

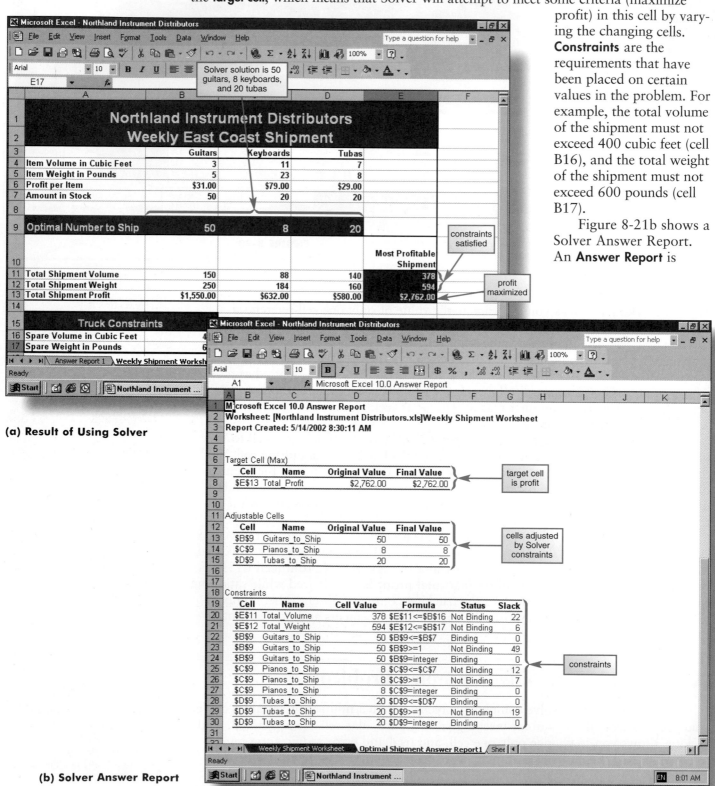

(a) Result of Using Solver

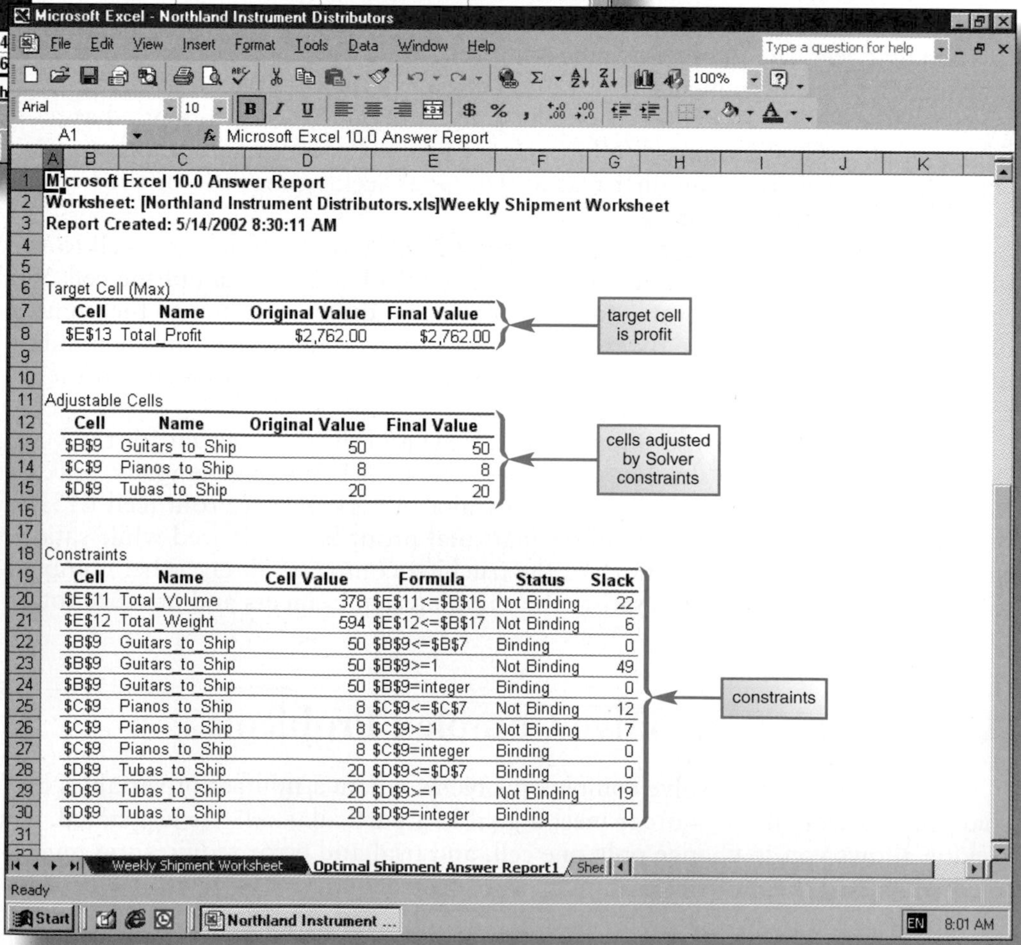

(b) Solver Answer Report

FIGURE 8-21

a worksheet that displays the results of a Solver calculation in a concise format. The report satisfies the requirement to document the results of the shipment analysis.

Using Solver to Find the Optimal Combination of Instruments

The Tools menu contains the **Solver command**, which starts Solver. If the Solver command does not display on the Tools menu, then you must use the Add-Ins command on the Tools menu to add it. The cell that is the target for Solver is the total profit cell, E13. The goal is to maximize the value in that cell. The cells that can be changed by Solver to accomplish this goal are cells B9, C9, and D9, which contain the number of each instrument type. The constraints are summarized in Table 8-3.

The following steps show how to use Solver to solve the Weekly Shipment Worksheet within the given constraints.

TABLE 8-3 Additional Constraints for Solver

CELL	OPERATOR	CONSTRAINT
B9	<=	Value of cell B7
B9	>=	1
B9	int	
C9	<=	Value of cell C7
C9	>=	1
C9	int	
D9	<=	Value of cell D7
D9	>=	1
D9	int	
E11	<=	Value of cell B16
E12	<=	Value of cell B17

Steps To Use Solver to Find the Optimal Combination

1 **Click Tools on the menu bar and then point to Solver.**

The Tools menu displays (Figure 8-22).

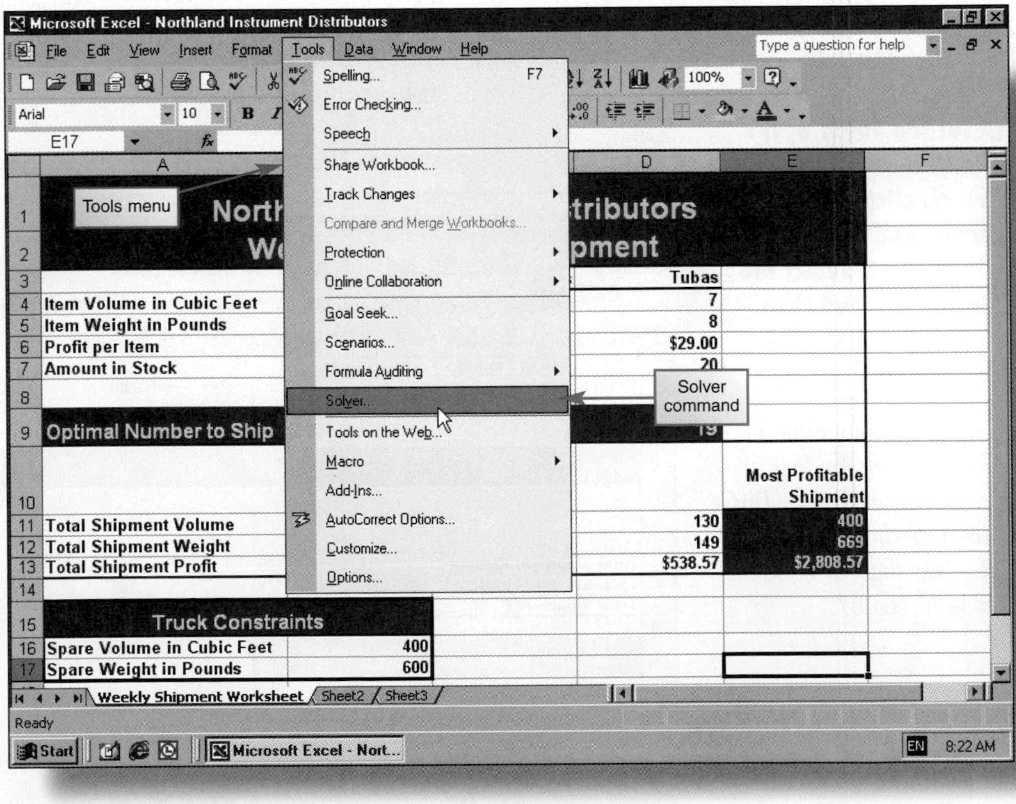

FIGURE 8-22

2 Click Solver. When the Solver Parameters dialog box displays, click cell E13 to set the target cell. Click the By Changing Cells box and select the range B9:D9. Point to the Add button.

*Excel displays the **Solver Parameters dialog box** as shown in Figure 8-23. The Set Target Cell box displays cell E13.*

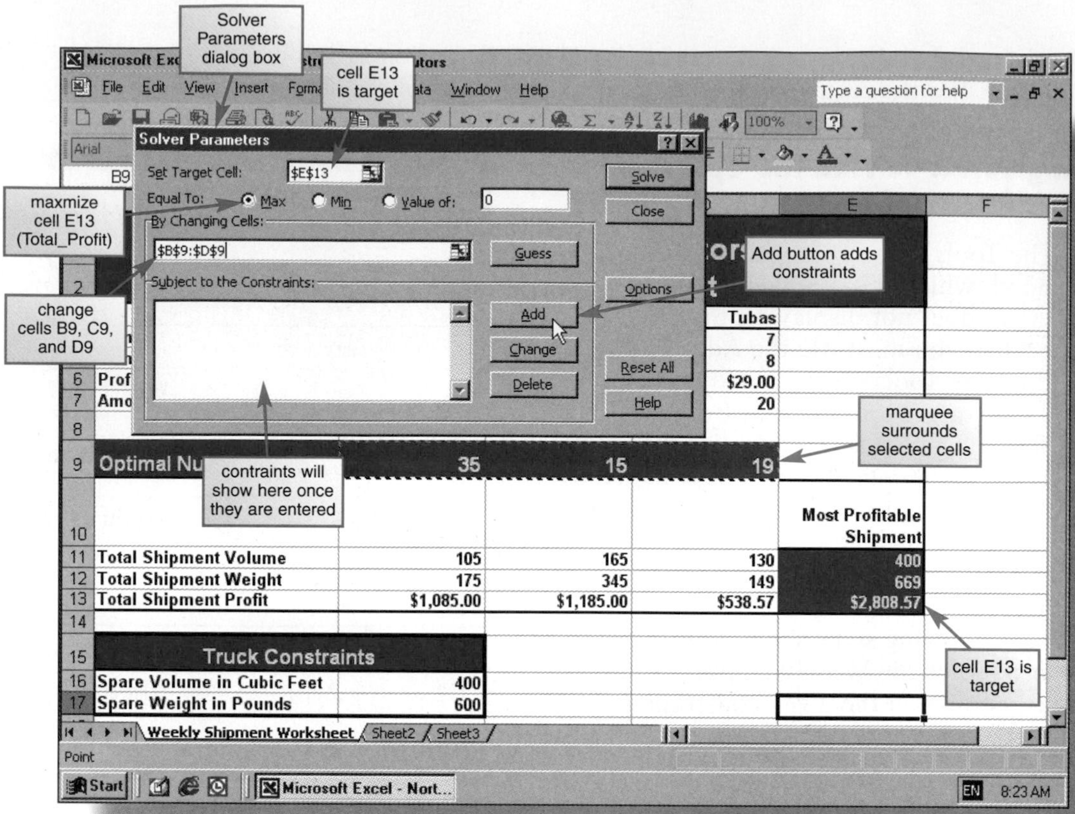

FIGURE 8-23

3 Click the Add button. Click cell B9 to set the value of the Cell Reference box. If necessary, click the middle box arrow and then select <= in the list. Select the Constraint box and then click cell B7. Point to the Add button.

*The **Add Constraint dialog box** displays with the first constraint (Figure 8-24). This constraint means that cell B9 must be less than or equal to the value in cell B7.*

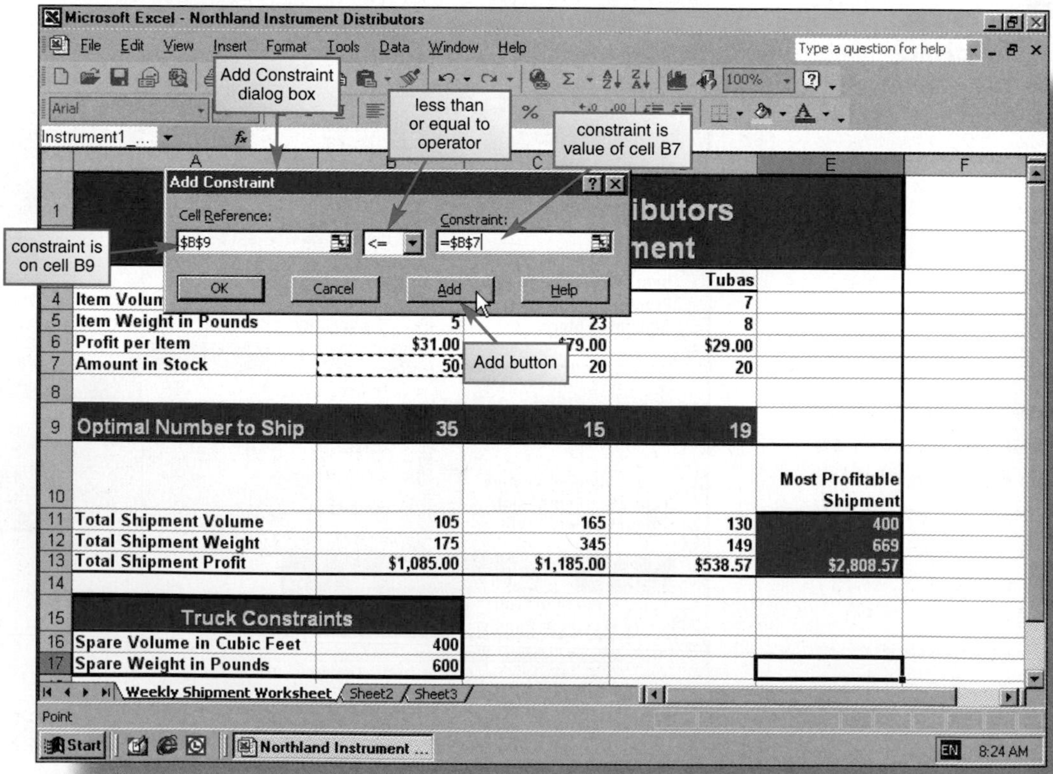

FIGURE 8-24

4 **Click the Add button. Click cell B9 to set the value of the Cell Reference box. Click the middle box arrow and then select >= in the list. Type 1 in the Constraint box and then point to the Add button.**

The values for the second constraint display (Figure 8-25). This constraint means that cell B9 must be greater than or equal to 1.

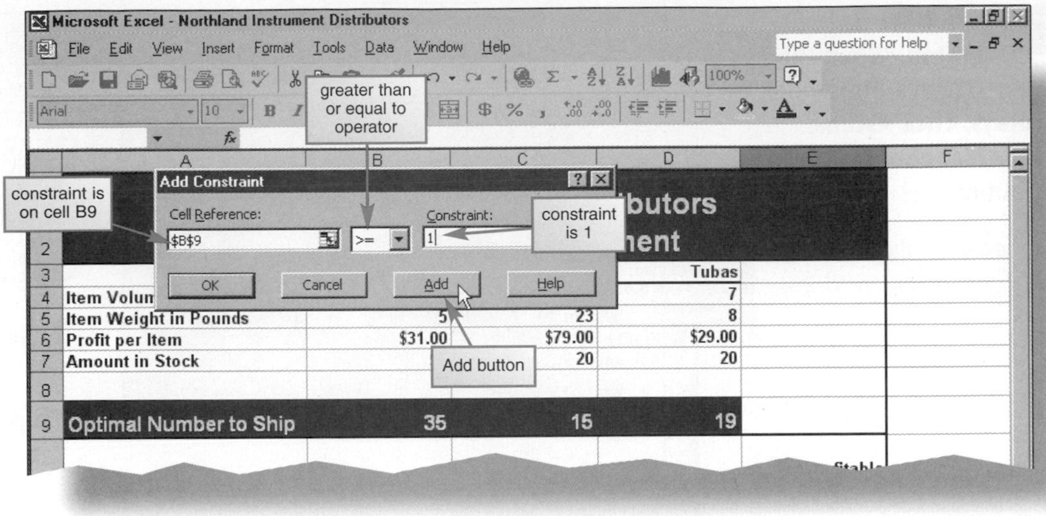

FIGURE 8-25

5 **Click the Add button. Click cell B9 to set the value of the Cell Reference box. Click the middle box arrow and then select int in the list. Point to the Add button.**

The values for the third constraint display (Figure 8-26). This constraint means that cell B9 must be assigned an integer.

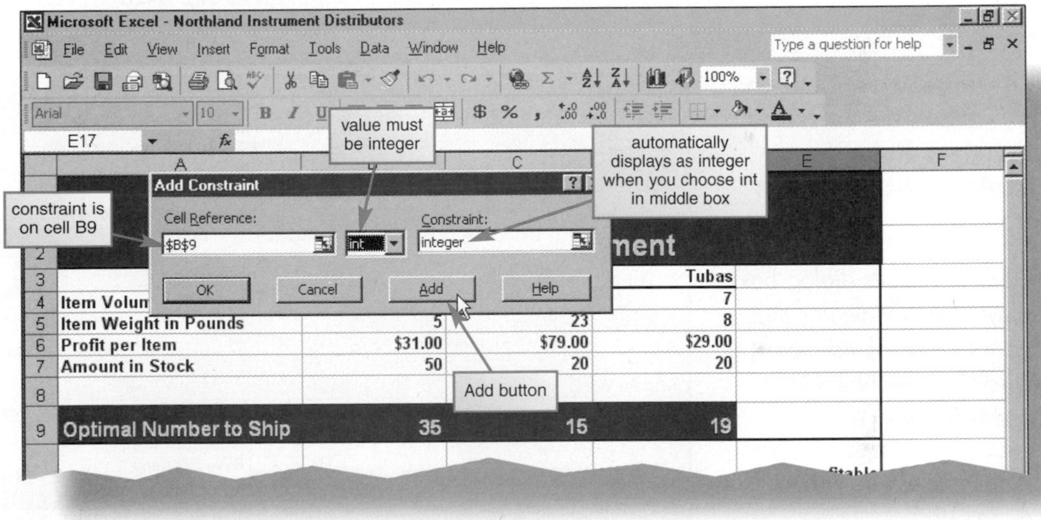

FIGURE 8-26

6 **Click the Add button. Enter the remaining constraints shown in Table 8-3 on page E 8.25 beginning with the constraints for cell C9. When finished with the final constraint, click the OK button in the Add Constraint dialog box. When the Solver Parameters dialog box redisplays, point to the Options button.**

Excel displays all of the constraints in the Subject to the Constraints list (Figure 8-27).

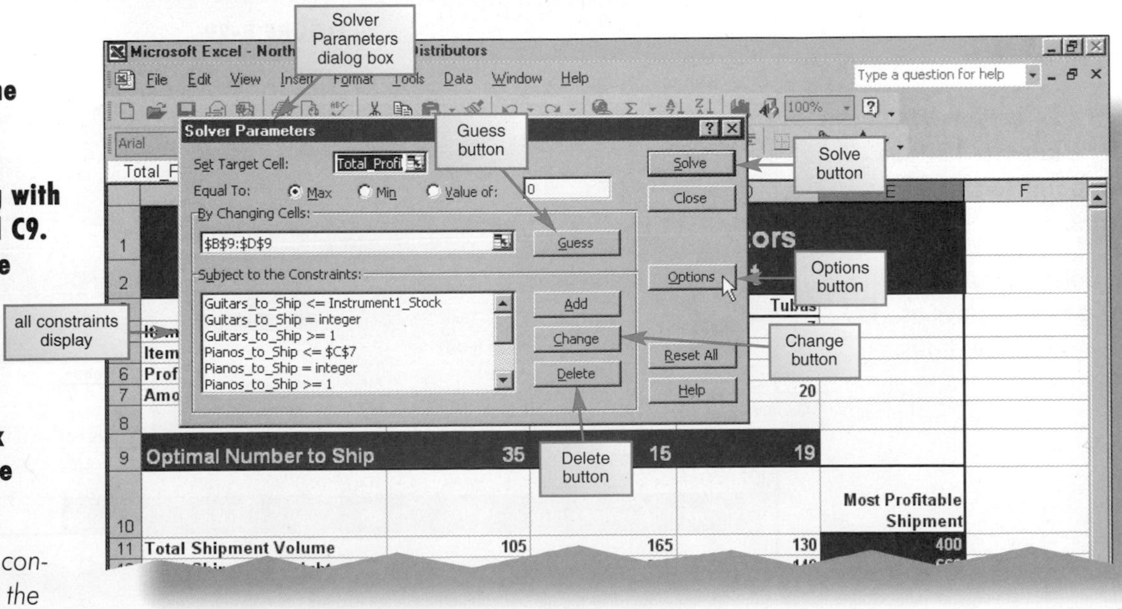

FIGURE 8-27

7 **Click the Options button. When the Solver Options dialog box displays, click Assume Linear Model. Point to the OK button.**

The Solver Options dialog box displays (Figure 8-28).

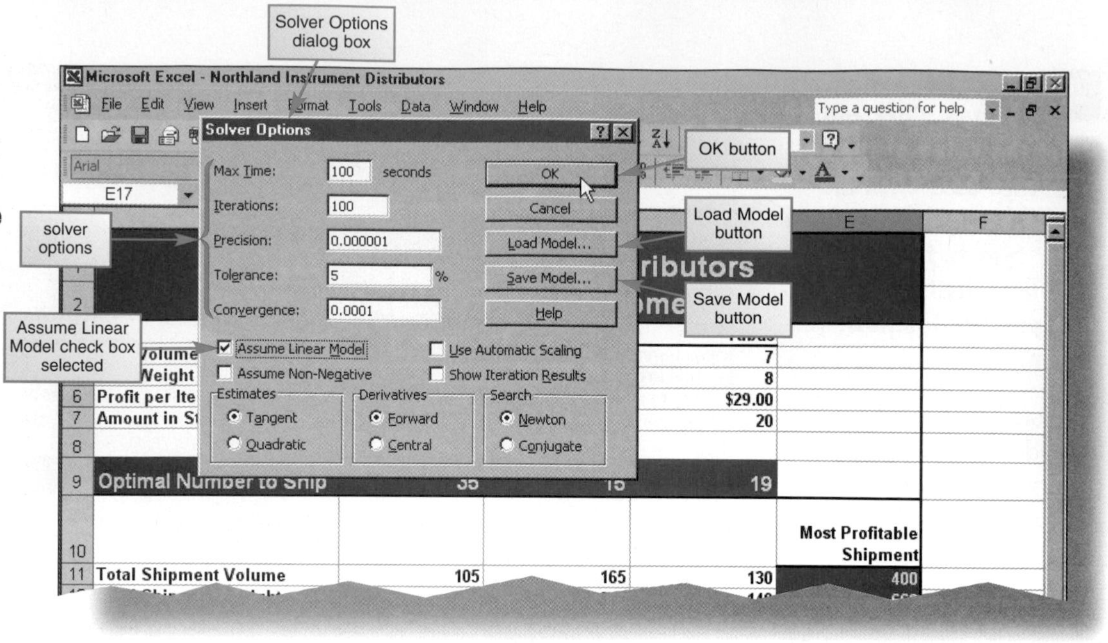

FIGURE 8-28

8 **Click the OK button. When the Solver Parameters dialog box redisplays, click the Solve button.**

The Solver Results dialog box displays. Excel indicates that it has found a solution to the problem as shown in Figure 8-29.

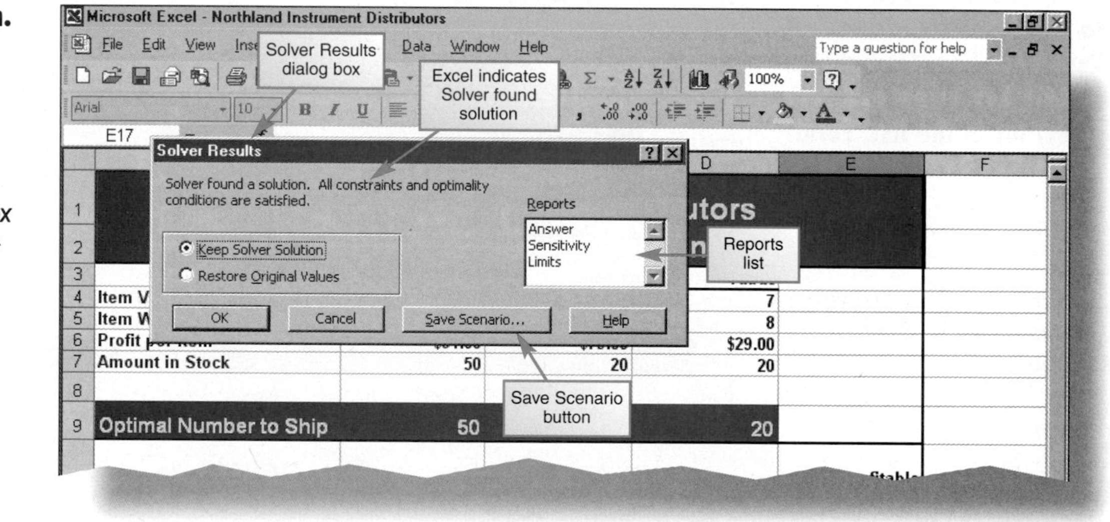

FIGURE 8-29

9 **Select Answer in the Reports list and then point to the OK button.**

The Solver Results dialog box displays as shown in Figure 8-30.

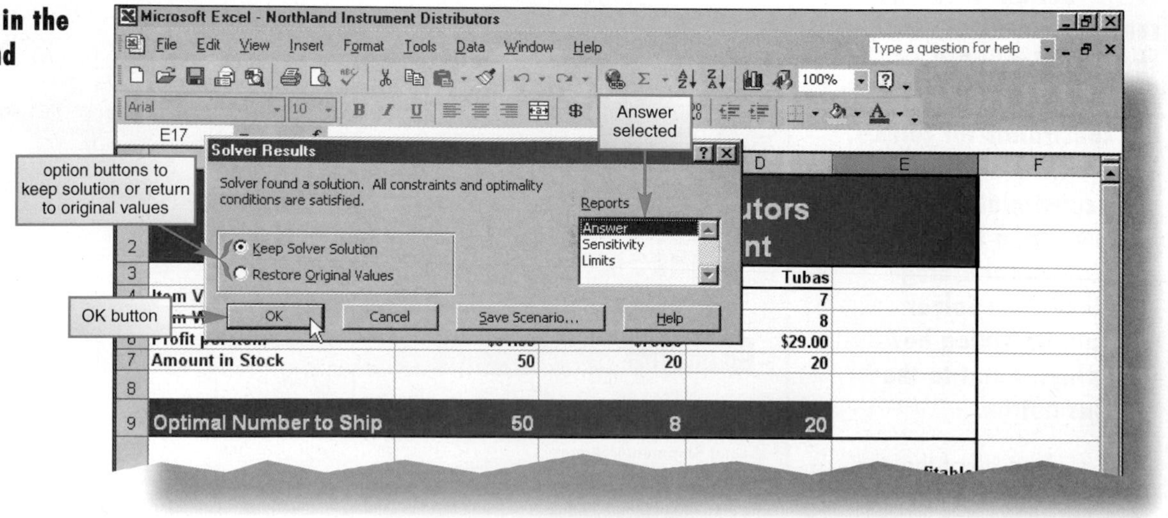

FIGURE 8-30

10 **Click the OK button.**

Excel displays the values found by Solver and recalculates the totals (Figure 8-31). All of the constraints of the problem have been satisfied.

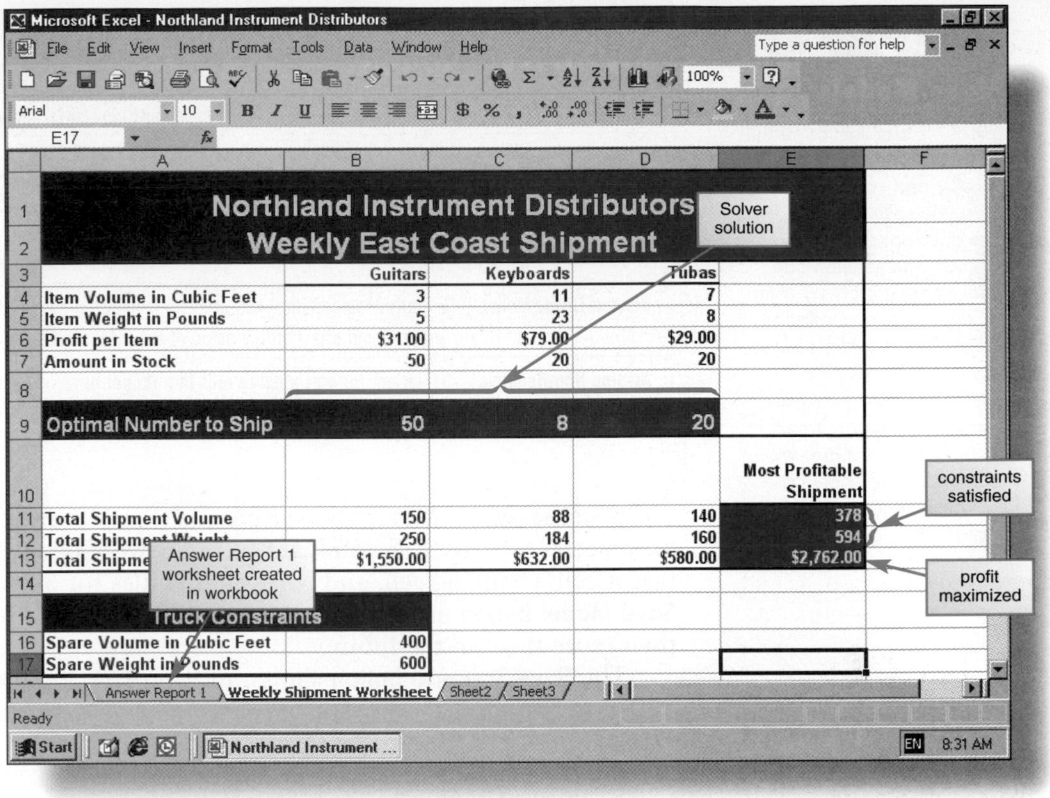

FIGURE 8-31

Other Ways

1. Press ALT+T, V
2. In Voice Command mode, say "Tools, Solver"

Figure 8-31 shows that all of the constraints in the problem have been satisfied. The profit is $2,762.00 for the shipment, which is the only solution thus far that both meets the constraints and maximizes profit.

When adding constraints, as shown in Figure 8-24 on page E 8.26, Solver allows you to enter a cell reference followed by an operator. If the operator is <=, >= or =, you enter the constraint value in the **Constraint cell box**. The constraint can be a value or a cell reference. The other valid operators are **int**, for an integer value, or **bin**, for cells that contain only one of two values, such as yes/no or true/false.

Rather than selecting the range B9:D9 as the changing cells in Step 2 clicking the **Guess button** in the Solver Parameters dialog box (Figure 8-27 on page E 8.27) would have Solver try to determine which cells affect the target cell. The button works much the same way as the Trace Precedents button does on the Formula Auditing toolbar. Solver searches the formula in the target cell to determine which cells are precedents of the target cell and then adds these cells to the **By Changing Cells box** for you. The Guess button is not always accurate, however, which then would require a change to the cells selected by Solver.

The **Change button** and **Delete button** in the Solver Parameters dialog box in Figure 8-27 allow you to edit the constraints that display in the Subject to the Constraints list.

The Solver Options dialog box in Figure 8-28 contains several technical parameters that allow you to configure the inner workings of Solver. Many of the other parameters are beyond the scope of this discussion. Usually, you already have the information for a problem that lets you determine which parameters you need to vary. Table 8-4 on the next page shows the meaning of some of the parameters that you may use from time to time.

More *About*

Solver Parameters

Sometimes Solver will give you a message telling you that the target cell values do not converge. This means that Solver can meet all of the constraints, but the target value, such as the Total Profit in cell E13 in Figure 8-31, can be increased or decreased indefinitely. Usually, this means that you have not specified enough constraints.

More About

Solver Models

A model is a collection of the data in the target cell, changing cells, and constraints. When you save a model, Excel does not save the solution itself. The solution can be saved separately by using the Save Scenario option in the Solver Results dialog box shown in Figure 8-29 on page E 8.28. When saving a model, the data is saved in an area you select in a worksheet. You should note carefully where you save models, because Excel does not label or mark the model in any way.

More About

Solver Scenarios

When you click the Save Scenario button in the Solver Results dialog box, Solver creates a record of the values of the changing cells that solved the problem. You can name this result and then be able to recall it in the future. It is important to note that the target cell value is not changed, just the changing cells' values.

More About

Other Solver Reports

The Sensitivity Report shows how sensitive the Solver solution is to changes in the constraints and the target cell. The Limits Report shows the upper and lower values that the changing cells can have and still solve the problem given the constraints. Both of these reports are generated as separate worksheets in the current workbook, the same way the Answer Report is.

TABLE 8-4 Commonly Used Solver Parameters in the Solver Options Dialog Box

PARAMETER	MEANING
Max Time	The total time that Solver should spend trying different solutions expressed in seconds.
Iterations	The number of different combinations of possible answer values that Solver should try.
Tolerance	Instructs Solver how close it must come to the target value in order to consider the problem to be solved. For example, if the target value is 100 and the Tolerance is 5%, then 95 is an acceptable answer.
Assume Linear Model	If selected, assume that this problem is linear in nature. That is, the changing values have a proportional effect on the value of the target cell.
Assume Non-Negative	If selected, for all changing cells that do not have constraints on them, Solver should keep these numbers positive.

Excel saves the current Solver parameters automatically. Only the most recent parameters are saved. If you want to use new values in Solver and want to save the target cell, changing cell, and constraint values for Solver, the **Load Model button** and **Save Model button** in the Solver Options dialog box allow you to save the values and then reuse them in the future.

The **Save Scenario button** shown in Figure 8-29 on page E 8.28 allows you to save the results of Solver in a separate area in your workbook. Scenarios are discussed in detail later in this project.

When using Solver, two other issues must be kept in mind. First, some problems do not have solutions. The constraints may be constructed in such a way that an answer cannot be found that satisfies all of the constraints. Second, sometimes multiple answers solve the same problem. Solver does not indicate when this is the case, and you will have to use your own judgment to determine if this is the case. As long as you are confident that you have given Solver all of the constraints for a problem, however, all answers should be equally valid.

Viewing a Solver Answer Report

The **Solver Answer Report** summarizes the problem that you have presented to Solver. It shows the original and final values of the target cell along with the original and final values of the cells that Solver adjusted to find the answer. Additionally, it lists all of the constraints that you imposed on Solver.

The Answer Report documents that a particular problem has been solved correctly. Because it lists all of the relevant information in a concise format, you use the Answer Report to make certain that you have entered all of the constraints and allowed Solver to vary all the cells necessary to solve the problem. You also can use the report to reconstruct the Solver model in the future.

Perform the following steps to view the Solver Answer Report.

Steps To View the Answer Report

1 Click the Answer Report 1 tab at the bottom of the window.

The Solver Answer Report displays (Figure 8-32).

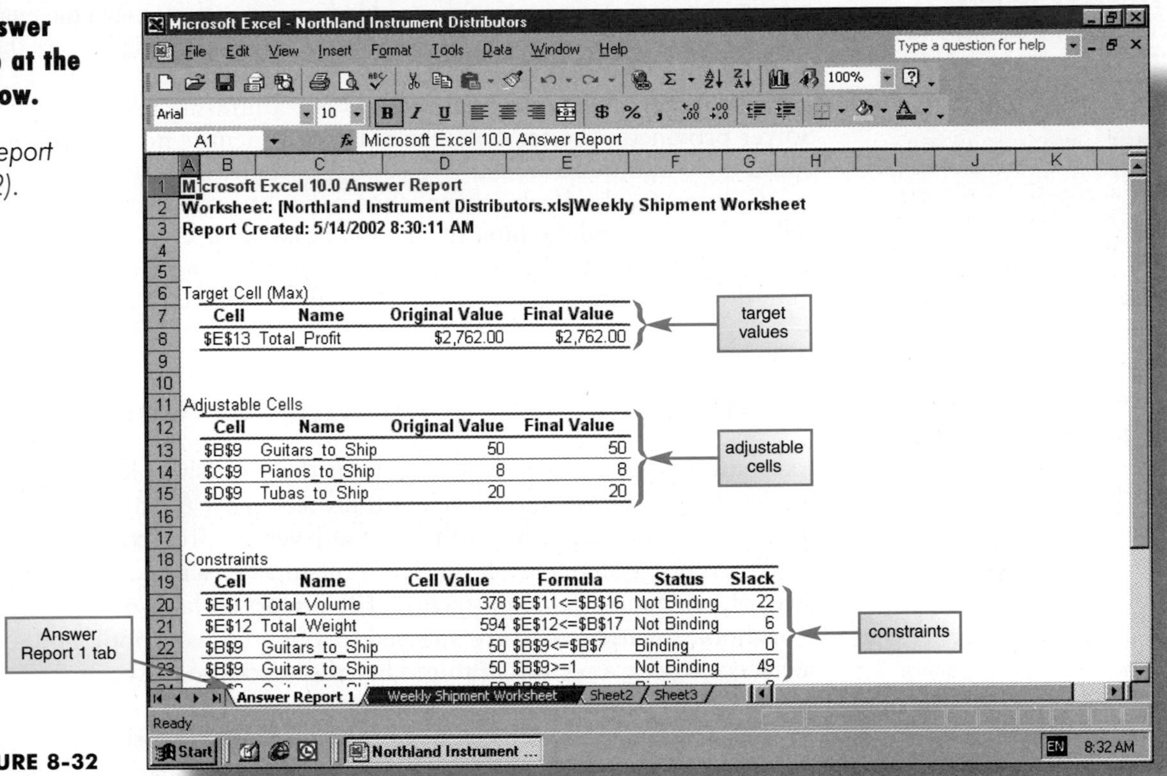

FIGURE 8-32

2 Double click the Answer Report 1 tab and type `Optimal Shipment Answer Report1` **as the worksheet name. Select cell A1. Right click the Optimal Shipment Answer Report1 tab and then click Tab Color on the shortcut menu. Select the color red in column 1, row 3 on the Color palette and then click the OK button. Drag the tab to the right of the Weekly Shipment Worksheet tab. Use the down scroll arrow to scroll down to view the remaining cells of the Answer Report.**

The tab shows the new worksheet name, and the remainder of the Answer Report displays (Figure 8-33).

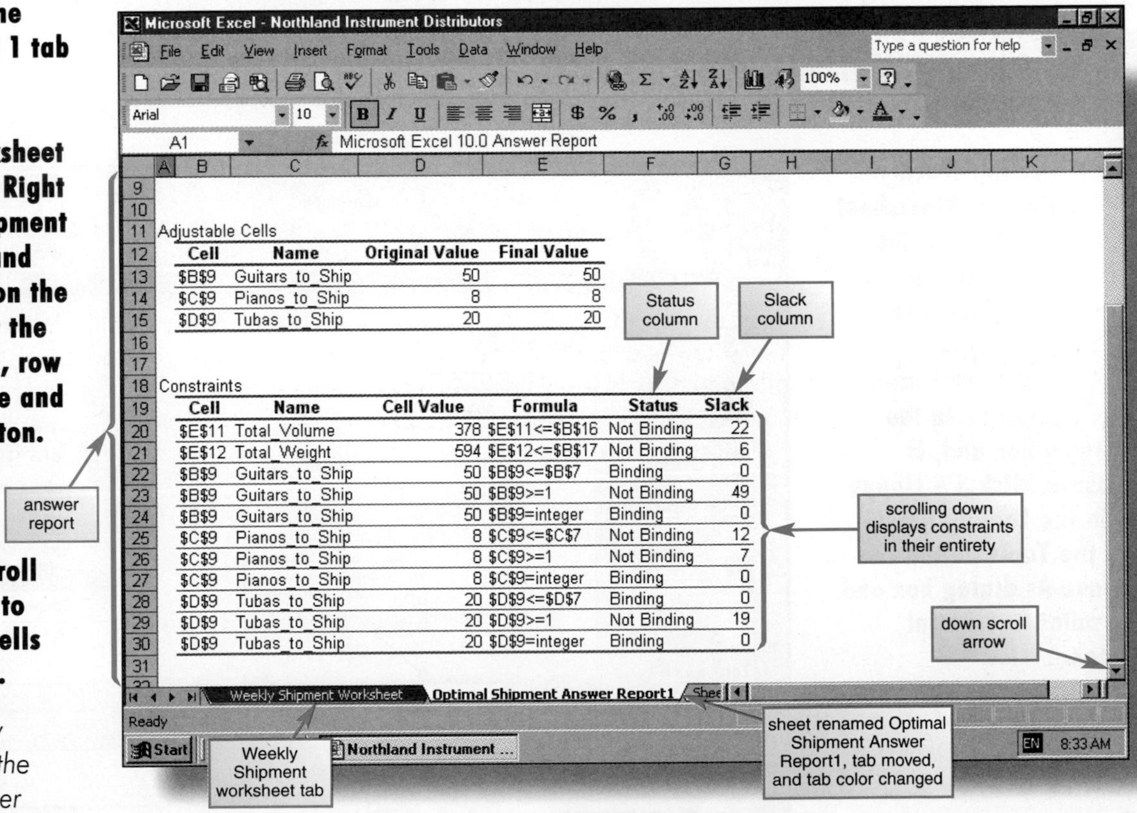

FIGURE 8-33

More About

Answer Reports

The slack value in the Answer Report tells you where you may have some flexibility in the answer that Solver has found. The less slack that a changing cell has, the less you can change it and still meet the constraints of the problem. Slack tells you where you still have options in the Solver answer.

Figure 8-33 on the previous page displays additional information about the constraints that you placed on the problem and how the constraints were used to solve the problem. Column F, the **Status column**, indicates whether the constraint was binding or not. A constraint that is **binding** is one that limited the final solution in some way. For example, the total number of guitars to ship is binding because the solution maximizes the amount of guitars that are in stock. No more guitars could possibly be shipped. A constraint that is **not binding** is one that was not a limiting factor in the solution that Solver provided. The total weight of the shipment is not binding because the solution could have had more weight if necessary to meet the other constraints.

Column G, the **Slack column**, shows the difference between the value in the cell in that row and the limit of the constraint. Cell G20 shows that the slack for the Total_Volume is 22. This means that the solution contains 22 fewer cubic feet of items than the maximum allowed in the constraints. Cells that are binding have zero slack.

More About

File Protection

Once you have protected your workbook with a password, it is important to write the password down or memorize it for future reference. Once you have saved the file with a password, it always will be a password-protected file; no way exists to bypass the requirement for a password.

Saving the Workbook with Passwords

Excel allows you to protect your data at the worksheet level, workbook level, and file level. At the worksheet level, you protect cells. At the workbook level, you protect the Excel window. Both of these levels of protection are available through the Protection command on the Tools menu as described in Project 7. The highest level of protection is file protection. **File protection** lets you assign a password to a workbook for users who are allowed to view the workbook and a separate password for users who are permitted to modify the workbook. Recall that a password is case-sensitive and can be up to 15 characters long.

File protection is performed when Excel saves a workbook. Even though you are the workbook creator, you will be prompted for the passwords when you open the workbook later. The following steps save the workbook with passwords.

Steps To Save the Workbook with Passwords

1 Click the Weekly Shipment Worksheet tab at the bottom of the window. Click File on the menu bar and then click Save As. Type Northland Instrument Distributors2 **in the File name box and, if necessary, click 3½ Floppy (A:) in the Look in list. Click the Tools button in the Save As dialog box and then point to General Options.**

The Save As dialog box and Tools menu display (Figure 8-34).

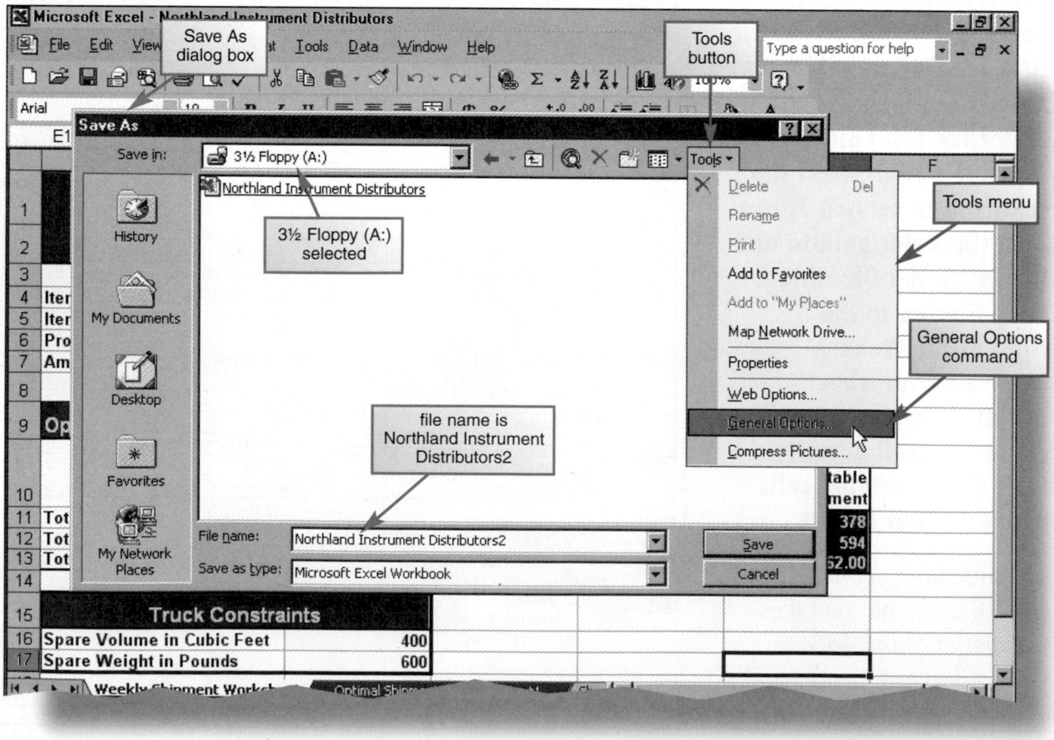

FIGURE 8-34

2 **Click General Options. Type** `maxprofit` **in the Password to open text box. Type** `maxprofit` **in the Password to modify text box. Point to the OK button.**

The Save Options dialog box displays. Excel displays asterisks in place of the password, maxprofit, in both instances so that no one is able to see the password you typed (Figure 8-35).

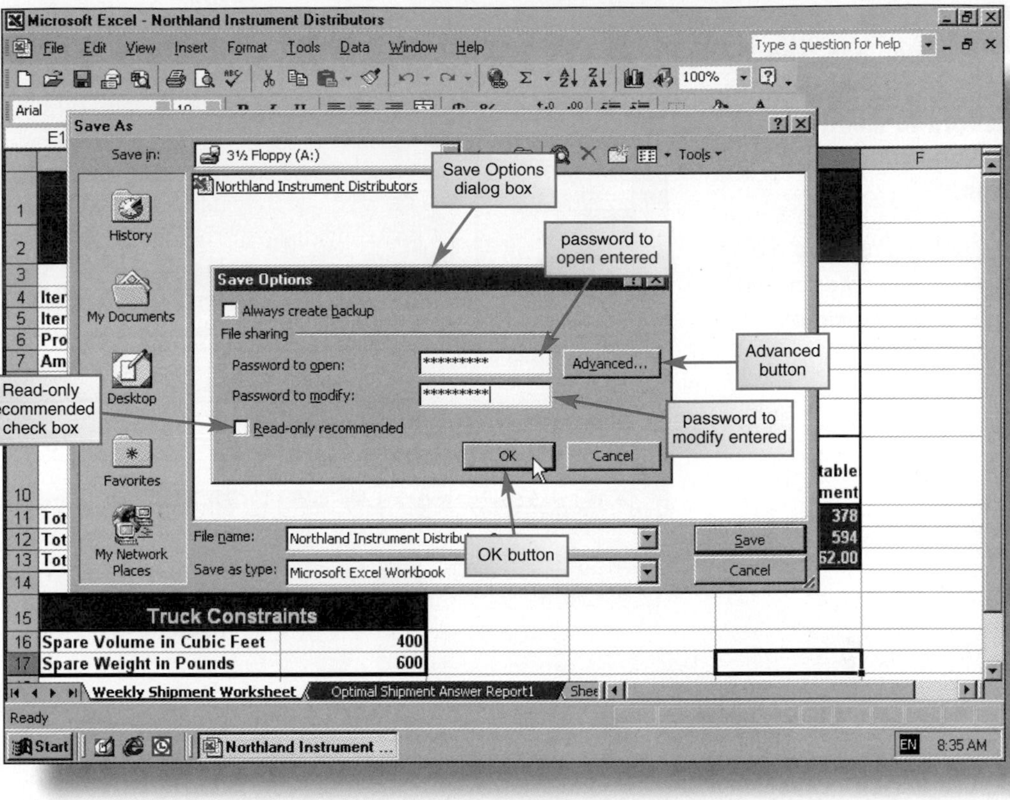

FIGURE 8-35

3 **Click the OK button and type** `maxprofit` **in the Reenter password to proceed text box. Point to the OK button.**

The Confirm Password dialog box displays. Again, Excel displays asterisks in place of the password, maxprofit (Figure 8-36).

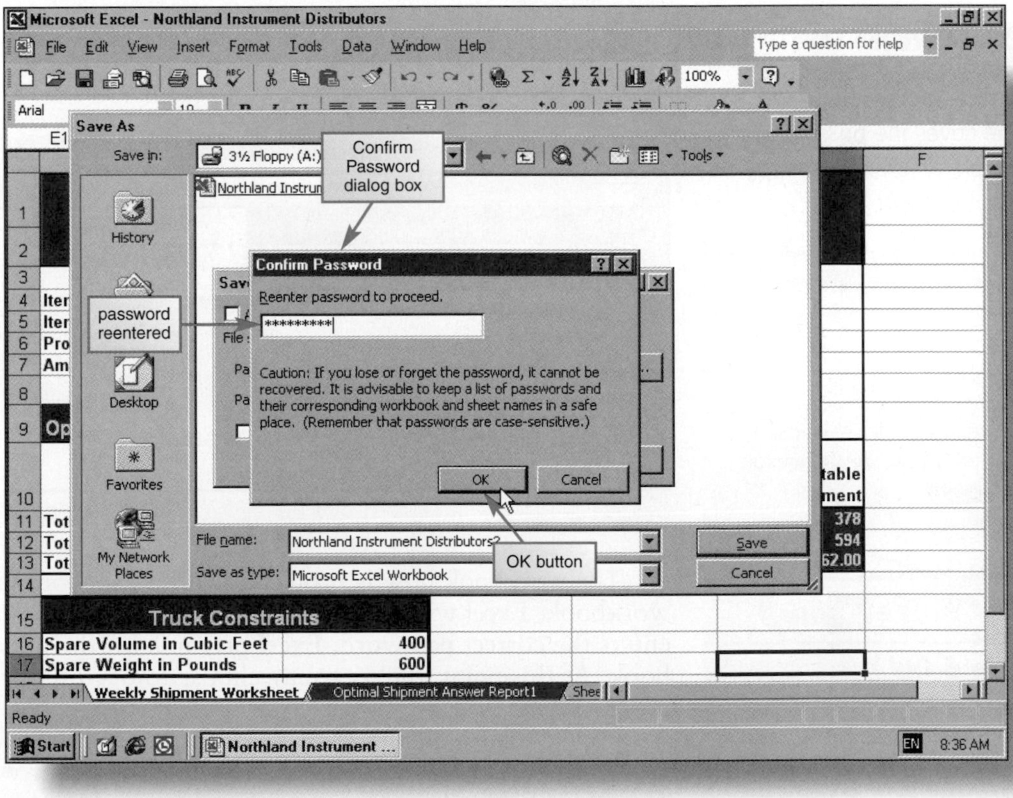

FIGURE 8-36

4 **Click the OK button and type** `maxprofit` **in the Reenter password to modify text box. Point to the OK button.**

The Confirm Password dialog box displays for the password to modify the workbook (Figure 8-37).

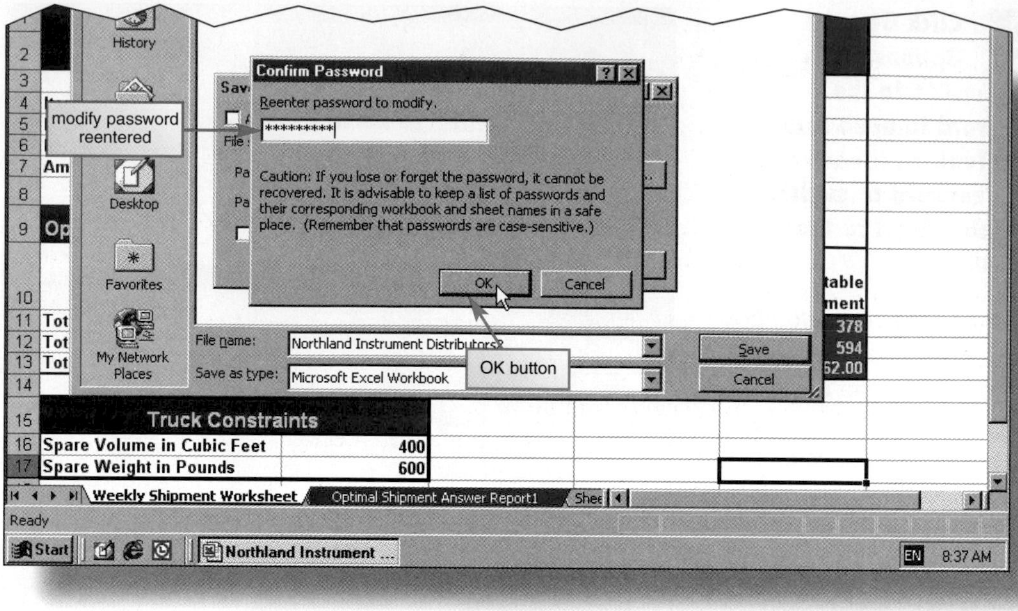

FIGURE 8-37

5 **Click the OK button and then point to the Save button in the Save As dialog box (Figure 8-38).**

6 **Click the Save button.**

Excel saves the password protected file on the floppy disk in drive A.

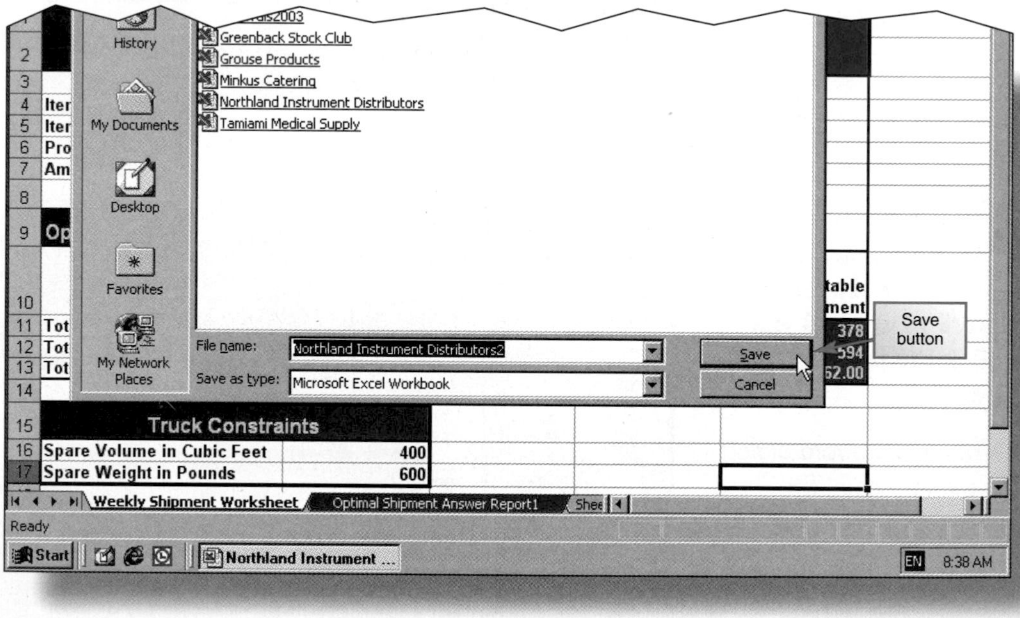

FIGURE 8-38

Other Ways

1. With Save As dialog box open, press ALT+L, G
2. With Save As dialog box open, in Voice Command mode, say "Tools, General Options"

The workbook now is protected with a password, and when a user opens the workbook, Excel will prompt for a password to view the workbook. If the user enters the correct password, Excel prompts for the password to modify the workbook. At this point, the user may choose to open the workbook as read-only, meaning that the user can only view the contents of the workbook and not modify the workbook. The **Read-only recommended check box** shown in Figure 8-35 on the previous page allows you to notify users who open your workbook that it is best to open the workbook as read-only. The **Advanced button** shown in Figure 8-35 allows you to select a method for encrypting the file. **Encryption** allows you to store the file in a secure manner so that malicious users cannot view or alter the contents of your file without a great deal of effort.

More About

Read-Only

You can save a file and recommend read-only access to others who open the worksheet. This is not a guarantee that the user will follow the recommendation. To ensure that the worksheet truly is read-only, use a file password and keep it to yourself.

Using Scenario Manager to Analyze Data

Excel's **Scenario Manager** allows you to record and save different sets of what-if assumptions (data values) called scenarios. For example, each different shipment being analyzed (guitars or accordions) can be considered a scenario. A shipment containing guitars and meeting the other constraints is the first scenario. The second scenario consists of a shipment that contains accordions, which has different volume, weight, profit, and amount in stock. Each set of values in these examples represents a what-if assumption. The primary uses of Scenario Manager are to:

1. Create different scenarios with multiple sets of changing cells
2. Build summary worksheets that contain the different scenarios
3. View the results of each scenario on your worksheet

The remainder of this project shows how to use Scenario Manager for each of the three uses listed above. Once you create the scenarios, you can instruct Excel to build the summary worksheets, including a Scenario Summary and a Scenario PivotTable.

More About

Scenario Manager

Worksheets are used primarily for what-if analysis. You enter values into cells, and instantaneously the results change in the dependent cells. As you continue to change values in the key cells, you lose the previous results. If you want to go back, you have to reenter the data. Scenario Manager allows you to store the different sets of values (called scenarios) so you can redisplay them easily with a few clicks of the mouse. Each scenario can have up to 32 sets of changing cells.

Saving the Current Data as a Scenario

The current data on the worksheet consists of the Guitars scenario and contains the values that correctly solve one of the problems presented. These values can be saved as a scenario that can be accessed later or compared side by side with other scenarios. The steps on the next page create the Accordion scenario using the **Scenarios command** on the Tools menu.

Steps To Save the Current Data as a Scenario

1 Click Tools on the menu bar and point to Scenarios.

The Tools menu displays (Figure 8-39).

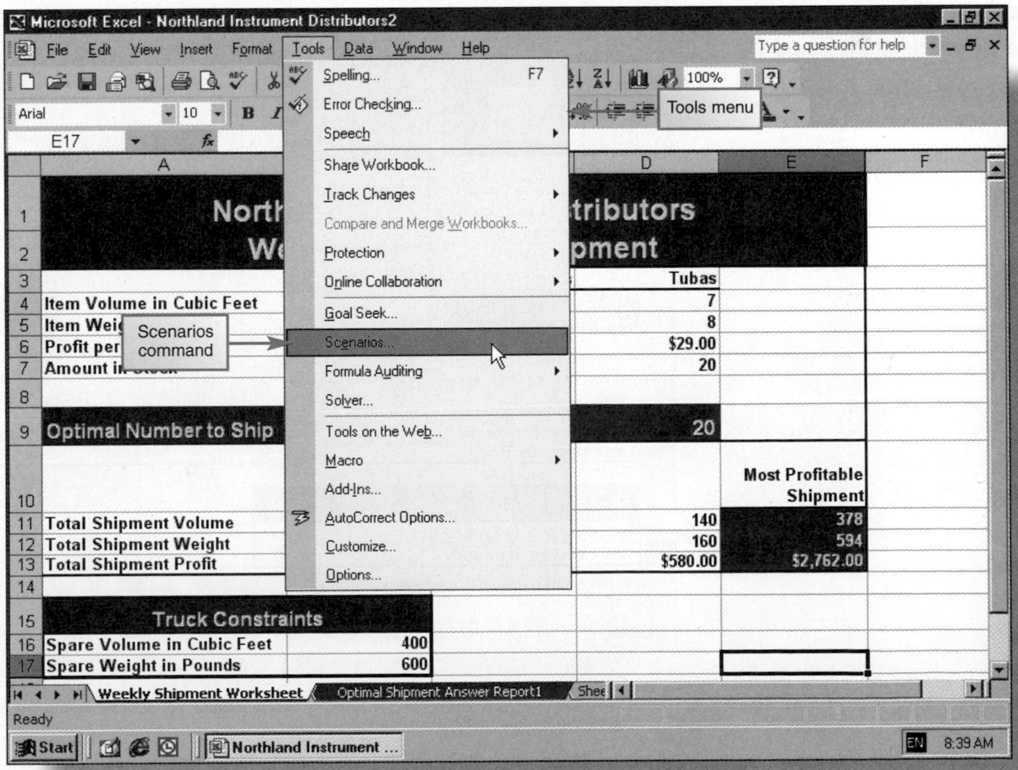

FIGURE 8-39

2 Click Scenarios. When the Scenario Manager dialog box displays, point to the Add button.

The Scenario Manager dialog box displays indicating that no scenarios are defined (Figure 8-40). It also instructs you to choose Add to add scenarios.

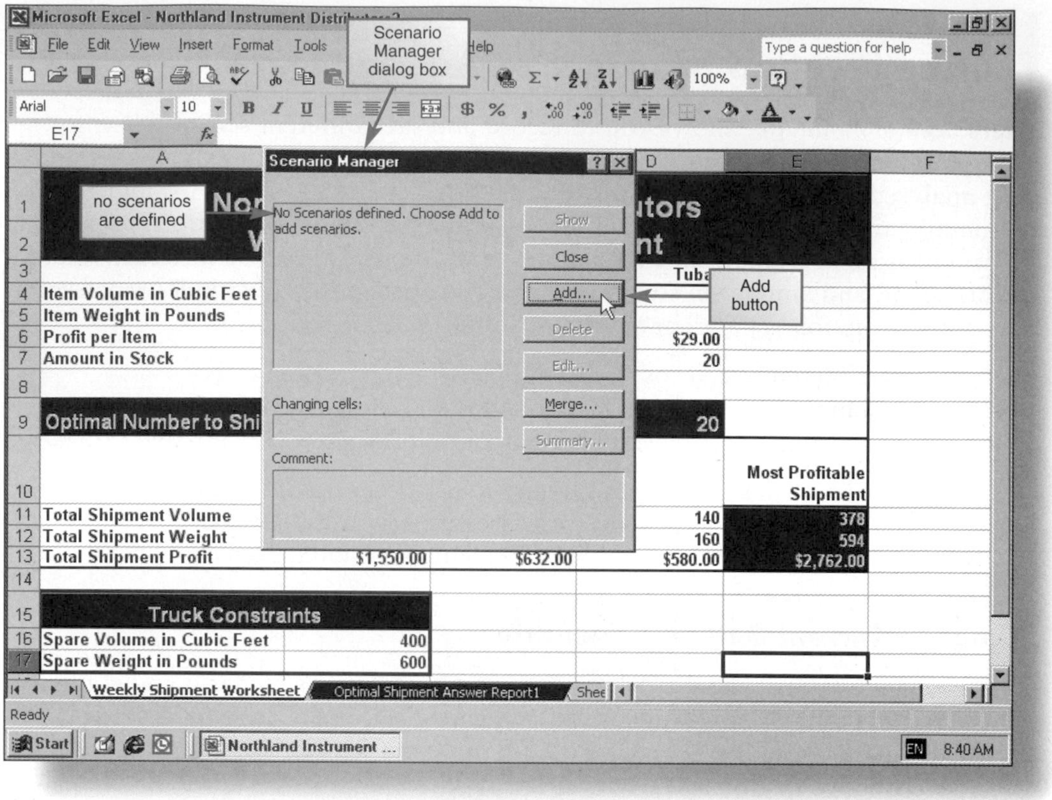

FIGURE 8-40

3 Click the Add button. When the Add Scenario dialog box displays, type `Guitars` **in the Scenario name text box. Point to the Collapse Dialog button.**

The Add Scenario dialog box displays (Figure 8-41).

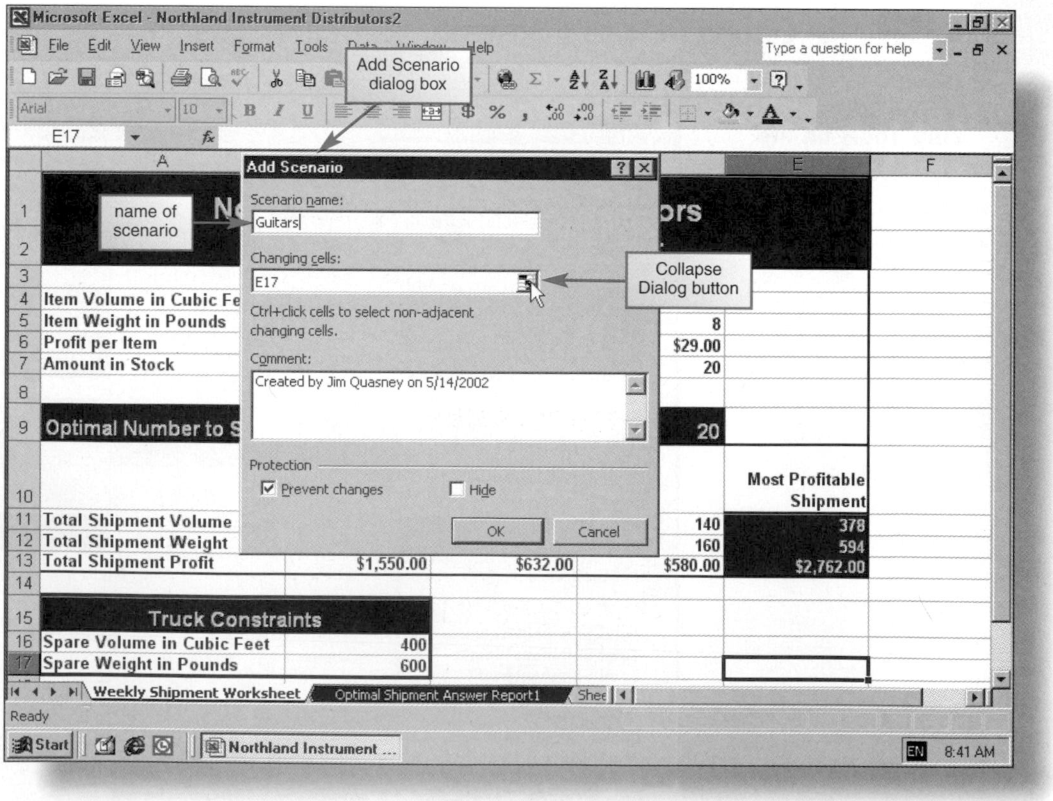

FIGURE 8-41

4 Click the Collapse Dialog button. When the Add Scenario - Changing cells dialog box displays, click cell B3, hold down the CTRL key, and then click cells B4, B5, B6, B7, B9, C9, D9, B16, and B17. Release the CTRL key. Point to the Collapse Dialog button in the Add Scenario - Changing cells dialog box.

A marquee displays around the selected cells. Excel assigns the cells to the Changing cells text box (Figure 8-42).

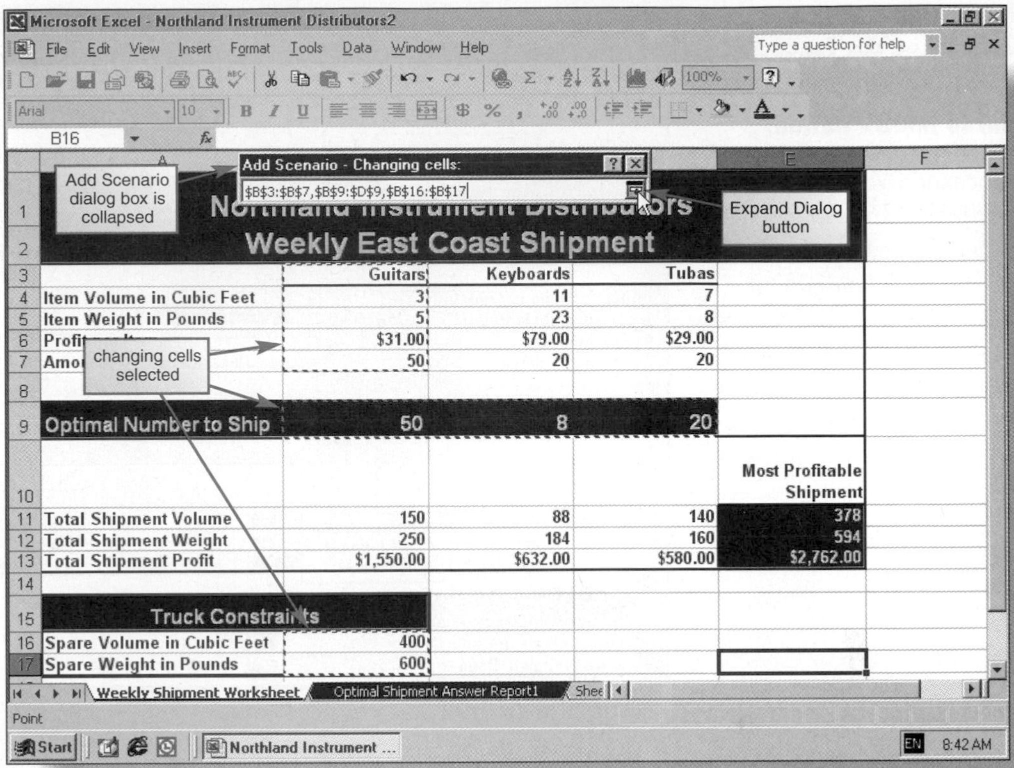

FIGURE 8-42

5 Click the Expand Dialog button. When the Edit Scenario dialog box displays, point to the OK button.

The Add Scenario dialog box changes to the ***Edit Scenario dialog box*** *(Figure 8-43).*

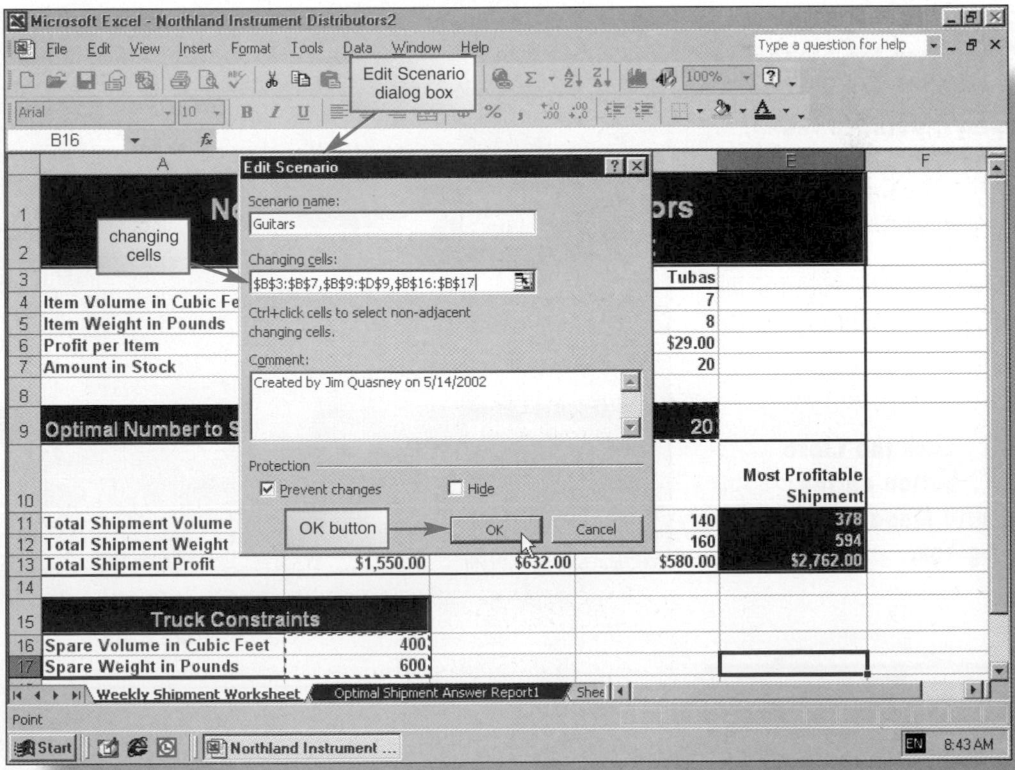

FIGURE 8-43

6 **Click the OK button. When the Scenario Values dialog box displays, point to the OK button.**

The Scenario Values dialog box displays. The cell names selected display in a numbered list with their current values (Figure 8-44). Because names were assigned to these cells when the worksheet was created, the cell names, rather than cell references, display in the numbered list.

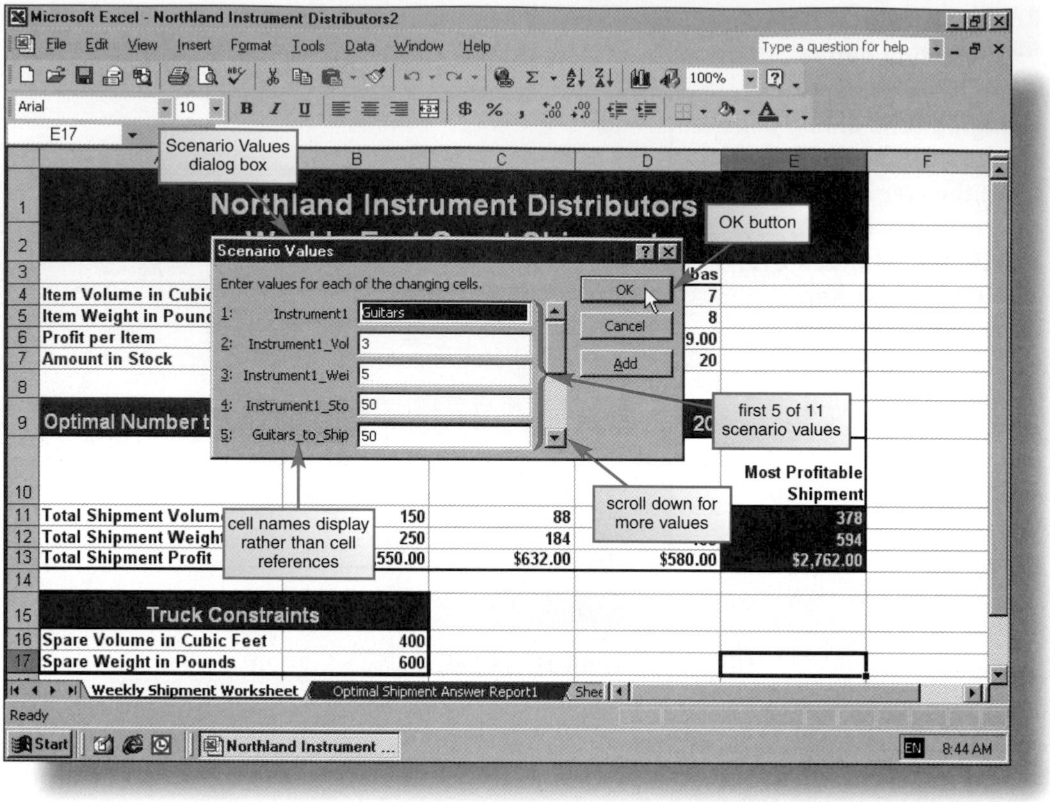

FIGURE 8-44

7 **Click the OK button. When the Scenario Manager dialog box displays, point to the Close button.**

The Guitar scenario displays in the Scenarios list (Figure 8-45). Excel displays the names of the changing cells in the Changing cells text box.

8 **Click the Close button on the Scenario Manager dialog box.**

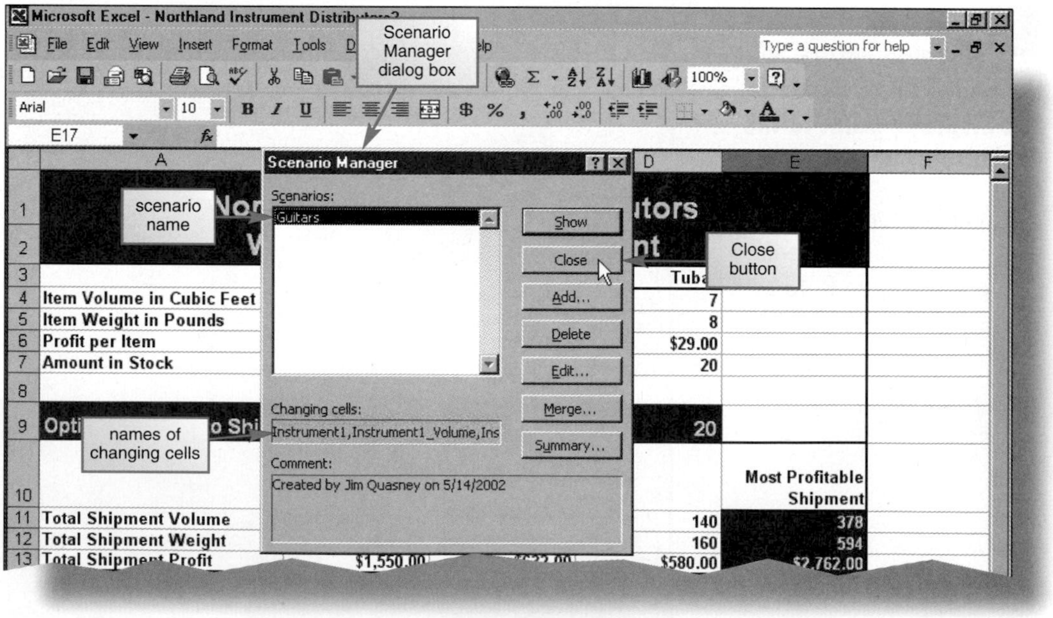

FIGURE 8-45

Other Ways

1. Press ALT+T, E
2. In Voice Command mode, say "Tools, Scenarios"

Once the scenario has been saved, you can recall it at any time using Scenario Manager. In Figure 8-44, the values of the cells in the Scenario Values dialog box are defaulted to the current changing cells in the worksheet. By changing the text boxes next to the cell names, you can save different values in the scenario from what is shown in the worksheet.

The next step is to change the values on the worksheet to show the data when using accordions as a subsitute for guitars.

Creating a New Scenario

Because the Guitar scenario is saved, you can enter the data for the Accordion scenario directly in the worksheet and then use Solver to solve the Accordion scenario (Figure 8-46a) in the same way that you solved the Guitar scenario. The same constraints apply for both scenarios, so Solver does not require you to reenter all of the constraints. The Answer Report (Figure 8-46b) meets the requirement that you create supporting documentation for your answer. After solving the Accordion scenario, you should save the scenario in the same manner that you saved the Guitar scenario.

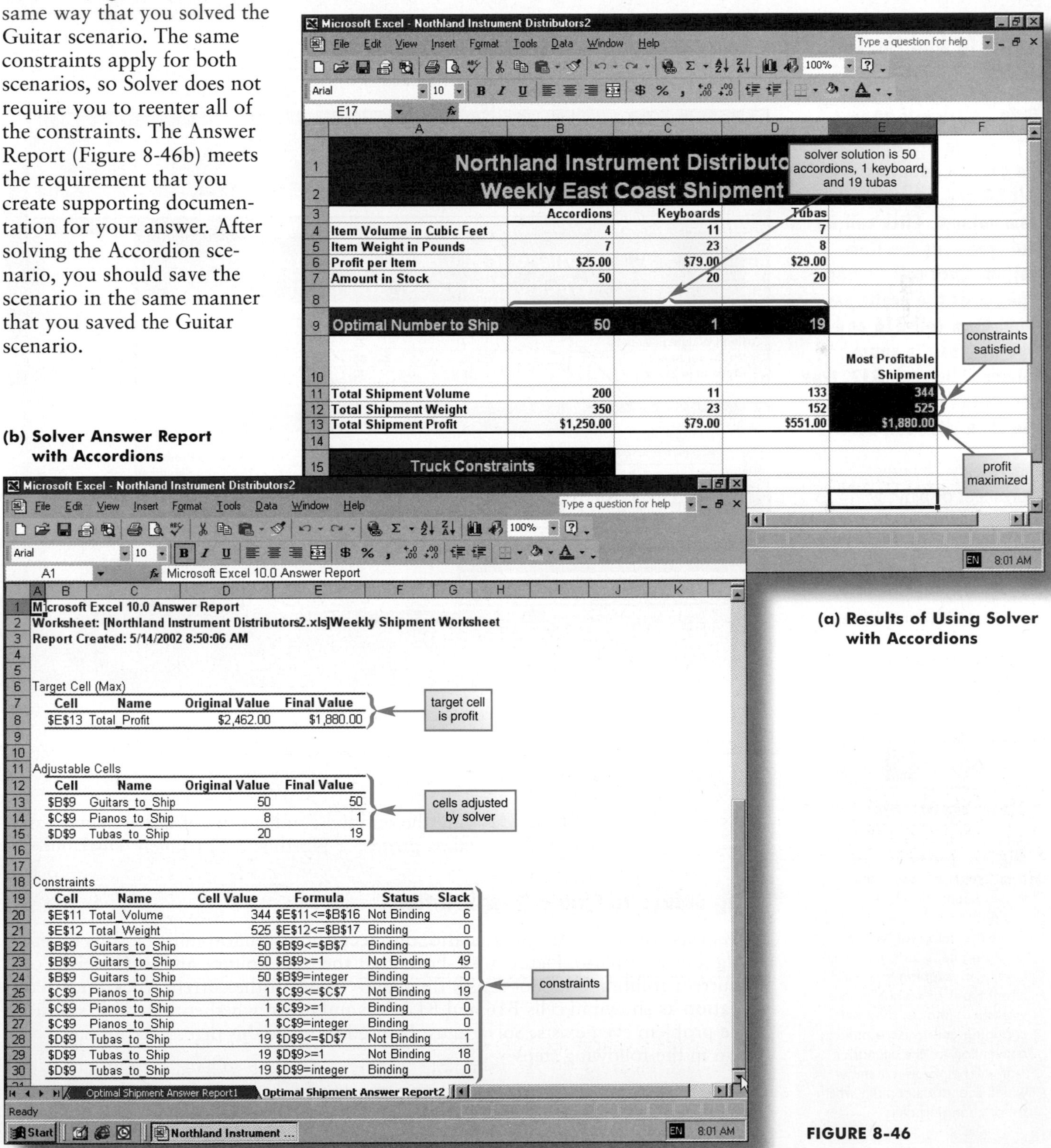

(a) Results of Using Solver with Accordions

(b) Solver Answer Report with Accordions

FIGURE 8-46

The relevant information for the Accordion scenario (Figure 8-46a on the previous page) is that accordions take four cubic feet, weigh seven pounds, contribute $25.00 to profit per item, and 50 are in stock. The truck that is available in the following week for this shipment has 350 cubic feet free and 525 pounds of capacity available. These values must be entered into the appropriate cells before you can use Solver.

Perform the following step to add the data for a new scenario.

Steps To Add the Data for a New Scenario

1 Click cell B3 and type Accordions **as the column heading. Click cell B4 and type** 4 **as the item volume. Click cell B5 and type** 7 **as the item weight. Click cell B6 and type** 25 **as the profit per item. Click cell B16 and type** 350 **as the spare volume. Click cell B17, type** 525 **as the spare weight, and then click cell E17.**

The Weekly Shipment Worksheet displays with accordions replacing guitars (Figure 8-47).

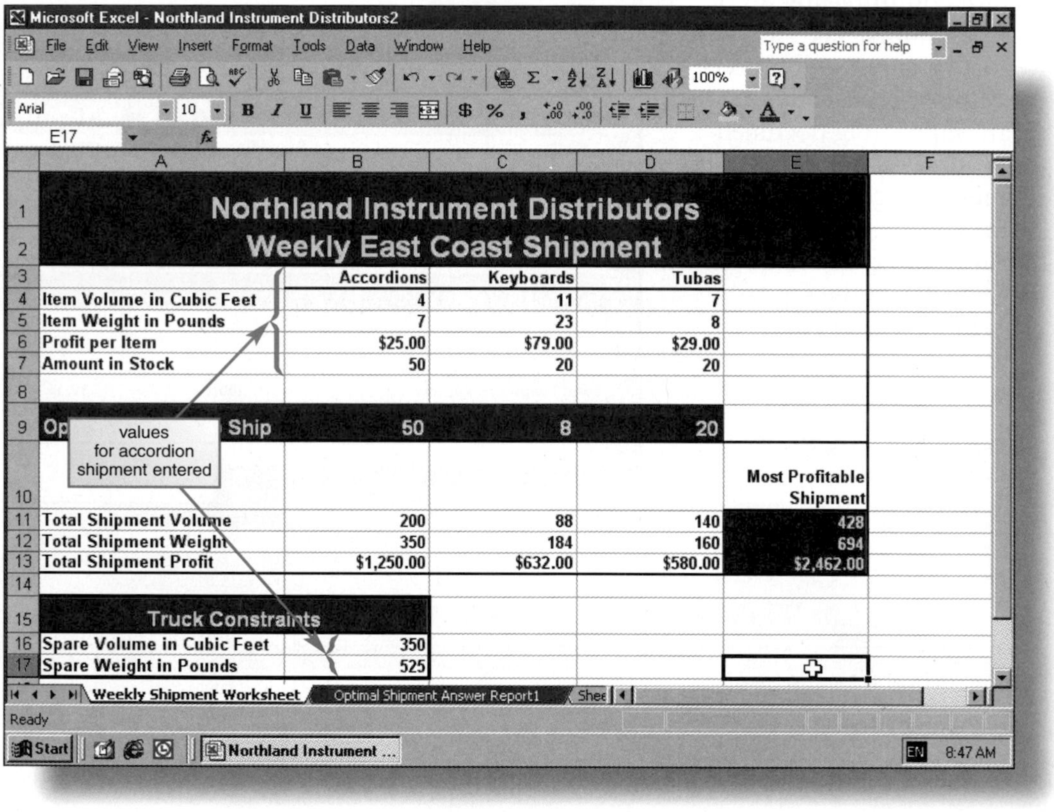

FIGURE 8-47

More About

New Scenarios

A few guidelines can help in organizing scenario data. First, create a base scenario that contains the original values of the worksheet. Second, name the cells that will be changing cells and result cells. Finally, if you plan to save different types of scenarios in a worksheet (that is, different changing cells), use a naming convention for the scenarios that will help you remember which scenarios contain which set of changing cells.

Next, Solver must be used to find the optimal combination of instruments that satisfies the constraints and maximizes profit for Northland Instrument Distributors.

Using Solver to Find a New Solution

As was true of the Guitar scenario, the Accordion scenario must be solved before saving it as a scenario. Figure 8-47 shows that the total volume and total weight of the current solution does not satisfy the requirements of the current truck under consideration as shown in cells B16 and B17. It is unknown whether a possible solution to the problem even exists. Solver must be used to make this determination, as shown in the following steps.

Steps To Use Solver to Find a New Solution

1 Click Tools on the menu bar and then point to Solver (Figure 8-48).

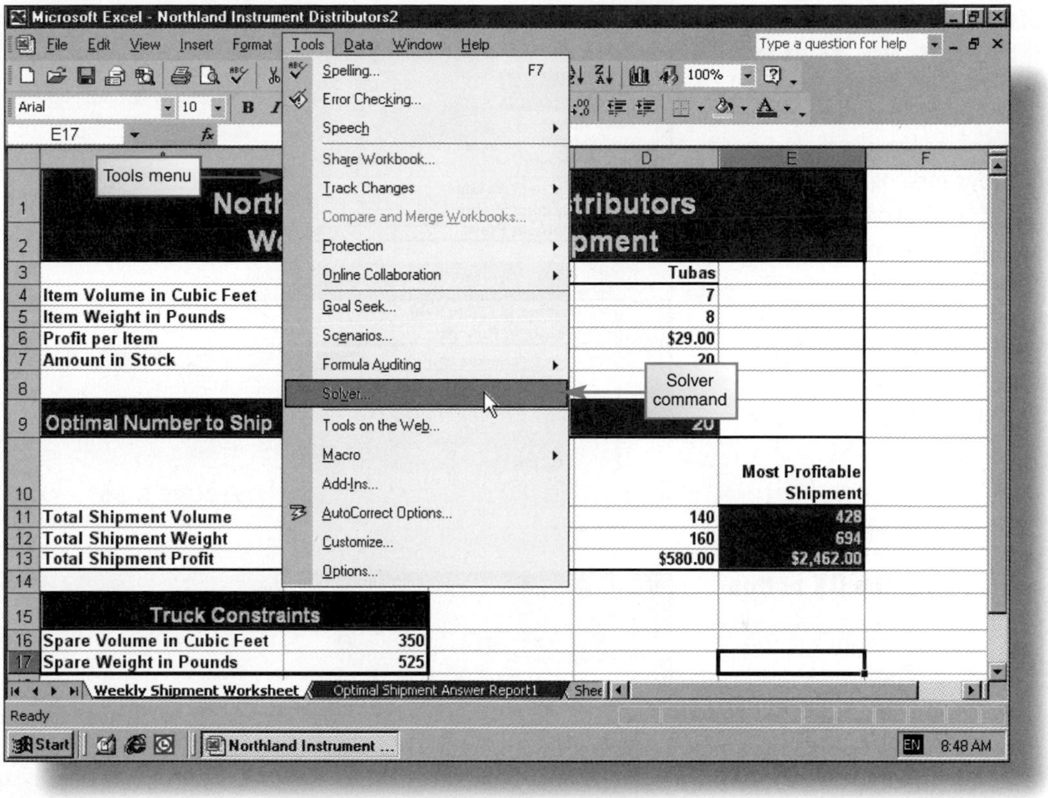

FIGURE 8-48

2 Click Solver. When the Solver Parameters dialog box displays, point to the Solve button.

The Solver Parameters dialog box displays with the previous target cell and constraints (Figure 8-49). Because the constraints remain the same for accordions as they were for guitars, no additional entries are required in the Solver Parameters dialog box.

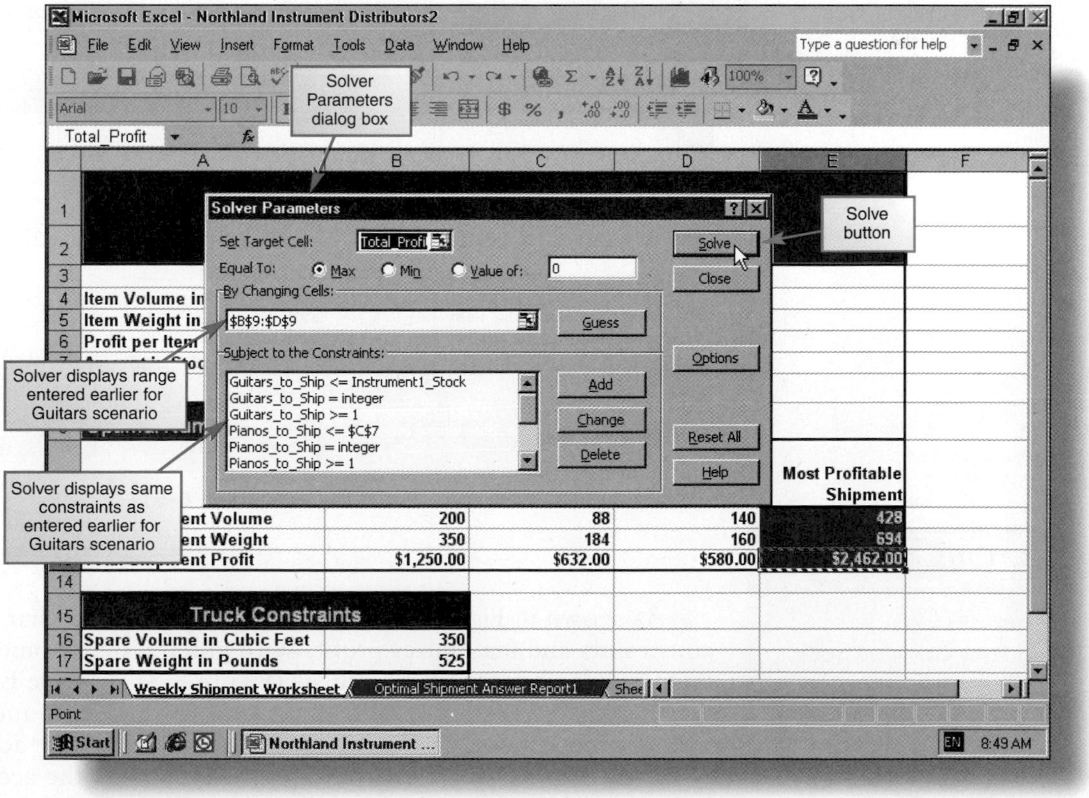

FIGURE 8-49

3 Click the Solve button. When the Solver Results dialog box displays, click Answer in the Reports list. Point to the OK button.

The Solver Results dialog box displays indicating that Solver found a solution to the problem (Figure 8-50).

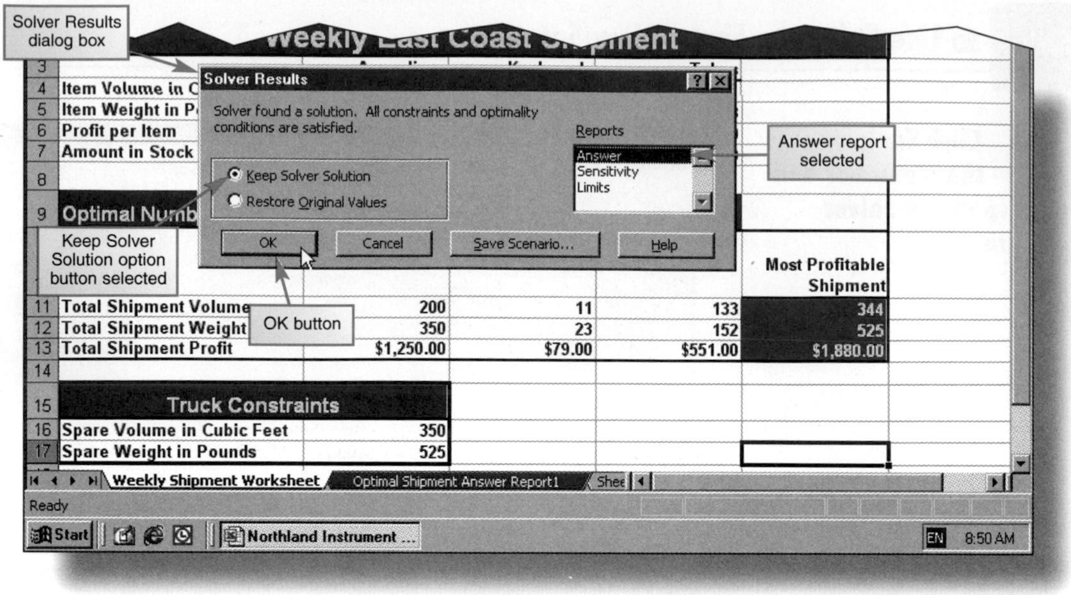

FIGURE 8-50

4 Click the OK button.

The solution displays in the worksheet. The constraints have been satisfied (Figure 8-51).

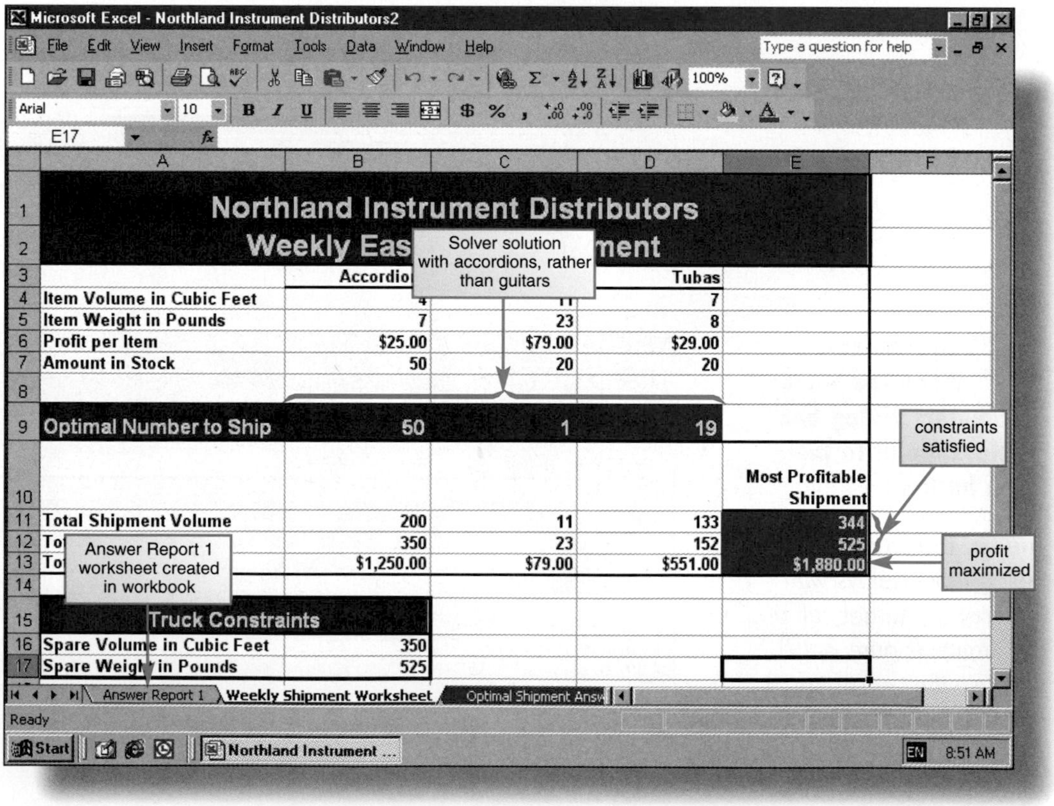

FIGURE 8-51

Other Ways

1. Press ALT+T, V
2. In Voice Command mode, say "Tools, Solver"

As shown in Figure 8-51, Solver found a solution that satisfies all of the constraints and maximizes profit. With guitars, the shipment breakdown was 50 guitars, 8 keyboards, and 20 tubas (Figure 8-31 on page E 8.29). With accordions, the shipment breakdown is 50 accordians, 1 keyboard, and 19 tubas (Figure 8-51). The profit for guitars was $2,762.00. The profit for the accordions is $1,880.00.

The next step is to view the Answer Report for the accordion solution that will be presented to the trucking company.

Steps To View the Second Answer Report

1 **Click the Answer Report 1 tab at the bottom of the window.**

The accordion Solver Answer Report displays (Figure 8-52).

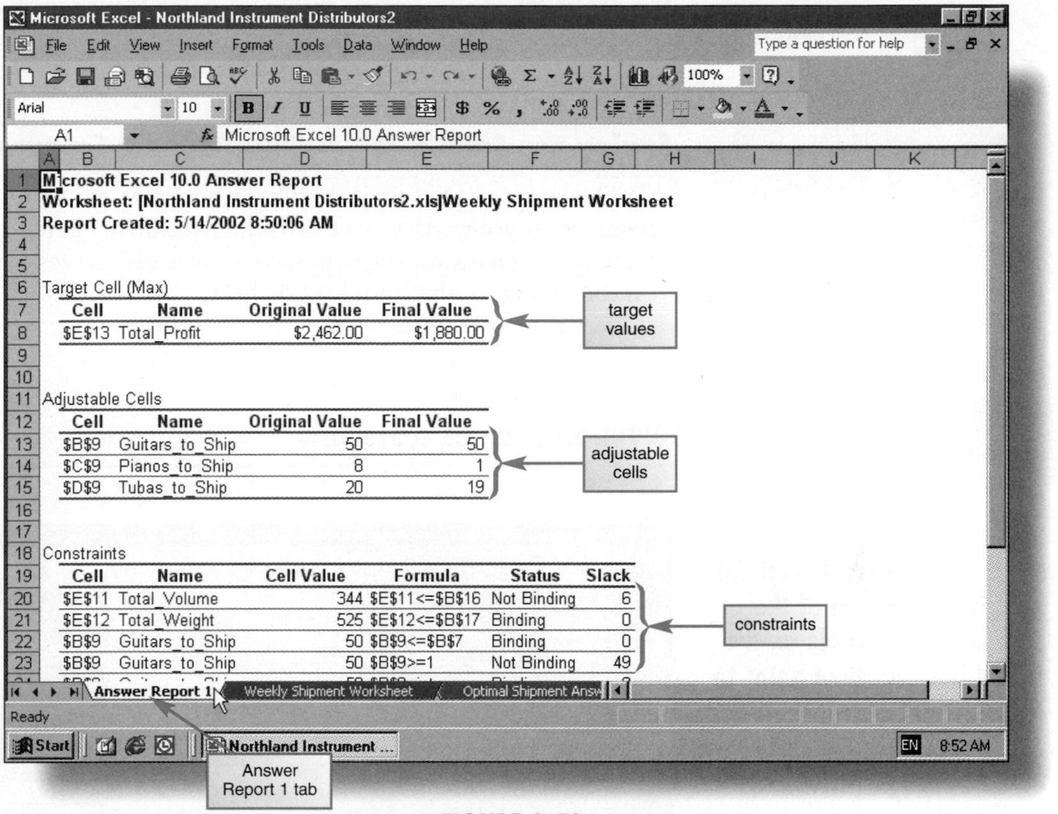

FIGURE 8-52

2 **Double click the Answer Report 1 tab and type** `Optimal Shipment Answer Report2` **as the worksheet name. Select cell A1. Right-click the Optimal Shipment Answer Report2 tab and then click Tab Color on the shortcut menu. Select the color yellow in column 3, row 4 on the Color palette and then click the OK button. Drag the tab to the right of the Optimal Shipment Answer Report1 tab. Use the down scroll arrow to scroll down to view the remaining cells of the accordion answer report.**

The worksheet is renamed, and the remainder of the answer report for the accordion scenario displays (Figure 8-53).

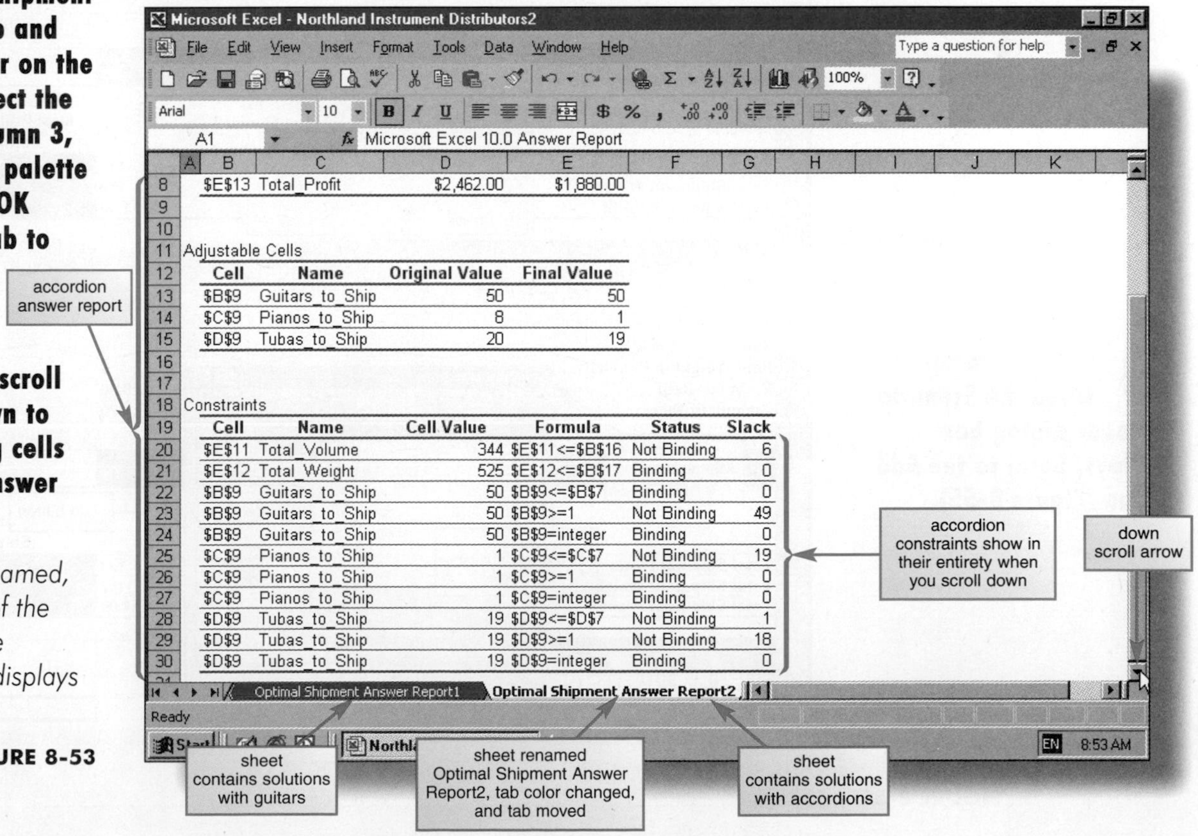

FIGURE 8-53

More About

Quick Reference

For a table that lists how to complete the tasks covered in this book using the mouse, menu, shortcut menu, and keyboard, see the Excel Quick Reference Summary at the back of this book or visit the Office XP Web page (www.scsite.com/offxp/qr.htm), and then click Microsoft Excel 2002.

The Answer Report indicates that the shipment has six fewer cubic feet of volume than the maximum allowed, and exactly the amount of weight allowed. The shipment is clearly very close to filling the available truck space. Furthermore, the profit on the accordian shipment is far less than that of the guitar shipment.

The next step is to save the accordion solution as a scenario so that it can be referenced in the future.

Saving the Second Solver Solution as a Scenario

The power of Scenario Manager becomes evident when you begin adding scenarios to your worksheet. Multiple scenarios can be compared side by side. Using multiple scenarios on the same worksheet also saves time by recycling the work that you did to create the initial worksheet.

Perform the following steps to save the second Solver solution as a scenario.

Steps To Save the Second Solver Solution as a Scenario

1 **Click the Weekly Shipment Worksheet tab at the bottom of the window. Click Tools on the menu bar and then point to Scenarios (Figure 8-54).**

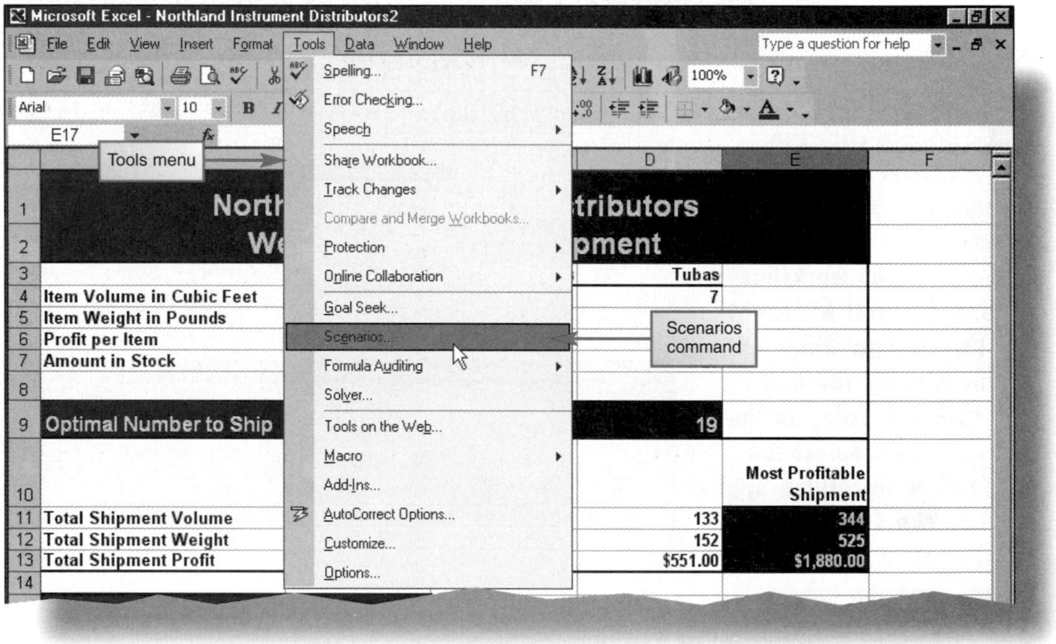

FIGURE 8-54

2 **Click Scenarios. When the Scenario Manager dialog box displays, point to the Add button (Figure 8-55).**

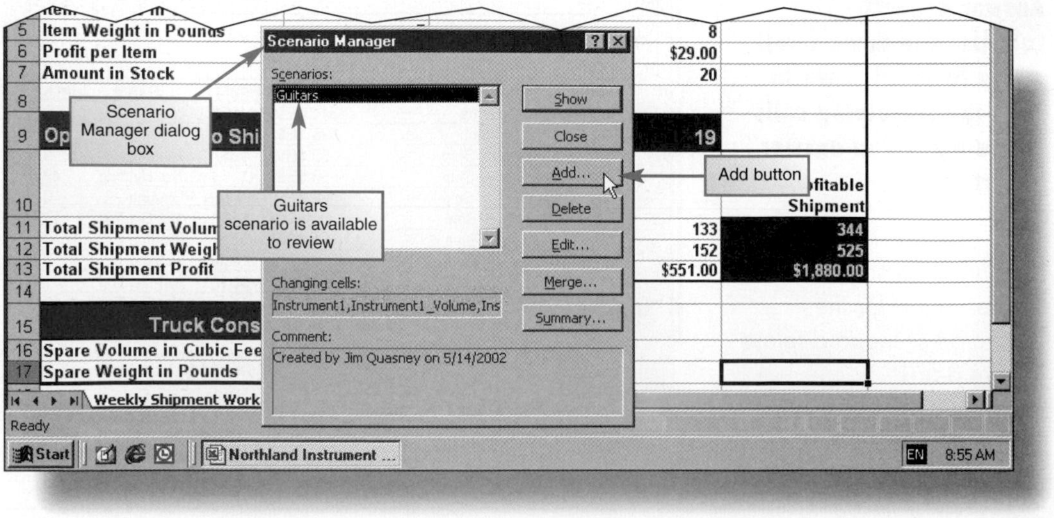

FIGURE 8-55

3 Click the Add button. Type `Accordions` **in the Scenario name text box and then point to the OK button.**

The Add Scenario dialog box displays. The Changing cells box defaults to the previous values used in the Guitars scenario (Figure 8-56).

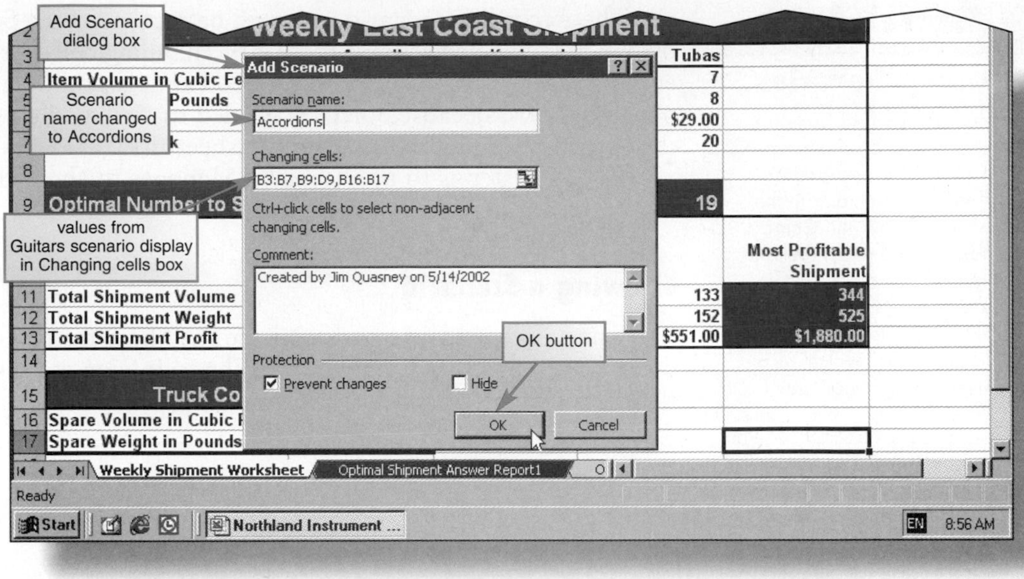

FIGURE 8-56

4 Click the OK button. When the Scenario Values dialog box displays, point to the OK button.

The Scenario Values dialog box displays with the values from the worksheet (Figure 8-57).

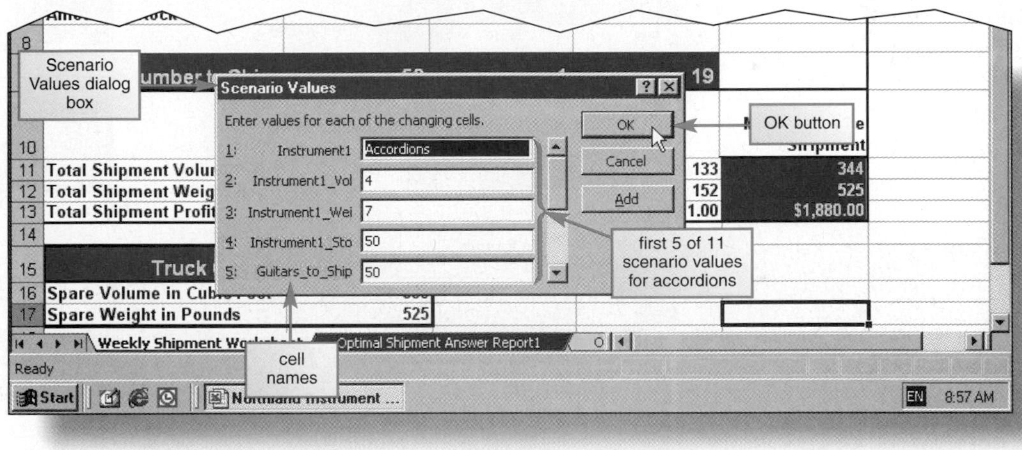

FIGURE 8-57

5 Click the OK button. When the Scenario Manager dialog box displays, point to the Close button.

Accordions displays along with Guitars in the Scenarios list (Figure 8-58). Each name represents a different scenario.

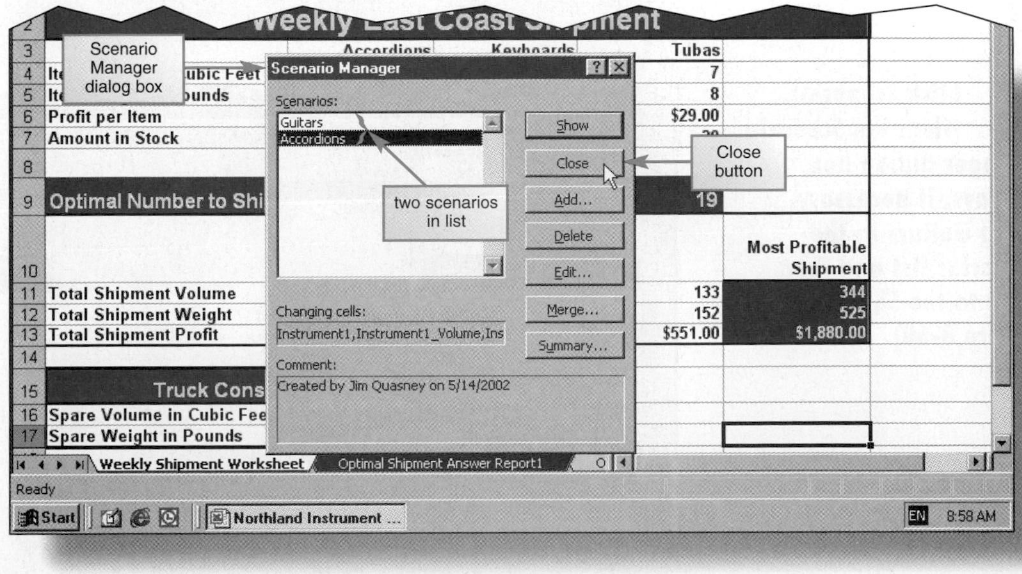

FIGURE 8-58

More About

Showing Scenarios

You can add a list of scenarios to your toolbar by using the Customize command on the Toolbars command in the View menu. Click the Commands tab and select tools. Drag the item named Scenario: with the drop-down arrow up to a toolbar. You then can quickly switch between scenarios on your worksheet.

The Accordion scenario now can be recalled using Scenario Manager. Figure 8-57 on the previous page shows the list of changing cells for the scenario. Instead of entering the data in the worksheet, you simply could enter values here for adding new scenarios. Because Solver is needed to find a solution to the scenario, however, the values were entered on the worksheet first.

The next step is to use Scenario Manager to show the Guitars scenario in the worksheet.

Showing a Scenario

Once a scenario is saved, you use the **Show button** in the Scenario Manager dialog box to display the scenario. The following steps show you how to apply the Guitars scenario created earlier directly to a worksheet.

Steps To Show a Saved Scenario

1 **Click Tools on the menu bar and then point to Scenarios (Figure 8-59).**

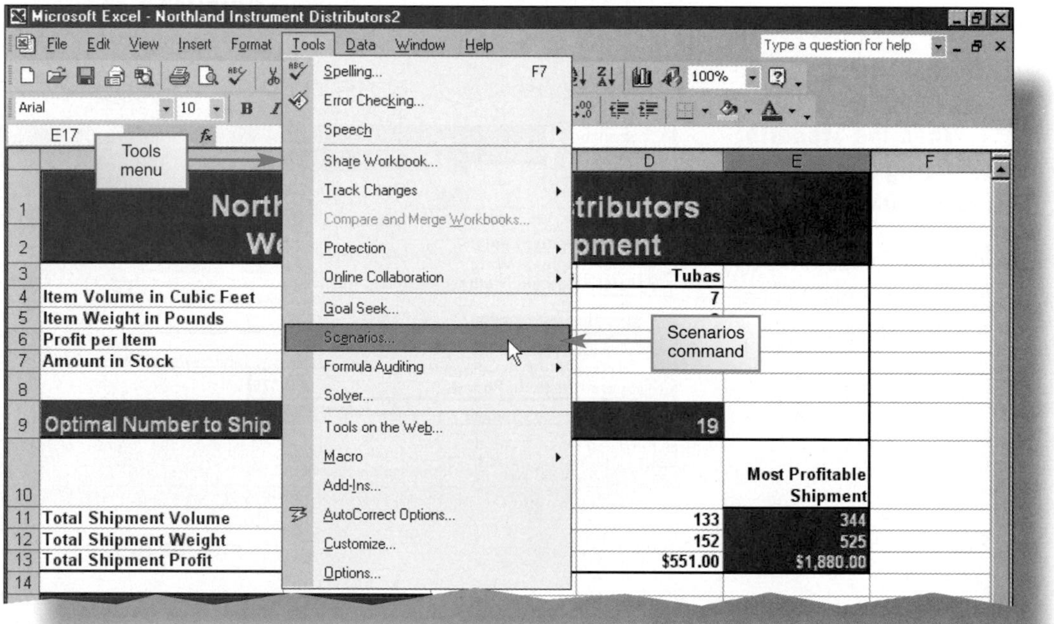

FIGURE 8-59

2 **Click Scenarios. When the Scenario Manager dialog box displays, if necessary, select Guitars in the Scenarios list and then point to the Show button (Figure 8-60).**

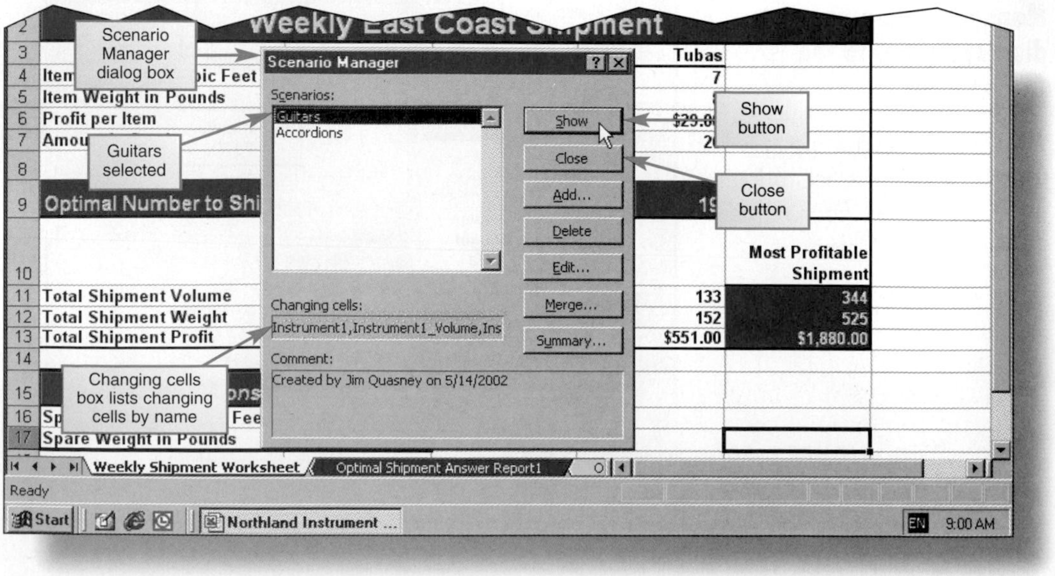

FIGURE 8-60

3 Click the Show button and then click the Close button.

Excel displays the data in the worksheet for the Guitars scenario (Figure 8-61).

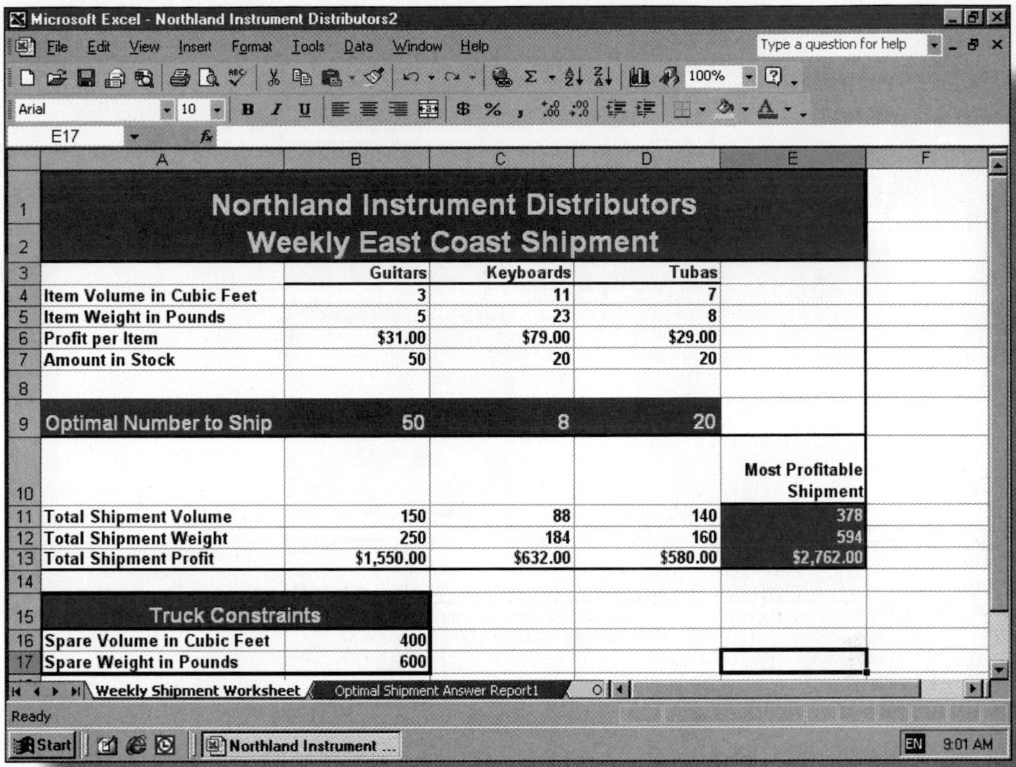

FIGURE 8-61

Other Ways

1. Press ALT+T, E, double-click the scenario name
2. In Voice Command mode, say "Tools, Scenario", click the scenario name, say "Show"

You can undo the scenario results by clicking the Undo button on the Standard toolbar. If desired, you then can click the Redo button on the Standard toolbar to display the scenario results again. If you had several saved scenarios, you could display each one and then use the Undo and Redo buttons to switch between them.

Scenario Manager is an important what-if tool for organizing assumptions. Using Scenario Manager, you can define different scenarios with up to 32 changing cells per scenario. Once you have entered the scenarios, you can show them one by one, or you can create a Scenario Summary worksheet or a Scenario PivotTable worksheet as described in the next section.

Summarizing Scenarios

This section creates a Scenario Summary worksheet and a Scenario PivotTable worksheet. These concise reports allow you to view and manipulate several what-if situations side by side to assist decision making. The **Scenario Summary worksheet** generated by the Scenario Manager actually is an outlined worksheet (Figure 8-62a on the next page) that you can print and manipulate just like any other worksheet. An **outlined worksheet** is one that contains symbols (buttons) above and to the left, which allows you to collapse and expand rows and columns.

The **PivotTable worksheet** (Figure 8-62b on the next page) generated by the Scenario Manager also is a worksheet that you can print and manipulate like other worksheets. A **PivotTable** is a table that summarizes large amounts of information and can be manipulated to show the data from different points of view. The Scenario PivotTable compares the results of scenarios.

More About

Report Manager

Report Manager is an Add-In that allows you to print several scenarios at once. Report Manager is available for download on Microsoft's Web site. Typically, you would need to use the Show command on the Scenario Manager dialog box for each scenario you want to print and then print the worksheet. By using Report Manager, which displays on the View menu, you simply select the scenarios that you want to print; you then can print them all at once.

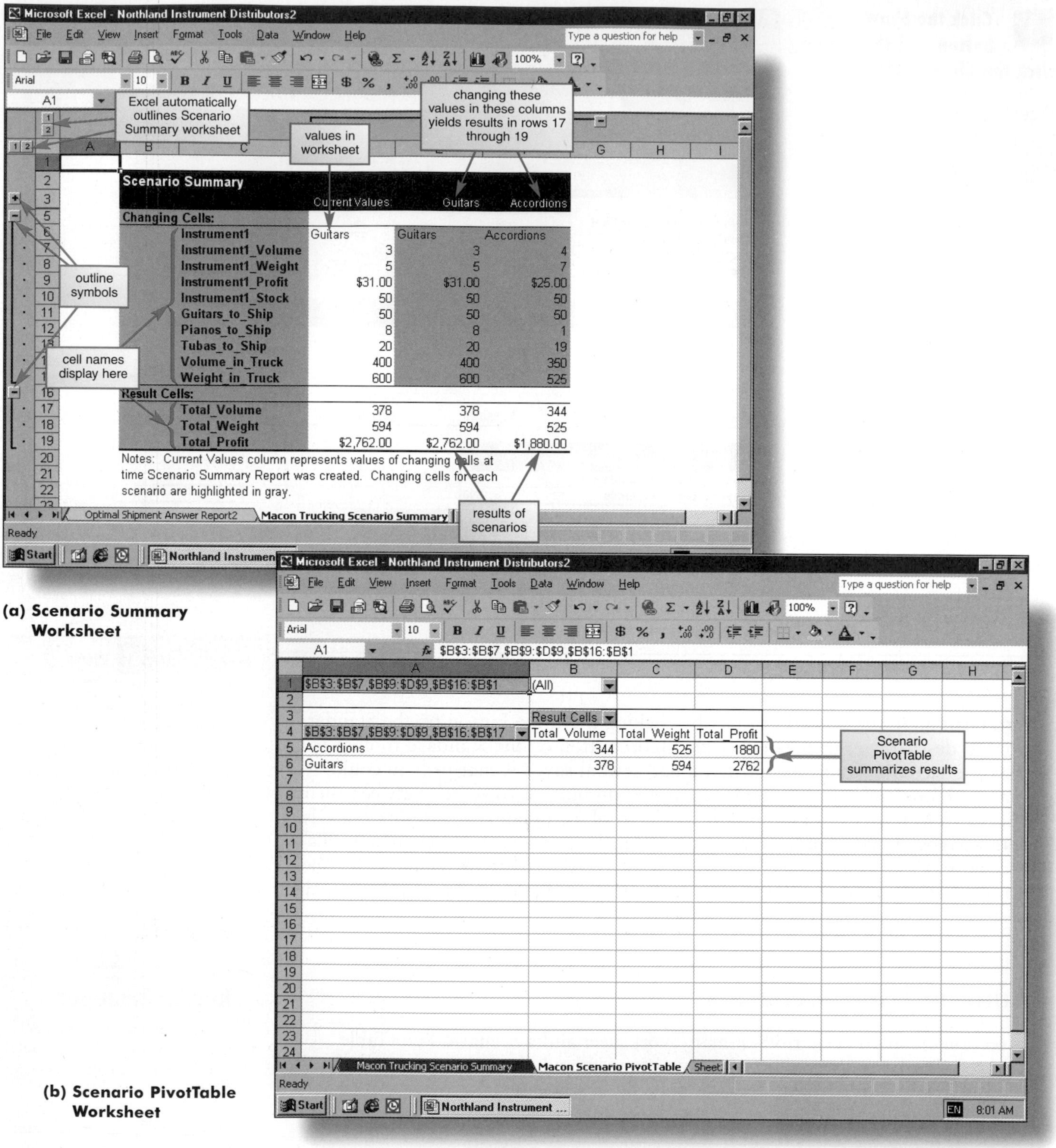

(a) Scenario Summary Worksheet

(b) Scenario PivotTable Worksheet

FIGURE 8-62

Creating a Scenario Summary Worksheet

The Scenario Summary worksheet in Figure 8-62a displays the total volume, total weight, and total profit for the current worksheet values and the two scenarios. The optimal number of instruments of each type calculated by Solver are shown for shipments that include either guitars or accordions.

Perform the following steps to create a Scenario Summary worksheet.

Steps To Create a Scenario Summary

1 Click Tools on the menu bar and then point to Scenarios (Figure 8-63).

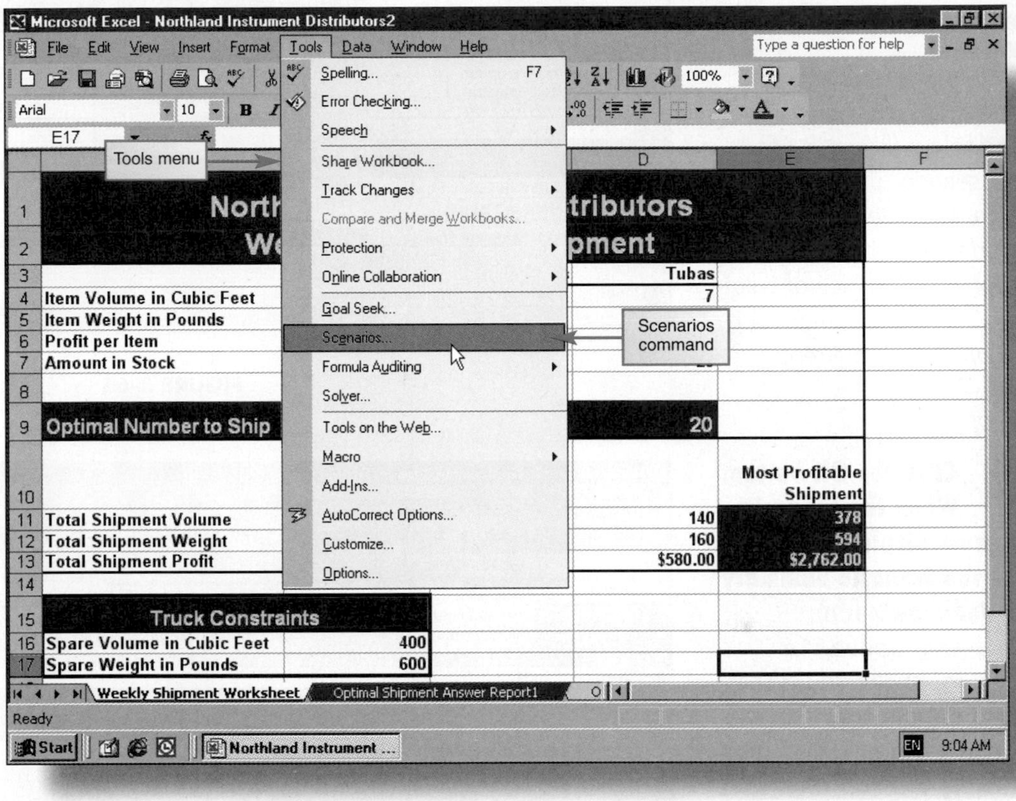

FIGURE 8-63

2 Click Scenarios. When the Scenario Manager dialog box displays, if necessary, select Guitars, then point to the Summary button.

The Scenario Manager dialog box displays (Figure 8-64).

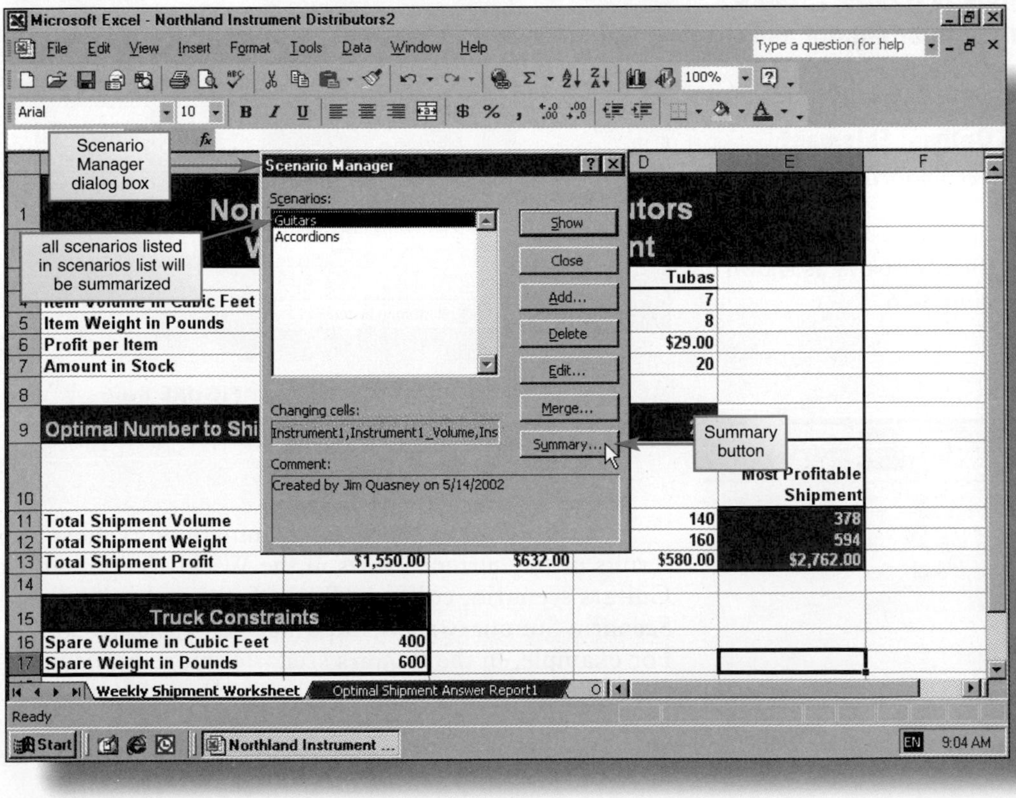

FIGURE 8-64

3 Click the Summary button. When the Scenario Summary dialog box displays, point to the OK button.

The Scenario Summary dialog box displays (Figure 8-65). The Scenario summary option button is selected in the Report type area. The dialog box offers the choice of creating a Scenario summary or a Scenario PivotTable report.

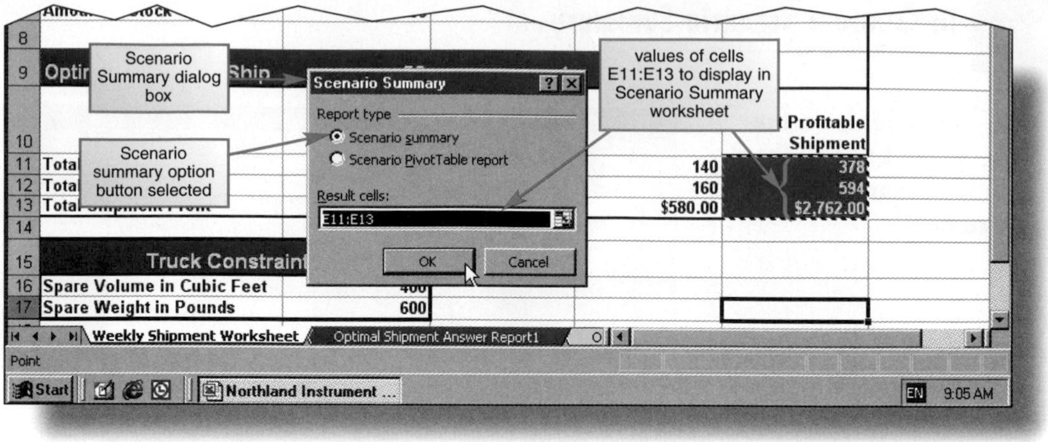

FIGURE 8-65

4 Click the OK button. When the Scenario Summary displays, double-click the Scenario Summary tab and type `Macon Trucking Scenario Summary` **as the worksheet name. Right-click the Macon Trucking Scenario summary tab and then click tab color on the shortcut menu. Select the color purple in column 1, row 4 on the color palette and then click the OK button. Drag the tab to the right of the Optimal Shipment Answer Report2 tab.**

The Scenario Summary worksheet displays as shown in Figure 8-66.

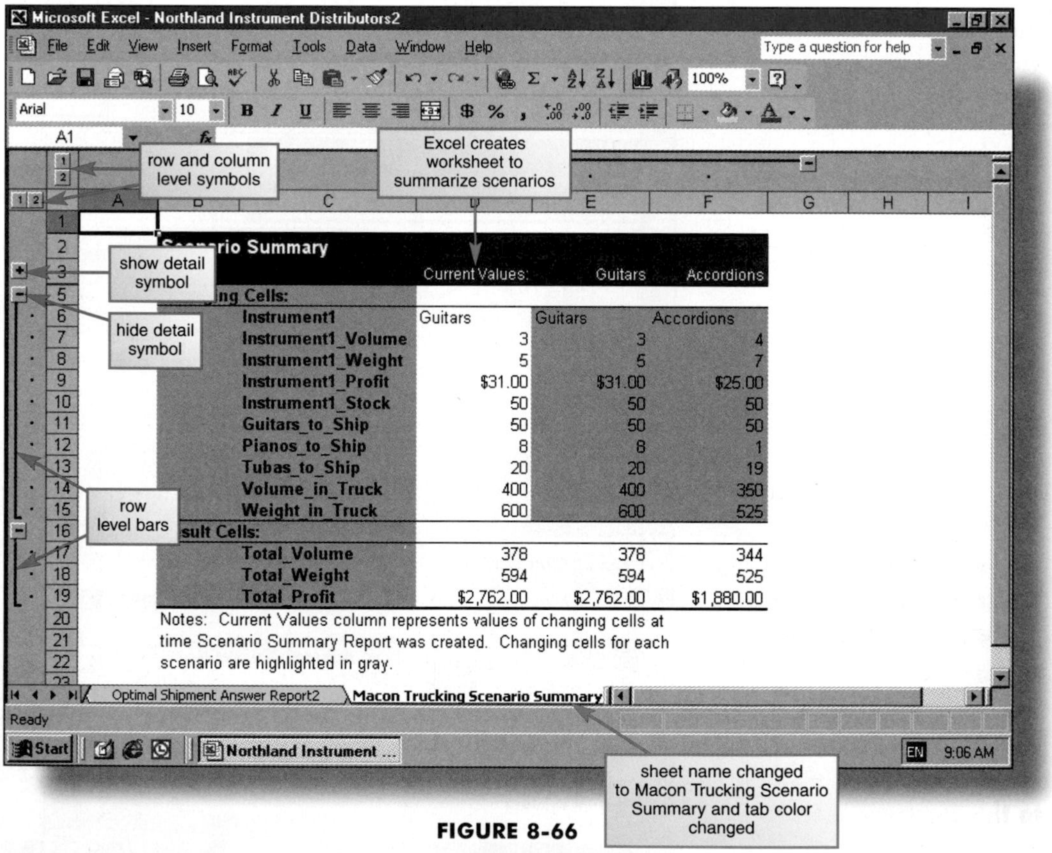

FIGURE 8-66

Other Ways

1. Press ALT+T, E
2. In Voice Command mode, say "Tools, Scenarios"

Column D in the Scenario Summary worksheet in Figure 8-66 shows the results of the current values in the Weekly Shipment Worksheet, which is the Guitars scenario; columns E and F show the results of the two scenarios. The Scenario Summary worksheet makes it easier to compare the results of the scenarios. For example, in the Guitars scenario, more profit is possible due to the higher profit margin on guitars. Subsequently, Northland Instrument Distributors stands to make a better profit if there is more demand for guitars. Perhaps this indicates how the Northland Instrument Distributors should go about marketing its instruments to its customers.

Working with an Outlined Worksheet

Excel automatically outlines the Scenario Summary worksheet. The outline symbols display above and to the left of the worksheet (Figure 8-66). You click the outline symbols to expand or collapse the worksheet. For example, if you click the **show detail symbol**, Excel displays additional rows or columns that are summarized on the displayed row or column. If you click a **hide detail symbol**, Excel hides any detail rows that extend through the length of the corresponding row level bar or column level bar. You also can expand or collapse a worksheet by clicking the **row level symbol** or **column level symbol** above and to the left of row title 1.

An outline is especially useful when working with large worksheets. To remove an outline, point to Group and Outline on the Data menu and then click Clear Outline on the Group and Outline submenu.

More About

Outlined Worksheets

You can outline any worksheet by using the Auto Outline command on the Group and Outline submenu. To access outlining features, click Data on the menu bar, point to Group and Outline, and then click Auto Outline on the Group and Outline submenu.

Creating a Scenario PivotTable

Excel also can generate Scenario PivotTables to help analyze and compare the results of multiple scenarios. A **Scenario PivotTable** gives you the ability to summarize the scenario data and then rotate the table's row and column titles to obtain different views of the summarized data. The PivotTable to be created in this project is shown in Figure 8-62b on page E 8.48. The table summarizes the Guitar and Accordion scenarios and displays the result cells for the two scenarios for easy comparison.

PivotTables are powerful data analysis tools because they allow you to view the data in various ways by interchanging or pairing the row and column fields by dragging the buttons located on cells A1, A4, and B3 in Figure 8-62b. The process of rotating the field values around the data fields will be discussed in the next project.

To create the PivotTable shown in Figure 8-62b, perform the following steps.

More About

Scenario PivotTables

A Scenario PivotTable is a powerful analysis tool for comparing the results of scenarios when the differences and causes of the differences among scenarios are not completely obvious. You can compare scenarios side by side, perform sorts and filters on the values of the result cells, and rotate rows and columns of the table to gain a different perspective on the results.

Steps To Create a Scenario PivotTable

1 **Click the Weekly Shipment Worksheet tab at the bottom of the window. Click Tools on the menu bar and then click Scenarios. When the Scenario Manager dialog box displays, if necessary, select Guitars, then point to the Summary button.**

The Scenario Manager dialog box displays (Figure 8-67).

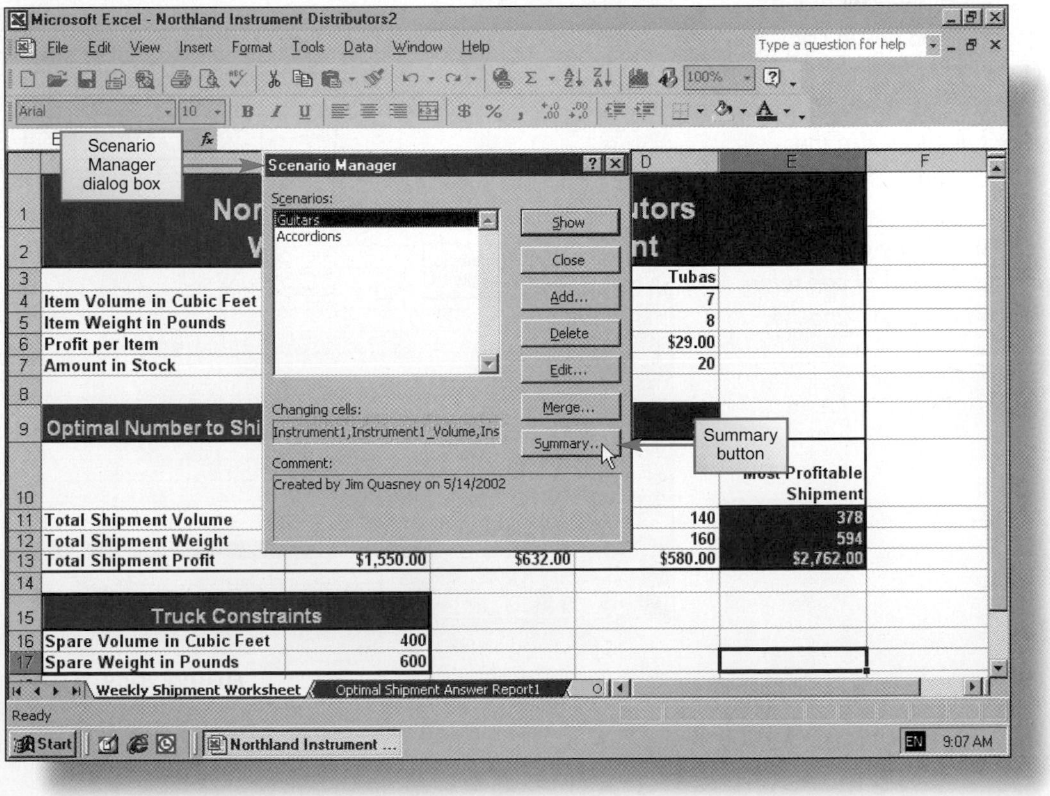

FIGURE 8-67

2 **Click the Summary button. When the Scenario Summary dialog box displays, click Scenario PivotTable report in the Report type area. Point to the OK button.**

The Scenario Summary dialog box displays as shown in Figure 8-68. The range E11:E13 displays in the Results cells box because these cells were specified the last time this dialog box displayed.

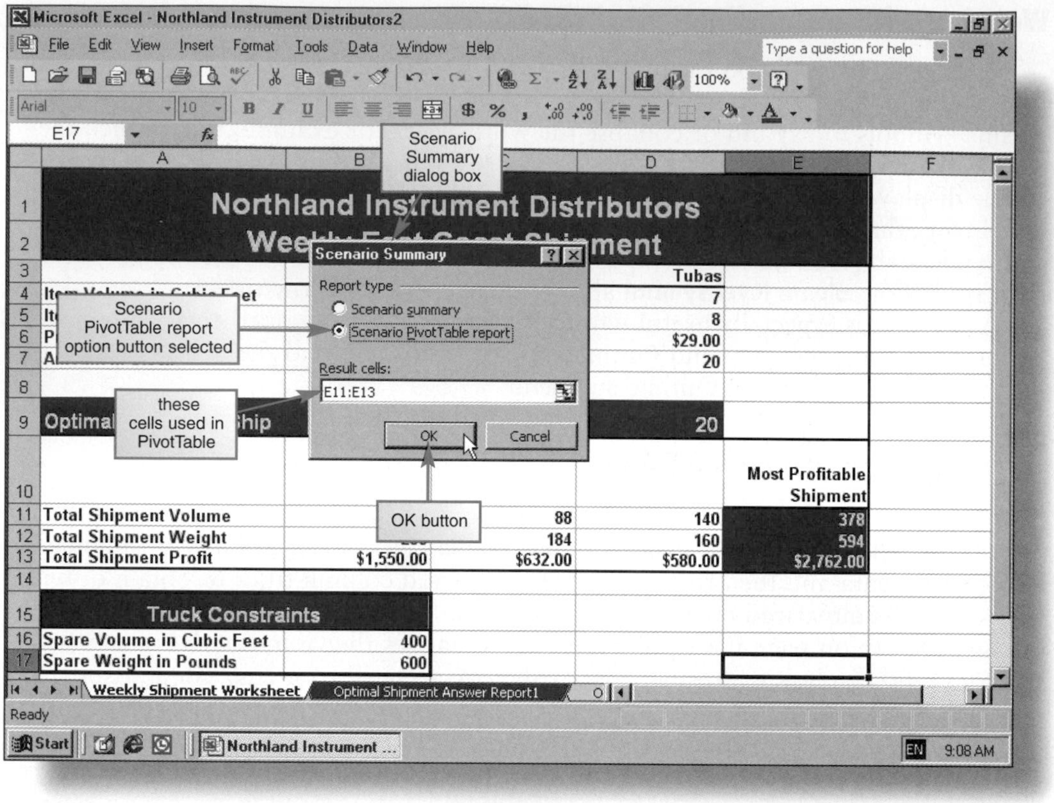

FIGURE 8-68

3 **Click the OK button.**

The Scenario PivotTable worksheet displays with the cell references of the changing values in column A (Figure 8-69). Your worksheet may display differently; you may have to resize the column width of column A if it appears too large. Your worksheet may also have cell names instead of cell references in cells A1 and A4.

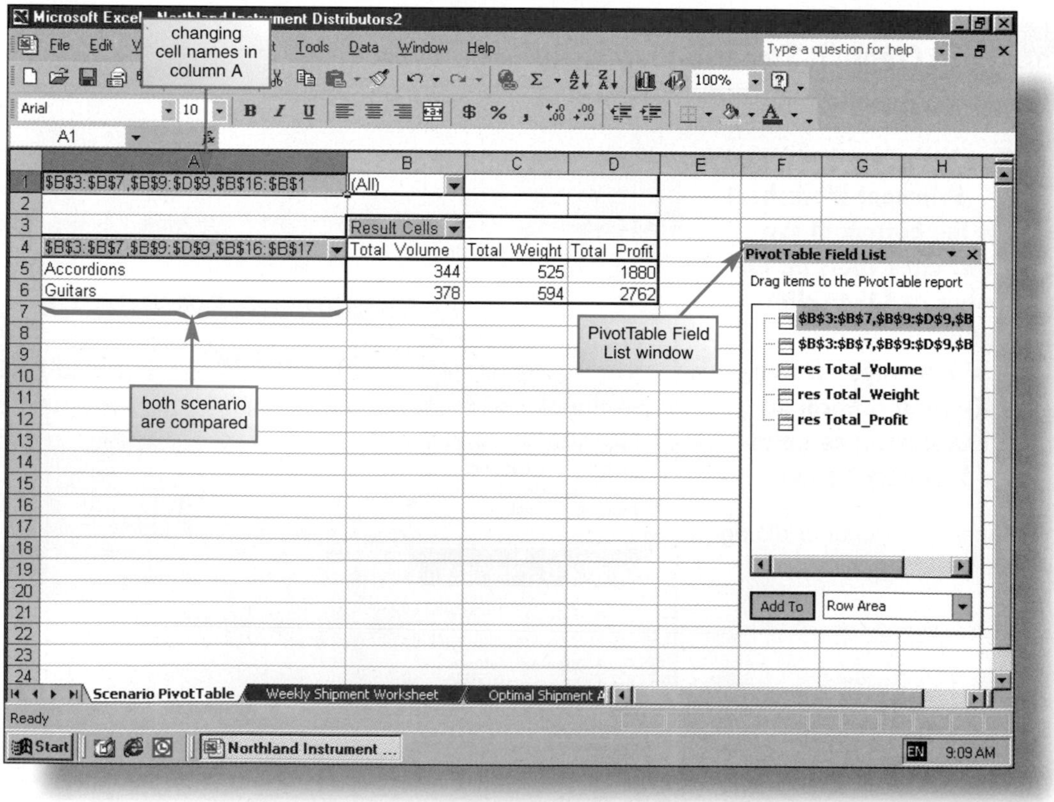

FIGURE 8-69

4 **Point to the boundary to the right side of the column A heads and drag to resize the column as shown in Figure 8-70. Double-click the Scenario PivotTable tab and type** `Macon Scenario PivotTable` **as the worksheet name. Click cell A8. Right-click the Macon Scenario PivotTable tab and then click Tab Color on the shortcut menu. Select the color green in column 4, row 4 on the Color palette and then click the OK button. Drag the tab to the right of the Macon Trucking Scenario Summary tab.**

The Scenario PivotTable displays within the viewable area of the worksheet. The result cells of the two scenarios display in rows 5 and 6, as shown in Figure 8-70.

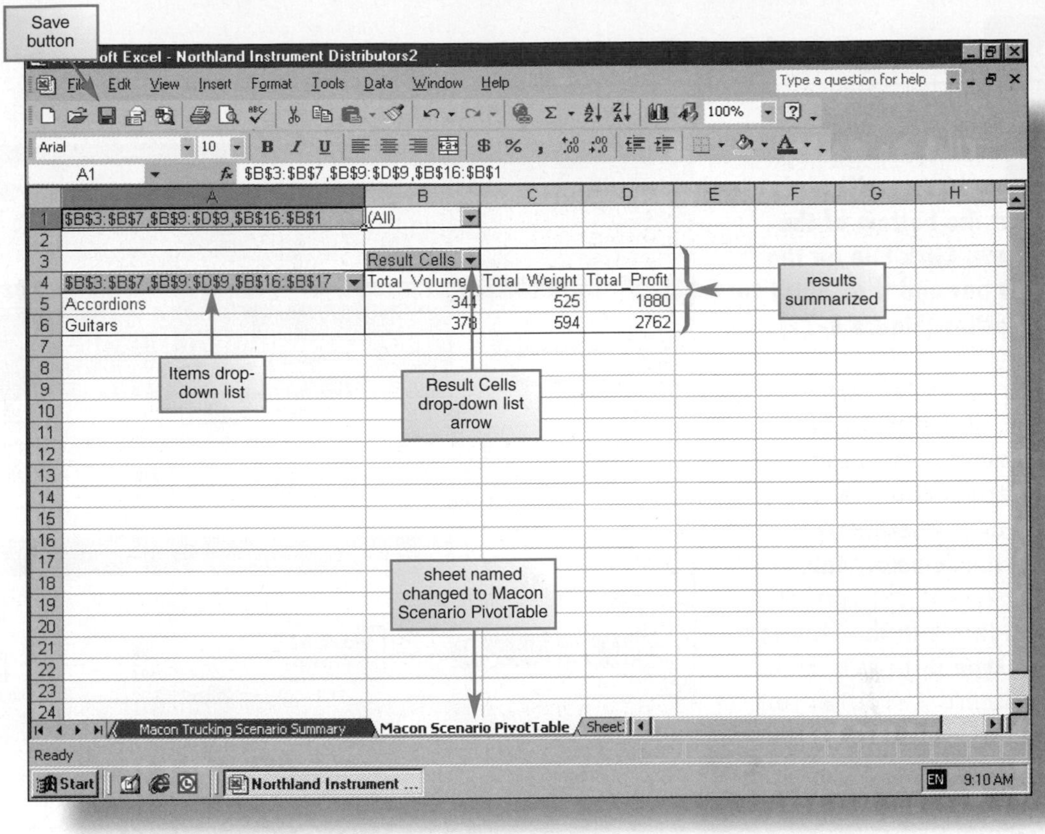

FIGURE 8-70

5 **Click the Save button on the Standard toolbar to save the workbook using the file name, Northland Instrument Distributors2.**

Other Ways

1. Press ALT+T, E
2. In Voice Command mode, say "Tools, Scenarios"

Once the PivotTable is created, you can treat it like any other worksheet. Thus, you can print or chart a PivotTable. If you update the data in one of the scenarios, click the **Refresh Data command** on the Data menu. If you show a scenario and merely change values on the scenario worksheet, it is not the same as changing the scenario. If you want to change the data in a scenario, you must use Scenario Manager.

Changing the Properties on a Workbook

Excel allows you to store a variety of information about each workbook. This information collectively is called **workbook properties**, and it is useful when workbooks will be used by many people or if you need to save pertinent data about the purpose of the workbook for future reference.

The Northland Instrument Distributors workbook obviously will be very useful in the future if Macon Trucking or other shipping firms require similar analysis for a shipment. The steps on the next page save relevant information about the Northland Instrument Distributors2 workbook for future reference.

More About

Workbook Properties

Workbook properties can be viewed from Windows Explorer by right-clicking an Excel file and then clicking Properties on the shortcut menu. This makes it easy to determine the contents and purpose of a workbook without opening it. If the user has the View as Web Page option selected in Windows Explorer and the Save preview picture option is selected in the Summary tab, then they can see a preview of the workbook.

Steps To Change Workbook Properties

1 **Click the Weekly Shipment Worksheet tab at the bottom of the window. Click File on the menu bar and then point to Properties (Figure 8-71).**

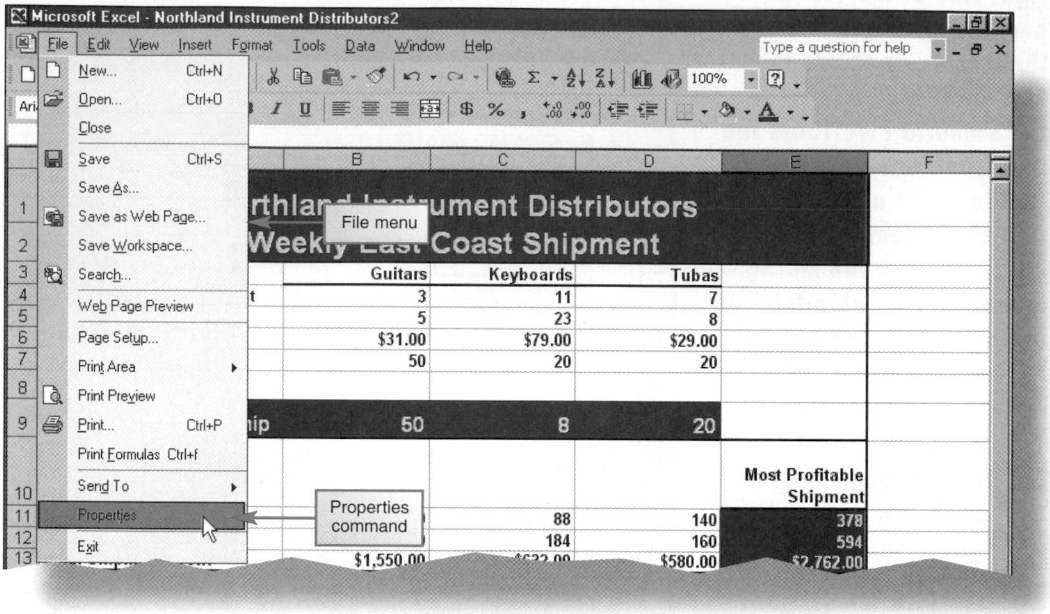

FIGURE 8-71

2 **Click Properties. When the Northland Instrument Distributors2 Properties dialog box displays, if necessary, click the Summary tab. Type** `Weekly Shipment Worksheet` **in the Title text box. Type** `Optimal Truck Shipment Calculation` **in the Subject text box. Type** `Marsha Gresham` **in the Manager text box. Type** `Shipment planning for East coast shipments for May 2002, week 3. Shipping conditions met for Macon Trucking.` **in the Comments text box. Point to the OK button.**

The summary fields display in the Northland Instrument Distributors2 Properties dialog box as shown in Figure 8-72.

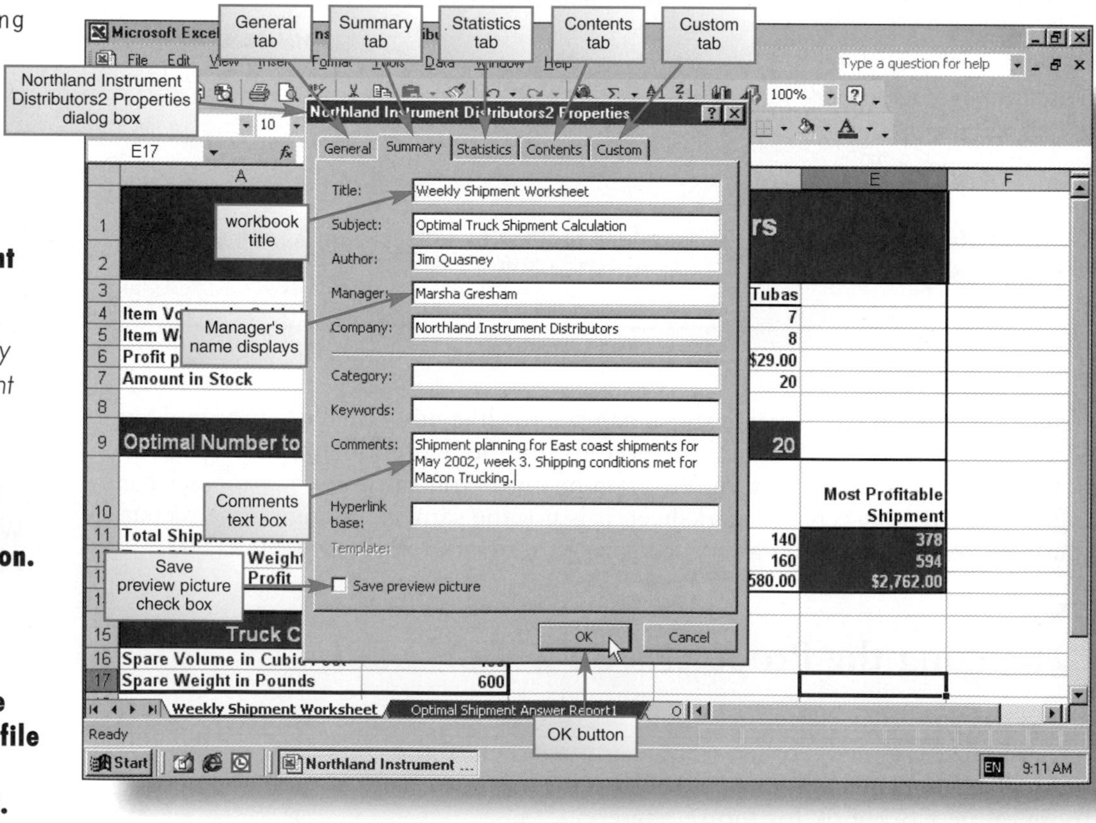

FIGURE 8-72

3 **Click the OK button.**

4 **Click the Save button on the Standard toolbar to save the workbook using the file name, Northland Instrument Distributors2.**

Other Ways

1. Press ALT+F, I
2. In Voice Command mode, say "File, Properties"

The **Workbook Properties dialog box** contains other useful information about the workbook. The **General sheet** displays data about the workbook file, including the size of the file, creation date, date modified, and the date the file last was accessed. The **Save preview picture check box** selected on the **Summary sheet** saves an image of the current worksheet that will be visible in the Open dialog box when the file is selected by the user. The **Statistics sheet** displays some of the file data from the General sheet in addition to a record of when the file last was opened and modified.

The **Contents sheet** displays a list of all the worksheets and charts contained in the workbook. This feature allows you to search large workbooks quickly that contain many worksheets and charts when you are looking for a particular worksheet or chart.

The **Custom sheet** allows you to create your own workbook properties. For example, you can add fields such as document number, editor, your telephone number, division, group, owner, or any other field you want to store with the workbook. For each item you define, you can set the data type for the value. Valid data types are Text, Date, Number, and Yes or No.

More About

Custom Properties

In addition to using text fields, you can set up custom properties that link to cells in your workbook. For example, you can have a property that contains the value in the total profit cell in the Track Team worksheet.

Quitting Excel

The project is complete. To exit Excel, follow the steps below.

TO QUIT EXCEL

1. Click the Close button on the right side of the title bar.
2. If a Microsoft Excel dialog box displays, click the No button.

CASE PERSPECTIVE SUMMARY

With the two solved scenarios developed in this project, Marsha Gresham is convinced that the company is shipping the best combination of instruments to its customers within the constraints of the shipping method the company has chosen. She also has the confidence that Northland Instrument Distributors is maximizing its profit when making its weekly shipment to the East coast. The worksheet can be used in the future to analyze any potential shipment.

Project Summary

In this project, you learned how to use a number of techniques to approach problem solving, including trial and error, goal seek, and Solver. You learned how to analyze a worksheet using the Formula Auditing toolbar. You learned how to use data validation on cells and inform the user about the validation rules. You also learned how to manage different problems on the same worksheet using Scenario Manager and then summarize the results of the scenarios with a Scenario Summary and a Scenario PivotTable. Finally, you learned how to save a workbook file with passwords and modify the properties of a workbook.

What You Should Know

Having completed this project, you should now be able to perform the following tasks:

- Add Data Validation *(E 8.16)*
- Add the Data for a New Scenario *(E 8.40)*
- Change Workbook Properties *(E 8.54)*
- Create a Scenario PivotTable *(E 8.51)*
- Create a Scenario Summary *(E 8.49)*
- Display the Formula Auditing Toolbar *(E 8.10)*
- Quit Excel *(E 8.55)*
- Remove the Trace Dependents Arrows *(E 8.14)*
- Remove the Trace Precedents Arrows *(E 8.12)*
- Save the Second Solver Solution as a Scenario *(E 8.44)*
- Save the Current Data as a Scenario *(E 8.35)*
- Save the Workbook with Passwords *(E 8.32)*
- Show a Saved Scenario *(E 8.46)*
- Start Excel, Open a Workbook, and Customize Excel *(E 8.08)*
- Trace Dependents *(E 8.13)*
- Trace Precedents *(E 8.11)*
- Use Solver to Find the Optimal Combination *(E 8.25)*
- Use Solver to Find a New Solution *(E 8.41)*
- Use the Goal Seek Command to Attempt to Solve a Complex Problem *(E 8.21)*
- Use Trial and Error to Attempt to Solve a Complex Problem *(E 8.19)*
- View the Second Answer Report *(E 8.43)*
- View the Answer Report *(E 8.31)*

More About

Microsoft Certification

The Microsoft Office User Specialist (MOUS) Certification program provides an opportunity for you to obtain a valuable industry credential — proof that you have the Excel 2002 skills required by employers. For more information, see Appendix D or visit the Shelly Cashman Series MOUS Web page at www.scsite.com/offxp/cert.htm.

Learn It Online

Instructions: To complete the Learn It Online exercises, start your browser, click the Address bar, and then enter `scsite.com/offxp/exs.htm`. When the Office XP Learn It Online page displays, follow the instructions in the exercises below.

1 Project Reinforcement TF, MC, and SA

Below Excel Project 8, click the Project Reinforcement link. Print the quiz by clicking Print on the File menu. Answer each question. Write your first and last name at the top of each page, and then hand in the printout to your instructor.

2 Flash Cards

Below Excel Project 8, click the Flash Cards link. When Flash Cards displays, read the instructions. Type 20 (or a number specified by your instructor) in the Number of Playing Cards text box, type your name in the Name text box, and then click the Flip Card button. When the flash card displays, read the question and then click the Answer box arrow to select an answer. Flip through Flash Cards. Click Print on the File menu to print the last flash card if your score is 15 (75%) correct or greater and then hand it in to your instructor. If your score is less than 15 (75%) correct, then redo this exercise by clicking the Replay button.

3 Practice Test

Below Excel Project 8, click the Practice Test link. Answer each question, enter your first and last name at the bottom of the page, and then click the Grade Test button. When the graded practice test displays on your screen, click Print on the File menu to print a hard copy. Continue to take practice tests until you score 80% or better. Hand in a printout of the final practice test to your instructor.

4 Who Wants to Be a Computer Genius?

Below Excel Project 8, click the Computer Genius link. Read the instructions, enter your first and last name at the bottom of the page, and then click the Play button. Hand in your score to your instructor.

5 Wheel of Terms

Below Excel Project 8, click the Wheel of Terms link. Read the instructions, and then enter your first and last name and your school name. Click the Play button. Hand in your score to your instructor.

6 Crossword Puzzle Challenge

Below Excel Project 8, click the Crossword Puzzle Challenge link. Read the instructions, and then enter your first and last name. Click the Play button. Work the crossword puzzle. When you are finished, click the Submit button. When the crossword puzzle redisplays, click the Print button. Hand in the printout.

7 Tips and Tricks

Below Excel Project 8, click the Tips and Tricks link. Click a topic that pertains to Project 8. Right-click the information and then click Print on the shortcut menu. Construct a brief example of what the information relates to in Excel to confirm you understand how to use the tip or trick. Hand in the example and printed information.

online

8 Newsgroups

Below Excel Project 8, click the Newsgroups link. Click a topic that pertains to Project 8. Print three comments. Hand in the comments to your instructor.

9 Expanding Your Horizons

Below Excel Project 8, click the Articles for Microsoft Excel link. Click a topic that pertains to Project 8. Print the information. Construct a brief example of what the information relates to in Excel to confirm you understand the contents of the article. Hand in the example and printed information to your instructor.

10 Search Sleuth

Below Excel Project 8, click the Search Sleuth link. To search for a term that pertains to this project, select a term below the Project 8 title and then use the Google search engine at google.com (or any major search engine) to display and print two Web pages that present information on the term. Hand in the printouts to your instructor.

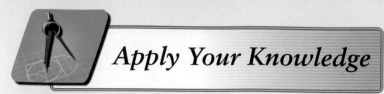

Apply Your Knowledge

1 Determining the Optimal Servings for a Meal

Instructions: Minkus Catering has been asked to create custom meals for a local minor league baseball team. Follow the steps below to use trial and error, and then Solver to find the optimal servings mix that should make up a meal with no more than 400 calories and 20 grams of fat based on the current product costs and prices. The items requested to be included in the meals include potatoes, pork, and carrots. The meal must include at least one serving of each item and no more than four.

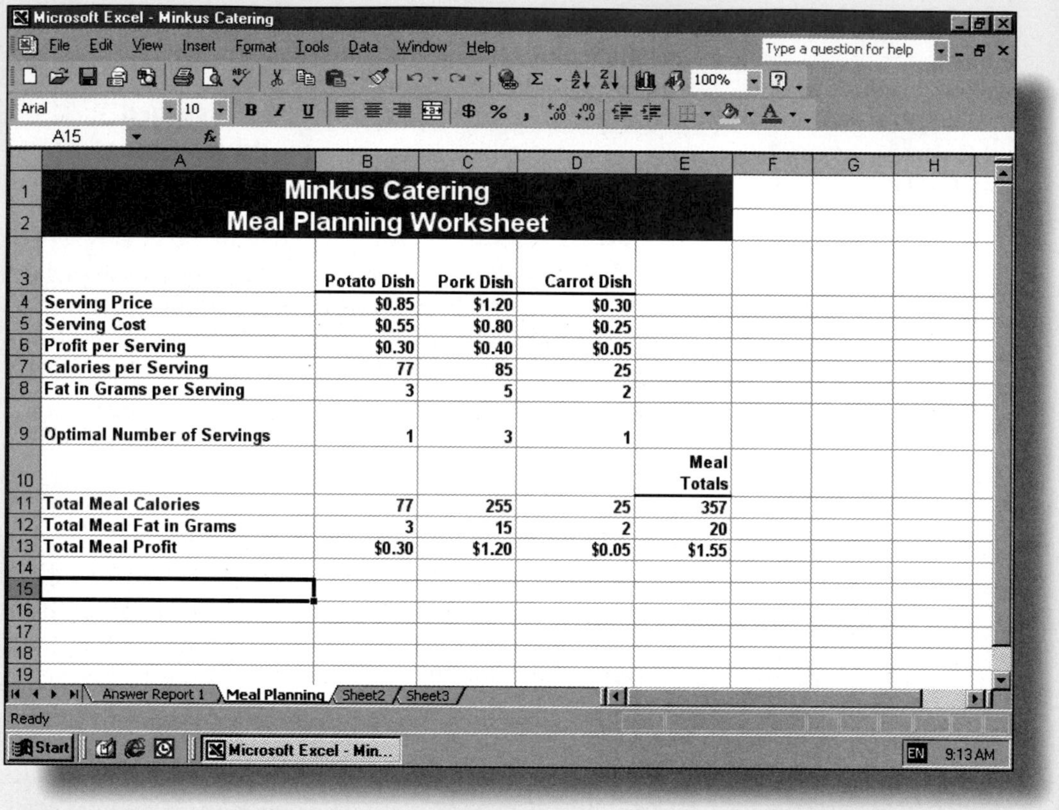

FIGURE 8-73

1. Open the workbook Minkus Catering from the Data Disk. If you do not have a copy of the Data Disk, see the inside back cover of this book.
2. Enter your name, course, laboratory assignment number (Apply 8-1), date, and instructor name in the range A15:A19.
3. Using trial and error, enter values in cells B9, C9, and D9 to try to solve the problem.
4. Use Solver to find a solution to the problem so that the profit on the meal is maximized. Allow Solver to change cells B9, C9 and D9. The total calories of the meal should not exceed 400 and the total fat should not exceed 20 grams. The results in B9, C9, and D9 should be integer values. Also, use the Assume Linear Model option in Solver.
5. Instruct Solver to create the Answer Report for your solution. Solver should find the answer as shown in Figure 8-73.
6. Go into the workbook properties on the File menu and enter a title for the workbook of Minkus Catering Custom Meal Workbook. Enter your name in the Author field and your instructor's name in the Manager field.
7. Print the worksheet and the Answer Report 1 worksheet. Hand in the two printouts to your instructor.

In the Lab

1 Gaining Confidence in the Greenback Stock Club Workbook

Problem: You have been given the task of taking over the job of another employee who has retired. Your first task is to learn about some of the Excel workbooks for which you now are responsible.

Instructions: Start Excel and perform the following tasks.

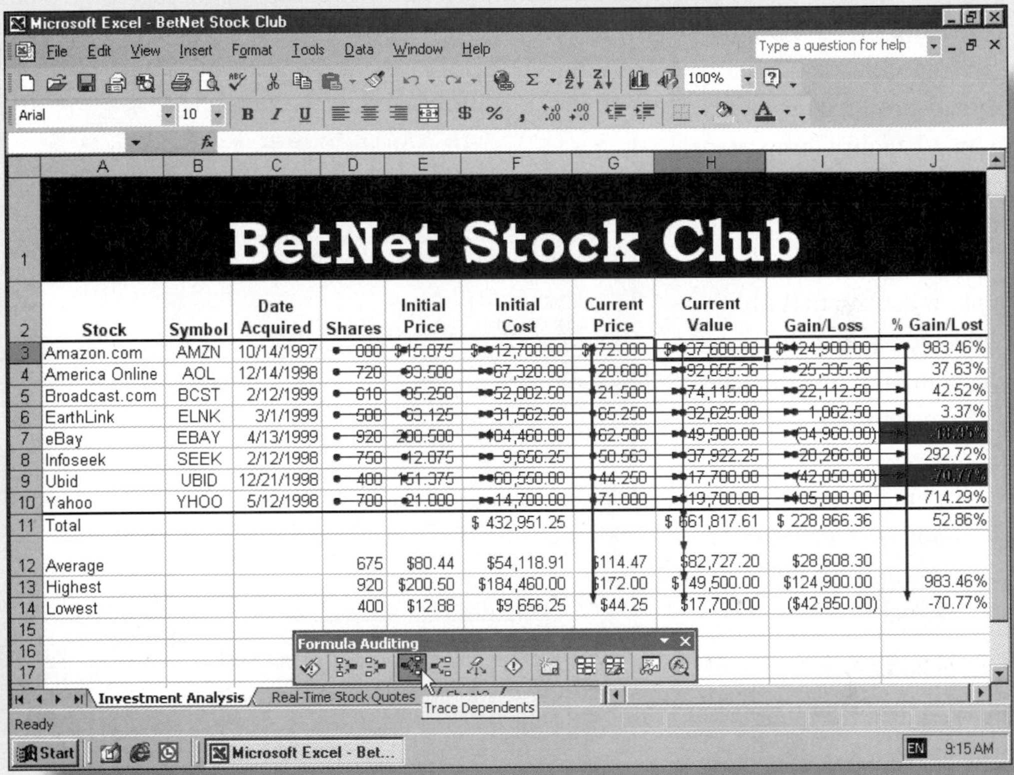

FIGURE 8-74

1. Open the BetNet Stock Club workbook from the Data Disk. See the inside back cover of this book for instructions for downloading the Data Disk or see your instructor for information on accessing the files required in this book.
2. Display the Formula Auditing Toolbar. Trace four levels of precedents for cell J14. Trace one level of the precedents for cell G14. Trace one level of the dependents for cell H3. The worksheet should display as shown in Figure 8-74.
3. Enter your name, course, laboratory assignment number (Lab 8-1), date, and instructor's name in the range A16:G20. Print the worksheet.
4. Remove all trace arrows. Enter the value of zero in cell D5.
5. Use the Trace Error button to trace the error in cell J5. Use the Trace Error button to trace the error in cell J14. Print the worksheet.
6. Select the range D3:D10. Open the Data Validation dialog box. Create a validation rule that forces the user to enter a positive whole number in the cells in the selected range. Clear the Ignore blank check box.
7. Click the Error Alert tab and create an error message with the title `Number of Shares` that contains the message `Enter a positive whole number for the number of shares.` Click the OK button.
8. Reenter the value of zero in cell D5 and press the ENTER key to view the error message. Select Retry and then enter 300 in cell D5. Print the worksheet. Hand in the three printouts to your instructor.

In the Lab

2 Finding the Best Production Mix

Problem: Grouse Products assembles four types of compressors in its factory. Each type of compressor requires a different amount of labor input and a different amount of materials to produce a single compressor. As the production manager, it is your job to determine the best mix of compressors to produce based on the amount of available labor and material for a given week. The company should produce no more than 12 Light Compressor and Medium Compressor units in a week due to a high level of inventory. Due to contractual obligations with a distributor, the company must always produce at least 20 Heavy Compressor units each week. Finally, the company does not wish to produce more than 50 of any item in a week.

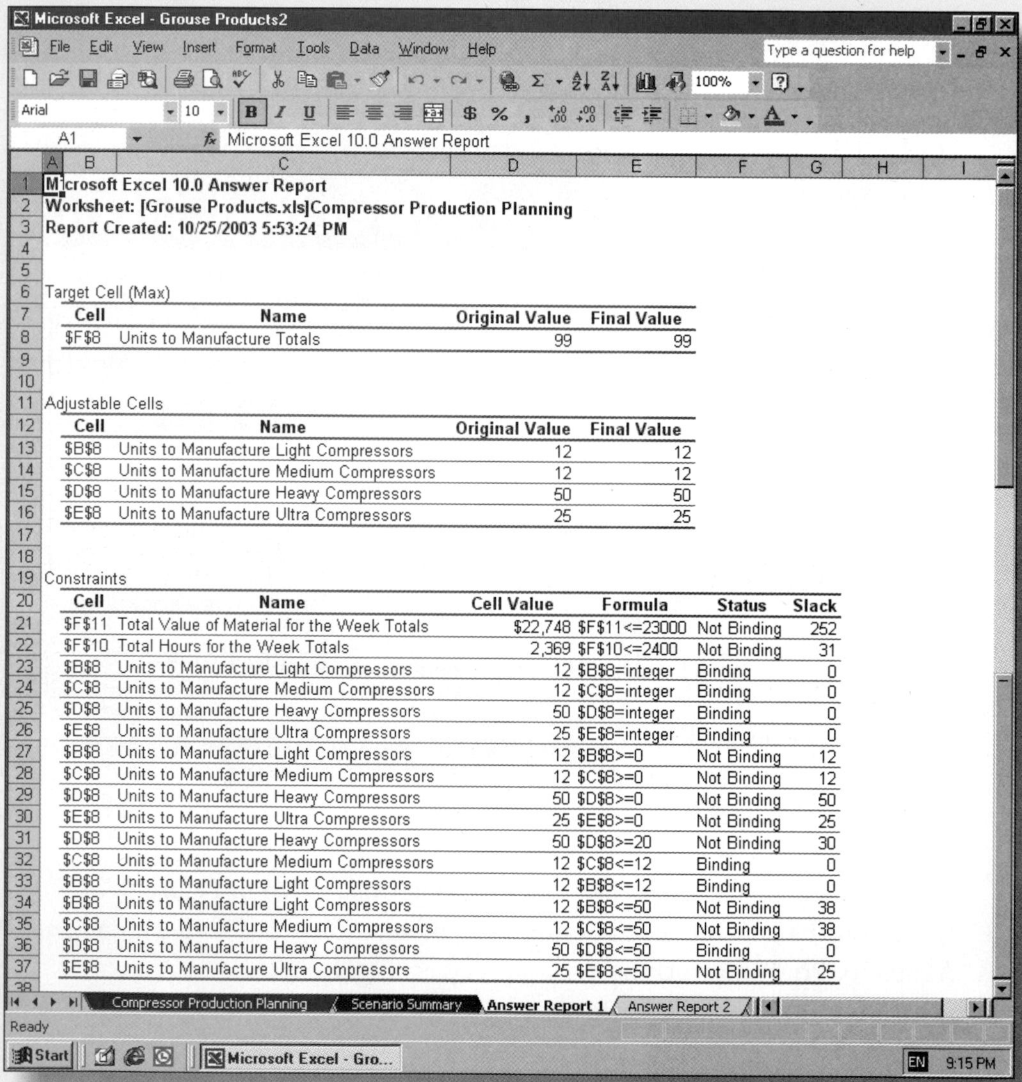

Microsoft Excel - Grouse Products2

Microsoft Excel 10.0 Answer Report
Worksheet: [Grouse Products.xls]Compressor Production Planning
Report Created: 10/25/2003 5:53:24 PM

Target Cell (Max)

Cell	Name	Original Value	Final Value
$F$8	Units to Manufacture Totals	99	99

Adjustable Cells

Cell	Name	Original Value	Final Value
$B$8	Units to Manufacture Light Compressors	12	12
$C$8	Units to Manufacture Medium Compressors	12	12
$D$8	Units to Manufacture Heavy Compressors	50	50
$E$8	Units to Manufacture Ultra Compressors	25	25

Constraints

Cell	Name	Cell Value	Formula	Status	Slack
$F$11	Total Value of Material for the Week Totals	$22,748	$F$11<=23000	Not Binding	252
$F$10	Total Hours for the Week Totals	2,369	$F$10<=2400	Not Binding	31
$B$8	Units to Manufacture Light Compressors	12	$B$8=integer	Binding	0
$C$8	Units to Manufacture Medium Compressors	12	$C$8=integer	Binding	0
$D$8	Units to Manufacture Heavy Compressors	50	$D$8=integer	Binding	0
$E$8	Units to Manufacture Ultra Compressors	25	$E$8=integer	Binding	0
$B$8	Units to Manufacture Light Compressors	12	$B$8>=0	Not Binding	12
$C$8	Units to Manufacture Medium Compressors	12	$C$8>=0	Not Binding	12
$D$8	Units to Manufacture Heavy Compressors	50	$D$8>=0	Not Binding	50
$E$8	Units to Manufacture Ultra Compressors	25	$E$8>=0	Not Binding	25
$D$8	Units to Manufacture Heavy Compressors	50	$D$8>=20	Not Binding	30
$C$8	Units to Manufacture Medium Compressors	12	$C$8<=12	Binding	0
$B$8	Units to Manufacture Light Compressors	12	$B$8<=12	Binding	0
$B$8	Units to Manufacture Light Compressors	12	$B$8<=50	Not Binding	38
$C$8	Units to Manufacture Medium Compressors	12	$C$8<=50	Not Binding	38
$D$8	Units to Manufacture Heavy Compressors	50	$D$8<=50	Binding	0
$E$8	Units to Manufacture Ultra Compressors	25	$E$8<=50	Not Binding	25

Compressor Production Planning / Scenario Summary / Answer Report 1 / Answer Report 2

FIGURE 8-75a Answer Report

Instructions: Start Excel and perform the following tasks.

1. Open the Grouse Products workbook from the Data Disk. If you do not have a copy of the Data Disk, then see the inside back cover of this book.
2. Use Solver to determine the mix of products that maximizes the number of units produced in the week. The total amount of labor hours available in the first week of November is 2,400 hours, and $23,000 worth of materials is available. Use the Assume Linear Model option in Solver. Instruct Solver to create an answer report if it can find a solution to the problem. Figure 8-75a shows the values that Solver should find. If necessary, change the assumptions for the Hours of Labor per Unit in cells B5:E5 to show the values of 15 for Light Compressors, 22 for Medium Compressors, 25 for Heavy Compressors, and 27 for Ultra Compressors.

In the Lab

3. Save the current worksheet as a scenario named `November, Week 1`. The Changing cells are B5:E6 and B8:E8.
4. Enter your name, course, laboratory assignment number (Lab 8-2), date, and instructor's name in the range A13:A17. Print the worksheet.
5. The company president feels that perhaps the assumptions about how many labor hours it takes to produce certain products is not correct. The new assumptions are that Light Compressors takes 17 labor hours to produce, Medium Compressors takes 15 hours to produce, 31 for Heavy Compressors, and Ultra Compressors takes 25 hours to produce. Enter these new values in the worksheet.
6. Use Solver to find a solution to the problem. Instruct Solver to create an Answer Report if it can find a solution to the problem. Solver should report that the optimal number of units of Light Compressors 1 is 12, of Medium Compressors is 12, of Heavy Compressors is 24, and of Ultra Compressors is 38.
7. Save the current worksheet as a scenario named `November, Week 2`. Print the worksheet and the Answer Report (Figure 8-75a).
8. Create a Scenario Summary (Figure 8-75b) showing the two scenarios that you have saved in Scenario Manager.
9. Save the workbook with the password, lab8-2, and with the file name, Grouse Products2. Print the Scenario Summary worksheet.

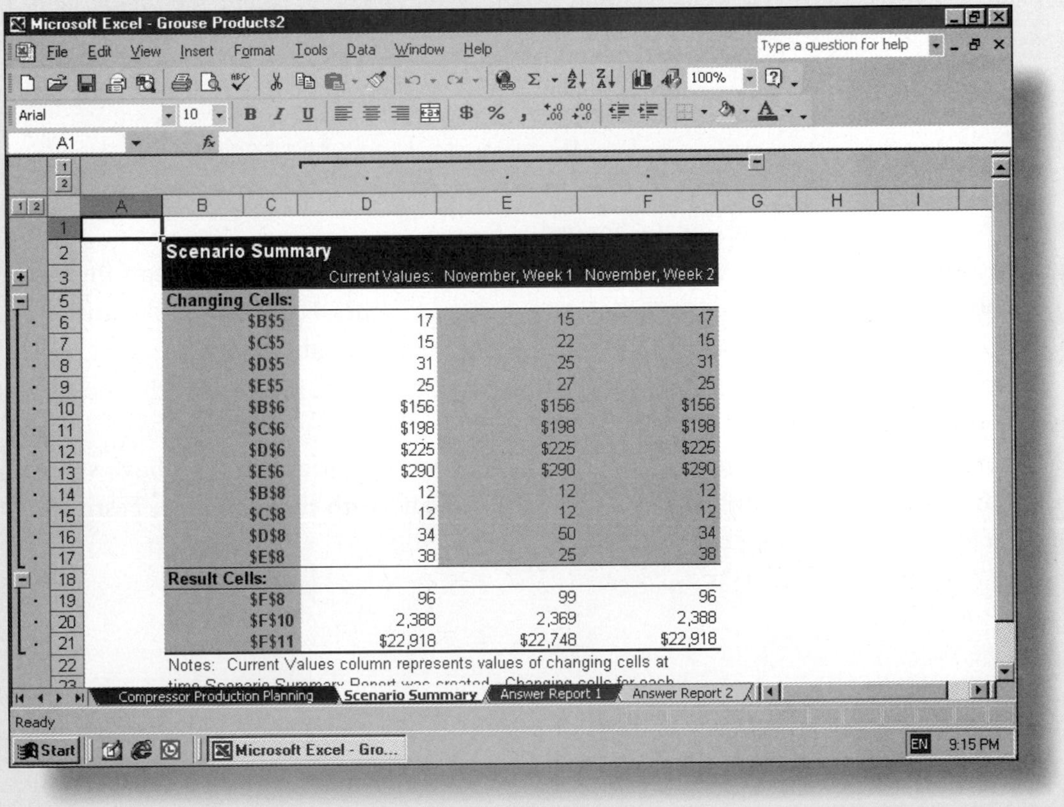

Scenario Summary

	Current Values:	November, Week 1	November, Week 2
Changing Cells:			
$B$5	17	15	17
$C$5	15	22	15
$D$5	31	25	31
$E$5	25	27	25
$B$6	$156	$156	$156
$C$6	$198	$198	$198
$D$6	$225	$225	$225
$E$6	$290	$290	$290
$B$8	12	12	12
$C$8	12	12	12
$D$8	34	50	34
$E$8	38	25	38
Result Cells:			
$F$8	96	99	96
$F$10	2,388	2,369	2,388
$F$11	$22,918	$22,748	$22,918

Notes: Current Values column represents values of changing cells at

FIGURE 8-75b Scenario Summary

In the Lab

3 Finding the Optimal Advertising Mix

Problem: Your town holds two annual festivals each summer, one in June and one in August. The town manager would like you to help determine how to best promote the events through advertisements in a variety of media. The town board has identified a local newspaper, a local radio station, and the local cable television station as advertising targets. Each type of media claims to be able to target a certain number of individuals in the town's target audience with each advertisement. The town hopes to attract as many people from other local communities as from the town itself. Each media type has a limit on how many advertisements can be placed each month leading up to the festival and the prices vary from month to month.

Instructions: Start Excel and perform the following tasks.

1. Open the Festivals2003 workbook from the Data Disk.
2. Use Solver to determine the best mix of advertising for the festival in the June. The advertising budget for the first festival is $10,500. The newspaper allows a maximum of fourteen ads per week, the radio station allows a maximum of thirty advertisement spots per week, and the cable television station allows a maximum of twenty one advertisements per week. The costs for the month of June are already in the worksheet. Use the Assume Linear Model option in Solver. Instruct Solver to create an answer report if it can find a solution to the problem. Figure 8-76a shows the values that Solver should find for this situation.
3. Save the current worksheet as a scenario named `June 2003 Festival`. The Changing cells are B6:D6 and B9:D9.
4. Enter your name, course, laboratory assignment number (Lab 8-3), date, and instructor's name in the range B15:B19. Print the worksheet and the Answer Report.
5. The festival in August is much larger and is allocated a budget of $23,500. Radio advertisements will cost $355 each for that month and cable television advertisements will also cost $850 for that week. The cost of newspaper advertisements remains unchanged.
6. Use Solver to solve the problem. Instruct Solver to create an answer report if it can find a solution to the problem. Solver should find that the optimal combination reaches 187,000 people, and includes fourteen newspaper advertisements, one radio advertisements, and twenty cable television advertisements.
7. Save the current worksheet as a scenario named `August 2003 Festival`. Print the worksheet and the Answer Report (Figure 8-76a).
8. Create a Scenario Summary (Figure 8-76b) showing the two scenarios that you have saved in Scenario Manager. Save the workbook with the password, lab8-3, and with the file name, Festivals2003-2. Print the Scenario Summary.

In the Lab

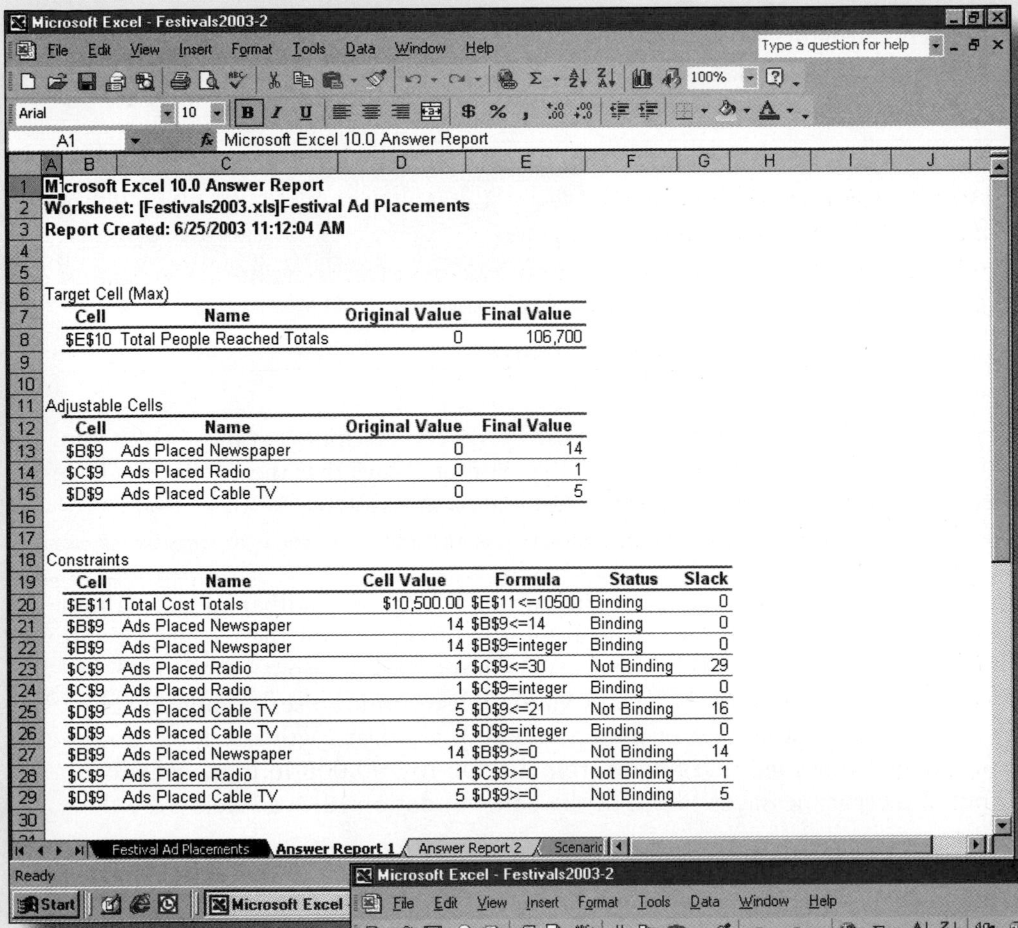

Target Cell (Max)

Cell	Name	Original Value	Final Value
$E$10	Total People Reached Totals	0	106,700

Adjustable Cells

Cell	Name	Original Value	Final Value
$B$9	Ads Placed Newspaper	0	14
$C$9	Ads Placed Radio	0	1
$D$9	Ads Placed Cable TV	0	5

Constraints

Cell	Name	Cell Value	Formula	Status	Slack
$E$11	Total Cost Totals	$10,500.00	$E$11<=10500	Binding	0
$B$9	Ads Placed Newspaper	14	$B$9<=14	Binding	0
$B$9	Ads Placed Newspaper	14	$B$9=integer	Binding	0
$C$9	Ads Placed Radio	1	$C$9<=30	Not Binding	29
$C$9	Ads Placed Radio	1	$C$9=integer	Binding	0
$D$9	Ads Placed Cable TV	5	$D$9<=21	Not Binding	16
$D$9	Ads Placed Cable TV	5	$D$9=integer	Binding	0
$B$9	Ads Placed Newspaper	14	$B$9>=0	Not Binding	14
$C$9	Ads Placed Radio	1	$C$9>=0	Not Binding	1
$D$9	Ads Placed Cable TV	5	$D$9>=0	Not Binding	5

(a) Answer Report

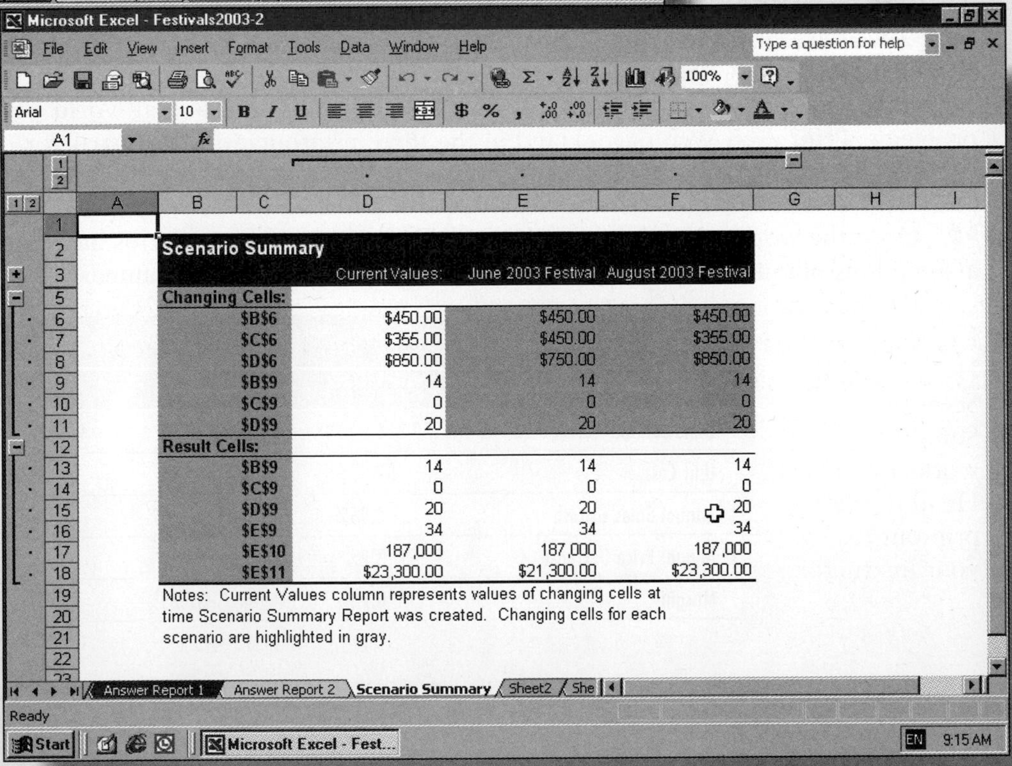

	Current Values:	June 2003 Festival	August 2003 Festival
Changing Cells:			
$B$6	$450.00	$450.00	$450.00
$C$6	$355.00	$450.00	$355.00
$D$6	$850.00	$750.00	$850.00
$B$9	14	14	14
$C$9	0	0	0
$D$9	20	20	20
Result Cells:			
$B$9	14	14	14
$C$9	0	0	0
$D$9	20	20	20
$E$9	34	34	34
$E$10	187,000	187,000	187,000
$E$11	$23,300.00	$21,300.00	$23,300.00

Notes: Current Values column represents values of changing cells at time Scenario Summary Report was created. Changing cells for each scenario are highlighted in gray.

(b) Scenario Summary

FIGURE 8-76

Cases and Places

The difficulty of these case studies varies:
◗ are the least difficult; ◗◗ are more difficult; and ◗◗◗ are the most difficult.

1 ◗ Cillan Snacks has purchased access to 21 square feet of shelf space in a local grocery store to test market two new items to local consumers. Table 8-5 shows the two items, their profitability per item, and how much space each item takes up. The marketing department wants to be sure that at least 15 of each item are on the shelf. If one of the items sells rapidly, the marketing department wants to be certain that the most profitable combination of items is on the shelf as well. Create a worksheet with the necessary information and use Solver to determine the most profitable combination of items to place on the shelves. Create an Answer Report that shows that the constraints have been met. Print the worksheet and Answer Report and hand them in to your instructor.

TABLE 8-5 Snack Marketing Information

SNACK NAME	PROFIT PER ITEM	SQUARE FEET PER ITEM
Banana Mango Chips	$1.52	.23
Papaya Chips	$1.79	.34

2 ◗ Open the workbook Hyperlink on the Data Disk. Use the Formula Auditing toolbar to learn about the worksheet. Trace 4 levels of precedents for cell H14, the Total Net Income. Print the worksheet with the arrows and hand it in to your instructor. Use Data Validation to limit a user's input on cell B19, the Commission, to a decimal value between 1 and 12. Use Data Validation to limit a user's input on cell B22, the Revenue for Bonus, to a decimal value greater than 5,000,000. Use Data Validation to allow the worksheet user to select a Bonus from a list that ranges from 50,000 to 100,000 in increments of 10,000. Add appropriate input and error messages for all of the data validation rules as well. Save the worksheet as Hyperlink2.

3 ◗ Using a browser search engine, such as Yahoo!, type the keywords Linear Programming. Visit three Web pages that discuss how Linear Programming is used in real world situations to solve business problems. Print each Web page. Hand in the three printouts to your instructor.

4 ◗◗ Open the workbook e-book on the Data Disk. Create four scenarios based on four different planning assumptions outlined in Table 8-6. Create a Scenario Summary that summarizes the result cells of B17, C17, D17, E17, F17, G17, and H17. Print the Scenario Summary worksheet. Hand in the printout to your instructor.

TABLE 8-6

ASSUMPTION	SCENARIO 1	SCENARIO 2	SCENARIO 3	SCENARIO 4
Units Sold in Year 2002	9,372,859	8,322,338	9,492,016	8,322,338
Unit Cost	$7.23	$7.23	$8.34	$8.34
Annual Sales Growth	5.95%	6.25%	3.45%	5.25%
Annual Price Decrease	3.2%	3.2%	5.5%	2.40%
Margin	40.75%	37.75%	37.75%	42.5%

Microsoft Excel 2002

PROJECT 9

Importing Data, Routing Changes, PivotCharts, PivotTables, and Trendlines

OBJECTIVES

You will have mastered the material in this project when you can:

- Import data from a text file
- Import data from an Access database
- Import data from a Web page
- Import data from spreadsheet XML
- Replicate formulas
- Insert, edit, and remove a comment
- Explain collaboration techniques
- Track changes and share a workbook
- Route a workbook to other users
- Accept and reject tracked changes made to a workbook
- Create and format a PivotChart and PivotTable
- Analyze worksheet data using a PivotChart
- Analyze worksheet data using a PivotTable
- Analyze worksheet data using a trendline
- Merge shared workbooks
- Add a trendline to a chart
- Explain the concept of exporting data from a workbook

From Dots and Dashes to the Internet

Electronic Data Transfer From Morse Code to the Internet

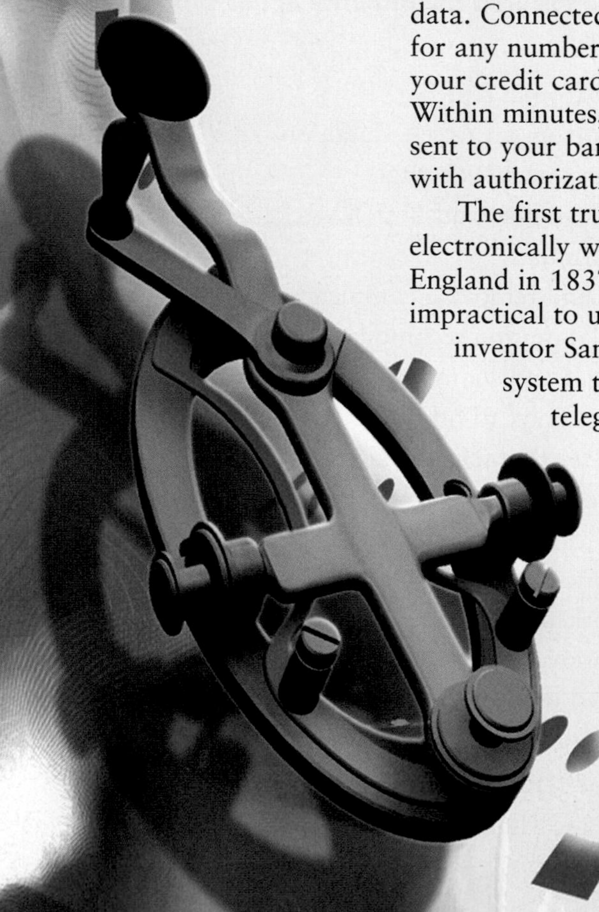

In recent years, daily Internet transactions have become commonplace, making it possible for people to transfer electronically vast amounts of critical business and personal data. Connected to the Web, you can conduct a quick search for any number of online businesses, place orders, and enter your credit card information in a form on a Web page. Within minutes, the data necessary to complete your order is sent to your bank for verification, returned to the e-retailer with authorization codes, and your order is complete.

The first truly successful system for transmitting data electronically was the telegraph, which began operating in England in 1837. The complexity of this system made it impractical to use on a large scale. Not until American inventor Samuel Morse developed a simpler telegraph system that required only a single wire was the telegraph widely used across the United States.

Morse's system enabled an operator to use a device to create or break a flow of electric current between a telegraph machine's battery and its receiver. On the receiving end, the electric current powered an electromagnet that attracted a small armature when a signal was received. The armature produced a series of dots and dashes that could be decoded by a telegraph operator using Morse code, which Morse himself developed.

To create this code, Morse studied a printer's type box to determine the most frequently used letters in English. He assigned these letters the shortest possible patterns of dots and dashes. The letter, e, for instance, is represented by a single dot. The letter, t, is signified by a single dash. In this way, Morse created a code that enabled telegraph operators to send messages across vast distances easily and decode messages reliably.

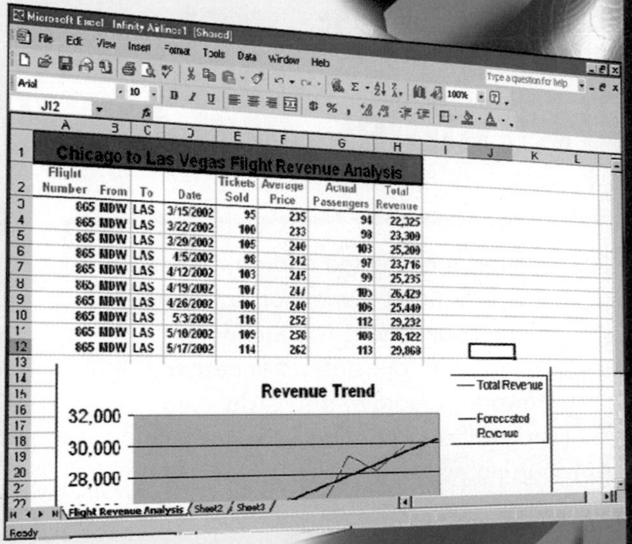

By 1837, Morse sent a signal across ten miles. Gradually, transmission signals reached greater distances. On May 24, 1844, Morse sent a message over the first official telegraph link, which ran between Baltimore, Maryland, and Washington, D.C. His message simply said, "What hath God wrought!"

Although the Internet has far outpaced the telegraph in terms of its capability of sending and receiving all kinds of data, its basic purpose remains the same: it enables people to send and receive data electronically with a minimum of error.

Today, companies such as Triangle Environmental rely on the Internet to transmit critical business data across the nation. Triangle Environmental field technicians use the company's testing equipment to verify that gas station storage tanks meet federal environmental regulations. Field technicians enter test results into Excel worksheets using notebook computers. When a test is complete, technicians upload the data via a Web page. The data is received and handled by lab technicians who use the data to prepare reports for the state to certify compliance with current regulations. Electronic data transfer is the heart of the company.

In the connected world of the twenty-first century, the ability to use and analyze data from a variety of sources is a necessity, and the Internet has provided an important means to move that data reliably from person to person, place to place.

Microsoft Excel 2002

Importing Data, Routing Changes, PivotCharts, PivotTables, and Trendlines

PROJECT

9

CASE PERSPECTIVE

Gene Curry created and now manages a not-for-profit foundation called the Curry Foundation. The foundation operates in four states: Minnesota, Nevada, Georgia, and Oklahoma. The state offices coordinate various fund-raising activities, including phonathons, direct-mail campaigns, and a yearly banquet. Gene suspects that the effectiveness of certain activities is changing.

Gene has requested the individual Curry Foundation state offices send information regarding each office's fund-raising efforts along with other profile information. Gene has asked you, his assistant, to gather this information and produce some supporting documentation that will either confirm or reject his suspicions. Gene would like the data in a concise, easy-to-read format so he can share the findings with the board of directors. Each state has sent its information in different formats, because each state office operates independently of the foundation headquarters.

With your Excel background, you realize that PivotTables and PivotCharts would be helpful. Gene also has requested an analysis of expenses over the past years, which you know can be analyzed with a trendline.

Introduction

In today's diverse business environment, the ability to use and analyze data from a wide variety of sources is a necessity. In this project, you will learn how to **import**, or bring, data from various external sources into an Excel worksheet (Figure 9-1f) and then analyze that data.

Suppose you routinely conduct business with an organization that stores data in text format (Figure 9-1a on page E 9.06) rather than in a workbook. To make use of that data, you first input the data, and then format and manipulate it. Businesses also receive data in various database formats, such as Microsoft Access tables (Figure 9-1b), and from Web pages (Figure 9-1c). Finally, businesses routinely receive data in various XML formats, such as spreadsheet XML (Figure 9-1d).

Businesses often create charts to represent data visually. One way to analyze data visually is through the use of PivotCharts, PivotTables, and trendlines. A **PivotChart** (Figure 9-1g) is an interactive chart that provides the user with ways to graphically analyze data by varying the fields and categories to present different views. For example, if the Curry Foundation wanted to display a pie chart showing percentages of donations from each state, a PivotChart could display that percentage using any field such as total donations for a year or total donations for certain campaign types for a year.

Excel creates and associates a PivotTable with every PivotChart. A **PivotTable** (Figure 9-1h) is an interactive view of worksheet data that gives you the ability to summarize the database and then rotate the table's row and column titles to show different views of the summarized data. An inexperienced user with little knowledge of formulas, functions, and ranges can employ powerful what-if analyses of the data simply by clicking a field from a list of fields in a PivotChart or PivotTable. A **trendline** is a visual way to show how some particular data is changing over time. Excel can overlay a trendline on any chart, including a PivotChart.

Other techniques introduced in this project apply to issues of multiple users of the same workbook, including routing, tracking changes, and comments. If you want several people to look at a workbook and make comments, you can **route** it, or pass the workbook around, electronically. You can **track changes** to a workbook by displaying who changed what data, in which cell, and when. **Comments**, or descriptions, which do not regularly display as part of the worksheet data, can be added to the workbook itself to alert the recipients to special instructions, and later edited or deleted. Workbooks that have been saved and copied to others also can be merged. **Merging** allows you to bring together copies of workbooks that others have worked on independently.

Project Nine — Curry Foundation Analysis

From your meeting with Gene Curry, you have accumulated the following workbook specifications:

Need: Import data from the four states in which the Curry Foundation operates (Figures 9-1a, 9-1b, 9-1c, and 9-1d on the next two pages) into a worksheet containing headings and formulas, but no data (Figure 9-1e on the next page). Once the data is imported, the formulas in cells H3 and I3 must be copied to each row of data (Figure 9-1f on page E 9.07). After the import is complete, the data in the worksheet requires verification by the state coordinators. A PivotChart (Figure 9-1g on page E 9.07) and its associated PivotTable (Figure 9-1h on page E 9.07) allow interactive views of the data from the worksheet.

Source of Data: The four state coordinators for the Curry Foundation will submit data from their respective states via a text file (Minnesota), an Access database (Nevada), a Web page (Georgia), and spreadsheet XML (Oklahoma).

Calculations: The formulas used to calculate average donation per donor in the 2004 and 2003 are in cells H3 and I3 of the worksheet (Figure 9-1d). The formulas divide donation amounts for each year by the number of donor for a particular fund raising campaign each year. After importing the data, the formulas need to be copied down for all rows of data.

Special Requirements: Before creating the PivotChart and PivotTable, route the workbook with the imported data (Figure 9-1f) to the four state coordinators for verification and then accept tracked changes.

Chart Requirements: Create a PivotChart (Figure 9-1g) and associated PivotTable (Figure 9-1h) that analyze donations based on any combination of states and campaigns.

More About

External Data

Imported data that maintains a refreshable link to its external source is called external data. When you use external data, your worksheet also will update whenever a change is made to the original file. You can choose when and how the data is refreshed.

More About

Importing Data

If your system contains only a minimum installation of Excel, the first time you use one of the import features, Excel may attempt to install MSQuery. MSQuery is the supplemental application included in Microsoft Office XP, used to retrieve data from external data sources.

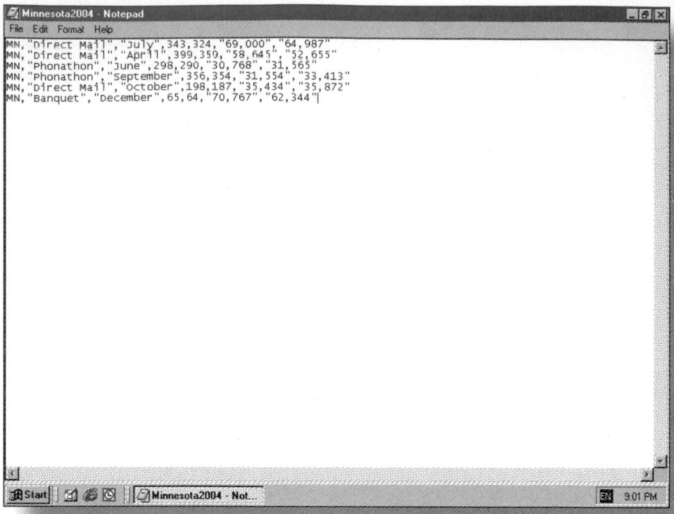
Minnesota2004 - Notepad
File Edit Format Help
MN,"Direct Mail","July",343,324,"69,000","64,987"
MN,"Direct Mail","April",399,359,"58,645","52,655"
MN,"Phonathon","June",298,290,"30,768","31,565"
MN,"Phonathon","September",356,354,"31,554","33,413"
MN,"Direct Mail","October",198,187,"35,434","35,872"
MN,"Banquet","December",65,64,"70,767","62,344"
Start
Minnesota2004 - Not...
9:01 PM

(a) Text File

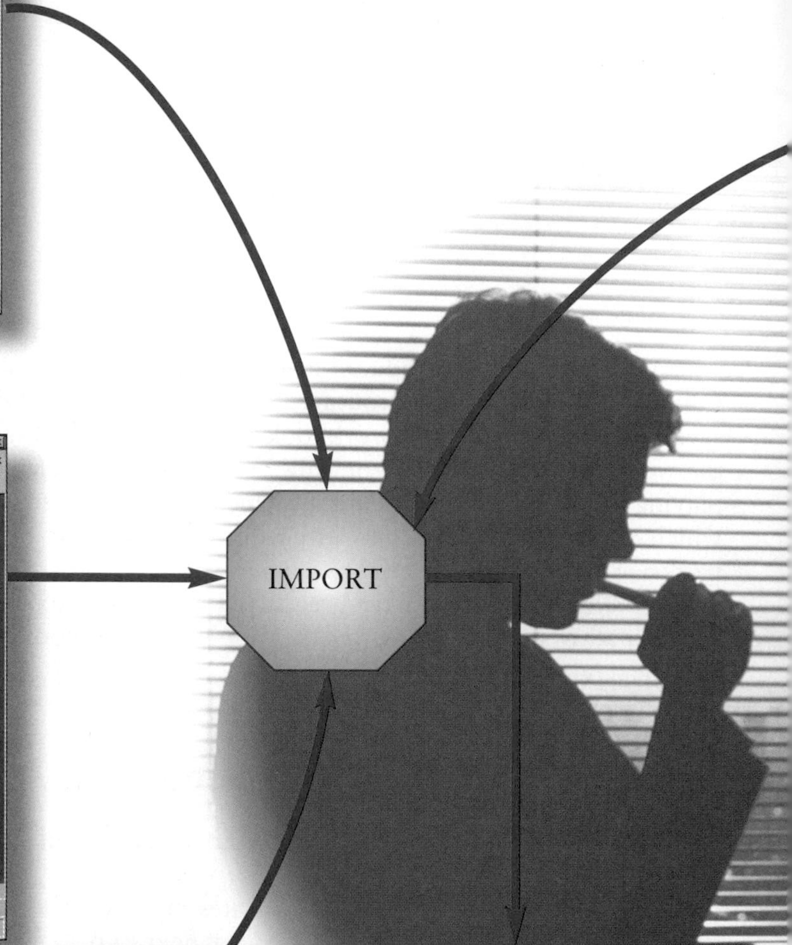
IMPORT

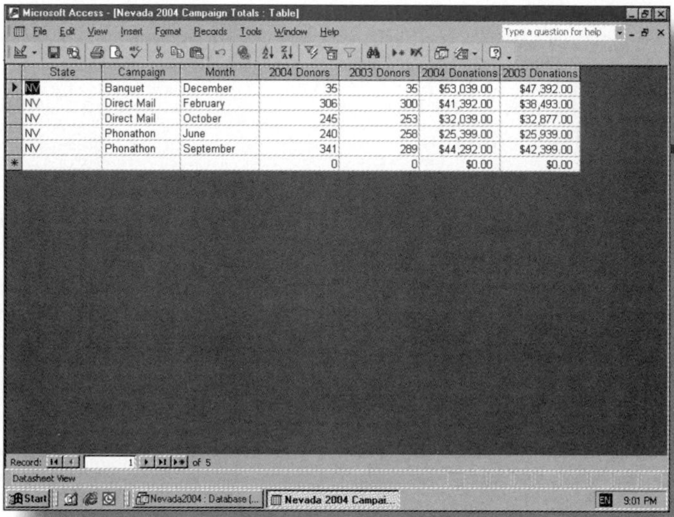
Microsoft Access - [Nevada 2004 Campaign Totals : Table]
File Edit View Insert Format Records Tools Window Help
Type a question for help
State | Campaign | Month | 2004 Donors | 2003 Donors | 2004 Donations | 2003 Donations
NV | Banquet | December | 35 | 35 | $53,039.00 | $47,392.00
NV | Direct Mail | February | 306 | 300 | $41,392.00 | $38,493.00
NV | Direct Mail | October | 245 | 253 | $32,039.00 | $32,877.00
NV | Phonathon | June | 240 | 258 | $25,399.00 | $25,939.00
NV | Phonathon | September | 341 | 289 | $44,292.00 | $42,399.00
0 | 0 | $0.00 | $0.00
Record: 1 of 5
Datasheet View
Start
Nevada2004 : Database (...
Nevada 2004 Campai...
9:01 PM

(b) Access File

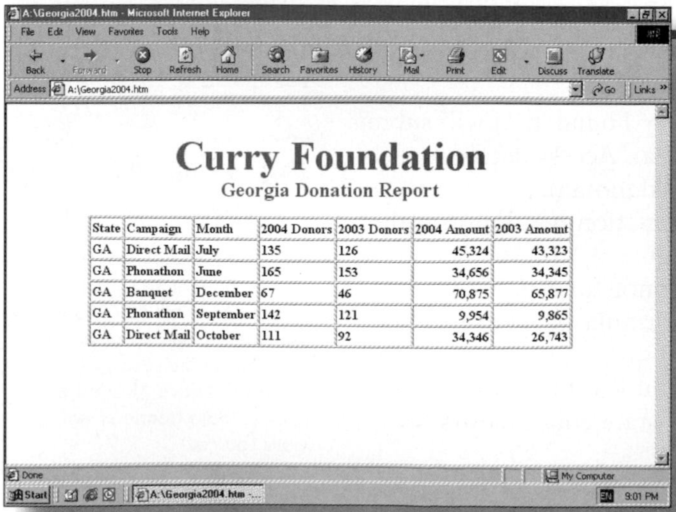
A:\Georgia2004.htm - Microsoft Internet Explorer
File Edit View Favorites Tools Help
Back Forward Stop Refresh Home Search Favorites History Mail Print Edit Discuss Translate
Address A:\Georgia2004.htm
Go Links
Curry Foundation
Georgia Donation Report
State | Campaign | Month | 2004 Donors | 2003 Donors | 2004 Amount | 2003 Amount
GA | Direct Mail | July | 135 | 126 | 45,324 | 43,323
GA | Phonathon | June | 165 | 153 | 34,656 | 34,345
GA | Banquet | December | 67 | 46 | 70,875 | 65,877
GA | Phonathon | September | 142 | 121 | 9,954 | 9,865
GA | Direct Mail | October | 111 | 92 | 34,346 | 26,743
Done
My Computer
Start
A:\Georgia2004.htm -...
9:01 PM

(c) HTML File

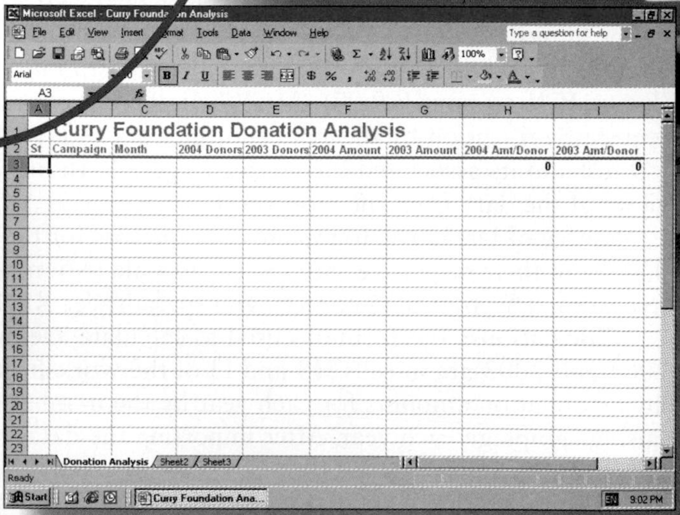
Microsoft Excel - Curry Foundation Analysis
File Edit View Insert Format Tools Data Window Help
Type a question for help
Arial
A3
Curry Foundation Donation Analysis
St | Campaign | Month | 2004 Donors | 2003 Donors | 2004 Amount | 2003 Amount | 2004 Amt/Donor | 2003 Amt/Donor
0
0
Donation Analysis / Sheet2 / Sheet3
Ready
Start
Curry Foundation Ana...
9:02 PM

(e) Worksheet Has No Data

FIGURE 9-1

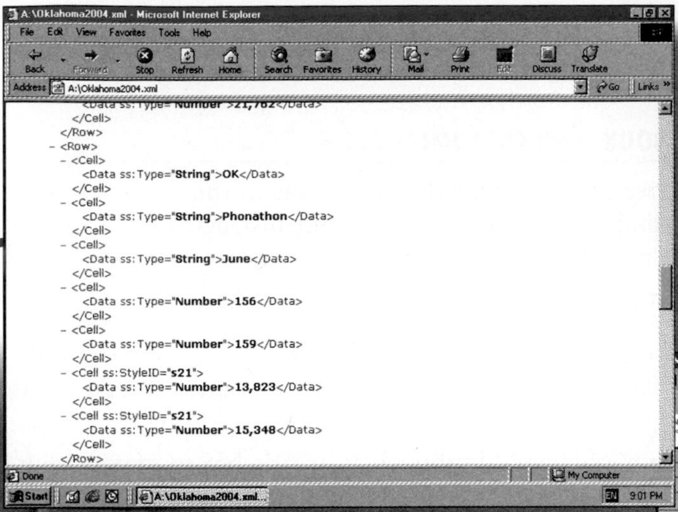

(d) Spreadsheet XML

(h) PivotTable

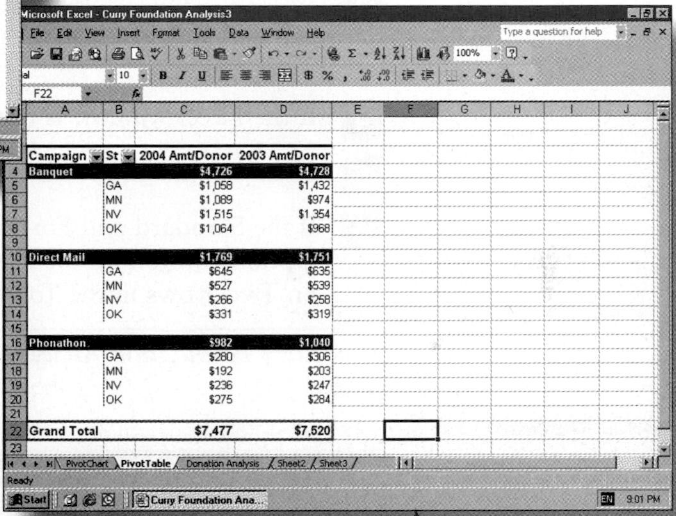

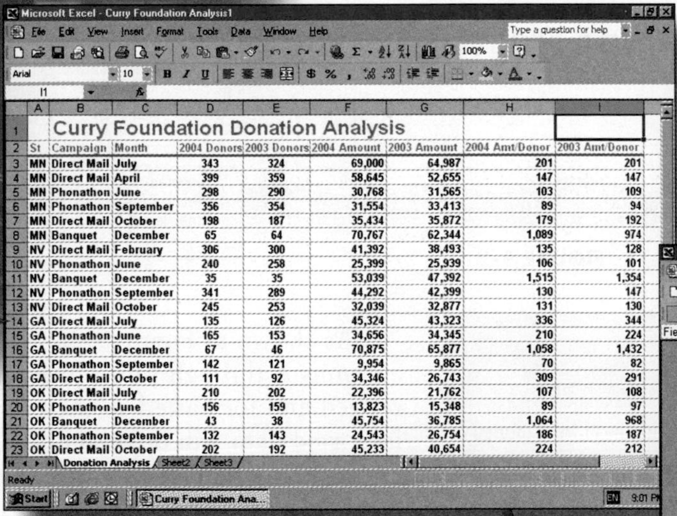

(f) Data Imported into Worksheet

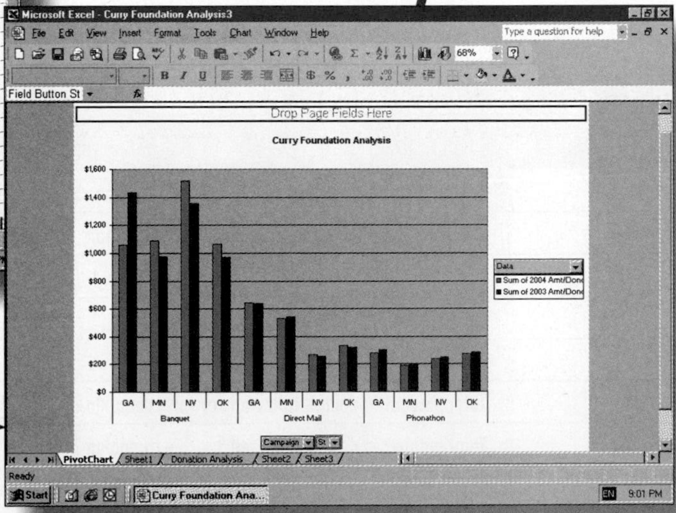

(g) PivotChart

Starting Excel and Opening a Workbook

Perform the following steps to start Excel, open the empty workbook, Curry Foundation Analysis, from the Data Disk, and reset the toolbars.

TO START EXCEL, OPEN A WORKBOOK, AND CUSTOMIZE EXCEL

1. Insert the Data Disk in drive A. See the inside back cover of this book for instructions for downloading the Data Disk or see your instructor for information on accessing the files required in this book.
2. Click the Start button on the taskbar and then click Open Office Document.
3. When the Open Office Document dialog box displays, click the Look in box arrow and then click 3½ Floppy (A:). Double-click Curry Foundation Analysis in the Look in list.
4. If the Excel window is not maximized, double-click its title bar to maximize it.
5. If the Language bar displays, click its Minimize button.
6. If the Standard and Formatting toolbars display on one row, click the Toolbar Options button on the right side of either toolbar and then click Show Buttons on Two Rows in the Toolbar Options list.

The Curry Foundation Analysis workbook displays in the Excel window (Figure 9-2).

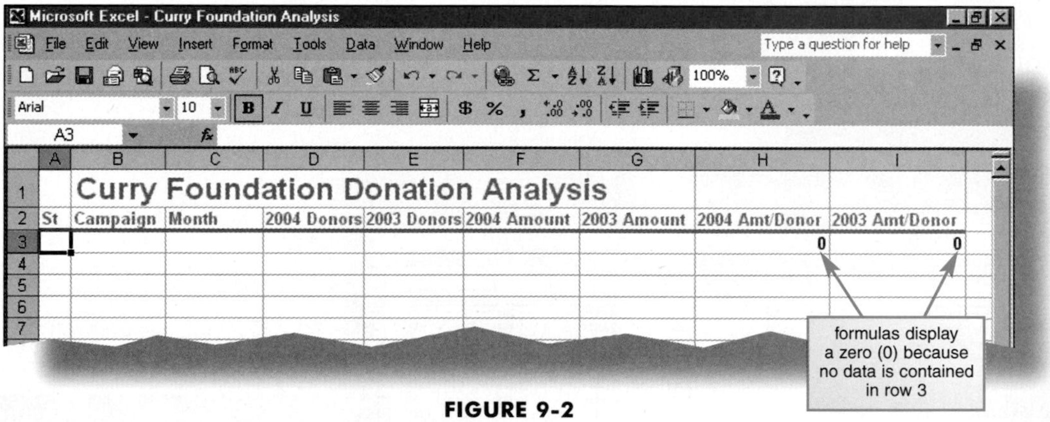

FIGURE 9-2

As shown in Figure 9-2, columns A through I have been resized and formatted so the imported data will be readable. Table 9-1 shows a summary of the data fields.

When you import data into a formatted worksheet, Excel formats the incoming data using the formats assigned to the cells as best it can.

Table 9-1 Curry Foundation Analysis Data Fields

NAME OF FIELD	*DATA DESCRIPTION*
St	Standard postal abbreviation for the name of the state in which the office is located
Campaign	The type of fundraising campaign (i.e., Phonathon, Banquet, or Direct Mail)
Month	Month in which the campaign occurred
2004 Donors	Number of donors for this campaign in 2004
2003 Donors	Number of donors for this campaign in 2003
2004 Amount	Total amount in dollars collected for this campaign in 2004
2003 Amount	Total amount in dollars collected for this campaign in 2003
2004 Amt/Donor	Average donation per donor for this campaign (2004 Amount/2004 Donors)
2003 Amt/Donor	Average donation per donor for this campaign (2003 Amount/2003 Donors)

Importing Files

Data may come to you from a variety of sources. Even though many users keep data in databases such as Microsoft Access, it is common to receive text files with fields of data separated by commas, especially from mainframe computer users. Also, with the increasing popularity of the World Wide Web, more companies are posting data on the Web. XML quickly is becoming a very popular format for data exchange. The ability to download data from the Web into an Excel worksheet is required. Importing data into Excel, rather than copying and pasting the data, also can create a refreshable link you may use to update data whenever the original file changes.

> **More About**
>
> **Opening a Text File in Excel**
>
> If you open a text file, such as Minnesota2004.txt, in Excel, the Text Import Wizard will start automatically. You then could make the same choices shown in the previous set of steps to import the data from the text file. To open a text file in Excel, you must choose Text Files or All Files in the Files of type box in the Open dialog box.

Importing Text Files

A **text file** contains electronic data created with little or no formatting. Many software applications, including Excel, offer an option to import data from a text file, also called an ASCII text file. **ASCII** stands for the American Standard Code for Information Interchange.

In text files, commas, tabs, or other characters often separate the fields. Alternately, the text file may have fields of equal length in columnar format. Each record usually exists on a separate line. A **delimited file** contains a selected character, such as a comma, to separate data fields. A **fixed width file** contains data fields of equal length in the records. In the case of a fixed width file, a special character need not separate the data fields. During the import process, Excel provides a preview to help you identify the type of text file with which you are working.

The following steps import a comma-delimited text file into the Curry Foundation Analysis workbook using the **Text Import Wizard**. The text file on the Data Disk contains data about fundraising campaigns in Minnesota for 2003 and 2004 (Figure 9-1a on page E 9.06).

Steps To Import Data from a Text File into a Worksheet

1 With the Curry Foundation Analysis worksheet active and the Data Disk in drive A, click cell A3, if necessary. Click Data on the menu bar. Point to Import External Data and then point to Import Data on the Import External Data submenu.

The Data menu and the Import External Data submenu display (Figure 9-3).

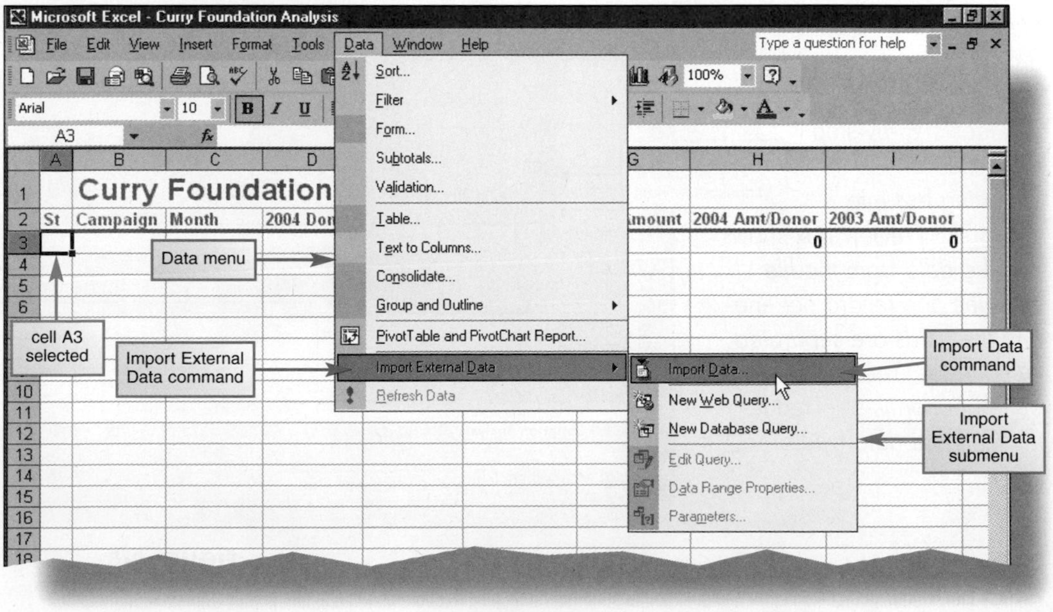

FIGURE 9-3

2 Click Import Data. When the Select Data Source dialog box displays, click the Look in box arrow, and then click 3½ Floppy (A:). Point to Minnesota2004.

The files on drive A display (Figure 9-4).

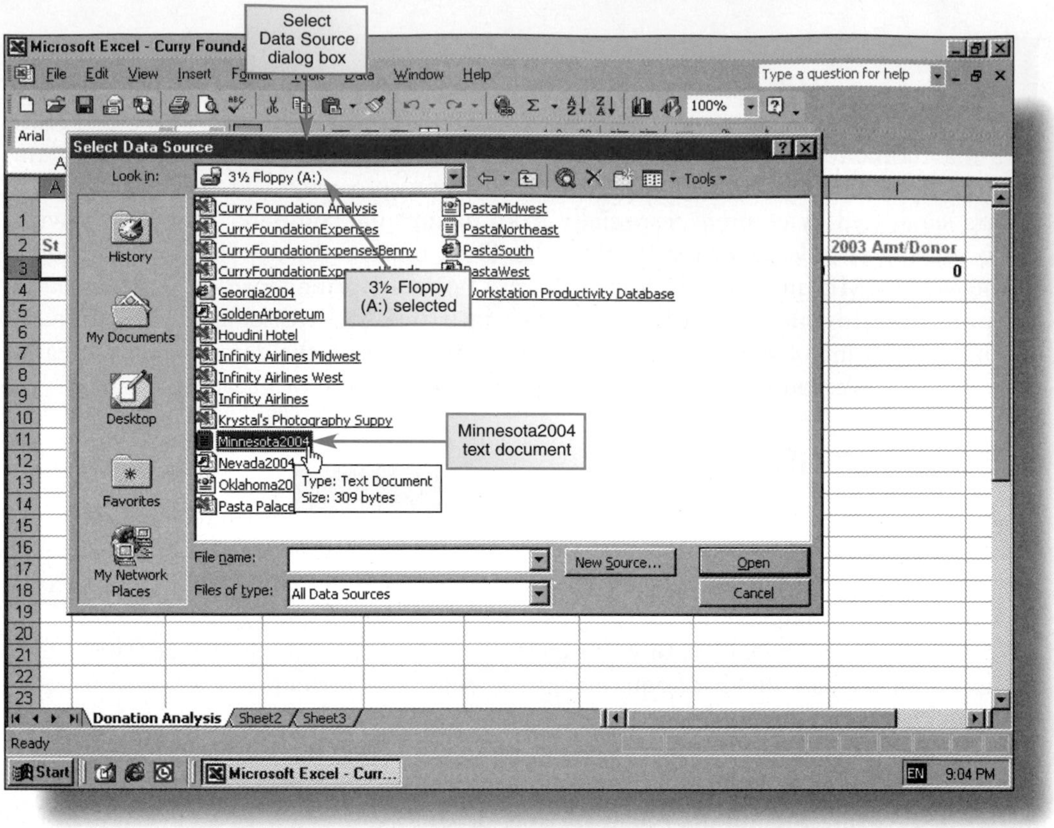

FIGURE 9-4

3 Double-click Minnesota2004. When the Text Import Wizard - Step 1 of 3 dialog box displays, point to Next button.

*Excel displays the Text Import Wizard - Step 1 of 3 dialog box (Figure 9-5). The **Text Import Wizard** provides step-by-step instruction on importing text into Excel. The Preview box shows that the data from the file contains one record per line and the fields are separated by commas. The Delimited option button is selected in the Original data type area.*

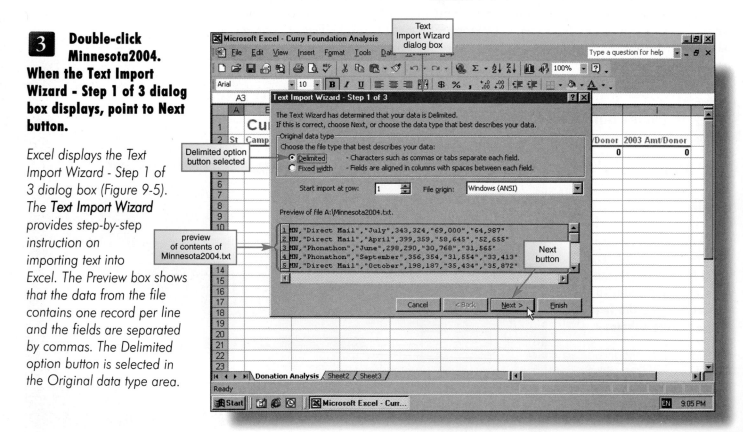

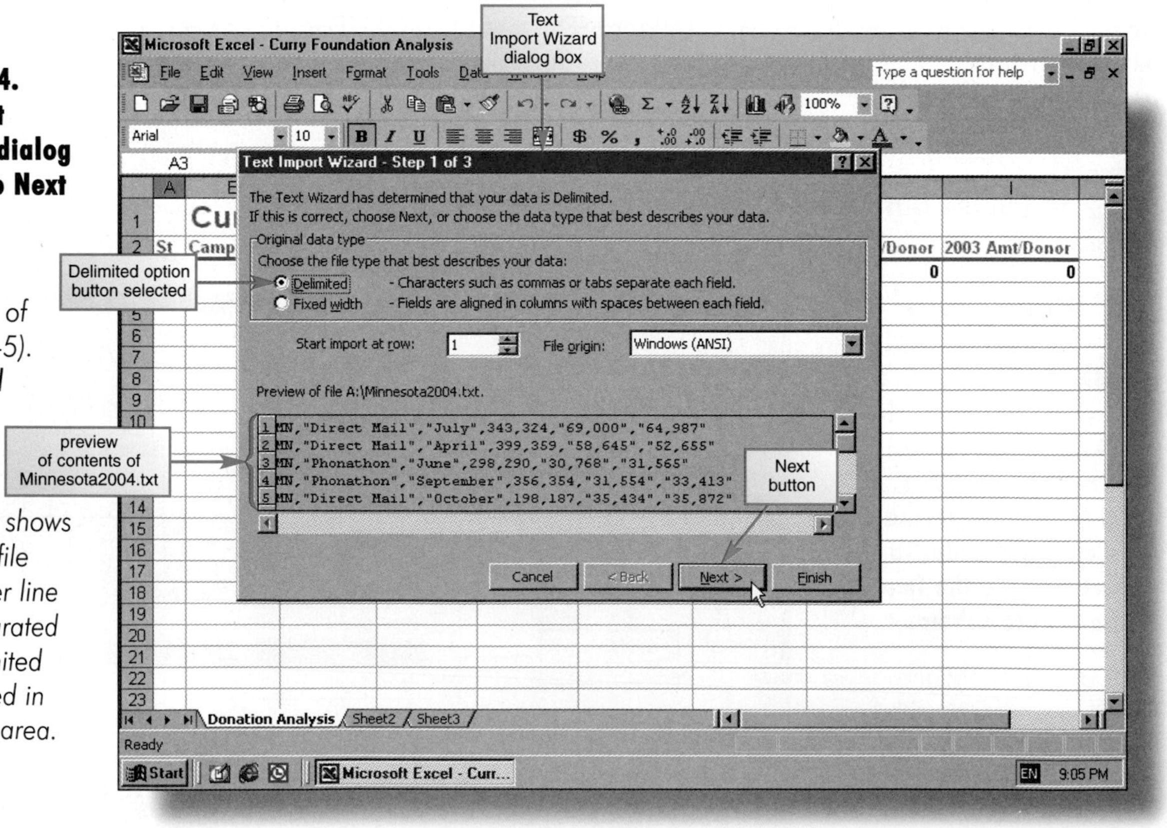

FIGURE 9-5

4 Click the Next button. When the Text Import Wizard - Step 2 of 3 dialog box displays, click Comma in the Delimiters area. Click Tab in the Delimiters area to clear the check box. Point to the Next button.

The Data preview area reflects the change (Figure 9-6). Excel correctly shows the fields of data in the Data preview area.

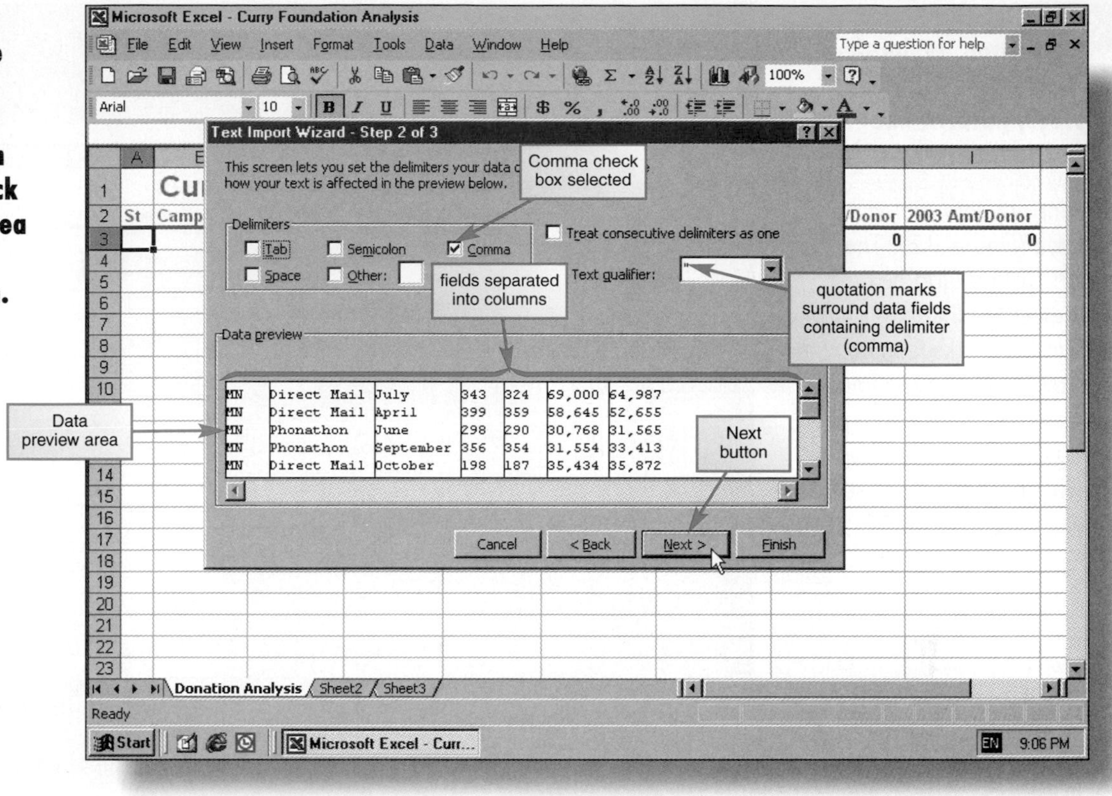

FIGURE 9-6

5 Click the Next button. When the Text Import Wizard - Step 3 of 3 dialog box displays, point to the Finish button.

The third dialog box of the Text Import Wizard displays (Figure 9-7). Step 3 allows you to select the format of each column of data. General is the default selection. The Data preview area shows the data separated based on the comma delimiter.

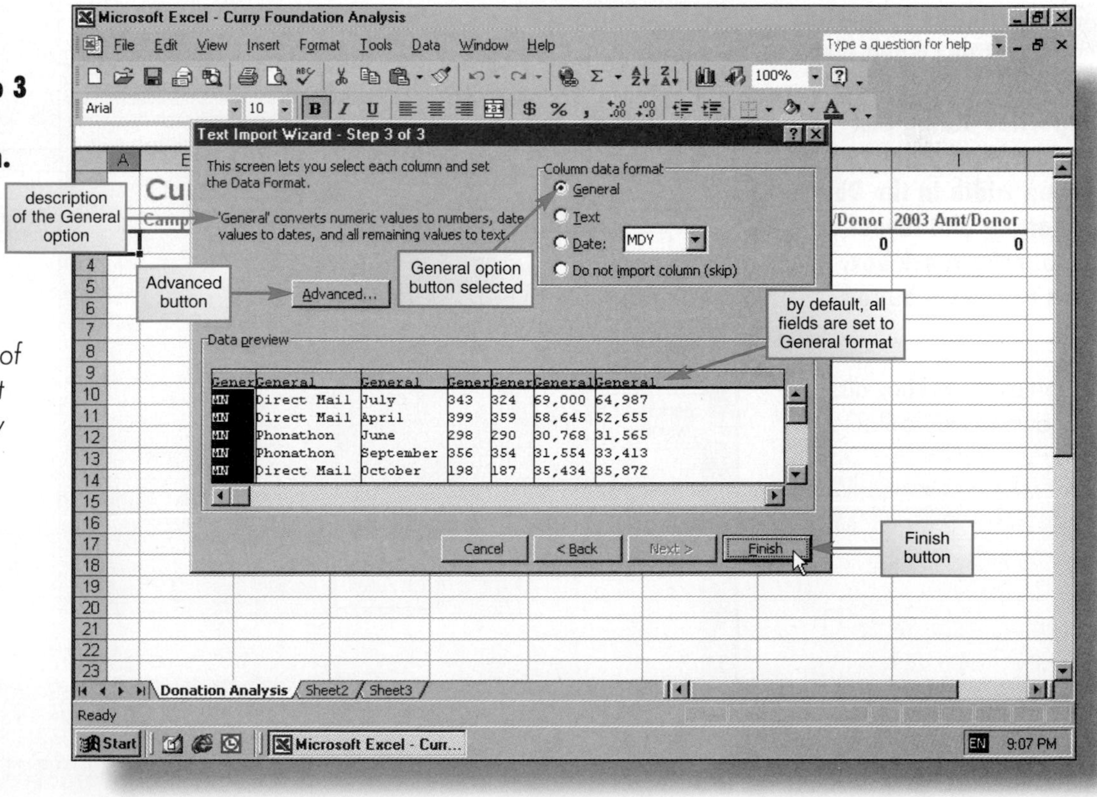

FIGURE 9-7

6 **Click the Finish button. When the Import Data dialog box displays, point to the Properties button.**

The Import Data dialog box displays (Figure 9-8). The Import Data dialog box lets you select the location of the data in the worksheet, as well as providing a way to tailor the data before importing it. Data will be imported beginning at cell A3. A marquee displays around cell A3.

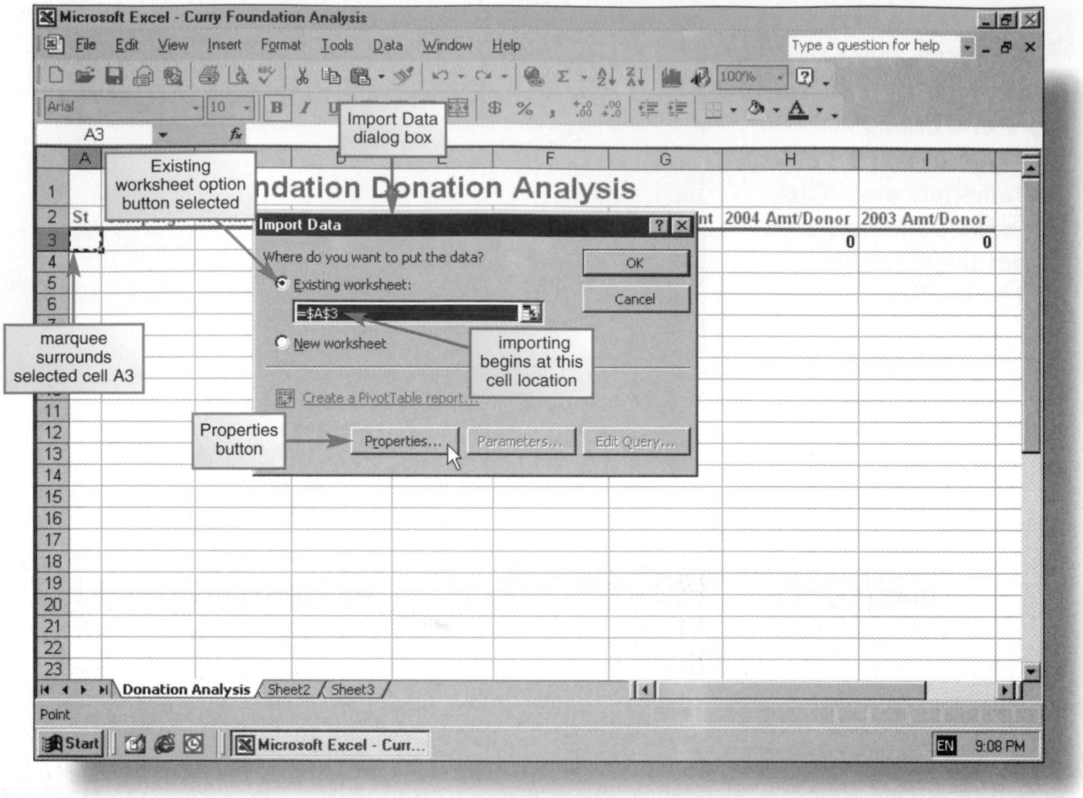

FIGURE 9-8

7 **Click the Properties button. When the External Data Range Properties dialog box displays, click Adjust column width in the Data formatting and layout area to clear the check box. Point to the OK button.**

The External Data Range Properties dialog box displays as shown in Figure 9-9.

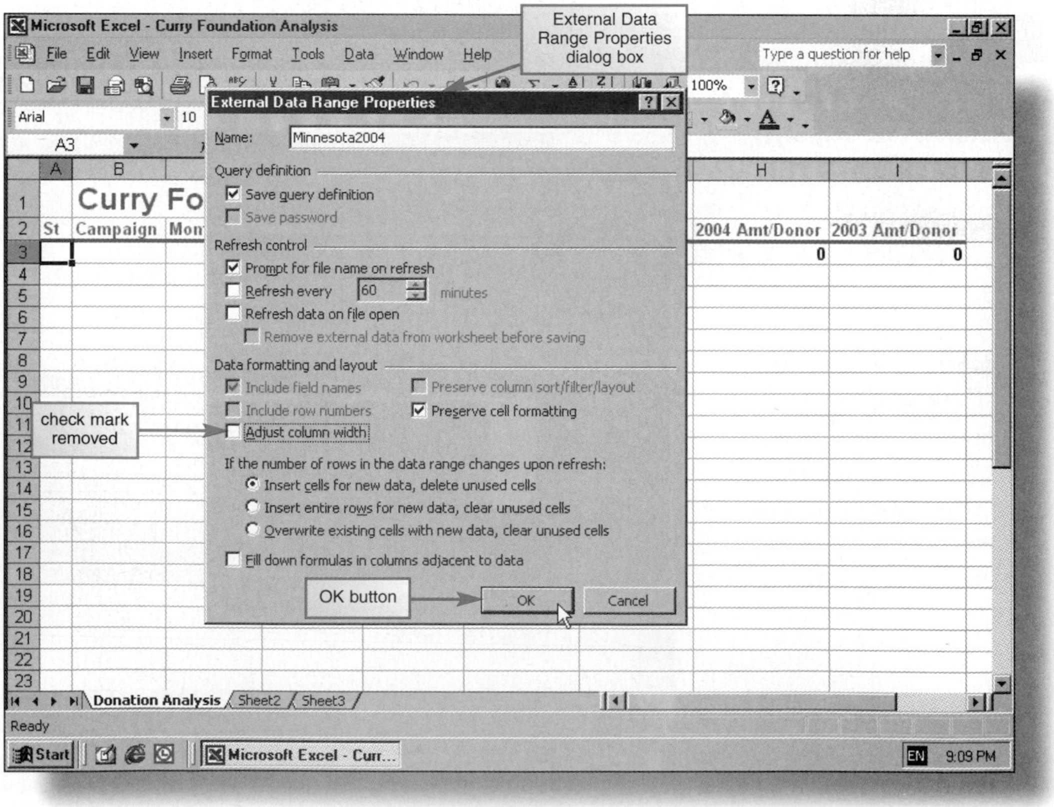

FIGURE 9-9

8 Click the OK button. When the Import Data dialog box displays, click the OK button. If the External Data toolbar displays on your screen, click its Close button.

Excel imports the data into the worksheet beginning at cell A3 (Figure 9-10).

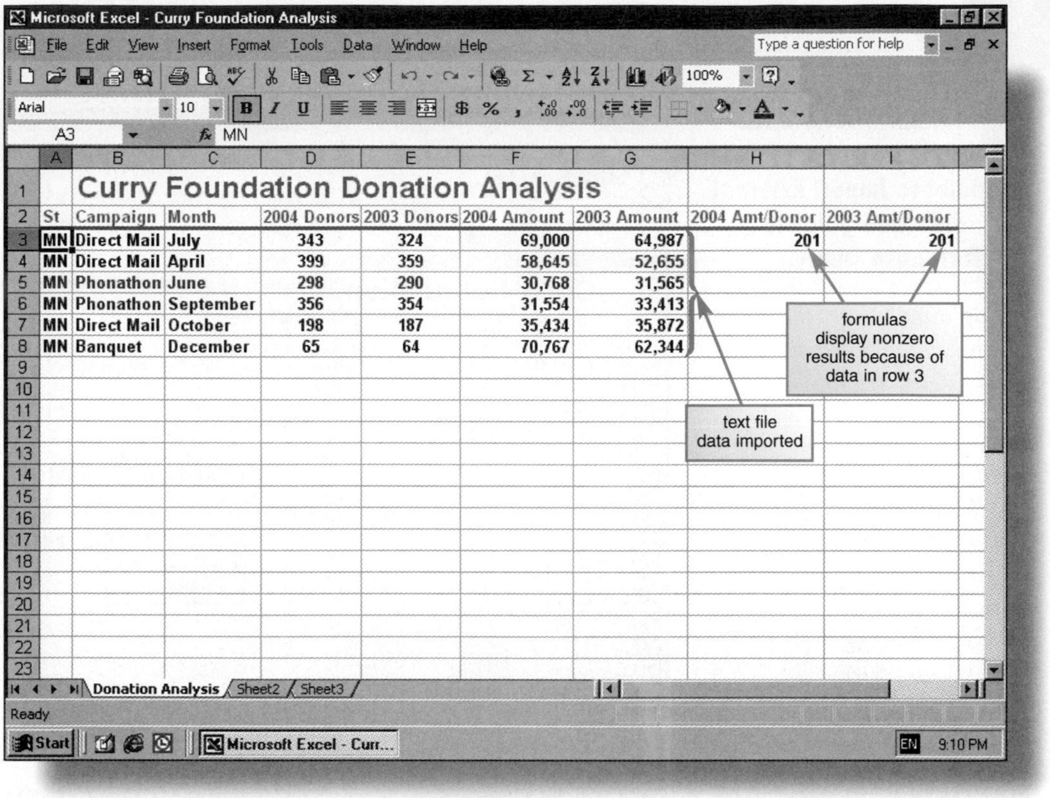

FIGURE 9-10

Other Ways

1. Press ALT+D, D, D
2. In Voice Command mode, say "Data, Import External Data, Import Data"

The commas in the last two columns of numbers in the Data preview area (Figure 9-7 on page E 9.11) are not considered to be delimiters because each of these data values was surrounded by quotation marks when the text file was created.

By default, the cell that is active when you perform the text import will become the upper-left cell of the imported range. If you want to import the data to a different location, you can specify the location in the Import Data dialog box (Figure 9-8).

By importing the text file, Excel can **refresh**, or update, the data whenever the original text file changes using the **Refresh Data command** on the Data menu.

Importing Access Tables

When you import data from an Access database, you start by making a query of the data. A **query** is a way to qualify the data you want to import by specifying a matching condition or asking a question of a database. You may choose to import the entire file or only a portion. For example, you can make a query to import only those records that pass a certain test, such as records containing numeric fields greater than a specific amount, or records containing text fields matching a specific value.

The following steps import an entire table from an Access database using the **Query Wizard**. The table in the Access database on the Data Disk contains data about fundraising campaigns in Nevada for 2003 and 2004 (Figure 9-1b on page E 9.06).

More About

Dragging and Dropping a Text File

You also can drag a text file to Excel. Simply drag the file name or the icon from its location to a blank worksheet. You then can format the data easily using the Text to Columns command on the Data menu. The data does not maintain a refreshable link to the text file.

Steps To Import Data from an Access Table into a Worksheet

1 Click cell A9. Click Data on the menu bar, point to Import External Data, and then point to New Database Query.

The Data menu and the Import External Data submenu display (Figure 9-11).

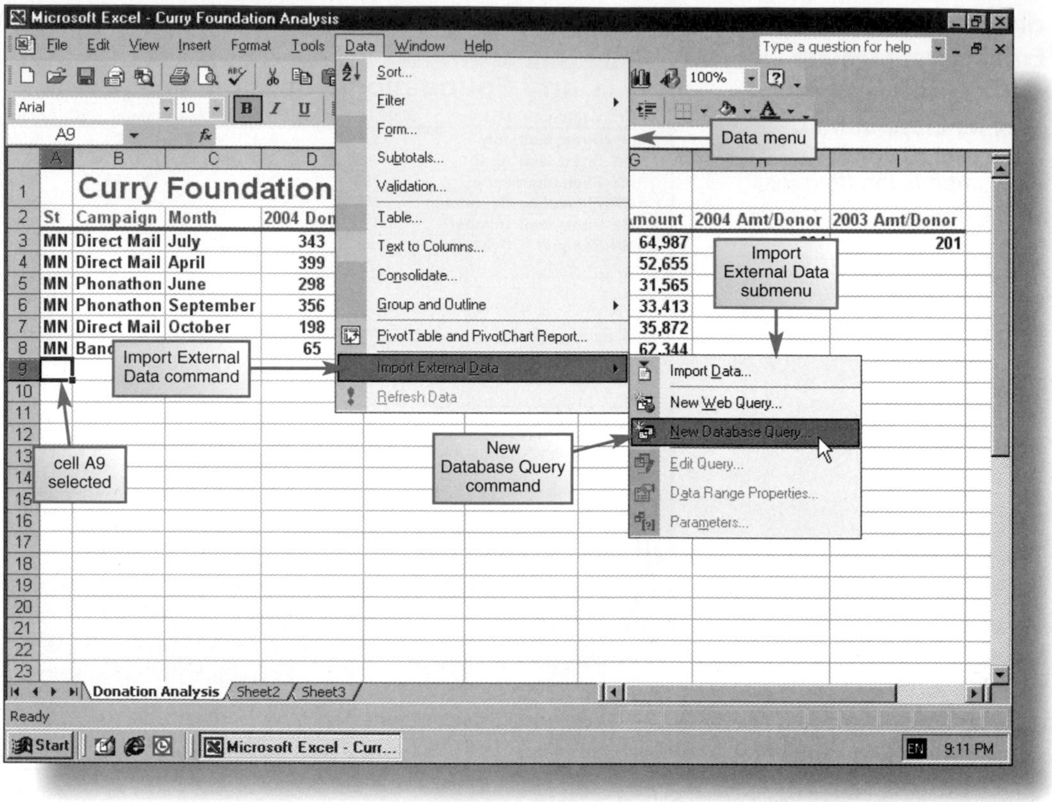

FIGURE 9-11

2 Click New Database Query. When the Choose Data Source dialog box displays, if necessary, click the Databases tab, and then click MS Access Database* in the list. Point to the OK button.

The Choose Data Source dialog box displays several database application formats (Figure 9-12). This list may differ on your computer. A check mark displays in the Use the Query Wizard to create/edit queries check box.

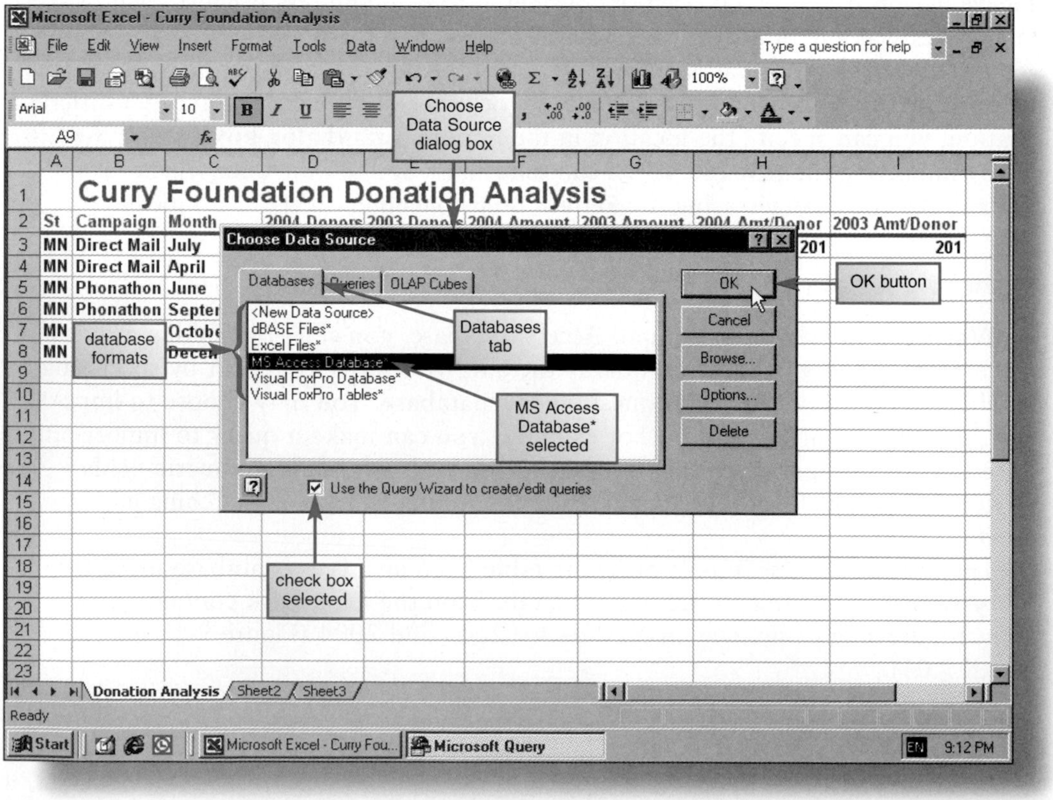

FIGURE 9-12

3 Click the OK button. When the Select Database dialog box displays, click the Drives box arrow and then click a. Point to nevada2004.mdb in the Database Name list.

The Select Database dialog box displays (Figure 9-13). Your system may not display the Connecting to data source progress box.

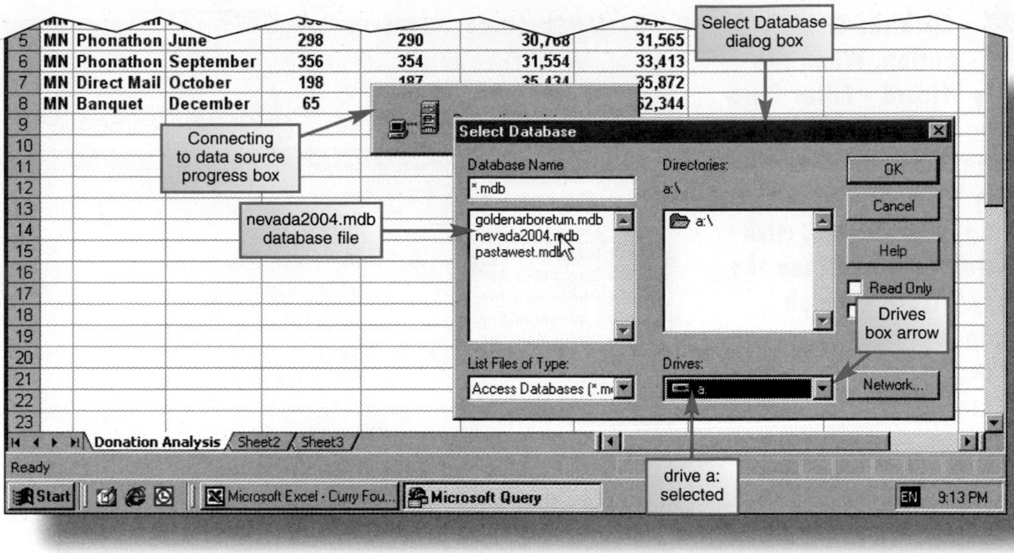

FIGURE 9-13

4 Double-click nevada2004.mdb. When the Query Wizard - Choose Columns dialog box displays, select the Nevada 2004 Campaign Totals table and then point to the Add Table button (Figure 9-14).

The database contains only one table to add to the query, which is listed in the Available tables and columns list.

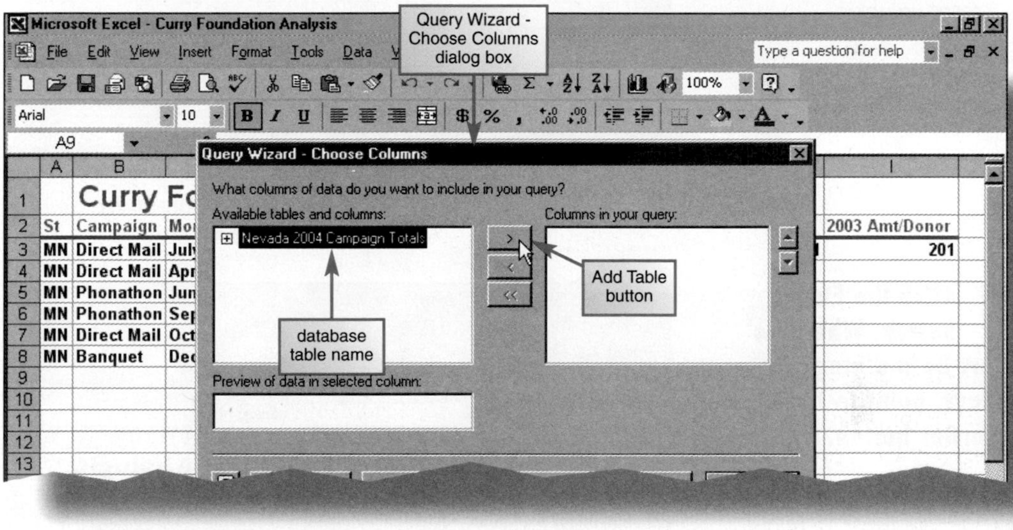

FIGURE 9-14

5 Click the Add Table button and then point to the Next button.

The fields of the Nevada 2004 Campaign Totals table display (Figure 9-15).

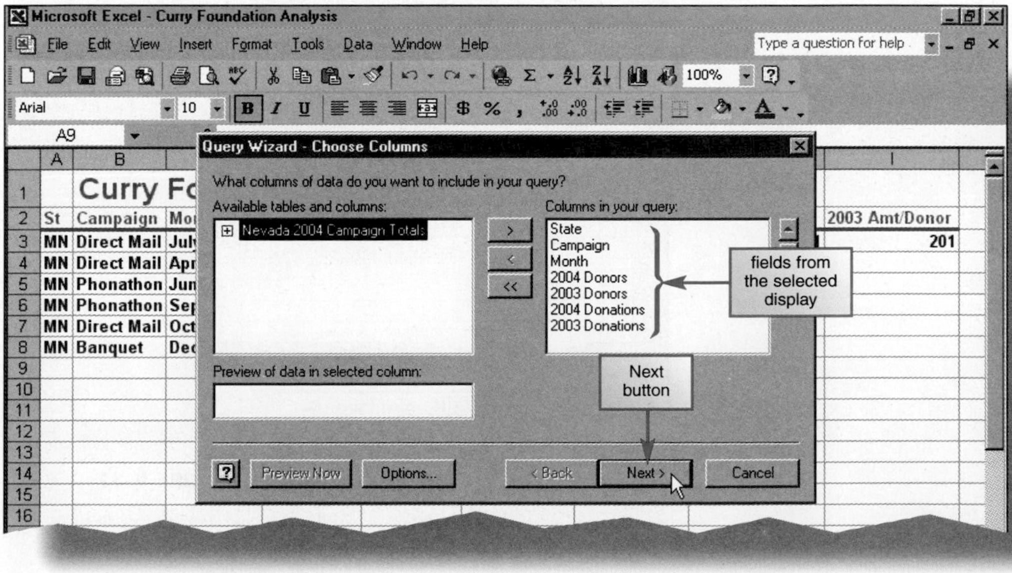

FIGURE 9-15

6 Click the Next button. When the Query Wizard - Filter Data dialog box displays, click the Next button. When the Query Wizard - Sort Order dialog box displays, click the Next button. When the Query Wizard - Finish dialog box displays, point to the Finish button (Figure 9-16).

Because the entire table is being imported without a specific query, clicking the Next button in each of the wizard dialog boxes accepts the preset values.

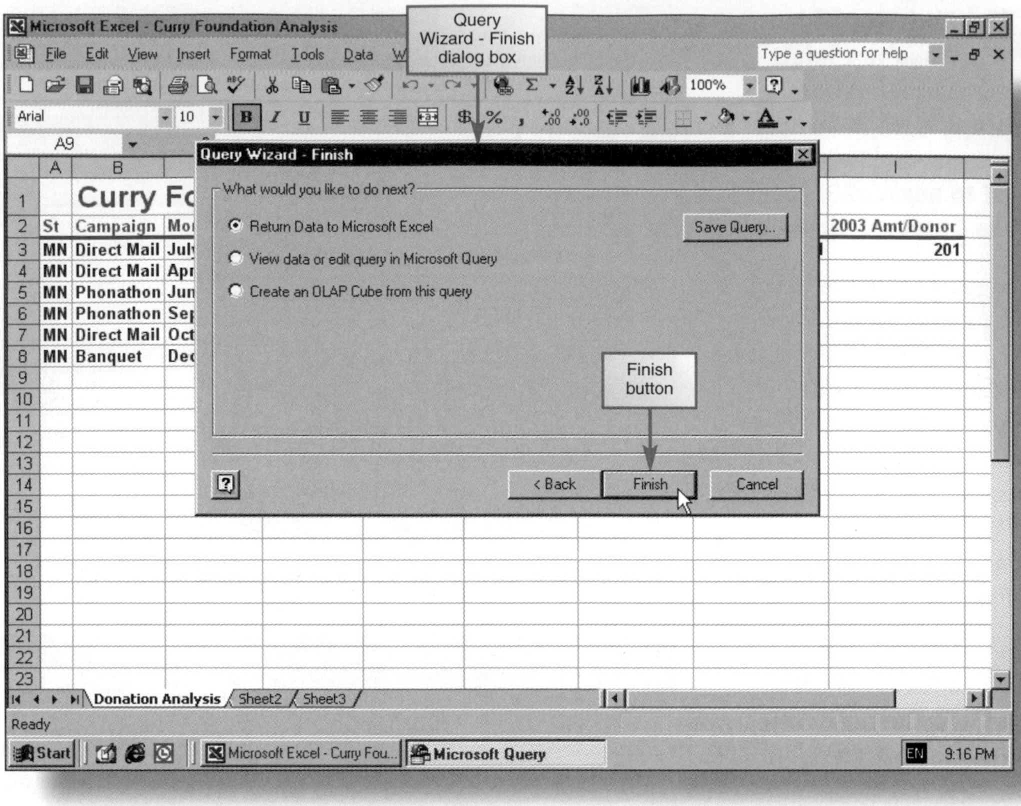

FIGURE 9-16

7 Click the Finish button. When the Import Data dialog box displays, point to the Properties button.

The Import Data dialog box displays (Figure 9-17). Data will be imported beginning at cell A9. A marquee displays around cell A9.

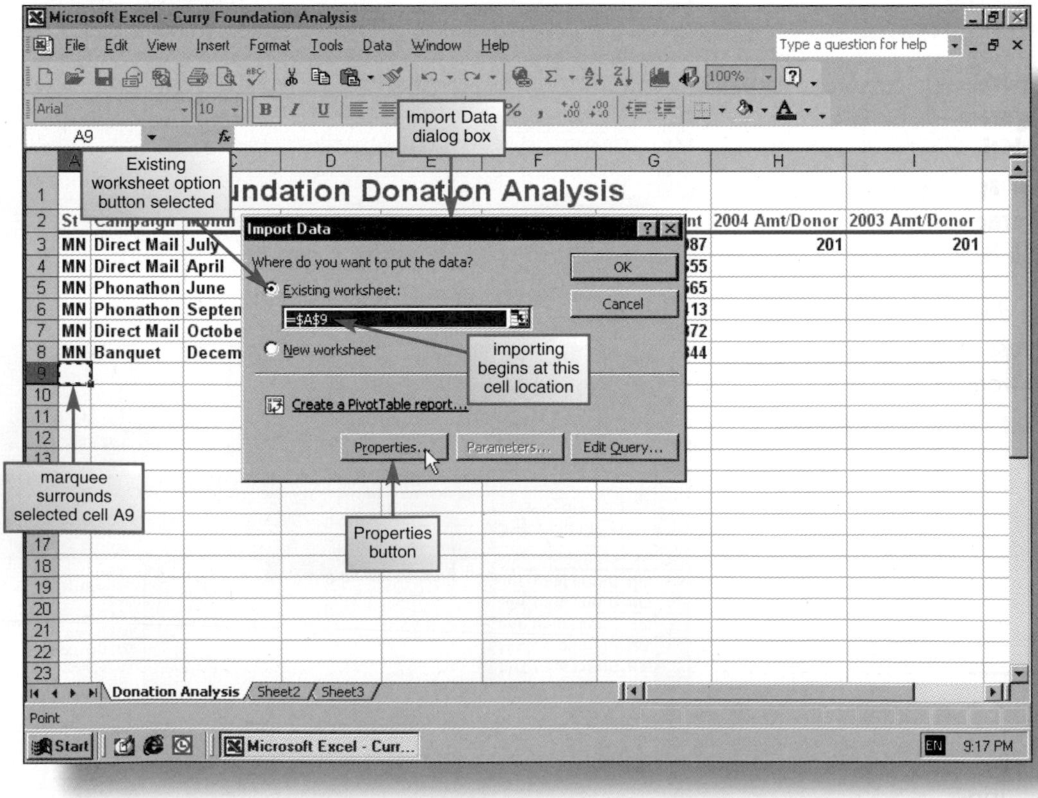

FIGURE 9-17

8 **Click the Properties button. When the External Data Range Properties dialog box displays, click Include field names and Adjust column width in the Data formatting and layout area to clear the check boxes. Point to the OK button.**

The External Data Range Properties dialog box displays (Figure 9-18). With the two check marks removed, Excel will not import the field names or adjust column widths in Excel.

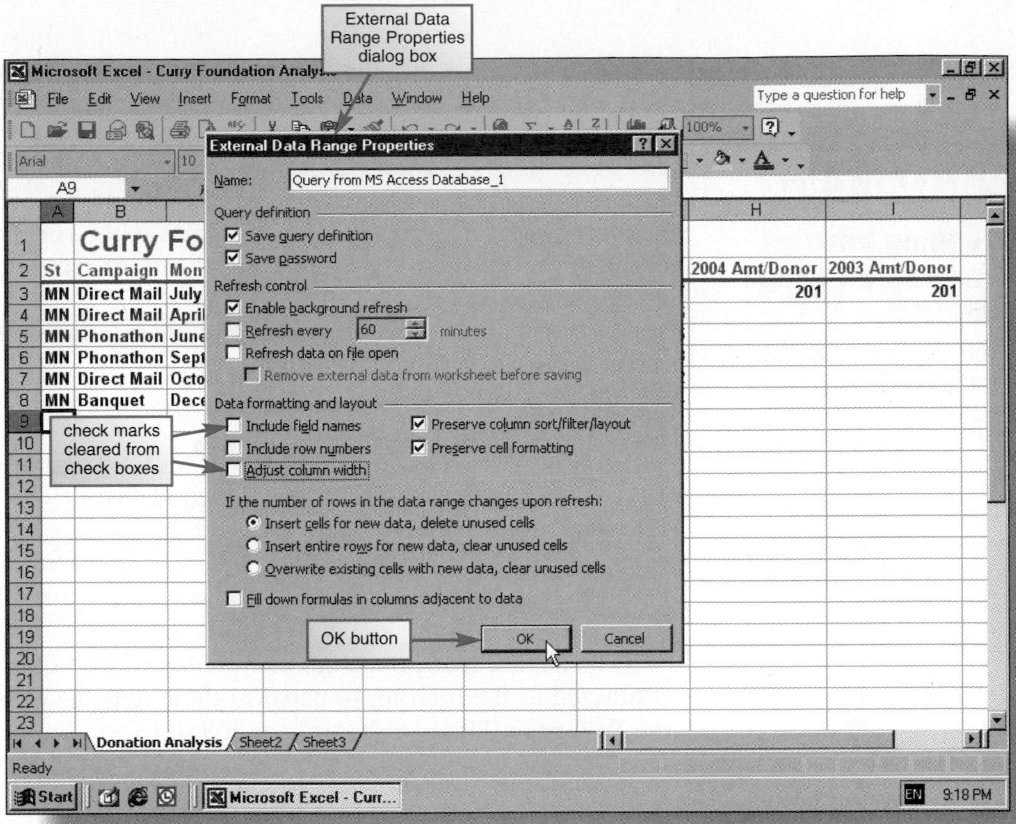

FIGURE 9-18

9 **Click the OK button. When the Import Data dialog box (Figure 9-17) redisplays, click the OK button. If your system displays the External Data toolbar, click its Close button.**

The data imported from the Access database displays in the worksheet (Figure 9-19).

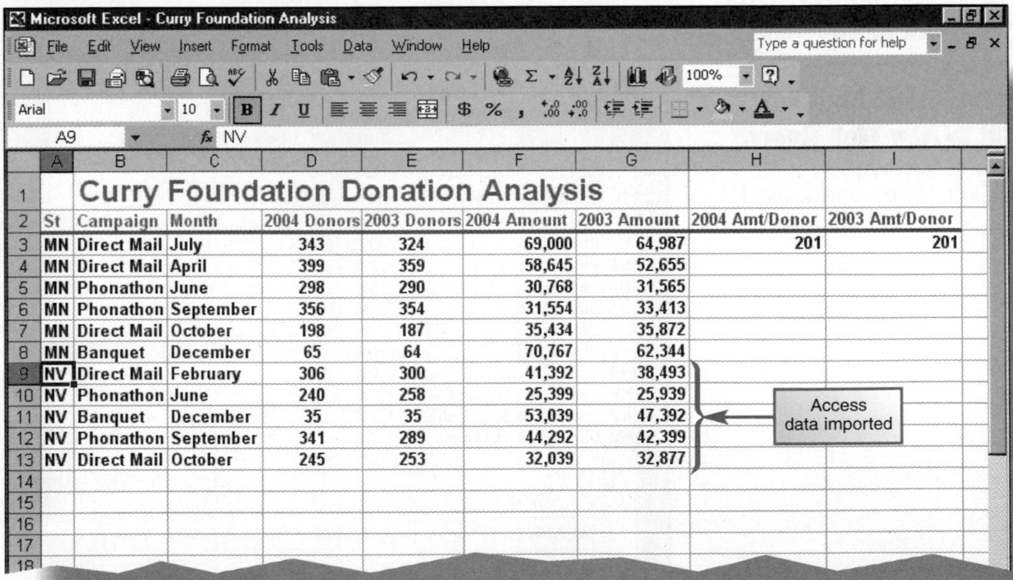

FIGURE 9-19

By default, the cell that is active when you perform the database query becomes the upper-left cell of the imported range. If you want to import the data to a different location, you specify the location in the Returning External Data to Microsoft Excel dialog box (Figure 9-17).

Other Ways

1. Press ALT+D, D, N
2. In Voice Command mode, say "Data, Import External Data, New Database Query"

More About

Dragging and Dropping an Access File

If you have both Excel and Access open on your desktop, you can drag and drop an entire table or query from Access to Excel. Select the table or query you want to transfer in the database window and drag it to the location in the worksheet.

The Access file, nevada2004.mdb, contains only one table, Nevada 2004 Campaign Totals. The table contains seven fields that correspond to the columns in the worksheet. The Add Table button shown in Figure 9-14 on page E 9.15 added all the columns of data. The second step of the Query Wizard allows you to **filter**, or specify, which records from the database should be included in the result set, using operators such as is-greater-than or begins-with. For example, you can filter the data in the previous example by specifying to import records that have 100 or more donors in 2003.

With the data from Minnesota and Nevada imported, the next step is to import the Georgia data from a Web page.

Importing Data from a Web Page

A Web page uses a file format called HTML. **HTML** stands for **Hypertext Markup Language**, which is a language that Web browsers can interpret. A Web page allows you to import data into preformatted areas of the worksheet. You specify which parts of the Web page you want and how much of the HTML formatting you want to keep.

The next sequence of steps creates a new Web query. You do not have to be connected to the Internet to perform these steps because the Data Disk includes the Web page (Figure 9-1c on page E 9.06).

Steps To Import Data from a Web Page into a Worksheet

1 Click cell A14. Click Data on the menu bar, point to Import External Data, and then point to New Web Query.

The Data menu and Import External Data submenu display (Figure 9-20).

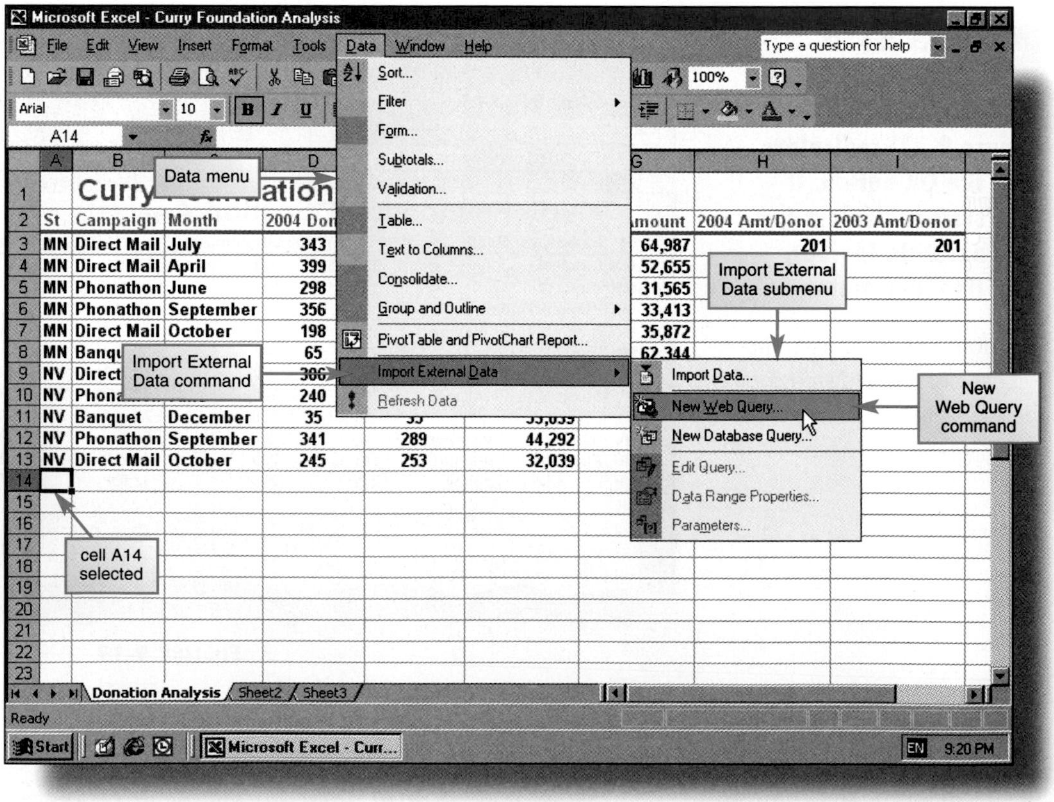

FIGURE 9-20

2 Click New Web Query. When the New Web Query dialog box displays, type `a:\georgia2004.htm` **in the Address box and then click the Go button. Point to the second Select a Table arrow.**

The file location displays in the Address box at the top of the New Web Query dialog box, and the Web page displays in the preview area (Figure 9-21). Excel appends file :// to the beginning of the address to indicte that the address points to a local file.

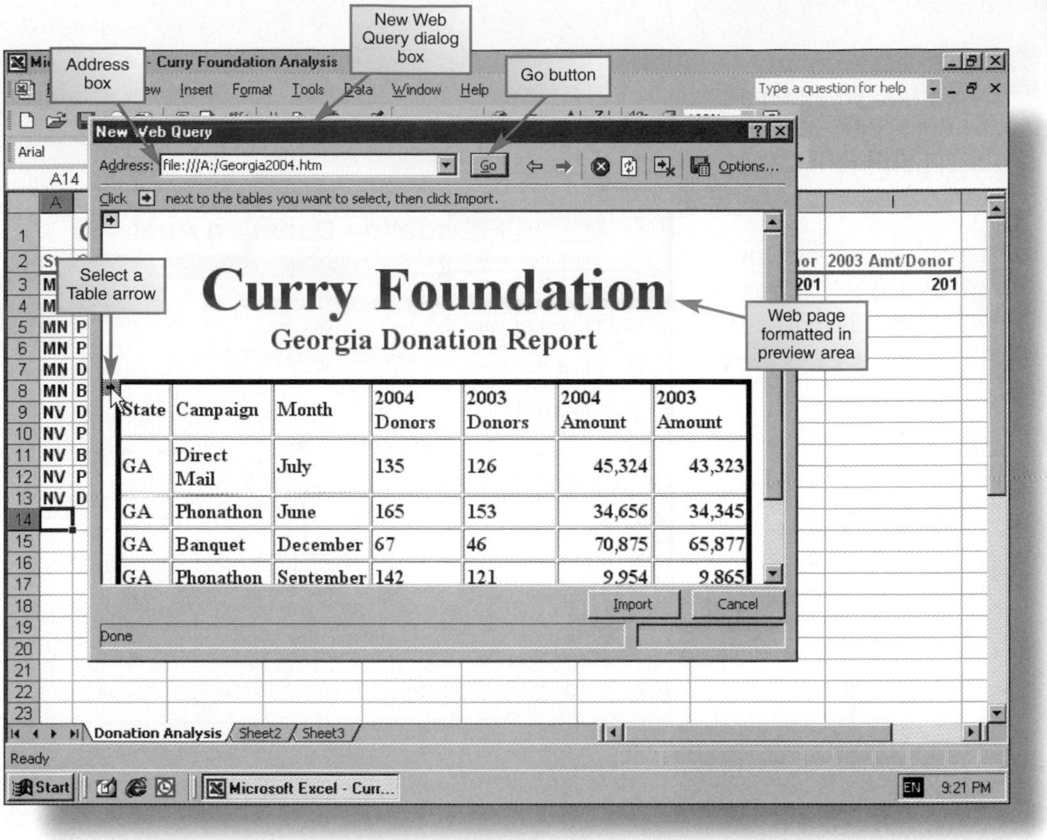

FIGURE 9-21

3 Click the Select a Table arrow and point to the Import button.

The table containing the Georgia Donation Report is selected as shown in Figure 9-22.

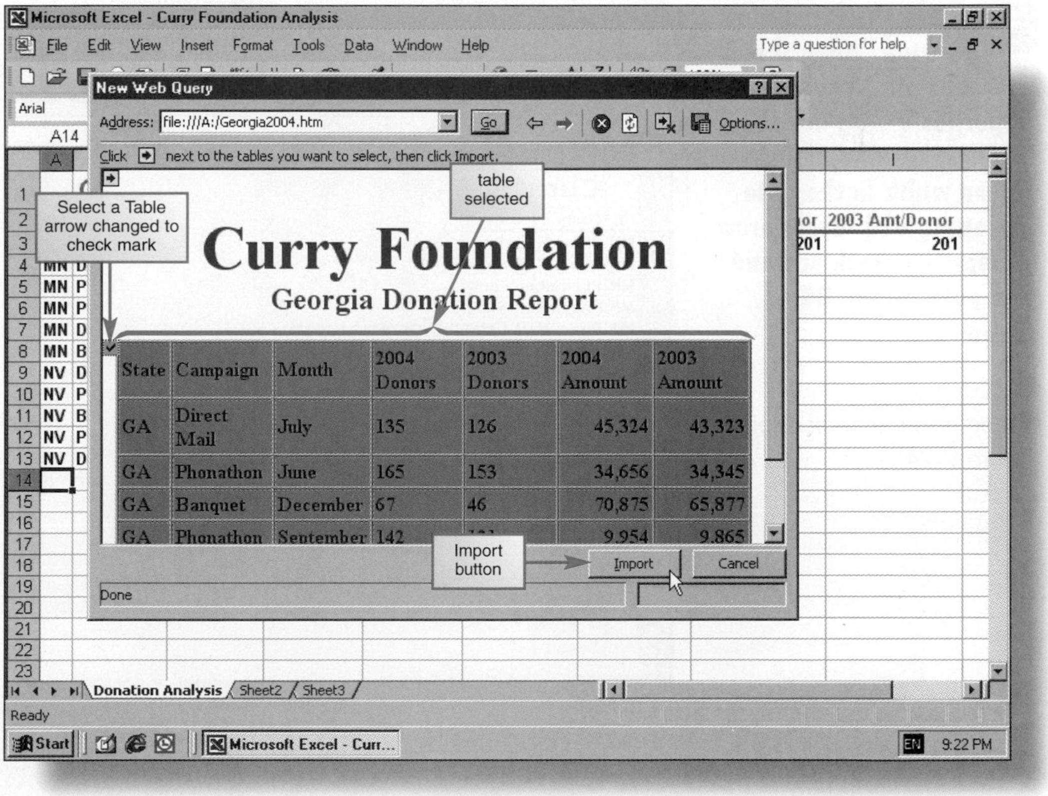

FIGURE 9-22

4 Click the Import button. When the Import Data dialog box displays, point to the Properties button.

The Import Data dialog box displays (Figure 9-23). Data will be imported beginning at cell A14. A marquee displays around cell A14.

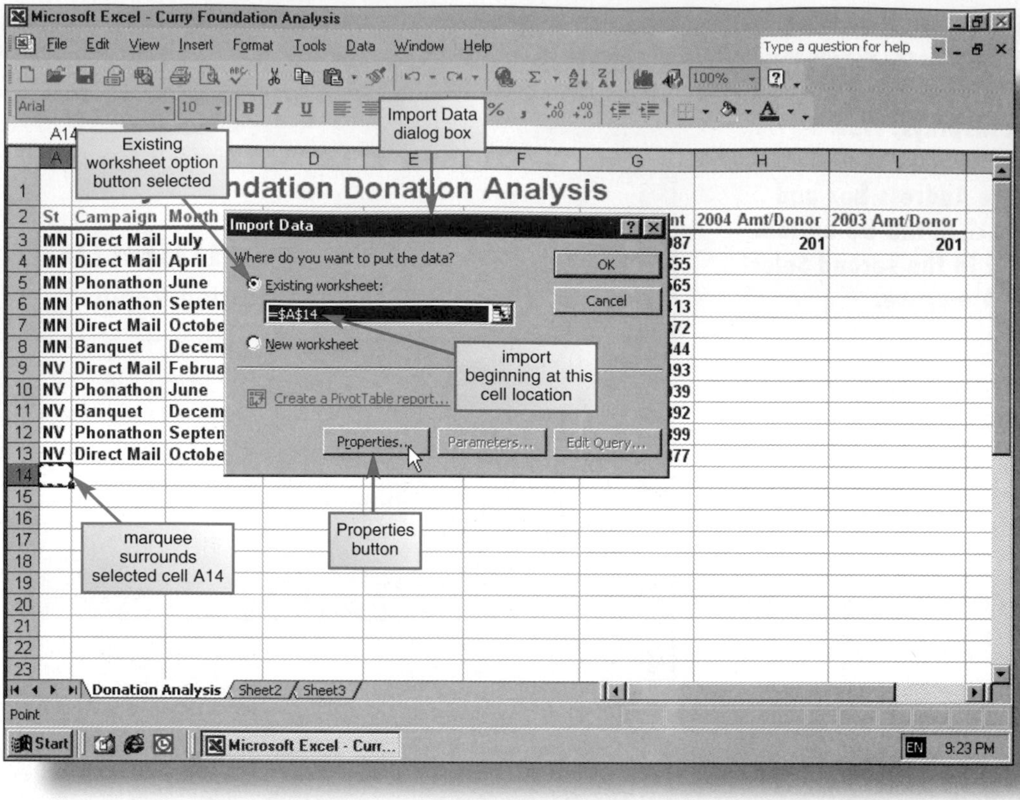

FIGURE 9-23

5 Click the Properties button. When the External Data Range Properties dialog box displays, click Adjust column width in the Data formatting and layout area to clear the check box and then point to the OK button.

The External Data Range Properties dialog box displays (Figure 9-24).

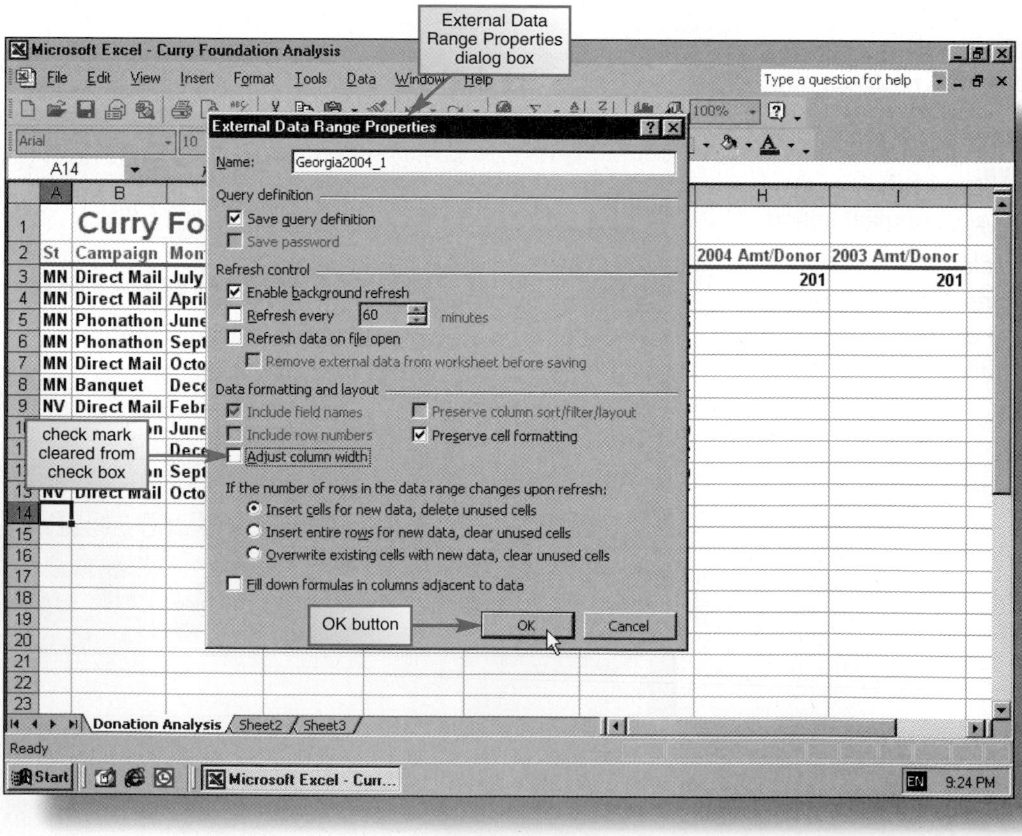

FIGURE 9-24

6 **Click the OK button. When the Import Data dialog box displays, click the OK button. If the External Data toolbar displays on your screen, click its Close button.**

The data displays in the worksheet (Figure 9-25).

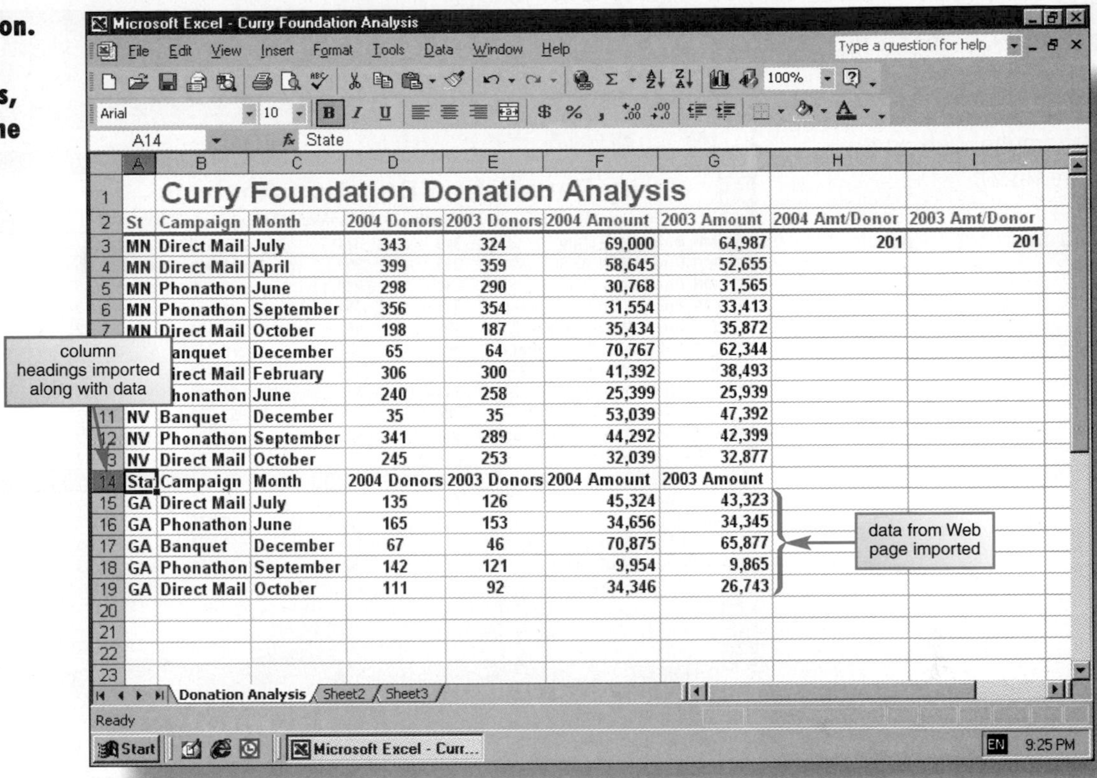

FIGURE 9-25

7 **Right-click row heading 14. Point to Delete on the shortcut menu.**

The shortcut menu for the selected row displays (Figure 9-26). You will delete these extra column headings from the Web page table.

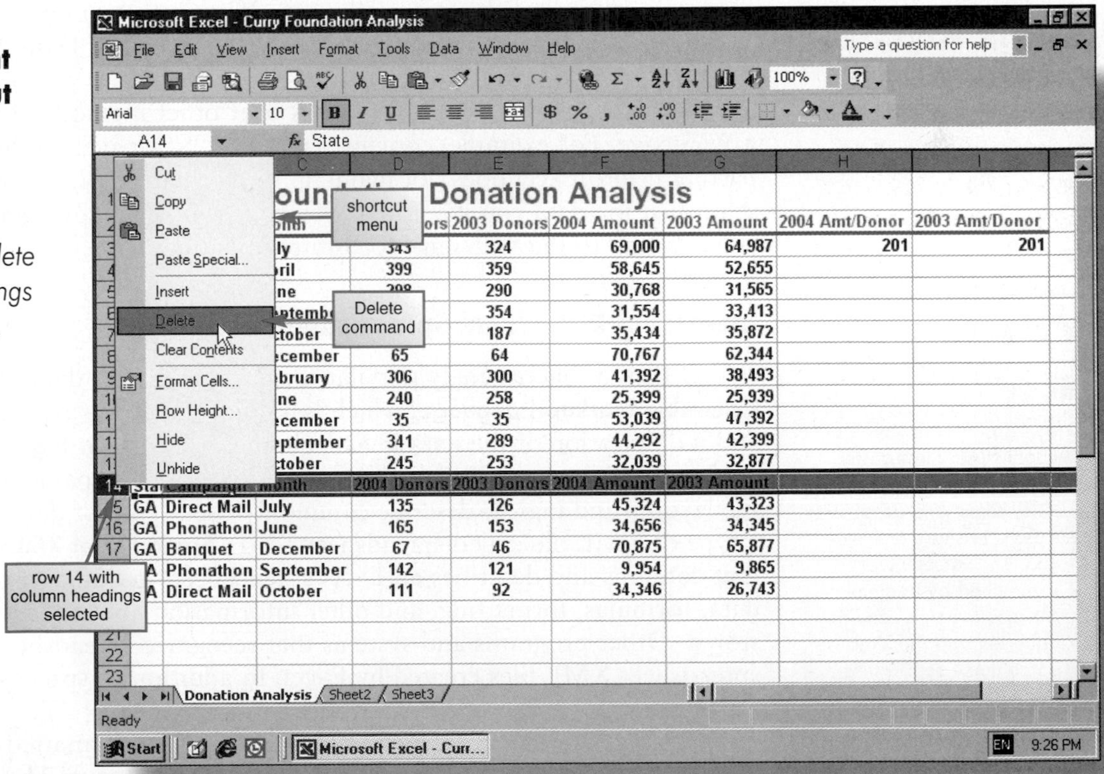

FIGURE 9-26

8 Click Delete.

Excel deletes row 14, which contained the column headings from the Web page (Figure 9-27).

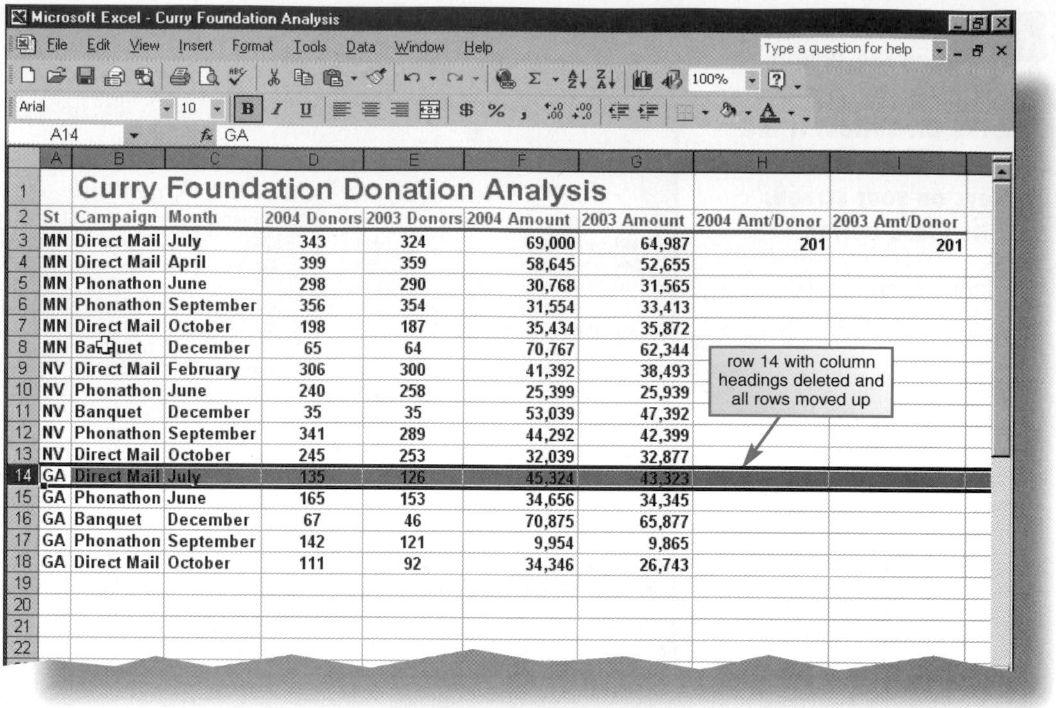
Microsoft Excel - Curry Foundation Analysis
File Edit View Insert Format Tools Data Window Help
Type a question for help
Arial
10
100%
A14
GA
Curry Foundation Donation Analysis
St Campaign Month 2004 Donors 2003 Donors 2004 Amount 2003 Amount 2004 Amt/Donor 2003 Amt/Donor
MN Direct Mail July 343 324 69,000 64,987 201 201
MN Direct Mail April 399 359 58,645 52,655
MN Phonathon June 298 290 30,768 31,565
MN Phonathon September 356 354 31,554 33,413
MN Direct Mail October 198 187 35,434 35,872
MN Ba quet December 65 64 70,767 62,344
NV Direct Mail February 306 300 41,392 38,493
NV Phonathon June 240 258 25,399 25,939
NV Banquet December 35 35 53,039 47,392
NV Phonathon September 341 289 44,292 42,399
NV Direct Mail October 245 253 32,039 32,877
GA Direct Mail July 135 126 45,324 43,323
GA Phonathon June 165 153 34,656 34,345
GA Banquet December 67 46 70,875 65,877
GA Phonathon September 142 121 9,954 9,865
GA Direct Mail October 111 92 34,346 26,743
row 14 with column headings deleted and all rows moved up

FIGURE 9-27

Other Ways

1. Press ALT+D, D, W
2. In Voice Command mode, say "Data, Import External Data, New Web Query"

By default, the cell that is active when you perform the Web query will become the upper-left cell of the imported range. If you want to import the data to a different location, you can specify the location in the Import Data dialog box (Figure 9-23 on page E 9.20).

Using a Web query has advantages over other methods of importing data from a Web page. For example, copying data from Web pages to the Clipboard and then pasting it into Excel does not maintain the formatting. In addition, it is tedious to select just the data you want in a Web page. Finally, copying and pasting does not create a link to the Web page for future updating.

More About

XML

XML can describe any type of data. Banks use it to transfer financial information among various systems, and graphic artists use it to share multimedia data. The versatility of XML is matched by its simplicity. XML also is being used to make queries over the Web using a common set of rules available to any user. For example, a user can send an XML query to a travel Web site and receive the current information for a specific flight in XML format.

Importing Data from Spreadsheet XML

XML is an increasingly popular format for sharing data. **XML** stands for **Extensible Markup Language**, which is a language that is used to encapsulate data and a description of the data in a single file, or **XML file**. **Tags** are used in XML files to describe data items. Industry organizations and companies create standard XML file layouts and tags to describe commonly used types of data. Microsoft has defined a type of XML file called spreadsheet XML. **Spreadsheet XML** is a type of XML file that contains and describes an Excel spreadsheet. In addition to containing the cell data, formulas, formatting, and other information about the workbook also is stored. Other programs and systems that recognize spreadsheet XML can read spreadsheet XML files created by Excel. In addition to spreadsheet XML, any other XML file can be imported into Excel.

An XML file allows you to import data into preformatted areas of the worksheet. You specify which parts of the XML file you want. The next sequence of steps creates a new XML Web query. You do not have to be connected to the Internet to perform these steps because the Data Disk includes the XML file (Figure 9-1c on page E 9.06).

Steps To Import Data from Spreadsheet XML into a Worksheet

1 Click cell A19. Click Data on the menu bar, point to Import External Data, and then point to New Web Query.

The Data menu and Import External Data submenu display (Figure 9-28).

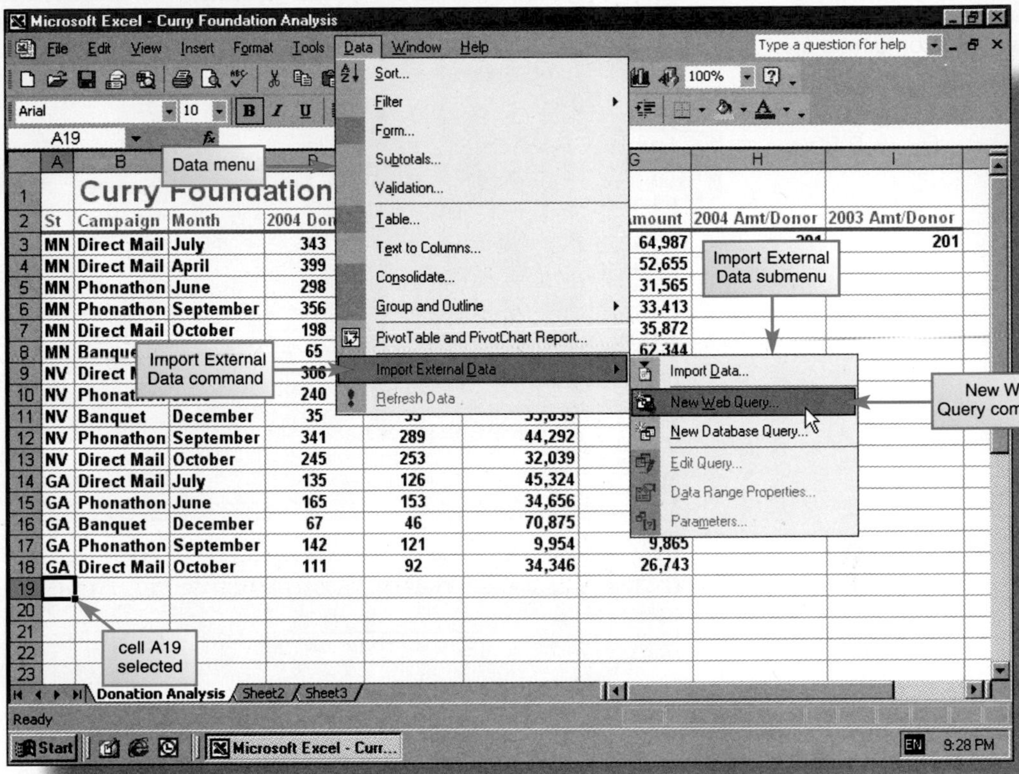

FIGURE 9-28

2 Click New Web Query. When the New Web Query dialog box displays, type `a:\Oklahoma2004.xml` **in the Address box and then click the Go button. Point to the Select a Table arrow.**

The file location displays in the Address box at the top of the New Web Query dialog box, and the XML file contents display in the preview area (Figure 9-29). Excel appends file :// to the address to indicate that the address points to a local file.

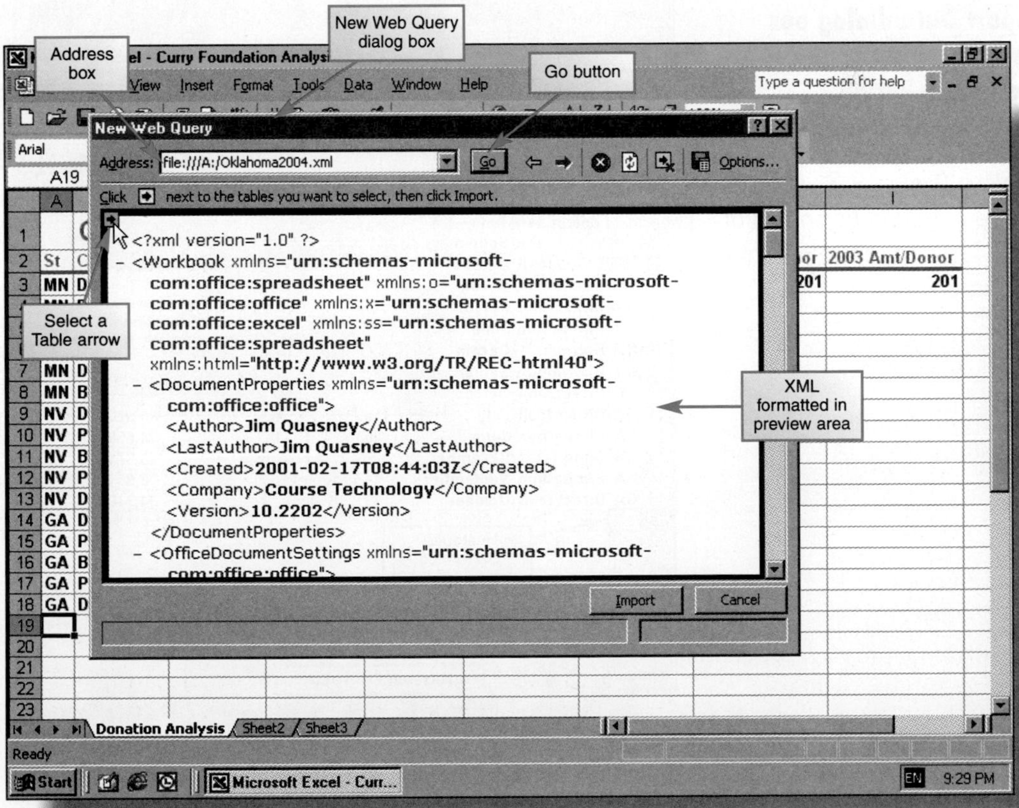

FIGURE 9-29

3 Click the Select a Table arrow and point to the Import button.

The table containing the Oklahoma 2004 donation XML data is selected as shown in Figure 9-30.

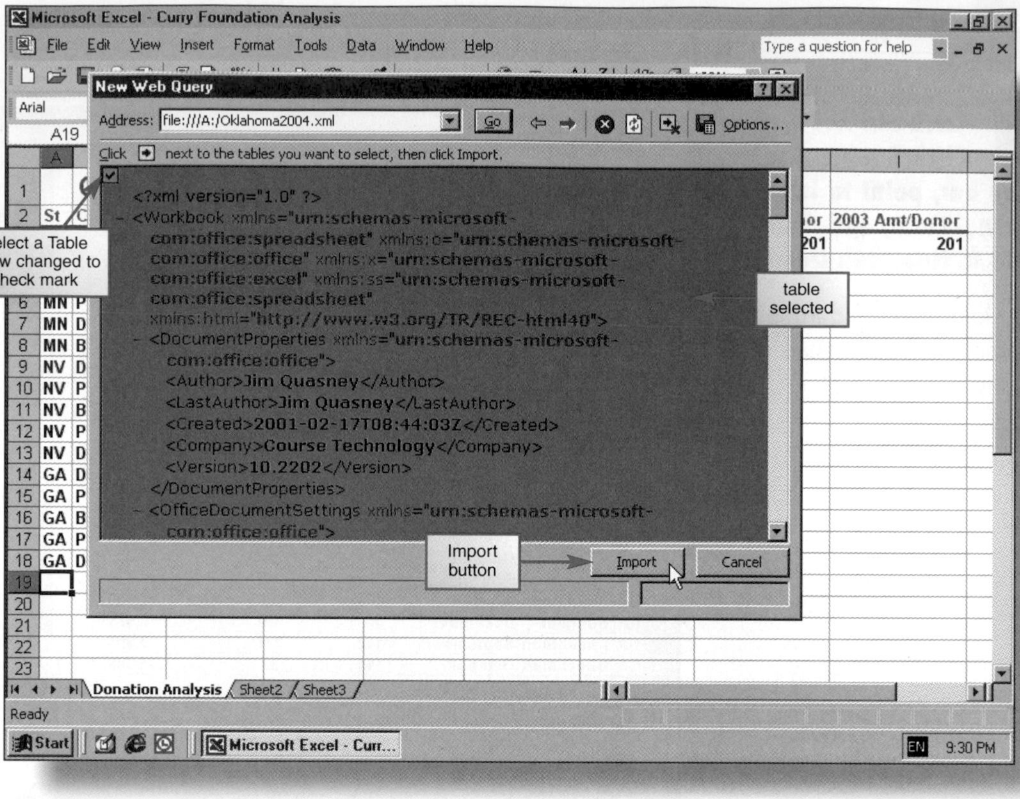

FIGURE 9-30

4 Click the Import button. When the Import Data dialog box displays, point to the Properties button.

The Import Data dialog box displays (Figure 9-31). Data will be imported beginning at cell A19. A marquee displays around cell A19.

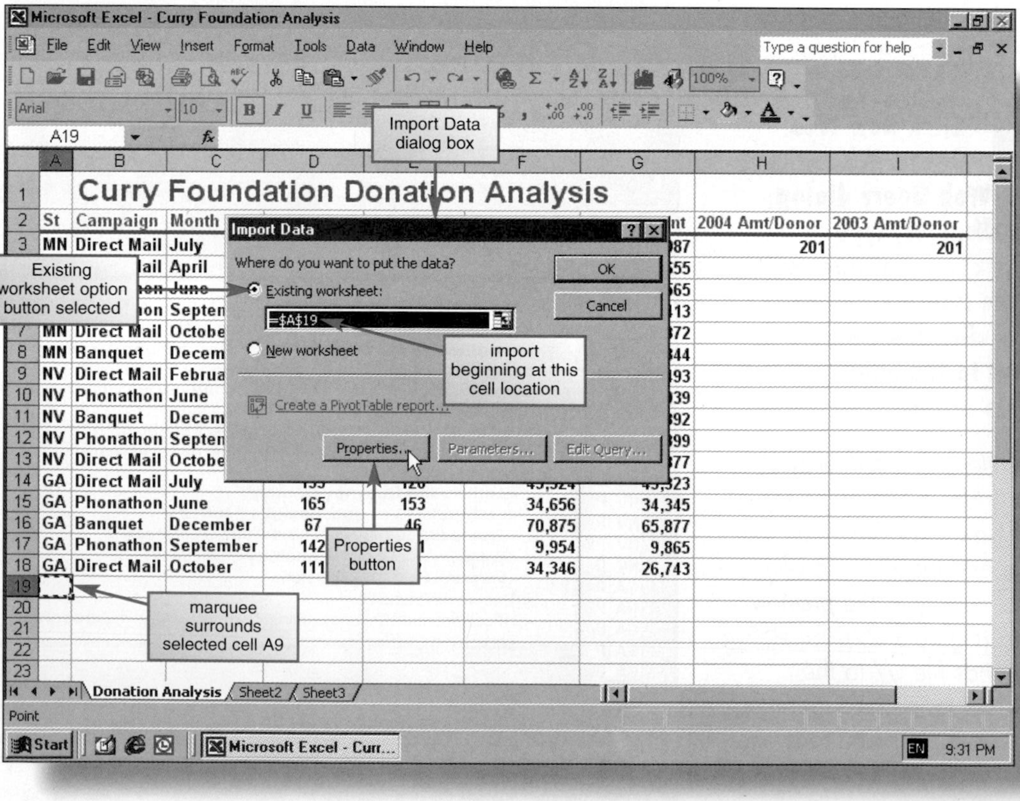

FIGURE 9-31

5 Click the Properties button. When the External Data Range Properties dialog box displays, click Adjust column width in the Data formatting and layout area to clear the check box and then point to the OK button.

The External Data Range Properties dialog box displays (Figure 9-32).

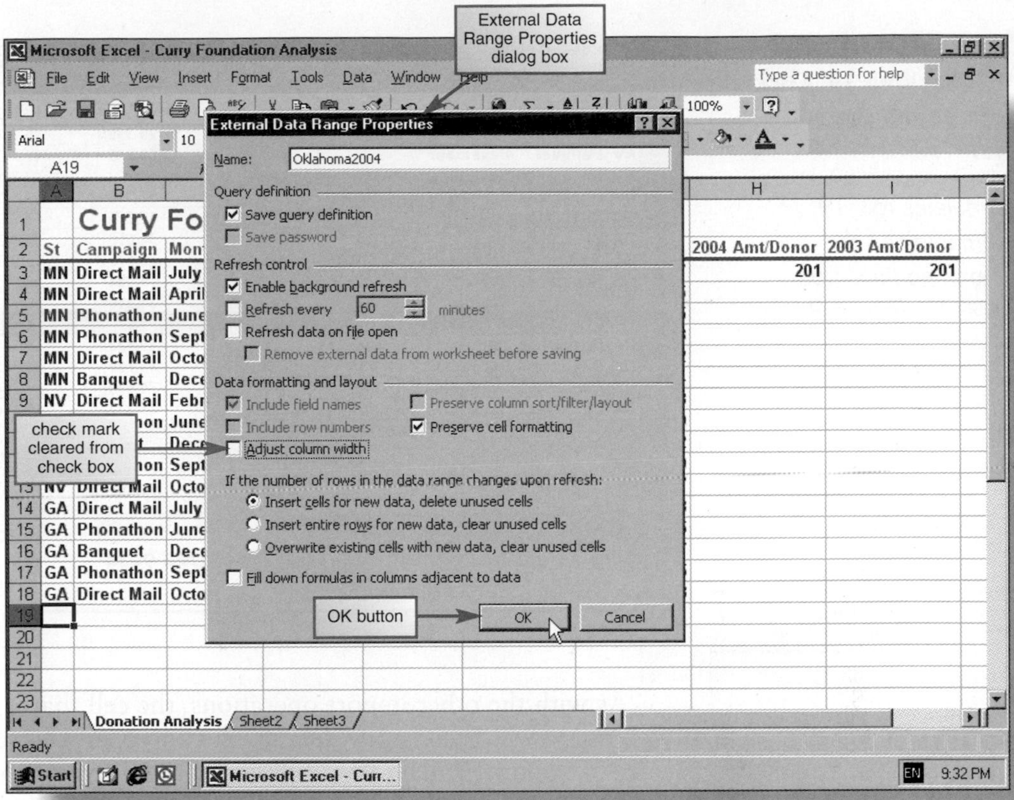

FIGURE 9-32

6 Click the OK button. When the Import Data dialog box displays, click the OK button. If the External Data toolbar displays on your screen, click its Close button.

The data displays in the worksheet (Figure 9-33).

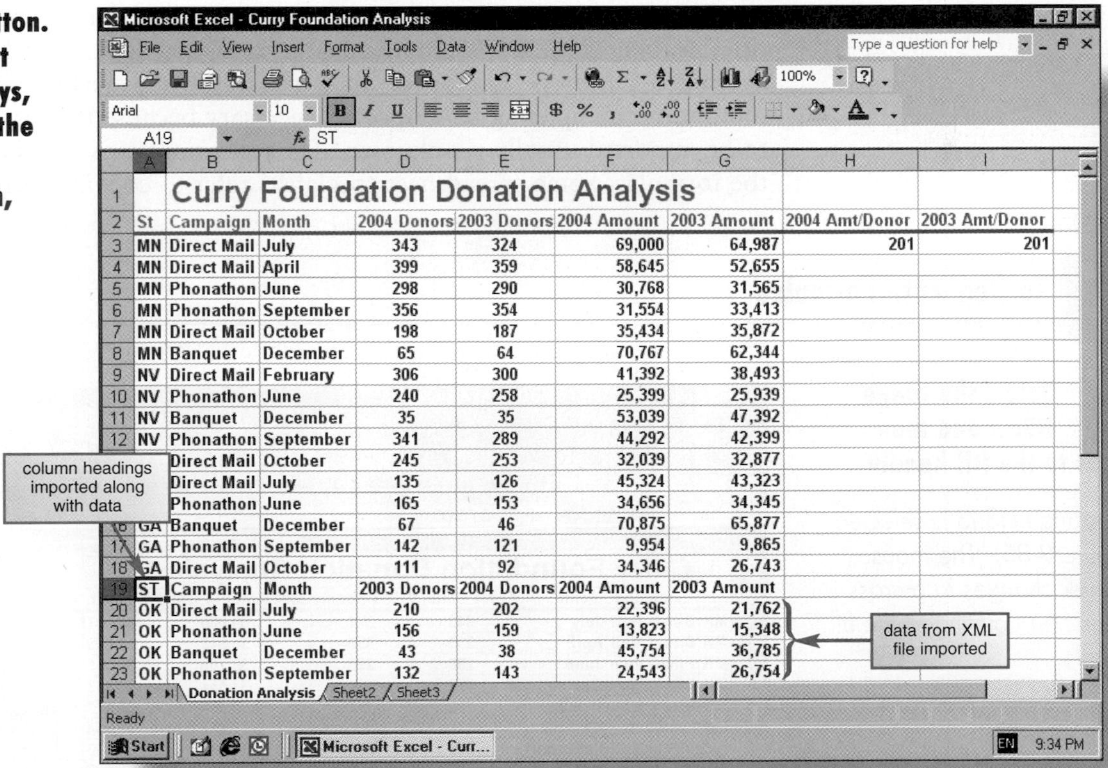

FIGURE 9-33

7 Right-click row heading 19. Click Delete on the shortcut menu.

Excel deletes row 19, which contained the column headings from the XML file (Figure 9-34).

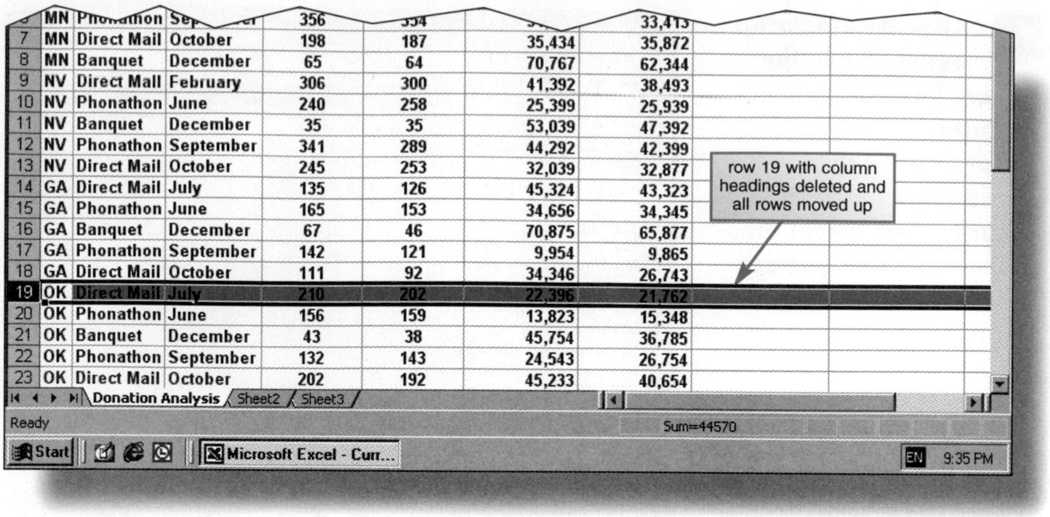

FIGURE 9-34

Other Ways

1. Press ALT+D, D, W
2. In Voice Command mode, say "Data, Import External Data, New Web Query"

As with the other import operations, the cell that is active when you perform the Web query will become, by default, the upper-left cell of the imported range. If you want to import the data to a different location, you can specify the location in the Import Data dialog box (Figure 9-31 on page E 9.24).

Replicating Formulas

The workbook opened at the beginning of this project contained a worksheet title, headings for each column, and formulas in cells H3 and I3 to calculate the average donation per donor for 2004 and 2003. This technique of copying the formulas after completing the import is necessary because the total number of records to be imported usually is unknown. The following steps use the fill handle to copy the formulas. Some spreadsheet specialists refer to copying formulas as **replication**.

Steps To Replicate Formulas

1 Select the range H3:I3 and then point to the fill handle.

The range H3:I3 is selected (Figure 9-35). The mouse pointer changes to a cross hair when pointing to the fill handle.

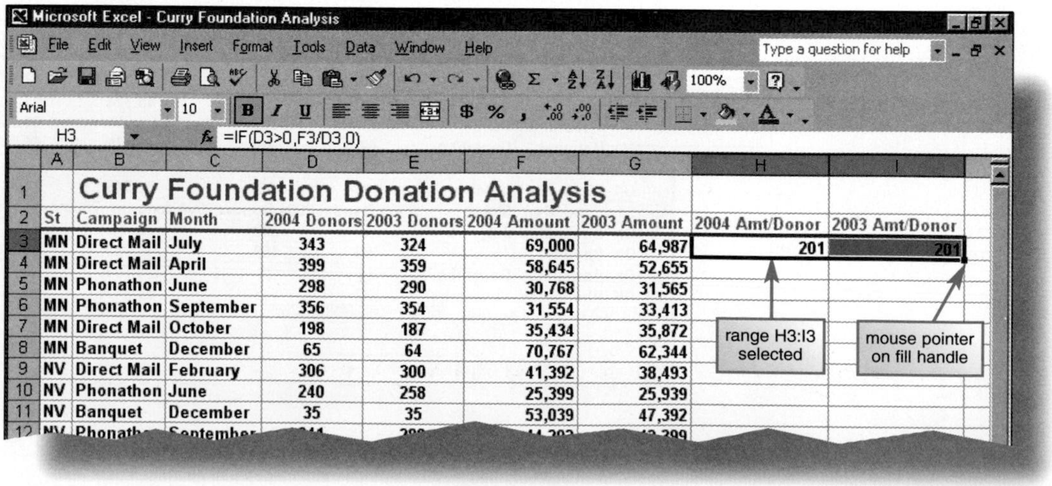

FIGURE 9-35

2 Drag the fill handle down through row 23.

Excel copies the two formulas to the range H4:I23 and displays the new values for the Amt/Donor columns (Figure 9-36).

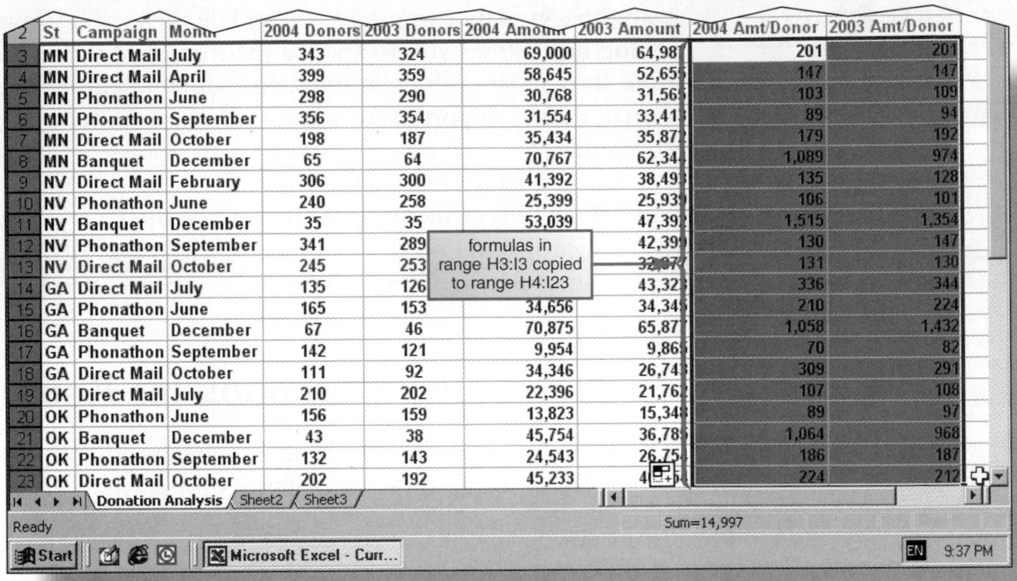

FIGURE 9-36

Other Ways

1. Click Copy button on Standard toolbar, click Paste button on Standard toolbar
2. On Edit menu click Copy, on Edit menu click Paste
3. Press CTRL+C, press CTRL+V
4. Click Copy on shortcut menu, click Paste on shortcut menu
5. In Voice Command mode, say "Copy," select destination area, in Voice Command mode, say "Paste"

Recall that when you copy, or replicate, a formula, Excel adjusts the cell references so the new formulas contain references corresponding to the new locations. It then performs calculations using the appropriate values. If you want an exact copy without replication, you must hold down the CTRL key while dragging the fill handle. Holding down the SHIFT key while dragging the fill handle inserts new cells rather than overwriting the existing data.

Saving the Workbook with a New File Name

Perform the following steps to save the workbook with the file name Curry Foundation Analysis1.

TO SAVE THE WORKBOOK WITH A NEW FILE NAME

1. Click File on the menu bar and then click Save As.
2. When the Save As dialog box displays, type `Curry Foundation Analysis1` in the File name text box.
3. If necessary, click 3½ Floppy (A:) in the Save in list.
4. Click the Save button in the Save As dialog box.

Excel saves the workbook on the Data Disk in drive A using the file name, Curry Foundation Analysis1.

More About

Replicating Formulas

The External Date Range Properties dialog box includes a check box labeled Fill down formulas in columns adjacent to data. You can use this check box as an alternative to replicating formulas when importing data.

Exporting Structured Data from Excel

In addition to importing data, Excel allows you to export data in a variety of formats. Exporting is the process of saving data in a format that can be read by another application, such as a database program or a word processor. You export data by

More About

Importing External Data

Excel assigns a name to each external data range. You can view these names by clicking the Name box arrow in the formula bar. External data ranges from text files are named with the text file name. External data ranges from databases are named with the name of the query. External data ranges from Web queries are named with the name of the Web page from which the data was retrieved.

More About

Selecting External Data

If you want to view which part of your spreadsheet is imported, or if you want to format or delete an external data range, click the arrow next to the Name box on the formula bar, and then click the external data range name.

using the Save As command on the File menu. The Save as type box on the Save As dialog box allows you to specify the format of the exported data. Some commonly used formats are tab delimited text, comma delimited text, and spreadsheet XML. Often, data is exported for use on other computer systems, such as mainframe computers.

If you wish to export the Curry Foundation Donation Analysis worksheet to a tab delimited text file in order to send to the Curry Foundation's accounting firm, you select Save As on the File menu. Select Text (Tab delimited) in the Save as type box, and click the OK button.

Preparing the Workbook for Routing

The next step is to add a routing comment and then verify the accuracy of the data by routing it to the state coordinators for review.

Inserting Comments

Comments are used to describe the function of a cell, a range, a sheet, or an entire workbook, or they may be used to clarify entries that might otherwise be difficult to understand. Multiple users or people reviewing the workbook often use comments to communicate suggestions, tips, and other messages. Gene suspects that the donation amount in cell F12 from Nevada is incorrect, and thus will add a comment to the cell before routing the workbook to the four state coordinators as shown in the following steps.

Steps To Insert a Comment

1 Right-click cell F12. Point to Insert Comment on the shortcut menu.

The shortcut menu displays (Figure 9-37).

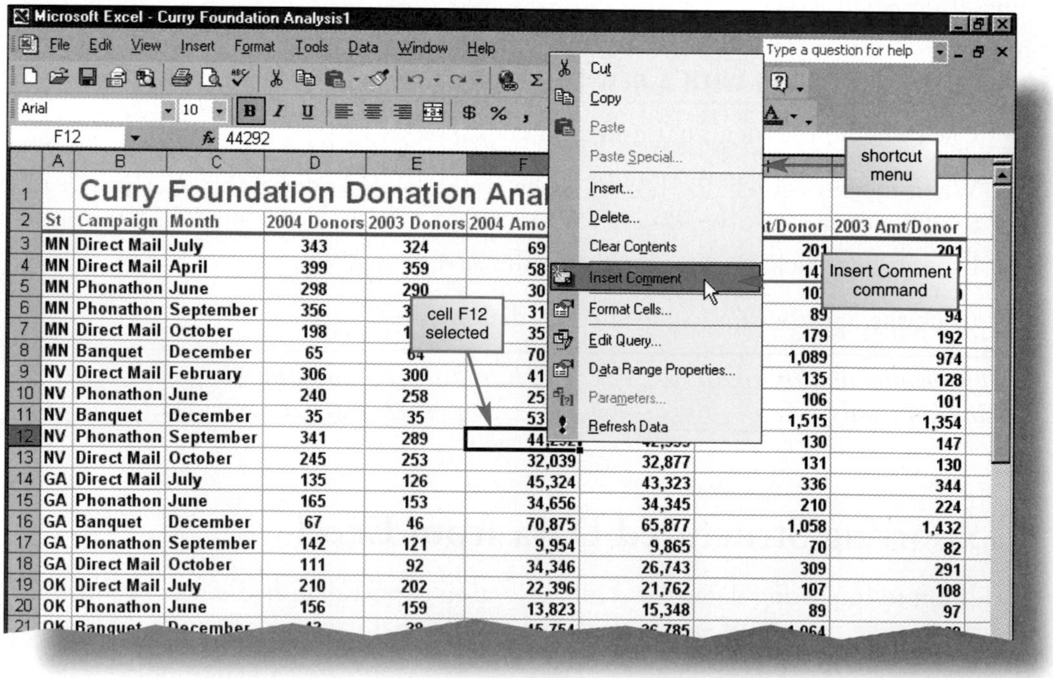

FIGURE 9-37

2 Click Insert Comment. When the comment box displays, enter the comment as shown in Figure 9-38.

Excel opens a comment box *next to the selected cell (Figure 9-38). The insertion point displays in the comment box below the system user name. Your system user name will differ from this figure. Excel adds a small red triangle, called a* comment indicator*, to cell F12. A small black arrow attached to the comment box points to the comment indicator.*

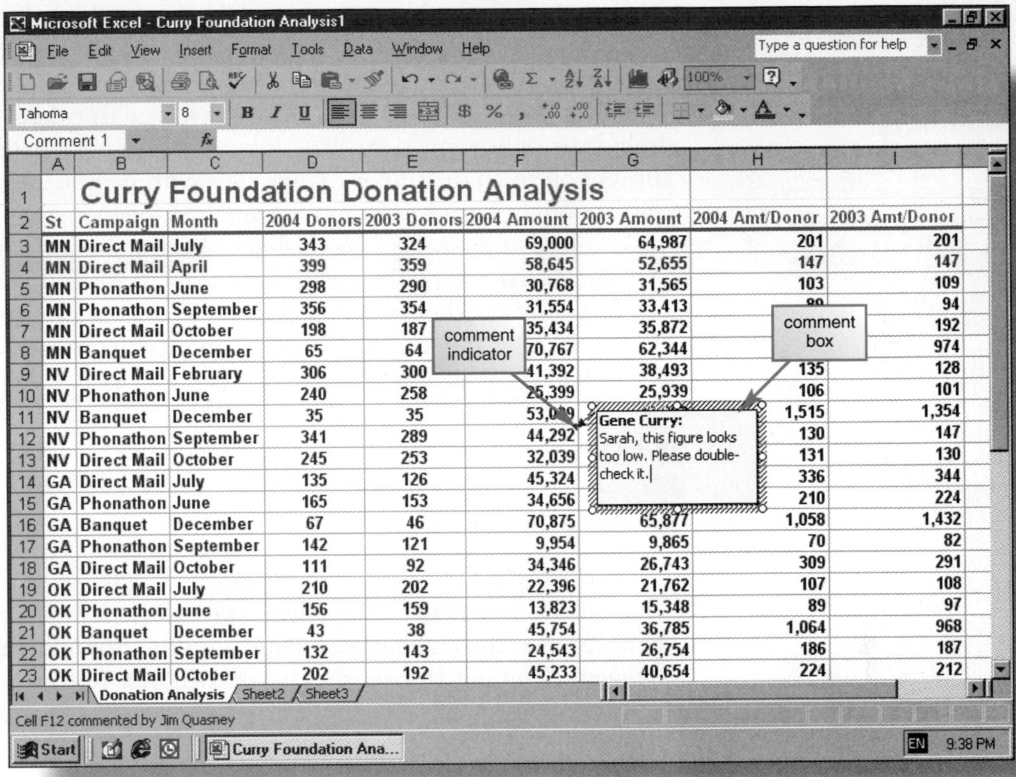

FIGURE 9-38

3 Click anywhere outside the comment box and then click the Save button on the Standard toolbar to save the workbook using the file name, Curry Foundation Analysis1.

Other Ways

1. On Insert menu click Comment
2. Press ALT+I, M
3. In Voice Command mode, say "Insert, Comment"

When Excel closes the comment box and returns to the workbook window, the comment disappears from the screen. If you want to redisplay the comment, simply point to the cell containing the red comment indicator.

If you want to print the comments where they display on the sheet, click Comments on the View menu, move and resize the comments as necessary, and then print in the normal way. If you want to print the comments at the end of the worksheet, on the File menu click Page Setup, and then click the Sheet tab. Click At end of sheet in the Comments box.

Collaborating on Workbooks

If you plan to have others edit your workbook or suggest changes, Excel provides four ways to collaborate with others. **Collaborating** means working together in cooperation on a document with other Excel users.

First, you can **distribute** your workbook to others, physically on a disk or through e-mail using the Send To command on the File menu. With the Send To command, you may choose to embed the document as part of the e-mail message or attach the file as an e-mail attachment, which allows recipients of the e-mail message to open the file if the application is installed on their system.

Second, you can **route** your workbook to a list of people who pass it along from one to another on the routing list using e-mail. The Send To command on the File menu includes a Routing Recipient command. A routing slip displays in which you

More About

Collaboration

Another way to collaborate on workbooks is by using an Exchange folder. If you send the workbook to an Exchange folder, others working on the same project have a central location where they can go to locate project information. Because it saves time, this method is preferred if many revisions need to be circulated. Project members can look at what is relevant to them instead of going through numerous project-related e-mails.

More About

Excel's Routing Capability

To e-mail or route a workbook as an attachment in Excel format, you need Excel 2002 and one of the following e-mail programs: Outlook, Outlook Express, Microsoft Exchange Client, Lotus cc:Mail or another compatible program with the Messaging Application Programming Interface (MAPI). To receive a routed workbook, you need Excel 97 or a later version.

can specify e-mail addresses. Excel handles creating the e-mail message with routing instructions. It even reminds people who open the document to pass it along to the next person in the routing list when they are finished.

Third, you can **collaborate** interactively with other people through discussion threads or online meetings. The integration of **NetMeeting** with Microsoft Office XP allows you to share and exchange files with people at different sites. When you start an online meeting from within Excel, NetMeeting automatically starts in the background and allows you to share the contents of your file(s).

Fourth, you can collaborate by sharing the workbook. **Sharing** means more than simply giving another user a copy of your file. Sharing implies that multiple people can work independently on the same workbook at the same time if you are in a networked environment.

With any of the collaboration choices, you should keep track of the changes that others make to your workbook.

Tracking Changes

Tracking changes means that Excel, through the **Track Changes command** on the Tools menu, will display the edited cells with a comment indicating who made the change, when the change was made, and the original value of the cell that was changed. Tracking and sharing work together. When you turn on one, the other is enabled by default. The following steps turn on track changes.

Steps To Turn on Track Changes

1 Click Tools on the menu bar, point to Track Changes, and then point to Highlight Changes.

The Tools menu and the Track Changes submenu display (Figure 9-39).

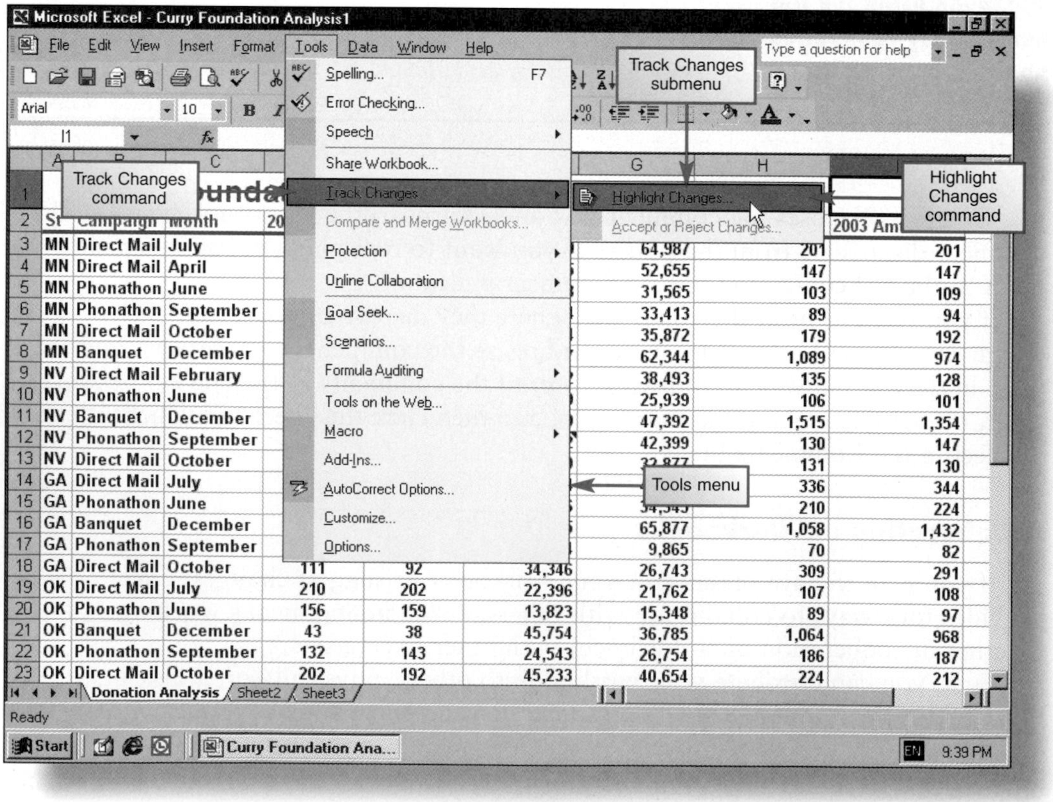

FIGURE 9-39

2 Click Highlight Changes. When the Highlight Changes dialog box displays, click Track changes while editing. If necessary, clear all of the check boxes in the Highlight which changes area. Point to the OK button.

The Highlight Changes dialog box displays (Figure 9-40). Clicking the Track changes while editing check box also shares the workbook. The When, Who, and Where check boxes and list boxes play no role when you first enable track changes.

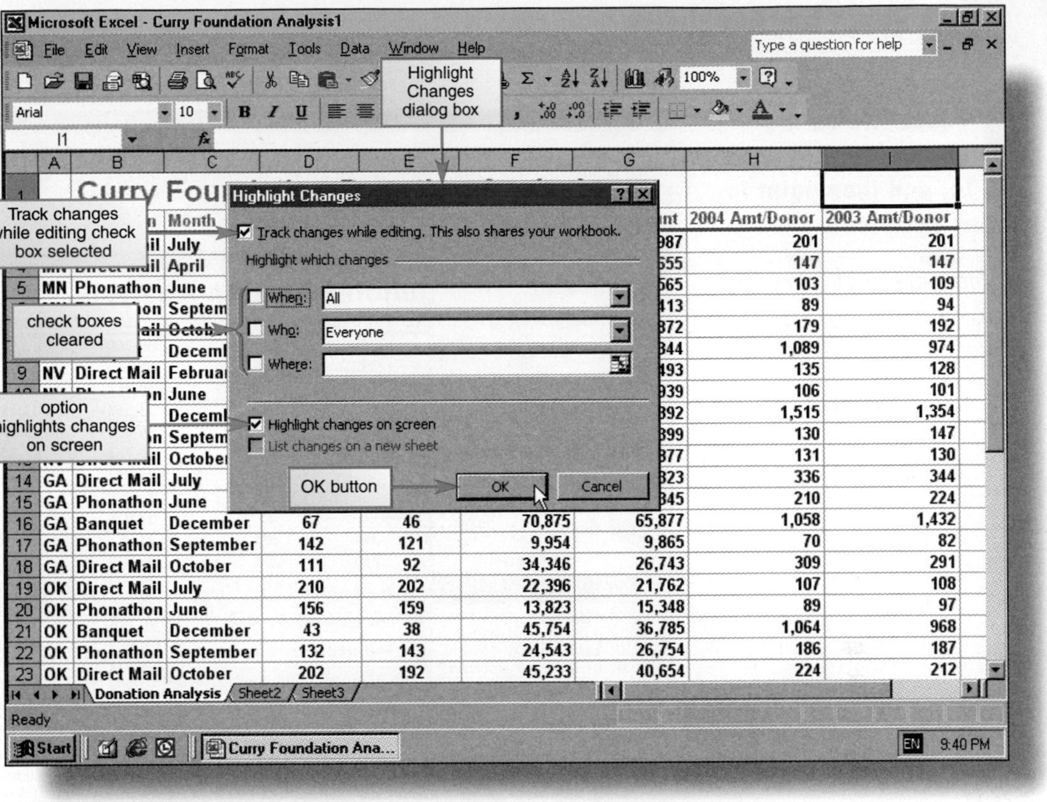

FIGURE 9-40

3 Click the OK button. When the Microsoft Excel dialog box displays asking if you want to continue by saving, click the OK button to save the workbook.

The title bar indicates this workbook is shared (Figure 9-41).

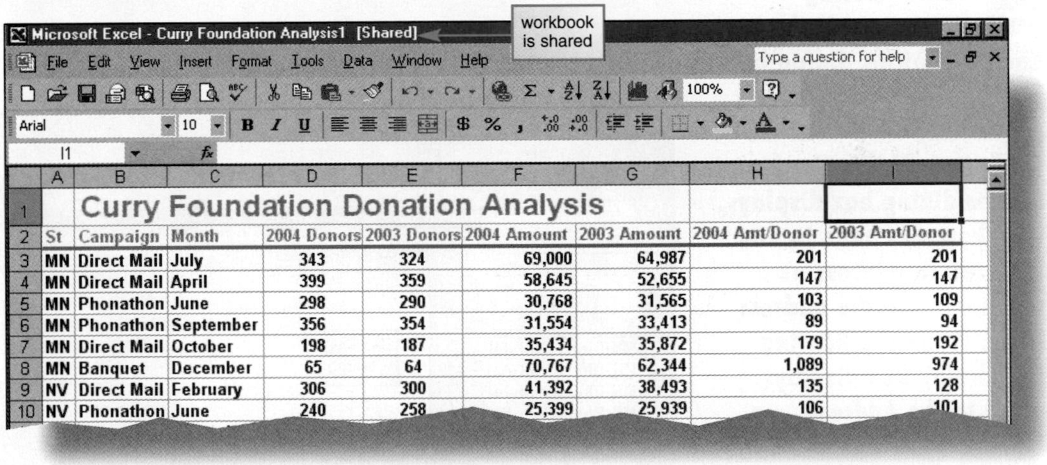

FIGURE 9-41

Routing the Workbook

The next step is to route the workbook to the four state coordinators for the Curry Foundation. If you are completing this project on a PC, you will be prompted to choose the e-mail addresses of the routing recipients. If you plan actually to execute the routing, substitute the e-mail addresses shown with e-mail addresses from your address book or class. Your return e-mail contact information must be valid as well, in order to round trip the file back to yourself. The term **round trip** refers to sending a document to recipients and then receiving it back at some point in time.

Perform the steps on the next page to route the workbook.

Other Ways

1. Press ALT+T, T, H
2. In Voice Command mode, say "Tools, Track Changes, Highlight Changes"

Steps To Route the Workbook

1 Click File on the menu bar, point to Send To, and then point to Routing Recipient.

The File menu and Send To submenu display (Figure 9-42).

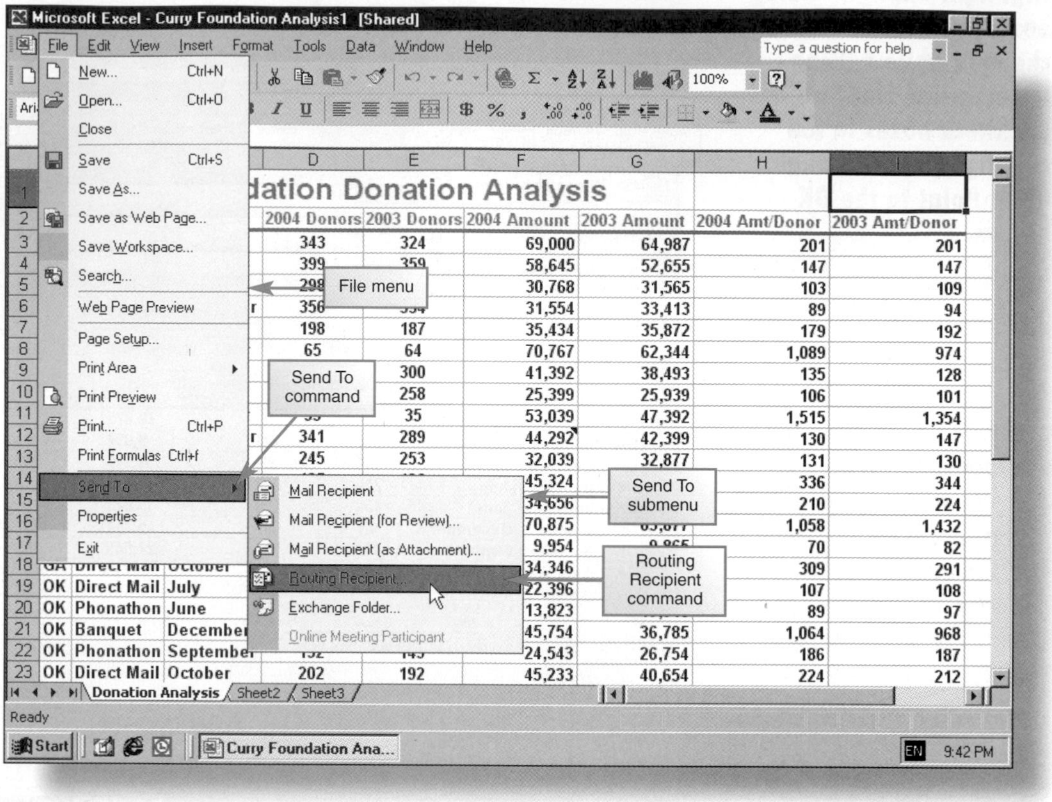

FIGURE 9-42

2 Click Routing Recipient. If the Choose Profiles dialog box displays, choose your user profile and then click the OK button. If the Check Names dialog box displays, you then may have to add your return address as a new listing to the address book. When the Routing Slip dialog box displays, point to the Address button.

*A **routing slip** displays that allows you to specify the recipient, subject, and message similar to an e-mail message (Figure 9-43). Your routing slip will display a different name in the From area. If you are working on a networked system, see your instructor or network administrator for the correct e-mail account to use.*

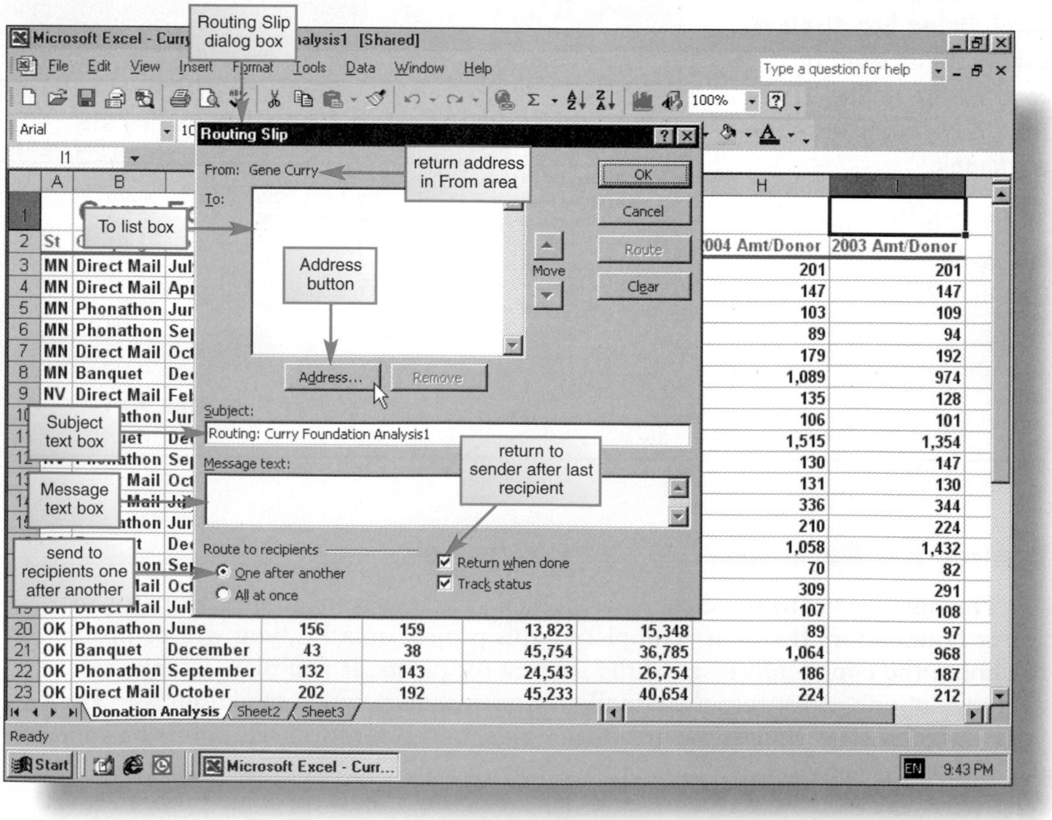

FIGURE 9-43

3 **Click the Address button. When the Address Book dialog box displays, click an address in your list, and then click the To button. Repeat the process for three more recipients. Point to the OK button.**

If no addresses display in your address list, you may leave the recipients blank for the purposes of this project. To add new e-mail recipients, you would click the New Contact button and then enter the correct information (Figure 9-44).

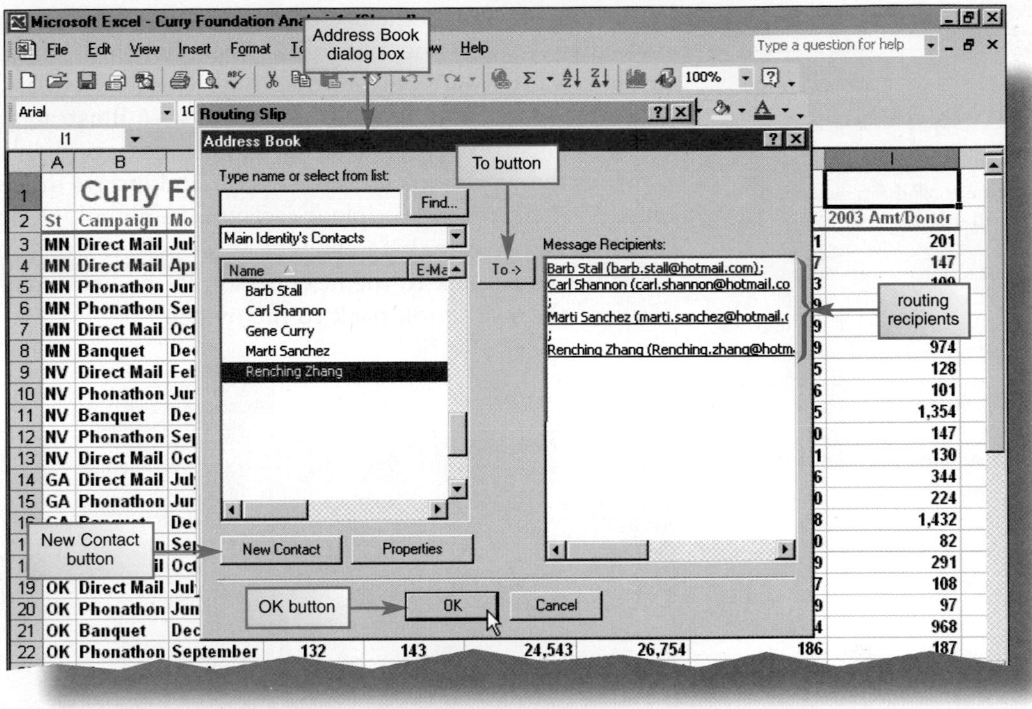

FIGURE 9-44

4 **Click the OK button. When the Routing Slip dialog box is visible again, click the Message text box. Type** `Please review the attached worksheet and make corrections as necessary. When you are finished reviewing, route to the next recipient. Thank you.` **Point to the Route button.**

The Routing Slip *dialog box displays the addresses, subject, and message (Figure 9-45).*

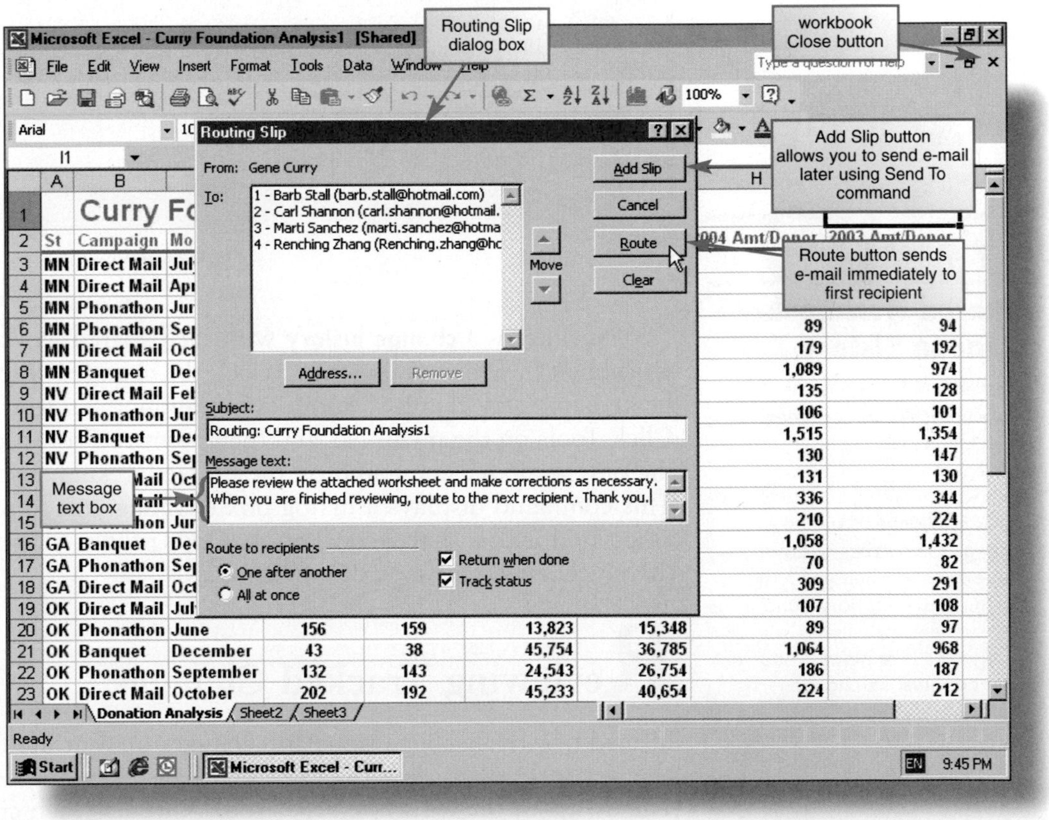

FIGURE 9-45

5 **Click the Route button.**

6 **Click the Save button on the Standard toolbar to save the workbook using the file name Curry Foundation Analysis1. Click the workbook Close button on the menu bar.**

Excel saves a copy of the workbook on the floppy disk and closes the workbook.

Other Ways

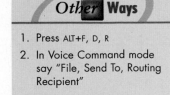

1. Press ALT+F, D, R
2. In Voice Command mode say "File, Send To, Routing Recipient"

More About

Routing Slips

The e-mail addresses you use in the routing slip must be a valid address from your Contacts folder. Your own name and e-mail address must be in the Contacts folder as well, if you want to "round trip" the workbook. To add an address, in the Routing Slip dialog box, click the Address button, and then click the New button in the Address Book dialog box.

In the previous sequence of steps, the e-mail to the first recipient was sent immediately when you clicked the **Route button**. If you had clicked the **Add Slip button** instead of the Route button, then Excel would have asked if it should send the e-mail when the workbook was closed. Figure 9-46 illustrates the e-mail received by the third recipient, Marti Sanchez. A sample message displays and Excel automatically attaches the workbook to the message and inserts instructions to the routing recipients. As each routing recipient receives the e-mail, he or she opens the workbook and looks it over, making changes as necessary. Excel reminds each recipient to forward the workbook to the next person in the list. Excel prompts the last recipient to forward the workbook back to the owner.

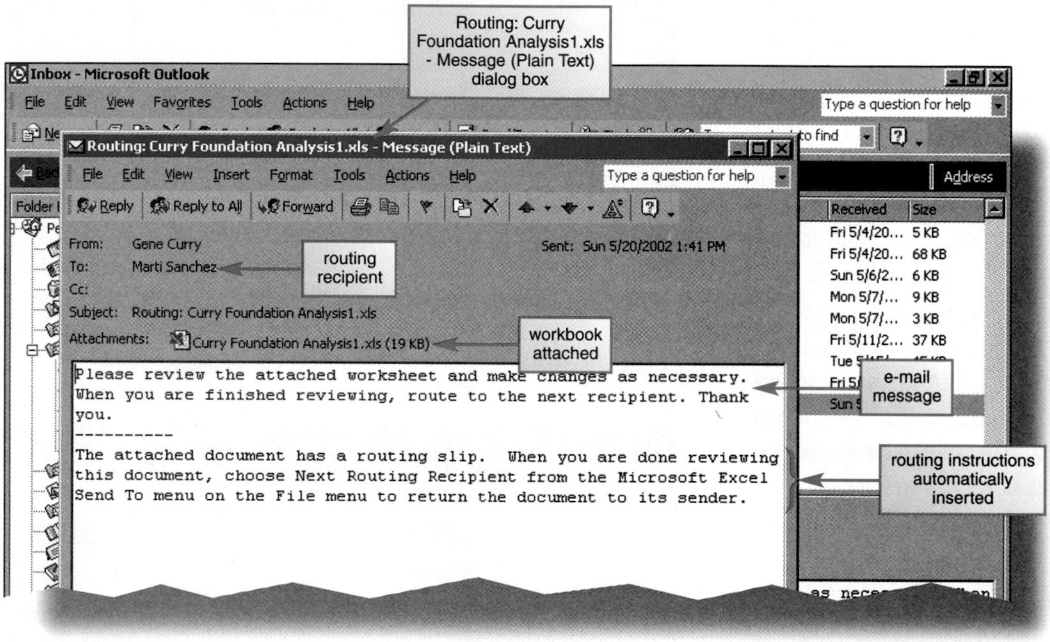

FIGURE 9-46

More About

Shared Workbook Change History

Shared workbooks usually are current, active spreadsheets. Excel maintains a preset change history of 30 days. If you want more time to keep track of changes, you may change the number of days. For example, when you turn on the change history but are not sure exactly when the merge will take place, you can preserve the change history by setting a large number of days to maintain the change history, up to the maximum of 32,767 days.

Excel keeps a **change history** with each shared workbook. In the case of a shared workbook in which you want to track the changes, Excel provides a way for users to make data entry changes, but does not allow them to modify the change history. Click Tools on the menu bar and then point to Protection. In a shared workbook, the only available command on the Protection submenu is **Protect Shared Workbook.** This command displays a dialog box enabling you to protect the change history associated with a shared workbook. Once protected, no one can unprotect, and thereby change, it except the owner.

Reviewing Tracked Changes

Instead of writing suggestions and changes on a printed draft copy, Excel's track changes feature allows users to enter suggested changes directly on the workbook. The owner of the workbook then looks through each change and makes a decision about whether or not to accept it.

Reviewing the Routed Workbook

After a routed workbook has progressed through the entire routing list, it is returned to the owner. Because Highlight Changes was enabled for the Curry Foundation Analysis1 workbook, the file has come back to you with each recipient's changes, corrections, and comments. As the owner, you review those changes and make decisions about whether or not to accept the changes. A tracked workbook named Curry Foundation Analysis2 is stored on the Data Disk. The following steps use this workbook to illustrate reviewing the changes.

Steps To Open a Routed Workbook and Review Tracked Changes

1 With Excel active, click the Open button on the Standard toolbar. When the Open dialog box displays, if necessary click the Look in box arrow and then click 3½ Floppy (A:). Double-click the Curry Foundation Analysis2 workbook. When the workbook displays, click Tools on the menu bar, point to Track Changes, and then point to Highlight Changes.

The Curry Foundation Analysis2 workbook displays, as do the Tools menu and Track Changes submenu (Figure 9-47).

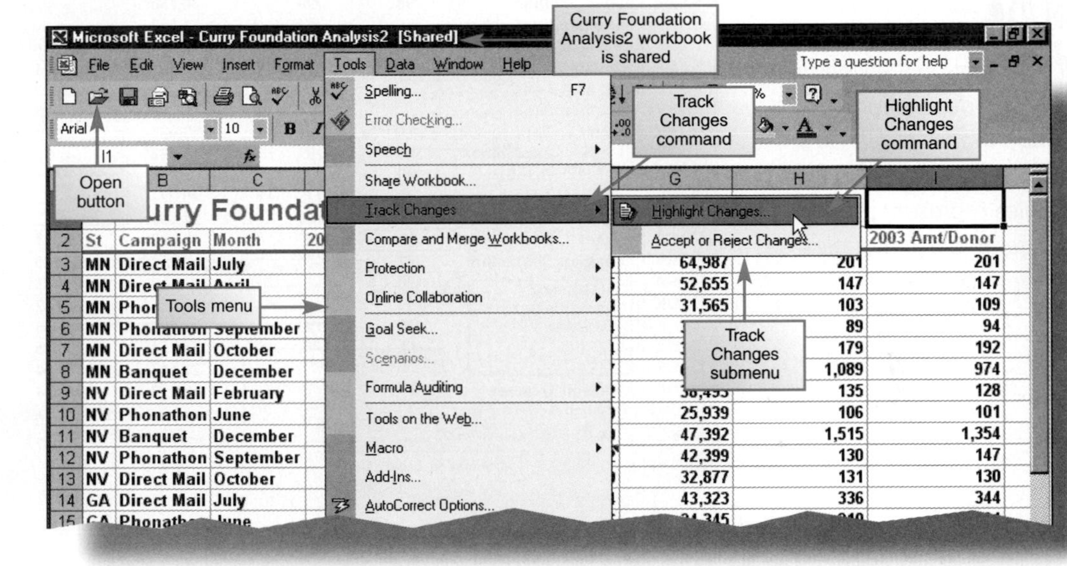

FIGURE 9-47

2 Click Highlight Changes. When the Highlight Changes dialog box displays, click When to clear the check box. Point to the OK button.

The Highlight Changes dialog box displays (Figure 9-48). Removing the check mark from the When check box indicates you want to review all changes in the history file.

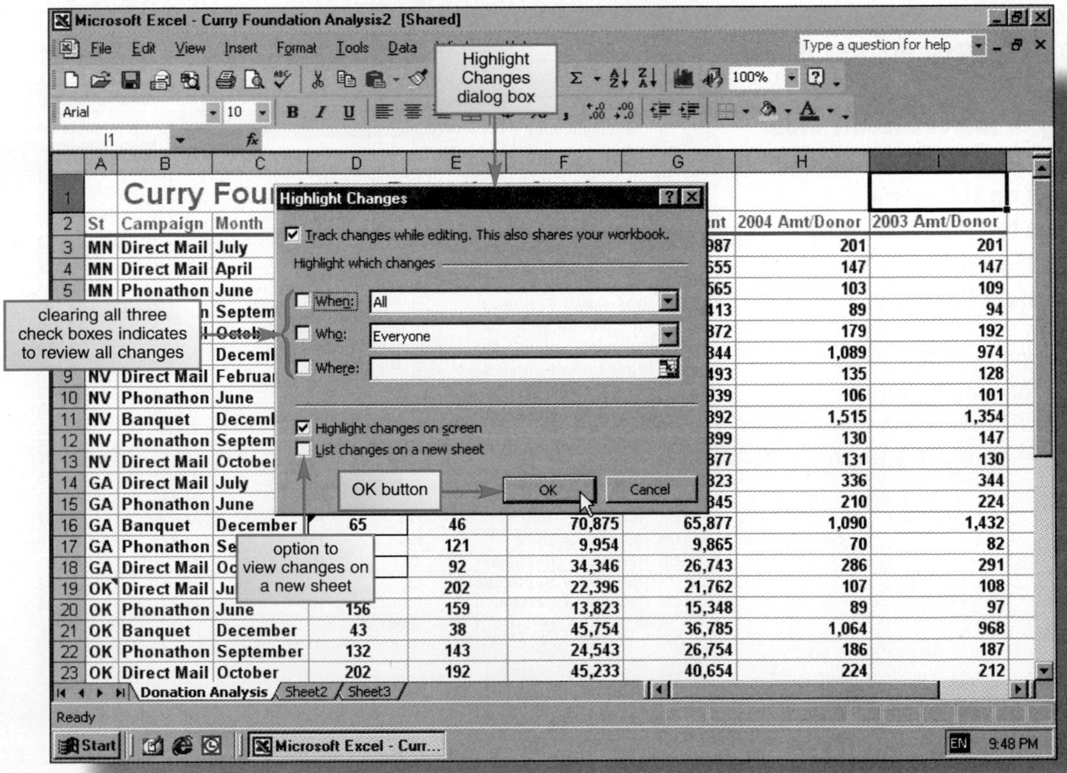

FIGURE 9-48

3 Click the OK button. Click Tools on the menu bar and then click Options. If necessary, click the View tab and then click Comment & indicator in the Comments area. Click the OK button. Point to cell D18.

All comments in the worksheet display. A description of the change made to cell D18 displays (Figure 9-49). Blue triangles represent a data change, and red triangles represent comments.

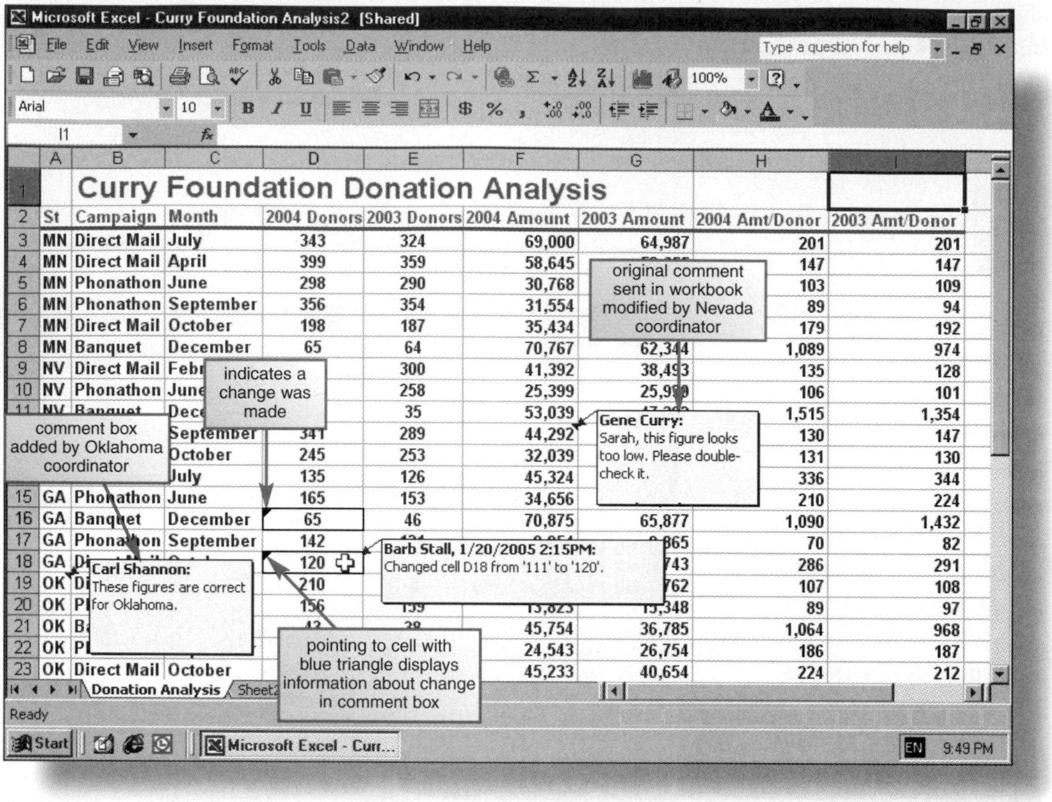

FIGURE 9-49

4 Click Tools on the menu bar and then click Options. If necessary, click the View tab and then click Comment indicator only in the Comments area. Click the OK button. Click Tools on the menu bar, point to Track Changes, and then point to Accept or Reject Changes.

All comments are hidden. The Tools menu and the Track Changes submenu again display (Figure 9-50).

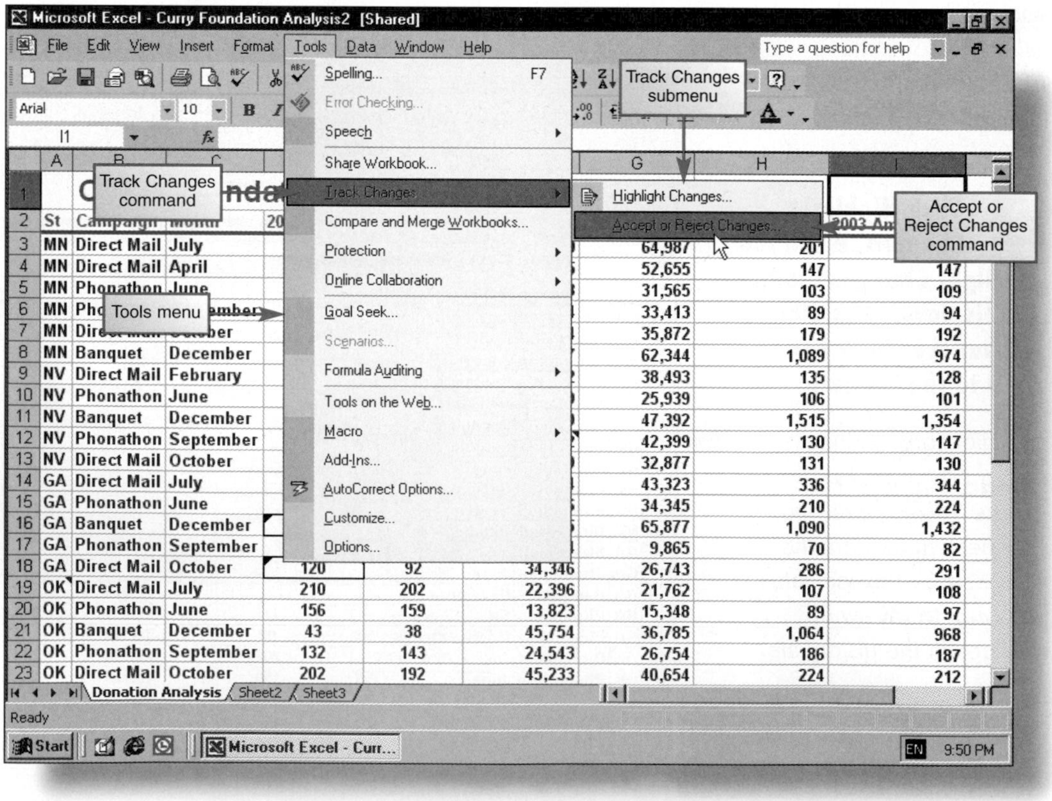

FIGURE 9-50

5 Click Accept or Reject Changes. When the Select Changes to Accept or Reject dialog box displays, if necessary, clear the check boxes and then point to the OK button.

The *Select Changes to Accept or Reject dialog box* allows you to specify the types of changes you want to review (Figure 9-51).

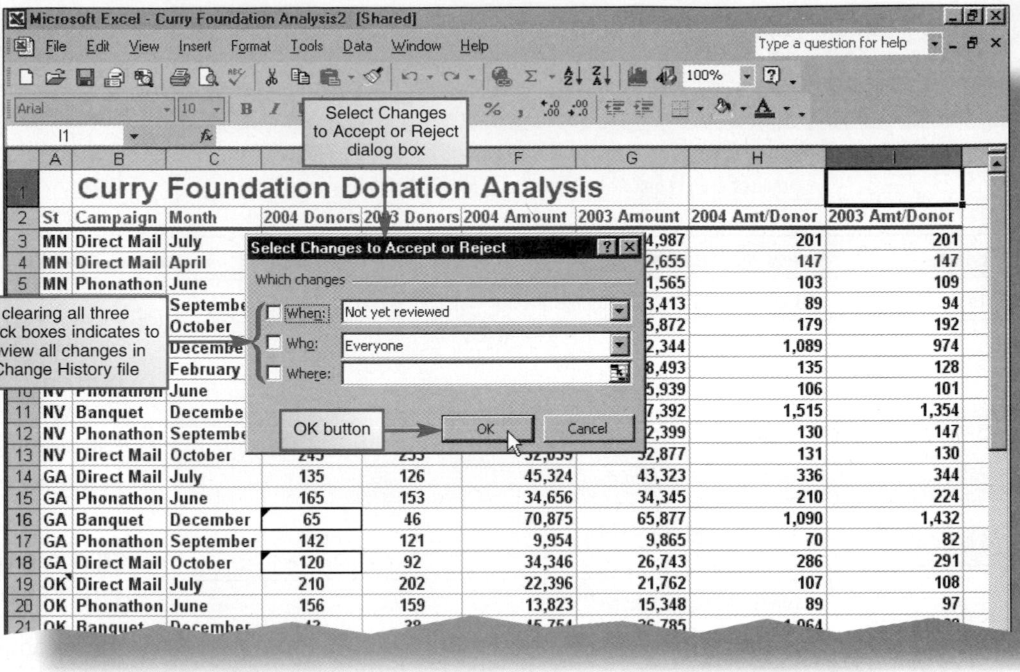

FIGURE 9-51

6 Click the OK button. When the Accept or Reject Changes dialog box displays Change 1, point to the Accept button.

One change at a time displays in the *Accept or Reject Changes dialog box* (Figure 9-52). The cell with the change displays with a marquee. Excel allows you to accept or reject the changes one at a time, or all at once.

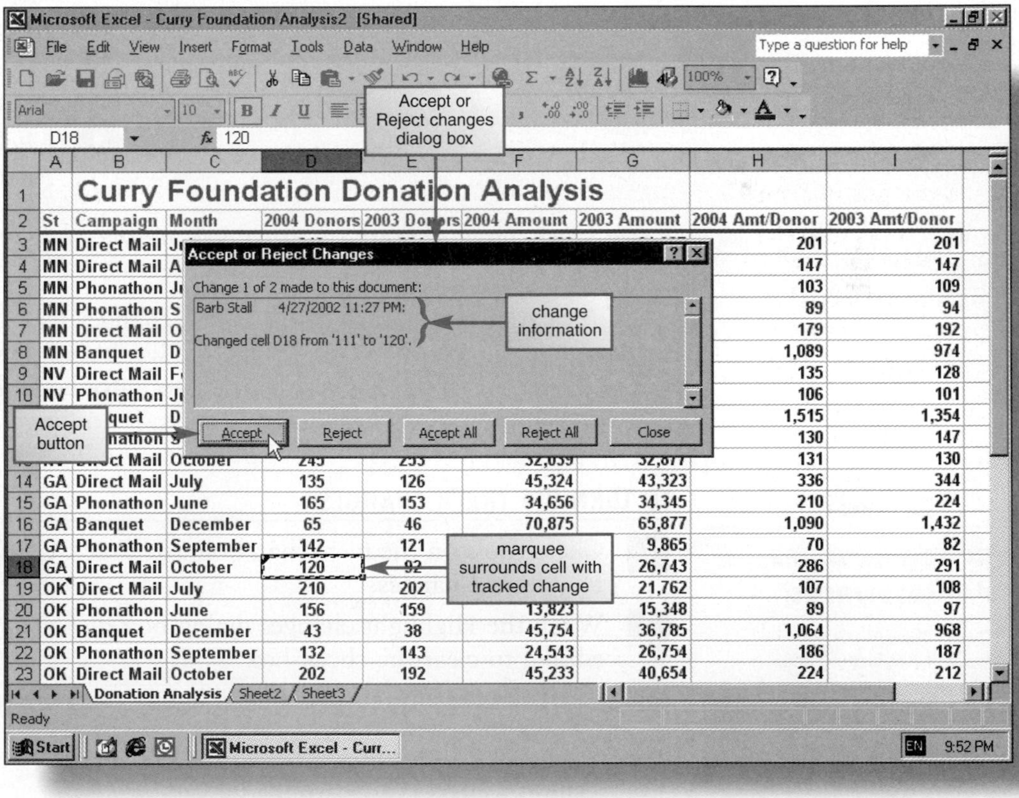

FIGURE 9-52

7 Click the Accept button. As each change displays, click the Accept button. Right-click cell A19 and then click Delete Comment on the shortcut menu. Right-click cell F12 and then click Delete Comment on the shortcut menu.

The process of reviewing and accepting the changes to the workbook is complete.

Table 9-2 Categories of Changes in the Select Changes to Accept or Reject Dialog Box

CHECK BOX	DESCRIPTION
When	Select when you want to review changes within a time interval; the four choices are (1) Since I Last Saved; (2) All; (3) Not Yet Reviewed; and (4) Since Date
Who	View changes based on who made them
Where	View changes made to a range of cells

Table 9-3 Buttons in the Accept or Reject Changes Dialog Box

BUTTON	DESCRIPTION
Accept	Accepts the current change
Reject	Rejects the current change
Accept All	Accepts all changes
Reject All	Rejects all changes
Close	Closes the Accept or Reject Changes dialog box and terminates the procedure

As shown in Figure 9-51 on the previous page, you can select the category of changes in the change history that you want to accept or reject. Table 9-2 summarizes the three check boxes.

For each tracked change, Excel displays the Accept or Reject Changes dialog box (Figure 9-52 on the previous page) with five buttons from which to choose. Table 9-3 summarizes the five buttons.

With the changes accepted, the following steps save the workbook using a new file name.

TO SAVE THE TRACKED CHANGES IN A WORKBOOK WITH A NEW FILE NAME

1. Click File on the menu bar and then click Save As.
2. When the Save As dialog box displays, type `Curry Foundation Analysis3` in the File name text box.
3. If necessary, click 3½ Floppy (A:) in the Save in list.
4. Click the Save button in the Save As dialog box.

Excel saves the workbook on drive A using the file name, Curry Foundation Analysis3.

The next step is to turn off the track changes feature. Excel denies access to features such as the PivotChart while the workbook is shared. Perform the following steps to turn off track changes, which also automatically turns off sharing and saves the workbook as an exclusive one. That is, it no longer is a shared workbook.

TO TURN OFF TRACK CHANGES

1. Click Tools on the menu bar, point to Track Changes, and then click Highlight Changes.
2. When the Highlight changes dialog box displays, click Track Changes while editing to clear the check box.
3. Click the OK button in the Highlight Changes dialog box.
4. When the Microsoft Excel dialog box displays asking you to make the workbook exclusive, click the Yes button.

The workbook displays without the word, Shared, on the title bar. Excel disables track changes.

When you turn off track changes, you turn off sharing as well. At the same time, Excel erases the change history. The workbook automatically resaves as an exclusive workbook. An **exclusive workbook** can be opened only by a single user.

More About

Tracking Changes with Passwords

If you want to make sure others will not turn off the change history or reduce the number of days in the history, you can protect a shared workbook with a password. On the Tools menu click Protection, and then click Protect and Share Workbook. Passwords may be added only if the workbook is unshared at the time of protection.

The imports and changes complete the Curry Foundation Analysis workbook. The next step is to analyze the data using PivotCharts and PivotTables to better understand the information gathered.

Creating and Formatting PivotCharts and PivotTables

A **PivotChart** is an interactive chart used to analyze data graphically by varying the fields and categories to present different views. After you create a PivotChart, you may view different levels of detail, reorganize the layout of the chart by dragging its fields, or display and hide items in drop-down lists. While you usually create a PivotChart on a separate worksheet in the same workbook containing the data you are analyzing, you can create a PivotChart on the same worksheet as the data.

When you create a PivotChart, Excel creates and associates a PivotTable automatically. A **PivotTable** is an interactive view of worksheet data that gives you the ability to summarize data in the database, and then rotate the table's row and column titles to show different views of the summarized data.

More About

PivotTables

The PivotTable is one of the most powerful analytical tools available in Excel. PivotTables are used to show the relationships among the data in a list or a database. These tables allow you to use drag and drop to examine the data from different views.

Creating a PivotChart

The **PivotChart command** on the Data menu starts the **PivotTable and PivotChart Wizard**, which guides you through creating a PivotChart. The wizard does not modify the data in any way; it simply uses the data to generate information on a new worksheet.

The required PivotChart for this project is shown in Figure 9-53. It summarizes 2003 and 2004 total amounts per donor information by fundraising campaign type within state for the Donation Analysis worksheet. The x-axis displays categories by fundraising campaign within state. The y-axis displays the series values for the total amount per donor for each year. The interactive buttons allow the user to choose which fields to display. The legend displays the color coding for each year.

To create the PivotChart shown in Figure 9-53, perform the steps on the next page.

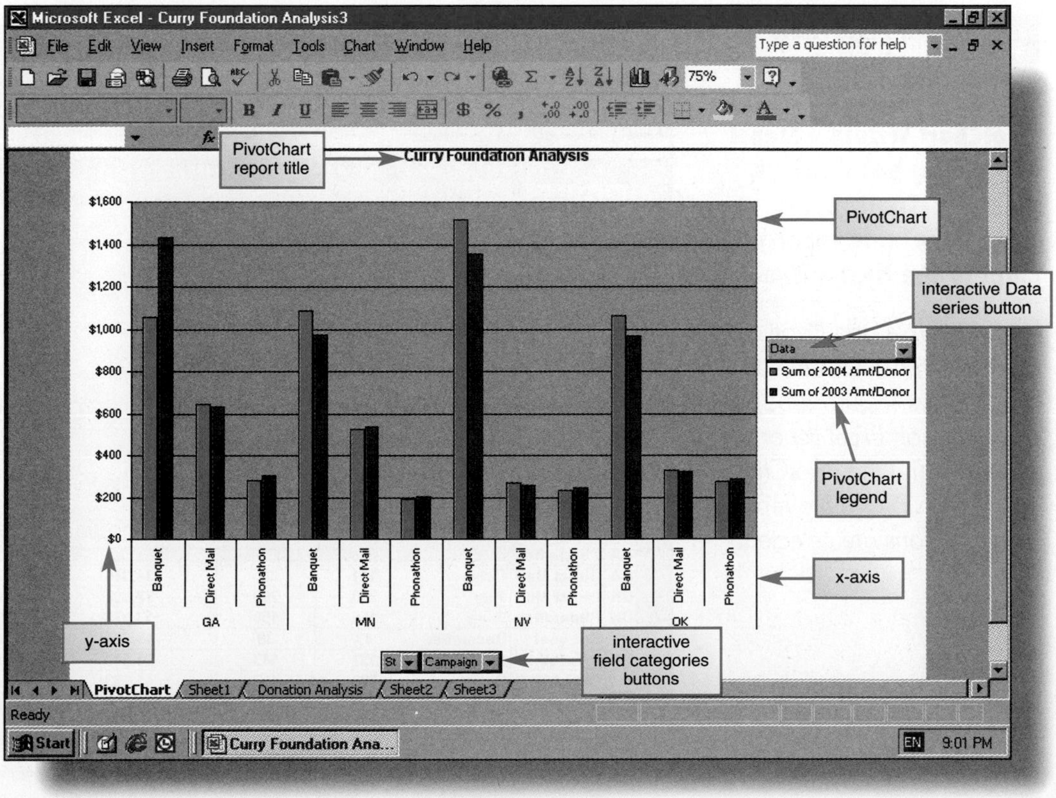

FIGURE 9-53

Steps To Create a PivotChart

1 Scroll to and then click cell A3. Click Data on the menu bar and then point to PivotTable and PivotChart Report (Figure 9-54).

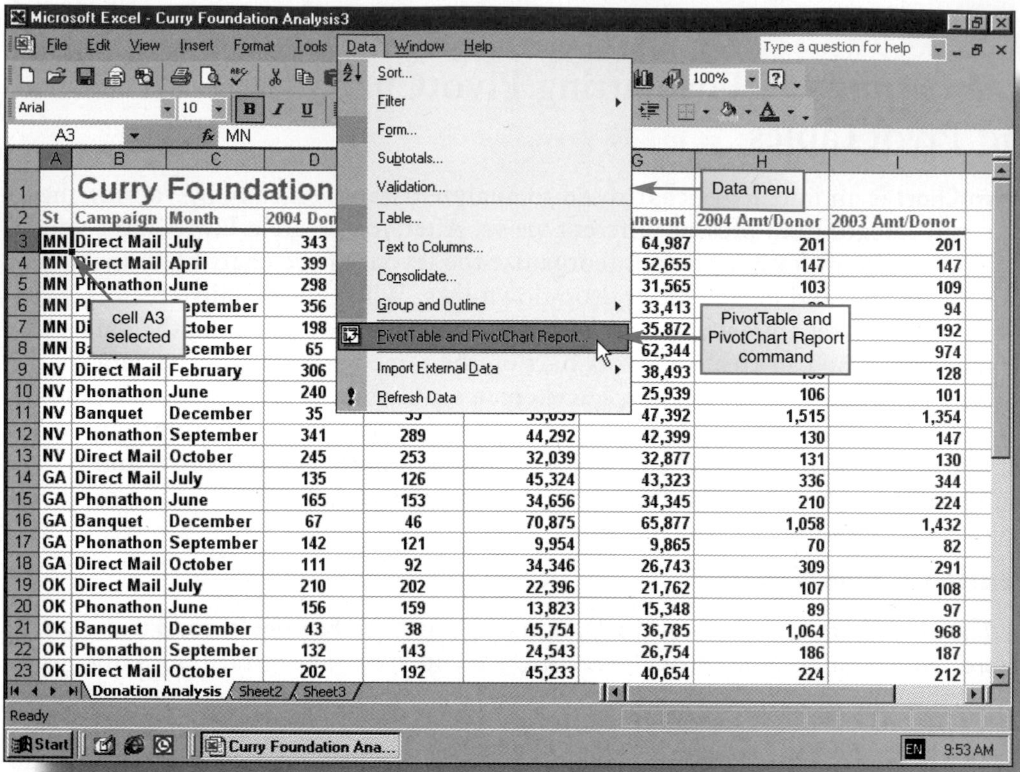

FIGURE 9-54

2 Click PivotTable and PivotChart Report. When the PivotTable and PivotChart Wizard - Step 1 of 3 dialog box displays, click PivotChart report (with PivotTable report). Point to the Next button.

The PivotTable and PivotChart Wizard - Step 1 of 3 dialog box displays (Figure 9-55). The Microsoft Excel list or database and the PivotChart report (with PivotTable report) option buttons are selected.

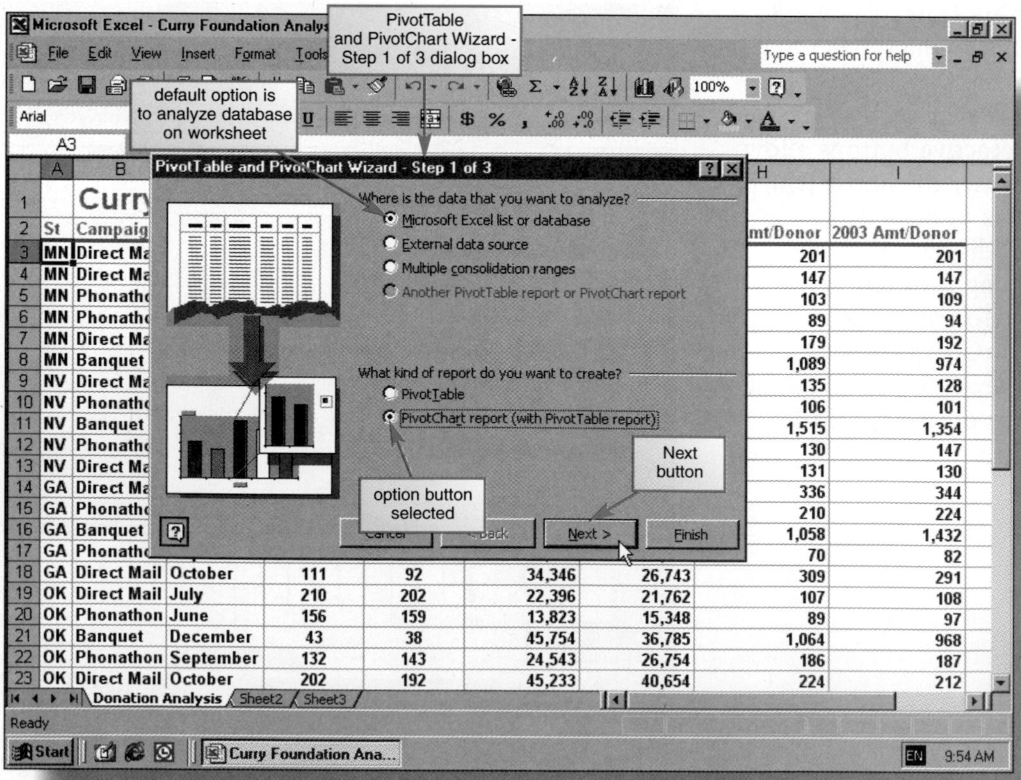

FIGURE 9-55

3 Click the Next button.

The PivotTable and PivotChart Wizard - Step 2 of 3 dialog box displays. The range A2:I23 automatically is selected (Figure 9-56). A marquee surrounds the data on the worksheet.

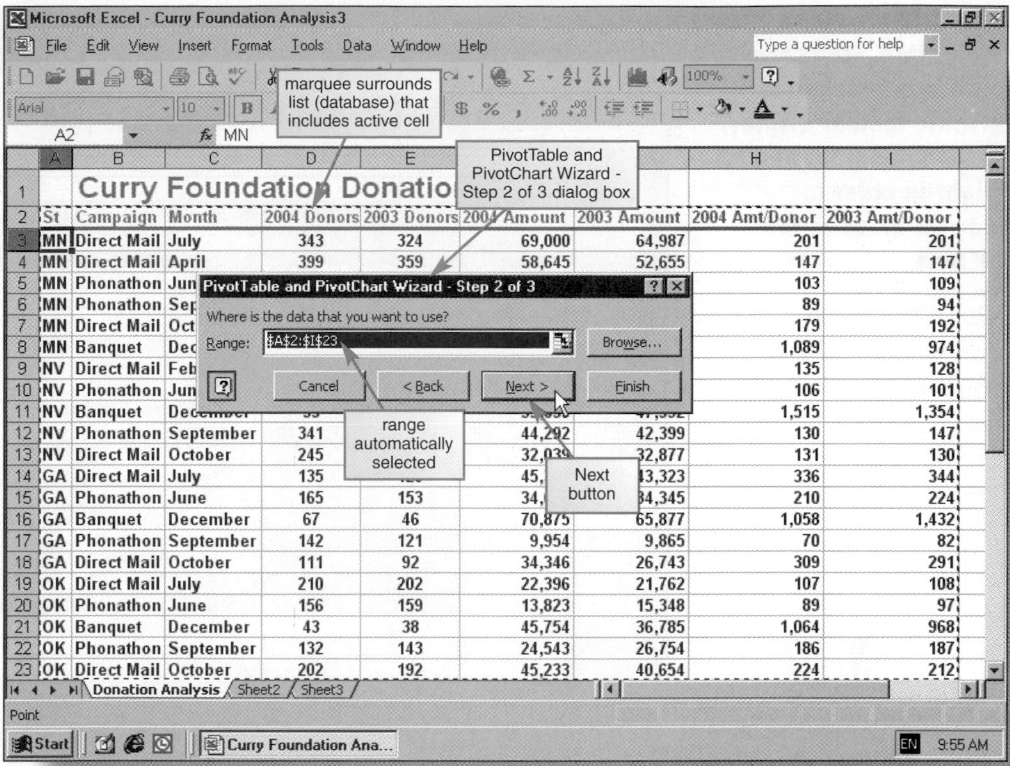

FIGURE 9-56

4 Click the Next button. When the PivotTable and PivotChart Wizard - Step 3 of 3 displays, if necessary, click New worksheet and then point to the Finish button.

The wizard will place the chart and table on separate worksheets in the workbook (Figure 9-57).

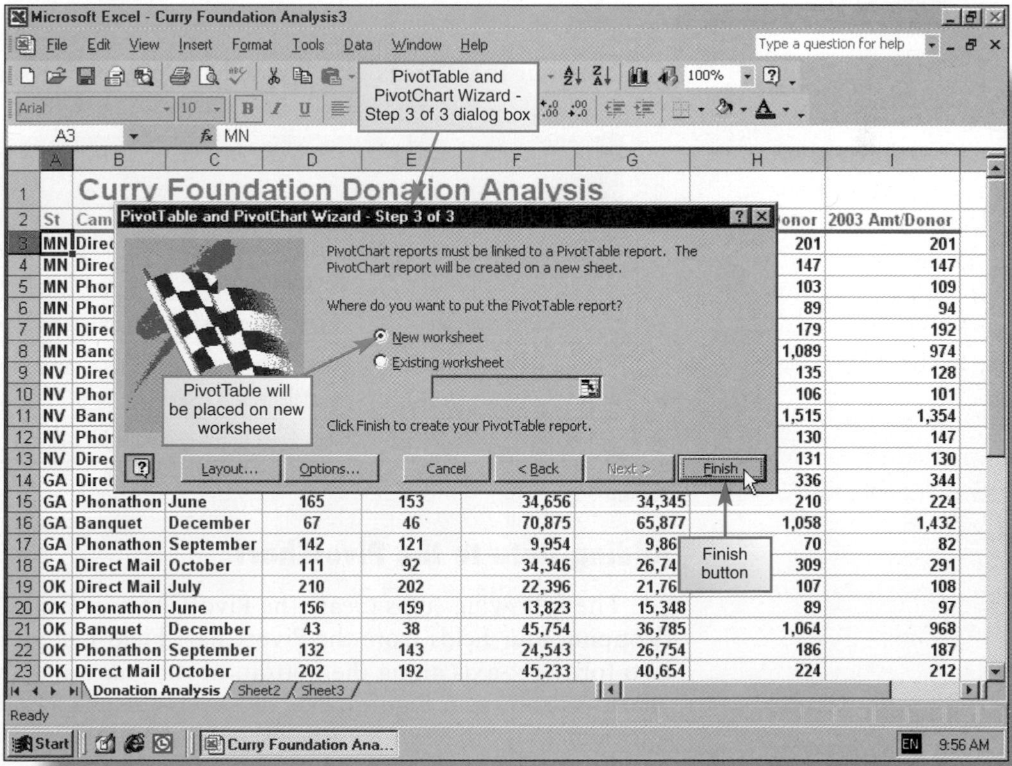

FIGURE 9-57

5 Click the Finish button. When the PivotChart area and the PivotTable toolbar display, drag the toolbar up and to the right in order to display all areas of the PivotChart.

*The PivotChart displays on a new worksheet (Figure 9-58). The **PivotTable toolbar** also displays. Fields from the list of data display in the PivotTable Field List window.*

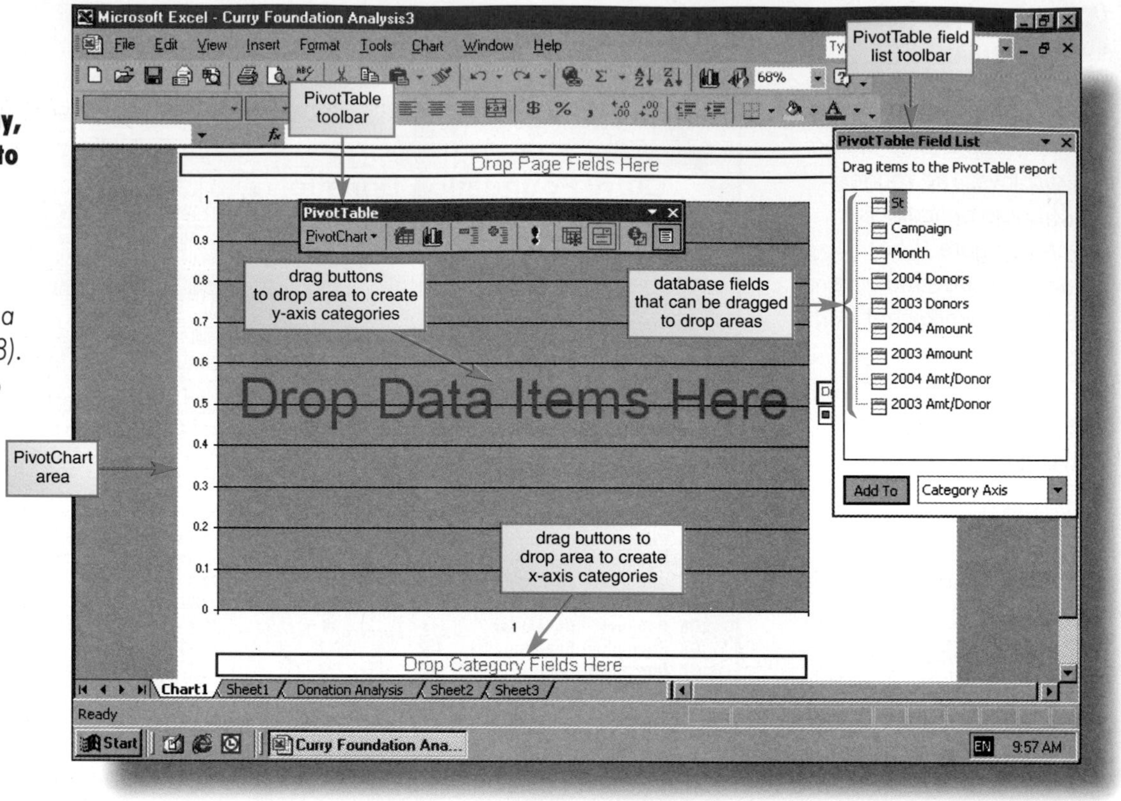

FIGURE 9-58

Other Ways

1. Press ALT+D, P
2. In Voice Command mode, say "Data, PivotTable"

The four main areas of a PivotChart (Figure 9-58) are described in Table 9-4.

Table 9-4 PivotChart Drop Areas

PIVOTCHART DROP AREA	DESCRIPTION OF DATA
Drop Page Fields Here	Data fields that categorize the entire chart
Drop Data Items Here	Data fields plotted on the chart, summarizing the detail of the database cells
Drop Series Fields Here	Multiple data items plotted as a series, summarizing the detail columns of the database cells (y-axis)
Drop Category Fields Here	Data fields to categorize on the x-axis

Adding Data to the PivotChart

The following steps create the PivotChart in Figure 9-53 on page E 9.39 by dropping four fields from the PivotChart Field List window in the PivotChart area: two for the x-axis along the bottom of the chart and two for the data series in the chart. As shown in Figure 9-53, the x-axis displays campaign within state. The y-axis includes the two data fields 2003 Amt/Donor and 2004 Amt/Donor.

Steps To Add Data to the PivotChart

1 Drag the St (state) button from the PivotTable Field List window to the Drop Category Fields Here area. Drag the Campaign button from the PivotTable Field List window and drop it to the right of the St (state) button. Point to the 2003 Amt/Donor button.

The State and Campaign field buttons display at the bottom of the chart (Figure 9-59).

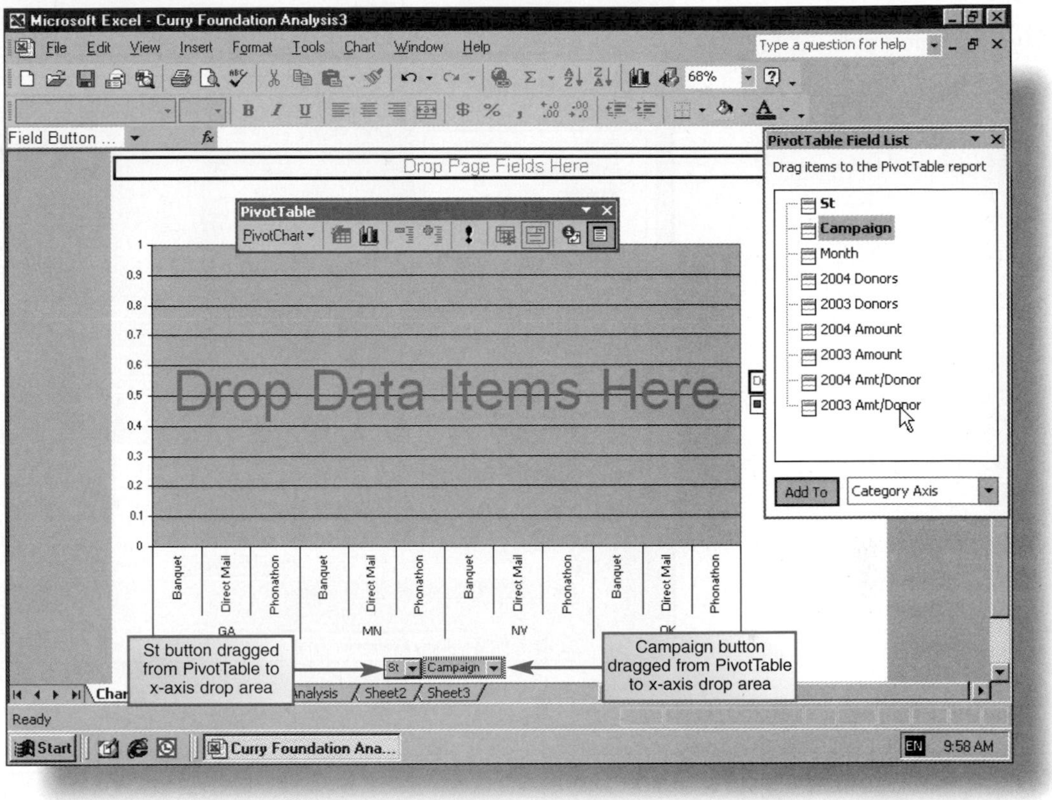

FIGURE 9-59

2 Drag the PivotTable Field List window to the left side of the screen. Drag the 2003 Amt/Donor button to the Drop Data Items Here area in the center of the chart area. Drag the 2004 Amt/Donor button to the same area.

The data fields display in the PivotChart (Figure 9-60). Because multiple fields have been added to the chart, a field Data button displays in the categories area at the bottom of the chart.

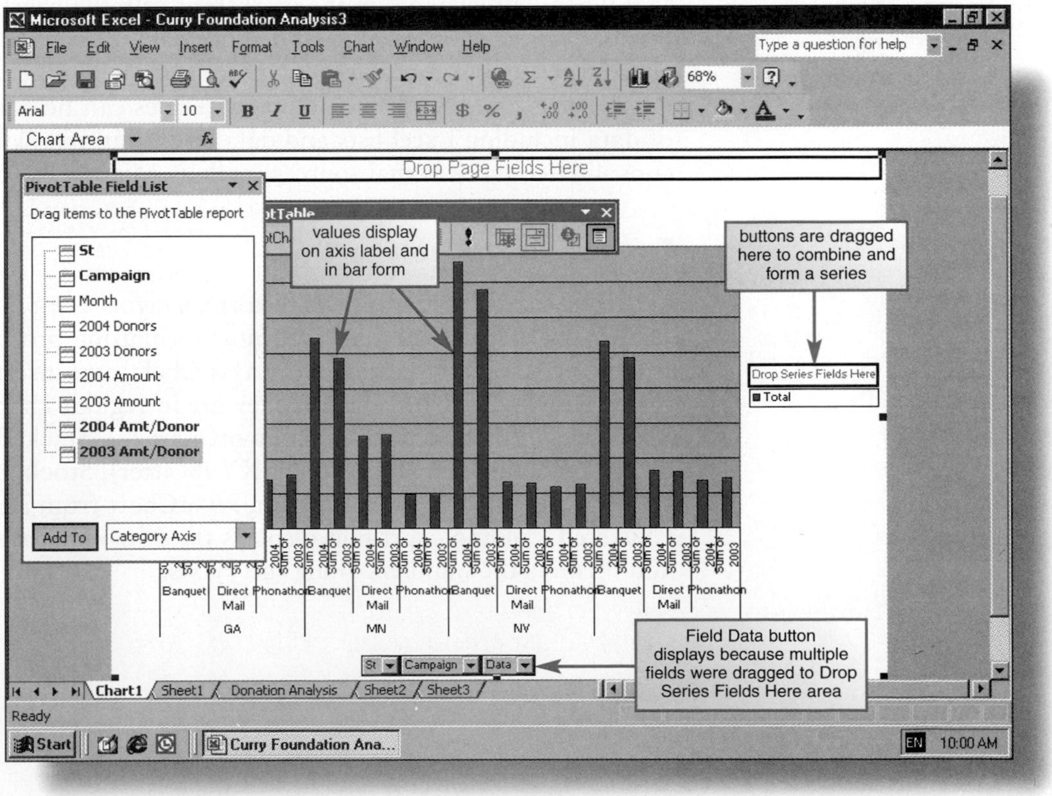

FIGURE 9-60

3 Drag the Field Data button to the Drop Series Fields Here area.

The two data fields display stacked (Figure 9-61).

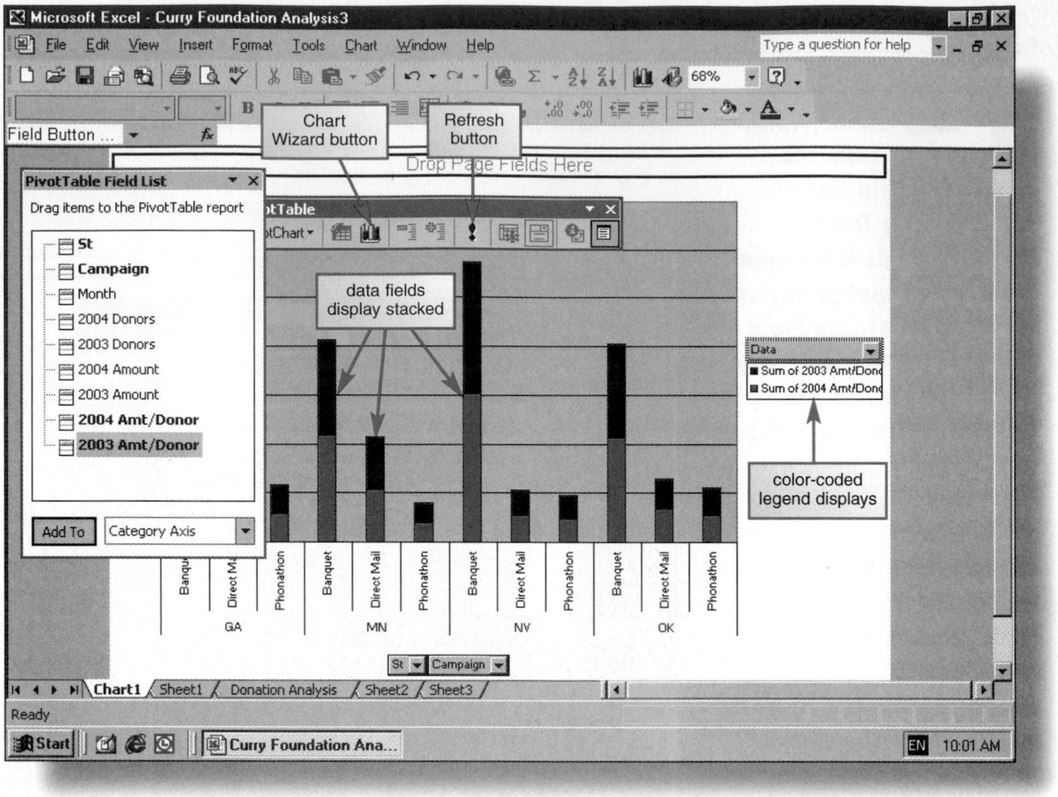

FIGURE 9-61

Other Ways

1. In PivotTable and PivotChart Wizard - Step 3 of 3 dialog box, click Layout button

Regular charts in Excel are linked directly to worksheet cells, which means that when data changes in the worksheet cell, the chart is updated automatically. PivotCharts are not linked to worksheet cells. The PivotTable toolbar contains a Refresh button (Figure 9-61) to update data when it changes on the worksheet. PivotCharts and their associated PivotTables can be based on several different types of data including Excel lists and databases, multiple data ranges that you want to consolidate, and external sources, such as Microsoft Access databases.

Formatting a PivotChart

Excel provides many ways to format PivotCharts. If you are familiar with regular charts, you will find that most formatting processes, such as choosing a chart type, displaying category or axis labels, and inserting titles, are performed the same way in PivotCharts as they are in regular charts.

The default chart type for a PivotChart is a Stacked Column chart. PivotCharts can display any chart type except XY (Scatter), Stock, or Bubble. The following steps change the Curry Foundation PivotChart from a Stacked Column chart to a Clustered Column chart that displays the two-year data side by side, adds a title, and formats the numbers along the y-axis.

Steps To Change the PivotChart Type and Format the Chart

1 Click the Chart Wizard button (shown in Figure 9-61) on the PivotTable toolbar. When the Chart Wizard - Step 1 of 4 - Chart Type dialog box displays, click the Clustered Column chart in the top row of the Chart sub-type box. Point to the Next button.

The Chart Type dialog box allows you to choose the type of chart and its subtype (Figure 9-62). Clicking the Press and Hold to View Sample button produces a preview.

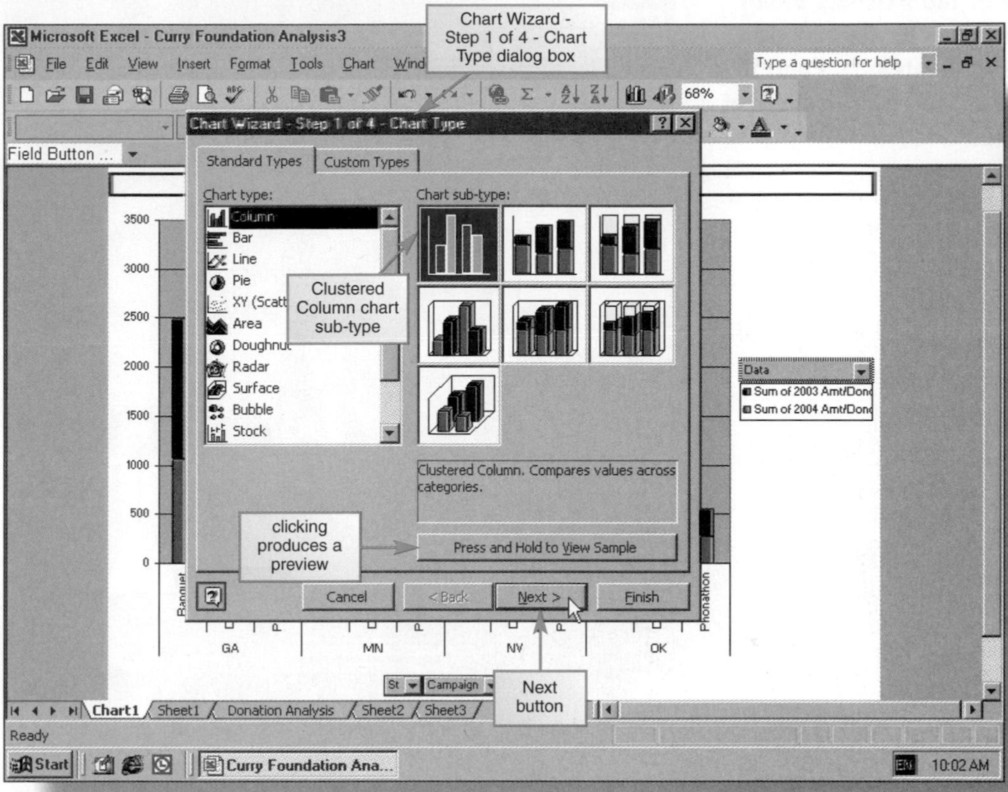

FIGURE 9-62

2 Click the Next button. When the Chart Wizard - Step 3 of 4 - Chart Options dialog box displays, if necessary, click the Titles tab. Click the Chart title text box, type `Curry Foundation Analysis` **and then point to the Finish button.**

The Chart Options dialog box displays as shown in Figure 9-63.

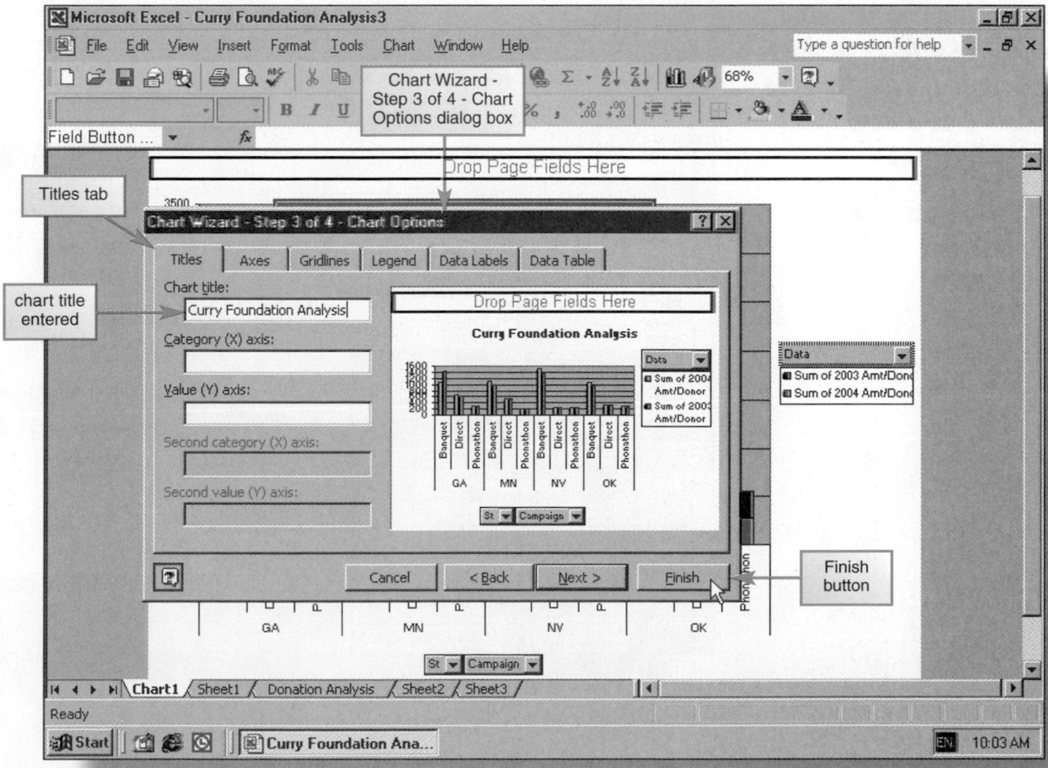

FIGURE 9-63

3 **Click the Finish button. Right-click any of the numbers along the y-axis on the left side of the PivotChart. Point to Format Axis on the shortcut menu.**

The Chart Wizard closes and the shortcut menu displays (Figure 9-64). Clicking the Finish button accepted the default values for the rest of the Chart Wizard.

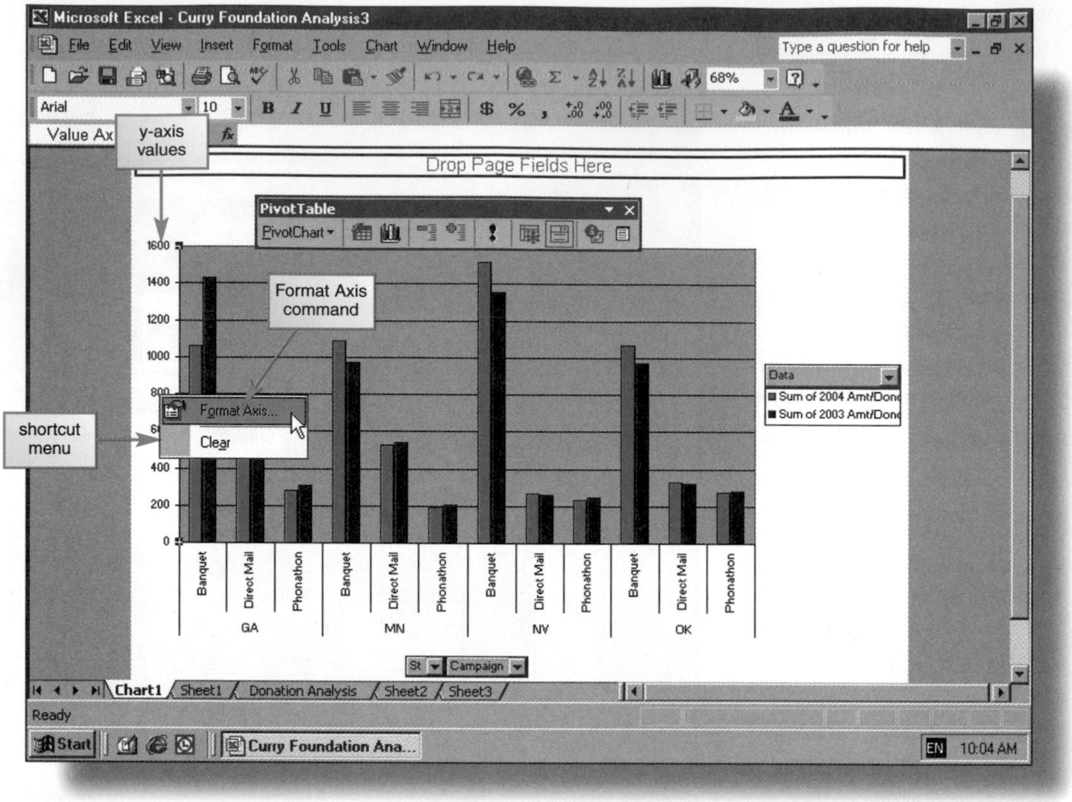

FIGURE 9-64

4 **Click Format Axis. When the Format Axis dialog box displays, click the Number tab, and then click Currency in the Category list. Type** 0 **in the Decimal places box. Point to the OK button.**

*The **Format Axis dialog box** displays as shown in Figure 9-65.*

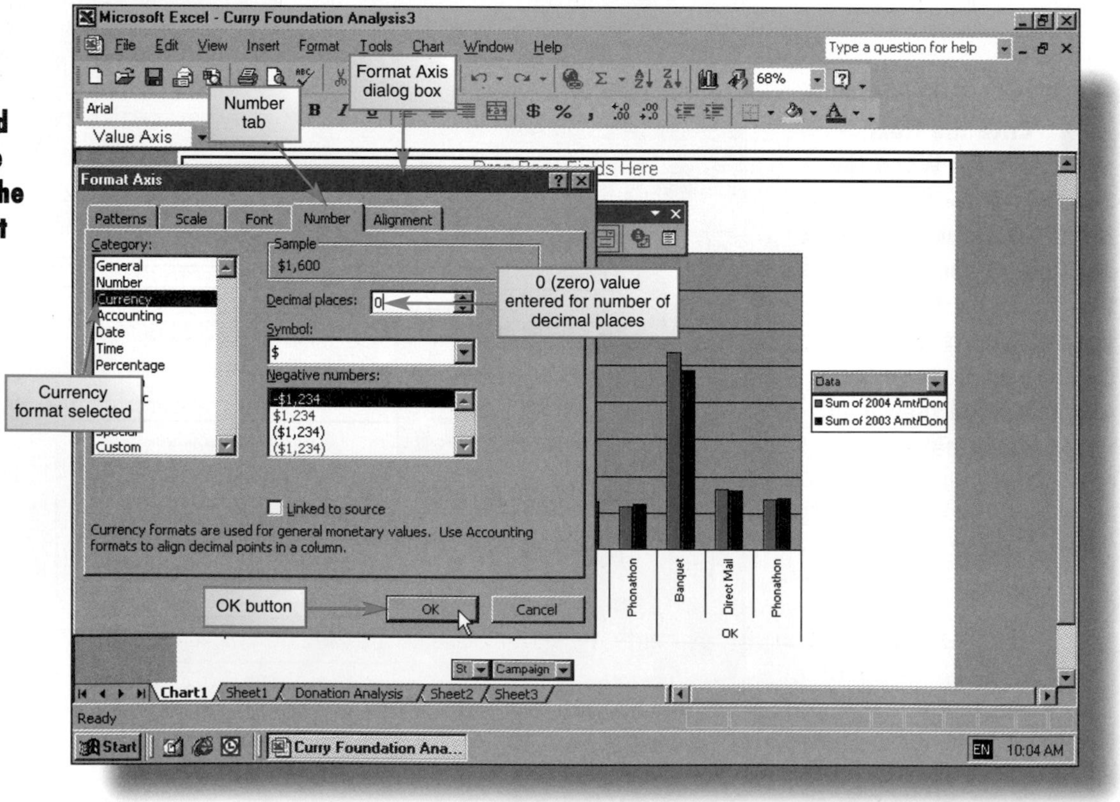

FIGURE 9-65

5 Click the OK button. Double-click the Chart1 sheet tab at the bottom of the workbook. Type `PivotChart` and then press the ENTER key to rename the sheet.

The numbers along the y-axis display using the Currency format (Figure 9-66).

6 Click anywhere on the chart to deselect the y-axis. Click the PivotTable toolbar Close button and then click the Save button on the Standard toolbar.

Excel saves the workbook with the PivotChart on drive A.

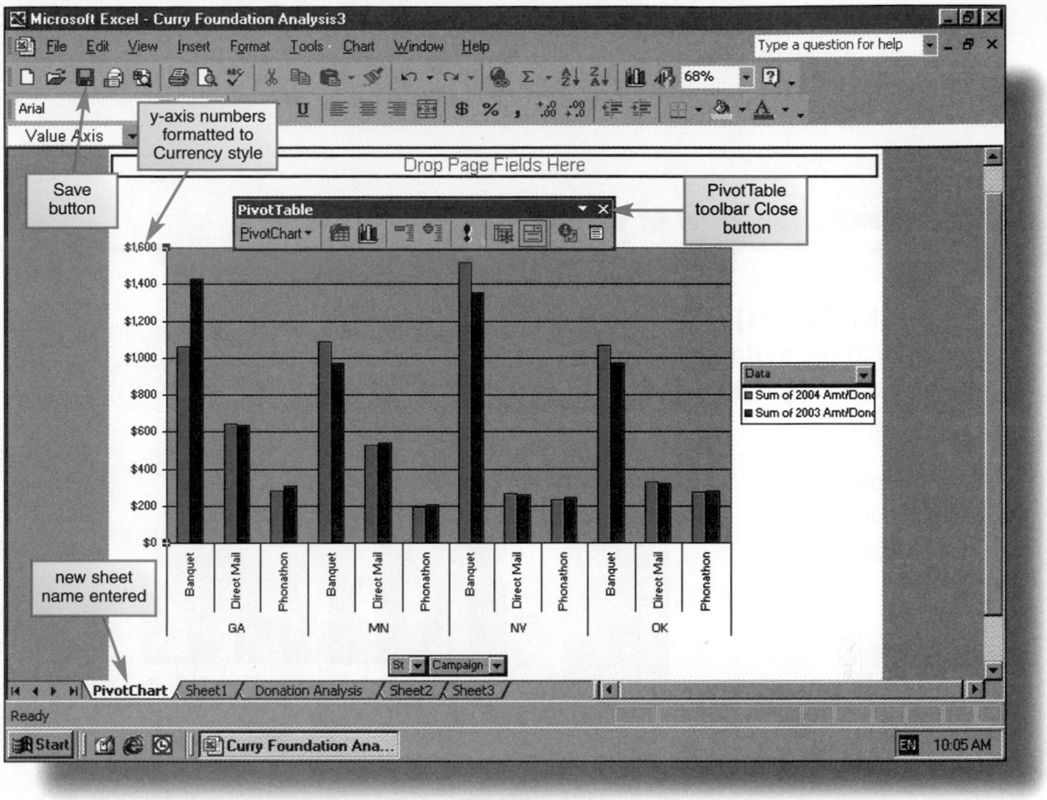

FIGURE 9-66

Other Ways

1. Click PivotChart button on PivotTable toolbar, click Options
2. Click Chart Wizard button on PivotTable toolbar, apply formatting in each wizard step

With the chart completed and formatted appropriately, the chart can be manipulated and the data analyzed in a variety of views.

Changing the View of a PivotChart

With regular charts, you must create one chart for each view of the data summary that you want to see. With a PivotChart, you are able to create a single chart and view the summaries several ways just by using the mouse. The PivotChart provides a powerful interactive summarization of data with the visual appeal and benefits of a chart.

The Curry Foundation PivotChart currently displays the amount per donor for each year within campaign type within state (Figure 9-66).

It is easy to see common trends, such as that banquets seem to have declining amounts given per donor while other event types are increasing in the amount given for each donor. You also can see that in general, Georgia is experiencing better growth than the other states. You may wish to view the data in other ways, such as just looking at one year's worth of information. If you want to compare the data in different combinations, you can use the interactive buttons in the categories area at the bottom of the chart.

Because Minnesota and Oklahoma have similar target audiences for the Curry Foundation fundraising efforts, you might want to view the data and compare only those two states rather than all four. Moving the two data ranges next to each other in the worksheet would be tedious; in the PivotChart, however, you may choose which categories to display by using the interactive buttons at the bottom of the chart.

If you want to isolate two years to compare to one another, for instance, you use the interactive buttons in the series area on the right of the chart.

Perform the following steps to interact with the PivotChart categories and series of data.

Steps To Change the View of a PivotChart

1 Drag the St (state) button at the bottom of the chart to the right of the Campaign button

Notice the locations are grouped by campaign now, rather than by states (Figure 9-67).

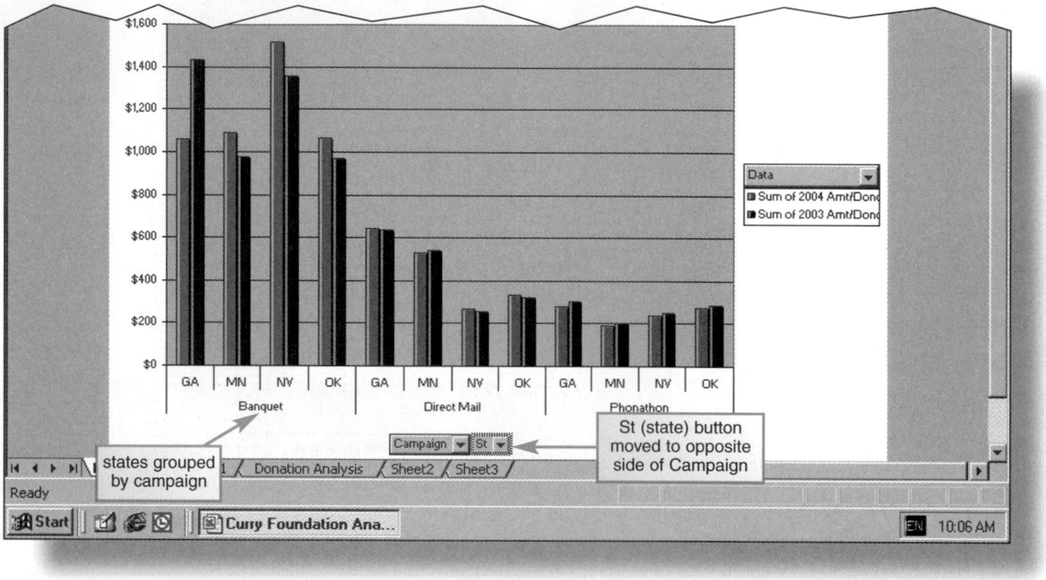

FIGURE 9-67

2 Click the Data button arrow on the right of the chart. When the list displays, click the check box next to Sum of 2003 Amt/Donor to clear the check box. Point to the OK button.

The list of fields of data on the chart displays (Figure 9-68).

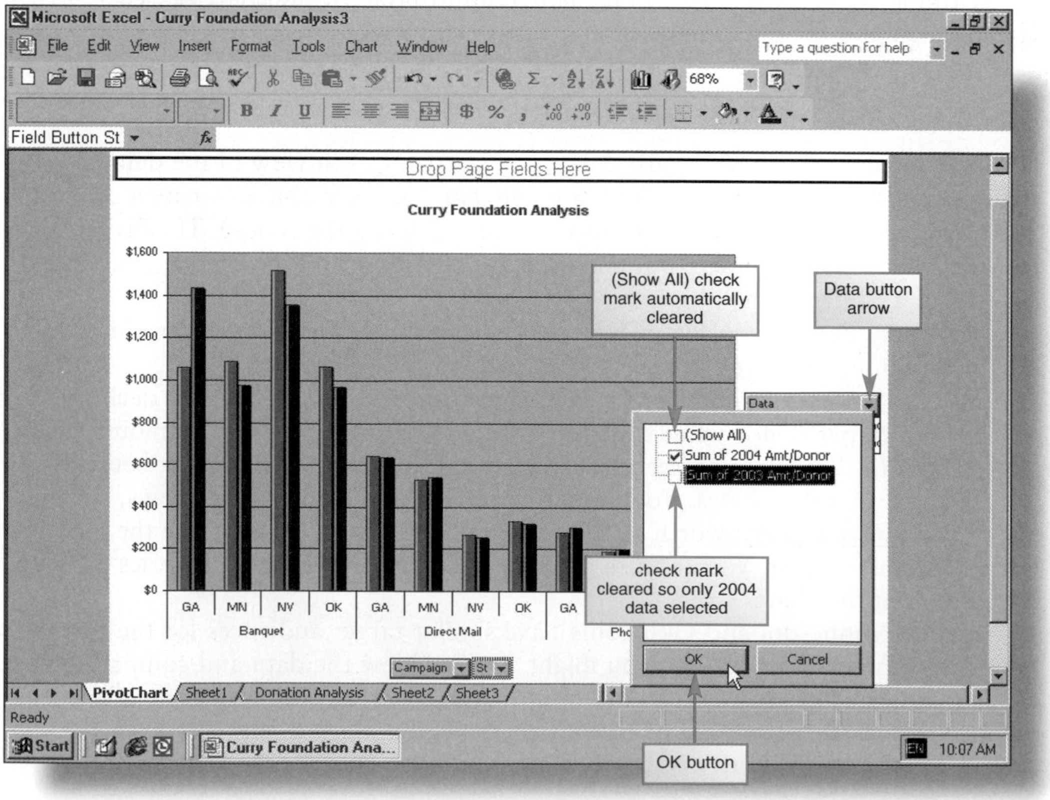

FIGURE 9-68

3 Click the OK button. Point to the Undo button on the Standard toolbar.

Only the data for 2004 displays (Figure 9-69). The Sum of 2004 Amt/Donor becomes a field for the entire page.

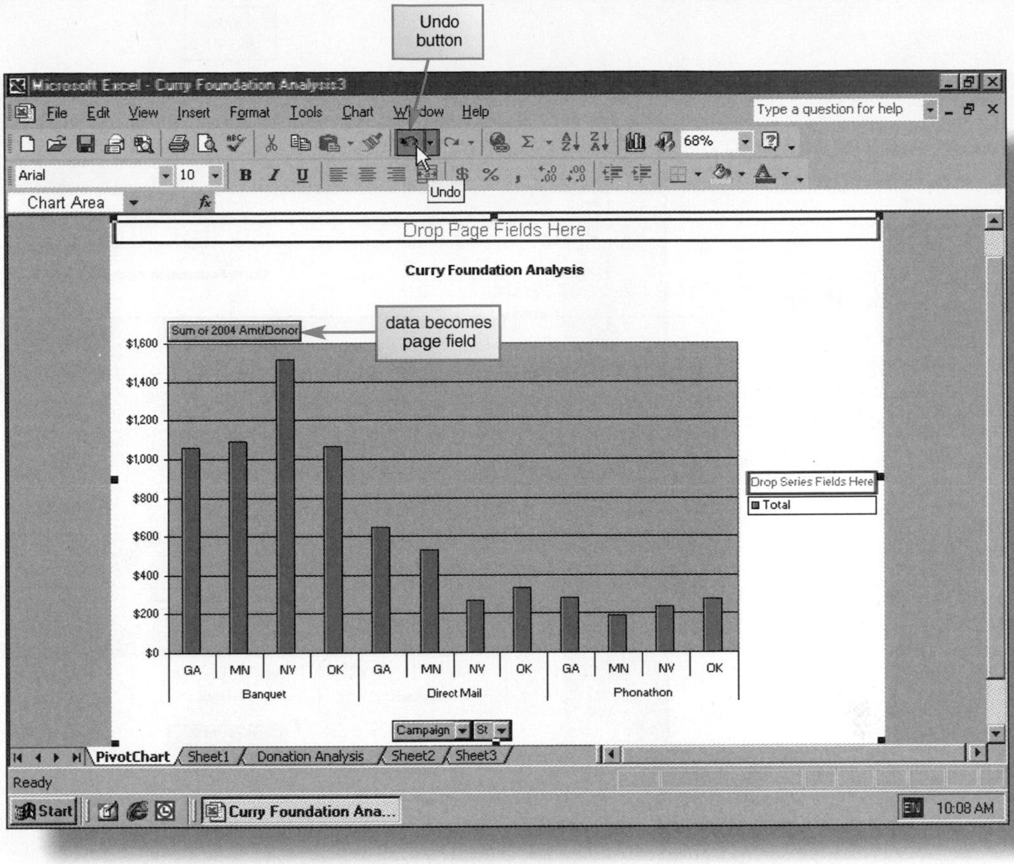

FIGURE 9-69

4 Click the Undo button on the Standard toolbar. Click the arrow on the St (state) interactive button, click the check boxes for Georgia (GA) and Nevada (NV) to clear them, and then point to the OK button.

The data fields in the St (state) button display (Figure 9-70). The 2003 data again displays in the PivotChart.

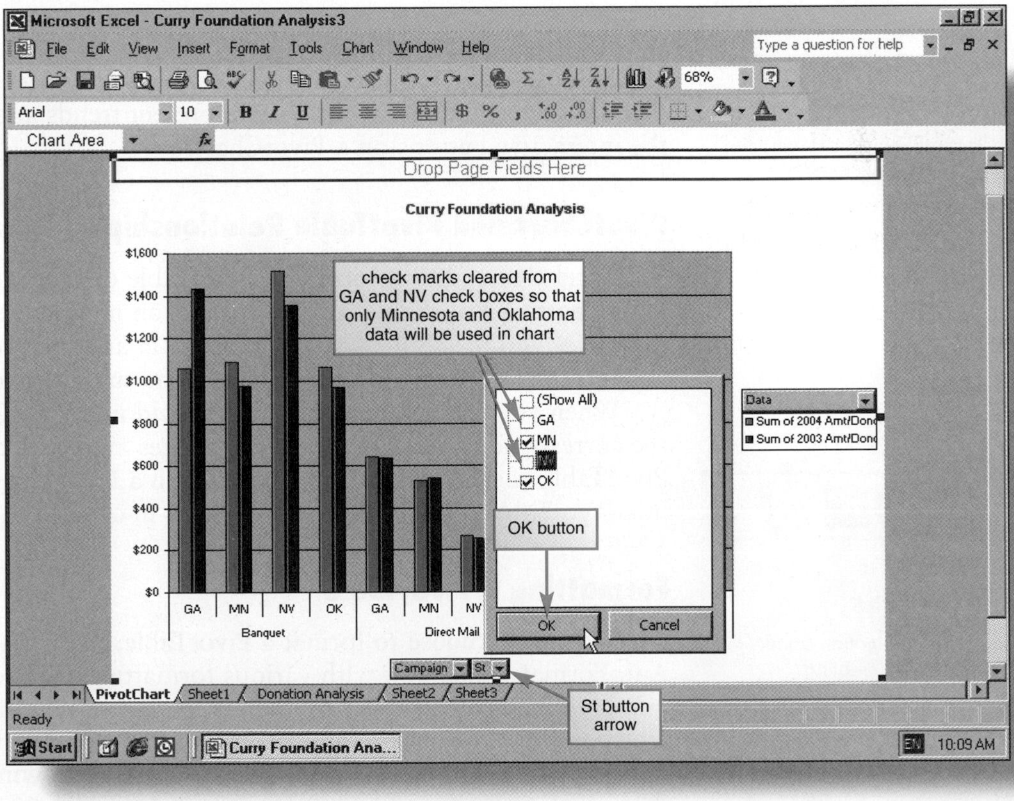

FIGURE 9-70

5 Click the OK button.

Only the data for Minnesota and Oklahoma displays (Figure 9-71).

6 Click the Undo button on the Standard toolbar.

The data for all states displays (Figure 9-67 on page E 9.48).

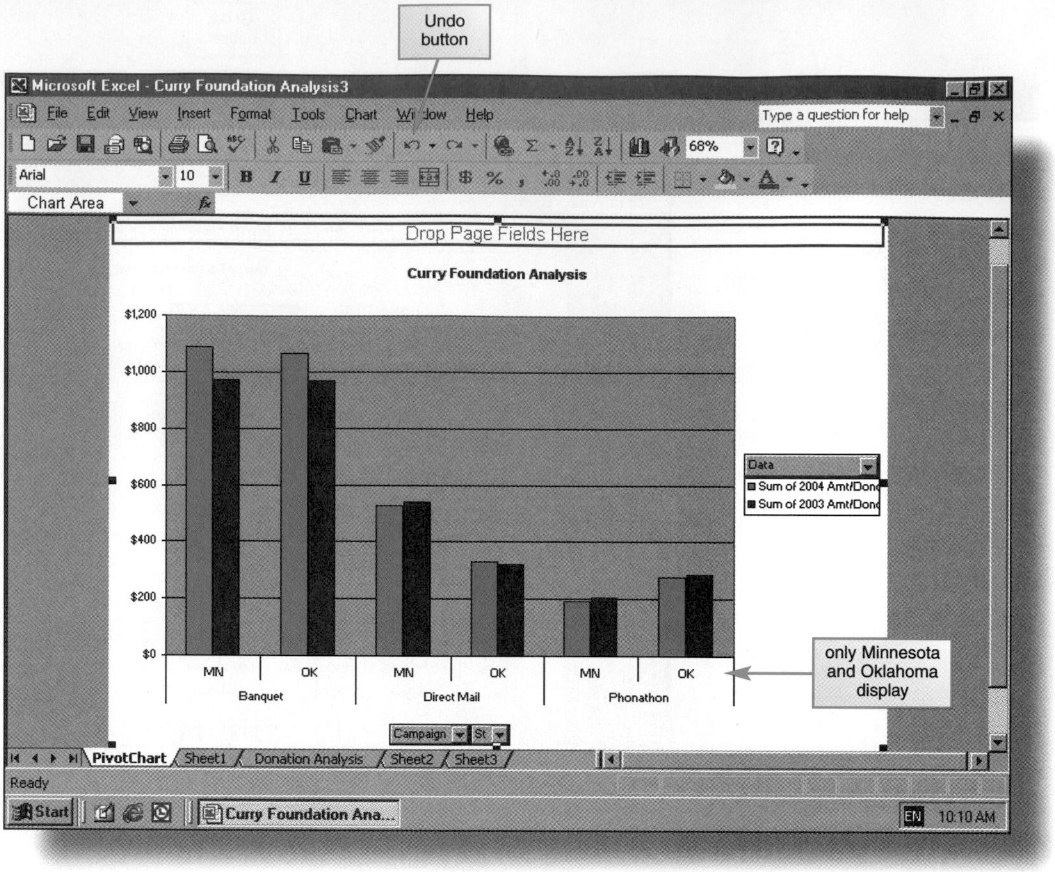

FIGURE 9-71

Other Ways

1. To remove data, drag button off chart
2. To add data, drag field from PivotTable Field List window to desired location
3. Right-click field button and then click Remove Field on the shortcut menu

You can employ powerful data summarization techniques using PivotCharts. Choosing which kinds of data best represent trends and comparisons is easy with the interactive buttons on a PivotChart.

PivotChart and PivotTable Relationships

Excel creates and associates a PivotTable on a separate sheet with every PivotChart. A PivotTable (Figure 9-72) is an interactive view of worksheet data that gives you the ability to summarize data and then rotate the table's row and column titles to show different views of the summarized data.

When you change the position of a field in a PivotChart or PivotTable, the corresponding field in the other changes automatically. **Row fields** in a PivotTable correspond to category fields in a PivotChart, while **column fields** in a PivotTable correspond to series fields in charts.

More About

Creating PivotTables

For more information about the process of creating PivotTables, visit the Excel 2002 More About Web page (scsite.com/ex2002/more.htm) and then click PivotTables.

Formatting a PivotTable

When you choose to format a PivotTable, Excel displays samples in the AutoFormat dialog box with various formatting applied to the cells, borders, and numbers. You can choose from colors, patterns, alignments, fonts, and borders, which apply to the entire table. You also may apply any of the wide range of Excel's normal formats to individual cells. The following steps choose a format that contains color and borders to enhance the data.

Steps To Format a PivotTable

1 Double-click the Sheet1 tab at the bottom of the workbook. Type `PivotTable` and then press the ENTER key to rename the sheet. Right-click a toolbar and click PivotTable on the shortcut menu to display the PivotTable toolbar. Point to the Format Report button on the PivotTable toolbar.

The PivotTable, created by Excel and associated with the PivotChart, displays (Figure 9-72). If the PivotTable toolbar does not display, right-click the toolbar and click PivotTable.

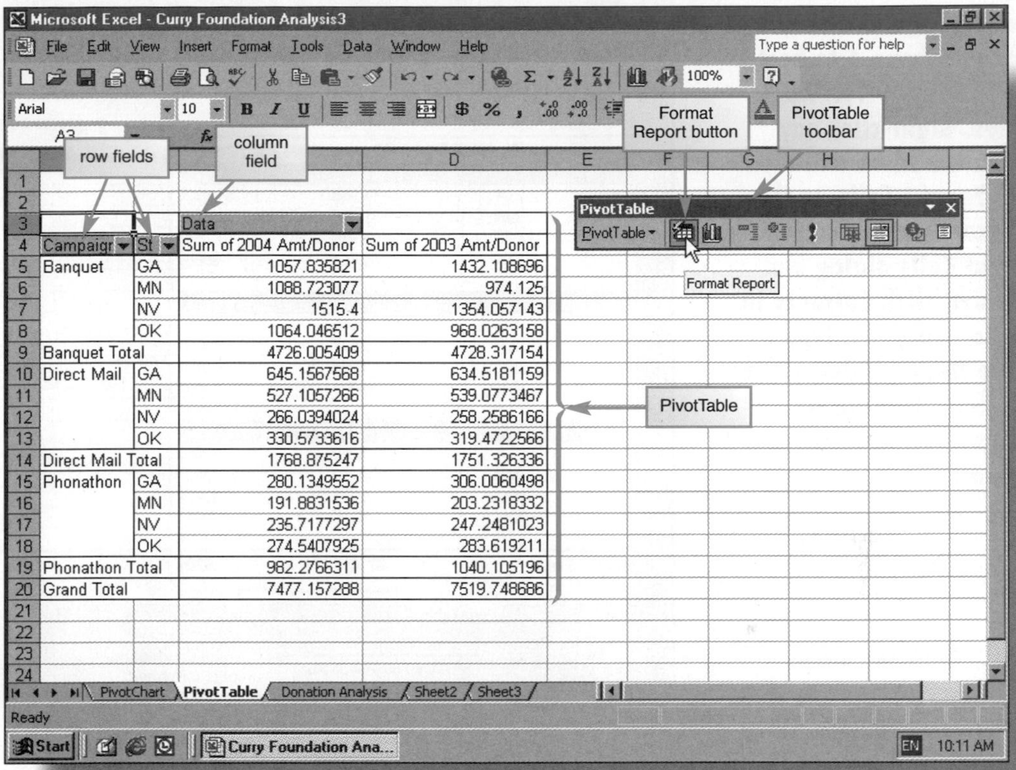

FIGURE 9-72

2 Click the Format Report button. When the AutoFormat dialog box displays, if necessary, scroll to display Report 6. Click Report 6 and then point to the OK button.

The AutoFormat dialog box displays report formats you can use to add color and variety to the PivotTable (Figure 9-73).

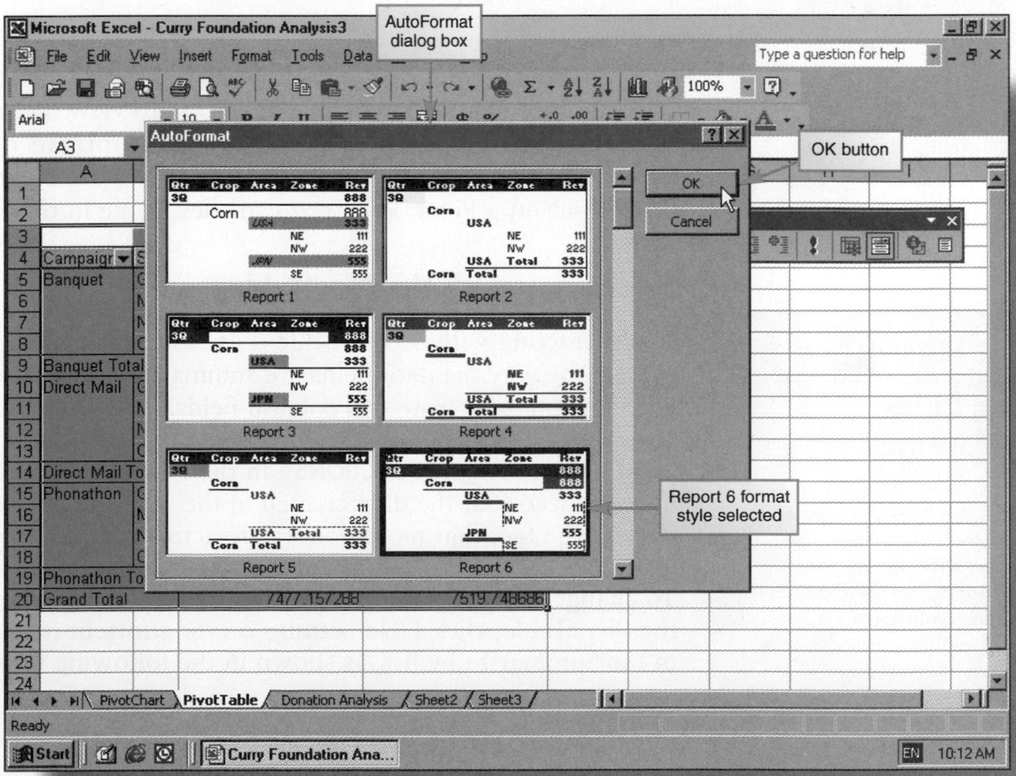

FIGURE 9-73

3 **Click the OK button. Double-click the border between column headings A and B to change column A to best fit. Click the Select All button. Right-click any cell in the table and then click Format Cells on the shortcut menu. When the Format Cells dialog box displays, click Currency in the Category list, type 0 in the Decimal places box, and then click the OK button. Click cell F22 to deselect the worksheet.**

The PivotTable displays as shown in Figure 9-74.

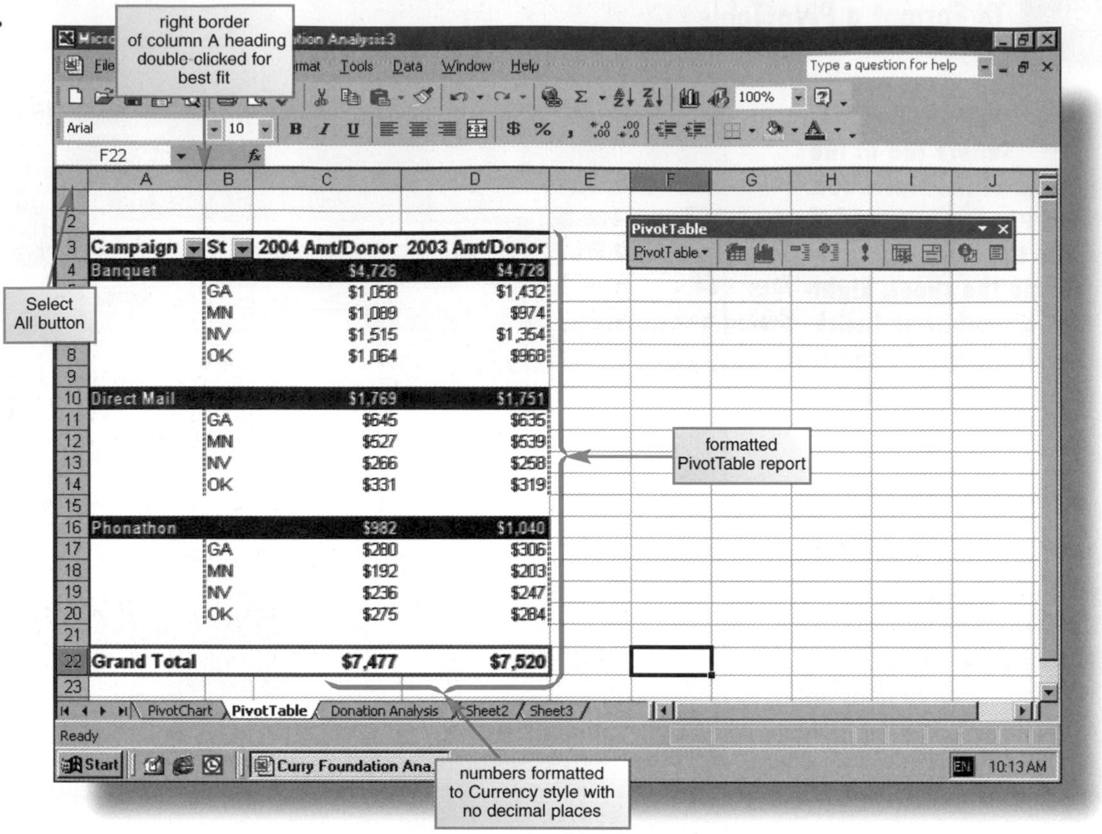

FIGURE 9-74

4 **Click the Save button to save the workbook using the file name, Curry Foundation Analysis3.**

Other Ways

1. Press ALT+O
2. Select table, in Voice Command mode, say "Format, Autoformat"

The AutoFormat dialog box shown in Figure 9-73 on the previous page includes 12 customized formats. Use the scroll box to view the formats that do not display in the dialog box. Each one of these customized formats offers a different look. The one you choose depends on the worksheet you are creating. If you want to remove the format on a PivotTable, you can click None in the list of formats.

More About

The Quick Reference

For a table that lists how to complete the tasks covered in this book using the mouse, menu, shortcut menu, and keyboard, see the Excel Quick Reference Summary at the back of this book or visit the Office XP Web page (www.scsite.com/offxp/qr.htm), and then click Microsoft Excel 2002.

Interacting with the PivotTable

Interacting with a PivotTable is as easy as it is with the PivotChart. You can change the way the data fields are summarized, add new fields to the analysis, or you can rotate the row and column fields.

SWITCHING SUMMARY FUNCTIONS In the Curry Foundation PivotChart, you may have realized that the data created in the chart illustrates the sum of the amount per donor. The fact that more donors are active in Nevada will skew the figures if you just look at the sums. An average might be a better way to compare the campaigns. To change the field setting from sum to average, you simply right-click the field in the PivotTable, click Field Settings on the shortcut menu, and then choose Average in the Summarize by list, as shown in the following steps.

Steps To Switch Summary Functions in a PivotTable

1 Right-click cell C3. Click Field Settings on the shortcut menu. When the PivotTable Field dialog box displays, click Average in the Summarize by list. Click the OK button.

The numbers in column C change from sums to averages.

2 Right-click cell D3. Click Field Settings on the shortcut menu. When the PivotTable Field dialog box displays, click Average in the Summarize by list. Click the OK button.

The numbers in column D change from location sums to location averages (Figure 9-75).

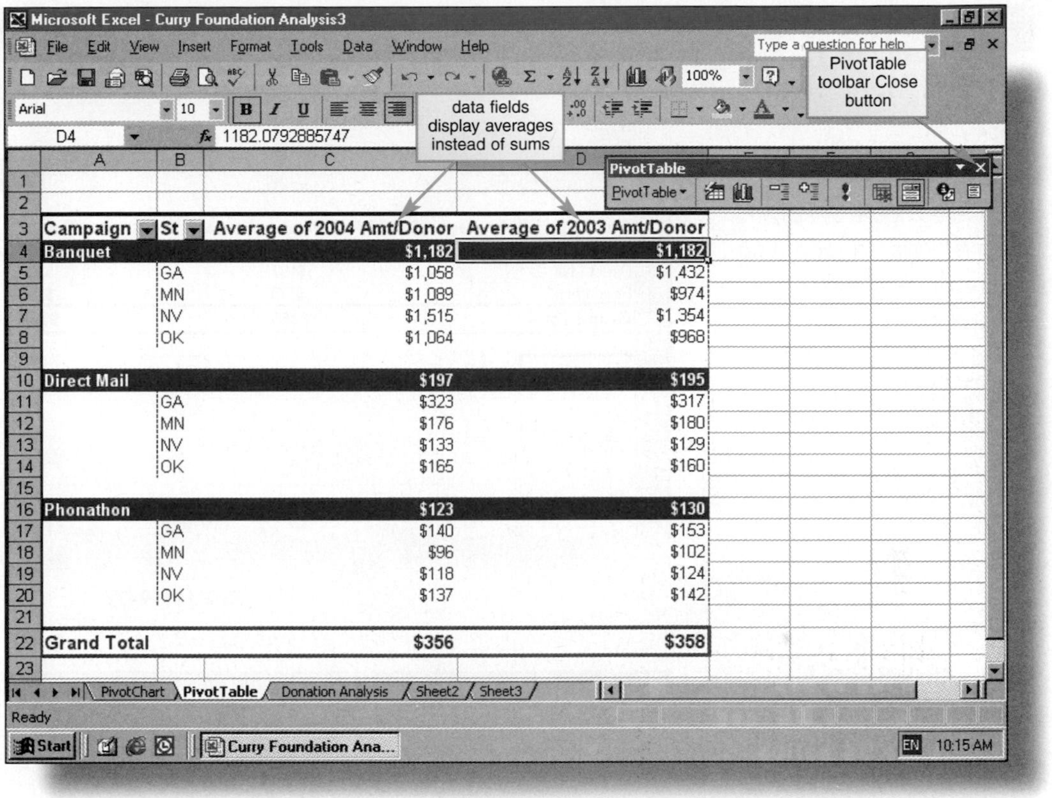

FIGURE 9-75

3 Click the PivotTable toolbar Close button.

Table 9-5 lists the summary functions from which you may choose through the Field Settings command on the shortcut menu to analyze your data in PivotCharts and PivotTables.

CHANGING THE VIEW OF A PIVOTTABLE You can rotate the row and column fields around the data field by dragging the buttons to different locations on the PivotTable. For example, if you drag the St (state) button to the Drop Page Fields Here area at the top of the table (above row 1 in the worksheet), you change the view of the PivotTable, as shown in the steps on the next page.

Table 9-5 Summary Functions for PivotChart and PivotTable Data Analysis

SUMMARY FUNCTION	DESCRIPTION
Sum	Sum values; this is the default function for numeric source data
Count	The number of items
Average	The average of the values
Max	The largest value
Min	The smallest value
Product	The product of the values
Count Nums	The number of rows that contain numeric data
StdDev	An estimate of the standard deviation of all the data to be summarized
StdDevp	The standard deviation of all of the data to be summarized
Var	An estimate of the variance of all of the data to be summarized
Varp	The variance of the data to be summarized

Steps To Change the View of a PivotTable

1 Drag the St button above row 1. Select cell A9.

Excel displays a new, different view of the PivotTable (Figure 9-76), which is easier to read than the PivotTable shown in Figure 9-75.

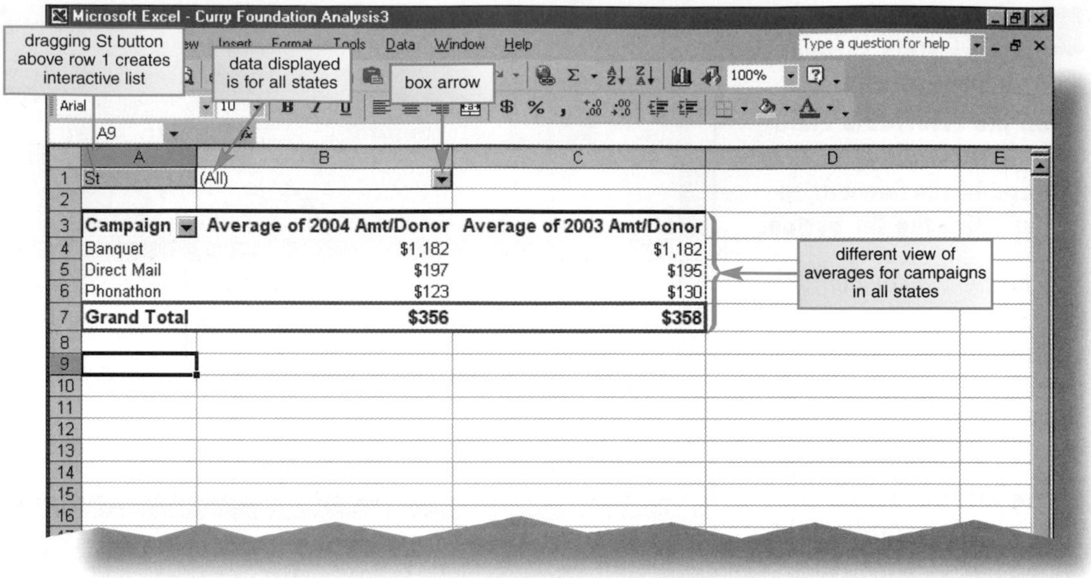

FIGURE 9-76

2 Click the St box arrow, click MN, and then click the OK button.

Excel displays the averages for each campaign type in the state of Minnesota (Figure 9-77).

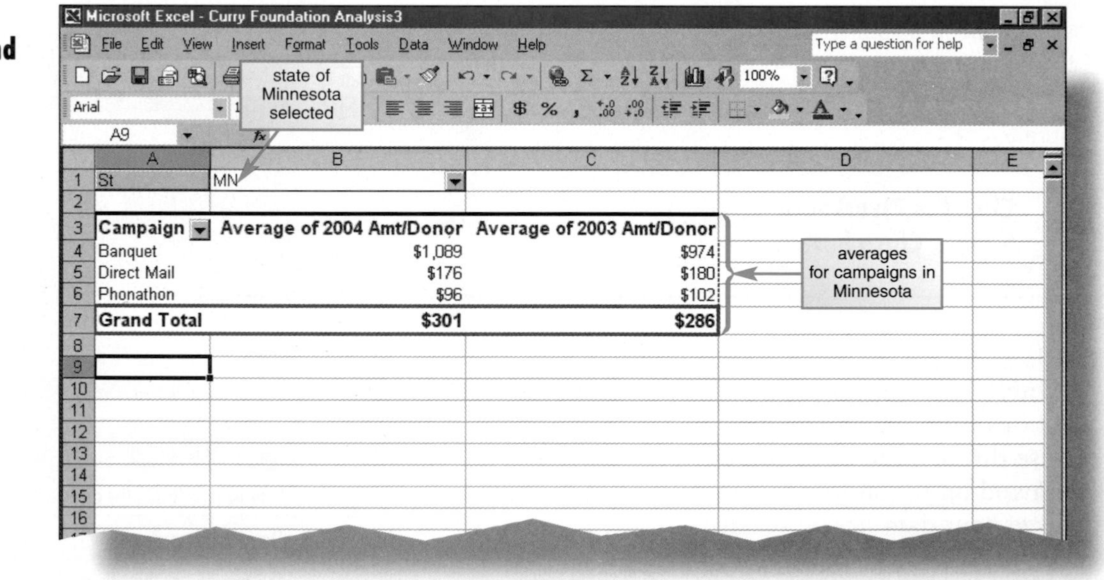

FIGURE 9-77

In Figure 9-76, a box and box arrow display to the right of the St button. Click the box arrow to display the St list box and select specific states whose averages you want to view.

PivotTables are powerful data analysis tools because they allow you to view the data in various ways by interchanging or pairing up the row and column fields. You can print a PivotChart or PivotTable just as you would any other worksheet. If you update the data on the Donation Analysis sheet, click **Refresh Data** on the Data menu or click the **Refresh button** on the PivotTable toolbar to update the corresponding PivotTable and PivotChart.

The donation analysis is complete. To close the Curry Foundation Anaysis3 workbook, follow the step below.

TO CLOSE THE WORKBOOK

1. Click the Curry Foundation Anaysis3 Close window button on the right side of the menu bar.

Merging Workbooks

Instead of tracking all of the changes to a single copy of a workbook, it sometimes is necessary to merge copies of the same workbook. This may be because multiple users are entering data or because new data has come in from a different source. To merge the changes from one workbook into another, both workbooks must satisfy the following requirements:

- You must make the original workbook shared, before making copies, and each workbook must be a copy of the same workbook.
- When you make copies, track changes or sharing must be turned on (which keeps a change history of the workbook).
- The Share Workbook command on the Tools menu displays a dialog box with a tab for recording the number of days to record the change history. Shared workbooks must be merged within that time period.
- If you use passwords, all workbooks involved in the merge must have the same password.
- When the copies come back, each must have a different file name.

When you have all the copies of the workbook together, you open the copy of the shared workbook into which you want to merge changes from another workbook file on disk. Then, on the Tools menu, click **Merge Workbooks**, which will display choices for you to choose a workbook or workbooks to merge. Not only is the data merged, but if comments are recorded, they display one after another in the given cell's comment box.

If Excel cannot merge the two workbooks, you still can incorporate the information from one workbook into the other, by copying and pasting the information from one workbook to another.

The Curry Foundation maintains historical foundation expense information in a workbook that has been shared and copied to two other members of the staff for review. The Curry Foundation Expenses worksheet also contains a chart that shows total expenses over the past five years. The steps on the next pages merge the changes from the other members of the staff with the original workbook, CurryFoundationExpenses.

More About

Changing PivotTables

At any time while the workbook containing a PivotTable is active, you can click the tab of the sheet containing the PivotTable, and then click PivotTable and PivotChart on the Data menu to display the PivotTable and PivotChart Wizard - Step 3 of 3 dialog box (Figure 9-57 on page E 9.41). Use the Layout button in this dialog box as an alternative to using drag and drop to change the view of the PivotTable.

More About

Merging

If you are not sure of the time period that will elapse before you merge workbooks that you send out for changes, set a large number of days to keep change history. You can set the number of days to be as large as 32,767 days.

More About

Microsoft Certification

The Microsoft Office User Specialist (MOUS) Certification program provides an opportunity for you to obtain a valuable industry credential — proof that you have the Excel 2002 skills required by employers. For more information, see Appendix D or visit the Shelly Cashman Series MOUS Web page at scsite.com/offxp/cert.htm.

Steps To Merge Workbooks

1 Open the file named, CurryFoundationExpenses, from the Data Disk.

The Curry Foundation Expenses worksheet displays as shown in Figure 9-78. The title bar indicates that the workbook is shared.

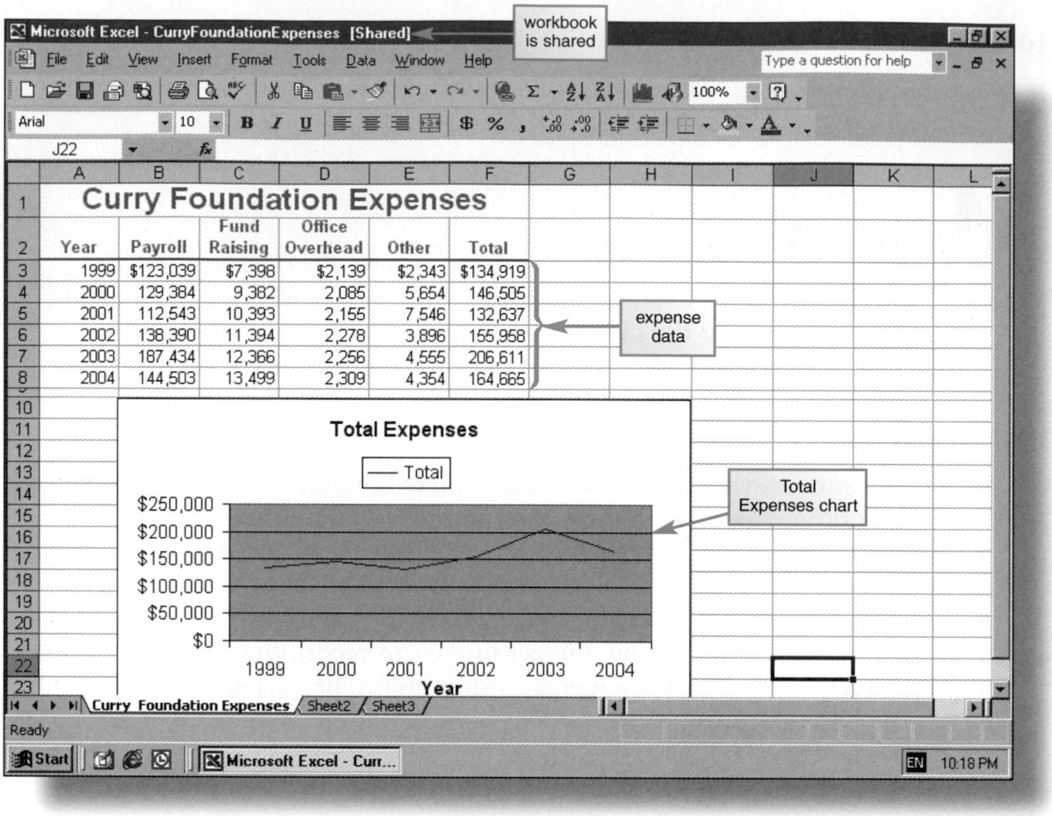

FIGURE 9-78

2 Click Tools on the menu bar and then point to Compare and Merge Workbooks.

The Tools menu displays (Figure 9-79).

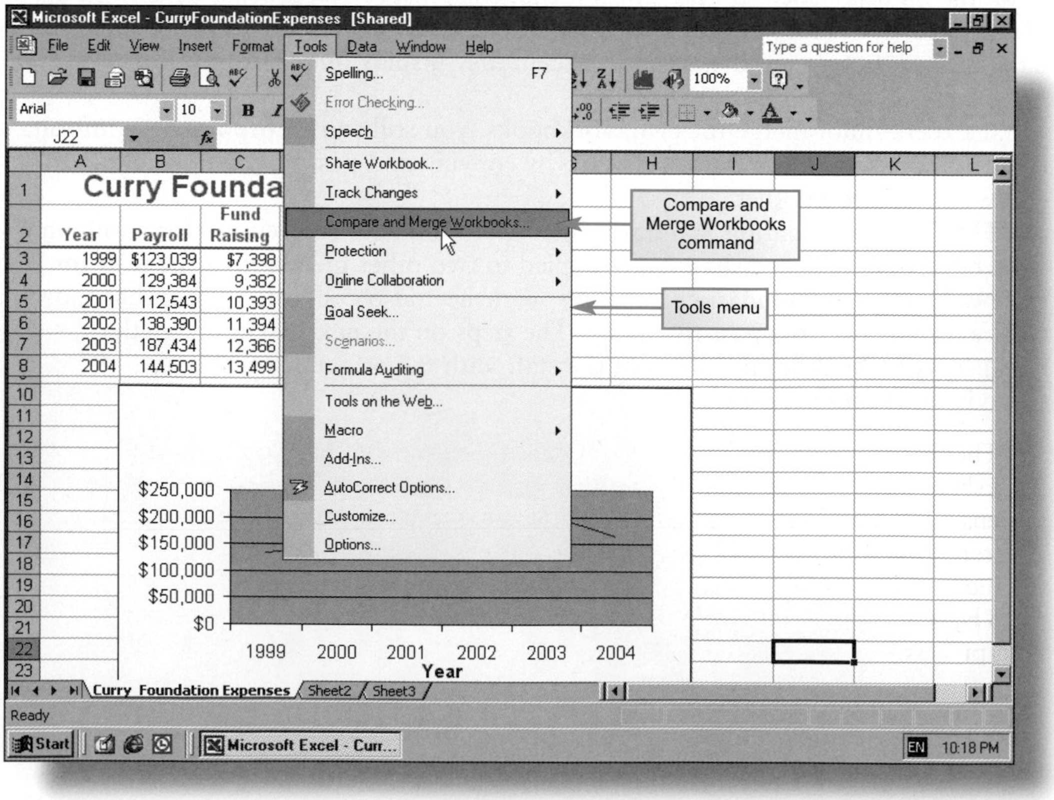

FIGURE 9-79

3 **Click Compare and Merge Workbooks. Click 3½ Floppy (A:), if necessary, in the Look in box. Drag through the workbooks CurryFoundation ExpensesBenny and CurryFoundation ExpensesWanda and then point to the OK button.**

The Select Files to Merge Into Current Workbook dialog box displays. The two workbooks to be merged are selected as shown in Figure 9-80.

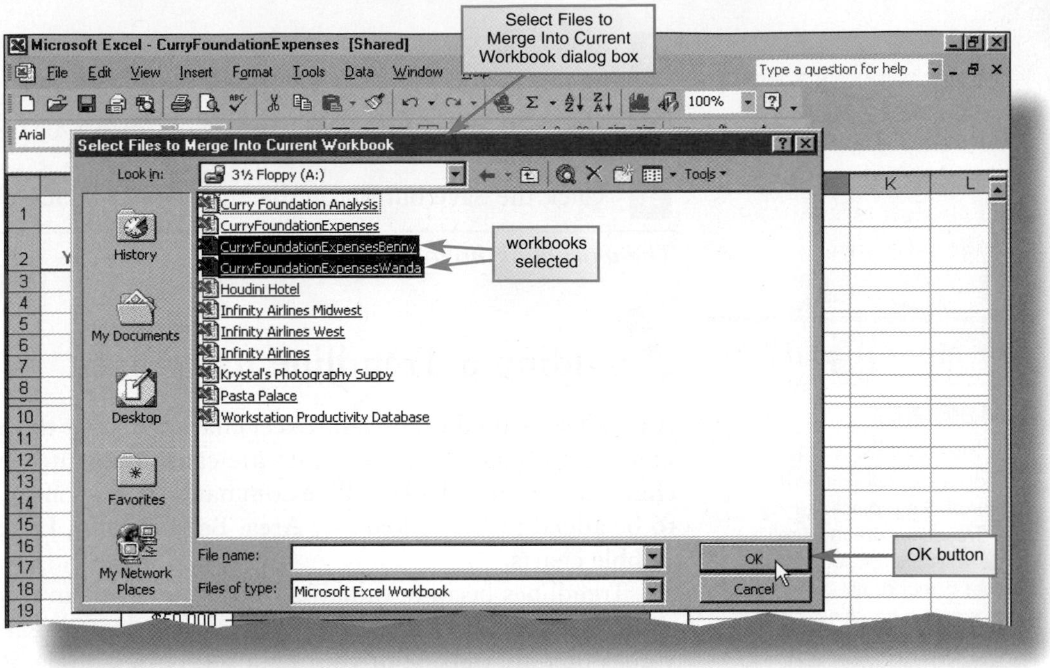

FIGURE 9-80

4 **Click the OK button.**

The workbooks are merged and cells that were changed by Benny and Wanda are changed in the Curry Foundation Expenses worksheet (Figure 9-81).

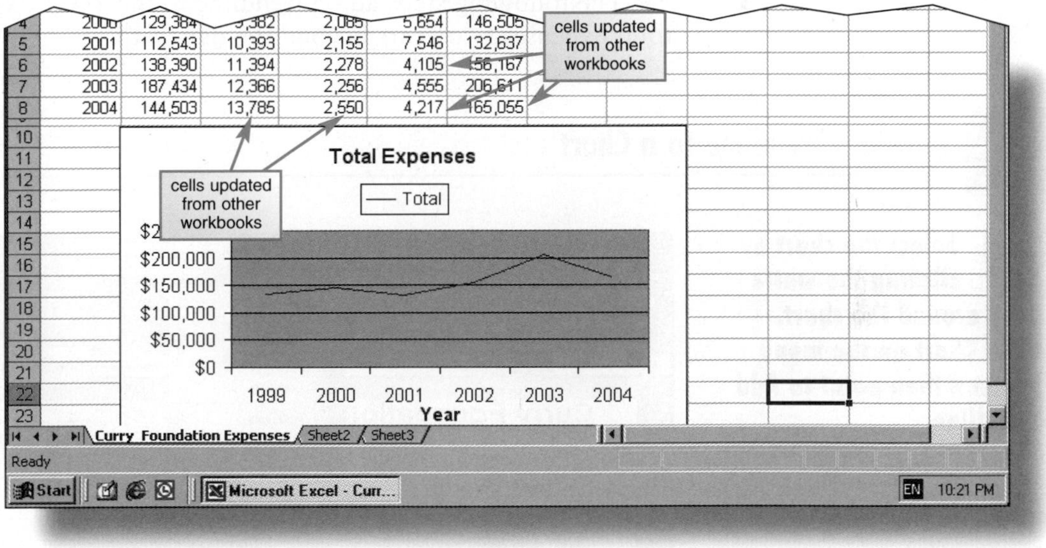

FIGURE 9-81

Other Ways

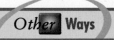

1. Press ALT+T, W
2. In Voice Command mode, say "Tools, Compare and Merge Workbooks"

The workbooks have been merged, and the Curry Foundation Expenses worksheet reflects the changes from Benny and Wanda. Excel also updated the Total Expenses historical chart. If Benny and Wanda had changed a common cell with different values, Excel would have prompted you to select which change to keep in the merged workbook.

The next step is to turn off workbook sharing so that the chart can be manipulated.

TO TURN OFF WORKBOOK SHARING AND SAVE THE WORKBOOK

1 Click Tools on the menu bar and then select Share Workbook on the Tools menu.

2 When the Share Workbook dialog box displays, clear the check box on the Editing page.

3 Click the OK button. When the Microsoft Excel dialog box displays, click the Yes button.

4 Click the Save button on the Standard toolbar.

The workbook no longer is shared.

More About

Trendlines

The R-squared value of a trendline can tell you how accurate the projection may be. Trendlines are most reliable when their R-squared values are at or near 1. When you create a trendline, Excel automatically calculates the R-squared value. You then can display this value on your chart.

Adding a Trendline to a Chart

A **trendline** is used on certain Excel charts to show the general tendency of how data in a chart is changing. Trendlines are calculated automatically and overlaid onto charts using the Add Trendline command on the Chart menu. Excel allows trendlines to be added to Unstacked 2-D Area, Bar, Column, Line, Stock, XY (Scatter), and Bubble charts.

Trendlines become valuable when you use them to project data beyond the values of a data set. This process is called forecasting. **Forecasting** helps predict data values that are outside of your data set. For example, if your data is for a 10-year period and the data shows a trend in that 10-year period, Excel can predict values beyond that period or tell you what the values may have been before that period.

The following steps add a trendline to the Total Expenses chart and predict the total expenses two years beyond the data set.

Steps To Add a Trendline to a Chart

1 **Select the chart by clicking the white area around the chart. Click Chart on the menu bar and then point to Add Trendline.**

The Chart menu displays (Figure 9-82).

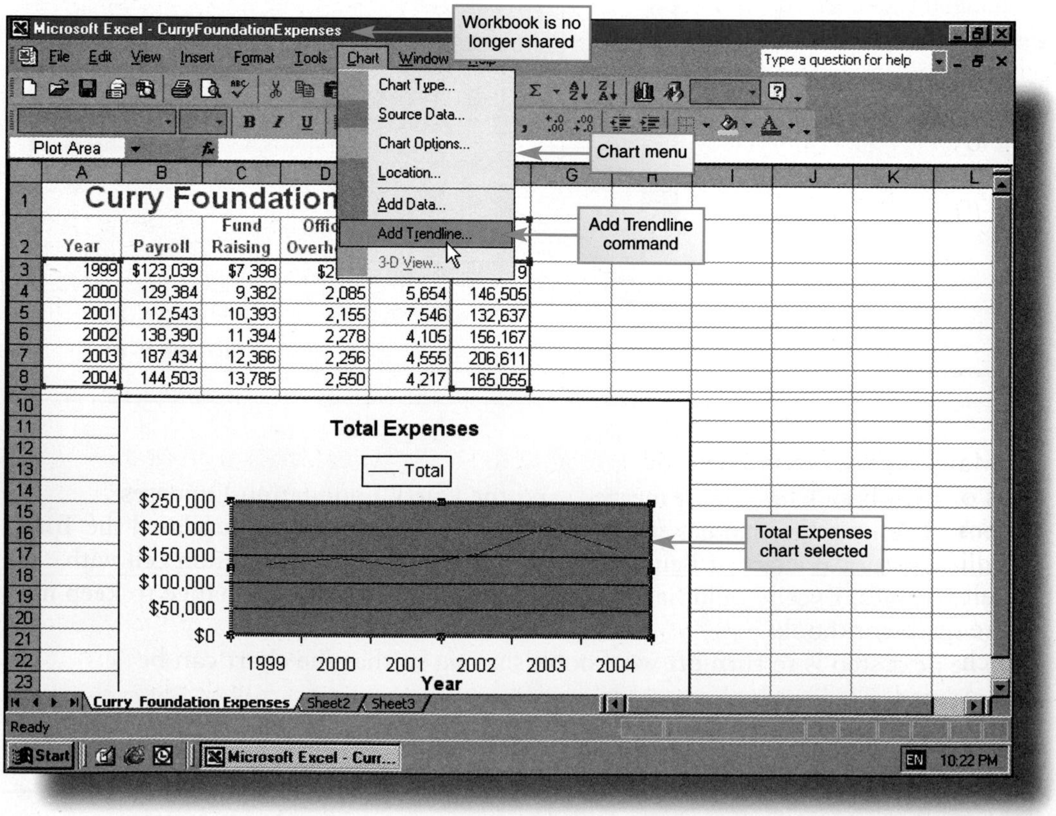

FIGURE 9-82

2 Click Add Trendline. When the Add Trendline dialog box displays, if necessary, click the Options tab. Click the Forward text box in the Forecast area and type 2**. Point to the OK button**

The Add Trendline dialog box displays, and the option is set to forecast two periods forward on the trendline as shown in Figure 9-83.

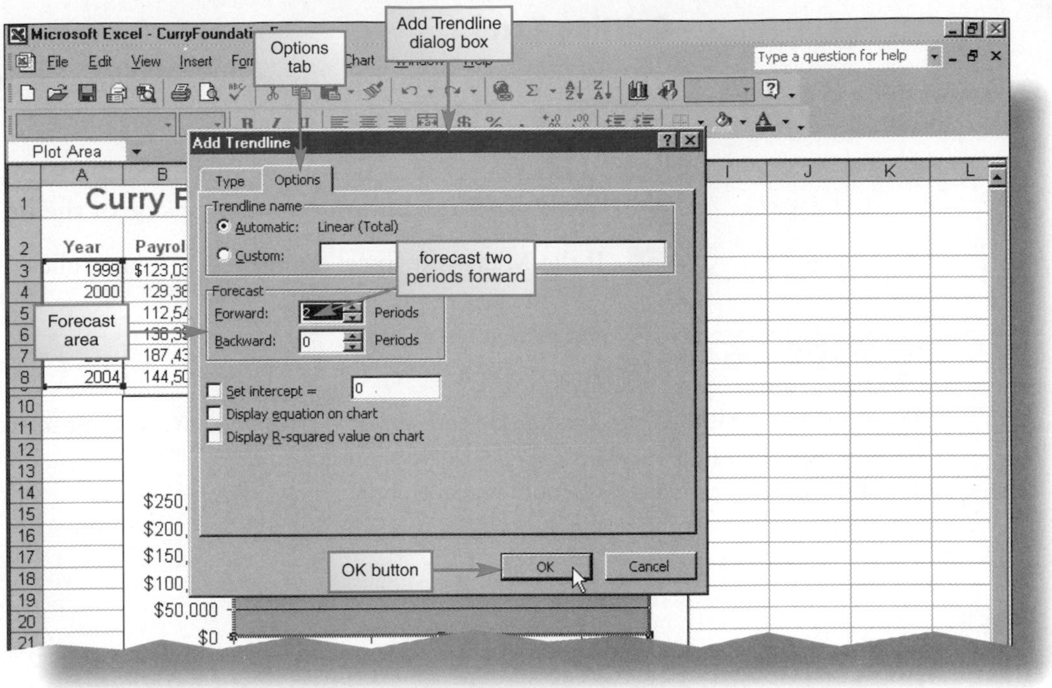

FIGURE 9-83

3 Click the OK button. Drag the legend sub-title of the chart to the left to align it under the Total Expenses chart title.

The trendline displays on the chart, and two additional data points are added to the chart to reflect projected values in the years 2005 and 2006 (Figure 9-84).

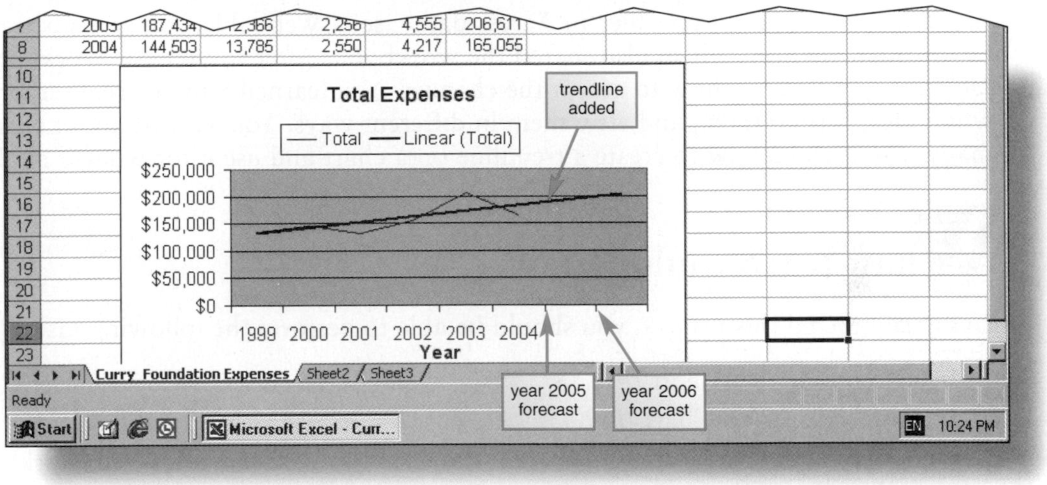

FIGURE 9-84

Other Ways

1. Select the chart, press ALT+C, R
2. Select the chart, in Voice Command mode, say "Chart, Add Trendline"

Many types of trendlines and several options are available for the trendline. The types of trendlines and when to use type each is beyond the scope of this book. The **Options tab** allows you to customize the trendline that you are adding to a chart. The Trendline name area allows you to specify a name for the trendline or accept the default name automatically selected by Excel. The Forecast area determines how far before or after your data values to project the trendline on the chart. If the Set intercept checkbox is checked, Excel draws the trendline so that the trendline intercepts the y-axis at the location specified in the Set intercept = box. Excel displays an equation of the form y = mx + b for linear trendlines when the Display equation on chart check box is checked. If another trendline type is being used, Excel displays the corresponding equation for the data being analyzed. When the Display R-squared value on chart check box is checked, Excel displays the statistical correlation of the data values with which the trendline is associated.

Quitting Excel

The project is complete. To quit Excel, follow the steps below.

TO QUIT EXCEL

1. Click the Close button on the right side of the title bar.
2. If the Microsoft Excel dialog box displays, click the No button.

CASE PERSPECTIVE SUMMARY

With the imported data, the PivotChart, and the PivotTable developed in this project, Gene Curry can view and analyze the donation data in a variety of ways. Links to the external data will update automatically when he refreshes his tables. Gene now can prepare his annual report with the knowledge the he has the best data available to him and will be able to better share his vision.

Project Summary

In this project, you learned how to import data in different formats into a worksheet, track changes, route workbooks, and create visual representations of the data in a worksheet. Using a preformatted worksheet, you learned how to import a text file, an Access database, a Web table, and spreadsheet XML. You then learned how to track changes, which also shared the workbook. After routing the workbook to the coordinator from each state, you learned how to accept the changes. You learned how to create interactive PivotChart and PivotTables, format them, and view them in different ways. You learned about sharing and merging workbooks. Finally, you learned how to create a trendline on a chart and use it for what-if analysis.

What You Should Know

Having completed this project, you should be able to perform the following tasks:

- Add a Trendline to a Chart *(E 9.58)*
- Add Data to the PivotChart *(E 9.43)*
- Change the PivotChart Type and Format the Chart *(E 9.45)*
- Change the View of a PivotChart *(E 9.48)*
- Change the View of a PivotTable *(E 9.54)*
- Close the Workbook *(E 9.55)*
- Create a PivotChart *(E 9.40)*
- Format a PivotTable *(E 9.51)*
- Import Data from a Text File into a Worksheet *(E 9.09)*
- Import Data from a Web Page into a Worksheet *(E 9.18)*
- Import Data from an Access Table into a Worksheet *(E 9.14)*
- Import Data from Spreadsheet XML into a Worksheet *(E 9.23)*
- Insert a Comment *(E 9.28)*
- Merge Workbooks *(E 9.56)*
- Open a Routed Workbook and Review Tracked Changes *(E 9.35)*
- Quit Excel *(E 9.60)*
- Replicate Formulas *(E 9.26)*
- Route the Workbook *(E 9.32)*
- Save the Workbook with a New File Name *(E 9.27)*
- Save the Tracked Changes in a Workbook with a New File Name *(E 9.38)*
- Start Excel, Open a Workbook, and Customize Excel *(E 9.08)*
- Switch Summary Functions in a PivotTable *(E 9.53)*
- Turn off Track Changes *(E 9.38)*
- Turn off Workbook Sharing and Save the Workbook *(E 9.57)*
- Turn on Track Changes *(E 9.30)*

Learn It Online

Instructions: To complete the Learn It Online exercises, start your browser, click the Address bar, and then enter `scsite.com/offxp/exs.htm`. When the Office XP Learn It Online page displays, follow the instructions in the exercises below.

1 Project Reinforcement TF, MC, and SA

Below Excel Project 9, click the Project Reinforcement link. Print the quiz by clicking Print on the File menu. Answer each question. Write your first and last name at the top of each page, and then hand in the printout to your instructor.

2 Flash Cards

Below Excel Project 9, click the Flash Cards link. When Flash Cards displays, read the instructions. Type 20 (or a number specified by your instructor) in the Number of Playing Cards text box, type your name in the Name text box, and then click the Flip Card button. When the flash card displays, read the question and then click the Answer box arrow to select an answer. Flip through Flash Cards. Click Print on the File menu to print the last flash card if your score is 15 (75%) correct or greater and then hand it in to your instructor. If your score is less than 15 (75%) correct, then redo this exercise by clicking the Replay button.

3 Practice Test

Below Excel Project 9, click the Practice Test link. Answer each question, enter your first and last name at the bottom of the page, and then click the Grade Test button. When the graded practice test displays on your screen, click Print on the File menu to print a hard copy. Continue to take practice tests until you score 80% or better. Hand in a printout of the final practice test to your instructor.

4 Who Wants to Be a Computer Genius?

Below Excel Project 9, click the Computer Genius link. Read the instructions, enter your first and last name at the bottom of the page, and then click the Play button. Hand in your score to your instructor.

5 Wheel of Terms

Below Excel Project 9, click the Wheel of Terms link. Read the instructions, and then enter your first and last name and your school name. Click the Play button. Hand in your score to your instructor.

6 Crossword Puzzle Challenge

Below Excel Project 9, click the Crossword Puzzle Challenge link. Read the instructions, and then enter your first and last name. Click the Play button. Work the crossword puzzle. When you are finished, click the Submit button. When the crossword puzzle redisplays, click the Print button. Hand in the printout.

7 Tips and Tricks

Below Excel Project 9, click the Tips and Tricks link. Click a topic that pertains to Project 9. Right-click the information and then click Print on the shortcut menu. Construct a brief example of what the information relates to in Excel to confirm you understand how to use the tip or trick. Hand in the example and printed information.

online

8 Newsgroups

Below Excel Project 9, click the Newsgroups link. Click a topic that pertains to Project 9. Print three comments. Hand in the comments to your instructor.

9 Expanding Your Horizons

Below Excel Project 9, click the Articles for Microsoft Excel link. Click a topic that pertains to Project 9. Print the information. Construct a brief example of what the information relates to in Excel to confirm you understand the contents of the article. Hand in the example and printed information to your instructor.

10 Search Sleuth

Below Excel Project 9, click the Search Sleuth link. To search for a term that pertains to this project, select a term below the Project 9 title and then use the Google search engine at google.com (or any major search engine) to display and print two Web pages that present information on the term. Hand in the printouts to your instructor.

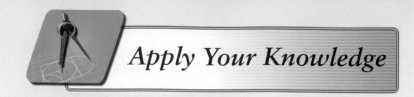

Apply Your Knowledge

1 Merging Workbooks and Creating a Trendline

Instructions: Start Excel and perform the following tasks.

1. Open the workbook, Infinity Airlines, from the Data Disk. See the inside back cover of this book for instructions for downloading the Data Disk or see your instructor for information on accessing the files required in this book. The worksheet displays as shown in Figure 9-85. The worksheet contains revenue information for one of Infinity Airlines flights that departs each week. The worksheet also contains a graph of the total revenue from each week. The workbook is shared.
2. Merge the workbooks Infinity Airlines West and Infinity Airlines Midwest into the Infinity Airlines workbook.
3. Turn off sharing of the workbook. Print the Flight Revenue Analysis worksheet.
4. Add a trendline to the chart on the worksheet. Forecast the total revenue two weeks forward. Resize the chart so the legend and the chart do not overlap. Print the worksheet.
5. Right-click the trendline and then click Format Trendline on the shortcut menu. Click the Options tab and forecast four weeks forward. Resize the chart so the legend and the chart do not overlap. Print the worksheet.
6. Right-click the trendline and then click Format Trendline on the shortcut menu. Click the Options tab and use a custom trendline name of Forecasted Revenue. Forecast eight weeks forward. Resize the chart so the legend and the chart do not overlap. Print the worksheet.
7. Save the workbook as Infinity Airlines1.

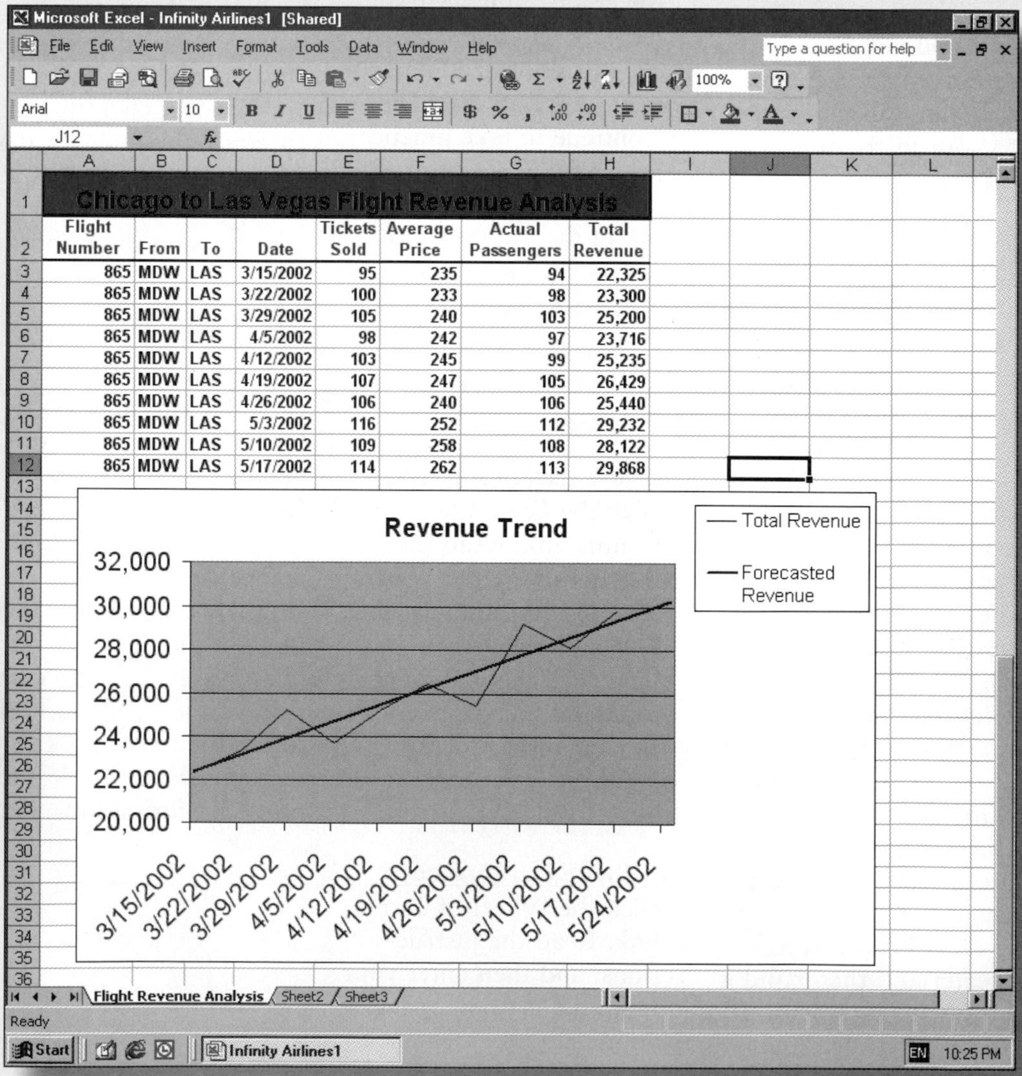

FIGURE 9-85

In the Lab

1 Importing Data into an Excel Worksheet

Problem: You work in the strategic planning department for a small chain of fast food restaurants. You have asked each of the regional managers to send you historic data for sales of french fries over the past five years. Each manager has sent the required data, but each is in a different format. The northeast region sent a text file with fields separated by commas. The west region uses an Access database to maintain its data, and queried it, creating a table to send to you. The south region posted its data to the company's intranet site as a Web page. The Midwest region uses spreadsheet XML to communicate its data to other entities.

Instructions: Perform the following tasks.

1. Open the workbook Pasta Palace (Figure 9-86a on the next page) from the Data Disk. See the inside back cover of this book for instructions for downloading the Data Disk or see your instructor for information on accessing the files required in this book.
2. In cell J3, enter the formula =SUM(E3:I3).
3. Click cell A3. From the Data Disk, import the text file, PastaNortheast. It is a comma delimited text file. In step 2 of the Text Import Wizard, click the Comma check box; otherwise accept the default settings. When the Import Data dialog box displays, click the Properties button. When the External Data Range Properties dialog box displays, clear the Adjust the column width check box.
4. Click cell A8. From the Data Disk, import the Access database file, PastaWest. Add all the fields from the West Region French Fries table. Accept all of the default settings. When the Import Data dialog box displays, click the Properties button. When the External Data Range Properties dialog box displays, clear the Adjust the column width and Include field names check boxes.
5. Click cell A13. From the Data Disk, import the HTML file, PastaSouth. Accept the default settings for the New Web Query. When the Import Data dialog box displays, click the Properties button. When the External Data Range dialog box displays, clear the Adjust the column width check box. Manually delete the column headings imported from the HTML file.
6. Click cell A18. From the Data Disk, import the spreadsheet XML file, PastaMidwest. Accept the default settings for the New Web Query. When the Import Data dialog box displays, click the Properties button. When the External Data Range Properties dialog box displays, clear the Adjust the column width check box. Manually delete the column headings imported from the XML file.
7. Replicate the formula from cell J3 to fill the range J4:J23 (Figure 9-87b on the next page). Format all cells with dollar amounts so that they display with a comma, no decimal places, and no currency symbol.
8. Enter your name, course, computer laboratory exercise (Lab 9-1), date, and instructor name in the range A25:A29.
9. On the File menu, click Page Setup. When the Page Setup dialog box displays, click Landscape in the Orientation area on the Page sheet. Print a copy of the worksheet.
10. Save the workbook using the file name, Pasta Palace1.
11. Export the French Fry Analysis worksheet by selecting Save As on the File menu. When the Save As dialog box appears, select Text (Tab delimited)(*.txt) in the Save as type box. Click Save.

(continued)

In the Lab

Importing Data into an Excel Worksheet *(continued)*

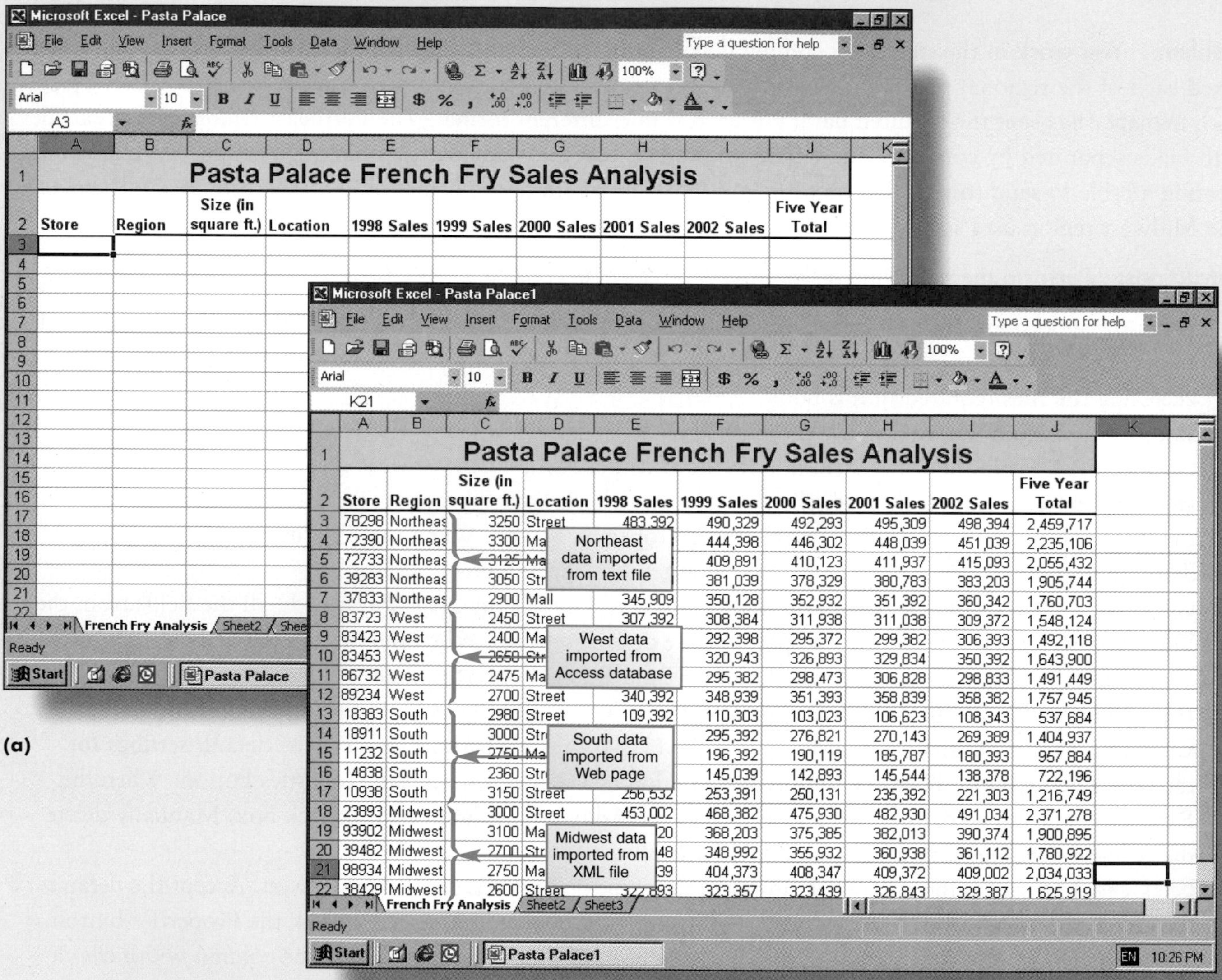

(a)

(b)

FIGURE 9-86

2 Routing Workbooks, Tracking Changes, and Inserting Comments

Problem: This problem requires collaboration with two other classmates. Make sure that you can send e-mail to other classmates before completing this exercise.

You work as an assistant in the accounting department of Krystal's Photography Supply. The head of the accounting department has asked you to verify inventory amounts so that she can finish her quarterly reports. To do so, you must ask the warehouse managers to review the numbers that are in the current Inventory Summary worksheet (Figure 9-87).

In the Lab

Instructions: Perform the following tasks:

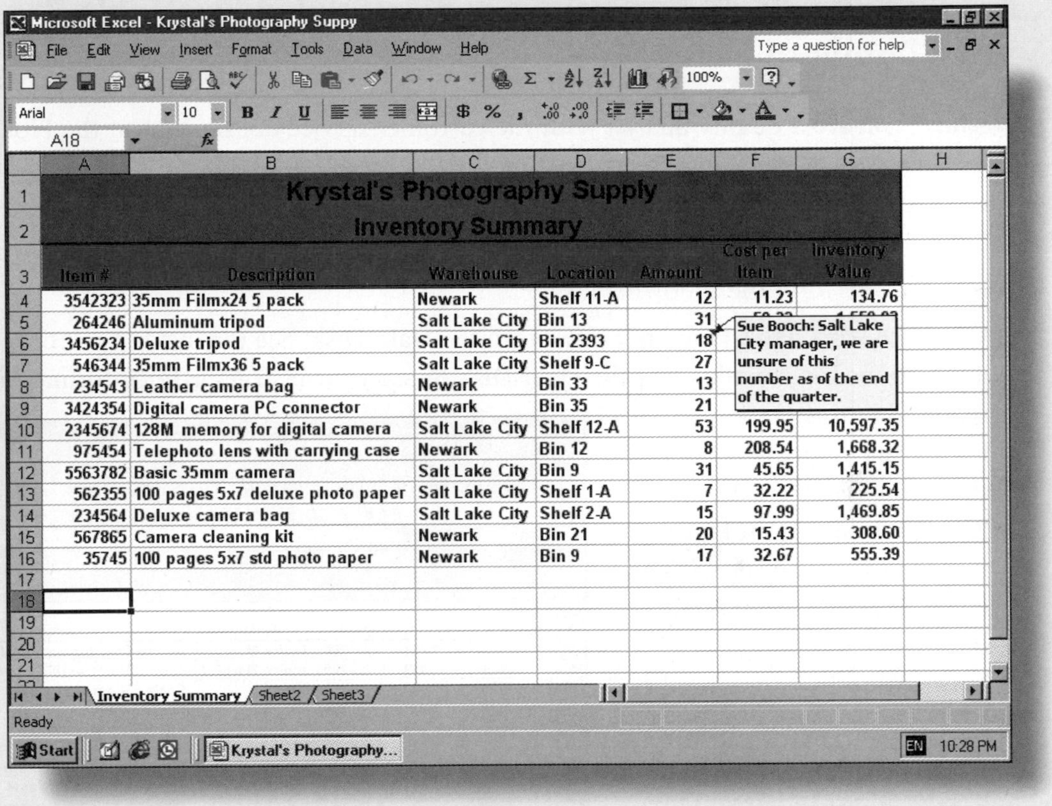

	A	B	C	D	E	F	G
1	Krystal's Photography Supply						
2	Inventory Summary						
3	Item #	Description	Warehouse	Location	Amount	Cost per Item	Inventory Value
4	3542323	35mm Filmx24 5 pack	Newark	Shelf 11-A	12	11.23	134.76
5	264246	Aluminum tripod	Salt Lake City	Bin 13	31		
6	3456234	Deluxe tripod	Salt Lake City	Bin 2393	18		
7	546344	35mm Filmx36 5 pack	Salt Lake City	Shelf 9-C	27		
8	234543	Leather camera bag	Newark	Bin 33	13		
9	3424354	Digital camera PC connector	Newark	Bin 35	21		
10	2345674	128M memory for digital camera	Salt Lake City	Shelf 12-A	53	199.95	10,597.35
11	975454	Telephoto lens with carrying case	Newark	Bin 12	8	208.54	1,668.32
12	5563782	Basic 35mm camera	Salt Lake City	Bin 9	31	45.65	1,415.15
13	562355	100 pages 5x7 deluxe photo paper	Salt Lake City	Shelf 1-A	7	32.22	225.54
14	234564	Deluxe camera bag	Salt Lake City	Shelf 2-A	15	97.99	1,469.85
15	567865	Camera cleaning kit	Newark	Bin 21	20	15.43	308.60
16	35745	100 pages 5x7 std photo paper	Newark	Bin 9	17	32.67	555.39

FIGURE 9-87

1. Open the workbook Krystal's Photography Supply from the Data Disk. See the inside back cover of this book for instructions for downloading the Data Disk or see your instructor for information on accessing the files required in this book.
2. Add a comment to cell E6 as shown in Figure 9-87.
3. Track changes to the workbook. On the Tools menu, click Track Changes and then click Highlight Changes. Click Track changes while editing and clear the three check boxes in the Highlight which changes area.
4. Route the workbook to two classmates. On the File menu, point to Send To and then click Routing Recipient. Select the e-mail addresses of two classmates and enter `Krystal's Photography Inventory Verification` as the Subject. Enter appropriate message text requesting that each classmate add comments to at least one cell and change the contents of two cells. Click the Route button.
5. Ask a classmate to route the workbook to you as well. When you receive the e-mail, print it. Enter comments in at least one cell and change the contents of at least two cells before sending the workbook to the next routing recipient.
6. When you receive your workbook back after it has been routed to all recipients, point to Track Changes on the Tools menu, and then click Accept or Reject Changes. Reject one change and accept all others.
7. Select Page Setup on the File menu. Click the Sheet tab and then select As displayed on sheet in the Comments list box in the Print area. This allows comments to print when you print the worksheet.
8. Enter your name, course, computer laboratory exercise (Lab 9-2), date, and instructor name in the range, B18:B22. Print the worksheet. Save the workbook using the file name, Krystal's Photography Supply1.

In the Lab

3 Creating a PivotChart Report and Associated PivotTable Report for a Customer Service Database

Problem: You are a quality analyst with the customer service department of the Houdini Hotel. You have been assigned the task of creating a PivotChart and PivotTable from the company's customer complaint database (Figure 9-88a). Records are added to this database whenever a refund is given to a customer due to a complaint. The PivotChart and PivotTable are shown in Figure 9-88b and 9-88c.

Instructions: Perform the following tasks:

1. Open the workbook Houdini Hotel from the Data Disk. See the inside back cover of this book for instructions for downloading the Data Disk or see your instructor for information on accessing the files required in this book.
2. Create the PivotChart shown in Figure 9-88b and PivotTable shown in Figure 9-88c on separate sheets. The PivotChart and PivotTable summarize refund amount information by room number and complaint date. Use the PivotTable and PivotChart Report Wizard to create the PivotChart and associated PivotTable.
3. Add the title shown in Figure 9-88b.
4. Format the y-axis labels to currency with no decimal places.
5. Rename the Chart 1 sheet tab PivotChart. Rename the Sheet1 sheet tab PivotTable.

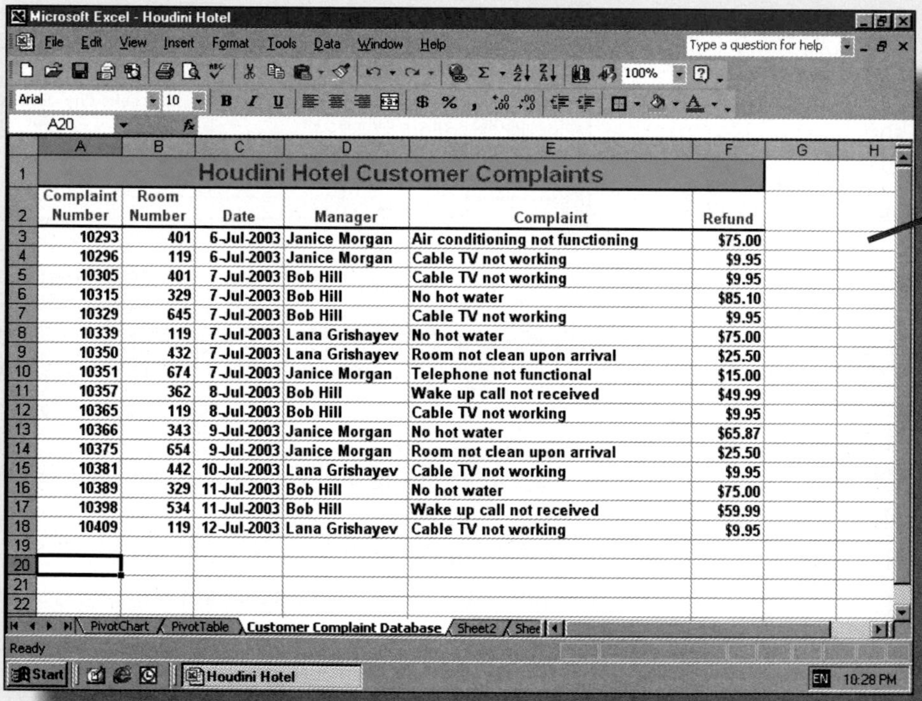

Houdini Hotel Customer Complaints

Complaint Number	Room Number	Date	Manager	Complaint	Refund
10293	401	6-Jul-2003	Janice Morgan	Air conditioning not functioning	$75.00
10296	119	6-Jul-2003	Janice Morgan	Cable TV not working	$9.95
10305	401	7-Jul-2003	Bob Hill	Cable TV not working	$9.95
10315	329	7-Jul-2003	Bob Hill	No hot water	$85.10
10329	645	7-Jul-2003	Bob Hill	Cable TV not working	$9.95
10339	119	7-Jul-2003	Lana Grishayev	No hot water	$75.00
10350	432	7-Jul-2003	Lana Grishayev	Room not clean upon arrival	$25.50
10351	674	7-Jul-2003	Janice Morgan	Telephone not functional	$15.00
10357	362	8-Jul-2003	Bob Hill	Wake up call not received	$49.99
10365	119	8-Jul-2003	Bob Hill	Cable TV not working	$9.95
10366	343	9-Jul-2003	Janice Morgan	No hot water	$65.87
10375	654	9-Jul-2003	Janice Morgan	Room not clean upon arrival	$25.50
10381	442	10-Jul-2003	Lana Grishayev	Cable TV not working	$9.95
10389	329	11-Jul-2003	Bob Hill	No hot water	$75.00
10398	534	11-Jul-2003	Bob Hill	Wake up call not received	$59.99
10409	119	12-Jul-2003	Lana Grishayev	Cable TV not working	$9.95

(a) Worksheet Database

6. Click the PivotChart sheet tab. Drag the Refund button to the Drag Data Items Here area (y-axis). Drag the Room Number and the Date buttons to the Drop Category Fields Here area (x-axis).
7. Select the Customer Complaint Database and PivotTable sheets. Enter your name, course, computer laboratory exercise (Lab 9-3), date, and instructor in the rage A21:A25. Hold down the SHIFT key and then click the Customer Complaint Database tab.
8. Print the worksheet, PivotChart, and PivotTable. Save the workbook using the file name, Houdini Hotel1.
9. Click the Date box arrow to deselect the date 7-Jul-2003. Print the PivotChart and PivotTable. Add the 7-Jul-2003 date back in.
10. Remove the Room Number from the x-axis, and add the Manager button to the right of the Date button. Print the PivotChart and PivotTable.

In the Lab

11. Close Houdini Hotel1 without saving changes and then reopen it. Click the PivotTable tab. Drag the buttons to create three different views. Print the PivotTable for each view. Close the workbook without saving changes.

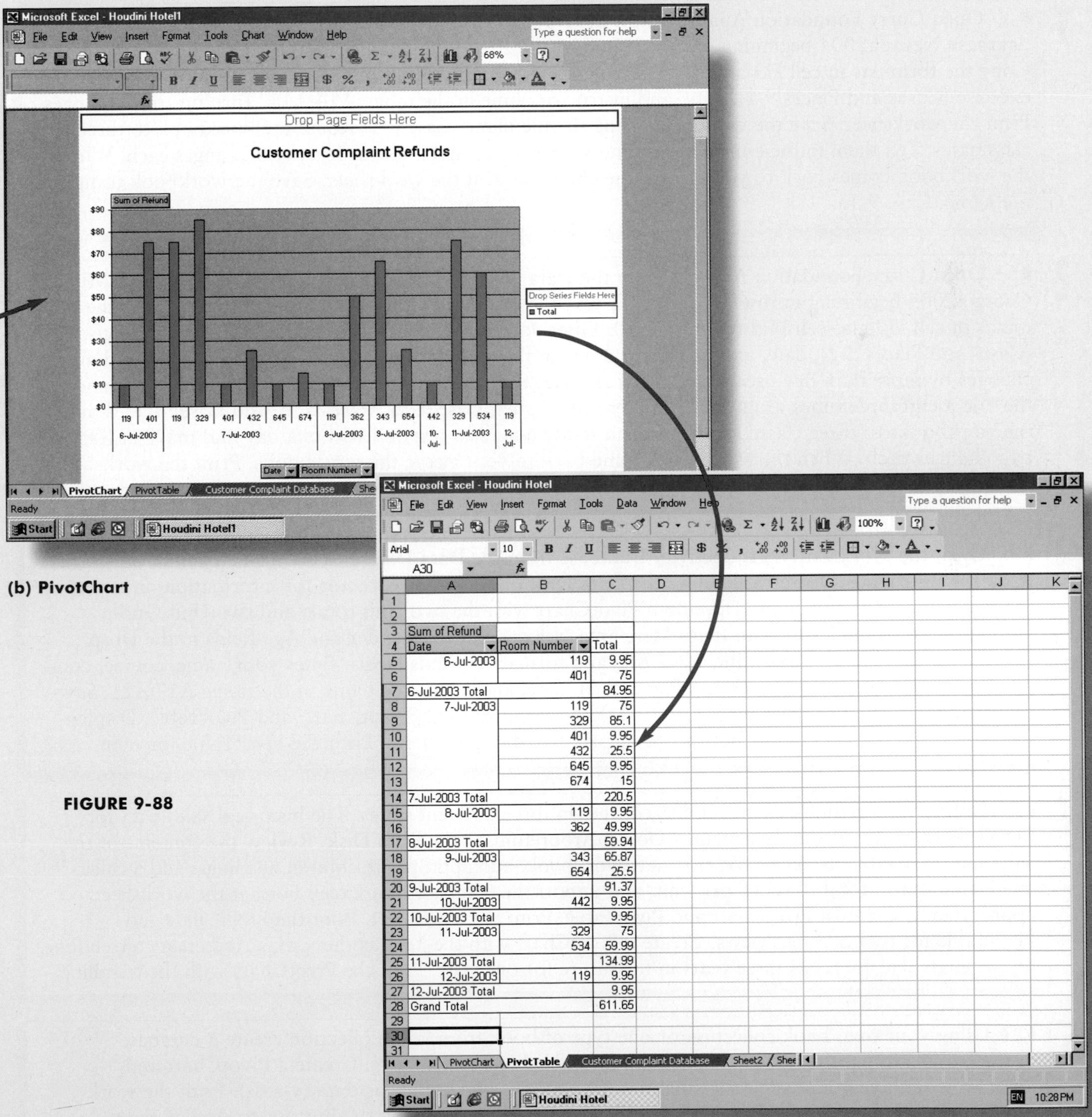

Sum of Refund		
Date	Room Number	Total
6-Jul-2003	119	9.95
	401	75
6-Jul-2003 Total		84.95
7-Jul-2003	119	75
	329	85.1
	401	9.95
	432	25.5
	645	9.95
	674	15
7-Jul-2003 Total		220.5
8-Jul-2003	119	9.95
	362	49.99
8-Jul-2003 Total		59.94
9-Jul-2003	343	65.87
	654	25.5
9-Jul-2003 Total		91.37
10-Jul-2003	442	9.95
10-Jul-2003 Total		9.95
11-Jul-2003	329	75
	534	59.99
11-Jul-2003 Total		134.99
12-Jul-2003	119	9.95
12-Jul-2003 Total		9.95
Grand Total		611.65

(b) PivotChart

FIGURE 9-88

(c) PivotTable

Cases and Places

The difficulty of these case studies varies:
◗ are the least difficult; ◗◗ are more difficult; and ◗◗◗ are the most difficult.

1 ◗ Open Curry Foundation Analysis from the Data Disk. Import data from the table in the Access database Nevada2004 beginning in row 3. Import the XML file Oklahoma2004 beginning in row 7. Copy the formulas in cell H3 and cell I3 through row 10. Enter your name, course, computer laboratory exercise (Cases and Places 9-1), date, and instructor name in the range A14:A18. Turn on track changes. Print the worksheet. Save the workbook using the file name, Case 9-1. Route the workbook to three classmates. Tell them in the e-mail to respond within a day and make at least two changes each. When the workbook comes back to you, accept the changes. Print the worksheet. Save the workbook using the file name, Case 9-1a.

2 ◗ Open Curry Foundation Analysis from the Data Disk. Import data from the table in the HTML file Georgia2004 beginning in row 3. Import the text file Minnesota2004 beginning in row 7. Copy the formulas in cell H3 and cell I3 through row 10. Enter your name, course, computer laboratory exercise (Cases and Places 9-2), date, and instructor name in the range A14:A18. Share the workbook and allow changes by more than one user. Print the worksheet. Save the workbook using the Save As command on the File menu three times using three different file names: Case 9-2a, Case 9-2b, and Case 9-2c. E-mail the workbooks to three classmates. Tell them in the e-mail to respond within a day and make at least two changes each. When the workbooks come back to you, merge the workbooks. Print the worksheet. Save the workbook using the file name, Case 9-2d.

3 ◗◗ Open the Workstation Productivity Database from the Data Disk. See the inside back cover of this book for instructions for downloading the Data Disk or see your instructor for information on accessing the files required in this book. Develop a PivotChart with the two Unit totals and two Unit Quota amount fields in the Drop Data Items Here area (y-axis) and the Gender and Age fields in the Drop Category Fields Here (x-axis). Include a title and formatted y-axis labels. Enter your name, course, computer laboratory exercise (Cases and Places 9-3), date, and instructor name in the range A17:A21. Save the workbook using the file name, Case 9-3. Print the worksheet, PivotChart, and PivotTable. Display the PivotTable sheet. Drag the buttons to display five different views. Print the PivotTable for each.

4 ◗◗ Golden Arboretum sells medium-sized trees in three different states. The historical sales data for five years is an Access database named GoldenArboretum on the Data Disk. Review the contents of the SalesSummary table in Access. Open a new workbook, add appropriate column headings, add a calculated column for Total Revenue per Unit, and import the database into Excel. Format the worksheet appropriately. Create a PivotChart and PivotTable. Print the worksheet. Print the PivotChart and PivotTable for two different views. Create a PivotChart with the Year as the x-axis, and create a trendline on the chart that forecasts three years in the future for one state. Print the PivotChart with the trendline.

5 ◗◗◗ Using your own book collection or one type of book from your collection create a database of the book titles, authors, year of publication, publishers, and subject. Create a PivotChart and PivotTable with year and subject as the x-axis categories and author as data (y-axis). Print the worksheet, PivotChart, and PivotTable. Display the PivotTable sheet. Drag the buttons to display three different views. Print the PivotTable for each.

Microsoft Excel 2002

Creating a PivotTable List Web Page Using Excel

CASE PERSPECTIVE

JetMassage, Inc. sells a water powered personal body massager through infomercials on television in select countries. The company rents several warehouses throughout the world where it stores and ships its product. Sales districts are broken down by warehouse locations, which are located in four countries: the United States, Canada, Mexico, and the United Kingdom.

After receiving complaints from upper management about the high cost of maintaining inventory in many warehouses, Catherine Cay has been keeping an Excel spreadsheet regarding that state of inventory in each warehouse. Catherine needs to analyze this data in a more comprehensive and flexible manner in order to make some critical decisions.

As the spreadsheet specialist at JetMassage, Inc., Catherine has asked you to take warehouse data supplied in a worksheet and make it available to the upper management in an easy-to-use format. From your experience with Excel 2002, you know that you can create interactive Web pages. You also know that PivotTables are an ideal tool for analyzing data. You decide the best solution is to develop an interactive PivotTable list Web page.

Introduction

Excel 2002 allows you to save a workbook, a worksheet, a range of cells, or a chart as a Web page using the Save as Web Page command on the File menu. Excel also allows you to save worksheet data as a PivotTable list. A **PivotTable list** is a Web page that lets you analyze data using your Web browser, rather than Excel. Similar to a PivotTable report, a PivotTable list is an interactive table that allows you to change the view of data, filter data, and create summaries of the data. The difference between the two PivotTables is that a PivotTable report is manipulated in Excel, whereas a PivotTable list is manipulated in your Web browser.

To create a PivotTable list, you start with an Excel workbook (Figure 1a on the next page). You use the Save as Web Page command on the File menu to create the PivotTable list (Figure 1b on the next page). Once you display the PivotTable list in your Web browser, you can change the view of the data as shown in Figures 1c and 1d on the next page. Figure 1c shows the data in Figure 1b summarized by the warehouse's country within Drain. The Drain column is used to indicate that management has decided to close the warehouse and will no longer ship any product to that location. When a warehouse has no more in ventory, it is said to be drained, and is subsequently ready to be shut down. Figure 1d illustrates the filtering capabilities of a PivotTable list, showing only the rows that represent all warehouses in the USA except those in the West area. The other records in the list (Figure 1b) are hidden.

For other users to interact with a PivotTable list, they must have the Office Web components installed, and they must be using Microsoft Internet Explorer 4.01 or later. The Office Web components are installed automatically as part of the Office XP installation process.

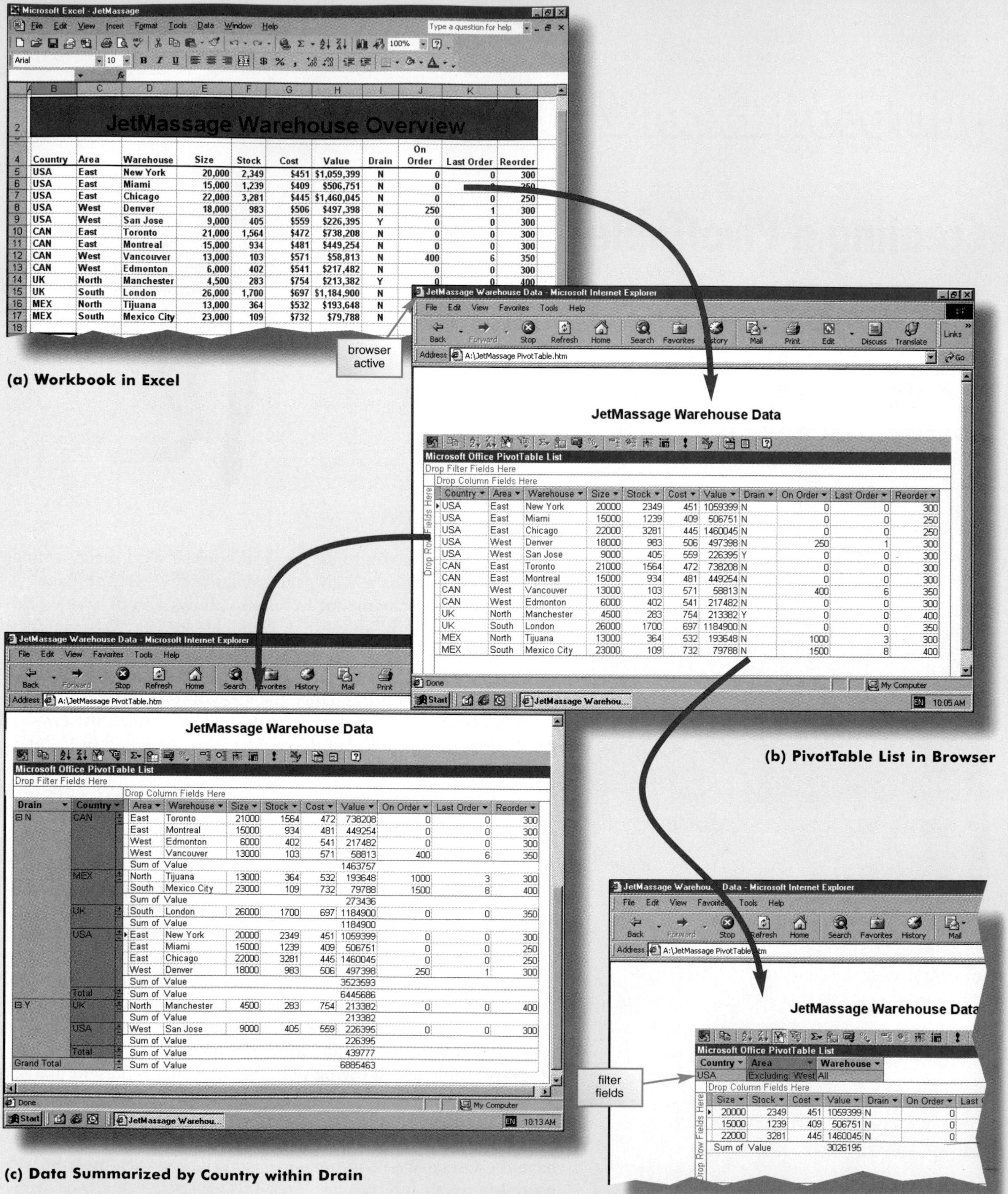

(a) Workbook in Excel

(b) PivotTable List in Browser

(c) Data Summarized by Country within Drain

(d) All Warehouses in the USA Except West Area Display

FIGURE 1

Saving a Worksheet Database as a PivotTable List

The first step in this project is to open the JetMassage workbook (Figure 1a) and save the database in the range B4:L17 as a PivotTable list that can be viewed and manipulated in a browser.

More About

PivotTables

For more information on PivotTables, visit the Excel 2002 More About Web page (scsite.com/ex2002/more.htm) and click PivotTables.

Steps To Save a Worksheet Database as a PivotTable List

1 Insert the Data Disk in drive A. Start Excel and then open the workbook JetMassage on drive A. See the inside back cover of this book for instructions for downloading the Data Disk or your instructor for information on accessing the files required in this book. Reset your toolbars as described in Appendix C. Select the range B4:L17. Click File on the menu bar and then point to Save as Web Page.

The File menu displays (Figure 2).

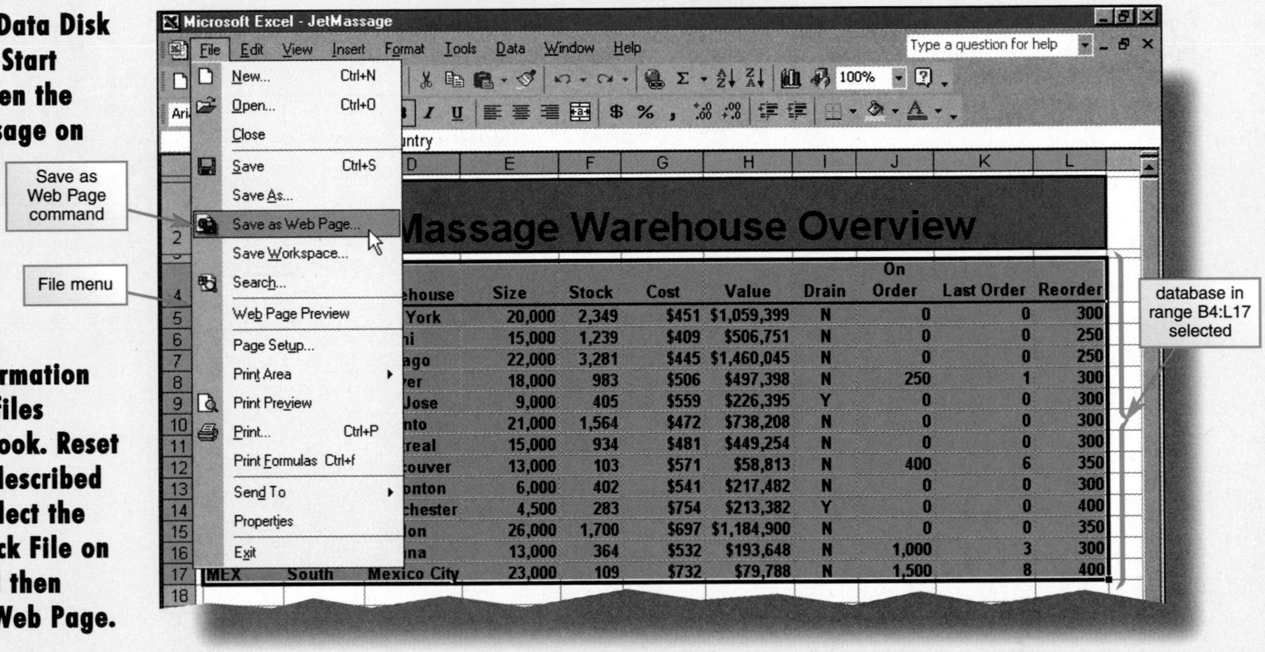

FIGURE 2

2 Click Save as Web Page. When the Save As dialog box displays, type `JetMassage PivotTable` **in the File name text box and then, if necessary, click the Save in box arrow and click 3½ Floppy (A:). Point to the Publish button.**

The Save As dialog box displays as shown in Figure 3.

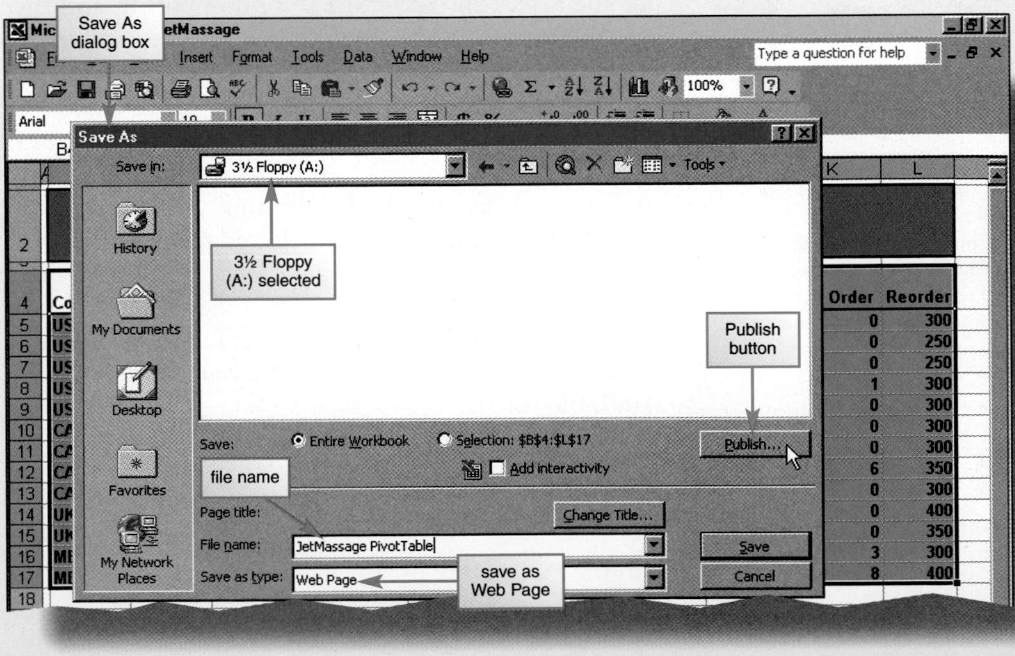

FIGURE 3

3 **Click the Publish button. Click the Add interactivity with check box, click the Add interactivity with box arrow, and then click PivotTable functionality. Click the Change button. When the Set Title dialog box displays, type** `JetMassage Warehouse Data` **in the Title text box. Point to the OK button.**

The Publish as Web Page and Set Title dialog boxes display as shown in Figure 4.

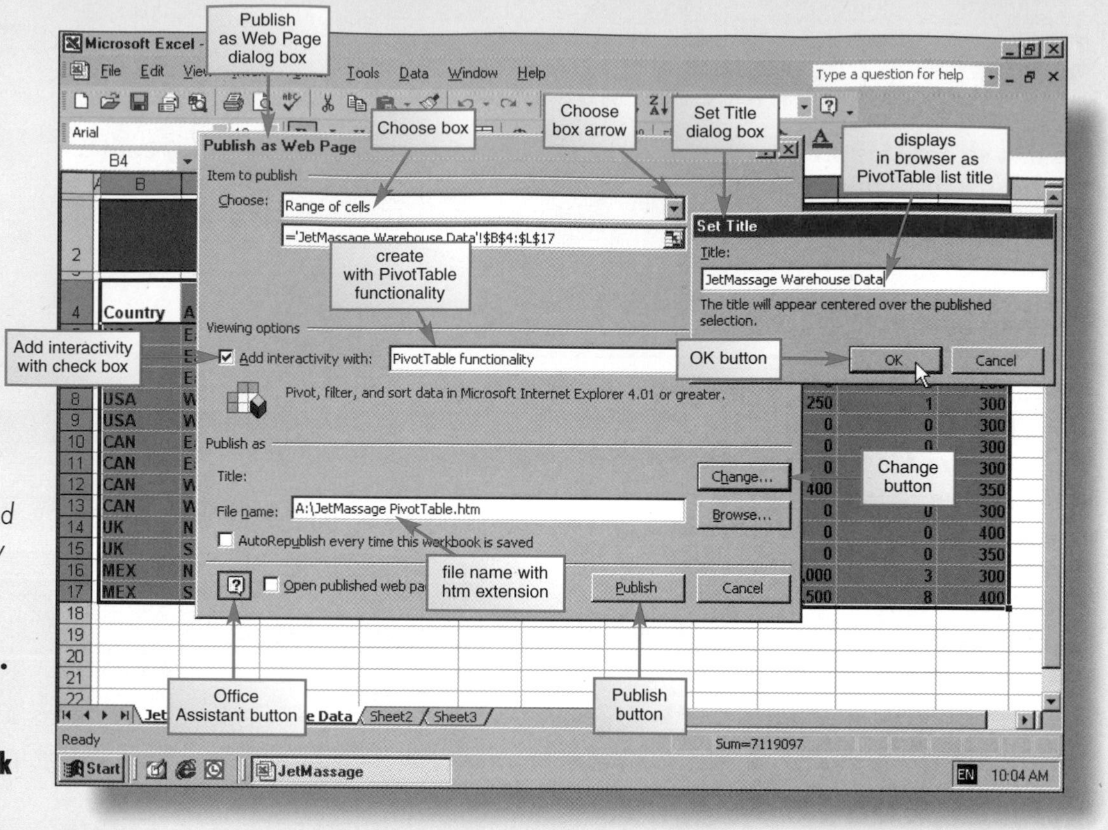

FIGURE 4

4 **Click the OK button. Click the Publish button in the Publish as Web Page dialog box. Click the Close button on the right side of the Excel title bar. If your browser opens, click the close button on the right side of the browser title bar.**

Excel saves the PivotTable list in HTML (hypertext markup language) format to drive A.

> **More About**
>
> **PivotTable Lists and Associated Charts**
>
> Along with a PivotTable list, you can include a chart that displays the same data graphically. If you display the PivotTable list in your browser and change the view, you will see the same changes in the chart.

If you click the Save button in the Save As dialog box shown in Figure 3 on the previous page, Excel saves the entire workbook as a noninteractive Web page. If you click the Selection: $B$4:$L$17 option button and then click the Save button, Excel saves the selected range B4:L17 as a noninteractive Web page. If you click the Add interactivity check box, then Excel saves the range B4:L17 as an **interactive Web page**. An interactive Web page allows you to change the values in the cells in your browser, but it does not give you the ability to rotate fields the way a PivotTable list does.

When you use the Publish button, you must tell Excel what you want to publish. In Figure 4, the range of cells selected on the worksheet is selected in the Choose list box. In the Viewing options area, once you add a check mark to the Add interactivity with check box, the list box becomes active. The list box gives you two choices — Spreadsheet functionality or PivotTable functionality. The Change button in Figure 4 displays the **Set Title dialog box**, which allows you to add a title to the PivotTable list.

Viewing the PivotTable List Using Your Browser

With the PivotTable list saved as an HTML file, the next step is to view it using your browser, as shown in the following steps.

Steps To View a PivotTable List Using Your Browser

1 **Click the Launch Internet Explorer Browser button on the taskbar.**

2 **When the Internet Explorer window displays, type** `a:\JetMassage PivotTable.htm` **in the Address bar, and then press the ENTER key.**

The PivotTable list, JetMassage PivotTable.htm, displays (Figure 5).

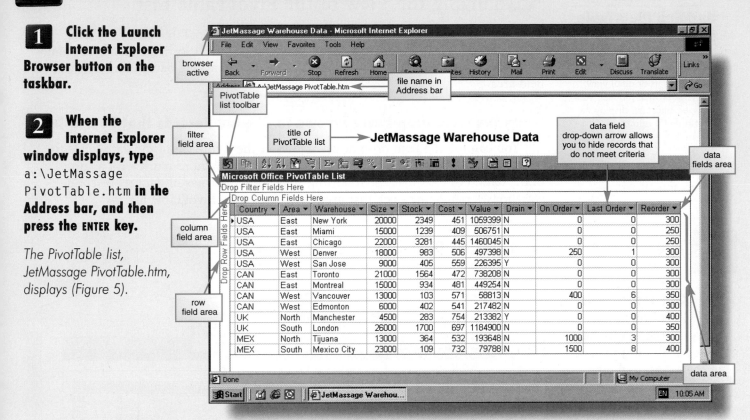

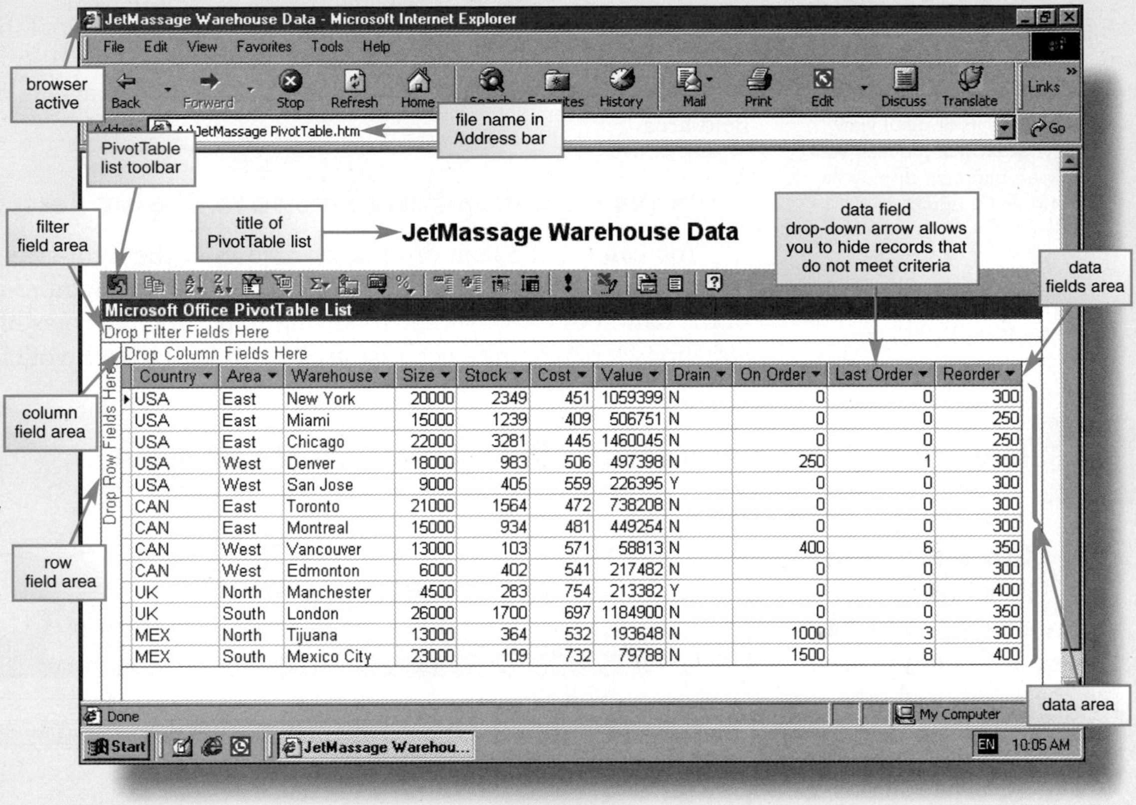

FIGURE 5

The PivotTable list Web page in Figure 5 resembles an Excel worksheet with the column and row structure. The Address bar displays the URL. The title above the columns and rows is the same as the entry made in the Set Title dialog box in Figure 4. The toolbar immediately below the title includes buttons that allow you to complete tasks quickly, such as copy, sort, filter, calculate summaries, and move fields. Figure 6 identifies the buttons on the PivotTable list toolbar.

The area below the toolbar is divided into five areas as shown in Figure 5: (1) data area; (2) data fields; (3) row field area; (4) column field area; and (5) filter field area. The data area contains the data. Each entry in the data area is called an item. The data fields at the top of each column identify the data below them. For example, the Stock data field identifies the amount of product in stock in the same column. Each data field contains a field drop-down arrow that allows you to set up filters to display only records that meet certain criteria. You drag data fields to the row field area on the left side of the PivotTable list and the column field area at the top of the PivotTable list to display different views of the data. You also can drag data fields to the filter field area to display different views of the data using filtering techniques.

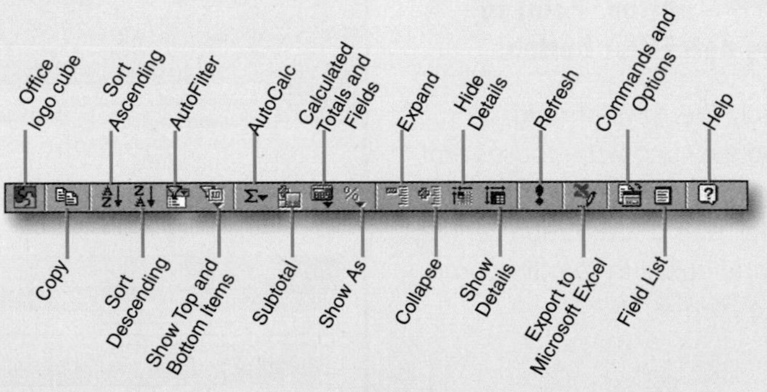

FIGURE 6

More About

Undoing PivotTable List Changes

If you make several changes to a PivotTable list and wish to restore it to its original view, quit your browser, launch your browser, and then display the PivotTable list again.

Changing the View of the PivotTable List

This section shows you how to change the view of the PivotTable list by (1) using the field drop-down arrows; (2) adding summary totals; (3) sorting columns of data; (4) dragging data fields to the row field area; and (5) dragging data fields into the filter field area.

Using the Field Drop-Down Arrows to Display Records that Pass a Test

You can use the field drop-down arrows at the right-side of the data fields to hide rows of data that do not pass a test. This allows you to work with a subset of the data. For example, the following steps hide the rows of data representing warehouses remaining open that are displaying in the PivotTable list.

Steps To Use Field Drop-Down Arrows to Display Records that Pass a Test

1 Click the Drain data field drop-down arrow, click the check box labeled N (for no) to clear the check box, and then point to the OK button.

A list of the different items in the Drain column of data display as check boxes along with a check box titled All (Figure 7). The N check box does not have a check mark. The AutoFilter button on the toolbar is selected.

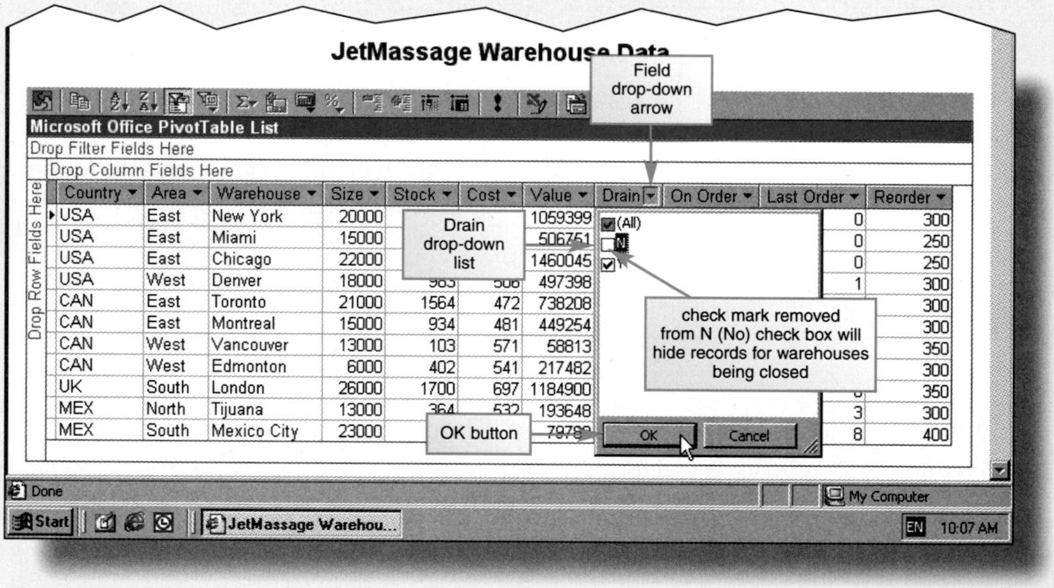

FIGURE 7

2 Click the OK button. Point to the AutoFilter button.

Only the rows of data representing warehouses that are closing display (Figure 8). The rows of data representing warehouses to remain open are hidden.

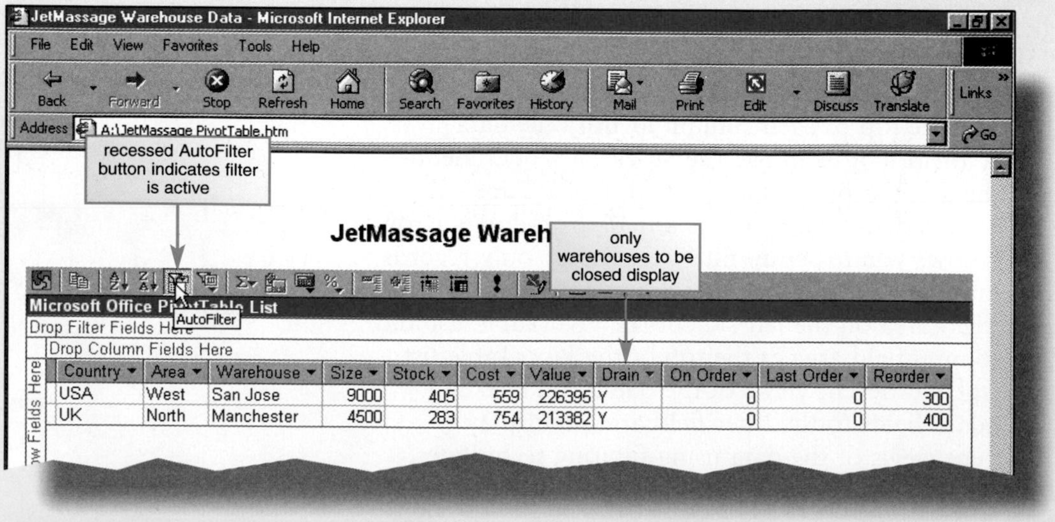

FIGURE 8

3 Click the AutoFilter button on the toolbar.

The filter is disabled and all rows of data display (Figure 9).

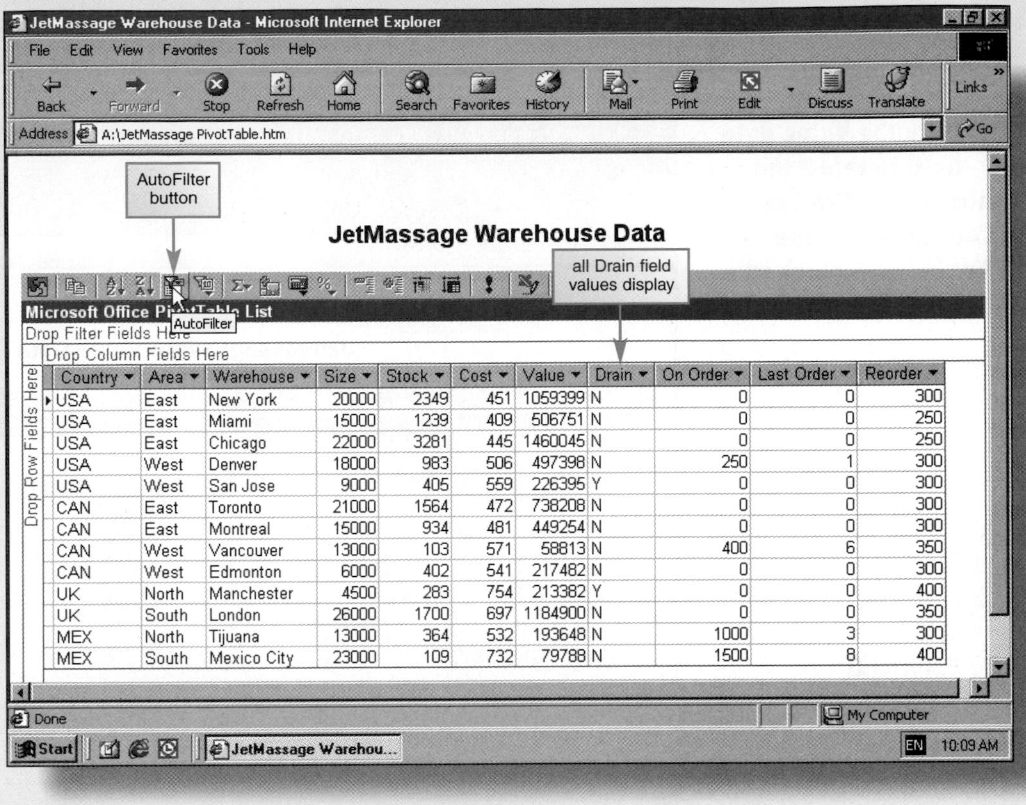

FIGURE 9

When you use a field drop-down arrow to filter the data, the arrow changes to the color blue. It remains blue until you disable the filter using the AutoFilter button or select the All check box in the Drain field drop-down list (Figure 7). You can add additional filters by using other field drop-down arrows. Thus, you can display a subset of a subset. For example, after applying the filter as shown in Figure 8, you can apply a second filter to the Country field that only displays warehouses in the USA. If you disable the filter by clicking the AutoFilter button and then select new filters, the original disabled filter is lost.

Adding Summary Totals

A PivotTable list is more useful if you add summaries to key columns of data. For example, you can add a summary to the Value column in Figure 9. The Value column indicates the total value of the current inventory at a specific warehouse. Nine summary functions are available through the AutoCalc button on the toolbar. The nine **summary functions** are Sum, Count, Min, Max, Average, Standard Deviation, Standard Deviation Population, Variance, and Variance Population. The steps on the next page add the Sum summary function to the Value column of data.

More About

Summary Functions

The type of data in a field determines whether a summary function is available or not. For example, if a field contains dates, then the Sum function is not available. If a field contains text, you cannot use the Sum, Min, or Max function, but you can use Count.

Steps **To Add a Summary Total to a Column of Data**

1 **Click the Value data field to select the entire column. Click the AutoCalc button on the PivotTable list toolbar and point to Sum.**

The PivotTable list displays as shown in Figure 10.

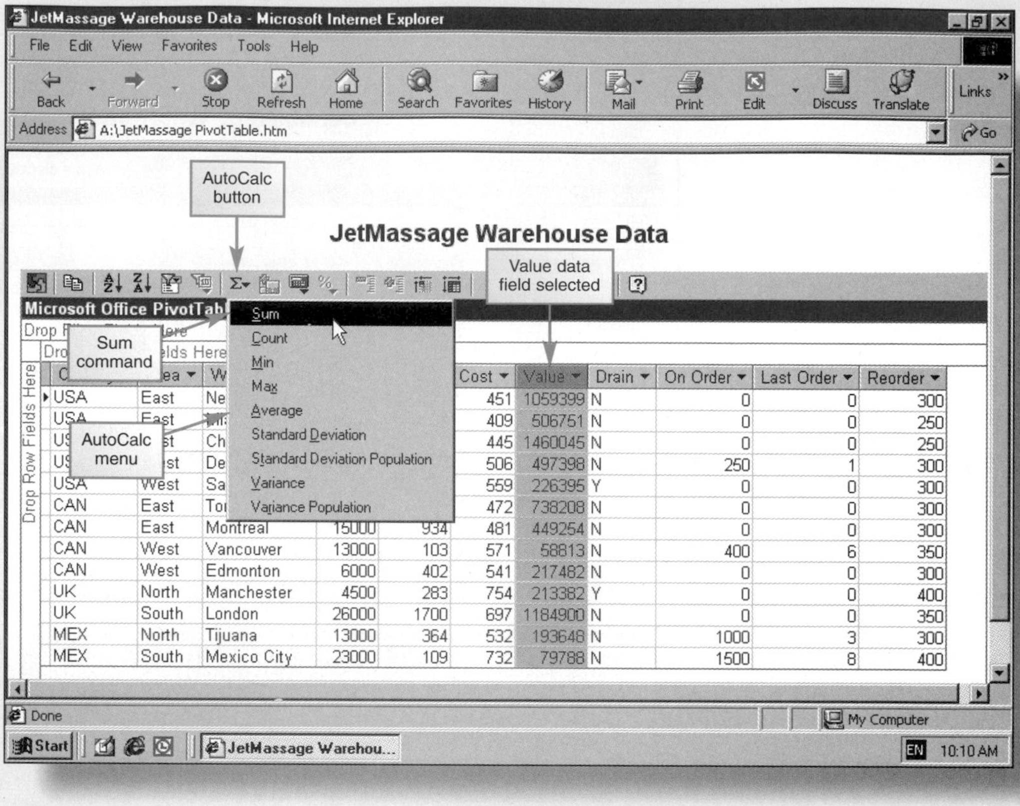

FIGURE 10

2 **Click Sum.**

A grand total displays below the Value column of data (Figure 11).

JetMassage Warehouse Data

Microsoft Office PivotTable List

Drop Filter Fields Here

Drop Column Fields Here

Country ▼	Area ▼	Warehouse ▼	Size ▼	Stock ▼	Cost ▼	Value ▼	Drain ▼	On Order ▼	Last Order ▼	Reorder ▼
USA	East	New York	20000	2349	451	1059399	N	0	0	300
USA	East	Miami	15000	1239	409	506751	N	0	0	250
USA	East	Chicago	22000	3281	445	1460045	N	0	0	250
USA	West	Denver	18000	983	506	497398	N	250	1	300
USA	West	San Jose	9000	405	559	226395	Y	0	0	300
CAN	East	Toronto	21000	1564	472	738208	N	0	0	300
CAN	East	Montreal	15000	934	481	449254	N	0	0	300
CAN	West	Vancouver	13000	103	571	58813	N	400	6	350
	West	Edmonton	6000	402	541	217482	N	0	0	300
	North	Manchester	4500	283	754	213382	Y	0	0	400
	South	London	26000	1700	697	1184900	N	0	0	350
MEX	North	Tijuana	13000	364	532	193648	N	1000	3	300
MEX	South	Mexico City	23000	109	732	79788	N	1500	8	400
Sum of Value						6885463				

Summary data area

grand total displays in summary data area

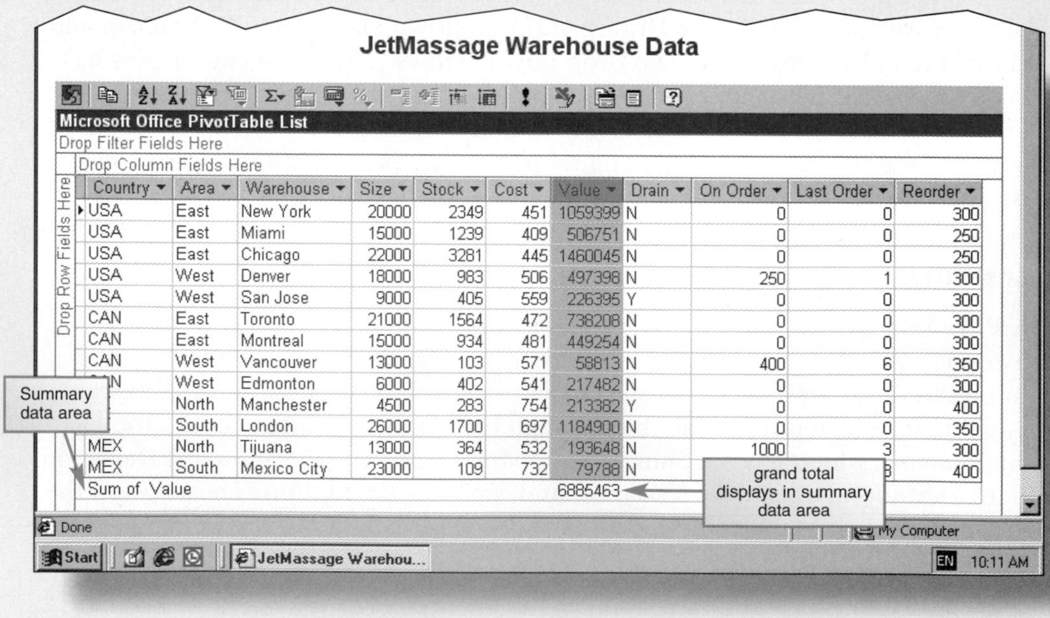

FIGURE 11

You can select, one at a time, all nine of the summary functions shown in the drop-down list in Figure 10. Each time you select a summary function, a new summary line is added to the summary data area.

Sorting Columns of Data

The data in a PivotTable is easier to work with and more meaningful if you arrange the data sequentially based on one or more fields. The sort routine available with a PivotTable list is similar to Excel in that it sorts the data using the current order of the records. Thus, if you need to sort on more than one column of data, sort the minor field first, progressing to the major field.

The following step sorts the PivotTable list in ascending sequence by the On Order amount.

> **More About**
>
> **Sort Order**
>
> The order in which numbers, text, and special characters are sorted depends on the source data and your regional settings in the Windows Control Panel.

Steps To Sort Columns of Data

1 Click the On Order data field and then click the Sort Ascending button on the toolbar.

The data in the PivotTable list is sorted first by country and then the number of items on order at each warehouse (Figure 12).

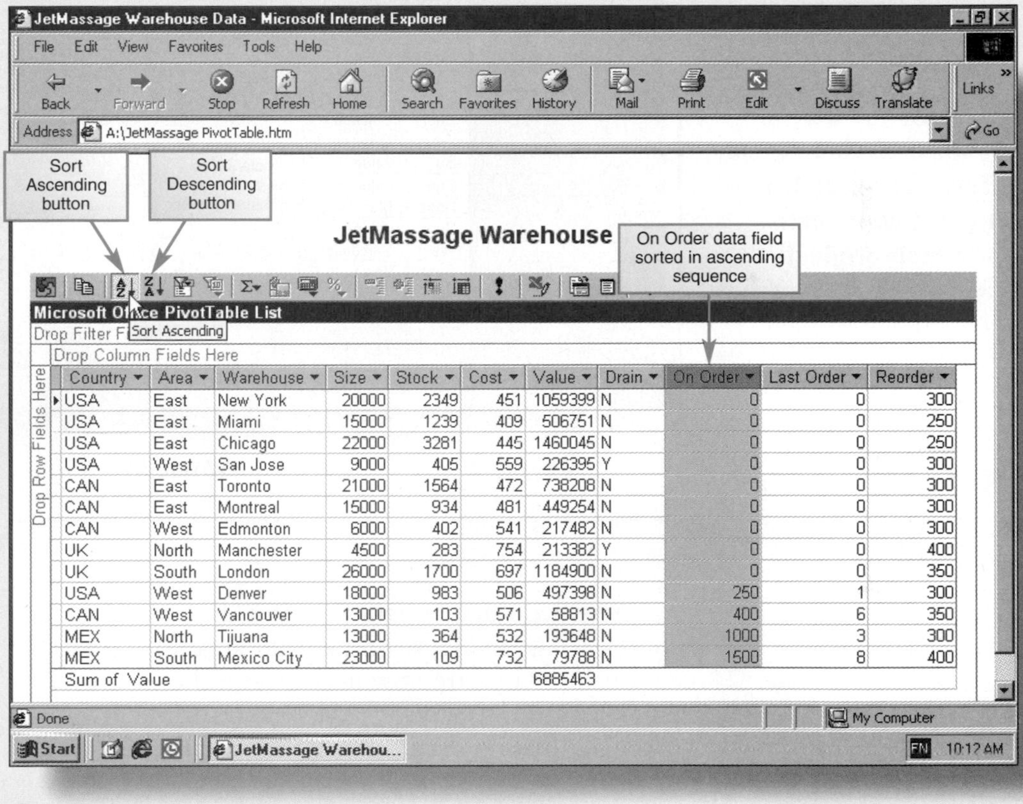

FIGURE 12

With the data sorted by the On Order value, you now can change the view of the data by moving data fields to the drop areas to change the view of the PivotTable list.

> **More About**
>
> **Sorting**
>
> To undo a sort and return the data to its previous order, click the recessed Sort Ascending or Sort Descending button.

Dragging Data Fields to the Row Field Area

Moving data fields to the drop areas changes the view. The **drop areas** are to the left and above the data area. The steps on the next page drag the Drain and Country data fields to the row field area on the left side of the PivotTable list to generate a new view. The last step returns the PivotTable list to its original view.

Steps To Drag Data Fields to the Row Field Area

1 Drag the Drain data field to the row field area. Drag the Country data field to the row field area and to the right of the Drain field.

The PivotTable list changes dramatically, showing subtotals for each country category and each drain category (Figure 13).

2 When you are finished viewing the PivotTable list, drag the Drain and Country data fields to their original locations in the data area.

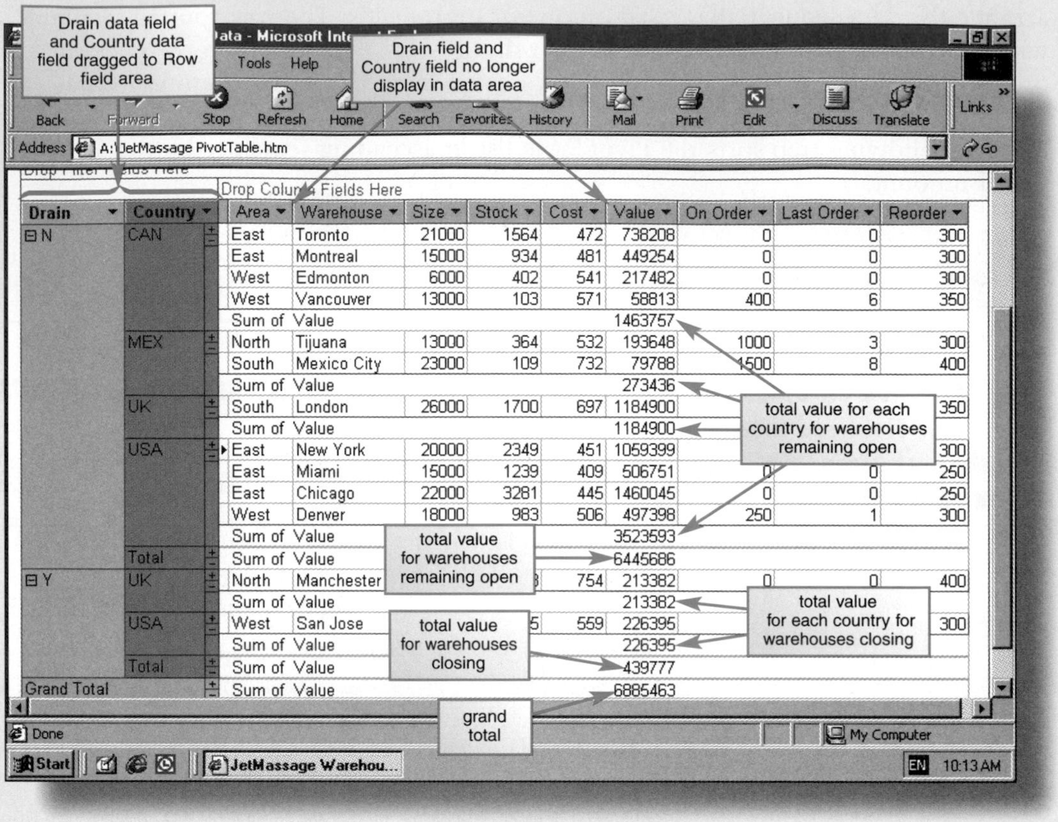

FIGURE 13

When you drag a data field to a drop area, the data field is moved rather than copied. Thus, in Figure 13 the data area no longer contains the Drain and Country data fields. They are now in the row field area. In Figure 12 on the previous page, only one total displayed at the bottom of the PivotTable list. In Figure 13, after dragging the two data fields, eight subtotals and one grand total display, and the rows of data are divided into categories based on their respective Drain and Country values.

More About

Dragging Fields to Drop Areas

When you drag a data field to the row field area, each unique data item within the field displays down the rows of the PivotTable list. When you drag a data field to the column field area, each unique data item within the field displays across the columns of the PivotTable list.

Dragging Data Fields to the Filter Field Area

Another way to manipulate the view of the PivotTable is to drag data fields to the filter field area at the top of the PivotTable list. When you drag a data field to this drop area, the data field maintains the field drop-down arrow, which allows you to apply a filter to the data. The following steps drag the Country, Area, and Warehouse data fields to the filter field area and then apply a filter.

Steps To Drag Data Fields to the Filter Field Area and Apply a Filter

1 Drag the Country data field to the filter field area. Drag the Area data field to the right of the Country filter field. Drag the Warehouse data field to the right of the Area filter field.

The PivotTable list displays as shown in Figure 14.

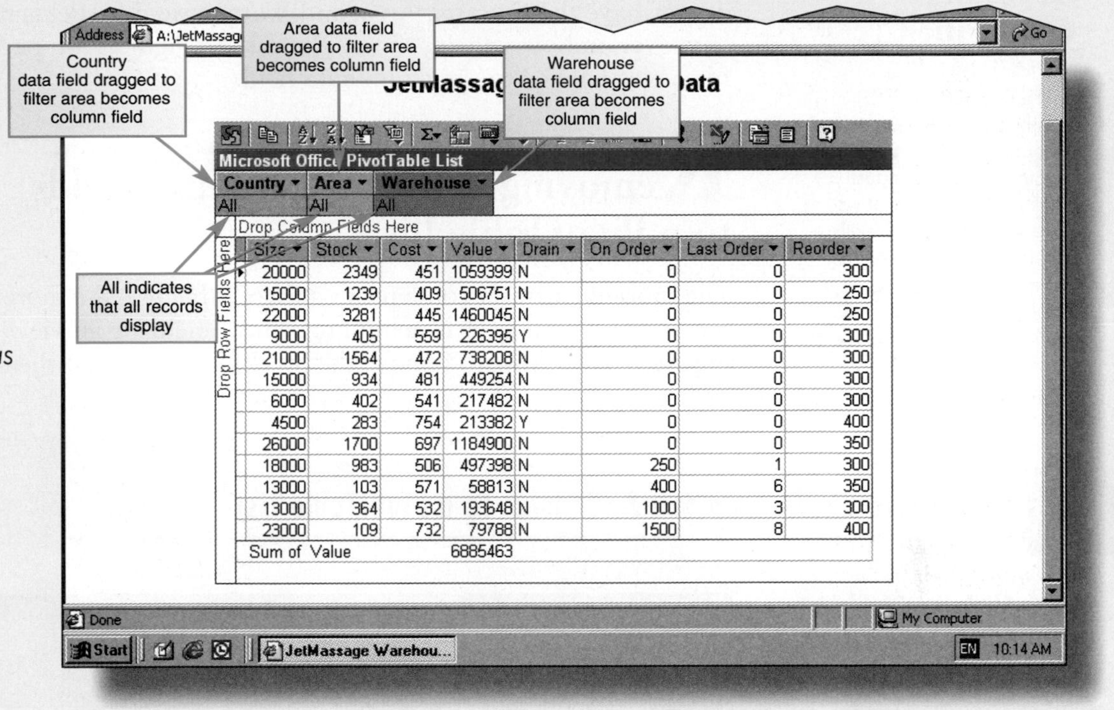

Country	Area	Warehouse
All	All	All

Size	Stock	Cost	Value	Drain	On Order	Last Order	Reorder
20000	2349	451	1059399	N	0	0	300
15000	1239	409	506751	N	0	0	250
22000	3281	445	1460045	N	0	0	250
9000	405	559	226395	Y	0	0	300
21000	1564	472	738208	N	0	0	300
15000	934	481	449254	N	0	0	300
6000	402	541	217482	N	0	0	300
4500	283	754	213382	Y	0	0	400
26000	1700	697	1184900	N	0	0	350
18000	983	506	497398	N	250	1	300
13000	103	571	58813	N	400	6	350
13000	364	532	193648	N	1000	3	300
23000	109	732	79788	N	1500	8	400
Sum of Value			6885463				

FIGURE 14

2 Click the Country data field drop-down arrow and click check boxes for CAN, MEX, and UK to unselect them. Click the Area data field drop-down arrow and click the check box labeled West.

Only three rows of data display (Figure 15). The remaining rows of data failed to pass the test of belonging to all USA areas except the West.

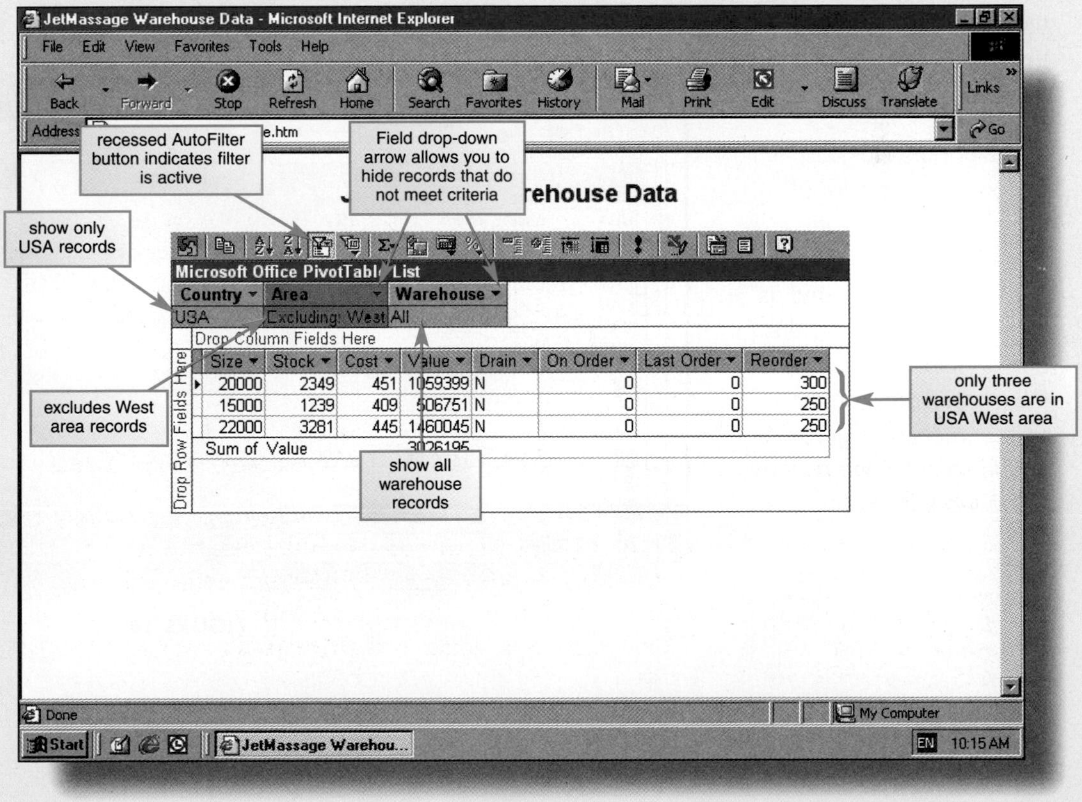

Country	Area	Warehouse
USA	Excluding: West	All

Size	Stock	Cost	Value	Drain	On Order	Last Order	Reorder
20000	2349	451	1059399	N	0	0	300
15000	1239	409	506751	N	0	0	250
22000	3281	445	1460045	N	0	0	250
Sum of Value			3026195				

FIGURE 15

3 When you are finished viewing the PivotTable list in its current form, click the AutoFilter button on the toolbar to disable the filter. One at a time, drag the three filter fields back to their original position in the data area.

More About

Microsoft Certification

The Microsoft Office User Specialist (MOUS) Certification program provides an opportunity for you to obtain a valuable industry credential —proof that you have the Excel 2002 skills required by employers. For more information, see Appendix D or visit the Shelly Cashman Series MOUS Web page at scsite.com/offxp/cert.htm.

You could have applied the filters to the data fields in the data area, rather than dragging them to the filter field area. By dragging these fields to the filter field area, however, the rows that pass the test are cleaner and easier to read. For example, you do not have the Country, Area, and Warehouse data fields repeating the same numbers over and over again, as was the case in Figure 7 on page EW 2.06 when the filter was applied to the Drain data field.

Removing Fields and Adding Fields to a PivotTable List

The more data fields you have in a PivotTable list, the more difficult it is to interpret the data. Sometimes it is helpful to remove fields from view temporarily. The following steps show how to remove the Stock data field and then add the field back to the data area.

Steps To Remove Fields from and Add Fields to a PivotTable List

1 Click the Field List button on the PivotTable list toolbar to display the PivotTable Field List window. Right-click the Stock data field. When the shortcut menu displays, point to Remove Field.

The PivotTable Field List window displays a list of all the data fields in the PivotTable list (Figure 16). The Stock data field and its data are selected, and the shortcut menu displays. Most of the commands on the shortcut menu in Figure 16 are the same as the buttons on the toolbar.

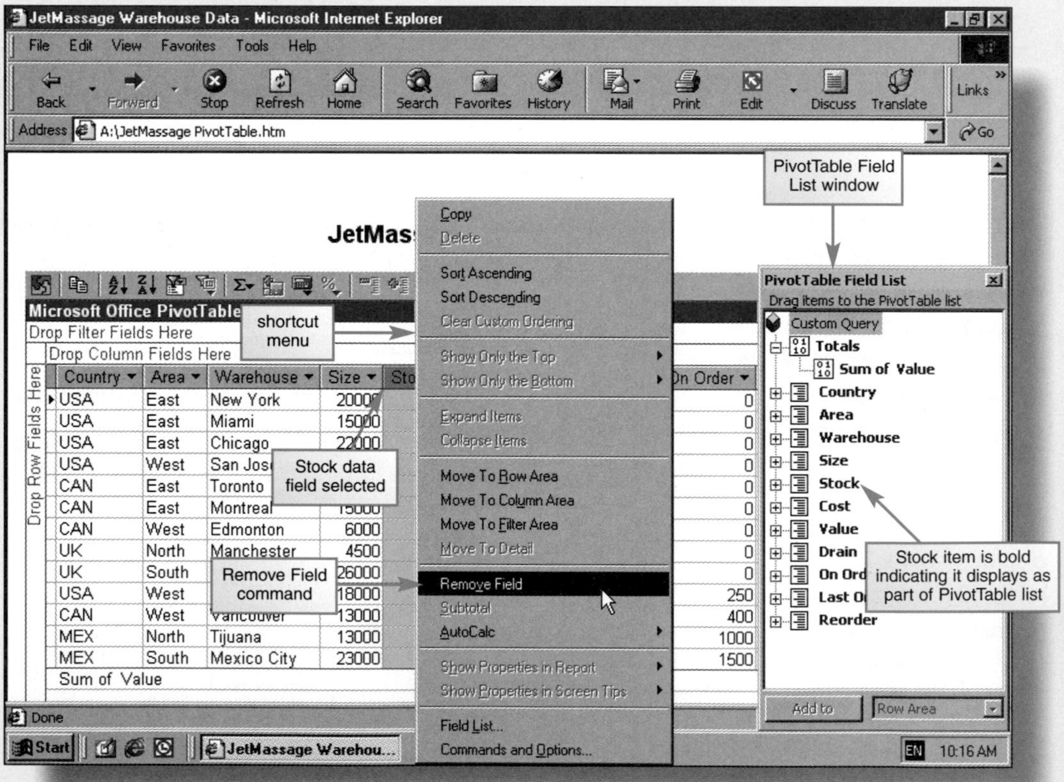

FIGURE 16

2 Click Remove Field.

The Stock data field and its column of data are hidden. The word, Stock, in the PivotTable Field List window is regular font style, whereas the active data fields are bold in the PivotTable Field List window (Figure 17).

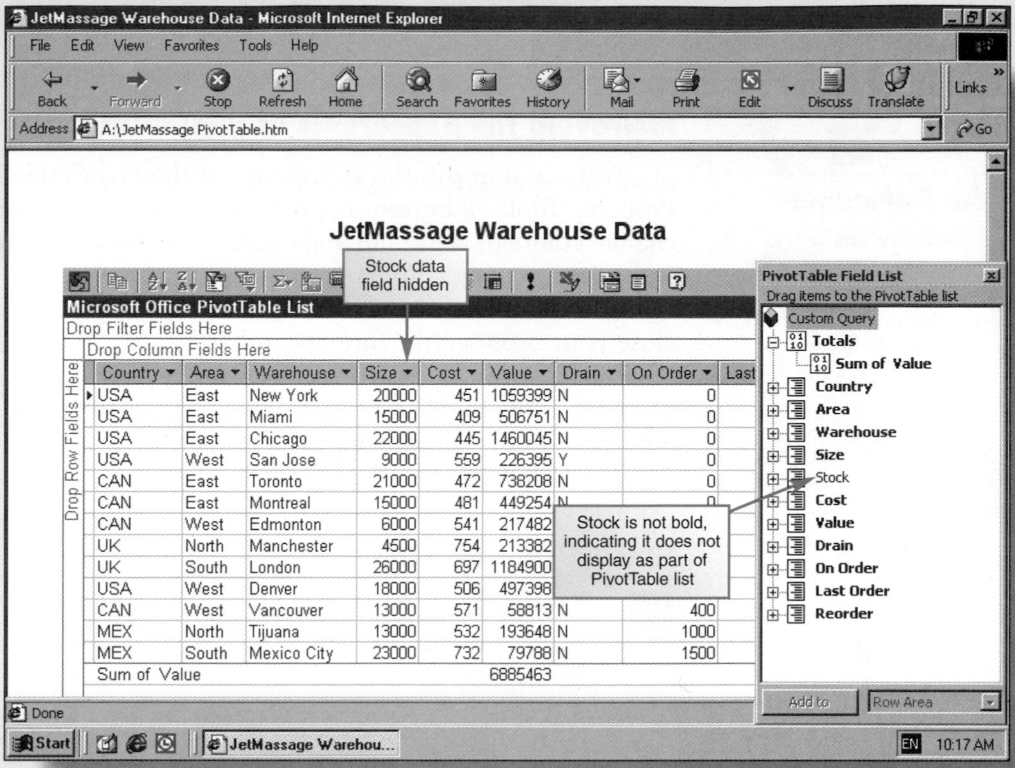

FIGURE 17

3 Drag the Stock data field from the PivotTable Field List window to its original location between the Size and Cost data fields.

The Stock data field is added to the data area in the PivotTable list (Figure 18). The word, Stock, now is bold in the PivlotTable Field List window.

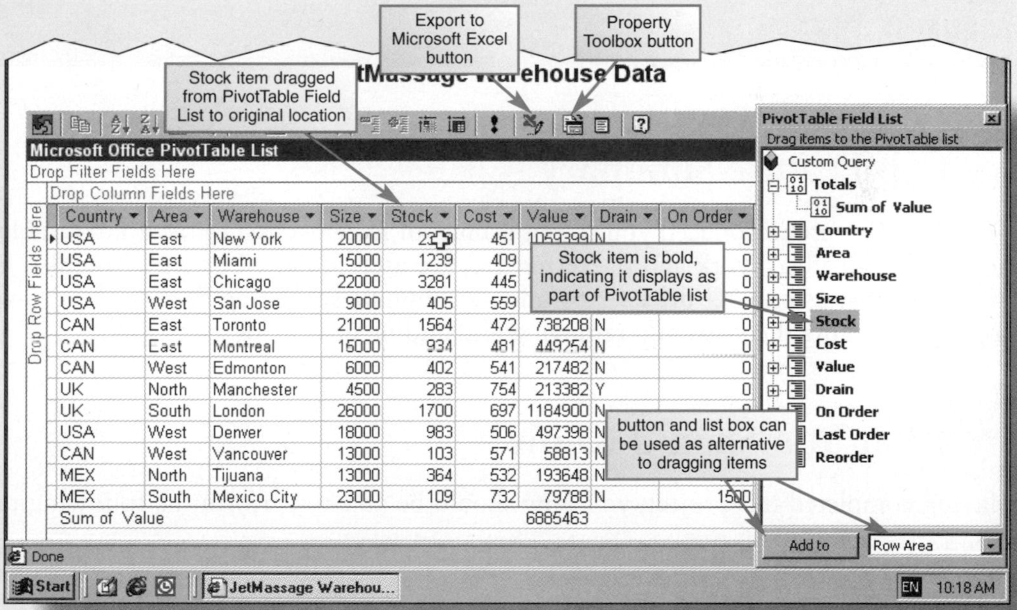

FIGURE 18

You can remove (hide) as many data fields as you want from the data area to simplify the PivotTable list. When you add data fields, you can insert them at any location. For example, you could have added the Stock data field anywhere in the data area. You cannot duplicate a data field. That is, the Stock data field can show up only once in the data area.

Besides removing fields and adding fields, you can move data fields from one location in the data area to another by dragging.

More About

Quick Reference

For a table that lists how to complete tasks covered in this book using the mouse, menu, shortcut menu, and keyboard, see the Quick Reference Summary at the back of this book or visit the Shelly Cashman Series Office XP Web page (scsite.com/offxp/qr.htm) and then click Microsoft Excel 2002.

Improving the Appearance of a PivotTable List

You can improve the appearance of the PivotTable list through the use of the Property Toolbox button. For example, you can change the font, format numbers, change colors of cells, and align text. You also can increase or decrease the column width by dragging column borders as you did in Excel. Any formatting you do to the PivotTable list remains effective as long as you do not close your browser. Once you close your browser, the formats are lost.

Finally, you can export the PivotTable list to Excel. In Excel, the PivotTable list becomes a PivotTable report. You can format the PivotTable report using Excel's powerful formatting capabilities and then save it as a PivotTable list.

The following step closes your browser.

TO CLOSE YOUR BROWSER

1. Click the Close button on the right side of the browser's title bar.

CASE PERSPECTIVE SUMMARY

Catherine Cay will be pleased with the PivotTable list capabilities. It will serve as the first step towards keeping the management team up to date on warehouse information. The managers and executives will be able to analyze the warehouse data by displaying different views. More importantly, they will be able to analyze the data using their browsers, rather than using Excel.

Web Feature Summary

This Web Feature introduced you to publishing an Excel worksheet as a PivotTable list Web page. You learned how PivotTable lists work and the terms that are used to describe them. You also learned how to enhance a PivotTable list using your browser by adding summaries, filtering data so only rows that pass a test display, sorting, changing the view, and removing and adding data fields.

What You Should Know

Having completed this project, you now should be able to perform the following tasks:

- Add a Summary Total to a Column of Data *(EW 2.08)*
- Close Your Browser *(EW 2.14)*
- Drag Data Fields to the Filter Field Area and Apply a Filter *(EW 2.11)*
- Drag Data Fields to the Row Field Area *(EW 2.10)*
- Remove Fields from and Add Fields to a PivotTable List *(EW 2.12)*
- Save a Worksheet Database as a PivotTable List *(EW 2.03)*
- Sort Columns of Data *(EW 2.09)*
- Use Field Drop-Down Arrows to Display Records that Pass a Test *(EW 2.06)*
- View a PivotTable List Using Your Browser *(EW 2.05)*

In the Lab

1 Creating the Korvin Sales Force PivotTable List

Problem: You are a spreadsheet specialist for Korvin Distributors, a distributor of truck engine parts with a national sales force. You have been asked to make information about the company's sales force available to management on the company's intranet. You decide to use a PivotTable list to distribute information across the company's intranet so that it can be analyzed using a browser.

Instructions: Start Excel and open the workbook, Korvin Distributors, from the Data Disk. If you do not have a copy of the Data Disk, then see the inside back cover of this book. Save the range B4:J14 as a PivotTable list to drive A using the file name, Korvin Distributors PivotTable. Add the title, Korvin Distributors Sales Analysis, as shown in Figure 19 before publishing the Web page. Close Excel and open your browser. Display the PivotTable list by entering `a:\Korvin Distributors PivotTable.htm` in the Address bar and then print the PivotTable list. Print the PivotTable list for each of the following:

1. Add a total to the Sales column. Sort the PivotTable list on Sales in descending sequence.
2. Sort in ascending sequence Educ within Gender. Drag the Gender data field to the filter field area (Figure 19). Use the Gender drop-down arrow to display rows for all males (M in the Gender field).

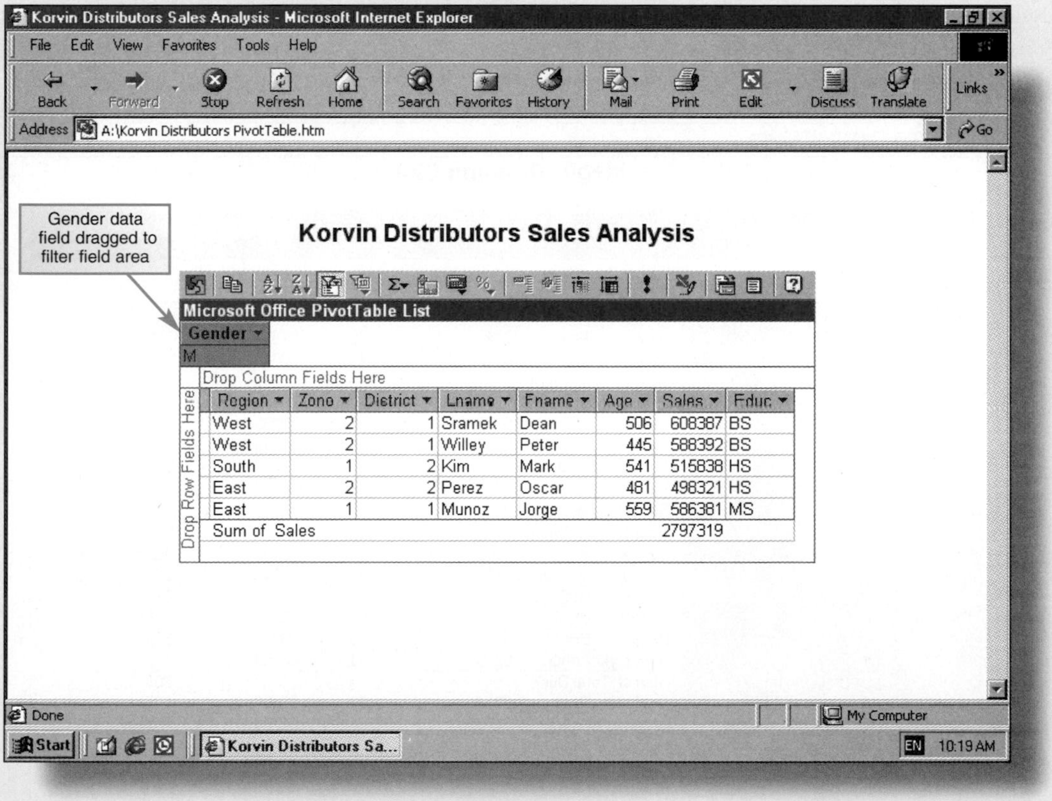

FIGURE 19

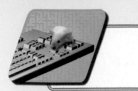

In the Lab

2 Creating the Ideolix Running Club PivotTable List

Problem: You are a member of a local running club. The members would like to access online the club's database, which includes each member's name, age, gender, zip code, preferred race type, total dues paid, and number of years in the club. You have been asked to use your Excel skills to create a PivotTable list from the database so it can be manipulated remotely using a browser.

Instructions: Start Excel and open the workbook, Ideolix Running, from the Data Disk. If you do not have a copy of the Data Disk, then see the inside back cover of this book. Save the range B4:J17 as a PivotTable list to drive A using the file name, Ideolix PivotTable. Add the title `Ideolix Running Club` as shown in Figure 20 before publishing the Web page. Close Excel and open your browser. Display the PivotTable list by entering the `a:\Ideolix PivotTable.htm` in the Address bar and then print the PivotTable list. Print the PivotTable list for each of the following:

1. Add a total to the Total Dues column. Display only club members who prefer 5k races.
2. Show all Preferred Race Types. Sort in ascending sequence on Preferred Race within Gender. Drag the Gender and Preferred Race data fields to the row field area as shown in Figure 20.

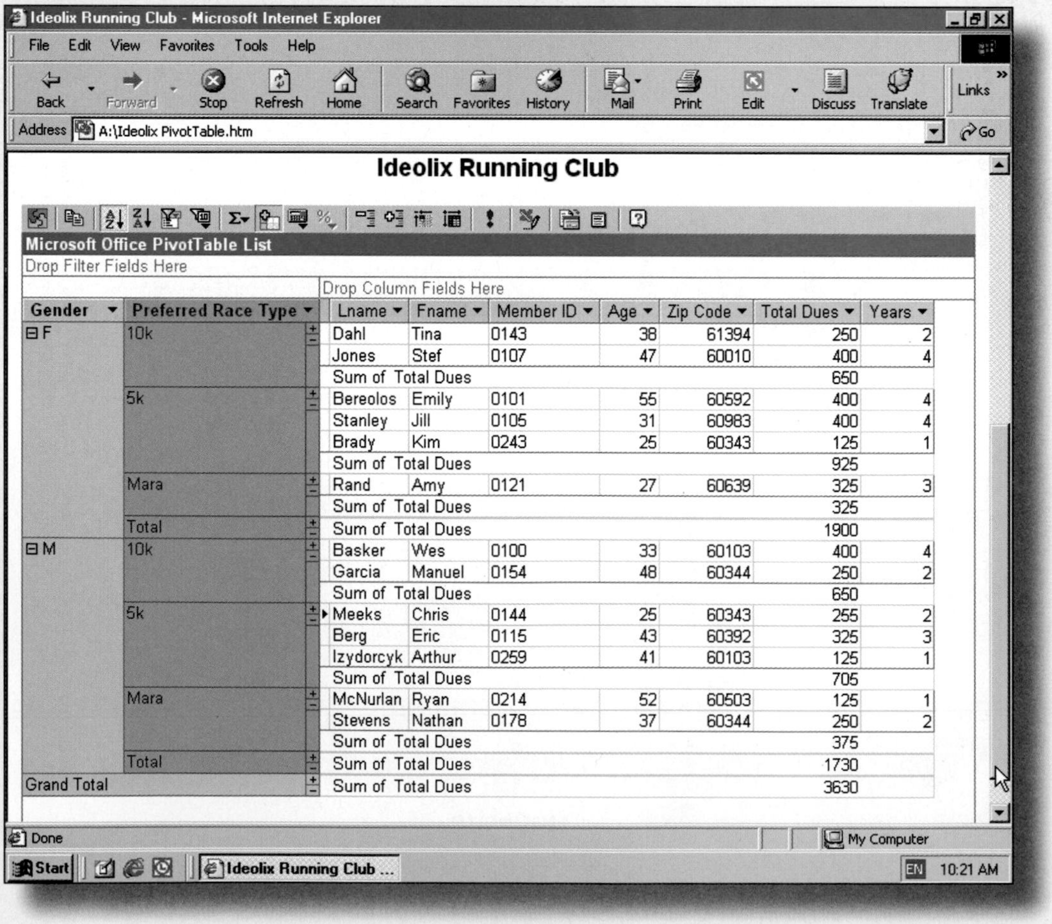

FIGURE 20

Microsoft Access 2002

PROJECT 7

Creating a Report Using Design View

OBJECTIVES

You will have mastered the material in this project when you can:

- Open a database
- Create additional tables
- Import data from an ASCII text file
- Change the layout of a table
- Relate several tables
- Change join properties
- Change field properties in a query
- Filter a query's recordset using Filter By Selection and Filter By Form
- Create and run a parameter query
- Create queries for reports
- Create a report
- Group and sort in a report
- Add fields to a report
- Add a subreport to a report
- Modify and move a subreport
- Add a date and page number
- Bold data
- Add a title
- Change margins
- Create and print mailing labels

Step Right Up!

Data Management Just Got Easier

In August of 1835, newspaper readers were transfixed by a series of articles in the New York Sun concerning "great astronomical discoveries" made by one of the more famous astronomers of the day, Sir John Herschel. According to the reports, Herschel used a sophisticated new telescope to view details on the moon that included mountains, lakes, vegetation, and animal and bird life, as well as a population of furry, winged men resembling bats. It seemed as if the world was on the verge of a new era. With the publication of the articles, the Sun was able to claim the largest circulation of any newspaper in the world: 19,360. The articles, of course, were fabrications.

When the hoax was exposed, people generally were amused. Moreover, they did not seem to lose interest in the Sun, which never lost its increased circulation. Throughout the 1800s, people read with amazement stories of petrified humans, discoveries of prehistoric remains, and plots to overthrow the government. Even well-known authors Edgar Allen Poe and Mark Twain got in on the fun. In 1850, Poe wrote an article detailing a bogus transatlantic hot air balloon crossing. A few years later, Twain wrote an article detailing the discovery of a petrified man in Nevada. It seemed that the man's body had been lying there for at least 100 years. Twain later explained that he created the hoax in order to poke fun at the many petrification stories that were all the rage in the papers at that time. Twain once said, "Truth is the most valuable thing we have. Let us economize it."

Into this climate of amusement and humbug strode a man who arguably was the all-time giant of American entertainment. For 60 years, Phineas Taylor Barnum

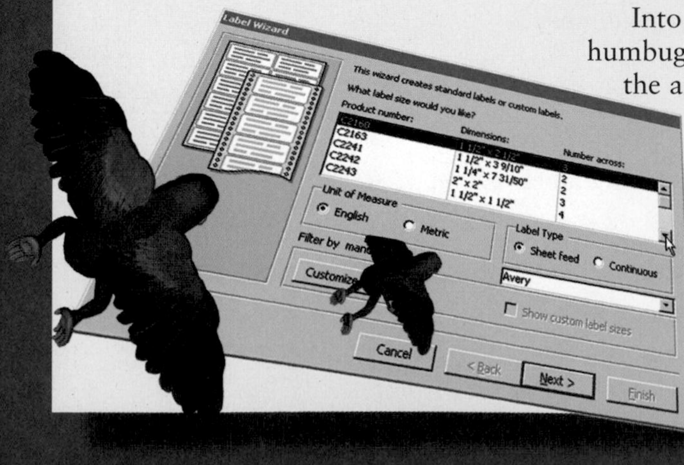

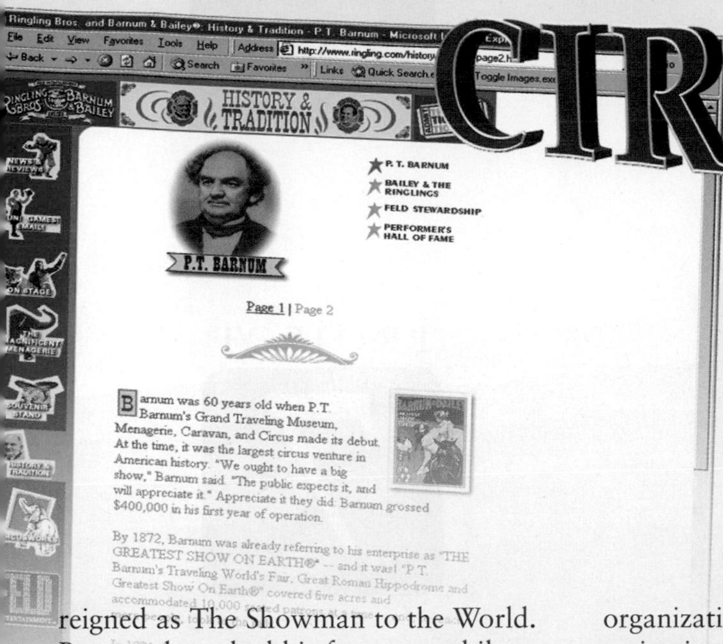

CIRCUS

reigned as The Showman to the World. Barnum launched his famous mobile circus in 1871, publicized as the The Greatest Show on Earth. The Barnum circus promoted some of the more outrageous oddities America and the world have ever seen, most of them legitimate, others born of Barnum's abundant imagination and love for the prank.

After it became known that P.T. Barnum was a master of absurdities, crowds flocked to see the infamous sideshows. The public not only expected the unusual from him, but also required it. Barnum's name became a household word. As a master presenter, Barnum preceded each new attraction with a concentrated public relations campaign. The news media ate it up, and attendance under the Big Top soared. Barnum loved the sensational, and above all, he loved people. Now, more than 100 years later, the show of shows still goes on. You can visit the Barnum Museum online (www.barnum-museum.org).

In all likelihood, you may never have the opportunity to manage an event of such magnitude as a grand-scale Barnum circus. In your professional career, however, you are likely to oversee the day-to-day operations of a business or head a large corporation that requires you to keep the organization's data centralized and maintained. With the working knowledge you have gained thus far of the powerful database management capabilities of Access 2002, you have acquired many of the skills you will need.

In this project, the more advanced concepts and techniques of Access are presented that illustrate report design from scratch using the Report Design window, inserting page numbers on a report, and creating mailing labels using the Label Wizard. If this type of application had existed in the days of P.T. Barnum, he might have used an Access database to handle the vast amounts of information required to organize the acts, maintain inventories, monitor schedules, and keep records for such a huge undertaking. The publishers of the New York Sun could have used Access to keep track of their rapidly expanding circulation list. In this century, those who take advantage of using the right tools will find themselves equipped to step right up and manage the big events successfully.

Microsoft Access 2002

Creating a Report Using Design View

PROJECT 7

CASE PERSPECTIVE

The management of Alisa Vending Services has determined that they need to expand their database. They want to include information on open work orders; that is, uncompleted requests for service. These work orders are to be categorized by the requested type of service (for example, coin handling repair). Once the work orders and service categories have been added to the database, they want a query created that enables them to find open work orders for all customers, for a single customer, or for a range of customers (for example, customers whose number is between CN21 and GS29). Management also wants a report that lists for each driver, each of the driver's customers along with all open work orders for the customer. Finally, they want to be able to produce mailing labels for the drivers. Your task is to fulfill these requests.

Introduction

This project creates the report shown in Figure 7-1a and the labels shown in Figure 7-1b. The report is organized by driver. For each driver, it lists the number, first name, and last name. Following the driver number and name, it lists data for each customer served by the driver. The customer data includes the customer number, name, address, city, state, zip code, telephone number, customer type, amount paid, and current due. It also includes any open work orders (requests for service) for the customer. For each such work order, the report lists the location of the vending machine to be serviced, the category of service (for example, preventive maintenance), a description of the problem, and the status of the request. Additional work order data includes the estimated hours to rectify the problem, the hours spent so far, and the date of the next scheduled service for the work order.

The project also creates mailing labels for the drivers. These labels, which are shown in Figure 7-1b, are designed perfectly to fit the type of labels that Alisa Vending Services has purchased.

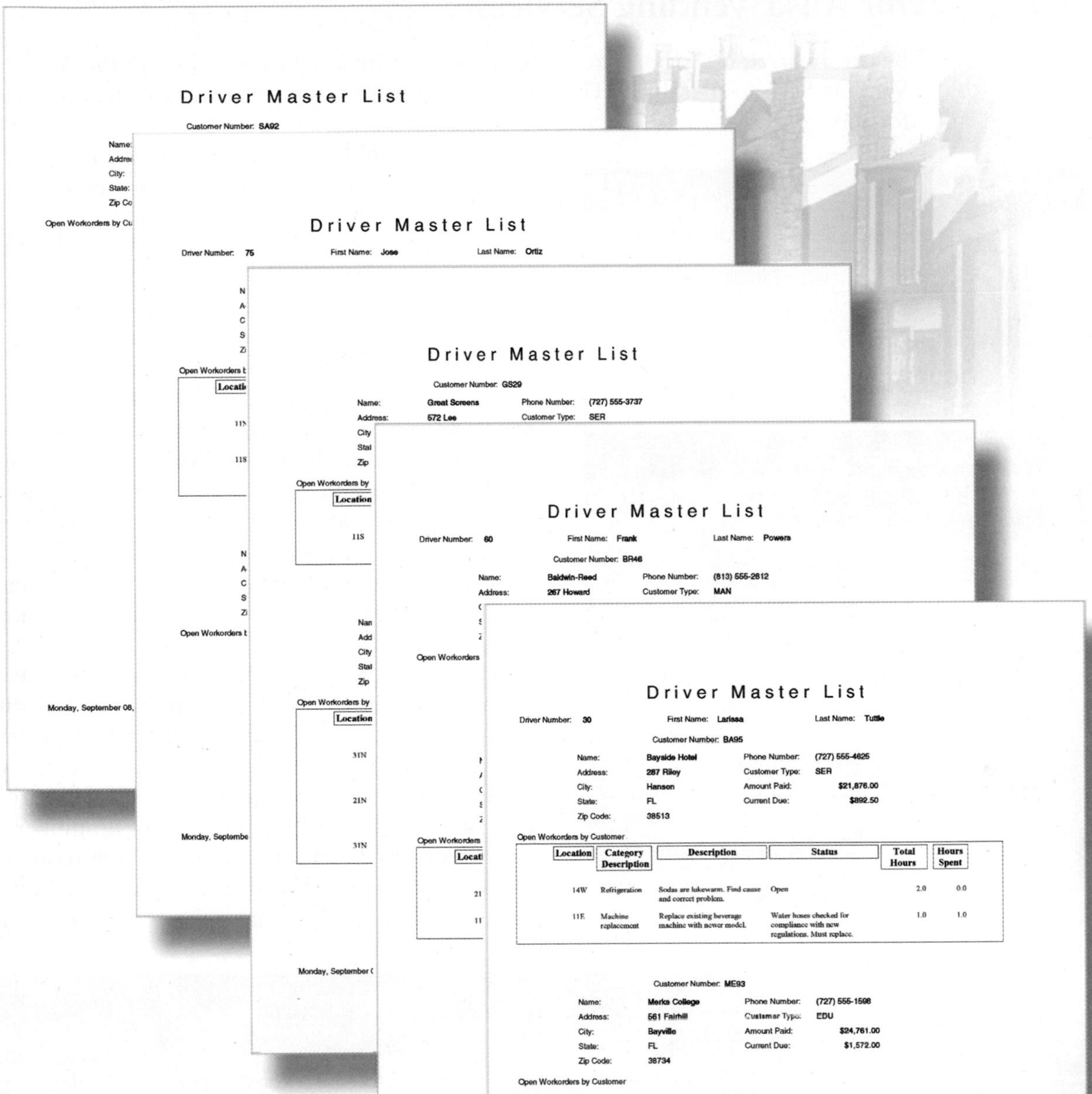

Driver Master List

Driver Number: 30 First Name: Larissa Last Name: Tuttle

Customer Number: BA95

Name: Bayside Hotel Phone Number: (727) 555-4625
Address: 287 Riley Customer Type: SER
City: Hanson Amount Paid: $21,876.00
State: FL Current Due: $892.50
Zip Code: 38513

Open Workorders by Customer

Location	Category Description	Description	Status	Total Hours	Hours Spent
14W	Refrigeration	Sodas are lukewarm. Find cause and correct problem.	Open	2.0	0.0
11E	Machine replacement	Replace existing beverage machine with newer model.	Water hoses checked for compliance with new regulations. Must replace.	1.0	1.0

Customer Number: ME93

Name: Merks College Phone Number: (727) 555-1598
Address: 561 Fairhill Customer Type: EDU
City: Bayville Amount Paid: $24,761.00
State: FL Current Due: $1,572.00
Zip Code: 38734

Open Workorders by Customer

Page 1

FIGURE 7-1a

Frank Powers
57 Ravenwood
Gillmore, FL 37572

Jose Ortiz
341 Pierce
Douglas, FL 37613

Larissa Tuttle
7562 Hickory
Laton Springs, FL 37891

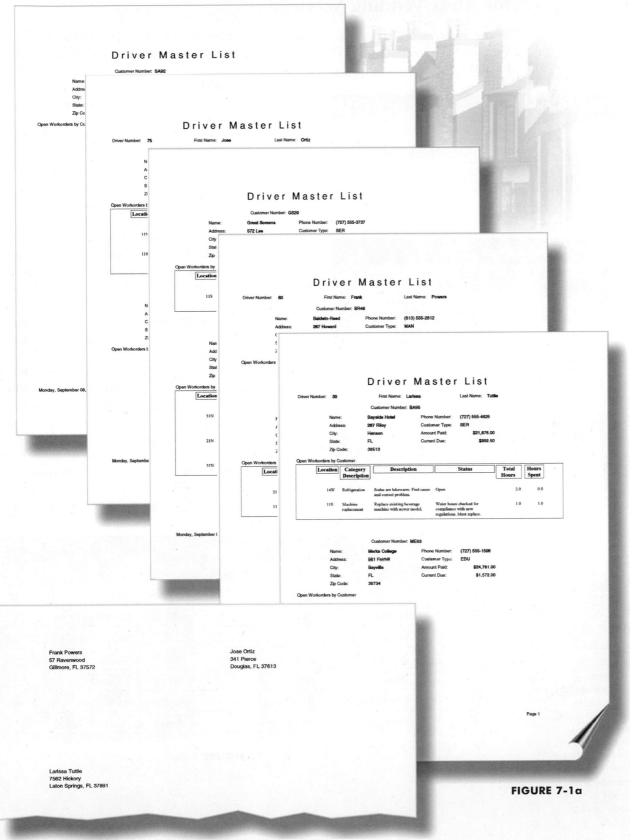

FIGURE 7-1b

Project Seven — Creating a Report Using Design View for Alisa Vending Services

Before creating the reports and labels, you first must add two tables to the Alisa Vending Services database. These tables help Alisa track open work orders (requests for service).

The first table, Category, is shown in Figures 7-2a and 7-2b. This table is used to categorize the open work orders. Figure 7-2a, which shows the structure of the table, indicates that there are two fields, Category Number (the primary key) and Category Description. Figure 7-2b shows the data in the table. The figure indicates, for example, that category 1 is an installation, category 2 is preventive maintenance, category 3 is refrigeration, and so on.

The second table, Open Workorders, is shown in Figures 7-3a and 7-3b. Figure 7-3a, the structure, indicates that the table contains a customer number and a location. The location, which is assigned by the customer, indicates the placement of the vending machine (for example, a building and placement within the building, such as 11E). The next field, Category Number, indicates the category of the service being requested. The Description field, a memo field, gives a description of the problem. The Status field, also a memo field, indicates the status of the request. The Total Hours (est) field gives an estimate of the total number of hours that will be required to satisfy the request. The Hours Spent field indicates how many hours already have been spent by a driver on the request.

Structure of Category table

NAME	TYPE	SIZE	DESCRIPTION
Category Number	Text	2	Category Number (Primary Key)
Category Description	Text	50	Description of Category

FIGURE 7-2a

Data for Category table

CATEGORY NUMBER	CATEGORY DESCRIPTION
1	Installation
2	Preventive maintenance
3	Refrigeration
4	Coin handling repair
5	Food or beverage dispensing repair
6	Electrical systems
7	Machine replacement
8	Heating

FIGURE 7-2b

Structure of Open Workorders table

NAME	TYPE	SIZE	DESCRIPTION
Customer Number	Text	4	Customer Number (Portion of Primary Key)
Location	Text	6	Location (Portion of Primary Key)
Category Number	Text	2	Category Number (Portion of Primary Key)
Description	Memo	-	Description of Problem
Status	Memo	-	Status of Work Request
Total Hours (est)	Number	-	Estimate of Total Number of Hours Required
Hours Spent	Number	-	Hours Already Spent on Problem

FIGURE 7-3a

More About

Microsoft Certification

The Microsoft Office User Specialist (MOUS) Certification program provides an opportunity for you to obtain a valuable industry credential — proof that you have the Access 2002 skills required by employers. For more information, see appendix E or visit the Shelly Cashman Series MOUS Web page at scsite.com/offxp/cert.htm.

Date for Open Workorders table

CUSTOMER	LOCATION	CATEGORY NUMBER	DESCRIPTION	STATUS	TOTAL HOURS (EST)	HOURS SPENT
BA95	11E	7	Replace existing beverage machine with newer model.	Water hoses checked for compliance with new regulations. Must replace.	1	1
BA95	14W	3	Sodas are lukewarm. Find cause and correct problem.	Open	2	0
CN21	11E	4	Exact change indicator light will not turn off.	Service call has been scheduled.	1	0
CN21	21W	2	Clean refrigeration condensers. Lubricate mechanical parts.	Open	1	0
FR28	11S	5	Dispenses too much coffee per cup. Leak under machine.	Driver has determined that control valve is rusty. Must still determine source of leak.	2	1
FR28	11N	1	Check necessary water, drainage, and electricity. Install new machine.	Electricity and water hook-ups okay. Drainage is very slow. Check for blockage and correct.	3	1
GS29	11S	6	Machine does not appear to be receiving any power.	Outlets and power cord checked and okay. Electrical specialist called.	2	1
LM22	21N	5	All items on row 2 will not drop into merchandise chute.	Open	1	0
LM22	31N	2	Check handles, springs, plungers, and merchandise chutes. Lubricate mechanical parts.	Must replace two plungers. Need parts.	2	1
LM22	31N	8	Hot beverages are cold. Find cause and correct problem.	Service call has been scheduled.	1	0

FIGURE 7-3b

Figure 7-3b gives the data. For example, the first record shows that customer BA95 has requested service. The location of the vending machine to be serviced is location 11E. The service is in category 7, machine replacement, as indicated in Figure 7-2b. The description of the problem is "Replace existing beverage machine with newer model." The status is "Water hoses checked for compliance with new regulations. Must replace." The driver has estimated that one hour total will be required on the problem. So far, one hour of work already has been spent.

If you examine the data in Figure 7-3b, you see that the Customer Number field cannot be the primary key. The first two records, for example, both have a customer number of BA95. Location also cannot be the primary key. The first and third records, for example, both have location of 11E. (Both customers have locations with the same number within their facilities and the vending machines in these locations currently require service.) In addition, the combination of customer number

More About

The Access Help System

Need help? It is no further than the Ask a Question box in the upper-right corner of the window. Click the Ask a Question box (it contains the text, Type a question for help), type `help` and then press the ENTER key. Access will respond with a list of items you can click to learn about obtaining help on any Access-related topic. To find out what is new in Access 2002, type `what's new in Access` in the Ask a Question box.

and location cannot be the primary key. The last two records both have LM22 as the customer number and 31N as the location. The primary key for the Open Workorders table is actually the combination of the Customer Number field, the Location field, and the Category Number field. No combination of customer number, location, and category number can occur on more than one row.

After creating the tables and loading the data, you will create three queries. You first will create a query to join the Customer and Open Workorders tables. Then you will modify the join properties to ensure that all customers display, even if they have no open work orders. You will modify the field properties of two of the fields and also filter the **recordset** (results) of the query. Then you will change the query to a **parameter query**, one that prompts the user for input when the query is run. Finally, you will create two queries that will be used in the report in Figure 7-1a on page A 7.05.

The report shown in Figure 7-1a contains a **subreport**, which is a report that is contained within another report. The subreport in the report in Figure 7-1a is the portion that lists the open work orders. You will create the report shown in the figure from scratch; that is, you will use Design view instead of the Report Wizard You will create mailing labels for the drivers as shown in Figure 7-1b on page A 7.05.

You are to create the tables, queries, report, and mailing labels requested by the management of Alisa Vending Services.

Opening the Database

Before you complete the steps in this project, you must open the database. Perform the following steps to complete this task.

TO OPEN A DATABASE

1. Click the Start button, click Programs on the Start menu, and then click Microsoft Access on the Programs submenu.
2. Click Open on the Database toolbar and then click 3½ Floppy (A:) in the Look in box. Make sure the database called Alisa Vending Services is selected.
3. Click the Open button.

The database opens and the Alisa Vending Services : Database window displays.

Creating the Additional Tables

Before creating the queries, report, and mailing labels required by Alisa Vending Services, you need to create the two additional tables shown in Figures 7-2a, 7-2b, 7-3a, and 7-3b on pages A 7.06 and A 7.07.

Creating the New Tables

The steps to create the new tables are identical to those you have used in creating other tables. Perform the following steps to create the new tables.

Steps To Create the New Tables

1 Click the Tables object. Right-click Create table in Design view, and then click Open on the shortcut menu. Maximize the window and then enter the information for the fields in the Category table as indicated in Figure 7-2a on page A 7.06. Be sure to select the Category Number field and click the Primary Key button to make Category Number the primary key. Close the window containing the table by clicking its Close button. Click the Yes button to save the changes. Type `Category` **as the name of the table, and then click the OK button.**

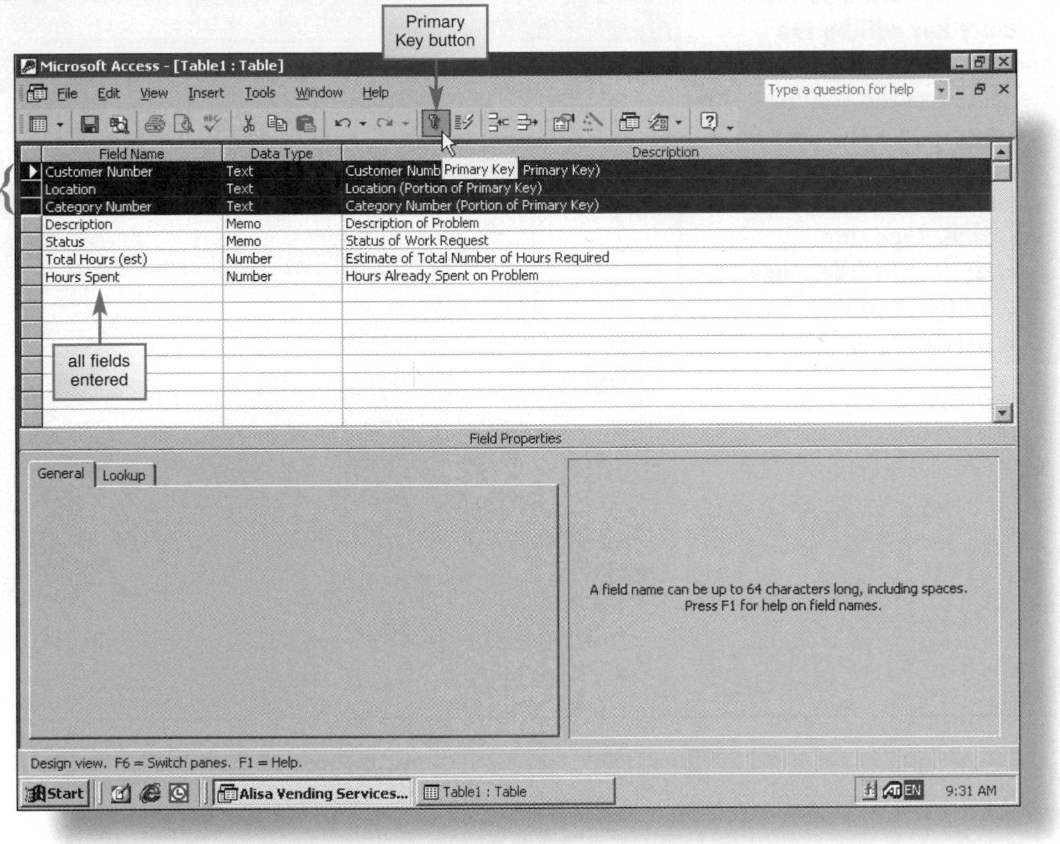

FIGURE 7-4

2 Right-click Create table in Design view, and then click Open on the shortcut menu. Enter the information for the fields in the Open Workorders table as indicated in Figure 7-3a on page A 7.06.

3 Click the row selector for the Customer Number field. Hold down the SHIFT key and then click the row selector for the Location field and the row selector for the Category Number field so all three fields are selected. Point to the Primary Key button on the Table Design toolbar.

The Customer Number, Location, and Category Number fields are all selected (Figure 7-4).

4 **Click the Primary Key button so the primary key will be the combination of the three fields. Close the window by clicking its Close button. Click the Yes button to save the table. Type** `Open Workorders` **as the name of the table and then point to the OK button.**

The Save As dialog box displays (Figure 7-5). The first three fields comprise the primary key.

5 **Click the OK button to save the table.**

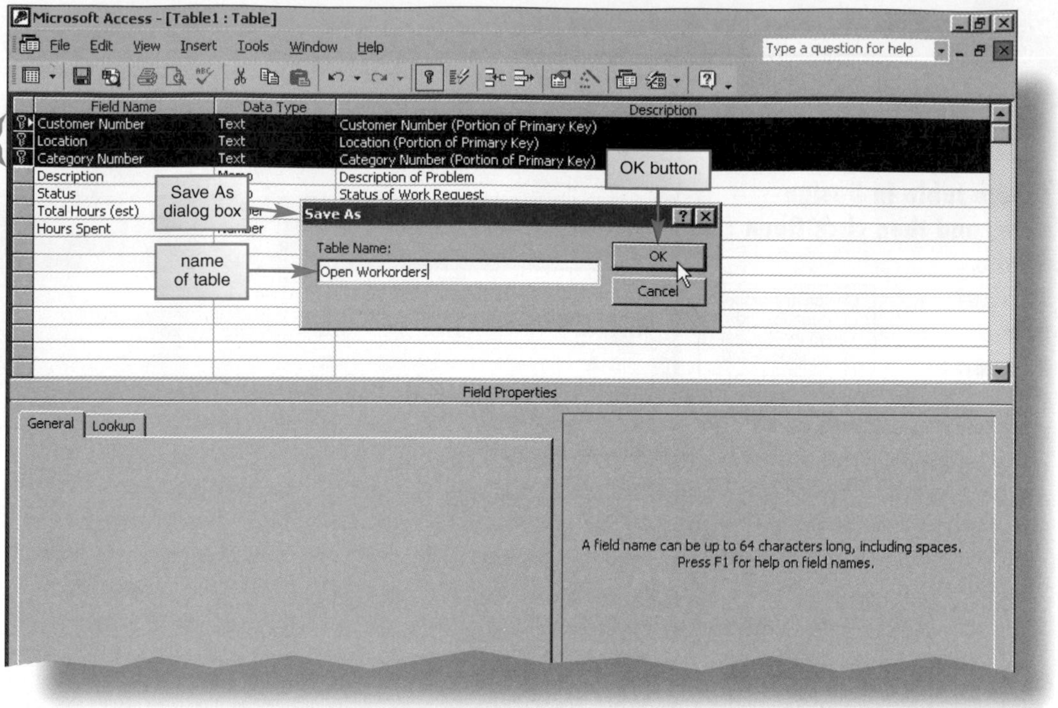

FIGURE 7-5

Importing the Data

Now that the tables have been created, you need to add data to them. You either could enter the data, or if the data is already in electronic form, you could import the data. The data for the Category and Open Workorders tables are on your Data Disk as text files. Use the following steps to import the data.

> **More About**
>
> ### Importing Data
>
> When importing text files, you have several options concerning how the data in the various fields are separated. For more information about importing data, visit the Access 2002 More About page (scsite.com/ac2002/more.htm) and then click Import Data.

TO IMPORT THE DATA

1. With the Alisa Vending Services database open, right-click the open space in the Database window, and then click Import on the shortcut menu.
2. Click the Files of type box arrow in the Import dialog box, and then select Text Files. Select 3½ Floppy (A:) in the Look in list. Make sure the Category text file is selected. Click the Import button.
3. When the Import Text Wizard dialog box displays, click the Next button. Click the First Row Contains Field Names check box, and then click the Next button again.
4. Click the In an Existing Table option button and then click the In an Existing Table box arrow. Select the Category table from the list. Click the Next button, click the Finish button, and then click the OK button.
5. Repeat Steps 1 through 4 to import the Open Workorders text file.

The data for the Category and Open Workorders tables are imported.

Changing the Layout

Now that the tables contain data, you need to adjust the column sizes to best fit the data. Perform the following steps to change the layouts of the tables.

Steps To Change the Layout

1 **Right-click the Category table, and then click Open on the shortcut menu. Double-click the right boundary of the field selector for each field to resize the columns to best fit the data.**

2 **Close the window containing the table. When asked if you want to save the changes to the layout, click the Yes button.**

The changes to the layout for the Category table are saved.

3 **Right-click the Open Workorders table, and then click Open on the shortcut menu. Drag the lower boundary of the row selector for the first record to the approximate position shown in Figure 7-6. Resize the columns to the approximate sizes shown in the figure by dragging the right boundaries of their field selectors.**

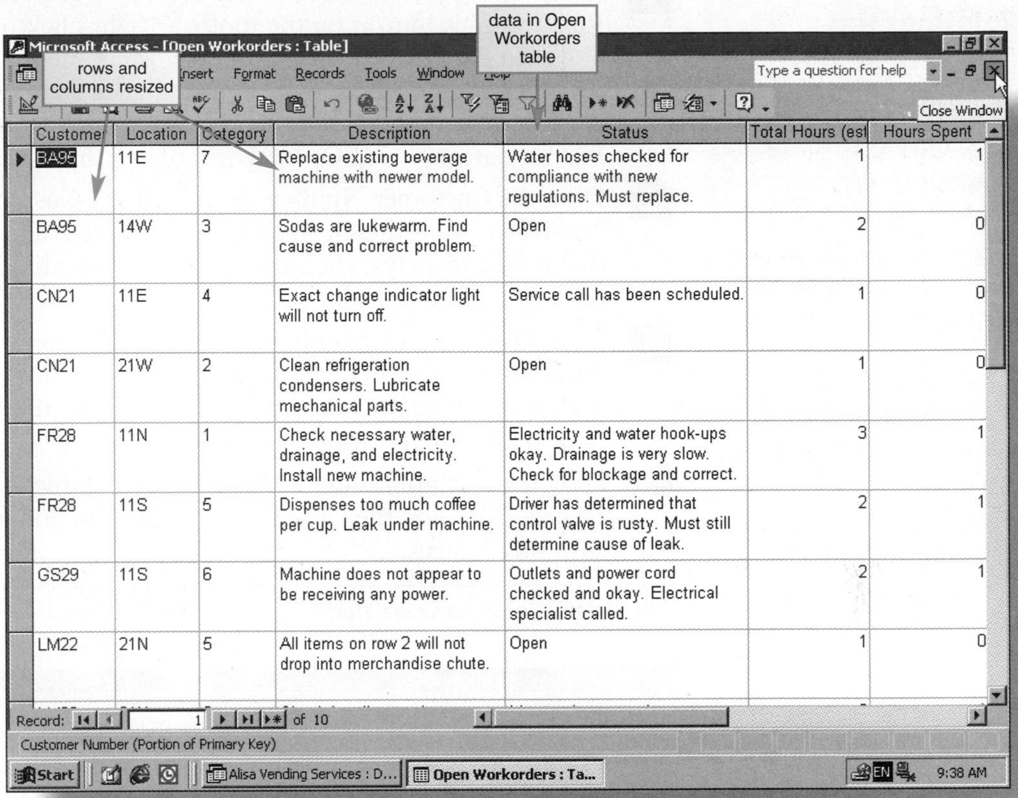

FIGURE 7-6

4 **Close the window containing the table. When asked if you want to save the changes to the layout, click the Yes button.**

The changes to the layout for the Open Workorders table are saved.

Relating Several Tables

Now that the tables have been created they need to be related to the existing tables. The Customer and Open Workorders tables are related through the Customer Number fields in both. There is a one-to-many relationship between the two tables, that is, one customer can have many open work orders. The Category and Open Workorders tables are related through the Category Number fields in both. A one-to-many relationship exists between the two tables because one service category can be on many work orders. Perform the steps on the next page to relate the tables.

More About

Relationships (Many-to-Many)

If the primary key of the Open Workorders table contains the primary keys for both the Customer table and the Category table, there is a many-to-many relationship between customers and categories. (A customer can have many categories of service scheduled to be performed, and a service can be scheduled to be performed for many customers.) For more information, visit the Access 2002 More About page (scsite.com/ac2002/more.htm) and then click Many-to-Many Relationships.

TO RELATE SEVERAL TABLES

1. Close any open datasheet on the screen by clicking its Close button. Click the Relationships button on the toolbar. Right-click in the Relationships window and then click Show Table on the shortcut menu. If necessary, click the Category table, click the Add button, click the Open Workorders table, click the Add button again, and then click the Close button. Resize the Field lists for the Category and Open Workorders tables so all fields are visible.
2. Drag the Customer Number field from the Customer table to the Customer Number field in the Open Workorders table. When the Edit Relationships dialog box displays, click the Enforce Referential Integrity check box, and then click the Create button.
3. Drag the Category Number field from the Category table to the Category Number field in the Open Workorders table. When the Edit Relationships dialog box displays, click the Enforce Referential Integrity check box, and then click the Create button.
4. Drag the Category and Open Workorders tables to the positions shown in Figure 7-7. Click the Close Window button, and then click the Yes button to save the changes.

The relationships are created.

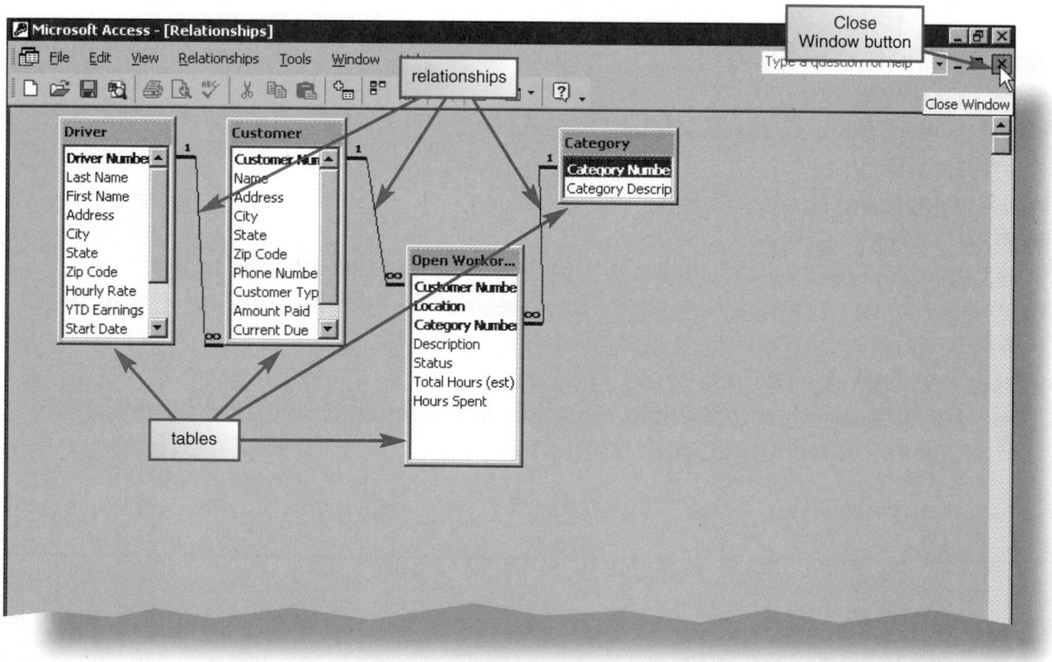

FIGURE 7-7

More About

Relationships (One-to-One)

Two tables have a one-to-one relationship when the primary key for a record in the first table matches the primary key for a record in the second table. For more information, visit the Access 2002 More About page (scsite.com/ac2002/more.htm) and then click One-to-One Relationships.

Creating Joins in Queries

Creating the required queries involves creating join queries. In the first query, the process also involves the modification of appropriate properties.

Creating a Query

Creating the initial query follows the same steps as in the creation of any query that joins tables. Perform the following steps to create a query that joins the Customer and Open Workorders tables.

Steps To Create a Query

1 **If necessary, in the Database window, click Tables on the Objects bar, and then click Customer. Click the New Object: AutoForm button arrow on the Database toolbar. Click Query. Be sure Design View is selected, and then click the OK button. If necessary, maximize the Query1 : Select Query window. Resize the upper and lower panes and the Customer field list so all the fields in the Customer table display.**

2 **Right-click any open area in the upper pane, click Show Table on the shortcut menu, click the Open Workorders table, click the Add button, and then click the Close button in the Show Table dialog box. Resize the Open Workorders field list so all the fields in the Open Workorders table display. Double-click the Customer Number and Name fields from the Customer table. Double-click the Location, Description, Status, and Total Hours (est) fields from the Open Workorders table. If necessary, click the right scroll arrow to shift the fields in the Design grid to the left, and then double-click the Hours Spent field.**

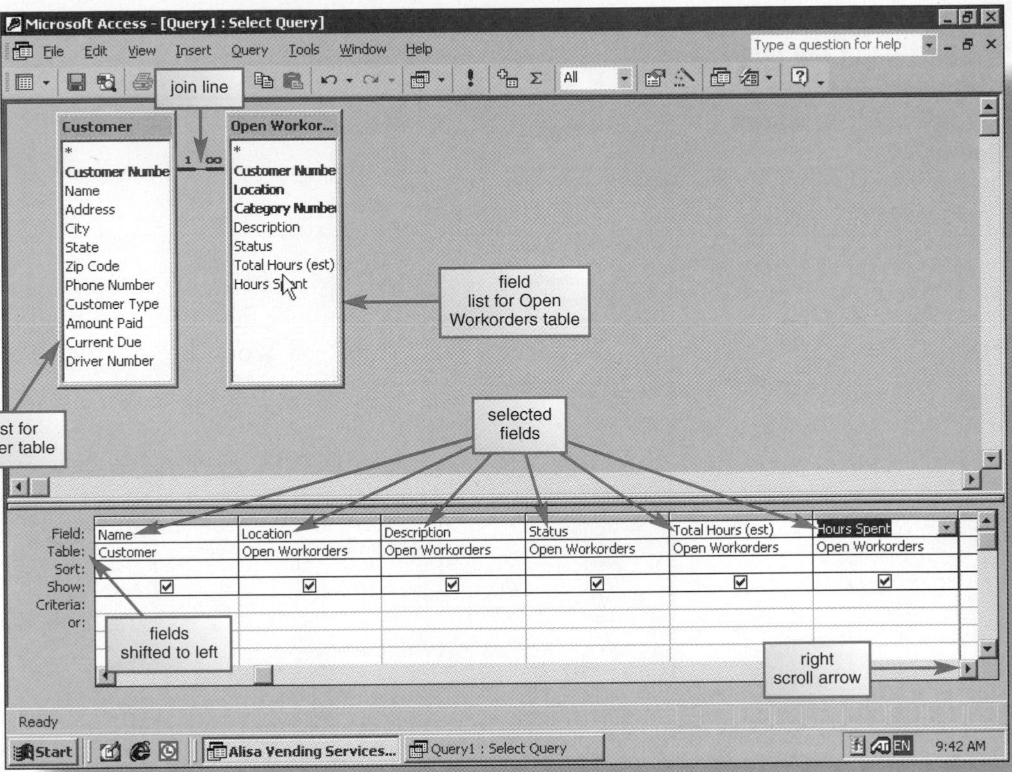

FIGURE 7-8

The tables are related and the fields are selected (Figure 7-8). The fields are shifted to the left.

Other Ways

1. Click Show Table button on toolbar
2. On Query menu click Show Table
3. In Voice Command mode, say "Show Table"

Changing Join Properties

Normally records that do not match will not display in the results of a join query. A customer for whom there are no work orders, for example, would not display. In order to cause such a record to display, you need to change the **join properties** of the query, which are the properties that indicate which records display in a join. Perform the steps on the next page to change the join properties.

Steps To Change Join Properties

1 **Point to the middle portion of the join line (the portion of the line that is not bold) as shown in Figure 7-9.**

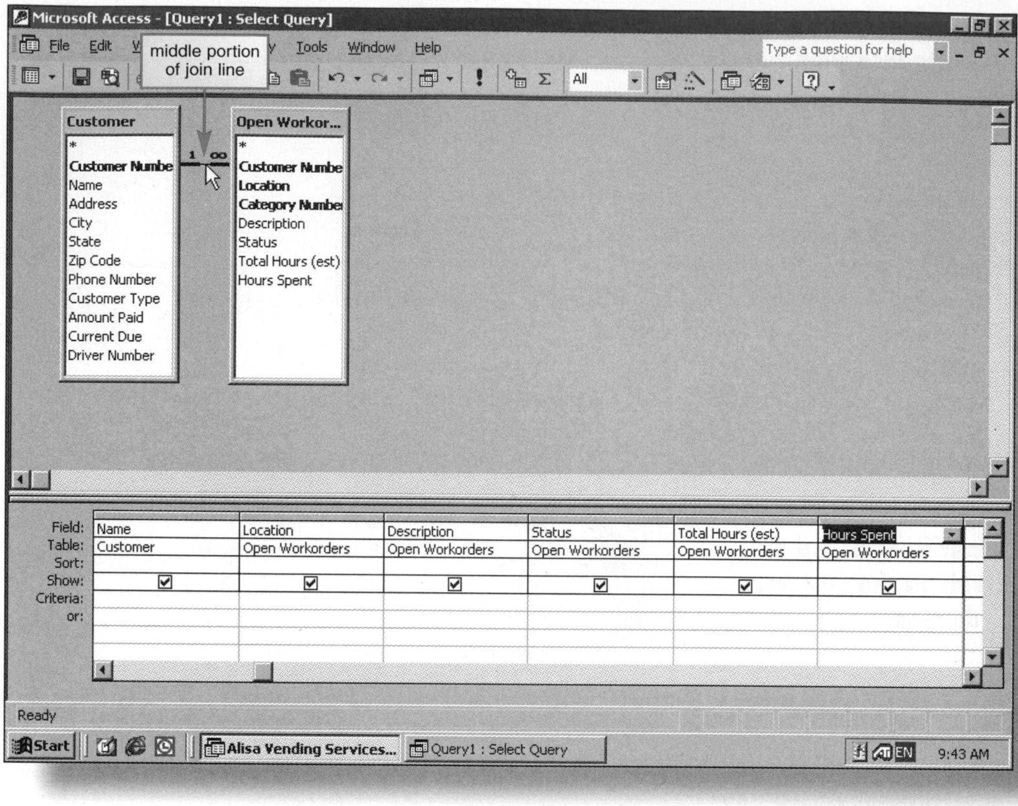

FIGURE 7-9

2 **Right-click the middle portion of the join line, and then point to Join Properties on the shortcut menu (Figure 7-10). (If Join Properties does not display on your shortcut menu, you did not point to the appropriate portion of the join line.)**

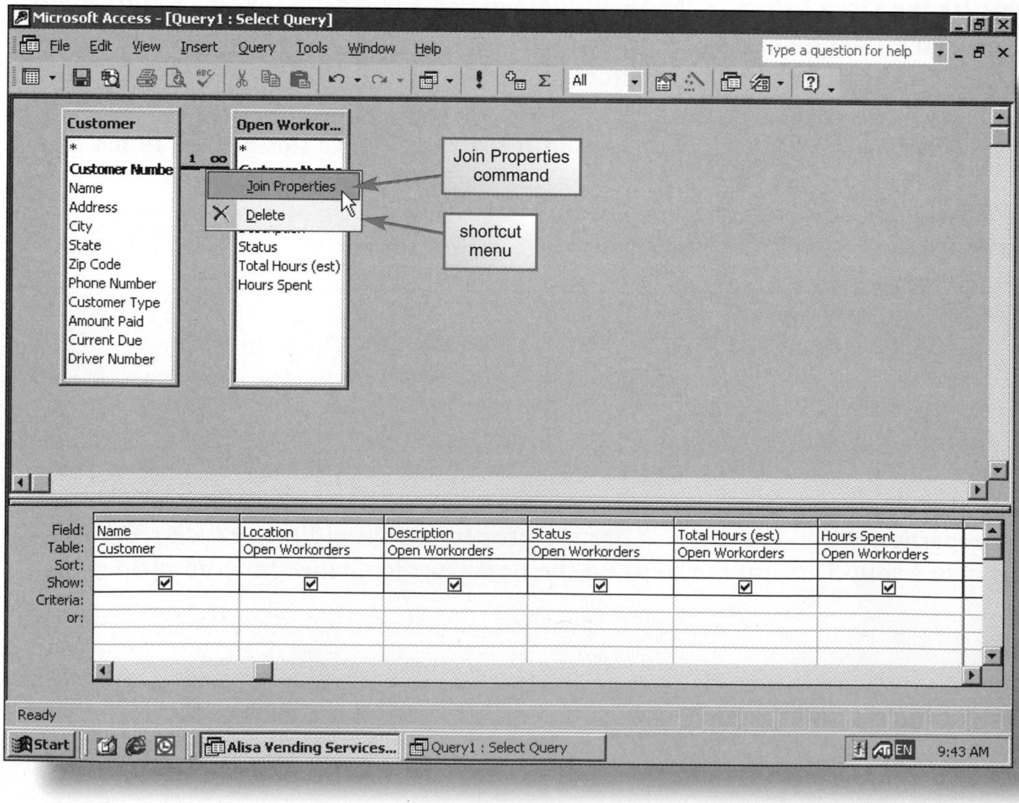

FIGURE 7-10

3 Click Join Properties on the shortcut menu and then point to option button 2.

The Join Properties dialog box displays (Figure 7-11).

4 Click option button 2 to include all records from the Customer table regardless of whether or not they match any open work orders. Click the OK button.

The join properties are changed.

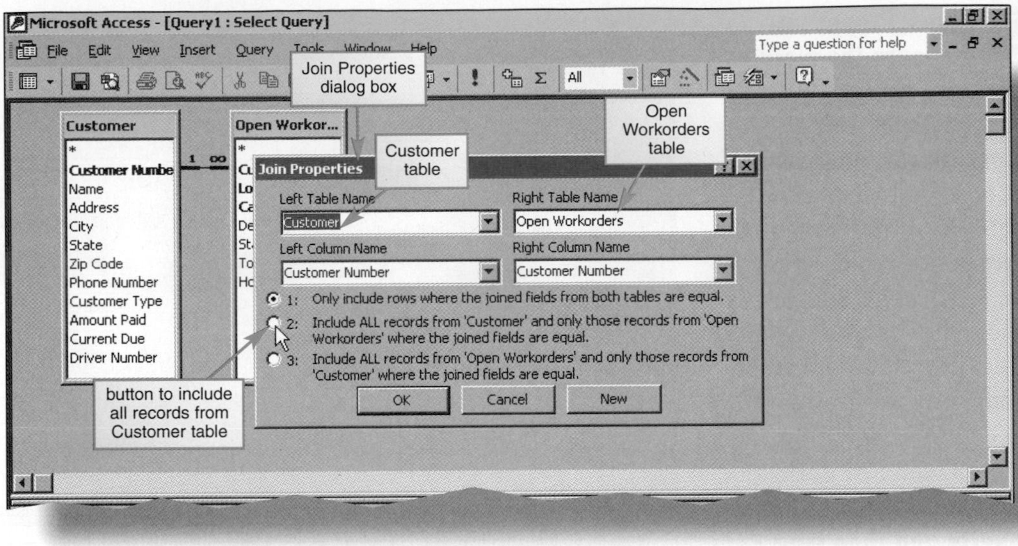

FIGURE 7-11

Other Ways

1. On View menu click Join Properties
2. In Voice Command mode, say "View, Join Properties"

Changing Field Properties

You can change field properties within a query by using the Properties command, and then changing the desired property in the field's property sheet. The following steps change the Format and Decimal Places properties to modify the way the contents of the Total Hours (est) and Hours Spent fields display. The steps also change the Caption properties so the **captions** (column headings) are different from the field names.

Steps To Change Field Properties

1 Right-click the Total Hours (est) column, and then point to Properties on the shortcut menu (Figure 7-12).

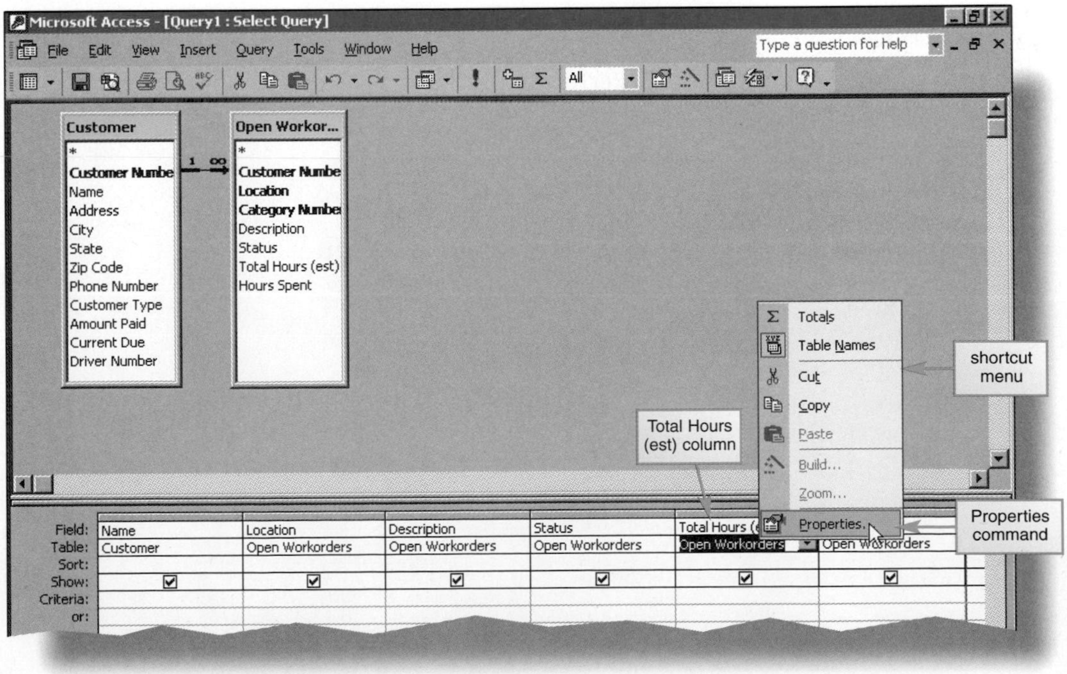

FIGURE 7-12

2 **Click Properties. Be sure the Field Properties property sheet displays. If the Query Properties property sheet displays, close it and right-click in the column again. Click the Format property, click the arrow to display the list of available properties, and then select Fixed. Click the Decimal Places property and type** `1` **as the number of decimal places. Click the Caption property and then type** `Est Hours` **as the caption. Point to the Close button in the Field Properties property sheet.**

The changed properties display (Figure 7-13).

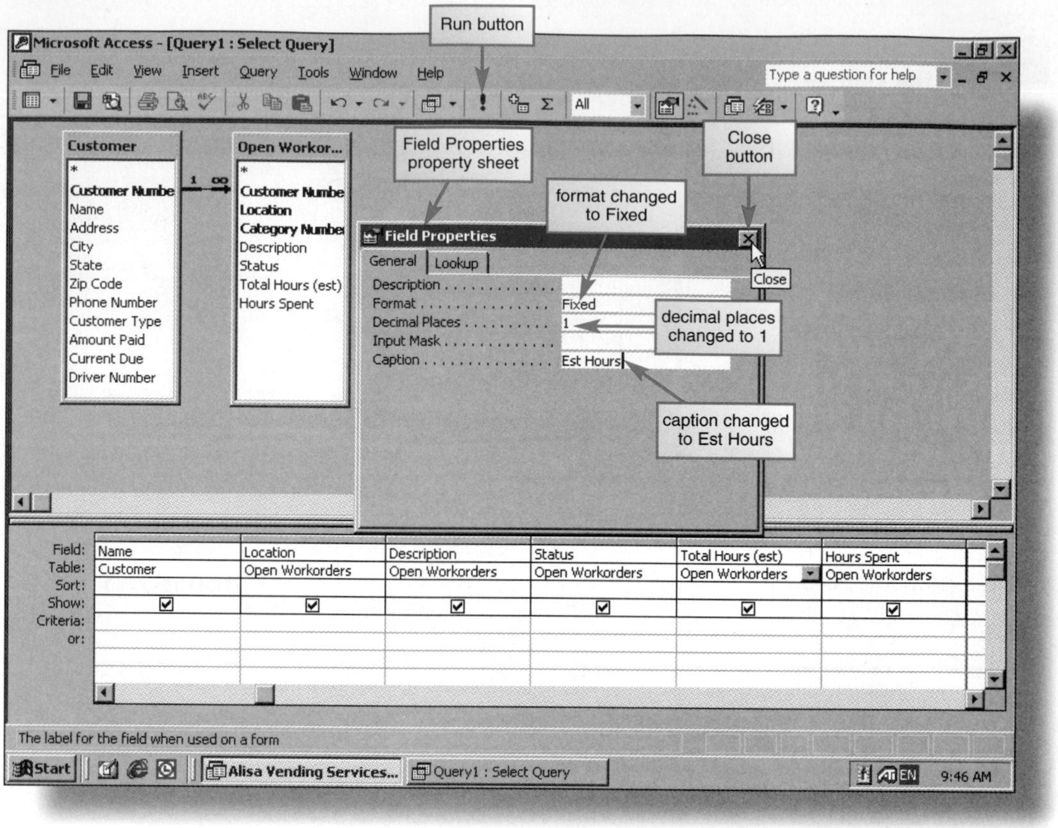

FIGURE 7-13

3 **Click the Close button.**

4 **Use the same technique to change the Format property for the Hours Spent field to Fixed, the number of decimal places to 1, and the caption to Spent Hours.**

Running the Query and Changing the Layout

Perform the following step to run the query and change the layout.

Steps To Run the Query and Change the Layout

1 Click the Run button on the toolbar. Resize the columns to the sizes shown in Figure 7-14 and then resize the rows by dragging the lower boundary of the row selector for the first record to the position shown in the figure.

The results display. Customer BR46 displays, even though the customer has no open work orders. The captions for the Total Hours (est) and Hours Spent fields have been changed. Both fields display with precisely one decimal place.

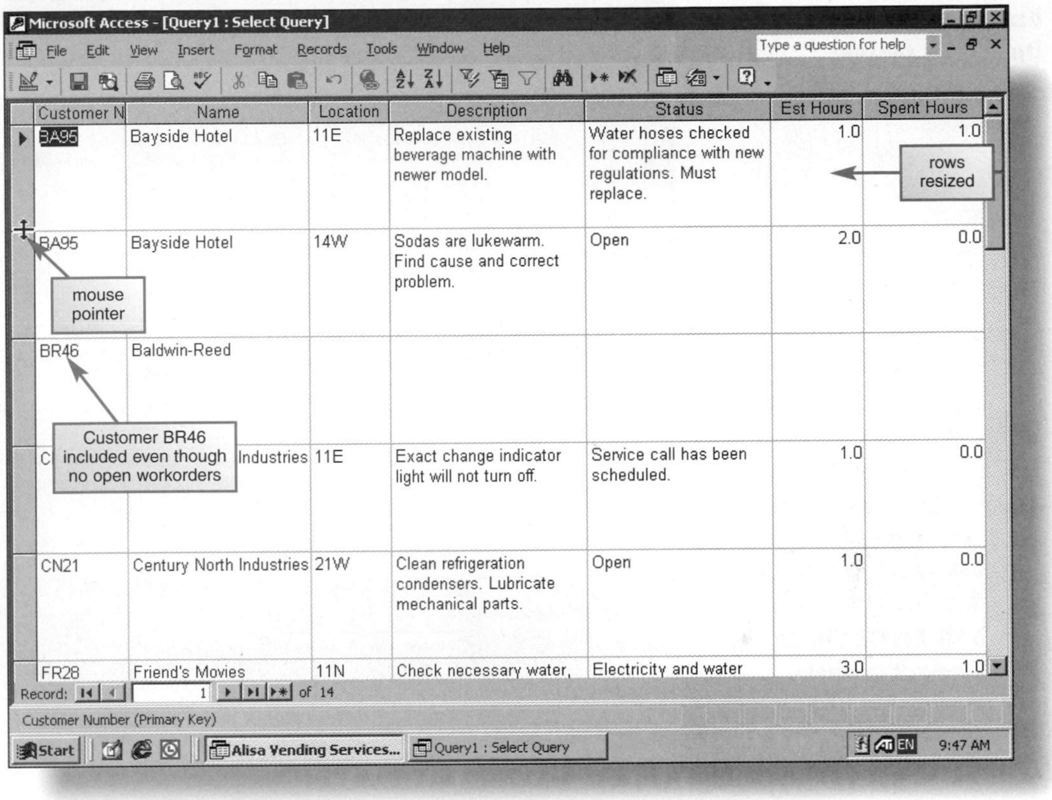

FIGURE 7-14

Filtering the Query's Recordset

You can filter the recordset (that is, the results) of a query just as you can filter a table. The following steps, for example, use Filter By Selection to restrict the records displayed to those on which the number of spent hours is 0.0.

Steps To Filter a Query's Recordset

1 Click the Spent Hours field on the second record to indicate 0.0 as the number of spent hours. Point to the Filter By Selection button on the Query Datasheet toolbar (Figure 7-15).

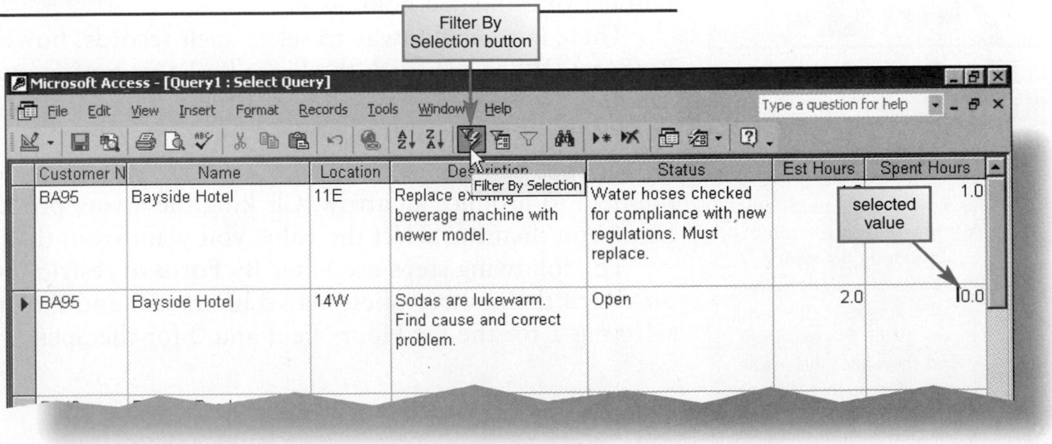

FIGURE 7-15

2 **Click the Filter By Selection button. Point to the Remove Filter button on the Query Datasheet toolbar.**

Only those records on which the number of spent hours is 0.00 display (Figure 7-16). Baldwin-Reed, which had no open work orders, does not display because there was no value in the Spent Hours field.

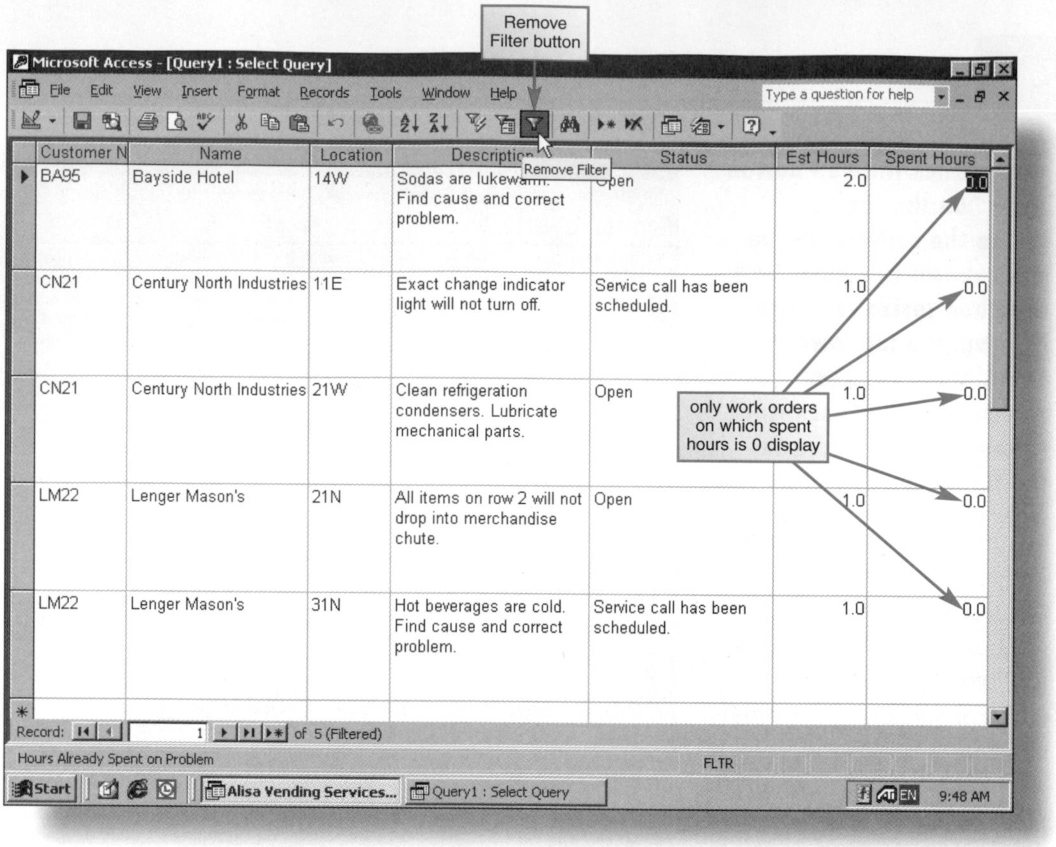

FIGURE 7-16

3 **Click the Remove Filter button so all records once again display. Close the Query by clicking its Close Window button. Click the Yes button in the Microsoft Access dialog box to save the query. Type** `Work Orders by Customer` **as the name of the query in the Save As dialog box and then click the OK button.**

The query is saved.

Other Ways

1. On Records menu click Filter, click Filter By Selection
2. In Voice Command mode, say "Filter By Selection"

More About

Filtering a Query's Recordset

Sometimes, when querying a database, an existing query is similar to what you need, but is missing a single criterion. You could modify the query, adding the extra criterion. In some cases, however, it would be simpler to run the existing query and then filter the resulting recordset, thus incorporating the additional criterion.

Using Filter By Form

If you have multiple criteria (for example, the number of estimated hours is 2 and the number of spent hours is 0), you can apply Filter By Selection twice. That is, you could first use Filter By Selection to select those records on which the number of spent hours is 0. You could then use Filter By Selection on the results of the first Filter By Selection to restrict further the records displayed to those on which the number of estimated hours is 2.

There is a simpler way to select such records, however, and that is to use Filter By Form. When you click the Filter By Form button, you are presented with a blank view of the datasheet. (If you were viewing the data in Form view, you would be presented with a blank view of the form, instead.) You then can select values in as many fields as you want. To select a value, you can type the value. You also can click the field to produce an arrow. Clicking the arrow produces a list of values for that field. You then can select the value you want from the list.

The following steps use Filter By Form to restrict the records displayed to those on which the number of estimated hours is 2 and the number of spent hours is 0 by selecting 2 for the Est Hours field and 0 for the Spent Hours field.

Steps To Use Filter By Form

1 If necessary, click Queries on the Objects bar. Right-click the Work Orders by Customer query, and then click Open on the shortcut menu. Point to the Filter By Form button on the Query Datasheet toolbar.

The query results display in Datasheet view (Figure 7-17).

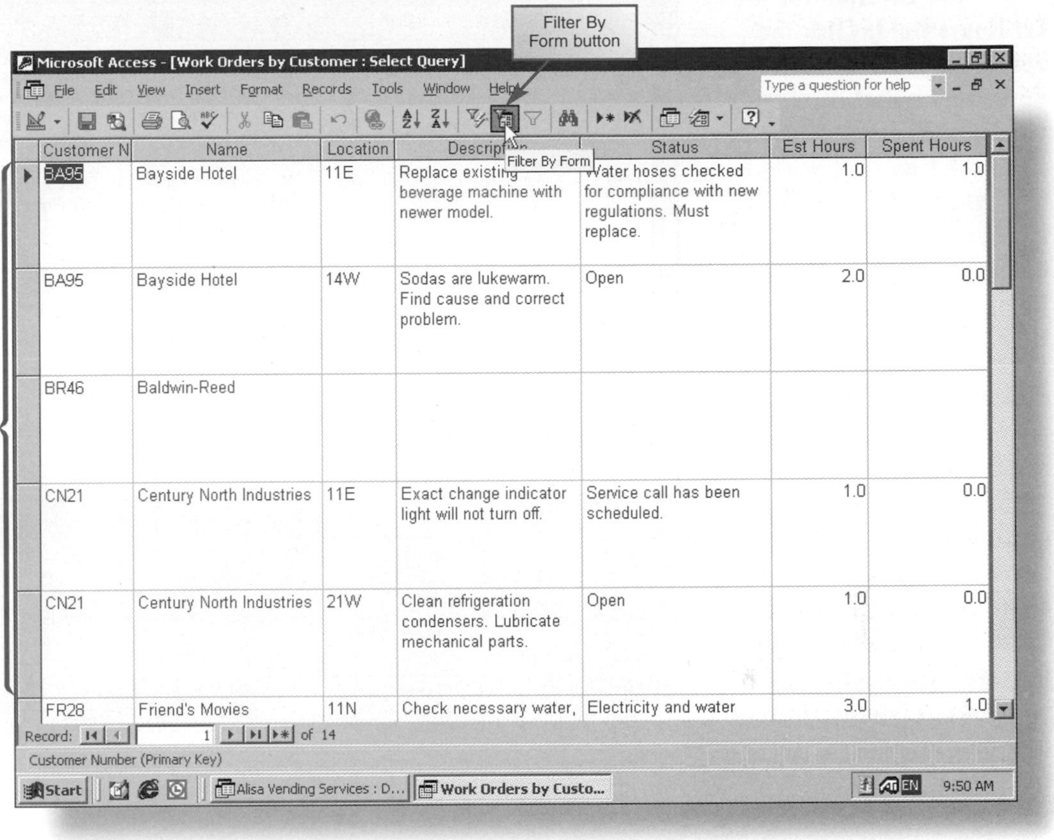

FIGURE 7-17

2 Click the Filter By Form button. Click the Est Hours field, click the down arrow that displays, and then point to 2.

A blank view of the datasheet displays (Figure 7-18). The list of values for the Est Hours field displays.

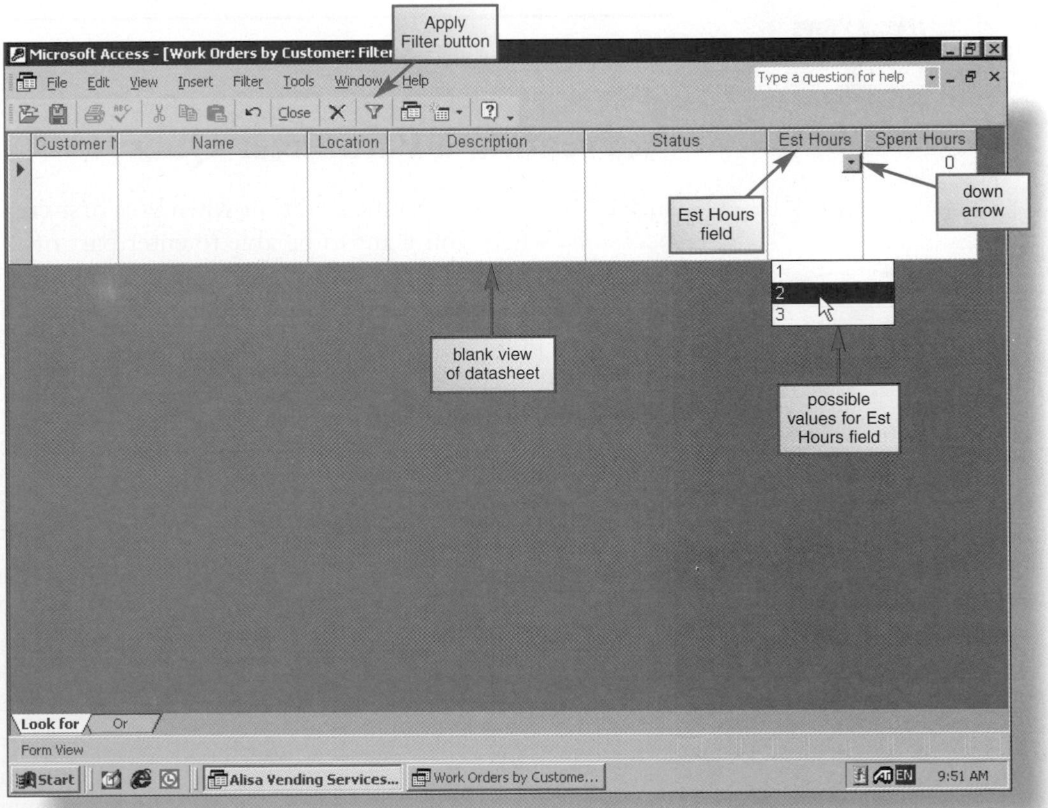

FIGURE 7-18

3 **Click 2 to select 2 as the criterion for the Est Hours field. Click the Spent Hours field, click the down arrow that displays, and then click 1 to select 1 as the criterion for the Spent Hours field. Click the Apply Filter button and then point to the Remove Filter button.**

Only those records on which the number of estimated hours is 2 and the number of spent hours is 1 display (Figure 7-19).

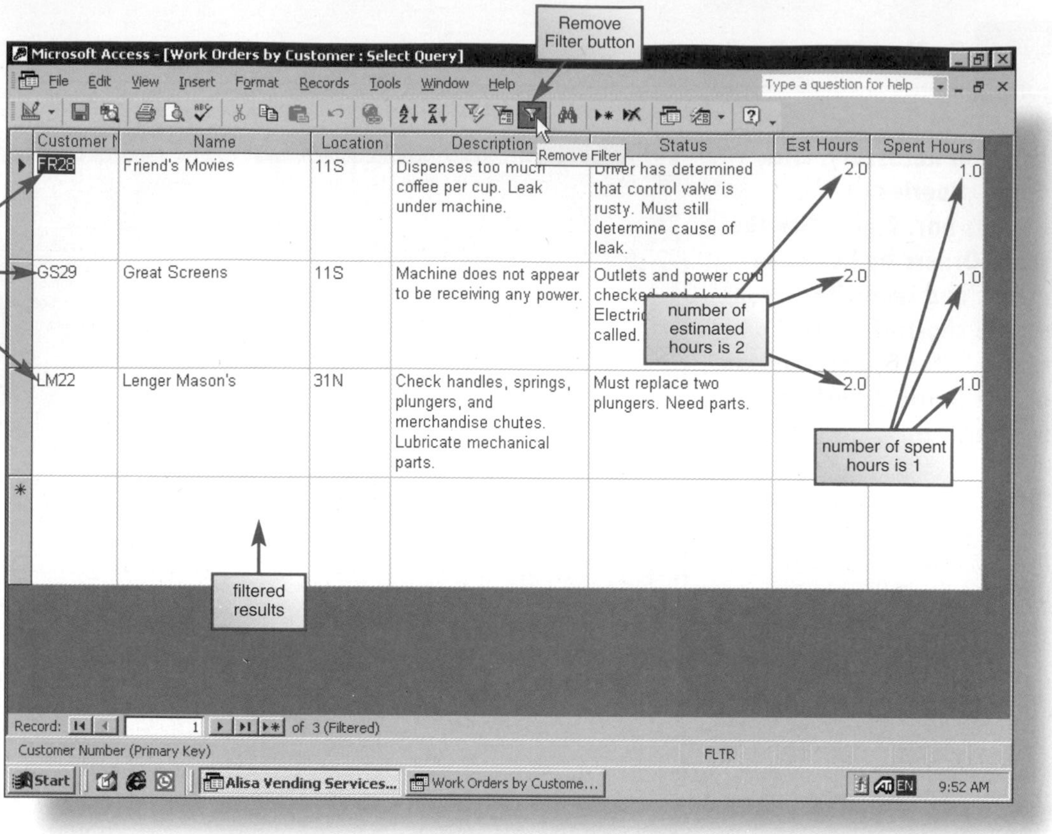

FIGURE 7-19

4 **Click the Remove Filter button so all records once again display. Close the Query by clicking its Close Window button. Do not save your changes.**

The query results no longer display.

Other Ways

1. On Records menu click Filter, click Filter By Form
2. In Voice Command mode, say "Filter By Form"

More About

Parameter Queries

Parameter queries are especially useful in cases where the same query is run frequently with slight changes to one or more of the query's criteria. By using parameters rather than specific values, you can enter the values for the criterion as the query is run, rather than having to change the query design. For more information about parameter queries, visit the Access 2002 More About page (scsite.com/ac2002/more.htm) and then click Parameter Queries.

Creating a Parameter Query

Instead of giving a specific criterion when you first create the query, there are occasions where you want to be able to enter part of the criterion when you run the query, and then have the appropriate results display. For example, to display all the customers located in Hansen, you could enter Hansen as a criterion in the City field. From that point on, every time you ran the query, only the customers in Hansen would display. If you wanted to display all the customers in Fernwood, you would need to create another query.

A better way is to allow the user to enter the city at the time the query is run. Thus a user could run the query, enter Hansen as the city, and then see all the customers in Hansen. Later, the user could run the same query, but enter Fernwood as the city, and then see all the customers in Fernwood. In order to do this, you create a **parameter query**, a query that prompts for input whenever it is run. You enter a parameter, rather than a specific value as the criterion. You create one by enclosing a value in a criterion in square brackets (like you enclose field names), but where the value in the brackets does not match any field. For example, you could place [Enter city] as the criterion in the City field.

You can include more than one parameter in a query. At Alisa, for example, they want to be able to enter a beginning and ending customer number, and then display all the records in the Customer table for which the customer number is between the two values entered. If the user enters AA00 and ZZ99 as the beginning and ending numbers, the display will include all customers. If the user enters FR28 as both the beginning number and the ending number, only those work orders for customer FR28 will display. If the user enters FR28 as the beginning number and GS29 as the ending number, only those work orders on which the customer number is between FR28 and GS29 will display.

In order to allow users to enter two values, there will be two values in the criterion enclosed in square brackets, that is, two parameters, as in the following steps.

Steps To Create a Parameter Query

1 **In the Database window, if necessary, click Queries on the Objects bar, and then right-click Work Orders by Customer. Click Design View on the shortcut menu. If necessary, maximize the Work Orders by Customer : Select Query window.**

2 **Right-click the Criteria row under the Customer Number field, and then point to Zoom on the shortcut menu.**

The shortcut menu displays (Figure 7-20).

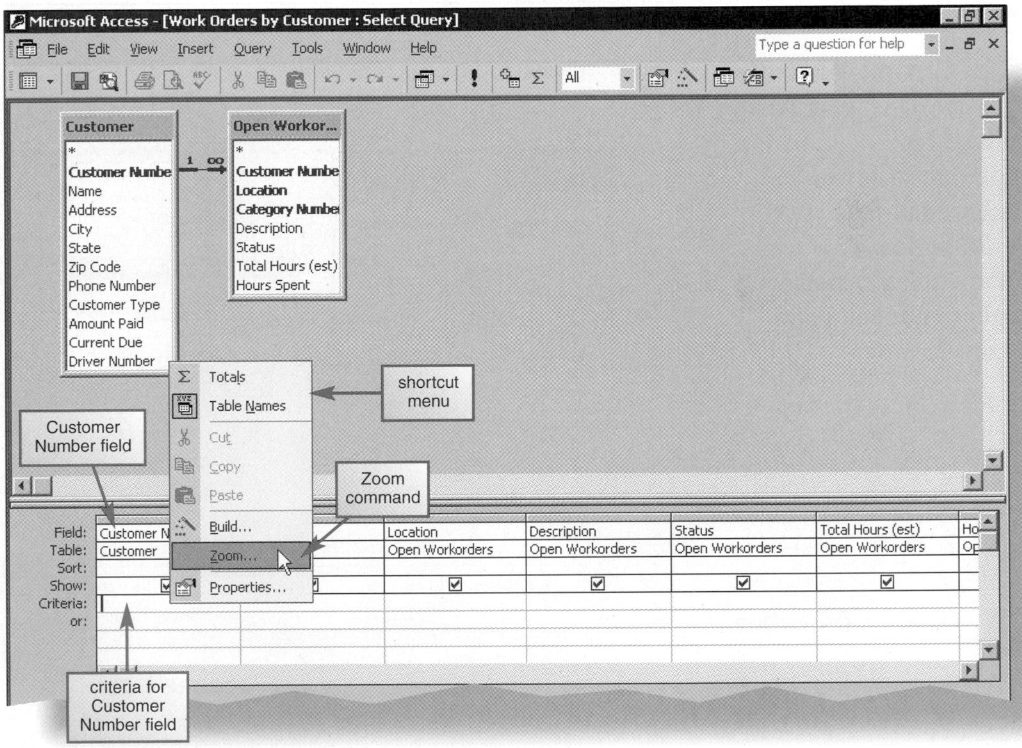

FIGURE 7-20

3 **Click Zoom, and then type** `Between [Beginning customer number] and [Ending customer number]` **in the Zoom dialog box. Point to the OK button.**

The Zoom dialog box displays (Figure 7-21).

4 **Click the OK button.**

The criterion is entered.

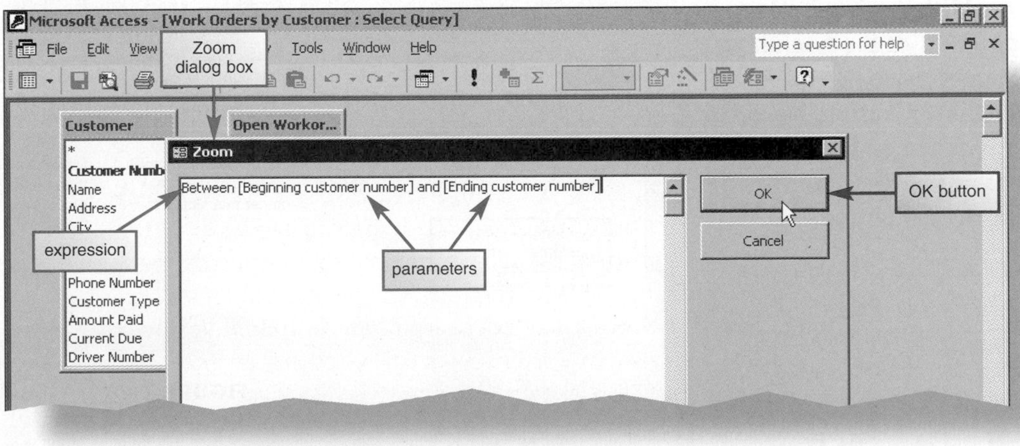

FIGURE 7-21

Running a Parameter Query

You run a parameter query similarly to any other query. The only difference is that when you do, you will be prompted for values for any parameter in the query; that is, the values for any expression enclosed in square brackets other than field names. For this query that means the values for both the beginning customer number and the ending customer number. Once you have furnished these values, the appropriate results then will display. The following steps run the query from the query Design view. If you ran the query from the Database window, you would be prompted for the same parameter values.

Steps To Run a Parameter Query

1 **Click the Run button on the Query Design toolbar. Type** AA00 **as the beginning customer number, and then click the OK button. Type** ZZ99 **as the ending customer number and then point to the OK button.**

The Enter Parameter Value dialog box displays and ZZ99 has been entered as the Ending Customer Number (Figure 7-22).

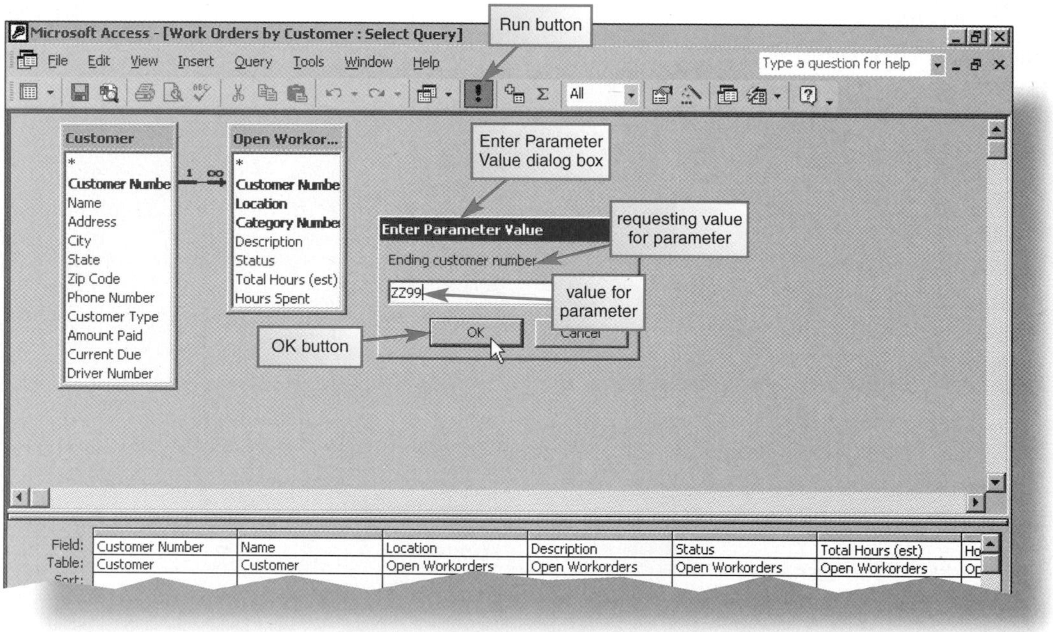

FIGURE 7-22

2 **Click the OK button.**

All records display.

3 **Click the View button to return to Design view. Click the Run button. Type** FR28 **as the beginning customer number, and then click the OK button. Type** FR28 **as the ending customer number, and then click the OK button.**

Only those work orders on which the customer number is FR28 display (Figure 7-23).

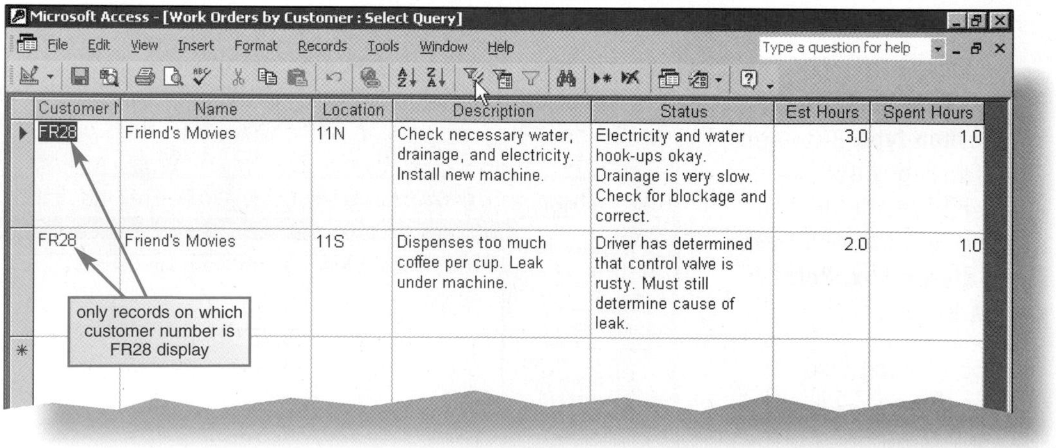

FIGURE 7-23

4 **Close the query by clicking its Close Window button. Click the Yes button to save the changes.**

Creating a Report

Creating the report shown in Figure 7-1a on page A 7.05 from scratch involves creating the initial report in Report Design view, indicating any grouping or sorting, adding the fields, adding the subreport, modifying the subreport separately from the main report, and then making the final modifications to the main report.

Creating Queries for Reports

The report you will create requires two queries. The first query relates drivers and customers and the second query relates categories and work orders. The following steps create the necessary queries.

TO CREATE QUERIES FOR REPORTS

1. In the Database window, if necessary, click Tables on the Objects bar, and then click Driver. Click the New Object: Query button arrow on the Database toolbar. Click Query. Be sure Design View is selected, and then click the OK button. If necessary, maximize the Query1 : Select Query window. Resize the upper and lower panes and the Driver field list so all the fields in the Driver table display.
2. Right-click any open area in the upper pane, click Show Table on the shortcut menu, click the Customer table, click the Add button, and then click the Close button in the Show Table dialog box. Resize the Customer field list so all the fields in the Customer table display. Double-click the Driver Number, First Name, and Last Name fields from the Driver table. Double-click the Customer Number, Name, Address, City, State, Zip Code, Phone Number, Customer Type, Amount Paid, and Current Due fields from the Customer table.
3. Close the query by clicking its Close Window button. Click the Yes button to save the query. Type `Drivers and Customers` as the name of the query, and then click the OK button.
4. If necessary, click Tables on the Objects bar, and then click Category. Click the New Object: Query button arrow on the Database toolbar. Click Query. Be sure Design View is selected, and then click the OK button. If necessary, maximize the Query1: Select Query window. Resize the upper and lower panes and the Category field list so all fields in the Category table display.
5. Right-click any open area in the upper pane, click Show Table on the shortcut menu, click the Open Workorders table, click the Add button, and then click the Close button in the Show Table dialog box. Resize the Open Workorders field list so all the fields in the Open Workorders table display. Double-click the following fields in the order shown from the Open Workorders and Category field lists: Customer Number, Location, Category Description, Description, Status, Total Hours (est), and Hours Spent fields.
6. Close the query by clicking its Close Window button. Click the Yes button to save the query. Type `Workorders and Categories` as the name of the query, and then click the OK button.

The queries are saved.

More About

Queries

If you create an expression in a query in which a field name enclosed in brackets is misspelled, Access will assume that the brackets contain a parameter. When you run the query, it will ask you for a value. If this happens, notice the name specified in the dialog box, check the spelling, and then make the necessary changes.

Grouping and Sorting in a Report

When you want to create a report from scratch, you begin with the same general procedure as when you want to use the Report Wizard to create the report. The difference is that you will select Design View instead of Report Wizard. If you want to group data in a report you create in Design View, use the Sorting and Grouping dialog box and select the desired fields.

When specifying Sorting and Grouping, the data will be sorted on the fields you select. If you select two fields, for example, Driver Number and Customer Number, the first field will be the major key and the second will be the minor key. If you also want data to be grouped on a selected field, simply indicate that you want to display a group header, group footer, or both for the field.

It is possible for a group header to print at the bottom of one page and the first detail record in the group to print at the top of the next page. In order to prevent this from happening, you can change the value of the Keep Together property for the group. If you would like to have the group header and as many detail records as possible print on the same page, you should change the value to Whole Group. If you change the value to With First Detail instead of Whole Group, then Access only will print the group header on a page if it also can fit at least one detail record on the page.

Perform the following steps to create the initial version of the Driver Master List and to indicate that the data is to be sorted and grouped by the Driver Number field. There should be a group header and the group header should be kept together with the records in the group. In addition, within the records with the same driver number, the data is to be sorted further by the Customer Number field.

More About

Adding Objects

You can add various types of objects to reports in two ways. You can use the Object command on the Insert menu, select the desired type of object (for example, a bitmap image), and then select the specific object you wish to insert (for example, a specific bitmap image on your disk). You also can click the Unbound Object Frame tool on the toolbar and then click the position on the report you wish to place the object. As with the Object command on the Insert menu, you then select the desired type of object and then the specific object you wish to insert.

Steps To Group and Sort in a Report

1 If necessary, in the Database window, click Queries on the Objects bar, and then click Drivers and Customers. Click the New Object: Query button arrow on the Database toolbar, and then click Report. Be sure Design View is selected and then click the OK button.

2 If necessary, dock the toolbox at the bottom of the screen. Be sure the field list displays. If it does not, click the Field List button on the Report Design toolbar. Point to the lower boundary of the field list.

A blank report displays in Design view (Figure 7-24). A field list displays.

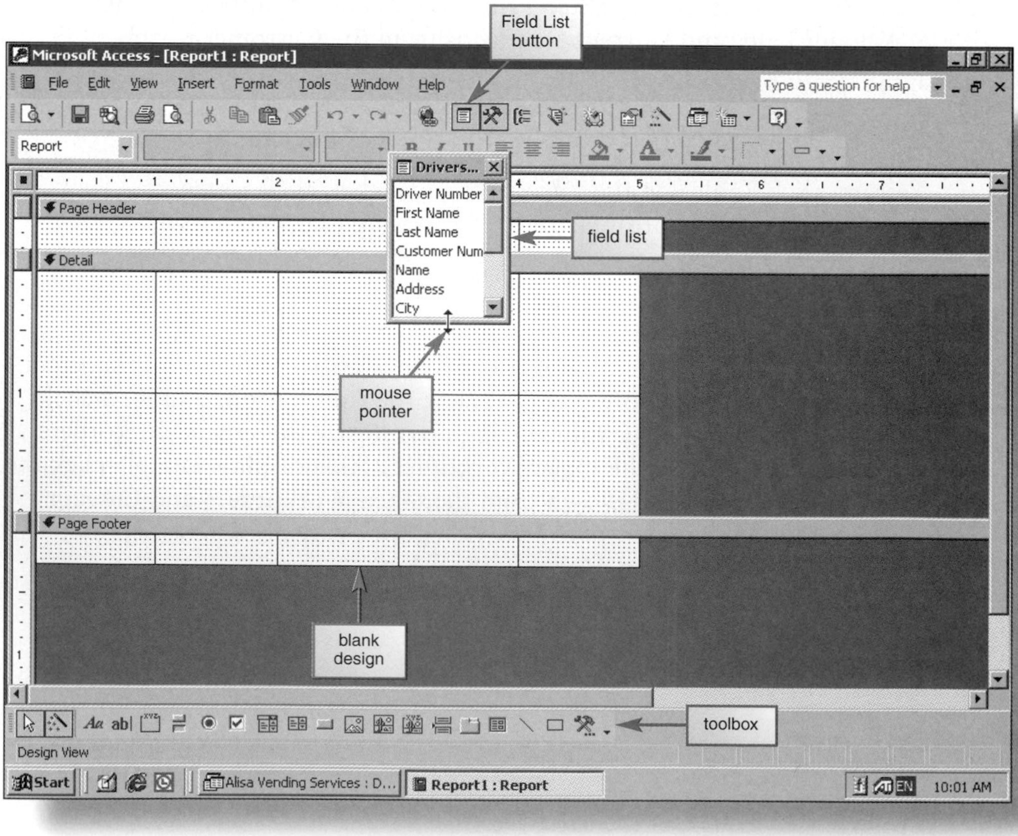

FIGURE 7-24

3 Drag the bottom boundary of the field list down so all fields display. Move the field list to the lower-right corner of the screen by dragging its title bar. Right-click any open area of the Detail section of the report, and then point to Sorting and Grouping on the shortcut menu.

The field list is moved and the shortcut menu displays (Figure 7-25).

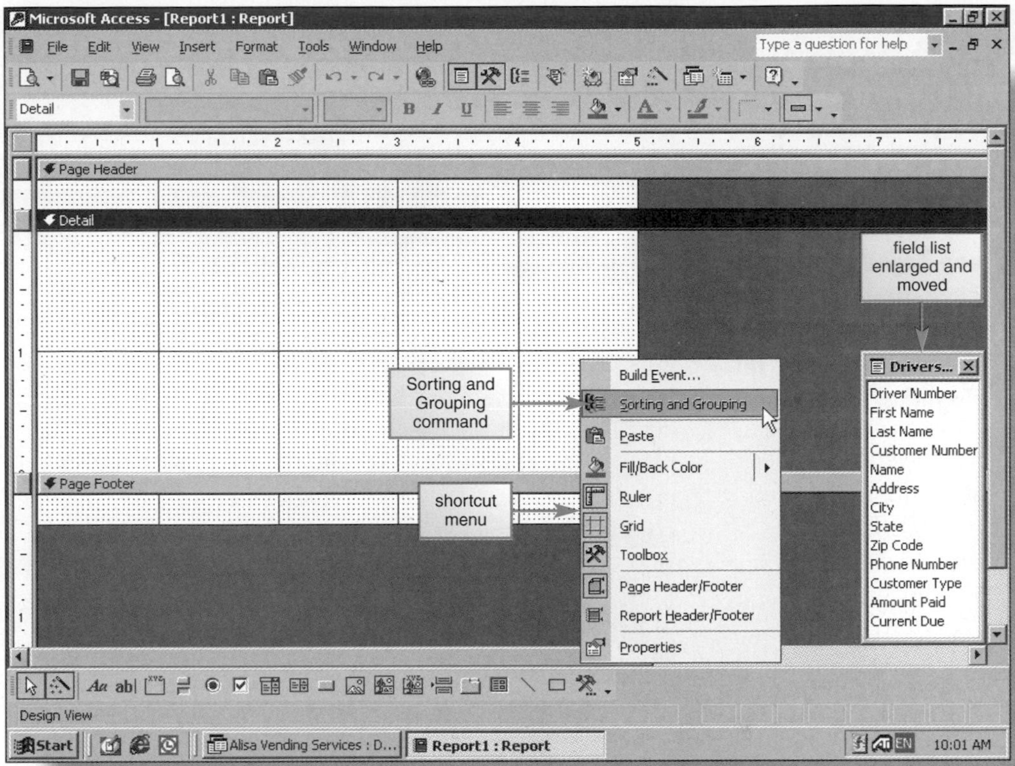

FIGURE 7-25

4 Click Sorting and Grouping, click the down arrow in the Field/Expression box, and then point to Driver Number.

The Sorting and Grouping dialog box displays (Figure 7-26). The list of available fields displays.

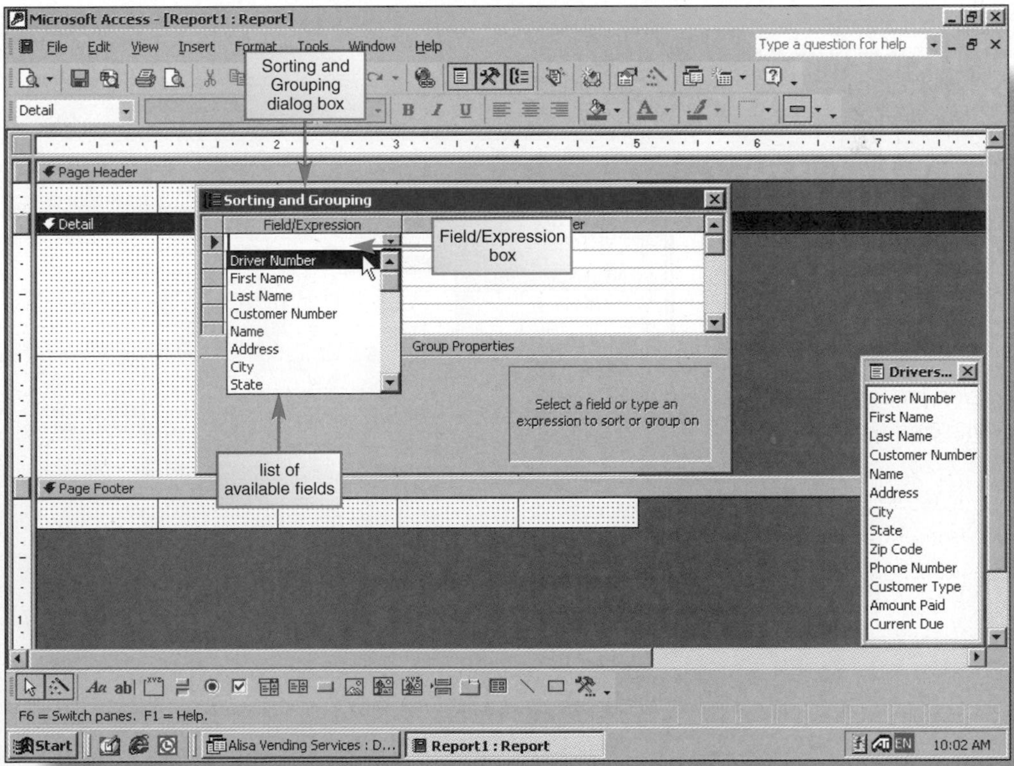

FIGURE 7-26

5 **Click Driver Number, click the Group Header property box, click the Group Header property box arrow, and then click Yes. Click the Keep Together property, click the Keep Together property box arrow, and then point to Whole Group in the list of available values for the Keep Together property.**

The Group Header property is changed from No to Yes (Figure 7-27). The list of values for the Keep Together property displays.

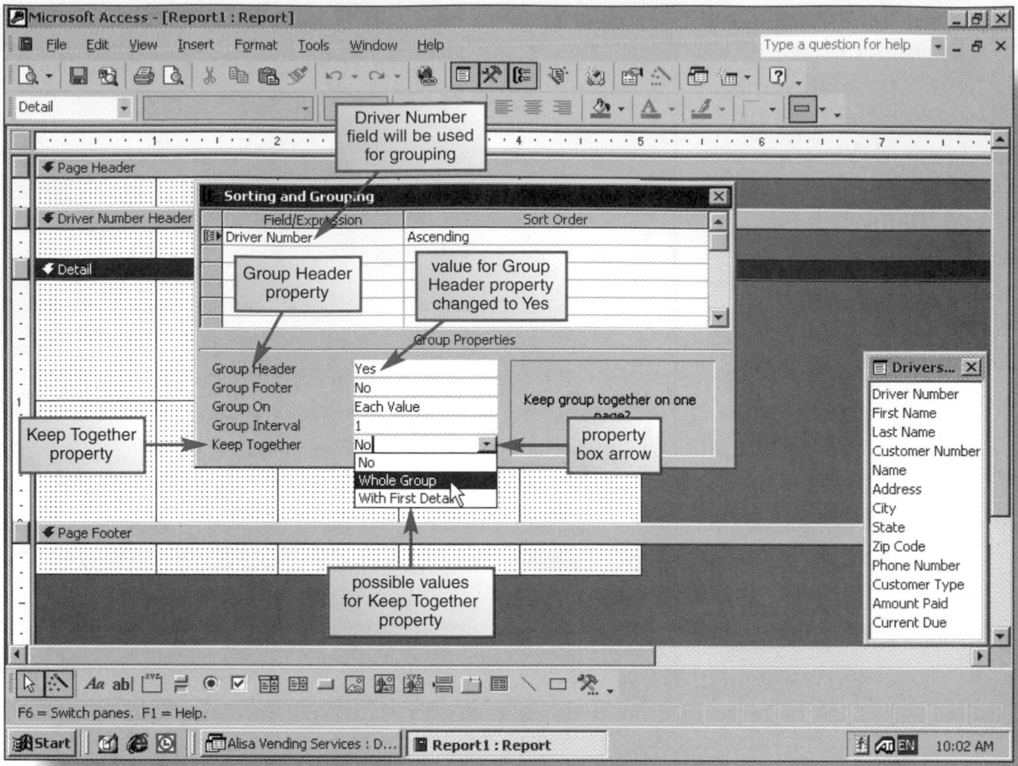

FIGURE 7-27

6 **Click Whole Group, and then click the Field/Expression box on the second row (the row under Driver Number), click the down arrow that displays, and then click Customer Number in the list of fields that displays. Point to the Close button.**

The fields are selected for grouping and sorting (Figure 7-28).

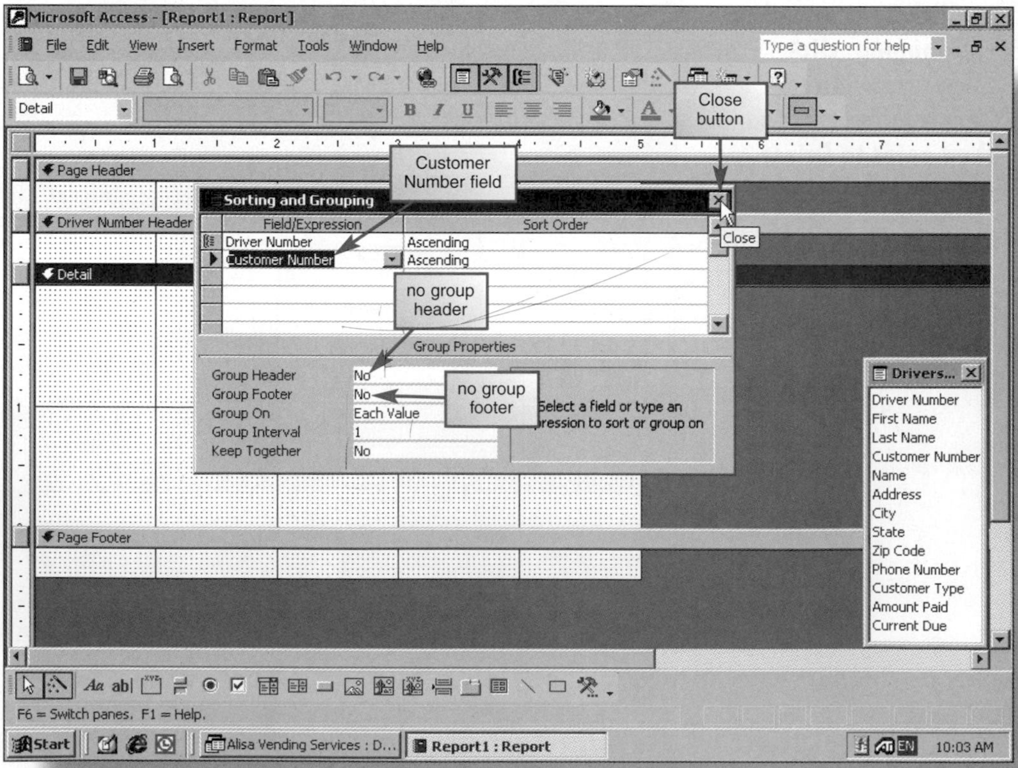

FIGURE 7-28

7 **Click the Close button to close the Sorting and Grouping dialog box. Point to Driver Number in the field list (Figure 7-29).**

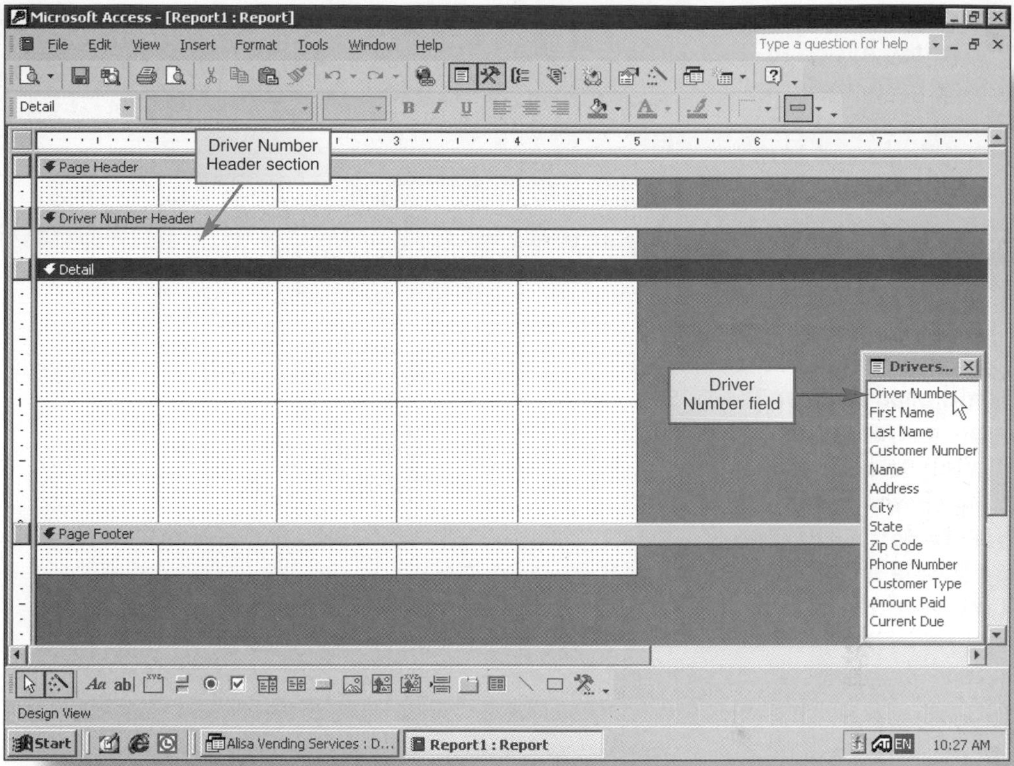

FIGURE 7-29

Other Ways

1. Click Sorting and Grouping button on Report Design toolbar
2. On View menu click Sorting and Grouping
3. In Voice Command mode, say "View, Sorting and Grouping"

Adding the Fields

You can add the fields to the report by dragging them from the field list to the appropriate position on the report. The following steps add the fields to the report.

Steps To Add the Fields

1 **Drag the Driver Number field to the approximate position shown in Figure 7-30.**

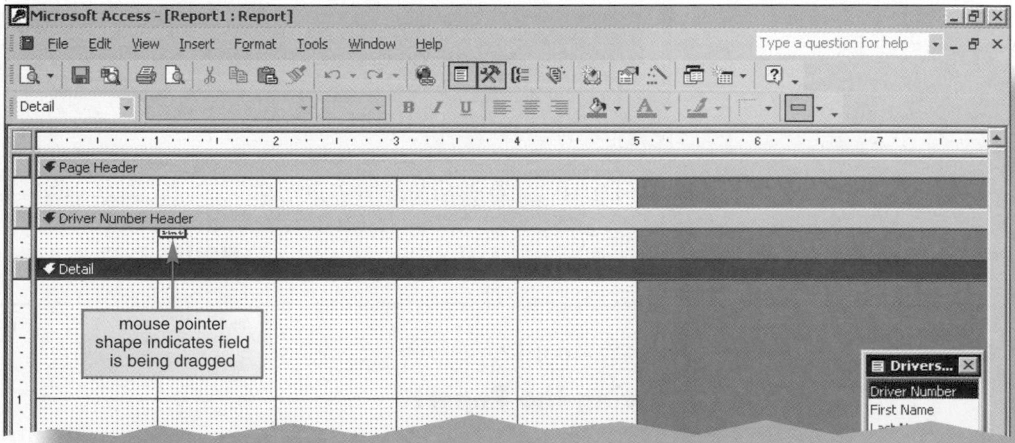

FIGURE 7-30

2 **Release the left mouse button to place the field. Use the same techniques to place the First Name and Last Name fields in the approximate positions shown in Figure 7-31. If any field is not in the correct position, drag it to its correct location. You also will need to move the controls and/or labels separately to achieve the spacing shown in the figure. To do so, drag the large handle in the upper-left corner of the control or label.**

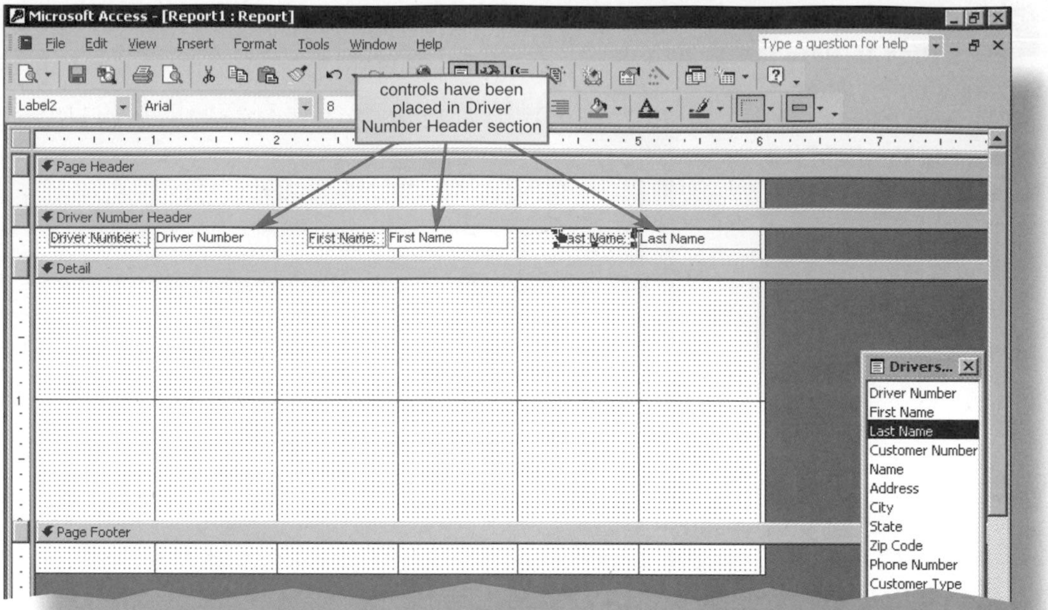

FIGURE 7-31

3 **Place the remaining fields in the positions shown in Figure 7-32 and then point to the Close button in the field list.**

4 **Close the field list by clicking its Close button.**

The fields are placed. The field list no longer displays.

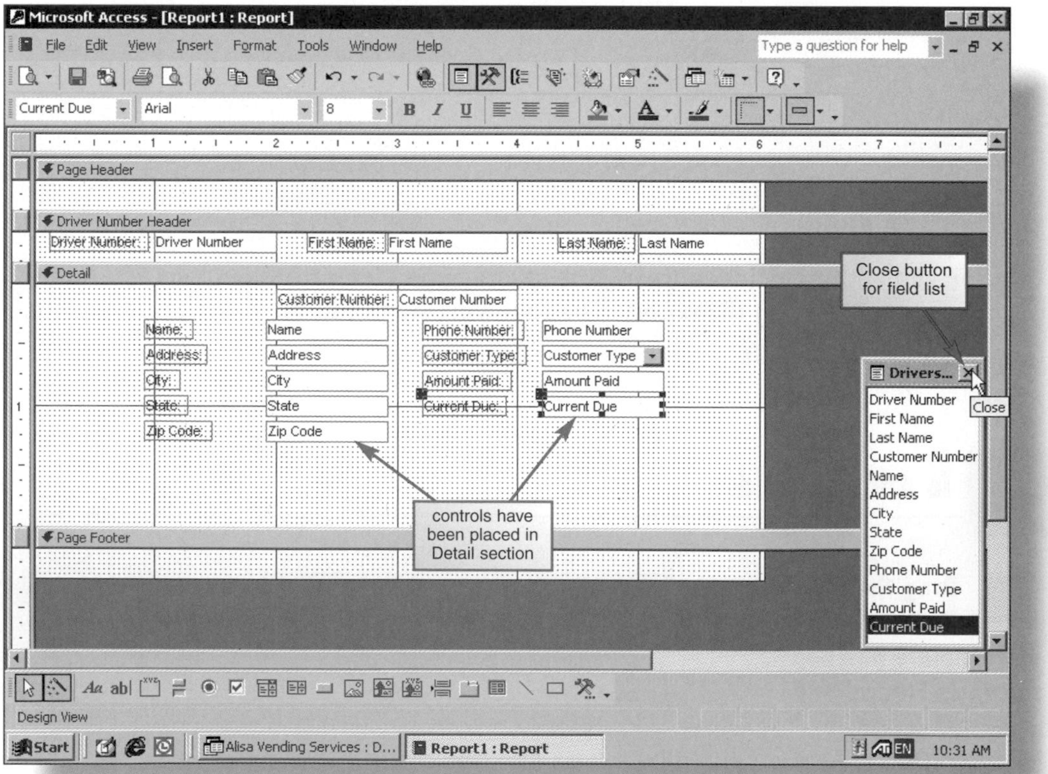

FIGURE 7-32

Saving the Report

Before proceeding with the next steps in the modification of the report, it is a good idea to save your work. Perform the following steps to save the current report.

Steps To Save the Report

1 Point to the Save button on the Report Design toolbar (Figure 7-33).

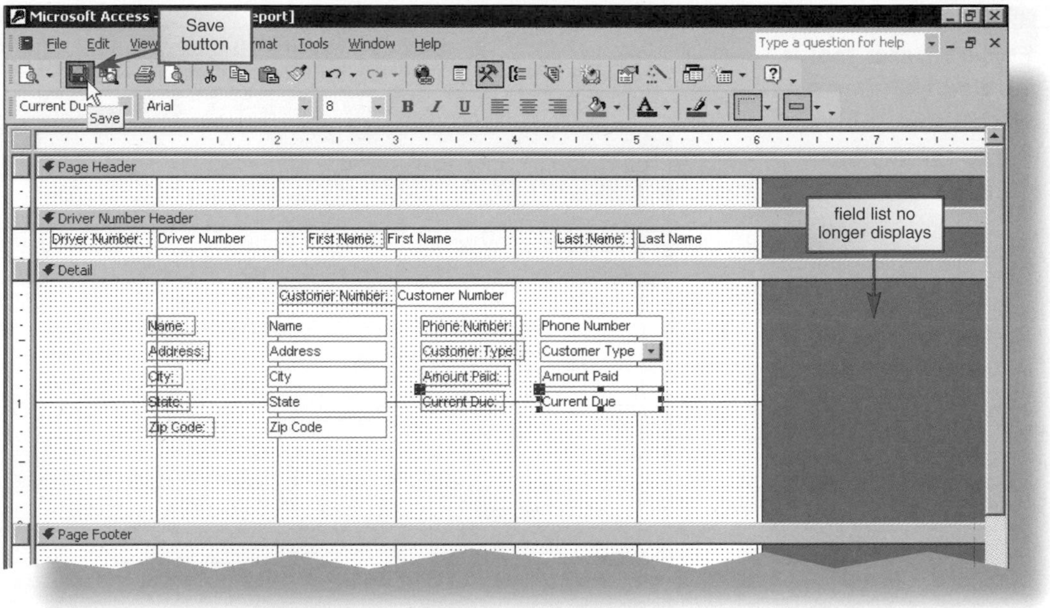

FIGURE 7-33

2 Click the Save button, and then type `Driver Master List` **as the report name. Point to the OK button.**

The Save As dialog box displays (Figure 7-34).

3 Click the OK button.

The report is saved. The name is Driver Master List.

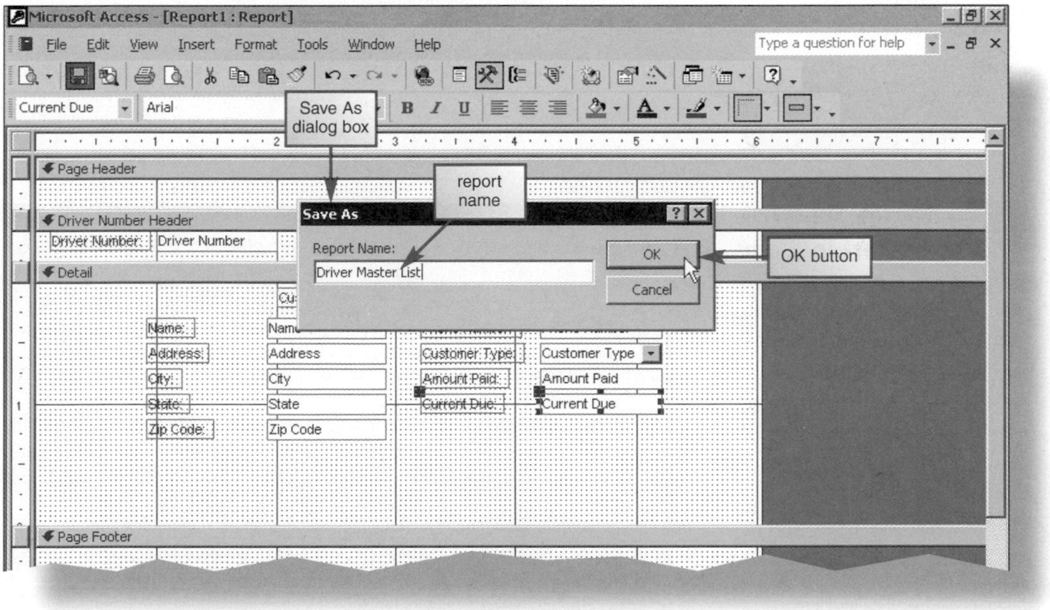

FIGURE 7-34

Adding a Subreport

To add a subreport to a report, you use the Subform/Subreport tool in the toolbox. Provided the Control Wizards tool is selected, a wizard will guide you through the process of adding the subreport as shown in the steps on the next page.

Steps To Add a Subreport

1 **Be sure the Control Wizards tool is selected and then point to the Subform/Subreport tool in the toolbox (Figure 7-35).**

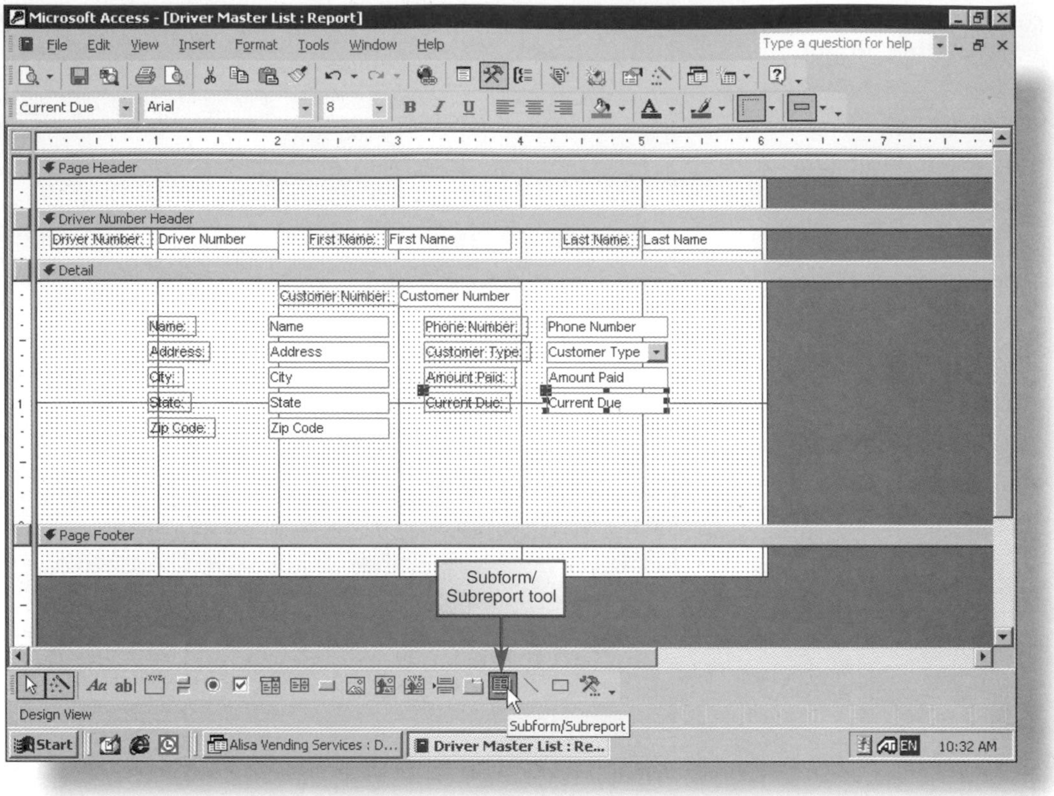

FIGURE 7-35

2 **Click the Subform/ Subreport tool and move the pointer, which has changed to a plus sign with a subreport, to the approximate position shown in Figure 7-36.**

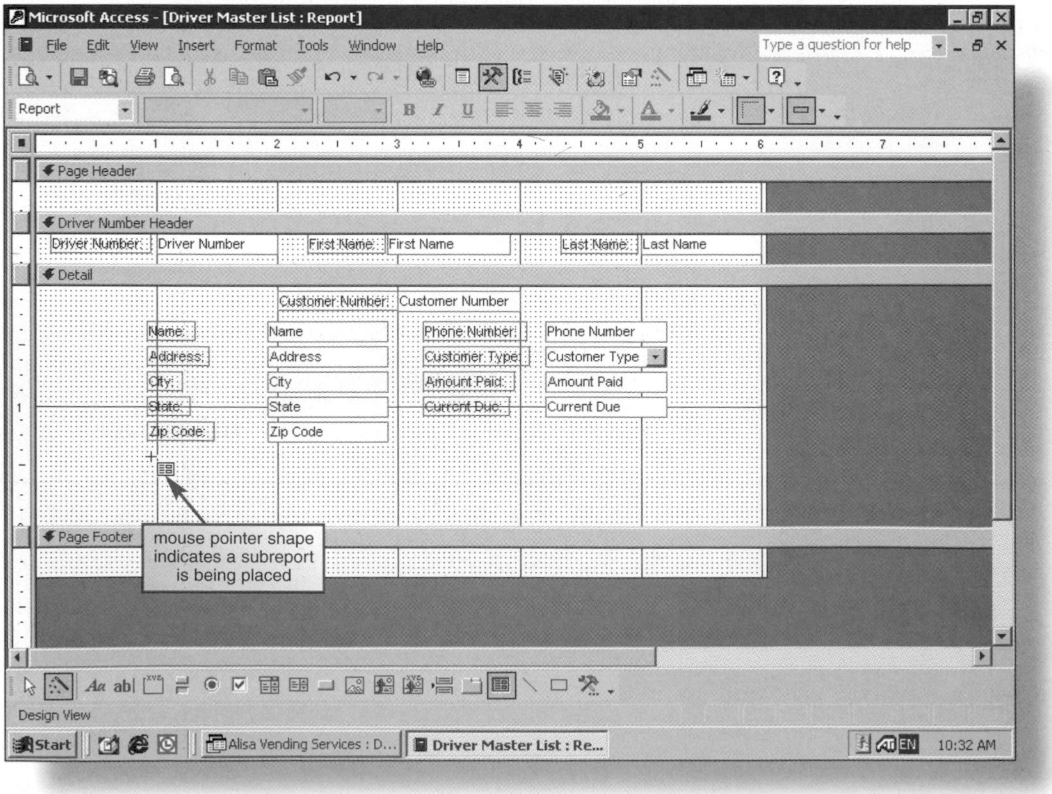

FIGURE 7-36

3 **Click the position shown in Figure 7-36. Be sure the Use existing Tables and Queries option button is selected in the SubReport Wizard dialog box, and then point to the Next button.**

The SubReport Wizard dialog box displays (Figure 7-37).

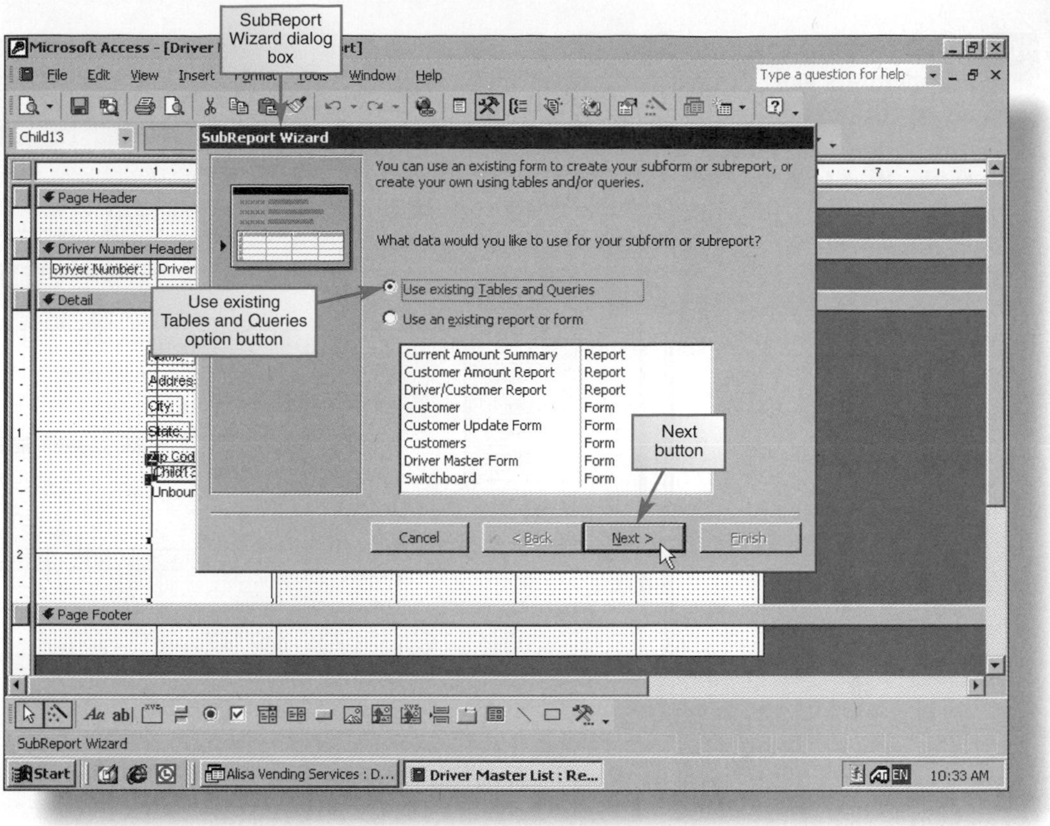

FIGURE 7-37

4 **Click the Next button. Click the Tables/Queries box arrow, and then point to Query: Workorders and Categories (Figure 7-38).**

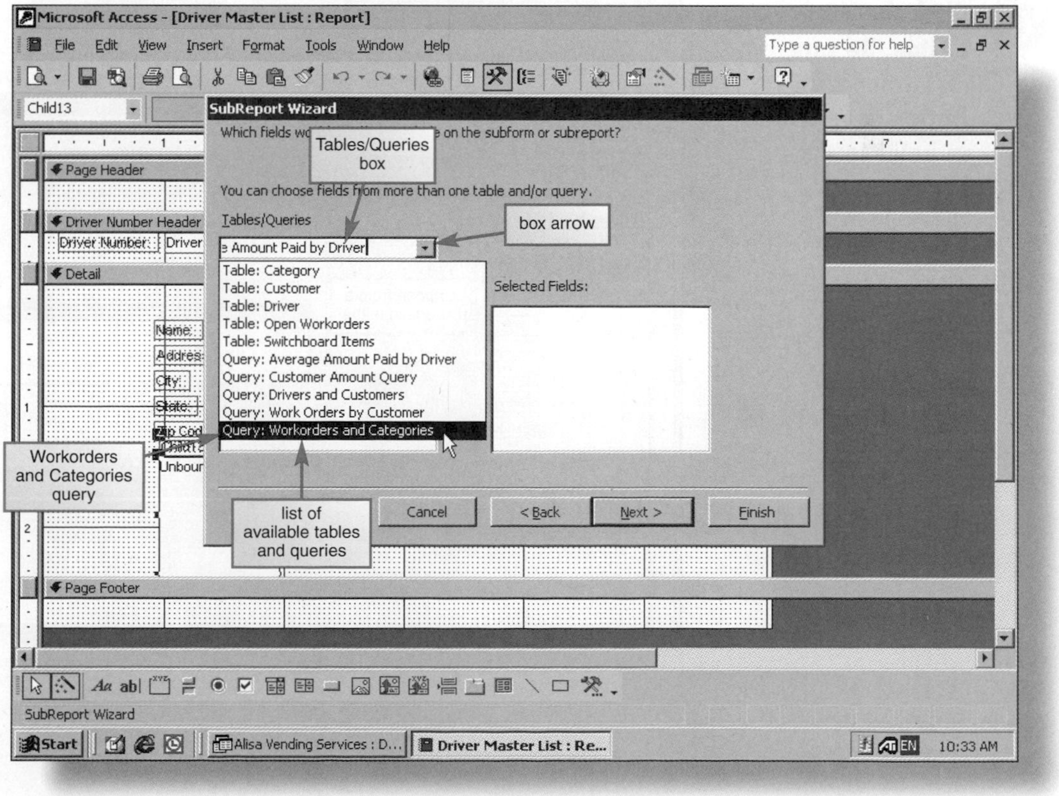

FIGURE 7-38

5 **Click Query: Workorders and Categories, click the Add All Fields button, and then point to the Next button.**

All the fields in the query are selected (Figure 7-39).

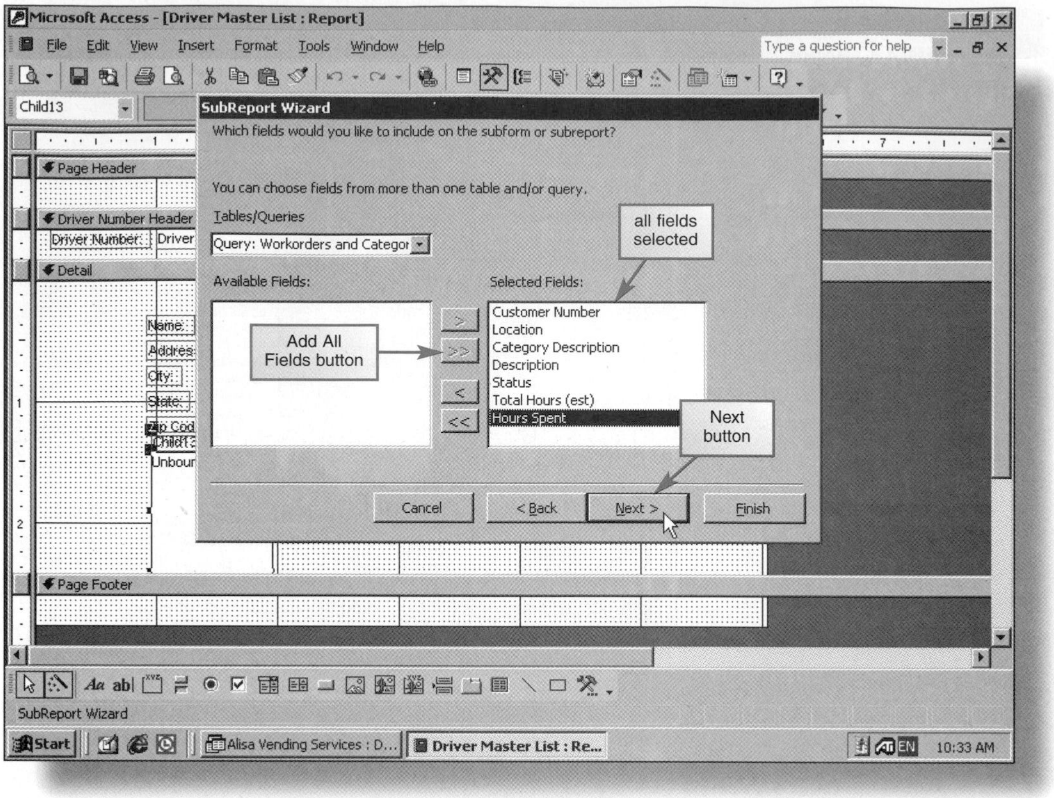

FIGURE 7-39

6 **Click the Next button. Be sure the Choose from a list option button is selected, and then point to the Next button.**

The SubReport Wizard dialog box displays (Figure 7-40). You use this dialog box to indicate the fields that link the main report (referred to as "form" in the sentence) to the subreport (referred to as "subform"). If the fields have the same name, as they often will, you can simply select Choose from a list, and then accept the selection Access already has made.

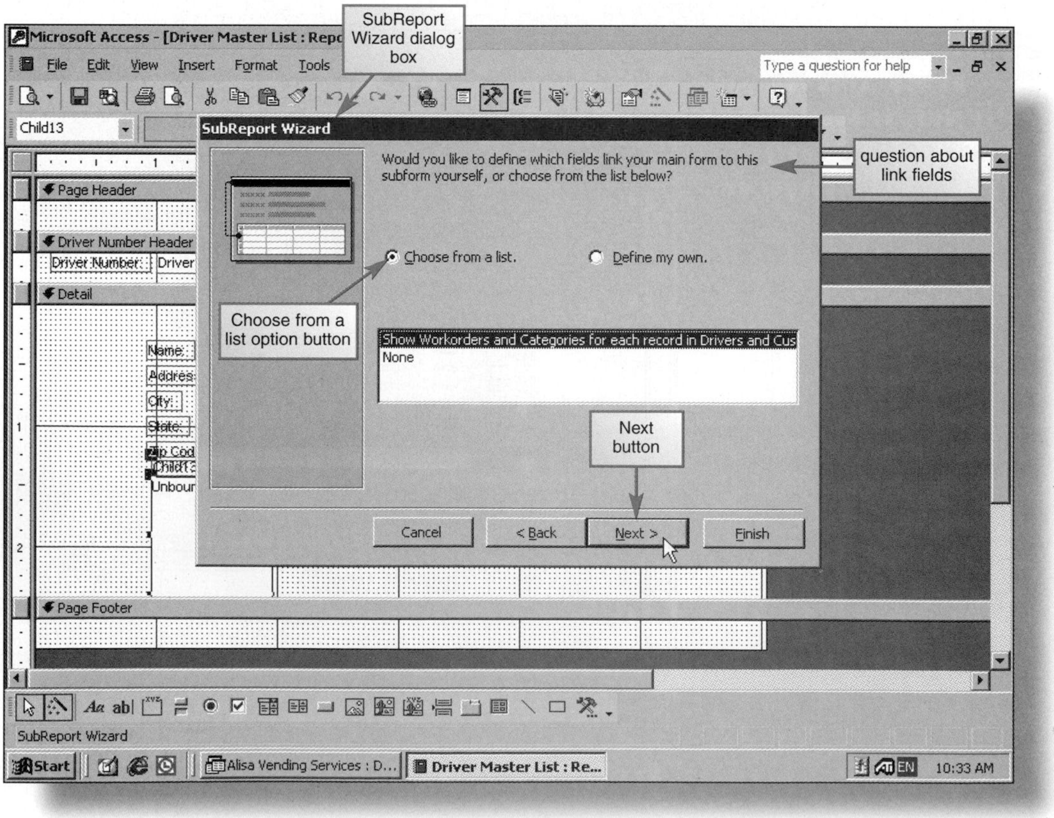

FIGURE 7-40

7 **Click the Next button. Type** `Open Workorders by Customer` **as the name of the subreport, and then point to the Finish button (Figure 7-41).**

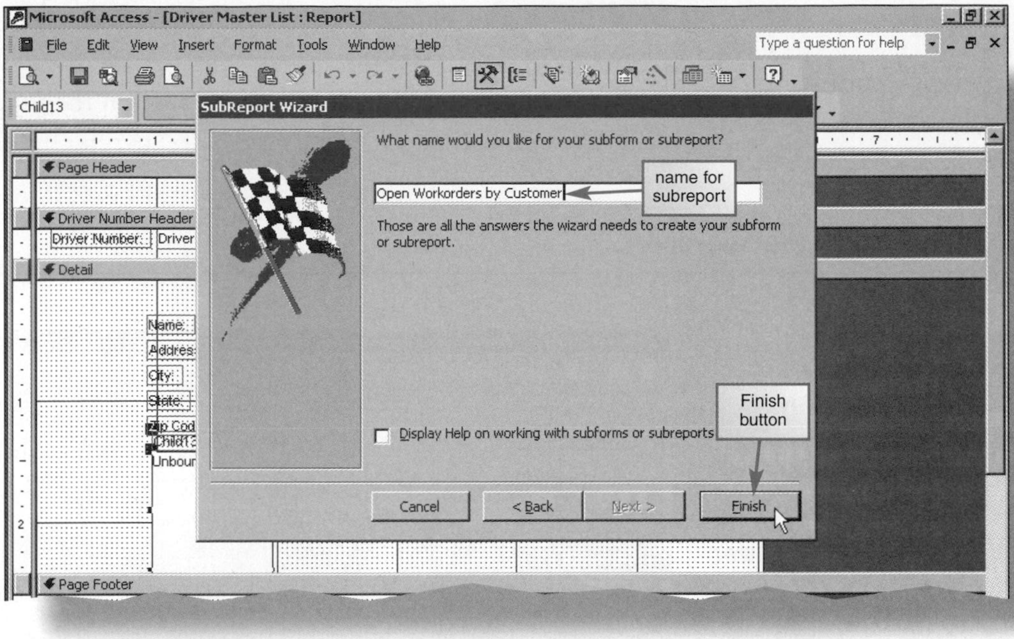

FIGURE 7-41

8 **Click the Finish button. It is possible that the window containing the report design no longer may be maximized. If it is not, click the Maximize button to maximize the window. If the field list displays, click its Close button. If necessary, click the subreport to select it, and then drag it to the approximate position shown in Figure 7-42. Point to the Close Window button.**

The subreport is created and placed in the report design.

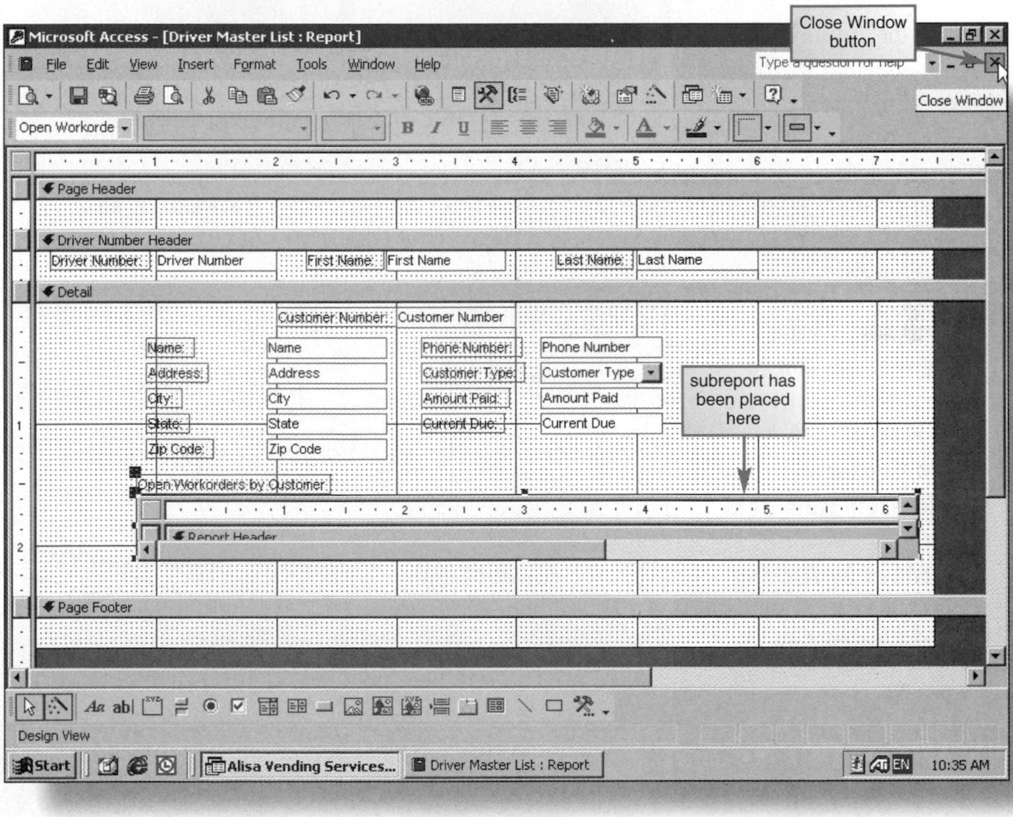

FIGURE 7-42

9 **Click the Close Window button to close the report design. Click the Yes button to save the changes.**

The report is saved. The Database window displays.

Modifying the Subreport

The subreport displays as a separate report in the Database window. It can be modified just like any other report. Perform the following steps to modify the subreport.

Steps To Modify the Subreport

1 Be sure the Reports object is selected, right-click Open Workorders by Customer, and then click Design View on the shortcut menu that displays. Point to the lower boundary of the Report Header section. (The font and style of your headings may be different.)

The design for the subreport displays (Figure 7-43). The mouse pointer shape changes to a two-headed vertical arrow with a crossbar.

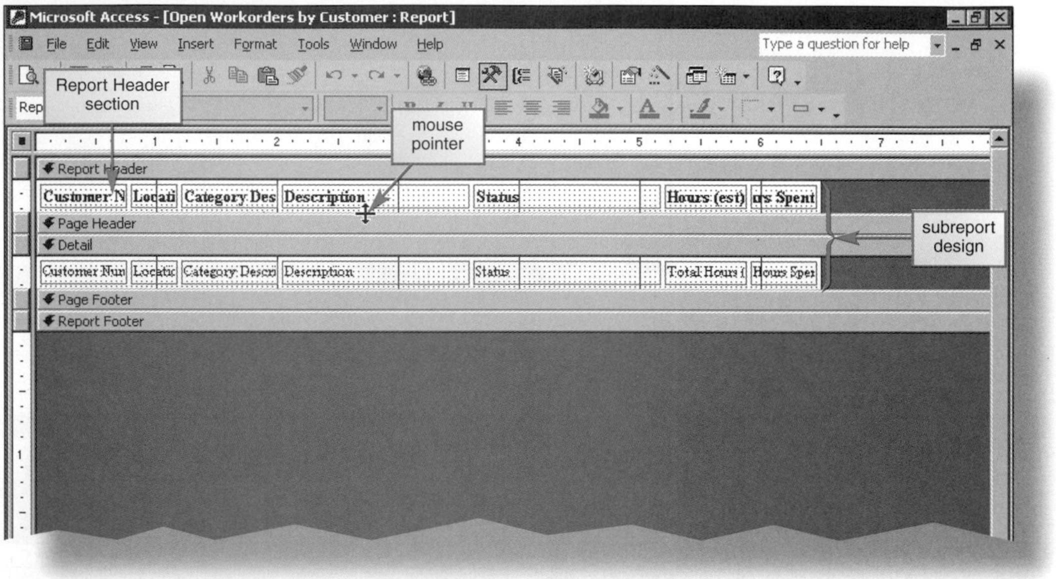

FIGURE 7-43

2 Drag the lower boundary of the Report Header section to the approximate position shown in Figure 7-44. Delete the Customer Number controls from both the Report Header and Detail sections by clicking each control and then pressing the DELETE key. Change the labels in the Report Header section to match those shown in the figure. (To extend a heading over two lines, press SHIFT+ENTER. To move a label, click the label to select it and then drag it to the desired location. To resize a label, click the label to select it, unless it already is selected, and then drag the appropriate sizing handle.)

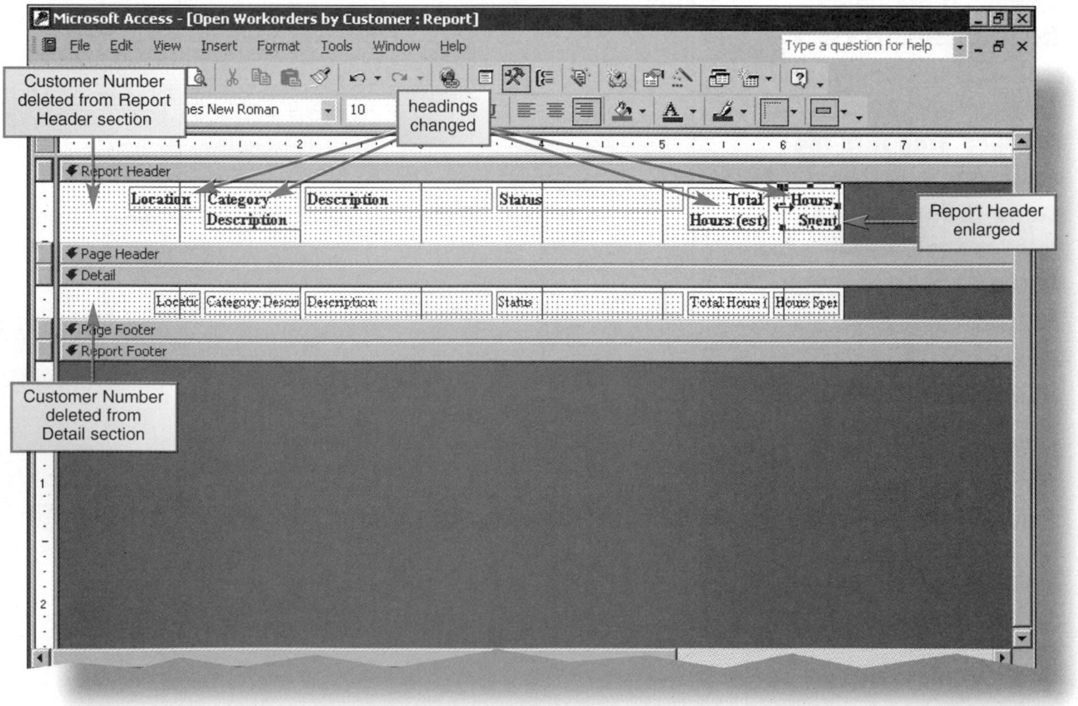

FIGURE 7-44

3 **Point to the ruler in the position shown in Figure 7-45.**

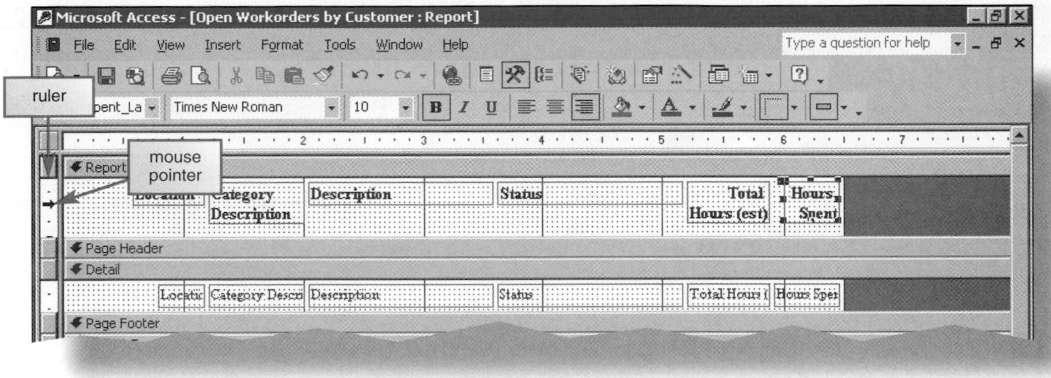

FIGURE 7-45

4 **Click the position shown in Figure 7-45.**

All the header labels are selected (Figure 7-46).

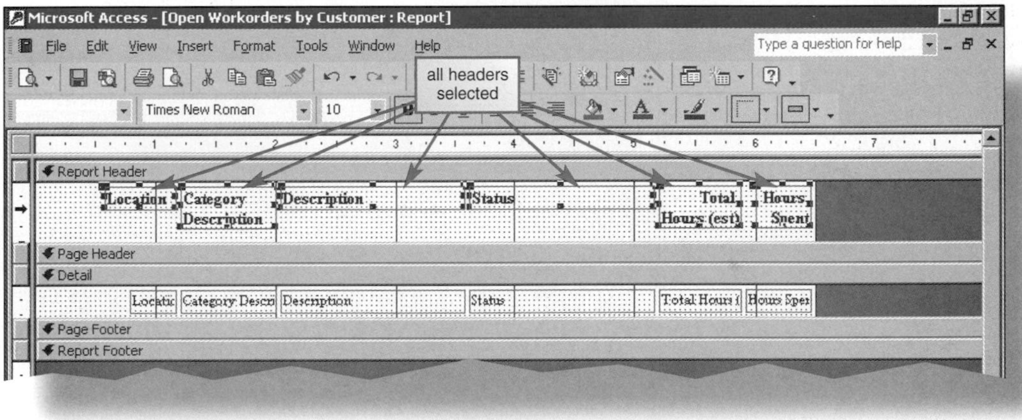

FIGURE 7-46

5 **Right-click any of the selected labels, and then click Properties on the shortcut menu. If necessary, click the All tab. Click the down scroll arrow to display the Border Style property. Click the Border Style property, click the Border Style property box arrow, and then point to Solid.**

The Multiple selection property sheet displays (Figure 7-47). The list of available border styles displays.

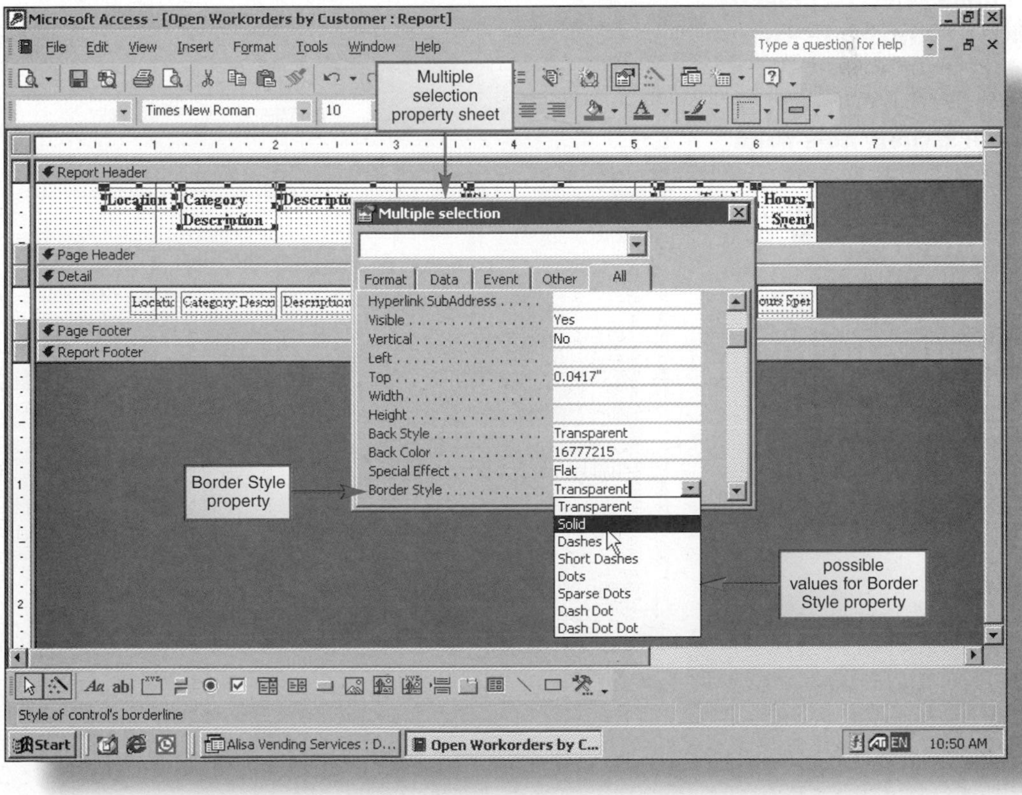

FIGURE 7-47

6 **Click Solid. Click the down scroll arrow so the Text Align property displays. Click the Text Align property, click the Text Align property box arrow, and then point to Center.**

The Multiple selection property sheet displays (Figure 7-48). The list of options for the Text Align property displays.

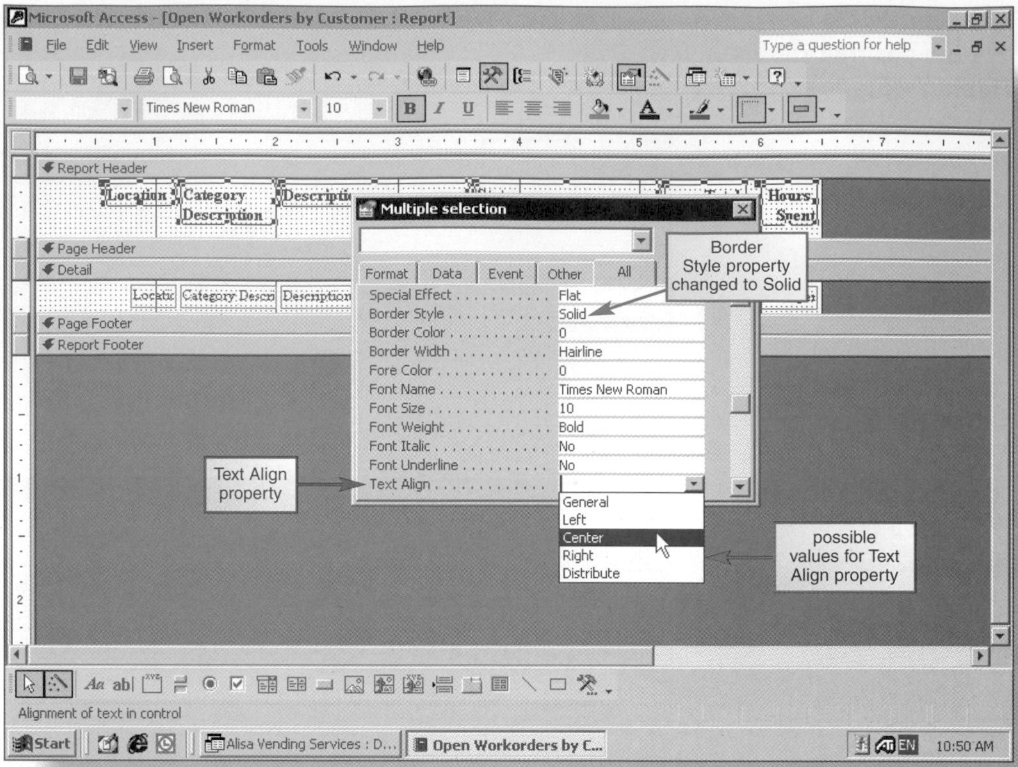

FIGURE 7-48

7 **Click Center, and then close the Multiple selection property sheet by clicking its Close button. Click the Total Hours (est) control in the Detail section. Hold down the SHIFT key, and then click the Hours Spent control in the Detail section. Right-click either of the selected controls and then point to Properties on the shortcut menu (Figure 7-49).**

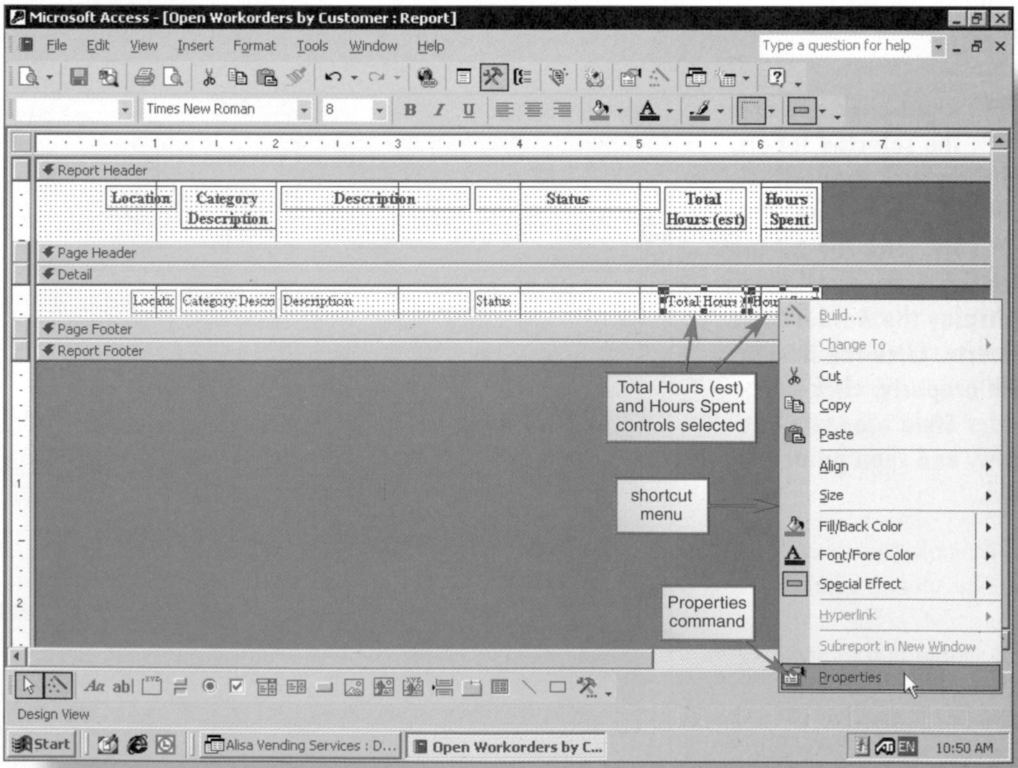

FIGURE 7-49

8 **Click Properties, click the Format property, click the Format property box arrow, and then select Fixed. Click the Decimal Places property, click the Decimal Places property box arrow, and then click 1. Point to the Close button.**

The format is changed to Fixed and the number of decimal places is changed to 1 (Figure 7-50).

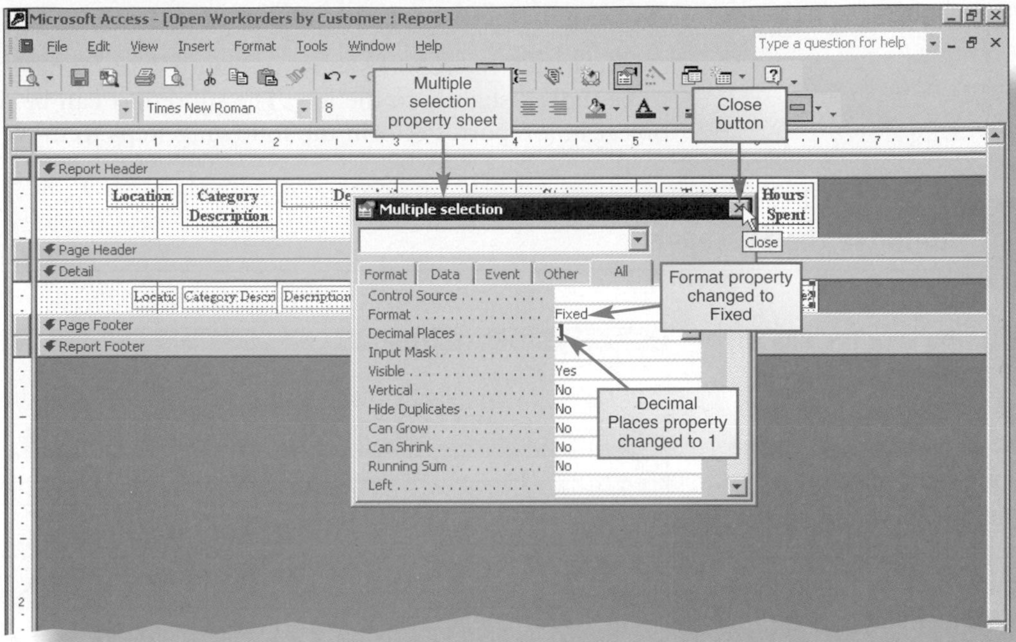

FIGURE 7-50

9 **Click the Close button for the Multiple selection property sheet. Right-click the Category Description control in the Detail section and then click Properties on the shortcut menu. Click the Can Grow property, click the Can Grow property box arrow, and then click Yes. Point to the Close button for the Text Box: Category Description property sheet.**

The value for the Can Grow property has been changed to Yes (Figure 7-51). Category Description will be spread over several lines.

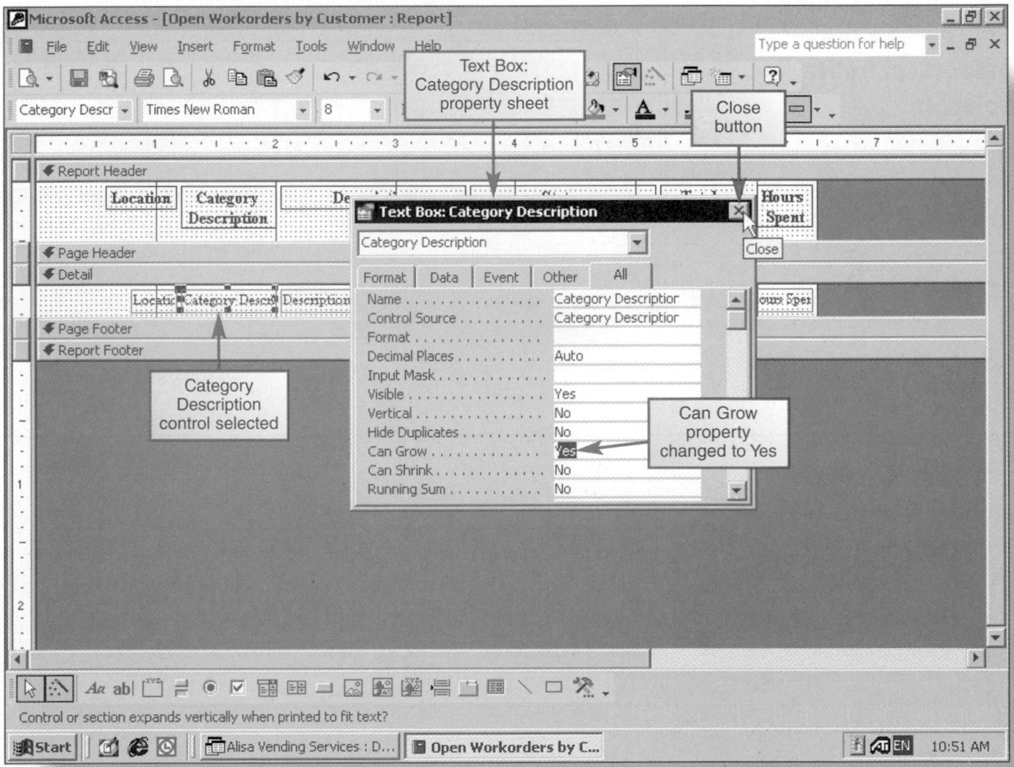

FIGURE 7-51

10 **Click the Close button for the property sheet, and then close the subreport by clicking its Close Window button. Click the Yes button to save the changes.**

The changes are saved and the report is removed from the screen.

Moving the Subreport

To match the report shown in Figure 7-1a on page A 7.05, the subreport needs to be moved slightly to the left. The subreport can be dragged just like any other object in a report. Perform the following steps to move the subreport.

Steps To Move the Subreport

1 **Be sure the Reports object is selected, right-click Driver Master List, and then click Design View on the shortcut menu. Drag the subreport to the position shown in Figure 7-52 and then drag the right sizing handle to the position shown in the figure.**

2 **Click anywhere outside the subreport control to deselect it.**

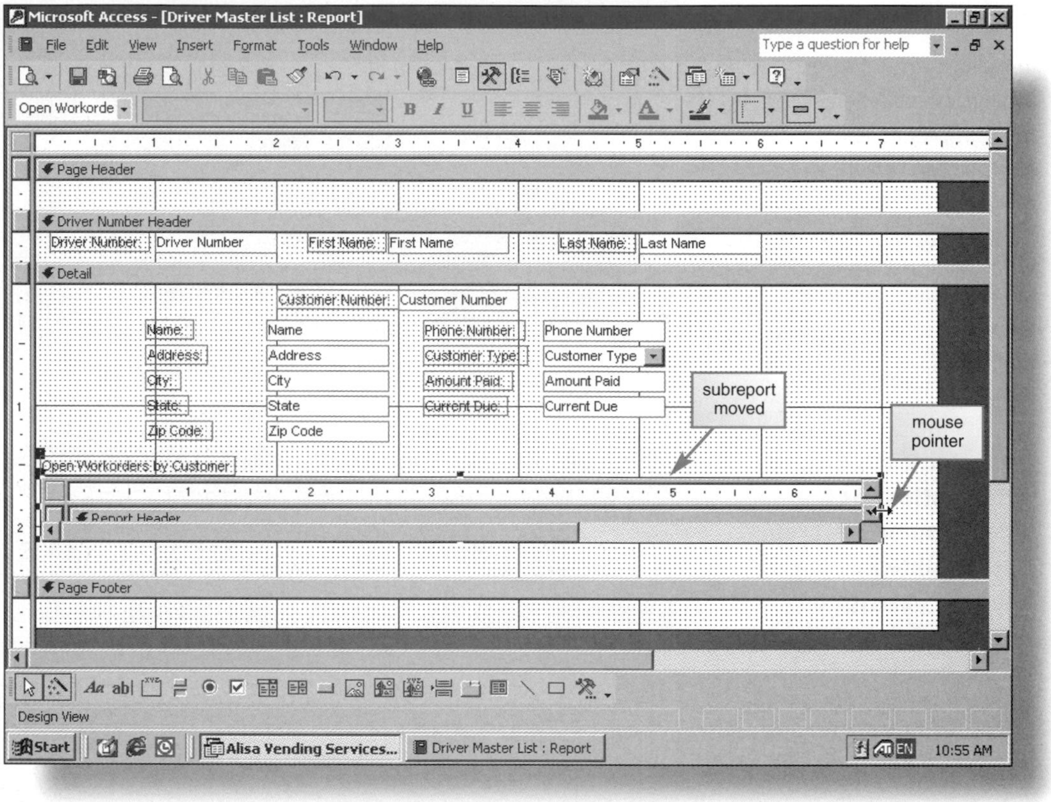

FIGURE 7-52

More About

Adding a Date

After adding a date to a report, you can change the format used to display the date by right-clicking the date control and then clicking Properties on the shortcut menu. You then can select a format for the date and/or the time by changing the value for the Format property.

Adding a Date

To add a date to a report, use the Date and Time command on the Insert menu. When you do, you will be given a choice of a variety of date and time formats. After adding the date, you can drag it into the desired position. Perform the following steps to add the date.

Steps To Add a Date

1 **Click Insert on the menu bar, and then click Date and Time on the Insert menu. Point to the Include Time check box in the Date and Time dialog box.**

The Date and Time dialog box displays (Figure 7-53).

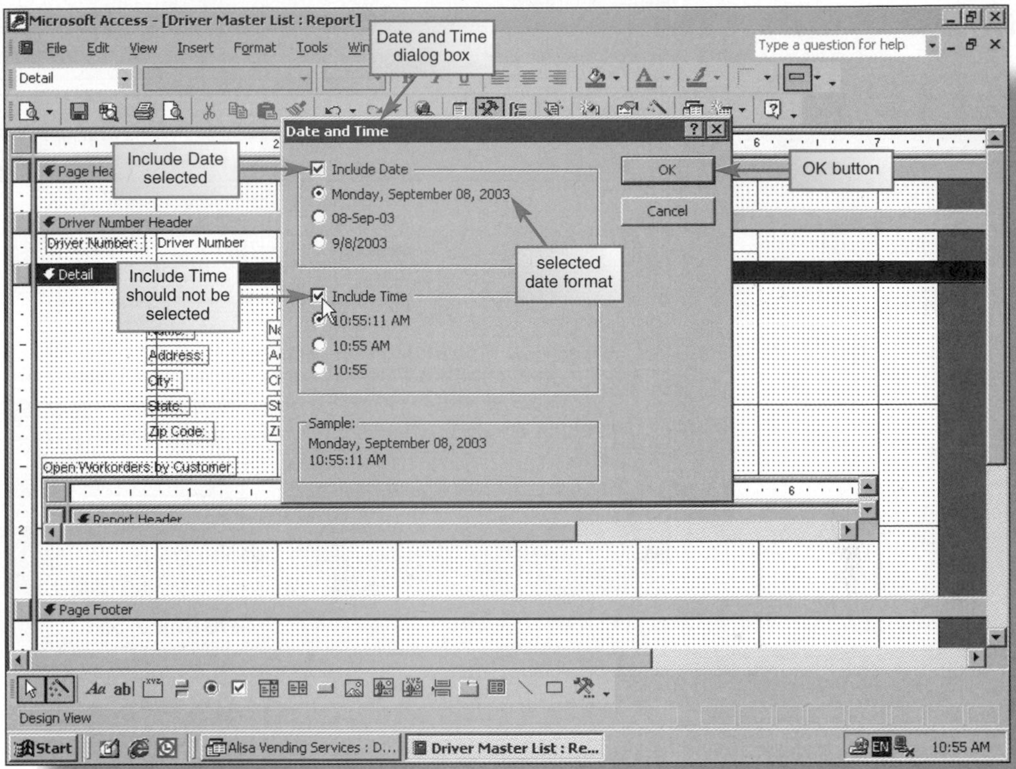

FIGURE 7-53

2 **Click the Include Time check box to remove the check mark. Be sure that Include Date is checked and that the date format selected is the first of the three options. Click the OK button to add the date. Click the Date control and point to the boundary of the newly-added Date control away from any of the handles. The pointer shape changes to a hand as in Figure 7-54.**

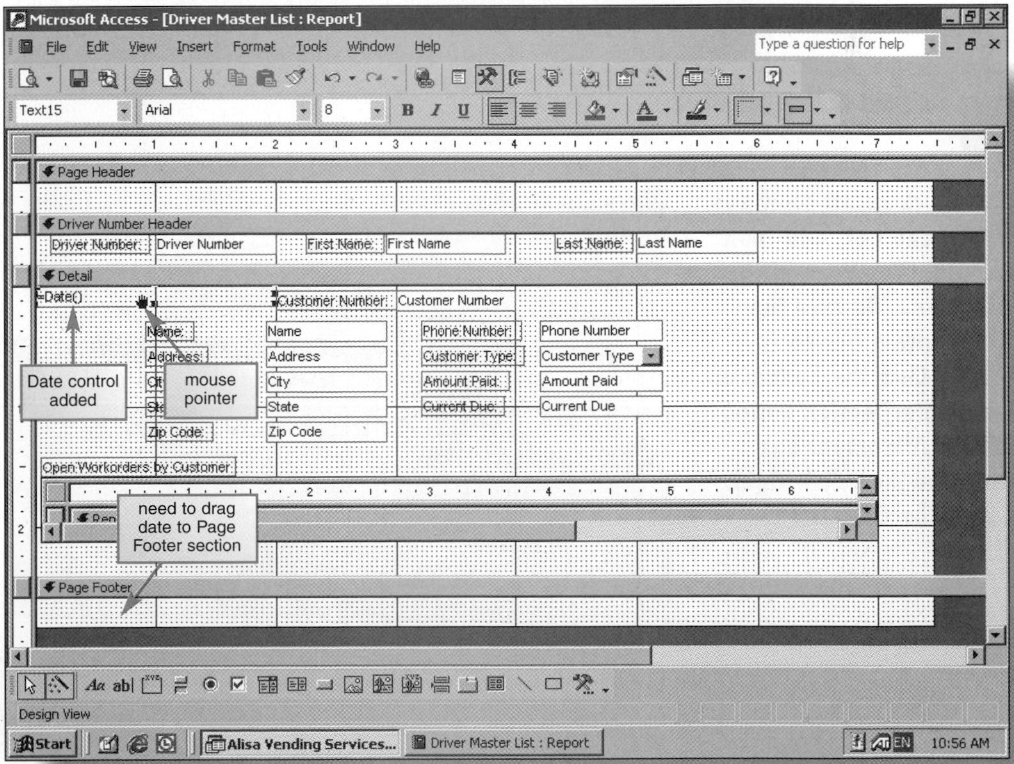

FIGURE 7-54

3 Drag the Date control to the position shown in Figure 7-55.

The date is added to the report.

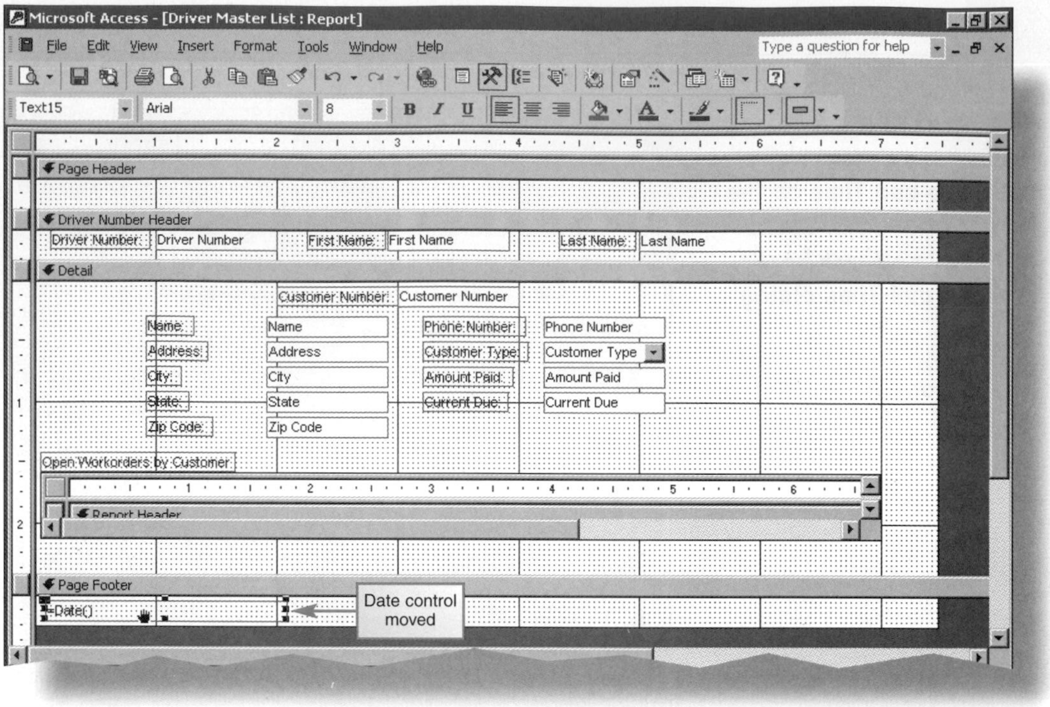

FIGURE 7-55

Other Ways

1. In Voice Command mode, say "Insert, Date and Time"

Adding a Page Number

To add a page number to a report, use the Page Numbers command on the Insert menu. When you do, you will be given a choice of a variety of page number formats and positions. Perform the following steps to add a page number.

Steps To Add a Page Number

1 Click Insert on the menu bar, and then click Page Numbers on the Insert menu. Be sure the Page N option button is selected. Click the Bottom of Page [Footer] option button. Click the Alignment box arrow, and then click Right. Point to the OK button.

The Page Numbers dialog box displays (Figure 7-56). The selected format for the page number is Page N. The page number will display at the bottom of the page and be right-aligned.

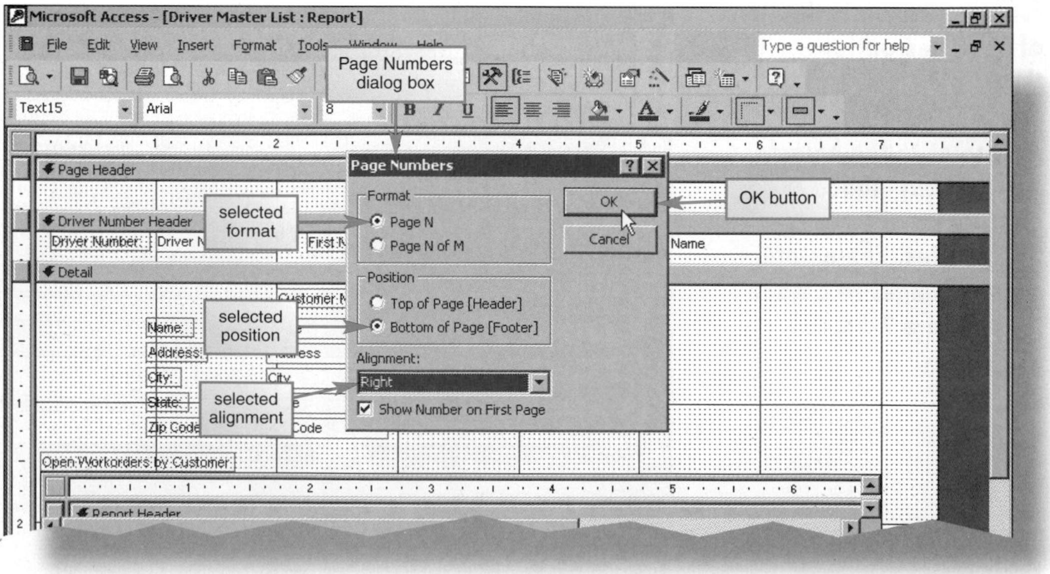

FIGURE 7-56

2 **Click the OK button to add a page number. Drag the Page Number control to the position shown in Figure 7-57.**

The page number is added.

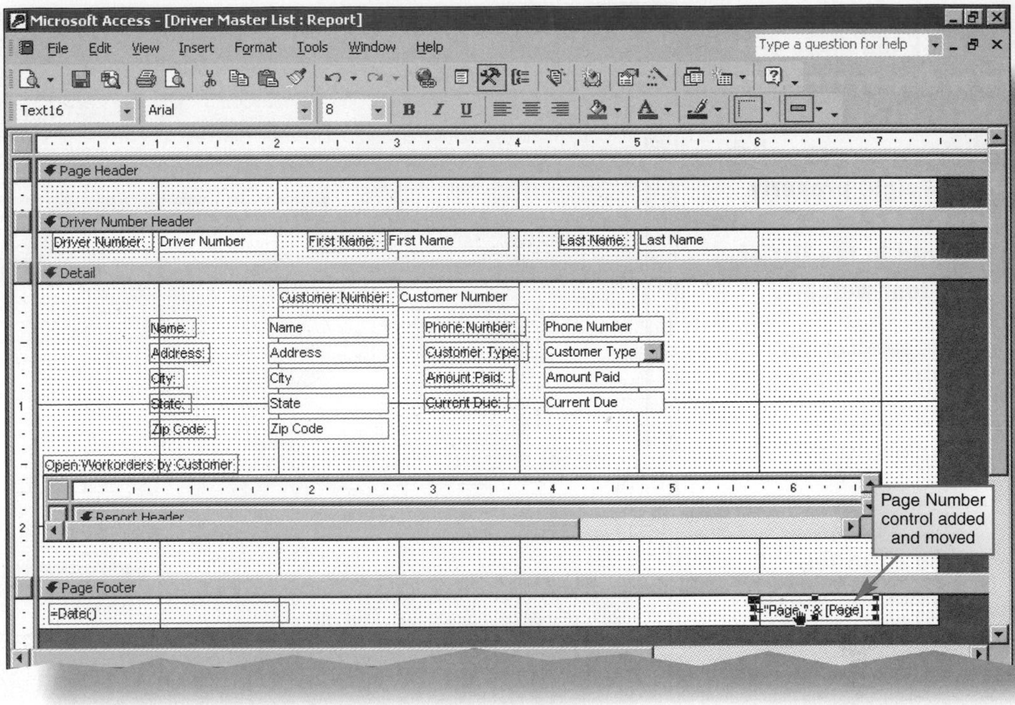

FIGURE 7-57

Other Ways

1. In Voice Command mode, say "Insert, Page Numbers"

Bolding Data

In the report shown in Figure 7-1a on page A 7.05, the data is semi-bold, which is slightly lighter than bold. To change the data in a control to semi-bold, change the Font Weight property. Perform the following steps to select all the controls, and then change the Font Weight property to Semi-bold.

Steps To Bold Controls

1 **Click the Driver Number control to select it. Hold down the SHIFT key while selecting each of the other controls as shown in Figure 7-58. Right-click any of the selected controls and then point to Properties on the shortcut menu.**

The shortcut menu displays (Figure 7-58). Depending on which control you right-clicked, the shortcut menu may be in a different location.

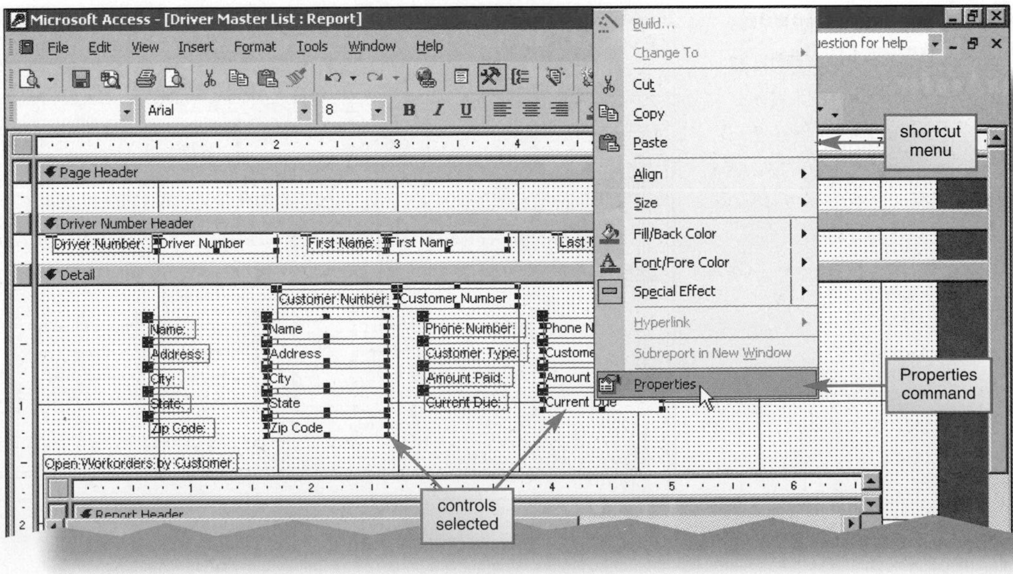

FIGURE 7-58

2 Click Properties. Click the down scroll arrow to display the Font Weight property. Click the Font Weight property, click the Font Weight property box arrow, and then point to Semi-bold in the list of available font weights.

The Multiple selection property sheet displays (Figure 7-59). The list of available font weights displays.

3 Click Semi-bold and then close the Multiple selection property sheet by clicking its Close button.

The data are all semi-bold.

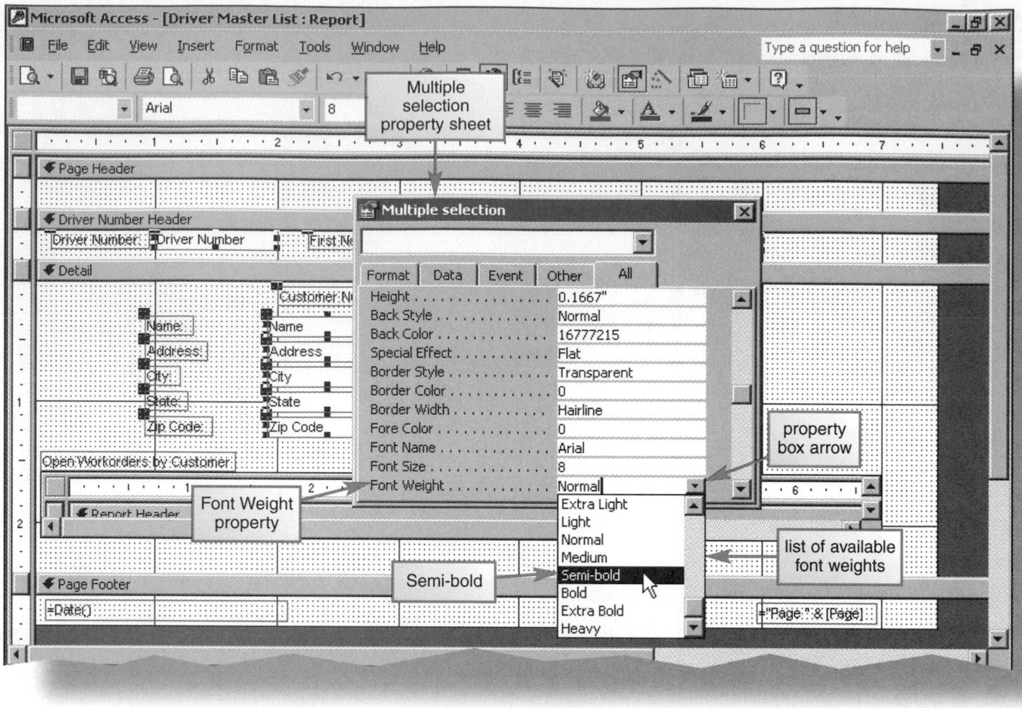

FIGURE 7-59

Adding a Title

A report title is added as a label. Assuming that the title is to display on each page, it should be added to the page header. (If it is to display only once at the beginning of the report, it instead would be added to the report header.) Perform the following steps to add a title to the page header.

Steps To Add a Title

1 Point to the lower boundary of the page header.

The pointer changes to a double-pointing arrow (Figure 7-60).

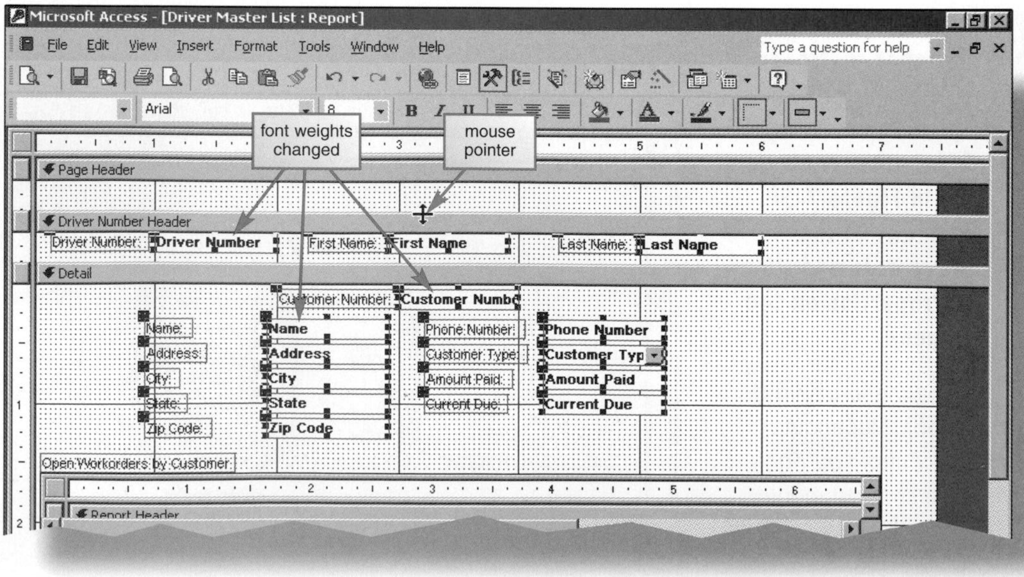

FIGURE 7-60

2 **Drag the lower boundary of the page header to the approximate position shown in Figure 7-61 and then point to the Label tool in the toolbox.**

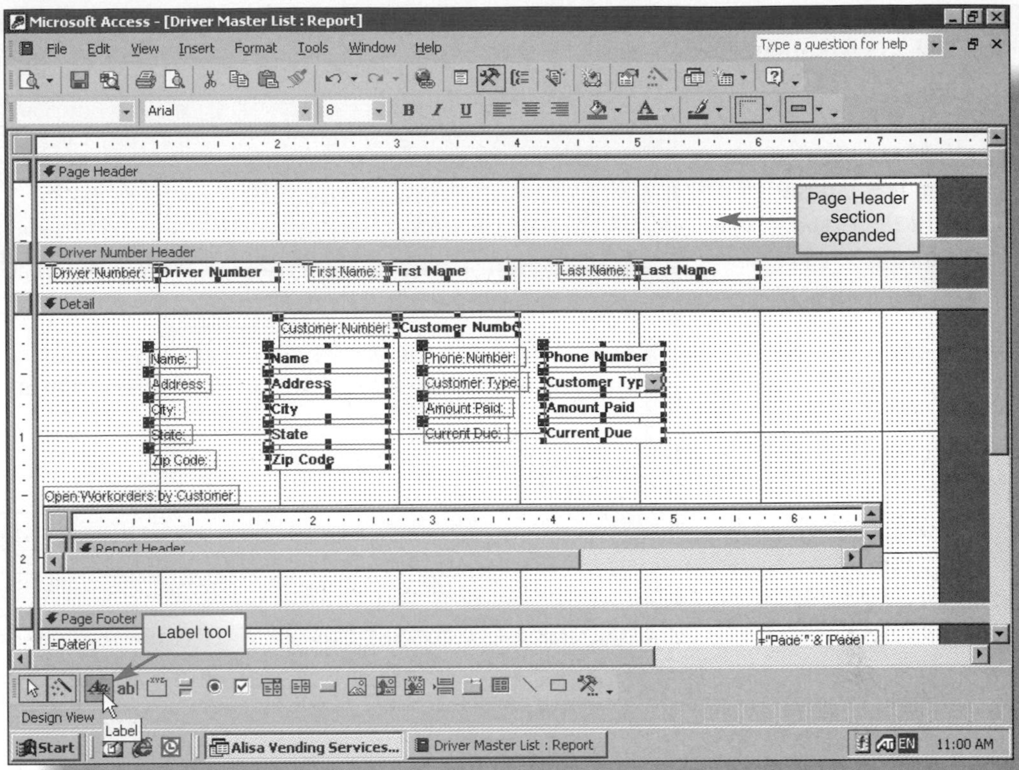

FIGURE 7-61

3 **Click the Label tool and then move the mouse pointer, which has changed to a plus sign with a label, to the position shown in Figure 7-62.**

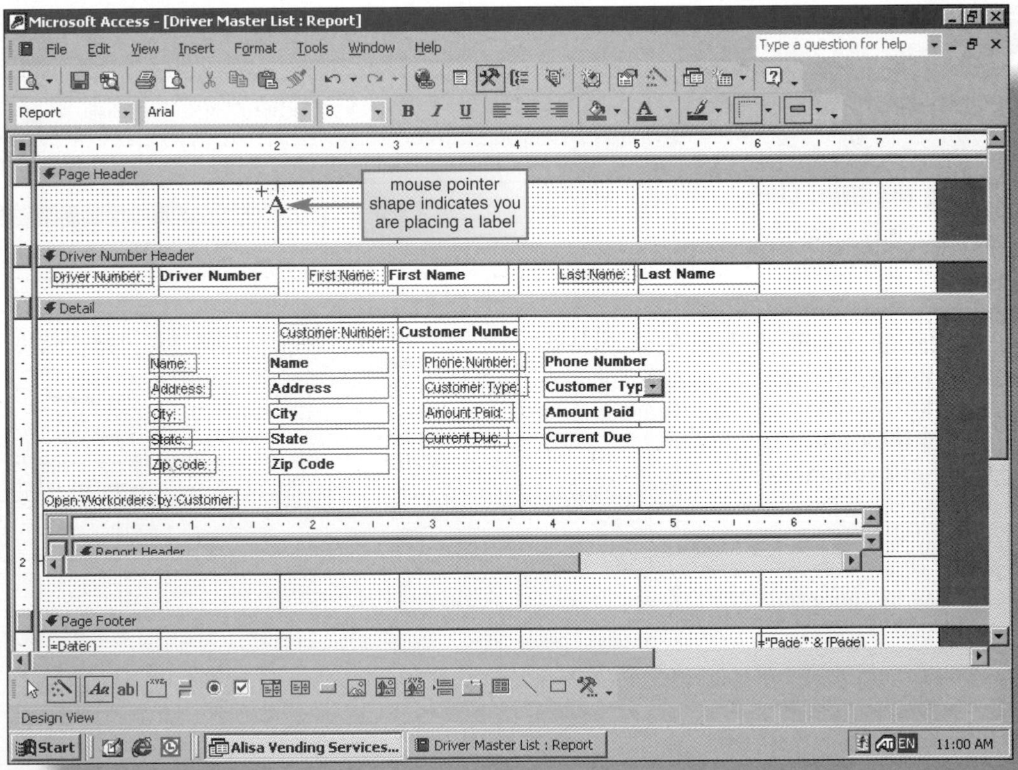

FIGURE 7-62

4 **Drag the pointer to the lower-right corner of the label to the approximate position shown in Figure 7-63, release the left mouse button, and then type** `Driver Master List` **as the title.**

The title is entered.

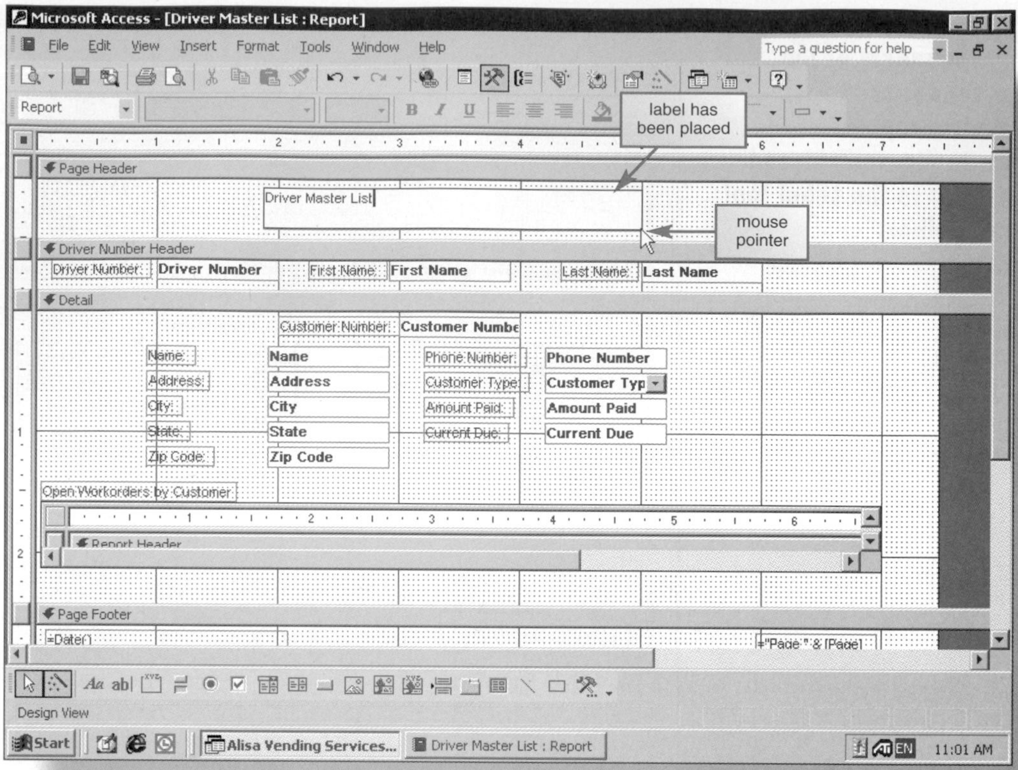

FIGURE 7-63

5 **Click somewhere outside the label containing the title to deselect the label. Next, right-click the label containing the title. Click Properties on the shortcut menu. Click the down scroll arrow so the Font Size property displays. Click the Font Size property, click the Font Size property box arrow, and then point to 18 in the list of available font sizes.**

The Label: Label17 (your number may be different) property sheet displays (Figure 7-64). The list of available font sizes displays.

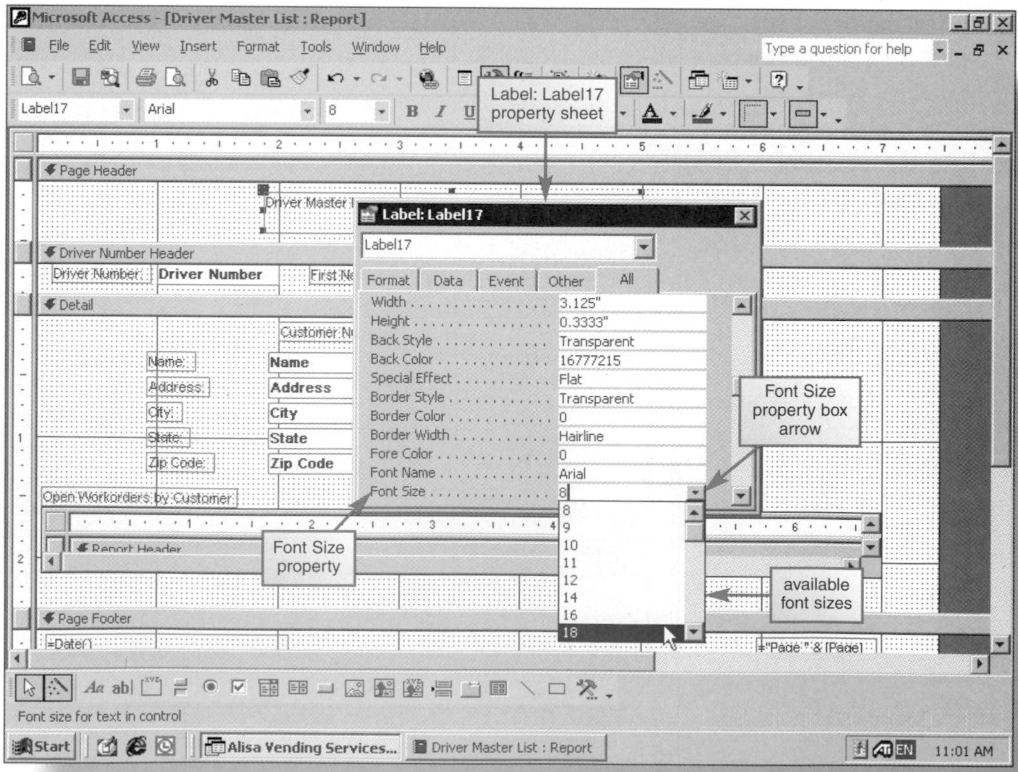

FIGURE 7-64

6 **Click 18 as the new font size. Click the down scroll arrow so the Text Align property displays. Click the Text Align property, click the Text Align property box arrow, and then point to Distribute.**

The list of available values for the Text Align property displays (Figure 7-65).

7 **Click Distribute as the new Text Align property. Close the property sheet by clicking its Close button.**

The format of the title is changed.

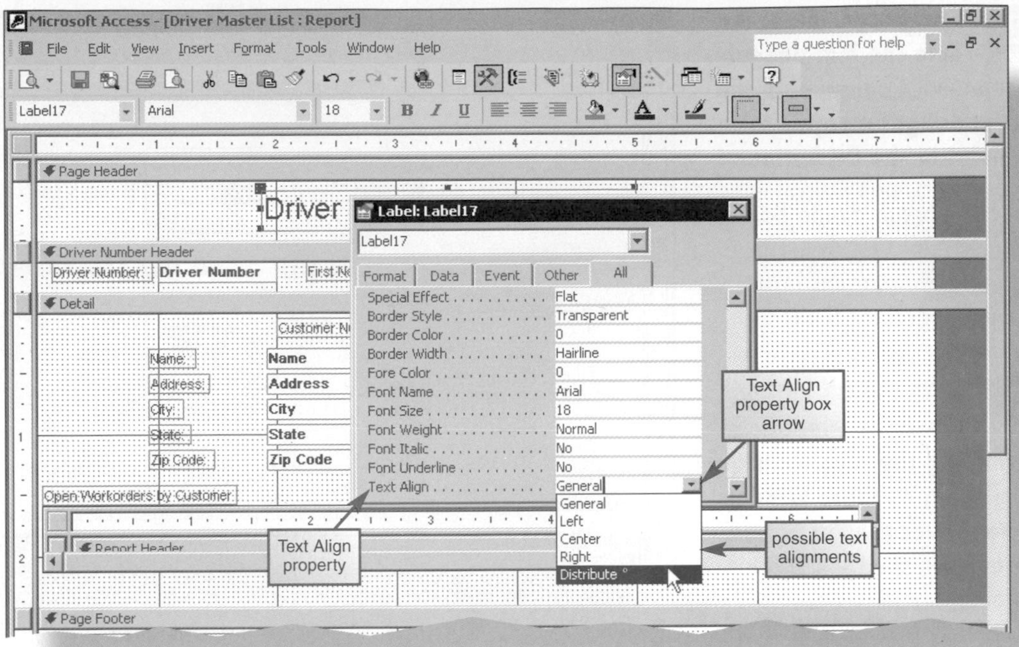

FIGURE 7-65

Changing Margins

The report just created is slightly too wide to print across the width of the page. You could modify the report to decrease the width. If, however, you do not need to reduce it by much, it usually is easier to adjust the margins. To do so, use the Page Setup command as in the following steps, which reduces both the left and right margins to 0.5 inch.

Steps To Change the Margins

1 **Click File on the menu bar, and then point to Page Setup on the File menu.**

The File menu displays (Figure 7-66).

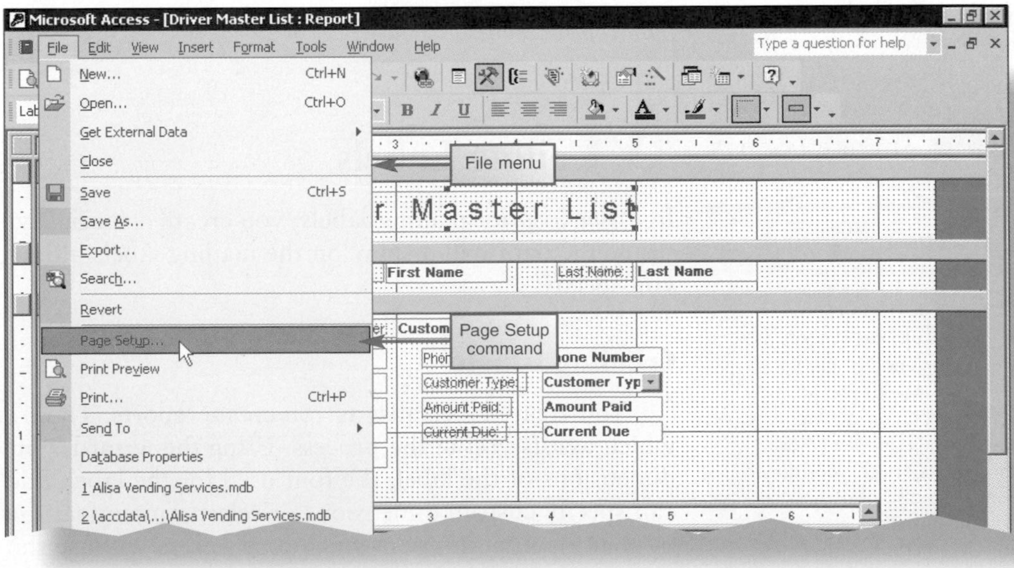

FIGURE 7-66

2 Click Page Setup. Be sure the Margins tab is selected. Change both the Left and Right margins to .5. Point to the OK button.

The Page Setup dialog box displays (Figure 7-67). The left and right margins have been changed to .5.

3 Click the OK button. Close the window containing the report design by clicking its Close Window button. Click the Yes button to save the changes.

The changes are saved. The completed report will look like the one shown in Figure 7-1a on page A 7.05.

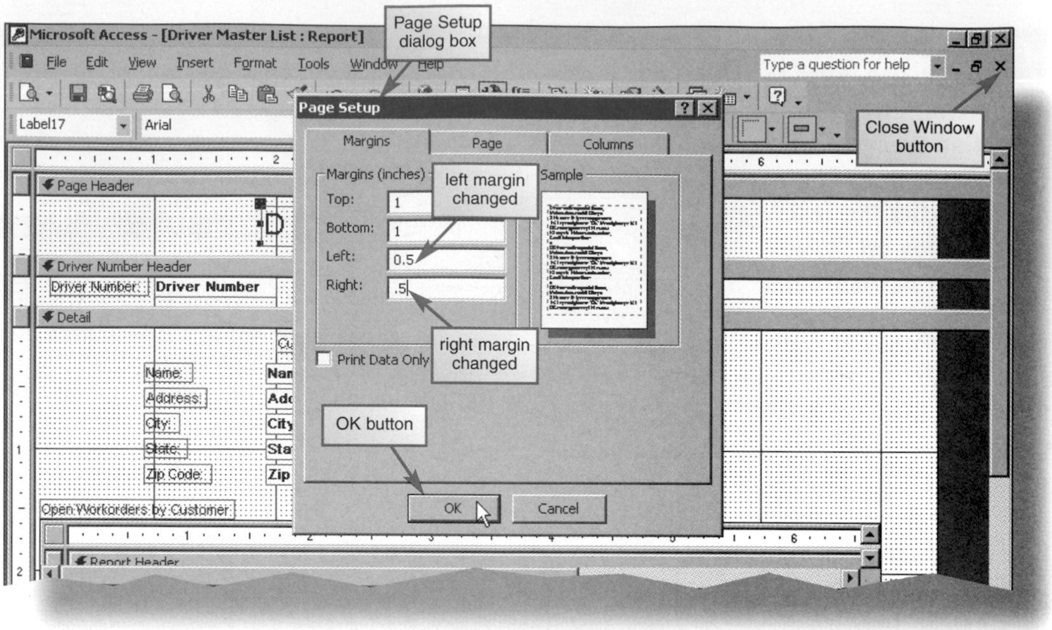

FIGURE 7-67

Other Ways

1. In Voice Command mode, say "File, Page Setup"

More About

Margins

If you find you make the same changes to the margins on all your reports, you may wish to change the default margins. To do so, click Tools on the menu bar, click Options on the Tools menu, click the General tab, and then specify the desired margins.

More About

Mailing Labels

If you need to print labels that are not included in the list of available labels, you have two options. You can attempt to find labels in the list whose dimensions match your dimensions. You also can click the Customize button and specify precisely the dimensions you need.

Printing a Report

To print a report, right-click the report in the Database window, and then click Print on the shortcut menu. Perform the following steps to print the Driver Master List.

TO PRINT A REPORT

1. If necessary, in the Database window, click the Reports object. Right-click Driver Master List.
2. Click Print on the shortcut menu.

The report prints.

Mailing Labels

In order to print mailing labels, you create a special type of report. When this report prints the data will display on the mailing labels all aligned correctly and in the order you specify.

Creating Labels

You create labels just as you create reports. There is a wizard, the Label Wizard, which assists you in the process. Using the wizard, you can specify the type and dimensions of the label, the font used for the label, and the contents of the label. You can specify custom dimensions or select a manufacturer and a specific label produced by that manufacturer, in which case Access will use the appropriate dimensions.

Perform the following steps to create the labels.

Steps To Create Labels

1 In the Database window, click Tables on the Objects bar, and then click Driver. Click the New Object : Report button arrow on the Database toolbar, and then click Report. Click Label Wizard in the New Report dialog box, and then point to the OK button.

The New Report dialog box displays (Figure 7-68).

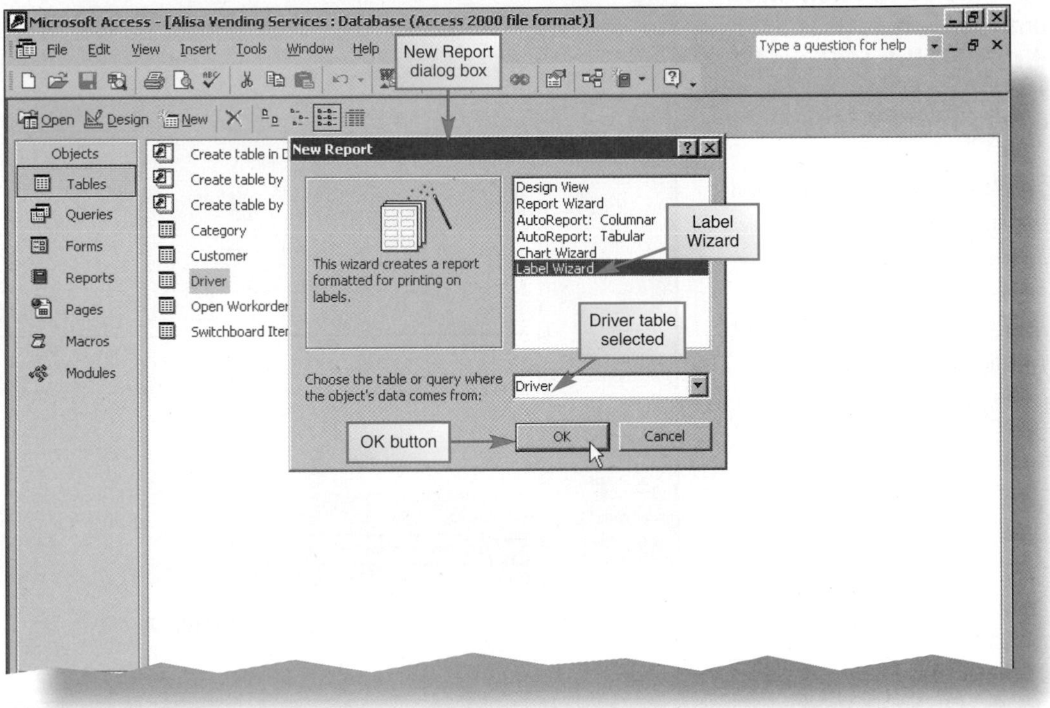

FIGURE 7-68

2 Click the OK button.

The Label Wizard dialog box displays (Figure 7-69).

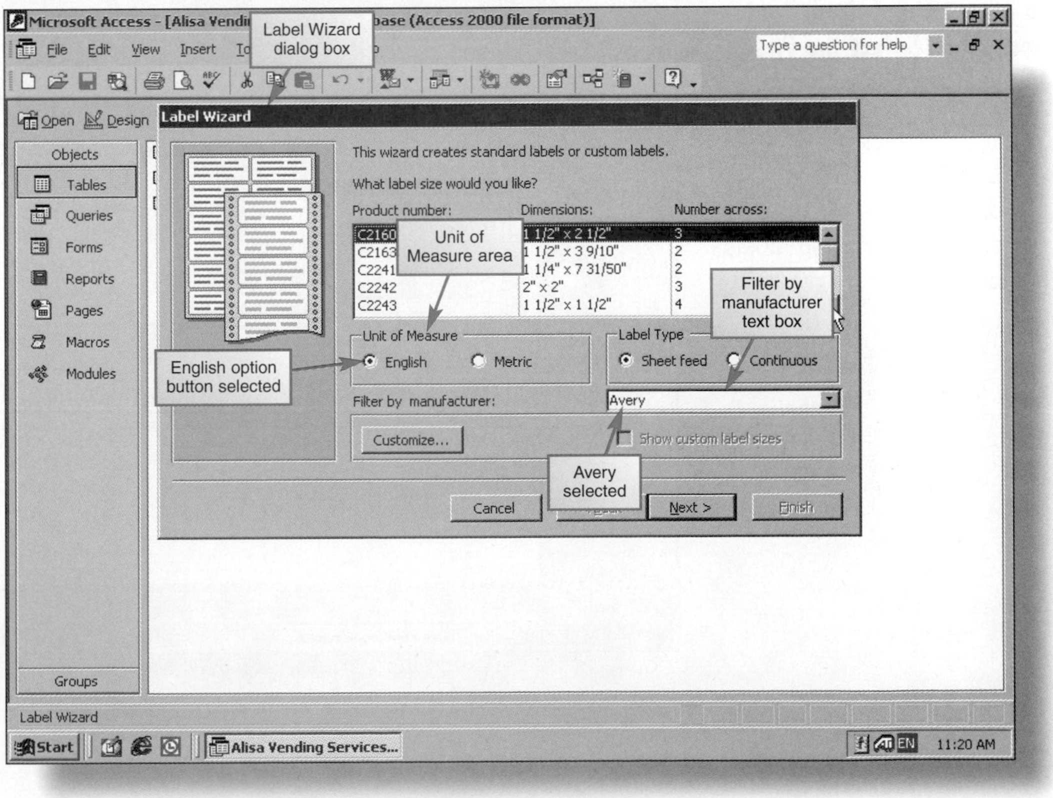

FIGURE 7-69

3 **Be sure the English option button is selected and that Avery is selected in the Filter by manufacturer text box. Click the down scroll arrow until Product number 5095 displays, click 5095, and then point to the Next button.**

The Label Wizard dialog box displays (Figure 7-70). English is the unit of measure, and Avery is selected as the manufacturer. The list of Avery labels displays, and product number 5095 is selected.

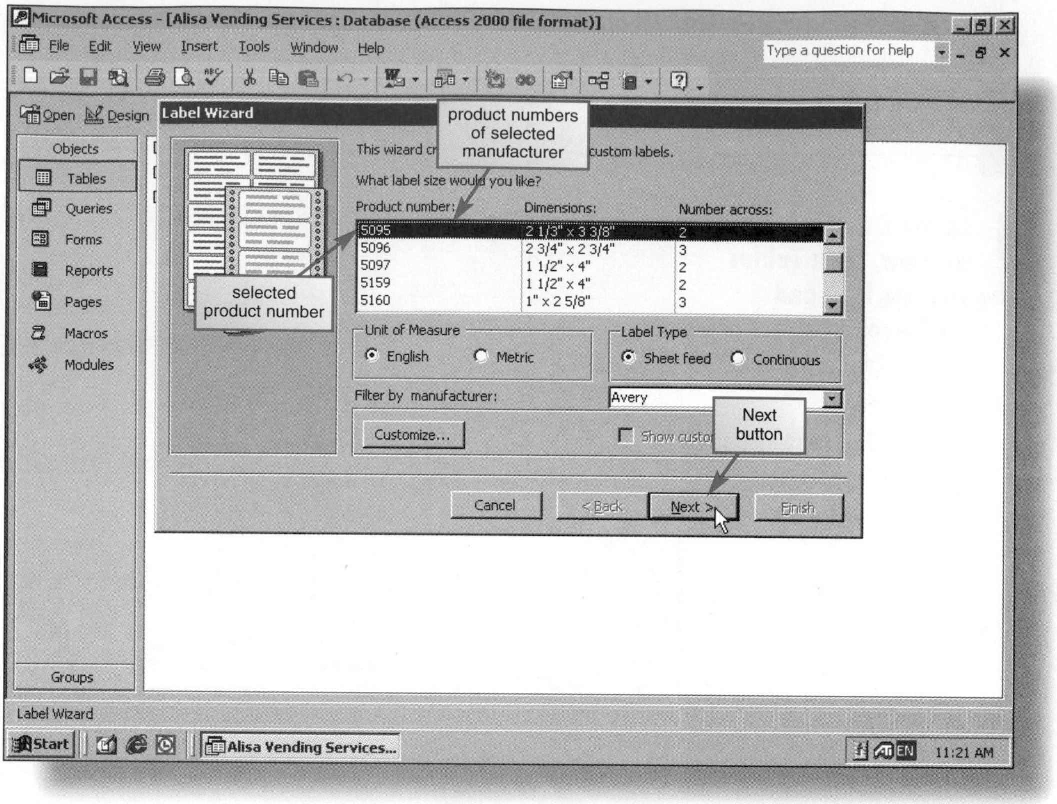

FIGURE 7-70

4 **Click the Next button. Click the Next button a second time to accept the default font and color. Select the First Name field and point to the Add Field button.**

The Label Wizard dialog box displays asking for the contents of the mailing labels (Figure 7-71).

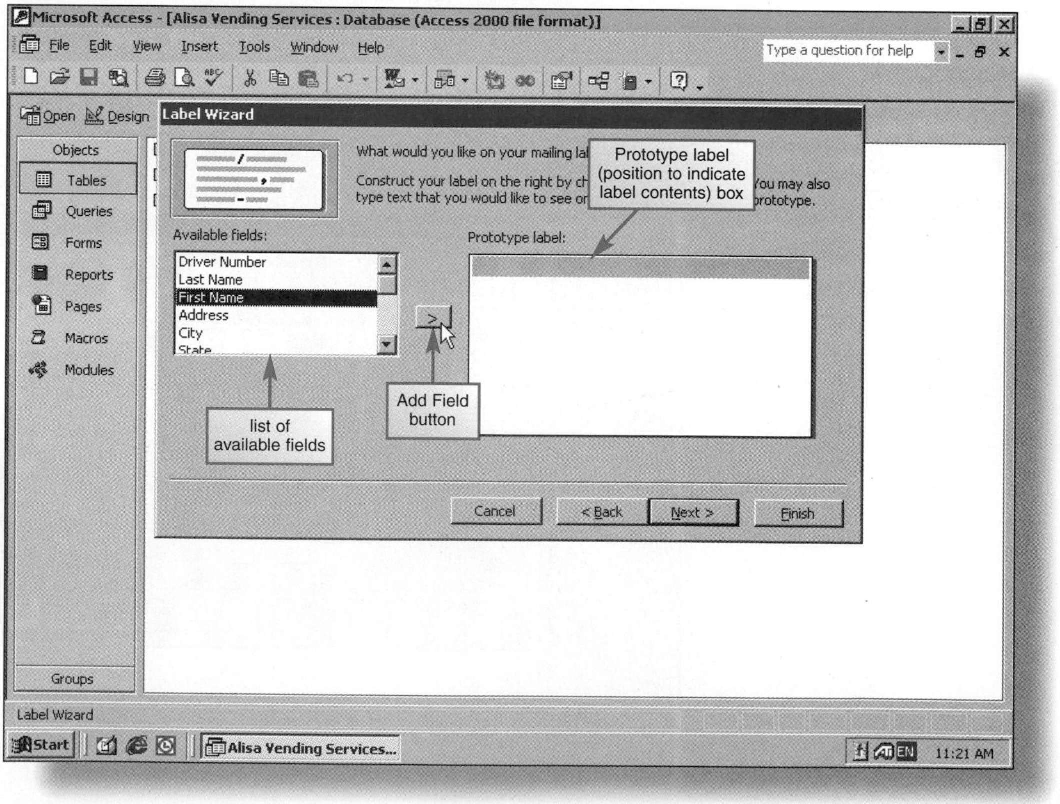

FIGURE 7-71

5 **Click the Add Field button, press the SPACEBAR, select the Last Name field, and then click the Add Field button. Click the second line in the label, and then add the Address field. Click the third line of the Prototype label. Add the City field, type , (a comma), press the SPACEBAR, add the State field, press the SPACEBAR twice, and then add the Zip Code field. Point to the Next button.**

The contents of the label are complete (Figure 7-72).

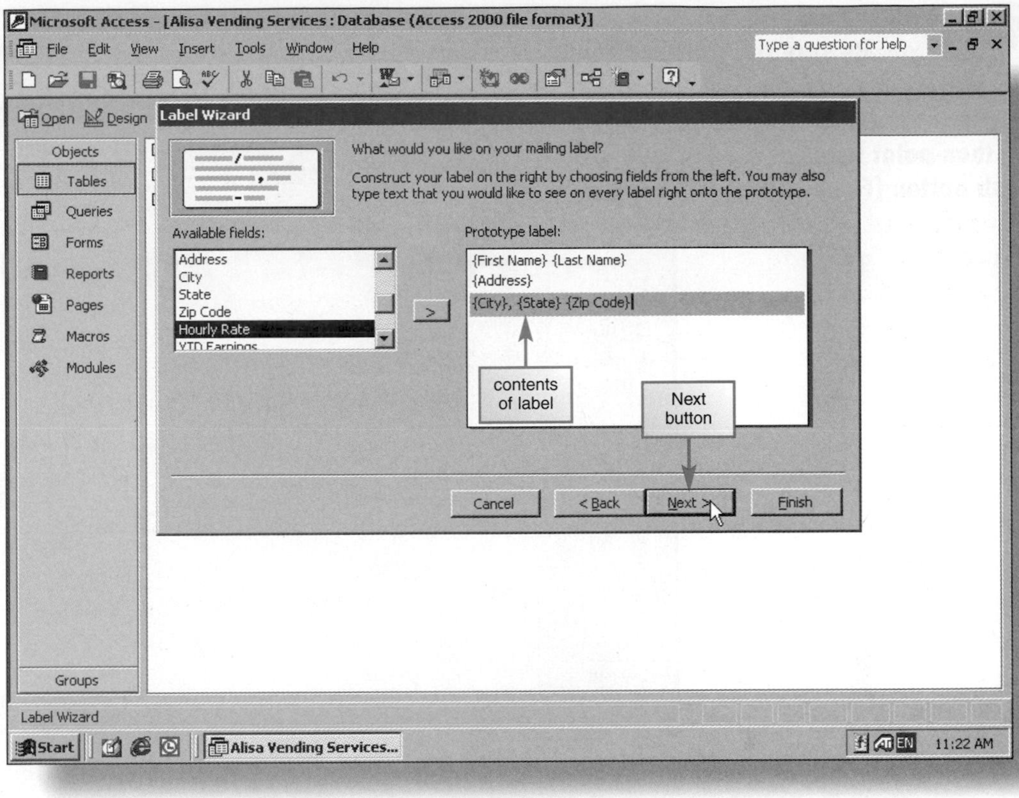

FIGURE 7-72

6 **Click the Next button. Select the Zip Code field as the field to sort by, and then click the Add Field button. Point to the Next button.**

The Zip Code field is selected as the field by which to sort (Figure 7-73).

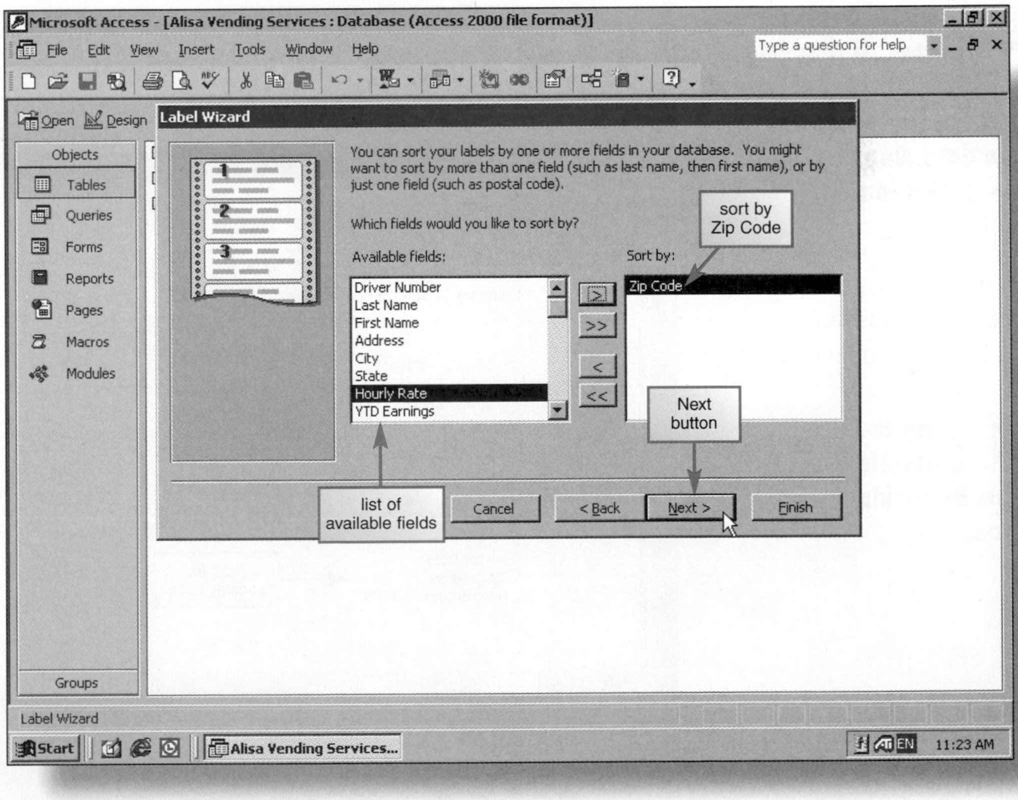

FIGURE 7-73

7 **Click the Next button. Be sure the name for the report (labels) is Labels Driver, and then point to the Finish button (Figure 7-74).**

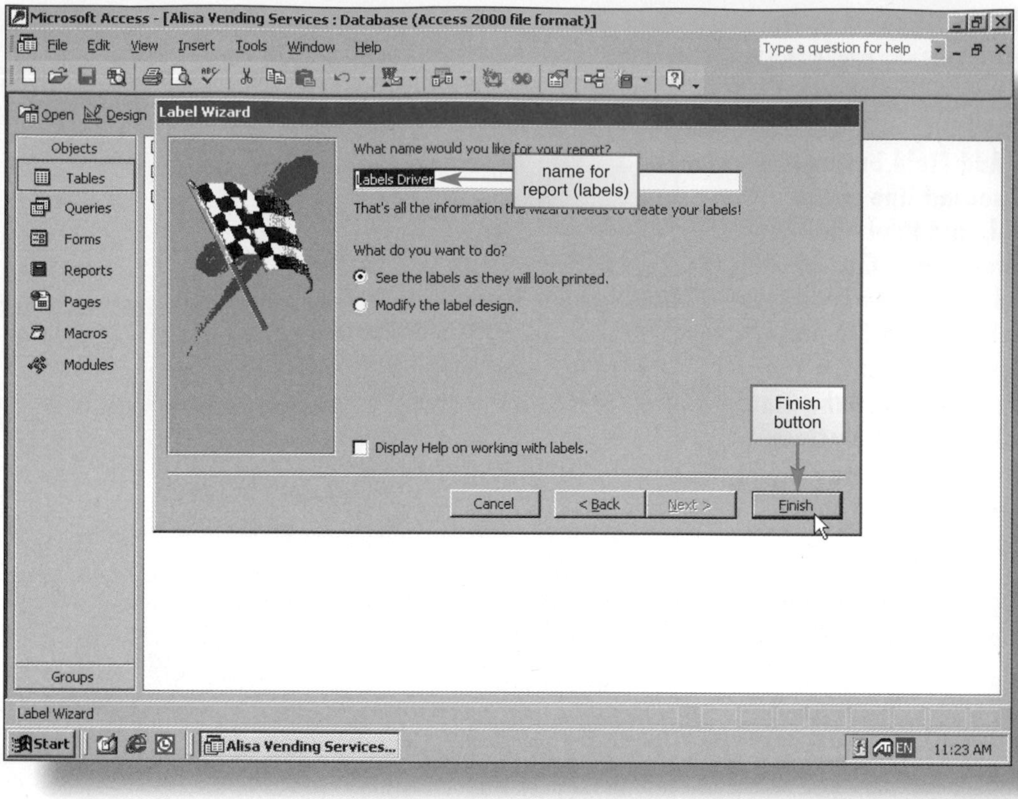

FIGURE 7-74

8 **Click the Finish button. If a Microsoft Access dialog box displays with the message, Some data may not display, click the OK button.**

The labels display (Figure 7-75). They are similar to the ones in Figure 7-1b on page A 7.05.

9 **Close the window containing the labels by clicking its Close button.**

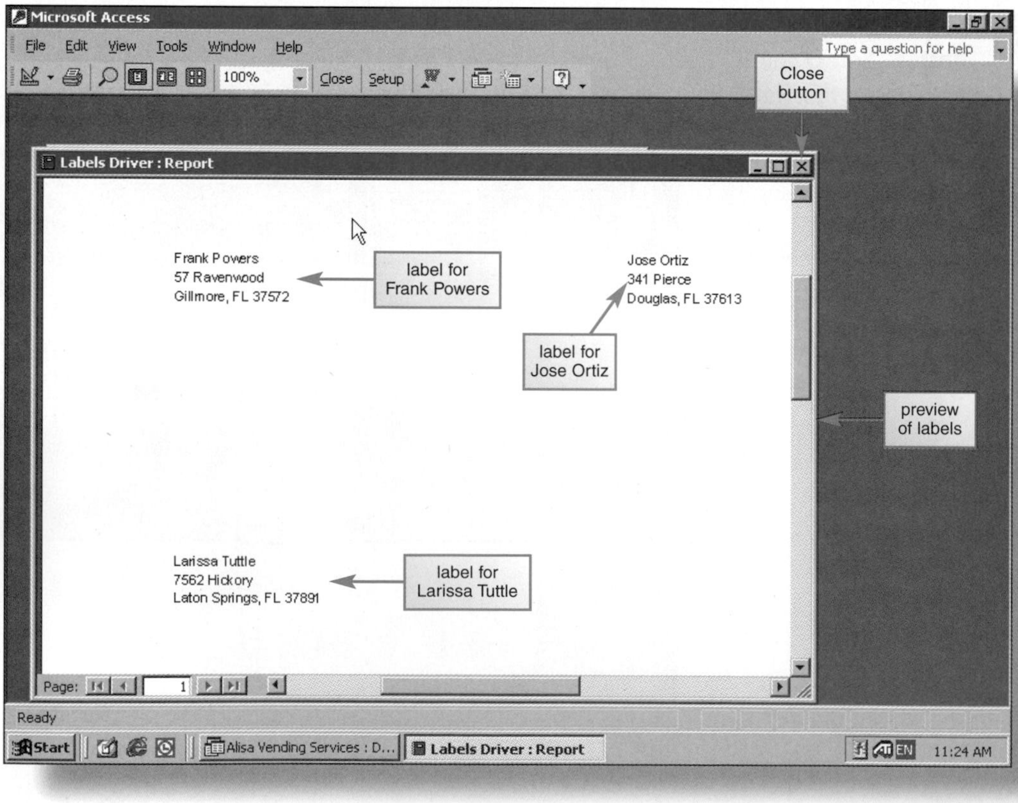

FIGURE 7-75

Printing the Labels

To print the labels, right-click the label report in the Database window, and then click Print on the shortcut menu. Perform the following steps to print the labels just created.

More About

Printing Labels

If you are printing labels on a dot-matrix or tractor-feed printer, you may have to make some changes to the page size in order to have the labels print correctly. To do so, click the Start button on the Windows desktop, click Settings, and then click Printers. Right-click your printer, click Properties, click the Paper tab, and then click the Custom icon. You then can make whatever changes might be necessary.

TO PRINT LABELS

1. If necessary, in the Database window, click the Reports object. Right-click Labels Driver.
2. Click Print on the shortcut menu. If a warning message displays, click the OK button.

The labels print.

Closing the Database

The following step closes the database by closing its Database window.

TO CLOSE A DATABASE

1. Click the Close button for the Alisa Vending Services : Database window.

CASE PERSPECTIVE SUMMARY

In Project 7, you assisted the management of Alisa Vending Services by helping them add the Category and Open Workorders tables to their databases. You created a parameter query for them so they could examine easily the open work orders for any customers in which they were interested. You created a detailed report that lists all drivers, customers, and open work orders. Finally, you created mailing labels for the drivers at Alisa.

Project Summary

In Project 7, you added two new tables to the Alisa Vending Services database. You then related these new tables to the existing tables. You created a query in which you changed the join properties as well as some field properties. You filtered the query's recordset two different ways. You transformed the query to a parameter query. You also created queries to be used by the report. You then created the report from scratch, using Design view instead of the Report Wizard. In the report, you used grouping and sorting, and also included a subreport. Finally, you created mailing labels for the Driver table.

More About

Quick Reference

For a table that lists how to complete tasks covered in this book using the mouse, menu, shortcut menu, and keyboard, see the Quick Reference Summary at the back of this book, or visit the Shelly Cashman Series Office XP Web page (scsite.com/offxp/qr.htm) and then click Microsoft Access 2002.

What You Should Know

Having completed this project, you now should be able to perform the following tasks:

- Add a Date *(A 7.39)*
- Add a Page Number *(A 7.40)*
- Add a Subreport *(A 7.30)*
- Add a Title *(A 7.42)*
- Add the Fields *(A 7.27)*
- Bold Controls *(A 7.41)*
- Change Field Properties *(A 7.15)*
- Change Join Properties *(A 7.14)*
- Change the Layout *(A 7.11)*
- Change the Margins *(A 7.45)*
- Close a Database *(A 7.51)*
- Create a Parameter Query *(A 7.21)*
- Create a Query *(A 7.13)*
- Create Labels *(A 7.47)*
- Create Queries for Reports *(A 7.23)*
- Create the New Tables *(A 7.09)*
- Filter a Query's Recordset *(A 7.17)*
- Group and Sort in a Report *(A 7.24)*
- Import the Data *(A 7.10)*
- Modify the Subreport *(A 7.34)*
- Move the Subreport *(A 7.38)*
- Open a Database *(A 7.08)*
- Print a Report *(A 7.46)*
- Print Labels *(A 7.51)*
- Relate Several Tables *(A 7.12)*
- Run a Parameter Query *(A 7.22)*
- Run the Query and Change the Layout *(A 7.17)*
- Save the Report *(A 7.29)*
- Use Filter By Form *(A 7.19)*

Learn It Online

Instructions: To complete the Learn It Online exercises, start your browser, click the Address bar, and then enter `scsite.com/offxp/exs.htm`. When the Office XP Learn It Online page displays, follow the instructions in the exercises below.

1 Project Reinforcement TF, MC, and SA

Below Access Project 7, click the Project Reinforcement link. Print the quiz by clicking Print on the File menu. Answer each question. Write your first and last name at the top of each page, and then hand in the printout to your instructor.

2 Flash Cards

Below Access Project 7, click the Flash Cards link. When Flash Cards displays, read the instructions. Type `20` (or a number specified by your instructor) in the Number of Playing Cards text box, type your name in the Name text box, and then click the Flip Card button. When the flash card displays, read the question and then click the Answer box arrow to select an answer. Flip through Flash Cards. Click Print on the File menu to print the last flash card if your score is 15 (75%) correct or greater and then hand it in to your instructor. If your score is less than 15 (75%) correct, then redo this exercise by clicking the Replay button.

3 Practice Test

Below Access Project 7, click the Practice Test link. Answer each question, enter your first and last name at the bottom of the page, and then click the Grade Test button. When the graded practice test displays on your screen, click Print on the File menu to print a hard copy. Continue to take practice tests until you score 80% or better. Hand in a printout of the final practice test to your instructor.

4 Who Wants to Be a Computer Genius?

Below Access Project 7, click the Computer Genius link. Read the instructions, enter your first and last name at the bottom of the page, and then click the Play button. Hand in your score to your instructor.

5 Wheel of Terms

Below Access Project 7, click the Wheel of Terms link. Read the instructions, and then enter your first and last name and your school name. Click the Play button. Hand in your score to your instructor.

6 Crossword Puzzle Challenge

Below Access Project 7, click the Crossword Puzzle Challenge link. Read the instructions, and then enter your first and last name. Click the Play button. Work the crossword puzzle. When you are finished, click the Submit button. When the crossword puzzle redisplays, click the Print button. Hand in the printout.

7 Tips and Tricks

Below Access Project 7, click the Tips and Tricks link. Click a topic that pertains to Project 7. Right-click the information and then click Print on the shortcut menu. Construct a brief example of what the information relates to in Access to confirm you understand how to use the tip or trick. Hand in the example and printed information.

online

8 Newsgroups

Below Access Project 7, click the Newsgroups link. Click a topic that pertains to Project 7. Print three comments. Hand in the comments to your instructor.

9 Expanding Your Horizons

Below Access Project 7, click the Articles for Microsoft Access link. Click a topic that pertains to Project 7. Print the information. Construct a brief example of what the information relates to in Access to confirm you understand the contents of the article. Hand in the example and printed information to your instructor.

10 Search Sleuth

Below Access Project 7, click the Search Sleuth link. To search for a term that pertains to this project, select a term below the Project 7 title and then use the Google search engine at google.com (or any major search engine) to display and print two Web pages that present information on the term. Hand in the printouts to your instructor.

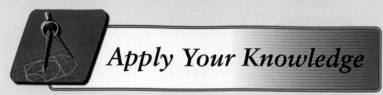

Apply Your Knowledge

1 Adding Tables to and Creating Queries for the Beyond Clean Database

Instructions: For this assignment, you will use two files: Beyond Clean.mdb, and Cleaning Accounts.xls. If you are using the Microsoft Access 2002 Comprehensive text, use the Beyond Clean database that you used in Project 6. Otherwise, see the inside back cover for instructions for downloading the Data Disk or see your instructor for information about accessing the files required for this book. Cleaning Accounts.xls is an Excel workbook that is on the Data Disk. Be sure that the database and the workbook are on the same disk before starting this assignment. If you do not know how to do this, see your instructor for assistance.

You will create two new tables for the Beyond Clean database. The Fee table contains information on the fee that each client pays for cleaning. The structure and data for the Fee table are shown in Figure 7-76. There is a one-to-one relationship between the Client table and the Fee table. The Service table contains information on when the cleaning was performed during the current week. Some clients use Beyond Clean on a daily basis while others use the company less frequently. For each record to be unique, the primary key for the Service table must be the combination of client number and service date. There is a one-to-many relationship between the Client table and the Service table. The structure and data for the Service table are shown in Figure 7-77. Perform the following tasks.

1. Start Access. Open the Beyond Clean database and create the Fee table using the structure shown in Figure 7-76. Use Fee as the name for the table.
2. Import the Fees worksheet to the database. The worksheet is in the Cleaning Accounts workbook and it should be on the same disk as the Beyond Clean database. When the Import Spreadsheet Wizard dialog box displays, be sure the Fees worksheet is selected. Be sure to select the First Row Contains Column Headings check box. Open the table in Datasheet view and resize the columns to best fit the data. Save the changes to the layout of the table.
3. Print the Fee table.

Structure of Fee table

FIELD NAME	*DATA TYPE*	*FIELD SIZE*	*PRIMARY KEY?*	*DESCRIPTION*
Client Number	Text	4	Yes	Client Number (Primary Key)
Fee	Currency			Fee Charged for Cleaning

Data for Fee table

CLIENT NUMBER	*FEE*
AD23	$30.00
AR76	$35.00
CR67	$50.00
DL61	$30.00
GR36	$55.00
HA09	$30.00
ME17	$40.00
R045	$50.00
ST21	$45.00

FIGURE 7-76

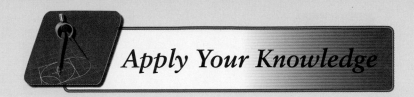

Apply Your Knowledge

4. Create the Service table using the structure shown in Figure 7-77. The primary key is the combination of Client Number and Service Date. Use Service as the name for the table.

Structure of Service table				
FIELD NAME	*DATA TYPE*	*FIELD SIZE*	*PRIMARY KEY?*	*DESCRIPTION*
Client Number	Text	4	Yes	Client Number (Portion of Primary Key)
Service Date	Date/Time (Change the Format property to Short Date)		Yes	Date that Cleaning was Performed (Portion of Primary Key)

Data for Service table	
CLIENT NUMBER	*SERVICE DATE*
AD23	8/25/2003
AR76	8/26/2003
CR67	8/29/2003
GR36	8/28/2003
HA09	8/25/2003
HA09	8/26/2003
HA09	8/28/2003
ME17	8/28/2003
ME17	8/29/2003
RO45	8/26/2003
ST21	8/27/2003

FIGURE 7-77

5. Import the Services worksheet to the database. The worksheet is in the Cleaning Accounts workbook and it should be on the same disk as the Beyond Clean database. When the Import Spreadsheet Wizard dialog box displays, be sure the Services worksheet is selected. Be sure to select the First Row Contains Column Headings check box. Open the table in Datasheet view and resize the columns to best fit the data. Save the changes to the layout of the table.
6. Print the Service table.
7. Click the Relationships button in the Database window, and add the Fee and Service tables to the Relationships window. Create a one-to-one relationship between the Client table and the Fee table. Create a one-to-many relationship between the Client table and the Service table. Create a one-to-many relationship between the Fee table and the Service table. Print the Relationships window by making sure the Relationships window is open, clicking File on the menu bar, and then clicking Print Relationships.
8. Create a query that joins the Client and Service table. All records in the Client table should display regardless of whether there is a matching record in the Service table. Display the Client Number, Name, and Service Date in the query results. Change the caption for Service Date to Cleaning Date.
9. Run the query and print the results.
10. Filter the recordset to find only those clients who had cleaning performed on August 28, 2003.
11. Print the results.
12. Create a parameter query that joins the Client table and the Fee table to enter a beginning client number and an ending client number. The query should display the client number, name, address, telephone number, and fee. Change the caption for the Fee field to Cleaning Fee. Run the query to find the records for clients with client numbers between AR76 and GR36.
13. Print the results.

In the Lab

1 Creating Queries, a Report, and Mailing Labels for the Wooden Crafts Database

Problem: Jan Merchant would like to track craft products that are being reordered from suppliers. She must know when a product was ordered and how many were ordered. She may place an order with a supplier one day and then find that she needs to order more of the same product before the original order is filled. She also would like to be able to query the database to find out whether a product is on order. Finally, she would like a report that displays supplier information as well as information about the craft product and its order status.

Instructions: If you are using the Microsoft Access 2002 Comprehensive text, use the Wooden Crafts database that you used in Project 6. Otherwise, see the inside back cover for instructions for downloading the Data Disk or see your instructor for information about accessing the files required for this book. Perform the following tasks.

1. Create a table in which to store the reorder information using the structure shown in Figure 7-78. Use Reorder as the name for the table.
2. Add the data shown in Figure 7-78 to the Reorder table.
3. Print the table.
4. Add the Reorder table to the Relationships window and establish a one-to-many relationship between the Product table and the Reorder table. Print the Relationships window by making sure the Relationships window is open, clicking File on the menu bar, and then clicking Print Relationships.
5. Create a query that joins the Product, Reorder, and Supplier tables. The query should display all products in the Product table whether or not they are on reorder. Display the Product Id, Description, Date Ordered, Number Ordered, Cost, First Name, and Last Name. Change the caption for Number Ordered to On Order. Run the query and print the results.
6. Use Filter By Selection to display only those records where the supplier is Antonio Patino. Print the results.

Structure of Reorder table

FIELD NAME	DATA TYPE	FIELD SIZE	PRIMARY KEY?	DESCRIPTION
Product Id	Text	4	Yes	Product Id (Portion of Primary Key)
Date Ordered	Date/Time (Change the Format property to Short Date)		Yes	Date Product Ordered (Portion of Primary Key)
Number Ordered	Number			Number of Products Ordered

Data for Reorder table

PRODUCT ID	DATE ORDERED	NUMBER ORDERED
AD01	9/05/2003	15
BF01	8/10/2003	5
BF01	9/02/2003	10
BL23	8/12/2003	2
BL23	9/04/2003	2
FT05	8/24/2003	4
LB34	8/28/2003	5
MR06	9/05/2003	4

FIGURE 7-78

7. Create a parameter query that joins the Product and Reorder tables. The user should be able to enter a beginning and ending product id. Display the Product Id, Description, Date Ordered, and Number Ordered. Change the caption for Date Ordered to Order Date and the caption for Numbered Ordered to On Order. Run the query to find all records where the product id is between FT05 and MR06. Print the results.

In the Lab

8. Run the query again to find all records where item number is BL23. Print the results.
9. Create the report shown in Figure 7-79. The report uses the Suppliers and Products query that was created in Project 2 as the basis for the main report and the Reorder table as the basis for the subreport. Be sure to include the current date and page numbers on the report. Use the name Supplier Master Report for the report. The report is in the same style as that demonstrated in the project.
10. Print the report.
11. Create mailing labels for the Supplier table. Use Avery labels 5095 and format the label with first name and last name separated by a space on the first line, address on the second line, and city, state, and zip code on the third line. There is a comma and a space after the city and 2 spaces between the state and the zip code.
12. Print the mailing labels.

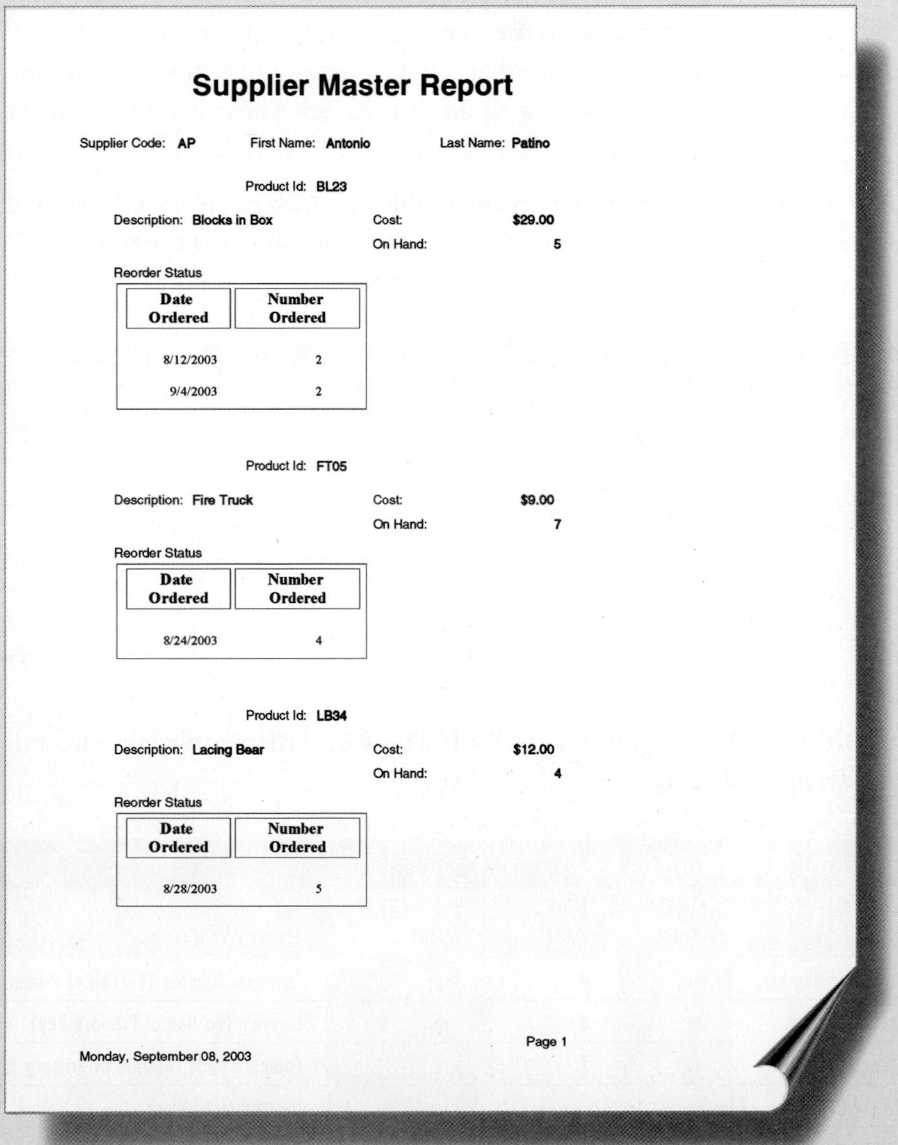

Supplier Master Report

Supplier Code: **AP** First Name: **Antonio** Last Name: **Patino**

Product Id: **BL23**

Description: **Blocks in Box** Cost: **$29.00**
On Hand: **5**

Reorder Status

Date Ordered	Number Ordered
8/12/2003	2
9/4/2003	2

Product Id: **FT05**

Description: **Fire Truck** Cost: **$9.00**
On Hand: **7**

Reorder Status

Date Ordered	Number Ordered
8/24/2003	4

Product Id: **LB34**

Description: **Lacing Bear** Cost: **$12.00**
On Hand: **4**

Reorder Status

Date Ordered	Number Ordered
8/28/2003	5

Monday, September 08, 2003 Page 1

FIGURE 7-79

In the Lab

2 Creating Queries, a Report, and Mailing Labels for the Restaurant Supply Database

Problem: Because the restaurant supply company sells paper and soap products, they also provide and install the dispensers in which to store paper towels, liquid soap, toilet paper, cups, and so on. When a dispenser malfunctions or breaks, it is the company's responsibility to repair or replace the item. The company wants to maintain data on those restaurants that require dispenser service. The company also wants to query the database to find which restaurants require service. Finally, they want a report that lists the sales rep, the restaurants that the sales rep handles, and a list of any dispenser repairs.

Instructions: For this assignment, you will use two files: Restaurant Supply.mdb, and Active Work Requests.txt. If you are using the Microsoft Access 2002 Comprehensive text, use the Restaurant Supply database that you used in Project 6. Otherwise, see the inside back cover for instructions for downloading the Data Disk or see your instructor for information about accessing the files required for this book. The Active Work Requests.txt file is a text file that is on the Data Disk. Be sure that the database and the text file are on the same disk before starting this assignment. If you do not know how to do this, see your instructor for assistance. Perform the following tasks.

1. Open the Restaurant Supply database and create a table in which to store the service category information using the structure shown in Figure 7-80. Use Category as the name for the table.
2. Add the data shown in Figure 7-80 to the Category table.

Structure of Category table

FIELD NAME	*DATA TYPE*	*FIELD SIZE*	*PRIMARY KEY?*	*DESCRIPTION*
Category Code	Text	1	Yes	Category Code (Primary Key)
Category Description	Text	50		Description of Service Category

Data for Category table

CATEGORY CODE	*CATEGORY DESCRIPTION*
1	Installation
2	Replacement
3	Repair

FIGURE 7-80

3. Print the table.
4. Create the Workorders table shown in Figure 7-81. The Workorders table contains information on the type of work the restaurant needs done.

Structure of Workorders table

FIELD NAME	*DATA TYPE*	*FIELD SIZE*	*PRIMARY KEY?*	*DESCRIPTION*
Customer Number	Text	4	Yes	Customer Number (Portion of Primary Key)
Location	Text	3	Yes	Location (Portion of Primary Key)
Category Code	Text	1	Yes	Category Code (Portion of Primary Key)
Description	Memo			Description of Work

FIGURE 7-81

In the Lab

5. Import the Active Work Requests text file into the Workorders table. Be sure to check the First Row Contains Column Headings box. The data is in delimited format with each field separated by tabs.
6. Open the Relationships window and establish a one-to-many relationship between the Category table and the Workorders table and between the Customer table and the Workorders table. Print the Relationships window by making sure the Relationships window is open, clicking File on the menu bar, and then clicking Print Relationships.
7. Open the Workorders table in Datasheet view and resize the columns to best fit the data. Save the changes to the layout of the table.
8. Print the table.
9. Create a query that joins the Customer and the Workorders table. All Customers should display whether or not they have active accounts. Display the Customer Number, Name, Address, Location, and Description.
10. Run the query and print the results.
11. Filter the query results to find all records where the location is KIT.
12. Print the results.
13. Remove the filter and return to Design View. Add the Category Code field to the query and create a parameter query to enter a category code.
14. Run the query to find all records where the category code is 2. Print the results.
15. Create the report shown in Figure 7-82. The report is grouped by Sales Rep Number and includes a subreport. It is in the same style as that demonstrated in the project. Note that the label for first name has been changed and that there is no label for the last name. Be sure to include the current date and page numbers on the report. Use Sales Rep Master Report as the name for the report. (***Hint:*** Create queries for both the main report and the subreport.)

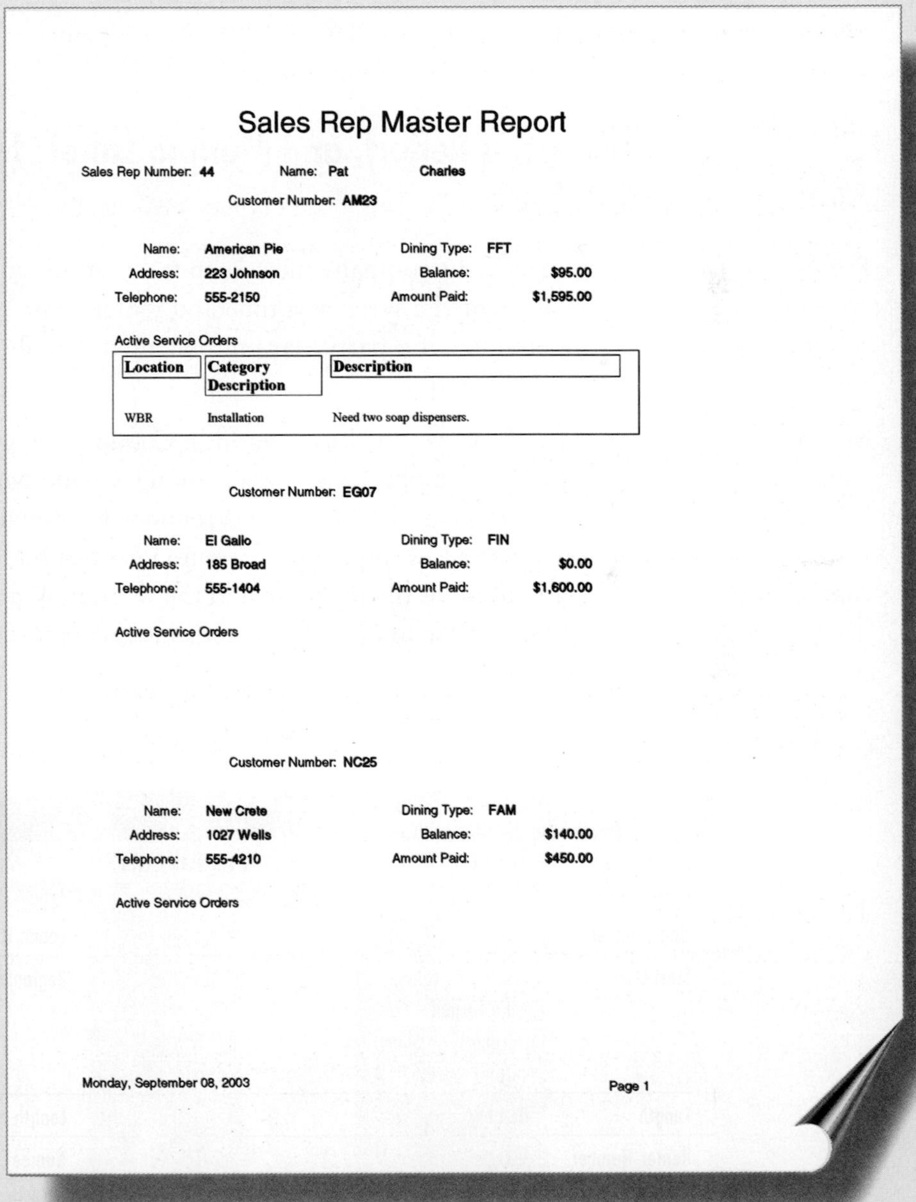

Sales Rep Master Report

Sales Rep Number: 44 Name: Pat Charles

Customer Number: AM23

Name: American Pie Dining Type: FFT
Address: 223 Johnson Balance: $95.00
Telephone: 555-2150 Amount Paid: $1,595.00

Active Service Orders

Location	Category Description	Description
WBR	Installation	Need two soap dispensers.

Customer Number: EG07

Name: El Gallo Dining Type: FIN
Address: 185 Broad Balance: $0.00
Telephone: 555-1404 Amount Paid: $1,600.00

Active Service Orders

Customer Number: NC25

Name: New Crete Dining Type: FAM
Address: 1027 Wells Balance: $140.00
Telephone: 555-4210 Amount Paid: $450.00

Active Service Orders

Monday, September 08, 2003 Page 1

FIGURE 7-82

continued

In the Lab

Creating Queries, a Report, and Mailing Labels for the Restaurant Supply Database, *continued*

16. Print the report.
17. Create mailing labels for the Sales Rep table. Use Avery labels 5095 and format the label with first name and last name on the first line, address on the second line, and city, state, and zip code on the third line. There is a comma and a space after the city and two spaces between the state and the zip code.
18. Print the mailing labels.

3 Creating Queries, a Report, and Mailing Labels for the Condo Management Database

Problem: The condo management company must keep track of the units that are rented and the individuals who rent the units. Units are rented a week at a time and rentals start on Saturday. They also need to be able to query the database to determine if a particular unit is rented. Finally, they need to prepare reports for the owners that display rental information.

Instructions: For this assignment, you will use two files: Condo Management.mdb and Rentals.xls. If you are using the Microsoft Access 2002 Comprehensive text, use the Condo Management database that you used in Project 6. Otherwise, see the inside back cover for instructions for downloading the Data Disk or see your instructor for information about accessing the files required for this book. Rentals.xls is an Excel workbook that is on the Data Disk. Be sure that the database and the workbook are on the same disk before starting this assignment. If you do not know how to do this, see your instructor for assistance. Perform the following tasks.

1. Create the Current Rentals table using the structure shown in Figure 7-83. Use the name Current Rentals for the table.

Structure of Current Rentals table

FIELD NAME	DATA TYPE	FIELD SIZE	PRIMARY KEY?	DESCRIPTION
Unit Number	Text	3	Yes	Condo Unit Number (Portion of Primary Key)
Start Date	Date/Time (Change the Format property to Short Date)		Yes	Beginning Date of Rental (Portion of Primary Key
Length	Number			Length of Time in Weeks of Rental
Renter Number	Text	4		Number of Renter

FIGURE 7-83

2. Import the Rentals workbook into the Current Rentals table. The workbook is on the Data Disk. In the Import Spreadsheet Wizard dialog box, click the Show Named Ranges options and select the Rentals range. Be sure to select the First Row Contains Column Headings check box.

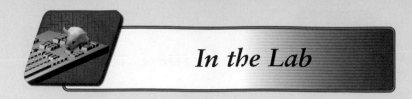

In the Lab

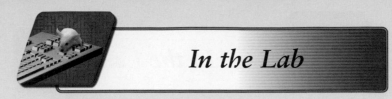

3. Create the Renter table using the structure shown in Figure 7-84. Use Renter as the name for the table.

Structure of Renter table				
FIELD NAME	*DATA TYPE*	*FIELD SIZE*	*PRIMARY KEY?*	*DESCRIPTION*
Renter Number	Text	4	Yes	Renter Number (Primary Key)
First Name	Text	10		First Name of Renter
Last Name	Text	15		Last Name of Renter
Telephone Number	Text	12		Telephone Number (999-999-9999 version)

FIGURE 7-84

4. Import the Rentals workbook into the Renter table. The workbook is on the Data Disk. In the Import Spreadsheet Wizard dialog box, click the Show Named Ranges option button and select the Renters range. Be sure to select the First Row Contains Column Headings check box.
5. Open the Relationships window and establish a one-to-many relationship between the Renter table and the Current Rentals table. Establish a one-to-many relationship between the Condo table and the Current Rentals table. Print the Relationships window by making sure the Relationships window is open, clicking File on the menu bar, and then clicking Print Relationships.
6. Open the Current Rentals table in Datasheet view, resize the columns to best fit the data, save the changes, and print the table.
7. Open the Renter table in Datasheet view, resize the columns to best fit the data, save the changes, and print the table.
8. Create a join query for the Condo and Current Rentals tables. All condo units should display in the result regardless of whether the unit is rented. Display the Unit Number, Weekly Rate, Start Date, and Length. Change the caption for the Length field to Weeks Rented. Run the query, resize the columns to best fit the data, and print the results.
9. Filter the query results to find all units that rent for $1,100 per week and have a start date of 12/6/2003. Print the results.
10. Create a parameter query to enter a beginning start date and an ending start date. The query should display the Unit Number, Start Date, Length, and the first and last name of the renter. Change the caption for the Length field to Weeks Rented. Run the query to find all records where the start date is between 11/22/2003 and 11/29/2003. Print the results.
11. Run the query again to find all records where the start date is 12/20/2003. Print the results.
12. Create the report shown in Figure 7-85 on the next page. The report includes a subreport. Group the report by owner id.
13. Print the report.
14. Create mailing labels for the Owner table. Use Avery labels 5095 and format the label with first and last name on the first line, address on the second line, and city, state, and zip code on the third line. There is a comma and a space after the city and two spaces between the state and the zip code.
15. Print the mailing labels.

In the Lab

Creating Queries, a Report, and Mailing Labels for the Condo Management Database, *continued*

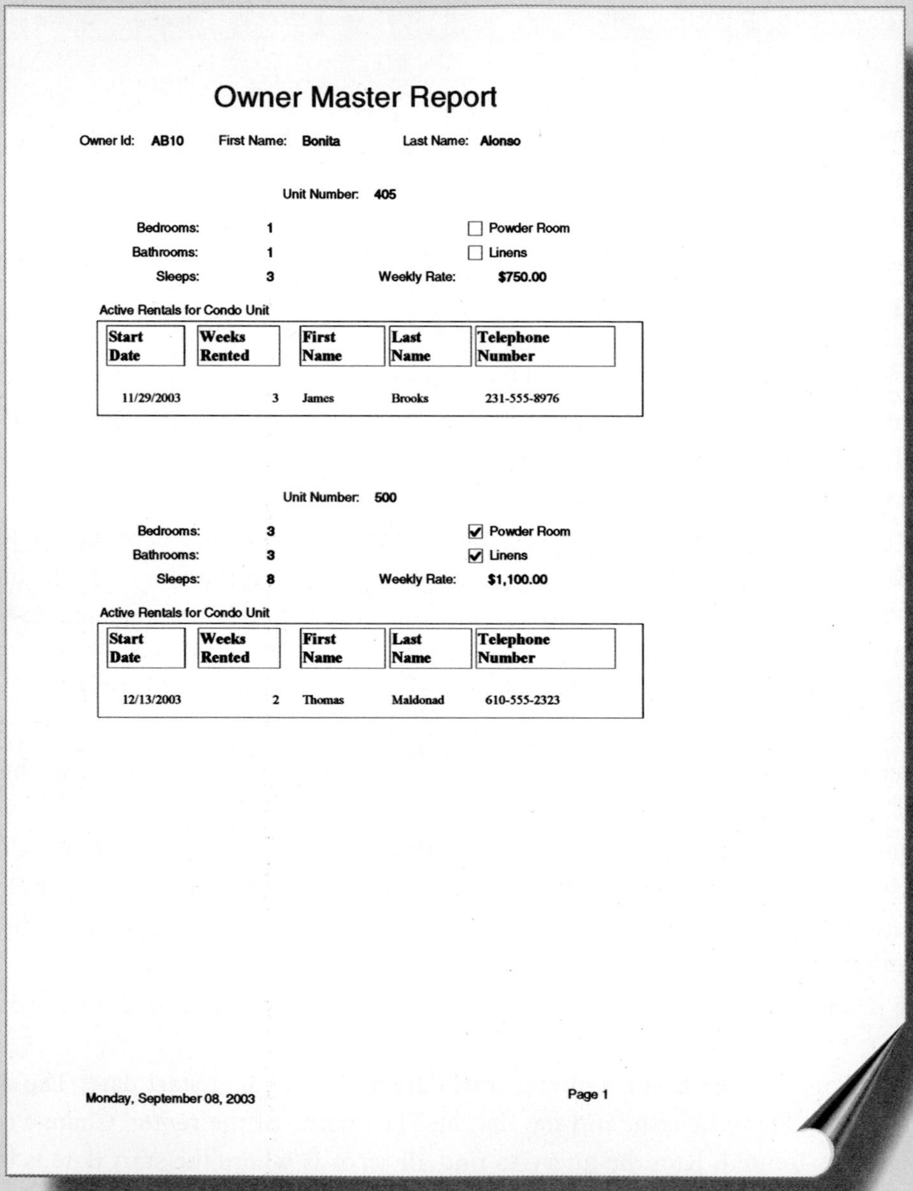

Owner Master Report

Owner Id: **AB10**   First Name: **Bonita**   Last Name: **Alonso**

Unit Number: **405**

Bedrooms:	1	☐	Powder Room
Bathrooms:	1	☐	Linens
Sleeps:	3	Weekly Rate:	$750.00

Active Rentals for Condo Unit

Start Date	Weeks Rented	First Name	Last Name	Telephone Number
11/29/2003	3	James	Brooks	231-555-8976

Unit Number: **500**

Bedrooms:	3	☑	Powder Room
Bathrooms:	3	☑	Linens
Sleeps:	8	Weekly Rate:	$1,100.00

Active Rentals for Condo Unit

Start Date	Weeks Rented	First Name	Last Name	Telephone Number
12/13/2003	2	Thomas	Maldonad	610-555-2323

Monday, September 08, 2003   Page 1

FIGURE 7-85

Cases and Places

The difficulty of these case studies varies:
◗ are the least difficult; ◗◗ are more difficult; and ◗◗◗ are the most difficult.

1 ◗ For this assignment, you will use two files: CompuWhiz.mdb and Computer Workorders.xls. If you are using the Microsoft Access 2002 Comprehensive text, use the CompuWhiz database that you used in Project 6. Otherwise, see the inside back cover for instructions for downloading the Data Disk or see your instructor for information about accessing the files required for this book. Computer Workorders.xls is an Excel workbook that is on the Data Disk. Be sure that the database and the workbook are on the same disk before starting this assignment. If you do not know how to do this, see your instructor for assistance. CompuWhiz has determined that they need to expand their database. They need to include information on open service requests, that is, uncompleted requests for service. Create two tables in which to store the open service request information. The structure of these two tables is identical to the Category and Open Workorders tables (see Figure 7-2a and Figure 7-3a on page A 7.06). The data for the tables is in the Computer Workorders workbook. Update the CompuWhiz database to include these tables and establish the relationships between the tables. Use Category and Open Workorders as the table names. Print the tables. When you enter the table structure data, be sure to change Customer Number in the Open Workorders table to Client Number. Create a join query for the Client and Open Workorders tables. All clients should display in the query result. Print the query results.

2 ◗ Use the CompuWhiz database and create a report that is similar in style to the report demonstrated in the project. The report groups the data by technician. Within technician, the data is sorted by client number. The report includes a subreport for the work orders information.

Cases and Places

3 ▶▶ If you are using the Microsoft Access 2002 Comprehensive text, use the Hockey Shop database that you used in Project 6. Otherwise, see the inside back cover for instructions for downloading the Data Disk or see your instructor for information about accessing the files required for this book. The Hockey Shop needs to add a table to the database that tracks the reorder status of items. The structure of the Reorder table and the data for the table are shown in Figure 7-86. There is a one-to-many relationship between the Item table and the Reorder table. You may need to change the layout of the table. Print the Reorder table. Create a query that joins the Item, Reorder, and Vendor tables. Display Item Id, Description, Date Ordered, Number Ordered, Cost, and Name. Include a calculated field, Reorder Cost, that is the result of multiplying Cost and Number Ordered.

Data for Reorder table

ITEM ID	*DATE ORDERED*	*NUMBER ORDERED*
3663	9/05/2003	15
4563	8/10/2003	5
4593	9/02/2003	10
4593	8/12/2003	5
6189	9/04/2003	6
6343	8/24/2003	4
7810	8/28/2003	5
7810	9/05/2003	4

Structure of Reorder table

FIELD NAME	*DATA TYPE*	*FIELD SIZE*	*PRIMARY KEY?*	*DESCRIPTION*
Item Id	Text	4	Yes	Item Id (Portion of Primary Key)
Date Ordered	Date/Time (Change the Format property to Short Date)		Yes	Date Item Ordered (Portion of Primary Key)
Number Ordered	Number			Number of Items Ordered

FIGURE 7-86

4 ▶▶ Create a report for the Hockey Shop database that is similar in style to the report created for Alisa Vending Services. The report should group data by vendor and display the vendor code and name in the group header. For each vendor, display information about each item sorted in item id order, and include a subreport for the reorder information. Add a picture or clip art to the Page Header for the report. To add a picture or clip art to a report, you use the Image tool in the toolbox. (See More About Adding Objects on page A 7.24.) You can use the clip art that comes with Microsoft Office or download clip art from the Web.

5 ▶▶▶ Use the copy and rename features of Windows to copy the Hockey Shop database and rename it as Hockey Pro Store database. The shop now buys some of the same items from more than one vendor. For example, baseball caps now can be purchased from Arnie Cheer or from Logo Great. Modify the design of the Ice Hockey database to allow for multiple vendors for an item.

Microsoft Access 2002

PROJECT

8

Using Visual Basic for Applications (VBA) and Advanced Form Techniques

OBJECTIVES

You will have mastered the material in this project when you can:

- Add buttons, controls, and combo boxes to forms
- Modify Access-generated VBA code
- Use VBA
- Create functions in a standard module
- Test functions
- Use the functions in a query
- Associate code with an event
- Create Sub procedures
- Create a function to run a command
- Create a form using Design view
- Add a tab control
- Add a subform control to a form
- Add a chart to a form
- Add an ActiveX control to a form

Shopping Made Simple

Online Grocers Offer Convenience and Savings

Ten years ago, you might have thought it strange to visit a Web site. Today, you probably use the Web every day to search for information, connect with friends and family, and shop for many popular purchases, such as books, software, music, clothing, and electronics. The reasons people turn to the Web to shop are numerous, but more than 75 percent of online consumers agree that convenience is the primary motivation. Many shoppers also enjoy the lack of sales pressure, the time saved, and the abundance of information about companies and their products available on the Web. No matter the reasons, online purchases have grown steadily over the last five years. In 2000 alone, online spending amounted to $354 billion. Analysts predict that upward trends will continue, with expectations that a billion people will generate online sales of more than $5 trillion annually by the year 2005.

Industry experts indicate that online grocery sales will take part in this booming market and should represent 15 percent of total grocery sales by the year 2005. For many individuals, shopping on the Web has simplified this mundane task. Consider that a trip to the grocery store requires 66 minutes on average. From hunting for a parking space to waiting in long check-out lines, the entire experience often is tiring and frustrating.

Since 1998, consumers in five metropolitan areas of the United States have been shopping at Peapod.com, an online grocer that offers convenient and customer-friendly service.

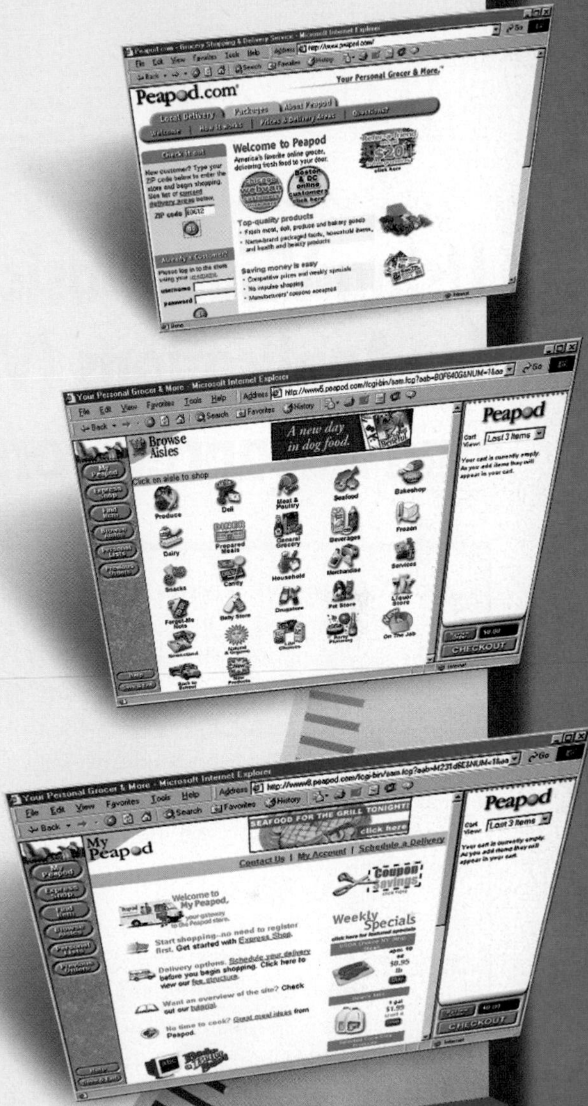

Entering data into Peapod Personal Grocer online forms, shoppers place their orders from work or home, day or night. Peapod offers convenient features such as Express Shop, which allows you to locate all the items in your grocery list at once. You also can review your most recently ordered items at any time, indicate whether or not Peapod can substitute items when necessary, and even specify that you want only green bananas!

Shoppers enter the store online, select, and then purchase items on their computers via forms and buttons. These forms and buttons are similar to the ones you will modify and create using advanced form techniques in this Access 2002 project. Forms are powerful database tools that allow Peapod users to place their orders, find items, create shopping lists, and then add the items to their shopping carts with a simple click of a button on the Web page.

Details such as the price and nutritional content of each item are kept in a database that is integrated with a billing system and a customer database. The products database is updated daily as prices change, new items are added to the stores' shelves, and unpopular items are removed. Produce prices change weekly.

A nutrition-conscious shopper can query the database to display a picture of the product, view its nutrition facts, and sort items by nutritional content. Selective shoppers instantly can compare prices in the database to find the best deals. Buyers can view items in their shopping carts, check subtotals any time to stay within a budget, redeem manufacturer and electronic coupons, and designate a delivery time.

Once an order is placed, Peapod can deliver groceries as soon as the next day. You can choose the delivery time so that groceries arrive while you are at home or, alternately, specify a safe location to leave items if you desire to have the groceries delivered while no one is at home. Peapod even can package your delivery so that frozen and chilled items remain perfectly cooled even when they are left unattended in a safe location. Customers report top-quality products, competitive pricing, and convenience as their main reasons for using the Peapod service. The primary customer base consists of two-income families with children, individuals with disabilities, and the elderly. These groups find that the convenience of being able to order at any time and place gives them flexibility in their busy lifestyles, independence, and less stress.

Peapod aims to become the leading provider of interactive grocery shopping services. With more than three million orders fulfilled, it is well on its way.

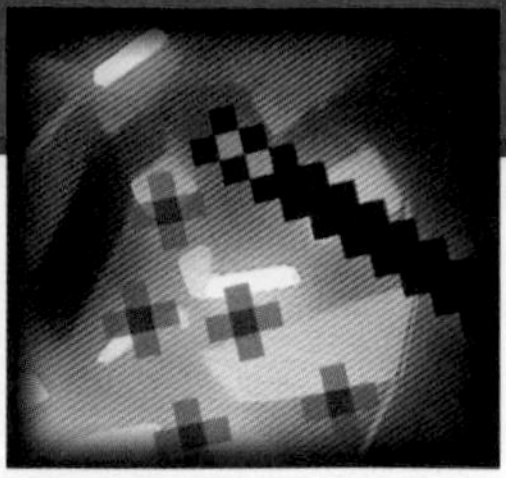

Microsoft Access 2002

Using Visual Basic for Applications (VBA) and Advanced Form Techniques

PROJECT 8

CASE PERSPECTIVE

Alisa Vending Services requires improvements to the Customer Update Form, including placing buttons on the form to allow moving to next and previous records, adding and deleting a record, and closing the form. They want users of the form to be able to search for a customer given the customer's name.

Periodically, they run promotions. Each customer receives a promotion factor based on customer type. The promotion amount is the result of multiplying the current due amount by the appropriate promotion factor. The form should display both the promotion amount and the promotion factor. Alisa must be able to hide this information whenever necessary. They require a query that shows the promotional amounts that can be run from the form.

Alisa Vending Services also needs a form that lists the number and name of drivers, with a subform listing open work orders for the driver, two charts that illustrate the hours spent by the driver in each service category, and a Web browser to display the company's home page. Your task is to modify the Customer Update Form and to create the new driver form.

Introduction

By including both command buttons and a combo box that allows users to search for customers by name, you will enhance the Customer Update Form created earlier (Figure 8-1a). When you add the command buttons and the combo box to the form, you will use appropriate Access wizards. The **wizards** create the button or the combo box to your specifications, place it on the form, and create an event procedure for the button or the combo box. An **event procedure** is a series of steps that Access will carry out when an event, such as the clicking of a command button, occurs. For example, when you click the Delete Record button, the steps in the event procedure created for the Delete Record button will execute. This procedure will cause the record to be deleted. Event procedures are written in a language called **Visual Basic for Applications**, or **VBA**. This language is a standard throughout Microsoft applications.

Generally, you do not even need to be aware that these event procedures exist. Access creates and uses them automatically. Occasionally, however, you may want to make changes to an event procedure. Without making changes, for example, clicking the Add Record button blanks out the fields on the form so you can enter a new record. Yet, it would not produce an insertion point in the Customer Number field. You would have to take special action, such as clicking the Customer Number field, before you could begin entering data. You can rectify this by making a change to the event procedure for the Add Record button.

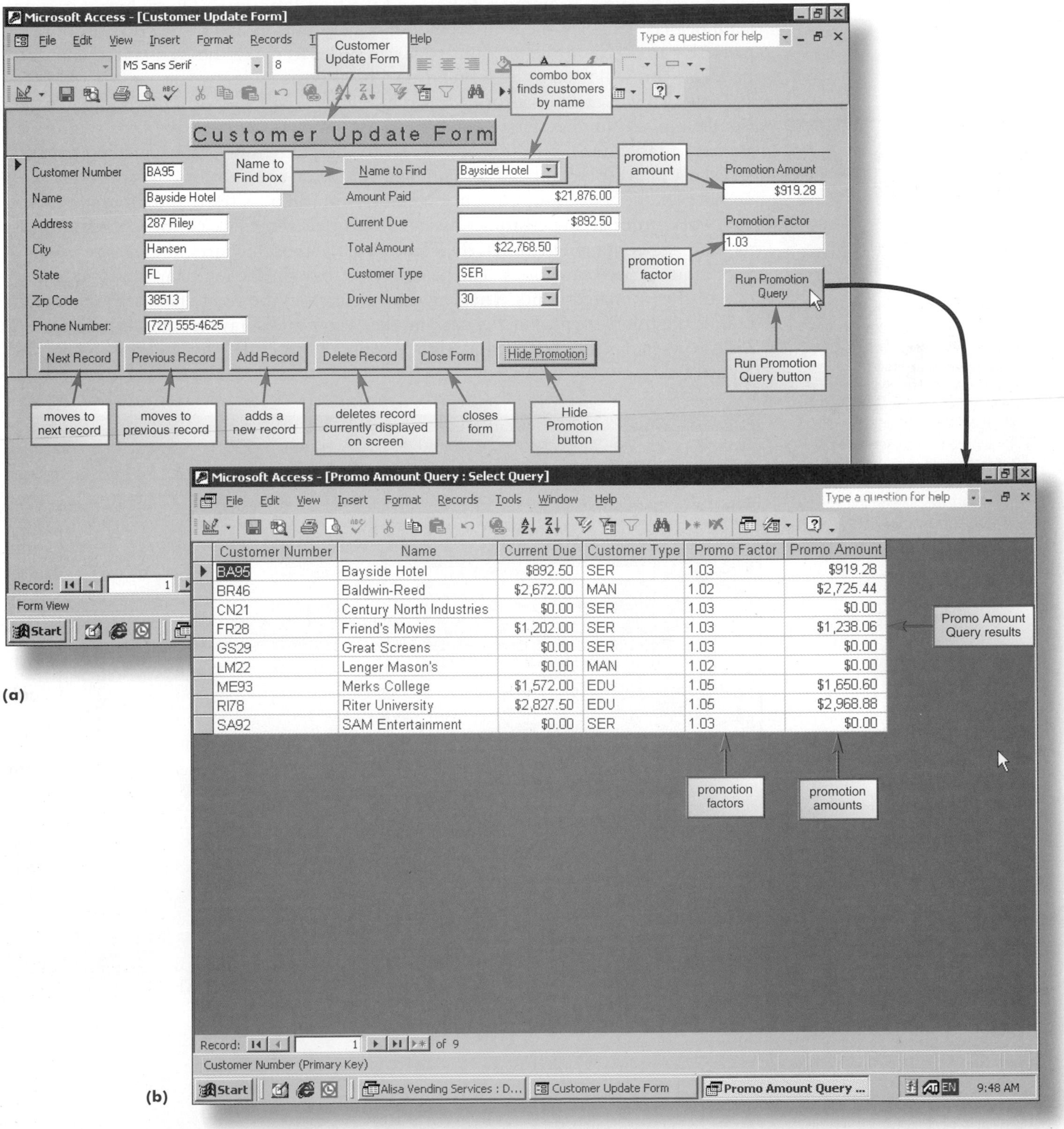
Microsoft Access - [Customer Update Form]
Customer Update Form
combo box finds customers by name
Customer Update Form
Name to Find box
promotion amount
promotion factor
Run Promotion Query button
moves to next record
moves to previous record
adds a new record
deletes record currently displayed on screen
closes form
Hide Promotion button
(a)
Microsoft Access - [Promo Amount Query : Select Query]
Promo Amount Query results
promotion factors
promotion amounts
(b)

FIGURE 8-1

Also on the form shown in Figure 8-1a on the previous page are the promotion amount, promotion factor, and two additional buttons. One is labeled Hide Promotion. Clicking this button will hide the promotion amount, the promotion factor, and the Run Promotion Query button. In addition, the caption on the button will change to Show Promotion. Clicking the Show Promotion button will cause the promotion amount, promotion factor, and the Run Promotion Query button to once again display. Clicking the Run Promotion Query button will display the promotion query (Figure 8-1b on the previous page). In order to make these enhancements to the form, you will need to learn to create Visual Basic code.

You also will create the form shown in Figure 8-2a. The form in Figure 8-2a lists the Driver Number, First Name, and Last Name fields from the Driver table. It contains a tab control allowing you access to three different pages. Clicking the Datasheet tab displays a page containing a subform. The subform lists the Customer Number, Name, Location, Category Number, Total Hours (est), and Hours Spent for each work order at any customer assigned to the driver. Clicking the Charts tab displays a page containing two charts (Figure 8-2b). In both charts, the bars represent the various service categories. The height of the bars in the left chart represents the total of the estimated hours. The height of the bars in the right chart represents the total of the hours spent. Finally, clicking the Web tab displays a page containing a Web browser. The home page for Alisa Vending Services displays in the browser (Figure 8-2c).

More About

The Access Help System

Need Help? It is no further than the Ask a Question box in the upper-right corner of the window. Click the box that contains the text, Type a question for help (Figure 8-2b), type `help`, and then press the ENTER key. Access will respond with a list of items you can click to learn about obtaining help on any Access-related topic. To find out what is new in Access 2002, type `what's new in Access` in the Ask a Question box.

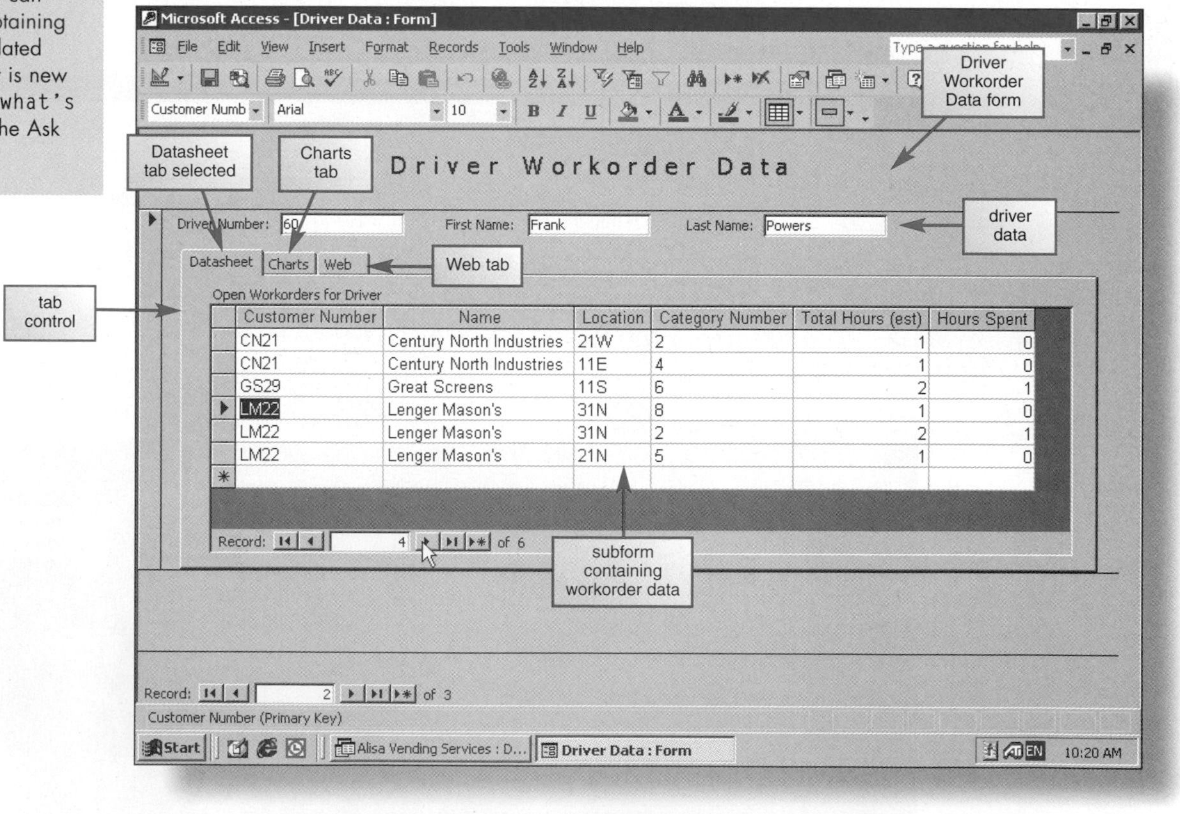

FIGURE 8-2a

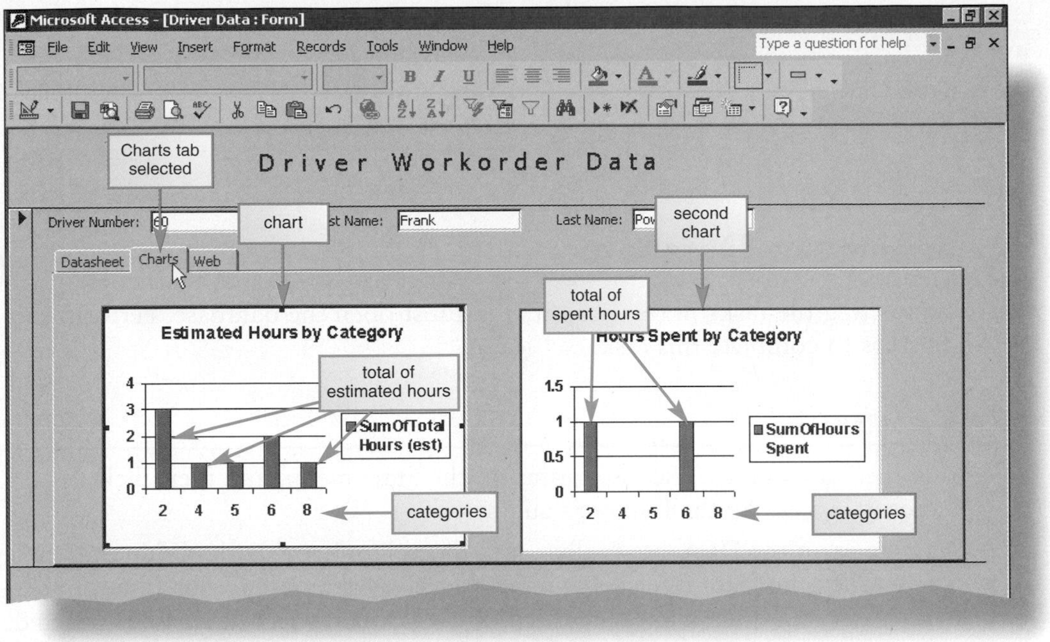

FIGURE 8-2b

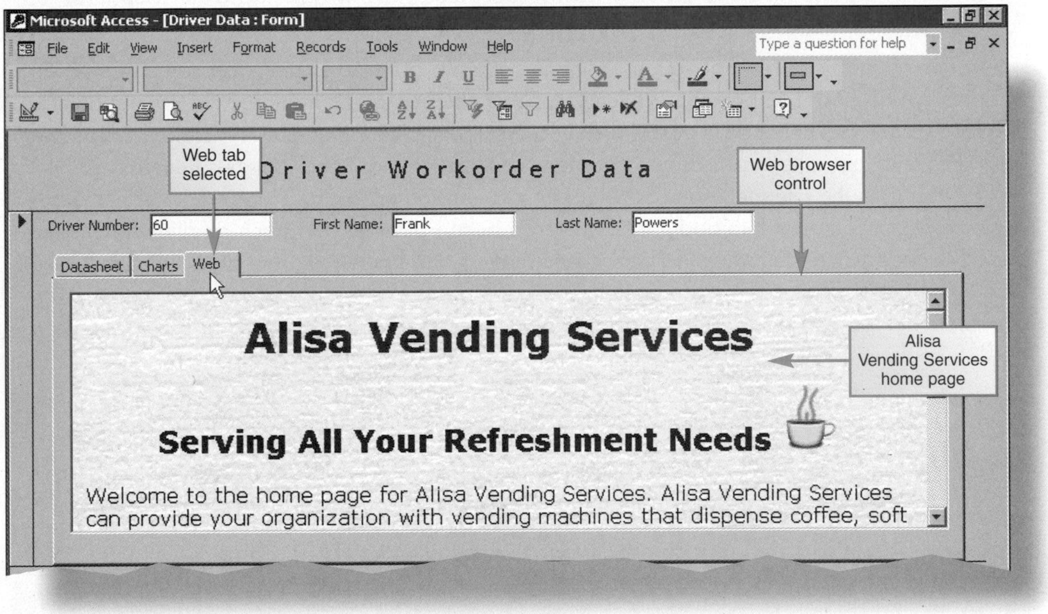

FIGURE 8-2c

Project Eight — Using Advanced Form Techniques and Visual Basic for Applications

You begin this project by adding the necessary buttons to the Customer Update Form. Then, you add the combo box that allows users to find a customer given the customer's name. You will add the controls and buttons to support the promotional requirements Alisa has given you and create appropriate Visual Basic for Applications (VBA) code to give your form the necessary functionality. You will create queries that will be used on the forms you will create. You then create a form from scratch using Design view. You will add a tab control, a subform, two charts, and a Web Browser control to this form.

Note: This project assumes that your databases are located in a folder called data on drive C. If your database is on a floppy disk (drive A), copy your database to drive C or to a network drive. If you do not have access to drive C or a network drive, do not attempt to do the activities in this project. You will not have enough room on your disk.

Opening the Database

Before completing the tasks in this project, you must open the database. Perform the following steps to complete this task.

TO OPEN A DATABASE

1. Click the Start button, click Programs on the Start menu, and then click Microsoft Access on the Programs submenu.
2. Click Open on the Database toolbar, and then click Local Disk (C:) in the Look in box. Click the Data folder (assuming that your database is stored in a folder called Data), and then make sure the Alisa Vending Services database is selected.
3. Click the Open button.

The database opens and the Alisa Vending Services : Database window displays.

Note: This project requires that you make many changes to the Customer Update Form including changes to VBA code. To prevent problems, such as deleting a command button but not deleting the accompanying VBA code, you may want to have multiple versions of the Customer Update Form. For example, after you add the command buttons for Next and Previous Records, you can click Save As on the File menu and save the form as Customer Update Form v1, and then use Customer Update Form v1 to add the Add Record button. As you add each additional button or add VBA code, save the form with the succeeding version number and use the newest version for the next steps. That way, if you make a mistake instead of deleting an incorrect button or other control, you can return to the previous version and continue your work.

Enhancing the Form

You now will enhance the form you created by adding command buttons and a combo box. In addition, you will place a rectangle around the combo box.

More About

Command Buttons

With the Control Wizards tool and the Command Button tool, you can create more than 30 different types of command buttons. For example, you can create command buttons to print the current record, edit or apply a filter, find a specific record, and update form data. You even can create a command button to dial a telephone number.

Adding Command Buttons to a Form

To add command buttons, you will use the Control Wizards tool and Command Button tool in the toolbox. Using the series of Command Button Wizard dialog boxes, you must provide the action that should be taken when the button is clicked. Several categories of actions are available.

In the **Record Navigation category**, you will select the Go To Next Record action for one of the buttons. From the same category, you will select the Go To Previous Record action for another. Other buttons will use the Add New Record and the Delete Record actions from the **Record Operations category**. The Close Form button will use the Close Form action from the **Form Operations category**.

Perform the following steps to add command buttons to move to the next record, move to the previous record, add a record, delete a record, and close the form.

Steps To Add Command Buttons to a Form

1 **Click Forms on the Objects bar, right-click Customer Update Form, and then point to Design View on the shortcut menu.**

The shortcut menu displays (Figure 8-3).

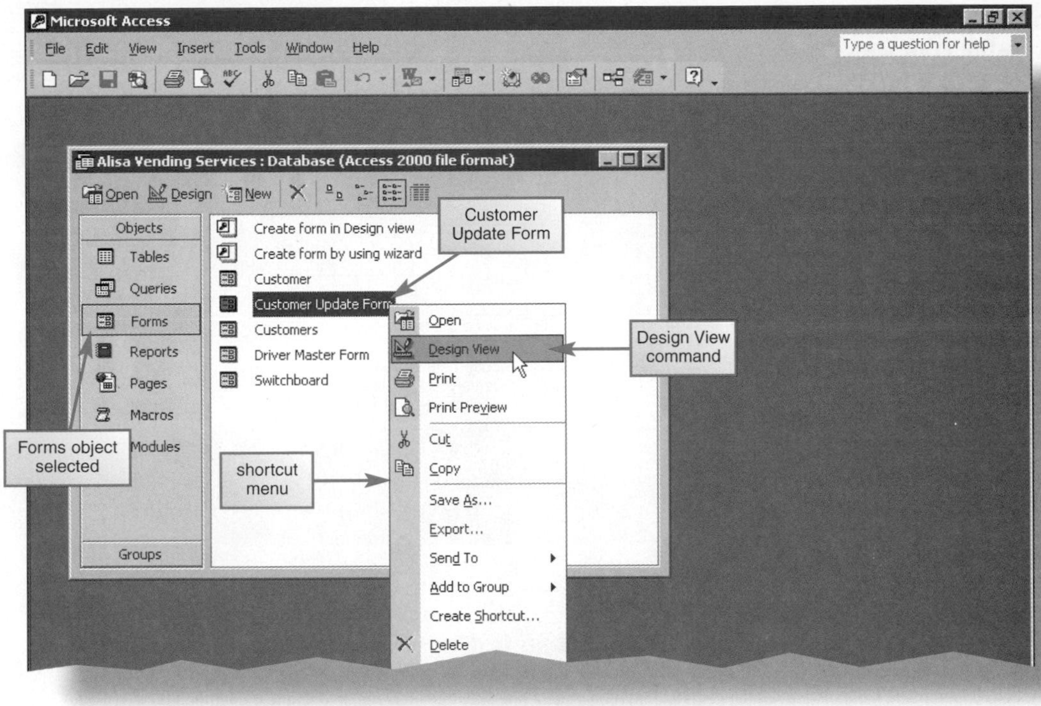

FIGURE 8-3

2 **Click Design View on the shortcut menu, and then, if necessary, maximize the window. Be sure the toolbox displays and is docked at the bottom of the screen. (If it does not display, click the Toolbox button on the toolbar. If it is not docked at the bottom of the screen, drag it to the bottom of the screen to dock it there.) If a field list displays, remove it by clicking its Close button. Make sure the Control Wizards tool is selected, and then point to the Command Button tool in the toolbox.**

The design of the form displays in a maximized window (Figure 8-4).

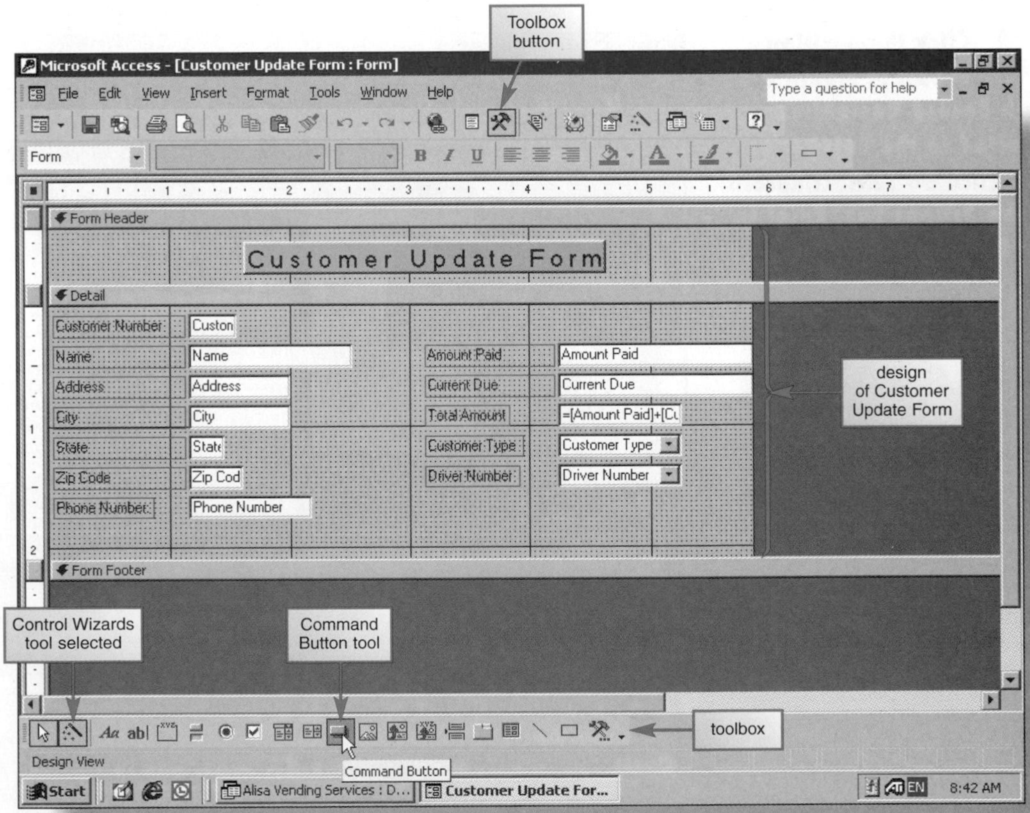

FIGURE 8-4

3 Click the Command Button tool and move the mouse pointer, whose shape has changed to a plus sign with a picture of a button, to the position shown in Figure 8-5.

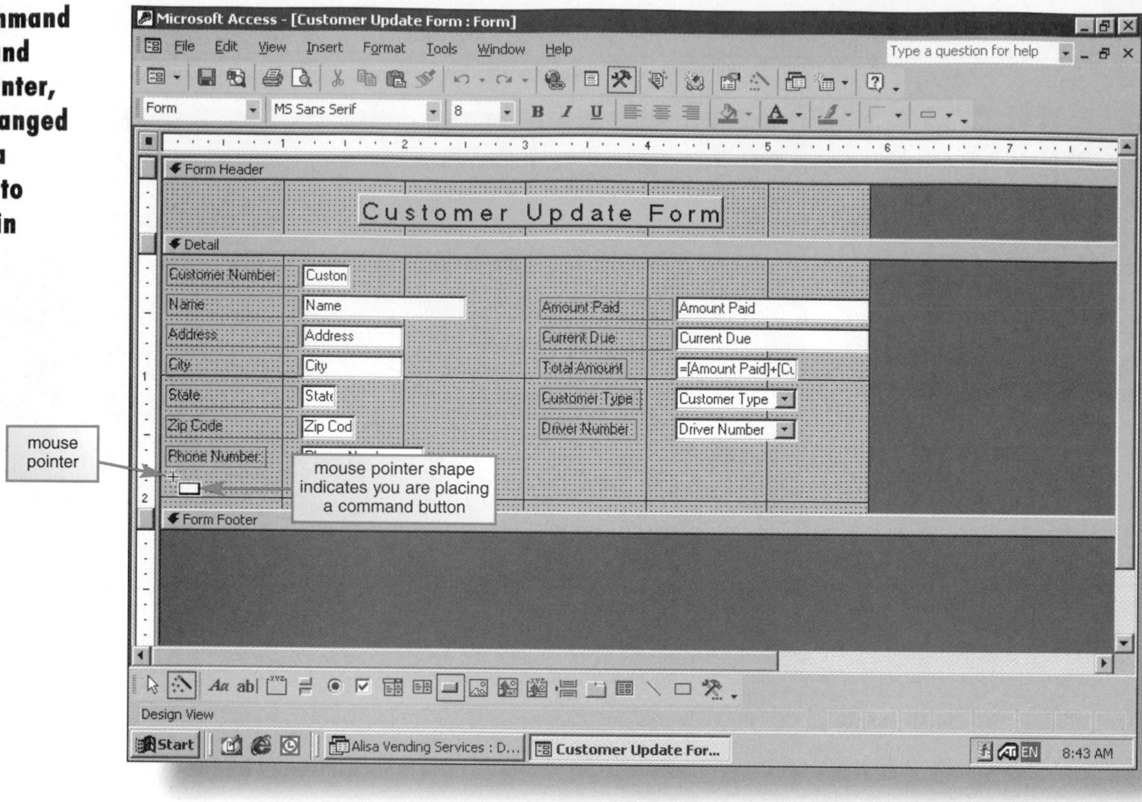

FIGURE 8-5

4 Click the position shown in Figure 8-5. With Record Navigation selected in the Categories box, click Go To Next Record in the Actions box. Point to the Next button.

The Command Button Wizard dialog box displays (Figure 8-6). Go To Next Record is selected as the action. A sample of the button displays in the Sample box.

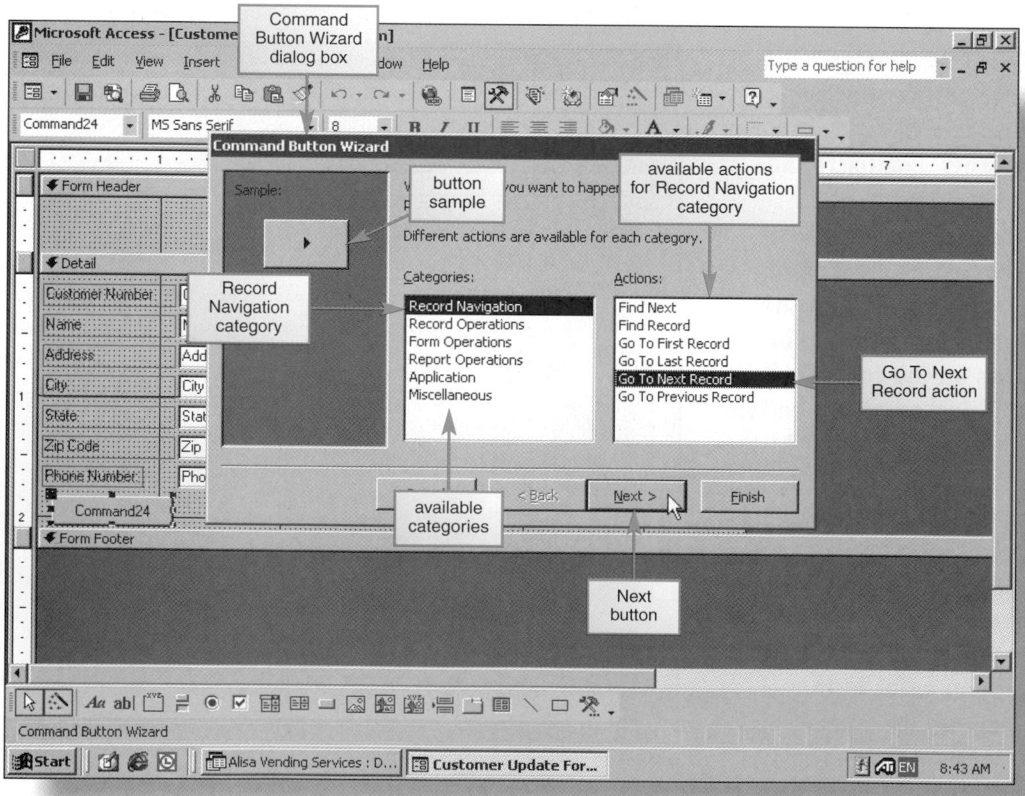

FIGURE 8-6

5 Click the Next button. Point to the Text option button.

The next Command Button Wizard dialog box displays, asking what to display on the button (Figure 8-7). The button can contain either text or a picture.

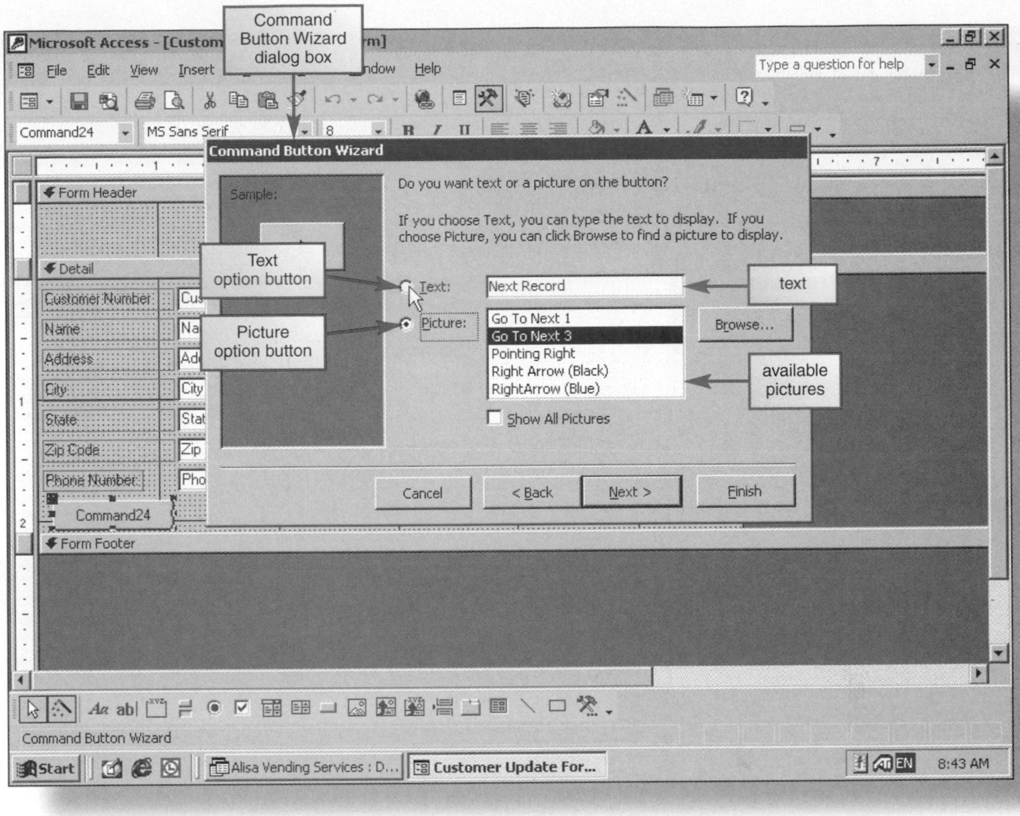

FIGURE 8-7

6 Click the Text option button. Next Record is the desired text and does not need to be changed. Click the Next button, and then type `Next Record` **as the name of the button. Point to the Finish button.**

The name of the button displays in the text box (Figure 8-8).

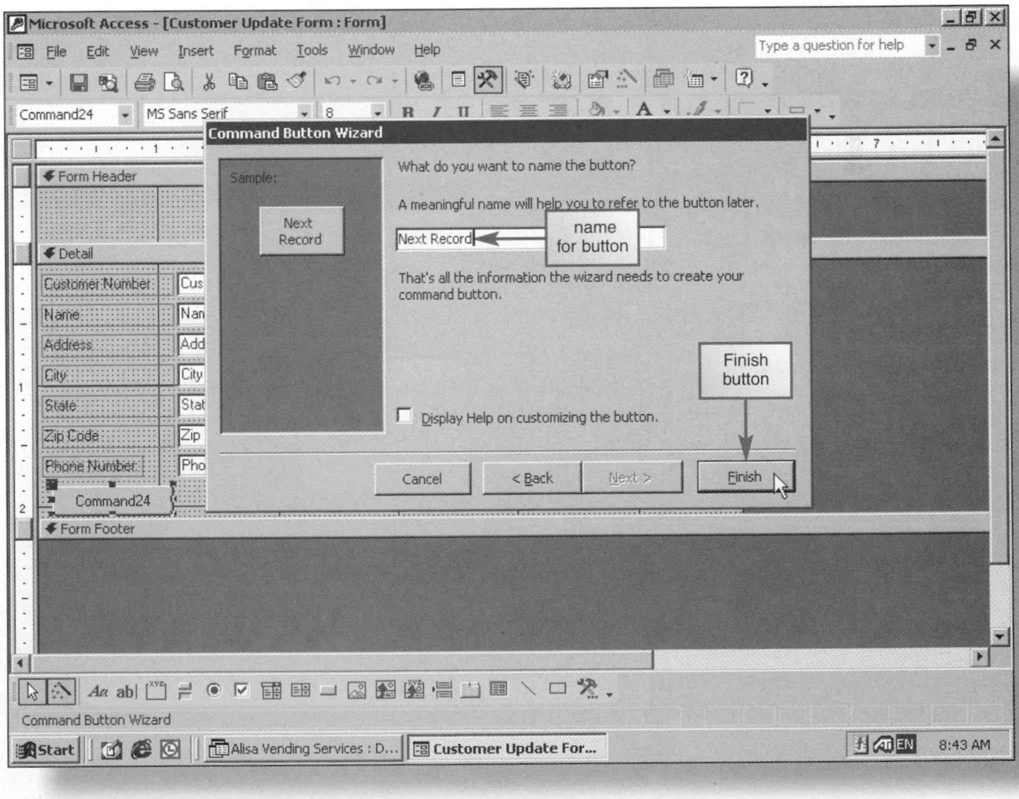

FIGURE 8-8

7 **Click the Finish button and then use the techniques in Steps 3 through 7 to place the Previous Record button directly to the right of the Next Record button. You must click Go To Previous Record in the Actions box, and then type** `Previous Record` **as the name of the button.**

8 **Place a third button directly to the right of the Previous Record button. Click Record Operations in the Categories box. Add New Record is the desired action. Point to the Next button.**

The Command Button Wizard dialog box displays with the selections (Figure 8-9).

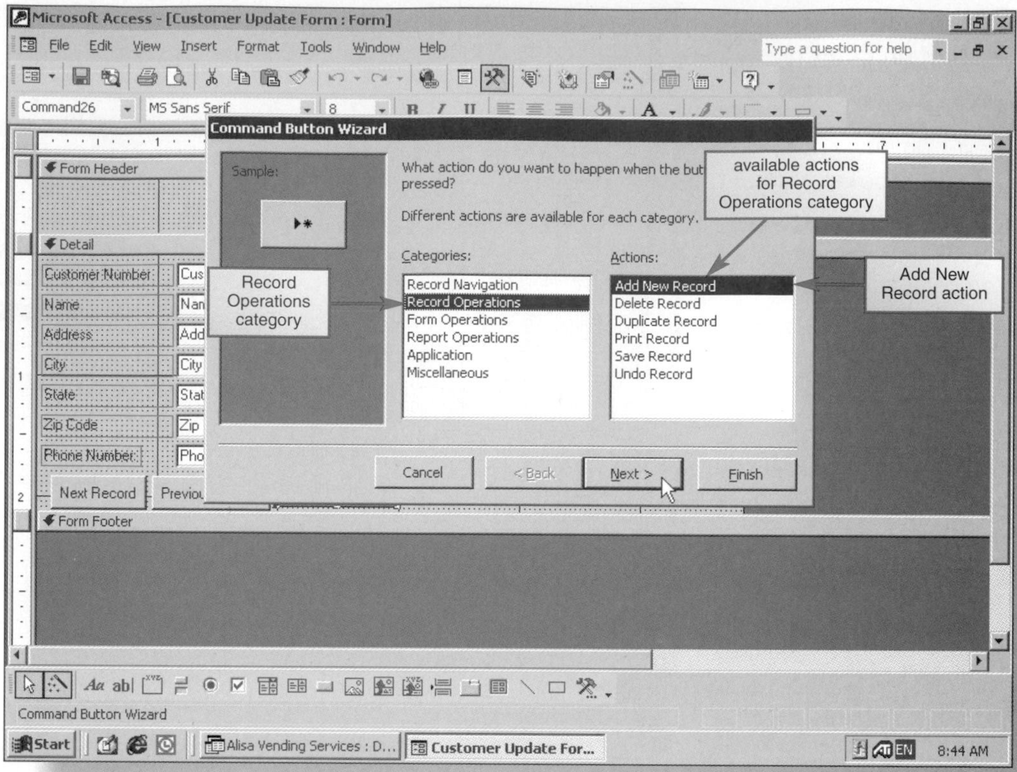

FIGURE 8-9

9 **Click the Next button, and then click the Text option button to indicate that the button is to contain text (Figure 8-10). Add Record is the desired text. Click the Next button, type** `Add Record` **as the name of the button, and then click the Finish button.**

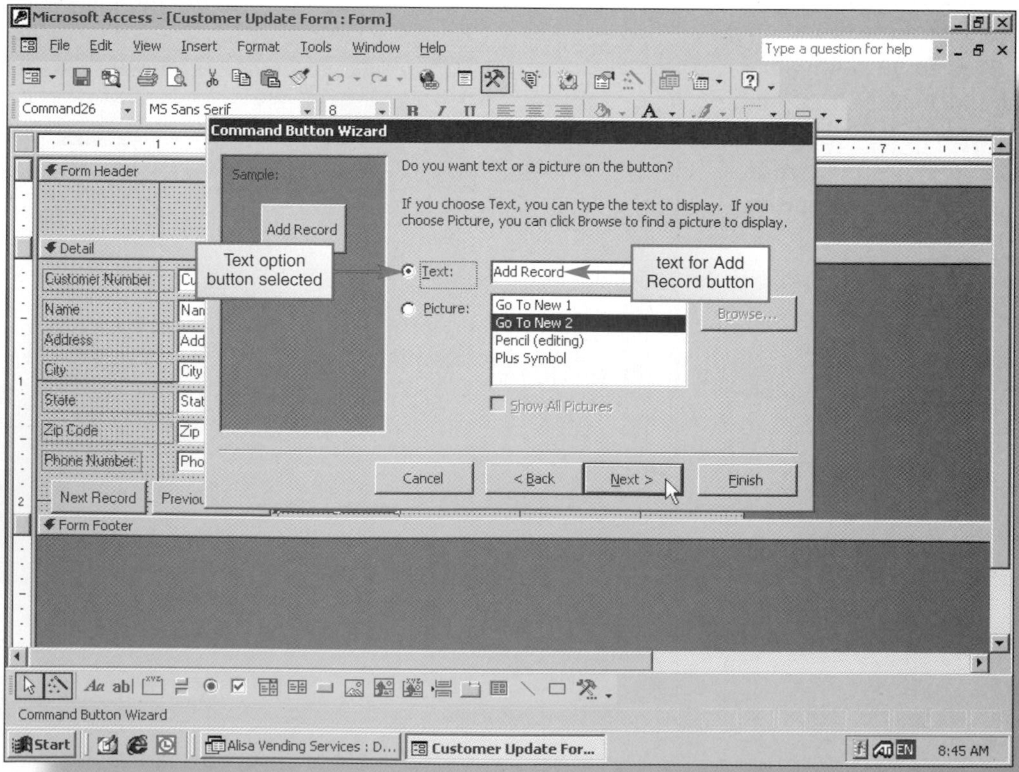

FIGURE 8-10

10 Use the techniques in Steps 3 through 7 to place the Delete Record and Close Form buttons in the positions shown in Figure 8-11. For the Delete Record button, the category is Record Operations and the action is Delete Record. For the Close Form button, the category is Form Operations and the action is Close Form. (If your buttons are not aligned properly, you can drag them to the correct positions.)

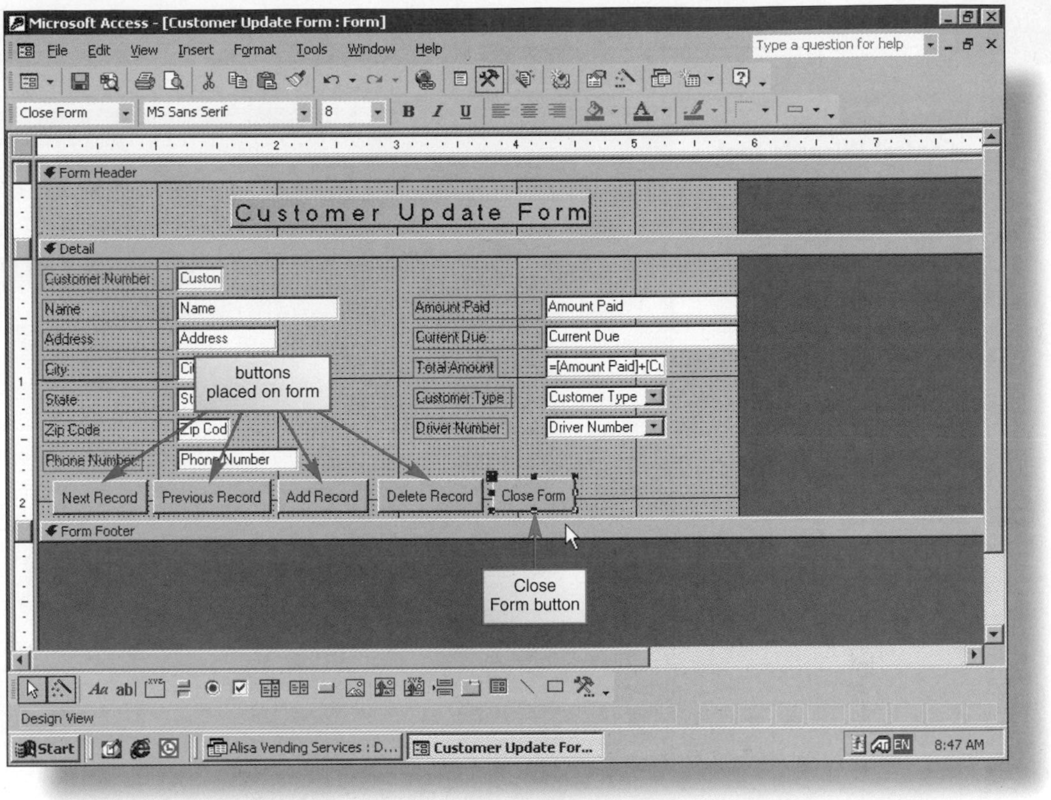

FIGURE 8-11

Creating and Using Combo Boxes

A **combo box**, such as the one shown in Figure 8-1a on page A 8.05, combines the properties of a **text box**, a box into which you can type an entry, and a **list box**, a box you can use to display a list. You could type the customer's name directly into the box. Alternatively, you can click the Name to Find box arrow, and Access will display a list of customer names. To select a name from the list, simply click the name.

Creating a Combo Box

To create a combo box, use the Combo Box tool in the toolbox. The Combo Box Wizard then will guide you through the steps of adding the combo box. Perform the steps on the next page to place a combo box for names on the form.

Steps To Create a Combo Box

1 **Make sure the Control Wizards tool is selected, and then point to the Combo Box tool in the toolbox (Figure 8-12).**

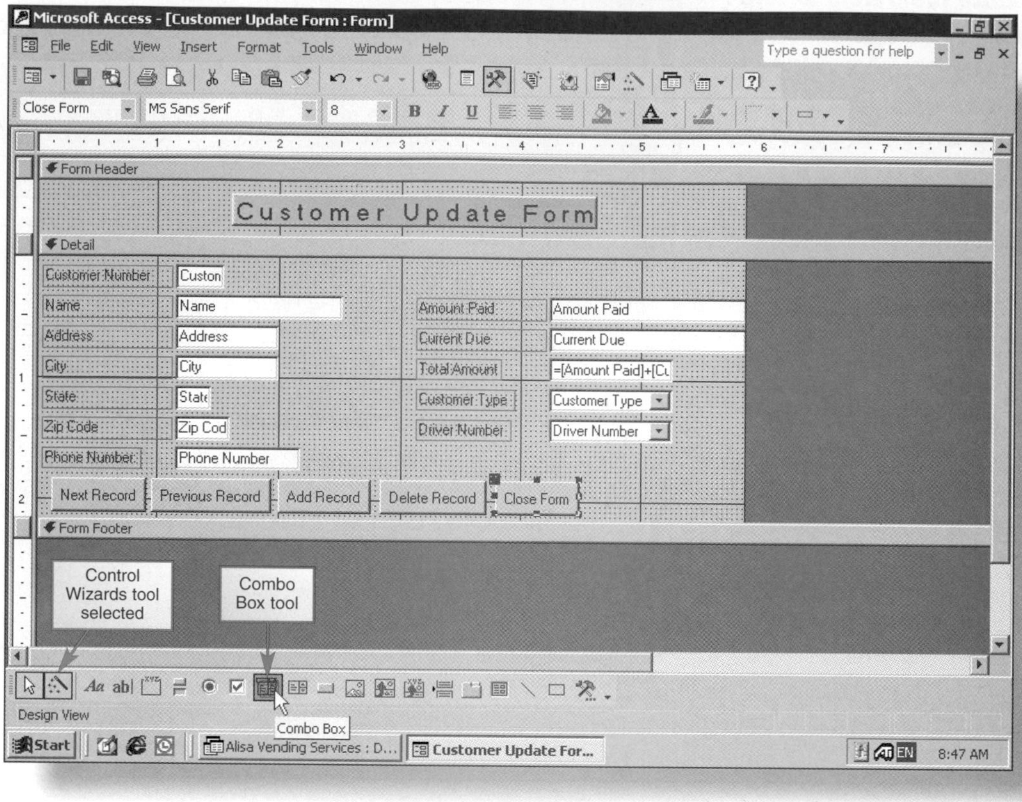

FIGURE 8-12

2 **Click the Combo Box tool and then move the mouse pointer, whose shape has changed to a small plus sign with a combo box, to the position shown in Figure 8-13.**

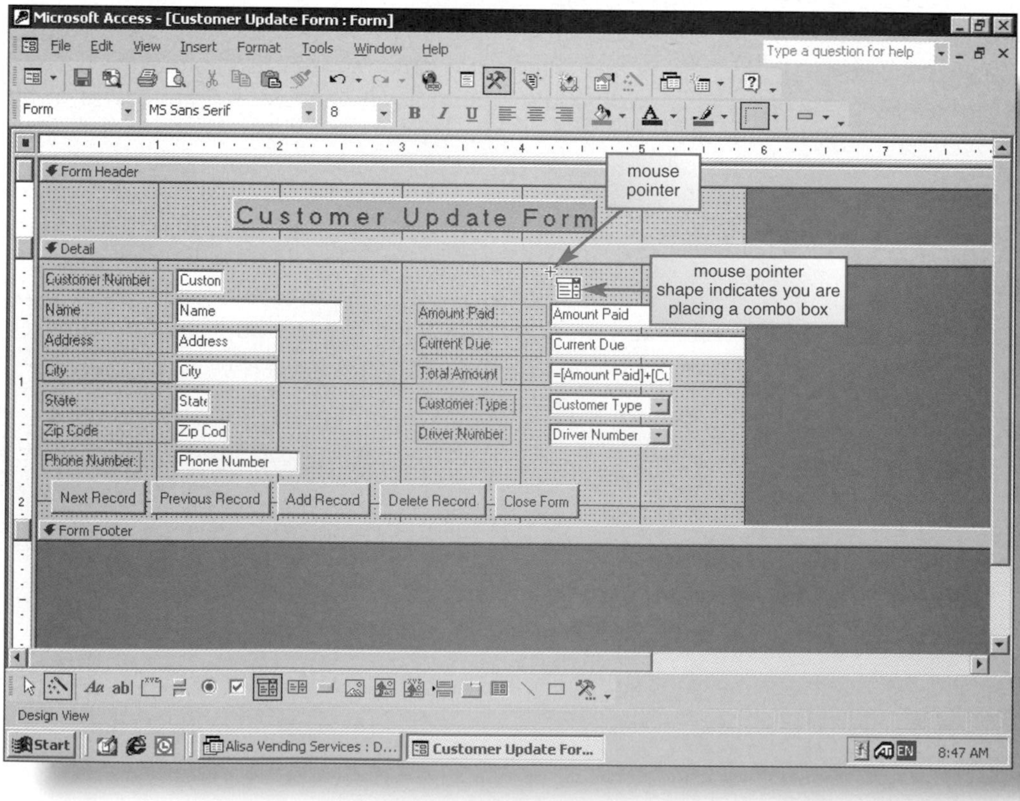

FIGURE 8-13

3 Click the position shown in Figure 8-13 to place a combo box. Click the Find a record on my form based on the value I selected in my combo box option button. Point to the Next button.

The Combo Box Wizard dialog box displays, instructing you to indicate how the combo box is to obtain values for the list (Figure 8-14).

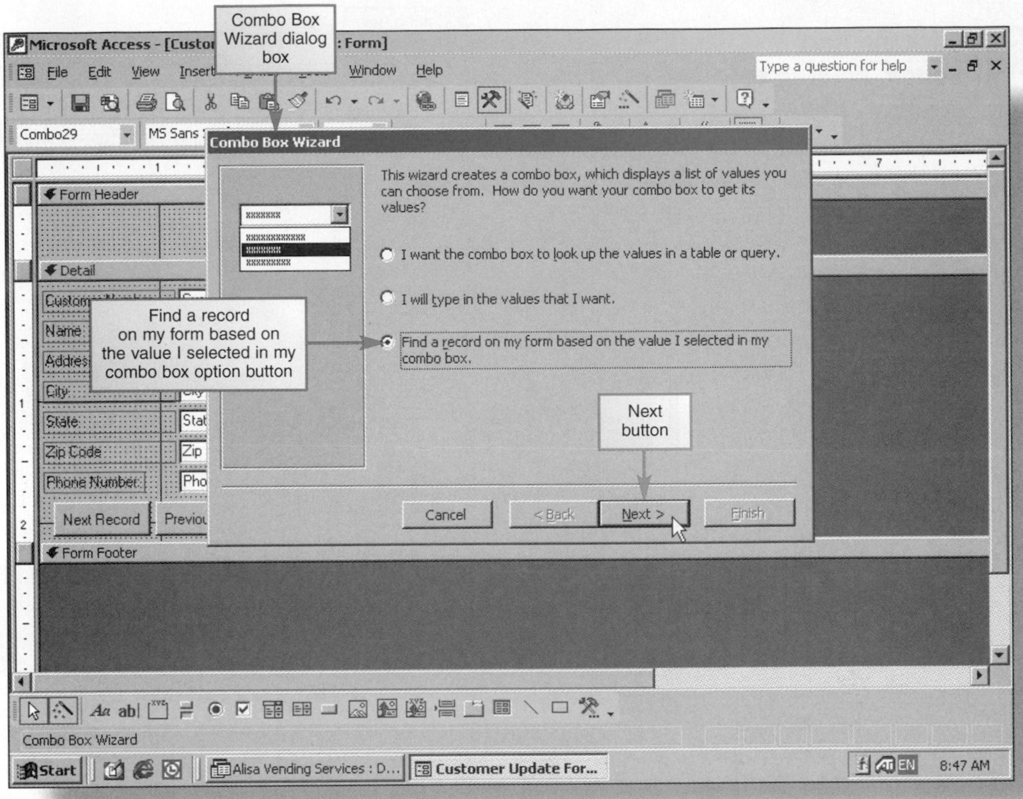

FIGURE 8-14

4 Click the Next button, click the Name field, and then click the Add Field button to add Name as a field in the combo box. Point to the Next button.

The Name field is selected (Figure 8-15).

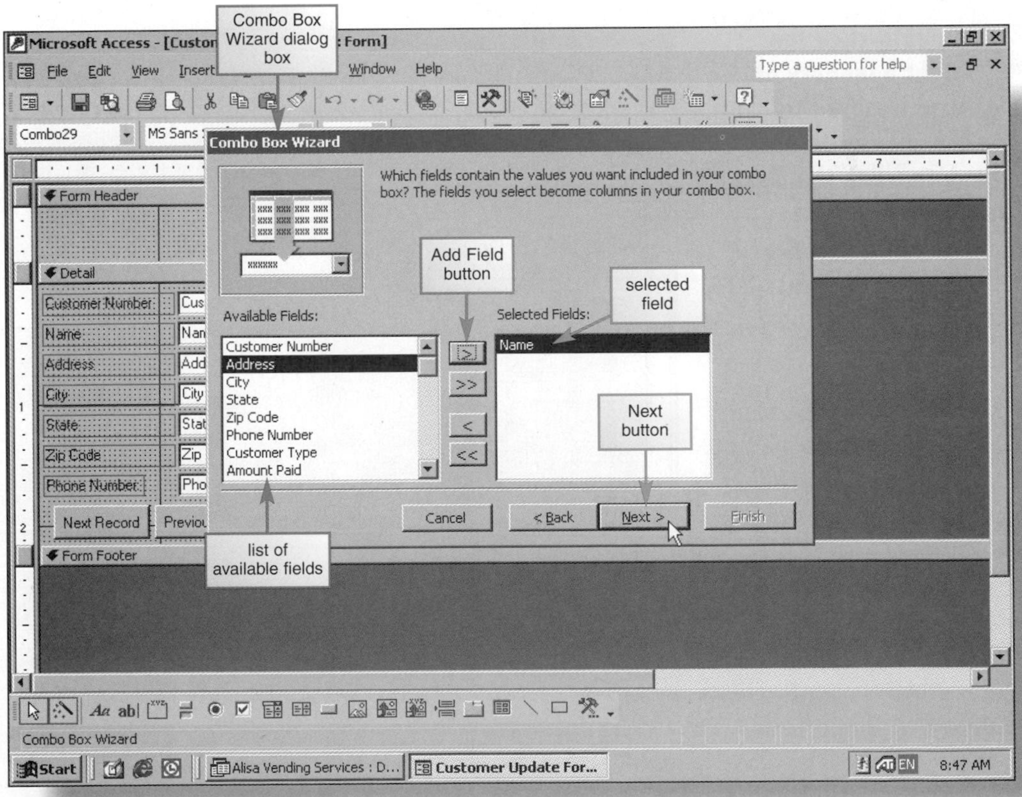

FIGURE 8-15

5 Click the Next button. Point to the right boundary of the column heading.

The Combo Box Wizard dialog box displays (Figure 8-16), giving you an opportunity to resize the columns in your combo box.

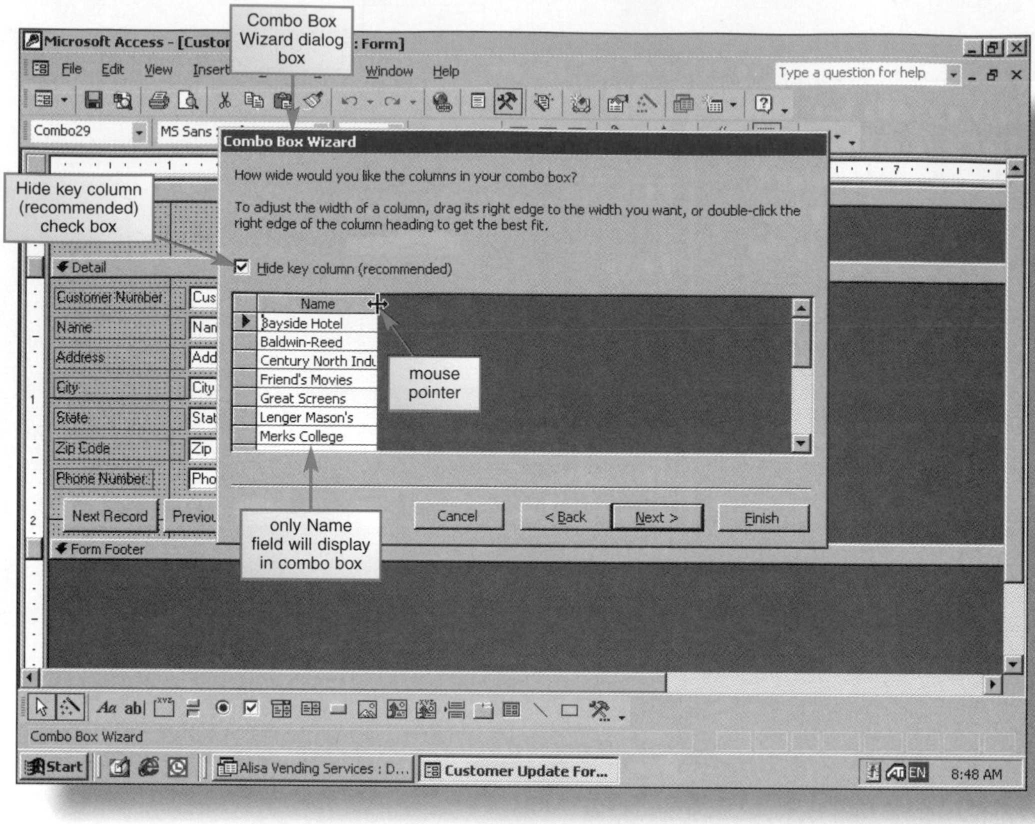

FIGURE 8-16

6 Double-click the right boundary of the column heading to resize the column to best fit the data, click the Next button, and then type `&Name to Find` **as the label for the combo box. Point to the Finish button.**

The label is entered (Figure 8-17). The ampersand (&) in front of the letter N indicates that users can select the combo box by pressing ALT+N.

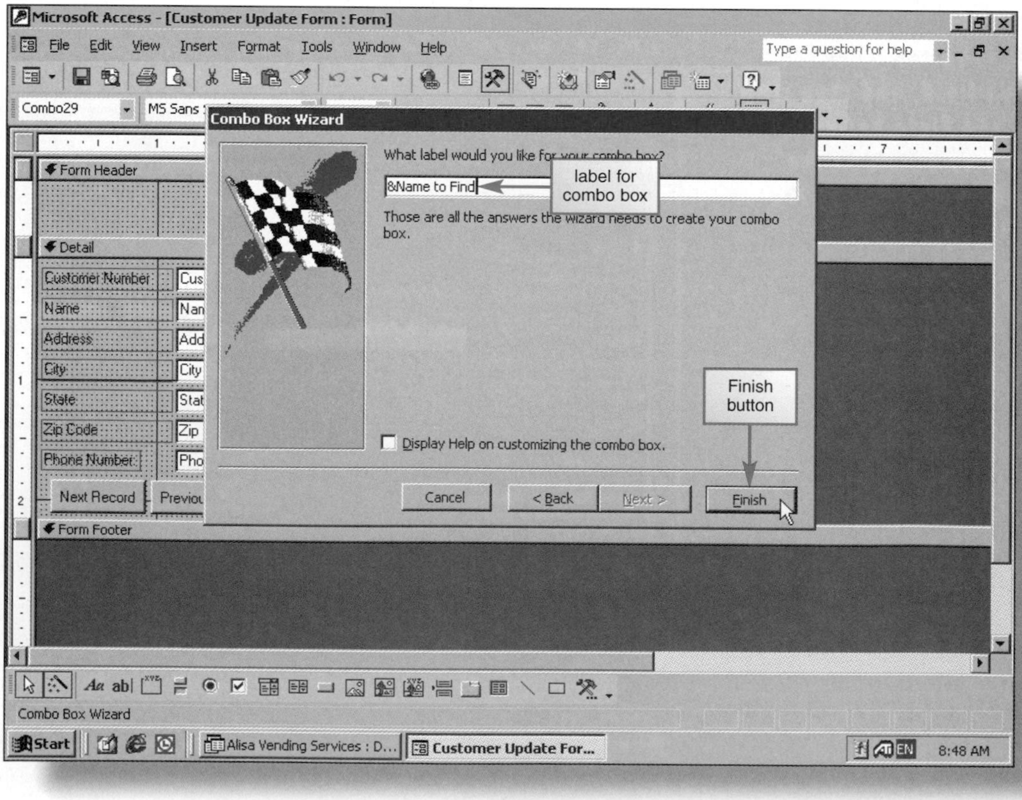

FIGURE 8-17

7 Click the Finish button. If necessary, drag the control to the approximate position shown in Figure 8-18.

The combo box is added. The N in Name is underlined indicating that you can press ALT+N to select the combo box.

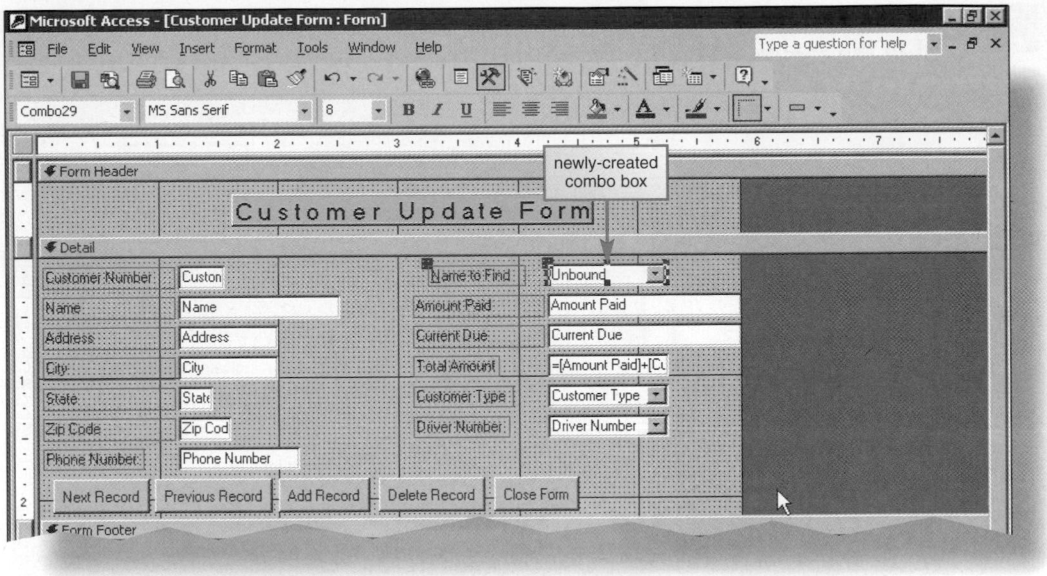

FIGURE 8-18

Placing a Rectangle

In order to emphasize the special nature of the combo box, you will place a rectangle around it. To do so, use the Rectangle tool in the toolbox as in the following steps.

More About

Rectangles

To change the line style (dots, dashes, double, and so on) of a rectangle's border, right-click the rectangle, click Properties on the shortcut menu to open the property sheet, and then click a border style in the BorderStyle property box.

Steps To Place a Rectangle

1 Point to the Rectangle tool in the toolbox (Figure 8-19).

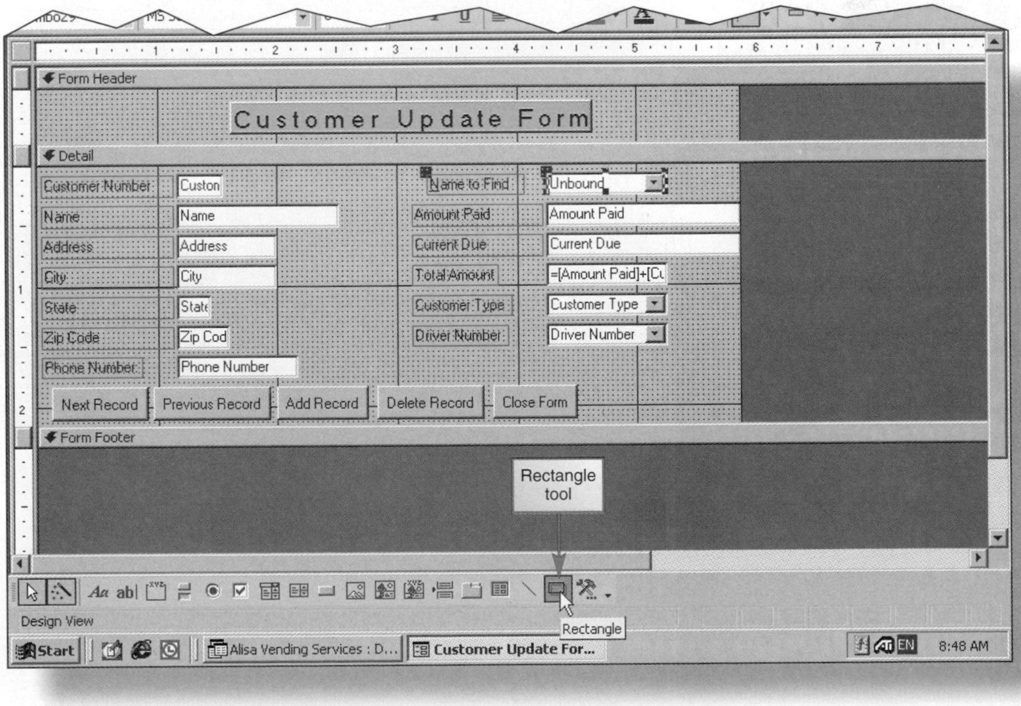

FIGURE 8-19

2 **Click the Rectangle tool in the toolbox and then move the mouse pointer, whose shape has changed to a plus sign accompanied by a rectangle, to the approximate position shown in Figure 8-20.**

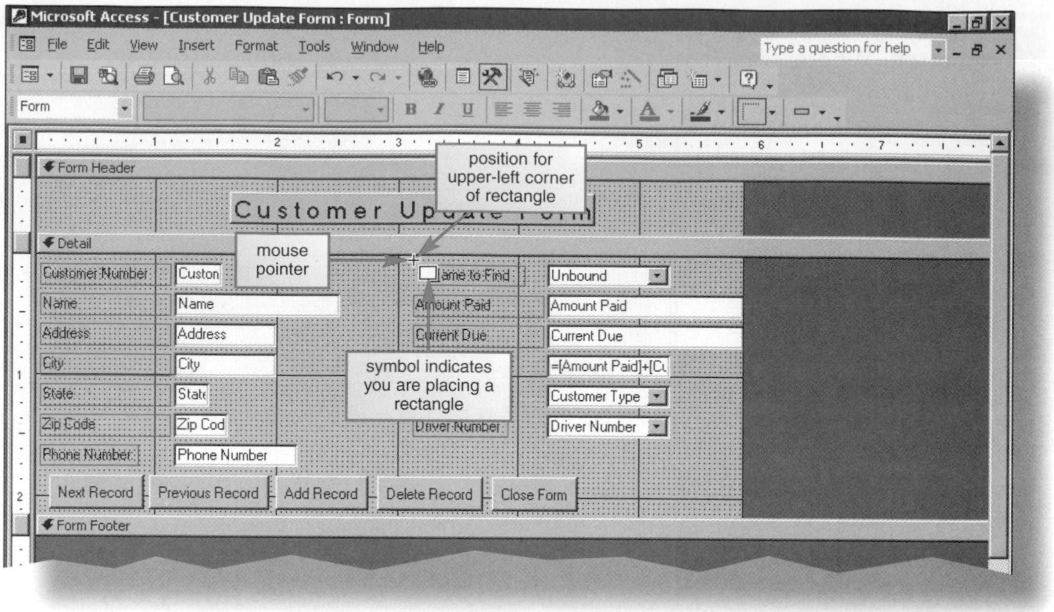

FIGURE 8-20

3 **With the mouse pointer in the position shown in Figure 8-20, drag the mouse pointer to the approximate position shown in Figure 8-21 and then release the left mouse button.**

4 **Point to the border of the newly-created rectangle, right-click, and then click Properties on the shortcut menu. Change the value of the Special Effect property to Raised. Make sure the value of the Back Style property is Transparent, so the combo box will display within the rectangle. (If the value is not Transparent, the rectangle would completely cover the combo box and the combo box would not be visible.)**

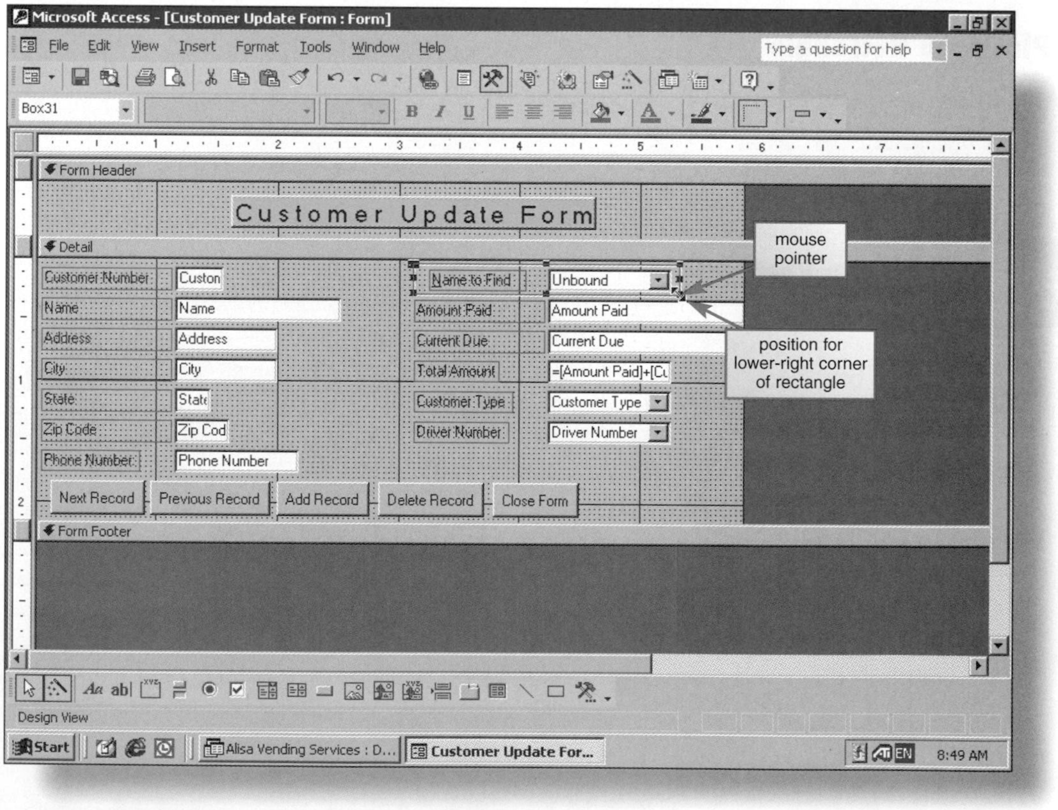

FIGURE 8-21

5 **Close the Rectangle property sheet by clicking its Close button.**

Closing and Saving a Form

To close a form, close the window using the window's Close button. Then indicate whether you want to save your changes. Perform the following step to close and save the form.

TO CLOSE AND SAVE A FORM

1. Click the Customer Update Form : Form window's Close Window button to close the window, and then click the Yes button to save the design of the form.

> **More About**
>
> **Saving**
>
> If you want to have multiple versions of the Customer Update Form, click Save As on the File menu and then save the form as Customer Update Form v1. Then, open Customer Update Form v1 in Design view and continue with the steps in the next section. Use the Save As command to save a new version of the form after each change to the form design. For example, after you modify the Add Record button, use the Save As command to save the form as Customer Update Form v2.

Opening a Form

To open a form, right-click a form in the Database window, and then click Open on the shortcut menu. The form will display and can be used to examine and update data. Perform the following step to open the Customer Update Form.

Steps To Open a Form

1. **With Forms selected on the Objects bar, right-click the Customer Update Form to display the shortcut menu. Click Open on the shortcut menu, and then point to the Add Record button.**

The form displays with the added buttons (Figure 8-22).

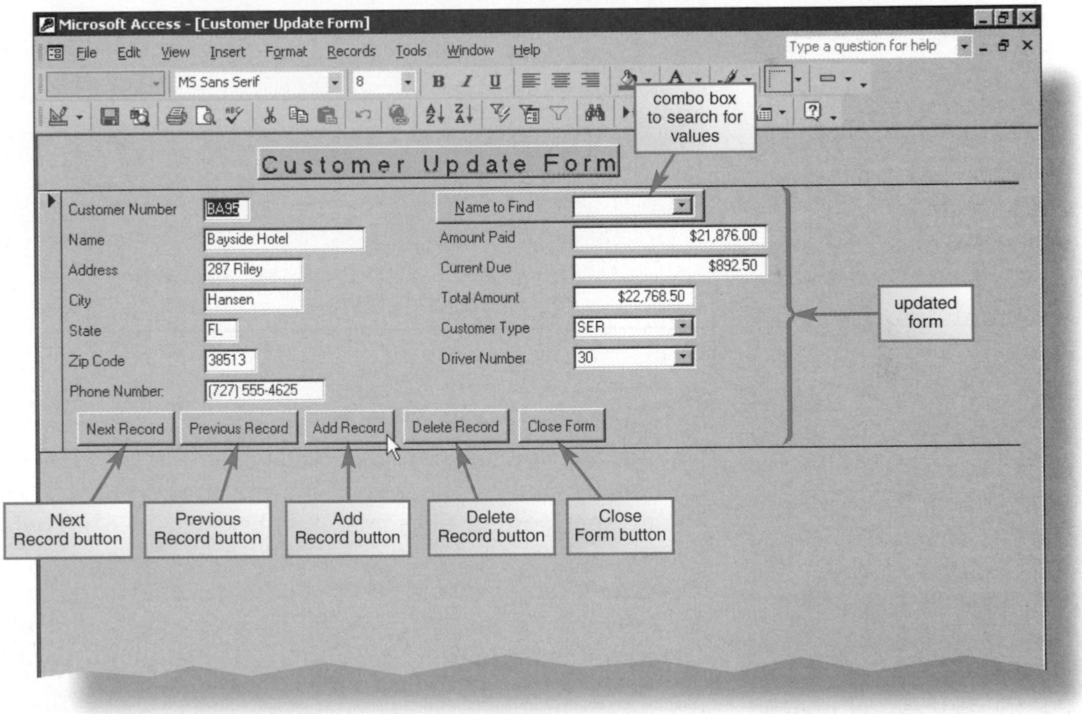

FIGURE 8-22

> **Other Ways**
>
> 1. Select form, click Open button on Database toolbar
> 2. Double-click form
> 3. In Voice Command mode, select form, say "Open"

Using the Buttons

To move around on the form, you can use the buttons to perform the actions you specify. To move to the next record, click the Next Record button. Click the Previous Record button to move to the previous record. Clicking the Delete Record button will delete the record currently on the screen. You will get a message requesting you to verify the deletion before the record actually is deleted. Clicking the Close Form button will remove the form from the screen.

Clicking the Add Record button will clear the contents of the form so you can add a new record. Perform the following step to use the Add Record button.

Steps To Use the Add Record Button

1 Click the Add Record button.

The contents of the form are cleared in preparation for adding a new record (Figure 8-23).

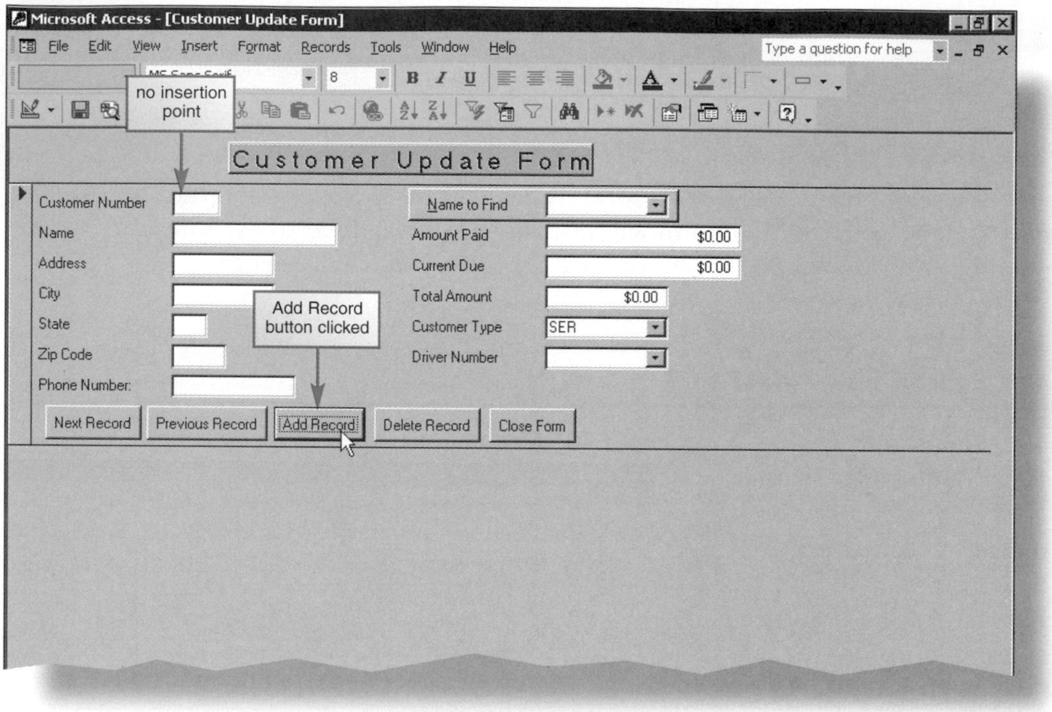

FIGURE 8-23

On the form in Figure 8-23, the contents are cleared, but an insertion point does not display. Therefore, to begin entering a record, you would have to click the Customer Number field before you can start typing. To ensure that an insertion point displays in the Customer Number field text box when you click the Add Record button, you must change the focus. A control is said to have the **focus** when it becomes active; that is, when it becomes able to receive user input through mouse or keyboard actions. At any point in time, only one item on the form has the focus. The Add Record button needs to update the focus to the Customer Number field.

> **More About**
>
> **The Add Record Button**
>
> If your spelling was not consistent, you will get an error message when you click the Add Record button. To correct the problem, return to the form design. Check to make sure the name you gave to the Customer Number control and then name in the SetFocus command are both the same (Customer_Number).

Using the Combo Box

Using the combo box, you can search for a customer in two ways. First, you can click the combo box arrow to display a list of customer names, and then select the name from the list by clicking it. Alternatively, you can begin typing the name. As you type, Access will display automatically the name that begins with the letters you have typed. Once the correct name is displayed, select the name by pressing the TAB key. Regardless of the method you use, the data for the selected customer displays on the form once the selection is made.

The following steps first locate the customer whose name is Friend's Movies, and then use the Next Record button to move to the next customer.

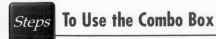

Steps To Use the Combo Box

1 Click the Name to Find box arrow and then point to Friend's Movies.

The list of names displays (Figure 8-24). The list is not in alphabetical order.

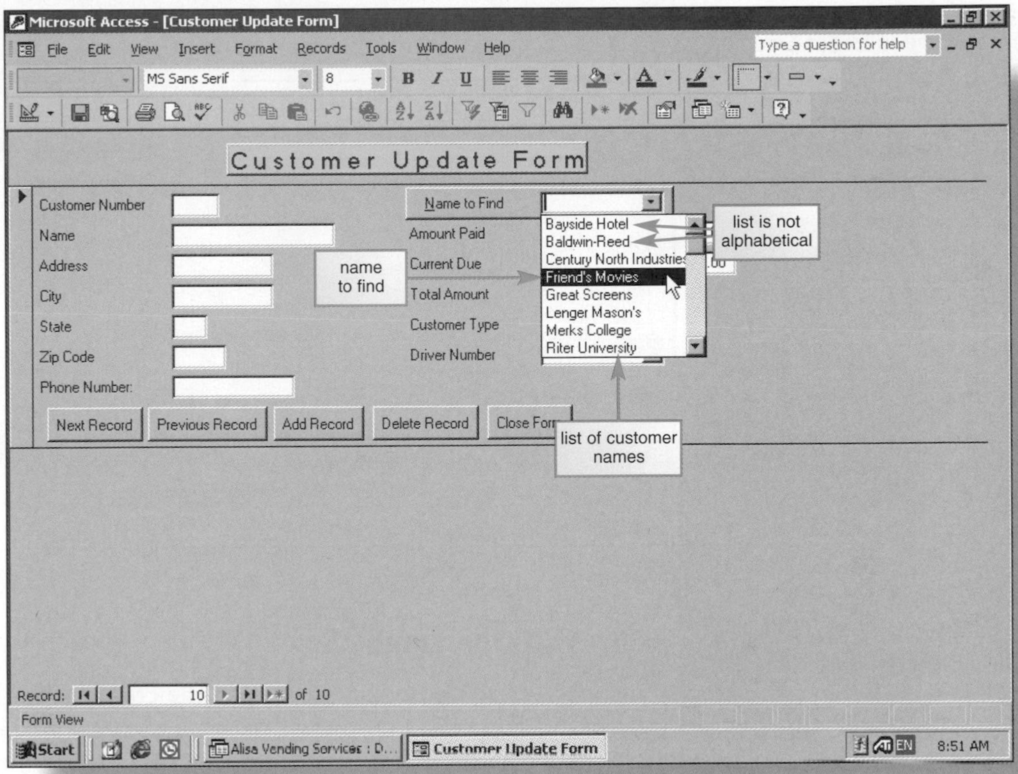

FIGURE 8-24

2 Click Friend's Movies and then point to the Next Record button.

The data for the customer whose name is Friend's Movies displays on the form (Figure 8-25).

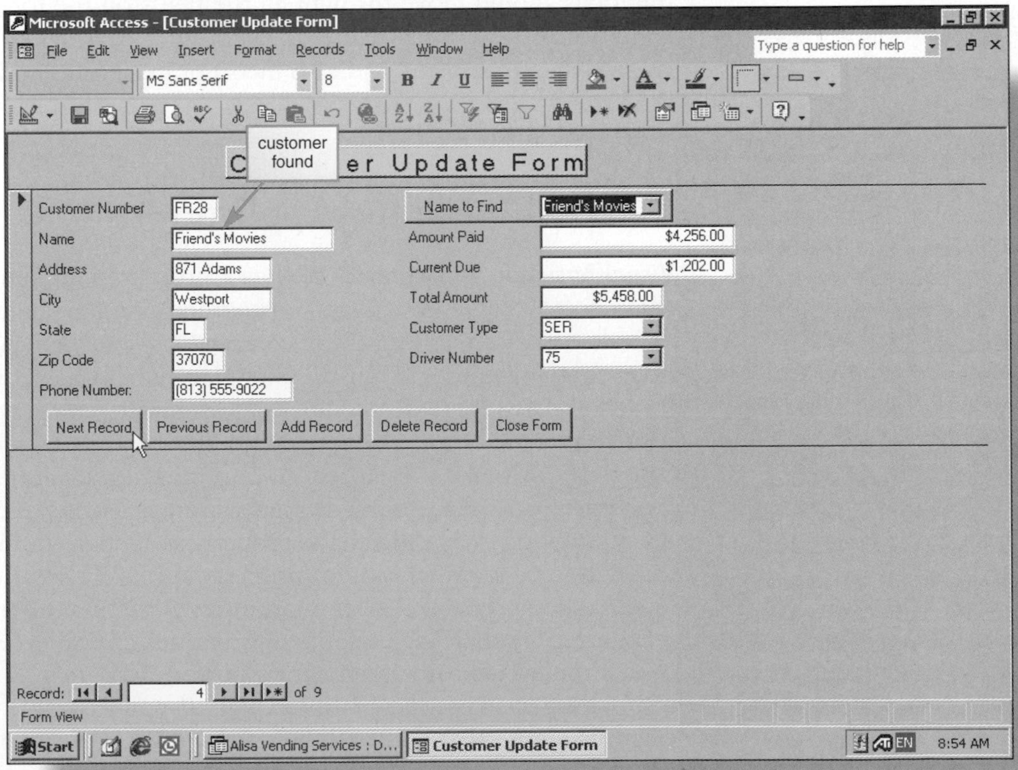

FIGURE 8-25

3 Click the Next Record button.

The data for the customer whose name is Great Screens displays on the form (Figure 8-26). The combo box still contains Friend's Movies.

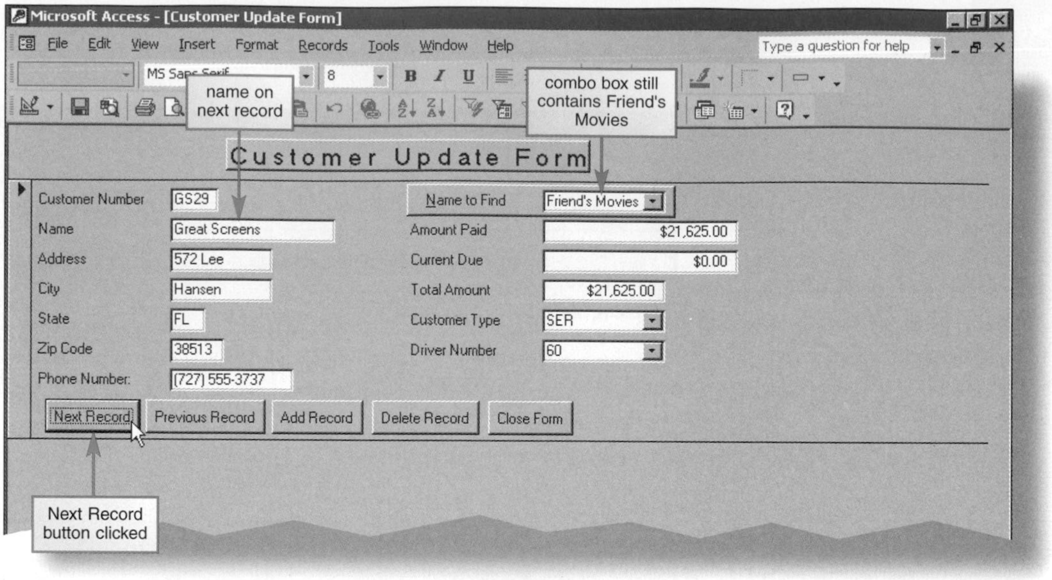

FIGURE 8-26

Issues with the Combo Box

Consider the following issues with the combo box. First, if you examine the list of names in Figure 8-24, you will see that they are not in alphabetical order (Bayside Hotel comes before Baldwin-Reed). Second, when you move to a record without using the combo box, the name in the combo box does not change to reflect the name of the customer currently on the screen. Third, one way to change the focus from one field to another is to press the TAB key. As you repeatedly press the TAB key, the focus should move through all the fields on the form. It should not move to the combo box, however, because that does not represent a field to be updated. You will correct these problems and also incorporate several additional features in the next section.

More About

VBA and Office XP

The VBA programming language also can be used with Excel, Word, PowerPoint, Publisher, and Outlook. For more information about using VBA in other Office XP products, visit the Access 2002 More About page (scsite.com/ac2002/more.htm) and then click VBA and Office XP.

Visual Basic for Applications (VBA)

Visual Basic for Applications (**VBA**) is a programming language that can be used with Microsoft Access. As with other programming languages, programs in VBA consist of **code**; that is, a collection of **statements**, also called **commands**, which are instructions that will cause actions to take place when the program is executed.

An Access database is composed of objects that have properties and that are in turn composed of other objects. Tables, for example, have properties and are in turn composed of fields, which also have properties. (The field properties are shown in the lower pane in the Table Design window.) Forms and reports have properties and contain controls that also have properties. You are familiar with these objects through your manipulation of property sheets.

The key properties when working with VBA deal with **events**, which are actions recognized by these objects. Such properties are called event properties. For example, one of the events associated with a button on a form is clicking the button. The corresponding event property is On Click. If you associate VBA code with the On Click event property, that code will be executed whenever the user clicks the button. This approach is referred to as **event-driven programming**.

Table 8-1 shows some events associated with actions a user can take and Table 8-2 shows some events associated with data updates.

Table 8-1 Events Associated with User Actions

EVENT	*WHEN OCCURS*
Activate	Form or report receives focus (that is, is activated)
Click	User presses and releases left mouse button
DblClick	User presses and releases left mouse button twice rapidly
Deactivate	Form or report loses focus (that is, is deactivated)
Enter	Just before a control receives focus
Exit	Just before a control loses focus
GotFocus	Control receives focus
LostFocus	Control loses focus
MouseDown	User presses either mouse button
MouseMove	User moves the mouse
MouseOver	User moves the mouse over the control
MouseUp	User releases mouse button

Table 8-2 Events Associated with Data Updates

EVENT	*WHEN OCCURS*
AfterDelConfirm	User responds Yes when asked to confirm deletion
AfterInsert	New record added to database
AfterUpdate (control)	Value in control changed
AfterUpdate (form)	Record changed in database
BeforeDeleteConfirm	Record deleted, but user has not yet responded when asked to confirm deletion
BeforeInsert	Contents of record entered, but record not yet added to database
BeforeUpdate	Contents of record changed on screen, but update not yet reflected in database
Delete	Record removed from database

Names in VBA

Names in Visual Basic can be up to 255 characters long. They must begin with a letter and can include letters, numbers, or underscores (_). Unlike names in Access, they cannot contain spaces. There are two principal ways of handling the restriction on spaces when the name you wish to use contains more than one word. The first is to avoid the space, but place an initial cap on each word. For example, if you wanted the name Show Promotion, you would instead use ShowPromotion. The second is to use an underscore instead of the space. For example, if you wanted the name Current Due, you would instead use Current_Due. In this project, you will use the second method for any name that represents a field in the database and the first method for all others.

There also are some generally accepted conventions for naming specific items on forms. Names of command buttons begin with cmd, names of text boxes begin with txt, and names of labels begin with lbl. For example, you will use cmdPromo as the name of the command button for showing or hiding promotion data. You will use txtPromoAmount as the name of the text box that contains the promotion amount and lblPromoAmount as the name of its attached label.

More About

Events

An event can be caused by a user action or by a VBA statement, or it can be triggered by the system. Using properties associated with events, you can tell Access to run a macro, call a Visual Basic function, or run an event procedure in response to an event.

Statements in VBA

Statements in VBA use **variables**, which are named locations in computer memory. You can place a value in a variable, change the value in a variable, and use the value in a variety of ways, such as computations and comparisons.

The **assignment** statement is used to assign a value to a variable and also to change the value in a variable. For example, the statement on line 1 in Table 8-3 assigns the value 1.05 to a variable called PromoFactor. The statement on line 2 multiplies (*) this value by the value in Current_Due and assigns the result to the variable called PromoAmount.

Table 8-3 Assignment Statement

LINE	*STATEMENT*
1	`PromoFactor = 1.05`
2	`PromoAmount = PromoFactor * Current_Due`

Table 8-4 Simple If Statement

LINE	STATEMENT
1	`If Customer_Type = "EDU" Then`
2	`    PromoFactor = 1.05`
3	`End If`

The **If** statement performs a test and then takes action. The action to be taken depends on the results of the test. The simplest form of the If statement is illustrated in Table 8-4. In this statement, if the customer type is equal to EDU, PromoFactor will be set to 1.05. If the customer type is not equal to EDU, no action will be taken. (Because EDU is a text value, it must be enclosed in quotation marks.)

Table 8-5 If Statement with Else

LINE	STATEMENT
1	`If Customer_Type = "EDU" Then`
2	`    PromoFactor = 1.05`
3	`Else`
4	`    PromoFactor = 1`
5	`End If`

An If statement also can contain the word Else as illustrated in Table 8-5. In this statement, if the customer type is equal to EDU, PromoFactor will be set to 1.05. If the customer type is not equal to EDU, PromoFactor will be set to 1.

An If statement also can contain ElseIf to perform multiple tests as illustrated in Table 8-6. In this statement, if the customer type is equal to EDU, PromoFactor will be set to 1.05. If the customer type is equal to SER, PromoFactor will be set to 1.03. If the customer type is MAN, PromoFactor will be set to 1.02. If the customer type is not equal to any of these values, PromoFactor will be set to 1.

Table 8-6 If Statement with ElseIf

LINE	STATEMENT
1	`If Customer_Type = "EDU" Then`
2	`    PromoFactor = 1.05`
3	`ElseIf Customer_Type = "SER" Then`
4	`    PromoFactor = 1.03`
5	`ElseIf Customer_Type = "MAN" Then`
6	`    PromoFactor = 1.02`
7	`Else`
8	`    PromoFactor = 1`
9	`End If`

In the above examples, some lines were indented four spaces. This is not necessary, but is done to make the statement more readable.

Comments in VBA

You can include **comments** in VBA code to describe the purpose of the code. To indicate that the text you are entering is a comment and not a VBA statement, place an apostrophe before the comment. The comment can be on a line by itself as on line 1 of Table 8-7. It also can display on the same line with code as on line 3 of the table. Comments are a valuable tool to help make the code more readable.

Table 8-7 Contents of Promo Modules Standard Module

LINE	STATEMENT
1	`' Determine PromoFactor based on Customer Type`
2	`If Customer_Type = "EDU" Then`
3	`    PromoFactor = 1.05 ' Promo factor for Educational customers`
4	`End If`

Procedures in VBA

In VBA, a group of statements that accomplishes some specific task is called a **procedure**. There are two different types of procedures. A **function procedure**, which usually is simply called a **function**, typically calculates and returns a value. You can use the function in an expression anywhere that you can use expressions (for example, in queries, in controls on forms and reports, in Visual Basic code). The value calculated by the function then will be used in the expression.

Table 8-8 shows a sample function. It begins with the word Function followed by the name of the function and ends with End Function. The name of the function in the table is PromoFactor. Within the function, PromoFactor is treated as if it were a variable. The purpose of the function is to calculate a value for PromoFactor. The If statement in this function will set PromoFactor to 1.05 if the customer type is EDU and to 1 otherwise.

The variable in parentheses (Customer_Type) is called a **parameter** and allows you to furnish data to the function to be used in calculating the function value. To use the function, you type the name of the function and then in parentheses, specify

Table 8-8 PromoFactor Function

```
Function PromoFactor(Customer_Type)
    ' Determine PromoFactor based on Customer Type
    If Customer_Type = "EDU" Then
        PromoFactor = 1.05 ' Promo factor for Educational customers
    Else
        PromoFactor = 1 ' Promo factor for others
    End If

End Function
```

the value for this parameter. The item that furnishes this value is called an **argument**. For example, if you specified PromoFactor ("EDU"), "EDU" would be the argument. During the execution of the PromoFactor function, Customer_Type would be EDU and thus PromoFactor would be set to 1.05. It would be more common to use a database field as the argument as in PromoFactor ([Customer Type]). In this case if the current value in the Customer Type field were EDU, the function would calculate a value of 1.05. If instead, the current value in the field is MAN, the function would calculate a value of 1.

The other type of procedure is a Sub procedure. Unlike functions, **Sub procedures**, also called **subroutines**, do not return a value and cannot be used in expressions. Table 8-9 includes a sample Sub procedure that you will create and use later in this project. It makes the controls containing the promotional amount and promotional factor, as well as the button to run the promotion query, visible. By placing the statements to accomplish this in a procedure, you can use them from a variety of places within the VBA code. All you need to do is include the name of the procedure wherever you want the commands executed.

Table 8-9 ShowPromotion Sub Procedure

```
Public Sub ShowPromotion()
    txtPromoAmount.Visible = True
    txtPromoFactor.Visible = True
    cmdPromoQuery.Visible = True
End Sub
```

Modules in VBA

In VBA, you group procedures in a structure called a **module**. There are two types of modules. A **standard module** contains procedures that are available from anywhere in a database. A **class module** contains procedures for a particular form or report. When you create a procedure for an object on a form or report, Access automatically places the procedure in the class module for that form or report. If you create additional procedures, you can place them in either a standard module or a class module. If the only way the procedure will be used is in connection with a form or report, you should place the procedure on the form's or report's class module. If it will be used more widely than that, placing it in a standard module is the appropriate action. For example, if a function is used both by a control on a report and in a query, it should be in a standard module.

Compilation

In order for Access to execute your programs, they must be translated from Visual Basic into a language that Access can understand and run. This process is called **compilation**. Translating a program formally is called **compiling** a program and the tool that performs the translation is called a **compiler**. When a procedure is run that has not been translated previously, the compiler first will attempt to compile (translate) the procedure. Assuming it is successful, the compiled version then is run. If, however, the compiler finds an error, that is, some aspect of the procedure that does not follow the rules of Visual Basic, it will not complete the translation. Instead it will report the error. You first must correct the error and then you can try to run the procedure again. If you have an error, compare the statement very carefully with a similar statement from one of the examples in the book to determine the problem and then correct the problem.

Instead of waiting for these errors to be reported when the procedure is run, you can have Access immediately compile a procedure as soon as you have created it by clicking Debug on the menu bar in Visual Basic and then clicking Compile on the Debug menu. The compiler then will attempt to compile the procedure. If it is successful, Access will use the compiled version the next time the procedure is to be run without requiring the compilation step to take place. If there are errors, they are reported immediately and can be corrected while you are still working on the procedure.

Help on VBA

The help available through the Microsoft Visual Basic Help system is extensive. Just as with other help systems, if you select the Contents tab, several books are available. By clicking the plus sign in front of the book icon, you can "open" the book to view all the topics contained within it. The books you may find particularly useful are Visual Basic User Interface Help (how to use the interface to create and modify Visual Basic code), Visual Basic Conceptual Topics (general concepts concerning Visual Basic), Visual Basic How-To Topics (how to accomplish various tasks in Visual Basic), and Visual Basic Language Reference (rules for forming various Visual Basic statements).

Using Visual Basic for Applications (VBA)

In the next sections, you will use VBA to accomplish several tasks. In particular, you will do the following:

1. You will modify the Access-generated code associated with clicking the Add Record button by adding a VBA command to change the focus. This will ensure that an insertion point displays in the Customer Number control after the Add Record button is clicked.
2. You will modify the combo box for searching for a name so the names display in alphabetical order. You also will update the code associated with the On Current event property of the form so whenever a user moves to another customer, the combo box will be updated to contain the correct name.
3. You will create functions in a standard module to calculate the promotion factor and the promotion amount.
4. You will test the functions you just created to ensure they work correctly.
5. You will use the functions you just created in a query.
6. You will add buttons and controls associated with the promotion amounts to the Customer Update Form.
7. You will associate code with the cmdPromo_Click Event, that is, the event of clicking the Show Promotion button. If the button currently reads Show Promotion, the promotion data currently does not display. Clicking the button will cause the promotion data to display and also change the caption

More About

Typing VBA Code

When you press the ENTER key to insert a new line in the Code window, the insertion point is positioned automatically at the beginning of the previous line of text. If the previous line of text was indented, then the inserted line also will be indented. To indent text, press the SPACEBAR or TAB key. If you do not want to indent text, press the BACKSPACE key or SHIFT+TAB.

of the Show Promotion button to Hide Promotion. Clicking the button a second time will hide the promotion data and also change the caption back to Show Promotion. Associated with this change, you also will need to create the ShowPromotion and HidePromotion procedures.

8. You will create the code necessary to update the controls that show promotion data. The data will be updated whenever the user moves to a different customer on the form, the user updates the customer type, or the user updates the current due amount.
9. You will create code that will be executed when the form first is loaded to hide the promotion data.
10. You will create a function to run a query and associate this function with the Run Promotion Query button.
11. You will examine the complete programs.

More About

When to Use VBA

You can accomplish many of the same tasks in Access using either macros or VBA. Your database, however, will be easier to maintain if you use VBA. Because macros are separate objects from the objects that use them, a database containing many macros that respond to events on form and report objects can be difficult to maintain. Visual Basic event procedures are built into the object's definition. If you move a form or report from one database to another, the event procedures built into the form or report object move with it.

Modifying the Add Record Button

To display an insertion point automatically when you click the Add Record button, you need to change the focus. In order to do so using Visual Basic for Applications (VBA), you first must change the name of the control for the Customer Number field to a name that does not contain spaces, because spaces are not permitted in names in VBA. You will replace the space with an underscore (_) giving the name Customer_Number. Next, you must add a statement to the VBA code that Access creates automatically for the button click event. The added statement, Customer_Number.SetFocus, will move the focus to the control for the Customer Number field as soon as the button is clicked.

Perform the following steps to change the name of the Customer Number control to Customer_Number and then add an additional statement to the VBA code that will set the focus to Customer_Number.

More About

Focus

Access provides a visual way to determine which object on the screen has the focus. If a field has the focus, an insertion point will display in the field. If a button has the focus, a small rectangle will display inside the button.

Steps To Modify the Add Record Button

1 Click the View button on the toolbar to return to Design view. Right-click the control for the Customer Number field (the white space, not the label), and then click Properties on the shortcut menu. If necessary, click the Name property, use the DELETE or BACKSPACE key to erase the current value, and then type `Customer_Number` **as the new name. Point to the Close button in the property sheet.**

The name is changed (Figure 8-27).

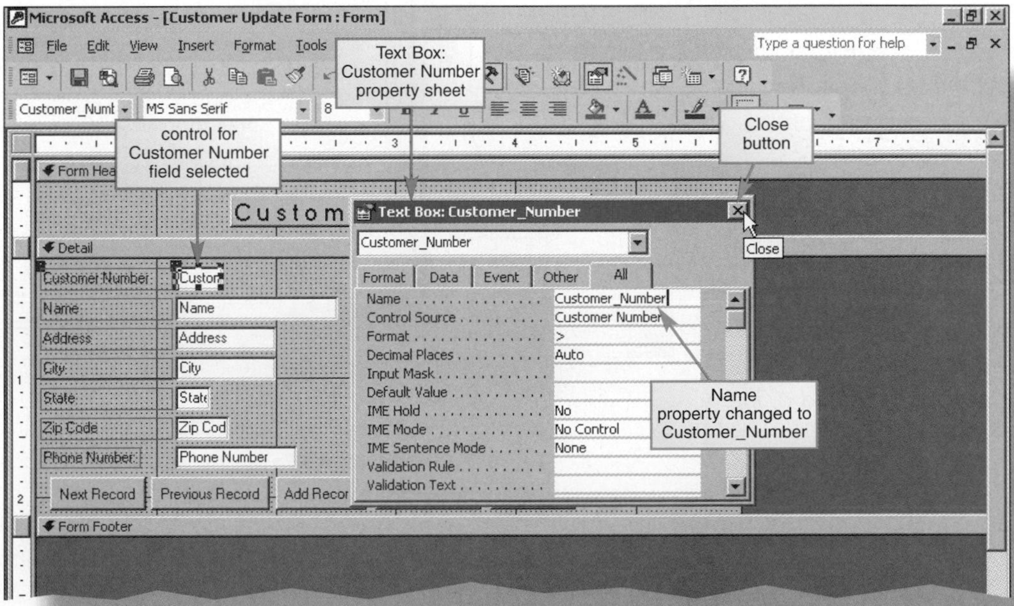

FIGURE 8-27

2 Click the Close button to close the Text Box: Customer Number property sheet. Right-click the Add Record button. Point to Build Event on the shortcut menu.

The shortcut menu displays (Figure 8-28).

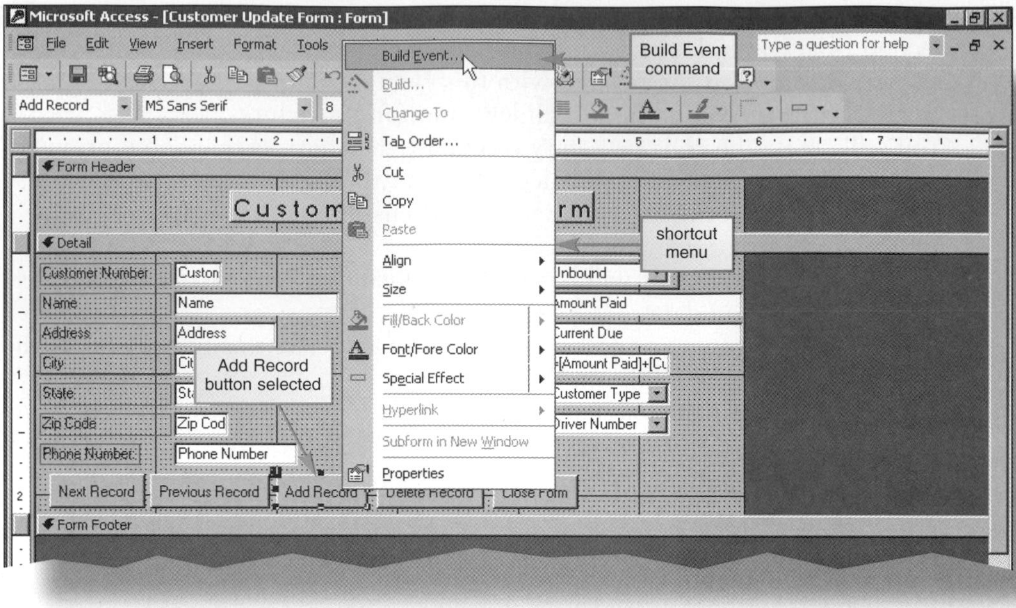

FIGURE 8-28

3 Click Build Event on the shortcut menu. If necessary, click the Maximize button.

The VBA code for the Add Record button displays (Figure 8-29). The important line in this code is DoCmd, which stands for Do Command. Following DoCmd, is the command, formally called a method, that will be executed; in this case GoToRecord. Following GoToRecord are the arguments, which are items that provide information that will be used by the method. The only argument necessary in this case is acNewRec. This is a code that indicates that Access is to move to the new record at the end of the table; that is, the position where the new record will be added. This command will not set the focus to any particular field automatically, however, so an insertion point still will not be produced. The Project Explorer window displays to the left of the Code window. The Project Explorer window may not be visible on your screen.

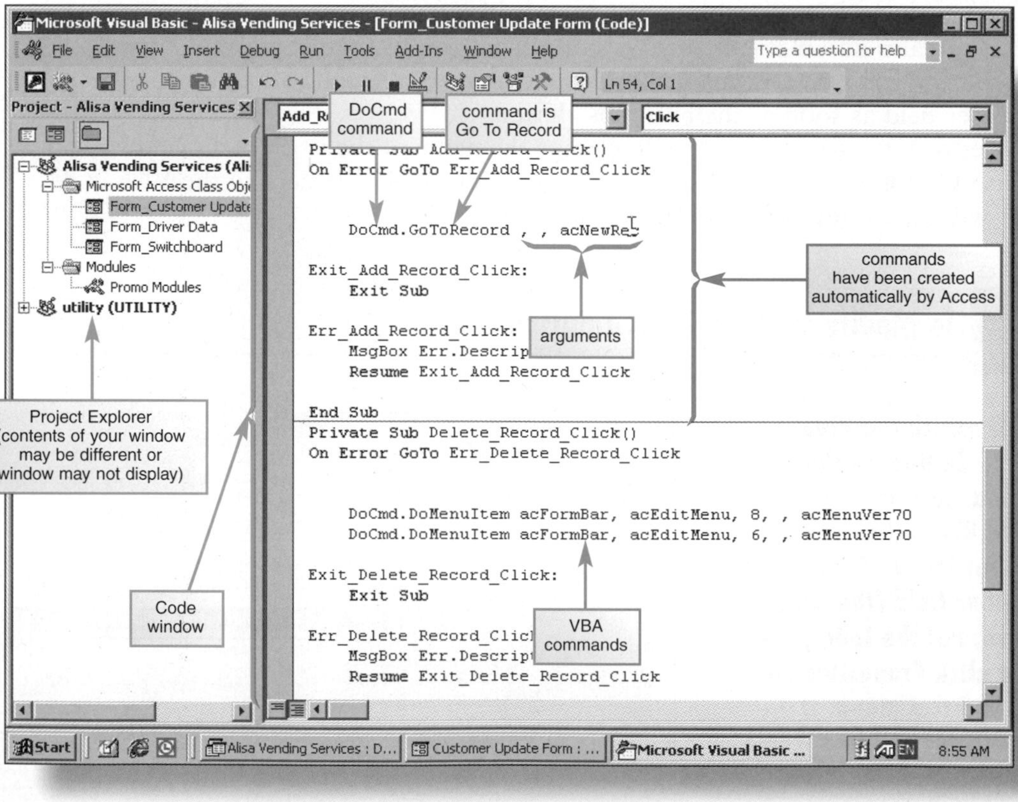

FIGURE 8-29

4 **Press the DOWN ARROW key four times, press the TAB key, and type** `Customer_Number.SetFocus` **as the additional statement. Press the ENTER key.**

The statement is entered (Figure 8-30). While typing, a box may display indicating selections for the statement. You may ignore this list. This statement will set the focus in the control named Customer_Number as soon as the previous statement (GoToRecord) is executed.

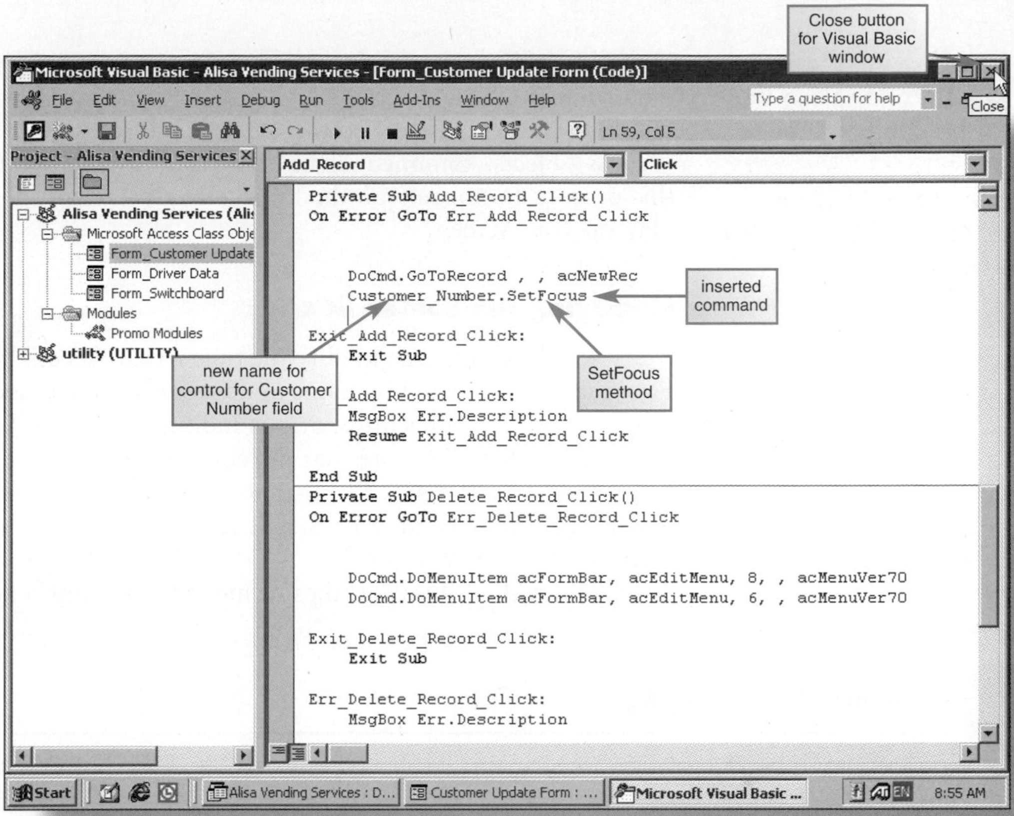

FIGURE 8-30

5 **Close the Microsoft Visual Basic - Alisa Vending Services - [Form_Customer Update Form (Code)] window. Click the View button on the toolbar, click Form View, and then click the Add Record button.**

An insertion point displays in the Customer Number field (Figure 8-31).

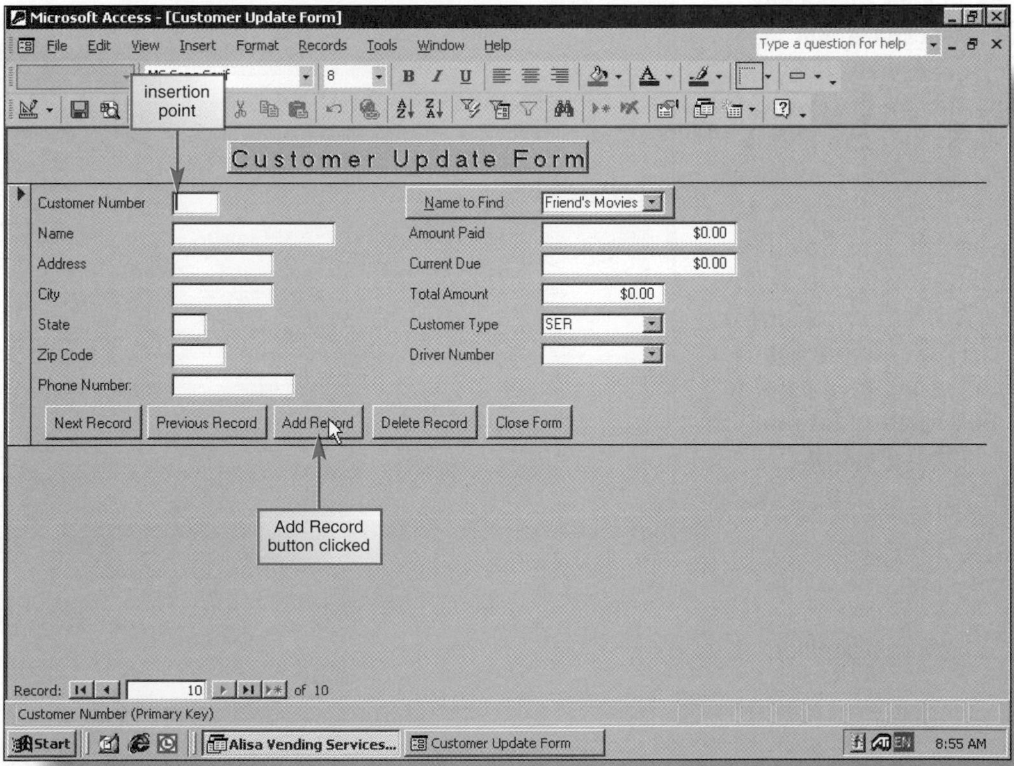

FIGURE 8-31

The large window on the right in Figure 8-29 on page A 8.28 is called the **Code window**. This is the area where you create and modify Visual Basic code. The window on the left is called the **Project Explorer**, which allows you to navigate among various objects contained in the database on which you are working. The steps in this project do not rely on the Project Explorer and the window may or may not display on your screen.

Modifying the Combo Box

The following steps modify the query that Access has created for the combo box. First the data is sorted by name and then the code associated with the On Current event property of the entire form is modified. The modification to the On Current event property will ensure that the combo box is kept current with the rest of the form; that is, it contains the name of the customer whose number currently displays in the Customer Number field. The final step changes the Tab Stop property for the combo box from Yes to No.

Perform the following steps to modify the combo box.

Steps To Modify the Combo Box

1 Click the View button on the toolbar to return to the design grid. Right-click the Name to Find combo box (the white space, not the label), and then click Properties on the shortcut menu. Be sure the All tab is selected. Note the number of your combo box, which may be different from the one shown in Figure 8-32, because it will be important later. Click the Row Source property, and then point to the Build button for the Row Source property.

The Combo Box: Combo29 property sheet displays (Figure 8-32). The combo box number is 29 (Combo29). (Yours may be different.) The Row Source property is selected. Depending on where you clicked the Row Source property, the value may or may not be highlighted.

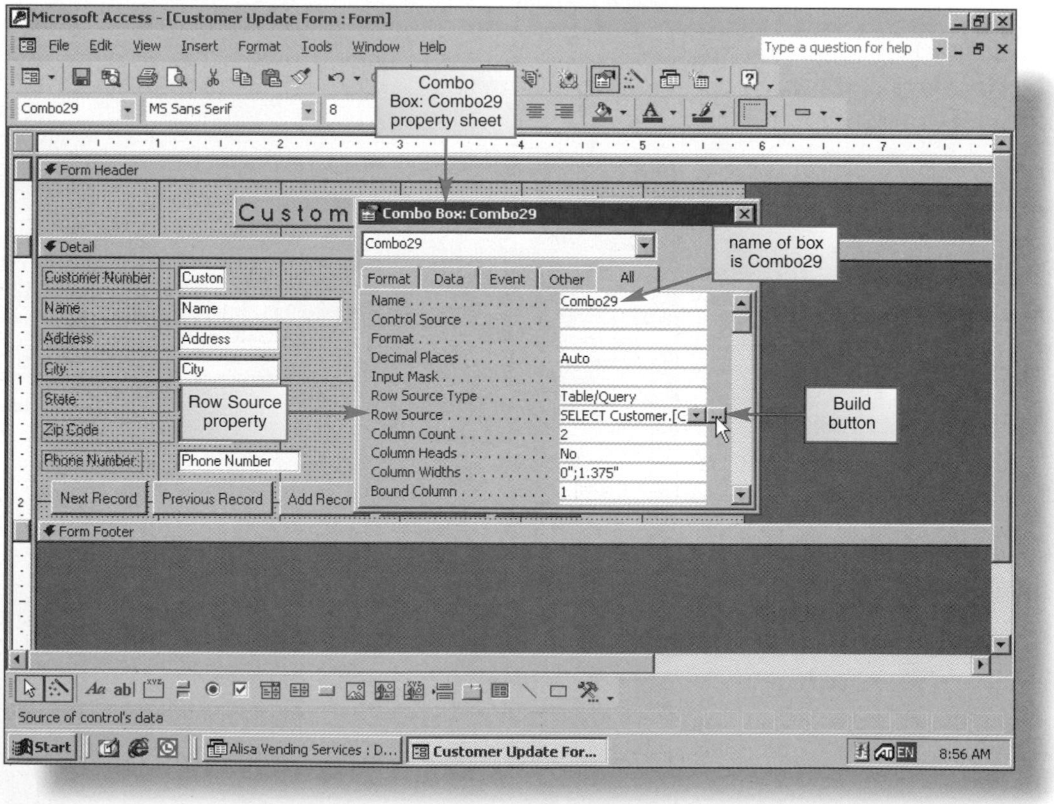

FIGURE 8-32

2 Click the Build button. Point to the Sort row under the Name field.

The SQL Statement : Query Builder window displays (Figure 8-33). This screen allows you to make changes just as you did when you created queries.

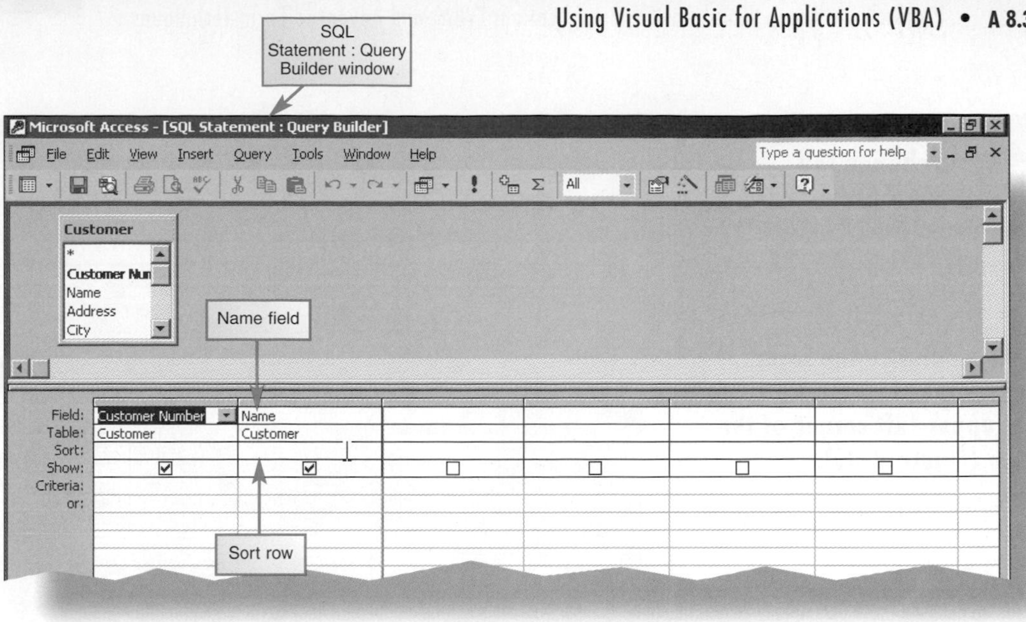

FIGURE 8-33

3 Click the Sort row in the Name field, click the box arrow that displays, and then click Ascending. Point to the Close Window button for the SQL Statement : Query Builder window.

The sort order is changed to Ascending (Figure 8-34).

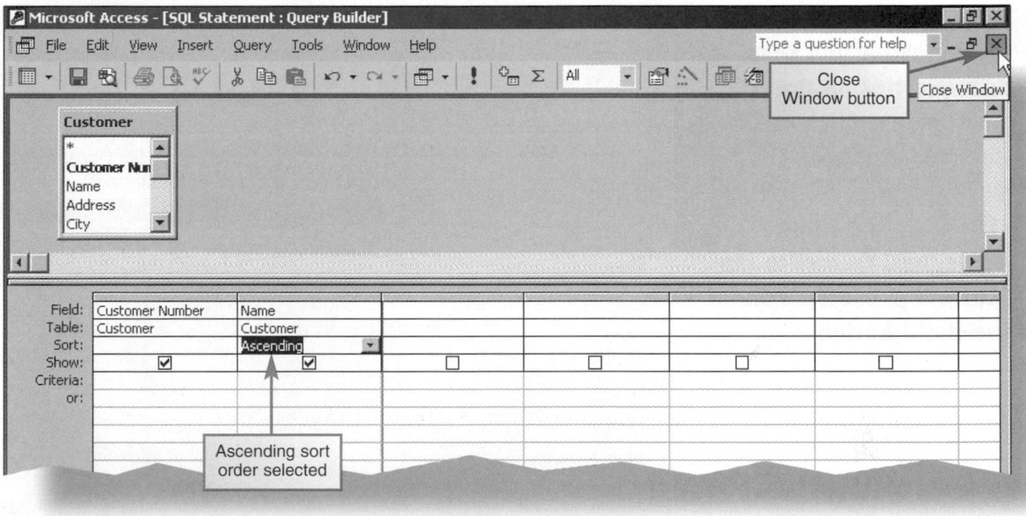

FIGURE 8-34

4 Close the SQL Statement : Query Builder window by clicking its Close Window button. Point to the Yes button.

The Microsoft Access dialog box displays (Figure 8-35).

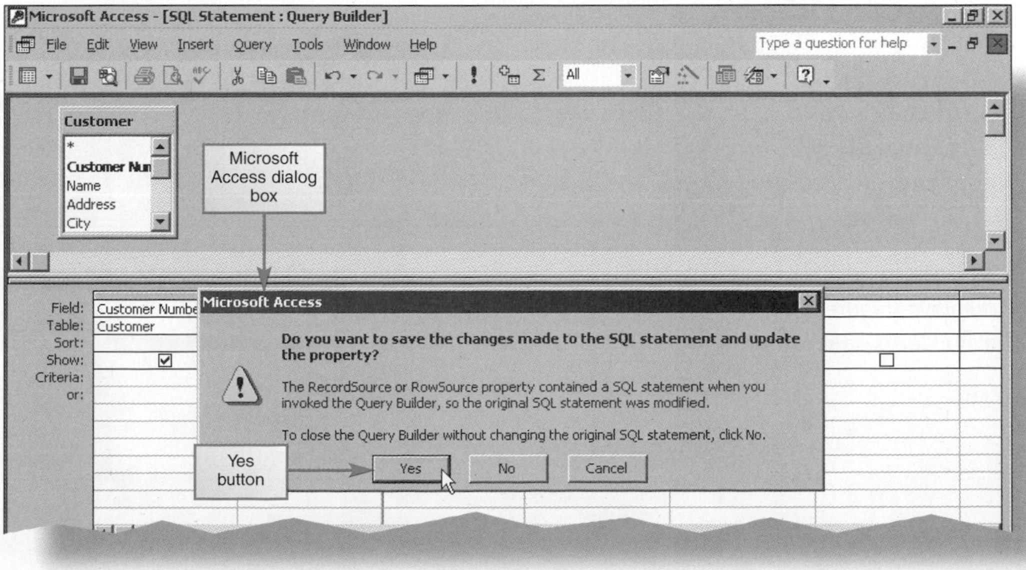

FIGURE 8-35

5 **Click the Yes button to change the property, and then close the Combo Box: Combo29 property sheet.**

6 **Point to the form selector, the box in the upper-left corner of the form (Figure 8-36).**

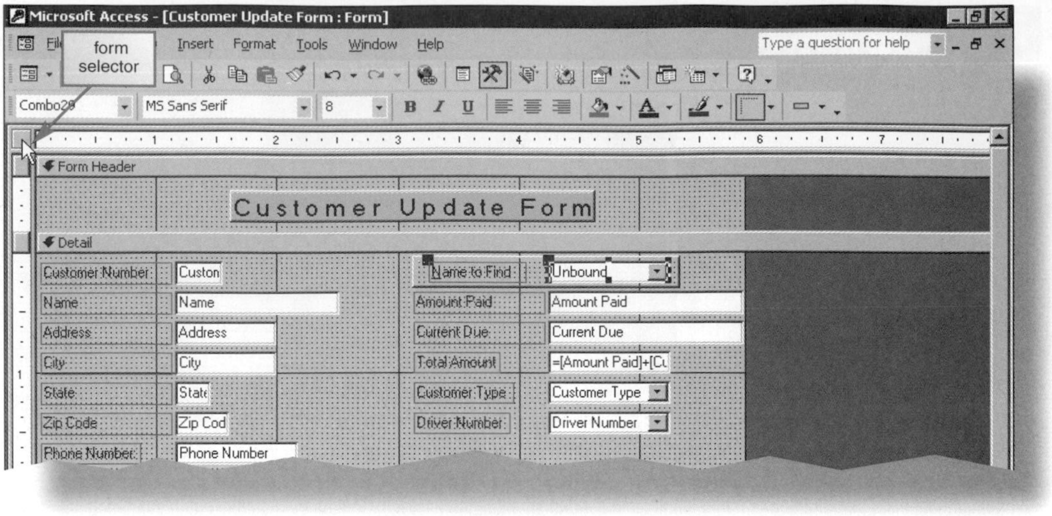

FIGURE 8-36

7 **Right-click the form selector, and then click Properties on the shortcut menu. Click the down scroll arrow on the Form property sheet until the On Current property displays, and then click the On Current property. Point to the Build button.**

The Form property sheet displays (Figure 8-37).

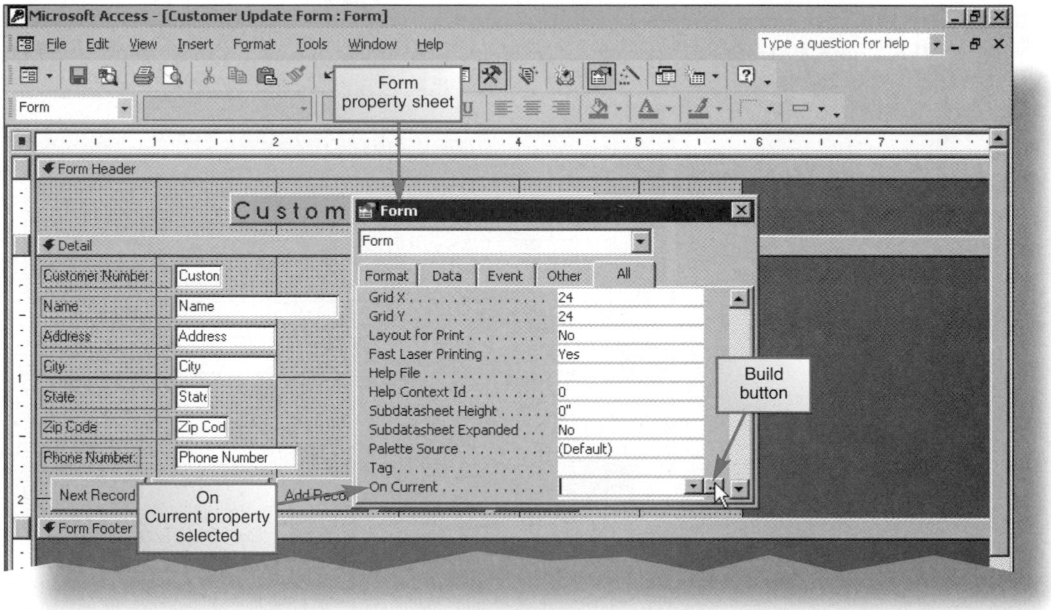

FIGURE 8-37

8 **Click the Build button, click Code Builder, and then point to the OK button.**

The Choose Builder dialog box displays (Figure 8-38). Code Builder is selected.

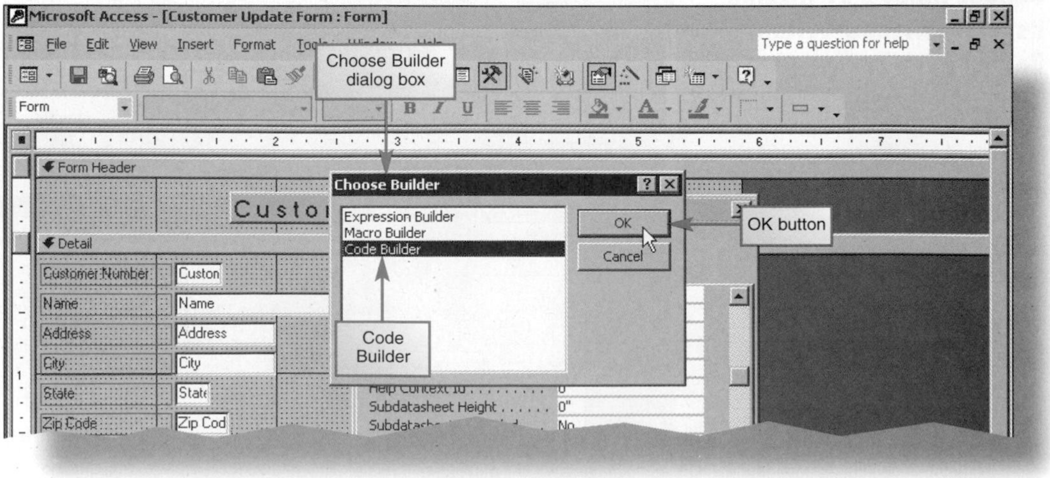

FIGURE 8-38

9 Click the OK button.

The code generated by Access for the form displays (Figure 8-39).

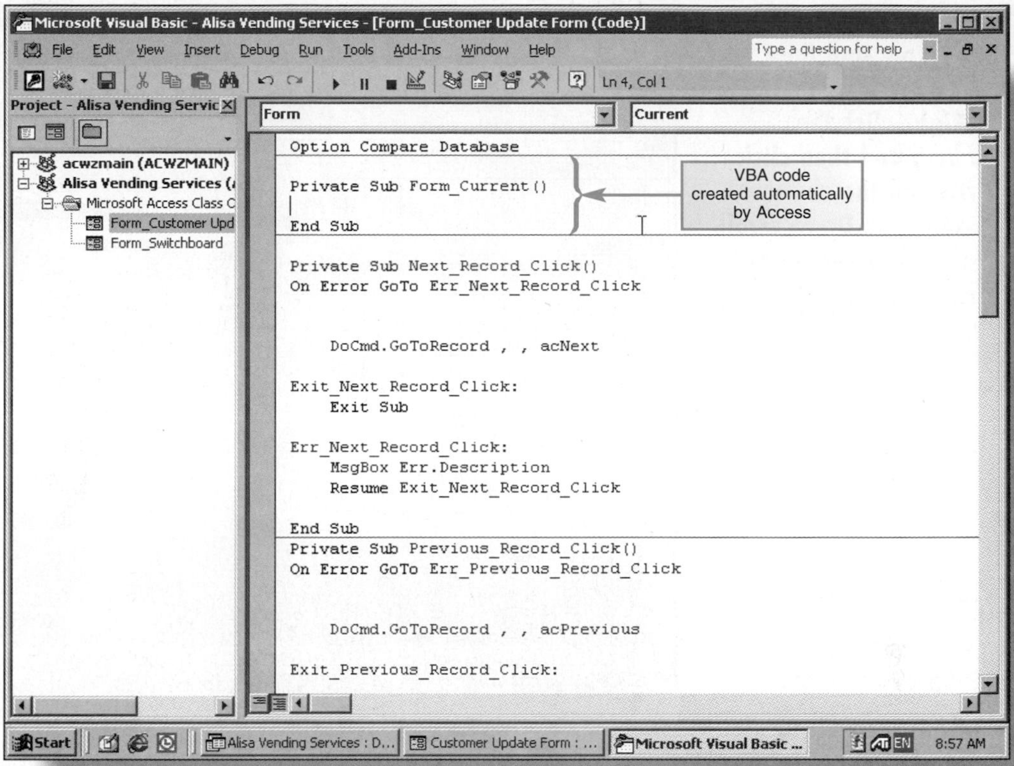

FIGURE 8-39

10 Press the TAB key and then type `Combo29 = Customer_Number ' Update the combo box` **in the position shown in Figure 8-40. Point to the Close button.**

This statement assumes your combo box is Combo29. If yours has a different number, use your number in the statement instead of 29. This statement will update the contents of the combo box using the customer number currently in the Customer_Number control. The portion of the statement following the apostrophe is a comment, describing the purpose of the statement.

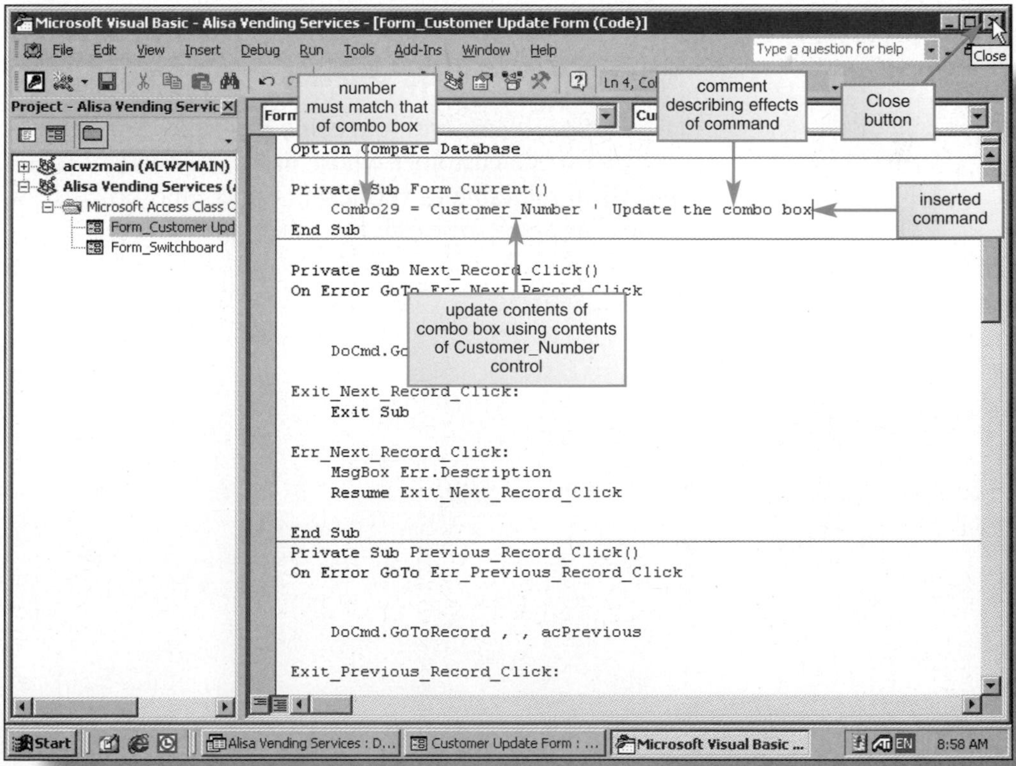

FIGURE 8-40

11 **Click the Close button, and then close the Form property sheet. Right-click the combo box, and then click Properties on the shortcut menu. Click the Down scroll arrow until the Tab Stop property displays, click the Tab Stop property, click the Tab Stop property box arrow, and then point to No (Figure 8-41).**

12 **Click No, and then close the Combo Box: Combo29 property sheet.**

The modifications to the combo box are complete.

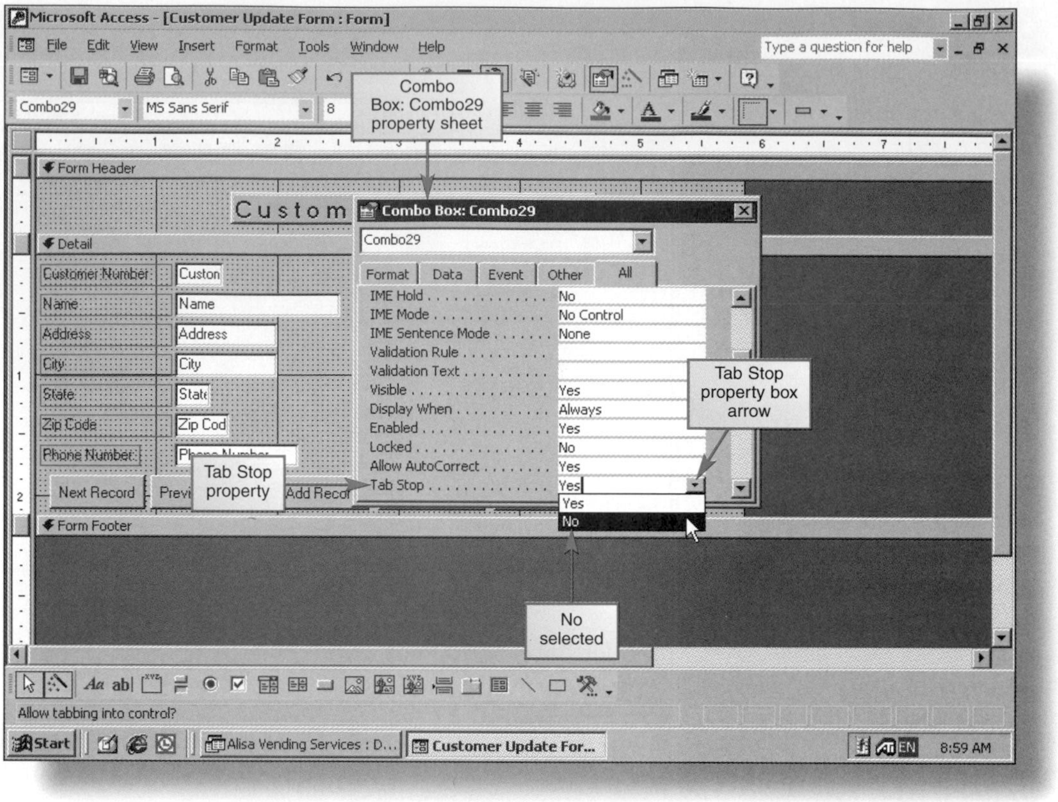

FIGURE 8-41

Using the Modified Combo Box

The problems with the combo box now are corrected. The following steps first search for the customer whose name is Friend's Movies, and then move to the next record in the table to verify that the combo box also will be updated. Perform the following steps to search for a customer.

Steps To Use the Modified Combo Box to Search for a Customer

1 Click the View button on the toolbar to display the Customer Update Form in Form view, and then click the Name to Find box arrow.

A list of names displays (Figure 8-42). The list is in alphabetical order. (Baldwin-Reed does not display, because the name on the first record, Bayside Hotel, comes after Baldwin-Reed. If you clicked the Up scroll arrow to move up to the first element in the list, Baldwin-Reed would display immediately above Bayside Hotel.)

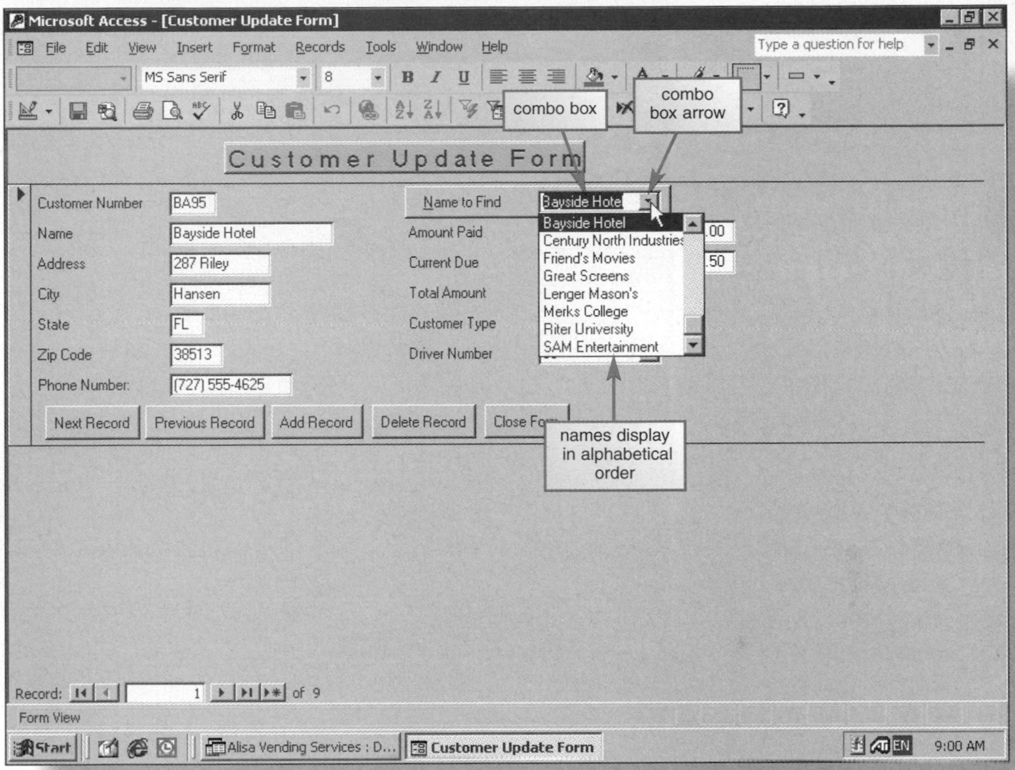

FIGURE 8-42

2 Click Friend's Movies and then point to the Next Record button.

Customer FR28 displays on the form (Figure 8-43).

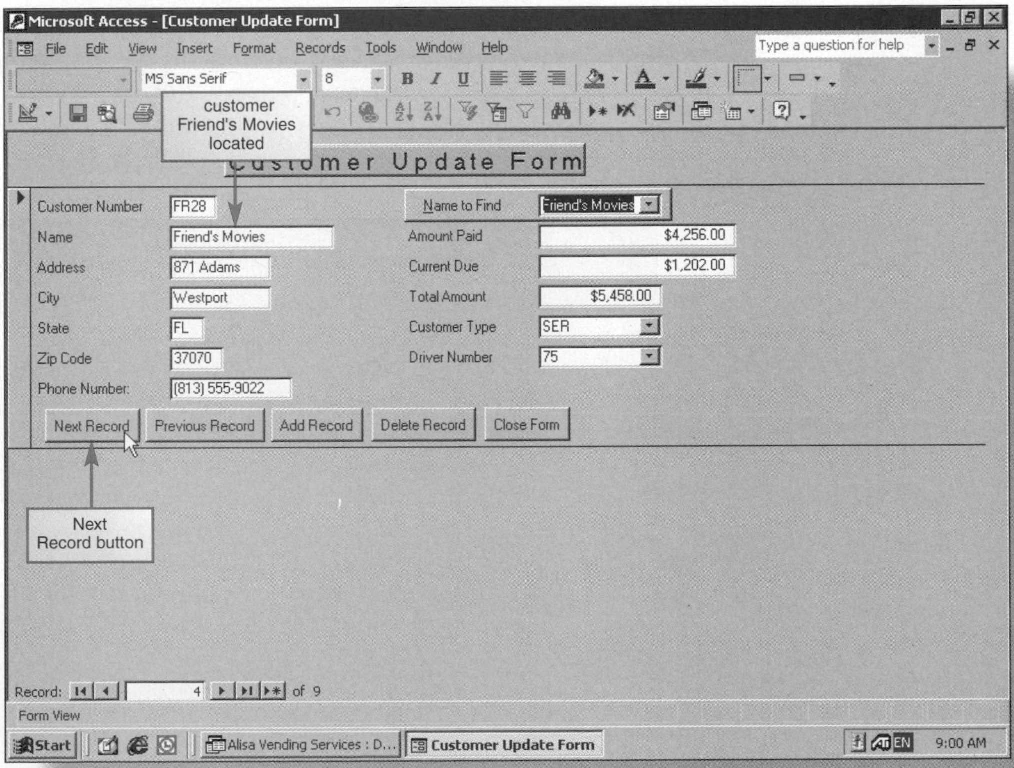

FIGURE 8-43

3 **Click the Next Record button.**

Customer GS29 displays on the form (Figure 8-44). The customer's name also displays in the combo box.

4 **Close the form by clicking its Close Window button, and then click the Yes button to save the changes.**

The changes are saved.

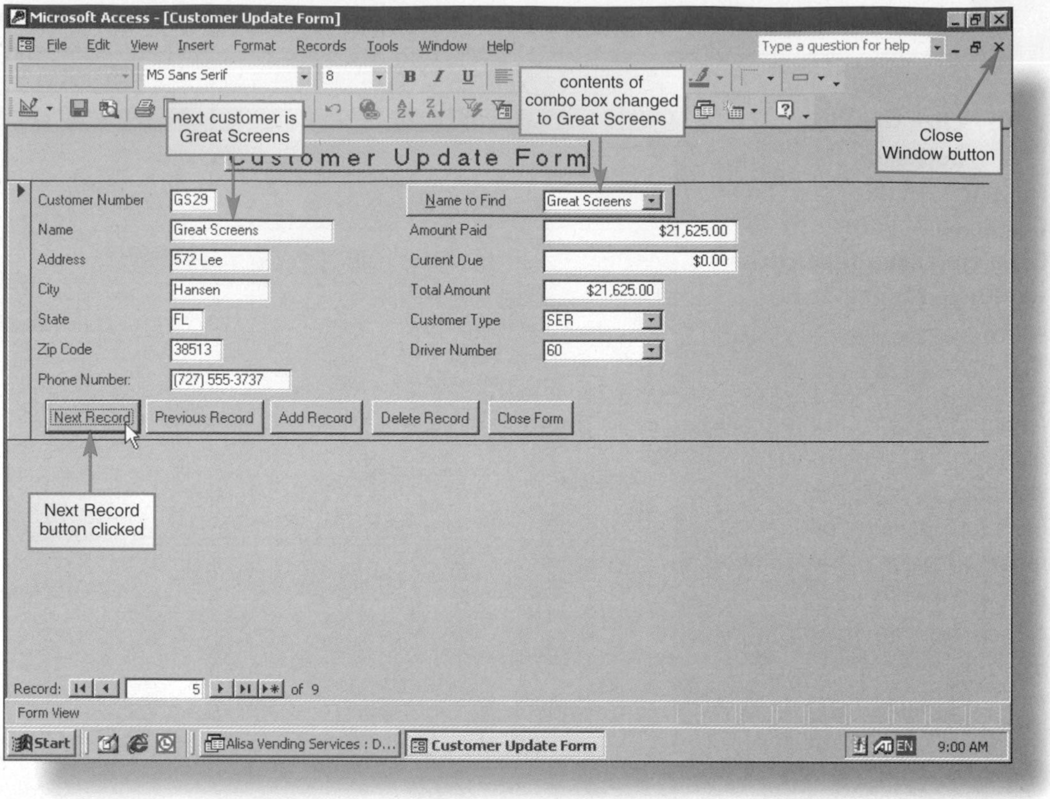

FIGURE 8-44

Creating Functions in a Standard Module

The functions that calculate the promotional factor and promotional amount should be available to be used throughout the database. In this project, for example, you will use these functions in a query and also from within a form. In order to have functions widely available, they are placed in a standard module. The function to calculate the promotional factor is called PromoFactor and is shown in Table 8-10.

Table 8-10 PromoFactor Function

STATEMENT

```
Function PromoFactor(Customer_Type)
    ' Determine PromoFactor based on Customer Type
    If Customer_Type = "EDU" Then
        PromoFactor = 1.05 ' Promo factor for Educational customers
    ElseIf Customer_Type = "SER" Then
        PromoFactor = 1.03 ' Promo factor for Service customers
    ElseIf Customer_Type = "MAN" Then
        PromoFactor = 1.02 ' Promo factor for Manufacturing customers
    Else
        PromoFactor = 1 ' Promo factor for others (should not be any)
    End If

End Function
```

The following is an explanation of the lines in the PromoFactor function:

Line 1. The Function statement indicates that the code between the word Function and the End Function statement (line 13) forms a function. This function is called PromoFactor and has an argument of Customer_Type. The statement within this function will assign an appropriate value to PromoFactor.

Line 2. This line is a comment because it begins with an apostrophe. It indicates the purpose of the function.

Line 3. This line begins an If statement. This particular If statement checks to see if the Customer_Type is EDU.

Line 4. This line will be executed if the Customer_Type is EDU. It will set PromoFactor to 1.05. The portion following the apostrophe is a comment describing the fact that this is the appropriate value for customers whose type is EDU.

Line 5. This line checks to see if the Customer_Type is SER.

Line 6. This line will be executed if the Customer_Type is SER. It will set PromoFactor to 1.03, the appropriate value for customers whose type is SER.

Line 7. This line checks to see if the Customer_Type is MAN.

Line 8. This line will be executed if the Customer_Type is MAN. It will set PromoFactor to 1.02, the appropriate value for customers whose type is MAN.

Line 9. There is no test on this line. This final ELSE indicates the action to be taken if all the previous tests failed; that is, if the customer type is something other than EDU, SER, or MAN.

Line 10. This line will be executed if all the other tests failed. It will set the PromoFactor to 1. As the comment indicates, no customers should fall into this category. This is put here just in case a customer happened to get into the database with an invalid customer type.

Line 11. This line indicates the end of the If statement.

Line 12. This line is intentionally left blank for readability.

Line 13. This line marks the end of the function.

The function to calculate the promotional amount is called PromoAmount and is shown in Table 8-11.

Table 8-11 PromoAmount Function

LINE	*STATEMENT*
1	`Function PromoAmount(Customer_Type, Current_Due)`
2	`    ' Determine PromoAmount based on Customer Type and Current Due`
3	`    PromoAmount = PromoFactor(Customer_Type) * Current_Due`
4	
5	`End Function`

The following is an explanation of the lines in the PromoAmount function:

Line 1. The Function statement indicates that the code between the word Function and the End Function statement (line 5) forms a function. This function is called PromoAmount and has two arguments, Customer_Type, and Current_Due. The statement within this function will assign an appropriate value to PromoAmount.

Line 2. This line is a comment because it begins with an apostrophe. It indicates the purpose of the function.

Line 3. This line will calculate the appropriate value for PromoAmount. It uses the PromoFactor function to find the appropriate factor for a customer with the given type. It multiplies this factor by the current due amount, and then sets PromoAmount equal to the result.

Line 4. This line is intentionally left blank for readability.
Line 5. This line marks the end of the function.

The following steps create these functions in a standard module that will be saved with the name Promo Modules.

Steps To Create Functions in a Standard Module

1 Click Modules on the Objects bar in the Database window and then point to the New button in the Database window.

The Modules object is selected (Figure 8-45).

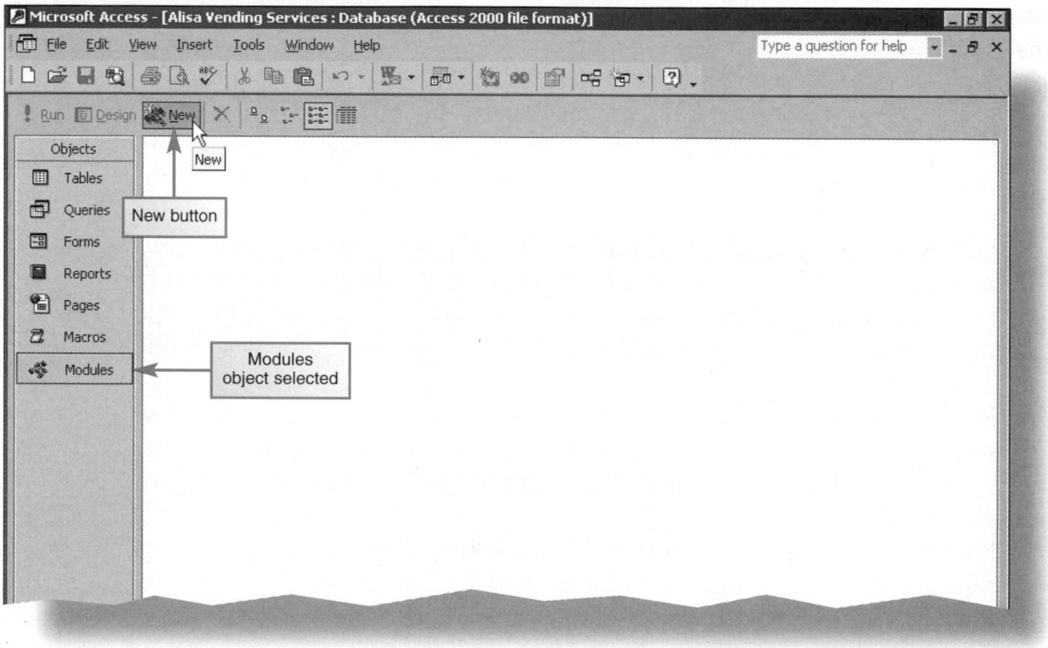

FIGURE 8-45

2 Click the New button on the Database toolbar and be sure the window is maximized.

The Alisa Vending Services – Module1 (Code) window displays (Figure 8-46).

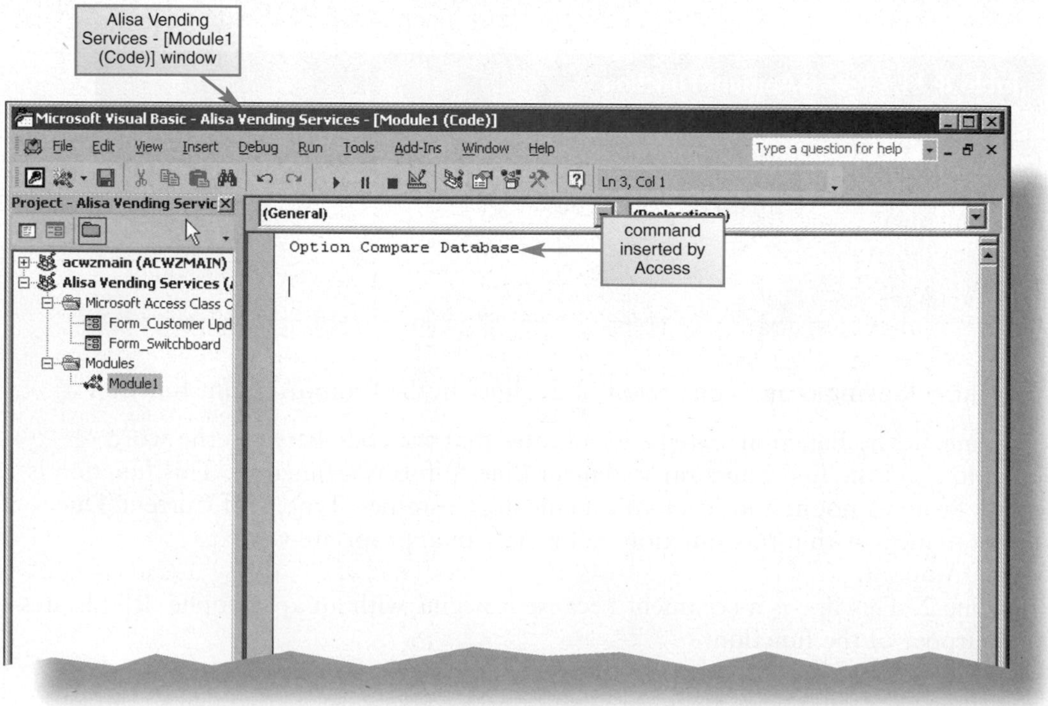

FIGURE 8-46

3 **Type** `Function PromoFactor (Customer_Type)` **and then press the ENTER key.**

Visual Basic creates a function and adds the End Function statement (Figure 8-47). The insertion point is positioned between the Function statement and the End Function statement.

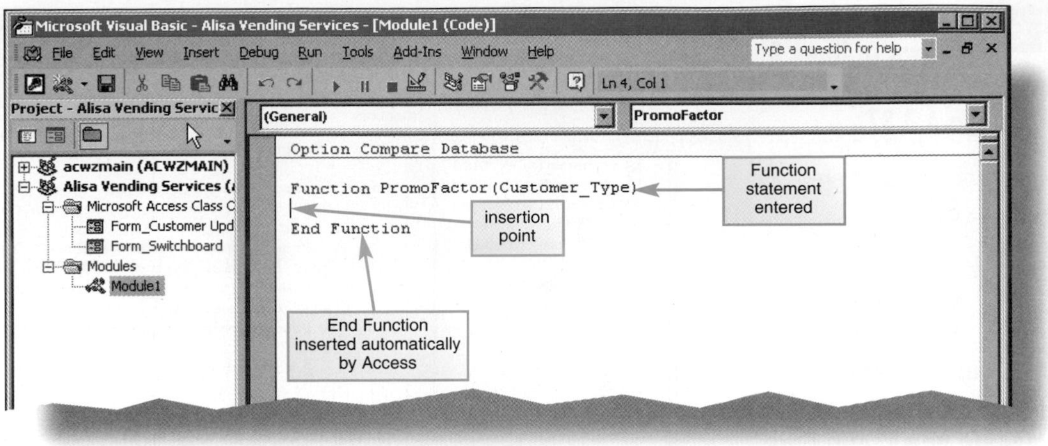

FIGURE 8-47

4 **Type the statements shown in lines 2 through 12 of Table 8-10 on page A 8.36.**

The function is entered (Figure 8-48).

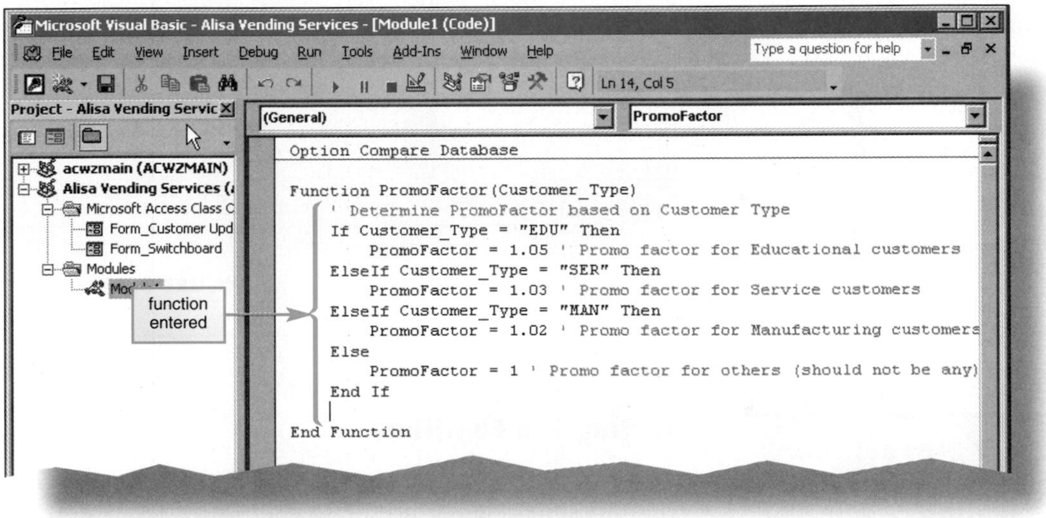

FIGURE 8-48

5 **Use the DOWN ARROW key to move the insertion point below the End Function statement. Type** `Function PromoAmount(Customer_Type, Current_Due)` **and then press the ENTER key.**

Visual Basic creates a function and adds the End Function statement (Figure 8-49). The insertion point is positioned between the Function statement and the End Function statement.

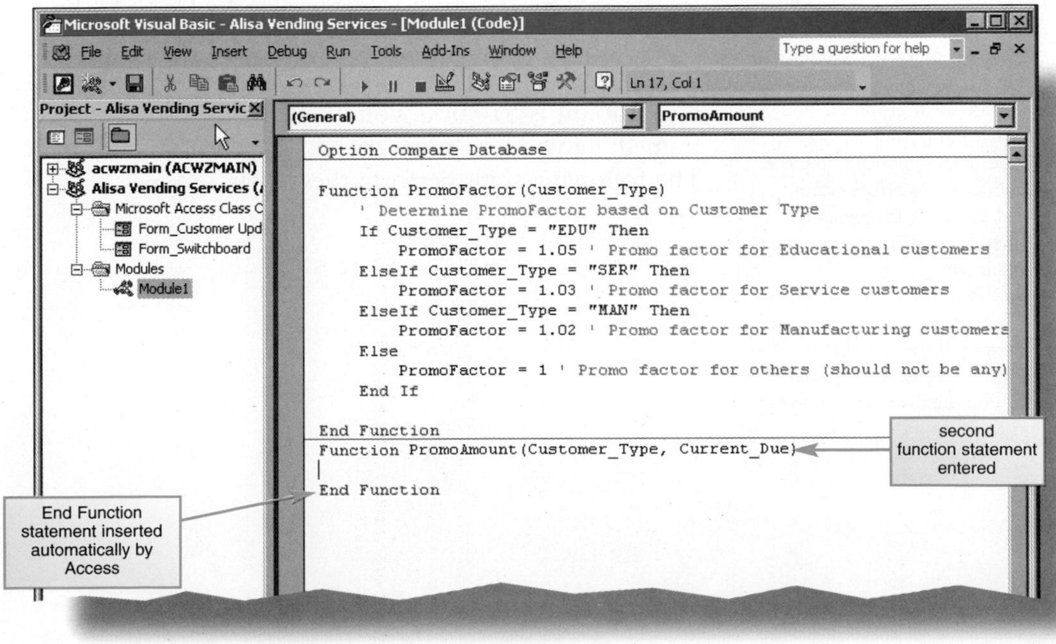

FIGURE 8-49

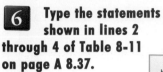

6 Type the statements shown in lines 2 through 4 of Table 8-11 on page A 8.37.

The function is entered (Figure 8-50).

7 Click the Save button on the Standard toolbar, type `Promo Modules` **as the module name, and then click the OK button.**

The module is saved as Promo Modules.

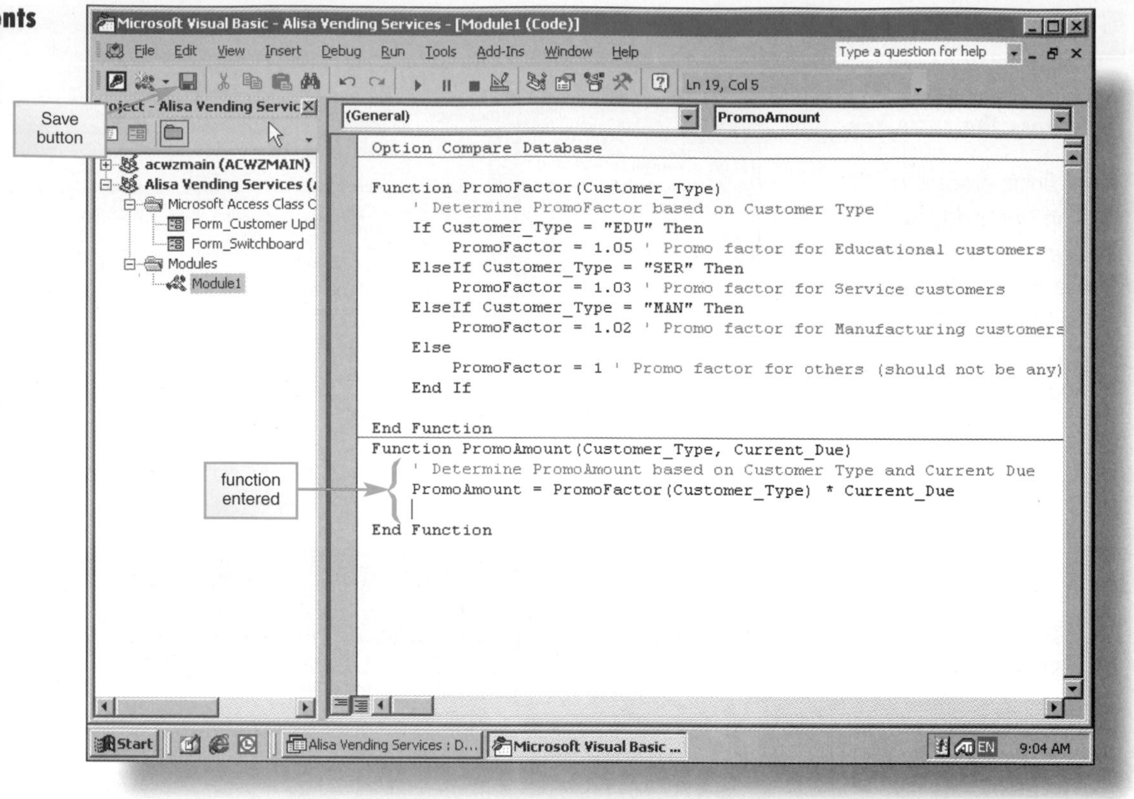

FIGURE 8-50

More About

Testing

Testing is only one piece of a larger process known as debugging. Debugging is the process of locating and fixing errors in a program. Compile-time errors usually are caused by mistakes in grammar and punctuation (syntax errors) or by mistakes in constructing the code. Run-time errors occur when the code is executed. An example of a run-time error is attempting to divide by zero. Logic errors occur when the program does not perform as intended and produces incorrect results. Testing will help you uncover both run-time and logic errors.

Testing the Functions

Visual Basic provides an easy way to test functions and procedures. You can use the Immediate window. When you do so, you can type a question mark, followed by the procedure name along with values for any arguments. To test if the PromoFactor function calculates the right value for customers of type EDU, for example, you would type `?PromoFactor("EDU")` in the Immediate window, press the ENTER key, and then see if the correct value is displayed. To test if the PromoAmount function calculates the right amount for a customer whose type is EDU and whose current due amount is $10,000, you would type `?PromoAmount("EDU",10000)` in the Immediate window, press the ENTER key, and see if the correct value is displayed. The following steps perform these tests.

Steps To Test the Functions

1 **Click View on the menu bar, and then click Immediate Window on the View menu. Type** ?PromoFactor("EDU") **in the Immediate window, and then press the ENTER key.**

Visual Basic displays 1.05, which is the correct factor for a customer type of EDU (Figure 8-51).

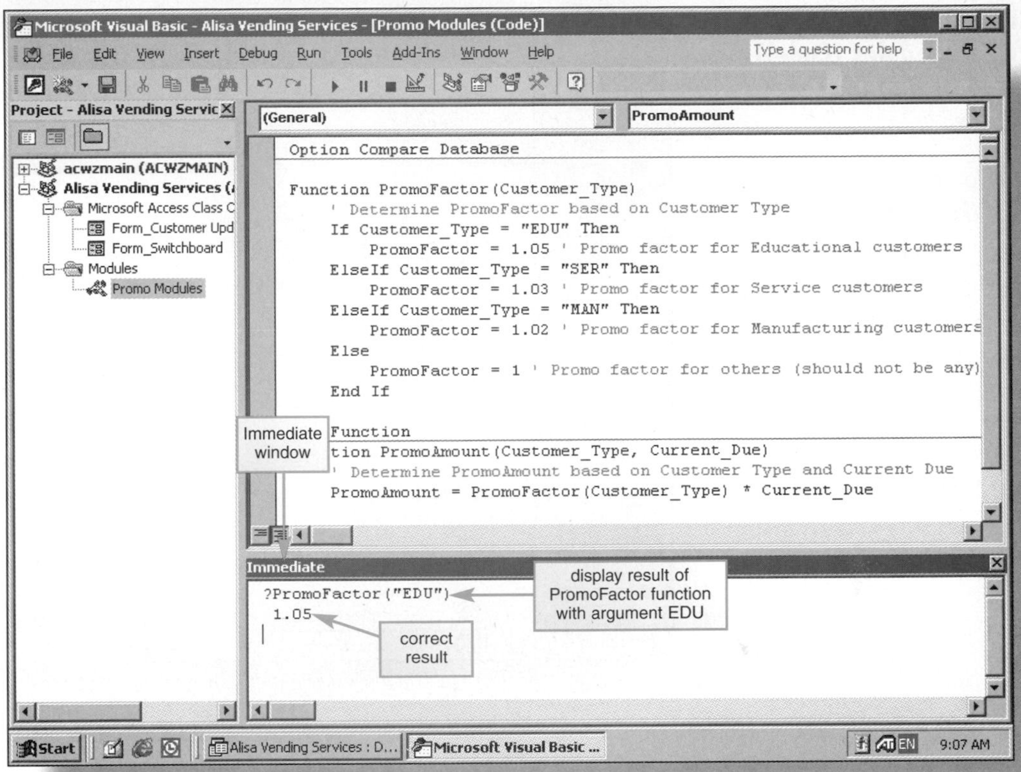

FIGURE 8-51

2 **Type** ?PromoAmount ("EDU",10000) **in the Immediate window, and then press the ENTER key.**

Visual Basic displays 10500 ($10,500), which is the correct amount for a customer type of EDU and a current due amount of 10000 ($10,000) (Figure 8-52).

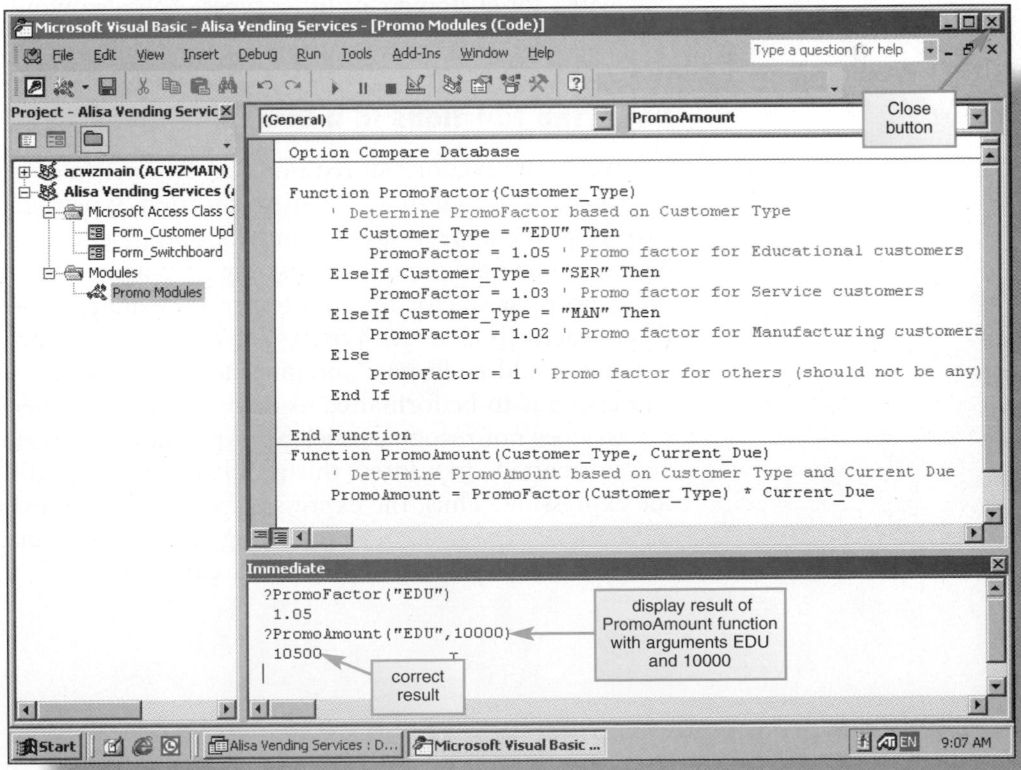

FIGURE 8-52

3 Click the Close button for the Microsoft Visual Basic – Alisa Vending Services – [Promo Modules (Code)] window to close the window.

The Database window displays (Figure 8-53).

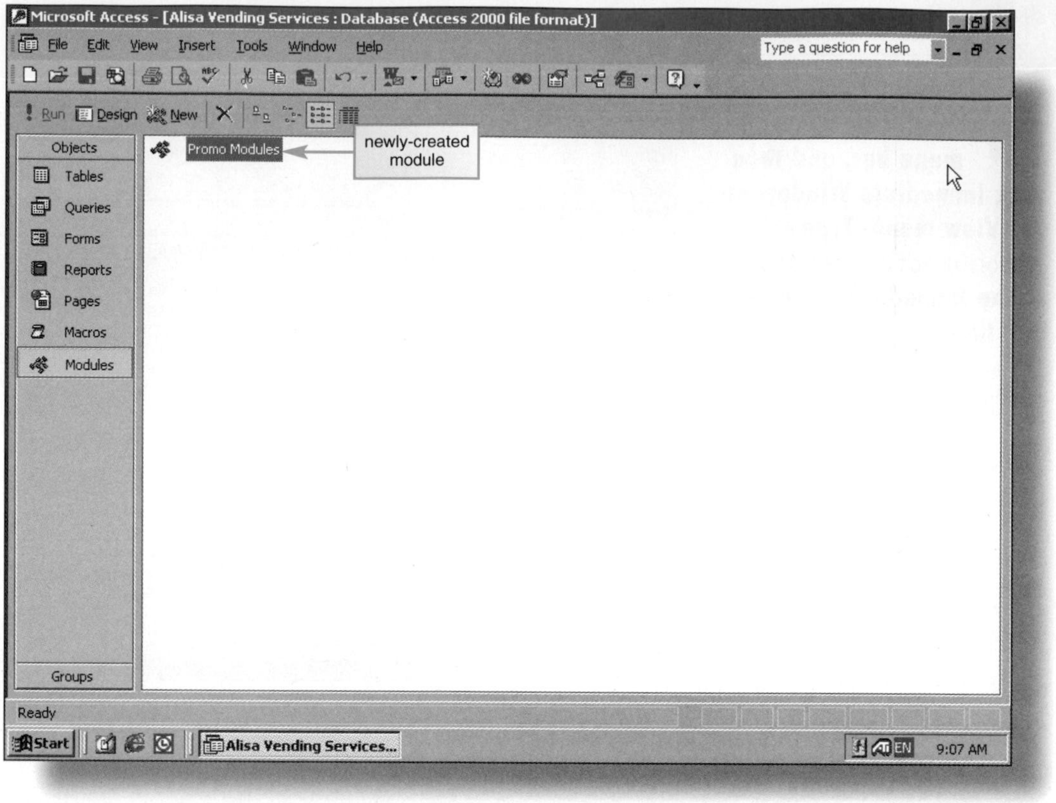

FIGURE 8-53

To complete the tests, you would use similar steps to see if the correct values are calculated for customers of other types. You also would test with an invalid value, for example, “NON”.

Using the Functions in a Query

With the functions stored in a standard module, they are available to be used anywhere in the database. To use a function, type the name of the function and then place the appropriate argument or arguments in parentheses. If the arguments happen to be field names, enclose the field names in square brackets. To calculate the appropriate factor for a customer, for example, the expression would be PromoFactor([Customer Type]). The appropriate expression for the promotion amount would be PromoAmount([Customer Type],[Current Due]). In addition, this expression is to be formatted as currency with two decimal places. In some cases, Access does not recognize such an expression as returning a numeric value that can be reformatted. To address this problem, you can multiply the function by 1.00 in the expression. Thus, the expression would be PromoAmount([Customer Type], [Current Due]) * 1.00. The following steps use the functions in a query and also reformat the promotional amount as currency.

Steps To Use the Functions in a Query

1 In the Database window, click Tables on the Objects bar, and then click Customer. Click the New Object: AutoForm button arrow on the Database toolbar. Click Query. Be sure Design View is selected, and then click the OK button. If necessary, maximize the Query1 : Select Query window. Resize the upper and lower panes and the Customer field list so all the fields in the Customer table display. One-by-one double-click the Customer Number, Name, Current Due, and Customer Type fields. Right-click the column following Customer Type, and then click Zoom on the shortcut menu. Type `Promo Factor:PromoFactor([Customer Type])` **and then point to the OK button.**

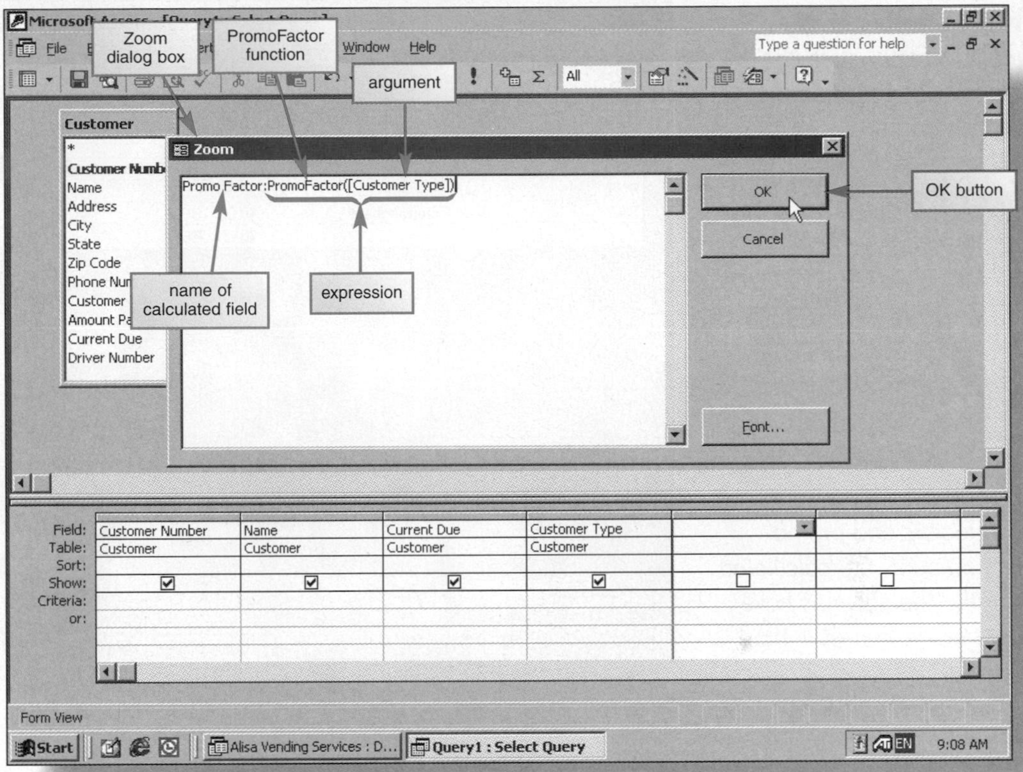

FIGURE 8-54

The expression for the Promo Factor is entered in the Zoom dialog box (Figure 8-54).

2 Click the OK button. Right-click the column following Promo Factor, and then click Zoom on the shortcut menu. Type `Promo Amount:PromoAmount([Customer Type], [Current Due])*1.00` **and then point to the OK button.**

The expression for the Promo Amount is entered in the Zoom dialog box (Figure 8-55).

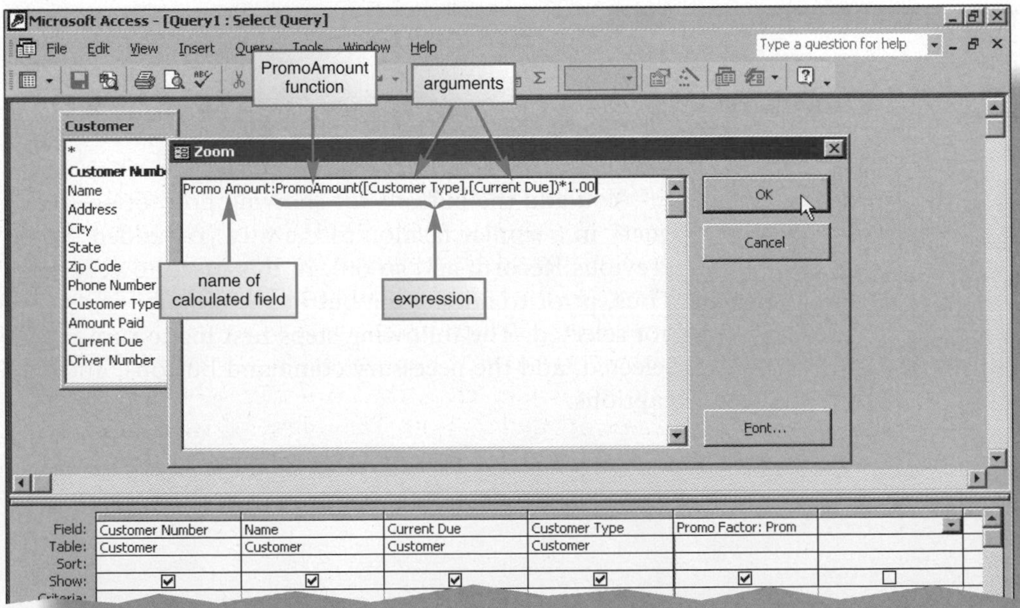

FIGURE 8-55

3 **Click the OK button. Right-click the PromoAmount column, click Properties on the shortcut menu, click the Format property, click the Format property box arrow, and then click Currency. Close the property sheet by clicking its Close button. Run the query, resize each column to best fit the data by double-clicking the right border of the column heading.**

The results display (Figure 8-56). The promotional factors and promotional amounts are calculated correctly. The columns have been resized to best fit the data. The format of the PromoAmount column is changed.

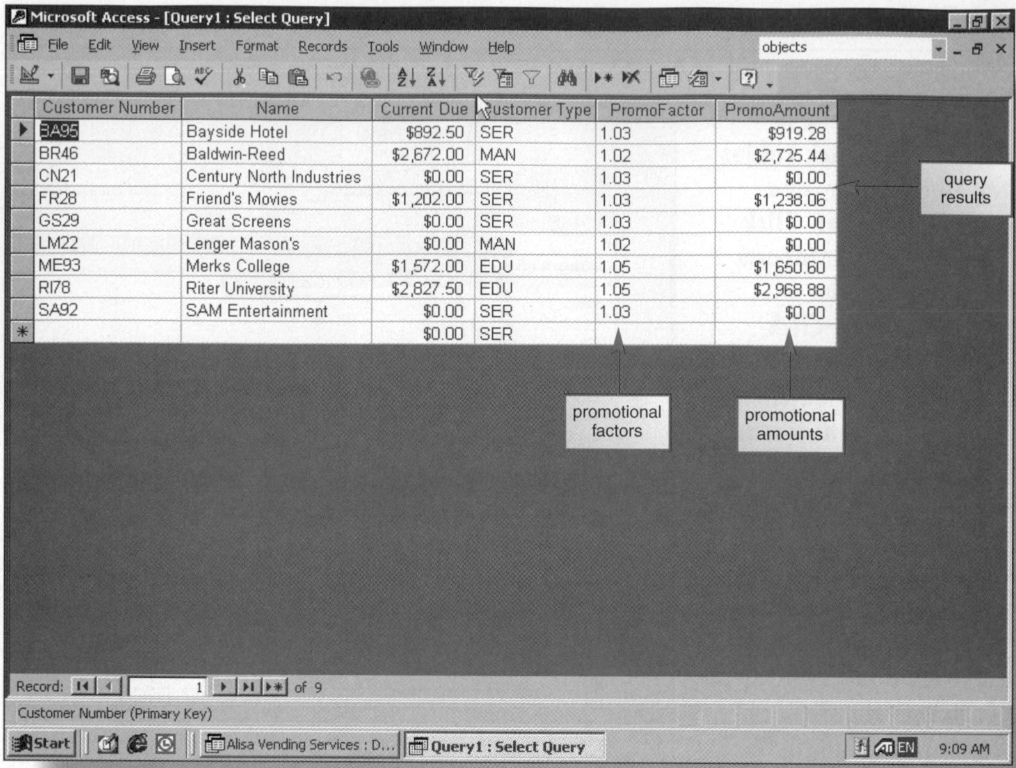

FIGURE 8-56

4 **Close the window containing the query by clicking its Close Window button, click the Yes button to save the query, type** `Promo Amount Query` **as the name, and then click the OK button.**

The query is created and saved.

Adding Buttons to the Customer Update Form without the Control Wizards

You add the buttons for showing promotion data and running the promotion query in a similar fashion to the way you added the previous buttons (Next Record, Previous Record, and so on). In this case, however, you will not use the wizard. Thus, prior to adding the buttons you must make sure the Control Wizards tool is not selected. The following steps first make sure the Control Wizards tool is not selected, add the necessary command buttons, and then change the names and captions.

Steps To Add Buttons to the Customer Update Form without the Control Wizards

1 Click Forms on the Objects bar, right-click the Customer Update Form, click Design View on the shortcut menu, and then maximize the window if it already is not maximized. If the field list displays, click its Close button. Be sure the toolbox displays and is docked at the bottom of the screen, and then point to the Control Wizards tool in the toolbox.

The Customer Update Form displays (Figure 8-57).

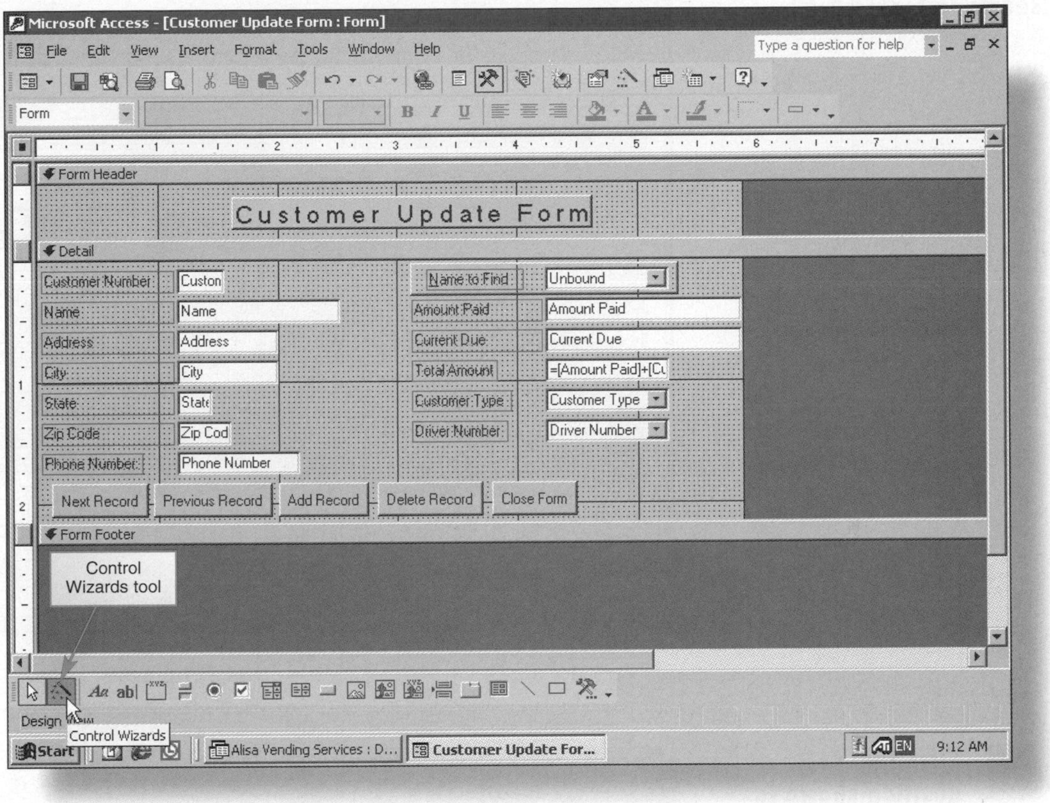

FIGURE 8-57

2 If the Control Wizards tool currently is selected, click the tool so it is no longer selected. Point to the Command Button tool.

The Control Wizards tool is not selected (Figure 8-58).

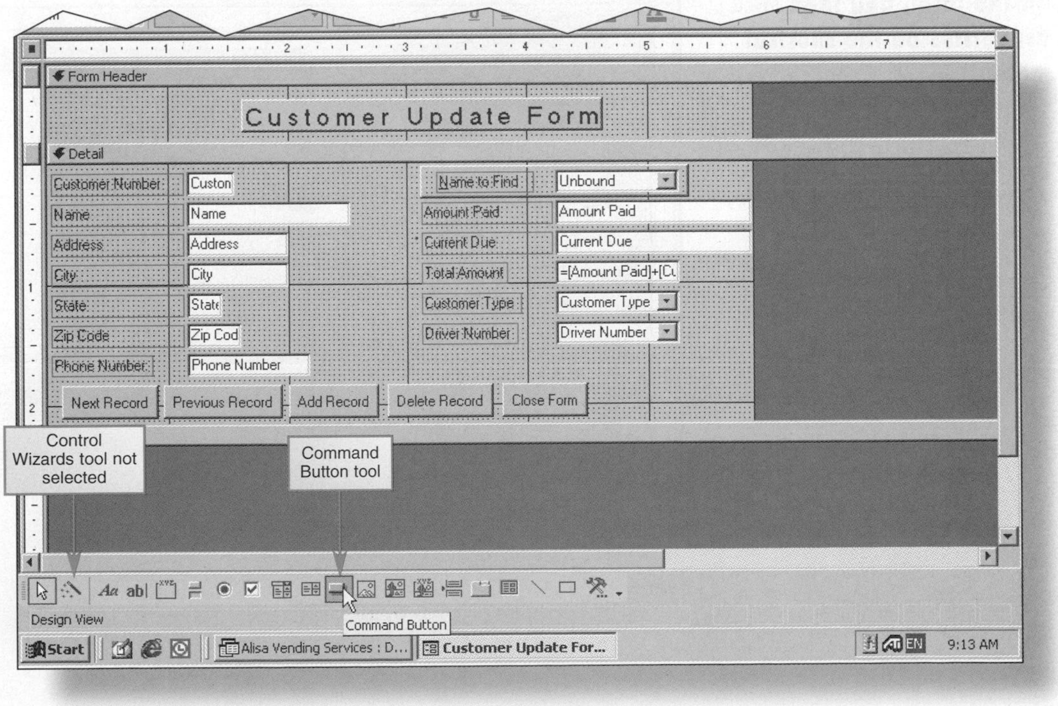

FIGURE 8-58

3 Click the Command Button tool and then move the pointer to the approximate position shown in Figure 8-59.

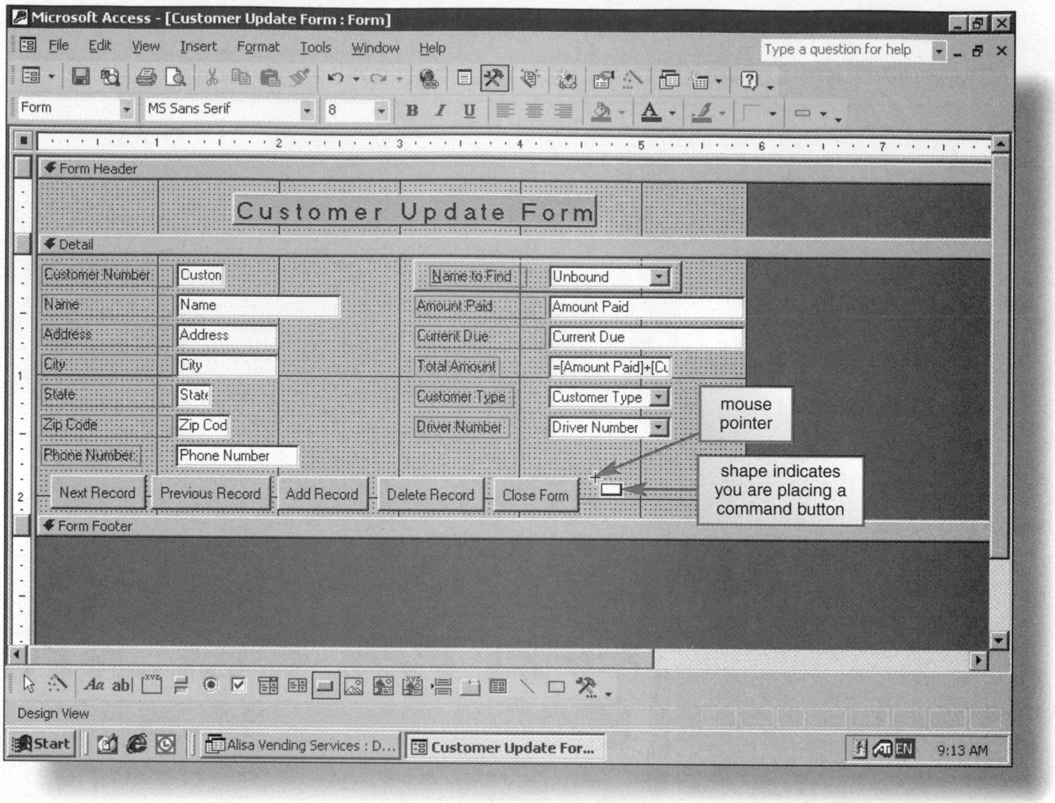

FIGURE 8-59

4 Click the position shown in Figure 8-59, right-click the button that is placed on the form, and then click Properties on the shortcut menu.

The property sheet for the new button displays (Figure 8-60). Your command button name may have a different number.

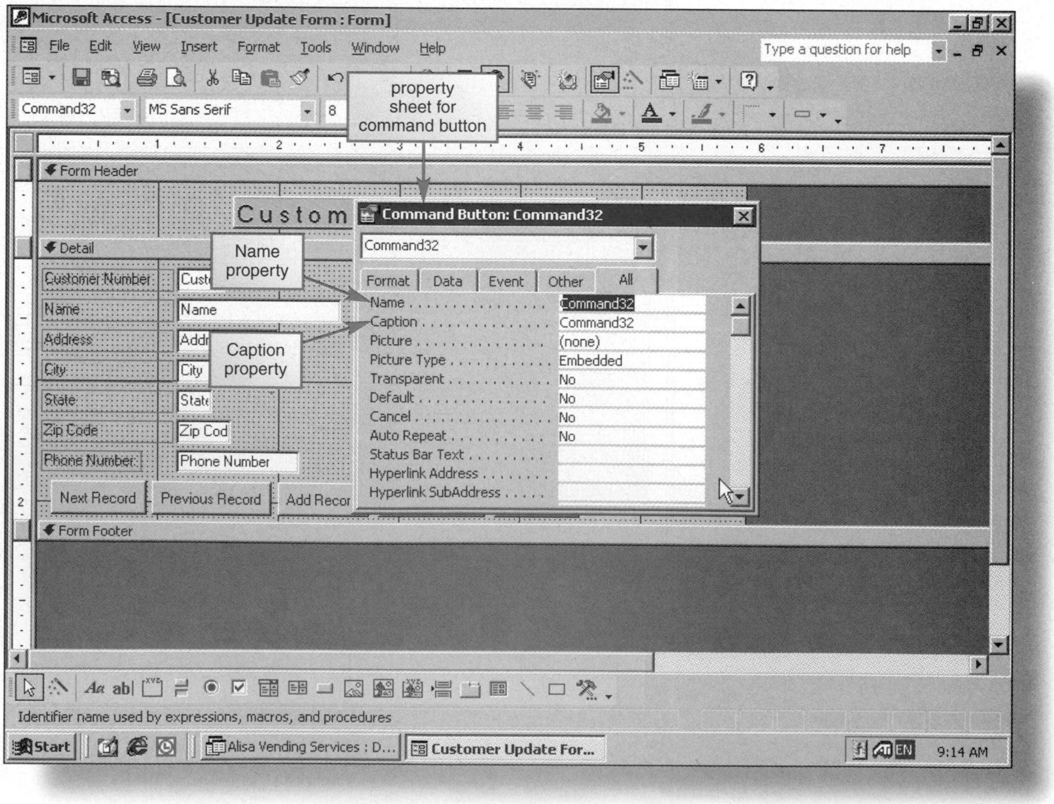

FIGURE 8-60

5 **Change the Name property to cmdPromo and then change the Caption property to Show Promotion. Point to the Close button for the property sheet.**

The name and caption are changed (Figure 8-61).

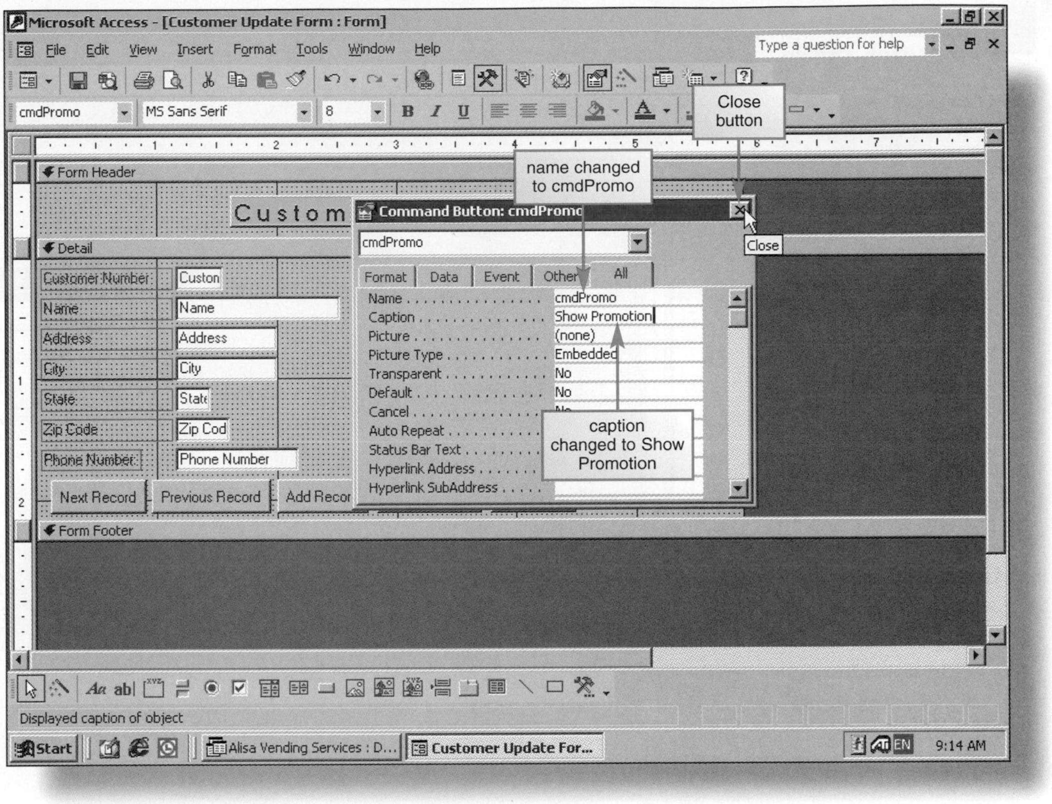

FIGURE 8-61

6 **Click the Close button for the property sheet, click the Command Button tool in the toolbox and then move the pointer to the approximate location shown in Figure 8-62.**

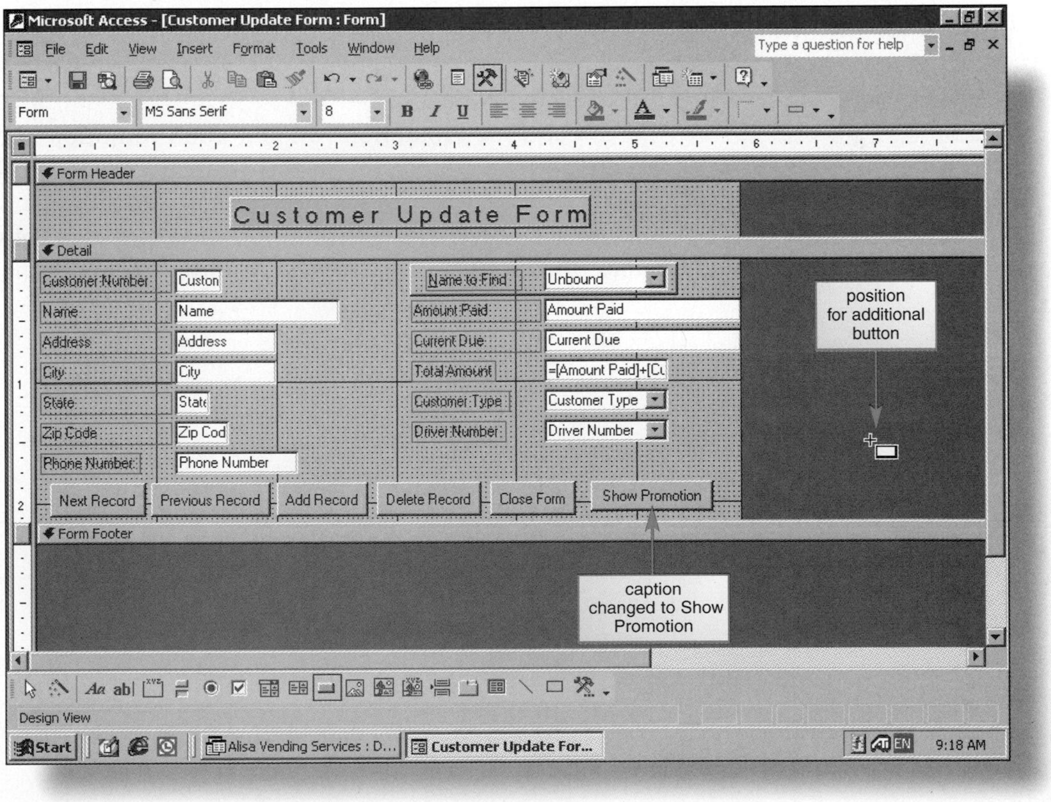

FIGURE 8-62

7 **Click the position shown in Figure 8-62 on the previous page, right-click the button that is placed on the form, and then click Properties on the shortcut menu. Change the Name property to cmdPromoQuery and then change the Caption property to Run Promotion Query. Click the Close button for the property sheet. Drag the lower sizing handle for the button so the entire caption (Run Promotion Query) displays.**

The button is added (Figure 8-63). The entire caption displays.

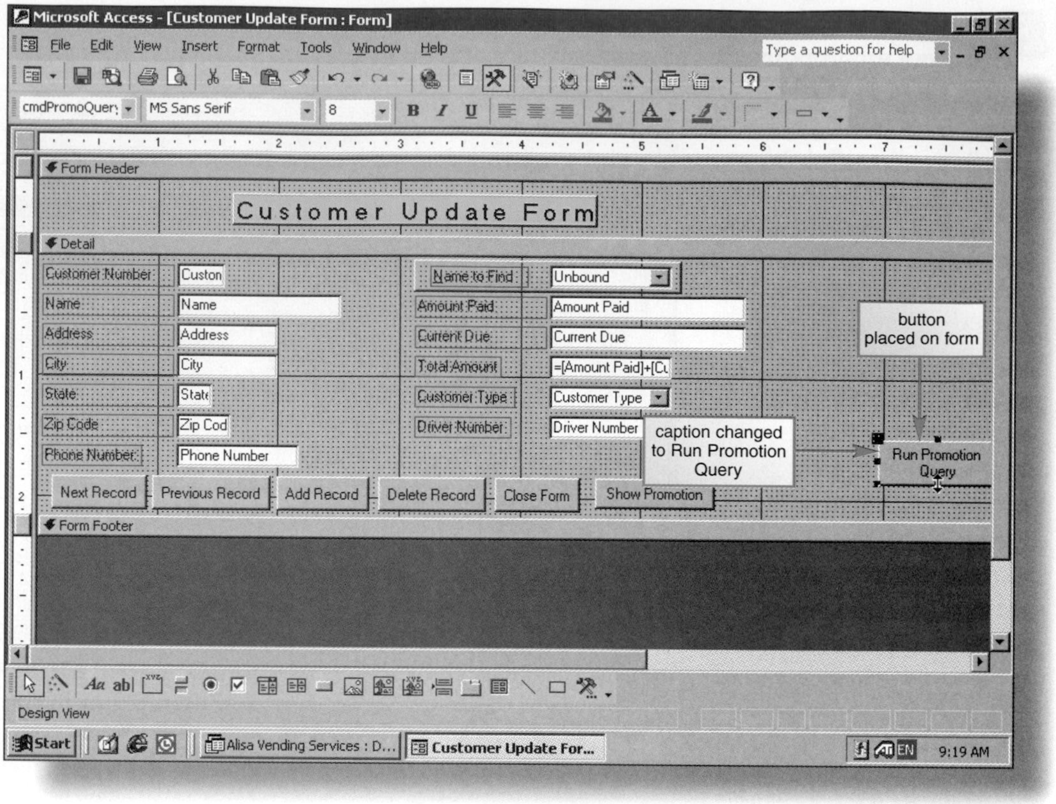

FIGURE 8-63

Adding Controls to the Customer Update Form

You add the Promotion Amount and Promotion Factor controls to the Customer Update Form as text boxes, just as you have done on other forms. The following steps add the necessary controls. Once you have added them, you will move the attached label so it is above the control rather than to the left of it. The steps also change the names of the controls and attached labels, as well as the captions of the labels.

Steps To Add Controls to the Customer Update Form

1 **Point to the Text Box tool in the toolbox (Figure 8-64).**

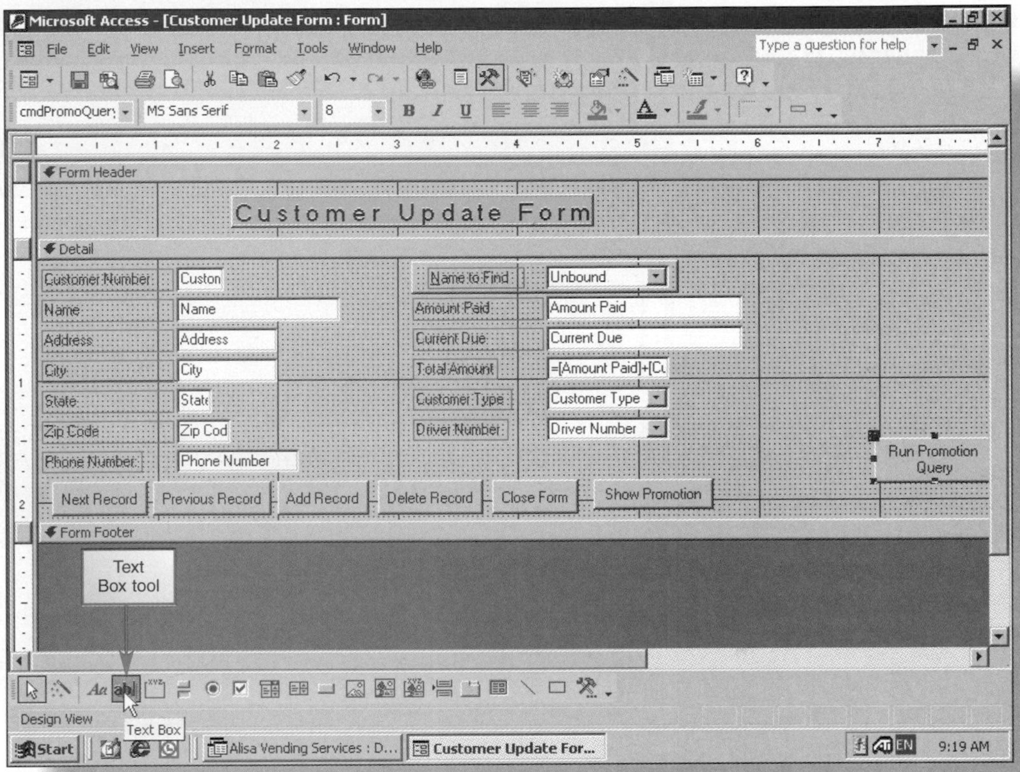

FIGURE 8-64

2 **Click the Text Box tool and then move the pointer to the approximate position shown in Figure 8-65.**

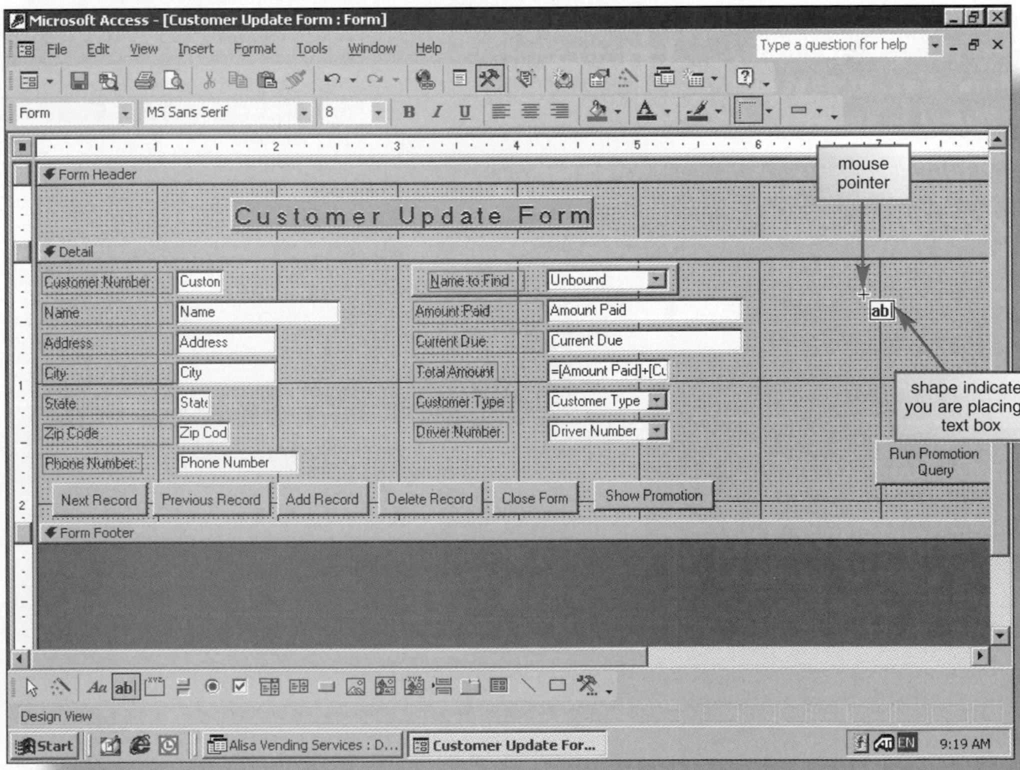

FIGURE 8-65

3 **Click the position shown in Figure 8-65 on the previous page, point to the Move handle for the label, and then drag the label to the position shown in Figure 8-66.**

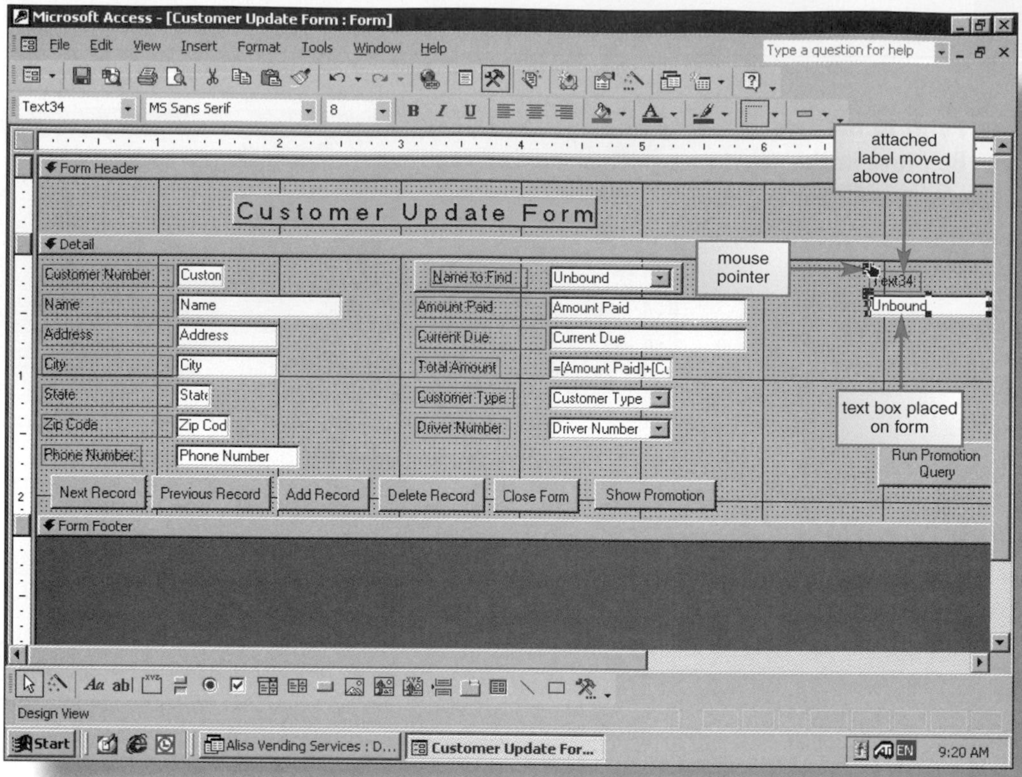

FIGURE 8-66

4 **Right-click the control (the white space, not the label), click Properties on the shortcut menu, change the name to txtPromoAmount, change the format to Currency, change the number of decimal places to 2, and then point to the Close button for the property sheet.**

The property sheet for the control displays (Figure 8-67). The name is changed to txtPromoAmount, the format is changed to Currency, and the number of decimal places is changed to 2.

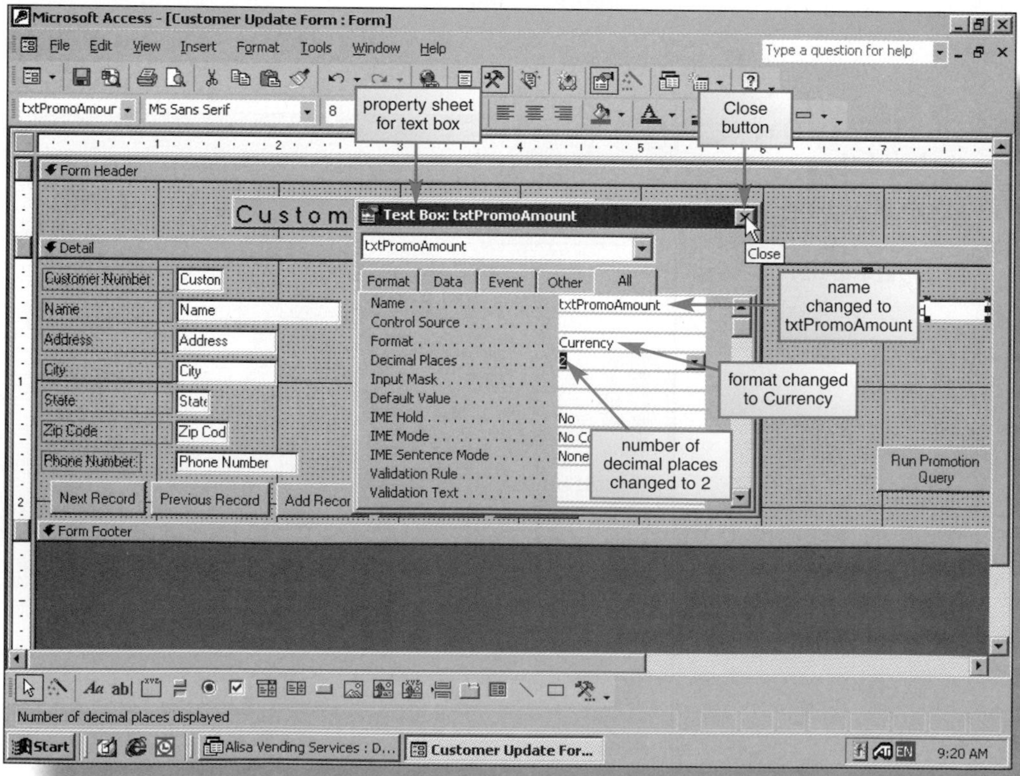

FIGURE 8-67

5 Close the property sheet for the control, right-click the label, and then click Properties on the shortcut menu. Change the name to lblPromoAmount and the caption to Promotion Amount. Point to the Close button for the property sheet.

The property sheet for the label displays (Figure 8-68). The name is changed to lblPromoAmount and the caption is changed to Promotion Amount.

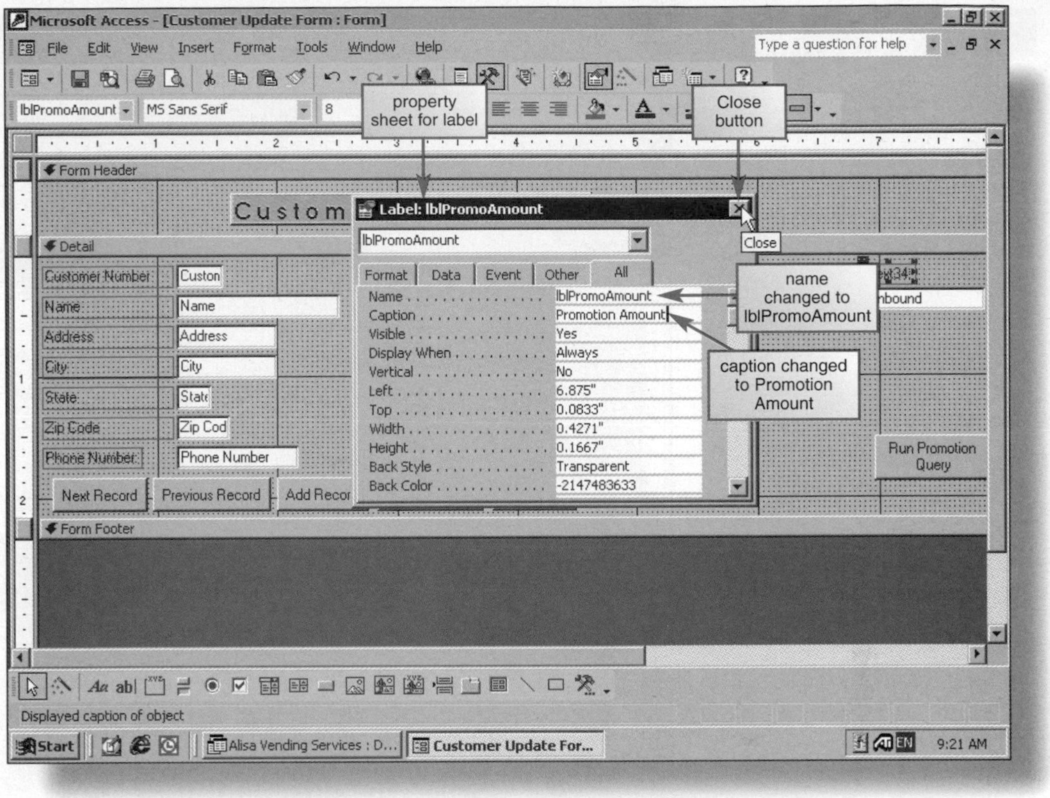

FIGURE 8-68

6 Close the property sheet, double-click the right-sizing handle for the label so the entire label displays, and then point to the Text Box tool in the toolbox.

The label is changed (Figure 8-69).

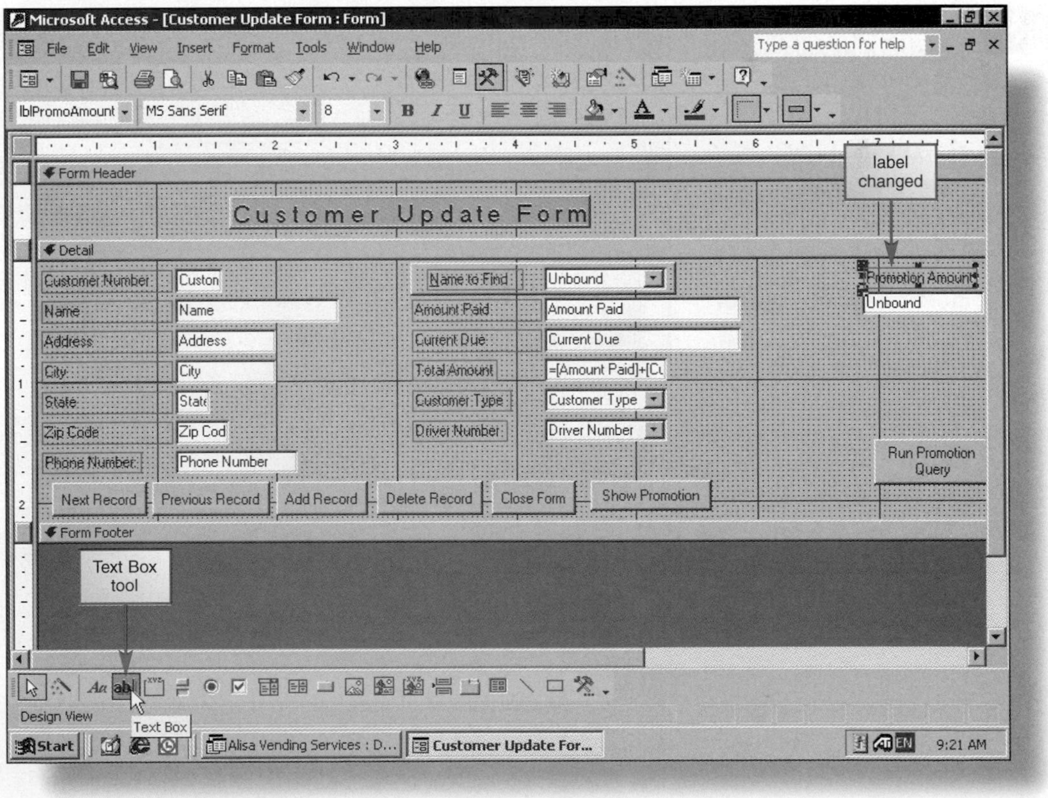

FIGURE 8-69

7 **Click the Text Box tool in the toolbox and then move the pointer to the approximate position shown in Figure 8-70.**

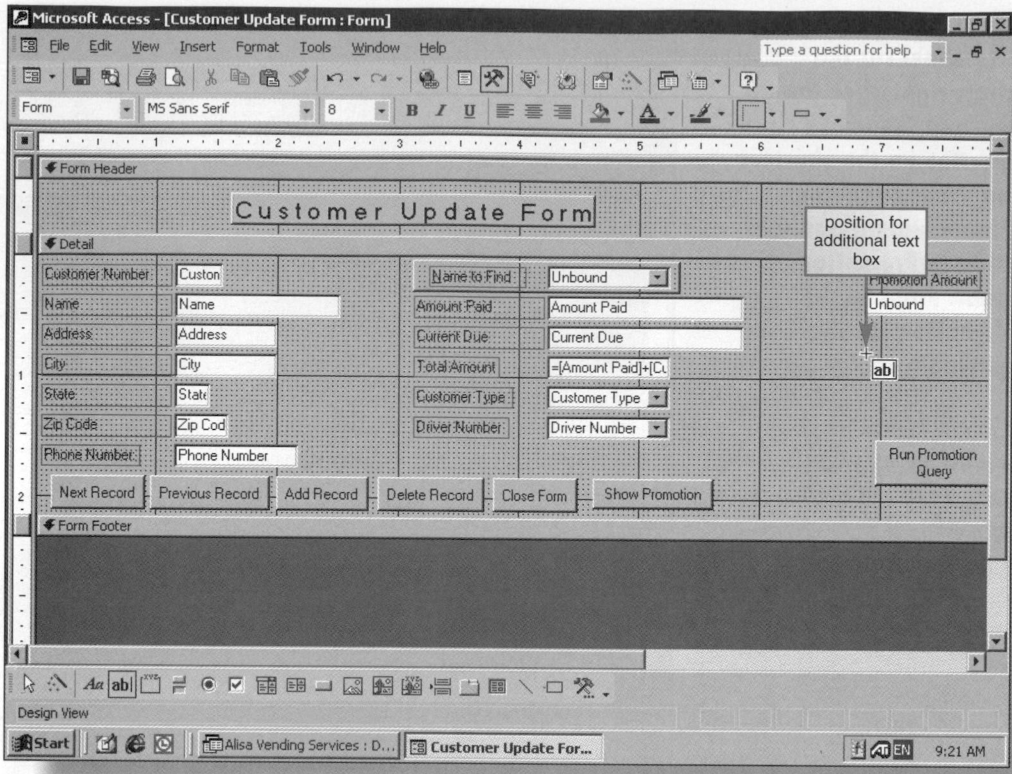

FIGURE 8-70

8 **Click the position shown in Figure 8-70, move the label so it is above the control, right-click the control, click Properties on the shortcut menu, change the name to txtPromoFactor, the number of decimal places to 2, and then point to the Close button for the property sheet.**

The label is moved above the control (Figure 8-71). The property sheet displays. The name and number of decimal places are changed.

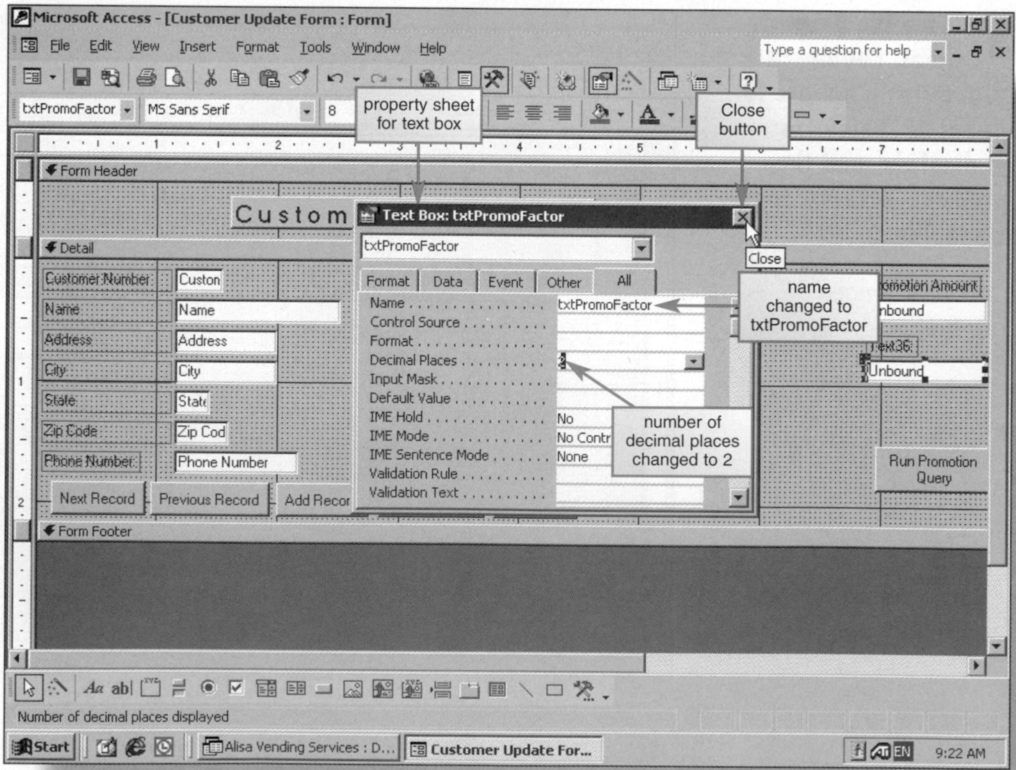

FIGURE 8-71

9 **Close the property sheet by clicking its Close button. Right-click the label, click Properties on the shortcut menu, change the name to lblPromoFactor, and the caption to Promotion Factor. Close the property sheet and then resize the label so the entire label displays. Click the Run Promotion Query button and then point to the border of the button.**

The label is changed (Figure 8-72). The Run Promotion Query button is selected and the pointer shape has changed to a hand.

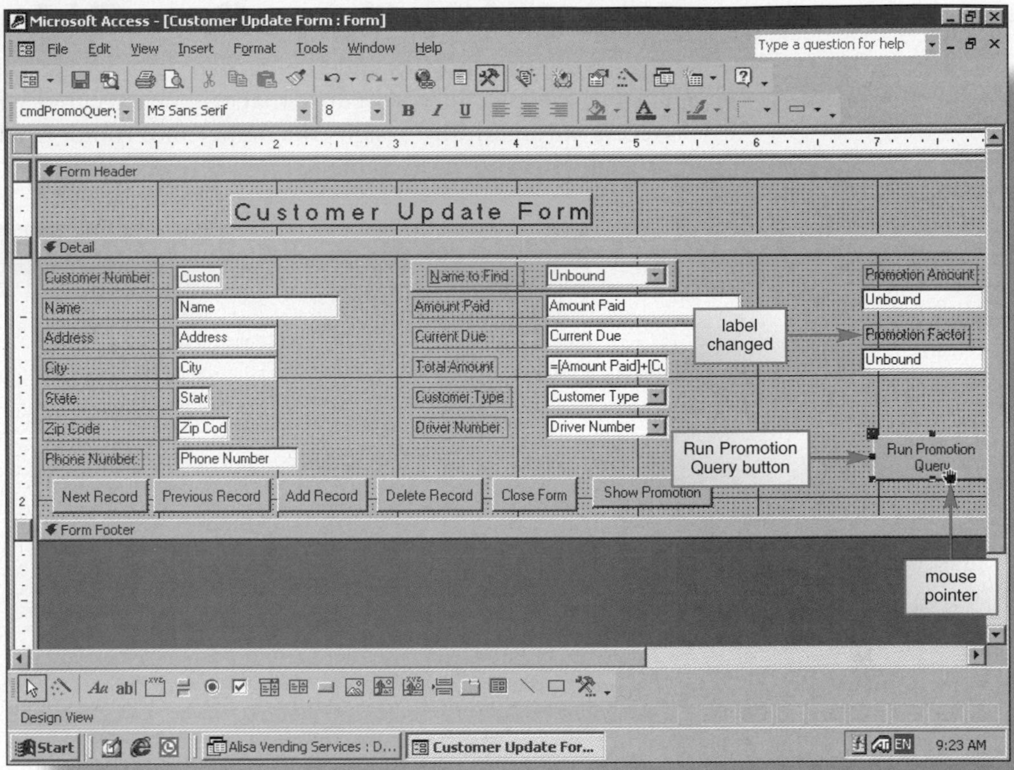

FIGURE 8-72

10 **Move the Run Promotion Query button so it lines up under the newly-added controls (Figure 8-73).**

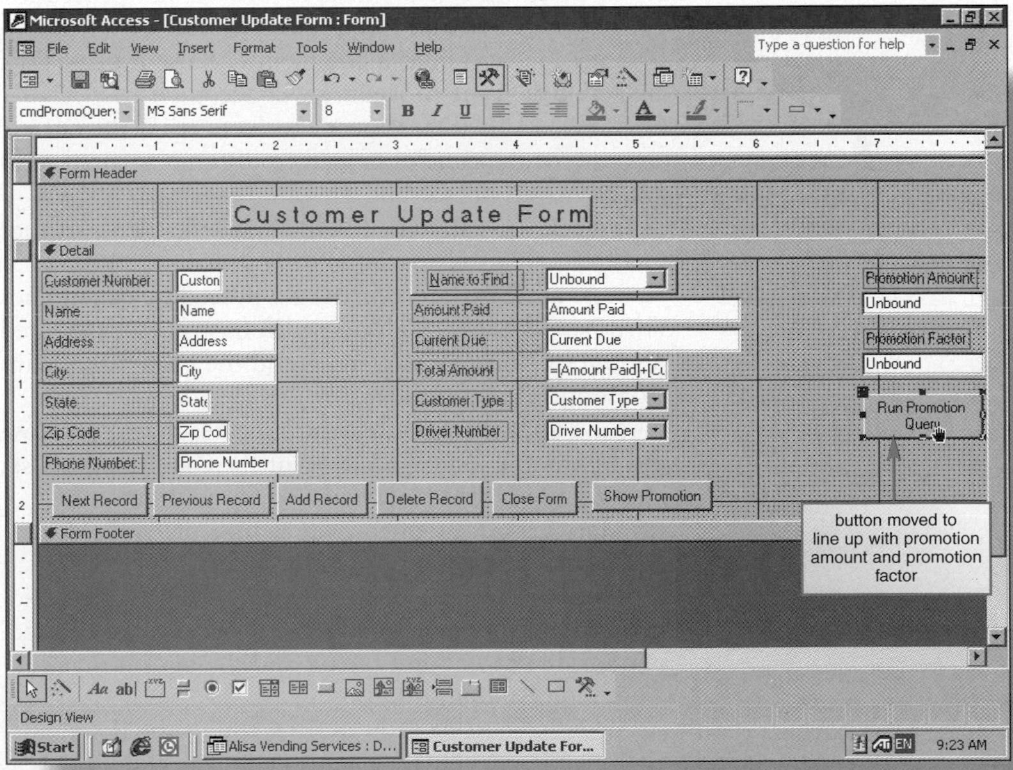

FIGURE 8-73

Associating Code with the cmdPromo_Click Event

In order to show or hide the promo data by clicking the cmdPromo button, you need to create a Sub procedure that will be executed when the user clicks the button. Access automatically assigns the name cmdPromo_Click to this procedure. The procedure is shown in Table 8-12.

Table 8-12 cmdPromo_Click Sub Procedure

LINE *STATEMENT*

```
1   Private Sub cmdPromo_Click()
2       ' Update button caption and take appropriate action
3       If cmdPromo.Caption = "Show Promotion" Then
4           cmdPromo.Caption = "Hide Promotion"
5           ShowPromotion ' Display promotion info
6       Else
7           cmdPromo.Caption = "Show Promotion"
8           HidePromotion ' Hide promotion info
9       End If
10
11  End Sub
```

The following is an explanation of the lines in the cmdPromo_Click Sub procedure:

Line 1. The Sub statement indicates that the code between the word Sub and the End Sub statement (line 11) forms a Sub procedure. This procedure is called cmdPromo_Click and has no arguments.

Line 2. This line is a comment because it begins with an apostrophe. It indicates the action that the procedure will accomplish.

Line 3. This If statement checks to see if the current value in the Caption property of the control named cmdPromo is equal to Show Promotion. If so, the statements on lines 4 and 5 will be executed.

Line 4. This statement will change the value of the Caption property for the cmdPromo control to Hide Promotion.

Line 5. This statement runs a procedure called ShowPromotion. The ShowPromotion procedure, which has yet to be created, will display the promotion amount, the promotion factor, and the button that can be clicked to run the Promotion Amount query.

Line 6. The Else statement indicates that the following statements (lines 7 and 8) are to execute in the event the condition is false; that is, the caption for the cmdPromo button is *not* equal to Show Promotion.

Line 7. This statement will change the value of the Caption property for the cmdPromo control to Show Promotion.

Line 8. This statement runs a procedure called HidePromotion. The HidePromotion procedure, which has yet to be created, will hide the promotion amount, the promotion factor, and the button that can be clicked to run the Promotion Amount query.

Line 9. This line indicates the end of the If statement.

Line 10. This line is intentionally left blank for readability.

Line 11. This line marks the end of the Sub procedure.

The following steps create the necessary code and associate it with the On Click property.

Steps To Associate Code with the cmdPromo_Click Event

1 Right-click the cmdPromo button (the button whose caption is Show Promotion), click Properties on the shortcut menu, scroll down so the On Click property displays, click the On Click property, and then point to the Build button.

The property sheet for the cmdPromo button displays (Figure 8-74). The On Click property is selected.

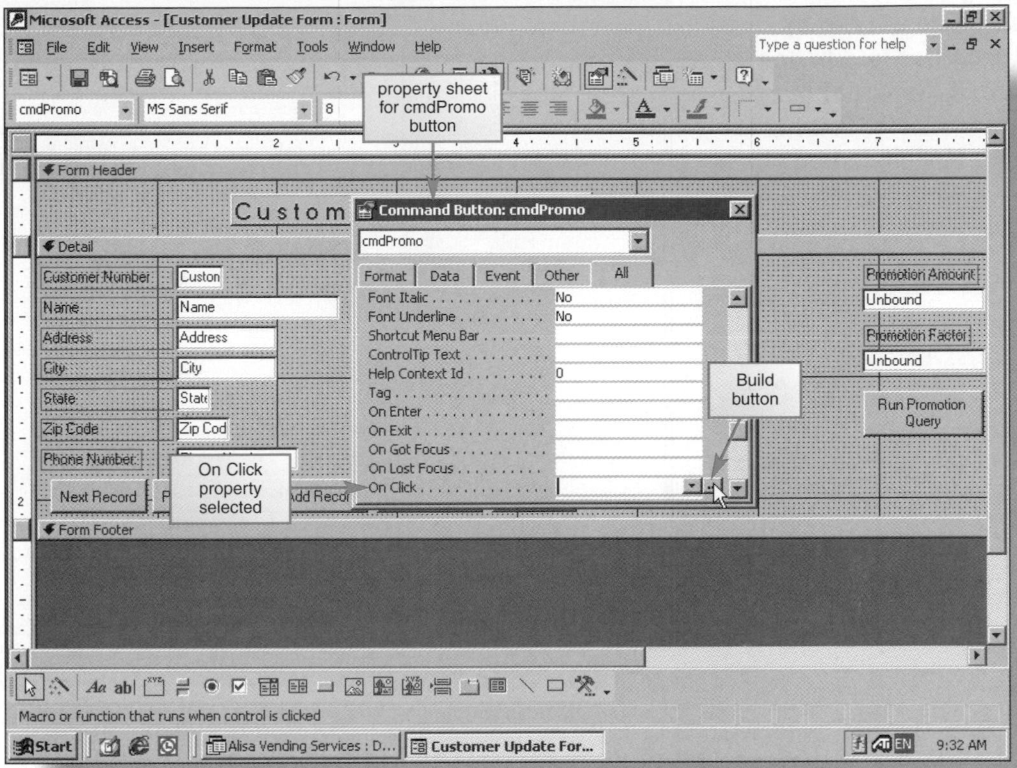

FIGURE 8-74

2 Click the Build button, click Code Builder in the Choose Builder dialog box, and then click the OK button.

The code for cmdPromo_Click, that is, clicking the cmdPromo button, displays (Figure 8-75). The Immediate window, which may be blank, displays beneath the Code window.

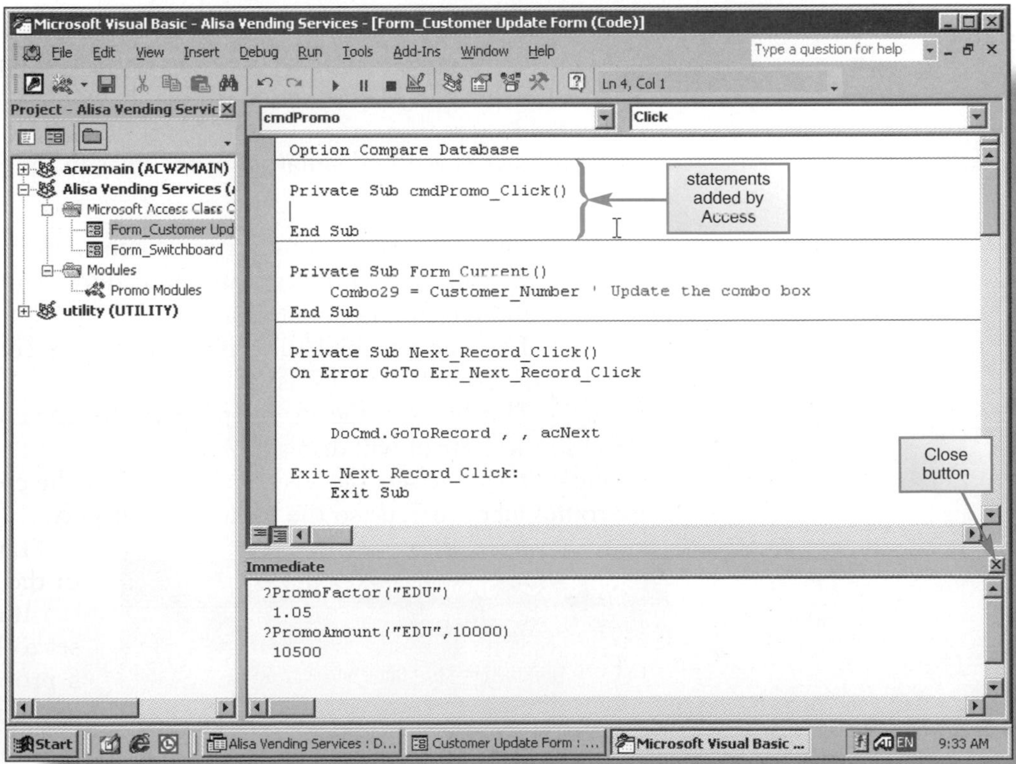

FIGURE 8-75

3 Type the statements shown in Table 8-12 on page A 8.54. Close the Immediate window by clicking its Close button so more of the Visual Basic code is visible. Point to the Insert Module button.

The code for the cmdPromo_Click event is entered (Figure 8-76). The Immediate window no longer displays. A Properties window may display below the Project Explorer window. You will not use either the Project Explorer or the Properties windows.

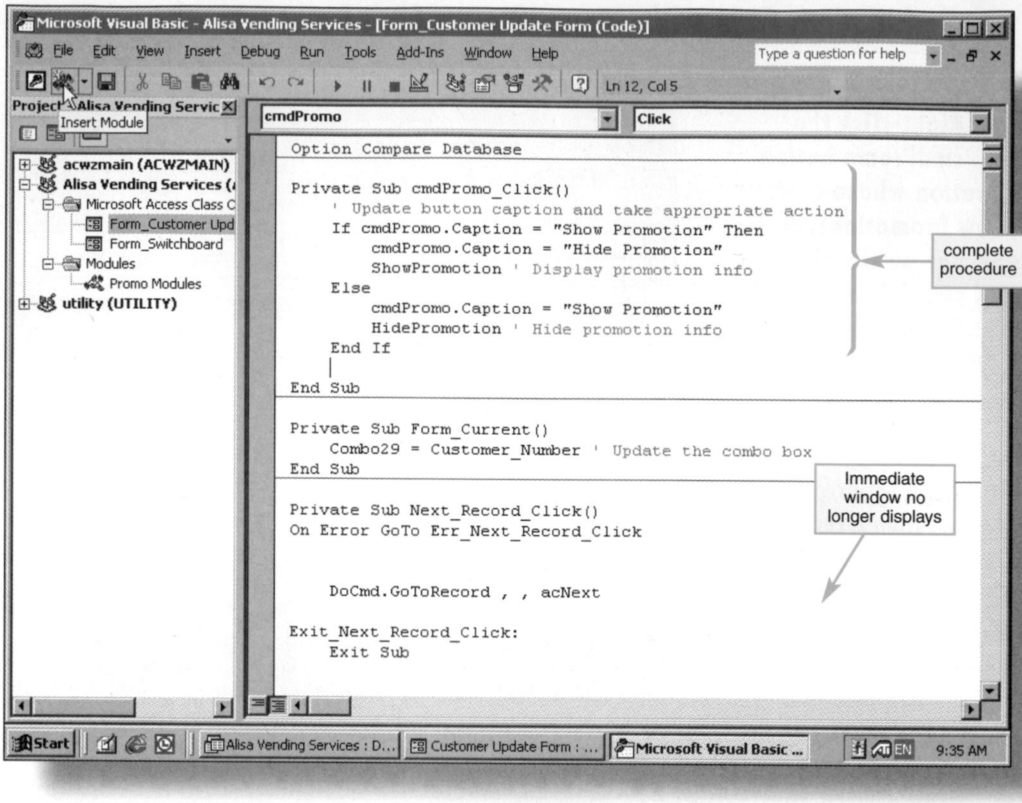

FIGURE 8-76

Creating the ShowPromotion and HidePromotion Sub Procedures

An item on a form will display, that is, be visible, if its Visible property is set to True. Thus, a procedure to make the promotion amount, the promotion factor, and the button to run the promotion query visible would contain the statements shown in Table 8-13.

The following is an explanation of the lines in the Show Promotion Sub procedure:

Line 1. The Sub statement indicates that the code between the word Sub and the End Sub statement (line 5) forms a Sub procedure. This procedure is called Show Promotion and has no arguments.

Line 2. This line sets the Visible property for the control named txtPromoAmount to True so the control will display.

Line 3. This line sets the Visible property for the control named txtPromoFactor to True so the control will display.

Line 4. This line sets the Visible property for the command button named cmdPromoQuery to True so the button will display.

Line 5. This line marks the end of the Sub procedure.

If an item's Visible property is set to False, it will not display. Thus, a procedure to hide the promotion amount, the promotion factor, and the button to run the promotion query would contain the statements shown in Table 8-14.

Table 8-13 ShowPromotion Procedure

LINE	*STATEMENT*
1	`Public Sub ShowPromotion()`
2	`    txtPromoAmount.Visible = True`
3	`    txtPromoFactor.Visible = True`
4	`    cmdPromoQuery.Visible = True`
5	`End Sub`

The following is an explanation of the lines in the HidePromotion Sub procedure:

Table 8-14 HidePromotion Procedure

LINE	STATEMENT
1	`Public Sub HidePromotion()`
2	`    txtPromoAmount.Visible = False`
3	`    txtPromoFactor.Visible = False`
4	`    cmdPromoQuery.Visible = False`
5	`End Sub`

Line 1. The Sub statement indicates that the code between the word Sub and the End Sub statement (line 5) forms a Sub procedure. This procedure is called HidePromotion and has no arguments.

Line 2. This line sets the Visible property for the control named txtPromoAmount to False so the control will not display.

Line 3. This line sets the Visible property for the control named txtPromoFactor to False so the control will not display.

Line 4. This line sets the Visible property for the command button named cmdPromoQuery to False so the button will not display.

Line 5. This line marks the end of the Sub procedure.

Perform the following steps to create these procedures as part of the VBA code for the form.

Steps To Create the ShowPromotion and HidePromotion Sub Procedures

1 **Click the Insert Module button arrow on the Standard toolbar, and then point to Procedure (Figure 8-77).**

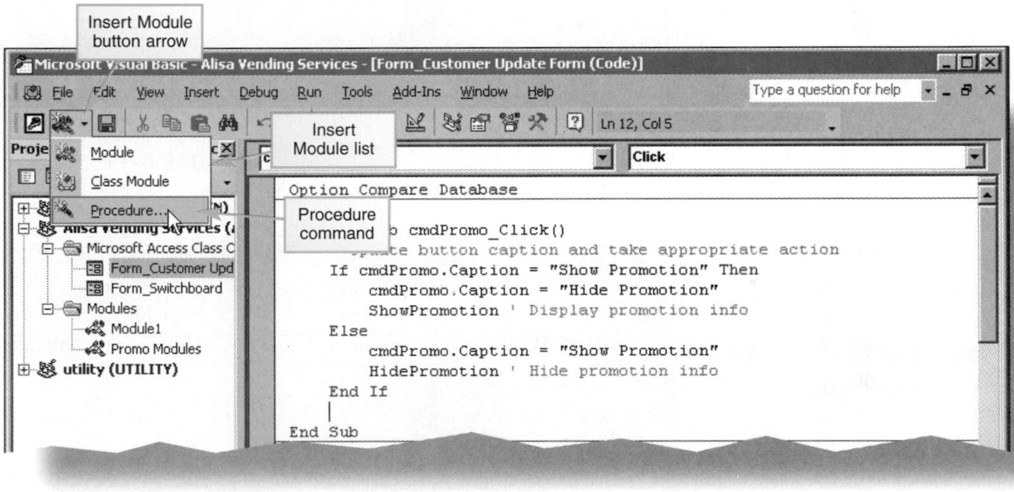

FIGURE 8-77

2 **Click Procedure. Type** `ShowPromotion` **as the name of the procedure in the Add Procedure dialog box, and then point to the OK button.**

The Add Procedure dialog box displays (Figure 8-78). The type (Sub) and scope (Public) already selected are acceptable.

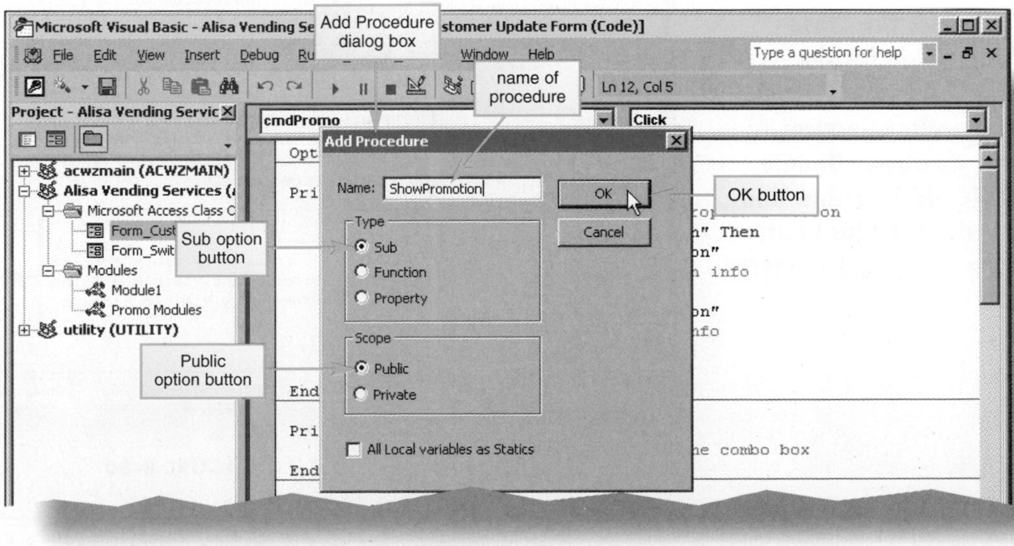

FIGURE 8-78

3 Click the OK button and then type the statements on lines 2 through 4 for the ShowPromotion procedure shown in Table 8-13 on page A 8.56.

The code for the ShowPromotion procedure is entered (Figure 8-79).

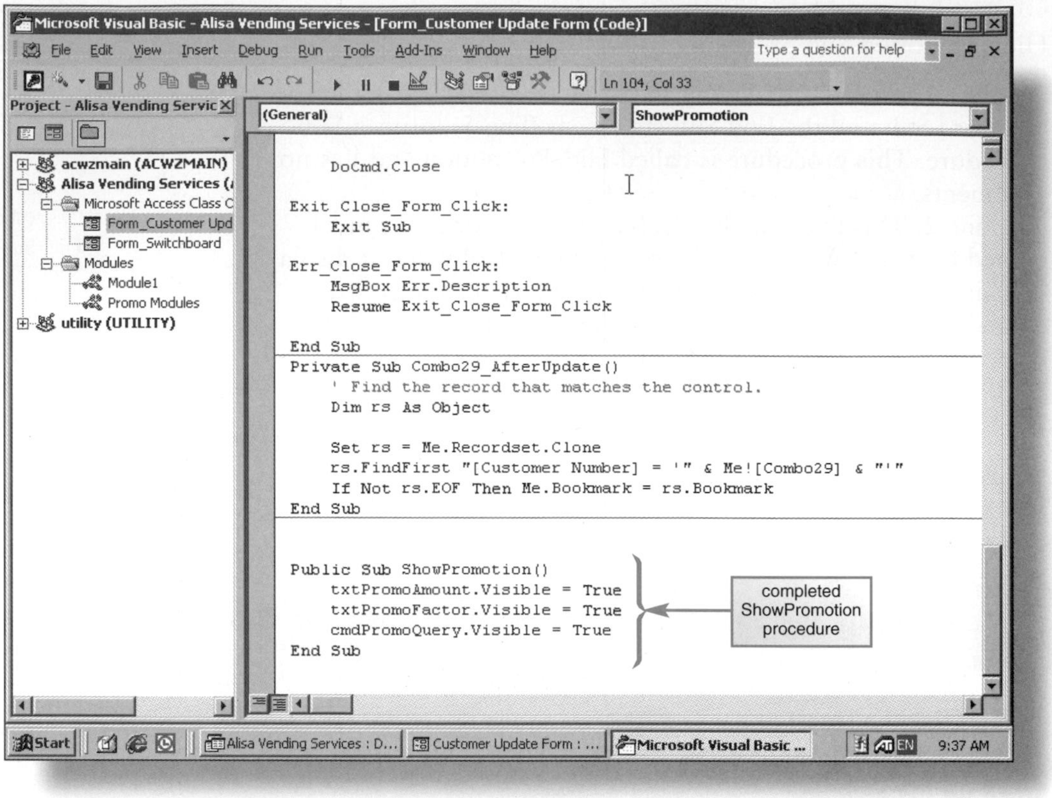

FIGURE 8-79

4 Use the techniques in Steps 1 to 3 to create the HidePromotion procedure from Table 8-14 on the previous page.

The code for the HidePromotion procedure is entered (Figure 8-80).

5 Click the Close button for the Microsoft Visual Basic – Alisa Vending Services – [Form_Customer Update Form (Code)] window and then click the Close button for the cmdPromo property sheet.

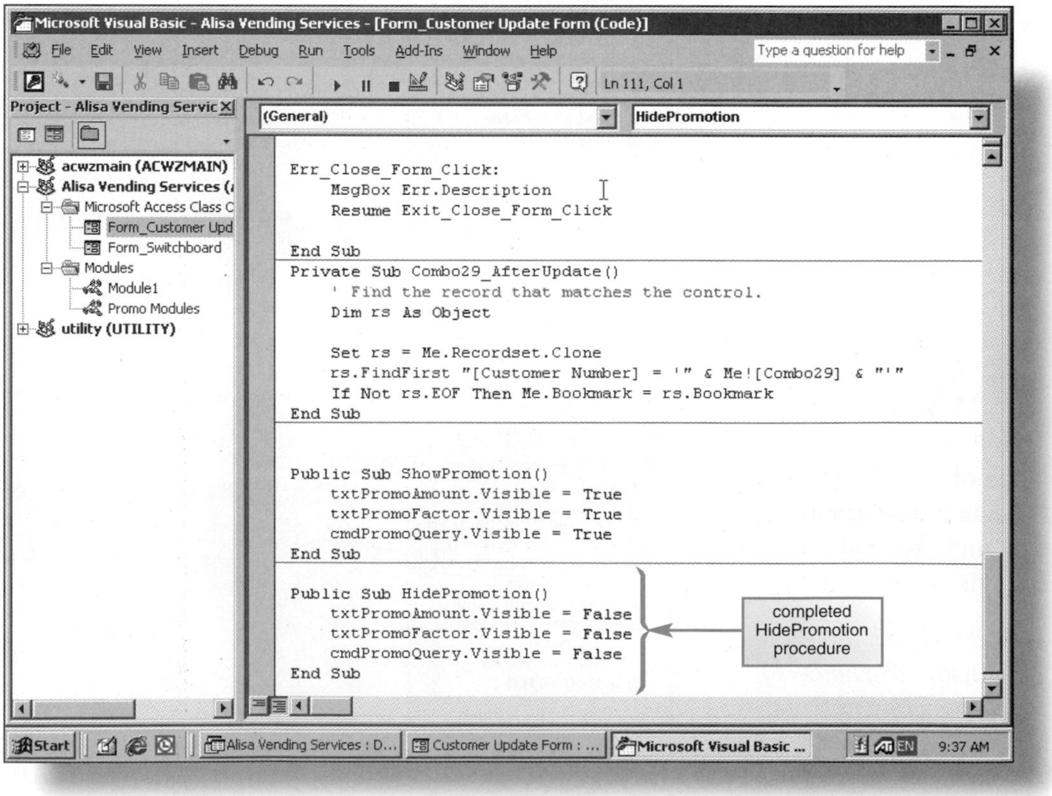

FIGURE 8-80

Creating Code to Update the Controls

To update the promotion amount and the promotion factor, set the Value property for the txtPromoAmount to the result calculated by the PromoAmount function and set the txtPromoFactor to the value calculated by the PromoFactor function. The complete procedure is shown in Table 8-15.

Table 8-15 UpdatePromoData Procedure

LINE	*STATEMENT*
1	`Public Sub UpdatePromoData()`
2	`    txtPromoAmount.Value = PromoAmount([Customer Type], [Current Due])`
3	`    txtPromoFactor.Value = PromoFactor([Customer Type])`
4	`End Sub`

The following is an explanation of the lines in the UpdatePromoData Sub procedure:

Line 1. The Sub statement indicates that the code between the word Sub and the End Sub statement (line 4) forms a Sub procedure. This procedure is called UpdatePromoData and has no arguments.

Line 2. This line uses the PromoAmount function to calculate the appropriate amount for the given customer type and current due amount. It then changes the Value property of the txtPromoAmount control to the result of this calculation.

Line 3. This line uses the PromoFactor function to calculate the appropriate factor for the given customer type. It then changes the Value property of the txtPromoFactor control to the result of this calculation.

Line 4. This line marks the end of the Sub procedure.

Once this procedure is created, it can be called (used) from other procedures. In particular it could be used in the Form_Current procedure, which guarantees the promotional data will be updated whenever you move from one customer to another. It also could be used from other procedures. For example, using it in a Current_Due_AfterUpdate procedure would guarantee that the values would be updated immediately whenever a user changed the current due amount. Using it in an AfterUpdate procedure for the Customer Type combo box would guarantee that the values would be updated immediately whenever a user changes the Customer Type. Perform the steps on the next page to include a statement to call the UpdatePromoData procedure in the Form_Current procedure and then create the UpdatePromoData procedure. The steps also include statements to call the UpdatePromoData procedure from within both the Combo29_AfterUpdate and Current_Due_After update procedures.

Steps To Create Code to Update the Controls

1 Right-click the form selector (the small box in the upper-left corner of the form), click Properties, click the On Current property, and then point to the Build button.

The property sheet for the form displays (Figure 8-81). The On Current property is selected. The current value, Event Procedure, indicates that an event procedure already has been created for this property. The procedure to which this refers is the one you created when you updated the On Current property to ensure the combo box always contained the correct name.

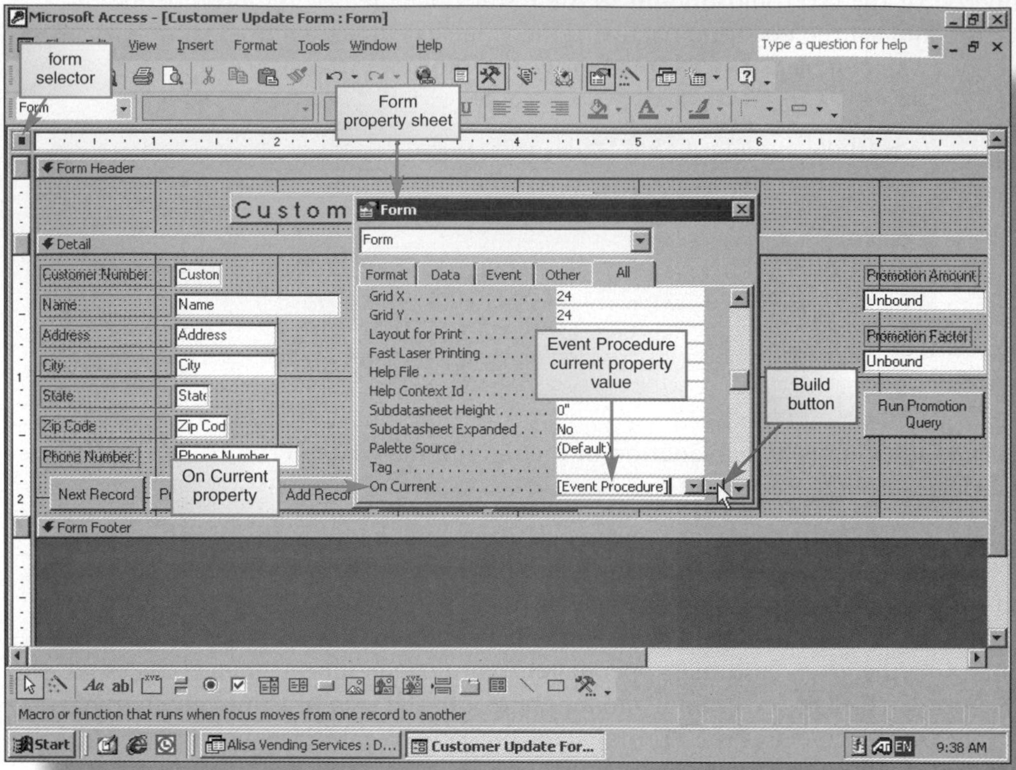

FIGURE 8-81

2 Click the Build button.

The code for the Form_Current procedure displays (Figure 8-82). It contains the statement added earlier to update the combo box.

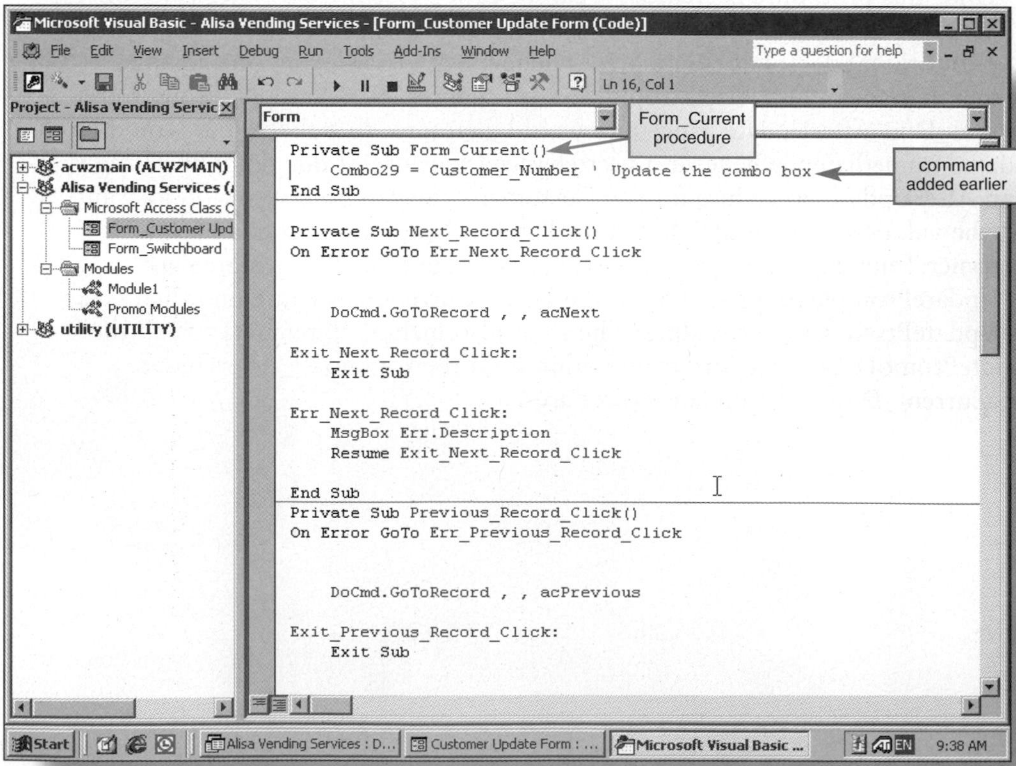

FIGURE 8-82

3 Add the additional statement shown in Figure 8-83.

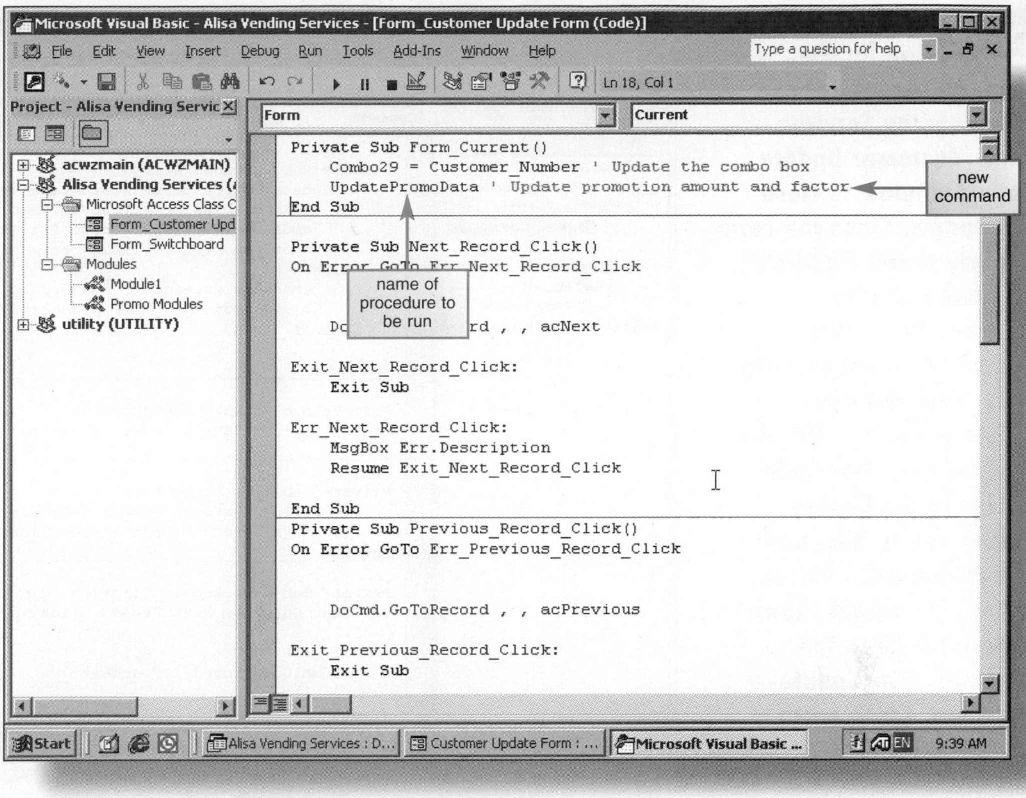

FIGURE 8-83

4 Click the Insert Procedure button arrow on the Standard toolbar, click Procedure, be sure the Sub and Public option buttons are selected in the Add Procedure dialog box, type `UpdatePromoData` **as the name of the procedure, and then click the OK button. Type the statements for the UpdatePromoData procedure shown in Table 8-15 on page A 8.59.**

The code for the UpdatePromoData is entered (Figure 8-84). In the figure, the final parenthesis in the first statement does not display.

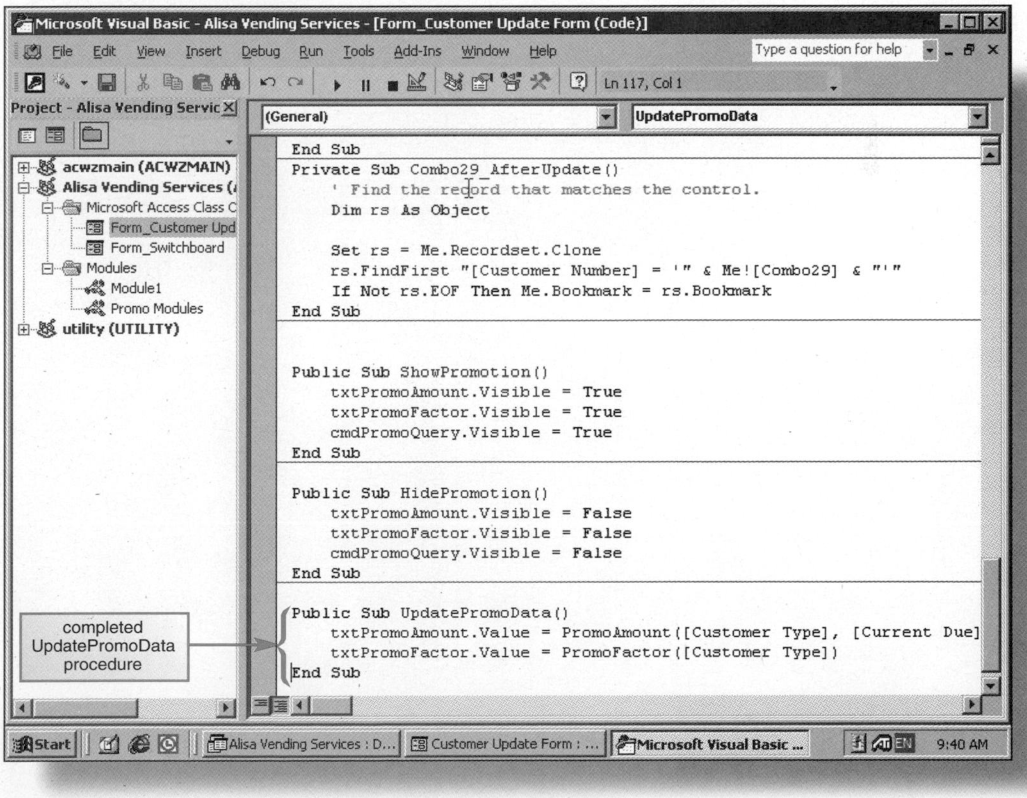

FIGURE 8-84

5 **Click the Close button for the Microsoft Visual Basic – Alisa Vending Services – [Form_Customer Update (Code)] window to close the window. Close the Form property sheet. Right-click the combo box for Customer Type, click Properties on the shortcut menu, click the After Update property, click the Build button, click Code Builder in the Choose Builder dialog box, and then click the OK button. Add the statement shown in Figure 8-85 to the Combo18_AfterUpdate procedure. (Your number may be different.)**

The procedure for updating promotion data after the value in the combo box has been changed is entered.

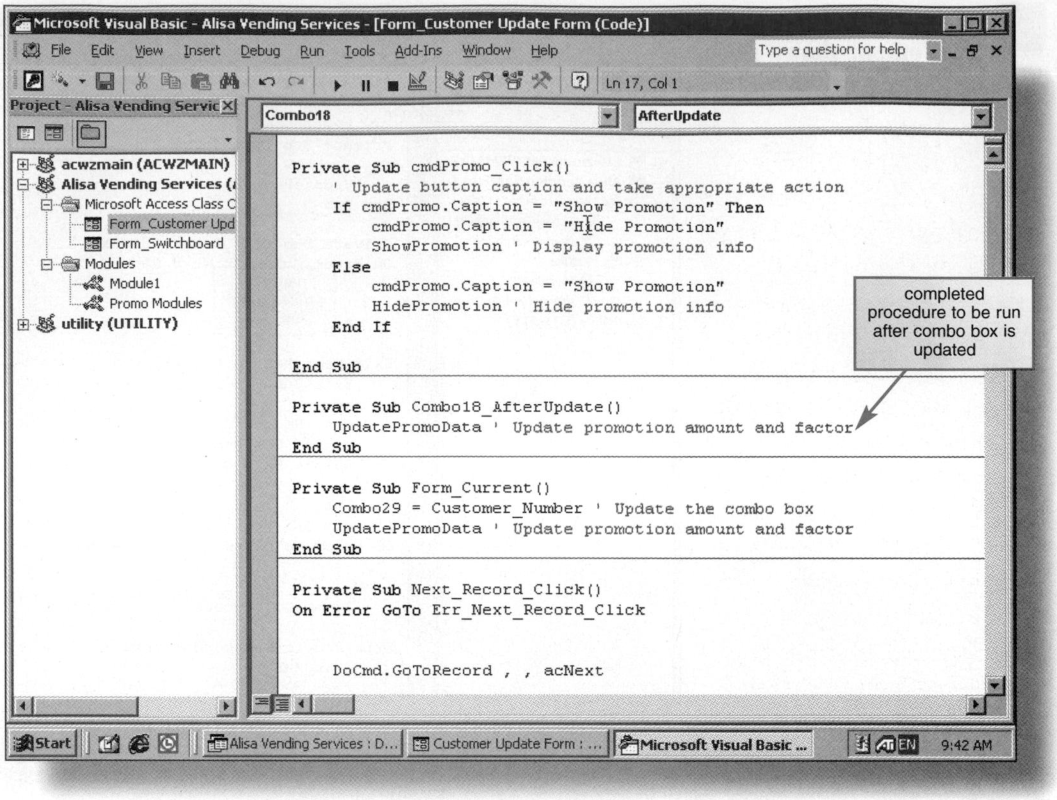

FIGURE 8-85

6 **Click the Close button for the Microsoft Visual Basic – Alisa Vending Services – [Form_Customer Update (Code)] window to close the window. Click the Close button for the Combo Box: Combo 19 property sheet. Right-click the control for the Current Due field (the white space, not the label), click Properties on the shortcut menu, click the After Update property, click the Build button, click Code Builder in the Choose Builder dialog box, and then click the OK button. Add the statement shown in Figure 8-86 to the Current_Due_AfterUpdate procedure.**

The procedure for updating promotion data after the value in the Current Due field has been changed is entered.

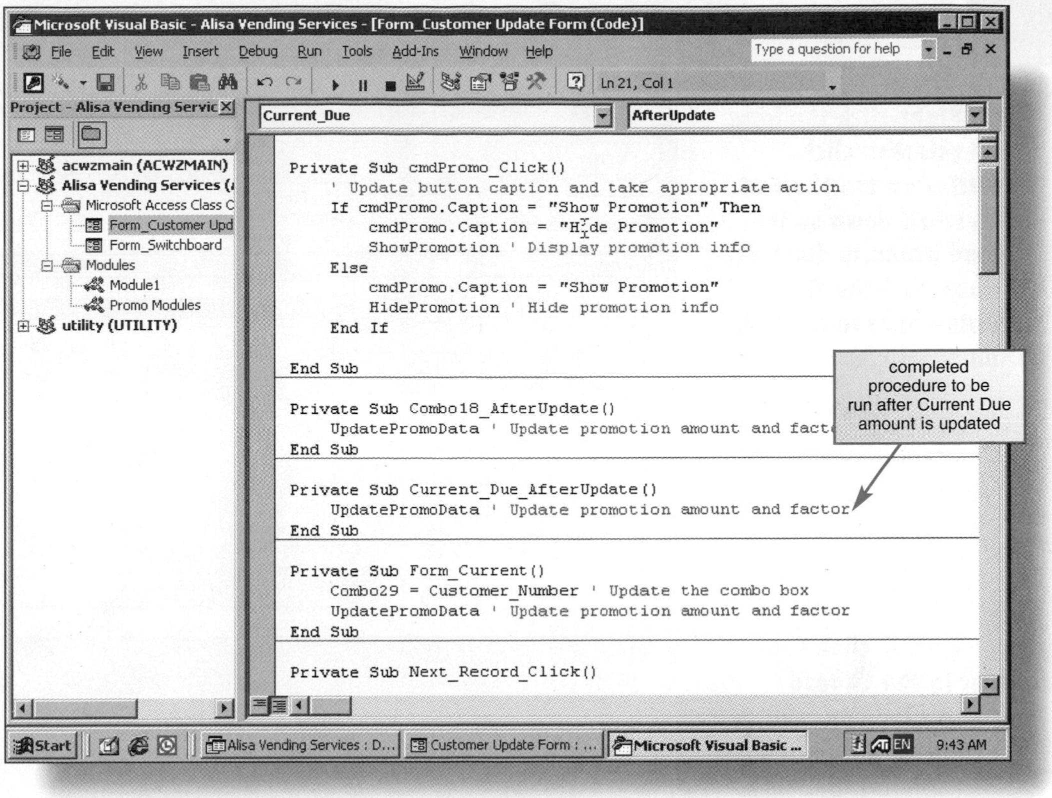

FIGURE 8-86

7 **Click the Close button for the Microsoft Visual Basic – Alisa Vending Services – [Form_Customer Update (Code)] window to close the window and then close the Text Box: Current Due property sheet.**

The Visual Basic window is closed and the form design again displays.

Creating a Form Load Event Procedure

There are occasions where there is some special action to be taken when a form first loads into memory. Such an action would be included in a Form Load event procedure, that is, a procedure executed when the Form Load event occurs. For this form, the promotion amount, the promotion factor, and the button to run the Promotion Amount query should all be hidden when the form first displays. To accomplish this, create a Form Load Event procedure containing the single statement, HidePromotion. Perform the steps on the next page to create such a procedure.

Steps To Create a Form Load Event Procedure

1 Right-click the form selector, click Properties on the shortcut menu, scroll down so the On Load property displays, and then click the On Load property. Point to the Build button.

The property sheet for the form displays (Figure 8-87). The On Load property is selected.

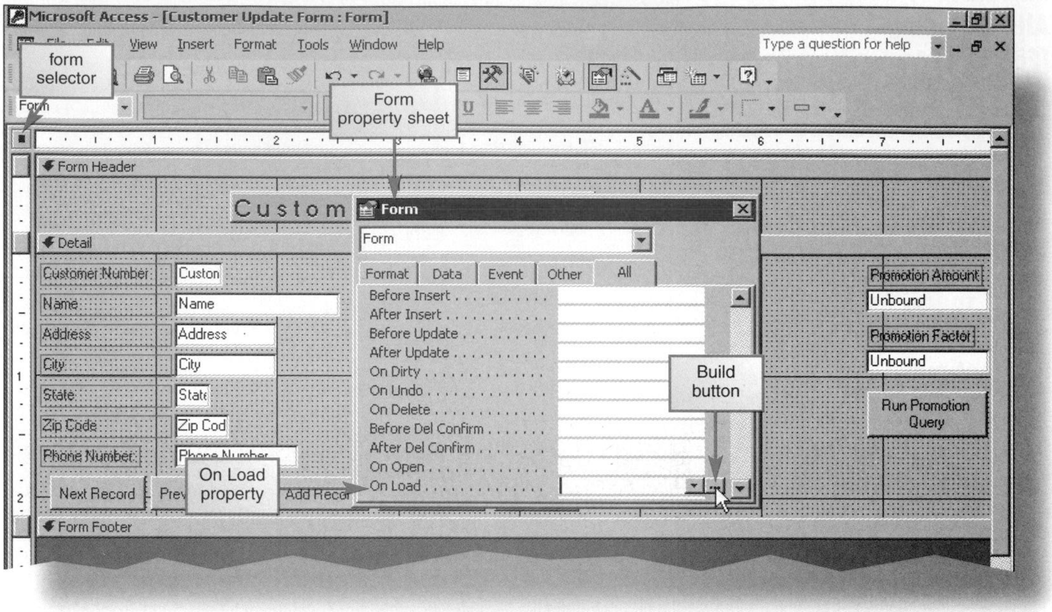

FIGURE 8-87

2 Click the Build button, click Code Builder in the Choose Builder dialog box, and then click the OK button. Type `HidePromotion` **as the statement in the Form_Load procedure.**

The Form_Load procedure is created (Figure 8-88).

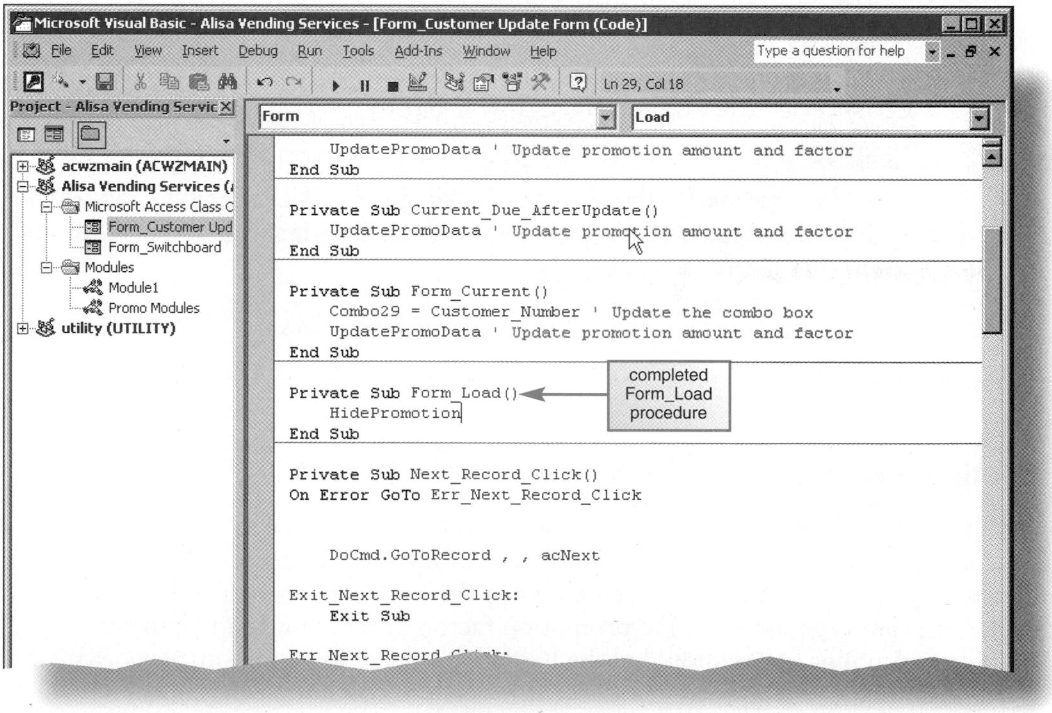

FIGURE 8-88

3 Click the Close button for the Microsoft Visual Basic – Alisa Vending Services – [Form_Customer Update Form (Code)] window to close the window, and then close the Form property sheet.

The Visual Basic window is closed and the form design again displays.

4 Click the Close Window button for the window containing the form design. When asked if you want to save your changes, click the Yes button.

The form design no longer displays. The changes are saved.

Creating a Function to Run a Query

You learned earlier to carry out actions using macros. You can carry out the same actions within VBA code by using DoCmd. (You encountered this function earlier in the Access-generated code for the Add Record button.)

To use DoCmd, type `DoCmd` followed by a period and then the action. Any arguments are listed after the action separated by commas. Formally, DoCmd is an **object** and the action to be carried out is a **method**. Some of the most common methods you can use with the DoCmd object are shown in Table 8-16. To determine the appropriate arguments for any of these methods, use Help and search for the method. To determine the arguments for the OpenQuery method, for example, use Help and search for OpenQuery.

Table 8-16 Common Methods for DoCmd

METHOD	*PURPOSE*
ApplyFilter	Sets a filter
Close	Closes open object (form, report, table, query)
FindRecord	Locates a record
GoToRecord	Moves to a specific record
Maximize	Maximizes a window
OpenForm	Opens a form
OpenQuery	Opens a query
OpenReport	Opens a report
Printout	Prints object
RunCommand	Runs a command
ShowAllRecords	Removes filter

The RunPromoAmountQuery function is shown in Table 8-17. The key statement in it is the DoCmd statement on line 4, which uses the OpenQuery method to run a query. The remaining statements are included for **error handling**. If an error occurs, for example, someone deletes the query so there is no query to run when you click the button, your program will abruptly terminate. Instead of terminating, it would be better for the program to handle the error by displaying a message indicating the problem that has occurred, having the user click an OK button, and then continuing. The additional statements handle any errors that may occur in this fashion.

The following is an explanation of the lines in the RunPromoAmountQuery function:

Table 8-17 RunPromoAmountQuery Function

LINE *STATEMENT*

```
1   Function RunPromoAmountQuery()
2   On Error GoTo RunPromoAmountQuery_Err
3
4       DoCmd.OpenQuery "Promo Amount Query", acNormal, acReadOnly
5
6   RunPromoAmountQuery_Exit:
7       Exit Function
8
9   RunPromoAmountQuery_Err:
10      MsgBox Error$
11      Resume RunPromoAmountQuery_Exit
12
13  End Function
```

Line 1. The Function statement indicates that the code between the word Function and the End Function statement (line 13) forms a function. This function is called RunPromoAmountQuery. It has no arguments.

Line 2. This line indicates that if an error occurs while the function is running, Access is to immediately move to line 9, the line labeled RunPromoAmountQuery_Err.

Line 3. This line is intentionally left blank for readability.

Line 4. This line runs the OpenQuery method of the DoCmd object. The arguments are the name of the query (Promo Amount Query), the view in which the results are to be displayed (acNormal, which means Datasheet view), and the data mode (acReadOnly). ReadOnly indicates that the users cannot change data when running this query; they can simply view the results.

Line 5. This line is intentionally left blank for readability.

Line 6. This is a label. It is used by the statement in line 11.

Line 7. This line terminates the function; that is, when this line is executed, the function is complete.

Line 8. This line is intentionally left blank for readability.

Line 9. This is the label that is referenced in the On Error statement in line 2. If an error occurs while this procedure is running, Access will move immediately to this line.

Line 10. This line uses the MsgBox statement to display the contents of Error$, a special variable that automatically contains a description of the error that occurred, and then force the user to click the OK button to continue.

Line 11. This line resumes the running of the procedure at the line with the specified label. In this case, the line with this label is line 6 so the next action to be taken is the action specified on line 7, which is to terminate the function. Thus, as soon as the user has reviewed the error message and clicked the OK button the function terminates and the user would be returned to the form.

Line 12. This line is intentionally left blank for readability.

Line 13. This line marks the end of the function.

Perform the following steps to create this function and then use it to run the query whenever the Run Promotion Query button is clicked.

Steps To Create a Function to Run a Query

1 Click Modules on the Objects bar in the Database window, right-click Promo Modules, and then click Design View on the shortcut menu. If necessary, maximize the window. Click below the End Function for the second function (PromoAmount), type `Function RunPromoAmountQuery ()`**, and then press the ENTER key.**

Visual Basic creates a function and adds the End Function statement (Figure 8-89). The insertion point is positioned between the Function statement and the End Function statement.

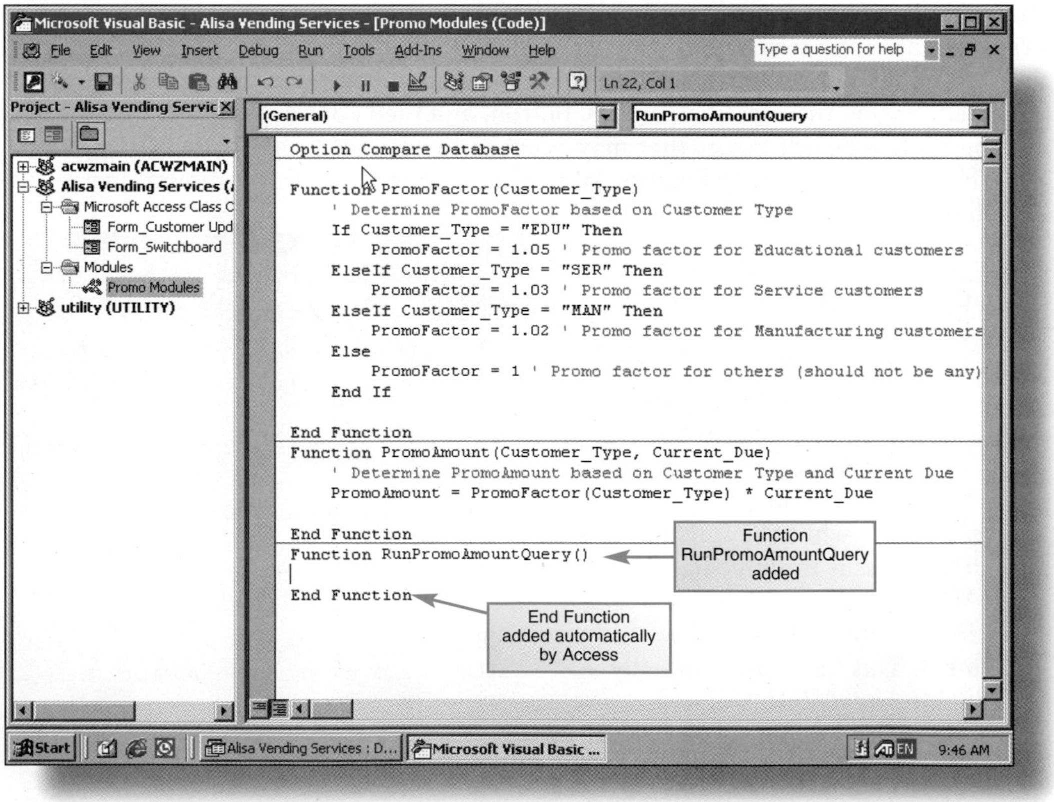

FIGURE 8-89

2 Type the statements on lines 2 through 12 shown in Table 8-17 on page A 8.65.

The statements for the RunPromoAmountQuery are entered (Figure 8-90).

3 Click the Close button for the Microsoft Visual Basic – Alisa Vending Services – [Promo Modules (Code)] window to close the window.

The Visual Basic window is closed and the Database window displays.

4 Click Forms on the Objects bar in the Database window, right-click the Customer Update Form, click Design View on the shortcut menu, and then maximize the window if it already is not maximized. Right-click the button whose caption is Run Promotion Query, click Properties on the shortcut menu, click the On Click property in the Command Button: cmdPromoQuery property sheet, and then type =RunPromoAmountQuery() **as the value for the On Click property.**

The value for the On Click property is entered (Figure 8-91). Only the final portion currently displays.

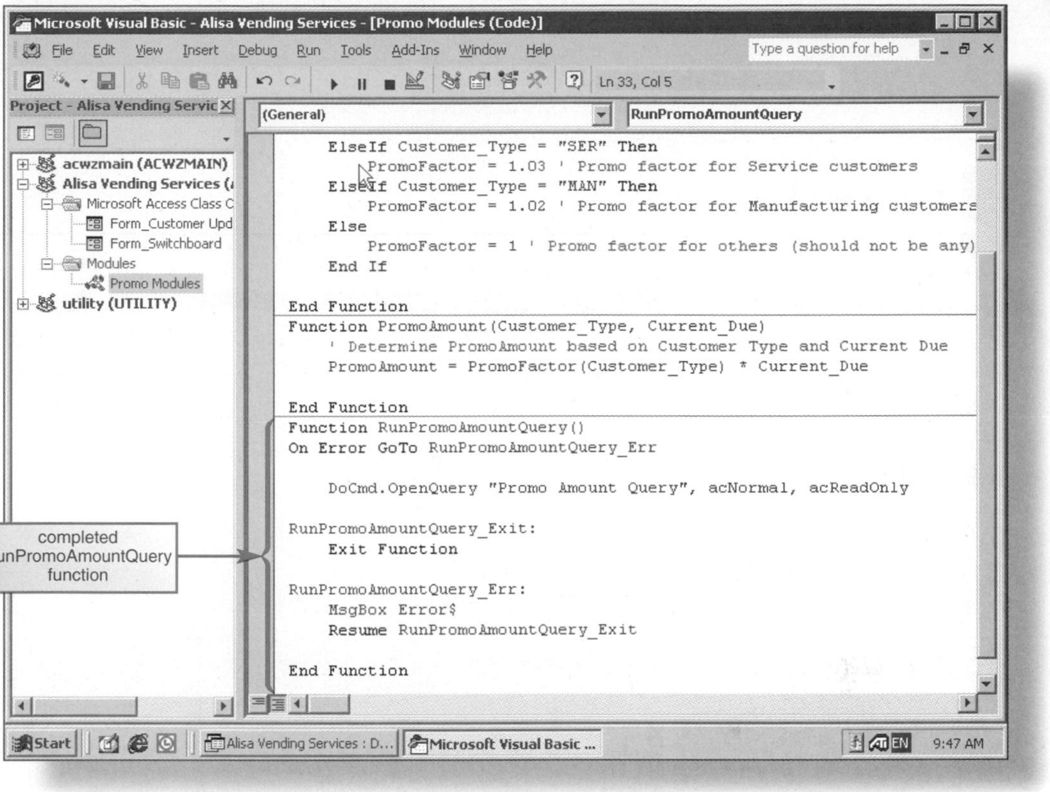

FIGURE 8-90

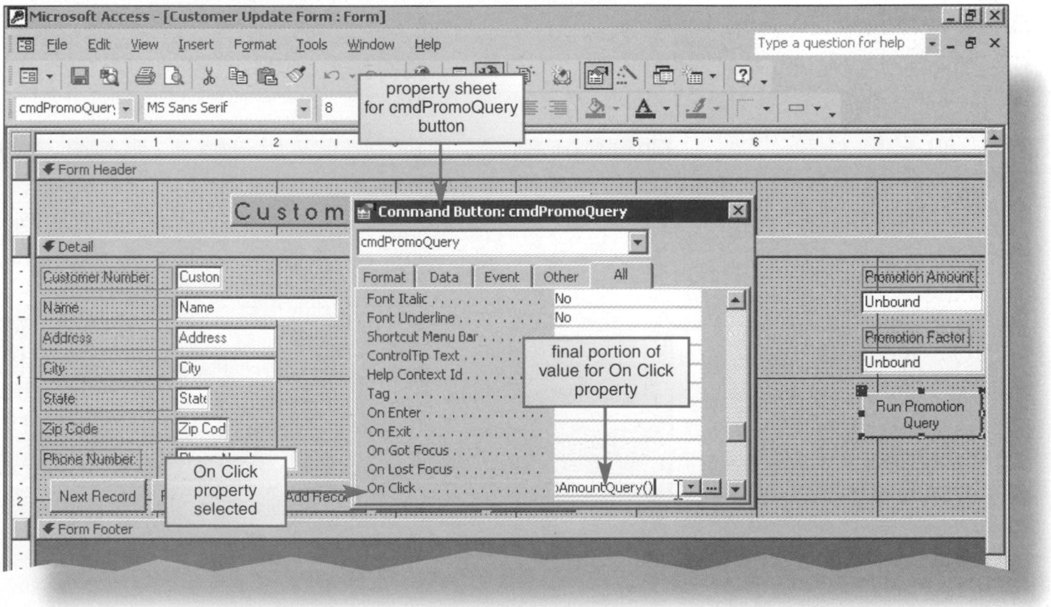

FIGURE 8-91

5 Close the property sheet by clicking its Close button, and then click the Close Window button for the window containing the form design. When asked if you want to save your changes, click the Yes button.

The form design no longer displays. The changes are saved.

Using the Form

The form now can be used like any other form. Perform the following steps to open the form and use the newly-added buttons and controls.

Steps To Use the Form

1 **With the Database window displaying and the Forms object selected, right-click the Customer Update Form, and then click Open on the shortcut menu. Point to the Show Promotion button.**

The form displays (Figure 8-92). The promotion data and Run Promotion Query buttons do not display.

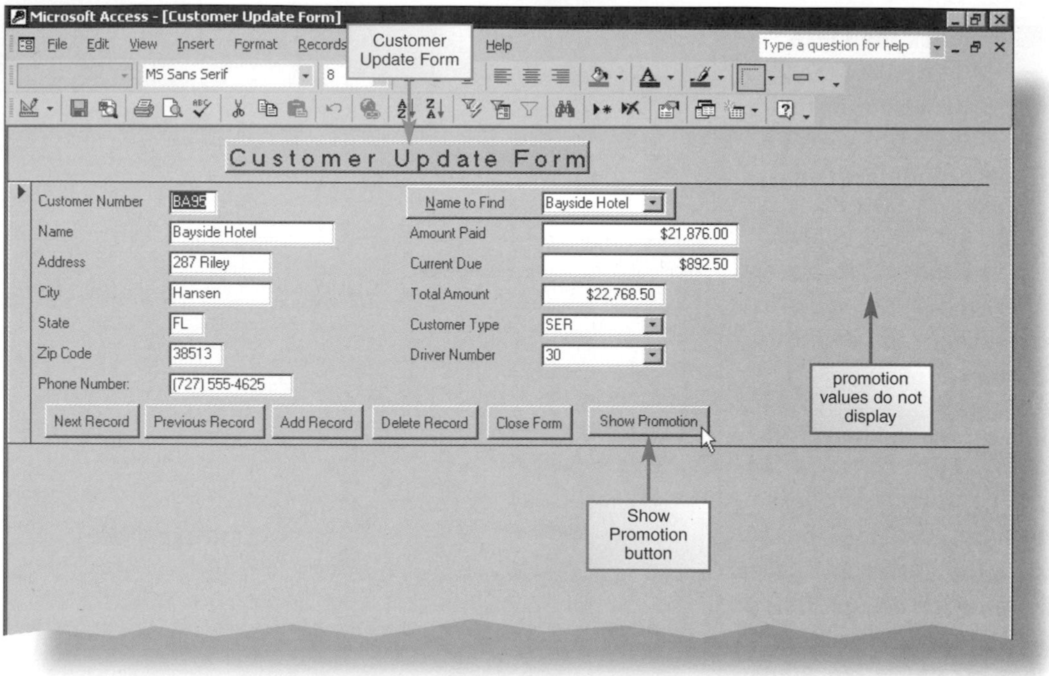

FIGURE 8-92

2 **Click the Show Promotion Query button. Point to the Run Promotion Query button.**

The promotion data and Run Promotion Query buttons display (Figure 8-93). The caption that had read Show Promotion now reads Hide Promotion. The Promotion Amount and Promotion Factor values have been calculated appropriately.

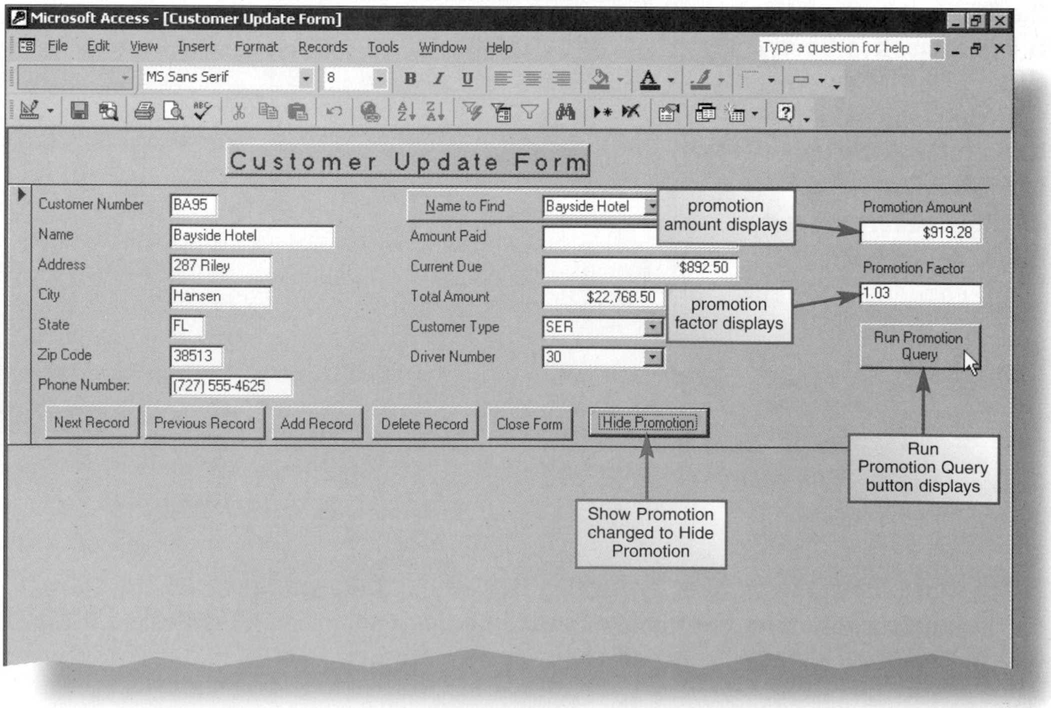

FIGURE 8-93

3 Click the Run Promotion Query button.

The query results display (Figure 8-94).

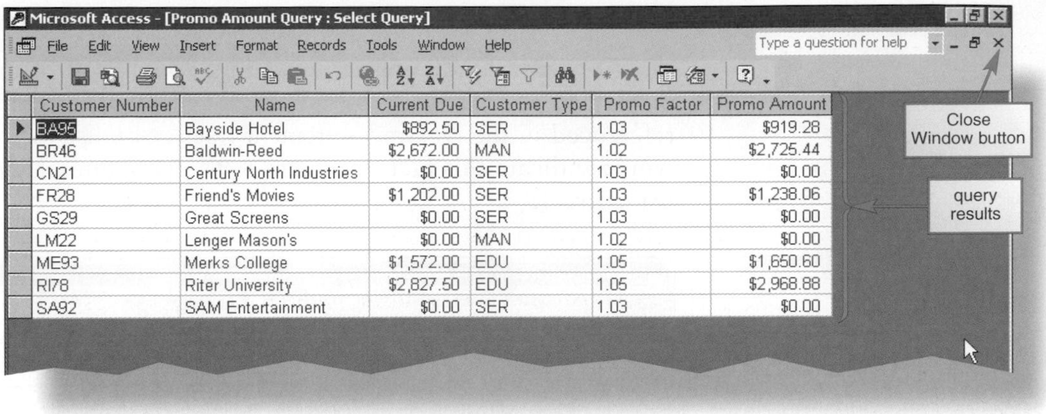

FIGURE 8-94

4 Close the window containing the query by clicking its Close Window button. Use the Customer Type combo box to change the customer type for Bayside Hotel to EDU. Point to the Hide Promotion button.

The query no longer displays (Figure 8-95). Bayside Hotel displays on the form with the customer type changed to EDU. The Promotion Amount and Promotion Factor values have been updated appropriately.

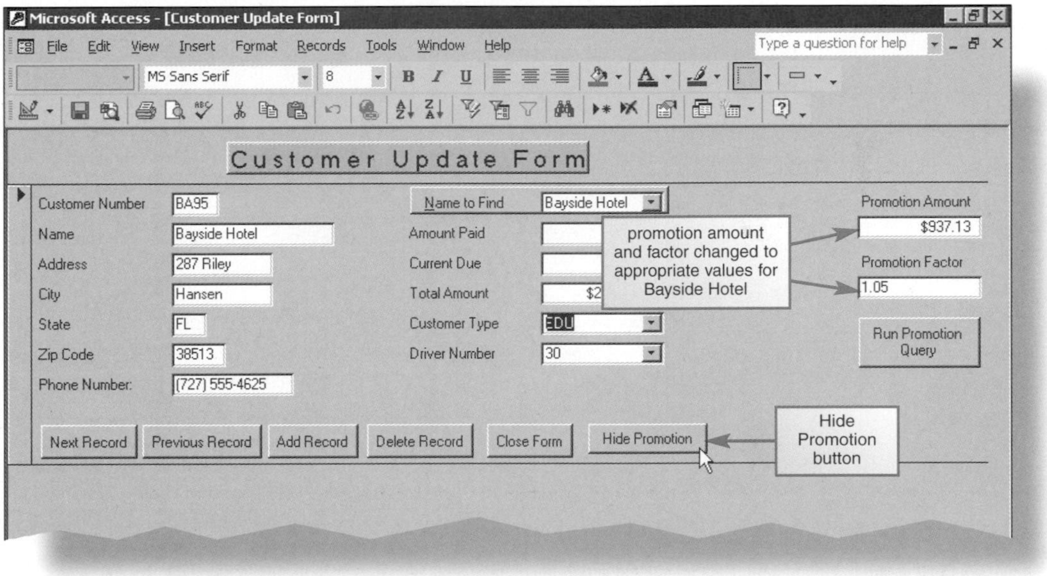

FIGURE 8-95

5 Click the Hide Promotion button.

The promotion data and Run Promotion Query buttons no longer display (Figure 8-96).

6 Close the form by clicking the Close Form button.

The form no longer displays.

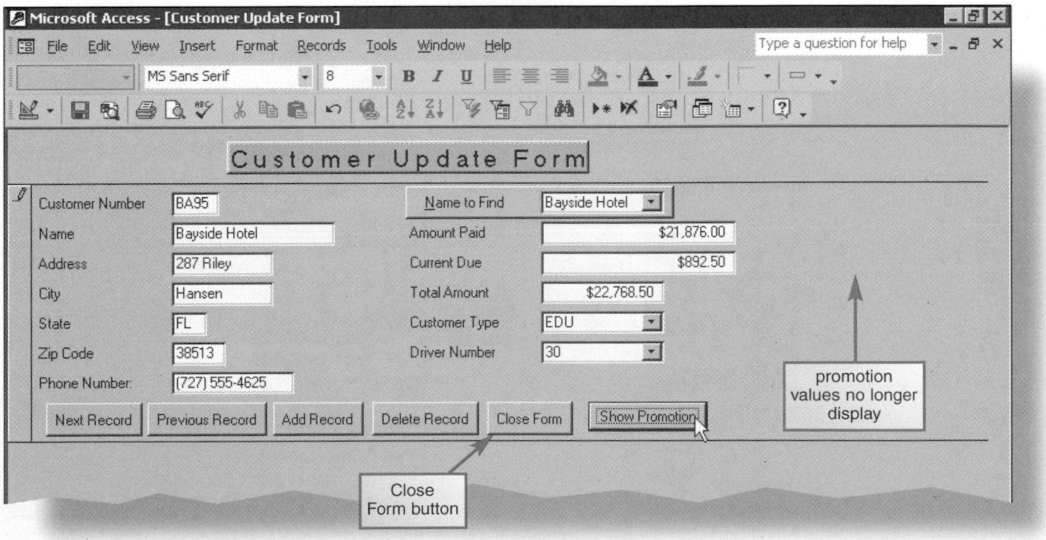

FIGURE 8-96

Error Handling

The error handling statements in the RunPromoAmountQuery function will display an appropriate message in case there is an error. If, for example, the query referenced in the DoCmd statement does not exist for some reason, the message would indicate this fact. In Figure 8-97, the name of the query, Promo Amnt Query, is incorrect.

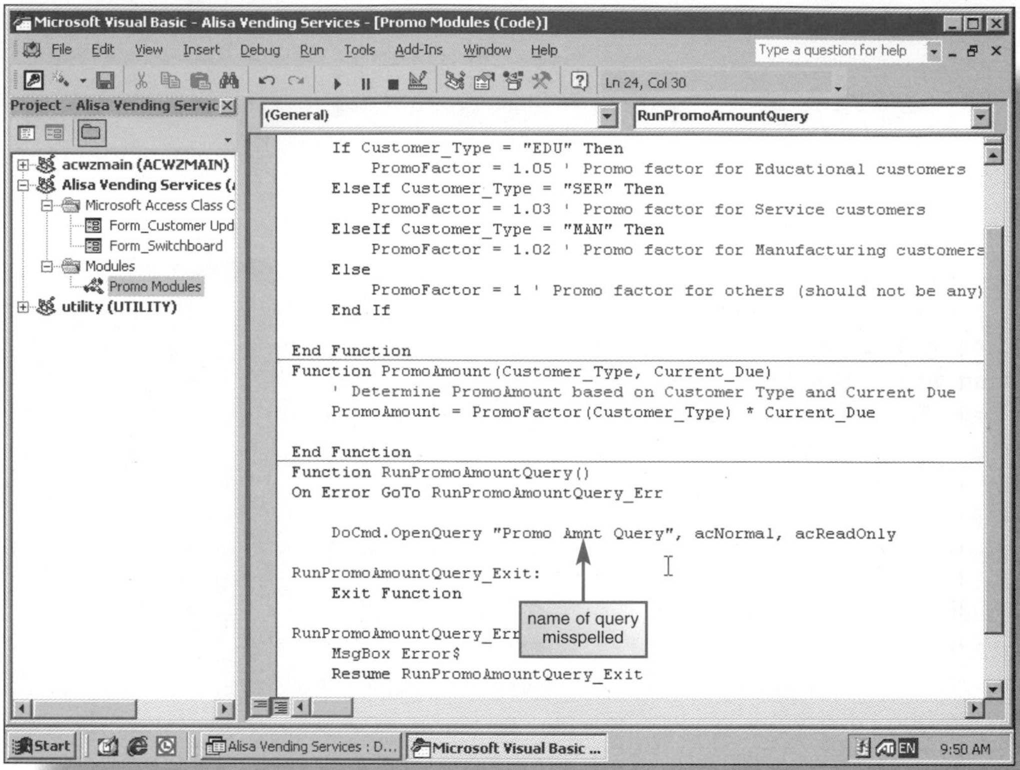

FIGURE 8-97

If a user of the form clicked the Run Promotion Query button with this error, Access would display the message shown in Figure 8-98.

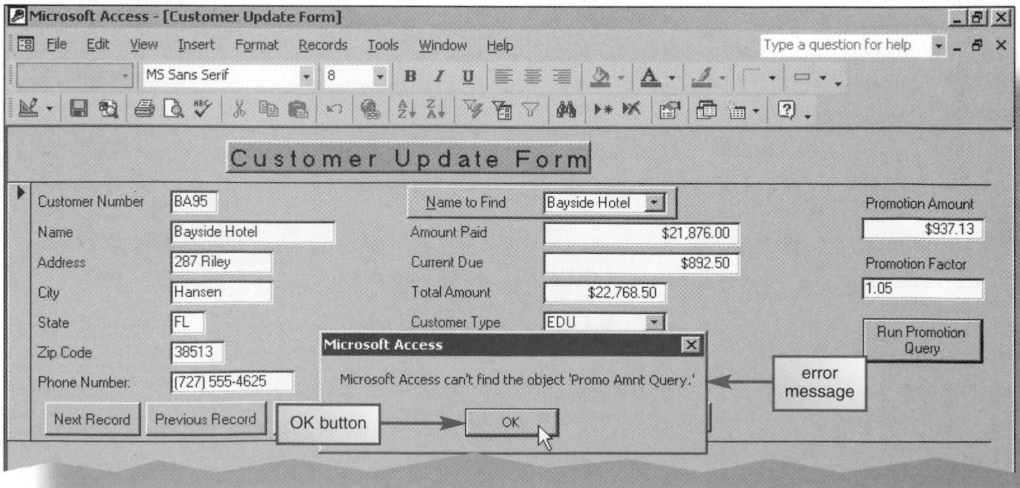

FIGURE 8-98

The Complete Programs

The complete programs are shown in Table 8-18, which shows the standard module, and Table 8-19 on the next page, which shows the form's class module, that is, the code associated with the form.

Table 8-18 Contents of Promo Modules Standard Module

LINE *STATEMENT*

```
1   Option Compare Database
2
3   Function PromoFactor(Customer_Type)
4       ' Determine PromoFactor based on Customer Type
5       If Customer_Type = "EDU" Then
6           PromoFactor = 1.05 ' Promo factor for Educational customers
7       ElseIf Customer_Type = "SER" Then
8           PromoFactor = 1.03 ' Promo factor for Service customers
9       ElseIf Customer_Type = "MAN" Then
10          PromoFactor = 1.02 ' Promo factor for Manufacturing customers
11      Else
12          PromoFactor = 1 ' Promo factor for others (should not be any)
13      End If
14
15  End Function
16
17  Function PromoAmount(Customer_Type, Current_Due)
18      ' Determine PromoAmount based on Customer Type and Current Due
19      PromoAmount = PromoFactor(Customer_Type) * Current_Due
20
21  End Function
22
23  Function RunPromoAmountQuery()
24  On Error GoTo RunPromoAmountQuery_Err
25
26      DoCmd.OpenQuery "Promo Amount Query", acNormal, acReadOnly
27
28  RunPromoAmountQuery_Exit:
29      Exit Function
30
31  RunPromoAmountQuery_Err:
32      MsgBox Error$
33      Resume RunPromoAmountQuery_Exit
34
35  End Function
```

The following is an explanation of the lines in the table:

Line 1. This line is inserted automatically. It indicates the method to be used to compare and sort text data. The Database option, which is the one Access includes automatically, means that normal alphabetical order will be used.

Lines 3-15. This is the PromoFactor function. It was discussed on page A 8.37.

Lines 17-21. This is the PromoAmount function. It was discussed on page A 8.37.

Lines 23-35. This is the RunPromoAmountQuery function. It was discussed on pages A 8.65 and A 8.66.

Table 8-19 Code Associated with Customer Update Form

STATEMENT

```
Option Compare Database

Private Sub cmdPromo_Click()
    ' Update button caption and take appropriate action
    If cmdPromo.Caption = "Show Promotion" Then
        cmdPromo.Caption = "Hide Promotion"
        ShowPromotion ' Display promotion info
    Else
        cmdPromo.Caption = "Show Promotion"
        HidePromotion ' Hide promotion info
    End If

End Sub

Private Sub Combo29_AfterUpdate()
    UpdatePromoData ' Update promotion amount and factor
End Sub

Private Sub Current_Due_AfterUpdate()
    UpdatePromoData ' Update promotion amount and factor
End Sub

Private Sub Form_Current()
    Combo31 = Customer_Number ' Update the combo box
    UpdatePromoData ' Update promotion amount and factor
End Sub

Private Sub Form_Load()
    HidePromotion
End Sub

Private Sub Next_Record_Click()
On Error GoTo Err_Next_Record_Click


    DoCmd.GoToRecord , , acNext

Exit_Next_Record_Click:
    Exit Sub

Err_Next_Record_Click:
    MsgBox Err.Description
    Resume Exit_Next_Record_Click

End Sub
Private Sub Previous_Record_Click()
On Error GoTo Err_Previous_Record_Click


    DoCmd.GoToRecord , , acPrevious

```

Table 8-19 Code Associated with Customer Update Form *(continued)*

LINE *STATEMENT*

```
Exit_Previous_Record_Click:
    Exit Sub

Err_Previous_Record_Click:
    MsgBox Err.Description
    Resume Exit_Previous_Record_Click

End Sub
Private Sub Add_Record_Click()
On Error GoTo Err_Add_Record_Click


    DoCmd.GoToRecord , , acNewRec
    Customer_Number.SetFocus

Exit_Add_Record_Click:
    Exit Sub

Err_Add_Record_Click:
    MsgBox Err.Description
    Resume Exit_Add_Record_Click

End Sub
Private Sub Delete_Record_Click()
On Error GoTo Err_Delete_Record_Click


    DoCmd.DoMenuItem acFormBar, acEditMenu, 8, , acMenuVer70
    DoCmd.DoMenuItem acFormBar, acEditMenu, 6, , acMenuVer70

Exit_Delete_Record_Click:
    Exit Sub

Err_Delete_Record_Click:
    MsgBox Err.Description
    Resume Exit_Delete_Record_Click

End Sub
Private Sub Close_Form_Click()
On Error GoTo Err_Close_Form_Click


    DoCmd.Close

Exit_Close_Form_Click:
    Exit Sub

Err_Close_Form_Click:
    MsgBox Err.Description
    Resume Exit_Close_Form_Click
```

Table 8-19 Code Associated with Customer Update Form *(continued)*

LINE	*STATEMENT*
103	End Sub
104	Private Sub Combo31_AfterUpdate()
105	' Find the record that matches the control.
106	Dim rs As Object
107	
108	Set rs = Me.Recordset.Clone
109	rs.FindFirst "[Customer Number] = '" & Me![Combo31] & "'"
110	If Not rs.EOF Then Me.Bookmark = rs.Bookmark
111	End Sub
112	
113	Public Sub ShowPromotion()
114	txtPromoAmount.Visible = True
115	txtPromoFactor.Visible = True
116	cmdPromoQuery.Visible = True
117	End Sub
118	
119	Public Sub HidePromotion()
120	txtPromoAmount.Visible = False
121	txtPromoFactor.Visible = False
122	cmdPromoQuery.Visible = False
123	End Sub
124	
125	Public Sub UpdatePromoData()
126	txtPromoAmount.Value = PromoAmount([Customer Type], [Current Due])
127	txtPromoFactor.Value = PromoFactor([Customer Type])
128	End Sub

The following is an explanation of the lines in the table:

Line 1. This line is inserted automatically. It indicates the method to be used to compare and sort text data. The Database option, which is the one Access includes automatically, means that normal alphabetical order will be used.

Lines 3-13. This is the cmdPromo_Click procedure. It was discussed on page A 8.54.

Lines 15-17. This is the procedure to update promotion data after the data in the Customer Type combo box is changed. It was discussed on page A 8.61.

Lines 19-21. This is the procedure to update promotion data after the data in the Current Due control is changed. It was discussed on page A 8.63.

Lines 23-26. This is the procedure that will be executed whenever a different record displays (for example, after the Next Record button is clicked). The statement on line 24, which updates the combo box with the correct customer's name, was discussed on page A 8.33. The statement on line 25, which runs the UpdatePromoData procedure to update the promotion amount and promotion factor, was discussed on page A 8.61.

Lines 28-30. This is the procedure that will be executed when the form is loaded. The statement on line 29 runs the procedure to hide the promotion amount, the promotion factor, and the button to run the Promotion Amount query. It was discussed on page A 8.54.

Lines 32-45. This is the procedure that will be executed when the Next Record button is clicked. It was added automatically by Access and was not changed.

Lines 46-59. This is the procedure that will be executed when the Previous Record button is clicked. It was added automatically by Access and was not changed.

Lines 60-74. This is the procedure that will be executed when the Add Record button is clicked. It was added automatically by Access. The statement on line 65 updates the focus to display an insertion point in the control for the Customer Number field. It was discussed on page A 8.29.

Lines 75-89. This is the procedure that will be executed when the Delete Record button is clicked. It was added automatically by Access and was not changed.

Lines 90-103. This is the procedure that will be executed when the Close Form button is clicked. It was added automatically by Access and was not changed.

Lines 104-111. This is the procedure that will be executed when the combo box for finding a customer is updated. It was added automatically by Access and was not changed.

Lines 113-117. This is the ShowPromotion procedure. It was discussed on page A 8.56.

Lines 119-123. This is the HidePromotion procedure. It was discussed on page A 8.57.

Lines 125-128. This is the UpdatePromoData procedure. It was discussed on page A 8.59.

> **More About**
>
> **Charts**
>
> At least one of the fields used in a chart must have a data type that stores only numbers. The use of charts in Access is not restricted to forms. You also can place a chart on a report or on a data access page. The steps involved in placing such charts are the same as those for placing charts on forms. For more information about charts, visit the Access 2002 More About page (scsite.com/ac2002/more.htm) and then click Charts.

Creating a Form Using Design View

You have used the Form Wizard to create a variety of forms. You also can create a form without the wizard by simply using Design view. You will be presented with a blank form on which you can place all the necessary controls. On the form you create in this project, you will need to place a subform and two charts.

Creating a Query for the Subform

The subform is based on data in a query, so you first must create the query. Perform the following steps to create the query for the subform.

TO CREATE THE QUERY FOR THE SUBFORM

1. If necessary, in the Database window click Tables on the Objects bar, and then click Customer. Click the New Object: AutoForm button arrow on the Database toolbar. Click Query. Be sure Design View is selected, and then click the OK button. Maximize the Query1 : Select Query window. Resize the upper and lower panes and the Customer field list so all the fields in the Customer table display.
2. Right-click any open area in the upper pane, click Show Table on the shortcut menu, click the Open Workorders table, click the Add button, and then click the Close button. Resize the Open Workorders field list so all the fields in the Open Workorders table display. Double-click the Driver Number field from the Customer table.
3. Double-click the Customer Number and Name fields from the Customer table. Double-click the Location, Category Number, Total Hours (est), and Hours Spent fields from the Open Workorders table.
4. Select Ascending as the sort order for both the Driver Number and Customer Number fields.

5 Close the query by clicking its Close Window button. Click the Yes button to save the query. Type `Customers and Workorders by Driver` as the name of the query, and then click the OK button.

The query is created.

Creating the Form

When you want to create a form from scratch, you begin with the same general procedure as when you want to use the Form Wizard. The difference is that you will select Design View instead of Form Wizard. Perform the following steps to create the form.

Steps To Create the Form

1 **If necessary, in the Database window click Tables on the Objects bar, and then click Driver. Click the New Object: Query button arrow on the Database toolbar. Click Form. Be sure Design View is selected, and then click the OK button.**

2 **Be sure the field list displays and the window is maximized. (If it does not, click the Field List button on the Form Design toolbar.) Drag the Driver Number, First Name, and Last Name fields to the approximate positions shown in Figure 8-99. Move the attached labels for the First Name and Last Name fields to the positions shown in the figure by dragging their Move handles. Point to the Close button in the field list.**

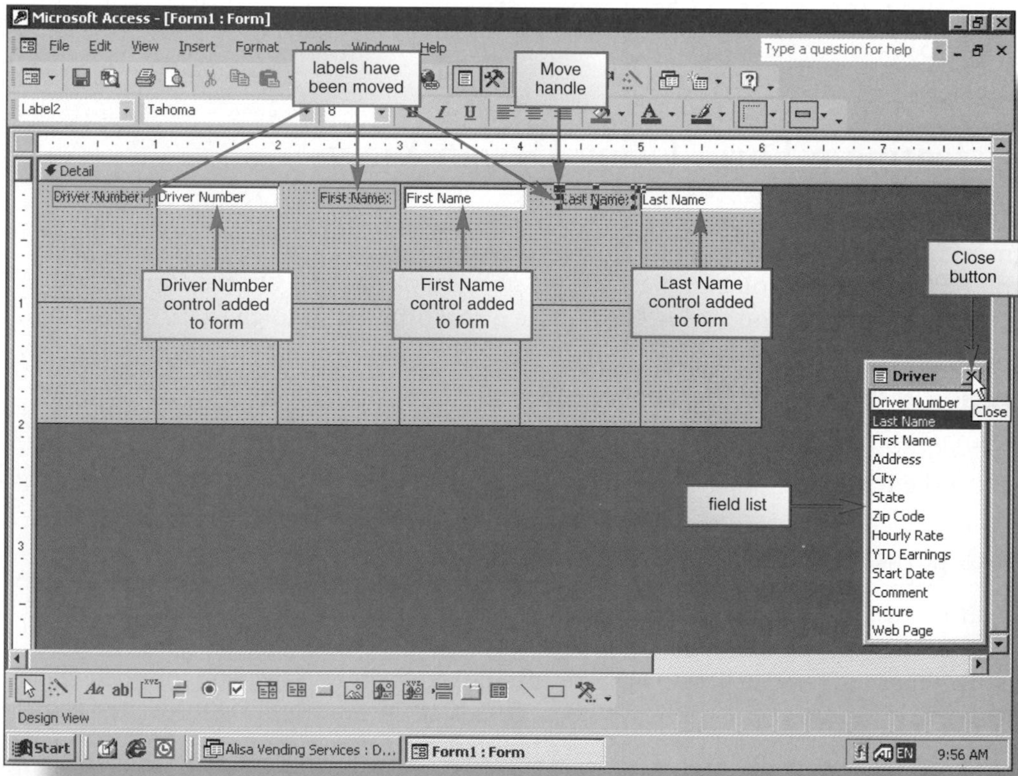

FIGURE 8-99

3 **Close the field list by clicking its Close button.**

The field list no longer displays.

Other Ways

1. Click Forms on Objects bar, click New button, click Design View
2. Click Forms on Objects bar, double-click Create form in Design view
3. On Insert menu click Form, click Design View
4. In Voice Command Mode, say "Forms, New"

Using Tab Controls to Create a Multi-Page Form

You can create a **multi-page form**, a form that includes more than a single page, by inserting a page break at the desired location. An alternative that produces a nice-looking and easy to use multi-page form is to insert a tab control. Once you have done so, users can change from one page to another by clicking the desired tab. Perform the following steps to insert a tab control with three tabs — Datasheet, Charts, and Web. Users will be able to click the Datasheet tab in the completed form to view work order data in Datasheet view. Clicking the Charts tab will display two charts representing work order data. Clicking the Web tab will display a Web browser showing the Alisa Vending Services home page.

Steps To Use Tab Controls to Create a Multi-Page Form

1 Point to the Tab Control tool in the toolbox (Figure 8-100).

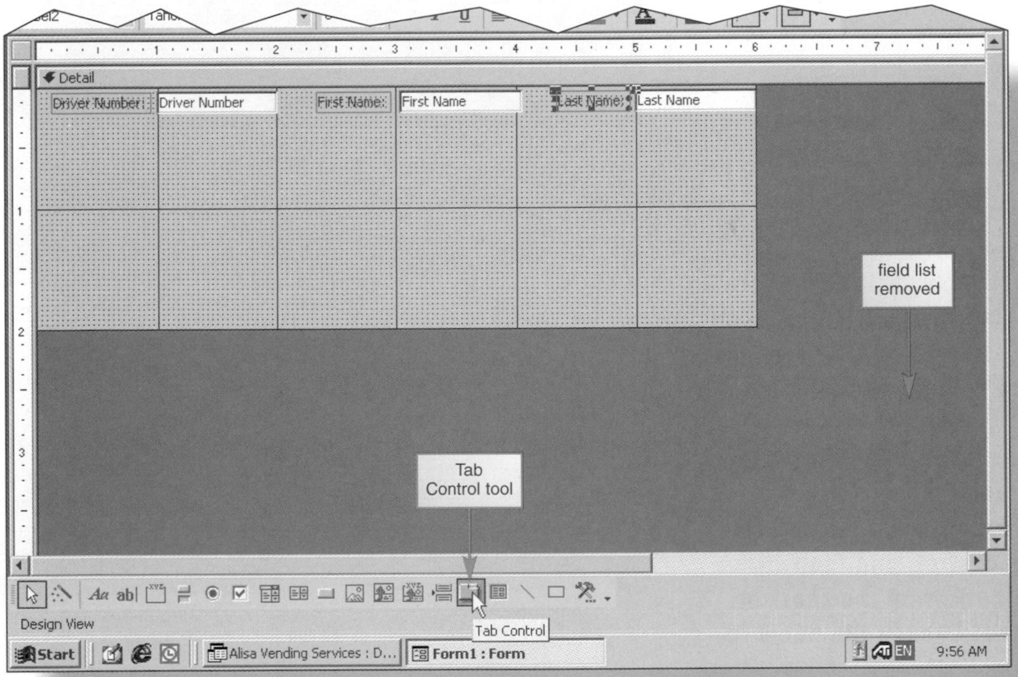

FIGURE 8-100

2 Click the Tab Control tool and move the mouse pointer to the approximate location shown in Figure 8-101.

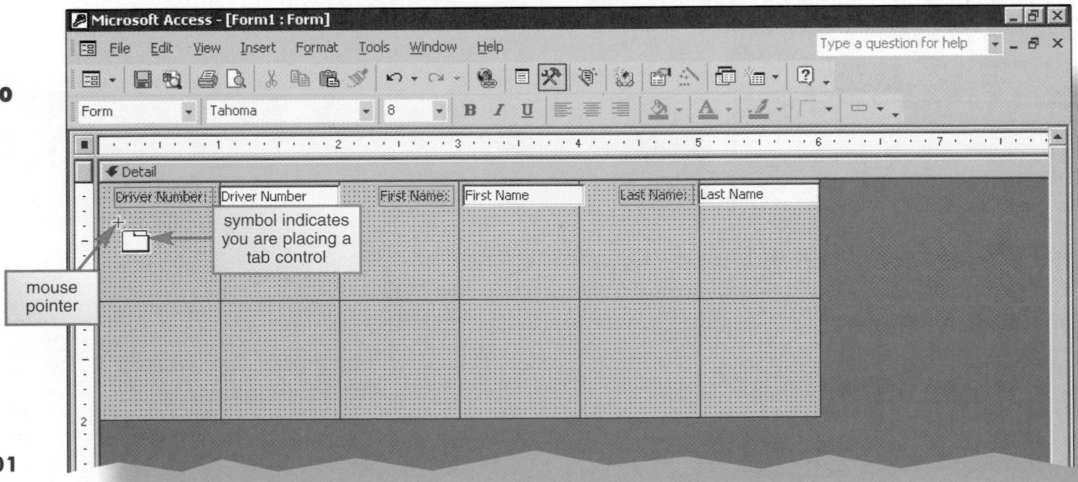

FIGURE 8-101

3 Click the position shown in Figure 8-101 on the previous page.

A tab control displays on the form (Figure 8-102). There currently are two tabs on the control. (Yours may have different numbers.)

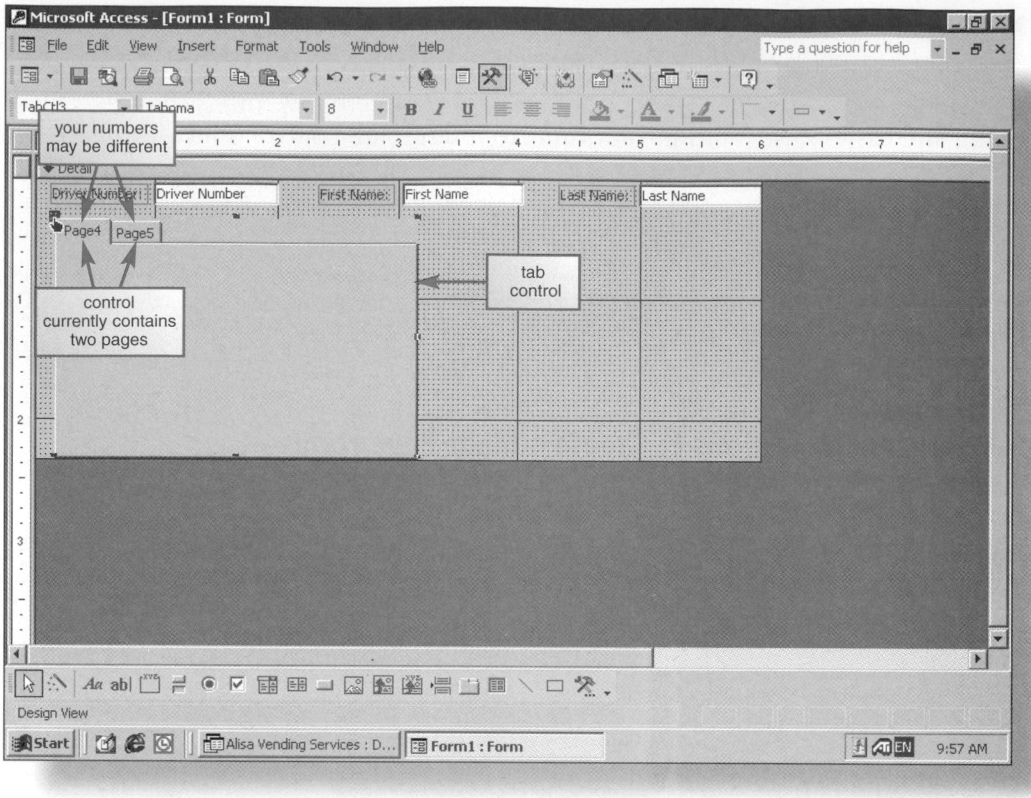

FIGURE 8-102

4 Right-click the tab control, and then click Insert Page on the shortcut menu. Click the leftmost tab, right-click the tab control, and then click Properties on the shortcut menu. Change the name to Datasheet.

The property sheet displays (Figure 8-103). The leftmost tab is selected. The name is changed to Datasheet.

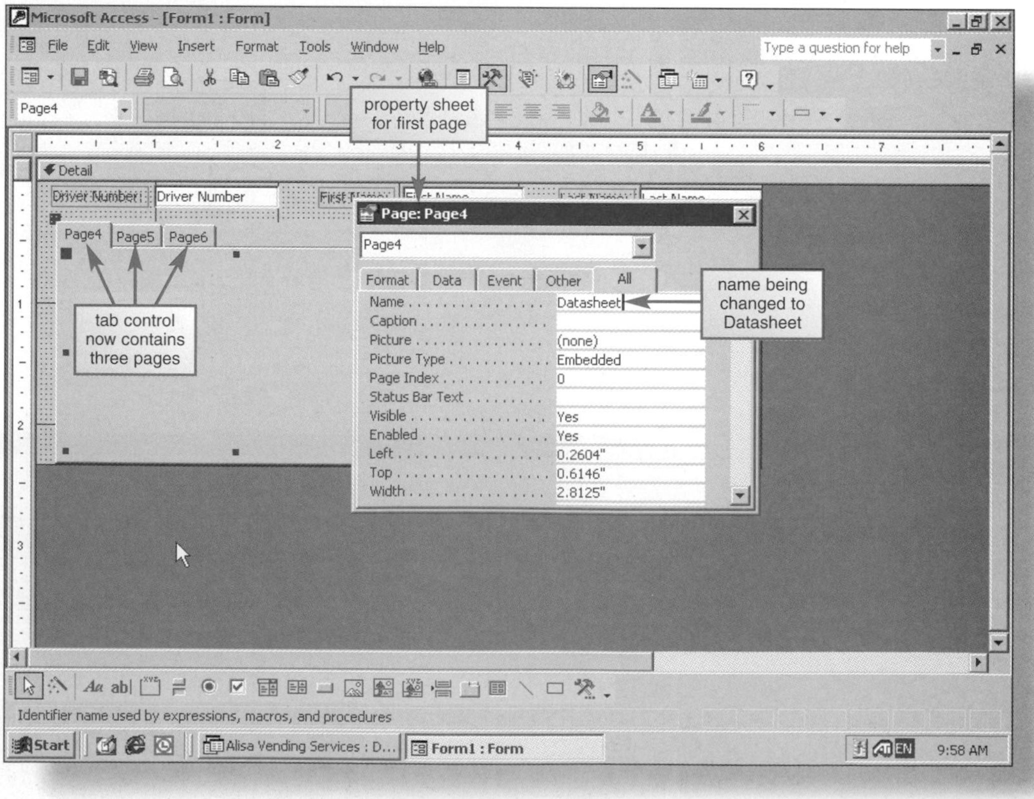

FIGURE 8-103

5 **Close the property sheet by clicking its Close button. Right-click the middle tab, click Properties on the shortcut menu, change the name to Charts, and then close the property sheet. Right-click the rightmost tab, click Properties on the shortcut menu, change the name to Web, and then close the property sheet. Click the leftmost tab. Resize the tab control to the approximate size shown in Figure 8-104 by dragging the appropriate sizing handles. Point to the Subform/Subreport tool in the toolbox.**

The tab names are changed and the tab control is resized. The leftmost tab is selected.

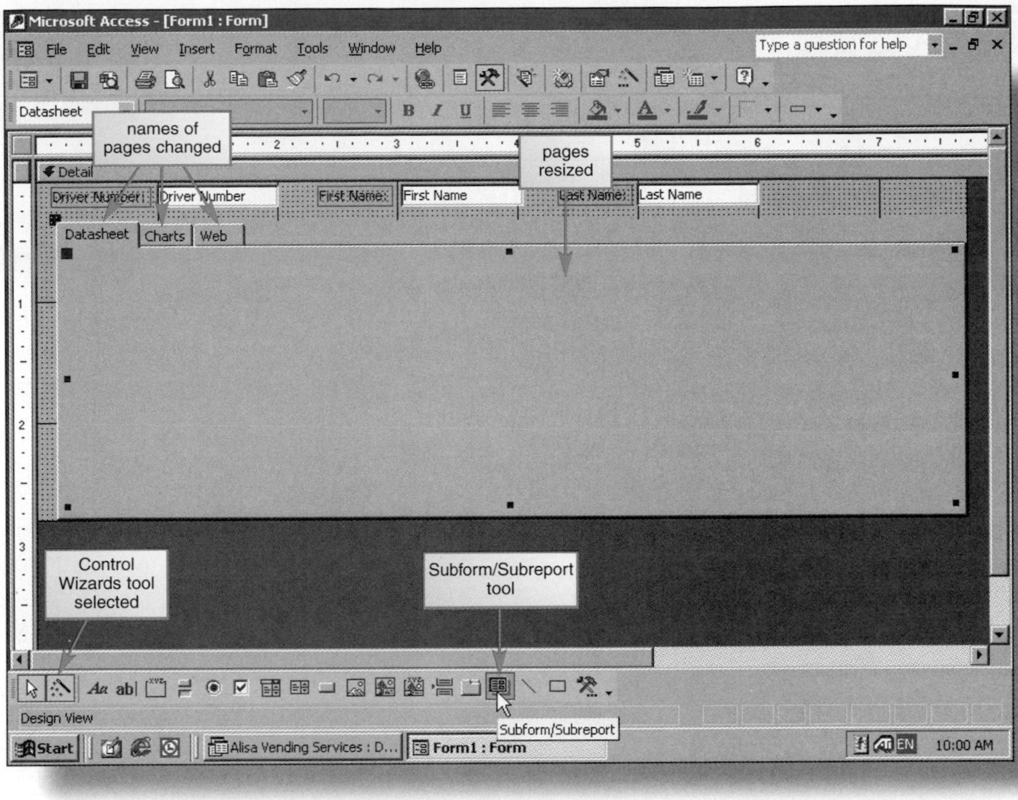

FIGURE 8-104

Placing a Subform

To place a subform on a form, you use the Subform/Subreport tool in the toolbox. Provided the Control Wizards tool is selected, a wizard will guide you through the process of adding the subform as in the following steps.

More About

Quick Reference

For a table that lists how to complete tasks covered in this book using the mouse, menu, shortcut menu, and keyboard, see the Quick Reference Summary at the back of this book, or visit the Shelly Cashman Series Office XP Web page (scsite.com/offxp/qr.htm) and then click Microsoft Access 2002.

Steps To Place the Subform

1 **Be sure the Control Wizards tool is selected, click the Subform/Subreport tool in the toolbox, and then move the mouse pointer to the approximate position shown in Figure 8-105.**

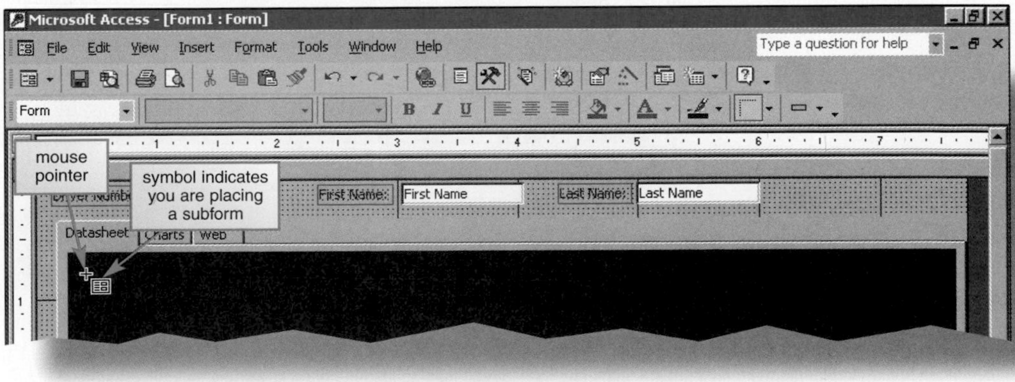

FIGURE 8-105

2 Click the position shown in Figure 8-105 on the previous page. Be sure the Use existing Tables and Queries button is selected and then point to the Next button.

The Subform Wizard dialog box displays (Figure 8-106).

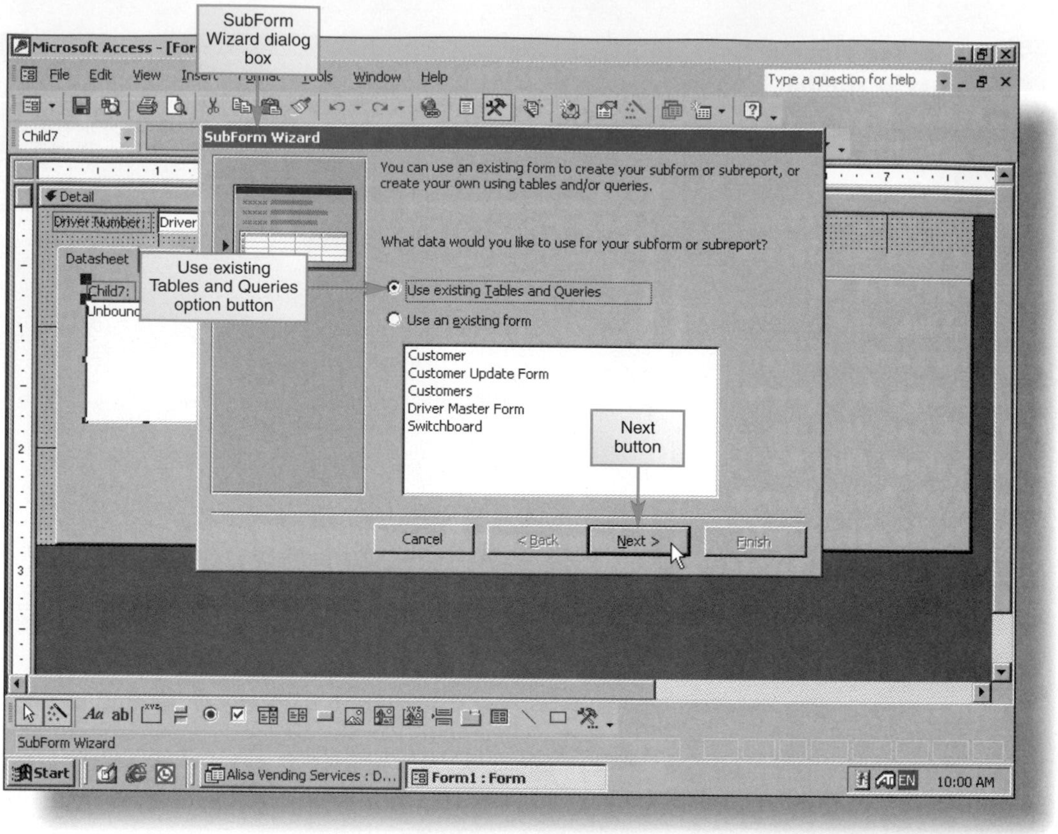

FIGURE 8-106

3 Click the Next button. Click the Tables/Queries box arrow and then click the Customers and Workorders by Driver query. Click the Add All fields button and then point to the Next button.

The Customers and Workorders by Driver query is selected (Figure 8-107). All fields are selected.

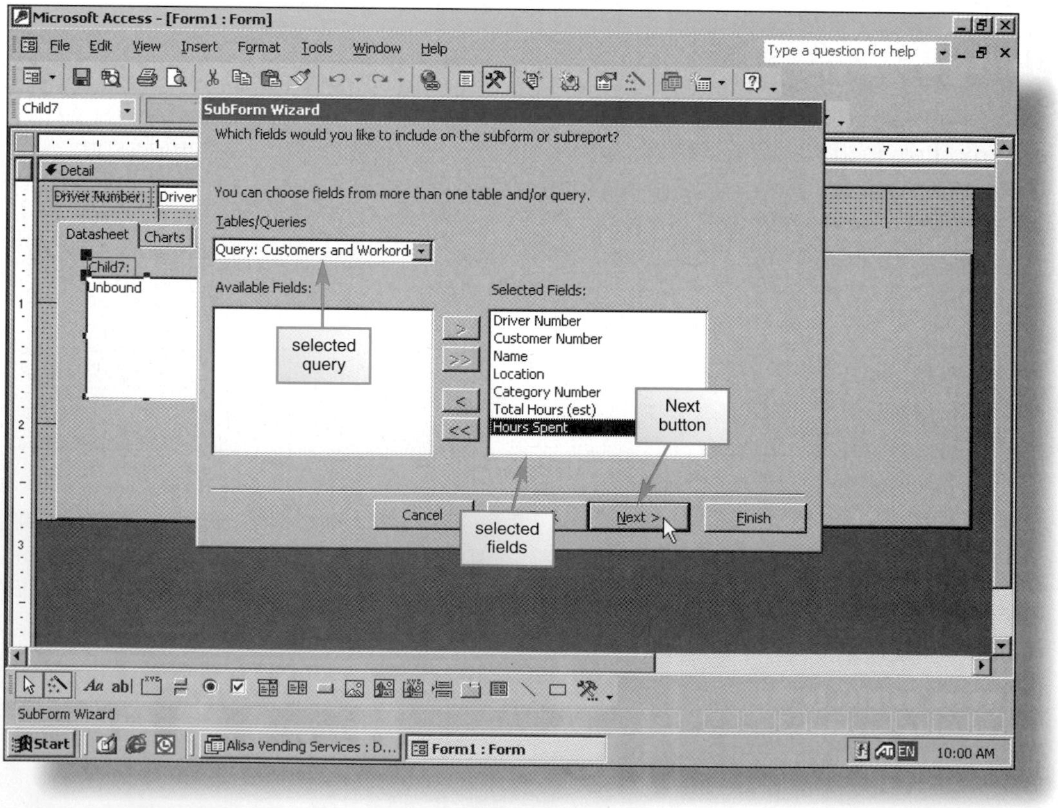

FIGURE 8-107

4 **Click the Next button. Be sure the Choose from a list option button is selected and then point to the Next button (Figure 8-108).**

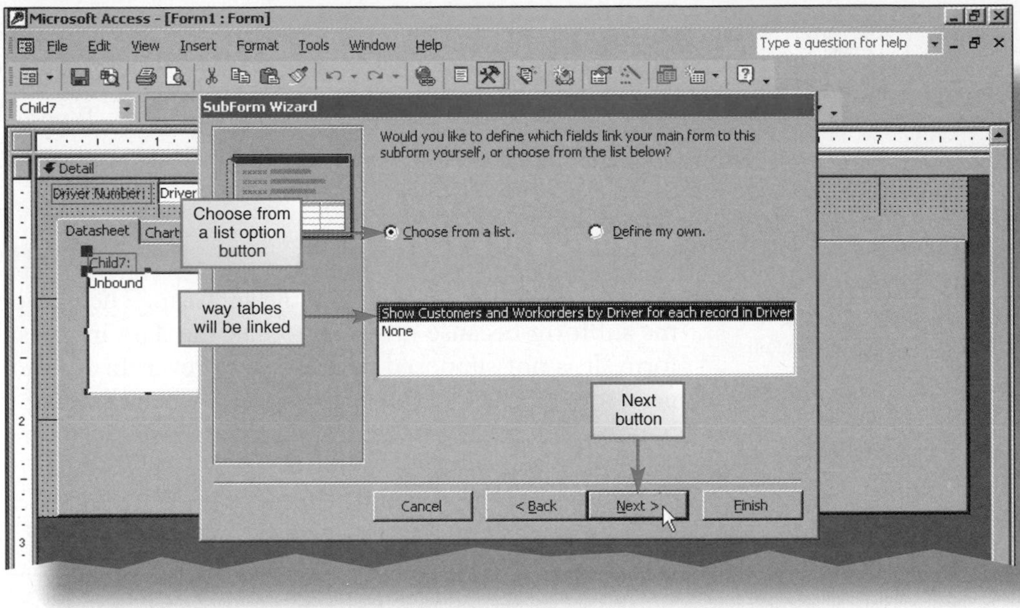

FIGURE 8-108

5 **Click the Next button. Type** `Open Workorders for Driver` **as the name of the subform and then click the Finish button. If the window is no longer maximized, maximize the window. If the field list displays, close the field list. Resize the subform to the approximate size shown in Figure 8-109 by dragging the appropriate sizing handles, and then point to the Close Window button for the window containing the form design.**

The subform is added to the Datasheet page of the tab control.

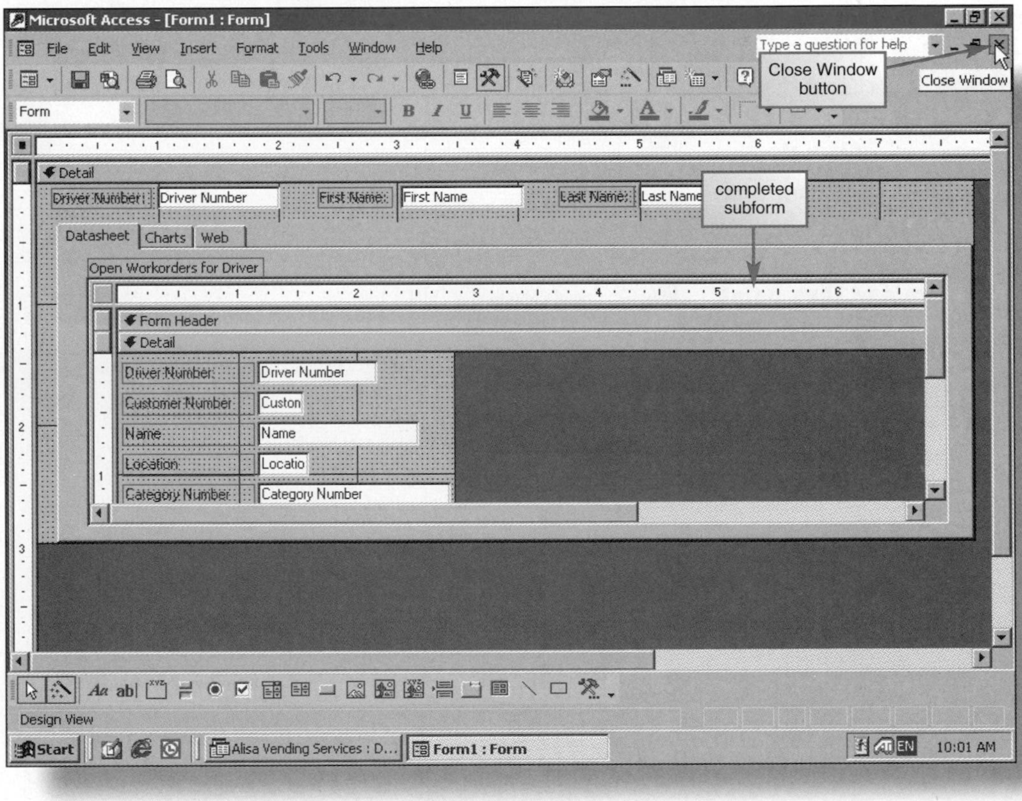

FIGURE 8-109

Closing and Saving the Form

To close a form, close the window using the Close Window button. Then indicate whether you want to save your changes. Perform the steps on the next page to close and save the form.

More About

Subforms

A main form does not need to be based on a table or query. If the main form is not based on a table or query, it still can contain one or more subforms. It simply serves as a container for the subforms, which then have no restrictions on the information they must contain.

TO CLOSE AND SAVE THE FORM

1. Close the form by clicking its Close Window button.
2. Click the Yes button to save the changes. Type `Driver Data` as the name of the form and then click the OK button.

Modifying the Subform

The next task is to modify the subform. The Driver Number field needed to be in the subform because it is used to link the data in the subform to the data in the main form. It is not supposed to display, however. In addition, the remaining columns need to be resized to appropriate sizes. The following steps first remove the Driver Number field and then convert to Datasheet view to resize the remaining columns.

Steps To Modify the Subform

1. **In the Database window, click Forms on the Objects bar, right-click the Open Workorders for Driver form, and then click Design View on the shortcut menu. Click the Driver Number control, and then press the DELETE key to delete the control. Click the View button and then point to the right boundary of the field selector for the Customer Number field.**

The subform displays in Datasheet view (Figure 8-110). The Driver Number field has been removed. The mouse pointer has changed shape indicating that the column can be resized.

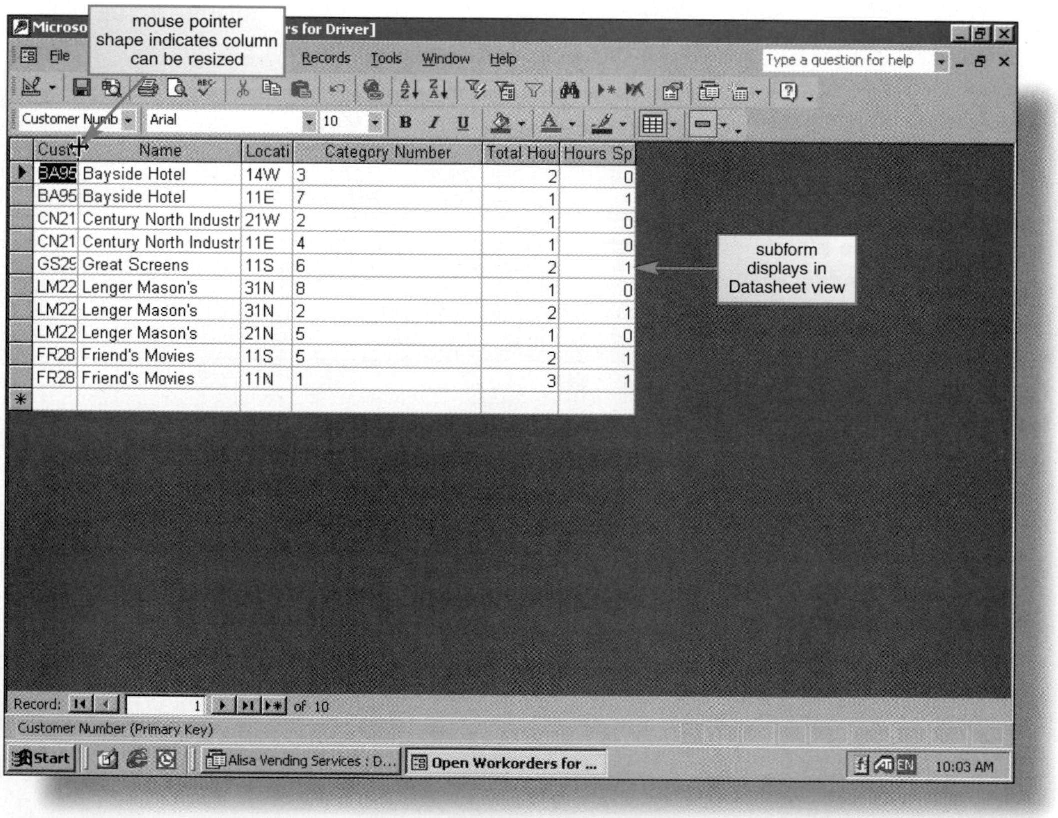

FIGURE 8-110

2. **Resize each column to best fit the data by double-clicking the right boundary of the column's field selector. Close the subform by clicking its Close Window button. Click the Yes button to save the changes.**

The subform has been changed.

Inserting Charts

To insert a chart, use the Chart command on the Insert menu. The Chart Wizard then will ask you to indicate the fields to be included on the chart and the type of chart you wish to insert. Perform the following steps to insert a chart.

Steps To Insert Charts

1 In the Alisa Vending Services: Database window, be sure Forms is selected on the Objects bar, right-click Driver Data and then click Design View on the shortcut menu. If necessary, maximize the window and close the field list. Click the Charts tab, click Insert on the menu bar, and then point to Chart.

The Insert menu displays (Figure 8-111).

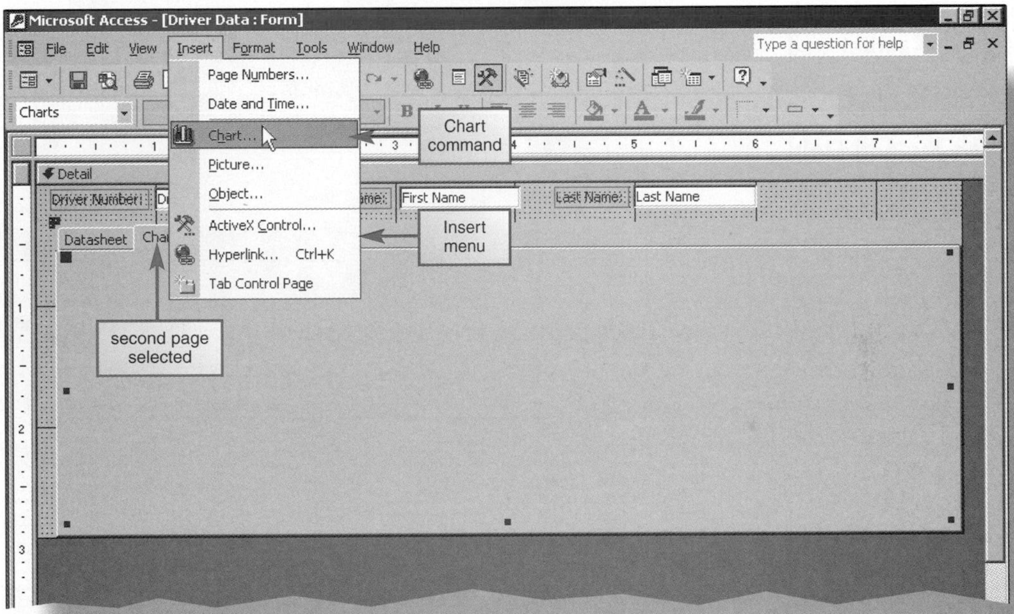

FIGURE 8-111

2 Click Chart and then move the pointer to the approximate position shown in Figure 8-112.

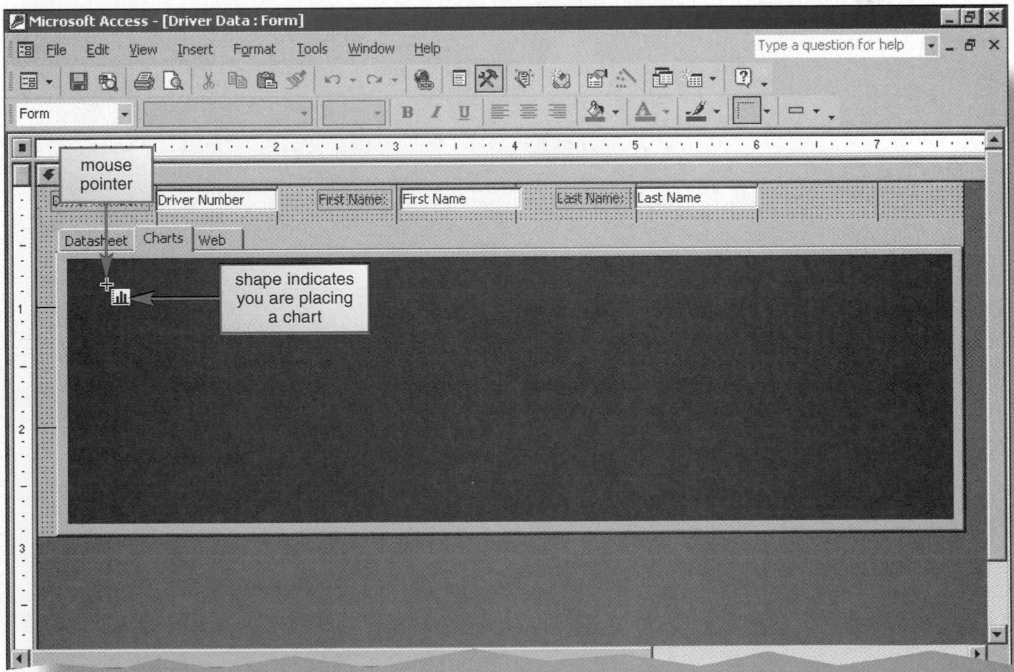

FIGURE 8-112

3 Click the position shown in Figure 8-112 on the previous page. Click the Queries option button in the Chart Wizard dialog box, click the Customers and Workorders by Driver query, and then click the Next button. Select the Category Number and Total Hours (est) fields by clicking them and then clicking the Add Field button. Point to the Next button.

The Chart Wizard dialog box displays (Figure 8-113). The fields for the chart have been selected.

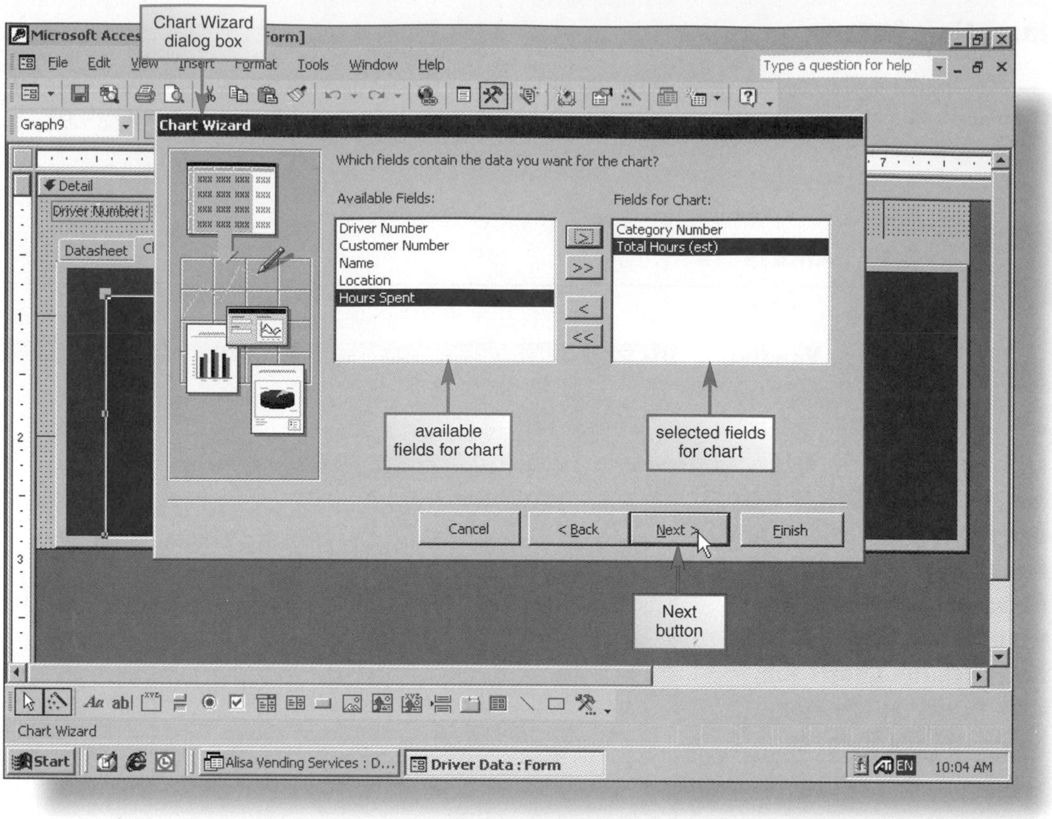

FIGURE 8-113

4 Click the Next button. Be sure the chart in the upper-left corner is selected and then point to the Next button.

The Chart Wizard dialog box displays (Figure 8-114). Use this box to select the type of chart you want to produce. A description of the selected chart type displays in the dialog box.

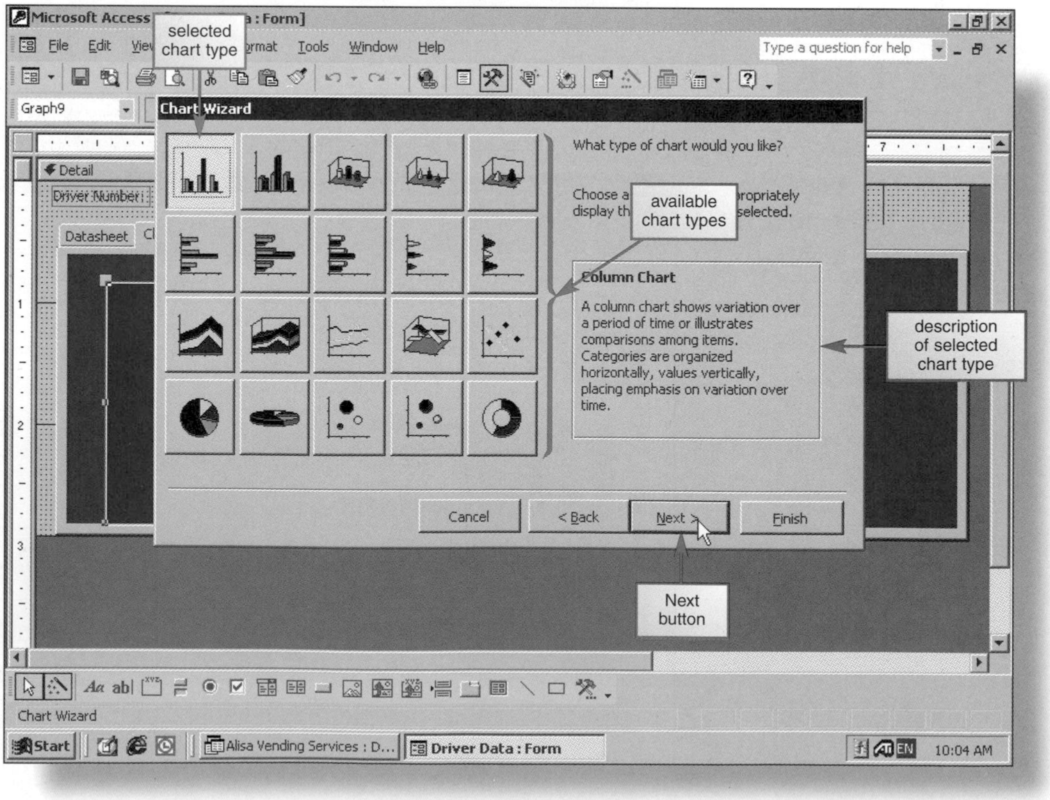

FIGURE 8-114

5 Click the Next button.

The Chart Wizard dialog box displays (Figure 8-115). The correct items have been placed on the chart in the correct positions. (If not, you could drag the items to the correct positions.)

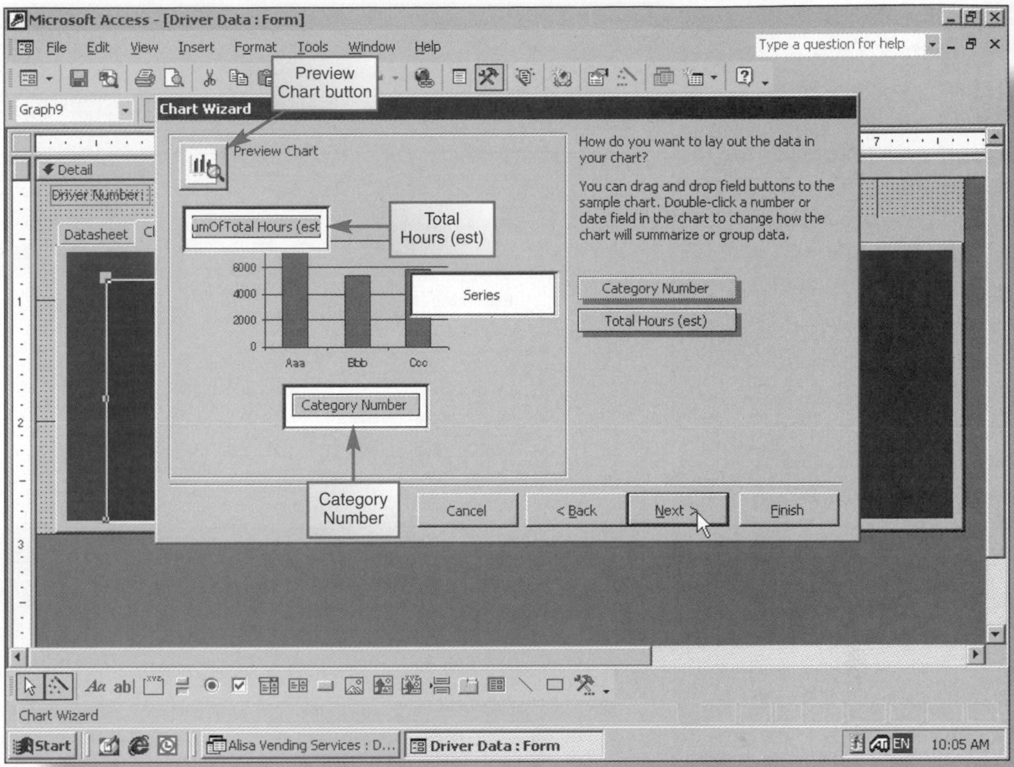

FIGURE 8-115

6 Click the Next button.

The Chart Wizard dialog box displays, indicating the fields that will be used to link the document and the chart (Figure 8-116). Linking the document and the chart ensures that the chart will reflect accurately the data for the correct driver, that is, the driver who currently is displayed on the form.

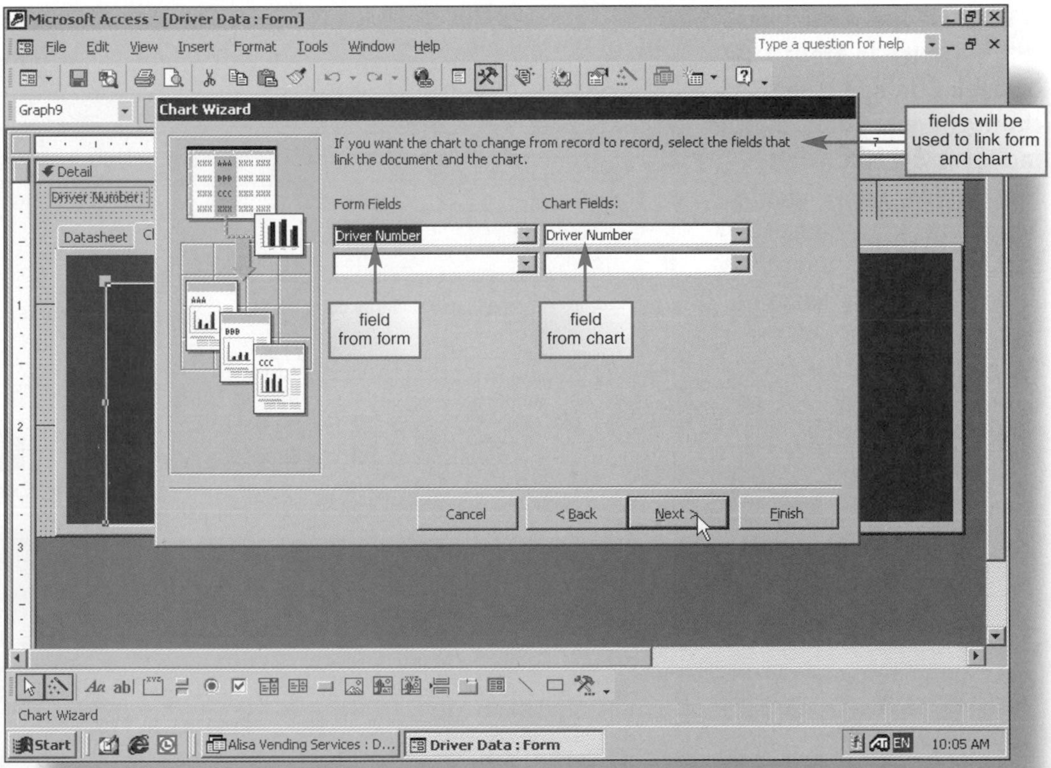

FIGURE 8-116

7 **Click the Next button. Type** `Estimated Hours by Category` **as the name of the chart and then click the Finish button.**

The chart displays (Figure 8-117). The data in it is fictitious. It simply represents the general way the chart will look.

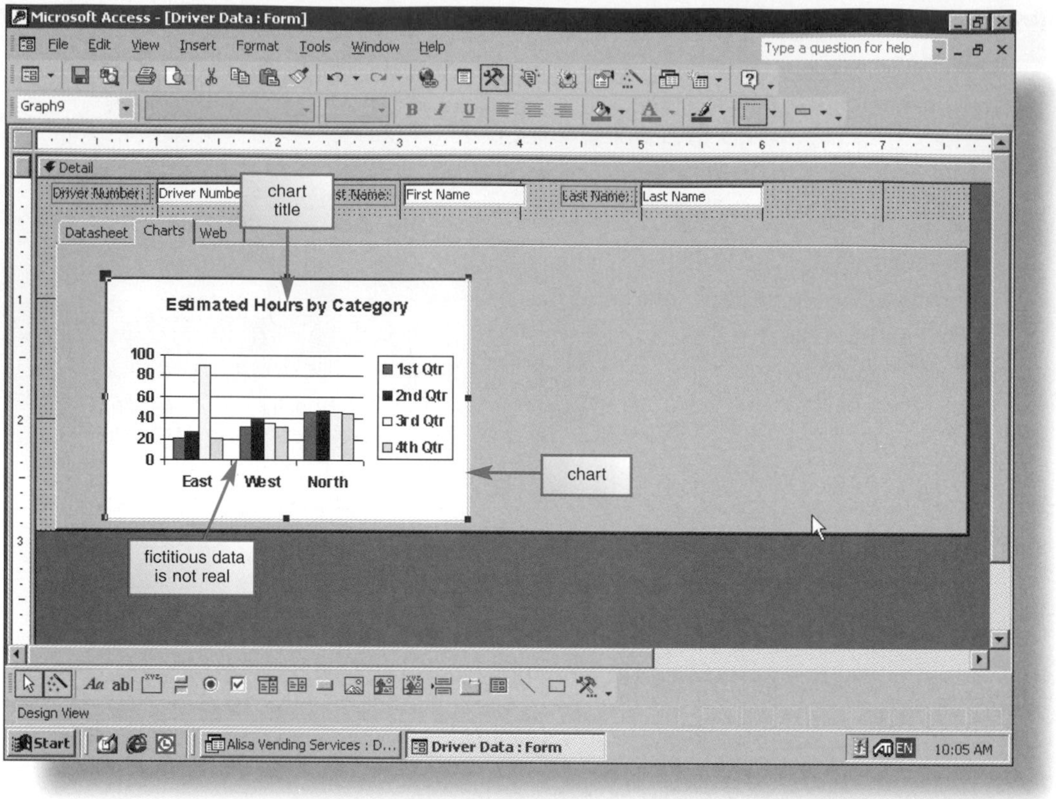

FIGURE 8-117

8 **Use the techniques shown in Steps 1 through 7 to add a second chart at the position shown in Figure 8-118. In this chart, select Hours Spent instead of Total Hours (est) and type** `Hours Spent by Category` **as the name of the chart instead of Estimated Hours by Category.**

The chart is inserted.

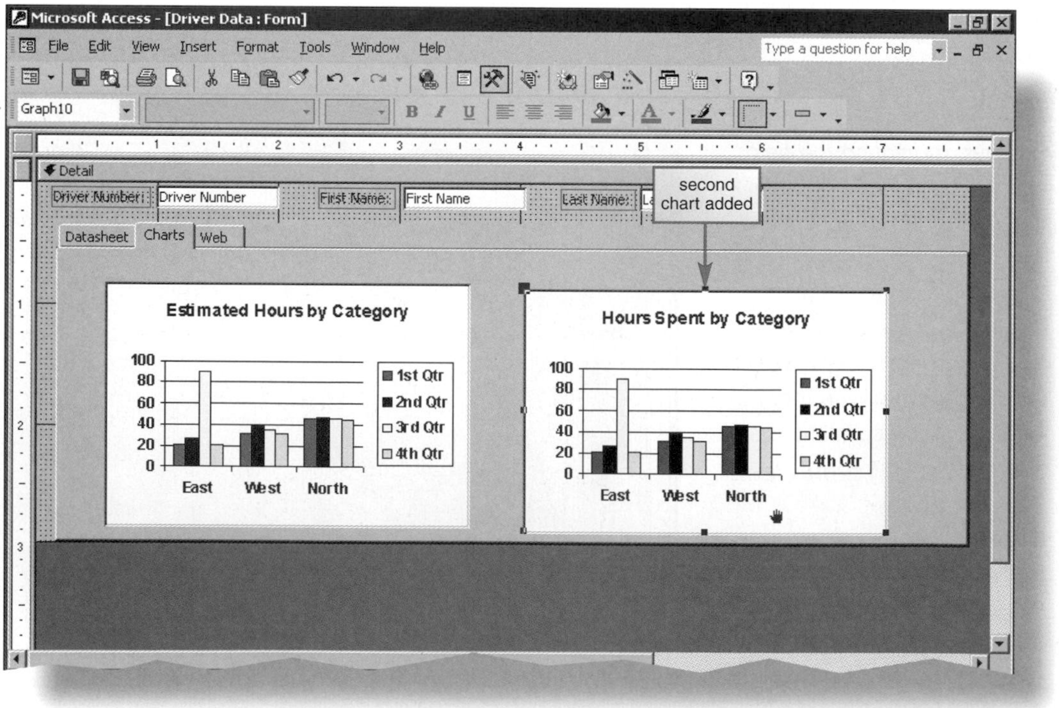

FIGURE 8-118

Other Ways

1. In Voice Command mode, say "Insert, Chart"

Adding an ActiveX Control

When you created forms, you worked with several of the special built-in Microsoft Access controls. These included: text box, label, command button, combo box, rectangle, and so on. Many additional controls, called **ActiveX controls**, also are available. These controls are similar to the others except that they are not part of Access and typically have been developed to work with a variety of applications. There are a wide variety of ActiveX controls available, both from Microsoft and from other sources. In general, to find how to use a particular control, consult the documentation provided with the control.

Many ActiveX controls are installed automatically along with Office. One of the most popular of these is the Calendar control, which enables you to display a calendar on a form. The following steps use another popular control, the Microsoft Web Browser control, to display a Web page on a form. To use the Microsoft Web Browser control you first add it to the form by selecting it from a list of available ActiveX controls. This places the control on the form. You also will indicate during the loading of the form the Web page that should be displayed.

To indicate the Web page, include a statement similar to the following in the Form_Load procedure: me!WebBrowser1.navigate followed by the URL for the Web page to be displayed. For example, you will use the statement me!WebBrowser1.navigate "http://www.scsite.com/ac2002/alisa.htm" in the procedure that will be executed when the form is loaded. In this statement, the me keyword followed by the exclamation point simply indicates that what follows is part of the current object, that is, the form that is being loaded. The name following the exclamation point is the name of the control. The navigate method of the control is used to open the indicated Web page.

Perform the following steps to add the Web Browser control to the form and to make the necessary change to the Form_Load procedure.

More About

ActiveX Controls

ActiveX controls are objects with embedded code usually written in the Visual Basic or the C++ programming language. ActiveX controls can be used by many different applications in the Windows environment. The slider boxes and counters used on Web pages are other examples of ActiveX controls. ActiveX controls are similar in concept and implementation to Java applets. For more information about ActiveX controls, visit the Access 2002 More About page (scsite.com/ac2002/more.htm) and then click ActiveX Controls.

More About

The Me Keyword

The Me keyword always refers to the current object. If used within a form, Me is the simplest way to reference the form.

Steps To Add an ActiveX Control

1 Click the third tab, the one labeled Web on the tab control. Click Insert on the menu bar, and then click ActiveX Control on the Insert menu to display the Insert ActiveX Control dialog box. Select Microsoft Web Browser in the select an ActiveX control list and then click the OK button. Click the Web Browser control, if necessary, and then point to the right sizing handle.

The Microsoft Web Browser is added to the Web page on the tab control (Figure 8-119).

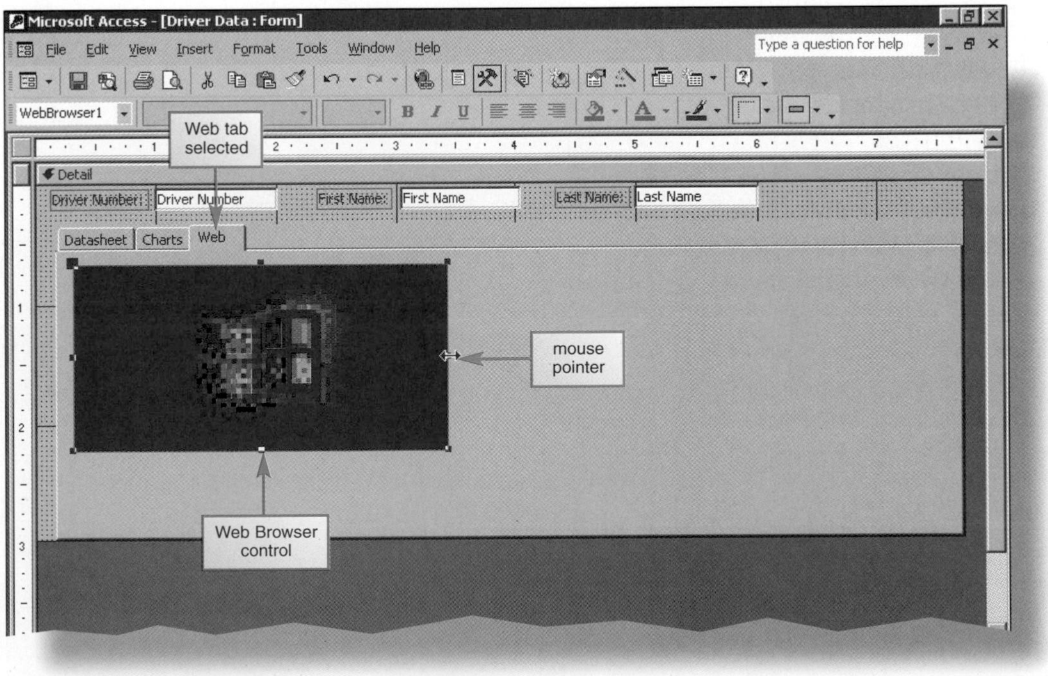

FIGURE 8-119

2 Drag the right sizing handle and then drag the lower sizing handle to change the size of the Web Browser control to the one shown in Figure 8-120. Right-click the control and then click Properties on the shortcut menu to display the property sheet. In the figure, this already has been done.

The property sheet for the Web Browser control displays. The name of the control is WebBrowser1 (yours may be different).

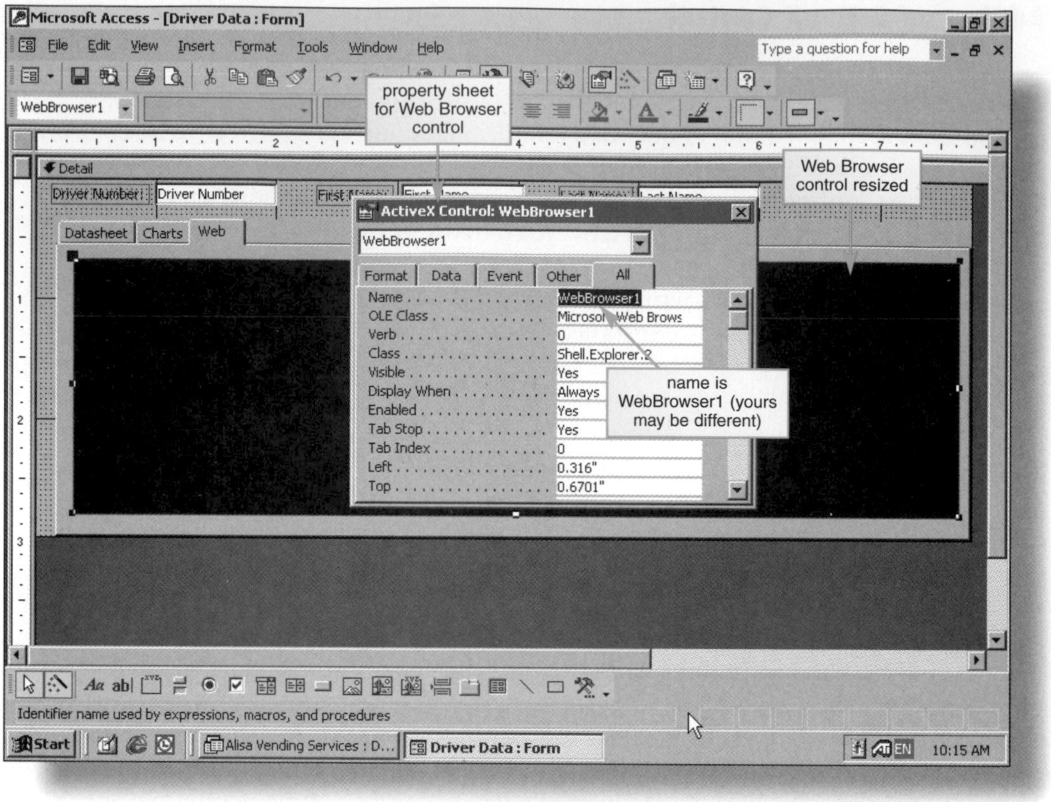

FIGURE 8-120

3 **Note the number of your Web Browser control, which may be different from the one shown in Figure 8-120. Click the Close button for the property sheet. Right-click the form selector, click Properties on the shortcut menu, scroll down so the On Load property displays, and then click the On Load property. Click the Build button, click Code Builder in the Choose Builder dialog box, and then click the OK button. Type** `me!WebBrowser1 .navigate "http:// www.scsite.com/ ac2002/alisa.htm"` **as the statement in the Form_Load procedure.**

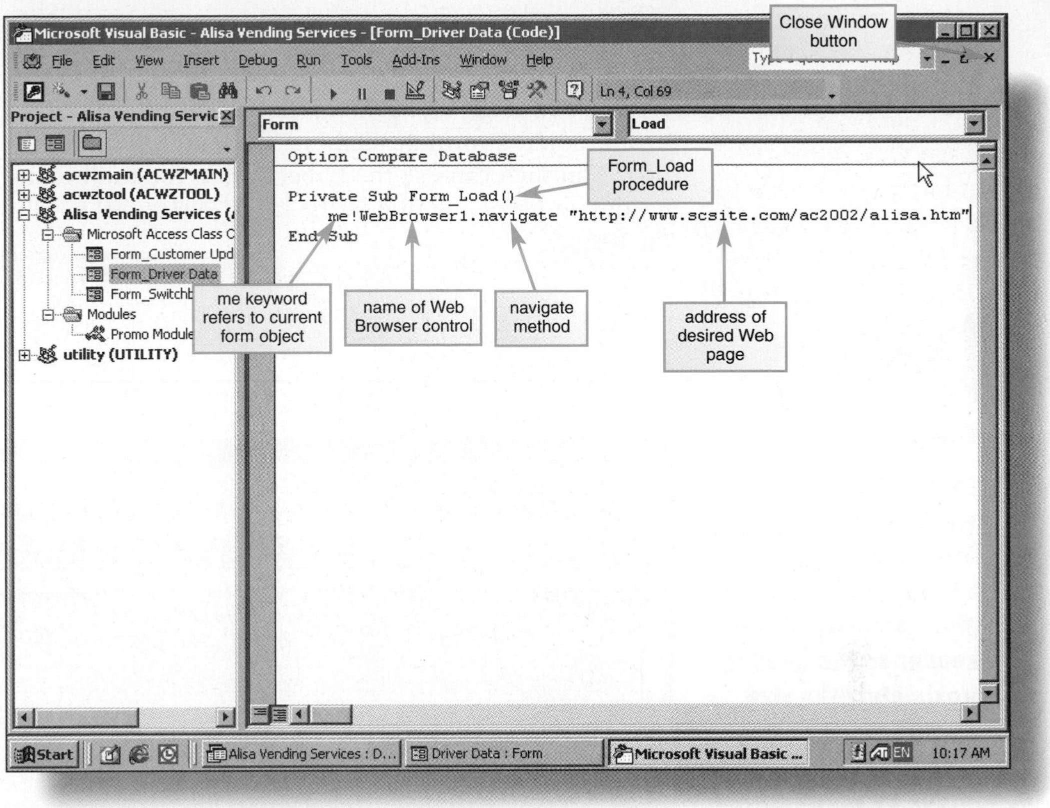

FIGURE 8-121

The Form_Load procedure is created (Figure 8-121). If the name of your Web Browser control is not WebBrowser1, substitute the name of your control for WebBrowser1 in the statement. If you do not have access to the Internet, you can replace the http address with the version furnished with your Data Disk (for example, "a:\alisa.htm").

4 **Click the Close button for the Microsoft Visual Basic – Alisa Vending Services – [Form_Driver Data (Code)] window to close the window. Click the Close button for the property sheet.**

The Visual Basic window and the property sheet are closed and the form design again displays.

Other Ways

1. In Voice Command mode, say "Insert, ActiveX Control"

Adding a Title

The form in Figure 8-2a on page A 8.06 contains a title. To add a title to a form created in Design view, first click the Form Header/Footer command on the View menu to add a form header. Next, expand the form header to allow room for the title. You then can use the Label tool in the toolbox to place the label in the form header and type the title in the label. Perform the following steps to add a title to the form.

Steps To Add a Title

1 Click the Datasheet tab, click View on the menu bar, and then click Form Header/Footer on the View menu. Drag the lower boundary of the form header so the header is approximately the size shown in Figure 8-122. Point to the Label tool in the toolbox as shown in the figure.

The form header is expanded. The subform displays in such a way that only the name displays. (Yours may display the subform design instead of a name.)

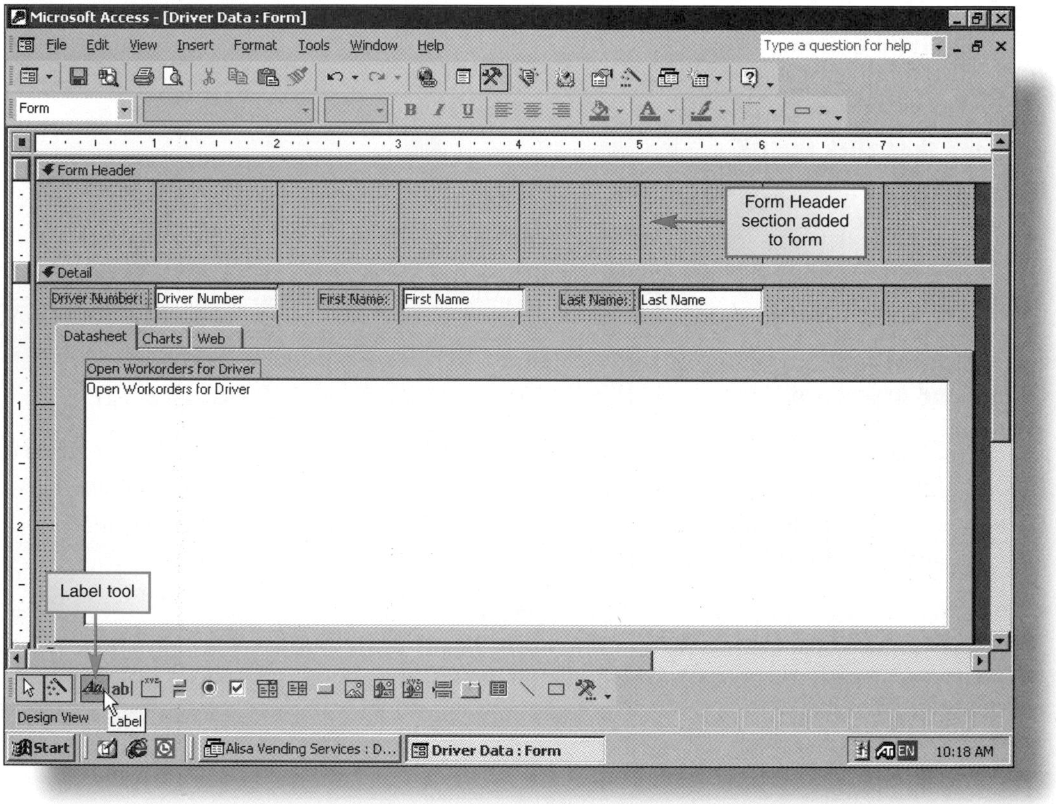

FIGURE 8-122

2 **Click the Label tool in the toolbox, click the approximate upper-left corner of the label for the title shown in Figure 8-123, drag the pointer so the label has the approximate size of the one shown in the figure, and then type** `Driver Workorder Data` **as the title.**

3 **Click outside the label to deselect it, right-click the label, and then click Properties on the shortcut menu. Change the value of the Font Size property to 14 and the value of the Text Align property to Distribute. Close the property sheet.**

The changes to the title are complete.

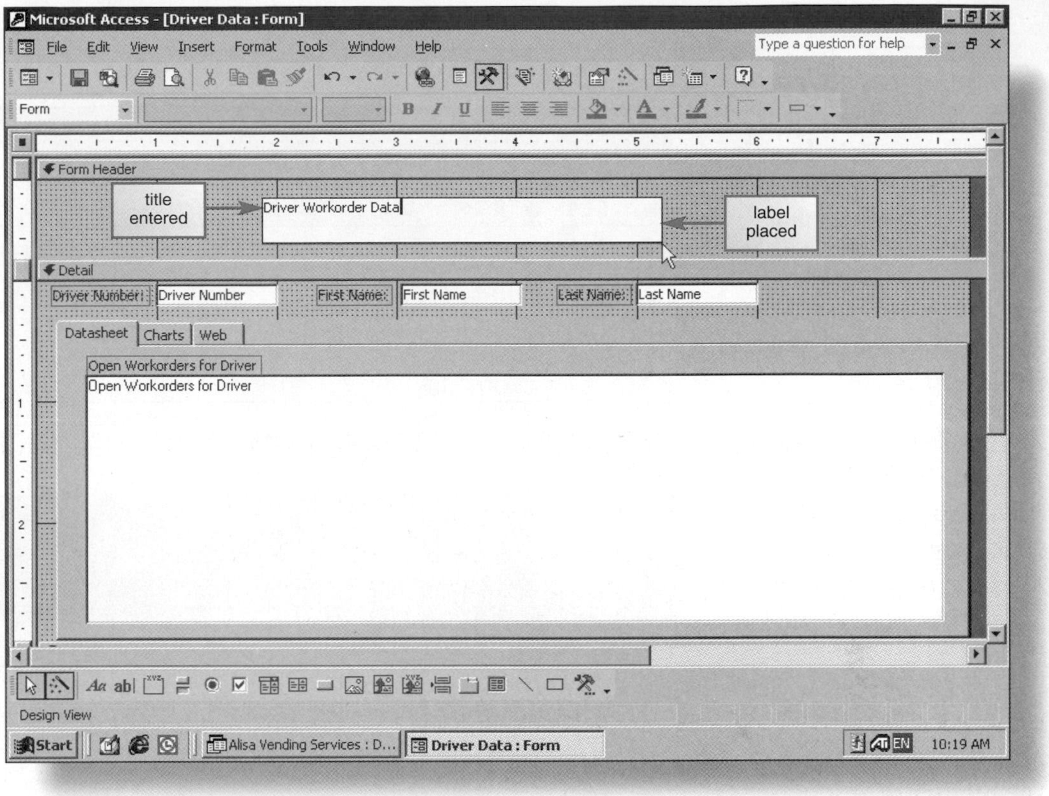

FIGURE 8-123

4 **Close the form by clicking its Close Window button. When asked if you want to save your changes, click the Yes button.**

The form is closed and the changes are saved.

Using the Form

You use this form, just like the other forms you have created and used. To move from one tabbed page to another, simply click the desired tab. The corresponding page then will display. Perform the steps on the next page to use the form.

More About

Microsoft Certification

The Microsoft User Specialist (MOUS) Certification program provides an opportunity for you to obtain a valuable industry credential —proof that you have the Access 2002 skills required by employers. For more information, see Appendix E or visit the Shelly Cashman Series MOUS Web page at scsite.com/offxp/cert.htm.

Steps To Use the Form

1 **Right-click the Driver Data form in the Database window, and then click Open on the shortcut menu. Point to the Next Record button.**

The completed form displays (Figure 8-124).

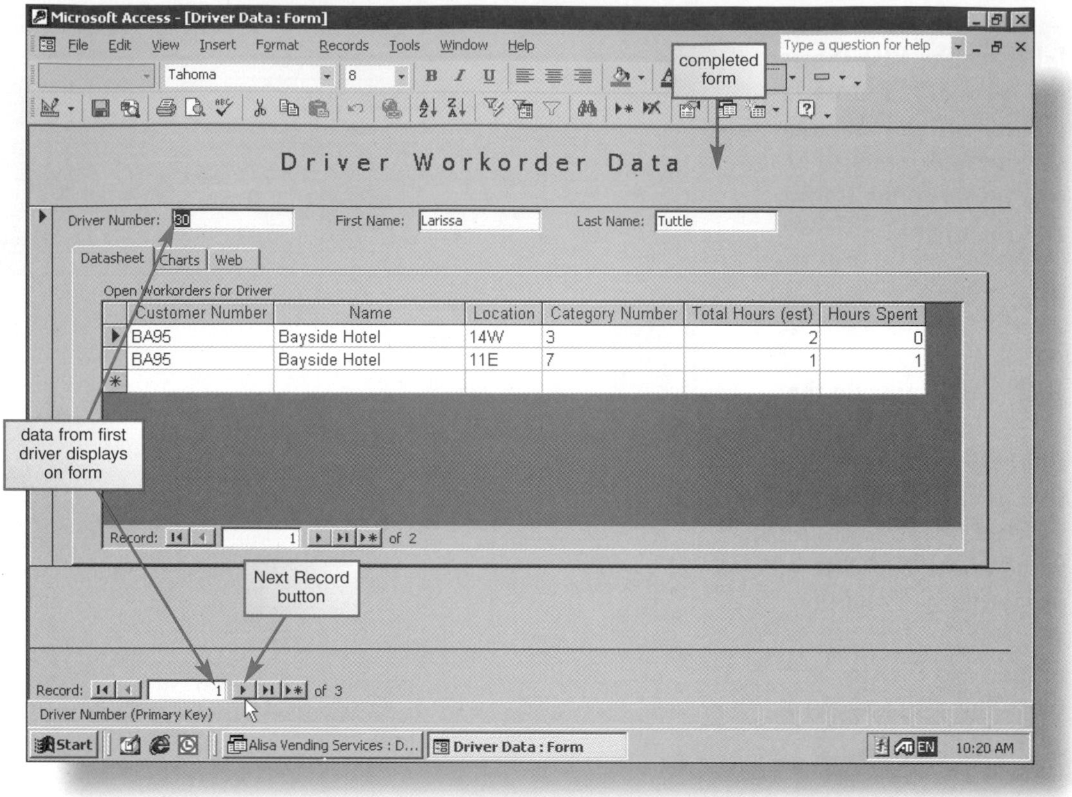

FIGURE 8-124

2 **Click the Next Record button for drivers (the one in the set of navigation buttons at the bottom of the screen) to move to the second driver. Click the Next Record button for Open Workorders (the one in the navigation buttons under the subform) three times.**

The second driver displays on the form (Figure 8-125). The fourth work order for this driver is highlighted.

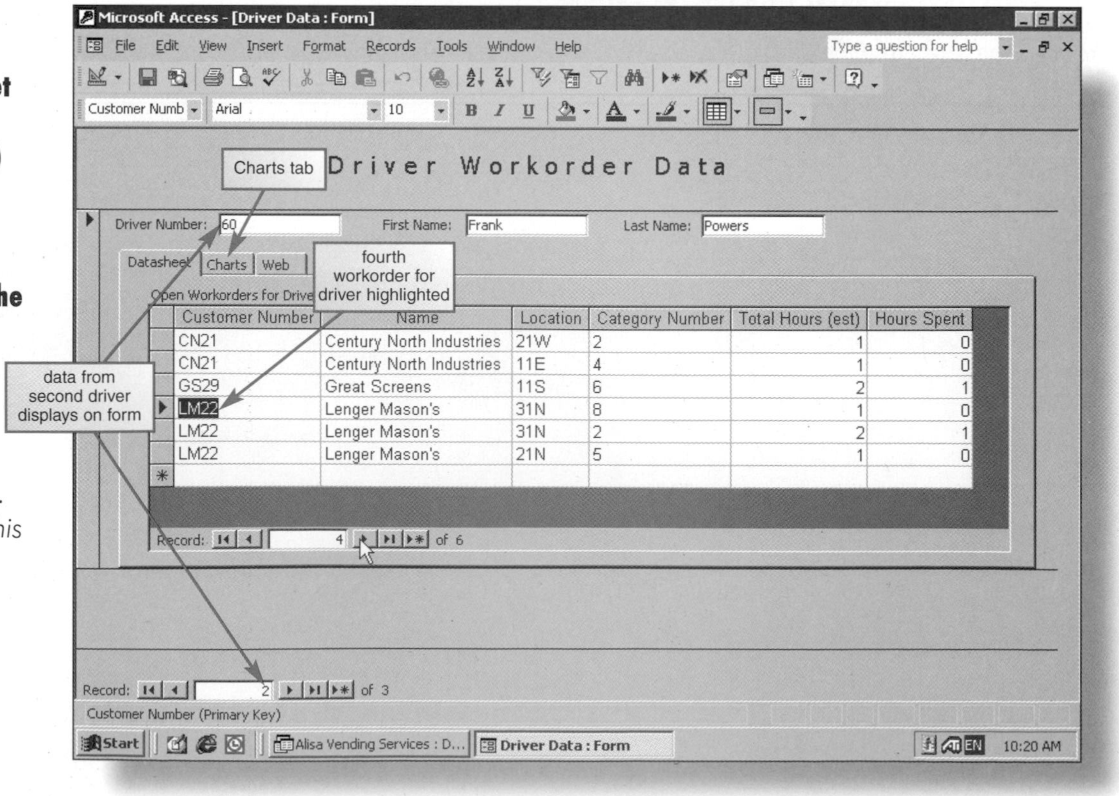

FIGURE 8-125

3 Click the Charts tab.

The charts for the second driver's work order data display (Figure 8-126). Across the bottom of the charts are the categories (2, 4, 5, 6, and 8 for this driver). The height of the bars represents the total hours. For category 2, for example, the bar has a height of 3 in the first chart, indicating the driver has a total of 3 estimated hours for services in category 2. The height of the corresponding bar in the second chart is 1, indicating that the driver already has spent 1 hour for services in this category.

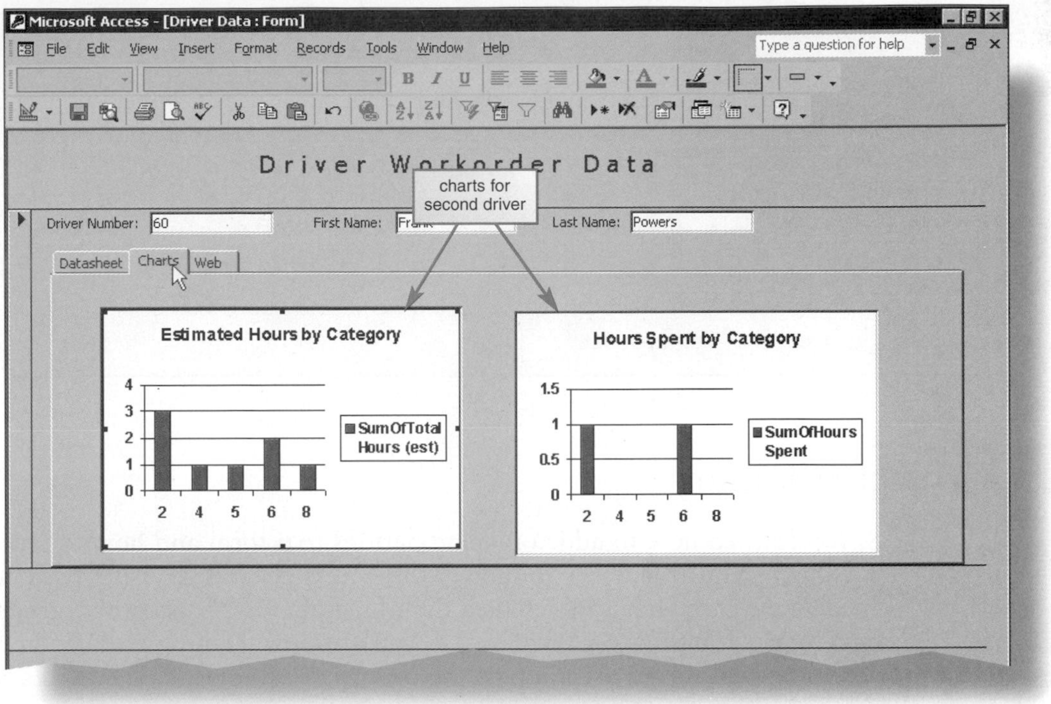

FIGURE 8-126

4 Click the Web tab.

The Web page for Alisa Vending Services displays (Figure 8-127). If you are not connected to the Internet, you may see a message indicating the Web page is unavailable.

5 Close the form by clicking its Close Window button.

The form no longer displays.

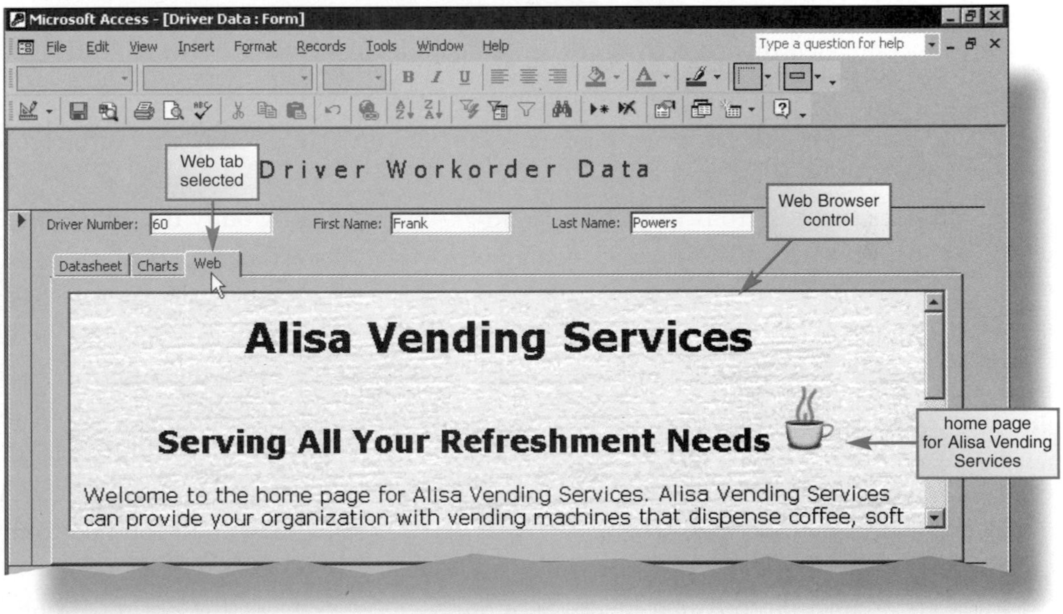

FIGURE 8-127

Closing the Database

The following step closes the database by closing its Database window.

TO CLOSE A DATABASE

1. Click the Close button for the Alisa Vending Services : Database window.

CASE PERSPECTIVE SUMMARY

In Project 8, you assisted the management of Alisa Vending Services by modifying the Customer Update Form to include special buttons as well as a combo box that can be used to search for a customer based on the customer's name. You also included controls to display data associated with a promotion that Alisa periodically runs. You provided the ability to hide this promotion data as well as to run a query from the form. You also created a form listing the number and name of drivers. The form included a tab control with three tabs. One tab displayed a subform listing details concerning open work orders for the driver. A second displayed two charts that graphically illustrate the number of hours spent by the driver in each of the service categories. The third displayed the homepage for Alisa Vending Services in a Web browser.

Project Summary

In Project 8, you learned how to add command buttons to a form and how to create a combo box that can be used for searching. You learned how to modify the Access-generated Visual Basic for Applications (VBA) code as well as to create your own code. You created both functions and procedures, grouped procedures in a module, and used these to accomplish a variety of tasks. You also learned how to create forms from scratch using Design view. You also modified a form by adding a tab control, a subform, charts, and a Web Browser control.

What You Should Know

Having completed this project, you now should be able to perform the following tasks:

- Add an ActiveX Control *(A 8.87)*
- Add Buttons to the Customer Update Form without the Control Wizards *(A 8.45)*
- Add Command Buttons to a Form *(A 8.09)*
- Add Controls to the Customer Update Form *(A 8.49)*
- Add a Title *(A 8.90)*
- Associate Code with the cmdPromo_Click Event *(A 8.55)*
- Close and Save a Form *(A 8.19, A 8.82)*
- Close a Database *(A 8.93)*
- Create a Combo Box *(A 8.14)*
- Create a Form Load Event Procedure *(A 8.64)*
- Create a Function to Run a Query *(A 8.66)*
- Create Code to Update the Controls *(A 8.60)*
- Create Functions in a Standard Module *(A 8.38)*
- Create the Form *(A 8.76)*
- Create the Query for the Subform *(A 8.75)*
- Create the ShowPromotion and HidePromotion Sub Procedures *(A 8.57)*
- Insert Charts *(A 8.83)*
- Modify the Add Record Button *(A 8.27)*
- Modify the Combo Box *(A 8.30)*
- Modify the Subform *(A 8.82)*
- Open a Database *(A 8.08)*
- Open a Form *(A 8.19)*
- Place a Rectangle *(A 8.17)*
- Place the Subform *(A 8.79)*
- Test the Functions *(A 8.41)*
- Use the Add Record Button *(A 8.20)*
- Use the Combo Box *(A 8.21)*
- Use the Modified Combo Box to Search for a Customer *(A 8.35)*
- Use the Form *(A 8.68, A 8.92)*
- Use the Functions in a Query *(A 8.43)*
- Use Tab Controls to Create a Multi-Page Form *(A 8.77)*

Learn It Online

Instructions: To complete the Learn It Online exercises, start your browser, click the Address bar, and then enter `scsite.com/offxp/exs.htm`. When the Office XP Learn It Online page displays, follow the instructions in the exercises below.

1 Project Reinforcement TF, MC, and SA

Below Access Project 8, click the Project Reinforcement link. Print the quiz by clicking Print on the File menu. Answer each question. Write your first and last name at the top of each page, and then hand in the printout to your instructor.

2 Flash Cards

Below Access Project 8, click the Flash Cards link. When Flash Cards displays, read the instructions. Type 20 (or a number specified by your instructor) in the Number of Playing Cards text box, type your name in the Name text box, and then click the Flip Card button. When the flash card displays, read the question and then click the Answer box arrow to select an answer. Flip through Flash Cards. Click Print on the File menu to print the last flash card if your score is 15 (75%) correct or greater and then hand it in to your instructor. If your score is less than 15 (75%) correct, then redo this exercise by clicking the Replay button.

3 Practice Test

Below Access Project 8, click the Practice Test link. Answer each question, enter your first and last name at the bottom of the page, and then click the Grade Test button. When the graded practice test displays on your screen, click Print on the File menu to print a hard copy. Continue to take practice tests until you score 80% or better. Hand in a printout of the final practice test to your instructor.

4 Who Wants to Be a Computer Genius?

Below Access Project 8, click the Computer Genius link. Read the instructions, enter your first and last name at the bottom of the page, and then click the Play button. Hand in your score to your instructor.

5 Wheel of Terms

Below Access Project 8, click the Wheel of Terms link. Read the instructions, and then enter your first and last name and your school name. Click the Play button. Hand in your score to your instructor.

6 Crossword Puzzle Challenge

Below Access Project 8, click the Crossword Puzzle Challenge link. Read the instructions, and then enter your first and last name. Click the Play button. Work the crossword puzzle. When you are finished, click the Submit button. When the crossword puzzle redisplays, click the Print button. Hand in the printout.

7 Tips and Tricks

Below Access Project 8, click the Tips and Tricks link. Click a topic that pertains to Project 8. Right-click the information and then click Print on the shortcut menu. Construct a brief example of what the information relates to in Access to confirm you understand how to use the tip or trick. Hand in the example and printed information.

online

8 Newsgroups

Below Access Project 8, click the Newsgroups link. Click a topic that pertains to Project 8. Print three comments. Hand in the comments to your instructor.

9 Expanding Your Horizons

Below Access Project 8, click the Articles for Microsoft Access link. Click a topic that pertains to Project 8. Print the information. Construct a brief example of what the information relates to in Access to confirm you understand the contents of the article. Hand in the example and printed information to your instructor.

10 Search Sleuth

Below Access Project 8, click the Search Sleuth link. To search for a term that pertains to this project, select a term below the Project 8 title and then use the Google search engine at google.com (or any major search engine) to display and print two Web pages that present information on the term. Hand in the printouts to your instructor.

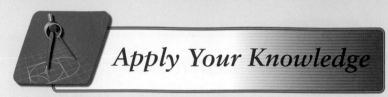

Apply Your Knowledge

1 Applying Advanced Form Techniques to the Beyond Clean Database

Instructions: Start Access. If you are using the Microsoft Access 2002 Comprehensive text, open the Beyond Clean database that you used in Project 7. Otherwise, see the inside back cover for instructions for downloading the Data Disk or see your instructor for information about accessing the files required for this book. Perform the following tasks.

1. Modify the Client Update Form to create the form shown in Figure 8-128. The form includes command buttons and a combo box to search for clients by name. Be sure to sort the names in ascending order, place a rectangle around the combo box, and update the combo box. The user should not be able to tab to the combo box. When the Add Record button is clicked, the insertion point should be in the Client Number field.

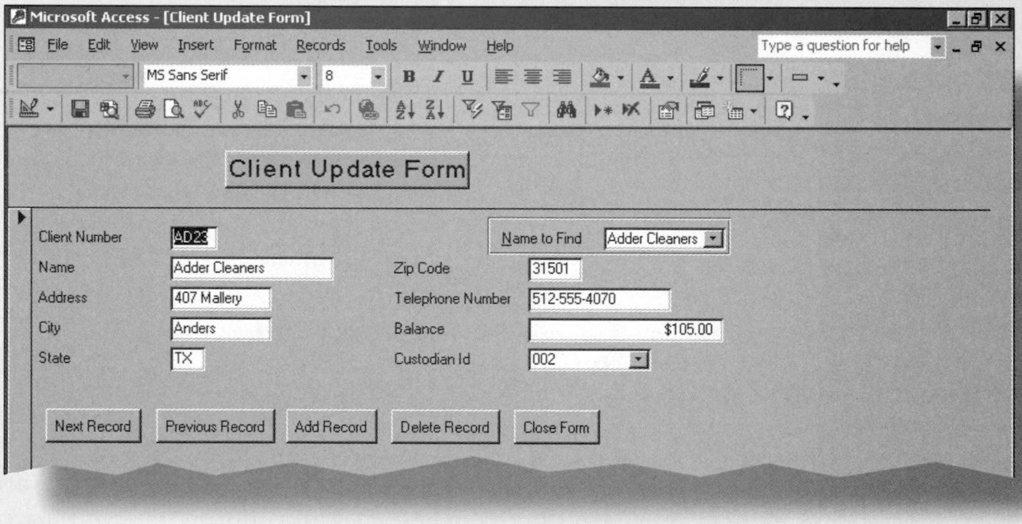

FIGURE 8-128

2. Save and print the form. To print the form, open the form, click File on the menu bar, click Print, and then click Selected Record(s) as the print range. Click the OK button.
3. Create the query shown in Figure 8-129. The query joins the Fee and Service tables. Save the query as Total Fees by Client. The caption for the column that sums the fees should be Total Fees.
4. Add a command button to the Client Update Form you modified in Step 1 that will run the Total Fees by Client query. Place the button to the right of the Name to Find combo box. The button should display Run Total Fees Query as the caption. The function that you create for the button should be part of a standard module called Total Fees Module and should include error handling. Save the changes to the form.
5. Open the form and click the Run Total Fees Query button and print the query results.
6. Create a query that joins the Client and Fee table. Include the Custodian Id, Client Number, Name, and Fee in the query results. Sort the query in ascending order by Custodian Id and Client Number. Save the query as Clients and Fees by Custodian.

Apply Your Knowledge

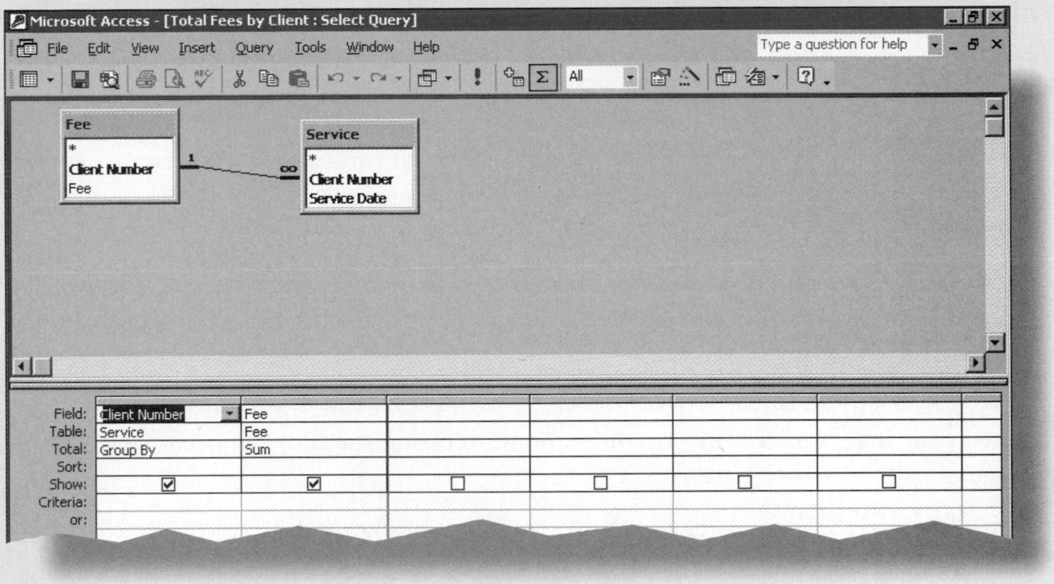

FIGURE 8-129

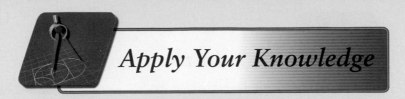

7. In Design view, create the Custodian Data form shown in Figure 8-130. The subform that displays in the Datasheet tab uses the Clients and Fees by Custodian query. Use the Alisa Vending Services home page for the Web tab.

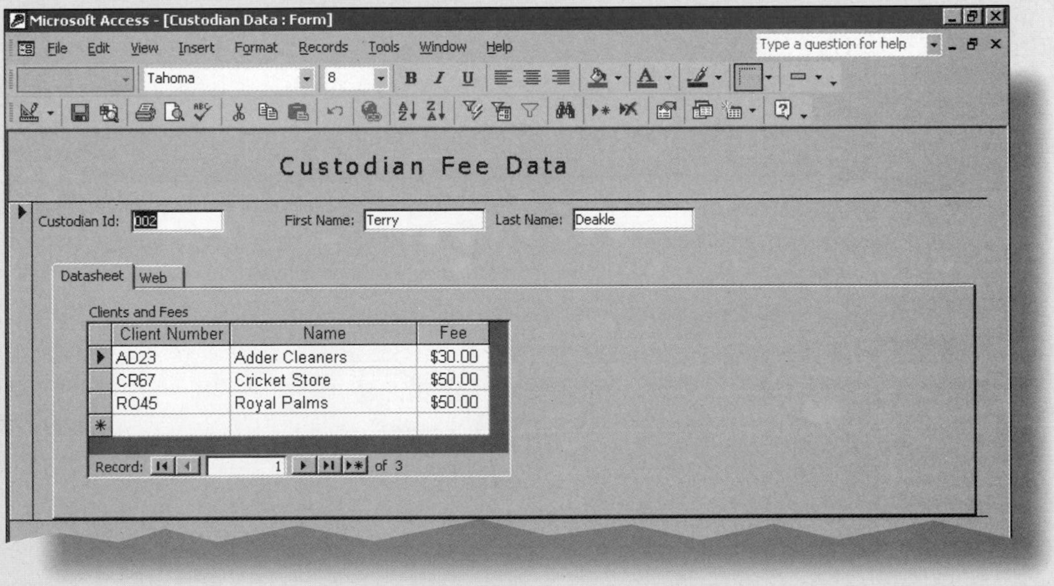

FIGURE 8-130

8. Save and print the form shown in Figure 8-130. To print the form, open the form, click File on the menu bar, click Print, and then click Selected Record(s) as the Print Range. Click the OK button.

In the Lab

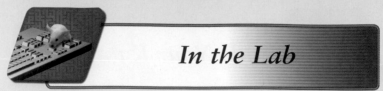

1 Applying Advanced Form Techniques to the Wooden Crafts Database

Problem: Jan Merchant has some additional requests. First, she would like some improvements to the Product Update Form. This includes placing buttons on the form to make it easier to perform tasks such as adding a record and closing the form. She also wants an easier way to search for a product given its description. Because she gives a 10 percent discount to all senior citizens, she wants a button added to the form that will display the discounted selling price. She also wants an additional form, one that lists the supplier code and name as well as any products that are on order with the supplier. The form should include a chart that graphically illustrates the total number ordered for each item.

Instructions: Start Access. If you are using the Microsoft Access 2002 Comprehensive text, open the Wooden Crafts database that you used in Project 7. Otherwise, see the inside back cover for instructions for downloading the Data Disk or see your instructor for information about accessing the files required for this book. Perform the following tasks.

1. Modify the Product Update Form to create the form shown in Figure 8-131. To create this form, you will need to do the following:
   a. Add command buttons to move to the next record, to move to the previous record, to add a new record, to delete a record, and to close the form. When the Add Record button is clicked, the insertion point should be in the Product Id field.
   b. Add a combo box to search for products by description. Be sure to sort the product description in ascending order and update the combo box. The user should not be able to tab to the combo box.
   c. Create a function in a standard module to calculate the discounted amount.
   d. Create a control to display the discounted amount and create the code necessary to update the control. The data will be updated whenever the user moves to a different product on the form or the user updates the selling price.

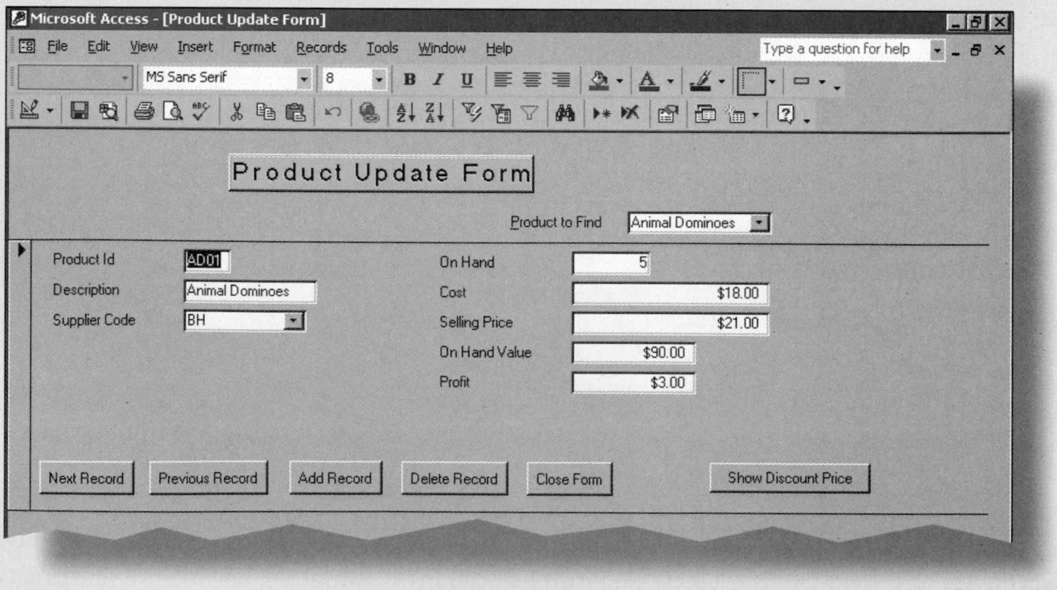

FIGURE 8-131

In the Lab

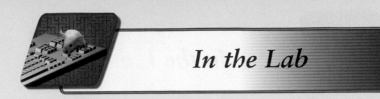

e. Add a button to show the discount price. If the button currently reads Show Discount Price, the discount amount does not display and clicking the button will cause the discount amount to display and the caption for the button to change to Hide Discount Price. Clicking the button a second time will hide the discount amount and also change the caption back to Show Discount Price.

f. Create code that will be executed when the form first is loaded to hide the discount amount.

2. Save and print the form shown in Figure 8-131. To print the form, open the form, click File on the menu bar, click Print and then click Selected Record(s) as the print range. Click the OK button.
3. Use the Next Record button to move to the record for product id, CC14. Click the Show Discount Price button and print the form.
4. Change the selling price for the record to $20.00 and print the form again.
5. Create a query that joins the Product, Reorder, and Supplier tables. Display the Supplier Code, First Name, Last Name, Product Id, Description, Date Ordered, and Number Ordered fields. Save the query as Reorder Items by Supplier.
6. In Design view, create the Open Reorders by Supplier form shown in Figure 8-132. The subform uses the Reorder Items by Supplier query. The Product Id, Description, Date Ordered, and Number Ordered fields display in Datasheet view when the Datasheet tab is pressed. The chart uses the Reorder Items by Supplier query and displays the product id on the x-axis and the sum of the number ordered on the y-axis. Save the form.

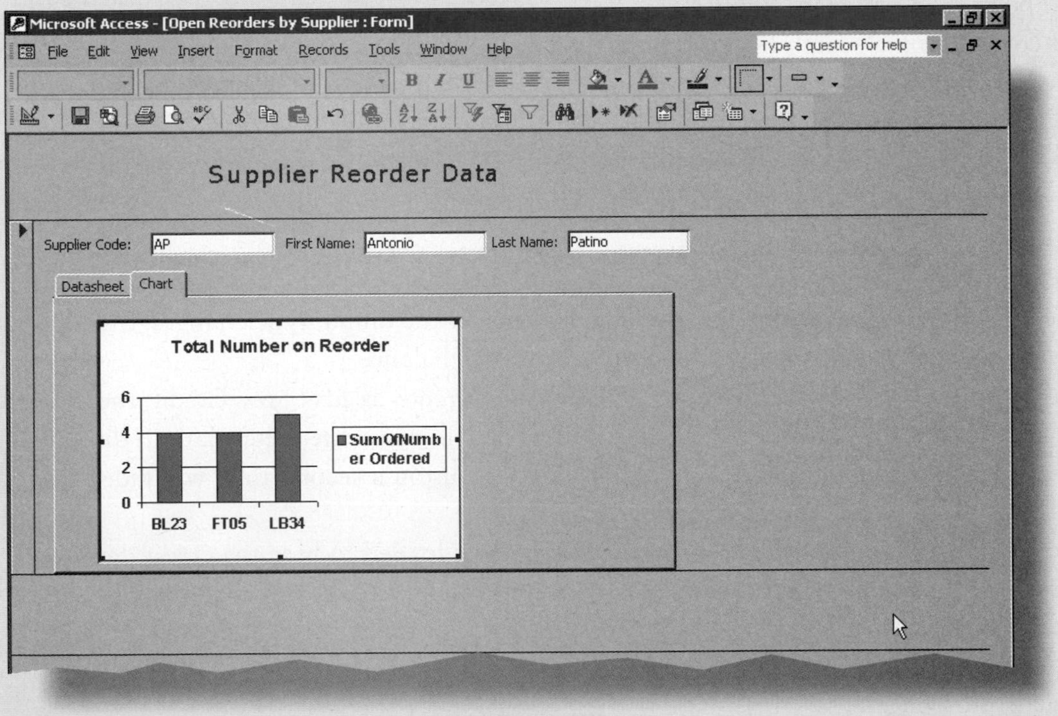

FIGURE 8-132

7. Open the Open Reorders by Supplier form and move to the record for Bert Huntington. Click the Datasheet tab and print the form.
8. Click the Chart tab and print the form.

In the Lab

2 Applying Advanced Form Techniques to the Restaurant Supply Database

Problem: The restaurant supply company has some additional requests. First, they would like some improvements to the Customer Update Form. This includes placing buttons on the form to make it easier to perform tasks such as adding a record or closing the form. They also want a simple way of searching for a customer given its name. Occasionally, the company offers incentives to it customers by discounting prices or by applying a credit to customer balances. The company wants to be able to display the credit amount on the form. The credit factor is determined by the restaurant type. Finally, the company would like a form that lists the sales rep number and name as well as any open work orders for the sales rep. The user should be able to access the company's Web page from the form.

Instructions: If you are using the Microsoft Access 2002 Comprehensive text, open the Restaurant Supply database that you used in Project 7. Otherwise, see the inside back cover for instructions for downloading the Data Disk or see your instructor for information about accessing the files required for this book. Perform the following tasks.

1. Modify the Customer Update Form to create the form shown in Figure 8-133. To create this form, you will need to do the following:
   a. Add command buttons to move to the next record, to move to the previous record, to add a new record, to delete a record, and to close the form. When the Add Record button is clicked, the insertion point should be in the Customer Number field.
   b. Add a combo box to search for customers by name. Be sure to sort the name in ascending order and update the combo box. The user should not be able to tab to the combo box.
   c. Create two functions in a standard module to calculate the credit factor and the amount to credit to the customer's balance. Customers with a dining type of FFT receive 1 percent credit; customers with a dining type of FAM receive a 2 percent credit; and customers with a dining type of FIN receive a 3 percent credit.
   d. Create controls to display the credit factor and the credit amount and then create the code necessary to update the controls. The data will be updated whenever the dining type changes, the user moves to a different customer on the form, or the user updates the balance.
   e. Add a button to show the credit data. If the button currently reads Show Credit, the credit factor and credit amount do not display and clicking the button will cause the credit data to display and the caption for the button to change to Hide Credit. Clicking the button a second time will hide the credit data and also change the caption back to Show Credit.
   f. Create code that will be executed when the form first is loaded to hide the credit data.
2. Save and print the form shown in Figure 8-133. To print the form, open the form, click File on the menu bar, click Print, and then click Selected Record(s) as the print range. Click the OK button.
3. Use the Next Record button to move to the record for customer number CM09. Click the Show Credit button and print the form.
4. Change the dining type for customer CM09 to FIN and print the form again.

In the Lab

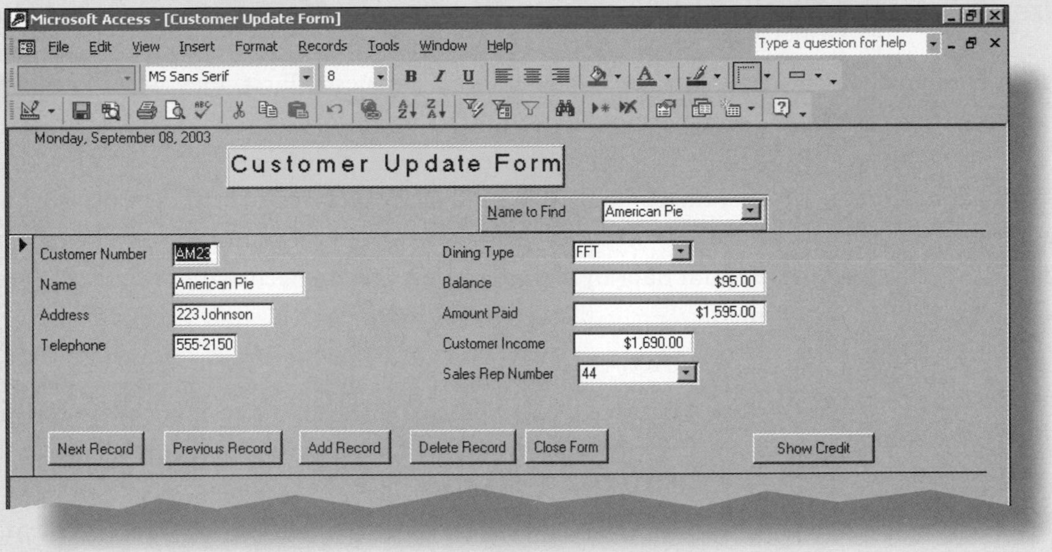

FIGURE 8-133

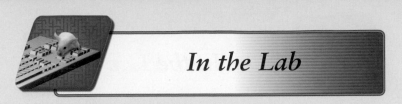

5. Create a query that joins the Customer, Workorders, and Category tables. Include the Sales Rep Number, Customer Number, Name, Location, and Category Description in the results. Sort the query in ascending order by sales rep number and customer number. Save the query as Customers and Workorders by Sales Rep.
6. In Design view, create the form shown in Figure 8-134. The subform uses the Customers and Workorders by Sales Rep query. Use the Alisa Vending Services Web page for the Web Browser control.

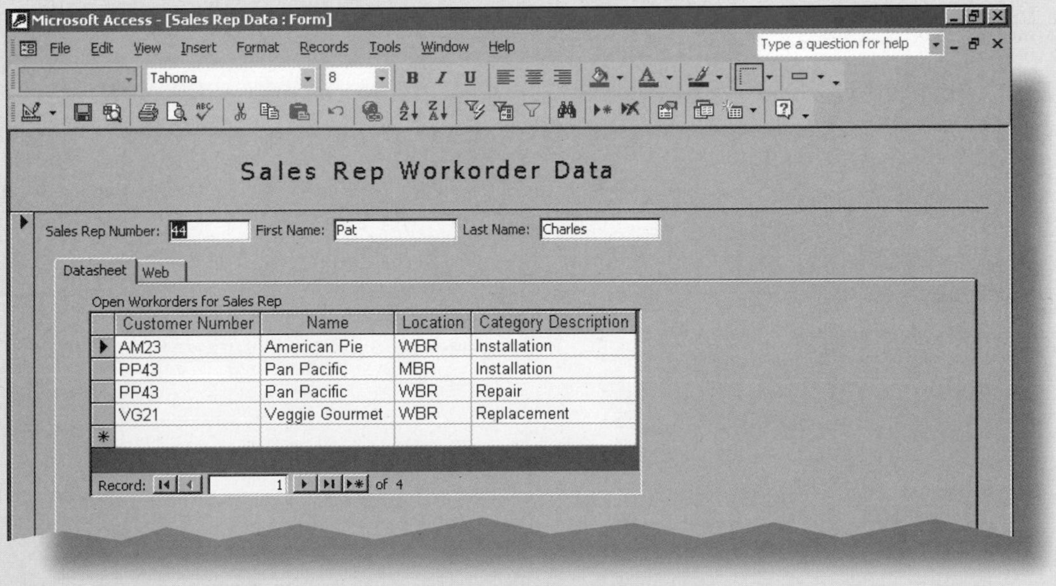

FIGURE 8-134

7. Save and print the form shown in Figure 8-134. To print the form, open the form, click File on the menu bar, click Print, and then click Selected Record(s) as the Print Range. Click the OK button.

In the Lab

3 Applying Advanced Form Techniques to the Condo Management Database

Problem: The condo management company has some additional requests. First, they want some improvements made to the Condo Update Form. This includes placing buttons on the form to make it easier to perform tasks such as adding a record, printing a record, and closing the form. They also want a simple way to search for a unit. Because most units are not for sale, the company would like to hide this data and display it only as necessary. When the for sale data does display, they want to be able to open the Owner Master Form. Finally, the company needs a form that will show rental data by owner and display a chart that graphically illustrates the total number of weeks each unit is rented.

Instructions: If you are using the Microsoft Access 2002 Comprehensive text, open the Condo Management database that you used in Project 7. Otherwise, see the inside back cover for instructions for downloading the Data Disk or see your instructor for information about accessing the files required for this book. Perform the following tasks.

1. Modify the Condo Update Form to create the form shown in Figure 8-135. To create this form, you will need to do the following:
   a. Add command buttons to move to the next record, to move to the previous record, to add a new record, to delete a record, and to close the form. When the Add Record button is clicked, the insertion point should be in the Unit Number field.
   b. Add a combo box to search for condo units. The user should not be able to tab to the combo box.
   c. Move the For Sale and Sales Price controls to the position shown in Figure 8-135.
   d. Create a command button that when clicked, will open the Owner Master Form. Use a VBA function that includes an error routine to open the form. (*Hint*: See Table 8-16 on page A 8.65 for the method to open a form.)

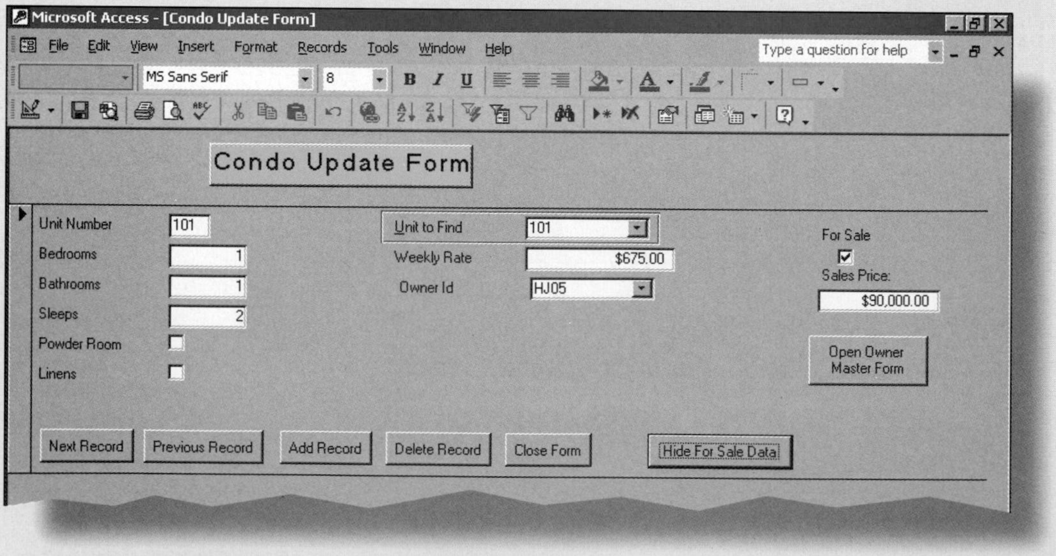

FIGURE 8-135

In the Lab

e. Add a button to show the for sale data. If the button currently reads Show For Sale Data, the For Sale control and the Sales Price control do not display and clicking the button will cause the for sale data to display and the caption for the button to change to Hide For Sale Data. Clicking the button a second time will hide the for sale data and also change the caption back to Show For Sale Data.

f. Create code that will be executed when the form first is loaded to hide the for sale data.

2. Save the form and then open the form.
3. Click the Show For Sale Data button and print the form. To print the form, open the form, click File on the menu bar, click Print and then click Selected Record(s) as the print range. Click the OK button.
4. Click the Open Owner Master Form button and print the form.
5. Close the Owner Master Form and then click the Hide For Sale Data button and print the form again.
6. Create a query that joins the Current Rentals, Owner, Condo, and Renter tables. Include the Owner Id, Unit Number, Start Date, Length, and First Name and Last Name of the renter in the results. Sort the query in ascending order by unit number within owner id. Save the query as Active Rentals by Owner.
7. In Design view, create the form shown in Figure 8-136. The subform uses the Active Rentals by Owner query. The chart should display the unit number on the x-axis and total number of weeks rented on the y-axis. Save the form as Owner Rental Data.
8. Open the form and then click the Next Record button to display owner BR18. Click the Datasheet tab and print the form. To print the form, open the form, click File on the menu bar, click Print, and then click Selected Record(s) as the Print Range. Click the OK button.
9. Click the Charts tab and print the form again.

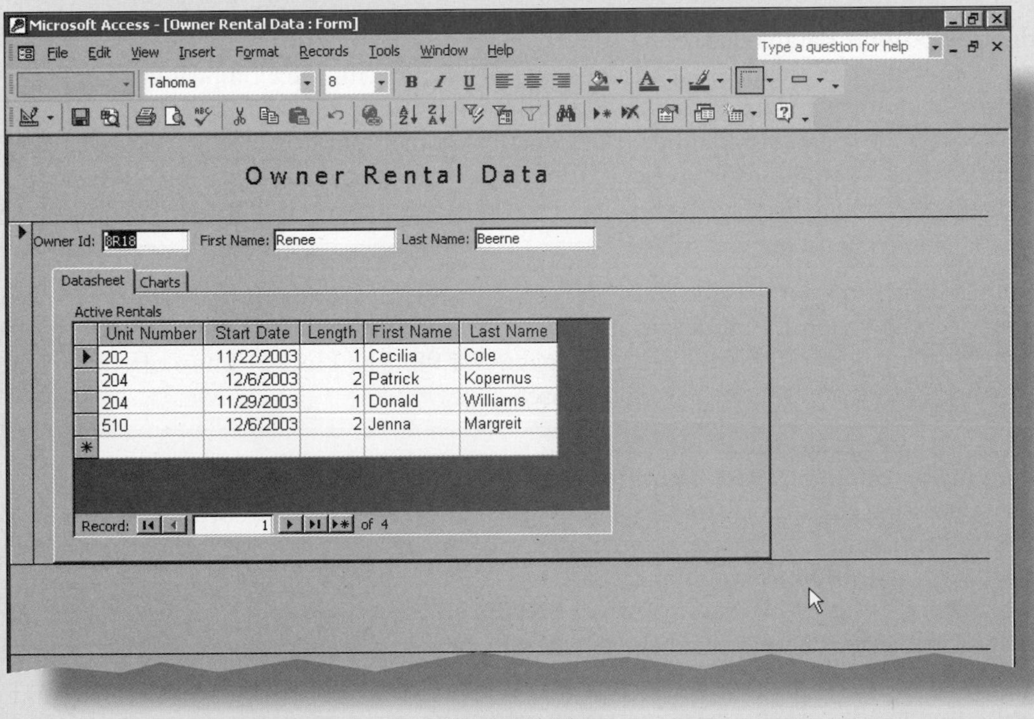

FIGURE 8-136

Cases and Places

The difficulty of these case studies varies:
◗ are the least difficult; ◗◗ are more difficult; and ◗◗◗ are the most difficult.

1 ◗ Use the CompuWhiz database used in Project 7 for this assignment or see your instructor for information about accessing the files required for this book. Modify the Client Update Form to create a form similar to that shown in Figure 8-133 on page A 8.101. To create this form, you will need to do the following:

a. Add command buttons to move to the next record, to move to the previous record, to add a new record, to delete a record, and to close the form.
b. Add a combo box to search for clients by name.
c. Create two functions in a standard module to calculate the credit factor and the amount to credit to the client's balance. Clients with a client type of DIN receive 2 percent credit; clients with a client type of SER or RET receive a 3 percent credit; and clients with a client type of MFG receive a 4 percent credit.
d. Create controls to display the credit factor and the credit amount and then create the code necessary to update the controls. The data will be updated whenever the client type changes, the user moves to a different client on the form, or the user updates the balance.
e. Add a button to show the credit data. If the button currently reads Show Credit, the credit factor and credit amount do not display and clicking the button will cause the credit data to display and the caption for the button to change to Hide Credit. Clicking the button a second time will hide the credit data and also change the caption back to Show Credit.
f. Create code that will be executed when the form first is loaded to hide the credit data.

2 ◗ Use the CompuWhiz database used in Project 7 for this assignment or see your instructor for information about accessing the files required for this book. Create a form for the CompuWhiz database that is similar to the Driver Data form created in Project 8 and shown in Figures 8-2a, 8-2b, and 8-2c on pages A 8.06 and A 8.07. The subform should be based on a query that joins the Client and Open Workorders tables and the datasheet should display Client Number, Name, Category, Total Hours (est), and Hours Spent. Use the Alisa Vending Services Web page for the Web tab or select your own Web page reference.

3 ◗◗ Use the Hockey Shop database used in Project 7 for this assignment or see your instructor for information about accessing the files required for this book. Modify the Item Update Form to create a form that is similar to that shown in Figure 8-131 on page A 8.98. The Hockey Shop offers a 15 percent discount to youth groups that make team purchases.

4 ◗◗ Use the Hockey Shop database used in Project 7 for this assignment or see your instructor for information about accessing the files required for this book. Create an Open Reorders by Vendor form that is similar in format to Figure 8-132 on page A 8.99. Add a picture to the form header. To add a picture to a form, use the Image tool in the toolbox. You can use the clip art that is included with Microsoft Office, download free clip art from the Web, or create your own picture in Microsoft Paint.

5 ◗◗◗ Add two buttons to the form that you created in Cases and Places 4. One button should close the form and the other button should print the Vendor/Items report.

Microsoft Access 2002

PROJECT

9

Administering a Database System

You will have mastered the material in this project when you can:

OBJECTIVES

- Convert a database to an earlier version of Access
- Use the Table Analyzer, Performance Analyzer, and Documenter
- Use an input mask
- Specify referential integrity options
- Set startup options
- Set and remove passwords
- Encrypt a database
- Use replication
- Create PivotTables and PivotCharts
- Create and run SQL queries
- Split a Database
- Create an MDE File
- Specify user-level security

Incentive Program

Interactive Workout Puts Fitness Goals Within Reach

Great job! You are working at 80 percent of your target. Try adding five pounds for the next two reps.

Imagine getting these messages from a piece of equipment at your local health club. That just might happen if your fitness center has FitLinxx installed on its machines.

The FitLinxx Interactive Fitness Network acts like a personal trainer. It monitors your workouts with a Personal Digital Assistant-sized personal computer

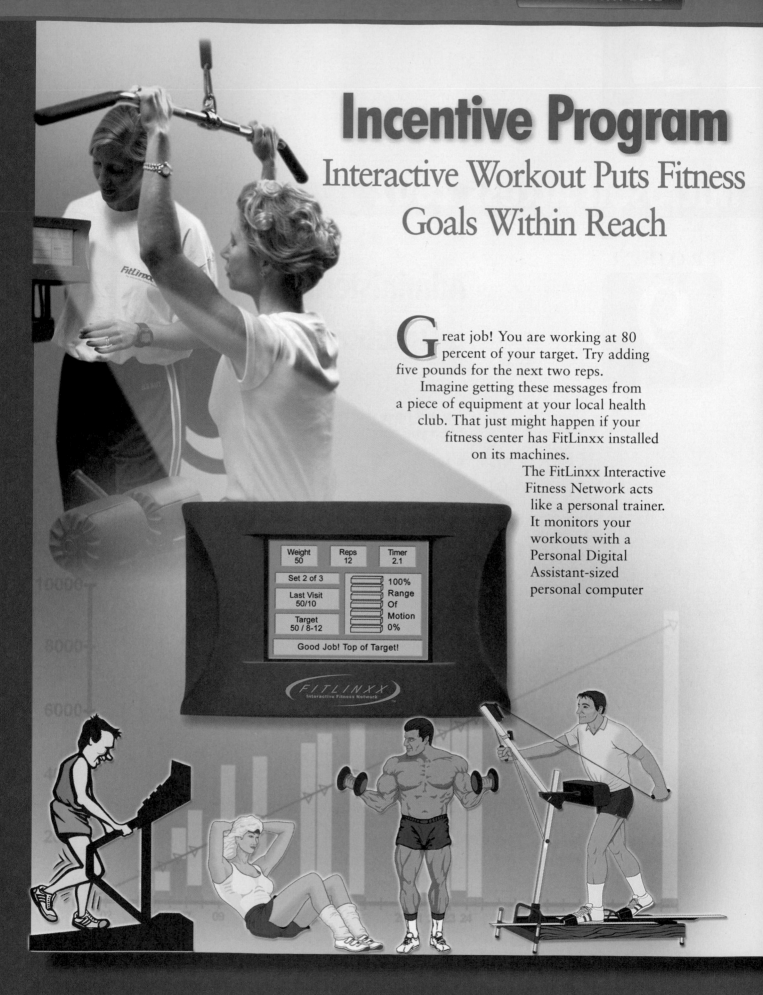

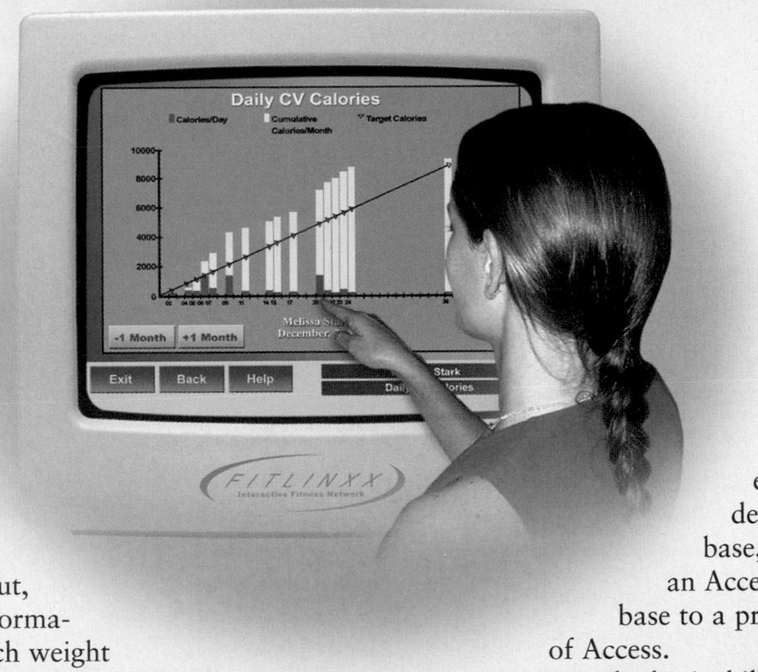

and an optical sensor system attached to each piece of weight training and cardio equipment. As you work out, the system detects information such as how much weight you are lifting, your range of motion, distance traveled, calories burned, your heart rate, and other data on a form that resembles the forms you have created in projects in this book.

At the end of your workout, the FitLinxx network sends the data to a Microsoft Access or Microsoft SQL Server database. This database is connected to a touch-screen kiosk, so you can log in and obtain reports and graphs of your progress.

Fitness trainers traditionally use pencils and clipboards to track their clients' improvement; with FitLinxx they can log into their own computers, view a record of every workout, track trends, and create an individual's specific exercise plan. The system even tells the trainers which members have not been coming to the fitness center, and the trainers can send motivating e-mail messages to those people.

These fitness trainers perform activities related to the administration of the FitLinxx database. They help create database passwords, optimize database performance, and use add-in tools to help fitness center members optimize their exercise sessions. You will perform similar database administration actions in this project. You will replicate databases, use indexes and data type formats, set startup options, encrypt and decrypt a database, and convert an Access 2002 database to a previous version of Access.

FitLinxx is the brainchild of Keith Camhi and Andy Greenberg, who were friends at Cornell University and MIT where they studied physics, computer science, electrical engineering, and business. Camhi had joined a health club in 1991, and within six months was losing interest and thinking of quitting. He realized the value of exercise and wanted to continue the workouts, so he thought about why he was having the problem. He and Greenberg figured that software might help with the motivation factor.

They worked on a prototype system in Camhi's mother's basement beginning in 1993. A year later, they introduced a beta system in the New York Knicks basketball team's training center and a community center in Stamford, Connecticut, where FitLinxx is headquartered. Since then, they have installed their systems in more than 400 health clubs, YMCAs, wellness centers, and hospitals.

FitLinxx helps make your workouts more effective and efficient by guiding you through your own personalized exercise routine, tracking your performance, and motivating you to ensure continued success. With the help of this database workout partner, your fitness goals are well within reach.

Microsoft Access 2002

Administering a Database System

PROJECT 9

CASE PERSPECTIVE

The management of Alisa Vending Services is so pleased with your work that they have decided to put you in charge of database system administration and have asked you to determine precisely what this would entail. You found many activities that the individual in charge of administering the database must perform. These include analyzing tables for possible duplication, analyzing performance to see where improvements could be made, and producing complete system documentation. The administrator should specify necessary integrity constraints to make sure the data is valid. Security is another issue. The administrator should consider the use of both passwords and encryption to protect the database from unauthorized use. Alisa wants more users to have remote access to the database, so administration would include the creation of replicas. They also want to analyze data using PivotTables and PivotCharts. You also learned how important the language called SQL has become in a database environment and determined that the administrator should be familiar with the language and its use. Alisa also wants you to investigate other ways of protecting their data.

Introduction

Administering a database system encompasses a variety of activities (Figure 9-1). It can include conversion of a database to an earlier version. It usually includes such activities as analyzing tables for potential problems, analyzing performance to see if changes are warranted to make the system perform more efficiently, and documenting the various objects in the database. It also includes integrity issues, that is, taking steps to ensure that the data in the database is valid. These steps can include the creation of custom input masks and also the specification of referential integrity options. Securing the database through the use of passwords and encryption also is part of the administration of a database system as is the setting of startup options. Supporting remote users through replication (making copies of the database for remote use) also falls in the category of administering a database as does assisting users in analyzing data through the creation of PivotTables and PivotCharts.

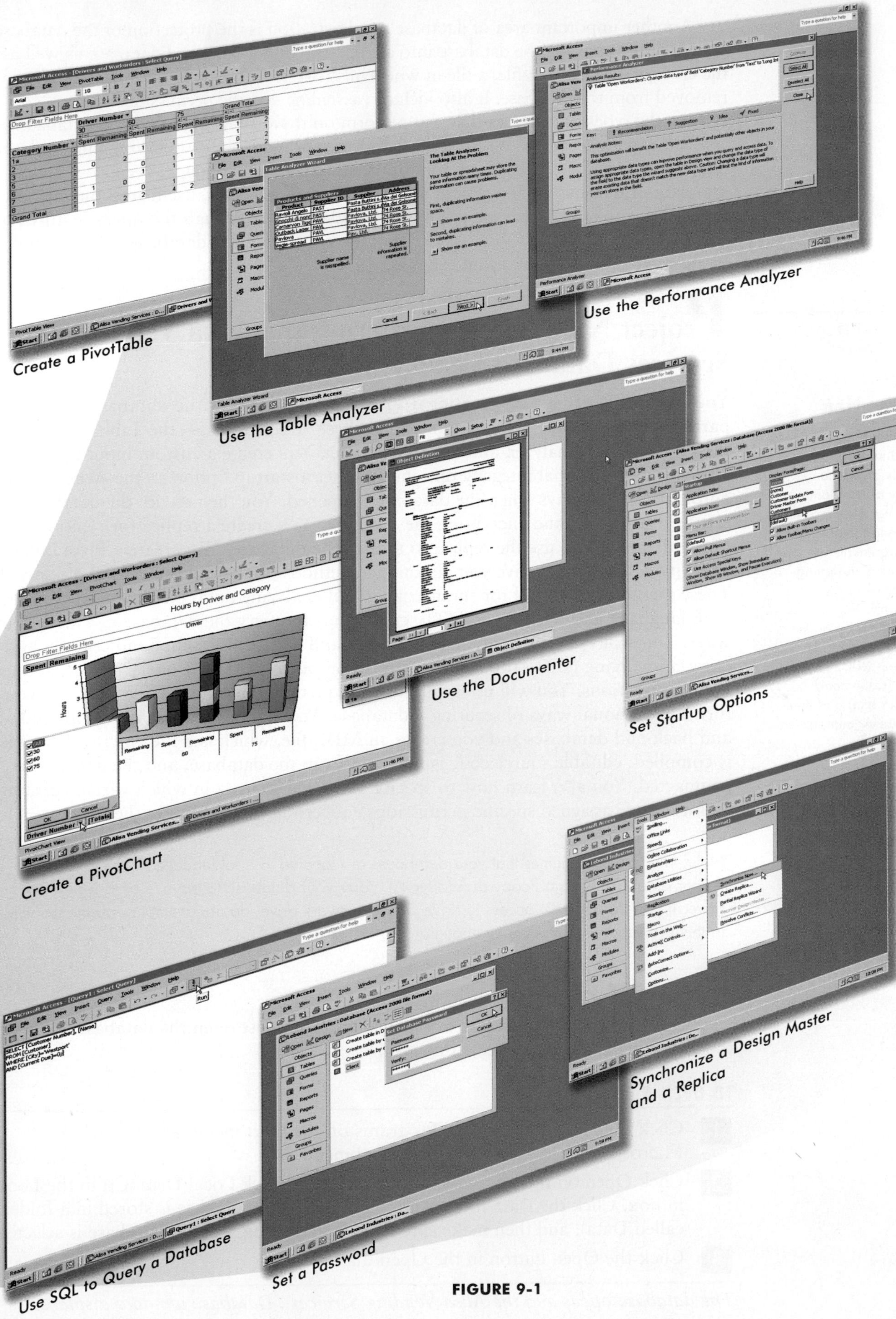
Create a PivotTable
Use the Table Analyzer
Use the Performance Analyzer
Use the Documenter
Set Startup Options
Create a PivotChart
Synchronize a Design Master
and a Replica
Use SQL to Query a Database
Set a Password

FIGURE 9-1

Another important area of database administration is the protection of the database. This includes splitting the database into a front-end and a back-end database as well as the creation of an MDE file, a file in which all VBA source code is compiled and then removed from the database. It also includes assigning specific permissions to users concerning the types of activities they can perform on the various objects in the database.

The language called SQL is a very important language for querying and updating databases. It is the closest thing to a universal database language, because the vast majority of database management systems, including Access, use it in some fashion. Although many users will query and update databases through the query features of Access instead of SQL, those in charge of administering the database system should be familiar with this important language.

Project Nine — Administering the Alisa Vending Services Database System

You begin this project by creating an Access 97 version of the database for a particular user who needs it. You next use three Access tools — the Table Analyzer, the Performance Analyzer, and the Documenter. You create a custom input mask and also specify referential integrity options. You set a startup option so the switchboard automatically displays when the database is opened. You then secure the database by setting a password and encrypting the database. You create a replica for remote users of the database and use the replica to update the database. You create a PivotTable and PivotChart, which give you alternative methods of viewing the data in a query. These methods are useful for summarizing and analyzing data. Next, you turn to the SQL language and write several SQL commands to query the database in a variety of ways. You will use criteria involving number and text fields, compound criteria, and criteria involving NOT. You also will use a computed field, sort query results, and use built-in functions. You will use grouping in a query and also join tables. Finally, you turn to additional ways of securing a database. You split a database into front-end and back-end databases and you create an MDE file, which is a file where VBA code is compiled, editable source code is removed from the database, and the database is compacted. You also learn how to specify user-level security in which various groups and users are assigned specific permissions concerning the objects in the database.

More About

Database Administration

Database administration (DBA) is the individual or group of individuals given the responsibility of maintaining and controlling a company's database management system (DBMS) environment. The DBA function includes designing and implementing databases as well as controlling access. For more information on the responsibilities of the DBA, visit the Access 2002 More About page (scsite.com/ac2002/more.htm) and then click Database Administration.

Note: This project assumes that your databases are located in a folder called Data on drive C. If your database is on a floppy disk (drive A), copy your database to drive C or to a network drive. If you do not have access to drive C or a network drive, do not attempt to do the activities in this project. You will not have enough room on your disk.

Opening the Database

Before completing the tasks in this project, you must open the database. Perform the following steps to complete this task.

TO OPEN A DATABASE

1. Click the Start button, click Programs on the Start menu, and then click Microsoft Access on the Programs submenu.
2. Click Open on the Database toolbar, and then click Local Disk (C:) in the Look in box. Click the Data folder (assuming that your database is stored in a folder called Data), and then make sure the Alisa Vending Services database is selected.
3. Click the Open button in the Open dialog box.

The database opens and the Alisa Vending Services : Database window displays.

Using Microsoft Access Tools

Microsoft Access has a variety of tools that are useful in administering databases. These include tools to convert a database to an earlier version of Access, to analyze table structures, to analyze performance, and to create detailed documentation.

More About

The Access Help System

Need help? It is no further than the Ask a Question box in the upper-right corner of the window. Click the box that contains the text, Type a question for help (Figure 9-2), type `help`, and then press the ENTER key. Access will respond with a list of items you can click to learn about obtaining help on any Access-related topic. To find out what is new in Access 2002, type `what's new in Access` in the Ask a Question box.

Converting a Database to an Earlier Version

If you have stored your database in the default Access 2000 format, any user of Access 2000 can access the database. Occasionally, you might encounter someone who needs to use your database, but who uses Access 97. Such a user cannot access the data directly. You need to convert the database to the earlier version in order for the user to access it. Once you have done so, the user can use the converted version. To convert the database, use the Convert Database command as in the following steps.

Steps To Convert a Database to an Earlier Version

1. **Click Tools on the menu bar, click Database Utilities on the Tools menu, click Convert Database on the Database Utilities submenu, and then point to To Access 97 File Format (Figure 9-2).**

2. **Click To Access 97 File Format. Type** `Alisa Vending Services 97` **as the name of the file and then click the Save button in the Convert Database Into dialog box. If a warning message displays, click the OK button.**

The Access 97 version of the database is created and available for use.

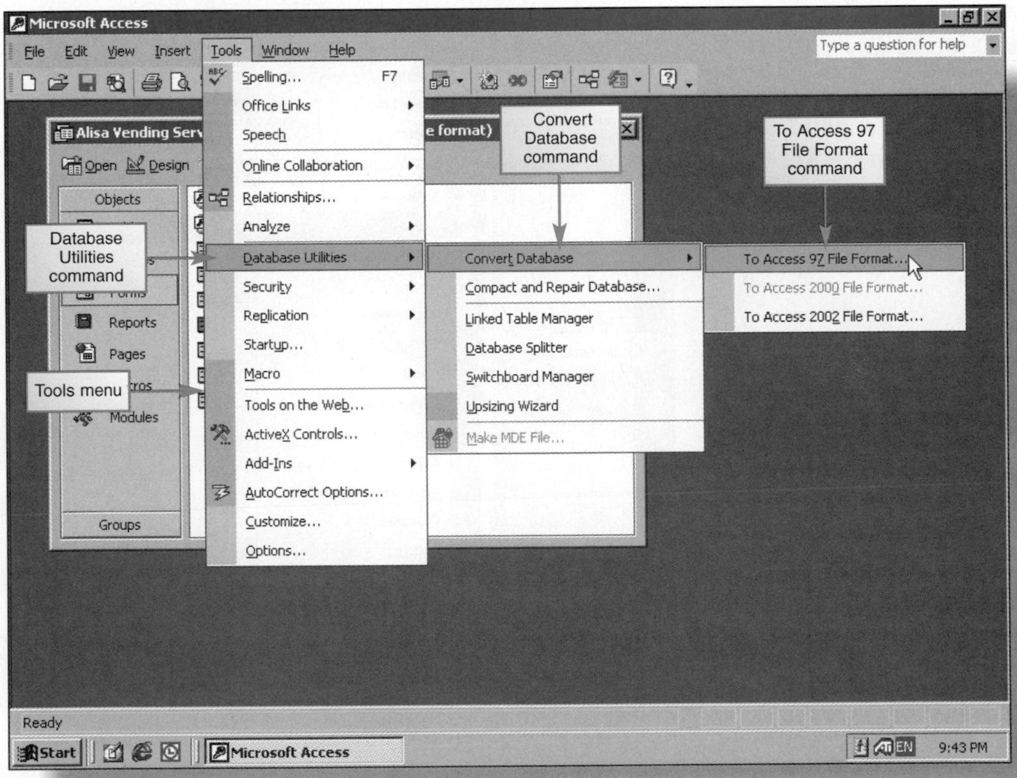

FIGURE 9-2

Other Ways

1. In Voice Command mode, say "Tools, Database Utilities, Convert Database, To Access 97 File Format"

It is important to realize that any changes made in the converted version, will not be reflected in the original. Assuming the original version still is going to be used, the converted version should be used for retrieval purposes only. Otherwise, if you make changes they will display in one version and not the other, making your data inconsistent.

> **More About**
>
> **Redundancy**
>
> Normalization is a special technique for identifying and eliminating redundancy. For more information about normalization, visit the Access 2002 More About page (scsite.com/ac2002/more.htm) and then click Normalization.

Using the Analyze Tool

Access contains an Analyze tool that performs three separate functions. It can analyze tables while looking for potential redundancy (duplicated data). It also can analyze performance. It will check to see if there is any way to make queries, reports, or forms more efficient. It then will make suggestions for possible changes. The final function of the analyzer is to produce detailed documentation of the various tables, queries, forms, reports, and other objects in the database.

Using the Table Analyzer

The Table Analyzer examines tables for **redundancy**, which is duplicated data. If found, the Table Analyzer will suggest ways to split the table in order to eliminate the redundancy. Perform the following steps to use the Table Analyzer.

Steps To Use the Table Analyzer

1 Click Tools on the menu bar, click Analyze on the Tools menu, and then point to Table (Figure 9-3).

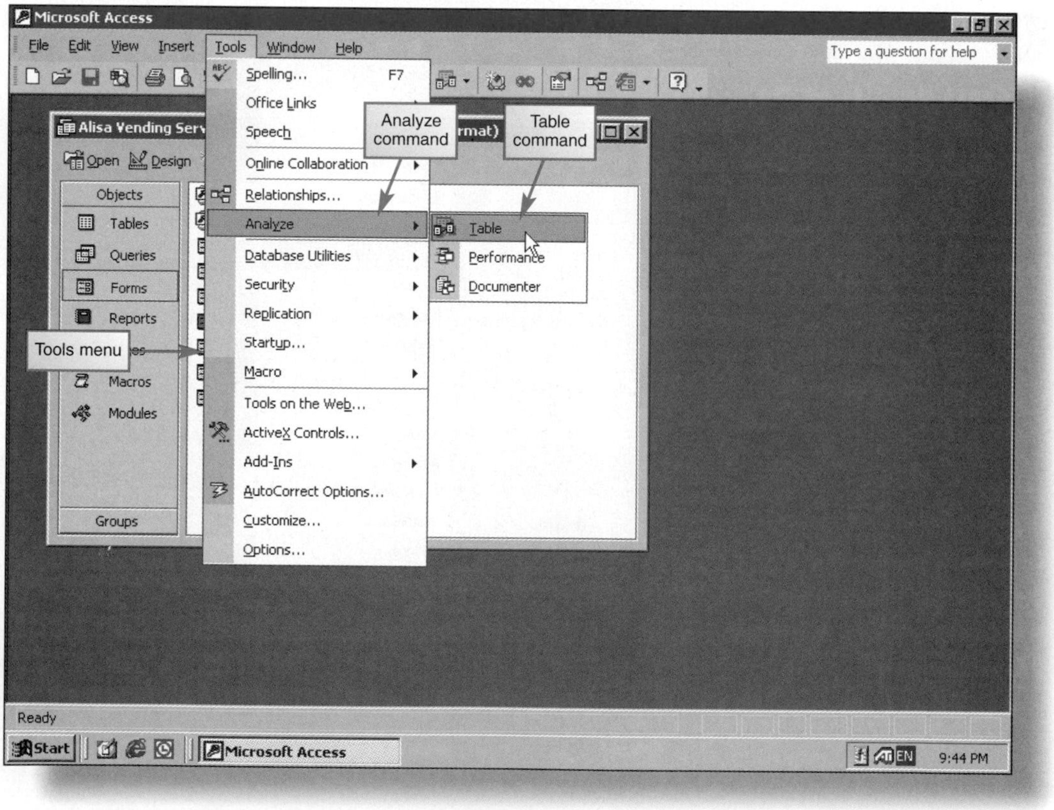

FIGURE 9-3

2 Click Table. Point to the Next button.

The Table Analyzer Wizard displays (Figure 9-4). The message indicates that tables may store duplicate information, which can cause problems.

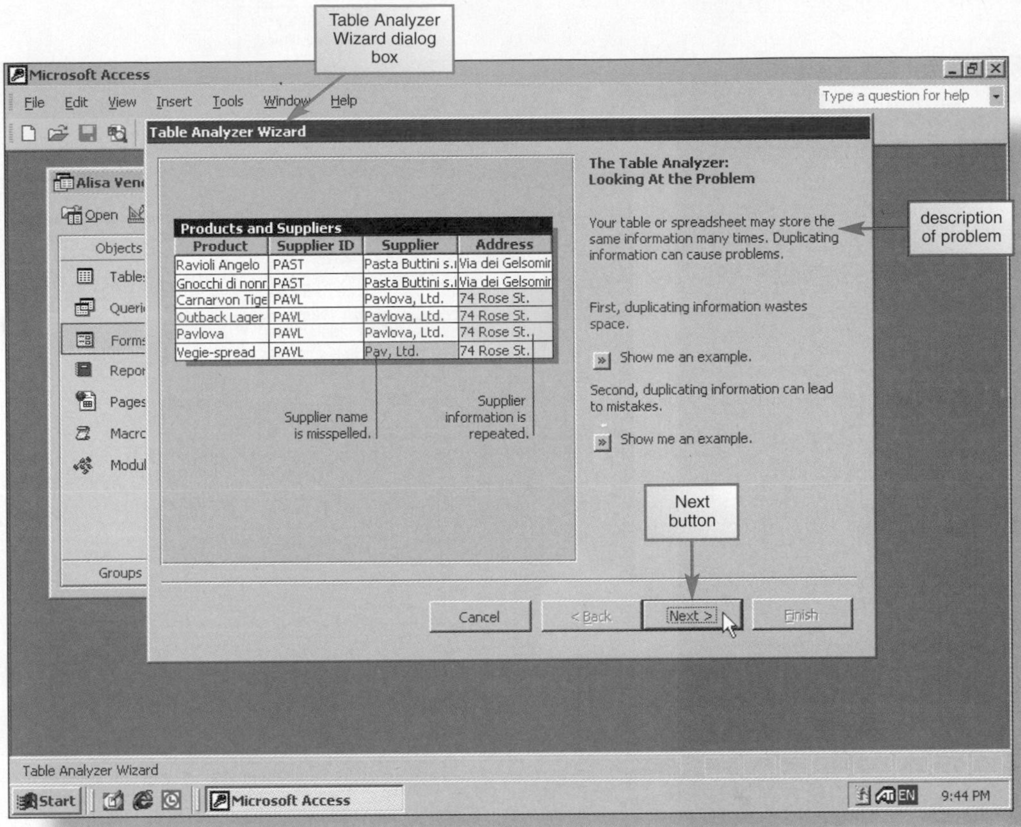

FIGURE 9-4

3 Click the Next button and then point to the Next button.

The Table Analyzer Wizard displays (Figure 9-5). The message indicates that the wizard will suggest ways to split the original table to remove duplicate information.

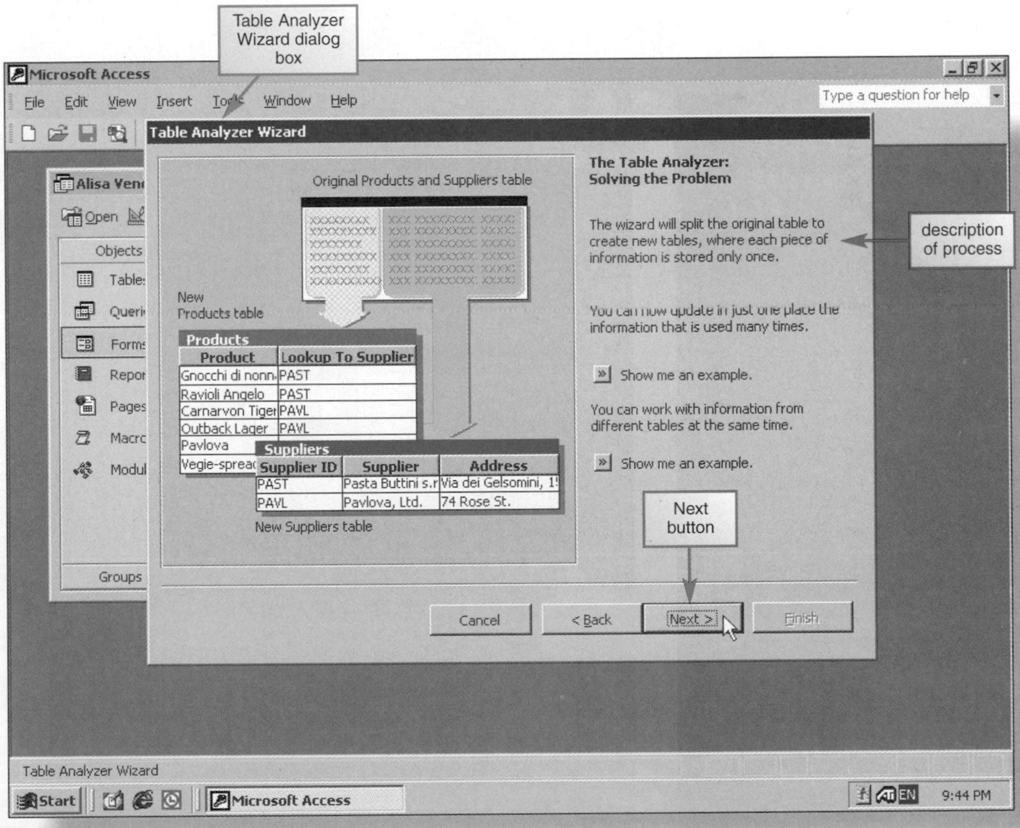

FIGURE 9-5

4 Click the Next button. Click the Customer table and then point to the Next button.

The Customer table is selected (Figure 9-6).

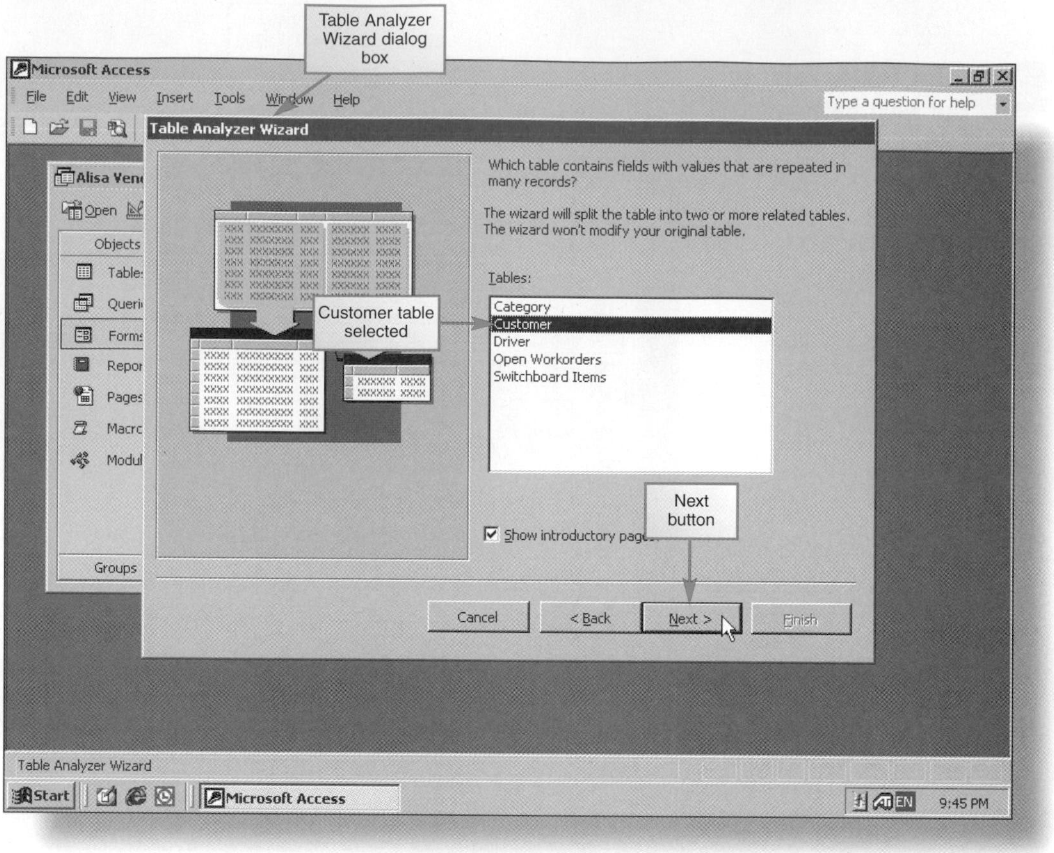

FIGURE 9-6

5 Click the Next button. Be sure the Yes, let the wizard decide option button is selected and then point to the Next button (Figure 9-7).

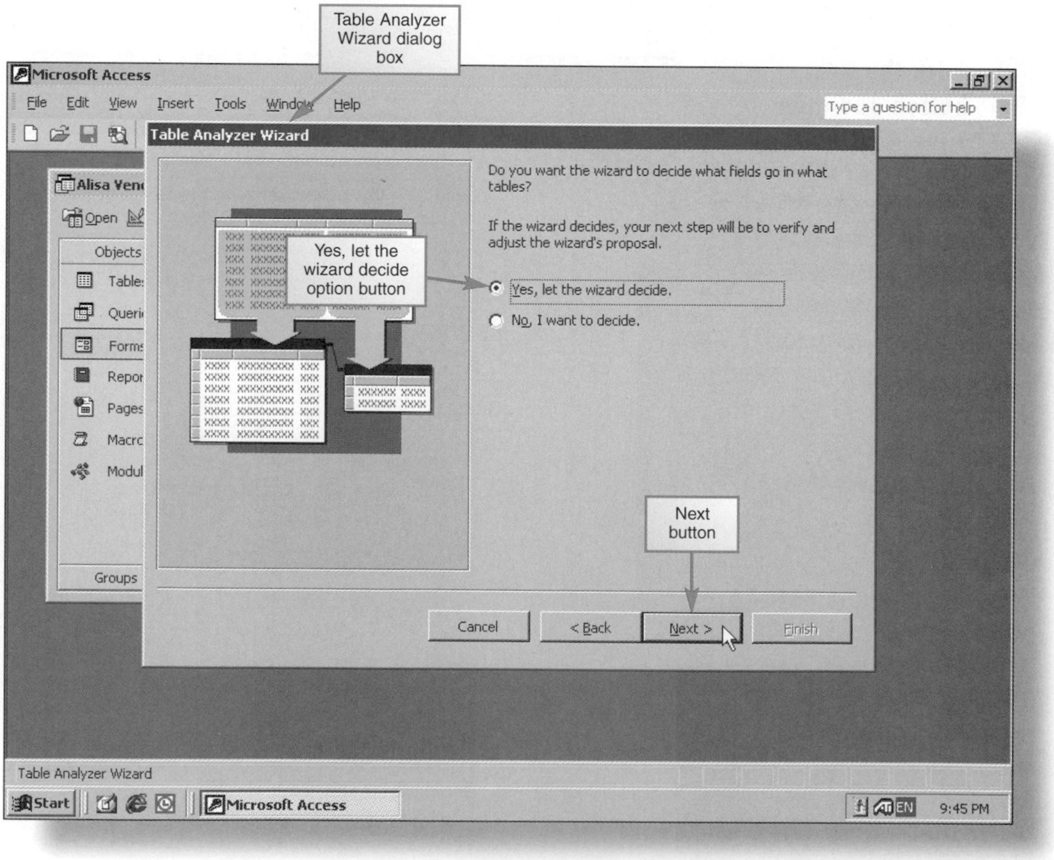

FIGURE 9-7

6 Click the Next button. Point to the Cancel button.

The Table Analyzer Wizard dialog box displays (Figure 9-8). It indicates duplicate information (for example, City, State, Zip Code). Your screen may be different.

7 Because the type of duplication identified by the analyzer does not pose a problem, click the Cancel button.

The structure is not changed.

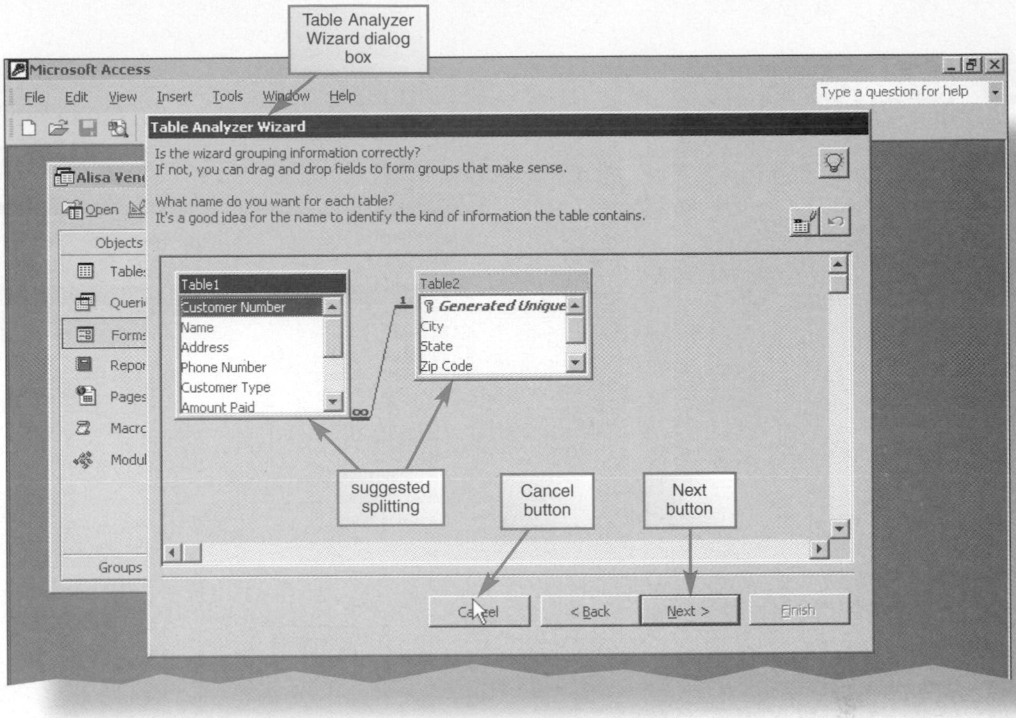

FIGURE 9-8

Using the Performance Analyzer

The Performance Analyzer will examine the tables, queries, reports, forms, and other objects in your system, looking for changes that would improve the efficiency of your database. This could include changes to the way data is stored as well as changes to the indexes created for the system. Once it has finished, it will make recommendations concerning possible changes. Perform the following steps to use the Performance Analyzer.

Other Ways

1. Click Analyze button arrow on Database toolbar, click Analyze Table
2. In Voice Command mode, say "Analyze, Analyze Table"

Steps To Use the Performance Analyzer

1 Click Tools on the menu bar, click Analyze on the Tools menu, and then point to Performance (Figure 9-9).

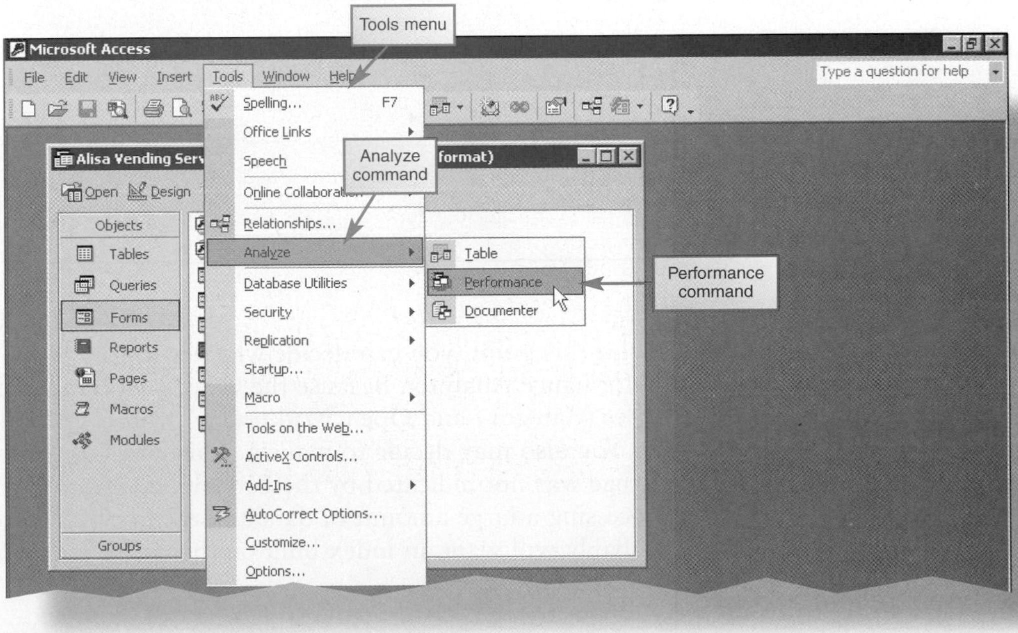

FIGURE 9-9

2 **Click Performance and then click the Tables tab. Point to the Select All button.**

The Performance Analyzer displays (Figure 9-10). The Tables tab is selected so all the tables display.

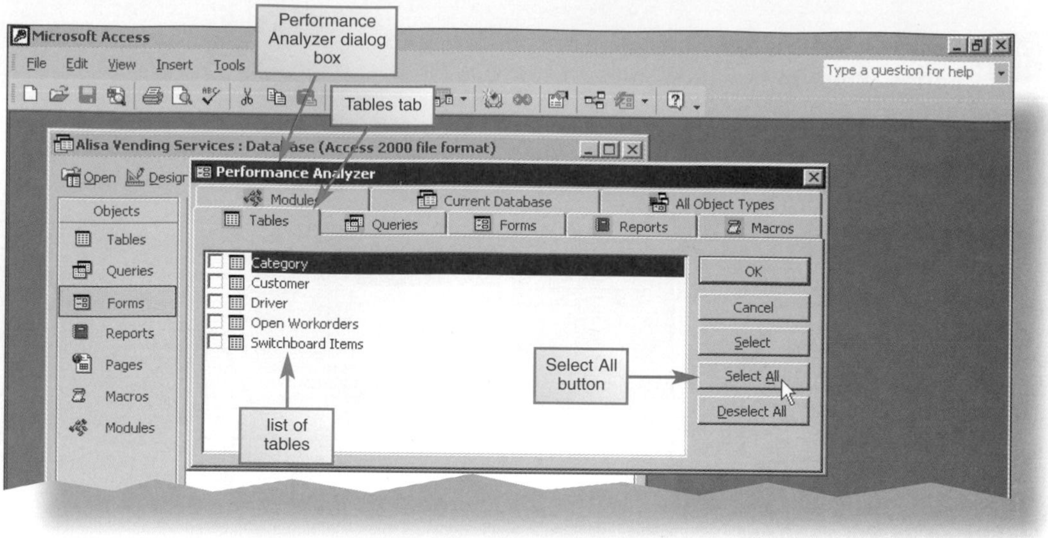

FIGURE 9-10

3 **Click the Select All button to select all tables. Click the Queries tab and then click the Select All button to select all queries. Click the OK button. Point to the Close button.**

The Performance Analyzer displays the results of its analysis (Figure 9-11). It indicates that you might consider changing the data type of the Category Number field from Text to Long Integer, which is an efficient number format for both computations and data storage.

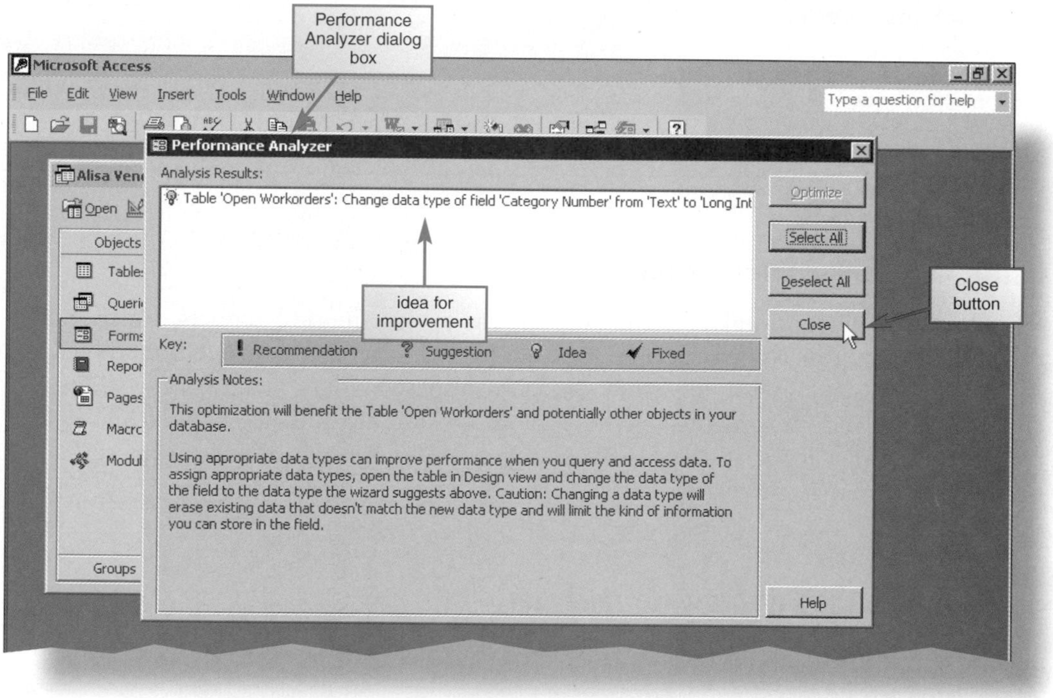

FIGURE 9-11

4 **Click the Close button.**

The Performance Analyzer no longer displays.

Other Ways

1. Click Analyze button arrow on Database toolbar, click Analyze Performance
2. In Voice Command mode, say "Analyze, Analyze Performance"

At this point, you can decide whether to follow the advice given by the Performance Analyzer. Because the Category Number field is used to relate tables (Category and Open Workorders), you cannot make the suggested change.

You also may decide to make a change to improve performance even though the change was not indicated by the Performance Analyzer. If you have a query that is processing a large amount of data and the query is sorted on a particular field, you probably will want an index built on that field. If one already does not exist, you should create it.

Using the Documenter

The Documenter allows you to produce detailed documentation of the various tables, queries, forms, reports, and other objects in your database. Figure 9-12 shows a portion of the documentation of the Customer table. The complete documentation is much more lengthy than the one shown in the figure. In the actual documentation, all fields would have as much information displayed as the Customer Number field. In this documentation, only those items of interest are shown for the other fields.

Notice that the documentation of the Phone Number field includes the input mask. Notice also the documentation of the Customer Type field contains the default value, the description, and the row source associated with the Lookup information for the field. The documentation for both the Customer Type and Amount Paid fields contain validation rules and validation text.

The following steps use the Documenter to produce documentation for the Customer table.

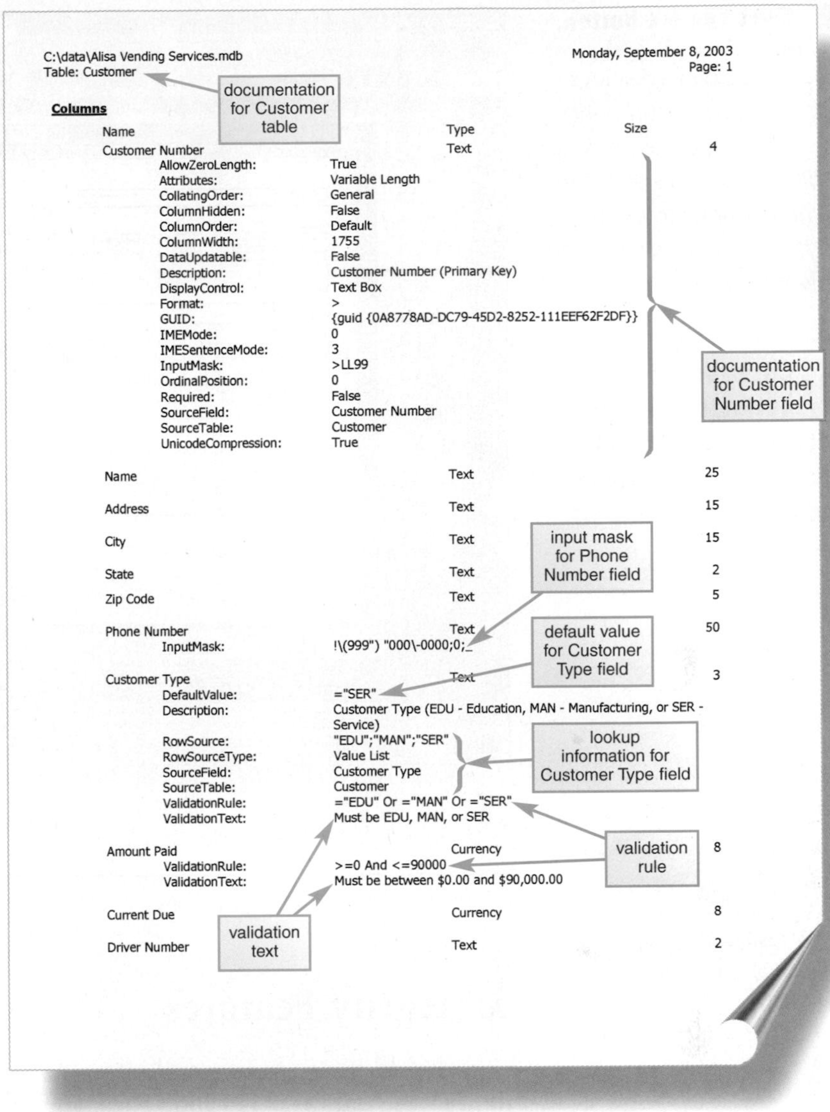

FIGURE 9-12

Steps To Use the Documenter

1 **Click Tools on the menu bar, click Analyze on the Tools menu, and then click Documenter. Click the Tables tab, click the Customer check box, and then point to the OK button.**

The Documenter displays (Figure 9-13).

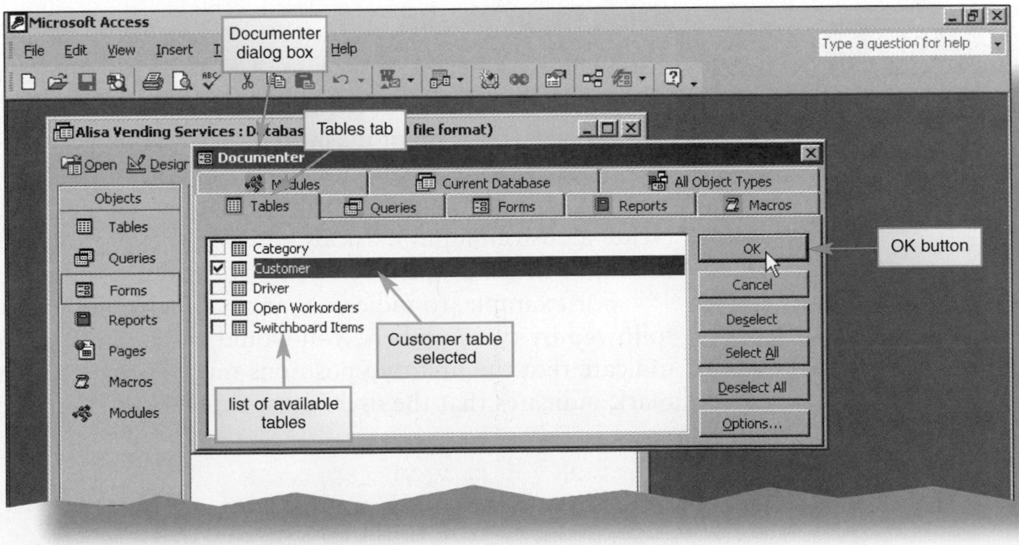

FIGURE 9-13

2 **Click the OK button.**

The documentation displays (Figure 9-14). You can print the documentation by clicking the Print button. You also can save the documentation by using the Export command on the File menu.

3 **Click the Print button on the Print Preview toolbar to print the documentation. Close the window by clicking its Close button.**

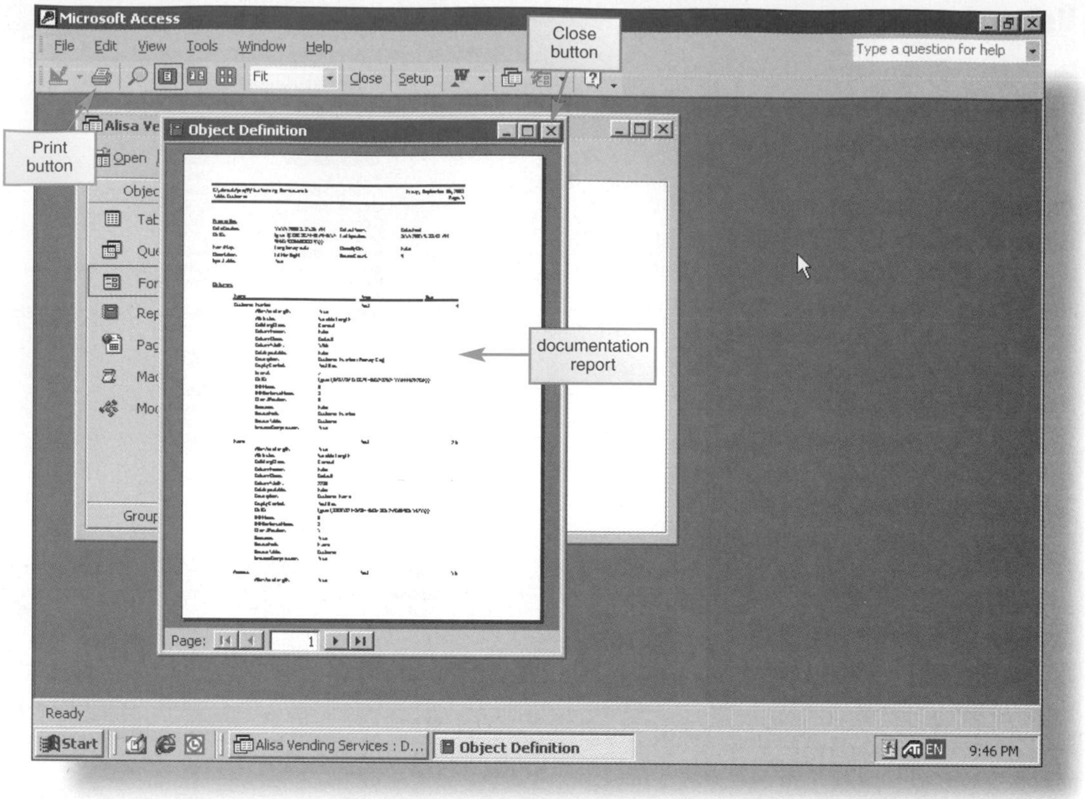

FIGURE 9-14

Other Ways

1. Click Analyze button arrow on Database toolbar, click Documenter
2. In Voice Command mode, say "Analyze, Documenter"

More About

Data Types

Access provides several data types. In some cases, more than one data type might be appropriate. To select the best choice for your particular circumstance, you need to know the advantages and disadvantages associated with each. For more information, visit the Access 2002 More About page (scsite.com/ac2002/more.htm) and then click Data Types.

Integrity Features

You should have used several integrity features already, that is, features to ensure the data in the database is valid. These include creating validation rules and text, specifying relationships and referential integrity, using the Input Mask Wizard to create an input mask, and creating a Lookup Wizard field. In this section, you will specify a custom input mask and also specify properties associated with referential integrity.

Using Input Masks

An input mask specifies how data is to be entered and how it will display. You may have used the Input Mask Wizard to create an input mask. Using the wizard, you can select the input mask that meets your needs from a list. This often is the best way to create the input mask.

If the input mask you need to create is not similar to any in the list, you can create a custom input mask by entering the appropriate characters as the value for the Input Mask property. In doing so, you use the symbols from Table 9-1.

For example, to indicate that customer numbers must consist of two letters followed by two numbers, you would enter LL99. The Ls in the first two positions indicate that the first two positions must be letters. Using L instead of a question mark indicates that the users must enter these letters; that is, they are not optional.

With the question mark, they could leave these positions blank. The 9s in the last two positions indicate that the users must enter digits (0 through 9). Using 9 instead of 0 indicates that they could leave these positions blank; that is, they are optional. Finally, to ensure that any letters entered are converted to uppercase, you would use the > symbol at the beginning of the input mask. The complete mask would be >LL99.

Perform the following steps to enter an input mask for the Customer Number field.

Table 9-1 Input Mask Symbols

SYMBOL	TYPE OF DATA ACCEPTED	DATA ENTRY OPTIONAL
0	Digits (0 through 9) without plus (+) or minus (-) sign. Positions left blank display as zeros.	No
9	Digits (0 through 9) without plus (+) or minus (-) sign. Positions left blank display as spaces.	Yes
#	Digits (0 through 9) with plus (+) or minus (-) sign. Positions left blank display as spaces.	Yes
L	Letters (A through Z).	No
?	Letters (A through Z).	Yes
A	Letters (A through Z) or digits (0 through 9).	No
a	Letters (A through Z) or digits (0 through 9).	Yes
&	Any character or a space.	No
C	Any character or a space.	Yes
<	Converts any letters entered to lowercase.	Does not apply
>	Converts any letters entered to uppercase.	Does not apply
!	Characters typed in the input mask fill it from left to right.	Does not apply
\	Character following the slash is treated as a literal in the input mask.	Does not apply

Steps To Use an Input Mask

1 Click the Tables object, if necessary, to be sure the tables display. Right-click Customer and then click Design View on the shortcut menu. Maximize the window.

2 With the Customer Number field selected, click the Input Mask property and then type >LL99 as the value (Figure 9-15).

3 Close the window containing the design by clicking its Close Window button. When prompted to save the changes, click the Yes button.

The changes are saved

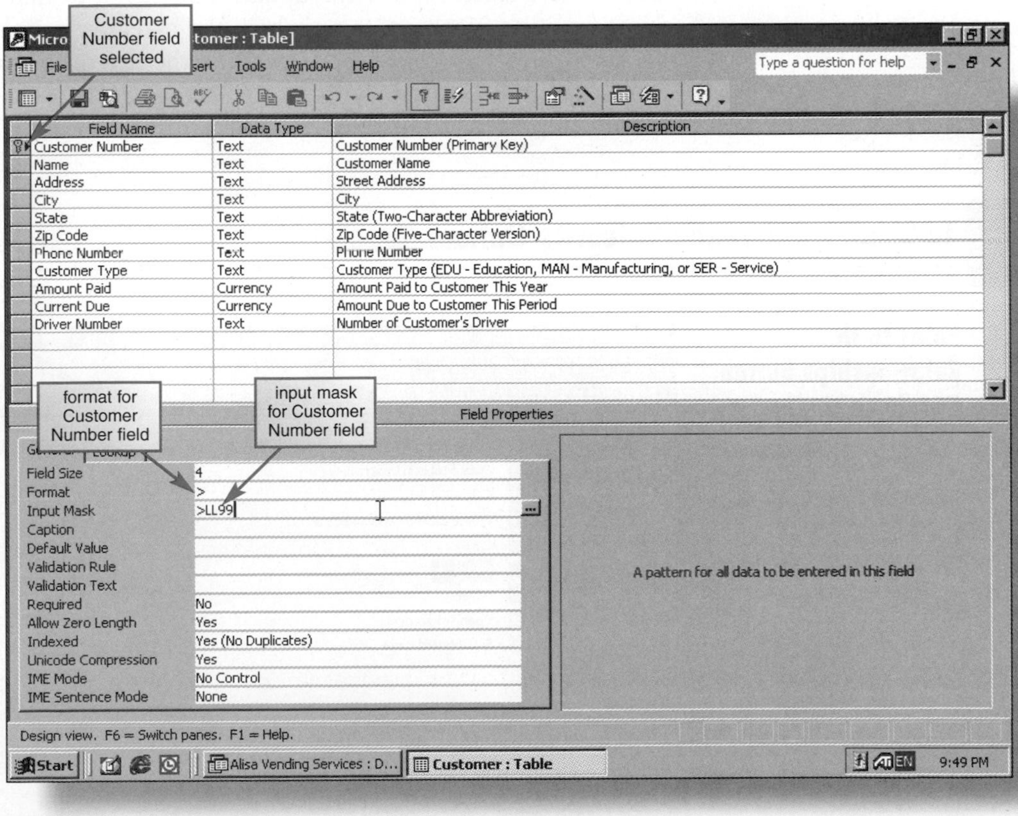

FIGURE 9-15

From this point on, anyone entering a customer number will be restricted to letters in the first two positions and numeric digits in the last two. Further, any letters entered in the first two positions will be converted to uppercase.

In Figure 9-15, the Customer Number field has both a custom input mask and a format. Technically, you do not need both. When the same field has both an input mask and a format, the format takes precedence. Because the format specified for the Customer Number field is the same as the input mask (uppercase), it will not affect the data.

More About

Referential Integrity

Referential integrity is an essential property for databases, but providing support for it proved to be one of the most difficult tasks facing the developers of relational database management systems. For more information, visit the Access 2002 More About page (scsite.com/ac2002/more.htm) and then click Referential Integrity.

Specifying Referential Integrity Options

The property that ensures that the value in a foreign key must match that of another table's primary key is called **referential integrity**. When specifying referential integrity, there are two ways to handle deletion. In the relationship between customers and open work orders, for example, deletion of a customer for which open work orders exist, such as customer number CN21, would violate referential integrity. Any open work orders for customer number CN21 would no longer relate to any customer in the database. The normal way to avoid this problem is to prohibit such a deletion. The other option is to **cascade the delete**, that is, have Access allow the deletion but then automatically delete any work orders related to the deleted customer.

Two ways are available to update the primary key. In the relationship between categories and open work orders, for example, changing the category number for category 1 in the Category table from 1 to 1a would cause a problem. There are open work orders on which the category number is 1. These work orders would no longer relate to any existing category. Again, the normal way of avoiding the problem is to prohibit this type of update. The other option is to **cascade the update**; that is, have Access allow the update but then automatically make the corresponding change on any work order on which the category number was 1.

The following steps specify cascade the delete for the relationship between customers and open work orders. The steps also specify cascade the update for the relationship between categories and open work orders.

Steps To Specify Referential Integrity Options

1 Point to the Relationships button on the Database toolbar (Figure 9-16).

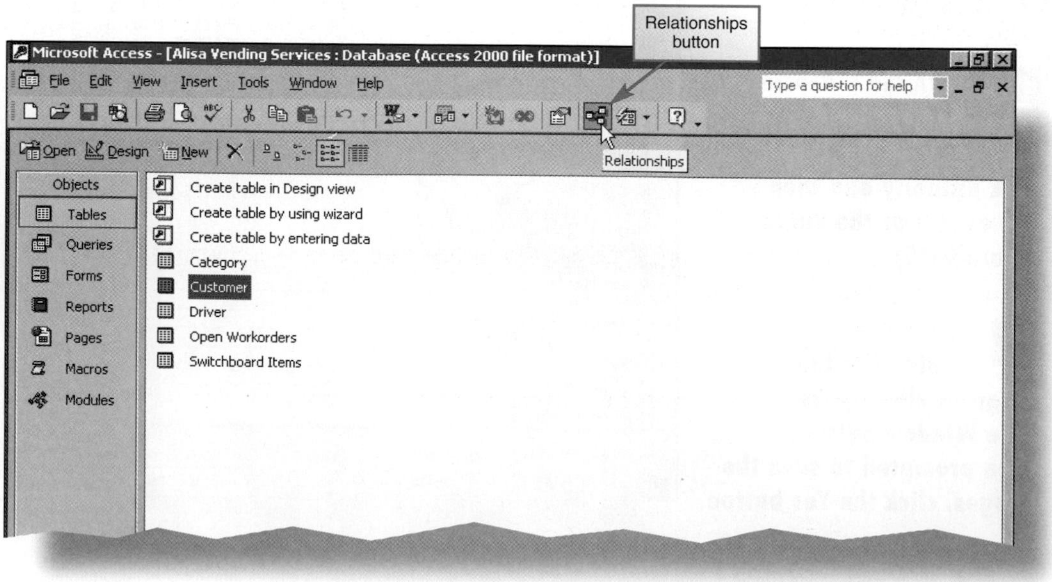

FIGURE 9-16

2 Click the Relationships button. Right-click the line joining Customer and Open Workorders and then point to Edit Relationship on the shortcut menu.

The relationship between Customer and Open Workorders is selected (Figure 9-17).

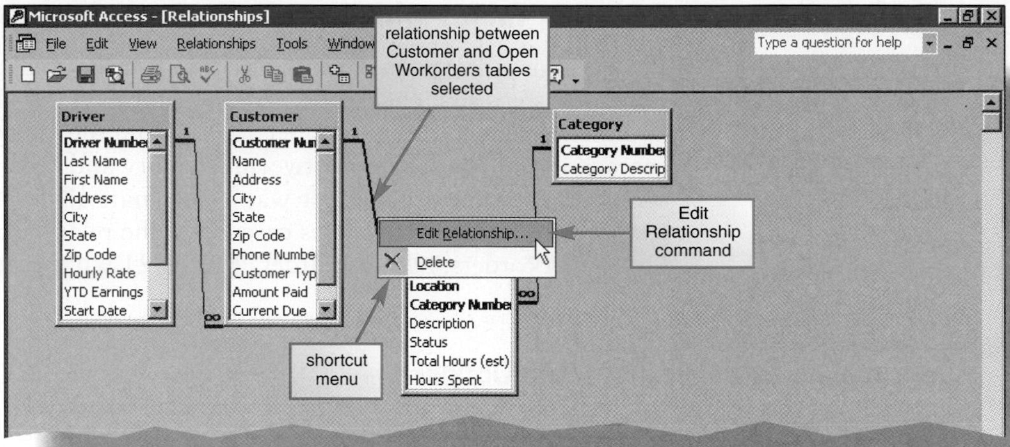

FIGURE 9-17

3 Click Edit Relationship on the shortcut menu. Click the Cascade Delete Related Records check box and then point to the OK button (Figure 9-18).

4 Click the OK button.

5 Right-click the line joining the Category and Open Workorders tables, click Edit Relationship on the shortcut menu, click the Cascade Update Related Fields check box, and then click the OK button.

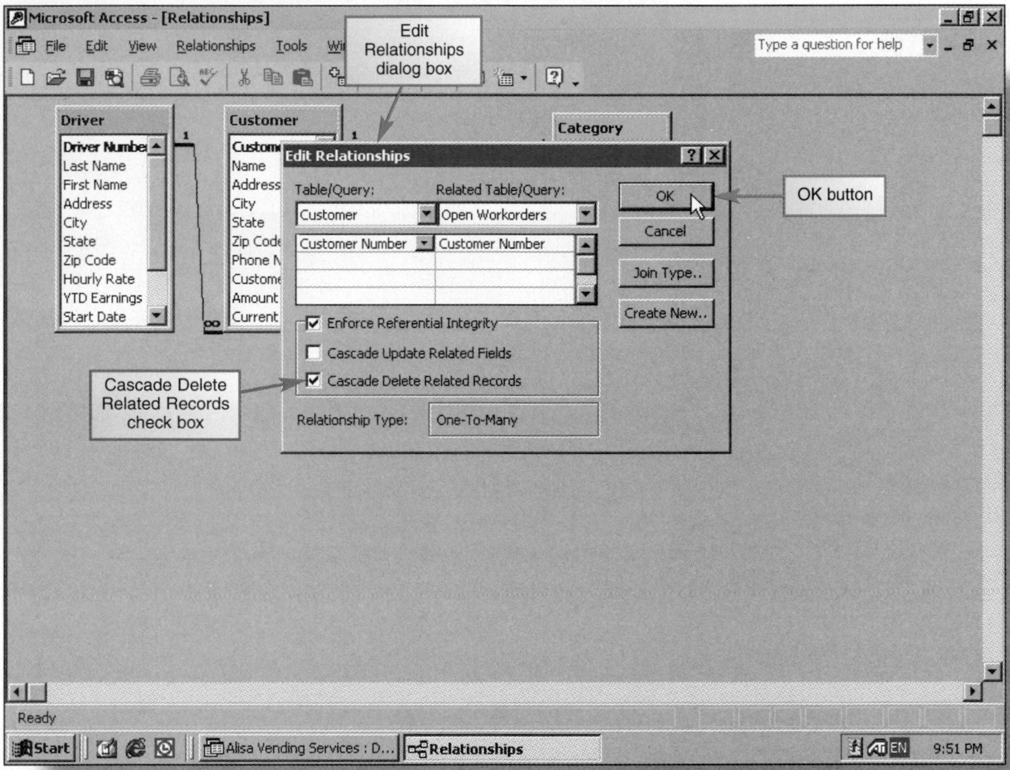

FIGURE 9-18

6 Click the Close Window button for the Relationships window. If the Microsoft Access dialog box displays prompting you to save the changes, click the Yes button to save the changes.

The relationship changes are saved.

Other Ways

1. On Tools menu click Relationships
2. In Voice Command mode, say "Relationships"

Updating Tables with Cascade Options

The Cascade options have a direct impact on updates to the database. The following steps first change a category number in the Category table from 1 to 1a and then delete customer number CN21 from the Customer table. Because updates cascade in the relationship between Category and Open Workorders, all work orders on which the category number was 1 automatically will have the category number changed to 1a. Because deletes cascade in the relationship between Customer and Open Workorders, all work orders for CN21 will be deleted.

Steps To Update a Table with Cascade Options

1 Open the Category table and change the category number on the first record to 1a (Figure 9-19).

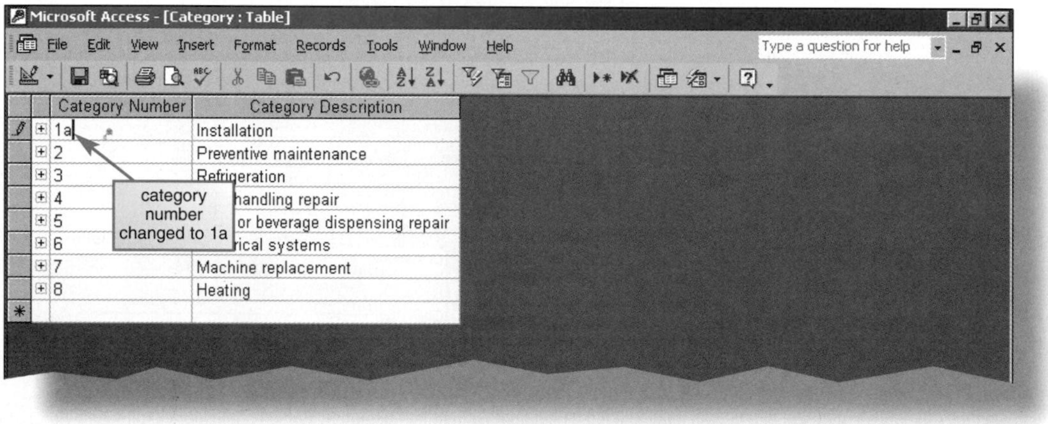

FIGURE 9-19

2 Close the Category table and open the Open Workorders table.

The category number on the work order for customer number FR28, location 11N has been changed automatically to 1a (Figure 9-20).

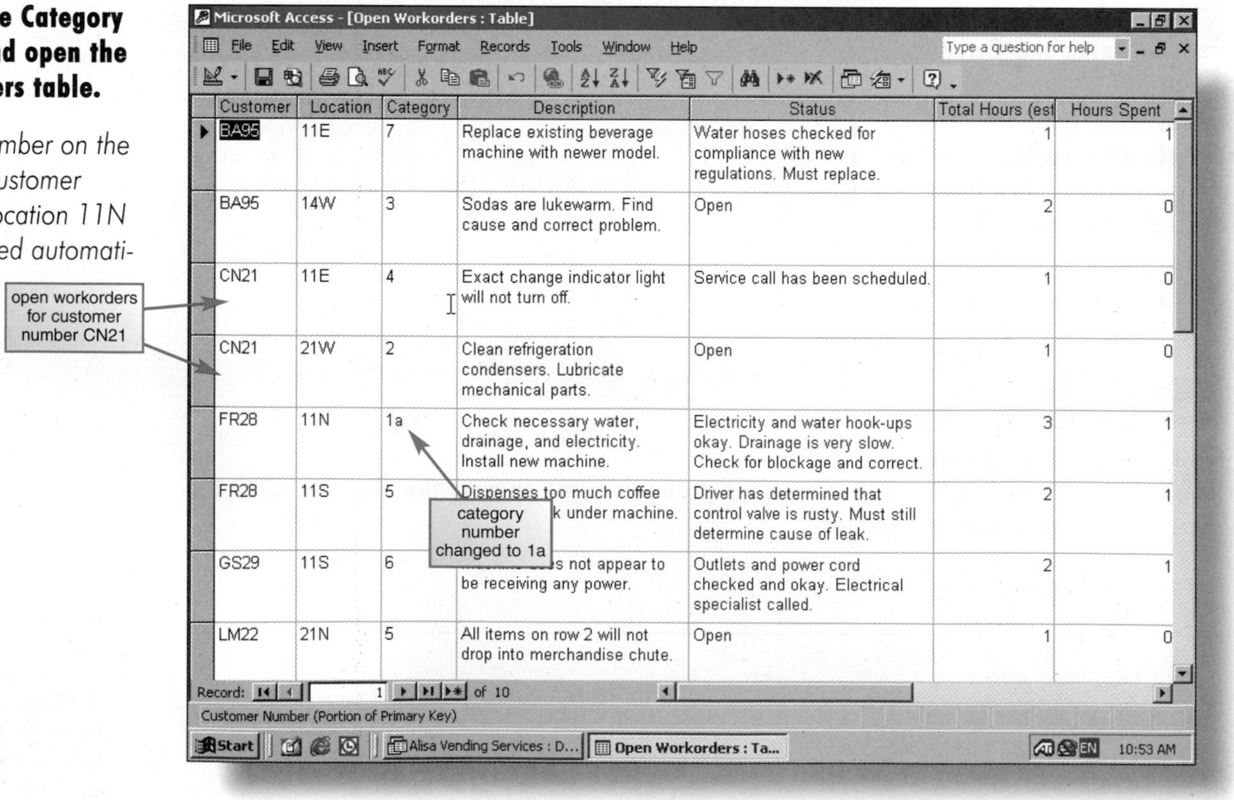

FIGURE 9-20

3 Close the Open Workorders table. Open the Customer table and then click the record selector for customer number CN21.

Customer number CN21 is selected (Figure 9-21).

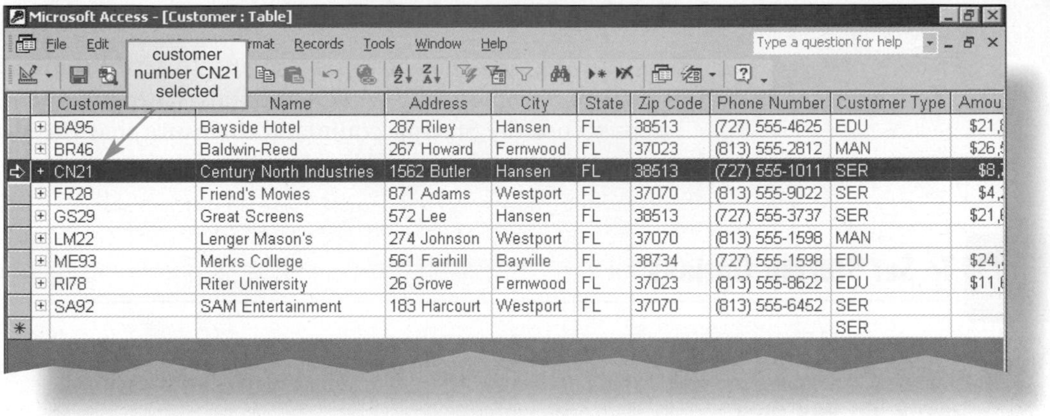

FIGURE 9-21

4 Press the DELETE key to delete customer number CN21 and then point to the Yes button.

The Microsoft Access dialog box displays (Figure 9-22). It indicates that a record in a related table also will be deleted.

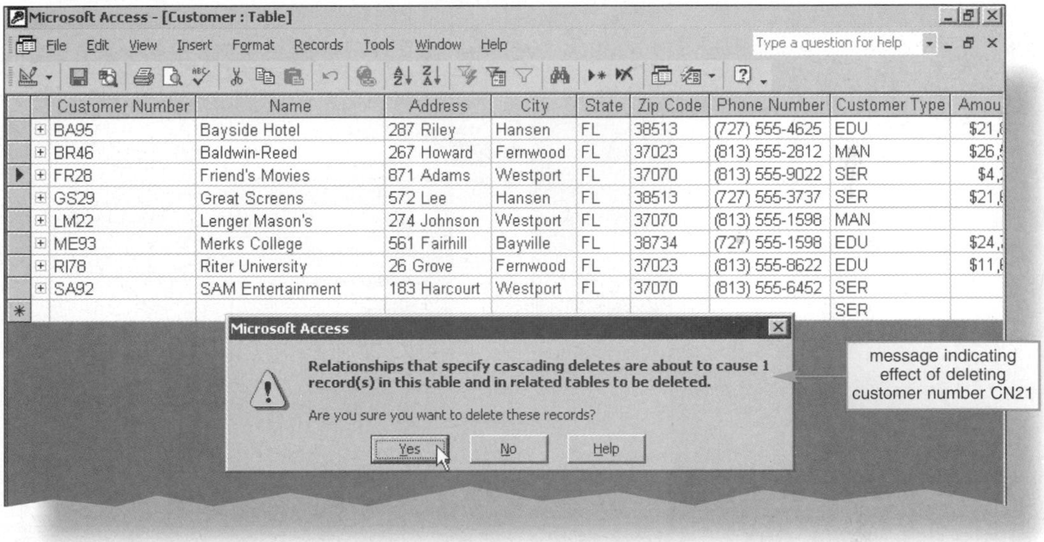

FIGURE 9-22

5 Click the Yes button. Close the Customer table and open the Open Workorders table.

The work orders for customer number CN21 (see Figure 9-20) have been deleted (Figure 9-23).

6 Close the Open Workorders table by clicking the Close Window button.

The table no longer displays.

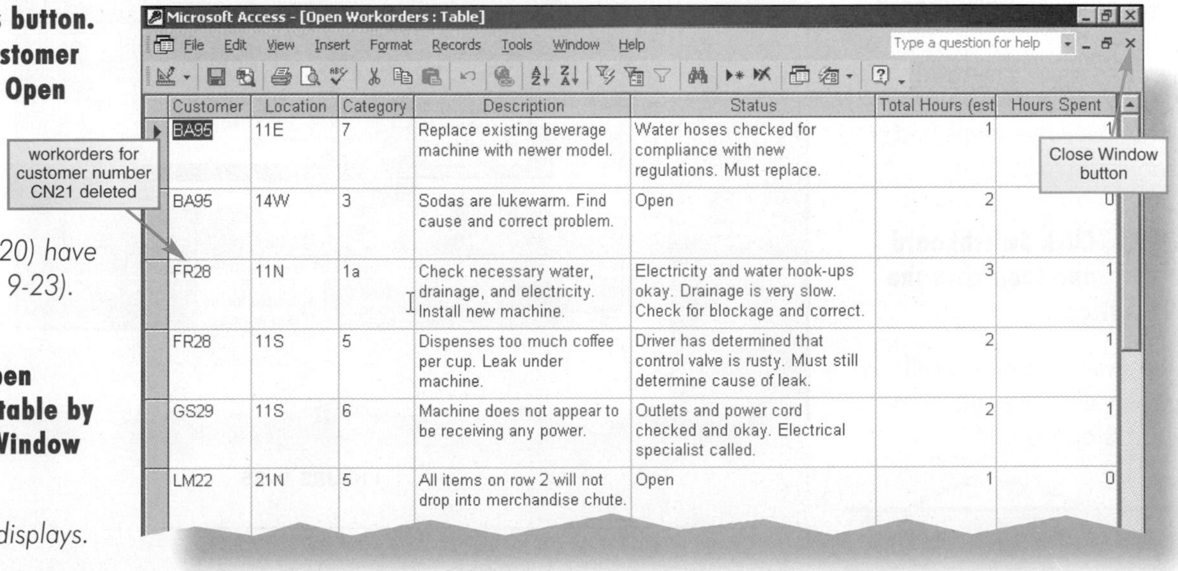

FIGURE 9-23

Setting Startup Options

You can use the Startup command to set **startup options**, that is, actions that will be taken automatically when the database first is opened. Perform the following steps to use the Startup command to ensure that the switchboard displays automatically when the Alisa Vending Services database is opened.

Steps To Set Startup Options

1 Click Tools on the menu bar and then point to Startup (Figure 9-24).

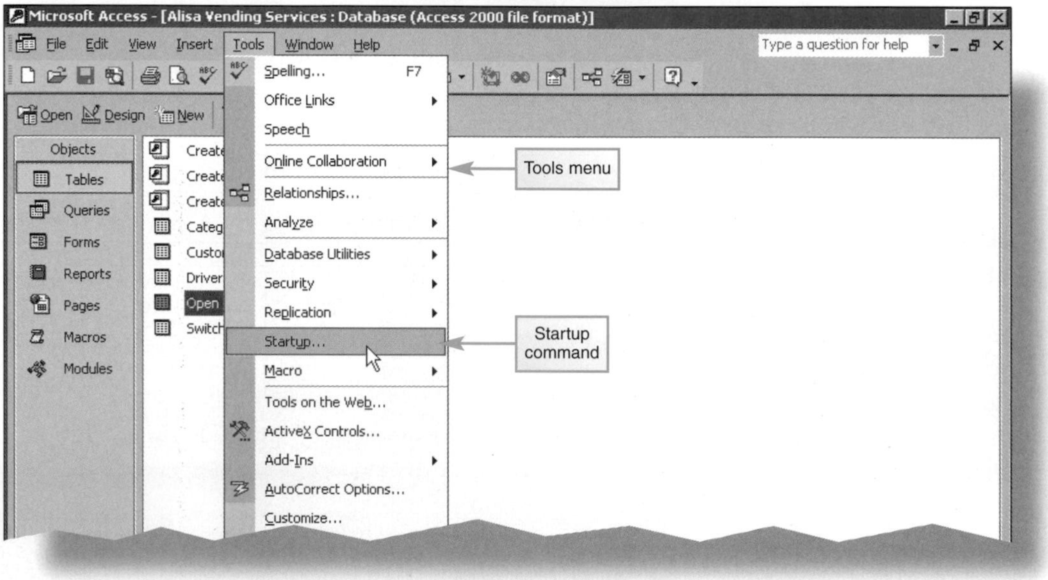

FIGURE 9-24

2 Click Startup, click the Display Form/Page box arrow, and then point to Switchboard.

The Startup dialog box displays (Figure 9-25). The list of available forms and pages displays.

3 Click Switchboard and then click the OK button.

The switchboard now will display whenever the database is opened.

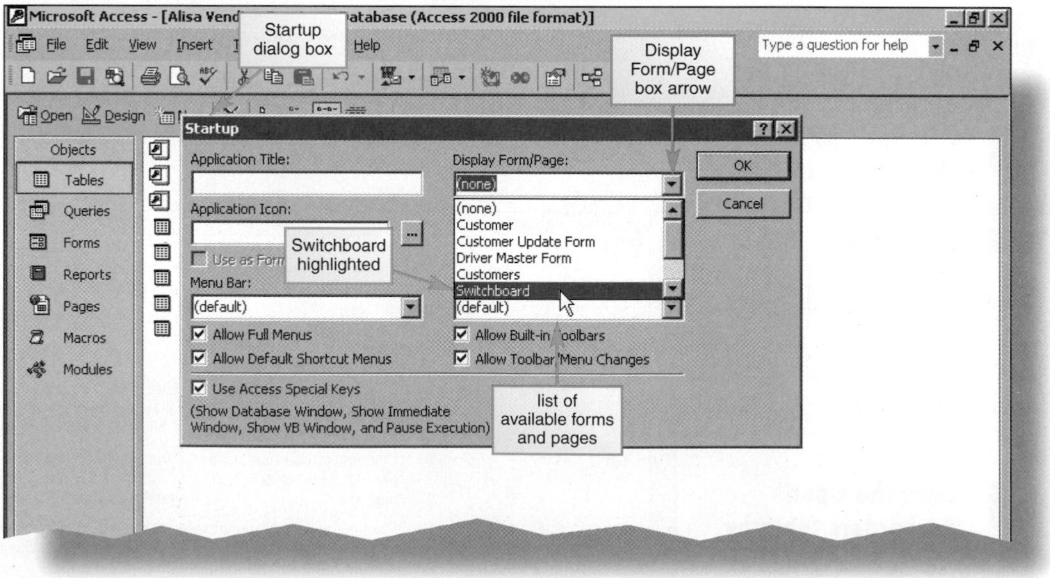

FIGURE 9-25

Other Ways

1. In Voice Command mode, say "Tools, Startup"

Setting Passwords

In order to set a password, the database must be open in exclusive mode. The following steps open the Lebond Industries database in exclusive mode in preparation for setting a password.

More About

Passwords

It is possible to set different passwords for different users. In addition, each password can be associated with a different set of privileges concerning accessing the database. If you forget your database password, you will be unable to access the database. Unlike other systems, such as email systems, there is no way to reset the password.

TO OPEN A DATABASE IN EXCLUSIVE MODE

1. Close the Alisa Vending Services : Database window.
2. Click the Open button on the Database toolbar.
3. If necessary, click Local Disk (C:) in the Look in box and then click the Data folder (assuming your database is stored in a folder called Data). Make sure the Lebond Industries database is selected.
4. Click the Open button arrow (not the button itself). Click Open Exclusive in the list that displays.

The database opens in exclusive mode and the Lebond Industries : Database window displays.

With the database open in exclusive mode, perform the following steps to set a password.

Steps To Set a Password

1 Click Tools on the menu bar, click Security on the Tools menu, and then point to Set Database Password (Figure 9-26).

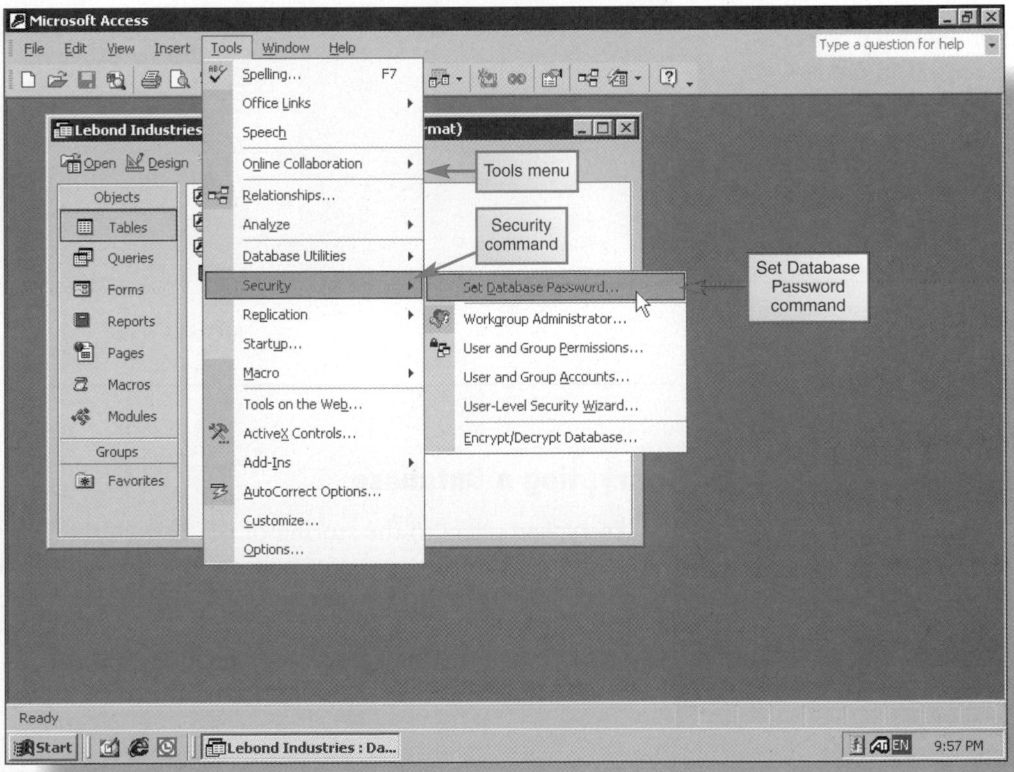

FIGURE 9-26

2 Click Set Database Password. Type your password in the Password text box in the Set Database Password dialog box. Asterisks, not the actual characters, display as you type your password. Press the TAB key and then type your password again in the Verify text box. Point to the OK button. Be sure to remember the password that you type. You will use it again in the next sections.

The password is entered in both the Password text box and the Verify text box (Figure 9-27).

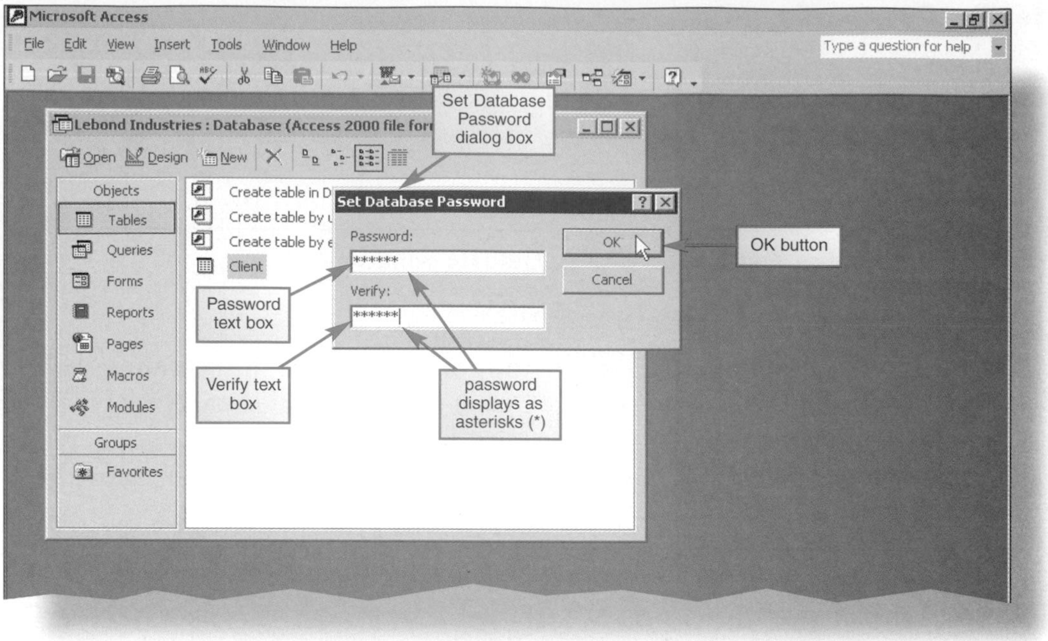

FIGURE 9-27

3 Click the OK button.

The password is entered. From this point on, whenever a user opens the database, the user will be required to enter the password in the Password Required dialog box (Figure 9-28).

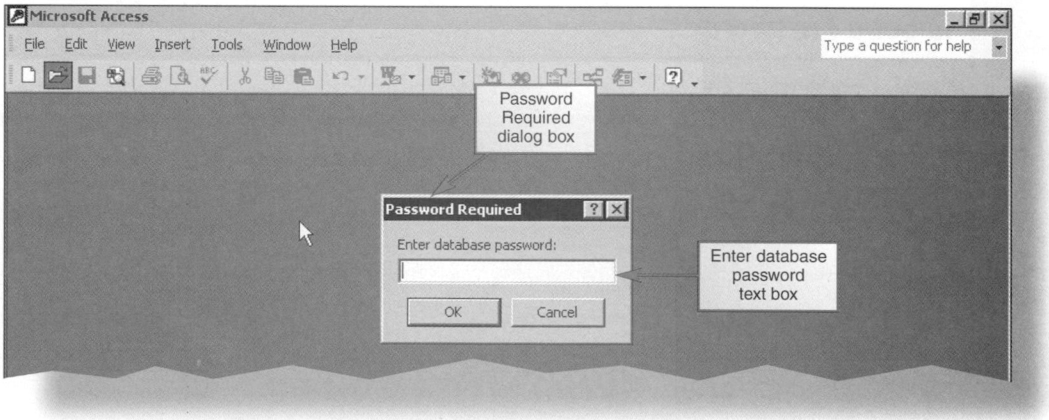

FIGURE 9-28

Other Ways

1. In Voice Command mode, say "Tools, Security, Set Database Password"

Encrypting a Database

Encryption refers to the storing of the data in the database in an encrypted (encoded) format. Any time a user stores or modifies data in the database, the database management system (DBMS) will encrypt the data before actually updating the database. Before a legitimate user retrieves the data via the DBMS, the data will be decrypted. The whole encryption process is transparent to a legitimate user; that is, he or she is not even aware it is happening. If an unauthorized user attempts to bypass all the controls of the DBMS and get to the database through a utility program or a word processor, however, he or she will be able to see only the encrypted, and unreadable, version of the data.

In order to encrypt/decrypt a database, the database must be closed. To encrypt a database, use the Encrypt/Decrypt Database command as in the following steps.

Steps To Encrypt a Database

1 Close the database by clicking the Lebond Industries : Database window Close button. Click Tools on the menu bar, click Security on the Tools menu, and then point to Encrypt/Decrypt Database (Figure 9-29).

2 Click Encrypt/Decrypt Database. Select the Lebond Industries database, click OK, enter your password, and then click the OK button in the Password Required dialog box. Type `Lebond Industries Enc` **as the file name in the File name box and then click the Save button. Enter your password again, and then click the OK button in the Password Required dialog box.**

The database is encrypted. The encrypted version is called Lebond Industries Enc.

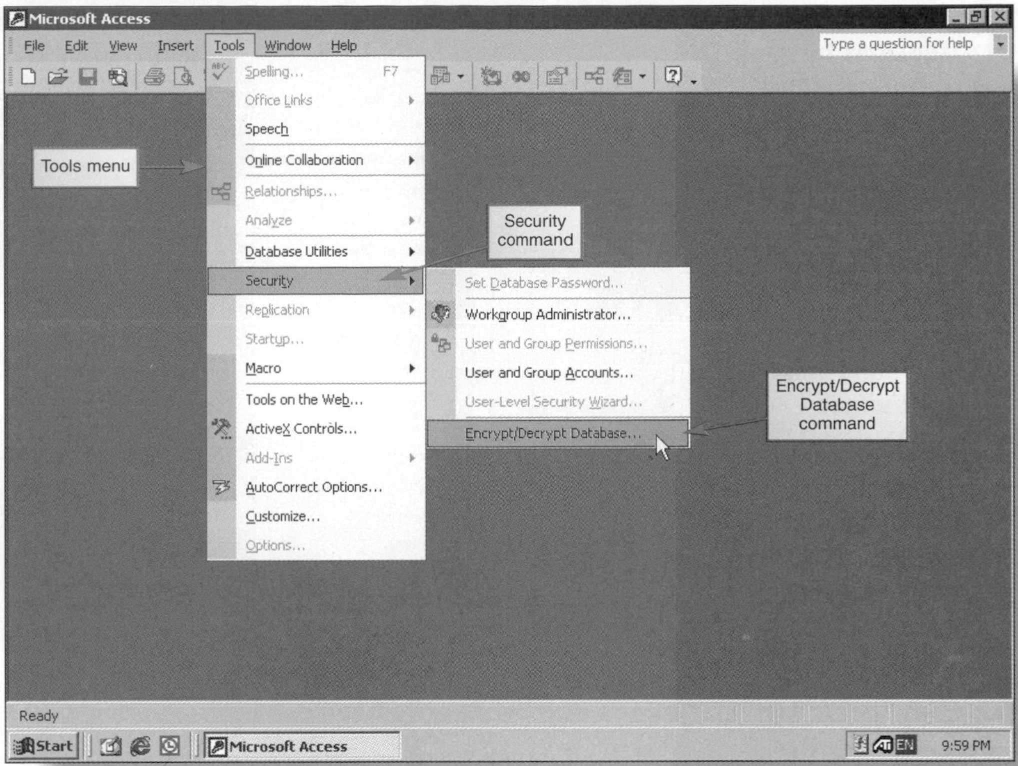

FIGURE 9-29

Other Ways

1. In Voice Command mode, say "Tools, Security, Encrypt Decrypt Database"

Removing a Password

If you no longer feel a password is necessary, you can remove it by using the Unset Database Password command as in the steps on the next page.

Steps To Remove a Password

1 Open Lebond Industries in exclusive mode (see the steps on page A 9.21). Enter your password when requested.

2 Click Tools on the menu bar, click Security on the Tools menu, and then point to Unset Database Password (Figure 9-30).

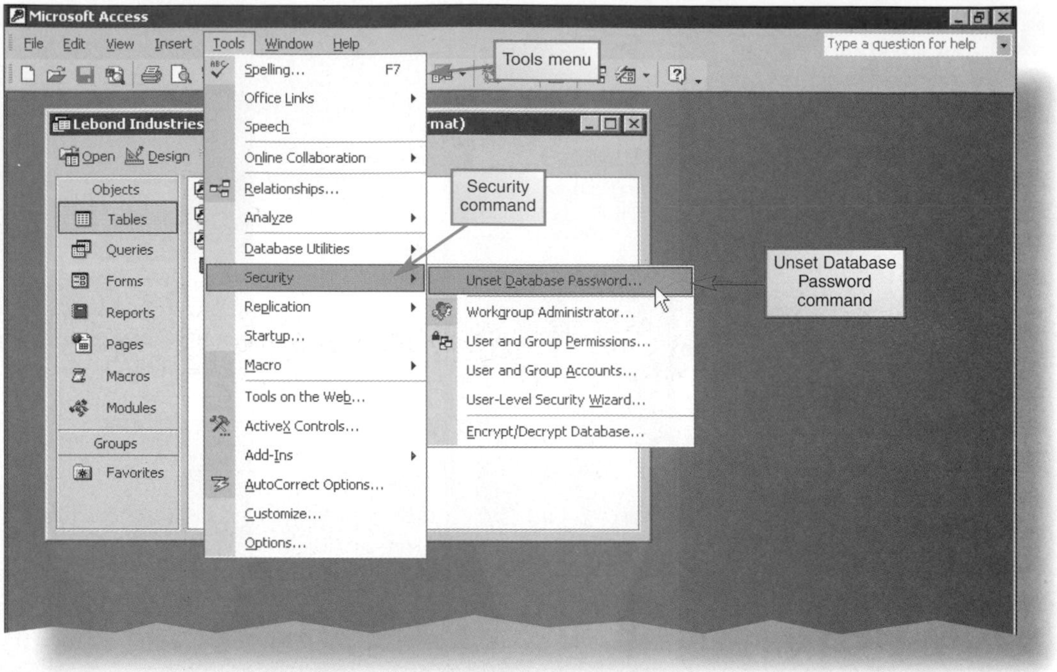

FIGURE 9-30

3 Click Unset Database Password. Type the password in the Unset Database Password dialog box and then point to the OK button.

The Unset Database Password dialog box displays (Figure 9-31).

4 Click the OK button.

The password is removed.

5 Close the Lebond Industries database, and then click the Close button for the Microsoft Access window.

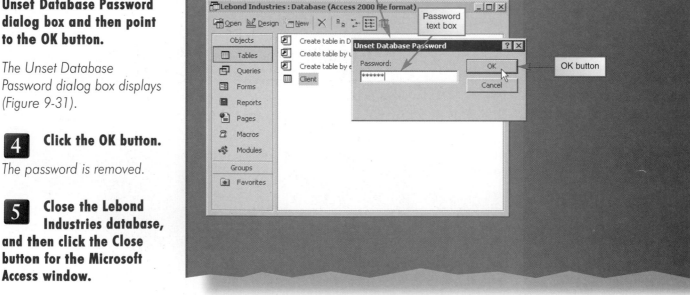

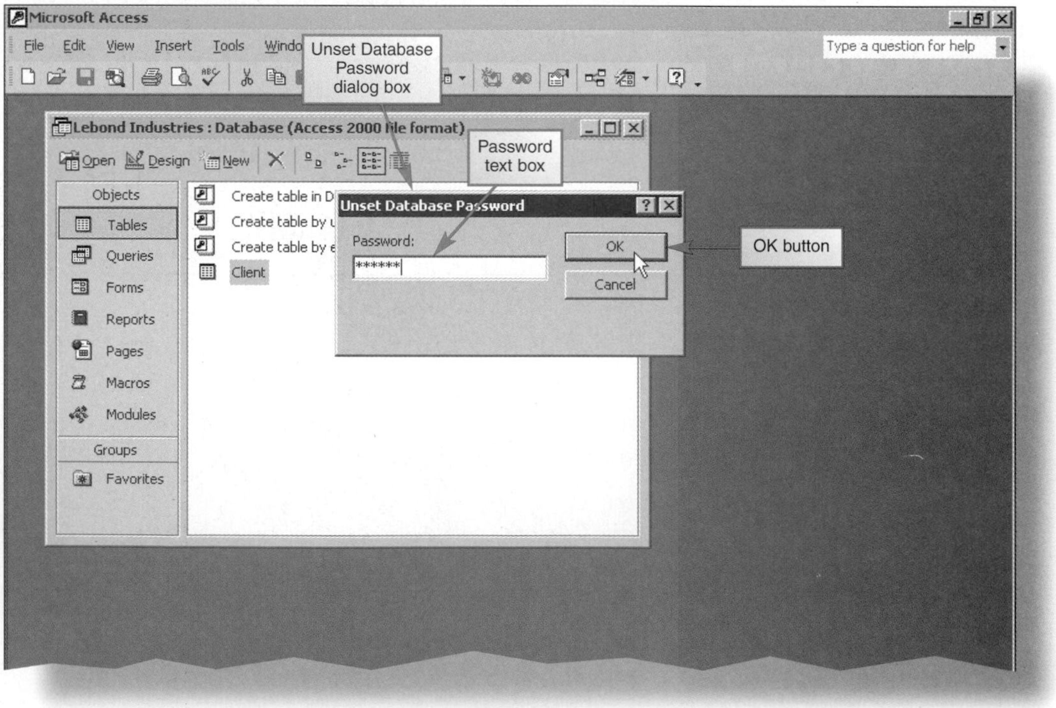

FIGURE 9-31

Other Ways

1. In Voice Command mode, say "Tools, Security, Unset Database Password"

Using Replication

Replication is the process of making multiple copies, called **replicas**, of a database. The original database is called the **Design Master**. The replicas then can be used at different locations. To make sure the Design Master reflects the changes made in the various replicas, the Design Master and the replicas will be **synchronized** periodically. This ensures that all databases reflect all the changes that have been made.

Creating a Replica

To create a replica, use the Briefcase feature of Windows. In order to use this, there must be a Briefcase icon on the Windows desktop. If not, provided this feature is installed, you can display such an icon by right-clicking any open area of the Windows desktop, clicking New on the shortcut menu, and then clicking Briefcase on the New submenu.

Note: Check with your instructor to make sure the feature is installed and appropriate for you to use before completing the following steps.

TO CREATE A REPLICA

1. Use either My Computer or Windows Explorer to open a window for the Data folder on drive C. Drag the Lebond Industries database from this window to the Briefcase icon.
2. When the message indicating that Briefcase is making the database replicable displays, asking if you want to continue, click the Yes button.
3. When the message asking if you want Briefcase to make a backup copy of your database displays, click the No button.
4. When the message asking if you want to be able to make design changes in the original copy or the Briefcase copy displays, be sure that the Original Copy option button is selected and then click the OK button.
5. Click the Finish button.
6. Close the Data window.

The replica is created and placed in the New Briefcase folder.

Using a Replica

You can use a replica similar to any other database, except that you cannot change the structure of any of the objects in your database. Perform the steps on the next page to add a record and change one of the names in the replica, which is stored in the New Briefcase folder.

More About

Replication

When many users are each using their own replicas, potential problems in synchronizing the data exist. A user adding a work order for a customer in one replica, while another user is deleting the same customer from a different replica would pose problems during synchronization. For more information concerning replication, visit the Access 2002 More About page (scsite.com/ac2002/more.htm) and then click Replication.

More About

Encryption

The encryption process requires Access to make an additional copy of the database, which is called the encrypted version. Once the process is complete, the original will be deleted. During the process, however, there must be sufficient disk space available for both versions of the database. If not, the process will fail.

Steps To Use the Replica

1 **Click the Start button, click Programs on the Start menu, and then click Microsoft Access on the Programs submenu. Click Open on the Database toolbar, and then click New Briefcase in the Look in box. Make sure the Lebond Industries database is selected and then click the Open button. If your briefcase is on the desktop, you will need to click Desktop in the Look in box to locate New Briefcase.**

2 **Right-click Client and then point to Open on the shortcut menu.**

The shortcut menu displays (Figure 9-32). The symbol in front of Client indicates that it is a replica.

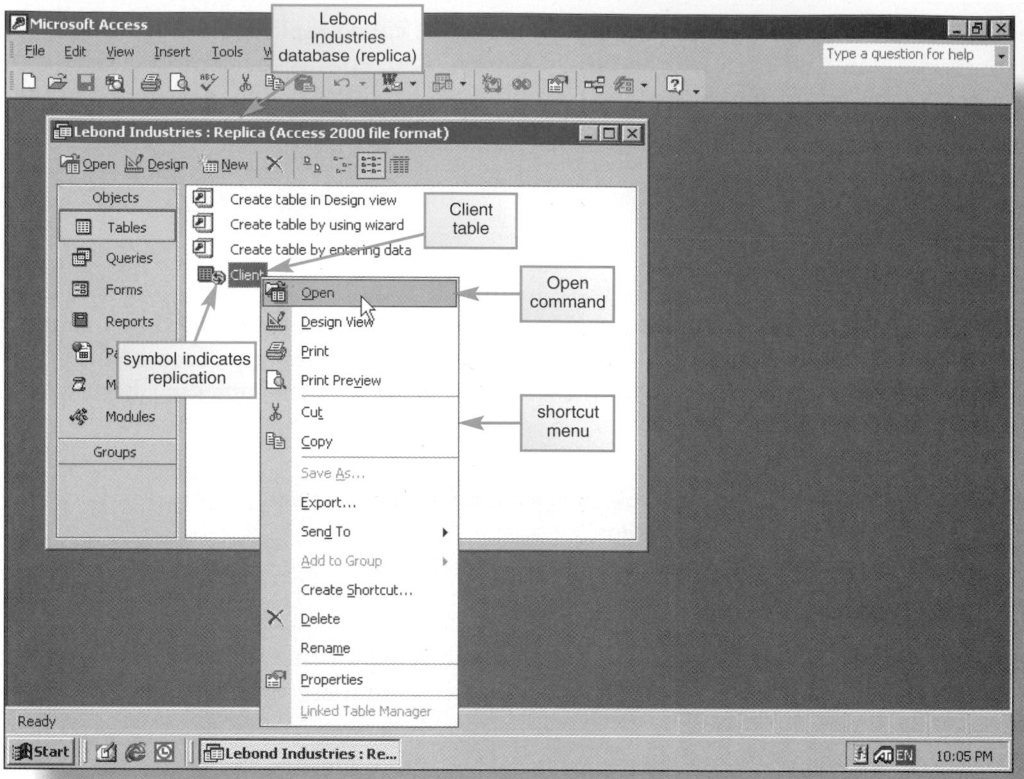

FIGURE 9-32

3 **Click Open and then click the New Record button. Type the final record shown in Figure 9-33.**

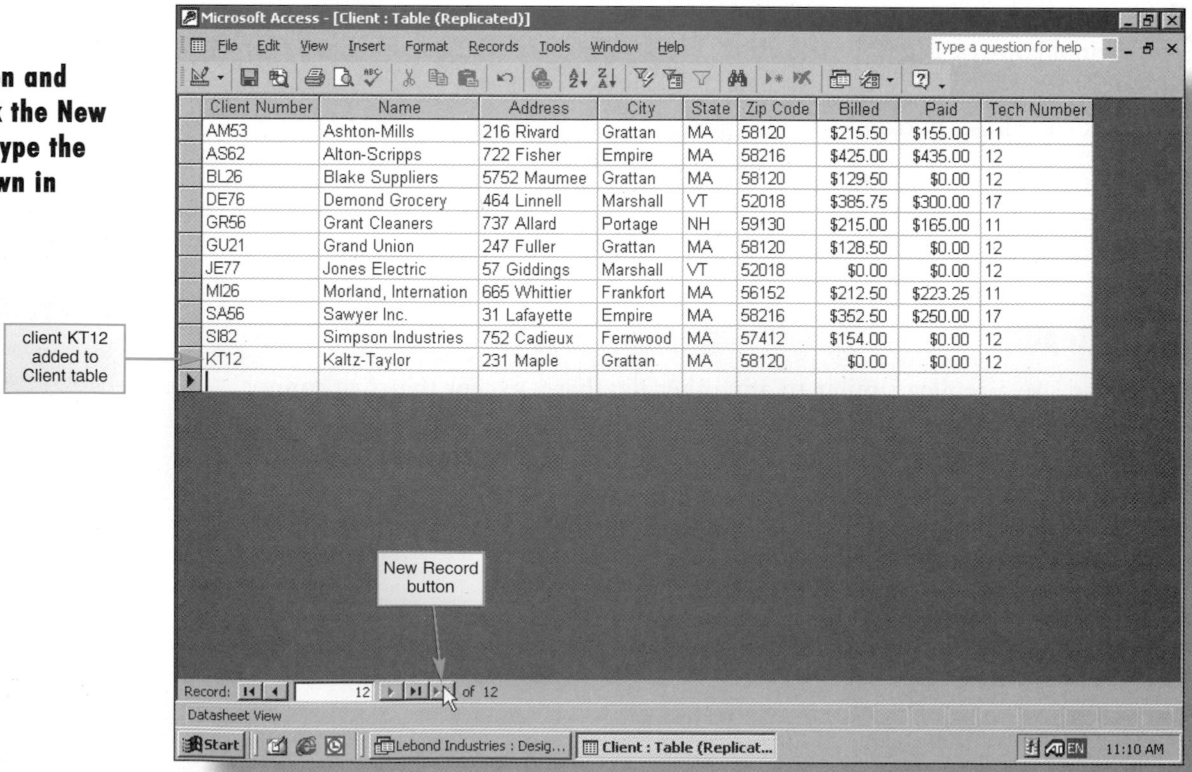

FIGURE 9-33

4 Click the name of client number BL26, and then change the name from Blake Suppliers to Blake Supply.

The changes are made (Figure 9-34).

5 Click the Close button for the window containing the Client table.

The table no longer displays.

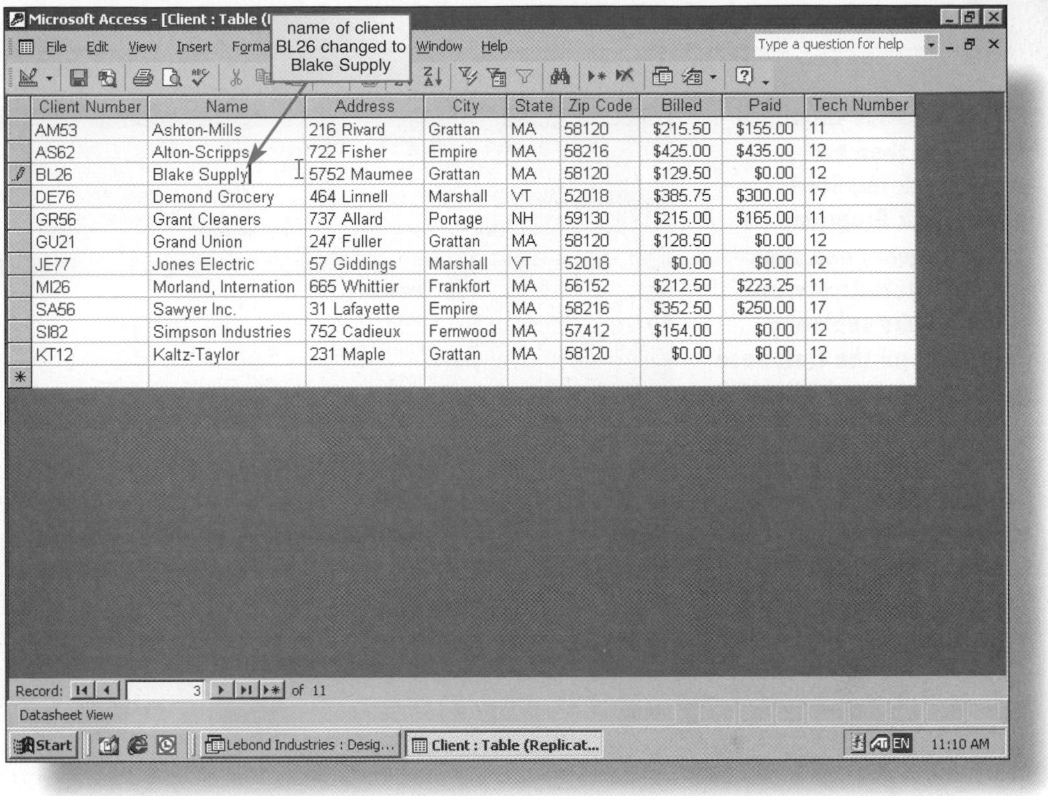

FIGURE 9-34

Synchronizing the Design Master and the Replica

Now that the replica has been updated, the data in the Design Master and the data in the replica no longer match. In order for them to match, the updates to the replica also must be made to the Design Master. Microsoft Access will make these updates automatically, using a process called **synchronization**. Perform the steps on the next page to synchronize the Design Master and the replica.

Steps To Synchronize the Design Master and the Replica

1 Close the database and then exit Access. Click the Start button, click Programs on the Start menu, and then click Microsoft Access on the Programs submenu. Click Open on the Database toolbar, click Local Disk (C:) in the Look in box, and then click the Data folder. Make sure the Lebond Industries database is selected.

2 Click the Open button arrow (not the button itself). Click Open Exclusive in the list that displays.

The database opens in exclusive mode and the Lebond Industries : Database window displays.

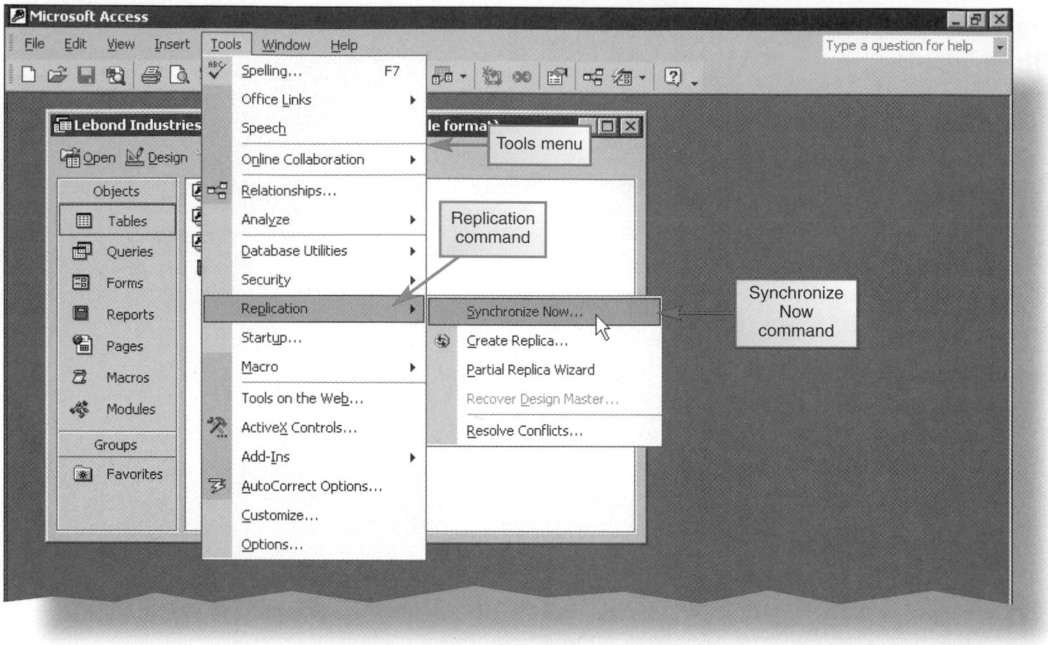

FIGURE 9-35

3 Click Tools on the menu bar, click Replication on the Tools menu, and then point to Synchronize Now on the Replication submenu (Figure 9-35).

4 Click Synchronize Now. If necessary, click the Directly with Replica option button in the Synchronize Database 'Lebond Industries' dialog box and then click the OK button. When a message displays indicating that Microsoft Access must close the database in order to perform the synchronization, click the Yes button.

The databases are synchronized. Access displays the message shown in Figure 9-36 when the process is complete.

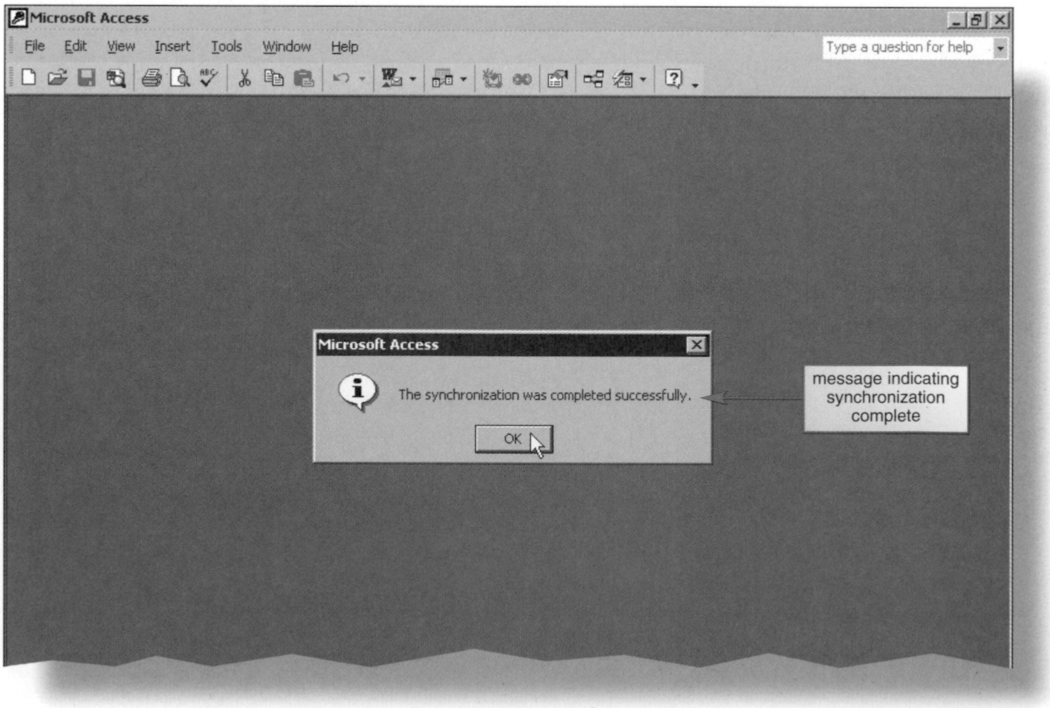

FIGURE 9-36

The data in the replicated database (the Design Master) now incorporates the changes made earlier to the replica, as shown in Figure 9-37.

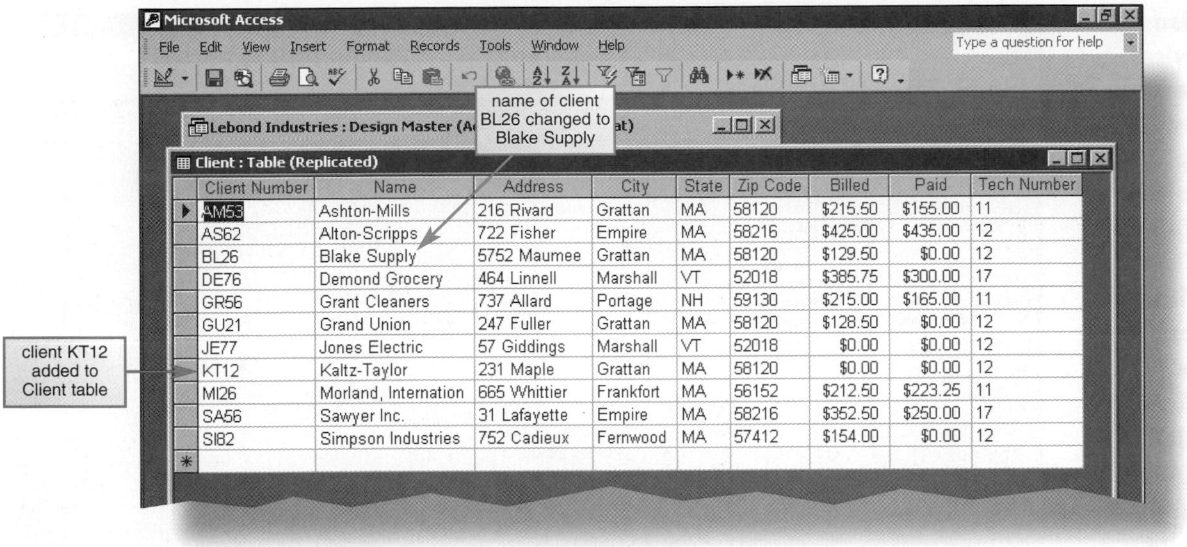

Client Number	Name	Address	City	State	Zip Code	Billed	Paid	Tech Number
AM53	Ashton-Mills	216 Rivard	Grattan	MA	58120	$215.50	$155.00	11
AS62	Alton-Scripps	722 Fisher	Empire	MA	58216	$425.00	$435.00	12
BL26	Blake Supply	5752 Maumee	Grattan	MA	58120	$129.50	$0.00	12
DE76	Demond Grocery	464 Linnell	Marshall	VT	52018	$385.75	$300.00	17
GR56	Grant Cleaners	737 Allard	Portage	NH	59130	$215.00	$165.00	11
GU21	Grand Union	247 Fuller	Grattan	MA	58120	$128.50	$0.00	12
JE77	Jones Electric	57 Giddings	Marshall	VT	52018	$0.00	$0.00	12
KT12	Kaltz-Taylor	231 Maple	Grattan	MA	58120	$0.00	$0.00	12
MI26	Morland, Internation	665 Whittier	Frankfort	MA	56152	$212.50	$223.25	11
SA56	Sawyer Inc.	31 Lafayette	Empire	MA	58216	$352.50	$250.00	17
SI82	Simpson Industries	752 Cadieux	Fernwood	MA	57412	$154.00	$0.00	12

FIGURE 9-37

Closing the Database

The following step closes the database by closing its Database window.

TO CLOSE A DATABASE

1 Click the Close button for the Lebond Industries : Design Master window.

Other Ways

1. In Voice Command mode, say "Tools, Replication, Synchronize Now"

PivotTables and PivotCharts

There are two alternatives to viewing data in Datasheet view or Form view. **PivotTable view** presents data as a **PivotTable**, that is, an interactive table that summarizes or analyzes data. In a PivotTable you can show different levels of detail easily as well as change the organization or layout of the table by dragging items. You also can filter data by checking or unchecking values in drop-down lists. **PivotChart view** presents data as a **PivotChart**, that is, a graphical representation of the data. In a PivotChart, just as in a PivotTable, you can show different levels of detail or change the layout by dragging items. You also can filter data by checking or unchecking values in drop-down lists. You can change the type of chart that displays as well as customize the chart by adding axis titles, a chart title, and a legend. In this section, you will create a PivotTable and a PivotChart. Both the PivotTable and the PivotChart are based on a query.

Creating a Query

Because the PivotTable and PivotChart you will create will be based on a query, you first must create the query. The steps on the next page create the necessary query.

Steps To Create the Query

1 **Open the Alisa Vending Services database. When the Main Switchboard window displays, close it by clicking its Close button. If necessary, click Tables on the Objects bar, and then click Driver. Click the New Object: AutoForm button arrow on the Database toolbar. Click Query. Be sure Design View is selected, and then click the OK button. If necessary, maximize the Query1 : Select Query window. Resize the upper and lower panes and the Driver field list so all the fields in the Driver table display.**

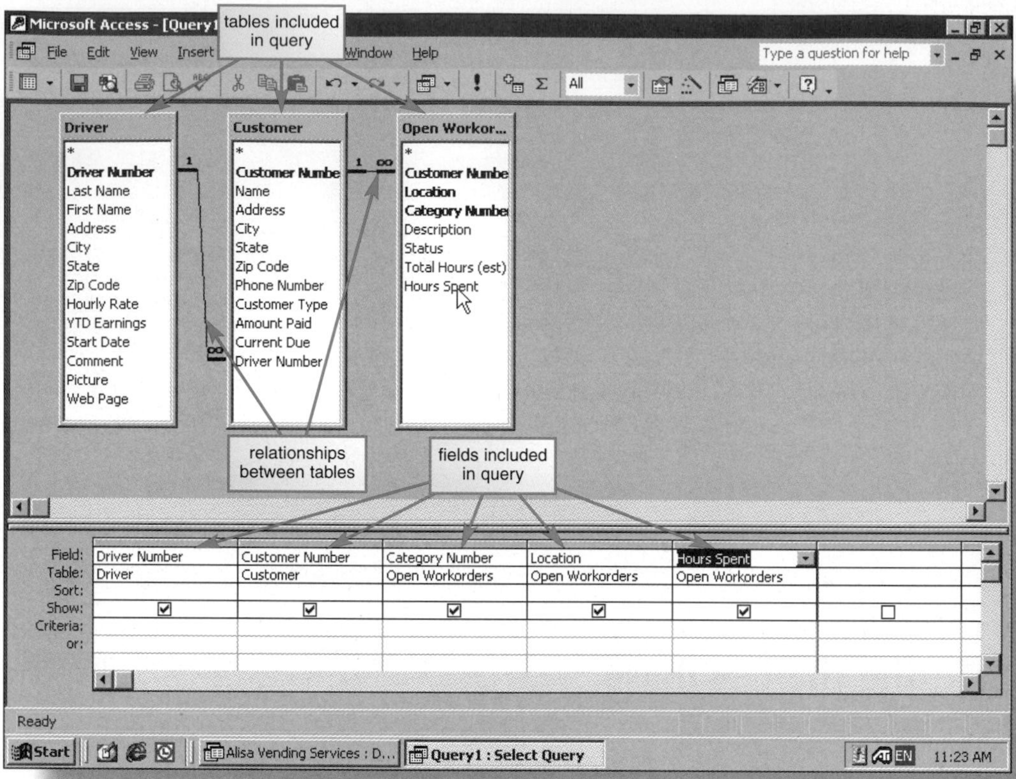

FIGURE 9-38

2 **Right-click any open area in the upper pane, click Show Table on the shortcut menu, click the Customer table, click the Add button, click the Open Workorders table, click the Add button, and then click the Close button in the Show Table dialog box. Resize the Customer and Open Workorders field lists so all the fields display. Double-click the Driver Number field from the Driver table and the Customer Number field from the Customer table. Double-click the Category Number, Location, and Hours Spent fields from the Open Workorders table.**

The tables are related and the fields are selected (Figure 9-38).

3 **Right-click the Field row in the first open column, click Zoom on the shortcut menu, type** `Hours Remaining:[Total Hours (est)]-[Hours Spent]` **in the Zoom dialog box, and then point to the OK button.**

The expression for Hours Remaining is entered (Figure 9-39).

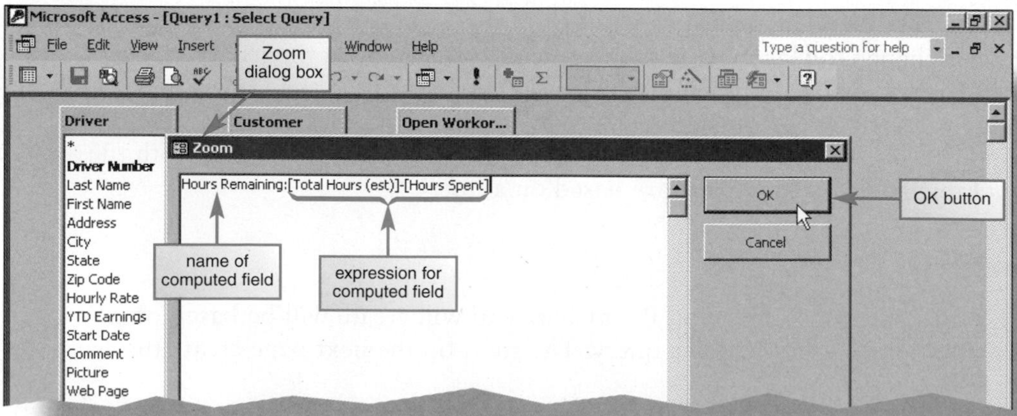

FIGURE 9-39

4 Click the OK button, click the Run button on the Query Design toolbar to ensure your results are correct, click the Close Window button for the window containing the query results, and then point to the Yes button.

The query results display (Figure 9-40). (If your results do not look like the ones shown in the figure, return to the query design and make any necessary changes, before attempting to close and save the query.)

5 Click the Yes button, type `Drivers and Workorders` **as the name of the query, and then click the OK button.**

The query is saved.

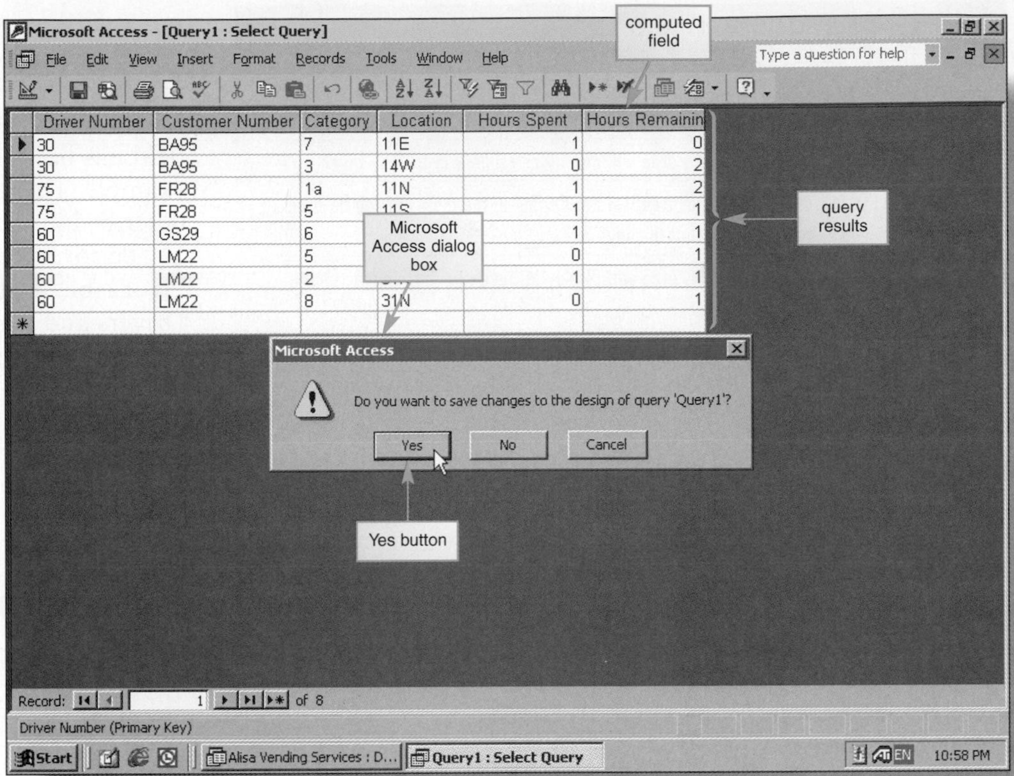

FIGURE 9-40

PivotTables

Figure 9-41 shows a sample PivotTable. The rows in the table represent the service categories. The columns represent the driver numbers. Each column is subdivided into the total of the hours spent and the total of the hours remaining for work orders for those customers assigned to the driver. The last column shows the grand total for the items in each row. The last row shows the grand total for items in each column.

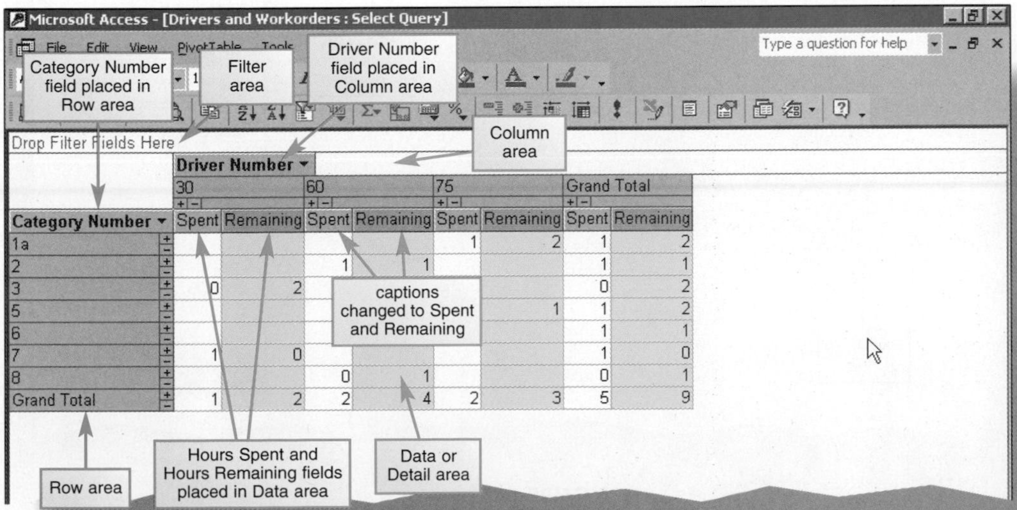

FIGURE 9-41

Table 9-2 PivotTable Drop Areas	
AREA	PURPOSE
Row	Data from fields in this area will display as rows in the table.
Column	Data from fields in this area will display as columns in the table.
Filter	Data from fields in this area will not display in the table but can be used to restrict the data that displays.
Detail	Data from fields in this area will display in the detail portion (the body) of the table.
Data	Summary data (for example, a sum) from fields in this area will display in the detail portion (the body) of the table. Individual values will not display.

To create the PivotTable, you place fields in predefined areas of the table called **drop areas**. In the PivotTable in Figure 9-41 on the previous page, the Category Number field has been placed in the Row area, for example. The drop areas are listed and described in Table 9-2.

Perform the following steps to create a PivotTable using the PivotTable view of the Drivers and Workorders query and to place fields in appropriate drop areas.

Steps To Create a PivotTable

1 Click Queries on the Objects bar, right-click the Drivers and Workorders query, and then click Open on the shortcut menu. Click the View button arrow, and then point to PivotTable View.

The query displays in Datasheet view (Figure 9-42).

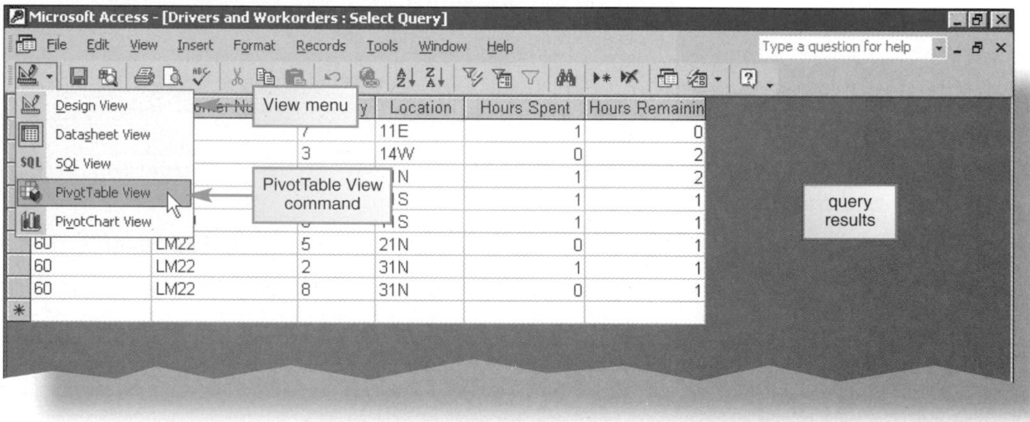

FIGURE 9-42

2 Click PivotTable View. If the PivotTable Field List does not display, click the Field List button on the PivotTable toolbar to display the field list. Click Category Number in the field list, be sure Row Area displays next to the Add to button, and then point to the Add to button.

The PivotTable displays (Figure 9-43). Category Number is selected in the field list and Row Area is selected.

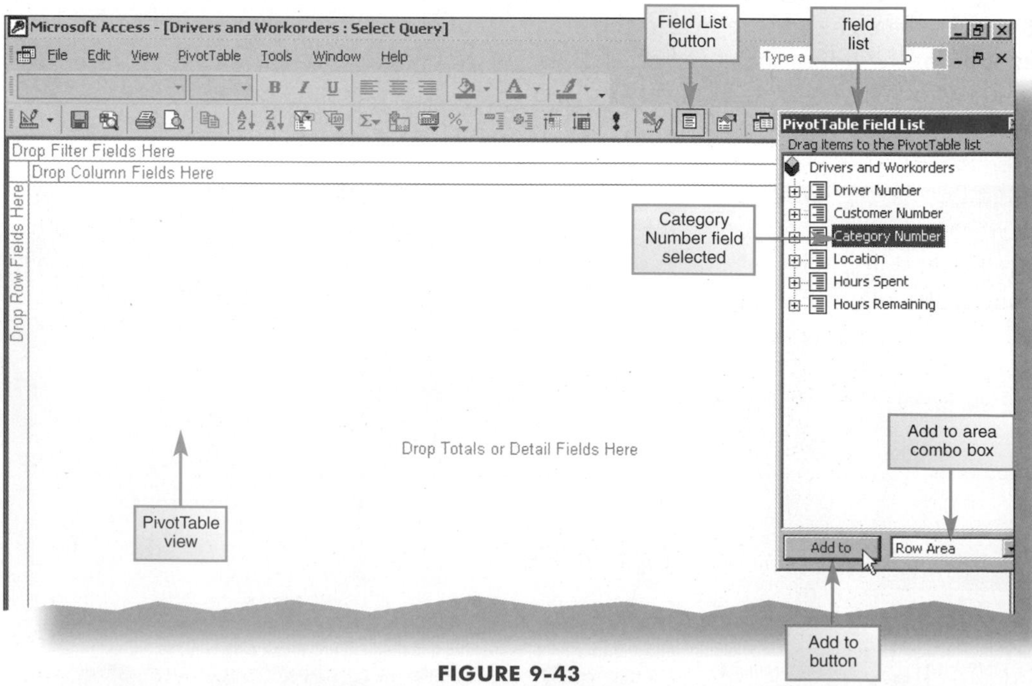

FIGURE 9-43

3 **Click the Add to button to add the Category Number field to the Row area. Click the Driver Number field, click the arrow to display the list of available areas, and then point to Column Area.**

The list of available areas displays (Figure 9-44). The Driver Number field is selected.

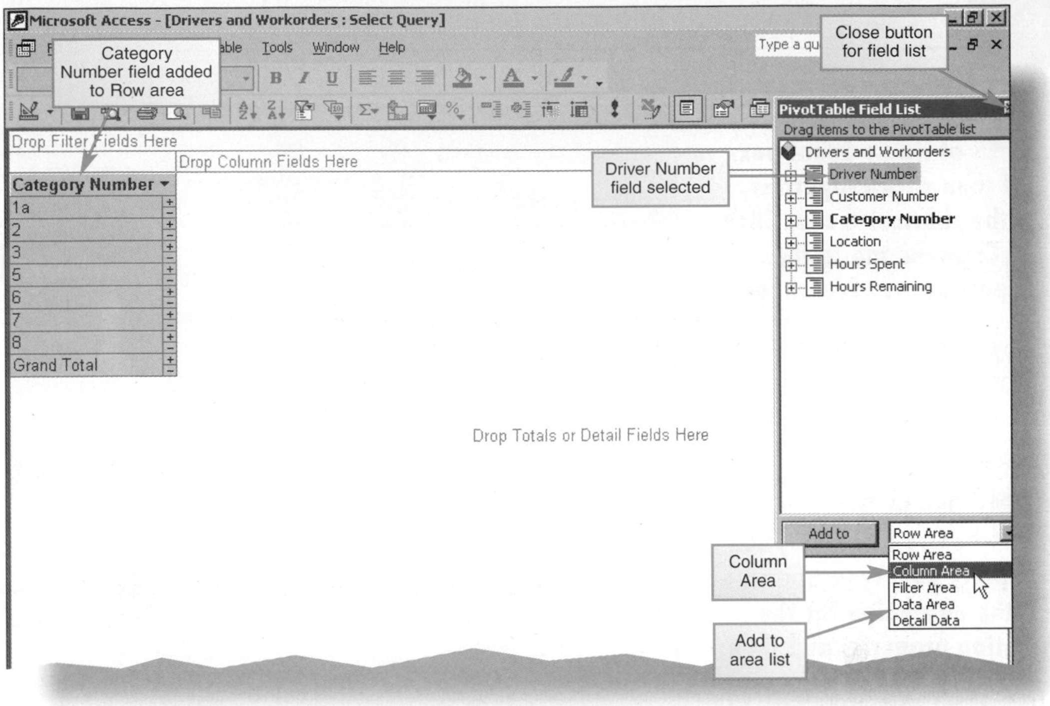

FIGURE 9-44

4 **Click Column Area, and then click the Add to button to add the Driver Number field to the Column area. Click Hours Spent, click the arrow to display the list of available areas, click Data Area, and then click the Add to button to add the Hours Spent field to the Data area. Use the same technique to add the Hours Remaining field to the Data area. Close the PivotTable Field List by clicking its Close button. Point to the Sum of Hours Spent box under driver number 30.**

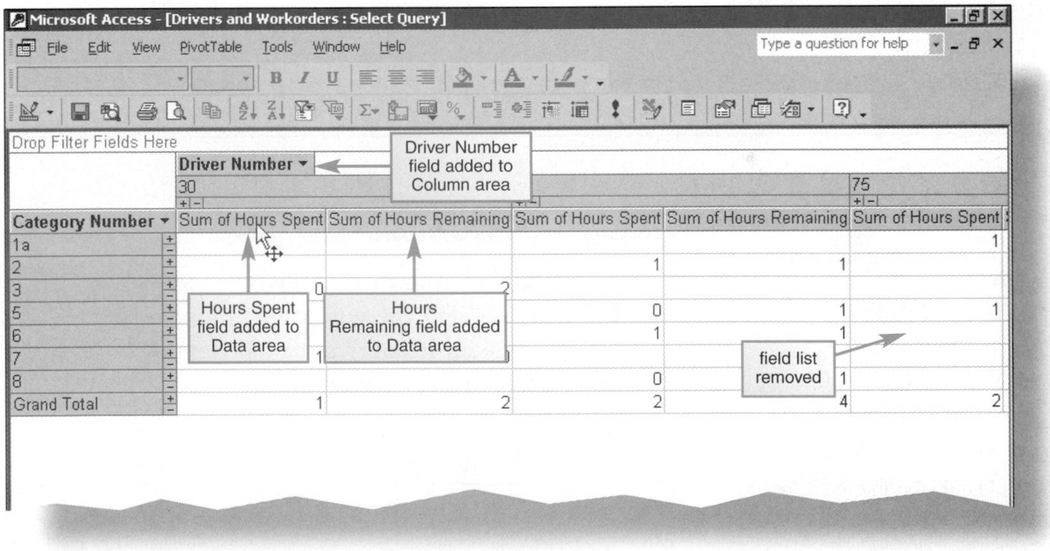

FIGURE 9-45

The fields have been added to appropriate areas of the PivotTable (Figure 9-45).

Changing Properties in a PivotTable

You can use the property sheet for the objects in a PivotTable to change characteristics of the objects. The steps on the next page use the appropriate property sheet to change the caption for Sum of Hours Spent to Spent and for Sum of Hours Remaining to Remaining in order to reduce the size of the columns in the PivotTable.

Other Ways

1. On View menu click PivotTable View
2. In Voice Command mode, say "View, PivotTable View"

Steps To Change Properties in a PivotTable

1 Right-click the Sum of Hours Spent box, and then click Properties on the shortcut menu. Click the Captions tab in the Properties property sheet.

The property sheet and the Caption property display (Figure 9-46).

2 Delete the current entry in the Caption property box, type `Spent` **as the new value for the Caption property, and then close the property sheet. Use the same technique to change the caption for the Sum of Hours Remaining box to Remaining.**

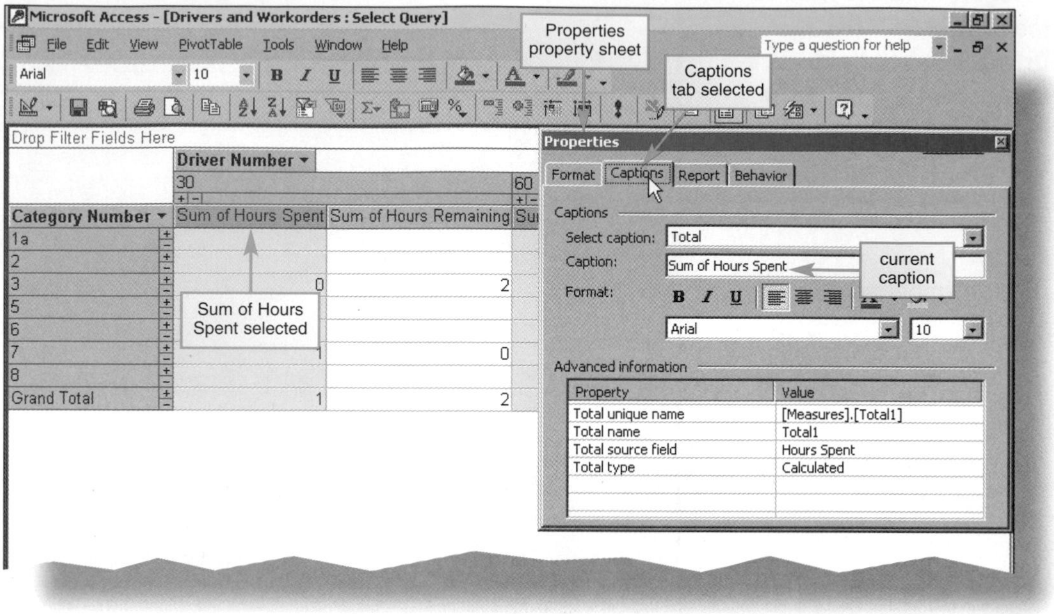

FIGURE 9-46

The captions are changed and match the ones shown in Figure 9-41 on page A 9.31.

More About

PivotTables

PivotTable views are a new feature of Access 2002. You do not need to create a query to view fields in PivotTable view. To display data in a table in PivotTable view, open the table in Datasheet view, click the View button arrow on the Table Datasheet toolbar, and then click PivotTable View in the list.

Saving the PivotTable Changes

To save the changes to the PivotTable view of the query, you save the query. You can do so, by closing the window containing the PivotTable and then clicking the Yes button when asked if you want to save your changes. The following steps close the window and then save the changes.

TO CLOSE AND SAVE THE PIVOTTABLE CHANGES

1. Click the Close Window button for the window containing the PivotTable.
2. Click the Yes button in the Microsoft Access dialog box.

The changes to the layout of the query are saved. In particular, the changes to the PivotTable view of the query are saved.

Using a PivotTable

To use a PivotTable, you must open it. If the PivotTable is associated with a query, this would involve opening the query and then switching to PivotTable view. You then can click appropriate plus (+) or minus (–) signs to hide or show data. You also can click appropriate arrows and then check or uncheck the various items that display to restrict the data that displays. You can drag items from one location to another to change the layout of the PivotTable. Perform the following steps to use the PivotTable view of the Drivers and Workorders query.

Steps To Use a PivotTable

1 If necessary, click Queries on the Objects bar, right-click the Drivers and Workorders query, and then click Open on the shortcut menu. Click the View button arrow, and then click PivotTable View. Click the plus sign (+) under driver number 30.

The PivotTable displays (Figure 9-47). Data for driver number 30 is hidden, that is, it does not display. The column heading is changed to No Details. By clicking the appropriate plus sign, you also can hide the data for category numbers or the Grand Total data.

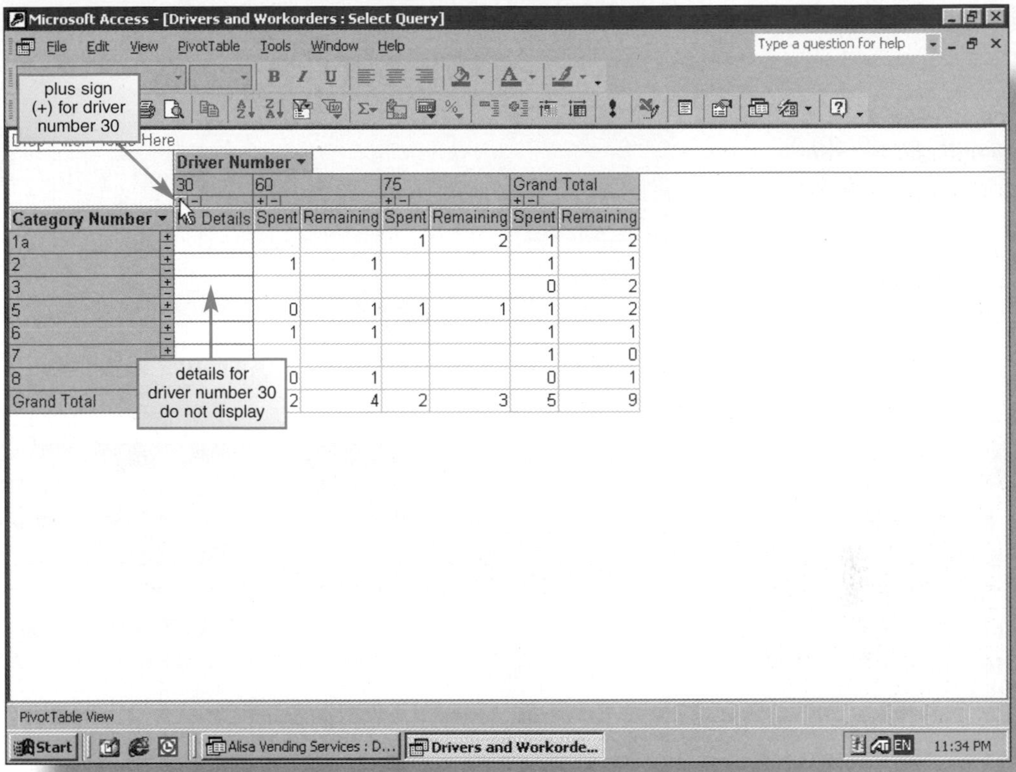

FIGURE 9-47

2 Click the minus sign (–) under driver number 30 to again display data for driver number 30. Click the Driver Number arrow.

The list of available driver numbers displays (Figure 9-48). Removing a check mark on a driver number causes that driver to be hidden, that is, the driver number will not display.

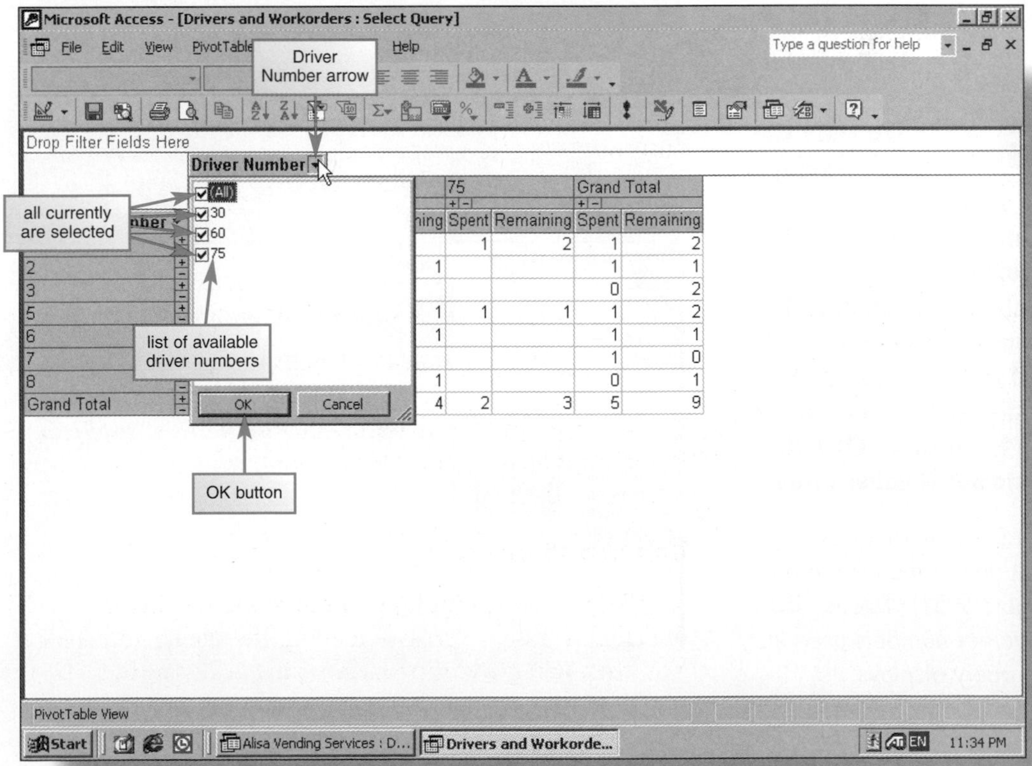

FIGURE 9-48

3 Click the check box for driver number 60 to remove the check mark and then click the OK button.

Driver number 60 does not display (Figure 9-49).

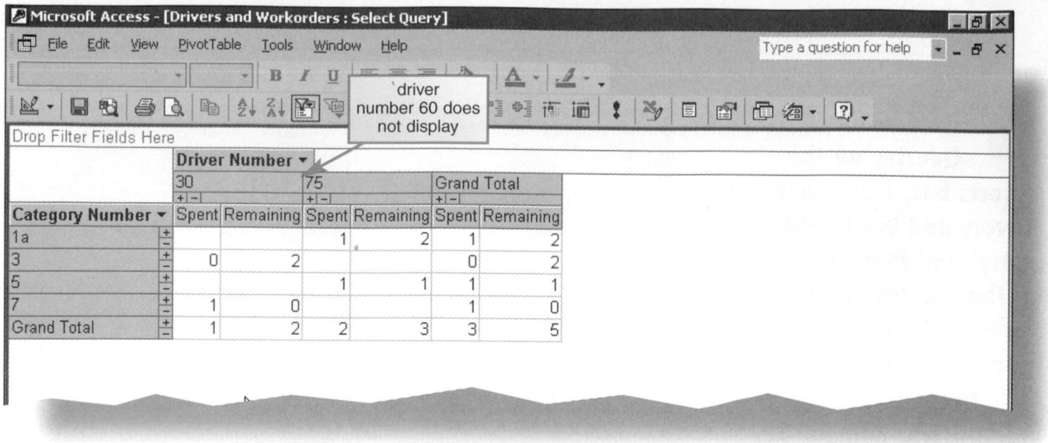

FIGURE 9-49

4 Click the Driver Number arrow, click the All check box to display all driver numbers, click the OK button, and then point to the Field List button on the PivotTable toolbar.

All driver numbers display (Figure 9-50).

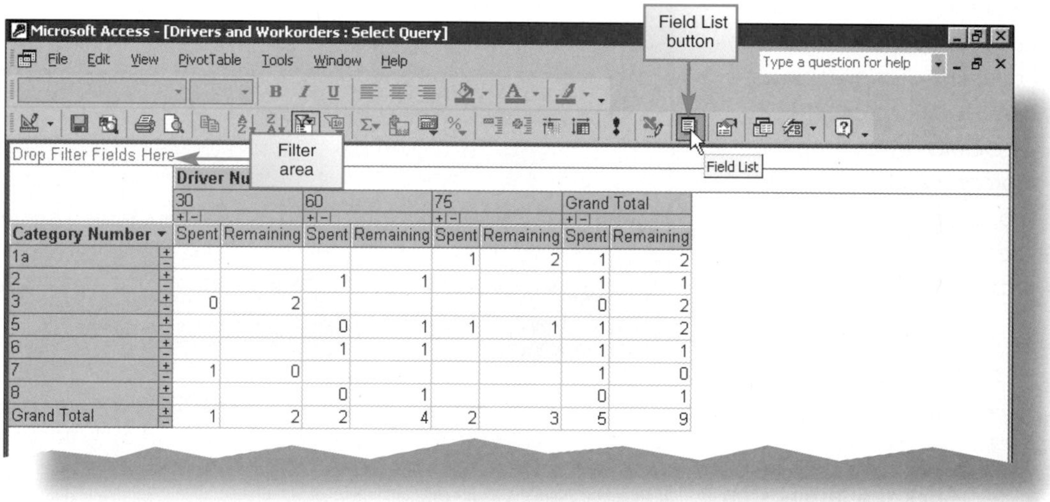

FIGURE 9-50

5 Click the Field List button to display the field list. Click Customer Number, click the arrow to display a list of available areas, click Filter Area, and then click the Add to button to add the Customer Number field to the Filter area. Click the Customer Number arrow.

The Customer Number field is added to the Filter area (Figure 9-51). The list of customer numbers used in the query displays.

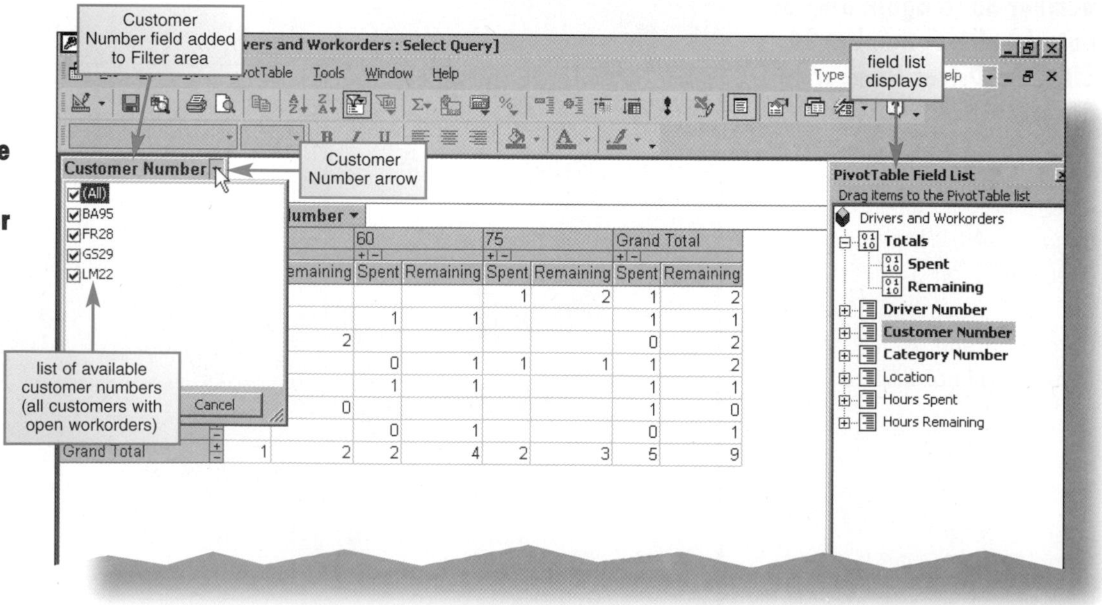

FIGURE 9-51

6 Click the check boxes in front of customers GS29 and LM22 to remove the check marks, and then click the OK button.

The data displaying in the PivotTable is changed (Figure 9-52). The data displaying does not include any amounts for customers GS29 or LM22.

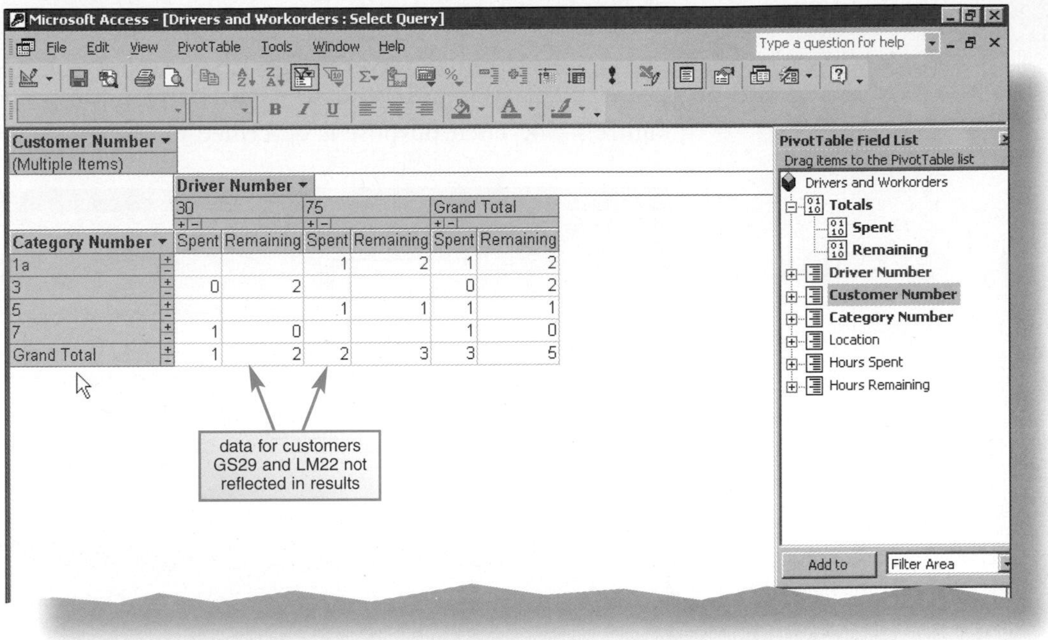

FIGURE 9-52

7 Click the Customer Number arrow, click the (All) check box, and then click the OK button to display data for all customers. Drag the Driver Number field from the Row area to the Column area, and then drag the Category Number field from the Column area to the Row area.

The rows and columns in the PivotTable are reversed (Figure 9-53).

8 Click the Close Window button for the window containing the PivotTable. Click the No button when asked if you want to save your changes.

The PivotTable is closed. The changes are not saved. The next time you open the PivotTable, the changes you just made will not be reflected.

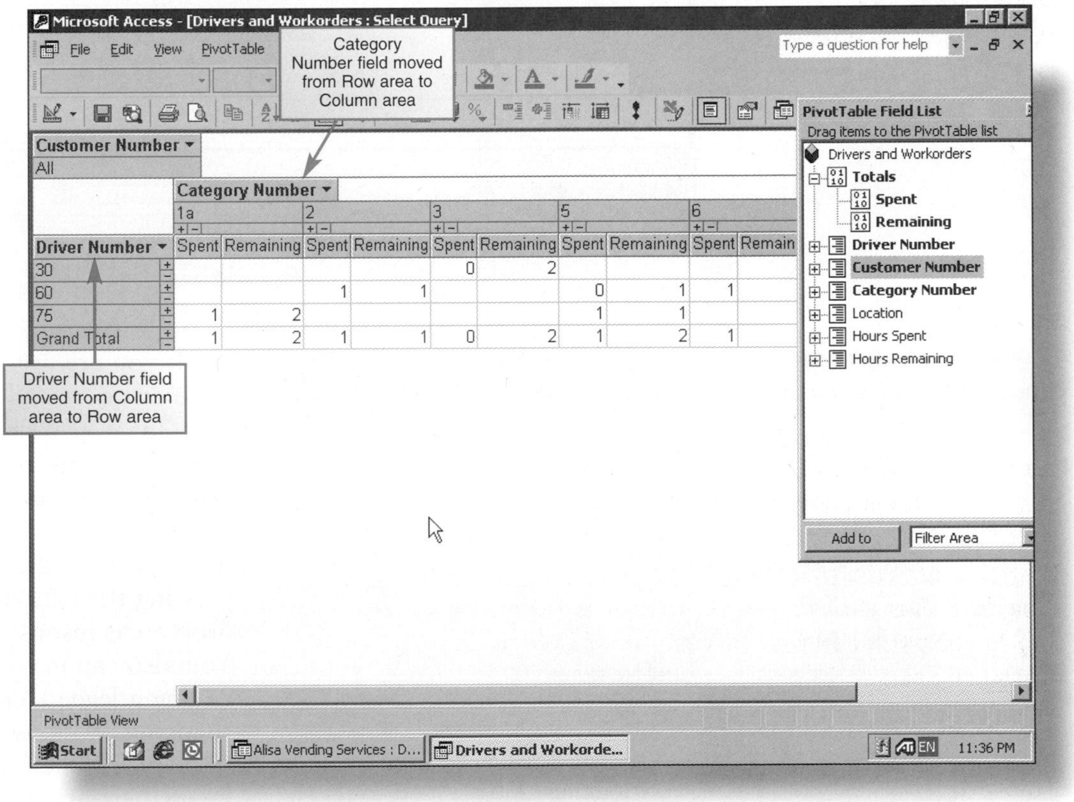

FIGURE 9-53

PivotCharts

You can create a PivotChart from scratch by placing fields in appropriate drop areas just as you did when you created a PivotTable. The drop areas are shown in Figure 9-54. Their purpose is described in Table 9-3.

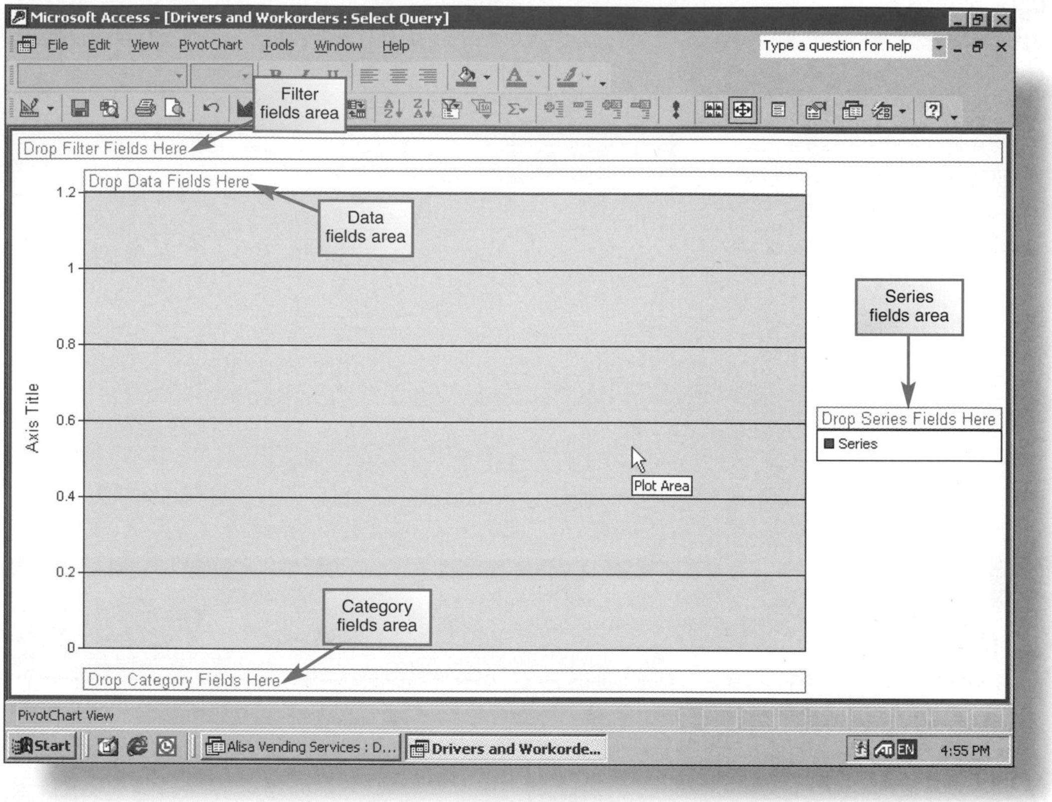

FIGURE 9-54

Table 9-3 PivotChart Drop Areas

AREA	*PURPOSE*
Series	Data from fields in this area will display as data series, which are represented by colored data markers such as bars. Related markers constitute a series and are assigned a specific color. The names and colors appear in the chart legend.
Category	Data from fields in this area will display as categories, that is, related groups of data. Category labels display across the x-axis (horizontal) of the chart provided the graph type selected has such an axis.
Filter	Data from fields in this area will not display in the chart but can be used to restrict the data that displays.
Data	Data from fields in this area will be summarized within the chart.

If you are using the PivotChart view of a table or query and already have modified the PivotTable view, much of this work already is done. The same information is used wherever possible. You can, of course, modify any aspect of this information. You can remove fields from drop areas by clicking the field name and then pressing the DELETE key. You can add fields to drop areas just as you did with the PivotTable. You also can make other changes, including adding a legend, changing the chart type, changing captions, and adding titles.

Perform the following steps to create a PivotChart using PivotChart view of the Drivers and Workorders query and to add a legend.

Steps To Create a PivotChart and Add a Legend

1 If necessary, click Queries on the Objects bar, right-click the Drivers and Workorders query, and then click Open on the shortcut menu. Click the View button arrow, and then click PivotChart View. If the Chart Field List displays, close the field list by clicking its Close button. Point to the Show Legend button on the PivotChart toolbar.

The PivotChart displays (Figure 9-55). It represents the same data specified in the PivotTable.

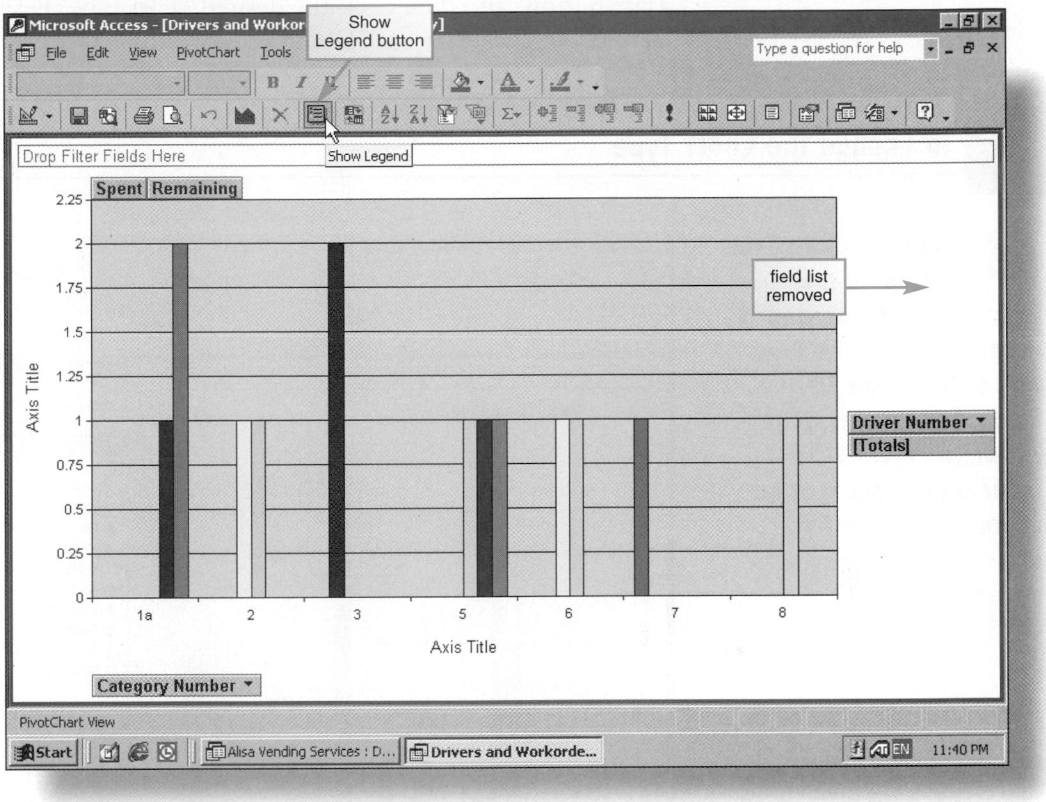

FIGURE 9-55

2 Click the Show Legend button, and then point to the Chart Type button on the PivotChart toolbar. If the Chart Type button is dimmed, click the white space in the chart. The Chart Type then will be available.

A legend displays (Figure 9-56).

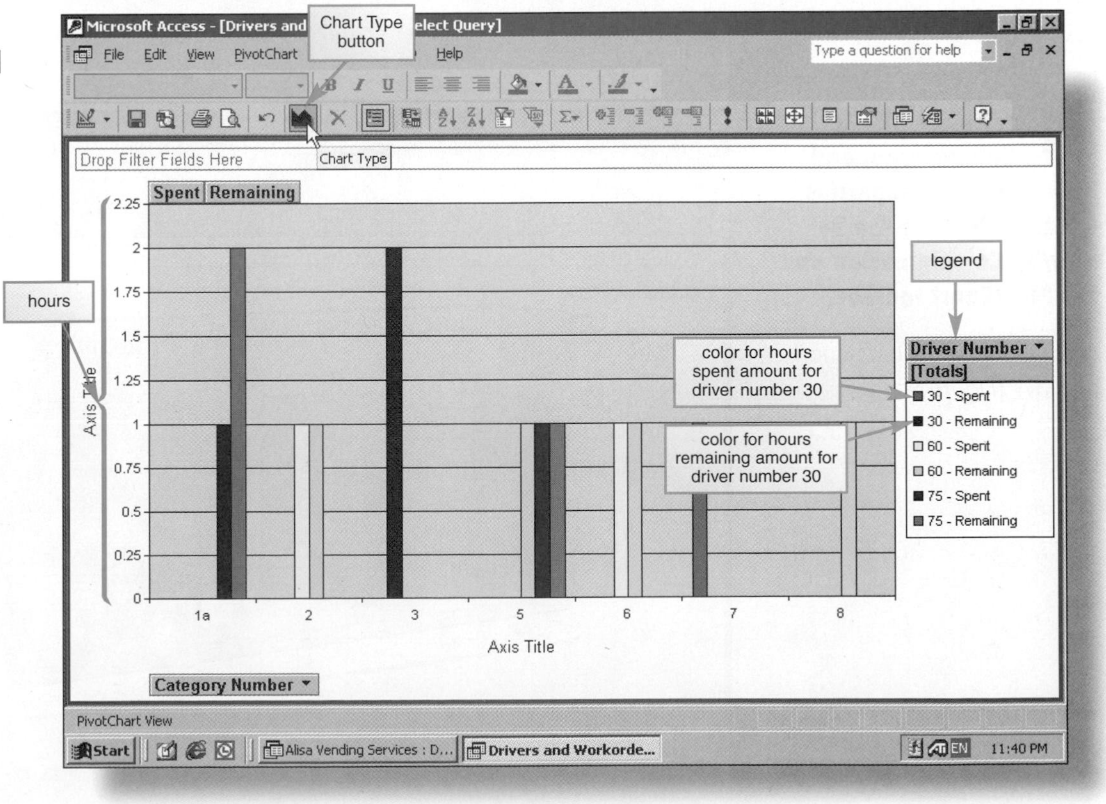

FIGURE 9-56

Changing the Chart Type

Several types of charts are available. To change the chart type, click the Chart Type button, and then click the desired chart type. Perform the following steps to change the chart type to 3D Stacked Column.

Steps To Change the Chart Type

1 **Click the Chart Type button on the PivotChart toolbar, and if necessary, click the Type tab. Point to the 3D Stacked Column type as shown in Figure 9-57 (your chart types may be arranged differently).**

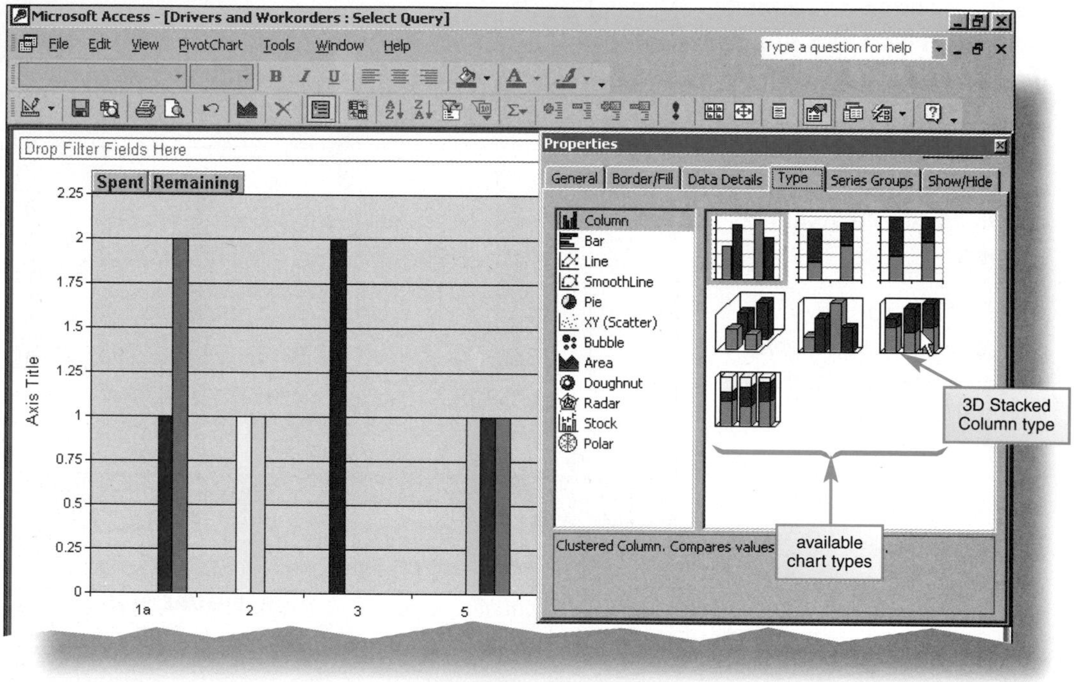

FIGURE 9-57

2 **Click the 3D Stacked Column type, and then close the Properties window. Point to the By Row/By Column button on the PivotChart toolbar.**

A 3D Stacked Column chart displays (Figure 9-58).

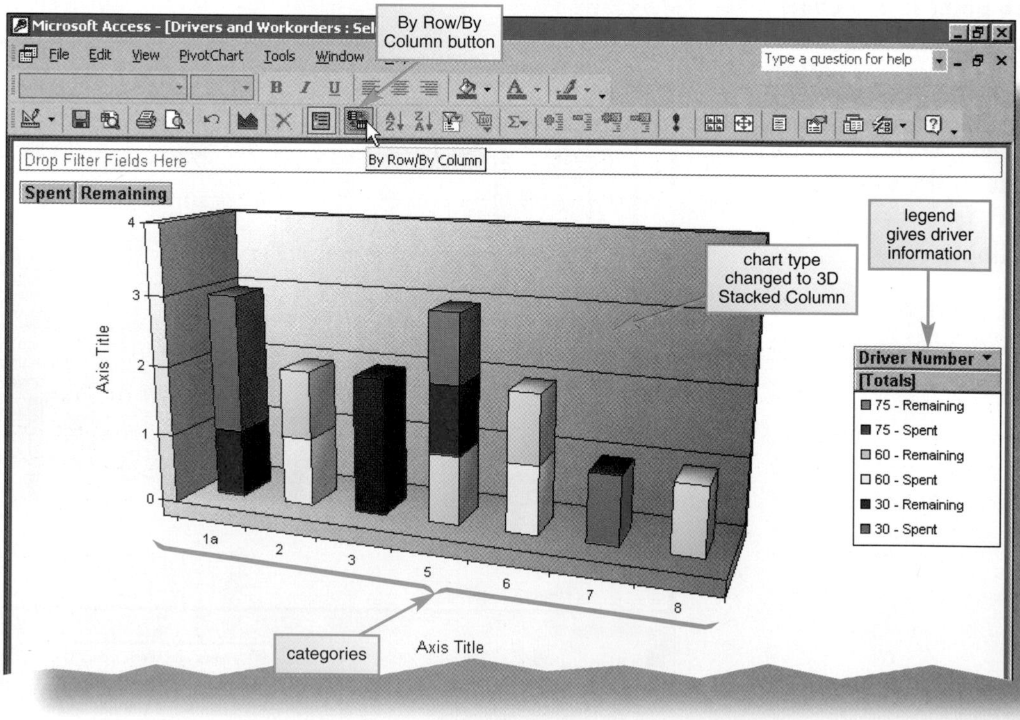

FIGURE 9-58

Changing PivotChart Organization

The chart in Figure 9-58 has the category numbers along the horizontal axis and driver numbers in the legend. The heights of the bars represent the total number of hours for each category. Within a bar, the colors represent the driver and whether the amount represents hours remaining or hours spent (see legend). To change the orientation, you can click the By Row/By Column button. Perform the following step so the driver numbers display along the horizontal axis and the categories display in the legend.

Steps To Change PivotChart Organization

1 Click the By Row/By Column button on the PivotChart toolbar.

The driver numbers now display along the x-axis and the categories display in the legend (Figure 9-59).

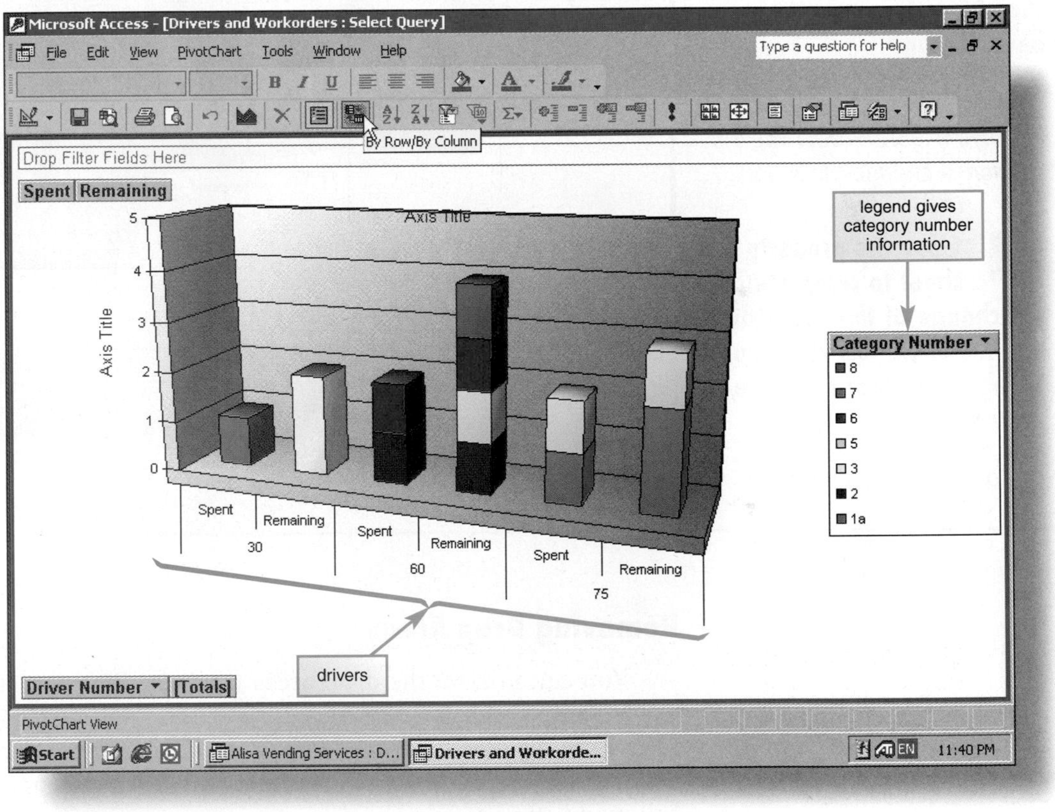

FIGURE 9-59

Assigning Axis Titles

You can assign titles to an axis by right-clicking the Axis Title box for the axis you want to change, clicking Properties on the shortcut menu, and then changing the Caption property to the title you want to assign. Perform the steps on the next page to change the two axis titles to Hours and Driver.

Steps To Assign Axis Titles

1 **Right-click the Axis Title to the left of the chart, and then click Properties on the shortcut menu. Click the Format tab in the Properties property sheet, click the Caption property box, use the BACKSPACE or DELETE key to delete the caption, and then type** `Hours` **as the new caption.**

The Properties property sheet displays (Figure 9-60). The caption is changed to Hours.

2 **Close the property sheet to complete the change of the axis title. Use the same technique to change the other axis title to Driver.**

The axis titles are changed.

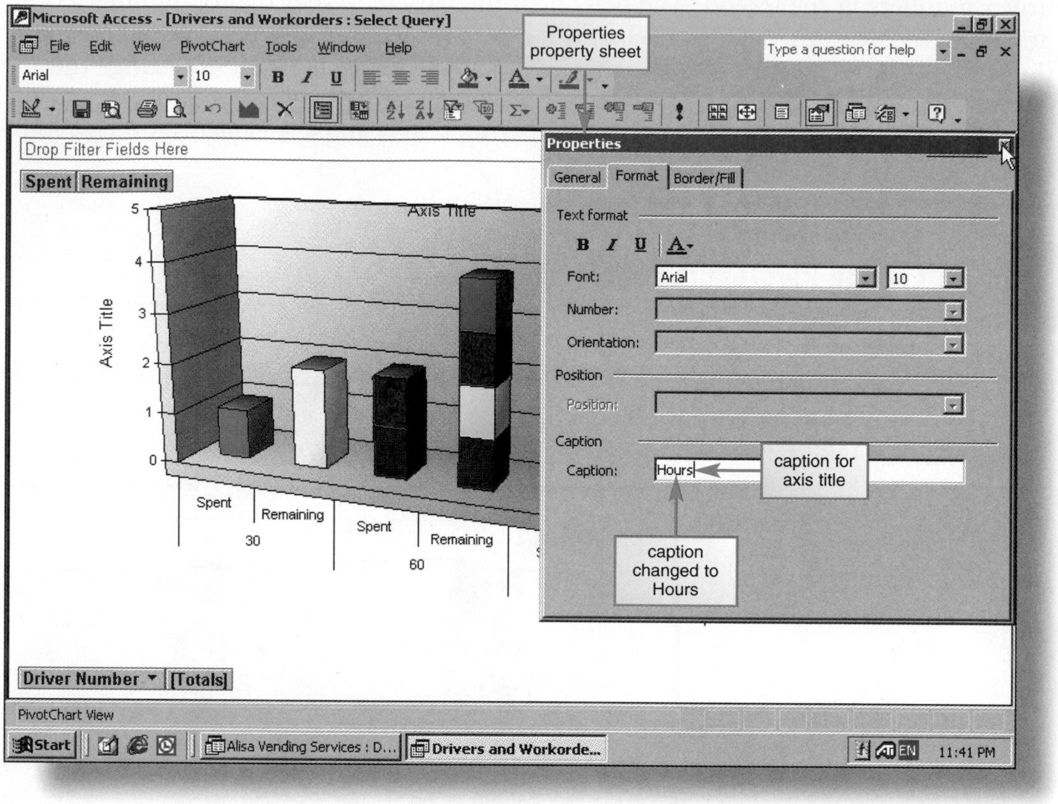

FIGURE 9-60

Removing Drop Areas

You can remove the drop areas from the PivotChart to give the chart a cleaner look. To do so, click the Drop Areas command on the View menu. If you later need to use the drop areas to perform some task, you can return them to the screen by clicking the Drop Areas command on the View menu a second time. Perform the following steps to remove the drop areas.

Steps To Remove Drop Areas

1 Click View on the menu bar, and then point to the Drop Areas command on the View menu (Figure 9-61).

2 Click Drop Areas on the View menu.

The drop areas no longer display.

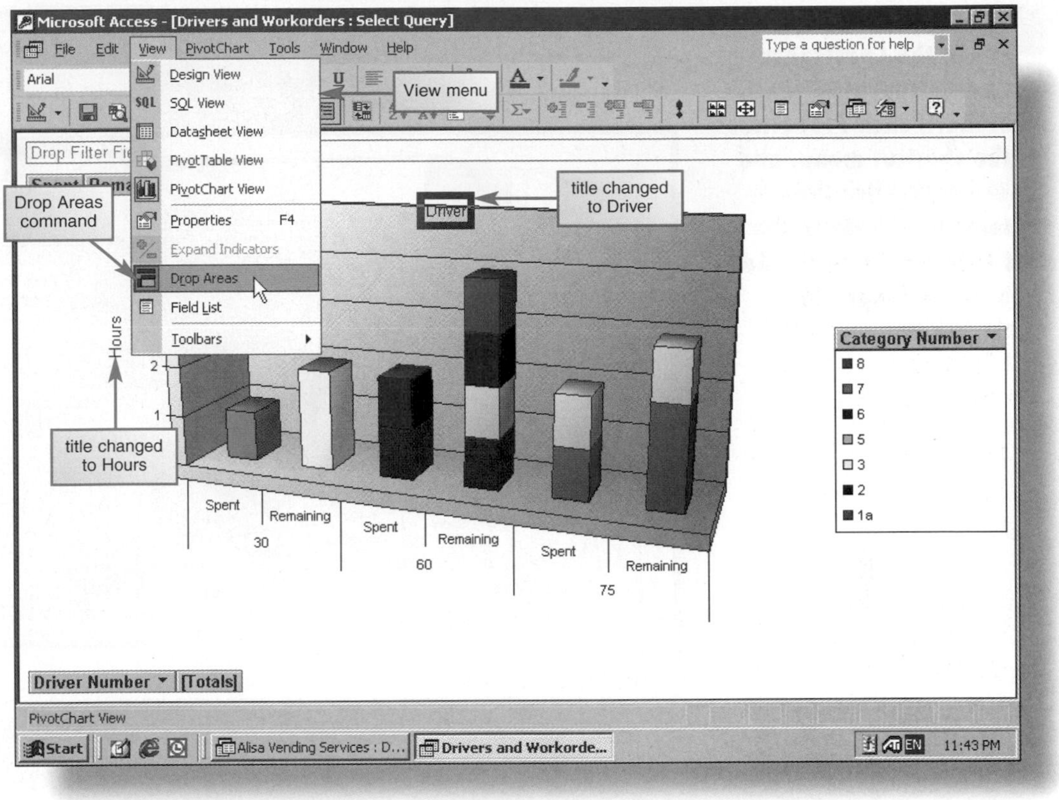

FIGURE 9-61

Adding a Chart Title

You can add a title to a PivotChart by clicking the Add Title button in the property sheet for the chart. You then can change the Caption property for the newly-added title to assign the title of your choice. Perform the steps on the next page to add a title to the PivotChart and then change the title's Caption property to Hours by Driver and Category.

Steps To Add a Chart Title

1 **Right-click anywhere in the Chartspace (the white space) of the PivotChart, click Properties on the shortcut menu, and if necessary, click the General tab. Point to the Add Title button in the Add area in the Properties property sheet.**

The property sheet displays (Figure 9-62). The General tab is selected.

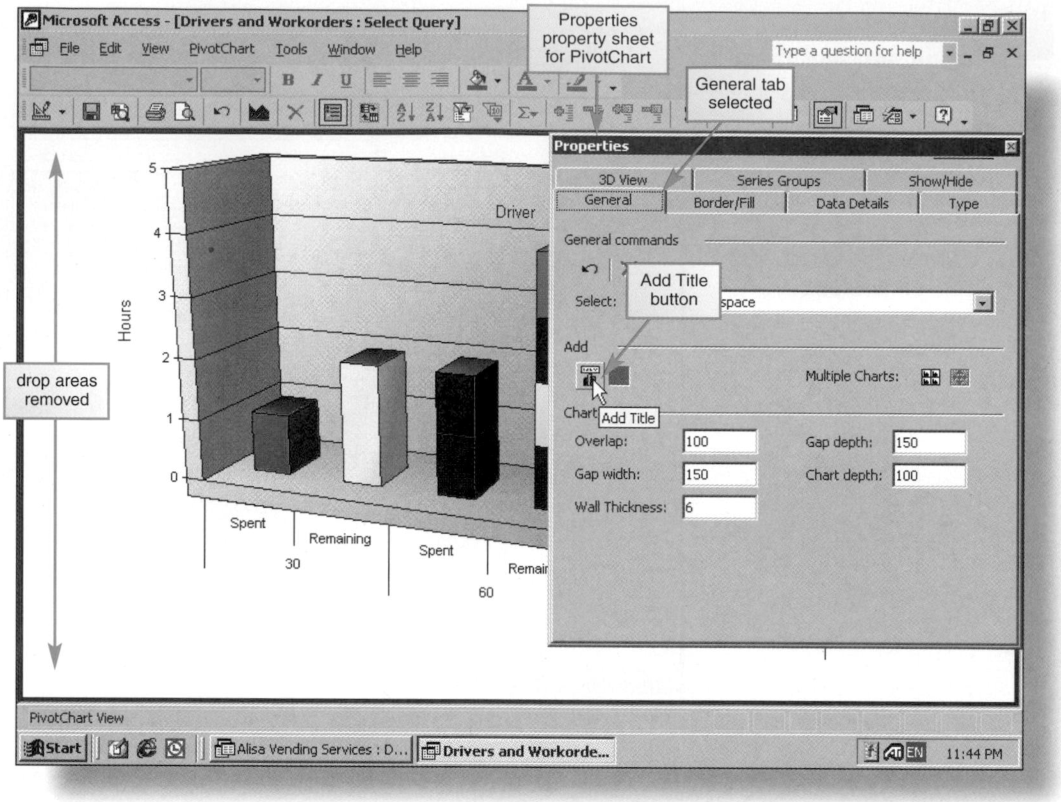

FIGURE 9-62

2 **Click the Add Title button, close the Properties property sheet, right-click the newly-added title, and click Properties on the shortcut menu. When the Properties property sheet displays, click the Format tab, and then type** `Hours by Driver and Category` **as the new caption. Point to the Close button for the property sheet.**

The property sheet displays (Figure 9-63). The caption is changed.

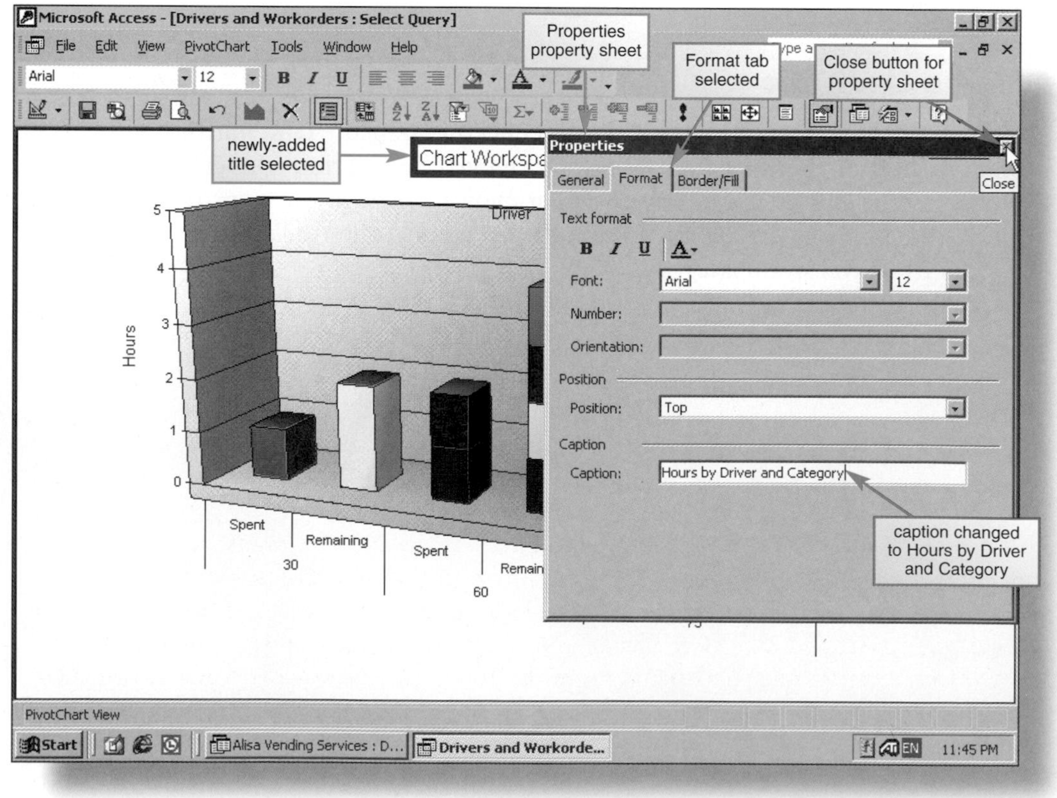

FIGURE 9-63

3 **Close the property sheet by clicking its Close button.**

The chart has a title (Figure 9-64).

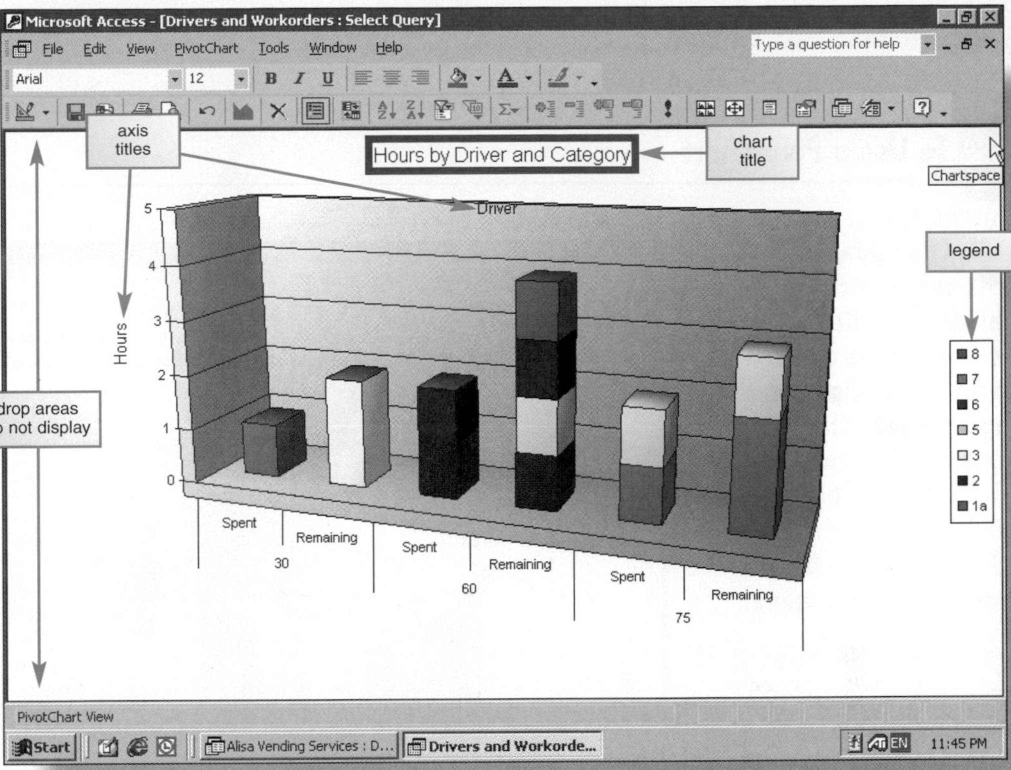

FIGURE 9-64

Other Ways

1. On View menu click PivotChart View
2. In Voice Command mode, say "View, PivotChart View"

Saving the PivotChart Changes

To save the changes to the PivotChart view of the query, you save the query. You can do so, by closing the window containing the PivotChart and then clicking the Yes button when asked if you want to save your changes. The following steps close the window and then save the changes.

TO CLOSE AND SAVE THE PIVOTCHART CHANGES

1 Click the Close Window button for the window containing the PivotChart.

2 Click the Yes button in the Microsoft Access dialog box.

The changes to the layout of the query are saved. In particular, the changes to the PivotChart view of the query are saved.

More About

PivotCharts

PivotChart views are a new feature of Access 2002. You do not need to create a query to view fields in PivotChart view. To display data in a table in PivotChart view, open the table in Datasheet view, click the View button arrow on the Table Datasheet toolbar, and then click PivotChart View in the list.

Using a PivotChart

To use a PivotChart, you first must open it. If the PivotChart is associated with a query, this would involve opening the query and then switching to PivotChart view. You then can click appropriate arrows and check or uncheck the various items that display to restrict the data that displays. In order to do so, the drop areas must display. If they do not, click Drop Areas on the View menu to display them. You then can click the arrows. You also can drag fields to the drop areas.

You can make the same types of changes you made when you first created the PivotChart. You can change the chart type. You can change the orientation by clicking the By Row/By Column button. You can add or remove a legend. You can change titles.

Perform the following steps to use the PivotChart view of the Drivers and Workorders query.

Steps To Use a PivotChart

1 Click Queries on the Objects bar, right-click the Drivers and Workorders query, and then click Open on the shortcut menu. Click the View button arrow, and then click PivotChart View. Click View on the menu bar and then point to Drop Areas on the View menu.

The PivotChart and View menu display (Figure 9-65). The drop areas currently do not display.

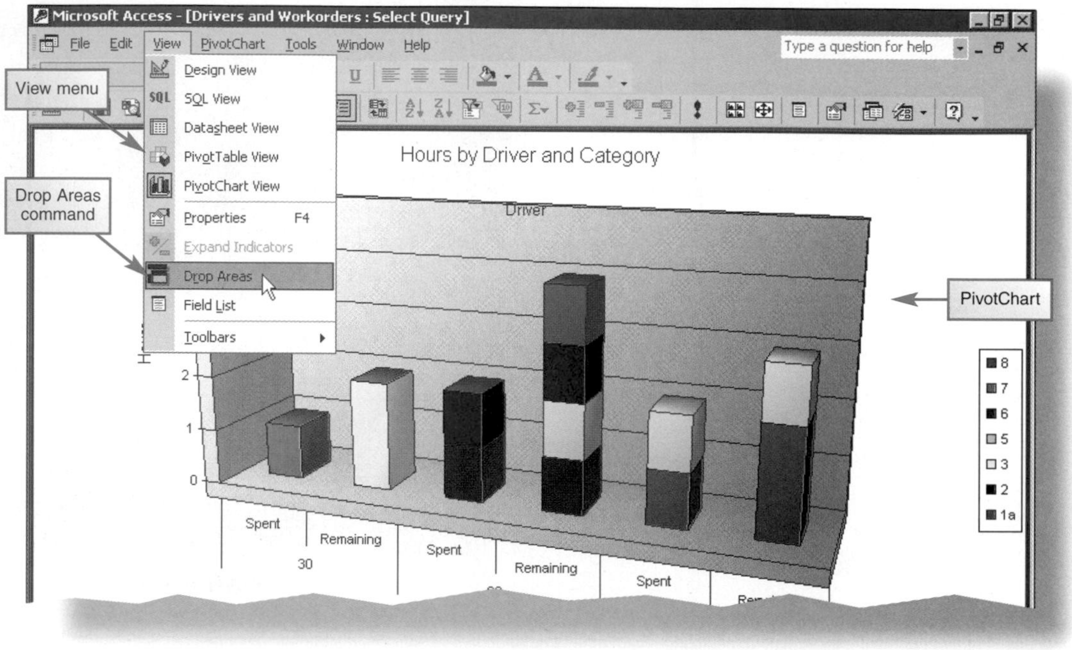

FIGURE 9-65

2 Click Drop Areas on the View menu. Click the Driver Number arrow.

The list of available drivers displays (Figure 9-66).

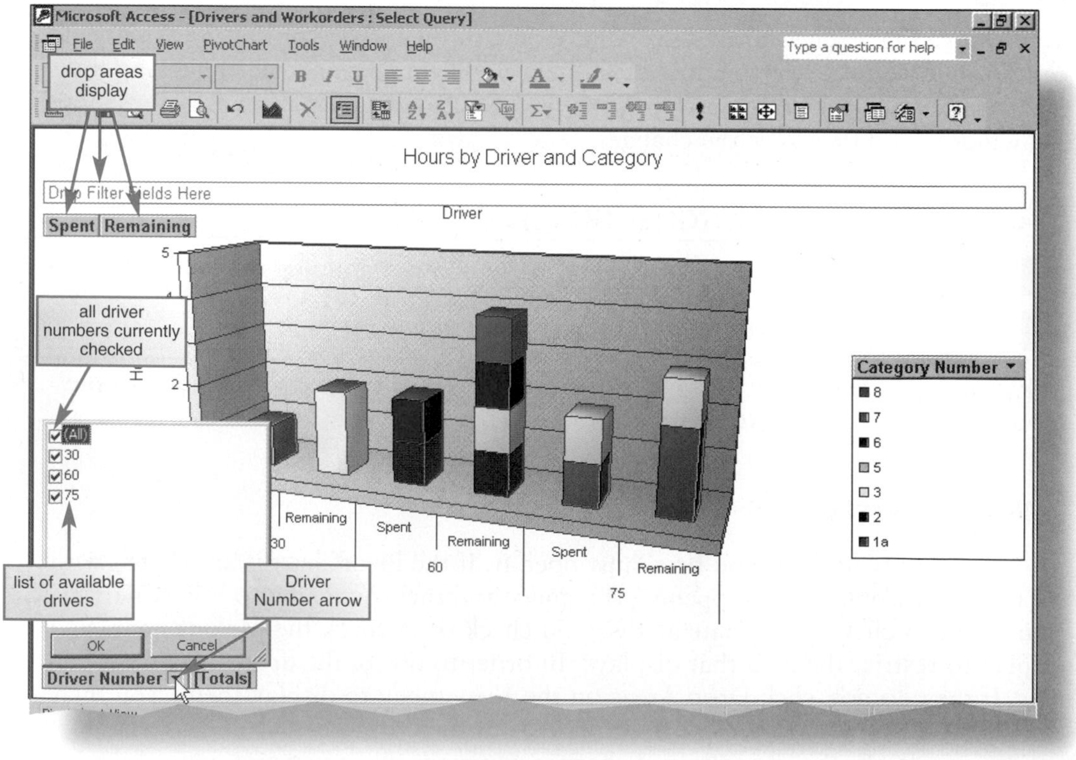

FIGURE 9-66

3 Click the check box for driver number 75 to remove the check mark, and then click the OK button.

Driver number 75 no longer displays on the PivotChart (Figure 9-67).

4 Click the Close Window button for the window containing the PivotChart. Click the No button when asked if you want to save your changes.

The PivotChart is closed. The changes are not saved. The next time you open the PivotChart, the changes you just made will not be reflected.

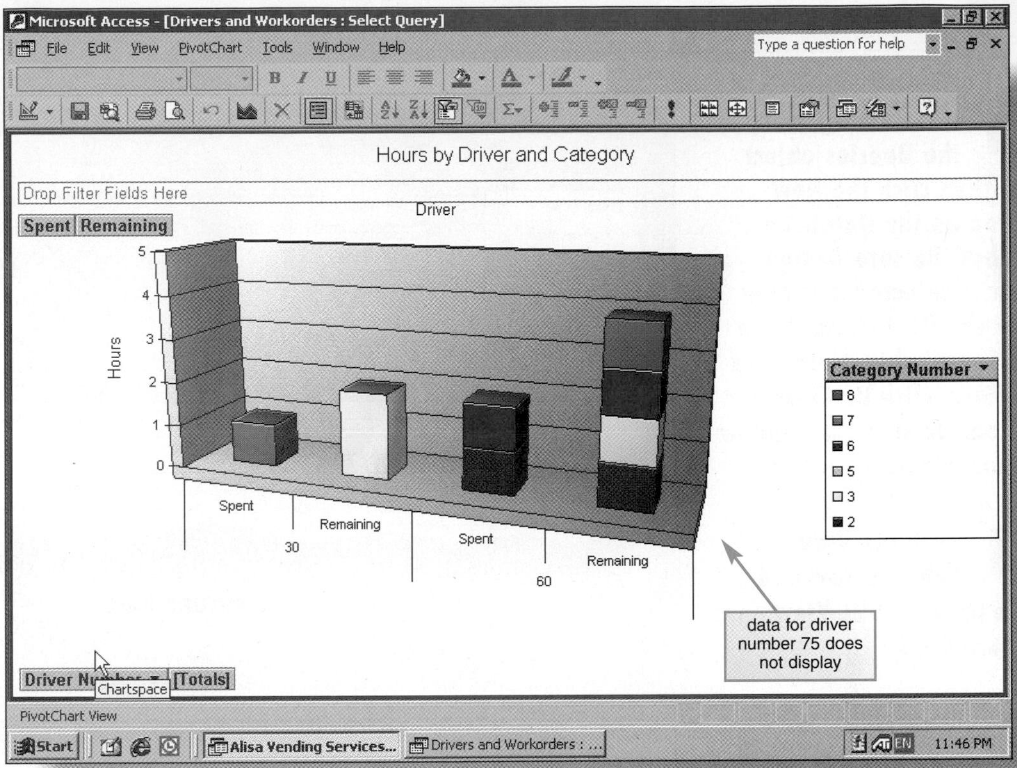

FIGURE 9-67

SQL

This section examines the language called **SQL** (**Structured Query Language**). Similar to creating queries in Design view, SQL furnishes users a way of querying relational databases. In SQL, you must type commands to obtain the desired results, however, instead of making entries in the design grid.

SQL was developed under the name SEQUEL at the IBM San Jose research facilities as the data manipulation language for IBM's prototype relational model DBMS, System R, in the mid-1970s. In 1980, it was renamed SQL to avoid confusion with an unrelated hardware product called SEQUEL. It is used as the data manipulation language for IBM's current production offerings in the relational DBMS arena — SQL/DS and DB2. Most relational DBMS's, including Microsoft Access, use a version of SQL as a data manipulation language.

More About

SQL

The American National Standards Institute (ANSI) has developed standards for SQL. These standards are reviewed continually, and new and improved standards periodically are proposed and accepted. For more information concerning these standards, visit the Access 2002 More About page (scsite.com/ac2002/more.htm) and then click SQL Standards.

Creating a New SQL Query

You begin the creation of a new **SQL query**, which is a query expressed using the SQL language, just as you begin the creation of any other query in Access. The only difference is that you will use SQL view instead of Design view. Perform the steps on the next page to create a new SQL query.

Steps To Create a New SQL Query

1 **If necessary, click the Queries object and then click the New button on the Database toolbar. Be sure Design View is selected and then click the OK button. When the Show Table dialog box displays, click its Close button. Be sure the window is maximized.**

2 **Click the View button arrow and then point to SQL View (Figure 9-68).**

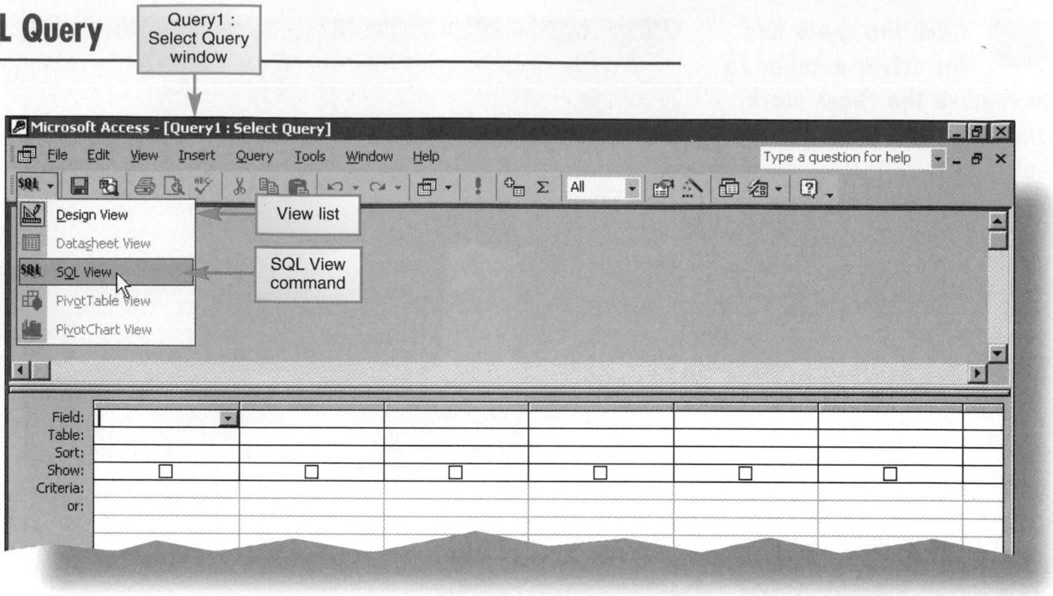

FIGURE 9-68

3 **Click SQL View.**

The Query1 : Select Query window displays in SQL view (Figure 9-69).

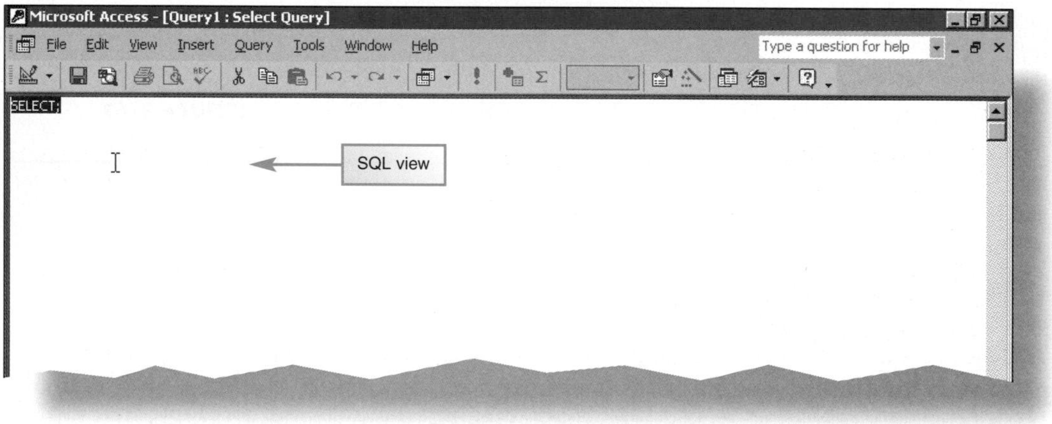

FIGURE 9-69

Other Ways

1. On View menu click SQL View
2. In Voice Command mode, say "View, SQL View"

The basic form of an SQL expression is quite simple: SELECT-FROM-WHERE. After the SELECT, you list those fields you wish to display. The fields will display in the results in the order in which they are listed in the expression. After the FROM, you list the table or tables involved in the query. Finally, after the WHERE, you list any criteria that apply to the data you want to retrieve. The command ends with a semicolon (;).

There are no special format rules in SQL. In this text, you place the word FROM on a new line, then place the word WHERE, when it is used, on the next line. This makes the commands easier to read. Words that are part of the SQL language are entered in uppercase and others are entered in a combination of uppercase and lowercase. Because it is a common convention, and necessary in some versions of SQL, place a semicolon (;) at the end of each command.

Unlike some other versions of SQL, Microsoft Access allows spaces within field names and table names. There is a restriction, however, to the way such names are used in SQL commands. When a name containing a space displays in SQL, it must be enclosed in square brackets. For example, Customer Number must display as [Customer Number] because the name includes a space. On the other hand, City does not need to be enclosed in square brackets because its name does not include a space. In order to be consistent, all names in this text will be enclosed in square brackets. Thus, the City field would display as [City] even though the brackets are technically not required.

Including Only Certain Fields

To include only certain fields, list them after the word SELECT. If you want to list all rows in the table, you do not need to include the word WHERE. The following steps list the number, name, amount paid, and current due amount of all customers.

Steps To Include Only Certain Fields

1 **Type** `SELECT [Customer Number], [Name], [Amount Paid], [Current Due]` **as the first line of the command. Press the ENTER key and then type** `FROM [Customer];` **as the second line. Point to the Run button on the Query Design toolbar.**

The command is entered (Figure 9-70).

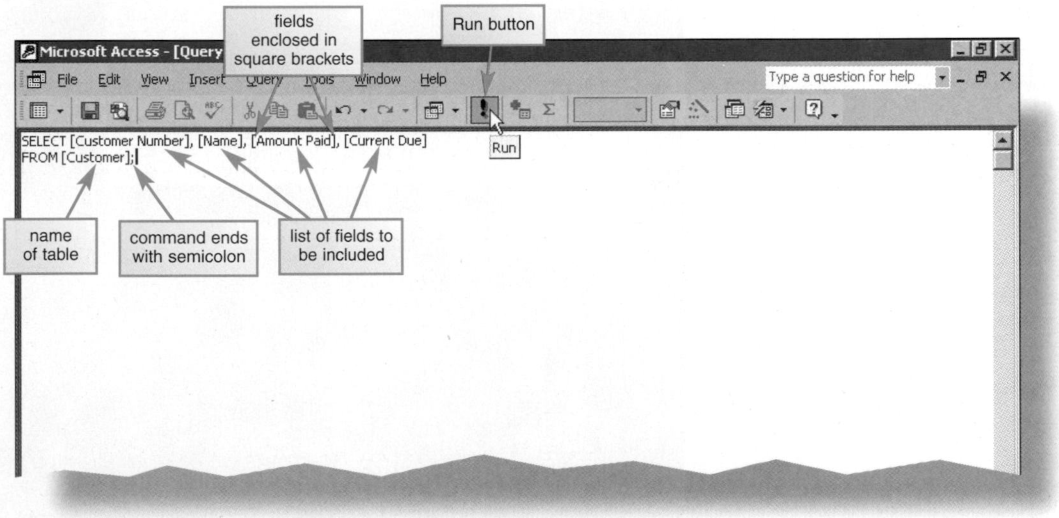

FIGURE 9-70

2 **Click the Run button.**

The results display (Figure 9-71). Only the fields specified are included.

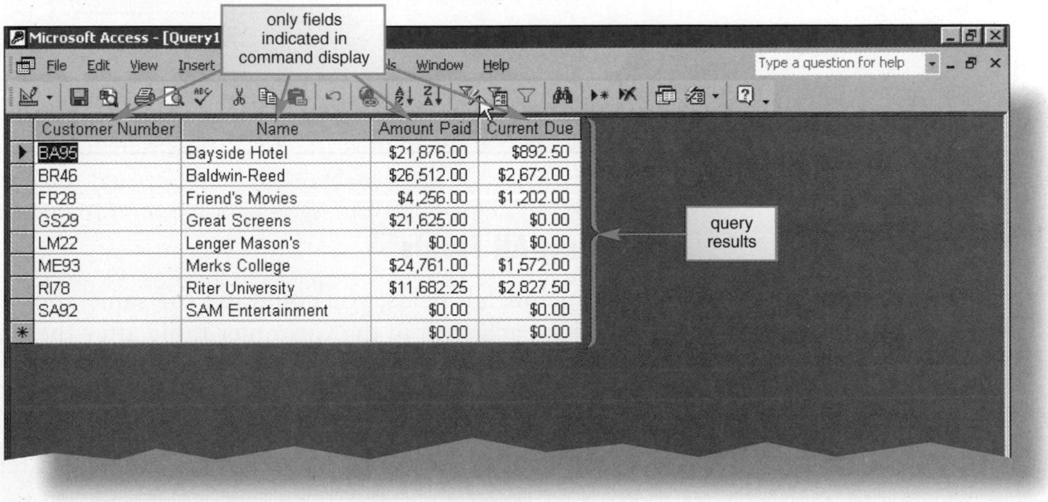

Customer Number	Name	Amount Paid	Current Due
BA95	Bayside Hotel	$21,876.00	$892.50
BR46	Baldwin-Reed	$26,512.00	$2,672.00
FR28	Friend's Movies	$4,256.00	$1,202.00
GS29	Great Screens	$21,625.00	$0.00
LM22	Lenger Mason's	$0.00	$0.00
ME93	Merks College	$24,761.00	$1,572.00
RI78	Riter University	$11,682.25	$2,827.50
SA92	SAM Entertainment	$0.00	$0.00
*		$0.00	$0.00

FIGURE 9-71

Preparing to Enter a New SQL Command

To enter a new SQL command, you could close the window, click the No button when asked if you want to save your changes, and then begin the process from scratch. A quicker alternative is to use the View menu and select SQL View. You then will be returned to SQL view with the current command displaying. At that point, you could erase the current command and then enter a new one. (If the next command is similar to the previous one, it may be simpler to modify the current command instead of erasing it and starting over.)

Perform the following steps to prepare to enter a new SQL command.

Steps To Prepare to Enter a New SQL Command

1 Click the View button arrow and then point to SQL View (Figure 9-72).

2 Click SQL View.

The command once again displays in SQL view.

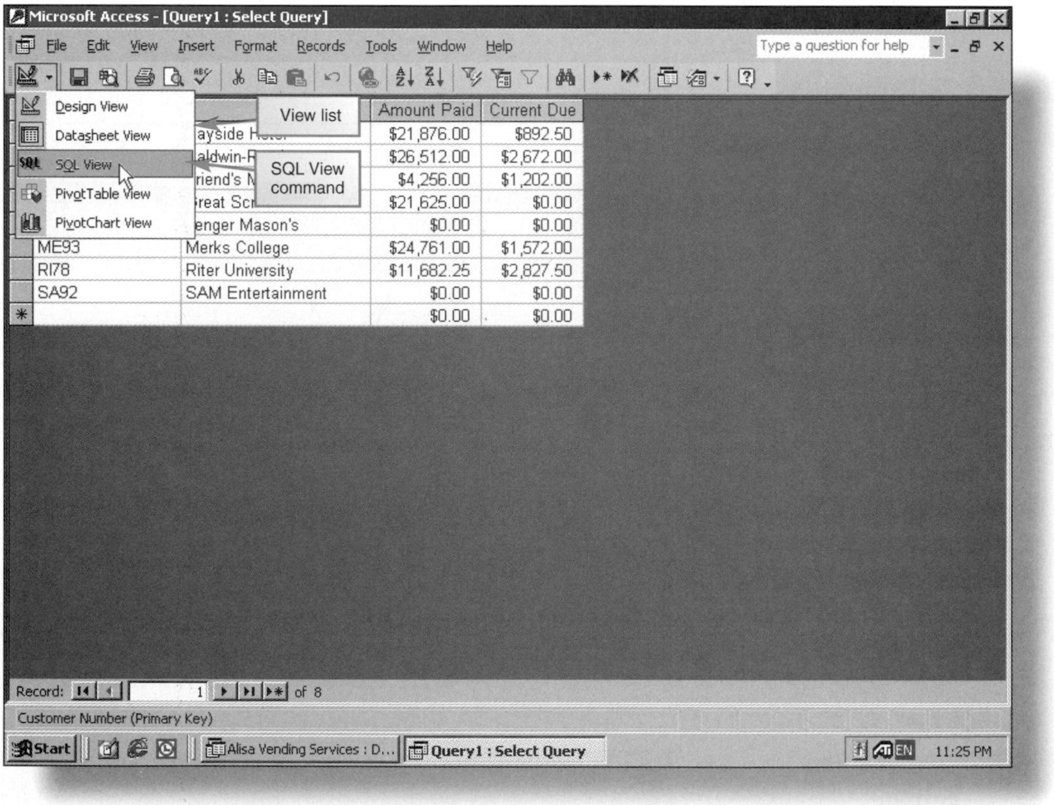

FIGURE 9-72

Including All Fields

To include all fields, you could use the same approach as in the previous steps, that is, list each field in the Customer table after the word SELECT. There is a shortcut, however. Instead of listing all the field names after SELECT, you can use the asterisk (*) symbol. This indicates that you want all fields listed in the order in which you described them to the system during data definition. To list all fields and all records in the Customer table, use the following steps.

Steps To Include All Fields

1 Erase the current command, and then type `SELECT *` **as the first line of the command. Press the ENTER key and then type** `FROM [Customer];` **as the second line. Point to the Run button.**

The command is entered (Figure 9-73).

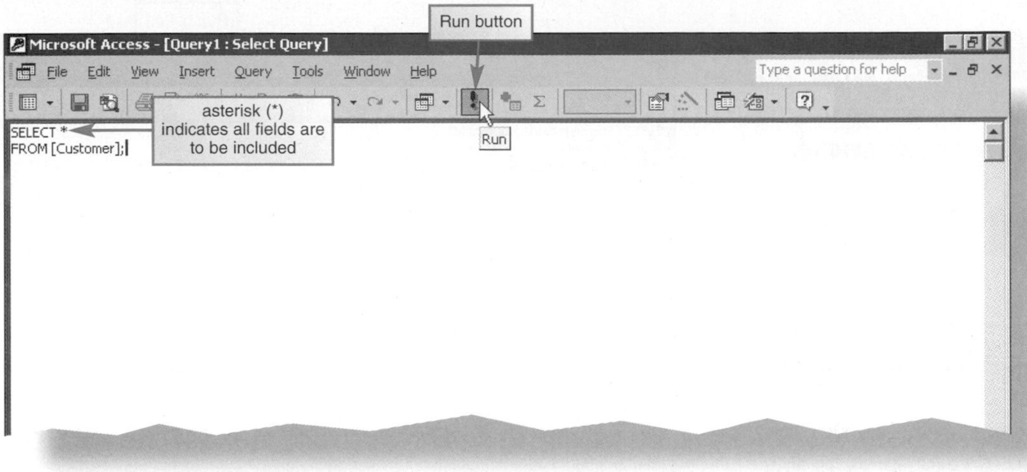

FIGURE 9-73

2 Click the Run button.

The results display (Figure 9-74). All fields specified are included.

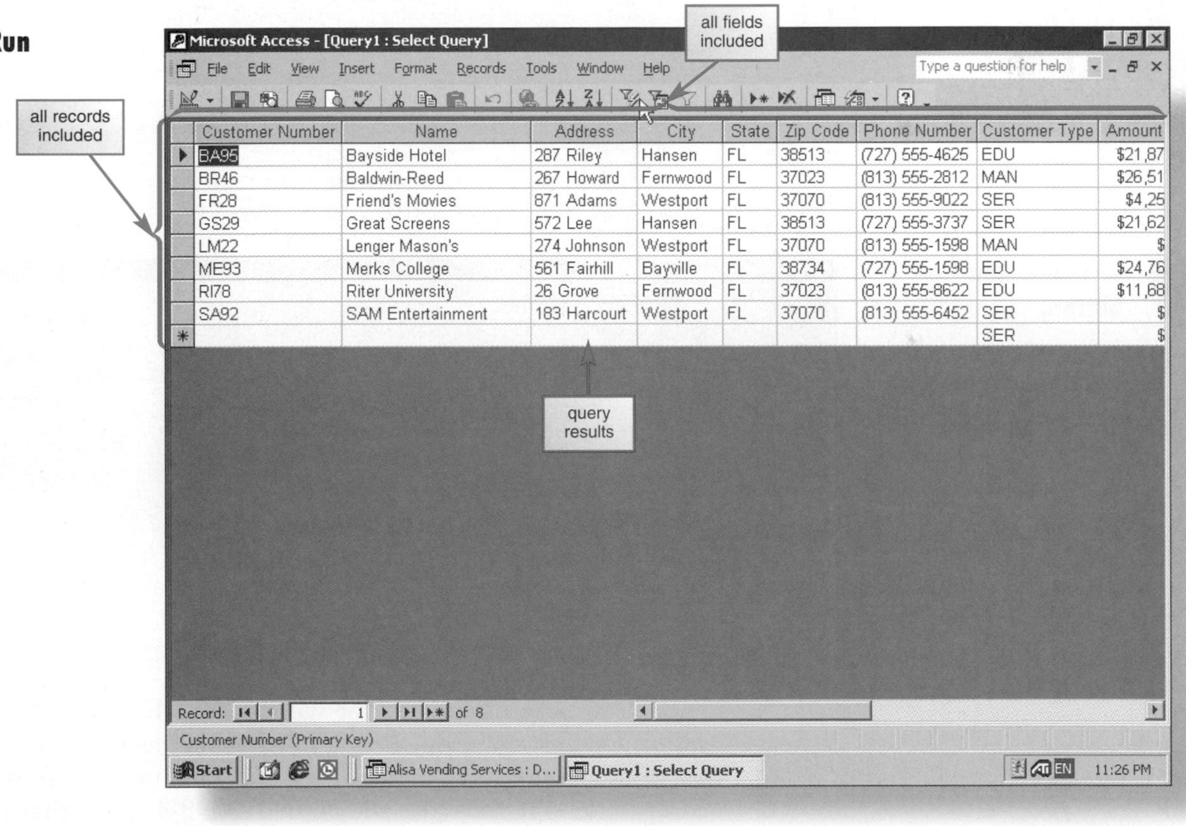

Customer Number	Name	Address	City	State	Zip Code	Phone Number	Customer Type	Amount
BA95	Bayside Hotel	287 Riley	Hansen	FL	38513	(727) 555-4625	EDU	$21,87
BR46	Baldwin-Reed	267 Howard	Fernwood	FL	37023	(813) 555-2812	MAN	$26,51
FR28	Friend's Movies	871 Adams	Westport	FL	37070	(813) 555-9022	SER	$4,25
GS29	Great Screens	572 Lee	Hansen	FL	38513	(727) 555-3737	SER	$21,62
LM22	Lenger Mason's	274 Johnson	Westport	FL	37070	(813) 555-1598	MAN	$
ME93	Merks College	561 Fairhill	Bayville	FL	38734	(727) 555-1598	EDU	$24,76
RI78	Riter University	26 Grove	Fernwood	FL	37023	(813) 555-8622	EDU	$11,68
SA92	SAM Entertainment	183 Harcourt	Westport	FL	37070	(813) 555-6452	SER	$
							SER	$

FIGURE 9-74

Using a Criterion Involving a Numeric Field

To restrict the records to be displayed, include the word WHERE followed by a criterion as part of the command. If the field involved is a numeric field, you simply type the value. To list the customer number and name of all customers whose current due amount is 0, for example, you would type `[Current Due]=0` as the condition as in the steps on the next page.

Steps To Use a Criterion Involving a Numeric Field

1 **Click the View button arrow, click SQL View, and then erase the current command.**

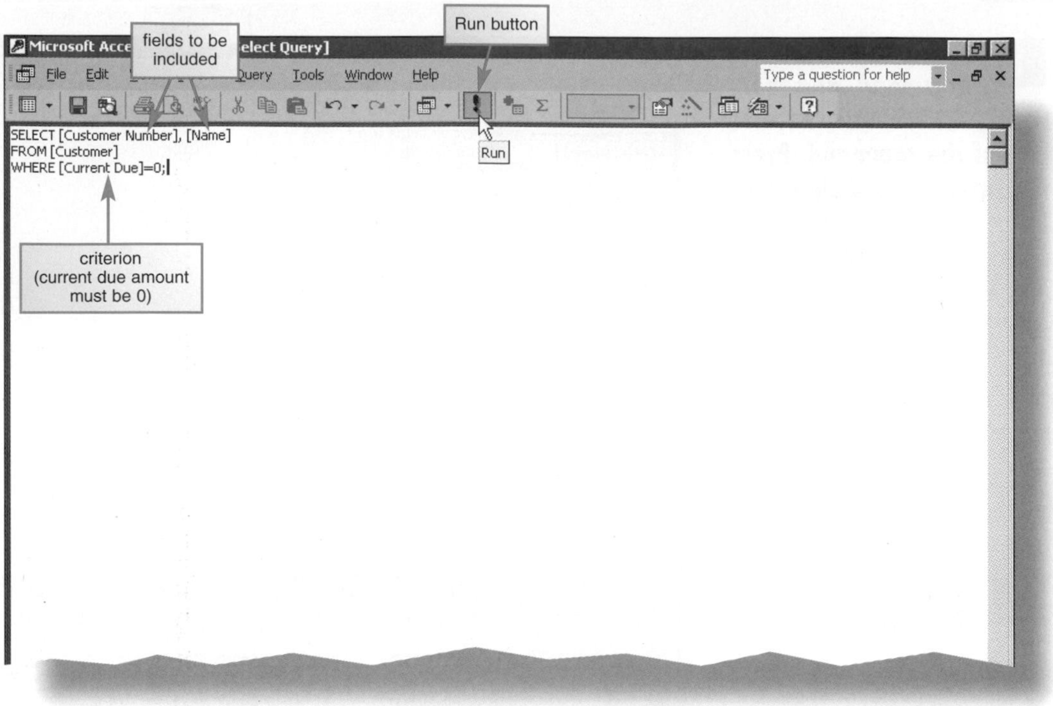

FIGURE 9-75

2 **Type** `SELECT [Customer Number], [Name]` **as the first line of the command. Press the ENTER key and then type** `FROM [Customer]` **as the second line. Press the ENTER key and then type** `WHERE [Current Due]=0;` **as the third line. Point to the Run button.**

The command is entered (Figure 9-75).

3 **Click the Run button.**

The results display (Figure 9-76). Only those customers for which the current due amount is 0 are included.

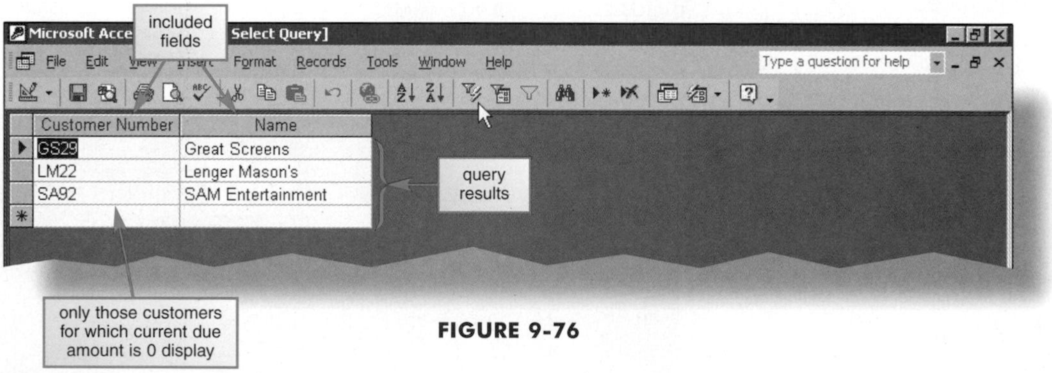

FIGURE 9-76

The criterion following the word WHERE in the preceding query is called a simple criterion. A **simple criterion** has the form: field name, comparison operator, then either another field name or a value. The possible comparison operators are shown in Table 9-4. Note that there are two different versions for "not equal to" (<> and !=). You must use the one that is right for your particular implementation of SQL. If you use the wrong one, your system will let you know instantly. Simply use the other.

Table 9-4 Comparison Operators

COMPARISON OPERATOR	MEANING
=	Equal to
<	Less than
>	Greater than
<=	Less than or equal to
>=	Greater than or equal to
<>	Not equal to

Using a Criterion Involving a Text Field

If the criterion involves a text field, the value must be enclosed in single quotation marks. The following example lists all customers located in Westport, that is, all customers for whom the value in the City field is Westport.

Steps To Use a Criterion Involving a Text Field

1 Click the View button arrow, click SQL View, and then erase the current command.

2 Type `SELECT [Customer Number], [Name]` **as the first line of the command. Press the ENTER key and then type** `FROM [Customer]` **as the second line. Press the ENTER key and then type** `WHERE [City]='Westport';` **as the third line. Point to the Run button.**

The command is entered (Figure 9-77).

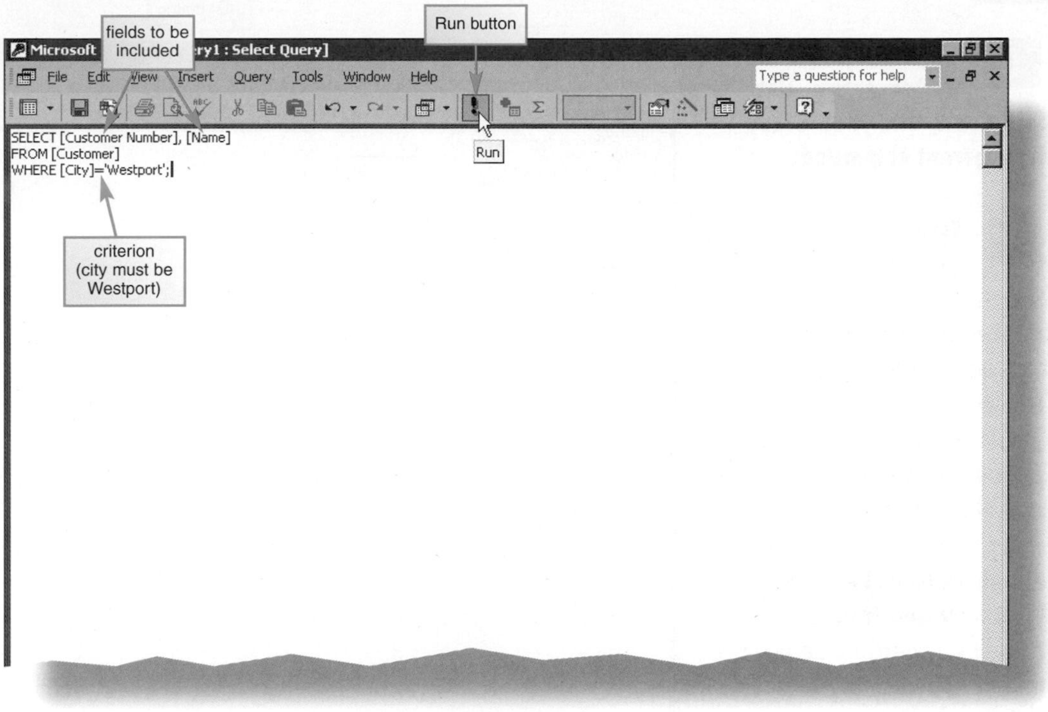

FIGURE 9-77

3 Click the Run button.

The results display (Figure 9-78). Only those customers located in Westport are included.

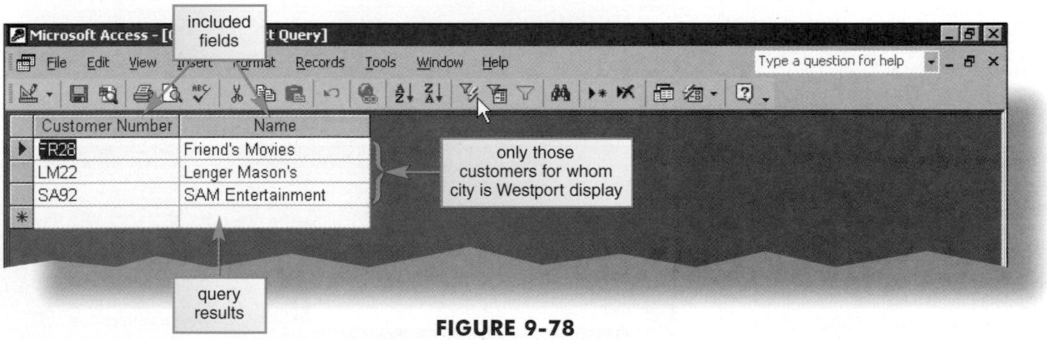

FIGURE 9-78

Using Compound Criteria

The criteria you have seen so far are called simple criteria. The next examples require compound criteria. **Compound criteria** are formed by connecting two or more simple criteria using AND, OR, and NOT. When simple criteria are connected by the word AND, all the simple criteria must be true in order for the compound criterion to be true. When simple criteria are connected by the word OR, the compound criterion will be true whenever any of the simple criteria are true. Preceding a criterion by NOT reverses the truth or falsity of the original criterion. That is, if the original criterion is true, the new criterion will be false; if the original criterion is false, the new one will be true.

The steps on the next page use compound criteria to display the names of those customers located in Westport and for whom the current due amount is 0.

Steps To Use a Compound Criterion

1 Click the View button arrow, click SQL View, and then erase the current command.

2 Type `SELECT [Customer Number], [Name]` **as the first line of the command. Press the ENTER key and then type** `FROM [Customer]` **as the second line. Press the ENTER key and then type** `WHERE [City]='Westport'` **as the third line. Press the ENTER key and then type** `AND [Current Due]=0;` **as the fourth line. Point to the Run button.**

The command is entered (Figure 9-79).

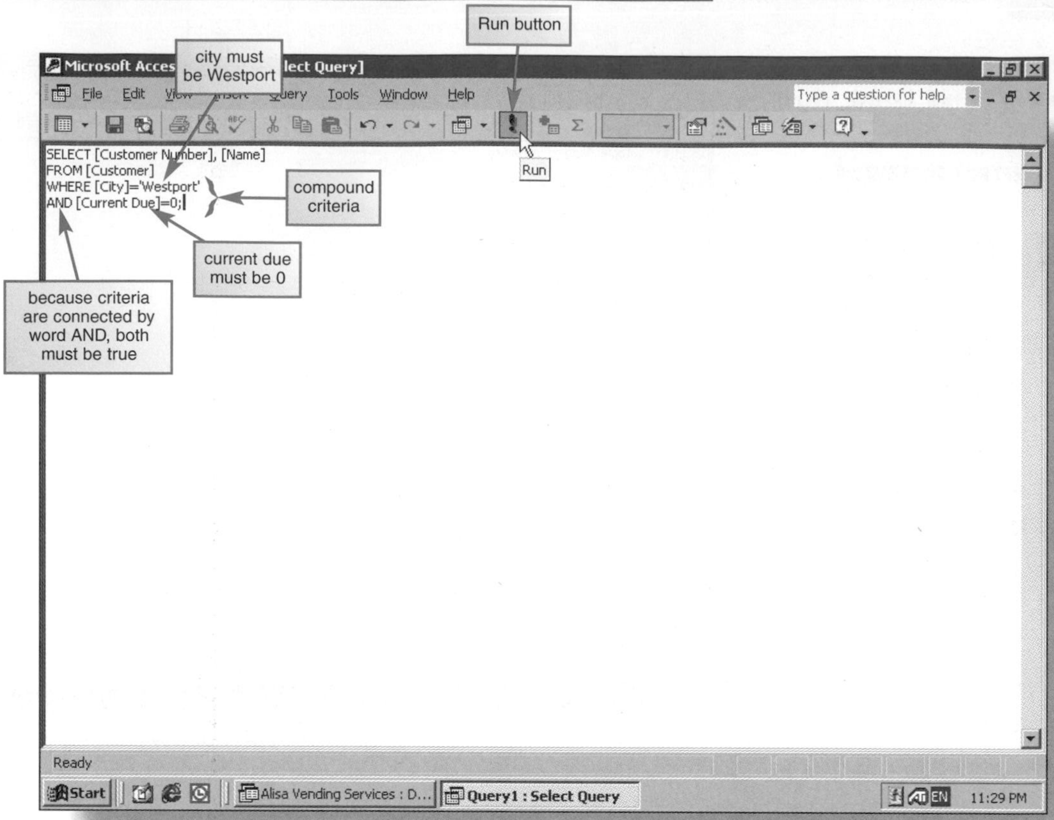

FIGURE 9-79

3 Click the Run button.

The results display (Figure 9-80). Only those customers located in Westport and with a current due amount of 0 are included.

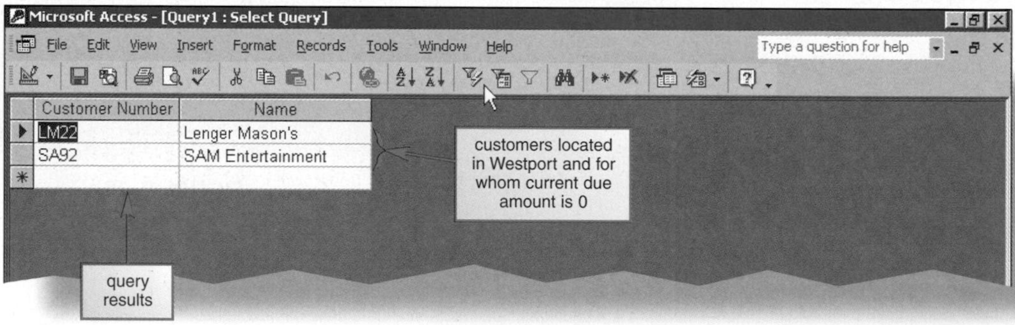

FIGURE 9-80

You use the same method to form compound criteria involving OR. Simply use the word OR instead of the word AND. In that case, the results would contain those records that satisfied either criterion.

Using NOT in a Criterion

To use NOT in a criterion, precede the criterion with the word NOT. Perform the following steps to list the numbers and names of the customers not located in Westport.

Steps To Use NOT in a Criterion

1 **Click the View button arrow, click SQL View, and then erase the current command.**

2 **Type** `SELECT [Customer Number], [Name]` **as the first line of the command. Press the ENTER key and then type** `FROM [Customer]` **as the second line. Press the ENTER key and then type** `WHERE NOT [City]='Westport';` **as the third line. Point to the Run button.**

The command is entered (Figure 9-81).

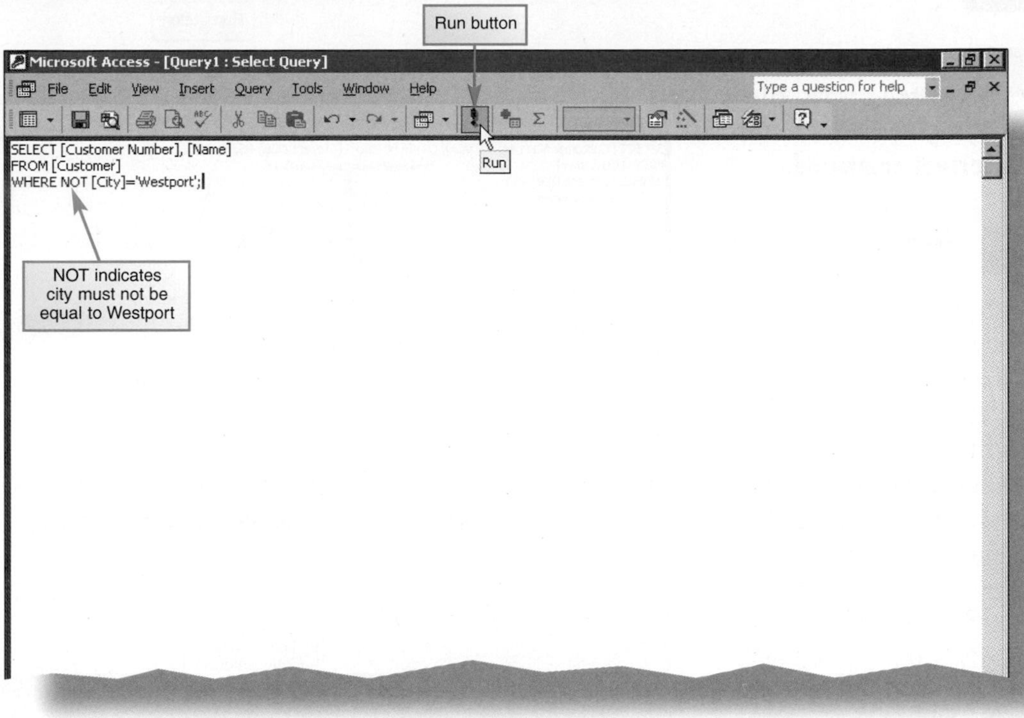

FIGURE 9-81

3 **Click the Run button.**

The results display (Figure 9-82). Only those customers not located in Westport are included.

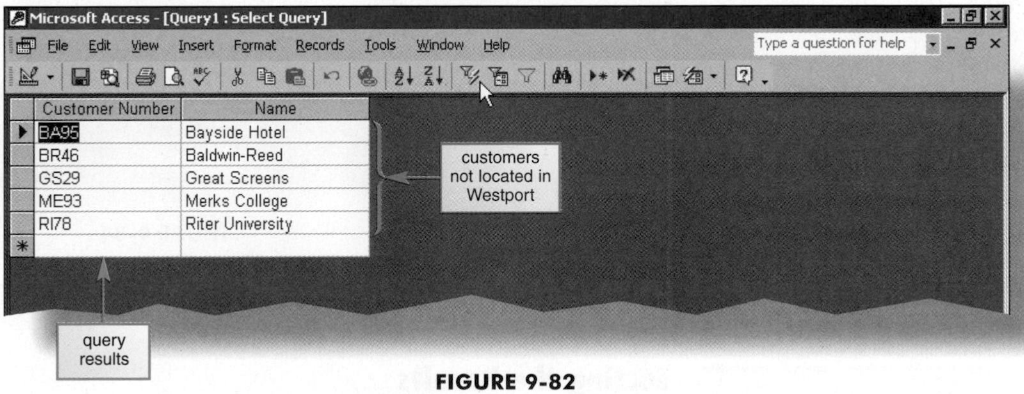

FIGURE 9-82

Using Computed Fields

Just as with queries created in Design view, you can include fields in queries that are not in the database, but that can be computed from fields that are. Such a field is called a **computed** or **calculated field**. Such computations can involve addition (+), subtraction (–), multiplication (*), or division (/). The query in the following steps includes the total amount, which is equal to the amount paid amount plus the current due amount.

To name the computed field, follow the computation with the word AS and then the name you wish to assign the field. The steps on the next page assign the name Total Amount to the computed field. They also list the Customer Number and Name for all customers for which the current due amount is greater than 0.

Steps To Use a Computed Field

1 **Click the View button arrow, click SQL View, and then erase the current command.**

2 **Type** SELECT [Customer Number], [Name], [Amount Paid]+ [Current Due] AS [Total Amount] **as the first line of the command. Press the ENTER key and then type** FROM [Customer] **as the second line. Press the ENTER key and then type** WHERE [Current Due]>0; **as the third line. Point to the Run button.**

The command is entered (Figure 9-83).

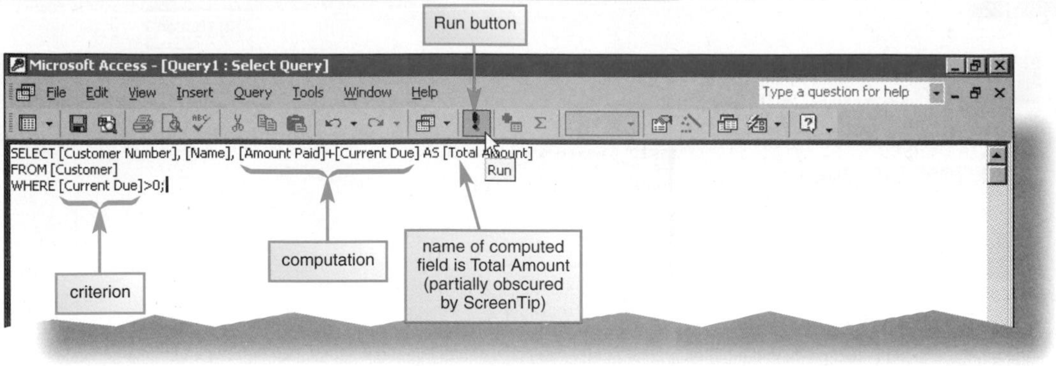

FIGURE 9-83

3 **Click the Run button.**

The results display (Figure 9-84). The total amount is calculated appropriately. Only those customers with a current due amount greater than 0 are included.

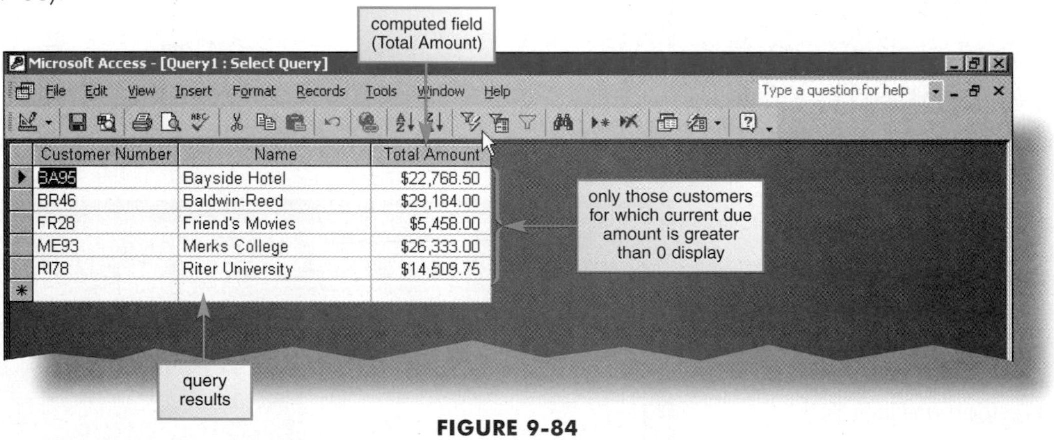

FIGURE 9-84

More About

Sorting in SQL

In SQL, you can sort in descending order by following the sort key with DESC in the ORDER BY clause. If you have two sort keys, you could choose to sort one in descending order and the other in ascending order. For example, ORDER BY [Driver Number], [Current Due] DESC; would sort on ascending Driver Number and descending Current Due.

Sorting the Results

The field on which data is to be sorted is called a **sort key**, or simply a **key**. If the data is to be sorted on two fields, the more important key is called the **major sort key** (also referred to as the **primary sort key**) and the less important key is called the **minor sort key** (also referred to as the **secondary sort key**). To sort the output, you include the words ORDER BY, followed by the sort key. If there are two sort keys, the major sort key is listed first.

The following steps list the customer number, name, amount paid amount, current due amount, and driver number for all customers. The data is to be sorted by driver number. Within the customers having the same driver number, the data is to be further sorted by amount paid amount. This means that the Driver Number field is the major (primary) sort key and the Amount Paid field is the minor (secondary) sort key.

Steps To Sort the Results

1 Click the View button arrow, click SQL View, and then erase the current command.

2 Type SELECT [Customer Number], [Name], [Amount Paid], [Current Due], [Driver Number] **as the first line of the command. Press the ENTER key and then type** FROM [Customer] **as the second line. Press the ENTER key and then type** ORDER BY [Driver Number], [Amount Paid]; **as the third line. Point to the Run button.**

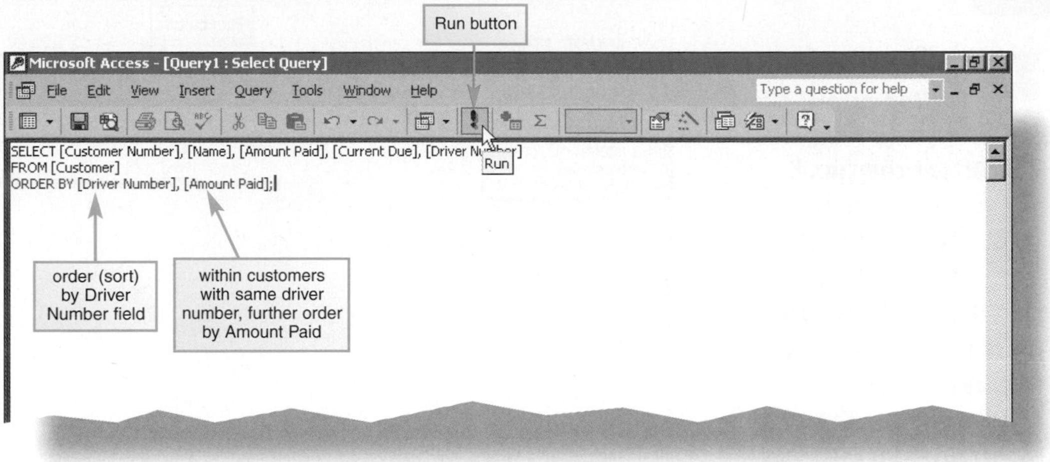

FIGURE 9-85

The command is entered (Figure 9-85). By default, the records will be sorted in ascending order.

3 Click the Run button.

The results display (Figure 9-86). The customers are sorted by driver number. Within the customers of a particular driver, the results further are sorted by amount paid.

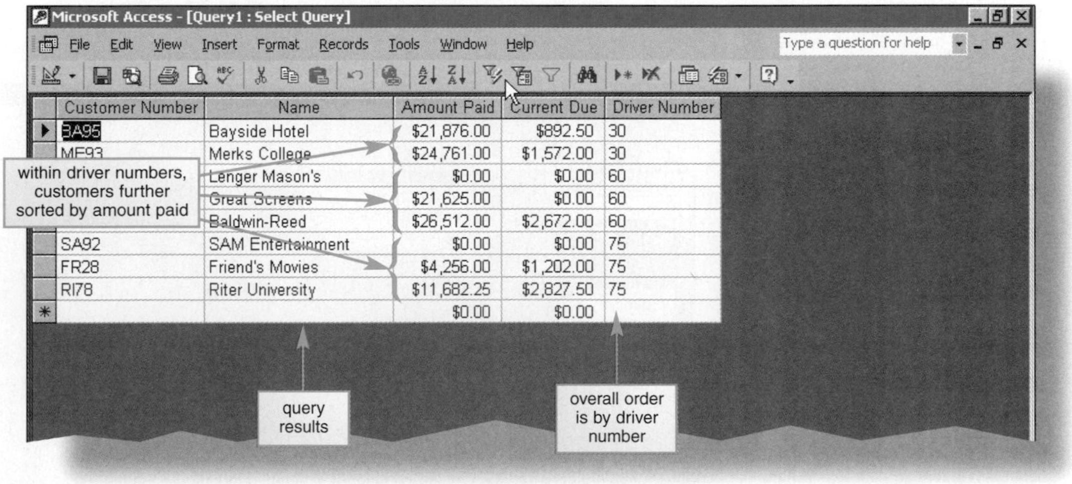

FIGURE 9-86

Using Built-In Functions

SQL has **built-in** functions (also called **aggregate** functions) to calculate the number of entries, the sum or average of all the entries in a given column, and the largest or smallest of the entries in a given column. In SQL, these functions are called COUNT, SUM, AVG, MAX, and MIN, respectively.

The steps on the next page count the number of customers assigned to driver number 60. To do so, use the COUNT function with an asterisk (*).

Steps To Use a Built-In Function

1 Click the View button arrow, click SQL View, and then erase the current command.

2 Type `SELECT COUNT(*)` **as the first line of the command. Press the ENTER key and then type** `FROM [Customer]` **as the second line. Press the ENTER key and then type** `WHERE [Driver Number]='60';` **as the third line. Point to the Run button.**

The command is entered (Figure 9-87).

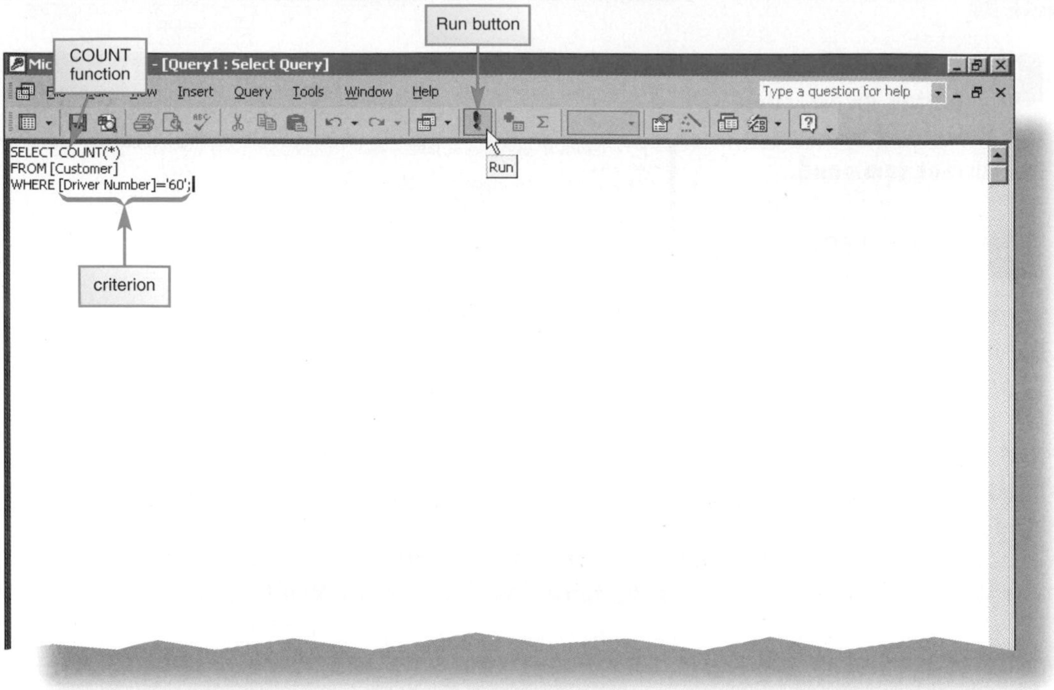

FIGURE 9-87

3 Click the Run button.

The results display (Figure 9-88). The heading Expr1000 is a default heading assigned by Access.

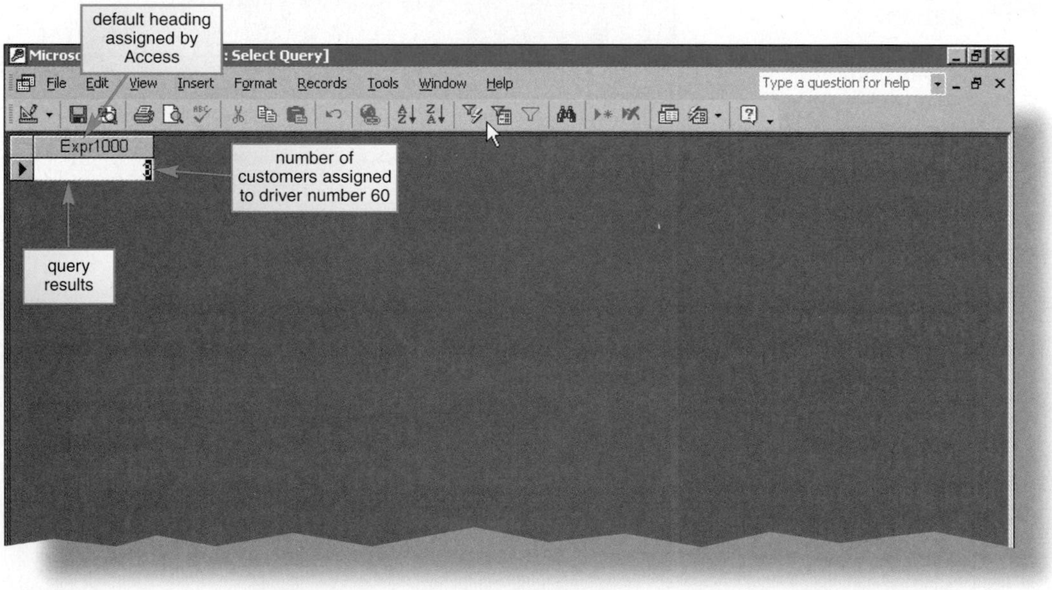

FIGURE 9-88

Using Multiple Functions in the Same Command

The only differences between COUNT and SUM, other than the obvious fact that they are computing different statistics, are that first, in the case of SUM, you must specify the field for which you want a total, instead of an asterisk (*) and second, the field must be numeric. You could not calculate a sum of names or addresses, for example. The following steps use both the COUNT and SUM functions to count the number of customers and calculate the SUM (total) of their Amount Paid amounts.

Steps To Use Multiple Functions in the Same Command

1 **Click the View button arrow, click SQL View, and then erase the current command.**

2 **Type** `SELECT COUNT(*), SUM([Amount Paid])` **as the first line of the command. Press the ENTER key and then type** `FROM [Customer];` **as the second line. Point to the Run button.**

The command is entered (Figure 9-89).

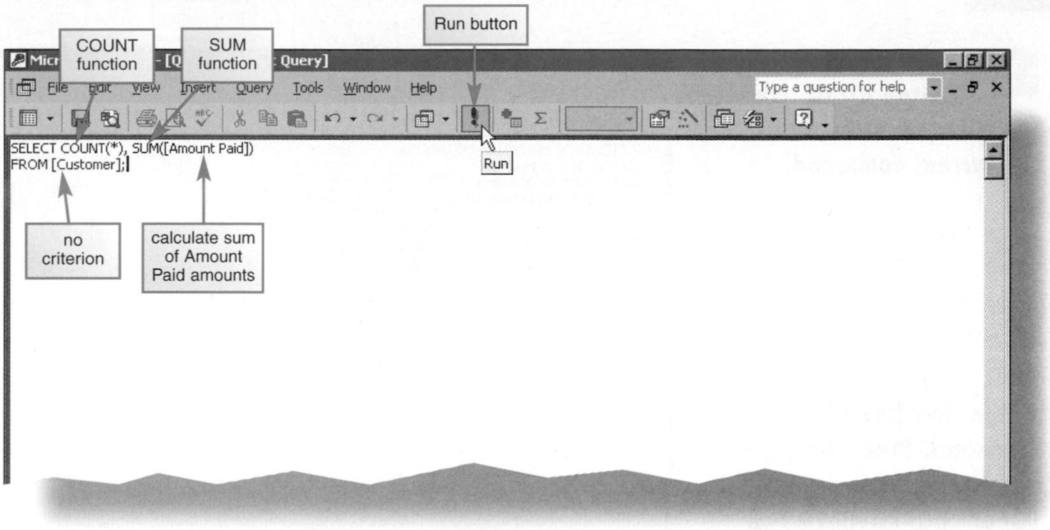

FIGURE 9-89

3 **Click the Run button.**

The results display (Figure 9-90). The number of customers (8) and the total of the amounts paid ($110,712.25) both display.

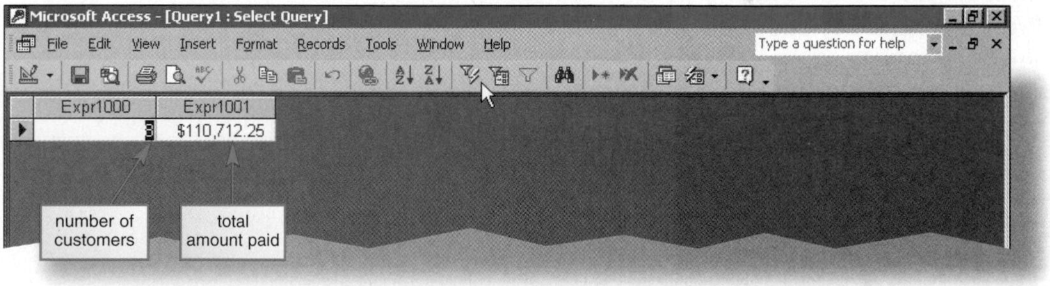

FIGURE 9-90

The use of AVG, MAX, and MIN is similar to SUM. The only difference is that a different statistic is calculated.

Using Grouping

Grouping means creating groups of records that share some common characteristic. In grouping work orders by customer number, for example, the work orders of customer BA95 would form one group, the work orders of customer FR28 would be a second, the work orders of customer GS29 would form a third, and so on.

The following steps calculate the totals of the Total Hours (est) and the Hours Spent fields for each customer. To calculate the totals, the command will include the SUM([Total Hours (est)]) and SUM([Hours Spent]). To get individual totals for each customer the command also will include the words GROUP BY followed by the field used for grouping, in this case Customer Number.

Including GROUP BY Customer Number will cause the work orders for each customer to be grouped together; that is, all work orders with the same customer number will form a group. Any statistics, such as totals, displaying after the word SELECT will be calculated for each of these groups. It is important to note that using GROUP BY does not imply that the information will be sorted. To produce the results in a particular order, you also should use ORDER BY as in the steps on the next page.

Steps To Use Grouping

1 Click the View button arrow, click SQL View, and then erase the current command.

2 Type `SELECT [Customer Number], SUM([Total Hours (est)]), SUM([Hours Spent])` **as the first line of the command. Press the ENTER key and then type** `FROM [Open Workorders]` **as the second line. Press the ENTER key and then type** `GROUP BY [Customer Number]` **as the third line. Press the ENTER key and then type** `ORDER BY [Customer Number];` **as the fourth line. Point to the Run button.**

The command is entered (Figure 9-91).

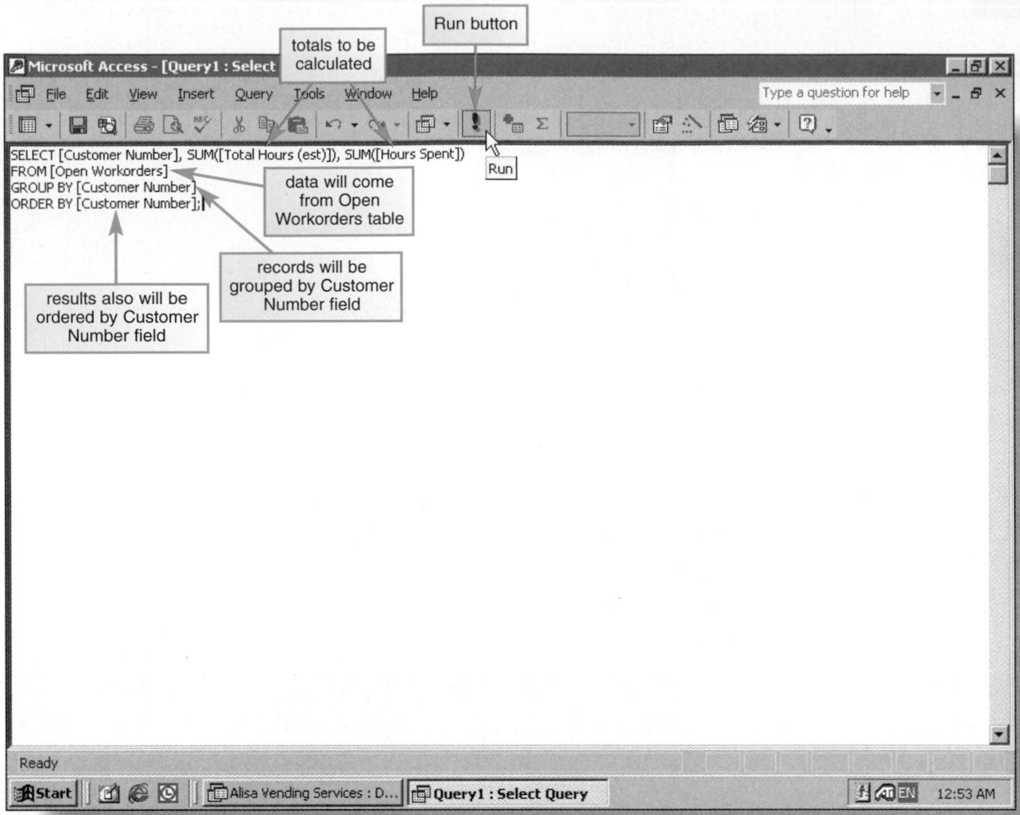

FIGURE 9-91

3 Click the Run button.

The results display (Figure 9-92). The first row represents the group of work orders for customer BA95. For these work orders, the sum of the Total Hours (est) amounts is 3 and the sum of the Hours Spent amounts is 1. The second row represents the group of work orders for customer FR28. For these work orders, the sum of the Total Hours (est) amounts is 5 and the sum of the Hours Spent amounts is 2.

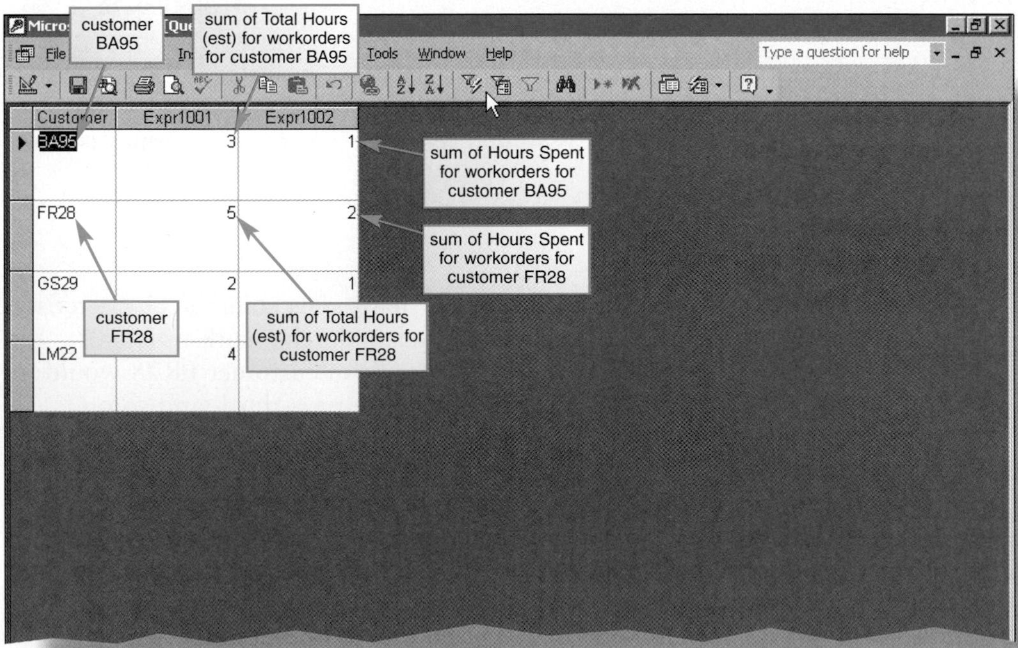

FIGURE 9-92

When rows are grouped, one line of output is produced for each group. The only things that may display are statistics calculated for the group or fields whose values are the same for all rows in a group. For example, it would make sense to display the customer number, because all the work orders in the group have the same customer number. It would not make sense to display the start date, because the start date will vary from one row in a group to another. (SQL could not determine which start date to display for the group.)

Restricting the Groups that Display

In some cases you only want to display certain groups. For example, you may want to display only those customers for which the sum of Total Hours (Est) is greater than 3. This restriction does not apply to individual rows, but instead to groups. Because WHERE applies only to rows, it is not appropriate to accomplish the kind of selection you have here. Fortunately, there is a word that is to groups what WHERE is to rows. It is the word HAVING and it is used in the following steps.

Steps To Restrict the Groups that Display

1 Click the View button arrow, and then click SQL View.

2 Move the insertion point to the beginning of the fourth line (ORDER BY [Customer Number];) and click. Press the ENTER key, click the beginning of the new blank line, and then type `HAVING SUM([Total Hours (est)])>3` **as the fourth line. Point to the Run button.**

The command is entered (Figure 9-93).

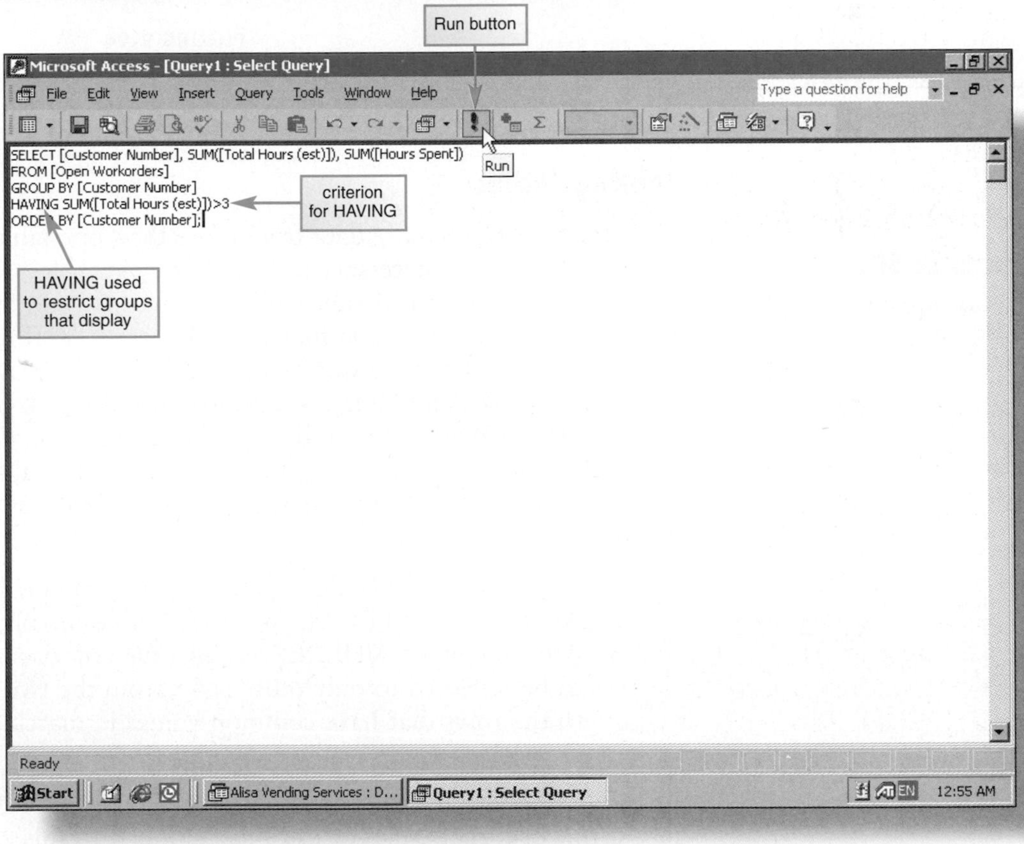

FIGURE 9-93

3 Click the Run button.

The results display (Figure 9-94). Only those groups for which the sum of the Total Hours (est) is greater than 3 display.

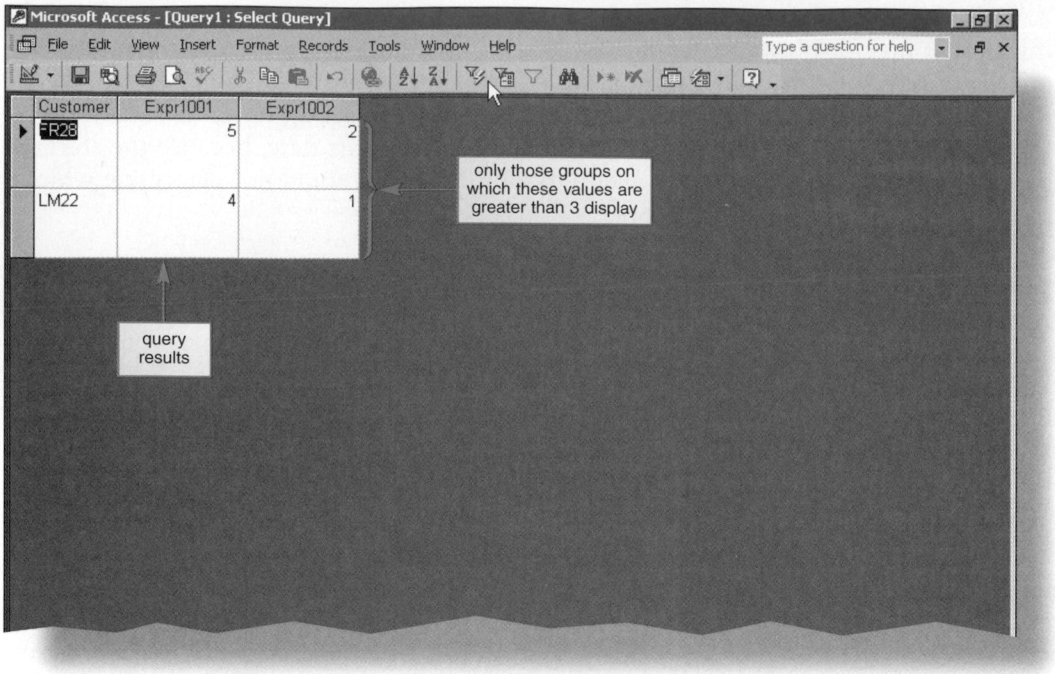

FIGURE 9-94

More About

Joins in SQL

Different types of joins can be implemented in SQL. For example, in joining customers and work orders in such a way that a customer will display even if it has no open work orders, you would need to perform a type of join called an outer join. For more information, visit the Access 2002 More About page (scsite.com/ac2002/more.htm) and then click Joins in SQL.

Joining Tables

Many queries require data from more than one table. Just as with creating queries in Design view, it is necessary to be able to **join** tables, that is, to find rows in two tables that have identical values in matching fields. In SQL, this is accomplished through appropriate criteria following the word WHERE.

If you wish to list the Customer Number, Name, Location, Category Number, Total Hours (est), and Hours Spent fields for all work orders, you need data from both the Open Workorders and Customer tables. The Customer Number field is in both tables, the Name field is only in the Customer table, and all other fields are only in the Open Workorders table. You need to access both tables in your SQL command, as follows:

1. After the word SELECT, you indicate all fields you wish displayed.
2. After the word FROM, you list all tables involved in the query.
3. After the word WHERE, you give the criterion that will restrict the data to be retrieved to only those rows from the two tables that match, that is, to the rows that have common values in matching fields.

There is a problem, however. The matching fields are both called Customer Number. There is a field in Customer called Customer Number, as well as a field in Open Workorders called Customer Number. In this case, if you only enter Customer Number, it will not be clear which table you mean. It is necessary to **qualify** Customer Number, that is, to specify which field in which table you are referring to. You do this by preceding the name of the field with the name of the table, followed by a period. The Customer Number field in the Open Workorders table is [Open Workorders].[Customer Number]. The Customer Number field in the Customer table is [Customer].[Customer Number].

Perform the following steps to list the Customer Number, Name, Location, Category Number, Total Hours (est), and Hours Spent fields for all work orders.

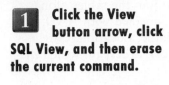

Steps To Join Tables

1 Click the View button arrow, click SQL View, and then erase the current command.

2 Type `SELECT [Open Workorders].[Customer Number], [Name], [Location], [Category Number], [Total Hours (est)], [Hours Spent]` **as the first line of the command. Press the ENTER key and then type** `FROM [Open Workorders], [Customer]` **as the second line. Press the ENTER key and then type** `WHERE [Open Workorders].[Customer Number]=[Customer].[Customer Number];` **as the third line. Point to the Run button.**

The command is entered (Figure 9-95).

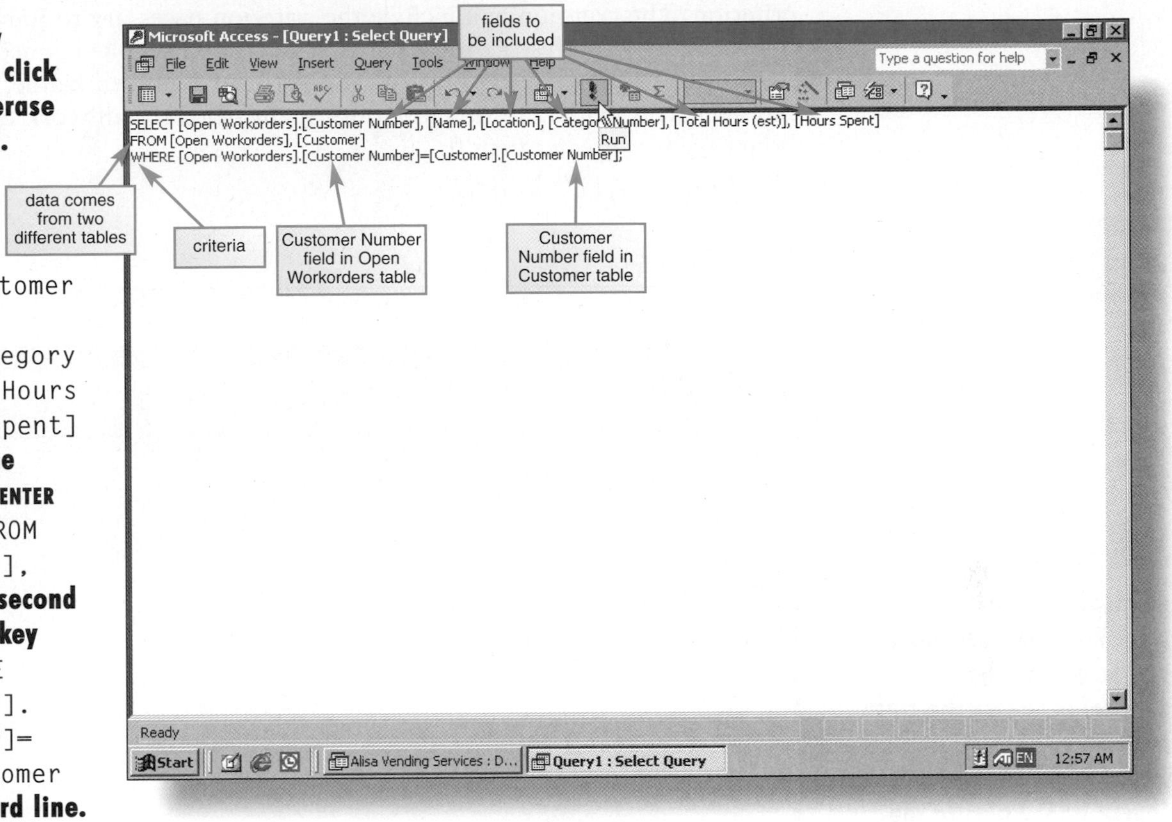

FIGURE 9-95

3 Click the Run button.

The results display (Figure 9-96). They include the appropriate data from both the Open Workorders table and the Customer table. The row spacing for the results may display differently on your screen.

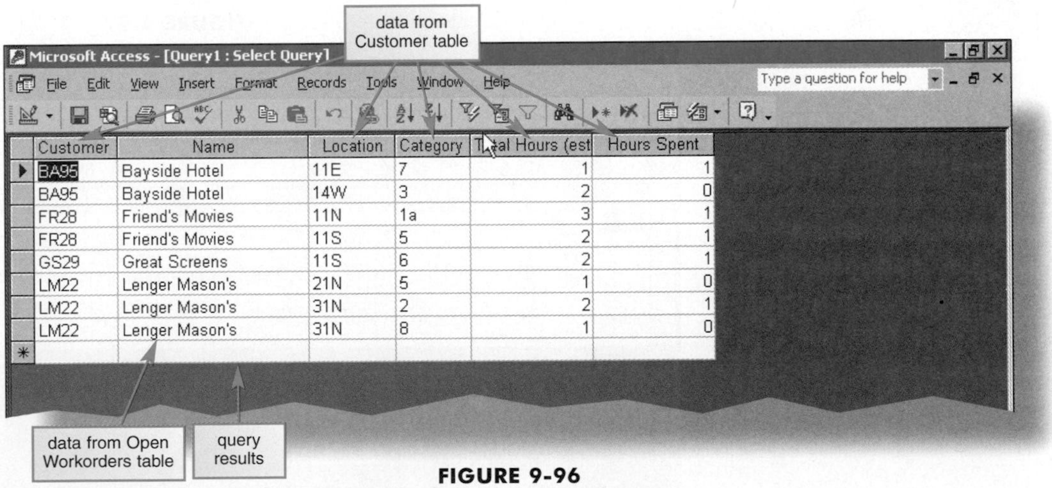

FIGURE 9-96

Note that whenever there is potential ambiguity, you must qualify the fields involved. It is permissible to qualify other fields as well, even if there is no confusion. For example, instead of [Name], you could have typed [Customer].[Name] to indicate the Name field in the Customer table. Some people prefer to qualify all fields and this is not a bad approach. In this text, you only will qualify fields when it is necessary to do so.

Restricting the Records in a Join

You can restrict the records to be included in a join by creating a compound criterion. The criterion will include the criterion necessary to join the tables along with a criterion to restrict the records. The criteria will be connected with AND. Perform the following steps to list the Customer Number, Name, Location, Category Number, Total Hours (est), and Hours Spent fields for all work orders on which the hours spent is greater than 0.

Steps To Restrict the Records in a Join

1 Click the View button arrow, and then click SQL View.

2 Click immediately after the semicolon on the third line. Press the BACKSPACE key to delete the semicolon. Press the ENTER key and then type `AND [Hours Spent]>0;` **as the fourth line. Point to the Run button.**

The command is entered (Figure 9-97).

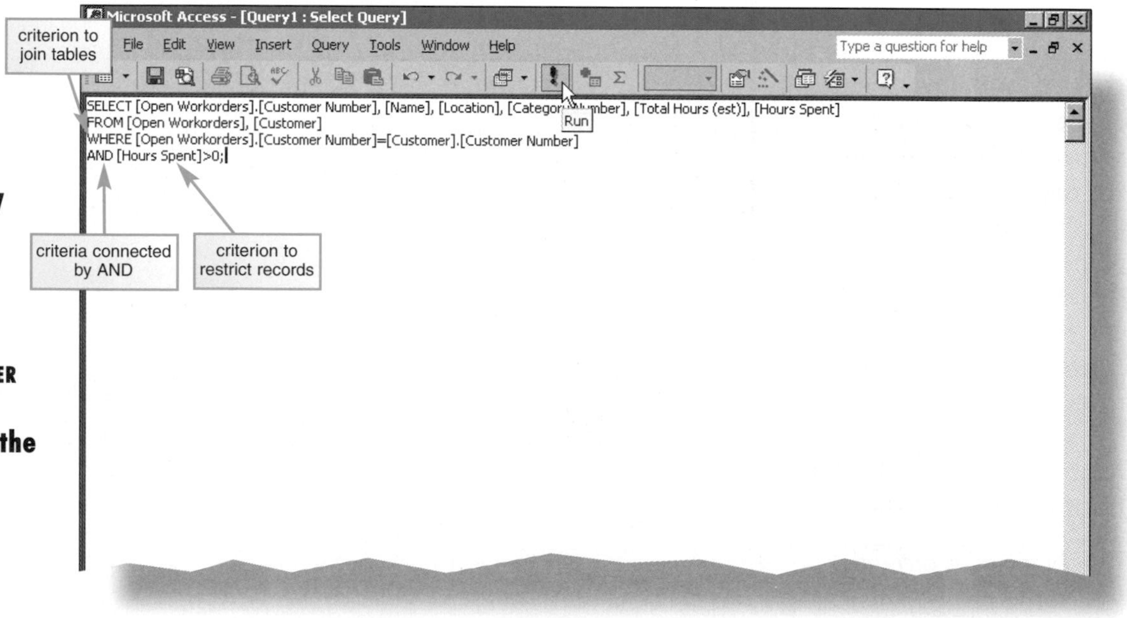

FIGURE 9-97

3 Click the Run button.

The results display (Figure 9-98). Only those work orders for which the hours spent is greater than 0 display. The row spacing for the results may display differently on your screen.

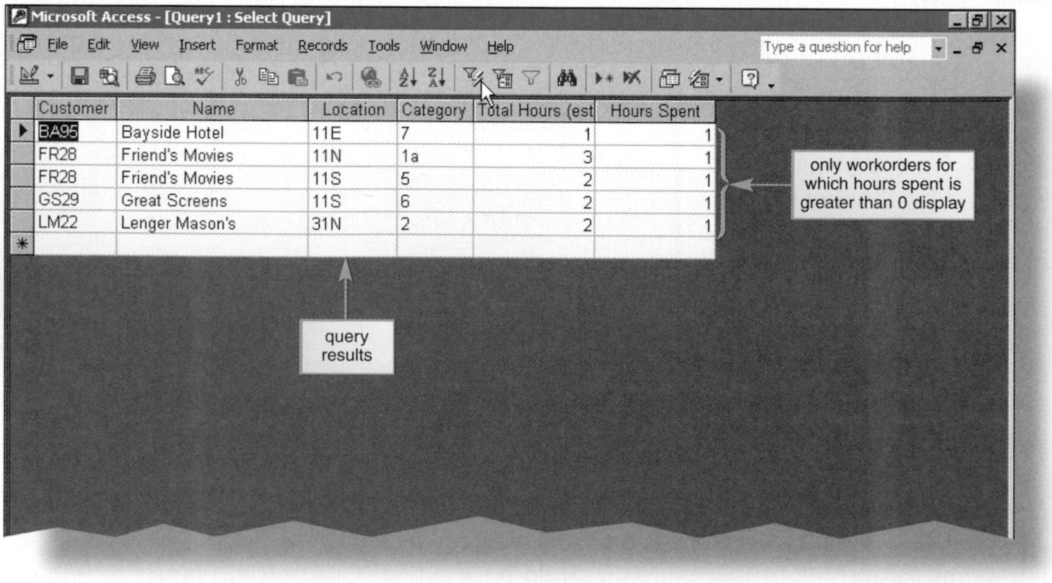

FIGURE 9-98

Joining Multiple Tables

In some cases, you will need data from more than two tables. The following steps, for example, include all the data from the previous query together with the category description, which is found in the Category table. Thus, the Category table also must be included in the query as well as a condition relating the Category and Open Workorders tables. The condition to do so is [Open Workorders].[Category Number]=[Category].[Category Number]. The following steps produce the desired results.

Steps To Join Multiple Tables

1 Click the View button arrow, click SQL View, and then erase the current command.

2 Type `SELECT [Open Workorders].[Customer Number], [Name], [Location], [Category].[Category Number], [Category Description], [Total Hours (est)], [Hours Spent]` **as the first line of the command. Press the ENTER key and then type** `FROM [Open Workorders], [Customer], [Category]` **as the second line. Press the ENTER key and then type** `WHERE [Open Workorders].[Customer Number]=[Customer].[Customer Number]` **as the third line. Press the ENTER key and then type** `AND [Open Workorders].[Category Number]=[Category].[Category Number]` **as the fourth line. Press the ENTER key and then type** `AND [Hours Spent]>0;` **as the fifth line. Point to the Run button.**

The command is entered (Figure 9-99).

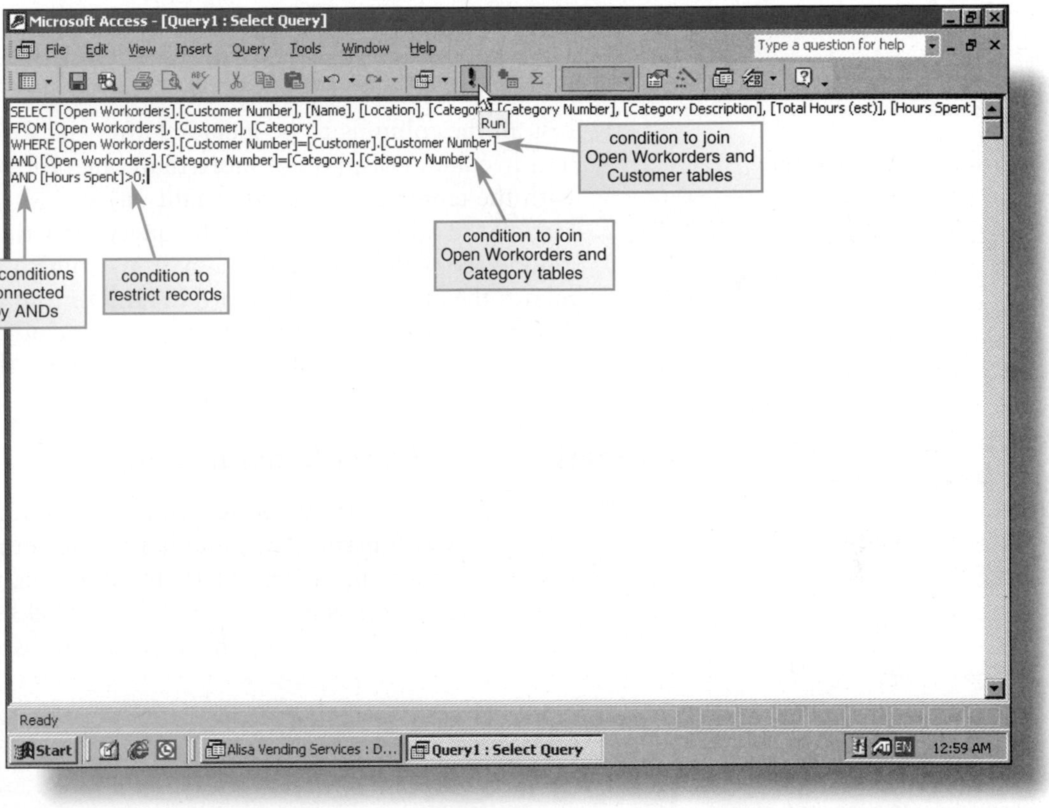

FIGURE 9-99

3 Click the Run button. If necessary, reduce the size of the Category Number column so all columns display.

The results display (Figure 9-100). The row spacing for the results may display differently on your screen.

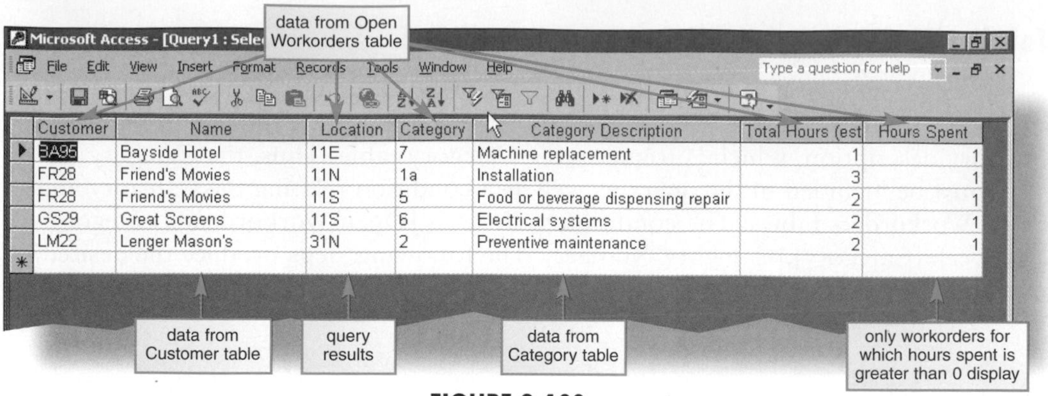

FIGURE 9-100

To create an SQL command that joins data from more than two tables, it is best to take it one step at a time, as follows:

1. List all the columns to be included after the word SELECT. If the name of any column displays in more than one table, precede the column name with the table name (that is, qualify it).
2. List all the tables involved in the query after the word FROM.
3. Taking the tables involved one pair at a time, put the condition that relates the tables after the word WHERE. Join these conditions with AND. If there are any other conditions, include them after the word WHERE and connect them to the others with the word AND.

Comparison with Access-Generated SQL

When you create a query in Design view, Access automatically creates a corresponding SQL command that is similar to the commands you have created. The Access query shown in Figure 9-101, for example, includes the Customer Number and Name. There is a criteria in the City field (Westport), but the City field will not display in the results. The View menu displays in the figure.

More About

Access-Generated SQL

After creating an SQL command, you can move to Design view. Access automatically fills in the design grid appropriately to match your SQL command. You then can return to SQL view and once again see your command. If you make any changes in the design grid before returning to SQL view, however, Access will reformat your command as an Access-Generated SQL command.

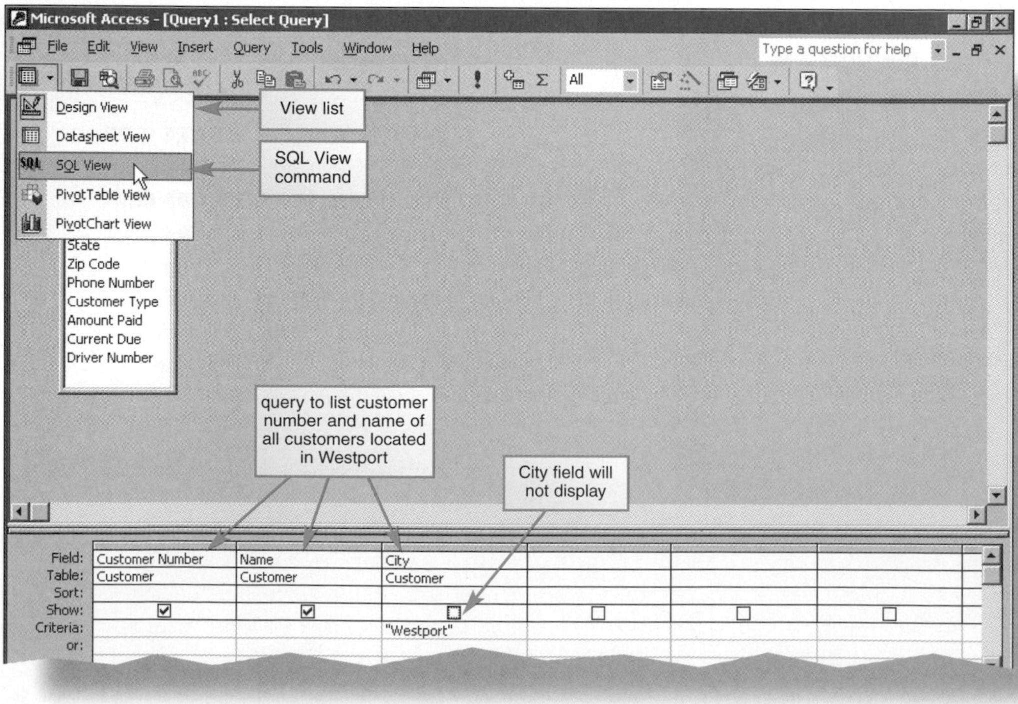

FIGURE 9-101

The corresponding SQL query is shown in Figure 9-102. It is very similar to the queries you have entered, but there are three slight differences. First, the fields are qualified (Customer.[Customer Number] and Customer.Name), even though they do not need to be. (There only is one table involved in the query, so no qualification is necessary. Second, the Name field is not enclosed in square brackets. It is legitimate not to enclose it in square brackets because there are no spaces or other special characters in the field name.) Finally, there are extra parentheses in the criteria.

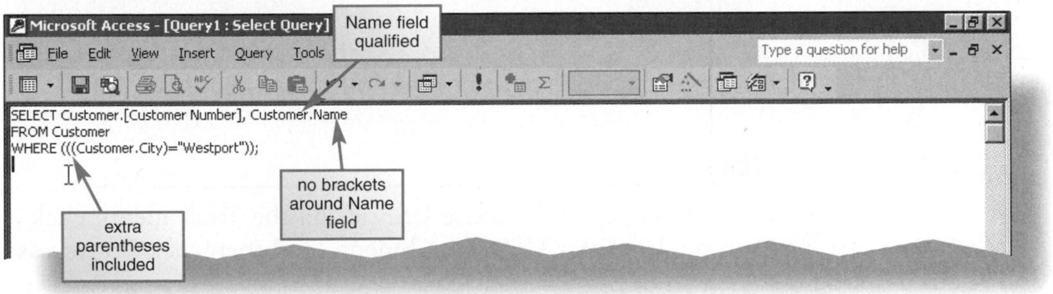

FIGURE 9-102

Both the style used by Access and the style you have been using are legitimate. The choice of style is a personal preference.

Closing the Query

The following step closes the query by closing the Query Datasheet window.

TO CLOSE A QUERY

1. Click the Close Window button for the Microsoft Access - [Query1 : Select Query] window and then click the No button when asked if you want to save your changes.

Protecting a Database through Splitting and Creating MDE Files

In many cases, users would like to develop their own custom forms, reports, queries, or other objects. If each user develops such custom objects, the database can become cluttered and confusing. There could be many reports, for example, each developed by a different user for a different purpose. Further, unless some special action is taken, there is nothing to protect one user's object (for example, a report or form) from modification by another user.

A better approach is to **split** the database into two databases, one called the **back-end database** that contains only the tables data, and another database called the **front-end database** that contains the other objects. While there only would be a single copy of the back-end database, each user could have his or her own copy of the front-end database. A user would create the desired custom objects in his or her own front-end database, thereby not interfering with any other user. In addition, if additional security is desired, front-end databases can be secured using the advanced security techniques described later in this project.

If a database has Visual Basic for Applications (VBA) code associated with it, you can protect this code by saving your database as an **MDE file**. In an MDE version, all VBA code is compiled and then the source code (that is, the original code) is removed from the database. This makes the database smaller and also prevents any modifications to the VBA code.

More About

MDE Files

If the database is replicated, you first must remove replication before creating an MDE file. When you do create an MDE file, users still will be able to update data and run reports but they will not be able to view, create, or modify forms or reports in Design view. Users also cannot import or export forms or reports.

It is very important that you save your original database in case you ever need to make changes to the VBA code. Because the VBA code is removed from the MDE file, you cannot use it to make such changes.

More About

Access File Formats

By default, Access creates a new database in Access 2000 format. A file in Access 2000 file format can be opened in both Access 2000 and Access 2002. This allows you to share your database with users who do not have Access 2002. You can open a file in Access 2002 format only in Access 2002. Certain features, such as creating MDE files, are not available if the database is in Access 2000 file format.

Converting to 2002 Format

You can split a database in Access 2000 format. To create an MDE file, however, the database must be stored in 2002 format. To prepare for the activities in this section, you will create a version of the Alisa Vending Services database in Access 2002 format called Alisa Vending Services2002. To do so, use the Convert Database command on the Database Utilities submenu as in the following steps.

TO CONVERT TO 2002 FORMAT

1. Click Tools on the menu bar, click Database Utilities on the Tools menu, click Convert Database on the Database Utilities submenu, and then click To Access 2002 File Format.
2. Be sure the Save in text box contains the location where you wish to store the converted file, type `Alisa Vending Services2002` as the file name, and then click the Save button.
3. Click the OK button in the Microsoft Access dialog box.
4. Click the Close button for Alisa Vending Services : Database window.

The database is converted. The name of the resulting database is Alisa Vending Services2002.

Splitting the Database

To split a database, make sure the database to be split is open, and then select the Database Splitter command on the Database Utilities submenu. You then will identify a name and location for the back-end database that will be created by the splitter. Perform the following steps to split the Alisa Vending Services2002 database.

Steps To Split the Database

1 Open the Alisa Vending Services2002 database that you created in the previous steps. When the Main Switchboard window displays, close it by clicking its Close button. With the Database window displaying, click Tools on the menu bar, click Database Utilities on the Tools menu, and then point to Database Splitter (Figure 9-103).

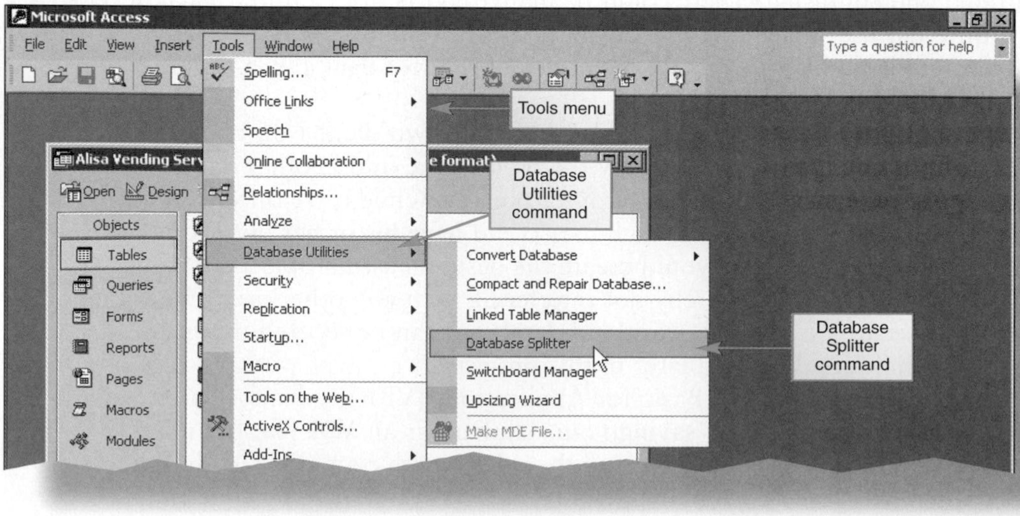

FIGURE 9-103

2 **Click Database Splitter on the Database Utilities submenu, and then point to the Split Database button in the Database Splitter dialog box.**

The Database Splitter dialog box displays (Figure 9-104). The message indicates the effect of splitting a database and some reasons for doing so.

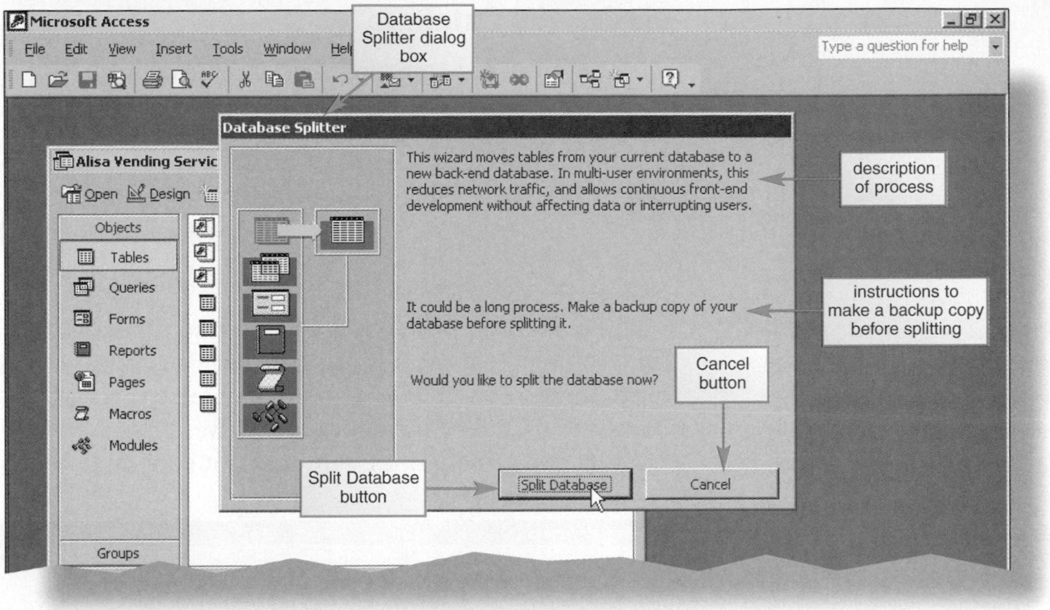

FIGURE 9-104

3 **Click the Split Database button. Be sure the file name in the Create Back-end Database dialog box that displays is Alisa Vending Services2002_be.mdb, and then click the Split button. Point to the OK button.**

The Database Splitter message box displays (Figure 9-105).

4 **Click the OK button.**

The database is split.

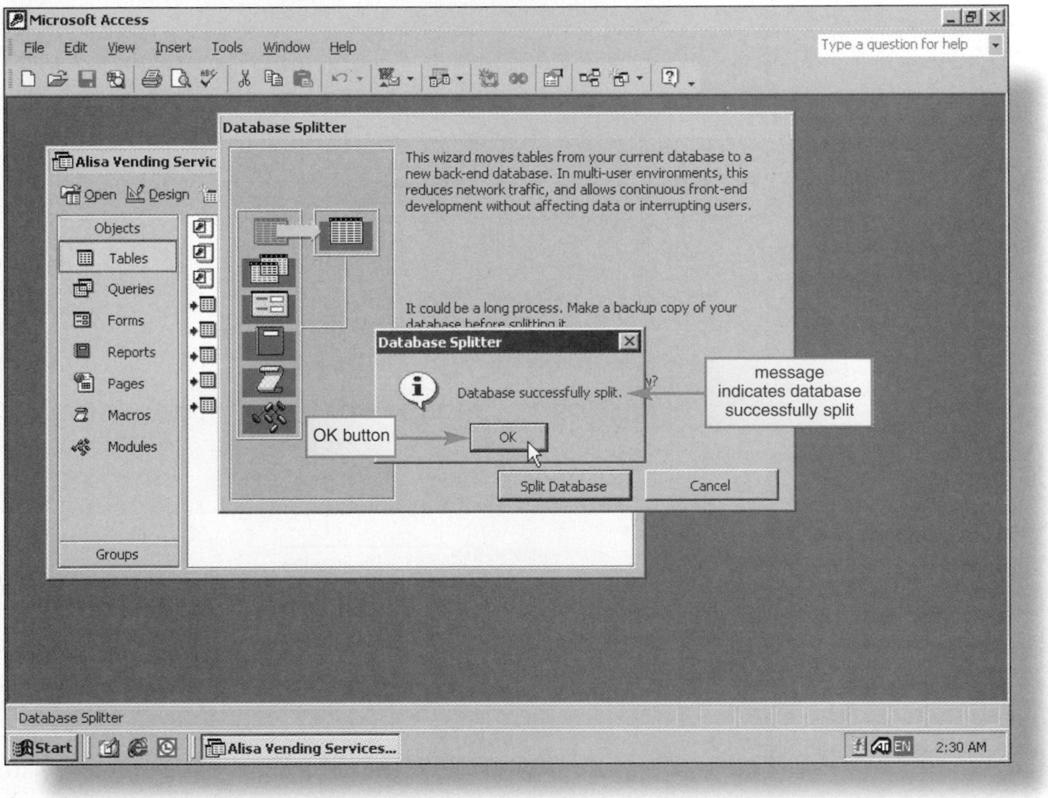

FIGURE 9-105

Other Ways

1. In Voice Command mode, say "Tools, Database Utilities, Database Splitter"

Closing the Database

The following step closes the database by closing its Database window.

TO CLOSE A DATABASE

1. Click the Close button for the Alisa Vending Services : Database window.

The Front-End and Back-End Databases

The database now has been split into separate front-end and back-end databases. The front-end database is the one that you will use. It contains all the queries, reports, forms, and so on, from the original database. It only contains links to the tables, however, instead of the tables themselves (Figure 9-106). The back-end database contains the actual tables, but does not contain any other objects.

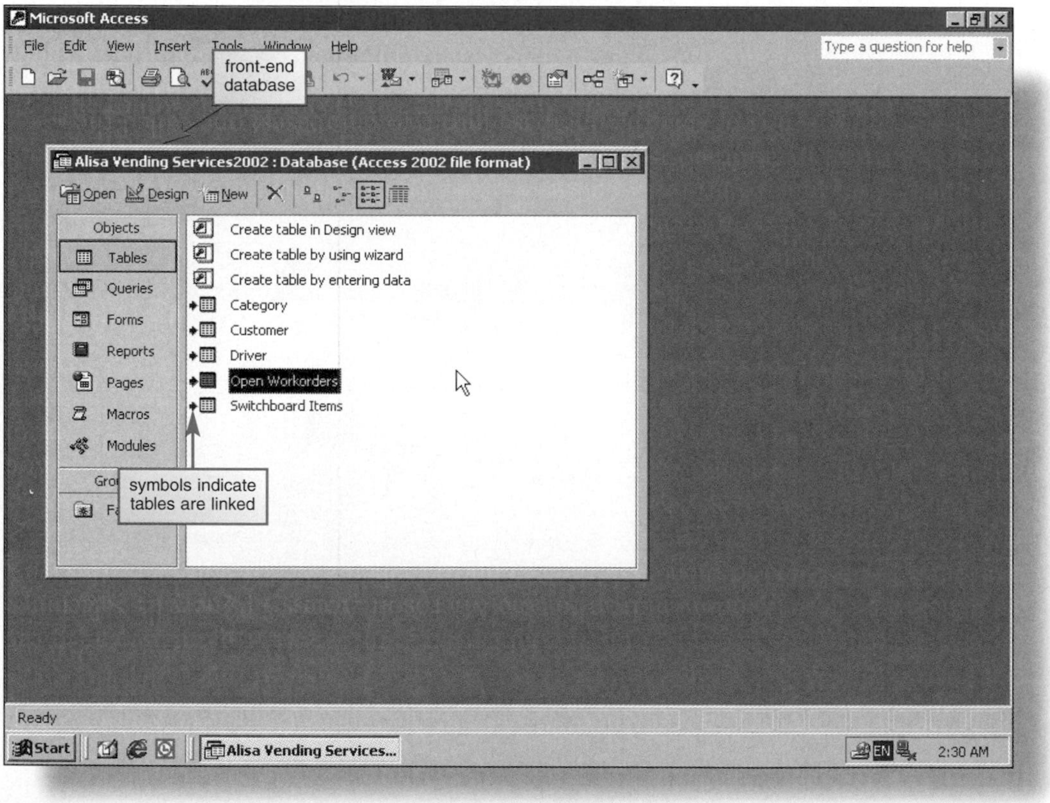

FIGURE 9-106

Creating an MDE File

To create an MDE file, the database needs to be stored in 2002 format. Provided that it is, you create the MDE file by using the Make MDE File command on the Database Utilities submenu of the Tools menu. Perform the following steps to create an MDE file for the Alisa Vending Services2002 database.

Steps To Create an MDE File

1 Click Tools on the menu bar, click Database Utilities on the Tools menu, and then point to Make MDE File (Figure 9-107).

2 Click Make MDE File. Double-click Alisa Vending Services2002 in the Database to Save as MDE dialog box. When the Save MDE As dialog box displays, be sure the Save as type box contains MDE Files. Click the Save button.

The MDE file is created.

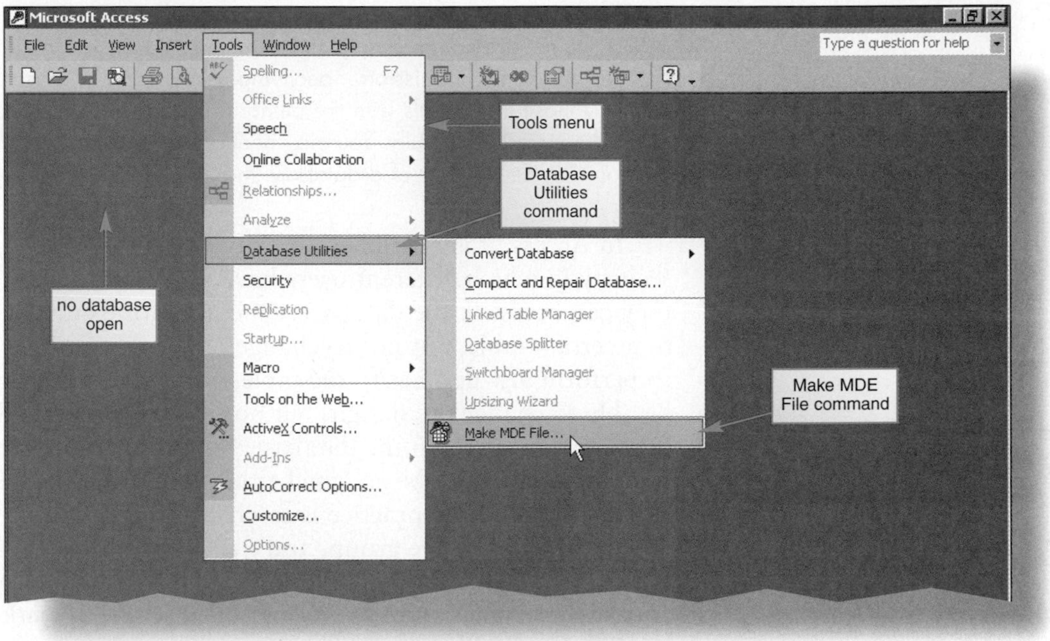

FIGURE 9-107

Using the MDE File

You use an MDE file just as you use the databases with which you now are familiar with two exceptions. First, you must select MDE files in the Files of type box when opening the file. Second, you will not be able to modify any source code because the source code has been removed. If you clicked Modules, for example, and then right-clicked Promo Modules, you would find that the Design View command on the shortcut menu is dimmed, as are most other commands (Figure 9-108).

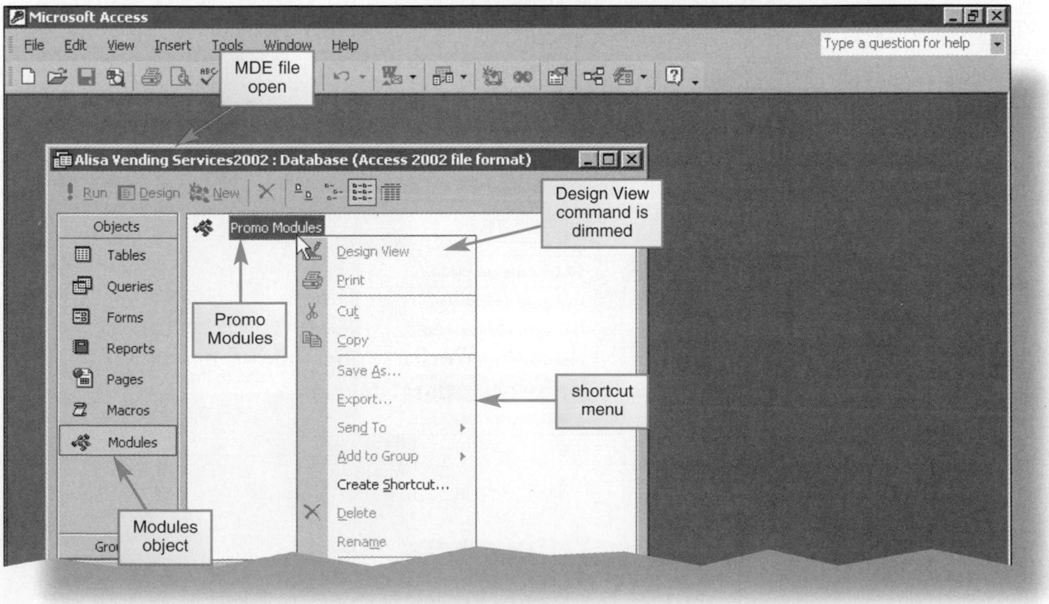

FIGURE 9-108

More About

Security

Permissions are a set of attributes that specify what kind of access a user has to data or objects in a database. A workgroup is a group of users in a multi-user environment who share data and the same workgroup information file.

Advanced Security

Note: Do not attempt to do any of the activities described in the next section unless your instructor has given you permission. Specifying user-level security is a task that should be performed only by those individuals with the authority and responsibility to do so. You should, however, read the material carefully. You may need to perform database administration duties in the future or you may be the user of a database that has user-security levels implemented.

In Access, it is possible to specify **user-level security**, that is, an approach to security in which different users have different permissions concerning the objects they can access in the database. One user, for example, may be able to add records to a certain table, but not to change or delete existing records. Another may be able to perform any updates to the table, but not change the table's design. A third may be able to change the design, but not update the data. The same types of permissions apply to all objects in the database: tables, queries, forms, reports, and other objects.

Permissions can be assigned either to individual users or to entire groups of users. One common practice is to create groups, called **workgroups**, assign appropriate permissions to the group, and then assign each user to an appropriate workgroup based on the permissions the user requires. Information about workgroups, users, and permissions is stored in a special file, called a **workgroup information file**.

When using user-level security, each user is identified by a personal ID and password. Before accessing the database, the user must furnish the ID and password. If either is invalid, the user will not be able to access any data in the database. If both are valid, the user can perform any actions for which he or she has permission.

User-Level Security Wizard

You used the Security submenu on the Tools menu earlier to set a database password and to encrypt a database. Other options on this menu allow an individual to administer workgroups, set permissions, and manage user and group accounts (Figure 9-109). The User-Level Security Wizard command on the Security submenu allows you to use a wizard to perform many of these tasks in a guided fashion.

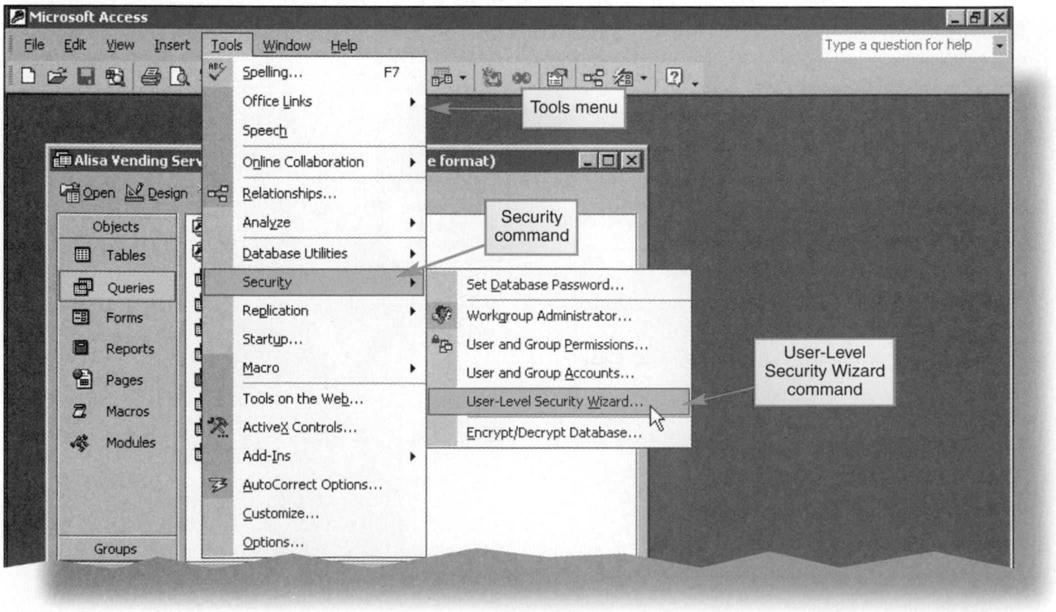

FIGURE 9-109

When you use the Security Wizard, you first must decide which workgroup information file you wish to use. You can create a new file or modify your current file, provided that you have permission to do so. In order to create a new workgroup information file, make sure the Create a new workgroup information file option button is selected before you click the Next button (Figure 9-110).

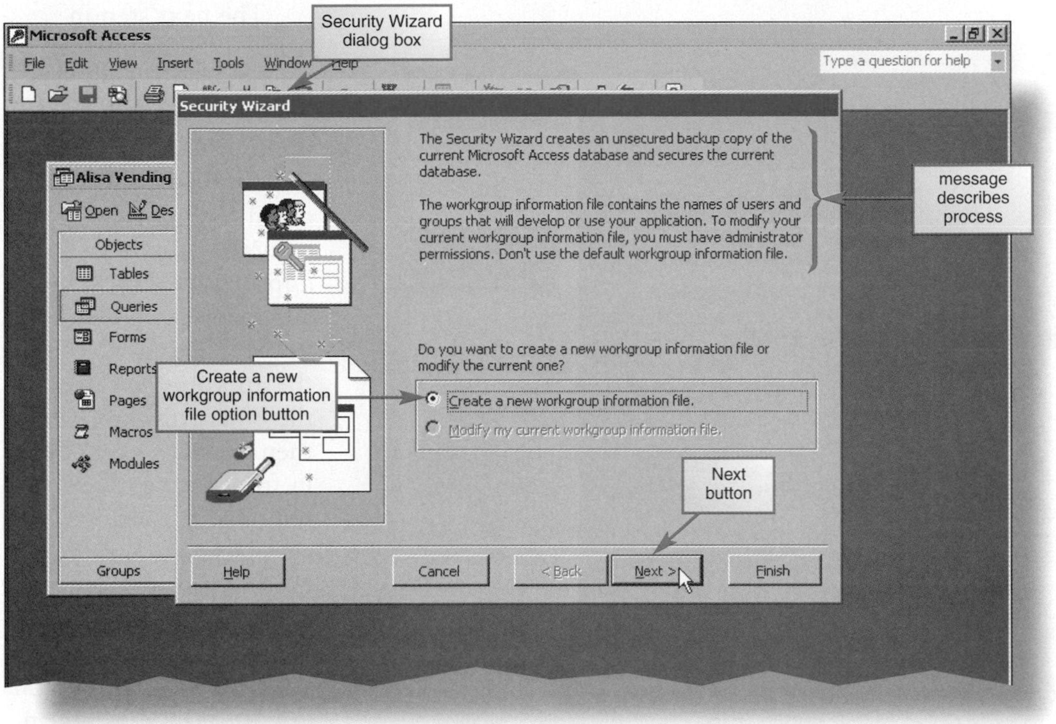

FIGURE 9-110

In the next step, you identify the name and location for the file containing workgroup information (Figure 9-111). You also need to enter a **workgroup ID** (**WID**). As the information in the Security Wizard dialog box indicates, the WID is a unique alphanumeric string that is 4-20 characters in length. You can accept the one that the wizard is suggesting or, if you prefer, change it to some other value. In either case, it is critically important that you record this ID somewhere so you have it for future reference. If there is any problem with the workgroup file, you will need this information to make the necessary corrections.

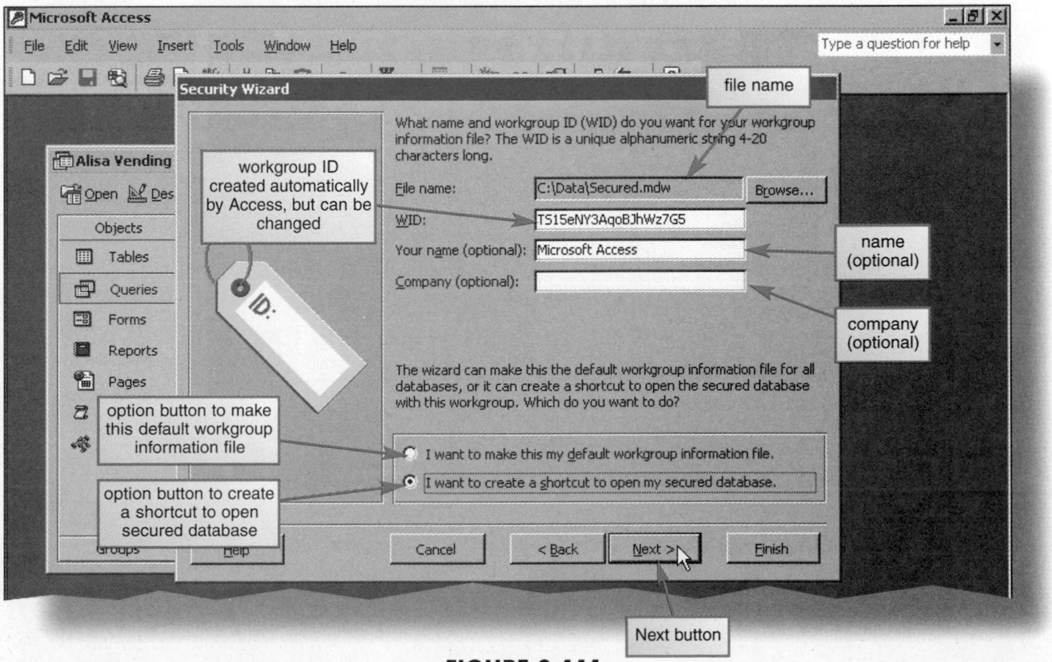

FIGURE 9-111

In this dialog box, you also indicate whether this workgroup file is to become your **default workgroup information file**, the file that will be used whenever you start Access. As an alternative, you can create a shortcut to open the database you are securing. When you use this shortcut, the database will be opened using the workgroup you have just created. If the information in the workgroup is specific to this database, creating a shortcut is typically the approach you will want to take.

The next step in using the wizard is to decide whether all objects in the database are to be secured (Figure 9-112). By default, all objects are secured. Usually this is appropriate. If you have some object, that you do not want secured, click the appropriate tab so the object displays, and then click the check box in front of the object to remove the check mark.

Access has several built-in groups that automatically are assigned appropriate collections of permissions (Figure 9-113). You can select any of these groups that you feel would be appropriate for your security needs by placing a check mark in the check box in front of the group. The wizard creates a group ID for any group you select automatically. You can, if desired, change the group ID. The available groups and corresponding permissions are shown in Table 9-5.

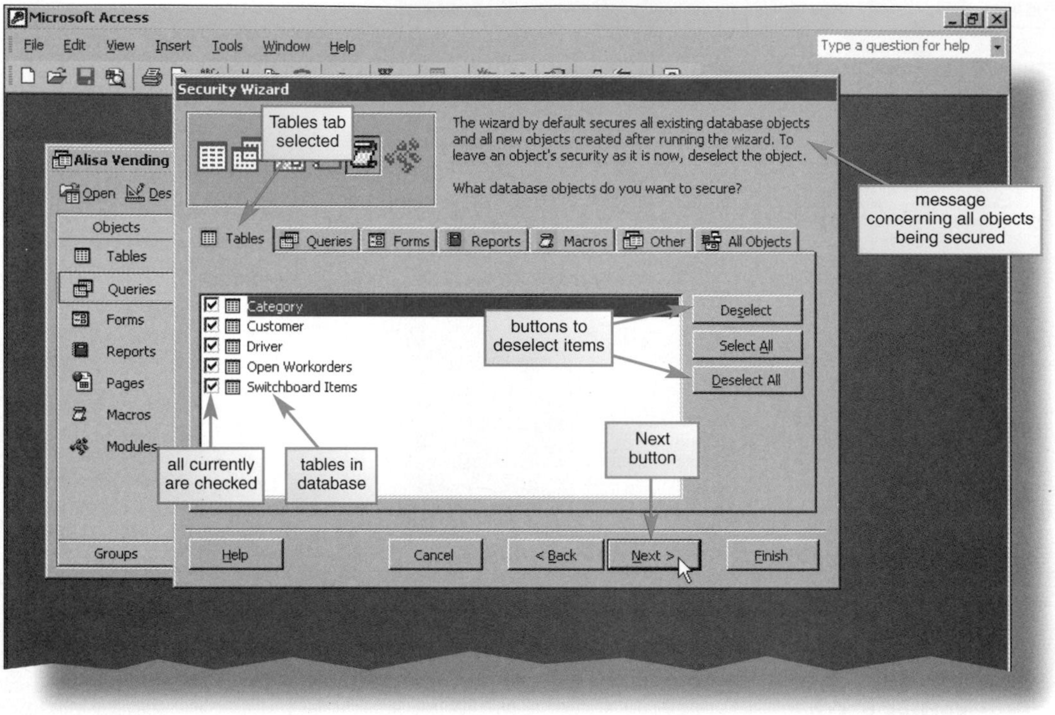

FIGURE 9-112

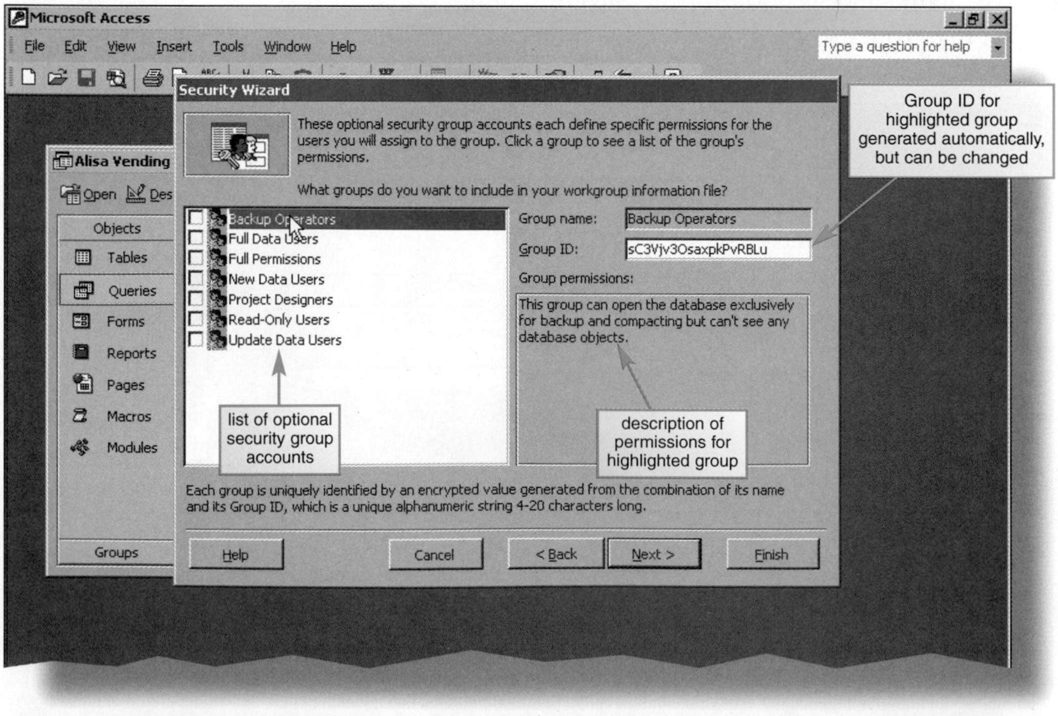

FIGURE 9-113

The next step in using the wizard is to decide whether or not to assign permissions to the Users group (Figure 9-114). There is a default Users group in every workgroup information file. All users automatically belong to this group, whether or not they belong to any other group. Thus, every user would automatically receive any permissions assigned to the Users group. Typically, you do not want to grant any permissions to this group. Rather, you grant permissions to the other groups you specify. You also may grant permissions directly to certain specific users.

Table 9-5 Groups and Associated Permissions

GROUP	PERMISSIONS
Backup Operators	Open database exclusively to perform backup and compacting operations, but cannot view any objects.
Full Data Users	Edit data, but cannot alter any object's design.
Full Permissions	Full permissions for all objects, but cannot assign permissions to anyone else.
New Data Users	Read and insert data, but cannot update or delete data. Cannot alter any object's design.
Project Designers	Edit data and object. Cannot alter tables or relationships.
Read-Only Users	Read data. Cannot alter data or any object's design.
Update Data Users	Read and update data, but cannot insert or delete data. Cannot alter any object's design.

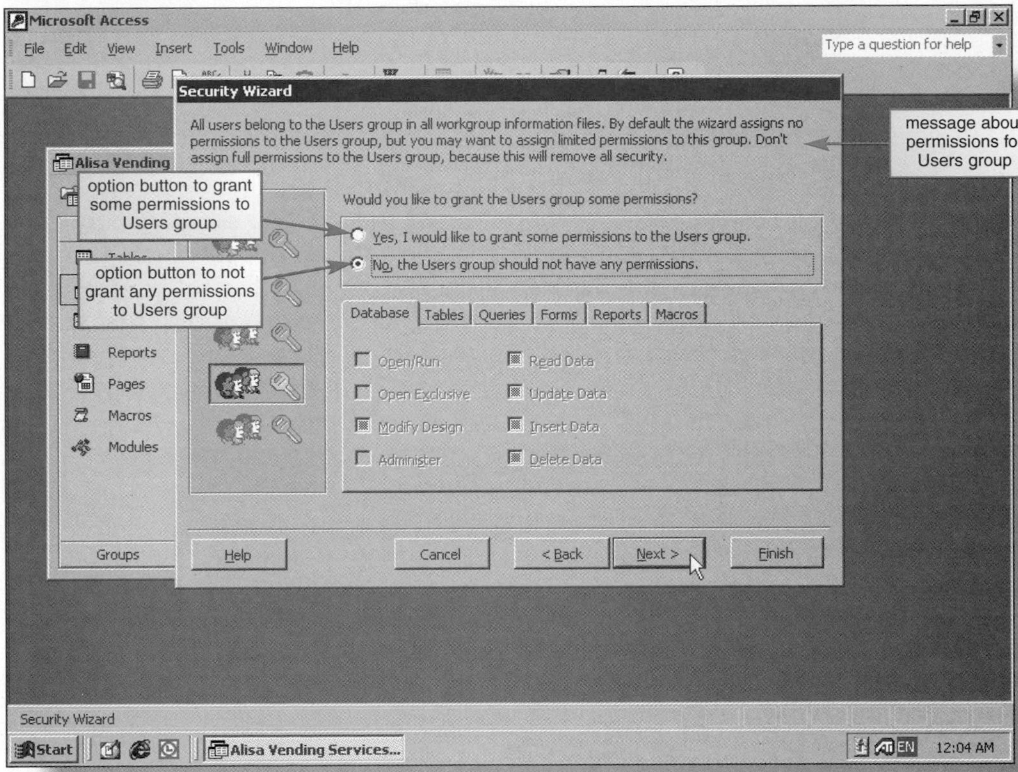

FIGURE 9-114

The next step is to add new users (Figure 9-115). To add a user, select Add New User, and then type the user name and password. You either can accept the Personal ID (PID) that the wizard has assigned or assign one of your own. Once you have made these changes, click the Add This User to the List button to add the user. In the figure, user Pratt has been added. The Administrator user was created automatically.

More About

Quick Reference

For a table that lists how to complete tasks covered in this book using the mouse, menu, shortcut menu, and keyboard, see the Quick Reference Summary at the back of this book or visit the Shelly Cashman Series Office XP Web page (scsite.com/offxp/qr.htm) and then click Microsoft Access 2002.

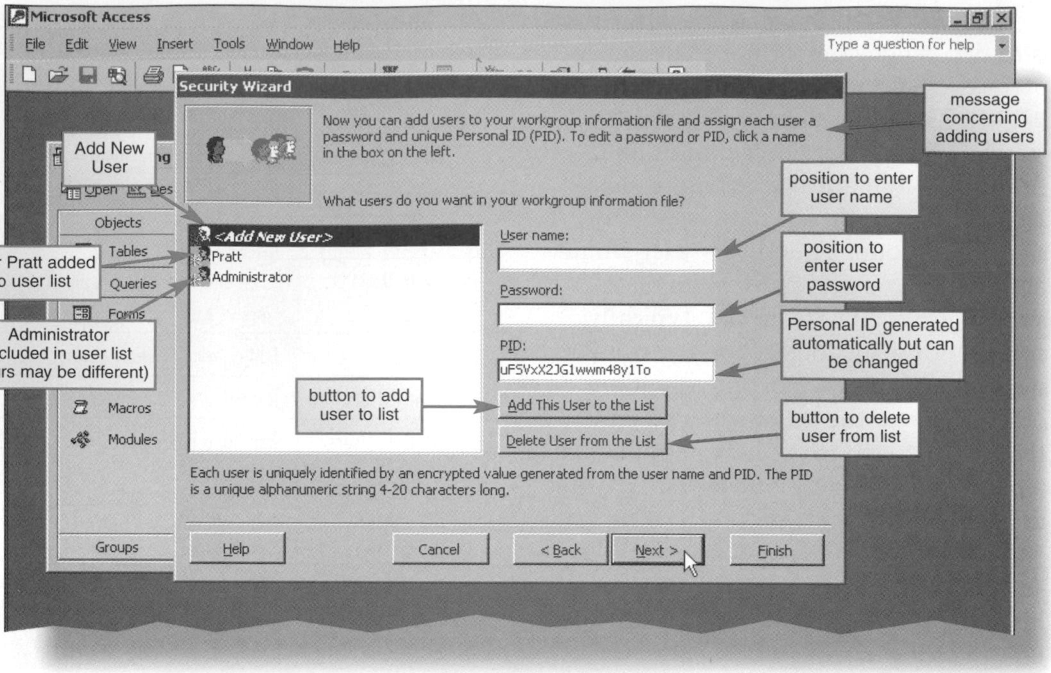

FIGURE 9-115

The next step is to assign users to groups (Figure 9-116). You can do so in one of two ways. You first can select a user and then select the groups to which the user is to be assigned. Alternatively, you first can select a group and then select all the users to be assigned to the group. To carry out either of these operations, first select the option button that corresponds to the approach you want to take. Then, make the appropriate selections.

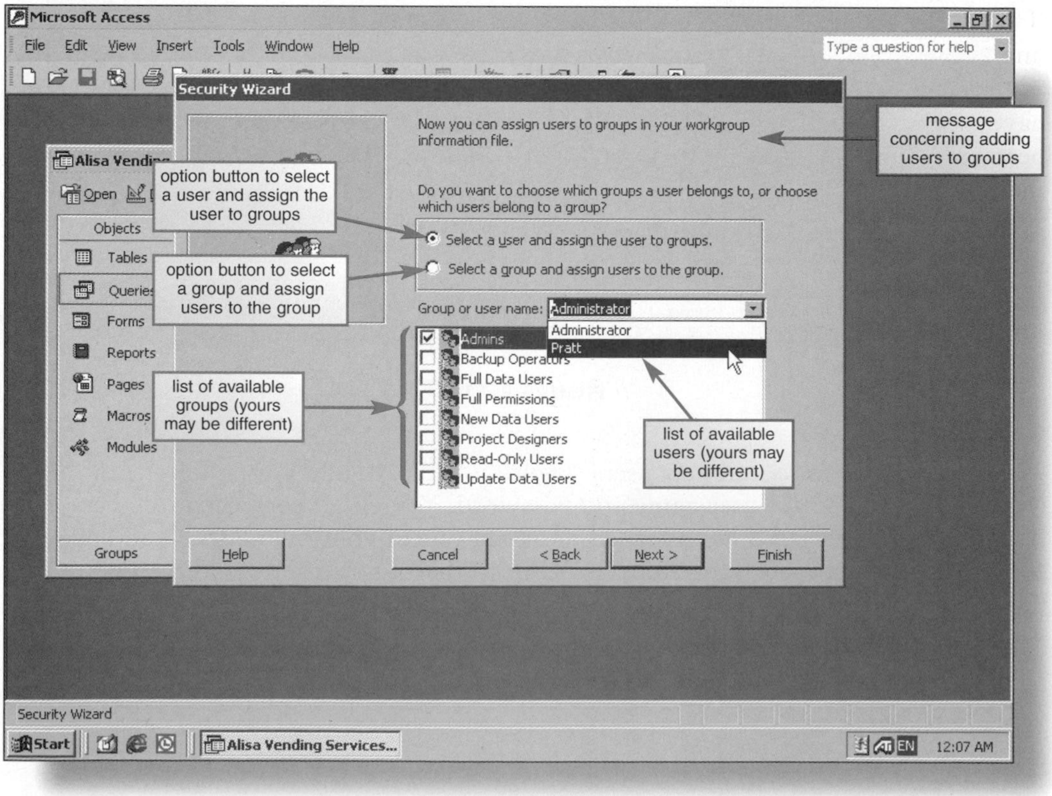

FIGURE 9-116

To complete the process, you need to indicate the location and name for the backup copy of the unsecured database (Figure 9-117). After you have done so and clicked the Finish button, the wizard will create the backup database and encrypt the secured database. It also will update the workgroup information file to reflect the users, groups, and permissions you have assigned. Finally, it will generate and display a report giving detailed information about the users and groups in the workgroup information file. You should print and save this report in case there is ever a problem with the workgroup information file. You will need the information in this file to correct the problem. Once the process is complete, you will need to restart Access in order for the security you specified to take effect.

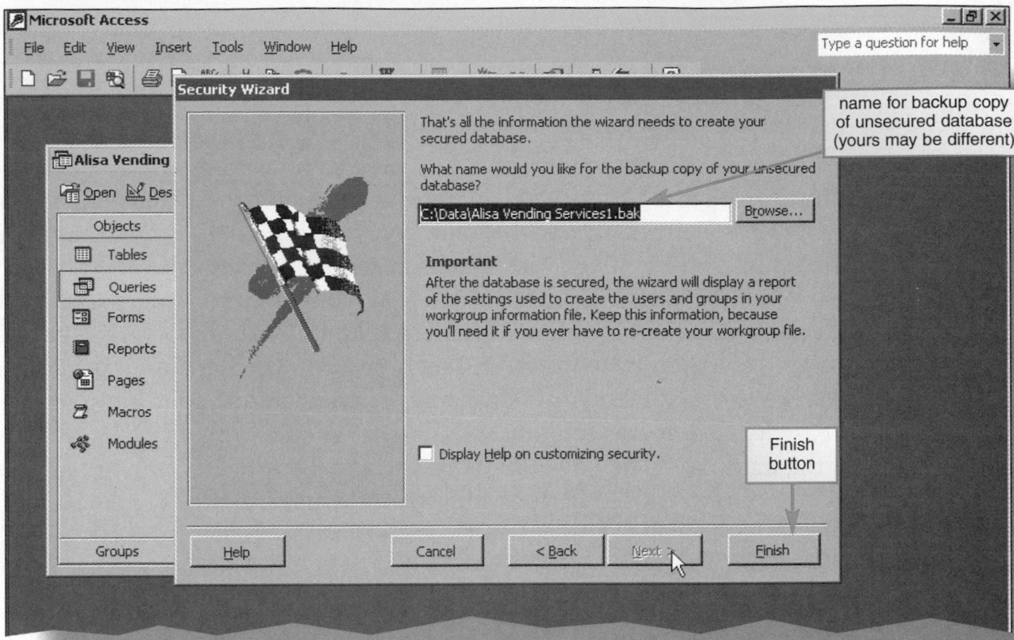

FIGURE 9-117

> **More About**
>
> **Microsoft Certification**
>
> The Microsoft Office User Specialist (MOUS) Certification program provides an opportunity for you to obtain a valuable industry credential — proof that you have the Access 2002 skills required by employers. For more information, see Appendix E or visit the Shelly Cashman Series MOUS Web page at scsite.com/offxp/cert.htm.

Working with a Secured Database

When you open a secured database, you will be asked for a name and password. If you are not able to enter a valid name and password combination, you will be unable to open the database. A valid combination identifies you as a legitimate user of the database. You then can take the actions corresponding to the permissions you have been assigned. If you try to take an action for which you have not been granted permission, Access will display an error message and will not allow you to take the action.

CASE PERSPECTIVE SUMMARY

In Project 9, you assisted the management of Alisa Vending Services by becoming the administrator of their database system. You converted their database to a prior version of Access for a user who needed to query the database and did not have the current version available. You analyzed both tables and performance and produced important documentation. You also specified important integrity constraints involving an input mask and referential integrity. You made sure the database was secure by setting a password and by encrypting the database. You created a replica of the database for use by a remote user and then synchronized that replica with the Design Master. You created a PivotTable and PivotChart. You also learned the importance of the SQL language and used it in several queries. You then investigated additional ways of protecting a database. These included splitting the database into separate front-end and back-end databases as well as creating an MDE file version of the database in which source code is compiled and then removed. You also investigated how to specify special permissions for both users and groups concerning access to the various objects in the database.

Project Summary

In Project 9, you learned how to create an Access 97 version of the database. You used the Table Analyzer, the Performance Analyzer, and the Documenter. You created a custom input mask and also specified referential integrity options. You ensured that the switchboard automatically displays when the database is opened by setting startup options. You set a password and encrypted the database. You created a replica for remote users of the database, updated the replica, and synchronized the replica with the Design Master. You also created PivotTables and PivotCharts. You wrote several SQL commands to query the database. You used criteria involving both number and text fields, compound criteria, and criteria involving NOT. You also used a computed field, sorted query results, and used built-in functions. You used grouping in a query and also joined tables. You also investigated ways of protecting the database. These included splitting the database into a front-end and a back-end database as well as creating an MDE file, a file in which all VBA source code is compiled and then removed from the database. They also included assigning specific permissions to users concerning the types of activities they can perform on the various objects in the database.

What You Should Know

Having completed this project, you now should be able to perform the following tasks:

- Add a Chart Title *(A 9.44)*
- Assign Axis Titles *(A 9.42)*
- Change PivotChart Organization *(A 9.41)*
- Change Properties in a PivotTable *(A 9.34)*
- Change the Chart Type *(A 9.40)*
- Close a Database *(A 9.29, A 9.70)*
- Close a Query *(A 9.67)*
- Close and Save the PivotChart Changes *(A 9.45)*
- Close and Save the PivotTable Changes *(A 9.34)*
- Convert a Database to an Earlier Version *(A 9.07)*
- Convert to 2002 Format *(A 9.68)*
- Create a PivotChart and Add a Legend *(A 9.39)*
- Create a PivotTable *(A 9.32)*
- Create a New SQL Query *(A 9.48)*
- Create a Replica *(A 9.25)*
- Create an MDE File *(A 9.71)*
- Create the Query *(A 9.30)*
- Encrypt a Database *(A 9.23)*
- Include All Fields *(A 9.51)*
- Include Only Certain Fields *(A 9.49)*
- Join Multiple Tables *(A 9.65)*
- Join Tables *(A 9.63)*
- Open a Database *(A 9.06)*
- Open a Database in Exclusive Mode *(A 9.21)*
- Prepare to Enter a New SQL Command *(A 9.50)*
- Remove a Password *(A 9.24)*
- Remove Drop Areas *(A 9.43)*
- Restrict the Groups that Display *(A 9.61)*
- Restrict the Records in a Join *(A 9.64)*
- Set a Password *(A 9.21)*
- Set Startup Options *(A 9.20)*
- Sort the Results *(A 9.57)*
- Specify Referential Integrity Options *(A 9.16)*
- Split the Database *(A 9.68)*
- Synchronize the Design Master and the Replica *(A 9.28)*
- Update a Table with Cascade Options *(A 9.18)*
- Use a Built-In Function *(A 9.58)*
- Use a Compound Criterion *(A 9.54)*
- Use a Computed Field *(A 9.56)*
- Use a Criterion Involving a Numeric Field *(A 9.52)*
- Use a Criterion Involving a Text Field *(A 9.53)*
- Use a PivotChart *(A 9.46)*
- Use a PivotTable *(A 9.35)*
- Use an Input Mask *(A 9.15)*
- Use Grouping *(A 9.60)*
- Use Multiple Functions in the Same Command *(A 9.59)*
- Use NOT in a Criterion *(A 9.55)*
- Use the Documenter *(A 9.13)*
- Use the Performance Analyzer *(A 9.11)*
- Use the Replica *(A 9.26)*
- Use the Table Analyzer *(A 9.08)*

Learn It Online

Instructions: To complete the Learn It Online exercises, start your browser, click the Address bar, and then enter `scsite.com/offxp/exs.htm`. When the Office XP Learn It Online page displays, follow the instructions in the exercises below.

1 Project Reinforcement TF, MC, and SA

Below Access Project 9, click the Project Reinforcement link. Print the quiz by clicking Print on the File menu. Answer each question. Write your first and last name at the top of each page, and then hand in the printout to your instructor.

2 Flash Cards

Below Access Project 9, click the Flash Cards link. When Flash Cards displays, read the instructions. Type 20 (or a number specified by your instructor) in the Number of Playing Cards text box, type your name in the Name text box, and then click the Flip Card button. When the flash card displays, read the question and then click the Answer box arrow to select an answer. Flip through Flash Cards. Click Print on the File menu to print the last flash card if your score is 15 (75%) correct or greater and then hand it in to your instructor. If your score is less than 15 (75%) correct, then redo this exercise by clicking the Replay button.

3 Practice Test

Below Access Project 9, click the Practice Test link. Answer each question, enter your first and last name at the bottom of the page, and then click the Grade Test button. When the graded practice test displays on your screen, click Print on the File menu to print a hard copy. Continue to take practice tests until you score 80% or better. Hand in a printout of the final practice test to your instructor.

4 Who Wants to Be a Computer Genius?

Below Access Project 9, click the Computer Genius link. Read the instructions, enter your first and last name at the bottom of the page, and then click the Play button. Hand in your score to your instructor.

5 Wheel of Terms

Below Access Project 9, click the Wheel of Terms link. Read the instructions, and then enter your first and last name and your school name. Click the Play button. Hand in your score to your instructor.

6 Crossword Puzzle Challenge

Below Access Project 9, click the Crossword Puzzle Challenge link. Read the instructions, and then enter your first and last name. Click the Play button. Work the crossword puzzle. When you are finished, click the Submit button. When the crossword puzzle redisplays, click the Print button. Hand in the printout.

7 Tips and Tricks

Below Access Project 9, click the Tips and Tricks link. Click a topic that pertains to Project 9. Right-click the information and then click Print on the shortcut menu. Construct a brief example of what the information relates to in Access to confirm you understand how to use the tip or trick. Hand in the example and printed information.

online

8 Newsgroups

Below Access Project 9, click the Newsgroups link. Click a topic that pertains to Project 9. Print three comments. Hand in the comments to your instructor.

9 Expanding Your Horizons

Below Access Project 9, click the Articles for Microsoft Access link. Click a topic that pertains to Project 9. Print the information. Construct a brief example of what the information relates to in Access to confirm you understand the contents of the article. Hand in the example and printed information to your instructor.

10 Search Sleuth

Below Access Project 9, click the Search Sleuth link. To search for a term that pertains to this project, select a term below the Project 9 title and then use the Google search engine at google.com (or any major search engine) to display and print two Web pages that present information on the term. Hand in the printouts to your instructor.

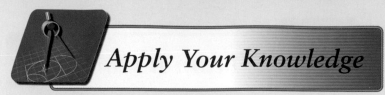

Apply Your Knowledge

1 Administering the Beyond Clean Database

Instructions: Start Access. If you are using the Microsoft Access 2002 Comprehensive text, open the Beyond Clean database that you used in Project 8. Otherwise, see the inside back cover for instructions for downloading the Data Disk or see your instructor for information about accessing the files required for this book. Perform the following tasks.

1. Use the Table Analyzer to analyze the Client table. On your own paper, list the results of the analysis.
2. Use the Performance Analyzer to analyze all the tables and queries in the Beyond Clean database. On your own paper, list the results of the analysis.
3. Use the Documenter to produce documentation for the Fee table. Print the documentation.
4. Create a custom input mask for the Client Number field in the Client table. The first two characters of the client number must be uppercase letters and the last two characters must be digits. No position may be blank. On your own paper, list the input mask you created.
5. Open the Relationships window and edit the relationship between the Client table and the Custodian table. Cascade the update so any changes made to the Custodian Id field in the Custodian table will result in a change in the Custodian Id field in the Client table. Save the changes to the Relationships window.
6. Open the Custodian table in Datasheet view and change the custodian id for custodian 002 from 002 to 005. Close the table.
7. Print the Client table.
8. Open the Total Fees by Client query and switch to PivotChart view. Create the PivotChart shown in Figure 9-118. Save the changes to the layout of the query.
9. Print the PivotChart in landscape orientation.
10. Use SQL to create a query that joins the Client table and the Service table. Include the Client Number, Name, and Service Date fields in the query results. Run the query and print the results.

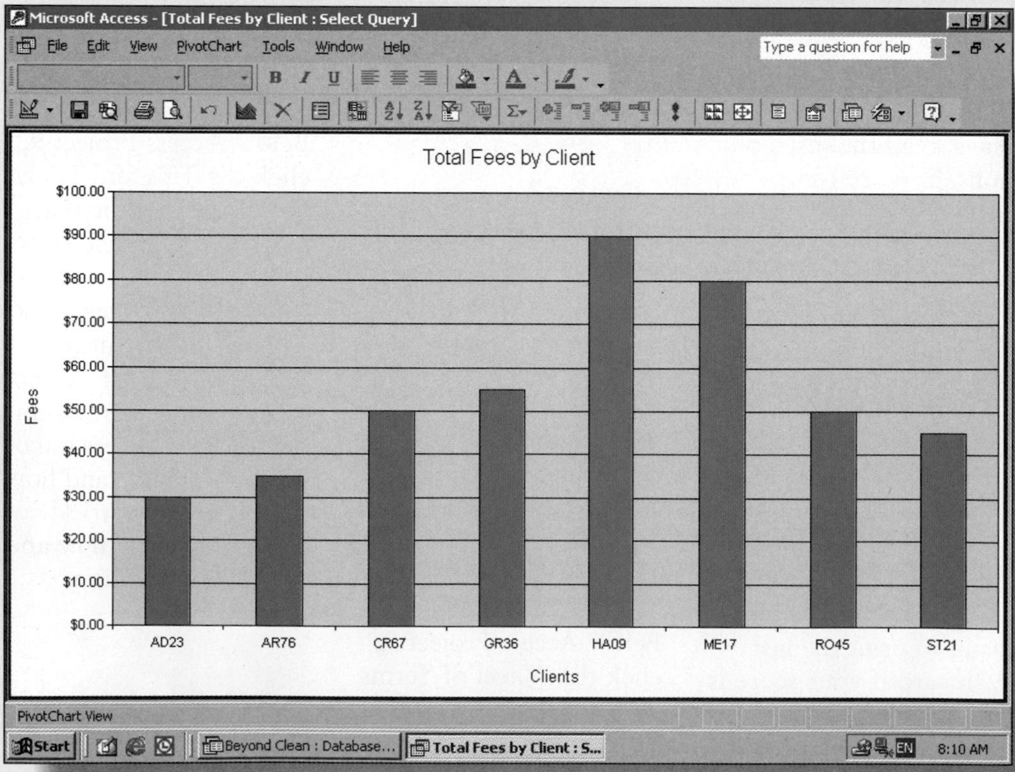

FIGURE 9-118

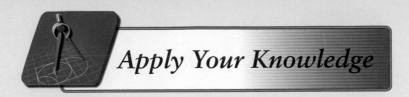

Apply Your Knowledge

11. Return to the SQL window, highlight the SQL command you used in Step 10 above and click Copy on the Query Design toolbar.
12. Start Microsoft Word, create a new document, type your name at the top of the document, and then click Paste on the Standard toolbar.
13. Print the Word document containing the SQL command.
14. Quit Word and Access.

In the Lab

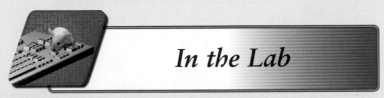

1 Administering the Wooden Crafts Database

Problem: Jan Merchant has placed you in charge of administering her database system. A database administrator must perform activities such as analyzing the performance of the DBMS, specifying integrity constraints, protecting the database from unauthorized use, creating PivotTables and PivotCharts, and using SQL.

Instructions: If you are using the Microsoft Access 2002 Comprehensive text, open the Wooden Crafts database that you used in Project 8. Otherwise, see the inside back cover for instructions for downloading the Data Disk or see your instructor for information about accessing the files required for this book. Perform the following tasks.

1. Use the Performance Analyzer to analyze all the tables and queries in the Wooden Crafts database. On your own paper, list the results of the analysis.
2. Use the Documenter to print the documentation for the Reorder table.
3. Supplier Code is a field in both the Product and Supplier tables. Create an input mask for the Supplier Code field in both tables. On your own paper, list the input mask that you created.
4. Edit the relationship between the Reorder table and the Product table so a product may be deleted from the Product table and then automatically deleted from the Reorder table.
5. Edit the relationship between the Supplier table and the Product table so a change to the Supplier Code field in the Supplier table will result in the same change to the Supplier Code field in the Product table.
6. Open the Supplier table and change the supplier code for Bert Huntington to AH.
7. Print the Product table.
8. Open the Product table and delete product MR06.
9. Print the Product table and the Reorder table.
10. Open the Reorder Items by Supplier query and switch to PivotTable view. Create the PivotTable shown in Figure 9-119 on the next page. Save the changes to the layout of the query.
11. Print the PivotTable.
12. Hide the details for supplier code PL and print the PivotTable again. Do not save the changes to the layout of the query.

(continued)

In the Lab

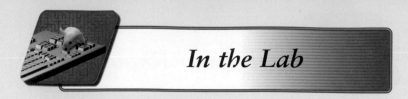

Administering the Wooden Crafts Database *(continued)*

13. Open Microsoft Word, create a new document, and then type your name at the top. With both Access and Word open on the desktop, create the queries in Steps 14 through 17 in SQL. For each query, run the query, print the query results and copy the SQL command to the Word document. To copy the SQL command, highlight the command, click Copy on the Query Design toolbar, switch to Word, and then click Paste on the Standard toolbar.

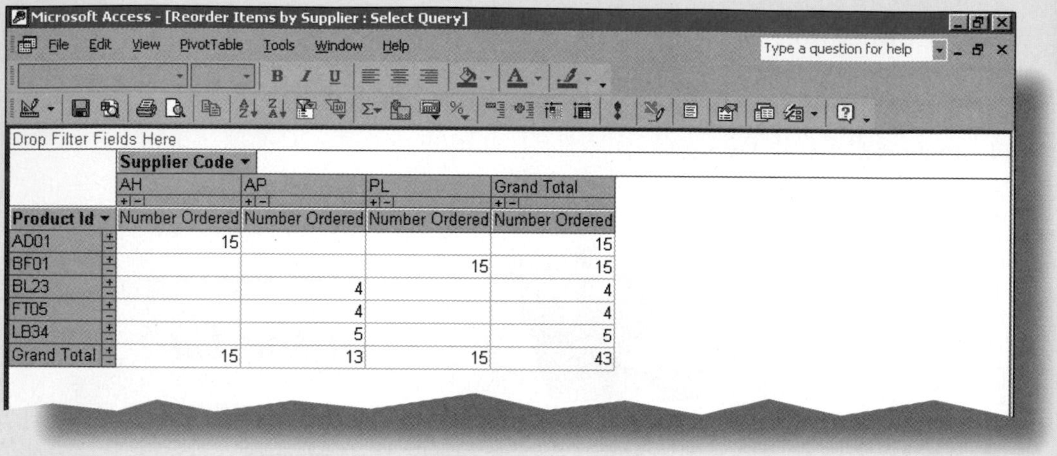

Product Id	AH Number Ordered	AP Number Ordered	PL Number Ordered	Grand Total Number Ordered
AD01	15			15
BF01			15	15
BL23		4		4
FT05		4		4
LB34		5		5
Grand Total	15	13	15	43

FIGURE 9-119

14. Find all records in the Product table where the difference between the cost of the product and the selling price of the product is less than $4.00. Display the product id, description, cost, and selling price.
15. Join the Reorder table and the Product table. Display the product id, description, number ordered, cost, and total cost (cost * number ordered). Be sure to name the computed field, Total Cost.
16. Join the Product and Reorder tables. Display the product id, description, and number ordered for all products where the number ordered is less than 5.
17. Find the total number of reordered products for each product. Display the product id and total number ordered.
18. Print the Word document that includes the 4 SQL commands used above.

2 Administering the Restaurant Supply Database

Problem: The restaurant supply company has placed you in charge of administering their database system. A database administrator must perform activities such as analyzing the performance of the DBMS, specifying integrity constraints, protecting the database from unauthorized use, creating PivotTables and PivotCharts, and using SQL.

Instructions: If you are using the Microsoft Access 2002 Comprehensive text, open the Restaurant Supply database that you used in Project 8. Otherwise, see the inside back cover for instructions for downloading the Data Disk or see your instructor for information about accessing the files required for this book. Perform the following tasks.

1. Use the Performance Analyzer to analyze all the tables and queries in the Restaurant Supply database. On your own paper, list the results of the analysis.
2. Use the Documenter to print the documentation for the Category table.

In the Lab

3. Sales Rep Number is a field in both the Customer and Sales Rep tables. Create an input mask for the Sales Rep Number field in both tables. On your own paper, list the input mask that you created.
4. Edit the relationship between the Workorders table and the Customer table so a customer may be deleted from the Customer table and then automatically deleted from the Workorders table.
5. Edit the relationship between the Sales Rep and the Customer table so a change to the Sales Rep field in the Sales Rep table will result in the same change to the Sales Rep field in the Customer table.
6. Open the Sales Rep table and change the sales rep number for Jose Ortiz to 53.
7. Print the Customer table.
8. Open the Customer table and delete customer AM23.
9. Print the Customer table and the Workorders table.
10. Open the Sales Rep and Customers query and switch to PivotTable view. Create the PivotTable shown in Figure 9-120. Note that the Grand Total details are hidden. Save the changes to the layout of the query.
11. Print the PivotTable.

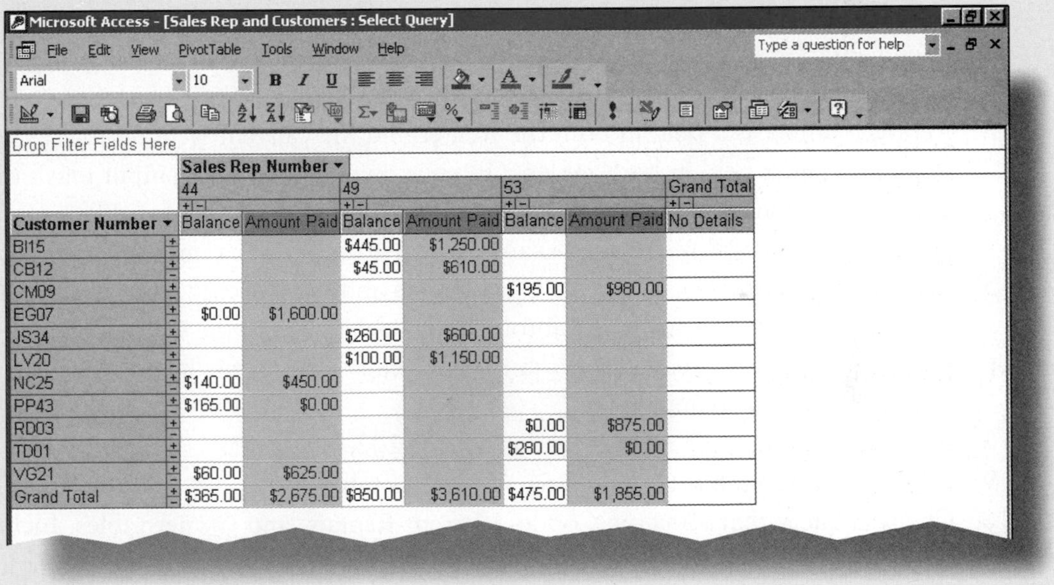

	Sales Rep Number						
	44		49		53		Grand Total
Customer Number	Balance	Amount Paid	Balance	Amount Paid	Balance	Amount Paid	No Details
BI15			$445.00	$1,250.00			
CB12			$45.00	$610.00			
CM09					$195.00	$980.00	
EG07	$0.00	$1,600.00					
JS34			$260.00	$600.00			
LV20			$100.00	$1,150.00			
NC25	$140.00	$450.00					
PP43	$165.00	$0.00					
RD03					$0.00	$875.00	
TD01					$280.00	$0.00	
VG21	$60.00	$625.00					
Grand Total	$365.00	$2,675.00	$850.00	$3,610.00	$475.00	$1,855.00	

FIGURE 9-120

12. Open Microsoft Word, create a new document, and then type your name at the top. With both Access and Word open on the desktop, create the queries in Steps 13 through 17 in SQL. For each query, run the query, print the query results and copy the SQL command to the Word document. To copy the SQL command, highlight the command, click Copy on the Query Design toolbar, switch to Word, and then click Paste on the Standard toolbar.
13. Display the Customer Number and Name fields for all customers that do not have a dining type of FFT.
14. Display the Customer Number, Name, Address, and Telephone fields for all customers who have a balance greater than the amount paid.
15. Display the sales rep's First Name and Last Name, Customer Number, Name, and Description fields for all work orders where the category code is 1. Order the records by sales rep's last name.
16. Display the customer number, name, and total amount (balance + amount paid) for all customers that have a dining type of FAM.
17. Group the work orders by customer and count the number of work orders for each customer.
18. Print the Word document that includes the five SQL commands used above.
19. Modify the startup options so the switchboard opens automatically when the Restaurant Supply database is open.

In the Lab

3 Administering the Condo Management Database

Problem: The condo management company has placed you in charge of administering their database system. A database administrator must perform activities such as analyzing the performance of the DBMS, specifying integrity constraints, protecting the database from unauthorized use, creating PivotTables and PivotCharts, and using SQL.

Instructions: If you are using the Microsoft Access 2002 Comprehensive text, open the Condo Management database that you used in Project 8. Otherwise, see the inside back cover for instructions for downloading the Data Disk or see your instructor for information about accessing the files required for this book. Perform the following tasks.

1. Use the Performance Analyzer to analyze all the tables and queries in the Condo Management database. On your own paper, list the results of the analysis.
2. Use the Documenter to print the documentation for the Current Rentals table. Print page 1 of the documentation by clicking Print on the File menu, and then clicking the Pages button. Enter 1 in both the From and To boxes.
3. Renter Number is a field in both the Renter and the Current Rental tables. Create an input mask for the Renter Number field in both tables. On your own paper, list the input mask that you created.
4. Edit the relationships between the Renter and the Current Rentals table so a change to the renter number in the Renter table will result in the same change to the renter number in the Current Rentals table.
5. Edit the relationship between the Condo table and the Current Rentals table so a condo unit may be deleted from the Condo table and then automatically deleted from the Current Rentals table.
6. Open the Renter table and then change the renter number for Jenna Margreit to R006.
7. Print the Current Rentals table.
8. Open the Condo table and delete condo unit 202.
9. Print the Condo table and the Current Rentals table.
10. Create a query that joins the Condo, Current Rentals, and Owner tables. Include the Owner Id, Unit Number, and Length fields in the query. Save the query as Rentals by Owner and Unit.
11. Open the Rentals by Owner and Unit query and switch to PivotTable view. Create the PivotTable shown in Figure 9-121. Print the PivotTable.

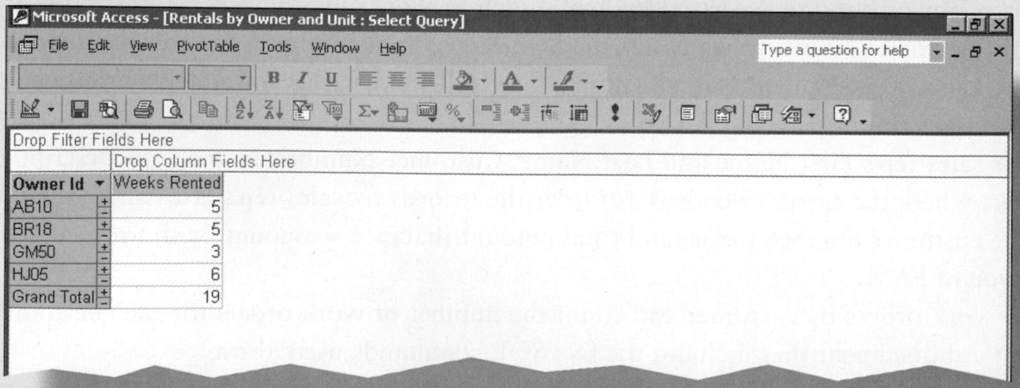

FIGURE 9-121

In the Lab

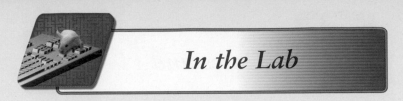

12. Switch to PivotChart view and then create the PivotChart shown in Figure 9-122. Print the PivotChart in landscape orientation.
13. Open Microsoft Word, create a new document, and then type your name at the top. With both Access and Word open on the desktop, create the queries in Steps 14 through 20 in SQL. For each query, run the query, print the query results and copy the SQL command to the Word document. To copy the SQL command, highlight the command, click Copy on the Query Design toolbar, switch to Word, and then click Paste on the Standard toolbar.

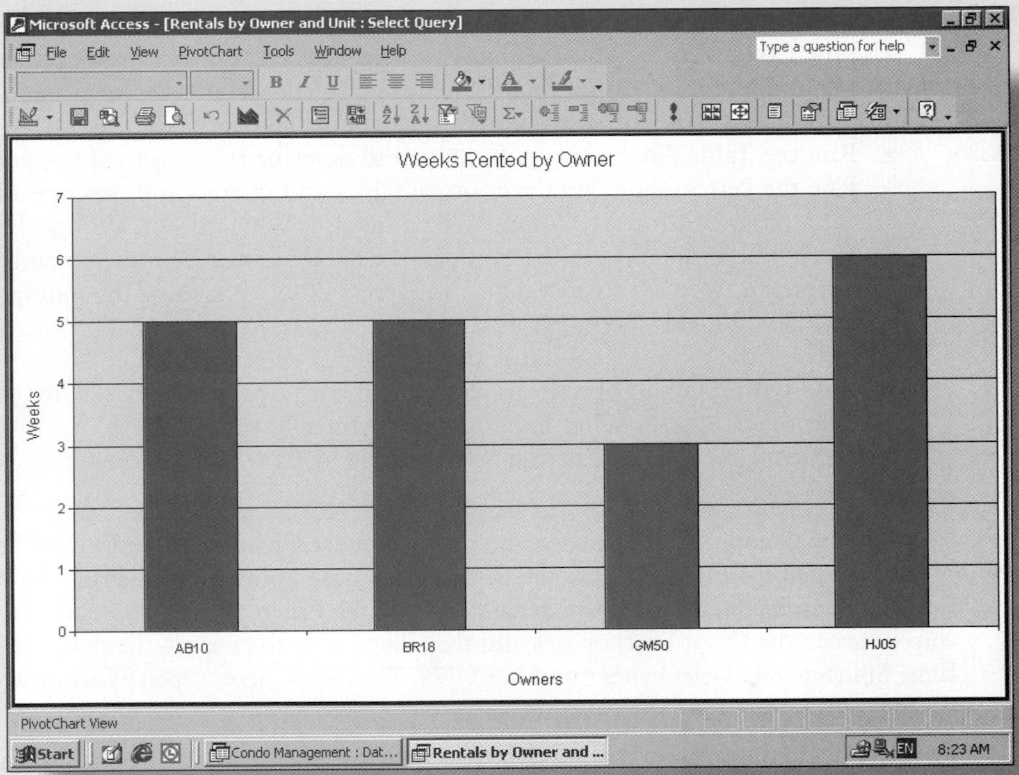

FIGURE 9-122

14. Display and print the unit number, renter first name and last name, and total amount owed (weekly rate * length) for all current rentals.
15. Display and print the average weekly rate by owner. Be sure to sort the records in ascending order.
16. Modify the query you created in Step 15 to only those records where the average weekly rate is greater than $1,000.00.
17. Display and print unit number, start date, length, and renter first and last name for all current rentals.
18. Display and print the owner's first and last name, the unit number, and the weekly rate for all condos that provide linens. (***Hint:*** Search Yes/No fields by using True and False as the criterion.)
19. Display and print the unit number, bedrooms, sleeps, and weekly rate for all records. Sort the records in descending order by bedrooms within sleeps. (***Hint:*** Use the reserved word DESC after the sort key.)
20. Display and print the unit number, bedrooms, and weekly rate for all units that have more than one bedroom and more than one bathroom and a powder room.
21. Print the Word document that includes the seven SQL commands used above.
22. Modify the startup options so the switchboard opens automatically when the Condo Management database is open.

Cases and Places

The difficulty of these case studies varies:
▶ are the least difficult; ▶▶ are more difficult; and ▶▶▶ are the most difficult.

1 ▶ Use the CompuWhiz database that you used in Project 8 for this assignment or see your instructor for information about accessing the files required for this book. Perform the following database administration tasks and answer the questions about the database.

a. Run the Table Analyzer on all tables and describe the results of the analysis.
b. Run the Performance Analyzer on all tables and queries and describe the results of the analysis.
c. Set a password for the CompuWhiz database. Why did you choose that particular password? What will happen if you try to open the database and cannot remember your password?
d. Create an Access 97 version and an Access 2002 version of the CompuWhiz database. Why would you need to convert a database to an earlier version?
e. Encrypt the database. What is the purpose of encryption?
f. Modify the startup options so the switchboard opens automatically.
g. Split the database. What happens when you split the database?
h. Create an MDE file. What happens to VBA code when you create an MDE file?

2 ▶ Use the CompuWhiz database and create a query, PivotTable, and PivotChart that are similar to the objects created for the Alisa Vending Services database in the project. Print the PivotTable and PivotChart. Edit the relationship between the Technician and the Client tables to cascade the update. Edit the relationship between the Open Workorders and the Client table to cascade the delete. Change the technician id for Irene Smith to 91. Delete client number CJ78. Print the Client, Open Workorders, and Technician tables.

3 ▶▶ Replicate the CompuWhiz database. Use the replica and add yourself as a client. Create a work order for yourself and add the data to the Open Workorders table. Synchronize the master and the replica. Use the master to print the updated tables.

4 ▶▶ Use the Hockey Shop database that you used in Project 8 for this assignment or see your instructor for information about accessing the files required for this book. Create and run the following SQL queries. Print the query results, copy the SQL commands to a Word document, and then print the Word document.

a. Find the total cost (units on hand * cost) of all items.
b. Find the average cost by vendor.
c. Display the item id, description, reorder date, reorder number, and vendor name for all items that are on reorder.
d. Display the item id, description, cost, and selling price of all items where the difference between the selling price and cost is more than $3.00.
e. Find the total number of reordered items for each item. Display the item id and total number ordered.
f. Display the item id and description for all records where the description starts with the letter S. (***Hint***: Use the LIKE operator and a wildcard to solve this problem.)
g. Display the average cost by vendor for those items that have an average cost less than $20.00.

5 ▶▶▶ If you have your instructor's permission, use the User-Level Security Wizard to create user-level security for the Hockey Shop database.

Microsoft Access 2002

Grouped Data Access Pages, PivotTables, and PivotCharts

CASE PERSPECTIVE

Alisa Vending Services has requests for data to be accessible on the Web. They realize this means placing the data on data access pages. The first request is to make a list of drivers available on the Web. When viewing this data, they would like the option of displaying all the customers for one or more of the drivers on the data access page. In addition, they have found both the PivotTable and the PivotChart you created for them to be very useful and would like to be able to view a PivotTable and a PivotChart on the Web. They want you to take the steps necessary to place both a PivotTable and a PivotChart on data access pages.

Introduction

In this feature, you will create the data access pages shown in Figures 1a, 1b, and 1c on the next page. Figure 1a shows a grouped data access page. The data is grouped by driver number. Clicking the plus sign (+) in front of a driver displays all the customers associated with that driver. When the customers associated with a driver display, the plus sign changes to a minus sign (–). Clicking the minus sign will hide the customers associated with the driver.

The data access page in Figure 1b contains a PivotTable. The Driver Number field is in the Filter area and can be used to restrict the data shown in the PivotTable to only customers associated with certain drivers. The Customer Number and Location fields are both in the Row area. The Category Number field is in the Column area. The Hours Spent and Hours Remaining fields are in the Detail area with their captions changed to Spent and Remaining, respectively. Sums of both the Hours Spent and Hours Remaining also are included in the PivotTable.

The data access page in Figure 1c contains a PivotChart. The PivotChart is a 3D Stacked Column chart and includes a legend. The bar heights represent total hours. The x-axis (horizontal axis) shows the driver numbers subdivided into hours spent and hours remaining. The Customer Number field is added to the Filter area and can be used to restrict the data in the PivotTable to only work orders associated with certain customers.

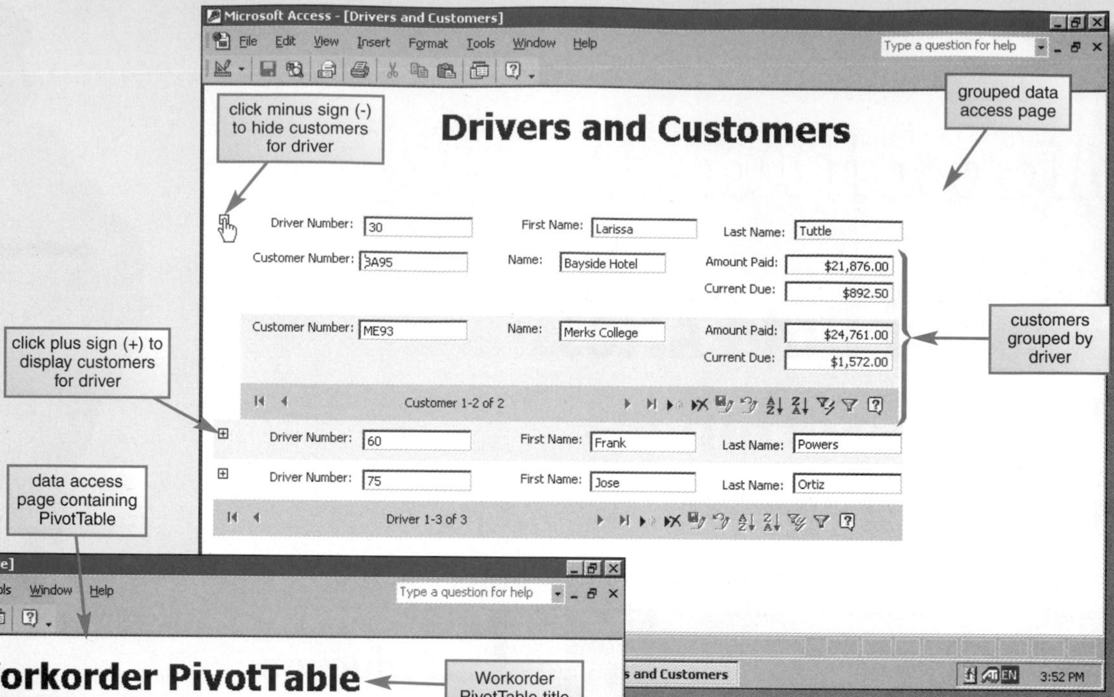

FIGURE 1a

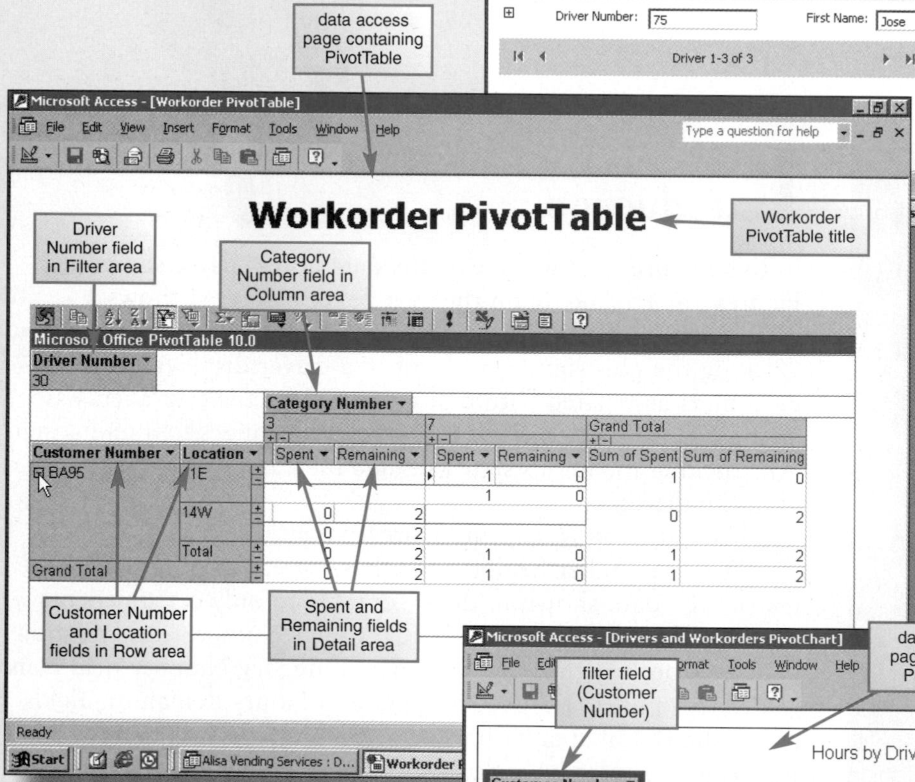

FIGURE 1b

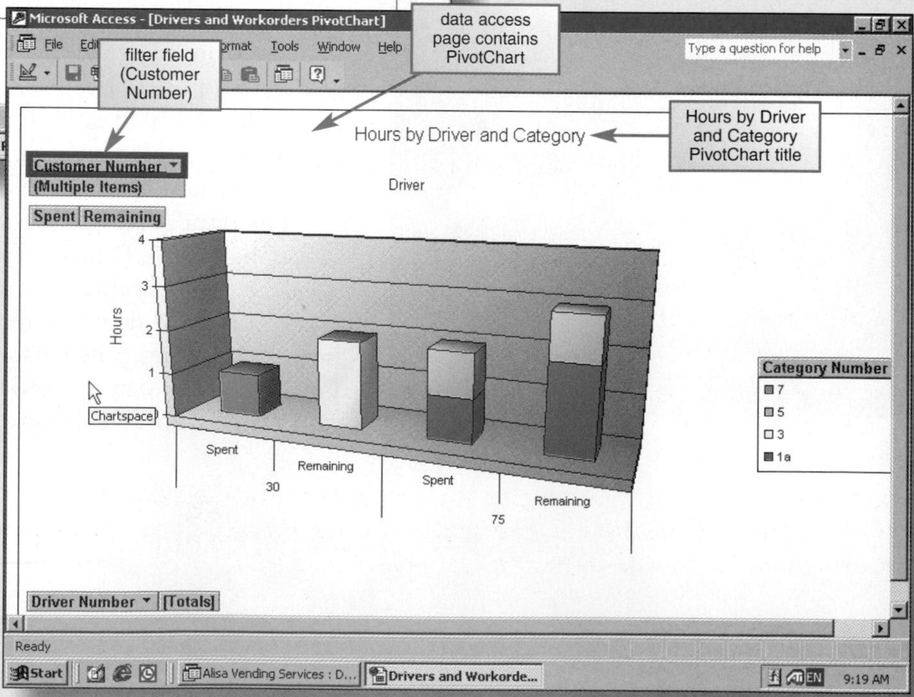

FIGURE 1c

Opening the Database

Before carrying out the steps in this project, you first must open the database. To do so, perform the following steps.

TO OPEN A DATABASE

1. Click the Start button, click Programs on the Start menu, and then click Microsoft Access.
2. Click Open on the Database toolbar, and then click Local Disk (C:) in the Look in box. Click the Data folder (assuming that your database is stored in a folder called Data), and then make sure the Alisa Vending Services database is selected.
3. Click the Open button. When the switchboard displays, close it by clicking its Close button.

The database opens and the Alisa Vending Services : Database window displays.

More About

The Access Help System

Need help? It is no further than the Ask a Question box in the upper-right corner of the window. Click the box that contains the text, Type a question for help (Figure 1a), type help, and then press the ENTER key. Access will respond with a list of items you can click to learn about obtaining help on any Access-related topic. To find out what is new in Access 2002, type what's new in Access in the Ask a Question box.

Grouped Data Access Pages

A data access page is an HTML document that can be bound directly to data in the database. You can group records on a data access page that have some common characteristic. For example, you could group customers by driver number, as in the data access page shown in Figure 1a. Thus, the customers of driver number 30 form one group, the customers of driver number 60 form a second, and the customers of driver number 75 form a third. In the data access page, you can show or hide any of these groups.

To create this type of data access page, you can use a wizard. When you do, the wizard will give you an opportunity to specify grouping levels. You also can group in a data access page you are creating in Design view. To create a database in Design view, perform the following steps.

TO CREATE A DATA ACCESS PAGE IN DESIGN VIEW

1. Click Pages on the Objects bar and then click the New button on the Database toolbar.
2. Be sure Design View is selected in the New Data Access Page dialog box, and then click the OK button.
3. When a message displays indicating that you will not be able to open this data access page in Design view in Access 2000, click the OK button.
4. If a field list does not display, click the Field List button on the Page Design toolbar to display a field list. If the Alignment and Sizing toolbar displays, click its Close button.
5. Maximize the window containing the data access page by clicking its Maximize button. If the Maximize button is hidden by the field list, you can maximize the window by double-clicking its title bar.

The data access page and field list display in a maximized window (Figure 2 on the next page).

More About

Data Access Pages

When you save a data access page in Design view, all supporting files, such as bullets and graphics are organized in a supporting folder. If you move or copy your data access page to another location, you also must move the supporting folder.

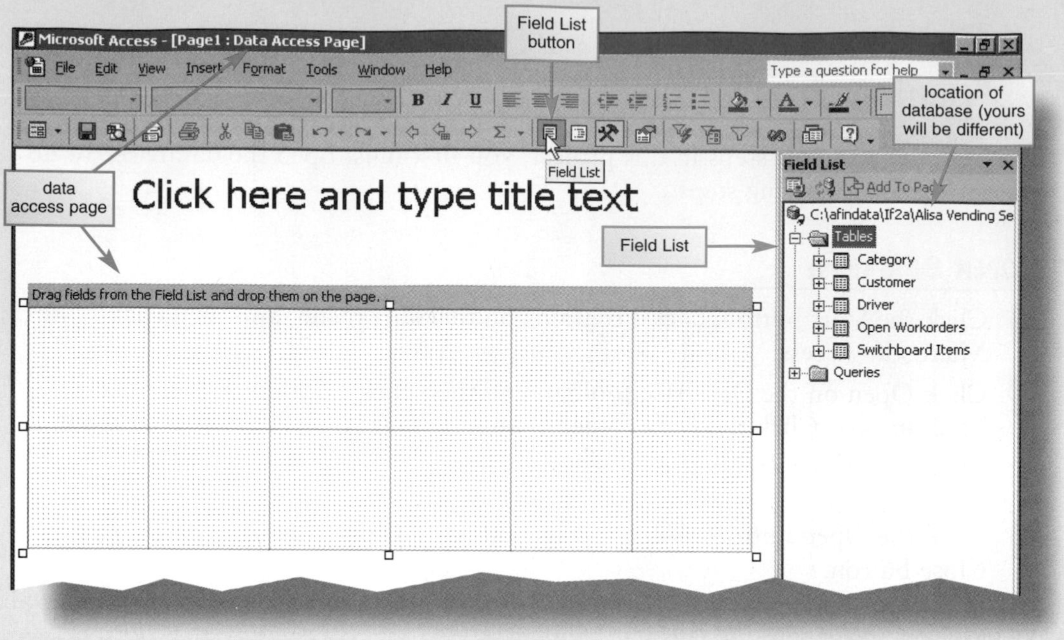

FIGURE 2

Adding the Fields and Grouping

To group in a data access page, you first include the fields by dragging them from a field list to the desired position. Then, you indicate grouping by clicking the Group by Table button on the Page Design toolbar. For example, to indicate grouping by the Driver table, you first will select the Driver Number field and the Customer Number field, and then click the Group by Table button. This will add a section for Driver above a section for Customer. Driver fields will be in the Driver section and Customer fields will be in the Customer section. Perform the following steps to add the fields and to specify grouping.

Steps To Add the Fields and Grouping

1 Click the plus sign in front of Customer in the field list. When the Customer fields display, click the plus sign in front of Related Tables, and then click the plus sign in front of the Driver table listed in the Related Tables section.

The fields in the Driver table display (Figure 3).

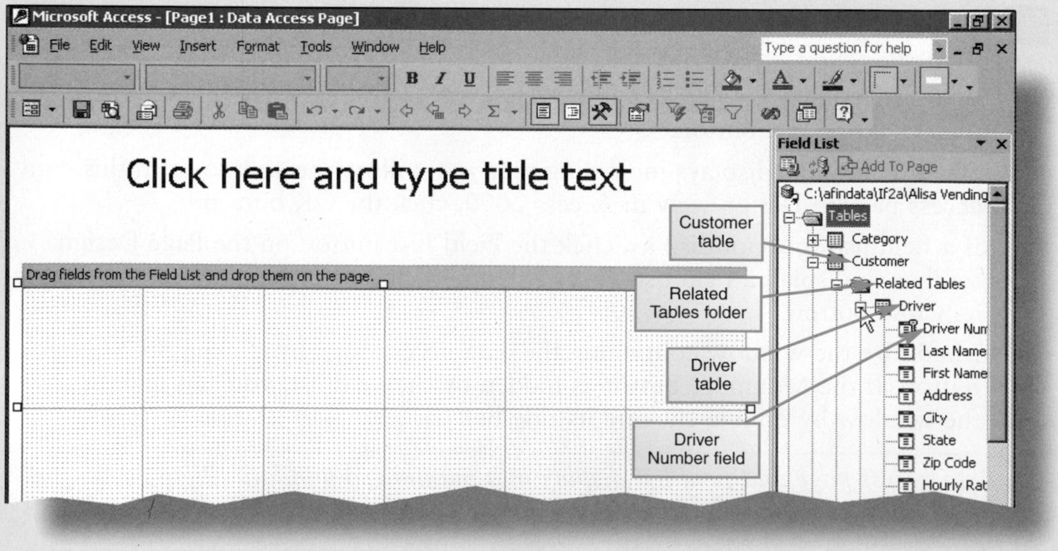

FIGURE 3

2 **Drag the Driver Number field to the approximate position shown in Figure 4.**

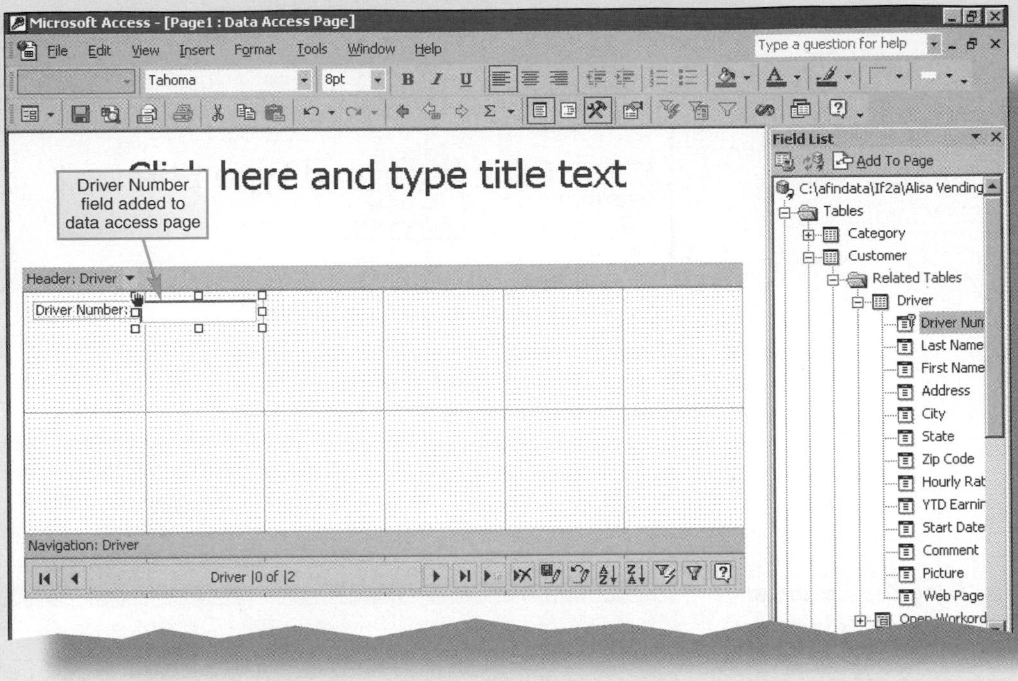

FIGURE 4

3 **Drag the First Name and Last Name fields to the approximate positions shown in Figure 5. Drag the labels for the First Name and Last Name fields to the positions shown in the figure. Click the minus sign (–) in front of the Driver table so the fields no longer display, and then drag the Customer Number field to the position shown in the figure. If the Layout Wizard dialog box displays, be sure Columnar is selected and then click the OK button. Click the Driver Number field on the data access page to select it, and then point to the Group by Table button on the Page Design toolbar.**

The First Name, Last Name, and Customer Number fields are added. The Driver Number field is selected.

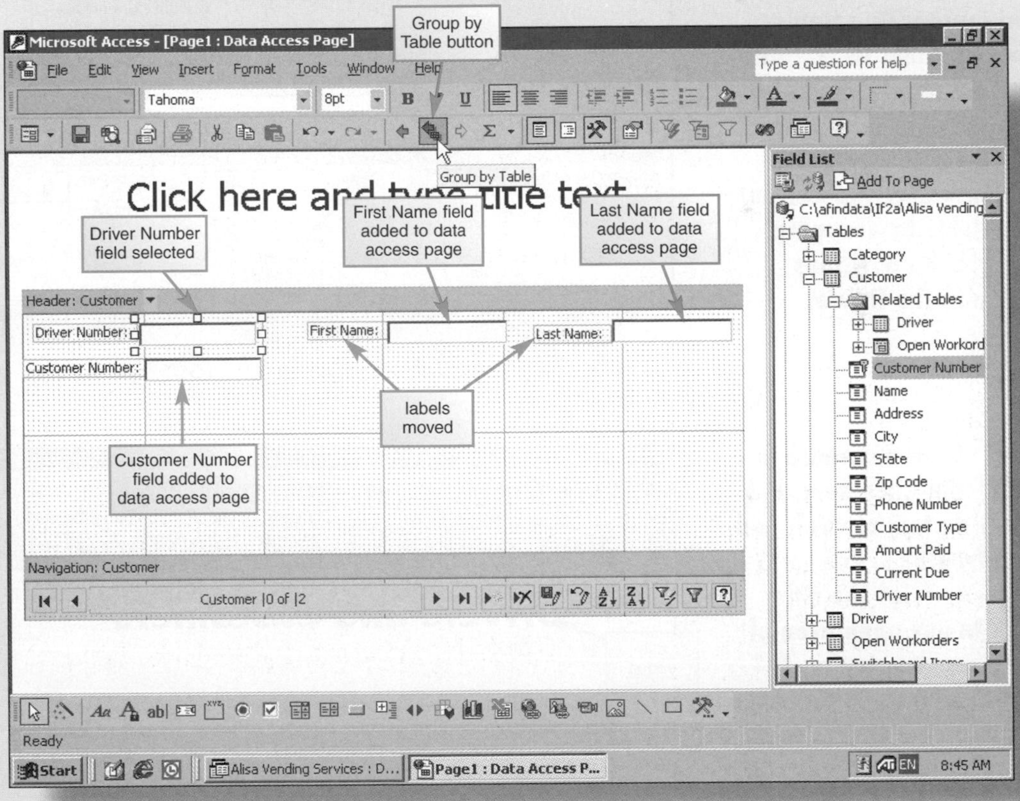

FIGURE 5

4 Click the Group by Table button.

The data is grouped by driver (Figure 6). A header for the Driver table is added above the header for the Customer table.

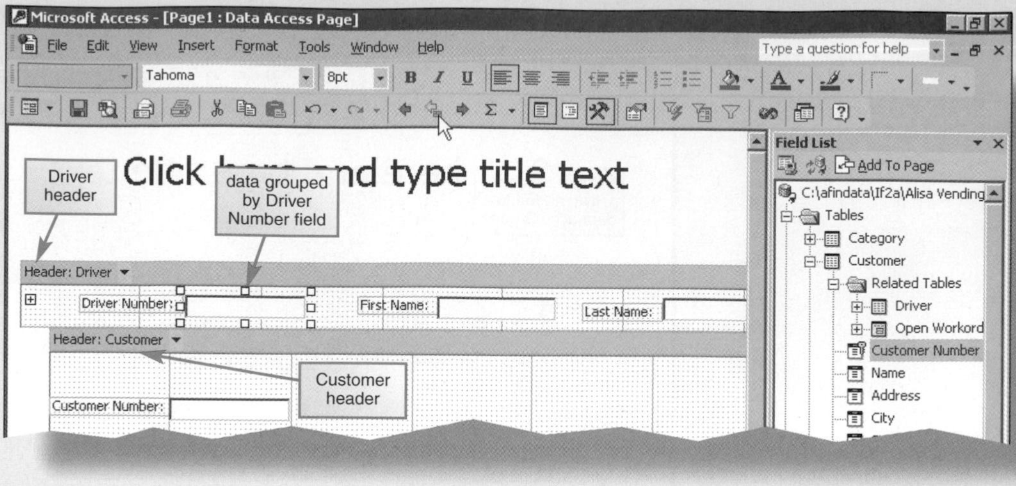

FIGURE 6

5 Drag the Customer Number field to the approximate position shown in Figure 7. Drag the Name, Amount Paid, and Current Due fields from the field list to the approximate positions shown in the figure. Adjust the labels for the Name, Amount Paid, and Current Due fields by dragging them to the positions shown in the figure.

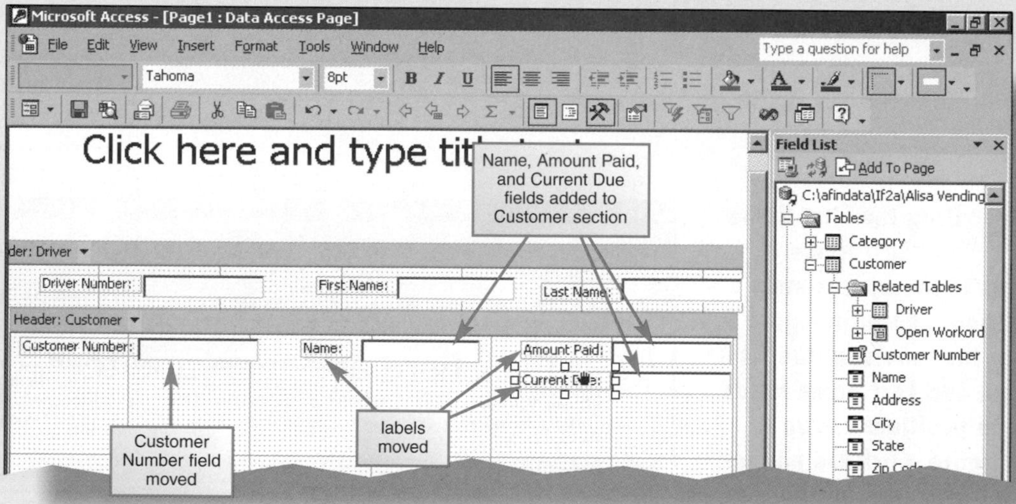

FIGURE 7

6 Click anywhere in the Click here and type title text control, and then type `Drivers and Customers` **as the title. Click in any open area of the Customer section to select the section, and then drag the lower sizing handle to the approximate position shown in Figure 8.**

The title is added and the Customer section is resized.

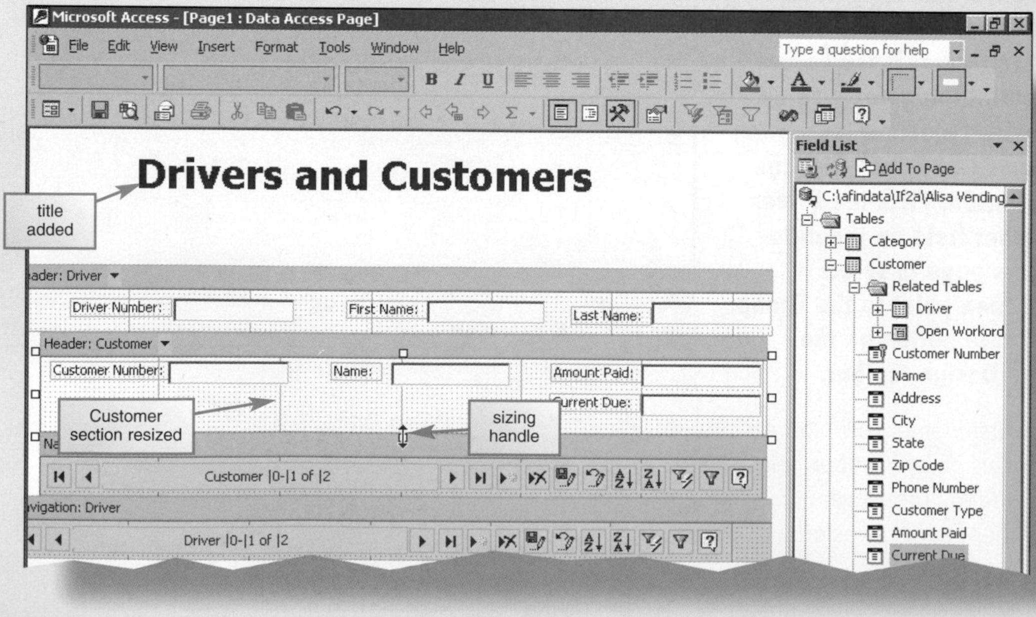

FIGURE 8

7 **Close the window containing the data access page by clicking its Close Window button. Click the Yes button when asked if you want to save your changes, type** `Drivers and Customers` **as the file name for the data access page, and then click the Save button in the Save As Data Access Page dialog box. If you see a message similar to the one in Figure 9, click the OK button because the file location you specified is acceptable. (This message indicates that you will need to specify a UNC (Universal Naming Convention) address, instead of the file location you have specified if you want the page to be accessible over a network.)**

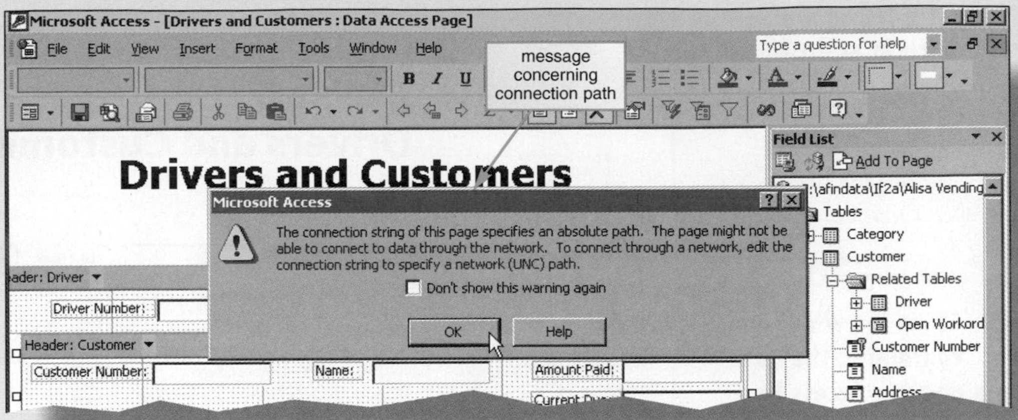

FIGURE 9

The data access page is created.

Other Ways

1. In Voice Command mode, say "Group by Table"

Using the Data Access Page

While in Access, you can preview what the page will look like in the browser by using Web Page Preview on the File menu. You also can open the data access page. In either case, you work with the page in the same manner. The following steps open the data access page that was just created and then view all the customers of the driver by clicking the plus sign in front of driver number 30.

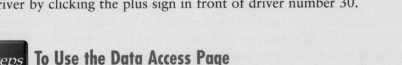

Steps To Use the Data Access Page

1 **With the Database window displaying, be sure the Pages object is selected, right-click Drivers and Customers, and then click Open on the shortcut menu. Point to the plus sign in front of driver number 30.**

The data access page displays (Figure 10). Customers currently do not display.

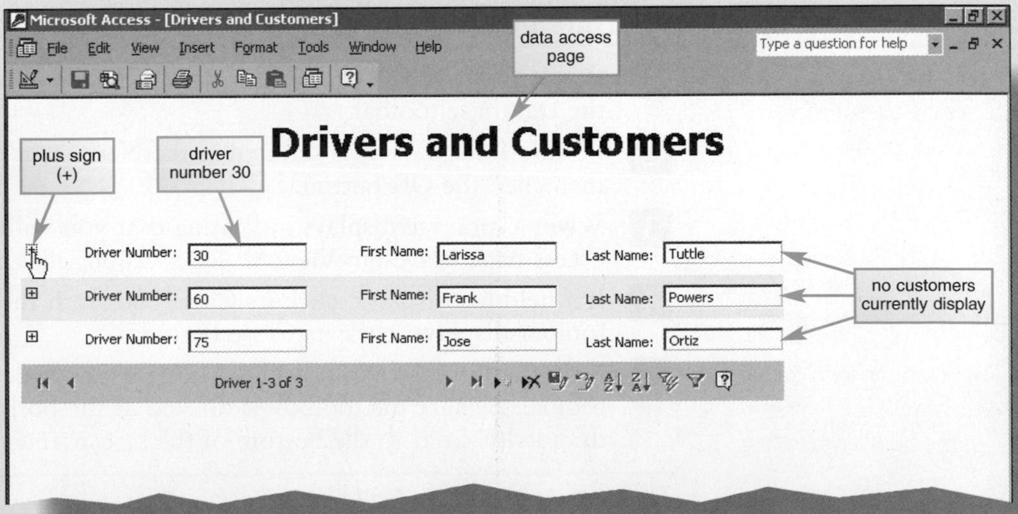

FIGURE 10

2 Click the plus sign in front of driver number 30.

The customers of driver number 30 display underneath driver number 30 (Figure 11).

3 Close the window containing the data access page in Access by clicking its Close Window button.

The page no longer displays.

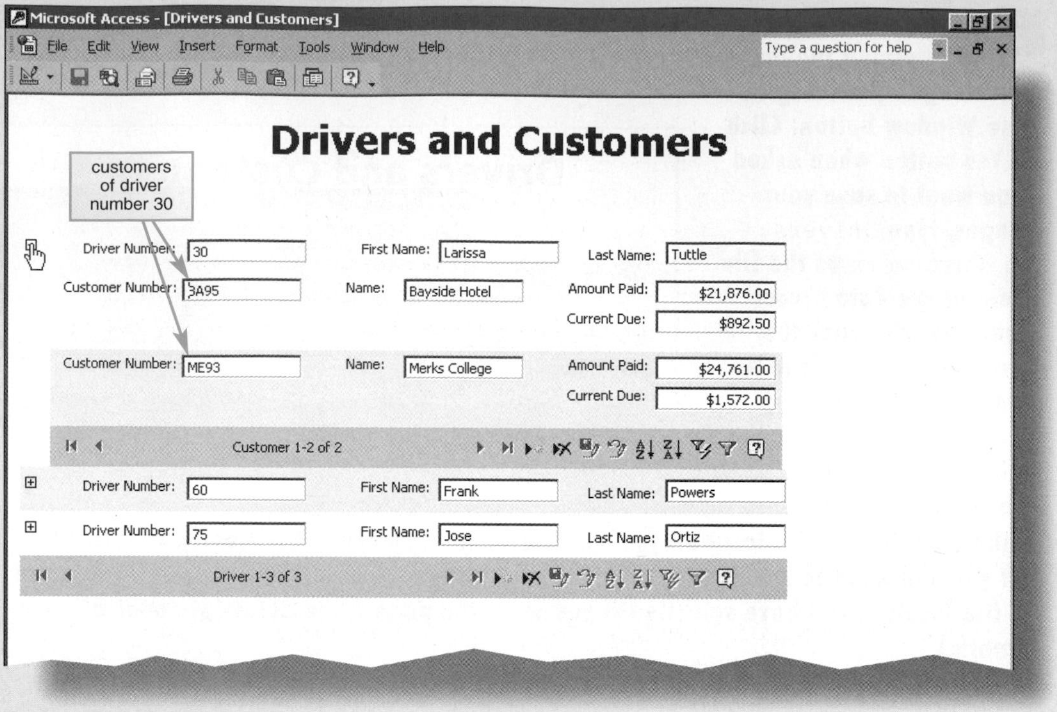

FIGURE 11

PivotTables in Data Access Pages

There are two ways to create a PivotTable in a data access page. You can create a PivotTable view of a table or query and then save the PivotTable as a data access page. Alternatively, you can create a data access page in Design view, place a PivotTable on the data access page, and then place the desired fields in appropriate areas of the PivotTable as you did when you created a PivotTable in Project 9. For the second approach you first must create a data access page in Design view as in the following steps.

TO CREATE A DATA ACCESS PAGE IN DESIGN VIEW

1. If necessary, click Pages on the Objects bar and then click the New button on the Database toolbar.
2. Be sure Design View is selected in the New Data Access Page dialog box, and then click the OK button.
3. When a message displays indicating that you will not be able to open this data access page in Design View in Access 2000, click the OK button.
4. If a field list displays, click its Close button. If the Alignment and Sizing toolbar displays, click its Close button.
5. If the toolbox does not display, click the Toolbox button on the Page Design toolbar. Be sure the toolbox is docked at the bottom of the screen. If it is not, drag its title bar to the bottom of the screen and release the left mouse button.

The data access page displays in Design view.

Creating a PivotTable on a Data Access Page

To create a PivotTable on a data access page, click the Office PivotTable tool in the toolbox and then click the position at which you would like to place the PivotTable. Select the table or query that will form the basis of the PivotTable, display a field list, and then drag the fields for the PivotTable to the appropriate areas. You also can add statistics, such as Sum and Average to the PivotTable.

Occasionally, you will place more than one field in either the Row or the Column area. The PivotTable in Figure 1b on page AI 2.02, for example, has both the Customer Number and Location fields in the Row area. The one to the left is called the **outer field** and the one to the right is called the **inner field**. In the example, the Customer Number field is the outer field and the Location field is the inner field. The overall organization is by the outer field, so the PivotTable in the example is organized by customer number. If the order of the fields were reversed, the PivotTable would be organized by location. Thus, it is critical that the fields be positioned appropriately. If you find that you have placed the fields incorrectly, you can correct the problem by dragging the field or fields to the correct location. If, for example, you placed the Location field to the left of the Customer Number field, you could drag the Location field to the right of the Customer Number field and then release the left mouse button.

Perform the following steps to create the PivotTable on the data access page.

More About

PivotTables

When you add a PivotTable to a grouped data access page, a PivotTable Field List displays for each group and contains only those records for the group. For example, on a data access page grouped by driver number with a PivotTable containing work order data, there is a PivotTable list for each driver containing only the work order data for that driver. You cannot display the PivotTable Field List for more than one group at a time.

Steps To Create a PivotTable on a Data Access Page

1 Click the Office PivotTable tool in the toolbox and then point to the approximate position shown in Figure 12.

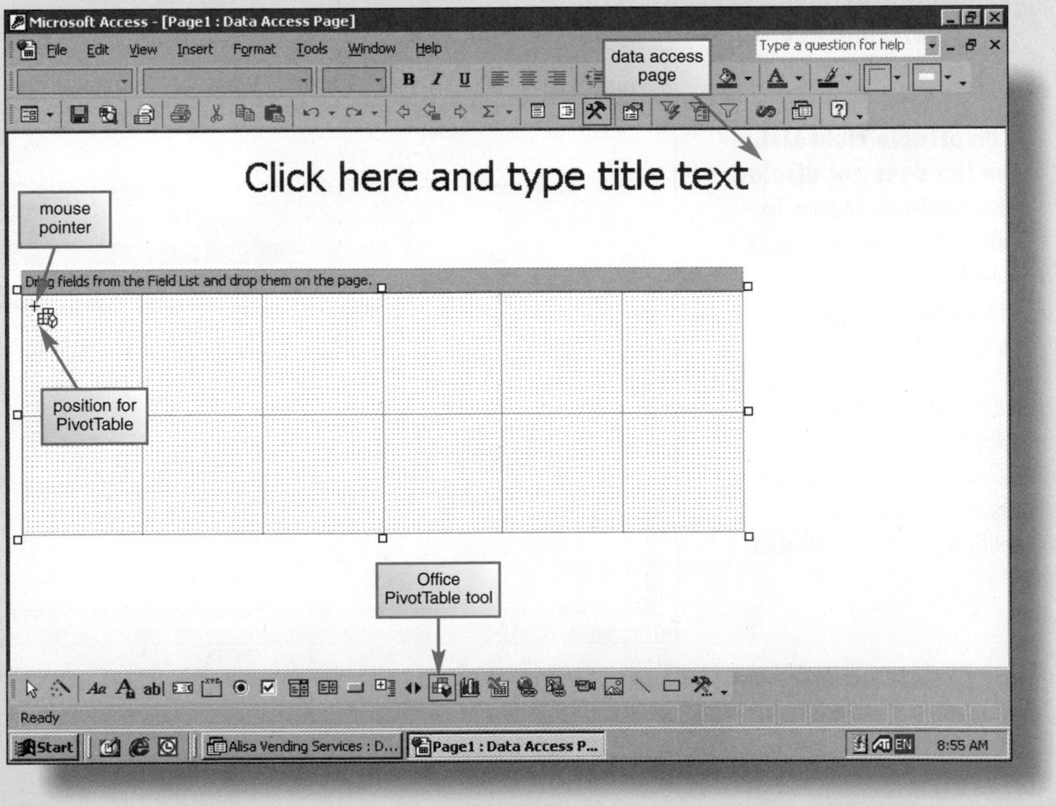

FIGURE 12

2 **Click the position shown in Figure 12 on the previous page to place the PivotTable. A field list may redisplay. If it does close it by clicking its Close button. Right-click the PivotTable, click Commands and Options on the shortcut menu, click the Data member, table, view, or cube name option button, click the arrow, select the Drivers and Workorders query. Click the Close button in the Commands and Options dialog box. Resize the PivotTable to the approximate size shown in Figure 13 by dragging its lower and right sizing handles.**

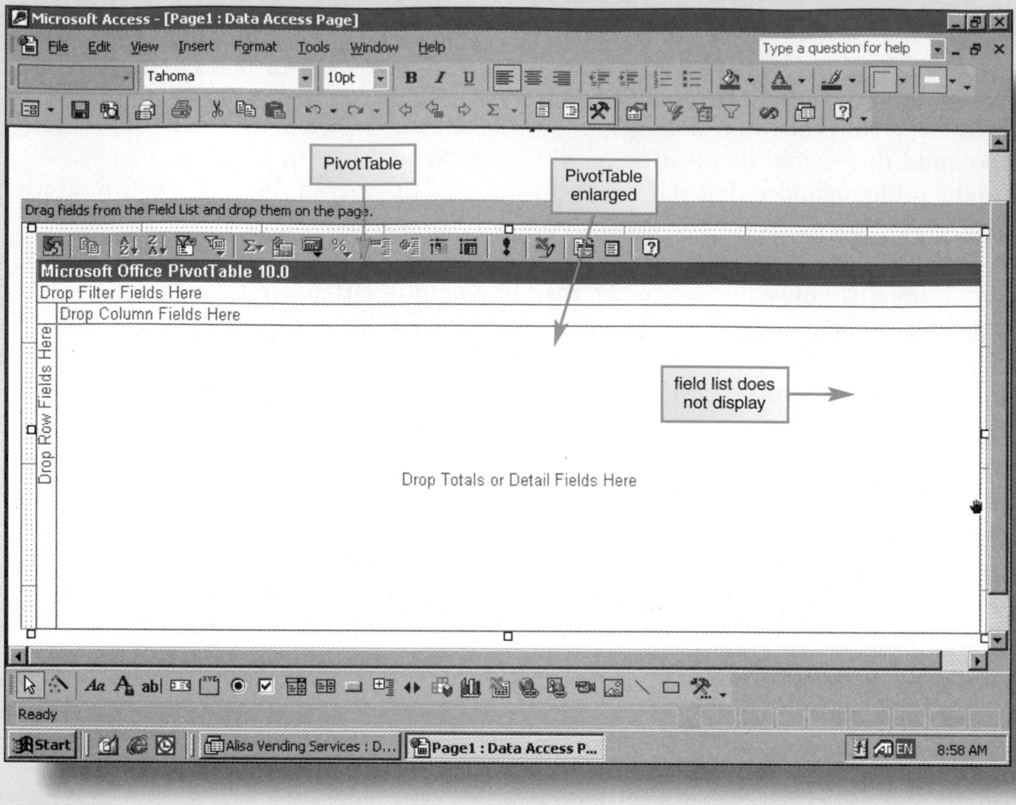

FIGURE 13

3 **Right-click the PivotTable, and then click Field List on the shortcut menu to display the PivotTable Field List. If the list does not display in the position shown in Figure 14, move the field list to the indicated position by dragging its title bar.**

The PivotTable Field List displays. It contains only the Drivers and Workorders query, the query you identified for the PivotTable.

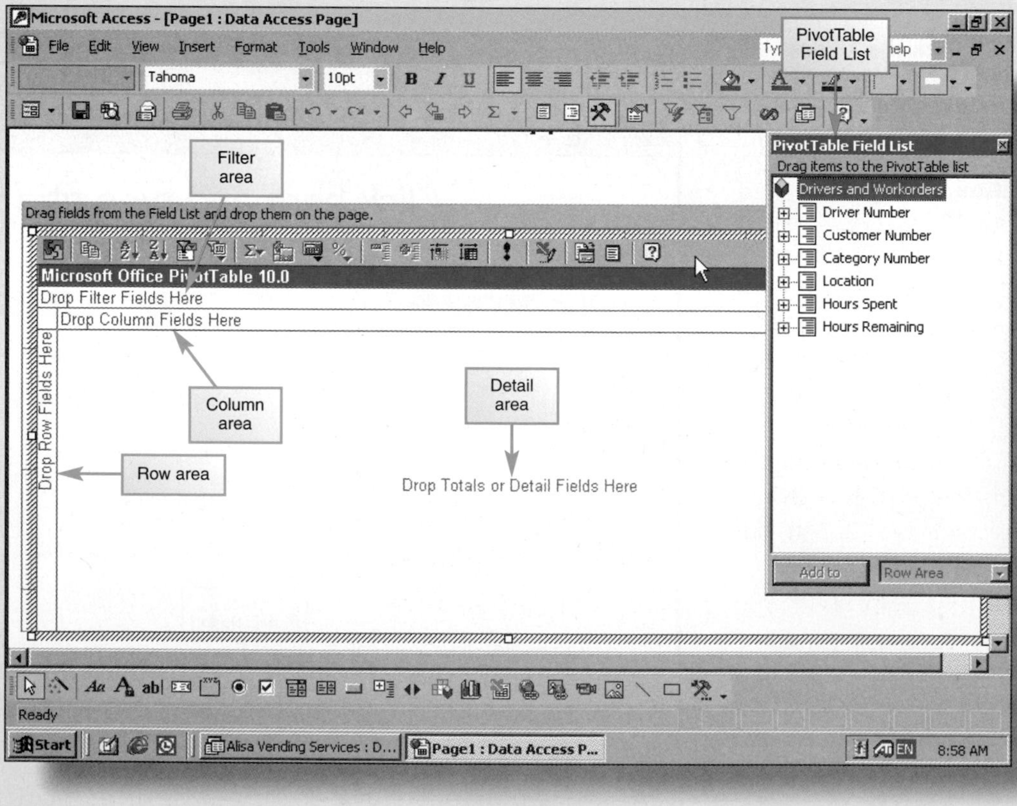

FIGURE 14

4 Drag the Customer Number field to the Row area, and then drag the Location field to the Row area to the right of the Customer Number field. Drag the Category Number field to the Column area. Drag the Driver Number field to the Filter area. Drag the Hours Spent and Hours Remaining fields to the Detail area. The Location field should be to the right of the Customer Number field in the Row area. If it is not, drag it to the right of the Customer Number field. Similarly, the Hours Remaining field should be to the right of the Hours Spent field in the Detail area. If it is not, drag the Hours Remaining field to the right of the Hours Spent field.

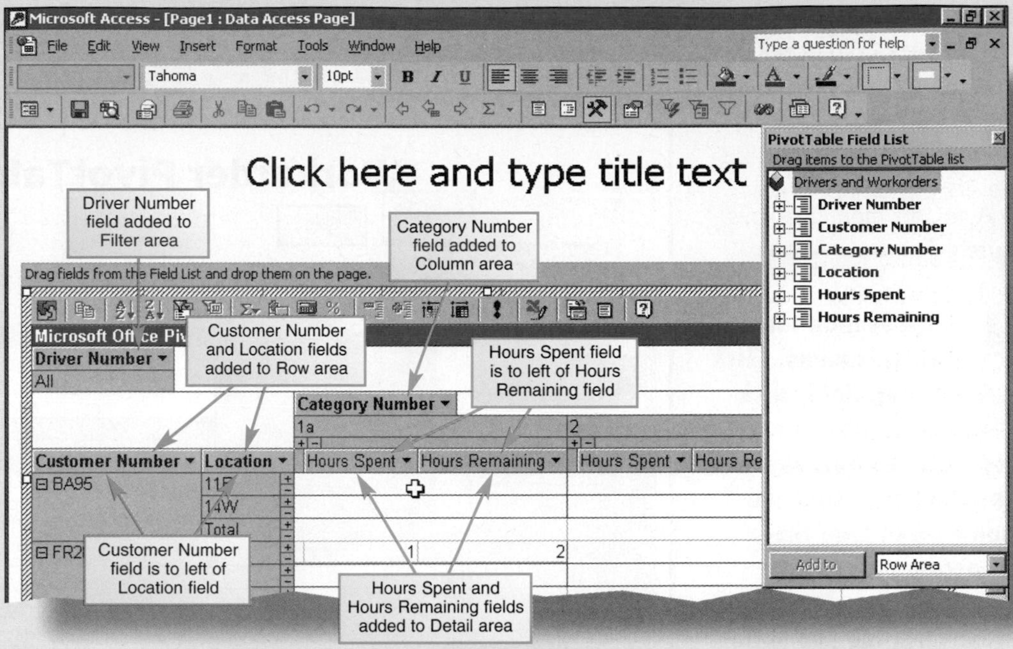

FIGURE 15

The Customer Number and Location fields are added to the Row area (Figure 15). The Category Number field is added to the Column area. The Driver Number field is added to the Filter area. The Hours Spent and Hours Remaining fields are added to the Detail area.

5 Close the PivotTable Field List by clicking its Close button. Right-click the Hours Spent field, click Commands and Options on the shortcut menu, click the Captions tab, erase the current caption, and then type `Spent` **as the new caption. Using the same technique, change the caption for Hours Remaining to Remaining. Click Click here and type title text, and then type** `Workorder PivotTable` **as the title.**

The caption for the Hours Spent field is changed to Spent (Figure 16). The caption for the Hours Remaining field is changed to Remaining. The title is changed to Workorder PivotTable.

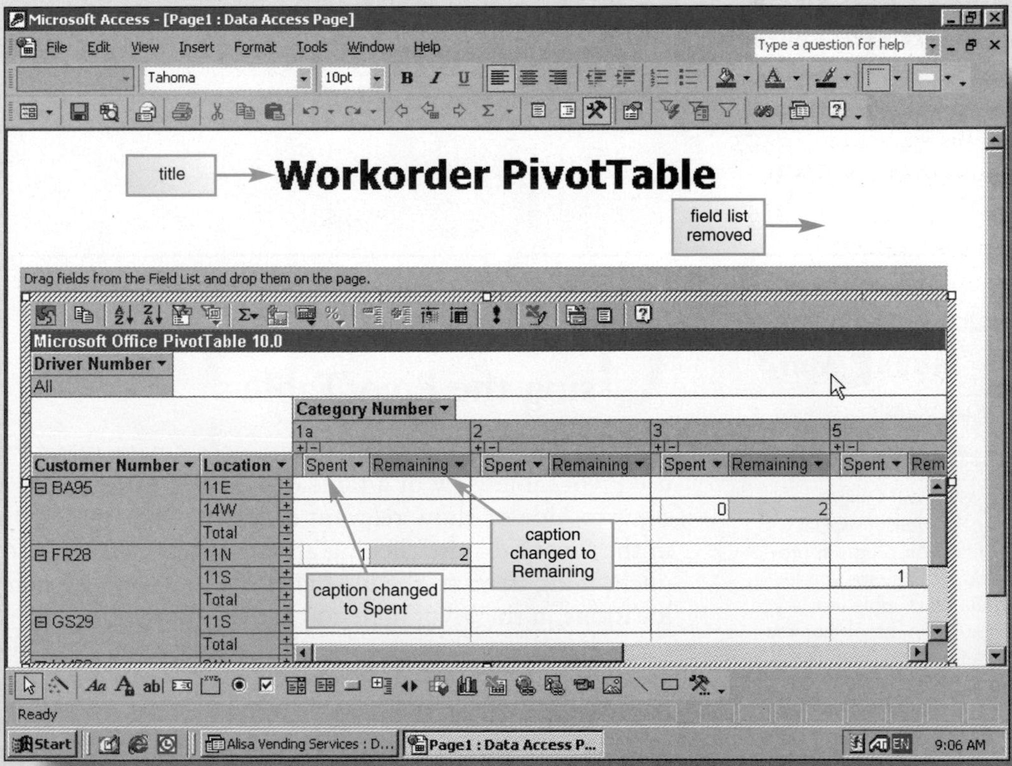

FIGURE 16

6 **Click the Spent caption, click the AutoCalc button on the PivotTable toolbar, and then point to Sum.**

The AutoCalc menu displays (Figure 17).

7 **Click Sum on the AutoCalc menu. Click the Remaining field, click the AutoCalc button on the PivotTable toolbar, and then click Sum. Close the window containing the data access page by clicking its Close Window button. Click the Yes button when asked if you want to save your changes, type** `Workorder PivotTable` **as the file name in the Save As Data Access Page dialog box, and then click the Save button. If you see a message like the one in Figure 9 on page AI 2.07, click the OK button because the file location you specified is acceptable.**

The data access page is created.

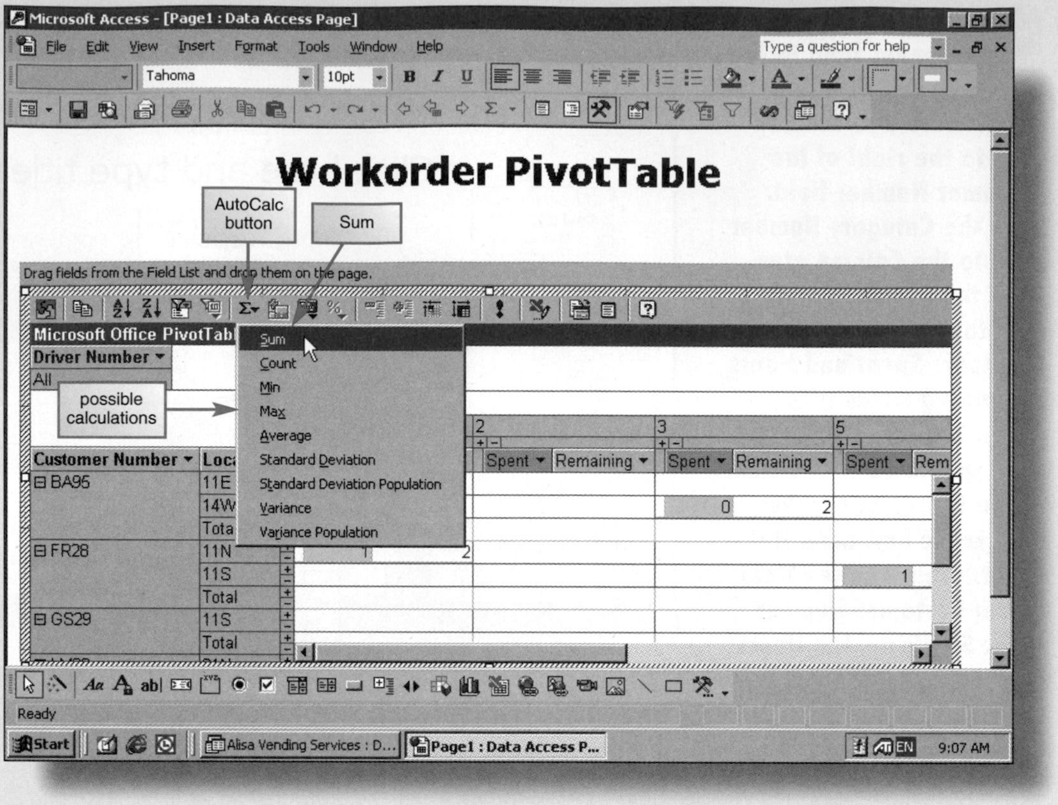

FIGURE 17

More About

Microsoft Certification

The Microsoft Office User Specialist (MOUS) Certification program provides an opportunity for you to obtain a valuable industry credential —proof that you have the Access 2002 skills required by employers. For more information, see Appendix E or visit the Shelly Cashman Series MOUS Web page at scsite.com/offxp/cert.htm.

Using the PivotTable

You use the PivotTable in the data access page in a similar manner to the way you use PivotTable view of a table or query. You can click appropriate plus or minus signs to hide or show relevant data. You can restrict the data that will be reflected in the PivotTable by clicking an appropriate down arrow and then checking or unchecking items in the list that displays. You also can drag the fields to different locations in the PivotTable to change its organization. Perform the following steps to open the data access page, restrict the data reflected in the table to only workorders for customers of driver number 30, and then hide the individual locations for the customer that displays.

Steps To Use the PivotTable

1 With the Database window displaying, if necessary click the Pages object. Right-click Workorder PivotTable, and then click Open on the shortcut menu. Click the Driver Number arrow, remove the check marks from all driver numbers except driver number 30, and then click the OK button. Point to the minus sign in front of customer number BA95.

The data access page displays (Figure 18). The only customer of driver number 30 currently to have open workorders, customer number BA95, displays. Both locations for workorders for customer number BA95 display.

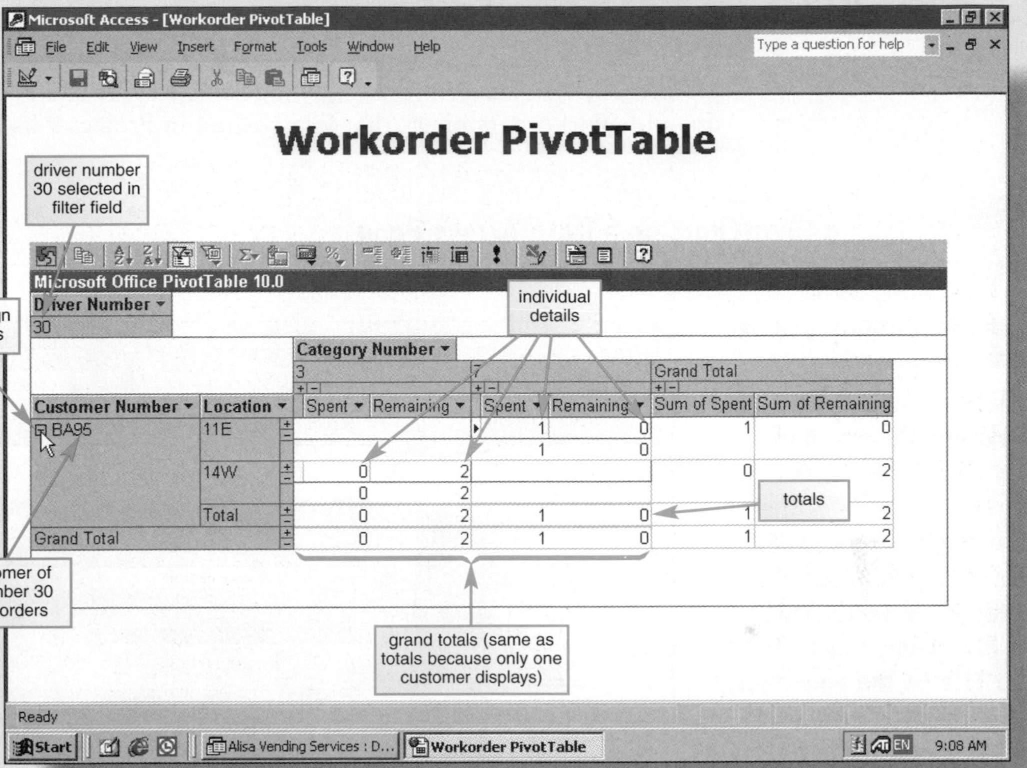

FIGURE 18

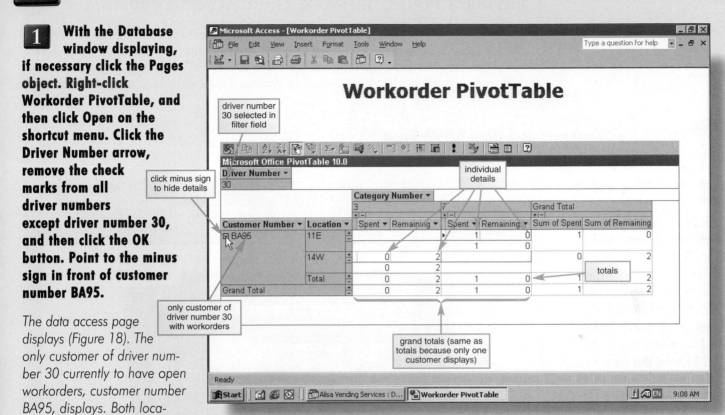

2 Click the minus sign in front of customer number BA95.

The individual locations for customer number BA95 do not display (Figure 19). The data for these locations is combined into a single row.

3 Close the window containing the data access page in Access by clicking its Close Window button.

The page no longer displays.

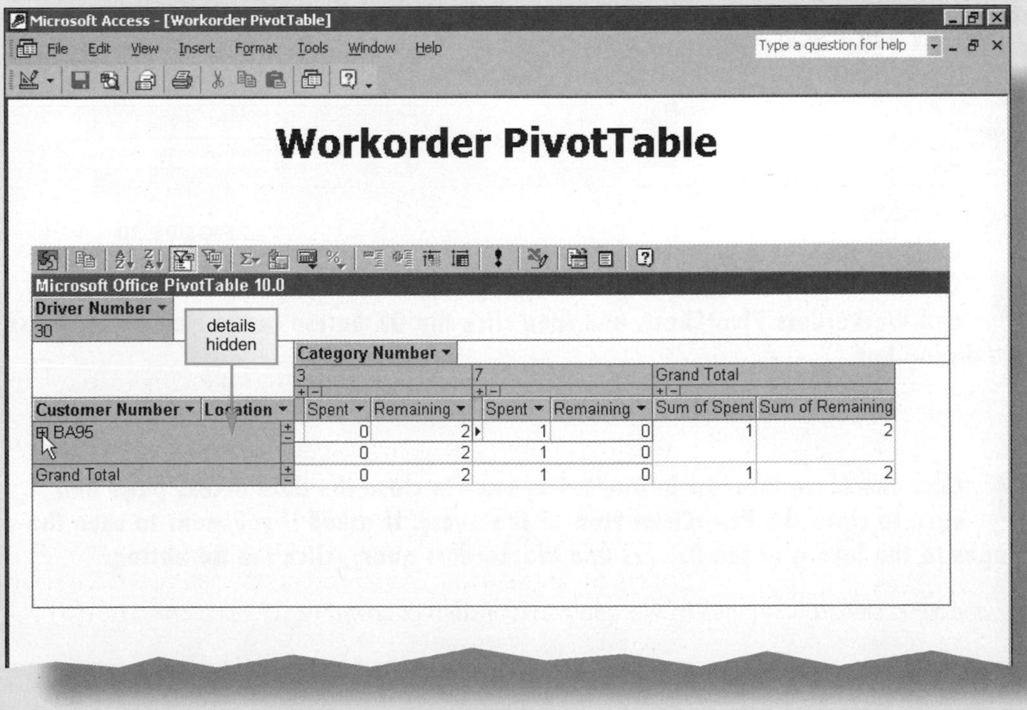

FIGURE 19

Saving a PivotChart as a Data Access Page

You can create a PivotChart on a data access page by first creating the PivotChart as the PivotChart view of a table or query and then saving the PivotChart as a data access page. Perform the following steps to save the PivotChart view of the Drivers and Workorders query that you created in Project 9 as a data access page.

Steps To Save a PivotChart as a Data Access Page

1 Click Queries on the Objects bar, right-click the Drivers and Workorders query, and then click Open on the shortcut menu. Click the View button arrow, and then click PivotChart View on the View menu. With the PivotChart displaying, click File on the menu bar, and then click Save As on the File menu. Change the name from Drivers and Workorders to Drivers and Workorders PivotChart, click the arrow in the As text box, and then select Data Access Page. Point to the OK button.

The PivotChart displays (Figure 20). The Save As dialog box displays.

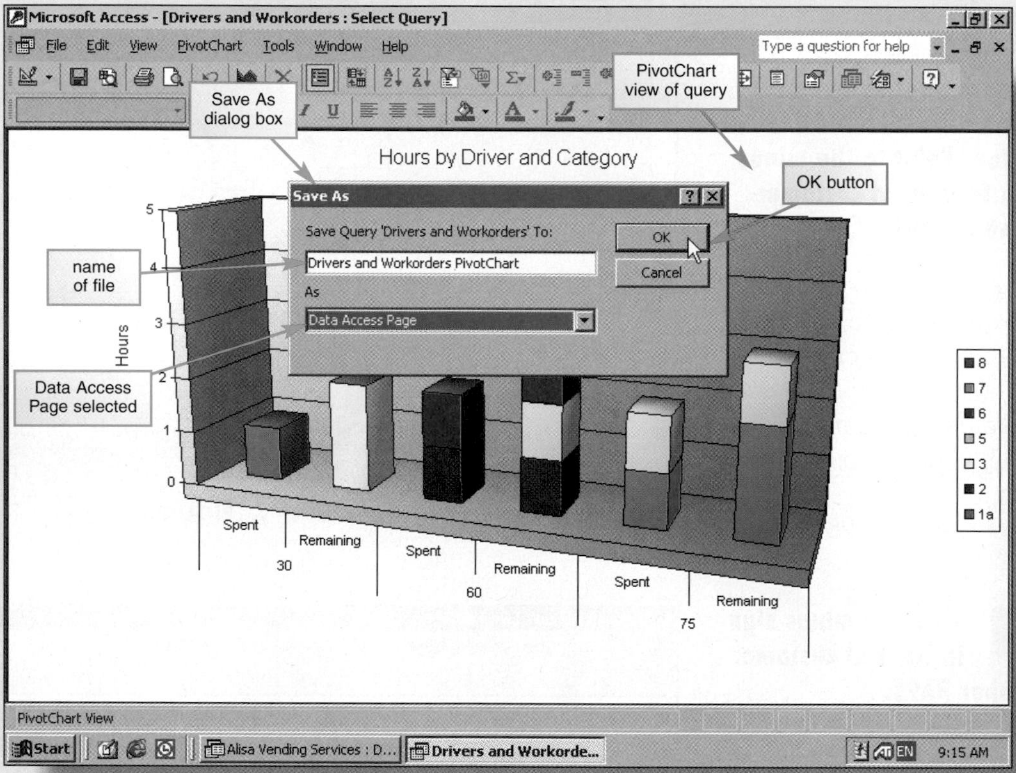

FIGURE 20

2 Click the OK button in the Save As dialog box, be sure the file name is Drivers and Workorders PivotChart, and then click the OK button in the New Data Access Page dialog box.

The data access page is created.

3 Click the Close Window button twice, once to close the data access page and once to close the PivotChart view of the query. If asked if you want to save the changes to the layout of the Drivers and Workorders query, click the No button.

The window is closed. Changes to the query layout are not saved.

Using the Data Access Page

You use the PivotChart in the data access page in a similar manner to the way you use PivotChart view of a table or query. You can display the drop areas and then use them to restrict the data that will be reflected in the PivotChart. You also can display the PivotChart toolbar and use it to change the chart type, to change the chart organization, to show or hide a legend, and so on. Perform the following steps to open the data access page, display a field list, display the drop areas, place the Customer Number field in the Filter Fields area, and then use the Customer Number control to restrict the customers whose data is reflected in the PivotChart.

More About

Quick Reference

For a table that lists how to complete tasks covered in this book using the mouse, menu, shortcut menu, and keyboard, see the Quick Reference Summary at the back of this book or visit the Shelly Cashman Series Office XP Web page (scsite.com/offxp/qr.htm) and then click Microsoft Access 2002.

Steps To Use the Data Access Page

1 With the Database window displaying, click the Pages object. Right-click Drivers and Workorders PivotChart, and then click Open on the shortcut menu. Right-click any open area of the PivotChart and then point to Field List on the shortcut menu.

The PivotChart displays (Figure 21). The shortcut menu for the PivotChart displays.

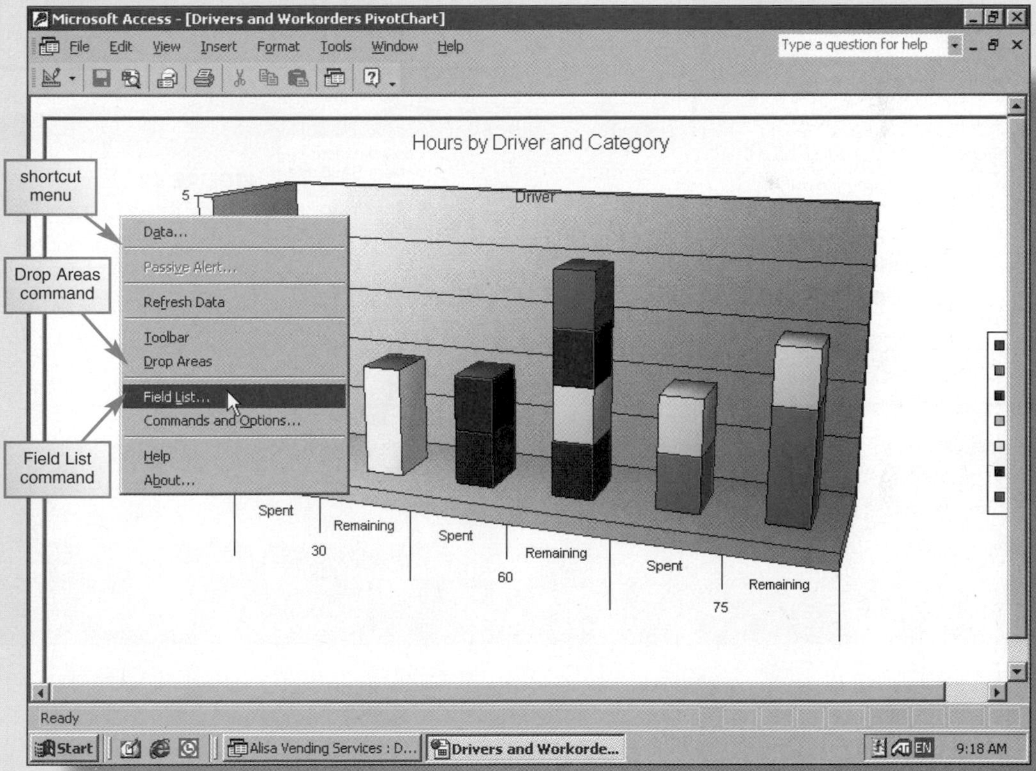

FIGURE 21

2 **Click Field List on the shortcut menu to display a field list. Right-click any open area of the PivotChart, and then click Drop Areas on the shortcut menu. Drag the Customer Number field to the Filter Fields area, and then close the field list by clicking its Close button. Click the Customer Number arrow, and then remove the check marks from Customer Number GS29 and Customer Number LM22. Click the OK button.**

The PivotChart displays (Figure 22). Only workorders for customers BA95 and FR28 are reflected in the chart.

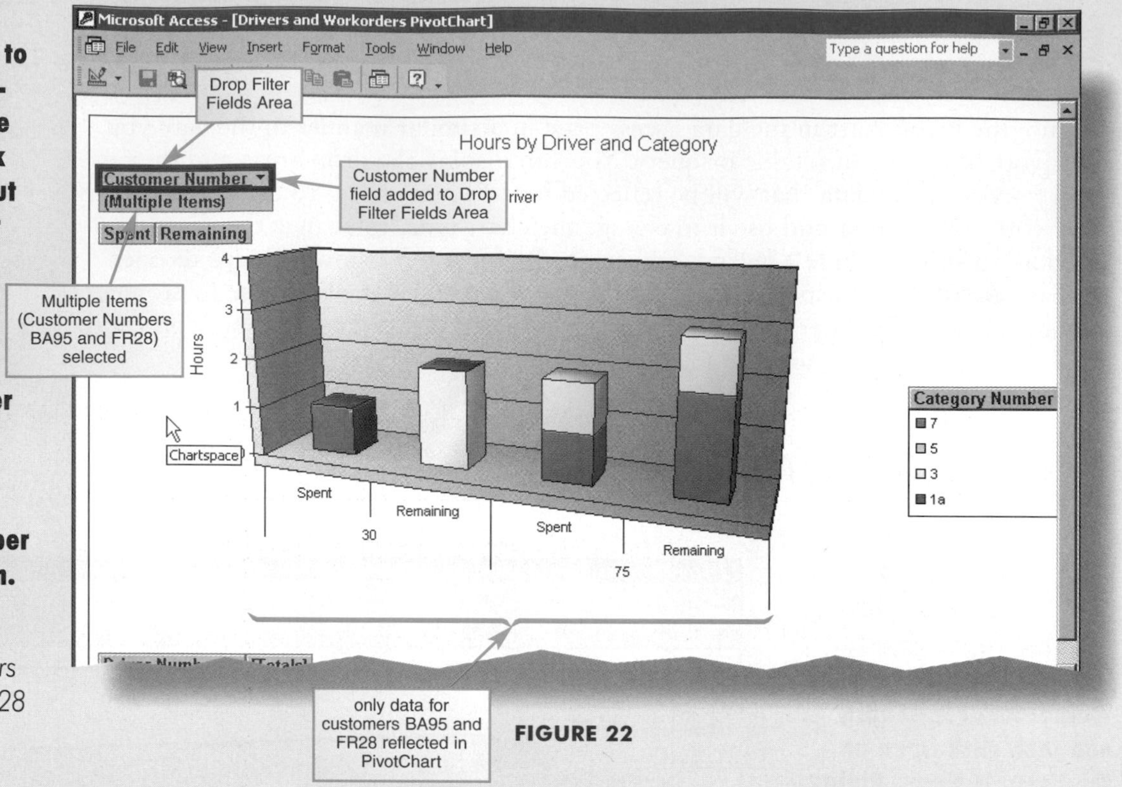

FIGURE 22

3 **Close the window containing the data access page in Access by clicking its Close Window button.**

The page no longer displays.

CASE PERSPECTIVE SUMMARY

In this Integration Feature, you created a grouped data access page that grouped customers by drivers. You also placed a PivotTable and a PivotChart on data access pages. Alisa Vending Services now can view these pages using the Internet.

Integration Feature Summary

In this Integration Feature, you created and used a grouped data access page that grouped customers by driver. You created a data access page in Design view, and then created a PivotTable on the data access page. You saved a PivotChart that you created earlier as a data access page. You also saw how to use each of the data access pages you created.

What You Should Know

Having completed this Integration Feature, you now should be able to perform the following tasks:

- Add the Fields and Grouping *(AI 2.04)*
- Create a Data Access Page in Design View *(AI 2.03, AI 2.08)*
- Create a PivotTable on a Data Access Page *(AI 2.09)*
- Open a Database *(AI 2.03)*
- Save a PivotChart as a Data Access Page *(AI 2.14)*
- Use the Data Access Page *(AI 2.07)*
- Use the PivotTable *(AI 2.13)*

In the Lab

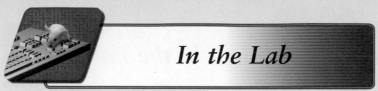

1 Creating Data Access Pages for the Beyond Clean Database

Instructions: Start Access. Open the Beyond Clean database that you used in Project 9 for this assignment or see your instructor for instructions about accessing the files required for this book. Perform the following tasks.

1. Create the grouped data access page shown in Figure 23. The page groups customers by custodian.

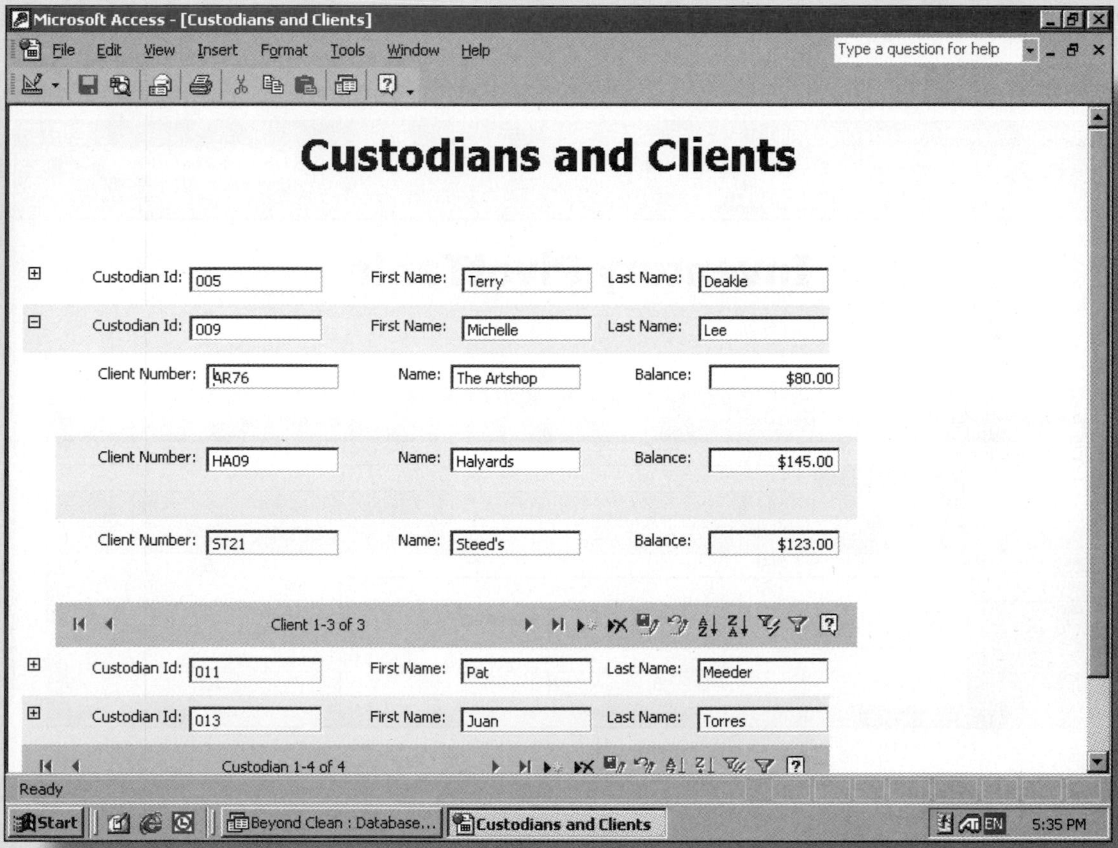

FIGURE 23

2. Open the data access page and then click the Last Name field. Click the Sort Ascending button to sort the records in order by last name.
3. Print the data access page. To print the page, click File on the menu bar, and then click Print.
4. Click the plus sign in front of custodian 009 and then print the page again. Close the data access page.
5. Open the Total Fees by Client query and then switch to PivotChart view. Save the PivotChart as a data access page. Name the data access page Total Fees by Client PivotChart. Press the PRINT SCREEN key.
6. Start Microsoft Word, create a new document, type your name at the top of the document, and then click Paste on the Standard toolbar.
7. Print the Word document containing the PivotChart.
8. Quit Word and Access.

In the Lab

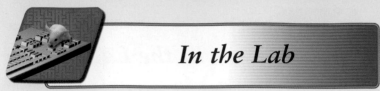

2 Creating Data Access Pages for the Wooden Crafts Database

Instructions: Start Access. Open the Wooden Crafts database that you used in Project 9 for this assignment or see your instructor for instructions about accessing the files required for this book. Perform the following tasks.

1. Open the Reorder Items by Supplier Query that was created previously in Design view.
2. Add the On Hand field to the query and save the query.
3. Create the data access page shown in Figure 24. The PivotTable uses the modified Reorder Items by Supplier Query.

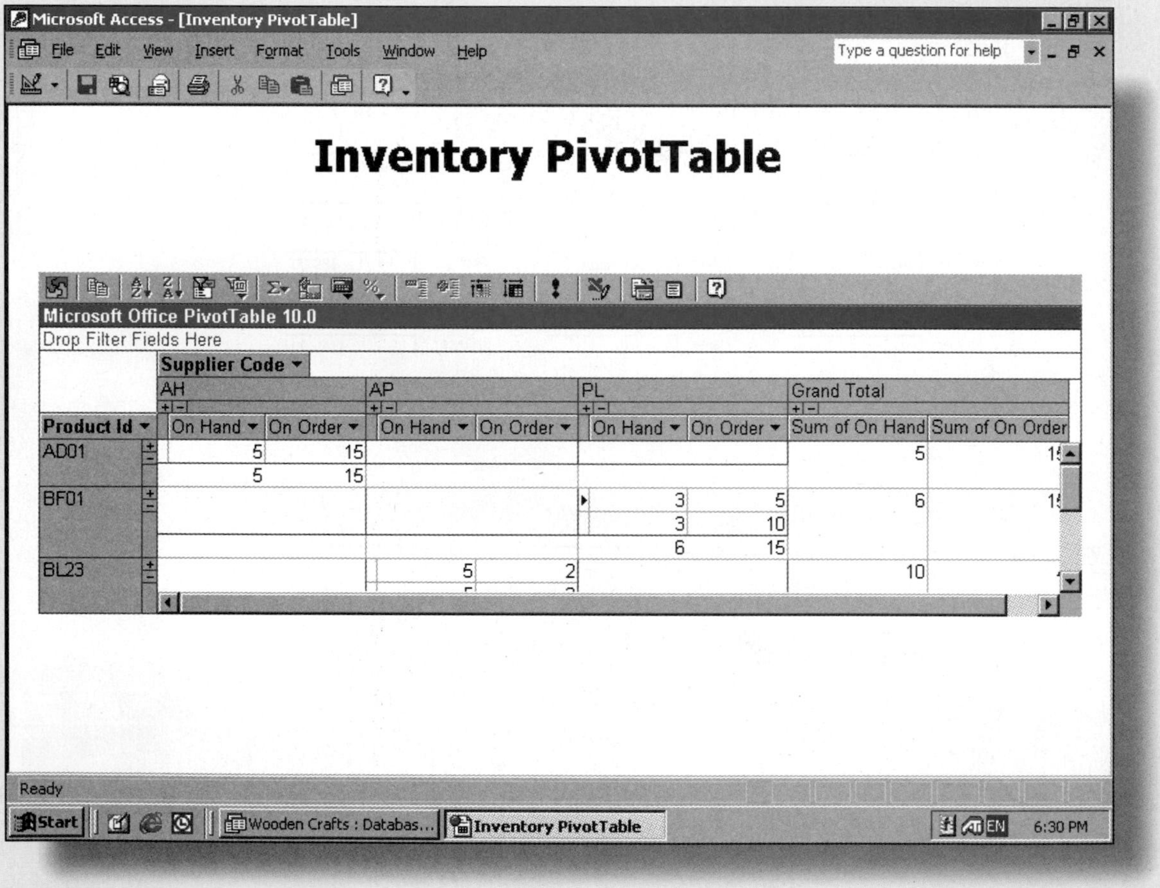

FIGURE 24

4. Save the data access page as Inventory PivotTable. With the PivotTable displaying, press the PRINT SCREEN key.
5. Start Microsoft Word, create a new document, type your name at the top of the document, and then click Paste on the Standard toolbar.
6. Print the Word document containing the PivotTable.
7. Quit Word and Access.

Microsoft PowerPoint 2002

PROJECT

5

Working with Macros and Visual Basic for Applications (VBA)

OBJECTIVES

You will have mastered the material in this project when you can:

- Create a toolbar
- Customize a toolbar by adding buttons
- Use the macro recorder to create a macro
- Customize a menu by adding a command
- Open a presentation and print it by executing a macro
- Create a form to customize a presentation
- Create a user interface
- Add controls, such as command buttons and combo boxes, to a form
- Assign properties to controls
- Write VBA code to create a unique presentation

The Perfect Portfolio

Customized and Creative

After all your hard work as a student, you are ready to leap into a profession in your chosen field of study. Many college graduates search for career choice information at campus placement centers and job fairs and in employment classified advertisements in local papers and career Web sites.

As you read job descriptions and begin interviewing for positions, you will discover that computer skills are an important priority with employers. CareerLab®, an online occupation advisement Web site, indicates that a high number of middle- and upper-level management job seekers do not own a computer, cannot create a word-processed document or copy a disk, and never have used the Internet. These individuals are at a disadvantage in the job market.

People with up-to-date computer skills are in high demand, and top executives are expected to take their notebook computers on the road. Many employers look for candidates with more than a basic knowledge

of computers; they desire individuals proficient in the latest version of software, especially Microsoft Word, Microsoft Excel, and Microsoft PowerPoint. An added bonus for employers is a candidate who has become certified as a Microsoft Office User Specialist (MOUS). When writing your cover letter and resume, emphasize your competency in these and any other programs in which you are proficient.

After you receive a call to schedule an interview, you must prepare for presenting yourself in the most persuasive manner. Career books and Web sites abound with advice on what questions to expect, what questions to ask, and what clothes to wear. In the typical 30-minute interview, you will be judged on your communications skills, leadership ability, maturity, and intelligence.

No doubt you also will be asked questions about your computer expertise. While you can list these skills on your resume and discuss them with the interviewer, nothing is more persuasive than actually demonstrating your proficiency. One of the most influential methods of showing this technological knowledge is with an electronic portfolio.

The portfolio concept is not new; artists, architects, and journalists routinely bring binders, scrapbooks, and folders to interviews to showcase their drawings, plans, and writings. Today, technology-savvy students have transformed these tangible notebooks to electronic notebooks using PowerPoint to display their projects, describe their experiences, and demonstrate their skills.

In this project, you will develop an electronic career portfolio slide show for Bernie Simpson, an elementary education major who is seeking a position teaching middle school science. The presentation highlights Bernie's teaching and leisure activities using video clips and digital photographs. With a form developed in Visual Basic for Applications, a programming language that extends PowerPoint's capabilities, the slide show can be tailored for each prospective school district.

Eye-catching, professional-looking electronic portfolios provide employment candidates with cutting-edge skills recruiters seek. The techniques you will learn in this project, coupled with organized interview plans and a well-thought-out portfolio, will benefit you as you embark on your chosen career path.

Microsoft PowerPoint 2002

Working with Macros and Visual Basic for Applications (VBA)

PROJECT 5

CASE PERSPECTIVE

Creative job seekers are developing innovative methods of presenting their educational background and work experiences. One of these techniques is running an electronic career portfolio slide show on a notebook computer during an interview. Your classmate, Bernie Simpson, has asked you to help him develop such a slide show. Bernie is an elementary education major and is seeking a position teaching science at a middle school. He wants to tailor his slide show for each prospective school district for several interviews next month. He has two video clips and three digital photos highlighting his teaching and leisure activities.

After examining the information Bernie wants to emphasize, you determine that the best method for customizing each presentation is to use a form you develop using Visual Basic for Applications. Bernie's responses on the form will create a unique slide show for each interview. You also will create a toolbar and add buttons and then add a command to the File menu to simplify the related tasks he must perform: saving the presentation as a Web page, using the Pack and Go Wizard, printing a handout, and displaying the form.

Introduction

Before a computer can take an action and produce a desired result, it must have a step-by-step description of the task to be accomplished. This series of precise instructions is called a **procedure**, which also is called a **program** or **code**. The process of writing a procedure is called **computer programming**. Every PowerPoint command on a menu and button on a toolbar has a corresponding procedure that executes when the command or button is clicked. When the computer **executes** a procedure, it carries out the step-by-step instructions. In a Windows environment, the instructions associated with a task are executed when an **event** takes place, such as clicking a button, an option button, or a check box.

Because a command or button in PowerPoint does not exist for every possible task, Microsoft has included a powerful programming language called **Visual Basic for Applications** (**VBA**). This programming language allows you to customize and extend the capabilities of PowerPoint.

In this project, you will learn how to create macros using a code generator called a **macro recorder**. A **macro** is a procedure composed of VBA code that automates multi-step tasks. By simply executing a macro, the user can perform tasks that otherwise would require many keystrokes. You also will learn how to add buttons to toolbars. You will add a command to a menu and associate it with a print macro. Finally, you will learn the basics of VBA as you create an interface, set properties, and write the code.

The slide show you create in this project is intended to help the user, Bernie Simpson, in his job search. The goal is that he will open the Teaching Portfolio file on his notebook computer at each job interview, open the form, and then make selections on the form to indicate which slide template, video clip, and picture to insert. VBA will create the presentation corresponding to these selections. Two possible slide shows are shown in Figures 5-1a through 5-1h.

Presentation 1

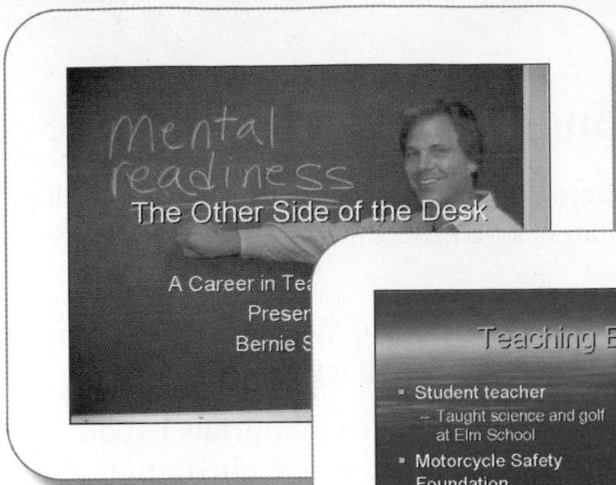

(a) Slide 1

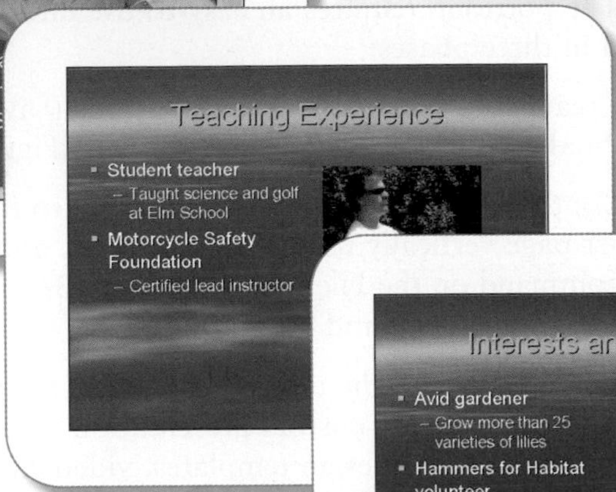

(b) Slide 2

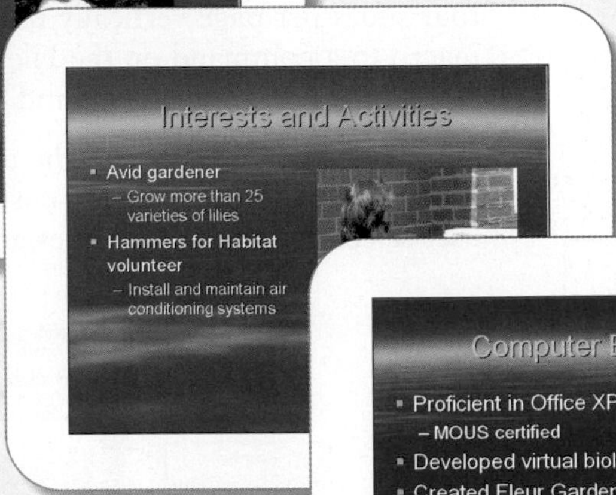

(c) Slide 3

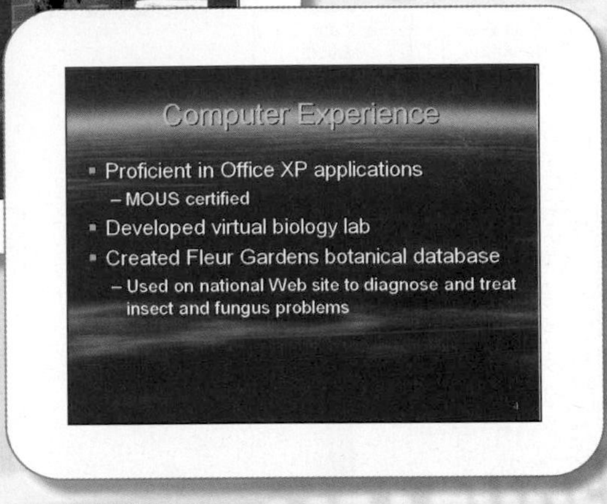

(d) Slide 4

Presentation 2

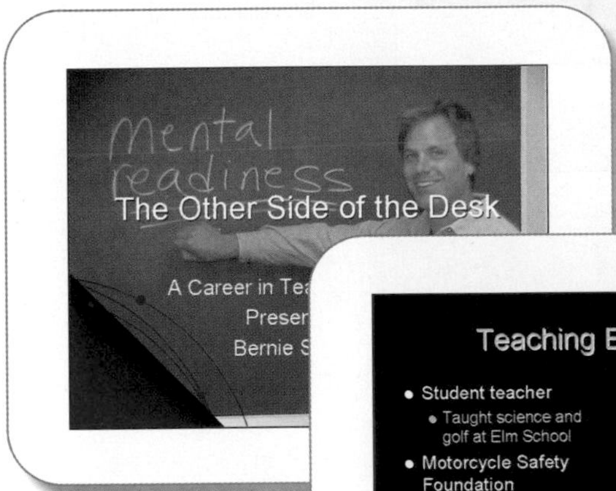

(e) Slide 1

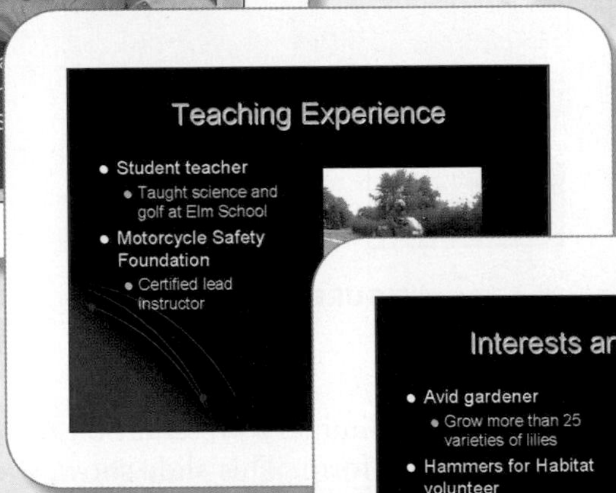

(f) Slide 2

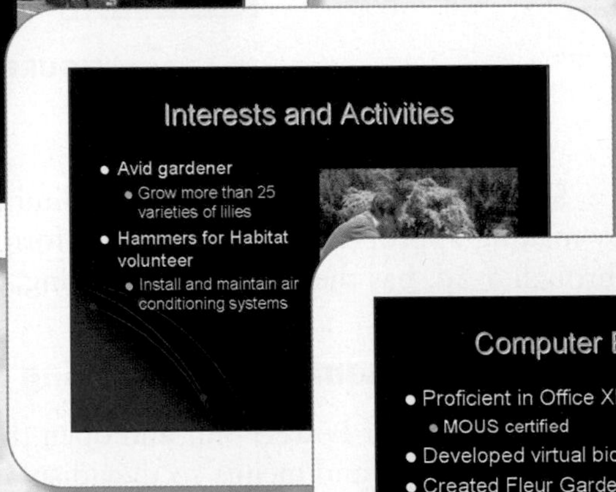

(g) Slide 3

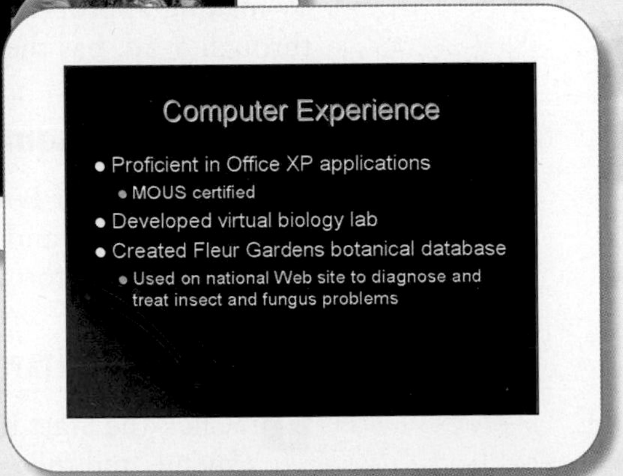

(h) Slide 4

FIGURE 5-1

Project Five — Creating an Electronic Resume

The following requirements are necessary to create the Teaching Portfolio:

Needs: The portfolio requires an easy-to-use interface. This interface will be implemented in three phases:

Phase 1 — Create a toolbar and add two buttons (Save as Web Page and Pack and Go) that normally do not display on any toolbar (Figure 5-2).

Phase 2 — Use the macro recorder to create a macro that prints handouts that display four slides per page vertically using the Pure Black and White option. Assign the macro to a command on the File menu (Figure 5-3) so the user can execute the macro by clicking the command.

Phase 3 — Add a button to the toolbar created in Phase 1 that displays a form allowing the user to design a custom presentation (Figure 5-4). This form lets the user select one of two slide design templates, video clips, and pictures.

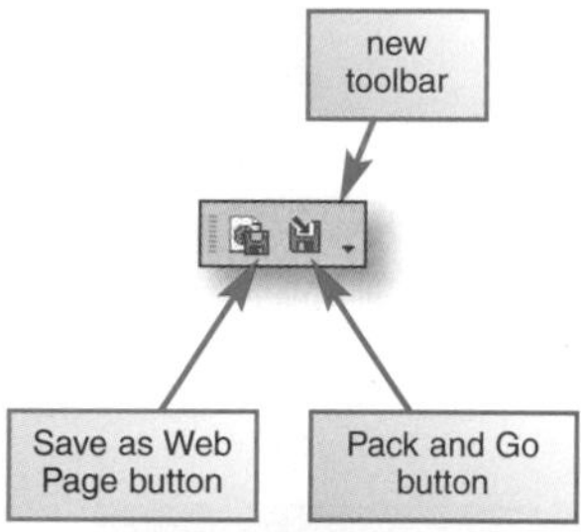

FIGURE 5-2

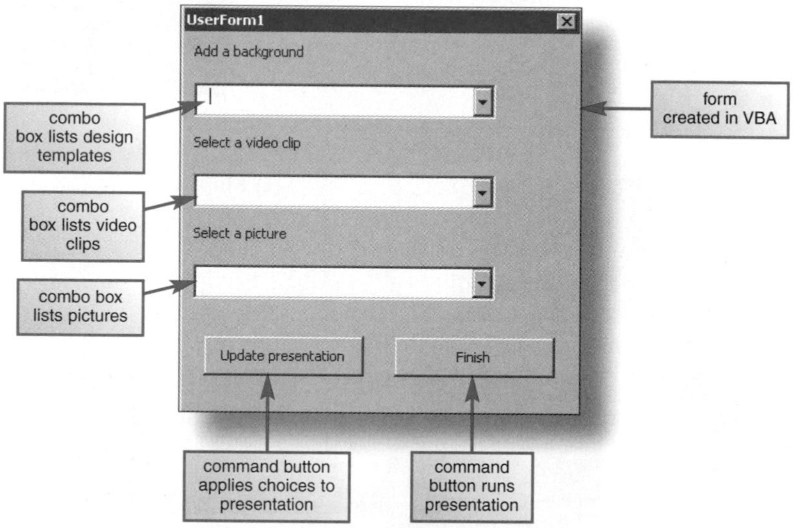

FIGURE 5-4

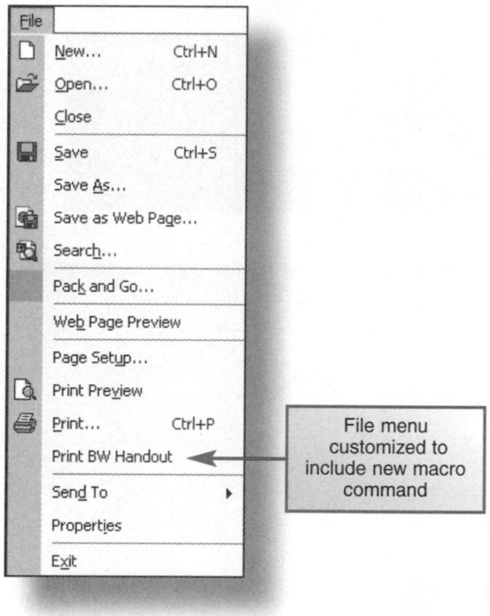

FIGURE 5-3

Source of Data: You develop a preliminary presentation the user will complete by making appropriate selections on a form. This slide show, shown in Figures 5-5a through 5-5d, has the file name, Teaching, and is located on the Data Disk.

Opening a Presentation and Saving It with a New File Name

To begin, start PowerPoint and open the Teaching file on the Data Disk. Then reset the toolbars and menus so they display exactly as shown in this book (see Appendix D). Perform the following steps.

TO OPEN A PRESENTATION AND SAVE IT WITH A NEW FILE NAME

1. Click the Start button on the Windows taskbar, point to Programs on the Start menu, and then click Microsoft PowerPoint on the Programs submenu.

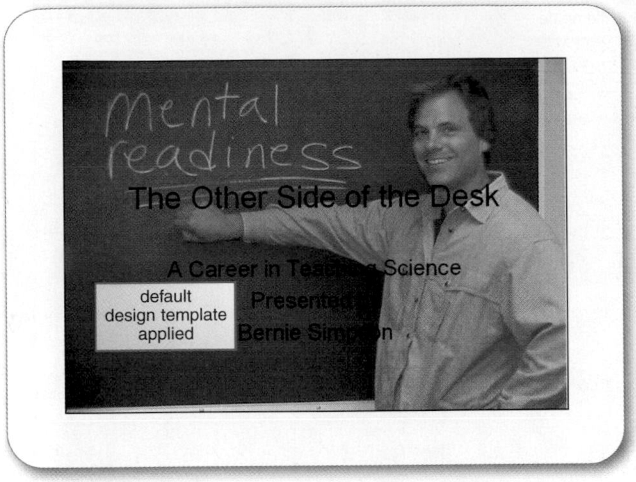

(a) Slide 1

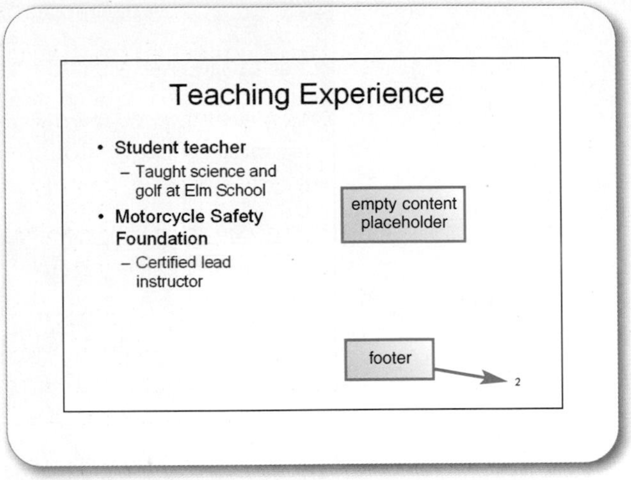

(b) Slide 2

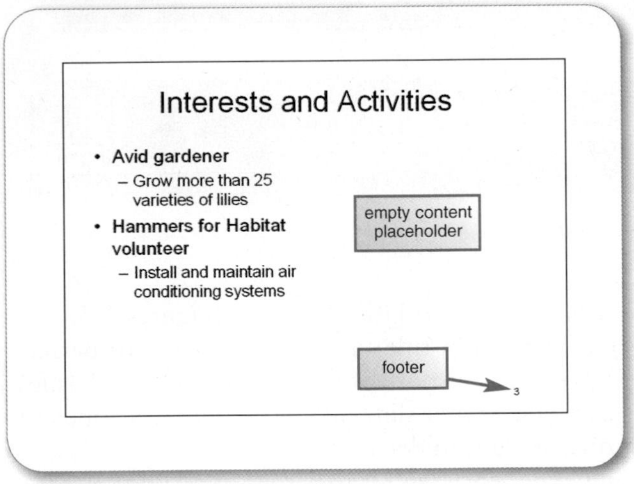

(c) Slide 3

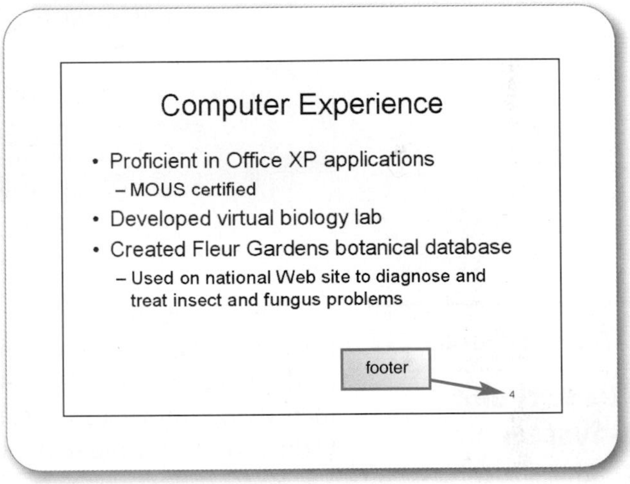

(d) Slide 4

FIGURE 5-5

2 If the New Presentation task pane displays, click the Show at startup check box to remove the check mark and then click the Close button on the task pane title bar.

3 If the Language bar displays, click its Minimize button.

4 If the Standard and Formatting toolbars display on one row, click the Toolbar Options button on the right side of either toolbar and then click Show Buttons on Two Rows on the Toolbar Options menu.

5 Open the presentation, Teaching, from the Data Disk. See the inside back cover of this book for instructions for downloading the Data Disk or see your instructor for information about accessing the files required for this book.

6 Save the presentation with the file name, Teaching Portfolio.

The presentation is saved with the file name, Teaching Portfolio (Figure 5-6 on the next page).

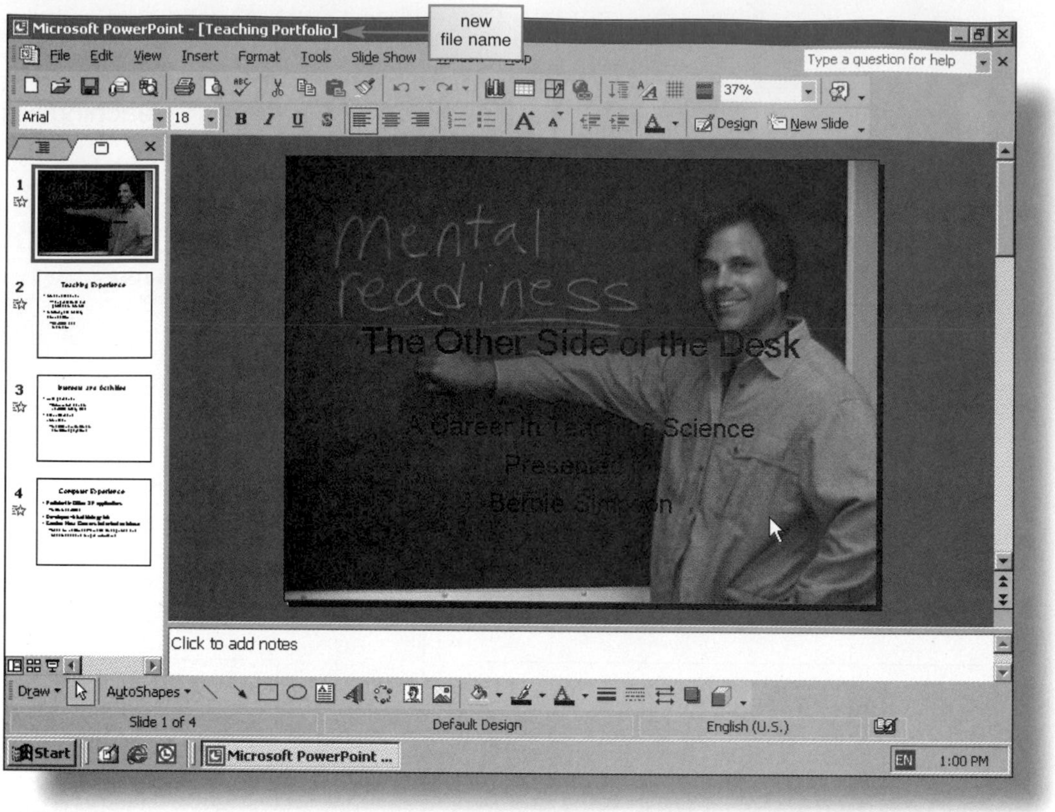

FIGURE 5-6

More About

The PowerPoint Help System

Need Help? It is no further than the Ask a Question box in the upper-right corner of the window. Click the box that contains the text, Type a question for help (Figure 5-6), type `help`, and then press the ENTER key. PowerPoint will respond with a list of items you can click to learn about obtaining help on any PowerPoint-related topic. To find out what is new in PowerPoint 2002, type `what's new in PowerPoint` in the Ask a Question box.

The Teaching Portfolio presentation is composed of four slides (Figures 5-5a through 5-5d on the previous page). The first is a title slide with a picture of Bernie as the background. The subtitle text gives the purpose of the slide show and Bernie's identifying information. You will select one of two slide design templates, Clouds or Orbit, to format the text and position the placeholders.

Slide 2 describes Bernie's teaching experience, and it uses the Title, Text, and Content slide layout. The content placeholder is empty, but it will contain one of two possible video clips, golf or motorcycle, based on the selection made in the Visual Basic form. A digital video camera was used to shoot this video, and then later it was edited and the clips were compressed to use in this presentation.

Slide 3 highlights Bernie's interests and activities. One of his pastimes is gardening, growing many types of lilies, and another is volunteering at the local Hammers for Habitat organization, which builds and repairs low-income housing for community residents. The slide also uses the Title, Text, and Content slide layout; one of two photos of Bernie gardening or testing an air conditioning unit will be inserted into the content placeholder.

Slide 4 emphasizes Bernie's computer expertise and his Microsoft Office User Specialist (MOUS) certification in Office XP. His accomplishments include creating a virtual lab for biology classes and developing the botanical database for Fleur Gardens, which are emphasized in the presentation.

Slides 2, 3, and 4 have a footer that contains the slide number, as seen in Figure 5-7. In addition, they use the Float animation scheme. Slide 1 automatically advances in 10 seconds or when you click the mouse, and Slides 2, 3, and 4 advance 15 seconds after they display or when you click the mouse.

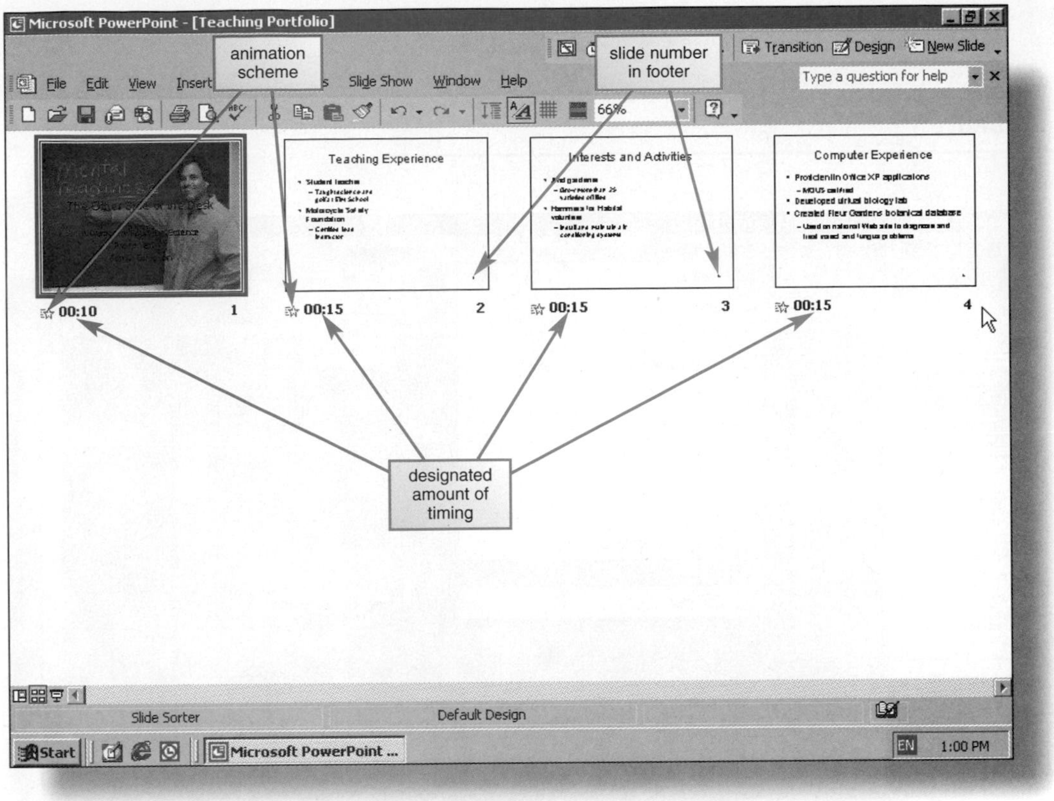

FIGURE 5-7

Phase 1 — Creating a Toolbar and Adding Two Buttons

The first phase of this project creates a toolbar that displays in the lower-right corner of the screen beside the Drawing toolbar. PowerPoint provides more than a dozen toolbars for a variety of purposes. A **custom toolbar**, however, allows you to display the buttons specific to your needs.

> **More About**
>
> **Job Hunting**
>
> Are you looking for a job or do you need information about a career? Turn to the Internet for a wealth of information about the fastest-growing careers, employment databases, salaries, freelance work, and resume writing. For more information, visit the PowerPoint 2002 More About Web page (scsite.com/pp2002/more.htm) and then click Jobs.

Creating and Customizing a Toolbar

One of the buttons you will add to the custom toolbar is the Save as Web Page button. Although users can save a file as a Web page by clicking the Save as Web Page command on the File menu, they also can click a button to make the presentation available for potential employers to view on the Internet. The second button you will add to the custom toolbar in this phase of the project will launch the Pack and Go Wizard. Users can click this button to compress and store the presentation files. They then can transport the presentation on floppy disks to show on a computer at the interviewing site, rather than view it on their notebook computers.

You can customize toolbars and menus by adding, deleting, and changing the function of buttons and commands. Once you add a button to a toolbar or a command to a menu, you can assign a macro to the button or command. You customize a toolbar or menu by invoking the **Customize command** on the Tools menu. The key to understanding how to customize a toolbar or menu is to recognize that when the Customize dialog box is open, PowerPoint's toolbars and menus are in edit mode. **Edit mode** allows you to modify the toolbars and menus.

Perform the following steps to create a custom toolbar.

Steps To Create a Custom Toolbar

1 Click Tools on the menu bar and then point to Customize.

The Tools menu displays (Figure 5-8).

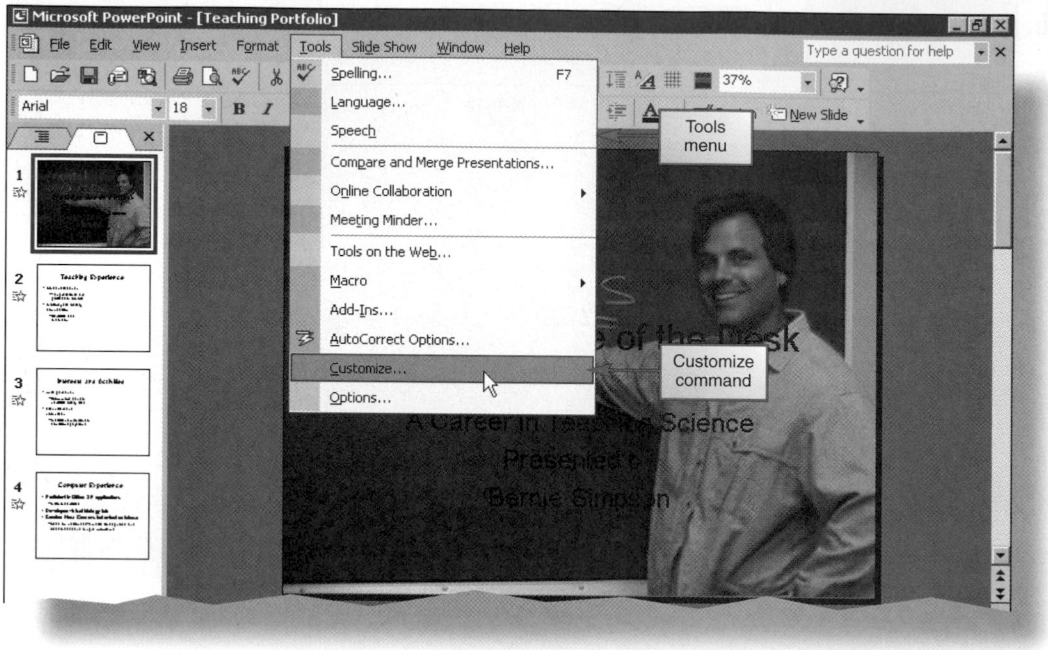

FIGURE 5-8

2 Click Customize. When the Customize dialog box displays, if necessary, click the Toolbars tab, and then point to the New button.

The Toolbars sheet in the Customize dialog box displays (Figure 5-9).

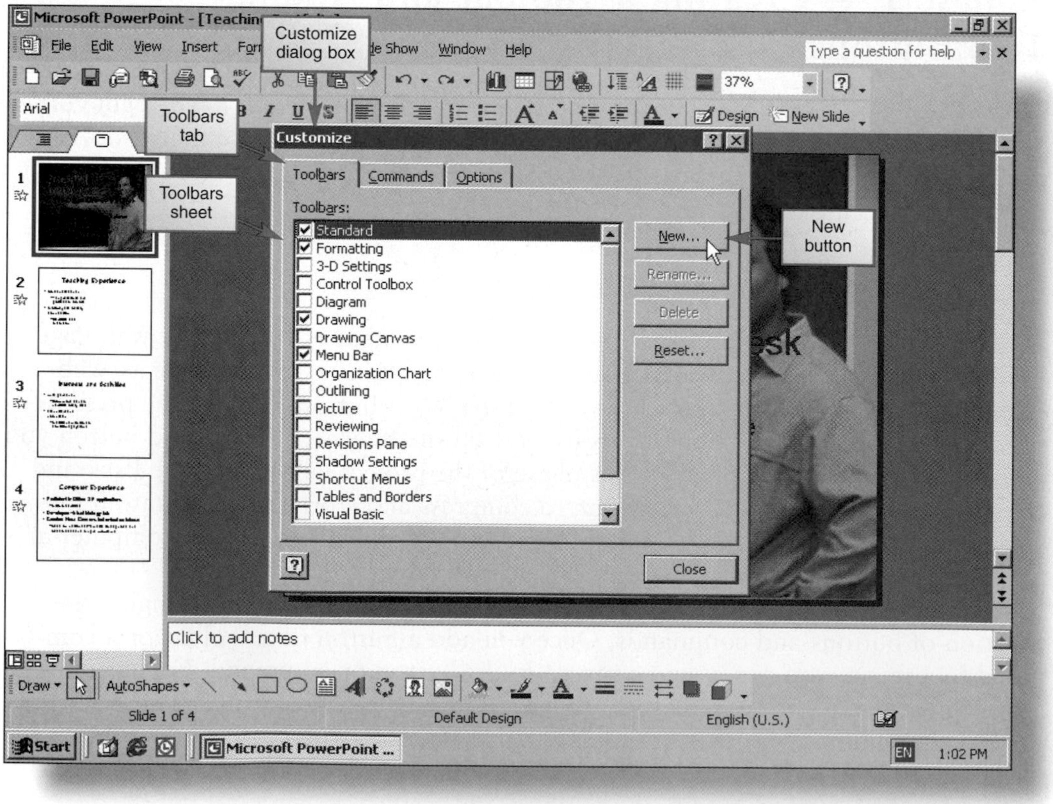

FIGURE 5-9

3 Click the New button. When the New Toolbar dialog box displays, type `Resume` **in the Toolbar name text box and then point to the OK button.**

Resume will be the name of the new toolbar (Figure 5-10).

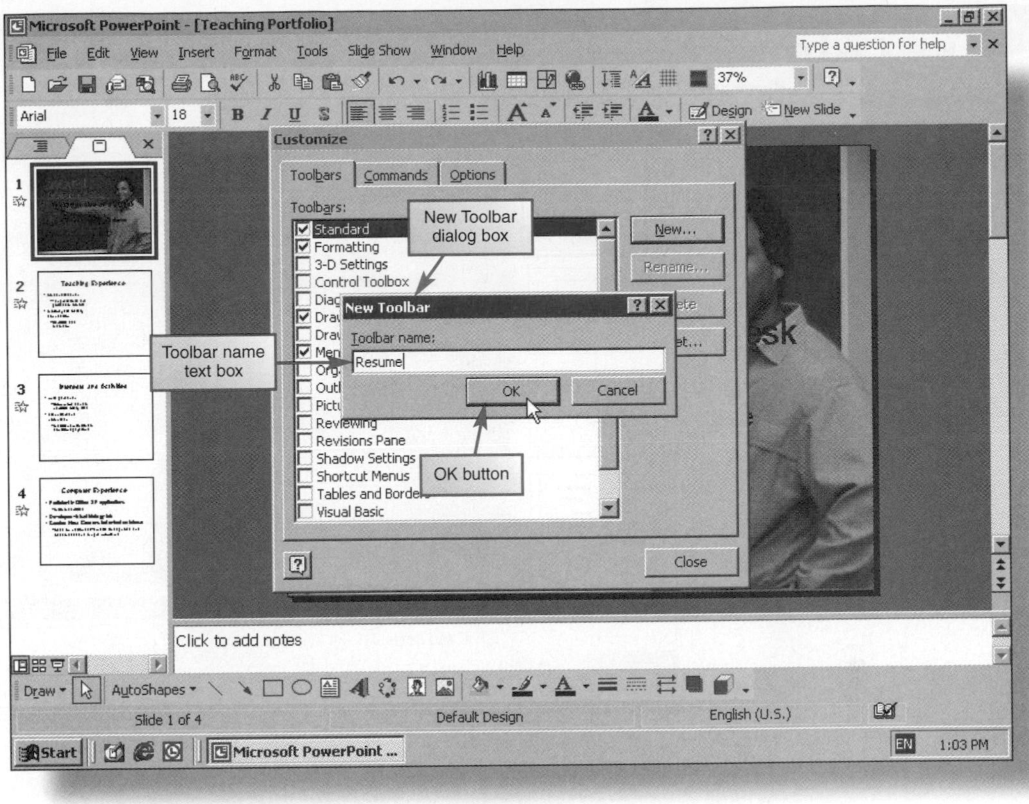

FIGURE 5-10

4 Click the OK button and then point to the Close button in the Customize dialog box.

The Resume toolbar displays (Figure 5-11).

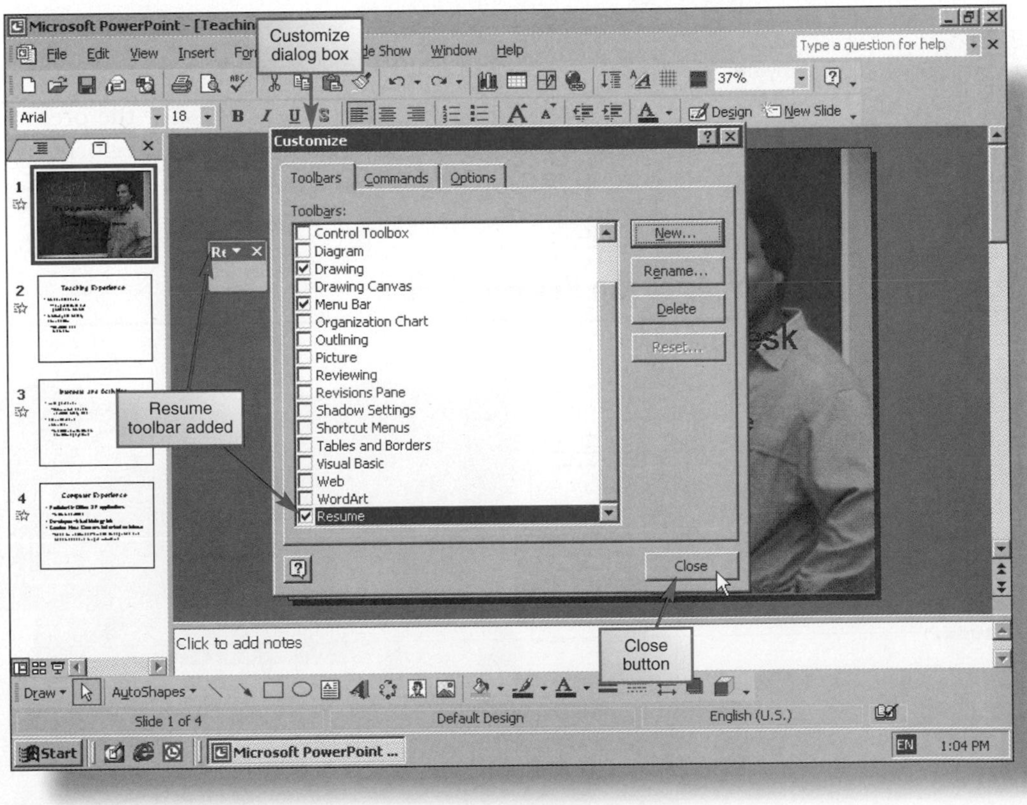

FIGURE 5-11

5 Click the Close button, and then click the toolbar and drag it to the bottom-right corner of the screen beside the Drawing toolbar.

The Resume toolbar displays in the desired location (Figure 5-12). The toolbar title does not display.

FIGURE 5-12

Other Ways

1. Right-click a toolbar, click Customize on shortcut menu, click Toolbars tab, click New button
2. Click More buttons on a toolbar, click Add or Remove buttons, click Customize, click Toolbars tab, click New button

The Resume toolbar is positioned beside the Drawing toolbar. The next step is to add two buttons to it. One button will save the presentation as a Web page, and the second will start the Pack and Go Wizard. Perform the following steps to add these buttons to the Resume toolbar.

Steps To Add Two Buttons to the Resume Toolbar

1 Click the Toolbar Options button on the new toolbar, point to Add or Remove Buttons, and then point to Customize on the Add or Remove Buttons submenu.

The Add or Remove Buttons submenu displays (Figure 5-13).

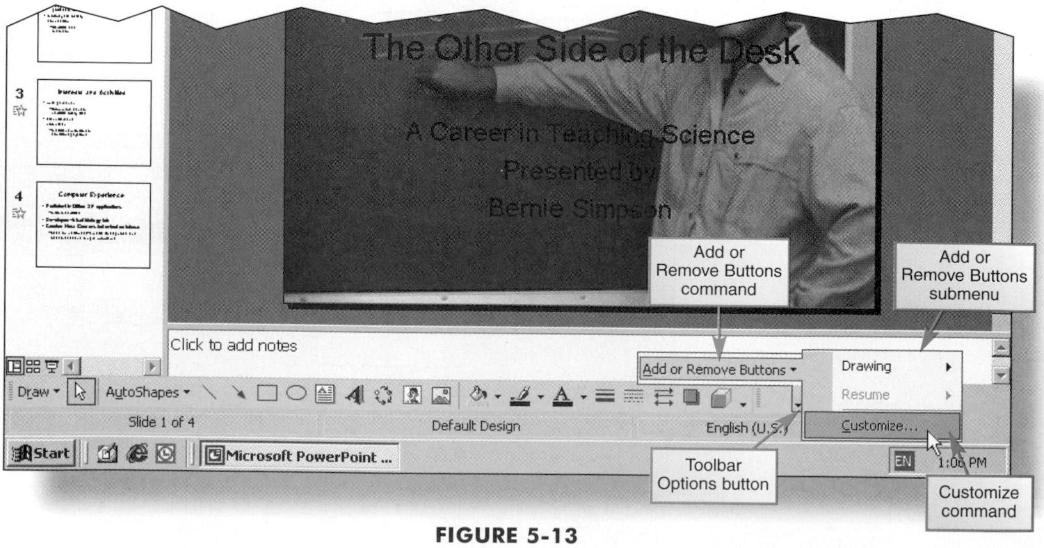

FIGURE 5-13

2 Click Customize. When the Customize dialog box displays, click the Commands tab. Scroll down in the Commands list and then click Save as Web Page.

You can select buttons from several categories, and each category has a variety of commands (Figure 5-14). File is the default category. Some commands have images associated with them.

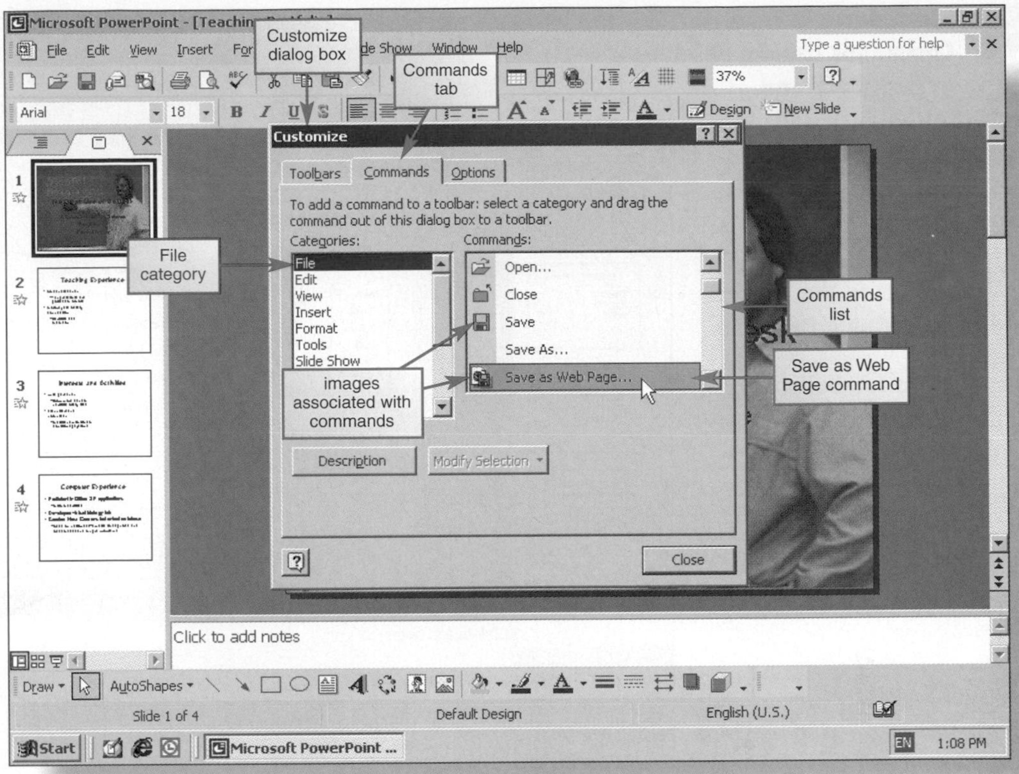

FIGURE 5-14

3 Drag the Save as Web Page command from the Commands list to the new Resume toolbar.

The Save as Web Page button displays with an image on the Resume toolbar (Figure 5-15). The heavy border surrounding the button indicates PowerPoint is in edit mode.

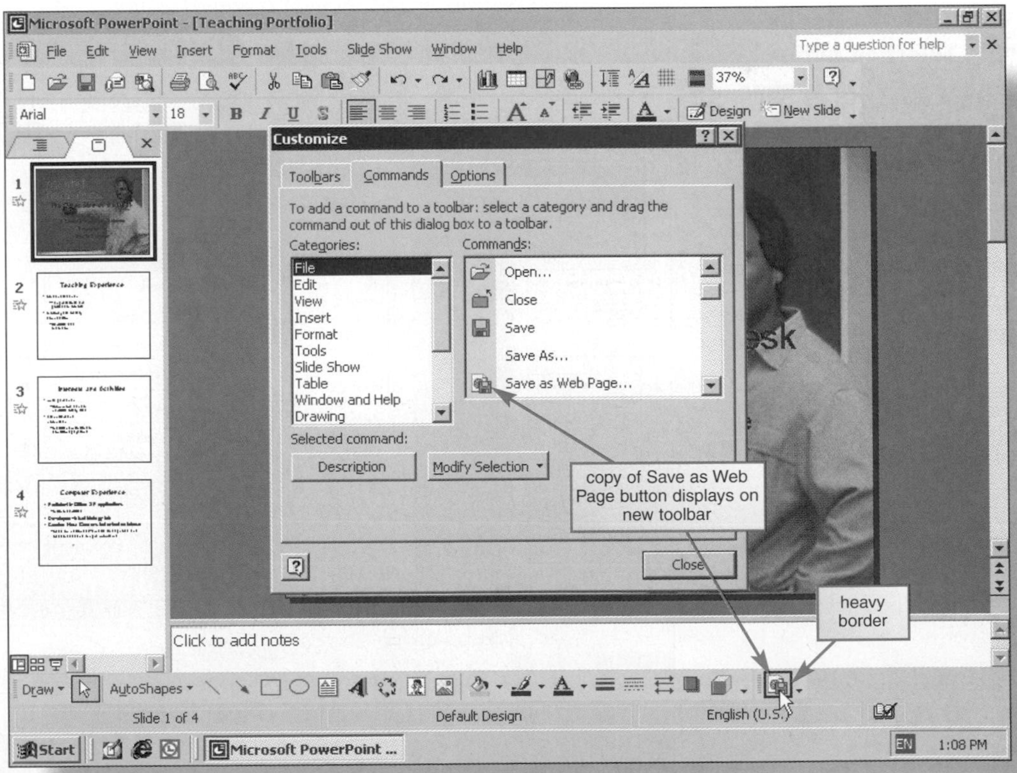

FIGURE 5-15

4 **Scroll down in the Commands list and then click Pack and Go. Drag the Pack and Go command from the Commands list to the right of the Save as Web Page button on the Resume toolbar. Point to the Modify Selection button.**

The Pack and Go button displays on the Resume toolbar with its name displaying on the face of the button (Figure 5-16). A heavy border surrounds the button, indicating that PowerPoint is in edit mode.

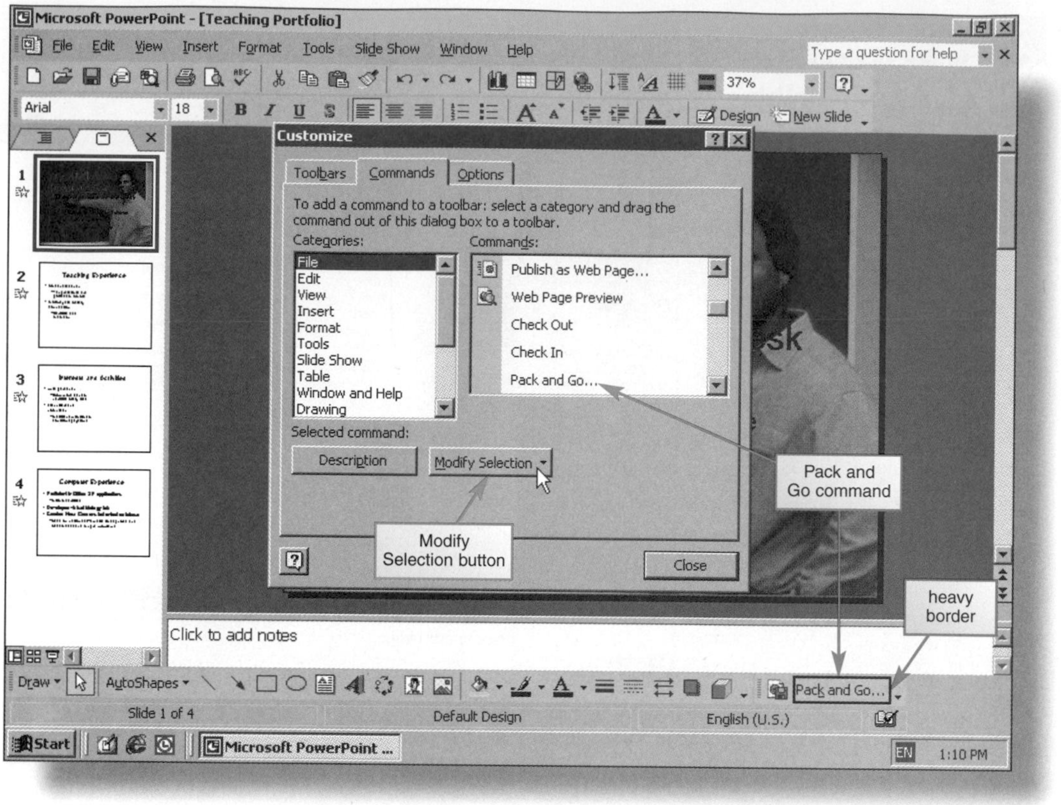

FIGURE 5-16

5 **Click the Modify Selection button and then point to Change Button Image. When the Change Button Image palette displays, point to the button with a blue arrow pointing toward a floppy disk (row 1, column 6).**

PowerPoint displays a palette of button images from which to choose (Figure 5-17).

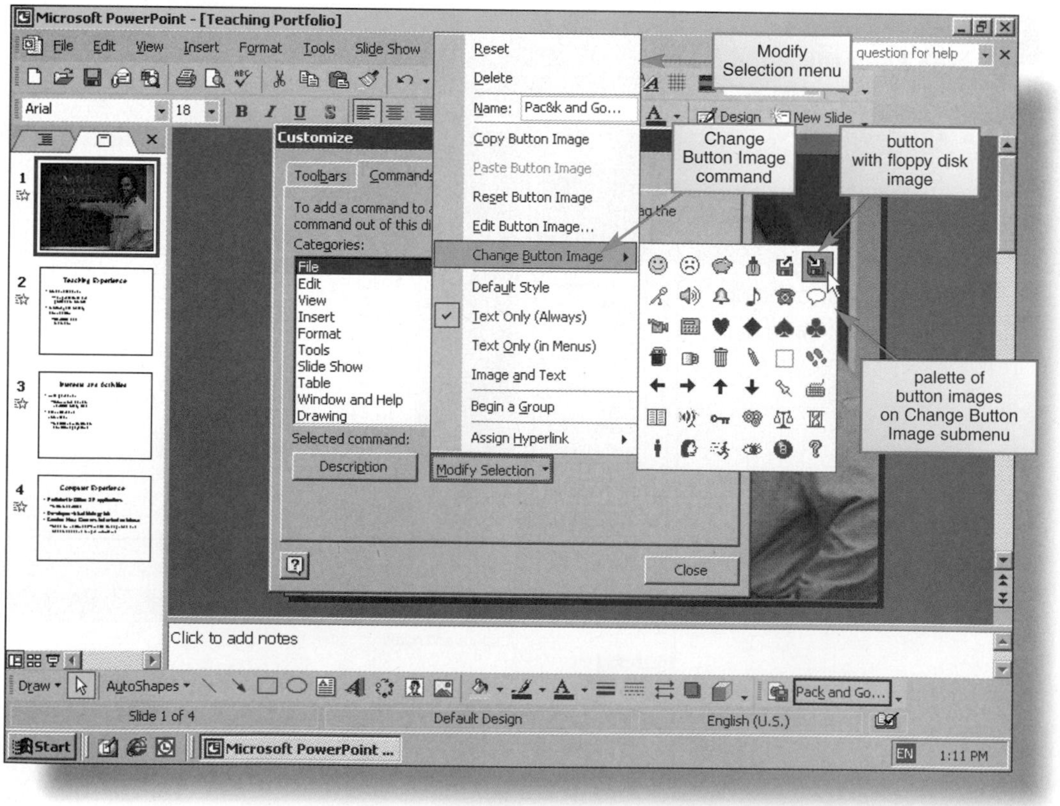

FIGURE 5-17

6 Click the button with the floppy disk image. Point to the Modify Selection button.

The Pack and Go button displays on the toolbar with the floppy disk image and the text, Pack and Go (Figure 5-18).

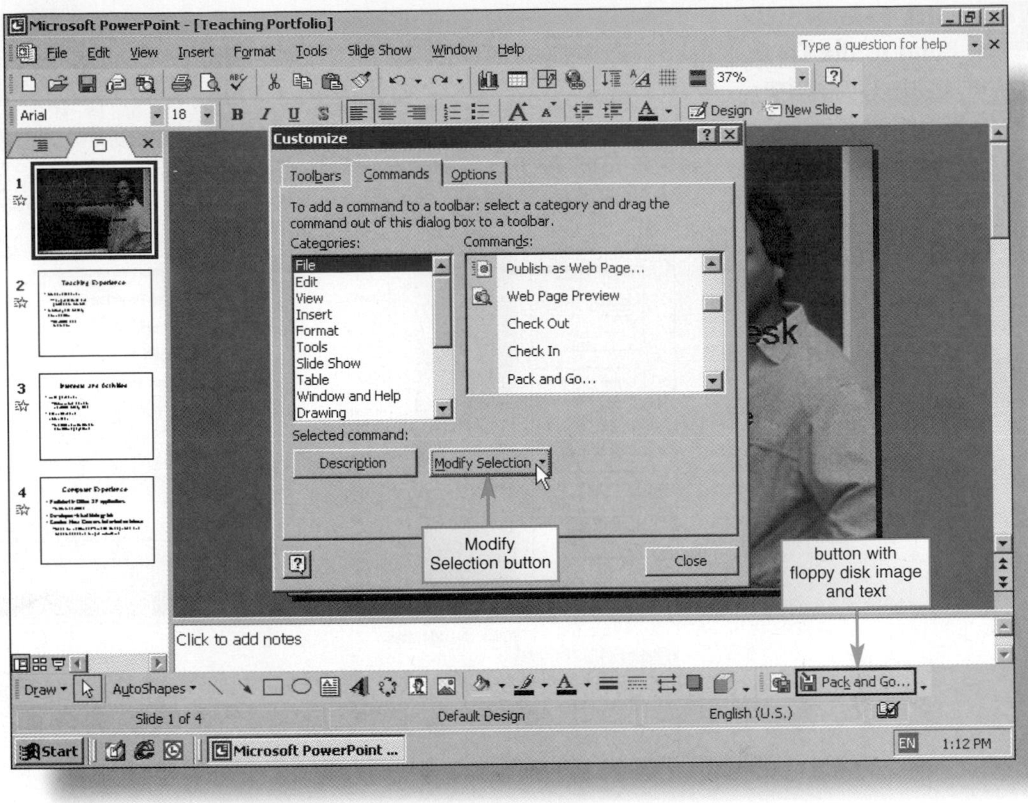

FIGURE 5-18

7 Click the Modify Selection button and then point to Default Style.

The default style includes only the image, not text (Figure 5-19). The ampersand in the Name box, Pac&k and Go, underlines the letter k on the button, indicating a keyboard shortcut.

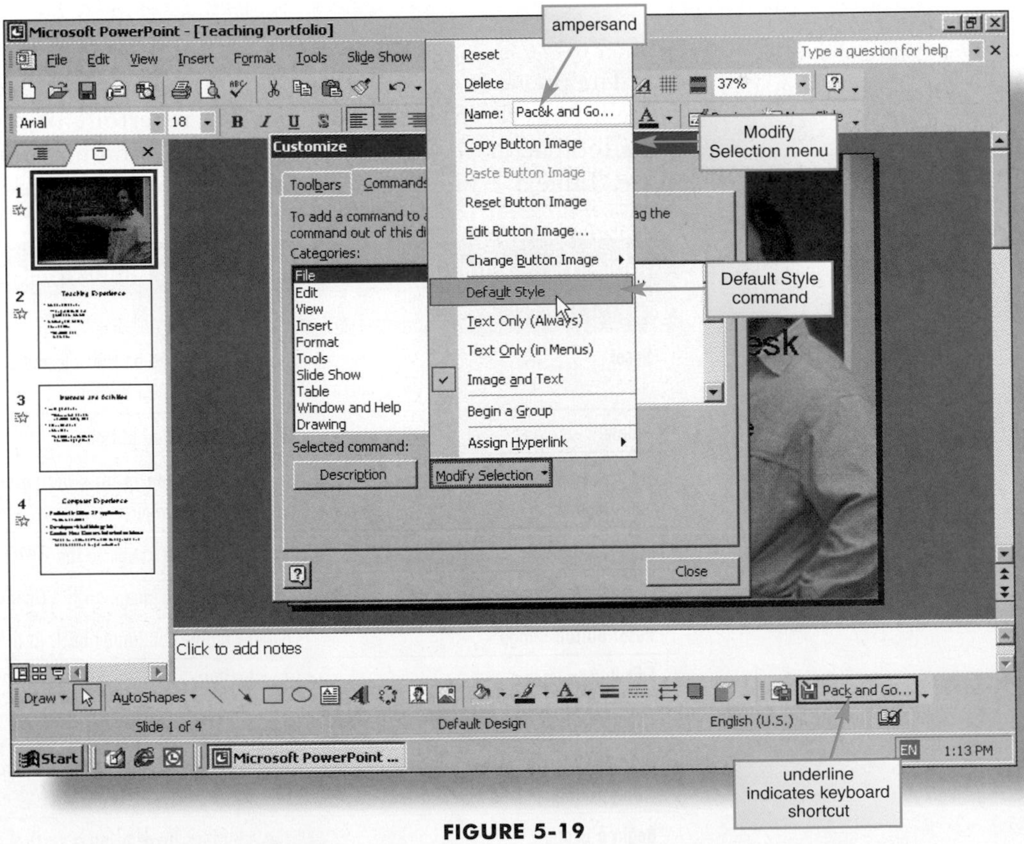

FIGURE 5-19

8 Click Default Style. Point to the Close button in the Customize dialog box.

The Pack and Go button image displays with the floppy disk only (Figure 5-20).

9 Click the Close button.

PowerPoint quits edit mode.

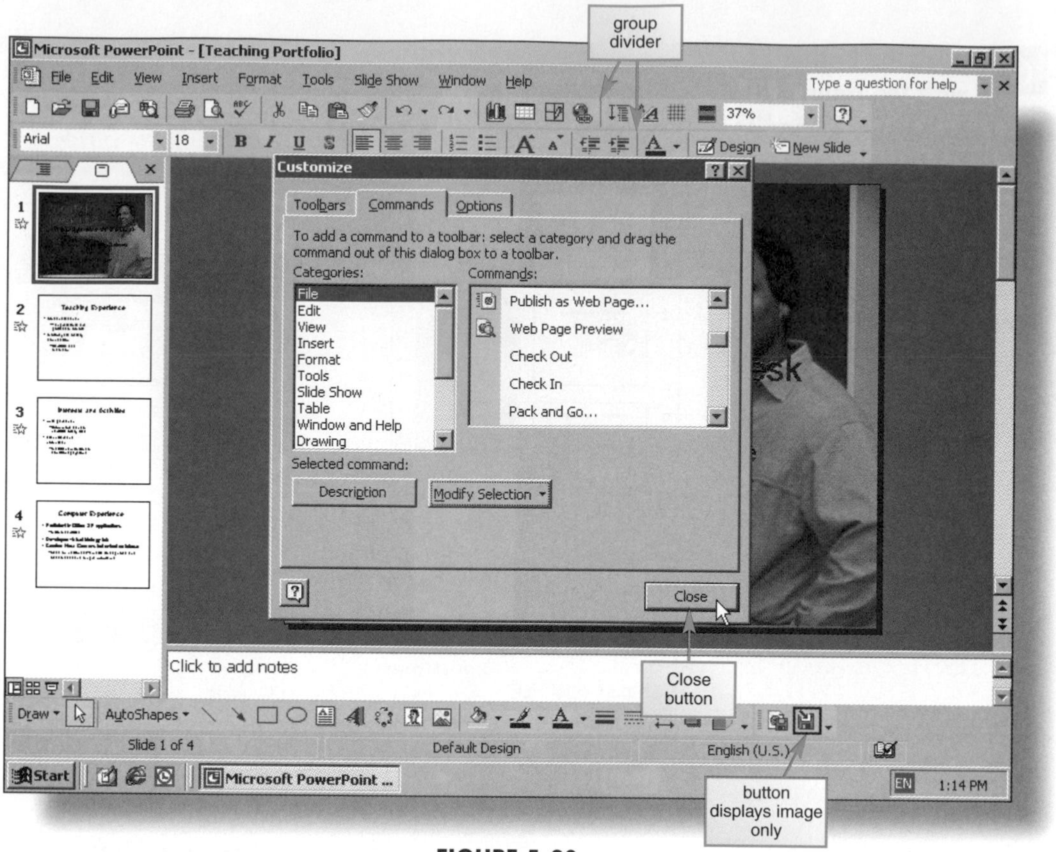

FIGURE 5-20

The previous steps illustrate how a toolbar is created easily and how buttons are added. PowerPoint includes a complete repertoire of commands for editing buttons on a toolbar, as shown on the Modify Selection menu in Figure 5-19 on the previous page. Table 5-1 briefly describes each of the commands on this menu.

Table 5-1 Summary of Commands on the Modify Selection Menu

COMMAND	DESCRIPTION
Reset	Changes the image on the selected button to the original image and disassociates the macro with the button
Delete	Deletes the selected button
Name box	Changes the ScreenTip for a button and changes the command name for a command on a menu
Copy Button Image	Copies the button image to the Office Clipboard
Paste Button Image	Pastes the button image on the Office Clipboard onto selected button
Reset Button Image	Changes the button image back to the original image
Edit Button Image	Edits the button image
Change Button Image	Chooses a new button image
Default Style; Text Only (Always); Text Only (in Menus); Image and Text	Chooses one of the four styles to indicate how the button should display
Begin a Group	Groups buttons by drawing a vertical line (divider) on the toolbar (see the group dividing lines in Figure 5-20)
Assign Hyperlink	Assigns a hyperlink to a Web page or document

You can add as many buttons as you want to a toolbar. You also can change any button's function. For example, when in edit mode with the Customize dialog box displaying, you can right-click the Save button on the Standard toolbar and assign it a macro or hyperlink. The next time you click the Save button, the macro will execute, so PowerPoint will launch the application associated with the hyperlink rather than save the presentation.

Reset the toolbars to their installation default by clicking the Toolbars tab in the Customize dialog box, selecting the toolbar in the Toolbars list, and clicking the Reset button. Because it is so easy to change the buttons on a toolbar, each project in this book begins by resetting the toolbars.

More About

Modifying Buttons

If the Change Button Image palette does not contain an image to your liking, you can modify one of the icons or draw a new one. Click the Edit Button Image command and then design a unique image using the Button Editor dialog box.

Saving the Presentation

The changes to Phase 1 of the presentation are complete. Perform the following step to save the presentation before recording a macro in Phase 2 of this project.

TO SAVE A PRESENTATION

1 Click the Save button on the Standard toolbar.

PowerPoint saves the presentation by saving the changes made to the presentation since the last save.

Phase 2 — Recording a Macro and Assigning It to a Menu Command

The second phase of the project creates a macro to print a handout displaying four slides per page vertically using the Pure Black and White option. The default PowerPoint print setting is Slides, with one slide printing on each sheet of paper. When the Print what setting is changed to handouts, the default setting is six slides per page in a horizontal order, meaning Slides 1 and 2 display at the top of the page, Slides 3 and 4 display in the middle of the page, and Slides 5 and 6 display at the bottom of the page. The user can distribute a one-page handout, shown in Figure 5-21, of the four slides in this presentation printed using the Pure Black and White option and displayed vertically, meaning Slides 1 and 3 display on the top, and Slides 2 and 4 display below.

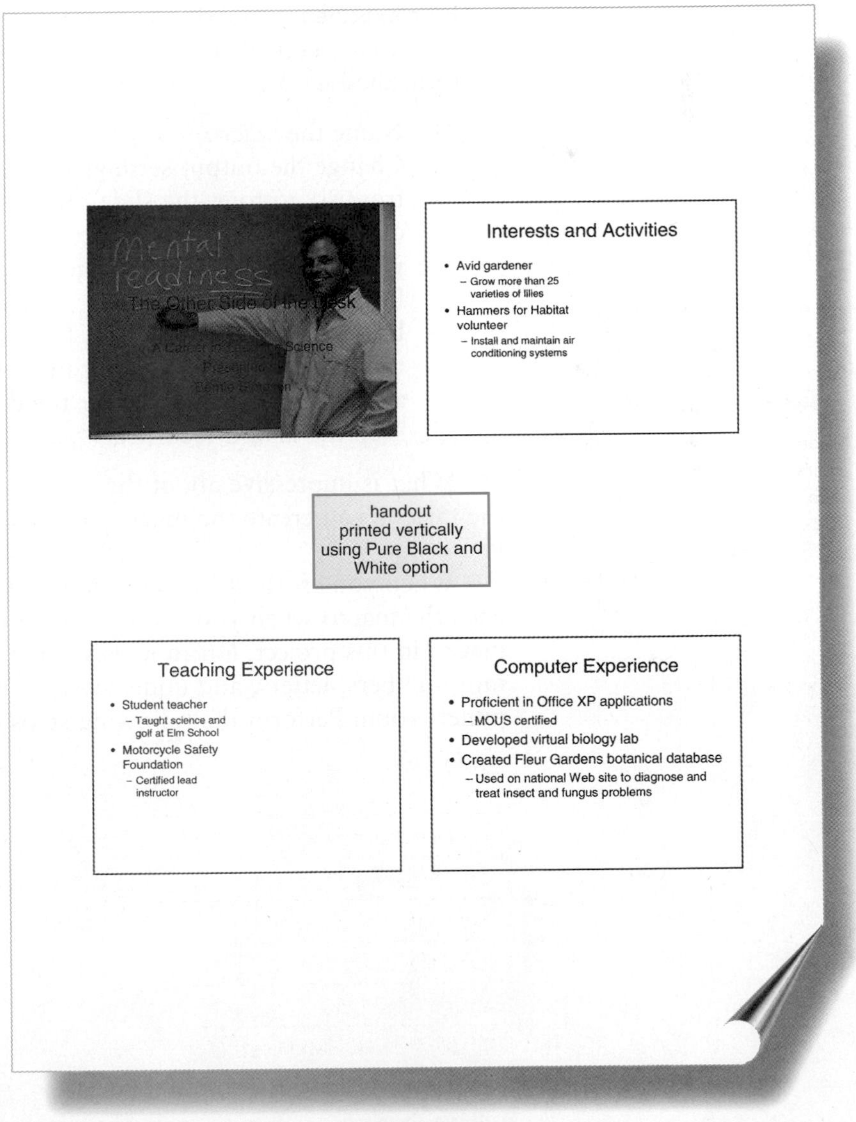

FIGURE 5-21

More About

Deleting Toolbars

You may decide to delete a toolbar once you have created it. To delete a custom toolbar, click Tools on the menu bar, click Customize, and then click the Toolbars tab. Select the custom toolbar in the Toolbars list that you want to delete, and then click the Delete button. You cannot delete a built-in toolbar. If you select a built-in toolbar in the Toolbars list, the Reset button displays. When you click the Reset button, PowerPoint restores that toolbar to its default buttons, menus, and submenus.

The planned macro will change the output from slides to handouts and will change the slide order on the handout from horizontal to vertical. The handout will print using the Pure Black and White option instead of Grayscale or another default setting on your computer, so all shades of gray will change to either black or white. The macro then will reset the Print dialog box to its original settings.

With the macro, users can print a one-page handout by executing a single command, rather than performing the several steps otherwise required. They can click the Print button on the Standard toolbar and change the settings in the Print dialog box to print these handouts, or they can execute the macro to print the handout. Once the macro is created, it will be assigned to a command on the File menu.

Recording a Macro

PowerPoint has a **macro recorder** that creates a macro automatically based on a series of actions performed while it is recording. Like a tape recorder, the macro recorder records everything you do to a presentation over a period of time. The macro recorder can be turned on, during which time it records your activities, and then turned off to stop the recording. Once the macro is recorded, it can be **played back** or **executed** as often as desired.

It is easy to create a macro. All you have to do is turn on the macro recorder and perform these steps:

1. Name the macro.
2. Change the output settings from slides to handouts, the slides per page from six to four, the slide order on the handout from horizontal to vertical, and the print option from Grayscale (or the default print setting on your computer) to Pure Black and White.
3. Print the handout.
4. Restore the output settings from four slides per page to six, from vertical to horizontal slide order, from handouts to slides, and from Pure Black and White to Grayscale (or the default print setting on your computer).
5. Stop the macro recorder.

More About

Undoing Macros

Occasionally, you may want to undo the changes created by a macro you have executed. Clicking the Undo button on the Standard toolbar once often does not reverse all the changes. You probably will need to click the Undo button arrow and then select several commands in the list.

What is impressive about the macro recorder is that you actually step through the task as you create the macro. You will see exactly what the macro will do before you use it.

When you create the macro, you first must name it. The name is used to reference the macro when you want to execute it. The name PrintHandout is used for the macro in this project. **Macro names** can be up to 255 characters long; they can contain numbers, letters, and underscores; and they cannot contain spaces and other punctuation. Perform the following steps to record the macro.

Steps To Record a Macro to Print Handouts in Vertical Slide Order in Pure Black and White

1 Click Tools on the menu bar, point to Macro, and then point to Record New Macro on the Macro submenu.

The Tools menu and Macro submenu display (Figure 5-22).

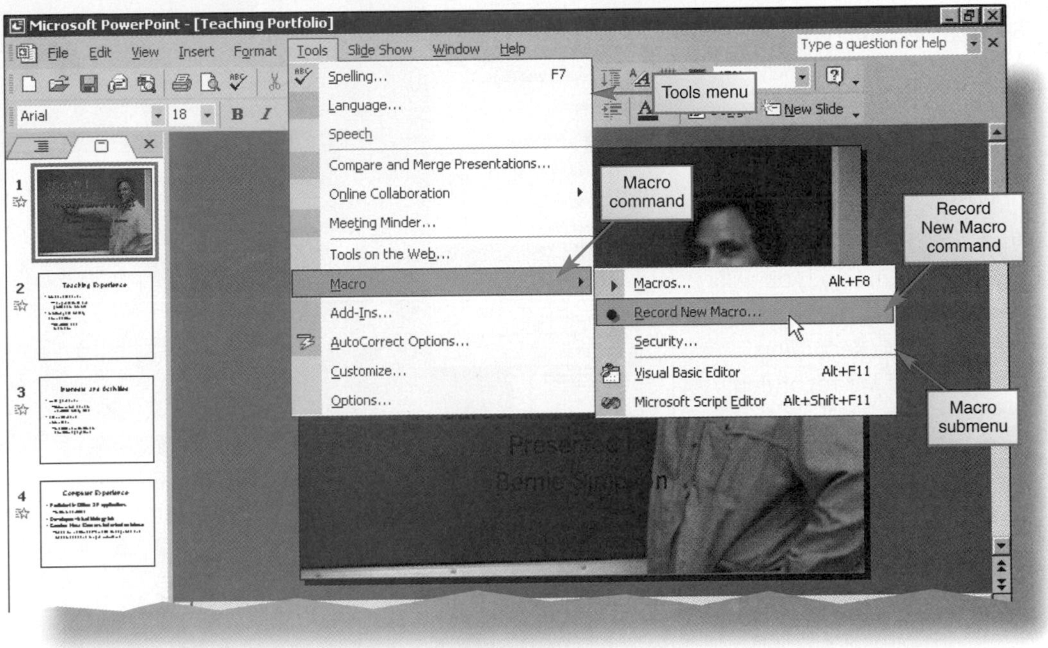

FIGURE 5-22

2 Click Record New Macro. When the Record Macro dialog box displays, type `PrintHandout` **in the Macro name text box. Type** `Macro prints Pure Black and White handouts in vertical slide order` **in the Description text box. Make sure the Store macro in text box displays Teaching Portfolio. Point to the OK button.**

The Record Macro dialog box displays as shown in Figure 5-23.

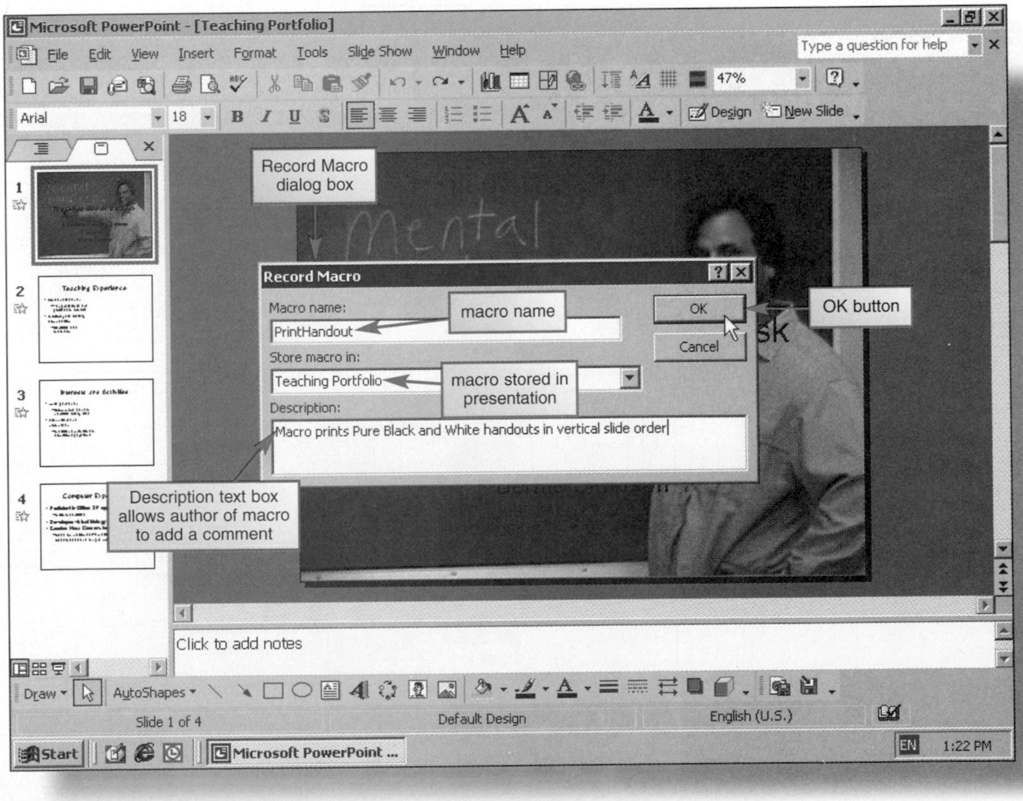

FIGURE 5-23

3 Click the OK button. Click File on the menu bar and then point to Print.

The Stop Recording toolbar and the File menu display (Figure 5-24). Any task you perform after the Stop Recording toolbar displays will be part of the macro. When you are finished recording the macro, you will click the Stop Recording button on the Stop Recording toolbar to end the recording.

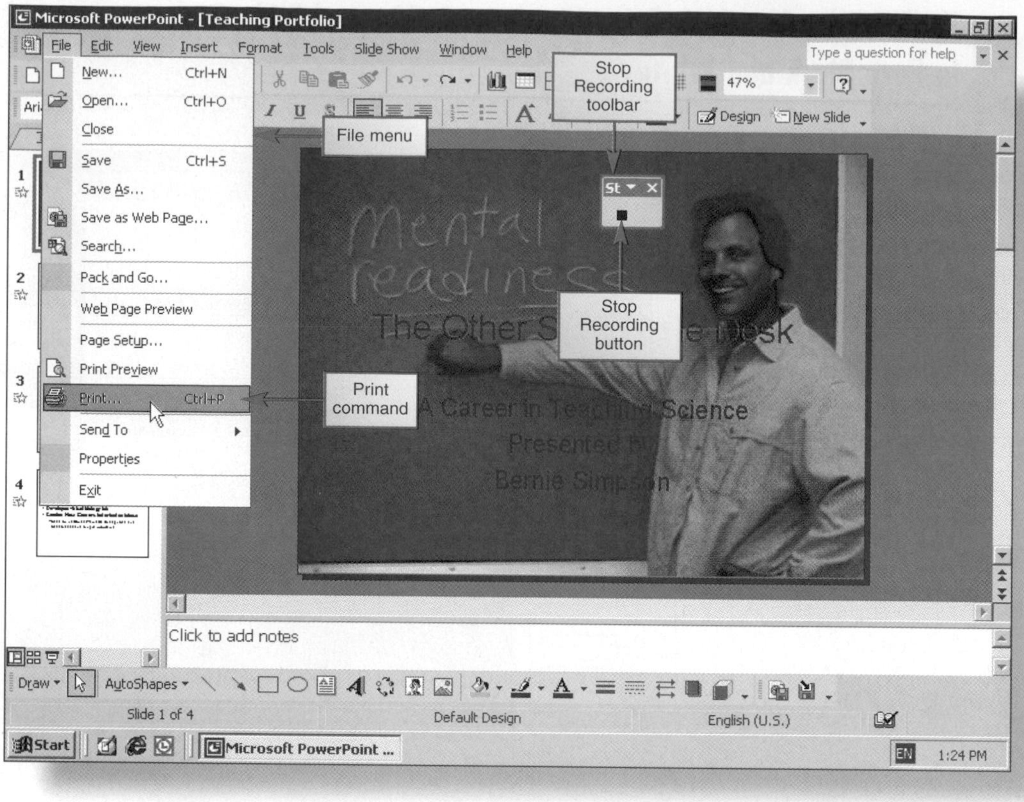

FIGURE 5-24

4 Click Print. When the Print dialog box displays, click the Print what box arrow and click Handouts, click the Slides per page box arrow in the Handouts area and click 4, click Vertical order in the Handouts area, click the Color/grayscale box arrow, click Pure Black and White, and then point to the OK button.

The Print dialog box displays as shown in Figure 5-25.

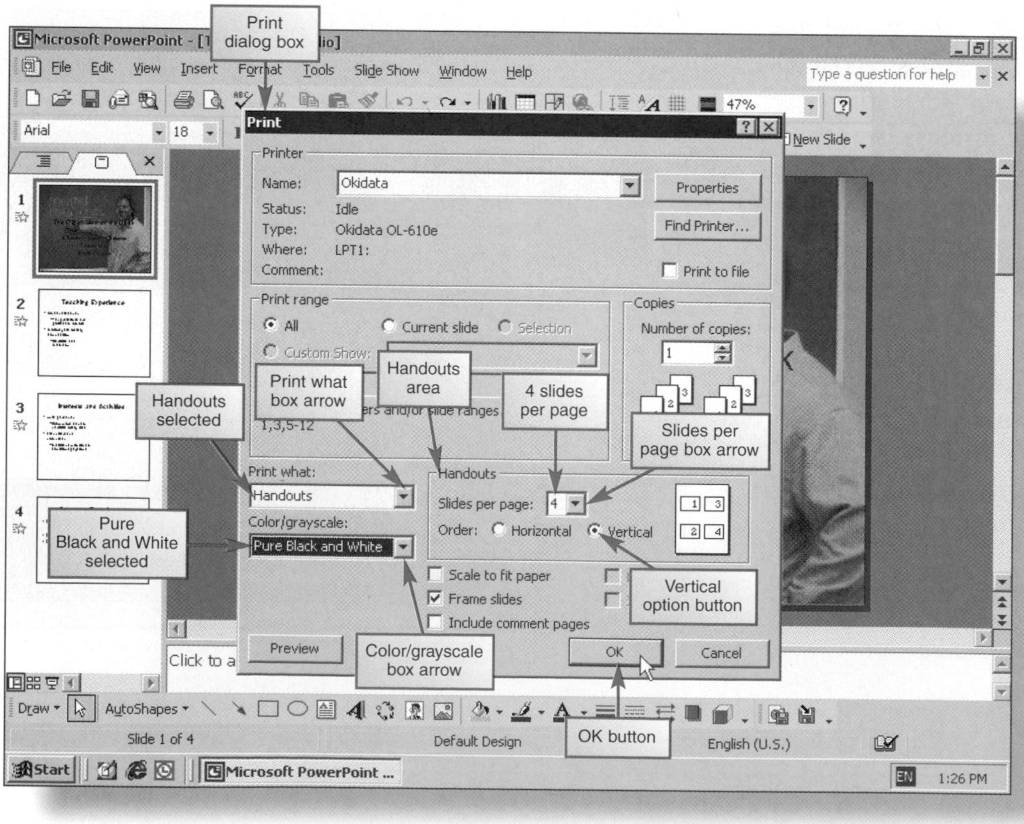

FIGURE 5-25

5 Click the OK button. Click File on the menu bar and then click Print. When the Print dialog box displays, click the Color/grayscale box arrow and then click Grayscale, click the Slides per page box arrow in the Handouts area and click 6, click Horizontal order in the Handouts area, click the Print what box arrow and click Slides, and then point to the OK button.

The Print dialog box displays as shown in Figure 5-26. Your computer is restored to its default print settings. The printout resembles the handout shown in Figure 5-21 on page PP 5.17.

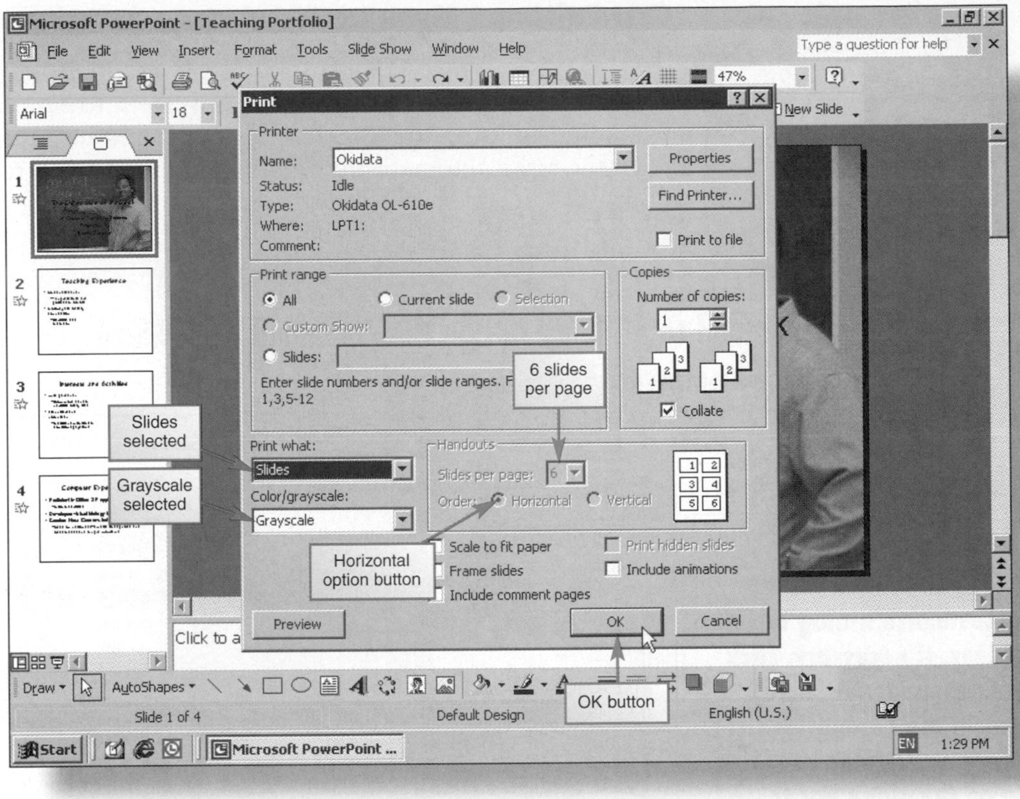

FIGURE 5-26

6 Click the OK button. Point to the Stop Recording button.

The Print dialog box closes (Figure 5-27). The four slides in the presentation print in grayscale or your computer's default print option.

7 Click the Stop Recording button.

PowerPoint stops recording the printing activities and hides the Stop Recording toolbar.

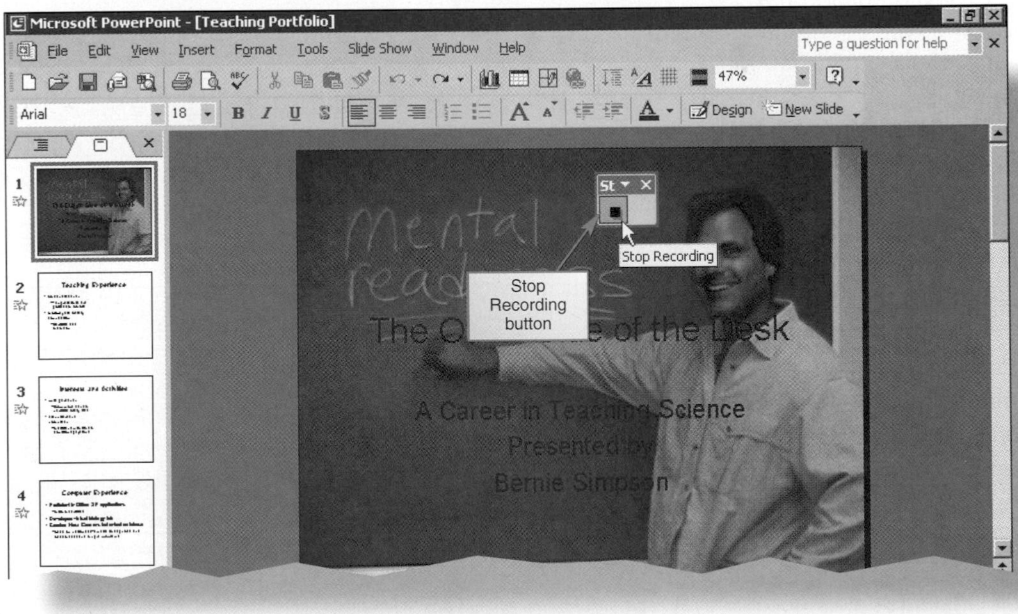

FIGURE 5-27

Other Ways

1. Click Record Macro button on Visual Basic toolbar
2. Press ALT+T, press M, press R
3. In Voice Command mode, say "Tools, Macro, Record New Macro"

If you recorded the wrong actions, delete the macro and record it again. You delete a macro by clicking Tools on the menu bar, pointing to Macro on the Tools menu, and then clicking Macros on the Macro submenu. When the Macro dialog box displays, click the name of the macro (PrintHandout), and then click the Delete button. Then record the macro again.

Customizing a Menu

As you use PowerPoint to create presentations and print handouts, you may find yourself repeating many steps. It is convenient to simplify these repetitive processes by adding a button to a toolbar or a command to a menu that you can click to perform the tasks automatically. PowerPoint allows you to add commands to a button or to a menu. The following steps show how to add a command to the File menu to execute the PrintHandout macro.

Steps To Add a Command to a Menu, Assign the Command to a Macro, and Invoke the Command

1 **Click Tools on the menu bar and then click Customize. When the Customize dialog box displays, if necessary, click the Commands tab. Scroll down in the Categories list and then click Macros. Click File on the menu bar to display the File menu.**

The Customize dialog box and File menu display (Figure 5-28). A heavy border surrounds the File menu name, indicating PowerPoint is in edit mode.

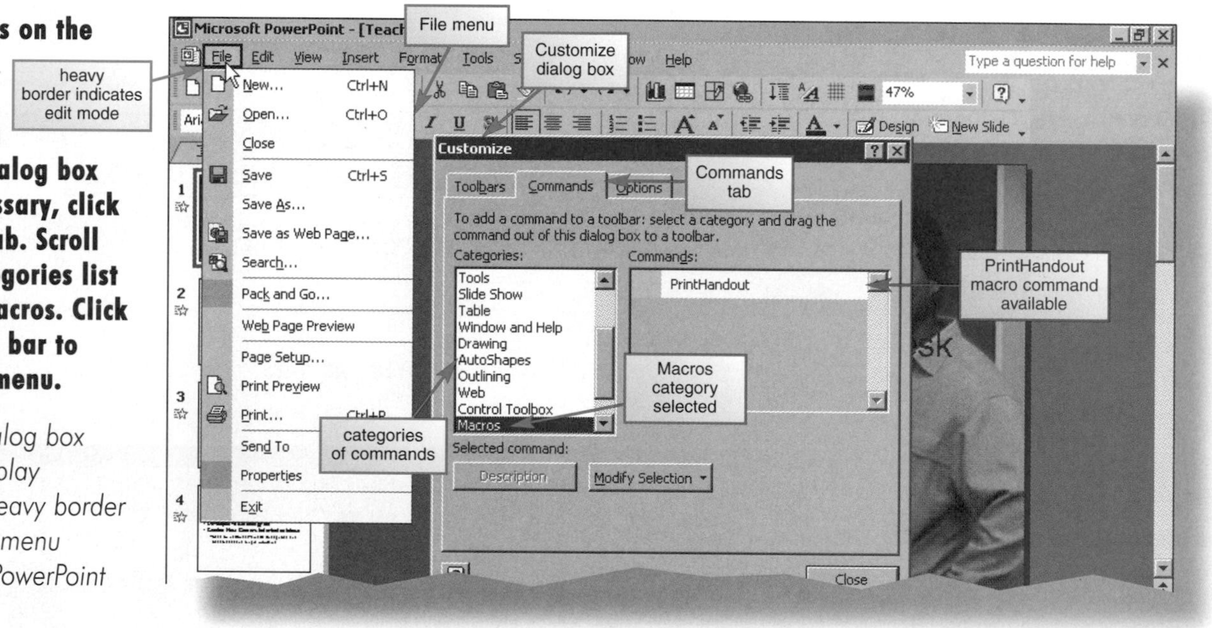

FIGURE 5-28

2 **Drag the PrintHandout entry from the Commands list in the Customize dialog box immediately below the Print command on the File menu.**

PowerPoint adds PrintHandout to the File menu (Figure 5-29). The heavy border surrounding PrintHandout on the File menu indicates edit mode.

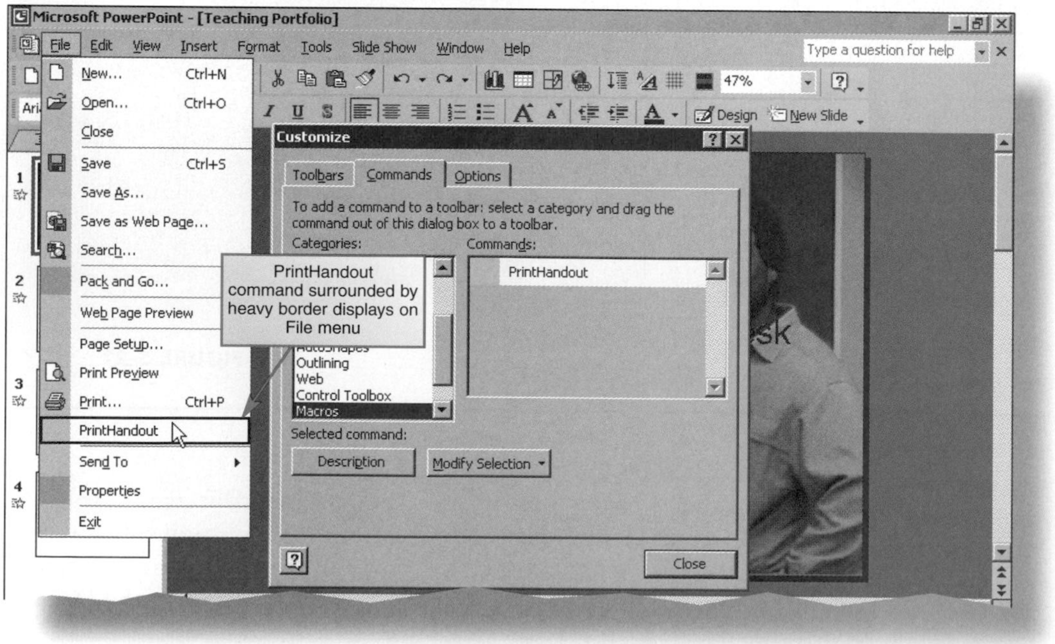

FIGURE 5-29

3 Right-click PrintHandout on the File menu and then click the Name box on the shortcut menu. Type `Print BW Handout` **as the new name of this command. Point to the Close button at the bottom of the Customize dialog box.**

The shortcut menu displays with the new command name in the Name box (Figure 5-30).

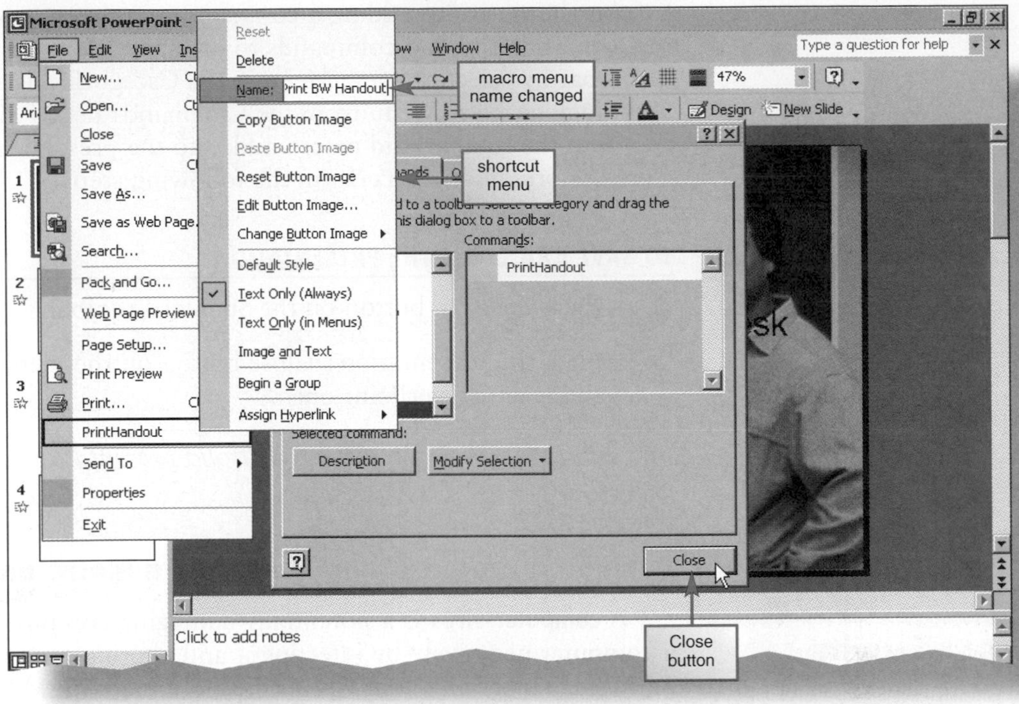

FIGURE 5-30

4 Click the Close button. Click File on the menu bar and then point to Print BW Handout.

PowerPoint quits edit mode. The File menu displays with the new command, Print BW Handout, on the menu (Figure 5-31).

5 Click Print BW Handout on the File menu.

After several seconds, the handout and slides print as shown in Figures 5-5 and 5-21 on pages PP 5.07 and PP 5.17.

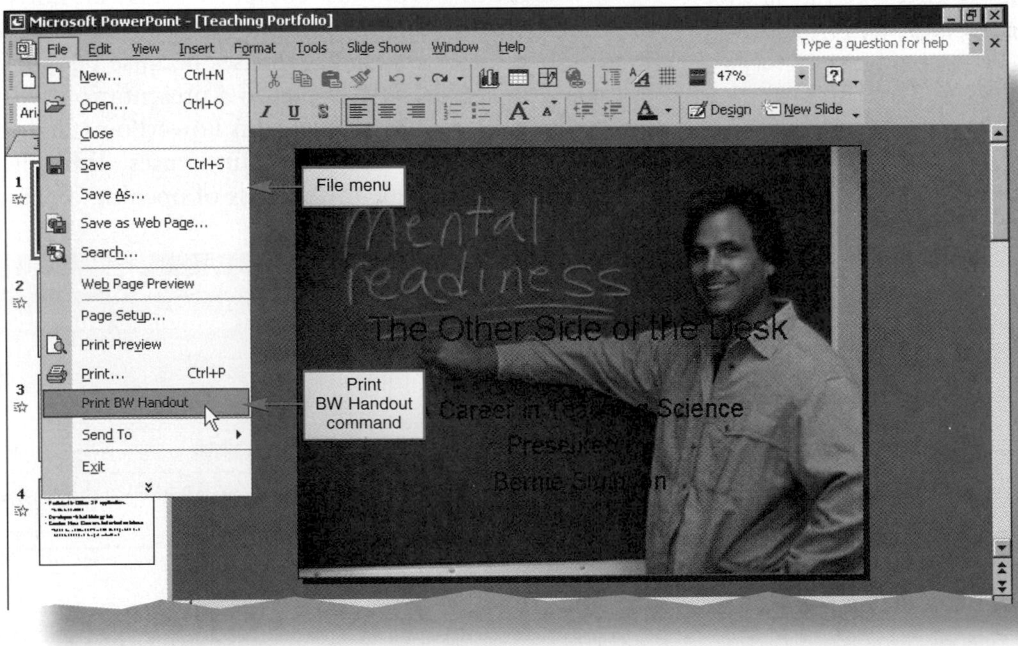

FIGURE 5-31

Other Ways

1. Right-click toolbar, click Customize on shortcut menu, click Commands tab
2. On View menu click Toolbars, click Customize, click Commands tab
3. In Voice Command mode, say "View, Toolbars, Customize, Commands"

You have the same customization capabilities with menus as you do with toolbars. All of the commands described in Table 5-1 on page PP 5.16 apply to menus as well. Any command specific to buttons pertains to editing the button on the left side of a command on a menu.

An alternative to adding a command to a menu is to add a new menu name to the menu bar and add commands to its menu. You can add a new menu name to the menu bar by selecting New Menu in the Categories list of the Customize dialog box and dragging New Menu from the Commands list to the menu bar.

With the toolbar and macro added to the presentation, save the file and then close the presentation. Perform the following steps.

TO SAVE AND CLOSE THE PRESENTATION

1. Click the Save button on the Standard toolbar.
2. Click the presentation's Close button on the menu bar to close the presentation and leave PowerPoint open.

PowerPoint saves the Teaching Portfolio presentation on drive A and then closes the presentation.

More About

Macro Security

If you change the macro security setting for a PowerPoint file, that setting takes effect only for PowerPoint presentations. It does not apply to Microsoft Word and Excel files. You can specify different security levels for the three Office applications.

Opening a Presentation Containing a Macro and Executing the Macro

A **computer virus** is a potentially damaging computer program designed to affect a computer negatively by infecting it and altering the way it works without the user's knowledge or permission. Currently, more than 13,000 known computer viruses exist, and an estimated six new viruses are discovered each day. The increased use of networks, the Internet, and e-mail has accelerated the spread of computer viruses.

To combat this evil, most computer users run antivirus programs that search for viruses and destroy them before they ever have a chance to infect the computer. Macros are a known carrier of viruses because people can add code easily to them. For this reason, each time you open a presentation with a macro associated with it, PowerPoint may display a Microsoft PowerPoint dialog box warning that a macro is attached and that macros can contain viruses. Table 5-2 summarizes the buttons users can use to continue the process of opening a presentation with macros.

Table 5-2 Buttons in the Microsoft PowerPoint Dialog Box When Opening a Presentation with Macros

BUTTONS	*DESCRIPTION*
Disable Macros	Macros are unavailable to the user
Enable Macros	Macros are available to the user to execute
More Info	Opens the Microsoft PowerPoint Help window and displays information on viruses and macros

If you are confident of the source (author) of the presentation and macros, click the Enable Macros button. If you are uncertain about the reliability of the source, then click the Disable Macros button. For more information on this topic, click the More Info button.

The following steps open the Teaching Portfolio presentation to illustrate the Microsoft PowerPoint dialog box that displays when a presentation contains a macro. The steps then show how to execute the recorded macro, PrintHandout.

Steps To Open a Presentation with a Macro and Execute the Macro

1 With PowerPoint active, click File on the menu bar and then click Open. When the Open dialog box displays, click the Look in box arrow, and if necessary, click 3½ Floppy (A:). Double-click the file name Teaching Portfolio.

The Microsoft PowerPoint dialog box displays (Figure 5-32).

2 Click the Enable Macros button. When Slide 1 of the Teaching Portfolio displays, click File on the menu bar and then click Print BW Handout.

PowerPoint opens the Teaching Portfolio presentation, executes the macro, and then prints the handout and the four slides shown in Figures 5-5 and 5-21 on pages PP 5.07 and PP 5.17.

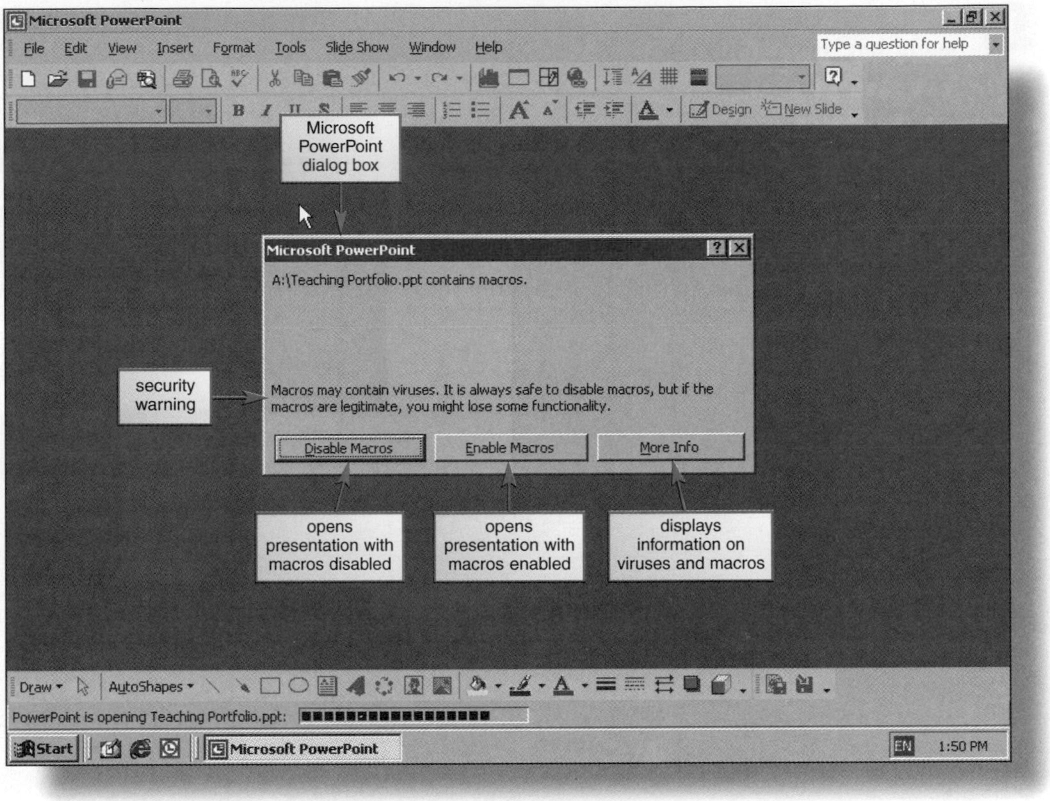

FIGURE 5-32

Other Ways

1. Click Run Macro button on Visual Basic toolbar
2. On Tools menu point to Macro, click Macros, double-click macro name
3. Press ALT+F8, double-click macro name
4. In Voice Command mode, say "Tools, Macro, Macros"

If you are running antivirus software, you may want to turn off the security warning shown in Figure 5-32. You can turn off the security warning by clicking Tools on the menu bar, pointing to Macro, and then clicking Security on the Macro submenu. When the Security dialog box displays, click the Low button. Then, the next time you open a presentation with an attached macro, PowerPoint will open the presentation immediately, rather than display the dialog box shown in Figure 5-32.

Viewing a Macro's VBA Code

As described earlier, a macro is composed of VBA code, which is created automatically by the macro recorder. You can view the VBA code through the Visual Basic Editor. The **Visual Basic Editor** is used by all Office applications to enter, modify, and view VBA code.

Steps To View a Macro's VBA Code

1 **Click Tools on the menu bar, point to Macro, and then point to Macros on the Macro submenu.**

The Tools menu and Macro submenu display (Figure 5-33).

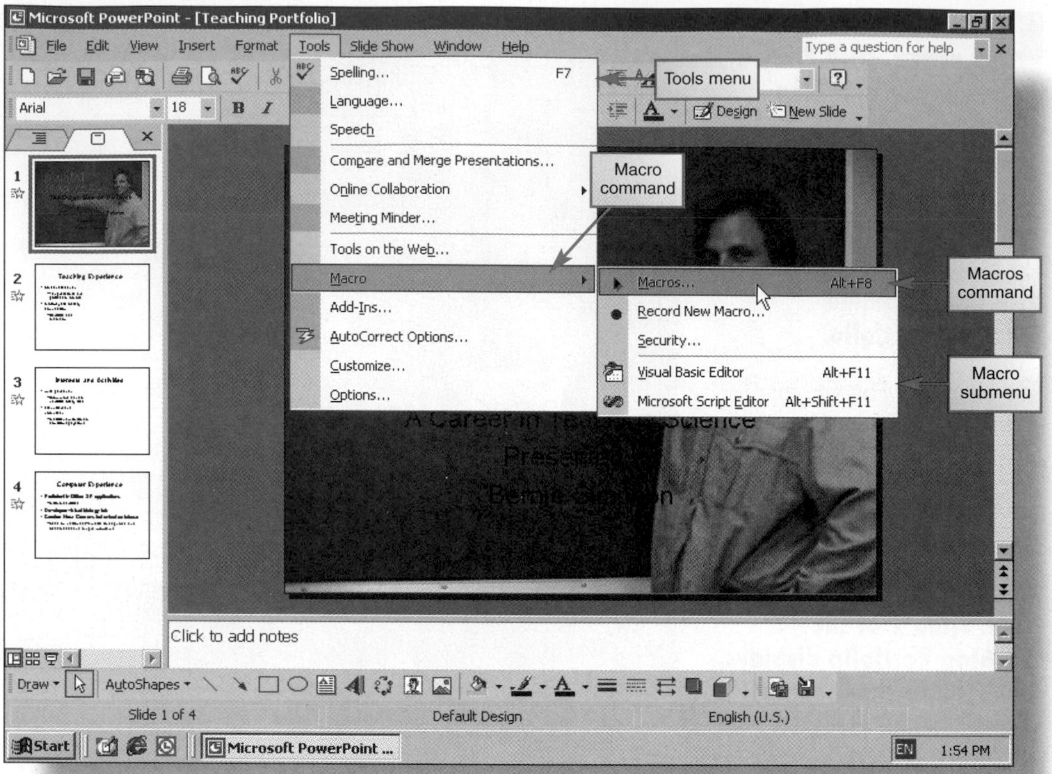

FIGURE 5-33

2 **Click Macros. When the Macro dialog box displays, if necessary click PrintHandout in the list, and then point to the Edit button.**

The Macro dialog box displays (Figure 5-34).

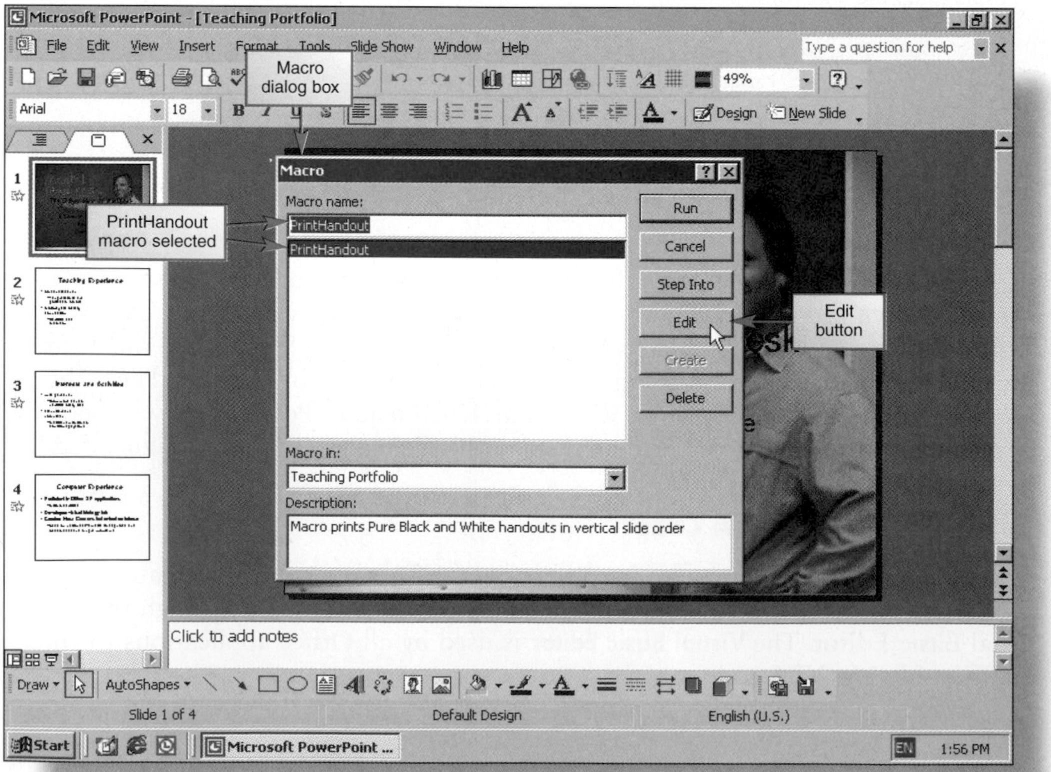

FIGURE 5-34

3 **Click the Edit button.**

The Visual Basic Editor starts and displays the VBA code in the PrintHandout macro (Figure 5-35).

4 **Scroll through the VBA code. When you are finished, click the Close button on the right side of the Microsoft Visual Basic – Teaching Portfolio title bar.**

The Visual Basic Editor closes, and Slide 1 in the Teaching Portfolio presentation displays.

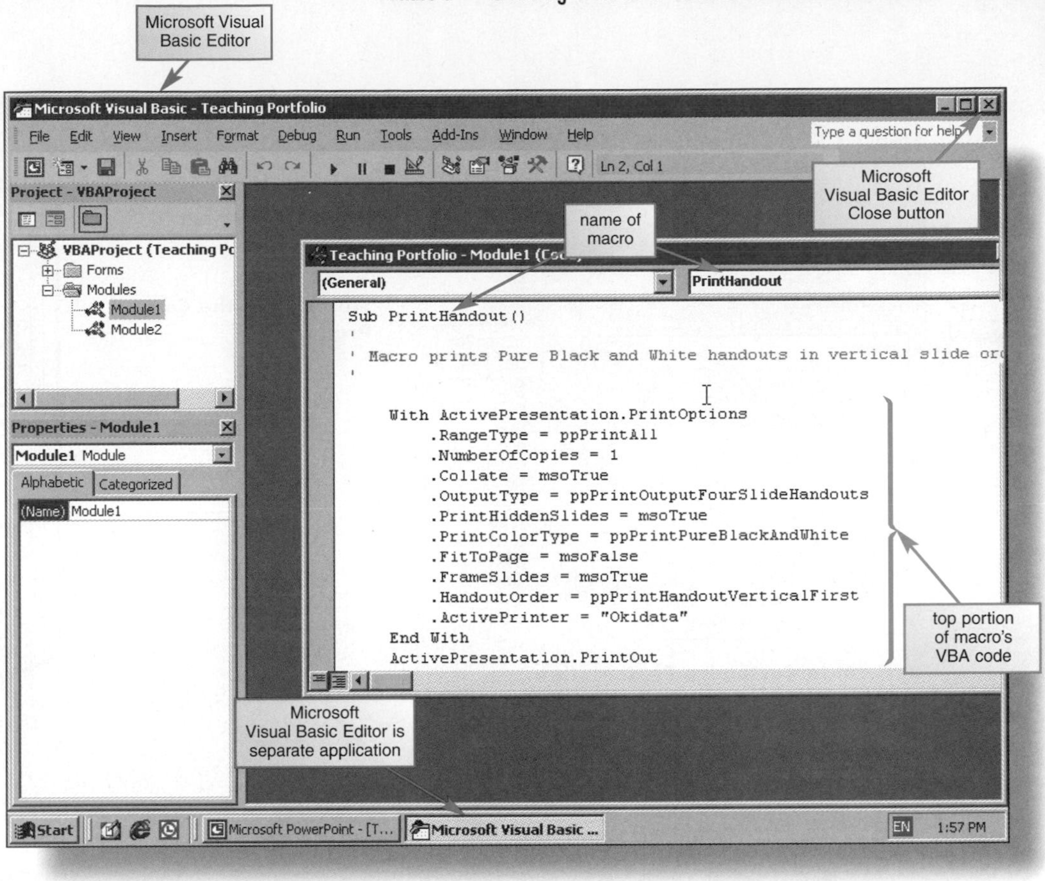

FIGURE 5-35

Other Ways

1. Click Visual Basic Editor button on Visual Basic toolbar
2. Press ALT+T, press M, press V

This set of instructions, beginning with line 1 in Figure 5-35 and continuing sequentially to the last line, executes when you invoke the macro. By scrolling through the VBA code, you can see that the macro recorder generates many instructions. In this case 32 lines of code are generated to print the handout vertically using the Pure Black and White option.

Phase 3 — Creating a Form to Customize the Presentation

With a toolbar and buttons added and the macro recorded to print handouts, you are ready to develop a form that allows users to design custom presentations for each interview. This form, called a **user interface**, allows users to input data and then display results. The user interface and the step-by-step procedure for its implementation are called an **application**. Thus, Microsoft created the name Visual Basic for Applications (VBA) for its programming language used to customize PowerPoint and other Office XP programs.

Programmers build applications using the three-step process shown in Figures 5-36a through 5-36c (on the next page): (1) create the user interface; (2) set the properties; and (3) write the VBA code.

More About

Narration

Add audio and video narration to your slides with add-ins that several companies, including Microsoft and RealNetworks, have developed. These powerful and inexpensive tools can make your presentations powerful and dynamic. Simply start these programs, run your slide show, and speak into a microphone or look into a camera. You then can broadcast the integrated presentation over the Web. For more information, visit the PowerPoint 2002 More About Web page (scsite.com/pp2002/more.htm) and then click Narration.

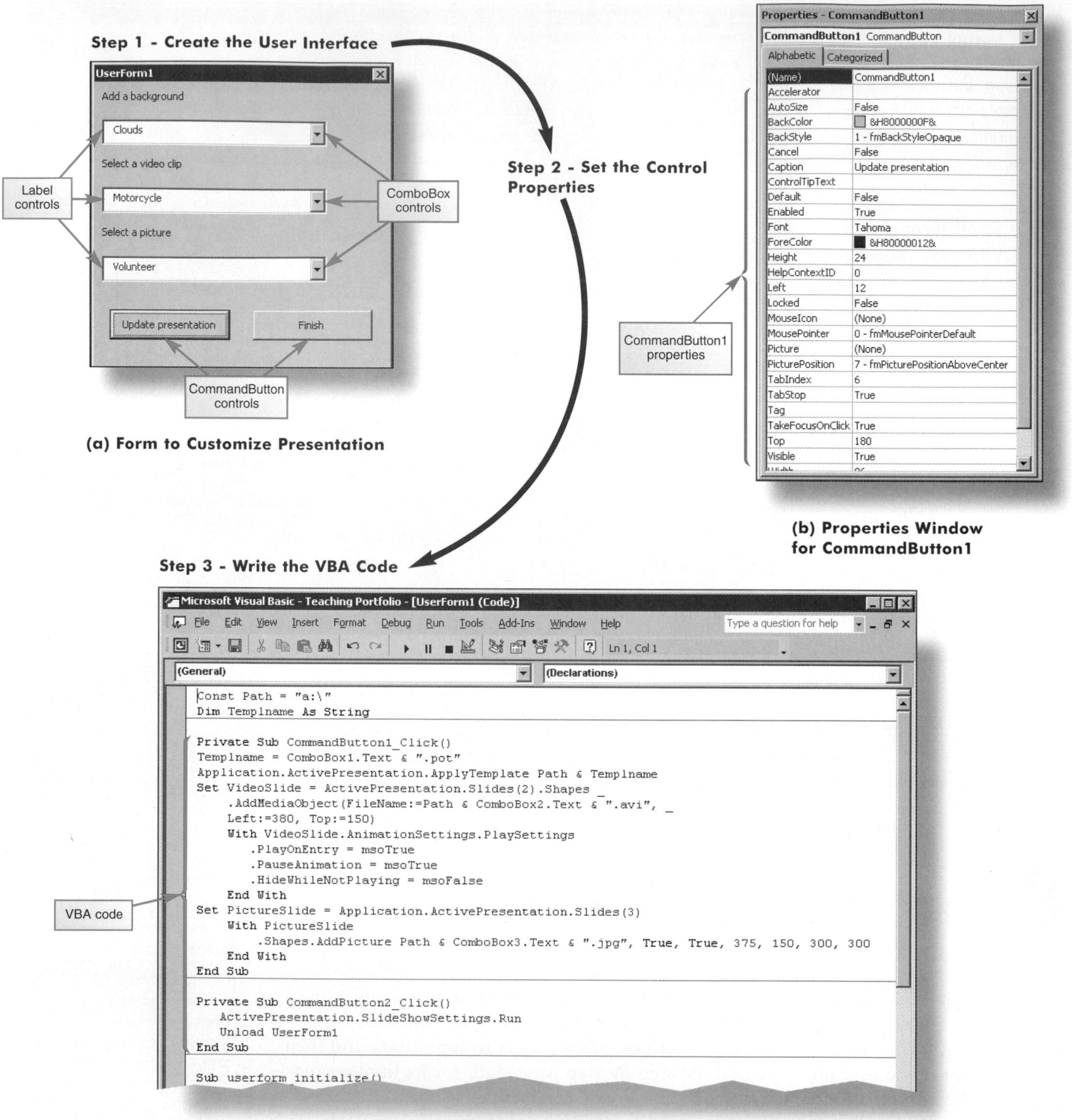

(a) Form to Customize Presentation

(b) Properties Window for CommandButton1

(c) VBA Code Associated with Command Buttons

FIGURE 5-36

Step 1 – Create the User Interface

The form shown Figure 5-36a displays the application's user interface. The **interface** allows the user to specify a template, video clip, and digital picture and place them in the presentation. The form contains three label controls, three combo box controls, and two command button controls. The **labels** identify the contents of the combo boxes. Each **combo box** allows a choice of two items. The **command buttons** update the presentation, close the interface form, and run the presentation.

The first element on the form is a label indicating the use of the combo box directly below the label. The label instructs the user to select one of two slide design templates listed in the combo box. This label-and-combo-box set is repeated twice. The second set allows the user to select one of two video clips, and the final set tells the user to choose one of two photos. The two command buttons at the bottom of the form execute the VBA procedure. The **Update presentation button** applies the design template and inserts the video clip and picture into the slides, and the **Finish button** hides the user form, unloads it from memory, and runs the presentation.

Creating the interface consists of sizing the form, adding each of the controls to the form, and adjusting their sizes and positions. When beginning to create a user interface, position the controls as close as possible to their final locations on the form; after setting the properties, you can finalize their positions. As you create the form, try to locate the controls as shown in Figure 5-36a.

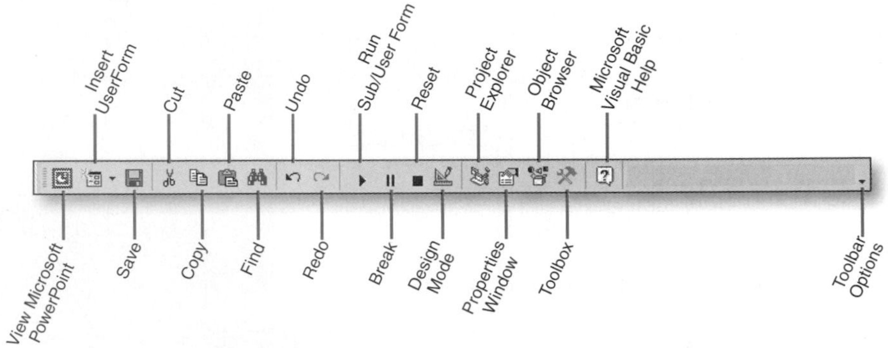

FIGURE 5-37 - VBA Standard Toolbar

The Standard toolbar (Figure 5-37) displays when you use VBA. Alternately, you can right-click a toolbar and then click Standard on the shortcut menu to display it.

Opening the Visual Basic IDE and a New Form

Before you begin creating the interface, you must start the **Visual Basic integrated development environment (IDE)**, which contains nine different windows and four toolbars. The windows can be **docked**, or anchored, to other windows that are dockable, and the four toolbars can be docked or can float in their own windows. Perform the following steps to open the Visual Basic IDE and open a new form.

More About

Docking

To customize the Visual Basic environment, you can move, dock, and resize a toolbar, a window, or the toolbox. To move an element, click the title bar and then drag the object to the desired location. This element will dock, or attach itself, to the edge of another window. To see more content in a docked element, drag one of its borders.

Steps To Open the Visual Basic IDE and a New Form

1 With the Teaching Portfolio presentation still open, click Tools on the menu bar, point to Macro, and then point to Visual Basic Editor.

The Tools menu and Macro submenu display (Figure 5-38).

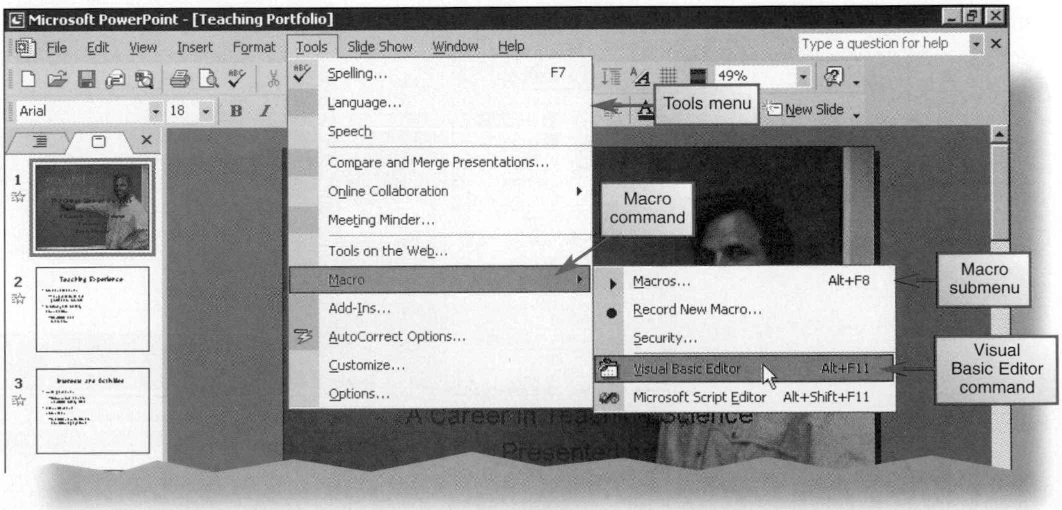

FIGURE 5-38

2 Click Visual Basic Editor. Click Insert on the menu bar and then point to UserForm.

The Visual Basic Editor opens and displays a Project window and a Properties window. The Insert menu displays (Figure 5-39).

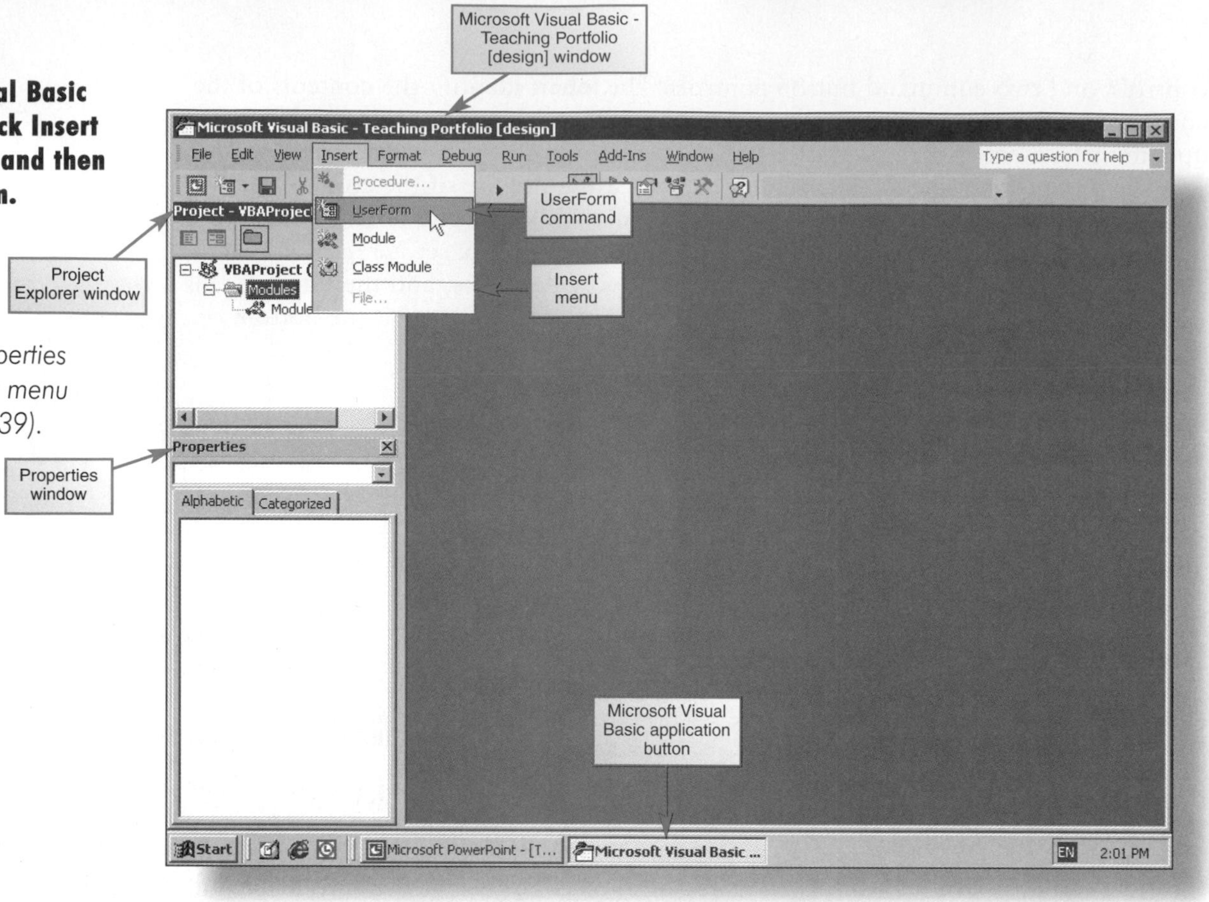

FIGURE 5-39

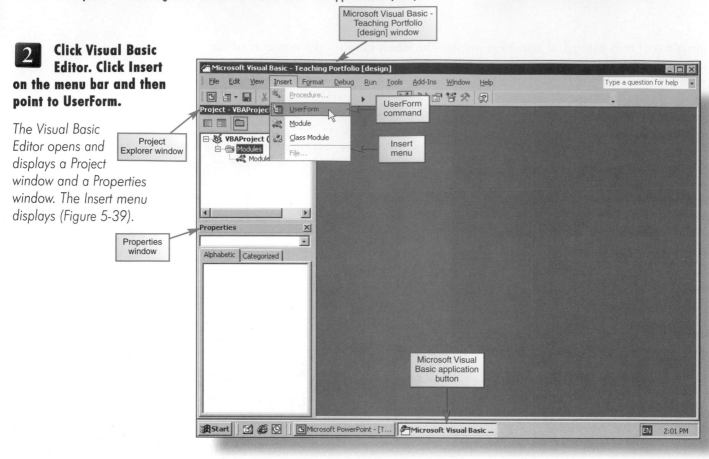

3 Click UserForm. If the Toolbox does not display, click the Toolbox button on the Standard toolbar.

A new form, UserForm1, opens and the Toolbox displays (Figure 5-40). Your form may display in a different location, and your Toolbox may have a different shape.

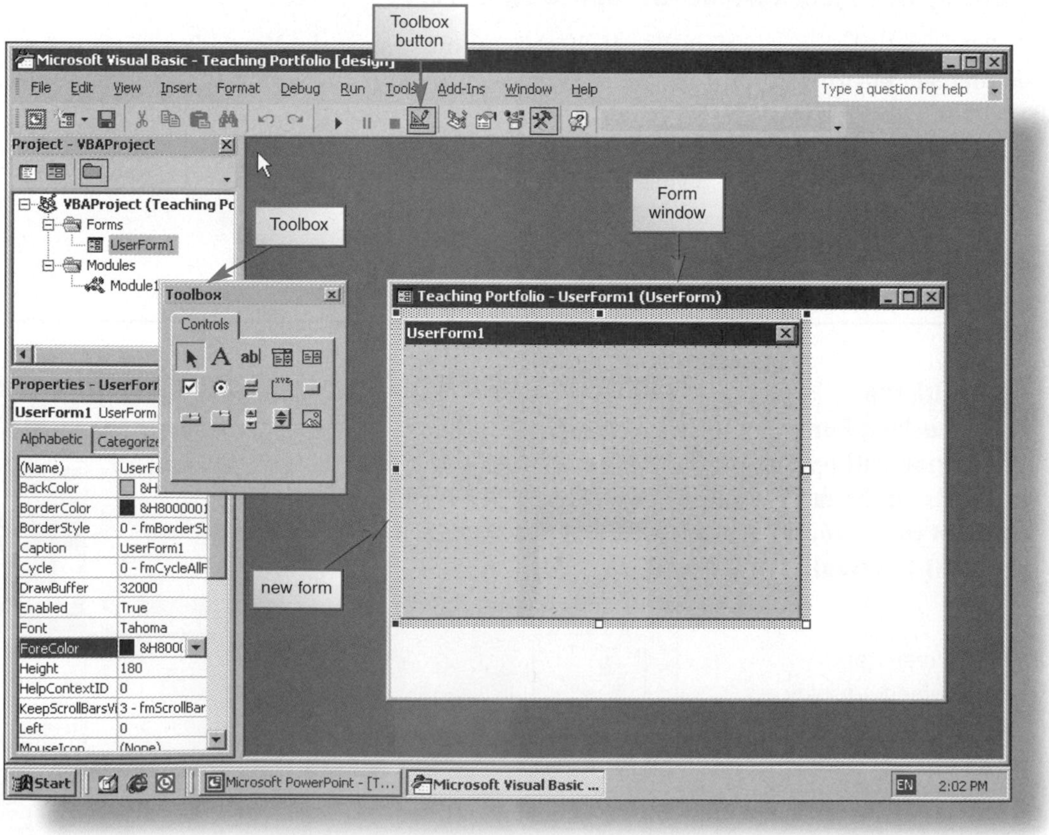

FIGURE 5-40

Changing the Form Size and the Toolbox Location

In design mode, you can resize a form by changing the values of its **Height property** and **Width property** in the Properties window, and you can change a form's location on the screen by changing the values of its **Top property** and **Left property.** You also can resize a form by dragging its borders and change its location by dragging and dropping. Perform the following steps to set the size of the form by dragging its borders and set the location by dragging and dropping.

More About

File Names

If you modify a macro, you need to resave it to preserve the changes. To see the file name that will be used, point to the Save button on the Standard toolbar. The ScreenTip will display the current file name.

Steps To Change the Form Size and the Toolbox Location

1 Point to the form window's bottom border. Without releasing the mouse button, drag the window border down.

Dragging the bottom border increases the height of the form window (Figure 5-41). The mouse pointer displays as a two-headed arrow.

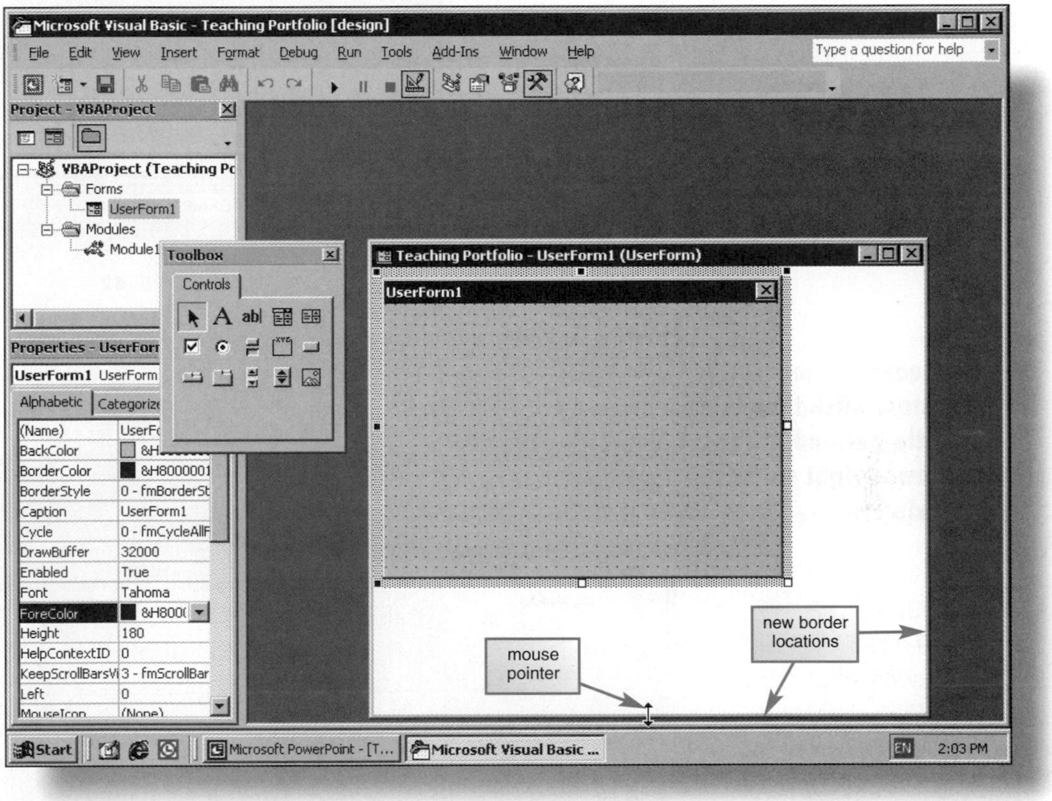

FIGURE 5-41

2 Release the mouse button. Point to the form's bottom-center sizing handle. Without releasing the mouse button, drag the form border down.

Dragging the border of the form increases the height of the form. The mouse pointer displays as a two-headed arrow (Figure 5-42).

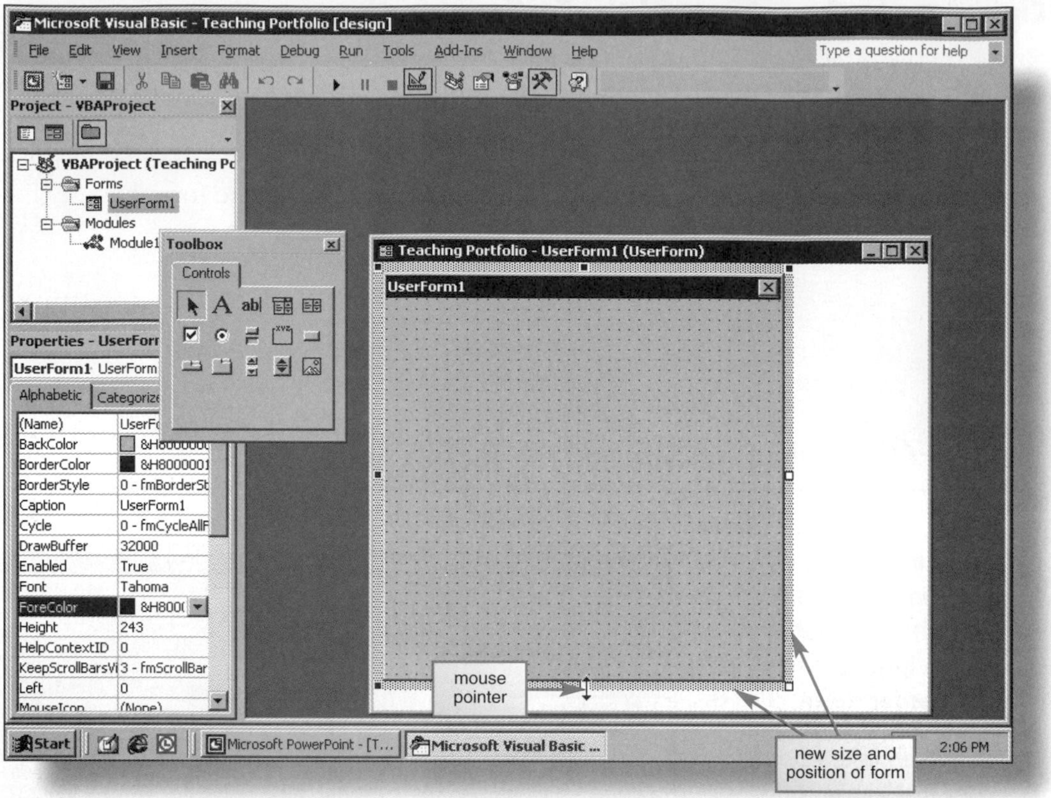

FIGURE 5-42

3 Release the mouse button. Click the Toolbox title bar and drag it to the lower-right side of the form window.

The form's size displays as shown in Figure 5-43. The Toolbox displays to the right of the form window.

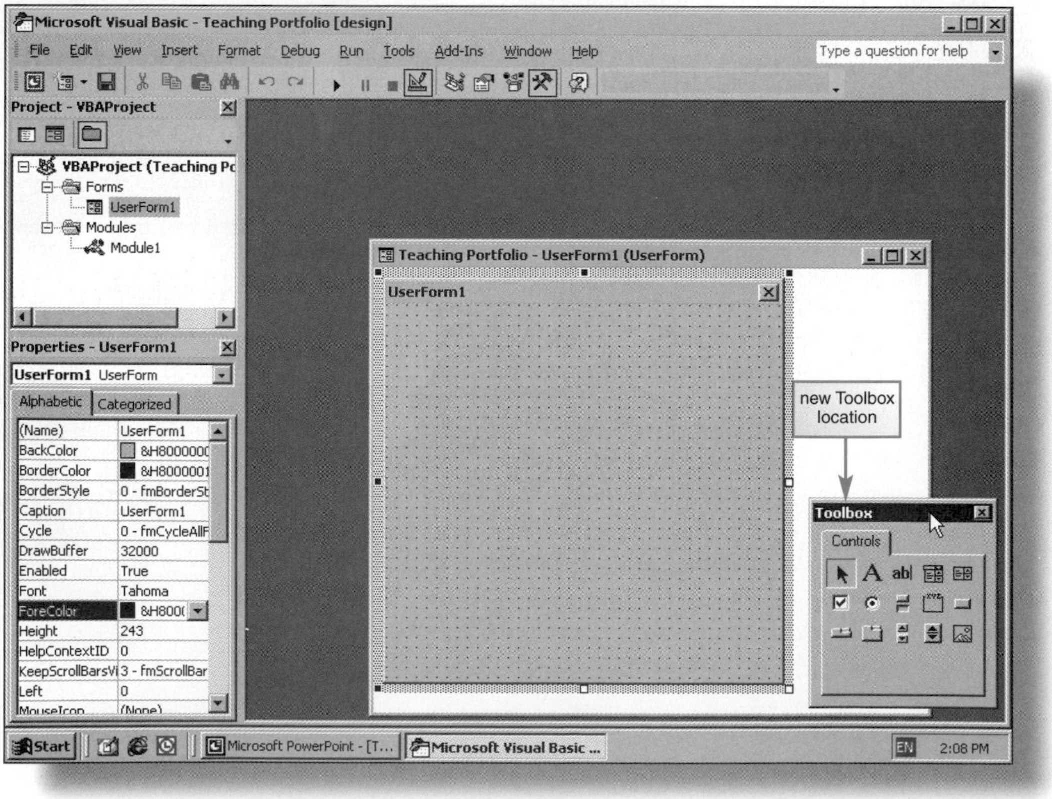

FIGURE 5-43

Adding Controls

Graphical images, or objects, in Windows applications include buttons, check boxes, tabs, and text boxes. Visual Basic calls these objects **controls**. The user form in this project contains three types of controls (see Figure 5-36a on page PP 5.28). Table 5-3 describes these controls and their functions.

You add controls to a form using tools in the **Toolbox**. To use a tool, you click its respective button in the Toolbox. Table 5-4 identifies the Toolbox buttons.

Table 5-3 VBA Controls Used in UserForm1

CONTROL	DESCRIPTION
Label	Displays text such as the words, Company Name, on a form. At run time, the user cannot change the text on a label.
ComboBox	Presents a list of choices. When an item is selected from the list by clicking it, the item displays in a highlighted color.
CommandButton	Represents a button that initiates an action when clicked.

Table 5-4 Summary of Buttons in the Toolbox

BUTTON	NAME	FUNCTION
	Select Objects pointer	Draws a rectangle over the controls you want to select
	Label	Adds a label control
	TextBox	Adds a text box control
	ComboBox	Adds a custom edit box, drop-down list box, or combo box on a menu bar, toolbar, menu, submenu, or shortcut menu
	ListBox	Adds a list box control
	CheckBox	Adds a check box control
	OptionButton	Adds an option button control
	ToggleButton	Adds a toggle button control
	Frame	Creates an option group or groups controls with closely related contents
	CommandButton	Adds a command button control
	TabStrip	Contains a collection of one or more tabs
	MultiPage	Contains a collection of one or more pages
	ScrollBar	Adds a scroll bar control
	SpinButton	Adds a spin button control
	Image	Adds an image control

ADDING LABEL AND COMBO BOX CONTROLS The next steps are to add the three label and combo box controls shown in Figure 5-36a on page PP 5.28. Perform the steps on the next page to add these controls to the form.

Steps To Add Label and Combo Box Controls to a Form

1 Click the Label button in the Toolbox. Position the mouse pointer in the upper-left corner of the form.

The Label button in the Toolbox is selected, and the mouse pointer changes to a cross hair and a copy of the Label button when it is over the form (Figure 5-44). The upper-left corner of the Label control will be positioned in this location.

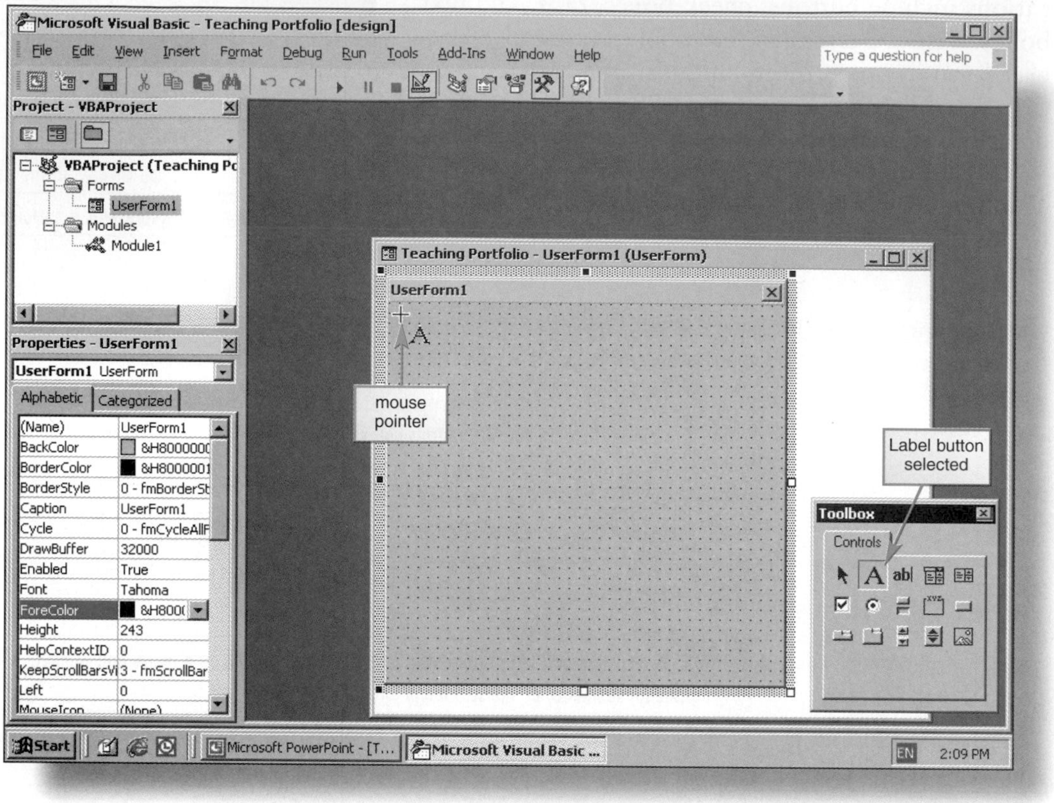

FIGURE 5-44

2 Click the mouse button. Point to the ComboBox button in the Toolbox.

The label displays on the form with the default caption, Label1 (Figure 5-45). The label is surrounded by a selection rectangle and sizing handles.

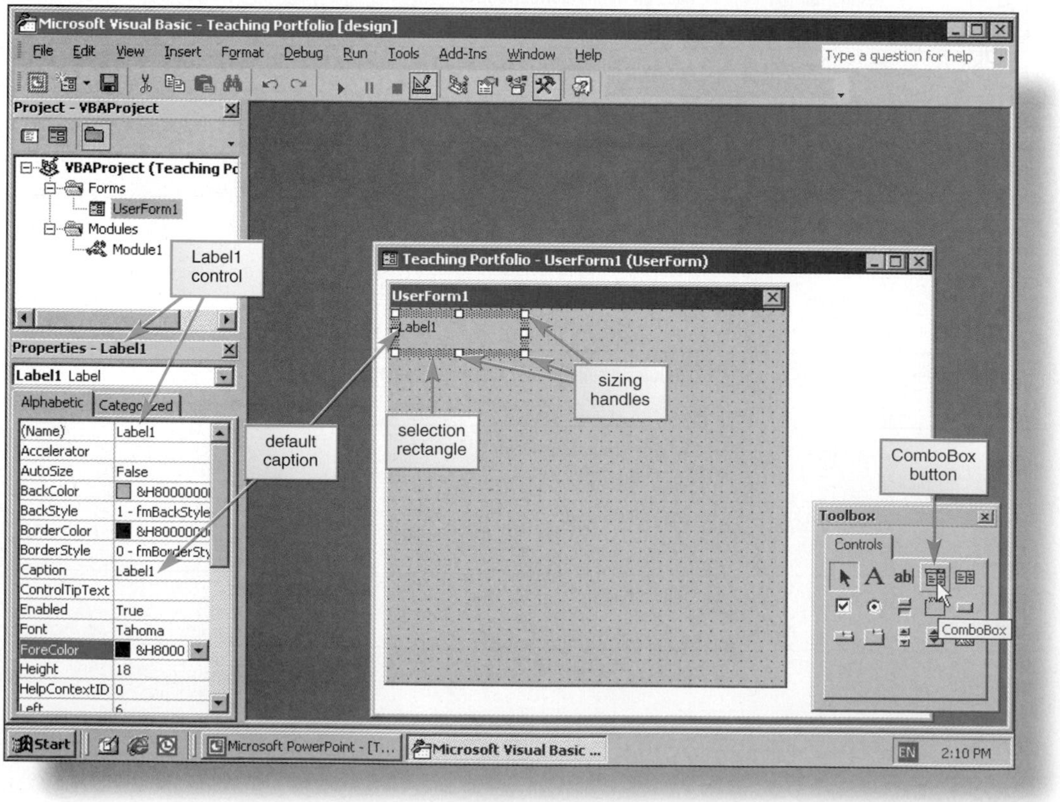

FIGURE 5-45

3 Click the ComboBox button in the Toolbox. Position the mouse pointer below the Label1 control.

The ComboBox button in the Toolbox is recessed, and the mouse pointer changes to a cross hair and a copy of the ComboBox button when it is over the form (Figure 5-46). The upper-left corner of the ComboBox control will be positioned in this location.

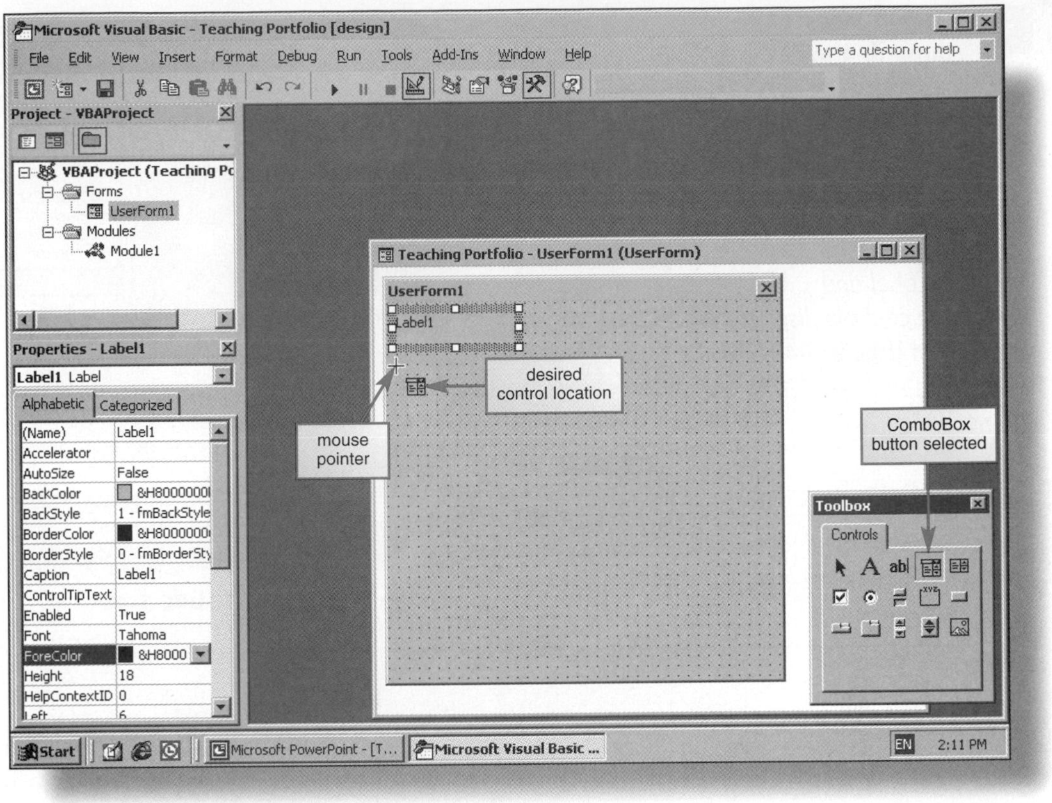

FIGURE 5-46

4 Click the mouse button.

The ComboBox control is added to the form (Figure 5-47).

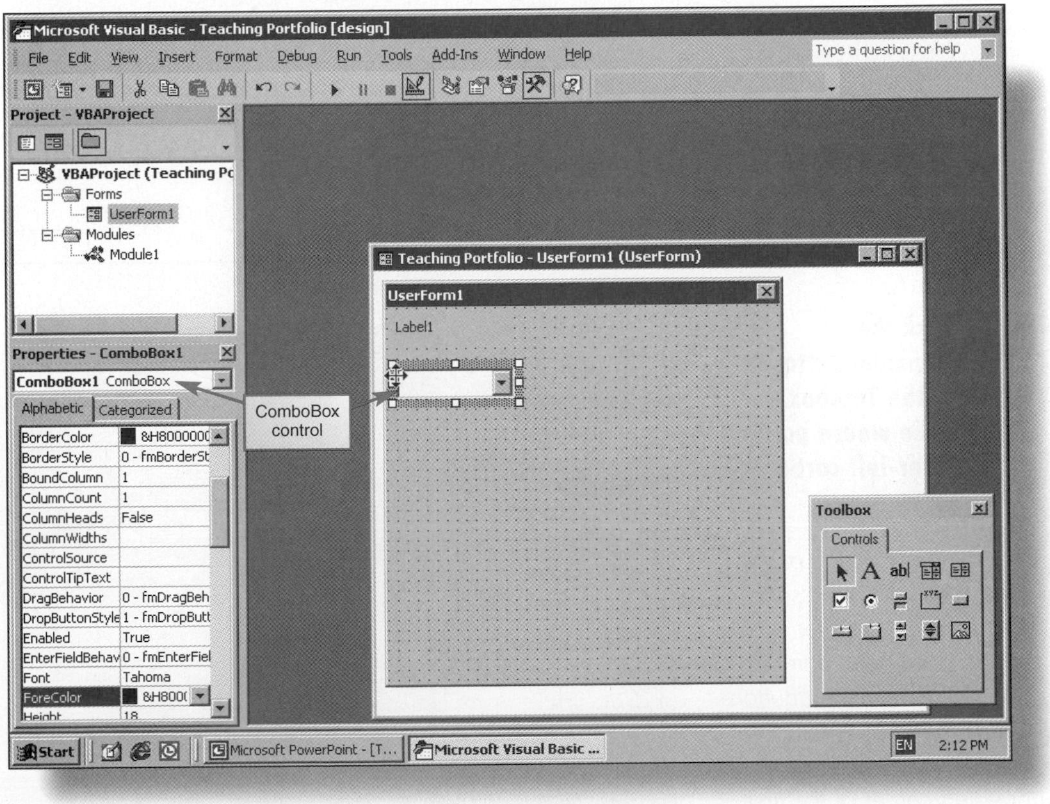

FIGURE 5-47

5 **Repeat Steps 1 through 4 to add the second and third Label controls and second and third ComboBox controls to the form as shown in Figure 5-48.**

The three Label and ComboBox controls display on the form (Figure 5-48).

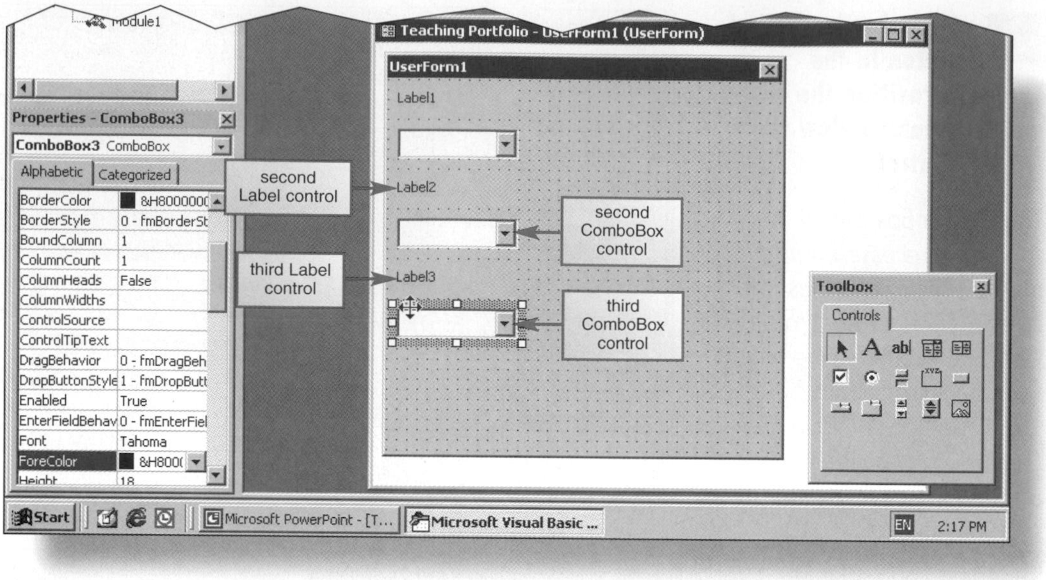

FIGURE 5-48

With the labels and combo boxes added to the form, the next step is to add the two CommandButton controls below the third ComboBox control.

ADDING COMMAND BUTTON CONTROLS When users finish making selections on the form, they can click the Update presentation button to assemble the presentation by applying the design template and inserting the video clip and picture into the slides. After clicking the Update presentation button, they can click the Finish button to hide the user form, unload it from memory, and run the presentation. Perform the following steps to add these two command button controls to the form.

Steps To Add Command Button Controls to a Form

1 **Click the CommandButton button in the Toolbox. Position the mouse pointer in the lower-left corner of the form.**

The CommandButton button in the Toolbox is recessed, and the mouse pointer changes to a cross hair and a copy of the CommandButton button when it is over the form (Figure 5-49). The upper-left corner of the first command button control will be positioned in this location.

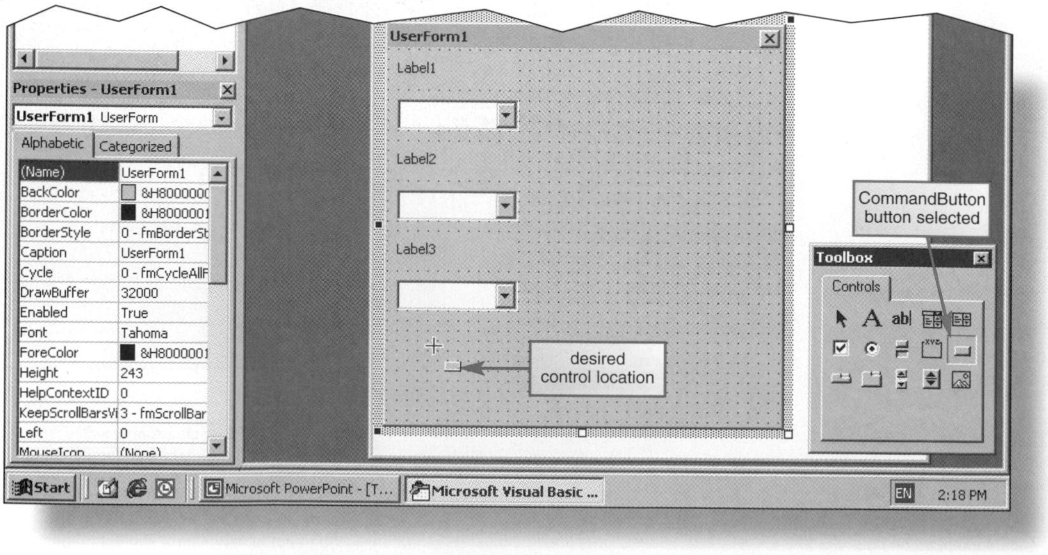

FIGURE 5-49

2 Click the mouse button.

The CommandButton1 control is added to the form (Figure 5-50).

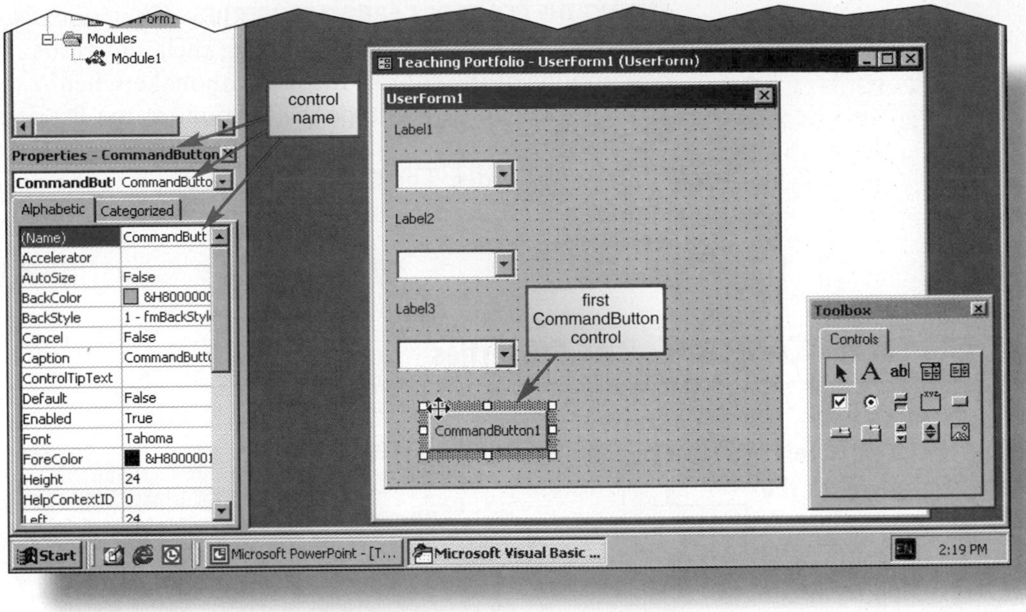

FIGURE 5-50

3 Repeat Steps 1 and 2 to add a second CommandButton control, CommandButton2, as shown in Figure 5-51.

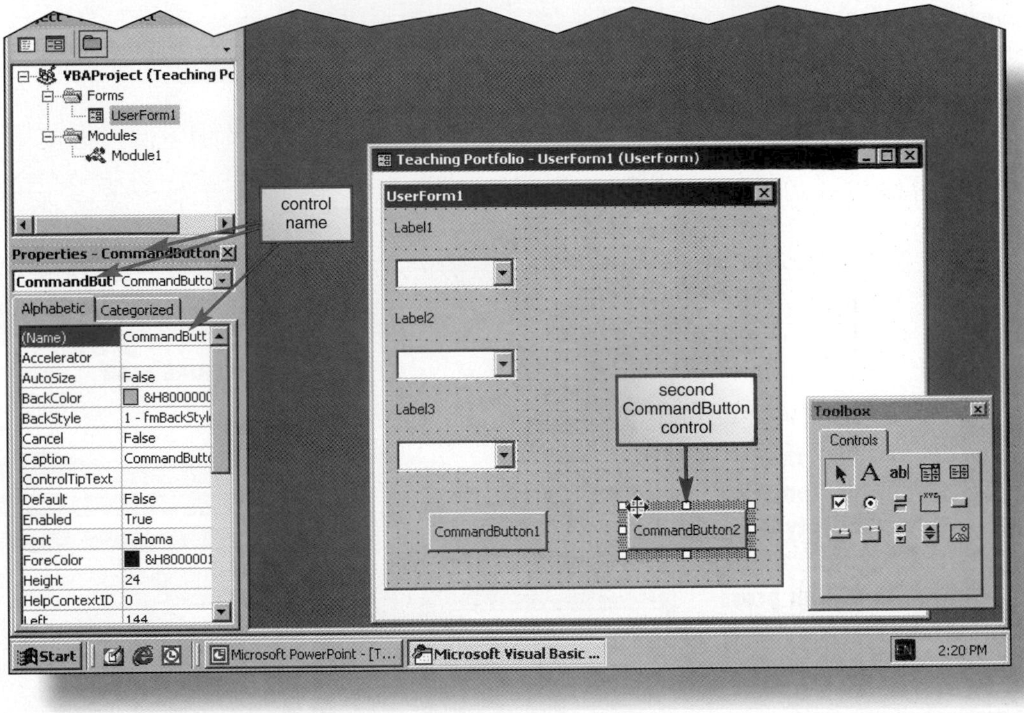

FIGURE 5-51

Step 2 – Set Control Properties

Controls have several different **properties** (Figure 5-52 on the next page), such as caption (the words on the face of the button), background color, foreground color, height, width, and font. Once you add a control to a form, you can change any property to improve its appearance and modify how it works.

SETTING THE CONTROL CAPTION PROPERTIES The controls on the form are not very informative because they do not state their functions. You must provide meaningful descriptions of the choices the user can make when using the form. These descriptions are called **captions**. You type the captions in the Properties window. This window has two tabs, Alphabetic and Categorized. The **Alphabetic list** displays the properties in alphabetical order. The **Categorized list** displays the properties in categories, such as appearance, behavior, font, and miscellaneous. The following steps change the controls' caption properties.

Steps To Set the Controls' Caption Properties

1 **Click the Label1 control. With the Label1 control selected, click Caption on the Alphabetic tab in the Properties window.**

The Properties window for the Label1 control displays (Figure 5-52). The default Caption property is Label1. Sizing handles indicate Label1 is selected.

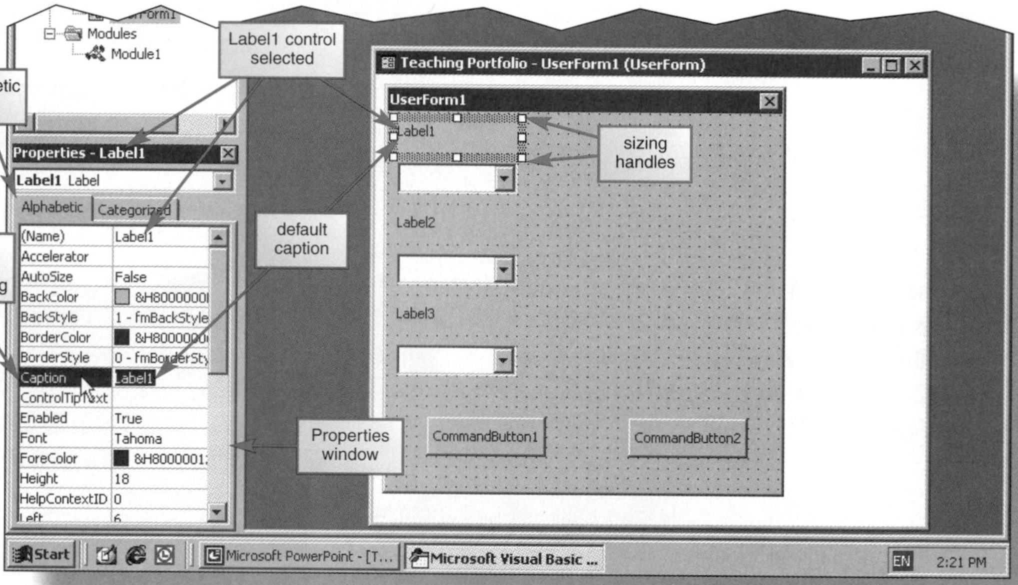

FIGURE 5-52

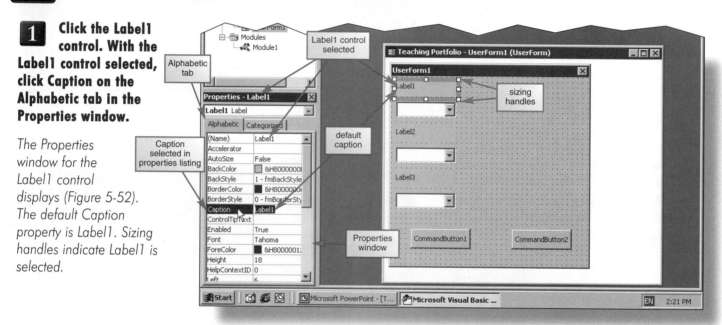

2 **Double-click the current caption, Label1, to select it, type** `Add a background` **as the caption, and then press the ENTER key.**

Add a background is the new caption for Label1 (Figure 5-53). The new caption displays on the form.

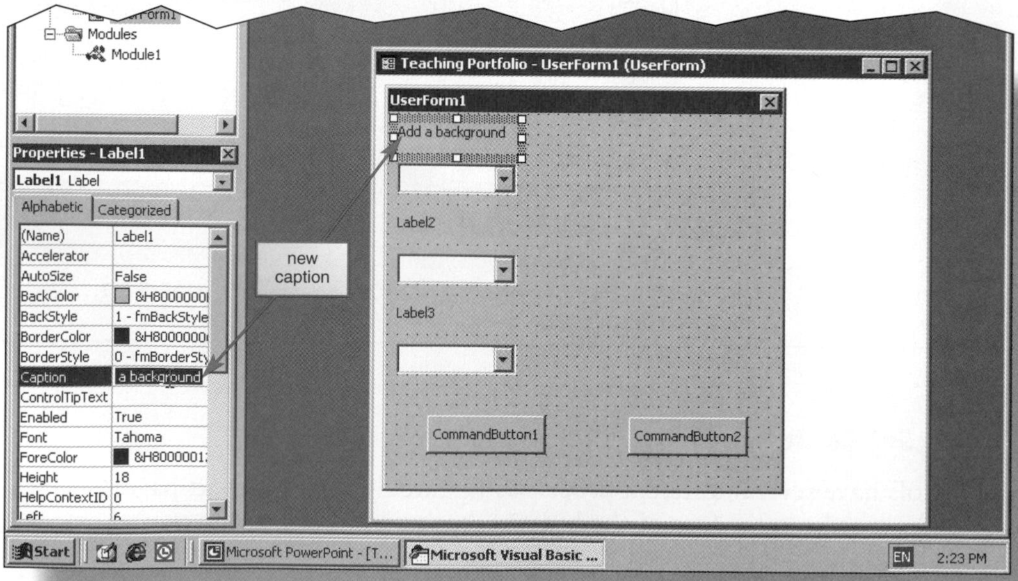

FIGURE 5-53

3 Change the captions for the remainder of the controls on the form using Table 5-5.

The captions for the form display (Figure 5-54).

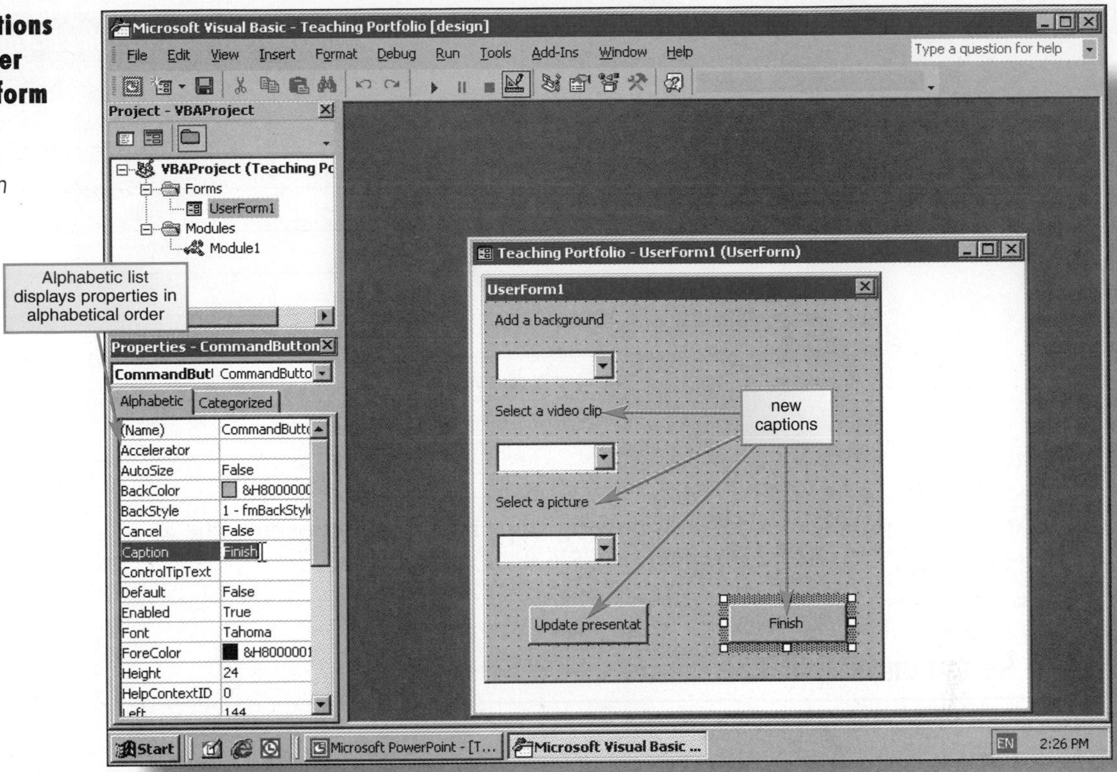

FIGURE 5-54

Table 5-5 Control Captions	
CONTROL CAPTION	NEW CAPTION
Label2	Select a video clip
Label3	Select a picture
CommandButton1	Update presentation
CommandButton2	Finish

FINE-TUNING THE USER INTERFACE After setting the properties for all the controls, you can fine-tune the size and location of the controls on the form. You can reposition a control in three ways:

1. Drag the control to its new location.
2. Select the control and use the arrow keys to reposition it.
3. Select the control and set the control's Top and Left properties in the Properties window.

To use the third technique, you need to know the distance the control is from the top of the form and the left edge of the form in points. One point is equal to 1/72 of an inch. Thus, if the Top property of a control is 216, then the control is 3 inches (216 / 72) from the top of the form.

Controls also may require resizing. You need to increase the size of the CommandButton1 control so the entire caption displays. You can resize a control in two ways:

1. Drag the sizing handles.
2. Select the control and set the control's Height and Width properties in the Properties window.

As with the Top and Left properties, the Height and Width properties are measured in points. Table 5-6 on the next page lists the exact points for the Top, Left, Height, and Width properties of each of the controls on the form.

More About

Electronic Portfolios

Electronic portfolios help emphasize a job seeker's accomplishments and strengths. The presentations are shown during interviews, mailed to potential employers along with a paper resume, and posted on personal home pages. Employers are impressed with the creativity and efforts these interviewees display in these presentations. For more information, visit the PowerPoint 2002 More About Web page (scsite.com/pp2002/more.htm) and then click Portfolios.

Table 5-6 Exact Locations of Controls on the Form

CONTROL	TOP	LEFT	HEIGHT	WIDTH
Label1	6	6	18	96
Label2	60	6	18	96
Label3	114	6	18	96
ComboBox1	30	6	20	180
ComboBox2	84	6	20	180
ComboBox3	138	6	20	180
CommandButton1	180	12	24	96
CommandButton2	180	126	24	96

The following steps resize and reposition the controls on the form using the values in Table 5-6.

Steps To Resize and Reposition Controls on a Form

1 Click the Label1 control, Add a background. Change its Top, Left, Height, and Width properties in the Properties window to those listed in Table 5-6.

The Label1 control Properties window displays (Figure 5-55).

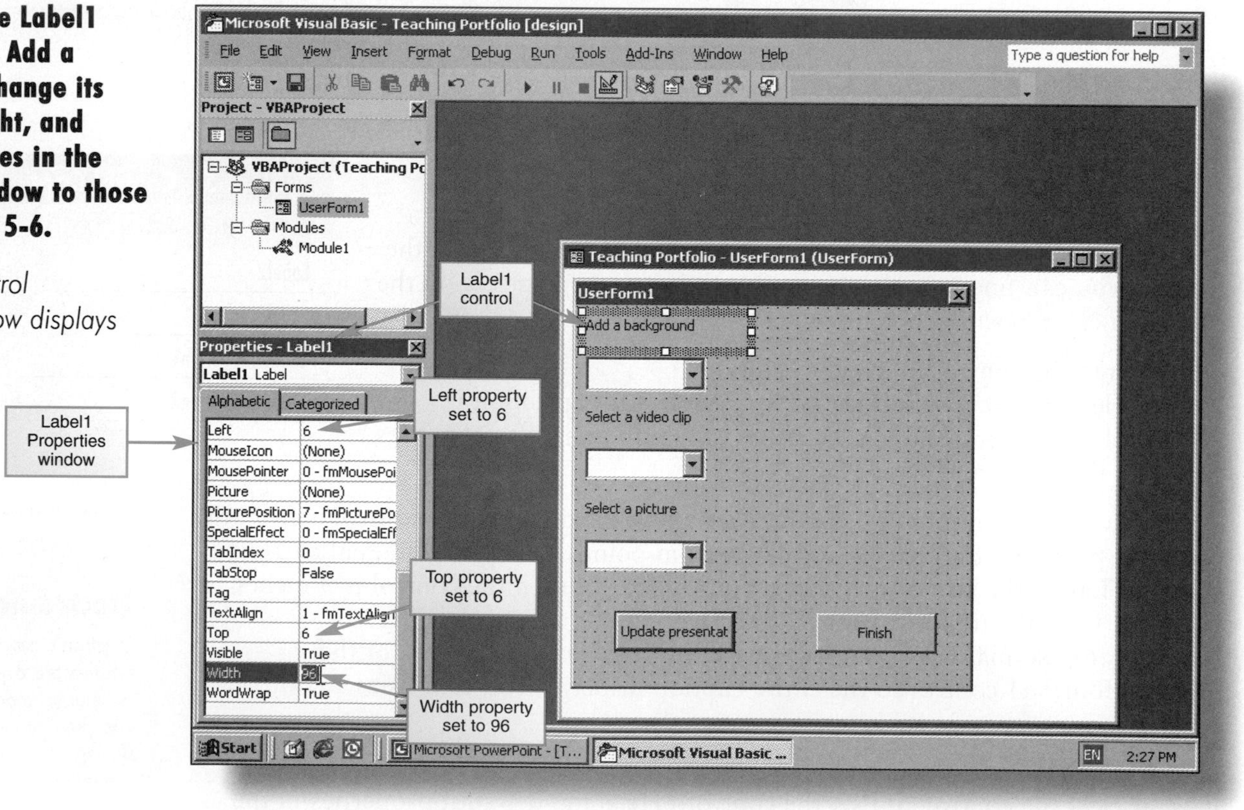

FIGURE 5-55

2 **One at a time, select the controls and change their Top, Left, Height and Width properties to those listed in Table 5-6.**

The form displays with the resized and repositioned controls (Figure 5-56).

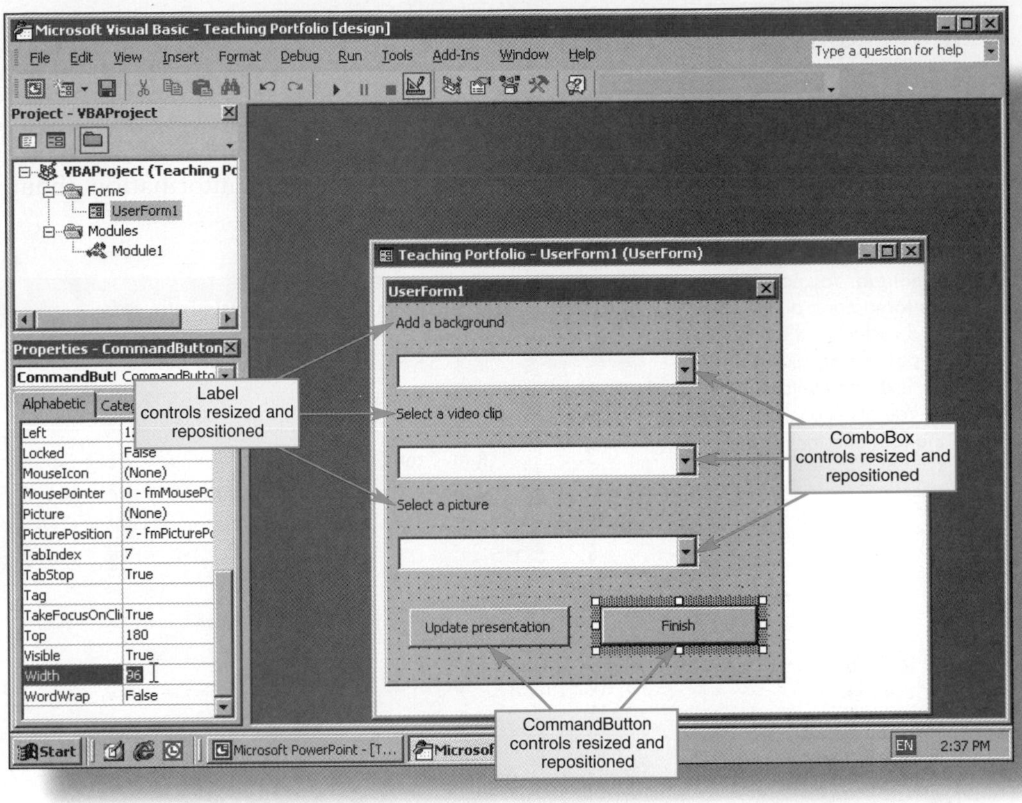

FIGURE 5-56

Step 3 – Write the VBA Code

You have created the interface and set the properties of the controls for this project. The next step is to write and then enter the procedure that will execute when you click the Create Presentation button on the Resume toolbar. You will create this button near the end of this project. Clicking this button is the event that triggers execution of the procedure that assembles the custom presentation. As mentioned earlier, Visual Basic for Applications (VBA) is a powerful programming language that can automate many activities described thus far in this book. The code for this project will include events and modules. The events in this program are the buttons on the form. To begin the process, you need to write a module that will serve as a macro that will display the form.

PLANNING A PROCEDURE When you trigger the event that executes a procedure, PowerPoint steps through the Visual Basic statements one at a time beginning at the top of the procedure. When you plan a procedure, therefore, remember that the order in which you place the statements in the procedure is important because the order determines the sequence of execution.

Once you know what you want the procedure to do, write the VBA code on paper in a similar format as that shown in Table 5-7 on the next page. Then, before entering the procedure into the computer, test it by putting yourself in the position of PowerPoint and stepping through the instructions one at a time. As you do so, think about how the instructions affect the slide show. Testing a procedure before entering it is called **desk checking**, and it is an important part of the development process.

More About

VBA Topics

The Microsoft Visual Basic for Applications Home Page gives information geared toward independent software vendors and corporate developers. The site includes VBA news and related topics that help programmers customize their applications. To view this page, visit the PowerPoint 2002 More About Web page (scsite.com/pp2002/more.htm) and then click VBA Topics.

More About

Customizing the VBA Appearance

To customize the appearance of VBA code, click Tools on the VBA menu bar, click Options, and then click the Editor Format tab. You can specify the foreground and background colors used for different types of text, such as Comments Text and Syntax Error Text. You also can change the font and font size.

Adding comments before a procedure will help you remember its purpose at a later date. In Table 5-7, the first seven lines are comments. **Comments** begin with the word Rem or an apostrophe ('). These comments contain overall documentation about the procedure and may be placed anywhere in the procedure. Most developers place comments before the Sub statement. Comments have no effect on the execution of a procedure; they simply provide information about the procedure, such as name, creation date, and function.

Table 5-7 Create Presentation Procedure

LINE	*VBA CODE*
1	`' Create Presentation Procedure          Author: Lakesha Helms`
2	`' Date Created: 12/1/2003`
3	`' Run from: Click Update presentation button`
4	`' Function: When executed, this procedure accepts data that causes`
5	`'           PowerPoint to build a custom presentation that adds`
6	`'           a template, video clip, and digital picture.`
7	`'`
8	`Sub createpresentationteaching()`
9	`  UserForm1.userform_initialize`
10	`  UserForm1.Show`
11	`End Sub`

A procedure begins with a **Sub statement** and ends with an **End Sub statement** (lines 8 and 11 in Table 5-7). The Sub statement begins with the name of the procedure. The parentheses following the procedure name allow the passing of data values, or arguments, from one procedure to another. Passing arguments is beyond the scope of this project, but the parentheses still are required. The End Sub statement signifies the end of the procedure and returns PowerPoint to normal view.

The first executable statement in Table 5-7 is line 9, which calls the userform_initialize procedure on the form, indicated by the object name, UserForm1. You use the UserForm1 object name, so VBA can find the userform_initalize procedure. Line 10, issues the command to display the form in the PowerPoint normal view window. Again, you must use the form name so VBA knows which form to display. Line 11 is the end of the procedure. Every procedure must conclude with an End Sub statement.

More About

VBA Help

Microsoft offers a variety of VBA help on its Web site. Topics include understanding VBA syntax, setting References, using Object Variables, and writing efficient code. To view this site, visit the PowerPoint 2002 More About Web page (scsite.com/pp2002/more.htm) and then click VBA Help.

To enter a procedure, use the Visual Basic Editor. To activate the Visual Basic Editor, you can click the **View Code button** in the VBA Project window or click the **Module command** on the Insert menu.

The Visual Basic Editor is a full-screen editor, which allows you to enter a procedure by typing the lines of VBA code as if you were using word processing software. At the end of a line, press the ENTER key to move to the next line. If you make a mistake in a statement, you can use the arrow keys and the DELETE or BACKSPACE key to correct it. You also can move the insertion point to previous lines to make corrections.

USING THE VISUAL BASIC EDITOR TO ENTER A PROCEDURE The following steps activate the Visual Basic Editor and create the procedure for the Create Presentation module.

Steps To Enter the Create Presentation Procedure

1 Click the Insert UserForm button arrow on the Standard toolbar and then point to Module.

The Insert UserForm list displays (Figure 5-57).

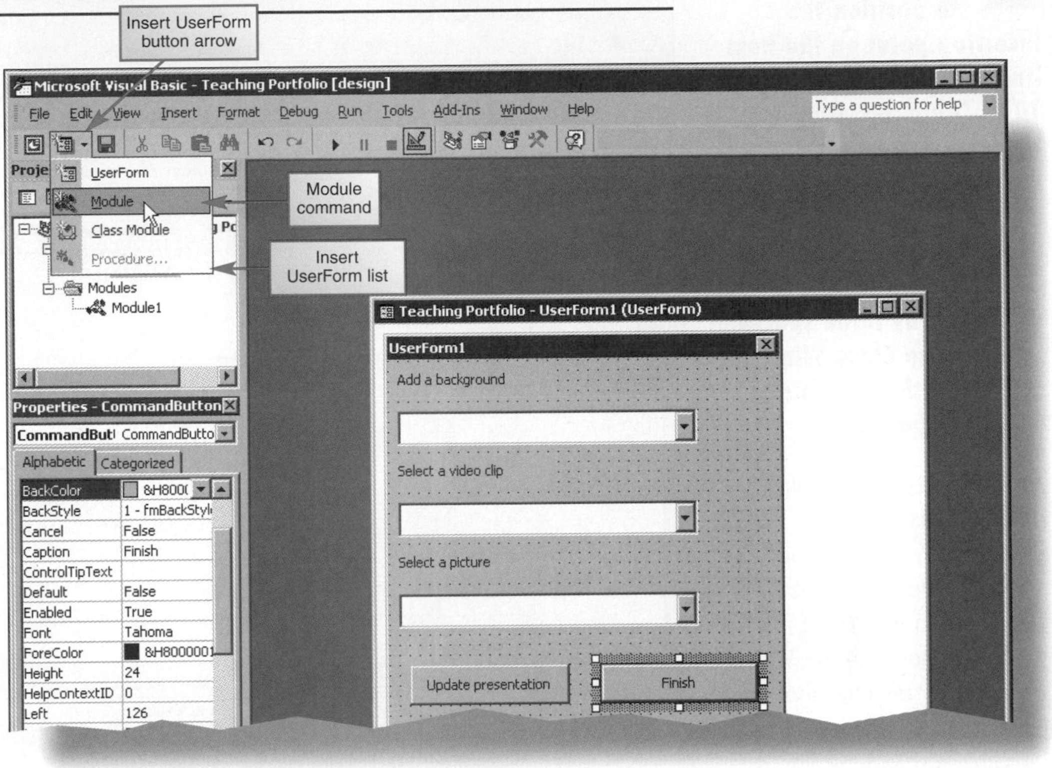

FIGURE 5-57

2 Click Module in the Insert UserForm list. When the Visual Basic Editor opens, click the maximize button in the Teaching Portfolio – Module2 (Code) window. Type the seven comment statements (lines 1 through 7) in Table 5-7. Be certain to enter an apostrophe at the beginning of each comment line.

PowerPoint starts the Visual Basic Editor, adds Module2, and displays the Microsoft Visual Basic window (Figure 5-58). The comment lines display in green. Module1 contains the code for the Print BW Handout macro you recorded in Phase 2 of this project.

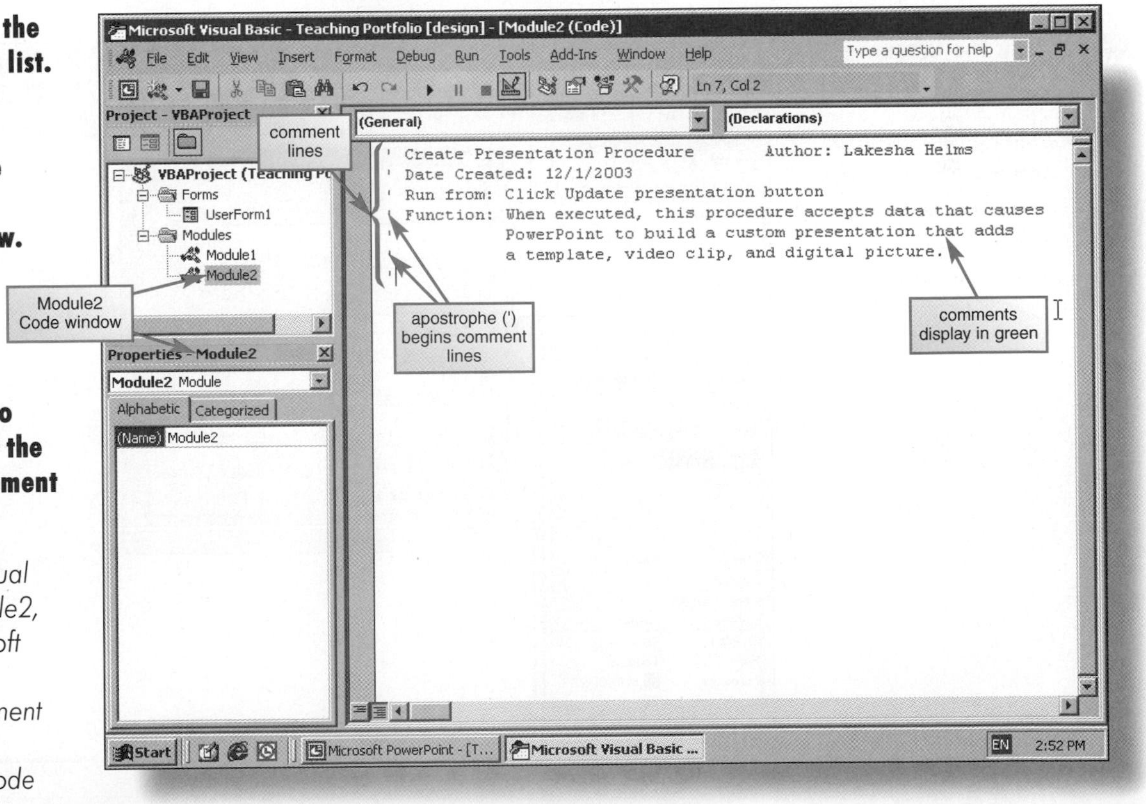

FIGURE 5-58

3 Press the ENTER key to position the insertion point on the next line. Enter lines 8 through 10 in Table 5-7. Do not enter the End Sub statement (line 11). For clarity, indent all lines between the Sub statement and End Sub statement by three spaces. Point to the Close Window button on the right side of the menu bar.

The Create Presentation procedure is complete (Figure 5-59). You do not need to enter the End Sub statement in line 11 of Table 5-7 because the Visual Basic Editor displays that line automatically when you type the Sub statement in line 8.

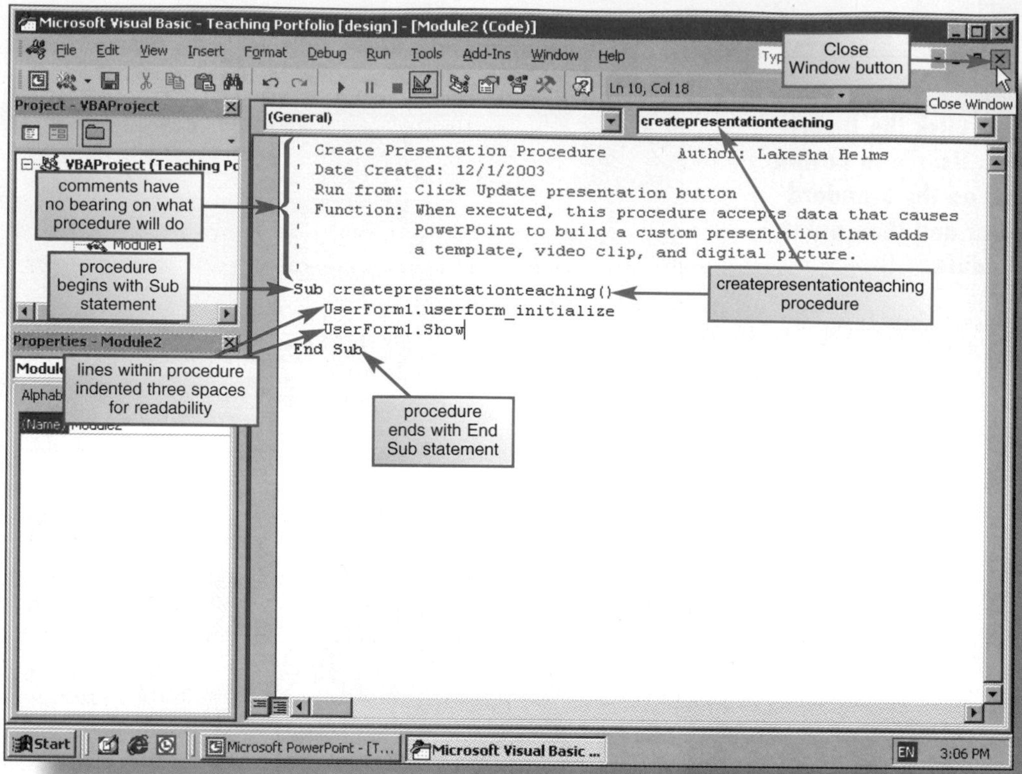

FIGURE 5-59

4 Click the Close Window button.

The Module2 Code window closes, and the form displays in the UserForm1 window (Figure 5-60). The UserForm1 window is maximized.

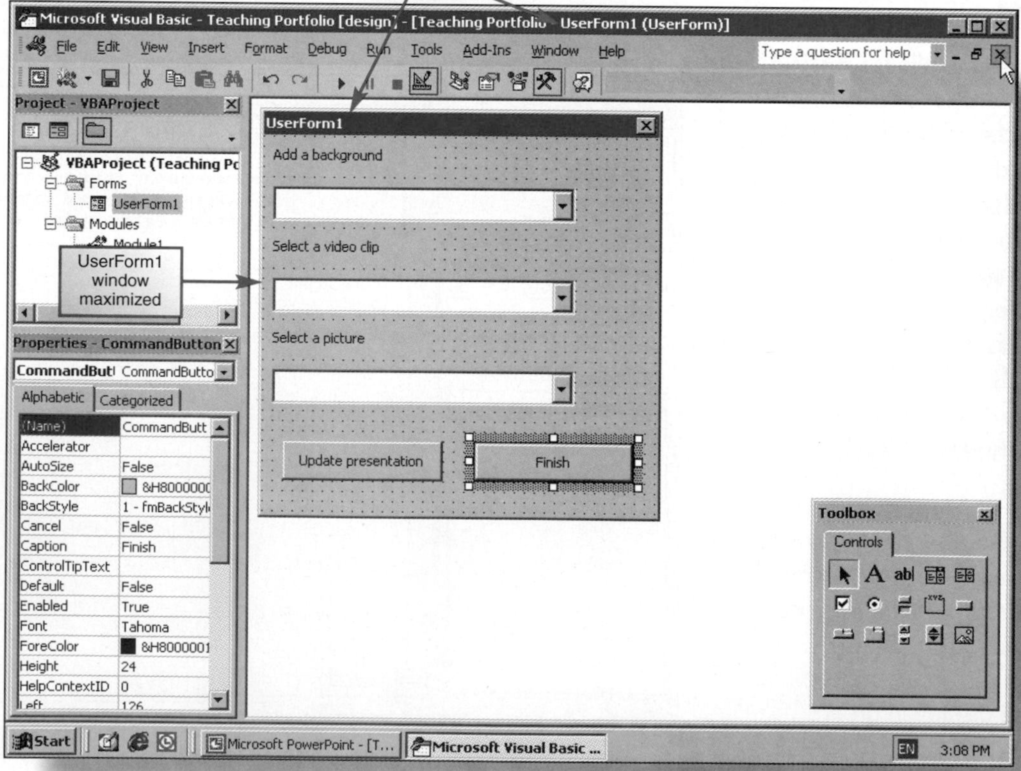

FIGURE 5-60

Other Ways

1. On Insert menu click Module
2. Press ALT+I, press M

More About Visual Basic for Applications

Visual Basic for Applications uses many more statements than those presented here. Even this simple procedure, however, should help you understand the basic makeup of a Visual Basic statement. Lines 9 and 10 in the procedure shown in Figure 5-59 include a period. The entry on the left side of the period tells PowerPoint which object you want to affect.

An **object** is a real-world thing. Your textbook, your car, your pets, and even your friends are objects. Visual Basic uses objects in its association with applications. This technique is described as **object-oriented** (**OO**). When it refers to programming it is called **Object-Oriented Programming** (**OOP**). The development of OOP provides a way to represent the world in conceptual terms that people understand. People relate to their everyday objects and easily can understand that these objects can have properties and behaviors.

An object is described by its properties. **Properties** are attributes that help differentiate one object from another. For example, your car has a color, a certain body style, and a certain type of interior. These properties are used to describe the car. The Visual Basic programming language has specific rules, or **syntax**. In Visual Basic syntax, you separate an object and its property with a period. For example, car.color, specifies a car object and the property color. You would write the statement, car.color = “red”, to set the value of the color property to red.

An object also has certain behaviors, or methods. A **method** is a function or action you want the object to perform or an action that will be performed on an object. You can write your own functions, or you can use the built-in methods supplied with Visual Basic. Methods associated with car, pet, and friend objects might be drive, feed, and talk, respectively. The drive method would be written, car.drive, just as in the statement, UserForm1.Show, where UserForm1 is the object and Show is the method.

The following example shows that you can change an object’s property value during execution of a procedure. Similar statements often are used to clear the properties of controls or to set them to initial values. This process is called **initialization**. The object in this case is a text box control.

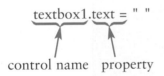

textbox1.text = " "

control name — textbox1; property — text

More About

VBA Web Sites

The Internet contains a variety of Visual Basic information. Many Web sites offer information on coding, magazines, games, and tips. To view these sites, visit the PowerPoint 2002 More About Web page (scsite.com/pp2002/more.htm) and then click VBA Web Sites.

More About

Variables

When variables are initialized, a numeric variable is initialized to zero, a variable-length string is initialized to a zero-length string (" "), which also is called a null string, and a fixed-length string is filled with zeros.

WRITING THE FORM’S INITIALIZATION PROCEDURE The next step is to write the procedure to initialize some of the control properties. Recall in Step 2 – Set Control Properties of this project that you added the controls to the form and then set some of the properties. With respect to VBA, PowerPoint has two modes: design mode and run mode. In **design mode**, you can resize controls, assign properties to controls, and enter VBA code. In **run mode**, all controls are active. That is, if you click a control, it triggers the event, and PowerPoint executes the procedure associated with the control.

Properties such as the label and command button caption properties were set in Step 2 of this project at design time. Data items can be added to a combo box at run-time using the AddItem method. The **AddItem method** is used to add items to a combo box. Table 5-8 shows the general form of the AddItem method.

Table 5-8 AddItem Method Format

General Form:	`ComboBox1.AddItem "item name"`
Comment:	The AddItem method places the item name string into the text list of the combo box.

Example:	`ComboBox1.AddItem "Clouds"`
	`ComboBox1.AddItem "Golf"`
	`ComboBox3.AddItem "Volunteer"`

Table 5-9 General Form of the Clear Method

General Form:	`ComboBox1.Clear`
Comment:	All the items in the combo box are deleted.
Example:	`ComboBox2.Clear`

Table 5-10 Initialize Form Procedure

LINE	*VBA CODE*
1	`Sub userform_initialize()`
2	`' Initialize the drop down list choices`
3	`ComboBox1.Clear`
4	`ComboBox2.Clear`
5	`ComboBox3.Clear`
6	`ComboBox1.AddItem "Clouds"`
7	`ComboBox1.AddItem "Orbit"`
8	`ComboBox2.AddItem "Motorcycle"`
9	`ComboBox2.AddItem "Golf"`
10	`ComboBox3.AddItem "Garden"`
11	`ComboBox3.AddItem "Volunteer"`
12	`End Sub`

A good practice is to issue the **Clear method** before adding items to the combo box. Table 5-9 shows the general form of the Clear method to clear all the items in a combo box.

The initialize procedure code in Table 5-10 sets some controls' property values during run mode. The **Initialize Form procedure** ensures the combo boxes are clear and adds the text items to the combo boxes. To add items to a combo box, use the AddItem method. Before adding items to a combo box, the Initialize Form procedure clears the entries in the combo boxes.

The statements in lines 3, 4, and 5 use the Clear method to make sure the combo boxes are empty. Lines 6 through 11 use the AddItem method to add the items to the combo boxes. To complete the section of code for the InitializeForm() procedure, an End Sub statement closes the procedure at line 12.

Steps To Enter the InitializeForm() Procedure

1 Point to the View Code button at the top of the Project Explorer window.

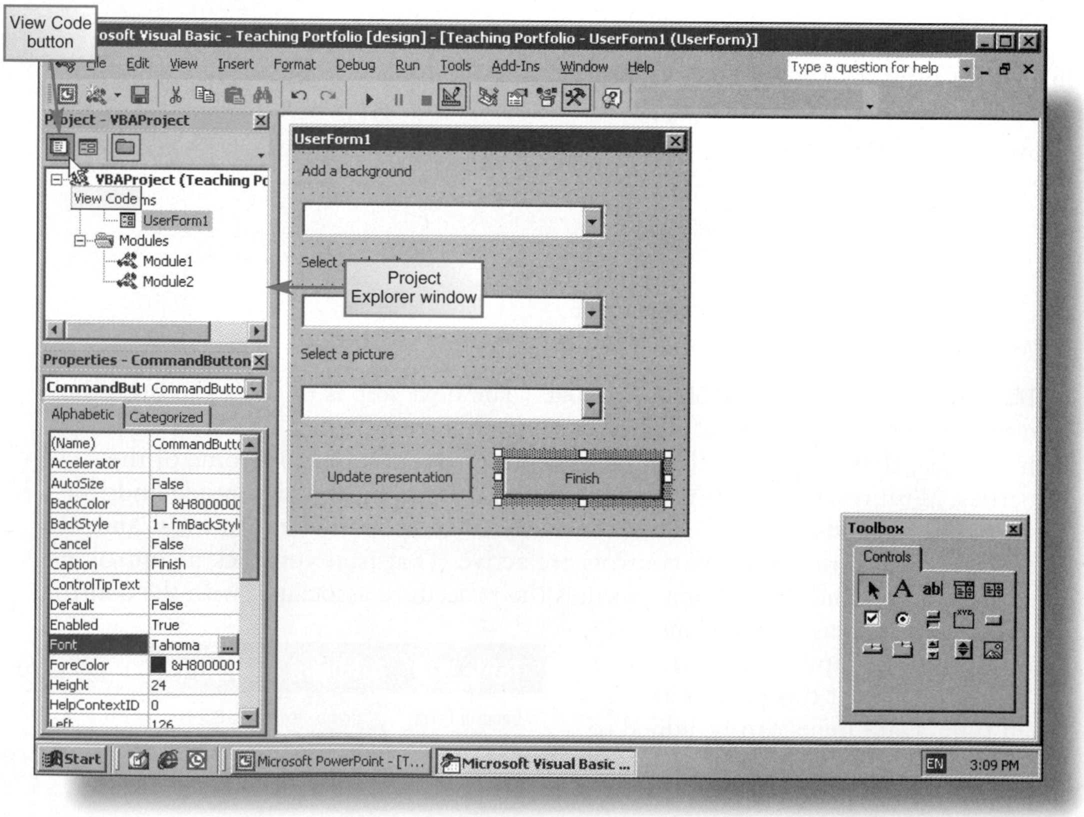

FIGURE 5-61

2 Click the View Code button. Enter the VBA code shown in Table 5-10.

The initialize procedure displays in the Code window (Figure 5-62). The word, UserForm, displays in the Object box, and the word, initialize, displays in the Procedure box.

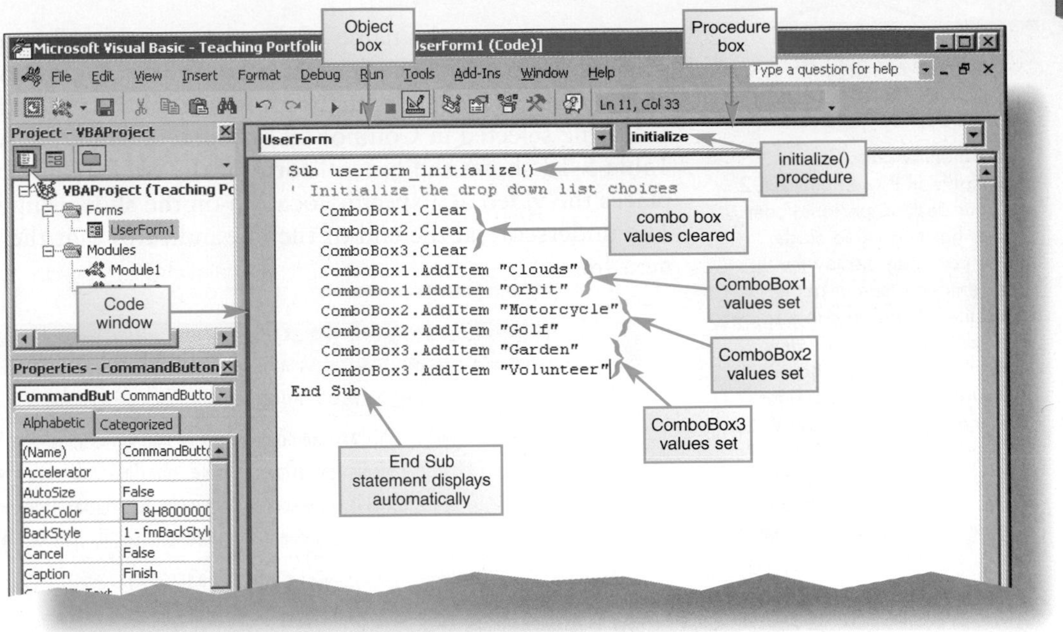

FIGURE 5-62

WRITING THE COMMANDBUTTON1 PROCEDURE Whenever you need to work with an object's properties or methods in more than one line of code, you can use the With statement to eliminate some coding. The **With statement** accepts an object as a parameter and is followed by several lines of code that pertain to this object. You therefore do not need to retype the object name in these lines. Table 5-11 describes the general form of the With statement.

The next step is to write the code for the CommandButton1 procedure as shown in Table 5-12. The CommandButton1 procedure is activated when the user clicks the Update Presentation button on the form. The code for this procedure is associated with the Click event.

Table 5-11 With Statement Format

General Form:	`With object`
	`  Visual Basic code`
	`End With`

Comment:	Object is any valid Visual Basic or user-defined object

Example:	`With textbox1`
	`  .text = ""`
	`End With`

Table 5-12 CommandButton1 Procedure

LINE	VBA CODE
1	`Templname = ComboBox1.Text & ".pot"`
2	`Application.ActivePresentation.ApplyTemplate Path & Templname`

3	`Set VideoSlide = ActivePresentation.Slides(2).Shapes _`
	`  AddMediaObject(FileName:=Path & ComboBox2.Text & ".avi", _`
	`  Left:=380, Top:=150)`

4	`  With VideoSlide.AnimationSettings.PlaySettings`
5	`    PlayOnEntry = msoTrue`
6	`    PauseAnimation = msoTrue`
7	`    HideWhileNotPlaying = msoFalse`
8	`  End With`
9	`Set PictureSlide = Application.ActivePresentation.Slides(3)`
10	`  With PictureSlide`
11	`    .Shapes.AddPicture Path & ComboBox3.Text & ".jpg", True, True, 375, 150, 300, 300`
12	`  End With`

More About

Presenter View

Dual-monitor capability is available in PowerPoint 2002 if your desktop personal computer has two video cards. One card can display the presentation to your audience, and the other card can display PowerPoint's Presenter view, which helps you navigate through the slides. Presenter view allows you to show slides out of sequence, read speaker notes with an enlarged font size, preview the text that is going to display on the next slide, and black out the screen.

Line 1 defines the name of the template. Line 2 assigns the template to the presentation object. The Set statement in line 3 does several things. It sets an object name, VideoSlide, that represents Slide 2. The statement then assigns the video file selected in ComboBox2 to Slide 2 using the **AddMediaObject() method**. Table 5-13 shows the general form of the AddMediaObject() method. The method places the video at a specific location on the slide using the Left and Top coordinates. The underscore at the end of the line indicates that the statement continues on the next line.

Table 5-13 AddMediaObject() Method Format

General Form:	`Shape_Object.AddMediaObject(FileName, Left, Top, Width, Height)`
Comment:	Shape_Object is the name of the shape on the slide. The file name is required and is the name of the media file. If a path is not specified, the current working folder is path. Left and Top are the positions (in points) of the upper-left corner of the media location relative to the upper-left corner of the document. You also may supply optional Width and Height positions.
Example:	`ActivePresentation.Slides(2).Shapes.AddMediaObject(FileName:= "golf.avi", Left:=380, Top:=150)`

More About

Controls

If you press the F1 key when you are running your presentation, PowerPoint displays a list of controls that help you navigate through the slide show. For example, the list describes which keys to press or actions to take to return to the first slide, change the mouse pointer to a pen, and stop and restart an automatic slide show.

Lines 4 through 8 use the same object, VideoSlide, and assign the animation and play settings. The **PauseAnimation property** set to True indicates the animation will pause when the user clicks the shape. When the user clicks the shape again, the animation will continue to play. The **HideWhileNotPlaying property** is set to False, so the video displays and stays on the slide even when not running.

Line 9 sets Slide 3 to a new object called PictureSlide. Lines 10 through 12 add the picture selected from the Picture combo box to the specific coordinates using the **AddPicture method**. Table 5-14 shows the general form of the AddPicture method.

Table 5-14 AddPicture Method Format

General Form:	`Shape_Object.AddPicture(FileName, LinkToFile, SaveWithDocument, Left, Top, Width, Height)`
Comment:	The file name is required and represents the file from which the OLE object is created. LinkToFile value is True, to link the picture to the file or False to make the picture an independent copy of the file. SaveWithDocument value True saves the linked picture with the presentation or False to store only the linked information in the document. If LinkToFile is False, this value must be True. Left and Top are the points location for the picture, and Width and Height are the width and height of the picture.
Example:	`.Shapes.AddPicture "mypicture.jpg", True, True, 375, 150, 300, 300`

Steps To Enter the CommandButton1 Procedure

1 Click the Object box arrow at the top of the Code window, and then point to CommandButton1 in the Object list (Figure 5-63).

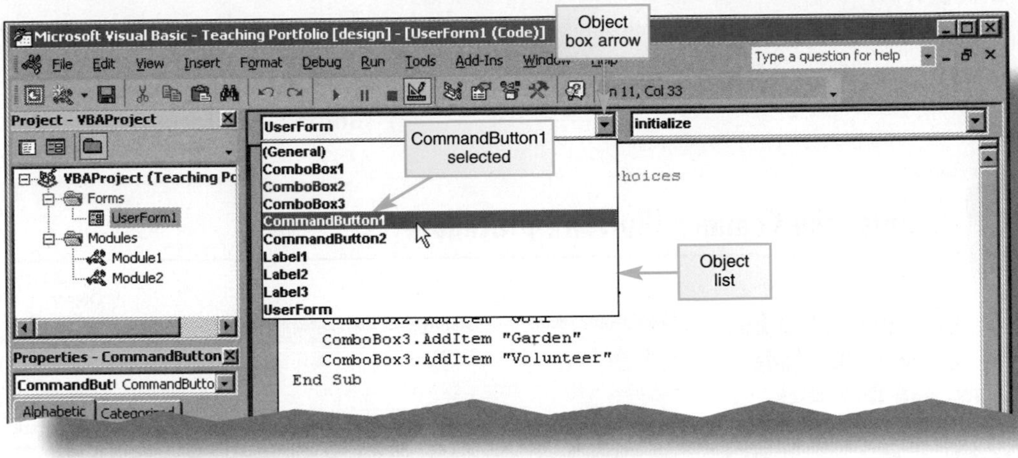

FIGURE 5-63

2 Click CommandButton1. Make sure Click is in the Procedure box.

The Visual Basic Editor displays the Sub and End Sub statements for the CommandButton1 procedure and positions the insertion point between the two statements (Figure 5-64).

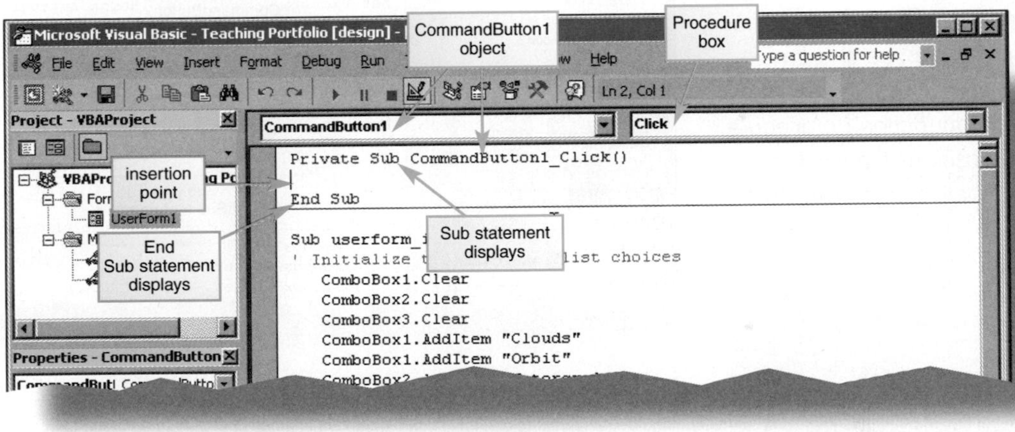

FIGURE 5-64

3 Enter the VBA code shown in lines 1 through 12 in Table 5-12. Do not press the ENTER key after typing the End With statement in line 12.

CommandButton1_Click() displays as the procedure (Figure 5-65).

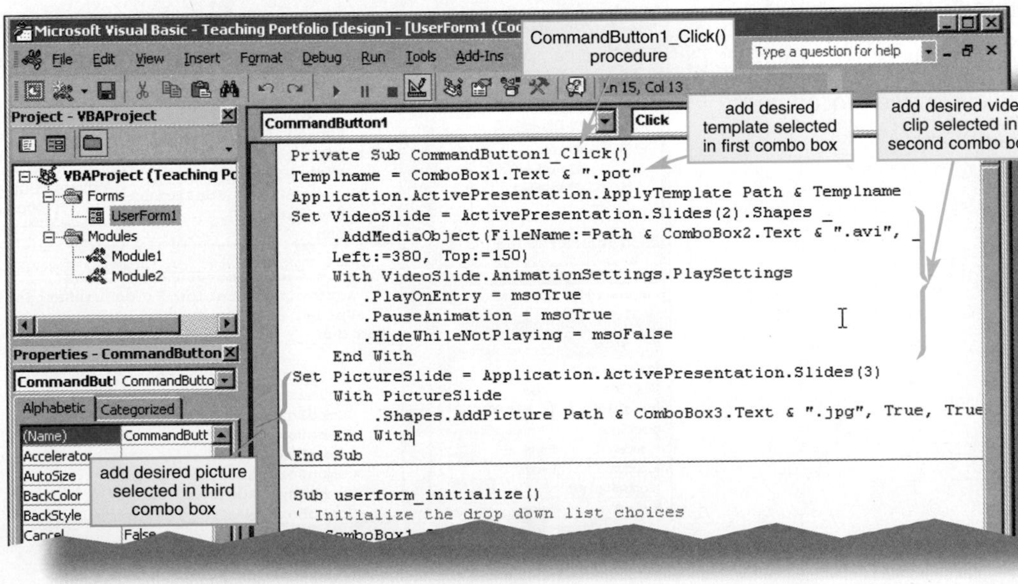

FIGURE 5-65

Table 5-15 CommandButton2 Procedure

LINE	VBA CODE
1	`ActivePresentation.SlideShowSettings.Run`
2	`Unload UserForm1`

WRITING THE COMMANDBUTTON2 PROCEDURE The next step is to write the CommandButton2 procedure. This procedure executes when the user clicks the Finish button. The procedure hides and unloads the form and starts the presentation.

Line 1 starts the current active presentation. Line 2 unloads the form (UserForm1).

Steps To Enter the CommandButton2 Procedure

1 Click the Object box arrow in the Code window, and then click CommandButton2 in the Object box. Make sure Click is in the Procedure box.

The Visual Basic Editor displays the Sub and End Sub statements for the CommandButton2 procedure and positions the insertion point between the two statements (Figure 5-66).

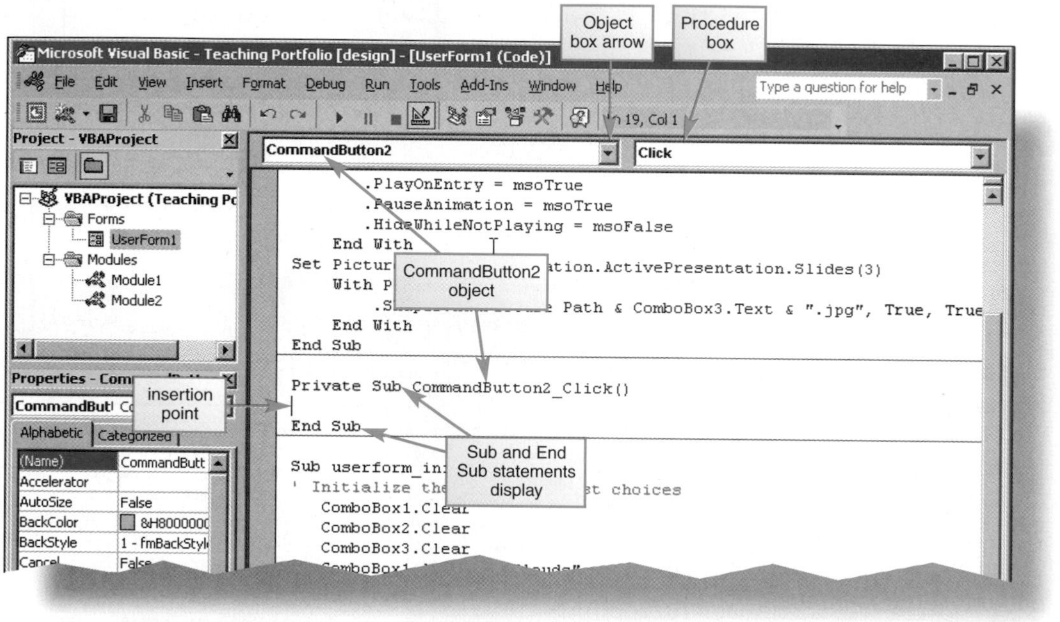

FIGURE 5-66

2 Enter the VBA code shown in Table 5-15.

CommandButton2_Click() displays as the procedure (Figure 5-67).

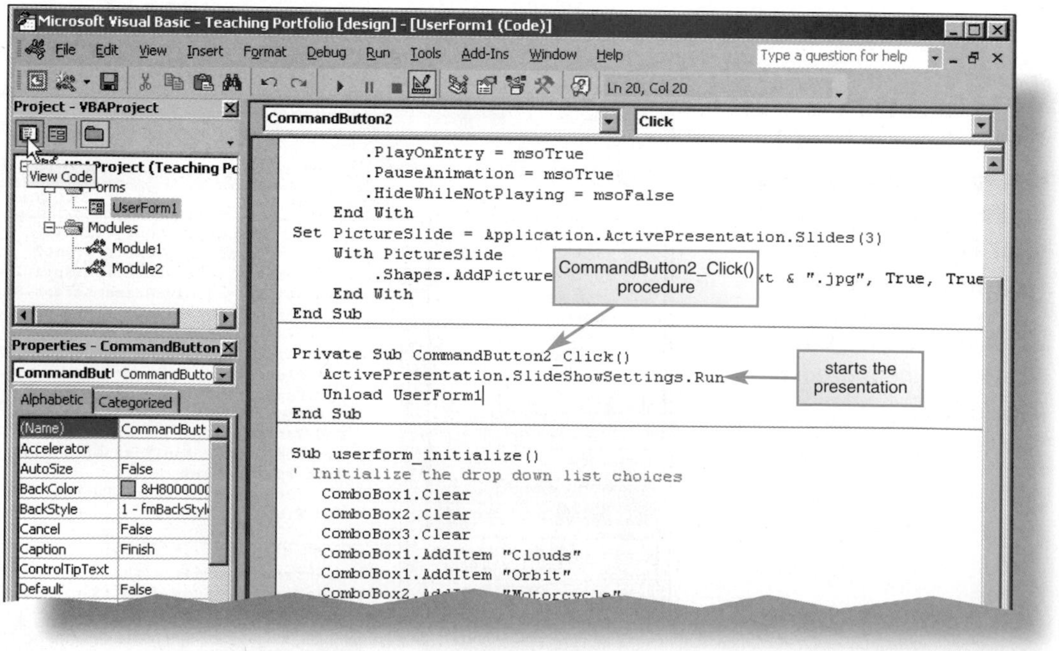

FIGURE 5-67

WRITING THE GENERAL DECLARATIONS At the beginning of a Visual Basic program, it may be necessary to declare some variables or constant values. In this application, a **Path constant** is declared, which tells PowerPoint where to find files on a disk. PowerPoint needs to locate the templates, video, and digital images. The basic form of a **Constant statement** is shown in Table 5-16.

Table 5-16	Constant Statement Format
General Form:	`Public | Private] Const constname [As type] = expression`
Comment:	Public or Private indicates whether the value is available to all Visual Basic modules or just the current module. The constname must be a valid Visual Basic identifier and type must be a valid Visual Basic data type. The expression can be any valid Visual Basic expression.
Examples:	`Const Path = "a:\"` `Const Tax = 0.065`

Similar to the Const statement is the Dim statement. The general form of the Dim statement is shown in Table 5-17.

This project uses the Path constant because the video clip and digital images used are too large to fit on a floppy disk. By assigning the Path value once, the Path constant can be used in several modules as needed. If the location of the files changes, the programmer need only change the value of the Path constant. This procedure reduces the possibility of errors. To initialize a Path constant, perform the following steps.

Table 5-17	Dim Statement Format
General Form:	`Public | Private] DIM VariableName [As type] = expression`
Comment:	Public or Private indicates whether the value is available to all Visual Basic modules or just the current module. The VariableName must be a valid Visual Basic identifier and type must be a valid Visual Basic data type. The expression can be any valid Visual Basic expression.
Examples:	`Dim Area As Single` `Dim Templname As String`

Steps To Initialize a Path Constant

1 Click the Object box arrow and then click (General).

(General) displays in the Object box, and (Declarations) displays in the Procedure box (Figure 5-68).

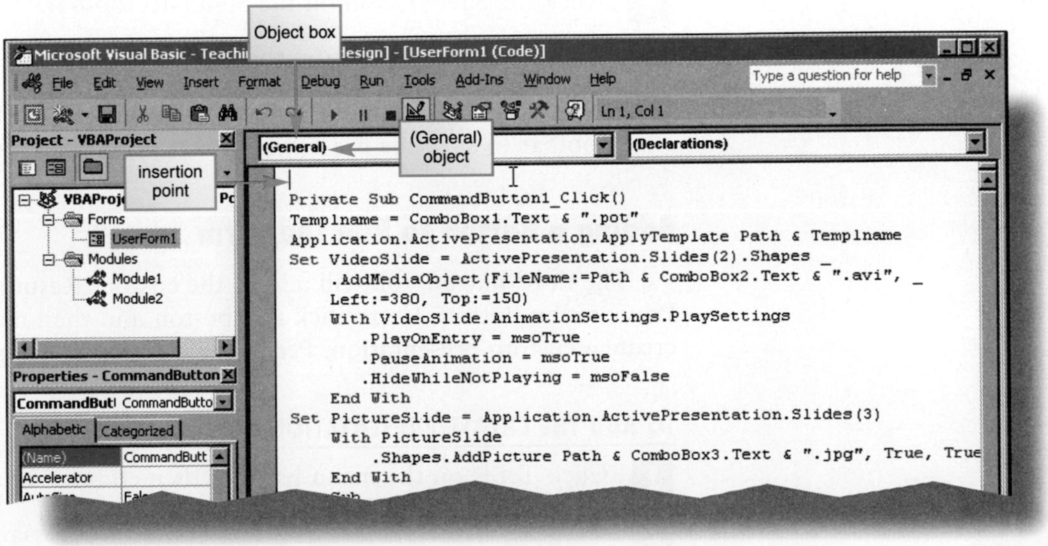

FIGURE 5-68

2 **Type** `Const Path = "a:\"` **and then press the ENTER key. Type** `Dim Templname As String` **and then press the ENTER key.**

The constant and variable are declared for all procedures. A line displays and separates the General Declarations from the CommandButton1 procedure (Figure 5-69). You need to specify the location of your files.

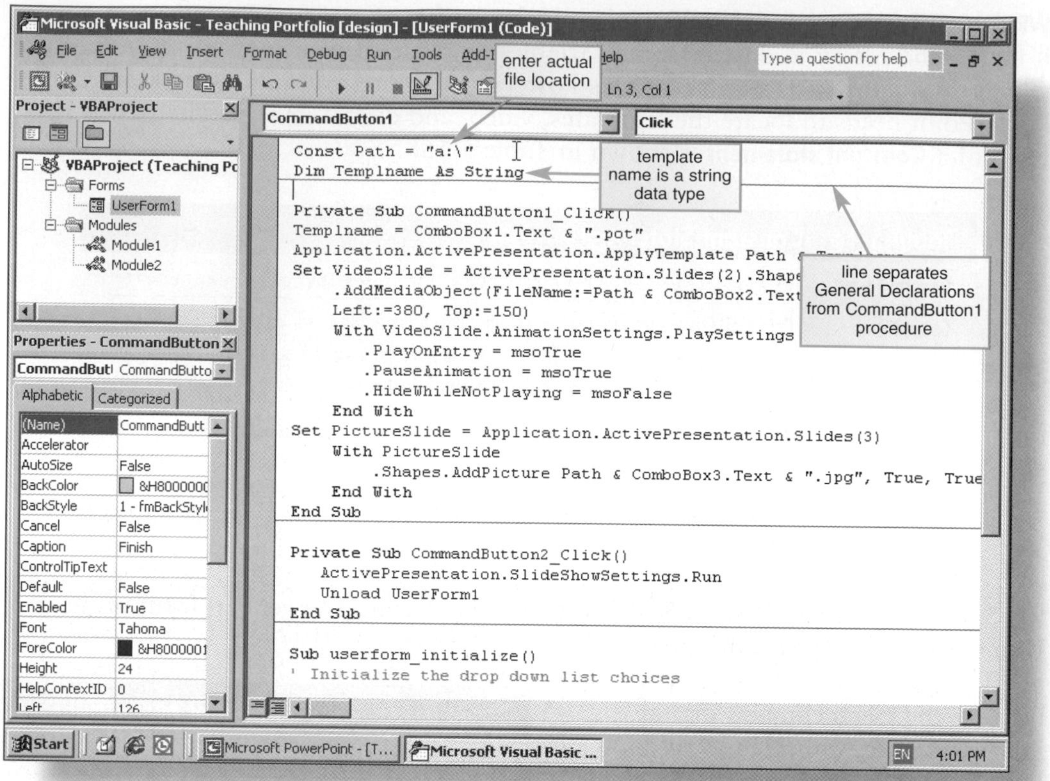

FIGURE 5-69

Other Ways

1. Click File on menu bar, click Close and Return to Microsoft PowerPoint
2. Press ALT+Q
3. Press ALT+F, press C

The VBA code is complete. The next step is to close the Visual Basic Editor and save the presentation. Before closing the Visual Basic Editor, you should verify your code by comparing it to Figures 5-58 through 5-69.

TO SAVE THE VISUAL BASIC CODE, CLOSE THE VISUAL BASIC EDITOR, AND SAVE THE PRESENTATION

1. Click the Save button on the Standard toolbar.
2. Click the Close button on the right side of the Visual Basic Editor title bar.
3. When the PowerPoint window displays, click the Save button on the Standard toolbar to save the presentation using the file name, Teaching Portfolio.

Adding a Button to Run the Form

The third button you will add to the custom Resume toolbar is the Create Presentation button. Users click this button and then make selections on the form to create a custom presentation. Perform the following steps to add this button.

TO ADD THE CREATE PRESENTATION BUTTON

1. Click Tools on the menu bar and then click Customize.
2. When the Customize dialog box opens, if necessary, click the Commands tab. Scroll down in the Categories box and then click Macros. Click createpresentationteaching in the Commands box.

3 Drag the createpresentationteaching entry from the Commands list in the Customize dialog box to the right of the Pack and Go button on the Resume toolbar.

4 Click the Modify Selection button and then point to Change Button Image on the submenu. When the Change Button Image palette displays, click the button with a key (row 6, column 3).

5 Click the Modify Selection button and then click Name on the shortcut menu. Type `Create Presentation` as the new name of this button.

6 Click Default Style on the submenu.

7 Click the Close button in the Customize dialog box.

The Create Presentation button displays with a key image (Figure 5-70).

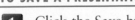

FIGURE 5-70

Saving the Presentation

The changes to the presentation are complete. Perform the following step to save the finished presentation before testing the controls.

TO SAVE A PRESENTATION

1 Click the Save button on the Standard toolbar.

PowerPoint saves the presentation by saving the changes made to the presentation since the last save.

Testing the Controls

The final step is to test the controls on the form. Use the following data: Orbit design template; Motorcycle video clip; and Volunteer picture. Perform the steps on the next page to test the controls.

More About

Quick Reference

For a table that lists how to complete tasks covered in this book using the mouse, menu, shortcut menu, and keyboard, see the Quick Reference Summary at the back of this book, or visit the Shelly Cashman Series Office XP Web page (scsite.com/offxp/qr.htm) and then click Microsoft PowerPoint 2002.

Steps To Test the Control on the Form

1 Click the Create Presentation button on the Resume toolbar. When the form displays, click the Add a background box arrow and then click Orbit. Click the Select a video clip box arrow and then click Motorcycle. Click the Select a picture box arrow and then click Volunteer. Point to the Update presentation button.

The form displays as shown (Figure 5-71).

2 Click the Update Presentation button and then click the Finish button.

The Teaching Portfolio slide show runs automatically.

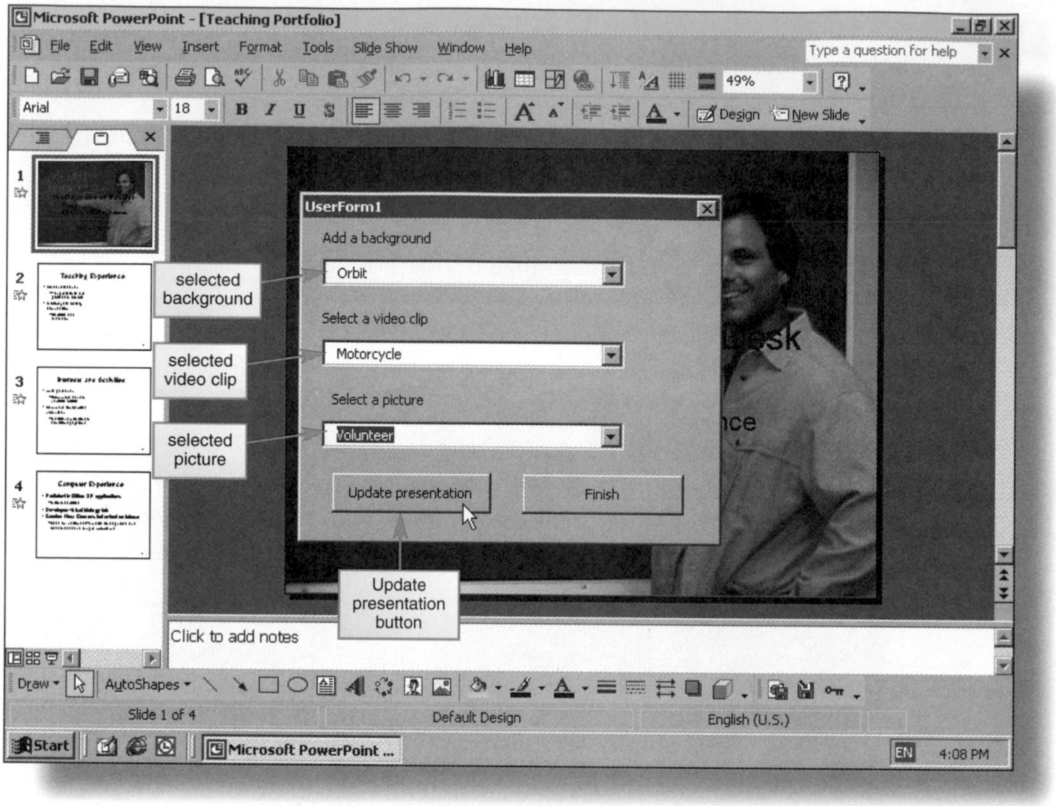

FIGURE 5-71

3 Click the black slide to end the slide show. Print the four slides and a handout.

More About

Microsoft Certification

The Microsoft Office User Specialist (MOUS) Certification program provides an opportunity for you to obtain a valuable industry credential — proof that you have the PowerPoint 2002 skills required by employers. For more information, see Appendix E or visit the Shelly Cashman Series MOUS Web page at scsite.com/offxp/cert.htm.

The Orbit design template is applied to the presentation, the motorcycle video displays on Slide 2, and the air conditioning digital picture displays on Slide 3. If the slides do not display as shown, then click Tools on the menu bar, point to Macro, and then click Visual Basic Editor. Click the View Code button on the VBA Project toolbar, and then check the controls' properties and VBA code. Save the presentation again and repeat Steps 1 and 2 above.

Quitting PowerPoint

The project is complete. To quit PowerPoint, perform the following steps.

TO QUIT POWERPOINT

1. Click the Close button on the title bar.
2. If the Microsoft PowerPoint dialog box displays, click the Yes button to save changes made since the last save.

PowerPoint closes.

CASE PERSPECTIVE SUMMARY

The Teaching Portfolio slide show should assist Bernie with his job search. The form you developed using Visual Basic for Applications allows him to create a unique presentation for each interview. He can select a template, video clip, and digital picture. In addition, the buttons on the Resume toolbar you created and the new command on the File menu easily allow him to save the presentation as a Web page, to use the Pack and Go Wizard to transport this file, and to print a handout for the interviewer. Bernie's extraordinary and professional custom presentation should impress interviewers and help him land the best job possible.

Project Summary

Project 5 presented the principles of customizing a presentation. In Phase 1, you learned how to create a toolbar and add two buttons, Save as Web Page and the Pack and Go Wizard. In Phase 2, you learned how to use the macro recorder to create a macro that prints handouts displaying four slides per page and assign this macro to a command on the File menu. In Phase 3, you learned how to create a form composed of label controls, combo box controls, and command button controls. In this phase, you also learned how to write VBA code.

What You Should Know

Having completed this project, you now should be able to perform the following tasks:

- Add a Command to a Menu, Assign the Command to a Macro, and Invoke the Command *(PP 5.22)*
- Add Two Buttons to the Resume Toolbar *(PP 5.12)*
- Add Command Button Controls to a Form *(PP 5.36)*
- Add Label and Combo Box Controls to a Form *(PP 5.34)*
- Add the Create Presentation Button *(PP 5.52)*
- Change the Form Size and the Toolbox Location *(PP 5.31)*
- Create a Custom Toolbar *(PP 5.10)*
- Enter the CommandButton1 Procedure *(PP 5.49)*
- Enter the CommandButton2 Procedure *(PP 5.50)*
- Enter the Create Presentation Procedure *(PP 5.43)*
- Enter the InitializeForm() Procedure *(PP 5.46)*
- Initialize a Path Constant *(PP 5.51)*
- Open a Presentation and Save It with a New File Name *(PP 5.06)*
- Open a Presentation with a Macro and Execute the Macro *(PP 5.25)*
- Open the Visual Basic IDE and a New Form *(PP 5.29)*
- Quit PowerPoint *(PP 5.54)*
- Record a Macro to Print Handouts in Vertical Slide Order in Pure Black and White *(PP 5.19)*
- Resize and Reposition Controls on a Form *(PP 5.40)*
- Save a Presentation *(PP 5.17, PP 5.53)*
- Save and Close the Presentation *(PP 5.24)*
- Save the Visual Basic Code, Close the Visual Basic Editor, and Save the Presentation *(PP 5.52)*
- Set the Controls' Caption Properties *(PP 5.38)*
- Test the Control on the Form *(PP 5.54)*
- View a Macro's VBA Code *(PP 5.26)*

Learn It Online

Instructions: To complete the Learn It Online exercises, start your browser, click the Address bar, and then enter `scsite.com/offxp/exs.htm`. When the Office XP Learn It Online page displays, follow the instructions in the exercises below.

1 Project Reinforcement TF, MC, and SA

Below PowerPoint Project 5, click the Project Reinforcement link. Print the quiz by clicking Print on the File menu. Answer each question. Write your first and last name at the top of each page, and then hand in the printout to your instructor.

2 Flash Cards

Below PowerPoint Project 5, click the Flash Cards link. When Flash Cards displays, read the instructions. Type 20 (or a number specified by your instructor) in the Number of Playing Cards text box, type your name in the Name text box, and then click the Flip Card button. When the flash card displays, read the question and then click the Answer box arrow to select an answer. Flip through Flash Cards. Click Print on the File menu to print the last flash card if your score is 15 (75%) correct or greater and then hand it in to your instructor. If your score is less than 15 (75%) correct, then redo this exercise by clicking the Replay button.

3 Practice Test

Below PowerPoint Project 5, click the Practice Test link. Answer each question, enter your first and last name at the bottom of the page, and then click the Grade Test button. When the graded practice test displays on your screen, click Print on the File menu to print a hard copy. Continue to take practice tests until you score 80% or better. Hand in a printout of the final practice test to your instructor.

4 Who Wants to Be a Computer Genius?

Below PowerPoint Project 5, click the Computer Genius link. Read the instructions, enter your first and last name at the bottom of the page, and then click the Play button. Hand in your score to your instructor.

5 Wheel of Terms

Below PowerPoint Project 5, click the Wheel of Terms link. Read the instructions, and then enter your first and last name and your school name. Click the Play button. Hand in your score to your instructor.

6 Crossword Puzzle Challenge

Below PowerPoint Project 5, click the Crossword Puzzle Challenge link. Read the instructions, and then enter your first and last name. Click the Play button. Work the crossword puzzle. When you are finished, click the Submit button. When the crossword puzzle redisplays, click the Print button. Hand in the printout.

7 Tips and Tricks

Below PowerPoint Project 5, click the Tips and Tricks link. Click a topic that pertains to Project 5. Right-click the information and then click Print on the shortcut menu. Construct a brief example of what the information relates to in PowerPoint to confirm you understand how to use the tip or trick. Hand in the example and printed information.

8 Newsgroups

Below PowerPoint Project 5, click the Newsgroups link. Click a topic that pertains to Project 5. Print three comments. Hand in the comments to your instructor.

9 Expanding Your Horizons

Below PowerPoint Project 5, click the Articles for Microsoft PowerPoint link. Click a topic that pertains to Project 5. Print the information. Construct a brief example of what the information relates to in PowerPoint to confirm you understand the contents of the article. Hand in the example and printed information to your instructor.

10 Search Sleuth

Below PowerPoint Project 5, click the Search Sleuth link. To search for a term that pertains to this project, select a term below the Project 5 title and then use the Google search engine at google.com (or any major search engine) to display and print two Web pages that present information on the term. Hand in the printouts to your instructor.

online

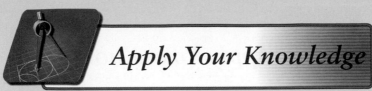

Apply Your Knowledge

1 Creating a Macro and Customizing a Menu and Toolbar

Instructions: Start PowerPoint. Open the presentation, Beach, from the Data Disk. See the inside back cover of this book for instructions for downloading the Data Disk or see your instructor for information on accessing the files required for this book. Perform the following tasks.

1. Use the Record New Macro command to create a macro that exports the presentation outline to Microsoft Word. Call the macro ExportWord. Change the name of the author in the Description box to your name. Make sure the Store macro in box displays Beach Vacation. Click the OK button. When the Stop Recording toolbar displays, do the following:
   (a) Click File on the menu bar and then click Save As. (b) When the Save As dialog box displays, type `Beach Outline` in the File name box. (c) Click the Save as type box arrow and then click Outline/RTF in the Save as type list. (d) Be certain the Save in box location is 3½ Floppy (A:). (e) Click the Save button. (f) Click the Stop Recording button on the Stop Recording toolbar.
2. Add a button to the Standard toolbar (Figure 5-72a) and a command to the File menu (Figure 5-72b on the next page). Use the image of a pencil (row 4, column 4) and the Default Style for the button. Change the macro name on the File menu to Export to Word.
3. View the ExportWord's VBA code. When the Visual Basic Editor displays the macro (Figure 5-72c on the next page), click File on the menu bar, click Print, and then click the OK button. Close the Visual Basic Editor.
4. Run the macro as follows: (a) Click the button you added to the Standard toolbar. (b) Click File on the menu bar and then click the Export to Word command.
5. Save the presentation with the file name, Beach Vacation.

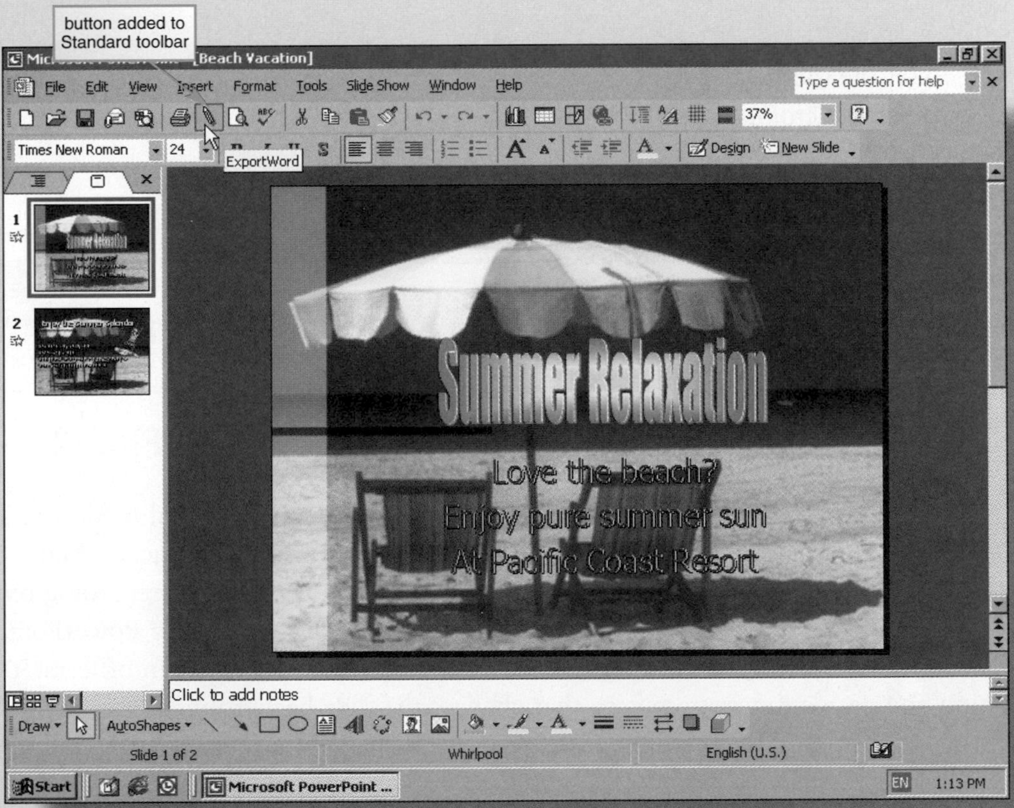

FIGURE 5-72a

(continued)

Apply Your Knowledge

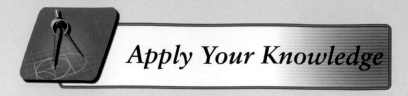

Creating a Macro and Customizing a Menu and Toolbar *(continued)*

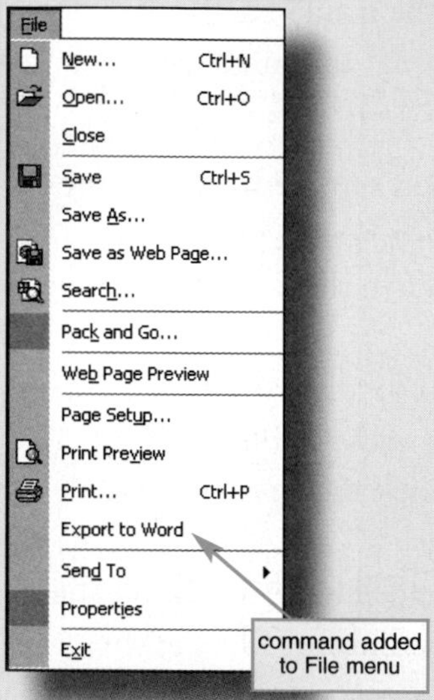

FIGURE 5-72b

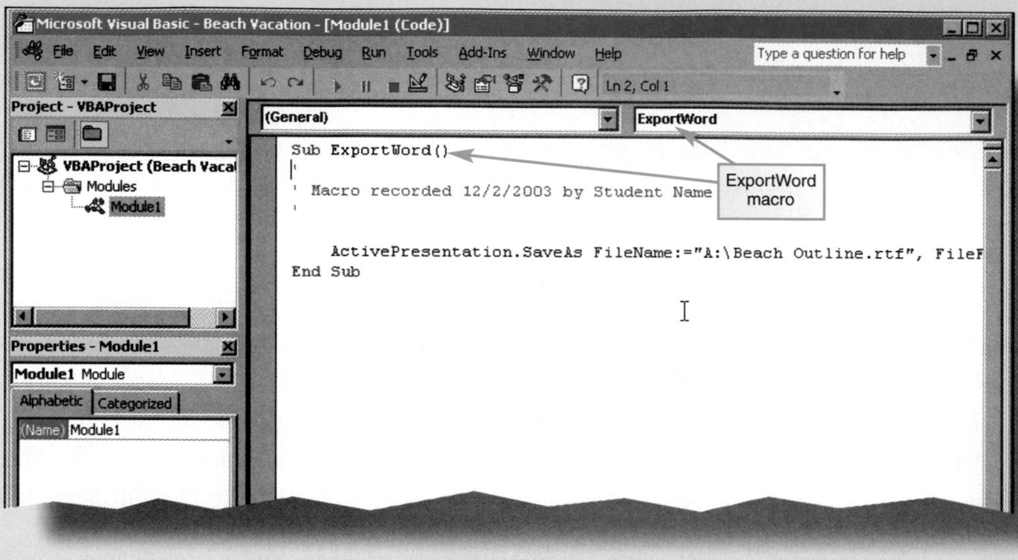

FIGURE 5-72c

6. Reset the toolbars to their installation settings (see Appendix D). Quit PowerPoint. Hand in the printout to your instructor.

In the Lab

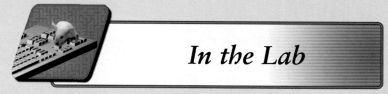

1 Create a New Toolbar, Record New Macros, and Place New Macros on a Toolbar

Problem: You are employed as an administrative assistant at the local bank. Part of your job responsibilities includes greeting customers and arranging appointments with loan officers. Many of the customers are in the process of applying for used car loans, and they have many questions regarding buying these vehicles efficiently and obtaining the best price. Your manager has asked you to prepare a PowerPoint presentation for these customers to view as they are waiting for their appointments with the loan officers. You agree to create this presentation and decide to write a macro that changes the slide backgrounds. You also add a button to save the presentation using the Pack and Go Wizard. A third macro prints Notes Pages for handouts to distribute to these customers. Slide 1 and the new buttons display in Figure 5-73.

Instructions: Start PowerPoint and perform the following tasks with a computer.

1. Open the file, Road Tips, from your Data Disk. Save the presentation with the file name, Road Tips Revised.

In the Lab

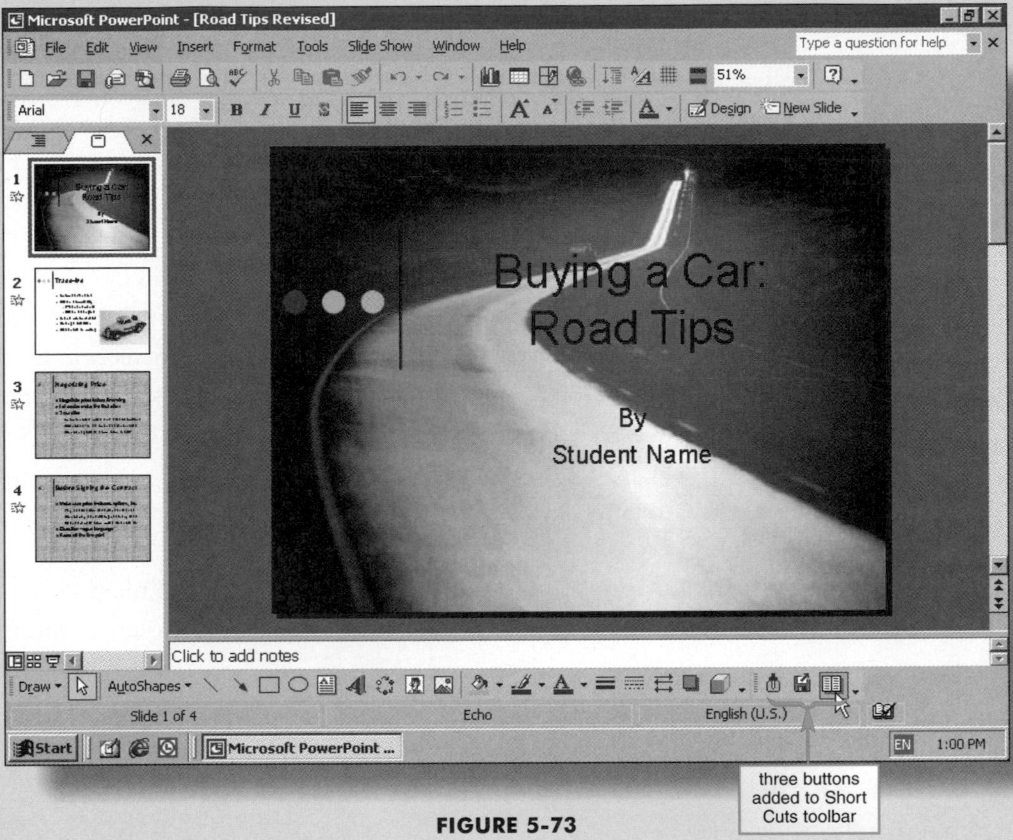

FIGURE 5-73

2. Create a new toolbar and name it Short Cuts. Place the new toolbar next to the Drawing toolbar.
3. Use the Record New Macro command to create a macro that changes the backgrounds on Slides 3 and 4. Name the macro, Background, change the name of the author in the Description box to your name, and then store the macro in the Road Tips Revised file.
4. With the Stop Recording toolbar on the screen, do the following: (a) Select Slides 3 and 4 on the Slides tab. (b) Click Format on the menu bar and then click Background. (c) Click the Background fill area arrow in the Background dialog box, click Fill Effects, click the Texture tab, click Papyrus, click the OK button, and then click the Apply button in the Background dialog box. (d) Click the Stop Recording button on the Stop Recording toolbar.
5. Use the Record New Macro command to create a macro that saves the presentation using the Pack and Go Wizard. Call the macro, PackandGo, change the name of the author in Description box to your name, and store the macro in the Road Tips Revised file.
6. With the Stop Recording toolbar displaying, perform the following steps: (a) Click File on the menu bar and then click Pack and Go. (b) Follow the instructions for the Pack and Go Wizard using the active presentation and save it on your Data Disk. Do not include linked files, embedded True Type fonts, or the Viewer. (c) Click the Stop Recording button on the Stop Recording toolbar.
7. Use the Record New Macro command to create a macro that prints Notes Pages. Call the macro, PrintNotes, change the name of the author in Description box to your name, and then store the macro in the Road Tips Revised file.

(continued)

In the Lab

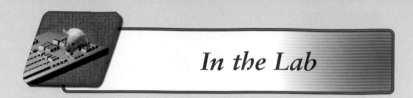

Create a New Toolbar, Record New Macros, and Place New Macros on a Toolbar *(continued)*

8. With the Stop Recording toolbar displaying, perform the following steps: (a) Click File on the menu bar and then click Print. (b) In the Print what box, click Handouts. (c) In the Slides per page box, click 4; make sure Order is Horizontal; and then click the OK button. (d) After the handouts print, click File on the menu bar and then click Print. (e) In the Slides per page box, click 6. (f) In the Print what box, click Slides. (g) Click the OK button. (h) After the four slides print, click the Stop Recording button on the Stop Recording toolbar.
9. Add the three macros to the new Short Cuts toolbar. Modify the selection for the Background macro, and change the image to the ink bottle icon (row 1, column 4). On the Modify Selection menu, select the Default Style. Change the image icon for the PackandGo macro to the floppy disk with the arrow pointing out (row 1, column 5). Select the Default Style on the Modify Selection menu. Modify the selection for the PrintNotes macro and change the image to the book pages (row 6, column 1).
10. Add the PrintNotes macro to the File menu above the Print menu command. Change the Name to Print Notes.
11. Save the presentation again. Print the macro code for all three macros. Reset the menus and toolbars to their installation settings (see Appendix D). Quit PowerPoint. Hand in the macro code and Notes Pages to your instructor.

2 Creating a New Toolbar and Writing a Visual Basic Program to Add Preset Gradient Backgrounds

Problem: You are a summer intern at New Century Credit Union working in the Information Technology (IT) department. The IT director wants you to work with Shalanda Green, who is developing a presentation on investing. Shalanda will be giving the presentation several times to various groups and wants the presentation to have a different look each time. You tell Shalanda you can write a Visual Basic program to display a form (Figure 5-74a) and let her change the background to preset gradient colors. The two of you agree to change the background on Slides 2 and 4. To streamline the process, you will create a toolbar and place a Start button for the Visual Basic program on the new toolbar (Figure 5-74b).

Instructions: Start PowerPoint and perform the following tasks.

1. Open the Investing presentation on the Data Disk. Save the presentation with the file name, New Century.
2. Create a new toolbar with the name, Invest. Place this toolbar to the right of the Formatting toolbar.
3. Open the Visual Basic Editor and insert a new module.
4. Click the View Code button. In the General Declarations window, enter the code from Table 5-18, which will run the Visual Basic program. The End Sub statement will display automatically after entering line 1.
5. Close the Visual Basic Editor. Add this module, createpresentationInvesting(), to the new toolbar as a button.

Table 5-18 General Declarations

LINE	*VBA CODE*
1	`Sub createpresentationInvesting()`
2	`  UserForm1.UserForm_Initialize`
3	`  UserForm1.Show`

In the Lab

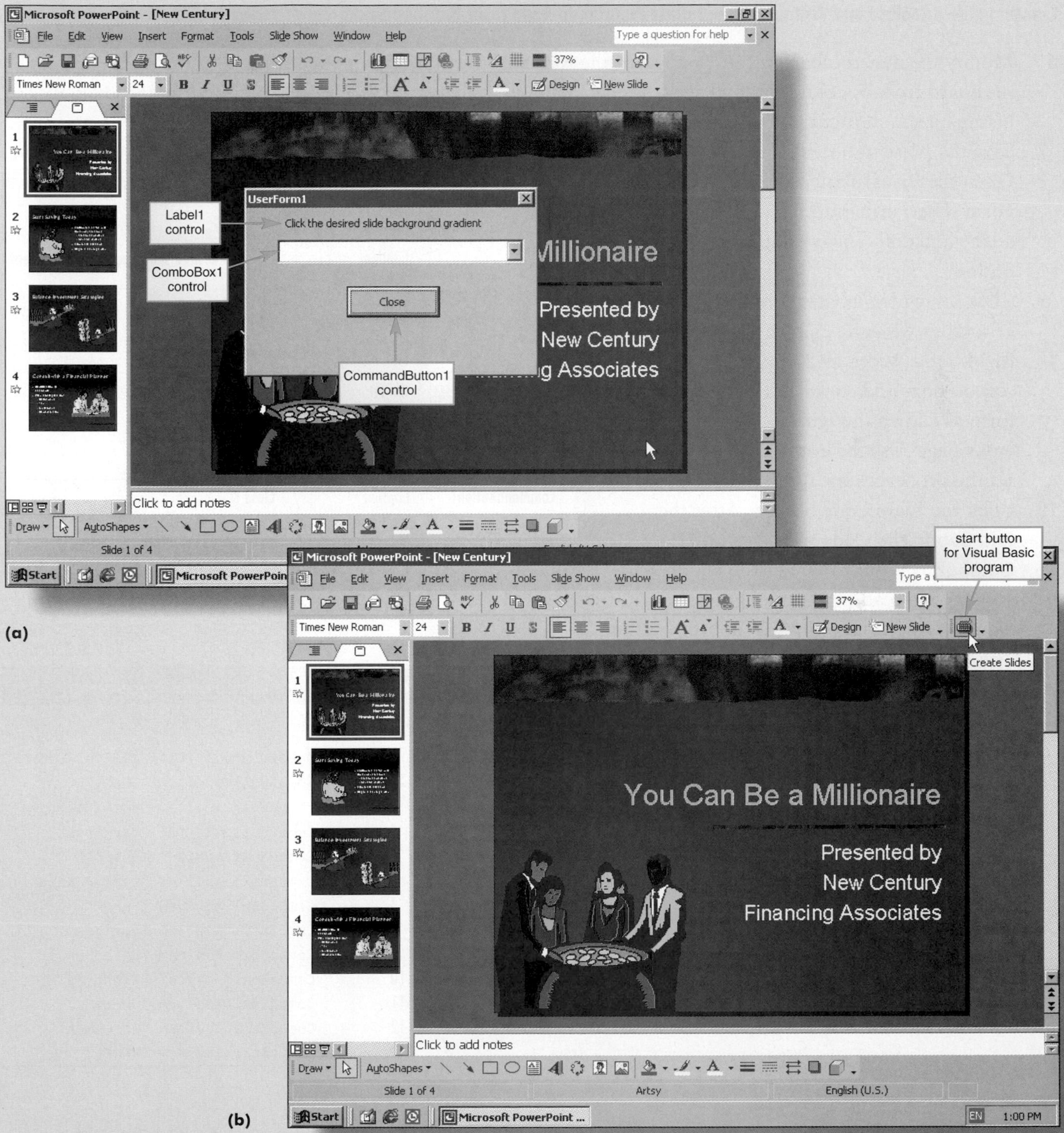

FIGURE 5-74

(continued)

In the Lab

Creating a New Toolbar and Writing a Visual Basic Program to Add Preset Gradient Backgrounds *(continued)*

6. Modify the new toolbar button by clicking the Modify Selection button. Change the button image to the keyboard (row 5, column 6) and select the Default style. Click the Modify Selection button and then click Name on the shortcut menu. Change the name of this button to Create Slides.
7. Save the presentation again.
8. Open the Visual Basic Editor. A new User Form (UserForm1) already exists. Add a label, a combo box, and a command button.
9. Click anywhere in UserForm1. In the Properties window, change the Height to 147 and Width to 230. Place a label, combo box, and command button on the form as shown in Figure 5-74a on the previous page. Use the data in Table 5-19 to set the properties for these controls.
10. Click the View Code button. After the End Sub in the Code window for the ComboBox1 control, enter the code from Table 5-20 to add the preset gradient names to the combo box (ComboBox1). The End Sub will display automatically.
11. Click the Object box arrow and then select CommandButton1. Make sure Click is in the Procedure box. Enter the code in Table 5-21 between the Sub and End Sub statements.

Table 5-19 Control Properties

CONTROL	PROPERTY	VALUE
Label1	Caption	Click the desired slide background gradient
	Height	18
	Width	222
	Top	6
	Left	30
ComboBox1	Height	18
	Width	192
	Top	24
	Left	24
CommandButton1	Caption	Close
	Height	24
	Width	72
	Top	60
	Left	78

Table 5-20 Initialize Form Procedure

LINE	VBA CODE
1	`Sub UserForm_Initialize()`
2	`ComboBox1.AddItem "Brass"`
3	`ComboBox1.AddItem "Calm Water"`
4	`ComboBox1.AddItem "Day Break"`
5	`ComboBox1.AddItem "Desert"`
6	`ComboBox1.AddItem "Early Sunset"`
7	`ComboBox1.AddItem "Fire"`
8	`ComboBox1.AddItem "Horizon"`
9	`ComboBox1.AddItem "Late Sunset"`
10	`ComboBox1.AddItem "Night Fall"`
11	`ComboBox1.AddItem "Ocean"`
12	`ComboBox1.AddItem "Parchment"`
13	`ComboBox1.AddItem "Wheat"`

Table 5-21 CommandButton1 Procedure

LINE	VBA CODE
1	`ActivePresentation.SlideShowSettings.Run`
2	`UserForm1.Hide`
3	`Unload UserForm1`
4	`End`

12. Save the Visual Basic code. Close the Visual Basic Editor. Run the presentation.
13. Print the presentation. Print the form and the Visual Basic code by clicking File on the menu bar and then clicking Print, clicking Current Project in the Range area, making sure the Form Image and Code boxes are checked in the Print What area, and then clicking the OK button. Quit PowerPoint. Hand in the printouts to your instructor.

In the Lab

3 Writing a Visual Basic Program to Place Picture Images as the Background

Problem: You are working part time for the Community Park District. The director, Fernando Leva, wants a kiosk to display a PowerPoint presentation listing the monthly activities the park district offers. The kiosk will display in the foyer of the town hall, and the presentation will be started every morning. Fernando wants to show a different background picture every day. For the month of July, the district has these programs scheduled: a trip to see a major league soccer game; a golf outing; a fishing trip; a visit to the zoo; a trip to a remote beach; and a nature photography course. You tell Fernando that you can create a Visual Basic program with a form that allows him to select a background picture. Fernando wants to see a prototype before you complete the entire project.

Instructions: Start PowerPoint and then perform the following tasks.

1. Open the Park presentation on the Data Disk. Save the presentation with the file name, Park District.
2. Open the Visual Basic Editor.
3. Create the form shown in Figure 5-75a on page PP 5.65. Position the controls as shown in the figure, and then change the properties for each control as indicated in Table 5-22.
4. Write the Visual Basic code for the OptionButton1 control. Double-click the OptionButton1 control and enter the code from Table 5-23 between the Private Sub and End Sub statements.

Table 5-23 OptionButton1 Procedure

LINE | VBA CODE

```
With ActiveWindow.Selection.SlideRange
      .FollowMasterBackground = msoFalse
      .DisplayMasterShapes = msoTrue
      With .Background
       .Fill.Visible = msoTrue
       .Fill.Transparency = 0#
       .Fill.UserPicture "a:\soccer.jpg"
      End With
End With
```

Table 5-22 Control Properties

CONTROL	PROPERTY	VALUE
Label1	Caption	Select Background Pictures
	Height	18
	Width	114
	Top	24
	Left	66
OptionButton1	Caption	Soccer
	Height	18
	Width	108
	Top	60
	Left	6
OptionButton2	Caption	Golfing
	Height	18
	Width	108
	Top	90
	Left	6
OptionButton3	Caption	Fishing
	Height	18
	Width	108
	Top	126
	Left	6
OptionButton4	Caption	Zoo
	Height	18
	Width	108
	Top	60
	Left	126
OptionButton5	Caption	Beach
	Height	18
	Width	108
	Top	90
	Left	126
OptionButton6	Caption	Photography
	Height	18
	Width	108
	Top	90
	Left	126
CommandButton1	Caption	Run Show
	Height	24
	Width	72
	Top	156
	Left	78

(continued)

In the Lab

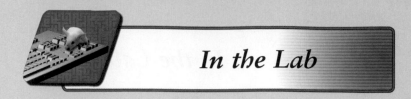

Writing a Visual Basic Program to Place Picture Images as the Background *(continued)*

5. Repeat the process for option buttons 2 through 5. Change the file name for the picture in line 7 for each option button as indicated in Table 5-24.

Table 5-24 Option Button File Names	
CONTROL	*VALUE*
OptionButton2	A:\golf.jpg
OptionButton3	A:\fishing.jpg
OptionButton4	A:\zoo.jpg
OptionButton5	A:\beach.jpg
OptionButton6	A:\camera.jpg

6. Create a new toolbar with the name, Park District. Place the toolbar to the right of the Drawing toolbar.
7. With the Visual Basic Editor still open, insert a new module.
8. Click the View Code button. In the General Declarations window, enter the code from Table 5-25, which will run the Visual Basic program. The End Sub statement will display automatically after entering line 1.

Table 5-25 General Declarations	
LINE	*VBA CODE*
1	`Sub ParkDistrictStart()`
2	` UserForm1.userform_initialize`
3	` UserForm1.Show`
4	`End Sub`

9. Add this module, ParkDistrictStart(), to the new toolbar as a button.
10. Click the Modify Selection button to modify the new toolbar button. Change the button image to the runner (row 7, column 3) and use the Default Style (Figure 5-75b). Change the button name to Run Show.
11. Save the Visual Basic code.
12. Print the form and the Visual Basic code by clicking File on the menu bar and then clicking Print. Click the Current Project in the Range area. Make sure the Form Image and Code boxes are checked in the Print What area. Click the OK button. Close the Visual Basic Editor and reset the toolbars to their installation settings (see Appendix D). Quit PowerPoint. Hand in the printouts to your instructor.

In the Lab

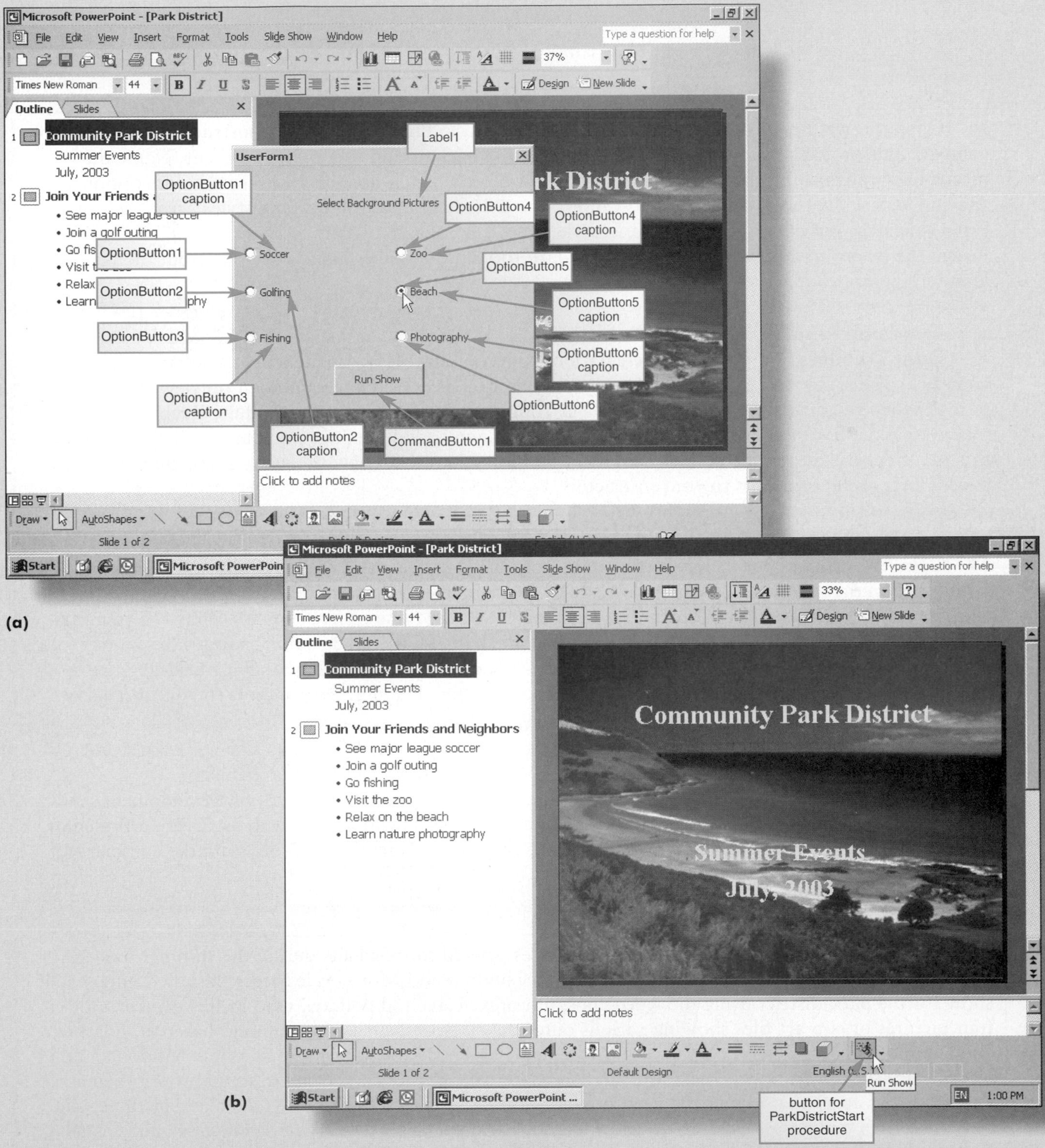

FIGURE 5-75

Cases and Places

The difficulty of these case studies varies:
◗ are the least difficult; ◗◗ are more difficult; and ◗◗◗ are the most difficult.

1 ◗ Open the Wellness Institute presentation you created in Project 3. See your instructor if you did not complete this project. Record a macro that changes the background to a preset gradient. Name the macro BWGradient. On the Gradient tab in the Fill Effects dialog box, click the Two colors option. Assign Color 1 the color, light blue and Color 2 the color, white. In the Shading styles area, click the From title style and click the first Variants style (row 1, column 1). Apply the background to all slides. Assign the macro to a new button on the Standard toolbar. View the macro and then print the code. Hand in the printouts to your instructor.

2 ◗ Open The Blues about the Flu presentation from the Data Disk. Create a new toolbar with the name, Flu Tools. Record a macro to save the presentation as a Web page and then preview the Web pages. Assign the macro to a button on the Flu Tools toolbar to execute this module. Record a second macro to add a footer with today's date, your school's name, and the page number on all slides except the title slide. Assign the macro to a command on the View menu. View the macros and then print the code. Hand in the printouts to your instructor.

3 ◗◗ Open The Blues about the Flu presentation from the Data Disk and delete the clips on Slides 4 and 5. Create a form that allows the user to select one of five templates from a combo box. Slides 3 and 4 have clip art, and the user can select one of five clips for Slide 3 and one of five clips for Slide 4. These five images may be used as choices for both slides. Write the Visual Basic module that executes this form. Name the module, AddTemplates_ClipArt, and then add a button on the Formatting toolbar to execute this module. Print the form, the Visual Basic code, and the presentation. Hand in the printouts to your instructor.

4 ◗◗ Using Microsoft Internet Explorer, go to the Microsoft Office Developer's Web site: msdn.microsoft.com/library/. In the Table of Contents frame, click Office Solutions Development, and then click Microsoft PowerPoint. Click the links and find a technical article, such as Create a Presentation from a Word Document. Read and summarize the article. Hand in the article and the summary to your instructor.

5 ◗◗ Your local park district is expanding the classes offered for residents during the summer months. Two of the new classes are Golf Fundamentals for Children and Motorcycle Safety Basics. Create a slide show for the park district using the video clips, motorcycle.avi and golf.avi, used in this project. Add four pictures or clip art files showing various outdoors activities, such as swimming, baseball, boating, and camping. Create a new toolbar with the name, Classes. Record a macro that prints handouts and notes. Place this macro on the new toolbar, and change the text of the button to an appropriate image. Next, create a form that allows the user to modify the slides to select various video clips, pictures, clip art, and design templates. Execute the print macro, and then display the form. Print slides, the Visual Basic code, and the form. Submit the printouts to your instructor.

Cases and Places

6 ▶▶▶ PowerPoint cannot record a macro for every keystroke. For example, PowerPoint will not record the keystrokes to make a Summary Slide automatically. Open the completed Enjoy Spring Break presentation you created in Project 2. See your instructor if you did not complete this project. Write a Visual Basic module that creates a new blank slide at the end of the slide sequence and reads the title text of Slides 2 through the end of the slides. By incorporating the Count method and using Visual Basic For/Next statements, you can create this slide.

(a) Start a new subroutine for this module called SummarySlide().

(b) In the General Declarations window, enter the code from Table 5-26 to declare the variables used in the module.

(c) Type `Sub Summary_Slide()` and then press the ENTER key. The End Sub statement should display automatically.

(d) Enter the Visual Basic code in Table 5-27 to determine the total number of slides in the presentation. Do not press the ENTER key after typing the End With statement in line 12.

Table 5-26 General Declarations

LINE	*VBA CODE*
1	`Dim mySlide As Integer`
2	`Dim SumText As String`
3	`Dim SummarySlideLines(5) As String`

Table 5-27 Determine Slide Count Procedure

LINE	*VBA CODE*
4	`' Determine the total number of slides`
5	`With ActivePresentation.Slides`
6	`  SlideCount = .Count + 1`
7	`End With`

(e) Enter the Visual Basic code in Table 5-28 to collect the titles from every slide.

Table 5-28 Collect Titles Procedure

LINE	*VBA CODE*
8	`' Collect the titles from every slide`
9	`For mySlide = 2 To SlideCount - 1`
10	` Set myPresentation = ActivePresentation.Slides(mySlide)`
11	` SummarySlideLines(mySlide) = myPresentation.Shapes.Title.TextFrame.TextRange.Text`
12	`Next mySlide`

(f) Add the Visual Basic code from Table 5-29 to add a slide at the end of the presentation and then insert the slide title.

Table 5-29 Add Summary Slide Procedure

LINE	*VBA CODE*
13	`' Add the summary slide`
14	`Set SumSlide = ActivePresentation.Slides.Add(SlideCount, ppLayoutText).Shapes`
15	`' Insert the title for the summary slide`
16	`SumSlide.Title.TextFrame.TextRange.Text = "In Conclusion"`

(continued)

Cases and Places

(g) Using the For/Next loop in Table 5-30, collect the slide titles into one long string of text. Press the ENTER key at the end of each title so the titles will display on separate lines in the slide.

Table 5-30 Collect Slide Titles Procedure

LINE	VBA CODE
17	`For mySlide = 2 To SlideCount - 1`
18	`SumText = SumText & SummarySlideLines(mySlide) & Chr(13)`
19	`Next mySlide`

(h) Insert the SumText module in Table 5-31 that places text into the text placeholder.

Table 5-31 Insert Summary Text Procedure

LINE	VBA CODE
20	`' Insert the titles in the slide text placeholder`
21	`SumSlide.Placeholders(2).TextFrame.TextRange.Text = SumText`
22	`End Sub`

(i) Create a button on the Formatting toolbar to execute the Summary_Slide() module.

(j) Save the Visual Basic code, and then save the presentation with the file name, Spring Break Update.

(k) Execute the Visual Basic program. Print the Visual Basic code and the slides using the Pure Black and White option. Quit PowerPoint.

7 ▶▶▶ Open the Teaching Portfolio presentation you created in this project. You would like to share the layout of your form with various colleagues to obtain their feedback on the forms layout. With the Visual Basic Editor open, search the Help files for the code to write a module that prints the form. Save the module as PrintThisForm. Using the Customize command on the Tools menu, locate your module in the Macro commands. Drag the PrintThisForm entry to the right of the Create Presentation button on the Resume toolbar. Modify this new button using the open pages image (row 6, column 1) on the Change Button Image palette. Name the button Print Form and then set the new button to the default style. Execute and then print the macro. Hand in the printouts to your instructor.

Microsoft PowerPoint 2002

PROJECT 6

Creating a Self-Running Presentation Containing Interactive Documents

OBJECTIVES

You will have mastered the material in this project when you can:

- Insert a slide from another presentation
- Add action buttons and action settings to slides
- Use guides to position an object
- Format action buttons by adding fill color, shadows, and lines
- Add captions to action buttons
- Format action button caption text
- Insert, size, and format a Radial diagram
- Add text to Radial diagram shapes
- Insert and format an AutoShape
- Add and format AutoShape text
- Apply a motion path animation effect to an AutoShape
- Create a self-running presentation
- Set slide show timings manually
- Start the self-running presentation and view interactive documents

Innovative Images Create Meaningful Messages

Films of the silent era launched the motion picture industry in the early twentieth century. Movies consisted of one-reel films only a few minutes long. At first a novelty, and then increasingly an art form, silent films reached greater intricacy and length in the early 1910s. Even without sound, these films portrayed numerous types of emotions and messages. Humans have relied on imagery to communicate since the beginning of time. Images play a vital role in relaying messages and promoting communication.

Individuals long have used pictures, or graphics, as guides for building structures involving complex spatial relationships. Imagine trying to build the pharaohs' pyramids without a plan drawn out on papyrus or a Boeing jet without engineering drawings.

Yet, in recent years, graphics, onscreen presentations, self-running presentations, online meetings, presentations on the Web, overhead transparencies, and 35mm slide shows have played an even greater role in the art of communication. People understand more easily when visual elements are combined. From sales presentations, to impressive slide shows in courtroom dramas, to disseminating information in kiosks, people turn to images to persuade others, to influence buying choices, or to adopt

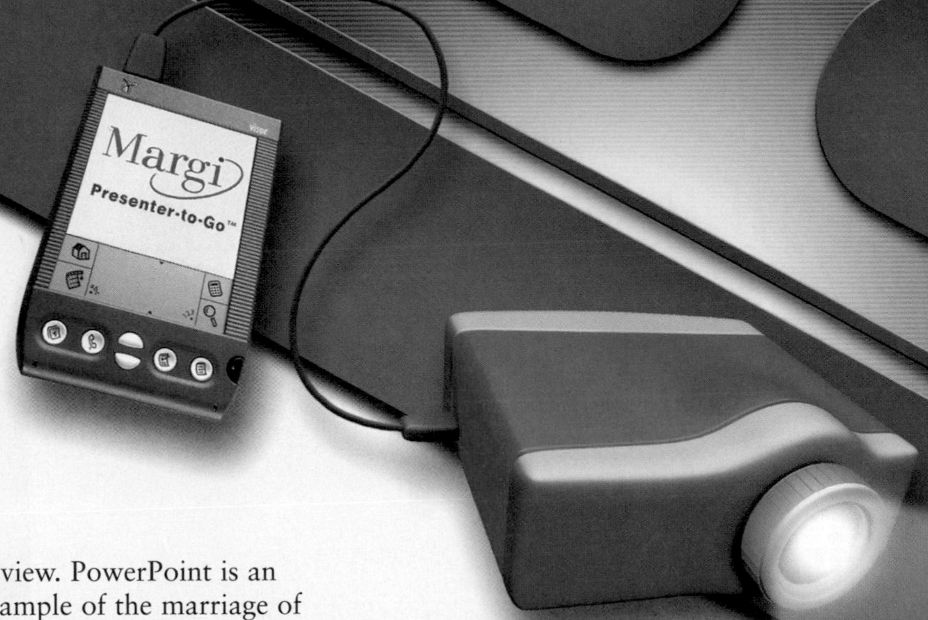

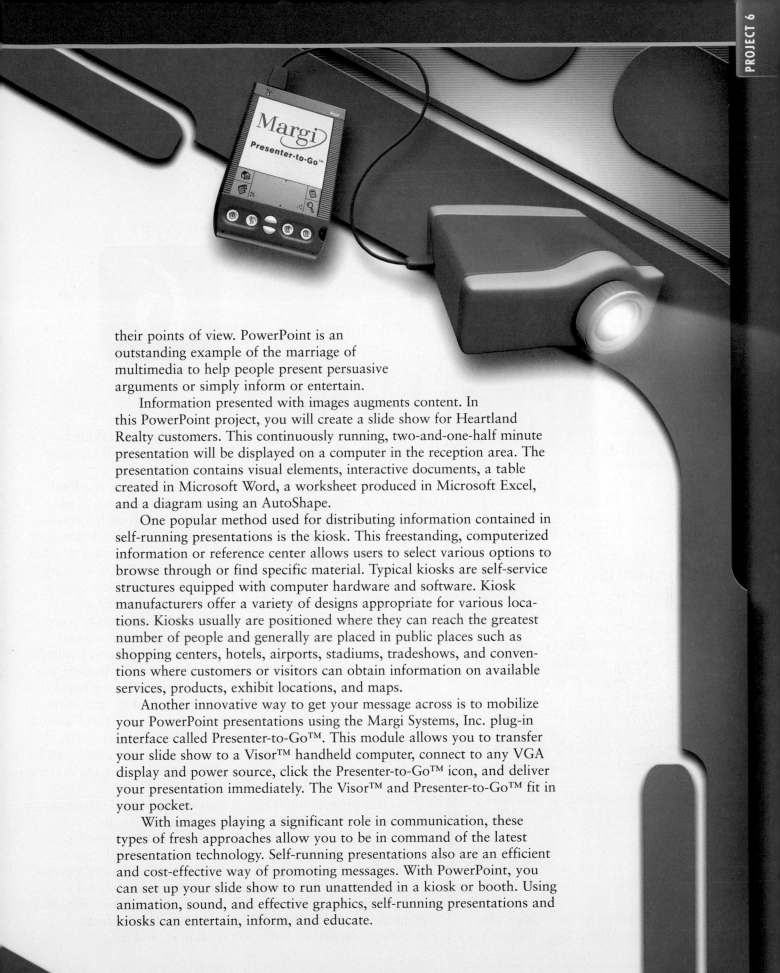

their points of view. PowerPoint is an outstanding example of the marriage of multimedia to help people present persuasive arguments or simply inform or entertain.

Information presented with images augments content. In this PowerPoint project, you will create a slide show for Heartland Realty customers. This continuously running, two-and-one-half minute presentation will be displayed on a computer in the reception area. The presentation contains visual elements, interactive documents, a table created in Microsoft Word, a worksheet produced in Microsoft Excel, and a diagram using an AutoShape.

One popular method used for distributing information contained in self-running presentations is the kiosk. This freestanding, computerized information or reference center allows users to select various options to browse through or find specific material. Typical kiosks are self-service structures equipped with computer hardware and software. Kiosk manufacturers offer a variety of designs appropriate for various locations. Kiosks usually are positioned where they can reach the greatest number of people and generally are placed in public places such as shopping centers, hotels, airports, stadiums, tradeshows, and conventions where customers or visitors can obtain information on available services, products, exhibit locations, and maps.

Another innovative way to get your message across is to mobilize your PowerPoint presentations using the Margi Systems, Inc. plug-in interface called Presenter-to-Go™. This module allows you to transfer your slide show to a Visor™ handheld computer, connect to any VGA display and power source, click the Presenter-to-Go™ icon, and deliver your presentation immediately. The Visor™ and Presenter-to-Go™ fit in your pocket.

With images playing a significant role in communication, these types of fresh approaches allow you to be in command of the latest presentation technology. Self-running presentations also are an efficient and cost-effective way of promoting messages. With PowerPoint, you can set up your slide show to run unattended in a kiosk or booth. Using animation, sound, and effective graphics, self-running presentations and kiosks can entertain, inform, and educate.

Microsoft PowerPoint 2002

Creating a Self-Running Presentation Containing Interactive Documents

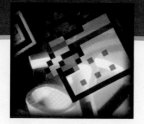

PROJECT 6

CASE PERSPECTIVE

Owning a home is the ultimate dream for many people, but buying the right home can be complicated. Potential buyers must be financially qualified, and they need to understand mortgage options and how much money they can afford to buy a house. Buyers often use worksheets to determine their eligibility in order to investigate various lending options.

At Heartland Realty, you assist real estate agents in scheduling workshops on financing options and loan documentation. They want to conduct a workshop for first-time home buyers, but no slide show exists on that topic. You decide to use your PowerPoint skills to create this presentation. The slide show will consist of one slide from an existing presentation and three new slides to cover prequalification review, the maximum affordable home price, and the benefits of home ownership. You will create an interactive slide show that includes a program to determine the debt-to-income ratio, a worksheet created in Microsoft Excel that allows buyers to determine the maximum selling price, a table created in Microsoft Word that shows the interest rate factor, and a diagram using an AutoShape that shows the benefits of home ownership.

Introduction

People thirst for information. From catching the breaking news on cable television to downloading their latest e-mail messages, individuals keep up with the day's events.

One method used for disseminating information is a **kiosk**. This freestanding, self-service structure is equipped with computer hardware and software and is used to provide information or reference materials to the public. Some have a touch screen or keyboard that serves as an input device and allows users to select various options to browse through or find specific information. Kiosks frequently are found in public places, such as shopping centers, hotels, museums, libraries, and airport terminals.

Every presentation is created for a specific audience. Sometimes, when running a slide show, you want to open another application to show more detailed information about a particular topic. For example, when presenting mortgage information, you may want to show an estimated affordable home price based on the buyer's income and debts and the percentage and term of the loan. PowerPoint allows you to show these figures without leaving the presentation by using interactive documents. An **interactive document** is a file created in another application, such as Microsoft Word or Excel, and then opened during the running of a slide show.

In this project, you will create a slide show for Heartland Realty customers. This show will run continuously on a computer in the reception area, so potential first-time home buyers can view five slides during the brief two-and-one-half-minute presentation that gives them information on purchasing a property. The five presentation slides are shown in Figures 6-1a, 6-1b, 6-1d, 6-1f, and 6-1h. The users also can advance the slides manually to interact with the presentation. The interactive documents are shown in Figures 6-1c, 6-1e, and 6-1g.

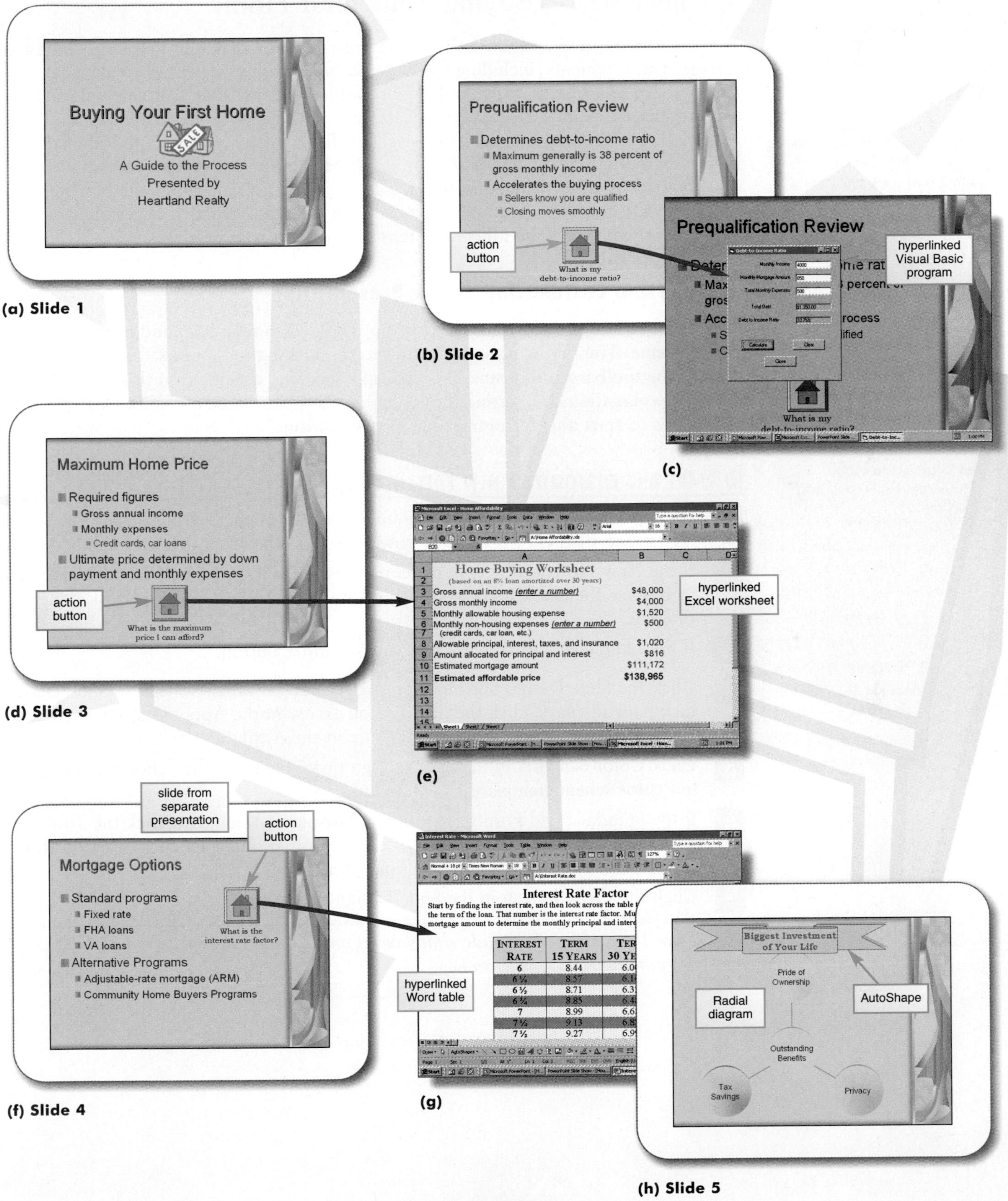
Buying Your First Home
SALE
A Guide to the Process
Presented by
Heartland Realty
(a) Slide 1
Prequalification Review
Determines debt-to-income ratio
Maximum generally is 38 percent of gross monthly income
Accelerates the buying process
Sellers know you are qualified
Closing moves smoothly
action button
What is my debt-to-income ratio?
(b) Slide 2
hyperlinked Visual Basic program
(c)
Maximum Home Price
Required figures
Gross annual income
Monthly expenses
Credit cards, car loans
Ultimate price determined by down payment and monthly expenses
action button
What is the maximum price I can afford?
(d) Slide 3
Home Buying Worksheet
(based on an 8% loan amortized over 30 years)
Gross annual income (enter a number) $48,000
Gross monthly income $4,000
Monthly allowable housing expense $1,520
Monthly non-housing expenses (enter a number) $500
(credit cards, car loan, etc.)
Allowable principal, interest, taxes, and insurance $1,020
Amount allocated for principal and interest $816
Estimated mortgage amount $111,172
Estimated affordable price $138,965
hyperlinked Excel worksheet
(e)
slide from separate presentation
action button
Mortgage Options
Standard programs
Fixed rate
FHA loans
VA loans
Alternative Programs
Adjustable-rate mortgage (ARM)
Community Home Buyers Programs
What is the interest rate factor?
(f) Slide 4
Interest Rate Factor
hyperlinked Word table
(g)
Biggest Investment of Your Life
Pride of Ownership
Radial diagram
AutoShape
Outstanding Benefits
Tax Savings
Privacy
(h) Slide 5

FIGURE 6-1

Project Six — Buying Your First Home

More About

Kiosks

Kiosks allow customers to place orders, make payments, and access the Internet. Many kiosks have multimedia devices for playing sound and video. Military bases have installed kiosks that allow personnel to conduct personal business and communicate with friends and family by sending video clips and photographs. Governments worldwide have installed kiosks that provide Internet access to public services and information. For more information, visit the PowerPoint 2002 More About Web page (scsite.com/pp2002/more.htm) and then click Kiosk.

The self-running two-and-one-half-minute presentation created in Project 6 contains several visual elements, including three action buttons that hyperlink to a Visual Basic program, an Excel chart, and a Word table. The last slide contains a Radial diagram and an AutoShape that emphasize the advantages of home ownership. Automatic slide timings are set so these slides display after a desired period of time. The presentation then is designated to be a self-running presentation so that it restarts when it is finished. As with other PowerPoint presentations, the first steps are to create a new presentation, select a design template, create a title slide, and save the presentation. The following steps illustrate these procedures.

Starting and Customizing a New Presentation

To begin, create a new presentation, apply a design template, and change the color scheme. The following steps review accomplishing these tasks. You also need to reset the toolbars and menus so they display exactly as shown in this book. For a detailed explanation of resetting the toolbars and menus, see Appendix D. Perform these steps to start and customize a new presentation.

TO START AND CUSTOMIZE A NEW PRESENTATION

1. Click the Start button on the Windows taskbar, point to Programs on the Start menu, and then click Microsoft PowerPoint on the Programs submenu.
2. If the New Presentation task pane displays, click the Show at startup check box to remove the check mark and then click the Close button on the task pane title bar.
3. If the Language bar displays, click its Minimize button.
4. Click the Slide Design button on the Formatting toolbar. When the Slide Design task pane displays, click the down scroll arrow in the Apply a design template list, and then click the Kimono template in the Available For Use area.
5. Click Color Schemes in the Slide Design task pane, and then click the bottom-left color scheme template (row 4, column 1).
6. If the Standard and Formatting toolbars display on one row, click the Toolbar Options button on the right side of either toolbar and then click Show Buttons on Two Rows on the Toolbar Options menu.
7. Click the Close button in the Slide Design task pane.

Slide 1 has the desired Title Slide slide layout and Kimono design template with a revised color scheme (Figure 6-2).

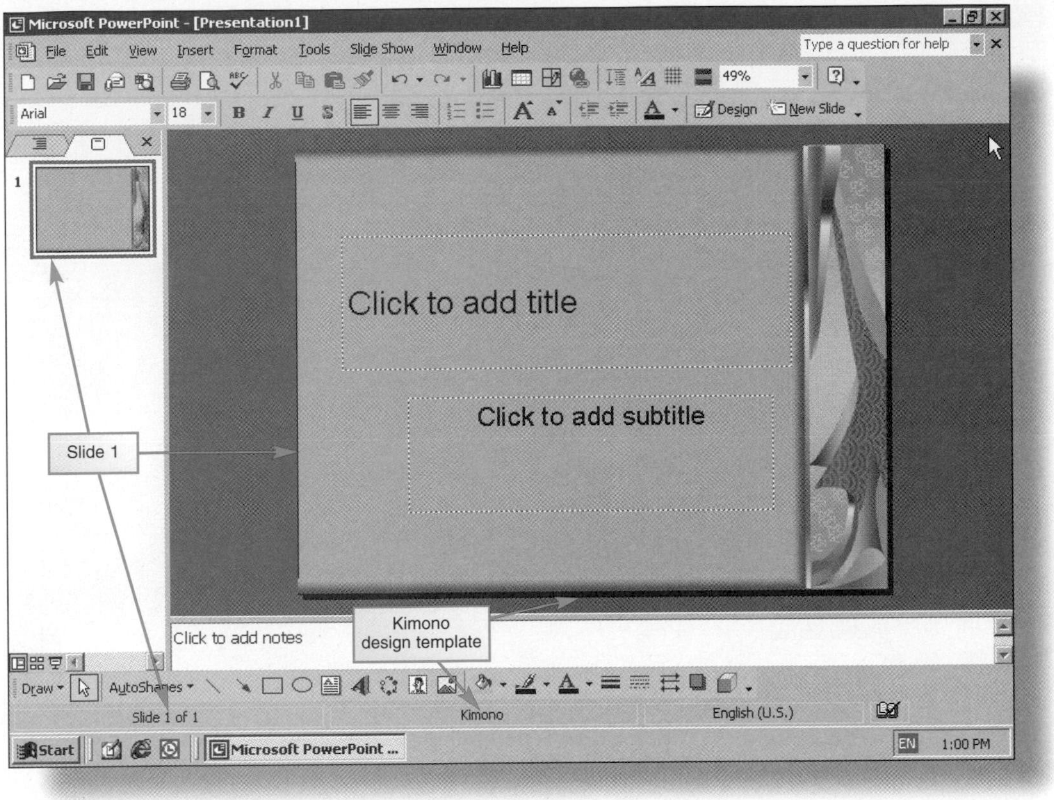

FIGURE 6-2

Creating the Title Slide

The purpose of this presentation is to guide potential homeowners through the buying process. The slide show will give helpful pointers to enhance their meetings with real estate agents. The opening slide should introduce this concept. Perform the following steps to create a title slide.

TO CREATE A TITLE SLIDE

1. Click the title text placeholder to select it.
2. Type `Buying Your First Home` in the title text placeholder.
3. Press CTRL+ENTER to move the insertion point to the subtitle text placeholder.
4. Type `A Guide to the Process` and then press SHIFT+ENTER to create a line break.
5. Type `Presented by` and then press SHIFT+ENTER.
6. Type `Heartland Realty` but do not press the ENTER key.

The title text and subtitle text display on Slide 1 as shown in Figure 6-3 on the next page.

More About

The PowerPoint Help System

Need Help? It is no further than the Ask a Question box in the upper-right corner of the window. Click the box that contains the text, Type a question for help (Figure 6-2), type `help`, and then press the ENTER key. PowerPoint will respond with a list of items you can click to learn about obtaining help on any PowerPoint-related topic. To find out what is new in PowerPoint 2002, type `what's new in PowerPoint` in the Ask a Question box.

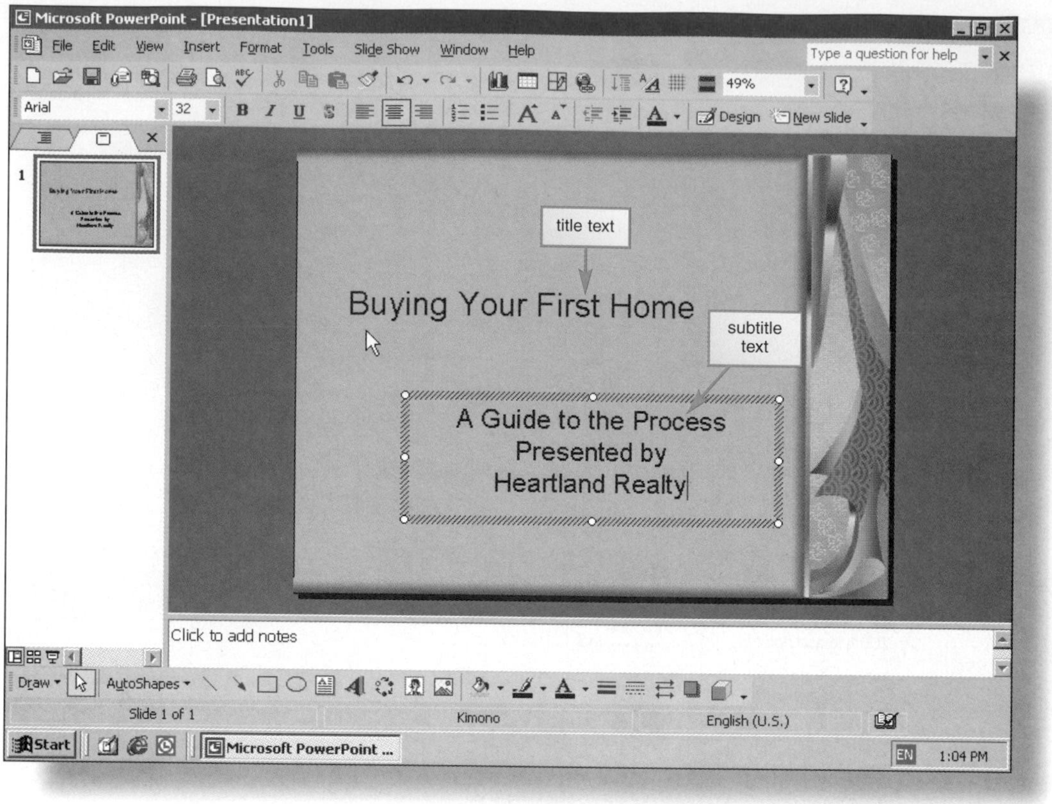

FIGURE 6-3

Creating Slide 2

The **prequalification review process** gives potential home buyers an accurate idea of the maximum home price they can afford. As a standard real estate industry guideline, lenders desire monthly debt to not exceed 38 percent of monthly income. When buyers meet this financial requirement, they can shop for a home with confidence, and sellers can appreciate they are dealing with serious buyers. This debt-to-income ratio is described on the second slide in the presentation. It contains a button that runs a Visual Basic program that allows users to determine if their debt-to-income ratio exceeds 38 percent. Perform the following steps to create Slide 2.

More About

Home Buying

First-time house buyers can find a wealth of information on the Internet. Web sites offer information about mortgages, inspections, closings, and checklists. For more information, visit the PowerPoint 2002 More About Web page (scsite.com/pp2002/more.htm) and then click Home Buying.

TO CREATE SLIDE 2

1. Click the New Slide button on the Formatting toolbar.
2. Type `Prequalification Review` in the title text placeholder.
3. Press CTRL+ENTER to move the insertion point to the body text placeholder.
4. Type `Determines debt-to-income ratio` and then press the ENTER key.
5. Press the TAB key. Type `Maximum generally is 38 percent of gross monthly income` and then press the ENTER key.
6. Type `Accelerates the buying process` and then press the ENTER key.
7. Press the TAB key. Type `Sellers know you are qualified` and then press the ENTER key.

8 Type `Closing moves smoothly` but do not press the ENTER key. Point to the New Slide button on the Formatting toolbar.

The Slide 2 title text and body text display (Figure 6-4).

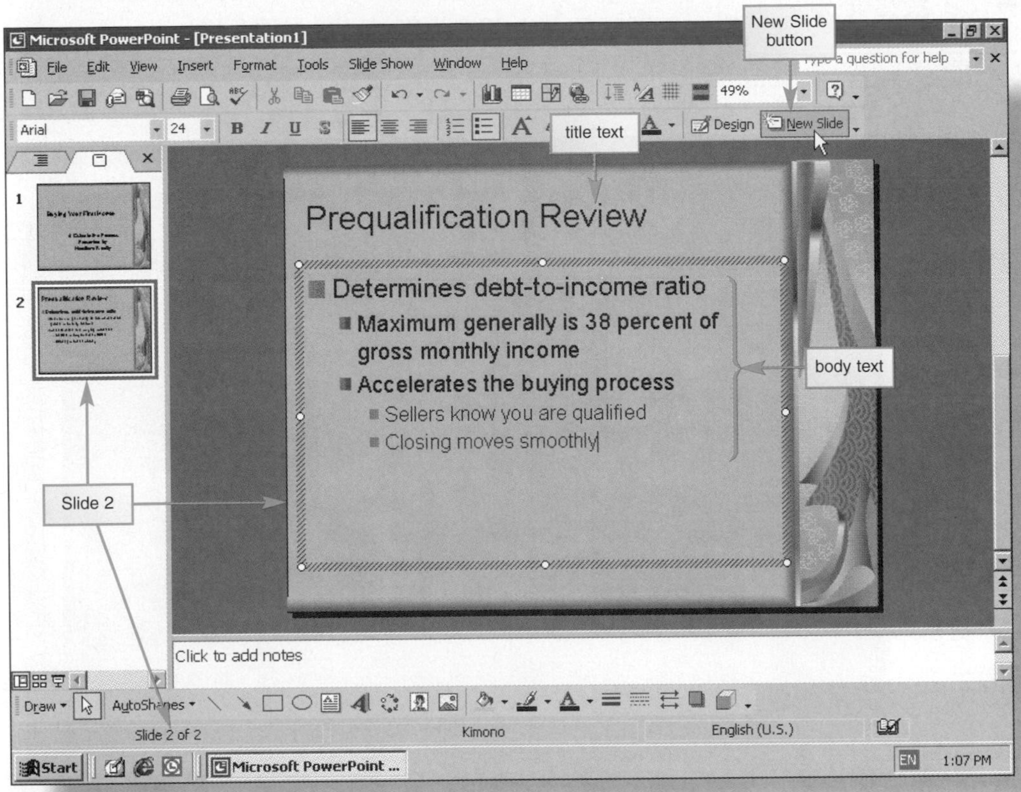

FIGURE 6-4

Creating Slide 3

The maximum home price is computed based on the buyer's monthly annual income; housing expenses, such as utilities and repairs; non-housing expenses, such as tuition loans, credit card payments, and car loans; housing obligations, including taxes and insurance; and mortgage payment. The third slide in the presentation describes the maximum home price. It contains a button that displays an Excel worksheet allowing buyers to compute their estimated affordable home price. Perform the following steps to create Slide 3.

TO CREATE SLIDE 3

1. Click the New Slide button on the Formatting toolbar.
2. Type `Maximum Home Price` in the title text placeholder.
3. Press CTRL+ENTER to move the insertion point to the body text placeholder.
4. Type `Required figures` and then press the ENTER key.
5. Press the TAB key. Type `Gross annual income` and then press the ENTER key.

More About

Inserting Slide Numbers

Slide numbers help organize the slides. To insert a slide number on every side except the title slide, click Insert on the menu bar and then click Slide Number. When the Header and Footer dialog box displays, click Date and time in the Include on slide area, click Slide number, click Footer, click Don't show on title slide, and then click the Apply to All button.

6 Type `Monthly expenses` and then press the ENTER key.

7 Press the TAB key. Type `Credit cards, car loans` and then press the ENTER key.

8 Press SHIFT+TAB two times. Type `Ultimate price determined by down payment and monthly expenses` but do not press the ENTER key.

The Slide 3 title text and body text display (Figure 6-5).

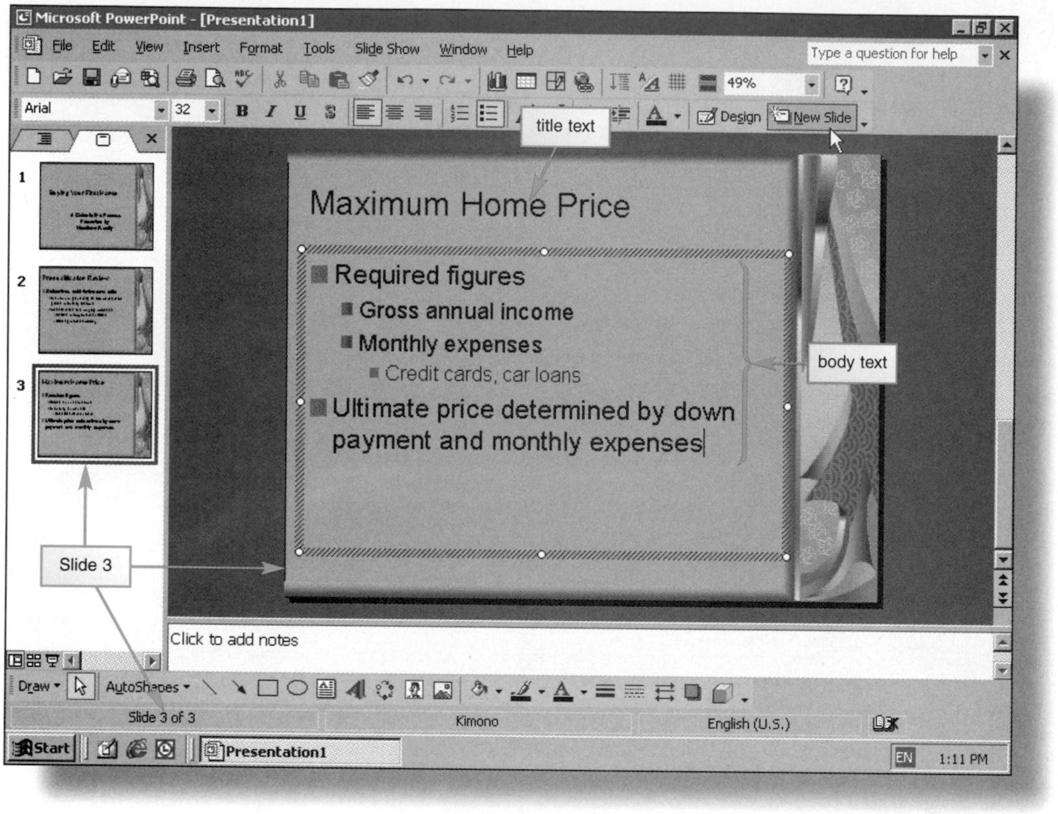

FIGURE 6-5

Adding a Presentation within a Presentation

Occasionally, you may need a slide from another presentation in the presentation you are creating. PowerPoint makes it easy to insert one or more slides from other presentations.

More About

Audiences

A relaxed and refreshed audience often is willing to listen to new concepts. Researchers suggest that audiences are most prone to feel these emotions on Sundays, Mondays, and Tuesdays. Viewers generally have less time to consider the major points of a presentation at the end of the week.

Inserting a Slide from Another Presentation

The PowerPoint presentation with the file name, Mortgage Basics, describes various mortgage types. It contains four slides, and the third slide, shown in Figure 6-6c, lists standard and alternative mortgage types. The Mortgage Basics file is on your Data Disk. See the inside back cover of this book for instructions for downloading the Data Disk or see your instructor for information on accessing the files required for this book. The steps on page PP 6.12 demonstrate how to insert Slide 3 from that file into your presentation.

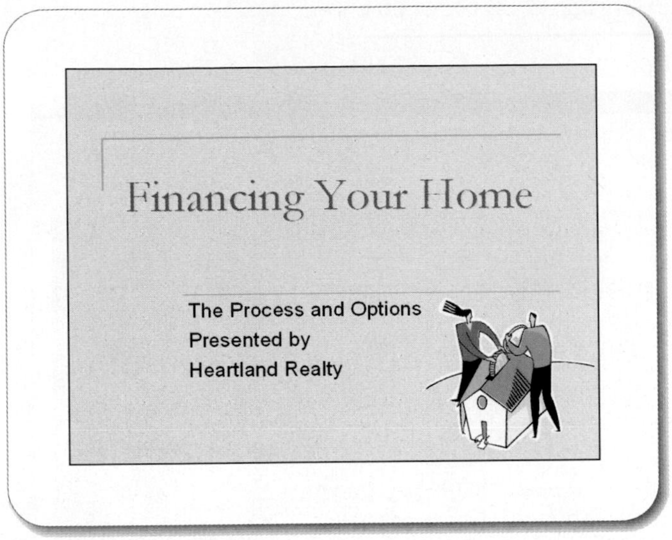

(a) Slide 1

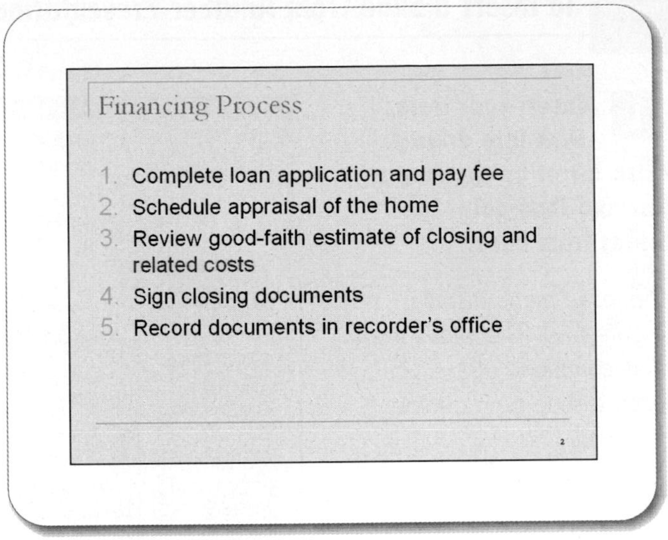

(b) Slide 2

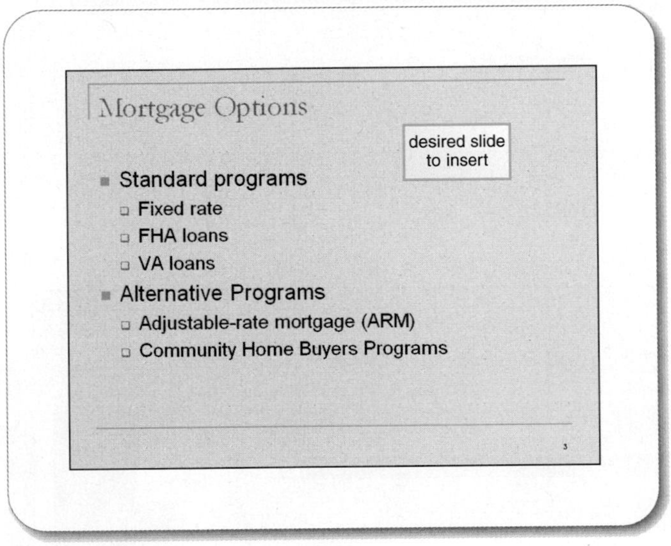

(c) Slide 3

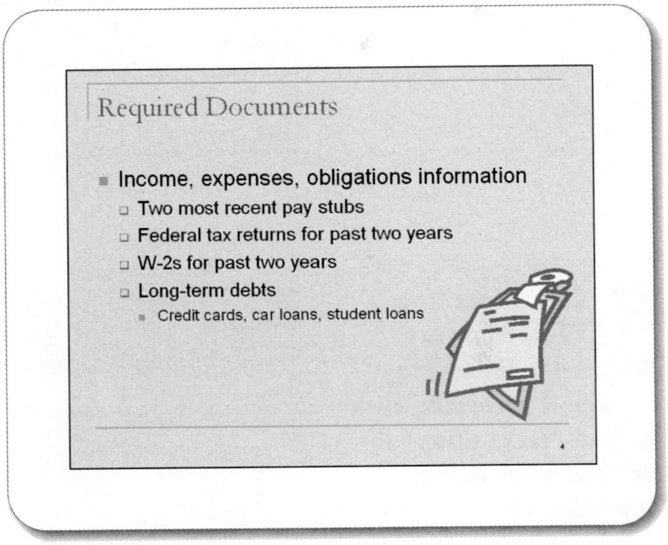

(d) Slide 4

FIGURE 6-6

Steps To Insert a Slide from Another Presentation

1 Insert your Data Disk into drive A. Click Insert on the menu bar and then point to Slides from Files.

The Insert menu displays (Figure 6-7). The ***Slides from Files command*** *allows you to insert a slide from another PowerPoint file.*

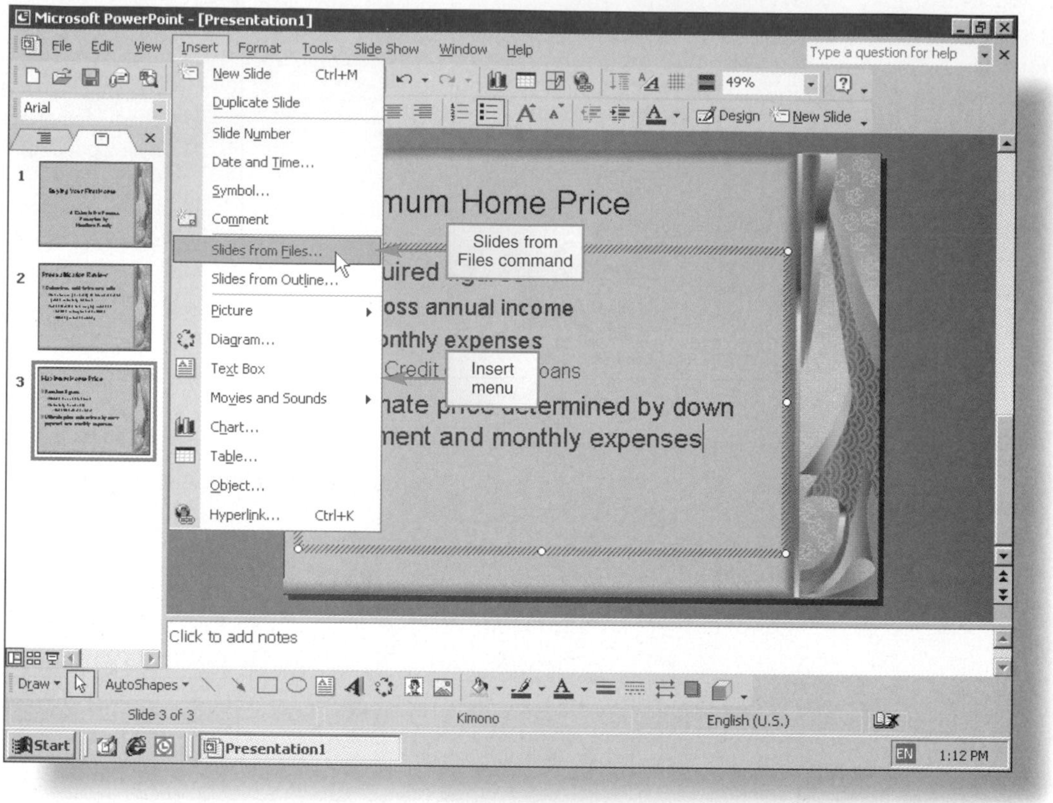

FIGURE 6-7

2 Click Slides from Files. When the Slide Finder dialog box displays, if necessary, click the Find Presentation tab and then point to the Browse button.

The Slide Finder dialog box displays (Figure 6-8). If you use several presentations on a regular basis, you can add them to your List of Favorites so you can find them easily.

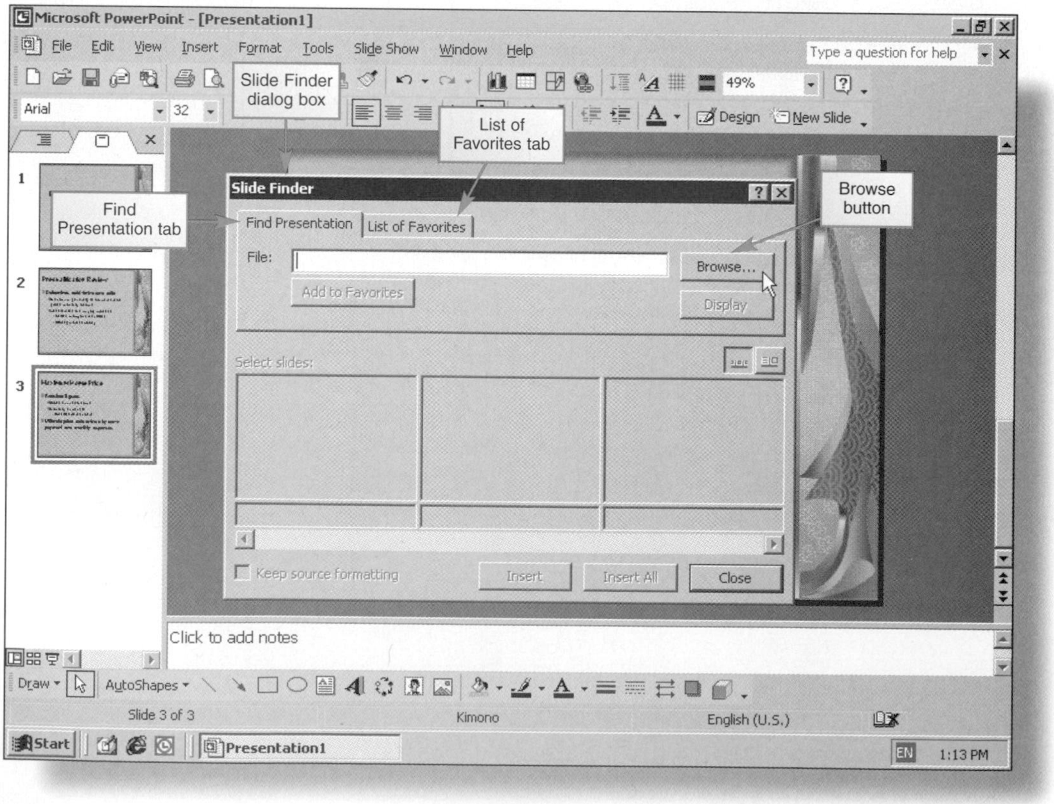

FIGURE 6-8

3 Click the Browse button. Click the Look in box arrow and then click 3½ Floppy (A:). Click Mortgage Basics in the list. Point to the Open button.

The Browse dialog box displays (Figure 6-9). A list displays the files that PowerPoint can open. Your list of file names may vary. Mortgage Basics is the file that contains the slide you will insert.

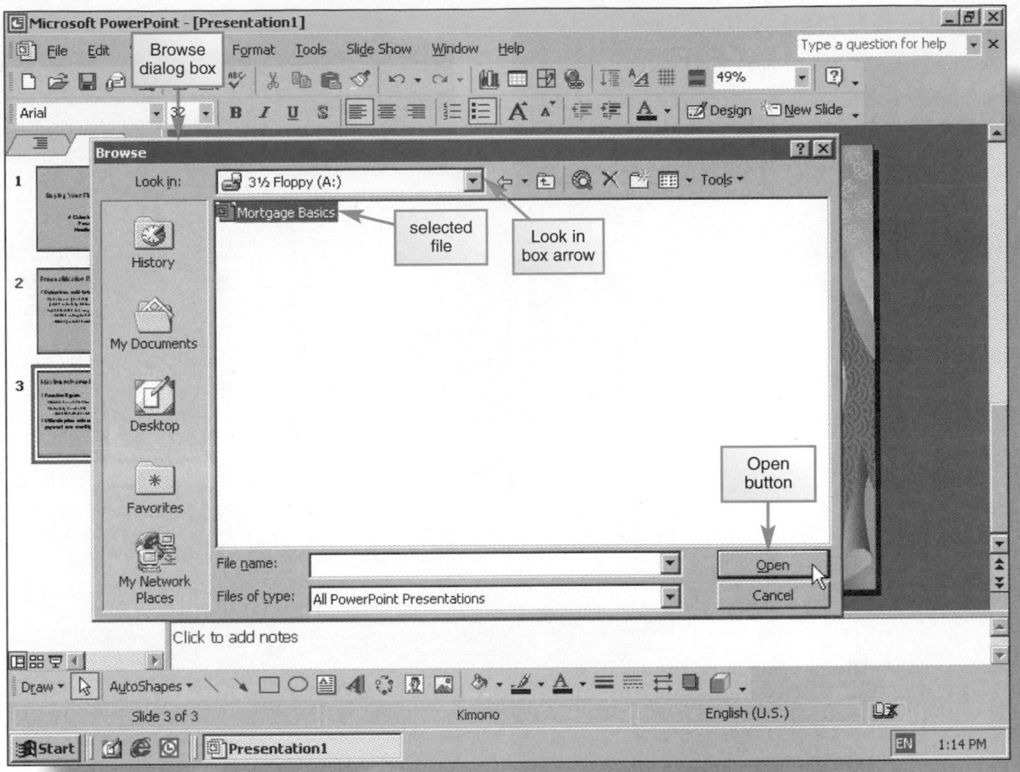

FIGURE 6-9

4 Click the Open button. Click the Slide 3 image, Mortgage Options, in the Select slides area. Point to the Insert button.

The Slide Finder dialog box displays (Figure 6-10). The selected file, A:\Mortgage Basics.ppt, displays in the File text box. Slide 3 of this presentation is the slide to insert in your presentation.

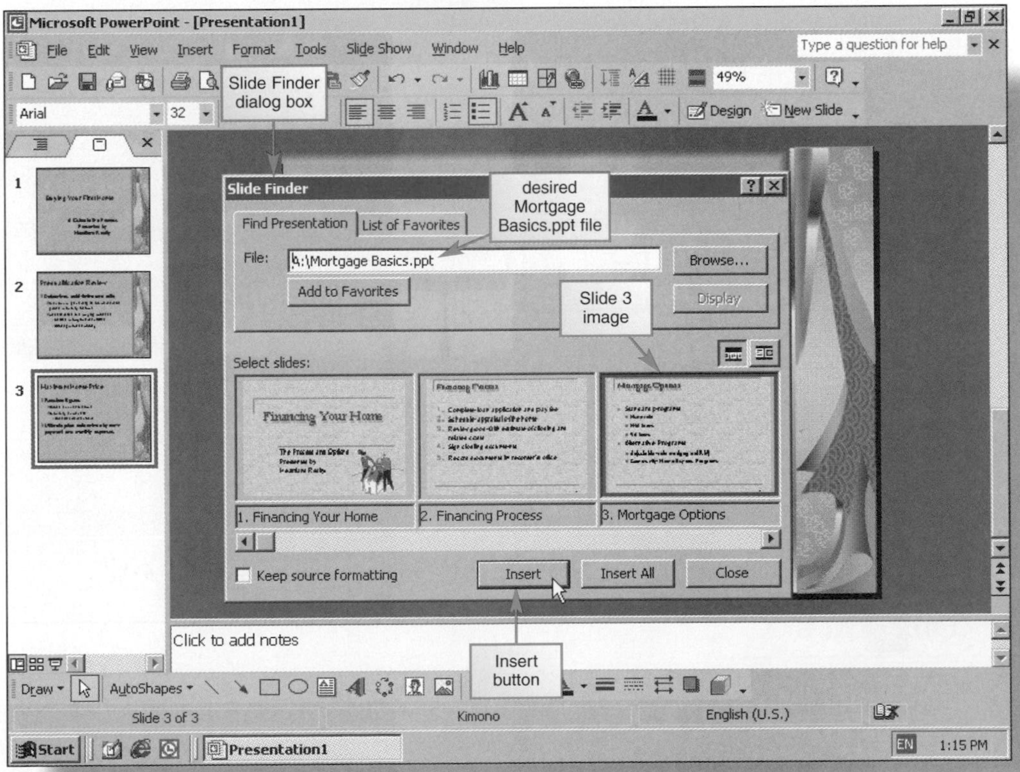

FIGURE 6-10

5 Click the Insert button. Point to the Close button.

PowerPoint inserts the Mortgage Basics Slide 3 in your presentation (Figure 6-11). The Slide Finder dialog box remains open to allow you to insert additional slides.

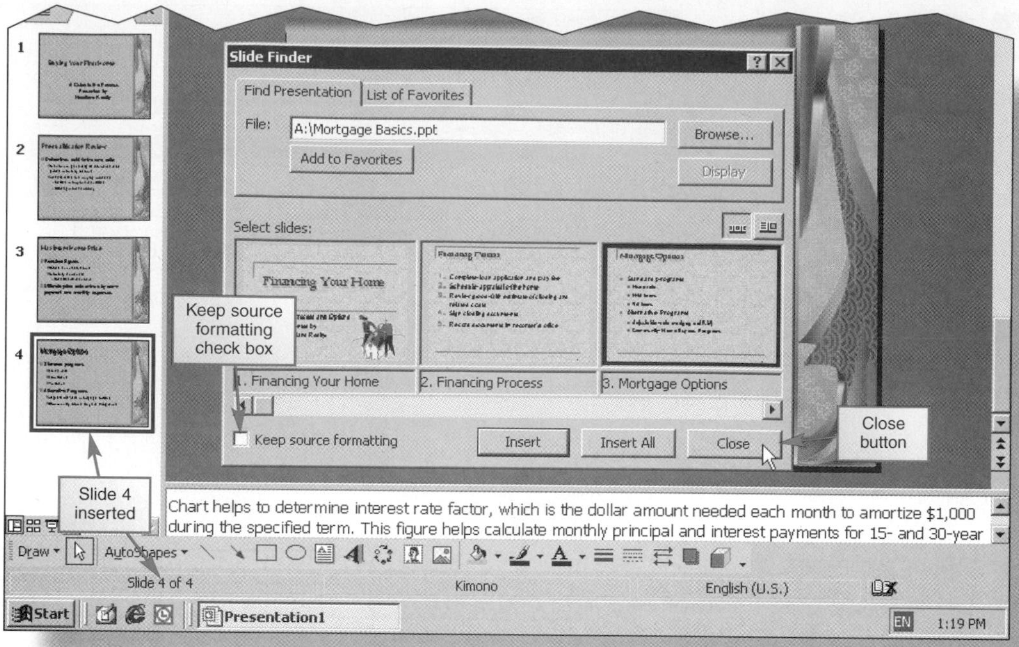

FIGURE 6-11

6 Click the Close button.

Your presentation consists of four slides (Figure 6-12).

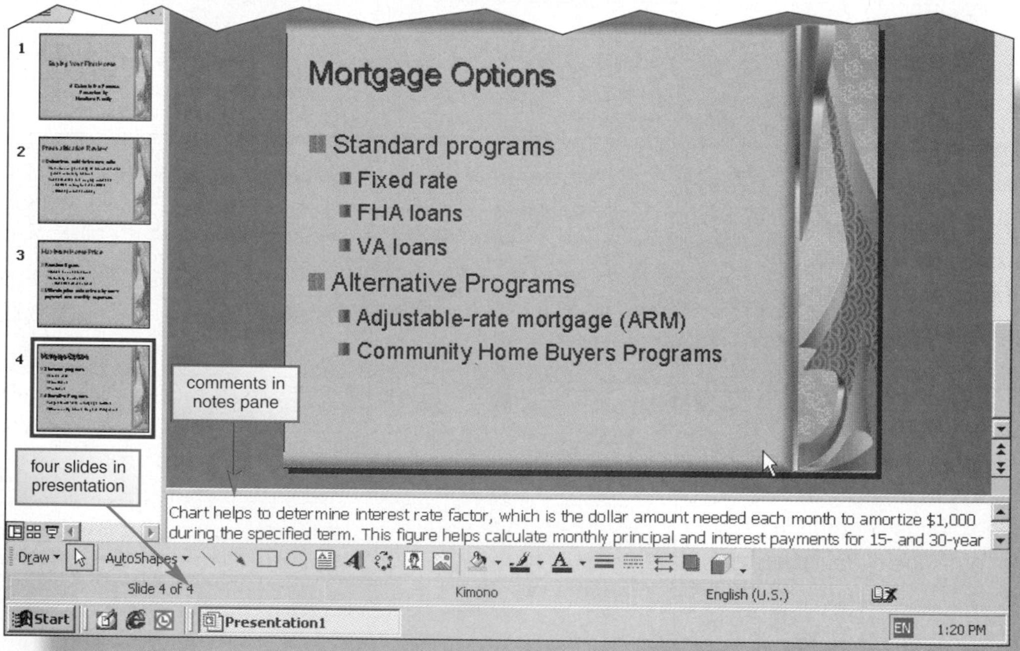

FIGURE 6-12

Other Ways

1. Press ALT+I, press F, press ALT+B, select desired file, press ALT+O, select desired slide, press I, press ESC
2. In Voice Command mode, say "Insert, Slides from Files, Browse, [type file name], Open, [select slide], Insert, Close"

The Kimono design template and revised color scheme are applied to the new Slide 4. To retain the Edge design template that is applied to the Mortgage Basics slides, you would click Keep source formatting in the Slide Finder dialog box. If desired, you could have selected additional slides from the Mortgage Basics presentation or from other slide shows. If you might use the Mortgage Basics file later, you can add that file to your Favorites folder so it is accessible readily.

Adding Notes to Slides

In this project, Slides 2 and 4 have comments. Slide 4 retains the comments that were inserted for the Mortgage Basics presentation. Perform the following step to add text to the notes pane on Slide 2.

TO ADD NOTES

1 Click the Slide 2 slide thumbnail in the tabs pane, click the notes pane, and then type `A prequalification review is a simple, quick process that tells only how much of a loan a potential buyer can afford.`

The information in this note supplements the text in the slide (Figure 6-13).

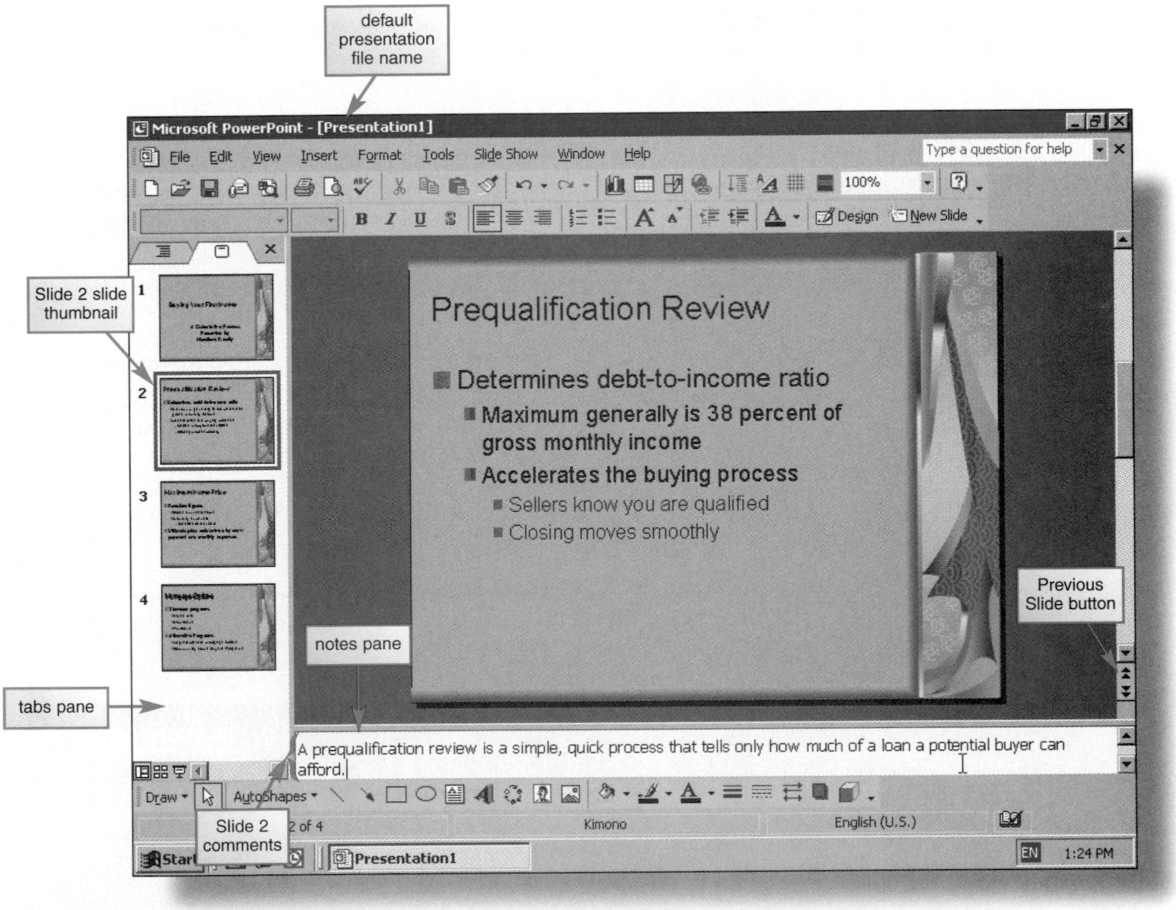

FIGURE 6-13

Saving the Presentation

You now should save your presentation because you have done a substantial amount of work. The following steps save the presentation.

TO SAVE A PRESENTATION

1 Click the Save button on the Standard toolbar.

2 Type `House Buying` in the File name text box.

3. Click the Save in box arrow. Click 3½ Floppy (A:) in the Save in list.
4. Click the Save button in the Save As dialog box.

The presentation is saved on the floppy disk in drive A with the file name, House Buying. This file name displays on the title bar.

The presentation contains four slides with text. The next section inserts a clip and adds timings to Slide 1.

Inserting, Sizing, and Moving a Clip on a Slide

With all the desired text added to the slides in the presentation, the next step is to add the animated house clip to Slide 1. Perform the following steps to add and size this clip and then move it to the center of the slide.

TO INSERT, SIZE, AND MOVE A CLIP ON A SLIDE

1. Click the Previous Slide button to display Slide 1. Click the Insert Clip Art button on the Drawing toolbar. When the Insert Clip Art task pane displays, type `for sale` in the Search text text box and then click the Search button. Click the animated pink and gray house or another appropriate clip. Click the Close button on the Insert Clip Art task pane title bar.
2. Right-click the clip and then click Format Picture on the shortcut menu. If necessary, click the Size tab when the Format Picture dialog box displays. Double-click the Height text box in the Scale area and then type `250` in the box. Click the OK button.
3. If necessary, use the arrow keys to move the clip to the center of the slide between the title text and the subtitle text.

The selected clip is inserted into Slide 1, sized, and moved to the desired location (Figure 6-14).

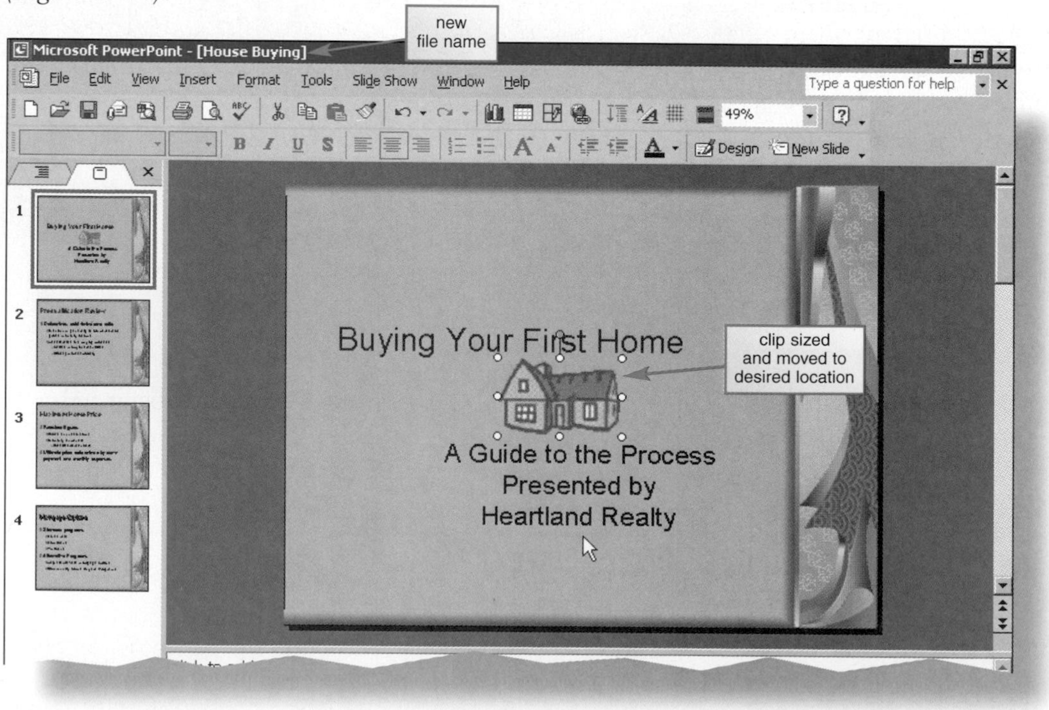

FIGURE 6-14

Creating an Interactive Document

The next step in customizing the House Buying presentation is to edit slides so they connect to three files with additional information. You edit Slides 2, 3, and 4 to contain three hyperlinks: one to a Visual Basic program, debtratio; another to a Microsoft Excel worksheet, Home Affordability; and a third to a Microsoft Word document, Interest Rate. These files are stored on the Data Disk. Figure 6-1(b) on page PP 6.05 contains an action button to reference the debtratio program. This program determines the buyer's debt-to-income ratio.

An **action button** is a built-in 3-D button that can perform specific tasks such as display the next slide, provide help, give information, and play a sound. In addition, the action button can activate a **hyperlink**, which is a shortcut that allows users to jump to another program, in this case Visual Basic, Microsoft Excel, and Microsoft Word, and load a specific file. A hyperlink also allows users to move to specific slides in a PowerPoint presentation or to an Internet address. In this slide, you will associate the hyperlink with an action button, but you also can use text or any object, including shapes, tables, or pictures. You specify which action you want PowerPoint to perform by using the **Action Settings** command on the Slide Show menu.

When you run the House Buying presentation and click the action button on Slide 2, PowerPoint runs the Visual Basic program. Once you have finished running the Visual Basic program, you will return to Slide 2 by clicking the Close button on the Debt-to-Income Ratio form.

Creating the slide requires several steps. First, add an action button and create a hyperlink to the Visual Basic program. Then, scale the button, add color, and add a caption. The next several sections explain how to add an action button and an action setting to the slide.

Adding an Action Button and Action Settings

You will display additional information about qualifying for a mortgage by running the Visual Basic program without quitting PowerPoint. To obtain details on the buyer's debt-to-income ratio, you will click the action button. When you click the button, a coin sound will play. The next section describes how to create the action button and place it on Slide 2.

More About

Activating Hyperlinks

In this presentation, you activate a hyperlink by clicking an action button. You also have the option of activating the hyperlink by placing the mouse pointer over the button. To specify this option, click the Mouse Over tab in the Action Settings dialog box and then select the desired controls.

More About

Visual Basic

Millions of developers worldwide use the Visual Basic language and programming system to create computer software components and applications. This set of tools and technologies is an extremely powerful, versatile, and complex system for Windows desktop applications, reusable software components for building other applications, and applications targeted for the Internet and intranets. For more information, visit the PowerPoint 2002 More About Web page (scsite.com/pp2002/more.htm) and then click Visual Basic.

Steps To Add an Action Button and Action Settings

1 **Click the Next Slide button to display Slide 2. Click Slide Show on the menu bar, point to Action Buttons, and then point to Action Button: Home on the Action Buttons submenu.**

The Action Buttons submenu displays 12 built-in 3-D buttons (Figure 6-15).

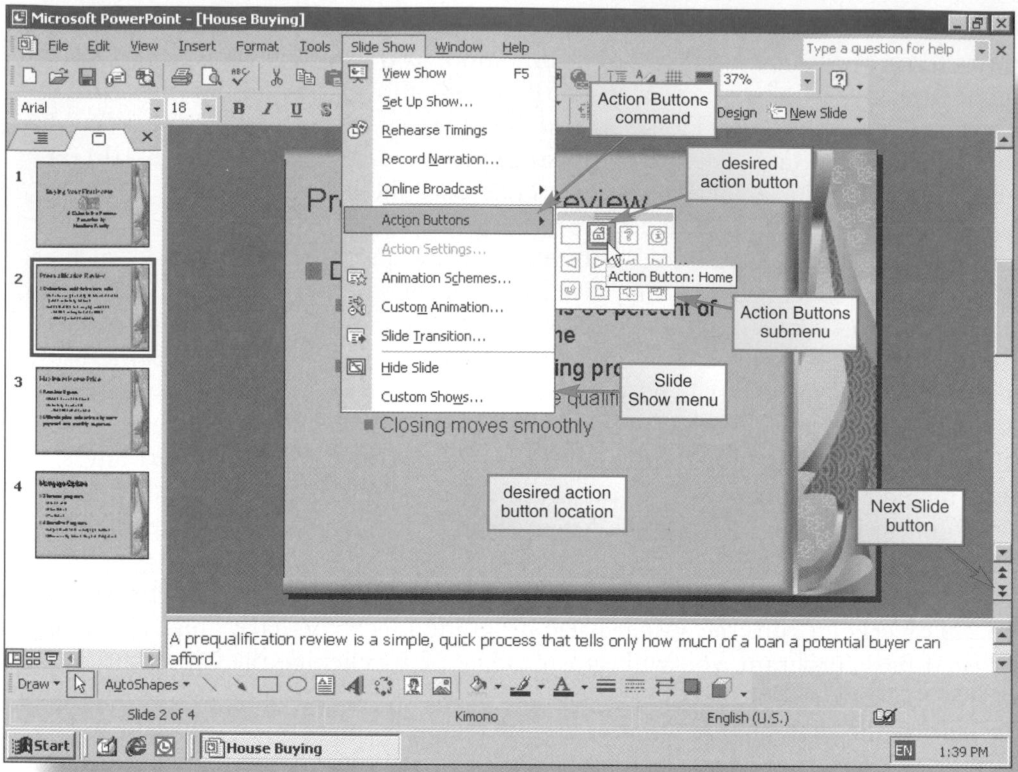

FIGURE 6-15

2 **Click Action Button: Home. Click the bottom center of Slide 2 below the last text paragraph. When the Actions Settings dialog box displays, if necessary, click the Mouse Click tab. Point to the Hyperlink to box arrow.**

The Action Settings dialog box displays (Figure 6-16) with the action button placed on Slide 2. Hyperlink to is the default Action on click.

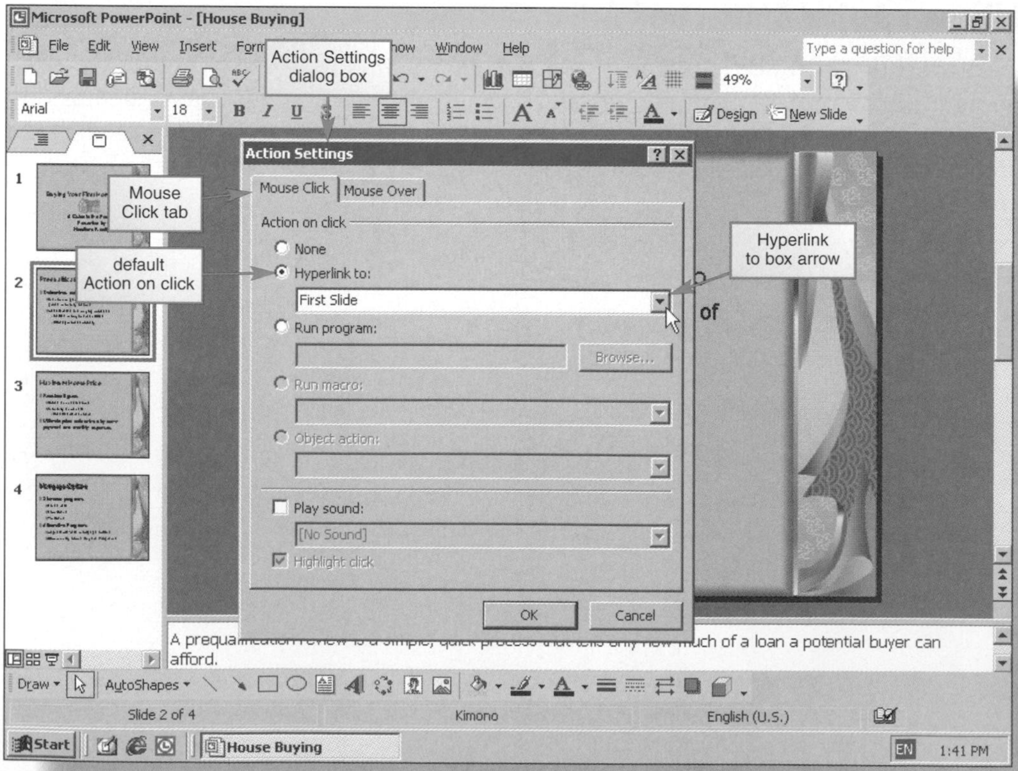

FIGURE 6-16

3 Click the Hyperlink to box arrow, click the down scroll arrow to scroll through the list of locations, and then point to Other File.

The list box displays the possible locations in the slide show or elsewhere where a hyperlink can be established (Figure 6-17). Other File is selected.

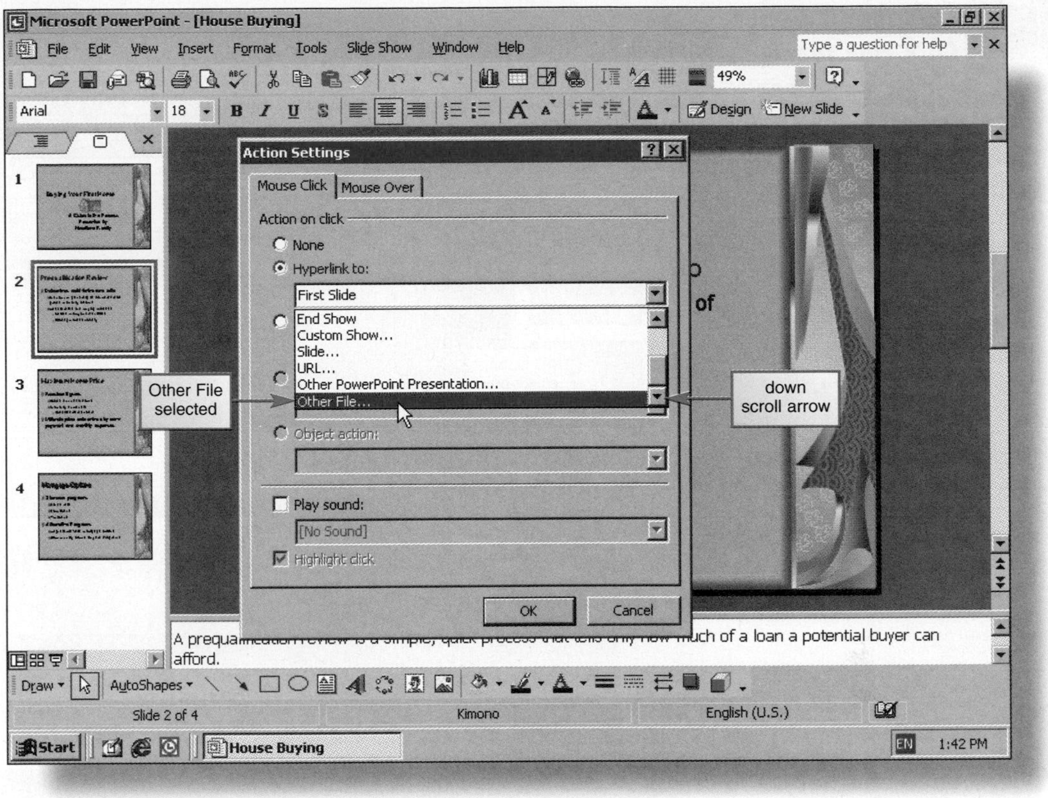

FIGURE 6-17

4 Click Other File. When the Hyperlink to Other File dialog box displays, if necessary, click the Look in box arrow and then click 3½ Floppy (A:). Click debtratio. Point to the OK button.

The debtratio file name is the Visual Basic file you will link to the action button (Figure 6-18). Your list of file names may vary.

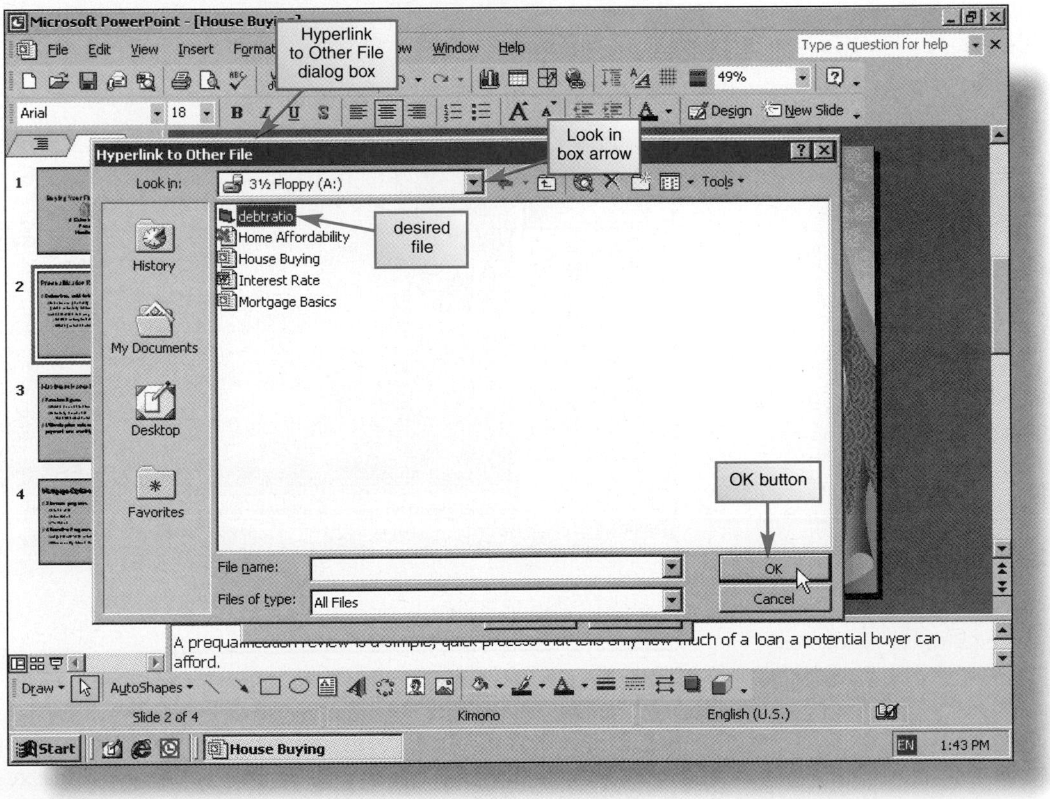

FIGURE 6-18

5 Click the OK button. Click Play sound, click the Play sound box arrow, click the down scroll arrow, and then point to Coin.

The Hyperlink to box displays the Visual Basic program file name, debtratio (Figure 6-19). A check mark displays in the Play sound check box. The Play sound list displays sounds that can play when you click the action button.

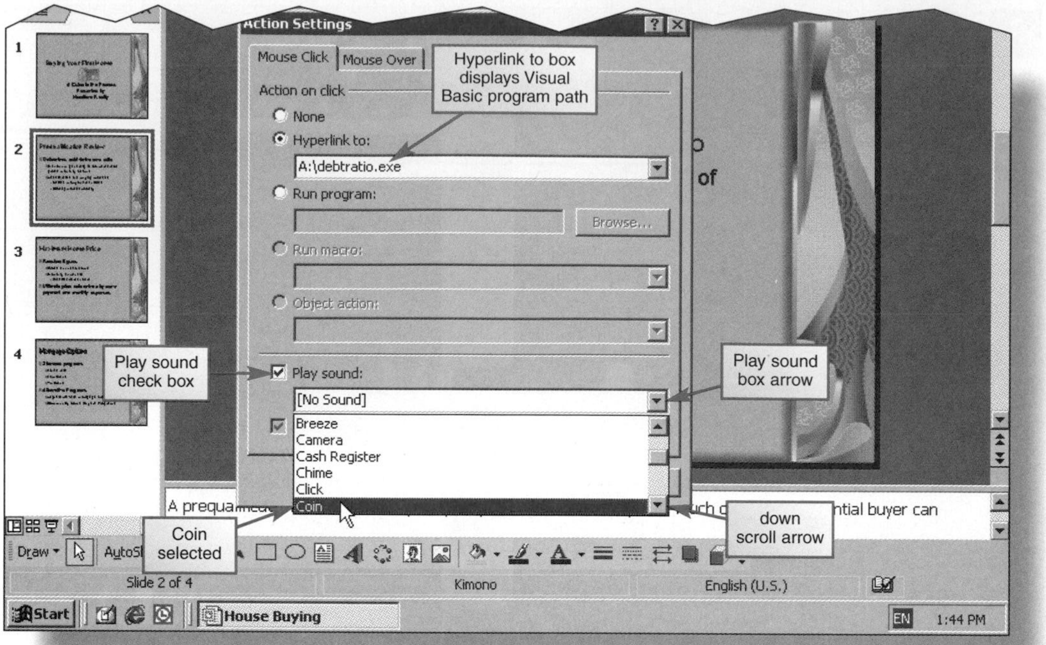

FIGURE 6-19

6 Click Coin. Click the OK button.

The action button is selected on Slide 2 as indicated by the sizing handles (Figure 6-20).

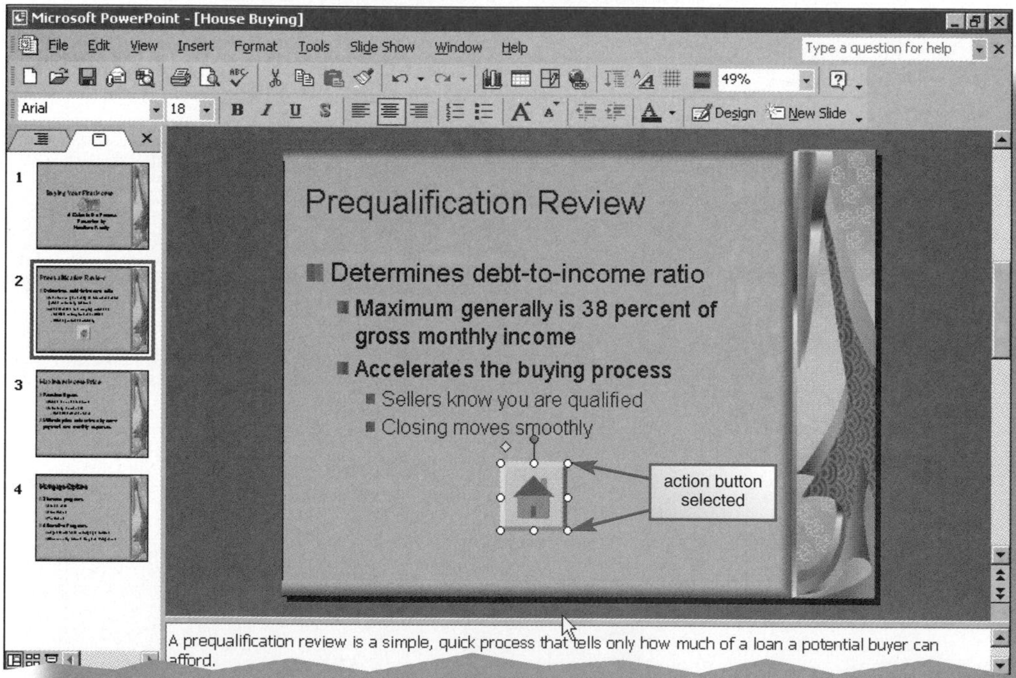

FIGURE 6-20

Other Ways

1. Click AutoShapes button on Drawing toolbar, on AutoShapes menu point to Action Buttons, on Action Buttons submenu click desired action button
2. Press ALT+D, press I
3. In Voice Command mode, say "Slide Show, Action Buttons"

With the action button created and linked to the Visual Basic program, debtratio, you need to repeat the procedure for the Excel worksheet action button on Slide 3 and the Word table action button on Slide 4. Perform the following steps to create action buttons on Slides 3 and 4 and to hyperlink the Excel and Word documents to the PowerPoint presentation.

TO CREATE ADDITIONAL ACTION BUTTONS AND HYPERLINKS

1. Click the Slide 3 slide thumbnail in the tabs pane. Click Slide Show on the menu bar, point to Action Buttons, and then click Action Button: Home on the Action Buttons submenu.
2. Click the bottom center on Slide 3 below the last text paragraph.
3. Click the Hyperlink to box arrow in the Action Settings dialog box, click the down scroll arrow to scroll through the list of locations, and then click Other File.
4. Double-click Home Affordability in the list.
5. Click Play sound. Click the Play sound box arrow, click the down scroll arrow, and then click Typewriter.
6. Click the OK button.
7. Click the Slide 4 slide thumbnail in the tabs pane. Click Slide Show on the menu bar, point to Action Buttons, and then click Action Button: Home on the Action Buttons submenu.
8. Click the area to the right of the first first-level paragraph on Slide 4.
9. Click the Hyperlink to box arrow, click the down scroll arrow, and then click Other File.
10. Double-click Interest Rate in the list.
11. Click Play sound. Click the Play sound box arrow, and then scroll down and click Cash Register.
12. Click the OK button.

Slides 3 and 4 display with the action buttons for the Excel worksheet and Word document hyperlinks (Figure 6-21).

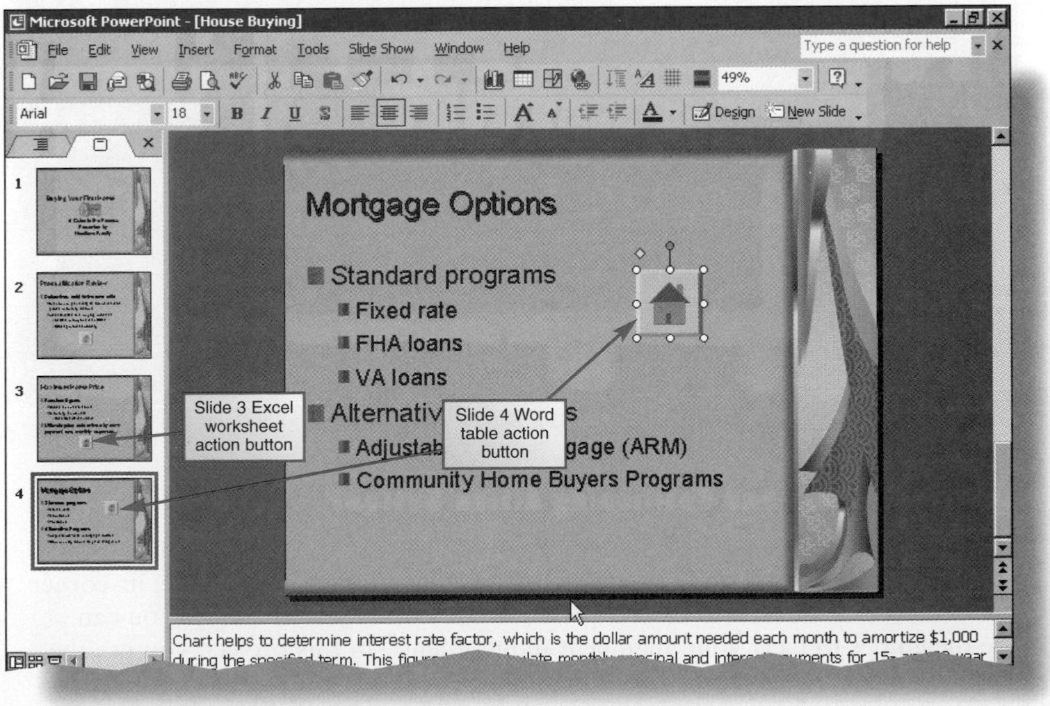

FIGURE 6-21

When you select a file in the Look in list, PowerPoint associates the file with a specific application, which is based on the file extension. For example, when you select the Home Affordability file with the file extension **.xls**, PowerPoint recognizes the file as a Microsoft Excel file. Additionally, when you select the Interest Rate file with the file extension **.doc**, PowerPoint recognizes the file as a Microsoft Word file.

Scaling Action Buttons

The size of the action buttons can be increased. Perform the following steps to scale the three action buttons.

TO SCALE ACTION BUTTONS

1. With Slide 4 active, right-click the action button and then click Format AutoShape on the shortcut menu.
2. If necessary, click the Size tab. Click Lock aspect ratio in the Scale area and then double-click the Height text box. Type 110 in the Height box.
3. Click the OK button.
4. Repeat these steps for the action buttons on Slides 2 and 3.

The action buttons are resized to 110 percent of their original size (Figure 6-22).

Other Ways

1. On Format menu click AutoShape, click Size tab, click Lock aspect ratio
2. Press ALT+O, press O, RIGHT ARROW
3. In Voice Command mode, say "Format, AutoShape, Size, Lock aspect ratio"

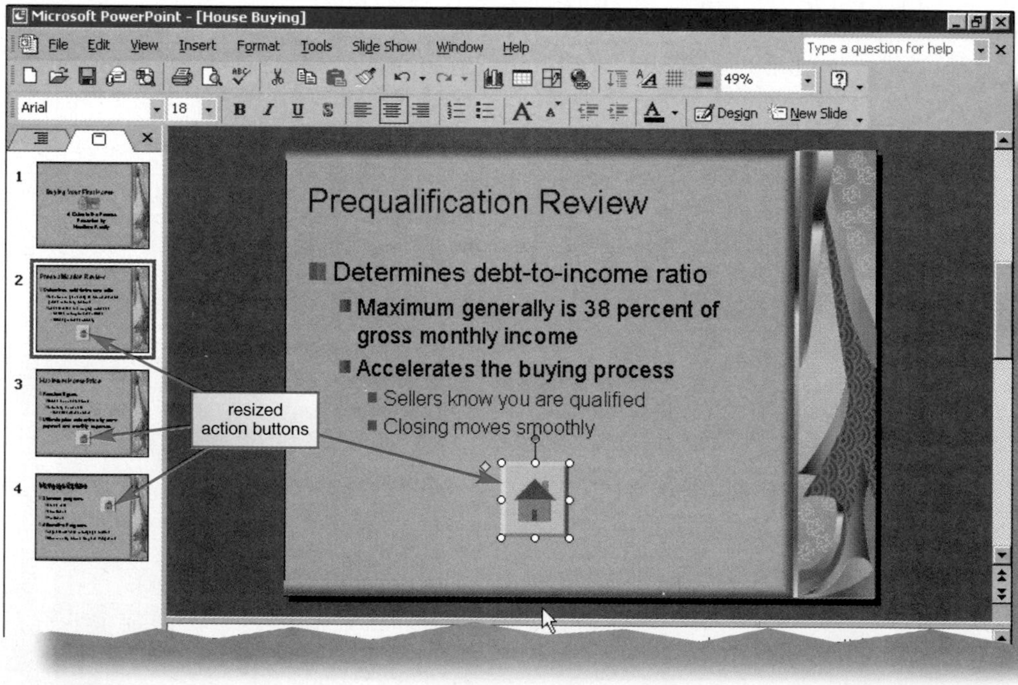

FIGURE 6-22

More About

Sounds

The sounds that play when you click an action button fit a variety of applications. You can, however, add custom sounds, such as a human voice, music, or sound effects, to a slide show. Many Web sites on the Internet provide these sound files, which have the file extension .wav, and allow you to download them free. For an example of one of these Web sites, visit the PowerPoint 2002 More About Web page (scsite.com/pp2002/more.htm) and then click Sounds.

Displaying Guides and Positioning Action Buttons

PowerPoint guides are used to align objects. The **guides** are two straight dotted lines, one horizontal and one vertical. When an object is close to a guide, its corner or its center (whichever is closer) **snaps**, or attaches itself, to the guide. You can move the guides to meet your alignment requirements. In this project, you use the vertical and horizontal guides to help position the action buttons and captions on Slides 2, 3, and 4. The center of a slide is 0.00 on both the vertical and the horizontal guides. You position a guide by dragging it to a new location. When you point to a guide and then press and hold the mouse button, PowerPoint displays a ScreenTip containing the exact position of the guide on the slide in inches. An arrow displays below the guide position to indicate the vertical guide either left or right of center. An arrow displays to the right of the guide position to indicate the horizontal guide either above or below center. Perform the following steps to display the guides and position the action button on Slide 2.

Steps To Display Guides and Position the Slide 2 Action Button

1 With Slide 2 selected, right-click anywhere in the gray area of the slide except the title text or body text placeholders or the action button. Point to Grid and Guides on the shortcut menu (Figure 6-23).

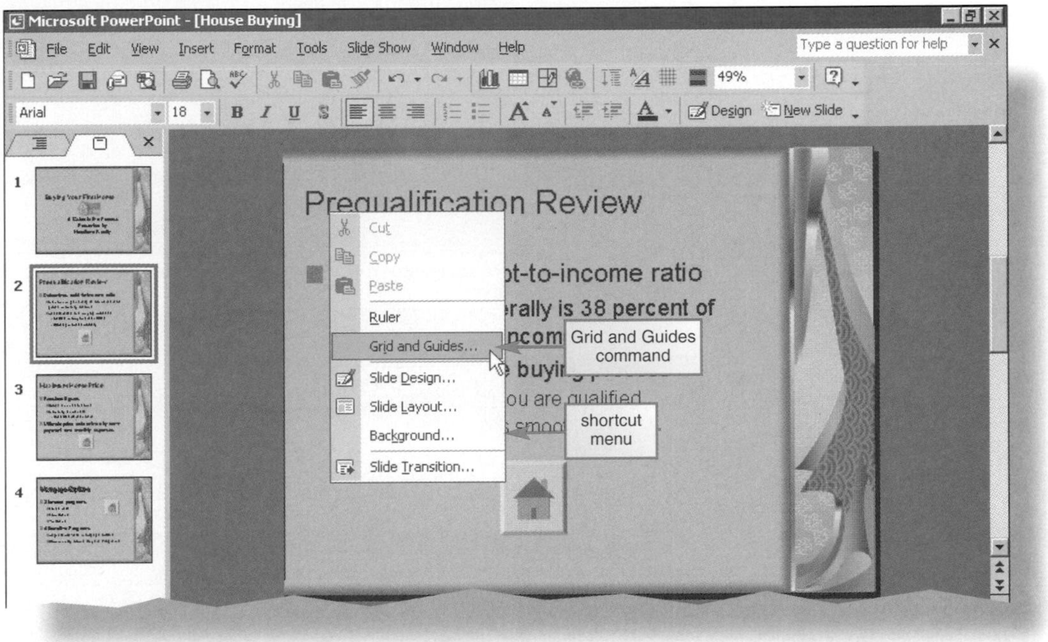

FIGURE 6-23

2 Click Grid and Guides. When the Grid and Guides dialog box displays, click Display drawing guides on screen in the Guide settings area and then point to the OK button.

The Snap objects to grid check box indicates the action buttons and other objects will snap to the drawing guides that display on the screen (Figure 6-24).

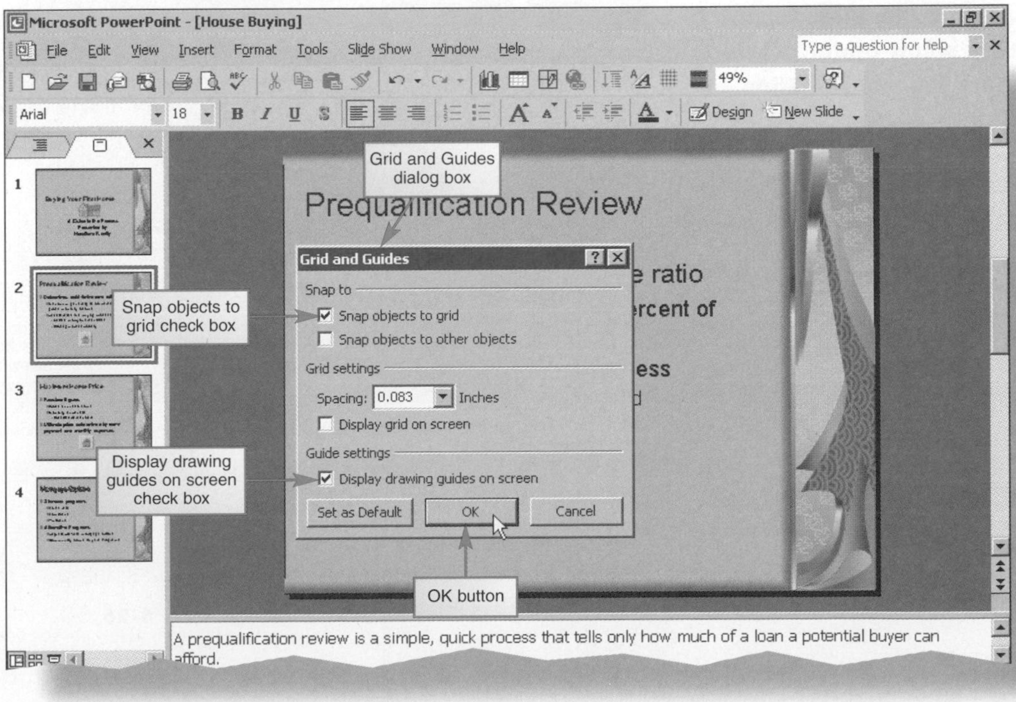

FIGURE 6-24

3 Click the OK button.

The horizontal and vertical guides display (Figure 6-25).

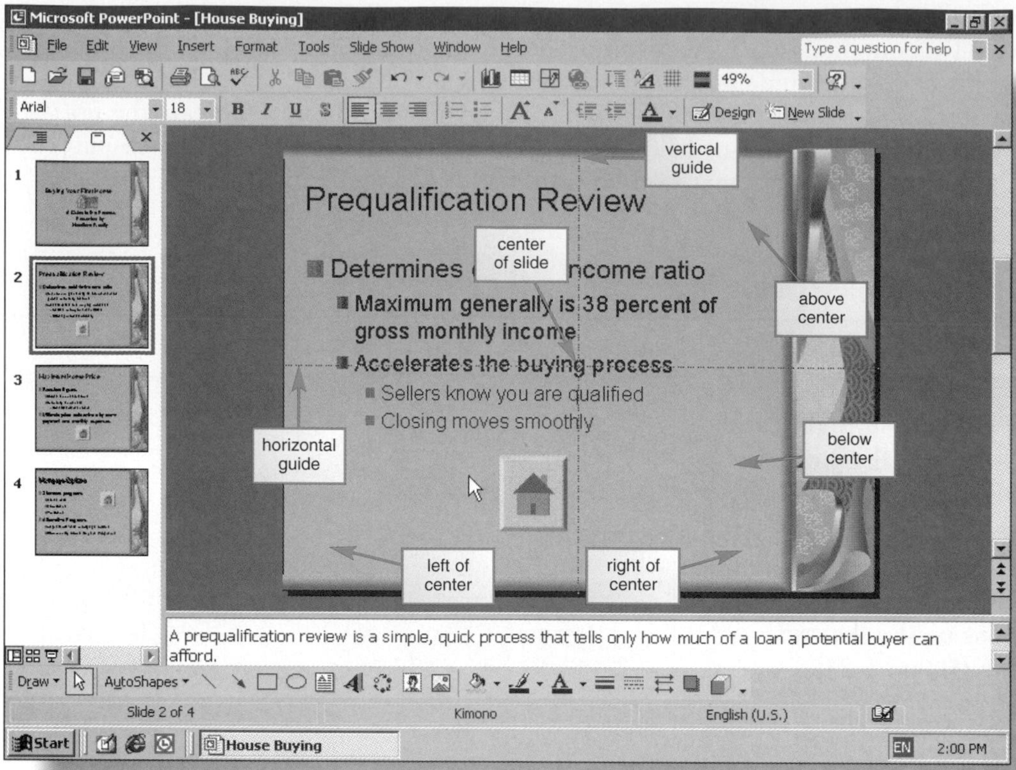

FIGURE 6-25

4 Point to the horizontal guide anywhere in the gray area of the slide except the title text or body text placeholders. Click and then drag the guide to 1.50 inches below center. Do not release the mouse button.

While holding down the mouse button, a ScreenTip displays indicating the position of the horizontal guide (Figure 6-26). This guide will be used to position the top edge of the action button.

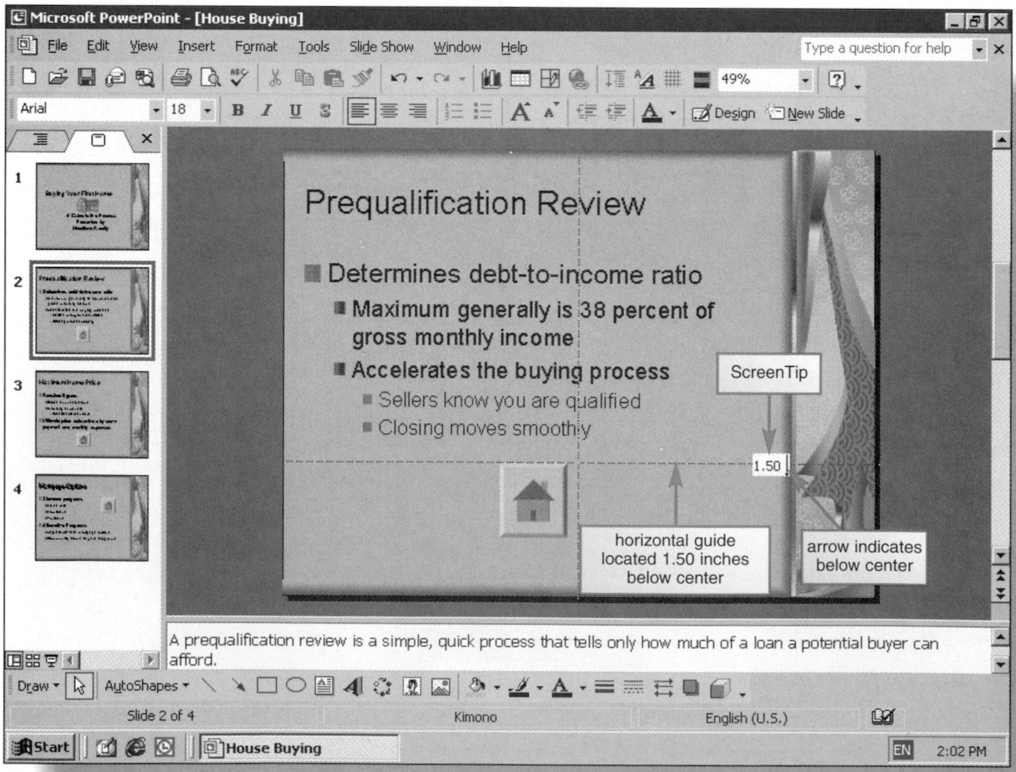

FIGURE 6-26

5 **Release the mouse button. Drag the action button until the top edge snaps to the horizontal guide and the right edge snaps to the vertical guide.**

The top of the action button aligns with the horizontal guide, and the right edge of the button aligns with the vertical guide (Figure 6-27).

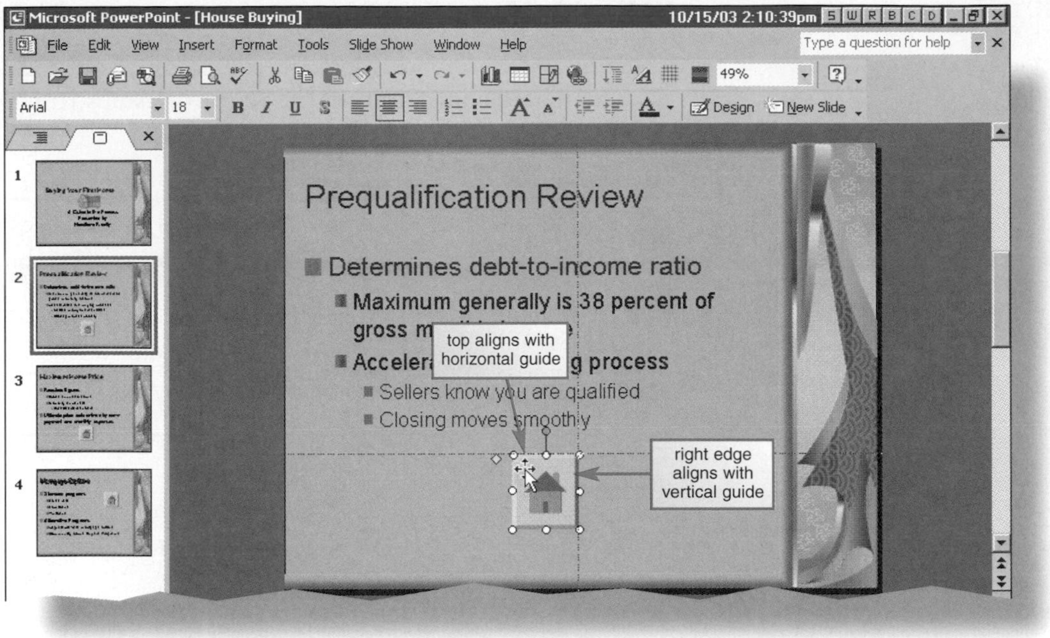

FIGURE 6-27

The Slide 2 action button displays in the desired location. Perform the following steps to align the action buttons on Slides 3 and 4.

Other Ways

1. On View menu click Grid and Guides, click Display drawing guides on screen
2. Press ALT+V, press I, press I
3. In Voice Command mode, say "View, Grid and Guides, Display drawing guides on screen"

TO POSITION THE SLIDE 3 AND SLIDE 4 ACTION BUTTONS

1 Click the Next Slide button to display Slide 3. Drag the action button until the top edge snaps to the horizontal guide and the right edge snaps to the vertical guide.

2 Click the Next Slide button to display Slide 4. Drag the horizontal guide to 0.75 inches above center. Drag the vertical guide to 1.25 inches right of center.

3 Drag the action button until the bottom edge snaps to the horizontal guide and the left edge snaps to the vertical guide.

The action buttons for Slides 3 and 4 display in the desired locations (Figure 6-28).

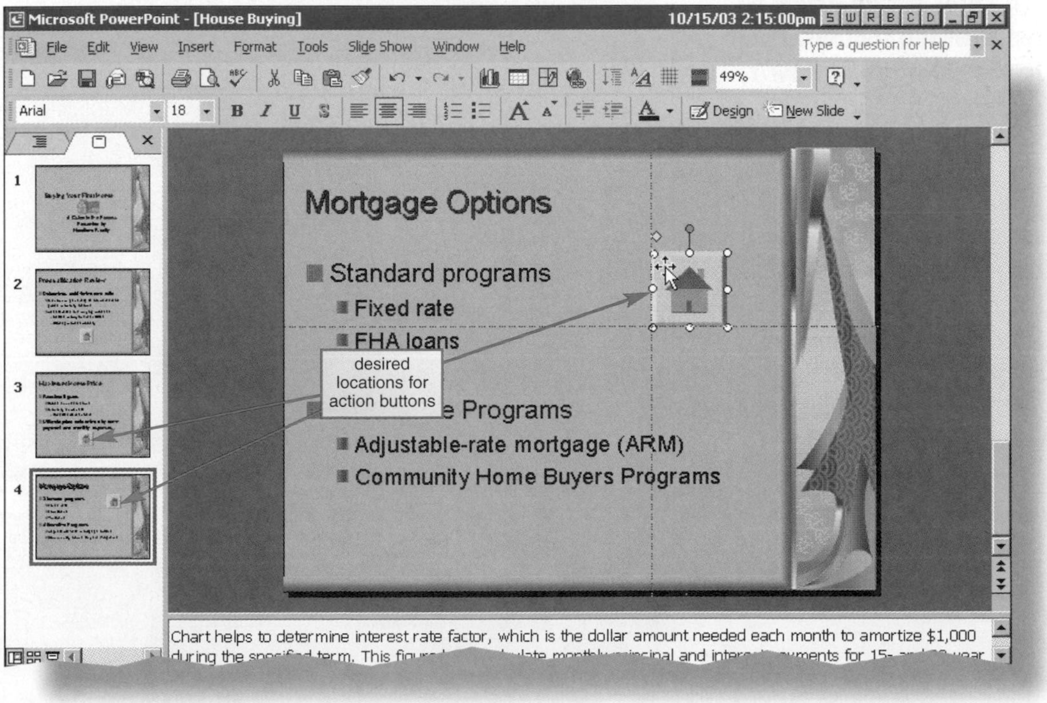

FIGURE 6-28

Hiding Guides

When you no longer want to control the exact placement of objects on the slide, you can **hide guides**. Perform the following steps to hide guides.

TO HIDE GUIDES

1. Right-click Slide 4 anywhere except the title or body text placeholders or the action buttons. Click Grid and Guides on the shortcut menu.
2. When the Grid and Guides dialog box displays, click Display drawing guides on screen in the Guide settings area.
3. Click the OK button.

The guides are hidden.

Other Ways

1. On View menu click Grid and Guides, click Display drawing guides on screen
2. Press ALT+V, press I, press I
3. In Voice Command mode, say "View, Grid and Guides, Display drawing guides on screen"

The action buttons are positioned in the desired locations. Changing the fill color, shadow, and lines can enhance them.

Adding a Fill Color to the Action Buttons

To better identify the action buttons from the slide background, you can add fill color. **Fill color** is the interior color of a selected object. Perform the following steps to add fill color to the action button on Slide 4.

Steps To Add a Fill Color to the Slide 4 Action Button

1 With Slide 4 active, click the action button and then click the Fill Color button arrow on the Drawing toolbar. Point to the color green (row 1, column 6).

The Fill Color list displays (Figure 6-29). Automatic is selected, indicating that beige is the current default fill color based on the Kimono design template color scheme. Green is the default Follow Accent Scheme Color.

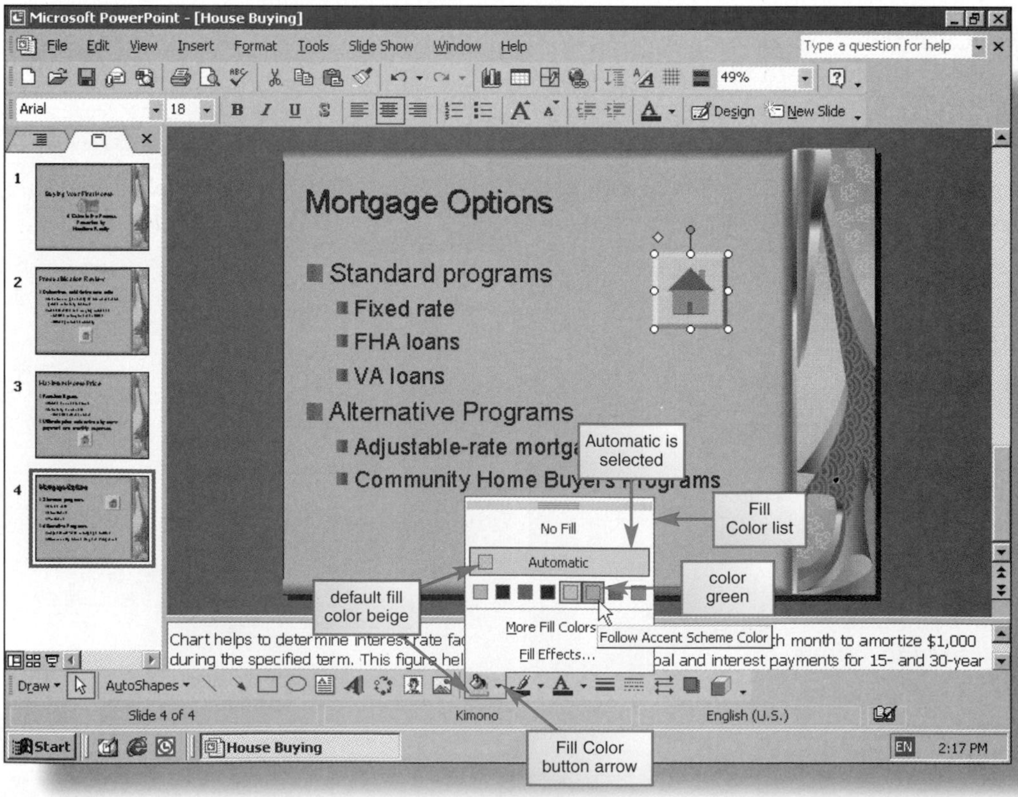

FIGURE 6-29

2 Click the color green.

The action button displays filled with the color green (Figure 6-30).

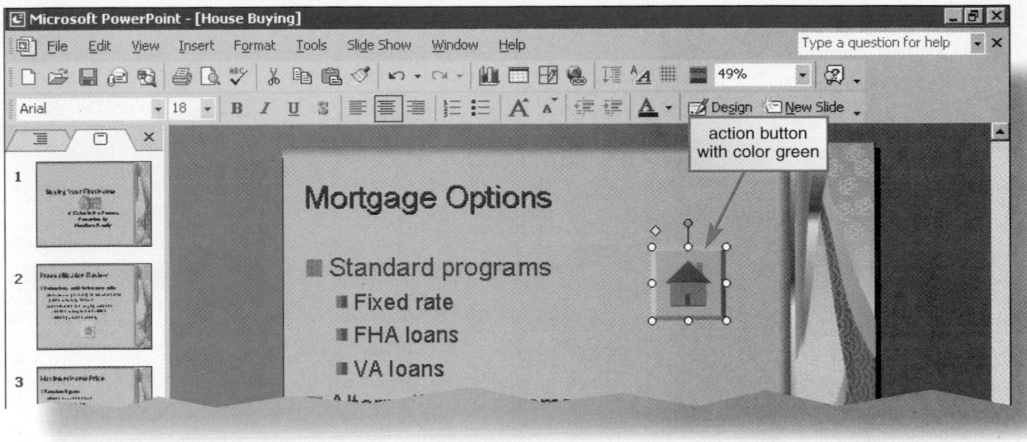

FIGURE 6-30

Other Ways

1. On Format menu click AutoShape, click Colors and Lines tab
2. Right-click action button, click Format AutoShape on shortcut menu, click Colors and Lines tab
3. Press ALT+O, press O
4. In Voice Command mode, say "Format, AutoShape, Colors and Lines"

The Slide 2 action button is filled with the color green. The fill color now is set to this color. Perform the following steps to change the fill color of the action buttons on Slides 2 and 3 to this color.

TO ADD A FILL COLOR TO THE SLIDE 2 AND SLIDE 3 ACTION BUTTONS

1. Click the Previous Slide button to display Slide 3. Click the action button and then click the Fill Color button on the Drawing toolbar.
2. Repeat Step 1 for the Slide 2 action button.

The action buttons on Slides 2 and 3 display filled with the color green (Figure 6-31).

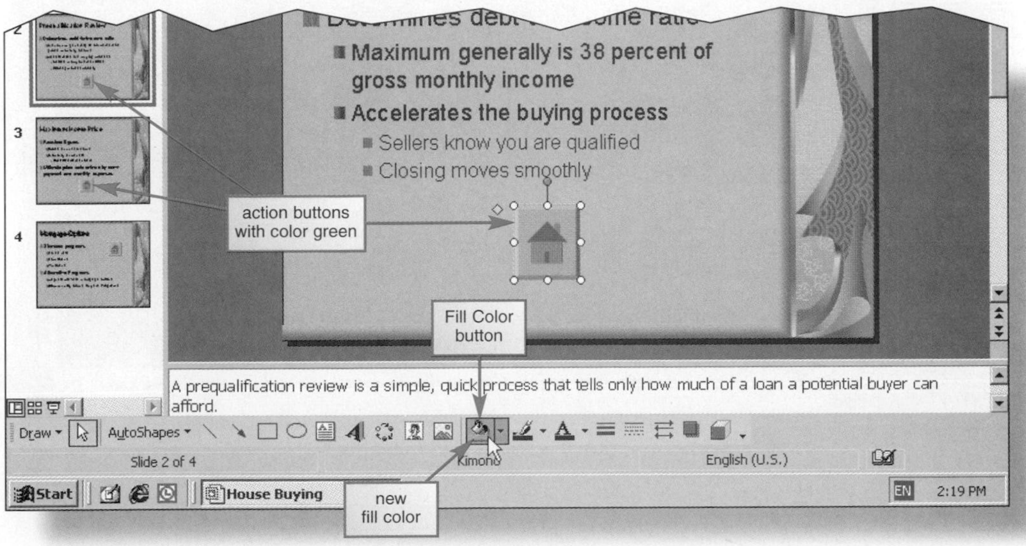

FIGURE 6-31

Adding a Shadow to the Action Buttons

To add depth to an object, you **shadow** it by clicking the Shadow button on the Drawing toolbar. Perform the steps on the next page to add a shadow to the three action buttons.

Steps To Add a Shadow to the Action Buttons

1 With the Slide 2 action button selected, click the Shadow Style button on the Drawing toolbar. Point to Shadow Style 14 (row 4, column 2) in the Shadow Style list.

Twenty shadow styles display along with a No Shadow option (Figure 6-32).

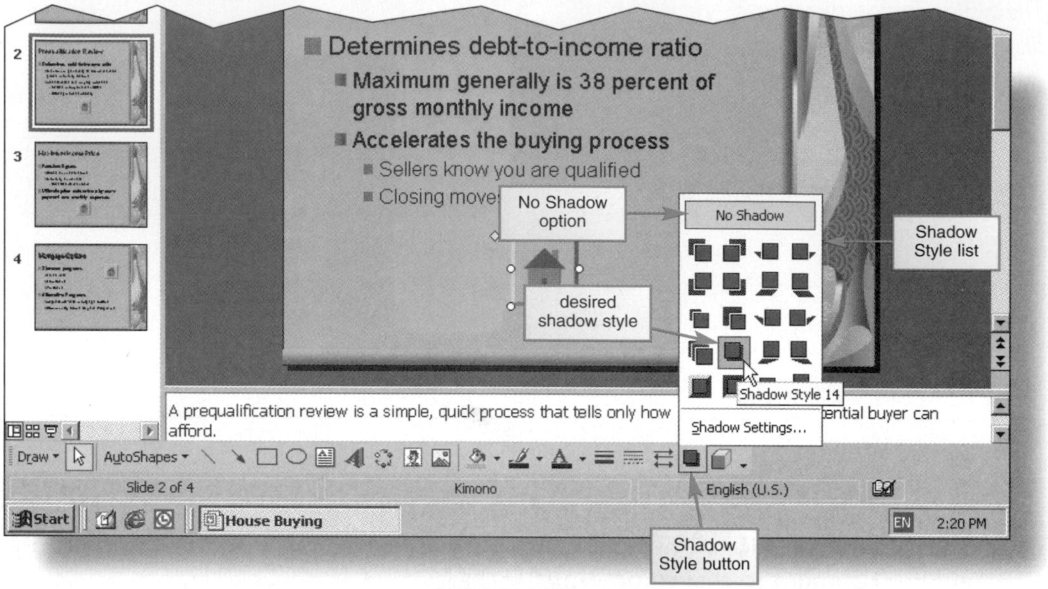

FIGURE 6-32

2 Click Shadow Style 14.

PowerPoint adds the shadow effect to the action button (Figure 6-33).

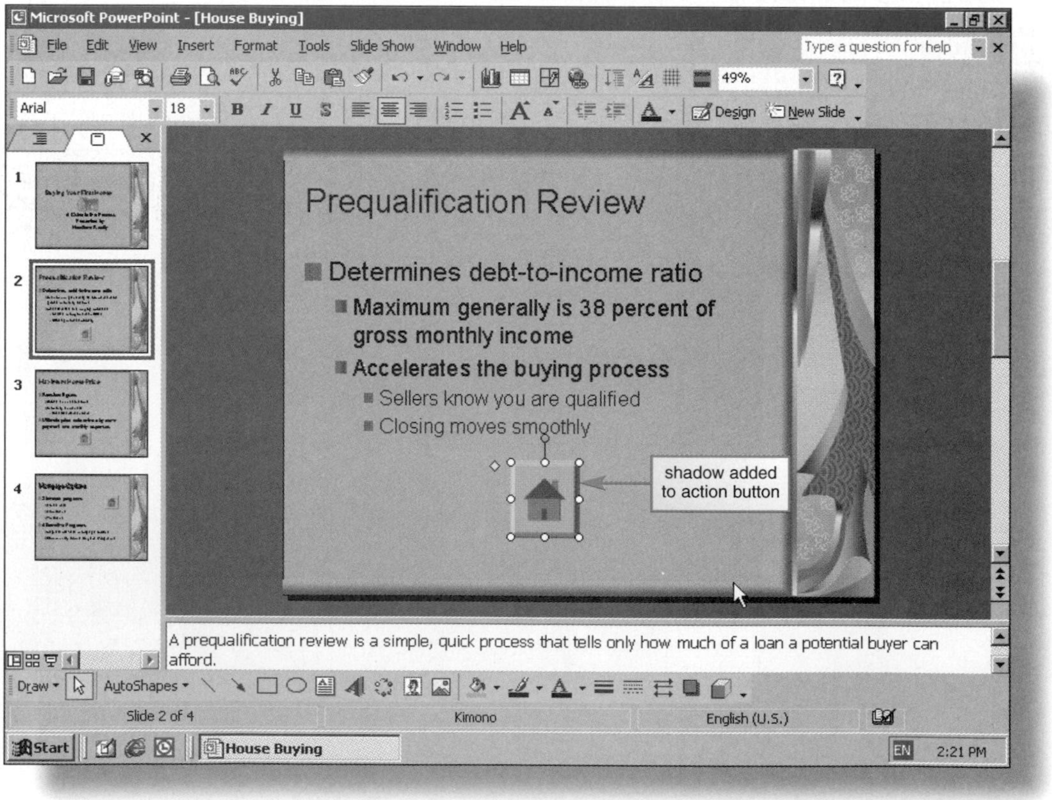

FIGURE 6-33

Slide 2 is defined with a green fill color and shadow. The buttons on Slides 3 and 4 also will be modified with shadows. Perform the following steps to add shadow effects to the remaining action buttons on Slides 3 and 4.

TO ADD A SHADOW TO THE SLIDE 3 AND SLIDE 4 ACTION BUTTONS

1. Click the Next Slide button to display Slide 3. Click the action button, click the Shadow Style button on the Drawing toolbar, and then click Shadow Style 14 (row 4, column 2).
2. Repeat Step 1 for the Slide 4 action button.

The action buttons on Slides 3 and 4 display with shadows (Figure 6-34).

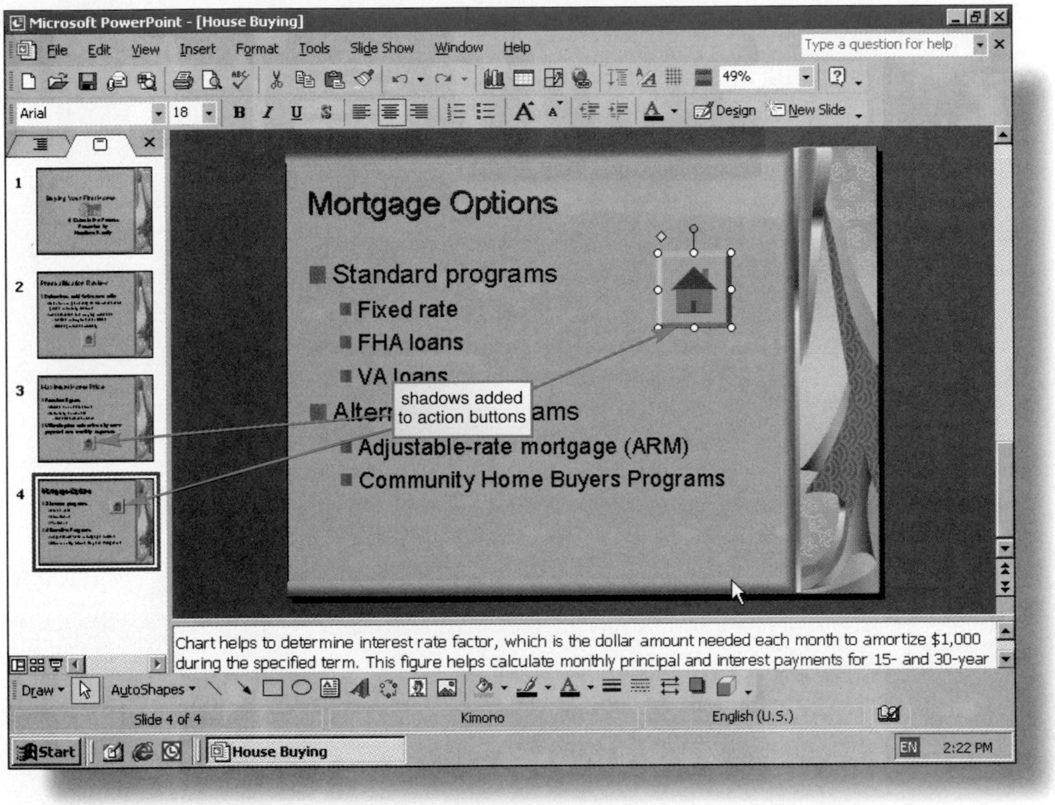

FIGURE 6-34

The green color and shadows help to identify the buttons. Lines further identify their shapes. The next section describes how to add lines to the action buttons.

Adding Lines to the Action Buttons

Lines define the edges of a shape. To add lines, click the Line Style button on the Drawing toolbar. Thirteen line styles are available, and you can modify them by clicking More Lines and then changing colors, size, and positions. Perform the steps on the next page to add lines to the three action buttons.

More About

Action Buttons

The 12 action buttons in the Action Buttons submenu are a subset of PowerPoint's AutoShapes, which are convenient visuals designed to add visual interest to slides. To add an action button with one of these other AutoShapes, click the AutoShapes button on the Drawing toolbar, select one of the categories of shapes, such as lines, connectors, basic shapes, flowchart elements, stars and banners, and callouts, click an AutoShape, and then click the slide in the location where you want the AutoShape to display.

Steps To Add Lines to the Slide 4 Action Button

1 With the Slide 4 action button selected, click the Line Style button on the Drawing toolbar and then point to the ¾ pt line style in the Line Style list.

PowerPoint provides 13 line styles (Figure 6-35).

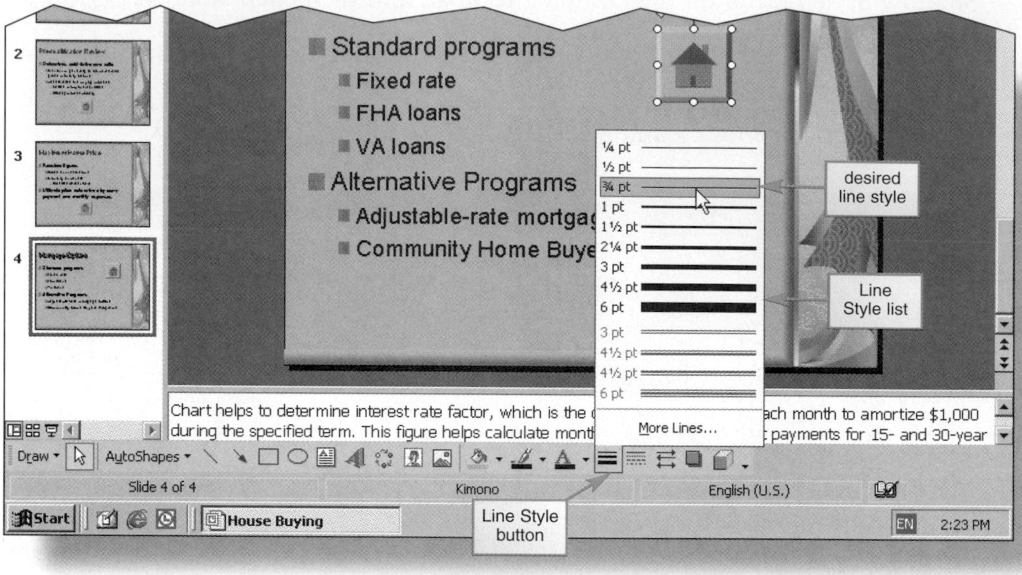

FIGURE 6-35

2 Click the ¾ pt style.

PowerPoint adds lines to the Slide 4 action button (Figure 6-36).

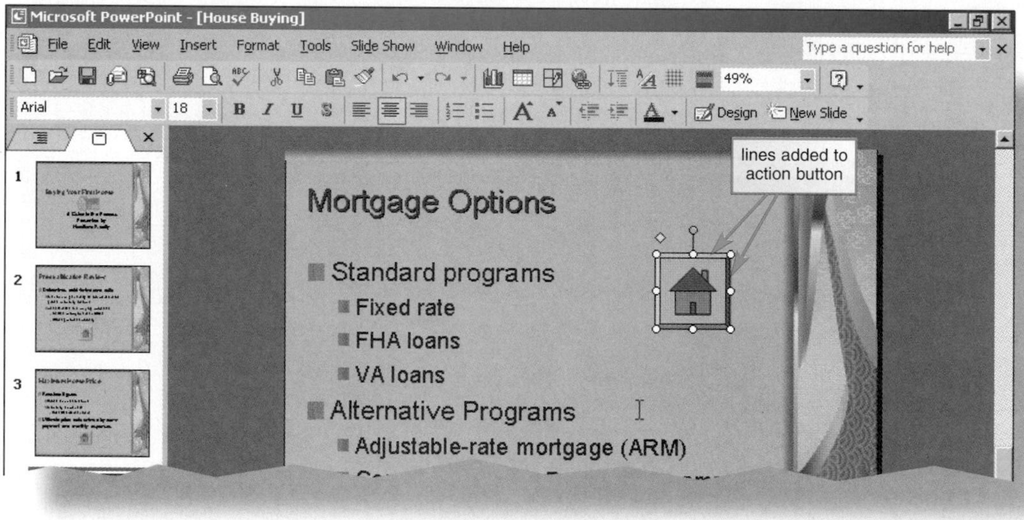

FIGURE 6-36

Other Ways

1. On Format menu click AutoShape, click Colors and Lines tab
2. Right-click action button, click Format AutoShape on shortcut menu, click Colors and Lines tab
3. Press ALT+O, press O
4. In Voice Command mode, say "Format, AutoShape, Colors and Lines"

The Slide 4 action button is enhanced with lines. The buttons on Slides 2 and 3 also will be modified. Perform the following steps to add lines to the action buttons on Slides 2 and 3.

TO ADD LINES TO THE SLIDE 2 AND SLIDE 3 ACTION BUTTONS

1. Click the Previous Slide button to display Slide 3. Click the action button, click the Line Style button on the Drawing toolbar, and then click the ¾ pt style.
2. Repeat Step 1 for the Slide 2 action button.

The action buttons on Slides 2 and 3 display with lines (Figure 6-37).

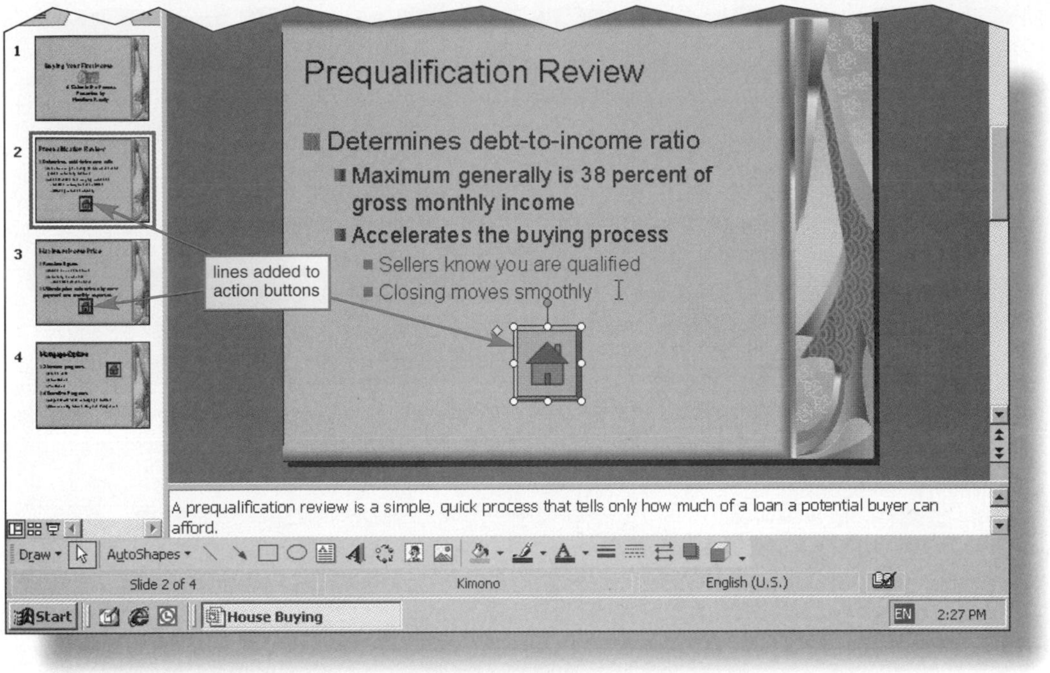

FIGURE 6-37

The three action buttons are distinguished from the background with a new fill color, shadows, and lines. Captions will identify their functions to users, as discussed in the following section.

Adding Captions to the Action Buttons

Captions for the three action buttons are the final components that need to be added to Slides 2, 3, and 4. Perform the following steps to add a caption to the action button on Slide 2.

More About

Hiding Slides

As a presenter, you can decide whether to show a particular slide. To hide a slide, click the Slide Sorter View button at the lower left of the PowerPoint window, right-click the desired slide, and then click Hide Slide on the shortcut menu. The null sign, a square with a slash, displays over the slide number to indicate the slide is hidden. When you no longer want to hide a slide, change views to slide sorter view, right-click the slide, and then click Hide Slide on the shortcut menu. This action removes the square with a slash surrounding the slide number. When you run the presentation, the hidden slide does not display unless you press the H key when the slide preceding the hidden slide is displaying. You skip the hidden slide by clicking the mouse and advancing to the next slide.

Steps To Add a Caption to the Slide 2 Action Button

1 With Slide 2 displaying, click the Text Box button on the Drawing toolbar and then point to the area below and to the left of the action button.

The Text Box button is selected (Figure 6-38). The mouse pointer is positioned where the left edge of the text box will be located.

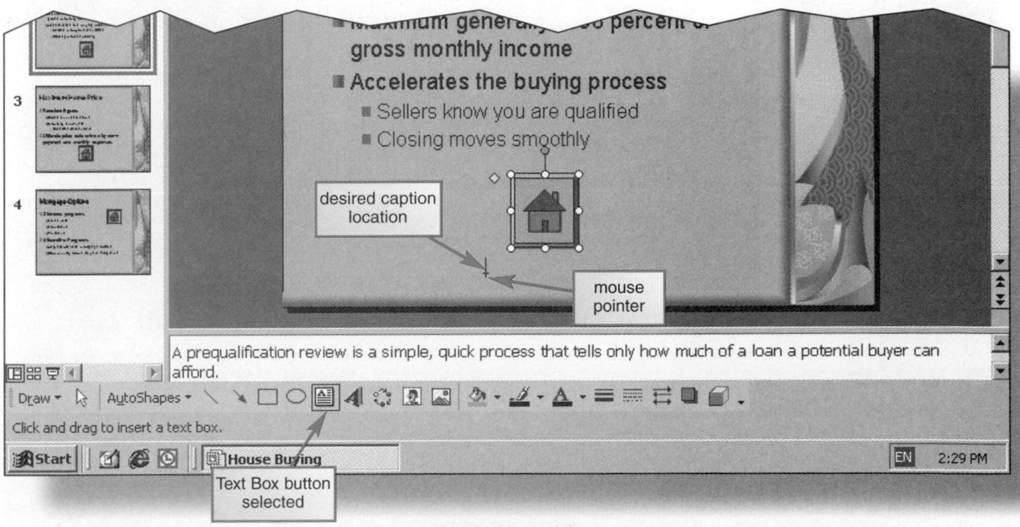

FIGURE 6-38

2 **Click the slide at this location. Type** `What is my` **and then press SHIFT+ENTER. Type** `debt-to-income ratio?` **as the second caption line.**

The caption for the Slide 2 action button displays (Figure 6-39).

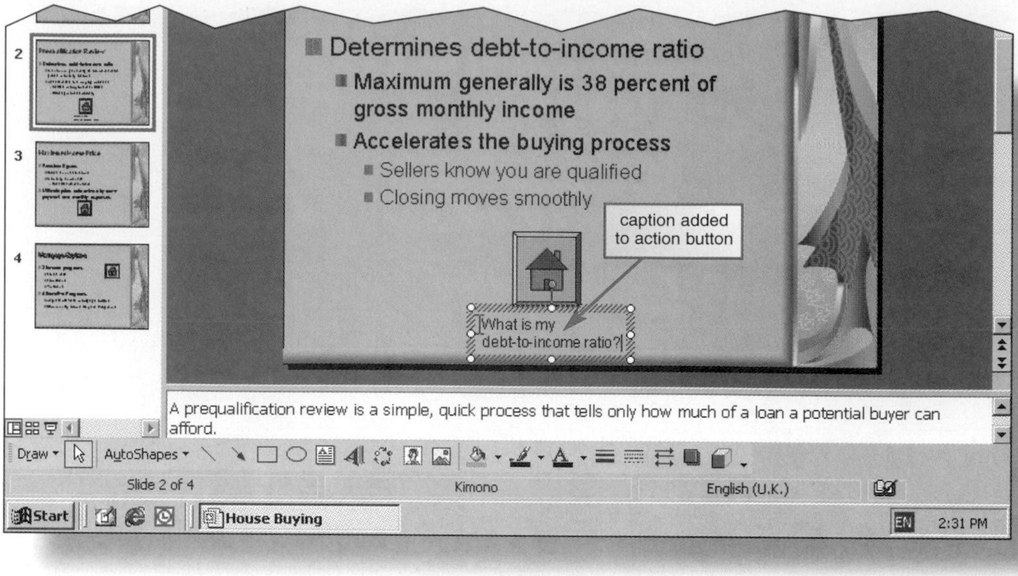

FIGURE 6-39

Other Ways

1. On Insert menu click Text Box
2. Press ALT+I, press X
3. In Voice Command mode, say "Insert, Text Box"

A caption helps identify the Slide 2 action button. The buttons on Slides 3 and 4 also need captions. Perform the following steps to add captions to the action buttons on Slides 3 and 4.

TO ADD CAPTIONS TO THE SLIDE 3 AND SLIDE 4 ACTION BUTTONS

1 Click the Next Slide button to display Slide 3. Click the Text Box button on the Drawing toolbar and then click below and to the left of the action button. Type `What is the maximum` and then press SHIFT+ENTER. Type `price I can afford?` as the second caption line.

2 Click the Next Slide button to display Slide 4. Click the Text Box button on the Drawing toolbar and then click below and to the left of the action button. Type `What is the` and then press SHIFT+ENTER. Type `interest rate factor?` as the second caption line.

The captions for the Slide 3 and Slide 4 action buttons display (Figure 6-40).

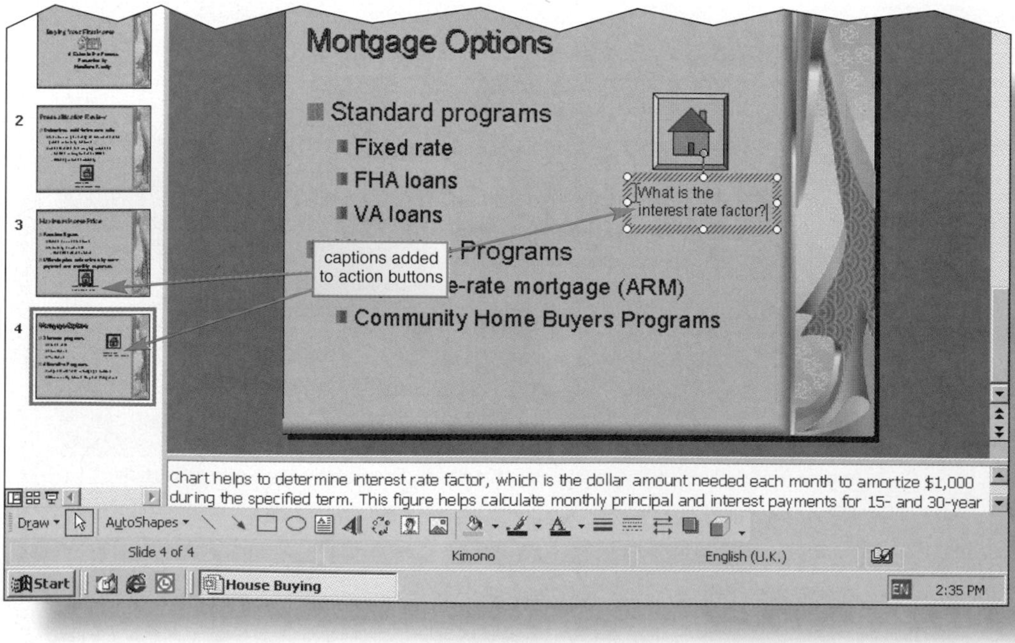

FIGURE 6-40

The three captions are added to the slides. To enhance the display, you can format the text by changing the font, font size, and font color.

Formatting the Action Button Caption Text

Changing the characteristics of the caption text adds visual appeal to the action buttons. The following steps format the captions by changing the font to Bookman Old Style, increasing the font size to 20, and changing the font color to gold.

More About

Black Slides

A black slide may help an audience focus on the speaker. To create this slide, click the New Slide button on the Standard toolbar, select the Blank slide layout, click Format on the menu bar, click Background, click the Background fill box arrow, and then click the color black.

Steps To Format the Slide 4 Action Button Caption Text

1 If necessary, click the Slide 4 action button caption text and then click the Center button on the Formatting toolbar. Click Edit on the menu bar and then point to Select All.

The caption text is centered in the text box and the Edit menu displays (Figure 6-41). The Select All command will select all letters in the caption by highlighting them.

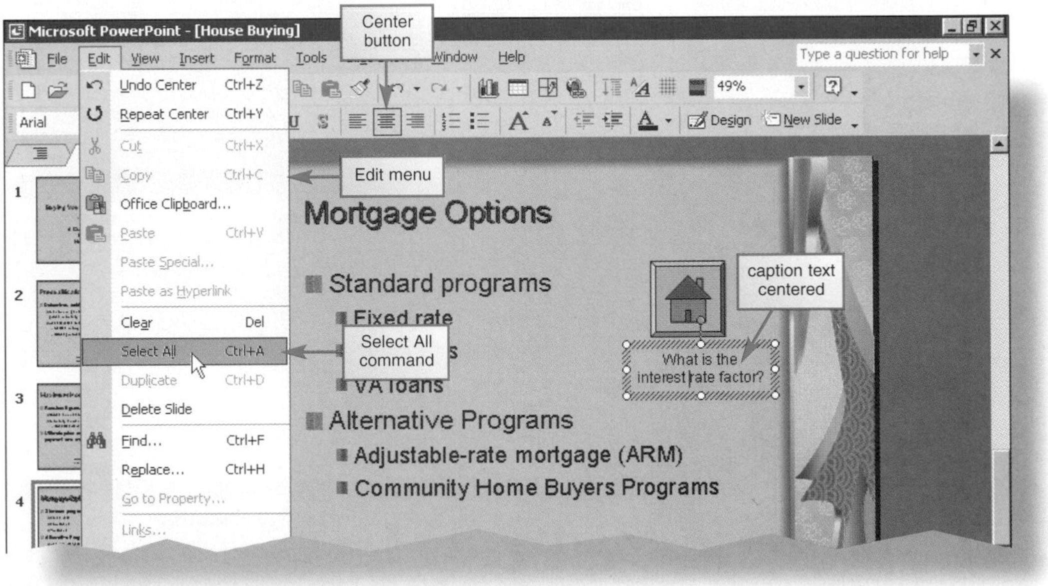

FIGURE 6-41

2 Click Select All. Right-click the caption text and then click Font on the shortcut menu. When the Font dialog box displays, click the down scroll arrow in the Font list and then click Bookman Old Style in the Font list. Click 20 in the Size list. Point to the Color box arrow.

Bookman Old Style displays in the Font box, and 20 displays in the Size box (Figure 6-42).

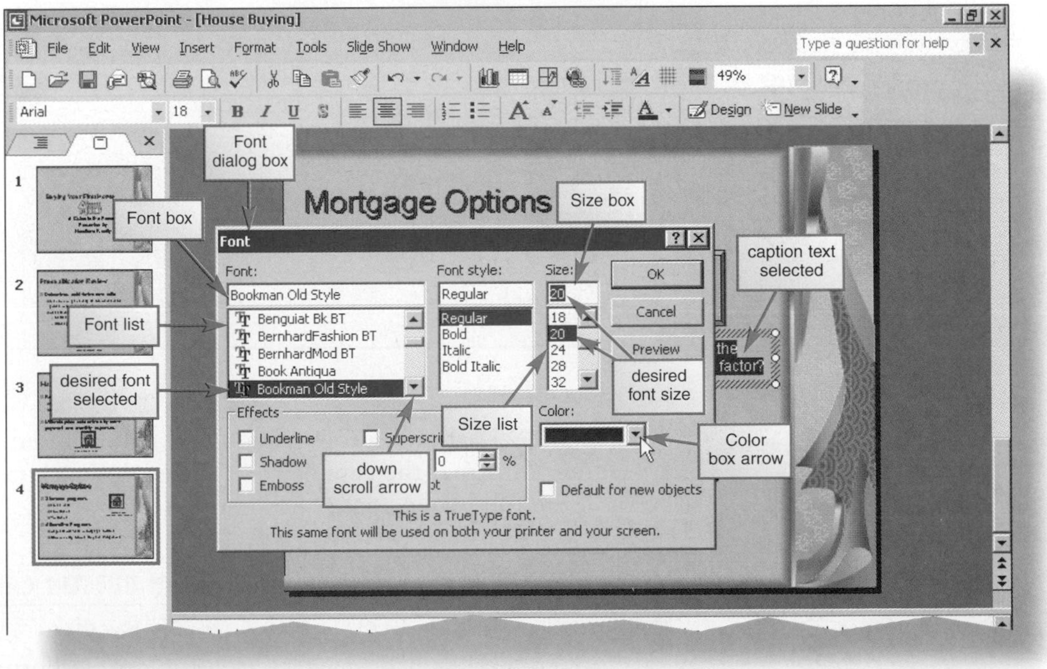

FIGURE 6-42

3 Click the Color box arrow and then click the color gold (row 1, column 7). Point to the OK button.

The color gold is the Follow Accent and Hyperlink Scheme Color in the Kimono design template color scheme (Figure 6-43). The color gold displays in the Color box.

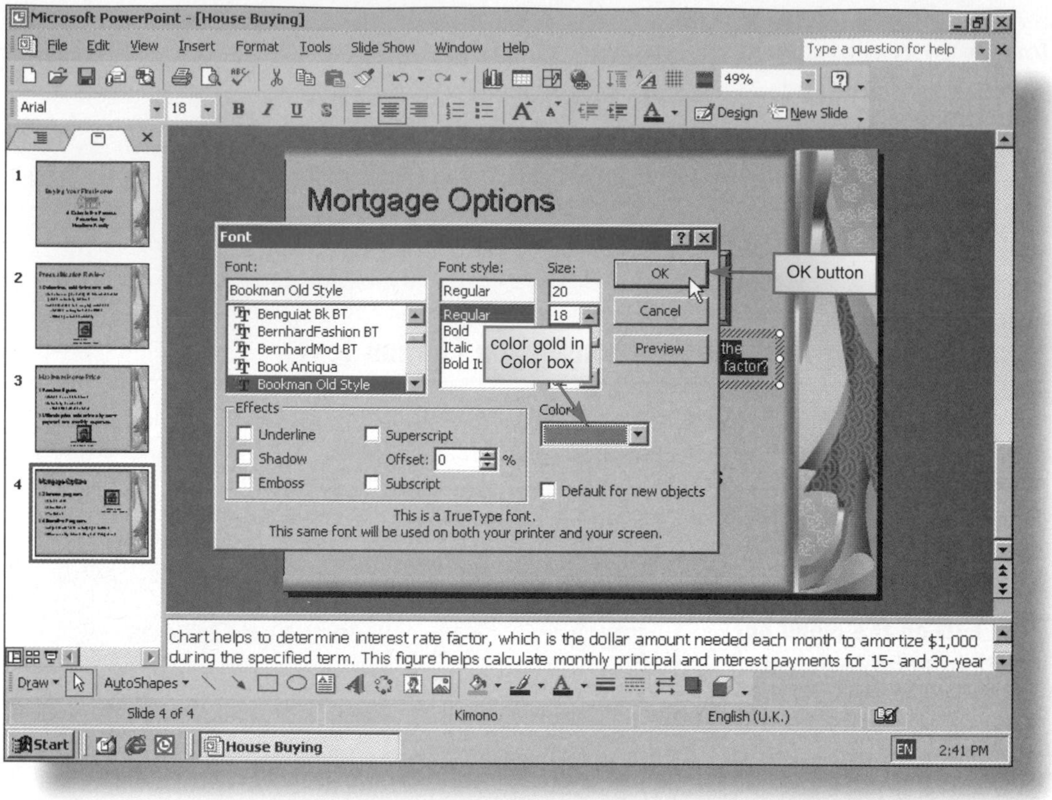

FIGURE 6-43

4 Click the OK button and then click anywhere on the slide other than the title and body text placeholders.

PowerPoint displays the Slide 4 caption with the Bookman Old Style font, a font size of 20, and the color gold (Figure 6-44).

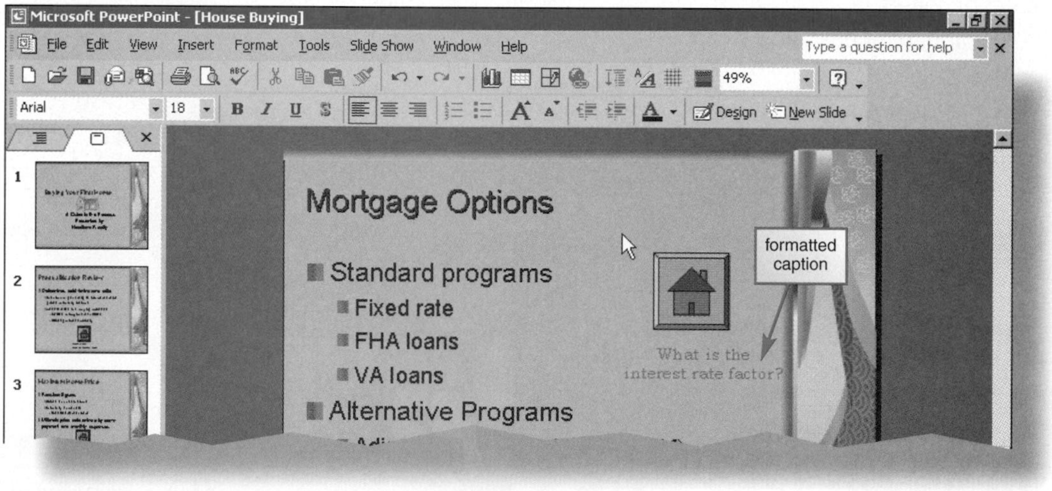

FIGURE 6-44

The Slide 4 action button caption text is formatted, and you need to repeat the procedure to format the caption text for the action buttons on Slides 2 and 3. Perform the following steps to format these captions.

TO FORMAT THE SLIDE 2 AND SLIDE 3 ACTION BUTTON CAPTION TEXT

1. Click the Previous Slide button to display Slide 3. Click the action button caption and then click the Center button on the Formatting toolbar. Press CTRL+A.

2 Right-click the text and then click Font on the shortcut menu. When the Font dialog box displays, click the down scroll arrow in the Font list and then click Bookman Old Style.

3 Click 20 in the Size list.

4 Click the Color box arrow and then click the color gold (row 1, column 7).

5 Click the OK button and then click anywhere on a blank area of the slide.

6 Repeat these steps for Slide 2 in the presentation.

Slides 2, 3, and 4 are complete (Figure 6-45).

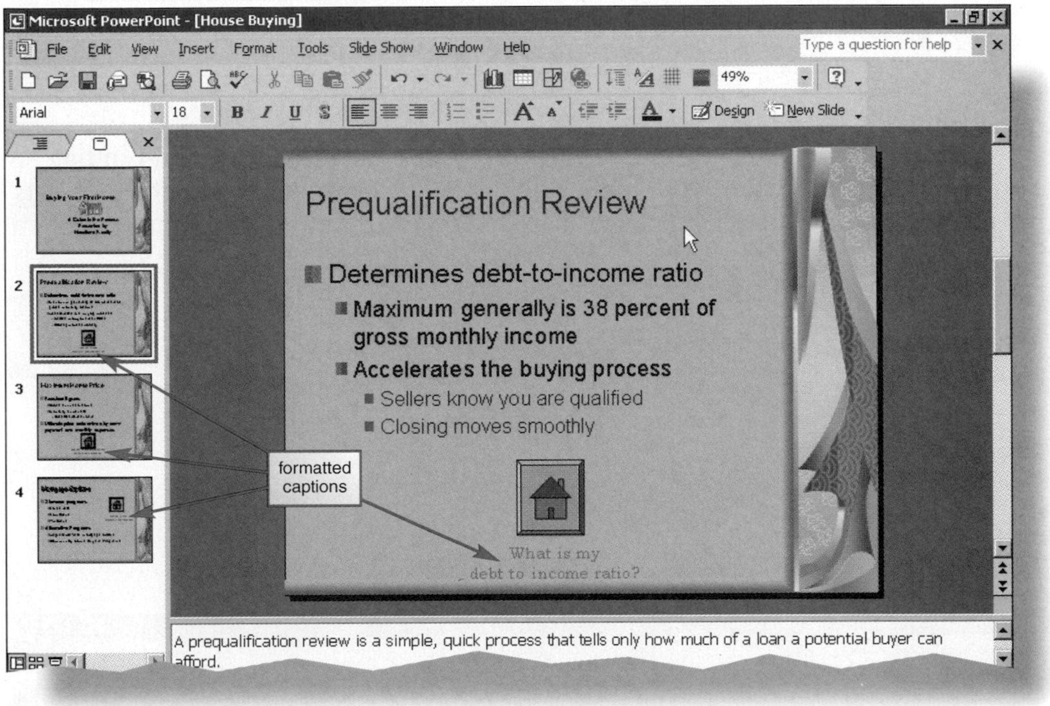

FIGURE 6-45

The captions are added and formatted, and you may need to make slight modifications to center their placements below the action buttons. If so, click a caption, click the border, and use the arrow keys to position the text box as shown in Figure 6-45.

You now should save your presentation because you have done a substantial amount of work.

Inserting, Formatting, and Animating a Diagram

Diagrams help users understand concepts by showing the relationship among parts of a process or visualizing how something works. One of the new features in PowerPoint 2002 is the capability of inserting predesigned diagrams by clicking the Insert Diagram or Organization Chart button on the Drawing toolbar or by selecting the slide layout with a content placeholder and then clicking the Insert Diagram or Organization Chart button in the content placeholder. The five diagram types are described in Table 6-1 on the next page.

More About

Fonts

Designers have developed hundreds of unique fonts that you can download and then use in your presentations. Many of these fonts are available free. For examples of these fonts, visit the PowerPoint 2002 More About Web page (scsite.com/pp2002/more.htm) and then click Fonts.

Table 6-1 Diagram Types and Functions

TYPE	NAME	FUNCTION
	Cycle	Shows process with continuous action
	Pyramid	Shows relationship between elements based on a foundation
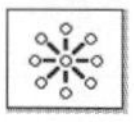	Radial	Shows elements relating to a core element
	Target	Shows steps leading to a goal
	Venn	Shows overlap between and among different elements

More About

Summary Slides

A summary slide contains bulleted titles from selected slides and can be used to recap the main points of the presentation or as an agenda of topics. To add a summary slide in slide sorter view, select the slides you want to include in the summary and then click the Summary Slide button on the Slide Sorter toolbar. You then can rearrange the summary slide by moving it to the end of the presentation.

Diagrams have a **drawing space** around them that extends to the non-printing border and drawing handles. More drawing space can be added if additional objects are needed, or this space can be reduced to fit tightly around the diagram.

Inserting a Radial Diagram

PowerPoint inserts a **Radial diagram** composed of a central core element and three related elements. You easily can add elements by using the Diagram toolbar buttons. Perform the following steps to insert the Radial diagram.

Steps To Insert a Radial Diagram

1 Click the Slide 4 slide thumbnail in the tabs pane and then click the New Slide button on the Formatting toolbar to insert a new slide. Click Format on the menu bar and then click Slide Layout. When the Slide Layout task pane displays, point to the Content slide layout in the Content Layouts area.

The Slide Layout task pane displays (Figure 6-46). The new Slide 5 displays with Title and Text layout.

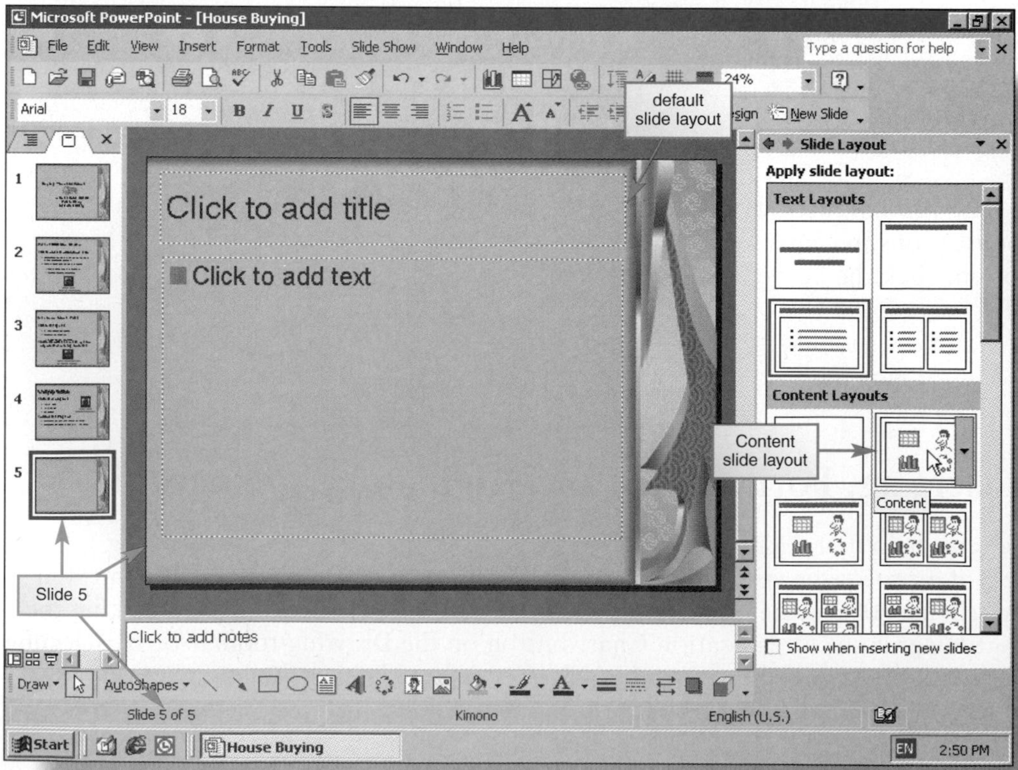

FIGURE 6-46

2 Click the Content slide layout. Point to the Insert Diagram or Organization Chart button in the content placeholder.

The Insert Diagram or Organization Chart button is selected (Figure 6-47). A ScreenTip describes its function.

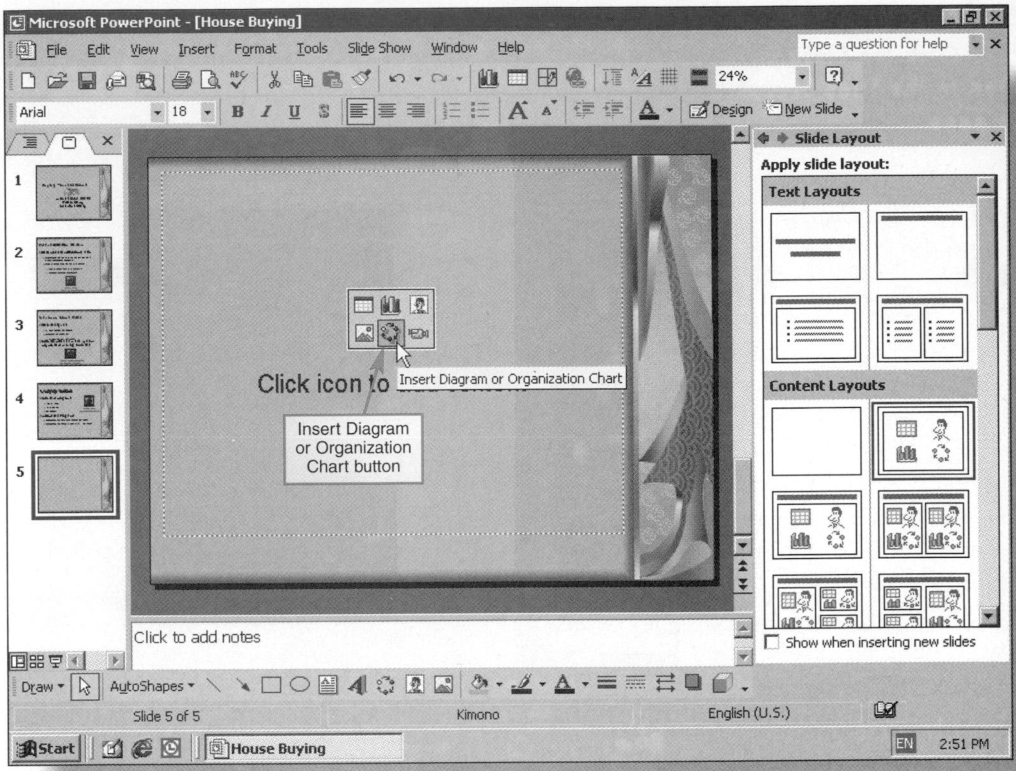

FIGURE 6-47

3 Click the Insert Diagram or Organization Chart button. When the Diagram Gallery dialog box displays, click the Radial Diagram diagram type. Point to the OK button.

Radial Diagram is selected (Figure 6-48).

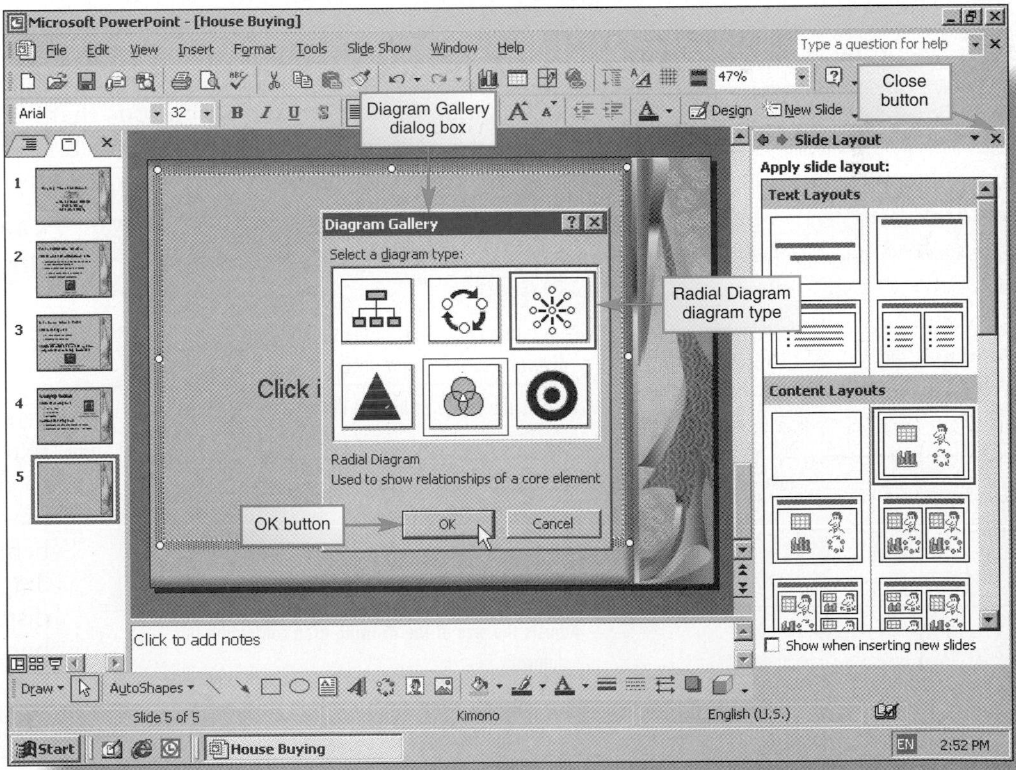

FIGURE 6-48

4 **Click the OK button. Click the Close button in the Slide Layout task pane.**

The Radial diagram and Diagram toolbar display (Figure 6-49).

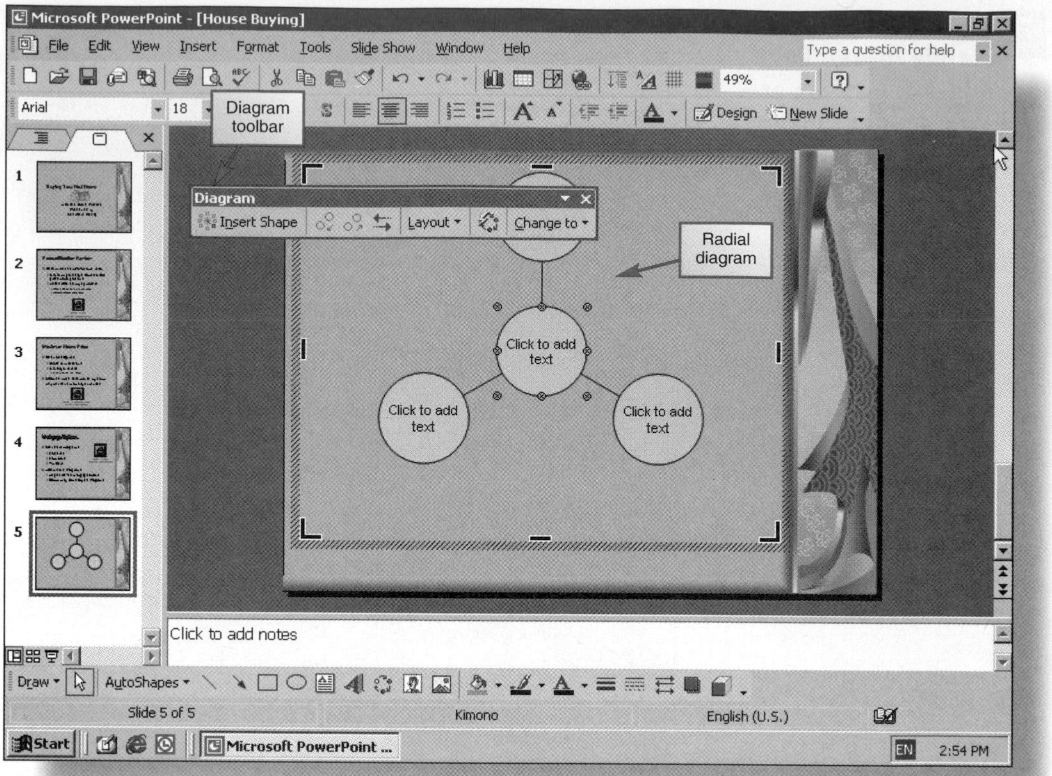

FIGURE 6-49

Other Ways

1. Click Insert Diagram or Organization Chart button on Drawing toolbar
2. On Insert menu click Diagram
3. Press ALT+I, press G
4. In Voice Command mode, say "Insert, Diagram"

The Diagram toolbar displays automatically when you select any diagram other than an organization chart. It contains buttons that allow you to create and design a diagram. Table 6-2 describes the functions of each button on the Diagram toolbar.

Table 6-2 Diagram Toolbar Buttons and Functions

BUTTON	NAME	FUNCTION
Insert Shape	Insert Shape	Adds a new shape next to the selected shape in the diagram, such as a new level to a Pyramid diagram
	Move Shape Backward	Rotates the shape within the diagram
	Move Shape Forward	Rotates the shape within the diagram
	Reverse Diagram	Reverses the order of shapes in the diagram
Layout	Layout	Adjusts the size of the drawing area containing the diagram
	AutoFormat	Customizes the overall style of a diagram with a preset design scheme in the Diagram Style Gallery dialog box
Change to	Change to	Converts the diagram to another type of diagram or chart, such as from a Radial diagram to a Venn diagram

Changing the Radial Diagram Size

Each object inserted into a slide is placed on a drawing layer. Each **drawing layer** is stacked on top of each other and can be rearranged, in a manner similar to shuffling a deck of cards, so that it displays in front of or behind other objects. The Radial diagram drawing layer should display as the top layer of Slide 5, but it is too large. The diagram can be sized and scaled in the same manner as clip art and other objects are sized. Perform the following steps to scale the diagram.

Steps To Change the Radial Diagram Size

1 Right-click the gray slide background in the drawing area and then point to Format Diagram on the shortcut menu.

The shortcut menu displays and a border displays around the drawing area (Figure 6-50).

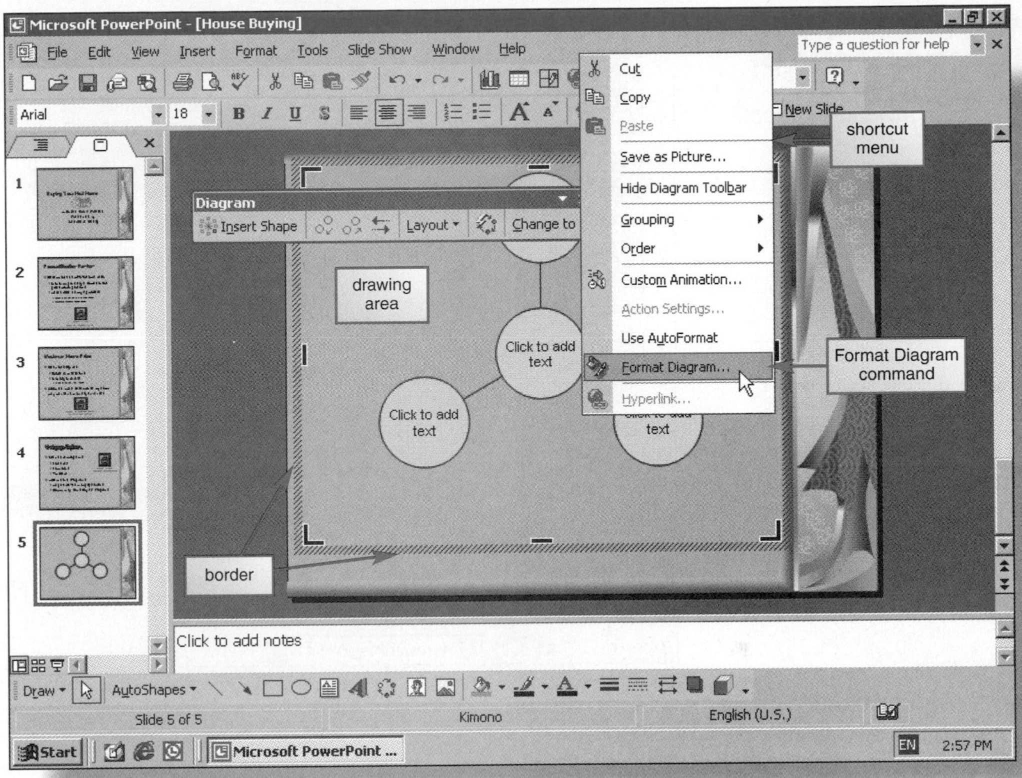

FIGURE 6-50

2 Click Format Diagram. When the Format Diagram dialog box displays, if necessary, click the Size tab and then click and hold down the Height box up arrow in the Scale area until 120 % displays. Point to the OK button.

Both the Height and Width boxes in the Scale area display 120 % (Figure 6-51).

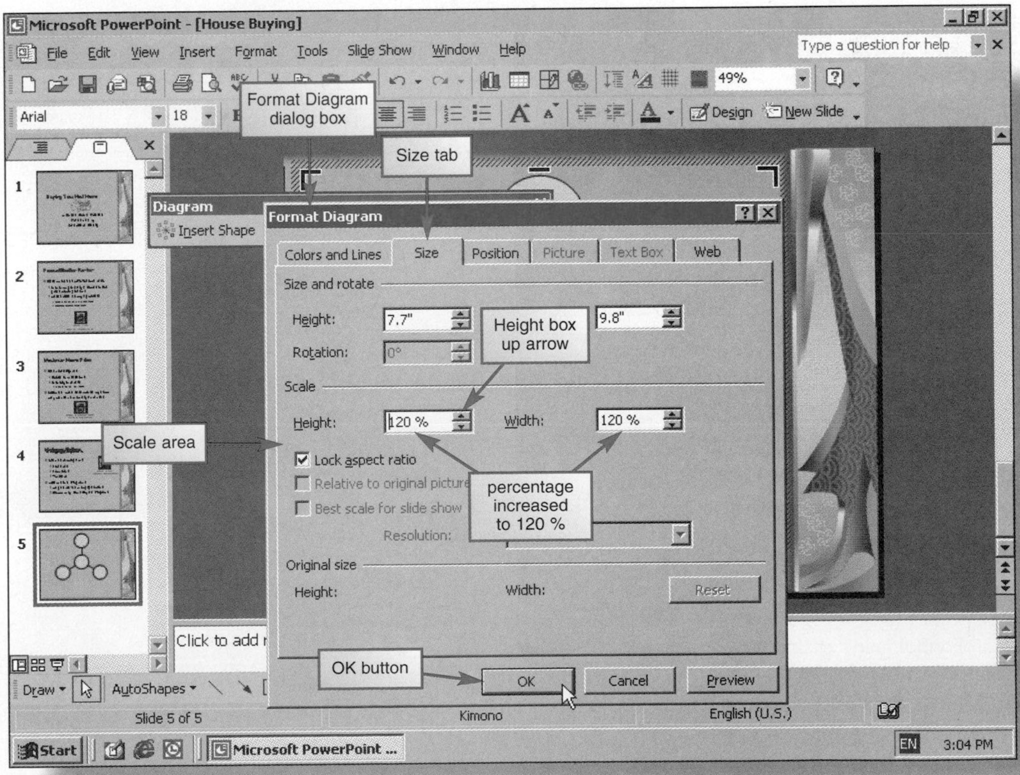

FIGURE 6-51

3 Click the OK button. Click the Layout button on the Diagram toolbar and then point to Fit Diagram to Contents.

The Fit Diagram to Contents command reduces the unnecessary space around the diagram (Figure 6-52).

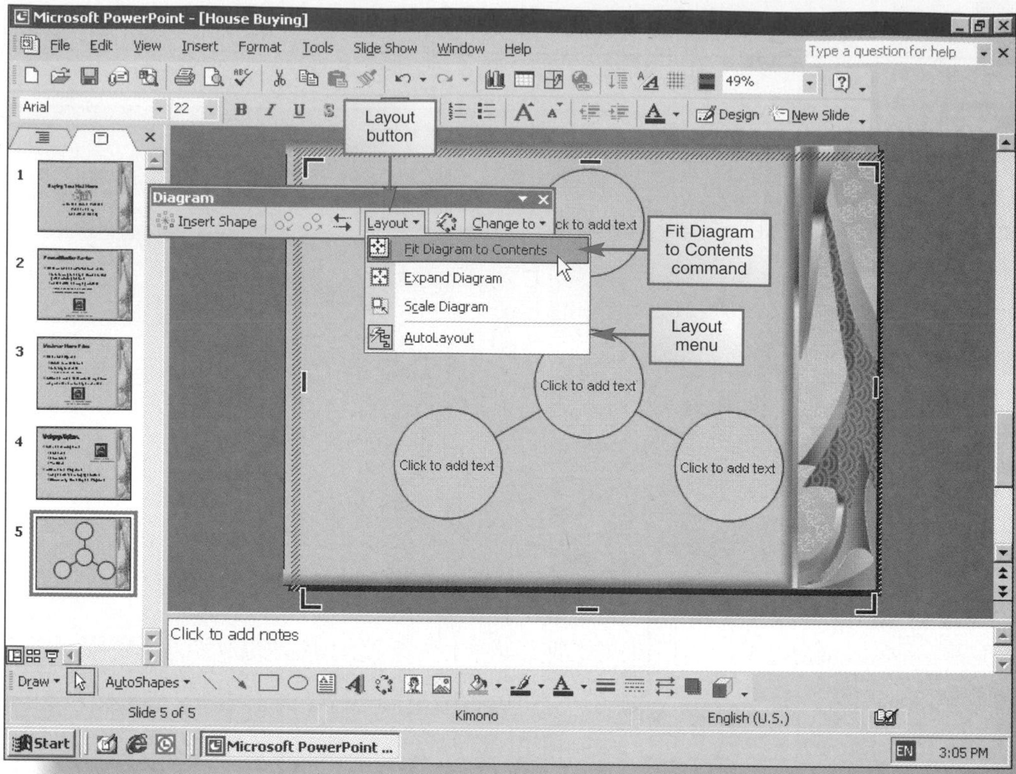

FIGURE 6-52

4 Click Fit Diagram to Contents. Click the border of the diagram and then drag the border down and to the center of the gray area.

The Radial diagram is the desired size and is positioned in the correct location (Figure 6-53).

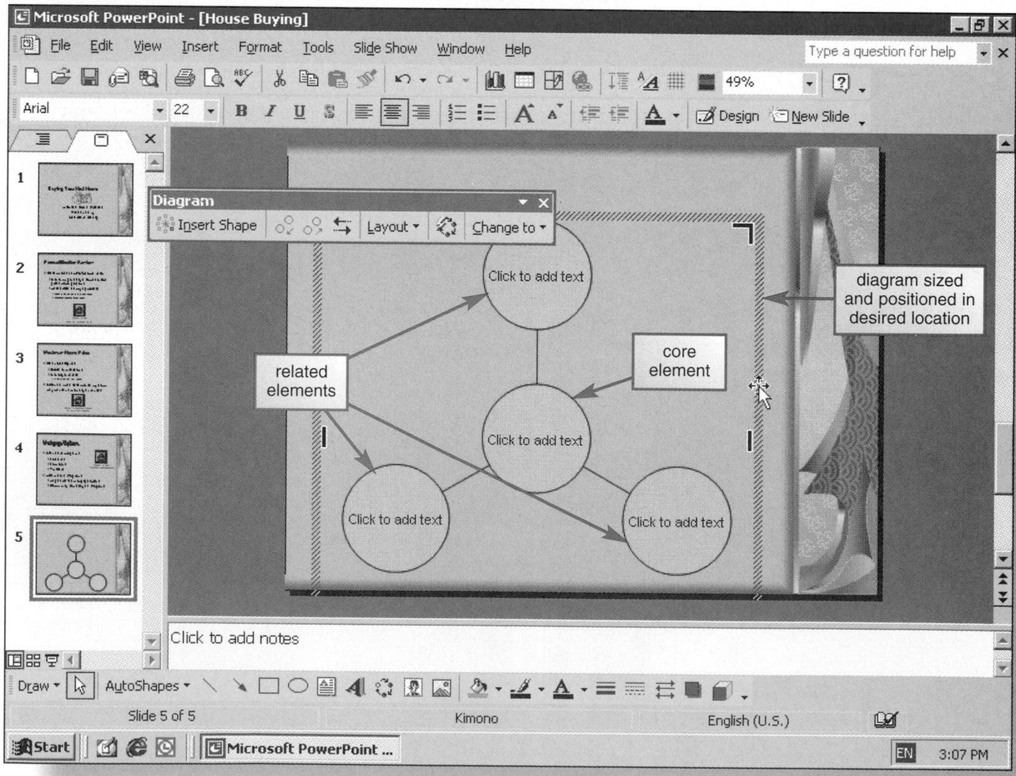

FIGURE 6-53

Other Ways

1. On Format menu click Diagram, click Size tab
2. Press ALT+O, press D, press D
3. In Voice Command mode, say "Format, Diagram, Size"

The Radial diagram displays in the center of Slide 5. It consists of a central core element and three related elements. If necessary, you can use the Diagram toolbar to add and connect additional elements to the core element and to move them forward or backward in the diagram. You also can delete elements by selecting them and then pressing the DELETE key.

More About

Adding Text

In the Target and Cycle diagrams, you can add text only to the text boxes provided. In the other diagrams, you can add text by inserting a text box.

Adding Text to the Diagram Shapes

Text helps users identify the relationships among these objects. Because buying a home has many advantages, placing the words, Outstanding Benefits, in the Radial diagram core element is appropriate and carries the most weight. Three major benefits of home ownership are pride, tax savings, and privacy. These three concepts will be placed in the three shapes connected to the core element. Perform the following steps to add text to the four shapes in the Radial diagram.

Steps To Add Text to the Radial Diagram Shapes

1 Click the center shape. Type `Outstanding` **and then press the ENTER key. Type** `Benefits` **and then point to the top shape.**

The desired text is added to the core element (Figure 6-54).

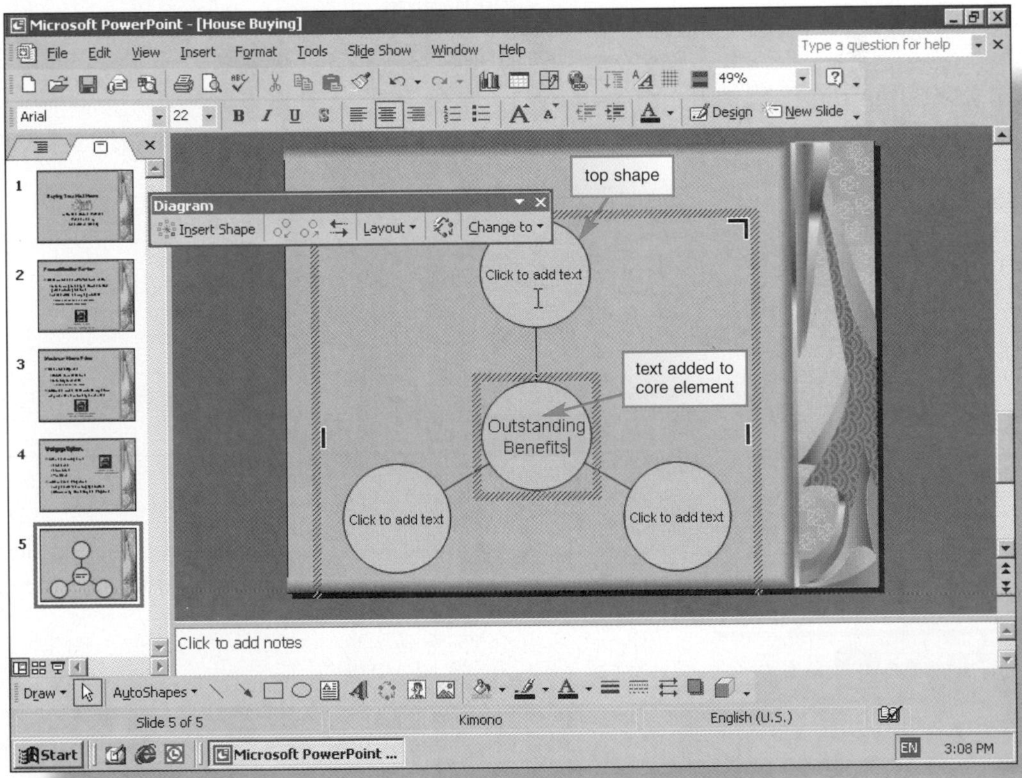

FIGURE 6-54

2 **Click the top shape. Type** `Pride of` **and then press the ENTER key. Type** `Ownership` **and then point to the left shape.**

The text for the first benefit of home ownership is described in the top shape.

3 **Click the left shape. Type** `Tax` **and then press the ENTER key. Type** `Savings` **and then point to the right shape.**

The text for the second benefit of home ownership is described in the left shape.

4 **Click the right shape. Type** `Privacy` **and then point to the AutoFormat button on the Diagram toolbar.**

The text for the third benefit of home ownership is described in the right shape (Figure 6-55).

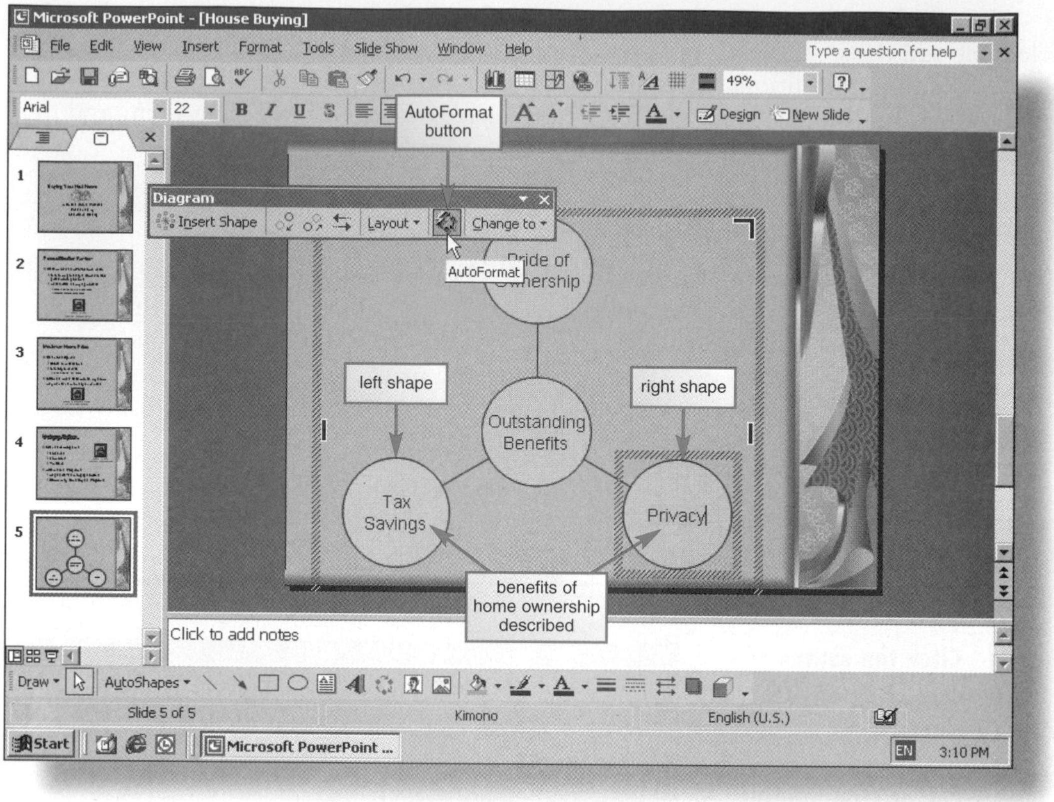

FIGURE 6-55

All elements of the Radial diagram have been added. Formatting the diagram would create visual interest. The next section describes the preset design schemes that can enliven a presentation.

> **More About**
>
> **Adding Sound**
>
> You can add sound to a diagram to direct focus to different pieces of a diagram during a presentation. You can, for example, have PowerPoint play the sound of applause as an element displays.

Formatting the Radial Diagram

PowerPoint provides nine preset styles in addition to the default style in the **Diagram Style Gallery**. These styles use assorted colors, shadows, and lines to add interest and variety. You also can custom format the diagram by adding color, changing the line style and weight, changing the fill color, inserting a background, and adding texture. The following steps show how to format the diagram by applying the 3-D Color diagram style.

Steps To Format the Radial Diagram

1 Click the AutoFormat button on the Diagram toolbar. When the Diagram Style Gallery dialog box displays, click the 3-D Color diagram style. Point to the Apply button.

Diagram Style names display in the list. When you click a name, PowerPoint previews that style (Figure 6-56).

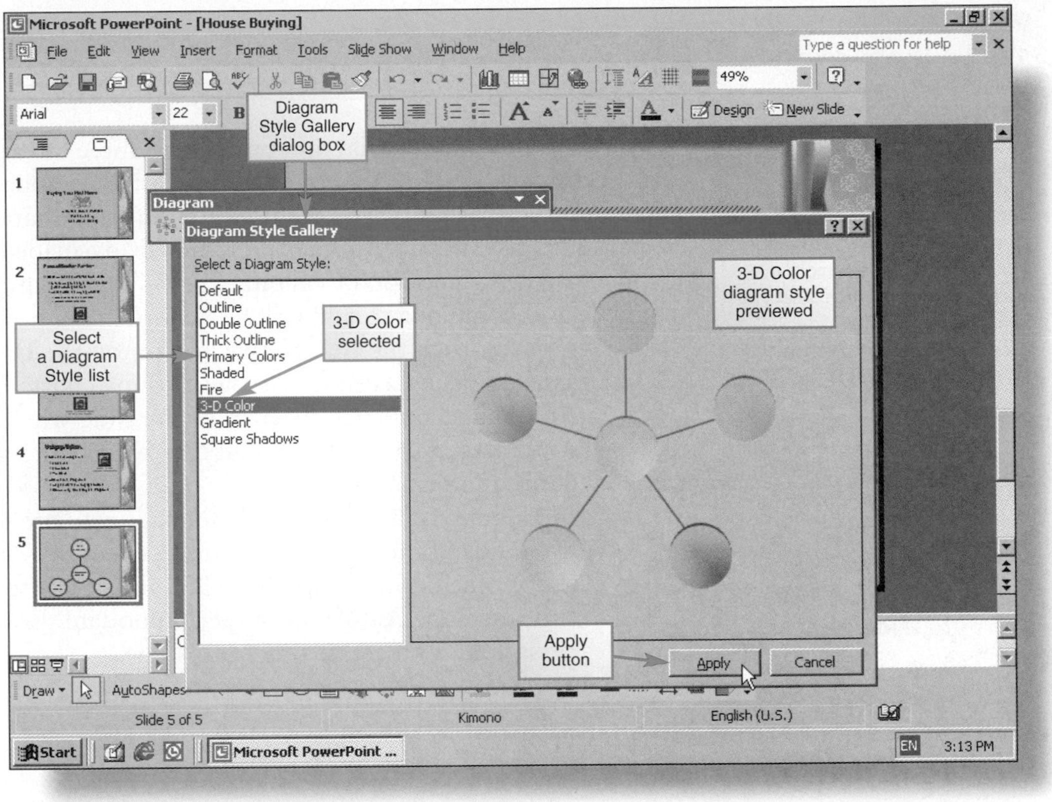

FIGURE 6-56

2 Click the Apply button. Click a gray area of the slide not in the diagram placeholder.

PowerPoint applies the 3-D Color diagram style to the Radial diagram (Figure 6-57).

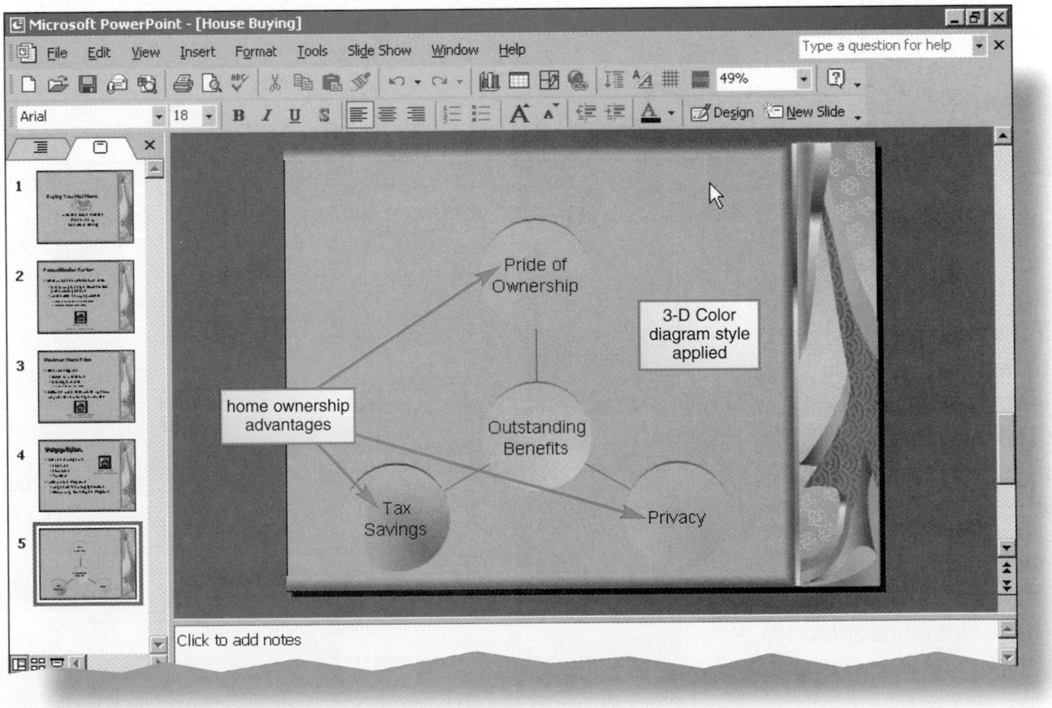

FIGURE 6-57

More About

Transforming AutoShapes

After you insert and format one AutoShape, you may decide to substitute a different AutoShape. Rather than delete the AutoShape, convert it to the shape you desire by selecting the object, clicking the Draw button on the Drawing toolbar, clicking Change AutoShape, and then selecting the new AutoShape on the Change AutoShape submenu.

The elements of the Radial diagram are complete. If you want to move one of the shapes, select that shape and then click the Move Shape Forward or Move Shape Backward button on the Diagram toolbar.

Inserting and Formatting an AutoShape

As shown in the Radial diagram on Slide 5, three advantages of owning a home are pride of ownership, tax savings, and privacy. To emphasize the value of the investment and these benefits, you want to add an AutoShape that calls attention to this remarkable investment. An **AutoShape** is a ready-made object, such as a line, star, banner, arrow, connector, or callout. These shapes can be sized, rotated, flipped, colored, and combined to add unique qualities to a presentation.

You click the AutoShapes button on the Drawing toolbar to select a category, such as Block Arrows or Flowchart. Then, you choose the desired AutoShape and click the area of the slide where you want to insert the AutoShape. You then can add text by clicking the AutoShape and typing the desired information.

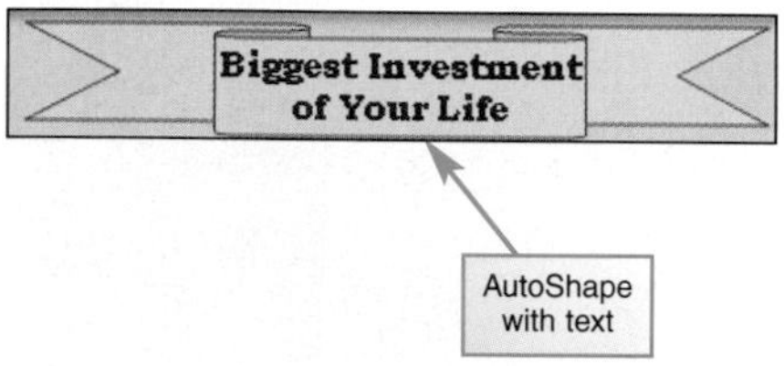

FIGURE 6-58

Figure 6-58 shows the AutoShape you are to create to accompany the Radial diagram. Creating this object requires several steps. First, you must choose the desired AutoShape and insert it into the slide. You then add text and resize the AutoShape to accommodate this text. The next several sections explain how to create this AutoShape.

Inserting an AutoShape

PowerPoint has a variety of AutoShapes organized in the categories of Lines, Connectors, Basic Shapes, Block Arrows, Flowchart, Stars and Banners, Callouts, and Action Buttons. In addition, the More AutoShapes category displays AutoShapes in the Clip Gallery. The first step in creating the AutoShape object is to select the desired shape. Perform the following steps to insert an AutoShape into Slide 5.

Steps To Insert an AutoShape

1 Click the AutoShapes button on the Drawing toolbar, point to Stars and Banners, and then point to Down Ribbon (row 3, column 2) on the Stars and Banners submenu.

The Stars and Banners submenu displays (Figure 6-59). The desired AutoShape, Down Ribbon, is selected.

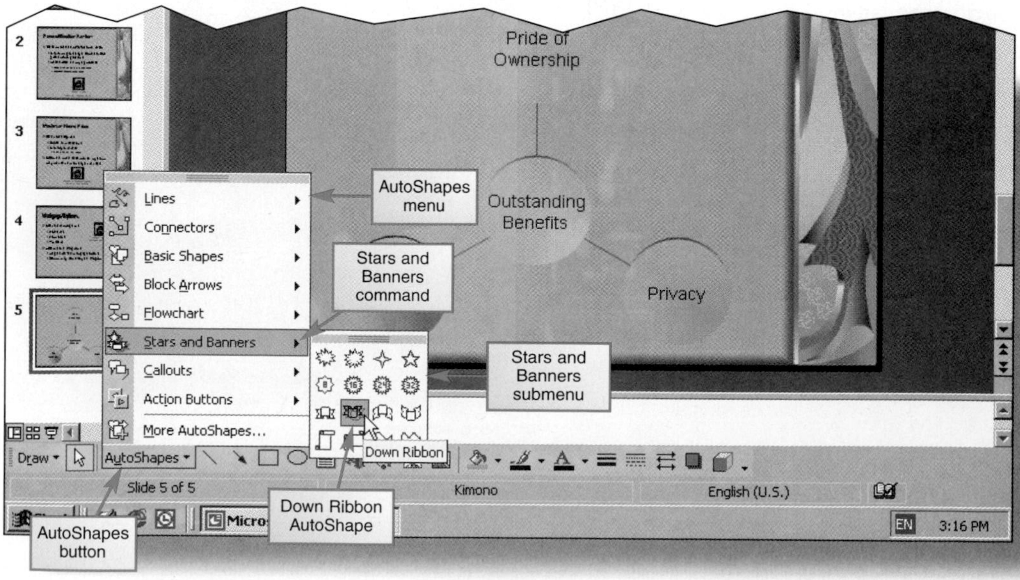

FIGURE 6-59

2 Click Down Ribbon. Point to the gray area at the top of the slide above the Pride of Ownership object.

The mouse pointer changes shape to a cross hair (Figure 6-60). The AutoShape will display in this area of the slide.

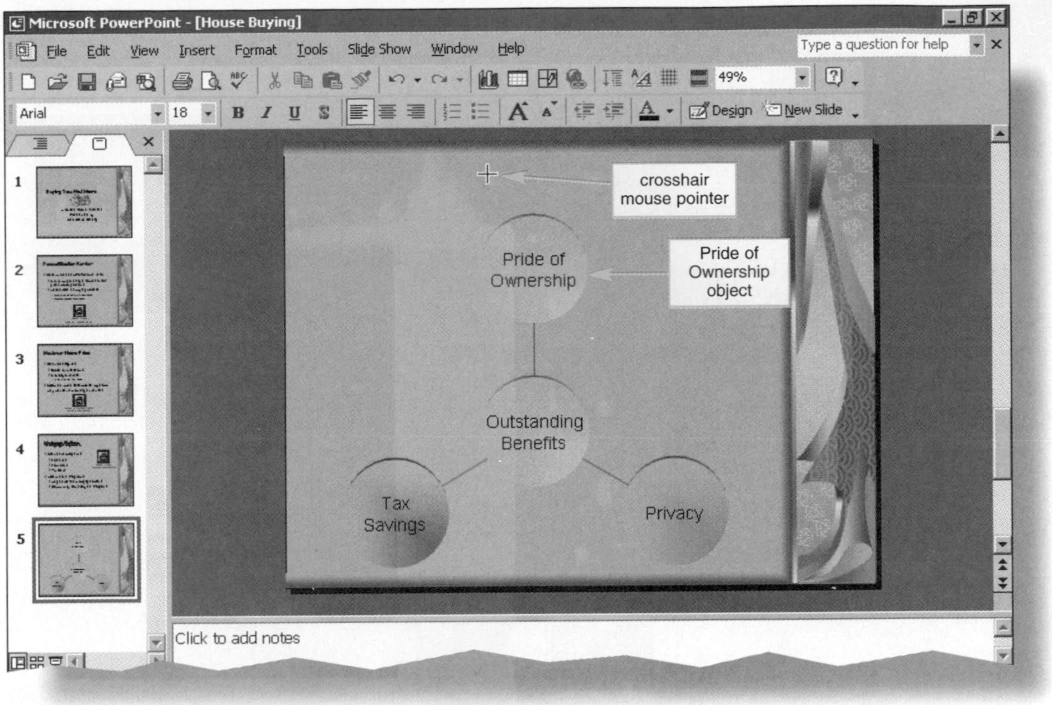

FIGURE 6-60

3 Click the area at the top of the slide.

The Down Ribbon AutoShape displays in the desired location (Figure 6-61).

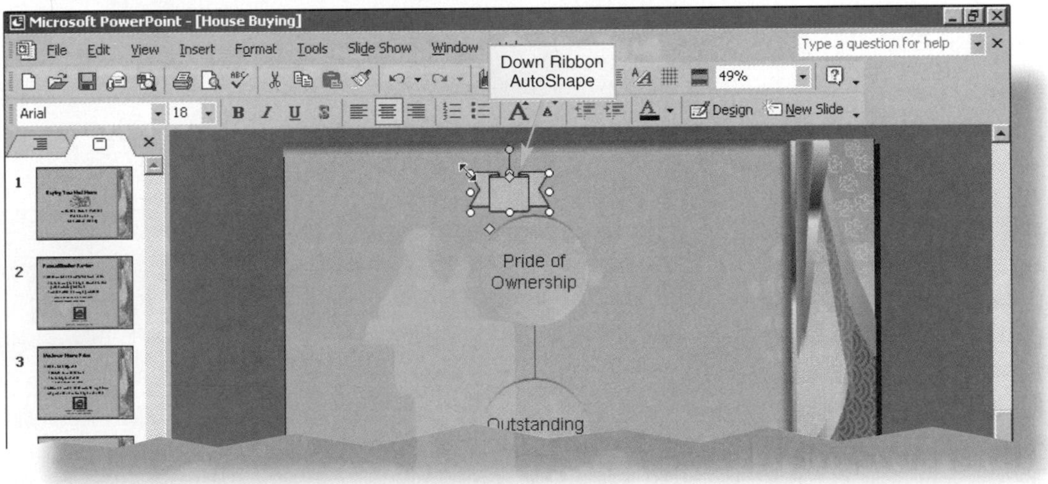

FIGURE 6-61

Other Ways

1. Press ALT+U
2. In Voice Command mode, say "AutoShapes, Stars and Banners, Down Ribbon"

If desired, you now could add special effects and text to the AutoShape. One special effect, for example, is a shadow you can create by clicking Shadow Settings in the Shadow Style list. To allow you to accomplish this, PowerPoint displays the Shadow Settings toolbar containing buttons to turn the shadow on or off, to nudge the shadow up, down, left, or right, and to change the shadow color. Another addition is text. The next section describes adding text to the AutoShape.

Adding Text to an AutoShape

The AutoShape displays on Slide 5 in the correct location. The next step is to add text stating that buying a house is a tremendous investment. The steps on the next page describe how to add this information.

Steps To Add Text to an AutoShape

1 With the AutoShape selected, type Biggest Investment **and then press SHIFT+ENTER. On the next line, type** of Your Life **as the text.**

The AutoShape text displays on two lines (Figure 6-62). Pressing SHIFT+ENTER creates a line break, which moves the insertion point to the beginning of the next line and does not create a new paragraph.

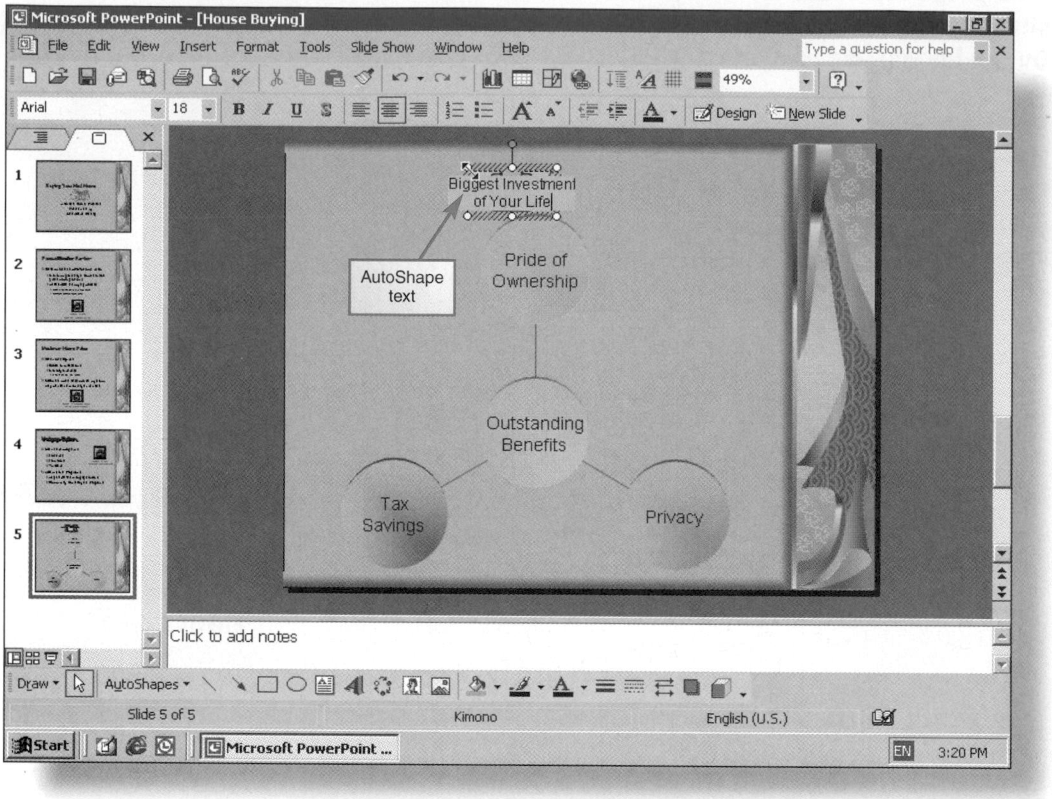

FIGURE 6-62

2 Right-click the AutoShape, click Format AutoShape on the shortcut menu, and then click the Text Box tab in the Format AutoShape dialog box. Click Resize AutoShape to fit text and then point to the OK button.

The Text Box sheet in the Format AutoShape dialog box displays (Figure 6-63). The default text placement is in the middle of the object, as indicated by the entry in the Text anchor point box. You can click the Preview button to see the resized AutoShape.

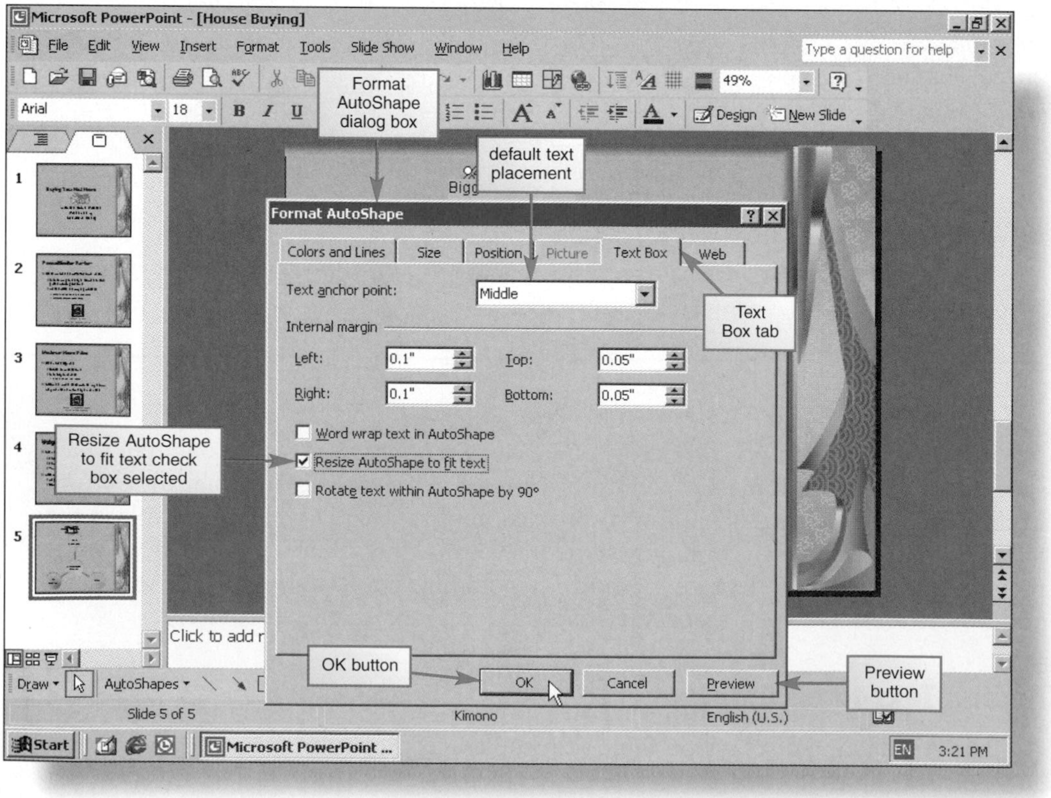

FIGURE 6-63

3 Click the OK button. Click the AutoShape border and drag the object so it is centered above the Pride of Ownership shape.

PowerPoint changes the size of the AutoShape automatically based on the amount of text entered and the amount of space allocated for the AutoShape's margins. The AutoShape displays in the desired location (Figure 6-64). Press the arrow keys to adjust the location.

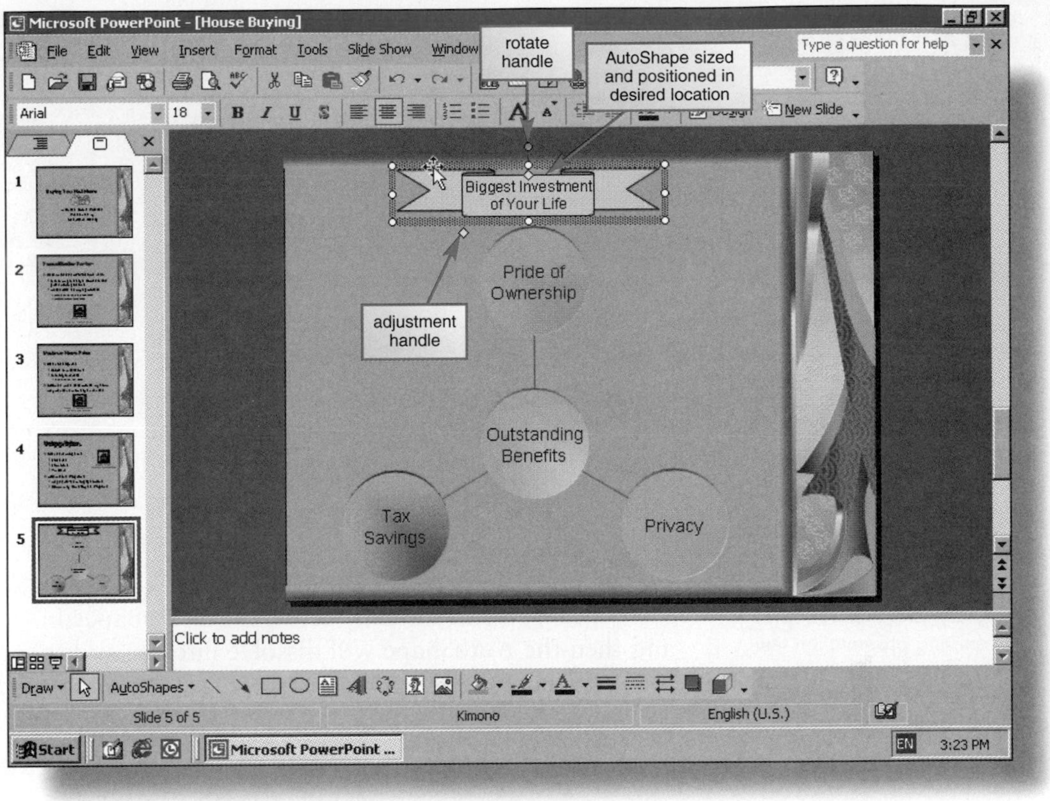

FIGURE 6-64

Other Ways

1. Type desired text, on Format menu click AutoShape, click Text Box tab, click Resize AutoShape to fit text, click OK button
2. Type desired text, press ALT+O, press O, press CTRL+TAB to select Text Box tab, press TAB to select Resize AutoShape to fit text check box, press SPACEBAR, press ENTER
3. Click AutoShape object, drag a sizing handle until object is desired shape and size

You can rotate the AutoShape by dragging the green **rotate handle** on the object in the desired direction. The shape also contains two yellow, diamond-shaped **adjustment handles** that allow appearance changes to the most prominent features of the object. For example, you can change the width of the front part of the ribbon by dragging the bottom adjustment handle to the right or to the left to reduce or expand this area.

Applying an AutoShape Entrance Animation Effect

The next steps in creating Slide 5 are to animate the AutoShape object. Perform the following steps to apply an entrance effect.

TO APPLY AN AUTOSHAPE ENTRANCE ANIMATION EFFECT

1. With the AutoShape selected, click Slide Show on the menu bar, click Custom Animation, and then click the Add Effect button in the Custom Animation task pane.
2. Point to Entrance and then click Dissolve In on the More Effects menu.
3. Click the Start box arrow and then click After Previous in the Add Entrance Effect dialog box.
4. Click the Speed box arrow and then click Slow.

The AutoShape will display slowly in the presentation using the Dissolve In animation effect during the slide show (Figure 6-65 on the next page).

Other Ways

1. Right-click AutoShape, Click Custom Animation on shortcut menu, click Add Effect button
2. Press ALT+D, press M
3. In Voice Command mode, say "Slide Show, Custom Animation, Add Effect, Entrance"

More About

AutoShape Defaults

AutoShapes automatically have a medium shade of green and a thin black border. To change these defaults, double-click a shape to open the Format AutoShape dialog box, make line and color modifications, and then click the Default for new objects check box in the lower-left corner of the Colors and Lines tab. Click the OK button to return to the slide. This formatting will apply to every new AutoShape you insert into a slide. To return to the default settings, click Format on the menu bar, click Apply Design Template, and then reapply the existing presentation template. These settings will override the new default settings.

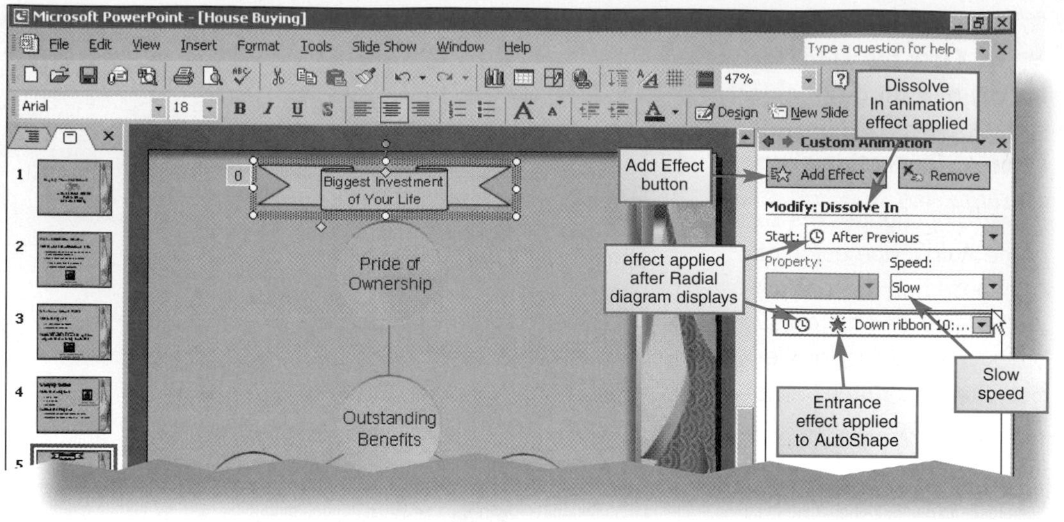

FIGURE 6-65

When you run the slide show, the four shapes in the Radial diagram will display, and then the AutoShape will dissolve into the slide. The next section describes how the AutoShape will move in a triangular pattern around the top object.

Applying a Motion Path Animation Effect to an AutoShape

The next step is applying a motion path to the AutoShape. A **motion path** is a pre-drawn path the shape will follow. In this presentation, the shape will display and then move on the slide in a triangular shape. Perform the following steps to apply a motion path animation effect.

Steps To Apply a Motion Path Animation Effect to an AutoShape

1 With the AutoShape selected, click the Add Effect button in the Custom Animation task pane. Point to Motion Paths and then point to More Motion Paths on the Motion Paths submenu.

The effects in your list may differ (Figure 6-66).

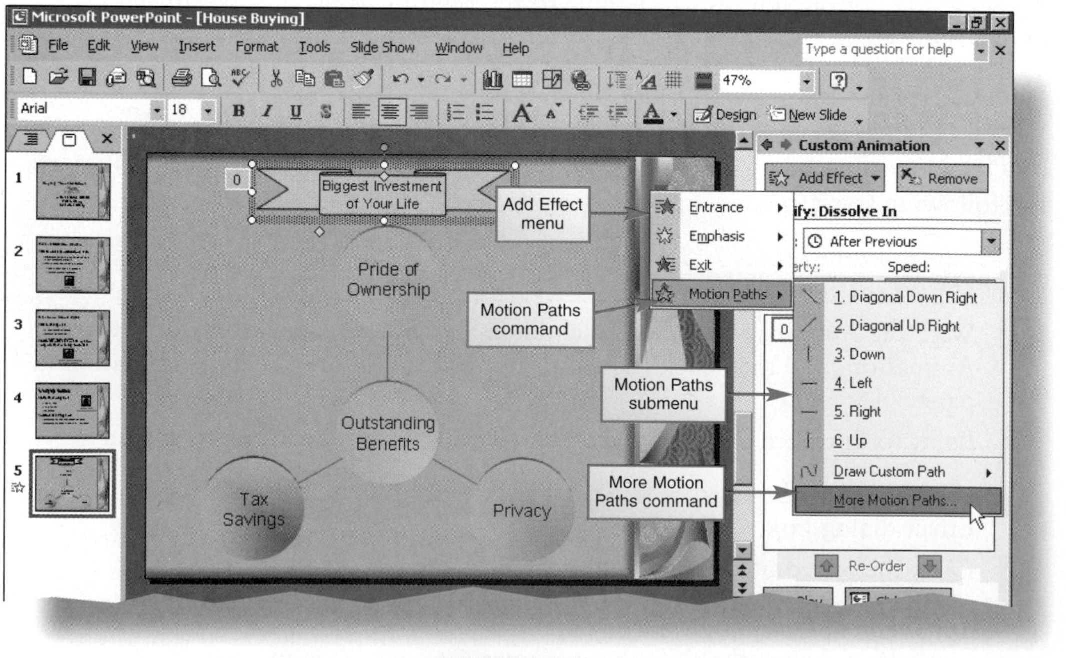

FIGURE 6-66

2 Click More Motion Paths. When the Add Motion Path dialog box displays, click Equal Triangle in the Basic category and then point to the OK button.

The Equal Triangle effect is previewed on Slide 5 behind the dialog box because the Preview Effect check box is selected (Figure 6-67).

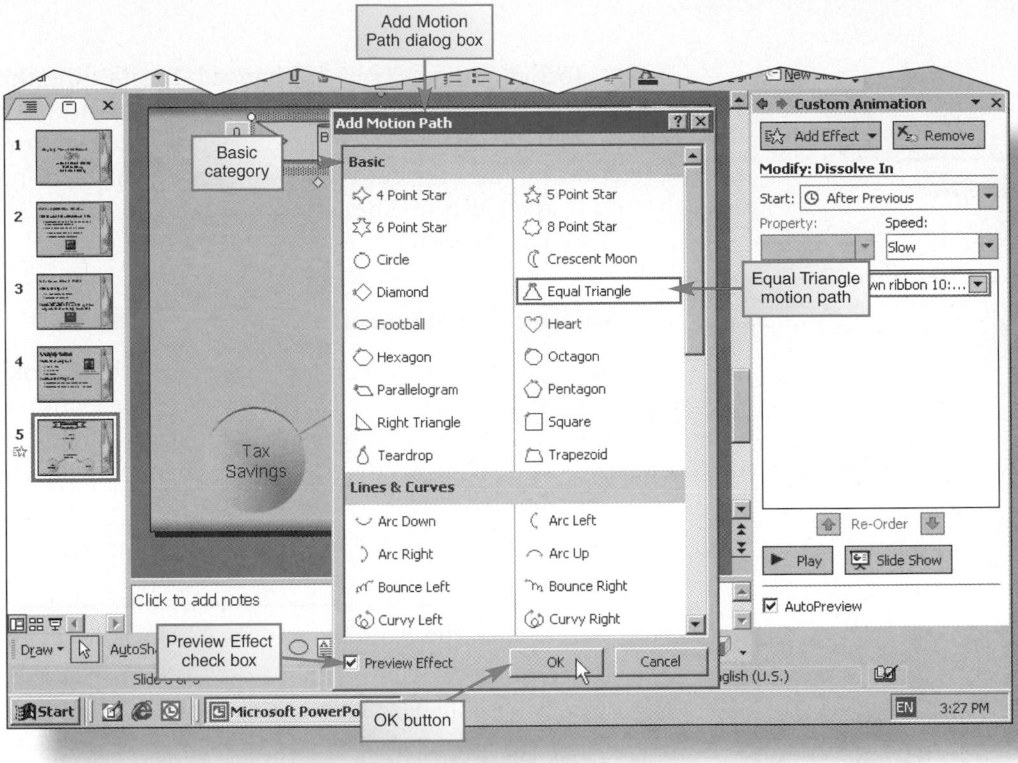

FIGURE 6-67

3 Click the OK button. Click the Start box arrow in the Custom Animation task pane and then click After Previous. Click the Speed box arrow and then click Very Slow.

The Equal Triangle motion path is applied (Figure 6-68).

4 Click the Close button in the Custom Animation task pane.

The AutoShape will move very slowly in a triangular path after the Radial diagram displays.

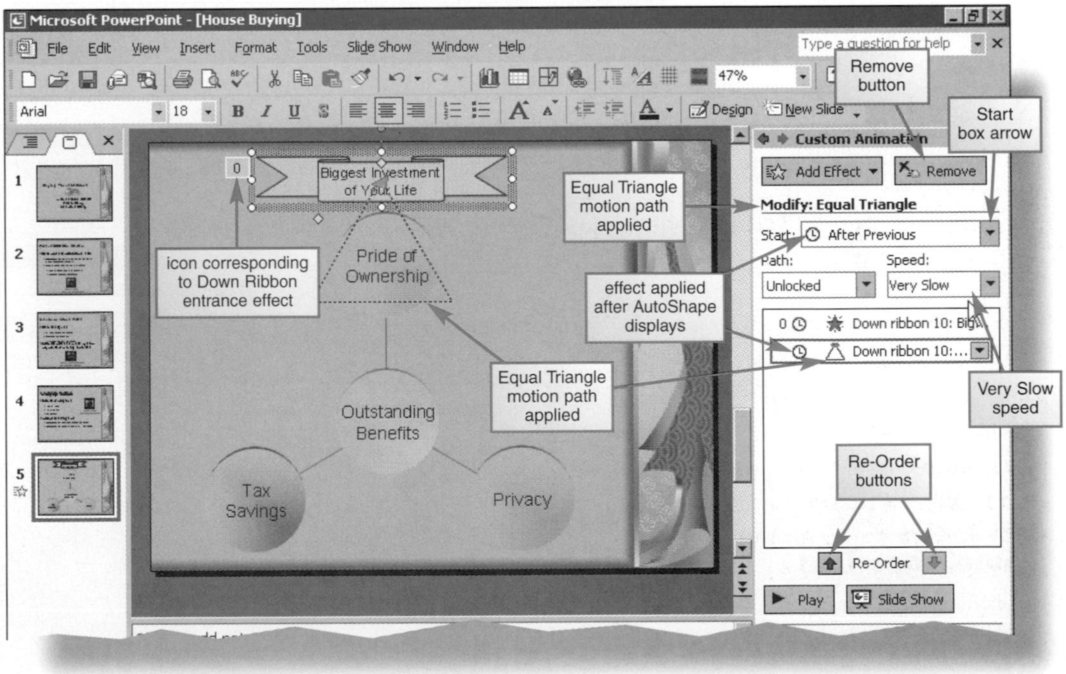

FIGURE 6-68

Effects display in the Custom Animation list in the order they were applied to the slide. This animation sequence can be changed easily by clicking the item you want to move in the list and either dragging it to another position or clicking the Re-Order buttons. The changes are reflected in the renumbered list and in the corresponding icons attached to the placeholders. To remove an effect, click the animation item in the Custom Animation list and then click the Remove button.

A motion path also can be changed. Positioning the mouse pointer over the path and then dragging the path to the desired area on the slide, for example, changes its location. To reverse the movement, right-click the path and then click Reverse Path Direction on the shortcut menu. To apply a different motion path, click the Change button in the Custom Animation task pane, point to Motion Paths, and then click the desired animation.

More About

Graphics

The art field has expanded with the emergence of computer-generated graphics. Web sites profile artists and their works. They also provide resources for computer artists, designers, and technicians. To view these graphics, visit the PowerPoint 2002 More About Web page (scsite.com/pp2002/more.htm) and then click Graphics.

Formatting AutoShape Text

The Kimono design template determines the AutoShape's text attributes. You can, however, change these characteristics. For example, you can modify the font color, change the font, increase the font size, and add bold and italic styles and underline and shadow effects. Perform the following steps to change the AutoShape's font, font size, and font style.

TO FORMAT AUTOSHAPE TEXT

1. Triple-click the AutoShape text. Click the Font box arrow and then click Bookman Old Style.
2. Click the Font Size box arrow and then click 24.
3. Click the Bold button on the Formatting toolbar.
4. Click the slide in an area other than the AutoShape or placeholders.

The bold AutoShape text has the Bookman Old Style font and a font size of 24 (Figure 6-69).

Other Ways

1. Right-click AutoShape, click Custom Animation on shortcut menu, click Add Effect button
2. Press ALT+D, press M
3. In Voice Command mode, say "Slide Show, Custom Animation, Add Effect, Motion Paths"

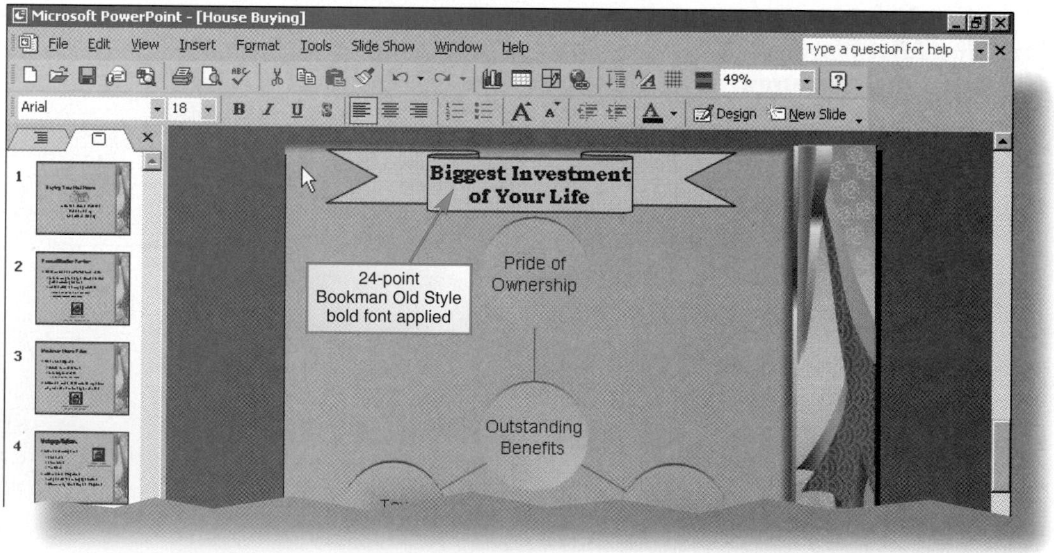

FIGURE 6-69

More About

AutoShape Text

AutoShape text displays in 24-point Times New Roman font. To change the default formatting of text, select the text or AutoShape, click Format on the menu bar, click Font, and then choose a font style, size, color, and effect. Then, click the Default for new objects check box in the lower-right corner of the Font dialog box. Click the OK button to return to the slide.

Text added to an AutoShape becomes part of the shape, which means that it increases font size if the AutoShape is enlarged or that it rotates or flips if the shape is rotated or flipped. If you do not want to attach text to the object, add text instead by using the Text Box button on the Drawing toolbar and then placing the text on top of the object.

All slide elements have been added to the presentation. The next section describes how to set the controls so the slide show runs automatically without user intervention.

Creating a Self-Running Presentation

The House Buying presentation is designed to run unattended. When the last slide in the presentation displays, the slide show **loops**, or restarts, at Slide 1.

PowerPoint has the option of running continuously until a user presses the ESC key. The following steps explain how to set the slide show to run in this manner.

Steps To Create a Self-Running Presentation

1 Click Slide Show on the menu bar and then point to Set Up Show.

The Set Up Show options let you decide how much control, if any, you will give to your audience (Figure 6-70).

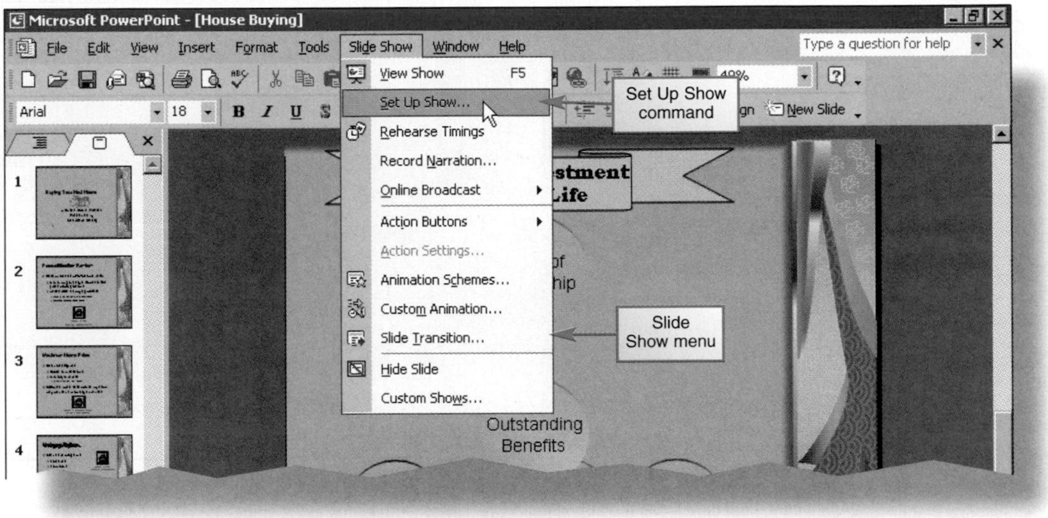

FIGURE 6-70

2 Click Set Up Show. When the Set Up Show dialog box displays, point to Browsed at a kiosk (full screen) in the Show type area.

The Set Up Show dialog box displays (Figure 6-71). The default show type is Presented by a speaker (full screen). The Set Up Show dialog box is used to specify the show type, which slides to display, how to advance slides, how multiple monitors are used, and performance enhancements.

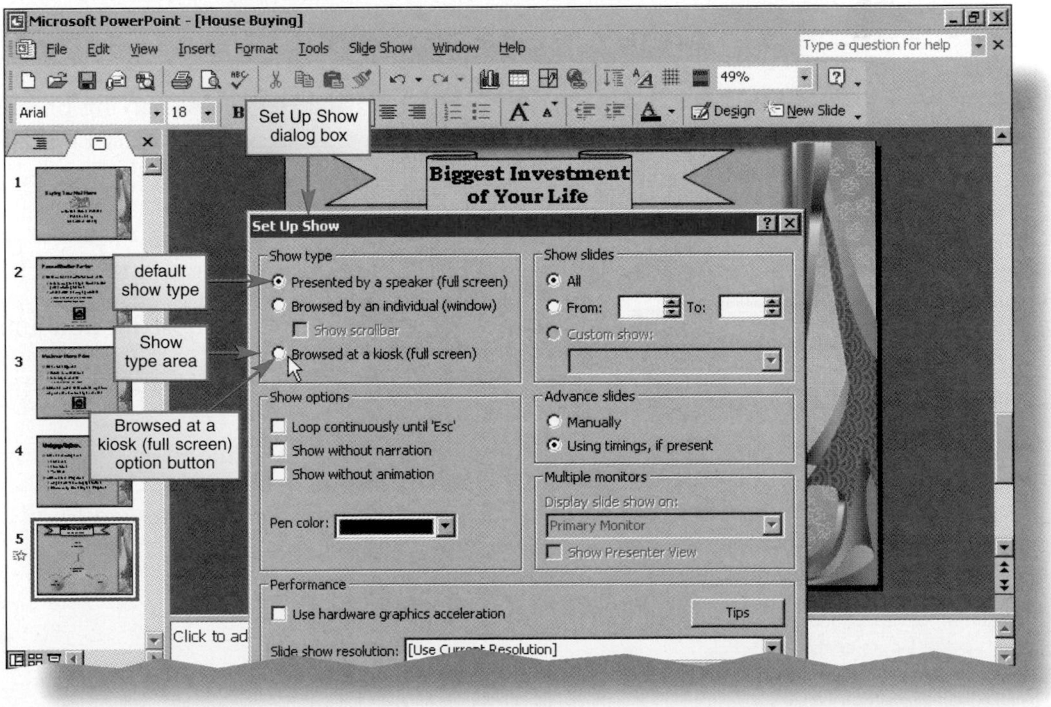

FIGURE 6-71

3 Click Browsed at a kiosk (full screen). Point to the OK button.

A check mark displays in the Loop continuously until 'Esc' check box, and the text box and label are dimmed (Figure 6-72). The slides will advance automatically based on the timings you specify.

4 Click the OK button.

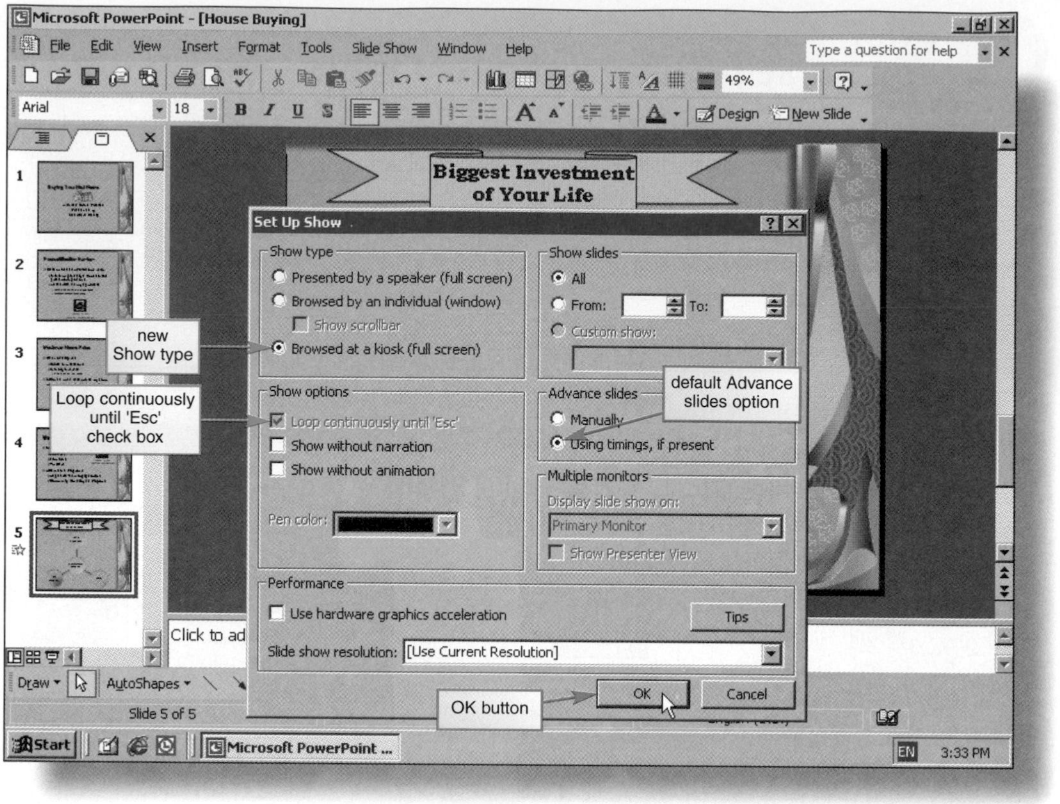

FIGURE 6-72

Other Ways

1. Press ALT+D, press S, press ALT+K, press ENTER
2. In Voice Command mode, say "Slide Show, Set Up Show, Browsed at a kiosk, OK"

This slide show will run by itself without user intervention. The user can, however, advance through the slides manually and click the action buttons.

Adding an Animation Scheme

The next step in preparing the House Buying presentation is to add an animation scheme. Perform the following steps to add the Ellipse motion animation scheme.

TO ADD AN ANIMATION SCHEME

1. Click Slide Show on the menu bar and then click Animation Schemes.
2. Scroll down and then click the Ellipse motion animation scheme in the Exciting category.
3. Click the Apply to All Slides button.
4. Click the Close button on the Slide Design task pane title bar.

The Ellipse motion animation scheme is applied to all slides in the presentation (Figure 6-73).

More About

Quick Reference

For a table that lists how to complete tasks covered in this book using the mouse, menu, shortcut menu, and keyboard, see the Quick Reference Summary at the back of this book or visit the Shelly Cashman Series Office XP Web page (scsite.com/offxp/qr.htm) and then click Microsoft PowerPoint 2002.

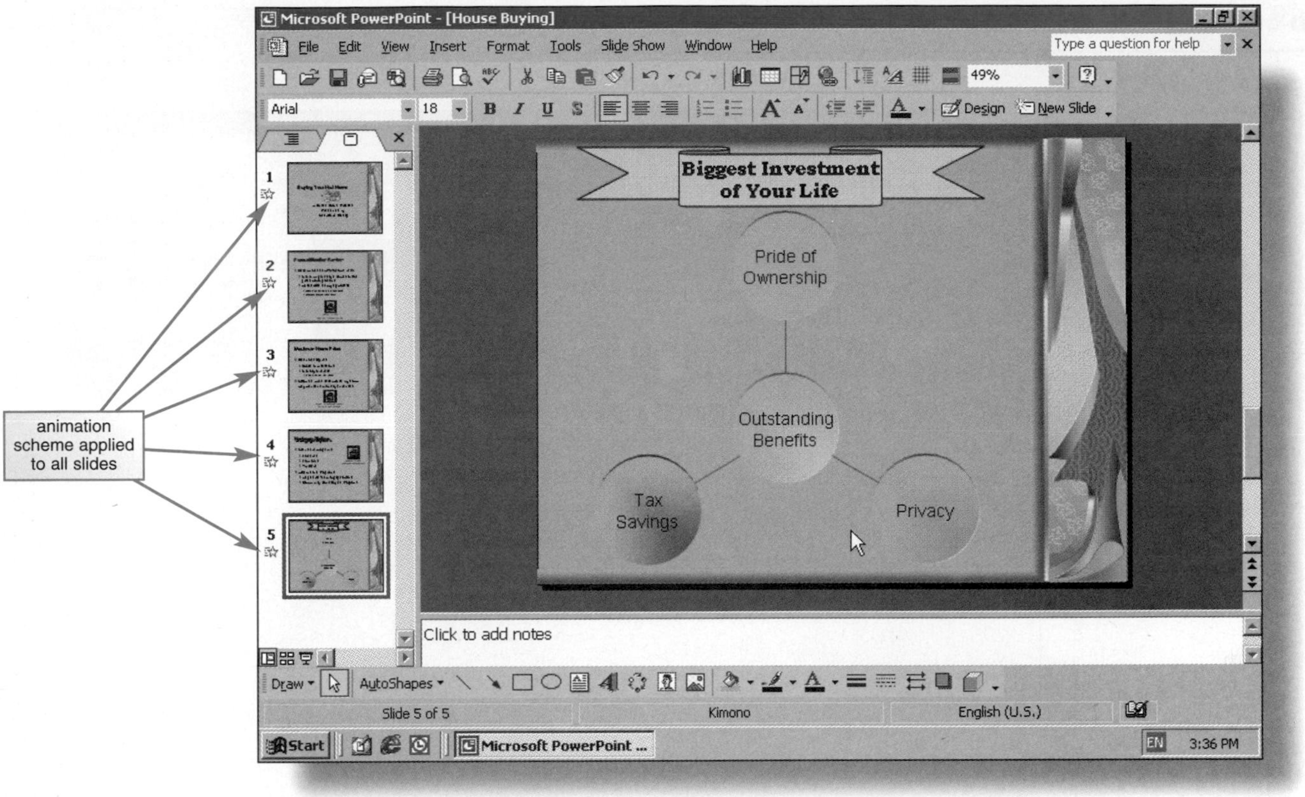

FIGURE 6-73

Setting Slide Show Timings Manually

The slide show is designed to loop continuously at a kiosk for two-and-one-half minutes unless the user moves through the slides manually. Consequently, you must determine the length of time each slide will display on the screen. You can set these times in two ways. One method is to use PowerPoint's **rehearsal** feature, which allows you to advance through the slides at your own pace, and the amount of time you view each slide is recorded. The other method is to set each slide's display time manually. You will use this second technique in the steps on the next page.

More About

Effective Presentations

Major corporations hire graphic designers and speech coaches who work together and develop guidelines that help executives develop effective presentations. These individuals focus on aesthetically pleasing presentations and a fluent delivery. For more information, visit the PowerPoint 2002 More About Web page (scsite.com/pp2002/more.htm) and then click Guidelines.

Steps To Set Slide Show Timing Manually for Slide 1

1 Click the Slide Sorter View button. Right-click Slide 1 and then point to Slide Transition.

Slide 1 is selected (Figure 6-74).

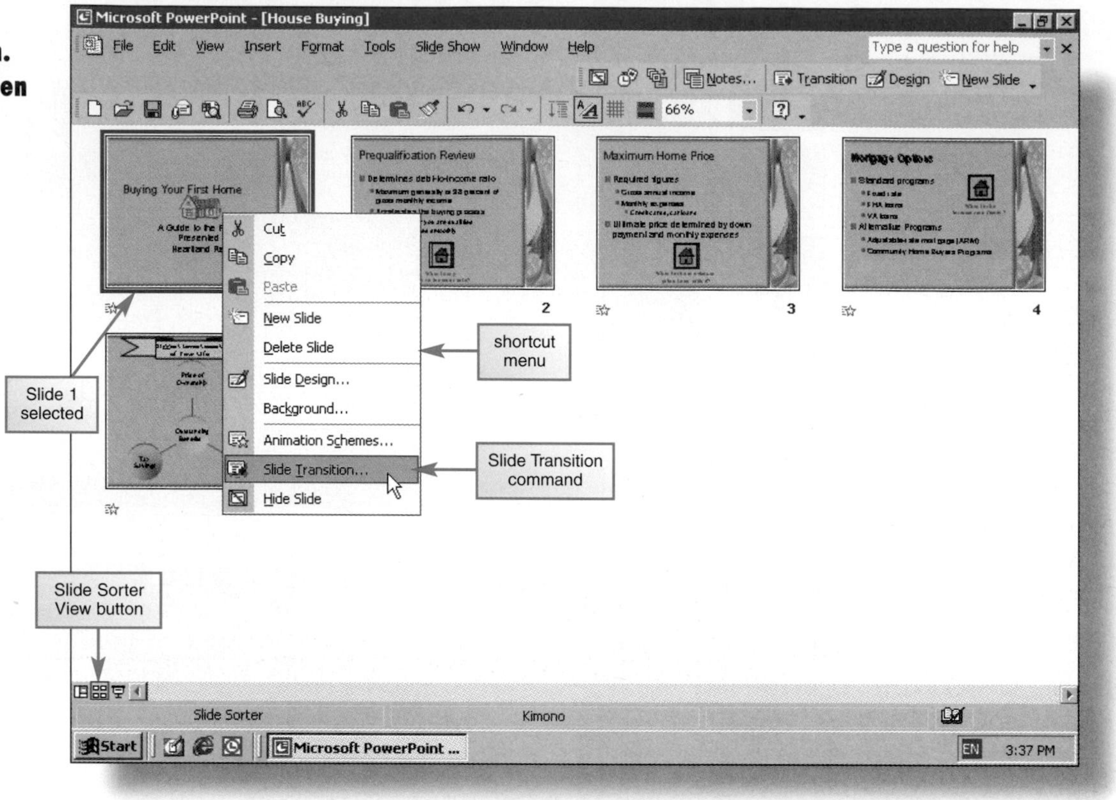

FIGURE 6-74

2 Click Slide Transition. Point to Automatically after in the Advance slide area.

The Slide Transition task pane displays (Figure 6-75). The On mouse click check box is selected. A speaker generally uses this default setting to advance through the slides in a presentation. The Strips Right-Down transition effect is part of the Ellipse motion animation scheme.

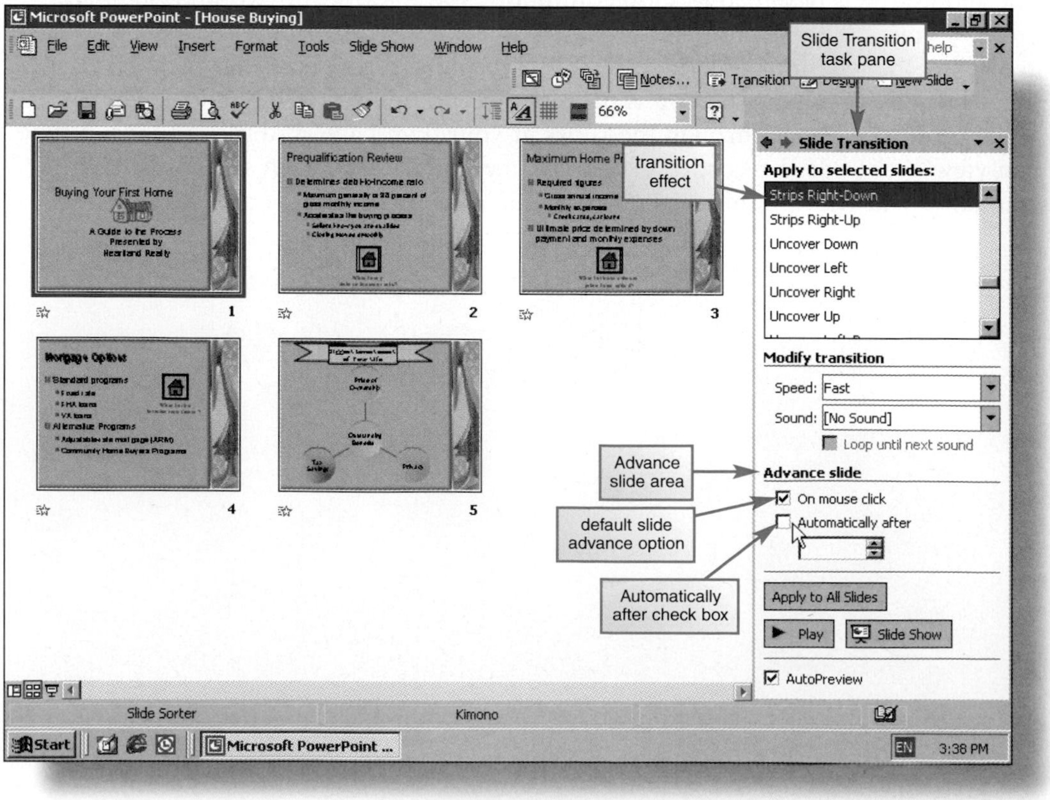

FIGURE 6-75

3 Click Automatically after and then point to the Automatically after box up arrow.

This slide show advances the slide automatically after it has displayed for a designated period or allows users to display the slides manually (Figure 6-76). You specify the length of time you want the slide to display in the Automatically after text box.

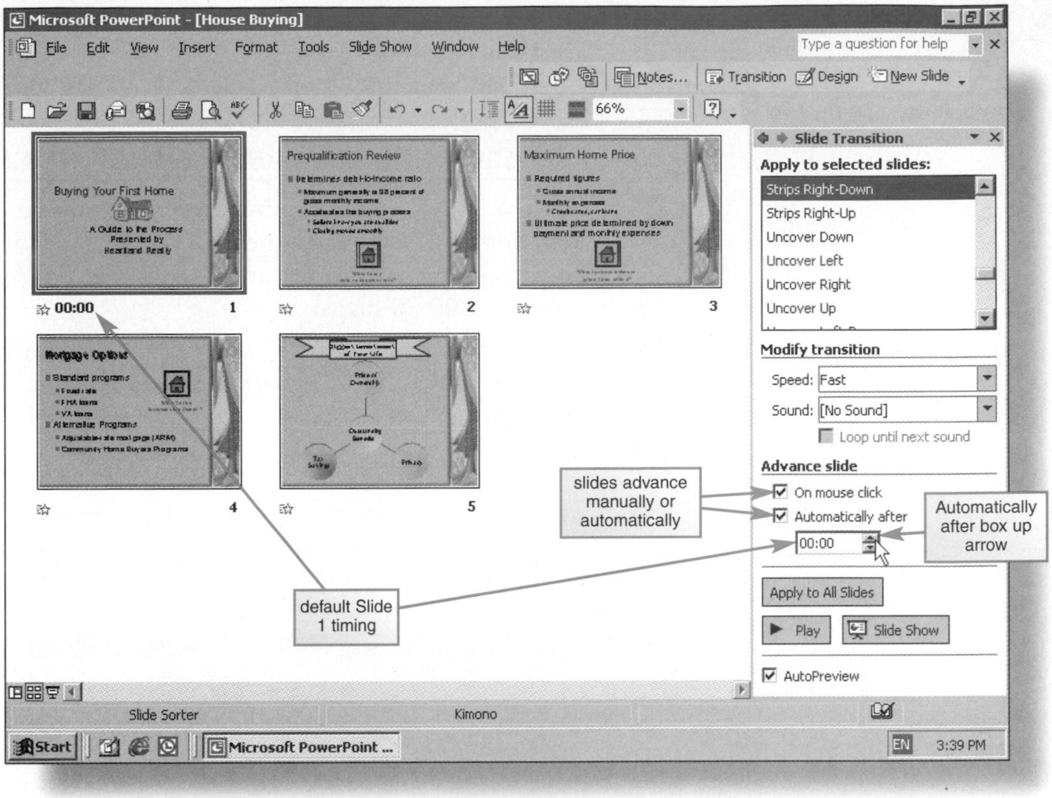

FIGURE 6-76

4 Click and hold down the mouse button on the Automatically after box up arrow until 00:15 displays and then point to the Play button.

The Automatically after text box displays 00:15 seconds (Figure 6-77). Another method of entering the time is to type the specific number of minutes and seconds in the text box.

5 Click the Play button.

The Strips Right-Down slide transition displays in the Slide 1 slide thumbnail. Below Slide 1, 00:15 displays indicating the designated slide timing.

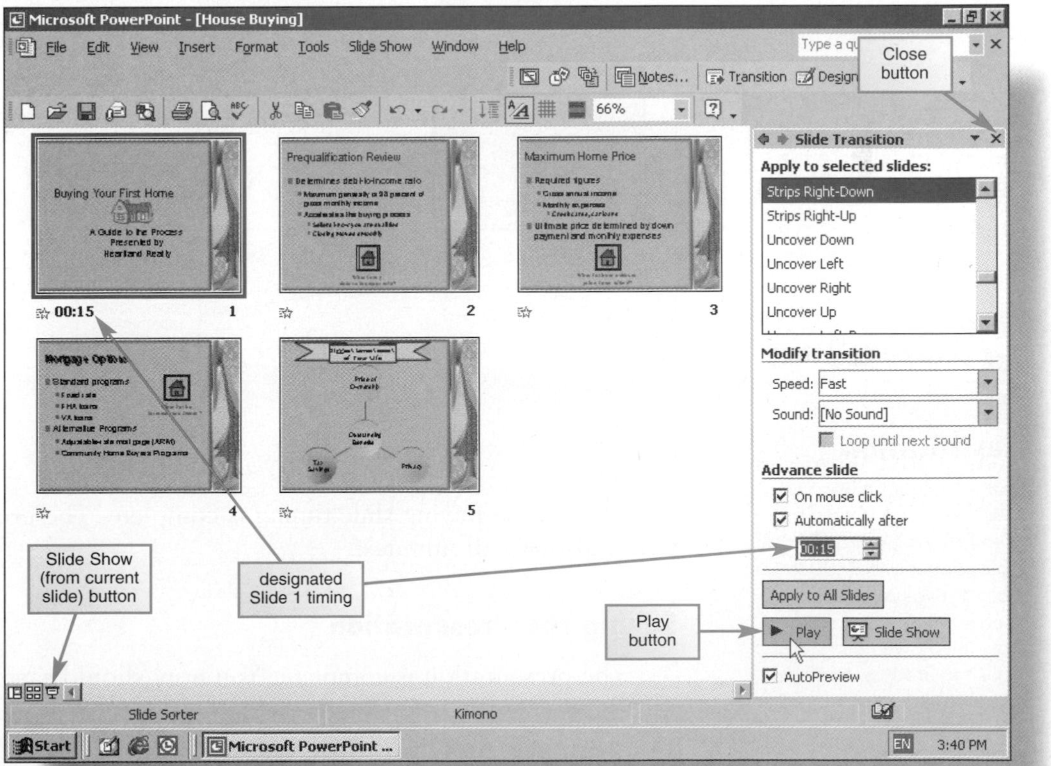

FIGURE 6-77

Other Ways

1. On Slide Show menu click Slide Transition, click Automatically after, click Automatically after box up arrow, click Apply button
2. Press ALT+D, press T, type desired time, press ENTER
3. In Voice Command mode, say "Slide Show, Slide Transition, Automatically after, [type time], Close"

The timing for Slide 1 is complete. You need to repeat this procedure for Slides 2 through 5 in the House Buying presentation. Perform the following steps to set these timings.

TO SET SLIDE SHOW TIMINGS MANUALLY FOR THE REMAINING SLIDES

1. Click the Slide 2 slide thumbnail, press and hold down the SHIFT key, and then click Slide 4. Click Automatically after in the Advance Slide area in the Slide Transition task pane. Click and hold down the Automatically after box up arrow until 00:30 displays.
2. Click the Slide 5 slide thumbnail. Click Automatically after in the Advance Slide area in the Slide Transition task pane. Click and hold down the Automatically after box up arrow until 00:45 displays.
3. Click the Play button.
4. Click the Close button in the Slide Transition task pane title bar.

Each slide's timing displays in the lower-left corner (Figure 6-78).

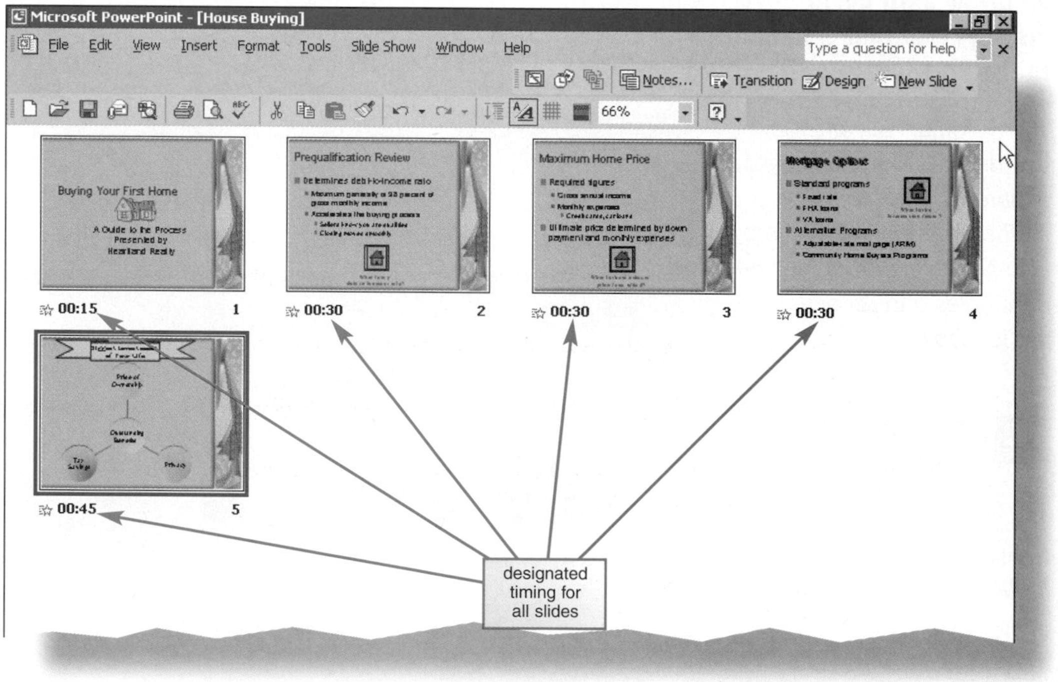

FIGURE 6-78

The House Buying slide timing is complete. The presentation will run for two-and-one-half minutes.

Saving the Presentation

The presentation is complete. You now should save it again.

Starting the Self-Running Presentation

Starting a self-running slide show basically is the same as starting any other slide show. Perform the following steps to run the presentation.

More About

Microsoft Certification

The Microsoft Office User Specialist (MOUS) Certification program provides an opportunity for you to obtain a valuable industry credential — proof that you have the PowerPoint 2002 skills required by employers. For more information, see Appendix E or visit the Shelly Cashman Series MOUS Web page at scsite.com/offxp/cert.htm.

TO START THE SELF-RUNNING PRESENTATION

1. Click Slide 1 and click the Slide Show (from current slide) button.
2. When Slide 2 displays, click the action button. If a security warning displays, click the OK button. Type 4000 in the Monthly Income text box. Click the Monthly Mortgage Amount text box and then type 850 in the box. Click the Total Monthly Expenses text box and then type 500 in the box. Click the Calculate button.
3. Click the OK button, click the Clear button and then enter 2500 in the Monthly Income text box, 650 in the Monthly Mortgage Amount text box, and 500 in the Total Monthly Expenses text box. Click the Calculate button. Click the OK button. Click the Close button.
4. When Slide 3 displays, click the action button. If necessary, maximize the Microsoft Excel window when the worksheet displays. Click the Gross annual income figure (cell B3) and then type 48000 in that cell. Press the ENTER key. Click the Monthly non-housing expenses figure (cell B6) and then type 500 in that cell. Press the ENTER key.
5. After you review the figures, including the Estimated affordable price, click the Gross annual income figure (cell B3) and then type 30000 in that cell. Press the ENTER key. Click the Monthly non-housing expenses figure (cell B6) and then type 500 in that cell. Press the ENTER key.
6. After you review the figures, click the Close button on the Microsoft Excel title bar to return to the presentation.
7. When Slide 4 displays, click the action button. If necessary, maximize the Microsoft Word window when the table displays. Review the table and then click the Close button on the Microsoft Word title bar to return to the presentation.
8. When Slide 5 displays, review the information on the diagram.
9. When Slide 1 displays, press the ESC key to stop the presentation.

The presentation will run for two-and-one-half minutes, and then it will loop back to the beginning and start automatically.

Printing Slides as Handouts

Perform the following steps to print the presentation slides as handouts, three slides per page.

TO PRINT SLIDES AS HANDOUTS

1. Ready the printer.
2. Click File on the menu bar and then click Print.
3. Click the Print what box arrow and then click Handouts in the list.
4. Click the Slides per page box arrow in the Handouts area and then click 3 in the list.
5. Click the OK button.

The handouts print as shown in Figure 6-79 on the next page.

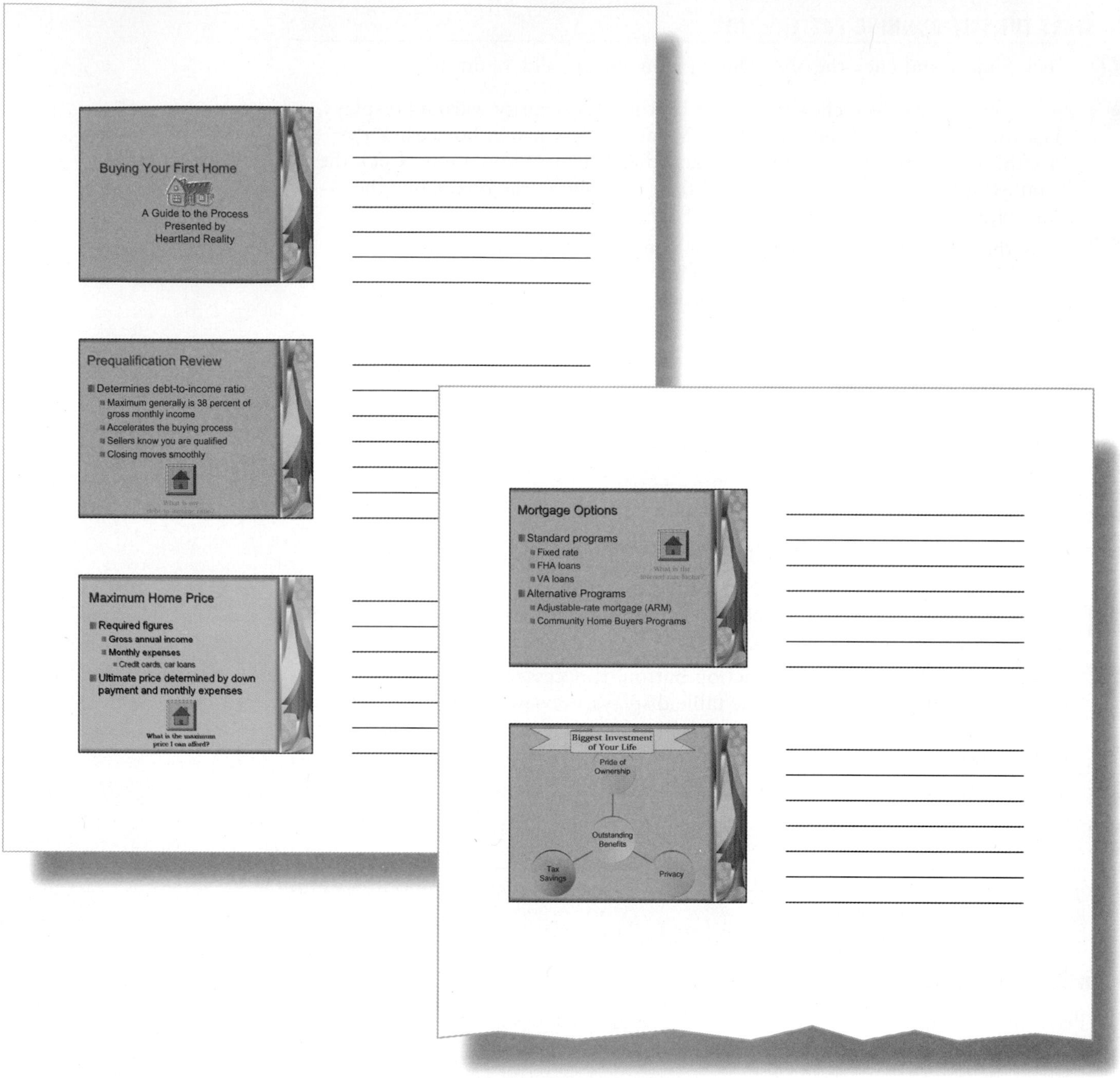

FIGURE 6-79

The House Buying presentation now is complete. If you made any changes to your presentation since your last save, you now should save it again before quitting PowerPoint.

CASE PERSPECTIVE SUMMARY

The House Buying slide show should help first-time buyers understand the process of purchasing real estate. When they arrive for their appointments at Heartland Realty, they can view your presentation at a kiosk and learn the basics of prequalification, determine the approximate home price they can afford, preview mortgage options, and understand the advantages of owning a home. The real estate agents should find your presentation beneficial for introducing their customers to the house-buying process.

Project Summary

Project 6 presented the principles of creating a self-running presentation that can run at a kiosk. You began the project by starting a new presentation and then inserting a slide from another presentation. Next, you embedded a Visual Basic program, an Excel worksheet, and a Word table. You then inserted, formatted, and animated a Radial diagram. Next, you inserted and formatted an AutoShape and added text and a motion path animation effect. You then added an animation scheme and set automatic slide timings to display each slide for a designated period of time. Finally, you printed your presentation slides as handouts with three slides displaying on each page.

What You Should Know

Having completed this project, you now should be able to perform the following tasks:

- Add a Caption to the Slide 2 Action Button *(PP 6.31)*
- Add a Fill Color to the Slide 2 and Slide 3 Action Buttons *(PP 6.27)*
- Add a Fill Color to the Slide 4 Action Button *(PP 6.26)*
- Add a Shadow to the Action Buttons *(PP 6.28)*
- Add a Shadow to the Slide 3 and Slide 4 Action Buttons *(PP 6.29)*
- Add an Action Button and Action Settings *(PP 6.18)*
- Add an Animation Scheme *(PP 6.52)*
- Add Captions to the Slide 3 and Slide 4 Action Buttons *(PP 6.32)*
- Add Lines to the Slide 2 and Slide 3 Action Buttons *(PP 6.30)*
- Add Lines to the Slide 4 Action Button *(PP 6.30)*
- Add Notes *(PP 6.15)*
- Add Text to an AutoShape *(PP 6.46)*
- Add Text to the Radial Diagram Shapes *(PP 6.41)*
- Apply a Motion Path Animation Effect to an AutoShape *(PP 6.48)*
- Apply an AutoShape Entrance Animation Effect *(PP 6.47)*
- Change the Radial Diagram Size *(PP 6.39)*
- Create a Self-Running Presentation *(PP 6.51)*
- Create a Title Slide *(PP 6.07)*
- Create Additional Action Buttons and Hyperlinks *(PP 6.21)*
- Create Slide 2 *(PP 6.08)*
- Create Slide 3 *(PP 6.09)*
- Display Guides and Position the Slide 2 Action Button *(PP 6.23)*
- Format AutoShape Text *(PP 6.50)*
- Format the Radial Diagram *(PP 6.43)*
- Format the Slide 2 and Slide 3 Action Button Caption Text *(PP 6.34)*
- Format the Slide 4 Action Button Caption Text *(PP 6.33)*
- Hide Guides *(PP 6.26)*
- Insert a Radial Diagram *(PP 6.36)*
- Insert a Slide from Another Presentation *(PP 6.12)*
- Insert an AutoShape *(PP 6.44)*
- Insert, Size, and Move a Clip on a Slide *(PP 6.16)*
- Position the Slide 3 and Slide 4 Action Buttons *(PP 6.25)*
- Print Slides as Handouts *(PP 6.57)*
- Save a Presentation *(PP 6.15)*
- Scale Action Buttons *(PP 6.22)*
- Set Slide Show Timing Manually for Slide 1 *(PP 6.54)*
- Set Slide Show Timings Manually for the Remaining Slides *(PP 6.56)*
- Start and Customize a New Presentation *(PP 6.06)*
- Start the Self-Running Presentation *(PP 6.57)*

Learn It Online

Instructions: To complete the Learn It Online exercises, start your browser, click the Address bar, and then enter `scsite.com/offxp/exs.htm`. When the Office XP Learn It Online page displays, follow the instructions in the exercises below.

1 Project Reinforcement TF, MC, and SA

Below PowerPoint Project 6, click the Project Reinforcement link. Print the quiz by clicking Print on the File menu. Answer each question. Write your first and last name at the top of each page, and then hand in the printout to your instructor.

2 Flash Cards

Below PowerPoint Project 6, click the Flash Cards link. When Flash Cards displays, read the instructions. Type 20 (or a number specified by your instructor) in the Number of Playing Cards text box, type your name in the Name text box, and then click the Flip Card button. When the flash card displays, read the question and then click the Answer box arrow to select an answer. Flip through Flash Cards. Click Print on the File menu to print the last flash card if your score is 15 (75%) correct or greater and then hand it in to your instructor. If your score is less than 15 (75%) correct, then redo this exercise by clicking the Replay button.

3 Practice Test

Below PowerPoint Project 6, click the Practice Test link. Answer each question, enter your first and last name at the bottom of the page, and then click the Grade Test button. When the graded practice test displays on your screen, click Print on the File menu to print a hard copy. Continue to take practice tests until you score 80% or better. Hand in a printout of the final practice test to your instructor.

4 Who Wants to Be a Computer Genius?

Below PowerPoint Project 6, click the Computer Genius link. Read the instructions, enter your first and last name at the bottom of the page, and then click the Play button. Hand in your score to your instructor.

5 Wheel of Terms

Below PowerPoint Project 6, click the Wheel of Terms link. Read the instructions, and then enter your first and last name and your school name. Click the Play button. Hand in your score to your instructor.

6 Crossword Puzzle Challenge

Below PowerPoint Project 6, click the Crossword Puzzle Challenge link. Read the instructions, and then enter your first and last name. Click the Play button. Work the crossword puzzle. When you are finished, click the Submit button. When the crossword puzzle redisplays, click the Print button. Hand in the printout.

7 Tips and Tricks

Below PowerPoint Project 6, click the Tips and Tricks link. Click a topic that pertains to Project 6. Right-click the information and then click Print on the shortcut menu. Construct a brief example of what the information relates to in PowerPoint to confirm you understand how to use the tip or trick. Hand in the example and printed information.

8 Newsgroups

Below PowerPoint Project 6, click the Newsgroups link. Click a topic that pertains to Project 6. Print three comments. Hand in the comments to your instructor.

9 Expanding Your Horizons

Below PowerPoint Project 6, click the Articles for Microsoft PowerPoint link. Click a topic that pertains to Project 6. Print the information. Construct a brief example of what the information relates to in PowerPoint to confirm you understand the contents of the article. Hand in the example and printed information to your instructor.

10 Search Sleuth

Below PowerPoint Project 6, click the Search Sleuth link. To search for a term that pertains to this project, select a term below the Project 6 title and then use the Google search engine at google.com (or any major search engine) to display and print two Web pages that present information on the term. Hand in the printouts to your instructor.

online

Apply Your Knowledge

1 Designing a Title Slide Using AutoShapes

Instructions: Members of the astronomy club, the Moonstrucks, have asked you to help them promote their organization. Perform the following tasks to create the title slide shown in Figure 6-80 on the next page.

1. Start PowerPoint. Create a new presentation using the Title Slide slide layout and the Fireworks design template. Apply the color scheme in row 2, column 1.
2. Type the text for the title slide as shown in Figure 6-80. Add a shadow to the title text by selecting the text and clicking the Shadow button on the Formatting toolbar. Bold and italicize the subtitle text.
3. Display the drawing guides. Click the AutoShapes button on the Drawing toolbar, point to Basic Shapes, and then click Moon (row 6, column 4) on the Basic Shapes submenu. Click the slide to display the moon object.
4. Right-click the moon object and then click Format AutoShape on the shortcut menu. If necessary, click the Size tab. Click Lock aspect ratio, scale the moon to 200 %, and then click the OK button.
5. Click the Fill Color button arrow on the Drawing toolbar and then click the color white in the row of available colors.
6. Drag the horizontal guide to 1.50 inches above center and the vertical guide to 3.25 inches left of center. Drag the moon to the upper-left corner of the slide so the top and bottom edges snap to the guides.
7. Click the AutoShapes button on the Drawing toolbar, point to Stars and Banners, and then click 4-Point Star (row 1, column 3). Click the slide to display the star object.
8. Click the Fill Color button arrow on the Drawing toolbar, and then click the color yellow in the row of available colors.
9. Click the Fill Colors button arrow again and then click Fill Effects. If necessary, click the Gradient tab, and then click the lower-left variant sample in the Variants area. Click the OK button in the Fill Effects dialog box.
10. Right-click the 4-Point Star AutoShape, and then click Format AutoShape on the shortcut menu. If necessary, click the Size tab. Click Lock aspect ratio, scale the star to 175 %, and then click the OK button.
11. Drag the horizontal guide to 2.00 inches below center and the vertical guide to 3.25 inches right of center. Drag the star to the lower-right corner of the slide so the top and left edges snap to the guides.
12. Click the AutoShapes button on the Drawing toolbar, point to Basic Shapes, and then click Lightning Bolt (row 6, column 2). Click the slide to display the lightning bolt object.
13. Right-click the lightning bolt object, and then click Format AutoShape on the shortcut menu. If necessary, click the Size tab. Scale the lightning bolt to 200 % without clicking Lock aspect ratio, and then click the OK button.
14. Drag the vertical guide to 3.75 inches left of center and the horizontal guide to 0.42 inch below center. Drag the lightning bolt so the left and top points align with the guides.
15. Click the Insert WordArt button on the Drawing toolbar. Choose the WordArt style in row 3, column 1, and then click the OK button. Enter the club information shown in the bottom of the slide, and substitute your name for the words, Student Name. Click the OK button in the Edit WordArt Text dialog box. Click the WordArt Shape button on the WordArt toolbar, and then apply the Inflate shape (row 4, column 1). Scale the text to 110 %.

(continued)

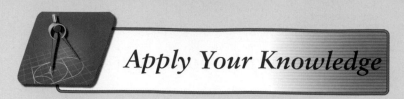

Apply Your Knowledge

Designing a Title Slide Using AutoShapes *(continued)*

FIGURE 6-80

16. Drag the vertical guide to 2.00 inches left of center and the horizontal guide to 2.00 inches below center. Align the top and left edges of the WordArt object with these guides. You might need to make minor adjustments with the scaling to accommodate your name.
17. Apply the Flash bulb animation scheme. Save the presentation with the file name, Moonstrucks. Print the slide using the Pure Black and White option. Quit PowerPoint.

In the Lab

1 Formatting Backgrounds, Linking Slides, and Inserting a Diagram

Problem: The Tri-Circle Ranch has expanded its activities for vacationers. In the past year, the owners have added a variety of hikes through the Rocky Mountains, fishing lessons and trips, and white-water rafting. You have visited the ranch during your summer vacations, and you agree to help the owners market their new programs. You develop a self-running PowerPoint presentation to display at trade shows throughout the country. To make the slide show useful and interesting, you add clip art, hyperlinks to slides within the presentation, and a slide with a Venn diagram. You create the presentation shown in Figures 6-81a through 6-81f on the next page.

Instructions: Start PowerPoint and perform the following tasks. If the picture and clip art images are not available on your computer, see your instructor for copies of these files or substitute similar objects and a picture.

1. Open a new presentation and apply the Title Slide slide layout and the Default Design design template.
2. Create the title slide shown in Figure 6-81a by inserting the picture as a background and moving the placeholder locations. Use the Garamond font. Bold the text, and use a font size of 54 for the title text and 36 for the subtitle text. The title text font color is dark blue, and the subtitle color is white.
3. Insert a new slide and then apply the Blank slide layout. Insert the Venn diagram and then apply the Thick Outline AutoFormat. Scale the Venn diagram to 170 %, click the Layout button on the Diagram toolbar, and then click Fit Diagram to Contents. Center the Venn diagram on the slide.
4. Add a caption shown in Figure 6-81b to each of the areas marked, Click to add text. Apply the Blue tissue paper texture to the Slide 2 background.
5. Add the AutoShape shown in Figure 6-81b by clicking the AutoShapes button on the Drawing toolbar, pointing to Stars and Banners, and then clicking 8-Point Star (row 2, column 1). Insert the AutoShape in the center of the Venn diagram. Type `Tri-Circle Ranch` and then change the font to Garamond and the font size to 32. Bold this text. Right-click the AutoShape, click Format AutoShape on the shortcut menu, and then click the Text Box tab when the Format AutoShape dialog box displays. Click Resize AutoShape to fit text, and then click the OK button.
6. Add the Circle entrance animation effect and the Circle motion path to the AutoShape.
7. Insert a new slide and apply the Title Only slide layout. Type the title text shown on Slide 3 (Figure 6-81c).
8. Insert a new slide and apply the Title and Text slide layout. Type the text shown on Slide 4 (Figure 6-81d). Repeat this step to create Slides 5 and 6.
9. Insert the clips shown. Scale the clip on Slide 4 to 270 %, Slide 5 to 170 %, and Slide 6 to 285 %.
10. Create the slide backgrounds for Slides 3 through 6 by pressing and holding down the SHIFT key and then clicking the Slide 3 slide thumbnail on the Slides tab. Right-click the Slide 3 slide thumbnail, and then click Background on the shortcut menu. When the Background dialog box displays, click the Background fill arrow, and then click Fill Effects. If necessary, click the Gradient tab in the Fill Effects dialog box. Click From title in the Shading styles area. Click the Color 1 box arrow, and then click the color dark blue in the row of available colors. Click the OK button, and then click the Apply button.
11. Change the font color for all text on Slides 3, 4, 5, and 6 to light blue. Apply the Big title animation scheme to all slides.

(continued)

In the Lab

Formatting Backgrounds, Linking Slides, and Inserting a Diagram *(continued)*

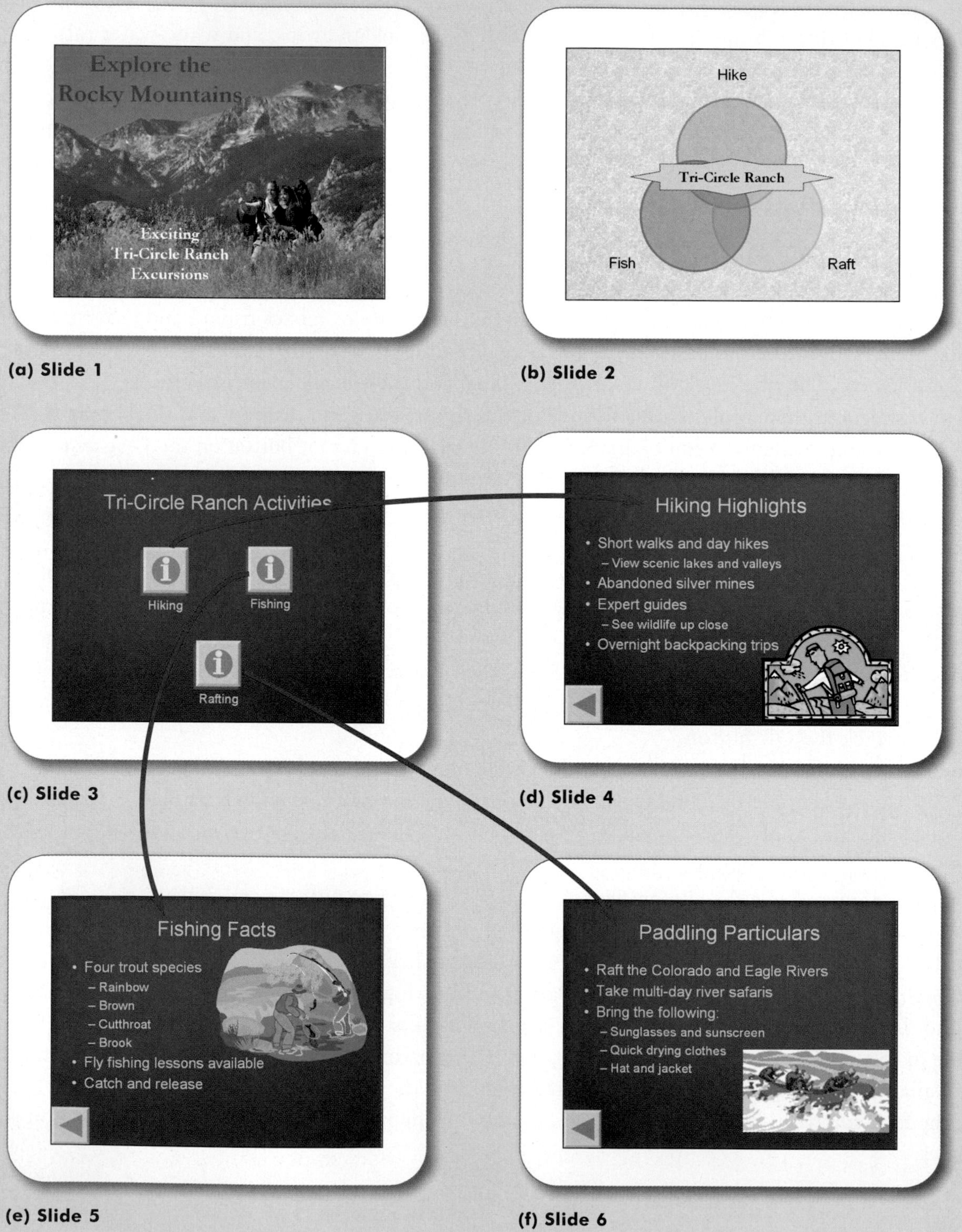

FIGURE 6-81

In the Lab

12. Add the three action buttons and captions shown in Figure 6-81c to Slide 3. Hyperlink the Hiking action button to the Next Slide. Hyperlink the Fishing action button to Slide 4 by clicking the Hyperlink to arrow, clicking Slide, clicking 4. Hiking Highlights, and then clicking the OK button. Hyperlink the Rafting action button to Slide 5. Scale the action buttons to 120 % and apply Shadow Style 5. Change the font to light blue and change the font size to 28 point.
13. Add an action button to the lower-left corner of Slides 4, 5, and 6, and hyperlink each action button to the Previous Slide.
14. Save the presentation with the file name, Rocky Mountains. Run the slide show. When Slide 3 displays, click the Hiking action button to jump to Slide 4. When Slide 4 displays, click the action button to return to Slide 2. Click the Fishing action button to jump to Slide 5. When Slide 5 displays, click the action button to return to Slide 2. Click the Rafting button to jump to Slide 6. When Slide 6 displays, click the slide anywhere except the action button. When Slide 1 displays, press the ESC key.
15. Print the six presentation slides as a handout with two slides per page. Quit PowerPoint.

2 Linking Slides, Inserting an AutoShape, and Setting Timings

Problem: Wireless technology has taken the world by storm. From cellular telephones to notebook computers with high-speed Internet access, these devices have simplified and expanded communication capabilities. Asia and Europe have emerged as global leaders in wireless device use, and during the next few years more than 1.2 billion of these products will be used in most areas of the world. Technology experts gather several times a year to learn about the latest wireless trends and to view new products. One of these conferences is scheduled for San Francisco, and you have offered to create a PowerPoint presentation to help publicize the event. You decide a self-running interactive slide show would be the best vehicle to share information. Develop the presentation shown in Figures 6-82a through 6-82f.

Instructions: Start PowerPoint and perform the following tasks.

1. Open a new presentation and apply the Satellite Dish design template. Add the Golden Gate Bridge picture to the Slide 1 background.
2. On Slide 1, enter the title and subtitle text shown in Figure 6-82a. Bold the text and change the font color of the title text to white and the subtitle text to green (color 8 in the row of available colors). Add the animated cellular telephone clip and scale it to 300 %.
3. Insert a new slide and apply the Title and Text slide layout. Enter the title and bulleted list shown in Figure 6-82b. Add an action button and hyperlink it to the Wireless Use worksheet (Figure 6-82c) on your Data Disk. See the inside back cover of this book for instructions for downloading the Data Disk or see your instructor for information on accessing this file. Play the Voltage sound when the mouse is clicked.
4. Change the button fill color to green, scale it to 90 %, and apply Shadow Style 5. Display the drawing guides and then drag the horizontal guide to 0.58 inch left of center and the vertical guide to 1.75 inches below center. Position the upper-left corner of the button at the intersection of these guides. Add the caption shown in Figure 6-82b and change the font size to 20 point.

(continued)

In the Lab

Linking Slides, Inserting an AutoShape, and Setting Timings *(continued)*

(a) Slide 1

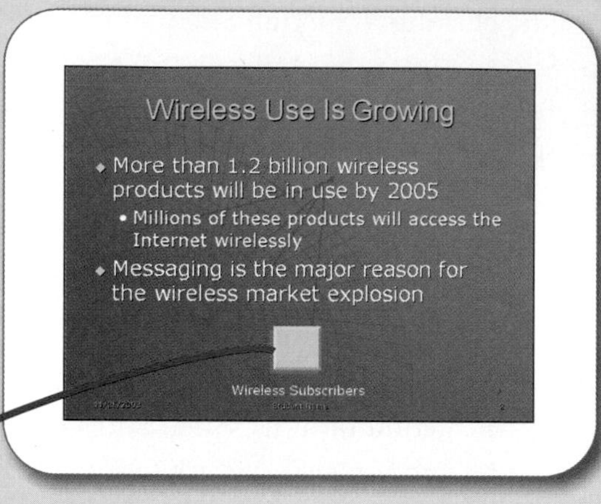

(b) Slide 2

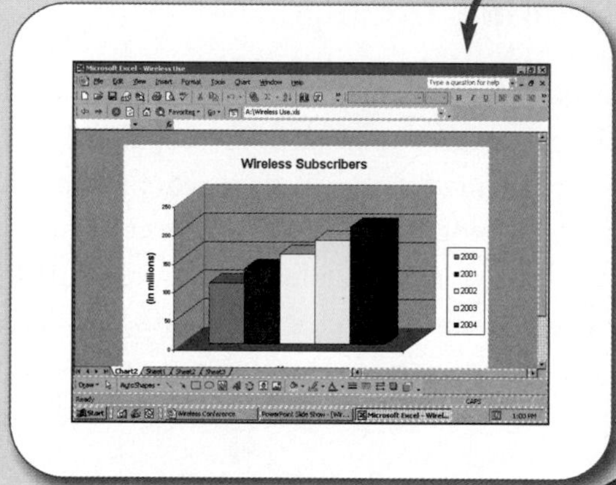

(c) Wireless Use Worksheet

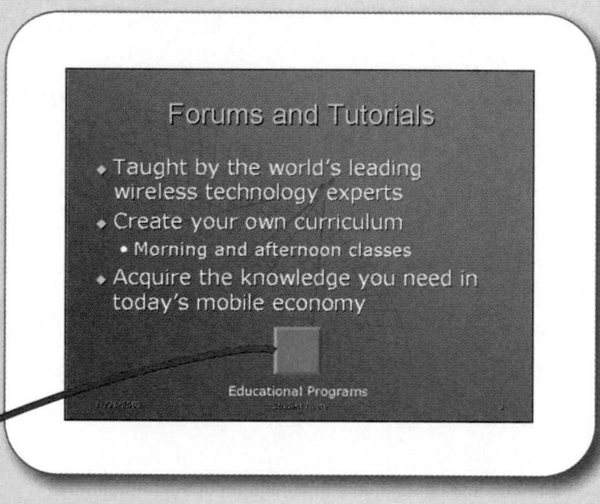

(d) Slide 3

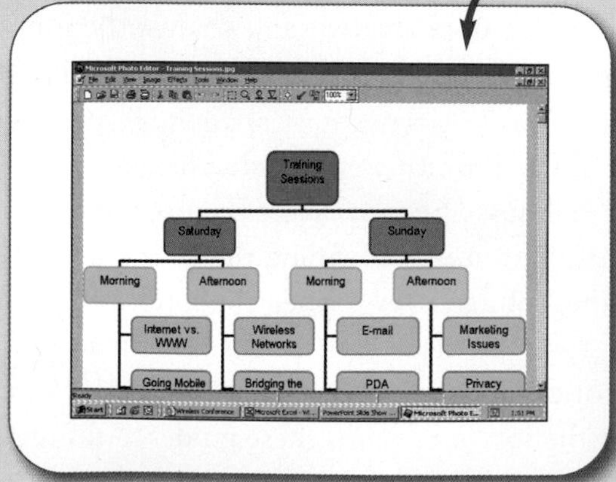

(e) Training Sessions Picture

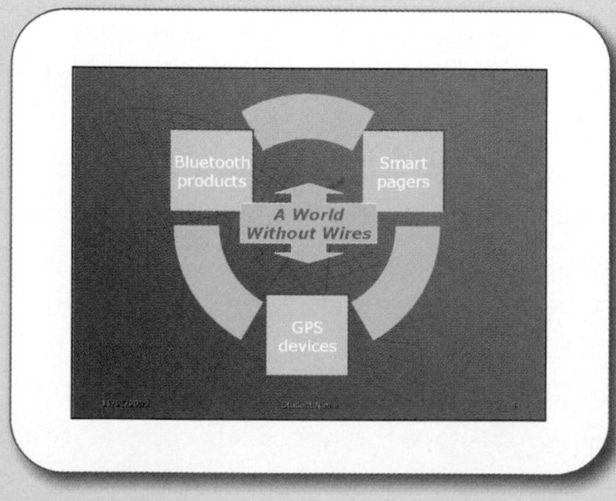

(f) Slide 4

FIGURE 6-82

In the Lab

5. Insert a new slide and then enter the title and bulleted list shown in Figure 6-82d. Add an action button and hyperlink it to the Training Sessions picture (Figure 6-82e) on your Data Disk. Play the Wind sound when the mouse is clicked.
6. Change the button fill color to aqua, scale it to 90 %, and apply Shadow Style 6. Position the upper-left corner of the button at the intersection of the guides used for Slide 2. Add the caption shown in Figure 6-82d and change the font size to 20 point. Hide the guides.
7. Insert a new slide and apply the Blank slide layout. Insert the Cycle diagram, scale it to 130 %, and position it in the center of the slide. Add the text shown in Figure 6-82f to each of the areas marked, Click to add text. Apply the Square Shadows diagram style.
8. Click the AutoShapes button on the Drawing toolbar, point to Block Arrows, and then click Up-Down Arrow Callout (row 7, column 2). Click the center of the Cycle diagram, and then add the text shown in Figure 6-82f. Increase the font to 24 point and italicize the text. Change the font color to dark green (color 3 in the list) and then resize the AutoShape to fit the text. Add the Spinner entrance effect and 8 Point Star motion path to the AutoShape.
9. Set the slide timings to 30 seconds for Slide 1 and 15 seconds for the other three slides.
10. Set the show type as Browsed at a kiosk.
11. Add your name, today's date, and the slide number to the slide footer.
12. Apply the Float animation scheme to all slides. Save the presentation with the file name, Wireless Conference.
13. Run the slide show. When Slide 2 displays, click the action button to view the Excel chart. Click the Close button on the Wireless Use title bar to return to the presentation. When Slide 3 displays, click the action button to view the class schedule. If necessary, click the maximize button on the Training Sessions title bar. After you have viewed the training sessions, click the Close button on the Training Sessions title bar. When Slide 4 displays, review the information and wait for Slide 1 to display. When Slide 1 displays, press the ESC key.
14. Print handouts with two slides per page. Quit PowerPoint.

3 Inserting a Slide and Adding AutoShapes and Diagrams

Problem: Triathlon Training Techniques (T^3) holds camps in Orlando, Florida, during the summer and winter months for athletes preparing to participate in triathlons. The training sessions feature quality instruction from world-class athletes and include demonstrations and lectures. Many camp participants compete in the Calumet Triathlon, which is held annually in November. T^3 trainers have asked you to prepare a short slide show promoting their training camp. They have given you a file composed of four slides promoting the Calumet Triathlon, and they want you to insert one slide from that presentation in your new T^3 presentation.

Instructions Part 1: Start PowerPoint and open the Calumet Triathlon presentation from the Data Disk. Slides 2 and 4 have information that can be presented visually using diagrams. Perform the tasks on the next page to modify these slides as shown in Figures 6-83a through 6-83d on the next page.

(continued)

In the Lab

Inserting a Slide and Adding AutoShapes and Diagrams *(continued)*

(a) Slide 1

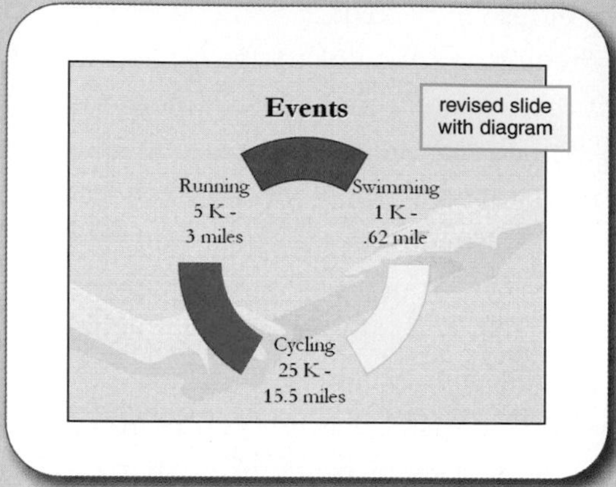

(b) Slide 2

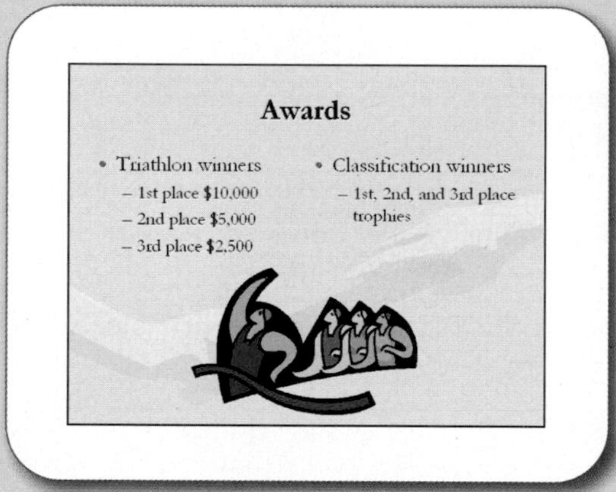

(c) Slide 3

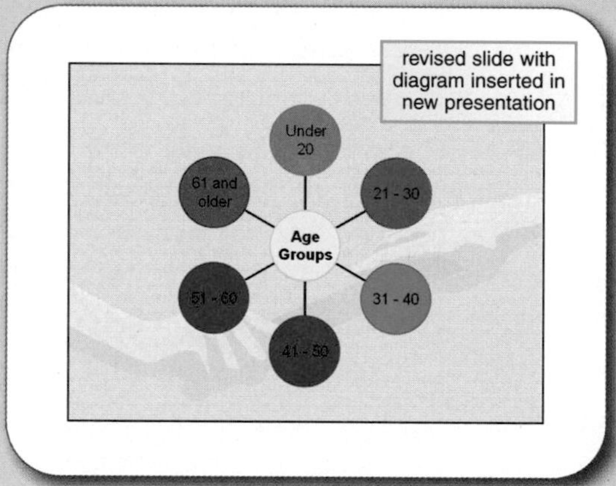

(d) Slide 4

FIGURE 6-83

1. Save the presentation with the new file name, Revised Calumet Triathlon. Click the Next Slide button to display Slide 2. Apply the Title Only slide layout and then delete the text placeholder. Insert a Cycle diagram and then add the text shown in Figure 6-83b to each of the areas marked, Click to add text. Change the font size to 32 point. Apply the Primary Colors diagram style. Scale the diagram to 125 %. Fit the diagram to contents.
2. Click the Slide 4 slide thumbnail on the Slides tab. Apply the Blank slide layout and then delete the title text and two text placeholders. Insert a Radial diagram. Click the Insert Shape button on the Diagram toolbar three times. Add the text shown in Figure 6-83d to each of the areas marked, Click to add text. Change the font to Arial. Bold the center core element. Apply the Primary Colors diagram style. Scale the diagram to 130 %. Fit the diagram to contents. Save the presentation again.

Instructions Part 2: Perform the following tasks to create the presentation shown in Figures 6-84a through 6-84d.

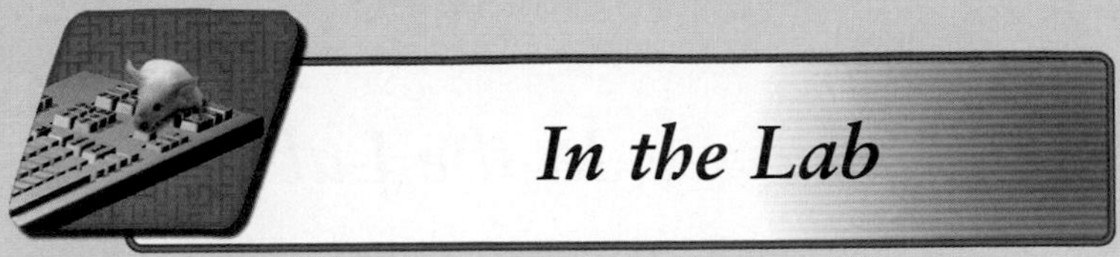

In the Lab

1. Click the New button on the Formatting toolbar to create a new presentation. Save the presentation with the file name, Triathlon Camps. Apply the Pixel design template. Type the Slide 1 title and subtitle text shown in Figure 6-84a.
2. Create the T^3 AutoShape by clicking the AutoShape button on the Drawing toolbar, pointing to Flowchart, and then clicking the Flowchart: Manual Operation shape. Insert the shape in the white area above the title text placeholder. Size the AutoShape to a height of 1.75 inches and a width of 1.83 inches. Type T3 and then increase the font size to 72. Change the font to Bookman Old Style. Select the number 3. Superscript the number 3 by clicking Format on the menu bar and then clicking Font. When the Font dialog box displays, click Superscript in the Effects area and then click the OK button. Apply the Blinds entrance effect and have the effect Start After Previous. Apply the Spin emphasis effect and have the effect Start After Previous. Apply the Curvy Left motion path. Display the guides. Drag the horizontal guide to 3.25 inches above center and the vertical guide to 0.25 inch right of center. Drag the AutoShape so the top-left corner snaps to the guides.

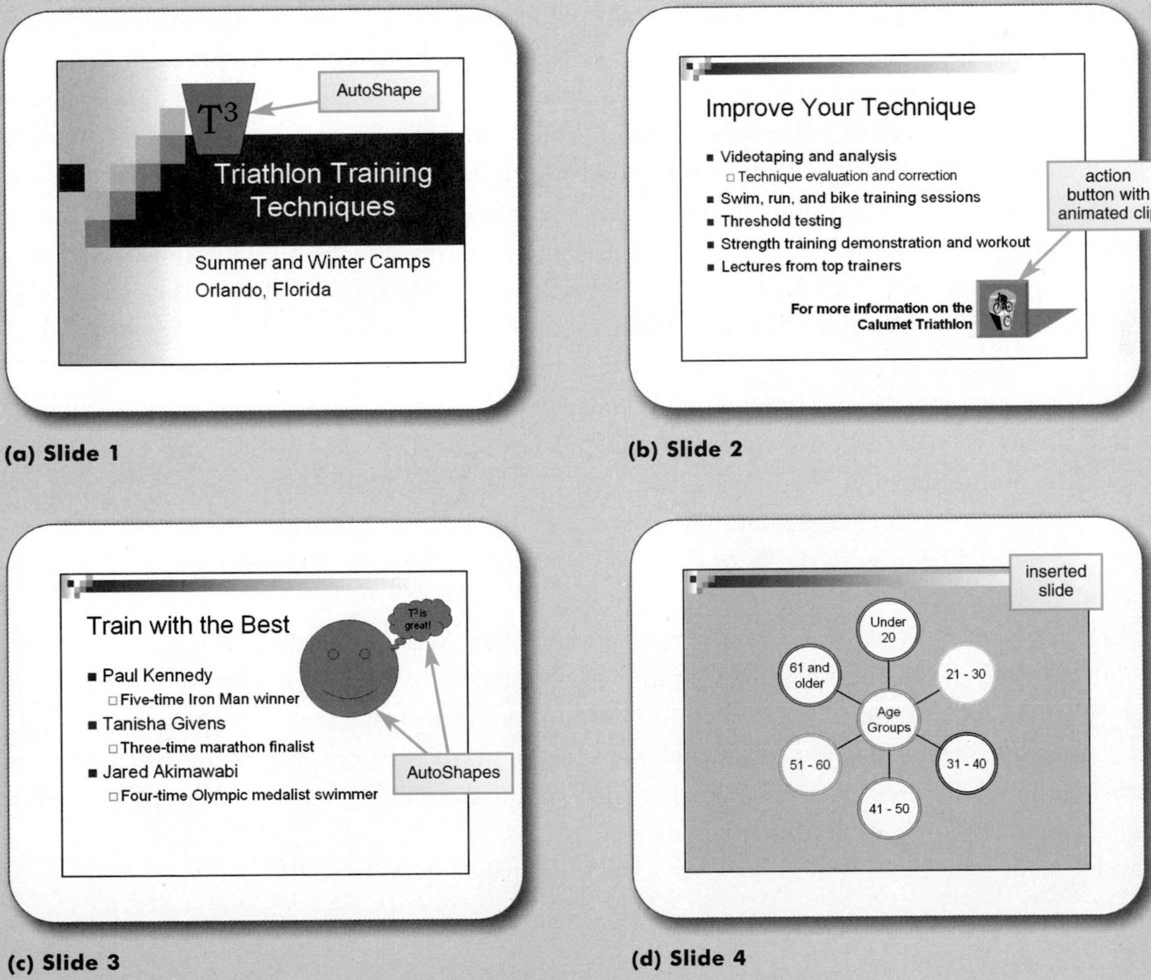

(a) Slide 1 **(b) Slide 2**

(c) Slide 3 **(d) Slide 4**

FIGURE 6-84

(continued)

In the Lab

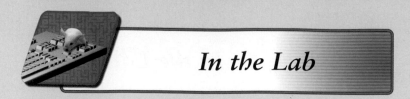

Inserting a Slide and Adding AutoShapes and Diagrams *(continued)*

3. Insert a new slide and then enter the title and body text shown in Figure 6-84b on the previous page. Add the Custom action button (row 1, column 1), and then hyperlink it to the Revised Calumet Triathlon presentation. When the Hyperlink to Slide dialog box displays, click 1. Calumet Triathlon and then click the OK button. Play the Drum Roll sound when the mouse is clicked. Size the button to 120 %. Apply Shadow Style 4 (row 1, column 4). Insert the animated bike clip, size it to 125 %, and then drag it to the middle of the action button. Group the action button and the clip.
4. Add the action button caption shown in Figure 6-84b. Click the Align Right button on the Formatting toolbar, select the caption text, and then bold the text and change the font size to 24 point.
5. Insert a new slide and then enter the title and body text shown in Figure 6-84c on the previous page. Insert the Smiley Face AutoShape (row 5, column 1) in the Basic Shapes category and size it to 250 %. If the AutoShape size is not correct, be certain the Lock aspect ratio check box in the Scale area is checked. Drag the horizontal guide to 2.58 inches above center and the vertical guide to 0.92 inch right of center. Drag the AutoShape so the top and left edges snap to the guides. Insert the Cloud Callout AutoShape (row 1, column 4) in the Callouts category and size it to 175 %. If the AutoShape size is not correct, be certain the Lock aspect ratio check box in the Scale area is checked. Drag the horizontal guide to 3.08 inches above center and the vertical guide to 3.08 inches right of center. Drag the AutoShape so the top and left edges snap to the guides. Add the text shown in Figure 6-84c to the Cloud Callout AutoShape. Hide the guides.
6. Insert Slide 4 from the Revised Calumet Triathlon presentation. Click the Radial diagram and then change the AutoFormat to Double Outline. Right-click the slide in an area other than the Radial diagram and then click Background on the shortcut menu. When the Background dialog box displays, click the Background fill box arrow, click the color light blue (color 8 in the row of available colors), and then click the Apply button.
7. Apply the Spin animation scheme to all slides in the new presentation. Save the presentation again. Display the Revised Calumet Triathlon presentation and then delete Slide 4. Right-click the runners clip on Slide 3, click Hyperlink on the shortcut menu, click Triathlon Camps in the Look in list, click the Address text box, and then type `#Train with the Best` at the end of the address so that the entire hyperlink address is Triathlon Camps.ppt#Train with the Best. Click the OK button. Save the Revised Calumet Triathlon presentation again.
8. Display and then run the Triathlon Camps presentation. When Slide 2 displays, click a blue area of the action button to run the Revised Calumet Triathlon presentation. After you have reviewed Slide 3 in the Calumet Triathlon presentation, click the clip to return to Slide 3 of the Triathlon Camps presentation. When the complete Slide 3 displays, right-click the slide, point to Pointer Options on the shortcut menu and then click Pen on the Pointer Options submenu. Click and make a check mark in front of each of the solid blue bullets, and then circle each athlete's name.
9. Print handouts for both presentations with two slides per page. Quit PowerPoint.

Cases and Places

The difficulty of these case studies varies:
◗ are the least difficult; ◗◗ are more difficult; and ◗◗◗ are the most difficult.

1 ◗ This past summer you joined the Midwest SUV Club. This organization sponsors many road rallies throughout the summer. At the early spring meeting, the members discuss and plan the first summer rally for June. You volunteer to help publicize the club's activities. You create two presentations, one with the file name, Off-Road Rally, and the second with the file name, Rally Information. The Off-Road Rally presentation contains two slides; Slide 2 contains four action buttons linking to one of four slides in the Rally Information slide show. The captions for these four action buttons are: Who sponsors the rally? What distance is covered? Where does the rally start? How is the scoring conducted? The first action button should link to Rally Information Slide 2, which has the title text, Midwest SUV Club. The body text states that Tanaka Kobiashi and Kenny Park founded the organization, which is composed of conscientious owners of off-road vehicles. Another item on this slide states that the members are safety minded, with excitement in mind. They hold yearly road rallies and vehicle exhibitions. The last item emphasizes that rallies bring friends together and help form new friendships. The second action button links to Slide 3, which has the title text, The Rally. The bulleted text states that a road rally is held each Saturday in June or on Sunday if the weather is inclement. Each rally's distance is approximately 300 miles. The winner is determined at the end of the month and is the individual with the most points. The third action button links to Slide 4, which has the title, Rally Departure Information. It states that the departure point is the Avery High School parking lot. Registration begins at 7:00 a.m., and technical information is provided from 7:30 a.m. to 8:00 a.m. The first car departs at 8:01 a.m. Awards are given at the end of the rally. The fourth action button links to Slide 5, which has the title, Scoring Points. This slide explains that each team consists of two members: a driver and a navigator. These two people may switch places if they are fatigued. Points are based on distance, time, and accomplishment. Accomplishment is defined as the number of directions that are followed. Road speed is not a factor. Slides 2, 3, 4, and 5 in the Rally Information slide show have an action button that hyperlinks back to Slide 2 of the Off-Road Rally slide show. Using the techniques introduced in this project, create these two slide shows. Enhance the presentations with sound and art clips and animation schemes.

2 ◗ Many employees telecommute, meaning they work some hours in an office and other hours at home. A recent survey found that 21 percent of telecommuters work at home at least 40 hours weekly, 10 percent between 30 to 39 hours, 24 percent between 20 to 29 hours, 31 percent between 10 to 19 hours, and 14 percent fewer than 10 hours. Sixty-one percent of employees say they would take a pay cut to work at home. Teleworkers cite many reasons for using this flexible employment option, including reduced gasoline or public transportation costs, less stress, the ability to work during unconventional hours, fewer distractions from office workers, and fewer clothing purchases and cleaning bills. The work practice has its negative aspects, however. They include lack of supervision, reduced contact with managers and co-workers, technical problems, and fewer opportunities for career advancement and raises. The highest proportions of telecommuters are in the New England, Mountain, and Pacific states. Using the techniques introduced in this project, create a slide show describing the telecommuting practice. Use a Target diagram to present the advantages of telecommuting and a Pyramid diagram to present the disadvantages. Create a Word table containing the hours employees spend telecommuting and an Excel table showing the growing trend in the number of telecommuters. Insert action buttons into one slide to hyperlink to these tables. Add an animation scheme and appropriate clips.

Cases and Places

3 ▶▶ Many home owners find satisfaction when they tackle remodeling and building projects themselves. The local home improvement store, Yancy's Home Center, sponsors several Do It Yourself (DIY) clinics throughout the year. As a part-time employee, you agree to help publicize these workshops by creating a short slide show that will run continuously at a kiosk near the service desk. The next clinic is designed to help customers select materials to build decks. Possible materials are cypress, cedar, and synthetics. Cypress is inexpensive and has a soft, even texture. It installs easily and accepts stains and preservatives easily. One negative aspect is that it requires periodic maintenance. Cedar, particularly Western Red Cedar, resists decay naturally and is a very stable, beautiful softwood. It stays flat, resists checking, is lightweight, and is easy to install. Both clear and knotty boards are available. Synthetics are durable because they are created from recycled wood and polymers. They are maintenance free and do not require staining. They will not split or rot and are resilient to weather. Synthetics are excellent to use around pools and hot tubs. Create a presentation using this information, and include an animation scheme and appropriate clips. Use the 32-Point Star AutoShape in your title slide and a footer with the current date, your name, and the slide number on all slides except the title slide. Include an action button to hyperlink to the Excel worksheet, Deck Estimator, which is on your Data Disk. Yancy's has several other PowerPoint presentations on a variety of topics that you can view. Locate the presentation, Yancy, which is on your Data Disk. Insert Slides 2 and 3 from this presentation into your slide show.

4 ▶▶ Recycling is a common practice in many households. Paper, plastics, and glass often are separated and disposed in special bins or bags. Electronic equipment, too, can be recycled. Your county has developed a special program for broken or obsolete computers and peripherals, office equipment and products, small home appliances, and entertainment equipment. These items include personal computers, printers, telephones, toasters, televisions, videocassette recorders, and video games. County officials will be collecting these items during the next two Saturdays at your local high school and a nearby shopping center. They will not accept air conditioners, humidifiers, and hazardous wastes. Develop a short slide show that can be viewed at kiosks throughout the county. Emphasize that recycling is important because electronic products' short useful lives produce waste, these items may contain hazardous materials, and many components can be salvaged. Include a slide with clips of acceptable products, and insert a green arrow AutoShape on this slide to call attention to these items. Include another slide with unacceptable products, and insert a red "No Symbol" AutoShape to emphasize that these products are not included in this recycling project.

5 ▶▶▶ Your economics instructor has assigned a project comparing three cellular telephone services. This task requires you to research monthly fees, the cost of minutes during peak and off-peak hours, current incentives, and the service area range. Then, you must develop a persuasive PowerPoint presentation showing the service with the most favorable plan for your needs. Create this slide show and include the following components: an action button to an Excel worksheet showing fees for various packages; an action button to a Word document promoting the features of a cellular telephone included in these packages; an action button to an Excel chart comparing the talk time and range; and a Cycle diagram showing the three best features of the service you selected. Set the slide timings to 10 seconds for Slide 1 and 15 seconds for the other slides in the presentation. Set the show type as Browsed at a kiosk. Include an animation scheme and appropriate clips.

Microsoft PowerPoint 2002

Importing Templates and Clips from the Microsoft Web Site

CASE PERSPECTIVE

Chippy's Computer Shop in your town specializes in assembling custom computer systems and repairing and upgrading existing computers and peripherals. Chip Phillips, the owner, realizes he can attract new customers and maintain relationships with existing customers by having a Web site. He is soliciting bids for developers to create Web pages for him next summer. One of the required components of the bid package is a timeline showing when each phase of the Web site creation will occur. You have decided to submit a bid and need to develop this timeline. You browse the templates and the AutoContent Wizard and do not find any timelines. Knowing that Internet access is built into PowerPoint 2002, you decide to browse the Microsoft Office Template Gallery Web site for a suitable timeline. In addition, you view the animated clips in the Microsoft Design Gallery Live Web site for a new clip of a computer and a modem sound to add to this timeline.

Introduction

Although the design templates included in PowerPoint 2002 are varied and versatile, they sometimes do not fit your needs. The Microsoft Clip Organizer likewise has a wide variety of picture images, but at times these images are not exactly to your liking. Microsoft has created the Template Gallery and the Design Gallery Live, which are sources of additional templates, pictures, sounds, and movie clips on the World Wide Web. To access the Template Gallery, you click the Templates on Microsoft.com hyperlink in the New Presentation task pane. To access the Design Gallery Live, you click the Clips Online hyperlink in the Insert Clip Art task pane. If you have an open connection to the Internet, PowerPoint connects you directly to the Template Gallery or the Design Gallery Live home pages (Figures 1a and 1b on the next page).

In this Web Feature, you download the three-month timeline and then modify the slide by adding an animated clip of a computer and a sound file from the Web, as shown in Figure 1c on the next page.

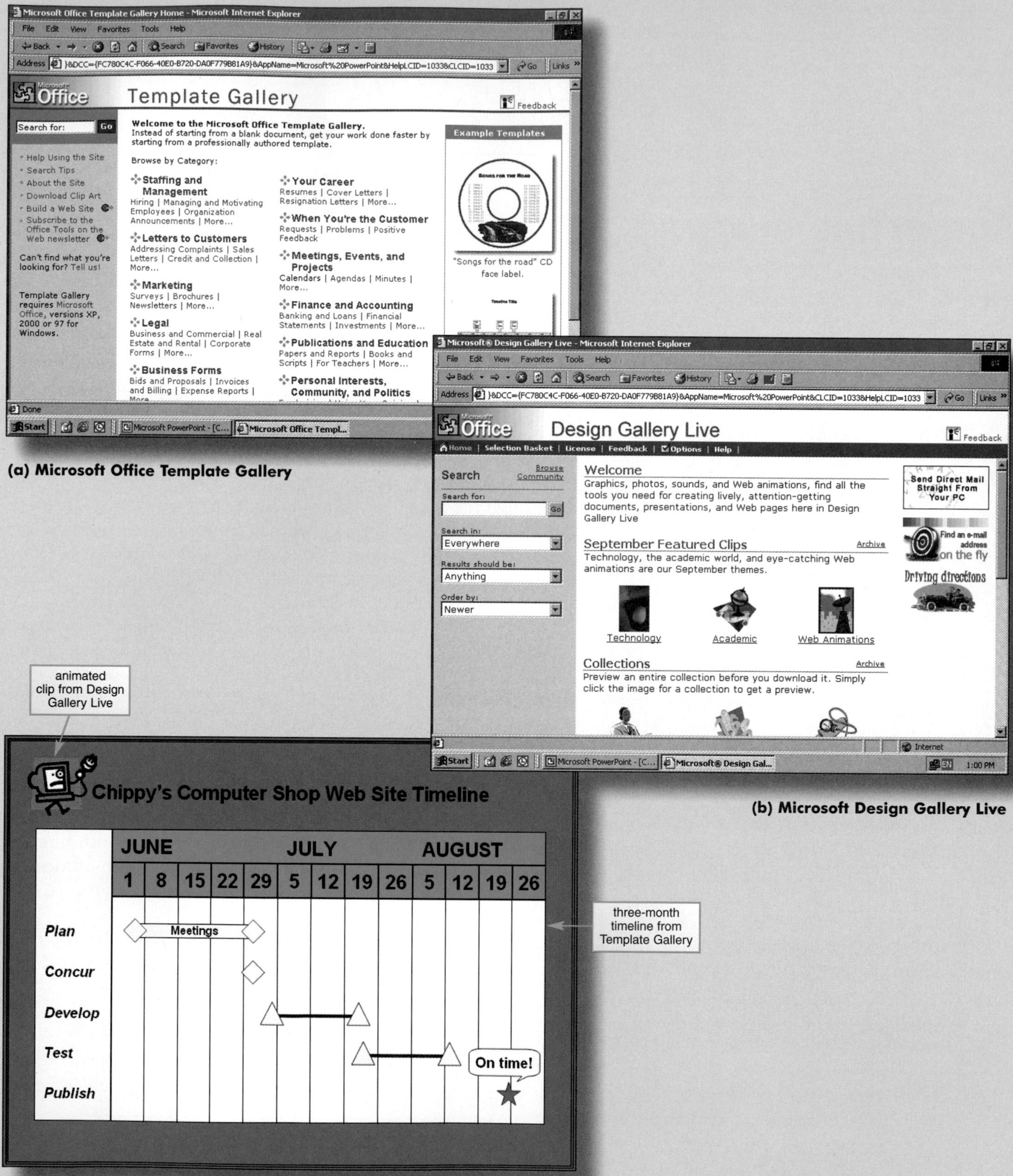

(a) Microsoft Office Template Gallery

(b) Microsoft Design Gallery Live

(c) Slide 1

FIGURE 1

Importing a Design Template from the Microsoft Office Template Gallery on the World Wide Web

Downloading a template from the Microsoft Office Template Gallery is an easy process. To begin, perform the following steps to start and customize a new PowerPoint presentation.

More About

Templates

Microsoft states that users frequently visit the Office Update Web site to request templates. The initial templates in the Template Gallery were created based on this customer feedback, and Microsoft promises to continue to add new templates to the Web site. If you need a specific template, request one using the Suggestion/Feedback area of the Template Gallery.

TO START AND CUSTOMIZE A NEW PRESENTATION

1. Click the Start button on the Windows taskbar, point to Programs on the Start menu, and then click Microsoft PowerPoint on the Programs submenu.
2. If the Language bar displays, click its Minimize button.
3. If the Standard and Formatting toolbars display on one row, click the Toolbar Options button on the right side of either toolbar and then click Show Buttons on Two Rows on the Toolbar Options menu.

A new presentation titled Presentation1 displays in the PowerPoint window.

Content experts have developed hundreds of templates for PowerPoint, Word, Excel, and Access. The templates are arranged in a variety of categories, including Staffing and Management, Marketing, Legal, Your Career, and Publications and Education. These categories are subdivided into organized groupings. For example, the Stationery, Labels, and Cards category is subdivided into the Business Cards, Labels, Fax and Transmission Covers, Cards and Binders, Letterhead and Envelopes, and For the holidays categories. Three timelines are included in the Calendars subcategory within the Meetings, Events, and Projects category.

To use the Microsoft Office Template Gallery and Design Gallery Live Web sites, you must have access to the World Wide Web through an **Internet service provider** (**ISP**) and then use **Web browser** software to find the Microsoft site. This project uses **Microsoft Internet Explorer** for the Web browser. If you do not have Internet access, your instructor will provide the template used in this part of the project. To simplify connecting to the Template Gallery, the New Presentation task pane contains a Templates on Microsoft.com hyperlink to connect directly to the Template Gallery Web site.

Connecting to the Microsoft Office Template Gallery Web Site

You want to use a template with a three-month timeline. Once you connect to the Web, the Microsoft Office Template Gallery Live home page displays. A **home page** is a specially designed page that serves as a starting point for a Web site. Microsoft updates this home page frequently to reflect additions and features.

Perform the steps on the next page to open the New Presentation task pane, if necessary, connect to the World Wide Web, and then display the Microsoft Office Template Gallery home page.

More About

Creating Templates

Microsoft partnered with industry leaders to create the hundreds of templates on the Template Gallery Web site. For example, Avery Dennison helped create templates that work with Avery brand labels and other printing supplies, ranging from business cards to CD-ROM labels. Lawoffice.com designed the legal forms and documents and the connection to local attorneys who can provide legal advice in using these forms.

Steps To Connect to the Microsoft Office Template Gallery Web Site

1 If the New Presentation task pane does not display, click File on the menu bar and then point to New.

The File menu displays (Figure 2). You want to open the New Presentation task pane and then connect to the Microsoft Web site.

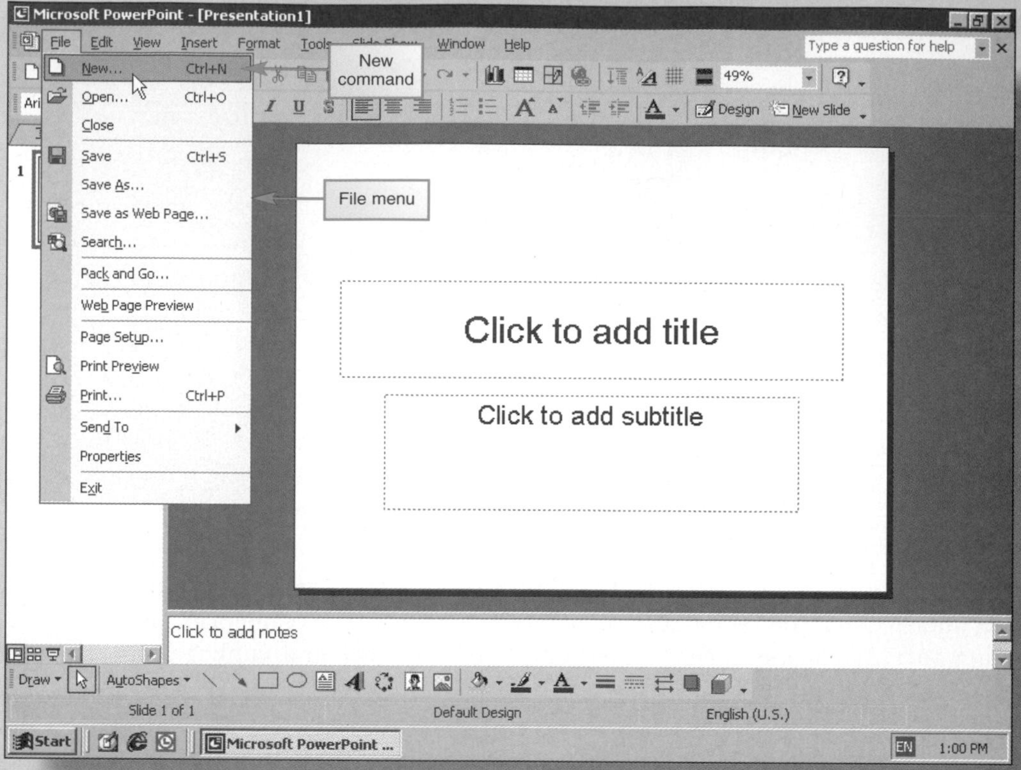

FIGURE 2

2 Click New. When the New Presentation task pane displays, point to Templates on Microsoft.com in the New from template area.

The New Presentation task pane displays (Figure 3). If the Templates on Microsoft.com hyperlink does not display, point to the down arrow at the bottom of the task pane.

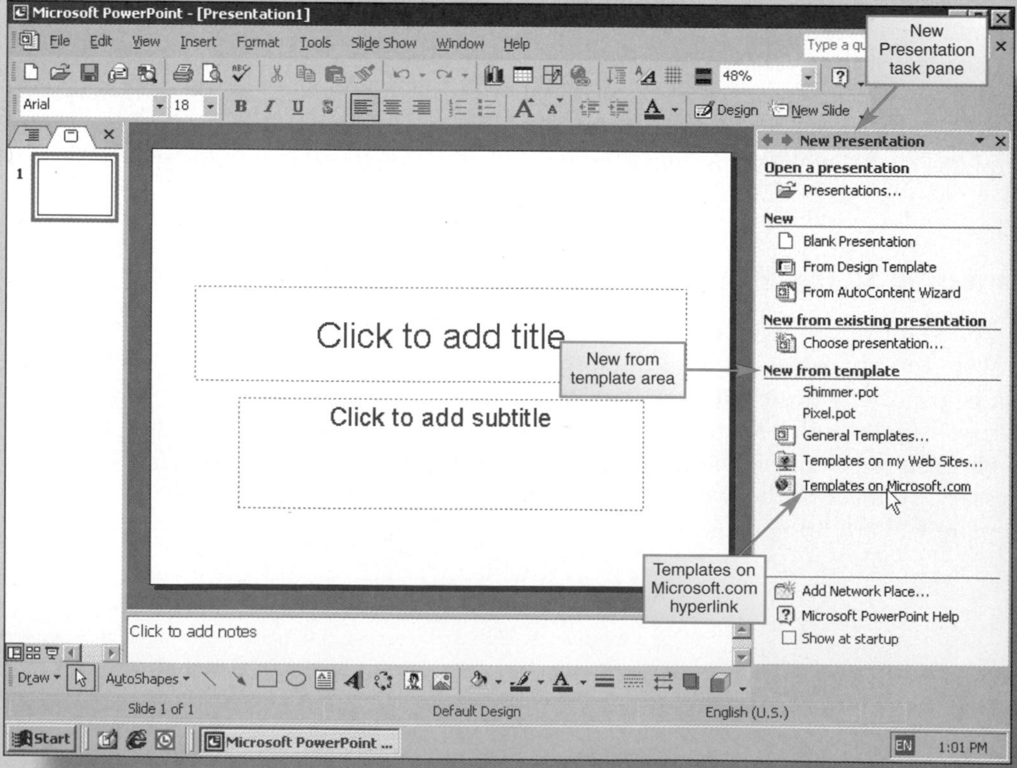

FIGURE 3

3 Click Templates on Microsoft.com. Connect to the World Wide Web as required by your browser software and ISP. Point to the Calendars hyperlink in the Meetings, Events, and Projects category.

If you are using a modem, a dialog box displays that connects you to the Web via your ISP. If you are connected directly to the Web through a computer network, the dialog box does not display. Microsoft Internet Explorer displays the Microsoft Office Template Gallery home page, which contains information about Microsoft Office Template Gallery features (Figure 4). The Calendars link is underlined and has the font color red.

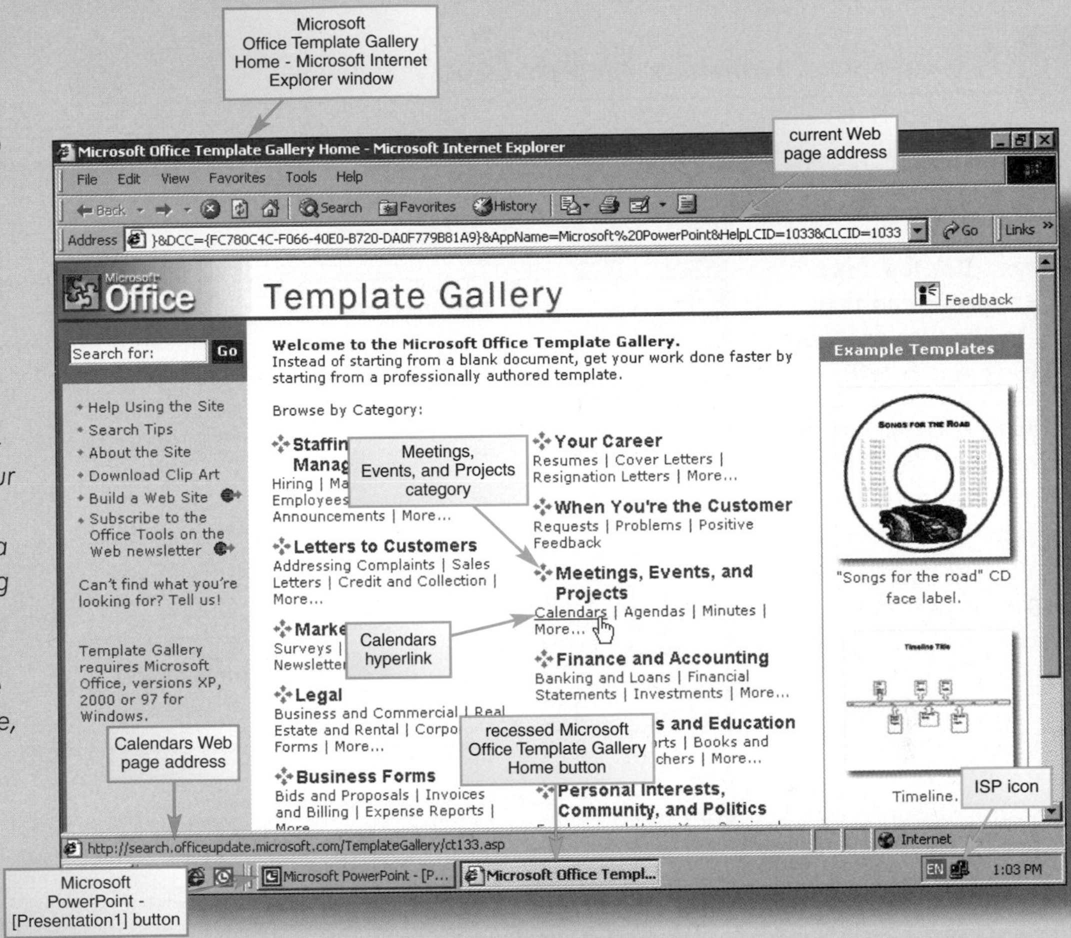

FIGURE 4

The Template Gallery contains hundreds of templates. To find a specific template, you can browse the categories or perform a search by typing a description of the content you want to find. When you locate a desired template, preview the template and then click the Edit in Office button to jump to a Microsoft Office program. You then can customize and edit the template. When you open this new document, the Template Gallery displays a list of hyperlinks in your Web browser. This list may have links to related templates, Help topics about using the Template Gallery, features in the template, and sign-up information to learn about new templates.

Locating and Downloading a Template

Templates are located by browsing the categories or by using keywords to search for a particular type of file. In this Web feature, you will locate a timeline template by browsing the Calendars subcategory in Meetings, Events, and Projects category.

When you find a template to add to your presentation, you can **download**, or copy, it instantly by previewing the template and then clicking the Edit in Microsoft PowerPoint button. Perform the steps on the next page to locate and download the three-month timeline template in the Template Gallery.

More About

Templates

Although many varieties of design templates are available in PowerPoint 2002 and the Microsoft Office Template Gallery, many more are available on Web sites. Designers create these templates and allow you to download and then apply them to your presentations. To view some of these templates, visit the PowerPoint 2002 More About Web page (scsite.com/pp2002/more.htm) and then click Templates.

Steps To Locate and Download a Template Gallery Template

1 Click the Calendars subcategory. When the Calendars page displays, click the down arrow to scroll and then point to Timeline for three months (PowerPoint).

The Timeline for three months template is required for this project (Figure 5). Other PowerPoint templates in the Calendar subcategory are timelines for six and twelve months.

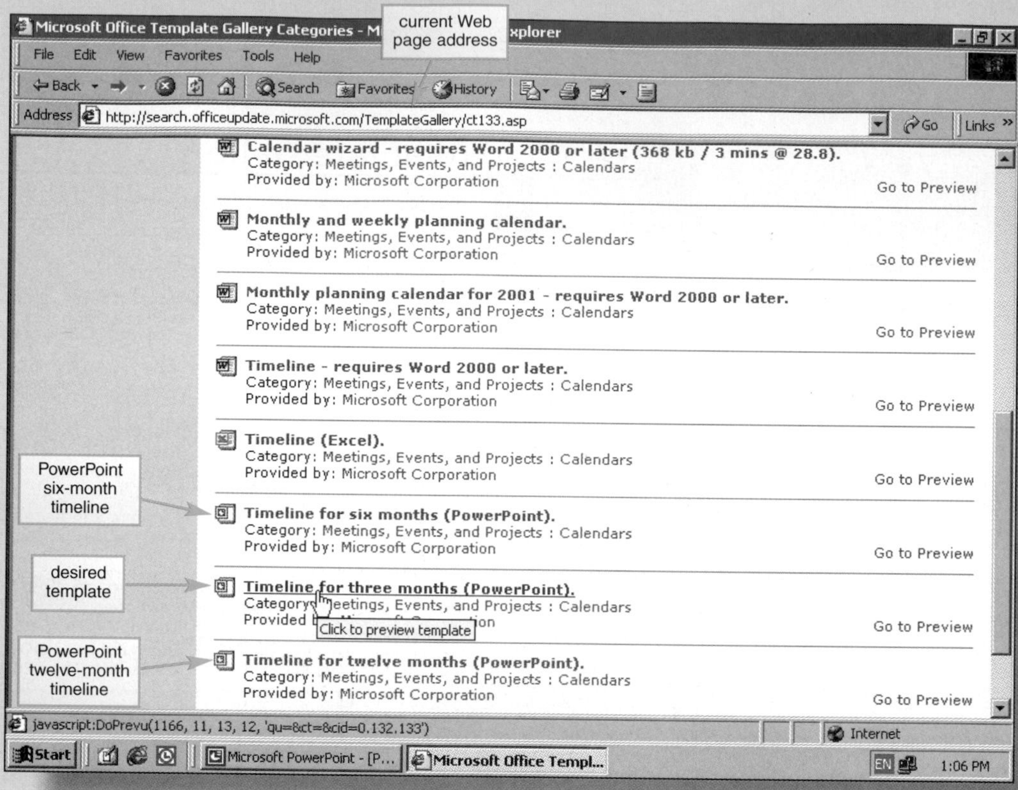

FIGURE 5

2 Click Timeline for three months (PowerPoint). If the Security Warning dialog box displays asking you to install and run "Microsoft Office Tools on the Web Control," click the Yes button. If the End-User License Agreement for Templates displays, read the agreement and then click the Accept button. Point to the Edit in Microsoft PowerPoint hyperlink.

Once connected to the Web, the Microsoft Office Template Gallery Live home page displays the Microsoft End-User License Agreement. When you click the Accept button, the Microsoft End-User License Agreement area no longer displays. The Timeline for three months template is previewed in the Web page (Figure 6).

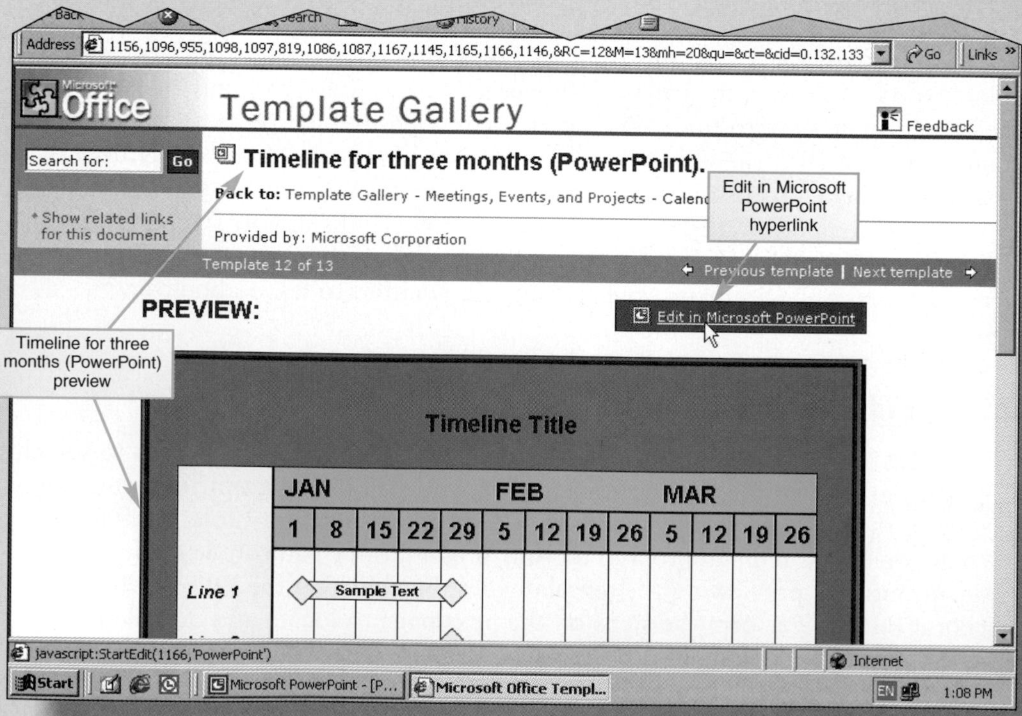

FIGURE 6

3 Click the Edit in Microsoft PowerPoint hyperlink. Click the Close button in the New Presentation task pane.

PowerPoint opens a new presentation, downloads the Timeline for three months (PowerPoint) template, and displays it in Slide 1 (Figure 7).

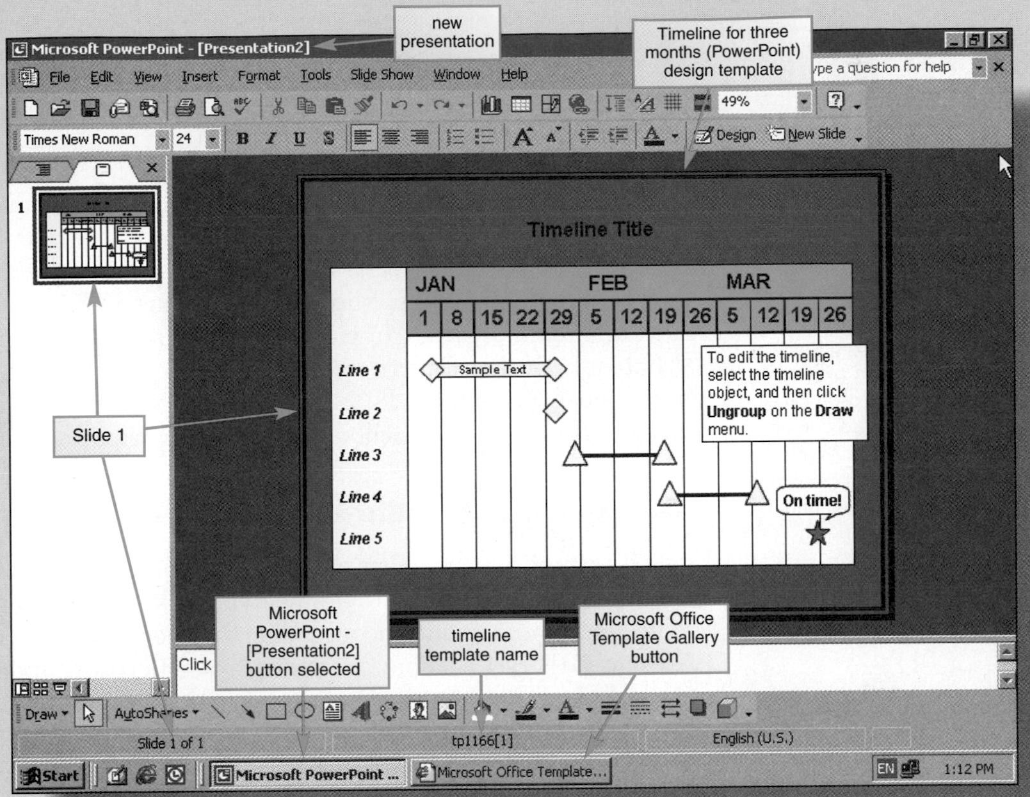

FIGURE 7

Saving the Presentation

You now should save the presentation because you applied a design template. The following steps summarize how to save a presentation.

TO SAVE A PRESENTATION

1. Click the Save button on the Standard toolbar.
2. Type `Chippy Timeline` in the File name text box.
3. Click the Save in box arrow. Click 3½ Floppy (A:) in the Save in list.
4. Click the Save button in the Save As dialog box.

The presentation is saved on the floppy disk in drive A with the file name Chippy Timeline. This file name displays on the title bar.

The Chippy Timeline displays in Slide 1. The next section describes downloading clips from the Microsoft Design Gallery Live Web site.

More About

The End-User License Agreement

When you view the Microsoft Office Template Gallery for the first time, you may be asked to read the Microsoft End-User License Agreement (EULA). When you click the Accept button, you agree to abide by the copyright restrictions Microsoft imposes to protect the use of its software. Read the EULA to see what rights and restrictions you have to use the templates found at this site. For more information, visit the PowerPoint 2002 More About Web page (scsite.com/pp2002/more.htm) and then click EULA.

More About

Downloaded Clips

The clips you download while working on your PowerPoint presentation can be used in other Microsoft Office applications. For example, the computer you import in this project can be part of a flyer created in Microsoft Word, and the modem sound can play while users view a Microsoft Excel chart. The clips also can be used and reused in Microsoft Publisher, Microsoft FrontPage, Microsoft PhotoDraw, and Microsoft Works.

Importing Clips from the Microsoft Design Gallery Live on the World Wide Web

The Microsoft Clip Organizer is a useful source for drawings, photographs, sounds, video, and other media files. Many companies provide clip art images on the Web; some sites offer clips free of charge, and others charge a fee.

For additional clips, Microsoft maintains a Web site called the Design Gallery Live that contains clips of pictures, photographs, sounds, and videos. To use the Microsoft Design Gallery Live Web site, as with the Template Gallery Web site, you must have access to an ISP and then use a Web browser. If you do not have Internet access, your instructor will provide the two clips used in this part of the project.

Connecting to the Microsoft Design Gallery Live Web Site

To simplify connecting to the Design Gallery Live Web site, the Insert Clip Art task pane contains a Clips Online hyperlink. You want to insert a motion clip of a computer and a sound file into Slide 1. Once you connect to the Web, the Microsoft Design Gallery Live home page displays. Microsoft updates this home page frequently to reflect seasons, holidays, new collections, artists, special offers, and events.

Perform the following steps to open the Insert Clip Art task pane, connect to the World Wide Web, and then display the Microsoft Design Gallery Live home page.

Steps To Connect to the Microsoft Design Gallery Live Web Site

1 Click the Insert Clip Art button on the Drawing toolbar. Point to Clips Online in the Insert Clip Art task pane.

The Insert Clip Art task pane displays (Figure 8).

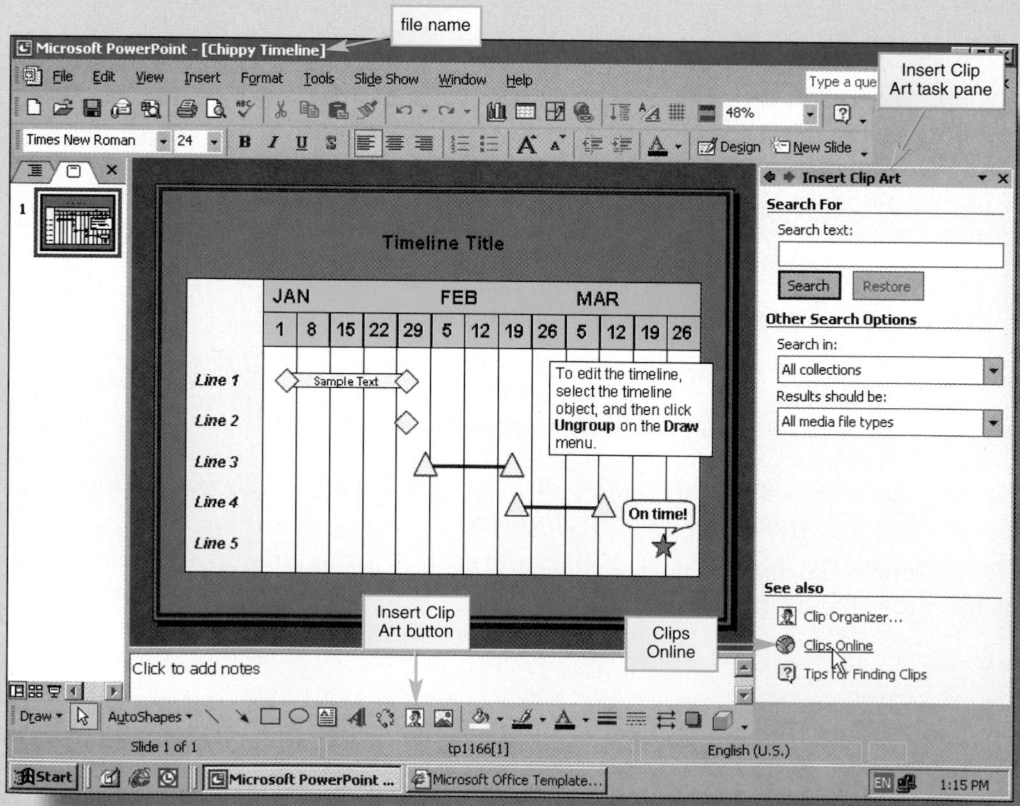

FIGURE 8

2 Click Clips Online. If necessary, click the OK button in the Connect to Web for More Clip Art, Photos, Sounds dialog box and connect to the Internet. When the Microsoft Design Gallery Live home page displays, if necessary maximize the screen, read the Addendum to the Microsoft End-User License Agreement, and then click the Accept button.

If you are using a modem and are not already connected to the Web, a dialog box displays that connects you to the Web via your ISP. If you are connected directly to the Web through a computer network, the dialog box does not display. Once connected to the Web, the Microsoft Design Gallery Live home page displays the Addendum to the Microsoft End-User License Agreement. When you click the Accept button, the Microsoft End-User License Agreement area no longer displays. The home page displays information about the Microsoft Design Gallery Live features and boxes to locate specific types of clips (Figure 9).

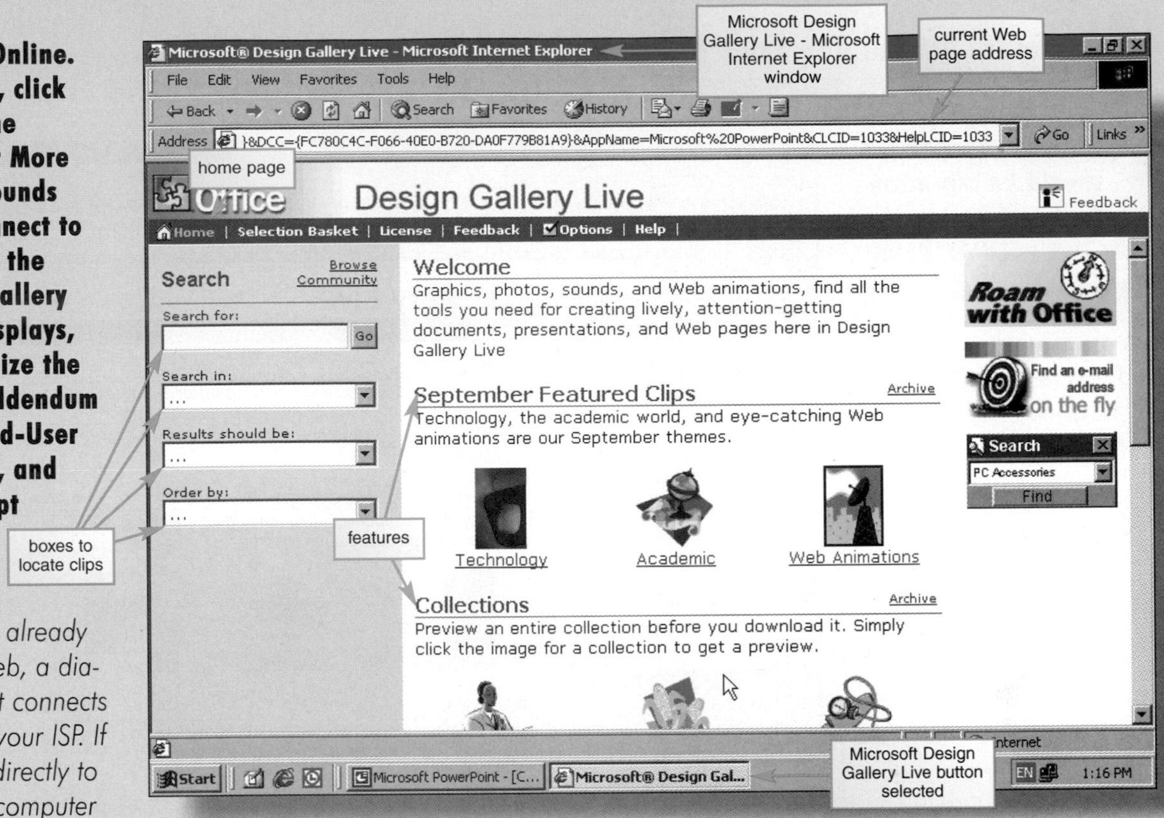

FIGURE 9

Searching for and Downloading Microsoft Design Gallery Live Clips

The Microsoft Design Gallery Live is similar to the Microsoft Office Template Gallery and the Microsoft Clip Organizer in that you can use keywords to search for clips. You want to locate a motion clip animating a computer and a sound clip containing the sound of a modem. You first will search the Microsoft Design Gallery Live for motion files with the keyword, computers. Then, you will search for sound files with the keyword, technology.

When you find a clip to add to your presentation, you can download it instantly to the Microsoft Clip Organizer on your computer by clicking the Immediate Download icon below the desired clip. You also can select several clips individually and then download them simultaneously. In this project, you want to download motion and sound clips, so you will choose a motion file and then select the check box below the clip to add the file to the selection basket. The **selection basket** holds your selections temporarily until you are ready to add them to your presentation. You then will add the sound clip to the selection basket. The downloaded clips will be added to the Microsoft Clip Organizer in the Downloaded Clips category. To remove a clip from the selection basket, clear the clip's check box.

Perform the steps on the next page to search for clips in the Microsoft Design Gallery Live Web site.

More About

Accepting the EULA

When you accept the terms of the Microsoft End-User License Agreement, your computer sends a message to the Microsoft Design Gallery Live Web site stating that you agree to the licensing restrictions. Microsoft, in turn, sends a message, called a cookie, to your computer so that you will not be asked to accept the EULA each time you visit this Web site. If you are using Internet Explorer 4.0 or later and are asked to accept the agreement each time you go to this site, your computer probably has been instructed not to accept cookies.

Steps To Search for and Download Microsoft Design Gallery Live Clips

1 Click the Results should be box arrow in the Microsoft Design Gallery Live window. Point to Motion in the list.

Microsoft groups the clips in five categories: Anything, Clip Art, Photos, Sounds, and Motion (Figure 10).

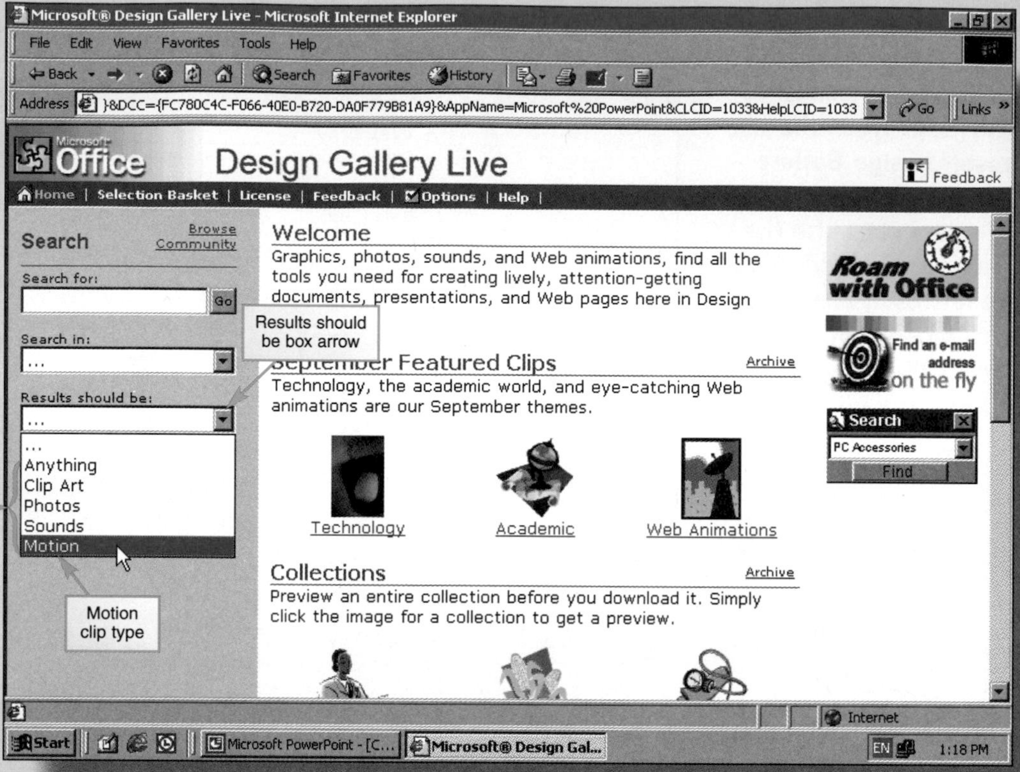

FIGURE 10

2 Click Motion. Click the Search for text box and type computer **in the box. Point to the Go button (Figure 11).**

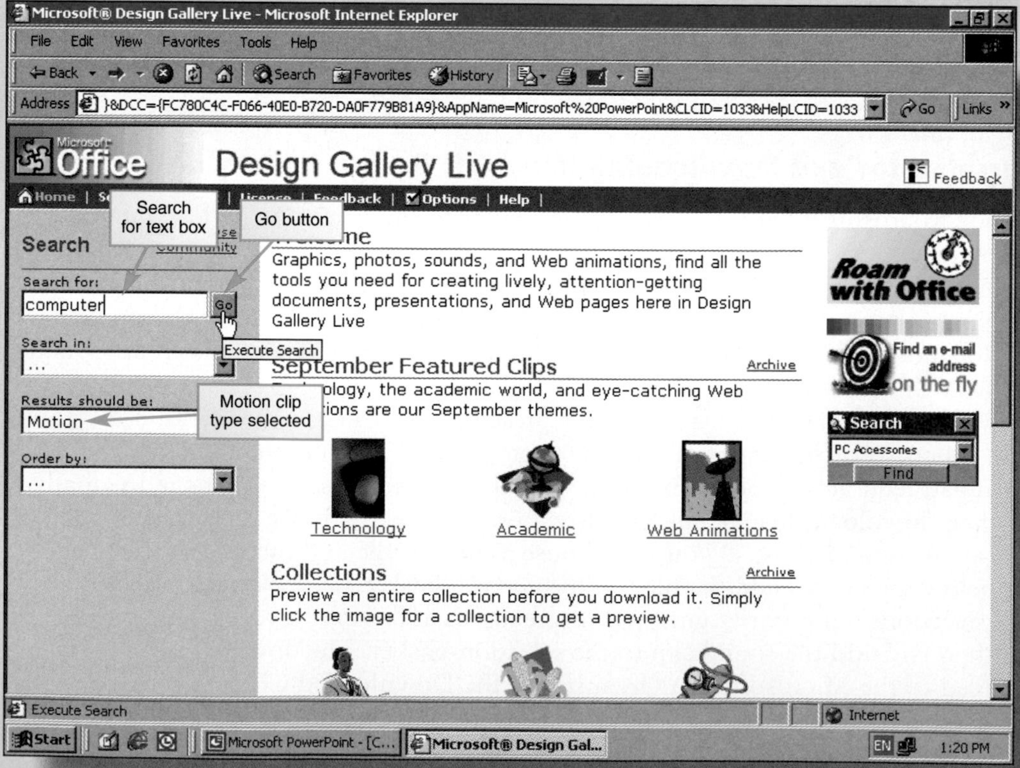

FIGURE 11

3 Click the Go button. When the search results display, click the check box below the purple animated walking computer and plug. Click the Results should be box arrow. Point to Sounds in the list.

Design Gallery Live executes the search and displays the results (Figure 12). When you click the check box associated with the thumbnail-sized clip, the motion clip is added to the selection basket, as indicated by the Download 1 Clip hyperlink. The search status displays at the upper-right corner of the page and indicates the number of pages of clips matching the search criteria. The number below each file name is the clip's file size.

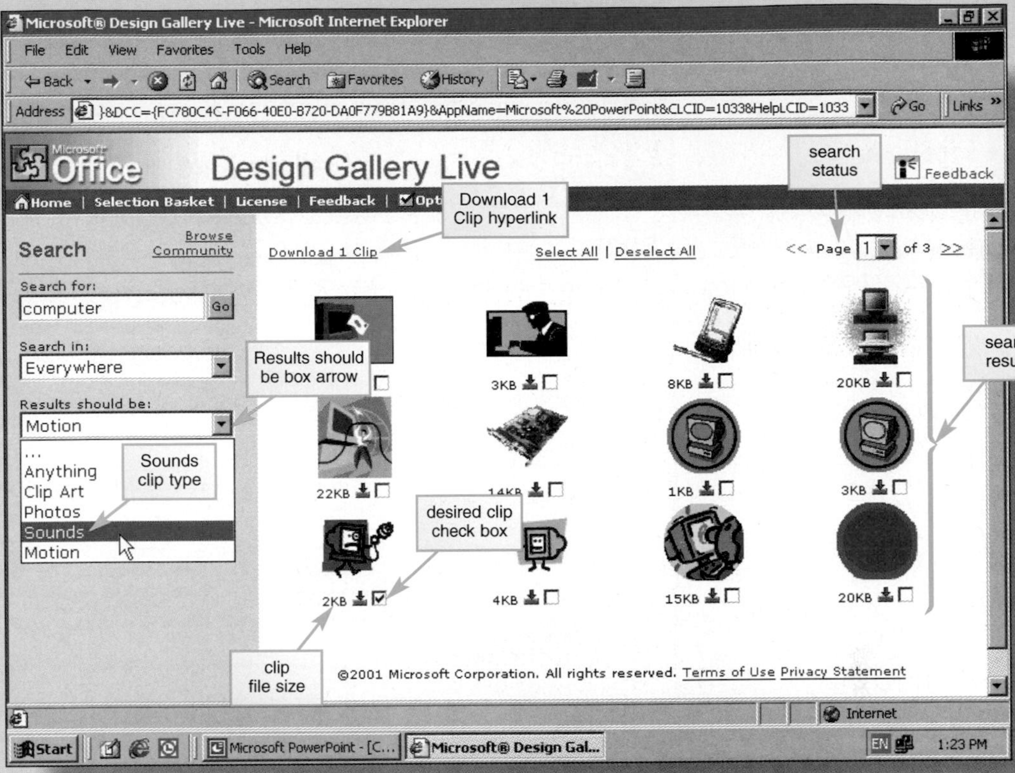

FIGURE 12

4 Click Sounds. Click the Search for text box, select the current text, and then type `technology` **in the box. Click the Go button.**

Design Gallery Live executes the search. After a few moments, several speaker icons with the keyword, technology, display (Figure 13). The speaker icons identify the sound clips. The hyperlink below each clip is its file name. The numbers below each file name are the clip's estimated download time and file size.

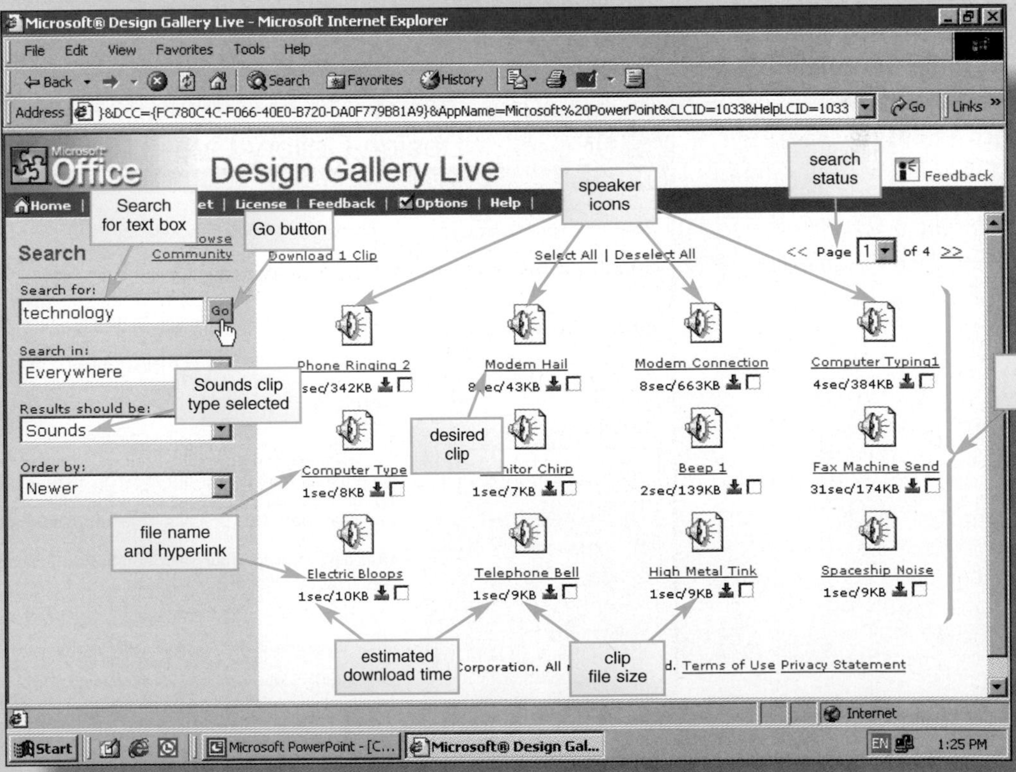

FIGURE 13

5 Click the check box below the clip with the file name, Modem Hail. Point to the Download 2 Clips hyperlink.

When you click the check box, the sound clip is added to the selection basket, as indicated by the underlined Download 2 Clips hyperlink that displays with the font color red (Figure 14).

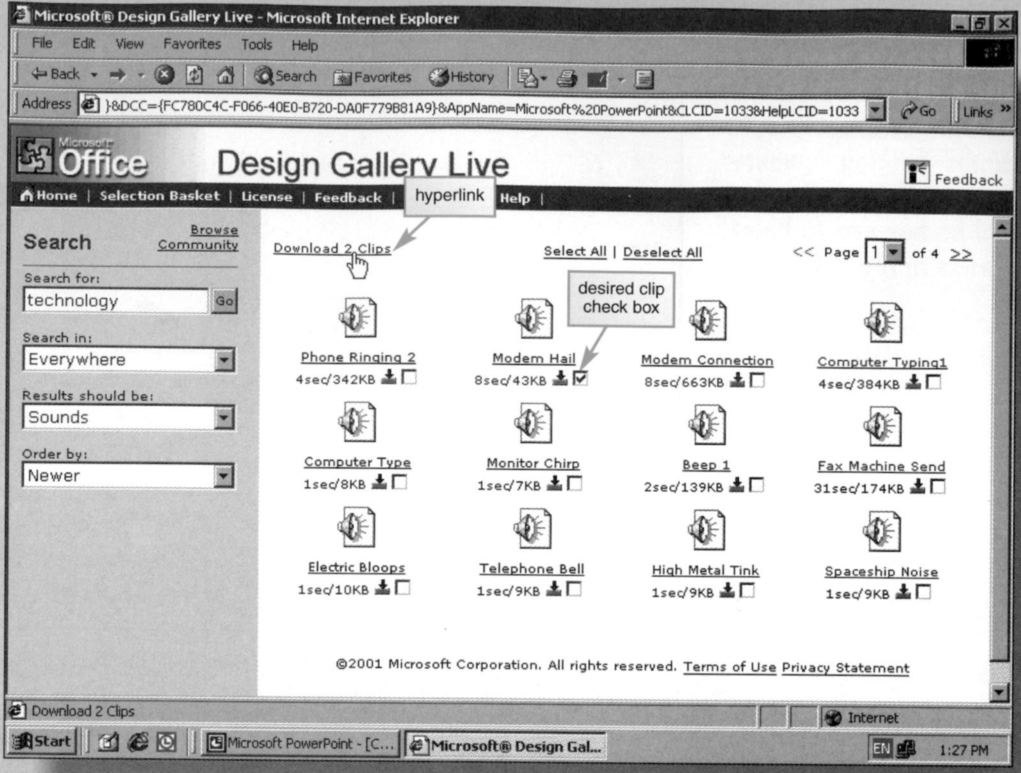

FIGURE 14

6 Click the Download 2 Clips hyperlink. Point to the Download Now! button in the Selection Basket sheet.

Clicking the button will download the two clips stored temporarily in the selection basket (Figure 15).

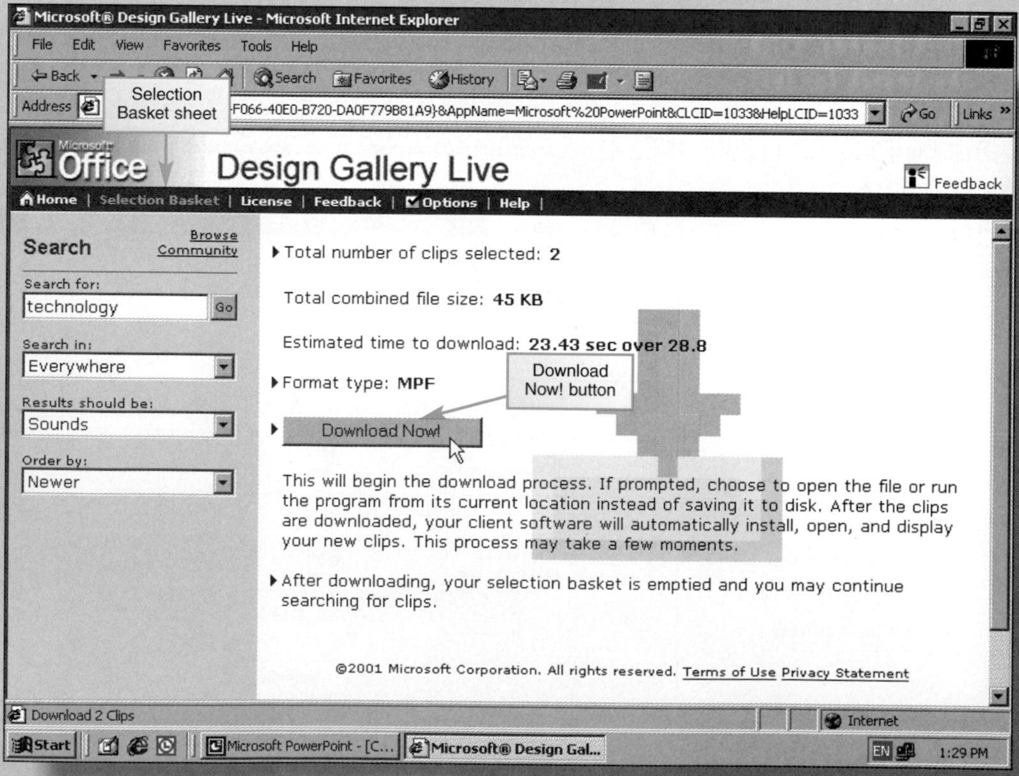

FIGURE 15

7 Click the Download Now! button. Point to the Microsoft PowerPoint - [Chippy Timeline] button on the taskbar.

PowerPoint downloads the two clips into the Science & Technology category of the Microsoft Clip Organizer (Figure 16).

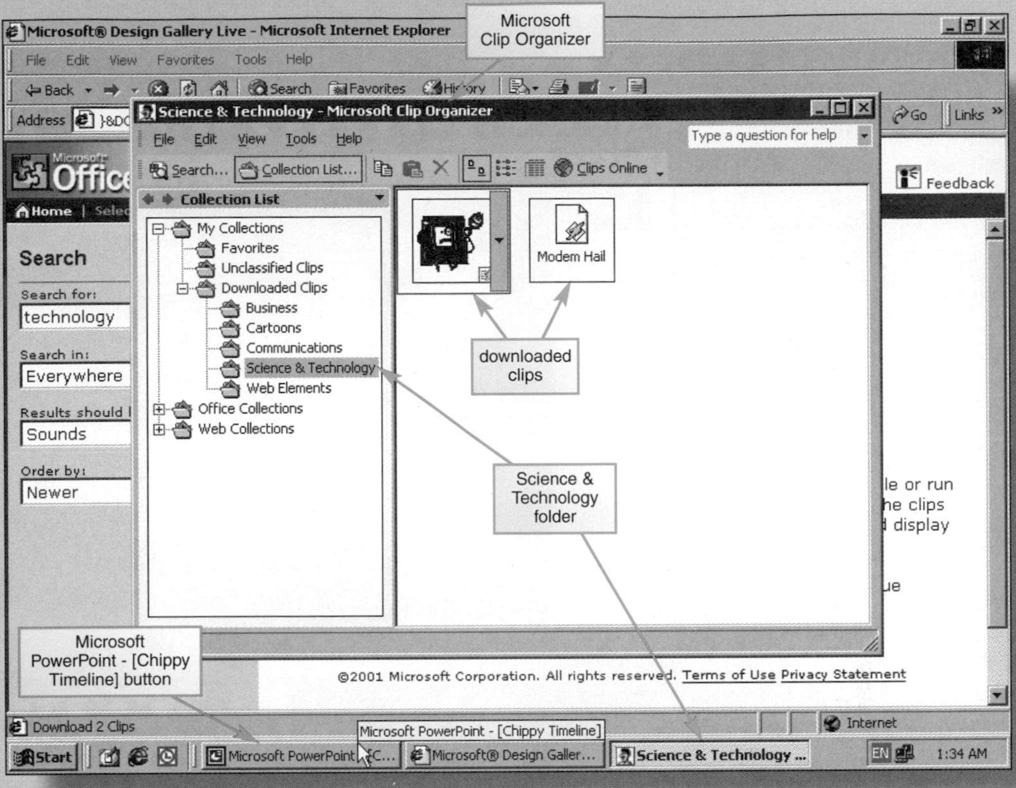

FIGURE 16

8 Click the Microsoft PowerPoint - [Chippy Timeline] button. Click the Search text text box in the Insert Clip Art task pane, type computer **and then point to the Search button (Figure 17).**

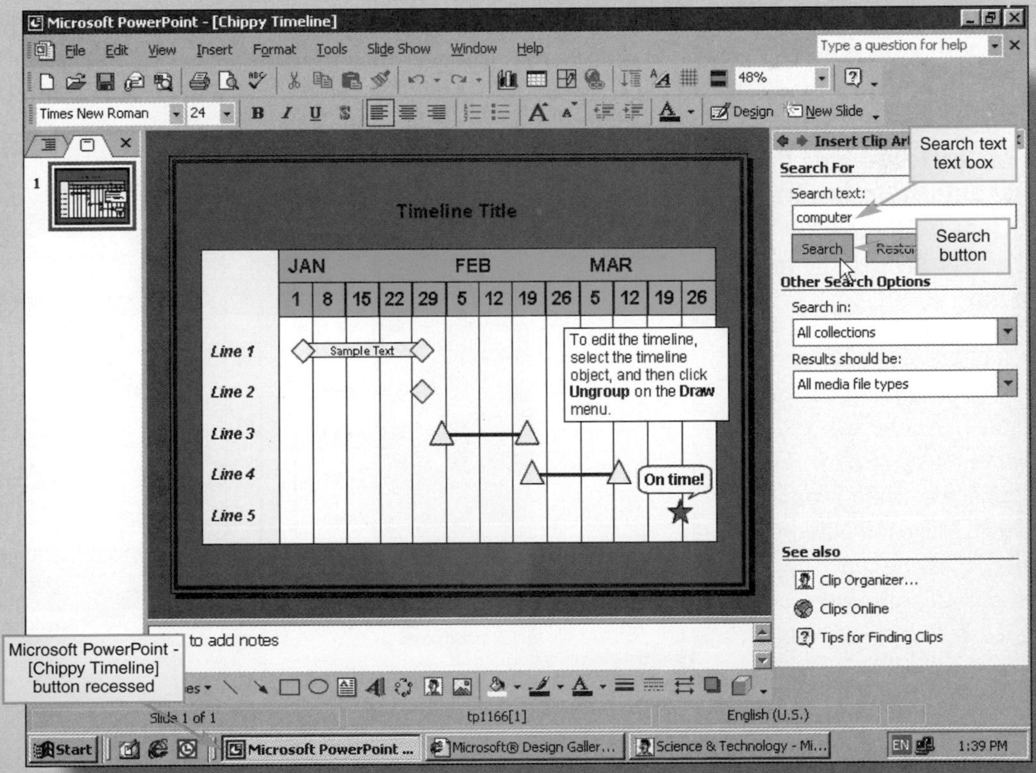

FIGURE 17

9 Click the Search button. Click the computer clip and then point to the Modem Hail thumbnail.

When you click the computer clip, PowerPoint inserts the clip into Slide 1 (Figure 18).

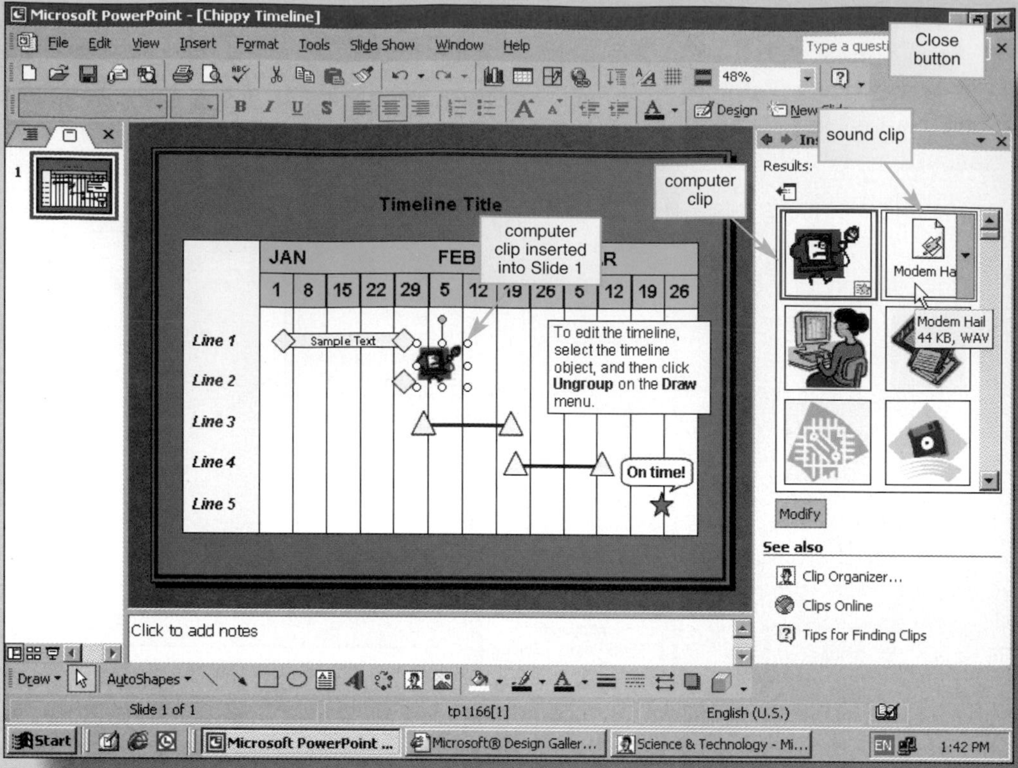

FIGURE 18

10 Click the Modem Hail clip. When the Microsoft PowerPoint dialog box displays, click the Yes button to play the sound automatically. Click the Close button on the Insert Clip Art task pane title bar.

The speaker icon displays on top of the animated computer in Slide 1 (Figure 19). You want the music to play automatically when Slide 1 displays. Microsoft Design Gallery Live and the Microsoft Clip Organizer Science & Technology folder still are open, and you are connected to the ISP.

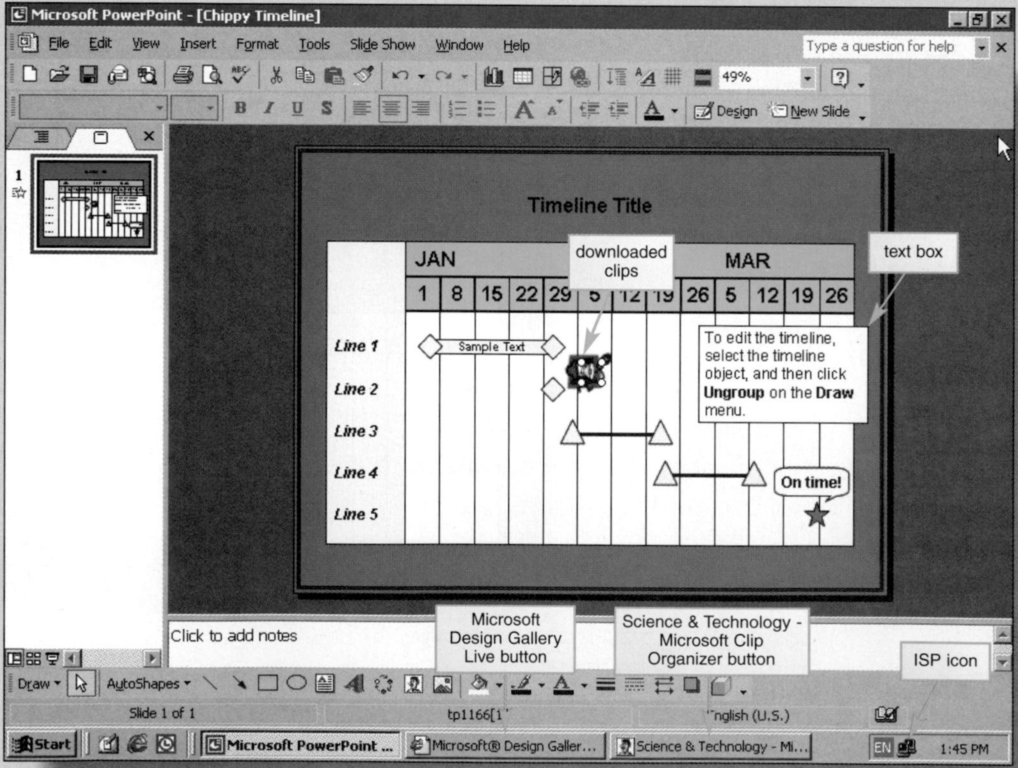

FIGURE 19

Quitting a Web Session

Once you have downloaded the template and clips, quit the Web session. Because Windows displays buttons on the taskbar for each open application, you quickly can quit an application by right-clicking an application button and then clicking the Close button on the shortcut menu. Perform the following steps to quit your current Web session.

TO QUIT A WEB SESSION

1. Right-click the Microsoft Design Gallery Live - Microsoft Internet Explorer button on the taskbar. If you are not using Microsoft Internet Explorer, right-click the button for your browser.
2. Click Close on the shortcut menu.
3. When the dialog box displays, click the Yes button to disconnect. If your ISP displays a different dialog box, terminate your connection to your ISP.
4. Right-click the Science & Technology - Microsoft Clip Organizer button on the taskbar.
5. Click Close on the shortcut menu.

The browser software and Microsoft Clip Organizer close, and the ISP connection is terminated.

Slide 1 displays with the two downloaded objects in the center of the timeline template. The speaker icon represents the Modem Hail sound file.

More About

Quick Reference

For a table that lists how to complete tasks covered in this book using the mouse, menu, shortcut menu, and keyboard, see the Quick Reference Summary at the back of this book, or visit the Shelly Cashman Series Office XP Web page (scsite.com/offxp/qr.htm) and then click Microsoft PowerPoint 2002.

Editing Text and Moving the Clips

You want to edit the default timeline text and then move the speaker icon to the lower-right corner of the slide and the computer to the upper-left corner. Perform the following steps to edit the text and move the clips to these respective locations.

TO EDIT TEXT AND MOVE THE CLIPS

1. Triple-click the text, Timeline Title, at the top of Slide 1 and then type `Chippy's Computer Shop Web Site Timeline` to replace the current text.
2. Click each of the text items in Slide 1 and replace the text with the words and numbers shown in Figure 20 on the next page.
3. Drag the speaker icon to the lower-right corner of Slide 1.
4. Scale the computer clip to 160 % and then drag it to the upper-left corner of Slide 1.
5. Click the text box with instructions of how to edit the timeline, click the text box border, and then press the DELETE key.

The revised text and downloaded clips display in the appropriate locations in the Slide 1 timeline (Figure 20).

More About

Common Questions

Many Web sites feature frequently asked questions (FAQs) about PowerPoint and provide a wealth of information and tips. They give answers to common PowerPoint questions, provide templates and add-ins, and contain tutorials. Some sites allow users to submit questions and to comment about the Web pages' content. To view some of these FAQs, visit the PowerPoint 2002 More About Web page (scsite.com/pp2002/more.htm) and then click FAQ.

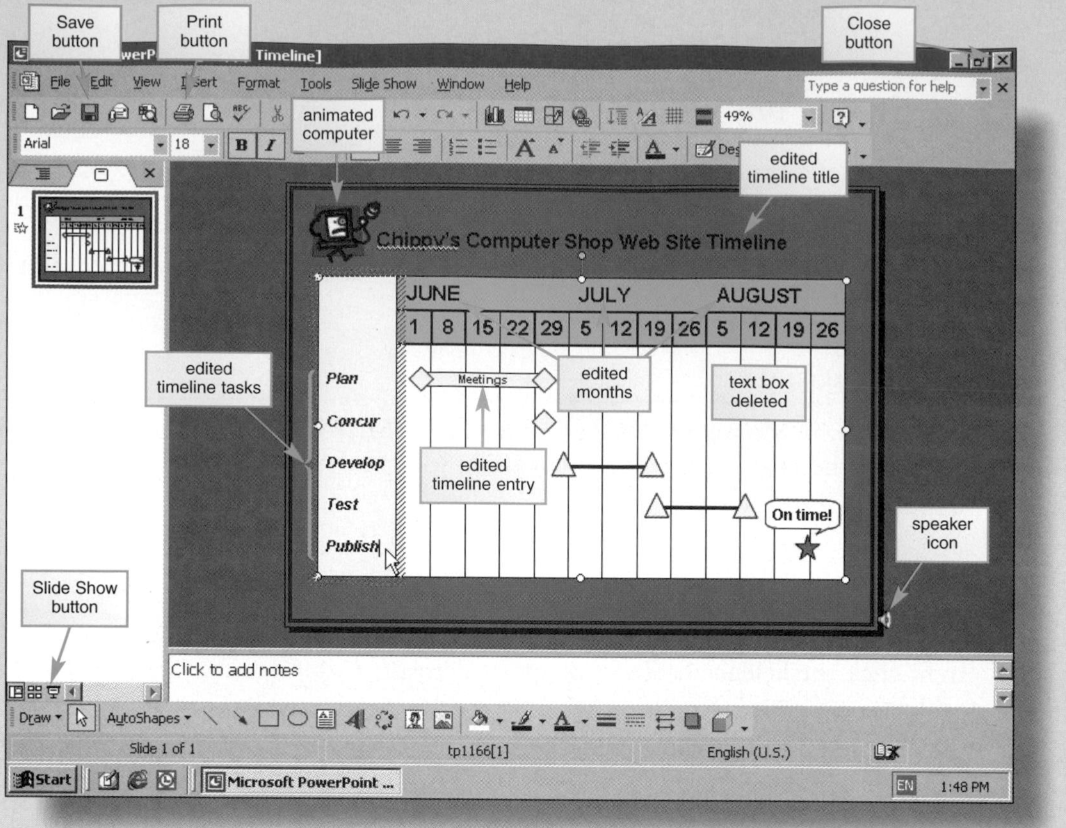

FIGURE 20

Running and Printing the Presentation

The changes to the presentation are complete. Save the presentation again before running the slide show.

Running a Slide Show

To verify the timeline looks as expected, run the presentation. Perform the following step to run the Chippy Timeline slide show.

More About

Microsoft Certification

The Microsoft Office User Specialist (MOUS) Certification program provides an opportunity for you to obtain a valuable industry credential — proof that you have the PowerPoint 2002 skills required by employers. For more information, see Appendix E or visit the Shelly Cashman Series MOUS Web page at scsite.com/offxp/cert.htm.

TO RUN A SLIDE SHOW

1. Click the Slide Show button in the lower-left corner of the PowerPoint window. When Slide 1 displays, click the slide anywhere except on the Pop-up menu buttons.

The presentation displays the animated computer, plays the sound file, and then returns to normal view when finished.

The presentation is complete. If the timeline elements do not display in the desired locations, you can move them on the slide. The next step is to print the presentation slide.

Printing a Presentation Slide

Perform the following step to print the timeline.

TO PRINT A PRESENTATION SLIDE

1. Click the Print button on the Standard toolbar.

Slide 1 prints.

Quitting PowerPoint

To quit PowerPoint, perform the following steps.

TO QUIT POWERPOINT

1. Click the Close button on the Microsoft PowerPoint title bar.
2. If the Microsoft PowerPoint dialog box displays, click the Yes button to save changes made since the last save.

PowerPoint closes.

CASE PERSPECTIVE SUMMARY

The timeline now has edited text, the modem sound, and an animated computer in Slide 1. The design template from the Template Gallery allowed you to create this timeline easily. The clips from the Microsoft Design Gallery Live Web site enhance the slide show and should catch Chip Phillips's attention.

Web Feature Summary

This Web Feature introduced importing design templates and sound and animation clips from the Microsoft Office Template Gallery and the Microsoft Design Gallery Live sites on the World Wide Web. You began by opening a new presentation and then accessing the Template Gallery home page by clicking the Templates on Microsoft.com hyperlink in the New Presentation task pane. You then downloaded the Timeline for three months (PowerPoint) design template. The next step was to access the Microsoft Design Gallery Live home page on the World Wide Web by clicking the Clips Online hyperlink in the Insert Clip Art task pane. Once connected to the Microsoft Design Gallery Live home page, you searched for an animated computer and a technology sound. Then you imported these clips to the Clip Organizer by downloading the files from the Web page. You moved the clips to appropriate locations in Slide 1, edited the timeline text, and then quit the Web session by closing the browser software and disconnecting from the ISP. Finally, you saved the presentation, ran the presentation in slide show view to check for continuity, printed the presentation slide, and quit PowerPoint.

What You Should Know

Having completed this Web Feature, you now should be able to perform the following tasks:

- Connect to the Microsoft Design Gallery Live Web Site *(PPW 3.08)*
- Connect to the Microsoft Office Template Gallery Web Site *(PPW 3.04)*
- Edit Text and Move the Clips *(PPW 3.15)*
- Locate and Download a Template Gallery Template *(PPW 3.06)*
- Print a Presentation Slide *(PPW 3.17)*
- Quit PowerPoint *(PPW 3.17)*
- Quit a Web Session *(PPW 3.15)*
- Run a Slide Show *(PPW 3.16)*
- Save a Presentation *(PPW 3.07)*
- Search for and Download Microsoft Design Gallery Live Clips *(PPW 3.10)*
- Start and Customize a New Presentation *(PPW 3.03)*

In the Lab

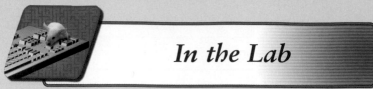

1 Importing a Template and Sound and Motion Clips

Problem: Real estate agents devote much time explaining the home-buying process to first-time buyers. The agents at Heartland Realty have asked you to enhance the presentation you created in Project 6. They believe a Personal Budget worksheet would help home buyers accurately assess their financial situations. In addition, they believe the sound of a coin dropping and an animated clip from the Microsoft Design Gallery Live Web site would make the presentation even more impressive. You decide to use the Microsoft Web Site to find appropriate clips and to modify Slides 3 and 5 of the House Buying presentation.

Instructions: Start PowerPoint and then perform the following steps.

1. Open the House Buying presentation shown in Figures 6-1a through 6-1h on page PP 6.05 that you created in Project 6. (If you did not complete Project 6, see your instructor for a copy of the presentation.)
2. Save the House Buying presentation with the new file name, Enhanced House Buying.
3. Display Slide 3, click View on the menu bar, click Task Pane, and then click Templates on Microsoft.com in the New Presentation task pane. If necessary, connect to the Internet. When the Template Gallery displays, download the Personal Budget worksheet from the Budgeting subcategory in the Finance and Accounting category. Save the worksheet with the file name, Personal Budget.
4. Click the Microsoft PowerPoint - [Enhanced House Buying] button on the taskbar. Add an action button to the upper-right corner of Slide 3 and hyperlink it to the Personal Budget file. Add the caption, What is my Personal Budget? Format the caption font to Bookman Old Style, the font size to 20 point, the font color to black, and no effects. Apply Shadow Style 14 to the action button with a ¾ pt line.
5. Display Slide 5. Click the Insert Clip Art button on the Drawing toolbar, and then click the Clips Online hyperlink in the Insert Clip Art task pane.
6. Search for motion clips with the keyword, money. Select a clip with a rotating coin. Then search for sound clips with the same keyword, money. Select the Coin Drops 1 clip. Download the two clips.
7. Click the Microsoft PowerPoint - [Enhanced House Buying] button on the taskbar. Insert the clips into Slide 5, and have the sound play automatically. Size the rotating coin clip to 300 %. Move the speaker icon to the lower-right corner of Slide 5, and then move the coin clip above the Tax Savings shape.
8. Disconnect from the Web and save the file again.
9. Run the slide show and then print Slides 3 and 5. Quit PowerPoint.

In the Lab

2 Importing a Template and Multiple Sound and Motion Clips

Problem: Administrators running the Triathlon Training Techniques (T^3) training camps are pleased with the Triathlon Camps presentation you developed in the In the Lab 3 exercise in Project 6. They want you to add more clips and an action button that hyperlinks to a weight-training log. You decide to search the Microsoft Design Gallery Live Web site for the clips and the Microsoft Office Template Gallery for a training log.

Instructions: Start PowerPoint and then perform the following steps.

1. Open the Triathlon Camps presentation shown in Figures 6-83a through 6-83d and 6-84a through 6-84d on pages PP 6.68 and PP 6.69 that you created in Project 6. (If you did not complete this exercise, see your instructor for a copy of the presentation.) Save the Triathlon Camps presentation with the new file name, Revised Triathlon Camps.
2. Click the Insert Clip Art button on the Drawing toolbar and then click Clips Online in the Insert Clip Art task pane. Search for a photo clip with the keyword, swimming, and select a clip with people swimming at a beach. Search for a motion clip with the keyword, marathons, and select a clip with a male runner. Search for a sound clip with the file name, splashes. Download these three clips.
3. Click the Microsoft PowerPoint - [Revised Triathlon Camps] button on the taskbar. Click View on the menu bar, click Task Pane, and then click Templates on Microsoft.com in the New Presentation task pane. If necessary, connect to the Internet. When the Template Gallery displays, download the Weight training log located in the Hobbies, Sports, and Collections subcategory of the Personal Interests, Community, and Politics category. Click the Edit in Microsoft Word button hyperlink, and then save the document with the file name, Weight Training Log.
4. Click the Microsoft PowerPoint - [Revised Triathlon Camps] button on the taskbar. Display Slide 2 and insert the swimming photo. Size the swimming photo to 60 %. Move the swimming clip to the upper-right corner of the slide. Insert the Splash sound clip into Slide 2 and have the sound play automatically. Move the speaker icon to the lower-left corner of Slide 2.
5. Click the Next Slide button to display Slide 3. Add an action button to the lower-left corner and hyperlink it to the Weight Training Log file. Add the caption, Weight Training Log, to the right of the action button. Format the caption font to Arial, the font size to 24 point, and the font color to black. Bold and left-align the text. Apply Shadow Style 3 to the action button.
6. Insert the marathon clip. Size the runner to 15 % and then drag the clip to the middle of the action button. If the clip image disappears, right-click the action button and then click Bring Forward on the shortcut menu. Group the action button and the clip.
7. Disconnect from the Web and save the file again.
8. Run the slide show and then print Slides 2 and 3. Quit PowerPoint.

In the Lab

3 Modifying a Personal Presentation

Problem: You have been asked to speak to the Campus Computer Club about the usefulness of Microsoft PowerPoint. You decide to prepare a slide show to enhance your speech and want the first slide to list your name and qualifications. The Microsoft Office Template Gallery has an appropriate template, so you download it, add clips from the Design Gallery Live, and then edit the text.

Instructions: Start PowerPoint and perform the following tasks.

1. Start a new presentation. Connect to the Microsoft Office Template Gallery Web site and then locate and download the Introducing and thanking a speaker template. This template is found in the Preparations subcategory of the Meetings, Events, and Projects category.
2. Search the Microsoft Design Gallery Live Web site for appropriate motion, picture, and sound clips. Add these clips to the slide.
3. Edit the Slide 1 text to reflect your qualifications.
4. Delete the text in the notes pane and then add information about yourself.
5. Save the presentation with the file name, Introducing Yourself.
6. Run the slide show and then print the slide. Quit PowerPoint.

APPENDIX A

Microsoft Office XP Help System

Using the Microsoft Office Help System

This appendix demonstrates how you can use the Microsoft Office XP Help system to answer your questions. At anytime while you are using one of the Microsoft Office XP applications, you can interact with the Help system to display information on any topic associated with the application. To illustrate the use of the Microsoft Office XP Help system, you will use the Microsoft Word 2002 application in this appendix. The Help systems in other Microsoft Office XP applications respond in a similar fashion.

As shown in Figure A-1, you can access Word's Help system in four primary ways:

1. Ask a Question box on the menu bar
2. Function key F1 on the keyboard
3. Microsoft Word Help command on the Help menu
4. Microsoft Word Help button on the Standard toolbar

If you use the Ask a Question box on the menu bar, Word responds by opening the Microsoft Word Help window, which gives you direct access to its Help system. If you use one of the other three ways to access Word's Help system, Word responds in one of two ways:

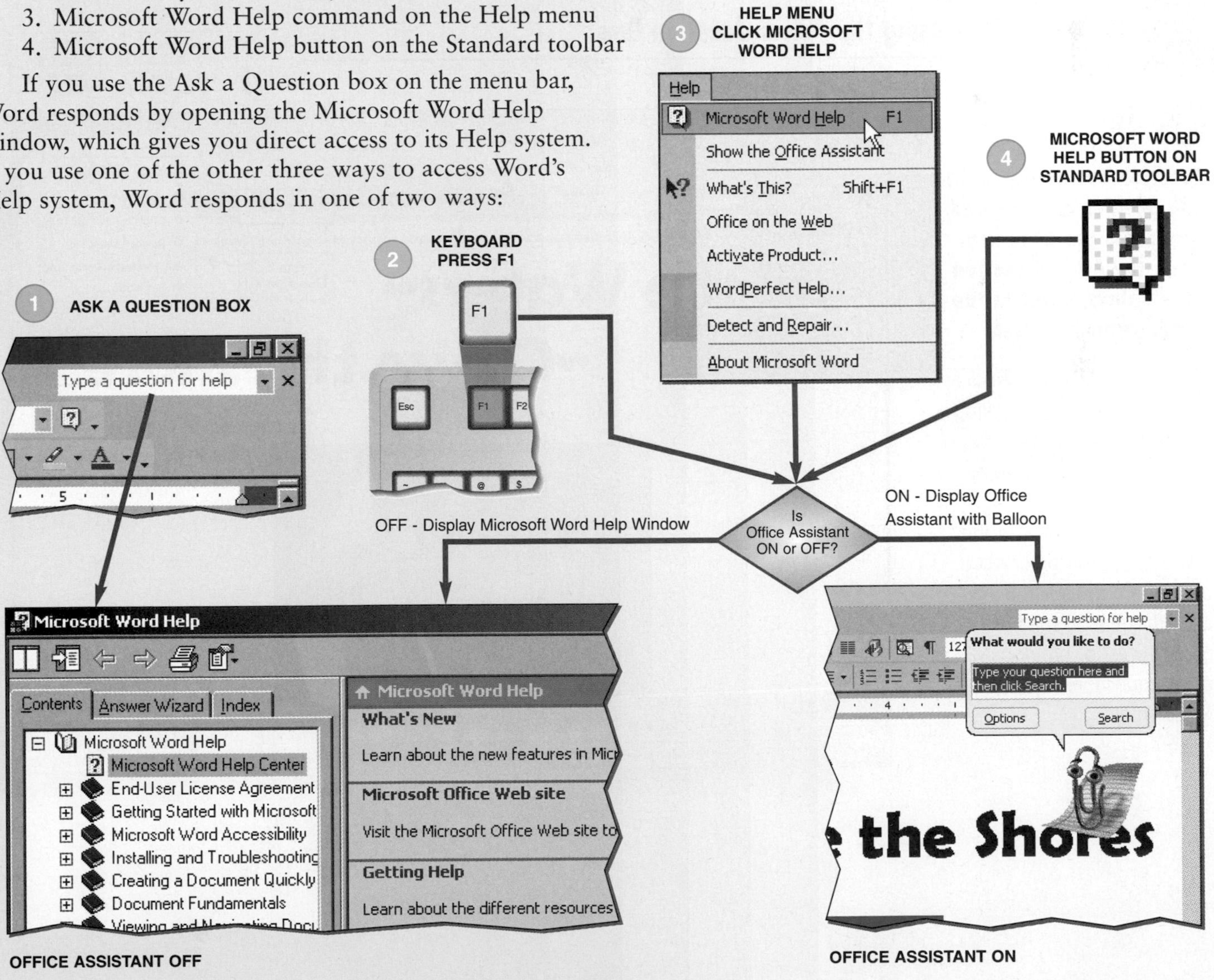

FIGURE A-1

1. If the Office Assistant is turned on, then the Office Assistant displays with a balloon (lower-right side in Figure A-1 on the previous page).
2. If the Office Assistant is turned off, then the Microsoft Word Help window displays (lower-left side in Figure A-1 on the previous page).

The best way to familiarize yourself with the Word Help system is to use it. The next several pages show examples of how to use the Help system. Following the examples are a set of exercises titled Use Help that will sharpen your Word Help system skills.

Ask a Question Box

The **Ask a Question box** on the right side of the menu bar lets you type questions in your own words, or you can type terms, such as template, smart tags, or speech. Word responds by displaying a list of topics related to the term(s) you entered. The following steps show how to use the Ask a Question box to obtain information about how smart tags work.

Steps To Obtain Help Using the Ask a Question Box

1 Type `smart tags` **in the Ask a Question box on the right side of the menu bar and then press the ENTER key. When the Ask a Question list displays, point to the About smart tags link.**

The Ask a Question list displays (Figure A-2). Clicking the See more link displays a new list of topics in the Ask a Question list. As you enter questions and terms in the Ask a Question box, Word adds them to its list. If you click the Ask a Question box arrow, a list of previously asked questions and terms will display.

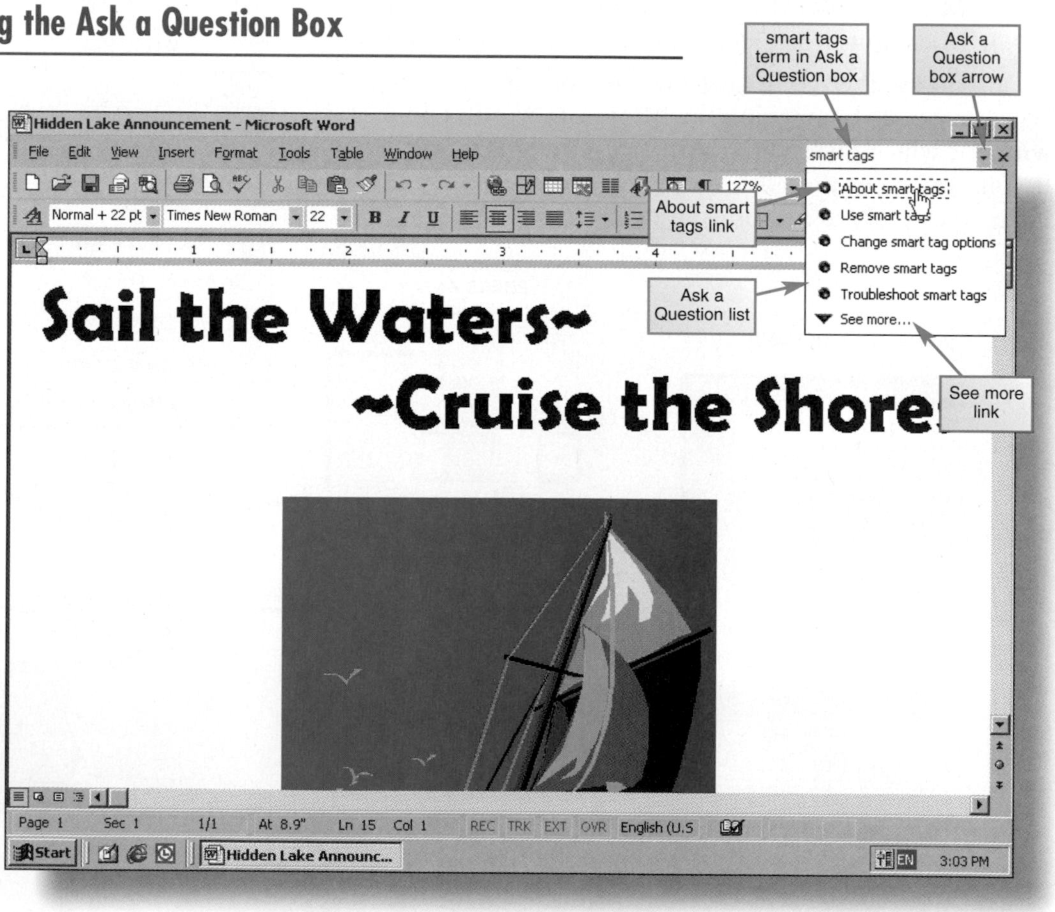

FIGURE A-2

2 Click About smart tags. When the Microsoft Word Help window displays, double-click its title bar to maximize it. If necessary, click the Contents tab.

Word displays and maximizes the Microsoft Word Help window (Figure A-3). A toolbar displays at the top of the window. The left side of the window contains the Contents, Answer Wizard, and Index tabs. The right side of the window contains the About smart tags topic.

3 Click th e Close button on the Microsoft Word Help window title bar.

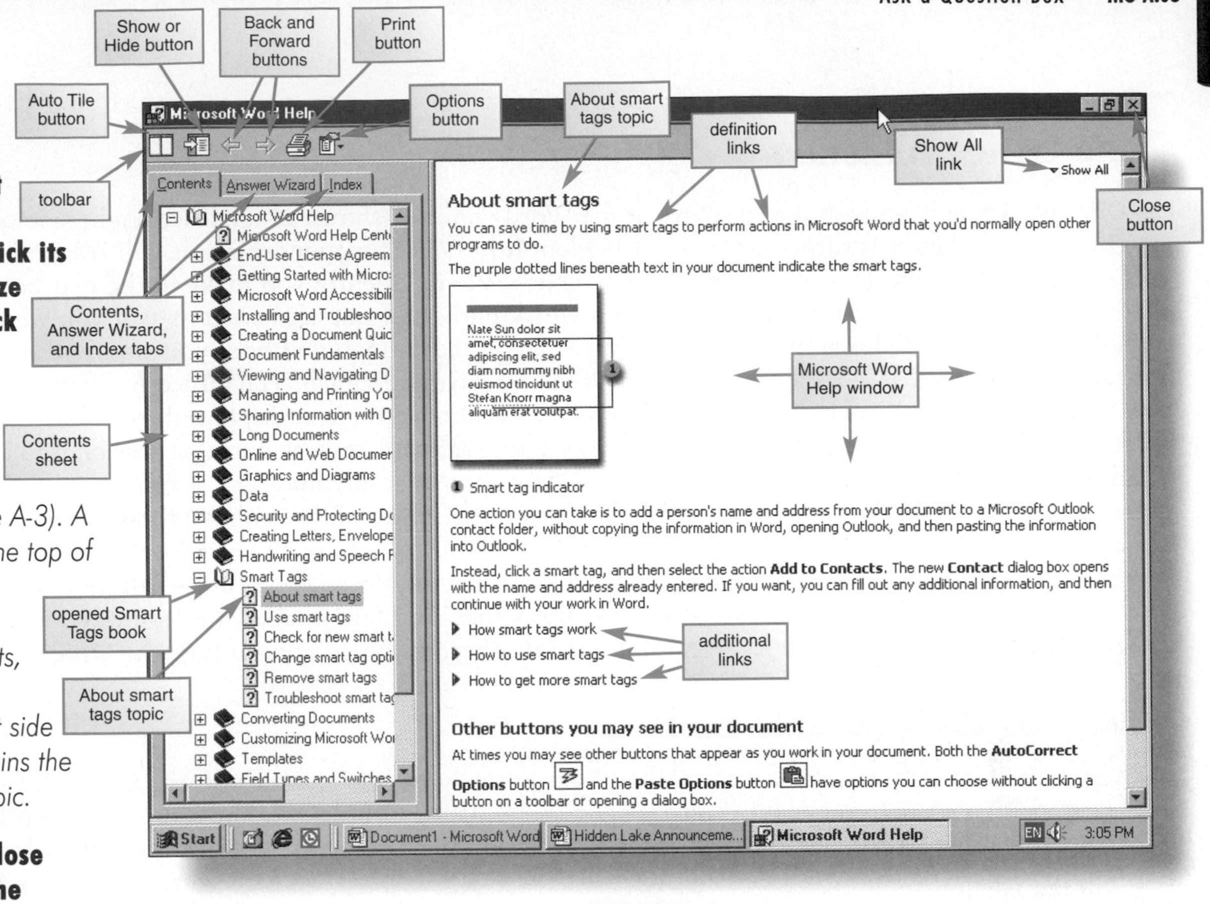

FIGURE A-3

The Microsoft Word Help window closes and the document window is active.

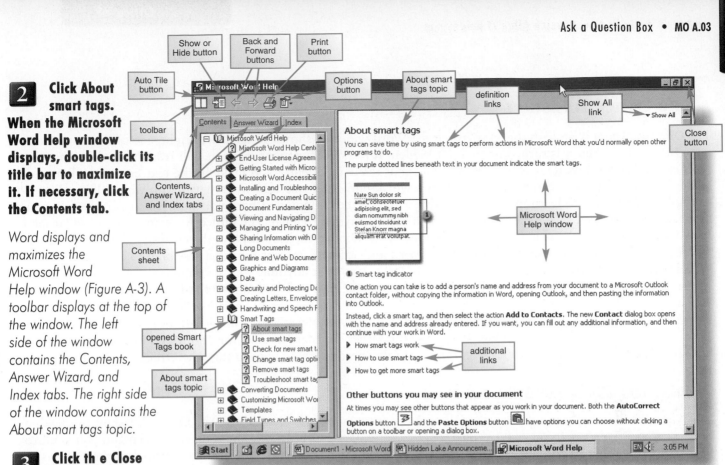

The right side of the Microsoft Word Help window shown in Figure A-3 contains the About smart tags topic. The two links at the top of the window, smart tags and actions, display in blue font. Clicking either of these links displays a definition in green font following the link. Clicking again removes the definition. The How smart tags work link, How to use smart tags link, and How to get more smart tags link also display on the right side of the window. Clicking one of these links displays additional information about the link. Clicking again removes the information. Clicking the Show All link in the upper-right corner of the window causes the text associated with each link to display. In addition, the Hide All link replaces the Show All link.

If the Contents sheet is active on the left side of the Microsoft Word Help window, then Word opens the book that pertains to the topic for which you are requesting help. In this case, Word opens the Smart Tags book, which includes a list of topics related to smart tags. If you need additional information about the topic, you can click one of the topics listed below the Smart Tags book name.

The six buttons on the toolbar in the Microsoft Word Help window (Figure A-3) allow you to navigate through the Help system, change the display, and print the contents of the window. Table A-1 lists the function of each button on the toolbar.

Table A-1 Microsoft Word Help Toolbar Buttons

BUTTON	NAME	FUNCTION
	Auto Tile	Tiles the Microsoft Word Help window and Microsoft Word window when the Microsoft Word Help window is maximized
or	Show or Hide	Displays or hides the Contents, Answer Wizard, and Index tabs
	Back	Displays the previous Help topic
	Forward	Displays the next Help topic
	Print	Prints the current Help topic
	Options	Displays a list of commands

The Office Assistant

The **Office Assistant** is an icon that displays in the Word window (shown in the lower-right side of Figure A-1 on page MO A.01) when it is turned on and not hidden. It has dual functions. First, it will respond in the same way the Ask a Question box does with a list of topics that relate to an entry you make in the text box at the bottom of the balloon. The entry can be in the form of a word, phrase, or question written as if you were talking. For example, if you want to learn more about saving a file, in the balloon text box, you can type any of the following terms or phrases: save, save a file, how do I save a file, or anything similar. The Office Assistant responds by displaying a list of topics from which you can choose. Once you choose a topic, it displays the corresponding information.

Second, the Office Assistant monitors your work and accumulates tips during a session on how you might increase your productivity and efficiency. You can view the tips at anytime. The accumulated tips display when you activate the Office Assistant balloon. Also, if at anytime you see a lightbulb above the Office Assistant, click it to display the most recent tip.

You may or may not want the Office Assistant to display on the screen at all times. You can hide it, and then show it at a later time. You may prefer not to use the Office Assistant at all. Thus, not only do you need to know how to show and hide the Office Assistant, but you also need to know how to turn the Office Assistant on and off.

Showing and Hiding the Office Assistant

When Word initially is installed, the Office Assistant may be off. You turn on the Office Assistant by clicking the **Show the Office Assistant command** on the Help menu. If the Office Assistant is on the screen and you want to hide it, you click the **Hide the Office Assistant command** on the Help menu. You also can right-click the Office Assistant to display its shortcut menu and then click the **Hide command** to hide it. You can move it to any location on the screen. You can click it to display the Office Assistant balloon, which allows you to request Help.

Turning the Office Assistant On and Off

The fact that the Office Assistant is hidden, does not mean it is turned off. To turn the Office Assistant off, it must be displaying in the Word window. You right-click it to display its shortcut menu (right side of Figure A-4). Next, click Options on the shortcut menu. When you click the **Options command**, the **Office Assistant dialog box** displays (left side of Figure A-4).

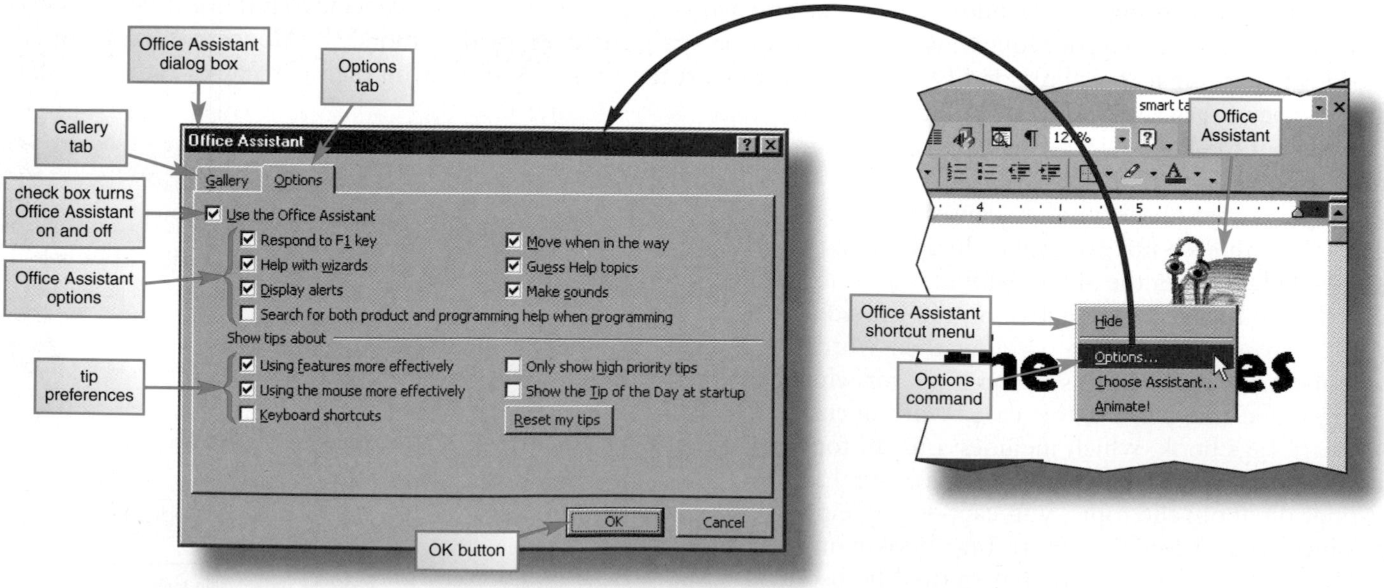

FIGURE A-4

In the **Options sheet** in the Office Assistant dialog box, the **Use the Office Assistant check box** at the top of the sheet determines whether the Office Assistant is on or off. To turn the Office Assistant off, remove the check mark from the Use the Office Assistant check box and then click the OK button. As shown in Figure A-1 on page MO A.01, if the Office Assistant is off when you invoke Help, then Word displays the Microsoft Word Help window instead of displaying the Office Assistant. To turn the Office Assistant on later, click the **Show the Office Assistant command** on the Help menu.

Through the Options command on the Office Assistant shortcut menu, you can change the look and feel of the Office Assistant. For example, you can hide the Office Assistant, turn the Office Assistant off, change the way it works, choose a different Office Assistant icon, or view an animation of the current one. These options also are available by clicking the **Options button** that displays in the Office Assistant balloon (Figure A-5).

The **Gallery sheet** (Figure A-4) in the Office Assistant dialog box allows you to change the appearance of the Office Assistant. The default is the paper clip (Clippit). You can change it to a bouncing red happy face (The Dot), a robot (F1), the Microsoft Office logo (Office Logo), a wizard (Merlin), the earth (Mother Nature), a cat (Links), or a dog (Rocky).

Using the Office Assistant

As indicated earlier, the Office Assistant allows you to enter a word, phrase, or question and then responds by displaying a list of topics from which you can choose to display Help. The following steps show how to use the Office Assistant to obtain Help on speech recognition.

Steps To Use the Office Assistant

1 If the Office Assistant is not turned on, click Help on the menu bar and then click Show the Office Assistant. Click the Office Assistant. When the Office Assistant balloon displays, type what is speech recognition **in the text box immediately above the Options button. Point to the Search button.**

The Office Assistant balloon displays and the question, what is speech recognition, displays in the text box (Figure A-5).

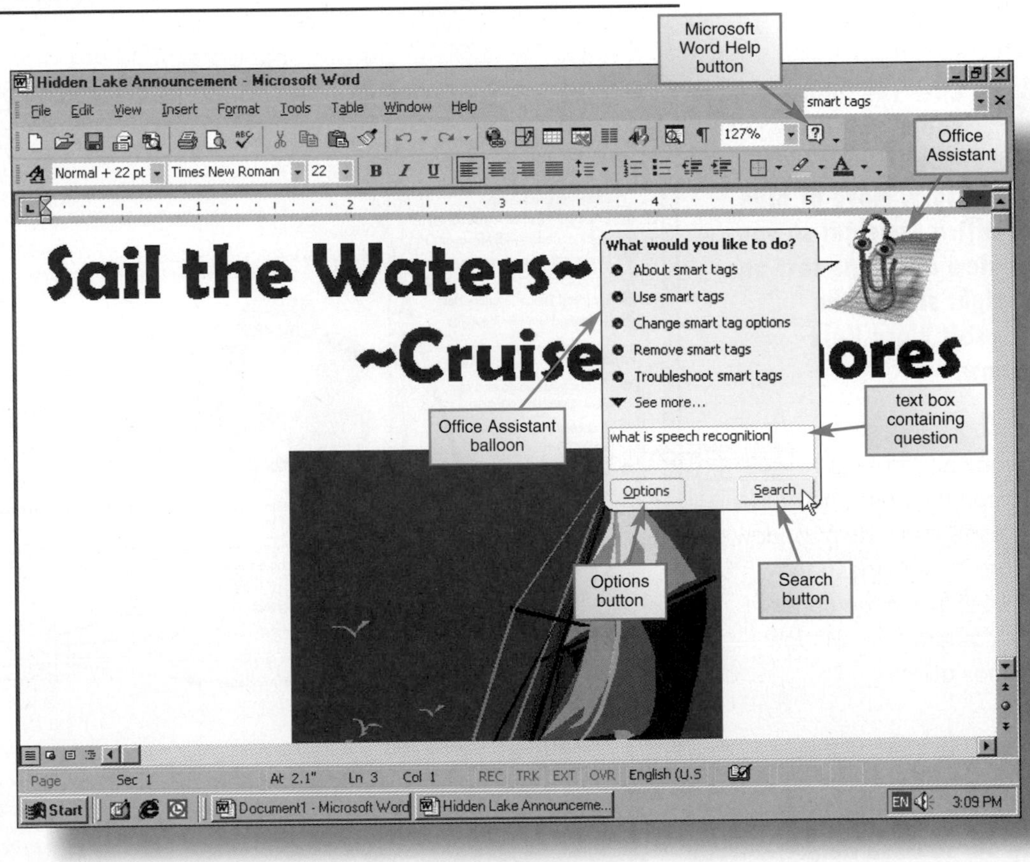

FIGURE A-5

2 Click the Search button. When the Office Assistant balloon redisplays, point to the topic, About speech recognition.

A list of links displays in the Office Assistant balloon (Figure A-6).

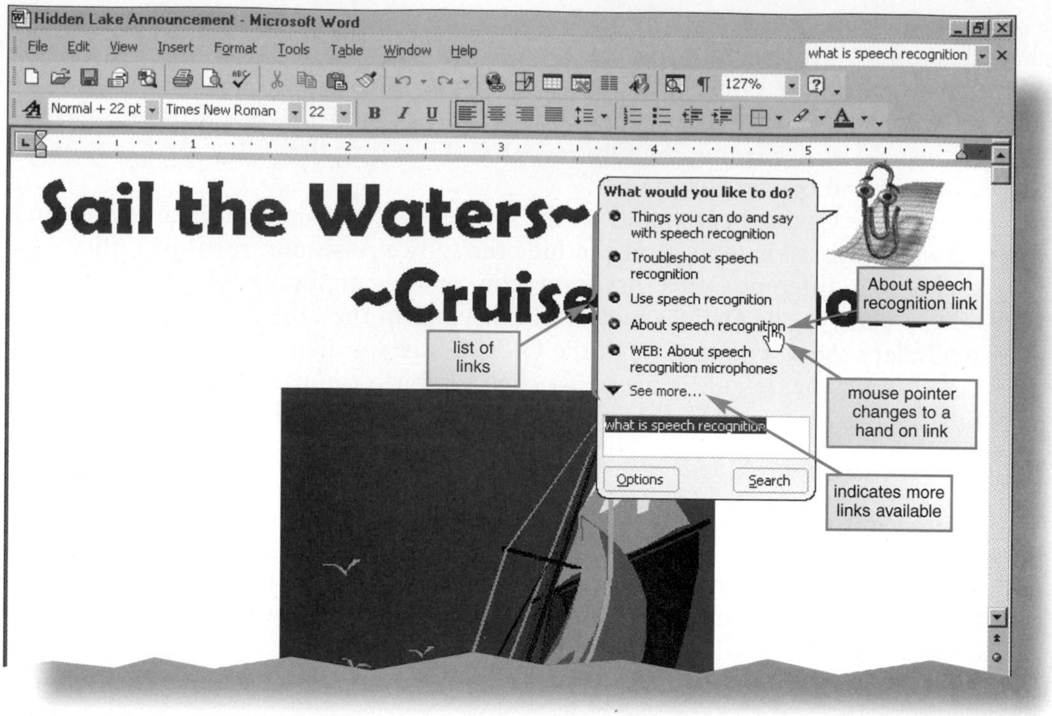

FIGURE A-6

3 Click the topic, About speech recognition (Figure A-7). If necessary, move or hide the Office Assistant so you can view all of the text on the right side of the Microsoft Word Help window.

The About speech recognition topic displays on the right side of the Microsoft Word Help window (Figure A-7). Clicking the Show All link in the upper-right corner of the window expands all links.

4 Click the Close button on the Microsoft Word Help window title bar to close Help.

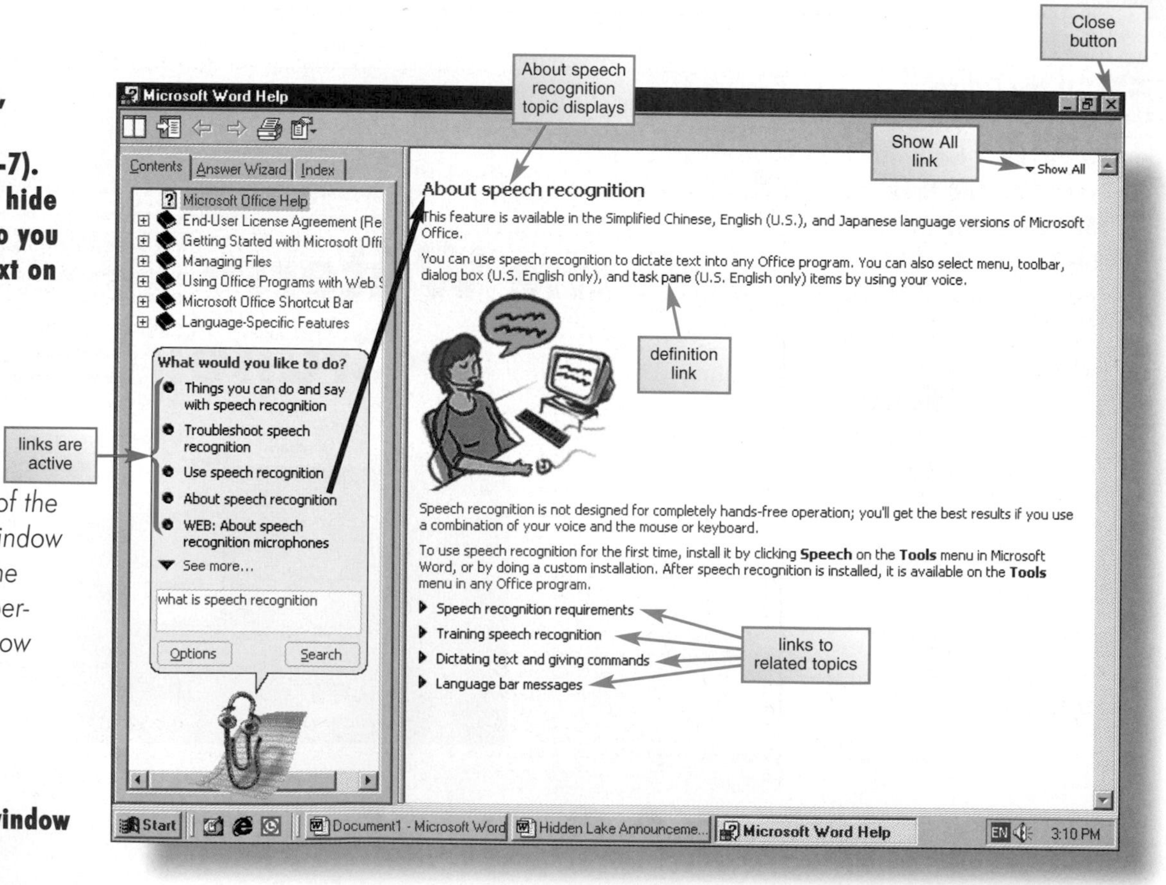

FIGURE A-7

The Microsoft Word Help Window

If the Office Assistant is turned off and you click the Microsoft Word Help button on the Standard toolbar, the Microsoft Word Help window displays (Figure A-8). The left side of this window contains three tabs: Contents, Answer Wizard, and Index. Each tab displays a sheet with powerful look-up capabilities.

Use the Contents sheet as you would a table of contents at the front of a book to look up Help. The Answer Wizard sheet answers your queries the same as the Office Assistant. You use the Index sheet in the same fashion as an index in a book to look up Help. Click the tabs to move from sheet to sheet.

Besides clicking the Microsoft Word Help button on the Standard toolbar, you also can click the Microsoft Word Help command on the Help menu, or press the F1 key to display the Microsoft Word Help window to gain access to the three sheets. To close the Microsoft Word Help window, click the Close button in the upper-right corner on the title bar.

Using the Contents Sheet

The **Contents sheet** is useful for displaying Help when you know the general category of the topic in question, but not the specifics. The following steps show how to use the Contents sheet to obtain information about handwriting recognition.

TO OBTAIN HELP USING THE CONTENTS SHEET

1. Click the Microsoft Word Help button on the Standard toolbar (shown in Figure A-5 on page MO A.05).
2. When the Microsoft Word Help window displays, double-click the title bar to maximize the window. If necessary, click the Show button to display the tabs.
3. Click the Contents tab. Double-click the Handwriting and Speech Recognition book in the Contents sheet. Double-click the Handwriting Recognition book.
4. Click the subtopic, About handwriting recognition, below the Handwriting Recognition book (Figure A-8).
5. Close the Microsoft Help window.

Word displays Help on the subtopic, About handwriting recognition (Figure A-8).

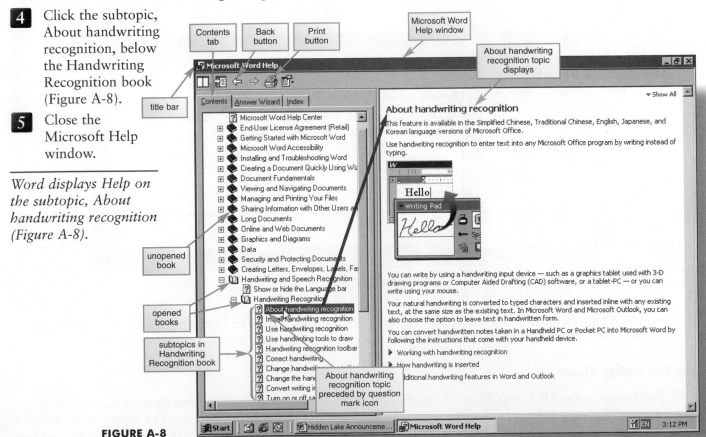

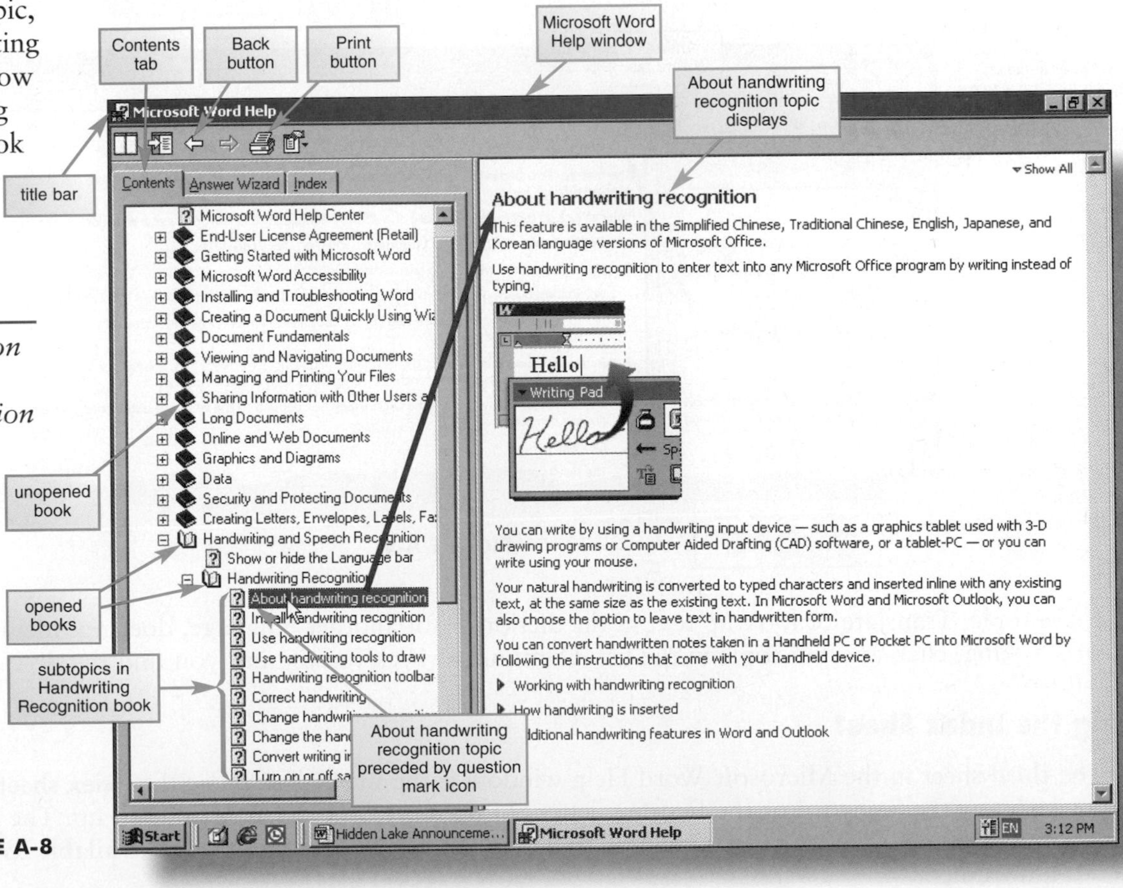

FIGURE A-8

Once the information on the subtopic displays, you can read it or you can click the Print button to obtain a printed copy. If you decide to click another subtopic on the left or a link on the right, you can get back to the Help page shown in Figure A-8 on the previous page by clicking the Back button.

Each topic in the Contents list is preceded by a book icon or question mark icon. A **book icon** indicates subtopics are available. A **question mark icon** means information on the topic will display if you double-click the title. The book icon opens when you double-click the book (or its title) or click the plus sign (+) to the left of the book icon.

Using the Answer Wizard Sheet

The **Answer Wizard sheet** works like the Office Assistant in that you enter a word, phrase, or question and it responds by listing topics from which you can choose to display Help. The following steps show how to use the Answer Wizard sheet to obtain Help on translating or looking up text in the dictionary of another language.

TO OBTAIN HELP USING THE ANSWER WIZARD SHEET

1. With the Office Assistant turned off, click the Microsoft Word Help button on the Standard toolbar (shown in Figure A-5 on page MO A.05).
2. When the Microsoft Word Help window displays, double-click the title bar to maximize the window. If necessary, click the Show button to display the tabs.
3. Click the Answer Wizard tab. Type `translation` in the What would you like to do? text box on the left side of the window. Click the Search button.
4. When a list of topics displays in the Select topic to display list, click Translate or look up text in the dictionary of another language (Figure A-9).
5. Close the Microsoft Help window.

Word displays Help on how to translate or look up text in the dictionary of a different language on the right side of the Microsoft Word Help window (Figure A-9).

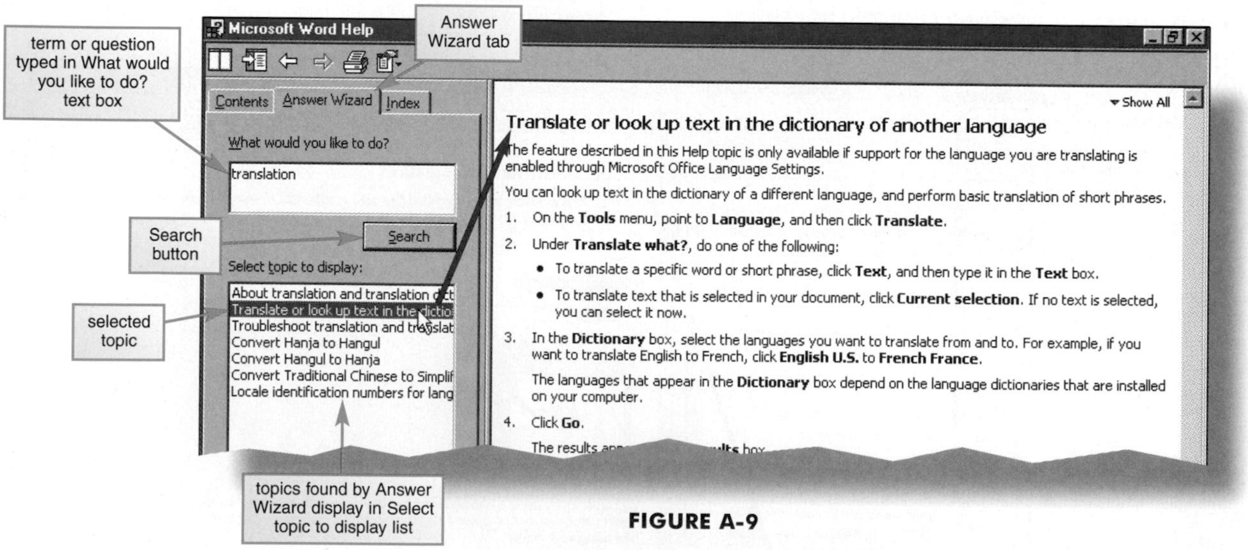

FIGURE A-9

If the topic, Translate or look up text in the dictionary of another language, does not include the information you are seeking, click another topic in the list. Continue to click topics until you find the desired information.

Using the Index Sheet

The third sheet in the Microsoft Word Help window is the Index sheet. Use the **Index sheet** to display Help when you know the keyword or the first few letters of the keyword you want to look up. The following steps show how to use the Index sheet to obtain Help on understanding the readability scores available to evaluate the reading level of a document.

TO OBTAIN HELP USING THE INDEX SHEET

1. With the Office Assistant turned off, click the Microsoft Word Help button on the Standard toolbar (shown in Figure A-5 on page MO A.05).
2. When the Microsoft Word Help window displays, double-click the title bar to maximize the window. If necessary, click the Show button to display the tabs.
3. Click the Index tab. Type `readability` in the Type keywords text box on the left side of the window. Click the Search button.
4. When a list of topics displays in the Choose a topic list, click Readability scores.
5. When the Readability scores topic displays on the right side of the window (Figure A-10), click the Show All link in the upper-right corner of the right side of the window.

Word displays information about readability scores and two links on the right side of the window (Figure A-10). Clicking the Show All link expands the two links and displays the Hide All link. As you type readability into the Type keywords box, Word recognizes and completes the word and automatically appends a semicolon to the keyword.

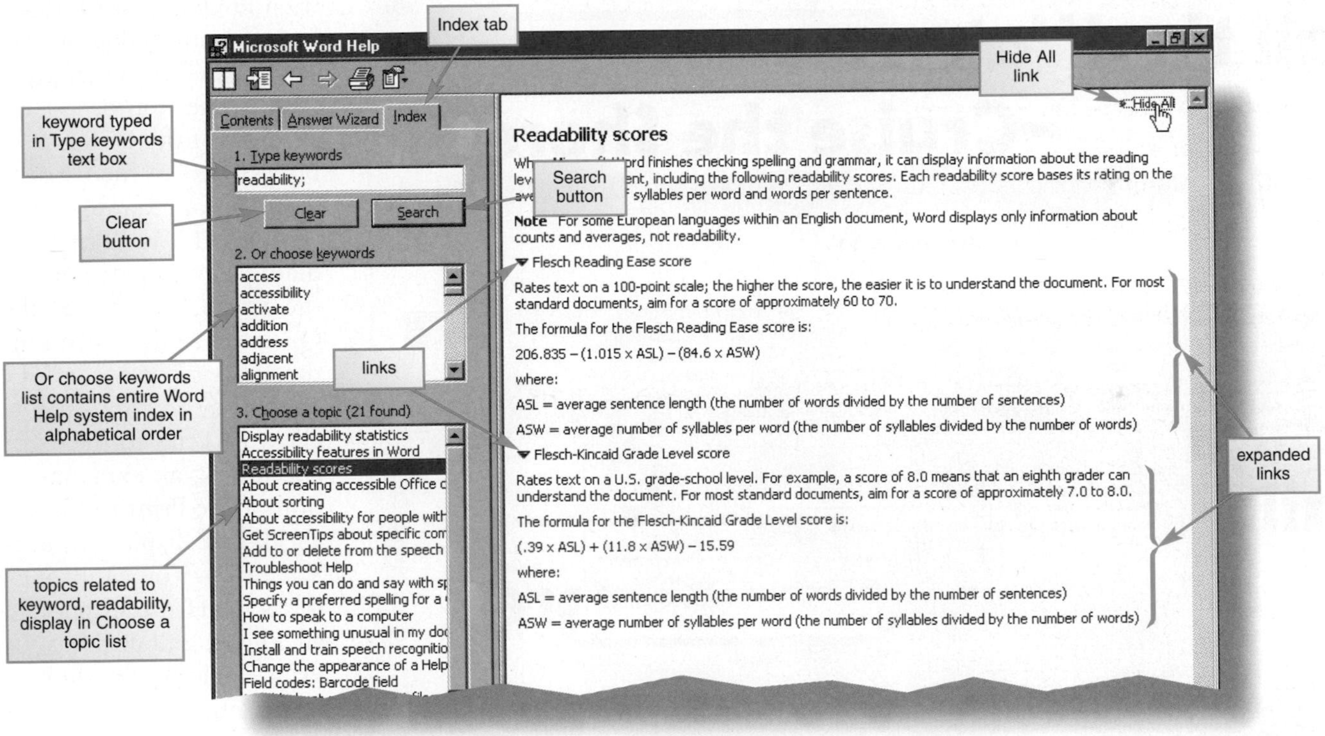

FIGURE A-10

An alternative to typing a keyword in the Type keywords text box is to scroll through the Or choose keywords list (the middle list on the left side of the window). When you locate the keyword you are searching for, double-click it to display Help on the topic. Also in the Or choose keywords list, the Word Help system displays other topics that relate to the new keyword. As you begin typing a new keyword in the Type keywords text box, Word jumps to that point in the middle list box. To begin a new search, click the Clear button.

What's This? Command and Question Mark Button

Use the What's This? command on the Help menu or the Question Mark button in a dialog box when you are not sure what an object on the screen is or what it does.

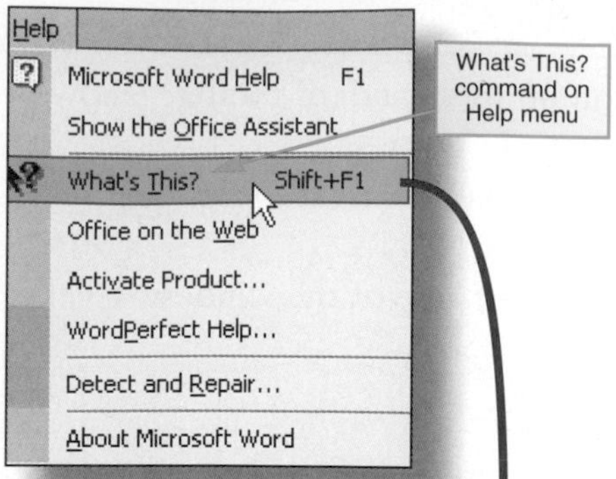

What's This? Command

You use the **What's This? command** on the Help menu to display a detailed ScreenTip. When you click this command, the mouse pointer changes to an arrow with a question mark. You then click any object on the screen, such as a button, to display the ScreenTip. For example, after you click the What's This? command on the Help menu and then click the Zoom box on the Standard toolbar, a description of the Zoom box displays (Figure A-11). You can print the ScreenTip by right-clicking it and then clicking Print Topic on the shortcut menu.

FIGURE A-11

Question Mark Button

Similarly to the What's This? command, the **Question Mark button** displays a ScreenTip. You use the Question Mark button with dialog boxes. It is located in the upper-right corner on the title bar of the dialog boxes, next to the Close button. For example, in Figure A-12, the Print dialog box displays on the screen. If you click the Question Mark button in the upper-right corner of the dialog box and then click the Print to file check box, an explanation of the Print to file check box displays in a ScreenTip. You can print the ScreenTip by right-clicking it and clicking Print Topic on the shortcut menu.

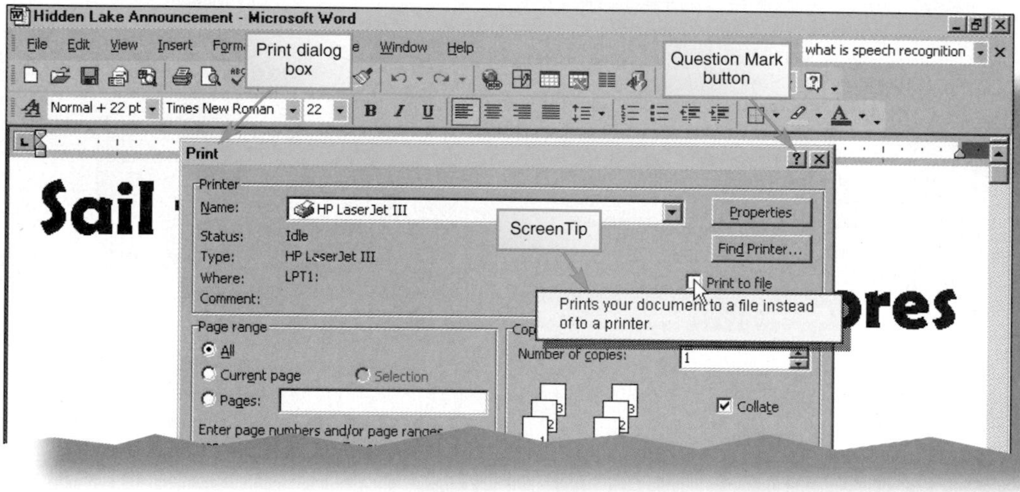

FIGURE A-12

If a dialog box does not include a Question Mark button, press SHIFT+F1. This combination of keys will change the mouse pointer to an arrow with a question mark. You then can click any object in the dialog box to display the ScreenTip.

Office on the Web Command

The **Office on the Web command** on the Help menu displays a Microsoft Web page containing up-to-date information on a variety of Office-related topics. To use this command, you must be connected to the Internet. When you invoke the Office on the Web command, the Assistance Center Home page displays. Read through the links that in general pertain to topics that relate to all Office XP topics. Scroll down and click the Word link in the Help By

Product area to display the Assistance Center Word Help Articles Web page (Figure A-14). This Web page contains numerous helpful links related to Word.

Other Help Commands

Four additional commands available on the Help menu are Activate Product, WordPerfect Help, Detect and Repair, and About Microsoft Word. The WordPerfect Help command is available only if it was included as part of a custom installation of Word 2002.

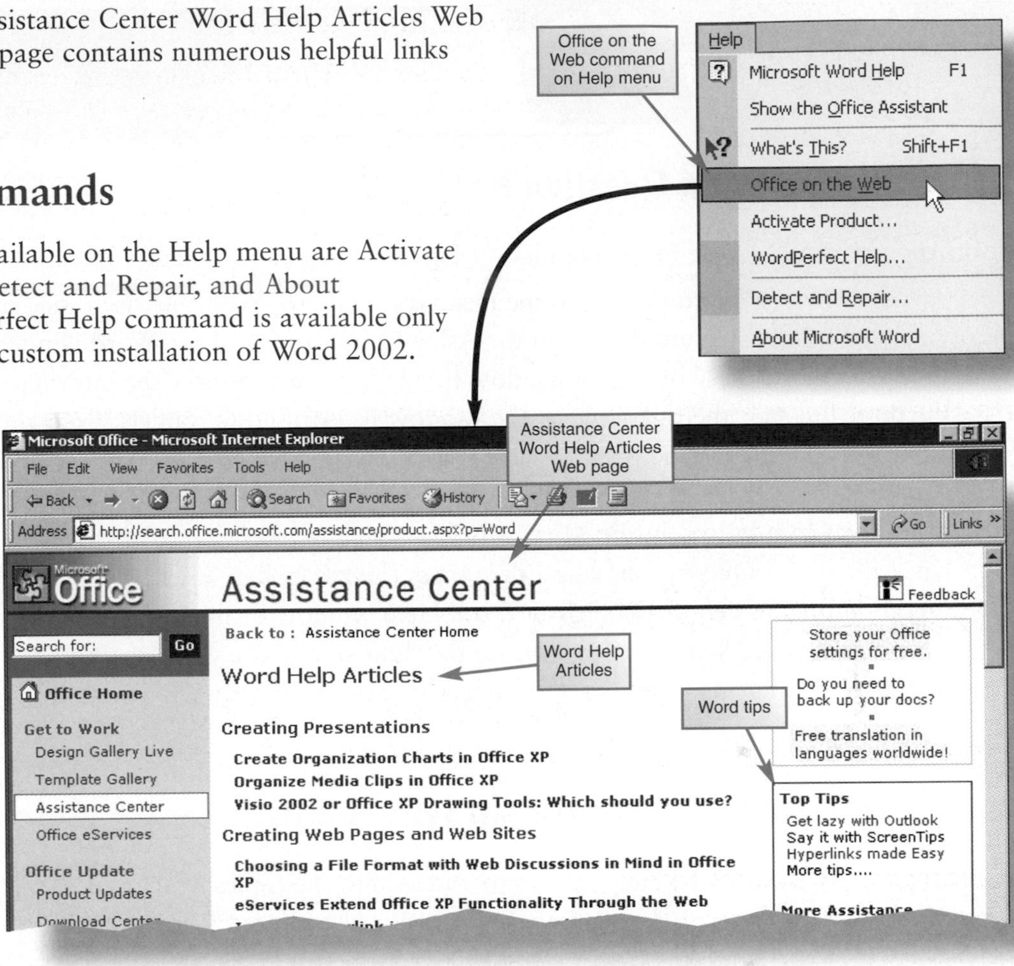

FIGURE A-14

Activate Product Command

The **Activate Product command** on the Help menu lets you activate your Microsoft Office subscription if you selected the Microsoft Office Subscription mode.

WordPerfect Help Command

The **WordPerfect Help command** on the Help menu offers assistance to WordPerfect users switching to Word. When you choose this command, Word displays the Help for WordPerfect Users dialog box. The instructions in the dialog box step the user through the appropriate selections.

Detect and Repair Command

Use the **Detect and Repair command** on the Help menu if Word is not running properly or if it is generating errors. When you invoke this command, the Detect and Repair dialog box displays. Click the Start button in the dialog box to initiate the detect and repair process.

About Microsoft Word Command

The **About Microsoft Word command** on the Help menu displays the About Microsoft Word dialog box. The dialog box lists the owner of the software and the product identification. You need to know the product identification if you call Microsoft for assistance. The three buttons below the OK button are the System Info button, Tech Support button, and Disabled Items button. The **System Info button** displays system information, including hardware resources, components, software environment, Internet Explorer 5, and Office XP applications. The **Tech Support button** displays technical assistance information. The **Disabled Items button** displays a list of items that were disabled because they prevented Word from functioning correctly.

Use Help

1 Using the Ask a Question Box

Instructions: Perform the following tasks using the Word Help system.

1. Click the Ask a Question box on the menu bar, and then type `how do I add a bullet`. Press the ENTER key.
2. Click Add bullets or numbering in the Ask a Question list. If the Word window is not maximized, double-click the Microsoft Word Help window title bar. Read and print the information. One at a time, click the three links on the right side of the window to learn about bullets. Print the information. Hand in the printouts to your instructor.
3. If necessary, click the Show button to display the tabs. Click the Contents tab to prepare for the next step. Click the Close button in the Microsoft Word Help window.
4. Click the Ask a Question box and then press the ENTER key. Click About bulleted lists in the Ask a Question box. When the Microsoft Word Help window displays, maximize the window. Read and print the information. Click the two links on the right side of the window. Print the information. Hand in the printouts to your instructor.

2 Expanding on the Word Help System Basics

Instructions: Use the Word Help system to understand the topics better and answer the questions listed below. Answer the questions on your own paper, or hand in the printed Help information to your instructor.

1. If the Office Assistant is on, right-click the Office Assistant. When the shortcut menu displays, click Options. Click Use the Office Assistant to remove the check mark, and then click the OK button.
2. Click the Microsoft Word Help button on the Standard toolbar. Maximize the Microsoft Word Help window. Click Getting Help on the right side of the window. Click the five links in the About getting help while you work topic. Print the information and hand in the printouts to your instructor. Close the Microsoft Word Help window.
3. Press the F1 key. Maximize the Microsoft Word Help window. Click the Answer Wizard tab. Type `help` in the What would you like to do? text box, and then click the Search button. Click Guidelines for searching Help. Click the four links on the right side of the window. Print the information and hand in the printouts to your instructor.
4. Click the Contents tab. Click the plus sign (+) to the left of the Document Fundamentals book. Click the plus sign (+) to the left of the Selecting Text and Graphics book. One at a time, click the three topics below the Selecting Text and Graphics book. Read and print each one. Close the Microsoft Word Help window. Hand in the printouts to your instructor.
5. Click Help on the menu bar and then click What's This? Click the E-mail button on the Standard toolbar. Right-click the ScreenTip, click Print Topic on the shortcut menu, and click the Print button. Click Format on the menu bar and then click Paragraph. When the Paragraph dialog box displays, click the Question Mark button on the title bar. Click the Special box. Right-click the ScreenTip, click Print Topic, and then click the Print button. Close the Paragraph dialog box and Microsoft Word window.

APPENDIX B

Speech and Handwriting Recognition and Speech Playback

Introduction

This appendix discusses how you can create and modify documents using Office XP's new input technologies. Office XP provides a variety of **text services**, which enable you to speak commands and enter text in an application. The most common text service is the keyboard. Two new text services included with Office XP are speech recognition and handwriting recognition. The following pages use Word to illustrate the speech and handwriting recognition capabilities of Office XP. Depending on the application you are using, some special features within speech or handwriting recognition may not be available.

When Windows was installed on your computer, you specified a default language. For example, most users in the United States select English (United States) as the default language. Through text services, you can add more than 90 additional languages and varying dialects such as Basque, English (Zimbabwe), French (France), French (Canada), German (Germany), German (Austria), and Swahili. With multiple languages available, you can switch from one language to another while working in an Office XP application. If you change the language or dialect, then text services may change the functions of the keys on the keyboard, adjust speech recognition, and alter handwriting recognition.

The Language Bar

You know that text services are installed properly when the Language Indicator button displays by the clock in the tray status area on the Windows taskbar (Figure B-1a) or the Language bar displays on the screen (Figure B-1b or B-1c). If the Language Indicator button displays in the tray status area, click it, and then click the **Show the Language bar command** (Figure B-1a). The Language bar displays on the screen in the same location it displayed last time.

You can drag the Language bar to any location in the window by pointing to its move handle, which is the vertical line on its left side (Figure B-1b). When the mouse pointer changes to a four-headed arrow, drag the Language bar to the desired location.

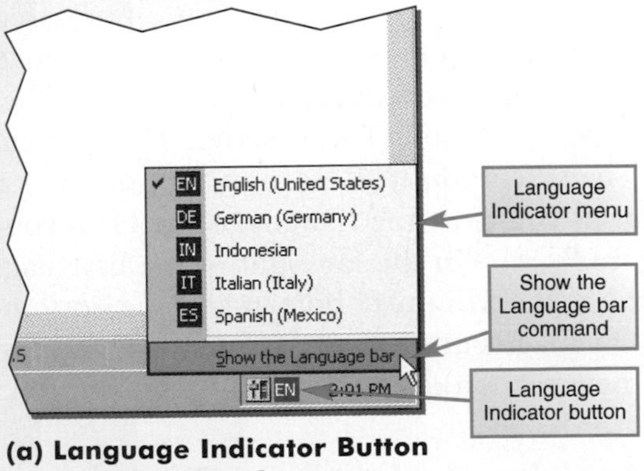

(a) Language Indicator Button in Tray Status Area on Windows Taskbar and Its Menu

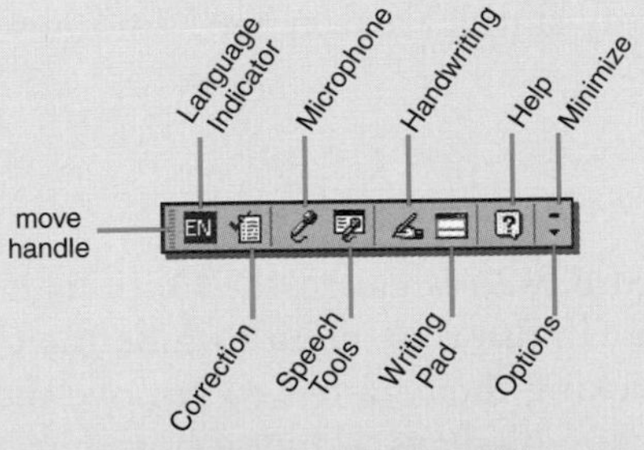

(b) Language Bar with Text Labels Disabled

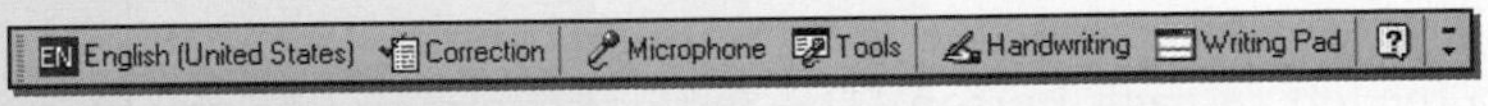

(c) Language Bar with Text Labels Enabled

FIGURE B-1

If you are sure that one of the services was installed and neither the Language Indicator button nor the Language bar displays, then do the following:

1. Click Start on the Windows taskbar, point to Settings, click Control Panel, and then double-click the Text Services icon in the Control Panel window.
2. When the Text Services dialog box displays, click the Language Bar button, click the Show the Language bar on the desktop check box to select it, and then click the OK button in the Language Bar Settings dialog box.
3. Click the OK button in the Text Services dialog box.
4. Close the Control Panel window.

You can perform tasks related to text services by using the **Language bar**. The Language bar may display with just the icon on each button (Figure B-1b on the previous page) or it may display with text labels to the right of the icon on each button (Figure B-1c on the previous page). Changing the appearance of the Language bar will be discussed shortly.

Buttons on the Language Bar

The Language bar shown in Figure B-2a contains nine buttons. The number of buttons on your Language bar may be different. These buttons are used to select the language, customize the Language bar, control the microphone, control handwriting, and obtain help.

When you click the **Language Indicator button** on the far left side of the Language bar, the Language Indicator menu displays a list of the active languages (Figure B-2b) from which you can choose. When you select text and then click the **Correction button** (the second button from the left), a list of correction alternatives displays in the Word window (Figure B-2c). You can use the Correction button to correct both speech recognition and handwriting recognition errors. The **Microphone button**, the third button from the left, enables and disables the microphone. When the microphone is enabled, text services adds two buttons and a balloon to the Language toolbar (Figure B-2d). These additional buttons and the balloon will be discussed shortly.

The fourth button from the left on the Language bar is the Speech Tools button. The **Speech Tools button** displays a menu of commands (Figure B-2e) that allows you to hide or show the balloon on the Language bar; train the Speech Recognition service so that it can better interpret your voice; add and delete words from its dictionary, such as names and other words not understood easily; and change the user profile so more than one person can use the microphone on the same computer.

The fifth button from the left on the Language bar is the Handwriting button. The **Handwriting button** displays the **Handwriting menu** (Figure B-2f), which lets you choose the Writing Pad (Figure B-2g), Write Anywhere (Figure B-2h), the Drawing Pad (Figure B-2i), or the on-screen keyboard (Figure B-2j). The **On-Screen Symbol Keyboard command** on the Handwriting menu displays an on-screen keyboard that allows you to enter special symbols that are not available on the On-Screen Standard Keyboard. You can choose only one form of handwriting at a time.

The sixth button indicates which one of the handwriting forms is active. For example, in Figure B-1a on the previous page, the Writing Pad is active. The handwriting recognition capabilities of text services will be discussed shortly.

The seventh button from the left on the Language bar is the Help button. The **Help button** displays the Help menu. If you click the Language Bar Help command on the Help menu, the Language Bar Help window displays (Figure B-2k). On the far right of the Language bar are two buttons stacked above and below each other. The top button is the Minimize button and the bottom button is the Options button. The **Minimize button** minimizes (hides) the Language bar so that the Language Indicator button displays in the tray status area on the Windows taskbar. The next section discusses the Options button.

Customizing the Language Bar

The down arrow icon immediately below the Minimize button in Figure B-2a is called the Options button. The **Options button** displays a menu of text services options (Figure B-2l). You can use this menu to hide the Correction, Speech Tools, Handwriting, and Help buttons on the Language bar by clicking their names to remove the check mark to the left of each button. The Settings command on the Options menu displays a dialog box that lets you customize the Language bar. This command will be discussed shortly. The Restore Defaults command redisplays hidden buttons on the Language bar.

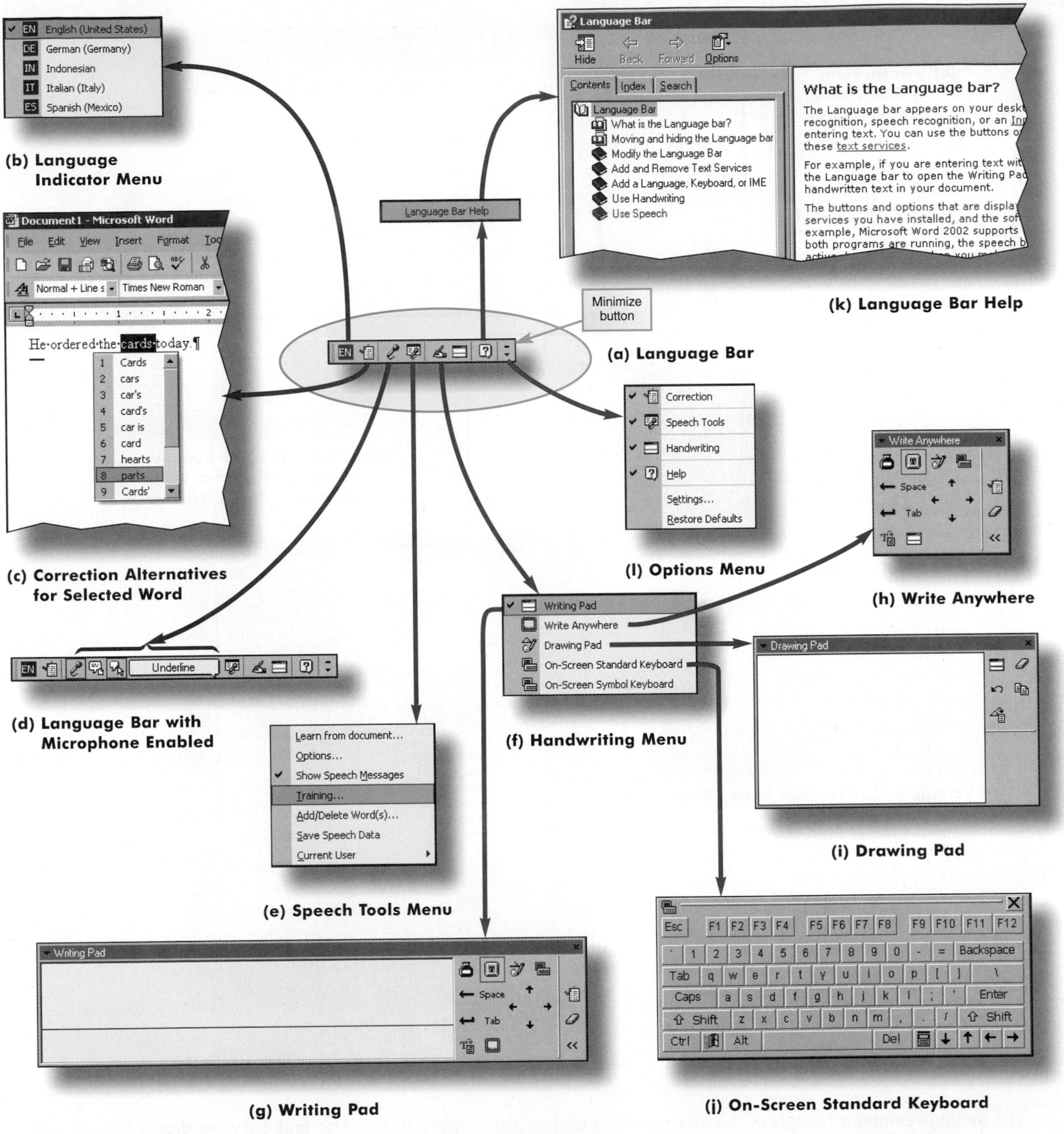

FIGURE B-2

If you right-click the Language bar, a shortcut menu displays (Figure B-3a on the next page). This shortcut menu lets you further customize the Language bar. The **Minimize command** on the shortcut menu minimizes the Language bar the same as the Minimize button on the Language bar. The **Transparency command** toggles the Language bar between being solid and transparent. You can see through a transparent Language bar (Figure B-3b). The **Text Labels command** toggles text labels on the Language bar on (Figure B-3c) and off (Figure B-3a). The **Additional icons in taskbar command** toggles between only showing the Language Indicator button in the tray status area and showing icons that represent the text services that are active (Figure B-3d).

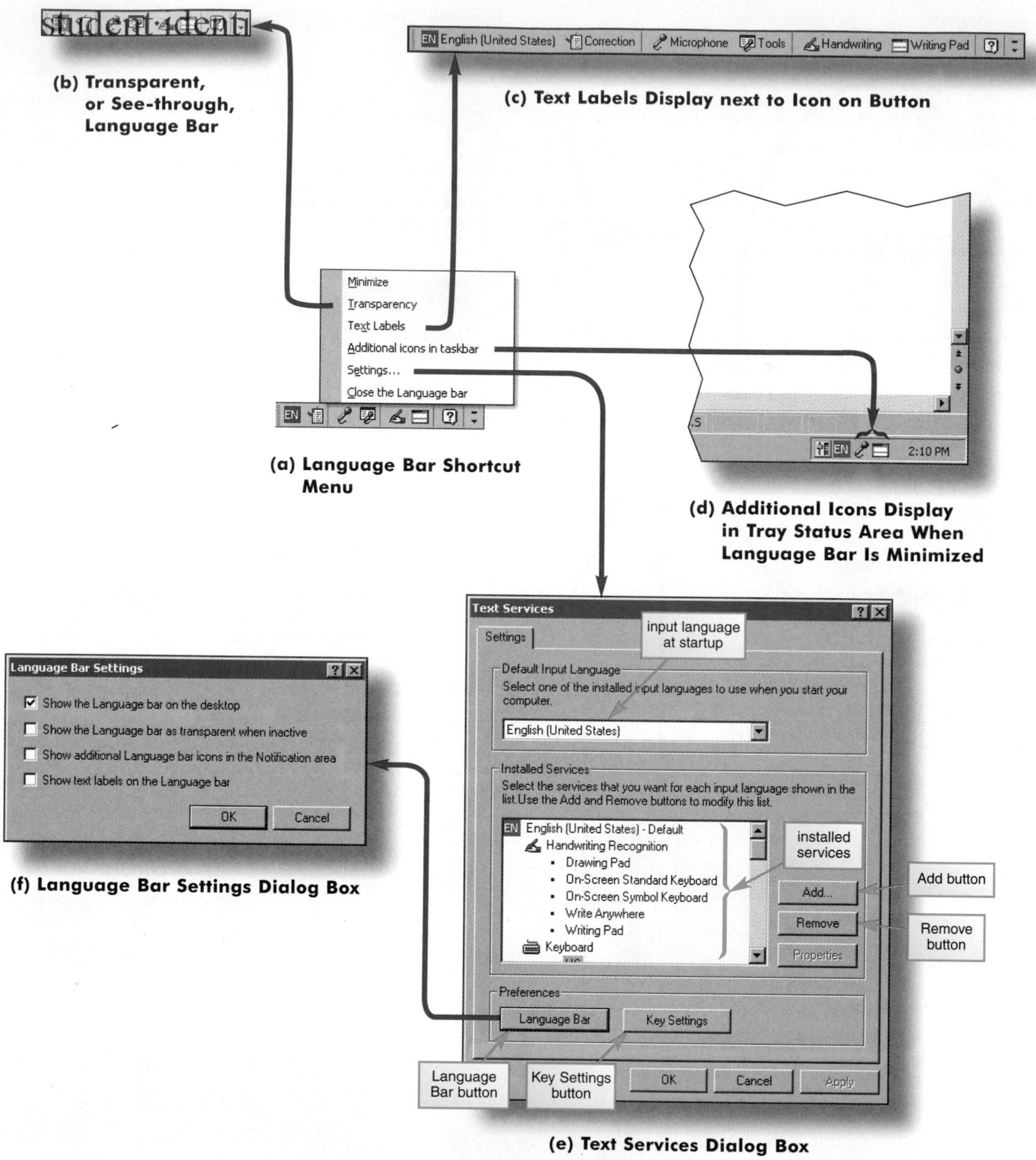

FIGURE B-3

The **Settings command** displays the Text Services dialog box (Figure B-3e). The **Text Services dialog box** allows you to select the language at startup; add and remove text services; modify keys on the keyboard; and modify the Language bar. If you want to remove any one of the entries in the Installed Services list, select the entry, and then click the Remove button. If you want to add a service, click the Add button. The Key Settings button allows you to modify the keyboard. If you click the **Language Bar button** in the Text Services dialog box, the **Language Bar Settings dialog box** displays (Figure B-3f). This dialog box contains Language bar options, some of which are the same as the commands on the Language bar shortcut menu described earlier.

The **Close the Language bar command** on the shortcut menu shown in Figure B-3a closes the Language bar and hides the Language Indicator button in the tray status area on the Windows taskbar. If you close the Language bar and want to redisplay it, follow the instructions at the top of page MO B.02.

Speech Recognition

The **Speech Recognition service** available with all Office XP applications enables your computer to recognize human speech through a microphone. The microphone has two modes: dictation and voice command. The example in Figure B-4 uses Word to illustrate the speech recognition modes of Office XP. You switch between the two modes by clicking the Dictation button and the Voice Command button on the Language bar. These buttons display only when you turn on Speech Recognition by clicking the **Microphone button** on the Language bar (Figure B-5 on the next page). If you are using the Microphone button for the very first time in Word, it will require that you check your microphone settings and step through voice training before activating the Speech Recognition service.

The **Dictation button** places the microphone in Dictation mode. In **Dictation mode**, whatever you speak is entered as text at the location of the insertion point. The **Voice Command button** places the microphone in Voice Command mode. In **Voice Command mode**, whatever you speak is interpreted as a command. If you want to turn off the microphone, click the Microphone button on the Language bar or in Voice Command mode say, "Mic off" (pronounced mike off). It is important to remember that minimizing the Language bar does not turn off the microphone.

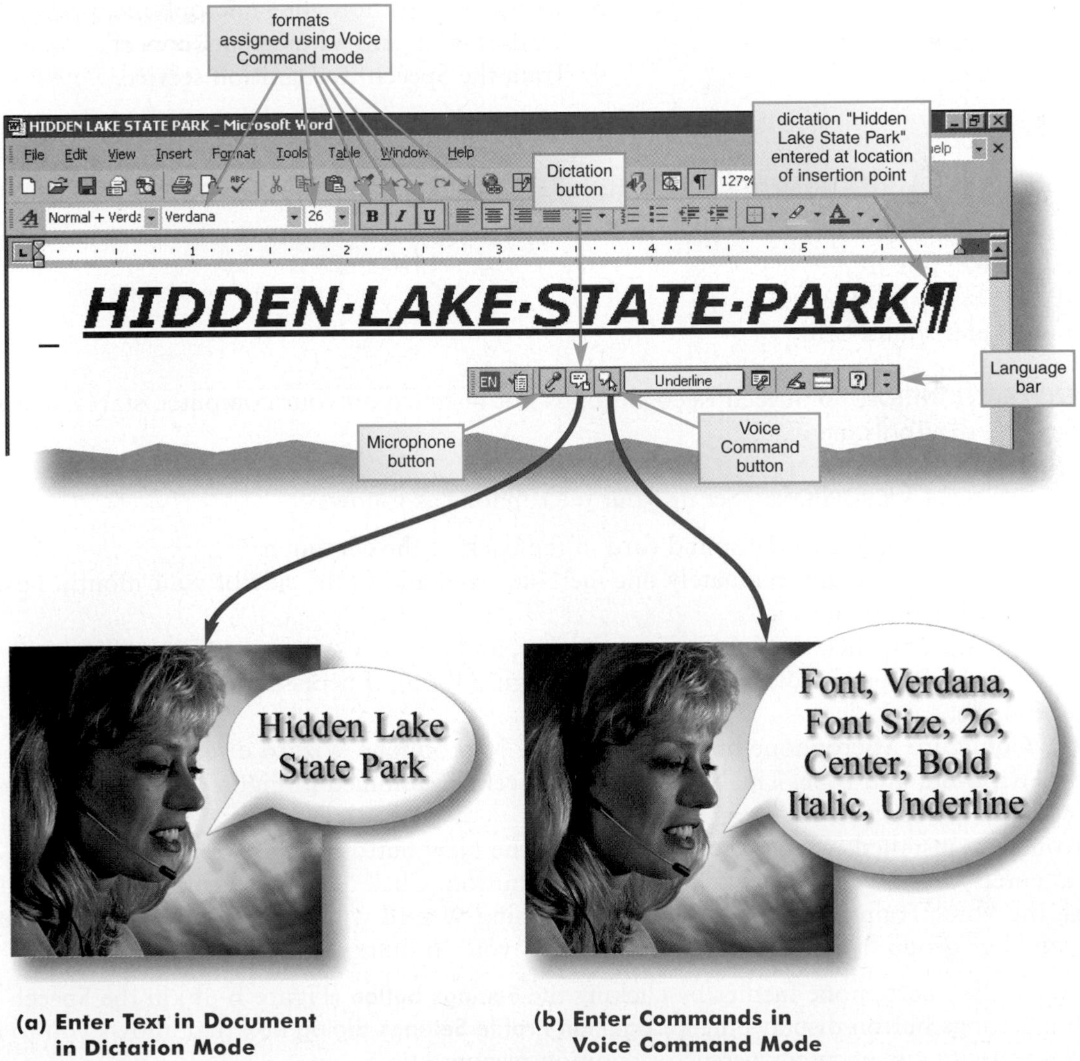

FIGURE B-4

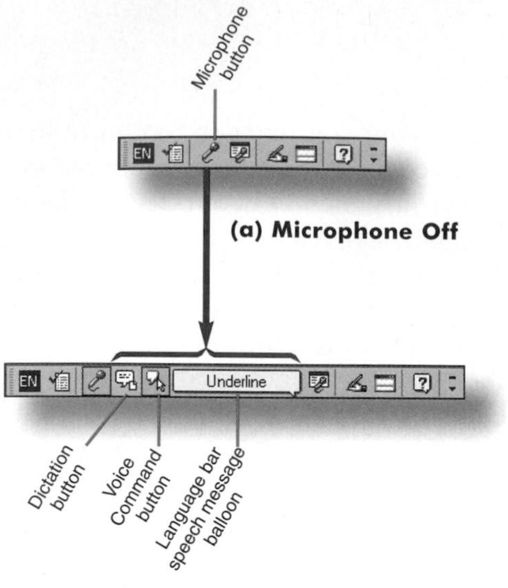

(b) Microphone On

FIGURE B-5

The **Language bar speech message balloon** shown in Figure B-5b displays messages that may offer help or hints. In Voice Command mode, the name of the last recognized command you said displays. If you use the mouse or keyboard instead of the microphone, a message will appear in the Language bar speech message balloon indicating the word you could say. In Dictation mode, the message, Dictating, usually displays. The Speech Recognition service, however, will display messages to inform you that you are talking too soft, too loud, too fast, or to ask you to repeat what you said by displaying, What was that?

Getting Started with Speech Recognition

For the microphone to function properly, you should follow these steps:

1. Make sure your computer meets the minimum requirements.
2. Install Speech Recognition.
3. Set up and position your microphone, preferably a close-talk headset with gain adjustment support.
4. Train the Speech Recognition service.

The following sections describe these steps in more detail.

SPEECH RECOGNITION SYSTEM REQUIREMENTS For Speech Recognition to work on your computer, it needs the following:

1. Microsoft Windows 98 or later or Microsoft Windows NT 4.0 or later
2. At least 128 MB RAM
3. 400 MHz or faster processor
4. Microphone and sound card

INSTALLING SPEECH RECOGNITION If Speech Recognition is not installed on your computer, start Microsoft Word and then click Speech on the Tools menu.

SET UP AND POSITION YOUR MICROPHONE Set up your microphone as follows:

1. Connect your microphone to the sound card in the back of the computer.
2. Position the microphone approximately one inch out from and to the side of your mouth. Position it so you are not breathing into it.
3. On the Language bar, click the Speech Tools button, and then click Options (Figure B-6a).
4. When the Speech Properties dialog box displays (Figure B-6b), if necessary, click the Speech Recognition tab.
5. Click the Configure Microphone button. Follow the Microphone Wizard directions as shown in Figures B-6c, B-6d, and B-6e. The Next button will remain dimmed in Figure B-6d until the volume meter consistently stays in the green area.
6. If someone else installed Speech Recognition, click the New button in the Speech Properties dialog box and enter your name and then click the Finish button. Click the Train Profile button and step through the Voice Training Wizard. The Voice Training Wizard will require that you enter your gender and age group. It then will step you through voice training.

You can adjust the microphone further by clicking the **Settings button** (Figure B-6b) in the Speech Properties dialog box. The Settings button displays the **Recognition Profile Settings dialog box** that allows you to adjust the pronunciation sensitivity and accuracy versus recognition response time.

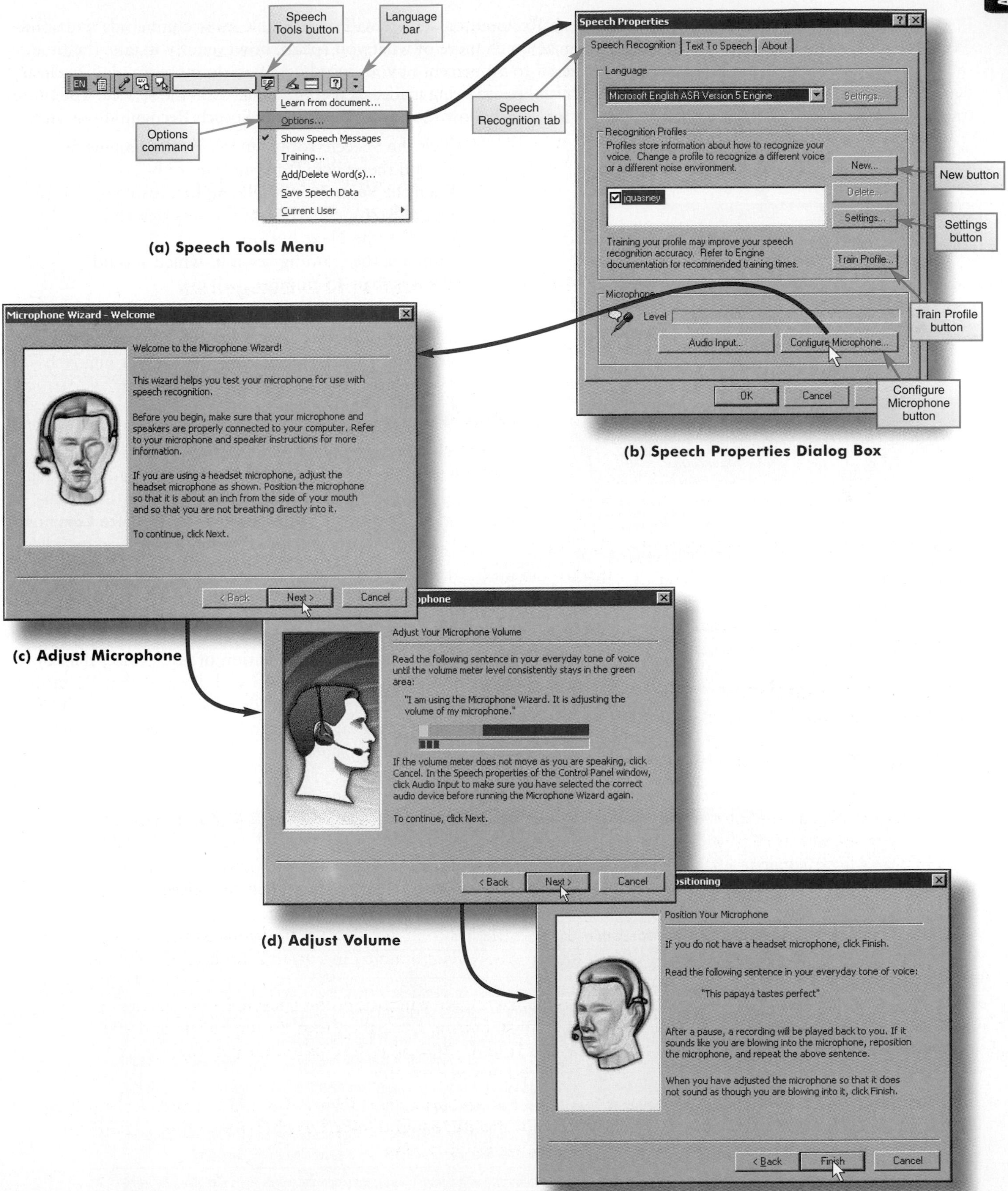

(a) Speech Tools Menu

(b) Speech Properties Dialog Box

(c) Adjust Microphone

(d) Adjust Volume

(e) Test Microphone

FIGURE B-6

TRAIN THE SPEECH RECOGNITION SERVICE The Speech Recognition service will understand most commands and some dictation without any training at all. It will recognize much more of what you speak, however, if you take the time to train it. After one training session, it will recognize 85 to 90 percent of your words. As you do more training, accuracy will rise to 95 percent. If you feel that too many mistakes are being made, then continue to train the service. The more training you do, the more accurately it will work for you. Follow these steps to train the Speech Recognition service:

1. Click the Speech Tools button on the Language bar and then click Training (Figure B-7a).
2. When the **Voice Training dialog box** displays (Figure B-7b), click one of the sessions and then click the Next button.
3. Complete the training session, which should take less than 15 minutes.

If you are serious about using a microphone to speak to your computer, you need to take the time to go through at least three of the eight training sessions listed in Figure B-7b.

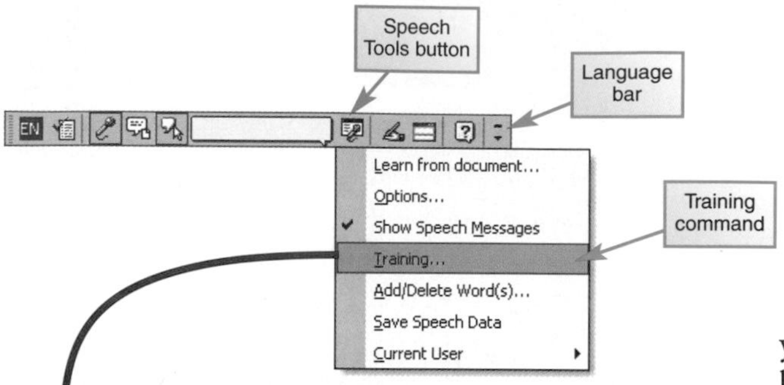

(a) Speech Tools Menu

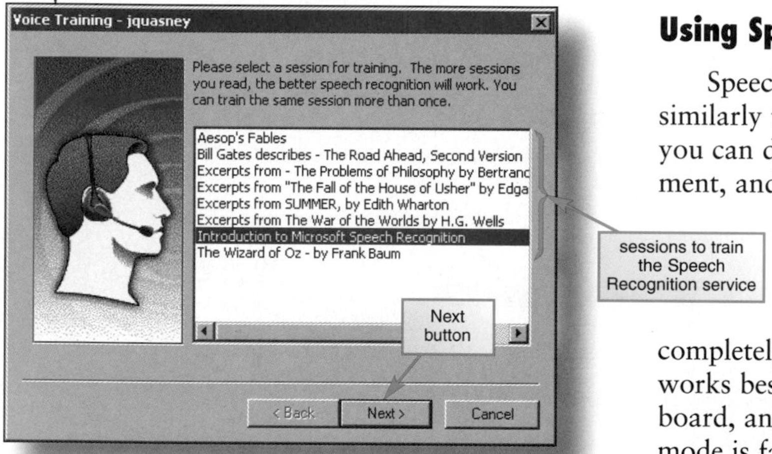

(b) Voice Training Dialog Box

FIGURE B-7

Using Speech Recognition

Speech recognition lets you enter text into a document similarly to speaking into a tape recorder. Instead of typing, you can dictate text that you want to display in the document, and you can issue voice commands. In **Voice Command mode**, you can speak menu names, commands on menus, toolbar button names, and dialog box option buttons, check boxes, list boxes, and button names. Speech Recognition, however, is not a completely hands-free form of input. Speech recognition works best if you use a combination of your voice, the keyboard, and the mouse. You soon will discover that Dictation mode is far less accurate than Voice Command mode. Table B-1 lists some tips that will improve the Speech Recognition service's accuracy considerably.

Table B-1 Tips to Improve Speech Recognition

NUMBER	TIP
1	The microphone hears everything. Though the Speech Recognition service filters out background noise, it is recommended that you work in a quiet environment.
2	Try not to move the microphone around once it is adjusted.
3	Speak in a steady tone and speak clearly.
4	In Dictation mode, do not pause between words. A phrase is easier to interpret than a word. Sounding out syllables in a word will make it more difficult for the Speech Recognition service to interpret what you are saying.
5	If you speak too loudly or too softly, it makes it difficult for the Speech Recognition service to interpret what you said. Check the Language bar speech message balloon for an indication that you may be speaking too loudly or too softly.
6	If you experience problems after training, adjust the recognition options that control accuracy and rejection by clicking the Settings button shown in Figure B-6b on the previous page.
7	When you are finished using the microphone, turn it off by clicking the Microphone button on the Language bar or in Voice Command mode say, "Mic off." Leaving the microphone on is the same as leaning on the keyboard.
8	If the Speech Recognition service is having difficulty with unusual words, then add the words to its dictionary by using the Learn from document command or Add/Delete Word(s) command on the Speech Tools menu (Figure B-8a). The last names of individuals and the names of companies are good examples of the types of words you should add to the dictionary.
9	Training will improve accuracy; practice will improve confidence.

The last command on the Speech Tools menu is the Current User command (Figure B-8a). The **Current User command** is useful for multiple users who share a computer. It allows them to configure their own individual profiles, and then switch between users as they use the computer.

For additional information on the Speech Recognition service, click the Help button on the Standard toolbar, click the Answer Wizard tab, and search for the phrase, Speech Recognition.

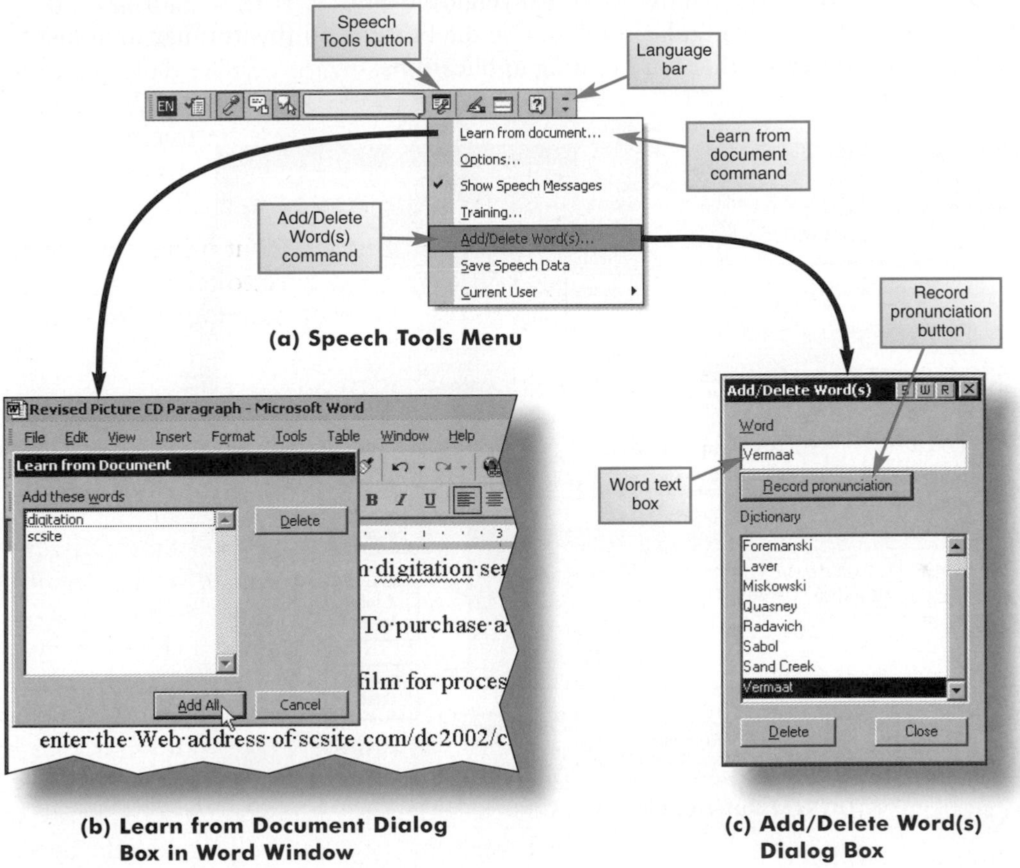

FIGURE B-8

Handwriting Recognition

Using the Office XP handwriting recognition capabilities, you can enter text and numbers into all Office XP applications by writing instead of typing. You can write using a special handwriting device that connects to your computer or you can write on the screen using your mouse. Four basic methods of handwriting are available by clicking the **Handwriting button** on the Language bar: Writing Pad, Write Anywhere, Drawing Pad, and On-Screen Keyboard. Although the on-screen keyboard does not involve handwriting recognition, it is part of the Handwriting menu and, therefore, will be discussed in this section. The following pages use Word to illustrate the handwriting recognition capabilities available in most Office XP applications.

If your Language bar does not include the Handwriting button (Figures B-1b or B-1c on page MO B.01), then for installation instructions click the Help button on the Standard toolbar, click the Answer Wizard tab, and search for the phrase Install Handwriting Recognition.

Writing Pad

To display the Writing Pad, click the Handwriting button on the Language bar and then click Writing Pad. The **Writing Pad** resembles a note pad with one or more lines on which you can use freehand to print or write in cursive. You can form letters on the line by moving the mouse while holding down the mouse button. With the **Text button** selected, the handwritten text is converted to typed characters and inserted into the document (Figure B-9a on the next page).

Consider the example in Figure B-9a. With the insertion point at the top of the document, the name, Millie, is written in cursive on the **Pen line** in the Writing Pad. As soon as the name is complete, the Handwriting Recognition service automatically converts the handwriting to typed characters and inserts the name into the document at the location of the insertion point.

With the **Ink button** selected, the text is inserted in handwritten form into the document. Once inserted, you can change the font size and color of the handwritten text (Figure B-9b).

To the right of the note pad is a rectangular toolbar. Use the buttons on this toolbar to adjust the Writing Pad, move the insertion point, and activate other handwriting applications.

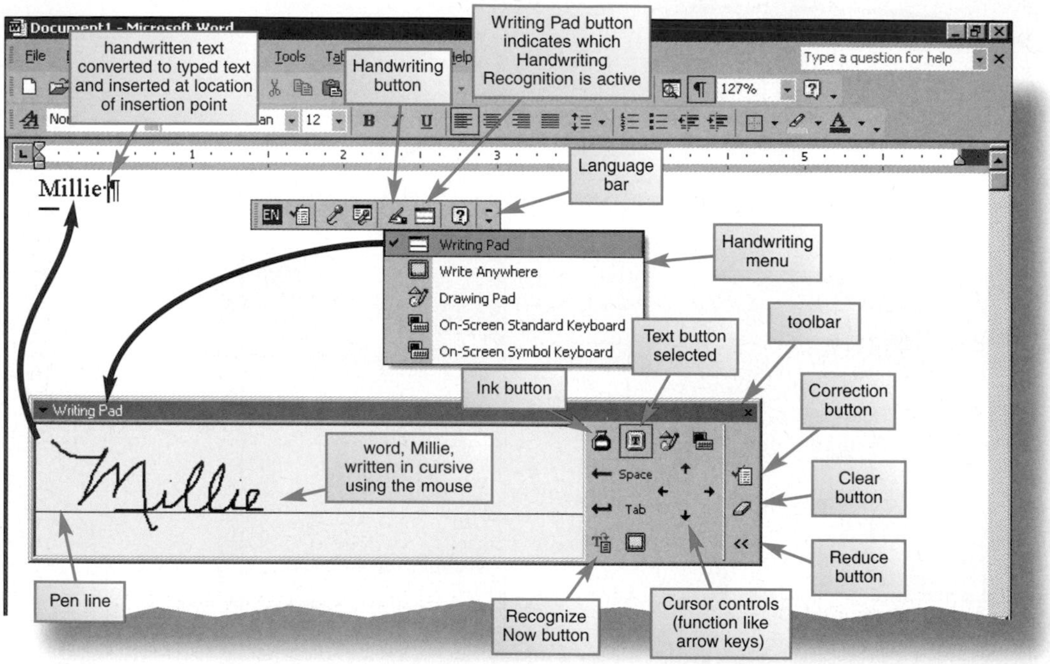

(a) Text Button Selected

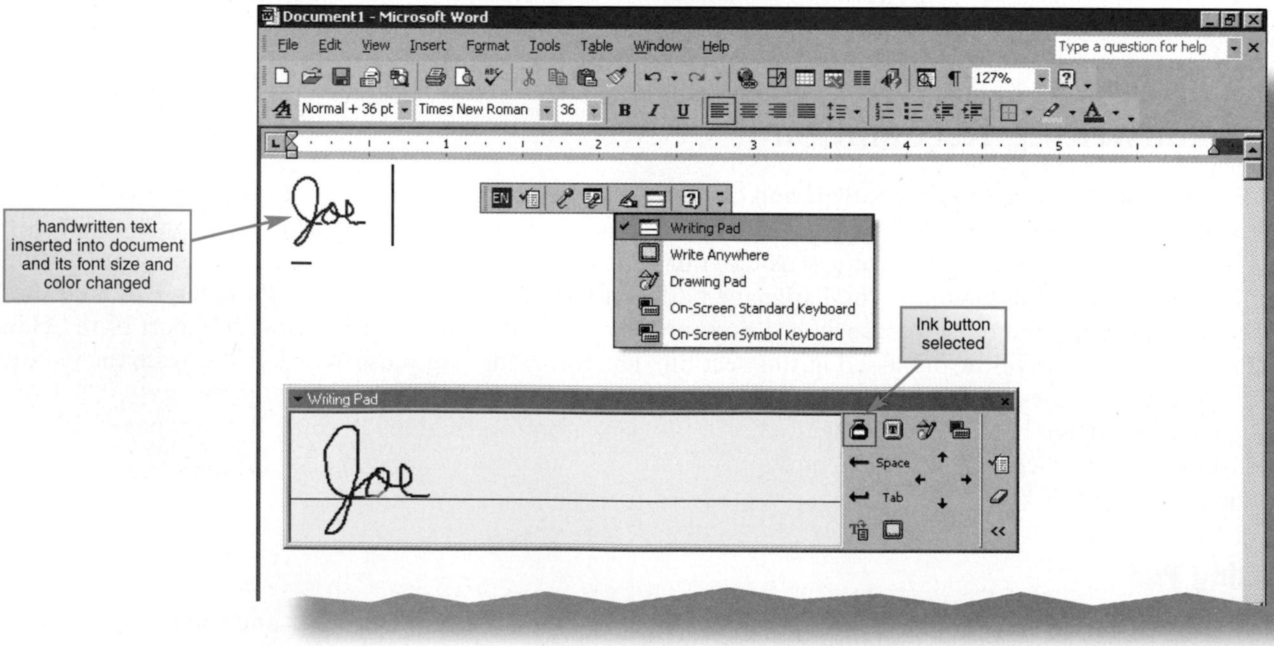

(b) Ink Button Selected

FIGURE B-9

You can customize the Writing Pad by clicking the **Options button** on the left side of the title bar and then clicking the Options command (Figure B-10a). Invoking the **Options command** causes the Handwriting Options dialog box to display. The **Handwriting Options dialog box** contains two sheets: Common and Writing Pad. The **Common sheet** lets you change the pen color and pen width, adjust recognition, and customize the toolbar area of the Writing Pad. The **Writing Pad sheet** allows you to change the background color and the number of lines that display in the Writing Pad. Both sheets contain a **Restore Default button** to restore the settings to what they were when the software was installed initially.

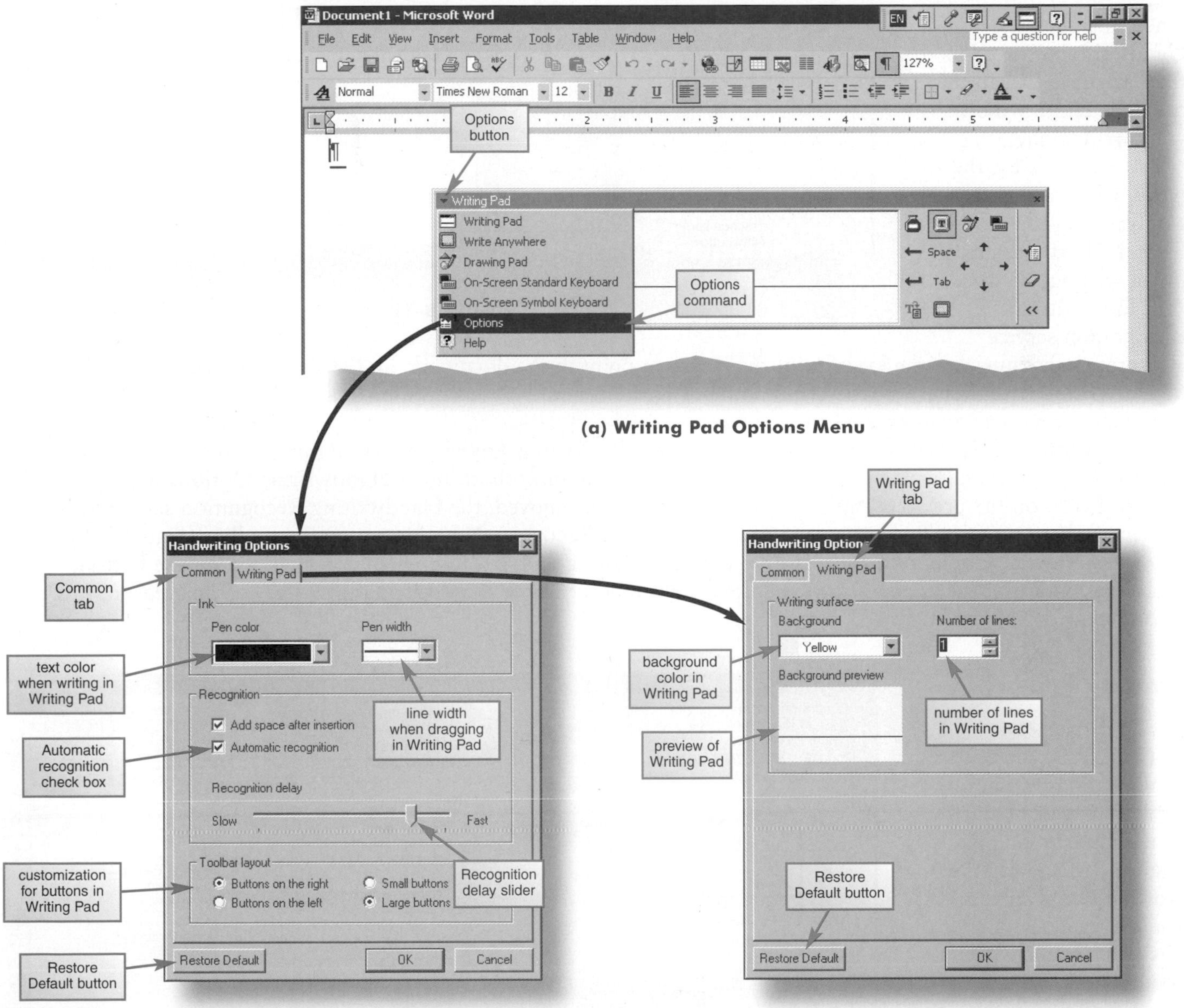

(a) Writing Pad Options Menu

(b) Handwriting Options Dialog Box with Common Sheet Active

(c) Handwriting Options Dialog Box with Writing Pad Sheet Active

FIGURE B-10

When you first start using the Writing Pad, you may want to remove the check mark from the **Automatic recognition check box** in the Common sheet in the Handwriting Options dialog box (Figure B-10b). With the check mark removed, the Handwriting Recognition service will not interpret what you write in the Writing Pad until you click the **Recognize Now button** on the toolbar (Figure B-9a). This allows you to pause and adjust your writing.

The best way to learn how to use the Writing Pad is to practice with it. Also, for more information, click the Help button on the Standard toolbar, click the Answer Wizard tab, and search for the phrase, Handwriting Recognition.

Write Anywhere

Rather than use a Writing Pad, you can write anywhere on the screen by invoking the **Write Anywhere command** on the Handwriting menu (Figure B-11) that displays when you click the Handwriting button on the Language bar. In this case, the entire window is your writing pad.

In Figure B-11, the word, Chip, is written in cursive using the mouse button. Shortly after you finish writing the word, the Handwriting Recognition service interprets it, assigns it to the location of the insertion point in the document, and erases what you wrote. Similarly to the Writing Pad, Write Anywhere has both an Ink button and a Text button so you can insert either handwritten characters or have them converted to typed text.

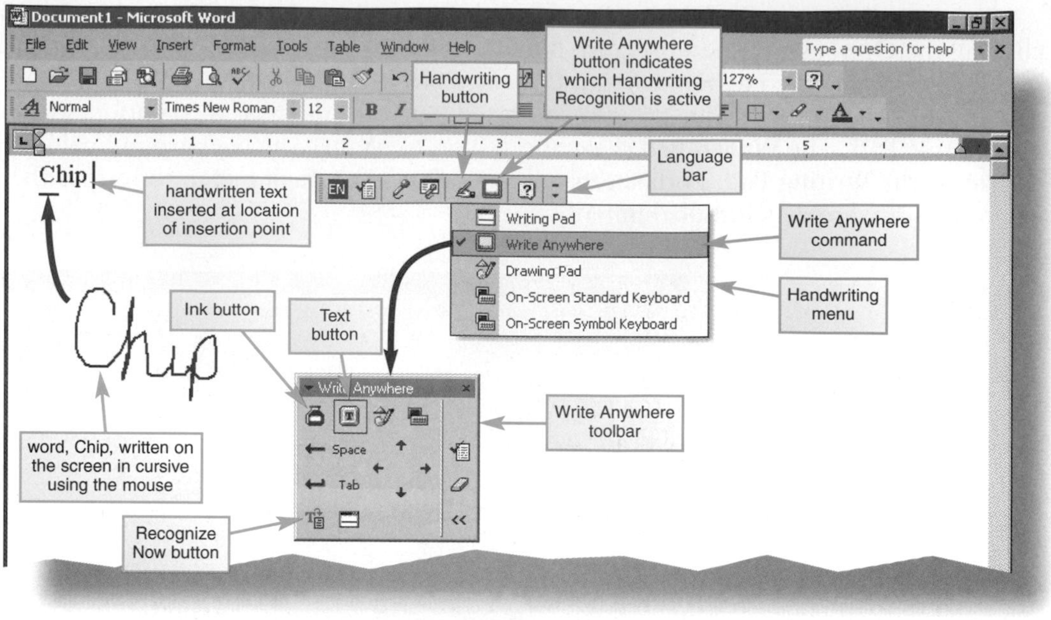

FIGURE B-11

It is recommended that when you first start using the Writing Anywhere service that you remove the check mark from the Automatic recognition check box in the Common sheet in the Handwriting Options dialog box (Figure B-10b on the previous page). With the check mark removed, the Handwriting Recognition service will not interpret what you write on the screen until you click the Recognize Now button on the toolbar (Figure B-11).

Write Anywhere is more difficult to use than the Writing Pad, because when you click the mouse button, Word may interpret the action as moving the insertion point rather than starting to write. For this reason, it is recommended that you use the Writing Pad.

Drawing Pad

To display the Drawing Pad, click the Handwriting button on the Language bar and then click Drawing Pad (Figure B-12). With the **Drawing Pad**, you can insert a freehand drawing or sketch into a Word document. To create the drawing, point in the Drawing Pad and move the mouse while holding down the mouse button.

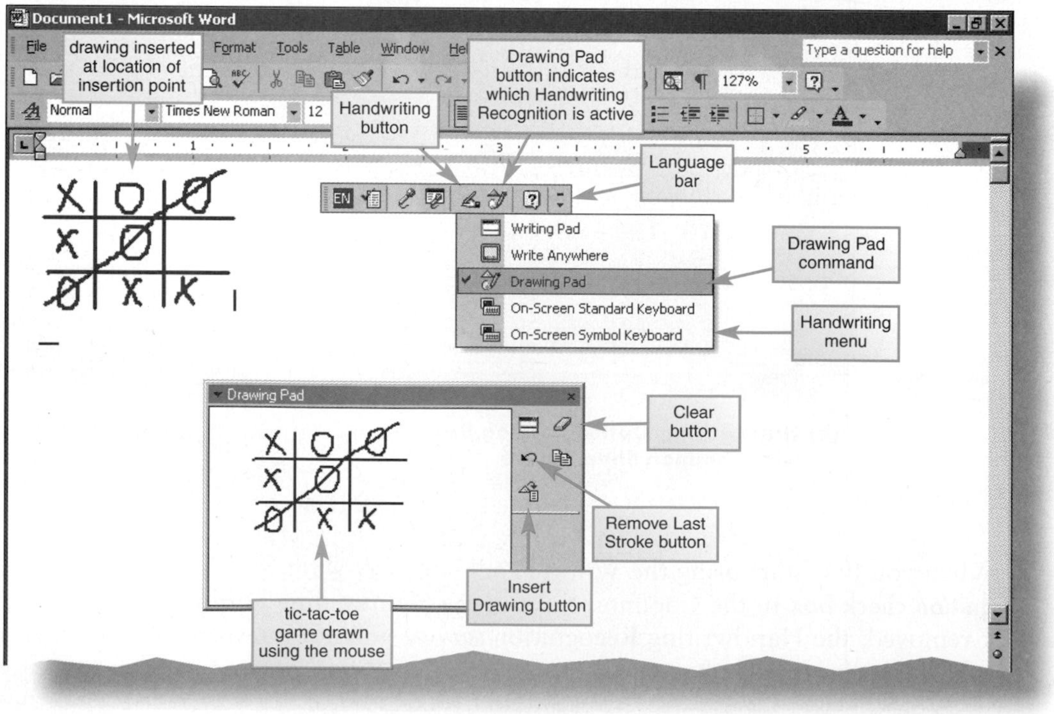

FIGURE B-12

In Figure B-12, the mouse button was used to draw a tic-tac-toe game in the Drawing Pad. To insert the drawing into the Word document at the location of the insertion point, click the Insert Drawing button on the rectangular toolbar to the right of the Drawing Pad. Other buttons on the toolbar allow you to erase a drawing, erase your last drawing stroke, copy the drawing to the Office Clipboard, or activate the Writing Pad.

You can customize the Drawing Pad by clicking the Options button on the left side of the title bar and then clicking the Options command (Figure B-13a). Invoking the **Options command** causes the Draw Options dialog box to display (Figure B-13b). The **Draw Options dialog box** lets you change the pen color and pen width and customize the toolbar area of the Drawing Pad. The dialog box also contains a Restore Default button that restores the settings to what they were when the software was installed initially.

The best way to learn how to use the Drawing Pad is to practice with it. Also, for more information, click the Help button on the Standard toolbar, click the Answer Wizard tab, and search for the phrase, Drawing Pad.

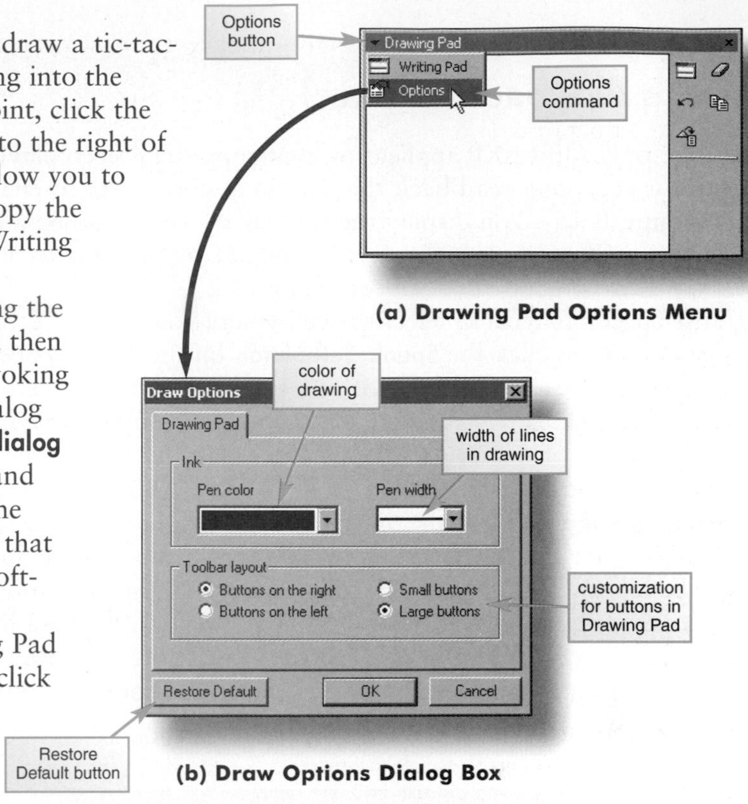

FIGURE B-13

On-Screen Keyboard

The **On-Screen Standard Keyboard command** on the Handwriting menu (Figure B-14) displays an on-screen keyboard. The **on-screen keyboard** lets you enter characters into a document by using your mouse to click the keys. The on-screen keyboard is similar to the type found on handheld computers.

The **On-Screen Symbol Keyboard command** on the Handwriting menu (Figure B-14) displays a special on-screen keyboard that allows you to enter symbols that are not on your keyboard, as well as Unicode characters. **Unicode characters** use a coding scheme capable of representing all the world's current languages.

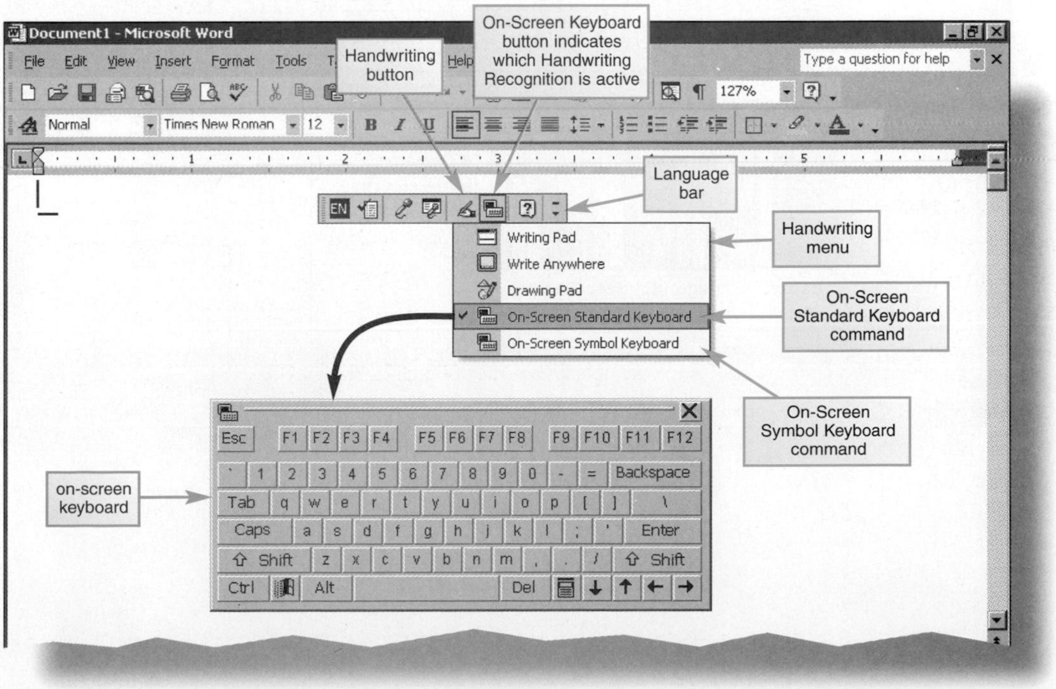

FIGURE B-14

Speech Playback in Excel

Excel is the only Office XP application that supports speech playback. With Excel, you can use **speech playback** to have your computer read back the data in a worksheet. To enable speech playback, you use the **Text To Speech toolbar** (Figure B-15). You display the toolbar by right-clicking a toolbar and then clicking Text To Speech on the shortcut menu. You also can display the toolbar by pointing to Speech on the Tools menu and then clicking Show Text To Speech Toolbar on the Speech submenu.

To use speech playback, select the cell where you want the computer to start reading back the data in the worksheet and then click the **Speak Cell button** on the Text To Speech toolbar (Figure B-15). The computer stops reading after it reads the last cell with an entry in the worksheet. An alternative is to select a range before you turn on speech playback. When you select a range, the computer reads from the upper-left corner of the range to the lower-right corner of the range. It reads the data in the worksheet by rows or by columns. You choose the direction you want it to read by clicking the **By Rows button** or **By Columns button** on the Text To Speech toolbar. Click the **Stop Speaking button** or hide the Text To Speech toolbar to stop speech playback.

The rightmost button on the Text To Speech toolbar is the Speak On Enter button. When you click the **Speak On Enter button** to enable it, the computer reads data in a cell immediately after you complete the entry by pressing the ENTER key or clicking another cell. It does not read the data if you click the Enter box on the formula bar to complete the entry. You disable this feature by clicking the Speak On Enter button while the feature is enabled. If you do not turn the Speak On Enter feature off, the computer will continue to read new cell entries even if the toolbar is hidden.

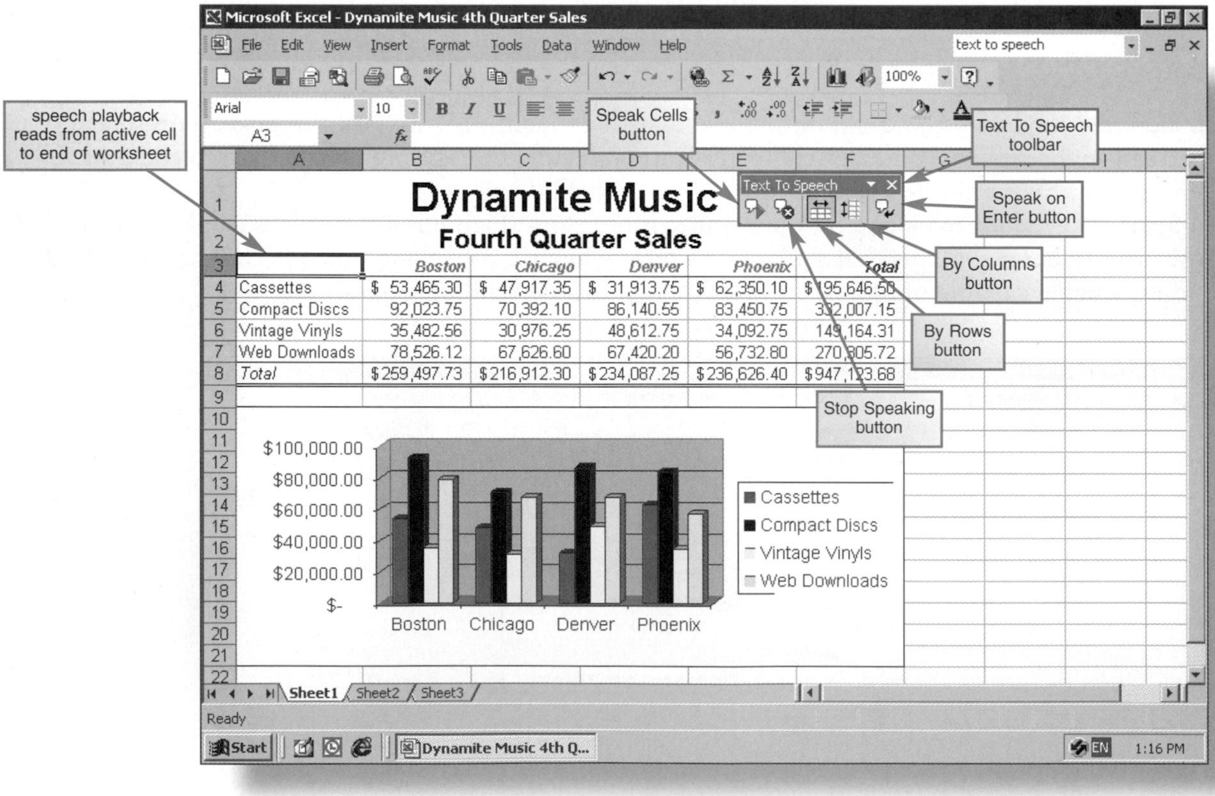

FIGURE B-15

Customizing Speech Playback

You can customize speech playback by double-clicking the **Speech icon** in the Control Panel window (Figure B-16a). To display the Control Panel, point to Settings on the Start menu and then click Control Panel. When you double-click the Speech icon, the Speech Properties dialog box displays (Figure B-16b). Click the Text To Speech tab. The Text To Speech sheet has two areas: Voice selection and Voice speed. The Voice selection area lets you choose between a male and female voice. You can click the Preview Voice button to preview the voice. The Voice speed area contains a slider. Drag the slider to slow down or speed up the voice.

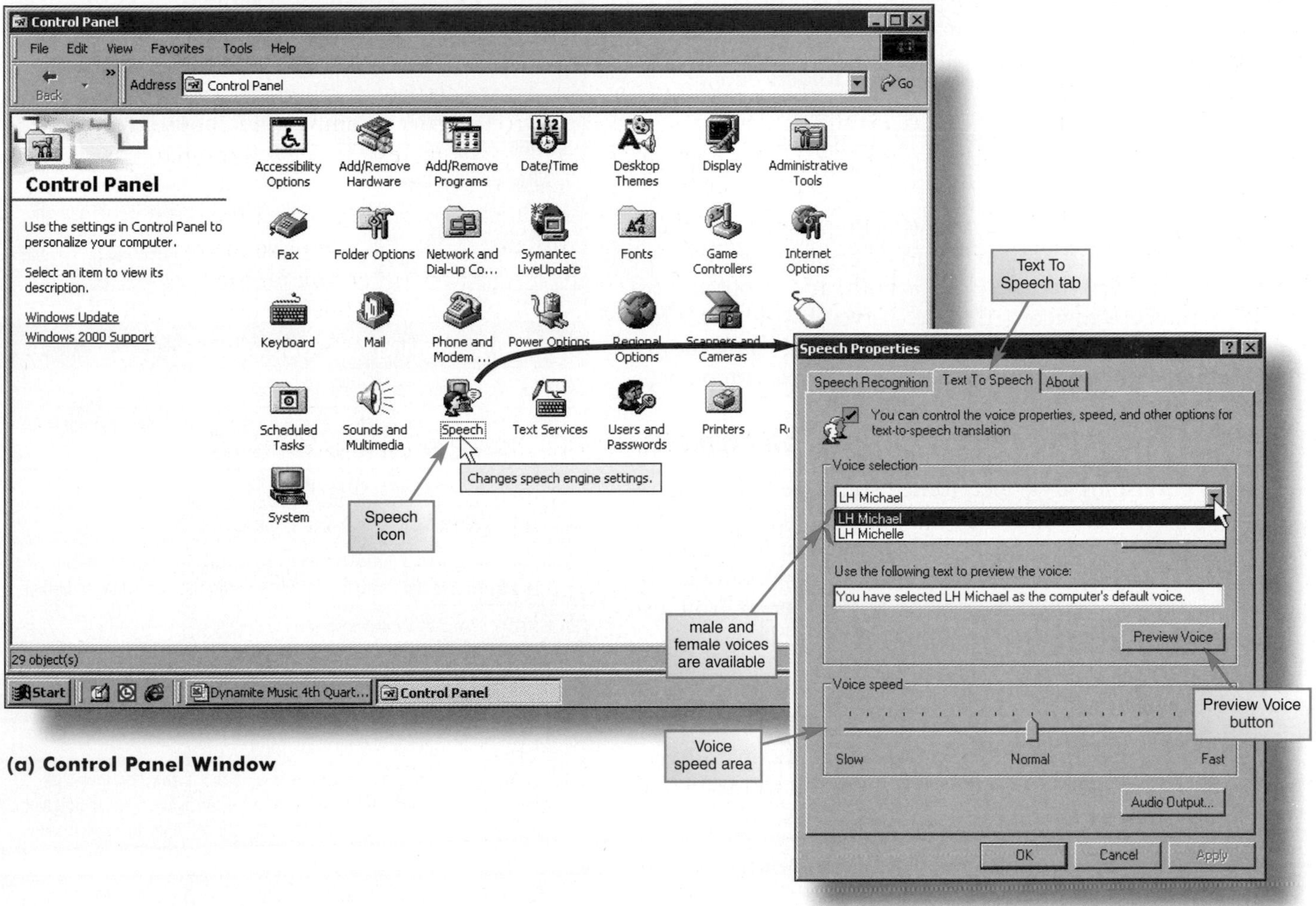

(a) Control Panel Window

(b) Speech Properties Dialog Box

FIGURE B-16

APPENDIX C

Publishing Office Web Pages to a Web Server

With the Office applications, you use the Save as Web Page command on the File menu to save the Web page to a Web server using one of two techniques: Web folders or File Transfer Protocol. A **Web folder** is an Office shortcut to a Web server. **File Transfer Protocol (FTP)** is an Internet standard that allows computers to exchange files with other computers on the Internet.

You should contact your network system administrator or technical support staff at your ISP to determine if their Web server supports Web folders, FTP, or both, and to obtain necessary permissions to access the Web server. If you decide to publish Web pages using a Web folder, you must have the Office Server Extensions (OSE) installed on your computer.

Using Web Folders to Publish Office Web Pages

When publishing to a Web folder, someone first must create the Web folder before you can save to it. If you are granted permission to create a Web folder, you must obtain the URL of the Web server, a user name, and possibly a password that allows you to access the Web server. You also must decide on a name for the Web folder. Table C-1 explains how to create a Web folder.

Office adds the name of the Web folder to the list of current Web folders. You can save to this folder, open files in the folder, rename the folder, or perform any operations you would to a folder on your hard disk. You can use your Office program or Windows Explorer to access this folder. Table C-2 explains how to save to a Web folder.

Using FTP to Publish Office Web Pages

When publishing a Web page using FTP, you first must add the FTP location to your computer before you can save to it. An **FTP location**, also called an **FTP site**, is a collection of files that reside on an FTP server. In this case, the FTP server is the Web server.

To add an FTP location, you must obtain the name of the FTP site, which usually is the address (URL) of the FTP server, and a user name and a password that allows you to access the FTP server. You save and open the Web pages on the FTP server using the name of the FTP site. Table C-3 explains how to add an FTP site.

Office adds the name of the FTP site to the FTP locations list in the Save As and Open dialog boxes. You can open and save files using this list. Table C-4 explains how to save to an FTP location.

Table C-1 Creating a Web Folder
1. Click File on the menu bar and then click Save As (or Open).
2. When the Save As dialog box (or Open dialog box) displays, click My Network Places (or Web Folders) on the Places Bar. Double-click Add Network Place (or Add Web Folder).
3. When the Add Network Place Wizard dialog box displays, click the Create a new Network Place option button and then click the Next button. Type the URL of the Web server in the Folder location text box, enter the folder name you want to call the Web folder in the Folder name text box, and then click the Next button. Click Empty Web and then click the Finish button.
4. When the Enter Network Password dialog box displays, type the user name and, if necessary, the password in the respective text boxes and then click the OK button.
5. Close the Save As or the Open dialog box.

Table C-2 Saving to a Web Folder
1. Click File on the menu bar and then click Save As.
2. When the Save As dialog box displays, type the Web page file name in the File name text box. Do not press the ENTER key.
3. Click My Network Places on the Places Bar.
4. Double-click the Web folder name in the Save in list.
5. If the Enter Network Password dialog box displays, type the user name and password in the respective text boxes and then click the OK button.
6. Click the Save button in the Save As dialog box.

Table C-3 Adding an FTP Location
1. Click File on the menu bar and then click Save As (or Open).
2. In the Save As dialog box, click the Save in box arrow and then click Add/Modify FTP Locations in the Save in list; or in the Open dialog box, click the Look in box arrow and then click Add/Modify FTP Locations in the Look in list.
3. When the Add/Modify FTP Locations dialog box displays, type the name of the FTP site in the Name of FTP site text box. If the site allows anonymous logon, click Anonymous in the Log on as area; if you have a user name for the site, click User in the Log on as area and then enter the user name. Enter the password in the Password text box. Click the OK button.
4. Close the Save As or the Open dialog box.

Table C-4 Saving to an FTP Location
1. Click File on the menu bar and then click Save As.
2. When the Save As dialog box displays, type the Web page file name in the File name text box. Do not press the ENTER key.
3. Click the Save in box arrow and then click FTP Locations.
4. Double-click the name of the FTP site to which you wish to save.
5. When the FTP Log On dialog box displays, enter your user name and password and then click the OK button.
6. Click the Save button in the Save As dialog box.

APPENDIX D

Resetting the Word Toolbars and Menus

Word customization capabilities allow you to create custom toolbars by adding and deleting buttons and to personalize menus based on their usage. Each time you start Word, the toolbars and menus display using the same settings as the last time you used it. This appendix shows you how to reset the Standard and Formatting toolbars and menus to their installation settings.

Steps To Reset the Standard and Formatting Toolbars

1 Click the Toolbar Options button on the Standard toolbar and then point to Add or Remove Buttons on the Toolbar Options menu.

The Toolbar Options menu and the Add or Remove Buttons submenu display (Figure D-1).

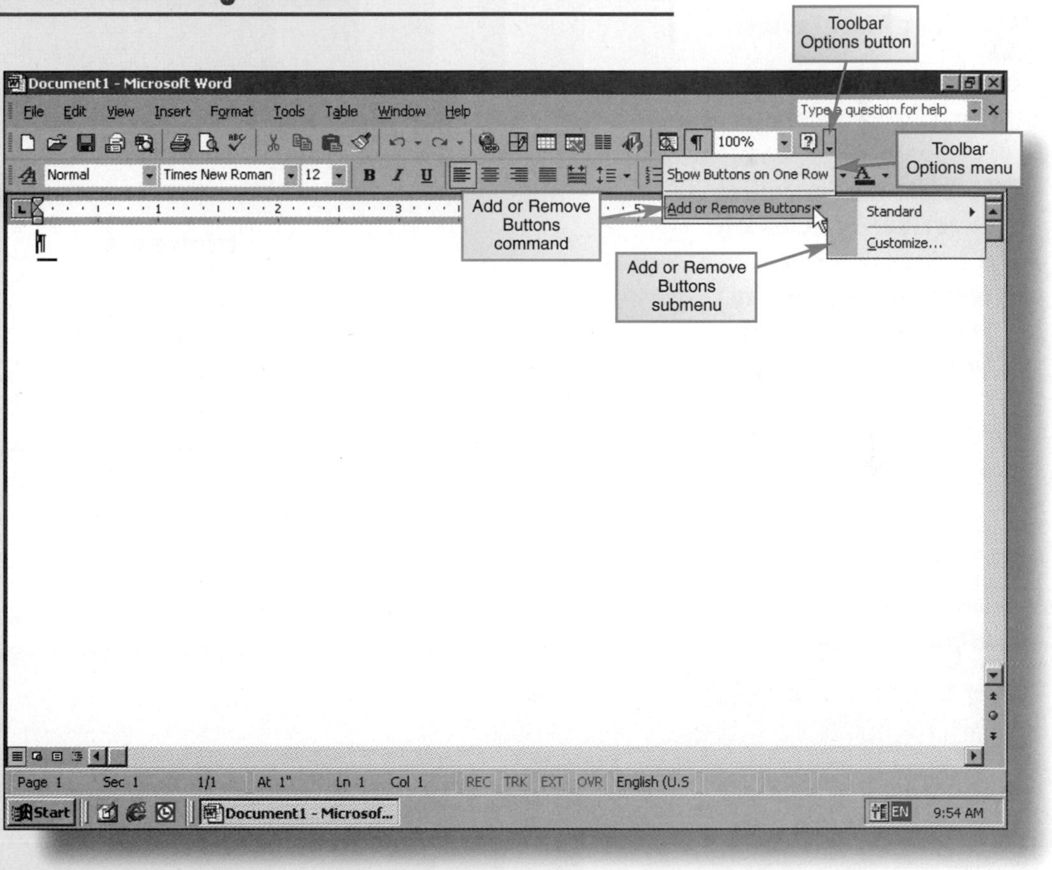

FIGURE D-1

2 Point to Standard on the Add or Remove Buttons submenu. When the Standard submenu displays, scroll down and then point to Reset Toolbar.

The Standard submenu displays indicating the buttons and boxes that display on the toolbar (Figure D-2). Clicking a button name with a check mark to the left of the name removes the check mark and then removes the button from the toolbar.

3 Click Reset Toolbar.

Word resets the Standard toolbar to its installation settings.

4 Reset the Formatting toolbar by following Steps 1 through 3 and replacing any reference to the Standard toolbar with the Formatting toolbar.

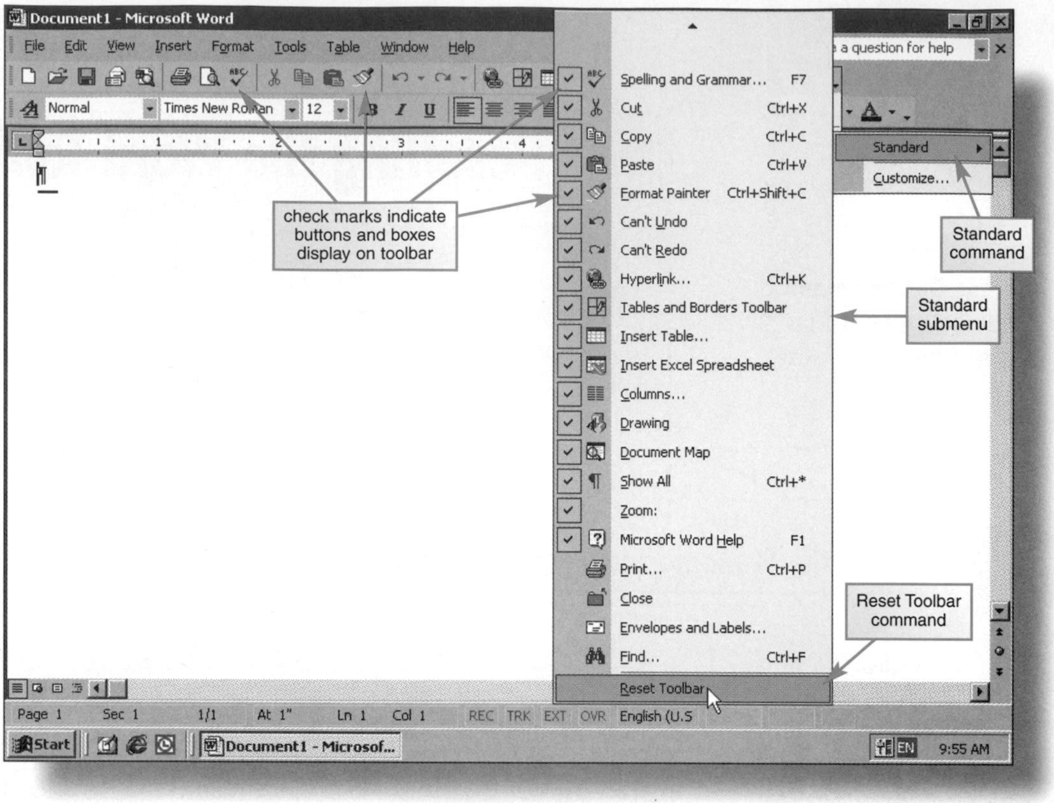

FIGURE D-2

Other Ways

1. On View menu point to Toolbars, click Customize on Toolbars submenu, click Toolbars tab, click toolbar name, click Reset button, click OK button, click Close button
2. Right-click toolbar, click Customize, click Toolbars tab, click toolbar name, click Reset button, click OK button, click Close button
3. In Voice Command mode, say "View, Toolbars, Customize, Toolbars, [toolbar name], Reset, OK, Close"

Steps To Reset Menus

1 Click the Toolbar Options button on the Standard toolbar and then point to Add or Remove Buttons on the Toolbar Options menu. Point to Customize on the Add or Remove Buttons submenu.

The Toolbar Options menu and the Add or Remove Buttons submenu display (Figure D-3).

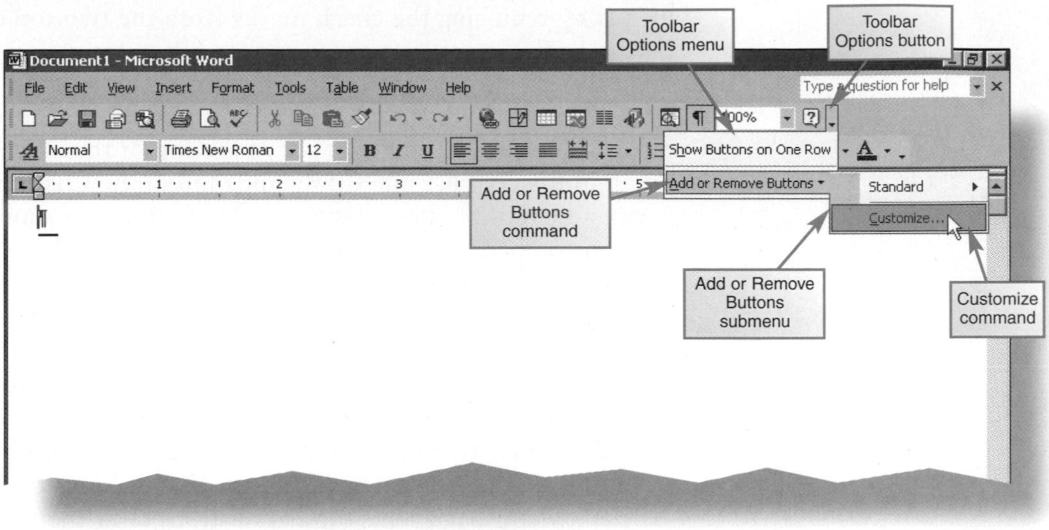

FIGURE D-3

2 Click Customize. When the Customize dialog box displays, click the Options tab and then point to the Reset my usage data button.

The Customize dialog box displays (Figure D-4). The ***Customize dialog box*** *contains three tabbed sheets used for customizing the Word toolbars and menus.*

3 Click the Reset my usage data button. When the Microsoft Word dialog box displays, click the Yes button. Click the Close button in the Customize dialog box.

Word resets the menus to the installation settings.

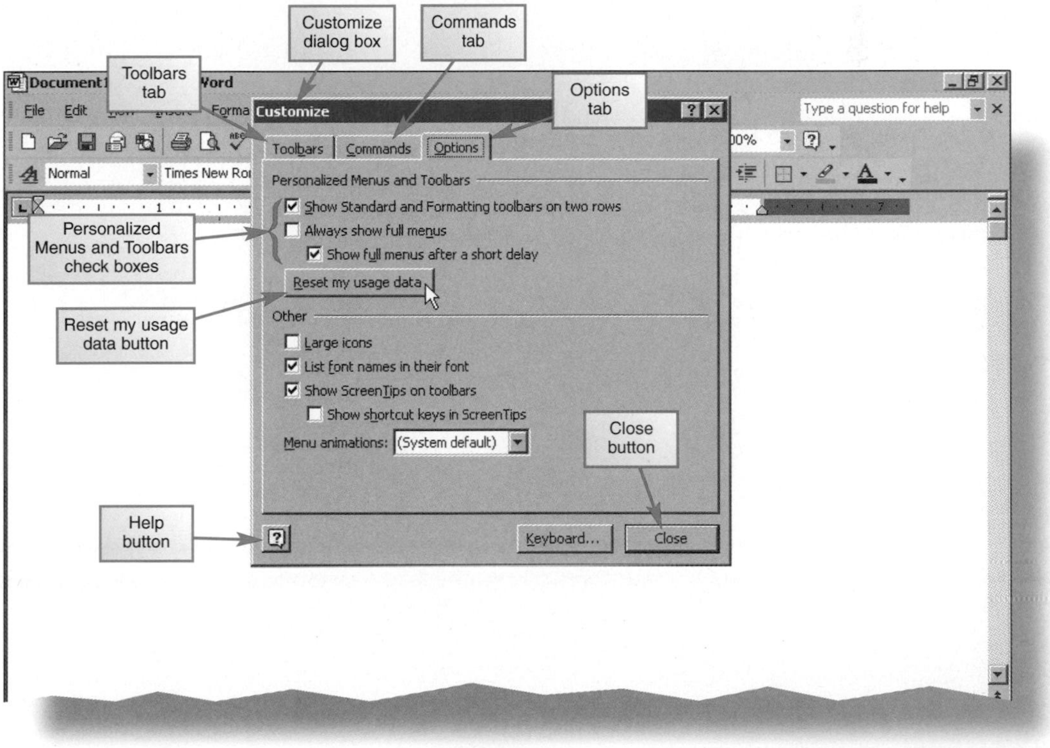

FIGURE D-4

Other Ways

1. On View menu point to Toolbars, click Customize on Toolbars submenu, click Options tab, click Reset my usage data button, click Yes button, click Close button
2. In Voice Command mode, say "View, Toolbars, Customize, Options, Reset my usage data, Yes, Close"

In the Options sheet in the Customize dialog box shown in Figure D-4 on the previous page, you can turn off toolbars displaying on two rows and turn off short menus by removing the check marks from the two top check boxes. Click the Help button in the lower-left corner of the Customize dialog box to display Help topics that will assist you in customizing toolbars and menus.

Using the Commands sheet, you can add buttons to toolbars and commands to menus. Recall that the menu bar at the top of the Word window is a special toolbar. To add buttons, click the Commands tab in the Customize dialog box. Click a category name in the Categories list and then drag the command name in the Commands list to a toolbar. To add commands to a menu, click a category name in the Categories list, drag the command name in the Commands list to the menu name on the menu bar, and then, when the menu displays, drag the command to the desired location in the menu list of commands.

In the Toolbars sheet, you can add new toolbars and reset existing toolbars. If you add commands to menus as described in the previous paragraph and want to reset the menus to their default settings, do the following: (1) Click View on the menu bar and then point to Toolbars; (2) click Customize; (3) click the Toolbars tab; (4) click Menu Bar in the Toolbars list; (5) click the Reset button; (6) click the OK button; and then (7) click the Close button.

APPENDIX E

Microsoft Office User Specialist Certification Program

What Is MOUS Certification?

The Microsoft Office User Specialist (MOUS) Certification Program provides a framework for measuring your proficiency with the Microsoft Office XP applications, such as Word 2002, Excel 2002, Access 2002, PowerPoint 2002, Outlook 2002, and FrontPage 2002. The levels of certification are described in Table E-1.

Table E-1 Levels of MOUS Certification

LEVEL	*DESCRIPTION*	*REQUIREMENTS*	*CREDENTIAL AWARDED*
Expert	Indicates that you have a comprehensive understanding of the advanced features in a specific Microsoft Office XP application	Pass any ONE of the Expert exams: Microsoft Word 2002 Expert Microsoft Excel 2002 Expert Microsoft Access 2002 Expert Microsoft Outlook 2002 Expert Microsoft FrontPage 2002 Expert	Candidates will be awarded one certificate for each of the Expert exams they have passed: Microsoft Office User Specialist: Microsoft Word 2002 Expert Microsoft Office User Specialist: Microsoft Excel 2002 Expert Microsoft Office User Specialist: Microsoft Access 2002 Expert Microsoft Office User Specialist: Microsoft Outlook 2002 Expert Microsoft Office User Specialist: Microsoft FrontPage 2002 Expert
Core	Indicates that you have a comprehensive understanding of the core features in a specific Microsoft Office XP application	Pass any ONE of the Core exams: Microsoft Word 2002 Core Microsoft Excel 2002 Core Microsoft Access 2002 Core Microsoft Outlook 2002 Core Microsoft FrontPage 2002 Core	Candidates will be awarded one certificate for each of the Core exams they have passed: Microsoft Office User Specialist: Microsoft Word 2002 Microsoft Office User Specialist: Microsoft Excel 2002 Microsoft Office User Specialist: Microsoft Access 2002 Microsoft Office User Specialist: Microsoft Outlook 2002 Microsoft Office User Specialist: Microsoft FrontPage 2002
Comprehensive	Indicates that you have a comprehensive understanding of the features in Microsoft PowerPoint 2002	Pass the Microsoft PowerPoint 2002 Comprehensive Exam	Candidates will be awarded one certificate for the Microsoft PowerPoint 2002 Comprehensive exam passed.

Why Should You Get Certified?

Being a Microsoft Office User Specialist provides a valuable industry credential — proof that you have the Office XP applications skills required by employers. By passing one or more MOUS certification exams, you demonstrate your proficiency in a given Office XP application to employers. With over 100 million copies of Office in use around the world, Microsoft is targeting Office XP certification to a wide variety of companies. These companies include temporary employment agencies that want to prove the expertise of their workers, large corporations looking for a way to measure the skill set of employees, and training companies and educational institutions seeking Microsoft Office XP teachers with appropriate credentials.

The MOUS Exams

You pay $50 to $100 each time you take an exam, whether you pass or fail. The fee varies among testing centers. The Expert exams, which you can take up to 60 minutes to complete, consists of between 40 and 60 tasks that you perform online. The tasks require you to use the application just as you would in doing your job. The Core exams contain fewer tasks, and you will have slightly less time to complete them. The tasks you will perform differ on the two types of exams.

How Can You Prepare for the MOUS Exams?

The Shelly Cashman Series® offers several Microsoft-approved textbooks that cover the required objectives on the MOUS exams. For a listing of the textbooks, visit the Shelly Cashman Series MOUS Web page at scsite.com/offxp/cert.htm and click the Shelly Cashman Series Microsoft Office XP-Approved MOUS Textbooks link (Figure E-1). After using any of the books listed in an instructor-led course, you will be prepared to take the MOUS exam indicated.

How to Find an Authorized Testing Center

You can locate a testing center by calling 1-800-933-4493 in North America or visiting the Shelly Cashman Series MOUS Web page at scsite.com/offxp/cert.htm and then clicking the Locate an Authorized Testing Center Near You link (Figure E-1). At this Web site, you can look for testing centers around the world.

Shelly Cashman Series MOUS Web Page

The Shelly Cashman Series MOUS Web page (Figure E-1) has more than fifteen Web sites you can visit to obtain additional information on the MOUS Certification Program. The Web page (scsite.com/offxp/cert.htm) includes links to general information on certification, choosing an application for certification, preparing for the certification exam, and taking and passing the certification exam.

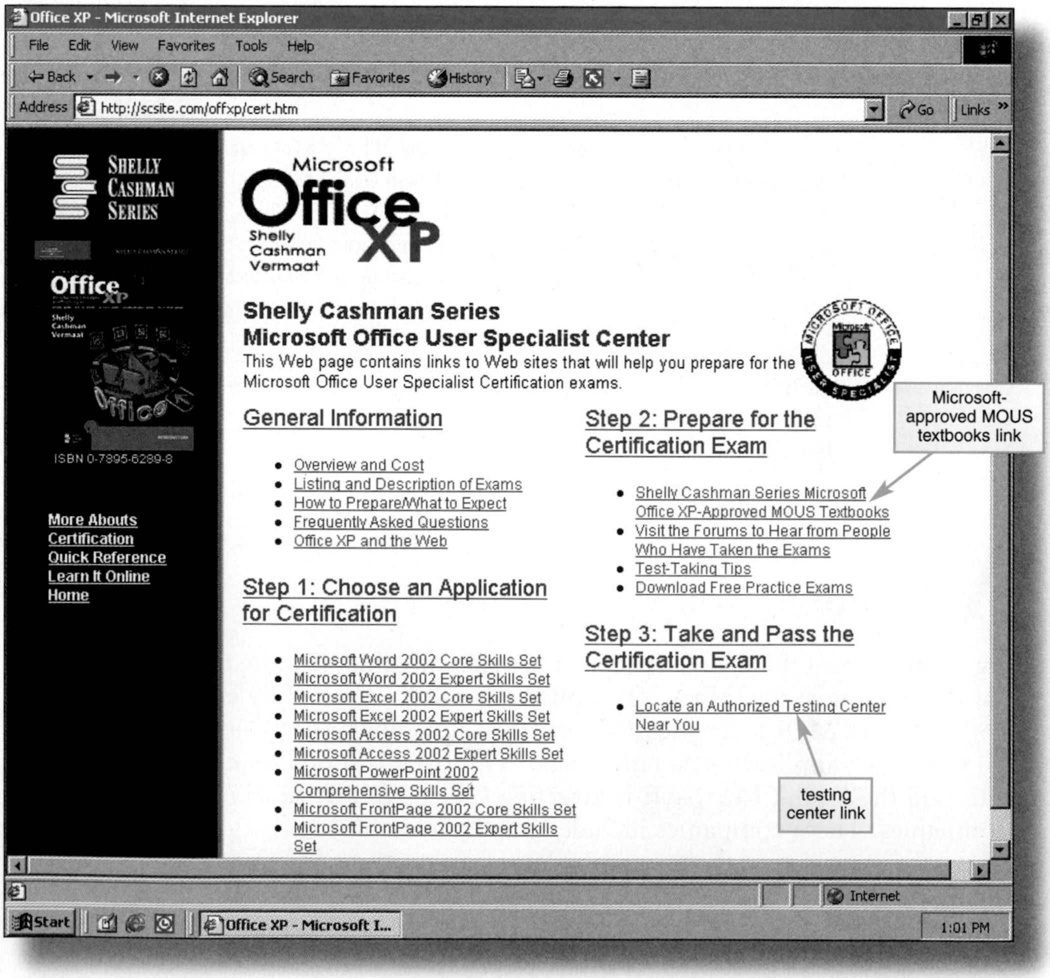

FIGURE E-1

Microsoft Office User Specialist Certification Map

The tables on the following pages list the skill sets and activities you should be familiar with if you plan to take one of the Microsoft Office User Specialist Certification examinations. Each activity is accompanied by page numbers on which the activity is illustrated and page numbers on which the activity is part of an exercise.

Microsoft Word 2002 Core and Expert Skill Sets and Activities

The Microsoft Word portion of *Microsoft Office XP: Introductory Concepts and Techniques* (ISBN 0-7895-6289-8 or 0-7895-6393-2 or 0-7895-6385-1) and *Microsoft Office XP: Advanced Concepts and Techniques* (ISBN 0-7895-6290-1 or 0-7895-6386-X) used in combination in a two-semester sequence of courses has been approved by Microsoft as courseware for the Microsoft Office User Specialist (MOUS) program. After completing the Word 2002 projects and exercises in these two books, students will be prepared to take the Core-level Microsoft Office User Specialist Exam for Microsoft Word 2002. Table E-2 lists the Microsoft Word 2002 Core Exam skill sets, activities, and page numbers on which the activities are demonstrated and can be practiced.

The Microsoft Word portion of *Microsoft Office XP: Post-Advanced Concepts and Techniques* (ISBN 0-7895-6291-X) used in combination with *Microsoft Office XP: Introductory Concepts and Techniques* (ISBN 0-7895-6289-8 or 0-7895-6393-2 or 0-7895-6385-1) and *Microsoft Office XP: Advanced Concepts and Techniques* (ISBN 0-7895-6290-1 or 0-7895-6386-X) in a three-semester sequence of courses has been approved by Microsoft as courseware for the Microsoft Office User Specialist (MOUS) program – Expert level. Table E-3 on page MO E.05 lists the skill sets, activities, and page numbers on which the activities are demonstrated and can be practiced.

Table E-2 Microsoft Word 2002 MOUS Core Skill Sets, Activities, and Locations in Book

SKILL SET	*ACTIVITY*	*ACTIVITY DEMONSTRATED IN BOOK*	*ACTIVITY EXERCISE IN BOOK*
I. Inserting and Modifying Text	A. Insert, modify, and move text and symbols	WD 1.21-26, WD 1.58, WD 2.20-24, WD 2.38-39, WD 2.46, WD 2.48-49, WD 3.19-20, WD 6.17-18, WD 6.36-37, WD 6.45-47	WD 1.64-65 (Steps 9, 13, 14), WD 2.57 (Steps 1-5), WD 2.59 (In the Lab 1 Step 2), WD 2.61-62 (In the Lab 2 Part 1 Step 2, Part 2 Step 4), WD 2.62-63 (In the Lab 3 Step 2), WD 3.64 (In the Lab 1 Step 2), WD 3.65 (In the Lab 2 Step 1), WD 6.77 (In the Lab 1 Steps 2, 6), WD 6.78 (In the Lab 2 Step 2), WD 6.79 (In the Lab 3 Step 2), WD 6.80 (Cases & Places 4)
	B. Apply and modify text formats	WD 1.20, WD 1.32, WD 1.35-36, WD 1.41, WD 1.43, WD 1.45, WD 3.28, WD 4.50-52, WD 6.28-29, WD 6.61-62	WD 1.66-67 (In the Lab 1 Steps 1, 5, 8-10), WD 1.67-68 (In the Lab 2 Steps 1, 5, 8-10), WD 1.68-69 (In the Lab 3 Steps 1, 5, 7, 9-10); WD 1.70-71 (Cases & Places 1-7), WD 2.57 (Apply Your Knowledge Steps 3, 7), WD 2.60-62 (In the Lab 2 Part 2 Steps 8-9), WD 3.65 (In the Lab 2 Step 1), WD 4.72-73 (In the Lab 1 Step 3a), WD 6.77 (In the Lab 1 Step 4), WD 6.78 (In the Lab 2 Step 4), WD 6.79 (In the Lab 3 Step 5)
	C. Correct spelling and grammar usage	WD 1.22, WD 1.27-29, WD 2.50-52	WD 1.64-65 (Apply Your Knowledge Steps 1-8), WD 1.66 (In the Lab 1 Step 3), WD 1.67-68 (In the Lab 2 Step 3), WD 1.68 (In the Lab 3 Step 3), WD 2.58-59 (In the Lab 1 Step 4), WD 2.60-61 (In the Lab 2 Step 4), WD 2.62 (In the Lab 3 Step 4)
	D. Apply font and text effects	WD 4.13-15, WD 4.38-39, WD 6.65-67	WD 4.72-73 (In the Lab 1), WD 4.74-75 (In the Lab 2), WD 4.76-78 (In the Lab 3), WD 6.80 (Cases & Places 1)
	E. Enter and format Date and Time	WD 3.43-44, WD 5.30-31	WD 3.65 (In the Lab 2 Step 2), WD 5.76-77 (In the Lab 2 Step 3), WD 5.80 (Cases & Places 1)
	F. Apply character styles		WD 5.76-77 (In the Lab 2 Step 3), WD 5.80 (Cases & Places 1) WD 4.72-73 (In the Lab 1 Step 3a)

(continued)

Table E-2 Microsoft Word 2002 MOUS Core Skill Sets, Activities, and Locations in Book *(continued)*

SKILL SET	*ACTIVITY*	*ACTIVITY DEMONSTRATED IN BOOK*	*ACTIVITY EXERCISE IN BOOK*
II. Creating and Modifying Paragraphs	A. Modify paragraph formats	WD 1.32, WD 1.37-38, WD 2.10, WD 2.17, WD 2.18 Table 2-2, WD 2.19, WD 2.36-38, WD 3.21, WD 3.37-38, WD 4.08-11, WD 6.26-27, WD 6.34-35, WD 6.39-40	WD 1.66-67 (In the Lab 1 Steps 6-7, 11), WD 1.67-68 (In the Lab 2 Steps 6-7, 11), WD 1.68-69 (In the Lab 3 Steps 6-8, 11); WD 1.70-71 (Cases & Places 1-7), WD 2.58-59 (In the Lab 1 Step 1), WD 2.60-62 (In the Lab 2 Step 1), WD 2.62 (In the Lab 1 Step 1), WD 3.64 (In the Lab 1 Step 2) WD 3.65 (In the Lab 2 Step 1), WD 4.72-73 (In the Lab 1, Step 1), WD 4.74-75 (In the Lab 2 Step 1), WD 4.76-78, In the Lab 3 Step 1), WD 6.77 (In the Lab 1 Steps 1, 6), WD 6.79 (In the Lab 3 Steps 3, 5)
	B. Set and modify tabs	WD 3.30-32, WD 3.42-43	WD 3.65 (In the Lab 2 Step 2), WD 3.66 (Cases & Places 5)
	C. Apply bullet, outline, and numbering format to paragraphs	WD 3.54-56, WD 5.38-41	WD 1.68 (In the Lab 3 Step 8), WD 3.64 (In the Lab 1), WD 3.65 (In the Lab 2), WD 3.66 (Cases & Places 5), WD 5.76-77 (In the Lab 2 Step 5), WD 5.80 (Cases & Places 1), WD 5.80 (Cases & Places 1)
	D. Apply paragraph styles	WD 5.41-42	WD 5.76-77 (In the Lab 2 Step 5), WD 5.80 (Cases & Places 1)
III. Formatting Documents	A. Create and modify a header and a footer	WD 2.11-15, WD 4.29-32	WD 2.58-59 (In the Lab 1 Step 1), WD 2.60-62 (In the Lab 2 Step 1), WD 2.62-63 (In the Lab 3 Step 1), WD 4.76-78 (In the Lab 3 Steps 6-8), WD 4.79-80 (Cases & Places 5-6)
	B. Apply and modify column settings	WD 6.23-35, WD 6.43-44, WD 6.48, WD 6.59-60	WD 6.77 (In the Lab 1 Steps 2-5), WD 6.78 (In the Lab 2 Steps 2-4), WD 6.79 (In the Lab 3 Steps 2-5), WD 6.80 (Cases & Places 1-4)
	C. Modify document layout and Page Setup options	WD 2.08, WD 2.14, WD 2.33, WD 4.22, WD 4.29-30, WD 5.66, WD 6.30	WD 2.59 (In the Lab 1 Steps 1-2), WD 4.72-73 (In the Lab 1 Step 2), WD 4.74-75 (In the Lab 2 Step 2), WD 4.76-78 (In the Lab 3 Steps 2, 6), WD 5.74-75 (In the Lab 1 Step 10), WD 5.76-77 (In the Lab 2 Step 10), WD 6.80 (Cases & Places 4)
	D. Create and modify tables	WD 3.49-54, WD 4.32-37, WD 4.53-63, WD 5.67	WD 3.63 (Apply Your Knowledge Steps 1-8), WD 3.65 (In the Lab 2), WD 4.70-71 (Apply Your Knowledge Steps 1-14), WD 4.72-73 (In the Lab 1 Step 3b), WD 4.73-74 (In the Lab 2 Step 3), WD 4.76-78 (In the Lab 3 Steps 4-5), WD 4.79-80 (Cases & Places 1-6), WD 5.74-75 (In the Lab 1 Step 10), WD 5.76-77 (In the Lab 2 Step 10)
	E. Preview and Print documents, envelopes, and labels	WD 1.54-55, WD 3.25-26, WD 3.57-58, WD 4.65	WD 1.64-65 ((Apply Your Knowledge Step 16), WD 1.66-67 (In the Lab 1 Step 15), WD 1.67-68 (In the Lab 2 Steps 13, 15), WD 1.68-69 (In the Lab 3 Steps 13, 15), WD 3.64 (In the Lab 1 Step 5), WD 3.65 (In the Lab 2 Steps 5, 6)
IV. Managing Documents	A. Manage files and folders for documents	WD 5.20-21	WD 5.74-75 (In the Lab 1 Step 4), WD 5.76-77 (In the Lab 2 Step 4), WD 5.78-79 (In the Lab 3 Step 3), WD 5.80 (Cases & Places 1-3)
	B. Create documents using templates	WD 3.08-14, WDW 1.05-08, WD 5.08-10	WD 3.64 (In the Lab 1 Steps 1-2), WD 3.66 (Cases & Places 1-5), WDW 1.14 (In the Lab 2), WD 5.74-75 (In the Lab 1 Steps 1-2), WD 5.76-77 (In the Lab 2 Steps 1-2), WD 5.78-79 (In the Lab 3 Steps 1-2)
	C. Save documents using different names and file formats	WD 1.30, WD 1.53-54, WDW 1.03	WD 1.65 (Apply Your Knowledge Step 15), WD 1.66-67 (In the Lab 1 Steps 4, 14), WD 1.67-68 (In the Lab 2 Steps 4, 14), WD 1.68-69 (In the Lab 3 Steps 4, 14)
V. Working with Graphics	A. Insert images and graphics	WD 1.46-49, WD 5.11-19, WD 6.55-57	WD 1.66-67 (In the Lab 1 Step 12), WD 1.67-68 (In the Lab 2 Step 12), WD 1.68-69 (In the Lab 3 Steps 12 -13), WD 1.70-71 (Cases & Places 1-7), WD 5.74-75 (In the Lab 1 Step 2), WD 5.76-77 (In the Lab 2 Step 2), WD 5.80 (Cases & Places 1-3), WD 6.78 (In the Lab 2 Step 2), WD 6.79 (In the Lab 3 Step 3)
	B. Create and modify diagrams and charts	WD 4.39-45, WD 6.49-54, WD 6.59 -60	WD 4.74-75 (In the Lab 2 Step 3), WD 4.76-78 (In the Lab 3 Step 5), WD 4.79-80 (Cases & Places 2-6), WD 6.78 (In the Lab 2 Step 4)
VI. Workgroup Collaboration	A. Compare and Merge documents	WD 6.71-73	WD 6.76 (Apply Your Knowledge Step 9)
	B. Insert, view, and edit comments	WD 6.68-71	WD 6.76 (Apply Your Knowledge Steps 1-7)
	C. Convert documents into Web pages	WDW 1.03, WDW 1.11	WDW 1.14 (In the Lab 1), WDW 1.14 (In the Lab 2)

Table E-3 Microsoft Word 2002 MOUS Expert Skill Sets, Activities, and Locations in Book

SKILL SET	*ACTIVITY*	*ACTIVITY DEMONSTRATED IN BOOK*	*ACTIVITY EXERCISE IN BOOK*
I. Customizing Paragraphs	A. Control Pagination	WD 4.46-48, WD 9.32-33	WD 4.76-78 (In the Lab 3 Steps 5-6), WD 4.79-80 (Cases & Places 2-6), WD 9.81-82 (Cases and Places 1-6)
	B. Sort paragraphs in lists and tables	WD 2.41-42, WD 5.52, WD 5.68	WD 2.60-62 (In the Lab 2 Step 3), WD 5.73 (In the Lab Step 4), WD 5.74-75 (In the Lab 1 Step 10), WD 5.76-77 (In the Lab 2 Step 10), WD 5.80 (Cases & Places 1)
II. Formatting Documents	A. Create and format document sections	WD 3.39, WD 4.12, WD 4.18-20, WD 4.23, WD 4.66-67, WD 5.19-20, WD 9.61-63	WD 4.70-71 (Apply Your Knowledge Step 17), WD 4.72-73 (In the Lab 1 Step 2), WD 4.74-75 (In the Lab 2 Step 2), WD 4.76-78 (In the Lab 3 Steps 2, 14), WD 5.74-75 (In the Lab 1 Step 3), WD 5.76-77 (In the Lab Step 3), WD 9.73-75 (In the Lab 1 Step 12), WD 9.78-80 (In the Lab 3 Steps 14-15)
	B. Create and apply character and paragraph styles	WD 2.27-31, WD 4.50-53, WD 5.41-42, WD 8.17-19	WD 2.60-62 (In the Lab 2 Part 2 Step 8), WD 4.72-73 (In the Lab 1 Step 3a), WD 5.76-77 (In the Lab 2 Step 5), WD 5.80 (Cases & Places 1), WD 8.73-74 (In the Lab 1 Step 4), WD 8.74-75 (In the Lab 2 Step 4), WD 8.76-77 (In the Lab 3 Step 4), WD 9.75-76 (In the Lab 1 Step 11)
	C. Create and update document indexes, tables of contents, figures, and authorities	WD 9.26-28, WD 9.30-32, WD 9.54-59, WD 9.67-69	WD 9.73-75 (In the Lab 1 Steps 2, 4, 9, 10, 14), WD 9.75-77 (In the Lab 2 Steps 4, 6, 10-13), WD 9.78-80 (In the Lab 3 Steps 2, 5, 11-13, 17)
	D. Create cross-references	WD 9.28-30	WD 9.73-75 (In the Lab 1 Step 3), WD 9.75-77 (In the Lab 2 Step 8) WD 9.78-80 (In the Lab 3 Step 4)
	E. Add and revise endnotes and footnotes	WD 2.24-32	WD 2.60-63 (In the Lab 2 Part 1 Step 2, Part 2 Steps 3-4, 7-9), WD 3.62-63 (In the Lab 3 Steps 3- 4), WD 2.64 (Cases & Places 1-5)
	F. Create and manage master documents and subdocuments	WD 9.36-48, WD 9.64-65	WD 9.73-75 (In the Lab 1 Steps 6-8), WD 9.78-80 (In the Lab 3 Steps 7-10), WD 9.81 (Cases & Places 2, 4-6)
	G. Move within documents	WD 2.43-44, WD 9.59-61, WD 9.66-67, WD 9.69	WD 2.62 (In the Lab 2 Part 2 Step 4), WD 9.75-77 (In the Lab 2 Step 14), WD 9.81 (Cases & Places 2, 4-6)
	H. Create and modify forms using various form controls	WD 7.08-47	WD 7.63-64 (In the Lab 1), WD 7.64-66 (In the Lab 2), WD 7.66-67 (In the Lab 3), WD 7.68-69 (Cases & Places 1-3)
	I. Create forms and prepare forms for distribution	WD 7.47-48, WD 7.57-59, WD 8.08, WD 8.61	WD 7.63-64 (In the Lab 1 Steps 8-9), WD 7.64-66 (In the Lab 2 Steps 9-11), WD 7.66-67 (In the Lab 3 Steps 8-10), WD 7.68-69 (Cases & Places 1-3), WD 8.73-74 (In the Lab 1 Steps 8-9), WD 8.74-75 (In the Lab 2 Steps 9,11), WD 8.76-77 (In the Lab 3 Steps 14-15)
III. Customizing Tables	A. Use Excel data in tables	WDI 2.04-12	WDI 2.14 (In the Lab 1), WDI 2.14 (In the Lab 2), WDI 2.14 (In the Lab 3)
	B. Perform calculations in Word tables	WD 4.33-34, WD 4.61	WD 3.63 (Apply Your Knowledge Step 4), WD 4.70-71 (Apply Your Knowledge Steps 1, 4, 9-10), WD 4.76-78 (In the Lab 3 Step 7)
IV. Creating and Modifying Graphics	A. Create, modify, and position graphics	WD 1.50-53, WD 3.29-30, WD 4.16, WD 4.40-41, WD 4.54-57, WD 5.11-18, WD 6.09-14, WD 6.21-22, WD 6.36-38, WD 6.41, WD 6.49, WD 6.51-54, WD 6.55-57, WD 6.59-60, WD 7.38-41, WD 8.19-21, WD 9.49-54	WD 1.67-68 (In the Lab 2 Steps 12-13), WD 1.68-69 (In the Lab 3 Steps 12-13), WD 4.72-73 (In the Lab 1 Steps 1, 3b), WD 4.74-75 (In the Lab 2 Steps 1, 3), WD 4.76-78 (In the Lab 3 Steps 1, 4, 7), WD 5.74-75 (In the Lab 1 Step 2), WD 5.76-77 (In the Lab 2 Step 2), WD 5.80 (Cases & Places 1-3), WD 6.77 (In the Lab 1 Steps 1, 6), WD 6.78 (In the Lab 2 Steps 1-2, 4), WD 6.79 (In the Lab 3 Steps 1, 3), WD 7.63-64 (In the Lab 1 Step 6), WD 7.64-66 (In the Lab 2 Steps 6-7), WD 7.66-67 (In the Lab 3 Step 6), WD 7.68-69 (Cases & Places 1-3), WD 8.74-75 (In the Lab 2 Step 3), WD 8.76-77 (In the Lab 3 Step 3), WD 8.78-79 (Cases & Places 1-3), WD 9.75-77 (In the Lab 2 Steps 4-5), WD 9.81-82 (Cases & Places 4-6)
	B. Create and modify charts using data from other applications	WD 4.45 (More About Charts), WDI 2.06-12	WDI 2.14 (In the Lab 1), WDI 2.14 (In the Lab 2), WDI 2.14 (In the Lab 3)

(continued)

Table E-3 Microsoft Word 2002 MOUS Expert Skill Sets, Activities, and Locations in Book *(continued)*

SKILL SET	ACTIVITY	ACTIVITY DEMONSTRATED IN BOOK	ACTIVITY EXERCISE IN BOOK
	C. Align text and graphics	WD 4.60, WD 4.62, WD 4.64-65, WD 6.11-13, WD 6.20-22, WD 6.28-29, WD 6.36-42, WD 6.55-57, WD 6.59-60 WD 7.41	WD 4.72-73 (In the Lab 1 Step 3b), WD 4.76-78 (In the Lab 3 Step 11), WD 4.79-80 (Cases & Places 2-6), WD 6.77 (In the Lab 1), WD 6.78 (In the Lab 2), WD 6.79 (In the Lab 3)
V. Customizing Word	A. Create, edit, and run macros	WD 8.23-27, WD 8.32-44, WD 8.46-50, WD 8.36-37, WD 8.51	WD 8.71-72 (Apply Your Knowledge), WD 8.73-74 (In the Lab 1 Steps 5-7), WD 8.74-75 (In the Lab 2 Steps 5-8), WD 8.76-77 (In the Lab 3 Steps 5-13), WD 8.78-79 (Cases & Places 1-3, 5-6)
	B. Customize menus and toolbars	WD 8.28-32	WD 8.76-77 (In the Lab 3 Steps 9, 13)
VI. Workgroup Collaboration	A. Track, accept, and reject changes to documents	WD 6.70, WD 9.11-23	WD 6.76 (Steps 2, 3, 5), WD 9.72-73 (Steps 1-12), WD 9.81-82 (Cases & Places 1)
	B. Merge input from several reviewers	WD 9.08-09, WD 9.21-23	WD 9.81-82 (Cases & Places 1)
	C. Insert and modify hyperlinks to other documents and Web pages	WD 2.39-40, WD 2.53, WD 3.40, WDW 1.04, WDW 1.10	WD 2.57 (Apply Your Knowledge Steps 6-7), WD 2.58-59 (In the Lab 1 Steps 3, 6), WD 2.60-61(In the Lab 1 Part 1 Steps 3, 6), WD 2.65 (In the Lab 2 Step 2), WDW 1.14 (In the Lab 2)
	D. Create and edit Web documents in Word	WDW 1.12-13, Appendix C	WDW 1.14 (In the Lab 1), WDW 1.14 (In the Lab 2), WD 7.66-67 (In the Lab 3 Step 10), WD 7.68-69 (Cases & Places 2)
	E. Create document versions	WD 9.16-17	WD 9.81-82 (Cases & Places 1)
	F. Protect documents	WD 7.47-48, WD 8.08, WD 8.61, WD 9.33-35, WD 9.40	WD 7.63-64 (In the Lab 1 Step 8), WD 7.64-66 (In the Lab 2, Step 9), WD 7.66-67 (In the Lab 3 Step 8), WD 7.68-69 (Cases & Places 1-3), WD 8.73-74 (In the Lab 1 Step 8), WD 8.74-75 (In the Lab 2 Step 9), WD 8.76-77 (In the Lab 3 Step 14), WD 9.81-82 (Cases & Places 1-6)
	G. Define and modify default file locations for workgroup templates	WDW 1.09, WDW 1.12-13, WD 7.57-58	WDW 1.14 (In the Lab 2), WD 7.66-67 (In the Lab 3 Step 10), WD 7.68-69 (Cases & Places 2), WD 8.78-79 (Cases & Places 6)
	H. Attach digital signatures to documents	WD 8.64-67	WD 8.74-75 (In the Lab 2 Step 10), WD 8.78-79 (Cases & Places 2-4)
VII. Using Mail Merge	A. Merge letters with a Word, Excel, or Access data source	WD 5.07-53, WDI 1.07-10	WD 5.73 (Apply Your Knowledge Step 5), WD 5.74-75 (In the Lab 1), WD 5.76-77 (In the Lab 2), WD 5.78-79 (In the Lab 3), WD 5.80-81 (Cases & Places 1-5), WDI 1.13 (In the Lab 1), WDI 1.13 (In the Lab 2), WDI 1.14 (In the Lab 3)
	B. Merge labels with a Word, Excel, or Access data source	WD 5.54-59	WD 5.74-75 (In the Lab 1 Step 8), WD 5.76-77 (In the Lab 2 Step 8), WD 5.78-79 (In the Lab 3 Step 7), WD 5.80-81 (Cases & Places 1-5)
	C. Use Outlook data as mail merge data source	WDI 1.05-10	WDI 1.13 (In the Lab 1), WDI 1.14 (In the Lab 3)

Microsoft Excel 2002 Core and Expert Skill Sets and Activities

The Microsoft Excel portion of *Microsoft Office XP: Introductory Concepts and Techniques* (ISBN 0-7895-6289-8 or 0-7895-6393-2 or 0-7895-6385-1) and *Microsoft Office XP: Advanced Concepts and Techniques* (ISBN 0-7895-6290-1 or 0-7895-6386-X) used in combination in a two-semester sequence of courses has been approved by Microsoft as courseware for the Microsoft Office User Specialist (MOUS) program. After completing the Excel 2002 projects and exercises in these two books, students will be prepared to take the Core-level Microsoft Office User Specialist Exam for Microsoft Excel 2002. Table E-4 lists the Microsoft Excel 2002 Core Exam skill sets, activities, and page numbers on which the activities are demonstrated and can be practiced.

The Microsoft Excel portion of *Microsoft Office XP: Post-Advanced Concepts and Techniques* (ISBN 0-7895-6291-X) used in combination with *Microsoft Office XP: Introductory Concepts and Techniques* (ISBN 0-7895-6289-8 or 0-7895-6393-2 or 0-7895-6385-1) and *Microsoft Office XP: Advanced Concepts and Techniques* (ISBN 0-7895-6290-1 or 0-7895-6386-X) in a three-semester sequence of courses has been approved by Microsoft as courseware for the Microsoft Office User Specialist (MOUS) program – Expert level. Table E-5 on the next page lists the skill sets, activities, and page numbers on which the activities are demonstrated and can be practiced.

Table E-4 Microsoft Excel 2002 MOUS Core Skill Sets, Activities, and Locations in the Book

SKILL SET	*ACTIVITY*	*ACTIVITY DEMONSTRATED IN BOOK*	*ACTIVITY EXERCISE IN BOOK*
I. Working with Cells and Cell Data	A. Insert, delete, and move cells	E 3.16, E 3.18, E 1.32	E 1.57 (Apply Your Knowledge), E 2.70 (In the Lab 1 Step 14), E 3.78 (In the Lab 3 Part 3)
	B. Enter and edit cell data including text, numbers, and formulas	E 1.08, E 1.16, E 1.19, E 1.21, E 1.49, E 1.51, E 2.07, E 2.16-23, E 2.33-38	E 1.58 (In the Lab 1 Steps 1, 10), E 1.60 (In the Lab 2 Step 5), E 2.70 (In the Lab 1 Steps 2-4), E 2.72 (In the Lab 2 Steps 5, 7-9, 13), E 3.70 (In the Lab 1 Step 7), E 3.77-78 (In the Lab 3 Steps 10-15)
	C. Check spelling	E 2.48-50	E 2.70 (In the Lab 1 Step 10), E 2.73 (In the Lab 2 Step 18)
	D. Find and replace cell data and formats	E 1.35-36, E 6.58-61	E 1.59-64, E 6.73 (In the Lab 2 Part 3)
	E. Work with a subset of data by filtering lists	E 5.35-39, E 5.40-47	E 5.53 (In the Lab 1 Part 2), E 5.57 (In the Lab 2 Part 3)
II. Managing Workbooks	A. Manage workbook files and folders	E 1.46, EW 1.06, E 6.62-64	E 1.57 (Apply Your Knowledge), EW 1.16 (In the Lab 1 Step 1)
	B. Create workbooks using templates	E 6.22-24	E 6.71 (In the Lab 1 Step 6), E 6.72 (In the Lab 2 Part 1)
	C. Save workbooks using different names and file formats	E 1.40-44, E 2.24-25, E 2.50, EW 1.06-08, E 6.12, E 6.24, E 6.65	E 1.58 (In the Lab 1 Step 8), EW 1.15-16 (In the Lab 1 Step 1, In the Lab 2 Step 2), E 6.71 (In the Lab 1 Step 6), E 6.72 (In the Lab 2 Steps 4, 6)
III. Formatting and Printing Worksheets	A. Apply and modify cell formats	E 1.28-35, E 2.26-43, E 3.32-43, E 4.07, E 4.09, E 4.36, E 6.12-21	E 1.58-59 (In the Lab 1 Step 5), E 2.68 (Apply Your Knowledge Step 5), E 2.72 (In the Lab 2 Steps 10, 13-15), E 3.69-71 (In the Lab 1 Steps 1-2, 8)
	B. Modify row and column settings	E 3.16-18, E 2.46, E 2.48, E 3.20, E 3.31	E 2.72 (In the Lab 2 Step 10), E 3.70 (In the Lab 1 Step 4), E 3.77 (In the Lab 3 Step 3), E 5.61 (In the Lab 3 Part 2)
	C. Modify row and column formats	E 2.32, E 2.43-48, E 5.08	E 2.70 (In the Lab 1 Steps 6 and 7), E 2.72 (In the Lab 2 Steps 10, 13), E 3.70 (In the Lab 1 Steps 2, 4), E 5.53 (In the Lab 1 Part 1)
	D. Apply styles	E 6.18-21	E 6.71 (Apply Your Knowledge Step 2)
	E. Use automated tools to format worksheets	E 1.33-35	E 1.59 (In the Lab 1 Step 5), E 1.60 (In the Lab 2 Step 5), E 1.61 (In the Lab 3 Step 4)
	F. Modify Page Setup options for worksheets	E 2.54, E 2.57, E 3.57, E 4.44-45, E 6.48-54	E 2.68 (Apply Your Knowledge Steps 8-9), E 2.73 (In the Lab 2 Step 19), E 3.71 (In the Lab 1 Step 10), E 6.70 (Apply Your Knowledge Step 5), E 6.73 (In the Lab 2 Step 6)
	G. Preview and print worksheets and workbooks	E 2.51-58, E 4.44-49, E 6.51, E 6.53	E 2.68 (Apply Your Knowledge Steps 8-9), E 2.70 (In the Lab 1 Steps 9-12), E 2.73 (In the Lab 2 Step 19), E 4.56 (Apply Your Knowledge Step 8), E 6.73 (In the Lab 2 Part 2)
IV. Modifying Workbooks	A. Insert and delete worksheets	E 6.24-25	E 6.71 (In the Lab 1 Step 3), E 6.73 (In the Lab 2 Step 2)
	B. Modify worksheet names and positions	E 3.54-56	E 3.71 (In the Lab 1 Part 2), E 3.74 (In the Lab 2 Step 11), E 3.75 (In the Lab 2 Part 2 Step 6)
	C. Use 3-D references	E 6.30-35, E 6.62, E 6.66-67	E 6.70 (Apply Your Knowledge Step 3, Part 2), E 6.73 (In the Lab 2 Step 4), E 6.75 (In the Lab 3 Step 5)

(continued)

Table E-4 Microsoft Excel 2002 MOUS Core Skill Sets, Activities, and Locations in the Book *(continued)*

SKILL SET	ACTIVITY	ACTIVITY DEMONSTRATED IN BOOK	ACTIVITY EXERCISE IN BOOK
V. Creating and Revising Formulas	A. Create and revise formulas	E 2.9-13, E 2.17, E 2.22, E 3.25-29, E 4.15-16, E 4.31	E 2.67 (Apply Your Knowledge Steps 1, 4), E 2.70 (In the Lab 1 Step 2), E 2.72 (In the Lab 2 Steps 5-9), E 3.70 (In the Lab 1 Step 7), E 3.74 (In the Lab 2 Step 7), E 4.56 (Apply Your Knowledge Steps 3-5), E 4.57 (In the Lab 1 Step 4), E 4.60 (In the Lab 2 Step 7), E 4.61 (In the Lab 3 Step 4)
	B. Use statistical, date and time, financial, and logical functions in formulas	E 1.23-24, E 1.27-28, E 2.16-24, E 3.22-24, E 3.27-28, E 4.15-16, E 4.31	E 2.70 (In the Lab 1 Step 4), E 2.72 (In the Lab 2 Steps 6-9), E 3.68 (Apply Your Knowledge Steps 1-4), E 3.69-70 (In the Lab 1 Steps 1 and 7), E 4.57 (In the Lab 1 Step 4), E 4.60 (In the Lab 2 Step 7)
VI. Creating and Modifying Graphics	A. Create, modify, position, and print charts	E 1.37-40, E 3.43-54, E 6.35-46, E 6.53-54	E 1.59 (In the Lab 1 Step 6), E 1.60 (In the Lab 2 Step 6), E 1.62 (In the Lab 3 Part 2), E 2.73 (In the Lab 2 Part 2), E 3.75 (In the Lab 2 Part 2)
	B. Create, modify, and position graphics	E 1.39, E 3.52-54, E 6.35-46	E 1.59 (In the Lab 1 Step 6), E 1.60 (In the Lab 2 Step 6), E 1.62 (In the Lab 3 Part 2), E 6.72-73 (In the Lab 2 Step 5)
VII. Workgroup Collaboration	A. Convert worksheets into Web pages	EW 1.04-05, EW 1.06-08, EW 1.10-12	EW 1.15 (In the Lab 1 Step 2), EW 1.16 (In the Lab 2 Part 1 Step 2)
	B. Create hyperlinks	E 4.39-44	E 4.60 (In the Lab 2 Step 10)
	C. View and edit comments	E 6.46-48, EI 1.10-14	E 6.71 (Apply Your Knowledge Step 3), E 6.73 (In the Lab 2 Step 6), EI 1.15 (In the Lab 1 Part 2, In the Lab 2 Part 2)

Table E-5 Microsoft Excel 2002 MOUS Expert Skill Sets, Activities, and Locations in Book

SKILL SET	ACTIVITY	ACTIVITY DEMONSTRATED IN BOOK	ACTIVITY EXERCISE IN BOOK
I. Importing and Exporting Data	A. Import data to Excel	E 9.9, E 9.14, E 9.18, E 9.23	E 9.63 (In the Lab 1)
	B. Export data from Excel	E 9.18, E 9.23, E 9.27	E 9.63 (In the Lab 1, Steps 5-6), E 9.63 (In the Lab 1, Step 11)
	C. Publish worksheets and workbooks to the Web	EW 1.04, Appendix C, EI 1.11, EW 2.03-04	EW 1.15 (In the Lab 1 Step 2), EW 1.16 (In the Lab 2 Part 1 Step 2), EI 1.15 (In the Lab 1 Part 1, In the Lab 2 Part 2), EW 2.15 (In the Lab 1), EW 2.16 (In the Lab 2)
II. Managing Workbooks	A. Create, edit, and apply templates	E 6.07-12	E 6.71 (In the Lab 1 Steps 1-8), E 6.72 (In the Lab 2 Part 1)
	B. Create workspaces	E 6.13-21, E 6.23-24, E 6.64-66	E 6.70 (Apply Your Knowledge Part 2), E 6.71 (In the Lab 1), E 6.72 (In the Lab 2 Part 1)
	C. Use Data Consolidation	E 6.30-35, E 6.62-67, E 9.56	E 6.70 (Apply Your Knowledge Parts 1-2), E 6.73 (In the Lab 2 Step 4), E 9.62 (In the Lab 2)
III. Formatting Numbers	A. Create and apply custom number formats	E 6.15-17	E 6.71 (Apply Your Knowledge Step 2)
	B. Use conditional formats	E 2.40-43, E 4.25-28	E 2.70 (In the Lab 1 Step 8), E 2.72 (In the Lab 2 Step 14), E 4.58 (In the Lab 1 Step 7)
IV. Working with Ranges	A. Use named ranges in formulas	E 4.12-13, E 4.47, E 5.09, E 5.18-20	E 4.56 (Apply Your Knowledge Steps 2-4), E 4.57 (In the Lab 1 Step 4), E 4.61 (In the Lab 3 Step 4)
	B. Use Lookup and Reference functions	E 4.15-16, E 5.15-18, E 5.48	E 4.56 (Apply Your Knowledge Steps 2-4), E 4.57 (In the Lab 1 Step 4), E 4.61 (In the Lab 3 Step 4), E 5.59 (In the Lab 2 Part 5), E 5.60 (In the Lab 3 Step 3), E 5.63 (Cases & Places 2)
V. Customizing Excel	A. Customize toolbars and menus	E 7.18-25	E 7.74 (Apply Your Knowledge), E 7.76 (In the Lab 1 Part 2 Step 5)
	B. Create, edit, and run macros	E 7.19-23, E 7.11-13, E 7.15-18, E 7.63-69	E 7.74 (Apply Your Knowledge), E 7.75-82 (In the Labs 1-3)
VI. Auditing Worksheets	A. Audit formulas	E 8.13	E 8.59 (In the Lab 1 Step 2)

Table E-5 Microsoft Excel 2002 MOUS Expert Skill Sets, Activities, and Locations in Book

SKILL SET	ACTIVITY	ACTIVITY DEMONSTRATED IN BOOK	ACTIVITY EXERCISE IN BOOK
	B. Locate and resolve errors	E 2.25, E 4.52-53, E 8.11	E 2.68 (Apply Your Knowledge Step 6), E 2.70 (In the Lab 1 Step 5), E 4.58 (In the Lab 1 Step 9), E 4.60 (In the Lab 2 Step 13), E 4.62 (In the Lab 3 Step 8), E 8.59 (In the Lab 2 Steps 2, 5)
	C. Identify dependencies in formulas	E 8.12-14	E 8.59 (In the Lab 1 Steps 2, 4)
VII. Summarizing Data	A. Use subtotals with lists and ranges	E 5.27-32	E 5.55 (In the Lab 1 Part 4)
	B. Define and apply filters	E 5.32-39, E 5.40-47	E 5.53 (In the Lab Part 2), E 5.57 (In the Lab Parts 3-4), E 5.61 (In the Lab Parts 4, 6)
	C. Add group and outline criteria to ranges	E 5.30-31	E 5.55 (In the Lab 1 Part 4)
	D. Use data validation	E 8.16-18	E 8.59 (In the Lab 1 Steps 6, 7, 8)
	E. Retrieve external data and create queries	E 9.23-26	E 9.63 (In the Lab 1)
	F. Create Extensible Markup Language (XML) Web queries	E 9.23-26	E 9.63 (In the Lab 1)
VIII. Analyzing Data	A. Create PivotTables, PivotCharts, and PivotTable/PivotChart Reports	E 9.34-39, E 9.51-52	E 9.66 (In the Lab 3)
	B. Forecast values with what-if analysis	E 9.58	E 9.62 (Apply Your Knowledge)
	C. Create and display scenarios	E 8.35-45	E 8.60-63 (In the Lab 2, In the Lab 3)
IX. Workgroup Collaboration	A. Modify passwords, protections, and properties	E 4.49-52	E 4.56 (Apply Your Knowledge Step 9), E 4.58 (In the Lab 1 Step 12), E 4.61 (In the Lab 2 Step 15), E 4.62 (In the Lab 3 Step 10)
	B. Create a shared workbook	E 9.30-31	E 9.64-65 (In the Lab 2)
	C. Track, accept, and reject changes to workbooks	E 9.30-31, E 9.35-37	E 9.64-65 (In the Lab 2)
	D. Merge workbooks	E 9.56-57	E 9.62 (Apply Your Knowledge)

Microsoft Access 2002 Core and Expert Skill Sets and Activities

The Microsoft Access portion of *Microsoft Office XP: Introductory Concepts and Techniques* (ISBN 0-7895-6289-8 or 0-7895-6393-2 or 0-7895-6385-1) and *Microsoft Office XP: Advanced Concepts and Techniques* (ISBN 0-7895-6290-1 or 0-7895-6386-X) used in combination in a two-semester sequence of courses has been approved by Microsoft as courseware for the Microsoft Office User Specialist (MOUS) program. After completing the Access 2002 projects and exercises in these two books, students will be prepared to take the Core-level Microsoft Office User Specialist Exam for Microsoft Access 2002. Table E-6 on the next page lists the Microsoft Access 2002 Core Exam skill sets, activities, and page numbers on which the activities are demonstrated and can be practiced.

The Microsoft Access portion of *Microsoft Office XP: Post-Advanced Concepts and Techniques* (ISBN 0-7895-6291-X) used in combination with *Microsoft Office XP: Introductory Concepts and Techniques* (ISBN 0-7895-6289-8 or 0-7895-6393-2 or 0-7895-6385-1) and *Microsoft Office XP: Advanced Concepts and Techniques* (ISBN 0-7895-6290-1 or 0-7895-6386-X) in a three-semester sequence of courses has been approved by Microsoft as courseware for the Microsoft Office User Specialist (MOUS) program – Expert level. Table E-7 on page MO E.11 lists the skill sets, activities, and page numbers on which the activities are demonstrated can be practiced.

Table E-6 Microsoft Access 2002 MOUS Core Skill Sets, Activities, and Locations in the Book

SKILL SET	*ACTIVITY*	*ACTIVITY DEMONSTRATED IN BOOK*	*ACTIVITY EXERCISE IN BOOK*
I. Creating and Using Databases	A. Create Access databases	A 1.11	A 1.64 (Cases & Places 6)
	B. Open database objects in multiple views	A 1.21, A 1.38, A 1.39, A 3.16, A 4.18, A 4.19, A 4.36, A 4.52	A 1.58-61 (In the Lab 2, In the Lab 3), A 3.51-57 (Apply Your Knowledge, In the Lab 1-3), A 4.56-60 (Apply Your Knowledge, In the Lab 1-3)
	C. Move among records	A 1.26, A 1.38, A 5.42	A 1.55 (Apply Your Knowledge Step 5), A 1.59 (In the Lab 2 Steps 9-10), A 1.61 (In the Lab 3 Step 10)
	D. Format datasheets	A 3.21, A 5.13, A 5.14	A 3.51 (Apply Your Knowledge Step 10), A 3.53 (In the Lab 1 Step 3), A 3.55 (In the Lab 2 Step 11), A 5.51-57 (Apply Your Knowledge, In the Lab 1-3)
II. Creating and Modifying Tables	A. Create and modify tables	A 1.13, A 1.15	A 1.63 (Cases & Places 3)
	B. Add a pre-defined input mask to a field	A 6.10	A 6.54 (In the Lab 1 Step 1), A 6.60 (Cases & Places 4)
	C. Create Lookup fields	A 6.07, A 6.08	A 6.56 (In the Lab 2 Step 1), A 6.60 (Cases & Places 1)
	D. Modify field properties	A 3.16, A 3.28, A 3.30, A 3.31, A 3.46, A 6.10	A 3.51-59 (Apply Your Knowledge Steps 2-6, In the Lab 1 Steps 2-3, 11, In the Lab 2 Steps 9, 12, In the Lab 3 Steps 2, 5, 9, Cases & Places 1-5), A 6.54 (In the Lab 1 Step 1), A 6.60 (Cases & Places 4)
III. Creating and Modifying Queries	A. Create and modify Select queries	A 2.06	A 2.44 (In the Lab 1 Step 2)
	B. Add calculated fields to Select queries	A 2.33	A 2.45 (In the Lab 1 Step 13), A 2.46 (In the Lab 2 Step 12), A 2.47 (In the Lab 3 Step 12), A 2.48 (Cases & Places 2 Part c)
IV. Creating and Modifying Forms	A. Create and display forms	A 1.38, A 4.34, A 5.21	A 1.56 (In the Lab 1 Step 8), A 1.58 (In the Lab 2 Step 8), A 1.61 (In the Lab 3 Step 12), A 4.56-62 (Apply Your Knowledge Step 3, In the Lab 1-3, Cases & Places 2, 4), A 5.51-58 (Apply Your Knowledge, In the Lab 1-3, Cases & Places 2, 4)
	B. Modify form properties	A 4.40, A 4.48, A 4.51, A 5.35	A 4.56-62 (Apply Your Knowledge, In the Lab 1-3, Cases & Places 2, 4), A 5.52-58 , (In the Lab 1-3, Cases & Places 2, 4)
V. Viewing and Organizing Information	A. Enter, edit, and delete records	A 1.21, A 1.27, A 3.06, A 3.14, A 3.20	A 1.54-64 (Apply Your Knowledge Step 1, In the Lab 1-3, Cases & Places 1-6), A 3.53 (In the Lab 1 Step 5), A 3.55 (In the Lab 2 Step 13), A 3.57 (In the Lab 3 Step 10), A 1.55 (Apply Your Knowledge Step 5), A 1.59 (In the Lab 2 Steps 9, 10), A 1.61 (In the Lab 3 Step 10), A 3.51 (Apply Your Knowledge Step 9), A 3.53 (In the Lab 1 Step 12), A 3.54 (In the Lab 2 Steps 7, 13), A 3.57 (In the Lab 3 Step 7), A 3.58 (Cases & Places 1-2)
	B. Create queries	A 2.06, A 3.39, A 3.45	A 2.44 (In the Lab 1 Step 2), A 3.59 (Cases & Places 5 Parts a, e)
	C. Sort records	A 2.25, A 3.41, A 3.42	A 3.51 (Apply Your Knowledge Step 15), A 3.53 (In the Lab 2 Step 6), A 3.56 (In the Lab 3 Step 3), A 2.44 (Apply Your Knowledge Step 14), A 2.46 (In the Lab 2 Step 12), A 2.47 (In the Lab 3 Steps 8-9) A 2.48 (Cases & Places 1 Part c, Cases & Places 2 Part e, Cases & Places 4 Part c)
	D. Filter records	A 3.13	A 3.51 (Apply Your Knowledge Step 13), A 3.55 (In the Lab 2 Step 16)
VI. Defining Relationships	A. Create one-to-many relationships	A 3.36-38	A 3.51 (Apply Your Knowledge Step 17), A 3.53 (In the Lab 1 Step 15), A 3.55 (In the Lab 2 Step 18), A 3.57 (In the Lab 3 Step 15), A 3.58-59 (Cases & Places 1-2, 4-5)
	B. Enforce referential integrity	A 3.36-38	A 3.51 (Apply Your Knowledge Step 17), A 3.53 (In the Lab 1 Step 15), A 3.55 (In the Lab 2 Step 18), A 3.57 (In the Lab 3 Step 15), A 3.58-59 (Cases & Places 1-2, 4-5)
VII. Producing Reports	A. Create and format reports	A 1.41, A 4.09, A 4.21	A 1.55 (Apply Your Knowledge Step 7), A 1.57 (In the Lab Step 9) A 1.59 (In the Lab 2 Step 12), A 1.61 (In the Lab 3 Step 12), A 4.56-62 (Apply Your Knowledge Step 1, In the Lab 1 Step 1, In the Lab 2 Steps 1, 3, In the Lab 3 Steps 1, 3, Cases & Places 1, 3, 5)

Table E-6 Microsoft Access 2002 MOUS Core Skill Sets, Activities, and Locations in the Book

SKILL SET	ACTIVITY	ACTIVITY DEMONSTRATED IN BOOK	ACTIVITY EXERCISE IN BOOK
	B. Add calculated controls to reports	A 4.33, A 6.20-21	A 4.57 (In the Lab 1, Steps 1, 3), A 4.62 (Cases & Places 3), A 6.60 (Cases & Places 3)
	C. Preview and print reports	A 1.46, A 4.20, A 4.33	A 1.55 (Apply Your Knowledge Step 7), A 1.57 (In the Lab Step 9) A 1.59 (In the Lab 2 Step 12), A 1.61 (In the Lab 3 Step 12), A 4.56-62 (Apply Your Knowledge Step 1, In the Lab 1 Step 1, In the Lab 2 Steps 1, 3, In the Lab 3 Steps 1 and 3, Cases & Places 1, 3, 5)
VIII. Integrating with Other Applications	A. Import data to Access	AI 1.05	AI 1.15 (In the Lab 1 Step 2), AI 1.16 (In the Lab 1 Step 5, In the Lab 1 Step 8)
	B. Export data from Access	AI 1.09, AI 1.11, AI 1.13	AI 1.17 (In the Lab 2 Step 1, In the Lab 2 Step 4), AI 1.18 (In the Lab 2 Step 7, In the Lab 2 Step 8)
	C. Create a simple data access page	AW 1.02	AW 1.10 (In the Lab 1)

Table E-7 Microsoft Access 2002 MOUS Expert Skill Sets, Activities, and Locations in Book

SKILL SET	ACTIVITY	ACTIVITY DEMONSTRATED IN BOOK	ACTIVITY EXERCISE IN BOOK
I. Creating and Modifying Tables	A. Use data validation	A 3.29, A 3.31	A 3.51-59 (Apply Your Knowledge Steps 2-6, In the Lab 1 Steps 2-3, 11, In the Lab 2 Steps 9, 12, In the Lab 3 Steps 2, 5, 9, Cases & Places 1-5)
	B. Link tables	AI 1.08	AI 1.16 (In the Lab 1 Step 8)
	C. Create lookup fields and modify Lookup field properties	A 6.07, A 6.08, A 6.14	A 6.56 (In the Lab 2 Step 1), A 6.60 (Cases & Places 1, 4)
	D. Create and modify input masks	A 6.10, A 9.15	A 6.54 (Apply Your Knowledge Step 1), A 6.60 (Cases & Places 4) A 9.80 (Apply Your Knowledge Step 4), A 9.81 (In the Lab 1 Step 3), A 9.83 (In the Lab 2 Step 3), A 9.84 (In the Lab 3 Step 3)
II. Creating and Modifying Forms	A. Create a form in Design view	A 8.76-89	A 8.97 (Apply Your Knowledge Step 7), A 8.99 (In the Lab 1 Step 6), A 8.101 (In the Lab 2 Step 6), A 8.102 (In the Lab 3 Step 7), A 8.104 (Cases & Places 2, 4)
	B. Create a Switchboard and set startup options	A 6.41, A 9.20	A 6.54-60 (In the Lab 1-3, Cases & Places 2, 5), A 9.85 (In the Lab 3 Step 22), A 9.86 (Cases & Places 1)
	C. Add Subform controls to Access forms	A 5.21, (using Form Wizard), A 8.79-81 (when creating a form in Design View)	A 5.51-60 (Apply Your Knowledge, In the Lab 1-3, Cases & Places 2, 4), A 8.97 (Apply Your Knowledge Step 7), A 8.99 (In the Lab 1 Step 6), A 8.101 (In the Lab 2 Step 6), A 8.102 (In the Lab 3 Step 7),A 8.104 (Cases & Places 2, 4)
III. Refining Queries	A. Specify multiple query criteria	A 2.23 (in Design View), A 2.24 (in Design View), A 9.54 (in SQL),	A 2.45 (In the Lab 1 Steps 8-9), A 2.46 (In the Lab 2 Steps 5, 7, 9), A 2.47 (In the Lab 3 Steps 4-5, 7), A 9.85 (In the Lab 3 Step 20)
	B. Create and apply advanced filters	A 3.13, A 7.17, A 7.19	A 3.51 (Apply Your Knowledge Step 13), A 3.55 (In the Lab 2 Step 16), A 7.55 (Apply Your Knowledge Step 10), A 7.56 (In the Lab 1 Step 6), A 7.59 (In the Lab 2 Step 11), A 7.61 (In the Lab 3 Step 9)
	C. Create and run parameter queries	A 7.21	A 7.55 (Apply Your Knowledge Step 12), A 7.57 (In the Lab 1 Step 7), A 7.59 (In the Lab 2 Step 13), A 7.61 (In the Lab 3 Step 10)
	D. Create and run Action queries	A 3.23, A 3.25, A 3.27	A 3.53 (In the Lab 1 Step 9), A 3.54 (In the Lab 2 Steps 3, 4, 5), A 3.58 (Cases & Places 2 Part b)

(continued)

Table E-7 Microsoft Access 2002 MOUS Expert Skill Sets, Activities, and Locations in Book *(continued)*

SKILL SET	ACTIVITY	ACTIVITY DEMONSTRATED IN BOOK	ACTIVITY EXERCISE IN BOOK
	E. Use aggregate functions in queries	A 2.36, A 9.58-59	A 2.45 (In the Lab 1 Steps 14-15), A 2.46 (In the Lab 2 Step 13), A 2.47 (In the Lab 3 Step 13, A 2.48 (Cases & Places 1 Parts d, e, f, Cases & Places 2 Part f, Cases & Places 4 Parts d, e, f, g), A 9.82 (In the Lab 1 Step 17), A 9.83 (In the Lab 2 Step 17), A 9.85 (In the Lab 3 Steps 15-16), A 9.86 (Cases & Places 4 Parts b, e, g)
IV. Producing Reports	A. Create and modify reports	A 7.24-46	A 7.57 (In the Lab 1 Step 9), A 7.59 (In the Lab 2 Step 15), A 7.61 (In the Lab 3 Step 12), A 7.62-63 (Cases & Places 2, 4)
	B. Add Subreport controls to Access reports	A 7.30-37	A 7.57 (In the Lab 1 Step 9), A 7.59 (In the Lab 2 Step 15), A 7.61 (In the Lab 3 Step 12), A 7.62-63 (Cases & Places 2, 4)
	C. Sort and group data in reports	A 7.24-26	A 7.57 (In the Lab 1 Step 9), A 7.59 (In the Lab 2 Step 15), A 7.61 (In the Lab 3 Step 12), A 7.62-63 (Cases & Places 2, 4)
V. Defining Relationships	A. Establish one-to-many relationships	A 3.36, A 7.12	A 3.51-58 (Apply Your Knowledge, In the Lab 1-3, Cases & Places 1-2), A 7.54-63 (Apply Your Knowledge, In the Lab 1-3, Cases & Places 1, 3)
	B. Establish many-to-many relationships	A 7.12	A 7.55 (Apply Your Knowledge Step 7), A 7.57 (In the Lab 1 Step 4), A 7.59 (In the Lab 2 Step 6), A 7.61 (In the Lab 3 Step 5), A 7.62-63 (Cases & Places 1, 3)
VI. Operating Access on the Web	A. Create and Modify a Data Access Page	AI 2.03-12	AI 2.17-18 (In the Lab 1-2)
	B. Save PivotTables and PivotCharts views to Data Access Pages	AI 2.08-12, AI 2.14	AI 2.17-18 (In the Lab 1-2)
VII. Using Access Tools	A. Import XML documents into Access	AI 1.08	AI 1.16 (In the Lab 1 Step 5)
	B. Export Access data to XML documents	AI 1.13	AI 1.18 (In the Lab 2 Step 8)
	C. Encrypt and decrypt databases	A 9.23	A 9.86 (Cases & Places 1)
	D. Compact and repair databases	A 5.48	A 5.56 (In the Lab 2 Step 7), A 5.58 (In the Lab 3 Step 6), A 5.59-60 (Cases & Places 2, 5)
	E. Assign database security	A 9.21, A 9.24, A 9.72-77	A 9.86 (Cases & Places 1, 5)
	F. Replicate a database	A 9.25, A 9.26, A 9.28	A 9.86 (Cases & Places 3)
VIII. Creating Database Applications	A. Create Access Modules	A 8.22-26, A 8.36-42, A 8.55-58, A 8.66-67	A 8.96-104 (Apply Your Knowledge, In the Lab 1-3, Cases & Places 1, 3, 5)
	B. Use the Database Splitter	A 9.68	A 9.86 (Cases & Places 1)
	C. Create an MDE file	A 9.71	A 9.86 (Cases & Places 1)

Microsoft PowerPoint 2002 Comprehensive Skill Sets and Activities

The Microsoft PowerPoint portion of *Microsoft Office XP: Introductory Concepts and Techniques* (ISBN 0-7895-6289-8 or 0-7895-6393-2 or 0-7895-6385-1) and *Microsoft Office XP: Advanced Concepts and Techniques* (ISBN 0-7895-6290-1 or 0-7895-6386-X) used in combination in a two-sequence course has been approved by Microsoft as courseware for the Microsoft Office User Specialist (MOUS) program. After completing the PowerPoint 2002 projects and exercises in these two books, students will be prepared to take the Comprehensive-level Microsoft Office User Specialist Exam for Microsoft PowerPoint 2002. Table E-8 lists the Microsoft PowerPoint 2002 Comprehensive Exam skill sets, activities, and page numbers on which the activities are demonstrated and can be practiced.

Table E-8 Microsoft PowerPoint 2002 MOUS Comprehensive Skill Sets, Activities, and Locations in Book

SKILL SET	ACTIVITY	ACTIVITY DEMONSTRATED IN BOOK	ACTIVITY EXERCISE IN BOOK
I. Creating Presentations	A. Create presentations (manually and using automated tools)	PP 1.10-11, PP 1.19-44, PP 2.07-45, PP 3.05-52, PP 4.06-10	PP 1.68 (Apply Your Knowledge Steps 1-5), PP 1.69-71 (In the Lab 1 Steps 1-3), PP 1.72-73 (In the Lab 2 Steps 1-3), PP 1.74-75 (In the Lab 3 Steps 1-4), PP 1.76-79 (Cases & Places 1-7), PP 2.56 (Apply Your Knowledge Step 1), PP 2.57-58 (In the Lab 1 Steps 1-3), PP 2.59-60 (In the Lab 2 Steps 1-3), PP 2.61-62 (In the Lab 3 Step 1), PP 2.64-66 (Cases & Places 1-7), PP 3.57 (Apply Your Knowledge Step 1), PP 3.58 (In the Lab 1 Steps 1-7), PP 3.59-60 (In the Lab 2 Steps 1-5), PP 3.60 (In the Lab 3 Steps 1-7), PP 3.62-63 (Cases & Places 1-7), PP 4.74-75 (In the Lab 1 Steps 1-9), PP 4.76-77 (In the Lab 2 Steps 1-5), PP 4.78-79 (In the Lab 3 Step 1), PP 4.80-82 (Cases & Places 1-7), PPW 2.39 (In the Lab 3)
	B. Add slides to and delete slides from presentations	PP 1.32-33, PP 1.37, PP 1.41, PP 2.12, PP 2.14-15, PP 2.17, PP 3.07-11, PP 4.31	PP 1.69-71 (In the Lab 1 Steps 1-3), PP 1.72-73 (In the Lab 2 Steps 1-3), PP 1.74-75 (In the Lab 3 Steps 1-3), PP 1.76-79 (Cases & Places 1-7), PP 2.57-58 (In the Lab 1 Steps 1-3), PP 2.59-60 (In the Lab 2 Step 1), PP 2.61-62 (In the Lab 3 Step 1), PP 2.64-66 (Cases & Places 1-7), PP 3.57 (Apply Your Knowledge Step 2), PP 3.59 (In the Lab 2 Step 1), PP 3.60 (In the Lab 3 Steps 1, 3), PP 3.62-63 (Cases & Places 1-7), PP 4.74-75 (In the Lab 1 Steps 1, 7), PP 4.76 (In the Lab 2 Steps 1, 3-5), PP 4.78 (In the Lab 3 Step 4)
	C. Modify headers and footers in the Slide Master	PP 4.09, PP 4.13-14	PP 4.72-73 (Apply Your Knowledge Step 8), PP 4.76-77 (In the Lab 2 Step 8), PP 4.78-79 (In the Lab 3 Step 1)
II. Inserting and Modifying Text	A. Import text from Word	PP 3.07-09	PP 3.57, PP 3.59 (In the Lab 2 Step 1), PP 3.60-61 (In the Lab 3 Step 1), PP 3.62 (Cases & Places 3)
	B. Insert, format, and modify text	PP 1.22-24, PP 1.26-28, PP 1.34-43, PP 1.58, PP 2.10-11, PP 2.13-17, PP 3.33-34, PP 4.26, PP 4.33, PP 4.39, PP 4.44, PP 4.48, PP 4.51-53	PP 1.68 (Apply Your Knowledge Steps 2-5), PP 1.69-71 (In the Lab 1 Steps 2-3), PP 1.72-73 (In the Lab 2 Steps 2-3), PP 1.74-75 (In the Lab 3 Steps 2-3), PP 1.76-79 (Cases & Places 1-7), PP 2.56 (Apply Your Knowledge Step 2), PP 2.57-59 (In the Lab 1 Steps 2-3), PP 2.59-60 (In the Lab 2 Steps 1-2), PP 2.61-62 (In the Lab 3 Step 1), PP 2.64-66 (Cases & Places 1-7), PP 3.58 (In the Lab 1 Step 2), PP 3.59-60 (In the Lab 2 Steps 2-5), PP 3.60-61 (In the Lab 3 Steps 3, 7), PP 3.62-63 (Cases & Places 1-7), PP 4.72-73 (Apply Your Knowledge Step 3), PP 4.74-75 (In the Lab 1 Steps 2-3, 8), PP 4.76-77 (In the Lab 2 Steps 2-5), PP 4.78-79 (In the Lab 3 Steps 1-2, 5-7), PP 4.80-82 (Cases & Places 1-7)
III. Inserting and Modifying Visual Elements	A. Add tables, charts, clip art, and bitmap images to slides	PP 2.24-30, PP 3.14, PP 3.30-49, PP 4.32-37	PP 2.56-57 (Apply Your Knowledge Steps 2-5), PP 2.57-59 (In the Lab 1 Steps 2, 4-6), PP 2.59-60 (In the Lab 2 Steps 2-5), PP 2.61-63 (In the Lab 3 Steps 2-7), PP 2.64-66 (Cases & Places 1-7), PP 3.57 (Apply Your Knowledge Steps 3-4), PP 3.58 (In the Lab 1 Steps 3, 5), PP 3.59-60 (In the Lab 2 Step 5), PP 3.60-61 (In the Lab 3 Steps 5, 7-8), PP 3.62-63 (Cases & Places 1-6), PP 4.74-75 (In the Lab 1 Step 9), PP 4.80-82 (Cases & Places 1-7)
	B. Customize slide backgrounds	PP 4.15-18	PP 4.74 (In the Lab 1 Step 1), PP 4.76-77 (In the Lab 2 Step 1), PP 4.82 (Cases & Places 5, 7)
	C. Add OfficeArt elements to slides	PP 4.18-25	PP 4.72 (Apply Your Knowledge Step 4), PP 4.74-75 (In the Lab 2 Step 6), PP 4.76-77 (In the Lab 2 Step 6), PP 4.78-79 (In the Lab 3 Step 3), PP 4.80-82 (Cases & Places 1-3)
	D. Apply custom formats to tables	PP 3.33-38	PP 3.59-60 (In the Lab 2 Step 5), PP 3.60-61 (In the Lab 3 Step 7), PP 3.62-63 (Cases & Places 2, 4, 6)

(continued)

Table E-8 Microsoft PowerPoint 2002 MOUS Comprehensive Skill Sets, Activities, and Locations in Book *(continued)*			
SKILL SET	*ACTIVITY*	*ACTIVITY DEMONSTRATED IN BOOK*	*ACTIVITY EXERCISE IN BOOK*
IV. Modifying Presentation Formats	A. Apply formats to presentations	PP 1.19-21, PP 2.06-07, PP 2.21-23, PP 3.49-51, PP 4.33-34, PP 4.44-45, PP 4.61-64	PP 1.68 (Apply Your Knowledge Step 1), PP 1.69-71 (In the Lab 1 Step 1), PP 1.72-74 (In the Lab 2 Step 1), PP 1.74-75 (In the Lab 3 Step 1), PP 1.76-79 (Cases & Places 1-7), PP 2.56 (Apply Your Knowledge Step 1), PP 2.57-58 (In the Lab 1 Step 1), PP 2.59-60 (In the Lab 2 Step 1), PP 2.61-63 (In the Lab 3 Step 1), PP 2.64-66 (Cases & Places 1-7), PP 3.57 (Apply Your Knowledge Step 1), PP 3.58 (In the Lab 1 Step 1), PP 3.59 (In the Lab 2 Step 2), PP 3.60-61 (In the Lab 3 Steps 2-3), PP 4.74-75 (In the Lab 1 Steps 3-5, 7-8), PP 4.76-77 (In the Lab 2 Steps 1, 3-5), PP 4.78-79 (In the Lab 3 Steps 6, 9)
	B. Apply animation schemes	PP 2.39-41, PP 3.52-53	PP 2.57 (Apply Your Knowledge Step 6), PP 2.59 (In the Lab 1 Step 8), PP 2.61 (In the Lab 2 Step 7), PP 2.62 (In the Lab 3 Step 9), PP 2.64-66 (Cases & Places 1-7), PP 3.57 (Apply Your Knowledge Step 6), PP 3.58 (In the Lab 1 Step 8), PP 3.59-60 (In the Lab 2 Step 6), PP 3.60 (In the Lab 3 Step 9), PP 3.62-63 (Cases & Places 2-5), PP 4.76-77 (In the Lab 2 Step 7)
	C. Apply slide transitions	PP 4.56-58	PP 4.72 (Apply Your Knowledge Step 6), PP 4.74-75 (In the Lab 1 Step 10), PP 4.76-77 (In the Lab 2 Step 7), PP 4.78-79 (In the Lab 3 Step 10), PP 4.80-82 (Cases & Places 2-5, 7)
	D. Customize slide formats	PP 1.26-28, PP 2.44-45, PP 4.61-64	PP 1.68 (Apply Your Knowledge Steps 2-5), PP 1.69-71 (In the Lab 1 Step 2), PP 1.72-73 (In the Lab 2 Steps 2-3), PP 1.74 (In the Lab 3 Steps 2-3), PP 1.76-79 (Cases & Places 1-7), PP 2.56-57 (Apply Your Knowledge Steps 2-5), PP 2.57-59 (In the Lab 1 Steps 2, 4-6), PP 2.59-61 (In the Lab 2 Steps 2-4, 8), PP 2.63 (In the Lab 3 Steps 2-7), PP 2.64-66 (Cases & Places 1-7), PP 3.59 (In the Lab 2 Step 2), PP 3.60-61 (In the Lab 3 Step 3), PP 4.72 (Apply Your Knowledge Step 5), PP 4.74-75 (In the Lab 2 Step 7), PP 4.78 (In the Lab 3 Step 9)
	E. Customize slide templates	PP 4.10-18	PP 4.74 (In the Lab Step 1), PP 4.76-77 (In the Lab 2 Steps 1-4), PP 4.78 (In the Lab 3 Step 6)
	F. Manage a Slide Master	PP 3.21-29, PP 4.13-14	PP 3.57 (Apply Your Knowledge Step 5), PP 3.59 (In the Lab 2 Step 3), PP 3.60 (In the Lab 3 Step 4), PP 4.76 (In the Lab 2 Step 5)
	G. Rehearse timing	PP 4.58-61	PP 4.78-79 (In the Lab 3 Step 11), PP 4.82 (Cases & Places 7)
	H. Rearrange slides	PP 3.51-52	PP 3.59-60 (In the Lab 2 Step 4), PP 3.60-61 (In the Lab 3 Step 6)
	I. Modify slide layout	PP 1.19-21, PP 2.06-07, PP 2.2-23, PP 3.11, PP 3.14, PP 4.18-20, PP 4.33-34, PP 4.38-39, PP 4.44-45	PP 1.68 (Apply Your Knowledge Step 1), PP 1.71 (In the Lab 1 Step 1), PP 1.73 (In the Lab 2 Step 1), PP 1.74 (In the Lab 3 Step 1), PP 1.76-79 (Cases & Places 1-7), PP 2.56 (Apply Your Knowledge Step 1), PP 2.58 (In the Lab 1 Step 1), PP 2.59 (In the Lab 2 Step 1), PP 2.61-62 (In the Lab 3 Step 1), PP 2.64-66 (Cases & Places 1-7), PP 3.57 (Apply Your Knowledge Step 1), PP 3.58 (In the Lab 1 Step 1), PP 3.59 (In the Lab 2 Step 2), PP 3.60-61 (In the Lab 3 Step 3), PP 4.74-75 (In the Lab 1 Steps 4-5), PP 4.76 (In the Lab 2 Step 5)
	J. Add links to a presentation	PP 4.49-51	PP 4.78-79 (In the Lab 3 Step 8), PP 4.80-82 (Cases & Places 1, 5, 7)
V. Printing Presentations	A. Preview and print slides, outlines, handouts, and speaker notes	PP 1.60-61, PP 2.47-51, PP 3.53, PP 4.65-67, PPW 2.09-14	PP 1.68 (Apply Your Knowledge Steps 7-9), PP 1.71 (In the Lab 1 Steps 6-7), PP 1.74 (In the Lab 2 Step 6), PP 1.74 (In the Lab 3 Step 6), PP 1.76-79 (Cases & Places 1-7), PP 2.56-57 (Apply Your Knowledge Step 8), PP 2.57-59 (In the Lab 1 Step 10), PP 2.59-61 (In the Lab 2 Step 10), PP 2.61-63 (In the Lab 3 Step 12), PP 2.64-66 (Cases & Places 1-7), PP 3.57 (Apply Your Knowledge Step 8), PP 3.58 (In the Lab 1 Step 10), PP 3.59-60 (In the Lab 2 Step 8), PP 3.60 (In the Lab 3 Step 10), PP 4.72 (Apply Your Knowledge Step 11), PP 4.74-75 (In the Lab 1 Step 14), PP 4.76 (In the Lab 2 Step 11), PP 4.78-79 (In the Lab 3 Step 14), PP 4.82 (Cases & Places 5), PPW 2.33 (In the Lab 1 Step 2), PPW 2.36 (In the Lab 2 Step 2), PPW 2.39 (In the Lab 3 Step 4)

Table E-2 Microsoft PowerPoint 2002 MOUS Comprehensive Skill Sets, Activities, and Locations in Book

SKILL SET	ACTIVITY	ACTIVITY DEMONSTRATED IN BOOK	ACTIVITY EXERCISE IN BOOK
VI. Working with Data from Other Sources	A. Import Excel charts to slides	PP 4.37-42	PP 4.78-79 (In the Lab 3 Step 6)
	B. Add sound and video to slides	PP 4.27-29	PP 4.72 (Apply Your Knowledge Step 7), PP 4.76 (In the Lab 2 Step 5), PP 4.78 (In the Lab 3 Step 6), PP 4.80-81 (Cases & Places 2-3)
	C. Insert Word tables on slides	PP 4.44-46	PP 4.76-77 (In the Lab 2 Step 4), PP 4.81-82 (Cases & Places 3, 5)
	D. Export a presentation as an outline	PP 4.67-68	PP 4.76 (In the Lab 2 Step 9), PP 4.78-79 (In the Lab 3 Step 14)
VII. Managing and Delivering Presentations	A. Set up slide shows	PP 4.58-61	PP 4.78-79 (In the Lab 3 Step 11), PP 4.82 (Cases & Places 7)
	B. Deliver presentations	PP 1.47-51, PP 2.45-47, PP 4.58-61, PP 4.68-69	PP 1.72-74 (In the Lab 2 Step 5), PP 1.74 (In the Lab 3 Step 4), PP 2.62 (In the Lab 3 Step 11), PP 4.74-75 (In the Lab 1 Step 13), PP 4.76 (In the Lab 2 Step 10), PP 4.78-79 (In the Lab 3 Steps 11, 13), PP 4.82 (Cases & Places 7)
	C. Manage files and folders for presentations	PP 4.29-30	PP 4.72 (Apply Your Knowledge Step 1), PP 4.76 (In the Lab 2 Step 9)
	D. Work with embedded fonts	PP 4.53-55, PPW 2.29	PP 4.72 (Apply Your Knowledge Step 9), PP 4.74-75 (In the Lab 1 Step 12), PP 4.76 (In the Lab 2 Step 9), PP 4.78-79 (In the Lab 3 Step 14), PPW 2.36 (In the Lab 2 Step 4)
	E. Publish presentations to the Web	PPW 1.03-05, Appendix C	PPW 1.12 (In the Lab 1 Steps 2-3, 6), PPW 1.12-13 (In the Lab 2 Steps 2-3, 6)
	F. Use Pack and Go	PPW 2.27-31	PPW 2.33 (In the Lab Step 9), PPW 2.36 (In the Lab 1 Step 4)
VIII. Workgroup Collaboration	A. Set up a review cycle	PPW 2.02-09	PPW 2.39 (In the Lab 3 Step 2)
	B. Review presentation comments	PPW 2.14-23	PPW 2.33-36 (In the Lab 1 Steps 2-6), PPW 2.36-39 (In the Lab 2 Step 2), PPW 2.39 (In the Lab 3 Steps 3-4)
	C. Schedule and deliver presentation broadcasts	PPW 2.24-27	PPW 2.33 (In the Lab 1 Step 7), PPW 2.39 (In the Lab 3 Step 1)
	D. Publish presentations to the Web	PPW 1.03-05, Appendix C	PPW 1.12 (In the Lab 1 Steps 2-3, 6), PPW 1.12-13 (In the Lab 2 Steps 2-3, 6)

Index

Microsoft Office XP
Quick Reference Summary

In the Microsoft Office XP applications, you can accomplish a task in a number of ways. The following four tables (one each for Word, Excel, Access, and PowerPoint) provide a quick reference to each task presented in this textbook. The first column identifies the task. The second column indicates the page number on which the task is discussed in the book. The subsequent four columns list the different ways the task in column one can be carried out. You can invoke the commands listed in the MOUSE, MENU BAR, and SHORTCUT MENU columns using Voice commands.

Table 1 Microsoft Word 2002 Quick Reference Summary

TASK	*PAGE NUMBER*	*MOUSE*	*MENU BAR*	*SHORTCUT MENU*	*KEYBOARD SHORTCUT*
1.5 Line Spacing	WD 2.18		Format | Paragraph | Indents and Spacing tab	Paragraph | Indents and Spacing tab	CTRL+5
ActiveX Control, Format	WD 8.56		Format | Control	Format | Control	
ActiveX Control, Insert	WD 8.52	Desired button on Control Toolbox toolbar			
ActiveX Control, Set Properties	WD 8.54	Properties button on Control Toolbox toolbar		Properties	
ActiveX Control, Write Code	WD 8.59	View Code button on Control Toolbox toolbar		View Code	
Animate Text	WD 6.66		Format | Font | Text Effects tab	Font | Text Effects tab	
AutoCorrect Entry, Create	WD 2.23		Tools | AutoCorrect Options | AutoCorrect tab		
AutoCorrect Options	WD 2.22	AutoCorrect Options button			
AutoShape, Add Text	WD 5.15			Add Text	
AutoShape, Format	WD 5.14	Double-click inside AutoShape	Format | AutoShape	Format AutoShape	
AutoShape, Insert	WD 5.12	AutoShapes button on Drawing toolbar	Insert | Picture | AutoShapes		
AutoText Entry, Create	WD 3.45		Insert | AutoText | New		ALT+F3
AutoText Entry, Insert	WD 3.47		Insert | AutoText		Type entry, then F3
Blank Line Above Paragraph	WD 2.18		Format | Paragraph | Indents and Spacing tab	Paragraph | Indents and Spacing tab	CTRL+0
Bold	WD 1.45	Bold button on Formatting toolbar	Format | Font | Font tab	Font | Font tab	CTRL+B
Bookmark, Add	WD 9.60		Insert | Bookmark		
Bookmark, Go To	WD 9.61	Select Browse Object button on vertical scroll bar	Edit | Go To		CTRL+G
Border, Bottom	WD 3.38	Border button arrow on Formatting toolbar	Format | Borders and Shading | Borders tab		
Border, Page	WD 6.63		Format | Borders and Shading | Page Border tab	Borders and Shading | Page Border tab	
Bulleted List	WD 3.54	Bullets button on Formatting toolbar	Format | Bullets and Numbering | Bulleted tab	Bullets and Numbering | Bulleted tab	* and then space followed by text, then ENTER

Table 1 Microsoft Word 2002 Quick Reference Summary *(continued)*

TASK	PAGE NUMBER	MOUSE	MENU BAR	SHORTCUT MENU	KEYBOARD SHORTCUT
Capitalize Letters	WD 2.18		Format | Font | Font tab	Font | Font tab	CTRL+SHIFT+A
Caption, Add	WD 9.26		Insert | Caption		
Caption, Update Caption Number	WD 9.27			Update Field	F9
Case of Letters	WD 2.18				SHIFT+F3
Center	WD 1.38	Center button on Formatting toolbar	Format | Paragraph | Indents and Spacing tab	Paragraph | Indents and Spacing tab	CTRL+E
Center Text Vertically	WD 4.19		File | Page Setup | Layout tab		
Character Formatting, Remove	WD 2.18		Format | Font | Font tab	Font | Font tab	CTRL+SPACEBAR
Character Style, Apply	WD 4.52	Style box arrow on Formatting toolbar	Format | Styles and Formatting		
Character Style, Create	WD 4.51	Styles and Formatting button on Formatting toolbar	Format | Styles and Formatting		
Chart, Change Chart Type	WD 4.43		Chart | Chart Type	Right-click chart, Chart Type	
Chart, Move Legend	WD 4.42		Select legend, Format | Selected Legend | Placement tab	Right-click legend, Format Legend | Placement tab	
Chart, Resize	WD 4.43	Drag sizing handles			
Chart Table	WD 4.40		Insert | Picture | Chart		
Clip Art, Insert	WD 1.46		Insert | Picture | Clip Art		
Clip Art, Insert from Web	WD 4.16		Insert | Picture | Clip Art		
Close All Open Documents	WD 5.70		SHIFT+File | Close All		
Close Document	WD 1.58	Close button on menu bar	File | Close		CTRL+W
Color Characters	WD 3.28	Font Color button arrow on Formatting toolbar	Format | Font | Font tab	Font | Font tab	
Column Break, Insert	WD 6.31		Insert | Break		CTRL+SHIFT+ENTER
Columns	WD 6.25	Columns button on Standard toolbar	Format | Columns		
Columns, Balance	WD 6.48		Insert | Break		
Columns, Format	WD 6.25		Format | Columns		
Comment, Delete	WD 9.18	Reject Change/Delete Comment button on Reviewing toolbar		Right-click comment reference mark in document window, click Delete Comment	
Comment, Insert	WD 6.69 WD 9.11	New Comment button on Reviewing toolbar	Insert | Comment		
Comment, Modify	WD 9.13	Double-click comment reference mark in document window	View | Comments	Right-click comment reference mark in document window, click Edit Comment	
Comment, Print	WD 9.13		File | Print | Options button		
Comment, Review	WD 9.18	Next button on Reviewing toolbar			
Compare and Merge Documents	WD 6.71 WD 9.21		Tools | Compare and Merge Documents		
Copy (Collect Items)	WD 3.33	Copy button on Standard toolbar	Edit | Copy	Copy	CTRL+C
Cross-Reference, Create	WD 9.29		Insert | Reference | Cross-reference		

Table 1 Microsoft Word 2002 Quick Reference Summary

TASK	PAGE NUMBER	MOUSE	MENU BAR	SHORTCUT MENU	KEYBOARD SHORTCUT
Count Words	WD 2.32	Recount button on Word Count toolbar	Tools | Word Count		
Data Source, Change Designation	WDI 1.05	Open Data Source button on Mail Merge toolbar	Tools | Letters and Mailings | Mail Merge Wizard		
Data Source, Type New	WD 5.23	Mail Merge Recipients button on Mail Merge toolbar	Tools | Letters and Mailings | Mail Merge Wizard		
Date, Insert	WD 3.43		Insert | Date and Time		
Delete (Cut) Text	WD 1.54	Cut button on Standard toolbar	Edit | Cut	Cut	CTRL+X
Demote List Item	WD 3.56	Decrease Indent button on Formatting toolbar			
Diagram, Add Segments	WD 6.51	Insert Shape button on Diagram toolbar		Insert Shape	
Diagram, AutoFormat	WD 6.52	AutoFormat button on Diagram toolbar			
Diagram, Insert	WD 6.49	Insert Diagram or Organization Chart button on Drawing toolbar			
Digitally Sign a File	WD 8.65		Tools | Options | Security tab		
Distribute Columns Evenly	WD 4.57	Distribute Columns Evenly button on Tables and Borders toolbar	Table | AutoFit | Distribute Columns Evenly		
Distribute Rows Evenly	WD 4.57	Distribute Rows Evenly button on Tables and Borders toolbar	Table | AutoFit | Distribute Rows Evenly		
Document Map	WD 9.66	Document Map button on Standard toolbar			
Document Window, Open New	WD 3.27	New Blank Document button on Standard toolbar		File | New | Blank Document	CTRL+N
Double-Space Text	WD 2.09	Line Spacing button on Formatting toolbar	Format | Paragraph | Indents and Spacing tab	Paragraph | Indents and Spacing tab	CTRL+2
Double Strikethrough Characters	WD 4.15		Format | Font | Font tab	Font | Font tab	
Double-Underline	WD 2.18		Format | Font | Font tab	Font | Font tab	CTRL+SHIFT+D
Drawing Canvas, Format	WD 5.18	Double-click edge of drawing canvas	Format | Drawing Canvas	Format Drawing Canvas	
Drawing Canvas, Resize	WD 5.17	Drag sizing handles	Format | Drawing Canvas | Size tab	Format Drawing Canvas | Size tab	
Drawing Object, 3-D Effect	WD 8.21	3-D Style button on Drawing toolbar			
Drawing Object, Fill	WD 7.42	Fill Color button arrow on Drawing toolbar	Format | AutoShape | Colors and Lines tab	Format AutoShape | Colors and Lines tab	
Drawing Object, Line Color	WD 7.43	Line Color button on Drawing toolbar	Format | AutoShape | Colors and Lines tab	Format AutoShape | Colors and Lines tab	
Drawing Object, Order	WD 7.41	Draw button on Drawing toolbar, Order	Format | AutoShape | Layout tab	Order	
Drawing Object, Shadow	WD 7.44	Shadow Style button on Drawing toolbar			
Drop Cap	WD 6.28		Format | Drop Cap		
Edit Field	WD 5.31			Edit Field	
E-Mail Document	WD 2.54	E-mail button on Standard toolbar	File | Send to | Mail Recipient		
E-Mail Document for Review	WD 9.08		File | Send To | Mail Recipient (for Review)		

Table 1 Microsoft Word 2002 Quick Reference Summary *(continued)*

TASK	PAGE NUMBER	MOUSE	MENU BAR	SHORTCUT MENU	KEYBOARD SHORTCUT
Emboss, Characters	WD 4.15		Format | Font | Font tab	Font | Font tab	
Engrave, Characters	WD 4.15		Format | Font | Font tab	Font | Font tab	
Envelope, Address	WD 3.57		Tools | Letters and Mailings | Envelopes and Labels | Envelopes tab		
Erase Table Lines	WD 4.56	Eraser button on Tables and Borders toolbar			
Field Code, Display	WD 5.45		Tools | Options | View tab	Toggle Field Codes	ALT+F9
Field Codes, Print	WD 5.46		Tools | Options | Print tab		
Find	WD 2.49	Select Browse Object button on vertical scroll bar	Edit | Find		CTRL+F
Find and Replace	WD 2.48	Double-click status bar to left of status indicators	Edit | Replace		CTRL+H
First-Line Indent	WD 2.19	Drag First Line Indent marker on ruler	Format | Paragraph | Indents and Spacing tab	Paragraph | Indents and Spacing tab	
Folder, Create	WD 5.21		File | Save As | Create New Folder button		CTRL+F12 | Create New Folder button
Font	WD 1.36	Font box arrow on Formatting toolbar	Format | Font | Font tab	Font | Font tab	CTRL+SHIFT+F
Font Size	WD 1.20	Font Size box arrow on Formatting toolbar	Format | Font | Font tab	Font | Font tab	CTRL+SHIFT+P
Footer	WD 4.31	Switch Between Header and Footer button on Header and Footer toolbar	View | Header and Footer		
Form, Add Help Text	WD 7.35	Double-click form field		Right-click form field, click Properties	
Form, Change Bookmark	WD 8.45	Double-click form field		Right-click form field, click Properties	
Form, Check Box Options	WD 7.25	Double-click check box form field		Right-click form field, click Properties	
Form, Drop-Down Form Field Options	WD 7.23	Double-click drop-down form field		Right-click form field, click Properties	
Form, Insert Check Box	WD 7.27	Check Box Form Field on Forms toolbar			
Form, Insert Drop-Down Form Field	WD 7.21	Drop-Down Form Field button on Forms toolbar			
Form, Insert Table	WD 7.15	Insert Table button on Forms toolbar	Table | Insert | Table		
Form, Insert Text Form Field	WD 7.17	Text Form Field button on Forms toolbar			
Form, Protect	WD 7.48	Protect Form button on Forms toolbar	Tools | Protect Document		
Form, Remove Field Shading	WD 7.37	Form Field Shading button on Forms toolbar			
Form, Save Data Only	WD 7.53		File | Save As | Tools | Save Options		
Form, Text Form Field Options	WD 7.19	Double-click text form field		Right-click form field, click Properties	
Format Characters, Font Dialog Box	WD 4.13		Format | Font| Font tab		

Table 1 Microsoft Word 2002 Quick Reference Summary

TASK	PAGE NUMBER	MOUSE	MENU BAR	SHORTCUT MENU	KEYBOARD SHORTCUT
Format Painter	WD 6.61	Format Painter button on Standard toolbar			
Footnote, Create	WD 2.25		Insert | Reference | Footnote		
Footnote, Delete	WD 2.31	Delete note reference mark in document window			
Footnote, Edit	WD 2.32	Double-click note reference mark in document window	View | Footnotes		
Footnotes to Endnotes, Convert	WD 2.32		Insert | Reference | Footnote		
Formatting, Clear	WD 3.39	Styles and Formatting button on Formatting toolbar or Style box arrow on Formatting toolbar			CTRL+SPACEBAR; CTRL+Q
Formatting Marks	WD 1.24	Show/Hide ¶ button on Standard toolbar	Tools | Options | View tab		CTRL+SHIFT+*
Formatting, Reveal	WD 2.36	Other Task Panes button on open task pane	Format | Reveal Formatting		
Full Menu	WD 1.14	Double-click menu name	Click menu name, wait few seconds		
Go To	WD 2.42	Select Browse Object button on vertical scroll bar	Edit | Go To		CTRL+G
Graph, Exit and Return to Word	WD 4.44	Click anywhere outside chart			
Graphic, Convert to Floating	WD 6.20	Text Wrapping button on Picture toolbar		Format | Picture | Layout tab	Format Picture | Layout tab
Graphic, Flip	WD 6.21	Draw button on Drawing toolbar			
Graphic Objects, Reorder	WD 6.57	Draw button on Drawing toolbar		Order	
GreetingLine Merge Field, Edit	WD 5.32			Edit Greeting Line	
Gridlines, Show	WD 7.17		Table | Show Gridlines		
Gutter Margin	WD 9.63		File | Page Setup | Margins tab		
Hanging Indent, Create	WD 2.37	Drag Hanging Indent marker on ruler	Format | Paragraph | Indents and Spacing tab	Paragraph | Indents and Spacing tab	CTRL+T
Hanging Indent, Remove	WD 2.18	Drag Hanging Indent marker on ruler	Format | Paragraph | Indents and Spacing tab	Paragraph | Indents and Spacing tab	CTRL+SHIFT+T
Header, Different from Previous	WD 4.29		View | Header and Footer		
Header, Display	WD 2.12		View | Header and Footer		
Headers, Alternating	WD 9.61	Page Setup button on Header and Footer toolbar	File | Page Setup | Layout tab		
Help	WD 1.59 and Appendix A	Microsoft Word Help button on Standard toolbar	Help | Microsoft Word Help		F1
Hidden Characters	WD 4.15		Format | Font | Font tab	Font | Font tab	
Highlight Text	WDW 1.09 WD 6.65	Highlight button on Formatting toolbar			
HTML Source	WDW 1.11		View | HTML Source		
Hyperlink, Convert to Regular Text	WD 3.40	AutoCorrect Options button | Undo Hyperlink		Remove Hyperlink	CTRL+Z
Hyperlink, Create	WD 2.40	Insert Hyperlink button on Standard toolbar		Hyperlink	Web address then ENTER or SPACEBAR

Table 1 Microsoft Word 2002 Quick Reference Summary *(continued)*

TASK	PAGE NUMBER	MOUSE	MENU BAR	SHORTCUT MENU	KEYBOARD SHORTCUT
Hyperlink, Edit	WDW 1.10	Insert Hyperlink button on Standard toolbar		Hyperlink	
IF Field, Insert	WD 5.36	Insert Word Field button on Mail Merge toolbar	Insert | Field		
Indent, Decrease	WD 2.18	Decrease Indent button on Formatting toolbar	Format | Paragraph | Indents and Spacing tab	Paragraph | Indents and Spacing tab	CTRL+SHIFT+M
Indent, Increase	WD 2.18	Increase Indent button on Formatting toolbar	Format | Paragraph | Indents and Spacing tab	Paragraph | Indents and Spacing tab	CTRL+M
Index, Build	WD 9.57		Insert | Reference | Index and Tables | Index tab		
Index, Update	WD 9.67			Right-click selected index, click Update Field	Select index, F9
Index Entry, Mark	WD 9.31		Insert | Reference | Index and Tables | Index tab		ALT+SHIFT+X
Insert File	WD 4.24		Insert | File		
Italicize	WD 1.41	Italic button on Formatting toolbar	Format | Font | Font tab	Font | Font tab	CTRL+I
Justify Paragraph	WD 6.26	Justify button on Formatting toolbar	Format | Paragraph | Indents and Spacing tab	Paragraph | Indents and Spacing tab	CTRL+J
Keep Lines Together	WD 4.47		Format | Paragraph | Line and Page Breaks tab	Paragraph | Line and Page Breaks tab	
Language Bar	WD 1.18	Language Indicator button in tray	Tools | Speech		
Last Editing Location	WD 4.25				SHIFT+F5
Leader Characters	WD 3.30		Format | Tabs		
Left-Align	WD 2.17	Align Left button on Formatting toolbar	Format | Paragraph | Indents and Spacing tab	Paragraph | Indents and Spacing tab	CTRL+L
Line Break, Enter	WD 3.21				SHIFT+ENTER
Link Copied Excel Data to Word Chart	WDI 2.08		Edit | Paste Link		
Link Copied Item	WD 6.45		Edit | Paste Special		
Link Excel Worksheet	WDI 2.04		Insert | Object | Create from File tab		
List Item, Demote	WD 5.41	Increase Indent button on Formatting toolbar			SHIFT+TAB
List Item, Promote	WD 5.41	Decrease Indent button on Formatting toolbar			TAB
Macro, Copy	WD 8.68	In Visual Basic Editor, Copy button on Standard toolbar, then Paste button on Standard toolbar	In Visual Basic Editor, Edit | Copy; then Edit | Paste	In Visual Basic Editor, Copy then Paste	In Visual Basic Editor, CTRL+C then CTRL+V
Macro, Delete	WD 8.68		Tools | Macro | Macros		
Macro, Record	WD 8.24	Double-click REC status indicator on status bar	Tools | Macro | Record New Macro		
Macro, Run	WD 8.27	Run Macro button on Standard toolbar in Visual Basic Editor	Tools | Macro | Macros		ALT+F8
Macro, Run on Exit	WD 8.51	Double-click form field		Right-click form field, click Properties	
Macro, View VBA Code	WD 8.38		Tools | Macro | Macros		ALT+F11
Mail Merge, Directory	WD 5.63	Main document setup button on Mail Merge toolbar	Tools | Letters and Mailings | Mail Merge Wizard		
Mail Merge, Envelopes	WD 5.60	Main document setup button on Mail Merge toolbar	Tools | Letters and Mailings | Mail Merge Wizard		

Table 1 Microsoft Word 2002 Quick Reference Summary

TASK	PAGE NUMBER	MOUSE	MENU BAR	SHORTCUT MENU	KEYBOARD SHORTCUT
Mail Merge, Mailing Labels	WD 5.54	Main document setup button on Mail Merge toolbar	Tools | Letters and Mailings | Mail Merge Wizard		
Mail Merge, Select Records	WD 5.49	Mail Merge Recipients button on Mail Merge toolbar			
Mail Merge, Sort Data Records	WD 5.52	Mail Merge Recipients button on Mail Merge toolbar			
Mail Merge Fields, Insert	WD 5.34	Insert Merge Field button on Mail Merge toolbar			
Mail Merge to New Document Window	WD 5.66	Merge to New Document button on Mail Merge toolbar			
Mail Merge to Printer	WD 5.48	Merge to Printer button on Mail Merge toolbar			
Mail Merged Data, View	WD 5.53	View Merged Data button on Mail Merge toolbar			
Mailing Label, Address	WD 3.58		Tools | Letters and Mailings | Envelopes and Labels | Labels tab		
Margins	WD 2.08	In print layout view, drag margin boundary on ruler	File | Page Setup | Margins tab		
Master Document, Open	WD 9.65	Open button on Standard toolbar, then Expand Subdocuments button on Outlining toolbar			
Menus and Toolbars, Reset	WD 2.07	Toolbar Options button on toolbar | Add or Remove Buttons | Customize | Options tab	View | Toolbars | Customize | Options tab		
Merge, Check for Errors	WDI 1.07	Check for Errors button on Mail Merge toolbar			
Merge to E-Mail Addresses	WDI 1.10	Merge to E-mail button on Mail Merge toolbar			
Move Selected Text	WD 2.46	Drag and drop	Edit | Cut; Edit | Paste	Cut; Paste	CTRL+X; CTRL+V
Nonbreaking Hyphen	WD 3.46		Insert | Symbol | Special Characters tab		CTRL+SHIFT+HYPHEN
Nonbreaking Space	WD 3.47		Insert | Symbol | Special Characters tab		ctrl+shift+spacebar
Note Pane, Close	WD 2.31	Close button in note pane			
Numbered List	WD 3.56	Numbering button on Formatting toolbar	Format | Bullets and Numbering | Numbered tab	Bullets and Numbering | Numbered tab	1. and then space followed by text, then ENTER
Office Clipboard Task Pane, Display	WD 3.33	Double-click Office Clipboard icon in tray	Edit | Office Clipboard		
Open Document	WD 1.56	Open button on Standard toolbar	File | Open		CTRL+O
Outline Numbered List	WD 5.38		Format | Bullets and Numbering | Outline Numbered tab	Bullets and Numbering | Outline Numbered tab	
Outline, Characters	WD 4.15		Format | Font | Font tab	Font | Font tab	
Outline, Create	WD 9.37	Outline View button on horizontal scroll bar	View | Outline		
Outline, Demote Heading	WD 9.45	Demote button on Outlining toolbar			TAB
Outline, Demote Heading to Body Text	WD 9.44	Demote to Body Text button on Outlining toolbar			TAB until style is Body Text
Outline, Promote Heading	WD 9.45	Promote button on Outlining toolbar			SHIFT+TAB

Table 1 Microsoft Word 2002 Quick Reference Summary *(continued)*

TASK	PAGE NUMBER	MOUSE	MENU BAR	SHORTCUT MENU	KEYBOARD SHORTCUT
Outline, Show First Line of Paragraphs	WD 9.46	Show First Line Only button on Outlining toolbar			
Page Alignment	WD 4.23		File | Page Setup | Layout tab		
Page Break	WD 2.35		Insert | Break		CTRL+ENTER
Page Numbers, Insert	WD 2.14	Insert Page Number button on Header and Footer toolbar	Insert | Page Numbers		
Page Numbers, Modify	WD 4.30	Format Page Number button on Header and Footer toolbar	Insert | Page Numbers | Format button		
Page Orientation	WD 5.66		File | Page Setup | Paper Size tab		
Paragraph, Change Format	WD 5.19	Click link in Reveal Formatting task pane	Format | Paragraph | Indents and Spacing tab	Paragraph | Indents and Spacing tab	
Paragraph Formatting, Remove	WD 2.18		Format | Paragraph | Indents and Spacing tab	Paragraph | Indents and Spacing tab	CTRL+Q
Paragraph Style, Apply	WD 5.42	Style box arrow on Formatting toolbar	Format | Styles and Formatting		
Password-Protect File	WD 9.34		File | Save As | Tools | Security Options		
Paste	WD 3.35	Paste button on Standard toolbar or click icon in Office Clipboard gallery in Office Clipboard task pane	Edit | Paste	Paste	CTRL+V
Paste Options, Display Menu	WD 2.47	Paste Options button			
Picture Bullets	WD 4.48		Format | Bullets and Numbering | Bulleted tab	Bullets and Numbering | Bulleted tab	
Print Document	WD 1.54	Print button on Standard toolbar	File | Print		CTRL+P
Print Preview	WD 3.25	Print Preview button on Standard toolbar	File | Print Preview		CTRL+F2
Promote List Item	WD 3.56	Increase Indent button on Formatting toolbar			
Propagate Labels	WD 5.58	Propagate Labels button on Mail Merge toolbar	Tools | Letters and Mailings | Mail Wizard		
Quit Word	WD 1.55	Close button on title bar	File | Exit		ALT+F4
Rectangle, Draw	WD 7.39	Rectangle button on Drawing toolbar			
Redo Action	WD 1.39	Redo button on Standard toolbar	Edit | Redo		
Repeat Command	WD 1.39		Edit | Repeat		
Resize Graphic	WD 1.51	Drag sizing handle	Format | Picture | Size tab	Format Picture | Size tab	
Resize Graphic, Format Picture Dialog Box	WD 4.17	Double-click graphic	Format | Picture | Picture tab	Format Picture | Picture tab	
Restore Graphic	WD 1.53	Format Picture button on Picture toolbar	Format | Picture | Size tab	Format Picture | Size tab	
Resume Wizard	WD 3.07		File | New | General Templates | Other Documents tab		
Reveal Formatting	WD 4.66		Format | Reveal Formatting		
Reviewer Initials, Change	WD 9.13		Tools | Options | User Information tab		
Right-Align	WD 1.37	Align Right button on Formatting toolbar	Format | Paragraph | Indents and Spacing tab	Paragraph | Indents and Spacing tab	CTRL+R
Ruler, Show or Hide	WD 1.13		View | Ruler		

Table 1 Microsoft Word 2002 Quick Reference Summary

TASK	PAGE NUMBER	MOUSE	MENU BAR	SHORTCUT MENU	KEYBOARD SHORTCUT
Save, All Open Documents	WD 5.70		SHIFT + File | Save All		
Save as Web Page	WDW 1.03		File | Save as Web Page		
Save Document - New Name	WD 1.54		File | Save As		F12
Save Document - Same Name	WD 1.53	Save button on Standard toolbar	File | Save		CTRL+S
Save New Document	WD 1.30	Save button on Standard toolbar	File | Save		CTRL+S
Save Version	WD 9.16		File | Versions		
Search for File	WD 6.67	Search button on Standard toolbar			
Section Break, Continuous	WD 6.24		Insert | Break		
Section Break, Next Page	WD 4.22		Insert | Break		
Security Level	WD 8.10		Tools | Macro | Security | Security Level tab		
Select Document	WD 2.45	Point to left and triple-click	Edit | Select All		CTRL+A
Select Graphic	WD 1.50	Click graphic			
Select Group of Words	WD 1.44	Drag through words			CTRL+SHIFT+RIGHT ARROW
Select Line	WD 1.40	Point to left of line and click			SHIFT+DOWN ARROW
Select Multiple Paragraphs	WD 1.34	Point to left of first paragraph and drag down			CTRL+SHIFT+DOWN ARROW
Select Nonadjacent Text	WD 4.37				CTRL, while selecting additional text
Select Paragraph	WD 2.45	Triple-click paragraph			
Select Sentence	WD 2.45	CTRL+click sentence			CTRL+SHIFT+RIGHT ARROW
Select Word	WD 1.42	Double-click word			CTRL+SHIFT+RIGHT ARROW
Shade Paragraph	WD 6.40	Shading Color button on Tables and Borders toolbar	Format | Borders and Shading | Shading tab	Borders and Shading | Shading tab	
Shadow, on Characters	WD 4.15		Format | Font | Font tab	Font | Font tab	
Single-Space	WD 4.58	Line Spacing button arrow on Formatting toolbar	Format | Paragraph | Indents and Spacing tab	Paragraph | Indents and Spacing tab	CTRL+1
Small Uppercase Letters	WD 2.18		Format | Font | Font tab	Font | Font tab	CTRL+SHIFT+K
Smart Tag Actions, Display Menu	WD 3.59	Point to smart tag indicator, click Smart Tag Actions button			
Sort Paragraphs	WD 2.41		Table | Sort		
Spelling and Grammar Check At Once	WD 2.51	Spelling and Grammar button on Standard toolbar	Tools | Spelling and Grammar	Spelling	F7
Spelling Check as You Type	WD 1.28	Double-click Spelling and Grammar Status icon on status bar		Right-click flagged word, click correct word on shortcut menu	
Strikethrough, characters	WD 4.15		Format | Font | Font tab	Font | Font tab	
Style, Create	WD 8.17	Styles and Formatting button on Formatting toolbar	Format | Styles and Formatting		
Style, Modify	WD 2.28	Styles and Formatting button on Formatting toolbar	Format | Styles and Formatting		
Styles and Formatting Task Pane, Display	WD 3.19	Styles and Formatting button on Formatting toolbar	View | Task Pane		
Subdocument, Break Connection	WD 9.46	Remove Subdocument icon on Outlining toolbar			

Table 1 Microsoft Word 2002 Quick Reference Summary *(continued)*

TASK	PAGE NUMBER	MOUSE	MENU BAR	SHORTCUT MENU	KEYBOARD SHORTCUT
Subdocument, Create	WD 9.43	Create Subdocument button on Outlining toolbar			
Subdocument, Delete	WD 9.46	Click subdocument icon, press DELETE			
Subdocument, Insert	WD 9.40	Insert Subdocument button on Outlining toolbar			
Subdocuments, Collapse	WD 9.42	Collapse Subdocuments button on Outlining toolbar			
Subdocuments, Expand	WD 9.42	Expand Subdocuments button on Outlining toolbar			
Subscript	WD 2.18		Format | Font | Font tab	Font | Font tab	CTRL+=
Superscript	WD 2.18		Format | Font | Font tab	Font | Font tab	CTRL+SHIFT+PLUS SIGN
Switch to Open Document	WD 3.32	Program button on taskbar	Window | document name		
Symbol, Insert	WD 6.17		Insert | Symbol	ALT+0 (zero) then ANSI code on numeric keypad	
Synonym	WD 2.50		Tools | Language | Thesaurus	Synonyms | desired word	SHIFT+F7
Tab Stops, Set	WD 3.31	Click location on ruler	Format | Tabs		
Table, Add a Row	WD 4.32	Insert Table button arrow on Tables and Borders toolbar	Table | Insert | Rows Above or Rows Below	Right-click selected row, Insert Rows	TAB in lower-right cell
Table, Adjust Row Height	WD 4.61	Drag row border	Table | Table Properties | Row tab	Table Properties | Row tab	
Table, Align Cell Contents	WD 4.62	Align button arrow on Tables and Borders toolbar	Table | Table Properties | Cell tab	Table Properties | Celll tab	
Table, AutoFormat	WD 3.53 WD 4.35	Table AutoFormat button on Tables and Borders toolbar	Table | Table AutoFormat		
Table, Convert Text	WD 5.65		Table | Convert | Text to Table		
Table, Draw	WD 4.54	Tables and Borders button on Standard toolbar	Table | Draw Table		
Table, Insert Empty	WD 3.49	Insert Table button on Standard toolbar	Table | Insert | Table		
Table, Insert Row	WD 3.16		Table | Insert | Rows Above/Below	Right-click selected row; Insert Rows	
Table, Resize Column	WD 3.54	Drag column boundary	Table | Table Properties | Column tab	Table Properties | Column tab	
Table, Resize Column to Contents	WD 3.52	Double-click column boundary	Table | AutoFit | AutoFit to Contents	AutoFit | AutoFit to Contents	
Table, Right-Align Cell Contents	WD 4.36	Align Right button on Formatting toolbar	Format | Paragraph | Indents and Spacing tab		CTRL+R
Table, Rotate Cell Text	WD 4.60	Change Text Direction button on Tables and Borders toolbar	Format | Text Direction	Text Direction	
Table, Select	WD 3.53	Click table move handle	Table | Select | Table		ALT+5 (on numeric keypad)
Table, Select Cell	WD 3.53	Click left edge of cell			Press TAB
Table, Select Column	WD 3.53	Click top border of column			
Table, Select Multiple Cells	WD 3.53	Drag through cells			
Table, Select Row	WD 3.53	Click to left of row			
Table, Shade Cells	WD 4.62	Shading Color button arrow on Tables and Borders toolbar	Format | Borders and Shading | Shading tab	Borders and Shading | Shading tab	

Table 1 Microsoft Word 2002 Quick Reference Summary

TASK	PAGE NUMBER	MOUSE	MENU BAR	SHORTCUT MENU	KEYBOARD SHORTCUT
Table, Sort	WD 5.68	Sort Ascending button on Tables and Borders toolbar	Table | Sort		
Table, Sum a Column	WD 4.34	AutoSum button on Tables and Borders toolbar	Table | Formula		
Table of Contents, Create	WD 9.58		Insert | Reference | Index and Tables | Table of Contents tab		
Table of Contents, Update	WD 9.67			Right-click selected table of contents, click Update Field	Select table of contents, F9
Table of Figures, Create	WD 9.55		Insert | Reference | Index and Tables | Table of Figures tab		
Task Pane, Close	WD 1.10	Close button on task pane	View | Task Pane		
Task Pane, Display Different	WD 1.49	Other Task Panes button on task pane			
Template, Create	WD 7.09		File | New | General Templates		
Template, Open	WD 3.41		File | New | General Templates		
Template, Use in Mail Merge	WD 5.08		Tools | Letters and Mailings | Mail Merge Wizard		
Text Box, Convert to a Frame	WD 9.28	Double-click text box	Format | Text Box	Format Text Box	
Text Box, Format	WD 6.38	Double-click text box	Format | Text Box	Format Text Box	
Text Box, Insert	WD 6.36	Text Box button on Drawing toolbar	Insert | Text Box		
Toolbar, Customize	WD 8.28		Tools | Customize	Customize	
Toolbar, Dock	WD 2.13	Drag toolbar to dock			
Toolbar, Float	WD 2.13	Double-click between two buttons or boxes on toolbar			
Toolbar, Show Entire	WD 1.16	Double-click move handle on toolbar			
Track Changes	WD 9.14	Double-click TRK status indicator on status bar	Tools | Track Changes		CTRL+SHIFT+E
Track Changes, Stop	WD 9.16	Double-click TRK status indicator on status bar	Tools | Track Changes		CTRL+SHIFT+E
Tracked Changes, Display	WD 9.14	Display for Review button arrow on Reviewing toolbar	View | Markup		
Tracked Changes, Review	WD 9.18	Click Next button on Reviewing toolbar		Right-click tracked change	
Underline	WD 1.43	Underline button on Formatting toolbar	Format | Font | Font tab	Font | Font tab	CTRL+U
Underline, in color	WD 7.31		Format | Font	Font	
Underline Words, not Spaces	WD 2.18		Format | Font | Font tab	Font | Font tab	CTRL+SHIFT+W
Undo Command or Action	WD 1.39	Undo button on Standard toolbar	Edit | Undo		CTRL+Z
Unprotect Document	WD 8.08	Protect Form button on Forms toolbar	Tools | Unprotect Document		
Vertical Rule	WD 6.34		Format | Borders and Shading | Borders tab		
Visual Basic Editor, Insert Procedure	WD 8.47	Insert UserForm button arrow on Standard toolbar	Insert | Procedure		

Table 1 Microsoft Word 2002 Quick Reference Summary *(continued)*

TASK	PAGE NUMBER	MOUSE	MENU BAR	SHORTCUT MENU	KEYBOARD SHORTCUT
Visual Basic Editor, Quit	WD 8.43	Close button on title bar	File | Close and Return to Microsoft Word		ALT+Q
Watermark	WD 4.64		Format | Background | Printed Watermark		
Web Page Frame, Resize	WDW 1.09	Drag frame border	Format | Frames | Frame Properties | Frame tab		
Web Page, View	WDW 1.11		File | Web Page Preview		
Web Page Wizard	WDW 1.05		File | New | General Templates | Web Pages tab		
White Space, Hide or Show	WD 3.15	Hide or Show White Space button	Tools | Options | View tab		
Widow/Orphan Setting	WD 9.33		Format | Paragraph	Paragraph	
WordArt Drawing Object, Format	WD 6.11	Format WordArt button on WordArt toolbar	Format | WordArt	Format WordArt	
WordArt Drawing Object, Insert	WD 6.09	Insert WordArt button on Drawing toolbar	Insert | Picture | WordArt		
WordArt Drawing Object, Shape	WD 6.13	WordArt Shape button on WordArt toolbar			
Wrap Text Around Graphic	WD 6.59	Text Wrapping button Picture or Diagram toolbar	Format | Picture or Diagram | Layout tab	Format Picture or Format Diagram | Layout tab	
Zoom Page Width	WD 1.19	Zoom box arrow on Formatting toolbar	View | Zoom		
Zoom Text Width	WD 3.18	Zoom box arrow on Formatting toolbar	View | Zoom		
Zoom Whole Page	WD 6.32	Zoom box arrow on Formatting toolbar	View | Zoom		

Table 2 Microsoft Excel 2002 Quick Reference Summary

TASK	PAGE NUMBER	MOUSE	MENU BAR	SHORTCUT MENU	KEYBOARD SHORTCUT
Advanced Filter	E 5.41		Data | Filter | Advanced Filter		ALT+D | F | A
Arrow, Add	E 6.44	Arrow button on Drawing toolbar			
AutoFilter	E 5.35		Data | Filter | AutoFilter		ALT+D | F | F
AutoFormat	E 1.33		Format | AutoFormat		ALT+O | A
AutoSum	E 1.23	AutoSum button on Standard toolbar	Insert | Function		ALT+= (equal)
Bold	E 1.29	Bold button on Formatting toolbar	Format | Cells | Font tab	Format Cells | Font tab	CTRL+B
Borders	E 2.30	Borders button on Formatting toolbar	Format | Cells | Border tab	Format Cells | Border tab	CTRL+1 | B
Center	E 2.32	Center button on Formatting toolbar	Format | Cells | Alignment tab	Format Cells | Alignment tab	CTRL+1 | A
Center Across Columns	E 1.32	Merge and Center button on Formatting toolbar	Format | Cells | Alignment tab	Format Cells | Alignment tab	CTRL+1 | A
Chart	E 1.37	Chart Wizard button on Standard toolbar	Insert | Chart		F11
Clear Cell	E 1.51	Drag fill handle back	Edit | Clear | All	Clear Contents	DELETE

Table 2 Microsoft Excel 2002 Quick Reference Summary *(continued)*

TASK	PAGE NUMBER	MOUSE	MENU BAR	SHORTCUT MENU	KEYBOARD SHORTCUT
Close All Files	E 6.67		SHIFT+File | Close All		SHIFT+ALT+F | C
Close All Workbooks	E 1.45		SHIFT+File | Close All		SHIFT+ALT+F | C
Close Workbook	E 1.45	Close button on menu bar or workbook Control-menu icon	File | Close		CTRL+W
Color Background	E 2.30	Fill Color button on Formatting toolbar	Format | Cells | Patterns tab	Format Cells | Patterns tab	CTRL+1 | P
Color Tab	E 3.55			Tab Color	
Column Width	E 2.44	Drag column heading boundary	Format | Column | Width	Column Width	ALT+O | C | W
Comma Style Format	E 2.34	Comma Style button on Formatting toolbar	Format | Cells | Number tab | Accounting	Format Cells | Number tab | Accounting	CTRL+1 | N
Command Button	E 7.28	Command Button button on Control Toolbox toolbar			
Comment	E 6.46		Insert | Comment	Insert Comment	ALT+I | M
Conditional Formatting	E 2.40		Format | Conditional Formatting		ALT+O | D
Copy and Paste	E 3.14	Copy button and Paste button on Standard toolbar	Edit | Copy; Edit | Paste	Copy to copy; Paste to paste	CTRL+C; CTRL+V
Custom Formats	E 6.15		Format | Cells | Number tab | Custom	Format Cells | Number tab | Custom	ALT+O | E | N
Currency Style Format	E 2.34	Currency Style button on Formatting toolbar	Format | Cells | Number tab | Currency	Format Cells | Number | Currency	CTRL+1 | N
Cut	E 3.16	Cut button on Standard toolbar	Edit | Cut	Cut	CTRL+X
Data Form	E 5.09		Data | Form		ALT+D | O
Data Table	E 4.18		Data | Table		ALT+D | T
Data Validation, Cell	E 8.16		Data | Validation		ALT+D | L
Date	E 3.22	Insert Function box on formula bar	Insert | Function		CTRL+SEMICOLON
Decimal Place Decrease	E 2.35	Decrease Decimal button on Formatting toolbar	Format | Cells | Number tab | Currency	Format Cells | Number tab | Currency	CTRL+1 | N
Decimal Place Increase	E 2.35	Increase Decimal button on Formatting toolbar	Format | Cells | Number tab | Currency	Format Cells | Number tab | Currency	CTRL+1 | N
Delete Rows or Columns	E 3.18		Edit | Delete	Delete	
Draft Quality	E 4.45		File | Page Setup | Sheet tab		ALT+F | U | S
Drop Shadow	E 3.40	Shadow Style button on Drawing toolbar			
Embed a Clip Art	E 4.39		Insert | Picture | Clip Art		ALT+I | P | C
E-Mail from Excel	E 2.63	E-mail button on Standard toolbar	File | Send To | Mail Recipient		ALT+F | D | A
File Passwords, Saving	E 8.32		File | Save As | Tools | General Options		ALT+F | A | ALT+L | G
Find	E 6.58		Edit | Find		CTRL+F
Fit to Print	E 2.56		File | Page Setup | Page tab		ALT+F | U | P
Folder, New	EW 1.06		File | Save As		ALT+F | A
Font Color	E 1.31	Font Color button on Formatting toolbar	Format | Cells | Font tab	Format Cells | Font tab	CTRL+1 | F
Font Size	E 1.30	Font Size box arrow on Formatting toolbar	Format | Cells | Font tab	Format Cells | Font tab	CTRL+1 | F
Font Type	E 2.28	Font box arrow on Formatting toolbar	Format | Cells | Font tab	Format Cells | Font tab	CTRL+1 | F
Footer	E 6.48		File | Page Setup | Header/Footer tab		ALT+F | U | H

Table 2 Microsoft Excel 2002 Quick Reference Summary *(continued)*

TASK	PAGE NUMBER	MOUSE	MENU BAR	SHORTCUT MENU	KEYBOARD SHORTCUT
Formula Auditing Toolbar, Display	E 8.10	Right-click any toolbar, click Formula Auditing	Tools | Formula Auditing | Show Formula Auditing Toolbar		ALT+T | U | S
Formula Checker	E 4.52		Tools | Error Checking		ALT+T | K
Formula Palette	E 2.19	Insert Function box on formula bar	Insert | Function		CTRL+A after you type function name
Formulas Version	E 2.56		Tools | Options | View tab | Formulas		CTRL+ACCENT MARK
Freeze Worksheet Titles	E 3.20		Window | Freeze Panes		ALT+W | F
Full Screen	E 1.12		View | Full Screen		ALT+V | U
Function	E 2.20	Insert Function box on formula bar	Insert | Function		SHIFT+F3
Go To	E 1.36	Click cell	Edit | Go To		F5
Goal Seek	E 3.63		Tools | Goal Seek		ALT+T | G
Gridlines	E 4.45		File | Page Setup | Sheet tab		ALT+F | U | S
Header	E 6.48		File | Page Setup | Header/Footer tab		ALT+F | U | H
Help	E 1.52 and Appendix A	Microsoft Excel Help button on Standard toolbar	Help | Microsoft Excel Help		F1
Hide Column	E 2.46	Drag column heading boundary	Format | Column | Hide	Hide	CTRL+0 (zero) to hide CTRL+SHIFT+ RIGHT PARENTHESIS to display
Hide Row	E 2.48	Drag row heading boundary	Format | Row | Hide	Hide	CTRL+9 to hide CTRL+SHIFT+ LEFT PARENTHESIS to display
Hyperlink	E 4.39	Insert Hyperlink on Standard toolbar	Insert | Hyperlink	Hyperlink	CTRL+K
In-Cell Editing	E 1.49	Double-click cell			F2
Import Data from Access Table	E 9.14		Data | Get External Data | New Database Query		ALT+D | D | N
Import Data from Text File	E 9.09		Data | Get External Data | Import Text File		ALT+D | D | T
Import Data from Web Page	E 9.18		Data | Get External Data | New Web Query		ALT+D | D | W
Import Data from Spreadsheet XML	E 9.23		Data | Get External Data | New Web Query		ALT+D | D | W
Insert Rows or Columns	E 3.16		Insert | Rows or Insert | Columns	Insert	ALT+I | R or C
Italicize	E 3.42	Italicize button on Formatting toolbar	Format | Cells | Font tab	Format Cells | Font tab	CTRL+I
Language Bar	E 1.16	Language Indicator button in tray	Tools | Speech | Speech Recognition		ALT+T | H | H
Link	EI 1.04		Edit | Paste Special		ALT+E | S
Link Update	E 6.67		Edit | Links		ALT+E | K
Macro, Execute	E 7.15	Run Macro button on Visual Basic toolbar	Tools | Macro | Macros		ALT+F8
Macro, Record	E 7.11		Tools | Macro | Record New Macro		ALT+T | M | R
Macro, View Code	E 7.17		Tools | Macro | Macros | Edit		ALT+F8
Margins	E 6.48		File | Page Setup | Margins		ALT+F | U | M
Menu, Customize	E 7.23		Tools | Customize | Commands tab	Customize | Commands tab	ALT+T | C | C
Merge Cells	E 1.32	Merge and Center button on Formatting toolbar	Format | Cells | Alignment tab	Format Cells | Font tab | Alignment tab	ALT+O | E | A
Move	E 3.16	Point to border and drag	Edit | Cut; Edit | Paste	Cut; Paste	CTRL+X; CTRL+V
Name Cells	E 1.36, E 4.12	Click Name box in formula bar and type name	Insert | Name | Create or Insert | Name | Define		ALT+I | N | D

Table 2 Microsoft Excel 2002 Quick Reference Summary

TASK	PAGE NUMBER	MOUSE	MENU BAR	SHORTCUT MENU	KEYBOARD SHORTCUT
Name Cells, Redefine	E 5.18		Insert | Name | Define		ALT+I | N | D
New Workbook	E 1.52	New button on Standard toolbar	File | New		CTRL+N
Open Workbook	E 1.46	Open button on Standard toolbar	File | Open		CTRL+O
Outline a Range	E 4.09	Borders button on Formatting toolbar	Format | Cells | Border tab	Format Cells | Border tab	CTRL+1 | B
Outline a Worksheet	E 5.30		Data | Group and Outline		ALT+D | G | A
Page Break	E 6.55		Insert | Page Break		ALT+I | B
Page Break, Remove	E 6.55		Insert | Remove Page Break		ALT+I | B
Percent Style Format	E 2.39	Percent Style button on Formatting toolbar	Format | Cells | Number tab | Percentage	Format Cells | Number tab | Percentage	CTRL+1 | N
PivotChart, Add Data to	E 9.43	Drag button from PivotTable toolbar to PivotChart			
PivotChart, Change View	E 9.48	Click interactive buttons on PivotChart			
PivotChart, Create	E 9.40		Data | PivotTable and PivotChart Report		ALT+D | P
PivotChart, Format	E 9.45	Chart Wizard button on PivotTable toolbar	Chart | Chart Type	Chart Type	ALT+C | T
PivotTable, Change View	E 9.54	Drag buttons to different locations on PivotTable			
PivotTable, Format	E 9.51	Format Report button on PivotTable toolbar	Format | AutoFormat	Format Report	ALT+O | A
PivotTable List, Add Fields	EW 2.12	Drag field from PivotTable Field List window			
PivotTable List, Add Summary Totals	EW 2.08	AutoCalc button on toolbar in browser			
PivotTable List, Change View	EW 2.10	Drag data fields to Row Field area in browser			
PivotTable List, Create	EW 2.03		File | Save as Web Page		ALT+F | G
PivotTable List, Filter	EW 2.06	Click field drop-down arrow and remove check marks			
PivotTable List, Remove Field	EW 2.12		Remove Field		
PivotTable List, Sort	EW 2.09	Sort Ascending button or Sort Descending button on toolbar in browser			
Preview Worksheet	E 2.51	Print Preview button on Standard toolbar	File | Print Preview		ALT+F | V
Properties, Set	E 7.31	Properties button on Control Toolbox toolbar			
Print Area, Clear	E 4.46		File | Print Area | Clear Print Area		ALT+F | T | C
Print Area, Set	E 4.45		File | Print Area | Set Print Area		ALT+F | T | S
Print Row and Column Headings	E 4.45		File | Page Setup | Sheet tab		ALT+F | U | S
Print Row and Column Titles	E 4.45		File | Page Setup | Sheet tab		ALT+F | U | S
Print Worksheet	E 2.51	Print button on Standard toolbar	File | Print		CTRL+P
Protect Worksheet	E 4.49		Tools | Protection | Protect Sheet		ALT+T | P | P
Quit Excel	E 1.45	Close button on title bar	File | Exit		ALT+F4

Table 2 Microsoft Excel 2002 Quick Reference Summary *(continued)*

TASK	PAGE NUMBER	MOUSE	MENU BAR	SHORTCUT MENU	KEYBOARD SHORTCUT
Range Finder	E 2.25	Double-click cell			
Redo	E 1.51	Redo button on Standard toolbar	Edit | Redo		ALT+E | R
Remove Precedent Arrows, Audit	E 8.12	Remove Precedent Arrows button on Auditing toolbar			
Remove Splits	E 3.61	Double-click split bar	Window | Split		ALT+W | S
Rename Sheet Tab	E 2.62	Double-click sheet tab		Rename	
Replace	E 6.60		Edit | Replace		CTRL+H
Rotate Text	E 3.08		Format | Cells | Alignment tab	Format Cells | Alignment tab	ALT+O | E | A
Route Workbook	E 9.32		File | Send To | Routing Recipient		ALT+F | D | R
Row Height	E 2.47	Drag row heading boundary	Format | Row | Height	Row Height	ALT+O | R | E
Save as Web Page	EW 1.06		File | Save as Web Page		ALT+F | G
Save Workbook – New Name	E 1.41		File | Save As		ALT+F | A
Save Workbook – Same Name	E 2.50	Save button on Standard toolbar	File | Save		CTRL+S
Scenario, Add	E 8.35	Add button in Scenario Manager dialog box	Tools | Scenarios		ALT+T | E | ALT+A
Scenario, Show	E 8.46	Show button in Scenario Manager dialog box	Tools | Scenarios		ALT+T | E | ALT+S
Scenario Manager	E 8.35		Tools | Scenarios		ALT+T | E
Scenario PivotTable	E 8.51	Summary button in Scenario Manager dialog box, choose Scenario PivotTable	Tools | Scenarios		ALT+T | E | ALT+U | ALT+P
Scenario Summary	E 8.49	Summary button in Scenario Manager dialog box, choose Scenario summary	Tools | Scenarios		ALT+T | E | ALT+U | ALT+S
Select All of Worksheet	E 1.52	Select All button on worksheet			CTRL+A
Select Cell	E 1.16	Click cell			Use arrow keys
Select Multiple Sheets	E 3.57	CTRL+click tab or SHIFT+click tab		Select All Sheets	
Search for File	E 6.62	Click Search button on Standard toolbar	File | Search		ALT+F | H
Series	E 3.08	Drag fill handle	Edit | Fill | Series		ALT+E | I | S
Shortcut Menu	E 2.28	Right-click object			SHIFT+F10
Solver	E 8.23		Tools | Solver		ALT+T | V
Solver, Solve Problem	E 8.25	Solve button in Solver Parameters dialog box*	Tools | Solver		ALT+T | V | ALT+S
Sort	E 5.22	Click Sort Ascending or Sort Descending button on Standard toolbar	Data | Sort		ALT+D | S
Spell Check	E 2.48	Spelling button on Standard toolbar	Tools | Spelling		F7
Split Cell	E 1.32	Merge and Center button on Formatting toolbar	Format | Cells | Alignment tab	Format Cells | Alignment tab	ALT+O | E | A
Split Window into Panes	E 3.60	Drag vertical or horizontal split box	Window | Split		ALT+W | S
Stock Quotes	E 2.58		Data | Import External Data | Import Data		ALT+D | D | D
Style, Add	E 6.18		Format | Style | Add button		ALT+O | S
Style, Apply	E 6.20		Format | Style		ALT+O | S
Subtotals	E 5.27		Data | Subtotals		ALT+D | B

Table 2 Microsoft Excel 2002 Quick Reference Summary

TASK	PAGE NUMBER	MOUSE	MENU BAR	SHORTCUT MENU	KEYBOARD SHORTCUT
Subtotals, Remove	E 5.31		Data | Subtotals | Remove All button		ALT+D | B | R
Switch Summary Functions	E 9.53	Field Settings button on PivotTable toolbar		Field Settings	
Task Pane	E 1.08		View | Task Pane		ALT+V | K
Text Box, Add	E 6.43	Text Box button on Drawing toolbar			
Toolbar, Customize	E 7.19		Tools | Customize | Commands tab	Customize | Commands tab	ALT+T | C | C
Toolbar, Dock	E 3.38	Drag toolbar to dock			
Toolbar, Reset	Appendix D	Toolbar Options, Add or Remove Buttons, Customize, Toolbars		Customize | Toolbars	ALT+V | T | C | B
Toolbar, Show Entire	E 1.14	Double-click move handle			
Toolbar, Show or Hide	E 3.38	Right-click toolbar, click toolbar name	View | Toolbars		ALT+V | T
Track Changes, Disable	E 9.38		Tools | Track Changes | Highlight Changes | remove check mark		ALT+T | T | H
Track Changes, Enable	E 9.30		Tools | Track Changes | Highlight Changes		ALT+T | T | H
Track Changes, Review	E 9.35	Point to blue triangle	Tools | Track Changes | Accept or Reject Changes		ALT+T | T | A
Trendline, Create	E 9.58		Chart | Add Trendline		ALT+C | R
Underline	E 3.42	Underline button on Formatting toolbar	Format | Cells | Font tab	Format Cells | Font tab	CTRL+U
Undo	E 1.52	Undo button on Standard toolbar	Edit | Undo		CTRL+Z
Unfreeze Worksheet Titles	E 3.32		Windows | Unfreeze Panes		ALT+W | F
Unhide Column	E 2.46	Drag column heading boundary to left	Format | Column | Unhide	Unhide	ALT+O | C | U
Unhide Row	E 2.48	Drag row heading boundary down	Format | Row | Unhide	Unhide	ALT+O | R | U
Unlock Cells	E 4.49		Format | Cells | Protection tab	Format Cells | Protection tab	CTRL+1 | SHIFT+P
Unprotect Worksheet	E 4.51		Tools | Protection | Unprotect Sheet		ALT+T | P | P
Visual Basic Editor	E 7.34	View Code button on Control Toolbox toolbar	Tools | Macro | Visual Basic Editor	View Code	ALT+F11
Web Page Preview	EW 1.03-04		File | Web Page Preview		ALT+F | B
WordArt	E 6.39	Insert WordArt button on Drawing toolbar	Insert | Picture | WordArt		ALT+I | P | W
Workbook Properties	E 8.54		File | Properties		ALT+F | I
Workspace File	E 6.64		File | Save Workspace		ALT+F | W
Zoom	E 3.58	Zoom box on Standard toolbar	View | Zoom		ALT+V | Z

Table 3 Microsoft Access 2002 Quick Reference Summary

TASK	PAGE NUMBER	MOUSE	MENU BAR	SHORTCUT MENU	KEYBOARD SHORTCUT
Add Chart	A 8.83	Chart tool	Insert | Chart		
Add Command Button	A 8.9	Command Button tool			
Add Combo Box	A 4.41, A 4.43	Combo Box tool			
Add Date	A 7.39		Insert | Date and Time		
Add Field	A 3.17	Insert Rows button	Insert | Rows	Insert Rows	INSERT
Add Fields Using Field List	A 7.27	Drag field			
Add Group of Records	A 3.25	Query Type button arrow | Append Query	Query | Append Query	Query Type | Append Query	
Add Label	A 4.46	Label tool			
Add Objects	A 7.45	Unbound Object Frame tool	Insert | Object		
Add Page Number	A 7.40		Insert | Page Number		
Add Record	A 1.21, A 1.27	New Record button	Insert | New Record		
Add Rectangle	A 8.17	Rectangle tool			
Add Subform	A 8.79	Subform / Subreport tool			
Add Subreport	A 7.30	Subform / Subreport tool			
Add Switchboard Item	A 6.46	New button			
Add Switchboard Page	A 6.44	New button			
Add Table to Query	A 2.30	Show Table button	Query | Show Table	Show Table	
Add Text Box	A 4.38	Text Box tool			
Apply Filter	A 3.13	Filter By Selection or Filter By Form button	Records | Filter		
Calculate Statistics	A 2.36	Totals button	View | Totals	Totals	
Change Field Properties in Query	A 7.15	Properties button	View | Properties	Properties	
Change Group of Records	A 3.23	Query Type button arrow | Update Query	Query | Update Query	Query Type | Update Query	
Change Join Properties in Query	A 7.14		View | Join Properties	Join Properties	
Change Margins	A 7.45		File | Page Setup | Margins tab		
Change Property	A 4.16	Properties button	View | Properties	Properties	F4
Change Referential Integrity Options	A 9.16		Relationships | Edit Relationship	Edit Relationship	
Change Tab Order	A 6.28		View | Tab Order	Tab Order	
Clear Query	A 2.15		Edit | Clear Grid		
Close Database	A 1.25	Close Window button	File | Close		
Close Form	A 1.36	Close Window button	File | Close		
Close Query	A 2.13	Close Window button	File | Close		
Close Table	A 1.25	Close Window button	File | Close		
Collapse Subdatasheet	A 3.40	Expand indicator (-)			
Compact a Database	A 5.48		Tools | Database Utilities | Compact and Repair		
Convert Database to Another Version	A 9.7		Tools | Database Utilities | Convert Database		
Create Calculated Field	A 2.34			Zoom	SHIFT+F2
Create Data Access Page	AW 1.02	New Object: AutoForm button arrow | Page	Insert | Page		

Table 3 Microsoft Access 2002 Quick Reference Summary

TASK	PAGE NUMBER	MOUSE	MENU BAR	SHORTCUT MENU	KEYBOARD SHORTCUT
Create Data Access Page in Design View	AI 2.03	Double-click Create Data Access Page in Design View	Insert | Page | Design View		
Create Database	A 1.11	New button	File | New		CTRL+N
Create Form	A 1.35, A 4.34	New Object: AutoForm button arrow | AutoForm	Insert | AutoForm		
Create Form Using Design View	A 8.76	Double-click Create Form in Design View	Insert | Form | Design View		
Create Input Mask	A 6.10	Input Mask property box			
Create Index	A 3.47	Indexes button	View | Indexes		
Create Labels	A 7.47	New Object button arrow | Report | Label Wizard	Insert | Report | Label Wizard		
Create Lookup Wizard Field	A 6.08	Text arrow | Lookup Wizard			
Create Macro	A 6.29	New Object button arrow | Macro	Insert | Macro		
Create MDE File	A 9.71		Tools | Database Utilities | Make MDE File		
Create PivotChart	A 9.39	View button arrow | PivotChart View	View | PivotChart View		
Create PivotTable	A 9.32	View button arrow | PivotTable View	View | PivotTable View		
Create PivotTable on Data Access Page	AI 2.09	Office PivotTable tool	Insert | Office PivotTable		
Create Query	A 2.06	New Object: AutoForm button arrow | Query	Insert | Query		
Create Replica	A 9.25		Tools | Replication | Create Replica		
Create Report Using Design View	A 7.24	Double-click Create Report in Design View	Insert | Report | Design View		
Create Snapshot	AI 1.13		File | Export	Export	
Create SQL Query	A 9.48	View button arrow | SQL View	View | SQL View	SQL View	
Create Standard Module	A 8.38	Module object | New button	Insert | Module		
Create Sub Procedure	A 8.57	Insert Module button arrow | Procedure	Insert | Procedure		
Create Switchboard	A 6.41		Tools | Database Utilities | Switchboard Manager		
Create Report	A 1.41	New Object AutoForm button arrow | Report	Insert | Report		
Create Table	A 1.15	Tables object | Create table in Design view or Create table by using wizard	Insert | Table		
Default Value	A 3.30	Default Value property box			
Delete Field	A 1.19, A 3.19	Delete Rows button	Edit | Delete	Delete Rows	DELETE
Delete Group of Records	A 3.26	Query Type button arrow | Delete Query	Query | Delete Query	Query Type | Delete Query	
Delete Record	A 3.14	Delete Record button	Edit | Delete Record	Delete Record	DELETE
Display Field List	A 7.24	Field List button	View | Field List		
Encrypt Database	A 9.23		Tools | Security | Encrypt/Decrypt Database		

Table 3 Microsoft Access 2002 Quick Reference Summary *(continued)*

TASK	PAGE NUMBER	MOUSE	MENU BAR	SHORTCUT MENU	KEYBOARD SHORTCUT
Exclude Duplicates	A 2.26	Properties button	View | Properties | Unique Values Only	Properties | Unique Values Only	
Exclude Field from Query Results	A 2.19	Show check box			
Expand Subdatasheet	A 3.40	Expand indicator (+)			
Export Data Using Drag and Drop	AI 1.11	Drag object to desired application			
Export Data Using Export Command	AI 1.10		File | Export	Export	
Field Size	A 1.18, A 3.16	Field Size property box			
Field Type	A 1.19	Data Type box arrow | appropriate type			Appropriate letter
Filter Query's Recordset	A 7.17	Filter by Selection or Filter by Form button	Records | Filter | Filter by Selection or Records | Filter | Filter by Form	Filter by Selection or Filter by Form	
Filter Records	A 3.13	Filter By Selection or Filter By Form button	Records | Filter | Filter by Selection or Records | Filter | Filter by Form	Filter by Selection or Filter by Form	
Format	A 3.32	Format property box			
Format a Calculated Field	A 2.33	Properties button	View | Properties	Properties	
Import Worksheet	AI 1.05		File | Get External Data | Import	Import	
Include All Fields in Query	A 2.14	Double-click asterisk in field list			
Include Field in Query	A 2.10	Double-click field in field list			
Key Field	A 1.18	Primary Key button	Edit | Primary Key	Primary Key	
Link Worksheet	AI 1.08		File | Get External Data | Link Tables	Link Tables	
Modify Switchboard Page	A 6.45, A 6.47	Edit button			
Move Control	A 4.36	Drag control			
Move to Design View	A 5.38	View button	View | Design View	Design View	
Move to First Record	A 1.26	First Record button			CTRL+UP ARROW
Move to Last Record	A 1.26	Last Record button			CTRL+DOWN ARROW
Move to Next Record	A 1.26	Next Record button			DOWN ARROW
Move to Previous Record	A 1.26	Previous Record button			UP ARROW
Open Database	A 1.25	Open button	File | Open		CTRL+O
Open Form	A 3.06	Forms object | Open button		Open	Use ARROW keys to move highlight to name, then press ENTER key
Open Table	A 1.21	Tables object | Open button		Open	Use ARROW keys to move highlight to name, then press ENTER key
Preview Table	A 1.29	Print Preview button	File | Print Preview	Print Preview	
Print Relationships	A 3.39		File | Print Relationships		
Print Report	A 1.46	Print button	File | Print	Print	CTRL+P
Print Results of Query	A 2.11	Print button	File | Print	Print	CTRL+P
Print Table	A 1.29	Print button	File | Print	Print	CTRL+P
Quit Access	A 1.49	Close button	File | Exit		ALT+F4
Relationships (Referential Integrity)	A 3.36	Relationships button	Tools | Relationships		
Remove Control	A 4.26	Cut button	Edit | Cut	Cut	DELETE

Table 3 Microsoft Access 2002 Quick Reference Summary

TASK	PAGE NUMBER	MOUSE	MENU BAR	SHORTCUT MENU	KEYBOARD SHORTCUT
Remove Filter	A 3.14	Remove Filter button	Records | Remove Filter/Sort		
Remove Password	A 9.24		Tools | Security | Unset Database Password		
Resize Column	A 3.21, A 5.13	Drag right boundary of field selector	Format | Column Width	Column Width	
Resize Control	A 5.29	Drag sizing handle			
Resize Row	A 5.13	Drag lower boundary of row selector	Format | Row Height	Row Height	
Resize Section	A 4.46	Drag section boundary			
Restructure Table	A 3.16	Tables object | Design button		Design View	
Return to Design View	A 2.12	View button arrow	View | Design View		
Run Query	A 2.11	Run button	Query | Run		
Save Form	A 1.36	Save button	File | Save		CTRL+S
Save Query	A 2.41	Save button	File | Save		CTRL+S
Save Table	A 1.20	Save button	File | Save		CTRL+S
Search for Record	A 3.09	Find button	Edit | Find		CTRL+F
Select Fields for Report	A 1.43	Add Field button or Add All Fields button			
Set Password	A 9.21		Tools | Security | Set Database Password		
Set Startup Options	A 9.20		Tools | Startup		
Sort Data in Query	A 2.25	Sort row | Sort row arrow | type of sort			
Sort Records	A 3.41	Sort Ascending or Sort Descending button	Records | Sort | Sort Ascending or Sort Descending	Sort Ascending or Sort Descending	
Specify Sorting and Grouping in Report	A 7.24	Sorting and Grouping button	View | Sorting and Grouping	Sorting and Grouping	
Specify User-Level Security	A 9.72		Tools | Security | User-Level Security Wizard		
Split a Database	A 9.68		Tools | Database Utilities | Database Splitter		
Switch Between Form and Datasheet Views	A 1.39, A 3.11	View button arrow	View | Datasheet View		
Synchronize Design Master and Replica	A 9.28		Tools | Replication | Synchronize Now		
Update Hyperlink Field	A 5.18	Insert Hyperlink	Insert | Hyperlink	Hyperlink | Edit Hyperlink	CTRL+K
Update OLE Field	A 5.15		Insert | Object	Insert Object	
Use AND Criterion	A 2.23				Place criteria on same line
Use Documenter	A 9.13	Analyze button arrow | Documenter	Tools | Analyze | Documenter		
Use OR Criterion	A 2.24				Place criteria on separate lines
Use Performance Analyzer	A 9.11	Analyze button arrow | Analyze Performance	Tools | Analyze | Performance		
Use Table Analyzer	A 9.8	Analyze button arrow | Analyze Table	Tools | Analyze | Table		
Validation Rule	A 3.29	Validation Rule property box			
Validation Text	A 3.29	Validation Text property box			

Table 4 Microsoft PowerPoint 2002 Quick Reference Summary

TASK	PAGE NUMBER	MOUSE	MENU BAR	SHORTCUT MENU	KEYBOARD SHORTCUT
Action Button, Add	PP 6.18	AutoShapes button on Drawing toolbar | Action Buttons	Slide Show | Action Buttons		ALT+D | I
Action Button, Caption (Text Box)	PP 6.31	Text Box button on Drawing toolbar	Insert | Text Box		ALT+I | X
Action Button, Fill Color	PP 6.26	Fill Color button on Drawing toolbar	Format | AutoShape | Colors and Lines tab	Format AutoShape | Colors and	ALT+O | O | Colors and Lines tab
Action Button, Lines	PP 6.30	Line Style button on Drawing toolbar	Format | AutoShape | Colors and Lines tab Lines tab	Format | AutoShape | Colors and Lines tab	ALT+O | O | Colors and Lines tab
Action Button, Scale	PP 6.22	Drag sizing handle	Format | AutoShape | Size tab	Format AutoShape | Size tab	ALT+O | O | Size tab
Action Button, Shadow	PP 6.28	Shadow Style button on Drawing toolbar			
Animate Text	PP 2.40		Slide Show | Custom Animation | Add Effect button		ALT+D | M
Animation Scheme, Add to Selected Slides	PP 3.52		Slide Show | Animation Schemes	Slide Design | Animation Schemes	ALT+D | C
AutoContent Wizard	PP 4.07		View | Task Pane | From AutoContent Wizard		
AutoShape, Add Text	PP 6.46		Type desired text | Format | AutoShape | Text Box tab | Resize AutoShape to fit text	Type desired text | Format AutoShape | Text Box tab | Resize AutoShape to fit text	Type desired text | ALT+O | O | CTRL+TAB | TAB | SPACEBAR
AutoShape, Apply Animation Effect	PP 6.48, 6.49		Slide Show | Custom Animation | Add Effect button	Custom Animation | Add Effect button	ALT+D | M
AutoShape, Insert	PP 6.45	AutoShapes button on Drawing toolbar			ALT+U
Bullet Character, Change	PP 3.24		Format | Bullets and Numbering | Bulleted tab | Customize	Bullets and Numbering | Bulleted tab | Customize	ALT+O | B | ALT+U
Bullet Color, Change	PP 3.28		Format | Bullets and Numbering | Bulleted tab | Color box	Bullets and Numbering | Bulleted tab | Color box	
Chart, Insert	PP 4.35	Insert Chart button in content placeholder or on Standard toolbar	Insert | Chart		ALT+I | H
Chart, Insert Excel	PP 4.40		Insert | Object | Create from file		ALT+I | O | ALT+F
Chart, Scale	PP 4.43		Format | Object	Format Object	ALT+O | O
Check Spelling	PP 1.56	Spelling button on Standard toolbar	Tools | Spelling		F7
Clip Art, Add Animation Effects	PP 2.42		Slide Show | Custom Animation		ALT+D | M
Clip Art, Change Size	PP 2.34	Format Picture button on Picture toolbar | Size tab	Format | Picture | Size tab	Format Picture | Size tab	ALT+O | I | Size tab
Clip Art, Insert	PP 2.25	Insert Clip Art button on Drawing toolbar	Insert | Picture | Clip Art		ALT+I | P | C
Clip Art, Ungroup	PP 3.17	Draw button on Drawing toolbar | Ungroup		Grouping | Ungroup	SHIFT+F10 | G | U
Clip Art, Move	PP 2.33	Drag			
Color Scheme, Change	PP 4.11	Slide Design button on Formatting toolbar | Color Schemes	Format | Slide Design | Color Schemes	ALT+O | D | DOWN ARROW	
Comment, Accept	PPW 2.15	Apply button on Reviewing toolbar			
Comment, Insert	PPW 2.05	Insert Comment button on Reviewing toolbar	Insert | Comment		ALT+I | M
Comment, Reject	PPW 2.15	Delete Comment button on Reviewing toolbar			

Table 4 Microsoft PowerPoint 2002 Quick Reference Summary

TASK	PAGE NUMBER	MOUSE	MENU BAR	SHORTCUT MENU	KEYBOARD SHORTCUT
Comment, Review	PPW 2.15	Next Item button on Reviewing toolbar			
Control, Add to Form	PP 5.34	Click Control in Toolbox			
Custom Background, Insert Picture	PP 4.15		Format | Background	Background	ALT+O | K
Delete an Object	PP 3.19	Select object | Cut button on Standard toolbar	Edit | Clear or Edit | Cut	Cut	ALT+E | A or DELETE or CTRL+X
Delete Slide	PP 3.10	Click slide icon | Cut button on Standard toolbar	Edit | Delete Slide	Delete Slide	ALT+E | D
Delete Text	PP 1.58	Cut button on Standard toolbar	Edit | Cut	Cut	CTRL+X or BACKSPACE or DELETE
Demote a Paragraph on Outline tab	PP 2.13	Demote button on Outlining toolbar	TAB or ALT+SHIFT+RIGHT ARROW		
Design Template	PP 1.19	Slide Design button on Formatting toolbar	Format | Slide Design	Slide Design	ALT+O | D
Design Template, Apply to Single Slide	PP 3.50	Slide Design button on Formatting toolbar | Arrow button on template | Apply to Selected Slides	Format | Slide Design | Arrow button on template | Apply to Selected Slides	Slide Design | Arrow button on template | Apply to Selected Slides	ALT+O | D Arrow button on template | S
Diagram, AutoFormat	PP 6.43	AutoFormat button on Diagram toolbar			
Diagram, Change Size	PP 6.39		Format | Diagram | Size tab	Format Diagram | Size tab	ALT+O | D | D | Size tab
Diagram, Insert	PP 6.36	Insert Diagram or Organization Chart button on Drawing toolbar	Insert | Diagram		ALT+I | G
Display a Presentation in Black and White	PP 1.58	Color/Grayscale button on Standard toolbar	View | Color/Grayscale | Pure Black and White		ALT+V | C | U
Edit Web Page through Browser	PPW 1.09	Edit button on Internet Explorer Standard Buttons toolbar	File on browser menu bar | Edit with Microsoft PowerPoint in browser window		ALT+F | D in browser window
E-Mail from PowerPoint	PP 2.52	E-mail button on Standard toolbar	File | Send To | Mail Recipient		ALT+F | D | A
Folder, Create	PP 4.30	Save button on Standard toolbar | Create New Folder button on Save As dialog box toolbar			
Font	PP 1.25 PP 4.52	Font box arrow on Formatting toolbar	Format | Font | Font tab	Font | Font tab	ALT+O | F, CTRL+SHIFT+F or ALT+O | F
Font Color	PP 1.25	Font Color button arrow on Formatting toolbar, desired color	Format | Font	Font | Color	ALT+O | F | ALT+C | DOWN ARROW
Font, Embed	PP 4.54		File | Save As | Tools | Save Options | Save tab | Embed TrueType fonts		ALT+F | A | ALT+L | S | E
Font Size, Decrease	PP 1.25	Decrease Font Size button on Formatting toolbar	Format | Font	Font | Size	CTRL+SHIFT+LEFT CARET (<)
Font Size, Increase	PP 1.27	Increase Font Size button on Formatting toolbar	Format | Font	Font | Size	CTRL+SHIFT+RIGHT CARET (>)
Footer, Modify on Title Master	PP 4.13	Normal View button + SHIFT | Footer Area | type text | Close Master View button on Slide Master View toolbar	View | Master | Slide Master		ALT+V | M | S | type text | ALT+C
Guides, Display	PP 6.23		View | Grid and Guides | Display drawing guides on screen	Grid and Guides | Display drawing guides on screen	ALT+V | I | I
Guides, Hide	PP 6.26		View | Grid and Guides | Display drawing guides on screen	Grid and Guides | Display drawing guides on screens	ALT+V | I | I

Table 4 Microsoft PowerPoint 2002 Quick Reference Summary *(continued)*

TASK	PAGE NUMBER	MOUSE	MENU BAR	SHORTCUT MENU	KEYBOARD SHORTCUT
Header and Footer, Add to Outline Page	PP 2.37		View | Header and Footer | Notes and Handouts tab		ALT+V | H | Notes and Handouts tab
Help	PP 1.62 and Appendix A	Microsoft PowerPoint Help button on Standard toolbar	Help | Microsoft PowerPoint Help		F1
Hyperlink, Add	PP 4.49	Hyperlink button on Standard toolbar	Insert | Hyperlink		ALT+I | I or CTRL+K
Insert Slide from Another Presentation	PP 6.12		Insert | Slides from Files | Find Presentation tab | Browse | Open | Insert | Close		ALT+I | F | ALT+B | select desired file | ALT+O | select desired slide| I | ESC
Italicize	PP 1.26	Italic button on Formatting toolbar	Format | Font | Font style	Font | Font style	CTRL+I
Language Bar	PP 1.18	Language Indicator button in tray	Tools | Speech | Speech Recognition		ALT+T | H | H
Macro, Create by Using Macro Recorder	PP 5.19	Record Macro button on Visual Basic toolbar	Tools | Macro | Record New Macro		ALT+T | M | R
Macro, View VBA Code	PP 5.26	Visual Basic Editor button on Visual Basic toolbar	Tools | Macro | Macros | Edit		ALT+T | M | V
Menu, Customize by Adding a Command	PP 5.22	More Buttons button on Standard toolbar | Add or Remove Buttons | Customize | Commands tab	Tools | Customize | Commands tab	Customize | Commands tab	
Merge Slide Shows	PPW 2.09		Tools | Compare and Merge Presentations		ALT+T | P
Microsoft Design Gallery Web Site, Connect to	PPW 3.XX	Insert Clip Art button on Drawing toolbar | Clips Online in Insert ClipArt task pane	Insert | Picture | Clip Art | Clips Online in Insert ClipArt task pane		ALT + I | P | C | TAB
Microsoft Template Gallery Web Site, Connect to	PPW 3.XX		File | New | Templates on Microsoft.com		ALT+F | N | TAB
Move a Paragraph Down	PP 2.09	Move Down button on Outlining toolbar			ALT+SHIFT+DOWN ARROW
Move a Paragraph Up	PP 2.09	Move Up button on Outlining toolbar			ALT+SHIFT+UP ARROW
New Slide	PP 1.32	New Slide button on Formatting toolbar	Insert | New Slide		CTRL+M
Next Slide	PP 1.46	Next Slide button on vertical scroll bar			PAGE DOWN
Normal View	PP 2.19	Normal View button at lower-left PowerPoint window	View | Normal		ALT+V | N
Online Broadcast, Set Up and Schedule	PPW 2.24		Slide Show | Online Broadcast | Schedule a Live Broadcast		ALT+D | O | S
Open an Outline as a Presentation	PP 3.08		Insert | Slides from Outline		ALT+I | L
Open Presentation	PP 1.53	Open button on Standard toolbar	File | Open		CTRL+O
Open Presentation and Print by Executing Macro	PP 5.25	Run Macro button on Visual Basic toolbar	File | Open | double-click file name | Enable Macros | File | click macro command		ALT+F8, double-click macro name
Organization Chart, Add Subordinate and Coworker Shapes	PP 3.43	Insert Shape button on Organization Chart toolbar			ALT+SHIFT+N
Organization Chart Design Scheme, Change	PP 3.48	Autoformat button on Organization Chart toolbar			ALT+SHIFT+C | RIGHT ARROW

Table 4 Microsoft PowerPoint 2002 Quick Reference Summary

TASK	*PAGE NUMBER*	*MOUSE*	*MENU BAR*	*SHORTCUT MENU*	*KEYBOARD SHORTCUT*
Organization Chart Diagram, Display	PP 3.39	Insert Diagram or Organization Chart button on Drawing toolbar	Insert | Picture | Organization Chart		ALT+I | P | O
Organization Chart Shape, Change	PP 3.46	Layout button on Organization Chart toolbar			ALT+SHIFT+L
Pack and Go Wizard	PPW 2.27		File | Pack and Go		ALT+F | K
Paragraph Indent, Decrease	PP 1.40	Decrease Indent button on Formatting toolbar			SHIFT+TAB or ALT+SHIFT+ LEFT ARROW
Paragraph Indent, Increase	PP 1.34	Increase Indent button on Formatting toolbar			TAB or ALT+SHIFT+RIGHT ARROW
Previous Slide	PP 1.46	Previous Slide button on vertical scroll bar			PAGE UP
Print a Presentation	PP 1.61	Print button on Standard toolbar	File | Print		CTRL+P
Print Comments	PPW 2.09		File | Print | Include comment pages		CTRL+P | TAB
Print Outline	PP 2.48		File | Print | Print what box arrow | Outline View		CTRL+P | TAB | TAB | DOWN ARROW | Outline View
Print Speaker Notes	PP 4.66		File | Print | Print what box arrow | Notes Pages		CTRL+P | ALT+W | DOWN ARROW
Promote a Paragraph on Outline tab	PP 2.14	Promote button on Outlining toolbar			SHIFT+TAB or ALT+SHIFT+LEFT ARROW
Quit PowerPoint	PP 1.52	Close button on title bar or double-click control icon on title bar	File | Exit		ALT+F4 or CTRL+Q
Rearrange Slides	PP 3.51	Drag slide thumbnail or slide icon to new location			
Redo Action	PP 1.23	Redo button on Standard toolbar	Edit | Redo		CTRL+Y or ALT+E | R
Regroup Objects	PP 3.20	Drag through objects | Draw button on Drawing toolbar | Regroup		Grouping | Regroup	SHIFT+F10 | G | O
Save a Presentation	PP 1.29	Save button on Standard toolbar	File | Save		CTRL+S
Save as Web Page	PPW 1.03		File | Save as Web Page		ALT+F | G
Save in Rich Text Format	PP 4.68		File | Save As | Save as type box arrow | Outline/RTF		ALT+F | A | ALT+T, DOWN ARROW
Self-Running Presentation, Create	PP 6.52		Slide Show | Set Up Show | Browsed at a kiosk (full screen)		ALT+D | S | ALT+K
Send Presentation for Review	PPW 2.08		File | Sent To | Mail Recipient (for Review)		ALT+F | D | C
Slide Background, Format	PP 4.62		Format | Background		ALT+O | K
Slide Layout	PP 2.22		Format | Slide Layout	Slide Layout	ALT+O | L
Slide Master, Display	PP 3.22		View | Master | Slide Master		SHIFT | Normal View
Slide Show Timings, Set Manually	PP 6.55		Slide Show | Slide Transition | Automatically after | Automatically after box up arrow	Slide Transition | Automatically after | Automatically after box up arrow	ALT+D | T | type desired time
Slide Show View	PP 1.48	Slide Show button at lower-left PowerPoint window	View | Slide Show		F5 or ALT+V | W
Slide Sorter View	PP 2.18	Slide Sorter View button at lower-left PowerPoint window	View | Slide Sorter		ALT+V | D
Slide Transition, Add	PP 4.57		Slide Show | Slide Transition	Slide Transition	ALT+D | T
Sound Effect, Add	PP 4.28		Insert | Movies and Sounds | Sound from File		ALT+I | V | N
Table, Format	PP 3.36	Table button on Tables and Borders toolbar | Select Table	Format | Table	Borders and Fill	ALT+O | T

Table 4 Microsoft PowerPoint 2002 Quick Reference Summary *(continued)*

TASK	PAGE NUMBER	MOUSE	MENU BAR	SHORTCUT MENU	KEYBOARD SHORTCUT
Table, Format Cell	PP 3.33	Click cell			
Table, Insert	PP 3.30 PP 4.45	Insert Table button on Standard toolbar	Insert | Table Insert | Object | Create from file		ALT+I | B, ALT+I | O | ALT+F
Table, Scale	PP 4.46		Format | Object	Format Object	ALT+O | O
Task Pane	PP 1.11		View | Task Pane		ALT+V | K
Timings, Rehearse	PP 4.59		Slide Show | Rehearse Timings		ALT+D | R
Title Text Placeholder, Delete	PP 4.19	Cut button on Standard toolbar	Edit | Cut		CTRL+X or DELETE
Toolbar, Add Button	PP 5.12	Toolbar Options button on toolbar | Add or Remove Buttons | Customize | Commands tab	Tools | Customize | Commands tab	Customize | Commands tab	
Toolbar, Create	PP 5.10	More Buttons button on Standard toolbar | Add or Remove Buttons | Customize | Toolbars tab | New button	Tools | Customize | Toolbars tab | New button	Customize | Toolbars tab | New button	
Toolbar, Display Reviewing	PPW 2.05		View | Toolbars | Reviewing	Any toolbar | Reviewing	ALT+V | T
Toolbar, Reset	Appendix D	Toolbar Options button on toolbar, Add or Remove Buttons, Customize, Toolbars tab		Customize | Toolbars tab	ALT+V | T | C | B
Toolbar, Show Entire	PP 1.12	Double-click move handle			
Undo Action	PP 1.23	Undo button on Standard toolbar	Edit | Undo		CTRL+Z or ALT+E | U
Visual Basic Editor, Close and Return to Microsoft PowerPoint	PP 5.52	Save button on Standard toolbar | Close button on Visual Basic Editor title bar	File | Return to Microsoft PowerPoint		ALT+Q
Visual Basic IDE, Open	PP 5.29		Tools | Macro | Visual Basic Editor		ALT+F11
Web Session, Close	PPW 3.XX			Microsoft Internet Explorer button on taskbar | Close | Yes	
WordArt, Height and Width	PP 4.24	Format WordArt button on WordArt toolbar | Size tab	Format | WordArt | Size tab	Format WordArt | Size tab	ALT+O | O | ALT+E
WordArt, Style	PP 4.21	Insert WordArt button on Drawing toolbar	Insert | Picture | WordArt		ALT+I | P | W
Zoom Percentage, Increase	PP 1.45	Zoom Box arrow on Standard toolbar	View | Zoom		ALT+V | Z